SPECIALIZED INDUSTRIES

THE INSTITUTIONS OF ACCOUNTING

THE LEGAL ENVIRONMENT

RESEARCH IN ACCOUNTING AND AUDITING

HANDBOOK OF ACCOUNTING AND AUDITING

Editors

John C. Burton, CPA

Arthur Young Professor of Accounting and Finance
Columbia University

Russell E. Palmer, CPA

Managing Partner and Chief Executive Officer
Touche Ross & Co.

Robert S. Kay, CPA

National Director of Professional Standards
—Accounting and Auditing
Touche Ross & Co.

WARREN, GORHAM & LAMONT

Boston • New York

Contributing Authors

A. RASHAD ABDEL-KHALIK
University of Florida
(*Chapter 47*)

BIPIN B. AJINKYA
University of Florida
(*Chapter 47*)

MICHAEL O. ALEXANDER
Financial Accounting Standards Board
(*Chapter 8*)

MARSHALL S. ARMSTRONG
Former Member
Financial Accounting Standards Board
(*Chapter 40*)

VICTOR H. BROWN
Standard Oil Company (Indiana)
(*Chapter 4*)

JOHN C. BURTON
Columbia University
(*Chapters 1 and 41*)

EDWARD B. DEAKIN III
University of Texas at Austin
(*Chapter 37*)

PATRICIA FAIRFIELD
Columbia University
(*Chapter 1*)

OSCAR S. GELLEIN
Former Member
Financial Accounting Standards Board
(*Chapter 2*)

R. JAMES GORMLEY
Bell, Boyd, Lloyd, Haddad & Burns
(*Chapter 46*)

RONALD D. GREENBERG
Columbia University
(*Chapter 45*)

DAVID D. HALE
Kemper Financial Services, Inc.
(*Chapter 6*)

EMERSON O. HENKE
Baylor University
(*Chapter 35*)

GERALD W. HEPP
Plante & Moran
(*Chapter 34*)

JAMES K. LOEBBECKE
University of Utah
(*Chapter 12*)

ARTHUR L. LITKE
United States General Accounting Office
(*Chapter 36*)

HARVEY L. PITT
Fried, Frank, Harris, Shriver &
  Kampelman
(*Chapter 44*)

JACK C. ROBERTSON
University of Texas at Austin
(*Chapter 11*)

LEONARD M. SAVOIE
University of Notre Dame
(*Chapter 5*)

JAMES H. SCHROPP
Fried, Frank, Harris, Shriver &
  Kampelman
(*Chapter 44*)

GORDON SHILLINGLAW
Columbia University
(*Chapter 42*)

DAVID SOLOMONS
University of Pennsylvania
(*Chapter 3*)

MIKLOS A. VASARHELYI
Columbia University
(*Chapter 48*)

And the following partners and management group personnel of Touche Ross & Co.:

RONALD A. BERMAN
(*Chapter 29*)

MICHAEL P. BOHAN
(*Chapter 19*)

DANE W. CHARLES
(*Chapter 21*)

W. DONALD GEORGEN
(*Chapter 10*)

ELI GERVER
(*Chapter 43*)

IRWIN GOLDBERG
(*Chapter 26*)

FLORENCE L. HAGGIS
(*Chapter 20*)

JAMES A. JOHNSON
(*Chapter 32*)

ROBERT S. KAY
(*Chapter 7*)

JAMES I. KONKEL
(*Chapter 28*)

NORMAN A. LAVIN
(*Chapter 33*)

KEVIN G. MILLER
(*Chapter 13*)

R. SCOTT MILLER
(*Chapter 24*)

JOHN F. MULLARKEY
(*Chapter 13*)

DOWLAN R. NELSON
(*Chapter 49*)

RICHARD A. NEST
(*Chapter 27*)

RUSSELL E. PALMER
(*Chapters 9 and 39*)

RAYMOND E. PERRY
(*Chapter 25*)

CHRIS E. PETERSON
(*Chapter 18*)

JOSEPH A. PUGLISI
(*Chapter 16*)

WILLIAM L. RABY
(*Chapter 43*)

JON C. RICHARDS
(*Chapter 38*)

ROBERT J. SACK
(*Chapter 31*)

NELSON H. SHAPIRO
(*Chapter 42*)

MICHAEL J. STYCZENSKI
(*Chapter 19*)

EUGENE G. TAPER
(*Chapter 23*)

ANN M. THORNTON
(*Chapter 14*)

JOHN VAN CAMP
(*Chapter 17*)

THOMAS B. WALL
(*Chapter 28*)

ROBERT N. WAXMAN
(*Chapter 22*)

BRUCE N. WILLIS
(*Chapter 30*)

KENT F. YARNALL
(*Chapter 15*)

Preface

In the course of careers encompassing professional practice, government service, and academe, we have been made keenly aware of the difficulty the professional auditor and the financial executive face in dealing with the multiplicity of sources affecting their day-to-day problems. For those not as intimate with the field (e.g., students, nonfinancial executives, and researchers from other disciplines), dealing systematically and comprehensively with a significant accounting problem is almost impossible.

Therefore, we were convinced of the need for a comprehensive, understandable reference source in accounting and auditing—one that is both practical and authoritative, contains ample references to relevant professional literature, and directs the user to additional sources from which to research a particular topic in depth.

Meeting this objective required more than a series of individually constructed articles on various topics. Such an approach inevitably leaves gaps and results in material of varying levels of sophistication. At the same time, a comprehensive work of this kind was beyond the expertise of any one author, since it of necessity requires diverse professional, technical, and business knowledge and skill.

Our solution was to employ the resources of a major international accounting and consulting firm, which necessarily maintains up-to-date expertise in all areas of professional accounting and auditing and related areas of practice; to supplement those resources with outside experts in specific areas; and to combine the resulting material into a finished product that is comprehensive, cross-referenced, and consistent. Bringing this about required an editorial commitment involving many levels of initial outlining and a detailed working and reworking of drafts over a period of more than two years.

A major problem in a reference work on accounting issues is that it soon becomes outdated in many respects. Accounting is not a set of absolute truths, but a social system that responds continuously to contemporary needs and pressures. And auditing, though fundamentally more conceptual, is today being subjected to new procedural pronouncements at a hectic pace. Although this *Handbook* was updated to within 120 days of publication, how to remain current *after* publication was of serious concern to us.

The conventional approach of a new edition every four or five years was unsatisfactory if we hoped to produce a book of continuing usefulness. We considered a loose-leaf service but felt that a book had many more advantages. Accordingly, we decided to use the handbook format, but to update it annually with a cross-referenced supplement, thus enabling a user to work with reasonably current information at all times. The first supplementary volume should appear early in 1982, and the entire *Handbook* will be revised from time to time to incorporate these supplements.

The *Handbook* comprises forty-nine chapters in seven part divisions:

- Part I deals with general issues of accounting measurement and disclosure.
- Part II provides an overview of auditing concepts and procedures.

- Part III covers specific areas of financial accounting, reporting, and auditing as they exist today (often with a prognosis about the future). This is the longest section and includes chapters on the components of financial statements, organized as much as possible according to the typical business-transaction flow. Also in this section are chapters on particular accounting problems such as partnerships, related-party transactions, consolidations, and uncertainties.

- Part IV deals with accounting for specialized industries: government, nonprofit enterprises, regulated industries, natural resources, and financial institutions.

- Part V describes and analyzes the major accounting institutions: the accounting profession, the FASB, the SEC, the CASB, and the IRS. These chapters are largely authored by persons who either are or were deeply involved with the institutions they describe.

- Part VI describes the legal environment within which accounting and auditing operate. The initial chapter in the section outlines the elements of the legal system that are of greatest interest to accountants, and the other two chapters cover accounting and auditing issues as they have been dealt with by the courts and the law (including the federal securities laws).

- Part VII provides an overview of accounting and auditing research in recent years. While some of this research may not be of immediate practical significance, it affects the future development of accounting and auditing. The first chapter of this section describes perhaps the most significant academic research area of the past decade— efficient market research and its implications for accounting theory and measurement. A second chapter provides an overview of other academic research, while the final chapter describes the research process in professional practice.

Many people are involved in a massive effort of this sort. When an international professional firm such as Touche Ross takes a leading role and devotes over 17,000 hours to the project, the number becomes almost too large to deal with in the limited space available for thanks.

However, special thanks must go to several people at Touche Ross: to managers Jim Johnson and Joe Puglisi, who shouldered the virtually full-time burden of technical coordination over the past two years; to Jonathan Yarmis and Leslie Manning, for their unstinting efforts in moving the chapter manuscripts, galleys, and page proofs through their countless stages; to Jim Martin, Margot Sheehan, and Karl Brown, for their skillful editorial removal of the fog that usually surrounds accountants' writing; and to Jonathan Kantrowitz, Esq., for reading the entire manuscript and pointing out legal quagmires, some of which we entered nonetheless.

In addition to the named authors, and those noted as providing particular assistance with individual chapters, we would like to express our gratitude to the entire National Accounting and Auditing Staff of Touche Ross & Co., who devoted their total effort to the project with only limited complaint. Authors were generally prompt with their manuscripts and patient with the delays in the editing process. The editors from Warren, Gorham & Lamont also demonstrated admirable restraint and cheerful cooperation in the process of getting out the book. We are deeply grateful to all.

John C. Burton
Russell E. Palmer
Robert S. Kay

January 1981

References

Throughout this *Handbook* there are countless references included directly in the text, avoiding the clutter of footnotes. A few words are in order about understanding these signals.

First, certain acronyms should be recognized:

GAAP	Generally accepted accounting principles
GAAS	Generally accepted auditing standards
FASB	Financial Accounting Standards Board
SFAS	Statement of Financial Accounting Standards
APB	Accounting Principles Board; predecessor of the FASB (usually shown with a release number, e.g., APB 16)
AICPA	American Institute of Certified Public Accountants
AcSEC	Accounting Standards Executive Committee of the AICPA
SOP	Statement of Position; issued by AcSEC
ARS	Accounting Research Study
AudSEC	Auditing Standards Executive Committee of the AICPA
SAS	Statement on Auditing Standards
SAP	Statement of Auditing Procedure; forerunner of SASs
SEC	Securities and Exchange Commission
ASR	Accounting Series Release; issued by the SEC upon commission approval
SAB	Staff Accounting Bulletin; issued by the chief accountant of the SEC without formal commission action
CAR	Commission on Auditors' Responsibilities (Cohen Commission)

There are, of course, many more acronyms that apply in specific chapters; these are explained when they are first encountered in the chapter.

Second, the *Handbook* contains a consolidated bibliography, permitting the use within the text of "telescope" citations consisting only of the author, year of publication, and page or paragraph numbers where applicable. For example: (Jones, 1974, pp. 19-26) or (AICPA, 1979s, par. 57). The letter accompanying the year of publication is used to identify a particular item where the author has more than one publication in a specific year.

The consolidated bibliography appears near the end of the *Handbook,* and items are located by finding the author's name. Where there are multiple listings for a single author, identify the specific item sought by locating the year, listed most recent year first (and alpha character if applicable). For example, an AICPA entry from 1979 might appear as:

AICPA. 1979s. *Report of the Special Committee on Audit Committees.* New York.

Finally, reference to the professional literature codified in *AICPA Professional Standards* is accomplished through citation of section and paragraph number. This type of reference is the most prevalent in the *Handbook*. Alphabetical prefixes refer to a particular section of the codification:

AC	Accounting Standards
AC B	FASB Technical Bulletins
AC U	Unofficial Accounting Interpretations by the AICPA
AR	Accounting and Review Services
AU	Auditing Standards
BL	AICPA Bylaws
ET	Professional Ethics
MS	Management Advisory Services
QC	Quality Control Standards
TX	Responsibilities in Tax Practice

Thus, AC 4053.006(b)(ii) refers to the classification of direct financing leases from the standpoint of the lessor; AU 335.02 defines related parties; and AC 5132-2.05 provides effective date and transitional accounting for an FASB interpretation (signified by the dash) of SFAS 12 (AC 5132), *Accounting for Certain Marketable Securities*.

Contents

Part IV   Specialized Industries

Part V   The Institutions of Accounting

Part VI   The Legal Environment

Part VII   Research in Accounting and Auditing

Part I

Financial Accounting – General

1

The Role of Financial Information

John C. Burton
Patricia Fairfield

NATURE OF FINANCIAL INFORMATION

Monetary Unit Representations

Gathering and disseminating financial information is a social process evolving in response to the need for communication of economic events. Our present structure of financial statements was originally created by Renaissance merchants who found that in order to communicate economic events in an understandable way, a common denominator for presentation was necessary—the monetary unit came to be that common denominator.

Since the owners of economic resources were primarily interested in keeping track of their ventures and measuring the success of their investments, the monetary unit was a logical choice. It was not unreasonable to present results in terms of the monetary unit, because the input and the output of the investment process is cash. People were able to comprehend cash measurements, because prices expressed in monetary terms were the means by which they made the resource allocation decisions in their daily lives between current consumption and deferred consumption (i.e., investment). The system of economic measurement that evolved in monetary terms thus can appropriately be described as financial accounting and reporting.

While the advantages of measuring and reporting economic events in financial terms are substantial, many weaknesses also result. Economic events themselves are inherently not financial. Goods, services, physical facilities, and human resources are tangible, multidimensional phenomena. While they may be exchanged for cash, they are not cash. Expressing them in monetary terms therefore requires a transformation function that is artificial, although it may be useful.

The danger of any accounting transformation function used for purposes of reporting is that some users of the reports begin to believe that the transformation designed to achieve communication actually transforms a variety of economic assets into cash. The early users of financial accounts were often intimately involved with the operations of the enterprise and had little difficulty distinguishing between representations on the balance sheet and the physical resources under their control. However, the financial statements prepared in our society are often read by persons having no direct connection with any of the physical resources of the enterprise. As a generalization, since most persons confront measurements expressed in cash primarily when their bank accounts are involved, people tend to think of monetary units in terms of dollar bills that can easily be converted into other goods and services. Thus, the present-day user of financial reporting may be acclimated to view the accountant as an alchemist who converts base metals into precious metals, even though the user has been told time and again that the accountant is a communicator using a humanly devised arbitrary system of measurement and presentation intended to assist users in making economic decisions. Said differently, there is a strong behavioral tendency in humans to equate the symbol for the monetary unit with money itself, particularly when the physical resources symbolized by the dollars are not under the direct control of the individual. Properly transforming goods and services into dollar values for reporting purposes does not ensure proper use of that information.

When such a misperception occurs, the user is misled rather than assisted in making economic decisions. An examination of the analysis of financial reports by users and of the use of accounting numbers in documents such as bank lending agreements, both of which cover real economic transactions, suggests that the misunderstanding is not trivial.

A system based on some other more arbitrary unit such as "utils" or on physical units, or a specially designed index of output or input, might avoid many of the problems inherent in using the accounting transformation model in a society characterized by complex systems of ownership. Nevertheless, the difficulties in developing the multiple transformations required to create a new model are staggering. The effort to convert monetary unit accounting into a system based on purchasing power units, a relatively simple mechanical step, illustrates the enormous problems confronting those seeking even more radical change. And the *net* benefits of such a change, if any, are far from clear.

Thus, it seems likely that financial accounting and reporting will continue to be the cornerstone of our economic measurement system. Continuous education of users in the conventions of the accounting model should mitigate the problems of misunderstanding and misuse. Informed users will then recognize that cash held by an individual or an enterprise represents an economic decision point between consumption and investment alternatives, whereas monetary representations in financial reports may not present either possibility.

Objectivity Versus Relevance

An additional problem created by the financial reporting process is the difficulty of establishing measures that are considered objective. The extent to which a measurement can be repeated with the same result is considered to be of paramount importance to the accountant, for obvious reasons. If the figures on a financial report are dependent entirely on who is doing the measuring, then the numbers are invalid for external use.

However, the extreme emphasis placed on objectivity in financial statements has also led to a situation in which types of financial information (interpretive analysis, forecasting) that are potentially most useful to investors are resisted by accountants because they lack the necessary objectivity. In this case, the interests of investors may not be served by the accounting profession's adherence to a single value.

More attention is due the trade-off between relevance and reliability in financial statements. What is the appropriate choice between information that is fundamentally sound, but of limited value for society's purposes, and information that is central for economic decision making, but unreliable? The traditional bias has been toward the former, but changing economic and social circumstances may shift that bias toward accepting more relevant, if unstable, information.

Complexity of the Social Environment

While the limitations of financial accounting and reporting are significant in the case of profit-seeking enterprises—those that have the ultimate objective of producing a cash outflow to the owner—the problems become more acute when dealing with the reporting problems of nonprofit and governmental enterprises, which are so prevalent in our society. The objective of the enterprise cannot be expressed in terms of ultimate cash flows to the owner or to the enterprise itself. Rather, the objective lies in a broader social goal, and a more segmented approach of measuring inputs and outputs in different units must be developed. Such measurement techniques are still in their infancy.

Problems also result from the nature of our social and capital structures, particularly with respect to the widespread separation of ownership and control and to the vast increase in public-sector responsibilities. As social structures evolve to encompass ever more complex and interdependent relationships between people and institutions, society's perspective on the financial reporting process must also change.

It is thus necessary to continually reexamine the answers to the following questions, which are the foundation of the financial accounting and reporting process:

1. How should the *objectives* of financial reporting be developed and articulated to correspond to the conditions and ideals of the society?
2. Who are the *participants* in the financial reporting process, and what are their information requirements and responsibilities?
3. What are the requirements for success of a *standard-setting body* in a complex environment, and are they understood by those responsible for the standards?
4. How do the characteristics of the *environment* in which financial information is used affect the parameters of the communication process?
5. Finally, how do the preceding concerns determine the form in which financial information is to be presented so that it may best serve its social purpose?

The sections that follow look at each of these problems, and explore ramifications of decisions that are shaping the communication of financial information in our society.

OBJECTIVES OF FINANCIAL ACCOUNTING AND REPORTING

If financial reporting is to be successful, its objectives must be understood. It is not sufficient simply to say that the purpose is to communicate economic facts and events. To become operational in any sense, objectives must specify *by whom, for whom,* and *for what purpose* financial reporting is to take place.

The different characteristics of commercial and nonprofit (including governmental) organizations necessitate the development of two sets of objectives, each reflecting the spirit of the underlying enterprise. The FASB inherited the responsibility for articulating the objectives of financial reporting in business enterprises and has recently assumed responsibility for defining objectives in nonprofit and public-sector reporting (FASB, 1980c).

Business Enterprises

The objectives of reporting by business enterprises have been expressed by the FASB (in SFAC 1; AC 1210) in relatively simple terms, given the complexity of the relationships that characterize a modern business organization: financial reporting is aimed at investors and creditors and is designed to assist them in predicting the amount, timing, and uncertainty of future cash flows *to them*—which can best be assessed by predicting the amount, timing, and uncertainty of future cash flows *to the firm.*

The current objectives of business financial reporting are the result of an evolutionary process, which is described at length in the next chapter. The original purpose of financial reporting was to account for the disposition of assets by managers in the interest of owners. This objective, described as stewardship accounting, derives from the English feudal system, under which the owner of an estate turned over his property to the supervision of a manager. The fundamental characteristic of this relationship was ownership retention—the owner was not likely to sell his property if he found the performance of the steward unsatisfactory; the more rational choice would be to hire a new manager for the estate.

In current contrast stands the development of increasingly sophisticated capital markets allowing for easy liquidation of traded investments, which represent much of the economic resources of our country. Thus it has become equally rational in today's society for an investor to elect to sell his property in the event of poor performance by his managers. It is not that he no longer holds management responsible for supervision of the assets, but he now considers other criteria in deciding whether to maintain his current ownership status.

The contrast between stewardship accounting and user-oriented accounting depends on one important distinction: the parameters of the owner's investment choice. Thus, in the case of stewardship accounting, a fair historical representation of the managers' actions is adequate to support a decision to keep those managers; the question the owner is seeking to answer is whether another manager could care for his property in a more responsible way. On the other hand, the modern stockholder is seeking an answer to a second question as well: would a different investment yield a higher return for the same risk? The property holdings (shares of stock) are no longer assumed to be stable, and therefore the investor seeks to predict not only future behavior of the managers but also future economic performance of his company. Stewardship accounting is insufficient for this purpose, and some information useful in predicting the future performance of the company must be provided.

The philosophy underlying the federal securities laws also suggests this kind of user orientation. It is broadly recognized that potential investors in publicly held companies have as much right to financial information as do current stockholders, and a heavy obligation rests on management to avoid prejudicing those rights in either direction.

The progression from stewardship to user-oriented financial reporting is therefore a reasonable response to changing ownership characteristics. Although this point in the objectives issue seems resolved, the evolution of financial reporting is not complete; users still lack some information that management could provide them in order to make rational economic decisions. But the recognition that the objectives of financial statements of business enterprises has changed is a sound beginning.

Nonbusiness Enterprises

Postulating nonbusiness enterprise financial reporting objectives is more complex; it involves more users and more purposes. The FASB's 1980 *Exposure Draft on Objectives of Financial Reporting by Nonbusiness Organizations* suggests that resource providers, constituents, governing and oversight bodies, and managers are all primary users of financial reporting and that the uses to which they would put the reports are numerous:

- Resource allocation decisions,
- Assessment of services and the ability to continue to provide them,
- Assessment of management stewardship and performance,

* Information about economic resources and obligations and changes therein, and
* Information about service efforts and accomplishments.

Considering that our society supports increasing numbers of public organizations, the problem of financial reporting in nonbusiness organizations is only beginning to receive the kind of attention it warrants. The accounting practices currently prevailing in governmental units (Chapter 34) and nongovernmental nonprofit organizations (Chapter 35) are not consistent among reporting entities, are frequently internally inconsistent, and in too many cases do not provide useful financial information. Numerous issues need to be resolved if an appropriate set of accounting standards is to be developed, not the least of which is whose responsibility it will be to establish those standards.

The FASB sponsored a research study on nonbusiness accounting (Anthony, 1978), following that up with the 1980 exposure draft. But these are only tentative steps toward undertaking a more ambitious project—gaining the confidence of managers of nonbusiness organizations. Despite the acceptance of the FASB in the private sector, there are many in the public sector who are very hesitant to expose themselves to a rigorous standard-setting mechanism. Strong opposition has developed to the FASB's intervention and an alternative structure featuring a Government Accounting Standards Board has been proposed.

Beyond the question of turf, there are many substantive issues to be resolved, most of them revolving around the fact that the purposes of nonprofit and governmental entities cannot be described by a "bottom line." A statement of operations may reflect the cost of operations and the methods of funding those costs, and the difference between them may represent a good measure of *generational transfer* between periods,[1] but it does not reflect success or failure. Resolution of these issues will have to take place in an interchange between the profession and the society it serves.

Trueblood Objectives

The objectives of financial reporting are shaped by the values and characteristics of the society, and thus must be periodically reexamined. One of the most ambitious attempts to establish a set of objectives for the profession culminated in the Trueblood Report in 1973. The report was issued in three parts: a monograph on conclusions, a volume of selected papers from the study group's deliberations, and a record of the entire proceedings.

The conclusions, contained in the *Report of the Study Group on Objectives of Financial Statements* (AICPA, 1973j), attest to the social role of financial accounting. The focus is on the needs of financial statement users, and particularly on the needs of those who have limited access to alternative sources of information. The goal of users was determined to be predicting, comparing, and evaluating potential cash flows—the product of an enterprise's earning power. Recognizing a user orientation,

---

[1] An excess of funding over cost represents building of capital for future use; an excess of cost over funding represents consumption of capital provided in the past or borrowing against the future.

the study group attempted to modify the accountant's traditional bias toward objectivity; it recommended that current values be reported when these are significantly different from historical cost, although the emphasis remained on reporting on factual aspects of enterprise transactions.

What may turn out to be the most significant points of the report, however, are two observations that may point the way toward the future of financial accounting. The first is that earnings forecasts are useful for the predictive process, thus opening the door for their inclusion in financial statements. The second is the suggestion that companies may be expected to report on aspects of their business that affect the goals of society in addition to the goals of their specific stockholders. The definition of user groups would be broadened considerably if and when this view becomes an accepted objective.

FASB Objectives

The FASB's statement on objectives (SFAC 1; AC 1210) does not diverge in most respects from the Trueblood Report, although two significant differences do exist. The first is that management forecasts are downplayed in favor of estimates and judgmental information. While the future orientation remains, an explicit recommendation that forecasts be presented as information that would assist investors in determining earning power thus has been omitted. More sharply noticed may be the fact that SFAC 1 omits all references to accounting for social goals.

It is fair to conclude that the FASB so far has failed to speak out in the two areas where its opinions could have some impact on the evolution of financial reporting. The other objectives identified by the FASB, while reasonable in themselves, do not establish a foundation for change, and in fact do little more than justify prevailing practice.

A Broader View

A further attestation to the social nature of the financial reporting process and to the role that society's values play in determining the objectives of financial reporting can be found in contrasting reporting rules in other countries. The FASB's emphasis on investors as the primary focus of financial reporting is not the primary objective in many countries of the world, even some of those in which businesses have similar capital structures. In many countries there is general acceptance of the proposition that many constituencies with diverse interests have a legitimate interest in financial reporting.

In the Common Market, for example, labor representatives have been active in shaping common reporting requirements with an employee orientation. The recent interest in the United Nations in reporting practices of multinational enterprises has emphasized the perspective of host countries, particularly developing countries, in the financial reporting process.

Even in the United States a developing school of thought holds that the responsibility of corporations to their stockholders represents only one of the numerous obligations the modern company accepts in this society. Many proponents of this viewpoint believe that the accounting profession must prepare for, and encourage, the development of *social accounting*. Broadly speaking, social accounting encompasses reporting on those activities of the firm that have an impact on the society at large but that are not necessarily represented by its traditional financial report.

One of the most articulate positions on the broader reporting responsibilities of business organizations is contained in *The Corporate Report,* prepared by the Accounting Standards Steering Committee of the Institute of Chartered Accountants in England and Wales in 1975. This publication has not received the attention it deserves, either in the United States or in the United Kingdom.

The Corporate Report takes what some consider a very radical position on the objectives of financial reporting. It expands the definition of user groups, the types of enterprises required to report, and the nature of their communication.

Regarding users, *The Corporate Report* defines any group that has a "reasonable right" to information as a legitimate user group. Identified as being among these users are stockholders, creditors, employees, customers and suppliers, financial analysts, government, and the public.

Any economically significant organization is considered responsible to the identified user groups. A size test is recommended for determining economic significance, but reporting enterprises would be expected to include partnerships, government agencies, professional associations, and nonprofit organizations.

The kinds of additional information mandated would include

- Employment report, possibly in the form of human resource accounting;
- Statement of corporate objectives;
- Statement of value added;
- Report on foreign currency transactions revealing balance of payments position;
- Forecast of future earnings, employment, and investment levels; and
- Accounting for various social objectives.

Though the full significance of these proposals is not likely to be felt for some time, it is interesting that much of the information proposed in *The Corporate Report* is already required by various government agencies, but it is frequently not publicly available.

PARTICIPANTS IN THE REPORTING PROCESS

The process of communicating financial information not only requires a clear statement of objectives, but also demands that the participants in the process be identified and that their particular contributions and needs be incorporated into the standards of reporting. Managers, auditors, the government, and investors all play an important part in the reporting process, and each has significant responsibilities and concerns attached to his role.

Management

Most observers of the financial reporting process would agree that management has a primary responsibility to keep its stockholders informed of the financial condition and results of operations of the corporation and at the same time seek to maximize their wealth. Unfortunately, however, fulfilling both these responsibilities suggests a conflict of interest.

On the one hand, management will wish to disclose enough information to creditors and investors to maintain their support and to cultivate potential new sources of capital. For a company in an unstable or unusual financial condition, disclosure of too much information could result in precisely the opposite: withdrawal of investor support and closing off of capital sources. At the same time, management must also be sensitive to the costs of disclosure—the direct costs of collecting, affirming, and distributing information and the indirect costs of competitive disadvantages of disclosure.

There is controversy about both types of disclosure costs. Estimates about the direct costs of providing certain types of information vary widely depending on the source of the estimates, as witnessed in the responses to the SEC's proposal that led to the promulgation of ASR 190 (disclosure of certain effects of replacement costs of property, plant, and equipment and inventories). There is even greater disagreement about the extent of the competitive disadvantage produced by certain disclosures, and the propriety of mandating such disclosures nationally, in an environment in which companies must compete on an international scale with others not subject to similar disclosure requirements.

It would be a mistake to cast this argument in terms of the stockholders' interests versus management's interests. Not only is it possible that certain competitively disadvantageous disclosures will ultimately reduce the value of the total stockholders' investment, but there is also a question whether all stockholders can be viewed as a homogenous group. Investors are likely to have different risk preferences and thus favor different amounts of disclosure at different costs; they also have varying investment horizons and thus react to the timing of disclosures as well as to their content. The stockholder group, broadly defined, also includes potential investors, who again may have very different preferences concerning disclosures.

A more reasoned approach to the question of management's responsibility in financial reporting is to consider the needs of various user groups in the context of the overriding economic objective—efficient allocation of resources throughout society. This macroeconomic goal will serve to check the demand for information where more or costlier resources are used to produce it than can be justified by the extent or incidence of the resulting values. The mechanism for efficient resource allocation operates within wide tolerances and over long time periods and thus cannot be counted on to make prompt fine tuning adjustments.

Auditors

The usefulness of financial information in society is dependent as much on the faith with which users accept the information as on the information itself. The user of a financial report must be satisfied that the auditor has understood and evaluated the information in the statements and that his testimony is a fair one. Therefore, the auditor has an initial responsibility to bring to his task a comprehensive knowledge of the accounting model, familiarity with the complexities of information systems, and understanding of the economic substance of the transactions of the enterprise. He has an additional responsibility, over and above the requirement of professional competence, to maintain his principal commitment to full and fair disclosure.

The auditor has another responsibility, often overlooked: not only must his performance and commitment be entirely professional, it must also appear so to the users of his information. Regardless of the degree of expertise and integrity he brings to his work, unless he can convince outsiders of the reliability of his work, it remains valueless to them.

The auditor, cannot, unfortunately, simply perform his particular task and present the results to users. He must instead assume the initiative of educating users about the nature and function of an audit and furthermore demand that the profession continually reaffirm, publicly and privately, its allegiance to the highest standards of accounting measurement and financial reporting.

The necessary relationship between auditor and client makes the accountant's responsibility for the professional appearance of his role particularly problematic. While the fee relationship between firm and client contributes to the conduct of an audit that is both economic and thorough and emphasizes the joint responsibility of management and auditor for the audit, it necessarily introduces doubt in the mind of the public about the independence of the accountant.

Certainly the most reliable way of guaranteeing auditor independence would be to establish a public authority, vest it with the responsibility for conducting audits, and charge all publicly held firms an annual fee for the service. However, the disadvantages of such a system might ultimately outweigh the benefits of guaranteeing auditor independence. In particular, economic pressure for audit efficiency would be reduced for both parties if the company were not paying directly for services rendered. The removal of the economic incentive for efficiency, and the presumed weakening of communication links between the assigned auditor and client, would likely contribute to more expensive and less thorough, albeit more demonstrably independent, financial reports.

Another problem that might be encountered were a third-party audit agency to be established is the loss of information currently obtained by the auditor from non-audit services to a company. This information has usually served to enhance the quality of an audit rather than compromise it. One might also speculate that a public audit agency, offering no other client services, might fail to attract the most qualified individuals to the profession.

If the option of a third-party auditor is compared with the current system, the advantages of the latter become clearer. Real independence is sacrificed when the audit fee is introduced, but the economic incentives for producing an efficient and fair report remain high. For example, the greater incidence of litigation against auditors in recent years has served to bolster the auditor's insistence on quality control in the audit process, since his firm's reputation and profits depend on it.

Apart from the immediate economic advantages in efficient allocation of resources derived by maintaining a financial relationship between auditor and client, it should be asked whether or not there might also be a social benefit in demanding joint responsibility for the financial report from management and auditor and permitting their professional relationship to develop beyond the boundaries of the audit process. Even at the present time it should be emphasized that the auditor has extensive responsibilities in the reporting process, and thus the term *auditor independence* is a misnomer. It is only through acknowledging his necessary ties to management and by insisting on their joint responsibilities in the reporting process as well as his primary professional commitment to proper financial reporting that the auditor could fully justify the absence of independence in the present fee arrangement relationship.

Much more on the role of the auditor and on his profession is provided in Chapters 9 and 39.

Government

Among the many users whose demands determine the type of financial information gathered, the government—especially federal—figures significantly and can be expected to figure even more prominently as the 1980s progress. The proliferation of regulatory agencies trying to implement social goals has caused a vast increase in the types and amount of accounting information disseminated by all kinds of enterprises.

In the last decade the requirements of equal employment legislation, environmental protection laws, the ERISA legislation, and the SEC have all contributed to the paperwork burden of private companies. Although it has been argued that the additional costs of such reporting are passed along to the consumer without any concomitant gains, there is currently insufficient evidence to make a final judgment on this issue. The Arthur Andersen study, prepared for the Business Roundtable (1977), concerning the incremental costs imposed by government regulations represents a first attempt to get a perspective on the true cost of government interference in the private sector, but the study does not attempt to address the question of social benefits to be gained from legislation.

More significantly, when considering the social desirability of government regulation, it is important to address not only the single issue of the cost-benefit trade-off of the government's demands for disclosure, but also the behavioral impacts of the monitoring and reporting process. To put it more succinctly, it is axiomatic that how you keep score will determine how you play the game. Thus, results will be achieved both through the coercive power of the federal government and through the more subtle method of changing the reporting rules.

Two important examples of the government's concern with the impact of the scorekeeping devices of the accounting profession occurred in the investment tax credit and oil and gas reporting incidents. Both times the government expressed a clear preference for an accounting method that it perceived would further its own ends: in the former case, the flow-through tax credit, and in the latter, reserve recognition accounting.

While society should recognize and take advantage of the possibilities for furthering its goals through legislation mandating certain disclosures or through stipulation of the methods of reporting certain economic facts, an even higher priority of all parties should be the maintenance of a measurement system that does not obscure or debase the reported transactions. The integrity of the capitalistic procedure for resource allocation requires a reliable reporting process; to jeopardize that process is to endanger the economic system on which it depends.

Investors

While there may be some dispute as to the exclusiveness or even the primacy of investors as users of information, there is no dispute that in a capitalist country they represent a very important category. Since so much has been done to tailor the reporting systems to this group of users, a closer look at who they are is warranted.

In the first place, investors are not a monolithic category. There are debt holders and stockholders, those with major interests and those with small, those who make their own decisions and those who rely on others, direct and indirect investors—and they possess a wide range of risk/return preferences.

The New York Stock Exchange (NYSE) periodically sponsors a survey of stockholders; the most recent was completed in 1975 (reported in the *New York Stock Exchange Fact Book,* 1980). Although there were a number of disquieting trends evinced by the shift in ownership from 1970 to 1975 (an increase in age and income bracket of the average shareholder and a decrease in the total number of individual shareholders), still the figures are a convincing testimonial to the existence of a shareholder democracy.

Roughly seven eighths of the dollar value of publicly held stock is traded on the NYSE; information about other holdings is available but has not been classified. Information on NYSE holdings indicates a very interesting shareholder demography. In 1975 over 18 million Americans, or 1 in 6 adults, owned stock in companies traded on the NYSE. The median age of these stockholders was 53, the average income $19,000 per household. Three and a half million adults in households with income under $10,000 owned over 14% of the shares held by individuals. Retired, unemployed, or nonemployed persons (e.g., housewives) were listed as owners of over 40% of the personally held stock; one third of the portfolios held by individuals were worth less than $5,000.

Approximately 35% of the stock listed on the NYSE is known to be held by institutional investors, and it has been suggested that if all institutional holdings could be estimated (presently excluded are bank-administered trust funds, private hedge funds, and nonbank trusts), the total institutional holdings would equal half the present publicly held stock.

In terms of transacting, institutional trading accounted for about 45% of all shares traded and about 55% of the market value of all trading. When NYSE-member firms' transactions are excluded, institutional trading accounted for 57% of all shares traded and 70% of all dollars traded.

In discussions of the responsibilities of financial reporting, one of the repeated refrains is the need to protect the "naive investor." Statistics on ownership cannot really identify the numbers of naive investors nor the extent of their naiveté. It is possible that the 40% of investors who have college degrees have no more sophisticated an understanding of the accountants' reports than the 7% who lack high school educations. However, in making commonsense hypotheses about the ability of different investor groups to make informed investment judgments, one encouraging fact does stand out. Pension fund holdings constitute almost one half of all institutional holdings; presumably administered by trained financial analysts, these investments are likely made on behalf of relatively naive investor groups. Thus the potential to protect even the most uninformed investor is there through the agency of the financial analyst. (The data needs and objectives of the financial analyst are discussed in Chapter 6.)

STANDARD SETTING IN A COMPLEX ENVIRONMENT

The process of developing reporting standards in a society characterized by complex economic and social organizations is necessarily a matter of interest to many groups. The accounting profession has accepted the role of the standard-setting body, but its efforts to fill this role have not been wholly successful. The more-than-occasional failure of the profession's representatives to recognize the political nature of this function and their reluctance to initiate changes in the reporting process in response to a changed environment have in the past led to criticism from other sectors of society. Only recently, with the creation of the FASB in 1973, has the profession assumed a truly leading role in developing standards for financial reporting.

Early Efforts

In 1917, in response to a suggestion from the Federal Trade Commission that regulatory powers be vested in the government and that a uniform code of accounting principles be drawn up to guide the profession, the AIA (American Institute of Accountants, forerunner of the AICPA) appointed a committee to study the problem. Led by George O. May, the committee succeeded in demonstrating to the federal authorities that the newly formed professional organization would serve as a control for audit practice. Furthermore, the committee shifted emphasis from the development of a uniform code of accounting, which was likely to have turned into a list of rules, to the promulgation of standard audit requirements and procedures. This bold move set the profession on an independent course directed away from government authority.

The second important development in the professionalization of audit practices in America was motivated by the 1929 stock market crash. The origins of generally accepted accounting principles—GAAP—can be traced to this period, when the United States accounting profession showed its first signs of professional maturity. In addition to having earlier reorganized itself into an active professional association, AIA, the profession also succeeded in establishing the broader parameters of audit responsibility and accounting regulations. Both these precedents significantly influenced the future development of financial reporting.

After the 1929 crash, pressures on the AIA to take the initiative in formulating general principles for accounting began to arise from within and without the organization. At the time of the enactment of the Securities Act of 1933, George O. May was serving as chairman of a committee of the AIA that was engaged in discussions on cooperation with members of the New York Stock Exchange. He considered the creation of the SEC (by the Securities Exchange Act of 1934) to be a clear mandate for definition of audit responsibilities, and in 1934 the institute published the results of the committee's negotiations.

The resulting document, *Audits of Corporate Accounts* (AIA, 1934) was actually the text of correspondence between the stock exchange and the AIA committee, along with a proposal for generalized accounting principles. The correspondence stressed the significance of professional judgment in determining audit procedures and focused on the importance of the income statement over the balance sheet. The most important characteristic of the document, however, was its discretion in limiting the principles of accounting to five very general statements (still applicable through ARB 43, Chapter 1A; each is in a different section of the AC codification). This commitment to actual principles rather than infinite rules masquerading as principles still guides the pronouncements of the FASB.

Committee on Accounting Procedure

In 1936 the AIA initiated a more formal attempt to delineate a set of accounting principles. A seven-member Committee on Accounting Procedure (CAP) was formed (later expanded in size and discretionary powers at the urging of George O. May) and immediately began to provoke controversy in the profession and the financial community. Its first publication, *A Statement of Accounting Principles* (Sanders, Hatfield, and Moore, 1938), was decried in the academic community as being little more than a codification of current accounting practice.

Those early criticisms of the CAP set the tone for two decades of commentary on the committee's endeavors. Because the committee was conceived in an atmosphere of threatened government regulation of financial reporting, many of its pronouncements were inspired by political considerations, which dictated that the committee's decisions be practical and quick as opposed to theoretical and slow.

Accountants review the CAP's history with varying degrees of disappointment or scorn. It is widely agreed that, lacking a theoretical framework to guide the formulation of GAAP, the committee left itself vulnerable to charges of inconsistency or to accusations that it was an apologist for prevailing corporate preferences. Certainly some of its decisions were theoretical disasters (ARB 2, *Unamortized Discount and Redemption Premium on Bonds Refunded* (AIA, 1939b) and ARB 5, *Depreciation on Amortization* (AIA, 1940)), but it is important to also acknowledge the contributions of the CAP. Chief among the benefits is that it accomplished the primary task of establishing an independent standard-setting body in the private sector, maintaining the essential support of the Securities and Exchange Commission and the private financial community. To have succeeded in establishing its professional authority during a period of rampant government regulation was no small task, and to view its record out of this context is to judge it unfairly.

During the decades following the Second World War, the American Accounting Association sponsored attempts to provide a conceptual framework for the standard-setting function. Among the most important of these was the monograph on *An Introduction to Corporate Accounting Standards* (Paton and Littleton, 1940).

Accounting Principles Board

Pressure on the CAP to develop a theoretical basis for its pronouncements was increased in the 1950s, but the committee's attempts to develop a comprehensive framework were short-lived. Criticism of the standard-setting body increased and was publicized through the efforts of some particularly dissatisfied academics and practitioners. Finally, in 1957, the new president of the AICPA, Alvin Jennings, proposed that a new research body be organized to study the theoretical assumptions of different accounting practices and to propose alternatives when deemed appropriate.

The Accounting Principles Board (APB), although fundamentally committed to a research orientation as the foundation of its pronouncements, was nonetheless subject to many of the same pressures that had troubled the CAP. Its first attempt to identify fundamental accounting postulates (ARS 1; Moonitz, 1962) and principles (ARS 3; Sprouse and Moonitz, 1962) was not well received, although dissenting opinions did not necessarily concur in their critiques.

The APB quickly adopted a more conservative stance toward the development of an accounting framework, and proceeded to examine prevailing practices with the objective of selecting appropriate principles from among those already in use. Needless to say, the board was not overwhelmingly successful in this task, a fact which contributed to its ultimate demise.

Probably the major failing of the APB was its unwillingness to acknowledge that its function was as much a political one as it was one of determining some unassailable truths. An incident early in the APB's life that is widely held responsible for the board's final dissolution bears testimony to this failure. The investment tax credit was a program designed by the Kennedy administration to encourage capital investment and arguably might have been more effective in achieving this objective if the APB had advocated the flow-through accounting method (see Chapter 25). The APB ruled in favor of a deferred treatment, however, and was then not supported by the SEC. The SEC's action served to erode the APB's flagging support, and by the beginning of the 1970s it became clear that the standard-setting process again had to be revitalized.

Financial Accounting Standards Board

The *Wheat Committee* was appointed in 1971 to examine the problems of the APB and to recommend solutions to them. Its findings (AICPA, 1972c) led to the formation of the FASB in 1973. The new standard-setting body, composed of both accountants and nonaccountants, reflects the profession's increased recognition of the changing environment of financial reporting. Although not free from controversy, the FASB's statements demonstrate its commitment to ascertaining and adequately addressing the needs of users of financial statements. Furthermore, the SEC's formal recognition in ASR 150 of GAAP as constituting "substantial authoritative support" under the securities acts has contributed to the authority of the FASB, and with a few notable exceptions the two organizations appear to be capable of maintaining a partnership, strengthened by open dialogue.

The challenges confronting the FASB in the 1980s will in large part concern its ability to recognize the political nature of the standard-setting process and assume a leading rather than reactionary role in balancing the interests of various parties, while at the same time resisting the attempts of different groups to debase the fundamental measurement system in pursuit of social goals.

The line between the recognition that GAAP is the product of a political process and the abandonment of any standards other than those dictated by majority rule is difficult to draw. Nonetheless, this is the task that the FASB must accomplish if it is to fulfill its own responsibility in the reporting process.

International Accounting Standards

While this volume is devoted primarily to accounting and auditing in the United States, substantial professional activities in these areas have been going on elsewhere in the world as well. In most of the English-speaking world, standard-setting bodies of the accounting profession have been at work for many years developing accounting, reporting, and auditing standards. It is fair to say that the United States has taken the lead in this respect, and its standards have had a substantial effect on international practice both because of its head start in the area and because U.S. business enterprise has played the leading role in international business in the postwar era.

In the early years of standard setting in the United Kingdom, Canada, Australia, and elsewhere, there was a strong tendency to follow the pronouncements of the American standard-setting bodies. In recent years, however, divergencies have become greater. In addition, as Western Europe has developed into a strong economic unit, it also has devoted more attention to accounting and reporting standards. Historically, the accounting professions in continental Europe had not been strong, and accounting standards to the extent they existed were largely embodied in the companies acts of each country rather than in professional pronouncements. Stronger economies, stronger capital markets, and the development of the Common Market all led to the need for better, more harmonized reporting standards in Europe. After several years of negotiation, the fourth directive of the European Economic Community (EEC) was adopted in 1979, and it spells out basic financial reporting requirements. The member countries are now in the process of conforming their laws to this directive. The EEC, meanwhile, is at work on additional accounting directives. The seventh directive, dealing with consolidation practices, is now in the drafting process.

In addition to this legally based effort at international harmonization in Europe, the worldwide accounting profession has also undertaken a major project to encourage voluntary harmonization. The first part of this effort focused on accounting standards and grew out of meetings following the International Congress of Accountants in Sydney, Australia, in 1972. At that time, under the leadership of Sir Henry Benson of the United Kingdom, the professional groups in the leading industrial countries of the world formed the International Accounting Standards Committee (IASC) and charged it with responsibility for articulating international standards. All of the member countries' professional organizations agreed to use their best efforts to ensure compliance with the standards adopted or at least disclosure of variations from the standards.

Since beginning to function in 1973, IASC has issued 13 international accounting standards covering such topics as disclosure of accounting policies (IAS 1), valuation and presentation of inventories (IAS 2), consolidated statements (IAS 3), depreciation accounting (IAS 4), accounting responses to changing prices (IAS 6), accounting for research and development (IAS 9), accounting for taxes on income (IAS 12), and presentation of current assets and liabilities (IAS 13). In addition, four exposure drafts were outstanding at the end of 1980. In general, international standards have been less proscriptive than those adopted by national bodies and have permitted alternative practices, so that conflicts with standards adopted in the U.S. and the U.K. have been minimized. While international standards have therefore not broken major new ground, they have been a step in the direction of international harmonization and have served as a useful articulation of standards in countries where no national body with standard-setting authority exists.

The relative success of voluntary association of international bodies in accounting standard setting encouraged further efforts at coordination between national professional bodies. At the International Congress in Munich in 1977, the national organizations in most leading nations agreed to the formation of a federation of accountancy bodies around the world. This federation, called IFAC, has assisted in international communication and has also created an international auditing standards committee, which has begun the process of developing standards with international application.

In a world that is more and more interrelated in both economic and social terms, it is encouraging to see the development of international institutions in accounting.

While national interests continue to be diverse and are reflected in the relatively slow progress made by these institutions, it is essential that vehicles for discussion among professionals with similar functional backgrounds exist, and this was the major accomplishment of the past decade. In the 1980s these institutions will undoubtedly evolve and include greater participation from the developing countries of the world as accounting is increasingly recognized as a vehicle for accelerating economic development.

ENVIRONMENTAL FACTORS

The characteristics of the environment in which financial information is used is an important factor impinging on the reporting process. In this society the market for securities is the focus of most efforts to determine those environmental characteristics, since the allocation of investors' resources is achieved through public trading.

Efficient Market Hypothesis

If there are sufficient analysts at work in the marketplace to absorb the data currently available and to assure by their own competition that the information is reflected in the price of the security, then all investors are protected by the fact that the security is fairly priced based on all currently known facts and expectations. This is a characteristic called an efficient market, and it is discussed in Chapter 47. There is considerable empirical evidence that the market for securities is such a market in many respects, and if so, less concern need be felt about developing disclosure rules and practices designed to simplify financial reporting.

If requirements for greater summarization of complex data aimed at improving the comprehensibility of the information for the "average investor" result in a diminution of the data available to the sophisticated analyst, it is likely that the interests of the "average investor" will be damaged rather than helped, since the efficient market cannot absorb data that is unavailable to buyers and sellers of securities. While the market prices may imply such data, empirical evidence suggests that the knowledge of actual "inside information" (i.e., not in the public domain) may allow those who possess it to earn abnormal returns; hence the market is not efficient with regard to such undisclosed data.

One of the results of efficient market research has been to push standard setters and government regulators in the direction of requiring more data aimed at the sophisticated analyst, even at a cost of diminished understandability to the layman. While summaries and explanations of complex data are encouraged and in some cases required, the thrust of disclosure has been in the direction of increased detail and complexity. There has been some advocacy of a policy of *differential disclosure* (covered in Chapter 4), which suggests different kinds of disclosure requirements aimed at different groups of users, but the evidence today does not indicate any major effort in the direction of simplification.

In addition to the research being done on the efficient market, there are in-

creasingly sophisticated attempts being made by the academic community to identify the consequences of reporting conventions. This research focuses both on
behavioral consequences (e.g., the change in an auditor's decision processes in
response to materiality definitions) and on the overall economic consequences of
accounting standards (e.g., the effect of SFAS 8 (AC 1083) on foreign currency
management practices).

Disclosure as a Check on Business Behavior

While the objectives of financial reporting in the United States are generally
expressed in terms of users' needs and the impact of the data on their behavior,
the legitimacy of an additional factor of disclosure policy must also be considered
—the impact of the disclosure requirements on those obligated to make the disclosure.

It is widely recognized that certain disclosure requirements have been established
by regulatory bodies primarily because they represent a check on the behavior of
managers. In 1913 Justice Brandeis noted in an often quoted opinion that "sunlight is said to be the best of disinfectants." The philosophy implicit in this statement has been extensively applied, sometimes to the point that managers have been
known to growl that too much sunlight causes cancer.

The SEC, for example, has extensive requirements regarding disclosure of compensation and fringe benefits of senior management that can only marginally be
justified in terms of investor decision making. Similarly, rules regarding environmental disclosure, disclosure of audit and nominating committees of boards, disclosure of auditor changes after disagreements over accounting principles, and
disclosure of the percentage of audit fees paid for nonaudit services are examples of
the commission imposing its judgments about corporate behavior through the vehicle
of disclosure requirements.

In its enforcement activities the SEC also uses the obligation for disclosure as
the means for enforcing a code of corporate behavior. In the mid-1970s the effort
to curtail the practice of illegal or improper corporate payments was based on
registrants' failure to have disclosed such practices, rather than on any direct attack
on the legality of the payments themselves.

If questionable business practices can be minimized through disclosure requirements, the public will benefit both by the elimination of the practice and by saving
the cost of investigations and litigation concerning such practices. At the same
time, however, care must be exercised to avoid indiscriminate use of a well-
developed disclosure system for purposes other than to meet the needs of investors.
There is always the danger that such expropriation will reduce the usefulness of
the system for investors by burying significant data among a mass of information
designed for other purposes.

If, for example, disclosures of environmental and equal employment opportunity
lawsuits must be made in detail regardless of their materiality, a disclosure document could become a multivolume affair. In addition, certain detailed disclosures
may have an anticompetitive impact or may cause management to avoid certain
actions that might be to the benefit of both the firm and society, simply because
management is unwilling to devote the time and emotional effort to deal with the

questions that might result. Disclosure requirements imposed for their behavioral impact are thus a two-edged sword and must be dealt with extremely carefully.

FORMS OF FINANCIAL REPORTING

The objectives developed for financial reporting, the identity of the participants in the reporting process, the standard-setting process, and the characteristics of the environment in which financial information is used are determinants of the form in which the information is to be presented.

The reporting model is evolving in response to the increased complexity of business enterprises, and both the requirements of an efficient market for information production and the needs of different types of users are being considered in modifications of the reporting process.

The original reporting model was designed to describe a simple trading enterprise and was frequently created for a single project. As business became continuous and encompassed manufacturing, more and more conventions were required to squeeze a more complex reality into the simple model. Today's world of corporate interrelationships—conglomerate enterprises operating across international boundaries and utilizing a wide variety of operating and financial techniques in an inflationary world—is beyond the capacity of any simple measurement and disclosure model to describe. Thus the model must be allowed to become more complex to reflect the business reality. At the same time, the costs to certain preparer groups of information gathering, and the need of investors for more future-oriented information, are forces for further changes in the reporting process.

Differentiation in Reporting Requirements

While the increased complexity of reporting requirements has significance for different groups of users, it also has implications for various classes of preparers of financial reports. Attention is therefore being directed toward the impact of the reporting form on the heterogeneous group of financial statement preparers.

A set of preparation requirements drafted with the circumstances of a complex multinational enterprise in mind may prove burdensome and perhaps irrelevant when applied to a small and relatively simple concern. Similarly, the demands of a particular industry situation may lead to specialized requirements that have no applicability elsewhere. Thus the increased complexity of financial reporting is leading as well to more specialized requirements for particular situations and acknowledgment of the need to recognize the unequal burden placed on the small enterprise.

The *Report of the Advisory Committee on Corporate Disclosure* (SEC, 1977a) recognized both these developments as being necessary and rational. The commission, in adopting this viewpoint, has begun in recent years to adopt industry-specific disclosure rules, to develop disclosure exemptions for small companies, and to apply certain of its rules only to very large enterprises.

The AICPA membership includes many practitioners who deal primarily or exclusively with small nonpublic companies and thus has been particularly concerned about the tendency of generally accepted accounting principles to address the problems of large public companies while imposing requirements on all. In 1974 a Committee on GAAP for Smaller and/or Closely Held Businesses was appointed. Its "little GAAP" report (AICPA, 1976e) cited as a major problem the unnecessary costs imposed on small businesses by requirements that they comply with all GAAP, necessitating the preparation of some information not useful to their financial statement users.

The "little GAAP" report identified the professional obligation of the CPA to be concerned with whether any financial statements with which he has been associated were prepared in accordance with GAAP. Even if the CPA judges that certain disclosures required by GAAP are irrelevant to the needs of the users of small business financial statements, this is not a professionally sustainable basis for noncompliance. His only alternative in such situations is to issue a modified opinion on the statements, which may be misinterpreted as an indication of problems in the financial condition of the business.

The committee seriously questioned a basic assumption underlying the requirement that financial statements be prepared in accordance with GAAP—the premise that users have similar needs, which are best served by a common set of financial statements. On the contrary, the "little GAAP" report concluded that the needs of the public investor and financial analyst, which have dictated many of the GAAP disclosure requirements (earnings per share for example), are very different from the needs of owners, owner/managers, and creditors in small or closely held businesses.

The committee did not recommend, however, that two or more different sets of generally accepted accounting principles be developed. Rather, it perceived a need to narrow the current parameters of GAAP and to differentiate between disclosures that provide additional or analytical data for some users and disclosures that should be reported by all organizations.

Some members of the committee also suggested that the use of the umbrella term *generally accepted accounting principles* be reconsidered and that different adjectives (*promulgated, required, established*) be used to describe various principles, depending on their source and manner of application. This suggestion came in response to specific concerns that SEC disclosure requirements were being incorporated into GAAP without consideration as to the consequences of such requirements on companies whose stock was not being publicly traded.

Rather than make wide-ranging proposals for the development of different accounting principles for different entities, the committee upheld the belief that standard measurement principles enhance the usefulness of all financial statements. Its more conservative recommendation to classify disclosures thus would preserve the integrity of the measurement process while at the same time relieve some of the disclosure burden that has fallen onto smaller and closely held companies.

Largely in response to the *Report of the Committee on Generally Accepted Accounting Principles for Smaller and/or Closely Held Businesses,* the FASB issued SFAS 21 (AC 2083) in 1978, suspending the effectiveness of segment reporting requirements (SFAS 14; AC 2081) and earnings per share requirements (APB 15; AC 2011) for nonpublic companies. The FASB also put the "big GAAP/little GAAP" subject on its agenda as part of the conceptual framework project. Subsequently, by specifying a size test as to applicability, its pronouncement on accounting for the effect of changing prices (SFAS 33; AC 1072), was made applicable only for large companies. Thus both size and ownership characteristics have recently been used in different situations to differentiate among disclosure requirements.

Financial Statements and Financial Reporting

The once-slow evolution of the communication of financial information is at last speeding up to respond to the wide-ranging implications of changes that have taken place in our society.

New Role of Supplementary Information. The FASB's project to examine the problems of differentiating between disclosures for smaller companies and those for larger companies is representative of the progress being made in developing responsive reporting models. As a project that has a much broader focus than that single issue, it represents a significant step in developments of the past decade that have resulted in diminution of the role of financial statements in financial reporting; instead, supplemental information is becoming the prime ingredient in meeting the reporting objectives.

Financial statements were once the totality of financial reporting. The typical annual report of the first half of the twentieth century was a set of financial statements with a brief uninformative transmittal letter from the chief executive. While consumer products companies sometimes used the annual report as a marketing device, seldom was much (if any) financial data presented outside the financial statements. Even footnotes to the statements were generally brief, and the need to briefly present more than a few was considered something of a sign of weakness in the statements themselves. GAAP focused almost exclusively on the methods of presenting numbers in the statements.

Since 1950, however, there has been a steady erosion in the perceived validity of financial statement numbers that are not explained and augmented. Among the factors that account for this are:

1. There was a long period of market enthusiasm in which "creative" use of accounting numbers, combined with investor overoptimism, resulted in some enterprises being materially overvalued. In many cases, values were based on earnings per share that substantially overstated the economic growth of the enterprise. Resulting adjustments tended to shake the previously evident faith in numbers.

2. Recognition of the fact that financial statements were primarily user oriented led to a greater emphasis on information bearing on the future. Users could not continue to be satisfied by historical data alone.

3. Businesses became more complex both in their operations and their financing, making any simple accounting model difficult to apply without explanation.

4. There was a substantial growth in the number and success of lawsuits challenging the adequacy of disclosure and imposing new liabilities on both preparers and auditors of financial information.

As a result, both regulators and private-sector standard-setting bodies began expanding disclosure requirements outside the basic financial statements, both in the notes (though defined as an integral part of the statements, notes are primarily narrative rather than tabular) and in other supplemental information. The SEC, for example, imposed line-of-business disclosures in the Description of Business section in SEC filing forms and substantially expanded the footnote disclosures required by Regulation S-X. And the APB issued opinions requiring increased pension disclosure and a statement of accounting policies in the notes, and dealt with interim reporting requirements for public companies apart from annual audited statements.

During most of this period, however, the private-sector standard-setting bodies continued to view the financial statements and the notes thereto as their principal responsibility. Rule 203 of the Code of Professional Ethics of the AICPA granted these bodies the authority to impose accounting standards on companies, to be enforced by independent public accountants who audited their financial statements, but no authority had been granted over supplemental disclosures.

It was a major step, therefore, when the FASB, in November 1978, issued its first statement of concepts (SFAC 1; AC 1210) describing the objectives of all financial reporting by business enterprises; the Board thereby staked out a vastly increased territory. The SEC, which previously had done all the specifying in this area, supported the Board's expanded domain, and the ethics rules and auditing standards of the AICPA were expanded to legitimize the FASB's authority. (See ET Appendix D, "Council Resolutions Designating Bodies to Promulgate Technical Standards" [re Rule 204, standards of disclosure of financial information outside financial statements].)

Now the FASB must face not only the issue of what measurement principles should be used in financial statements and what footnote disclosures should be required, but must also question what supplemental statement disclosure is needed and to whom such requirements should apply.

Framework for Differentiation. The FASB's first attempt to do this is found in *Invitation to Comment on Financial Statements and Other Means of Financial Reporting,* issued in May 1980, which presents a framework for looking at the issue. Unfortunately, the FASB did not provide any specific guidance as to what purposes were intended to be served by the various presentational forms of financial reporting.

In essence, the invitation to comment says that financial statements should include the data set forth in the definition of the elements of financial statements (see exposure draft on elements (FASB, 1979g)). It is not a revelation to say that statements should include those things generally included in statements. The FASB goes on to say that supplemental disclosure should include information based on a trade-off among relevance, reliability, and costliness (as presented in SFAC 2, *Qualitative Characteristics of Accounting Information*; AC 1220). One of the interesting aspects of the document is its suggestion that a new category of required public information might be established, to be made available on request but not routinely included in disclosure documents.

While this particular invitation to comment is notable only in that the significant issues are set forth, hopefully a more meaningful analysis will emerge after comments are received. Until all the other pieces of the conceptual framework are developed, it is understandable that conclusions regarding any one piece must be tempered. The following chapter on the conceptual framework describes its development and progress.

Future-Oriented Information. While it has long been recognized that financial statements were used to make estimates about the future, they were thought primarily to be representations of the past; financial statement preparers' responsibilities were limited to an accurate historical presentation. The securities acts placed a responsibility on preparers and auditors for full and fair disclosure, but did not require any statements about the future, and indeed for many years the SEC staff was vigilant in prohibiting and rooting out anything that had even the tinge of a forecast. In 1971 the commission began to move away from its historical opposition to forecasts, both in speeches by commissioners and in an *amicus curiae* brief filed with the Supreme Court in which it took the position that under certain circumstances a forecast was a mandatory disclosure.[2] In 1972 hearings were held on the forecast issue, and in 1973 a statement of policy was issued lifting the traditional ban.

Perhaps more importantly, in 1974 a new requirement was adopted (ASR 159) requiring management to provide an analysis of the summary of operations, pointing out the most significant changes reflected in the statement and disclosing any facts known to management that might make the historical results not indicative of what could be reasonably expected in the future. And in 1977 the Advisory Committee on Corporate Disclosure, chaired by A. A. Sommer, recommended an enlargement of the management analysis requirement and further encouragement of forecasts. The commission has since adopted a safe harbor rule to encourage forecasts by offering some protection against liability and has explicitly urged registrants to publish forecasts. In addition, rules were adopted in 1980 strengthening the future orientation of the management analysis requirement (see Chapter 4).

In SFAC 1 (AC 1210) the Board was quite explicit that in direct contrast to the Trueblood Report (AICPA, 1973j), it was unwilling to conclude that forecasts were data that would assist investors in predicting future cash flows. But the FASB clearly reemphasized the basic future orientation of financial reporting. Thus, both in supplemental disclosures and in the financial statements, there has been substantial movement in the direction of data with predictive implications in recognition of the business continuum being described. It seems likely that this direction will continue and that, ultimately, explicit forecasts will be part of the reporting package for external purposes (as they already are today in most internal reporting systems).

A Prognosis on Financial Reporting

It is apparent that the traditional accounting model covering financial statements cannot cope with the demands placed on it if financial statements are to be viewed as the core of financial reporting. At one level there is a demand for greater definitional precision and certainty in financial statements—to meet preparers' and auditors' concerns about liability and users' wishes for comparability of reported financial results and absence of undue bias by the statement issuers. The FASB's efforts in standard setting have moved in this direction, and statements have therefore become more objective.

---

[2] In *Gerstle v. Gamble-Skogmo,* discussed in Chapter 33, the court ruled that defendants were constrained in their disclosures by the SEC's steadfast opposition to forecasts.

At the same time both FASB objectives and SEC regulation have increased the demand for an orientation towards the future. This orientation is inevitably subjective and cannot be achieved within an objective model. Even in the presentation of historical data the multiple complexities and uncertainties of a business enterprise make it increasingly difficult to utilize a well-defined, single-valued consolidated model to describe results in a meaningful way. Thus we have a dual movement in financial reporting: in the direction of a better-defined, more circumscribed, and more objective (but also less useful) set of financial statements; and towards a more future-oriented, subjective, and expansive set of required supplementary disclosures. Both thrusts seem likely to continue.

The result will be a reporting package that no longer forces the same degree of trade-off between reliability and relevance in a single set of financial statements but rather permits reliability to be the dominant concern in one part of the reporting framework while relevance is the primary element in the other. This approach holds considerable promise, even though it also inevitably implies increased complexity and hence greater responsibility being placed on preparers, auditors, and users of financial reporting. The natural human longing of users for a simple "handle" to describe a complex reality must be put aside and replaced by a recognition that an analyst's role must necessarily include the construction of a complicated mosaic in order to achieve an understanding of an enterprise.

SUGGESTED READING

Carey, John. *The Rise of the Accounting Profession.* New York: AICPA, 1970. This is a partisan but thorough and intelligent history of the accounting profession in America.

Estes, Ralph. *Corporate Social Accounting.* New York: John Wiley & Sons, 1976. This book provides an introduction to the issues of social accounting.

Previts, Gary John, and Merino, Barbara. *A History of Accounting in America: An Historical Interpretation of the Cultural Significance of Accounting.* New York: John Wiley & Sons, 1979. This book is an ambitious attempt to present accounting in America in a broader historical perspective.

Ross, Howard. *The Elusive Art of Accounting.* New York: Ronald Press, 1966. This entertaining book debunks the myths of accounting.

2

The Conceptual Framework

Oscar S. Gellein

FINANCIAL ACCOUNTING CONCEPTS

A conceptual framework is intended to contribute order and thereby discipline. Concepts differ from percepts. Concepts are general; percepts are personal. A framework of concepts impounds the percepts that determine the bounds of a system and make it hang together. Engineering concepts, for example, permit construction of a bridge that will meet perceived standards of safety. Public expectation that those standards have been met underlies confidence that the bridge will stand, even against exceptional stresses. Similarly, belief that coordinated concepts underlie accounting standards bolsters confidence that the reporting is neutral and conforms with those standards.

Investors and lenders are concerned about amount, timing, and risk associated with return on investment and return of investment. The unique role of financial reporting is to furnish some of the information useful in the assessment of risk and return and thereby to contribute to maintenance of healthy capital markets, both public and private. Fulfilling that role requires identification of purposes and bounds of competence of financial reporting as well as compatible accounting concepts that further public understanding and public confidence.

HISTORICAL PERSPECTIVE

The progress of record keeping has been reasonably well documented for about 500 years. Only during the past 50 years have formal efforts been made in the United States to search out an underlying conceptual structure. An economist, John B. Canning, made a major effort in 1929 to articulate a conceptual focus for what accountants were doing. Canning's reference to the accountant's definition of an asset indicates the nature of his inquiry:

> What does the accountant mean by the term 'assets'? One who seeks an answer by searching the texts on accounting for formal definitions will first be surprised that many, perhaps most, of the writers offer none at all. Or he may find that what purports to be a definition confuses the nature of the thing with the measurement of it. He will not need to search far [to] find that the definitions given are confusingly diverse. If he tests an author's own use of the term, he will, in general, have no difficulty at all in finding things treated as assets that do not satisfy the definition given. Nor will he have difficulty in finding that many things literally within the formal definition fail to appear in the asset accounts and statements. The collecting of an extensive, not to say exhaustive, set of definitions does not repay the scissor-work. [1929, p. 12]

Since Canning, many have attempted a general theory of financial accounting, or have articulated its significant building blocks or concepts—Paton, Littleton, Gilman, Hendrickson, Chambers, Sterling, to name some. Their contributions and that of many others are substantive.

Past Philosophical Approaches

During the past half-century of standard setting for financial accounting in the United States, three philosophical approaches are discernible:

- First, 30 years of dealing with situations;
- Second, 14 years of searching for postulates and compatible principles, while continuing to deal with situations; and
- Third, 7 years of identifying objectives and attempting to establish a compatible conceptual framework, with concurrent attention to situations.

Present Approaches

What now is the prospect? Will the current efforts of the FASB build a conceptual structure that will be more than a dust-gathering symbol of good intentions?
It is important to recognize that general theories can be developed without con-

cern about their acceptance. Many have been. The long-run benefits of some of those efforts, often scoffed at by many when formulated but later respected by all, are easy to identify in other fields such as science, medicine, engineering, and economics. Human progress requires imagination and ingenuity, and depends especially on the courage to expose advanced ideas. Accounting progress is not different, it is just less dramatic. Scholarly inquiries about financial accounting have had their impact on attitudes and, in turn, on perceptions—the impact is persistent, even though measured in inches or millimeters.

It is also important to remember that human conduct will not accommodate great strides without unusual motivation. Unusual motivation stems from environmental events bordering on tragedy or from catastrophes with widespread effects, such as economic depression, war, or runaway inflation. In dealing with these problems, there is a persistent demand for advancement, order, and heightened performance. In accounting there must also be a sense of direction, a commitment to follow it, and perhaps of greatest importance, advancement in steps not large enough to stimulate excessive concern or fear or shock. Certainly, this is a delicate balance to maintain.

STAGES OF STANDARD SETTING

Early Correspondence Between the AICPA and NYSE

The first approach to standard setting started in the 1920s with concern about the annual reports of companies listed on the New York Stock Exchange. That concern resulted in an exchange of correspondence between a special committee of the American Institute of Accountants (now the AICPA), chaired by George O. May, and the Committee on Stock List of the New York Stock Exchange. The first letter (September 22, 1932) suggested the objectives the NYSE should keep in mind:

> In an earlier age it was possible to value assets with comparative ease and accuracy and to measure the progress made from year to year by annual valuations.
>
> As corporate organizations have become larger, more integrated, and more complex, periodic valuations have become increasingly impracticable.
>
> That circumstance has given rise to the need for conventions guiding the determination of the proportion of a given expenditure to be charged against the operations of a year and the proportion to be carried forward.
>
> ... there are few, if any, conventions which can fairly be claimed to be so inherently superior in merit to alternative conventions that they alone should be regarded as acceptable.
>
> ... the alternatives that suggest themselves are: (1) selection by a competent authority of detailed sets of rules that would be binding and (2) free choice by each corporation of its own methods within broad limits referred to in the letter, with required disclosure of the methods followed and consistency in their application from year to year. [American Institute of Accountants, 1934, pp. 4-10]

That May favored the latter "free choice within broad limits" seems evident from an exhibit to the letter; it set out five "broad principles" that still constitute part of the accounting profession's authoritative literature (ARB 43, Chapter 1). Some of them are concepts, some are standards, one is a rule.

One "broad principle" recognizes the sale, with some exceptions, as the point of profit realization and admonishes against recognition of unrealized profit. Another proscribes charges to capital surplus that should instead be made to income. A third deals with subsidiary earned surplus accumulated before acquisition and dividends declared from that earned surplus. The fourth principle acknowledges that treasury stock in some circumstances may be shown as an asset, but holds that dividends declared on treasury stock should not be included in income. The fifth, more a "rule" than a broad principle, requires receivables from officers, employees, and affiliates to be shown separately. Together, they are far short of a framework, or even the beginning of one.

A second exhibit concerned the statement that a corporation should make in its annual report regarding the accounting principles governing the classification of charges and credits between the balance sheet, the income statement, and the surplus statement.

Important parts of the correspondence were placed in evidence in a congressional hearing precedent to the enactment of the securities acts which are the origins of the Securities and Exchange Commission and the regulation of securities offerings and exchanges.

Committee on Accounting Procedure

The correspondence with the NYSE, and the Securities and Exchange Commission's conclusion that it would look to the accounting profession for the development of "generally accepted accounting principles," strongly influenced the establishment in 1938 of the Committee on Accounting Procedure (CAP) of the AICPA.

The CAP considered early on whether to attempt development of coordinated concepts and decided against it. And so 1938 marked the beginning of a 30- to 40-year period of addressing problems on a situation-by-situation basis. Immediacy transcended long-run purpose.

By 1958 many of those concerned about the course of financial reporting had concluded that a base of fundamentals was needed to advance financial reporting. The CAP, with its situational approach, ended its tenure with more unresolved major problems than it faced at its beginning. Even George O. May, the architect of the correspondence with the New York Stock Exchange, came to realize that a conceptual basis was essential. Paul Grady noted that "although Mr. May had probably caused the Committee on Accounting Procedure, when it was formed in 1938, to undertake consideration of separate questions, he had reached the view in 1958 that a coordinated approach was appropriate" (1962, p. 278).

The philosophy of the first 30-year period of standard setting may be summed up by quoting from the CAP's first release, ARB 1 (American Institute of Accountants, 1939a):

> ... problems have come to be considered more from the standpoint of the current buyer or seller in the market of an interest in the enterprise than from the standpoint of a continuing owner. [p. 1]
>
> One manifestation of it has been a demand for a larger degree of uniformity in accounting, although it may be pointed out that the change of emphasis itself is bound

to lead to the adoption of new accounting procedures, so that for a time diversity of practice is likely to be increased as new practices are adopted before old ones have become completely discarded. [p. 2]

Paul Grady (1962) added:

Under May's leadership the Committee on Accounting Procedure decided not to attempt an over-all coordinated statement of generally accepted accounting principles, but rather to deal with particular questions or subjects, as they seemed to require consideration. It was his view that this mode of operation for several years would produce the experience and pattern of decisions required for the development of a more comprehensive statement, if the latter then seemed necessary. [p. 122]

After issuance of 51 statements over about 20 years, the Committee on Accounting Procedure was terminated in October 1959. The comprehensive conceptual statement had not been written, but its need could surely be perceived.

Accounting Principles Board

Restiveness about the slow advance of financial reporting persisted. Some observers believed that the CAP's objective of narrowing areas of difference and inconsistency in accounting practice had not been sufficiently fulfilled. They believed that greater advances could be made only within a structure built on a cornerstone of coordinated postulates and principles, supported by extensive research.

Two bodies were formed to carry out the program: the Accounting Principles Board (APB), to make or authorize public pronouncements, and the Accounting Research Division of the AICPA, to conduct independent study of pertinent matters.

Postulates and Principles. Faithful to its charge, the APB soon arranged for two studies, the first to identify the postulates of accounting and the second to recommend a broad set of coordinated accounting principles. The first of those studies was made by Maurice Moonitz, who had been named Director of Accounting Research of the AICPA, and was completed in September 1961. The second was made by Robert T. Sprouse and Maurice Moonitz and was completed in April 1962.

The *postulates study* focused on the kinds of problems in the economic or political environment with which accountants are concerned. Moonitz concluded, however, that "relatively heavy reliance must be placed on deductive reasoning in the development of accounting postulates and principles. We must first recognize and define problems to be solved, then move to their solution by careful attention to what 'ought' to be the case, not what 'is' the case. Hopefully, the two, 'ought' and 'is,' will not be too far apart, but we have no reason to expect them to be identical" (1962, p. 6).

Moonitz identified three levels of postulates: (1) those deriving from analysis of the environment, (2) those concerning aspects of accounting itself, and (3) imperatives.

The *five environmental postulates* concern quantification, exchange, entities, time period, and unit of measure. The level of concreteness of those postulates can be seen from the one on entities:

> Economic activity is carried on through specific units or entities. Any report on the activity must identify clearly the particular unit or entity involved. [Moonitz, 1962, p. 52]

The *four accounting postulates* concern financial statements, market prices, entities, and tentativeness. Their firmness is also evident from the postulate on entities: "The results of the accounting process are expressed in terms of the specific units or entities" (Moonitz, 1962, p. 52).

The *five imperatives* concern continuity, objectivity, consistency, stable unit, and disclosure. Their concreteness is illustrated by the objectivity imperative:

> Changes in assets and liabilities, and the related effects (if any) on revenues, expenses, retained earnings, and the like, should not be given formal recognition in the accounts earlier than the point of time at which they can be measured in objective terms. [Moonitz, 1962, p. 53]

The study on *broad accounting principles* sought compatibility with the postulates identified in the earlier study and noted that accounting's proper functions "derive from the measurement of the resources of specific entities and of changes in those resources" (Sprouse and Moonitz, 1962, p. 23). The study went on to define financial statements, assets, cost, depreciation, liabilities, owners' equity, invested capital, retained earnings, net profit, net loss, revenue, expense, gains, and losses, thus comprehending elements of financial statements as then constituted.

The studies on postulates and principles soon had the APB's attention. The APB concluded (AC 1010.03-.04):

> While these studies are a valuable contribution to accounting thinking, they are too radically different from present generally accepted accounting principles for acceptance at this time.

The APB added, almost plaintively, that

> there is ample room for improvement in present generally accepted accounting principles and a need to narrow or eliminate areas of difference which now exist. . . . Some of the specific recommendations in these studies may prove acceptable to the Board while others may not.

The "postulates, principles" approach was off to a shaky start.

Not surprisingly, the APB found it necessary to follow the path marked by the Committee on Accounting Procedure—i.e., dealing with situations. It dealt with 35 situations, 31 through opinions that carried maximum authority and four through statements that were intended to be persuasive though not mandatory. That major effort lasted 14 years, until 1973.

Inventory of GAAP. The APB remained mindful throughout of the need for a broad conceptual basis for discharging its responsibilities. It found itself repetitively arguing basic issues. Significant resources were devoted to the pursuit of fundamentals. An APB-commissioned study, completed in 1965 by Paul Grady, director of accounting research for the AICPA, surveyed the then generally accepted practices. Grady's study dealt both with practices common to all industries and with specialized industries. Further, he summarized the status of accounting principles deemed to have reached accepted status in the United States in terms of broad objectives, standards of accounting performance and measurement, and standards of disclosure.

With Grady's work as a starting point, the APB in 1970 issued Statement 4, *Basic Concepts and Accounting Principles Underlying Financial Statements of Business Enterprises.* This APB statement dealt with the environment of financial accounting, uses of the information resulting from financial accounting, its objectives, and its basic elements. Despite the criticism leveled against it, the study was monumental.

Somewhat like Canning's analysis over 40 years earlier, APB Statement 4 deduced the fundamentals underlying generally accepted accounting principles from what was discerned in the practices of the times. If there were gaps or holes in the discernible concepts, they would show up—and they did. For example, in connection with perhaps the most fundamental of all notions, the nature of assets, the study indicated that assets shown in balance sheets consisted of

    a. economic resources that are recognized and measured in conformity with generally accepted accounting principles and

    b. certain deferred charges that are not resources but that are recognized in conformity with generally accepted accounting principles. [AC 1025.19]

Other basic financial statement elements, including liabilities, revenues, and expenses were also defined in part in terms of what was generally accepted at the time.

The APB Demise. The fact that the conceptual formulations were made to depend on what was generally accepted at the time was the focus of most of the critics of APB Statement 4 (AC 1021-1029). They asked how it would be possible to improve reporting by use of concepts that derived from the very practice intended to be improved. They overlooked the fact that, from practice, the APB was attempting to discern concepts, complete or incomplete, as a place to start, rather than to build a complete structure of concepts meeting objectives of financial accounting and financial statements as then perceived by the APB.

The Accounting Principles Board went into its final years well supplied with studies of concepts discernible from reporting practices and the solutions accorded problems by accountants. Unrest about the efficacy of those concepts continued, however, from both within and outside the APB. The APB found it difficult to sustain conclusions that were not anchored to purpose and concepts, and discontent with the APB's ability to narrow variations and limit alternatives in practice kept mounting. At the same time, of course, the APB was suffering from politically oriented efforts to thwart its work—but that factor, important as it was, is not the subject of this analysis.

The early period of standard setting committed to a philosophy of dealing with situations therefore was followed by a 14-year period of largely the same thing, although there was now a commitment to find a conceptual underpinning: it just did not come off.

By 1970, 11 years after the formation of the Accounting Principles Board, discontent with the state of corporate financial reporting and about the effectiveness of standard setting had reached a level of considerable concern within the accounting profession. The profession itself responded by initiating a fresh look. The outcome was the naming of two task forces in 1971: one to consider the structure for standard setting, the other to study objectives of financial reporting.

Financial Accounting Standards Board

The report on the first of those studies, called the Wheat Study after the name of the chairman of the study group, was issued in 1972. The AICPA quickly adopted the recommendation to replace the Accounting Principles Board with the Financial Accounting Standards Board under the auspices of the newly formed Financial Accounting Foundation. The particulars of this restructuring are discussed in Chapter 39.

Many factors have been mentioned as reasons the APB was not able to meet the perceived needs for standard setting. The Wheat Study, for example, refers to "doubts cast on the disinterestedness of a part-time board" (AICPA, 1972c) as the factor that troubled critics most. There was a perception that APB members with a continuing affiliation with firms or companies must inevitably find their loyalties divided. The study also questioned the efficiency of a large, part-time board.

The APB encountered considerable difficulty in developing and agreeing on solutions to problems. It also had problems in gaining support for some of its conclusions. The resistance manifested itself by efforts, with some success, to have certain APB proposals thwarted and conclusions overturned through action of regulatory or legislative authorities. The 1978 experiences of the FASB with its pronouncement on accounting for oil and gas production, where governmental intervention was actively sought, demonstrate that a full-time independent group is not free of the forces that caused the APB's problems. Full-time attention to reporting problems, with unobstructed public scrutiny, by an independent body that seeks views from interested parties and listens to those views is not sufficient to dampen attempts to upset a standard setter's conclusion. A structure based on those considerations alone will break down. There must also be a substantial acceptance of a public mission, a set of operational objectives, and a framework of compatible concepts to guide financial reporting evenhandedly.

Claims were made that the APB had conflicts of interest and was indecisive, in that it bent by modifying or relaxing its proposals as pressure was exerted. There is no need either to defend or to castigate the actions of the APB, for there was a factor far more significant that thwarted the APB's commitment to advance the written expression of GAAP. That factor was the need for a conceptual anchor, a base about which few would argue. Time after time, as the APB considered financial accounting problems, the discussion would focus on the building blocks. They were argued from the beginning each time, of course inconclusively. The result was inefficiency and difficulty in sustaining conclusions. Standard setting in the private sector must look to persuasion based on purpose, reason, and evenhandedness.

Setting standards primarily by assertion requires muscle for compliance, whereas conceptually based standards have a built-in persuasiveness. The APB's problems stemmed more from a missing anchor than from conflicts of interest and part-time attention.

THE POLITICAL CLIMATE

Standard setting for financial accounting is accomplished within an environment of shifting, swirling, conflicting forces, commonly characterized as a political climate. If the process is to be successful over the long term, those forces must be kept in balance. An implied consequence of the process is that some enterprises, perhaps many, will be required to change or modify their financial reporting practices. And each requirement to change will meet resistance, if only because resistance to change is an abiding human condition.

A conceptual framework that will effectively guide reporting, then, must take account of attitudes and should attempt both to influence and to accommodate them, but not to get too far ahead of them; above all, it must be—and be seen to be—evenhanded. Further, the results must be attainable at reasonable cost.

Development of a conceptual framework by a private standard-setting body has a further complexing constraint. Certain conventions, even certain concepts, must be taken as given. There are diverse views, of course, about what is given and about the order of reexamination of what is not. Some observers would have preferred that the FASB start its study with no assumptions about the continuation of financial reporting conventions. Yet if the FASB had chosen to brush aside all conventions, it is likely that the Board would not be permitted to build a framework at all.

The FASB started with objectives determined from preexisting conventions. Analysis of what is needed to fulfill those objectives led to the conclusion that many long-standing conventions are both compatible and useful. Basic to the reporting of business activities are a balance sheet, an earnings statement, a statement of changes in financial position, articulation of assets and liabilities, and changes in those elements manifested in revenues, expenses, gains, losses, and capital adjustments. In other words, conventions are more than assumptions—they grew out of efforts to meet initially perceived objectives.

A conspicuous FASB "given" is that a proprietary view, rather than an entity view, will continue. Perhaps the most significant implications of that assumption concern the nature of payments to creditors and of distributions to owners. An entity view might lead to the conclusion that by nature those payments and distributions are alike, that in both instances they are either a cost or a distribution of earnings. That matter should be reexamined sometime, but there is no pressing need to do so now.

The Framework

Desirable as it may be to treat coordinated concepts together, some partitioning is necessary; otherwise, the issues cannot be kept in focus by the diverse interests entitled to have a role in bringing about changes in financial reporting. The Financial Accounting Standards Board necessarily identified a hierarchy of conceptual considerations. At the peak are *objectives*—purposes to be served by financial reporting. Then there are the *elements*—the financial statement representations of the things (assets, liabilities, revenues, expenses, gains, losses, capital) for which accounting accounts. In addition, there are the *measurements* of the elements—the scales to be used and the attributes to be scaled—and the events or conditions giving rise to the *recognition* of the elements. Finally, there are the *qualitative characteristics* of financial accounting, which are the qualities of data entitled to be included in financial statements and the characteristics sought to be satisfied. These factors are fundamental, but there of course are others, still in earlier stages of FASB consideration: the way things are displayed; concern about flow of cash funds; and the scope of financial reporting, that is, reporting beyond the formal financial statements.

Figure 2.1 identifies the segments of the FASB's conceptual framework project and when each was or will be completed. This chapter touches on all these segments but does not discuss them in depth. The FASB publications listed at the end of the chapter will provide a discussion of greater depth.

Objectives. The objectives of financial reporting necessarily derive from the role of financial reporting in a society. That role in American society concerns alloca-

	Date	
Project Phase	*Placed on FASB's Agenda*	*Final Statement Expected**
Objectives of financial reporting by business enterprises	April 1973	Issued, 1978
Elements of financial statements of business enterprises	April 1973	1980
Qualitative characteristics	April 1973	Issued, 1980
Measurement—changing prices	April 1973	Issued, 1979
Changing prices—specialized assets	December 1978	1980
Accounting recognition criteria	April 1979	**
Reporting earnings	December 1977	1982
Funds flow and liquidity	December 1978	1982
Information in financial statements and in financial reporting other than financial statements	February 1978	***

* Taken from the FASB's *Status Report,* No. 106, October 7, 1980 (supplemented by other FASB releases).
** Prediction previously was 1982; no date presently set.
*** FASB has not determined date.

FIGURE 2.1   PHASES OF THE CONCEPTUAL FRAMEWORK PROJECT

tion of economic resources (goods and services) to enterprises, both those seeking a monetary return on investment and those not so concerned. For some business enterprises, this allocation process is facilitated by a public capital market, in which investors and creditors can, in effect, exchange holdings; for many others, mainly small enterprises, the capital allocation process results from direct negotiation of enterprises with investors and creditors. In either situation, the role of financial reporting concerns the use of financial data about enterprises as part of the basis for investing and lending choices.

In November 1978 the FASB issued a statement, *Objectives of Financial Reporting by Business Enterprises,* the first in a new series of Statements of Financial Accounting Concepts. It builds on the 1973 report of the AICPA Study Group on Objectives of Financial Statements, often referred to as the Trueblood Study. Highlights of the objectives in SFAC 1 (AC 1210) are that

- Financial reporting should provide information that is useful to present and potential investors and creditors and other users in making rational investment, credit, and similar decisions. The information should be comprehensible to those who have a reasonable understanding of business and economic activities and are willing to study the information with reasonable diligence.
- Financial reporting should provide information to help present and potential investors and creditors and other users in assessing the amounts, timing, and uncertainty of prospective cash receipts from dividends or interest and the proceeds from the sale, redemption, or maturity of securities or loans. Since investors' and creditors' cash flows are related to enterprise cash flows, financial reporting should provide information to help investors, creditors, and others assess the amounts, timing, and uncertainty of prospective net cash flows to the related enterprise.
- Financial reporting should provide information about the economic resources of an enterprise, the claims to those resources (obligations of the enterprise to transfer resources to other entities and owners' equity), and the effects of transactions, events, and circumstances that change its resources and claims to those resources.

The objectives are directed toward the common interests of many users concerned with financial reporting, and grow out of environmental needs. Accordingly, they are subject to change as the environment changes. But to make the objectives operational, the statement focuses on the information that investors and creditors (those with reasonable understanding) need to help them assess prospective enterprise net cash inflows (since those inflows determine—directly or indirectly—prospective cash flows to investors and creditors). Those information needs, in turn, concern the resources and obligations of the enterprise and the effects of changes therein (i.e., cash inflows or outflows).

Elements of Financial Statements. In December 1977 the FASB published a first exposure draft of its views about elements of financial statements (FASB, 1977c). Conceptual formulations of assets, liabilities, owners' equity, revenues, expenses, gains, losses, earnings—the elements of financial statements—are the essence of that publication, which probed the boundaries within which accounting could competently be performed. A second exposure draft, published in December 1979, modified some earlier views, and this draft (FASB, 1979g) will be the focus in this discussion.

The *Exposure Draft (Revised) on Elements of Financial Statements of Business Enterprises* and SFAC 1 (AC 1210) make it clear that the FASB views earnings as the sine qua non of financial accounting—that earnings on an accrual basis, better than other measures, are useful for assessing prospective enterprise net cash inflows and are therefore central to investor/creditor decisions.

Perceptions of Earnings. The financial reporting issue at the moment on which enlightened views seem to divide concerns the inferences that should be drawn from the earnings reported for a part of an enterprise's life. Should earnings reported for a period represent an expectation of what they might be in the future? That is, are current earnings a kind of barometric reading from which a judgment might be made about future earnings? Should the measure of earnings reflect only what is controllable? Should financial reporting have as an objective the presentation of a measure of enterprise value? Or is that an assessment to be otherwise made by those interested in its determination, or by the securities market itself? Should earnings, whatever the length of the period, manifest a change in enterprise wealth—a change in its ownings less owings?

Unfortunately, the 1979 exposure draft does not meet head-on the question of whether earnings for a period have the same nature as earnings for a lifetime. Introduction of the term *comprehensive income,* combined with the suggestion that earnings may be an intermediate measure or component that is a part of comprehensive income, blurs the matter. A notion as central as earnings cannot be left unresolved very long.

Financial statements are significant if they show what has happened during a period and sum up the circumstances of the enterprise at the end of that period. This assertion does not, of course, confine financial reporting to measures of historical cost to the enterprise. Happenings in the external environment during a period are historical too, and their effects may be significant to the enterprise.

If the notion that the earnings of a period have the same *nature* as the earnings for a lifetime is accepted, the definition of the elements of financial statements comes into sharp focus. Applying that notion, if the earnings for the full life of an enterprise are measured from cash to cash (assuming for the moment no change in the measuring unit, the dollar, by reason of inflation or deflation), then the earnings of a period shorter than full life should show a change in cash potential. Any deviation from that view requires introduction of a factor intended to make the earnings of a period different in nature from the earnings for a lifetime.

A business enterprise comprises resources, people, some common interests, and a central direction—nothing else. One essential quality of a resource is cash potential, either directly from sale or indirectly from use in conjunction with other resources. Earnings over the complete cycle represent increments in cash; earnings of a period represent increments in cash potential—that is the real world. Not all resources of a society represent resources of enterprises: society's resources in the aggregate are greater than the sum of the resources of enterprises and individuals, because not all resources are uniquely claimed by enterprises and individuals. Also, not all enterprise resources are recordable—some may not be measurable with sufficient accuracy. From every vantage point the definition of an asset is conceptually central. Even liabilities are secondary, since they represent claims of others that are to be satisfied with assets (if any). In a broad sense a liability can be viewed as the financial statement element necessary to recognize a delay in transferring or relinquishing a certain measure of assets.

Accepting that periodic earnings must have the same nature as lifetime earnings, the earnings of a period manifest additions to assets or reductions of liabilities. Earnings are therefore accompanied by resource increases. That view of earnings conforms with individuals' perceptions of their own earnings and of business managements' with respect to the enterprises they operate. Revenues result from receiving one asset in exchange for another or receiving an asset in exchange for services (or from some combination of assets and services). Costs or expenses result from selling an asset in exchange for another, using up an asset in production, giving an asset for services received, or again, some combination of these. Gains and losses have similar ties to assets. By any test, assets are conceptually central to financial accounting.

Assets. It is not surprising therefore that a conceptual formulation starts with assets.

Definitions. When Canning studied accounting practice of the 1920s and what accountants do, he inferred:

> An asset is any future service in money or any future service convertible into money (except those services arising from contracts the two sides of which are proportionately unperformed) the beneficial interest in which is legally or equitably secured to some person or set of persons. Such a service is an asset only to that person or set of persons to whom it runs. [1929, p. 22]

In 1962, Sprouse and Moonitz defined assets as "expected future benefits, rights to which have been acquired by the enterprise as a result of some current or past transaction" (1962, p. 8).

And in 1979, the FASB proposed to define assets in this way:

> Assets are probable future economic benefits obtained or controlled by a particular enterprise as a result of past transactions or events affecting the enterprise.... An asset has three essential characteristics: (a) a probable future benefit exists involving a capacity, singly or in combination with other assets, to contribute directly or indirectly to future net cash inflows, (b) the enterprise can obtain the benefit and control others' access to it, and (c) the transaction or other event giving rise to the enterprise's claim to or control of the benefit has already occurred. [FASB, 1979g, p. 8]

The following characteristics are common to the three definitions: (1) *future service or benefits* (related explicitly to cash realization in two definitions above and implicitly in the third); (2) *exclusive right to the benefit,* and (3) *a right secured or acquired in the past.* If things possessing characteristics other than these are to be termed assets, definitions never attempted will be needed.

First notion. There is a "first notion in the concepts" for every discipline— the one that goes undefined. For financial accounting it is economic resources, future benefits, potential services, or some variation of those terms. This first term can be talked about, but not defined, because no distinguishing term comes before it. It determines the bounds, the unique competence, of financial accounting.

All other elements relate to assets. Liabilities, revenues, expenses, equity—all other elements of financial statements can be defined in terms of the basic element: assets.

Again, Canning inferred a definition of liabilities:

> A liability is a service, valuable in money, which a proprietor is under an existing legal (or equitable) duty to render to a second person (or set of persons) and which is not unconditionally an agreed set-off to its full amount against specific services of equal or greater money value due from this second person to the proprietor. [1929, p. 55]

Sprouse and Moonitz defined liabilities as "obligations to convey assets or perform services, obligations resulting from past or current transactions and requiring settlement in the future" (1962, p. 8).

And in 1979 the FASB proposed to define liabilities in the following way:

> Liabilities are probable future sacrifices of economic benefits stemming from present legal, equitable, or constructive obligations of a particular enterprise to transfer assets or provide services to other entities in the future as a result of past transactions or events affecting the enterprise. . . . A liability has three essential characteristics: (a) a legal, equitable, or constructive duty or responsibility entails satisfaction or settlement by future transfer or use of assets at a specified or determinable date, on occurrence of a specified event, or on demand, (b) the duty or responsibility obligates a particular enterprise, leaving it little or no discretion to avoid the future sacrifice, and (c) the transaction or other event obligating the enterprise has already happened. [FASB, 1979g, pp. 9-10]

The 1979 draft includes a strange comment for a conceptual document: it suggests on page 11 that there may be need to display among liabilities certain inevitable future sacrifices of assets that are not yet owed by the enterprise to other entities. Even the examples (in paragraphs 172-177) do not clarify the limits.

Thus, since 1929, liabilities have had three distinguishing characteristics: (1) an *obligation* (legal or equitable—that is, another party or class of parties has a reasonable chance of sustaining a claim) (2) to *transfer assets* or *render services* in the future (3) because of an *existing duty* (that is, a responsibility resulting from a past event or circumstance).

Revenues are attended by asset additions or liability decreases, but so are capital contributions. Expenses are attended by asset decreases or liability increases, but so are capital distributions. To identify earnings, something else is needed. That something else concerns the very essence of a business: selling or serving, using up assets or services to acquire more assets, windfall increases in assets, externally imposed asset disposals—all these comprise revenues, expenses, gains, and losses. Each has a meaning in relation to assets (and in some cases, of course, to liabilities, which, as noted, have their meaning in relation to assets).

As Canning pointed out, revenues have fruition in assets but are not the fruit (1929, p. 10). By the same token, expenses use up the fruit, but are not the fruit consumed. Earnings, the difference between revenues and expenses (combined with the difference between any gains and losses), therefore also have fruition in assets. That is why earnings and its determinants, revenues, expenses, gains, and losses, are defined in terms of asset changes. If otherwise defined, the earnings for a period either are different by nature from the earnings for a lifetime or have fruition in something other than assets. Some observers apparently believe that earnings for a period may be different in nature from earnings for a lifetime, but no one seems to hold that earnings have fruition in other than cash, cash equivalents, or different kinds of assets.

A conceptual formulation of earnings in terms of asset fruition in no way requires, or even suggests, that the determination of earnings results from periodic asset revaluations. Fruition of assets results from transactions and events. It is the beauty of double-entry accounting that two aspects of transactions and effects of events are recorded: the fruition (sometimes negative) and the fruit. It is practicable and especially meaningful to display the fruition of earnings—useful concepts will not change that.

Measurement, Allocation, Recognition, and Matching. Assets and other financial statement elements can be defined without reference to their measure. Indeed, it is quite useful to separate definition from measurement. To do so is to break a complex subject into two manageable pieces: the thing to be measured, and its measure.

Most things have several properties that can be measured. For example, a few of the measurable physical properties of a table are its length, width, height, weight, and top surface area. The owner of the table could also measure its financial properties: its historical cost, its current cost, its depreciated historical cost, its depreciated current cost, its selling price, the replacement cost of a different table serving a similar function, or even the cost of some other item that would serve as a table, to name a few. Measures of financial statement elements—liabilities, revenues, expenses, gains, and losses—can be approached similarly.

Thus, measurement itself has two separable parts. The first concerns the *property to be measured*; the second concerns the *scale of measurement*. For example, the historical cost of an asset (its acquisition cost) is one of the financial properties that can be measured. The scale for measuring this historical cost could be money or units of general purchasing power. Conceivably, it could also be units of specific purchasing power or any unit that could be related in time to historical cost. The unit selected should be useful to the audience.

The FASB has identified a number of attributes[1] of assets and liabilities that have been considered for measurement, including historical cost/historical proceeds; current cost/current proceeds; current exit value in due course of business; expected exit value in due course of business; and present value of expected cash flows (1976b, p. 193).

Selection of the attribute to be applied in financial statements relates to usefulness, that is, to relevance and reliability, which are two important tests. What attribute best fits the purpose? Can it be *measured* reliably? The selection process

---

[1] The FASB chose the term *attribute* instead of *property* to avoid confusion with other accounting uses of the term *property*.

should therefore answer the question, What is the most relevant attribute that can be measured with reasonable reliability?

Measurements in financial statements in the United States are referred to as *historical cost* because of the way in which nonmonetary assets are measured when acquired. Monetary assets are usually measured at some form of realizable value when acquired, and liabilities are most often measured at historical proceeds or some form of amounts payable when incurred—certainly not at historical cost.

The FASB recently affirmed its intention to leave unchanged indefinitely the measures currently used in financial statements and to require them to be supplemented with current cost measures for certain kinds of assets, especially inventory and property, plant, and equipment, and with information about certain effects of using a scale based on general purchasing power. (See Chapter 8.)

Matching. Determination of earnings for periods shorter than a lifetime requires allocations. *Allocation* is an indispensable convention necessary to determine the revenues and expenses of a period by direct reference to happenings of the period, rather than by assessment of standing at the beginning of the period and again at the end. That focus may have obscured the nature of income; quite unintentionally it may have caused income to be viewed as an indicator, or barometer, of normal activity or controllable performance rather than the fruition of use of assets.

Nonetheless, allocation of measures of financial statement elements to periods has a significant role—without it, periodic determination of income may be impracticable. The issue of the day is to find the *limits* of the role of periodic allocation, rather than to eliminate it.

In their classic text on financial accounting, Paton and Littleton captured the need of the times when they stated:

> With acquisition and disposition prices measuring both the efforts to produce results and the results produced, the principal concern of accounting is the periodic matching of costs and revenues as a test-reading by which to gauge the effects of the efforts expended. [1940, p. 7]

This view of accounting as a practical necessity has had a tremendous influence on the development of financial reporting practices over the past 40 years.

Costs are viewed by many as "the fundamental data of accounting," as Paton and Littleton (1940) put it. Revenues are viewed as measurable by periods during which goods are sold or services rendered. Determination of periodic income involves "the division of the stream of costs incurred between the present and the future." One outcome of that emphasis has been a growing perception that "cost" is an asset. (More will be said about that later in this chapter.)

The matching notion, so well articulated by Paton and Littleton, ultimately came down to three aspects, as set forth in APB Statement 4 (AC 1026.20-.24):

1. *Associating Cause and Effect.* Some costs are recognized as expenses on the basis of a presumed direct association with specific revenues. . . . Recognizing them as expenses accompanies recognition of the revenue.

2. *Systematic and Rational Allocation.* . . . If an asset provides benefits for several periods its cost is allocated to the periods in a systematic and rational manner in the absence of a more direct basis for associating cause and effect.

3. *Immediate Recognition.* Some costs are associated with the current accounting period as expenses because (1) costs incurred during the period provide no discernible future benefits, (2) costs recorded as assets in prior periods no longer provide discernible benefits, or (3) allocating costs either on the basis of association with revenue or among several accounting periods is considered to serve no useful purpose.... The principle of immediate recognition also requires that items carried as assets in prior periods that are discovered to have no discernible future benefit be charged to expense, for example, a patent that is determined to be worthless.

Allocations, as well as matching costs and revenues, are practical necessities to determine periodic income. The emphasis on matching during the past 40 or more years, however, has not been without its frailties. There is some tendency to view it as an end in itself. Perceptions have developed concerning a "good" match. "Goodness of the match" has been judged at times in terms of minimized fluctuations in reported operating results. In what is perhaps the extreme view of "goodness of the match," revenue is recognized in proportion to the incurrence of costs intended to be covered by sales price, and is then factored into the establishment of that price.

There are several difficulties with this view, quite apart from the difficulties of attempting to attach revenues to cost (instead of the other way around) and tracing the costs. The principal conceptual difficulty is that revenue becomes a function of pricing instead of asset fruition, and therefore becomes a statistic instead of a manifestation of an addition to enterprise resources. Depreciation accounting, association with revenues of costs of goods sold and of services rendered, and periodic recognition of losses as the prospects of future benefits diminish or disappear are all essential aspects of financial accounting, and accordingly, matching has an important role to play in financial reporting. But whether it has a role for conceptualizing earnings is open to question.

A theory of matching could be developed that would place matching at the center of the concept of periodic earnings. It is difficult to see how that notion would conceptualize earnings for a lifetime, but it could conceptualize earnings for a period as an indicator. This approach would require conceptual development in a direction different from previous or current efforts. It would need to identify the elements and their measurement—somewhat different from those described in this chapter—qualifying for inclusion in financial statements.

Concepts of financial statement elements are intended to identify the characteristics that qualify elements for inclusion in the statements. If they do not, the conceptual framework is open-ended. Other considerations, commonly referred to as recognition criteria, determine when these elements should in fact be admitted to the financial statements. Recognition criteria are concerned with (1) events that trigger initial recording, (2) a change in measurement, and (3) whether a measure is reliable enough for recording. Indeed, recognition may be the watershed phase of the conceptual framework.

Qualitative Characteristics. Several groups have studied qualities or characteristics that make financial statement information useful, including an American Accounting Association committee, the Accounting Principles Board, the Trueblood study group, and the Accounting Standards Steering Committee of the

Institute of Chartered Accountants in England and Wales. (A description of these efforts may be found in FASB, 1976b, p. 148.) Relevance, reliability, verifiability, freedom from bias, understandability, materiality, consistency, comparability, and several other features are common to most of those studies though often expressed in different ways.

Some observers believe that a conceptual formulation for financial reporting should be confined largely to guidelines concerning the quality of data supplied, and that standards would necessarily be *ad hoc*. They argue that financial reporting is essentially pragmatic and, accordingly, not susceptible of conceptual analysis. The process of determining standards should start from the notion that at the outset there is an array of attitudes to be accommodated in establishing a standard. That array cannot be narrowed by adherence to concepts, because the underlying perceptions of the effects of the standard manifest a tangle of short-run, mid-term, and long-run interests. That tangle, so the argument goes, cannot be unsnarled by concepts, because concepts assume a truth, an ultimate verity, independent from attitudes and perceptions.

The solution these observers see is to identify a set of qualities against which data is tested—a number of "smell" tests, which, if met, will establish a level of reasonably good reporting. More significantly, this process, so it is argued, will follow only if the array of attitudes about reported data are accommodated by appeal to their qualities rather than to any concepts that must necessarily have a constraining effect.

There are great difficulties with aspects of this argument. Identification of the qualitative tests that data should meet is important, but some of the important qualitative tests are necessarily anchored in objectives and are operational only within a framework of concepts. Relevance of data, for example, concerns fitness for purpose. How can relevance be applied in standard setting if purposes are not sifted to determine those against which relevance will be tested? Concepts are needed to place limits on the information that qualifies for inclusion in financial statements or that even can be called a part of financial reporting. The universe of financial information is only a part of the larger universe of information reported by an enterprise. Financial accounting needs some bounds; objectives first, and concepts second, provide those bounds.

Materiality, timeliness, and verifiability are qualities essentially independent from concepts, because they concern properties of data relating to cost of preparation and user perceptions of satisfaction. Materiality, for example, concerns ranges of acceptable deviations. Whereas relevance concerns types of data or measurement—fitness for purpose—materiality concerns aberrations in or omissions of data otherwise determined to be helpful. (Materiality is discussed more fully in the next section of this chapter.)

Comparability and consistency are another class of qualities. If objectives and concepts are in place and operating, comparability and consistency should result— they are qualities inherent in the building blocks.

Because guidelines concerning the qualities of data can enhance the observance of concepts and the achievement of objectives, qualities should be identified and made a part of the total framework. At the same time, it should be recognized that an idea, which is essentially an abstraction, if made too concrete, ceases to be a concept or guideline and becomes a rule. There is no room for a rule in a conceptual framework.

In May 1980 the FASB issued Statement of Financial Accounting Concepts No. 2, *Qualitative Characteristics of Accounting Information* (AC 1220). The scope of the statement is broad, as would be expected of a concepts document; the hierarchy of qualities in SFAC 2 is shown in Figure 2.2. However described and ordered, there is a trade-off between relevance and reliability; there are conflicts in the features underlying these two criteria, which can be resolved only by balancing.

Materiality

Note that in Figure 2.2 materiality underlies all the characteristics. Though materiality is a quality existing quite apart from concept, it is so frequently mentioned as a concept in any discussion of financial accounting and reporting that some slight digression from this chapter's conceptual track is warranted.

If all events and balances were financially measurable with absolute precision and no errors were made in summarizing voluminous transactions into financial statements, then the financial statement amounts would be precisely stated. And if every possible qualitative disclosure were to be given along with those amounts, that combination would then be complete in the literal sense. But absolute precision in financial accounting and reporting is unattainable even if attempted.

The FASB discussion memorandum on materiality (FASB, 1975b) explored the subject from the following perspectives:

> Most presentations of financial information are the result of a process in which a large volume of data regarding the activities of an enterprise is analyzed, measured, recorded, classified, accumulated, and reported. Although the reported results of the accounting process may give the appearance of precision, accounting measurement does not possess the degree of precision associated with disciplines such as mathematics and engineering. Exact measurement, classification, and aggregation of the results of the large number of transactions representing the economic activities of an enterprise are rarely possible due to the "continuity, complexity, uncertainty, and joint nature of results inherent in economic activity." Accordingly, many aspects of an enterprise's economic activities must be estimated. [p. 6, quoting from APB Statement 4; AC 1025.10]
>
> Throughout the accounting process, decisions must be made involving not only estimates regarding the economic activities accounted for but also regarding the form and content of financial presentations. These decisions are based on the judgments of those responsible for such presentations and their advisers. If presentations of financial information are to be prepared economically on a timely basis and presented in a concise, intelligible form, the concept of materiality is crucial. Without such a concept, a great deal of time might be spent during the accounting process considering insignificant matters and the resulting financial presentations might contain data that tended to obscure more significant information. It is in this context that the concept of materiality is indispensable as well as pervasive. [p. 6]

If absolute precision is unattainable, how much leeway is permissible? There is no final answer, although the question has been raised in every authoritative pronouncement on accounting since the first one by the CAP in 1939. This stated:

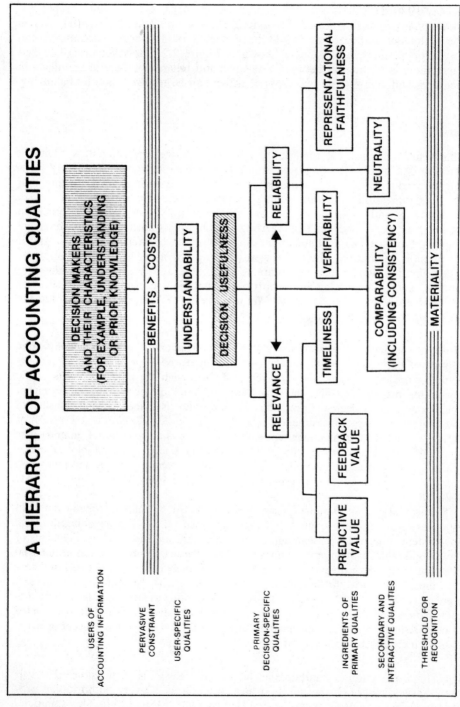

FIGURE 2.2   A HIERARCHY OF ACCOUNTING QUALITIES
Source: SFAC 2 (AC 1220.32).

The committee contemplates that its pronouncements will have application only to items large enough to be material and significant in the relative circumstances. It considers items of little or no consequence may be dealt with as expediency may suggest. [American Institute of Accountants, 1939a, p. 3]

"Large enough" suggests a quantitative limit, and in many respects the earlier materiality judgments were made within percentage ranges of appropriate bases. For example, some have said that if the enterprise's accounting and control process yields an earnings result within 10% of the "correct" amount, the result is fairly presented in all material respects. But there are many perceptions of the appropriate percentages and interrelationships, and there often is no agreement on the limits in specific situations.

The SEC has published percentage limits covering some matters, but they cannot be considered complete in and of themselves. This leads to an even more subjective facet of materiality—are some matters so important to financial statement users that virtually no leeway should be tolerated? Some observers have said that failure to disclose an illegal payment of $10,000 in a billion-dollar corporation is an omission of a material fact. If anything can be said about materiality perceptions in current practice it is that the quantitative leeway is ever-narrowing and the qualitative factors pointing to materiality are proliferating.

Materiality was on the FASB's early agenda because of the clamor for clarification that carried over from APB days. The FASB has now incorporated the completion of the materiality project into the conceptual framework by including it within the qualitative characteristics statement. Thus, the original FASB effort was not totally in vain, since the detailed exploration in the discussion memorandum has formed the basis for inclusion in the statement and has gone a long way in improving understanding of a complex subject. Indeed, better understanding of materiality may in itself serve the general need.

Applying Concepts

How could the concepts proposed by the FASB and discussed in this chapter have helped standard-setting groups over the years? Concepts, being neither rules nor standards, give no pat answers. They do, however, furnish a place to stand in deliberating standards, confining the things argued about and providing a better chance for order and fulfillment of financial reporting objectives.

Where asset considerations are involved, the steps in an analytical process might be described this way:

1. Is there an asset, i.e., is there (a) an expected future benefit (or service) that the enterprise can (b) exclusively claim as a result of (c) a transaction or an event that has occurred?
2. What measure of the asset should be used?
3. What is the event that triggers recording?
4. Is the uncertainty about the benefit or its measure so significant that the asset should not be included in financial statements?

Look for the *future benefit;* be sure there is an *exclusive claim* to the benefit; identify the *event* that gave rise to the exclusive claim; assess the *uncertainty* of realizing the benefit—and then decide on all those bases whether to record.

Where liability considerations are present, the steps could be described thus:

1. Is there a liability, i.e., is there (a) an obligation (equitable or otherwise) to others not acting as owners to (b) transfer assets as (c) a result of a past transaction, event, or circumstance?
2. What measure of the liability should be used?
3. What is the event triggering the recording?
4. Is the uncertainty about the obligation or its measure so great that the obligation should not be reported as an obligation?[2]

Look for the *obligation* (don't be too legalistic, because economic considerations may override) to *transfer* assets; identify the *event* that gave rise to the obligation; assess the *probability* and *estimability* of having to transfer assets—and then decide on all those bases whether to record.

For an indication of how sharper concepts aid specific standard setting, consider two brief examples discussed more thoroughly in other chapters: leases (Chapter 23) and casualty insurance reserves (Chapter 38).

Leases. For over 15 years, accounting for leases captured the attention of standard setters. The APB first focused on lessee accounting in 1964 and, after a span of some years, dealt separately with lessor accounting. The FASB issued a statement on accounting by both lessors and lessees in 1976. First the focus was on lessee liabilities and, incidentally, expenses; then it switched to lessor assets, mainly revenues. Finally the focus reached all of the financial statement elements of the two principal parties—lessee and lessor—on a coordinated basis.

Would accounting for leases today have been different if asset and liability concepts had been applied earlier? It might or might not, for reasons to be noted later, but one thing is certain: resolution of the problem would have suffered fewer false starts if those concepts had been recognized and applied as the matter was being considered.

Two views of leases are noted in SFAS 13, *Accounting for Leases* (AC 4053). The first is that "a lease that transfers substantially all of the benefits and risks incident to ownership of property should be accounted for as the acquisition of an asset and the incurrence of an obligation by the lessee and as a sale or financing by the lessor" (AC 4053.060). The second view states that "regardless of whether substantially all the benefits and risks of ownership are transferred, a lease, in transferring for its term the right to use property, gives rise to the acquisition of an asset and the incurrence of an obligation by the lessee" (AC 4053.063).

The first of those views emphasizes the physical property as the asset; the second emphasizes the services provided by the property, the benefits from use. Both views

---

[2] The recognition of liabilities at a lower level of reliability than for assets probably can be justified, since reaction to adverse surprises is more intense than to pleasant surprises. Conservatism, however, has no further conceptual basis. The proper aim is neutrality—neither conservatism nor liberalism—lest the interest of one group of investors or creditors—selling, holding, or buying—become unduly biased.

are compatible with the proposed concepts of assets and liabilities, the first by reference to substantially all the benefits and risks inherent in ownership, the second by reference to the right to use property. The second view focuses on services from use and recognizes that the total services of, or benefits produced by, a physical resource can be divided among several parties, a lease being one way of so dividing. The first view, however, is an all-or-nothing view—a physical asset is an asset because of its wholeness; it is an asset to one party, not several. Early on, the concepts would have settled the arguments about assets and liabilities with respect to leases. The standard of accounting for leases would then have been developed on the basis of relevance of information, reliability of measurement, and cost of assembling or compiling data.

Once accounting for leases had been developed this far, if a line were needed between leases to be capitalized and those to be treated as operating leases, it would have been drawn on grounds of practicality, not on ever-elusive concepts aimed at distinguishing the two.

Catastrophe Reserves. The liability concept came into play in resolving the accounting for catastrophe reserves of casualty insurance companies. In SFAS 5 (AC 4311) the FASB met head-on a long-standing simmering issue that by mid-1975 had resulted in charges to income for "future losses" of various kinds. Potential losses from catastrophes of the type covered by casualty insurance (hurricanes, floods, and the like) had come to be recognized as liabilities by a number of insurance companies. The FASB saw no conceptual problem with loss provisions for catastrophes that might occur within the terms of effective insurance policies, but concluded that the uncertainty of timing and amount of losses would not justify their recognition; the loss prospects did not appear to pass necessary tests of probability and estimability.

The substantive conceptual issue that the FASB faced concerned catastrophes that might occur after the end of the term of existing policies—catastrophes not covered by existing contracts. The FASB concluded that the characteristics of a liability were not present: there was no obligation to an outside party stemming from a past event or transaction; no outside party or class of parties could be identified that, based on existing relations, would have a reasonable basis for sustaining a claim against the insurance company. A new policy would have to be written (or an old one renewed) before a party could be identified who could sustain a claim. The liability tests were not met, and accordingly, the provision did not qualify for admission to financial statements.

Costs as Assets. Perhaps one of the most difficult classes of assets to analyze conceptually is that of costs of developing new business, training employees, moving, and similar activities, for which no separable economic resource can be identified. The discussion here focuses on concepts; the state of the art in accounting for "near-assets" is covered in Chapter 21. The difficulty relates to the notion of an asset as a resource, a potential service, or a future benefit with cash-flow prospects.

Moving, training, and business getting are activities not ordinarily perceived as resources, and accordingly, their costs are not deferrable simply on the plausibility that a company would not incur them without perceiving a benefit. Surely a cost is not per se an asset, although the presumption is not unreasonable that a cost is willingly incurred only if an asset (perhaps of very short life) is received in return.

But a cost incurred to obviate a future cash outflow otherwise required or to obtain benefits from other assets surely is a benefit even though a separable resource cannot be identified. With that thought in mind, the question of accounting for a cost incurred to move a plant to another location becomes one of identifying the asset, if any, to which the moving cost should be attached.

The reasons for the move need analysis. Consider three possibilities: (1) a move made primarily because of a local subsidy in the form of either a bargain purchase of a facility or reduced taxes for a specified period; (2) a move made to take advantage of a labor supply that, after adequate training, would result in relatively low wage rates, even after considering the cost of the move and training; (3) a move made to get out from under onerous local laws concerning environmental restraints.

One helpful way to view the accounting for the cost of moving is to test the results against the accounting for an enterprise that enjoys the same benefits but did not have to move to realize them. If one has an asset, surely the other one has; if one incurred a moving cost to acquire the asset and the other did not, one may have an amount to record, the other may not. For the three cases:

1. *As to the move made to take advantage of a local subsidy,* the asset is either the facility acquired at a bargain price or prepayment of an item in lieu of taxes. There is nothing in the asset concept that rules out recognition of moving costs as an asset in these situations.

2. *As to the move made to obtain access to certain labor skills,* the asset is a labor skill. The cost of the move and of training may well be part of the cost, paid in advance, of the service to the enterprise. A right to the benefits deriving from the talent or skill of people surely qualifies as an asset, and it ordinarily has a cost. There is nothing in the asset concept that proscribes recognition of these costs as an asset.

3. *As to the move to get out from under an onerous local law,* escaping a bad situation is not in itself an asset, despite its advantage. There is nothing in the asset concept that views relief from a bad situation as an asset, unless it obviates obligations otherwise requiring cash outflows.

In the above cases, especially the first two, considerations other than the asset concept would determine whether the asset is recordable. Without being definitive, some of these moves will give rise to recordable assets; some moving costs, therefore, are part of asset acquisition cost.

The activity of business getting may lead to asset recognition; the benefit may be enhancement of the opportunity to realize benefits from other assets. Again the asset concept, by itself, does not rule out asset recognition, but business getting may be the type of activity for which uncertainty as to the amount and timing of enhanced benefits rules out recognition on grounds of measurement unreliability.

The question of whether costs are assets is left with this methodology:

1. Determine the reason for incurring the cost.
2. Determine whether the cost can be identified with a previously recorded asset or with a recordable asset of any kind. The three asset tests should be applied in making this determination.

3. Assess the uncertainty of future benefits and their measurability to determine whether an asset identifiable from the first two steps meets the test for recording.

As a general observation, the word *cost* is often in the reporting caption of assets that are not exchangeable, or for which there is not a separable resource. Not very much has been done to describe assets that are not exchangeable individually but that enhance benefits obtainable from other assets—too often these assets have been characterized as if the cost itself were the asset.

Deferred Obligations as Liabilities. The liability facet of the cost question arises most often in connection with deferred maintenance for depreciable assets. Should the concept allow an expense and a liability on the financial statements if an activity, deemed ordinary in the conduct of the business, has been postponed and no commitment has been made to an outside party for performance of the activity? The liability concept speaks of an obligation to an outside party and is interpreted to mean that an event or circumstance has occurred that gives an outside party a basis for a claim that probably could be sustained. The liability concept also distinguishes between a commitment and a postponed commitment.

The issue of accounting for deferred repairs of a depreciable asset often intertwines with depreciation accounting. Accounting for major repairs should be compatible. A reserve for repairs, however, no more meets the liability test than a reserve for maintenance or other unperformed or uncommitted activities the timing of which may be discretionary.

THE MANY ROLES OF EARNINGS

Consider the following assertions: Earnings are the fruition of assets. Earnings measure performance. Earnings are the return on investment. Earnings are the remainder after provision has been made for maintaining enterprise capital. Capital has been maintained if the enterprise's operating capacity has been maintained (the *physical capital concept*). Capital has been maintained if value in money terms (historical cost, current cost, fair value, or other) has been maintained (the *financial capital concept*). Capital has been maintained only if recognition is given to changes in purchasing power of the monetary unit. There are net earnings, operating earnings, normal earnings, controllable earnings, sustainable earnings, distributable earnings.

A heterogeneous lot, to say the least. Are all of these assertions true? There are, of course, some very fundamental questions implicit in this array of notions about earnings, notions that are even difficult to classify. But there are at least three classes of issues:

1. *What is the nature of capital to be maintained in measuring earnings?* Whether capital is financial or physical is left untouched here. The FASB has postponed a decision on this very fundamental matter. A decision on capital maintenance must correlate to a decision on earnings. These decisions must be made early to get on with formulation of workable concepts.

2. *Should earnings through the "bottom line" include all of the earnings effects of events of the period and, if so, how should they be displayed?* This issue is not explored here, but is dealt with in Chapters 3 and 7. At present, the requirement is to show all current-period income effects in the same statement, the earnings statement, with rather limited sorting of kinds of effects. It may take a significant change in the display of earnings to furnish the information sought about the performance of an enterprise. Even display in several statements is a possibility, as partitioning might best communicate relations between earnings and enterprise financing, uncertainty, nearness to cash, recurrence, and all the other aspects of earnings sometimes comprehended in what is termed "quality of earnings." Attempting to unscramble those "qualities" is a venture worth considering.

3. *Should earnings and earnings determination be affected by liquidity or financing constraints?* This issue intertwines with notions of capital maintenance, but also extends beyond it. Ideas about displaying income deemed to be distributable or sustainable have a financing focus. But income determination and enterprise financing should not be confused. While liquidity considerations and information needs about financing requirements and constraints are important and should be given a prominent place in financial reporting, they are not determinants of income. There is something intrinsically wrong with the notion that what income is and how it is measured depends on needs for funds. There is nothing wrong with a display of earnings that focuses on liquidity, funds flows, and perception of needs for funds; indeed, that may be a beneficial advance in reporting. Proposals that cause income determination to depend in part on how an enterprise is leveraged, or on its debt-to-equity ratio, miss the mark. Those matters would be better considered in the FASB's project on liquidity and funds flow.

EPILOGUE

There is no place to end a discussion of conceptual matters, any more than there is a place to begin. But begin and end one must. Concepts are essential to order in financial reporting. Order and freedom are in a sense opposites but, paradoxically, are also dependent, because lack of order suppresses freedom. Without concepts to temper and control actions, freedom runs the risk of disorder and ultimate self-destruction.

Are the conceptual conclusions about assets, liabilities, expenses, revenues, and cost unreasonably inflexible? It should be remembered that they grow out of the concept that earnings are the fruition of assets and that period earnings have the same nature as lifetime earnings. A conceptual approach to accounting for earnings that builds on a notion different from asset fruition has not been constructed or proposed.

Many have said that earnings should not be distorted. In fact, accountants probably universally object to earnings distortion. But while some say distortion is gauged in relation to departure from the notion of asset fruition, others say distortion results from mismatching revenues and expenses. Because assets are basic, that is a distinction without a difference.

This issue—the definition of earnings—needs resolution not so much to solve current problems, but more to set the direction for future financial reporting. Unresolved, it leaves the door open to expanding alternatives. Is income asset fruition, or is it an indicator or index? If the latter, the charting of the conceptual framework for financial accounting and reporting has not yet begun.

In the final analysis, concern about the need for concepts depends on the role of financial reporting within the capital markets in the allocation of resources, in the operation of organized security markets, plus in all private investing and lending transactions. Financial reporting presumably has a bearing on these markets, including the public markets, even given some of the hypotheses based on stronger forms of the efficient market theory (Chapter 47).

One possible role for financial reporting is to assist those making decisions in these markets. Another is to attempt to influence the markets in certain ways. One role tries to be neutral, the other advocates; one helps those doing the allocating, the other allocates.

If the role is to assist others who make decisions affecting allocation of resources, as seems highly useful, the trick is to report in a way that does not influence behavior in a predetermined manner. There is no ultimate truth or reality to report. Financial reporting necessarily concerns choices of data based on perceptions of usefulness. The conceptual framework serves to make those choices purposeful and evenhanded.

SUGGESTED READING

AICPA. *Objectives of Financial Statements.* New York, 1973. This is the final report of the Study Group on Objectives of Financial Statements.

Cramer, Joe, and Sorter, George, eds. *Objectives of Financial Statements.* Volume 2. New York: AICPA, 1974. This volume contains selected papers considered by the Study Group on Objectives of Financial Statements.

Canning, John. *The Economics of Accountancy.* New York: Ronald Press, 1929. Republished by Arno Press, New York, 1978. Canning proceeded with great skill, and with considerable foresight of a growing need, to deduce the fundamentals underlying the accounting practices of his day. Even today the problem of identifying concepts continues to confuse the dialogue among sophisticated students of accounting.

APPENDIX 2   FASB PUBLICATIONS CONCERNING THE CONCEPTUAL FRAMEWORK

Discussion Memoranda

The FASB has published the following discussion memoranda (DM) on different components of the conceptual framework project in order to catalog the various issues, viewpoints, and implications surrounding the project. In general, DM are neutral; no one point of view is favored over others. The FASB uses DM to solicit written comments and recommendations from those interested in matters of financial accounting and reporting.

1. *Reporting the Effects of General Price-Level Changes in Financial Statements.* 1974.
2. *Conceptual Framework for Accounting and Reporting: Consideration of the Report of the Study Group on the Objectives of Financial Statements.* 1974.
3. *Criteria for Determining Materiality.* 1975.
4. *Conceptual Framework for Accounting and Reporting: Elements of Financial Statements and Their Measurement.* 1976.
5. *Reporting Earnings.* 1979.

Other FASB Publications

1. *Tentative Conclusions on Objectives of Financial Statements of Business Enterprises.* 1976. The FASB's initial conclusions resulting from its consideration of responses to the 1974 discussion memorandum.
2. *Scope and Implications of the Conceptual Framework Project.* 1976. A booklet summarizing the 1974 discussion memorandum and the Board's tentative conclusions.
3. *Exposure Draft on Objectives of Financial Reporting and Elements of Financial Statements of Business Enterprises.* 1977. A proposed statement of financial accounting concepts, this exposure draft reflected the FASB's conclusions on the objectives and elements phases of the conceptual framework project and solicited comments. After evaluating the responses, the Board determined that its conclusions regarding elements required modification and a second exposure draft was issued.
4. *Exposure Draft (Revised) on Elements of Financial Statements of Business Enterprises.* 1979. A proposed statement of financial accounting concepts, this exposure draft reflects the Board's conclusions regarding elements of financial statements and solicits comments on those conclusions.
5. *Exposure Draft on Qualitative Characteristics: Criteria for Selecting and Evaluating Financial Accounting and Reporting Policies.* 1979. This exposure draft provides guidance in choosing the one accounting and reporting alternative that produces the most useful information for decision-making purposes. This draft incorporates the materiality project (see Discussion Memoranda above).
6. *Exposure Draft on Financial Reporting and Changing Prices: Specialized Assets.* 1980. This exposure draft deals with applying the current cost measurement requirements of SFAS 33 to timber, mineral ore, oil and gas reserves, and income-producing real estate.

Final Releases

1. Statement of Financial Accounting Concepts No. 1, *Objectives of Financial Reporting by Business Enterprises.* 1978. This is a final statement of the Board's conclusions regarding financial reporting objectives and the first completed phase of the conceptual framework. This statement of concepts and others to follow will guide the Board in developing standards of financial accounting and reporting.
2. Statement of Financial Accounting Concepts No. 2, *Qualitative Characteristics of Accounting Information.* 1980. This is a final statement of the Board's views about properties of financial information to be reported.
3. Statement of Financial Accounting Standards No. 33, *Financial Reporting and Changing Prices.* 1979. This statement requires larger companies to supplement their historical cost financial statements with disclosures of the effects of changing prices and values. The statement was proposed in a 1978 exposure draft and a 1979 supplement.

3

The Basic Financial Statements

David Solomons

COMMUNICATING FINANCIAL INFORMATION

Though an enterprise can communicate financial information by means other than its basic external financial statements, those statements are the most widely used and the most comprehensive means of conveying such information. Whether the organization in question is a sole proprietorship, a partnership, a corporation, an association, a charitable group, or a governmental unit, whether it has profit-seeking or not-for-profit objectives, whether it is regulated or unregulated, it is primarily through its financial statements that it will report on its affairs. The nature and circumstances of the enterprise determine to whom it will report. It must always report to its owners, but it may also need to report to its employees, to certain creditors, to regulatory agencies, to taxation authorities, or to other constituents.

Different users of financial statements have different needs, and the selection of the information to be presented and the form of presentation must be adapted to meet those needs as fully as possible. Nevertheless, a general purpose form of statement has been developed and is widely used. It is addressed primarily to the needs of investors and creditors, who are the principal users of financial statements, but it goes a long way toward meeting the needs of others as well. This chapter will describe these general purpose statements, referred to as *basic financial statements,* and will review important types of variations therein.

The typical accounting entity is a profit-seeking enterprise, with its owners organized as a corporation; therefore, the illustrations used in this chapter pertain to corporations. However, other kinds of organizations have peculiar reporting problems and reflect them in the form and content of their statements. Other chapters in this *Handbook* are concerned with some of those organizations (e.g., partnerships in Chapter 27, governmental units in Chapter 34, not-for-profit entities in Chapter 35, and regulated industries in Chapter 36); thus their special reporting problems will not be discussed here. Since most accounting problems are common to a wide spectrum of enterprises, most of the following discussion, even when focused on business corporations, should be relevant to other enterprises as well.

Before discussing basic financial statements as they now are, one should recognize that their evolution happens quickly. Several FASB projects in process are mentioned throughout this chapter, but one of overriding significance bears mention here. In a May 1980 release, *Invitation to Comment on Financial Statements and Other Means of Financial Reporting,* the FASB considered the boundaries of financial statements, which are seen as part of the broad spectrum of information used in investment, credit, and similar decisions. Figure 3.1 displays the various sections of the information spectrum.

BASIC FINANCIAL STATEMENTS

The basic financial statements to be discussed here comprise four distinct but interrelated statements:

1. The balance sheet or statement of financial position,
2. The income statement or statement of earnings,
3. The statement of retained earnings or accumulated earnings, and
4. The statement of changes in financial position.

The purpose of the *balance sheet* (Figure 3.2) is to show the financial position of the enterprise at a particular moment of time in terms of its economic resources

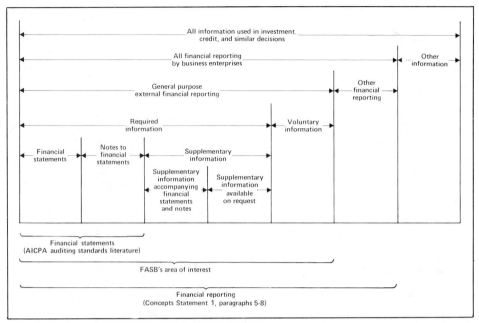

FIGURE 3.1 INFORMATION SPECTRUM

SOURCE: FASB, *Invitation to Comment on Financial Statements and Other Means of Financial Reporting* (Stamford, Conn., 1980), p. 2.

(assets), its economic obligations (liabilities), and the residual claims of its owners (the owners' equity). Assets and liabilities are usually shown in the order of their liquidity, with the most current shown first. By definition the total amount of owners' equity equals the total amount of assets less the total amount of liabilities.

The purpose of the *income statement* (Figure 3.3) is to show the results of operations for a given period of time. The significant types of income and expense are shown. The difference between income and expense, usually measured on the accrual basis of accounting, is the amount by which owners' equity changes as a result of the enterprise's operations.

The *statement of retained earnings* shows the increases and decreases in earnings retained by the company over a given period of time. These earnings usually include net income from operations and dividends declared or paid. Sometimes this statement is combined with the income statement. When changes in other capital accounts occur, the statement of retained earnings may be expanded into a *statement of stockholders' equity,* as shown in Figure 3.4.

The purpose of the *statement of changes in financial position* (Figure 3.5) is to show in one statement the sources and uses of the funds of the enterprise over a given period of time. Funds are usually defined as either cash or working capital.

Because three of the basic statements describe financial activity for the same period—that is, the period of time between the dates of two balance sheets—key figures reported in one statement correspond to balances included in the others.

Consolidated Balance Sheets | May 31

	1979	1978
	(In thousands)	
Assets		
Current assets:		
Cash (Note 5)	$ 8,415	$ 16,589
Marketable securities, at cost (approximates market)	29,294	20,060
Receivables, less allowance for doubtful accounts of $6.4 million and $6.1 million, respectively	274,352	236,848
Inventories (Note 3)	405,596	245,804
Advances on purchases	156,452	145,823
Prepaid expenses	32,453	15,466
Total current assets	906,562	680,590
Property, plant and equipment, net (Notes 4, 6 and 7):		
Parent company and nonrestaurant subsidiaries	310,823	176,352
Restaurant subsidiaries	430,693	310,157
	741,516	486,509
Net investment in direct financing leases (Note 7)	85,755	55,274
Intangibles	26,099	22,614
Investments and other assets	44,551	37,795
	$1,804,483	$1,282,782
Liabilities and Stockholders' Equity		
Current liabilities:		
Notes payable (Note 5)	$ 18,026	$ 18,582
Trade accounts payable	288,963	196,412
Advances on sales	133,471	121,764
Accrued liabilities	112,094	74,697
Taxes on income	49,645	31,567
Current portion of long-term debt	22,407	13,673
Total current liabilities	624,606	456,695
Long-term debt, noncurrent portion (Notes 6 and 7):		
Parent company and nonrestaurant subsidiaries	186,692	78,511
Restaurant subsidiaries (not guaranteed by The Pillsbury Company)	322,475	219,494
	509,167	298,005
Deferred taxes on income	75,387	62,945
Other deferrals	12,425	7,837
Stockholders' equity (Notes 1, 6 and 8):		
Preferred stock, without par value, authorized 500,000 shares, no shares issued		
Common stock, without par value, authorized 40,000,000 shares, issued 19,937,685 shares and 17,520,693 shares, respectively	212,187	131,366
Accumulated earnings retained and used in the business	383,423	326,908
Common stock in treasury at cost, 353,312 shares and 25,294 shares, respectively	(12,712)	(974)
Total stockholders' equity	582,898	457,300
	$1,804,483	$1,282,782

See Summary of Significant Accounting Policies and Notes to Consolidated Financial Statements.

FIGURE 3.2 SAMPLE BALANCE SHEET
SOURCE: The Pillsbury Company, 1979 Annual Report.

In other words, the four basic financial statements *articulate*. For example, in Figure 3.3, the net earnings reported in the 1979 earnings statement ($83,471,000) equal the amount of change in accumulated earnings from the enterprise's operations, as shown in the third column of the statement of stockholders' equity (Figure 3.4). When those net earnings are in turn adjusted for depreciation and other

Consolidated Statements of Earnings		Year ended May 31	
		1979	1978
		(In thousands except per share amounts)	
Net sales		**$2,165,982**	$1,704,914
Costs and expenses:			
Cost of sales		**1,538,236**	1,207,119
Selling, general and administrative expenses		**440,938**	336,667
Interest expense, net (Note 6)		**26,467**	18,964
		2,005,641	1,562,750
Earnings before taxes on income		**160,341**	142,164
Taxes on income (Note 9)		**76,870**	70,830
Earnings from continuing businesses		**83,471**	71,334
Gain on disposition of discontinued business,			
net of income tax of $1.2 million (Note 1)			1,179
Net earnings		**$ 83,471**	$ 72,513
Average number of shares outstanding		**18,078**	17,535
Earnings per share:			
Continuing businesses		**$4.62**	$4.07
Discontinued business			.07
Net earnings		**$4.62**	$4.14

See Summary of Significant Accounting Policies and Notes to Consolidated Financial Statements.

FIGURE 3.3   SAMPLE INCOME STATEMENT
SOURCE: The Pillsbury Company, 1979 Annual Report.

items not requiring use of working capital, the total ($152,453,000) equals the amount of change in financial position as a result of operations. (See Figure 3.5, first column. Note that funds are here defined as working capital.) The beginning and ending balances in the statement of stockholders' equity equal the corresponding balances in the stockholders' equity section in the balance sheets. The increase in working capital ($58,061,000) reported in the statement of changes in financial position equals the increase in the net current asset position (current assets less current liabilities) between the 1978 and 1979 balance sheets. Each of these basic financial statements is described further later in this chapter.

The footnotes and other supplementary information applicable to the statements in Figures 3.2 through 3.5 have not been reproduced here, but it must be noted that *footnotes* are an integral part of a complete set of financial statements. Certain information may be presented in either the main body of a statement or in the footnotes to it. An example is accumulated depreciation, which is commonly shown in the balance sheet as a deduction from the cost of property assets. An equally acceptable presentation is to show on the balance sheet only a net carrying amount for property, plant, and equipment (as in Figure 3.2) and to disclose accumulated depreciation in the footnotes. (Chapter 4 discusses the use of financial disclosures outside the tabular financial statements.)

Consolidated Statements of Stockholders' Equity

	Common shares outstanding	Common stock	Accumulated earnings	Treasury stock
		(In thousands)		
Balances at May 31, 1977	17,496	$130,843	$276,361	$ (366)
Net earnings			72,513	
Dividends declared:				
On common stock			(21,333)	
By pooled company prior to acquisition			(55)	
Change in year end of pooled company			(255)	
Stock issued for purchase of restaurant franchise	15	274		280
Stock issued under stock option plans	25	249	(323)	656
Purchase of treasury stock	(41)			(1,544)
Balances at May 31, 1978	17,495	131,366	326,908	(974)
Net earnings			83,471	
Dividends declared on common stock			(26,371)	
Stock issued for purchased companies	2,411	80,603		
Stock issued under stock option and performance unit plans	48	218	(585)	1,613
Purchase of treasury stock	(370)			(13,351)
Balances at May 31, 1979	19,584	$212,187	$383,423	$(12,712)

See Summary of Significant Accounting Policies and Notes to Consolidated Financial Statements.

FIGURE 3.4   SAMPLE STOCKHOLDERS' EQUITY STATEMENT
SOURCE: The Pillsbury Company, 1979 Annual Report.

Another integral part of published financial statements is the *auditor's report,* which states the auditor's opinion as to whether the statements are fairly presented in conformity with generally accepted accounting principles. See Chapter 16 for a complete discussion of the auditor's report.

Regulatory agencies such as the SEC may require disclosure of summarized financial information, or such information may be provided because it is useful to readers in interpreting financial statements (e.g., a ten-year summary of key figures, in an annual report). Generally, this information is presented outside the basic financial statements and is thus beyond the scope of this chapter. (See Chapter 4.)

PRINCIPLES OF FINANCIAL STATEMENT PRESENTATION

APB Statement 4, *Basic Concepts and Accounting Principles Underlying Financial Statements of Business Enterprises,* initially set forth (in paragraphs 191 to 201) 11 principles of financial statement presentation. Subsequently, APB 19 (AC 2021), which requires a statement of changes in financial position for profit-

Consolidated Statements of Changes in Financial Position	Year ended May 31	
	1979	1978
	(In thousands)	
Sources of working capital:		
Operations of continuing businesses:		
Earnings	**$ 83,471**	$ 71,334
Depreciation and amortization (Note 4)	**56,718**	46,091
Deferred taxes on income	**12,264**	11,066
Other		(193)
Total from continuing businesses	**152,453**	128,298
Gain on disposition of discontinued business (Note 1)		1,179
Total from operations	**152,453**	129,477
Increase in long-term debt	**154,751**	63,270
Disposals of property, plant and equipment	**13,074**	13,764
Transfer of property to direct financing leases	**35,056**	18,185
Current maturities of direct financing leases	**4,973**	2,980
Issuance of common stock for purchased companies	**80,603**	554
Issuance of common stock, other	**1,246**	582
Other, net	**521**	1,186
	442,677	229,998
Uses of working capital:		
Additions to property, plant and equipment	**230,257**	134,076
Transfer of property to direct financing leases	**35,056**	18,185
Cash dividends declared	**26,371**	21,388
Current maturities and retirements of long-term debt	**24,562**	32,452
Noncurrent net assets of purchased companies at time of acquisition (Note 1)	**54,529**	
Change in investments and other assets, net	**490**	15,027
Purchase of treasury stock	**13,351**	1,544
	384,616	222,672
Increase in working capital	**$ 58,061**	$ 7,326
Increase (decrease) in components of working capital (Note 1):		
Cash and marketable securities	**$ 1,060**	$ (51,150)
Receivables	**37,504**	45,103
Inventories	**159,792**	69,489
Other current assets	**27,616**	(7,794)
Notes payable and current portion of long-term debt	**(8,178)**	(6,259)
Accounts payable and accrued liabilities	**(141,655)**	(33,733)
Taxes on income	**(18,078)**	(8,330)
	$ 58,061	$ 7,326

See Summary of Significant Accounting Policies and Notes to Consolidated Financial Statements.

FIGURE 3.5 SAMPLE STATEMENT OF CHANGES IN FINANCIAL POSITION
SOURCE: The Pillsbury Company, 1979 Annual Report.

oriented business enterprises, increased the number of principles to 12. These are reproduced below (taken from AC 1027.17 through 1027.28, and listed in the same order), with a few modifications to conform to developments since October 1970, the issue date of Statement 4. To provide an overview, all 12 principles are listed; however, this chapter does not extensively deal with certain principles covered elsewhere as indicated by chapter references. The 12 principles are

1. *Basic financial statements.* A balance sheet, a statement of income, a statement of changes in retained earnings, a statement of changes in financial position, disclosure

of changes in other categories of stockholders' equity, descriptions of accounting policies, and related notes are the minimum presentation elements required to present fairly the financial position and results of operations of an enterprise in conformity with generally accepted accounting principles.

2. *Complete balance sheet.* The balance sheet or statement of financial position should include and properly describe all assets, liabilities, and classes of owners' equity as defined by generally accepted accounting principles.

3. *Complete income statement.* The income statement of a period should include and properly describe all revenue and expenses as defined by generally accepted accounting principles.

4. *Complete statement of changes in financial position.* The statement of changes in financial position of a period should include and properly describe all important aspects of the company's financing and investing activities.

5. *Accounting period.* The basic time period for which financial statements are presented is one year; interim financial statements (Chapter 5) are commonly presented for periods of less than a year.

6. *Consolidated financial statements.* Consolidated financial statements (Chapter 31) are presumed to be more meaningful than the separate statements of the component legal entities. Consolidated statements are usually necessary for fair presentation in conformity with generally accepted accounting principles if one of the enterprises in a group directly or indirectly owns over 50% of the outstanding voting stock of the other enterprises.

7. *Equity basis.* Unconsolidated subsidiaries, and investments in 50% or less of the voting stock of companies in which the investors have the ability to exercise significant influence over investees, should be presented on the equity basis (Chapter 21).

8. *Translation of foreign balances.* Financial information about the foreign operations of U.S. enterprises should be translated into U.S. dollars by the use of conventional translation procedures (Chapter 31) that involve foreign exchange rates.

9. *Classification and segregation.* Separate disclosure of the important components of the financial statements is presumed to make the information more useful. Examples in the income statement are sales or other sources of revenue, cost of sales, depreciation, selling and administrative expenses, interest expense, and income taxes. Examples in the balance sheet are cash, receivables, inventories, plant and equipment, payables, and categories of owners' equity.

   a. *Working capital.* Disclosure of components of working capital (current assets less current liabilities) is presumed to be useful in manufacturing, trading, and some service enterprises. Current assets and current liabilities are distinguished from other assets and liabilities.

   b. *Offsetting.* Assets and liabilities in the balance sheet should not be offset unless a legal right of setoff exists.

   c. *Gains and losses.* Revenue and expenses from other than sales of products, merchandise, or services may be separated from other revenue and expenses, and the net effects disclosed as gains or losses.

   d. *Extraordinary items.* Extraordinary gains and losses should be presented separately from other revenue and expenses in the income statement.

   e. *Net income.* The net income of an enterprise for a period should be separately disclosed and clearly identified in the income statement.

10. *Other disclosures.* In addition to informative classifications and segregation of data, financial statements should disclose all additional information that is necessary for fair presentation in conformity with generally accepted accounting principles. (Remainder of AC 1027.26 is omitted as it deals principally with the topic treated in Chapter 4.)

11. *Form of financial statement presentation.* No particular form of financial statements is presumed better than all others for all purposes, and several forms are used.

12. *Earnings per share.* Earnings per share information (Chapter 26) is most useful when furnished in conjunction with net income and its components and should be disclosed on the face of the income statement.

Although APB Statement 4 was issued in 1970, it still is designated by the FASB as a pronouncement that "will continue to serve [its] intended purpose—to describe objectives and concepts underlying standards and practices existing before the issuance of this Statement [SFAC 1]" (AC 1210.03). The Board's conceptual framework project, which has a multitude of subprojects (see Chapter 2) has not yet resulted in any conclusion about elements of financial statements and their recognition, measurement, and display (AC 1210, headnote preceding AC 1210.01), and until it does so, APB Statement 4 will continue to apply.

QUALITATIVE CHARACTERISTICS OF ACCOUNTING INFORMATION

As part of its study of the broad conceptual framework of financial accounting and reporting, the FASB has issued (May 1980) SFAC 2, *Qualitative Characteristics of Accounting Information* (AC 1220). SFAC 2 formally set forth the criteria the FASB will use in developing standards, and those same criteria should be used by preparers and users of financial statements in selecting and evaluating alternative accounting and reporting methods or disclosures.

Examples of accounting alternatives include methods of cost allocation (e.g., alternative depreciation or inventory-costing methods) and recognition of revenue (e.g., alternative treatment of long-term construction contracts and installment sales). Examples of reporting alternatives include showing more detail or less, aggregating or disaggregating accounting items, and showing related revenues gross or net.

The actual selection of accounting alternatives has to confront conflicting interests and needs. Judgment is required to balance these conflicts to provide the most useful information in a way that is meaningful to everyone involved. SFAC 2 presents a hierarchy of qualities of accounting information with *usefulness for decision making* as the primary criterion of choice. Figure 3.6 reproduces the chart (from SFAC 2) used by the FASB to frame its commentary; it is also the focus of the explanatory remarks that follow.

Relevance and Reliability

Information useful for decision making must be *understandable*. If the information is so complex or fragmented that it cannot be digested, it is of no use. But

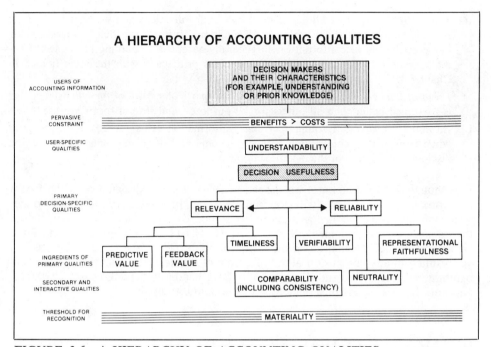

FIGURE 3.6   A HIERARCHY OF ACCOUNTING QUALITIES
SOURCE: FASB, SFAC 2, *Qualitative Characteristics of Accounting Information* (AC 1220).

information that cannot be understood by one user may be understood by another. Thus whether information is understandable depends on both the nature of the information and the understanding of the user.

The information must also be *relevant* and *reliable.* Information is relevant if it confirms or changes a decision maker's expectations and therefore contributes to his capacity to make decisions. What is relevant depends on the user's needs in relation to the decision to be made. If information is received by a user after a decision has been made, it cannot have an impact on the decision. Hence, *timeliness* is an aspect of relevance.

Information is reliable if it can be verified by agreement among a number of independent observers (i.e., is *verifiable*) *and* if it represents what it purports to represent (i.e., is *representationally faithful*). Reliability implies *completeness* and *neutrality* of information, allowing users to depend on it (1) to represent all the important conditions or events it is intended to represent and (2) to be free from bias deliberately or inadvertently introduced by the preparer.

Unfortunately, an accounting alternative that promises a gain in relevance may do so only at the expense of reliability. Different preparers (and users) will attach different relative values to these qualities, but unless information is minimally relevant *and* minimally reliable, it will be worthless. The preparer must use his own judgment as to what accounting choices will provide the best combination of relevance and reliability for the variety of users of the statements.

Comparability

One's knowledge about an organization is greatly increased if it can be compared in significant respects with other similar organizations. Comparison of the financial statements of two or more similar enterprises is one of the most widely used and most effective ways of gaining insights into the strengths and weaknesses of the enterprises. This can be achieved if the enterprises being compared are using uniform accounting methods or if disclosure is adequate to allow the user to make adjustments to a common basis. It would be useless to compare the current ratios of two manufacturing enterprises if one carried its inventory on a FIFO basis and the other on a LIFO basis.

Within a diversified organization, comparisons can be made between divisions or other segments, and the same considerations apply. In addition, if accounting methods are applied consistently over time, new insights may be gained from interperiod comparisons without looking for external benchmarks. From such comparisons it may be possible to detect significant trends or to interpret important fluctuations in operating results or in financial position. Thus, both *uniformity* in accounting methods and *consistency* in their application over time are essential to comparability.

But uniformity of method alone is not enough. Valid comparisons can be made only if the accounting methods used reflect, with reasonable completeness, the underlying economic activity being reported. To cite one of the FASB's examples, a comparison of the performance of two investment managers on the basis of their realized gains during a year could be carried out using completely uniform accounting methods, and yet, by ignoring unrealized gains made by one of them and not by the other, the comparison could fail altogether to reflect their relative success (AC 1220.118).

Likewise, consistency of method alone may not bring true comparability between two measurements if the measurements do not truly represent what they purport to represent. This can be exemplified by a series of sales figures prepared consistently and showing considerable growth from period to period. When price level changes are taken into account, however, the growth may be seen to be largely illusory.

Pervasive Qualities

A constraint overriding all these qualitative characteristics is the relative *cost and benefits* resulting from providing the accounting information. Information is costly to gather, process, report on, audit, interpret, and use. As with other commodities or services, new financial information should be supplied only if its benefits exceed its costs. Even though identification and measurement of these costs and benefits is extremely complex and subjective, their consideration is essential in selecting and evaluating accounting and reporting policies.

Another pervasive quality is *materiality*. This concept is discussed extensively in SFAC 2 (AC 1220.123-.132 and .161-.170). It is defined as "the magnitude of an omission or misstatement of accounting information that, in the light of surrounding circumstances, makes it possible that the judgment of a reasonable person relying on the information would be changed or influenced by the omission or misstatement."

An item of information can be relevant and yet be too small to matter. To be material, an item or a misstatement of an item must be of sufficient magnitude to make a difference to a decision maker. For that reason, materiality is shown in Figure 3.6 as the "threshold for recognition." Whether an item is material will depend on the circumstances surrounding it, and judgments must therefore be made on a case-by-case basis. The professional literature recognizes that in applying accounting standards, common sense demands a *de minimis* rule. Thus, each FASB statement bears this legend: "The provisions of this Statement need not be applied to immaterial items."

An item that may be immaterial in one set of circumstances may be material in another. Thus, an otherwise immaterial item may become material because it may result in a breach of covenant, or because it arises out of a related-party transaction, or because a taint of illegality attaches to it, or because it reverses an earnings trend. These are only a few examples of the kinds of circumstances that may lower a materiality threshold; many others could be cited.

Throughout this *Handbook* materiality is mentioned very often, and where it seems particularly important that materiality be understood in context, a cross-reference has been inserted to this chapter, to assure a consistency in the meaning of the term.

Materiality has many legal connotations, and a definition by the U.S. Supreme Court in *TSC Industries Inc. v. Northway Inc.,* CCH Fed. Sec. L. Rep. ¶ 95,615 (U.S. Sup. Ct. 1976), is in fact referred to in SFAC 2 (AC 1220.165) as "the most authoritative judicial definition of what constitutes a material omitted fact":

> An omitted fact is material if there is a substantial likelihood that a reasonable shareholder would consider it important in deciding how to vote. This standard is fully consistent with the ... general description of materiality as a requirement that "the defect have a significant *propensity* to affect the voting process." It does not require proof of a substantial likelihood that disclosure of the omitted fact would have caused the reasonable investor to change his vote. What the standard does contemplate is a showing of a substantial likelihood that, under all the circumstances, the omitted fact would have assumed actual significance in the deliberations of the reasonable shareholder. Put another way, there must be a substantial likelihood that the disclosure of the omitted fact would have been viewed by the reasonable investor as having significantly altered the "total mix" of information made available. [AC 1220.164]

Other judicial interpretations of materiality will be found in Chapters 44 through 46 dealing with the legal environment.

It is easier for an accountant to learn formal accounting rules than to learn how to form judgments about the degree of precision with which they should be applied or the rigor with which an audit test should be followed up. Research has thrown light on the way that materiality judgments have been made in practice in several different situations, and some success has been achieved in modeling these decisions' relation to materiality. Yet human judgment must still play an indispensable part in making such decisions, and the FASB has declined to promulgate general quantitative guidelines for determining questions of materiality, while recognizing that there may be specific situations where such guidance is appropriate. Indeed, the Board, in a small number of instances, has already specified materiality thresholds, and in other cases the SEC has done so. Some of the quantitative guidelines presently in force are set out in Appendix C of SFAC 2 (AC 1220.166).

BALANCE SHEET

Describing a balance sheet as a listing of assets, liabilities, and ownership interests may be straightforward, but determining what those terms cover is hardly simple. Only when the term *asset* has been defined can one logically distinguish between expenditures to be capitalized in the balance sheet and those to be written off in the income statement. Only when a *liability* has been defined can one distinguish between those future outlays that must be entered in the balance sheet (through charges to income) and those planned discretionary expenditures that should not be currently charged to income but provided for through reserves set aside by company management. For a conceptual discussion of assets and liabilities see Chapter 2; for purposes of this chapter, the definitions given in the *Exposure Draft (Revised) on Elements of Financial Statements of Business Enterprises* (FASB, 1979g) should suffice:

Assets are those probable future economic benefits obtained or controlled by a particular enterprise as a result of past transactions or events affecting the enterprise. [par. 17]

Liabilities are probable future sacrifices of economic benefits stemming from present legal, equitable, or constructive obligations of a particular enterprise to transfer assets or provide services to other entities in the future as a result of past transactions or events affecting the enterprise. [par. 22]

Cutoff Date

The balance sheet presents an enterprise's financial position as of a given moment in time. Accordingly, assets and liabilities (and the resulting owners' equity) are reflected in the balance sheet only if the event that gives rise to the asset or the liability has already occurred as of the balance sheet date. For instance, if a factory is completely destroyed by fire after the balance sheet date, the value of the factory recorded in the balance sheet would remain unchanged. If material, the amount of the loss would be disclosed in the footnote narrative. This reduction in assets would be first reflected in the balance sheet only upon its presentation *as of* a date after the fire. Likewise, anticipated capital expenditures, although already authorized by management or board action, would not be recorded as a liability in the balance sheet until the event that gave rise to the expenditure (e.g., receipt of building materials or design and labor services) had occurred.

Classification of Assets and Liabilities

The usefulness of a balance sheet is enhanced if the assets and liabilities in it are classified in a meaningful way as to current and noncurrent items. A number of relationships useful for financial analysis can then be obtained. The classification of assets has additional significance because GAAP sometimes requires different bases of measurement to be applied to different classes of assets.

One key problem for all enterprises is being able to meet their obligations as they arise. To provide information in this regard, a broad distinction has been made between current and noncurrent assets and between current and noncurrent liabilities (discussed in detail in AC 2031). Working capital (current assets less current liabilities) is a measure of an enterprise's ability to meet its current obligations. In the balance sheets in Figure 3.2, working capital has increased from $223,895 in 1978 to $281,956 in 1979.

Operating Cycle. In segregating noncurrent and current items, *operating cycle* refers to the time needed to convert cash first into materials and services, then into products, then by sale into receivables, and finally by collection back into cash. In some businesses in which products have to mature or age (e.g., distilleries or forest products), the cycle goes well beyond a year. In most businesses, however, there will be more than one cycle per year; in other businesses (e.g., service establishments) there is no recognizable operating cycle.

When an operating cycle does not exist or is shorter than a year, a one-year convention is used for both assets and liabilities. If the operating cycle exceeds a year, the longer period should be used; in practice it is common to use the longer period for current asset classification but apply the one-year convention to liabilities. This is done because extremely long cycles (e.g., shipbuilding) make it implausible to evaluate the extent to which noncurrent liabilities, such as long-term debt service, will be paid out of funds generated from the specific assets included in current assets.

Current Assets. Current assets include cash and other assets that are reasonably expected to be realized in cash or sold or consumed during one year, or within the normal operating cycle of the business if the operating cycle is longer than one year. Thus, current assets normally include

1. Cash, unless it is not available for current operations because it is segregated for some special purpose (e.g., the liquidation of a long-term debt);
2. Marketable securities available to be turned into cash as needed and not held for purposes of control or affiliation with another business;
3. Receivables, unless they arise from unusual circumstances such as transactions with affiliates or officers of the company and are not expected to be collected within 12 months of the balance sheet date;
4. Inventories of raw materials, work in process, finished goods, and operating and maintenance supplies; and
5. Prepaid expenses (e.g., insurance, rent, or advertising) that, though not realizable in cash, would involve an outlay of cash during the operating cycle if not prepaid.

Current Liabilities. Current liabilities in general are "obligations whose liquidation is reasonably expected to require the use of . . . current assets, or the creation of other current liabilities" (AC 2031.07). They include short-term obligations for items that have entered into the operating cycle, such as payables for materials and supplies, wages, expenses and taxes, and amounts collected in advance of the delivery of goods or services. As mentioned above, 12 months is the most common demarcation between current and noncurrent liabilities, but the operating cycle, if longer, is sometimes used. Current liabilities also include other obligations expected to be liquidated within 12 months, such as the short-term portion of notes relating to the acquisition of capital assets.

In SFAS 6 (AC 2033) the FASB considered the classification of short-term obligations expected to be refinanced. If refinanced when it becomes due, an obligation does not require the use of working capital. Accordingly, SFAS 6 provides that short-term obligations may be excluded from current liabilities if two conditions are met. The enterprise (1) must intend to refinance the obligation on a long-term basis and (2) must be able to do so (AC 2033.10 and .11). Some complicated situations have arisen in evaluating whether those conditions have been met, and they are discussed further in Chapter 22.

Effect on Measurement Methods. The significance of the distinction between current and noncurrent assets goes beyond the estimation of an enterprise's liquidity, because under GAAP different bases of measurement may apply to the two categories of assets. Broadly speaking, noncurrent assets are carried at cost, with a proportionate deduction for amortization of intangibles (and for depreciation in the case of depreciable assets) and a reduction (to "new cost") for any permanent diminution in value. Some current assets, such as receivables, are carried at their expected realizable value, the face value of the receivables being reduced by the deduction of allowances for uncollectible amounts and for discounts. Other current assets, such as inventories and certain marketable securities, are carried at the lower of cost or market value. The effect of the current/noncurrent classification on the carrying amounts of specific types of assets is discussed primarily in Chapters 17 through 21.

Asset contra accounts are used in reporting the carrying value of certain types of assets. In the balance sheets in Figure 3.2, depreciation (of $293,867,000 and $266,438,000 in 1979 and 1978 as disclosed in Note 4, not shown) is offset against the capitalized cost of plant and equipment, and the allowance for doubtful accounts (of $6.4 million and $6.1 million in 1979 and 1978) is offset against related receivables.

Owners' Equity

The excess of assets over liabilities in a balance sheet represents the owners' equity. This is the claim of the owners to their share in the entity's assets after its obligations have been met.

The claims of owners who are sole traders or partners may be satisfied by withdrawals of cash or other assets. The claims of stockholders in corporations are met through dividend payments and/or realization of the market value of the shares of the corporation's stock, for which cash proceeds may be obtained by sale of the shares. Also, corporations do from time to time buy back their own stock and hold it as treasury stock (pending possible reissue) or cancel it (thereby reducing the total number of owners' shares outstanding).

Not all of the owners' equity represents an indivisible residual claim to the net assets (and earnings) of the enterprise. A corporation may have preferred stock-holders, with higher priority but limited rights to share in the net assets and earnings. It is the common stockholders (in a corporation) who are entitled to the residual assets of the enterprise after all prior claims have been met. The various classes of stock are shown separately in the balance sheet, along with accumulated retained earnings, a typical example of which is shown in the balance sheets in Figure 3.2. In that example, note that (1) the preferred stock authorized has not been issued, (2) the cost of common stock purchased for the company's treasury is shown separately, and (3) the common stock in Figure 3.1 is not divided into separate accounts for par value and additional paid-in capital, because the common stock was issued without par value. (Equity capital is discussed further in Chapter 26.)

INCOME STATEMENT

The primary purpose of an income statement is to reflect an enterprise's operating performance, i.e., its net income (or loss). This shows whether the net worth of the owners' interests in the enterprise has increased or declined. The concepts underlying net income and its measurement are discussed in Chapter 7, and current reconsideration of the makeup of the income statement may cause changes. Current presentation practices are discussed below.

Format

The format of an income statement should show the significant components of net income, usually in their order of importance. For profit-seeking businesses, the principal elements of its operations are the revenues from the sales of its products or services and the costs at which those products or services are provided. Other factors that enter into the results of current operations are general administrative expenses, debt financing costs, taxes, and, usually, realized gains and losses on the disposal of assets.

The specific presentation of an income statement depends on the nature of the enterprise's operations. In selecting the most meaningful display, the preparer should consider the qualitative characteristics—the usefulness for decision making —discussed earlier. Figure 3.3 is a typical income statement in that earnings from continuing businesses are shown separately as part of net earnings. Reporting the effects on net income of discontinued operations is one of the special items for which accounting standards (APB 30; AC 2012) prescribe treatment. Other items for which treatment is prescribed are discussed later; they include extraordinary items, prior-period adjustments, and accounting changes.

Figure 3.3 also shows earnings per share (EPS) data on the face of the statement of earnings, a requirement of APB 15 (AC 2011.12); APB 15 also requires EPS data to be presented for various subcategories of earnings, including income before extraordinary items, continuing and discontinued operations, effects of accounting changes and pro forma computations of EPS assuming dilution from exercise of options, convertible securities, and similar items.

Aid in Assessing Cash Flow

One of the principal objectives of financial reporting, according to SFAC 1, is to help the users of financial reports assess the amounts, timing, and uncertainty of future cash flows to an enterprise, an intermediate step toward helping them to assess the cash distributions that the enterprise will make to its creditors and owners. A statement of cash receipts and disbursements is not a useful indicator of future cash flows, because it does not allow for matching current costs with the future revenues they may produce. Accrual accounting makes allowances for the uneven timing of the actual payments and receipts of cash, and better enables financial statement users to judge the future earning power of the enterprise.

Shortcomings in Accrual Basis. Net earnings determined using accrual accounting under GAAP do not reflect two factors affecting the future cash-flow potential of the owners' interests. One factor is the unrealized changes occurring during the reporting period in the value of assets and liabilities. The second is the change in the market's expectations regarding the enterprise's future cash flows; those expectations, more than any other factor, determine what an enterprise is worth. But financial statements are largely the reflection of *past* transactions and events—past acquisitions of assets, issues of capital, actual sales transactions, and expiration of costs. Even if important future developments are known with a considerable degree of certainty at the accounting date, they will not be directly reflected in the financial statements.

For example, suppose that two drug companies have incurred identical amounts of expenditures on research and development during the past year. One company knows that its efforts to develop a new drug have been unsuccessful to date and are not likely to succeed in the future. The other company knows that it has achieved a breakthrough and that substantial profitable sales of a new product are highly probable during the next few years. Though its future profits will not be indicated in its financial statements, the successful company will—and probably must under the federal securities laws—find ways to communicate its success to stockholders and the public. This could be done through management's letter to shareholders in the annual report, or in the management discussion and analysis comments required in SEC filings as discussed in Chapter 4. Nevertheless, research and development expenditures will be expensed in both companies' statements, while the results of the research will be reflected in neither's.

Extraordinary and Unusual Items

The usefulness of an earnings statement for predictive purposes is greatly enhanced if normal and recurrent items are distinguished from unusual and nonrecurrent items. The standards to achieve these purposes are contained in APB 9 (AC 2010.16-.18 and .25) and APB 30 (AC 2012), both entitled *Reporting the Results of Operations*. These pronouncements require that all items of profit and loss recognized during a period (except prior-period adjustments) be reflected in currently reported net income, and that extraordinary items (less related income taxes) be shown separately as an element of net income.

Where applicable, income from discontinued operations, along with any gain or loss on the sale or disposal of related facilities, less income taxes, should be reported separately, after income from continuing operations. The statement of operations in Figure 3.7 illustrates an income statement with both discontinued operations and an extraordinary item. Note that the loss from discontinued operations is shown separately from the loss on their disposal, both being shown net of applicable income tax benefits.

Extraordinary Items. The criteria laid down by the APB to identify extraordinary items (AC 2012.20-.24) are quite restrictive. The presumption is that an event or transaction is an ordinary and usual one unless there is clear evidence to the contrary. To be classified as extraordinary, an event or transaction must be material (in relation to reported earnings or the trend of earnings, or for other reasons); and it must be both unusual in nature and infrequent in occurrence.

Whether an event or transaction is unusual will depend in part on the nature of an enterprise and its environment. The event or transaction must be abnormal and significantly different from the ordinary activities of the enterprise, and what is abnormal for one enterprise may be normal for another. An event or transaction is to be regarded as infrequent in occurrence only if it is not reasonably expected to recur in the foreseeable future. Again, what is infrequent for one enterprise may not be infrequent for another.

APB 30 (AC 2012.23) lists a number of gains and losses that are specifically not to be regarded as extraordinary, and that are therefore to be included in net income before extraordinary items. They include

1. Asset writedowns,
2. Foreign exchange gains and losses (including the results of major devaluations and revaluations),
3. Gains or losses on the disposal of a segment of a business,
4. Gains or losses from sale or abandonment of business facilities,
5. Effects of a strike, and
6. Adjustment of accruals on long-term contracts.

If strictly applied, this definition would be so restrictive that extraordinary items would comprise little besides losses suffered through expropriation, revolutions, natural disasters, or exceptional legal actions. However, in March 1975, SFAS 4 (AC 2013) extended the category to include gains and losses resulting from the extinguishment of debt, whether at a scheduled maturity date or before.

Unusual Items. The income statement can usually be made more informative if items that are unusual or of infrequent occurrence (but not both) are shown separately as a component of income from continuing operations; this is required for material items, but, unlike items shown below operating income, they may not be reduced for applicable income taxes (AC 2012.26). This presentation allows users to understand a company's past performance better, and thus evaluate its future performance potential.

An example of unusual item presentation is shown in Figure 3.7, in which the nonrecurring cost of a European reorganization is separately identified.

Operating Versus Nonoperating Activities. Recurrent gains and losses from sources other than normal manufacturing or merchandising operations should pre-

Consolidated Statements of Operations

For the years ended December 31, 1977 and 1976

	1977	1976
Net sales	$96,148,000	$ 95,010,000
Cost of goods sold	66,414,000	69,340,000
Marketing, administration and general expense	20,948,000	25,256,000
Research and development expense	1,229,000	1,208,000
Interest expense	2,485,000	2,766,000
Non-recurring cost of European reorganization (Note 3)	—	2,100,000
Total costs and expenses	91,076,000	100,670,000
Income (loss) from continuing operations before income tax provision	5,072,000	(5,660,000)
Income tax provision (benefit) (Note 6)	2,413,000	(536,000)
Income (loss) before equity items and extraordinary credit	2,659,000	(5,124,000)
Equity in net income of affiliates	165,000	193,000
Minority interest	(193,000)	68,000
Income (loss) from continuing operations before extraordinary credit	2,631,000	(4,863,000)
Discontinued operations (Note 2):		
Loss from discontinued operations, net of $200,000 income tax benefits	—	(186,000)
Loss on disposal of discontinued operations, including provision of $875,000 for operating losses during phase-out period (net of $3,711,000 income tax benefits)	—	(4,772,000)
Income (loss) before extraordinary credit	2,631,000	(9,821,000)
Extraordinary credit from utilization of operating loss carry forward (Note 6)	662,000	—
Net income (loss)	$ 3,293,000	$ (9,821,000)
Income (loss) per share (Note 1):		
Continuing operations before extraordinary credit	$1.21	($2.24)
Loss from discontinued operations	—	(.08)
Loss on disposal of discontinued operations	—	(2.20)
Income (loss) before extraordinary credit	1.21	(4.52)
Extraordinary credit	.31	—
Net income (loss)	$1.52	($4.52)

(The notes to consolidated financial statements are an integral part of these statements)

FIGURE 3.7 INCOME STATEMENT WITH EXTRAORDINARY AND UNUSUAL ITEMS
SOURCE: The Ansul Company, 1977 Annual Report (EPS data omitted).

ferably be shown separately, if amounts are material. In Figure 3.8 this is accomplished by categorizing operating and nonoperating activities. Normally, income from investments, gains or losses on the sale of property, interest expense, and interest earned are examples of nonoperating activities. However, what is an operating activity for one enterprise may not be for another. For example, interest income and expense are operating activities for a bank but not for most manufacturing companies. Likewise, gains or losses on sales of securities are operating activities for a securities broker but not for most manufacturers.

Prior-Period Adjustments

The treatment of adjustments to the reported net income of earlier periods is regulated by SFAS 16 (AC 2014), which virtually proscribes such adjustments. In effect, almost every item of profit or loss that is recognized in a period, including changes in estimates that had entered into the determination of the income of an earlier period, is included in the current-period results. Only two exceptions to that principle are now permitted (AC 2014.11):

1. Correction of an error in the financial statements of a prior period, and
2. Adjustments that result from realization of income tax benefits of preacquisition operating loss carryforwards of purchased subsidiaries.

These two kinds of prior-period adjustments are to be shown as additions to or deductions from the opening balance of retained earnings, unless the financial statements of the prior period are presented together with those of the current period, in which case the earlier statements should be adjusted appropriately.

The distinction between an error and a change in accounting estimate was explained in APB 20:

> Errors in financial statements result from mathematical mistakes, mistakes in the application of accounting principles, or oversight or misuse of facts that existed at the time the financial statements were prepared. In contrast, a change in accounting estimate results from new information or subsequent developments and accordingly from better insight or improved judgment. Thus an error is distinguishable from a change in estimate. A change from an accounting principle that is not generally accepted to one that is generally accepted is a correction of an error for purposes of applying this opinion. [AC 1051.13]

Thus the information necessary for the correction of an error was available during the prior period, whereas the information necessary to revise an accounting estimate, such as the estimate of the life of an asset or the result of an income tax settlement relating to a prior year, was not available when the financial statements of the earlier period were originally issued.

The second type of prior-period adjustment permitted by SFAS 16 is that resulting from the realization of income tax benefits of preacquisition operating loss carryforwards of purchased subsidiaries. The tax effects of loss carryforwards will not be recognized as assets of a purchased subsidiary unless their realization is virtually assured. Thus, if not recognized as a type of receivable at the date of

CONSOLIDATED FINANCIAL STATEMENTS
STATEMENTS OF INCOME
(millions, except per share amounts)

	Notes	1974	1975	1976	1977	1978
Sales		$1,928	$1,900	$2,123	$2,320	**$2,609**
Operating expenses:						
Cost of goods sold		1,524	1,543	1,720	1,879	**2,092**
Selling and administration		181	183	177	194	**223**
Research and development		58	64	70	77	**83**
Total operating expenses	A	1,763	1,790	1,967	2,150	**2,398**
Operating income		165	110	156	170	**211**
Interest expense		(32)	(38)	(35)	(44)	**(48)**
Equity in net income of affiliates	B	8	4	4	8	**13**
Other income and expense		19	9	5	8	**14**
Gain on sale of assets	C	38	—	—	—	**—**
Income before taxes		198	85	130	142	**190**
Provision for income taxes	D	80	28	55	58	**61**
Income before minority interest		118	57	75	84	**129**
Minority interest	E	20	7	6	14	**17**
Income before cumulative effect of change in accounting principle		98	50	69	70	**112**
Cumulative effect of change in accounting principle		—	—	—	—	**43**
Net income		$ 98	$ 50	$ 69	$ 70	**$ 155**
Per share of common stock	F					
Income before cumulative effect of change in accounting principle:						
Primary		$ 6.78	$ 3.30	$ 4.67	$ 4.70	**$ 7.61**
Fully diluted		6.52	3.22	4.51	4.56	**7.36**
Net income:						
Primary		6.78	3.30	4.67	4.70	**10.62**
Fully diluted		6.52	3.22	4.51	4.56	**10.24**
Dividends		2.40	2.80	2.80	2.80	**2.85**
Pro forma income with 1978 change in accounting principle applied retroactively						
Net income		$ 97	$ 55	$ 74	$ 78	**$ 112**
Per share of common stock:						
Primary		6.68	3.67	5.04	5.27	**7.61**
Fully diluted		6.42	3.58	4.86	5.11	**7.36**

The accompanying notes are an integral part of these financial statements.

FIGURE 3.8 SEPARATION OF OPERATING AND NONOPERATING ACTIVITIES
SOURCE: Celanese Corporation, 1978 Annual Report.

acquisition but realized subsequently, acquisition goodwill will have been overstated, and amortization of goodwill during the interval between acquisition and the realization of the tax benefits will also have been overstated. Adjusting the original goodwill, including the correction of the goodwill amortization up to the time when the tax effects of the loss carryforwards were actually realized, is to be treated as a prior-period adjustment.

Accounting Changes

Great importance is attached to the consistent use of accounting procedures from period to period, for without consistency, interpretation of financial statements by comparing them over time would be useless. Therefore, a change from one accounting method to another can only be justified if management believes that the principle adopted after the change is to be preferred. Examples include a change in the method of inventory pricing, of depreciation, or of accounting for long-term contracts. The treatment of accounting changes is prescribed in APB 20 (AC 1051).

Requirements. When a change in an accounting principle is adopted, the nature of the change and management's justification for it must be disclosed in the financial statements of the period in which the change is made. The justification will explain why the new principle is thought to be preferable to the old one. (For SEC registrants, the auditor is also required to concur in the preferability justification, as discussed in Chapter 16.)

In general (AC 1051.19-.20) the cumulative effect of the change on retained earnings at the beginning of the period in which the change is made (including the income tax effect) should be shown between the captions "extraordinary items" and "net income" in the income statement for the period of the change. The effect on net income of the period of the change should also be disclosed, and per share information for the cumulative effect of the accounting change is required. When comparative financial statements for prior periods are shown, they should appear as originally reported.

A *pro forma statement*—i.e., what the effects would have been if the accounting change had been made retroactively—must also be shown for each year presented (AC 1051.21). This pro forma statement must show the effect on income before extraordinary items and on net income, and must include both the direct effect of the change and "non-discretionary adjustments of items based on income before taxes or net income," such as profit-based incentives or royalties; the related income tax effects must also be recognized (AC 1051.19(d), fn.7).

The statement of income in Figure 3.8 shows the cumulative effect of a change (from the deferral to the flow-through method of accounting for investment tax credits). The entire cumulative amount is included in net income of the period of change, but note the additional disclosure of the pro forma net income and EPS data for retroactive application of the change for each of the five years presented.

Restatement for Prior Periods. Though financial statements for prior periods are generally not to be restated for accounting changes, the APB accorded special treatment to three types of accounting change (AC 1051.27):

1. A change from LIFO inventory pricing to another method,
2. A change in the method of accounting for long-term construction-type contracts, and
3. A change to or from the full cost method of accounting in the extractive industries.

The board concluded that for those changes the financial statements of all periods presented should be restated. The nature and justification for the change, and the effect of the change on income before extraordinary items, net income, and the related per share amounts for all periods presented, must be disclosed either on the face of the income statement or in the notes (AC 1051.28).

APB 20 recognized that in some instances a future pronouncement on accounting principles might require retroactive application, and thus provided that any such pronouncement would take precedence over the APB 20 proscription. There have been numerous FASB statements issued since APB 20 that require retroactive application. In addition, in 1977, AICPA Statements of Position were granted the right to specify their manner of application (AC 1051-2.05).

When financial statements are issued prior to the effective date of an FASB statement, disclosure of pro forma financial data for application of the new provisions may be necessary if the effects of application will be material. Pro forma statements are also used for a variety of other purposes, including the accounting change disclosures discussed earlier. Their purpose is to show the effects of a major transaction occurring after the financial statement date, or the effects of a transaction that may or may not take place, e.g., a proposed merger of two or more companies. Pro forma disclosures normally include only pertinent key elements, such as sales, income, and EPS.

Occasionally, the effects may be so significant that disclosure can best be made by pro forma presentation of an entire statement. Figure 3.9 shows a pro forma balance sheet for 1978. In December 1978 the company sold substantially all of one of its divisions and received a note from the purchaser due on January 2, 1979. The pro forma balance sheet shows the effects of receipt and application of the proceeds as if the events had occurred as of December 31, 1978. Since the presence of such a large note-receivable balance is both unusual and short-lived, the pro forma presentation seems essential.

Future Developments

The FASB's conceptual framework is concerned not only with the measurement of income but also with the display of its various components. The distinction between those components that are routine and those that are unusual or nonrecurring is an important one when income statements are used as an aid in assessing future cash flows. The FASB's 1979 *Discussion Memorandum on an Analysis of Issues Related to Reporting Earnings* may be expected to lead to a somewhat more coherent presentation of results than is achieved by the form of income statement now in use.

STATEMENT OF RETAINED EARNINGS

The statement of retained earnings shows the changes that have taken place in owners' equity during a period, excluding changes as a result of capital contributions. Retained earnings are normally increased by the addition of net income and reduced by the payment of dividends. Less frequently, changes in retained earnings may arise from restatement of prior years' statements or from gains or losses on treasury stock transactions. The statement of retained earnings in Figure 3.10 shows changes caused by each of these. When the changes in retained earnings are simple and straightforward, the statements of income and retained earnings are often combined.

	Pro Forma December 31, 1978	December 31, 1978	December 31, 1977
Assets:	(Note 20)		(Note 6)
Current Assets:			
Cash and certificates of deposit of $1,300,000 in 1977 (Note 11)	$ 5,596,000	$ 7,946,000	$ 5,206,000
Accounts receivable, trade, less allowance for doubtful accounts of $872,000 and $472,000 (Note 10)	26,632,000	26,632,000	14,466,000
Notes and other accounts receivable (Notes 6 and 10)	1,211,000	75,647,000	1,968,000
Inventories (Notes 7 and 10)	46,612,000	46,612,000	25,737,000
Prepaid expenses (Note 6)	5,659,000	5,659,000	641,000
Current assets of discontinued operations (Note 6)	9,409,000	9,409,000	21,373,000
	95,119,000	171,905,000	69,391,000
Property, Plant and Equipment, at cost, less accumulated depreciation and depletion of $38,657,000 and $27,815,000 (Notes 9 and 10)	127,142,000	127,142,000	97,596,000
Investment in Unconsolidated Subsidiary (Note 4)	43,022,000	43,022,000	31,720,000
Undeveloped Real Estate, at cost (Note 10)	10,218,000	10,218,000	9,957,000
Intangible Assets, net of amortization of $806,000 and $539,000 (Note 8)	4,428,000	4,428,000	3,251,000
Other Assets (Note 6)	7,710,000	7,710,000	2,146,000
Non-Current Assets of Discontinued Operations (Note 6)	13,454,000	13,454,000	51,118,000
	$301,093,000	$377,879,000	$265,179,000

Liabilities and Stockholders' Equity:			
Current Liabilities:			
Portion of long-term debt due within one year (Note 10)	$ 8,948,000	$ 85,734,000	$ 1,400,000
Accounts payable	22,117,000	22,117,000	17,199,000
Accrued liabilities	12,161,000	12,161,000	5,264,000
Estimated warranty obligation (Note 16)	2,157,000	2,157,000	
Royalties payable	3,859,000	3,859,000	3,255,000
Deferred income taxes (Note 12)	11,787,000	11,787,000	283,000
Current liabilities of discontinued operations (Note 6)	5,370,000	5,370,000	12,311,000
	66,399,000	143,185,000	39,712,000
Long-Term Debt (less portion due within one year) (Note 10)	110,636,000	110,636,000	133,110,000
Deferred Income Taxes (Note 12)	8,047,000	8,047,000	4,643,000
Other Liabilities (Note 3)	10,081,000	10,081,00	2,648,000
Non-Current Liabilities of Discontinued Operations (Note 6)	7,678,000	7,678,000	10,324,000
	202,841,000	279,627,000	190,437,000

	Number of Shares 1978	Number of Shares 1977			
Stockholders' Equity:					
Common stock, par value $.10 (Note 13):					
Authorized	25,000,000	25,000,000			
Issued	9,467,000	7,827,000	947,000	947,000	783,000
Reserved for exercise of stock purchase warrants and stock options	842,000	1,014,000			
Paid-in capital			53,695,000	53,695,000	39,997,000
Retained earnings (Note 10)			43,697,000	43,697,000	34,049,000
Treasury stock, at cost	19,000	19,000	(87,000)	(87,000)	(87,000)
			98,252,000	98,252,000	74,742,000
Commitments and Contingencies (Note 17)					
			$301,093,000	$377,879,000	$265,179,000

FIGURE 3.9   PRO FORMA PRESENTATION OF SUBSEQUENT EVENT
SOURCE: Texas International Company, 1978 Annual Report.

Statement of Consolidated Retained Earnings
For the Years Ended December 31

	1979	1978*
Balance at beginning of year		
As previously reported		$1,084,980,000
Adjustment to reflect change in accounting for oil and		
gas exploration and producing activities (Note 2)		39,398,000
As restated	$1,193,527,000	1,124,378,000
Net income	507,116,000	138,898,000
Dividends		
Cash		
$3.50 cumulative convertible preferred stock	(11,701,000)	(19,459,000)
Common stock ($1.30 per share in 1979; $.95 per share in 1978)	(45,290,000)	(26,710,000)
Common stock — 2½%	(27,214,000)	(23,580,000)
Balance at end of year	$1,616,438,000	$1,193,527,000

*Restated. See Note 2.

See accompanying notes to consolidated financial statements.

FIGURE 3.10   SAMPLE RETAINED EARNINGS STATEMENT
SOURCE: Amerada Hess Corporation, 1978 Annual Report.

APB 12 requires "disclosure of changes in the separate accounts comprising stockholders' equity (in addition to retained earnings) . . ."; the disclosures "may take the form of separate statements or may be made in the basic financial statements or notes thereto" (AC 2042.02). When there are changes in several of the capital accounts, a separate statement of owners' equity (which usually includes retained earnings) is often presented. An example of a separate statement of owners' equity is shown in Figure 3.4.

STATEMENT OF CHANGES IN FINANCIAL POSITION

Changes in the financial position of an enterprise during a period can be seen by comparing the enterprise's balance sheet at the beginning and end of the period. Sometimes intelligent guesses can be made about the causes of the changes, but guesses are a poor substitute for reliable information about the transactions that have caused the changes to occur. An income statement covering the period between the two balance sheet dates shows those transactions relating to the enterprise's revenue-producing activities, but it will not show other kinds of transactions that materially affect liquidity, such as acquisitions of plant assets. It is the purpose of the statement of changes in financial position to summarize all the transactions, revenue-earning and others, that have changed the financial position shown in the balance sheet at the beginning of the period to the position shown in the balance sheet at the end of the period.

Since the issuance in 1971 of APB 19 (AC 2021), a business enterprise has had to include a statement of changes in financial position among its basic financial statements whenever it provides an income statement and balance sheet. The purpose of the statement is (1) to summarize the financing and investing activities of the entity, including the extent to which the enterprise has generated funds from operations during the period, and (2) to complete the disclosure of changes in financial position during the period (AC 2021.04).

The FASB is at work on a project on funds flow and liquidity as part of the conceptual framework project, with exposure of a proposed pronouncement expected in 1981. The eventual outcome of this effort will probably be a revision of the style and content of the statement of changes in financial position.

The present statement of changes in financial position (or *funds statement,* as it is sometimes called) can be drafted to focus on changes in cash or on changes in working capital. However, funds are more commonly identified with working capital than with cash, and this is how the term is used in the following discussion. In the statement reproduced in Figure 3.5 funds are defined as working capital. The statement shows an increase in working capital and the various sources and uses that led to it, and also presents the changes in the components of working capital.

In a profitable business, the primary source of working capital is usually the enterprise's net profit. However, some costs are expensed during a financial period without involving an expenditure. The most prominent of these costs is depreciation of assets. Here, the outflow of funds occurs when the assets are first acquired, so that no further outflows need be recognized as they are systematically expensed. Therefore, in calculating the amount of funds derived from operations, those expenses not requiring the use of funds must be added back to net profit.

Though depreciation is the most important nonfund expense, it is not the only one. Like depreciation, amounts written off intangible assets and bond discounts do not give rise to an outflow of funds. Another nonfund expense is deferred income tax. Timing differences between the accounting treatment of certain expenses and their tax treatment cause accounting profits and taxable profits to diverge, so that during a given financial period more is charged against profits for income tax than needs to be paid. Because the eventual liability is systematically expensed, profits are diminished—but no cash payment is made and no current tax liability is created (in most cases). Because the deferred tax liability is noncurrent, it does not diminish working capital. This does not apply, however, to timing differences between the accounting and tax treatment of current items such as installment sales, because any resulting deferred taxation is treated as a current liability, and working capital therefore is reduced by the provision for current deferred taxes.

In addition to funds generated by operations, the main sources of funds are disposals of fixed assets, issues of bonds and other noncurrent debt securities, and issues of equity capital and preference shares. The principal uses of funds are expenditures on the acquisition of property, plant, and equipment, purchases of investments to be held as noncurrent assets (e.g., investments in affiliates), retirement of debt, purchases of treasury stock, and the payment of dividends.

For certain transactions care must be taken to avoid double-counting in the funds statement. For instance, when capital assets are sold, the amount realized is normally more or less than the value at which they were recorded in the books. There will consequently be a gain or loss on sale, and this will go into the income statement as an addition to or a deduction from net income from operations. However, the sale of the asset increases working capital by the full amount realized on the sale. If the full sale price of the asset is shown as a source of funds, then the net income reported in the statement must be adjusted by eliminating from it any gain or loss from the sale of the asset. Alternatively, if net income from all sources is reported ih the statement (including gains and losses on the sale of capital assets), then the book value of assets, rather than the amount realized on the sale, must be shown as a source of funds.

Before APB 19 was issued, it was customary to include in a funds statement only transactions that gave rise to an inflow or an outflow of working capital (or of cash, if the statement was so defined). One of the results of APB 19 was to broaden the scope of the statement by including in it transactions that affect financial position even though no funds flows result (AC 2021.08). For example, a purchase of real estate paid for by an issue of securities or a conversion of debt securities into capital stock are examples of transactions that change a company's financial position without generating or using working capital.

SPECIAL PROBLEMS

Companies differ greatly among themselves, and consequently their financial statements vary considerably in their presentation. An individual financial statement reflects the unique circumstances of the entity on whose activities and condition it reports. It is impossible to identify and discuss all the countless special circumstances that have an effect on financial reporting, but in this section several special problems that arise from particular circumstances (and their effects on the presentation of financial statements) are discussed.

Development Stage Enterprises

In SFAS 7 (AC 2062), the FASB established special standards of financial reporting for development stage enterprises, which are defined as those that devote substantially all of their efforts to establishing a new business and in which either (1) planned principal operations have not commenced or (2) there have been no significant revenues therefrom (AC 2062.08). SFAS 7 requires the same generally accepted accounting principles for these companies as those that apply to established operating enterprises, e.g., costs that do not meet the usual definition of assets must be expensed as incurred (a practice generally *not* followed by development stage companies prior to SFAS 7). SFAS 7 also requires certain additional information (AC 2062.11):

1. A balance sheet, including any cumulative net losses reported with a descriptive caption such as "deficit accumulated during the development stage" in the stockholders' equity section.

2. An income statement, showing amounts of revenue and expenses for each period covered by the income statement and, in addition, cumulative amounts from the enterprise's inception.

3. A statement of changes in financial position, showing the sources and uses of financial resources for each period for which an income statement is presented and, in addition, cumulative amounts from the enterprise's inception.

4. A statement of stockholders' equity, showing from the enterprise's inception:
   a. For each issuance, the date and number of shares of stock, warrants, rights, or other equity securities issued for cash and for other consideration.
   b. For each issuance, the dollar amounts (per share or other equity unit and in total) assigned to the consideration received for shares of stock, warrants, rights, or other equity securities. Dollar amounts shall be assigned to any noncash consideration received.
   c. For each issuance involving noncash consideration, the nature of the noncash consideration and the basis for assigning amounts.

An example of an operating statement of a development stage enterprise is included in Figure 3.11. Note disclosure of cumulative amounts as required by (2) above. The other statements carry similar cumulative information, in this case "not reported on" by the auditors (as indicated in the column heading).

Parent Company Financial Statements

As indicated in ARB 51, when one company has controlling financial interests in another company there is a presumption that consolidated statements are more meaningful than separate statements; consolidated statements are therefore usually necessary for fair presentation (AC 2051.02). In some cases, parent company statements only may be needed to show the position of creditors or preferred stockholders of the parent or may be required in filings under the 1933 Securities Act. Consolidating statements, in which separate columns are used for the parent company and for various groups of subsidiaries, are often an effective way of presenting the relevant financial information. Matters concerned with consolidated financial statements are discussed further in Chapter 31.

Special Reports

In certain circumstances, a financial statement is prepared in accordance with a comprehensive but non-GAAP basis of accounting (e.g., an income tax basis, cash basis, or regulatory agency statutory basis). In those cases the titles of the statements and the classification of individual elements in the statements should reflect the basis being used. As stated in SAS 14, a cash basis financial statement might be titled *statement of assets and liabilities arising from cash transactions* or *statement of increases or decreases in funds arising from cash transactions,* and a financial statement prepared on a statutory or regulatory basis might be titled *statement of income—statutory basis* (AU 621.07). This subject is further covered in Chapter 16.

Voluntary Liquidation

Financial statements are normally based on the *going concern assumption,* i.e., that a business will continue to operate. Traditional accounting on a historical cost basis becomes inapplicable, however, when a company adopts a plan of liquidation. As stated in SFAC 1 (AC 1210.42, fn.10):

STATEMENTS OF OPERATIONS AND ACCUMULATED DEFICIT

	Cumulative Amounts From Inception to December 31, 1975	Year Ended December 31,	
		1975	1974
	(Not reported on)		
Operations:			
Ovitron management fees	$ 38,039		
Corporate salaries and expenses			
Officers' and directors' salaries	111,276	$ 19,500	$ 25,000
Other corporate expenses	37,261	9,510	6,676
Interest income	(120,309)	(18,273)	(30,693)
Acquisition costs written off	22,100		
Loss on disposition of assets	6,363		6,363
	56,681	10,737	7,346
Patent, research and development costs	2,479,360	13,611	33,287
Net Loss	$(2,574,080)	(24,348)	(40,633)
Accumulated deficit during the development stage (Note c)			
Beginning of year		(2,549,732)	(2,509,099)
End of year		$(2,574,080)	$(2,549,732)
Weighted average number of shares outstanding		370,732	388,449
Loss per common share (based on the weighted average number of shares outstanding; options and warrants have been excluded since they are anti-dilutive)		$(.07)	$(.10)

FIGURE 3.11 DEVELOPMENT STAGE COMPANY OPERATING STATEMENTS

SOURCE: Biological Preservation, Inc., 1975 Annual Report on Form 10-K.

Investors and creditors ordinarily invest in or lend to enterprises that they expect to continue in operation—an expectation that is familiar to accountants as "the going concern" assumption. Information about the past is usually less useful in assessing prospects for an enterprise's future if the enterprise is in liquidation or is expected to enter liquidation. Then emphasis shifts from performance to liquidation of the enterprise's resources and obligations. The objectives of financial reporting do not necessarily change if an enterprise shifts from expected operation to expected liquidation, but the information that is relevant to those objectives, including measures of elements of financial statements, may change.

The financial statements presented in a voluntary liquidation will include a statement of net assets in liquidation (which correspond to owners' equity in a going concern) and a statement of changes in net assets in liquidation. Figure 3.12 shows a statement of changes in net assets in liquidation. Not shown but accompanying this statement are

1. A statement of net assets in liquidation;
2. A statement of net earnings from operations, reporting on the significant activities continuing through the liquidation period; and
3. A statement of changes in cash and short-term investments, disclosing the results of liquidation activities, of which the two most significant typically are proceeds from sales of a business (or assets) and liquidating cash distributions.

Alternatively, disclosures of the results of operations and changes in cash and short-term investments might be included in the notes to the financial statements. While results of operations are the main point of interest in financial statements for a going concern, financial position is the focus when the statements describe a company in liquidation.

Bankrupt Companies[1]

When a company avails itself of the protection of the bankruptcy law, it must prepare specialized financial statements designed to meet the needs of the court of jurisdiction, general creditors and their committees, other creditor groups, stockholders, and regulatory agencies.

On October 1, 1979, a new Bankruptcy Code became effective, replacing the Bankruptcy Act of 1938, known as the Chandler Act. The former act gave us the chapter proceedings, the most familiar of which we have come to know as Chapter X (reorganization) and Chapter XI (arrangements). The new code now incorporates the former Chapters X, XI, and XII (which dealt with real estate liens) into a single Chapter 11 for business rehabilitation.

This section describes the financial statements[2] that contemplate the continua-

---

[1] The author expresses his appreciation to Howard S. Schwartz of Touche Ross & Co. for assistance in the bankruptcy topics discussed here.

[2] Editors' note: Other aspects of bankruptcy accounting and disclosure are also covered here, as this is the focal point for the topic in the *Handbook*.

	Year Ended December 31, 1978	January 1, 1977 Through December 31, 1978
Balance at beginning of period	$137,171	$685,391
Increase (decrease) during the period:		
Liquidation activities and other sales:		
Pretax gain (loss) on sales of businesses (Note C)	(5)	62,529
Pretax gain on sales of other assets	2,791	3,215
Liquidation (expenses) recoveries (Note E)	71	(20,547)
Write-down of certain Nonportfolio Assets to estimated net realizable value	—	(10,641)
Reduction of Nonportfolio Asset write-downs (Note H)	5,695	5,695
Income taxes applicable to liquidation activities (Note F)	—	(1,000)
Portfolio Stocks (Note B):		
Reduction to market value	—	(148,009)
Amount declared as a liquidating distribution	—	(426,086)
Reversal of deferred income taxes	—	29,926
Dividends received	—	6,808
Liquidating cash distributions	(86,342)	(143,904)
Net decrease due to liquidation activities and other sales	(77,790)	(642,014)
Net earnings from operations	9,415	24,638
Exercise of stock options	—	781
Balance December 31, 1978	$ 68,796	$ 68,796

FIGURE 3.12   STATEMENT OF CHANGES IN NET ASSETS IN LIQUIDATION
SOURCE: Kaiser Industries Corporation, 1978 Annual Report.

tion of the business enterprise and its eventual rehabilitation—the *fresh start* concept—rather than the straight Chapter 7 bankruptcy, wherein the purpose is an orderly liquidation and a distribution of the estate to the creditors according to their rank. Although the changes of the new code are sweeping, the types of financial statements required in Chapter 11 are not expected to change significantly from those under the old act.

Not even a brief synopsis of the complex bankruptcy laws is possible here, but to show what part the financial statements must play, a simplified scenario is presented as an example.

A debtor company is unable to meet its financial obligations as they fall due, i.e., it is insolvent. To forestall a disorderly liquidation of its debt or seizure of its property, it files a petition under Chapter 11 in federal court. This effectively stays its creditors. The court appoints a committee of creditors, which, upon being advised of the financial condition of the debtor, meets to formulate a feasible plan to pay some or all of the company's debts over a period of time while allowing its day-to-day operations to continue during negotiations. When a plan has been accepted by the committee, approved by a majority of the creditor body, and confirmed by the court, the debtor proceeds to pay its creditors an agreed-on amount over the period of time specified by the plan, and continues as a going concern.

The most common financial statements prepared in an insolvency arrangement deal with these basic events:

1. Filing the petition,
2. Demonstrating progress during the proceeding, and
3. Confirming the plan.

Filing the Petition. The filing of a petition under the Bankruptcy Code creates a fiduciary relationship. The debtor in possession or a trustee is charged with the responsibility of assembling, accounting for, and preserving the assets of the company. Assets are generally classified in the conventional balance sheet format except that disclosure must clearly indicate those assets pledged or encumbered by any liability.

The usual classification between current and long-term liabilities is irrelevant here since virtually every long-term debt agreement stipulates that the debt will automatically mature upon the filing of a petition in bankruptcy court. Rather, liabilities are classified by the following ranking: priority claims, fully secured liabilities, partially secured liabilities, and unsecured liabilities. Liabilities become fixed at the date of petition and are not commingled with debts incurred later.

Priority claims. By statute, certain unsecured debts have first claim on any unencumbered assets. These debts include wages and salaries unpaid for a statutory period of time (subject to maximum amounts); contributions due to employees and union benefit funds; and taxes and other liabilities to governments or subdivisions thereof.

Fully secured liabilities. These liabilities consist of debt secured by assets that, upon liquidation, would sufficiently satisfy the amount of indebtedness. Any amounts realized in excess of the related liabilities become free assets available to general creditors.

Partially secured liabilities. When encumbered assets are insufficient to satisfy the underlying indebtedness, the debt is partially secured and, to the extent of the deficiency, joins the unsecured creditors.

Unsecured liabilities. All other liabilities are unsecured. Under the code, the seven largest unsecured creditors (if willing to serve) constitute the creditors' committee, which has the primary responsibility to negotiate a plan of arrangement with the debtor.

Schedules. When the petition is filed it is accompanied by prescribed legal forms that provide detailed schedules of the debtor's assets and liabilities, a statement of executory contracts, and a series of 21 questions referred to as a statement of affairs (not to be confused with the *financial* statement known as the statement of affairs, discussed below). Inasmuch as a petition is often filed to forestall a pending legal proceeding or seizure of assets, the court usually grants a limited stay on the requirement for schedules, and the latest available financial statement accompanies the petition.

Figure 3.13 is a hypothetical illustration of a balance sheet classified in accordance with the ranking of liabilities as of the date of filing the petition. Every liability, including those that are contingent or disputed, is included, inasmuch as only "scheduled" liabilities can be discharged.

ALPHA BETA CORPORATION
STATEMENT OF FINANCIAL CONDITION
JUNE 16, 19XX

ASSETS

Current assets

Cash		$ 82,500
Accounts receivable—assigned, less allowance for doubtful accounts		1,468,300
Inventories		3,168,000
Prepaid claims and other current assets		32,700
		4,751,500
Property, plant, and equipment, less accumulated depreciation		6,430,000
Other assets		129,200
		$11,310,700

LIABILITIES AND STOCKHOLDERS' EQUITY (DEFICIT)

Priority claims

Wages and salaries payable	$ 138,000	
Due to employee benefit plans	173,000	
Taxes payable	176,000	
Total priority claims		$ 487,000
Fully secured liabilities		
Mortgage payable and accrued interest		2,687,400
Partially secured liabilities		
Notes payable—bank		1,500,000
Unsecured liabilities		
Notes payable	875,000	
Accounts payable	4,627,800	
Accrued expenses	316,900	
Deferred compensation payable	237,000	
Total unsecured liabilities		6,056,700
Stockholders' equity (deficit)		
Capital stock	100,000	
Paid-in capital	832,600	
(Deficit)	(353,000)	579,600
		$11,310,700

FIGURE 3.13   BANKRUPTCY PETITION BALANCE SHEET

Statement of affairs. This statement is the culmination of the process of presenting financial position for the purpose of enabling the court, the creditors, and the debtor to decide on the best course to follow. It presents all assets, tangible and intangible, booked and unbooked, at realizable values (rather than at historical cost, going concern values) and shows how much will be left for the unsecured creditors after the claims of priority, secured, and partly secured creditors have been met.

When approving the confirmation of a plan of arrangement, the court is required to determine that creditors obtain at least what liquidation would yield. Similarly, creditors must decide to what extent they are willing to grant partial forgiveness of indebtedness and/or future payments instead of moving for adjudication of bankruptcy and liquidation. The debtor must weigh the same information when formulating a plan for consideration by the creditors.

In Figure 3.14, the same information presented in the statement of financial condition is converted into a statement of affairs. Note that provision is made for estimated administration costs to be paid upon confirmation and for a projected deficiency to unsecured creditors of 50.6%.

Demonstrating Progress During the Proceeding. Certain statements are also required to demonstrate progress during the proceeding.

Monthly operating statements. The debtor in possession is required to provide the court with monthly operating statements, along with affidavits attesting to the timely payments of federal withholding taxes. These statements commence with the date of the filing of the petition and enable the court and other parties of interest to monitor the progress of operations and the extent of any deterioration of the debtor's assets. The form of these operating statements varies considerably among the federal court districts. Some jurisdictions require only a statement of cash receipts and disbursements, others are satisfied with simplified or condensed operating statements.

These statements vary so much in form and content that no purpose is served by presenting examples. They often diverge from GAAP. For example, interest is not accrued on prefiling unsecured debt, including priority claims such as delinquent taxes. Allocating lease payments on capitalized leases between interest and amortization of the obligation coupled with depreciation of the asset has little meaning to creditors and court, who are more concerned with the cash impact of the lease payments. Decisions to continue or disaffirm such leases can best be made on the basis of their cash-flow impact, which can be difficult to ascertain under GAAP. Since depreciation expense is not germane to the purpose of the statement, it is usually footnoted or omitted altogether. Payments on prefiling debt, although made rarely and only with the court's permission, should also be noted. The statement must be signed under oath by the debtor and filed with the court. Copies are usually presented to the creditors' committee.

Statutory annual filings of financial statements. During a lengthy period of debtor in possession, the company will often be required to issue full financial statements (e.g., in filings with the SEC on Form 10-K or with other government agencies).

Statements for the SEC are presented without regard to the date of filing the petition; the regular fiscal year of the company continues. Footnote disclosure will be lengthy, detailing the current status of the proceedings and indicating departures from generally accepted accounting principles. Auditors will often disclaim an opinion because of uncertainty as to the ability of the company to continue as a going concern.

The balance sheet of a debtor in possession presents a new layer of debt that

STATEMENT OF AFFAIRS
ALPHA BETA CORPORATION
JUNE 16, 19XX

Book Value	Assets	Estimated Fair Value	Estimated Loss	Expected to Realize for Unsecured Creditors
	Assets pledged with fully secured creditors			
$ 4,630,600	Land, building, and improvements (Net)	$3,750,000	$ 880,600	
	Less: Fully secured creditors (Contra)	2,687,400		$1,062,600
	Assets pledged with partially secured creditors			
1,468,300	Accounts receivable (net)	1,300,000	168,300	
87,100	Machinery and equipment	25,000	62,100	
		1,325,000		
	Free assets			
82,500	Cash	82,500		
3,168,000	Inventories	1,930,000	1,238,000	
32,700	Prepaid items and other current assets	8,000	24,700	
1,712,300	Machinery, equipment, and fixtures	750,000	962,300	
129,200	Other assets	10,000	119,200	
		2,780,500		
	Less: Priority claims (Contra)	487,000		
	Estimated administrative expenses (Contra)	275,000	275,000	
		762,000		2,018,500
$11,310,700			$3,730,200	$3,081,100

(figure continues)

FIGURE 3.14 EXAMPLE OF A STATEMENT OF AFFAIRS

		Expected to Rank	
Book Value	Liabilities and Stockholders' Equity (Deficit)	Secured or With Priority	Unsecured
	Priority claims		
$ 138,000	Wages and salaries payable	$ 138,000	
173,000	Dues to employee benefit plans	173,000	
176,000	Taxes payable	176,000	
	Total priority claims (Contra)	487,000	
-0-	Estimated administrative expenses (Contra)	275,000	
	Fully secured creditors		
2,687,400	Mortgage payable and accrued interest (Contra)	2,687,400	
	Partially secured creditors		
1,500,000	Notes payable, bank	1,500,000	
	Less: Assets pledged with partially secured creditors	1,325,000	$ 175,000
	Unsecured creditors		
875,000	Notes payable		875,000
4,627,800	Accounts payable		4,627,800
316,900	Accrued expenses		316,900
237,000	Deferred compensation payable		237,000
	Stockholders' equity		
100,000	Capital stock		
832,600	Paid-in capital		
(353,000)	(Deficit)		
	Total expected to rank		6,231,700
	Deficiency to creditors (50.6%)		
	Stockholders' equity	$ 579,600	
	Estimated loss on liquidation	(3,730,200)	(3,150,600)
$11,310,700			$3,081,100

FIGURE 3.14   CONT'D

has extrapriority impact. This is the debt incurred for services rendered or purchases made after the filing of the petition and during the proceedings. These administrative expenses come before any preexisting unsecured debt, including priority claims. The debtor in possession, with the permission of the court, can hypothecate unencumbered assets in order to secure the necessary credit to continue operations. Under the new Bankruptcy Code, the court is even empowered to substitute "the indubitable equivalent" of a secured creditor's interest in property if the court believes that this step is necessary to obtain financing when no other method will accomplish the result. As a result, these annual statements relegate prefiling debt to a secondary role; it is shown as a current liability, but presented below liabilities incurred after the filing of the petition.

Provisions for the estimated expenses to be incurred upon confirmation, e.g., professional, trustee, and court fees, should be accrued and included in the new priority category. Provision for losses resulting from the debtor's disaffirming executory contracts such as leases and performance contracts are generally included in prefiling debt unless some priority pertains through provision of law.

For a comprehensive example of a debtor in possession's financial statements filed with the SEC, refer to the Bowmar Instrument Corporation Proxy Statement of August 31, 1976, partially reproduced in Poloway and Charles, 1980, paragraph 4395. Of course this proxy statement does not reflect the provisions of the October 1979 change in the Bankruptcy Law.

Confirming the Plan. Upon confirmation, the debtor has returned to "normalcy." The complete terms of the plan of arrangement must be presented in the financial statements and explained in the footnote disclosures in accordance with generally accepted accounting principles, with particular reference to the following:

1. *Interest—taxes.* Whereas interest is not accrued on prefiling tax obligations during the proceedings (and would not constitute a claim upon adjudication and liquidation) the Supreme Court has ruled that the Treasury has a valid claim for interest on prefiling unpaid taxes upon confirmation. Thus such interest should be accrued at the date of confirmation.

2. *Interest—general.* Interest is not imputed on debt restructuring arrangements pursuant to the Bankruptcy Code since the issuance of SFAS 15 (AC 5363) in 1977. Previously, imputation of interest was required on any deferred-payment plans or the restructuring of equity securities and/or notes having a modification or alteration of its original terms. SFAS 15, *Accounting by Debtors and Creditors for Troubled Debt Restructurings,* is discussed in detail in Chapter 22.

3. *Forgiveness of debt.* In most plans of arrangement or reorganization, there is some forgiveness of debt. In the past, two positions were expounded. One was that forgiveness of debt constitutes income, albeit extraordinary. The other was that forgiveness of debt by the creditors as a result of bankruptcy proceedings when the creditors' body is to some extent in quasi control is a credit to donated or paid-in capital, created no differently from forgiveness of debt by a parent or officers/stockholders. This position was further bolstered by a specific provision in the Bankruptcy Act stating that forgiveness of debt neither constitutes income nor affects the net operating loss tax deductions carryforward available to the emerging debtor.

SFAS 15 speaks to this issue in clear terms. Gain shall be "classified as an extraordinary item, net of related income tax effect" (AC 5363.021). However, the statement contains a footnote that states that the statement will not apply "if under provisions of those Federal statutes or in a quasi-reorganization or corporate readjustment (ARB 43, Chapter 7, Section A) with which a troubled debt restructuring coincides, the debtor restates its liabilities generally" (AC 5363.010, fn. 4). It would appear that this footnote attempts to recognize an SEC view, expressed on numerous occasions, that a plan of reorganization under the bankruptcy laws that restructures equity and grants creditors substantial positions in the stock of a publicly traded company, is in reality a fresh start, and all deficit or retained earnings should be eliminated.

Net Operating Loss Carryforwards. In most Chapter 11 proceedings the debtor has available a net operating loss carryforward. To the extent that this tax benefit is utilized during the proceedings and after confirmation, the utilization should be presented as an extraordinary credit in the year of realization. However, in a quasi reorganization, any tax benefits realized from such loss carryforwards should be added to contributed capital because these benefits are attributable to periods prior to the quasi reorganization (AC 4091.49).

Other Reports. During a complex and lengthy proceeding, requests are made by parties-in-interest for cash-flow and operational forecasts, feasibility studies, and pro forma statements giving effect to the varied plans of arrangements that are being proposed. Furthermore, the new code requires the court in certain cases to appoint an examiner to investigate any allegations of fraud, dishonesty, incompetence, misconduct, mismanagement, or irregularity. Therefore, a myriad of special purpose reports may issue from insolvency and bankruptcy proceedings.

SUGGESTED READING

AICPA. *Illustrations of Reporting Accounting Changes.* Financial Report Survey 2. New York, 1974. This book, based on a NAARS survey of over 8,000 published annual reports, illustrates reporting under APB 20.

FASB. *Discussion Memorandum on an Analysis of Issues Related to Reporting Earnings.* Stamford, Conn., 1979. Because so much attention is focused on the earnings statement, the FASB is inquiring into the content and format improvements needed, and the role of financial forecasts.

————. *Objectives of Financial Reporting by Business Enterprises.* Statement of Financial Accounting Concepts No. 1. Stamford, Conn., 1978. To understand what the basic financial statements attempt to convey, it is essential to understand their overall objectives, as stated by the FASB. SFAC 1 firmly establishes the basic concept of usefulness in making business and economic decisions.

————. *Qualitative Characteristics of Accounting Information.* Statement of Financial Accounting Concepts No. 2. Stamford, Conn., 1980. This chapter touched only briefly on the qualities that make financial information useful. SFAC 2 is the culmination of a long deliberative process, which included the preparation of *Exposure Draft on Qualitative Characteristics: Criteria for Selecting and Evaluating Financial Accounting and Reporting Policies* (1979). The author of this chapter served as consultant to the Board and staff on the qualitative characteristics project.

Newton, Grant. *Bankruptcy and Insolvency Accounting.* New York: Ronald Press, 1975. This is probably the most comprehensive book on the subject, written by a CPA in a manner readily understood by accountants. The author is in process (1980) of preparing a revised edition to reflect the 1979 changes in bankruptcy laws.

4

Financial Disclosure

Victor H. Brown

DISCLOSURE EVOLUTION

In establishing objectives of financial reporting rather than objectives of financial statements, the FASB indicated that its concern extends to financial reporting beyond the statements themselves. In SFAC 1, *Objectives of Financial Reporting by Business Enterprises,* the Board concluded:

Although financial reporting and financial statements have essentially the same objectives, some useful information is better provided by financial statements and some is better provided, or can only be provided, by means of financial reporting other than financial statements. [AC 1210.05]

This chapter discusses financial data that should be disclosed outside of the basic financial statements discussed in Chapter 3.

Expanding the Boundaries

In recent years the quantity and variety of financial information made available to investors and creditors by business entities have expanded markedly. The greater complexity of business, the continuing refinement of accounting principles, and public demands for additional information are among the causes. The business community has voluntarily implemented many changes in reporting and disclosure practices, while standard-setting bodies and the SEC have established numerous additional requirements. These changes in the business and regulatory environment have led to evolution—some say revolution—in the disclosure area.

The trend toward significant expansion in the volume of information disclosed by business enterprises, in part in the form of financial disclosure, is clearly manifested in corporate annual reports. For example, from 1968 to 1977 the annual reports of ten industrial corporations—among the largest thirty in the "Fortune 500"—increased the average number of pages of notes to the financial statements from 2½ to 8½ pages, and the average number of pages of financial information from 9 to 17 pages. In most instances, the format of the basic financial statements did not change significantly. Therefore, most of the additional data is contained in footnotes, supplementary tables, and other narrative sections accompanying or related to the financial statements.

In addition to objective, or hard, financial data, information regarding productive capabilities or operating levels, purchase or sales commitments, and primary geographical areas of operations may be considered financially related. Financial disclosures thus are numerical (quantitative) as well as nonnumerical (qualitative). This material is often very complex, and providing it can easily become burdensome. As one company said about the complexity of footnotes in its annual management report: "Some material in the Notes to the Consolidated Financial Statements . . . is complex and, in the opinion of management, unnecessary to an understanding of the company. Such material is included only because it is mandatory, primarily due to government regulations and, to a lesser extent, the requirements of the public accounting profession" (excerpt from a Dan River Inc. annual report, AICPA, 1979m, p. 22).

At an early stage the basic financial statements, particularly the balance sheet, were the first to become more detailed. More information was provided in caption form, and information that was previously included in highly condensed form (such as property, plant, and equipment) was subdivided and given separate display within the statements. Eventually, however, it became apparent that the basic statements alone could not accommodate all the added detail. Consequently, much of the information began to appear first in footnotes, then in other supplementary and narrative forms.

The terms *supplementary* and *narrative* as used in this chapter encompass financially related information that is part of or an adjunct to the basic financial statements, both in annual reports to shareholders and in filings with the SEC. It is often referred to as financial disclosure or simply supplementary information. Of course, disclosure apart from the balance sheet, income statement, and funds statement can also appear in statement or tabular form; it need not be literally narrative, though it often is.

The nature of supplementary information has itself evolved. Financial disclosures were first used primarily to provide expanded detail on financial statement captions. For example, the total of long-term debt shown in the balance sheet would be detailed by principal issue in a supplementary footnote or schedule. Along with the expansion of historical information in recent years, supplementary information also began to exhibit new dimensions—in particular, a trend toward disclosures intended to enable users to better interpret and assess the historical information contained in the financial statements. The footnote disclosure of major accounting policies (APB 22; AC 2045) is an obvious example.

More recently, a new emphasis has become apparent. Many believe that financial disclosures should, in addition to merely expanding on historical data and assisting in their interpretation, provide greater assistance to investors and creditors in predicting future performance. Accordingly, disclosures of an analytical nature have become increasingly significant. For example, requirements for segment reporting (SFAS 14; AC 2081) and for the inclusion of a management discussion and analysis of financial condition and results of operations are intended to provide investors with a better appreciation of the composition of business assets and of underlying trends in enterprise profitability. This movement in turn has extended naturally to the question of disclosing more judgmental and future-oriented information, such as information on changing prices, replacement cost estimates, forecasts, and projections—although their desirability and utility will be debated for years to come.

There are no signs that the expanding disclosure movement will halt or reverse. Rather, the quantity and type of information disclosed is likely to continue to expand and evolve. Accordingly, financial statement preparers, auditors, and users must be well informed about the disclosure requirements of applicable professional organizations and the SEC, and financial information must be summarized and presented in a manner that will provide users with a base of data to facilitate informed decisions. As more soft, judgmental information is provided, there is an increasing need to exercise care in presentation, so as to minimize the risk of user misunderstanding.

Disclosure in the Context of Financial Reporting

At the outset a distinction must be made between financial statements and financial reporting. The previous chapter dealt with the *basic* financial statements, mostly to the exclusion of footnotes and supplementary data. The basic financial statements plus footnotes are generally referred to as *financial statements;* these plus other financially oriented disclosures make up *financial reporting.* The role of this chapter is to explore financial reporting apart from the basic financial statements, tying together the disclosure discussions contained in most of the other chapters in this *Handbook* so that the overall logic of the evolving disclosure structure can be seen.

SFAC 1, *Objectives of Financial Reporting by Business Enterprises,* discusses the above distinctions:

Financial statements are a central feature of financial reporting. They are a principal means of communicating accounting information to those outside an enterprise. Although financial statements may also contain information from sources other than accounting records, accounting systems are generally organized on the basis of the elements of financial statements (assets, liabilities, revenues, expenses, etc.) and provide the bulk of the information for financial statements. [AC 1210.06]

Financial reporting includes not only financial statements but also other means of communicating information that relates, directly or indirectly, to the information provided by the accounting system—that is, information about an enterprise's resources, obligations, earnings, etc. Management may communicate information to those outside an enterprise by means of financial reporting other than formal financial statements either because the information is required to be disclosed by authoritative pronouncement, regulatory rule, or custom or because management considers it useful to those outside the enterprise and discloses it voluntarily. Information communicated by means of financial reports other than financial statements may take various forms and relate to various matters. Corporate annual reports, prospectuses, and annual reports filed with the Securities and Exchange Commission are common examples of reports that include financial statements, other financial information, and nonfinancial information. News releases, management's forecasts or other descriptions of its plans or expectations, and descriptions of an enterprise's social or environmental impact are examples of reports giving financial information other than financial statements or giving only nonfinancial information. [AC 1210.07]

SEC Influence in Disclosure

The SEC, in assuming responsibility for adequate disclosure to investors, stated in ASR 4 (1938) that disclosure is not a substitute for proper accounting. Though ASR 4 suggests an environment of brevity, the SEC has imposed numerous disclosure requirements in addition to those required by GAAP, adding to the disclosure expansion and creating confusion about what is required by GAAP and what, in addition, is required by the SEC. The SEC's role in the disclosure area is placed in perspective here, and specific items are mentioned throughout this chapter.

SEC filings, of course, include primary financial statements, footnotes, a management discussion, and an analysis of financial condition and results of operations, as well as a great deal of other supplementary information. Disclosures required by the SEC are specified in Regulation S-X and in many cases go far beyond the information required by GAAP. The SEC's rules include both general and specific industry requirements.

The SEC has just revised (in ASR 280) Articles 3, 5, and part of 12 of Regulation S-X to

1. Eliminate rules that presently duplicate GAAP;
2. Effect changes to recognize predominant current practice and changes in circumstances;
3. Clarify and modify requirements that are presently subject to differing interpretations; and
4. Expand certain requirements to improve financial reporting.

The SEC also accomplished (in ASR 279) a major revision of Form 10-K, which is now designed to permit integrated disclosure concepts to be implemented to some extent with respect to all registered companies. Certain basic financial information would be in a registrant's annual report to shareholders and this information would be incorporated by reference in Form 10-K. In addition, the SEC has also

1. Amended Rules 14a-3 and 14c-3;
2. Expanded Regulation S-K to include three new items:
   a. Management's Discussion and Analysis of Financial Condition and Results of Operations,
   b. Selected Financial Data, and
   c. Market Price of the Registrant's Common Stock and Related Security Holder Matters;
3. Amended Regulation S-K, Item 1, Description of Business; and
4. Amended related forms, rules, and guides under the 1933 and 1934 acts.

With the foregoing changes, the annual shareholder's report becomes the pivotal document.

The 1980 changes are massive and cannot be adequately captured in any brief summary. However, to provide an indication of their magnitude, a generalized summary of the more substantive changes is provided later in this section. Before reviewing the SEC's current disclosure requirements, an understanding of the work of the Advisory Committee on Corporate Disclosure, discussed next, will provide the necessary context.

Advisory Committee on Corporate Disclosure. In the early 1970s the substance and effectiveness of the SEC-required disclosure system were being questioned. These questions evolved in light of forces such as the increasing institutionalization of the markets, the growth of interest in the random walk theory and the efficient market hypothesis (see Chapter 47), and increasing interest in assessing whether the required disclosure system was cost-effective. One area of question was the then-existing policy of the SEC to discourage, if not prohibit, the inclusion of soft information such as earnings projections in documents filed with the commission.

In response to these questions, an Advisory Committee on Corporate Disclosure was established in 1976 by the Securities and Exchange Commission. Its chairman was former SEC Commissioner A. A. Sommer, Jr. (thus it is often called the *Sommer Committee*). Its membership included representatives from government, academia, finance, accounting, and business. The major objectives of the committee, particularly those affecting narrative disclosures, were

- To identify the characteristics and functions of the present system of corporate disclosure and the SEC's role within that system;
- To do a cost-benefit analysis of the present system of corporate disclosure;
- To articulate the objectives of a system of corporate disclosure and to measure the commission's present disclosure policies against those objectives; and
- If necessary, to recommend to the commission adjustments to its policies to better effectuate those objectives.

In its report issued in November 1977, after almost two years of study, the committee concluded that the objective of corporate disclosure is to "assure the public availability in an efficient and reasonable manner and on a timely basis of reliable, firm-oriented information material to informed investment, and corporate suffrage decision-making. The Commission should not use disclosure solely to regulate corporate conduct unless expressly authorized to do so by the Congress" (CCH Fed. Sec. L. Rep. ¶ 81,300 at p. 88,477).

In order to meet its first objective, the committee identified six categories of participants in the system of corporate disclosure: corporations, security analysts, portfolio managers, information disseminators, registered representatives, and individual investors. Through a series of case studies and questionnaires, the committee attempted to understand the role of each group in the process of corporate disclosure and their views concerning the efficiency of the system and ways in which it could be improved.

The committee's recommendations dealing with disclosure, especially those encouraging the publication of analytical information, forecasts, projections, plans, and objectives, are particularly relevant to the consideration of narrative disclosure. The following is a brief summary of certain of the recommendations:

1. In addition to the disclosure of firm-oriented information, companies should be encouraged to discuss macroeconomic factors having a special or unique impact on their operations;
2. Disclosure guides for specific industries should be developed by the commission to encourage uniform disclosure of material items unique to those industries;
3. The SEC should issue a public statement to encourage disclosure of projections and forecasts in corporate annual reports and in filings with the commission;
4. The commission should encourage disclosure of other forward-looking information, such as planned capital expenditures and anticipated financing, management plans and objectives, and dividend policies and capital structure policies;
5. With respect to such forecasts, projections, and other forward-looking information, a safe harbor rule should be adopted to provide liability protection for management, unless such information was prepared without a reasonable basis or was disclosed other than in good faith;
6. Companies making projections should issue a statement clearly indicating the nature of the projections and cautioning investors against attributing undue certainty to them; and
7. Review of management's projections by third parties should be permitted but not required.

The last five recommendations above relate to forward-looking information. Although the committee was strongly in favor of future-oriented disclosures, it also recognized some of the potential problems. Accordingly, it did not recommend that such projections be required or that they should be subject to mandatory auditor review. Companies were also encouraged to make clear to investors the inherent limitations of forecasts and projections. Overall, the Sommer Committee's conclusions gave a major impetus to the projection disclosure trend, discussed later.

The first two recommendations above were clearly aimed at enhancing the ability of users to analyze profitability trends, and this concept had an important influence in the 1980 changes discussed next.

Regulation S-X. This regulation comprises the SEC's basic disclosure rules, and a general discussion of its content may be found in Chapter 41. Numerous references to this regulation are also given throughout this *Handbook*. In this chapter certain major changes made in Regulation S-X in late 1980 are highlighted, since they manifest the recommendations of the Sommer Committee and portend an even greater influence on GAAP disclosures than has been the case in the past.

The 1980 revision aims to eliminate rules in S-X that previously duplicated GAAP; all the remaining disclosure requirements in revised Regulation S-X, Articles 4 (Rules of General Application) and 5 (Commercial and Industrial Companies), other than supplementary schedules, are now to be included in the annual report to shareholders. Although certain of these items are not specifically GAAP disclosures, by custom they are frequently presented in annual reports. These disclosures include

1. Restrictions on the payment of dividends;
2. Domestic and foreign components of income before taxes;
3. Warrants and rights;
4. Separate presentation of and disclosures regarding redeemable preferred stock;
5. Excess of replacement or current cost over the stated LIFO value of inventories;
6. Five-year maturities of long-term debt;
7. Related-party transactions; and
8. Information regarding proved oil and gas reserves.

Regarding item 2 above, the SEC had proposed the disclosure of a reconciliation of book income and taxable income in the notes to the financial statements. Registrants would have had to reconcile pretax income and income tax expense for both their federal and foreign components, as reported in their financial statements, to federal (foreign) taxes shown in the income tax returns. A summary of the actual tax computation showing amounts taxed at various rates—statutory, capital gains, etc.—and the effect of offsetting credits would also have been required. There was considerable complaint about the excessive details in this proposal, and it was withdrawn upon finalization. All that is now additionally required is disclosure of the domestic and foreign components of income before taxes.

Regarding item 7 above, the SEC now requires more disclosure about related-party transactions via an integration of the disclosure requirements of SAS 6, *Related Party Transactions* (AU 335), into Regulation S-X. This integration was necessitated by the fact that GAAP contains almost no specification in this area (see Chapter 28) and the SEC could look only to the auditing literature to find some guidance.

Certain information is deemed to be important to investment advisers and analysts but not of prime importance to shareholders. The following are examples of this information, to be included in schedules:

1. Detailed information regarding marketable securities;
2. Details of certain borrowings by related parties and others, including employees;
3. Investments in and amounts due to or from affiliates;
4. Components of property, plant, and equipment;
5. Details of valuation accounts;
6. Information on short-term borrowings; and
7. Supplementary income information.

Certain other information would be treated as supplemental, i.e., as outside the financial statements. Based on the premise that information contained within the financial statements should be audited, the new rules remove from S-X the requirements relating to unaudited financial information concerning selected quarterly financial data and disclosures of oil and gas reserve information and place these requirements under Regulation S-K.

Form 10-K. This form is the basic annual reporting form for commercial and industrial companies, and, because of the disclosure requirements of S-X that exceeded GAAP, most companies in the past filed a 10-K that was separate from and in some ways different from an annual report for shareholders. Under the 1980 revisions, and with a maximum integration of the annual report and Form 10-K by the registrant, Form 10-K consists of the facing page; the annual report to shareholders (Parts I and II); the proxy or information statement (Part III); the information, if any, required by Part IV of the form (financial statement schedules and the exhibits); reports on Form 8-K; signatures; and a cross-reference sheet setting forth the item numbers and captions in Parts I, II, and III of the form and the page or pages in the referenced materials where the corresponding information appears.

The proposed requirement that the financial statements in the annual report be identical to the financial statements in the 10-K has brought much comment to the SEC, even from the FASB itself. This requirement would necessarily force annual report disclosures to comply with Regulation S-X, which, as discussed above, still contains certain specifications that exceed GAAP. It is too early to tell what kinds of problems this will cause in practice, even though the final rules allow some management discretion in what goes in the annual report and what is supplementary in the 10-K.

Under the new rules, a registrant may now combine all the information in Part I (Business, Properties, Legal Proceedings, and Security Ownership of Certain Beneficial Owners and Management) and Part II (Items 5 through 8) of the form by reference to the annual report to shareholders furnished to the SEC pursuant to Rule 14a-3 or Rule 14c-3.

In Part II of Form 10-K, Item 5 requires market price information for the registrant's securities and a statement of dividend policy. Although this item is new to Form 10-K and to Regulation S-X, its contents are similar to that of paragraph (8) of Rule 14a-3 (which requires market price information to be included in the annual report to shareholders), to Guide 26 (which requires a statement of a registrant's dividend policy), and to Item 9 of the previous form 10-K (which required information as to the approximate number of equity security holders). The principal change has been to move this item to Form S-K, where it can more easily be referenced into other forms.

The previous and familiar summary of operations has been deleted and in its place there has been inserted, as Item 6, a requirement calling for *Selected Financial Data*. This new requirement is designed to present significant five-year trend data relating to a registrant's revenues, income from continuing operations, liquidity, and capital resources. Although a registrant would be permitted to include other financial information in addition to that specified, it would be expected that any presentation of additional information would not necessarily emphasize income or revenues as opposed to liquidity or capital resources.

The deletion of the summary of operations is a consequence of two basic decisions. First, the SEC believes that five-year information is relevant primarily where it can be related to trends in the registrant's business. Many thought that the previous summary did not contain sufficient information about trends. The new Form 10-K also incorporates (in Item 7) an entirely restructured management's discussion and analysis as discussed later in a separate section of this chapter. As a result of the change of focus in this area to a discussion of the financial statements, the summary of operations is no longer the only subject of that discussion.

Under Item 8, Financial Statements and Supplementary Data, the SEC has (1) adopted uniform financial statement requirements (i.e., three-year income statements and statements of changes in financial position and two-year balance sheets for all filings) and (2) eliminated, to the extent possible, the differences between the requirements of GAAP and those of Regulation S-X.

Under Item 11, Exhibits, financial statements and schedules that previously had been required in Form 10-K but that are not now required in the annual report to shareholders under Rule 14a-3 or Rule 14c-3 are to be filed as exhibits to the form.

Effect of Disclosure on Small Businesses

With the proliferation of disclosure requirements, small and closely held companies have come under pressure to expend considerable amounts in producing information that they feel is not relevant to users. And if the small company is publicly held, it becomes subject to a host of SEC requirements designed, with few exceptions, to encompass all registrants. Even the privately held company does not fare much better, since an auditor reporting on its financial statements must require that all GAAP be followed in order to give a "clean" opinion—it can hardly be denied that in the last decade GAAP has institutionalized much that would seem responsive to the complexity of larger public companies.

Some relief has been granted, and perhaps more is on the way. The *Report of the Committee on Generally Accepted Accounting Principles for Smaller and/or Closely Held Businesses* (AICPA, 1976e) analyzed the problem at length and came to three major conclusions:

1. Measurement rules should be the same for everyone, but disclosures should be separated into those that are essential and those that merely provide additional or analytical data. The clear inference is that the latter group should not be required of all smaller and/or closely held businesses.
2. The SEC should restrain its ardor in drafting its requirements, avoiding implicit or explicit language suggesting that the requirements constitute GAAP.

3. The AICPA, in establishing auditing standards, should reconsider the nature of an independent accountant's association with unaudited interim and annual financial statements and those given on prescribed forms.

The FASB has since suspended the requirement for nonpublic companies to present earnings per share and segment information (SFAS 21; AC 2083) and has made SFAS 33, *Financial Reporting and Changing Prices* (AC 1072), applicable only to larger public companies. The FASB has incorporated the "big GAAP/little GAAP" issue in an invitation to comment, discussed in the next section.

Based at least in part on recommendations in the *Report of the Advisory Committee on Corporate Disclosure* (SEC, 1977a) the SEC has released a notice of proposed rule making, *Consideration of a System of Classifying Smaller Issuers for Purposes of Modifying Certain Reporting and Other Requirements* (Release 34-16866, June 2, 1980).

Required auditing procedures (SASs) multiplied for other reasons (see Chapter 39), causing a result much as recommended by the "little GAAP" committee—a separate series of pronouncements on accounting and review services and a revised SAS (14) on special reports (AU 621).

In the private sector there are at least two groups whose aim is to contain the spread of small business disclosure—the Small Business Committee of the Financial Accounting Standards Advisory Council and the Private Companies Practice Section of the AICPA Division for Firms. Small business is now getting some attention, but the questions are whether the problem is sufficiently delineated and the results responsive.

INFORMATION SPECTRUM

With the conceptual framework project well along, the FASB in mid-1980 released *Invitation to Comment on Financial Statements and Other Means of Financial Reporting*. Like a discussion memorandum in that it raised issues, it also expressed the Board's noncommittal thinking on segments that make up the information spectrum—that is, all information used in investment, credit, and similar decisions. This is shown in Figure 4.1.

In Chapter 3, the segment dealing with the basic financial statements alone—without the notes—was discussed. In this chapter the remainder of the FASB's area of interest will be reviewed. This includes

• Notes to financial statements,
• Supplementary financial information, and
• Voluntary financial information.

Not discussed are the rightmost two columns in Figure 4.1—the segments dealing with other financial reporting, such as financial information in company-sponsored magazines, newsletters, and press releases, disclosures of environmental or social impact, and other nonfinancial information that has a bearing on user decisions.

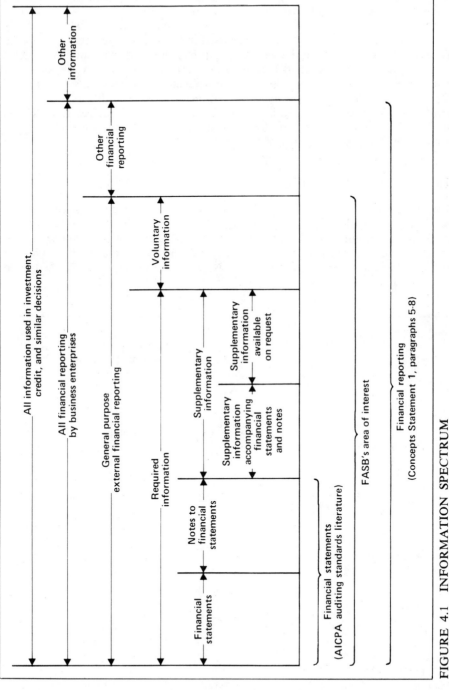

FIGURE 4.1 INFORMATION SPECTRUM

SOURCE: FASB, *Invitation to Comment on Financial Statements and Other Means of Financial Reporting* (Stamford, Conn., 1980), p. 2.

It only needs to be said that such information should not contradict the information contained in general purpose external financial reporting.

Another important visualization of the information spectrum is shown in Figure 4.2. It segregates the information discussed in this chapter according to whether all enterprises or only certain designated enterprises should provide it. The implications for smaller or closely held businesses are apparent, though at the same time the inference that larger companies should provide more information is troublesome.

The invitation to comment, therefore, essentially deals with *what, who,* and *where*—what information should be required, who should be required to provide it, and where it should be presented. Some of the FASB's tentative answers are interspersed throughout the remainder of this chapter.

Location of Financial Disclosure

Approaching disclosure from a location viewpoint facilitates definition of the general area to be addressed, but it also tends to overlook the practical problem of distinguishing information that might be better contained in the basic financial statements. This distinction is frequently blurred, and few rules are available. The preparer of a financial report has rather wide discretion, for example, as to whether de-

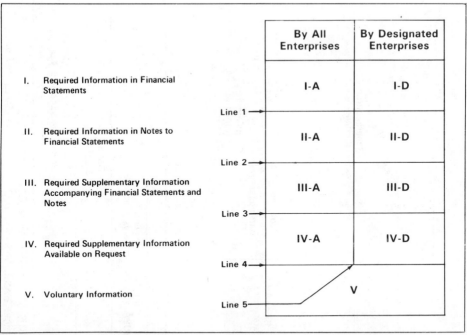

FIGURE 4.2   KINDS OF INFORMATION PROVIDED BY LOCATION AND APPLICABILITY

Source: FASB, *Invitation to Comment on Financial Statements and Other Means of Financial Reporting* (Stamford, Conn., 1980), p. 4.

tails of authorized and outstanding capital stock should be displayed as part of the caption within the balance sheet or in a separate schedule as part of the footnotes.

In general, it would seem desirable to present summarized information in the basic statements and details elsewhere, since this should enable the user to gain a broad overview of the financial position, results of operations, and changes in financial position. The user's comprehension can then be enlarged by studying supporting schedules and narrative disclosures. Moreover, many users desire only a general knowledge, and presenting relatively uncluttered basic statements should help them without detracting from the ability of more analytical users to gain a detailed understanding.

Once a decision has been reached on what goes into the basic financial statements, the issue of location of narrative disclosures must be addressed; again, few explicit rules exist. In distinguishing information to be presented in the footnotes from that disclosed in other locations apart from the basic financial statements, the qualitative characteristics of the data to be disclosed are important. Generally, information presented in the footnotes tends to be precise, objective, verifiable, and historical (frequently termed *hard data*). Conversely, information reported other than in the basic financial statements and footnotes is often judgmental, predictive, experimental, imprecise, uncertain, or unverifiable (frequently termed *soft data*).

The invitation to comment (FASB, 1980e) discussed earlier tries to make the distinction based on a *complete* perspective versus a *different* perspective. In the Board's tentative view the basic statements and footnotes should be *complete,* covering all the elements of financial statements from a single perspective—for example, historical costs measured in nominal units of currency. This definition would then classify as supplementary any information giving a different perspective, such as segment data or information about effects of inflation.

This approach may be useful to the FASB in making decisions on what supplementary information to require, but does not seem sufficiently clear to use as the primary guideline for making distinctions between supplementary information and the basic financial statements or for determining whether required supplementary information should accompany the financial statements and notes or should be available on request. These decisions should be made on the basis of optimizing relevance, reliability, and costliness—the three essential considerations applicable to all financial information.

FEI Reporting/Disclosure Model

The Financial Executives Institute (FEI) has defined a reporting and disclosure model to differentiate between formal and informal reporting systems. The principal attributes of this model are based on objectivity or reliability, as illustrated in Figure 4.3.

In general, the formal reporting model identified by the FEI deals almost entirely with hard auditable or verifiable information drawn directly from the historical accounting system. The FEI approach places footnote disclosures within this category. In contrast, the informal system is perceived as consisting of information that is less verifiable, more judgmental, and frequently experimental in nature. Disclosures classified here include projections and forecasts, detailed analytical information (such as management's discussion of results), and experimental information (such as that designed to portray the effects of inflation).

Formal System	Informal System
Factual and interpretive information	Subjective and uncertain information
Emphasis on numbers	Emphasis on words
Based on historical cost accounting	Alternative attributes
Subject to attestation	Subject to review
Focus on cash/earning power	Assessment of management
Financial Statements	**Supplemental Disclosures**
Balance Sheet	Future prospects
Income Statement	Contingencies
Funds Statement	Segment reporting
Footnotes	Management discussion and analysis
	Impact of inflation
	Business policy/strategy

FIGURE 4.3   FEI REPORTING/DISCLOSURE MODEL
SOURCE: FEI letter of December 15, 1977, to FASB in response to the December 2, 1976 *Discussion Memorandum on Elements of Financial Statements and Their Measurement.*

The similarities with the FASB's information spectrum are apparent, although the FASB has focused on subdividing the informal system area into the three categories shown in the third through fifth columns of Figure 4.1.

NOTES TO FINANCIAL STATEMENTS

APB Statement 4 (1970) recognized that it would be impossible to include all the necessary financial information into the basic financial statements—indeed, Statement 4 recognized what was true from the very origin of external financial reporting: ". . . information given on the face of the statements is largely restricted to that which can be represented by a number described by a very few words" (AC 1027.26).

Four categories of disclosure were required by APB Statement 4 (AC 1027.26):

1. Customary or routine disclosures—whatever the authoritative accounting literature requires, plus some traditional information (which has been shrinking as it becomes encompassed in the volumes of authoritative pronouncements since the issuance of Statement 4 in 1970);
2. Changes in accounting principles;
3. Subsequent events; and
4. Accounting policies.

The FASB has now reconfigured the concept of footnote disclosure, suggesting that it represents the "shadow" from the basic financial statements covering

a. Qualitative information about recognized elements (of financial statements) in general
b. Qualitative information about particular recognized elements
c. Quantitative information about particular recognized elements
d. Information about unrecognized elements . . . (oil and gas reserves, possible contingencies). [FASB, 1980e, p. 18]

While it may be possible to think in these abstract terms in building a financial disclosure model, it is difficult to translate them into current practice. The confusion has been contributed to by the FASB itself in requiring some data in notes (e.g., segment reporting) and some outside (e.g., oil and gas reserves). And the earlier SEC and Auditing Standards Board determinations to allow unaudited footnotes raised questions as to why the information was in the footnotes in the first place. The discussion that follows is based on current practice.

Characteristics of Footnote Disclosures

Information appearing in financial statements, including footnotes, tends to (but does not always) have certain characteristics. Among these are that

- Information entering the accounting processing system and included in the financial statements must be quantifiable in units of money. Data that cannot be quantified are generally not included within the body of the basic financial statements.
- The accounting process collects and reports information of a historical nature—the results of transactions that have occurred in the past. These transactions are denominated in terms of the exchange prices in effect at the date that the transactions were consummated.
- The information must be of a type subject to objective verification by independent accountants (though sometimes, as with contingencies, it may not be possible to verify).
- The elements of information should be similar to permit reasonable aggregation.

Since footnotes are directly influenced by the characteristics of the information presented in the basic financial statements, they usually deal with historical transactions denominated in monetary units, the terms of which are subject to reasonable verification. In addition, footnotes should also possess the general characteristics of readability, understandability, and relevance. Future-oriented information, subjective analyses, and disclosures of an experimental nature are typically not presented in the footnotes unless specifically required by GAAP or by the SEC.

Determining the Composition of Footnotes

Although it is reasonable as a general guideline to limit footnote disclosure to hard data, additional factors may need to be considered; differences in management judgment and in company circumstances will necessarily result in variations in presentation.

Influence of GAAP. Information required to be disclosed under GAAP is usually presented in the footnotes. Authoritative standards or regulations sometimes provide for soft information to be presented in the footnotes. For example, as discussed below, the SEC requires oil and gas producing companies to project future net revenues from proved oil and gas reserves using certain specified assumptions and to include this in SEC filings containing financial statements. Because of the precarious and soft nature of such projections and the fact that the FASB has not recognized these disclosures as GAAP, the SEC will not require, though they had so proposed, that the projections be audited by independent accountants for years ending after December 25, 1980.

Relationship to Basic Financial Statements. Information directly related to or expanding on amounts reported in the basic financial statements will generally be presented in the footnotes. General information relating to the activities of the reporting entity, economic conditions affecting operations, statistical data, descriptions of environmental impact matters, and other items that are not closely related to the basic financial statements should usually be disclosed outside the footnotes.

Degree of Auditor Involvement. Since data appearing in the footnotes are covered by the independent accountant's report unless marked unaudited, the susceptibility of information to audit is a consideration in determining where a particular element of information should be disclosed. Presentation in the footnotes conveys a greater sense of reliability and may lend additional emphasis to the information.

Types of Information in Footnotes

To a significant extent, footnote disclosures follow the four categories of disclosure mentioned above (AC 1027.26) and are made to comply with specified GAAP, the rules and regulations of the SEC, industry accounting and audit guides issued by the AICPA, and other semiauthoritative pronouncements, such as AcSEC SOPs. Thus footnote disclosures may be characterized as oriented towards compliance to a considerable degree.

Nevertheless, the specific information disclosed in the footnotes and the manner in which it is presented still depend heavily on management's judgment, the unique characteristics of the enterprise and the industry, and other matters that may be significant to users of the statements. A good illustration of this variety is provided by Figure 4.4, which shows the type of information frequently disclosed in a summary of accounting policies and the number of surveyed companies (out of a total of 600) disclosing such information.

Figure 4.4 indicates remarkable stability in the number of companies—in fact, most of those surveyed—reporting on the first seven categories. Predominant majorities considered each of these areas as deserving coverage in all years. On the other hand, the proportions disclosing their policies for earnings per share increased significantly over the four-year period, indicating the effect of the SEC's requirement for computational exhibit in Form 10-K. Finally, the number of companies reporting on foreign currency translation methods fell sharply in 1976, presumably because SFAS 8 (AC 1083) standardized accounting procedures in this area, leading many to conclude that repetition of the established principles was unnecessary. However, half the group surveyed apparently considered a discussion

	Number of Companies			
	1978	1977	1976	1975
Consolidation basis	589	584	584	578
Depreciation methods	589	581	586	583
Inventory pricing	555	557	556	556
Interperiod tax allocation	544	546	543	557
Property	514	504	505	497
Employee benefits	355	360	360	359
Amortization of intangibles	309	320	307	333
Earnings per share calculation	311	295	299	234
Translation of foreign currencies	213	238	301	401
Leasing transactions	116	N/C	N/C	N/C

N/C—not compiled.

FIGURE 4.4   DISCLOSURE OF ACCOUNTING POLICIES
SOURCE: AICPA, *Accounting Trends and Techniques* (New York, 1979), p. 43.

of this topic to be worthwhile, exhibiting the extent to which discretion determines the precise contents of footnote disclosure.

Footnote Preparation Considerations

Several factors to be considered in the preparation of footnotes follow:

* The notes should be grouped together in a separate section of the annual report adjacent to the financial statements of which they are an integral part;
* The notes should be individually numbered or clearly titled, as this is ordinarily necessary to facilitate cross-referencing to appropriate items in the financial statements;
* The section containing the notes should be identified as *Notes to Financial Statements* or something similar, to distinguish it from other sections in the report; and
* The notes should be legible and, for SEC filings, the minimum type size utilized must meet specified criteria.

The order in which the notes are presented varies greatly, but the notes should be in a logical sequence. Frequently they appear in the same order in which they are referred to in the financial statements. Sometimes they are in order of importance as perceived by the company. Also, the description of accounting policies, as required in APB 22 (AC 2045), generally appears as either the first note or as a separate statement immediately preceding the footnotes or basic financial statements. Required footnotes dealing with information on changing prices, and optional footnotes covering such items as quarterly financial data and other soft information, may be conveniently relegated to the end of the footnote section and clearly identified as unaudited. A few companies intersperse footnote data in an annual report financial review section, without specific cross-referencing within the financial statement.

As to footnote content, GAAP requires a large number of disclosures, and these are detailed in the relevant chapters throughout this *Handbook*.

In instances where financial statements for two or more fiscal years are presented, appropriate disclosures should be included for each year. This does not mean that all of the same disclosures are required for each year. Rather, judgment should be exercised in determining which disclosures relating to a prior year (if not mandatory for all years presented) remain meaningful and which are no longer relevant.

SUPPLEMENTARY DISCLOSURES

In recent years, supplementary disclosures have come to include more soft, or judgmental, information. This information first assisted users in interpreting the actual historical statements. Publication of detailed business segment information and the inclusion of the management discussion and analysis were key steps in that regard. Equipped with such details, investors are supposedly better able to understand the character and composition of a given business, to isolate unusual elements affecting the profitability of its individual components, and, accordingly, to develop an understanding of underlying trends that may have predictive value.

This approach essentially provides users with an enhanced ability to formulate their own projections, but the demand for additional analytical data to further improve these capabilities continues. In particular, with the SEC having attached a high priority to providing information that will enable users to better understand the impact of inflation on historical results, the FASB released SFAS 33, *Financial Reporting and Changing Prices* (AC 1072), which *requires* supplementary disclosure by larger publicly held companies. In a separate development, a growing number of observers believe that companies should communicate forecasts and other future-oriented information directly to users, and the SEC now *permits* it and has encouraged its publication through provision of a safe harbor for information issued in good faith and with a reasonable basis.

Required Disclosures

It is almost impossible to make a clean cut between required and voluntary information. The only supplementary information so far required by the FASB is SFAS 33 data (and that is required for some companies only). Oil and gas reserve quantity data are permitted by SFAS 25 to be in footnotes or to be given as supplementary data (AC 6022.06), but this was done in order to reconcile SFAS 25 with the SEC's override of SFAS 19 (AC 6021).

By its power to approve or disapprove registration of securities and other filings and its responsibility to oversee the operation of the securities markets, the SEC can and unquestionably does exert a major influence on the nature and extent of narrative disclosures. Traditionally, the SEC has encouraged the expansion of supplementary information, whether outside or within the footnotes, operating on the basic premise that competitive markets—if they are to function efficiently—

require full disclosure of all material facts. Accordingly, Regulation S-X had been patch-quilted over time to require extensive operating and financial information to be filed by most registrants. It was finally given a major overhaul late in 1980, as discussed earlier in this chapter.

Inflation-Related Disclosures. The impact of inflation on financial statements prepared on the historical cost basis of accounting has been of concern to accounting theoreticians for many years. In the 1970's, as rates of inflation in most Western countries increased, the distorting effects of inflation on reported financial results received greater attention.

Replacement cost data. A very significant disclosure development was the issuance in 1976 of ASR 190, in which the SEC required registrants meeting certain size criteria to disclose estimated current replacement costs for inventories and productive capacity in their Form 10-K filings. In addition, depreciation expense and cost of sales were to be indicated on a replacement cost basis.

The initial appearance of the replacement cost data in 1976 annual reports following the publication of ASR 190 was awaited with interest in the financial community. In particular, there was considerable speculation as to the impact that the information might have on the stock market. However, following the publication of annual reports, a number of empirical studies concluded that the availability of replacement cost data had no significant effect on relative equity prices (see Chapter 6). This suggests either that the stock market was already able to incorporate the impact of inflation through other means or that the replacement cost data were not helpful from a valuation perspective.

FASB standard. The FASB recognized a need nonetheless (somewhat at the strong insistence of the SEC) and in 1979 released SFAS 33, *Financial Reporting and Changing Prices* (AC 1072), which requires supplementary disclosures of constant dollar *and* current cost information by large publicly held enterprises, as fully described in Chapter 8. These FASB requirements were issued amid considerable controversy, with many believing that the FASB should have encouraged a wide range of experimentation for several years before making a mandatory selection. Thus, from the standpoint of narrative disclosures, this is likely to be an area of further expansion and heated debate. ASR 190 information will no longer be required after December 31, 1980, since at that point companies must begin to give current cost information under SFAS 33.

Oil and Gas Industry Disclosures. In SFAS 19 (AC 6021) the FASB had settled on successful efforts accounting (rejecting the full cost method) only to have this decision overturned by the SEC, which believed that a system could be devised to incorporate reserve values directly into the financial statements. (See Chapter 37 for a detailed discussion.) Pending the development of this method—reserve recognition accounting, or RRA—the SEC expressly permitted registrants to continue both successful efforts and full cost accounting, causing certain reconsiderations by the FASB of the location of reserve quantity disclosures.

Quantity data. By the time the FASB got around to taking action in response to the SEC override of SFAS 19, it had already issued SFAC 1 (AC 1210) on financial reporting objectives and thus was aiming at disclosure of supplementary data outside the financial statements (AC 6022.28). Accordingly, it changed the location of reserve *quantity* information, permitting its positioning as supplementary information accompanying but outside the financial statements (AC 6022.06). These proved reserve disclosures (AC 6021.050-.051) were retained as to quantities only, even though the SEC also requires a dollar valuation to be given, as discussed in the next paragraph.

Reserve recognition accounting. In concluding that neither the successful efforts method nor the full cost method was adequate, the SEC set out to develop a new method, which it terms *reserve recognition accounting,* a form of current value accounting. Under this approach, changes in discounted reserve values would be reflected in income as they occur, the total of discounted reserve values would be capitalized as an asset on the balance sheet, and all exploration and production expenses would be charged to income as they occur. The SEC has expressed the hope that RRA could replace the traditional historical cost methods in the primary financial statements during the early 1980's.

Specifically, the new requirements established by the SEC for fiscal years ending after December 25, 1979, call for oil and gas producing companies to report future net revenues from their proved reserves. Companies are required to estimate the future production from reserves, to apply year-end prices to obtain projected gross revenues, and then to subtract estimated future development and operating costs to arrive at what the SEC terms future net revenues. This cash-flow stream is to be both reported on an undiscounted basis and discounted at a prescribed 10%.

Development of such information requires many assumptions and estimates, and the results must be considered extremely judgmental and soft. Nevertheless, the disclosures represent a major element of an attempt by the SEC to develop a new, value-based form of accounting for the petroleum industry. Although many observers question the likelihood of the ultimate success of this experiment in the petroleum industry, it has generated wide concern in many other industries. In any event, the debate surrounding this requirement provides a good illustration of the controversy that the imposition of new narrative disclosures can create.

Voluntary Disclosures

The several items covered in this section are voluntary in the sense that they are not required of any companies as part of or accompanying financial statements prepared in conformity with GAAP. However, the SEC's recently revised Form 10-K calls for a management discussion and analysis of financial condition and results of operations and for the presentation of significant five-year trend data; so for SEC registrants, these certainly cannot be looked on as entirely voluntary.

Management's Discussion and Analysis. The importance of management's analysis and interpretation of reported financial information is summarized in SFAC 1 (AC 1210.54):

Management knows more about the enterprise and its affairs than investors, creditors, or other "outsiders" and can often increase the usefulness of financial information by identifying certain transactions, other events, and circumstances that affect the enterprise and explaining their financial impact on it. . . . Moreover, financial reporting often provides information that depends on, or is affected by, management's estimates and judgment. Investors, creditors, and others are aided in evaluating estimates and judgmental information by explanations of underlying assumptions or methods used, including disclosure of significant uncertainties about principal underlying assumptions or estimates. . . .

Clearly, there is an increasing awareness of the need to more fully communicate management's perceptions of operating results to investors. This approach necessarily involves the use of opinions, analytical data, and other soft information; however, a general consensus seems to have been reached that the potential utility of the information is sufficient to overcome its inherently imprecise nature.

Historical developments. A major step toward using narrative disclosures to aid financial statement users in identifying underlying trends in profitability occurred in 1974 with the issuance of ASR 159 by the SEC. This ASR required that reports filed with the commission contain a separate section entitled Management's Discussion and Analysis of the Summary of Operations, which would include

. . . a statement explaining (1) material changes from period to period in the amounts of the items of revenues and expenses, and (2) changes in accounting principles or practices or in the method of their application that have a material effect on net income as reported.

Although ASR 159 did not attempt to specify all the subjects that should be covered in the management discussion and analysis, it did list the following examples of matters that should be considered in its preparation:

- Material changes in product mix or in the relative profitability of lines of business;
- Material changes in advertising, research, development, product introduction, or other discretionary costs;
- The acquisition or disposition of a material asset other than in the ordinary course of business;
- Material and unusual charges or gains, including credits or charges associated with discontinuation of operations;
- Material changes in assumptions underlying deferred costs and the plan for amortization of such costs;
- Material changes in assumed investment return and in actuarial assumptions used to calculate contributions to pension funds; and
- The closing of a material facility or material interruption of business or completion of a material contract.

The release also provided the following guidelines regarding the manner in which the analysis was to be prepared:

The textual analysis should be presented in a manner that will best communicate the significant elements necessary to a clear understanding by the investor of the financial results. Favorable as well as unfavorable trends and changes should be discussed. Tables and charts may be used where appropriate. A mechanistic approach to this analysis which uses boilerplate or compliance jargon should be avoided.

This section of the financial report was intended to provide investors with management's analysis of the earnings data and to allow an assessment of the source and probability of the recurrence of earnings or losses. Although interpretations of financial data are necessarily subjective in nature, the data forming the basis for such interpretations in this instance would be based on historical transactions.

Subsequent to ASR 159, the Advisory Committee on Corporate Disclosure (SEC, 1977a) recommended the following in the management analysis area:

- Broader latitude should be given to registrants in making analytical disclosures and better directions are needed both as to quantitative analysis and as to the explanations and discussions needed to put the analytical disclosures into perspective; and
- The analysis should include a discussion of material facts, which, in the opinion of management, may make historical operations not indicative of future operations.

Current requirements. Late in 1980, the SEC made major changes to Form 10-K, incorporating an entirely restructured management discussion and analysis of financial condition and results of operations. The major provisions of this release are

1. The discussion is to be focused on the financial statements, and is no longer centered on the summary of operations, which has been eliminated as part of the same series of changes.
2. Discussion is to include three financial aspects of the registrant's business—liquidity, capital resources, and results of operations.
3. Favorable or unfavorable trends should be emphasized, and significant events or uncertainties identified.
4. Management discussion of segment information would be required only if, in the registrant's judgment, it would be appropriate to an understanding of the business.
5. Information concerning the effects of inflation and changing prices would be required for all registrants. However, those companies to which SFAS 33 is applicable may satisfy both the requirementts of SFAS 33 and the SEC with a single presentation.
6. The percentage tests and line-by-line analysis encouraged by the previous requirements have been eliminated. However, the causes for material changes in line items should be discussed.
7. Though projections or other forward-looking information is not specifically required, its presentation on a voluntary basis is encouraged.
8. There are no specific provisions with respect to the location of management's discussion, except for the general requirement that the discussion should be included within the annual shareholders' report.

At this point it appears that the basic framework for an illuminating management analysis of earnings is in place, although undoubtedly continuing efforts will be needed to ensure that the device is used to maximum advantage, and to reduce the amount of boilerplate that has been used in many management analyses in the past.

The SEC's rules do not specifically require auditor review or other association with information presented in the management discussion. However, as prescribed by SAS 8 (AU 550), the auditor should read the information appearing in this and other sections of the annual report or Form 10-K and consider whether it is materially inconsistent with that contained in the financial statements and related footnotes.

Financial Reviews. In addition to the financial statements section and management's discussion and analysis of earnings, annual reports to stockholders generally include a wide variety of other voluntary financial data, often presented in a financial review section.

Financial reviews have become increasingly popular in recent years, and many variations have appeared in practice. At one extreme some financial reviews contain only limited data, while at the other extreme the mandatory footnote information has been integrated with a large volume of statistical and operating data and with an extended narrative description of operations and results.

The financial review section can also accommodate a great variety of both general and industry-specific information pursuant to requirements established by the SEC, stock exchanges, and other regulatory bodies. Common disclosures include such items as comments by management on significant aspects of operations during the period, a description of major changes in productive facilities or assets, and data regarding changes in key members of management or the board of directors. Examples of mandatory industry-specific disclosures include reserve information for oil and gas producing companies, methods utilized in the determination of policy reserves for life insurance companies, and purchase order backlogs for government contractors.

Financial reviews generally include voluntary disclosures that can take many different forms. Indeed, almost every industry has certain unique characteristics on which managements may wish to elaborate in their annual reports. Examples include discussion of geographic regions served and quantities of aircraft, vehicles, or track mileage for transportation companies; timber resources for forest products companies; and acreage owned by land developers. A brief description of factors that may influence the extent of voluntary disclosures is given below:

- Data that management considers important to the understanding of the company's affairs and the business environment in which it operates;
- The extent to which competitors disclose voluntary information, together with the extent to which management may desire to adopt a progressive or leading disclosure role within its industry;
- The extent to which the general public may believe that additional information should be made available with respect to a particular industry's activities;
- Pressures from financial analysts for expanded operating and financial data;
- The extent to which disclosures made on a voluntary basis may preempt the establishment of more onerous reporting requirements by regulatory bodies; and

- The potential that exists to inform the public concerning industry problems, with the objective of improving consumer attitudes and the political climate in which business operates.

Clearly, not all the above factors are likely to be present for any single company at any given time. Also, individual companies will need to reassess their voluntary disclosure practices periodically, considering the likelihood that competitive and environmental considerations will fluctuate in importance from time to time.

Given the variety of different motivations behind providing voluntary disclosures, such disclosures are themselves extremely varied in practice. For example:

- Business has shown increasing concern over the growing costs of government regulation. Some companies have begun to include information on the costs of such regulation in their financial reviews (see Figure 4.5).
- A sizeable number of companies have discussed the effects of inflation on their operations, using various quantitative approaches. With the issuance of SFAS 33 (AC 1072), greater uniformity will occur for large public companies.
- Discussion of the effects of foreign exchange translation often extends well beyond the requirements imposed by SFAS 8 (AC 1083), particularly in the case of companies subject to large exposures.
- Some companies reported detailed information on business and geographic segments well in advance of SFAS 14 requirements (AC 2081).
- Petroleum companies have published very detailed operating and financial statistics for many years, in response to interest expressed by security analysts and the general public in their industry's activities.

The financial review section offers several clear advantages, but some possible drawbacks also exist. Care must be exercised to ensure that data included beyond those required by GAAP are not in any way contradictory of the mandatory disclosures. Further, the additional data will usually be subjected to testing and review by the independent accountants if the financial review is used in lieu of footnotes, and this may result in some additional audit costs. Also, the auditors may not be in a position to evaluate some of the financial review disclosures, causing some physical rearrangement of the information so that only parts of it will be specifically incorporated into the financial statements (usually by listing the applicable page numbers).

Future-Oriented Disclosures. While the AICPA is concerned primarily with providing accountants with standards for the review of a forecast and for attesting to the reasonableness of the assumptions underlying the forecast (see AICPA, 1979j, and Chapter 33), the SEC does not even formally distinguish between forecasts and projections. Instead, the SEC has recently become concerned with encouraging the availability and publication of forward-looking information that is not presently available to most external users of financial information.

In November 1978 the commission decided that its long-standing policy should be reversed to permit the disclosure of relevant, material forward-looking information that is reliable to an acceptable degree. In announcing this new position, the commission stated (in Release 33-5992):

R. J. Reynolds Industries' continuing study of the costs of government regulation to its shareholders showed that the company spent $34.3 million on compliance in 1978, nearly 19 percent higher than the dollar amount of the regulatory burden on RJR in 1977.

Expenditures for compliance reduced the company's earnings an estimated 11 cents per share during 1978. The bottom line effect would have been more pronounced except that more than one-third of the $34.3 million RJR spent to comply with regulations was for capital projects. Because only a fraction of the spending for capital assets is charged against earnings in any one year, most of the $12.4 million RJR spent in 1978 for regulatory-related capital projects did not reduce reported earnings per share. However, through depreciation charges, these capital costs will have a negative impact on earnings over the entire useful lives of the assets involved.

Once again, in 1978 by far the largest expense RJR incurred for regulatory compliance—approximately $22 million—was employee cost. The parent and operating companies expended nearly 738,000 man-hours filling out forms, filing reports and performing other essentially nonproductive tasks directly related to government regulation. This was an increase of more than 14 percent over the staff time devoted to compliance in the prior year.

The dramatic increase in regulatory costs brought to light by RJR's most recent study did not include similar costs at Del Monte Corporation, which was not yet part of Reynolds Industries in 1978. However, Del Monte's own survey revealed that its compliance costs also went up that year, to $15.5 million from $14.2 million in 1977, an increase of 9.2 percent.

The majority of the regulations encompassed by the study were issued by agencies or bureaus of the U. S. federal government. Conservative estimates were used for determining the cost of regulation whenever expenditures could not be precisely identified. Activities carried out primarily for operating reasons were totally excluded from the survey, even if their cost is heavily influenced by regulatory requirements. For example, RJR's survey did not cover the costs to the company of serving, in effect, as a collection agency for taxes payable by its employees.

One of the primary factors contributing to inflation in the United States is declining productivity. Regulation for its own sake has no economic benefit and, in fact, tends to depress productivity, creating a climate in which inflation is more apt to thrive.

If the 19 percent annual increase in compliance costs experienced by Reynolds Industries accurately reflects the increasing impact of regulation on the entire economy—and RJR believes it does—then it is clear this nonproductive sector not only is growing at a faster rate than inflation, but also exceeds by an even wider margin the rate of real growth in the U. S. economy.

Human and financial resources used up by regulation are not replaceable. Inevitably, if compliance costs continue to increase at the rates RJR has identified, the limited resources available for investments to improve productivity, job opportunities and, not incidentally, shareholder returns, will be further depleted.

In the past year, there have been some encouraging signs that the public and its elected representatives are beginning to understand the inflationary impact of government regulation. By quantifying the effect of regulation on the value of our shareholders' investment, Reynolds Industries hopes to demonstrate that there can be economic and social costs associated with government regulation that far outweigh any benefits to the consumer.

FIGURE 4.5   EXAMPLE OF VOLUNTARY DISCLOSURE—COST OF GOVERNMENT REGULATION

SOURCE: R. J. Reynolds Industries, 1979 Annual Report.

The availability of forward-looking and analytical information is important to an investor's assessment of a corporation's future earning power and may be material to informed investment decision making. Projections and other types of forward-looking information are generally available within the investment community and are obtained and used by investors and their advisers. . . .

In light of the significance attached to projection information and the prevalence of projections in the corporate and investment community, the Commission has determined to follow the recommendations of the Advisory Committee [on Corporate Disclosure] and wishes to encourage companies to disclose management projections in both their filings with the Commission and in general.

Safe harbor rule. Moreover, the SEC has adopted a safe harbor rule covering such projections. This rule indicates (in Release 33-6084):

A statement containing a projection of revenues, income (loss), earnings (loss) per share or other financial items shall be deemed not to be an untrue statement of a material fact, a statement false or misleading with respect to any material fact, an omission to state a material fact necessary to make a statement not misleading, or the employment of a manipulative, deceptive, or fraudulent device, contrivance, scheme, transaction, act, practice, course of business, or an artifice to defraud, as those terms are used in the Securities Act of 1933 or rules and regulations thereunder, if such statement (1) was prepared with a reasonable basis, and (2) was disclosed in good faith.

The safe harbor rule imposes specific responsibilities on management for the preparation of projections and other future-oriented information on a reasonable basis and the disclosure of such in good faith. However, future-oriented data should not be disclosed on a selective basis; that is, management has the responsibility to provide as clear and straightforward an assessment of the current prospects as is possible and present unfavorable as well as favorable information about future business prospects. Although the safe harbor rule does not specifically require the disclosure of the underlying assumptions on which the data are based, the SEC suggests that this is desirable.

Industry concerns. Industry response to the SEC's recommendations has been limited, undoubtedly reflecting serious concern as to the wisdom of making formal forward-looking projections. From the point of view of businesses, forward-looking disclosures entail a number of problems:

1. Projections may convey an unwarranted impression of accuracy. To attempt to mitigate this difficulty by providing ranges of estimates, as opposed to single-point forecasts, could entail elaborate explanations of the differential assumptions that would confuse many users.
2. Projections are virtually certain to become outdated very quickly. Therefore, to be useful and to avoid misleading the public, they would almost inevitably require frequent updating—in many cases on at least a monthly basis. A series of monthly profit projections could well display an erratic pattern of considerable variability that could confuse even sophisticated users unless very detailed, specific assumptions were

disclosed. However, reporting such detailed assumptions could potentially prejudice ongoing negotiations and other company interests.

3. Forecasts and projections may be used by competitors to the detriment of the reporting entity.

4. Management may feel compelled to meet published forecasts to the point of making short-run decisions that are not in the shareholders' best interests. For example, a high technology company might be tempted to cut its research and development spending to reduce expenses in the short run.

5. The disclosure of forecast assumptions by companies in certain highly concentrated industries could be perceived as being aimed at controlling the market. This could expose them to attack under the antitrust statutes.

6. Failure of the enterprise to meet its indicated projections could generate stockholder dissatisfaction and possibly litigation. In this regard, the safe harbor rule may afford insufficient protection. While the rule does indicate that the SEC will apply a generally reasonable standard in determining whether or not a violation may have occurred, it is not clear that it provides similar protection against charges made by third parties alleging injury. Legal opinion on this latter issue is divided and, until resolved, this uncertainty will continue to be a major impediment.

In view of these concerns, it is not surprising that no great increase in forward-looking disclosures has so far materialized. This reflects the fact that to most businesses the unresolved practical problems are seen to outweigh the more intangible benefits attributable to this variety of disclosure.

OTHER FINANCIAL DISCLOSURE MATTERS

Auditor's Perspective

Adequacy of disclosure is a primary concern to the auditor under the third GAAS standard of reporting, which says: "Informative disclosures in the financial statements are to be regarded as reasonably adequate unless otherwise stated in the report" (AU 150.02). This was further articulated in 1960 in SAP 30 and is now codified in AU 430 (as most recently amended by SAS 32):

The presentation of financial statements in conformity with generally accepted accounting principles comprehends the adequacy of disclosures involving material matters. These matters relate to the form, arrangement, and content of the financial statements with their appended notes including, for example, the terminology used, amount of detail given, classification of items in the statements, and bases of amounts set forth. Whether disclosure of a particular matter is required is for the independent auditor to consider in light of the circumstances and facts of which he is aware at that time. [AU 430.02]

The prerevision version also said that "verbosity should not be mistaken for adequate disclosure." Long footnotes do not necessarily mean better footnotes. Thus the nearly fourfold increase over the past ten years in the space consumed by footnotes has occurred despite efforts by financial statement issuers and auditors to truncate the verbiage.

A very significant part of the auditor's involvement always has been with hard objective information. GAAS never contemplated that any of the material with which the auditor would be associated would be less than objectively verifiable, and thus the citation above from SAS 32 hardly seems useful to such material. To compensate, the Auditing Standards Board has been issuing specific SASs to deal with soft data.

Audit Implications of Soft Disclosures

The independent accountant's responsibility traditionally extended only to the objectively verifiable historical data reported in the financial statements and footnotes. Of course, the auditor is required by SAS 8 (AU 550) to read other information in documents containing audited financial statements, such as the annual report, for reasonableness and consistency with that included in the financial statements, but such additional data are not mentioned in the auditor's report unless there is something negative to say. However, the growing importance of soft disclosure has begun to influence this traditional approach.

With respect to auditability of soft disclosures, existing professional standards require that there be sufficient competent evidence available to afford a reasonable basis for the auditor's opinion. Thus, soft disclosures must be examined on a case-by-case basis to assess the extent to which such evidence can be obtained. Forecasts and forward-looking projections depend substantially on management's plans and assessment of the future; even so, the AICPA has exposed procedures for forecast review (AICPA, 1979j) leading to the formulation of the CPA's opinion on the reasonableness of the forecast. (See Chapter 33.)

Auditability of inflation-related disclosures depends on the nature of the approach in question. For example, constant dollar financial statements can be audited to the same extent as the corresponding historical cost financial statements. On the other hand, replacement or current cost information depends on management's estimates and judgments to a very significant extent and poses limitations on the extent to which auditor corroboration is feasible. In the case of replacement cost disclosures, the SEC believed it was important to have at least some auditor review. As a result SAS 18 (AU 730) specified certain limited procedures. These were restricted to providing the auditor with a reasonable basis for considering (1) whether the replacement cost information was prepared and presented in accordance with Regulation S-X and (2) whether management's disclosures were consistent with responses given to certain inquiries made by the auditor. Thus, the audit role with respect to replacement cost disclosures has been essentially one of reviewing procedures and of calling attention to inconsistencies in the published information.

Given the likelihood of proliferation of supplementary data required to be a part of the financial reporting package, such as SFAS 33 (AC 1072) data, the Auditing Standards Board has issued SAS 27, *Supplementary Information Required by the Financial Accounting Standards Board* (AU 553). This provides that the auditor must apply certain limited procedures to supplemental information required by the FASB and that he must expand his standard auditor's report only to call attention to the omission of required supplemental information, improper measurement or presentation of such information, or inability to perform the procedures listed in the next paragraph. So far, explicit reporting on the review and results, absent deficiencies, is not permitted (AU 553.11).

The procedures the auditor should apply are (AU 553.07) to

a. Inquire of management regarding the methods of preparing the information, including (1) whether it is measured and presented within guidelines prescribed by the FASB, (2) whether methods of measurement or presentation have been changed from those used in the prior period and the reasons for any such changes, and (3) any significant assumptions or interpretations underlying the measurement or presentation.

b. Compare the information for consistency with (1) management's responses to the foregoing inquiries, (2) audited financial statements, and (3) other knowledge obtained during the examination of the financial statements.

c. Consider whether representations on supplementary information required by the FASB should be included in specific written representations obtained from management.

d. Apply additional procedures, if any, that other Statements prescribe for specific types of supplementary information required by the FASB.

e. Make additional inquiries if application of the foregoing procedures causes the auditor to believe that the information may not be measured or presented within applicable guidelines.

Note that SAS 27 applies to FASB requirements; thus it recognizes that the FASB is broadening into financial *information* as opposed to only financial statements. SAS 28, *Supplementary Information on the Effects of Changing Prices* (AU 554), adds specificity to the generalized requirements of SAS 27; this is further covered in Chapter 8.

One of the problems facing auditors is the prospect of liability for erroneous information under Section 11 of the 1933 Securities Act. Of course, this applies to all information in the financial statements, but the problem gets more difficult as to soft and/or unaudited data. In order to obtain accountants' reports on such data in registration statements, the SEC has been considering rules to exclude accountants from liability for reports issued in good faith—for example, reports on unaudited interim information are now specifically exempt. Others will be dealt with on a case-by-case basis.

Differential Disclosures

Among users of financial reports are those who have knowledge of economics, business, and reporting practices and who, as a result, are able to interpret and assess detailed quantitative data. Such users include professional analysts who desire to develop an in-depth understanding of corporate activity and operating results. On the other hand, some users have only a very limited understanding of information in financial reports. Such users generally do not have the time to study or the training necessary to fully understand such quantitative information. Between these two extremes, all shades of understanding exist.

Information users also vary widely in how they utilize financial statements in the decision-making processes. Some rely extensively on the analysis of quantitative data, while others base their conclusions on more subjective factors. Accordingly, whether information is of primary importance is a matter of how it is used.

Industry has generally attempted to meet the needs of all users by issuing a single set of general purpose financial statements and supplementary narrative disclosures in their annual reports to shareholders. However, the arrangement of financial information within annual reports suggests that many companies are aware of the varying levels of interest among users and attempt to accommodate these interests by careful presentation.

For example, many annual reports now include a highlights section that contains only a few key data series such as net income, earnings per share, capital expenditures, and so on—obviously a very basic level of detail. A second level consists of a compendium of trends in significant financial and operating data. Such summaries frequently extend to several pages and include information for five years. A third level of detail comprises the actual financial statements for the period. Although presentation practice varies, many companies prefer to keep the three primary statements relatively undetailed and to provide supplementary detail either in the footnotes or in a related financial review. Some very detailed or specialized information is excluded altogether from reports to shareholders and is published only in the Form 10-K reports filed with the SEC. (However, with the late-1980 changes in Form 10-K as discussed earlier in this chapter, this will change in some respects.)

One current concern is that the sheer volume of data included in financial reports is obscuring the important information. This has led some accountants to call for differential disclosure, namely the presentation of two or more types of reports or levels of information designed specifically for users with different levels of sophistication. For example, one level of disclosure could include detailed technical information that may be useful to the professional analyst. A second level could be condensed, containing less detailed information and more summarized data, which less sophisticated users could more readily understand.

The concept of differential disclosure poses a number of practical problems. One complication is classifying the user population into strata of varying sophistication in addition to deciding, in principle, what information to furnish each group. Supplying sophisticated (and, frequently, large) investors with more detailed information than that routinely supplied to smaller, less professional users would seem to be inherently inequitable. If the information is important to proper assessments by investors and creditors, it should arguably be made available to all without discrimination.

Both the SEC and the FASB appear to have adopted the general premise that disclosure should serve the needs of knowledgeable users. The SEC's Sommer Committee found evidence to suggest that individual investors are probably not as sophisticated in their information utilization as are financial analysts. However, they use the same types of information and engage in the same decision processes as do analysts and other professionals. As a result, the Sommer Committee recommended that

> . . . the Commission should not operate from the premise that filings with it must be directly usable by unsophisticated investors. Assumption of such a premise would almost inevitably result in only the most basic information being mandated. . . .
>
> The Commission's emphasis must be on ensuring the disclosure of that information

which will be of use to reasonably knowledgeable or sophisticated investors. Implementation of this emphasis in no way sacrifices the interests of unsophisticated investors. A major implication of the efficient market literature and research is that security prices reflect all information available to the market. All investors benefit from sophisticated information whether they can, themselves, understand and use it, or not, because security prices more fully reflect intrinsic values. . . . [SEC, 1977a, pp. 312-314]

The FASB reached a similar conclusion in SFAC 1:

Financial reporting should provide information that is useful to present and potential investors and creditors and other users in making rational investment, credit, and similar decisions. The information should be comprehensible to those who have a reasonable understanding of business and economic activities and are willing to study the information with reasonable diligence. [AC 1210.34] . . .

Financial information is a tool and, like most tools, cannot be of much direct help to those who are unable or unwilling to use it or who misuse it. Its use can be learned, however, and financial reporting should provide information that can be used by all—nonprofessionals as well as professionals—who are willing to learn to use it properly. Efforts may be needed to increase the understandability of financial information. Cost-benefit considerations may indicate that information understood or used by only a few should not be provided. Conversely, financial reporting should not exclude relevant information merely because it is difficult for some to understand or because some investors or creditors choose not to use it. [AC 1210.36]

These comments of the Sommer Committee and the FASB suggest that the test for inclusion of information in financial reports should be the usefulness of such information in the decision-making process and not the level of competence of the prospective user. This is the approach followed in the major revisions of Regulation S-X and Form 10-K in late 1980, discussed earlier in this chapter. Accordingly, it appears that the use of differential disclosure will probably not be significantly expanded unless the present financial reporting environment changes.

Future Trends

Narrative disclosures have expanded significantly in recent years and there is every indication that their role will continue to increase. The growing complexity of business and the environment within which it operates, the continuing refinement of accounting principles, and public demands for additional information all have contributed to this trend.

The character of narrative disclosures has also displayed a significant change in emphasis. Not only has there been a great increase in the disclosure of hard, quantitative information extracted from the historical accounting system, but attention has focused on providing users with assistance in interpreting available information and, in some cases, on making forward projections and other soft or judgmental data directly available. This changing emphasis in part reflects a belief that the greater relevance of soft information more than outweighs its reduced reliability. The continuing trend toward soft disclosures remains surrounded by controversy. The ultimate role of soft information within the system of narrative disclosure is as yet uncertain.

While required information in financial statements and in notes to financial statements should be the same for all business enterprises under generally accepted accounting principles, information required for some but not all business enterprises should preferably be designated as supplementary information. This distinction could be implemented in a manner completely consistent with the recommendations of the Committee on Generally Accepted Accounting Principles for Smaller and/or Closely Held Businesses discussed earlier. This would mean that information not required for smaller and/or closely held businesses would be designated as supplementary information.

Of course, specific criteria would be needed for determining which business enterprises are required to supply such information. This approach is illustrated by SFAS 33 and could be used in the future. Also, it might be appropriate for the FASB to review disclosure requirements under generally accepted accounting principles to see if there are some that should be restricted only to certain designated enterprises, such as publicly held companies, so that such disclosures can be redesignated as supplementary information. Whether specific information required as supplementary disclosures for a designated enterprise is to be audited or presented without audit must also be made.

It is hoped that both the decision to require supplementary information and the decision to require auditing thereof will be based on optimizing the major disclosure ingredients—relevance, reliability, and costliness.

SUGGESTED READING

AICPA. *Accounting Policy Disclosure*. Financial Report Survey 1. New York, 1972. This book, based on a NAARS survey of over 8,000 published annual reports, illustrates the application of APB 22.

————. *Disclosure of Unaudited Financial Information in Audited Financial Statements.* Financial Report Survey 13. New York, 1977. This NAARS survey shows disclosures relating to quarterly results (responsive to both ASR 177 and APB 28; AC 2071.31), replacement cost information (ASR 190), subsequent events, and numerous other matters.

————. *Management Reports on Financial Statements*. Financial Report Survey 19. New York, 1979. This NAARS survey shows management reports contained in annual reports. These management reports often contain statements on management's responsibility for financial statements; internal accounting controls; audit committees; and other matters. Management reports are becoming more prevalent, in part in response to the recommendations of the Cohen Commission and the AICPA Special Advisory Committee on Reports by Management.

————. *Updated Accounting Policy Disclosure*. Financial Report Survey 15. New York, 1978. This survey is based on a NAARS search of over 7,000 annual reports, and it aims for the types and extent of disclosure given in response to APB 22, *Disclosure of Accounting Policies* (AC 2045). Sections are classified by industry as well as by topic.

Burton, John C. "The Changing Face of Financial Reporting." *Journal of Accountancy,* February, 1976, pp. 60-63. This article discusses the varied interests of users of financial information and the development of differential reporting for different users.

Securities and Exchange Commission. *Report of the Advisory Committee on Corporate Disclosure*. Washington, D.C., 1977. (The forepart of report appears in CCH Fed. Sec. L. Rep. ¶ 81,300.) In addition to the aspects mentioned in this chapter, this report covers the SEC's objectives in administering the corporate disclosure system; rule-making and monitoring practices; segment reporting; disclosure of social and environmental information; proxy statement requirements; further integration of the 1933 and 1934 acts; reporting requirements under the 1934 act; special problems of small companies; and dissemination of information.

5

Interim Financial Statements

Leonard M. Savoie[1]

NEED FOR FREQUENT FINANCIAL INFORMATION

Precise financial information cannot be determined until a business has terminated and all its transactions are complete, but reporting at annual intervals has become accepted by custom and law because the users of financial information have been willing to sacrifice some precision for the sake of currentness. Reporting at less than annual intervals—*interim financial reporting*—has also become common, since decisions based on financial data are made daily and require current

---

[1] The author acknowledges with appreciation the assistance of Walter M. Hoff of Touche Ross & Co. in review standards and certain other aspects of this chapter.

financial information. Interim reporting is currently evolving toward continuous reporting.

For the most part, this chapter focuses on interim financial disclosures by publicly held companies, because that has been a *cause celebre* of professional standard-setting bodies and the SEC. It seems, however, that the evolution has carried into private companies as well, though at a slower rate. Many of the issues explored here may in due course also apply to private companies.

Evolution

Interim financial reporting began in 1902, when the United States Steel Corporation became the first corporation in the United States to publish quarterly financial information. In 1910 the New York Stock Exchange added to its listing agreement the requirement that all newly listed companies disclose quarterly financial information. By 1920, half of the companies on the exchange published this information.

Although it required, beginning in 1946, that most companies report quarterly sales figures, the SEC did not establish formal interim reporting requirements until 1970, when it issued Form 10-Q, which called for summarized quarterly information on operations and financial position. Then in 1973 the APB reacted to the need for interim information with APB 28 (AC 2071). Although earlier authoritative pronouncements had ruled on the applicability of certain accounting principles to interim reports, APB 28 was the first attempt at comprehensive coverage.

In 1973 the SEC also introduced Form 8-K, which was designed to achieve more timely reporting of unusual charges and credits to income and to assure the involvement of the independent auditor in the disclosure of these items (see ASR 138).

Another 1973 development was the publication by the New York Stock Exchange of a white paper (New York Stock Exchange, 1973) recommending, among other things, that companies (1) mail quarterly reports to shareholders, (2) include quarterly sales and earnings data in the highlight section of the annual report, (3) publish interim balance sheets and funds-flow data, and (4) consult with their auditors before publication of quarterly reports.

Under ASR 177 (1975) the disclosure requirements for quarterly reporting by publicly held companies were increased, and in addition auditors began to be publicly associated with the review of interim financial statements of public companies through optional identification in Form 10-Q. Reacting to the SEC moves, the AICPA issued SAS 10, *Limited Review of Interim Financial Information* (AICPA, 1975h), which set the standards and procedures to be followed by the independent accountant. This SAS was superseded in 1979 by SAS 24 (AU 712), which provided more detailed specifications.

In 1979 the AICPA Accounting and Review Services Committee resolved many of the problems occurring in interim financial reporting for private companies with the issuance of SSARS 1 (AR 100), as discussed further in Chapter 16.

Though these basic documents—Forms 10-Q and 8-K, APB 28, SAS 24, and SSARS 1—continue to be amended and interpreted by the AICPA, the FASB, and the SEC, many issues still cloud interim reporting. These issues center on the objectives and uses of interim financial data, on whether there is a need for greater precision in this data, on the extent of financial disclosures, and on the relative costs and benefits of the data.

Conceptual Issues

Timely release of interim results is very important in the financial community, but early release restricts the quality of measurement. Also, disclosures in addition to the basic financial statements often cannot be fully developed, and thus interim disclosures become limited in comparison with annual disclosures.

Financial information has both real and opportunity costs. Ideally, these costs should be incurred only if they are outweighed by the benefits provided by the information, but there is no objective way to measure either the benefits or the opportunity costs. Generally, it costs less to provide summarized data based on estimates than it does to produce complete financial statements based on a full closing of the books. For interim periods, moreover, the summarized data, supplemented with information contained in the previous annual report, may provide all the financial information reasonably needed for investment decisions. Users are likely to consider the opportunity loss caused by delay in receipt of current financial information more important than the benefit of the more detailed, accurate information received later.

Costs and benefits also affect how often a company should report interim results. For some businesses, the quarter is probably the most useful interval for reporting information; in more stable industries, information in greater detail but reported semiannually might be satisfactory. In still other sectors, on the other hand, it might be desirable to encourage very frequent reporting of certain kinds of data—automobile units sold or department store sales for example.

But the primary conceptual issue is whether the interim period is part of a longer period or is a period in itself. The former position is known as the *integral view,* the latter as the *discrete view.* Under the integral view, revenue and expenses for interim periods are based on estimates of total annual revenues and expenses. The discrete view holds that earnings for each period are not affected by projections of the annual results; the methods used to measure earnings are the same for any period, whether a quarter or a year. As a practical matter some elements of both positions are recognized in present reporting.

The example in Figure 5.1 (adapted from the theory section of the May 1973 CPA examination) illustrates the differing effects of these two views on interim financial statements.

FERF Report

An important research study by Michael Schiff, *Accounting Reporting Problems —Interim Financial Statements,* was published by the Financial Executives Research Foundation in 1978. Schiff deduces the SEC's views in this way:

> Interim income numbers are the important ones and the annual income number provides merely a confirmation of the previously reported numbers. . . . [T]he central thrust for the development of accounting reporting standards should be directed to interim reporting, and modifications in annual reporting standards should be made to accommodate the interim period. The interim period is a fraction of the annual period, much as the annual period is a fraction of the entity's life. The problem of integral vs. discrete is therefore viewed as a non problem . . . ." [pp. 10-11]

Assumptions	Units	Average Per Unit	Total
Sales:			
First quarter	100	$1.50	$ 150
Second quarter	200	2.00	400
Third quarter	200	2.00	400
Fourth quarter	500	2.00	1,000
Total	1,000		1,950
Costs:			
Variable:			
Manufacturing		$ .70	700
Selling and administrative		.25	250
		$ .95	950
Fixed:			
Manufacturing			380
Selling and administrative			220
			600
Total costs			1,550
Income before taxes			$ 400

Results Using the Integral Approach

	First	Second	Third	Fourth	Year
	\multicolumn{4}{c}{Quarter}	
Sales	$150	$400	$400	$1,000	$1,950
Variable costs (at 0.95 per unit)	95	190	190	475	950
Contribution margin	55	210	210	525	1,000
Fixed costs (Allocated on contribution margin)	33	126	126	315	600
Income before taxes	$ 22	$ 84	$ 84	$ 210	$ 400
Deferred fixed costs at end of period	$117	$141	$165	$ —	$ —

FIGURE 5.1   EXAMPLE OF INTEGRAL VS. DISCRETE MEASUREMENT OF INTERIM RESULTS

RESULTS USING THE DISCRETE APPROACH

	Quarter				
	First	Second	Third	Fourth	Year
Sales	$150	$400	$400	$1,000	$1,950
Variable costs					
(at 0.95 per unit)	95	190	190	475	950
Contribution margin	55	210	210	525	1,000
Fixed costs (as incurred)	150	150	150	150	600
Income (loss) before taxes	$(95)	$ 60	$ 60	$ 375	$ 400

No deferred fixed costs
at end of any period

FIGURE 5.1 CONT'D

Schiff recommends a modest approach that would have companies prepare interim reports with reporting standards applied on a consistent basis and report any accounting change in the interim period in which it occurs with disclosure equivalent to that practiced currently in annual reports. He also observed, prophetically, that this short-term strategy would allow the FASB to defer preparing an SFAS on interim reporting until it adopted a conceptual framework.

FASB Discussion Memorandum

The FASB's May 1978 *Discussion Memorandum on an Analysis of Issues Related to Interim Financial Accounting and Reporting* was an attempt to provide a neutral document that fully surveyed the conceptual and practical issues. The discussion memorandum examined five possible objectives of and uses for interim reporting:

• To estimate annual earnings,
• To make projections,
• To identify turning points,
• To evaluate management performance, and
• To supplement the annual report.

The discussion memorandum also explored the definitions of assets, liabilities, and earnings, the characteristics of useful information, and the various methods of determining net income for an interim period. The integral and discrete views were examined in great detail, as was the possibility of a third approach that would establish criteria to determine whether the integral or the discrete view should be applied for each particular revenue or expense item.

Finally, the discussion memorandum considered whether some companies should be exempt from interim disclosure standards, either on the basis of company size or because of nonpublic ownership, and tackled the question of how much information interim period reports should disclose. Three possibilities were examined:

- Disclose essentially the same information as annual financial statements;
- Add to or delete from the annual disclosure requirements, based on the application of certain criteria to the company; or
- Present selected financial items and a summary of other items in such a way that, when viewed together with the latest annual financial statements and the preceding interim statements, the information meets requirements for fair presentation.

Less than a year after releasing the discussion memorandum, the FASB indefinitely deferred further consideration of the issues surrounding interim reporting. A conceptual framework for assets and liabilities in annual reporting was being developed, and the FASB held that the issues in interim reporting hinge on those in annual reporting. Thus the FASB believed that issues in annual reporting had to be resolved before a conceptual framework could be developed for interim reporting. (See Chapter 2 for a discussion of the conceptual framework.)

Accounting Problems

Estimates and judgments are required for determining results of operations for any period, even a whole year. Normally, though, the shorter the period, the less precise the results, because the relative importance of estimates and judgments increases as the materiality base—e.g., the reported amounts—decreases. Further, to speed the release of interim results, companies simply must rely more heavily on estimates. Of course, the more sophisticated a company's accounting system and the stronger its internal control, the less it need rely on estimates.

For example, it is almost invariably considered impractical to count and price the inventory every quarter or every month, so estimates of gross profit must be used to determine cost of goods sold. Alternatively, the company may have perpetual inventory records integrated with the accounting records, allowing direct determination of cost of goods sold, but the perpetual records may not be verified by cycle counts, and some interim allowance will be needed for annual physical inventory adjustments. A great deal could be said about how to use the gross profit method to estimate interim cost of goods sold, but the subject has been so very well explored by Leonard Lorensen in a December 1975 *Journal of Accountancy* article, "Gross Profit Method and Interim Financial Information," that detailing will be omitted here. Note, however, that the accounting requirements of the Foreign Corrupt Practices Act (see Chapter 13) may be deemed to require the existence in publicly held companies of a system of internal controls that effectively assures the reasonableness of cost of goods sold and inventory balance amounts at interim dates; this might preclude the use of the gross profit method.

The inventory problem is further complicated for companies on LIFO, since these companies must estimate not only the gross profit on their sales but also the effect of inflation and the year-end inventory quantity level. Interim LIFO computations are described in detail in Chapter 19.

Companies fortunate enough to escape inventory problems are likely to encounter similar interim problems in other areas, such as income taxes—a complex area requiring considerable estimation. In order to calculate interim income taxes, a company must estimate such items as the annual pretax income, the annual investment tax credit, and other permanent differences for the full year. (See Chapter 25 for a detailed discussion of interim income taxes.) Interim accruals for various selling expenses, general and administrative expenses, allowances for doubtful accounts, and deferrals and contingencies are further illustrations of items that normally require companies to rely heavily on estimates.

Because investors have a tendency to project a full year's results on the basis of data given for the short period, random fluctuations (a one-time significant sale) or seasonal business (the Christmas sales quarter) that occurs in short periods, if not recognized, would lead to erroneous projections. Seasonal business also raises a question about matching revenues and expenses during the year. When revenues are confined to a short season and direct costs are incurred throughout the year, is it appropriate to spread these costs proportionate to revenues?

Although there is general agreement that the conceptual issues as well as the accounting problems need resolution, few accountants expect these issues to be settled in the near future. The present AICPA, FASB, and SEC guidelines, covering both public and private companies, are described in the following sections.

ACCOUNTING AND REPORTING STANDARDS

The basic authoritative literature for interim reporting is APB 28 (AC 2071), as amended by SFAS 3 (AC 2072), SFAS 18 (AC 2082), and FASB Interpretation No. 18 (AC 2071-1). These releases provide guidance on accounting and disclosure issues peculiar to interim reporting for all companies, and particularly mandate the minimum disclosure requirements for publicly traded companies.

The APB had to develop a transitional definition of the objective of interim information in order to release APB 28, and concluded that "interim financial information is essential to provide investors and others with timely information as to the progress of the enterprise. The usefulness of such information rests on the relationship that it has to the annual results of operations" (AC 2071.09). In other words, the APB concluded that the objective of interim reports is to convey information on the financial progress of the company between annual reports.

With this objective, APB 28 adopts the integral view—"each interim period should be viewed primarily as an integral part of an annual period" (AC 2071.09). Thus, the APB recognized that certain accounting principles and practices followed for annual reporting purposes may have to be modified for reporting at interim dates. However, the board also recognized that the integral view does not always provide for the proper matching of revenues and expenses at interim dates. The result is that GAAP requires interim financial statements to be prepared basically according to annual accounting policies—with certain noteworthy exceptions, described below.

Revenues

Revenue from products sold or services rendered should be recognized as earned during an interim period on the same basis as that followed for the full year. For example, when the percentage-of-completion method is used in accounting for contracts, that method should be used for interim periods as well as for the full year.

Costs and Expenses

Revenue-Associated. Costs and expenses associated with revenue should be charged against income in those interim periods in which the revenue is recognized. Examples are materials, wages and salaries and related fringe benefits, manufacturing overhead, and provision for warranties on products sold during the period.

Although APB 28 (AC 2071.13) states that costs and expenses associated with revenue for an interim period should be similar to those for an annual period, the method used to determine the cost of inventory may be different at the interim date. For example (AC 2071.14):

1. An estimated gross profit rate may be used to determine cost of goods sold during interim periods, and a physical inventory may be used at year-end. In this case the method used at interim dates should be disclosed.
2. When LIFO base inventories liquidated at an interim date are expected to be replaced by year-end, cost of goods sold for the interim period should include the cost of replacement.
3. Inventory losses from market declines should not be deferred beyond the interim period in which the decline occurs, unless the decline is temporary and no loss is expected to be incurred in the fiscal year.
4. Companies that use standard cost accounting systems for determining inventory and product costs generally should account for interim variances in the same manner as annual ones. Thus, planned variances at interim periods that are expected to be absorbed by year-end should ordinarily be deferred.

Seasonal businesses often have interpreted this requirement in APB 28 as a justification for the capitalization of costs and expenses associated with revenue during slack off-season periods. This practice is discussed later under Seasonal Revenue, Costs, or Expenses.

Other Than Revenue-Associated. Costs and expenses other than product costs should be charged against income in interim periods as incurred or be allocated among interim periods on some empirical basis (AC 2071.15(a)). These costs and expenses include selling and general and administrative expenses.

In applying the required accounting treatment to other costs and expenses, the FASB viewed the interim period as an integral part of the annual period. Thus, a specific item benefiting more than one interim period, though normally charged to expense in an annual period, may be allocated among those interim periods; but this allocation should not be made arbitrarily. Instead it should be based on an estimate of time expired, of benefit received, or of other activity associated with the period.

When costs and expenses are based on minimum levels (contingent rentals or quantity discounts), the accrual should be figured on the total estimated expense for the year. When costs and expenses incurred in a particular interim period cannot readily be identified with the activities of other interim periods, they should be charged off as incurred. Interim gains and losses should not be deferred to later interim periods within the same fiscal year if they are not deferrable at year-end.

APB 28 illustrates these points with examples in major repairs, quantity discounts, property taxes, interest, rent, and advertising costs (AC 2071.16). Additional examples could be given in foreign translation gains and losses and research and development expenses.

Costs and expenses other than product costs normally require estimation at the interim financial date, either for the timely release of interim data or because the benefit of greater accuracy is not worth the cost. Also, uncertainty of amount (such as pension expense, which is determined only once a year) is often a factor.

Additional guidance on interim accounting for income taxes, discontinued operations, extraordinary items, and contingencies is given below.

Income taxes. In a manner consistent with its conclusions on the accounting for other costs, the APB (AC 2071.19-.20) and later the FASB (AC 2071-1) have required income taxes for each interim period to be viewed as an integral part of the taxes due for the annual period. Chapter 25 details the requirements of accounting for income taxes in interim financial statements.

Discontinued operations and extraordinary items. Gains and losses from disposition of a business, discontinued operations, and extraordinary items should be disclosed separately in the income statement for the period in which they occur; they should not be prorated over the balance of the fiscal year (AC 2071.21). In determining materiality, extraordinary items should be related to the estimated income for the full year.

Contingencies. Contingencies and other uncertainties that could be expected to affect the fairness of presentation of financial data at an interim date should be accrued and/or disclosed in interim reports in the same manner required for annual reports (AC 2071.22 and AC 4311.08-.13). Again, the determination of significance should be judged in relation to annual financial statements.

Accounting Changes

Estimates. Since estimates provide much of the information presented in interim financial reporting, changes in estimates are common. The effect of any such change should be accounted for in the period in which the change is made, and the previously reported interim information should not be restated (AC 2071.26). Disclosure as to the nature and amounts of such changes, if material in relation to the interim amounts, should be made to avoid misleading comparisons. This conforms with the requirements for reporting estimate changes in year-end financial statements (AC 1051.33).

Cumulative Effect. SFAS 3 (AC 2072.09-.11) requires the cumulative effect (to the beginning of the fiscal year) of an accounting change made during the first interim period of a fiscal year to be included in net income of that period. However, if such an accounting change is made in a period other than the first interim period, the cumulative effect should not be included in the net income of the period of the change; instead, financial statements for interim periods before the change

ASSUMPTIONS

ABC company has 1,000,000 shares of common stock issued and outstanding, and no dilutive securities, in both 1979 and 1980. In 1980, the company decided to adopt the straight-line method of depreciation for manufacturing equipment. The amounts applicable to each quarter are shown below:

Period	Net Income on the Basis of Old Accounting Principle (Accelerated Depreciation)	Gross Effect of Change to Straight-Line Depreciation	Gross Effect Less Income Taxes (50%)	Net Effect After Incentive Compensation and Related Income Taxes
Before first quarter 1979		$ 20,000	$ 10,000	$ 9,000
First quarter 1979	$1,000,000	30,000	15,000	13,500
Second quarter 1979	1,200,000	70,000	35,000	31,500
Third quarter 1979	1,100,000	50,000	25,000	22,500
Fourth quarter 1979	1,100,000	80,000	40,000	26,000
Total at beginning of 1980	$4,400,000	$250,000	$125,000	$112,500
First quarter 1980	$1,059,500	$ 90,000	$ 45,000	$ 40,500
Second quarter 1980	1,255,000	100,000	50,000	45,000
Third quarter 1980	1,150,500	110,000	55,000	49,500
Fourth quarter 1980	1,146,000	120,000	60,000	54,000
	$4,611,000	$420,000	$210,000	$189,000

FIRST QUARTER CHANGE

If the change in the depreciation method was made in the first quarter of 1980, the manner of reporting the change is as follows:

	Three Months Ended March 31	
	1980	1979
Income before cumulative effect of a change in accounting principle	$1,100,000	$1,000,000
Cumulative effect of depreciation method change on prior years	125,000	—
Net income	$1,225,000	$1,000,000

FIGURE 5.2   INTERIM REPORTING OF ACCOUNTING CHANGES
ADAPTED FROM: Appendix A of SFAS 3 (AC 2072.17-.21).

Amounts per common share:
Income before cumulative effect of
a change in accounting principle $1.10 $1.00

Amounts per common share:		
Income before cumulative effect of a change in accounting principle	$1.10	$1.00
Cumulative effect of depreciation method change on prior years	.13	—
Net income	$1.23	$1.00
Pro forma amounts assuming the new depreciation method is applied retroactively:		
Net income	$1,100,000	$1,015,000
Net income per common share	$1.10	$1.02

THIRD QUARTER CHANGE

If the change had been made in the third quarter, the manner of reporting the change in the third quarter and year-to-date financial statements is as follows:

	Three Months Ended September 30		Nine Months Ended September 30	
	1980	*1979*	*1980*	*1979*
Income before cumulative effect of a change in accounting principle	$1,200,000	$1,100,000	$3,600,000	$3,300,000
Cumulative effect of depreciation method change on prior years	—	—	125,000	—
Net income	$1,200,000	$1,100,000	$3,725,000	$3,300,000
Amounts per common share:				
Income before cumulative effect of a change in accounting principle	$1.20	$1.10	$3.60	$3.30
Cumulative effect of depreciation method change on prior years	—	—	.13	—
Net income	$1.20	$1.10	$3.73	$3.30
Pro forma amounts assuming the new depreciation method is applied retroactively:				
Net income	$1,200,000	$1,125,000	$3,600,000	$3,375,000
Net income per common share	$1.20	$1.13	$3.60	$3.38

FIGURE 5.2   CONT'D

should be retroactively restated. The cumulative effect of the change on retained earnings at the beginning of the fiscal year should be included in the net income for the year-to-date amounts. Whenever financial information is given for interim periods earlier than the period of the change (but within the same fiscal year or trailing 12 months), it should be presented on the restated basis, as if the new accounting principle had been in effect during those periods. Prior years' interim income statements presented for comparative purposes should be restated on a pro forma basis. SFAS 3 (AC 2072.11) also calls for extensive disclosure of the effect of the change in all interim period reports for the fiscal year in which the change is made.

Figure 5.2 illustrates the requirements for reporting an accounting change that has a cumulative effect. APB 20 indicates there are some rare situations, principally a change to LIFO, in which the cumulative effect is not determinable, and it is therefore not possible to compute pro forma amounts (AC 1051.26). If this type of change is made in the first interim period, the disclosures required by SFAS 3 for accounting changes that have a cumulative effect should be made (AC 2072.12); but if the change is made in a later interim period, restatement of the interim periods before the change is also required (AC 2072.13).

Correction of Error. Previously issued interim financial statements must be restated for the correction of a material error. (See Chapter 3 for discussion of prior-period adjustments.) Materiality, again, is based on the estimated income for the full fiscal year and the trend of earnings.

Summarized Information

Certain minimum disclosures are required when publicly traded companies report summarized interim financial information to their shareholders (AC 2071.30-.33). There are no similar requirements for summarized interim information of privately held companies, but it is advisable that they follow the same guidelines as public companies.[2]

Publicly traded companies that report summarized financial information to their shareholders at an interim date must (under AC 2071.30) disclose at least the data indicated in Figure 5.3. When summarized financial data are regularly reported every quarter, the information in Figure 5.3 should be furnished for the current quarter and the current year to date (the last 12 months, or *trailing 12 months,* may be given), together with comparable data for the preceding year. The APB also encouraged public companies to publish balance sheets and funds-flow data at interim dates (AC 2071.33).

These minimum disclosures required by the APB do not meet the SEC requirements for quarterly reporting on Form 10-Q or in a footnote to the annual reports of certain public companies. The SEC's interim reporting requirements are discussed later in this chapter.

---

[2] Private companies may, however, issue unaudited financial statements that omit substantially all disclosures required under GAAP (AR 100.19-.21). This is discussed further in Chapter 16.

1. Sales or gross revenues, provision for income taxes, extraordinary items (including related income tax effects), cumulative effect of a change in accounting principles or practices, and net income
2. Primary and fully diluted earnings per share data for each period presented
3. Seasonal revenues, costs, or expenses
4. Significant changes in provisions for income taxes
5. Disposal of a segment of a business and extraordinary, unusual, or infrequently occurring items
6. Contingent items
7. Changes in accounting principles or estimates
8. Significant changes in financial position

FIGURE 5.3 SUMMARIZED INTERIM INFORMATION FOR DISCLOSURE TO SHAREHOLDERS OF PUBLIC COMPANIES

Of course, these minimum disclosures of interim financial data do not constitute fair presentation in conformity with GAAP. However, users of summarized interim financial data are presumed to have read the latest annual report, including the financial statements and related disclosures, and the management commentary concerning the annual financial results. The GAAP disclosure requirements for summarized interim information should be viewed in that context.

Special Disclosure Problems

Segment Information. SFAS 18, *Financial Reporting For Segments of a Business Enterprise—Interim Financial Statements* (AC 2082), requires that any segment information presented in interim financial statements be consistent with the requirements of SFAS 14 (AC 2081). However, the segment information originally called for by SFAS 14 in financial statements for interim periods is not required as a result of the SFAS 18 amendment.

Fourth Quarter Adjustments. In the absence of a separate fourth quarter report or the disclosure of that information in the annual report, disposals of segments of a business and extraordinary, unusual, or infrequently occurring items, as well as adjustments material to the results of that quarter, should be disclosed in a note to the annual financial statements (AC 2071.31).

Seasonal Revenues, Costs, or Expenses. To avoid the possibility that interim results with material seasonal variations may be used to extrapolate the results for a full year, businesses should disclose the seasonal nature of their activities. These companies should also consider supplementing their interim reports with information for the trailing twelve months for both the current and preceding years.

There is no authoritative guidance for seasonal businesses to follow in deciding whether to defer slack-period costs and expenses. Each set of circumstances must be viewed on its own merits, and industry practices often will govern. Seasonal businesses that do defer such costs and expenses should disclose their accounting policies and the nature of their activities in their interim financial statements. An example of such a disclosure might be:

> The interim results of ABC Baseball Team, Inc. are not necessarily indicative of the annual results of operations. Substantially all of the Company's revenue is earned during the regular baseball season, which except for postseason games, extends from the middle of April to the beginning of October. Expenses such as players' and coaches' salaries, stadium and game expenses, and broadcasting expenses, which are directly related to the playing of baseball, are deferred and will be amortized to expense on the basis of the number of games played. Expenses such as general and administrative expenses, public relations, scouting, player development, and spring training have been expensed as incurred.

Earnings Per Share. Each interim period stands alone for the calculation of earnings per share. Thus, total earnings per share for the combined interim periods will not necessarily equal the annual or year-to-date calculation. For example, because of changes in the market price of the stock, an option may be antidilutive in the calculation for the third quarter but dilutive in the calculation for the nine months then ended. Market price changes are probably the main cause of the four quarters' earnings per share not equaling the annual total; other changes—some applied retroactively—are summarized in AC U2011.039-.040.

SEC Requirements

The commission's requirements for quarterly reporting, first enumerated in ASR 177 (1975), provided for the filing of Form 10-Q and for the disclosure of quarterly information in a footnote to the annual financial statements. Based on September 1980 revisions, this data can be given outside the financial statements, since it is permitted to be unaudited. These requirements now exist under the Securities Exchange Act of 1934, and are discussed separately in the subsections that follow.

Under the Securities Act of 1933, companies registering securities must often include unaudited interim financial statements (called *stub statements*) in the offering prospectus. These usually coincide with the end of a fiscal quarter, and *capsule information* on sales and earnings figures for one or two subsequent months may also be given in the text following the earnings statement. The stub statements now must also conform to the requirements of Form 10-Q, so to that extent the commentary that follows is equally applicable. However, because of the responsibility of experts (including auditors) under Section 11(a) of the 1933 act (see Chapter 46) for false and misleading statements, until recently the relationship of the auditor had been quite different; he would not consent to the inclusion in the registration statement of his report (if he had issued one) on the stub statements. (AU 710 discusses this situation in greater detail.)

As a result of the issuance of ASR 274 in January 1980, Section 11 liability no longer applies to accountants' reports on interim financial information. Presumably, many more accountants' reports on quarterly data will appear as exhibits in both 1933 and 1934 act filings in 1980. The nature of this type of accountants' report, referred to as an *SAS No. 24 report* in ASR 274, is reviewed in more detail in Chapter 16, and later in this chapter under Review Standards.

Quarterly Reporting on Form 10-Q. Filed by all companies that file with the SEC, Form 10-Q is due within 45 days of the end of the company's quarter. The form is divided into two parts, financial information and other nonfinancial information.[3] Part I requires management's analysis of the quarterly results, along with the following financial statements:

- The income statement, presented for four periods: the most recent fiscal quarter, the year to date (except in a first quarter report), and the corresponding periods of the preceding fiscal year. The trailing 12 months may also be shown.
- The balance sheet, presented as of the end of the most recent fiscal quarter and the end of the corresponding period of the preceding fiscal year.
- The statement of source and application of funds, covering the period between the end of the last fiscal year and the end of the most recent fiscal quarter and the corresponding period(s) of the preceding year. The trailing 12 months may also be shown.

Companies engaged in the seasonal production and seasonal sale of a single-crop agricultural commodity may present comparative income statements for the trailing 12 months ended with the current interim quarter instead of for the current quarter and year-to-date information.

In general, interim financial statements for Form 10-Q are to be prepared in conformity with GAAP, but some condensation of captions from those called for in the SEC annual report (Form 10-K) is permitted under specific circumstances. In any event, raw materials, work in process, and finished goods must be separately disclosed when inventories are an important factor in operating results.

Form 10-Q follows APB 28 (AC 2071.30-.33) in that not all the detailed footnotes and schedules required in annual reports are necessary for the quarterly financial statement. The instructions to the form, however, warn that disclosures must be adequate to make the information presented not misleading. Of course, annual financial statements are also supposed to include all information to make them not misleading. This anomaly has resulted in the practice of many companies to include, by reference in Form 10-Q, the footnotes appearing in the annual financial statements. A trend toward more footnotes in the Form 10-Q filing has been developing, and many quarterly financial reports are now nearly as complete and extensive as annual financial reports.

In a proposal (Release 33-6236) outstanding at the time this *Handbook* went to press, the SEC gives more specifics as to what is needed in the 10-Q footnote disclosures, based on the general premises that (1) omission is proper of notes that substantially duplicate the most recent annual report and (2) events or circumstances having a material impact and occurring since the end of the most recent fiscal year should be disclosed in the 10-Q.

Note that the 10-Q need not be sent to shareholders; it must simply be filed with the SEC. Some companies still send only brief summaries to shareholders, based

---

[3] Part II is not discussed here. See proposed revised content, Parts I and II, in Release 33-6236, September 2, 1980.

on APB 28 (AC 2071.30-.33), but it is increasingly common to use the 10-Q for both SEC and shareholder reporting, and the SEC hopes to further encourage this by its outstanding proposal for 10-Q revision.

The form further requires that in the next quarterly report filed after the date of an accounting change, a letter from the company's independent accountant should be filed as an exhibit indicating whether the change is to a principle that, in his judgment, is preferable under the circumstances. The only exception is for a change made in response to a new FASB standard. This requirement has been very controversial because there are no authoritative standards by which the auditor can determine preferability (except the limited guidance inherent in SFAS 32; AC 1052). The preferability letter is further discussed in Chapter 16.

Part I of Form 10-Q also requires management to discuss and analyze material changes in financial position and results of operations. This analysis must explain the reasons for material changes between the most recent quarter and the quarter immediately preceding it, between the most recent quarter and the same calendar quarter in the preceding year, and between the current year to date and the same calendar period in the preceding year. The SEC proposal deletes the analysis explaining changes from the immediately preceding quarter even though the income statement for that quarter is not presented. These requirements are based on annual requirements for discussion and analysis, discussed in the preceding chapter.

The registrant company was also permitted to indicate whether the independent accountants made a limited review of the 10-Q financial statements, but such a representation had to include commentary on whether all adjustments or additional disclosures proposed by the independent accountants have been reflected—and if not, why not. Because this commentary is now included in an accountant's report under SAS 24 (AU 721), the 10-Q revision proposal will, when effective, require the accountant's report to be included as an exhibit to the 10-Q. This is further discussed under Accountant's Reports.

Quarterly Information in Annual Reports

In ASR 177 the SEC instituted a requirement that certain public companies disclose selected quarterly information in a footnote to the annual financial statements, both in filings with the SEC and in published annual reports. This data may be given outside the financial statements. The requirement (now in Item 12 of Regulation S-K) applies to companies listed on an exchange or traded over the counter that meet the Federal Reserve Board's margin requirements. Exempted are companies whose income (after taxes but before extraordinary items and the cumulative effect of a change in accounting) was less than $250,000 in each of the last three years and whose total assets were less than $200 million at their most recent fiscal year-end. The commission thus limited this reporting requirement to the larger and more actively traded companies.

For each quarter within the two most recent fiscal years and for any subsequent interim period for which income statements are presented, disclosure is required of net sales, gross profit, income before extraordinary items, the cumulative effect of a change in accounting, per-share data based on such income, and net income. Any amounts that differ from those previously reported on Form 10-Q must be reconciled and explained. The auditor's involvement in the review of this interim financial information is discussed under Review Standards below.

Current Updates

Form 8-K requires that a company report any significant event on a current basis. The report is to be filed within 15 days after the occurrence of the following specified events:

- Changes in control of the registrant,
- Acquisition and disposition of a significant amount of assets other than in the ordinary course of business,
- Appointment of a receiver of the registrant in a bankruptcy or similar proceeding,
- Changes in a registrant's certifying accountant, and
- Resignation of a director of the registrant.

The form requires specific information for each of these events. For example, the financial statements of a business acquired or disposed of must be included. And in the case of a change in the company's auditor, a letter from the replaced accountant is required (see Chapter 46).

The company may also use Form 8-K to report any other event that it believes significant to security holders. These reports on "other materially important events" are to be filed within ten days after the close of the month in which the event occurred. The SEC created this option because of the difficulties in defining *significance*. The option has been used by companies to report questionable or illegal payments as well as any material unusual charges or credits made to income.

REVIEW STANDARDS

When the SEC first proposed ASR 177 (Releases 33-5549 and 33-5579), the controversy that already surrounded the auditor's association with the interim financial data intensified. The commission at first stated it was not prepared to have the interim data in a footnote to the annual report labeled "unaudited," and the accounting profession believed that the vague involvement thus implied would burden practitioners with increased litigation. They doubted whether the courts would understand the limitations of a review, and feared that the costs to educate the courts would be enormous. The public companies, meanwhile, argued that the involvement of auditors in interim reports would unduly burden them with increased costs. Further, both accused the SEC of proposing this requirement in response to a few isolated abuses.

In a 1975 speech John C. Burton, then chief accountant of the SEC, listed the four objectives that had prompted the SEC's proposal (Burton, 1975a):

1. The commission's proposal is designed to emphasize the continuous nature of the reporting process. The commmission does not believe that some reports should have a degree of reliability significantly different than others, even though there may be differences in the precision of specific accounting estimates.

2. The objective of auditor involvement is primarily to include the professional accountant's reporting skill in the interim reporting process. Independent public accountants

are the professional experts of the reporting world. Their expertise and diversity of experience, if involved in the interim reporting process, should improve the quality of this reporting.

3. The involvement of auditors will lead the profession to devote more attention to the measurement problems associated with interim results. Public accountants and standard setters do not really have a full grasp of the communication problems associated with interim reporting, since they have not involved themselves in it.

4. An additional objective to the proposal is to change the auditor's outlook on auditing from one of auditing financial statements to that of auditing the company. Historically, the auditor has tended to look at an audit engagement as a discrete task aimed at rendering an opinion on a particular set of financial statements.

As finalized, ASR 177 allowed the annual report footnote containing eight (or more) quarters to be marked "unaudited," and made auditor association with Form 10-Q financial statements optional. Since then, the SEC has revised its rules to permit placement of this data outside the financial statements, and the accounting profession has developed standards for review and reporting on interim financial statements. These review standards, first enunciated in SASs 10 and 13 (AICPA, 1975h and 1976f), were revised in 1979 in SAS 24 (AU 721), which should be referred to for important details. Some progress has been made in the legal liability area; for example, as mentioned earlier, the SEC adopted a rule in January 1980 that exempts independent accountants from the Section 11 expert's liability, as defined in the 1933 act, for alleged false and misleading interim financial statements that are unaudited. This rule was adopted to encourage greater participation by independent accountants in the issuance of interim financial statements.

Objective and Timing

The objective of the review of interim financial information under SAS 24 (AU 721) is to provide the accountant[4] with the basis for reporting whether material modifications should be made to the interim report in order to conform with GAAP. Basically, the accountant performs the review by applying his knowledge of the company's financial reporting practices and internal control procedures to those significant accounting matters of which he has become aware through inquiry and analytical review procedures. The core of his ability to perform a review is his knowledge of the company's financial reporting practices and internal controls. This knowledge, commonly referred to as the *audit base,* is almost invariably needed to facilitate an interim review (AU 721.09, fn. 4).

The review can be performed either on a timely basis (directed to quarterly reports as released) or in conjunction with the annual audit (directed to the footnote or other presentation containing the comparative four quarters' data). SAS 24 seems to lean toward performance of the review on a timely basis, because it permits the early consideration of significant accounting matters.

---

[4] The use of *accountant* in nonaudit activities is meant to emphasize that the nature of the association is not that of an auditor.

Review Process

If the accountant has obtained the requisite knowledge through having an audit base, he would need only to identify the differences between the company's reporting practices and internal controls for annual financial statements and those for interim statements (AU 721.10). However, there are situations in which it is not possible to complete an annual audit before conducting a review. In that case, the accountant needs to consider, under the practical circumstances involved, whether he can acquire an adequate knowledge of the company's reporting practices and internal controls for a review of interim financial information (AU 721.09, fn. 4). Though SAS 24 does not say how this is to be done, many accountants believe that, normally, an audit base can be obtained only through the performance of a review and evaluation of the company's internal control system and a study of the degree of compliance with the system.

A possible problem implied in SAS 24 is that many companies use accounting and reporting procedures to determine interim data that are significantly different from the procedures they use for annual data. A common example is the extent of the closing of the books and records. Some accountants believe a company must complete a reasonably formal closing to prepare an interim financial statement, even if only summaries are to be reported to the public; but it might not be necessary to apply all the procedures, or to the full extent, used for an annual closing. The accountant, however, would usually require the books of original entry to be up to date and posted on a timely basis. All significant bank accounts and subsidiary ledgers would have to be reconciled, and certain complex accounts would have to be analyzed. None of this, however, is more than probably should be expected from a system of internal control meeting the requirements of the Foreign Corrupt Practices Act.

Just as he is required to understand the company's systems and procedures in an audit of financial statements, the accountant must also do so when he performs a review of interim financial statements. Significant weaknesses in internal accounting controls or in the financial reporting processes in an interim period may preclude the accountant from performing the review.

After the audit base (or equivalent) has been obtained, procedures for reviewing interim financial statements consist primarily of inquiries about and analyses of significant accounting matters affecting the financial information to be reported. SAS 24 suggests that the following procedures be performed (summarized from AU 721.06):

1. Inquire concerning (1) the accounting system, to obtain an understanding of the manner in which transactions are recorded, classified, and summarized in the preparation of interim financial information, and (2) any significant changes in the system of internal accounting control, to ascertain their potential effect on the preparation of interim information.
2. Apply analytical review procedures to interim financial information to identify and provide a basis for inquiry about relationships and individual items that appear to be unusual. (Analytical review procedures are described in Chapter 12 and Appendix 12-A.) In applying analytical procedures, the accountant should consider the types of matters that in the preceding year or quarters have required accounting adjustments.

3. Read the minutes of meetings of stockholders, board of directors, and committees of the board of directors to identify relevant actions.

4. Read the interim financial information to consider whether the information conforms with GAAP.

5. Obtain reports from other accountants, if any, who have been engaged to make a review of the interim financial information of significant components of the reporting entity, its subsidiaries, or other investees.

6. Inquire of officers and other executives having responsibility for financial and accounting matters concerning (1) whether the interim financial information has been consistently prepared in conformity with GAAP, (2) changes in the entity's business activities or accounting practices, (3) matters as to which questions have arisen in the course of applying the foregoing procedures, and (4) events subsequent to the date of the interim financial information that would have a material effect on its presentation.

7. Obtain written representations from management concerning its responsibility for the financial information, completeness of minutes, subsequent events, and other matters as appropriate.

The issue of which company locations the accountant should visit is ordinarily decided by considerations similar to those in an audit of the annual financial statements.

Caution must be used in applying SAS 24, because it does not cover the accountant's procedures concerning a review up to the effective date of a registration statement of interim financial statements contained therein. Such "bring-up" procedures are discussed in AU 710. (An exposure draft would extend coverage to 1933 act filings—see AICPA, 1980g.)

Accountant's Documentation

Although SAS 24 does not specify the form or content of the working papers, ordinarily the accountant should document the performance and results of the review procedures. This documentation is normally in the form of a review program, account analyses, and memoranda that summarize the inquiries and the responses.

An *engagement letter* is advisable to establish a clear understanding of the nature of the services to be performed and the responsibilities to be assumed. The letter should include (1) a general description of the procedures to be performed, (2) an explanation that these procedures are substantially narrower in scope than an examination made in accordance with GAAS, and (3) a description of the form of the report.

At the completion of the timely review, a *letter of representations* must be obtained. Representations pertaining to retrospective reviews are ordinarily included in the year-end audit letter. A sample letter of representations for a timely review is included in Figure 5.4.

Specific Problems

Secondary Accountants. On engagements involving secondary accountants on whom the lead accountant expresses reliance in his annual audit report, the lead accountant would also normally require a report from the secondary accountants

(Addressed to the independent accountants):

In connection with your limited review of the unaudited interim financial information to be included in the quarterly report to shareholders and in Form 10-Q for the quarter ended June 30, 19X1, we represent that, to the best of our knowledge and belief, the financial information included in the aforementioned documents is fairly presented in conformity with generally accepted accounting principles applied on a consistent basis with that of the interim report for the quarter ended June 30, 19X0, and substantially consistent with the audited financial statements as of and for the year ended December 31, 19X0. In preparing these interim financial statements, we believe we have complied with the applicable provisions of APB 28 as well as the applicable FASB opinions and interpretations.

(Any special representations that seem to be required by the particular engagement are inserted here.)

Further, we have made available to you

1. All financial records and related data.
2. All minutes of all meetings of stockholders, directors, and committees of directors, or summaries of actions of recent meetings for which minutes have not yet been prepared.

No matters have been discovered and no events have occurred since June 30, 19X1, that we believe would require adjustments to or additional disclosure in the financial information as of that date.

We understand that your limited review was not an examination in accordance with generally accepted auditing standards, and therefore cannot be relied on to disclose matters of significance with respect to the interim financial information.

(Signatures as appropriate)

FIGURE 5.4   REPRESENTATIONS LETTER FOR TIMELY INTERIM REVIEW

as a partial basis for his own report on the interim financial statements (AU 710.06(e), fn. 3). With companies required to publish quarterly data in their annual report, the secondary accountant can be expected to cooperate, at least to the extent of the minimum review of the four quarters required as part of the year-end audit. With companies not affected by ASR 177, however, some CPAs may decline to perform the review. In this case, the principal accountant will normally be unable to accomplish his own review.

Even if the principal accountant does not express reliance in his audit report, he still would normally request participation from the secondary accountant unless the segment is immaterial. When the amounts involved are not material, the principal accountant may be able to perform sufficient inquiry and analysis at the company's corporate level to dispense with the involvement of the secondary accountant.

Internal Auditors. As in year-end audit engagements, the accountant should consider work performed by the company's internal audit staff. Although he cannot substitute that work for his own interim review work, the internal auditor's activity may affect the scope of his review because of its relationship to internal controls. Both the scope of the internal audit staff's work and the extent of the independent accountant's review of it should be documented in the working papers. Authoritative guidance on the effect of an internal audit function on the scope of the independent auditor's examination is provided by AU 322 and is discussed extensively in Appendix 11-B.

Estimates. Since estimates are usually a critical factor in the preparation of interim financial statements, the accountant should understand the basis for all the estimates used, and he should review the company's methods of allocating costs to the various interim periods. The estimates and projections used should be both logical and reasonable. In reviewing the inventory calculation, for example, the accountant should understand the method used to arrive at the gross profit rate, the degree of accuracy achieved by the company in its previous gross profit estimates, and the company's plans for the remaining interim periods.

To review the provision for income taxes, the accountant must understand the calculation of the prior year's provision, the company's effective tax rate for the entire fiscal year, and the actual results to date. After he has grasped the mechanics of the tax provision calculation, he must challenge the variables for reasonableness.

Subsequent Events Review. Some period of time elapses between the date of an interim statement and the completion of the accountant's review. The accountant is generally required to perform a subsequent events review for this period. SAS 24 limits this to inquiry and written representations (AU 721.06(f) and (g)); but an accountant may also decide to perform some other subsequent events review procedures as set forth in AU 560.10, to evaluate whether postclosing transactions affect the reviewed financial statements or their disclosures.

Accountant's Reports

At present an accountant is not required to render a report on a review of interim financial statements. He must, however, perform a review of interim or "capsule" information included in filings with the SEC under the Securities Act of 1933, and the review procedures described in AU 710, not those above from AU 721, apply to these filings. (A current Auditing Standards Board proposal [AICPA, 1980g] would somewhat unify these procedures.)

However, a company may wish to include the accountant's review report in its reports on Form 10-Q. The company may also request the accountant to render a report solely for its board of directors or audit committee. If reference is made to the accountant's review in any public document, his report should be included in the document.

The form of an accountant's report on interim financial information that is presented outside of a note to audited annual financial statements is discussed in detail in Chapter 16. That chapter also gives examples of modifications to the report that should be used for special circumstances such as scope limitations, departures from GAAP, and inadequate disclosure. In outline, the accountant's report accompanying interim financial information should consist of (AU 721.17)

1. A statement that the review of interim financial information was made in accordance with the standards for such reviews,
2. An identification of the interim financial information reviewed,
3. A description of the procedures for a review of interim financial information,
4. A statement that a review of interim financial information is substantially narrower in scope than an examination in accordance with GAAS and therefore that no opinion based on these standards is expressed, and
5. A statement that the accountant is or is not aware of any material modifications that should be made to the accompanying financial information to bring it into conformity with GAAP.

In ordinary circumstances the accountant will be able to conclude his report with the following statement: "Based on our review, we are not aware of any material modifications that should be made to the accompanying financial statements for them to be in conformity with generally accepted accounting principles." This conclusion, which is allowed by SAS 24 (AU 721.18), is a much more positive statement than was previously permitted under the earlier authoritative pronouncements (SAS 10 and SAS 13).

The report may be addressed to the company, its board of directors, or its stockholders. Generally, the report should be dated as of the date of completion of the review. In addition, each page of the interim financial information should be clearly marked "unaudited."

When interim financial information designated as unaudited is presented in a note to audited annual financial statements, the auditor ordinarily need not modify his report on the audited financial statements to make reference to his review or to the selected interim financial information, because the interim financial information has not been audited and is not required for a fair presentation in conformity with GAAP. Chapter 16 describes reporting requirements when a review of interim financial information presented in a note to audited financial statements was not made or was limited in scope.

SUGGESTED READING

Bohan, Michael. "Interim Financial Reporting: Shall We Be Discrete?" *Journal of Accounting, Auditing, & Finance,* Winter, 1979, pp. 183-187. In this article the author reviews the implications of the integral and the discrete approaches in interim financial reporting and concludes the discrete approach is more logical.

Linett, Eugene. "LIFO: Conformity Requirement Applies to Interim Reports Forming Annual Report When Combined." *Tax Adviser,* May, 1978, pp. 317-318. This article reviews the various acceptable and unacceptable approaches to calculating inventory for interim periods for companies on LIFO.

Lorensen, Leonard. "Interim Financial Information—A Legal View." *Journal of Accountancy,* December, 1973, pp. 74-76. This article is a review of the implications of the *Republic Technology Fund, Inc. v. Lionel Corporation* (CCH Fed. Sec. L. Rep. ¶ 94,069) decision on the application of GAAP in the preparation of interim financial information.

6

The Financial Analyst's Approach

David D. Hale

THE CHANGING ROLE OF THE SECURITY ANALYST

Security Analysis

The basic objective of security analysis, both traditionally and today, is to determine a value for a company's securities through investigation of all the available information. However, there has been considerable evolution in how this objective is achieved in terms of the volume of information reviewed by analysts, the methods they use to interpret it, and the integration of their analysis into the investment decision-making process.

During the past decade an information explosion has occurred in the securities business. Because security analysts operate across the multiplicity of disciplines that affect information about a company, they must understand specific industry trends and broad economic changes and have a general comprehension of financial statements. In recent years, analysts often have felt overwhelmed by the need to absorb an increasing volume of nonfinancial information and to acquire a much broader general knowledge.

Today, most analysts find it necessary to keep generally informed about regulatory developments affecting specific industries and about public policy matters. Years ago, only analysts dealing with the utility and railroad industries were concerned with government regulations; now, those responsible for coverage of the petroleum, steel, and drug industries (among others) are interested too. Analysts also keep abreast of public policies pertaining to price controls, safety standards, pollution control, import restrictions, and more. A weekly newsletter from the capital is now a regular part of the analyst's reading, and the number of investment seminars held in Washington has greatly increased during the past decade.

Complementing the greater sensitivity to public policy and political developments is a growing awareness of litigation. Defenses against legal actions, including actions by the government, can have a major impact on a firm's business, as to both cost and result. Thus, the investment community in general and analysts in particular now frequently seek research advice on the potential business implications of corporate litigation long before a final verdict is handed down or a settlement reached. So too in accounting, the trend has been for analysts to seek the advice of outside consultants. Because of the many significant changes in accounting standards during recent years, analysts now turn to consultants, usually from academe, to help them understand and interpret the potential investment impact of these changes.

Computer Assistance. *Economic forecasting,* long a mainstay of the investment analyst, has also undergone substantial change since the 1960s. With the postwar development of macroeconomic forecasting and the current availability of low-cost, high-performance computer software, it is now possible for analysts to link their company sales and profit forecasts to larger models of industry sectors, the U.S. economy, or even the world economy. Analysts no longer have to rely solely on intuitive judgments about the potential impact of different economic scenarios for a particular company or industry. Instead, they can now test the company's possible sensitivity to future economic changes by linking their company forecasts to a macromodel and simulating different assumptions about growth, inflation, or other important variables.

Widespread use of the computer has enabled analysts to generate the streams of data and financial ratios needed to track a particular company's performance against trends in the economy, an industry, or competing firms. The computer also facilitates intensive analysis, comparison, and display of large volumes of security valuation data.

Stock Selection Methods. New data processing technology is also changing the way in which investment decisions are made. Analysts still supply fundamental research opinions about earnings and dividends to their organization's portfolio managers, but the process by which these managers integrate the analysts' conclusions into actual stock selection is becoming much more systematized and quantitative.

Analysts' estimates of earnings and dividend growth for individual stocks are fed into *valuation models,* which compare their expected rate of return to the market as a whole. These expected rates of return are then risk-adjusted quantitatively by the use of either historical measures of the stock's volatility or by *regression models,* which predict risk on the basis of changes in the company's financial condition and earning power. Attractive securities will have above-average rates of return relative to their risk; unattractive securities will have either low rates of return or rates of return inadequate to compensate for probable risk.

Quantitative stock selection models have by no means fully displaced intuition, qualitative judgment, or simple "market feel" as criteria for investing, but the poor performance of the stock market during the past decade and the impact of inflation on such traditional valuation criteria as the *price/earnings (P/E) ratio* have accelerated the acceptance of newer, more systematic methods of portfolio selection and evaluation. This trend has also been reinforced by ERISA (see Chapter 24), which mandates well-documented and easily verifiable systems of stock selection.

In many ways, the changes in the investment business during the past decade have enhanced the role of the security analyst. Because there is so much more information to absorb today, the need for evaluation by a specialist has increased. The greater use of formal valuation models, meanwhile, has added to the pressure for accurate earnings and dividend forecasts. Valuation models are only as good as the assumptions that are run through them, and analysts still provide the critical assumptions.

Demise of Portfolio Managers. If the changes in the investment business during the past decade have caused any particular group to lose influence, it is portfolio managers. In organizations that assign a high priority to formal valuation models, their role has become progressively less important. They have lost much of their traditional freedom to develop a personal investment style and are now often forced to rely on either their firm's official valuation model or its general investment criteria for stock selection. Hence, the role of many portfolio managers is becoming more that of an account administrator than an actual manager.

While this trend can only go so far before investment strategy becomes totally rigid, it still has important implications for the structure of power and careers in many investment organizations. Typically, the young analyst used to aspire to a job in portfolio management after a stint in research. In the future, he may enjoy equal seniority and salary without having to leave the research department for portfolio management responsibilities.

Equity Versus Fixed Income Security Analysis. Most of the discussion in the preceding paragraphs has focused on changes in equity analysis, but many of the trends apparent there also affect bond analysis. Government regulations, litigation, or economic developments that affect a firm's earning power can also influence its

financial soundness. In the early 1970s, for example, government-mandated investment in new pollution control facilities created a heavy drain on the liquidity of
some companies in basic intensively capitalized industries. Financial ratios that
appeared relatively prudent a few years earlier quickly deteriorated.

While the economic pressures of the past decade have caused equity analysts to
become more conservative (i.e., to focus more attention on balance sheet strength
or liquidity and less on growth), bond research has acquired a more speculative
flavor. Because of inflation, many investment firms have recently begun sponsoring
high-yield bond funds. These mutual funds invest in lower-quality bonds in order
to obtain the highest possible yield available from fixed-income instruments. Since
such bonds are by definition more speculative than high-grade paper, there is obviously considerable emphasis on close monitoring of the issuing firm's financial
condition. The analyst is on the lookout for any potential quality regrading in order
to avoid capital losses (or reap capital gains, if the rating change is positive).

There is nothing new about predicting rating changes in bond analysis, but the
volume of money now available for investment in lower-quality bonds is unprece-
dented.

Financial Analysis

Financial statements, like fundamental company research, play a vital role in
security analysis. For all their acknowledged drawbacks, they remain the basic
ingredient of financial analysis. In no other single place can the investor obtain so
much detailed information about a company's sales, earning power, liquidity, assets, and capital structure.

Analysts have never read financial statements exactly the way accountants prepare them to be read, and no doubt many accountants feel this is deliberate arro-
gance. Analysts have always adjusted reported income for items they do not regard
as significant to the sustainable trend of profitability. In recent years, high inflation
and new approaches to investment valuation have caused analysts to increase the
focus of attention to include concepts such as distributable income or free cash flow
rather than just income growth itself.

These analytical developments have tended to widen the acknowledged gap between the information desired by investors and the information included in financial
statements prepared in conformity with GAAP. However, pressure from regulatory
authorities, and a very busy FASB, have caused companies to expand disclosures
to meet changing investor needs. The footnotes to financial statements now contain
material about such matters as the replacement cost of assets (see Chapter 8) or
the sales and profits of business segments (see Chapter 32). With the FASB's
finalization of SFAC 1, *Objectives of Financial Reporting by Business Enterprises*
(AC 1210), the publication of economically meaningful information is now accepted as the official goal of the financial statements of U.S. companies. Thus,
while the mosaic of information used by investors today is probably broader and
more diverse than ever, financial statements continue to play a preeminent role.[1]

---

[1] The mosaic theory holds that there is no single piece of information used by investors to
the exclusion of all other information. Financial statement analysis requires using all the
bits—hence mosaic—of information to form an overall assessment.

EARNING POWER ANALYSIS

Adjustments to the Income Statement

Earning power has been the traditional focus of equity security analysis. As Graham, Dodd, and Cottle explained in their classic text (1962, p. 28):

> The most important single factor determining a stock's value is now held to be the indicated average future earning power, i.e., the estimated average earnings for a future span of years. Intrinsic value would then be found by first forecasting this earning power and then multiplying that prediction by an appropriate capitalization.

The problem for analysts is defining earning power and then computing an earnings number they can capitalize. Economists use a concept of income that measures the increase in a company's wealth, before dividend distributions, from one year to another. The concept was described by Hicks (1946, p. 172):

> The purpose of income calculations in practical affairs is to give people an indication of the amount they can consume without impoverishing themselves. Following out this idea it would seem that we ought to define a man's income as the maximum value which he can consume during a week and still expect to be as well off at the end of the week as he was at the beginning.

The net income reported by companies in their financial statements is supposed to serve this purpose, but practical considerations and accounting convention have heavily diluted its economic significance. As the editor of *The Financial Analysts Journal* explained in "The Problem with Earnings" (Treynor, 1972, p. 1):

> The accountant's concept of earnings dates from a time when specialization of labor within the investment industry had scarcely begun, and when indeed, ownership and management had not begun to separate. The accountant is, of course, the oldest of the professionals in the investment industry, and he continues to regard accounting earnings as his most important product. The accountant defines it as what he gets when he matches costs against revenues, making any necessary allocations of cost to time periods; or as the changes in the equity account over the accounting period, before capital transactions. These are not economic definitions of earnings, but merely descriptions of the motions the accountant goes through to arrive at an earnings number.

Unusual Gains and Losses. Analysts typically arrive at an earning power falling somewhere between reported income and cash flow. Their objective is to find an earnings figure that captures normal recurring income stripped of unusual gains and losses. The analyst does not want pure cash-flow accounting, since it would obscure the relationship between a firm's profitability and liquidity and would be impractical for industries with legitimate timing gaps between revenues and collections. What concerns analysts is the *noise* in conventional accounting, i.e., generally accepted financial accounting and reporting practices that produce income figures that frequently vary from sustainable cash-flow earnings.[2]

Analysts instinctively question such items as the reduction of expense through capitalization of soft costs (plant start-up losses) and deferred charges, the reduction of income through amortization of intangibles (especially goodwill), and instant recognition of profits from sales with long collection periods. Although all these items are acceptable to varying degrees under GAAP, they are often omitted from the analyst's definition of "real" earnings. The stock market, meanwhile, perceives such earnings to have low "quality" and assigns a below-average capitalization (low P/E ratio) to them.

Nonrecurring Items. Analysts also adjust reported income for items that they regard as being nonrecurring and thus of little consequence for future profitability. Such items might include gains or losses resulting from the disposal of certain assets, sales of securities, one-time write-downs of bad debts, repurchase of company bonds at prices below carrying value, strike losses, litigation settlements, and unusual hedging transactions.

What analysts define as recurring or nonrecurring depends on a company's business and history. If a firm has a frequent problem with strikes, there will be a tendency to make less of an adjustment for strike losses. If commodity-hedging gains or losses and debt write-downs are common, the same tendency to make less of an adjustment will follow. Every company's business risks differ, and the analyst will adjust for them accordingly. As the Financial Accounting Policy Committee of the Financial Analysts Federation explained in testimony to the FASB on the objectives of financial statements (Norby and Stone, 1972, p. 76):

> All these facets of earnings add up to "earning power" which we define as the ability of the company to produce continuing earnings from the operating assets of the business over a period of years. It encompasses the concepts of normality, stability, and growth. It is not fixed but will change with changes in management, the life cycle of industries and other long-term factors. The analyst is constantly on the alert to catch incipient shifts in the direction of earning power and, consequently, even small variations in earnings can have a magnified impact on investor expectations.

Inflation Complications. Normal recurring income aside, the problem of measuring earning power has been further complicated during the past decade by the use of historical cost accounting in a period of steadily and rapidly rising prices. This results in understatement of depreciation and most non-LIFO inventory costs of sales, thus inflating reported profits and increasing the effective tax burden on companies' real earnings.

Investors have responded to the inflation problem in two ways. First, security analysts are using more and more information from outside the formal financial statements to evaluate the quality of reported profits, including footnote replacement cost data and independently derived estimates of inflation's impact on depreciation and cost of goods sold. Second, inflation has strengthened the already-

---

[2] Investors' concepts of earnings are described in the FASB's *Discussion Memorandum on an Analysis of Issues Related to Materiality,* Stamford, Conn., 1975, pp. 119-125.

budding investor interest in the use of dividend discounting models to value securities. With inflation increasing a company's working capital needs and asset replacement costs, earnings growth is no longer an adequate proxy for dividend gains. The stock market has performed poorly since the 1960s, despite large gains in nominal profits. Hence, investors have shifted their focus from just forecasting profit expansion to analyzing the potential impact of it on returns to shareholders either through dividends or capital appreciation.

In summary, then, the analyst seeks to develop a measure of the average cash-generating capacity of the business sustainable in the long run. He does not want figures that are controlled by management, but at the same time he rejects a pure cash-flow approach as not reflective of long-run average trends. He recognizes that this measure of earning power is not a perfect predictor of the future, but is a point of reckoning.

Distributable Income

The inadequacies of conventional historical cost accounting, the greater volatility in reported earnings caused by such accounting changes as SFAS 8 (AC 1083) (see Chapter 31), and the growing use of discounted dividend streams to value securities have sharpened the investment community's interest in the concept of distributable income.

Not too long ago, it was common that analysts would take dividend policy for granted and concentrate on making good earnings forecasts. Dividends were either assumed to be unimportant compared to capital appreciation or expected to increase automatically in line with earnings. However, the shrinking effect of inflation on working capital, and ever-increasing asset replacement costs, have caused corporate dividend-payout ratios for the Standard and Poors' Index of 400 stocks to shrink from an average of 55% of earnings in the first two decades of the postwar period to only about 42% recently. In a sense, this phenomenon could be an indication of the declining quality of earnings, since a greater proportion must be retained simply to sustain the business. In any event, the lackluster performance of the stock market has caused investors to increase the importance attached to the dividend portion of total common stock return.

In a report for the clients of a major Wall Street brokerage house, Hawkins (1978, p. 2) outlined the main reasons security analysts are becoming more dividend oriented:

Many of the Financial Accounting Standards Board's accounting principles have contributed to the decline in earnings and the rise of dividends as the principal basis for evaluating stocks. For example, the Board's piecemeal adoption, since its creation, of the "changes in assets and liabilities" definition of income has made earnings more volatile, harder to predict, and less indicative of a company's future earnings power. In addition, the Board's decision not to adopt some form of required inflation adjusted financial reporting has made corporate earnings in periods of inflation poor indicators of a company's ability to pay dividends, finance corporate growth, or repay debt. And, currently, the Board's struggle to develop a conceptual framework upon which to base future corporate reporting practices has created a good deal of uncertainty about how future earnings figures will be computed, what they may represent conceptually, and what might be the investment significance of these unknown earnings figures. The net result of these Board actions is that the utility of the relative price-earnings approach to identifying over- and under-valued equities has declined because earnings and price/earnings multiples are not comparable over time.

Measuring Distributable Income. Measuring distributable income combines analysis of profitability with analysis of a company's liquidity, capital needs, and external fund-raising capacity. It requires a model for forecasting a company's sources and uses of funds.

Analysts have traditionally tried to forecast dividends by comparing projected capital spending with cash flows plus whatever amount the company could borrow from outside sources. The problem with this approach is that it does not distinguish between spending for growth and spending required simply to maintain existing productive capacity. It blurs expansion and necessity. Analysts are therefore starting to experiment with the use of replacement cost data (see Chapter 8) in dividend forecasting. Income is adjusted for replacement cost depreciation[3] and the replacement cost of goods sold. The analyst then subtracts projected increases in working capital from inflation-adjusted income in order to produce an estimate of the funds available. The company's total potential net funds inflow will be the sum of these internally generated funds and its borrowing capacity (Rappaport, 1979, pp. 92-96).

Borrowing capacity. Estimating a company's borrowing capacity involves numerous subjective judgments, and company treasurers, bank loan officers, and bond analysts have to make assumptions about how much a company can borrow without jeopardizing its bond ratings or credit standing. There is no reason equity analysts cannot construct tolerance ranges for new debt additions as well as bond analysts can.

Capital spending. Capital spending forecasts also require subjective evaluation, and company management is ordinarily very cooperative in helping analysts to develop such projections. Even without management assistance, though, analysts can determine minimum ranges for dividend growth by looking at a company's historical growth record and using sustainable growth formulas to project its potential future expansion. Dividend growth cannot exceed earnings growth indefinitely, so changes in sustainable growth rates provide important clues about potential dividend distributions.

Segment information. Although distributable income analysis requires a complete review of a company's income and growth characteristics, segment information can sometimes play an important role (see Chapter 32). Many firms have one or two divisions that are essentially mature, require little further incremental investment, and provide the other operations with cash. If the earnings perfor-

---

[3] Depreciation calculated on a replacement cost basis is appropriate for the portion of a company's productive facilities that its managers would choose to replace. But managers redeploy capital, including productive facilities, from low-profit investments to those offering a higher return. Depreciation on facilities such as these should be calculated on a current price level rather than replacement cost basis to determine distributable income.

mance of these "cash cows" were to deteriorate markedly or improve substantially, the impact on dividend policy would be more pronounced than if profitability were to change elsewhere in the firm.

Dividends thus become a function of expansion plans versus the funds available. If a company has aggressive capital spending plans and only limited ability to generate funds internally or obtain them externally, dividend growth will obviously be restricted. Conversely, if capital spending plans are limited or amply covered by external funds, dividend increases will be possible. Forecasting distributable income not only allows the analyst to project dividends, it is also a good check on the consistency of management's growth strategy with its wherewithal.

Income Statement Analysis

Income statement analysis has three primary objectives: (1) isolating the different components of profit change in a particular year; (2) identifying the underlying trend of profitability; and (3) determining the sensitivity of profits to various operating and economic factors.

Analysts break down the sources of earnings change because it is impossible to evaluate the quality of earnings without knowing the individual components, e.g., the contributions that came from sales volume changes, price increases, productivity improvement, control of administrative and marketing expenses, or nonoperating factors such as interest cost and income taxes.

The trend of profits is very important, because the stock market values companies on the basis of long-term earning power, not short-term fluctuations of income. A modest deterioration or improvement in a company's perceived earning power will have a far greater impact on the share rating than larger one-time income adjustments caused by nonrecurring events.

The definition of trend in profitability analysis will vary with each company and industry. In cyclical businesses, such as steel or paper, analysis of profit trends requires comparison of earnings growth and profit margins at similar stages of different business cycles; the pattern of profit performance during the first, second, and third years of economic expansion should be examined, not just the changes from year to year. For noncyclical businesses, such as fast food or computer manufacturing, analysts will be much more sensitive to annual or even quarterly fluctuations in earnings. Companies in these industries are expected to grow at high rates almost indefinitely; thus, any interruption of their expansion pattern or any failure to meet a minimum compound growth rate objective could provoke great concern that a longer-term profit deterioration had begun.

The variability of profit growth differs with each industry, and analysts evaluate trends accordingly. Large changes in profitability from one year to the next will not by themselves influence market perceptions of a company if analysts expect them. What matters is the magnitude of profit change relative to the profit growth normal standard deviation.[4]

---

[4] Normal standard deviation refers to the usual variation in corporate profits over the course of business cycle expansions and contractions. Analysts typically expect profits to rise and fall over the course of a business cycle; their expectations of by how much are based on the past (i.e., normal) standard deviation of profits from their trend growth rate. Thus, in a re-

Identifying the sensitivity of profits to operating, financial, and economic variables requires far more information than the income statement by itself can provide. However, the income statement and balance sheet together provide enough data for the analyst to qualitatively and quantitatively review many aspects of a company's profitability; and with other financial information provided, they are also the raw material for ratios that can give the analyst useful insights into a company's operating and profit characteristics.

Sales. Sales measure demand for a company's product; thus, this is where profit analysis typically begins. The analyst must answer many questions:

1. What portion of sales growth came from volume growth, and what portion came from price increases?
2. How stable is the growth rate?
3. Has the standard deviation of sales from the growth trend increased or decreased during recent years?
4. How do price changes affect demand for the product?
5. Is the company sensitive to the business cycle, or does it have a growth cycle all its own?
6. What is the company's market share, and how does it affect profitability?

Management is required to provide an analysis of the summary of earnings in SEC filings. This analysis may give some insight into these various factors, although the quality of this disclosure has not been entirely satisfactory, tending toward mechanical rather than meaningful answers to key questions.

Sales analysis by necessity is as much macroeconomically oriented as it is company-oriented. Companies control only some of the factors that determine demand for their products. The analyst's task is to identify how successful companies are in managing those factors they *can* influence, such as advertising, competitive pricing, and quality differentials.

Cost of Goods Sold. Analysts are concerned with (1) the impact of a firm's inventory accounting method on the cost of goods sold and (2) the components of cost of goods sold.

Analysts typically expect FIFO accounting to inflate profits by understating the replacement cost of goods sold. They expect LIFO accounting, on the other hand, to adjust for price changes during periods of inflation but to boost profits artificially during periods when inventory liquidation brings older cost layers of inventory into the income statement. They look at footnote disclosures for information about how inventory accounting may have affected the quality of reported income.

---

cession, analysts will not be surprised if steel industry profits decline. What will concern them is whether profits fall by the usual 20-25% or whether they fall by significantly more or less. If they fall by more, steel company shares could decline. If they fall by less, steel company shares could increase despite weak profits. For companies in volatile or cyclical industries, it is the standard deviation of profit performance, not just absolute gains or losses in profits over the short-term, that determines stock market valuation.

Companies seldom publish detailed information about their unit production costs. Analysts usually have to make inferences about them on the basis of management discussion of cost trends, data from trade journals, and other outside sources. Relying only on the information available from the financial statements, analysts can develop insights into a company's cost structure by constructing asset utilization and cost ratios, including ratios of wages to total production costs, sales to fixed assets, fixed assets to total assets, sales to other assets, and so on. Such ratios provide indications of a firm's relative exposure to fixed or variable costs and its resulting sensitivity to any changes in the rate of capacity utilization.

Depreciation. Analysts want to know the reasonableness of a company's depreciation policy and its impact on income taxation and reported profits. Common questions include:

1. How large a gap is there between tax depreciation and book depreciation?
2. Has the company changed depreciation policy recently?
3. If so, how did management explain that change, and what was the effect on reported earnings?
4. How does a particular company's depreciation method compare with the methods used by other firms in the same industry?
5. How do asset lives compare with the norms elsewhere in the business?

Historic cost depreciation is almost never an adequate basis on which to measure the cost of replacing the assets used in production. As a result, analysts are becoming more sensitive to the gap between historical-cost-based depreciation and estimates of replacement cost depreciation published in footnotes. A large gap between the two is commonly taken to indicate a lessening in the quality of reported profits. Nevertheless, when using replacement cost data, analysts have to make sure that the higher depreciation charges shown in footnotes do not exaggerate the problem by including assets that will not be replaced or by failing to properly adjust for the impact of technological change on asset replacement costs.

Selling, General, and Administrative Expense. The ratio of selling, general, and administrative (SGA) expense to sales is a useful analytical measure of company cost control. As a rule, investors expect SGA expense to grow on a trend basis, so any sharp fluctuations from the past trend of change are carefully scrutinized. If SGA is rising rapidly, analysts want to know if the increase is due to poor cost control, a new advertising campaign, or some other marketing/administrative investment that may not yield a return until later. Conversely, a sharp decline in the rate of SGA growth may be a sign that management is trying to manipulate earnings by sharply curtailing such an easily controllable expenditure as advertising. If companies fail to publish a detailed breakdown of SGA expense, analysts request it or seek to obtain it from trade publications.

In consumer-oriented industries, ratios of advertising to sales are very important analytical measures. Raw data on advertising costs are available in the supplementary income statement information (previously Schedule XVI but changed in late 1980 to Schedule XI) required in Part IV of Form 10-K filed with the SEC, as are data on royalties, maintenance and repairs, and other items that may be of significance in certain industries.

Interest Expense. This item is ordinarily analyzed in conjunction with a general review of a company's liquidity and capital structure. Common questions are:

1. How much does the company rely on variable rate debt that could increase sharply in cost during periods of restrictive monetary policy?
2. What are the prospects for reducing the volume of short-term debt and replacing it with fixed-cost long-term bonds?
3. Does the company have a large volume of older bonds that will have to be replaced at some point with higher-cost debt?
4. Is the ratio of cash (or cash equivalents) to sales large enough to absorb any surge in volume or price hikes without increasing bank borrowing?

Credit analysts are also very interested in ratios of interest coverage, i.e., the ratios of income to all interest expenses and to categories of interest expense related to specific debt instruments. (Debt ratios are described in more detail in Chapter 22.)

Concern about interest expense varies greatly with individual companies and different stages of the business cycle. Ordinarily, interest expense becomes a major problem for most companies only during the late stages of an economic expansion, when inflation is accelerating, interest rates are rising rapidly, and balance sheet liquidity has been strained.

Income Taxes. Taxes represent a very significant part of corporate results, since tax laws in the U.S. make the government nearly an equal partner in business success. In addition, tax laws provide incentives for various kinds of corporate activity, and these tax incentives may significantly affect business decisions. Finally, the accounting approach used to record income tax expense is not consistent with the current cash outlay for taxes and provides for a number of alternative treatments that can materially increase or decrease reported income. It is important, therefore, that the analyst approach the tax figures in the income statement and balance sheet with both understanding and care.

The tax laws generally provide that taxable income should be measured in accordance with sound accounting practices that fairly measure income, but there are a number of respects in which taxable income varies from conventional accounting measurement. These differences normally occur when conventional accrual accounting deviates substantially from cash flows; generally, taxable income more closely approximates cash flow and is usually a more conservative measure. Accordingly, some analysts believe that taxable profits are a more useful and comparable income concept than conventionally reported profit.

Allocation of tax expense. Generally accepted accounting principles in the U.S. provide for the comprehensive allocation of tax expense, which is a *normalization technique.* Tax expense is generally computed by applying the current tax rate to pretax book income, regardless of the actual tax to be paid in that period. To the extent that the amount of tax to be paid differs from tax expense, that difference is identified as *deferred income tax*. (For a detailed discussion of income tax accounting, see Chapter 25.)

There is considerable controversy over *the proper analytical approach to tax expense*. Some analysts prefer to ignore the deferred portion of tax expense altogether and to treat any deferred income tax on the balance sheet as an adjustment of equity. If, as is most commonly the case, the deferral is unlikely to be reversed in the near future and thus does not constitute a call on corporate cash until some undefined future period, there is much to be said for this approach. On the other hand, there are those who argue that if the analyst is trying to appraise the long-run earning power of the business, it is not proper to ignore the fact that income cannot be sheltered indefinitely by timing differences. In this case, a normalized approach is more realistic. Since the analyst is ultimately trying to measure cash-generating capacity, the best approach is to understand what is being done in the financial statements and then reach a judgment in each case about the likely cash outflows for taxes over five to ten years.

It is important for the analyst to recognize that there are significant *alternative accounting treatments* available for tax expense. For example, a company may accrue deferred tax expense on overseas earnings to reflect the tax that might ultimately be paid when those earnings are repatriated, or it may elect not to do so if it has no current plans for repatriation. The difference between these approaches may be material. Another example is the option available to companies to take the full benefit of the investment tax credit into reported income in the year when an eligible asset is placed in service, or to defer the benefit over the life of the asset. While these two examples are the most conspicuous, there are other ways in which companies may make accounting choices that affect their tax rates as reflected in published income statements.

Footnote disclosure. An important source of information about companies' tax accounting procedures is the footnote disclosure required by the SEC. The rules require that a company provide (1) a reconciliation of the amount of tax expense to the normalized tax expense that would be expected by applying the statutory tax rate to pretax income and (2) an analysis of the sources of book/tax timing differences reflected in deferred taxes. These disclosures allow the analyst to study the company's tax history over a period of years and ask questions of management regarding possible changes. Analysts also look at capital spending programs or other expenditures that generate large tax deferrals to see if they might change.

As a rule, analysts frown on companies that use tax policies that sacrifice cash flow to maintain or enhance reported profits. FIFO accounting for inventory is regarded as poor financial policy unless inventory turnover rates are so high as to make it immaterial. The same is true of cost deferrals if the accounting policy would result in higher current cash outlays for taxes.

Foreign Currency Adjustments. Under SFAS 8 (AC 1083) (see Chapter 31), U.S. companies must report the results of their overseas subsidiaries as if their business were being conducted in dollars, with no intermediate foreign currency playing a part. When foreign financial statements are translated into dollars, movements in the exchange rate can produce holding gains or losses on net asset exposures and therefore fluctuations in profit margins much larger than those reported in the foreign currency financial statements. To compound the analytical problem, not all financial statement items are translated at the same rate. For example, cost of goods sold is translated at a different rate than sales, with the magnitude of the difference, in the analyst's view, being a function of inventory turnover rates and the size of depreciation charges in relation to income.

Fluctuating exchange rates. Floating exchange rates are relatively new and SFAS 8 was issued only a few years ago; thus, analysts are still not agreed on how to interpret foreign translation gains and losses. As a rule, they try to ignore quarterly income fluctuations caused by currency translation in the hope that these fluctuations will net out to zero by year-end. Even the analysis of annual currency translation adjustments is complicated by the absence of uniform disclosure of the effects of rate changes on the reported results of operations, which is recommended but not required by SFAS 8 (AC 1083.033). Few companies report their exchange rate gains and losses separately by such categories as the adjustment produced by balance sheet translation, margin erosion or expansion resulting from translation of sales and cost of goods at differential rates, gains or losses from export contracts, and repatriated dividends.

While analysis of foreign currency exposure is still developing, the rules analysts use to assess its effects on sustainable earning power are unlikely to differ very much from the rules now used to evaluate other items of the income statement. Questions the analyst asks include:

1. Did the currency fluctuation cause a cash gain or loss or did it merely produce a translation adjustment?
2. Has the company hedged exposures in a particular currency?
3. Is the company risking cash losses in its hedging operations in order to protect reported income from noncash translation problems?
4. Are currency gains or losses material enough to affect dividend policy?

In general, currency adjustments affect investment valuation when they appear likely to have a material impact on cash flow and dividends, not when they cause temporary distortions in reported profits. SFAS 8 would be easier to work with if companies were to improve their disclosure of the individual components of translation and exchange gains or losses. This benefit is unlikely, however, because the FASB is reconsidering SFAS 8. A significantly different translation approach that would use current exchange rates and exclude translation gains and losses from income was issued for exposure and comment by the FASB in September 1980 (1980b). If major changes are made, analysts will have to go back to square one.

Pension Expense. APB 8 (AC 4063) helped to eliminate the large year-to-year fluctuations reported in pension expense, but analysts still find pension reporting to be one of the murkiest areas of corporate disclosure. The assumptions underlying pension fund contributions include expected rates of return on pension assets, projected inflation, methods of pension funding, and more. Analysts seldom receive sufficient information with which to compare these assumptions and consequently tend to ignore the issue unless a special development (a plant closing, for example) forces them to pay attention to it.

Because of ERISA (see Chapter 24), though, pension obligations are rapidly becoming an important topic for balance sheet analysis. The FASB's recent requirement for increased disclosure (AC 6110) and increased attention by analysts will ultimately help to improve disclosure of how pension expense is computed. In addition, the FASB's in-process evaluation of pension accounting by corporations should enhance comparability and understanding of the cost of pension obligations.

Measures of Profitability and Performance

Analysts use many different ratios to evaluate and compare company profitability. Typically, they measure operating performance with ratios of gross profit to sales, operating profit to sales, pretax income to sales, and net income to sales.

These ratios are used within all industries, but they cannot be used to compare companies in different industries, since each industry has its own pricing and volume characteristics. Some industries have consistently high ratios of income to sales; others have perpetually low margins. The analyst evaluates the ratios on the basis of industry norms and trends, not on the basis of whether they are high or low in absolute terms. Thus, figures such as sales per share mean little to professional analysts, despite the fact that they are commonly used in promotionally oriented research reports trying to identify companies with large potential earnings leverage from small margin adjustments.

Pretax Income. The most universally comparable measure of profitability is the ratio of pretax income before interest to total assets. Pretax income before interest expense divided by total assets measures the return on everything a company owns, not just the assets owned by equity shareholders. In analyzing profitability, investors are not concerned with the source of capital; what matters to them is the income generated by the total pool of capital.

Adjustment of Total Assets. In calculating return on total capital and other similar ratios, analysts sometimes adjust the total asset figures to exclude large or excessive cash balances, idle plant, or facilities under construction in order to measure the return only on assets in effective use. This is done to improve *interfirm comparability of asset returns,* not to get away from the basic concept that all assets have to pull their weight.

Return on Equity. This ratio is also a widely used measure of profitability, but comparisons of equity returns can be distorted by different leverage ratios. The more a company finances assets with debt, the greater the potential return on equity. As U.S. firms have increased their borrowing since the 1960s, equity ratios have become less and less useful.

Replacement Cost Data. Although most stock research reports still discuss only historical cost return on assets, high inflation is increasing analyst interest in the use of replacement cost data to generate inflation-adjusted profit return ratios. There are still many theoretical and technical problems with the use of replacement cost data for such a purpose; for example, one has to decide how to adjust for changes in the real value of debt and asset holding gains. However, some analysts are still prepared to overlook the theoretical problems and compute ratios of income to assets adjusted to include replacement cost of fixed assets, in order to obtain a more economically meaningful measure of profitability. (See Chapter 8.)

Segment Reporting

U.S. public companies are quite diversified, whether through conglomerate acquisitions or internal growth. Analysts need information about the sales, profit, and asset breakdown of business segments and international operations. Because each segment could have different growth cycles, profit characteristics, and capital requirements, it is impossible to analyze a diversified firm without knowing details of its business mix.

Prior to SFAS 14 (AC 2081) (see Chapter 32), analysts were generally dissatisfied with the extent of many companies' disclosures. They complained about failure to disclose a sufficient number of segments and about segment definitions that did not make economic sense (Duff and Phelps, 1976, pp. 63-66). SFAS 14 has not quieted all the critics, but it has improved the quality of disclosure enough to satisfy many analysts.

Reporting information about foreign operations has been one of the most neglected areas of corporate disclosure and investment research. The earnings fluctuations produced by floating exchange rates, as well as the sheer growth of multinational business since the 1950s, have encouraged more intensive analysis of foreign operations recently, which is made easier by SFAS 14 requirements for expanded disclosures in this area. However, although progress is being made, the overall quality of analysis of firms' international activities still lags far behind the analytical treatment of domestic operations.

THE BALANCE SHEET

Liquidity Analysis

Liquidity links analysis of the income statement with that of the balance sheet. It describes the extent to which the cash resources of the enterprise will meet the demands on those resources. While it has traditionally been viewed as a short-term concept, it is increasingly being applied in a longer time frame. Thus, analysts are interested in any information about the amounts, timing, and certainty of a company's future cash flows.

Liquidity is also a relative concept. A company's financial position might be satisfactory to a bank loan officer or credit analyst, yet leave an equity analyst dissatisfied because it was not strong enough to allow the company to obtain purchase discounts or take advantage of other expansion or cost reduction opportunities.

Traditionally, analysts have measured liquidity largely by monitoring changes in working capital and a variety of balance sheet ratios, including

- Current assets to current liabilities (the current ratio),
- Accounts receivable to sales,
- Cost of goods sold to inventory,

- Cash, cash equivalents, and accounts receivable to current liabilities (the quick ratio), and
- Cash and cash equivalents to current liabilities (cash-flow analysis).

Current Ratio. The *current ratio* is among the best known liquidity ratios, but analysts seldom use it without also reviewing the more cash-oriented working capital ratios. Inventory cannot readily be used to pay bills, so the cash ratios, which omit it, provide a better measure of a company's liquidity in the event of a downturn in the economy.

Accounts Receivable to Sales. The *ratio of receivables to sales* measures the "nearness" of sales to cash. It is a good quality check on receivables during periods of economic hesitation as well as an indicator of potential working capital strain. A high ratio means that a company provides a great deal of financing for its customers, a situation that could become trying during periods of high inflation, rapid growth, or tight money. Changes in this ratio could indicate a change in credit policy, greater difficulties in collection, or an unusual pattern of sales around the balance sheet date. Any such change should be a source of questions for the analyst.

Cost of Goods Sold to Inventory. *Inventory turnover ratios* (cost of products sold divided by inventory) also provide a useful measure of potential working capital strain. If the inventory turnover slows or falls below the industry average, it could mean that a company's stocks are obsolete, in weak demand, or otherwise unsalable at regular prices. Slower turnover would also increase the company's exposure to financing problems; the longer the inventory cycle, the more financing required.

In calculating the inventory turnover ratio, it is important to use data reflecting the current cost of inventories. If a company uses LIFO, the unadjusted balance sheet amount would give misleading results. In addition, the ratio should be computed using an average inventory amount to avoid seasonal impact, although unusual year-end levels should be questioned. Further, the analyst must ask if declining business activity has led to a substantial rundown of LIFO inventory and left older, undervalued cost layers of inventory on the balance sheet.

The Quick Ratio. Ratios are only as good as the numbers they are based on, so a qualitative analysis of the balance sheet is also an essential part of liquidity analysis. Investors will read the footnotes of the financial statements for any information about special factors affecting the major components of working capital. The *quick ratio*—cash, marketable securities, and net receivables—is an indicator of the immediate debt-paying ability of a company, and raises such questions as:

1. Are there restrictions on the use of cash, such as compensating balance requirements, advance appropriations for expenses such as construction projects, or obstacles to the repatriation of foreign earnings?
2. Do one or two customers dominate the accounts receivable?
3. If so, how credit worthy are these customers?

4. Has the company published any information about the due dates of payables and receivables?

Cash-Flow Analysis. In recent years, liquidity analysis has moved beyond the balance sheet to include much more cash-flow analysis. Balance sheet ratios are now regarded as useful but static measures of liquidity. They do not provide much information about the balance of cash inflows and outflows needed for the company to remain solvent. Among the ratios that analysts use to integrate cash flow into liquidity analysis are

- Current liabilities to cash flow,
- Cash and cash equivalents to annual cash expenses,
- Net noncash income to total net income, and
- Cash flow to annual cash expenses.

As noted in the earlier discussion of distributable income, analysts construct financial models of a company's funds flow to forecast dividend changes. The statement of source and application of funds can also play a role in liquidity analysis, but it is thought to have too strong a working capital orientation to fully satisfy analysts' needs. As the investment research firm Duff and Phelps (1976, pp. 81-82) explained in a recent study of financial reporting:

> The funds statement is an important analytical tool for investors. However, as these statements are generally presented, they are not much more than a miscellaneous collection of plus and minus changes in balance sheet items. . . . The predominant emphasis on working capital serves little purpose since working capital is not an important analytical figure. The primary value of the present funds statement to the analyst is the disclosure of capital expenditures and certain asset/liability transactions.

Changes in Liquidity Analysis. The increased use of cash-flow ratios in liquidity analysis has not happened by accident. It is the result of economic changes, particularly the much greater use of debt by corporations during the past two decades. Because of the growing dependence on *leveraging,* there has been a substantial deterioration in such traditional balance sheet ratios as the current ratio, the quick ratio, and total debt to equity ratio. Several statistical studies based on these ratios show the U.S. corporate sector as very illiquid today compared to the 1950s. However, the decline appears much less stark when cash-flow ratios are used. Economic growth and high inflation have forced companies to assume more debt, but these factors have also increased the stream of net cash inflows by enough to prevent corporate liquidity from becoming as precarious as balance sheet data alone might suggest.

The instability of the economy during the 1970s has also caused liquidity analysis to become more sophisticated. During the halcyon growth period of the 1950s and 1960s many analysts gradually forgot about liquidity, financial risk, and the constraints of limited resources on growth. Prosperity and expansion were so taken for granted that concern about possible adversity and dependence on leverage were regarded as old-fashioned. After a decade that has included three credit crunches and two recessions, a synthesis is now occurring between excessive emphasis on earnings growth and a healthy concern about solvency.

Asset Analysis

The most important categories of noncurrent assets on company balance sheets are long-term marketable investments, intangible assets, and tangible fixed assets. Each presents the investor with different analytical problems.

Long-Term Marketable Investments. The present method of accounting for marketable securities (see Chapter 17) is potentially confusing to investors because it allows companies to value identical assets in different ways.

Security dealers "mark to market" all securities held for resale or investment. Insurance companies carry bond investments at amortized cost, but carry common and nonredeemable preferred equities at market value. Commercial and industrial companies, meanwhile, are required to effectively carry noncurrent marketable equity securities at cost[5] unless there is a permanent decline in their value.

Companies must publish information about the market value of their securities, so the analytical problems posed by the differing accounting treatments of long-term investments are not great. But balance sheet ratios can be distorted when there is a large gap between market value and balance sheet carrying amount, as can occur in specialized industries or with respect to nonequity portfolios. Thus, investors should be cautious how they use the investment values reported in the financial statements.

Changing the valuation method for long-term marketable investments would require income statement recognition of security gains and losses, whether realized or unrealized. While constantly under pressure to change to an all-inclusive concept of income, banks use a reporting format that separates regular banking income from security transaction gains and losses. Similar reporting by other kinds of companies could be beneficial in performing financial analysis.

Intangible Assets. Analysts generally pay little attention to goodwill and deferred charges unless they seriously distort reported income or shareholders' equity (in which case the amortization or the balance, respectively, is subtracted). Deferred charges are usually scrutinized more carefully than goodwill, especially if the deferrals are large or used frequently to reduce the earnings impact of new plant start-up expenses or marketing programs.

Intangible assets such as patents, licenses, or other commercial rights are potentially of much greater importance. The problem for the analyst is putting a value on such assets. Their real worth is frequently bound up with the continued existence of the company and so is not readily transferable. Alternatively, the intangible asset might be salable, but management may have no such intentions, making any estimate of its real worth theoretical at best. Old motion pictures are perhaps one of the best examples of such an asset.

---

[5] Noncurrent marketable equity securities are shown in the balance sheet at the lower of cost or market, but any reduction to market is "dangled" in stockholders' equity rather than charged against earnings.

Fixed Assets. Because of high inflation and corporate takeover activity, analysts are now very interested in the current value of assets. Here, however, conventional financial statements are of limited use. Historic cost accounting ignores increased current values, and similar assets acquired only a few years apart can have widely divergent values. This distorts interfirm comparisons of asset value, return on assets, and other performance measures.

Until recently, analysts could do little to remedy this problem except make their own best informal estimates of current value using price indices, market data for plant and equipment sales, or takeover bids for similar companies. But the task has been made easier by replacement cost disclosure rules (ASR 190) and FASB requirements for supplementary footnote information about the effects of inflation. SFAS 33, *Financial Reporting and Changing Prices* (AC 1072), should prove to be even more helpful.

Current Value Information

The two principal alternatives to historical dollar cost accounting are *constant dollar* (i.e., price level adjustment) and *current value* accounting. Price level adjustments in financial statements are based on one overall index and account for changes in the value of money, not changes in the value of individual assets. A current value system, by contrast, accounts for changes in the current cost or actual value of assets, not changes in the value of money—except inasmuch as they contribute to specific value changes. (See Chapter 8 for a full discussion of constant dollar and current value accounting.)

The major problem with current value disclosure is the *nonstatic nature* of the current value concept. Current value is ultimately a function of profitability, which will fluctuate with the business cycle, industry trends, and the company's own management quality. Estimating the current or replacement cost of assets is a useful starting point, but no investor or takeover bidder has ever bought a company solely on the basis of replacement cost information. Buyers are attracted to assets by expectation of future cash flow, not by estimates of their replacement cost. Indeed, companies with asset replacement costs two or three times as great as their original cost have been known to write down historical cost asset values because of their low profit-generating ability. The size of the write-off would have been much larger if the assets had been carried on the books at replacement cost.

For all the comparability and technical problems posed by current value accounting, analysts receive information no less comparable than that now provided by historic cost accounts. And with time and effort, the information quality should steadily improve.

Liability Analysis and Capital Structure

Except for special issues such as lease and pension obligations, the liability side of balance sheets does not present as many interpretation and measurement problems to analysts as the asset side does. One million dollars of long-term debt is one million dollars that must be repaid, whatever happens to the value of money or, unless it is nonrecourse debt, to the value of the assets financed by the debt.

Liability analysis usually focuses on the suitability of a company's *capital struc-*

ture, given its asset mix, to its *long-term solvency.* Again, balance sheet and cash-flow ratios are among the principal tools of liability analysis.

Debt-to-Equity Ratios. The single most important balance sheet ratio is debt to equity (either long-term debt or all debt). Equity, the basic risk capital of the enterprise, needs neither to be paid back nor to earn a minimum rate of return for the company to remain solvent. The greater the ratio of equity to debt, the less vulnerable a company will be to financial problems resulting from earnings weakness, deteriorating economic conditions, and other adverse developments.

Asset Ratios. In addition to the overall relationship of equity to debt, analysts pay careful attention to how the debt/equity mix compares with a company's asset mix. Among the ratios commonly used for this purpose are

- Fixed assets to equity,
- Fixed assets to equity and long-term debt,
- Current liabilities to total liabilities,
- Bank loans to total liabilities, and
- Current assets to total debt.

Analysts expect companies to finance fixed assets with relatively permanent capital, whether long-term debt or equity. If the company is engaged in heavy capital spending or is in a regulated industry with assurance of minimum rates of return (the utility industry might be an example), analysts are not uncomfortable with a ratio of fixed assets to equity and long-term debt greatly in excess of 1.0. Over a longer period of time, however, they are concerned if a company relying heavily on short-term borrowing to finance growth has no plans to convert some of it into equity or bond financing. High ratios of fixed assets to equity or total permanent capital and high ratios of bank borrowings to total liabilities in heavily leveraged companies are usually interpreted as signs of overleveraged exposure and financial risk.

Cash-Flow Ratios. As with liquidity, cash-flow ratios are also used to monitor long-term solvency. They include

- Cash flow to long-term debt,
- Cash flow to interest expense,
- Net income before interest expense to interest expense (times interest earned), and
- Cash flow to fixed charges.

Which particular cash-flow ratio analysts emphasize depends on the purpose of their research. Equity analysts are typically interested only in general coverage trends and their implications for new borrowing capacity. Credit analysts, by contrast, are also concerned with specific earnings and cash-flow coverage of particular categories of debt—long-term bonds, senior notes, preferred stock, bank loans, and so on.

Considerable empirical work has been done in recent years in order to develop models and ratio tests for predicting corporate financial problems. In one study, William Beaver of Stanford University concluded that the best predictors of financial difficulty, in order of usefulness, were short-term and long-term ratios of cash flow to debt, capital structure ratios, liquidity ratios, and turnover ratios (Bernstein, 1974, p. 431).

Complex Liability Items. Although the liability side of the balance sheet has traditionally been easier for analysts to interpret than the asset side, in recent years two complex items have become more important in balance sheet analysis: leases and pension fund obligations.

Leases. Lease financing has expanded dramatically since early 1960, but attempts at unifying accounting for leases did not take hold until late 1976 with the issuance of SFAS 13 (AC 4053) (see Chapter 23). Companies must now record the asset and obligation under capital leases and adjust reported income for imputed interest and depreciation, instead of charging only level payment for lease rental expense. Capitalization of leases makes most balance sheets more comparable. Before lease capitalization, many companies, especially retailers, had balance sheet debt-to-equity ratios well below average; lease financing made them appear relatively unleveraged. However, the latitude in criteria for a capital lease under SFAS 13 is such that several large retailers have capitalized fewer leases than would have been expected based on disclosures made earlier under ASR 147. For these retailers partially, and for other companies more so, SFAS 13 lease rules correct this misimpression, showing such companies to be much more leveraged than previously reported.

Pension funds. Under ERISA (see Chapter 24), 30% of a company's equity can now be taken (under certain circumstances) to satisfy unfunded pension obligations. This law and the growth of pension benefits at many companies have made unfunded pensions increasingly important for both equity and credit analysts. To date, however, financial statement disclosure of pension obligations has been very inadequate. Although the amount of the unfunded obligation is disclosed, little additional detail is provided about the actuarial assumptions that went into determining that liability. Since pension expense can within limits be increased or decreased through changes in these assumptions, analysts have felt an inability to adequately evaluate the quality of management's pension accounting practices. The formal disclosure rules for pension liabilities are now undergoing change. For 1980, more comprehensive disclosures are required by SFAS 36 (AC 4065), which the FASB considers an interim standard (Chapter 24). The FASB has undertaken a comprehensive project to review and revise accounting and reporting of pension expense and obligations by companies. Analysts welcome these new rules. Meanwhile, companies can expect more questions from analysts about the assumptions underlying their pension obligations.

Investment Risk (Beta)

Investment valuation models have long attempted to adjust the expected rate of return on individual stocks for risk through beta coefficients. Beta relates the volatility of individual stock to the volatility of the stock market as a whole. A beta of

1.0 means that a stock should move with the market. A beta above 1.0 indicates more volatility, while a beta below 1.0 suggests less volatility.

Traditionally, beta has been computed on the basis of a stock's actual performance over a number of market cycles. It has been a function of the movement in a stock compared to swings in the market. But in recent years, analysts have begun to experiment with a new concept of beta aimed at predicting stock volatility on the basis of changes in a company's profitability and financial condition. These new predictive, or accounting, betas use financial information to project a change in the market's risk perception of a company instead of relying on past risk coefficients.

In a 1975 research paper on the prediction of investment risk, Barr Rosenberg of the University of California outlined some of the key factors used to develop predictive betas. They include (pp. 97-103)

- Earnings variability,
- Market capitalization of assets (market perception of company's success),
- Maturity of the company and its size,
- Company growth orientation,
- Financial structure and use of debt, and
- Industry characteristics.

Analysts have been using these same criteria to evaluate risk for many years, but in a more subjective and qualitative manner than is often the case today. Current attempts to quantify risk systematically for investment valuation purposes reinforce the importance of company accounts in the security analysis process. However, risk quantification through mathematical models also creates pressure for accounting information to be more economically meaningful and to provide comparable figures that can be used in models linking dozens of financial relationships among hundreds of companies.

INFORMATION AND DISCLOSURE: FINDING A BALANCE

There are many conflicting pressures at work in corporate disclosure and financial reporting today. The growing complexity of modern business has increased investors' need for information, although in recent years they have often felt overwhelmed by the volume of material already supplied to them. The company's problem of balancing the supply of and demand for information is further complicated by the many different categories of investors, each with varying capacities for absorbing and interpreting information. Some investors carefully analyze financial statements; others look at them only briefly; still others rely largely on intermediaries for information. The modern corporation must not only select the correct amount of information to provide in its shareholder reports, it must also find a balance between the different levels of analytical interest.

The solution to this information problem will vary with each company and its industry's level of complexity. Analysts, of course, prefer that corporate reporting aim at the trained investor, especially institutional security analysts. They represent the primary market for investment research, and the growing volume of money controlled by pension fund managers assures that they will remain so.

However, the existence of different levels of analytical interest leads logically to the argument that differential disclosure of information is acceptable. Companies can provide a certain amount of information in their annual reports and then publish additional data in supplementary statistical tables, 10-Ks, and other reports. If companies make sure that this information is available to everyone and advertise that fact, they should be able to serve the needs of all categories of investors. Such an approach may occasionally produce some information overload, but that will be less of a problem than too little disclosure.

The information gap between small and large investors comes from the greater degree of personal contact that the latter have with companies. It is relatively simple for companies to provide everyone with equal access to published information, including the transcripts of analyst society presentations. However, there is no way companies can provide individual contact with small shareholders as they do with large institutions — for example, telephone conversations between analysts and directors of corporate investor relations or company visits in which the analyst meets with senior management. Although the information provided by such meetings can eventually reach the general public through brokerage house reports, articles in the financial press, and other media, there is no uniformity in the timing and quality of such disclosure. And those who get the information earliest still have the opportunity to act first.

The situation is not totally one-sided, though. Institutional fund managers may have the advantage of being in regular contact with the companies on their research list, but they are often hindered in their ability to take advantage of information by the sheer volume of money they have to invest. It often takes several days, even weeks and months, to establish and liquidate large portfolio holdings. Thus, institutional investors can seldom beat the market simply through frequent contact with corporate management. They must also develop proprietary conclusions based on imaginative and original analysis of the information. And to be successful, they must develop those conclusions before the market as a whole does.

It is not pure information itself that determines the success or failure of an investment organization. The stock market is a reasonably efficient processor of public information (see Chapter 47). It is the ability to interpret information perceptively and then to integrate it into the investment decision process that determines good performance.

SUGGESTED READING

Bernstein, Leopold. *Understanding Corporate Reports*. Homewood, Ill.: Dow Jones-Irwin, 1974. Although this book is now out of print and somewhat out of date, it provides an extensive and detailed discussion of all aspects of financial statement interpretation by security analysts.

FASB. *Discussion Memorandum on an Analysis of Issues Related to Criteria for Determining Materiality*. Stamford, Conn., 1975. This document suffers from repetition, but it is so detailed and so thorough that it remains instructive.

Graham, Benjamin; Dodd, David; and Cottle, Sidney. *Security Analysis: Principles and Technique*. 4th ed. New York: McGraw-Hill Book Company, 1962. This book traditionally has been the bible of security analysis, so a look through it is a prerequisite for anyone interested in the field of investment research.

Rappaport, Alfred. "Measuring Company Growth Capacity During Inflation." *Harvard Business Review*, January-February, 1979, pp. 91-100. Accountants often complain that they do not understand how analysts can use inflation accounting information. This article provides an excellent discussion of how inflation accounting disclosures can be used to analyze a company's earning power and dividend policies. It will be useful for anyone interested in inflation accounting or the emphasis in the investment community today on dividend forecasting.

7

Earnings Measurement

Robert S. Kay

EARNINGS CONCEPTS

Earnings measurement problems have befuddled accountants for decades—from the time, after World War II, that the income statement took on more prominence for investors than the balance sheet. Chapters in this *Handbook* deal with revenue and expense recognition, unusual problems concerning gains and losses, how to reflect changing prices in financial statements, and how to make forecasts of future financial statements, just to mention a few individual and practical problems bearing on earnings measurement. This chapter presents an integrated and conceptually slanted discussion.

Though economic notions abound in this chapter, it is not heavily biased towards economic theory, nor does it dwell on economist's terms. Instead, the objective is to get the professional to focus on the underlying issues in earnings measurement when a problem comes up. Even if the problem is not unique, a good deal of thought may be needed about *why* a particular solution will be acceptable and, perhaps just as importantly, defensible.

In the sections that follow, this chapter describes basic perspectives on earnings, the elements of financial statements and what measurement bases are or could be used, and revenue and expense recognition criteria for both monetary and non-monetary exchanges. Finally, the chapter covers earnings reporting concepts, or how the income statement could be organized to properly report earnings phenomena, especially if a difference between net earnings and comprehensive income is established.

Earning Power

Earning power is defined in the Trueblood Report as "the enterprise's ability to be better off, to generate more cash, and to have earnings convertible into cash at some future date" (AICPA, 1973j, p. 23). The *ability to generate cash* is clearly a prerequisite to dividend and interest payments, and cash generation expectations are also a primary determinant of securities prices in the marketplace. It is the ability to generate cash and to pay dividends (periodic or liquidating) that must be present for common stocks to have value. Dividend payments need not be actually expected, but the *ability* to pay dividends at some time must be. An enterprise's earnings can affect market prices of equity securities that participate in those earnings simply by implying increasing or decreasing cash-generating and payout ability.

If earning power is so important, then so is the earning process that stands behind it. An enterprise's productive efforts and most of its exchange transactions with other entities are the ongoing major activities in the earning process, because the purpose of a business is to increase the value of goods or services by adding time, place, or form utility (FASB, 1979g, par. 40). If it does not cumulatively achieve this or repeat it more often than not, it will not be a successful enterprise.

The FASB further explains that despite differences in details, there are significant common characteristics among enterprises because they invest cash in noncash assets and services to earn a return and they assume a risk that no return may occur and that a part or all of the investment may be lost. All earning processes involve some combination of buying assets and services, combining and using those resources in ways that enhance their utility and value, charging a price or fee for the resulting output, and collecting the selling price or fee. The goal of each earning process is to bring more cash into an enterprise in the long run than the enterprise spends in the process. A return of investment alone is not sufficient; there must also be a return on the investment commensurate with the risks involved (FASB, 1979g, par. 41).

The income statement (or earnings statement, as it seems likely to be called in the future) is an attempt to measure the results of the earning process that took place in a given period. The analyst generally uses these statements over time as the principal means of evaluating the earning power, or long-run cash-generating capacity, of the enterprise. Any particular period's result as expressed in its earnings statement is therefore an attempt to estimate the long-run cash-generating capacity of the enterprise at its operating level during that period. This in essence is the result of the accrual accounting process: revenue recognition estimates the long-run average cash flow at the current level of activity, while recognition of expense is an estimate of the long-run average cash outflows needed to generate such inflows.

It must be recognized, however, that this conceptual construct must be made operational so as to be applied to the multiplicity of circumstances that are found in business activity. These are discussed in the remainder of this chapter. Problems of uncertainty, measurability, and abuse avoidance often lead to rules that supplement and sometimes are at variance with this theoretical approach.

Nevertheless, this basic concept of earnings is probably one most closely related to the FASB's objective for financial reporting, which provides that financial reporting should supply information helpful to the investor in predicting the amount, timing, and uncertainty of future cash flows to the firm. An enterprise with a record of stable or increasing earnings will generally be thought to have substantial earning power (assuming there is a consensus on the continued need for the enterprise's products or services). It will therefore attract investment, or at least make investment units already in the hands of owners transferable to others who may wish to participate in the process. The essential element of the earnings measurement—revenue and expense recognition—is thus extremely important.

Conceptual Framework

A brief initial review of the earnings measurement issue in the context of the FASB's conceptual framework project (discussed in Chapter 2) should be helpful. Five phases are the major ingredients:

1. What are the *objectives* of financial reporting? (Answered in SFAC 1; AC 1210.)
2. What *qualitative characteristics* should accounting information possess? (Answered in SFAC 2; AC 1220.)

3. What are the *elements* of financial statements—e.g., what is an asset or a liability?

4. How does one obtain a *measurement* of those elements—in dollars, units of purchasing power, intrinsic value in terms of gold bullion, meters, inches, or whatever?

5. Once the preceding four answers are available, what events and transactions, and what degrees of finality in each, should result in entries into the financial statements—i.e., what should be given *recognition?*

Ideally, these phases should be accomplished in the order indicated. However, pressures on the FASB for production in particular areas of current difficulty have caused the sequence to be disrupted.

In the unfinished elements category, the Board issued *Discussion Memorandum on Elements of Financial Statements and Their Measurement* (FASB, 1976b) and an initial and revised exposure draft on the search for elements (FASB, 1977c and 1979g, respectively), but has not yet issued a final statement on elements (expected near the end of 1980).

A comprehensive treatment of the measurement project would have considered various possible bases (five are described later in this chapter), but because of the proddings of the SEC that the FASB deal with the issue of inflation accounting, a partial consideration was necessary. This resulted in the issuance of SFAS 33, *Financial Reporting and Changing Prices* (AC 1072), along with three supplemental statements: SFAS 39 (AC 1073), dealing with changing prices for oil and gas and mining companies; SFAS 40 (AC 1074), covering timber resources; and SFAS 41 (AC 1075), for income-producing real estate. By approaching measurement in this way, the FASB may have been forced to prejudge the issue of supplementary versus basic financial statement inclusion of amounts displayed on a basis other than historical cost, and the broader issues in measurement have had to be deferred.

In the recognition project, research reports are due (late in 1980 or early in 1981) on asset and liability recognition (by Yuri Ijiri) and on present practices in the recognition of revenues, expenses, gains, and losses (by Henry Jaenicke). The FASB staff is also at work on a discussion memorandum to explore the conceptual issues. When these are released, the recognition phase of the conceptual framework project can finally be considered launched.

In addition, the FASB has embarked on a subsidiary piece of the conceptual framework project—how earnings are to be displayed in financial statements, covered by the *Discussion Memorandum on an Analysis of Issues Related to Reporting Earnings* (FASB, 1979a). In resolving these issues, some questions of measurement and recognition may be preempted, but only temporarily.

With the good progress already made in the conceptual framework project, it would be wrong to suggest that the FASB should delay pieces of it in order to resolve the remaining issues in exactly the right order. Previous standard-setting bodies were too intense on this point, ultimately contributing to their demise. Even now, it is all too common for the FASB to indicate that a particular standards issue will not be resolved until a designated portion of the conceptual framework is completed (e.g., interim financial reporting problems are awaiting completion of the elements phase). If many detailed standards must be delayed awaiting finalization of the conceptual framework, it would be doubly distracting to have the concepts work not proceed apace, albeit in a mixed-up order. To the FASB's credit, it is light-years further on concepts than any of its predecessors, fortifying the idea that the FASB will indeed be able to make the necessary retrospective adjustments when all the conceptual framework phases have been traversed at least once.

Economist's View

Perhaps the most frequently quoted definition of economic income is that by Hicks (1946, p. 172):

> The purpose of income calculations in practical affairs is to give people an indication of the amount they can consume without impoverishing themselves. Following out of this idea, it would seem that we ought to define a man's income as the maximum value which he can consume during a week and still expect to be as well off at the end of the week as he was at the beginning.

That is a very comprehensive view of income, but it could be broadened beyond its quantitative intent to include all monetary, nonmonetary, and personal satisfactions, whether related to a transaction or to an external event that simply had some effect on "well-offness." It is thus consumption and utility based rather than business oriented in the above formulation.

Certain accounting measurements aim for the economist's quantitative view of income, but it is impossible to measure all of the qualitative ingredients, at least in a way that will generally satisfy a variety of users. Not the least of the problems in this endeavor is the absence of standards to measure and recognize human or personal values or to recognize synergies in business enterprises (e.g., the improvement in earning power because a company has achieved optimal organization and therefore can earn extra returns, in contrast with a disorganized situation that impairs earning power).

The ultimate conclusion might be that each company would have a value represented by the discounted cash flow of *all* of its net future cash inflows. Of course, this is not accurately measurable, though in some simple businesses a reasonable guess could be made.

The uncertainties involved in predicting the future cause obvious problems for government economists who provide advice to the administration. Likewise, uncertainties about the future cause severe problems for the accountant, who is sometimes expected to transcend these difficulties and develop economic valuations that approach the ultimate.

Taxation View

Keeping the economist's definition in mind, it is interesting to note that the federal government in its taxation policies has never been much bothered by economics. As discussed more fully in Chapters 43 and 45, the income tax is a levy on income determined according to any method of accounting that clearly reflects income. However, by evolution this now means simply that the IRS may apply its judgment against that of a taxpayer concerning a particular issue for which there is vague specification (if any) in the tax regulations. In general, the tax law's view of income is more closely related to short-run cash flows than is normal accounting practice. This is based on a concept of equity that recognizes that tax cannot be paid until the cash is available to do so.

Thus, there are peculiarities in income tax accounting (in comparison with financial accounting) whereby some types of advance payments that may be refundable must be included in taxable income when received although the refund may be tax deductible when it is refunded, and certain multiyear expenses paid in advance may be fully tax deductible at the time they are paid.

More sophisticated examples of income tax differences lie in the use of income tax as a means of administering social benefits—that is, to redistribute income in a certain way, to stimulate certain areas of economic growth, to penalize certain transactions considered less desirable for the common good, and for other reasons.

For example, accelerated depreciation and asset depreciation range (ADR) approaches may be accepted without question for tax purposes, but most often these are substituted by straight-line depreciation in financial reporting, giving rise to deferred taxes (see Chapter 25). Accelerated depreciation indeed has a place in financial accounting when such an allocation of the asset cost properly corresponds with the utility expiration of the asset. Ordinarily, ADR lives are shorter than the physical—even useful—lives of assets for financial accounting purposes, often by a substantial amount. They are simply a means of establishing write-off lives that need not be challenged by the IRS, regardless of method of depreciation used; thus they really have nothing to do with financial accounting except by coincidence.

Another example is the investment tax credit (ITC) in its initial form (a reduction in the depreciable basis of the asset); the APB said it was to be deferred and amortized over the depreciable life of the asset. But it was not treated that way after Congress legislated that no one could be required to account for ITC in a prescribed manner. Naturally, whatever accounting treatment was chosen would not affect cash flow, but deferral would reduce immediate reported income, a result deemed by Congress to be inconsistent with the economic stimulant intended by the ITC.

Accountant's View

Accountants have been accused of being especially unappreciative of economic reality in financial accounting and reporting. The accountant's view of earnings is based on the improbable premise that (1) the value of the medium of exchange (cash or currency) is stable and (2) all business transactions eventually devolve to cash. Thus, what comes in is some kind of investment or revenue, what goes out is some kind of return of capital or expense, and what is left after deducting expenses from revenues (all measured in static currency units) is earnings. The approach fails to recognize changing prices and values and perhaps was never intended to be anything other than pragmatic—for surely the problems with historical cost basis accounting mentioned below had to have been recognized at the dawn of commercial record keeping.

Over the years, accountants have been quite content with an accounting model that cannot measure, in any objective way, many of the events and transactions that cause changes in the value of the business and the stability of the monetary unit. It has only been in the last ten years that the creeping misapplication of certain aspects of the accrual method of accounting has caused a noticeable anxiety about the limited measurement capabilities of the accounting model.

The historical cost model for businesses usually operates on the accrual basis— that is, resources and obligations are recognized when they have reached a "degree" of measurability and irreversibility. As is well known, however, the degree is very subjective, depending on the area, and stretch analogies resulting in overly ambitious recognition of income (which later turns out not to have had a large measure of irreversibility) have been all too frequent.

What now bothers accountants most, it seems, is the erratic (and mostly declining) value of the unit of measure—the dollar or whatever other national currency may be involved. In the U.S. the value or buying power of one unit of measure, considered only in relation to the country in which it is legal tender, has constantly decreased. For companies that operate around the world, currencies have values in relation to each other that depend in substantial measure on the perceptions of the fiscal condition of the country. There have been times when the value of the U.S. dollar has steadily risen in relation to major world currencies, but these may be periods of fond memory, since this has not happened in the past decade. Thus, the declining value of the measurement unit in terms of the goods and services it can command is a problem of world-wide scope.

ELEMENTS OF FINANCIAL STATEMENTS

A discussion of earnings measurement requires definitions of asset, liability, revenue, expense, gain, and loss that will apply regardless of which unit of measure is adopted.

According to the *Exposure Draft (Revised) on Elements of Financial Statements of Business Enterprises* (FASB, 1979g):

Assets are probable future economic benefits obtained or controlled by a particular enterprise as a result of past transactions or events affecting the enterprise. [par. 17]

Liabilities are probable future sacrifices of economic benefits stemming from present legal, equitable, or constructive obligations of a particular enterprise to transfer assets or provide services to other entities in the future as a result of past transactions or events affecting the enterprise. [par. 22]

Revenues are inflows or other enhancements of assets of an enterprise or settlements of its liabilities (or a combination of both) during a period from delivering or producing goods, rendering services, or other activities that constitute the enterprise's ongoing major or central operations. [par. 56]

Expenses are outflows or other using up [sic] of assets or incurrences of liabilities (or a combination of both) during a period from delivering or producing goods, rendering services, or carrying out other activities that constitute the enterprise's ongoing major or central operations. [par. 58]

Gains (or other appropriately descriptive terms) are increases in owners' equity (net assets) from peripheral or incidental transactions of an enterprise and from all other transactions and other events and circumstances affecting the enterprise during a period except those that result from revenues or investments in the enterprise by owners. [par. 60]

Losses (or other appropriately descriptive terms) are decreases in owners' equity (net assets) from peripheral or incidental transactions of an enterprise and from all other transactions and other events and circumstances affecting the enterprise during a period except those that result from expenses or distributions by the enterprise to owners. [par. 61]

The definitions of asset and liability (which will likely be modified when the SFAC on elements is finalized by early 1981) are footnoted with the explanation that probable future benefits and sacrifices

... may be less than certain but must be likely to some degree. The degree of probability or likelihood of a future benefit [sacrifice] that is needed to recognize it as an asset [liability] and the degree to which its amount can be measured or estimated with reasonable reliability are matters of recognition and measurement that are beyond the scope of this Statement.

Two views on how the elements defined above intertwine in earnings measurement are discussed below.

Asset/Liability Basis

This view has some resemblance to economic theory. It holds that the difference between owners' equity (assets less liabilities) at two points in time, adjusted for transactions with owners, constitutes "results of operations," whether that is called net earnings or something else. The balance sheet and income statement *articulate*—a net change in one has a corresponding change in the other.

Under the asset/liability view, a cost that does not meet the definition of an asset cannot temporarily rest in the balance sheet and must be charged against current operations. This approach results in a balance sheet that usually contains harder rather than softer (e.g., exchangeable versus nonexchangeable) assets and liabilities and avoids deferral of soft costs for matching against future revenues.

Revenue/Expense Basis

Another view, however, is that the most important goal of financial accounting is the measurement of earnings, and therefore amounts received in advance of "being earned" and costs incurred that will benefit future periods regardless of their lack of hardness or exchangeability should not enter the income statement at the time of the transaction, but should be deferred until they are properly matched with applicable costs and revenues, respectively. This approach results in various deferred charges (see Chapter 21) being classified as assets in the balance sheet, but indeed could result in an income statement more logical to the business manager given that he often views some of his expenses as "investments."

Reconciliation of Bases

Although practicing CPAs would likely choose the asset/liability basis because it is less subjective, there are perhaps other ways of looking at the problem. Many of the proponents of the revenue/expense view might come to accept the asset/

liability view if earnings were defined as something other than the difference between net assets at a point in time (as adjusted for transactions with owners). This
is indeed what the FASB is currently considering in its postulation of a *comprehensive income* concept, of which net earnings would only be a part, albeit the
major one. The FASB has proposed this definition:

> Comprehensive income is the amount by which an enterprise is better or worse off at
> the end of a period than at the beginning as a result of all transactions and other events
> and circumstances affecting it during the period except for owners' investments in the
> enterprise and distributions by the enterprise to owners. Specifically, comprehensive
> income results from (a) exchange transactions and other transfers between the enter-
> prise and other entities that are not its owners, (b) the enterprise's productive efforts,
> and (c) price changes, casualties, and other effects of interactions between the enter-
> prise and the economic, legal, social, political, and physical environment of which
> it is part. [FASB, 1979g, par. 39]

This may be the substance of the economist's view as given by Hicks (1946, cited
earlier), restated to a length suitable for accountants. With comprehensive income,
the asset/liability proponents achieve their desired articulation, while the revenue/
expense proponents retain their "net earnings."

There is a temptation to view this debate as semantic, but it may be much more:
accounting is now on the threshold of having the technology and disciplines available to much more deeply measure the events and transactions that affect a business
enterprise. It is inevitable that matters such as valuation changes resulting from
fluctuations in interest and discount rates, inflation, and supply and demand relative
to the net resources held by a company will enter the broad area of financial reporting, if not the financial statements themselves. At the very least, those ingredients
of comprehensive income caused by events not within the direct control of the enterprise or not attendant to a specific transaction entered into by the enterprise
might not be considered part of net earnings. Once all companies account in this
fashion, ideally all extraneous but impactive events would then be uniformly recognized; this would permit a rational comparison among companies of how their
managements employed the assets entrusted by the owners.

Whether such categorizations of elements of comprehensive income and comparisons of companies could encompass all the variable factors is debatable. An
astute management will take measures to enhance, preserve, hedge, or adjust the
mix of net assets that are exposed to valuation declines due to events not within
its direct control. Thus, a management that constantly readjusts to the environment will usually do a reasonable job of predicting the future as it affects the company's net assets. Some other managements may not operate this way, and thus
will obtain different results in the area of events "not within management's control." Further research is needed to see if the distinction can be sharpened.

The revised exposure draft on elements, by proceeding down the comprehensive
income path, minimizes the asset/liability versus the revenue/expense debate. However, accountants are persistent as well as consistent, and many proponents on
either side of this debate are disappointed that the FASB has written an exposure
draft on elements that (if it becomes a final SFAC) will accommodate just about
anything presently practiced, resulting in no progress on concepts.

Accrual Method

Under the accrual method of accounting, many elements of financial statements are recognized prior to their being settled in cash transactions. This is done on the basis of "sufficient" achievement of the applicable recognition criteria and a probability of irreversibility (i.e., the transaction will "stick"). For example, the sale of a tried and true product to a continuing customer who has never had a credit-rating problem results in recognition of revenue and a receivable at the time of the transaction, even though the transaction in the broad sense is not finally complete until the customer pays the amount owed. On the seller's side, he may not have paid obligations incurred in obtaining or manufacturing the goods, but they were nevertheless recorded as inventory and subsequently as cost of sales. It is readily agreed that accrual basis accounting is more reflective of the economics of a transaction than a cash-only basis.

Some transactions consummated totally in cash have been found to use cash as a fungible commodity, simply moving it around where needed; the substance of the transaction lay in other side agreements, accommodations, or an "I owe you one" understanding. Thus, too much focus should not be placed on the objectivity of cash, at least until other uncertainties—known or suspected—about a particular transaction are reduced to a minimal level.

The FASB has been said to be leaning in the direction of the cash basis by virtue of its resolutions on research and development (SFAS 2; AC 4211) and contingencies (SFAS 5; AC 4311). This is not a correct conclusion, but it is true that, apart from these two SFASs, the FASB is aiming towards assessments of cash flows to the enterprise (and by inference, therefore, cash flows to financial statement users —investors and creditors). To this extent, the FASB wants accrual basis numbers stated as much as possible in terms of cash-flow potential, and the Board may have to eventually reconsider SFAS 2 and SFAS 5 to bring them in line with emerging concepts.

Time Segments

When accrual basis accounting is combined with the need to report at specified intervals on the progress and condition of the business, problems multiply. Under the accrual method, numerous transactions at any given reporting date are not totally completed in that they have not had their ultimate cash consequences. A longer-term example is the investment in plant, which is intended to be realized by allocations to product costs for a period of up to 40 years.

Of course, if no report were required of a business entity until it had totally completed its operations and liquidated itself through distributions to its owners, an accurate determination of earnings in terms of the unadjusted monetary unit could then be made. A separate computation, however, would still be required to approximate the unrecorded ingredient in the enterprise's lifetime earnings—the change in the value of the unit of measure. The dollars invested by owners simply are not the same dollars returned.

Periodic reporting, despite the problems it presents, is necessary and required. Public companies must report annually and quarterly and must file current reports within 15 days of significant transactions, financial or otherwise, affecting the enterprise. And the trend is towards even more discreteness in reporting; some proponents of *continuous reporting* believe an enterprise should be able to report, given today's computer technology and measurement systems, on a daily basis if it is deemed useful for them to do so (some financial institutions have long done this internally). However, doing this may not be based on improvements in reporting ability; it may manifest the type of reporting now done on an annual basis, but simply done much faster. It may not improve the quality of the information reported, which could deteriorate because insufficient time might be available for the judgmental aspects of accounting measurement. And continuous reporting would certainly aggravate the problem of earnings measurement by requiring that those measurements be made for shorter and shorter periods. What must be recognized in any reporting system is that each period is part of a business continuum, and the allocation methodology used must be helpful in allowing a user to understand that continuum and its economic implications.

Periodic reporting is simply one of the problems that needs to be diminished by the development of better measurement and recognition methods and rules. This will improve consistency, which is certainly necessary as the reporting period becomes truncated.

MEASUREMENT APPROACHES

General

As indicated earlier, revenue recognition cannot be fully accomplished without deciding on the scale of measurement to be used. In the accounting area, there are five basic approaches (each having many possible permutations) that commonly have been recognized in writings on the subject:

1. *Historical cost,*
2. *Current cost,*
3. *Current exit value in orderly liquidation,*
4. *Expected exit value in due course of business,* and
5. *Discounted cash flows.*

These five bases can be classified in the various ways shown in Figure 7.1. (They are discussed at length in Chapters 2 and 8.)

Basis	*Temporality*	*Entry/Exit Value*	*Factuality*
Historical cost	Past	Entry	Actual
Current cost	Present	Entry	Hypothetical
Current exit value	Present	Exit	Hypothetical
Expected exit value	Future	Exit	Expected
Discounted cash flows	Future	Exit	Expected

FIGURE 7.1 CLASSIFICATION OF MEASUREMENT BASES

A good indication of the way these measurement bases can be intermixed is shown in *The Accounting Response to Changing Prices—Experimentation with Four Models* (AICPA, 1979b). Twenty-three major public companies recast their earlier financial statements according to one or more of these models:

Model A. Condensed financial statements based on historical costs but stated in units of general purchasing power (general price-level statements).

Model B. Historical cost financial statements incorporating inventories based on LIFO and with depreciation based on the current cost of depreciable assets.

Model C. Financial statements based partially on historical cost and partially on current costs and values (generally relying on replacement costs) and distinguishing between operating income and value changes.

Model D. Current value financial statements applying either replacement cost or various current values (such as exit values and discounted cash flow) to all resources and obligations as appropriate for each item and recognizing the effect of changes in the general level of prices on shareholders' equity.

Sample financial statements for each model are presented, along with portions of statements from the participating companies as needed to illustrate specific applications.

Constant Dollars. It is interesting that *constant dollars* do not make the list of measurement bases. This approach, described in SFAS 33 (AC 1072) and required as a supplementary presentation for large companies, represents a basically mechanical translation of initial entry (historical) costs into hypothetical amounts reckoned in terms of the purchasing power of today's dollars. (Refer to Model A above.) Nothing more than a change in the valuation of currency is involved. But the cost of various items does not rise symmetrically; purchasing power changes affect one item differently than another. Thus, constant dollar accounting is a grand averaging scheme that, in restating the entire financial statements, provides information of questionable usefulness, and analysts generally find this data unrevealing and distracting. (This point was emphatically made in a roundtable on inflation accounting; see Touche Ross & Co., 1980b.)

However, none of the measurement methods discussed below directly concern themselves with the changing value of the dollar. Thus, a second calculation is sometimes needed to separate this ingredient from other specific value changes. For example, in the SFAS 33 requirements for stating current cost, effects of increases in the general price level are to be shown separately (AC 1072.056).

Capital Maintenance. A decision needs to be made on how a business enterprise should maintain its capital and on whether there should be a charge against operations for doing so. *Physical capital* is determined in units of productivity; those who take a physical capital approach maintain capital at whatever amount of current cost is necessary to sustain the productive capacity or service potential of the enterprise. The *financial capital* approach, which the FASB favors, would require maintaining the total dollars of capital, adjusted for changes in the value of those dollars. Should financial capital not be so maintained, a partial liquidation of the business would be occurring. Thus, the question is: In addition to undistributed earnings inuring to the benefit of shareholders, does stockholders' equity become simply the repository for the net effect of changes in values (however measured) during the year, or should stockholders' equity first be "maintained" by a charge deducted from earnings and credited to capital?

The FASB almost dealt with the capital maintenance charge issue when it considered capitalization of interest. The *Discussion Memorandum on Accounting for Interest Costs* (FASB, 1977a) contained several advisory issues along these lines. If interest is a cost of a certain kind of capital (debt) and is deemed capitalizable in the development of certain assets (up to the time they are ready to produce in a normal way), then why not treat the other kind of capital (equity) in the same manner? Does it not have a cost as well, which should be charged against earnings or capitalized and deferred (in the same manner as SFAS 34 (AC 5155) finally concluded with respect to interest on debt capitalization)? These issues eventually will require resolution.

Historical Cost

This is defined as the amount paid to acquire an asset (less subsequent amortization) or the amount received when a liability was incurred (FASB, 1976b, p. 16). It should be noted that, even though current basic financial statements are said to be prepared on the historical cost basis, there are several kinds of adjustments based on some other method, such as inventories written down to lower of cost or market or assets fair valued in nonmonetary exchanges. By and large, however, current financial statement amounts can be pinned to a previous inflow or outflow of cash or monetary assets. Historical cost is often referred to as *initial entry value* or *original entry value,* thus signifying that these are the amounts at which the amounts entered the financial statements.

The main advantage of the historical cost method is its objectivity; its major defect is that it often lacks relevance because (1) it does not keep pace with changes in the value of the measurement unit; (2) it does not recognize that the value of those constant dollars changes irregularly in relation to different kinds of assets and liabilities; and (3) it does not account for many external events (as contrasted with transactions directly entering the financial statements) having an effect on the value of enterprise net assets and thus on the measurement of its earnings.

Because of its objectivity, historical cost will not be quickly supplanted by some other measurement method, although it is already being supplemented, via SFAS 33 (AC 1072), with hypothetical information about measurements made on a current cost basis and with translations into constant dollars.[1]

Current Cost

Also sometimes called the *replacement cost* or *current entry value* method, this approach restates the assets and liabilities of an enterprise at the number of monetary units (dollars) it would take to acquire or incur them today. There has been

---

[1] Though many academics believe historical cost is not informative, an engaging parody that comes to its defense is found in Robert Jensen, "Truth Versus ΦIKTION Versus Something," *Accounting Review,* October, 1975, pp. 871-873.

some dispute over whether replacement cost of assets should be figured in terms of productive capacity (new assets of equivalent operating capacity) or service potential (identical assets, generally). In ASR 190 the SEC had required productive capacity. But the FASB, in SFAS 33, chose the more objective existing service potential, and the SEC has now accepted it also.

Replacement cost data is viewed by many as an improvement over the historical cost basis and the constant dollar approach because it gives recognition to specific changes (relative to each asset and liability) in the value of the measurement unit. Thus, inflation is presumably recognized in the specific circumstances of the enterprise. And replacement cost statements, if they contain higher amounts than could be realized by the company in the production process and/or in the price obtainable in the market therefor, must reflect a reduction of that overvaluation (see SFAS 33; AC 1072.062).

A major drawback, however, is that it is quite hypothetical. An enterprise would not normally replace many or all of its assets and refund all of its liabilities at once. The fact that it owns and uses certain assets means that the benefits from continuing to own them are estimated to exceed the cash inflow that realistically could be achieved from selling them. This assessment by management does not mean that the assets currently provide a good return on investment; there currently may be other limiting factors that make replacement unrealistic, such as the complexity of a major restructuring or the availability of funds.

Nonetheless, current cost data would seem desirable for financial analysts and other serious users of financial statements, because of the reasonably sharper picture provided as to the specific effects of inflation. The first full year in which major companies were required to disclose information on a current cost basis was 1980, and early in 1981 a large amount of information will be available. Partial results based on 1979 voluntary reporting provide some interesting statistics; for example, based on a 1980 Price Waterhouse survey, income from continuing operations for a composite of industrial companies, as a percentage of historical cost, was 60% on a constant dollar basis and 63% on a current cost basis (related statistics are given in Figure 7.2). A 1980 Arthur Young & Co. survey of 279 nonfinancial companies (only 108 of which gave current cost information for 1979) showed (pp. 8-9) an even greater reduction in income from continuing operations—57% in constant dollars and 51% at current cost.

Current Exit Value

A substitute name more familiar to accountants may be *net realizable value*—the amount of cash that could be obtained by selling an asset in orderly liquidation or the amount required currently to eliminate an obligation (FASB, 1976b, p. 17). Marketable equity securities (SFAS 12; AC 5132) are already accounted for on this basis, and it is the method used when evaluating whether inventories are appropriately stated at the lower of cost or market. (Net realizable value for inventories is defined by ARB 43, Chapter 4, as the estimated selling price in the ordinary course of business less reasonably predictable costs of completion and disposal (AC 5121.08).)

The problem, of course, is that not every asset or liability in a balance sheet has an exit value, much less such a value in orderly liquidation. The going concern concept that underlies GAAP does not reasonably accommodate the orderly liqui-

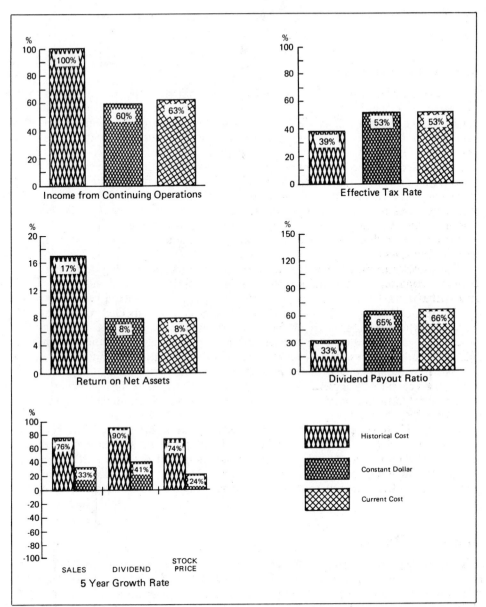

FIGURE 7.2   1979 RESULTS RESTATED IN CONSTANT DOLLARS AND AT
CURRENT COST FOR A COMPOSITE OF INDUSTRIAL COMPANIES
SOURCE: Price Waterhouse & Co., *Disclosure of the Effects of Inflation: An Analysis—Financial Reporting and Changing Prices* (New York, 1980), p. 7.

dation approach, and therefore it is doubtful that serious consideration will be given by the FASB to current exit value, at least as a broad basis method for measurement.[2]

Expected Exit Value

This is the nondiscounted amount of cash into which an asset is expected to be converted or at which a liability is expected to be satisfied—all in the due course of business. The major difference between this basis and the preceding one is that due course of business is substituted for orderly liquidation, with the latter term implying a forced removal from business perhaps just short of panic. The expected exit value approach would tolerate the normal length of time, even years, it might take for an asset to be converted to or a liability liquidated by cash. This presents particular problems in case of long-term capital assets, which, of course, the enterprise does not hold for liquidation except indirectly through the allocation of cost in some rational and systematic manner (a vague phrase, discussed below) to the cost of products or services; in a way, this results in an exit value in the due course of business.

The inability to disaggregate or separate a group of assets doing one thing (e.g., a plant complex) creates major problems in attempting to value individual assets at expected exit values. The method, of course, is also hampered by the fact that not all separable assets will have an exit value or can be expected to have an exit value anywhere near as high as the value in use to the business. For example, intangibles such as patents may be useless if they are separated from the physical plant or the human resources (such as the creative capacity of the inventor) necessary to turn the advantage of the intangible into cash flows. Liabilities, however, are rather easy to disaggregate, except possibly where there is nonrecourse debt related to a particular asset or a contingent obligation such as might be found after a troubled debt restructuring.

If the FASB after experimentation chooses a valuation basis other than historical cost or current cost, it is quite possible the choice might be expected exit value in due course of business. It has most of the advantages of the discounted cash flow basis discussed next, but less of the complications: it would not have to deal with fluctuations in the discount rate, nor with earnings on reinvestment of future cash flows.

Discounted Cash Flow

This is also called present value of expected cash flows, and the FASB describes it as "the discounted amount of net cash inflows pertaining to an asset or the discounted amount of net cash outflows required to eliminate a liability" (FASB, 1976b, p. 17). GAAP already requires that long-term receivables and payables be

---

[2] However, the subject has a certain amount of academic interest. For example, see James McKeown, "Usefulness of Exit-Value Accounting Statements in Satisfying Accounting Objectives," in *Objectives of Financial Statements,* Vol. 2, *Selected Papers,* edited by Joe Cramer, Jr. and George Sorter (New York: AICPA, 1974), pp. 161-177.

discounted at an appropriate rate of interest, and that the discount be accreted on the interest method (AC 5361) over the period between initiation and realization. A good example of discounted cash flow accounting (for capital leases) can be found in SFAS 13 (AC 4053). (See Chapter 22 for a discussion of discounting under APB 21, and Chapter 23 regarding leases.)

In its fullest measure, discounted cash flow provides the overall value of the business currently, discounted at an appropriate rate of return. Thus it would seem to be exactly what the FASB is calling for in SFAC 1, *Objectives of Financial Statements,* when it speaks about users' interest in cash flows to the business and, indirectly, in cash flows to themselves (AC 1210.39). However, there are major uncertainties involved in arriving at discounted cash flow. Three major problems are discussed below:

1. What discount rate should be used?
2. How are future cash flows from present nonmonetary assets to be dealt with?
3. Is disaggregation of assets possible or even necessary?

Discount Rate. The rate selected should vary according to some indication of return relative to the risk in a particular situation. A starting point might be the market average rate of return for all stocks on the New York Stock Exchange, available from CRSP and other databases. Assigning a risk factor is problematic, of course, since risk in an investor's assessment is dependent on at least these factors:

1. Assumptions underlying expected cash flows,
2. Whether the variability of expected cash flows differs significantly from the variability of alternative investment cash flows,
3. Degree of uncertainty associated with realization of the cash flows, and
4. Degree of control the company has over realization of the cash flows.

Further, the assessment would change over time. Thus, throughout the duration of a reporting period, the overall values of a business could change—up or down— by significantly more than the accretion of the discount using the rate at the beginning of the period simply because the risk-adjusted rate had changed.

Reinvestment. An assumption needs to be made that as nonmonetary assets are converted into cash, the net inflows are either returned to the shareholders or reinvested in the business or that some combination of the two occurs. Apart from short-term forecasts, it may not be possible to predict what management will do with the net cash inflow, since the alternative uses to be available later will be speculative. Therefore, the simple (and unrealistic) assumption is often made that such cash flow is invested in U.S. government treasury securities.

Disaggregation. As with expected exit value in the due course of business, it is not realistic to disaggregate an individual asset from an integrated operation for the purpose of determining its future cash flow. Thus, large segments of the business—

in some cases virtually the entire enterprise—will have to be forecast as to future operations, and the cash flows resulting from the aggregation of the segment's assets then subjected to discounting.

The resulting financial statements would not be in today's conventional format. However, this is not a unique result, because most of the measurement methods already discussed would require significant changes in financial statement presentation. SFAS 33 (AC 1072) has already introduced new categories necessary for these modes of measurement at current cost and translation in constant dollars.

Relevant Accounting

This proposed measurement methodology with a voguish name is based on the discounted cash flow (DCF) valuation described above but, recognizing the impracticability of disaggregating DCF, provides for the specific advantage of a firm to be shown in a separate column of the balance sheet. To the extent some disaggregation is possible, it could be shown. *Specific advantage* is the extent to which DCF exceeds exit values in orderly liquidation. Thus the total DCF, or economic value, of the enterprise is the sum of its exit values and the specific advantage. In addition, the balance sheet shows a *specific residual,* which is an indication of the market assessment of the company.

An abbreviated balance sheet is shown in Figure 7.3. In this example, the net assets of the company at 12/31/01 were $25,455 on a DCF basis, and the market value of the stock was $15,000. This shows that investors considered a certain *beta* (specific risk factor in relation to average market risk factor) as applicable and that they further discounted the company's net assets by $10,455. In other words, the market (assuming it is efficient)—for reasons such as past errors by the company in forecasting or the risky nature of the business—would value the company at less than management values it. On the other hand, if this sample company had an aggregate market value of $30,000, the specific residual would be negative by $4,545, and the efficient market would theoretically be saying that management is ultraconservative in its valuations. The market value of the stock is shown in the stockholders' equity section of the balance sheet both in the exit value column and the economic value (DCF) column.

Earnings measurement under relevant accounting becomes more complex. The historical cost portion of the income statement shown in Figure 7.4 can be articulated with its counterpart in the balance sheet (Figure 7.3); but economic income requires a further statement—called (for the sake of truth in labeling and not for "catchiness") *realizations and derealizations*, a kind of funds-flow statement shown in Figure 7.5.

There are numerous other statements and reports in the relevant accounting system, since it tries to present something for everyone: cash values, historical costs, exit values, use values, and benefit amounts classified according to their degree of certainty. Because it is multidimensional, it does not attempt to provide a single figure that can be called net income—and that may be its strongest point, because it is not truly possible to capture the results of economic activity in a single number.

There are some obvious problems with this approach in addition to having some of the drawbacks of each of the five methods described earlier; in particular, relevant accounting implicitly assumes that the market is strongly efficient (it is not; see

FIGURE 7.3 RELEVANT ACCOUNTING BALANCE SHEET

	Historical Cost		Exit Values		Specific Advantage and Residual		Total Economic Value	
Assets	12/31/00	12/31/01	12/31/00	12/31/01	12/31/00	12/31/01	12/31/00	12/31/01
Short term:								
Monetary	$ 5,570	$ 5,570	$ 5,600	$ 5,600			$ 5,600	$ 5,600
Nonmonetary	2,650	3,350	2,200	4,210			2,200	4,210
Long term—								
Nonmonetary	30,000	33,800	30,200	33,800			30,200	33,800
Specific advantage					$11,000	$12,875	11,000	12,875
Total Assets	$38,220	$42,720					$49,000	$56,485
Liabilities and Stockholders' Equity								
Liabilities (monetary) :								
Short term	$ 1,950	$ 6,030	$ 1,950	$ 6,030				
Long term	24,000	24,000	25,000	25,000				
Total liabilities	25,950	30,030	26,950	31,030			$26,950	$31,030
Equity:								
Stock:								
Contributed capital	10,000	10,000						
Retained earnings	2,270	2,690						
	12,270	12,690	13,050	15,000			13,050	15,000
Specific residual					$ 9,000	$10,455	9,000	10,455
Total	$38,220	$42,720					$49,000	$56,485

ADAPTED FROM: Joshua Ronen and George Sorter, "Relevant Accounting," *Journal of Business*, April, 1972, pp. 266-267.

	Historical Income		Economic Income	
	Expected	Unexpected	Expected	Unexpected
Inflows (sales)	$5,000	$ 200	$5,000	$ 200
Outflows:				
Values of goods sold:				
On conversion:				
Inputs	3,000	100	2,000	200
Value added			1,800	
On sales:				
Additional inputs	700		800	
Value added			400	
	(3,700)	(100)	(5,000)	(200)
	1,300	100	-0-	-0-
Interest revenue	20		4,900	
Interest expense	(1,000)		(2,695)	
	(980)		2,205	
Revision of expectations				1,200
Total	$ 320	$ 100	$2,205	$1,200
Interest appropriation			$2,205	

FIGURE 7.4   RELEVANT ACCOUNTING INCOME STATEMENT
SOURCE: Ronen and Sorter, 1972, p. 272.

Chapter 47). Another problem is a fluctuation in the overall market risk assessment, caused by exogenous factors such as direction of government policy; managements would have to continually reforecast the effects of the same factors in order to maintain their assessment on the same basis as the market's.

Setting aside these major details, the various relevant accounting reports (and the difference between the market's expectations of the company's future cash flows compared with the management's expectations) will be as sharp a rating of management as can be imagined from an accounting system. This may be desirable, but further research is needed before it is incorporated into financial reporting, to make sure it gives credible signals.

An unhurried reading of the entire treatise on relevant accounting (Ronen and Sorter, 1972) is suggested for researchers who want to acquire a better understanding and perhaps further develop it. For an example of how relevant accounting could impact business combination accounting, see the theory section of Chapter 30.

RECOGNITION OVERVIEW

Authoritative Rules

How does an acknowledged element of financial statements, measured in accordance with the foregoing bases, merit recognition in financial statements? The accounting literature is sparse in the area of recognition criteria for income statement elements—those that impact earnings measurement. The basic premise is contained in ARB 43, Chapter 1A (AC 4010.01), or alternatively in APB Statement 4 (AC 1026.11-.32), which is based on ARB 43.

ARB 43 indicates: "Profit is deemed to be realized when a sale in the ordinary course of business is effected, unless the circumstances are such that the collection of the sale price is not reasonably assured." The paragraph goes on to talk about certain industry market valuation methods.

APB Statement 4 builds on this scant inclusion in the early professional literature, in the following ways:

Revenue is generally recognized when both of the following conditions are met: (1) the earning process is complete or virtually complete and (2) an exchange has taken place. [AC 1026.14]

Revenue from services rendered is recognized ... when services have been performed and are billable. Revenue from permitting others to use enterprise resources ... is recognized as time passes or as the resources are used. [AC 1026.15]

Expenses are the costs that are associated with the revenue of the period, often directly but frequently indirectly through association with the period to which the revenue has been assigned. [AC 1026.19]

Since the point in time at which revenue and expense are recognized is also the time at which changes in amounts of net assets are recognized, income determination is interrelated with asset valuation. [AC 1026.11]

These few specifications have been built into numerous accounting guides, AcSEC SOPs, SEC Accounting Series Releases, and some FASB statements and interpretations. With so little specification, it is no wonder that revenue and expense recognition rules are eclectic. The FASB is aiming to fix that, but it has already warned that a Statement of Financial Accounting Concepts on recognition criteria will not actually answer the numerous difficult questions that plague accountants currently; as with the other SFACs, it will simply be a roadmap by which the FASB plans to arrive at consistent solutions to analogous problems. Whether the political environment in the future (see Chapter 39) will allow the "perfect" and "consistent" solution to be installed is another matter.

Definitions

Although in the recognition process it is not necessary to make a significant distinction between revenues and gains or between expenses and losses (definitions

	Net Cash Assets		Other (Net)		Specific Advantage	
	Expected	*Unexpected*	*Expected*	*Unexpected*	*Expected*	*Unexpected*
Realizations:						
From exit values—noncash to exit values—cash:						
Sales	$ 5,000	$ 200	$(5,000)	$ (200)		
Interest revenue	20		(20)			
	5,020	200	(5,020)	(200)		
From specific advantage to exit values:						
Value added			2,200		$(2,200)	
Changes in exit values of net current assets:						
On conversion			300		(300)	
At year end			150		(150)	
			2,650		(2,650)	
Derealizations:						
From net cash assets to exit values:						
Purchases:						
Current assets	(3,200)	(400)	3,200	400		
Fixed assets	(5,000)	300	5,000	(300)		
Interest expense	(1,000)		1,000			
	(9,200)	(100)	9,200	100		

From exit values to specific advantage:						
Purchase loss			(100)	(20)	100	$ 20
Changes in exit value of fixed assets (net)			(1,000)		1,000	
			(1,100)	(20)	1,100	20
Total realizations	5,020	200	(2,370)	(200)	(2,650)	
Total derealizations	(9,200)	(100)	8,100	80	1,100	20
Net	$(4,180)	$ 100	5,730	$ (120)	(1,550)	20
Net change in assets	(4,080)		5,610		(1,530)	
From the income statement:						
Imputed interest					2,205	
Revisions of expectations					1,200	
Net change in specific advantage					$ 1,875	

FIGURE 7.5 RELEVANT ACCOUNTING REALIZATIONS AND DEREALIZATIONS STATEMENT

SOURCE: Ronen and Sorter, 1972, p. 274.

were given earlier in this chapter, under Elements of Financial Statements), the FASB revised exposure draft (FASB, 1979g) does so.

A discussion in the exposure draft of the characteristics of gains and losses suggests that these result from events and circumstances stemming from the environment that may be largely beyond the control of individual enterprises and their managements (paragraph 62).

This section of the chapter will not make a significant distinction between revenues/gains or expenses/losses, as current accounting practice includes these items in arriving at the "bottom line" (i.e., net earnings), at least so long as these elements are based on transactions of the enterprise and on those events that would be reflected in the financial statements under present GAAP. This attitude is adopted because recognition criteria—whether for earnings or for comprehensive income—will have to depend on the same concepts. Nevertheless, there is a high probability that a distinction will be made during the 1980s between comprehensive income and net earnings, and gains and losses may be segregated into a category below net earnings that will resemble (in placement, if not in content) the "special items" category of the 1950s and 1960s. Such display matters are discussed in the last part of this chapter.

Issues

Recognition Scales. As a way of visualizing revenue recognition (as well as the concomitant expense recognition), imagine a scale of 1 to 100, whereby it takes a rating of 60 for an executory transaction to be recognized as recordable in financial statements. If, however, after recognition but before final cash realization, uncertainties arise, perhaps the scale has to drop to 50 in order to reverse the prior recognition. As another illustration, when an item achieves, say, 20 on the scale, it is time for disclosure as financial information outside the financial statements, and when 40 is reached, it moves into the disclosures in financial statement notes.

Consider a note receivable collaterized by and for the sale of a plant at well above its carrying amount. If it is deemed probable (more than 60) that collection will occur (e.g., because the down payment criteria set by the AICPA (1974a) have been met), the transaction is recorded as a profit-generating (or loss-generating) transaction. However, should some question arise later because the buyer stops servicing the debt and/or the collateral drops in value (between 50 and 60), the transaction would not be reversed. Should this trend continue down to 40, there may have to be a loss recorded based on repossession of the collateral or provision for less than full recovery on the note.

Coming in the other direction, if the plant is a very major asset and negotiations are in process to sell it (perhaps 25 on the scale), it might be desirable to discuss it in the president's letter or in the management discussion and analysis section of the annual report; and if an agreement in principle has been reached with a party of known integrity and creditworthiness (say a 45) subject to conditions precedent, there may need to be a footnote on the matter.

The analogy above is clumsy, of course, and does not deal with the countless variations that could be shown. Still, its simplicity should make it easy to keep in mind as recognition criteria are considered in the following sections.

Ultimately the FASB may have to group items signifying various levels of recognition criteria—the 20s, 40s, 60s, and so on—to arrive at standards pronouncements, though undoubtedly numerical demarcations are not plausible. The Board already has categories in an unadvertised, unstructured way in some of its pronouncements; for example, SFAS 5 (AC 4311) requires disclosure of contingent liabilities if recording conditions are not achieved.

Recognition by Disclosure. It can be readily argued that disclosure is not an issue relevant to recognition criteria. However, the FASB already realizes that some threshold has to be set for information to enter the financial statements (or to enter supplementary information required to accompany the financial statements). The Board might as well approach the broader rather than the narrower subject. Even if recording in the financial statements were the major focus, the FASB would inevitably have to deal with whether items that do not meet the recognition criteria should at some point be disclosed; so it is merely a question of which end of the problem will be the starting point. This issue is recognized in the FASB *Invitation to Comment on Financial Statements and Other Means of Financial Reporting* (FASB, 1980e), discussed at length in Chapter 4.

Uncertainties. Another way of visualizing the measurement scale is in terms of a spectrum of certainty/uncertainty. The Trueblood study group (AICPA, 1973j, p. 33) pointed out that information in financial statements should be segregated, to the extent possible, according to factual data and interpretive data, which are akin to certainty and uncertainty. Factual data is objectively measurable, and recognition is made easier by facts. Interpretive data is subjective and hard to quantify. But there are infinite gradations; there may be a mixture of fact and interpretation in a given transaction. Thus, even in what is considered "hard" information—a characteristic of most financial statement amounts—there are significant variations in tensility. Classifying financial statement amounts as to mostly factual or mostly interpretive may seem impossible, but it is worthy of further research because of the communications improvements that could result.

Criteria for revenue recognition might be grouped in a similar manner: broad criteria (uncertain) and specific criteria (certain). An example in the broad category might be that revenue should be recognized only after a particular transaction has occurred; in the specific category, that revenue should be recognized in a transaction resulting in a receivable if there are certain demonstrable characteristics assuring collectibility (one such characteristic might be the ability to discount the receivable without recourse at a financial instiution). Another certainty/uncertainty issue has to do with how strong each chosen criterion must be: convincing (very factual), persuasive ("moderately" factual), or suggestive ("substantially" uncertain, but contributing some value in the recognition process).

Another important issue is the association of costs with revenues. The so-called matching concept (AC 1026.11, fn. 6) is really quite uncertain in many applications, and as a result has been dealt a number of significant blows by the FASB. For example, SFAS 2 recognized that expenditures for research and development were clearly aimed at matching with future revenues to be derived from the results of such R&D; but the Board chose to require write-off of those expenditures in view of the larger issue: the inability to demonstrate with any degree of consistency that positive and beneficial results would be obtained (AC 4211.49). Thus, while there usually is no question about the concept of matching, the element of uncertainty is an overriding concern.

Criteria for Earnings Recognition

Transactions and Events. A decision needs to be made as to whether only transactions, or both transactions and events (and which ones), are to be admitted to financial statements. Present generally accepted accounting principles are substantially transaction oriented, although some events are used to modify the amounts resulting from recording transactions at historical cost. (A good review of transaction-based accounting recognition can be found in Horngren, 1965.)

Transactions. Transactions include exchanges of assets or services with parties outside the business entity, as well as transfers or use of assets or services within it. (For example, see AU 320.20.) A transaction arising as a result of relations with an outsider is an *external* transaction; one resulting from the expiration of cost, or by an accrual, transfer, or allocation of income or expense, is an *internal* transaction (see Kohler, 1975, p. 269). The distinction between internal and external transactions is somewhat dependent on one's perception of the boundaries of the business enterprise.

Internal transactions will not have an effect on the financial statements if they merely represent movements between categories that are classified together for financial reporting purposes. For example, the inventory caption on the balance sheet ordinarily will not be affected by a transfer in classification between work-in-process subaccounts. Other internal transactions, however, can affect the financial statements because they represent the recording of estimates as to realizability of assets and extent of liabilities not yet fixed through external exchanges.

Events. Events, on the other hand, do not require, and mostly will not involve, any direct participation by the affected business enterprise; they occur outside the enterprise. Events currently used to modify transactions recorded at historical cost include the lower of cost or market value for inventories where some external event reduces the value of inventory (e.g., commodities); or a write-down to scrap value of a single-purpose plant whose product has been substantially outlawed (e.g., cyclamates at the time they were banned by the federal government).

Applicable Qualitative Characteristics. By referring to SFAC 2, *Qualitative Characteristics of Accounting Information* (AC 1220), there are several characteristics of financial information that can be transferred to a discussion of earnings recognition criteria.

Relevance. All transactions are relevant, although some are not of a significance (quality) or size (quantity) to merit specific identification in a financial statement. The level at which external events become relevant in earnings recognition is even more difficult to attack; it seems logical, then, that some cutoff would have to be set, based on the proximity of the event to the enterprise. For example, an increase in the cost of energy (an event) is not a transaction until the enterprise purchases the energy. However, if the increase is significant, and if substantial amounts of energy are used in the production process, consideration has to be given to whether selling prices can be sufficiently increased to recover the increased energy cost. If not, the event might cause some accounting recognition, such as to reflect a decrease in utility of the plant.

Reliability. This characteristic applies to both transactions and events and suggests that the information conveyed can be accepted and that there are no substantial probabilities of the transaction or event becoming undone. In many transactions there are "strings," both visible and invisible. In a simple department store transaction a customer may have the right to return a purchase for no reason whatever (if that is the store's policy). The extent to which history demonstrates this will occur will be a major factor in deciding on the appropriate manner in which to recognize revenues.

On the murkier side, a transaction involving the sale of real estate with an unstated obligation on the part of the seller to repurchase the real estate at some future date is indeed a transaction. But some question must be raised about the reliability of the information conveyed by the recording of this transaction without full disclosure; and if full disclosure is given, one must wonder about usefulness to the reader. According to the FASB, "the reliability of a measure rests on the faithfulness with which it represents what it purports to represent, coupled with an assurance for the user, which comes through verification, that it has that representational quality" (AC 1220.059).

Verifiability. APB Statement 4 provides this definition: "Verifiable financial accounting information provides results that would be substantially duplicated by independent measurers using the same measurement methods" (AC 1024.18). A verifiable transaction has substantial credibility because the measurement can be duplicated over and over again. Note that this criterion controls the bias of the measurer but will not compensate for defects in the measurement method, even assuming all the independent measurers are using the same methodology.

There are also degrees of verifiability. Purely factual material, even if complex, can presumably be verified over and over by persons having the requisite skills to make the kind of measurement called for. Taking a simpler example, the answer to What is 2 + 2? is likely to be verified by almost everyone.[3] On the other hand, subjective data such as oil and gas reserve quantities can be "verified" by different geologists, all of whose estimates may differ; and all the estimates will be wrong in fact when the reservoir production is completed and the final count is in.

Representational faithfulness. "Representational faithfulness is correspondence or agreement between a measure or description, and the phenomenon it purports to represent. In accounting, the phenomena to be represented are economic resources and obligations and the transactions and events that change those resources

---

[3] Abraham Briloff in *Unaccountable Accounting,* 1972, pp. 1-2, tells an anecdote suggesting that professional accountants are not competent to make this computation.

and obligations" (AC 1220.063). An ingredient of representational faithfulness is its degree of certainty versus uncertainty, or how much precision there is in the information about the transaction. The more certain and precise that information, the more likely the transaction is to merit earnings recognition.

SFAC 2 notes that representational faithfulness is what behavioral scientists often call *validity*. The FASB would have preferred to use this term, but felt constrained because the scientific context of the word had to be kept in mind when using it.

There are, again, degrees of representational faithfulness. A single asset purchased for cash conveys a precise answer, but a business acquisition acquired for stock raises questions as to what the cost was in total and what was paid for each individual asset. Another example is the question of whether the Consumer Price Index for All Urban Consumers gives a satisfactory representation of constant dollar information for a company's specific assets. The answer has to be no, and only an approximation of the variance can be made based on current cost recomputations.

A particular problem having to do with representational faithfulness is the issue of substance versus form, discussed at length in Chapter 28. A related-party transaction with concealed facts can be represented to be something different than it really is, in order to obtain a desired accounting treatment. But even when all the facts are available, a question inevitably arises about how to portray a transaction in view of the related-party involvement. A large proportion of revenue recognition problems can be traced to those related-party transactions that are not representationally faithful to the underlying nature of the transaction (i.e., their form is different than their substance).

Neutrality. Information should be free from bias toward a predetermined result. However, that does not mean that there should not be some *purpose* for the way in which a certain accounting rule requires that a transaction be recorded. To be neutral, accounting information must report economic activity as faithfully as possible, without coloring the image it communicates for the purpose of influencing the behavior in *some particular direction* (AC 1220.099-.100).

Other qualities. Comparability, and therefore comparison, of a transaction or event to a similar type of transaction or event may be useful in adjudging the appropriateness of revenue recognition; likewise, consistent treatment from transaction to transaction and event to event is required, in order that the reported results of all similar transactions can be understood as having been produced applying the same standards.

There is also the matter of "completeness," at least within the bounds of what is material and feasible considering the cost. The more complete the information, the more relevant it is. However, it may cost far too much to improve the information to be virtually complete, so some trade-offs will be necessary.

Degrees of Achievement of Criteria. Transactions usually have a larger measure of the foregoing qualitative characteristics than external events do. For example, what does one do with a rumored event that could have a significant effect on the business? How much less credibility (degree of achievement) does that have compared with an event that has received affirmation in the press or an event specifically evident on a first-hand basis? Or, if there are related parties involved in the transaction, what proportion, if not all, of representational faithfulness will be discounted for that fact? Present accounting literature (see Chapter 28) aims at this problem via disclosure and in some cases, profit recognition deferral, but should there be some other uniform way to deal with degrees in these cases?

If a scale could be drawn for each qualitative characteristic, and a certain proportion of achievement required before recognition is permitted, most problems in earnings measurement would be solved. The scales would be hypothetical, and arbitrary at best, but the approach should not be dismissed out of hand.

Monetary and Nonmonetary Transactions

A major variable in revenue recognition is the extent, if any, to which a transaction is nonmonetary. For example, a machine purchased for cash is a monetary transaction to the purchaser as well as to the seller; one gives cash and the other gets cash. Adding a trade-in to that transaction may make it partly nonmonetary. Swapping one machine for another similar machine with little or no cash involved is an entirely nonmonetary transaction, and special accounting rules described later in this chapter govern such transactions.

Determining the extent to which the earning process is complete or substantially complete would seem to require the selection of some critical event in the earning process to permit any revenue to be recognized, and in current practice this largely depends on whether the transaction is monetary or nonmonetary, as discussed in the following two sections.

EARNINGS RECOGNITION FOR MONETARY TRANSACTIONS

There are at least five basic ways revenue recognition is applied under current GAAP, and they are reviewed in relation to monetary transactions:

Sale of Product
Performance of Service
Percentage of Completion
Installment Method
Cost Recovery Method

GAAP encompasses the accrual method of accounting; additional methods could be stated if cash basis accounting and certain value-based accounting practices were admitted.

The *critical event,* as that term is explained in Myers (1959), is not always recognized in current GAAP, since reliability often overshadows relevance. The critical event in a product sale may be its manufacture; in a service transaction it may be the performance of the most difficult action. In percentage-of-completion recognition, the critical event is even more elusive and indeed may not exist until the project is accepted by the customer as meeting the specifications.

Product Sales

Revenue is ordinarily recognized at the time the purchaser of the product is vested with ownership rights. For convenience, and historically for legal reasons, this point is deemed to be when title passes. Most manufacturers ship their products FOB factory, and thus a sale is ordinarily recorded at the time of shipment of merchandise. However, there can be many other timing arrangements. For example, the customer can have the merchandise placed aside in a segregated area, such as a bonded warehouse in the producer's factory, and if there are no other unusual uncertainties about whether a sale has been consummated, the transfer of specified goods into the segregated area will result in sale recording. Or goods may be shipped FOB destination or sold "on the high seas," as in the case of oil in tankers already en route to a particular port but without a specific customer having purchased the oil at the time of the tanker's departure.

The "delivery" of ownership title is, perhaps, better than possession as the sale event. For example, if the goods are shipped on consignment, the recipient has the complete right to return them, and the goods are therefore considered inventory of the seller. Likewise, if there is a right of return, an assessment must be made of the extent to which returns are likely, and the enterprise must have a track record by which to indicate the amounts are not material or are appropriately provided for as revenue reductions. (See further discussion in Chapter 18.)

Examples of product transaction types that are different from a simple over-the-counter product transaction, in addition to those mentioned above, are

1. Some product financing arrangements, in whole or in part (see Chapter 23);
2. Involuntary conversions (discussed below);
3. Rental of premises (partly a service and partly a percentage-of-completion-type transaction);
4. Sales-type leases;
5. Construction industry activities, as to the items constructed (however, many features in the construction industry are services; see Chapter 19);
6. Extractive industry sales, such as oil and gas products, hard minerals, and forest products (see Chapter 37);
7. Agricultural commodity sales (see National Society of Accountants for Cooperatives, 1974); and
8. Franchising, to the extent that services are required to be purchased by the franchisee from the franchisor.

The recognition issue gets particularly complicated when a transaction consists of a mixture of products and services and there is a period of time over which the transaction occurs. In such cases, what proportion of the transaction may be considered completed at a given interim point?

A transaction that makes the point is a lease. To the extent that the lessor conveys to the lessee the use of the property for virtually its entire useful life and recovers his cost plus a reasonable rate of return thereon, the transaction is considered a product sale. However, if the lease is short and the lessor will have to re-lease or otherwise dispose of the product at the end of the primary lease term, the transaction with the original lessee is then considered a service transaction—

that is, an operating lease. It is also, in these latter circumstances, deemed to result in the recognition of revenue by prorating the gross rental over the lease term.

When the lease qualifies as a sales-type lease, there is an element of service income involved—that is, the financial income that will be earned by the lessor at a constant rate applied against the diminishing unpaid balance. An operating lease, of course, contains this same factor, but under SFAS 13 it is accounted for differently.

Real estate sales are mostly sale of product and, apart from an outright cash sale (not common), various earnings recognition methods will be found in practice, including the percentage-of-completion method, installment method, and the cost recovery method, covered below. Because there are so many divisible rights in real estate, nonresidential transactions rarely transfer all of the rights in fee. A whole hierarchy of rules has been created to deal with this problem, as discussed in Chapter 18.

Service Performance

Because of the intangibility of services, it has been exceedingly difficult to ascertain, in many situations, when a service consisting of more than a single act has been satisfactorily provided so as to warrant recognition of revenue. AcSEC undertook a lengthy project in this area, which resulted in an exposure and a re-exposure draft of a proposed SOP. The re-exposure draft was taken up by the FASB and reissued as its first invitation to comment (FASB, 1978e). The large number of negative responses sent to the FASB resulted in the entire project being deferred, and it was incorporated into the recognition phase of the conceptual framework. (For a full discussion of the numerous problems in accounting for service transactions, see Chapter 18.)

The most important ingredient in determining when a service transaction has been completed is whether *substantial performance* has occurred. Performance as defined by the invitation to comment (I/C) is "the execution of a defined act or acts or occurs with the passage of time" (FASB, 1978e, p. 11). Because there are so many different kinds of service transactions, the I/C suggested four possible groupings to account for them:

1. Specific performance method;
2. Proportional performance method;
3. Completed performance method; and
4. Collection method.

This spectrum encompasses the percentage-of-completion method of accounting as well as the installment and collection methods.

Percentage of Completion

As discussed in Chapter 19, this method is mostly used in the construction industry and requires an estimation of total costs and total revenues in those longer-term transactions that afford evidence adequate for measuring progress towards completion. Progress may be based on physical evaluations, but perhaps more commonly is based on cost inputs to date versus the current estimate of total cost on the project (the "cost to cost" method). In the service area, AcSEC had described this approach as the *proportional performance method*.

The *program method* of accounting is rationalized by analogy to the operation of the percentage-of-completion method. Under the program method, a company that expends considerable resources in developing a product believed to have a broad market will sometimes, in the process of costing the sale of individual units of production, defer certain costs without a contract in hand assuring their recovery. The Lockheed L-1011 is a well-known example of the application of the program cost method, as shown in the footnote disclosure in Figure 7.6. It has been applied in less fortunate circumstances where the anticipation of further government contracts for a particular product did not materialize, resulting in substantial losses from having to write off earlier deferred costs (see Talley Industries, ASR 173).

The profession has not yet spoken on the appropriate use of the program method, and it is uncertain that current efforts will see the light of day, as there are strong traditionalist views among AICPA committee members who are responsible for clearing this matter.

Other Practices

In a footnote to APB 10, the installment method and collection method are sanctioned as exceptions to the basic realization principle:

> The Board recognizes that there are exceptional cases where receivables are collectible over an extended period of time and, because of the terms of the transactions or other conditions, there is no reasonable basis for estimating the degree of collectibility. When

---

Studies indicate a TriStar program of 300 aircraft should recover the December 29, 1974 inventory and provide a gross profit. Management believes there is a potential market of over 300 aircraft (including those already delivered) of the basic TriStar model and proposed improvements (which should not involve significant development costs), with production and deliveries extending into the 1980's. Based on current delivery projections, final recovery of the initial planning and tooling and of unrecovered production costs of previously delivered aircraft is expected to extend into the 1980's.

Recovery of the December 29, 1974 TriStar inventory is dependent on the number of aircraft ultimately sold (aircraft previously delivered, firm and second buy orders on hand, plus additional orders, less cancellations, if any), and actual selling prices and costs. Of the TriStar gross inventory as of December 29, 1974, the recovery of approximately $500 million is dependent on the receipt of future firm orders beyond the 157 received through December 29, 1974. Continued financing will be required until the TriStar inventory is substantially liquidated.

FIGURE 7.6 DISCLOSURE OF PROGRAM METHOD OF ACCOUNTING
SOURCE: Lockheed Aircraft Corporation, 1974 Form 10-K, portion of Note 5, "Inventories—TriStar Program."

such circumstances exist, and as long as they exist, either the installment method or the cost recovery method of accounting may be used. (Under the cost recovery method, equal amounts of revenue and expense are recognized as collections are made until all costs have been recovered, postponing any recognition of profit until that time.) [AC 4020.01, fn. 1]

Differentiating their use is not easy, but the AICPA 1974 guide, *Accounting for Profit Recognition on Sales of Real Estate,* indicates:

Since default on loans secured by real estate usually results in recovery of the real estate sold, the installment method would usually be appropriate. Where there is (a) uncertainty as to whether all or even a portion of cost will be recovered upon default by the purchaser or (b) cost has already been recovered in the sale and collection of further proceeds is uncertain, the cost recovery method is appropriate rather than the installment method. [par. 36]

Under any of these methods of accounting for sales using deferred recognition, caution should be exercised that the recorded asset amounts less deferred profit, if any, do not exceed the depreciated values had the property not been sold. It would be inappropriate to avoid charging losses in value to income by accomplishing a thinly financed "sale" under which the risk of losses in value continues to rest with the seller. Under these circumstances, the transaction is probably not in substance a sale.... [par. 37]

Installment Method. Under the installment method the purchaser is obligated to make specified payments over a period of time. This approach is used when there is some uncertainty about whether the entire transaction will be totally paid out. To the extent there is an excess of total proceeds over cost, each installment is deemed to bear the same proportion of profit and that profit is recognized when it is received.

Cost Recovery Method. Under this method all proceeds received are deemed to apply to the carrying amount of the asset being conveyed to the buyer until the carrying amount has been recovered; thereafter all proceeds are considered profit. This method is to be used when there is substantial uncertainty about whether the sale proceeds will be realized or whether there indeed will be any profit.

The SEC recently dealt with this subject in SAB 30, *Interpretation Regarding Divestitures in Connection with a Sale of a Subsidiary.* The situation described in this SAB, which is one of the few places a description of the use of the cost recovery method can be found, dealt with circumstances indicating that a "sale" had not occurred. As more fully discussed in Chapter 31 (under Continuing Involvement in a Sold Business), not even a deferred gain should be shown in the balance sheet.

Another example might be the sale of a distressed operating division to its management, where the only realistic means of payment would be from the operating profits and cash flow of the sold division. Of course in any such situations, a careful analysis needs to be made of whether or not the asset to be sold requires a write-down to estimated net realizable value. (See discussion of asset impairment later in this chapter.)

Collection Method. This is akin to the cost recovery method, except that a single payment is expected. Thus, if a product or service is "sold" to someone and there is no way of estimating to what extent payment will be received, revenue should then be recorded only when collection occurs. Although the result may be the same, it is not the cash method; it merely signifies that the uncertainty is so great as to not warrant recording of a receivable. An example (which ignores the fact that lawyers use cash basis accounting) might be legal services provided on a contingent fee basis; in such a case an uncontested judgment in favor of the lawyer's client may be adequate to reflect revenue.

EARNINGS RECOGNITION FOR NONMONETARY TRANSACTIONS

APB 29, *Accounting for Nonmonetary Transactions* (AC 1041), governs the accounting for transactions that are entirely or partly nonmonetary, that is, where the assets exchanged between the buyer and seller are for the most part other than monetary. It is to the APB's credit that near the end of its term as standard setter it dealt with the long-standing and difficult problem of nonmonetary transaction accounting. Although APB 29 is a somewhat obscure opinion other than to accountants who need to apply it to complex transactions, it is a very good piece of accounting principles work, likely to stand for quite some time even as the FASB builds its conceptual framework. APB 29 has this durability simply because its answers are logical and seem harmonious with the conceptual framework as it evolves.

Definitions

Monetary assets and liabilities are those assets and liabilities whose amounts are fixed in terms of units of currency by contract or otherwise. Examples are cash, short- or long-term accounts and notes receivable in cash, short- or long-term accounts and notes payable in cash; nonmonetary assets are anything else. (Note 2 to AC 1041.03(a) refers the reader to AC 1072.208 for an up-to-date listing of monetary and nonmonetary items. Of interest is the fact that marketable securities are considered nonmonetary, even though, as explained in Chapter 17, the line between certain kinds of marketable securities and cash is a thin one.)

There are several additional definitions that must be kept in mind when considering nonmonetary transactions.

Productive Assets. These are assets held for or used in the production of goods or services by the enterprise. An investment in another entity is a productive asset if it is accounted for by the equity method, but an investment not so accounted for is not a productive asset. *Similar productive assets* are productive assets that are of the same general type, that perform the same function, or that are employed in the same line of business (AC 1041.03(e)).

Exchange. Also referred to as a *reciprocal transfer,* this is a transaction that occurs between an enterprise and another entity that results in the enterprise acquiring assets or services or satisfying liabilities by surrendering other assets or services or by incurring other obligations (AC 1041.03(c)).

Examples of reciprocal nonmonetary transactions (exchanges) include barter; accommodation transactions (whereby two parties holding fungible inventory such as crude oil, but in different places, swap so that each has the inventory where it needs it); and exchanges of similar productive assets (such as an interest in one oil property for an interest in another, or one parcel of real estate for another parcel of real estate).

Nonreciprocal Transfer. This is a transfer of assets or services in one direction, either *from an enterprise* to its owners (whether or not to acquire their ownership interests) or to another entity, or from owners or another entity *to the enterprise.* An example of a *monetary* nonreciprocal transfer *to owners* is an entity's reacquisition of its outstanding stock for cash (AC 1041.03(d)); it is nonreciprocal because no asset is received or liability liquidated in the transaction.

Examples of *nonmonetary* nonreciprocal transfers *with owners* might be marketable securities held by a corporation issued as a dividend in kind to shareholders, or marketable securities issued for treasury stock acquisitions. Also in this category are spin-offs (distribution of stock of a subsidiary corporation to the shareholders of a parent) and recisions of business combinations (whereby some or all of the stock issued in an earlier business combination is received in exchange for returning the previously acquired business to its original owners).

Examples of *nonmonetary* nonreciprocal transfers *with nonowners* would include a donation of a building to a charity or, going the other way, receipt of land from a government unit as an inducement for the company to locate a plant thereon.

Accounting Requirements

Applicability. APB 29 applies to most nonmonetary transactions, including those that are partly in cash. The only exceptions to its application are (AC 1041.04)

1. Business combinations (see Chapter 30);
2. Transactions between a parent and subsidiary or between companies under common control (see Chapters 28 and 31);
3. The issuance of capital stock for the acquisition of nonmonetary assets (see Chapter 20) or services (see Chapter 26);
4. Stock dividends or stock splits (see Chapter 26); and
5. Involuntary conversions of nonmonetary assets, even where the proceeds are reinvested in replacement property; this is a monetary transaction because the recipient is *not obligated* to reinvest the proceeds in other nonmonetary assets.

Despite the fact that APB 29 is quite clear about the monetary nature of involuntary conversions, the FASB has had to release Interpretation No. 30, *Accounting for Involuntary Conversions of Nonmonetary Assets to Monetary Assets* (AC 1041-1), because in practice some companies insisted on nonrecognition of gain or loss, accounting for the difference between carrying amount and the proceeds from insurance or eminent domain proceedings as an adjustment to the cost basis of the property.

The FASB interpretation reaffirmed that involuntary conversions are monetary exchanges and therefore that gain or loss should be recognized. However, in view of possible detriment to a LIFO election for tax purposes, a pragmatic decision was made to not require recognition of gain on involuntary conversion of LIFO inventories.

Basic Rules. Prior to the passage of APB 29 in May 1973, nonreciprocal transfers with owners were recorded at the carrying amount of assets given. Non-reciprocal transfers with nonowners were recorded at the fair value of the asset received or the cost or other carrying amount of the asset given. Nonmonetary exchanges (reciprocal transfers) had been accounted for in both ways, at fair value and at cost or other carrying amount, both when being given and received.

APB 29 states the basic principle that "in general, accounting for nonmonetary transactions should be based on the fair values of the assets (or services) involved, which is the same basis as that used in monetary transactions" (AC 1041.18).

Fair value of a nonmonetary asset should be determined by referring to estimated realizable values in cash transactions involving the same or similar assets, quoted market prices, independent appraisals, estimated fair values of assets or services received in exchange, and other available evidence (AC 1041.25). In offers to shareholders, the offeree sometimes is given the choice of receiving a nonmonetary asset or cash. In those cases, the amount of cash that could have been received *may be* evidence of the fair value of the nonmonetary asset exchanged. (Where one of the offeree's choices is biased to encourage its selection, the two choices should of course not be considered equivalent.)

In order to determine fair value, it is not necessary that the parties be totally at arm's length. That is, they need not have essentially opposing interests. Where fair values cannot be determined, the transaction should be based on recorded amounts.

In the subsections that follow, the specific fair valuing rules of APB 29 are described.

Exchanges. Where the asset received is not a similar productive asset, the exchange is considered the culmination of the earning process, and gain or loss should be recognized by comparing the fair value of the asset given with its cost or other carrying amount. Where the fair value of the asset received is more clearly evident, that fair value should be used. On the other side of the transaction, presumably the other party will do the same, and thus the two parties are not likely to use the same values. For example, if an excess plant site carried on the books for $500,000 is exchanged for a desired office building site, and the party owning the plant site prior to the exchange has a reliable appraisal indicating that it is worth $1 million, that party would record a gain of $500,000 on the transaction and record the cost of the new office building site at $1 million. The party holding the office building site may have a reliable appraisal indicating it is worth $1.2 million, though it is carried at $1.3 million. Impairment in the asset relinquished should be recorded prior to bringing the new asset onto the books; thus a loss of $100,000 will be recorded, and the new plant site will be recorded at $1.2 million. Symmetry can only be achieved if each party arrives at fair values in exactly the same way, and that is not often likely, because of value differentials caused by the use an owner may have for a particular nonmonetary asset.

If a reciprocal transfer does not culminate the earning process, the enterprise should value the asset received at the carrying amount of the asset relinquished, also subject to impairment considerations. The APB specified two types of nonmonetary exchange transactions that do not culminate the earning process (AC 1041.21):

a. An exchange of a product or property held for sale in the ordinary course of business for a product or property to be sold in the same line of business to facilitate sales to customers other than the parties to the exchange [such as swaps of crude oil in two different locations]; and

b. An exchange of a productive asset not held for sale in the ordinary course of business for a similar productive asset or an equivalent interest in the same or similar productive asset.

A good example of the latter situation is the exchange of a subsidiary for an equity interest in the company acquiring it. If the new equity interest merits accounting by the equity method, it is considered a similar productive asset. If equity method accounting for the new investment is not warranted, it would not be considered a similar productive asset, and gain or loss most likely would be recognized.

There will be close calls on whether or not an asset is a similar productive asset. In the example above, the company desiring the office building site for its own use may sustain the point that the developable property remaining after the previous plant construction is sufficiently dissimilar. There will be mixed views by accountants in such a case, and the closer a party is to being in the real estate development business, the more likely this transaction would be deemed a similar productive asset exchange.

Nonreciprocal Transfers. These transfers are often treated differently depending on whether owners or nonowners are involved.

Transfers to and from owners. Spin-offs and recisions of business combinations are to be reflected at the carrying amount of the assets relinquished; this is so whether the portion of the entity being divested has been presented in the financial statements on the equity method or fully consolidated. In a business combination earlier accounted for by the purchase method, the carrying amount includes the unamortized portion of the goodwill generated in the business combination.

Other nonreciprocal transfers of nonmonetary assets to owners are to be accounted for at fair value, if the fair value of the nonmonetary asset distributed is objectively measurable and clearly would have been realizable to the distributing entity in an outright sale at or near the time of distribution. This would cover such transactions as issuing marketable securities or other nonmonetary assets as a dividend or to acquire treasury stock. However, where the value of the treasury stock is more clearly evident than the value of the asset given, that more clearly evident value should be used to record the transaction.

Where an owner makes a nonreciprocal transfer to the enterprise (e.g., donating a parcel of land without receiving any stock or asset therefor), the accounting presents a challenge. If the owner owns all or substantially all of the enterprise, the fact that stock is not physically issued seems irrelevant. Consistent with the exclusion from APB 29 applicability of the issuance of stock for nonmonetary assets (AC 1041.04(c)), such a donation should be recorded as donated capital (no gain recognized) at the lower of fair value or the contributor's carrying amount. Fair value is often unknown in such cases, and the company's board of directors (if they can be objective under the circumstances) may have to resolve the valuation issue.

However, if the preceding example assumed a minority owner (say, under 20%), the transaction is covered by APB 29, and the asset received is recorded (again, as donated capital—no gain recognized) at fair value even if higher than the donor's carrying amount.

What to do between the levels of "substantially all ownership" and "no significant influence" cannot be specified; each transaction needs to be examined individually, and the objectivity of the value weighed against the relationship of the parties.

Transfers to and from nonowners. In the case of a donation to a nonowner by the enterprise, the fair value of the asset given shall be charged as a donation expense. If fair value differs from carrying amount, a gain or loss would be recognized and, if material, classified in the income statement separate from the donation.

In the case of nonreciprocal transfers from nonowners, such as land received from a government unit, gain should be recognized, in concept, based on the fair value of the asset received. In practice, though, it is sometimes considered donated capital.

Recording Impairments in Asset Values. In fair-valued exchanges, if the asset relinquished has a value less than its recorded amount, a loss on the exchange will be recognized. Underlying this accounting is the premise that cost of the new asset acquired is the fair value of the old asset given up (AC 1041.18). By the same token, if the fair value of the asset given up is greater than the recorded amount, a gain will be recognized.

Accounting literature is inconclusive on the issue of recording impairment on assets held for longer-term use, such as a plant operating with a chronic loss even though the company overall is in a satisfactory profit-making position. SFAS 5 states:

> In some cases, the carrying amount of an operating asset not intended for disposal may exceed the amount expected to be recoverable through future use of that asset even though there has been no physical loss or damage of the asset or threat of such loss or damage. For example, changed economic conditions may have made recovery of the carrying amount of a productive facility doubtful. The question of whether, in those cases, it is appropriate to write down the carrying amount of the asset to an amount expected to be recoverable through future operations is not covered by this Statement. [AC 4311.31]

Though GAAP for retained assets is still under development, in nonmonetary transactions (even those required to be recorded using the previous carrying amounts of the assets, such as one productive asset for a similar productive asset) losses for impairment are nonetheless to be recorded as a separate provision. This is so because it is illogical to bring in the new asset at the old carrying amount when a serious question exists about that value. The APB's intent is clear from a reading of requirements where cash is involved (see AC 1041.22 and next subsection).

The problem becomes acute when an incipient exchange transaction, in which a loss at fair value is indicated, is aborted. What should be done with the asset still retained, since it "almost" resulted in a loss? Different accountants might treat it differently, but the answer would seem to depend on

1. How certain it is that the loss is inherent;
2. The nature of the asset—whether it is an extraneous or integral part of the owner's business; and
3. The likelihood that the asset will again be offered for sale.

If the asset remains available for sale, then under GAAP it should be carried at net realizable value, and a loss should be recorded currently.

Partially Monetary Consideration. Sometimes cash, or *boot* (an income tax term), is given in a nonmonetary transaction, in addition to the exchange of two nonmonetary assets. Boot occasionally is a relatively large amount, even though the general discussion by the APB prior to the passage of APB 29 suggested that boot would be small.

In a nonmonetary transaction accounted for at fair value, the fact that boot is received does not affect the recognition of gain or loss on the transaction. If anything, it makes the fair-valuing process easier. For example, if land costing $500,000 and worth $1 million is exchanged for marketable securities having an aggregate quoted market value of $750,000 and cash of $300,000, the fair value of the assets received undoubtedly would be considered more clearly evident than the fair value of the asset relinquished; thus the new assets would be recorded at $1,050,000, and gain on the exchange would be recorded at $550,000. If, on the other hand, the land fair-valued at $1 million was exchanged for $750,000 in marketable securities and $200,000 in cash, a loss of $50,000 would be recognized by the previous landowner. But where the land was exchanged for an interest in an oil lease plus $200,000 in cash, the oil lease would probably be recorded at $800,000, assuming the fair value of the asset given (the land at $1 million) were deemed to be more clearly evident.

Where nonmonetary exchanges that include boot are required to be recorded at the carrying amounts of the assets exchanged, gain or loss is still recognized, as indicated below.

Gains. In a transaction otherwise to be based on recorded amount (e.g., land exchanged for similar land plus cash), the cost-of-sales portion of the asset given up is determined by the ratio of cash to the total value received (including cash). The cash received minus the cost-of-sales portion equals the gain. A hypothetical calculation is shown below:

Cost of land to be exchanged for similar land	$500,000
Cash received	100,000
Fair value of similar land	700,000
Total fair value received	800,000
Cost of sales ($100,000/$800,000 × $500,000)	62,500
Gain ($100,000 − $62,500)	38,500
Carrying amount of new land ($500,000 − $62,500)	$438,500

On the other hand, and again where the transaction is to be based on recorded amounts, the fair value of the asset given may be more readily determinable. In such case, the proportion of cash received to the fair value of asset given, multiplied by the recorded amount, equals the cost portion of the asset sold; the cash received minus that portion equals the gain. For example:

Cost of land to be exchanged for similar land	$500,000
Cash received	100,000
Fair value of asset given	600,000
Cost of sales for cash portion ($100,000/$600,000 × $500,000)	83,333
Gain ($100,000 − $83,333)	16,667
Carrying amount of new land ($500,000 − $83,333)	$416,667

Logic would suggest that the entire $100,000 cash receipt should be considered gain, because the fair value of the asset given less the cash received equals the previous carrying amount of the asset given. What takes precedence, however, is the fact that exchanges of similar productive assets are not intended to be fair valued.

As to the company giving up the cash, it records the asset received at the amount of cash paid, plus the recorded amount of the nonmonetary asset surrendered.

Losses. AC 1041.22 indicates: "If a loss is indicated by the terms of a transaction described in this paragraph [boot transactions] or in paragraph .21 [which describes exchanges that do not culminate an earning process], the entire indicated loss on the exchange should be recognized."

Using the arithmetic under the gains example, assume that the cash received is less than the cost portion allocable thereto, indicating a loss. What should be done—record only the loss indicated by the cash proportion of the transaction or extrapolate this loss to the entire transaction? For example, if $100,000 cash is received along with land having a fair value of $300,000, and the carrying amount of the asset relinquished is $500,000, this would suggest that one fourth of the carrying amount has been sold for cash. There is clearly a loss indicated of $25,000 on the cash portion. If that is all that is recorded, however, the new asset will be carried at $375,000 (old carrying amount of $500,000 less $125,000 cost allocated to cash portion), when it is already known that the new asset received has a fair value of $300,000. The APB says that in these circumstances, the entire loss, namely $100,000, should be recognized. This is an anomalous situation, since the APB seems to be saying that in boot transactions when losses are involved, use fair values but when gains are involved, use recorded amount if the transaction is not the culmination of an earning process.

EXPENSE RECOGNITION

While the focus of this chapter has so far been on revenue and gain aspects of earnings measurement, many of the same considerations apply to the question of reflecting expenses and losses. That the need for criteria for expense recognition is no less real than in the area of income recognition is clearly illustrated in the FASB 1978 *Invitation to Comment on Accounting for Certain Service Transactions*. The AcSEC task force that drafted the proposed SOP underlying the I/C found it impossible to deal with the question of revenue recognition without fully considering expense accounting as well.

Chapter 19 contains a full discussion of costs and expenses. A brief review is given here to emphasize their interrelationship with revenues in the process of earnings measurement.

Classification of Costs

Accounting literature recognizes two basic kinds of costs, direct and indirect. Direct costs are said to be those that are clearly associated with the production of revenue during a period or with the production of assets held for future sale (such as inventories). Indirect costs thus are all other costs.

These two categories can be further divided. Costs directly related to revenues of the period are considered expenses of the period, in that they arise in the same transaction or event in which revenue is recognized. These are usually thought of as "product costs," but there are others, such as sales commissions and allocated costs.

Costs such as salaries and periodic rent not related directly to particular revenues but related to a period on the basis of transactions or events occurring in that period, or costs providing no discernible future benefits, are also recognized as expenses when incurred.

Finally, there are those costs that jointly benefit several periods and require "systematic and rational allocation" (a most elusive phrase). Some of these costs intuitively seem to benefit several periods, but there is no way to be sure of the amount of the benefit, if any, or the timing of its arrival. A good example is research and development (SFAS 2; AC 4211), which accordingly is recognized as an expense when incurred.

Three Tiers of Costs. The Accounting Standards Executive Committee proposed a three-tiered classification of costs for service transactions (FASB, 1978e, pp. 13-14), paraphrased below so as to not refer exclusively to that type of transaction:

1. *Initial direct costs* are costs incurred that are directly associated with negotiating and consummating revenue transactions. They include, but are not necessarily limited to, commissions, legal fees, cost of credit investigations, and installment paper processing

fees. In addition, the portion of salespersons' compensation, other than commissions, and of the compensation of other employees that is applicable to the time spent in the activities described above with respect to revenue transactions are also included in initial direct costs. The portion of salespersons' compensation and of the compensation of other employees that is applicable to the time spent in negotiating revenue transactions that are not consummated are not included in initial direct costs. No portion of supervisory and administrative expenses or other indirect expense, such as rent and facilities costs, is included in initial direct costs. (Note that this was taken by AcSEC from SFAS 17 (AC 4054.08), which defines initial direct costs for lessees.)

2. *Direct costs* are costs that have a clearly identifiable beneficial or causal relationship (a) to the product produced for inventory or sold or to the services performed, or (b) to the level of services performed for a group of customers (e.g., servicemen's labor, repair parts included as part of a service agreement).

3. *Indirect costs* are all costs other than initial direct costs and direct costs. They include provisions for uncollectible accounts, general and administrative expenses, advertising expenses, and general selling expenses. Indirect costs also include the portion of salespersons' compensation and of the compensation of other employees that is applicable to the time spent in negotiating transactions that are not consummated, as well as all allocations of facility costs (depreciation, rentals, maintenance, and other occupancy costs).

There is a problem in segregating direct costs between initial direct costs and all other direct costs. Where an enforceable contract (oral or written) exists, it may be possible to observe whether the estimated future benefit is sufficient to permit deferral of the initial direct costs (or to advance the recognition of a portion of income on the contract) in an amount equal to the initial direct costs. To do otherwise would result in a loss, with the "remainder" of the transaction perhaps yielding a substantial profit. However, this approach does not solve the problems of how to account for costs during lengthy precontract negotiations. (The initial direct cost problem is an aspect of the future-benefit problem discussed below.)

Accounting literature is generally consistent in stating that indirect costs should be charged against operations as incurred if they have no arguable cause-and-effect relationship with future revenues (such as the salary of a mailroom clerk, just to pick a safe example). However, many allocations of indirect costs affect future periods; an example is the allocation of factory overhead to units of inventory produced during a period and remaining on hand at period-end. Thus, the most difficult problem about indirect costs is that many of them consist of allocations of long-term assets (e.g., depreciation of plant and equipment, discussed in Chapter 20 and highlighted next).

Allocation Process

Depreciation, depletion, amortization of intangibles, and similar internal transactions are allocation processes designed to spread the cost of an asset in a *systematic and rational manner* over the period of its usefulness or over the number of units expected to be achieved. For example, if a machine costs $1,000, is expected to last for ten years, will have no salvage value, and will produce 1,000 units over its life, most accounting approaches would charge one tenth of the asset cost against operations per year, although occasionally a provision for obsolescence or a shortening of life may be reflected. Some approaches might charge $1 per unit produced, with continual reevaluation of the remaining number of units to be produced for the purpose of allocating the remaining undepreciated cost.

Since there is no objective definition of systematic and rational allocation, some form of exit value may be the best approach in determining what proportion of the carrying amount of long-term assets should be charged against operations during a particular reporting period. The differential between the value of plant assets at the beginning and at the end of the period would be the amount entering the operating statement. That amount could be subdivided in several ways, to reflect changing prices, physical deterioration, enhancement due to scarcity, or other identifiable features.

The allocation process has been the subject of much writing and not too much standard-setting action. (For example, see Kay, 1976a; Kay and Johnson, 1979; and Chambers, 1979.) At the end of 1980, the Financial Accounting Standards Advisory Council was considering recommending that the FASB commence study of depreciation accounting—the major allocation item.

Future Benefits

The idea of matching costs with revenues has led, in the past, to treating some costs as assets, even though the resultant asset lacks attributes such as exchangeability or tangibility. Deferrals of such costs are based on the idea that future revenue is expected to be derived from current expenditures.

The FASB has shown some inclination to disallow costs as assets (e.g., SFAS 2; AC 4211), and the asset attribute of exchangeability seems to have become more prominent than matching.

The definition of assets in the revised exposure draft on elements (FASB, 1979g) would seem to reopen the question of whether costs are assets, because exchangeability is not proposed as an essential criterion of an asset (paragraph 19).

Nonetheless, if a cost other than R&D has a demonstrably high probability of resulting in an identifiable and direct future benefit greater than the cost, it should be deferred. Alternatively, it may be preferable to recognize as revenue that portion of the future revenues equal to the current costs. This would substitute acceleration of revenues for making a cost into an asset and thus may be preferable conceptually. Some would go further and allow a profit to be recognized on the currently deferred costs, just as a profit is earned on the mainstream activity.

Initial direct costs are a prominent example of matching. In leasing transactions the FASB requires that the initial direct costs on direct finance leases should be charged to expense, with an equal amount of lease revenue recorded at inception of the lease (see AC 4053.101). The FASB had initially proposed deferral of initial direct costs, but changed to "front-ending" because that was the practice in use in the leasing industry. Leasing companies complained that deferral and amortization was cumbersome and would require a great deal of systems rework.

Interdependence of Cost and Revenue Recognition

Some revenue transactions are deemed to earn revenue over a period of time. In construction accounting, this has been called the *percentage-of-completion method* (as contrasted with the *completed-contract method*); and in service transactions, AcSEC referred to this as the *proportional performance method*.

Where a proportional method of recognizing revenues is based on the extent of direct costs incurred, all costs should be charged against operations as incurred. However, where performance is measured in some other way, it will then be appropriate to defer some proportion of the costs, or accrue additional costs, so as to maintain a ratable gross margin (the profit percentage) throughout the period of preformance or production. This is further discussed in Chapter 19 as to long-term construction or production-type contracts and in Chapter 18 as to service transactions. Thus, costs do become assets (or liabilities) in transactions that "earn" over a period of time, depending on the revenue recognition measurement method in use.

REPORTING EARNINGS IN THE FUTURE

In mid-1979 the FASB released *Discussion Memorandum on an Analysis of Issues Related to Reporting Earnings*. The purpose of this DM, which is a part of the conceptual framework project, is to comprehensively review the form and content of earnings reports. The DM indicates (FASB, 1979a, p. i):

> The main criticisms of earnings reports is that they do not provide enough information about past earnings to help users' assessments of future earnings. . . . Current earnings statements invite an excessive emphasis on a single net earnings number (the "bottom line").

For a discussion of the income statement format presently in use and what it intends to convey, see Chapter 3 and Chapter 26. The discussion contained here will give a perspective on the major conceptual issues introduced in the DM, which contains nine issues plus two advisory issues, as shown in Figure 7.7. The FASB is not expected to issue an exposure draft until late 1981.

The entire focus in the discussion memorandum is whether and how reports of past earnings can be used as a basis for the assessment of *future earnings*. In a way, this is only half the job, in that an additional step is necessary to fulfill the basic objective of financial statements: providing a means for assessment of *future cash flows* to the enterprise. The DM recognizes that this second phase is needed and that it is included in the conceptual framework project on funds flow and liquidity. Therefore it is dealt with here only on an advisory basis.

Regular Versus Irregular Earnings

Currently the Board is focusing only on presentational aspects, aiming basically at a segregation between regular and irregular earnings (*Issue One*). Although no conclusion has been reached on the feasibility of making this distinction accurately, most of the questions in the discussion memorandum are framed on the assumption that such a distinction can be made and would isolate earning power.

Earning power is a term normally used to mean sustainable or maintainable

ISSUE ONE: Which criteria should be adopted for choices between alternative requirements for the disclosure of information on earnings?
   a. Usefulness in assessing revenues from the regular activities of the enterprise?
   b. Usefulness in assessing the way in which regular expenses are affected by changes in the volume of activity or by changes in prices?
   c. Usefulness in assessing the frequency of occurrence and amount of irregular revenues, expenses, gains, and losses?

ISSUE TWO: Disclosure requirements for information on earnings could use placement to distinguish differences in the reliability of information, to distinguish information required by most users from information required by only some users, or to distinguish some other characteristics of information. Disclosure requirements could be limited to minimum disclosures in the financial statements or could also specify what minimum disclosures should be made outside the financial statements. Which considerations should determine any requirements for the placement of information on earnings?

ISSUE THREE: What information should an enterprise disclose, for industry segments or in aggregate, in order to improve assessments of revenues from regular activities?

ISSUE FOUR: What information should an enterprise disclose, for industry segments or in aggregate, in order to improve assessments of regular expenses, taking account of the differing effects of price changes and changes in the volume of activity?

ISSUE FIVE: What criteria should be used to identify irregular revenues, expenses, gains, and losses that should be disclosed by an enterprise?

ISSUE SIX: Should an enterprise present its earnings statement in a multiple-step format, and if so, should each of the following steps be shown?
   a. Gross margin
   b. Contribution margin
   c. Operating earnings
   d. Regular earnings
   e. Earnings of the year
   f. Earnings before financing expenses and income tax expense.

ISSUE SEVEN: Should any components of earnings be excluded from the earnings statement for the current period and included in a separate statement or treated as direct adjustments to equity interest?

ISSUE EIGHT: Should an enterprise present a five-year summary of earnings information and, if so, which components of earnings should be shown?

ISSUE NINE: Should an enterprise report earnings per share and any other ratios?

ADVISORY ISSUE ONE: What aspects of the reporting of cash flows are critical to any of the other issues above?

ADVISORY ISSUE TWO: Should an enterprise publish a forecast of future earnings before the end of the period concerned, or is it sufficient to rely entirely on reports of past earnings as a basis for users to prepare their own assessments of future earnings?

FIGURE 7.7 SUMMARY OF ISSUES ON REPORTING EARNINGS
SOURCE: FASB, 1979a.

earnings, giving some indication about the normal level of earnings expected to be attained in the future. (Earning power is discussed briefly at the outset of this chapter.)

A variant of earning power is described by the phrase *quality of earnings*. However, it may not be much different: earnings from continuing activities may be said to have a higher quality simply because they are expected to recur. An ingredient of the quality of earnings is the extent to which earnings are realized in cash. The higher the proportion of earnings realized in cash, the higher the quality of earnings is said to be, because the uncertainty of earnings is resolved when conversion into cash occurs.

The FASB describes users' concerns this way: "Users perceive a need for additional information about the regular and irregular components of earnings as a basis for improved assessments of future earnings" (FASB, 1979a, par. 30). The Board admits the possibility that users' assessments may not be improved, because "evidence presently available tends to support the hypothesis that earnings follow a random walk. . . . If changes in earnings are random in nature, is it possible that additional disclosure may lead to improved assessment of future earnings?" (FASB, 1979a, par. 21).

A point of view not explored by the DM is that present financial statements confuse many users by their intermixture of relatively factual and objective information with relatively interpretive and subjective information; the user generally cannot (or does not wish to) sort these out. This view may already be implied in the FASB's focus on regular and irregular. For example, short-term monetary item inflow and outflow relating to operations is mostly factual. However, earnings statement components affected by inventories, allowances for bad debts, and allocation of the cost of depreciable assets introduce a considerable degree of interpretation and subjectivity, which may be appreciated only by financial statement users who are reasonably well versed in accounting principles. For the sake of those less expert, however, it may be desirable to separate factual from interpretive, or give some indication of the degree of factuality a particular financial statement representation contains.

The fact that revenues or expenses (as well as related assets and liabilities) are estimated probably should also be disclosed, by including the word *estimated* in the financial statement caption; a footnote might explain the degree of estimation. This is simply a matter of clarity of presentation; many of these items (e.g., income taxes) are now understood by experienced financial statement readers to be estimates.

Regular Revenues. In *Issue Three* the FASB is seeking to identify what kind of new data would help in assessing revenue from regular activities.

Information about the volume of sales of major product lines and services would seem to be an essential disaggregation of regular activities. (The importance of segment reporting has already been recognized in SFAS 14 (AC 2081).) Giving the *effects* of changes in sales volume and selling prices would add more relevance. To report only units, unit prices, and internal or external selling price indexes as implied in the DM complicates the task of the user; and presumably that information will be used to derive the effects in any event.

Furthermore, there are many ways in which internal indexes can be calculated. To assure comparability among indexes that the FASB may require to be disclosed, detailed rules would be needed governing both the types of indexes and their calculation. This would assure comparability but probably not relevance. It is unlikely that any one index or method of calculation for all enterprises would be considered equally relevant by a majority of users. Economic indexes are widely available, and it probably should be left to financial statement users to determine which indexes are needed for their varied decision processes.

Information about the levels of unused productive capacity might also be reported in future earnings statements, but the many assumptions required to measure this (e.g., the number of shifts and holidays, or the kind of unit in which it is to be measured in the case of a multiproduct or multiservice business) might make such information not meaningful to users.

Regular Expenses. The DM asks for views on what new information would improve assessments of regular expenses (*Issue Four*). The possible requirement for segregation of expenses between fixed and variable, or direct versus indirect, might cloud user interpretation by introducing highly subjective factors. Although classification of expenses based strictly on variability is not likely to be practicable, disclosure along functional lines might be helpful. Thus, both in the aggregate and by segment, selling expenses could be separated from general and administrative expenses, and cost of sales, financing costs, and discretionary items could be disclosed.

The reporting of internally or externally prepared indexes of prices of major resources used is also under consideration. Externally prepared indexes may not be very relevant to a particular enterprise due to geographical and quantity usage differences, the timing of purchases, or the volatility of resource prices. If internally developed indexes are reported, variations from externally available indexes may raise unnecessary questions.

Irregular Earnings. In order to identify irregular revenues, expenses, gains, and losses that should be disclosed by an enterprise (*Issue Five*), one must first reach the conclusion that "irregularity" in accounting can be defined. It is not simply the corollary of regularity, because that is not defined either.

Perhaps the major distinction should be between operating and nonoperating. Unusual and incidental activities, accounting changes, realized value increases, prior-period adjustments, financing costs, and income taxes might better be reported within the earnings statement as separate line items following net results of operations.

The DM suggests that revenues or expenses unusual in amount, expenses that fluctuate periodically, future-oriented expenses, expenses or revenues the amounts of which are largely dependent on chance factors, and expenses that result from changes in the law might be distinctions to make for purposes of classifying items on the earnings statement. Most of these distinctions could hamper the more important distinction of operating versus nonoperating. A distinction, however, between discretionary and nondiscretionary items might be a relevant distinction, and material items of a discretionary nature should merit disclosure.

Placement of Earnings Information

Related to the issue of what kind of classification—regular or irregular, subjective or factual—of information is chosen, a decision is also necessary as to where various kinds of earnings information should be presented (*Issue Two*). In the financial statements, there are at least three choices: in the earnings statement itself, in other financial statements yet to be developed, or in the notes. There is also the opportunity to include information in financial reports but outside the financial statements. (See the FASB *Invitation to Comment on Financial Statements and Other Means of Financial Reporting,* 1980e.) This approach has already been adopted with respect to supplementary information on changing prices and on oil and gas reserves.

The DM on earnings reporting points out that the placement of information will say something about the reliability of that information. The present understanding seems to be that information incorporated into the financial statements has more reliability than information included in the financial report but outside the financial statements; this understanding is not likely to change, at least not quickly.

Reliability is probably the most important characteristic needed to aid predictability. Although the Board recognizes the danger of being categorical about degrees of reliability, it would seem that the placement approach should remain a useful signal, at least in broad terms, for users of financial information.

Display Questions

In general, the multiple-step format for the earnings statement is more prevalent than the single-step format, which exaggerates the significance of the "bottom line." The multiple-step format provides additional information content because of the "steps" shown. Questions arise, however, as to whether each of the following steps should be shown (*Issue Six*):

1. Gross margin;
2. Contribution margin;
3. Operating earnings;
4. Regular earnings;
5. Earnings of the year; and
6. Earnings before financing expenses and income tax expense.

The reporting of gross margin and contribution margin is related to the reporting of fixed and variable expenses. Because it is not practical to distinguish variable (direct) from fixed (indirect) expense in a consistent manner, reporting gross margin may be subject to misinterpretation.

Also it may not be possible to uniformly define contribution margin. In segment reporting under SFAS 14, the operating profit or loss for a segment (AC 2081.10(d)) depends on allocations of overall enterprise expenses. This provides comparability of contribution margin from year to year, but not necessarily among enterprises.

Finally, there is an overlap in regular earnings and operating earnings, which suggests that only one should be chosen. Earnings before financing expenses and income tax expense seems unattractive. Financing expenses are a determinant of income tax and it would be confusing to make them a part of the same step.

The DM reconsiders the sanctity of the clean surplus approach (*Issue Six (e) and Seven*), but hopefully the FASB will not succumb to allowing entry of any components of earnings directly to equity. It may be useful, however, to distinguish between those items affecting prior-period earnings; thus "earnings of the year" could be shown as a separate step in the earnings statement, followed only by prior-period adjustments (as currently defined) and income taxes. Adjustments made necessary by changes in accounting principles and now reported as adjustments to the beginning balance of retained earnings should continue to be reported in that manner. All other "irregular" items, such as future-oriented expenses, exceptional maintenance costs, or certain gains and losses, are nevertheless items affecting the current period and should not be removed from the operations statement.

The DM asks whether an enterprise should present a five-year summary of earnings information, and which components of earnings should be shown in any such summary (*Issue Eight*). Many companies have given multiyear summaries, and their usefulness is well acknowledged. A five-year summary should now be required by the FASB, showing net results of operation, net nonoperating items excluding financing cost and income tax, financing cost, income taxes, and aggregate earnings. Note that the SEC is aiming in this direction with its requirement for a five-year summary of selected data called for by Item 6 of the new Form 10-K, effective for calendar-year 1980. The SEC selections are different and include net sales, income or loss from continuing operations (in total and per share), cash dividends per common share, total assets at year-end, and long-term obligations and redeemable preferred stock at year-end.

Earnings Per Share and Other Ratios

Earnings per share (*Issue Nine*) should continue to be disclosed, since many users look to this as an expected ratio. However, the accounting profession probably should not encourage the use of particular ratios, or ratios in general, until their relevance in meeting the objectives of financial statements has been demonstrated. Accounting numbers, which are inexact, are made to look exact when converted into precise ratios.

Cash-Flow Reporting

Some aspects of the reporting of cash flows (*Advisory Issue One*) seem critical. For example, the determination of a preferred concept of funds flow should not be separated from the determination of an earnings statement format. If the earnings statement and the funds-flow statement are not *integrated,* all the old arguments of proper funds-flow terminology and approach will remain unresolved. In addition, the articulated approach would make the funds-flow statement more readily understandable than the often cryptic statement of source and use of funds based on APB 19 (AC 2021).

Forecasts

The board asks (in *Advisory Issue Two*) whether an enterprise should publish a forecast of future earnings before the end of the period concerned or whether it is sufficient to rely entirely on reports of past earnings as a basis for users to prepare their own assessments of future earnings. As more fully discussed in Chapter 33, enterprises should be encouraged to experiment with the issuance of responsibly prepared forecasts; however, forecasts should not be mandated at the present time.

A Possible Result

It is hoped that all revenues and expenses will be reported in a single financial statement. Categorization will separate mostly factual from mostly interpretive elements and provide a database useful for predicting future operations. This will be enhanced by having aggregate earnings separated into

1. Short-term monetary inflows from operations,
2. Allocations and allowances pertaining to operations,
3. Other items of a nonoperating nature,
4. Realized value increases,
5. Prior-period adjustments,
6. Financing costs, and
7. Income taxes.

Attempts to make other distinctions will fail because they require too many arbitrary and controversial definitions and reporting rules to be formulated with little, if any, improvement in interpretive significance of the earnings statement.

SUGGESTED READING

AICPA. *Illustrations of Reporting the Results of Operations.* Financial Report Survey 3. New York, 1974. This book, based on a NAARS survey of over 8,000 published annual reports, illustrates reporting under APB 30.

————. *Objectives of Financial Statements.* Vol. 2, *Selected Papers.* New York, 1974. Although Volume 1 is quite brief, Volume 2 contains interesting longer papers that continue to have relevance, in particular Section 3 on "Valuation Methods"; several papers dealing with income in Section 2; and "The Conceptual Inquiry" and the paper on "Accounting for Social Costs and Benefits" by Joshua Ronen in Section 5. (Social costs and benefits have not been dealt with in this chapter, but attempts at measuring and recording them will undoubtedly accelerate in the '80s.)

American Accounting Association. "The Realization Concept" (Report of 1964 Concepts and Standards Research Study Committee—The Realization Concept). *The Accounting Review,* April, 1965, pp. 312-322. This paper presents a rather thorough review of the subject of degrees of achievement of recognition criteria. Though it is over 16 years old, it contains a very plausible discussion of holding gains and losses and recommends that these be recorded in financial statements. In 1979 the FASB finally chose to recognize such holding gains and losses in supplementary financial information prepared on a current cost basis. A large portion of the April 1965 *Accounting Review* is dedicated to earnings measurement and is a useful source for the serious student of this subject.

FASB. *Discussion Memorandum on an Analysis of Issues Related to Reporting Earnings.* Stamford, Conn., 1979. This DM is a lucid explanation of what current earnings statements present and of what various possible reconfigurations might convey.

————. *Invitation to Comment on Accounting for Certain Service Transactions.* Stamford, Conn., 1978. This document is quite useful in showing how revenue and expense recognition must often go hand in hand in earnings measurement. An invitation to comment (this was the first) is not a document forming a part of the FASB due process; thus the FASB can choose to take no direct action after all of the respondents' views have been considered. Because of strong objections from unified groups in the service industries, the subject of this invitation to comment will be incorporated in the forthcoming FASB discussion memorandum on recognition criteria, a part of the conceptual framework.

8

Effects of Changing Prices and Values

Michael O. Alexander

HISTORICAL COST DRAWBACKS

A Modern-Day Fable

Two merchants had an identical item in their shops. Each of them had paid $1 for it. One fine day, one of the merchants opened his shop for business while the other went fishing. The merchant who opened his shop sold his item for $2, making a profit of $1. On this profit he paid a tax of 50¢.

During the day, the wholesale cost of the item rose to $2. The hardworking merchant had sold his item for $2, but because he had paid 50¢ in taxes, he now had only $1.50 with which to replace the same item of inventory. He decided to go to the bank and borrow the additional 50¢ he needed.

At the end of the day he assessed the result. He had made a profit of $1, he had the same item in stock, and he owed the bank 50¢. Meanwhile, the other merchant had thoroughly enjoyed his day fishing, had done no work, and had made no profit. But he had the same item in stock and owed the bank nothing.

Apart from its obvious social message on work ethics, this anecdote demonstrates the important and basic dilemma in deciding what is income during times of inflation. If the hardworking merchant had decided that his profit was not the amount he made over the cost of the item when he bought it, but the amount over the cost of replacing it now, he would not have shown any profit at all. He would nonetheless have paid his taxes and borrowed from the bank.

Problems for Business

To a business, as to an individual, inflation means that it must pay more for the goods and services it needs just to stay even. Under the conventional method of determining profits, which matches the current prices at which a business sells its products with the original price it paid for them—their historical cost—the profits that it reports may be high. Actually, though, because it will have to pay current prices to replace its products and maintain the same business activity, not all these reported profits will be available for distribution as dividends to the investors or for new capital investment in the business. Yet the business is taxed on the full amount. This explains why, in recent years of high inflation, business liquidity has often declined and debt-to-equity ratios have increased despite rises in reported earnings.

The problem inflation causes for business is exemplified in the following chain of events:

1. As costs of goods and services used by a business rise, additional cash is needed to finance operations (e.g., inventories and plant and equipment).
2. Growing uncertainty about the magnitude of future cost and price changes for materials, labor, and capital equipment increases the cost of borrowing.
3. This increases the *hurdle rate*—the rate of expected return that justifies a new investment.
4. New capital projects must therefore bring a higher rate of return. This usually requires significant increases in selling prices, which may be difficult to impose because of competition or price controls. In many cases, new productive activity is curtailed.
5. The decline in new productive capacity contributes to an overall decline in productive activity throughout the economy, and thus results in a reduction in the growth of productivity and output necessary to offset the decline in the value of the currency and in general standards of living.

Historical-cost-based accounting fails to reflect the effects of inflation and changing prices on a business enterprise. To change the basis of accounting, or to add supplemental information showing the effects of inflation, increases the cost to business of providing accounting information, at least in the short run. It might also complicate the task of reading and interpreting financial reports. These adverse consequences of change are fairly easy to foresee. But what are the consequences of continuing to ignore the effects of inflation in financial reports?

The role of financial reporting is to provide relevant information in order that investors, creditors, labor, government, and the public can make decisions affecting individual enterprises and, ultimately, the allocation of resources within the economy. Decisions based on incomplete or misleading data are likely to be poor decisions.

Improving Decisions. The following are examples of ways in which inflation-adjusted information would assist decision making:

- In the capital markets, allocation of capital is achieved through the pricing mechanism. Prices based on financial information that is incomplete or misleading will result in poor pricing and allocation decisions. Inflation, especially at rates varying widely from year to year, introduces increased uncertainty into business activities. Most managements appreciate the need to consider inflation in making decisions; but communicating the effects of inflation is hindered by the lack of systematic and explicit recognition of inflation's effects in financial reports. A better understanding by the general public of the effect of inflation and changing prices on business will help to promote an environment with rates of return on capital that will attract investment.
- Management decisions may be influenced by the disclosure of "real" growth. Those with an interest in an enterprise will be better able to judge management performance and ask informed questions. This may result in changes in pricing policy and investment decisions and in incentives to improve productivity—and in some cases, in changes in management.
- Economic policy decisions concerning investment incentives, industry development schemes, and taxation are based in part on macroeconomic data; information about the effect of specific price changes on individual enterprises and by industry groupings are likely to provide insight to policy makers on the different effects of inflation on each industry. If public understanding is improved by disclosure of the effect of inflation on businesses, this may also affect government policy decisions.
- The general public's view of the business sector is mainly influenced by the price paid for goods and services. It is also affected by reports of record business earnings during inflation. To the extent that the public's understanding of the effects of inflation is enhanced, business may be viewed in a somewhat less critical perspective. The continued ability of the enterprise to supply goods and services and to provide employment and generate funds for new investment, new employment, and increased wealth is dependent on achieving an adequate return through prices charged.

Few understand the effects of inflation on a business enterprise in its role as a generator of society's wealth. For a democratic society, in which broad social and economic decisions are profoundly influenced by public opinion, lack of understanding can be a matter of enormous consequence. Accountants generally agree that the financial information they prepare should give a better presentation of the effects of inflation on business performance. The debate among them concerns how this should be done.

Ways of Looking at Inflation

There are two ways of looking at inflation. In one view it is seen as an erosion in the value of the monetary unit, a decline in the currency's purchasing power. In the other view it is seen as individual changes in the specific prices affecting a firm's operations, its capital, and its cash flow. These are the changes in price of the specific items and services a firm buys, makes, or sells. The aggregate of these individual changes for a specific firm is not necessarily equal to the general inflation rate for the total economy.

The accounting solution to the problem of inflation when it is seen as a decline in the currency's purchasing power is usually called *general price level accounting, current purchasing power accounting,* or, in the terminology of the FASB, *constant dollar accounting.* The method used in this solution is to adjust the monetary unit for the general inflation rate while continuing to use historical cost as a basis for valuation of assets and liabilities and related revenues and expenses. As more fully explained later, historical costs are translated into units of current purchasing power or constant dollars.

The accounting solution to the problem of inflation when it is seen as specific price changes is known as *current cost* or *current value* accounting. There are many methods for determining current costs and current values, but all depart in some way from the historical cost basis employed to value assets and liabilities under conventional GAAP. Current cost methods employ various approaches to measuring the cost of currently reproducing or replacing existing assets with identical or equivalent assets, costs sometimes referred to as *entry values.* Current value methods employ various approaches to determining the amounts obtainable or expected to be obtained on disposing of assets (including their consumption in the company's production process); these are sometimes referred to as *exit values* and include *net realizable value* and *present value of future cash flows.* Current value is sometimes used generically to refer to either current cost or current value as discussed above, but in this chapter current value refers to exit or disposition values only.

A third accounting solution is a combination approach that recognizes both general inflation in terms of constant dollars as measured by a broad price index, and specific price changes as measured by a current cost or current value method. The FASB's current cost approach in SFAS 33 (AC 1072) is one example of such a combination approach. The method of measurement of financial statement amounts is under study by the FASB in its conceptual framework project, discussed in depth in Chapter 2. SFAS 33 is seen as a step in the measurement project, not as the final solution.

GENERAL PRICE LEVEL ACCOUNTING

General price level accounting and constant dollar accounting are used in this chapter as generic terms to refer to the accounting approach that aims to translate historical cost values into units of equal purchasing power. In general price level accounting, the dollars used in historical cost financial statements are adjusted for changes in the purchasing power of the dollar, making it possible to compare amounts from different periods in units of equal purchasing power.

Under historical cost accounting, by contrast, revenues will usually be measured in dollars that have a different purchasing power from that of cost dollars; thus earnings may fail to represent a change in the purchasing power of the owner's equity. For example, if a company invests $1,000 in an asset, holds it for a year, and then sells it for $1,150, conventional accounting would record a $150 profit and a return of 15%. If the general inflation rate during the year had been 10%, however, $100 of the $150 nominal profit would be a decline in purchasing power.

General price level accounting removes the general inflation factor from all measurements, and reports assets, liabilities, revenues, and expenses in constant dollars. (The actual dollars used in conventional accounting are referred to in this chapter as *nominal dollars* to differentiate them from constant dollars.) To do this, nominal dollars are restated in constant dollars using a measure of the change in the general price level such as the Consumer Price Index or the Gross National Product Implicit Price Deflator.

General price level accounting is favored as the best approach to inflation accounting by those who see the problem of inflation as an increase in general price levels and a decline in the purchasing power of the currency. This approach is recognized as the more objective and practical method. For this reason preparers often assert that it is easier to apply than current cost and current value methods. It has the further advantage of being based on historical costs, the conventional accounting system presently in use, and does not involve the sometimes subjective measurements required by the current value and current cost methods.

Those who criticize constant dollar accounting point out that it fails to reflect the impact of individual price changes on a firm and that it may be more difficult to understand.

Experience

As the rate of inflation increased in recent years, accountants in several countries began to study general price level adjustment methods. In the United Kingdom, the Accounting Standards Committee issued an exposure draft entitled *Accounting for Changes in the Purchasing Power of Money* (1973), followed by *Provisional Statement of Standard Accounting Practice 7* (Institute of Chartered Accountants in England and Wales, 1974).

In the United States, the arrival of double-digit inflation led to the issuance in 1974 of an FASB exposure draft that called for certain supplementary disclosures based on financial reporting in units of general purchasing power. That exposure draft was based heavily on APB Statement 3, *Financial Statements Restated for General Price-Level Changes,* issued in June 1969 (AICPA, 1969a).

In Canada, Australia, New Zealand, and other countries, the profession adopted comparable measures. In Brazil and other South American countries, a similar method has been used for several years to make a monetary correction for the extremely high rates of inflation prevailing there. In these countries the approach is not limited to financial reporting, but is also incorporated in contracts, taxation, and day-to-day business operations.

Field testing with general price level adjustment for inflation has been conducted with U.S. companies both by the AICPA (Rosenfield, 1969) and the FASB

(1977d). In the United Kingdom, a number of companies responded to the provisional British standard issued in May 1974 by publishing supplementary general price level statements. In Canada, some companies published similar supplementary data.

The FASB field test that followed its 1974 exposure draft was organized through the Financial Executives Institute and the American Petroleum Institute. In this test, 101 companies were asked to restate their 1972, 1973, and 1974 financial results along the lines proposed. The report on the test was limited to a description of conceptual and implementation problems encountered and the data collected by the companies; it did not include opinions or conclusions on the usefulness or reliability of the data either to the user or the preparer. The results of the test were not disclosed by the companies themselves in their annual reports; instead, the information was submitted to the FASB on a confidential basis. Some companies commented on the usefulness of the data to management. As might have been expected, the comments ranged from praising the information as providing "new insight" to calling it "misleading."

Apart from the FASB field test, there has been little voluntary experimentation with general price level accounting in the United States. Prior to 1979 the approach had not been adopted in the annual reports of companies to any noticeable extent, and as a result, U.S. investors have had little experience in using constant dollar information. In the United Kingdom and Canada, however, some actual experience with disclosure of constant dollar data in annual reports is available. A number of companies in both countries applied the method and disclosed the results for a few years in the mid-1970s. The results, however, seem to have had little effect on the investor, on accountants, or on the companies themselves, and some of the companies discontinued the practice.

An AICPA experiment completed in 1978 involved application of four different methods, including general price level accounting, by a group of 23 companies (AICPA, 1979b). The participants gave the general price level method a low rating on usefulness and relevance, but higher marks on measurability and reliability.

An opinion survey conducted by the Financial Executives Research Foundation and based on interviews with preparers and users of financial statements found that the general price level method received little acceptance (Price Waterhouse & Co., 1974). Some preparers reported that it helped alert managers to the need for higher prices and hoped that it would support the case for tax relief. Others indicated that the manager learned nothing new from it.

A further opportunity to assess the usefulness of general-price-level-adjusted financial information has been afforded with the issue in September 1979 of SFAS 33, *Financial Reporting and Changing Prices* (AC 1072), summarized near the end of this chapter. This statement requires all large public companies (estimated at between 1,300-1,500) to include in their annual reports, beginning with 1979, certain constant dollar information, including income from continuing operations on a constant dollar basis. This is the first time that data will be made available for a large number of companies.

Methodology

General price level (GPL) accounting is applied in practice by adjusting assets, liabilities, and revenue and expense items for changes in the general purchasing power of the dollar. The method has evolved during recent years, but only in relatively minor ways. Most of the modifications have concerned the definition of monetary and nonmonetary items. Monetary items include cash and claims to cash that are fixed in terms of numbers of dollars, regardless of changes in prices. Liabilities fixed in amount are also monetary items. Recently, foreign currency amounts and deferred income tax balances were reclassified by SFAS 33 (AC 1072.208) as monetary items. Nonmonetary items include property, plant, and equipment, inventories, and other elements that are affected by price changes.

The method restates the historical amounts of nonmonetary assets and liabilities by multiplying by the ratio of the general purchasing power index at the end of the current period (the Consumer Price Index for All Urban Consumers is required in SFAS 33; AC 1072.039) to the index at the date on which the nonmonetary item originated. The results are the amounts in dollars of purchasing power at the end of the period, as shown in Figure 8.1. Alternatively, the numerator could be 100 instead of the index at the date on which the nonmonetary item originated, in order to present amounts in terms of purchasing power of the base year of the index (1967 in the case of the Consumer Price Index); or the numerator could be the average index for the current year, in order to present amounts in terms of average purchasing power for the current year.

In restated financial statements, monetary items at the end of the period are stated at the same amount as in a nominal dollar balance sheet; monetary items at other dates are restated to end-of-period dollars, and the impact of changes in purchasing power is reflected in the income statement.

To illustrate how the method works in practice, a simplified balance sheet and an income statement showing a comparison of historical cost with general price level indexed amounts is shown in Figures 8.2 and 8.3.

In the balance sheet in Figure 8.2, note that the monetary items—cash, accounts receivable, accounts payable, and other current and long-term liabilities—do not change, since they are already stated at their current purchasing power. The nonmonetary items, such as inventories, property, and capital stock, have been restated to reflect changes in the general price level.

The statement of earnings and retained earnings in Figure 8.3 shows that sales have been restated in constant dollars to reflect that they occurred throughout the period during which the purchasing power of the dollar varied. Other items on the earnings statement have been adjusted in a similar manner.

GENERAL RULE FOR GPL RESTATEMENT OF
HISTORICAL AMOUNTS OF NONMONETARY ASSETS
AND LIABILITIES TO END-OF-PERIOD DOLLARS

$$\text{Historical Cost of Nonmonetary Asset or Nominal Amount of Nonmonetary Liability} \times \frac{\text{Index at End of Current Period}}{\text{Index at Date Nonmonetary Item Originated}}$$

FIGURE 8.1 GPL RESTATEMENT FORMULA

	Historical Cost	Historical Cost Restated to Purchasing Power of Dollar at End of Period
Cash	$ 3,000	$ 3,000
Inventories	10,118	10,381
Accounts receivable	9,354	9,354
Property, plant, and equipment	11,262	17,524
Accumulated depreciation	(5,818)	(9,052)
Goodwill on consolidation	816	946
Total assets	$28,732	$32,153
Accounts payable	$ 2,000	$ 2,000
Other current and long-term liabilities	15,879	15,879
Capital stock—462 shares outstanding	566	1,085
Contributed surplus	45	83
Retained earnings	10,242	13,106
Total liabilities and stockholders' equity	$28,732	$32,153

FIGURE 8.2 EXAMPLE OF GPL RESTATED BALANCE SHEET

The gain or loss on holding monetary items arises from the reduction in value of, respectively, net monetary liabilities and assets held during the period. Most people recognize that holding cash or other monetary assets during inflation will result in a decline in purchasing power or value of these assets, and that obligations to repay debt in the future in dollars of lower purchasing power may offset this loss. Thus, the gain or loss on monetary items shown on the earnings statement is a reflection of the effects of inflation on the monetary components of an enterprise. Companies with large amounts of long-term debt often show a large purchasing power gain during inflation, while companies with net monetary assets show a purchasing power loss. The gain on net monetary items in the illustration is calculated by multiplying the change in the index for the year by the average balance of net monetary items held or owed during the year.

Comparisons of Different Periods

Another application of constant dollar accounting arises in the comparison of a company's measurements for different periods. This is done by restating each measurement in terms of a common price level, in the same way "real growth" in the economy, measured by gross national product data, is restated in dollars of a specified base year. Sales or revenues, net assets, stockholders' equity, earnings, and dividends are obvious candidates for such treatment.

A company whose sales and earnings in nominal dollars have doubled in the

	Historical Cost	Historical Cost Restated to Purchasing Power of Dollar at End of Period
Sales	$69,058	$72,373
Costs and expenses		
Cost of goods sold	50,390	53,582
Depreciation	786	1,199
Selling, general, and administrative	11,678	12,238
Gain on holding monetary items	—	(402)
Earnings before income taxes	6,204	5,756
Provision for income taxes	2,927	3,068
Net earnings	8,277	2,688
Retained earnings, beginning of year	7,939	11,392
Dividends	(974)	(974)
Retained earnings, end of year	$10,242	$13,106
Earnings per share	$ 7.09	$ 5.82

FIGURE 8.3   EXAMPLE OF GPL RESTATED STATEMENT OF EARNINGS AND RETAINED EARNINGS

last ten years might, to the unsophisticated investor, appear to be a growth company, though the general price level in the United States has roughly doubled during that period. Restatement of the nominal dollar measurements of such a company would show that current sales and earnings represent approximately the same purchasing power as those of ten years earlier. A five-year summary of this type is required by SFAS 33 (AU 1072.035), except that all earnings data have to be adjusted for the effects of inflation in each year by applying the general price level techniques discussed above, and such adjusted earnings data is then converted to a common base.

CURRENT COST AND CURRENT VALUE ACCOUNTING

The objective of current cost accounting is to measure specific price changes and their effects on a business. Some current cost methods are designed mainly to account for the effects of price changes on earnings and capital, others address the issues of liquidity and the ability of the firm to pay dividends.

It is generally agreed that the value of a business is the present value of its future net cash inflows. Since price changes affect the amount and timing of future cash flows, they also affect the value of the business. But are such changes in value, as measured by changes in the current costs of assets employed in the business, an integral part of earnings?

Some accountants argue that such changes in current costs impact earnings in two areas: (1) the cost of previously acquired assets consumed in currently producing and selling goods and services (e.g., cost of goods sold and depreciation expense) and (2) holding gains and losses on assets held for future use or sale.

Other accountants believe that the measurement of holding gains and losses is too subjective and too unreliable to be used in basic financial reporting. This group favors reflecting the impact of changing prices only on the costs of assets consumed in the operations of the business—i.e., on the cost of goods sold and depreciation expense. This approach, which would exclude holding gains and losses from earnings, is viewed by its proponents as sufficient to comply with one of the objectives of financial reporting as presented in SFAC 1: ". . . financial reporting should provide information to help investors, creditors, and others assess the amounts, timing, and uncertainty of prospective net cash inflows to the related enterprise" (AC 1210.37).

Still other accountants believe that holding gains and losses should be *included* in earnings if they are measured by an exit value method (net realizable value or present value of future cash flows) but *excluded* from earnings if they are measured by an entry value method (current replacement cost, current reproduction cost, etc.).

The debate over how best to communicate the effect of specific price changes on a business enterprise has given rise to several different methods of current cost and current value accounting. These methods will be described after a brief glance at their history.

History

Current cost accounting had its origins in an era of little or no inflation. In the Netherlands, N.V. Philips Gloeilampenfabrieken employed replacement cost accounting beginning in 1936 to reflect the impact of specific price changes on individual product costs. In Canada the Imperial Tobacco Company produced shareholder financial statements on a limited current cost basis for some years starting in 1961.

With the increased inflation levels of the early 1970s, the accountant's first response was to use general price level accounting. The first time a current cost method was widely advocated was in the 1975 report (the Sandilands Report) of the Inflation Accounting Committee in the United Kingdom; it recommended what it called "current-cost accounting" (Sandilands, 1975). This major event triggered accountants in many other countries to reevaluate their earlier steps and to examine in some detail a possible move toward current value methods. Thus, Australia, Canada, New Zealand, and the United Kingdom all issued proposed standards or discussion memoranda on various forms of current cost and current value accounting.

In the United Kingdom, Exposure Draft 18 (Accounting Standards Committee, 1976) suggested a comprehensive change in financial reporting whereby historical cost accounting would be replaced by current cost accounting, but the proposal was opposed by a majority vote of practitioners. This experience helped other countries recognize that a comprehensive departure from historical cost accounting was far too revolutionary to take in one step, and attempts were made to develop simplified methods of disclosing the impact of changing prices in statements supplemental to the basic historical cost information.

In the United States, current cost and current value accounting was resisted because of a serious concern about any move away from the historical cost basis for financial statements. Nevertheless, action was taken by the SEC, which began requiring disclosure of replacement cost data by major corporations in 1976 (ASR 190).

In Canada, a partial approach was recommended in June 1977 by the Ontario Committee on Inflation Accounting. A similar approach was proposed in the United Kingdom by the Hyde Committee (Accounting Standards Committee, 1977). And in September 1979 the FASB issued SFAS 33 (AC 1072), requiring partial disclosure of the effects of changing prices using a current cost method. Most recently, a binding statement on current cost accounting was released by the Accounting Standards Committee in the United Kingdom (The Institute of Chartered Accountants in England and Wales, 1980); this is discussed later in this chapter. The focus below is on general considerations underlying current costs and values.

Measurement of Current Costs and Values

Unlike general price level accounting, current value and current cost accounting requires a change in the basic principle used in the preparation of financial statements—that of recording assets at their original cost to the business. The essence of current cost accounting is that it records assets and liabilities at present-day costs and charges consumption or use of these assets to operations based on those revised costs. Various forms of current value (exit value) and current cost accounting have been proposed, and an important difference among them is the manner in which costs and values are determined.

The presentation of results of operations or earnings for current cost methods differs from the presentation that is appropriate with an exit value method. Earnings presentations under current cost methods are similar to those made on the historical cost basis; for example, sales and cost of sales are recognized when products or services are delivered, and the difference between the two represents the gross profit or loss realized on sales. However, as illustrated below under Value to the Business, cost of sales is stated at current cost rather than historical cost; depreciation expense is calculated based on current cost rather than historical cost; and the differences between historical cost and current cost of inventories and property, plant, and equipment being held for sale or use in the business are separately recognized as unrealized holding gains or losses. Holding gains and losses are also discussed in a separate section below. When an exit value method is used, changes in value of assets held by the business are recognized as they occur; no distinction is made between gross profit on operations and holding gains and losses. Depreciation expense is not recorded, but instead the net change in exit value of property, plant, and equipment used in the business is included as a component in each period's earnings statement. A format for presentation of earnings information under an exit value accounting approach is illustrated in Chapter 37 in the discussion of reserve recognition accounting in the oil and gas producing industry.

Economic Value. Economic value, sometimes known as *value in use,* is obtained by calculating the discounted value of net cash inflows expected to be derived from the use of an asset or group of assets. (Economic value is sometimes also referred to as *future exit value.*) Because this approach in theory can be applied to the business as a whole, many believe it is the only "pure" accounting approach, but it lacks the support of accountants and businessmen, because economic value generally is not determinable in an objective, reliable, auditable manner. Except in those limited circumstances when future cash flows can be predicted with a high degree of certainty, economic value clearly is the least objective of the various proposed approaches, and hence it is the most difficult to implement.

Net Realizable Value. Net realizable value is the amount for which an asset can be sold. The FASB defined it recently as "the amount of cash, or its equivalent, expected to be derived from sale of an asset [in the ordinary course of business] net of costs required to be incurred as a result of the sale" (AC 1072.063(a)). If an asset cannot be sold in the ordinary course of business, then its net realizable value would be the cash or equivalent the enterprise could otherwise obtain for it. Net realizable value is also referred to as *current exit value.*

Those who favor valuing assets at current exit value do so on the basis that it often is a more objective measure of value and that it better measures management decisions to hold or sell. In addition, it may indicate the degree to which the business can redeploy its resources—i.e., its adaptability. In a sense, current exit value gives an indication of the firm's commitment to physical or fixed (nonmonetary) assets compared to monetary assets. Businesses that hold substantial fixed assets with little or no resale value (e.g., steel makers and oil refiners) have minimal opportunity to adapt to changing economic and business conditions. Market prices may not be available for all items, but this apparently does not worry the proponents of this method, because the lack of a ready market indicates the lack of liquidity for that asset. The point is also made that by measuring all assets at their net realizable value, physical or fixed assets can be related to monetary assets on an equal basis.

Current Cost Methods. The objectives of current cost methods are to revalue the assets used in the business, primarily inventories and property, plant, and equipment, to reflect current prices that would be paid to acquire the assets. This is important because during periods of rapid price inflation the present-day prices for most resources are apt to be considerably higher than historical cost.

There are two general approaches to current cost—current reproduction cost and current replacement cost. Under *current reproduction cost,* assets are stated at the cost of acquiring or reproducing assets physically identical to the ones held by the business. Advocates of this method state that it is the most objective of the current cost approaches and deals directly with the actual assets, not hypothetically equivalent assets. Advocates of current replacement cost state that current reproduction cost values are unrealistic in those situations in which assets identical to the ones held by the business are no longer commercially available; even if they are, they would not be acquired by the business, because of the availability of technologically superior assets that will perform the same functions better.

Under *current replacement cost* methods, the objective is to value the existing assets by reference to either identical assets or, if the identical assets are unavailable or uneconomic, to *equivalent assets.* There are two schools of thought as to the approach that should be used in selecting an equivalent asset. One approach focuses on service potential of existing assets, the other focuses on their productive capacity.

The replacement of *existing service potential* is generally interpreted to mean using the replacement cost of identical assets if both available and economical. When substitute assets are used, they should be assets that will provide the same function as existing assets. In general, when improved levels of technology are currently employed in producing specified goods or services, the existing technology is nevertheless focused on for the purpose of determining equivalent service potential unless it is decisively uneconomic.

Where the current replacement cost of *productive capacity* is used, it is generally interpreted to relate to the lowest amount that would have to be paid in the normal course of business to obtain new assets of equivalent operating capacity, as measured by the ability of a company to produce and distribute a specified number of units of product or services presently produced or provided within a given time frame. Thus, when this approach is used, the assets being valued would in most cases be different from the existing assets.

Under either the existing service potential or productive capacity approaches, current cost depreciation must be adjusted to give effect to any operating advantages or disadvantages related to the assumed use of the equivalent asset compared with the existing owned asset.

In some instances current reproduction cost of existing assets, current replacement cost of service potential, and current replacement cost of productive capacity may be identical; or each may be a different amount that is clearly determinable and distinguishable. However, in many cases the differences from one approach to the other are not completely clear-cut, because of their inherent subjectivity. Accordingly, it is appropriate to view the differences among the three approaches as ranges in a continuum of current cost values, rather than as discrete valuations.

In SFAS 33 (AC 1072.057), the FASB defines the current cost of inventory as the cost of purchasing the goods or resources required to produce the goods. The current cost of property, plant, and equipment is defined as the current cost of acquiring the same service potential (i.e., an asset or group of assets with the same operating costs and capacity) as that embodied in the assets owned (AC 1072.058). If equivalent assets are substituted for owned assets, adjustments for different operating costs compared to existing assets are required, as mentioned above. Also, current cost is to be reduced to a lower recoverable value under certain circumstances, as discussed in the next section. This differs from the replacement cost concept adopted by the SEC in ASR 190, which is based on productive capacity but does not allow for adjustments for differences in operating costs.

It should be noted, however, that when the current cost of property, plant, and equipment is determined by reference to the price of acquiring an asset with the same service potential in the "used market," the market price will tend to reflect a discount for the improved technology and efficiency of new assets that perform the same function. Under these circumstances, current cost of service potential and current cost of productive capacity may be identical.

Value to the Business. Value to the business, a concept integrating economic value and net realizable value with current cost, is a basis for the approach used in SFAS 33, *Financial Reporting and Changing Prices* (AC 1072). Value to the business depends on how much better off a business is by owning a particular asset. This approach is also known as the *deprival value* approach, because the value of an item to a business can be regarded as equal to the adverse effect on cash flows that would result from the company's being deprived of the use of the asset.

Value to the business is also closely aligned with the actual manner in which business decisions are made. To the manager, value is not a simple notion, for the value of an item is related to its intended use. In most cases, his decisions regarding the use of an item take three different bases into account:

1. What the asset costs today (current cost),
2. What it can be sold for (net realizable value or market value), and
3. What it can earn (economic value or present value of its future cash flows).

It is not necessary to know the historical cost in order to make a decision to acquire or dispose of an asset, because current cost equals historical cost only at the date of acquisition; after that time historical cost is history only.

The manager seeks to maximize the present value of future cash flows; therefore, when considering the purchase of an asset, he must have some idea of how much it will earn over its life. If the present value of future cash flows exceeds current cost, he is likely to acquire the asset, provided the excess is commensurate with the anticipated risk, cost of money, and rate of inflation. Conversely, if the current cost exceeds the expected future cash flows, the investment generally will not make economic sense. If the net realizable value of an existing asset exceeds its present value of future cash flows, the manager will probably decide to sell it.

Occasionally investments may be made in assets when cost exceeds economic value, but only because other activities play a part or for other than economic reasons. A decision on one asset cannot be viewed in isolation from other aspects of the business or the firm's environment. And of course, when assets are physically interrelated, these decisions must be made for the group, not for its separate pieces.

The value of an asset to the business can then be described as its current cost, except when both net realizable value and the present value of its future cash flows are higher than current cost; in that case the manager would not replace the asset but would dispose of it at the higher net realizable value or would retain it to obtain its future cash flows. When current cost is less than either its net realizable value or its present value of future cash flows, it can be argued that the value to the business of that asset is limited to its current cost, because this is the minimum investment that would have to be made currently in order to obtain the future benefits of owning the asset.

Information about the relationship between current cost and the recoverable value of assets may provide insight into the reasons for capital formation in a certain industry or for the lack of it. As differences between costs and recoverable value occur, capital investment will shift to or from a particular industry. This information may be of considerable interest to investors and to other users of financial reports, and it is particularly important for an understanding of the capital formation process.

In practice, current cost will normally be used in determining value to the business, simply because it is the most objective of the choices. While recoverable value

—the higher of the present value of future cash flows or net realizable value—may be viewed as theoretically the most desirable basis of valuation, limited reliability predestines its current use in practice to only those situations where it is clearly lower than current cost.

The value-to-the-business method is illustrated in Figure 8.4, which presents a balance sheet and income statement comparing historical cost and current cost, and in Figure 8.5, a schedule of property, plant, and equipment showing the basis for valuation of each asset.

The income statement in Figure 8.4 shows cost of sales at $60,000 at current cost, $50,000 at historical cost. The reason for the difference is that the sales for the period have been costed at their current cost on the date of sale rather than at the original cost paid for the item. Also, depreciation expense is higher at current cost ($12,000) than at historical cost ($10,000), because it is based on the lower of current cost or recoverable value of depreciable assets. This process matches current costs with current revenues and results in excluding from income an amount often referred to as a *holding gain*—the amount by which costs have increased during the period in which the inventory was held for sale.

BALANCE SHEET

	Historical Cost	*Current Cost*
Inventory	$ 5,000	$ 7,000
Other current assets	10,000	10,000
Property, plant, and equipment	30,000	43,000
	$ 45,000	$ 60,000
Liabilities	$ 25,000	$ 25,000
Equity	20,000	35,000
	$ 45,000	$ 60,000

INCOME STATEMENT

	Historical Cost	*Current Cost*
Sales	$100,000	$100,000
Cost of sales	50,000	60,000
	50,000	40,000
Depreciation expense	10,000	12,000
Other expenses	20,000	20,000
Income before taxes	20,000	8,000
Taxes	10,000	10,000
Net income (loss)	$ 10,000	$ (2,000)

FIGURE 8.4   SUMMARY BALANCE SHEET AND INCOME STATEMENT UNDER THE VALUE-TO-THE-BUSINESS ACCOUNTING METHOD

In Figure 8.5, item A has a historical cost of $13,000. Its current cost of $26,000 is lower than one of the two approaches to recoverable value (present value of future cash flows and net realizable value). This means that the asset may be expected to generate present value cash flows that exceed the current cost. The value to the business or deprival value of that asset is $26,000, because this is the amount that would have been expended in order to earn the $50,000 of recoverable value. Items B and C illustrate a recoverable value lower than current cost.

Current Cost Earnings. Investors often try to assess the amounts, timing, and probability of a company's future cash flows in order to estimate what dividends the company can pay and the extent to which reinvestment of earnings by the company would increase future cash flows. Earnings are an important factor in predicting cash flows, but only if the effects of changing prices on them can be determined: relationships between current revenues and original costs will not provide the necessary insights into future net cash flows during a period of rapidly changing prices. For this purpose, the cost of goods sold, depreciation, and amortization can be calculated and charged to operations on the basis of the current cost of the assets sold or consumed.

However, if earnings are to coincide with changes in the balance sheet, the other side of the double entry for the inflation adjustments (the increase in current cost of assets held) also has to be recognized. These other entries are normally called *holding gains*. The extent to which such holding gains should be recognized in the financial statements is a matter of debate.

One view considers it wrong to reflect amounts in excess of historical cost in the balance sheet; holding gains, shown separately in the income statement, should exactly offset the additional charges to operating earnings for cost of goods sold and depreciation. The sum of operating earnings and holding gains would thus be equal to historical cost net earnings. Segregation on the income statement, however, indicates earnings from operations after charging current costs against current revenues, and thus would be useful for predicting future operating results. The holding gains recognized represent the increase in value of the firm's productive

Item	Historical Cost (Net of Accumulated Depreciation)	Value to the Business	Current Cost	Recoverable Value	
				Net Realizable Value	Present Value of Future Cash Flows
A	$13,000	$26,000	$26,000	$ 2,000	$50,000
B	9,000	10,000	15,000	1,000	10,000
C	8,000	7,000	10,000	7,000	4,000
	$30,000	$43,000			

FIGURE 8.5   SCHEDULE OF PROPERTY, PLANT, AND EQUIPMENT UNDER THE VALUE-TO-THE-BUSINESS ACCOUNTING METHOD

capacity, inventory, and property, plant, and equipment that was realized during the period through sale or consumption.

Other proponents of current cost accounting favor reflecting all holding gains, both realized and unrealized, in earnings. The unrealized portion would usually be the increase in the current cost of net property, plant, and equipment and items remaining in inventory at the end of the period. Still others would reduce the holding gains from inventory and property, plant, and equipment by a factor for general inflation and also recognize the gain or loss in the purchasing power of monetary items.

In addition to the foregoing variations regarding holding gains, the particular form of the earnings statement depends on views of capital maintenance, discussed in a later section of this chapter.

Funds Flow. As its name implies, the funds-flow approach focuses on current cash-flow measurement. Though earnings have always been the basic measure of performance (with due regard being given to traditional differences between earnings and funds flow), differences between cash and accrual results become exaggerated during periods of inflation. In fact, short-term funds flow and liquidity may become a more important and real indicator of the health of the business than accrual earnings reported during periods of inflation. When attention to funds flow is crucial and short-term liquidity problems are significant, it may be more meaningful to express the impact of changing prices by adjusting funds flow from continuing operations than to do so by adjusting earnings.

Such an approach was recommended by the Ontario Committee on Inflation Accounting in 1977, and is summarized near the end of this chapter. Figure 8.6 shows the 1977 results in this format for several Canadian corporations.

The statement discloses the funds available after maintenance of productive capacity (i.e., the equivalent of historical cost basis depreciation), thus giving the users of financial reports an indication of the amount of cash that can be reinvested for expansion or distributed to the owners of the business. Additional capital requirements because of the effects of changing prices on the assets of the business are reduced by the amount of additional borrowings, an amount that the owners will not be required to put up. The funds available from borrowings reflect the present capital structure of the firm based on the assumption that the companies would actually be able to obtain future debt financing in the amounts shown.

The funds-flow approach attempts to communicate with the layman, who may see business earnings as something very similar to the salary of an individual, usually received in cash. The public generally fails to recognize that historical cost earnings of a business determined by accrual can be materially different from funds flow, particularly during periods of rising prices.

Primary Recognition Versus Supplementary Disclosure

After several years of discussion, and after hearing numerous proposals by various governmental and accounting bodies on how to account for the effects of inflation, it now appears that changes will be introduced not in the basic financial statement but by supplementary disclosure. Perhaps the rate of change and the uncertainty caused by inflation make a comprehensive departure from historical costs just too large a step for the preparers and users of financial reports to take at one time.

(all figures are in $000 and are for the year ended December 31, 1977)

	Nu-West Development Corp. Ltd.	Du Pont of Canada Limited	Domtar Inc.	Westinghouse Canada Limited	Ford Motor Company of Canada, Limited	Noranda Mines Limited	Consolidated-Bathurst Limited	Fraser Companies Limited
Funds generated from operations	$24,402	$38,000	$68,170	$20,142	$139,900	$142,000	$66,338	$27,466
Funds required to finance original cost of productive assets	–	26,000	38,907	5,107	83,400	83,000	32,316	7,909
	24,402	12,000	29,263	15,035	56,500	59,000	34,022	19,557
Funds required to finance increased cost of assets:								
Inventories (1)	7,792	5,000	6,333	10,000	48,800	25,000	10,627	3,200
Fixed assets (2)	4,981	12,000	28,474	2,300	26,300	49,000	20,029	6,200
Other	15,281 (4)	–	–	–	16,700 (5)	–	–	–
	(28,054)	(17,000)	(34,807)	(12,300)	(91,800)	(74,000)	(30,656)	(9,400)
Additional funds available from borrowings (3)	22,163	8,000	5,917	2,950	42,400	37,000	12,434	5,300
Impact of inflation (6)	(5,891)	(9,000)	(28,890)	(9,350)	(49,400)	(37,000)	(18,222)	(4,100)
Funds available for distribution or expansion	$18,511	$ 3,000	$ 373	$ 5,685	$ 7,100	$ 22,000	$15,800	$15,457

Notes 1 The increased cost of replacing inventories represents the difference between the historical cost and the current cost of goods sold at the date of sale. (Applicable to most of these companies)

2 The increased cost of maintaining the operating capacity of productive assets represents the difference between depreciation determined on an historical cost basis and depreciation indexed for the effects of inflation, using the business investment component of the GNE Implicit Price Index. (Applicable to most of these companies)

3 The extent to which additional funds may be available from borrowings is based on the ratio of equity to non-equity capital at the beginning of the accounting period, on the assumption that this ratio is maintained. (Applicable to most of these companies)

4 Land under development, etc.

5 Special tools.

6 These companies have developed and reported this information based on the recommendations of the Ontario Committee on Inflation Accounting.

FIGURE 8.6   EXAMPLES OF IMPACT OF INFLATION ON FUNDS AVAILABLE FOR DISTRIBUTION OR EXPANSION
SOURCE: Touche Ross & Co. (Canada), *What's New in Accounting* (Toronto, 1979), p. 28.

The objectivity of the historical cost system is widely accepted, and in times of uncertainty and change this objectivity is something like a security blanket. For this reason it seems unlikely that accounting and reporting will move completely away from the historical cost base in financial statements, at least not for some time.

The current FASB conceptual framework project deals with what should be included within the financial statements and what should be outside them but still within the overall financial report (see Chapter 2). Such a distinction provides standard setters with the opportunity to introduce change experimentally and to be more selective in designating discrete groups who must follow certain new procedures. Supplementary data included in the financial report but outside the financial statements may also be subject to less verification by auditors, because these data are more subjective than financial statement ingredients.

Clearly there is a need for some flexibility and experimentation in the evolution of accounting measurement. Current cost and current value concepts are difficult to apply and are certainly not agreed on at this time. The FASB has stated that it believes that orderly, systematic experimentation is required and that SFAS 33 (AC 1072.011-.015) provides an optimum model for that experimentation. Thus, SFAS 33 (AC 1072.027) requires current cost information to be disclosed in supplementary schedules, as does the proposal under consideration in Canada (Canadian Institute of Chartered Accountants, 1979). In the United Kingdom the recently adopted SSAP 16 (Institute of Chartered Accountants in England and Wales, 1980) requires both historical cost and current cost financial information but leaves it up to the issuer to determine which set is primary and which is supplemental. The Canadian and U.K. developments are summarized near the end of this chapter.

It is impossible to predict what effects a change in accounting measurement will have on management and other users of financial information. If new methods prove to be more useful than old ones, and if they sufficiently satisfy the other qualitative characteristics of financial information such as reliability, objectivity, and verifiability, they may eventually find their way into the basic financial statements. The FASB has indicated (AC 1072.015) it may take up to five years to evaluate the usefulness of the information disclosed in accordance with SFAS 33.

CONCEPTUAL PROBLEMS

While there is some consensus on the necessity, if not the method, of adjusting earnings to reflect the higher current costs of earlier-acquired items consumed in the operations of a business, there remains a considerable disparity of views as to the appropriate treatment of the increase in the current cost of *capital assets* owned by the business. The alternatives largely depend on different views of capital maintenance.

Capital Maintenance

Accountants and economists have long attempted to distinguish between maintaining capital and reporting income. Income has been defined by Hicks (1946, p. 172) in this way:

The purpose of income calculations in practical affairs is to give people an indication of the amount they can consume without impoverishing themselves. Following out of this idea, it would seem that we ought to define a man's income as the maximum value which he can consume during a week and still expect to be as well off at the end of the week as he was at the beginning.

The same idea can be used to define the income of a company: "A company's profit for the year is the maximum value which the company can distribute during the year and still expect to be as well off at the end of the year as it was at the beginning" (Sandilands, 1975, p. 29).

Those who use financial reports as a basis for predicting future cash flows from a business may use the distinction between capital and income to evaluate the firm's ability to pay dividends or to provide for expansion. The original idea of capital maintenance was that revenue could only be spent after capital had been maintained. It may be argued that by itself the maintenance of capital gives little indication of potential future cash flows, but it does represent a base line from which to predict future income and capital increases or decreases.

Financial and Physical Capital. The money invested in a business is *financial capital*. Any amounts earned that exceed the amount invested are considered return on capital or appreciation in the value of capital. *Physical capital,* on the other hand, is plant, equipment, and other physical resources that enable a business to produce goods and services. Physical capital is considered to have been maintained only when productive capacity has been maintained; to accomplish this a business may need more or less money than the originally invested financial capital, especially during periods of rapidly rising prices.

As a basis for determining earnings, financial capital is usually the preferred concept, because investors are assumed to be interested primarily in the monetary return on their money. The nature of the business or industry will determine the degree of risk, and the risk will affect the rate of return expected by the investor. For example, if a steel company decides to diversify into chemicals or services in order to ensure a continued increase in the rate of return on financial capital invested by its stockholders, investors might take note of the added risk and, accordingly, adjust their return expectations. But their ultimate objective would still be to get a return on, and of, the money they invested.

The concept of physical capital, or maintenance of productive capacity, is sharply different. In the example above, it applies only if a commitment has been made to continue the production of steel. Earnings can be determined only after productive capacity has been maintained. In effect, this means that if the costs of maintaining the productive capacity of a steel mill or of maintaining necessary levels of steel inventory rise, a charge must be made against income for the additional cost of sales and depreciation necessary to reflect those higher costs. Under this concept, the steel mill will continue in operation at current capacity, because physical capital will not be eroded by failing to recognize the effect of rising prices.

In order to maintain productive capacity, however, it may be necessary to raise selling prices to levels that exceed the average market price for similar products, because other firms may base their selling price on historical cost or financial capital, or may simply be practicing price competition in the short run. As a result, maintaining productive capacity through direct translation of needed margin levels into selling price increases may not be possible.

Actually, many businesses are no more concerned with the maintenance of physical capital than their investors are. Active and growing enterprises are constantly looking for new and more profitable lines of business activity for expansion, diversification, and modernization, and are not unequivocally committed to current products.

When Physical Capital Is Important. Notwithstanding the general preference for the concept of financial capital, there are situations in which measurement of physical capital can be important in assessing the well-being of an enterprise:

1. If the enterprise is unable to maintain its productive capacity because of significantly higher costs of plant and equipment, or if these higher costs would require large amounts of additional capital, this information could be important in predicting future cash requirements and cash flows. Investors need to know whether they can expect future cash flows to come from existing lines of business or whether the rate of return is so low as to cause the enterprise to seek new areas of operation. Such information may affect their perception of the prospects for the enterprise and industry and the relative risk of investing in it instead of others.
2. The user of the goods or services provided by the enterprise is interested in the ability of the enterprise to continue to provide these goods and services, particularly when the enterprise is in a monopolistic environment. Examples are transportation companies, oil and gas companies, and utilities. In many of these industries current pricing policies are not sufficient to permit replacement of capacity without significant new financial capital investment.

Holding Gains

Sometimes the investors' capital is adjusted to reflect changes in the purchasing power of the dollar by methods such as constant dollar accounting. Income (amount available for consumption) is then shown after maintenance of the purchasing power of the investors' capital. Application of constant dollar accounting does not change the basic concept of financial capital, because changes in the value of assets owned by the corporation represent an integral part of earnings. If the value of assets acquired with the investors' capital increases, then the value of the owners' interest will also increase. Such increases are often termed *holding gains*.

There is a sharp divergence of opinion on the appropriate treatment of holding gains. Using economic value (discussed earlier in this chapter) and a concept of financial capital results in changes in the expected future cash flows from assets from one period to the next being recognized as a component of income (holding gain or loss). As observed above, however, economic value is not a practical solution at this time, as many people are not prepared to recognize current cost as a surrogate measure of economic value. Accordingly, they do not view the changes in current cost of assets held as a holding gain or loss. These people believe that an increase in current cost is just that—an increase in cost that represents an additional capital requirement. Rather than showing this as a gain, therefore, it would be shown as an allocation of retained earnings, representing a capital maintenance provision.

Those who accept current cost as a surrogate for economic value favor inclusion of the holding gains or losses in income. The argument in favor of deterining holding gains on a current cost basis stems from the fact that investment decisions are based on a comparison of current cost and expected cash flows. If the asset is available in the marketplace, then presumably firms are buying it, and therefore a reasonable return must be attainable. If the same held true at the time of purchase of the existing asset, and assuming the required rate of return has not decreased and the current cost of the asset has increased, it is logical to deduce that expected cash flows have increased. The extent to which these increased cash flows can be obtained with the existing asset is an element of "super profit," or holding gain.

Estimates of value limited to a current cost basis may overlook greater economic values, and certainly do not result in a determination of the value *of* the business. Valuing individual assets ignores the fact that a business is the synergistic product of its physical and human resources. Future cash flows will largely depend on the managerial knowledge used to employ the individual assets of the business in an effective harmony.

Monetary Items

Because items such as cash, receivables, payables, and debt are fixed in monetary terms, it can be argued that there is no gain or loss caused by price changes. Although adjustments for cost of goods sold and depreciation have a cash impact—more cash is required to replace goods sold or consumed—monetary items are denominated in units of money and are not represented by physical goods, making the impact of price changes more difficult to comprehend.

But it can also be argued that value changes in monetary items should be measured either in terms of a decline in the purchasing power of the monetary unit itself, or by reference to their discounted cash-flow value, usually market value. The purchasing power approach is mechanically simple and has been incorporated into many inflation accounting proposals. The latter approach is more complex and has not received much serious consideration.

Interest Cost. To decide on the handling of gains or losses on monetary items, the calculation and presentation of real interest cost must be resolved. It is generally acknowledged that during times of inflation, interest rates rise because investors increase their *hurdle rate,* the rate of expected return that justifies a new investment. To the extent that market forces permit investors to obtain this inflation premium, the nominal interest rate will include a true interest component and an inflation component. If inflation occurs at the rate of the inflation component assumed in the interest rate, the decline in the nominal value of the debt instrument will then be exactly offset by the inflation premium included in the nominal interest cost.

However, as we are all aware, inflation rates are difficult to predict accurately. Often there will be an unexpected gain to the lender or to the borrower, depending on whether the actual inflation rate is greater or less than the inflation premium charged. Because the nominal interest cost is cash and thus objectively determinable and the calculated inflation gain or loss is not, accountants have been reluctant to "contaminate" the basic measure of inflation-adjusted performance—income from continuing operations (which includes nominal interest cost)—with the inflation gain or loss on monetary items.

A compromise method is to calculate the basic measure of performance including nominal interest as income from continuing operations and to show the related inflation gain or loss separately. This is the approach followed in SFAS 33, *Financial Reporting and Changing Prices* (AC 1072.029).

United Kingdom Requirements. The treatment of debt and other monetary items is probably the most significant difference between SFAS 33 (AC 1072) in the United States and SSAP 16 (Institute of Chartered Accountants in England and Wales, 1980) in the United Kingdom. SSAP 16 does not measure the impact of inflation on monetary items by comparison to a general measure of inflation (a general price index) or to market value, but regards the relative benefit to the owners of a business from debt participation as being reflected through the increased current cost of the enterprise assets.

To the extent that a company uses debt to finance assets, its creditors are considered to have absorbed a portion of the increase in current costs of assets caused by inflation. Thus the aggregate increase in current cost of sales and depreciation (plus an allowance for increase in monetary working capital) is reduced by the ratio of net borrowings (basically, long-term debt less long-term receivables) to net operating assets (basically, working capital plus fixed assets); this is known as the *gearing adjustment*. The reduction in operating earnings from increased current costs is therefore limited to the amount that relates to operating assets financed by equity capital.

Under this concept, if there is no increase in the current cost of the assets owned by the business, there can be no inflation gain on debt.

The U.K. standard applies to many more companies than SFAS 33 does (the formula for coverage includes most companies with sales of more than £5,000,000), and requires, at a minimum, a full current cost income statement and a summarized current cost balance sheet. U.K. companies may elect to present the current cost financial statements as the primary statements, with supplementary historical cost basis financial statements; or they may even omit the historical cost financial statements, provided that a reconciliation between current cost and historical cost income is presented. An example of the U.K. approach, which is summarized near the end of this chapter, is presented in Figure 8.7. (For more detailed explanations refer to SSAP 16 and the related guidance notes; Accounting Standards Committee, 1980.)

Tax Allocation

Current taxation policy levies tax on income determined on a historical cost basis. To the extent that historical cost earnings contain an element of realized holding gains, this is also taxed. The problem is, therefore, whether to charge the full current-year tax provision against income from continuing operations or whether to allocate a portion of that charge to the amount segregated as realized holding gains.

Arguing against allocation, many commentators believe that one of the major effects of inflation is that business is being taxed on capital and that the effective rate of tax is much higher than the statutory rate. Presenting the current-year tax

Turnover		£20,000
Profit before interest and taxation on the historical cost basis		£ 2,900
Less current cost operating adjustments		1,000 (a)
Current cost operating profit		1,900
Gearing adjustment	£200 (b)	
Interest expense	570	370
Current cost profit before taxation		1,530
Taxation		665
Current cost profit attributable to shareholders		865
Dividends		400
Retained current cost profit for the year		£ 465

(a) Comprises:

Cost of sales	£ 300	
Monetary working capital	100	(c)
Fixed asset disposals	150	
Additional depreciation	450	
	£1,000	

(b) Average net borrowing (net monetary items excluding monetary working capital) to average net operating assets (working capital plus fixed assets) on a current cost basis = 20%; 20% multiplied by current cost adjustments of £1,000 = £200.

(c) Increase in monetary working capital (excess of trade receivables over trade payables) because of price increases based on an index reflecting increases in input prices.

FIGURE 8.7   EXAMPLE OF U.K. CURRENT COST ACCOUNTING PRESENTATION

provision as a charge against inflation-adjusted income from continuing operations discloses this fact.

The argument for allocation is based on the principle of matching costs with revenues; the tax on the holding gain should be charged against the holding gain. This treatment better supports the concept of income from continuing operations, because it eliminates the fluctuations in tax charges as a result of realized inflationary gains.

In computing the effective tax rate, it is generally not appropriate to compare tax expense including a deferred tax provision arising from accelerated depreciation for tax purposes with current cost pretax income. Such an approach would be misleading, since it would overstate the actual tax to be paid and hence not take into consideration the tax benefit of accelerated depreciation.

PRACTICAL PROBLEMS

Both general price level accounting and the various current value and current cost accounting methods pose problems of implementation. General price level accounting, though far easier to apply, is criticized for its alleged lack of relevance. Indeed, proponents of current value and current cost accounting might invoke the comment attributed to Lord Keynes: "It is better to be vaguely right than precisely wrong." Current value or current cost accounting is seen as "vaguely right" and thus more relevant, and general price level accounting is seen as "precisely wrong" and thus irrelevant.

Obtaining Accounting Measurements

General Price Level. The Consumer Price Index (CPI) and the Gross National Product Implicit Price Deflator, either of which may be used to convert financial statements to constant dollars, are easy to obtain from published government statistics. There are, however, some lags in publishing the data, which may cause problems for those who wish to use the most timely index in preparing financial reports. The CPI is better in this regard, as it is published monthly. This was one of the reasons for the adoption of the CPI in SFAS 33 (AC 1072.039).

The calculations themselves are quite simple and involve little if any judgment. Once the method has been set up, it can be systematically followed each year thereafter. The most costly part involves the process of aging assets to convert them to constant dollars. But once this has been done, the process involves a relatively simple roll-forward each year. A market test is necessary to ensure that assets are carried at the lower of their indexed historical cost and market value.

Simple as the calculations are, shortcut methods have been suggested in SFAS 33 (AC 1072.209-.240). They eliminate much of the burden of calculation and conversion.

Current Cost. The opposition to current cost accounting is based, for the most part, on the expected difficulties of implementation and on the perceived lack of objectivity and reliability of the measurements proposed. For many of those who have prepared the information, however, current cost accounting has proven to be practical. A variety of methods are used, including estimating and averaging shortcuts. They focus on the main components of the current cost approach discussed below: inventories; property, plant, and equipment; cost of sales; depreciation; and long-term debt and other monetary items.

A more detailed description of implementation problems, and practical guidance dealing specifically with SFAS 33, are presented in Touche Ross & Co.'s *Financial Reporting and Changing Prices—A Guide to Implementing FASB Statement 33* (New York, 1979b).

Inventories. Companies using a LIFO inventory valuation method will find that the balance sheet figure for inventories considerably understates current cost. Conversely, cost of sales is more likely to approximate current prices, because under this method the latest cost is associated with the sale. Inventories can be converted to current cost at the balance sheet date by use of an index or by specific item identification valued at current purchase prices or reproduction costs.

Cost of sales. The current cost basis for cost of sales can be determined by reference to LIFO results if available. LIFO may closely approximate current cost when prices rise. However, LIFO will not represent current cost if the volume of inventory falls during a period or if costs rise rapidly on slow-moving goods. The advantage of LIFO is that many companies already use it, and the cost of converting to current cost is therefore minimized.

Changes in current costs may also be determined from a variety of other sources, including official indices, internally generated indices, standard cost systems, suppliers' catalogues and invoice prices, current labor and salary agreements, and production information. An approach particularly suitable for the smaller business is an averaging method recommended in the United Kingdom for determining current cost of sales when it is impractical to determine current cost on a specific item basis. An example based on this method is shown in Figure 8.8; it assumes that changes in inventory volume occur evenly throughout the period and that changes in current cost also occur evenly throughout the period.

Property, plant, and equipment. Measuring the current value or cost of these assets presents the most difficult problems. Three possible measures are current cost, net realizable value, and present value of future cash flows. Predicting the future cash flows of a machine, a production line, or a plant is usually extremely subjective, because of the need to allocate costs and revenues out of those for an aggregation of assets, and because of the uncertainty about future events and appro-

---

Cost of input to inventory	$150,000
Decrease in inventory volume:	
Opening inventory —12,000 units at $8 each	
Closing inventory —10,000 units at $12 each	
Decrease — 2,000 units	

Average current cost of inventory per unit during the period:

$$\frac{(\$8 + \$12)}{2} = \$10$$

Average current cost of decrease in inventory volume over the period:

$10 × 2,000 units	20,000
Current cost of sales	$170,000

FIGURE 8.8   AVERAGING METHOD FOR DETERMINING CURRENT COST OF SALES

priate discount rates. Few nonmonetary assets lend themselves to accurate and reliable prediction of future cash flows. Those that do might include annuity contracts, rental real estate, and other lease rentals. Net realizable value may also be difficult to determine if there is no market for the asset. When major plants are bought and sold they are usually combined with other nonplant assets, making it difficult to value them alone.

Current cost of fixed assets is the most common accounting measurement used for property, plant, and equipment, but it too presents some problems. Often there is no current cost (new) for a particular asset because the asset is not available, at least not in the same form. Current cost could, however, be determined by reference to the price that would have to be paid for an asset of similar service potential, a used machine for example.

The basic techniques for estimating current cost include independent appraisals, the use of recent prices for similar assets with the same service potential, and the use of general, industry, or internally developed indices. SFAS 33 (AC 1072.057-.060) suggests the following types of evidence to support the current cost of property, plant, and equipment:

1. Direct pricing:
   a. Current invoice prices, and
   b. Vendors' firm price lists or other firm quotations or estimates.
2. Unit pricing: computing the current cost of assets such as buildings by estimating the construction cost per unit (square foot of building space, for example), and multiplying the number of units in the asset being measured.
3. Indexing:
   a. Externally (independently) generated price indices for the class of assets being measured, and
   b. Internally generated indices of cost changes for the class of assets being measured.

Depreciation. Generally speaking, current cost depreciation is determined by a mathematical extension of the normal depreciation method, taking into account the revaluation of the asset from historical cost to current cost. An exception may arise when depreciation policy has already been adjusted to reflect the impact of inflation. For example, depreciation may be accelerated by shortening estimated useful lives to show the effect of rising costs. If so, current cost depreciation should not be determined by extrapolating historical cost information. Some other appropriate estimate of useful life and depreciation rate should be used.

Long-term debt and monetary items. The valuation of long-term debt and net monetary items presents no significant problems for any of the methods proposed. Determining the gain or loss by using the general inflation rate—the method adopted by the FASB—is a purely mathematical exercise requiring the use of the Consumer Price Index and a calculation of the net monetary item position (cash, receivables, other monetary assets, payables, and other liabilities).

When a gearing adjustment (see Figure 8.7) is used, the valuation is also mechanical. The ratio of average net borrowings to average operating assets is applied to the monetary items. It can be determined readily from opening, closing, or average balance sheets during a period.

A third method of valuing liabilities requires recognizing the market price of long-term debt. A problem arises if there is no market, in which case an appropriate discount rate has to be estimated.

Objectivity

The deepest reservations about current cost (and current value) accounting arise over the subjectivity of its valuation processes, whereas one of the major advantages cited for general price level accounting is its objectivity. This is a familiar theme: relevance and reliability of information are often in conflict. Too much concern with the objectivity of financial information may reduce it to mechanical irrelevance and uselessness. A fact often overlooked is that the traditional historical cost basis also involves many subjective valuations: bad-debt provisions, inventory valuations at lower of cost or market, and depreciation are examples that have had to be assimilated over the decades.

The concern over the subjectivity of current cost accounting is understandable in view of accountants' brief experience with it, but more experience will probably reduce this concern and possibly pave the way for altering the historical basis financial statements.

Comparability

General price level accounting, which is based on historical costs, causes each enterprise to make the same adjustments; the results are comparable, in a sense, because the same indexes are applied to everyone's historical costs. However, if specific price changes are viewed as more relevant, then conversion by use of a general index will produce noncomparable data among companies. In this case, current cost accounting provides better comparability, because it states assets of different companies at their own current costs. This is far more useful for purposes of determining a current return on investment, though some would say that comparability between companies is reduced by the subjectivity inherent in the personal selections of methods of determining current cost.

SUMMARY OF ACCOUNTING PROPOSALS AND STANDARDS

Since the mid-1970s the development of an acceptable method of accounting for inflation has been a high priority for accountants in many countries. Various proposals have been put forward and rules and standards adopted, but so far no single method is acceptable to all. Some idea of the divergence of views can be gathered from the following summary of major proposals, rules, and standards.

United States

SFAS 33, *Financial Reporting and Changing Prices* (AC 1072):

- Retains the basic financial statements based on historical costs.
- Requires supplemental disclosure (see Figure 8.9) in financial reports of the effects of changing prices on "income from continuing operations," using two different bases—

current cost and historical cost restated to a constant dollar amount by applying a general price index. In addition, the effects of inflation on monetary assets and liabilities are reported by applying a general price index; and the changes in current costs (net of general inflation) of inventories and property, plant, and equipment balances are disclosed separately.

- Covers only large publicly owned companies, but encourages other companies and organizations to present such supplemental disclosure.
- Applies to calendar year 1979 financial reporting, but allows companies the option of deferring current cost reporting for a year.
- Recognizes the need for experimentation with reporting the effects of changing prices.

Statements of Earnings Adjusted for Changing Prices
Year Ended December 31, 1979

$ in millions	As Reported in the Primary Financial Statements (Historical Cost)	Adjusted for General Inflation (Average 1979 Dollars)	Adjusted for Changes in Specific Prices (Current Costs)
Net sales	**$2,039.4**	$2,039.4	$2,039.4
Costs and expenses:			
Cost of products and services sold, excluding depreciation	**1,343.4**	1,389.9	1,400.5
Operating expenses, excluding depreciation	**485.2**	485.2	485.2
Depreciation expense	**35.9**	47.9	52.5
Total costs and expenses	**1,864.5**	1,923.0	1,938.2
Operating earnings	**174.9**	116.4	101.2
Other expense—net	**18.0**	18.0	18.0
Earnings before income taxes	**156.9**	98.4	83.2
Provision for income taxes	**47.5**	47.5	47.5
Net earnings	**$ 109.4**	$ 50.9	$ 35.7
Unrecognized gain from excess of amounts owed over cash, securities and accounts receivable		$ 14.4	$ 14.4
Unrecognized gains on inventories and properties held during the year due to:			
Increases in the general price level			$ 119.8
Specific cost increases in excess of the general price level increases			59.9
			$ 179.7

Depreciation expense has been calculated using the same methods and rates of depreciation used in the historical financial statements.

Comparison of Selected Data Adjusted for Effects of Changing Prices
Year Ended December 31

$ in millions except per share amounts	1979	1978	1977	1976	1975
Sales:					
As reported	**$2,039.4**	$1,744.8	$1,490.3	$1,344.6	$1,160.5
Adjusted for general inflation	**2,039.4**	1,941.3	1,785.1	1,714.5	1,565.2
Net earnings per share:					
As reported	**$ 2.78**				
Adjusted for general inflation	**1.32**				
Adjusted for changes in specific prices	**.95**				
Net assets at year-end:					
As reported	**$ 730.7**				
Adjusted for general inflation	**851.7**				
Adjusted for changes in specific prices	**924.0**				
Dividends per share:					
As reported	**$ .77**	$ .65	$ .52	$ .385	$ .31
Adjusted for general inflation	**.77**	.72	.62	.49	.42
Market price per share at year-end:					
As reported	**$ 31½**	$ 26¼	$ 26⅝	$ 30¾	$ 29⅝
Adjusted for general inflation	**29¾**	28⅛	31⅛	38⅜	38¾
Average Consumer Price Index	**217.4**	195.4	181.5	170.5	161.2

Information adjusted for general inflation is expressed in average 1979 dollars.

FIGURE 8.9 EXAMPLE OF SFAS 33 DISCLOSURES
SOURCE: American Hospital Supply Corporation and Subsidiaries, 1979 Annual Report.

- Provides for the different treatment of certain assets in special industries, e.g., oil and gas reserves, timberlands, mining properties, and income-producing real estate.

SEC ASR 190:

- Requires disclosure in annual filings with the SEC of current replacement cost of inventories; current replacement cost of goods and services sold at the time the sales were made; current cost of replacing (new) productive capacity (property, plant, and equipment), together with current depreciated replacement cost; and depreciation, depletion, and amortization calculated on a replacement cost basis.
- Applies to large publicly owned companies.
- Applies to financial statements for fiscal years ending on or after December 25, 1976 (being phased out as SFAS 33 is implemented).

United Kingdom

Current Cost Accounting, Statement of Standard Accounting Practice 16 (Institute of Chartered Accountants in England and Wales, 1980):

- Requires current cost information, both profit and loss and balance sheet accounts, in addition to historical cost accounts.
- Specifies that the current cost profit and loss account should show operating profit derived after making depreciation, cost of sales, and monetary working capital adjustments and the current cost profit attributable to shareholders derived after making a gearing adjustment for debt financing.
- Specifies that in the current cost balance sheet, property, plant, and equipment and inventory should generally be included at their value to the business (normally depreciated current replacement cost).
- Applies to most large enterprises, listed and other. Certain businesses such as life insurance and investment trusts are excepted.
- Detailed guidance notes are supplied in a companion publication.

Canada

Ontario Committee on Inflation Accounting (Toronto, 1977):

- Recommends a separate statement of the effects of inflation to be included as part of the financial statements of a business, setting out the effects of inflation in terms of funds available for distribution, reinvestment, or repayment of debt. The purpose of this statement is to describe how funds from operations should be allocated to ensure the maintenance of business capital during inflation. The statement is to present funds generated from operations, funds required to finance the original cost of productive assets, additional funds required to finance the increased cost of maintaining operating capacity of productive assets and the extent to which these funds may be available from borrowings, and funds available for distribution or expansion.
- Suggests that greater use of relative measures of performance, such as return on investment, would help illustrate the effects of inflation on business.

- Calls on government to encourage all enterprises that are affected by inflation to disclose its impact on their operations.

Canadian Institute of Chartered Accountants:

- Proposes, in an exposure draft on current cost accounting (1979), a current cost accounting system substantially the same as that required in the United Kingdom under SSAP 16.
- Differs from the U.K. proposal by stating that:
  - •• The current cost presentations would be supplementary to the basic historical cost financial statements, which would still be regarded as the primary financial statements in all cases.
  - •• Current cost restatements relating to nonmonetary items would be required only for inventories, cost of sales, property, plant, and equipment, and depreciation. Comprehensive restatement would not be required.

AUDITOR'S REVIEW OF CURRENT COST AND CURRENT VALUE DATA

Supplementary financial information on changing prices required by SFAS 33 (AC 1072) is not part of the basic financial statements and is almost universally presented as unaudited supplementary information, although companies could choose to have the data audited. Despite its unaudited status, the auditor reporting on the basic financial statements is considered associated with the information and, accordingly, must perform a limited review. The auditor's responsibilities in connection with such a limited review are set forth in SAS 27, *Supplementary Information Required by the Financial Accounting Standards Board* (AU 553), and in SAS 28, *Supplementary Information on the Effects of Changing Prices* (AU 554).

The auditor's limited review of the unaudited supplementary information on changing prices includes primarily the following procedures:

- The auditor should read the supplementary data and consider whether any of the statements made are in conflict with the basic financial statements.
- The auditor should make inquiries of responsible management personnel to determine that the supplementary data appear to have been prepared on a reasonable basis. The inquiries should be directed primarily to the following factors:
  - •• The sources of information on which the disclosures are based,
  - •• The assumptions and judgments made in calculating the constant dollar and current cost amounts required, and
  - •• The completeness and propriety of the explanations concerning the current cost and constant dollar amounts included in the supplementary information.

If on the basis of the limited review the auditor has no reason to believe that the supplementary disclosures required by SFAS 33 are incomplete or improper, no mention of the review need be made in the auditor's report covering the basic financial statements. However, if as a result of the limited review the auditor becomes aware of the fact that the supplementary disclosures are incomplete or improper, he is then required to express a reservation in his report on the basic financial statements. Such a reservation is equivalent to an "exception" in an auditor's report with respect to audited data, as discussed in Chapter 16.

In those unusual cases where a company engages its independent auditor to perform an audit of the supplementary information on changing prices, the auditor would, of course, be required to go beyond the limited review procedures disclosed above. He would have to verify the calculations of the constant dollar and current cost data, and also examine the sources of information used as a basis for the computations, to determine that (1) the sources used were appropriate, (2) the procedures applied were appropriate, and (3) the entire compilation of the supplementary data was properly performed.

In performing these audit procedures the auditor would be entitled to rely on systems of internal control in order to limit the amount of substantive audit procedures (see Chapter 13). This is logical because the historical cost data to which current cost and constant dollar adjustments are made would be covered as part of the audit of the basic financial statements.

SUGGESTED READING

AICPA. *The Accounting Responses to Changing Prices.* New York, 1979. This study shows how 23 major public companies recast their financial statements to show the effects of changing prices. Four approaches to presenting information on changing prices are presented and discussed.

Sandilands, Francis. *Inflation Accounting—Report of the Inflation Accounting Committee.* London: Her Majesty's Stationery Office, 1975. This historic report by an English group recommended the introduction of current cost accounting for listed U.K. companies by the end of 1977 and progressive extension of current cost accounting to other companies. The report, known as the Sandilands Report, initiated inflation accounting programs and research in the U.K., the U.S., and many other countries throughout the world.

Scott, George. *Research Study on Current-Value Accounting Measurements and Utility.* New York: Touche Ross Foundation, 1978. This book reports on a study to compare the usefulness of historical cost and current value financial statements in predicting future cash flows in a number of simulated circumstances.

Touche Ross & Co. *Economic Reality in Financial Reporting.* New York, 1975. This is a comprehensive analysis of current value accounting, including an implementation program and illustrative current value financial statements and methodology.

————. *Financial Reporting and Changing Prices—A Guide to Implementing FASB Statement 33.* New York, 1979. This exhaustive analysis of all aspects of SFAS 33 includes detailed step-by-step application of all accounting and disclosure requirements for constant dollar and current value information.

Part II

Auditing–General

9

The Auditor's Role

Russell E. Palmer

ORIGINS

The word "audit" comes from the Latin *audire,* which means the act of hearing; literally, an "auditor" is a person who hears or listens. When we say that a student audits a class, we still use the word in its oldest sense; the auditor merely listens to the lectures without responsibility for the required classwork. As a tool of social and commercial control, however, auditing has concentrated on verifying the fulfillment of responsibility.

For centuries, audits were oral hearings in which people entrusted with fiscal responsibility justified their stewardship, a word that occurs frequently in any discussion of auditing. Two New Testament parables, for example, center around such events. In the parable of the unjust steward, a "certain rich man" learns that his steward has wasted the goods entrusted to him. Summoning the steward, the rich man demands an oral accounting. In the parable of the talents, the "man travelling into a far country" brings his servants together on his return to determine how they managed the wealth he had placed in their care.

Similarly, medieval audits took on the nature of ritual, attempting to prove the "personal integrity of stewards, not the quality of their accounts" (Chatfield, 1977, p. 112). In medieval England, audits were oral verifications of estate, manorial, and even royal accounts. The Chancellor of the Exchequer held oral audits twice a year around a table covered by a checkered cloth.

But audits do more than help to keep people honest. In the most general sense, they provide assurance in a wide variety of human endeavors. Hospitals carry out audits of their various services. Social programs are audited for compliance and effectiveness. And while most audits are no longer oral examinations, they remain public hearings in spirit. They are formal examinations systematically and objectively carried out by people expert in the subject under scrutiny.

AUDITING OF BUSINESS ENTERPRISES

There are three general categories of auditing that relate to business enterprises: financial auditing, operational auditing, and social auditing.

Financial Auditing

In financial auditing the focus of attention falls on the financial statements, management's primary communication with its various publics. In the United States, audits of financial statements are performed by independent, outside auditors. Independent verification provides a degree of assurance as required by shareholders, creditors, government agencies, suppliers, and others. Depending on the circumstances, financial statements may be subject as well to audits by regulatory auditors, bank examiners, state auditors, United States General Accounting Office (GAO) auditors, and others.

It might be useful at this point to distinguish between two separate but intimately related activities: accounting and auditing. Strictly speaking, the discipline of auditing includes accounting. Yet the tasks of auditor and accountant differ. Accountants prepare financial information; auditors check it. Put more formally, auditors perform independent examinations to evaluate the propriety of accounting procedures, measurements, and communications.

A financial audit requires a substantial input of professional time and talent to enable the auditor to develop the necessary understanding of the business and its systems in order to express an opinion on its financial reports. Such professional inputs should generally create audit outputs that can go beyond the report on financial statements. The financial audit, therefore, will generally result in recommendations to the client regarding the possible improvements in business systems, information presentation, internal controls, and tax savings. Some of these recommendations are summarized in the management letter that the auditor normally submits at the conclusion of an audit, but more may emerge from the day-to-day contacts between audit personnel and client management during an engagement. And of course, the audit inputs place the independent accountant in a position to perform special engagements in the various areas where recommendations for improvement are made based on the audit. While the primary objective of the financial audit must always remain the professional evaluation of financial reports by an expert third party, the other outputs of the service may substantially enhance its economic usefulness.

Thus, the audit services that independent CPAs provide a business are not restricted to the examination of financial statements. Other related services might include, just to pick a few examples, (1) reviews of financial records, business practices, and other aspects of companies under consideration for acquisition; (2) review and evaluation of the company's internal controls beyond that required for the examination of financial statements; (3) reviews of forecasts or projections; (4) performance of feasibility studies; (5) examinations of financial statements of employee benefit plans; and (6) assistance in development of an internal audit function. The list is long, and many other service areas are mentioned throughout this *Handbook*.

Independent CPAs are not the only professionals involved in financial auditing. For example, internal auditors may examine and evaluate their company's internal accounting controls, often carrying out substantive tests (see Chapter 12) in determining the effectiveness of control systems. Regulatory auditors furnish another example; they carry out a variety of financial audit services, often to verify compliance with specific regulations that affect financial statements.

Operational Auditing

Auditors in the private sector and in government may also carry out operational audits, reviewing such matters as the efficiency of an organization's operations. Outside auditors are not directly involved in operational auditing while they carry out the audits of a company's financial statements. Because of their familiarity with the organization, however, they can and usually do offer useful recommendations. Beyond this, independent CPA firms that maintain the necessary skills can be engaged to assist in developing and improving production planning, scheduling, and inventory management policies. They can advise an enterprise about improving the control and efficiency of operations.

Internal auditors usually play a more prominent role than outside auditors in operational auditing. Management will often use internal auditors primarily to study an organization's operating practices to increase efficiency and to search for errors and irregularities.

Finally, governmental auditing such as that performed by the GAO is usually oriented strongly toward operational auditing.

Social Auditing

As the AICPA's Committee on Social Measurement has noted, "every business action, if traced with sufficient care, will be found to have both economic and social consequences" (AICPA, 1977f, p. 3). Social auditing, a professional discipline that has received serious consideration only during the past few years, attempts to measure the consequences of corporate actions and estimate their costs to society. Matters considered might include the impact of an enterprise on ecology, its efforts toward improving the status of minority groups, and its possible involvement in monopolistic practices. Some observers of corporate performance would like to see the auditor's responsibilities extended to such matters. Does the auditor know enough to judge whether a corporation has discharged its social responsibility? Can the auditor speak with authority about management's performance in nonfinancial areas? A qualified yes may be an appropriate response to these questions, but only if objectively measurable standards are developed. So far, however, it seems that criteria cannot be articulated for most of the focal issues. Experimentation will require time, work, and the cooperation of other professions and experts. The federal government has led the way in social auditing, establishing specific programs to evaluate a service organization's effectiveness in meeting the goals of projects funded by government.

The remainder of this chapter will concentrate on the activities of independent CPAs in relation to the financial information presented by business enterprises. Government and nonprofit enterprises will be discussed only in passing. (For a more complete discussion, see Chapters 34 and 35.) In addition, this chapter will introduce an issue of extreme importance today: society's expectations of auditors.

DEVELOPMENT OF AUDITING IN THE UNITED STATES

Even a cursory glance at the events of the past 70 years will show that the profession's history is characterized by the assumption of increasing responsibility and by growing public demands and expectations.

As organized professional activities, auditing and accounting are relative newcomers. The development of auditing began in Great Britain during the nineteenth century, largely as a result of the industrial revolution, the growth of capital, and the attendant chaos in financial reporting. These British roots have profoundly influenced the evolution of the profession in the United States.

Rudimentary audits were carried out in the United States during the nineteenth century, mainly to satisfy bankers' needs for information about companies seeking loans. But as American business embarked on its phenomenal expansion late in the century, investors and lenders demanded greater assurance that a company's financial statements provided reliable information for making economic decisions.

Three other institutional influences have contributed as well: governmental regulation, rules made by professional bodies, and court decisions.

Many of the developments in auditing practices and standards grew out of specific economic problems. Credit problems of the early 1900s, for example, led to bankers' demands for certification of corporate balance sheets. In 1917, a rash of business failures and the lack of uniformity in financial statements prompted the Federal Reserve Board to issue the first audit guidelines. The stock market crash and the Depression led to the Securities Act of 1933 and the Securities Exchange Act of 1934, which created the Securities and Exchange Commission, opening the way for governmental regulation of the securities markets and the financial information used in those markets. The Depression also resulted in the New York Stock Exchange requirement for audits of listed corporations.

Other developments can be traced to initiatives taken by the accounting profession itself. The formation of the American Institute of Accountants in 1916— the forerunner of today's AICPA—was an important first step in creating a national professional body to develop uniform goals and standards. The profession developed the uniform CPA examination, which is used throughout the United States as the principal means to determine admission to the profession. The profession was and is instrumental in developing curricula that assure that prospective CPAs obtain an educational foundation appropriate to perform their responsibilities. The Committee on Accounting Procedure, the Accounting Principles Board, the Auditing Standards Executive Committee, and more recently, the Financial Accounting Standards Board and the Auditing Standards Board—all private, profession-sponsored organizations—have provided the standards of accounting and auditing through the years.

The profession has its roots in the broad issue of *accountability*. Without accountability, society cannot function. "Whoever has a responsibility to others for his actions and their consequences is accountable to them" the Trueblood Committee reported in 1973. "That responsibility may derive from law, contract, organization policy or moral obligation" (AICPA, 1973j, p. 25). Efforts to measure the degree to which that "responsibility to others"—that accountability—has been met have become a necessary social endeavor.

In business, accountability takes on crucial dimensions. Business is accountable to shareholders, creditors, suppliers, government, and other interested "publics." Corporate financial statements, prepared by management accountants, serve as reports of fiscal accountability. Independent audits of these reports are needed to assure that management has not biased economic information in its favor. The auditor, who enforces standards for the presentation of financial information and evaluates management's judgment in applying these standards, thus exerts a restraining influence. But the auditor's role is much more complex than that, as described in the next section.

THE AUDITOR'S ROLE IN FINANCIAL REPORTING

Although a CPA engages in many activities also performed by non-CPAs, when he performs an independent audit of financial statements he is acting in a capacity legally reserved for his profession.

Audited Financial Statements

An independent auditor performs an examination with the objective of issuing a report containing his opinion on his client's financial statements. (Chapter 12 discusses audit performance, and Chapter 16 describes auditor's reports.) Although the examination may take months—at some large corporations the examination is spread throughout the year—the report is generally brief. An analysis of the contents of a typical auditor's report makes one wonder about its brevity; according to standards established by the profession, the auditor must communicate specific information to readers, generally by using prescribed terminology. An example of an auditor's standard report, with special terms italicized and explained, follows:

Board of Directors and Shareholders
ABC, Incorporated
New York, New York

We have examined the consolidated balance sheets of ABC, Incorporated and subsidiaries as of December 31, 1979 and 1978, and the related statements of income, changes in shareholders' equity, and changes in financial position for the years then ended. Our examinations were made *in accordance with generally accepted auditing standards* and, accordingly, included such tests of the accounting records and such other auditing procedures as we considered necessary in the circumstances.

In our opinion, the consolidated financial statements referred to above *present fairly* the financial position of ABC, Incorporated and subsidiaries at December 31, 1979 and 1978, and the results of their operations and the changes in their financial position for the years then ended *in conformity with generally accepted accounting principles* applied on a consistent basis.

Touche Ross & Co.
Certified Public Accountants

New York, New York
February 28, 1980

In Accordance With Generally Accepted Auditing Standards. In this phrase the auditor is reporting that he has complied with standards adopted by the AICPA to ensure the quality of the performance by CPAs who are engaged in an independent examination of financial statements. Ten standards, falling in three categories described below, form the foundation of generally accepted auditing standards, or GAAS (AU 150.02).

General standards require that (1) examinations be conducted by qualified individuals, (2) auditors maintain an independent mental attitude, and (3) they exercise "due professional care."

Standards of field work require that (1) the examination be adequately planned and supervised, (2) a study and evaluation of internal control be incorporated in the examination, and (3) the auditor's opinion be based on sufficient, competent evidence.

Standards of reporting require that the auditor's report state whether (1) the financial statements are presented in accordance with GAAP, (2) GAAP has been consistently applied, and (3) adequate information disclosures are given in the

financial statements. Finally, (4) the auditor must express an opinion on the
financial statements or, if he is unable to express an opinion, state the reasons.

Although paraphrased above, the ten actual standards are expressed in fewer
than 350 words. The standards are not audit procedures; they do not instruct
auditors how to conduct a financial statement examination. The AICPA draws the
following distinction:

> Auditing standards differ from auditing procedures in that "procedures" relate to acts
> to be performed, whereas "standards" deal with measures of the quality of the per-
> formance of those acts and the objectives to be attained by the use of the procedures
> undertaken. *Auditing standards* as distinct from *auditing procedures* concern them-
> selves not only with the auditor's professional qualities but also with the judgment ex-
> ercised by him in the performance of his examination and in his report. [AU 150.01]

The Auditing Standards Board, a senior technical committee of the AICPA,
issues pronouncements known as Statements on Auditing Standards (SASs),
which amplify the ten basic standards and guide the auditor in certain significant
areas of the examination. For example, SAS 6 (AU 335) guides the auditor in his
approach to related-party transactions, and SAS 12 (AU 337) instructs the auditor
in the inquiry of his client's attorneys. SASs are as binding as the basic standards
and are part of GAAS. Although the guidance given by SASs is more concrete
than the broad principles of the basic standards, taken together as GAAS they
form only a framework and set of objectives the auditor must satisfy in his examination and report. The auditor selects the myriad steps and procedures necessary
to plan and conduct an audit using his professional judgment within the confines
of this broad framework. Chapter 11 contains a full discussion of GAAS.

In Conformity With Generally Accepted Accounting Principles. In this phrase
the independent auditor is reporting that the financial statements prepared by his
client comply with the accepted conventions of financial accounting and reporting.
Since its formation in 1974, the Financial Accounting Standards Board is the independent organization responsible for promulgating GAAP in its pronouncements,
known as Statements of Financial Accounting Standards (see Chapter 40).

What are principles? In 1972 a blue-ribbon committee appointed by the AICPA
admitted that " 'accounting principles' has proven to be an extraordinarily elusive
term . . . [connoting] things basic and fundamental, of a sort which can be expressed
in a few words, relatively timeless in nature, and in no way dependent upon
changing fashions in business or the evolving needs of the investment community"
(AICPA, 1972c, p. 13). Herein lies the misunderstanding of the term GAAP;
there are no immutable accounting truths, because accounting principles are
conventions that depend on acceptance.

Economic reality and GAAP. As conventions, accounting principles do not
necessarily parallel economic reality. For example, the balance sheet representation of a factory's historical cost (reduced by periodic depreciation charges) usually
differs significantly from the market value of the structure or the cost the company
would incur if it were to replace the structure. For the most part, accounting
principles have been oriented toward actual transactions that have occurred in the

past; as a result "the information provided by financial reporting largely reflects the financial effects of transactions and events that have already happened" (AC 1210.21).

The FASB is developing a conceptual framework for financial accounting and reporting to serve as a theoretical construct on which future accounting standards will be based and existing standards evaluated (see Chapter 2). As part of the project, the FASB has defined the objectives served by financial statements, which are, in part, that investors, creditors, and others need information in order to "assess the amounts, timing, and uncertainty of prospective net cash inflows to the . . . enterprise" (AC 1210.37). As part of the conceptual framework project, the FASB has released SFAS 33, *Financial Reporting and Changing Prices* (AC 1072), which requires large companies to supplement their basic financial statements with information about the effects of inflation and changing values (see Chapter 8). A closer synthesis of accounting principles and economic reality is beginning to occur.

Present Fairly. The auditor is reporting several pieces of information in this phrase. First he is reporting that while the financial statements capture the underlying events within an acceptable range of approximation, they remain summaries of innumerable transactions that cannot be exactly portrayed. Beyond this acceptable range, an error or misstatement is deemed to be *material*. Unfortunately the profession has not successfully articulated the boundary that separates material from immaterial items; as a result, the exact criteria—within accepted ranges— used by different accountants are based on individual judgments that critics have labeled as inconsistent or arbitrary.

"Present fairly" means that the accounting principles selected by the company are generally accepted and appropriate in the circumstances. "Present fairly" always is coupled with "in conformity with generally accepted accounting principles" in an auditor's report on an examination of financial statements. GAAP is the standard by which to measure fairness. "Fairness" in the abstract means all manner of beneficence conceivable by financial statement users, and litigation against accountants often focuses on plaintiffs' broad assertions of unfairness (see Chapter 46).

Because of contemporary misunderstandings, the meaning of "present fairly" became the subject of SAS 5 (AU 411). In spite of SAS 5, many contend that the phrase "present fairly" still has no specific meaning. In fact, the Commission on Auditors' Responsibilities (CAR)—often called the Cohen Commission—recommended its deletion from the auditor's report (CAR, 1978, p. 14). Although general purpose financial statements should be "fair" in the sense of being free from bias, the process of financial accounting involves continuous judgments and estimates on the part of those who prepare and audit financial statements. The process is inherently subjective, and critics maintain that the auditor's report should emphasize—not obscure—this fact.

The Auditing Standards Board is actively considering the content of the auditor's standard report and may revise it in 1980.

Significance of the Audit—Added Assurance. Investors and creditors risk funds based on their assessment of an enterprise's future. Financial statements serve two purposes in this assessment: existing financial statements provide some (though far from all) of the data needed for users to make the prediction; and financial statements will confirm or correct aspects of the prediction as the future unfolds. An audit and the auditor's report increase the user's confidence in the information contained in financial statements. But users of financial statements should understand that the auditor plans his examination economically and that the auditor cannot and should not check all transactions. Though the auditor plans his examination to locate problems, his conclusion could be wrong because of the sampling nature of an audit, because of procedural faults, or most devastatingly and infrequently because of the lack of integrity by management. Such erroneous conclusions by auditors are uncommon, but when they occur and involve large public companies, they receive widespread attention in the financial press, the courts, and recently in Congress.

Audit sampling. An auditor comes to his conclusions based on a sampling of the transactions related to the period under examination (see Chapter 14). To do otherwise—that is, to examine every transaction—would mitigate the usefulness of audits, because the cost of such examinations would radically exceed the total benefits to investors, creditors, and others.[1] But, by virtue of examining only a portion of the transactions, the auditor and those who read his report must accept an element of uncertainty about the auditor's conclusions. By understanding the types of transactions a company enters, by specializing in assessing systems of internal control, and by using a variety of sophisticated audit procedures and audit tools where appropriate, auditors are generally able to minimize risks associated with their sampling approach and are able to design an audit plan that balances the costs and benefits of an audit.

Procedural and performance errors. An auditor may mistakenly use an audit procedure inappropriate for discovering the error or misstatement, fail to properly perform a procedure through misunderstanding of instructions, fail to accurately evaluate the results of a procedure, or fail to recognize that his subordinates on the audit team have made these mistakes. To minimize these occurrences, the profession has established requirements for entry to and continued practice in it, and accounting firms utilize a hierarchical structure so that persons with the appropriate experience are designing, performing, and reviewing all phases of the audit. Nonetheless, audits are conducted by people, and errors may occur in isolated cases regardless of the complex safeguards designed to prevent them.

Management integrity. To many laymen, it is incomprehensible that auditors occasionally fail to detect a major fraud. But collusive fraud by management lacking integrity is extremely difficult (often impossible) to detect: fictitious receivables may pose as assets, and the auditor's confirmation procedures count for nought if those circularized cooperate with the fraud perpetrators; underlying documents may be forged; cash receipts from unexpected sources may not be recorded. In

---

[1] It is also a fallacy that an examination of every transaction would assure the correctness of the auditor's conclusion. The estimates and judgments involved in financial statement presentation, and the intentions and integrity of management, are substantially non-transaction-based.

SAS 16 the AICPA attempted to define the auditor's responsibility for detecting irregularities and concluded that "unless the auditor's examination reveals evidential matter to the contrary, his reliance on the truthfulness of certain representations[2] and on the genuineness of records and documents obtained during his examination is reasonable" (AU 327.12).

As discussed later in this chapter, society does not appear to be satisfied with this limitation of an auditor's responsibilities. The Commission on Auditors' Responsibilities recommended (in Section 4 of its report) that, at a minimum, the profession develop a standard of care for fraud detection so that an auditor's performance can be evaluated. The recommendation is currently under study. However, the responsibilities of the auditor cannot increase in this complicated area without a corresponding increase in the cost to society of performing audits. It must also be mentioned that while thousands of companies file audited financial statements with the Securities and Exchange Commission and many thousands more file with banks and others, there have been very few cases of audit failure. Therefore, the profession's current standards may already provide the public with the right level of protection without the necessity—and related costs—of revising the standards and increasing the amount of audit work performed.

Need for Audit Services

Generally, one or more of the following characteristics will exist when a company engages a CPA to perform an audit:

1. *Public companies* almost without exception require an annual audit of their financial statements. A public company is defined by the AICPA as one whose securities trade in a public market or that has filed with a regulatory agency in preparation for the sale of securities in a public market (AC 2071.06, fn. 1).
2. *Users' needs* often include the added assurance of an audit for financial statements of nonpublic companies as well as public ones. Instances when users often need such added assurance are listed below:
   a. The company has entered into a significant contractual arrangement with a bank or other creditor, a joint venture partner, a large vendor, a lessor, etc.
   b. The company has a fiduciary responsibility to the public or others. For example, mutual savings and loan associations, mutual life insurance companies, health maintenance organizations, charities, country clubs, and many other nonbusiness organizations have such a responsibility.
3. *Owner's needs* sometimes call for an audit; for example, the owner may have infrequent contact with the actual managers and thus desire added audit assurance. More frequently, the owner believes that the benefits of an audit, including recommendations for improved internal control and operating efficiencies, outweigh the added expense of an audit.

---

2 Examples include management representations dealing with intent, knowledge, and the completeness of records, as well as third-party confirmations from debtors, creditors, and banks.

Unaudited Financial Statements

Need for Nonaudit Services. Many companies require the expertise of the independent CPA in preparing periodic financial statements but do not need the added assurance of a report based on an audit.

Until recently, the independent CPA could perform a variety of functions involving unaudited financial statements, but the standards of the profession prevented him from describing the nature of his association. He could merely report that he had not performed an audit and that he had no opinion on the financial statements (AU 516.04). The Cohen Commission pointed out that a statement of what the auditor did not do merely left the reader guessing what it was that he did do. The commission recommended that "users should be informed about the work done and the assurances intended . . ." (CAR, 1978, p. 84).

In December 1978 the Accounting and Review Services Committee, a new senior committee of the AICPA, issued the first Statement on Standards for Accounting and Review Services (SSARS), *Compilation and Review of Financial Statements* (AR 100), which establishes standards for auditor's reports on unaudited financial statements of *nonpublic* companies. The provisions of SSARS 1 are summarized below and are discussed in Chapter 16.

Compilation of Financial Statements. A compilation is presenting in financial statement form information that is the representation of management. The CPA must have or gain a general understanding of his client's industry and business, but he is not required to "make inquiries or perform other procedures to verify, corroborate, or review information" supplied by his client (AR 100.12). His report mentions that a compilation has been performed, describes a compilation, and states that no opinion or other form of assurance is expressed on the financial statements.

Review of Financial Statements. The CPA must have or gain familiarity with his client's industry and business. He also makes inquiries and performs certain analytical and other procedures so that he has a reasonable basis for expressing limited assurance on the financial statements. If, in performing any of these procedures, the auditor becomes aware that any information is "incorrect, incomplete, or otherwise unsatisfactory, he should perform the additional procedures he deems necessary . . ." (AR 100.29).

The accountant's review report states that a review was performed in accordance with AICPA standards and that the information in the financial statements is the representation of management, and describes the nature of a review as distinct from an audit. The report gives the limited assurance that, based on the review, the CPA is not aware of any material modifications that should be made to the financial statements in order for them to be in conformity with GAAP.

Association With Unaudited Financial Statements of Public Companies. If the auditor issues a report (known as a disclaimer of opinion) stating that he did not examine the financial statements of a public company and does not express an opinion on them, he then has no responsibility to perform *any* procedures beyond reading the financial statements for obvious material errors (AU 504.05). Frequently, however, the auditor is engaged to perform limited procedures with regard to unaudited statements of a public company, and he may be able to issue a report other than a disclaimer.

Interim financial statement review. As discussed in Chapter 5, companies prepare interim financial statements to satisfy the requirements of the SEC or other regulatory agencies, to report on a quarterly basis to their stockholders, to satisfy creditors' needs for periodic information, and for use within the organization. The degree of the independent CPA's involvement with interim financial statements depends on circumstances that differ from company to company and (if the auditor has any involvement at all) ranges from informal consultation to a formal audit conducted with the objective of expressing an opinion on the financial statements taken as a whole. A common form of auditor involvement is a review conducted in accordance with SAS 24 (AU 721). The auditor uses the review as a basis for reporting whether material modifications are required to bring the interim financial statements into conformity with GAAP.

ASR 177, released by the SEC in 1975, required registrants to report four separate quarters' information in a footnote to their annual financial statements. Even though the footnote was permitted to be marked "unaudited," and even though the auditor had not issued a report on a quarterly review, the SEC presumed that the accountant had applied "appropriate professional standards and procedures [those stipulated in SAS 24] with respect to the data in the note" (Regulation S-X, [old] Rule 3-16(t)). (The requirement for presentation of quarterly data has now been moved to Item 12 of Regulation S-K as part of the SEC reorganization of its disclosure system in September 1980. This places it within the annual report but outside the financial statements in recognition of the fact that the information is unaudited.)

Comfort letters. When companies intend to sell securities to the public, they are required to file with the SEC a registration statement that often contains unaudited financial statements in addition to audited statements. Frequently the underwriters for the offering will request that the independent CPAs provide them with a letter dealing with

- The accountant's independence,
- Compliance with the requirements of the Securities Act of 1933 as to the form of audited financial statements included in the registration statement,
- Unaudited financial statements in the registration statement,
- Changes in financial statement items subsequent to the registration statement's most recent financial statements, and
- Other financial information.

Short of conducting an audit, the assistance the independent accountant can provide the underwriter is subject to limitation; as a result, auditors must carefully evaluate the nature of what is requested. *Letters for underwriters* (AU 630) are discussed further in Chapter 26.

Other Independent Auditor Activities

The CPA's qualifications and knowledge of his client's business enable him to provide significant accounting and audit-related services[3] in addition to reporting on financial statements. The accountant may provide additional services when he is engaged to report on financial statements, or he may provide these services independently of an audit, review, or compilation.

Letter of Recommendations. According to GAAS, the auditor must make a study and evaluation of his client's system of internal control when he performs an audit. As a result, he is in a position to recommend that the company modify or install elements of internal control that will strengthen management's ability to safeguard company assets or improve the reliability of the company's financial records (see Chapter 13). Normally the auditor communicates his suggestions in a letter of recommendations (also known as a *management letter*).

Often the letter will contain suggestions related to the efficiency of a company's operations. For example, an auditor experienced in retailing may suggest that his client consider physically redesigning its warehouse distribution center to provide a more efficient flow of goods, or an auditor of a geographically diverse fast-food chain might recommend the installation of a cash management system to increase average daily balances.

Special Reviews. A company will frequently engage an independent CPA to perform an in-depth review of all or a portion of its internal control system, or to originate or evaluate proposals designed to increase operating efficiency. These studies often stem from suggestions contained in the auditor's letter of recommendations.

Many public companies have asked independent CPAs to assist them in satisfying the requirements of the Foreign Corrupt Practices Act, signed in 1977. According to this law, discussed in Chapter 13, public companies must examine their internal accounting controls and record-keeping systems and correct important weaknesses identified by the examination.

Consultation on Appropriate Accounting Principles. Most companies prepare financial statements on the basis of GAAP when they are intended for use outside the company. Management normally will consult with the independent CPA before changing an existing accounting practice or adopting a new one (such as accounting for the company's first important transaction in a new area). In some situations it may not be clear whether or not a proposed practice really is generally accepted because the authoritative literature does not address the circumstances of the underlying transaction. The CPA can conceptually evaluate the proposed accounting treatment, survey how other companies account for similar transactions, and review nonauthoritative sources of guidance such as books and articles in reaching a conclusion.

Another reason companies consult with auditors on accounting principles is that

---

[3] Management advisory services are generally not discussed in this *Handbook*.

GAAP restricts changes (from one generally accepted principle to another) to those where the new principle is "preferable" (AC 1051.16). Finally, consultation is desirable because the CPA can help the company assess the financial statement impact and income tax effects of the proposed change.

Special Reports. The independent CPA may be engaged to perform appropriate procedures aimed at the issuance of a seemingly endless variety of special reports. Under guidelines issued by the AICPA in SAS 14 (AU 621), special reports have been grouped into four categories as listed below and discussed in Chapter 16:

1. Reports on financial statements prepared in accordance with a comprehensive basis of accounting other than GAAP,
2. Reports on specified elements, accounts, or items of a financial statement,
3. Reports on compliance with aspects of a contractual agreement related to audited financial statements, and
4. Reports on information presented in prescribed forms or schedules that require a prescribed form of auditor's report.

Income Taxes. Based on the knowledge of his client's business and his familiarity with tax regulations and rulings, the independent CPA will frequently be able to suggest ways his client can lawfully reduce or defer payment of income taxes. He may also be asked to prepare tax returns, and if he is conducting an audit, he will review the adequacy of the financial statement provision for income taxes (see Chapters 25 and 43). Because tax matters can be very complex, accounting firms often have a separate department consisting of tax specialists, and the auditors and tax personnel work jointly to serve clients' income tax needs.

THE AUDITOR'S ROLE AND SOCIETY'S EXPECTATIONS

In the past, CPAs have relied almost solely on the accounting and auditing standards (GAAP and GAAS) to define their responsibilities to preparers and users of financial information. But the harsh criticism of the profession in the early 1970s has given the CPA a new perspective—he now understands that professional standards must reach beyond his own view of the auditor's role and consider as well society's expectations of what it is the independent CPA should do.

Needs of Public Companies

Most managers of public companies recognize that their companies have a unique obligation to existing and potential investors and creditors, and a responsibility to society as well. As a result, the accounting profession is developing approaches to satisfy and report on those obligations that go beyond the boundaries of traditional audited financial statements.

Review of Supplementary Financial Data. Standard setters have started to encourage, even require, public companies to provide financial information that is more subjective than the data normally associated with audited financial statements.

The SEC, in annual reports on Form 10-K and in other filings, has long required descriptive company information apart from the audited financial statements (see Chapter 4). More recently, however, the commission has required larger companies to present financially oriented supplemental data. For example, until 1979 larger registrants were required by ASR 190 to disclose replacement cost information in order to show the effects of inflation.[4] Also, SEC registrants had to present the four quarters' interim financial information in a note to the annual financial statements, though this is now moved outside of the statements. The SEC wanted the CPA's involvement with this financial information, but at the time the rules were imposed the CPA did not have professional standards to follow in order to review it. As a compromise, although the replacement cost and interim disclosures were made in audited financial statements, the SEC permitted companies to mark the notes "unaudited." The CPA did not have to perform auditing procedures but rather reviewed the information, thereby reducing the cost of his involvement. In effect, the SEC said that this information is valuable to financial statement readers and that limited review procedures by an auditor are acceptable in order to minimize the cost burden on business enterprises.

While the FASB studies the question of what information various types of companies should report, it is also trying to differentiate "between information that should be disclosed in financial statements and information that should be disclosed in financial reporting otherwise . . ." (AC 2083.04). But before completing this project the FASB issued SFAS 33, *Financial Reporting and Changing Prices* (AC 1072), which requires the presentation of information about the effects of inflation and changing prices as a supplement to the company's financial statements, as discussed in Chapter 8. This data and other supplemental information that future accounting standards may require but that do not have to be audited are covered by new auditing standards (SAS 27; AU 553) that define the auditor's responsibility, thus permitting the SEC to desist in the "unaudited footnote" approach.

Internal Control and the Foreign Corrupt Practices Act. When Congress passed the Foreign Corrupt Practices Act in 1977, it demonstrated that public companies need "more than an audit" to satisfy society's expectations. The law upset the CPA's traditional view of the internal control systems of his audit clients. Before, faced with a company having a relatively weak system of controls, the auditor could usually compensate for the weaknesses by extending other audit procedures, so long as he had made proper study and evaluation of the problems.

Although his audit approach technically remains the same today, the auditor has another consideration: his client might be in violation of the law. According to one section of the law, the internal control systems of public companies should provide reasonable assurance that

- Transactions take place only when authorized,
- Transactions are recorded so as to maintain accountability for assets,

---

[4] In ASR 271, the SEC deleted this requirement for registrants who fully adopt the provisions of SFAS 33 for 1979 financial statements.

- Assets are accessible only under proper authorization, and
- Assets are compared to the records from time to time and a follow-up system exists for discrepancies.

CPAs recognize these factors as proper objectives of a system of control (in fact Congress took them from the professional literature). But the Foreign Corrupt Practices Act has converted conceptual objectives into legal requirements that may not be stated precisely enough to determine whether or not a specific element of control satisfies the provisions of the law. Unfortunately, clear standards may be established only when the law is tested in the courts.

Until these standards emerge, many accountants are advising clients to adopt a program that demonstrates compliance efforts. Such a program includes an assessment of the existing system, identification of areas in which weaknesses exist, evaluation of the costs and benefits of modifications to eliminate the weaknesses, and installation of a technique to monitor the ongoing system. Documentation proving these steps were performed is essential. CPAs, experienced in evaluating and improving internal control systems, are able to offer practical advice and assistance at each phase (see Chapter 13).

Other Areas. Closely related to reviewing internal control and the Foreign Corrupt Practices Act is the evolving subject of auditors' reporting on internal control weaknesses. The SEC is proposing that auditors report to the public on their review of a company's internal control. SAS 20, *Required Communication of Material Weaknesses in Internal Accounting Control* (AU 323), established standards for the auditors' reporting material weaknesses to management. One recent legal case involving auditors had as a focal issue the fact that the auditors reported weaknesses in internal control to management but did not report these weaknesses to the public. In July 1980 the Auditing Standards Board released SAS 30, *Reporting on Internal Accounting Control* (AU 642), which settles some of the hotly contested issues about reporting to the public, but it is still too soon to tell how well this will work.

Increasingly, users of financial statements are regarding them as not only a report of the historical transactions but also a prediction of the future. And it has been suggested that an auditor should warn the financial statement reader if, as a result of his audit, he concludes that the company is headed for difficult times. The Auditing Standards Board is addressing this question, at least in part. An exposure draft of a SAS has been released dealing with the auditor's responsibility for anticipating going concern problems. The exposure draft concludes that the auditor must consider whether threats to the company's financial future might affect the carrying value of the assets or the classification of the liabilities as reported on the balance sheet. But the proposed statement as drafted refuses to give the auditor any responsibility for making a judgment as to whether the historical financial statements are or are not reasonable predictors of the future.

Standards for Small Businesses

The accounting profession is exploring whether or not smaller and privately held businesses need to provide the same information in their financial statements that large publicly held companies provide. Society's expectations diverge on this point; regulators (such as the SEC) of the content of financial statements of public companies are demanding more information about companies' financial position and prospects, while the owners and managers of small businesses find such contemporary accounting and auditing requirements onerous and too often irrelevant. Until recently, the profession and the FASB had attempted to reconcile the different expectations or, failing that, had opted for the large-company view. Now, standard setters are beginning to work out mechanisms that can accommodate both sets of expectations.

Private Companies and GAAS. As accounting standards mandate expanded disclosure, upward pressure is put on the costs of a financial statement examination; simply put, the independent accountant has more information to audit. If the FASB's project to differentiate standards for closely held companies is successful, some of the pressure will be relieved. The AICPA's Auditing Standards Board (ASB) is also examining ways to reduce the burden on smaller enterprises:

- The ASB has appointed a task force to review all existing SASs. During the review, the task force intends to analyze the standards from the point of view of a small business.
- The Private Companies Practice Section of the AICPA's Division of Firms (discussed in Chapter 39) provides a forum for accounting firms who are close to the problems of small businesses.
- SSARS 1 has articulated how the CPA may perform less than full audit services and still offer limited assurance on financial statements through compilation or review services, as discussed earlier.

Private Companies and GAAP. By performing a limited review rather than a full-scope examination, CPAs can save companies much of the expense associated with an audit. However, if the company bases its unaudited financial statements on GAAP—as most companies do for external use—just complying with accepted accounting principles becomes a time-consuming and expensive proposition.

During its tenure (1959-1973) the APB issued 31 opinions. Its successor, the FASB, has issued in excess of that number in the six years following its commencement. The volume of new pronouncements is not the only problem; critics have charged that in some cases the costs of complying with the rules far outweigh the benefits users of the financial statements derive.

The FASB is cognizant of the problem. When it released SFAS 21 (AC 2083), it suspended for nonpublic companies the requirements to disclose extensive information about operations in different industries (segment information, Chapter 32) and earnings per share (Chapter 26). These requirements were suspended pending the results of an FASB project designed, in part, to distinguish "between information that all enterprises should be required to report and information that only designated types of enterprises should be required to disclose. Special attention will be given ... to the financial statements and financial reporting of small or closely held enterprises" (AC 2083.04).

Since the issuance of SFAS 21, the FASB has evidenced its intent in SFAS 33 (AC 1072), requiring only large publicly held companies to provide constant dollar and current cost data (Chapter 8).

Other Areas

The expectations of society are placing new demands on and providing new opportunities for the independent CPA. The Commission on Auditors' Responsibilities (Cohen Commission), in its 1978 *Report, Conclusions, and Recommendations,* identified many areas in which society is expecting more from auditors; significant areas and the profession's current response are identified below.

Responsibility for Financial Representations. Some critics of corporate financial reporting believe that the independent auditor should assume the responsibility of determining the representations a company makes to users of its financial reports. The Cohen Commission considered this viewpoint and concluded that management's responsibility for processing accounting information and issuing financial statements should continue. What is needed, instead, is a vehicle to better describe the respective responsibilities of management and the auditor to users of financial statements.

Management alone, through its day-to-day contact with the company and its industry, has the capability to take responsibility for financial representations. According to the Cohen Commission report (CAR, p. 9):

> Preparing financial statements requires an assessment of the probabilities and potential implications of uncertain future events. Management's knowledge and experience are necessary to make such estimates. It is management's responsibility to support the measurements made and the auditor's responsibility to challenge those measurements and evaluate the adequacy of management's support.

The Cohen Commission found that an important defect of the current standard auditor's report is that it blurs users' understanding of respective responsibilities. To better communicate who is responsible for what, it recommended that management write a report for inclusion in financial statements acknowledging and describing its responsibilities. In addition, the standard auditor's report could then be revised; each paragraph would cover a major element of the audit and describe the work the auditor performed and his findings.

Although the AICPA concluded that it could not require clients of CPA firms to issue management reports, the AICPA and other groups, such as the Financial Executives Institute, actively support the concept. As a result, many public companies are including management reports in annual reports to shareholders. And a task force of the ASB is studying ways to revise the auditor's standard report so that it communicates better.

Fraud Detection. It is rare for the management of a large company to mislead the investing public by engaging in fraud. However, when these activities come to light, one of the first questions usually heard is, Where were the auditors? In short, if intensity of criticism is one measure of society's expectations about the auditor's proper role, then society clearly expects—in fact, demands—auditors to accept an important measure of responsibility for the detection of fraud.

The Cohen Commission explored at length the auditor's responsibility for the detection of fraud. The commission distinguished between employee fraud (usually theft) and management fraud ("the use of deceptive practices to inflate earnings or to forestall the recognition of either insolvency or a decline in earnings" CAR, p. 32). These practices sometimes include

- Fictitious transactions,
- Transactions without substance, and
- Intentional misapplication of accounting principles.

The Cohen Commission concluded that the auditor "has a duty to search for fraud, and should be expected to detect those frauds that the exercise of professional skill and care would normally uncover" (CAR, p. 36). On the other hand, the commission pointed out that auditors cannot be expected to discover all frauds, including frauds involving collusion between management and ostensible third parties.

In order to reconcile these two conclusions and in order to clarify to the public the auditor's role in the detection of fraud, the commission decided that a standard clearly delineating the auditors' responsibilities should be formulated. The commission suggested that the standard include the following provisions (CAR, pp. 38-40):

1. *Investigate clients.* Auditors should have a systematic approach to investigating the reputation and integrity of a potential client and should periodically reassess existing clients.
2. *Take action when doubts about management's integrity arise.* Resignation or other action may be appropriate when an auditor cannot resolve doubts about the honesty, integrity, or good faith of management.
3. *Evaluate conditions suggesting a predisposition to management fraud.* Many conditions, such as insufficient working capital, may be indicators that an increased possibility of fraud exists. When planning the engagement, the auditor should take these warnings into account.
4. *Know the client's industry.* Most auditors recognize that knowledge of their client's business and industry is a prerequisite for undertaking an audit.
5. *Expand the study and evaluation of internal control.* Controls that may have a "significant bearing on the prevention and detection of fraud" should be evaluated. Further, the AICPA and public accounting firms should develop methods for exchanging information about frauds and their detection.
6. *Be aware of possible deficiencies in audit steps.* Traditional audit procedures do not always produce the intended assurances. For example, confirmations with outside parties may not reveal collusive fraud between management and those returning the confirmation to the auditors.
7. *Understand engagement limitations.* Special engagements usually provide far less assurance that fraud may be detected than do audits. The auditor and the client should be aware of the limitations of special engagements.

The accounting profession is actively pursuing many of these recommendations. In addition, the internal policies of many accounting firms have long required new-client investigations, an evaluation of conditions suggesting the possibility of fraud, and comprehensive knowledge on the part of the auditor of his client's industry.

Research is underway at many universities and several large accounting firms on the development of early warning signals and improved audit procedures designed to detect fraud.

Even before the Cohen Commission released its report, the AICPA had concluded that the auditor's responsibilities for the detection of fraud should be expanded. SAS 6 (AU 335) requires auditors to investigate material transactions and determine if management is directly or indirectly involved (see Chapter 28). And SAS 16 states that the auditor

> has the responsibility, within the inherent limitations of the auditing process . . . to plan his examination . . . to search for errors or irregularities that would have a material effect on the financial statements. . . . An independent auditor's standard report implicitly indicates his belief that the financial statements taken as a whole are not materially misstated as a result of errors or irregularities. [AU 327.05]

Corporate Legal Accountability. The general public's view of business was greatly altered in the early 1970s as press reports and congressional investigations revealed that some U.S. multinational corporations were engaging in illegal domestic political contributions and improper foreign payments, kickbacks, and bribes. Predictably, the altered views of society translated into new expectations regarding the proper role of the independent auditor.

The auditor's proper role for assessing the legality of his client's acts is complex. Simply stated, the auditor does not usually possess the skills to make a legal assessment. The Cohen Commission recognized this basic limitation:

> Auditors cannot reasonably be expected to assume responsibilities for detection or disclosure of a client's violations of law in general. Auditors are primarily accountants, trained and experienced in activities that are basically financial. They are not lawyers nor are they criminal investigators, and they do not possess the training or skills of either group. [CAR, pp. 44-45]

In spite of this basic limitation, an auditor may become aware of illegal or possibly illegal acts during the course of an audit through correspondence with attorneys, through inquiry, or through his own knowledge as an informed businessman. To clarify the auditor's responsibilities towards detection and disclosure of illegal acts, SAS 17 (AU 328) provides the following guidelines:

- During the audit, the auditor should be alert to the possibility that illegal acts may have occurred;
- When an illegal act—even one with no material consequences—comes to his attention, the auditor must apprise client personnel at the appropriate level within the organization; and
- If the auditor does not believe appropriate consideration has been given to an illegal act, he should consider withdrawing from the engagement and severing future relationships.

SAS 17 provides, generally, that the auditor has no need to notify anyone outside the organization, because this notification is management's responsibility. This is a contentious area that will no doubt be clarified as the auditor's legal position becomes better demarcated vis-à-vis his clients and the public (see Chapter 46).

Excessive Expectations

Although the auditor is successfully grappling with many of the more difficult expectations of society, there are other expectations the auditing profession may not be able to satisfy.

Constraints of the Accounting Framework. Some of the criticism aimed at auditors should really be directed at a wider target: the framework of generally accepted accounting principles. Critics have charged that

- GAAP permits unwarranted variability between the reported financial results of different companies;
- GAAP is incomplete—the professional literature is silent on the accounting for many types of transactions and activities; and
- GAAP does not specify the disclosure of all specific information that a financial statement user may consider important.

Because of the limitations of GAAP, preparers of financial statements must exercise judgment in choosing among accepted alternatives, in determining what constitutes an accepted accounting method, and in selecting the appropriate data for inclusion in financial reports from among the myriad of available relevant and irrelevant information about a company. The exercise of judgment will continue to be at the core of the financial accounting process, and auditors must evaluate management's exercise of judgment. It is unreasonable to expect that auditors, and others involved in financial accounting and reporting, could develop a system of financial accountability that both eliminates the need for judgment yet purports to communicate an understandable summary of business activities.

Uncertainties. Companies are no different than society at large—they operate in the face of an unknown future. General economic declines affect most businesses, although some companies may be more adversely affected than others.

Legislation may be passed, such as the ban on cyclamates, that affects only an industry or group of industries. A company also faces its own uncertainties—the outcome of specific litigation or the ability to continue operations when liquidity is impaired. From among this mixture of uncertainties, the auditor must evaluate those that are both substantial and designated by the professional standards as appropriate to cause him to qualify his opinion (see Chapters 16 and 29).

The present standards for reporting on uncertainties cause confusion among many readers. The Cohen Commission believes that when uncertainty is adequately described in the financial statement footnotes, no mention need be made in the auditor's report. Taking the opposite view, some spokesmen for creditor groups insist that the auditor's qualification is a critical warning sign and should not be eliminated. Regardless of how the reporting issue is ultimately resolved, readers must not be misled into believing that auditors are better equipped to predict the unknown future than anyone else. Many in society fail to realize that significant elements of historically based financial statements hinge on estimates of future occurrences. Auditors can only give an added degree of assurance that important estimates were reasonably made; they cannot guarantee that the future will unfold as forecast.

Materiality. Anyone familiar with the financial accounting process is aware of the concept of materiality, but he will be frustrated in attempts to locate much definition in the authoritative accounting and auditing literature. SFAC 2 attempts to define the essence of materiality in this way:

> the magnitude of an omission or misstatement of accounting information that, in the light of surrounding circumstances, makes it probable that the judgment of a reasonable person relying on the information would have been changed or influenced by the omission or misstatement. [AC 1220.171]

The FASB arrived at this depiction of materiality after considering past attempts by the accounting profession, the SEC, academia, and the courts to define the term. The FASB's reluctance to characterize its view on materiality as a definition underscores the elusiveness of the concept. Although many expect clear standards of materiality to be articulated, they will probably be frustrated, because materiality, as the FASB indicates, is based on assessing the probable behavior of unknown third persons.

EXTENDING THE AUDITOR'S ROLE

Changes in society's expectations are causing the independent auditor to challenge what it is he does and to expand his responsibilities when he conducts an examination of financial statements. At the same time his overall role is growing, and this section examines some of these longer-term trends.

Auditor of Record

In the future, the investing public will likely view a company's independent accountant as its auditor of record. According to this view, the independent auditor is the auditor of record from the moment he accepts an auditing engagement until his engagement is terminated. An important assumption lies behind the idea: the auditor can best serve society by extending his relationship with his clients.

Continuous Financial Reporting Cycle. Traditionally, the auditor's work has been seasonal; in companies of average size, it often begins at or near the end of the client's fiscal year, and ends shortly thereafter when the auditor completes his examination of the financial statements. Yet the complex nature of business requires a constant flow of timely financial information to satisfy the demands of regulators, creditors, and investors. If these demands are to be met, the auditor will have to maintain an overview involvement in the financial affairs of his client.

In a discussion of the auditor of record concept, John C. Burton notes that it requires a significant change in attitude on the part of the auditor. He must shift his "outlook ... from one of auditing financial statements to that of auditing the company" (1975a, p. 11). The Cohen Commission takes a similar approach. It suggests a new and more comprehensive definition of the audit, recommending that it be "considered a 'function' to be performed during *a period of time,* rather than an audit of a *particular set* of financial statements" (italics in original). As a result, the audit function will expand to include "all important elements of the financial reporting process" (CAR, p. 60). For example, the commission advocates the following:

- A comprehensive evaluation of a company's accounting systems and controls—the core of the extended audit function;
- An examination of a company's budgeting systems, earning plans, and the relationship between operating activities and management's expectations; and
- Timely involvement, particularly in reviewing interim financial reports, in the entire financial reporting process.

As the auditor's role evolves in these directions, he will learn a great deal about the details of his client's operations. Along with this knowledge will come new responsibilities. Burton (1974, p. 121) notes, perhaps overoptimistically, that in this extended role the auditor will have a "continuous responsibility to review all public communications to investors and shareholders on a timely basis." He will do so not to perform "an audit on interim and other data but to provide assurance that audited financial results are not being misused in press releases and annual reports. ..." The auditor will make sure, as well, "that accounting and measurement problems have been adequately aired prior to the publication of interim reports and other announcements."

Limits of the Auditor's Association. As the role of the independent CPA evolves into the auditor of record, it becomes even more critical that society understand the proper boundaries of his role. The prior lack of such an understanding, at least feigned in litigation, is perhaps the greatest deterrent in auditors' willingness to accept this extended role.

The Cohen Commission has suggested that auditors concern themselves specifically with information of a *financial* or *accounting* nature, information that lies firmly within their areas of competence. For example, if a question regarding a company's fair employment practices arises, the company's lawyers and personnel executives, not its auditors, should provide the needed assurance.

Degrees of Assurance. The auditor of record will be associated with a wide variety of financial information released by his clients, ranging from the audited annual report to news releases describing the financial effects of a contemplated acquisition. The degree of assurance the auditor of record can provide will obviously vary depending on the nature and significance of the information and the extent of his involvement. Even today, the independent accountant finds it difficult to communicate the extent of assurance his audit provides; tomorrow, the auditor of record is likely to face an even greater challenge.

Specific Areas of Extension

Although it will take a number of years for the auditor of record concept to fully evolve, and the specific responsibilities may differ from the views stated in this section, the auditor may soon expand his role in certain specific areas consistent with the overall concept.

Internal Controls. Currently, the auditor carries out his study of the client's internal accounting control systems to assess their reliability for purposes of determining the extent of other substantive audit procedures he considers appropriate. Because inadequate controls raise doubts about the recorded financial data, the auditor increases the extent of other procedures performed; effective controls suggest that the auditor may rely on the information and that other procedures may be appropriately restricted. However, if the auditor does not intend to rely on an aspect of his client's accounting control system,[5] he may properly choose to omit its study and evaluation in performing an audit in accordance with GAAS.

As a result of the Foreign Corrupt Practices Act of 1977 and related SEC action, there is now much more emphasis on the study and evaluation of internal control. To determine if they are in compliance with the Foreign Corrupt Practices Act, many companies are conducting intensive examinations of their systems of internal control. The SEC had considered requiring management to represent in annual reports to shareholders that its systems of internal control provide reasonable assurances that the broad objectives of internal accounting control are achieved "without regard to materiality of amounts" (Securities Act Release 34-15572). The SEC withdrew this proposal in ASR 274 (1980), but its very existence illustrates the tenor of the times. Independent auditors may be involved in two ways: first, they are now assisting their clients in conducting internal control evaluations, and second, the issuance of SAS 30 (AU 642) will bring more public reporting on controls.

Not surprisingly, the Cohen Commission has recommended that evaluation of internal control form the core of the extended audit function. The commission suggests that, during an audit, the auditor "review and test the entire accounting control system"—not just the aspects on which he plans to rely. His objective is to provide himself with the ability to judge whether controls "provide reasonable, though not absolute, assurance that the system is free of material weaknesses" (CAR, p. 61). Auditors can do more in the area of providing assurances about internal controls, short of absolutes and having some regard for materiality. The problem, as with any overall improvements to benefit society, is the cost and who will pay it. It is in the area of auditor association with internal control systems that the auditors' clients are most reluctant to pay increased fees—the cost of complying with a prospective regulatory requirement so far appears to overwhelm the direct benefits perceived by the client.

Interim Financial Information Review. Investors and creditors require timely financial information that will aid them in deciding how to employ their capital.

---

[5] An auditor may choose not to study an aspect of the system because it does not involve transactions that could have a material effect on the financial statements or because placing reliance on the system may be less efficient than other audit approaches.

Although annual financial statements often form the core of investment and credit decisions, yearly information is not enough. Interim financial reports, usually issued quarterly, have become important sources of timely financial information.

The nature of the auditor's involvement with interim reporting varies from company to company. The next step in the evolution of the audit function includes establishing requirements for the extent and timeliness of the auditor's review and report on interim financial information. While a formal audit is not called for, some level of evaluation of internal control, and attention to the manner in which management prepares estimates, would seem likely components of an interim review.

The added assurance auditors can provide on interim financial information should benefit the investing public. Yet there is some question about the overall costs of obtaining these benefits; greater audit fees will be required. Though some argue that this comprehensive association will actually reduce the cost of the audit itself by eliminating much of the time-consuming verification in an annual audit, this does not happen now, as audits are not simply a standard list of steps, but are a series of interdependent procedures not necessarily reduced when only one of the purposes of a procedure is eliminated. Efficiency should continue to improve, but not enough to offset the cost of greater involvement.

Financial Forecasts. Although interim financial reports reflect ongoing developments on a more timely basis than annual financial statements, this may not be enough. Information that gives insight into the future directions of a business, such as forecasts of a company's plans, projected earnings, and cash flow, is now under serious consideration. Under the best of conditions, predicting remains a risky undertaking, and because projections cannot be verified, forecasts are not comparable to other kinds of financial information.

To what degree should the auditor associate himself with the forecasting process? As discussed in Chapter 33, standards for forecast reviews have just been released by the AICPA, and this may give impetus to the SEC's encouragement that forward-looking information be presented. At present, the biggest barrier to auditor involvement in the forecasting process is the threat of litigation, though a "safe harbor" is provided for information attested to in SEC filings (assuming the data was prepared in good faith and with a reasonable basis). Eventually, these difficult issues should be resolved, and association with ongoing financial forecasts may take its place as one of the auditor's extended responsibilities.

Costs

How will these evolutionary proposals affect the cost of auditing? The direct cost of carrying out an audit can be determined with some certainty; it boils down to counting the hours the auditors spend on the job, calculating billing-rate extensions, adding expenses, and so on. The auditor can therefore say that the audit fee for XYZ Corporation is $100,000.

There has been some effort to apply cost-benefit analysis to the auditing process, but the results are not impressive. According to these analyses, *costs* include such factors as audit fees and the estimated related costs incurred by the organization buying the audit services. *Benefits* include the prevention of material misstatements in financial statements and the discovery or prevention of fraud. In theory, by balancing costs against benefits it should be possible to determine whether expected benefits justify the additional effort. As the Cohen Commission has noted, the "needed extent of auditing is achieved when the incremental cost of finding or preventing another misstatement or omission is equal to the loss that would be sustained by investors from not finding or deterring it" (CAR, p. 53).

Several factors hamper the application of a cost-benefit analysis. Many of the expected benefits of the auditors' extended role accrue to society at large: employees, investors, and creditors. Yet the direct costs of providing the services are borne by individual companies. If individual companies evaluate the public benefits differently or believe that providing social benefits is the responsibility of others, they may not be willing to pay the bill.

There also are societal factors influencing the evolving auditor's role that are beyond his control, and these factors are only coincidentally based on a rational assessment of costs and benefits. For example, the Foreign Corrupt Practices Act is the catalyst that may require auditors' involvement in internal control systems beyond what is needed to do an audit. Yet Congress did not investigate the costs and benefits; it seemed simply that the remedy was worth whatever the cost.

There is a real danger that the costs of any poorly conceived extension of the auditor's role will outweigh the benefits. Society's resources will then be consumed inefficiently, and participants in the financial accounting and reporting system may react with an unwillingness to see the auditor's role extended into other areas in which auditors' clients and the public can garner benefits in excess of costs.

A NOTE ON THE FUTURE

Certainly the profession faces risks and challenges, but all this attention should convince auditors of their crucial role in today's world—adding assurance to the information that serves as our commercial life's blood. Ultimately, auditors are public servants in the best sense of the phrase. Today's challenges, then, should be looked on as opportunities for both personal and professional growth—as opportunities to employ professional skills in solving numerous vexing problems. Taking advantage of these many opportunities, however, requires creativity, imagination, leadership, hard work, and sacrifice. In the past, the profession has demonstrated its willingness to step up to its responsibilities. It will do so in the future.

SUGGESTED READING

Burton, John C. "Fair Presentation: Another View." *CPA Journal,* June, 1975, pp. 13-19. This article reviews development and expansion of the phrase "present fairly in conformity with generally accepted accounting principles" at a time when the AICPA Auditing Standards Executive Committee had proposed a clarification in the auditor's report to the effect that "fairness" cannot exist outside the context of GAAP. The author asserts a far broader meaning.

Chatfield, Michael. *A History of Accounting Thought.* Huntington, N.Y.: Robert E. Krieger Publishing Company, 1977. This book was designed for students majoring in accounting, to show the relevance of history to current issues. Descriptions of early times are interestingly presented, and the contrast with the present is remarkable.

Commission on Auditors' Responsibilities. *Report, Conclusions, and Recommendations.* New York: AICPA, 1978. This commission was an independent group established by the AICPA in 1974 to "develop conclusions and recommendations regarding the appropriate responsibilities of independent auditors. It should consider whether a gap may exist between what the public expects or needs and what auditors can and should reasonably expect to accomplish. If such a gap does exist, it needs to be explored to determine how the disparity can be resolved" (p. xi). The late Manuel F. Cohen was the chairman, and thus the group is often referred to as the Cohen Commission. There is little doubt that the commission catalogued virtually all the problems and issues facing the contemporary auditor, and its tentative conclusions (1977) raised some concerns about moving too fast. (For example: Touche Ross & Co. *Response . . . to The Commission on Auditors' Responsibilities on its Report of Tentative Conclusions.* New York, 1977.) Subsequent to release of the final report in early 1978, many of the Cohen Commission's recommendations have been studied and implemented in a short time frame. Other events converging at the time cloud the issue of whether the commission's report was the cause or effect—or most likely some of both —of upheaval in the profession. (See Chapter 39 of this *Handbook* for a perspective.) The Cohen Commission report is "must" reading for any student of the accounting and auditing profession.

10

The Audit Committee

W. Donald Georgen

OVERVIEW AND EVOLUTION

The audit committee has become the focus of corporate accountability for publicly held companies,[1] responsible for overseeing the financial reporting function, understanding the function of and integrating their role with that of the outside and internal auditors, and, of late, overseeing corporate conduct in general.

The use of audit committees has powerful sponsors today, including the AICPA, the New York and American Stock Exchanges, the SEC, and Congress. There have been suggestions that the Congress should mandate corporate audit committees, their composition, and their duties. There are indications that such legislation might have strong proponents if introduced in the Congress today. And in 1978 the Commission on Auditors' Responsibilities gave a strong impetus to audit committees as a means of fortifying auditors' independence (CAR, p. 106).

Korn/Ferry International reported in 1973 that 72% of the primarily large industrial corporations that responded to its survey had audit committees; in 1979 the figure had risen to over 97%. Other surveys report similar results. Thus, audit committees now seem securely rooted in the corporate scene.

The origin of audit committees is obscure. Boards of banks and other financial institutions are among the earliest known to have had audit committees, perhaps because they were required by statute to conduct audits. The Prudential Insurance Company of America, for instance, has had an audit committee for 75 years. A few industrial companies also had audit committees quite early.

Audit committees first received outside attention in 1939 when the New York Stock Exchange report on the infamous *McKesson and Robbins* case (New York Stock Exchange, 1939) strongly endorsed audit committees as a means of assuring auditor independence: "Where practicable, the selection of the auditors by a special committee of the board composed of directors who are not officers of the company appears desirable." The SEC expressed a similar opinion about the case in 1940 (ASR 19).

Initially these early endorsements of audit committees by the New York Stock Exchange and the SEC had very little effect. In 1967 the AICPA recommended that publicly owned companies establish audit committees composed of outside directors (AICPA, 1967b), but by 1970 not much progress had been made; survey research indicated that the audit committee concept was not being widely used (Mautz and Neumann, 1970, p. 15). In 1977 the AICPA repeated its recommendation (AICPA, 1979f, p. 1) and urged its members to encourage their clients to establish audit committees, but the impetus was primarily in response to congressional pressures (see Chapter 39) aimed at laxities in corporate governance.

In addition to requiring audit committees as part of specific consent settlements,

---

[1] This chapter is written in the context of the audit committee of a publicly held company because the preponderance of discussion, proposals, and rules deal with public business enterprises. However, the chapter is equally applicable to fiduciary institutions that are not publicly traded companies (as that term is defined in AC 2071.06, fn. 1); numerous kinds of non-business enterprises, such as eleemosynary institutions or nonproprietary hospitals; and larger privately held businesses, especially if there are major outside lenders. Though the chapter encourages separate audit committees, if this is not feasible or desirable many of the guides and suggestions can be used directly by a board of directors or board of trustees.

the SEC has used its rule-making authority to encourage audit committee formation generally. It first required disclosure of the existence or nonexistence of audit committees in 1974 (ASR 165), and it strengthened those reporting requirements in its new corporate governance rules released in late 1978 (Release 34-15384). But a more persuasive force for creating audit committees has been the prospect that the SEC would adopt even more requirements. The SEC has been vocal about the idea that audit committees should be *required* if an audit is to be performed in accordance with GAAS.

The New York Stock Exchange policy (New York Stock Exchange, 1977) requiring all domestic companies with listed securities to establish and maintain audit committees effective June 30, 1978, was proposed shortly after NYSE Chairman William Batten received a letter strongly recommending the action from then SEC Chairman Roderick Hills. The NYSE rule requires that all audit committee members be nonmanagement directors—effectively outside directors only. Subsequently, SEC Chairman Harold Williams made a similar recommendation to the American Stock Exchange, but this was not adopted as a prerequisite to remain listed.[2]

ALLOCATING DIRECTORS' RESPONSIBILITIES

The "Corporate Director's Guidebook" states: "The fundamental responsibility of the individual corporate director is to represent the interests of the shareholders as a group, as the owners of the enterprise, in directing the business and affairs of the corporation within the law" (American Bar Association, 1976, p. 20). The guidebook goes on to state that while economic objectives play the primary role in corporate decision making (and the law only rarely holds the individual director responsible for other objectives), trends in society and law should also guide the individual director in monitoring and shaping corporate conduct (ABA, 1976, p. 20). A corporate director has a duty of loyalty to the enterprise and a duty of care, both imposed by federal and state statutes as interpreted by various regulatory agencies and the courts.

---

[2] American Stock Exchange Chairman Levitt appointed a Special Advisory Committee on Audit Committees to study the SEC's recommendation. The Amex board modified the committee's recommendations and adopted a policy recommending that the audit committees of all listed companies comprise entirely (rather than have a majority of) independent directors. The board also expanded its definition of independent director to include directors who "are free of any relationship that would interfere with the exercise of independent judgment" as well as nonofficers who are neither related to the company's officers nor represent concentrated family shareholdings. Approximately 75% of the companies whose stock is traded on the American Exchange have audit committees, but many do not exclude management directors from committee membership.

Amex rejected a rule like that of the New York Exchange, believing it would be unduly burdensome for small and medium-sized companies to comply. A number of such companies list their securities on the American Exchange, and in the absence of a similar requirement for over-the-counter companies, Amex felt it might have been competitively disadvantaged.

Thus the role of the director is constantly and significantly changing. As J. Wilson Newman stated in hearings before a congressional subcommittee: "Added responsibilities are being placed on directors and being demanded now; in terms of legal concept they have been there all the time, but now they have surfaced" (U.S. Congress, 1977, p. 128). In this post-Watergate era, directors are concerned with issues not likely to have been raised only a few years ago. Corporate conduct codes, illegal political contributions, bribery of foreign officials, and the environmental, social, and economic impact of all corporate activities are all regular topics for directors. The continuing challenge will be to anticipate the impact of new attitudes and interpretations so as to be prepared, which was not the case with foreign payoffs.

The Model Business Corporation Act, as amended in 1974, provides that "a director shall perform his duties as a director, including his duties as a member of any committee of the Board upon which he may serve, in good faith, in a manner he reasonably believes to be in the best interest of the corporation, and with such care as an ordinary prudent person in a like position would use under similar circumstances." The act entitles a director to rely on information, opinions, reports, or statements, including financial statements and other financial data prepared or presented by corporate employees, outside experts, or a board committee of which he is not a member, unless he has knowledge that would cause such reliance to be unwarranted. The director, then, is an overseer, challenging the company's alignment with broad objectives; he may rely on management and others to carry out charges and to measure success.

The expanded role of directors demands a greater time commitment from them than previously. A concurrent trend—increasing the proportion of nonmanagement directors—complicates the problem. This policy does, however, protect against the insularity possible when all directors are insiders, and directors with diverse backgrounds and expertise can expand the board's capacity to cope with expanding and complex responsibilities. Because outside directors have other time constraints, boards have developed various means, discussed below, to limit the time commitments required.

Coping With an Expanded Role

Three factors seem to contribute the most to board time efficiency gains: well-qualified members, improved board-support functions, and an expanded board committee structure.

Boards have aggressively sought qualified persons to add to their number, frequently engaging executive search firms and increasing directors' fees. In some cases, persons having particular backgrounds are sought; specialists can help the board to focus on the most important issues more quickly.

Greater support for board activities has sometimes resulted in more effective use of the board members' time. Information pertaining to matters under consideration by the board and its committees is routinely prepared and distributed. The internal audit function and members of operating management often undertake board-directed fact-finding tasks. One example of a report prepared especially for the board, that of the outside auditor's report for audit committees, is discussed later in this chapter.

Committee Structure

More and more board activities are conducted through committees. The board is able to increase its scrutiny of specific matters by assigning them to the committees. This increases the board's overall effectiveness, because the full board is able in a limited time to focus directly on the issues the committees identify as important. Effectiveness is also increased by placing members having specialized skills on committees where those skills are needed.

The committee structure also enables the board to take a more active role in supervising certain activities between board meetings. For example, audit committees often monitor adherence to company codes of conduct.

Finally, a corporation's public image can be improved through publicizing audit committees, perhaps improving the credibility of corporate financial disclosure and obviating questions about the auditor's independence.

Committee Authority

The formation of committees does not relieve other board members of responsibility for matters considered by those committees. In most jurisdictions there are legal restrictions on what can be delegated to committees. Ministerial or routine functions can be delegated, and so can some of the board's discretionary or judgmental powers. Usually the full board is responsible for areas such as amending or proposing amendments to bylaws; appointing or removing officers, directors, and committee members; determining to whom specific board powers can be delegated; and controlling possible abuse of delegated powers by committees. Possible areas of abuse include determining directors' salaries or fees and neutralizing the views of some board representatives by assigning only directors holding a certain view to committees having certain authority to act on the board's behalf.

Committees operate most effectively when there is a clear, preferably written delineation of their responsibilities and authority. The bylaws of a corporation usually specify some committees; others may be formed by formal board resolution or even by informal board action. Sometimes the board limits committee membership terms and staggers them to assure a reasonable degree of continuity. Other membership criteria are also used quite often. For example, senior management officials on the board often must make up the executive committee, and management directors are frequently precluded from audit committee membership (this is a NYSE requirement). Committees ordinarily summarize their activities in a report to the board indicating the actions they have undertaken and recommending solutions for the board to consider in areas reserved for the full board.

The Audit Committee's Responsibilities

Audit committees are formed to fulfill, not expand, existing board responsibilities. Yet it can be argued that having an audit committee increases the board's responsibility to identify and deal with problems warranting board-level attention by broadening the scope and consideration of financial matters coming within the board's purview. The corollary is that an audit committee reduces the board's ability to rely on others, because of the directors' increased personal knowledge of financial matters. Though these arguments can be raised, they cannot be sustained. It is a specious premise indeed that a board today will have less responsibility without an audit committee.

For openers, the pressures on boards to have audit committees are simply too great to ignore; not having an audit committee might in itself be enough to discredit a defense in a specific matter at issue. As a case in point, in 1975 the SEC publicly criticized the conduct* of the two outside directors of Stirling Homex (Release 34-11514) for failure to fulfill their responsibilities, though apparently neither director knew that the company's financial statements were false and misleading. The commission pointed to the infrequent and perfunctory nature of board meetings, the absence of an audit committee, and the directors' failure to become informed about and exercise control over the accounting principles in use as indications of inadequate care exercised by directors.

It is noteworthy that the SEC so far has refrained from imposing an audit committee requirement for registrants; this suggests that voluntary progress is at least meeting the threshold of SEC expectations.

In a case brought by the SEC (Litigation Release 8052), the court held that the Falstaff Brewing Company's 1977 proxy statement disclosure was materially false and misleading in that it gave the impression that the board of directors effectively exercised oversight of their company's accounting functions through an audit committee, whereas in fact that committee never met or functioned.

Although it is clear that the mere existence of an audit committee implies some level of activity and the recognition of at least general areas of responsibility, there are no specific requirements for activities the audit committee should undertake on behalf of the entire board. Thus, the functions assigned to audit committees as opposed to other board committees or reserved for the full board vary with the structure and philosophy of each board.

The dramatic increase in the percentage of companies having audit committees, the New York Stock Exchange's domestic company listing requirement, the Amex recommendation, and the SEC's disclosure requirements—all mentioned above— suggest that boards without audit committees may be hard pressed to defend their practice as meeting contemporary custom, especially if a previously undetected problem of the type ordinarily considered by audit committees arises.

PRINCIPAL AUDIT COMMITTEE ACTIVITIES

Traditionally, the activities of audit committees have included nominating or selecting outside auditors, approving their overall audit scope, reviewing the results of the audit, and reviewing the company's internal controls, including the activities of the internal audit staff. These functions (and some incidental activities) are reviewed in this section.

The SEC has recently influenced some companies to expand their audit committee activities beyond these traditional ones. For the most part, the SEC has spoken out on expanded audit committee activities, even in tangential releases. The SEC has also succeeded in having its more expansive ideas imposed on companies in consent decrees and litigation. The commission's litigation against Mattell (Litigation Release 6467), Lums (Litigation Release 6317), and Sanitas (Litigation Release 6952) resulted in the courts requiring those companies to establish audit committees with a broad range of authority.

Since the entry of final judgment in the SEC's case against Killearn Properties, Inc. (Litigation Release 6792), SEC officials have been touting it as the model audit committee. The Killearn case alleged misrepresentations and omissions in certain reports concerning transactions with another company in which officials of Killearn had financial or other interests. The ten activity areas in the Killearn consent decree go well beyond the usual audit committee scope. In addition to consenting to review all aspects of the independent auditors' examination, the internal audit function, and the company's accounting and reporting systems and practices, the Killearn audit committee agreed to undertake what the SEC has characterized as special duties, functions, and responsibilities: reviewing all financial disclosures to the press, the public, and the shareholders; approving the disposition of claims or litigation against officers, directors, employees, or controlling persons; and reviewing officers' and directors' activities. Appendix 10 contains a comprehensive summary of the Killearn audit committee's responsibilities.

In the following discussion of principal audit committee activities, the focus is on interaction with the outside auditor, whose diligence in anticipating the strengths and needs of the committee and its members and in fulfilling those needs can cause the committee to be a vital force rather than possibly an organizational formality. Recognize, however, that the audit committee can also interact with the internal audit function in the areas described below (except, of course, in the area of selecting auditors). The degree of internal audit involvement will vary more, company by company, than will the activities involving the outside auditors.

Nomination or Selection of Auditors

Audit Committee Authority. The audit committee may be authorized to nominate or select auditors directly, but usually the committee's responsibility is to make a recommendation for board action. Of course, a corporation may—and some do—provide in their bylaws that the stockholders appoint the auditors. In any event, many boards seek shareholder ratification of the auditor selection. A typical ratification proposal included in a proxy statement is shown in Figure 10.1.

Auditor Selection Considerations. The audit committee normally assesses (by observation and also formally) the auditors' qualifications. If an audit committee

---

SELECTION OF AUDITORS

The Board of Directors proposes and recommends the selection of Touche Ross & Co. to audit the accounts of the Company for the fiscal year ending July 25, 1981. That firm has audited the accounts of the Company since 1968 and the Company's principal predecessor continuously from 1938 until its merger into the Company in 1969. Representatives of Touche Ross & Co. intend to be present at the annual meeting and will have an opportunity to make a statement if they desire to do so. These representatives will also be available to respond to appropriate questions. The membership of the Audit Committee of the Board of Directors of the Company is set forth above under the heading "Information Concerning the Board and Its Committees."

FIGURE 10.1 TYPICAL AUDITORS' RATIFICATION
SOURCE: Alexander's, Inc., 1980 Proxy Statement.

is considering new auditors, it usually screens many firms and asks several to submit proposals. In addition to considering independence, the firm's reputation (including litigation against the firm), its quality control system (including reports on peer reviews), and fee estimates, the audit committee assesses qualifications in relation to the company's needs. For example, the committee considers the range of services the firm offers, and the level of industry and other technical expertise possessed by the firm and the individuals who would be assigned to the audit engagement. Audit committees of multilocation companies also consider whether the audit firms have offices in the countries and cities in which these companies operate.

Each year the audit committee should evaluate the past performance of the auditing firm: the quality of the professional services rendered, the firm's recommendations for improvements, the firm's efficiency and effectiveness in conducting the examination and providing other services, and the overall strength of the relationship. The evaluation is based partly on auditor/audit committee interaction, mostly at meetings, but it is principally dependent on input from management.

In making its evaluation, the audit committee must remain cognizant of the SEC requirements specifically dealing with auditors' independence on an ongoing basis, not just in conjunction with an initial appointment. In addition to determining that the firm and its members had no direct or material indirect interest in the company, the audit committee must evaluate whether the firm's independence has been impaired by other relationships. For example, the audit committee must remain aware of the possible impact on independence of nonaudit services[3] and clerical accounting assistance the audit firm may be asked to provide. Some audit committees request a letter from the auditors stating that they are independent and outlining how their independence determination was made.

Figure 10.2 summarizes the issues an audit committee should consider in evaluating an audit firm. The questions in Figure 10.2, as well as those in Figures 10.4-10.9, are illustrative rather than exhaustive, and some are deliberately phrased in a less-than-precise manner, as might be the case in actual situations. Note that the answers will not be facile; a great deal of work may be involved in answering, and the auditor should obviously do his homework.

Approval of Overall Audit Scope

A fundamental point about audit committees needs recognition here: the committee members need not have a detailed understanding of what the auditor does—his scope, the decisions he makes, how he performs his audit. Rather than attempt to check the adequacy of the auditor's scope, the audit committee can "audit" the auditor's system of quality control (for example, see QC 90).

---

[3] The SEC's regulations require that companies disclose in their proxy statements a description of each professional service provided by the principal auditor, whether each was approved in advance by the board or audit committee, and whether the possible impact on the accountant's independence of rendering the service was considered. The disclosure must include the percentage relationship of the fee for each nonaudit service to total fees if over 3%, and the full details of noncustomary fee arrangements (ASR 250, June, 1978). See Chapter 39 for a full discussion of scope of services.

QUESTIONS FOR AUDITORS

1. Is your firm a member of the SEC Practice Section of the AICPA Division of Firms? When was your firm last peer reviewed, and what was the nature of the report rendered?*

2. Does your firm meet all SEC Practice Section membership requirements? **

3. Is your firm independent of the company?

4. Have you been engaged to perform nonaudit services without advance general or specific approval of the audit committee as required by ASR 250?

5. What are the qualifications of your firm in our industry/locale and of the partner who would be in charge of our engagement?

6. Do you have offices in _____ (places where significant operations are located?)

7. What type of support services (newsletters, industry programs, etc.) and informative consultation can your firm provide us?

8. Do you regularly furnish suggestions for improvements in controls and operational efficiencies?

9. What is the range of tax, management, and other consulting services you can offer without affecting your independence?

10. How are your fees determined, and how would you propose to minimize them and still maintain your quality standards in this audit?

11. What would be the advantages/disadvantages of our changing to your audit firm?

12. How do you coordinate performance of the work of other offices, and to what extent does the engagement partner in charge participate in a review of their work?

QUESTIONS FOR MANAGEMENT

1. Have the auditors been responsive on a timely basis to requests for assistance and met preestablished deadlines?

2. Are the auditors sensitive to your organizational structure and do they communicate their observations, findings, recommendations, and criticisms at the appropriate management levels?

3. What is your assessment of the technical quality of the auditors' services?

4. Do the auditors appear to manage their work effectively to avoid incurring unnecessary time charges?

5. Does the audit partner devote sufficient time to the engagement?

* SEC Practice Section member firms must submit to a peer review once every three years. On completion of the review, the review team submits (1) a report containing its evaluation of whether the reviewed firm's quality control system and compliance therewith comports with professional standards and (2) written communication of matters the review team believes require corrective action.

** SEC Practice Section members must adhere to AICPA quality control standards, ensure that all professionals meet continuing professional education requirements, assign new audit partners to each SEC engagement of which another partner was in charge for five consecutive years, and have a partner other than the one in charge of each SEC engagement perform a preissuance review of the audit report. These and other requirements are reviewed in Chapter 39.

FIGURE 10.2 QUESTIONS AN AUDIT COMMITTEE MIGHT ASK IN ASSESSING AN AUDITOR'S QUALIFICATIONS

Of course the audit committee can benefit from having a depth of knowledge in accounting and auditing matters, though this is not a qualification for membership. For this reason, retired partners from CPA firms will probably be more frequently seen on audit committees in the future.

Usually, the audit committee should consider the overall audit plan and scope before a significant amount of work has been done, but it can also meet its responsibility by assessing after its completion whether the audit was appropriately performed.

Audit Scope Determinants. Typically, an audit committee, in reviewing the planned audit scope, considers external reporting requirements, financial and ac-counting policies, and organizational, operational, and business considerations, including their impact on processing and interpreting accounting information. When it considers external reporting requirements, the audit committee must be aware of groups such as the SEC having a special interest in the company's financial information and then understand the information that must be furnished to them. These groups might also include other regulatory agencies and governmental units imposing audit requirements, and lenders. Counsel, management, and the auditors can provide detailed input. The audit committee should be satisfied that the scope of the audit contemplated by the independent auditors adequately considers all important reporting needs and audiences.

Audit scope also depends on a company's financial and accounting policies. Generally, more audit procedures are performed if a company defers costs or revenues; the specific procedures depend on which acceptable accounting method the company adopts. Often, the considerations having the greatest impact on audit scope are those related to the industry, organization, operations, and business con-ditions of a particular company. These conditions affect not only the choice of accounting principles and methods but the manner in which accounting information is processed and the particular types of accounting information that might have a material impact on the financial statements. The number of operational units, the degree of local autonomy, the extent of vendor and customer concentration, the nature of the goods or services produced by the enterprise, the basis on which employees are compensated, and other factors all influence the audit approach taken. (See Chapter 12 for a discussion of audit scope.)

The audit committee should have the auditors explain the criteria they use to select locations to be visited and the type of audit coverage planned for each location. The committee should also understand the extent to which the auditor plans to rely on internal accounting controls and how the principal factors listed above influenced his planning.

The Audit Committee's Evaluation. In evaluating the auditors' approach, the au-dit committee should determine whether the audit plan will adequately cover all the areas with which the committee is concerned. For example, the committee may wish to have the audit cover selected areas in greater depth than the auditors' plan based on generally accepted auditing standards. Some audit committees routinely ask the auditors to review officers' expense accounts or to expand audit coverage at certain locations. The committee may also ask the auditors to perform special reviews of certain internal accounting control aspects not required for audit pur-poses, in order to assist it in monitoring compliance with specific corporate policies.

Ordinarily, these additional matters are considered at the same time as the audit requirements so that greater efficiency can be achieved by integrating extra-audit goals into the audit logistics.

Review of Audit Results

The board of directors must understand the issues involved in complex financial and accounting matters. Financial reporting requirements for companies cover a vast area and encompass GAAP, applicable regulatory reporting requirements, and industry practices. In addition, audit performance and reporting standards—GAAS—are involved. A director is not expected to be expert in all of these areas, but he should have some familiarity with them. An inquiring mind, broad knowledge about corporate matters (including experience in financial and general management functions), and sufficient time to gain an understanding of the specific requirements equip an audit committee member to fulfill his obligations.

Understanding the Issues. Ordinarily, audit committees acquire the knowledge they need to review the results of the audit by reading the financial statements, the forepart of the annual report on Form 10-K, and other data, and by briefings from management and the independent auditors on the impact of accounting principles especially important to the company. Additional sources of information are the financial press, directors' publications, and the newsletters prepared by large accounting firms that summarize new accounting, auditing, and regulatory developments and analyze their features. An audit committee need not probe all areas in depth, but each member should know factors influencing asset valuations, the recording of contingencies, or disclosure in the financial statements.

Once they understand the issues, audit committee members can define their specific information needs and obtain them from the independent auditors, the internal auditors, and financial management; and they can isolate the sensitive areas requiring their in-depth attention. They can then devote their time to obtaining a more thorough understanding of the issues in sensitive or important areas and to advising management on the way these issues should be handled. For example, the audit committee can question the auditors and management on matters such as whether the company's accounting practices comport with those of others in the company's industry, the basis for major judgments such as estimating inventory obsolescence or receivables collectibility, changes in accounting principles, and auditor-perceived pressures by management to contrive desired results.

Review of Internal Controls

Although review and oversight of a company's system of internal controls (see Chapter 13) has traditionally been viewed as part of the audit committee's function, the Foreign Corrupt Practices Act of 1977 has accentuated the board's responsibility for internal control matters.

The Foreign Corrupt Practices Act. As its title suggests, the FCPA designates as criminal offenses certain corporate activities that are intended to induce foreign officials (and specific others) to help obtain or retain business.

The act requires companies registered with the SEC to keep accurate and reasonably detailed records of transactions that occur, and to maintain internal controls sufficient to provide reasonable assurances that specified objectives are met. These objectives include that (1) transactions are executed in accordance with management's authorization; (2) records are sufficient to permit preparation of appropriate financial statements; (3) access to assets is limited to authorized persons; and (4) periodic checks are made of the existence of recorded assets, and differences resolved. In a 1976 report to Congress, the SEC attributed many of the questionable corporate payments revealed in the aftermath of Watergate to faulty internal control systems employed by the offending companies (SEC, 1976, p. 6).

The Foreign Corrupt Practices Act underscores the audit committee's obligation to the board to ensure that management maintains an appropriate internal control system. The committee should not simply coordinate the external audit function with internal activities but should understand (1) the specific manner in which the broad internal accounting control objectives are interpreted and applied within the company, (2) whether the control environment and specific control procedures could reasonably be expected to accomplish their specific control objectives, and (3) whether appropriate monitoring devices are in place to detect disfunctions.

To fulfill this role, the audit committee must know the manner in which decision-making authority is allocated among management and supervisory personnel and whether management measures the degree of organizational responsiveness to reported exceptions. The audit committee should inquire if management has rechallenged its organizational structure and control systems, to assure that they are aligned with board-established policies and delegated authority. This inquiry should determine who was involved in the reassessment efforts, how scope and findings were documented, and how misalignments were dealt with. The committee may ask the outside auditors to monitor the process and report findings to them.

In relation to its internal accounting control responsibilities, the audit committee should oversee the functioning of administrative controls as well, because these permeate the control environment. Administrative controls are broader in scope than the specific accounting control procedures designed to prevent and detect errors. They include controls that track development of laws and regulations and ensure compliance with them, and they encompass many aspects of financial and operational organization. Administrative controls include the ongoing measurement of the effectiveness of present controls and consideration of whether changes might result in improvements. Since the company's organizational structure defines the boundaries of administrative control, the audit committee will often approve changes made in financial management and the organizational structure prior to their occurrence.

Possible Management Reporting on Internal Control. The SEC had proposed that management provide, in annual reports to shareholders and annual reports on Form 10-K, a statement on whether or not the internal control systems in place during the year provided reasonable assurances that the internal accounting control objectives specified above were met, and that an independent public accountant examine and report on this statement by management.

In introducing the internal control reporting proposal, the commission noted that the board of directors' role includes overseeing the establishment and maintenance of a strong control environment and procedures for evaluating an internal control system. The SEC concurred with the AICPA Special Advisory Committee on

Internal Accounting Control's statement that "it is unlikely that management can have reasonable assurance that the broad objectives of internal accounting control are being met unless the company has an environment that establishes an appropriate level of control consciousness" (AICPA, 1979r). While this proposal was not adopted as a rule, the commission's intent to monitor and encourage expanded activity in this area is clear.

Other Audit Committee Activities

The board of directors may assign special projects to the audit committee to ensure that the overall corporate disclosure obligations are satisfied. These projects may include investigating for questionable payments, monitoring compliance with the corporate code of conduct, or evaluating acquisition candidates. Other activities in which audit committees engage are generally nonrecurring.

Most audit committees devote some of their meeting time to their own education, selecting certain aspects of the company's internal control systems and accounting principles employed, other financial reporting requirements, and generally accepted auditing standards to study in depth each year. The educational efforts may also address legal considerations and the impact of new nonfinancial laws and litigation matters. The audit committee's educational efforts may reveal areas and issues that should receive greater attention from them and from the board as a whole.

TYPES OF AUDIT COMMITTEE MEETINGS

Audit committees meet from two to six times a year, and most meet three or four times. The meetings are usually supplemented by occasional phone conversations and informal discussions at board and committee meetings. The scope of the auditor's examination is usually considered in a meeting held early in the year, before significant audit work has begun. Generally, another meeting is held after completion of the audit but before financial results are announced; the draft financial statements and accompanying auditor's report are usually reviewed in detail at this meeting. Another meeting might be devoted to a review of internal control considerations, and still another to the upcoming annual shareholders' meeting. Other meetings may cover a variety of topics at any time during the year.

In reviewing the discussion that follows about meetings, it might be helpful to keep in mind the practices that are believed to foster the audit committee's success, as shown in Figure 10.3.

Audit Scope Meeting

The principal discussion at the audit scope meeting is about the auditor's planned approach to the audit examination. The meeting may begin with a discussion of critical dates and plans for engagement timing, staffing, and the engagement budget. Broad aspects of the plan for conducting the engagement will ordinarily be discussed, including the auditor's engagement to perform a formal limited review of interim financial statements or other audit-related work known at the outset of the engagement.

Most Important Practices	Ranking By			
	Chief Executive Officers	Nonofficer Directors	Internal Auditors	Independent CPAs
Ready access by audit committee to independent auditors	1	1	1	1
Regular briefings of audit committee by independent auditors	2	2	3	2
Availability to audit committee of relevant information and prompt providing of data requested	3	4	2	4
Prompt notification to audit committee of problems by independent auditors	4 *	3		3
Prompt notification to audit committee of problems by management	4 *			
Ready access by audit committee to internal auditors		5	4	
Providing of agenda, written statement of pertinent issues, and related material in advance of meetings			5	5

* Indicates identical ranking score.

FIGURE 10.3　IMPORTANCE OF PRACTICES CONTRIBUTING TO SUCCESS OF CORPORATE AUDIT COMMITTEES

SOURCE: Robert Mautz and Fred Neumann, *Corporate Audit Committees: Policies and Practices* (Cleveland: Ernst & Whinney, 1977), p. 68.

Timing considerations include agreement on the schedule for subsequent audit committee meetings, and the ground rules for reporting unexpected events to the audit committee in between meetings should be understood. It is often helpful to have on hand a draft of the auditor's engagement letter to focus on the important parts of the engagement.

While the auditor's engagement letter sets forth in summary his understanding with his client as to the terms and objectives of the engagement, considerably greater detail is generally provided to the audit committee. At the audit scope meeting, the auditor explains his planned approach based on his analysis of the industry and business risk characteristics of the company, i.e., areas where the potential for errors or omissions might be material. Against this framework, the auditor relates his approach to determining the operating units and other areas to be covered, the depth of coverage to be employed, and his plan for coordinating with the internal audit function.

The auditor will normally have received and documented the system of internal accounting control in prior audits and will have identified areas where examination efficiencies can result from testing and relying on the system. His plan will also include a broad outline of the substantive procedures he plans to perform (see Chapter 12).

Especially when the enterprise is complex, time will not permit the auditor to explain all details of the audit. So instead, many audit committees explore at least one phase in great depth each year, most commonly by having the auditor explain his approach to auditing transactions processed through one of the major accounting cycles or systems. This in-depth analysis of the selected system should identify the major controls on which the auditor plans to rely as a basis for limiting substantive procedures. By following this approach, the audit committee can, over time, obtain a detailed understanding of the various systems of internal controls and accounting processes.

Analysis of a selected area may take place after the audit scope meeting; it may even take place after the auditor has completed his tests of the system, so that problems encountered may then be considered.

Figure 10.4 illustrates some questions an audit committee might ask about audit scope.

Financial Statements Meeting

At this meeting the audit committee formally approves the draft financial statements on behalf of the board or, as is more commonly the case, recommends that the board approve them. Financial management normally begins the meeting with its presentation of the draft financial statements. The discussion will center on the most significant matters depicted in the financial statements and on accounting judgment areas. The judgment areas and the attendant risks that management's estimates might ultimately prove to be in error are the object of most of the audit committee members' questions, but they are also interested in trends and changing patterns implicit in the financial statements.

Financial Statement Disclosures. The committee will devote significant attention to the disclosures in and accompanying the financial statements. Usually, the inquiry will begin with the accounting policy statement, and the committee will ask about changes in accounting principles or the methods of their application. They may also ask for a comparison of the company's accounting methods with those of the industry.

Disclosure of commitments and contingencies is also an area involving a significant amount of audit committee discussion. The committee members may wish to challenge whether the outcome of a particular contingency is sufficiently predictable to warrant recording in the accounts; if not, they will be concerned that the disclosure convey the appropriate level of uncertainty.

1. Have all of the company's consolidated and unconsolidated units been considered in formulating your planned audit scope? If not, which ones were excluded and why? Where there are several audit firms, have you participated in scoping the work of other auditors, and how will you satisfy yourselves as to its adequacy?
2. Has management attempted to restrict or, in fact, restricted your audit scope in any way?
3. Do you plan an audit scope significantly different than last year's? Do you plan significant modifications this year in the nature and extent of procedures to be performed in any major locations?
4. Have you identified possible indications of change in the character of our business? What areas do you intend to emphasize?
5. To what extent do you plan to rely on the company's systems of internal controls in conducting your examination?
6. What techniques and approach do you plan to employ with respect to our EDP systems?
7. How do you plan to work with the internal audit department in your audit approach?
8. Is there any area in which additional company assistance could significantly reduce the planned extent of your work?
9. Does the planned scope of your examination include a review of officers' expense accounts?
10. To what extent does your plan reflect expected changes in accounting principles and auditing standards?
11. Explain how your audit plan would uncover material (and perhaps less-than-material) employee defalcations or fraud, questionable payments, or violations of laws or regulations, if any?
12. What areas of the audit are deserving of special attention by the audit committee, and why?

FIGURE 10.4   QUESTIONS AN AUDIT COMMITTEE MIGHT ASK AUDITORS ABOUT AUDIT SCOPE

Supplemental Disclosures. In its review of financial statements (or when later available), the committee will want to cover management's discussion and analysis of the results of operations (see Chapter 4), required supplemental disclosures (e.g., changing prices data, discussed in Chapter 8), the chairman's and president's letters, and other disclosures and analyses normally included in the annual report to shareholders. Committee members will want to see whether these disclosures raise questions about the financial statements or about the disclosures themselves, and will want to eliminate any inconsistencies and wrong inferences.

The Auditors' Participation. The committee will ordinarily ask the auditors to explain the effects of new accounting and auditing standards and what matters they consider most sensitive. The auditors will recite or describe the nature of their report and fully explain any qualifications or unusual modifications. The auditors will also discuss unexpected conditions that caused them to modify their audit approach, and any other matters they believe the audit committee should know about the audit, the financial statements, and the related disclosures.

As in all aspects of audit committee operations, the outside auditors' candor and the comprehensiveness of their comments are important ingredients for audit committee effectiveness. But also, to conserve audit committee time, it is important that before the meeting the auditors and management discuss with each other the matters to be presented, so that redundancy is eliminated and possible disagreements are identified and dealt with appropriately if possible. Figures 10.5, 10.6, 10.7, and 10.8 illustrate questions the audit committee might ask about the financial

---

1. Are other companies in our industry giving more or less information than we are planning to give?

2. Have there been any significant changes in the company's accounting practices during the year? Do all of the company's accounting practices fall within generally accepted accounting principles? Where "free choice" alternative principles are available, which ones are being used by the company? What would be the impact of using the other available choices? Are the company's accounting practices appropriate for its specific needs? Are they consistent with predominant industry practice?

3. Were there any material unusual items reflected in the operating results for the year? Are any of our operations incurring a loss?

4. What are the reasons for excluding some subsidiary companies from full consolidation, and what are the prospects for mandated changes in this practice?

5. Were there any important transactions with nonsubsidiary affiliated or related companies?

6. How are earnings per share computed? Why don't the quarterly figures add up to the cumulative figure?

7. Are there any new or proposed FASB statements or SEC requirements that will materially affect the company's accounting methods or reported financial position in the near future? Has there been full compliance with existing statements and requirements?

8. Does the company follow any accounting principles contrary to the recommendations contained in AcSEC SOP's or AICPA audit and accounting guides?

9. Did you have any disagreements with management as to accounting, auditing, and reporting matters?

FIGURE 10.5 QUESTIONS AN AUDIT COMMITTEE MIGHT ASK ABOUT FINANCIAL STATEMENTS IN GENERAL

1. For what periods are the company's time deposits committed? What are the company's compensating balance requirements?

2. Has the quoted market of the company's short-term investments changed significantly since year-end?

3. Why is the allowance for doubtful receivables lower than last year despite an increase in receivables? What is the average age of accounts compared to a year ago, and how is the change explained? Is the company following an appropriate credit policy? Are there large individual amounts where collectibility is in question? Are any of these receivables for an extended time period? Have receivables been discounted or pledged? Are there receivables from officers or other management employees?

4. Are there adequate physical controls over inventory? Has the LIFO method of valuing inventories been considered?

5. What steps have the independent public accountants taken with respect to inventories at outside locations?

6. Does the company generate internal reports on the condition of inventories so that timely action can be taken with respect to possible obsolescence? Were any significant write-downs incurred? Generally, what have the outside auditors done to satisfy themselves that the inventory as stated on the balance sheet does not contain obsolete or excess stock?

7. What is the basis of valuation of long-term investments? Is the valuation more or less than quoted market?

8. How does the company's equity in foreign companies compare with cost? What is the total amount at risk when intercompany receivables and temporary advances are considered? How does the company effectively hedge its exposure?

9. Why does the company use accelerated methods of depreciation for some items but not for others? Why is the same method of depreciation used for book and tax purposes? Is the company's policy regarding the differentiation between capital and expense items responsive to its needs?

10. Does the company have any significant proposed leases that might require capitalization?

11. Is the company policy regarding amortization of intangible assets realistic? Should the company consider amortization of goodwill arising from acquisition before November 1, 1970?

12. Are there nonoperating properties or idle facilities, and why have they been retained?

FIGURE 10.6   QUESTIONS AN AUDIT COMMITTEE MIGHT ASK ABOUT ASSETS

1. What is the status of federal income taxes, such as open years and items in dispute? Does the accrual for federal income taxes appear to be adequate to cover possible assessments upon examination by the IRS?
2. Has the company complied with financially related debt indenture covenants, or have waivers been required? Have all significant restrictions been disclosed?
3. Are there any restrictions pertaining to senior stock issues that effectively limit company activities? Has the company purchased any treasury stock during the year, and, if so, for what purposes?
4. Are there any contingencies of a legal or other nature as to which the appropriate treatment is in doubt?
5. Has the company made any unusual commitments, e.g., the purchase of inventories or the acquisition or construction of property assets? How well does the company's capital budgeting system seem to be working?
6. What is the relationship between the company's funding of pension plans and the accounting provisions made for them? Has the company's funding policy changed? Can the funding policy be changed under the provisions of ERISA?

FIGURE 10.7 QUESTIONS AN AUDIT COMMITTEE MIGHT ASK ABOUT LIABILITIES AND STOCKHOLDERS' EQUITY

1. Did management attempt to or actually restrict your work in any way?
2. How cooperative were company personnel?
3. In what specific ways was your audit approach modified from the plan you discussed with us and why?
4. Will your report be nonstandard in any respect?
5. Did any possible improprieties come to your attention during the course of your examination? If so, how were they resolved?
6. What work did you do with respect to acquired businesses?
7. What is your opinion as to the quality of the accounting and financial staffs?
8. Were any important internal control deficiencies encountered after our meeting concerning internal controls?
9. At any time during the year were errors found that necessitated correction of previously reported quarterly results?
10. What was the nature and scope of your review of disclosures, other than the financial statements, in the annual report for shareholders and in Form 10-K?

FIGURE 10.8 QUESTIONS AN AUDIT COMMITTEE MIGHT ASK ABOUT AUDIT RESULTS

statements and the audit results. Depending on the company, many or most of the financial statement questions may be directed to financial management, with the auditor commenting and corroborating.

Comments and Recommendations Meeting

The principal topic at the comments and recommendations meeting will ordinarily be internal accounting controls. The Foreign Corrupt Practices Act and the SEC's related reporting proposals (Release 34-15572, withdrawn with an admonition that the SEC will monitor voluntary reporting) have heightened the awareness of directors to exceptions and errors reported by the system as possible indications of a need to make preventive systems changes. Today a more formal record of the management control process is demanded, and thus its review is a regular part of audit committee activities. Many committees now maintain a continuing dialogue with management about programs to maintain up-to-date systems documentation and to monitor compliance with administrative and internal accounting control requirements.

The FCPA has also increased recognition of the importance of internal audit, both as a significant factor in the control environment and as a means of monitoring the disciplines involved in the system; as a result, interaction of the audit committee and internal audit has increased greatly in the past few years. But most audit committees traditionally look to the independent auditors for pertinent facts and expert guidance at the comments and recommendations meeting.

Generally accepted auditing standards require that independent CPAs report to the board of directors or its audit committee "material internal control weaknesses" that come to their attention in the course of examining the financial statements.[4]

In addition to noting material weaknesses, if any, most audit firms inform clients of areas where they believe internal controls could be improved or operational efficiencies effected through modifications to the systems. In some cases, the auditors also provide summaries of internal control lapses found through the audit process. Typically, management will have met with the auditors prior to the audit committee's consideration of these matters and prepared a plan of action for dealing with each of the auditors' recommendations. In this fashion, the audit committee's time is not taken up while management and the auditors reconcile differing viewpoints, and neither management nor the auditors are embarrassed because they did not anticipate the other's position.

After having thoroughly discussed the issues, the audit committee should consider management's statement concerning its responsibility for the preparation of financial statements and for maintaining a satisfactory system of internal accounting controls.[5]

---

[4] The phrase *material internal control weakness* describes "a condition in which the auditor believes the prescribed procedures or the degree of compliance with them does not provide reasonable assurance that errors or irregularities in amounts that would be material in the financial statements being audited would be prevented or detected within a timely period by employees in the normal course of performing their assigned functions" (AU 320.68).

[5] The Commission on Auditors' Responsibilities recommended that managements report on their responsibilities for accounting and financial matters (CAR, 1978, pp. 76-77), and the Financial Executives Institute has urged its members to adopt the recommendation. Both the FEI (1978) and the AICPA (1979s) have developed reporting guidelines.

While memories are still fresh, plans might be made with respect to management's internal control system objectives for the next year. The discussion might include programmed systems changes, detailed reassessments of cost/benefit relationships in particular areas or the criteria for making them, internal control difficulties caused by organizational changes, DP-related concerns, and implementation of planned corrective activities in response to the auditor's findings and recommendations.

Figure 10.9 provides a list of questions that could be raised about internal control at the comments and recommendations meeting.

Annual Shareholders' Meeting

In recent years the tone of some annual shareholders' meetings has been acrimonious, with questions raised as challenges or accusations rather than as requests for information. A number of companies have mitigated such problems by anticipating questions and preparing well-thought-out responses in advance. Some chief executive officers have found that their taking the initiative in addressing the most important likely issues in prepared oral remarks, letters to shareholders, or the annual report or 10-K contributes to a constructive shareholder dialogue. This approach conveys management's intention to be forthright and also assures that answers are framed in the proper perspective. Evenhanded responses to caustic questions will ensure that most shareholders will recognize and shy away from obstructive and irrelevant inquiries.

Since many of the key issues addressed at shareholders' meetings are financial, the audit committee is often extensively involved in the preparation for shareholders' meetings. Also, the audit committee is in the best position to obtain the benefit of the audit firm's experience gained in attending annual meetings of other clients. In advance of each year's round of annual meetings, many of the larger CPA firms prepare written communications to their clients about the principal new issues. The auditors are usually especially helpful in identifying the questions they expect might be addressed to them. Quite often, questions shareholders ask of the auditors are more properly answered by management, but the auditors may need to furnish management with information appropriate to use in response.

Annual meeting planning should be done after the financial statements have been approved and the comments and recommendations meeting has been held. The financial statements, internal controls, and auditors' recommendations can generate numerous shareholders' questions. Proxy statements, other materials sent to shareholders, recent press releases, and SEC filings are likely to have caught some shareholder's eye, so these also are normally reviewed in advance of the annual meeting.

Other Typical Meeting Topics

Additional audit committee meetings may be held for the purpose of dealing with any of the audit committee functions and activities discussed above. Specifically, at one of the meetings—usually the one that "closes out" the previous audit year—the audit committee will decide on the retention of the incumbent auditors for the ensuing year, and will take that recommendation to the full board; in many instances the retention will be put to the shareholders for a ratification vote, as

1. Have you any material weaknesses to report in internal accounting control?

2. Have you found other matters in the system of internal accounting control that call for corrective action?

3. Has management taken appropriate action in response to comments and recommendations you have made in the past?

4. Has the company documented its systems of internal accounting controls so as to adequately support representations about them in the management's published report on its responsibility for the financial statements and the internal accounting controls?

5. Have you modified your planned audit approach based on the results of your tests of the system of internal accounting control?

6. Is the internal audit function adequately staffed and organized?

7. What activities would you recommend the audit committee undertake in connection with its oversight of internal control?

8. In your judgment, has the company succeeded in creating an environment conducive to achievement of the objectives of internal control?

9. Does the system in place provide reasonable assurance that errors and conditions contrary to policy are reported?

10. Does management do an adequate job of monitoring reported exceptions as possible indications of a need for improvement?

11. During the course of your examination, did any conditions come to your attention that may warrant in-depth investigation by management, the internal auditors, or the audit committee?

12. What are the critical internal control areas that warrant the attention of the audit committee, and why are they important?

13. What is your impression of the quality of the long-range planning and budgetary controls employed by the company?

14. Does the company use its electronic data processing equipment effectively?

15. Are the company's policy and procedure manuals reasonably formal and maintained on a current basis?

16. Do company procedures designed to avoid conflicts of interest seem adequate in the circumstances?

17. Do you know whether management has exceeded its authority in any matters prescribed by the directors or failed to comply with any resolution passed by the directors?

FIGURE 10.9 QUESTIONS AN AUDIT COMMITTEE MIGHT ASK AUDITORS ABOUT INTERNAL CONTROL

discussed earlier and depicted in Figure 10.1. In situations in which the incumbent auditors might not be retained, the timing pattern will change.

Meetings are sometimes held when a prospectus for the sale of securities is in preparation or when there are to be other major releases to the public on important developments or activities. Meetings may be held to consider merger or acquisition prospects, including tender offers or takeover bids; major lawsuits filed against the company; engagement of the auditors to perform significant nonaudit services; updates on important new accounting or auditing standards or SEC rules; major organizational changes within the company; and the audits of financial statements of unconsolidated related entities, such as pension plans and investees accounted for on the equity method. Also, events that raise questions concerning the integrity of management might be considered at special meetings.

Although the SEC required the Killearn audit committee to review and approve all public releases containing financial information (see Appendix 10), most audit committees do not plan such extensive involvement. But if quarterly results are not reasonably in line with budgets or plans, if past audits have revealed significant errors that escaped timely interim detection, or if the auditors encounter a significant problem in their limited review of the quarterly financial statements, most audit committees will become involved prior to the issuance of the quarterly statements.

One of the most important topics for the audit committee to consider is its own agenda in light of evolving public expectations. The committee may make recommendations to the board as to matters that should come within its purview, be transferred to other board committees, or be dealt with by the board as a whole.

One final consideration is whether the audit committee should publish a report on its activities. There is a high probability that during the 1980s at least the largest companies will do so, either directly or by reference in management's report. Figure 10.10 shows a sample audit committee report.

AUDITOR/AUDIT COMMITTEE INTERACTION

In earlier years the role of the audit committee was conceived as little more than coordinating the independent auditors' examination of the company's financial statements. The expanding board of directors' role, and the idea that an audit committee improves the board's ability to fulfill it, are felt not only by the audit committee but also by the auditor. Audit committees often view the auditors as their fact-finding arm and as surrogates in making evaluations requiring the auditors' expertise.

Auditor Communication With the Audit Committee

Independent CPAs are responsible for bringing certain matters to the attention of a client's board of directors; when an audit committee exists, it is normally the appropriate vehicle for auditor/board communications. In addition to participating in audit committee discussions relating to the planned agenda items discussed below, the auditors should discuss other matters, as applicable, with the audit committee, including disputes with management concerning the selection or application

**Audit Committee: Independent
assessments of audits of GE**

The Audit Committee, which includes only
Directors from outside the Company, maintains an ongoing appraisal of the effectiveness of audits and the independence of
the public accountants. It recommends, for
approval by the full Board and the share
owners, the appointment of the independent public accountants. It also reviews
accounting principles and internal accounting controls, and the Annual Report and
proxy materials.

In February, May and September, 1978,
the Committee met with partners of Peat,
Marwick, Mitchell & Co. At the February
meeting, we reviewed the firm's audit for
1977, and inquired into the degree of
cooperation received from General Electric
in carrying out the audit. In May, we reviewed the organization and makeup of the
firm's audit team assigned to GE, its plan
for conducting the 1978 audit, and other
services to be provided.

At our May and September meetings,
we also met with the manager of GE's
corporate audit staff to review the organization and scope of the Company's own
internal audits.

On the basis of these reviews, we were
able to report with confidence to the full
Board that the resources allocated to the
audit function both by the independent auditors and by General Electric itself are
adequate to provide the assurances required by the Board.

We conducted a number of other reviews, including a meeting with the Senior
Vice President–Finance and the Senior
Vice President–General Counsel and Secretary to examine the results of reviews
and audits covering the compliance of employees with key GE policies.

FIGURE 10.10   SAMPLE AUDIT COMMITTEE REPORT
SOURCE: General Electric Company, 1978 Annual Report.

of accounting principles; conditions or transactions known or thought possibly to
be in violation of laws, regulations, or corporate policies (excepting only clearly
inconsequential items); situations potentially reflecting on management's integrity
or possible conflicts of interest; and any other matters that might be of sufficient
importance to warrant the board of directors' attention.

It is the auditors' obligation to be sensitive and alert to the needs of particular audit committees, even when specific ground rules for surfacing issues have not been articulated. Audit committees mature at various rates (Mautz and Neumann, 1977, pp. 88-90), and the relative importance of issues varies from company to company. On the other hand, auditors should guard against the natural tendency to provide the audit committee with a comprehensive and precise dissertation on all factors pertinent to a particular accounting or auditing issue. Since most audit committee members have a limited foundation in accounting and auditing and thus lack detailed technical know-how, such presentations could add more confusion than enlightenment; they may simply waste the audit committee members' time.

As a matter of good practice, the auditors should prepare a written report to the audit committee highlighting the subjects to be brought up at the meeting, and this report should be distributed beforehand. It may be as formal or as informal as the nature of the topics requires. In addition, presentations on complex issues are often made simpler with visual aids; however, overpresentation may wrest control of the meeting away from the audit committee chairman and interfere with the committee's functioning.

The Audit Committee's Agenda

All of the matters within the audit committee's usual scope of activities are either financial or financially related. The auditor's knowledge base gives him a unique perspective and thus an obligation to advise his client's directors concerning their oversight of corporate financial matters. To do this well, the auditor must know the audit committee's current activities and future agendas.

Some auditors conduct surveys or prepare pamphlets and newsletters for their clients to keep them abreast of current board of directors' and audit committee developments. Many also provide specific input for the audit committee to use in formulating its upcoming agenda. They also provide advance reading materials on significant matters to assist committee members in preparing for meetings. Auditors must be careful to provide their advice in a manner that does not alter their advisory role.

Executive Sessions

Many audit committees arrange to meet annually with representatives of the audit firm not in the presence of management. This is usually done as part of a regularly scheduled audit committee meeting, and is referred to as an *executive session*. The audit committee should raise questions it might not feel comfortable asking in the presence of management, and auditors can respond on sensitive issues in perhaps a less formal manner than might otherwise be the case. Similarly, audit committees may meet independently with internal auditors and with senior financial management without other parties being present.

Auditor Communication With Management

The fact that an audit committee meets with the auditors in a closed session is by no means an indication that management's credibility is in doubt or that management is not ably performing its function. In fact, to conduct their examination, the auditors must maintain an open and candid relationship with management. Their obligation to discuss sensitive matters with the board of directors need not override their relationship with management; indeed it is incumbent on auditors to use good judgment and tact to avoid misunderstandings. The auditors should be guided primarily by common sense and basic discretion, and there are some techniques that they can employ to reduce the likelihood of misunderstandings.

First, the auditors should make certain that they have all the relevant facts at their disposal. For example, possible indications that an irregularity may have occurred or that officers may have acted in a manner that appears contrary to law does not automatically indict management or impugn their integrity—though it does require thorough follow-through by the auditors, and a discussion with the audit committee or full board in situations in which their concurrence may be an important audit step (see Chapter 28 for further discussion).

Similarly, management's expressed preference for and adoption of an accounting method that appears inappropriate to the auditors does not become a formal disagreement until it can be determined whether the auditors and management agree on all the facts. On the other hand, once it is determined that a disagreement has occurred on a material accounting, auditing, or reporting issue, the auditors are obliged to bring this to the attention of the audit committee (or the full board) under the rules of the AICPA's SEC Practice Section. (See Chapter 39 for a discussion of this requirement.) This kind of disagreement is also reportable in SEC filings, but only in the event of a change in auditors (ASR 165). This matter is defined in the article "Disagreements Under Accounting Series Release No. 165" (Kay, 1976b), and is further covered in Chapter 46.

In view of the potentially sensitive nature of these matters, it is vital to determine the facts and the positions of management concerning matters to be discussed with the audit committee, including topics the auditors expect will arise in executive session. All these matters should be discussed with management sufficiently in advance of the meeting to enable management to fully consider the issues and take a position. Certain matters the auditors may feel compelled to bring to the attention of the audit committee fall squarely within the province of management, and it may be better that management bring up the topic with the audit committee. A discussion with management does not compel the auditors to change their views that the audit committee should have the opportunity to deal with particular issues, but such discussion can prevent damage to the mutual trust and candor essential to all auditor/management relationships.

Representatives of the audit firm and management should discuss all the items on the audit committee's meeting agenda, covering the general thrust of the comments both auditors and management plan to make, the questions the audit committee is expected to raise, and the intended responses. Furthermore, the factors considered in the auditor/management planning meeting should not be restricted to agenda items; frequently, audit committees will field the most sensitive questions (e.g., What do you think of the financial vice-president?) in an executive session or an informal break.

Another outcome of the auditor/management planning session might be an agreement as to who is to prepare advance distribution materials on particular topics and who is to present them at the meeting. Some topics lend themselves well to joint presentation. When this mode is used, care should be taken that auditor and management responsibilities do not become confusingly mixed.

CONTEMPORARY ISSUES

The role of the audit committee, like other board committees, has continued to evolve, and several current issues concerning audit committees are discussed below.

Audit Committee Structure

Probably the most prominent issue is deciding who should be an audit committee member. Nearly all the audit committee literature recommends that the member have an inquiring mind and a broad business background in management or finance, and says that these characteristics are more important than a specific background in accounting or auditing. A more controversial issue is whether board members possessing these characteristics should be precluded from audit committee membership because of other relationships with the company.

New York Stock Exchange Policy. The NYSE requires that audit committees be "comprised solely of directors independent of management and free from any relationship that, in the opinion of its Board of Directors, would interfere with the exercise of independent judgment as a committee member" (New York Stock Exchange, 1977). Officers, employees, or affiliates of the company, and generally their close relatives, are specifically disqualified for audit committee membership, but former officers are not. Partners, officers, or directors of an organization having customary commercial, industrial, banking, or underwriting relationships with the company and directors who are paid for providing services directly for the board are not disqualified; however, directors who regularly serve as professional advisers, legal counsel, or management consultants would not qualify as audit committee members if the board considers such relationship to be material to the company.

Other Views on Membership Qualifications. A more extreme view is that audit committee members ought to be free of *any* relationships with the company or its officers, directors, and affiliates other than their directorship relationship; a more relaxed view is that management directors should be permitted to serve on audit committees. Many point out that overly strict audit committee membership qualifications work a special hardship on small and medium-sized firms, whose boards typically have few (if any) members having absolutely no other relationships with the company.

The difficulties in differentiating between independent and outside directors based on their relationships caused the NYSE to revise its more stringent proposed policy distinctions; and the SEC also deleted from its final release on corporate governance a proposed requirement (Release 33-5868) that directors be identified as "management," "affiliated nonmanagement," or "independent." In fact, in its final release (Release 33-5934), the SEC urged registrants who presently "label" their directors not to do so in the future. The SEC does require, however, disclosure of personal or economic relationships between directors and the registrant.

There are differing views about how long a director should remain an audit committee member. Most commentators advocate a staggered rotation scheme to provide a fresh approach and perspective but still maintain continuity.

Separation of Audit Committee and Management Roles. Most directors resist suggestions for structural changes that have the potential for blurring the distinction between the roles of management and the board. Strong management generally welcomes a strong audit committee. When financial management is weak, committees find it difficult to avoid crossing the fine line between oversight and interference. Directors and management alike should remain cognizant of financial management's need to make the decisions, allocate resources, and take risks within the guidelines established by the board. Well-functioning audit committees allow management to exercise operating authority without fear of audit committee encroachment; this does not prevent a participative stance in deliberations before management makes its decision. Concern that the fine balance between advice and encroachment might be disturbed has caused most directors to reject Arthur Goldberg's proposal that the board be provided with a staff of advisers,[6] which presumably would also be available to the audit committee. Similarly, many feel that any attempt to overstructure the audit committee's functions would damage the committee's ability to deal appropriately with the issues of greatest concern.

Need for Structural Flexibility

There are at least some who advocate that the audit committee has the responsibility for many of the board's activities, including reviewing all releases containing financial information prior to issuance, monitoring compliance with legal requirements, and performing all fact-finding activities (such as reviewing officers' expense accounts and perquisites). But none of these activities is *always* performed by audit committees. Flexibility is important, so that each board can appropriately

---

[6] Former Supreme Court Justice Arthur Goldberg has suggested establishing a committee of overseers composed of outside directors (to which would be assigned a small staff of experts and outside consultants operating outside management's control) who would report only to the board. In 1977, Goldberg resigned from TWA's board when his request for staff assistance was not granted. Goldberg told Senator Metzenbaum's Citizens' and Shareholders' Rights and Remedies Subcommittee: "The outside director is simply unable to gather enough independent information to act as a watchdog or sometimes even to ask good questions" (U.S. Congress, 1977, p. 100).

In Goldberg's view, "the major problem in the corporate director system is the gap between what the law decrees to be the governing role of the corporate director and the reality of management control of the corporation.... Contrary to legal theory, the boards of directors of most of our larger companies do not, in fact, control and manage their companies, nor are they equipped to do so. Instead, the management hired by the board, presumably to execute decisions of the board, in fact generally decides the course of operations and periodically asks the board to confirm the determinations of management" (U.S. Congress, 1977, p. 99). While Goldberg's observations of board activities are consistent with the board of the past described by most commentators, most of them seem to disagree with the contention implicit in his argument that the board of directors is inherently ineffectual.

shape its structure as needed to attend to the issues important to that particular company. Still, there is disagreement over whether specific activities, not just general authority, should be assigned to the board and its committees.

Audit Committees and the Internal Auditor

Most audit committees regularly review the internal audit function as a part of their review of internal accounting controls and operational efficiency, expecting that internal audit will delve into areas not included in the outside auditor's scope. But among the controversial activities possibly within the audit committee's charge is whether the general auditor (i.e., the chief internal auditor) should organizationally report directly to the audit committee chairman and serve as the committee's fact-finding arm. Such reporting lines are common in banks, where the director's role is defined in some detail by regulations. Recognition of the new importance of the internal auditor's role underlies this proposal, but it has not attracted many management or boardroom adherents.

Proponents of the traditional structure—where the internal auditor reports to senior management—point out the availability of the external auditor as the audit committee's resource for necessary fact finding. Audit committees regularly engage external auditors when special reviews or investigations are being undertaken, and internal auditors often work as a part of the team. Without regard to structural preferences, virtually everyone agrees that both management and the audit committee need access to both internal and external auditors.

Nonetheless, many companies have taken steps to ensure that (1) the general auditor has access to the board through its audit committee on both a scheduled and as-needed basis and (2) the management organization hierarchy does not hamper internal audit effectiveness.

For a further discussion of how the internal and external auditors can appropriately coordinate, see Appendix 11-B.

Threat of Litigation

The standards of board and audit committee performance are constantly evolving. Periodically, new species are born of court actions. The importance of the law to the future of the directional function cannot be overstated. As one author has said:

> Although only a relatively few may actually be sacrificed to the tortures of the litigation process as society forges new standards for directional responsibility, the sheer fact of exposure can be deeply disturbing to all directors. Our courts will hopefully be sensitive to the desirability of tempering this process in such a way to avoid a high rate of attrition among those best qualified to serve at the very moment when we need them most. [Estes, 1973, p. 114]

SUGGESTED READING

AICPA. *Illustrations of Management Reports on Financial Statements.* Financial Report Survey 19. New York, 1979. This survey, drawn from over 8,000 reports on NAARS, provides examples of disclosures of audit committee composition and duties in annual reports, and shows several separate published reports by audit committees.

American Bar Association, Subcommittee on Functions and Responsibilities of Directors. "Corporate Director's Guidebook." *The Business Lawyer,* November, 1976, pp. 5-52. This guidebook, prepared by an ABA committee, provides an overview of legal responsibilities of the board of directors, its committees, and its members.

Bacon, Jeremy, and Brown, James. *Corporate Directorship Practices: Role, Selection and Legal Status of the Board.* New York: The Conference Board, 1975. This publication provides a comprehensive summary of many aspects of the board of directors from legal and operational perspectives.

Choka, Allen. "The New Role of the Audit Committee." *The Practical Lawyer,* September, 1977, pp. 53-60. In this article, the author discusses the board of directors' legal considerations from the perspective of an audit committee member.

Lovdal, Michael. "Making the Audit Committee Work." *Harvard Business Review,* March-April, 1977, pp. 108-114. In this article, the author provides a pragmatic operational perspective on audit committees. He deals with how objectives can be met, not what they are.

Mautz, Robert, and Neumann, Fred. *Corporate Audit Committees: Policies and Practices.* Cleveland: Ernst & Ernst, 1977. This survey updates the authors' 1970 comprehensive study of audit committee practices and what is expected of the audit committee.

APPENDIX 10   SUMMARY OF REQUIREMENTS FOR AUDIT COMMITTEE OF KILLEARN PROPERTIES, INC.

Under a consent decree settlement with the SEC (Litigation Release 6792), Killearn was ordered to appoint a majority of outside directors to its board of directors and to maintain an audit committee comprising at least three board members who are outside directors. The order outlines seven areas of basic responsibility for the audit committee and three "special duties." The basic responsibilities are to

1. Review the engagement of the independent auditors, including the scope and general extent of their review, the audit procedures to be employed, and the fees to be paid.

2. Review with the independent auditors and the company's chief financial officer the company's policies and procedures as to internal auditing, accounting, and financial controls.

3. Review a series of items with the independent auditors on completion of the audit, including the auditor's report or opinion proposed to be rendered; their perceptions of the company's financial and accounting personnel; the cooperation the independent auditors received during the course of their work; the extent to which the resources of the company were and should be utilized to minimize the time spent by the independent auditors; any significant transactions that are not a normal part of the company's business; any change in the accounting principles; all significant adjustments proposed by the auditors; and any recommendations that the independent auditors may have with respect to improving internal financial controls, choice of accounting principles, or management reporting systems.

4. Inquire of appropriate company personnel and the independent auditors as to any instances of deviation from established codes of conduct of the company, and periodically review such codes.

5. Meet with the company's financial staff at least twice a year to review and discuss the scope of internal accounting and auditing procedures and whether recommendations made by the internal staff or by the independent auditors have been implemented.

6. Prepare and present to the company's board of directors a report summarizing its recommendations with respect to the retention or discharge of the independent auditors for the ensuing year.

7. Investigate any matter brought to its attention within the scope of its duties, retaining outside counsel if necessary.

In the special duty areas, the committee is to

1. Review all releases and other information to be disseminated by Killearn to the press, the public, or its shareholders that concern current and projected financial condition of the company.

2. Review the present and contemplated future activities of the company's officers and directors as they relate to the company, and take appropriate action if necessary.

3. Approve any settlement or disposition of claims or causes of actions arising after the date of the order, or any litigation pending by Killearn against any past or present officers, directors, employees, or controlling persons.

11

Auditing Standards

Jack C. Robertson

THE IMPORTANCE OF STANDARDS

    The theory of auditing includes basic concepts, fundamental principles, and a set of guiding standards. In everyday practice the standards are paramount, because they contain the criteria governing the overall quality of audit performance.

    Auditing standards remain the same for all audits. *Auditing procedures,* on the other hand, consist of detailed steps that vary depending on the complexity of an engagement, the nature of an accounting system, the type of business under audit, and other features of a particular job. Auditors conform to auditing standards by performing auditing procedures necessary in the circumstances.

This chapter focuses primarily on standards for external, independent audits performed by certified public accountants (CPAs). These ten standards, known as *generally accepted auditing standards,* were approved by vote of the membership of the AICPA in the late 1940s and early 1950s. Interpretations of these standards are issued in the form of binding Statements on Auditing Standards, which are promulgated by the Auditing Standards Board, a senior technical board of the AICPA. Somewhat different standards are recognized in two other major areas of auditing practice. Government auditors operate under the General Accounting Office (GAO) *Standards for Audit of Governmental Organizations, Programs, Activities and Functions,* issued by the comptroller general of the United States in 1972. Internal auditors operate under *Standards for the Professional Practice of Internal Auditing,* approved by the membership of the Institute of Internal Auditors (IIA) in 1978. There are other kinds of specialized auditors, and they are mentioned in other chapters.

Generally accepted auditing standards (GAAS) are not the only source of quality criteria for independent auditors. The AICPA has adopted a Code of Professional Ethics, and several of the rules in this code pertain directly to auditing practice. The AICPA also publishes auditing interpretations and audit guides. The interpretations, which are issued by the Auditing Standards Board, are specific responses to questions and problems that arise in the practical application of GAAS. The audit guides are books dealing with application of GAAS to special industry situations. Some typical audit guides are *Audits of Stock Life Insurance Companies, Audits of Colleges and Universities,* and *Audits of Savings and Loan Associations.*

CPAs in public practice perform services other than audits of financial statements. Their other areas of practice (taxation, management advisory services, and financial statement compilation and review services) are governed by other statements of practice standards. Senior technical committees of the AICPA periodically issue Statements of Responsibilities in Tax Practice, Statements on Management Advisory Services, Statements on Accounting and Review Services, and Statements on Quality Control Standards, which apply to broad areas of practice and are discussed later in this chapter.

THE GENESIS OF AUDITING STANDARDS

Independent Auditing Standards

The AICPA has been setting auditing standards for a long time. Its Committee on Auditing Procedure was formed in 1939 and functioned under that name until 1972, by which time it had issued 54 Statements on Auditing Procedure (SAPs) plus several codifications and special reports. When the Financial Accounting Standards Board (FASB) came into existence as an organization independent of the AICPA in the early 1970s, the AICPA reorganized its own auditing area and created an Auditing Standards Division. The Auditing Standards Executive Committee (AudSEC) took over the work of the Committee on Auditing Procedure. Turning its attention from procedures to standards, AudSEC and its successor, the

Auditing Standards Board, issued 31 Statements on Auditing Standards (SASs) from 1973 through mid-1980. SAS 1, which was issued in 1973, is a compilation (with a few wording changes of substance) of all existing SAPs, and a regularly updated codification of SASs is available with topics arranged by section number rather than by SAS number.

Throughout this 40-year period, and especially in the last decade, the SEC has been actively commenting on the direction of auditing standards, sometimes imposing a very significant influence on particular standards. (See Chapter 41.) AudSEC was born in a reorganization movement stemming from a need to meet the problems of establishing accounting principles. It died from external pressures exerted from two fronts. In 1977 a staff study entitled *The Accounting Estab-lishment* was published by the Congressional Subcommittee on Reports, Accounting and Management, chaired by the late Senator Lee Metcalf (U.S. Congress, Senate, 1976b). The *Metcalf Report* severely criticized the organization of the accounting profession and its mechanism for setting auditing standards and recommended governmental intervention in the establishment of auditing standards. At that time, AudSEC consisted of 21 professionals appointed by the AICPA chairman. The members, who received no compensation for serving on the committee, gave part-time attention to committee duties while they were engaged in their own practices.

At about the same time, the Commission on Auditors' Responsibilities (CAR), an independent study group appointed and funded by the AICPA in 1974 to consider whether there was any gap between what the public expected of or needed from auditors and what auditors could and should reasonably expect to accomplish (and if there was such a gap, how to close it), released its *Report of Tentative Conclusions* (CAR, 1977). The commission, chaired by the late Manuel F. Cohen, former chairman of the SEC, fully demonstrated its independence of the AICPA by the nature of many of its recommendations. In its final statement, *Report, Conclusions, and Recommendations* (CAR, 1978), the *Cohen Commission* called for several specific changes in the institutional structure for establishing auditing standards. In summary, it concluded (in Section 10) that

1. A standard-setting organization separate from the AICPA would create great economic and organizational problems.
2. AudSEC should be replaced by a smaller, full-time committee compensated by the AICPA.
3. A full-time committee would require a larger and highly qualified staff. Within a budget allocated by the AICPA, the committee should select its own staff and make all personnel decisions.
4. Participation in the setting of auditing standards by people outside the profession should be encouraged. Formal procedures for this outside participation in the process should be provided.

The AICPA did not adopt all the Cohen Commission's recommendations, but in late 1978 it created the Auditing Standards Board to replace AudSEC. The Auditing Standards Board has 15 part-time members appointed by the AICPA chairman. All board members must be members of the AICPA. The AICPA staff has been increased; one important addition is a research director serving under the head of the Auditing Standards Division. Most portions of the board meetings are now open to the public, and a 15-member advisory council has been appointed from the ranks of financial analysts, corporate managers, bankers, academics, government employees, and accountants in public practice. The board issued its first statement, SAS 24, *Review of Interim Financial Information* (AU 721), in March 1979 and is now up to SAS 32.

Hardly a step was missed between the death of AudSEC and the birth of the Auditing Standards Board, largely because 11 members of AudSEC, including the chairman, carried over to the board and continued their work on projects started earlier. Time will tell whether the new arrangement will be more successful in setting auditing standards appropriate to the times.

Governmental and Internal Auditing Standards

Standards for governmental and internal auditing have not drawn nearly so much attention as have those for CPAs in public practice. In 1972, after a considerable amount of staff work and thought, the U.S. comptroller general simply issued the GAO "Yellow Book," *Standards for Audit of Governmental Organizations, Programs, Activities and Functions* (Comptroller General of the United States, 1972). A great deal of GAO experience lies behind these standards, and they reflect practices characteristic of GAO assignments, but there was no elaborate committee structure, no public meetings, and little controversy among government auditors over the standards when they were issued.[1] The standards are, however, subject to review and amendment. When important changes are proposed, the comptroller general solicits the comments of professional organizations, public interest groups, government agencies at all levels, and other interested parties. The first such change was a 1979 publication of additional standards on computer auditing.

The IIA went through a somewhat more elaborate process in formulating its *Standards for the Professional Practice of Internal Auditing*. A professional standards and responsibilities committee was formed in 1974 to develop these standards. Over the three years of its work, the committee included members from industry, banking, government, insurance, and academia, along with several experienced consultants. After some exposure of several drafts and publication of a tentative set of standards, the IIA board of directors adopted the final version. The IIA plans to modify the standards from time to time. Most likely, modification will consist of periodic publication of explanatory material as well as new standards. It is unlikely that the IIA standard-setting process will be opened to wide participation by all persons interested in auditing.

---

[1] There was, however, some concern among independent public accountants engaged to audit government grant programs, because in addition to the usual audit of financial statements, the CPAs were effectively being asked to attest to operational efficiency and the extent to which the grantee may have achieved the social goals of the organization. Government auditors were not similarly constrained, because they were reporting to the government as employees, not as independent third parties. The issue was generally resolved by having government agencies state their requirements in terms that were objectively verifiable. For further information, see *Auditing Standards Established by the GAO—Their Meaning and Significance for CPAs, A Report* (AICPA, 1973d) and *Guidelines for CPA Participation in Government Audit Engagements to Evaluate Economy, Efficiency and Program Results* (AICPA, 1977e).

Organization of Auditing Standards

GAAS comprise ten standards in three categories: general standards, standards of field work, and reporting standards. The numbered SASs are interpretations of one or more of these standards and have the same binding force and effect. Thus, the SASs themselves are often called GAAS. This chapter discusses the ten standards one by one, turning to particular SASs for crucial passages that define how those standards have been officially interpreted. The ten GAAS (AU 150.02) are shown in Figure 11.1.

Since the GAO and IIA standards were written with the AICPA standards for reference, they have many points in common with GAAS. They display several

---

GENERAL STANDARDS

1. The examination is to be performed by a person or persons having adequate technical training and proficiency as an auditor.

2. In all matters relating to the assignment, an independence in mental attitude is to be maintained by the auditor or auditors.

3. Due professional care is to be exercised in the performance of the examination and the preparation of the report.

STANDARDS OF FIELD WORK

1. The work is to be adequately planned and assistants, if any, are to be properly supervised.

2. There is to be a proper study and evaluation of the existing internal control as a basis for reliance thereon and for the determination of the resultant extent of the tests to which auditing procedures are to be restricted.

3. Sufficient competent evidential matter is to be obtained through inspection, observation, inquiries, and confirmations to afford a reasonable basis for an opinion regarding the financial statements under examination.

STANDARDS OF REPORTING

1. The report shall state whether the financial statements are presented in accordance with generally accepted accounting principles.

2. The report shall state whether such principles have been consistently observed in the current period in relation to the preceding period.

3. Informative disclosures in the financial statements are to be regarded as reasonably adequate unless otherwise stated in the report.

4. The report shall either contain an expression of opinion regarding the financial statements, taken as a whole, or an assertion to the effect that an opinion cannot be expressed. When an overall opinion cannot be expressed, the reasons therefor should be stated. In all cases where an auditor's name is associated with financial statements, the report should contain a clear-cut indication of the character of the auditor's examination, if any, and the degree of responsibility he is taking.

FIGURE 11.1   GENERALLY ACCEPTED AUDITING STANDARDS

important differences as well, but these differences merely reflect the special characteristics of governmental and internal auditing. The similarities and differences will be briefly noted as the AICPA standards are discussed.

GENERAL STANDARDS

The second general standard, independence in mental attitude, is the place to begin an analysis of GAAS. The other nine standards will then be covered in order.

Independence

Independence is a central concept for CPAs engaged in public practice. The credibility conferred upon a financial report when it is independently audited can be completely destroyed by any compromise of the auditor's independence, for an audit has value to recipients of financial statements only insofar as the auditor is perceived as independent of the control of management, objectively reviewing and reporting on management's representations contained in the statements.

Independence may be defined as an auditor's ability to act with integrity and objectivity. *Integrity* is an individual's ability to make difficult ethical decisions of right and wrong by correctly applying categorical rules for behavior to particular cases and by weighing the costs and benefits of alternative actions from the viewpoint of all persons who may be affected. This is the same integrity that all professionals must possess in their work. *Objectivity* is an auditor's ability to be impartial. In performance of an audit, a CPA should act exclusively in the capacity of an auditor or reviewer, not as a business consultant bent on giving management advice (though helpful control and efficiency advice may be a by-product), not as a business partner, and not as an advocate of any special interest. Throughout the duration of the audit—often almost continuously—the CPA may also operate in a consulting role or an advocacy role (as in tax practice), but in the audit itself these roles are set aside. Of course, knowledge gained by the auditor in the course of performing nonaudit services must be taken into account during performance of the audit. These concepts underlie the straightforward dictum of the second AICPA general standard: "In all matters relating to the assignment, an independence in mental attitude is to be maintained by the auditor or auditors" (AU 220.01).

Two Aspects of Independence. Auditing standards further recognize two aspects of independence: (1) an auditor must be intellectually honest, acting with integrity and objectivity, and (2) an auditor must be *recognized* as independent, free from any obligation to or interest in the audit client, the company under audit, its management, or its owners. The first of these aspects is often called independence *in fact* (a mental attitude that only the auditor himself knows that he possesses), and the second is often called independence *in appearance* (the absence of connections that can more easily be seen by others). The appearance of independence is important to maintaining public respect for the auditing profession.

AICPA Rules of Conduct. Specific AICPA Rules of Conduct reinforce the independence auditing standard. Rule 101 requires: "A member [of the AICPA] or a firm of which he is a partner or shareholder shall not express an opinion on financial statements of an enterprise unless he and his firm are independent with respect to such enterprise" (ET 101.01). The rule gives examples of impairment of the appearance of independence if the auditor has a direct financial interest or a material indirect financial interest in the client, has served as a trustee, officer, underwriter, or promoter of the enterprise, or has other associations that would enable observers to wonder about his ability to be objective. (It is interesting to note that many years ago an auditor's direct financial interest was thought to be desirable, on the theory that he would operate in the best interests of all owners if he himself were one.) Additional interpretations of this rule cover many details, including the effect of family relationships, litigation involving auditor and client, and other problem areas that have needed clarification from time to time. The SEC has laid down a similar rule and issued a series of examples and interpretations over the years for the guidance of auditors.[2]

Auditors can be penalized for failing to observe the spirit of independence rules. To the credit of the profession, however, there have been few cases in which auditors were specifically accused of lack of independence.[3]

Independence Criticism. The profession as a whole, however, has recently been criticized for maintaining relationships that some see as impairing audit independence.

Scope of services. Some critics contend that when CPA firms perform a wide variety of management advisory services for an audit client, the consultancy bond is so close as to make the auditor's objectivity improbable. The Cohen Commission reviewed this criticism and concluded that it was generally unfounded. However, executive search services, in which CPA firms find and place financial executives with audit clients, have now been prohibited by rules of the SEC Practice Section of the AICPA as to publicly held companies (CAR, 1978, pp. 1-17). The profession's Public Oversight Board (POB) thoroughly examined suggestions for more general prohibitions of advisory services and concluded that only a few other services, not extensively provided in practice, should be proscribed until compelling objective evidence is produced proving that the services are indeed incompatible with the independent auditing role (1979).

The SEC requires disclosure in proxy statements of the proportion of fees represented by nonauditing work to the audit fee, and in ASR 264 the SEC has taken issue with the POB report's conclusions that restrictions on nonaudit services were not advisable. The scope-of-services issue is explored in depth in Chapter 39,

---

[2] Although independence is woven into many SEC rules and regulations, a periodic compilation of specific situations considered by the SEC is also released. See, for example, ASR 234 (1977).

[3] SEC Litigation Releases as well as ASRs are a source of information on independence problems of specifically identified CPAs associated with SEC filings. The AICPA semimonthly newsletter, *The CPA Letter,* publishes disciplinary notices that cover other subjects and other CPAs as well.

but it is interesting to note here that the perceptions of independence vary and are the subject of very serious debate.

Client fee dependence. Another criticism concerns *who pays the fee.* Some critics ask how an auditor can truly be independent when his fee is paid by the client audited. However, no one has suggested any preferable payment method that would be workable. Critics can be comforted in knowing that the penalties of exposure, litigation, and monetary loss that befall an auditor are far more severe than loss of an audit fee. One mitigating arrangement is for the auditor to be engaged by, and remain in direct contact with, an audit committee composed of outside members of the client's board of directors or the board as a whole. This practice is now virtually standard for publicly held companies. The audit committee arrangement is widely perceived as enhancing the auditor's insulation from pressures that might be exerted by the client's management. The New York Stock Exchange now requires listed companies to have audit committees composed of outside directors, and SEC requires disclosure of the existence or nonexistence of audit committees and certain information about the committee's activities. (See Chapter 10.)

Independence Monitoring. Auditing firms are generally required to have quality control procedures that monitor compliance with the independence standards and rules. Authoritative pronouncements known as Statements on Quality Control Standards, issued by the AICPA, give general guidance, and firms are expected to formulate specific policies and procedures. (Statements on Quality Control Standards are discussed later in this chapter.) Many firms conduct regular briefings for new professional employees, require annual "independence sign-offs" in which partners and employees attest to the absence of any conditions that might impair independence, distribute notification of new clients with directions for divestiture of financial interest, and provide counseling on independence problems. Some firms have policies that are more restrictive than AICPA rules.

Governmental and Internal Audit Independence. GAO independence standards require maintenance of an "independent attitude." However, when a government auditor does not possess the appearance of independence (e.g., when he is employed by the audited entity), a report can still be rendered if the auditor discloses prominently the relationship with the organization or officials being audited.

Internal auditors are required to "be objective in performing audits." This means that auditors should not subordinate their judgment to that of others; that they should have an honest belief in their work product; that they should not audit activities for which they had recent operating line authority or responsibility; and that they should not design, install, or operate information systems that they will later be assigned to audit. IIA standards do not, however, expressly prohibit financial and business interests.

For all auditors, competence is as important a key to independence as integrity is. Great difficulties arise in trying to remain impartial and objective when faced with a complex task beyond one's capabilities. Thus, independence is not a separate standard but goes hand in hand with other auditing standards, particularly those of technical proficiency and professional care.

Technical Training and Proficiency

Competence is indispensable for a quality audit, because the auditor who does not understand the significant aspects of his client's business or its complex transactions puts himself in jeopardy of error that could have serious repercussions. Thus, the AICPA's first general standard requires: "The examination is to be performed by a person or persons having adequate technical training and proficiency as an auditor" (AU 210.01).

Training. Auditing standards recognize that technical training and proficiency are obtained through a combination of formal education and on-the-job training, with emphasis on the latter. Auditors must first be very competent accountants who know the principles of accounting and how to apply them. They must also have a grasp of economics in order to perceive the elusive economic substance represented by, or sometimes disguised in, transactions and balances. In some situations, the accounting rules may produce results that fail to reflect this substance; the auditor is expected to recognize these situations if they are material. Another level of education involves general business awareness of such fields as finance, marketing, management, law, statistics, and electronic data processing. Last, but far from least, an auditor must know how to audit.

A typical university course in auditing combines auditing theory, professional ethics, and legal liability with technical material on the use of statistics and computers, reporting the results of auditing work, and procedures for audit planning and evidence gathering. With this technical material the student can begin to learn how to recognize problems, gather evidence about them, evaluate this evidence, and make a decision.

Proficiency as an auditor finally comes down to one's ability to make decisions based on evidence. Although formal education provides a valuable introduction, it can never cover the wide variety of problems found outside the classroom. Practical experience in facing many unique situations is an absolute necessity if an auditor is eventually to be considered truly proficient. Explanations of this auditing standard therefore contain admonitions that neophyte auditors ought to be well supervised in their initial practical experience in order to gain the most benefit from it.

After some period of experience (ranging from a few years to many, depending on the kind of exposure obtained), an auditor may be sufficiently experienced to supervise the progress of newly hired auditors.

Continuing Professional Education. Along with on-the-job experience, continuing professional education (CPE) in formal modes is required of most auditors. Over half the state CPA licensing boards require auditors to obtain an average of 40 hours of CPE credit a year to retain their license to practice. Most of the other states have voluntary CPE programs. The AICPA's Division for Firms requires professional staff in member firms to obtain a minimum of 120 hours of CPE credit over three years—effectively 40 hours each year. The AICPA and state CPA societies offer hundreds of courses, ranging in length from four hours to several days and covering a variety of topics that would make most college deans envious. In addition, all the larger CPA firms spend a great deal of money on their own in-house training programs.

The AICPA quality control standards require firms to establish policies and procedures assuring that persons hired possess characteristics that will enable them to perform competently. Typical procedures for screening candidates include interviews with recruiting personnel, checking of references and college transcripts, and orientation briefings. For professional staff too, the standards call for policies and procedures to assure that members of a firm will have the knowledge they need to fulfill their assigned responsibilities. Most CPA firms monitor each professional's CPE time, including specialized industry training, and take measures to provide varied on-the-job experience. New accounting and auditing pronouncements are distributed to professional staff, along with instructions on applying those pronouncements in the context of the firm's quality control system. A firm is also required to have policies and procedures assuring that promotion is based on qualification to assume more responsible duties, not simply on tenure. Staff performance evaluations, published promotion guidelines, and advancement counseling are considered good practices for quality control in promotion.

Internal Auditing. The IIA has released four standards that deal directly with technical training and proficiency. Two of them focus on the internal auditing department as a whole and require that the department provide assurance that its collective technical proficiency, educational background, knowledge, skill, and discipline are adequate to its responsibilities. The other two standards focus on individual auditors and require that they possess the requisite knowledge, skills, and disciplines and can communicate with people effectively.

The IIA standards include one stating: "Internal auditors should maintain their technical competence through continuing education." This standard recognizes that maintaining proficiency and keeping abreast of current developments can be satisfied by attending conferences, seminars, college courses, and in-house training programs and by participating in research projects.

Governmental Auditing. GAO standards state: "The auditors assigned to perform the audit must collectively possess adequate professional proficiency for the tasks required." This standard is parallel to the AICPA standard. Otherwise, GAO standards are silent on the subject of continuing professional education, but government auditors nevertheless recognize the need for it and participate frequently in a wide variety of programs.

Due Professional Care

Due professional care concerns what an auditor does on an engagement and how well he does it. The third general standard declares: "Due professional care is to be exercised in the performance of the examination and the preparation of the report" (AU 230.01). Other passages in the professional literature further explain that this standard is discharged in part by full observance of the field work and reporting standards (discussed in later sections of this chapter).

Whether due care has been exercised depends on all the facts and circumstances of a particular audit situation. Due care cannot be defined so precisely that its application to every case is clear. Indeed, in most large, complex audits its achievement is based on many, many factors. The concept is well understood nevertheless.

It is the opposite of negligence in the law, which is described by this classic passage from *Cooley on Torts* (cited in AU 230.03):

> Every man who offers his service to another and is employed assumes the duty to exercise in the employment such skill as he possesses with reasonable care and diligence. In all these employments where peculiar skill is prerequisite, if one offers his service, he is understood as holding himself out to the public as possessing the degree of skill commonly possessed by others in the same employment, and, if his pretensions are unfounded, he commits a species of fraud upon every man who employs him in reliance on his public profession. But no man, whether skilled or unskilled, undertakes that the task he assumes shall be performed successfully, and without fault or error. He undertakes for good faith and integrity, but not for infallibility, and he is liable to his employer for negligence, bad faith, or dishonesty, but not for losses consequent upon pure errors of judgment.

Auditors are expected to have keen auditing perceptions and the ability to make decisions or judgments that would escape the attention of others, but the *degree* of skill and diligence required of auditors (i.e., whether due professional care has been exercised) always comes into question when financial statements are disputed and audited businesses encounter serious financial difficulties. Mautz and Sharaf (1961) have elaborated the concept with these specific notions:

1. A prudent practitioner is presumed to
    a. Have a knowledge of the philosophy and practice of auditing,
    b. Have the degree of training, experience, and skill common to the average independent auditor,
    c. Have the ability to recognize indications of irregularities, and
    d. Keep abreast of developments in the perpetration and detection of irregularities.
2. Due audit care requires that the auditor
    a. Acquaint himself with the company under examination,
    b. Review the method of internal control operating in the company,
    c. Obtain any knowledge readily available that is pertinent to the accounting and financial problems of the company,
    d. Be responsive to unusual events and unusual circumstances,
    e. Persist until he has eliminated from his own mind any reasonable doubts he may have about the existence of material irregularities, and
    f. Exercise caution in instructing his assistants and reviewing their work.

AICPA Statements on Quality Control Standards contribute to fulfillment of the due care standard by requiring that firms establish policies and procedures for assigning personnel to engagements, providing consultation resources on audit problems, and performing effective supervision and inspection. No single auditor acting individually can solve every conceivable problem, so firms must have policies for providing consultation with persons of knowledge, experience, and authority who can contribute to a solution. Large CPA firms operate their own technical research services in their national or regional offices, which receive inquiries from the field. All AICPA members can avail themselves of the technical information service at the AICPA in New York. Consultation can take many forms, but every firm needs to keep lines of communication open so that the expertise available from professional personnel can be shared.

Policies and procedures for effective supervision and inspection augment those for consultation. At the highest level of supervision, firms provide for the involvement of a concurring partner to review the audit report and the performance of the audit as deemed necessary. This procedure is required for publicly held companies under the AICPA's SEC Practice Section rules; so also is the procedure of quality control review (inspection) of audit working papers. Supervision at other levels is carried out in the field in observance of the field work standards (described later in this chapter), and all these activities performed diligently synthesize into the accomplishment of due professional care.

GAO standards include one almost identical to the AICPA standard, and the explanation of the GAO standard parallels that of the AICPA standard (AU 230). One aspect, however, is expressly added to the GAO concept of due audit care: follow-up work on previous audit findings to determine whether appropriate corrective measures have been taken. In practice, of course, this procedure is followed by independent auditors, but it is not specified as a basic standard.

Internal auditors have followed suit with a standard worded almost identically, and the IIA explanation parallels those of the AICPA and GAO. Like GAO, IIA has set an additional standard that states: "Internal auditors should follow up to ascertain that appropriate action is taken on reported audit findings."

Errors, Irregularities, and Illegal Acts. The concept of due professional care has a specific application in the search for errors (mistakes), irregularities (fraud), and illegal acts in a clients' records and financial statements. The auditor's responsibilities in performing this function have undergone upheaval in recent years. (See Chapters 13 and 46.) But due care is inevitably the contested issue and thus deserves a brief review in this context.

In 1961 Mautz and Sharaf (pp. 44-46) reflected the times by expressing as one of the basic auditing assumptions: "There is no necessary conflict of interest between the auditor and the management of the enterprise under audit." They explained that both management and the auditor are interested in the long-run prosperity and progress of the enterprise. If auditors are unable to accept this assumption, they went on, audits would have to be so detailed and extensive as to become uneconomical, especially if managements are assumed at the outset to be untrustworthy. Though there is no *necessary* conflict of interest, when an auditor sees evidence that one indeed exists, appropriate action must be taken.

Due professional care is proper as a basic standard, but without specification it has turned out to mean "more" to the public and "less than more" to auditors, with the courts being resorted to for a decision in each contested situation.

Corporate failures, massive frauds, and disclosures of illegal payoffs in the 1970s have caused a strenuous public criticism of the business community, and auditors have been caught in the same net. Where were the auditors? was a popular question, as if to place the auditor in a policeman's role. This role has been considered by the courts in the *Geotek* matter (*SEC v. Arthur Young & Co.,* 590 F.2d 785 (9th Cir. 1979)) and rejected. (See Chapter 46.) The auditor is neither an adversary nor an advocate. He is a professional exercising an informed judgment, not an ally of management in communicating a particular picture of the business most favorable to its interest. His first duty is the responsibility to exercise a dispassionate professional judgment on the client's financial reporting.

Those who issue auditing standards have not simply waited for the storm of public criticism to pass. Several SASs collectively set forth an auditor's professional responsibilities for various misstatements in financial statements, i.e., how he should exercise due care in specific areas. Here is a brief review of three of these standards: related-party transactions; errors and irregularities; and illegal acts.

Related-party transactions. Several lawsuits against auditors involving materially misleading financial statements have resulted from the dealings of corporate officers with each other, with affiliated companies, with family members, or with shell companies. SAS 6 (AU 335) specifies procedures for determining the existence of related parties, identifying transactions with related parties, examining the identified transactions, and making appropriate disclosure in the financial statements.

Detection of errors and irregularities. *Errors* are usually defined as unintentional mistakes; *irregularities* are intentional distortions of financial statements. Persons who rely on financial statements look to an entity's internal controls and to independent audits for reasonable assurance that financial statements are not materially misstated as a result of errors or irregularities. Thus, SAS 16 (AU 327) gives the independent auditor the responsibility, within the inherent limitations of the auditing process, (1) to plan the examination to search for errors or irregularities that would have a material effect on the financial statements and (2) to exercise due skill and care in the conduct of that examination. SAS 16 goes on to say that the auditor's standard report implicitly indicates a belief that the financial statements taken as a whole are not materially misstated as a result of errors or irregularities.

The key terms used in this formulation require discussion. *Reasonable assurance* is a concept intended to take relative costs and benefits into account, but it remains vague in application because costs and benefits are difficult to evaluate. In the context of SAS 16, diligent efforts should be made to obtain evidence, but not by disregarding all cost and time constraints. *Inherent limitations of the auditing process* is a concept based not only on time and cost considerations but also on the fact that most audit evidence is persuasive, not conclusive. Audits are based on sampling (Chapter 14), and this inevitably raises some risk that errors or irregularities can escape detection.

Illegal acts by clients. Many of the corporate disclosures of the mid-1970s involved illegal or questionable payments. SAS 17 (AU 328) explains the auditor's need to consider whether illegal acts may have occurred and to report them if they have. Though an auditor is neither a legal expert nor an administrative enforcement agent, he should be generally familiar with business law and be able to recognize a possibly illegal act in the area of financially related transactions (those that enter into the accounting system, e.g., income tax transactions and selling prices controlled by legislation or administrative rules). Actions that exist outside the accounting system, such as violation of health and safety laws and environmental control laws, are much less likely to come to the auditor's attention.

SAS 17 explains some procedures that may help the auditor to identify possibly illegal acts by clients and directs him to seek legal counsel. If an illegal act is discovered, the auditor is directed to assess its materiality, with due regard to possible ramifications. For example, public disclosure of a relatively small bribe (say $100,000 in a billion-dollar company) might endanger a large contract, a business license, or the right to operate in a foreign country. Findings should be reported to a high level in the client organization, up to and including the audit committee, for appropriate action.

Governmental and Internal Auditing Standards. GAO standards state: "A review is to be made of compliance with legal and regulatory requirements." The context of this standard, however, differs from that of AICPA standards, since compliance with laws and regulations is particularly significant in governmental auditing. Government organizations, programs, and activities are creatures of law and have more specific rules and regulations to follow than do most private organizations.

Internal auditing standards contain two statements concerning errors, irregularities, and illegal acts. The first, made in explanation of the IIA due professional care standard, states: "Internal auditors should be alert to the possibility of intentional wrongdoing, errors and omissions, inefficiency, waste, ineffectiveness, and conflicts of interest [and] to those conditions and activities where irregularities are most likely to occur." The second statement requires internal auditors to "review the systems established to ensure compliance with those policies, plans, procedures, laws, and regulations which could have a significant impact on operations and reports, and [to] determine whether the organization is in compliance."

STANDARDS OF FIELD WORK

All audits are different, except that any audit of financial statements is generally understood to involve unrestricted access to all the client's accounting information pertaining to the financial statements. Independent auditors are engaged to express opinions on these financial statements, and GAAS apply to these engagements. If the engagement is an audit but not an audit of financial statements presented in conformity with GAAP, GAAS apply (AU 621.02).

Government auditors and internal auditors bring into the realm of audits certain services that go beyond the AICPA definition. GAO general standards essentially recognize four types or levels of audit scope:

1. An examination of financial transactions, accounts, and reports,
2. An evaluation of compliance with applicable laws and regulations,
3. A review of efficiency and economy in the use of resources, and
4. A review to determine whether desired results are effectively achieved.

These are generally known as financial audits, compliance audits, economy and efficiency (or management) audits, and program results audits. IIA standards describe basically the same set, though internal auditors have no standard that applies directly to financial audits.

Independent accountants also perform compliance, efficiency and economy, and program results engagements, often under the description management advisory services (MAS). In 1979 a large CPA firm undertook what has been called the largest single audit contract ever granted—a multimillion-dollar audit of major oil companies' compliance with federal oil- and gas-pricing regulations—but the job is essentially a compliance audit. For guidance in such engagements, CPAs in public practice generally look to those specific auditing standards that apply, as well as to MAS practice standards and other sources such as the AICPA Management Advisory Services Guideline Series. No. 6 in that series is entitled *Guidelines for CPA Participation in Government Audit Engagements to Evaluate Economy, Efficiency and Program Results* (1977e). Generally accepted auditing standards for field work are relevant to most areas of practice, at least in a conceptual sense, and these are discussed next.

Planning and Supervision

The auditing standards on planning and supervision are an extension of due professional care. The first field work standard declares: "The work is to be adequately planned and assistants, if any, are to be properly supervised" (AU 310.01).

Auditing standards point out that early appointment of the auditor is beneficial, so that time is available to plan the engagement in advance. Particularly helpful is the ability to perform some of the audit work before the fiscal year-end and to plan for early confirmation of receivables and observation of inventories. Auditors may accept late appointments near or after year-end, but auditing standards suggest particular attention in such cases to the problem of completing the audit satisfactorily. *Interim* audit work, which is performed before the client's fiscal year-end, is also encouraged as a means of spreading the firm's workload more evenly over the year and of making planning and supervision more effective.

SAS 22, *Planning and Supervision* (AU 311), contains many suggestions for effective field work and establishes three definite requirements:

1. A written audit program should be prepared;
2. The auditor should obtain a knowledge of the entity's business, its organization, and its operating characteristics; and
3. Assistants should be informed of their responsibility, the objectives of the procedures they are to perform, and the method by which they should document disagreements with the auditor in charge if they believe it necessary to be dissociated from the resolution of a disputed issue.

GAO standards covering planning and supervision are essentially the same as AICPA standards, but also emphasize the planning of necessary coordination with other government auditors who may be working on the same agency audit. IIA standards follow suit, calling upon the director of internal auditing to coordinate internal audit efforts with those of the independent CPA firm. The AICPA standards are not so explicit about requiring coordination of efforts with other auditors, but they do provide guidance (1) where other independent auditors are involved in parts of the examination (see Chapter 16) and (2) on how to use the work and assistance of internal auditors. In practice, independent CPAs regularly coordinate their audit efforts with those of the client's internal auditors and those of government auditors, to the extent possible.

Study and Evaluation of Internal Control

Internal accounting control is provided by the methods and procedures within an entity's accounting system that are designed to safeguard assets and to prevent, detect, and correct errors and irregularities that might occur in the processing of accounting data. This is, of course, very significant to auditors, because a satisfactory system of internal control reduces the probability that undetected errors and irregularities will occur in the accounting output and hence in the financial statements. In other words, financial records produced under a system of satisfactory internal accounting control are justifiably considered more reliable than records produced under an unsatisfactory system.

The client's internal control system is addressed by the second field work standard. It states: "There is to be a proper study and evaluation of the existing internal control as a basis for reliance thereon and for the determination of the resultant extent of the tests to which auditing procedures are to be restricted" (AU 320.01).

A proper study and evaluation of internal accounting control provides the auditor with a basis for specifying the nature, timing, and extent of his auditing procedures. Knowledge of the system is indispensable for planning the audit (see Chapter 12), and compliance testing is essential in determining the degree of reliance an auditor can place on a particular segment of the control system (see Chapter 13). When an internal control system is found to be good, auditing standards allow the auditor to limit or restrict substantive auditing procedures but not to eliminate them altogether.

What constitutes a *proper study and evaluation* is a matter of the auditor's judgment, with costs and benefits taken into account. Auditors may decide not to study and evaluate a particular element of a control system and thus not to rely on it for its accounting output, but in this case the substantive audit of account balances and totals must be more extensive.[4]

GAO and IIA standards provide guidance for the study and evaluation of internal control, and since both organizations recognize that the scope of their audits may include more than financial statements, their standards specifically deal with more goals or objectives of internal control than that of ensuring the reliability of financial statements. The GAO standard calls for evaluation of a system in order to assess the extent to which it can be relied on to ensure not only accurate information but also compliance with laws and regulations, and to provide for economical and effective operations. IIA standards require the internal auditor to evaluate the ability of systems to meet objectives of

1. Reliability and integrity of information,
2. Compliance with policies, plans, procedures, laws, and regulations,
3. Safeguarding of assets,

---

[4] Under the Foreign Corrupt Practices Act, publicly held companies are required to maintain systems that reasonably achieve the objectives of internal accounting control specified in the act (as taken from AU 320.28). Under discussion is the auditor's attest, if any, of a client's achievement. Thus, it might come about that auditors of public companies will have to study and test systems even though that may not be the most cost-effective audit approach. (See Chapter 13.)

4. Economical and efficient use of resources, and

5. Accomplishment of established objectives and goals for operations or programs.

Sufficient, Competent Evidence

Auditing is a *problem solving process* that can be viewed in four steps:

1. Formulate the problem so that evidence concerning it will permit a decision, either positive or negative,

2. Specify and perform procedures to collect such evidence,

3. Evaluate the sufficiency and competence of the evidence and determine whether its weight is positive or negative, and

4. Make the decision.

The first step in this process is crucial. Auditors must be able to formulate all the problems that are implied in management's statements of financial transactions and events. For example, the balance sheet caption "Buildings—net of $130,000 accumulated depreciation . . . . $70,000" actually contains several assertions, among them that the buildings exist and are useful in the business, that they cost $200,000, and that the depreciation is computed properly. Each assertion is taken as a hypothesis and thus presents the problem of whether it should be accepted or rejected.

Auditors can expect to find empirical evidence supporting or denying a hypothesis in only a limited number of cases. The hypothesis that certain buildings exist, for example, can be tested empirically by going to see the buildings. In other cases auditors can decide whether management's assertions are *warranted,* i.e., supportable by evidence and by reference to generally accepted criteria for the type of assertion under audit. For the depreciation of a building, for example, auditors can read the contract or purchase agreement stating the cost and review the useful-life and depreciation figures to decide whether management's figure is appropriate. Auditors will then consider whether the utility of the building is impaired, based on evidence from other procedures such as analytical review. These procedures only produce evidence that can be used to decide whether the assertion must be rejected, as it would be if it were not in conformity with generally accepted accounting principles for historical cost basis accounting and for calculating depreciation. This simple example makes its point that evidence is the crux of performing the audit. (This is discussed in detail in Chapter 12.)

The decision-making methodology described above forms the basis for the third field work standard in GAAS: "Sufficient, competent evidential matter is to be obtained through inspection, observation, inquiries, and confirmations to afford a reasonable basis for an opinion regarding the financial statements under examination" (AU 330.01). GAO and IIA standards for evidence parallel the AICPA standards.

Evidence is considered *sufficient* when an auditor has enough of it to make a decision. How much is enough is a matter of professional judgment. Evidence is *competent* when it is relevant to the decision problem, reasonably objective, and free from bias. Whether it meets these criteria is also a matter of professional judgment. The auditor's professional judgment, in turn, depends on his independence, due professional care, training and proficiency, planning and supervision, and knowledge of the internal control system. Thus, the AICPA general and field work standards constitute a coordinated system of theory that finds application in decision making based on evidence.

Consultation With Others

Auditors often call upon others for aid in the evidence gathering process, and several Statements on Auditing Standards provide guidance for this consultation. The standards briefly described below set forth considerations for using the work of internal auditors and specialists, for inquiry of the client's lawyers, and for representations from the client's managers.

Internal Auditors. SAS 9 (AU 322) states that independent auditors cannot substitute the work of internal auditors for their own. In fact, they are not even required to consult with a client's internal auditors. When internal auditors are involved in the client's internal control system, however, the independent auditor should acquire an understanding of the internal audit function insofar as this understanding contributes to his study and evaluation of internal control. Going somewhat further, if the independent auditor decides that the internal auditors' work may have a bearing on his own procedures, he should (1) consider the competence and objectivity of the internal auditors and (2) evaluate their work. Many CPA firms have policies on relations with a client's internal auditors, and an adaptation of one firm's policy is included as Appendix 11-B.

Internal audit personnel may perform procedures that would otherwise be performed by persons on the independent auditor's staff, but the independent auditor should supervise and test their work. All important audit judgments must be made by the independent auditor, never delegated to internal auditors.

Specialists. A *specialist* is a person or firm possessing special skills or knowledge in a field other than accounting or auditing. Auditors frequently consult actuaries, appraisers, attorneys, engineers, and geologists for such services as the valuation of art works, estimation of mineral resources, actuarial determination of life insurance reserves, and interpretation of laws and regulations. SAS 11 (AU 336) states that when using a specialist the auditor should conduct inquiries or otherwise obtain satisfaction as to the specialist's professional qualifications and reputation. The auditor should also gain a general understanding of the methods and assumptions used by the specialist, be sure that the data the specialist is considering are the same data the auditor wants assessed (i.e., they tie in to the books), and know enough about the work to determine what bearing the specialist's findings have on financial statement information. Some testing and review of the specialist's work may be appropriate. In general, specialists should be independent of the client, but this is not always possible. Other chapters discuss specialists that are frequently used in the accounting and auditing process.

Lawyers. Auditors are required to obtain written responses from clients' lawyers concerning litigation in progress and other matters that might be accounted for and disclosed as contingencies in accordance with SFAS 5, *Accounting for Contingen-*

cies (AC 4311). SAS 12 (AU 337) sets forth procedures for obtaining representations from management and corroboration from the lawyers, and contains an illustrative inquiry letter and the American Bar Association's Statement of Policy regarding lawyers' responses. (See Chapter 29.)

Management. Auditors are required to obtain written representations from management, not as substitutes for evidence obtainable through other procedures, but to complement other audit evidence. In a few cases management representations may be the primary source of information, e.g., those concerning related-party transactions and intentions to refinance short-term obligations on a long-term basis. SAS 19 (AU 333.04) gives an illustrative list of 20 points of information about which representations may be obtained. Representation letters are to be signed by responsible, informed members of management, normally the chief executive officer and the chief financial officer. The formality of this process is intended to impress upon management its primary responsibility for the financial statements and related disclosures.

STANDARDS OF REPORTING

Independent auditors' reports to the users of audited financial statements are of several types and have several variations. Chapter 16 explains these types and variations, and the auditor's standard report is shown in both Chapters 9 and 16.

There are four summary reporting standards in GAAS. The first three are

1. The report shall state whether the financial statements are presented in accordance with generally accepted accounting principles (AU 410.01);
2. The report shall state whether such principles have been consistently observed in the current period in relation to the preceding period (AU 420.01); and
3. Informative disclosures in the financial statements are to be regarded as reasonably accurate unless otherwise stated in the report (AU 430.01).

A major conceptual theme underlies these standards: the notion of *fair presentation* in financial reporting. Current practice reflects the auditors' assumption that consistent application of generally accepted accounting principles results in the fair presentation of financial position and the results of operations. As Mautz and Sharaf (1961, pp. 47-48) have pointed out, this assumption is necessary if auditors are to have the benefit of *any* criteria for appropriate accounting.

Management has important prerogatives in selecting the accounting principles, procedures, and methods that in their opinion best reflect the effect of financial transactions and economic events on their business. Indeed, management bears primary responsibility for the financial statements and the decisions that go into preparing them. The troublesome decisions for auditors revolve around whether management's financial statements "present fairly . . . in conformity with generally accepted accounting principles."

Fair Presentation

SAS 5, *The Meaning of "Present Fairly in Conformity with Generally Accepted Accounting Principles" in the Independent Auditor's Report* (AU 411), explains that the auditor's decision is based on his professional judgment as to whether

1. The accounting principles selected and applied have general acceptance,
2. The accounting principles are appropriate in the circumstances,
3. The financial statements are sufficiently informative,
4. The financial statement information is classified and summarized in a manner that is neither too detailed nor too condensed, and
5. The financial statements are presented within a range of acceptable limits that are reasonable and practicable to obtain.

"General acceptance" of accounting principles is established through *authoritative support,* which is automatically attributed to FASB statements and interpretations and to pronouncements issued by its predecessors, the Accounting Principles Board and the Committee on Accounting Procedure. If no official pronouncement exists, SAS 5 identifies numerous other formal sources that may provide guidance. But no amount of accounting pronouncements can cover every real-world condition properly, so auditors have the option to "break the rules." Rule 203 of the AICPA Rules of Conduct, quoted below, strongly acknowledges the role of officially pronounced accounting principles, but leaves some latitude for deviation, as the passage in italics indicates. The fact that only a few Rule 203 opinions have been issued on publicly held companies underscores the credence auditors place in GAAP.

> A member [of AICPA] shall not express an opinion that financial statements are presented in conformity with generally accepted accounting principles if such statements contain any departure from an accounting principle promulgated by the body designated by Council to establish such principles which has a material effect on the statements as a whole, *unless the member can demonstrate that due to unusual circumstances the financial statements would otherwise have been misleading. In such cases his report must describe the departure, the approximate effects thereof, if practicable, and the reasons why compliance with the principle would result in a misleading statement.* [ET 203.01; emphasis added]

To help auditors decide whether accounting principles are "appropriate in the circumstances," the standards provide that they should consider whether the substance of transactions differs materially from their form, because reporting the economic substance is recognized as important. However, the standards also state that individual auditors should not be expected to rule on the appropriateness of principles where alternatives exist (such as depreciation methods) and the FASB has not specified criteria for matching methods with circumstances. This area is a constant problem for auditors, because as the Cohen Commission observed (CAR, 1978, p. 13), users of audited statements expect auditors to "evaluate the disclosures made by management and determine whether financial statements are misleading, even if they technically conform with authoritative accounting pronouncements."

Auditor's Report

The last three considerations set forth in SAS 5 need little explanation. All of them enable auditors to cope with the fourth AICPA reporting standard, which consists of two basic requirements (AU 150.02).

The first is: "The report shall either contain an expression of opinion on the financial statements, taken as a whole, or an assertion to the effect that an opinion cannot be expressed. When an overall opinion cannot be expressed, the reasons therefor should be stated." This requirement divides opinion statements into two classes: opinions on statements taken as a whole (unqualified, qualified, or adverse opinions) and disclaimers of opinion. An "overall opinion" in the context of this standard is an unqualified opinion. Thus, when an unqualified opinion is not given, all the substantive reasons must be explained.

The second requirement, referring to both the scope paragraph and the opinion paragraph of the standard report, states: "In all cases where an auditor's name is associated with financial statements, the report should contain a clear-cut indication of the character of the auditor's examination, if any, and the degree of responsibility he is taking."

"In all cases" means precisely what it says. Every time auditors are associated by name or action with financial statements, they must report on their examination and their responsibility. The character of an audit examination is usually described in the auditor's standard report as an examination conducted in accordance with generally accepted auditing standards. However, if the audit was restricted in some way, or if the statements were not audited, the independent accountant must say so in the scope paragraph. This is especially important when an acountant is associated with unaudited financial statements for a publicly held client.

The "degree of responsibility" is indicated by the form of the opinion. Auditors take full responsibility for their belief that the financial statements are or are not fairly presented in conformity with GAAP when they give the unqualified or the adverse opinion. They take no such responsibility when giving the disclaimer of opinion. When giving a qualified opinion, they take responsibility for all matters except those mentioned as the reasons therefor. The various forms of opinions —unqualified, qualified, adverse, and disclaimer—are explained more fully in Chapter 16.

GAO and IIA Reporting Standards

GAO reporting standards contain all four AICPA reporting standards plus thirteen additional standards providing details on distribution, timing, and report content. The standards on report content serve as general quality criteria for reports that may involve anything from effectiveness of weapons systems to efficiency of a food distribution program.

The IIA summary reporting standard is brief: "Internal auditors should report the results of their audit work." Explanations of this standard include all of the report content standards set forth by GAO. Both government and internal auditors need broad reporting standards because their wide range of assignments is simply not amenable to a standard report.

QUALITY CONTROL FOR A CPA FIRM

Throughout this chapter there has been mention of Statements on Quality Control Standards (SQCSs) and some of their particular features. The 1979 inauguration of these standards, which are issued by a new senior technical committee of the AICPA, was intended to separate professional quality control requirements from the basic SASs, which focus on individual engagement quality but not on quality assurance per se. Prior to the establishment of the Quality Control Standards Committee, the Auditing Standards Executive Committee had issued SAS 4, *Quality Control Considerations for a Firm of Independent Auditors* (AU 160, December 1974), and the first SQCS brings in the SAS 4 elements as the starting point.

SQCS 1, *System of Quality Control for a CPA Firm* (QC 10), applies to all members of the AICPA's Division for Firms (both SEC and Private Practice Sections) and requires that a CPA firm shall have a system of quality control that includes, in a manner suitable to its organizational structure, the following elements (QC 10.07):

  a. *Independence.* Policies and procedures should be established to provide the firm with reasonable assurance that persons at all organizational levels maintain independence to the extent required by the Rules of Conduct of the AICPA.
  b. *Assigning Personnel to Engagements.* Policies and procedures for assigning personnel to engagements should be established to provide the firm with reasonable assurance that work will be performed by persons having the degree of technical training and proficiency required in the circumstances.
  c. *Consultation.* Policies and procedures for consultation should be established to provide the firm with reasonable assurance that personnel will seek assistance, to the extent required, from persons having appropriate levels of knowledge, competence, judgment, and authority.
  d. *Supervision.* Policies and procedures for the conduct and supervision of work at all organizational levels should be established to provide the firm with reasonable assurance that the work performed meets the firm's standards of quality.
  e. *Hiring.* Policies and procedures for hiring should be established to provide the firm with reasonable assurance that those employed possess the appropriate characteristics to enable them to perform competently.
  f. *Professional Development.* Policies and procedures for professional development should be established to provide the firm with reasonable assurance that personnel will have the knowledge required to enable them to fulfill responsibilities assigned.
  g. *Advancement.* Policies and procedures for advancing personnel should be established to provide the firm with reasonable assurance that the people selected will have the qualifications necessary for fulfillment of the responsibilities they will be called on to assume.
  h. *Acceptance and Continuance of Clients.* Policies and procedures should be estab-

lished for deciding whether to accept or continue a client in order to minimize the likelihood of association with a client whose management lacks integrity.

i. *Inspection.* Policies and procedures for inspection should be established to provide the firm with reasonable assurance that the procedures relating to the other elements of quality control are being effectively applied.

In addition, SQCS 1 requires (1) assignment of responsibilities to personnel to provide for effective implementation, (2) effective communication of the policies and procedures throughout the firm, and (3) monitoring so that the system retains its effectiveness.

On the basis of having such a system in place and described in a quality control document, a firm is able to undergo a peer review (see Chapter 39) as required by the rules of its respective AICPA practice section.

Although this chapter on auditing standards has focused on the ten basic GAAS and the continual binding interpretations thereof through SASs and SAPs, it is clear that audits are not performed in a vacuum; most are performed by firms of all sizes and kinds. The new SQCSs will standardize firm practices that each firm, prior to SAS 4, had to invent on its own.

FUTURE AUDITING STANDARDS

Predicting the course of future standards is a risky business. Nevertheless, some near-term future standards are not hard to foresee.

The above-mentioned quality control standards for firms are just a beginning. Many more aspects of firm-wide quality control will receive attention in the future. The companion standards for performance of peer reviews will likewise burgeon as the response of the accounting profession is reconciled with the demands of the SEC.

The SEC and FASB have created a relatively new subcategory of financial information, required supplemental information, which accompanies the basic financial statements. This supplemental information serves in part as a form of experimentation in the effort to develop new measurement and reporting techniques. The SEC had required the reporting of replacement cost information until the FASB substituted supplemental information on changing prices: constant dollar information and current cost information. These are only examples; much more is specified throughout this book, especially in Chapters 4 and 8. Independent auditors are associated with such information, and the Auditing Standards Board will have to decide in each situation the procedures and reporting formats to be used to reflect the nature and extent of auditors' involvement and responsibility.

In the development of Statements on Auditing Standards, the Auditing Standards Board has much to do. As financial information becomes broader and more subjective and future-oriented, the board will reconsider how this information can be efficiently and effectively reviewed, and this will affect most auditors. The board is also studying the effect of "soft" information on materiality. Essentially, if such information can only be quantified within ranges, the appropriate measure to be used in judging materiality in the context of audited financial statements needs to be better specified. The Auditing Standards Board has several other projects under way, including one dealing with the distinction, if any, between auditing standards for large and small companies.

The serious forecaster of future auditing standards could probably do well by studying all the recommendations (more than 40) made by the Cohen Commission in 1977 (finalized in 1978). A covey of AICPA committees and task forces are at work, grappling with implementation problems bypassed by the Cohen Commission. As with many recent SASs, the SEC's demands for achievement of the Cohen Commission's recommendations will probably result in evolutionary standards in particular areas.

Generally accepted auditing standards are not static. The Auditing Standards Board, representing the auditing profession, is committed to a course of adaptive change, and new Statements on Auditing Standards will emerge as interpretations and extensions of the summary ten.

SUGGESTED READING

AICPA. *Auditing Standards Established by the GAO—Their Meaning and Significance for CPAs, A Report.* New York, 1973. This committee report was issued immediately after the GAO standards were published. It gives a discussion of the GAO standards and how they may impact CPAs' practices.

————. *Guidelines for CPA Participation in Government Audit Engagements to Evaluate Economy, Efficiency and Program Results.* New York: 1977. No. 6 in the AICPA Management Advisory Services Guideline Series, this book offers practical advice on elements of government audits, on responding to a request for proposal, and on conducting evaluations of economy, efficiency, and program results.

American Accounting Association Committee on Auditing Concepts. "A Statement of Basic Auditing Concepts." *Accounting Review,* supplement to vol. 47 (1972), pp. 15-76. This committee report is a conceptual-theoretical treatment of auditing that reveals the philosophy behind many of the generally accepted auditing standards. The committee report builds upon the Mautz and Sharaf *Philosophy.*

Commission on Auditors' Responsibilities. *Report, Conclusions, and Recommendations.* New York: AICPA, 1978. The final report contains numerous observations on current auditing practices and recommendations for change.

Mautz, Robert, and Sharaf, Hussein. *The Philosophy of Auditing.* American Accounting Association Monograph No. 6. Sarasota, Fla: AAA, 1961. The *Philosophy* was the first major attempt to catalog and explain the basic theoretical structure of concepts and basic postulates underlying independent auditors' practices.

Pomeranz, Felix; Cancellieri, Alfred; Stevens, Joseph; and Savage, James. *Auditing in the Public Sector.* Boston: Warren, Gorham, & Lamont, 1976. This book covers many details of government-type engagements. Programs, questionnaires, and practical guides are covered in addition to general explanations.

Robertson, Jack. *Auditing.* Revised edition. Dallas: Business Publications, 1979. This textbook blends conceptual explanations of auditing standards with structured decision making.

Sawyer, Lawrence. *The Practice of Modern Internal Auditing.* Altamonte Springs, Fla: Institute of Internal Auditors, 1973. A most complete text on internal auditing, this book covers everything from the origination and establishment of an internal audit department through technical procedures and audit reports.

Stamp, Edward, and Moonitz, Maurice. *International Auditing Standards.* Englewood Cliffs, N.J.: Prentice-Hall International, 1978. Many accountants need to be acquainted with standards in other nations. This book discusses the state of standards in Australia, Canada, the Netherlands, France, West Germany, Japan, Brazil, the United Kingdom, and the United States of America.

APPENDIX 11-A STATEMENTS ON AUDITING STANDARDS

No.	Date Issued	Title	Codification Section
1	Nov. 1972	*Codification of Auditing Standards and Procedures*	
2	Oct. 1974	*Reports on Audited Financial Statements*	509
3	Dec. 1974	*The Effects of EDP on the Auditor's Study and Evaluation of Internal Control*	321
4	Dec. 1974	*Quality Control Considerations for a Firm of Independent Auditors*	160
5	July 1975	*The Meaning of "Present Fairly in Conformity with Generally Accepted Accounting Principles" in the Independent Auditor's Report*	411
6	July 1975	*Related Party Transactions*	335
7	Oct. 1975	*Communications Between Predecessor and Successor Auditors*	315
8	Dec. 1975	*Other Information in Documents Containing Audited Financial Statements*	550
9	Dec. 1975	*The Effect of an Internal Audit Function on the Scope of the Independent Auditor's Examination*	322
10	Dec. 1975	*Limited Review of Interim Financial Information* (superseded by SAS 24)	—
11	Dec. 1975	*Using the Work of a Specialist*	336
12	Jan. 1976	*Inquiry of a Client's Lawyer Concerning Litigation, Claims, and Assessments*	337
13	May 1976	*Reports on Limited Review of Interim Financial Information* (superseded by SAS 24)	—
14	Dec. 1976	*Special Reports*	621
15	Dec. 1976	*Reports on Comparative Financial Statements*	505
16	Jan. 1977	*The Independent Auditor's Responsibility for the Detection of Errors or Irregularities*	327
17	Jan. 1977	*Illegal Acts by Clients*	328
18	May 1977	*Unaudited Replacement Cost Information*	730
19	June 1977	*Client Representations*	333
20	Aug. 1977	*Required Communication of Material Weaknesses in Internal Accounting Control*	323
21	Dec. 1977	*Segment Information*	435

APPENDIX 11-B   EXAMPLE OF A CPA FIRM'S POLICY ON UTILIZATION OF INTERNAL AUDIT FUNCTION [5]

Policy

This section covers two aspects of the internal audit function and its role in the audit process:

A. The internal audit function as an internal control.
B. The internal audit function in providing assistance to us as outside auditors in performing our audit of the financial statements.

It serves to reinforce and clarify the requirements of SAS 9, *The Effect of an Internal Audit Function on the Scope of the Independent Auditor's Examination* (AU 322).

When either or both of these aspects are present in a particular audit engagement, we must make a formal, documented evaluation of the internal audit function.

A. This evaluation should begin as part of the planning process.
B. It must be supported by appropriate audit procedures. (Possible procedures are outlined below.)
C. It will specifically include the competence and objectivity of internal audit personnel, as well as their level of performance.
D. The results of the evaluation along with other factors will determine the degree to which we rely on the internal audit function as an internal control and/or use internal audit to assist us in our examination.

---

[5] Adapted from the Touche Ross & Co. *Auditing Practice Policies Manual.*

Discussion—Internal Audit as an Internal Control

Internal audit is part of a class of controls that operate across the basic units and accounting systems of a company to determine that the detailed systems-level controls are operating effectively. In other words, they are, in a real sense, controls of controls. Other common corporate-level controls are management budgeting, reporting and follow-up systems, and standard procedures manuals. Often, internal audit will relate to these other corporate-level controls, such as in performing follow-up of variances from budget or in determining that standard procedures manuals are in use. In other instances, internal audit will review the efficiency, effectiveness, and degree of compliance with systems-level controls as a direct objective, or indirectly by examining data processed by the systems for errors. This is extremely important in large systems where no single person oversees both the initiation and completion of transactions, so that unreasonable processing results are observed and corrected (e.g., where EDP is used extensively).

The form of reliance on internal audit will depend on the types of internal accounting control activities performed. In many companies, internal audit will review the performance of others performing control functions. For example, they will review processed transactions for correctness, observe segregation of duties, and investigate accounting problem areas. In these cases the effective performance of internal audit will reduce the likelihood of the types of potential errors the controls reviewed are intended to prevent or detect and correct. If we are satisfied that this entire control structure—including the initial controls and internal audit—is functioning effectively, we can rely on it to a greater extent in designing substantive procedures than we could on the initial controls alone.

In companies with multiunits or several locations, internal audit is frequently used to visit individual locations to evaluate whether the prescribed policies and procedures issued by the home office are being followed and whether accurate information is being reported to the home office by the individual locations. In this situation, particularly where other corporate-level controls are in effect, internal audit can provide very effective control.

Although reliance on internal audit and other corporate-level controls often allows us to reduce significantly the number of locations we visit and the amount of detailed work we perform, it is important to understand that once we determine the extent of such work necessary for our purposes, we cannot then improperly delegate it to the internal auditors to perform on our behalf; however, as discussed below, they can provide us with assistance.

Discussion—Internal Audit Assistance in Performing Auditing Procedures

The nature, timing, and extent of year-end-oriented substantive procedures are determined by the outside auditor's appraisal of the likelihood of various types of errors in the financial statements after completion of the systems-testing phase of the examination. Internal audit as an internal control may or may not have been a factor in that appraisal. In either case, the appraisal reached is a fixed point of reference for determining the remaining amount of work to be completed by the outside auditor.

Thus, the outside auditor is responsible for performing and evaluating several types of procedures at levels established by the logic of his audit plan. These are compliance procedures (observations and compliance tests of transactions) relating to controls being relied on and substantive procedures (tests of transactions, year-end-oriented substantive tests of details and analytical procedures) relating to financial statement amounts. Where internal audit is being relied upon as a control, compliance procedures will be applied to the internal audit function by the outside auditor. For compliance procedures of other controls and substantive procedures, internal audit assistance may be appropriate.

Although it may be appropriate for internal auditors to assist in performing these procedures, as indicated above, the outside auditor retains the final responsibility for them. The outside auditor will fulfill this responsibility by several means, including assuring the competence and objectivity of internal audit personnel relative to the assistance provided; restricting internal audit assistance to areas where there is less chance of significant error; adequately supervising and reviewing the work performed by the internal auditors in providing assistance; and, in some cases, reperforming a portion of the work done by internal auditors in providing assistance, particularly for larger and more complex items.

Discussion—Internal Auditor Competence and Objectivity

As indicated above, a significant portion of our evaluation of the internal audit function will focus on the competence and objectivity of its members.

Competence relates to the internal auditor's skill (i.e., knowledge and experience) in performing an assigned task. As will be seen below, a person may approach a task objectively, but if he does not have the skill to perform it, objectivity will suffer, and in addition, the job may not get done as intended.

Competence can be viewed at two levels: general competence and specific task-related skill. General competence relates to a person's basic intelligence, problem-solving capabilities, and communication skills. Specific task-related skill relates to finding and matching appropriate people to the tasks to be performed. In internal auditing, the following are examples of tasks that require specific skills:

A. Management of the internal audit function—requires extensive general audit experience; knowledge of current developments; extensive knowledge of the company and its business; strong communication skills; personnel and behavioral skills.

B. Review of data processing—requires understanding of EDP fundamentals; understanding of EDP controls; understanding of computer auditing and control evaluation techniques; working knowledge of EDP data access and testing techniques, including audit software.

C. Inventory observation—requires understanding of auditing principles underlying inventory observation; understanding the nature of inventory taking and the function of instructions, second counts, tag control, etc.; knowledge of the plant or warehouse location, the people involved, the products, and the underlying manufacturing process.

Objectivity relates to the internal auditor's ability to make an unbiased judgment, in terms of seeking necessary information, evaluating the information properly, and taking appropriate actions based on the results. Objectivity is a function of two factors: the basic attitude of the person involved and the environmental influences in the circumstances surrounding a particular judgment. A desirable basic attitude would be one formed where the person involved understands the purpose of his function and wants to fulfill his function in an unbiased fashion, i.e., he understands the nature and value of objectivity and internalizes it.

The environmental influences affecting the objectivity of internal audit judgments are primarily organizational in nature, i.e., the internal auditor is likely to be biased in the following situations:

A. He is judging the performance of a direct superior.

B. He is judging the results of systems and procedures he participated in developing.

C. He is not knowledgeable in the area and must rely on the person responsible for the area for extended guidance.

D. The internal audit function is organizationally weak (e.g., small, does not have total management support, or is "undercapitalized") and subject to second guessing by those criticized in its reports.

E. Because of the attitude of management, internal audit operates under significant pressure to justify its existence by identifying cost savings and/or to cover an excessive range of projects during the year.

Competence and objectivity are matters of degree relative to the circumstances. The external auditor has the responsibility to establish and support with evidence that both these characteristics are present to the degree the external auditor believes is necessary for the particular use he intends to make of the internal audit function—i.e., to rely on as an internal control to some planned extent and/or to assist in performing a specific task.

The general procedures for evaluating competence and objectivity of internal audit are inquiry, analysis, observation and review, and testing of work performed.

Procedures

Presented in this section are a general set of procedures that can be used to obtain evidence to support our evaluation of internal audit. The inclusion and extent of application of any one or combination of these procedures will depend on the circumstances of the engagement and the degree to which we rely on internal audit as an internal control and/or use them to assist us in our examination.

The general procedures are as follows:

A. Gather descriptive information about the internal audit function.

B. Evaluate the competence of internal audit personnel.

C. Evaluate the objectivity of internal audit personnel.

D. Plan the degree to which we will rely on internal audit as an internal control. Where reliance exists, evaluate the performance of internal audit during the year.

E. Plan the extent to which internal audit will provide assistance to us in our examination.

   1. The extent to which they will be available will usually be at the discretion of client management.

   2. Where they will provide assistance, identify the specific tasks they will perform and the procedures we will follow to evidence their competence and objectivity and to control their activities in assisting us.

F. Provide for proper documentation in our working papers of the planning and completion of the above procedures.

(Specific procedures to be considered in each of the above general areas are omitted from this appendix.)

Other Considerations

We will generally review internal audit reports developed during the year during the course of our review and evaluation of internal audit activities. Where we do this and note that significant control problems were encountered by internal audit, the corrective follow-up measures taken and an evaluation of how these control problems affected our year-end procedures should be discussed in our audit working papers.

We must always structure our approach to internal audit to recognize that it is an on-going function. Although the bulk of our procedures regarding internal audit will come at particular points in time, our evaluation must be of a continuous nature. We should become aware of significant changes that take place in internal audit and include the impact of such changes in our audit design.

12

Performing the Audit

James K. Loebbecke

AUDIT CONCEPTS

The audit is basically a problem-solving process. The subject of the problem is an enterprise that conducts financial activities and reports the results of those activities to interested parties in the form of financial statements. The broad purpose of the audit is to determine whether these financial statements present the enterprise's actual activities in conformity with the accounting standards established for the type of entity and the circumstances involved. The result of the audit is the auditor's report.

This chapter presents a highly simplified approach to performing the audit. In a way, this is the conceptual framework on which much of the material in the other chapters of this *Handbook* is built. Thus, there are numerous references given to those other chapters.

The fundamental concepts involved in the audit process are audit evidence, materiality, audit sampling, and internal control. These are discussed below. (Chapters immediately following this one are devoted specifically to sampling and internal control.)

Audit Objectives

The broad objective of the audit is to form a correct opinion as to whether the financial statements are fairly presented in conformity with generally accepted accounting principles, and it is met by achieving certain audit objectives through specific procedures aimed at obtaining and evaluating evidential matter. These audit objectives are derived from the five fundamental assertions embodied in all components of financial statements. As discussed in SAS 31, *Evidential Matter* (AU 330.03), these assertions, whether explicit or implicit, are the representations of management, and are as follows:

- Existence or occurrence,
- Completeness,
- Rights and obligations,
- Valuation or allocation, and
- Presentation or disclosure.

The seven audit objectives deriving from these assertions and that (with some exceptions) must be satisfied (with appropriate individual and cumulative tolerances of materiality for each element of the financial statements) before the audit is complete are to determine that

1. All recorded transactions actually took place (i.e., are valid), and all actual transactions are recorded (existence);
2. All assets are owned, and all liabilities owed (ownership);
3. All recorded amounts are reasonably accurate, and changes in economic circumstances that affect recorded amounts are reflected in the financial statements (valuation);
4. Amounts are recorded in the correct financial statement classification (classification);
5. Amounts are recorded in the proper period (cutoff);
6. Amounts are correctly posted to and summarized in the financial statements (mechanical accuracy); and
7. Adequate pertinent information is set forth in the financial statements so that the statements are not misleading (adequate disclosure).

Audit Evidence

The auditor achieves his audit objectives by obtaining and evaluating *audit evidence*—information about events supporting the amounts and disclosures in the financial statements. Audit evidence is gathered using *auditing procedures.*

Several types of evidence are commonly obtained in an audit, but they are seldom fully conclusive. Usually they are only more or less persuasive, depending on the circumstances. Thus, deciding what forms of evidence to gather, how much of it to gather, and how to evaluate it requires a high level of auditing experience and the careful exercise of professional judgment. Among other things, the auditor must consider the relative cost of obtaining alternative types of evidence likely to provide equal satisfaction of audit objectives. Seven types of audit evidence, to be used as the audit circumstances warrant, are physical examination, confirmation, documentation, observation, representations by the client, recomputations and postings, and comparisons of related account balances and other information.

Physical Examination. An *inspection* or *count* of tangible items is often carried out to obtain audit evidence on such assets as inventories, cash on hand, securities, and property, plant, and equipment. Frequently, documents representing assets and obligations, such as titles, deeds, and notes, are also physically examined. Inspection provides direct verification of the existence of tangible assets, is evidence of both their quantity and their description, and may also provide evidence of their condition or quality. It is one of the most reliable forms of audit evidence for these attributes, but usually not for the assertion that the assets belong to the company being audited. Documentation representing assets, on the other hand, may be a good indication of ownership but not of quality.

Confirmation. A confirmation is a written or oral statement from a third party, in response to the auditor's request, as to the accuracy of information. For a confirmation to be reliable for the auditor's needs, it must be obtained from a source who is believed to be independent and who will presumably act competently and with integrity. To the extent that the auditor cannot make a reasonable judgment of the source's independence, competence, or integrity, the confirmation is not reliable. Thus, the auditor always considers these factors in deciding whether to seek confirmation and the degree of reliance he will place on the response. A major use of confirmations is in the accounts receivable area. (See Chapter 18 for a discussion of their value and weaknesses in this area.)

Documentation. The documents that the auditor examines are those that provide evidence about transactions and information that is or should be in the audited company's financial statements.

Documents are either internal or external. An *internal document* is one that has been prepared by, and processed through, the company's system. It is retained by the company without going to an outside party (e.g., a customer or a supplier) or is distributed to an outside party who is not expected to act on it. An *external document* is one that has been prepared by, or has been in the hands of, someone outside the company's organization who is a party to the transaction being documented and who has acted on the document or is expected to do so.

The reliability of a document as audit evidence depends to a great extent on whether it is an internal or an external document. Since external documents have been in the hands of both the company and an active outside party, there is some indication that both parties are in agreement about the information contained in the document. The concurrence, usually by some action, of the outside party provides objectivity. External documents are therefore regarded as more reliable evidence than internal ones. Nevertheless, the reliability of both types of documents is affected by the reliability of the audited company's internal controls through which they are processed. When documents are processed through satisfactory internal controls, there is more assurance of their reliability as audit evidence than when they are processed with unsatisfactory internal controls.

Observation. Observations are made in order to assess the performance of controls or to obtain knowledge of operations. For example, the auditor may tour production facilities to learn about the company's operations, or may periodically observe the receiving department's count and inspection of incoming materials to assess the implementation of controls. Also, the auditor may periodically watch individuals perform accounting tasks to evaluate whether they are carrying out their assigned responsibilities. As a test of internal controls, observation is normally not adequate audit evidence by itself, and will generally be accompanied by other tests. Nevertheless, observation is useful and necessary in most parts of the audit.

Representations by the Client. Representations (both *oral* and *written*) by the client in response to the auditor's expressed or implied questions and requests for data will always constitute a large portion of evidence accumulated during an audit. The auditor realizes that this form of evidence is not provided by an independent source, and that therefore it could, and in some instances perhaps even should, be biased in the client's favor. When the auditor obtains express or implied representations from the client on significant areas, therefore, he should also obtain corroborating evidence by other more objective procedures.

Occasionally the *only* evidence available will be the representation by the client, which in this case should be in writing. An example is management's future plans and intentions that do not seem infeasible and are not controverted by other evidence possessed by the auditor. The auditor must consider carefully the integrity and motivation of the person(s) signing the representation. SAS 19 (AU 333) discusses in detail the evidential value of client representations.

Recomputations and Postings. Recomputations involve testing for mathematical accuracy and, where applicable, observing the compliance of computations with specified formulas. They include such procedures as extending sales invoices and inventory, adding figures in journals and subsidiary ledgers, and checking the calculation of depreciation charges and prepaid expenses. The checking of postings consists of tracing amounts to their source to be confident that transactions are correctly recorded in the proper accounts and at the correct amounts. Inasmuch as the results of these procedures are evidence directly developed by the auditor, such evidence is considered reliable; but it must be evaluated according to the procedural controls established by the auditor to assure himself that postings other than those checked have not affected those that were found to be recorded properly.

Comparisons of Related Account Balances and Other Information. The use of analytical review procedures for comparisons of related account balances, ratios, trends, and the like provides useful evidence of the reasonableness of account balances or transactions, or of their conformity with an expected trend, as in a seasonal business. An example of this form of evidence is a comparison of the current period's repair expense with that of the previous year; if the comparison suggests that the repair expense is unexpectedly high or low, the auditor will then investigate the cause. If the area is not material to the financial statements, the auditor may request the client to investigate and explain. SAS 23 (AU 318) discusses analytical procedures in detail, and Appendix 12 provides a brief discussion of analytical audit approaches. In many of the chapters in Part III of this *Handbook,* specific analytical procedures are illustrated.

Materiality

Management is responsible for preparing the financial statements of the reporting enterprise. These statements must be *reasonably* accurate. In practice it is virtually impossible for them to be precisely accurate, but they must be sufficiently accurate so as not to be misleading to users who have a reasonable understanding of business and economic activities and who are willing to study the information with reasonable diligence. The degree to which financial statements may be imprecise but not misleading is known as *materiality.* When a misstatement or omission is so great as to lead an informed user of the financial statements to make a different decision than he would if the defect did not exist, the deficiency is said to be material. The materiality of an item depends, therefore, not only on its size, but also on qualitative aspects such as whether it involves related parties or conflicts of interest or whether it appears irregular or even illegal. See Chapter 3 for further discussion of materiality.

The concept of materiality is important to management because it allows the preparation of acceptable financial statements without incurring inordinately high accounting and preparation costs in a vain effort to be exact. This concept is also applied by the auditor to control auditing costs, for it allows him to gather only enough competent evidence to provide reasonable assurance that the financial statements are not materially affected by errors or irregularities. Total certainty by the auditor is not economically feasible, and it is not required by professional standards nor even by the severest critics of the auditing profession.

Audit Sampling

The practice of audit sampling is an application of the concepts of materiality and reasonable (rather than absolute) assurance. Audit sampling, or testing as it is often called, occurs when an audit procedure is performed on less than 100% of the available items. It is discussed in detail in Chapter 14.

Internal Control

The financial statements are based on the enterprise's accounting process. This process consists of formal systems and controls. These should be designed to provide a level of discipline and reliability adequate to assure management that the financial statements are appropriately prepared, that the assets are safeguarded and their existence is periodically verified, and that transactions are executed only as authorized and recorded in a manner that maintains accountability for the assets.

The existence of formal systems and controls, commonly termed *internal controls,* provides the auditor with auditing options. In effect, the auditor can audit the results of processing (the financial statements), or he can audit the process itself (the accounting system). These two approaches are termed the *substantive approach* and the *reliance approach,* respectively. In practice, a combination of both approaches is usually used. The auditor seeks to design an optimal combination for any given audit, recognizing the quality of internal control, the relative effectiveness of available procedures and evidence, and the economies offered by various alternatives. Internal control is fully covered in Chapter 13.

Characteristics of Audited Enterprises

Certain characteristics of the audited enterprises affect the auditing process. Among the most important of these characteristics are size, ownership, data processing systems, and industry.

Size. The size of the entity will often affect the audit approach. Small companies usually have less sophisticated and less reliable systems and controls than large companies do, but audits of large companies require a greater logistic effort because of their complexity and volume of transactions. Because of these differences in reliability and volume, auditors tend to adopt a predominantly substantive approach in audits of small companies and a predominantly reliance approach in audits of large companies. The substantive approach minimizes the uncertainties about appropriate presentation of the financial statements that could arise from potentially weak controls; the reliance approach allows work to be performed over a longer period of time and prior to the close of the company's fiscal year. (For a consideration of some of the differences in auditor services to small and large companies, see Chapter 9.)

Ownership. Publicly held companies are subject to the provisions of the 1933 and 1934 securities acts (and in some cases other acts administered by the SEC), which place formidable reporting requirements on the companies and certification burdens on their auditors. The seriousness of these responsibilities is emphasized by the legal sanctions contained in the securities acts and interpreted by the courts (see Chapter 46) and by the regulations administered by the SEC. The potential massive losses to investors as a result of published false or erroneous financial information is the justification for the extensive demands made of publicly held companies and their auditors.

Because of the securities acts and their ramifications, auditors must be knowledgeable about the related regulations and must perform numerous additional steps in conducting audits of publicly held companies. Not only publicly held companies are regulated by the SEC; many other companies with a fiduciary responsibility to the public, such as financial institutions, are regulated and audited in much the same way. (SEC regulation is discussed in Chapter 41, and financial institutions in Chapter 38.)

Data Processing Systems. The great majority of today's business enterprises of any size use electronic data processing (EDP) equipment, either in-house or through service bureaus, for processing at least some of their financial information. And constantly decreasing per-unit processing costs has brought the computer within the reach of even the smallest of enterprises. The computer presents the auditor with both an opportunity and a challenge. The opportunity is to use this powerful tool to assist in performing a more effective and efficient audit. The challenge is to be adept with the more complex technology used in electronic processing of data, and to evaluate its impact on the audited company's systems and controls. Both the challenge and the opportunity are discussed in detail in Chapter 15.

Industry. In discussions of auditing such as this chapter, the typical application is to commercial or manufacturing companies, but many actual audits are of companies in industries with special characteristics. Banks, insurance companies, construction companies, health care organizations, securities brokers and dealers, and the extractive industries are a few examples of industries with special business characteristics that the auditor must understand because they usually require specific recognition in audit planning and performance. As specialized industries are discussed in this *Handbook,* unique auditing aspects are mentioned.

THE AUDIT PROCESS

The audit process is a logical sequence of steps taken (1) to design the audit to be both efficient and effective, (2) to perform the audit in accordance with that design, and (3) to assure compliance with applicable professional standards (i.e., GAAS). In this process, the company's circumstances are considered, and the plan for that client's audit is drawn up. The best combination of substantive procedures and reliance on systems and controls will vary, depending on the company as well as on the auditor's own circumstances, e.g., timing and staff availability.

A graphic overview of the audit process is shown in Figure 12.1. The process is divided into three distinct phases: planning, systems testing, and verification of financial statement balances. Within each phase there are several steps. Each step has a specific objective and result, and each result serves as a basis for planning the details of work to be done in one or more subsequent steps. Thus it is essential to maintain the schedule established for each step in the sequence, at least within sections of the audit that are mutually related. In other words, Phase II in a specific transaction cycle cannot be done before Phase I, but a cycle could be in Phase II or III at the same time the auditor is working through Phase I in another cycle.

The objective of Phase I is to understand the audited company's business and systems and to decide on what appears to be the optimal approach for achieving the audit objectives. This results in a formal and specific overall audit plan. The plan tentatively indicates the extent to which systems and controls will be relied on, how financial statement balances will be tested, and the nature and extent of the systems tests to be performed. Phase II either corroborates the logic and appropriateness of the preliminary audit plan or indicates that the plan must be changed because systems and controls are not what they were believed to be. Then, based on this information, appropriate tests of the financial statement balances themselves are designed and carried out in Phase III. These results are evaluated, and the auditor's report is then issued.

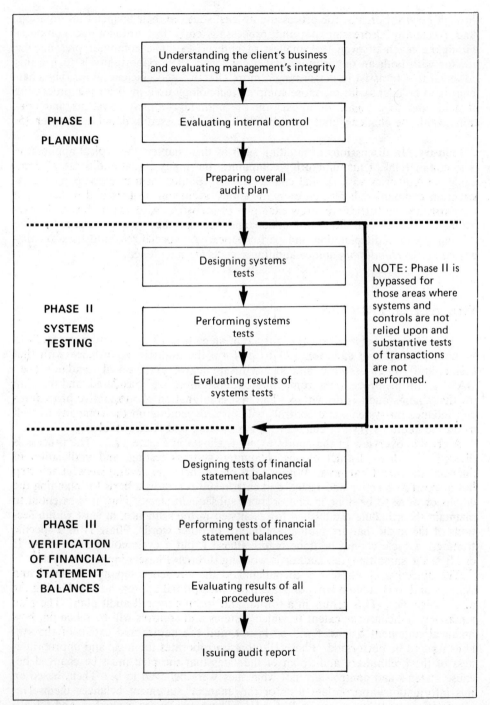

FIGURE 12.1   THE AUDIT PROCESS

Phase I: Planning

Understanding the Client's Business. The auditor is auditing a *business,* not just a set of books and records. Therefore, he must understand its operations in terms of its industry, products, markets, production processes, distribution systems, facilities, personnel, financing, and other relevant aspects.

There are several specific reasons this understanding should be kept in mind as information is obtained:

- To identify the degree of professional risk;
- To identify the need for special expertise in problem areas;
- To provide input about the client's systems;
- To provide a basis for assessment of accounting policies; and
- To provide the best possible client service.

These reasons are discussed below.

Identifying the degree of professional risk. When investors or creditors lose money, it is common for them to seek recovery through claims against auditors. The usual allegations in these cases, discussed in detail in Chapter 46, are that the investors and creditors relied on audited financial statements that failed to provide them with information that would have influenced their decisions and enabled them to avoid their losses. Such claims may or may not be valid, but the auditor must recognize that they present a professional risk. Since a client's economic downturn increases that risk, the auditor should identify early warning signs of potential economic downturns. Conventional forms of financial analysis are often used for this purpose (see Chapter 6).

A weak management organization or poor managerial performance or control can also result in economic downturn for the client, or may lead to defensive business decisions that are not in the company's best overall interest. Thus, in addition to using conventional financial analyses, including bankruptcy predictors (see Chapter 22), the auditor should consider conditions pointing to weaknesses in management performance or control.

Finally, the auditor must recognize that the integrity of management and its good faith in providing audit information are fundamental to the performance of an adequate audit. If management lacks integrity and good faith toward the auditor, it could circumvent controls established for the proper recording of transactions, and the resulting financial statements could be false or misleading. It is essential, therefore, that the auditor attempt to understand the motives of management and to identify conditions that might lead it to act without integrity or good faith. (Lack of integrity is often manifested through concealed related-party transactions, discussed at length in Chapter 28.)

The auditor's appraisal of professional risk is made on a continuing basis for existing clients and before an engagement is accepted with a new client. If the professional risk is high, the auditor will adjust his examination to compensate for it. In some cases, the auditor may decline to perform the audit examination. Several prominent factors that the auditor should consider in appraising professional risk are provided in Figure 12.2 as a convenient checklist, though the list should not be accepted as exhaustive.

GENERAL ECONOMIC AND FINANCIAL CONDITIONS

1. Insufficient working capital or credit lines to enable the business to operate at a profitable capacity.
2. Demands for new capital in excess of its availability.
3. Dependence on a single or relatively few products, customers, or transactions for the ongoing success of the business.
4. Violations or potential violations of debt restrictions (such as maintenance of working capital, coverage of interest charges, additional permissible debt) or of other terms of a loan agreement, trust indenture, or other contract.
5. The economic state of the industry. (For example, is it characterized by a large number of business failures?)
6. Excess capacity and high fixed costs.
7. Extremely rapid expansion of business or product lines.
8. Numerous acquisitions, particularly as a diversification into operations that are new to the client.
9. A long-term operating cycle for the company's products (long-term construction contracts, for example).
10. Chronically overoptimistic sales projections used to justify the continued deferral of start-up costs or expansion of new product lines.

ORGANIZATIONAL CONDITIONS

1. Significantly less profit than other companies in the industry.
2. A lack of strong leadership, or dissipation of strength at the top in power struggles.
3. High turnover in management positions, especially financial management.
4. Failure to develop managerial talent in proportion to the growth of the business.
5. Decentralized operations and transaction documentation, with a centralized management.
6. Diversified activities, each with its own accounting systems.
7. Overdependence on computer processing, effectively placing total operating reliance on these systems.
8. Inadequate internal audit.
9. Extensive use of different auditors for different segments of the business.
10. No outside counsel, or frequent changes in lawyer relationships.

MANAGEMENT'S INTEGRITY

1. Preoccupation with favorable earnings, perhaps because of a desire to support the company's share price or because of management profit-sharing agreements.
2. Desire for unrealistically low taxable income.
3. Desire for power (empire building).
4. Domination by one or a few individuals.
5. Questionable reputation outside the company.
6. Reputation for taking unusual or unnecessary risks.
7. Significant litigation, especially with shareholders.

FIGURE 12.2 FACTORS IN APPRAISING PROFESSIONAL RISK

Identifying the need for special expertise in problem areas. Auditing is normally a team effort. One reason for this is the sheer size of most audits, coupled with the need to perform all the required tasks by a deadline. Another reason is that certain tasks require special skills that not all auditors possess. When these skills are required, they must be identified, and someone to provide them must usually be arranged for in advance. The areas most commonly requiring special skills are industry expertise, advanced auditing methodology, and expertise in other professional disciplines, such as geology or actuarial science.

When the client is in an industry with unique accounting and auditing problems, a person with a knowledge of that industry should be involved. If this knowledge is not possessed by the engagement management team, a consultant may be required on a part-time basis. When the client is a publicly held company, there is generally a need for an auditor with SEC experience.

As discussed in Chapters 14 and 15, auditing firms have various philosophies about and approaches to the use of advanced auditing methods such as statistical sampling and computer audit techniques. Some firms use persons designated as specialists, who perform these tasks on several engagements with which they are not otherwise associated. Other firms train all their auditors to a sufficient level of expertise that the advanced methods can be applied by members of the engagement team, with consultation from a technical expert required only where necessary. Whatever the approach, persons with the requisite skills to apply these techniques properly must be brought into the engagement.

Outside experts or specialists are often needed on an engagement. Actuaries may be needed to review pension provision and funding computations; engineers, to measure bulk inventories or mineral reserves; gemologists, to determine the value of precious stones; appraisers, to value real estate; and lawyers, to interpret contracts and agreements. Whenever such specialists are used, the auditor must have a basic understanding of the special expertise being applied and must consider whether the specialist's findings support the related representations in the financial statements. The auditor must also make appropriate tests of accounting data provided by the client to the specialist (AU 336).

Providing input about the client's systems. A major portion of Phase I of the audit is the evaluation of internal control. Knowledge of the business will lead to the identification of the client's various systems and their relative significance to the audit examination. To identify the most important systems, the auditor first identifies the material types of transactions that take place in the business—the major economic events that are processed by the company's systems and that affect the financial statements. Those systems that process material types of transactions are very significant to the audit. Other systems are of interest, but need not be described in the detail necessary to support a critical evaluation by the auditor.

Whenever a transaction—material individually or as a type—is not processed by a formal system or by one of appropriate strength, it usually requires greater audit scrutiny than if it were subject to appropriate systems and controls. The auditor should always consider whether a material weakness in internal controls needs to be communicated to the client (SAS 20; AU 323).

Providing for assessment of accounting policies. An understanding of the business provides an important context for the judgments that the auditor will be making throughout his examination. The appropriateness of the accounting policies followed and their effect on and presentation in the financial statements, the need for and wording of specific financial statement disclosures, the reasonableness of client representations and explanations, and the broad implications of financial results as they are to be reported must all be viewed in terms of the client's business.

Assisting the auditor in providing the best possible client service. Although the auditor's primary objective is to render an opinion on the financial statements, a strong secondary objective is to provide helpful advice in the form of recommendations to management. In gaining an understanding of the client's business, the auditor will have an opportunity to recognize particular problems and suggest solutions to them. Based on the auditor's objectivity and broad business experience gained by auditing many companies, these recommendations may fall in operations areas as well as the financial area.

Information about the client's business is available to members of the audit team from a number of sources, including

1. Audit working paper files from prior years;
2. Visits to the client's locations and tours of facilities;
3. Discussions with client management and employees;
4. Industry publications, the business press, libraries, firm publications, professional institute publications, and annual reports of other companies in the same business;
5. Client publications such as annual reports, prospectuses, advertising literature, interim financial reports, and policy manuals; and
6. Management financial reports, budgets and forecasts, and directors' minutes.

Since this information is gathered by all the members of the audit team over a period of time, it is important that it be properly communicated within the team. To accomplish this, it should be assembled with forethought and made accessible to team members as needed.

The auditor's documented understanding of the business should include a summary of the following types of information (each type is accompanied by a few examples):

1. Long-range company plans—corporate objectives, targets for products or market share, financial goals in terms of profits or share price;
2. Organizational structure—operating divisions, diversification, management organization, departmentalization, decentralization;
3. Marketing—customer characteristics, major markets, potential markets, marketing strategy, future products;
4. Production—product lines, facilities and locations, purchasing, labor relations and policies, physical flow of materials, inventories and warehousing;
5. Sales—sales force, distribution system, commission policies, selling techniques;
6. Financial matters—banking relationships, financial resources, plans for future financing, profitability of the industry, stock exchange performance;
7. Ownership and management—principal stockholders, principal debt holders, directors and officers, key management personnel; and

8. Special relationships with other parties—common ownership or management, franchisers or franchisees, government relationships.

Evaluation of Internal Control. As a part of every audit, the auditor is required to make some evaluation of internal accounting control. The extent and nature of the evaluation will vary from audit to audit, but at a minimum the auditor must be satisfied that the client's system is auditable, i.e., that the system produces at least minimal documentation on economic events that affect the company. Such evidence is then examined in an appropriate manner to substantiate the resulting financial statement balances. In most audits, the internal control evaluation provides a basis for reducing the extent of substantive procedures to levels below those required when internal controls are not relied on.

The process of evaluating internal control often makes up a significant portion of the audit. The nature of internal control, the steps in evaluation, the various purposes of evaluation, the influence of the Foreign Corrupt Practices Act on publicly held companies, and related matters are discussed in depth in Chapter 13.

Objective of the evaluation. For purposes of the audit process, the objective of the evaluation of internal accounting control is to assess the likelihood of errors in the financial statements. If the auditor concludes that there is little likelihood that material errors exist, he can perform a satisfactory audit of the financial statement balances with less effort than if he strongly suspects the presence of such errors; in that case his procedures must be extensive enough to provide an approximation (within tolerances of materiality) of their amounts, thus enabling the client to record the adjustments proposed by the auditor as needed.

Evaluation steps. A brief summary of the steps in evaluating internal control follows:

1. *Identify the accounting systems* that process transactions having a material effect on the financial statements.
2. *Describe the systems.* This is normally done in a way that highlights the accounting controls contained in the systems and facilitates analysis. Many auditors use flow-charting for this purpose.
3. *Verify the systems descriptions.* Since systems descriptions usually come from secondary sources—procedures manuals, interviews with client's supervisory personnel—it is important to assure their validity by reference to actual client data. This is done by selecting one or a few transactions of each type being processed and "walking" them through the system.
4. *Identify the applicable objectives of internal control*—or their converse, error types—in detail. An analysis of each material transaction type is made to hypothesize what internal controls satisfy the objectives or, alternatively, what kinds of errors could occur that should be prevented or detected and corrected by internal controls.
5. *Identify the existing controls* for these objectives or error types. The systems descriptions are now analyzed to determine the characteristics and procedures that constitute effective controls—that is, the conditions and activities that the auditor believes will prevent or detect and correct errors on a timely basis, thus reducing the likelihood of their affecting the financial statements.

6. *Assess the likelihood of errors.* From the previous step, the auditor will know the set of controls for each specific error type. Based on this knowledge, the auditor can make a judgment on the likelihood that each error will occur. Together, these likelihoods constitute the auditor's evaluation of internal control, though the evaluation remains detailed in terms of each individual error type rather than aggregated in terms of the system as a whole. This is important because it allows the three phases of the audit to mesh effectively.

The form of the assessment has not been established by any predominant practice, and varies among auditors. One approach is to assess the likelihood of error as *low, moderate,* or *high,* defined as follows:

Low: the auditor expects few, if any, errors.
Moderate: the auditor expects errors, but believes they are not likely to be material.
High: the auditor expects errors and believes they may be material.

The auditor's use of the evaluation. The auditor uses the evaluation to set the approach for the overall audit plan. When control is not good and the likelihood of errors is high, the auditor must perform substantive tests to an extent sufficient to measure the errors in the financial statement balances within reasonable tolerances of materiality. If the system of internal controls is so poor that evidence for these substantive tests is not available, the entity is not auditable.

When control is moderate, the auditor can rely on the controls, but not as heavily as when control is good. Often, the systems tests in Phase II will be designed to look for errors in transactions as well as for indications of the application of control procedures. These substantive tests of transactions often allow the auditor to accomplish a portion of his substantive procedures more efficiently than if he performed them in Phase III after year-end.

When control is good and the likelihood of errors is low, the auditor is entitled to take a reliance approach. He will include tests of the controls being relied on in Phase II and reduce the substantive procedures performed in Phase III accordingly. Of course, he can take a substantive approach even when control is good, if he decides this will be more efficient.

Because the evaluation made at this step in the audit process is subject to later verification through audit procedures, it is called the *preliminary evaluation.*

Preparing an Overall Audit Plan. An overall audit plan is prepared as a basis for designing detailed audit procedures to be performed in Phases II and III. As procedures are performed and results obtained, the plan, along with the auditor's understanding of the client's business, provides a framework for making audit judgments. When the results obtained are as anticipated, the plan is validated, and the auditor proceeds on that basis. When unexpected results are obtained, the plan is used to determine the necessary changes in detailed procedures and approach.

Preparing the audit plan requires careful consideration of how to allocate materiality tolerances among the multitude of audit steps and procedures so that tests designed to identify material errors in a certain area do not overlook immaterial errors if there is a possibility that undetected immaterial errors in all audit areas could be material in total. The auditor's judgment is the primary ingredient in this decision—his experience, knowledge of transaction cycles and account interrelationships, and tendency to set test parameters conservatively all contribute to the judgment. Research is well underway by firms and academics on how to more formally structure the *shared materiality* of audit scope planning, and rudimentary decision models have already been devised for computer manipulation.

The audit plan should be written in such a way that it communicates the audit approach to the audit team. It is often the nucleus of the formal audit program containing the detailed procedures to be performed in order to complete the audit. A comprehensive audit plan consists of three main elements:

1. An identification of the major accounting systems and related transaction types, accompanied by a summary of the auditor's evaluation of the internal controls and likelihood of errors in each of them. As explained above, this information will suggest the available alternative audit approaches. Transaction cycles are the basic organizational framework for audit scope consideration. These cycles are described in Chapter 13, and certain chapters of the book are built around the transaction cycle approach, most notably Chapters 17-20.

2. An identification of important financial statement accounts, indicating approximate balances expected to exist at year-end and the relative audit significance or risk associated with each account. Since the auditor cannot perform a 100% examination of all details of all accounts, an allocation of effort is required. It is important to assign the greatest audit effort to the areas where the greatest payoff is expected. The evaluation of internal control will give information about the likelihood of errors from a transaction perspective. Further analysis will indicate the financial statement areas where those and other errors in significant amounts are likely to show up.

3. A statement of the planned approach, indicating for each account (a) the planned degree of reliance on internal controls; (b) the planned extent of substantive procedures in both Phase II and III; (c) the timing of Phase II procedures; (d) the timing of Phase III procedures; (e) for larger clients, the allocation of audit work among components; and (f) other major planning decisions, e.g., use of computer audit techniques or outside specialists.

Phase II: Systems Testing

All systems tests have one objective: to reach a formal assessment, supported by audit evidence, of the likelihood of errors in the accounts. One of the two basic types of systems tests is the *compliance test*. In this procedure, the auditor obtains evidence supporting his understanding of the way internal controls work. Such evidence is gathered by making observations of internal control procedures in operation and by examining documents for specific indication of properly applied internal controls. Compliance tests have the effect of converting the preliminary evaluation of internal accounting controls into a firmer evaluation.

The second basic type of systems test is the *substantive test of transactions*. By this procedure the auditor gains evidence about the correctness of the amounts resulting from transactions processed by the accounting systems and entered in the accounts. These tests can be performed at year-end just as well as during the second phase of the audit process. However, it is often efficient to combine a large proportion of the substantive tests with compliance tests, thereby broadening the results of the systems testing phase. Note that both types of tests are dual purpose, to an extent. Compliance tests often identify monetary errors, and substantive tests provide compliance evidence.

Although both types of tests contribute to an assessment of the likelihood of errors in the financial statements, compliance tests generally do this indirectly, and substantive tests of transactions do it directly. Compliance tests confirm or modify the auditor's understanding of internal controls, which he then uses to assess the likelihood of errors, whereas substantive tests of transactions measure the actual incidence of error. Of course, monetary errors found in compliance tests will be corrected as well, if other than trivial.

The assessment of likelihood of errors may be in the same form as that described above for evaluation of internal control—low, moderate, or high. When such an assessment has been made as part of the preliminary evaluation and that evaluation is supported by compliance tests, the auditor's assessment for the third phase remains the same. When compliance tests yield other results, the assessment will change accordingly. For error types addressed by substantive tests, the assessment will be the direct result of these tests. Generally, there will also be some error types identified but not assessed by systems tests. The assessment for these error types must remain unknown even if they have come under preliminary evaluation, for the auditor cannot rely on controls unless they are tested.

In practice, the lines between the phases in some transaction cycles are often not very distinct, especially between the second and third phases. This is so because a decision to use substantive procedures in Phase II is quite similar to using substantive procedures in Phase III.

Phase III: Verification of Financial Statement Balances

Designing Tests. The procedure for designing tests of financial statement balances consists of the following six steps:

1. For each important account, identify the set of transaction types that affect it.
2. For each transaction type affecting an account, identify the set of possible errors. Since each transaction type should affect two or more accounts, satisfactorily auditing one type of transaction usually contributes to the evidence supporting more than one account.
3. Recognize that each account has a set of audit objectives that must be supported by audit evidence.
4. Construct a matrix for each account in which the transaction/error types form the rows and the audit objectives form the columns.
5. Enter information on the likelihood that the account will contain the error types assessed in Phase II.
6. Select audit procedures to accomplish the applicable audit objectives, taking the likelihood of errors into consideration. Generally, when the likelihood is low or moderate, fewer or less extensive procedures will be required; when the likelihood is high or unknown, more procedures, or more extensive ones, will be required.

The matrix referred to in step 4 above can take various forms, but the purpose is to correlate transaction/error types—what can go wrong in the particular audit area—with the audit objectives applicable in the specific circumstances. (The seven detailed audit objectives are listed earlier in this chapter.) Using long-term debt as an uncomplicated example, Figure 12.3 identifies the detailed objectives and transaction error types applicable in a hypothetical situation. In the body of the matrix, procedure numbers are shown; although in Figure 12.3 these numbers are not further illustrated with an attached listing of the procedures, several of these matrices that do have accompanying listings are used in this *Handbook*. Note that often a single procedure accomplishes several objectives; it is important that the auditor consciously plan Phase III steps to avoid both omitting procedures and performing redundant procedures.

This analysis is a key part of the audit process. It connects the Phase II systems tests with the Phase III tests of financial statement balances. Without this analysis as part of preparing the audit program, the auditor runs the risk of omitting important procedures, misallocating audit effort, or overauditing and incurring unnecessary costs.

The possible audit procedures that may be performed on a given account are almost infinite. Each yields a certain type and quality of evidence, and each has its own cost characteristics. The selection of specific procedures is a matter of audit judgment and depends on the accounts and objectives involved, the nature and effectiveness of the evidence to be obtained, and the costs of the alternative tests that will produce the necessary level of auditor satisfaction. There is no standard audit program without exceptions and the need for modifications. It is up to the auditor to develop the optimal program for each audit examination.

Once the procedures are selected, their timing and extent must be decided as well. Although many Phase III procedures are performed as of the balance sheet date, many others are performed as of a date prior to year-end. This is pragmatic in terms of scheduling workloads and meeting completion dates, and is appropriate as long as procedures are performed to support the carryforward of the interim-date balances to year-end.

Phase III procedures are of two general types, *analytical tests* and *detailed tests of balances*. Analytical tests substantiate the reasonableness of account balances by use of comparisons with balances between years, with other accounts, and with industry data. Often the comparisons are in the form of ratios and trends. In some cases, mathematical techniques such as *regression estimation* and *discriminant analysis* are used for such tests. (See Appendix 12 for a more detailed discussion of financial analysis as an audit tool.) Analytical tests do not provide precise results, but are very helpful in two other ways: when they corroborate that the balance of an account is reasonable, they provide audit evidence, and when they indicate a possibly misstated balance, they provide direction for focusing detailed tests.

Detailed tests of balances are the most widely used procedures in auditing. They generally involve sampling. In designing samples, the number of items to test is only one important audit decision. The subject of sampling is discussed in detail in Chapter 14.

Performing Tests and Evaluating Results. After all the audit procedures and tests are properly planned, they must be performed by properly trained and supervised personnel, in accordance with GAAS. Supervision includes reviewing subordinates' work as well as giving direction.

A proper working paper record of work performed is essential. The media used for this purpose include audit programs, working paper schedules, copies of client documents, computer printouts, and memoranda. These papers, called the *audi-*

TRANSACTION – ERROR TYPE	AUDIT OBJECTIVE AND APPLICABLE PROCEDURES						
	VALIDITY	RECORDING	ACCURACY	CLASSIFI-CATION	CUT-OFF	MECHANICAL ACCURACY	ADEQUATE DISCLOSURE
BOOKS AND RECORDS Posting or addition errors in ledgers						1, 8, 9, 10, 11, 12, 15, 16	
Incorrect journal entries						1, 8, 10, 11, 12, 13, 14	
PAYMENTS Payments recorded but not made	2, 4, 17, 18, 19						
Payments made but not recorded		4, 6, 17, 18, 20, 21					
Payments amount recorded incorrectly			2, 4, 17, 18, 20, 21, 22				
Payments recorded in wrong period					2, 4, 17, 18, 20, 21, 22, 23, 24		
OTHER Improperly classified between short and long term				5			
Violation of covenants or lending agreements							6
Undisclosed debt		7					7

FIGURE 12.3　EXAMPLE OF AUDITING MATRIX—LONG-TERM DEBT

tor's documentation, are not to be confused with the *client's documentation* of its transactions, though the two often overlap, as when copies of client records are incorporated into the auditor's documentation. Some working papers are of a permanent nature, useful from one audit to the next, and are usually kept in separate files.

Audit procedures performed, and the results obtained, are indicated in the auditor's documentation using tick marks, footnote notations, narratives, and working paper structure. As documentation is prepared, it is initialed and dated by the preparer and later by the reviewer.

Critical aspects of performing individual tests of details of financial statement balances are that

1. The objectives of the test must be clearly stated;
2. The documentation developed must be in a form that relates the evidence gathered to the objectives; and
3. A conclusion must be achieved in terms relevant to the objectives.

When no errors are found through these tests, it is usually concluded that the objectives set for the tests have been met. When errors are found, the auditor must determine what they mean in relation to three auditing aspects. First, what weaknesses in accounting systems allowed the errors to occur? Second, what is the estimated magnitude of all such errors (found and not found), and is the aggregate material? Third, how should the audit approach be modified in view of these systems weaknesses and the materiality of error?

An approach taken by many auditors in answer to the second question is to classify known and estimated error amounts into these categories:

1. *Negligible amounts.* These errors are considered insignificant and require no further consideration, except that the company would be expected to correct known errors as a matter of good business practice.
2. *Material amounts.* These errors require an adjustment of the financial statements by the client in order for the auditor to render an opinion as to their conformity with generally accepted accounting principles.
3. *Individually immaterial amounts.* These errors are accumulated throughout the audit to determine whether or not they are material in the aggregate. Again, a client's correction of its records for known immaterial errors is advisable, even if these corrections are not worked into the financial statements.

In addition to procedures and tests concerning the amounts in the financial statements, the auditor is responsible for performing a review of the period from the balance sheet date to the date of his audit report (usually upon completion of virtually all audit procedures that could have an effect on the nature of the auditor's report). This step is termed a *post–balance sheet review,* and is designed to assess whether any significant events have occurred after the balance sheet date that should be disclosed in or cause revision of the financial statements.

Phase III procedures are complete when sufficient competent evidential matter has been obtained in support of all audit objectives for all accounts, when the post–

balance sheet review has been completed, and when appropriate representations have been obtained from management.

In addition, the auditor will review and corroborate footnote and supplementary disclosure data at this time if not accomplished as part of other procedures. Often such data is not incorporated in the formal accounting systems. Mention of the more prominent disclosures and their related audit approaches is provided throughout this *Handbook*.

The matters to be covered in the *letter of representations* are dictated by professional standards (SAS 19; AU 333). The letter is intended to assure that management accepts its responsibilities regarding the financial statements in general and the specific factual statements it has made to the auditors and understands the nature of the auditor's examination.

Issuing the Audit Report. The distillation of all the audit evidence gathered is the auditor's judgment of whether or not, within the bounds of materiality, the financial statement amounts are reasonably correct and the necessary disclosures are made in conformity with generally accepted accounting principles. This judgment will determine the nature of the auditor's report. The auditor's standard report, or unqualified report, is the hoped-for result, but in some cases the auditor will have to depart from the standard form. The most common types of qualifications are listed below:

1. The *qualified opinion* indicates, for example, that the financial statements are "subject to" the outcome of a material uncertainty.
2. The *exception* indicates that the auditor believes the financial statements are incorrect in a particular material respect.
3. The *adverse opinion* indicates that the financial statements are so materially misstated or misleading overall that they do *not* present fairly the financial position or results of operations in conformity with generally accepted accounting principles.
4. The *disclaimer of opinion* is used when the auditor is unable to obtain adequate evidence to support the client's presentation of financial position or results of operations. This may arise because of a significant limitation on the scope of the auditor's examination, the existence of unusual uncertainties of great magnitude, or for other reasons.

Auditors' reports are covered extensively in Chapter 16.

THE AUDIT PRACTICE

Although much of the profession's literature discusses auditing in terms of the *auditor,* audit examinations are in fact generally performed by audit *teams* who are partners and employees of auditing *firms*. Three important aspects of the audit practice are the team approach, the auditing firm's resources, and quality control.

The Audit Team

Auditing firms have several levels of experienced professionals. On an audit examination, the audit team comprises one or more persons from each level. The leader of the team is the audit partner. Since large auditing firms are almost invariably partnerships, the partner is an owner; and even when the firm has taken the form of a professional corporation, the actual operation is much the same. In any case, the partner in charge of the audit engagement has ultimate authority and responsibility for all important decisions and judgments made during the audit, including the nature of the audit opinion reached. The partner is also responsible for business matters with the client, such as fee determination. The partner and the engagement team will act in accord with specific policies of their firm, to the extent that such policies have been articulated in more detail than provided in professional standards and pronouncements.

On a day-to-day basis, the audit engagement is managed by an experienced auditor who is one to five years below the partner level. In many larger firms there are two positions that may exercise this responsibility: manager and supervisor. On large audits, there will be both managers and supervisors responsible for various elements of the engagement. More than one partner may also be on the team.

The manager or supervisor usually concerns himself with specific problem areas and management tasks. The performance of detailed procedures is usually under the direct control of audit seniors, who perform the more complex tasks and supervise staff assistants—team members with less than two or three years experience—in performing less complex tasks.

This hierarchical structure provides several advantages. First, all work performed is reviewed by the performer's superior, assuring that work is done properly and that the team members receive on-the-job training. Second, each member's capabilities are matched to the requirements of his task. More difficult tasks and judgments are reserved for more experienced auditors, and more routine activities are performed by those less experienced. Third, costs are minimized. Most of the time billed in the engagement is that of auditors who are lower in the hierarchy, because their tasks tend to be time-consuming by nature. Since these persons are newer to the firm and earn lower salaries, their billing rates are lower.

A major challenge for such a team, especially when some of its members are in different cities or even countries, is communication. To meet this challenge, the auditing firm must have a sound system of working paper documentation, so that as work is performed by individual auditors, it can be made available to and understood by other members of the team. Most audit firms prescribe the format for such documentation. For example, detailed procedures and other relevant information are presented in a program of examination. As work is performed, detailed working papers are prepared that summarize what was accomplished. Steps are usually signed off in the program as well. Finally, key matters—problems, judgments, findings—are often summarized in memoranda.

In addition, the audit involves a significant administrative operation, which is documented by time summaries and budgets, coordination and timing schedules, and correspondence.

Firm Resources

Most auditing firms provide important resources to support the audit team both in performing a particular engagement and in developing their professional competence as individuals.

Training Programs. Most firms have in-house training programs as well as access to the excellent programs offered by outside organizations. Because accounting and auditing is a field with a large and expanding body of technology, continuing professional education (CPE) is an essential part of every professional's development. Indeed, most states have CPE requirements for licensing. The AICPA's SEC Practice Section, whose membership comprises firms that audit publicly held companies, goes further: every professional in a member firm is required to devote 120 hours to accredited CPE over three years.

Manuals, Information Releases, and Forms. Auditing firms, like most organizations, set forth many of their policies and practices in firm manuals. This format facilitates training, implementation, and communication. Firms often have manuals covering administrative and operational matters as well as technical matters. With so much that is new or in the process of change in areas affecting accountants and auditors, information releases, such as technical newsletters or topical narratives, are commonplace in audit firms. Firms that do not maintain in-house information release systems obtain the material from the AICPA and voluntary associations of firms.

In addition to (and often as part of) manuals, many firms prescribe specific forms to standardize and control certain audit activities. These include administrative forms, examples of typical audit correspondence, internal control questionnaires, and generalized audit procedure lists.

Computer Tools. In today's audits, much company information is usually in the form of computer files. On-line systems present a particularly formidable challenge to the auditor in planning his procedures, because he must address company data in computer form during the limited time it is available. To meet these challenges, the auditor often has at his disposal computer software programs that are used to process this data in performing audit steps. The problems that computers raise in the audit, and their solutions, are discussed in Chapter 15.

In addition to special audit software tools, many auditors use computer time-sharing programs for such purposes as selecting random samples, evaluating sample results, making financial analyses, and performing lease computations. These computer applications are highlighted in Chapter 14 and in selected chapters involving timesharing routines that have been well established.

Research Materials and Sources. As in most disciplines, auditing involves knowing how to find and apply the right answer. Because the body of accounting and auditing knowledge is so large, many problems encountered during the audit must be researched. Audit firms provide such research facilities as libraries, topical information files, and data search and retrieval systems, often including microfiche and the National Automated Accounting Research System. Consultation with research staff members is another important resource. In larger firms these persons may be found at the local, regional, and national levels. Chapter 49 discusses professional research in detail.

Specialists. As previously noted, specialists in certain areas are often called on to participate in audit engagements. Industry specialists, technical specialists in areas such as data processing and statistics, tax specialists, and management consultants are among those frequently consulted. Some firms also have actuaries, appraisers, and other specialists on staff to assist the audit team in performing tests and making judgments in the complex areas of their expertise.

Quality Control

This chapter has focused on the individual audit engagement and, by inference, the individual auditor. But most audits are performed by firms. The AICPA has given special consideration to the problems of managing an audit practice and its effect on the quality of audit engagements. Statement on Quality Control Standards No. 1, issued in 1979, presents standards that cover a firm's entire professional auditing practice. These are listed and discussed in Chapter 11.

SUGGESTED READING

Arens, Alvin, and Loebbecke, James K. *Auditing—An Integrated Approach*. Englewood Cliffs, N.J.: Prentice-Hall, 1980. The audit process discussed in this chapter is explained in greater detail in this contemporary textbook.

Hershman, Arlene. "How to Figure Who's Going Bankrupt." *Dun's Review,* October, 1975. This article is a review of then-emerging mathematical books used to predict whether companies are in liquidity trouble.

Porter, W. Thomas, and Burton, John C. *Auditing: A Conceptual Approach*. Belmont, Calif.: Wadsworth Publishing Company, 1971. This is an introductory text on auditing that emphasizes a systems approach to the examination and relates the audit to the information system of the organization audited.

Robertson, Jack. *Auditing*. Revised edition. Dallas: Business Publications, 1979. Structured decision making is blended with conceptual explanations of auditing in this textbook.

APPENDIX 12 FINANCIAL ANALYSIS AS AN AUDIT TOOL

SAS 23 (AU 318), issued in October 1978, amended the auditing literature by formally recognizing analytical review procedures as a major ingredient of "sufficient competent evidential matter" (AU 320.69). In actuality, auditors have always intuitively analyzed data, and many auditors and audit firms have used formalized analysis systems of their own design or that were created as software by the audit firms or commercial timesharing vendors.

SAS 23 does not specify what should be analyzed, but assuming the auditor will determine that ingredient, all the rest of the guidance is there—nature, objectives, timing, and the investigation of significant fluctuations.

Ratios that auditors will often consider in analytical work on liquidity are discussed in Chapters 22 and 26. In addition, industry comparisons are easily made using the 14 significant financial ratios annually presented by Dun & Bradstreet, Inc. (in *Key Busi-*

ness Ratios) for 125 lines of retailing, wholesaling, manufacturing, and construction. Having this available facilitates timesharing analysis, as shown in an example below. The 14 Dun & Bradstreet ratios are:

Ratio	*Timesharing FINALY Abbreviation*
1. Current assets to current debt	CA/CD
2. Net profits to net sales	NP/NS
3. Net profits to tangible net worth	NP/TNW
4. Net profits to net working capital	NP/NWC
5. Net sales to tangible net worth	NS/TNW
6. Net sales to net working capital	NS/NWC
7. Collection period	CP
8. Net sales to inventory	NS/I
9. Fixed assets to tangible net worth	FA/TNW
10. Current debt to tangible net worth	CD/TNW
11. Total debt to tangible net worth	TD/TNW
12. Inventory to net working capital	I/NWC
13. Current debt to inventory	CD/I
14. Funded debts to net working capital	FD/NWC

Information for industry comparisons is available from many other sources. Management often regularly obtains annual reports of competitors and industry leaders for the purpose of ratio comparison. Trade associations and securities analysts publish extensive industry reports giving data on specific companies and the industry as a whole. Financial journals, such as *Barron's*, also publish this kind of data.

All of the financial ratios listed above involve computations of varying complexity using financial statement data. Since ratios are most meaningful when shown in trend format, the program[1] whose output is illustrated below computes 24 ratios for up to 20 years, with data maintained off line between years on a paper or magnetic tape. Output is in two formats: numerical trend and bar chart. The program also computes the long- and short-term liquidity trend ratios and all 14 Dun & Bradstreet ratios for the current period, and is usable for interim analysis by insertion of a fraction-of-year code.

The *long-term liquidity trend ratio* measures this trend using a mathematical technique known as the gambler's ruin prediction. Simply put, a mathematical model is used to determine the nature of year-to-year change in the liquidity of a company during the years preceding the evaluation date. From this it determines the probability that future negative trends could occur at a magnitude sufficient to absorb the net assets of the company, thus making it illiquid (see Wilcox, 1971).

The long-term liquidity trend ratio is expressed as a decimal fraction. If there is very little indication that the company could become illiquid within the ensuing five years,

---

[1] *FINALY*, © Touche Ross & Co., 1975. Written in BASIC and licensed for use through Tymshare, Inc.

the ratio will be close to zero. If there is a serious indication that it could, the ratio will be close to one. If there has been a negative change in liquidity over the entire period being considered (e.g., ten years), the ratio will be one. There are no established standards available for the value of the long-term liquidity trend ratio. Therefore, four examples are appended to give the reader an idea of possible results.

In producing the long-term liquidity trend ratio, the model used makes various assumptions that should be known to the user. First, there is the selection of the number of years' data to develop the trend. Wilcox believes the optimal number is nine, since this coincides with the average major business cycle. However, the model might also be useful with as few as five years, since this period probably covers a variety of conditions within the environment of most business enterprises.

Since the model deals with liquidity, assumptions must be made regarding the liquidation value of the various assets. These must by nature be arbitrary. In the program model illustrated below, the assumption has been made that current assets other than cash and marketable securities will be deflated to 70% and net tangible long-term assets to 50% of their recorded value upon liquidation.

The short-term liquidity trend ratio uses the technique of discriminant analysis with five key ratios:

1. Working capital to total assets,
2. Retained earnings to total assets,
3. Earnings before interest and taxes to total assets,
4. Market value equity to book value of total debt, and
5. Sales to total assets.

These ratios, computed as of the audit date, are mathematically combined to produce a *score value*. The score value can then be compared to a set of standard score values that have been empirically developed as indicators of short-term (one to two years) bankruptcy (see Altman and McGough, 1974). Figure 12.A.1 shows the trend numerical output, Figure 12.A.2 shows a portion of that output in bar chart format, and Figure 12.A.3 identifies the ratio formulas.

```
NAME OF COMPANY AND FISCAL YEAR
? COMPANY-A,197°

NAME OF DATA FILE CONTAINING INPUT DATA
? CMPNYA.BAS

HOW MANY YEARS DATA ARE INCLUDED (MAXIMUM 20)
? 11

   1   2   3   1969   1   2   3   1970   1   2   3   1971   1   2   3   1972   1   2   3
   1973   1   2   3   1974   1   2   3   1975   1   2   3   1976   1   2   3   1977   1   2
   3   1978   1   2   3   1979

IS CURRENT YEARS'S INPUT FOR FULL YEAR-Y OR N
? N

ENTER PORTION OF YEAR REPRESENTED AS DECIMAL
? .5

VISUAL DISPLAY FORM DESIRED-Y OR N
? Y

IS SHORT-TERM LIQUIDITY TREND RATIO DESIRED-Y OR
-
-RUN(TRC900)FINALY

            ******   FINALY   ******

FOR INSTRUCTIONS REFER TO BOOKLET AP-7, FINANCIAL ANALYSIS
AS AN AUDIT TOOL.    NOTE THAT NOW FASB13 IS IN EFFECT
IT IS RECOMMENDED THAT THE TERM NONCAPITALIZED FINANCING
LEASES BE READ TO MEAN OPERATING LEASES.


NAME OF COMPANY AND FISCAL YEAR
? COMPANY-A,1979

NAME OF DATA FILE CONTAINING INPUT DATA
? CMPNYA.BAS

HOW MANY YEARS DATA ARE INCLUDED (MAXIMUM 20)
? 11

   1   2   3   1969   1   2   3   1970   1   2   3   1971   1   2   3   1972   1   2   3
   1973   1   2   3   1974   1   2   3   1975   1   2   3   1976   1   2   3   1977   1   2
   3   1978   1   2   3   1979

IS CURRENT YEARS'S INPUT FOR FULL YEAR-Y OR N
? N

ENTER PORTION OF YEAR REPRESENTED AS DECIMAL
? .5

VISUAL DISPLAY FORM DESIRED-Y OR N
? N

IS SHORT-TERM LIQUIDITY TREND RATIO DESIRED-Y OR N
? Y

ENTER TOTAL MARKET VALUE OF EQUITY
? 8.9




      NOTE--CURRENT YEAR IS AN INTERIM PERIOD ONLY
RATIOS ANNUALIZED USING DECIMAL PORTION OF YEAR ENTERED
```

FIGURE 12.A.1   EXAMPLE OF FINANCIAL ANALYSIS NUMERICAL TREND OUTPUT

```
            ------VALUATION RATIOS-----
            CURRENT    QUICK     CASH
   YEAR     RATIO      RATIO     RATIO
   ----     -------    -------   -------
   1969      4.50       2.80      1.20
   1970      3.93       2.40      0.95
   1971      1.65       0.87      0.20
   1972      1.62       0.91      0.40
   1973      2.17       1.35      0.80
   1974      3.05       1.68      0.91
   1975      2.86       1.41      0.68
   1976      4.92       2.42      1.26
   1977      4.32       2.52      1.46
   1978      3.46       1.87      0.98
   1979      3.53       1.94      1.02


            ------------SHORT-TERM LIQUIDITY RATIOS------------
            ACTS REC  DAYS TO   INVTRY    DAYS TO   DAYS TO
   YEAR     TURNOVER  COLLECT   TURNOVER  SELL INV  CONVERT
   ----     --------  -------   --------  --------  --------
   1970      12.94     27.82     10.25     35.12     62.94
   1971      13.14     27.39     10.11     35.59     62.98
   1972      14.08     25.57      8.07     44.61     70.17
   1973      12.64     28.48      6.57     54.80     83.28
   1974      14.98     24.03      7.64     47.14     71.18
   1975      12.20     29.50      5.61     64.19     93.69
   1976      10.87     33.12      4.63     77.69    110.81
   1977      12.23     29.43      5.43     66.32     95.75
   1978      12.80     28.13      6.39     56.31     84.44
   1979      12.47     28.87      6.05     59.50     88.37

NOTE THAT THESE RATIOS ARE NOT AVAILABLE FOR 1969
BECAUSE BEGINNING YEAR BALANCES ARE NOT INCLUDED IN INPUT


            ------------LONG-TERM LIQUIDITY RATIOS------------
            DEBT TO   TNA TO    TIMES     TIMES INT&  TIMES INT
            EQUITY    EQUITY    INTEREST  LEASE PMTS  LP&PFD DIV
   YEAR     RATIO     RATIO     EARNED    EARNED      EARNED
   ----     -------   -------   --------  --------    --------
   1969      0.71      1.00      12.11     12.11       12.11
   1970      0.57      1.00       5.33      5.33        5.33
   1971      0.42      1.00      25.20     25.20        8.40
   1972      0.37      1.00      89.67     89.67       20.69
   1973      0.29      1.00       0.00      0.00       20.80
   1974      0.22      1.00       0.00      0.00       19.60
   1975      0.34      1.00       0.00     20.78        9.84
   1976      0.30      1.00      26.00      7.25        4.46
   1977      0.33      1.00      26.20      8.88        5.46
   1978      0.36      1.00      33.40     11.80        7.08
   1979      0.35      1.00      46.50     14.00        8.17


            ----OPERATING AND PERFORMANCE RATIOS-----
            EFFNCY    PROFIT    PFBLTY                BOOK
   YEAR     RATIO     MARGIN    RATIO     RTA         VALUE
   ----     -------   -------   --------  --------    --------
   1969      2.17      0.11      0.24      0.24        2.70
   1970      2.49      0.03      0.07      0.07        2.81
   1971      1.89      0.11      0.21      0.21        3.27
   1972      1.89      0.19      0.37      0.37        4.14
   1973      1.69      0.16      0.26      0.26        4.90
   1974      2.07      0.11      0.23      0.23        5.34
   1975      1.78      0.10      0.18      0.18        5.96
   1976      1.71      0.06      0.10      0.11        6.01
   1977      1.79      0.07      0.12      0.12        6.16
   1978      1.96      0.07      0.14      0.14        6.71
   1979      2.05      0.07      0.15      0.15        6.67
```

(figure continues)

FIGURE 12.A.1   CONT'D

```
---------------------------RETURN ON COMMON EQUITY-------------------------
                        ----------------LEVERAGE RECEIVED FROM---------------
              RETURN              OPERATING
     YEAR    BEF TAX   S-T DEBT    LEASES   L-T DEBT  OTHR LIA  FFD STK

     1969     0.37      0.04       0.00      0.09      0.00     0.00
     1970     0.09      0.01       0.00      0.01      0.00     0.00
     1971     0.34      0.08       0.00      0.02      0.00     0.03
     1972     0.59      0.16       0.00      0.00      0.00     0.06
     1973     0.39      0.09       0.00      0.00      0.00     0.03
     1974     0.32      0.06       0.00      0.00      0.00     0.02
     1975     0.26      0.06       0.01      0.00      0.00     0.01
     1976     0.13      0.02       0.00      0.00      0.00     0.00
     1977     0.16      0.02       0.00      0.01      0.00     0.00
     1978     0.19      0.03       0.00      0.01      0.00     0.00
     1979     0.21      0.04       0.00      0.01      0.00     0.01
```

```
*************************************************************************

THE LONG-TERM LIQUIDITY TREND RATIO AS OF THE END OF 1979 IS
   0.00000000

THE SHORT-TERM LIQUIDITY TREND RATIO AS OF THE END OF 1979 IS
   5.76506856

*************************************************************************


DO YOU WANT D & B RATIOS FOR CURRENT YEAR-Y OR N
? Y


D & B RATIOS ANNUALIZED FOR  1979  ARE :

        CA/CD      3.53
        NP/NS      0.04
        NP/TNW     0.10
        NP/NWC     0.18
        NS/TNW     2.78
        NS/NWC     5.01
        CP        29.35
        NS/I       8.47
        FA/TNW     0.58
        CD/TNW     0.22
        TD/TNW     0.31
        I/NWC      0.59
        CD/I       0.67
        FD/NWC     0.16


PROGRAM COMPLETE
```

FIGURE 12.A.1   CONT'D

```
                    ***********************************
                    *OPERATING AND PERFORMANCE RATIOS*
                    ***********************************


--------------------------------EFFICIENCY RATIO---------------------------------
   YEAR    VALUE                      VISUAL DISPLAY
   ----    -----                      --------------
   1969    2.17    ***********************************
   1970    2.49    *********************************************
   1971    1.89    ******************************
   1972    1.89    ******************************
   1973    1.69    **************************
   1974    2.07    *********************************
   1975    1.78    ****************************
   1976    1.71    **************************
   1977    1.79    ****************************
   1978    1.96    ********************************
   1979    2.05    **********************************

----------------------------------PROFIT MARGIN----------------------------------
   YEAR    VALUE                      VISUAL DISPLAY
   ----    -----                      --------------
   1969    0.109   **********************
   1970    0.029   *****
   1971    0.110   ***********************
   1972    0.195   ****************************************
   1973    0.155   *******************************
   1974    0.113   **********************
   1975    0.099   *******************
   1976    0.059   ************
   1977    0.066   *************
   1978    0.070   **************
   1979    0.074   ***************

-----------------------------------PFBLTY RATIO----------------------------------
   YEAR    VALUE                      VISUAL DISPLAY
   ----    -----                      --------------
   1969    0.236   *************************
   1970    0.072   *******
   1971    0.207   **********************
   1972    0.368   ***************************************
   1973    0.262   ****************************
   1974    0.235   *************************
   1975    0.176   ******************
   1976    0.101   ***********
   1977    0.117   ************
   1978    0.136   **************
   1979    0.153   ****************

--------------------------------------RTA----------------------------------------
   YEAR    VALUE                      VISUAL DISPLAY
   ----    -----                      --------------
   1969    0.236   *************************
   1970    0.072   *******
   1971    0.209   **********************
   1972    0.368   ***********************************************
   1973    0.262   ****************************
   1974    0.235   *************************
   1975    0.180   *******************
   1976    0.106   ***********
   1977    0.121   *************
   1978    0.139   **************
   1979    0.151   ***************
```

FIGURE 12.A.2   EXAMPLE OF FINANCIAL ANALYSIS BAR CHART OUTPUT (SELECTED RATIOS)

CURRENT RATIO $= \dfrac{\text{Current assets}}{\text{Current liabilities}}$

QUICK RATIO $= \dfrac{\text{Cash + marketable securities + net accounts receivable}}{\text{Current liabilities}}$

CASH RATIO $= \dfrac{\text{Cash + marketable securities}}{\text{Current liabilities}}$

AVERAGE ACCOUNTS RECEIVABLE TURNOVER

$= \dfrac{\text{Net sales}}{(\text{Beginning gross receivables + ending gross receivables}) \div 2}$

AVERAGE DAYS TO COLLECT

$= \dfrac{(\text{Beginning gross receivables + ending gross receivables}) \div 2}{\text{Net sales} \div 360}$

AVERAGE INVENTORY TURNOVER

$= \dfrac{\text{Costs of goods sold}}{(\text{Beginning inventory + ending inventory}) \div 2}$

AVERAGE DAYS TO SELL INVENTORY

$= \dfrac{(\text{Beginning inventory + ending inventory}) \div 2}{\text{Cost of goods sold} \div 360}$

AVERAGE DAYS TO CONVERT INVENTORY TO CASH

$=$ Average days to collect + average days to sell

DEBT TO EQUITY

$= \dfrac{\text{Current liabilities + long-term liabilities + present value of operating leases}}{\text{Stockholders' equity}}$

TANGIBLE NET ASSETS (TNA) TO EQUITY

$= \dfrac{\text{Stockholders' equity } - \text{ intangible assets}}{\text{Stockholders' equity}}$

TIMES INTEREST EARNED $= \dfrac{\text{Operating income}}{\text{Interest}}$

TIMES INTEREST AND LEASE PAYMENTS EARNED

$= \dfrac{\text{Operating income + lease payments}}{\text{Interest + lease payments}}$

TIMES INTEREST, LEASE PAYMENTS AND PREFERRED DIVIDENDS EARNED

$= \dfrac{\text{Operating income + lease payments}}{\text{Interest + lease payments} + \dfrac{\text{preferred dividends}}{1 - \text{tax rate}}}$

FIGURE 12.A.3   FINANCIAL ANALYSIS TIMESHARING FORMULAS

EFFICIENCY RATIO $= \dfrac{\text{Net Sales}}{\text{Tangible operating assets} + \text{present value of operating leases}}$

PROFIT MARGIN RATIO $= \dfrac{\text{Operating income}}{\text{Net sales}}$

PROFITABILITY RATIO $= \dfrac{\text{Operating income}}{\text{Tangible operating assets} + \text{present value of operating leases}}$

RETURN ON TOTAL ASSETS (RTA) $= \dfrac{\text{Income before interest and taxes}}{\text{Total assets} + \text{present value of operating leases}}$

RETURN (BEFORE TAXES) ON COMMON EQUITY

$= \dfrac{\text{Income before taxes} - \dfrac{\text{Preferred dividends}}{1 - \text{tax rate}}}{\text{Common equity}}$

LEVERAGE RECEIVED FROM SHORT-TERM DEBT

$= \dfrac{(\text{RTA} \times \text{current liabilities}) - \text{Interest attributable to current debt}}{\text{Common equity}}$

LEVERAGE RECEIVED FROM LONG-TERM DEBT

$= \dfrac{(\text{RTA} \times \text{long-term debt}) - \text{interest attributable to long-term debt}}{\text{Common equity}}$

LEVERAGE RECEIVED FROM OPERATING LEASES

$= \dfrac{(\text{RTA} \times \text{present value of operating leases}) - \text{Interest portion of lease payments}}{\text{Common equity}}$

LEVERAGE RECEIVED FROM OTHER LIABILITIES

$= \dfrac{\text{RTA} \times \text{other liabilities}}{\text{Common equity}}$

LEVERAGE RECEIVED FROM PREFERRED STOCK

$= \dfrac{(\text{RTA} \times \text{preferred stock}) - \dfrac{\text{Preferred dividends}}{1 - \text{tax rate}}}{\text{Common equity}}$

BOOK VALUE OF COMMON STOCK $= \dfrac{\text{Common equity}}{\text{Common shares}}$

(figure continues)

FIGURE 12.A.3   CONT'D

SHORT-TERM LIQUIDITY TREND RATIO

$$= .012X_1 + .014X_2 + .033X_3 + .006X_4 + .010X_5$$

Where,

$X_1 =$ Working capital/total assets

$X_2 =$ Retained earnings/total assets

$X_3 =$ Earnings before interest and taxes/total assets

$X_4 =$ Market value of equity/book value of total debt

$X_5 =$ Sales/total assets

LONG-TERM LIQUIDITY TREND RATIO $= (1 - X/1 + X)^Y$

Where:

$X = M/\sqrt{S+M^2}$

$Y = K/\sqrt{S+M^2}$

$S = \sum_1^N (L_i - M)^2 / N-1$

$M = \sum_1^N (L_i) / N$

$N =$ Number of years input

$K = A_N + .7B_N + .5C_N - D_N - E_N$

And where for year i:

$L_i = F_i - .5(G_i - H_i) - .3P_i - J_i$

$P_i = B_i - B_{i-1}$

$A_i =$ Cash + marketable securities

$B_i =$ Other current assets

$C_i =$ Other assets

$D_i =$ Current liabilities

$E_i =$ Long-term debt

$F_i =$ Earnings before special items

$G_i =$ Capital expenditures

$H_i =$ Depreciation expense

$J_i =$ Preferred and common dividends

However:

If $\Sigma(L_i)$ is a negative value, ultimately the company would become illiquid, and the ratio is therefore 1.0.

FIGURE 12.A.3   CONT'D

13

Internal Control

John F. Mullarkey
Kevin G. Miller

A NEW FOCUS OF INTEREST

Triggered by the passage of the Foreign Corrupt Practices Act (FCPA) in late 1977, companies and their auditors have noticeably increased the amount of attention given to internal accounting controls. The FCPA established a legal requirement that publicly held companies must maintain internal accounting controls sufficient to provide reasonable assurances as to the achievement of the objectives of such control—in short, the accuracy of accounting records. The act emerged as tangible evidence of congressional concern over the findings of the Watergate special prosecutor, which revealed that the existence of questionable or illegal payments by American businesses was more pervasive than had first appeared to be the case. Equally disconcerting was the fact that and the extent to which some companies had falsified entries in their own books and records.

These findings directly contributed to the renewed focus on internal accounting controls as a means of preventing recurrences. The path to prevention, however, is not very clear, as emphasized by the comment from a guide published by the American Bar Association (ABA) Committee on Corporate Law and Accounting "as an aid to corporate management, law practitioners, accountants, auditors and legal authorities as they embark upon the long-term task of incorporating the new requirements . . . into our corpus of law and practices" (ABA, 1978, p. 309). The guide correctly points out that

> just how the new accounting mandates of section 13(b)(2) of the 1934 Act will be applied in particular situations must ultimately await judicial interpretation. In the meantime, this Guide sets forth a set of roadmarkers that are grounded in the record of Congressional intent, and congruent with the realities of auditing and managerial practice. It is hoped that this Guide may prove of assistance to managers and practitioners, private and public, in this difficult and technical field where accounting and law are inextricably tangled. [ABA, 1978, p. 325]

As a result of the FCPA, the SEC in early 1979 proposed rules, subsequently withdrawn, that would effectively have required published annual reports to contain management representations and auditor attests on internal accounting control. Contemporaneously, a Special Advisory Committee on Internal Accounting Control issued a report (AICPA, 1979r) setting out its view of the differing responsibilities of management and the external auditors with regard to internal control, and in July 1980 the Auditing Standards Board of the AICPA issued SAS 30, *Reporting on Internal Accounting Control* (AU 642).

This chapter attempts to provide answers to several questions: What is internal accounting control? What is its function within the organization? Who is responsible for maintaining good internal accounting controls? How can there be an effective and efficient assurance that the necessary internal controls are in force? Who should report on internal accounting controls, and to whom? While concentrating primarily on internal accounting control as it affects the independent auditor, the discussion in this chapter is relevant to corporate management. In addition, such officers should look to discussions of internal accounting control as it specifically relates to their responsibilities.

Before entering into a detailed discussion of internal controls, consideration should be given to the SEC proposals, the special AICPA report, the SAS, and the formal definition of a material weakness. Though these subsections aim at definition, none succeeds in a workable way. And yet the concept of materiality is paramount in the audit approach described here. The reader must therefore do his best to personalize a definition.

Proposed SEC Requirements

The SEC proposed (Release 34-15772, April 30, 1979) rules that would have effectively required published annual reports to contain a representation by management that the objectives of internal accounting control stated in the FCPA (virtually the same as those found in AU 320.28) had been achieved, without regard to materiality of amounts. The proposed rules also required management's statement to be examined and reported on by an independent accountant, who would have had to express an opinion that management's representation was

- Consistent with the results of management's required evaluation of the system of internal accounting control, and
- Reasonable with respect to transaction and asset amounts that are material in relation to the financial statements.

The fact that the independent auditor's representation included the concept of materiality—material in relation to the financial statements—only emphasized that management's representation was not similarly limited. Essentially management would have been required to search for and, if uncorrected, report on any weakness that, on a cost/benefit basis, could have been corrected. This was one of the most controversial aspects of the proposal and, if adopted, would have been the most difficult to translate into practical terms. Reporting matters that have little significance confuses rather than enlightens users of financial statements, and may draw attention away from more significant matters, which is perhaps more serious. This proposal was originally intended to apply to calendar year 1979 reports, but was withdrawn by the commission in 1980 due to the widespread criticism it received and as a result of perceived private-sector initiatives for public reporting on internal accounting control. The SEC will monitor private-sector developments through the spring of 1982, at which time it will reconsider the subject. Certainly, as originally proposed, the release did not provide the criteria that management or auditors need to make a reasonable effort to comply with the FCPA or to form a basis for general reporting on internal accounting control (discussed at the end of this chapter).

AICPA Special Report

The *Report of the Special Advisory Committee on Internal Accounting Control* (AICPA, 1979r) made a particularly important contribution by emphasizing the importance of the internal accounting control environment and providing an interpretation of the applicability of concepts long used by auditors. The report identified how the broader concept of internal control could be segmented into aspects significant to controlling transactions, safeguarding assets, and permitting financial statements to be prepared with reasonable accuracy. Unfortunately, the report has an important flaw: it does not present a clear standard of materiality.

Material Weaknesses

A material weakness suggests the possibility that the company's system of internal accounting control will not prevent or detect an error that could materially misstate the financial statements. A material weakness does not mean that the financial statements will actually be incorrect, but only that the possibility exists. The AICPA defines *material weakness*[1] this way:

> ... a condition in which the specific control procedures or the degree of compliance with them do not reduce to a relatively low level the risk that errors or irregularities in amounts that would be material in relation to the financial statements being audited may occur and not be detected within a timely period by employees in the normal course of performing their assigned functions. [AU 320.68, as amended by SAS 30]

Auditing standards require that material weaknesses coming to the auditor's attention be communicated to senior management and the board of directors or its audit committee (AU 323.04). A material weakness will affect the audit examination, requiring the performance of tests to reasonably assure that the weakness has not actually resulted in a material error or irregularity in the financial statements. Senior management and the board of directors or its audit committee must be made aware of material weaknesses in internal accounting control because of their primary responsibilities for the financial statements. Because a material weakness could perhaps lead to a material misrepresentation in unaudited financial statements, management must take appropriate steps either to correct the weakness or to determine that, on a cost/benefit basis, correction is not justified.

---

[1] In connection with audits of brokers and dealers in securities the SEC has defined "[a] material inadequacy in the accounting system, internal accounting controls, procedures for safeguarding securities, and practices and procedures ... [as] any condition that has contributed substantially to or, if appropriate corrective action is not taken, could reasonably be expected to (i) inhibit a broker or dealer from promptly completing securities transactions or promptly discharging his responsibilities to customers, other broker-dealers or creditors; (ii) result in material financial loss; (iii) result in material misstatements in the broker or dealer's financial statements; or (iv) result in violations of the Commission's recordkeeping or financial responsibility rules to an extent that could reasonably be expected to result in the [proscribed] conditions ..." (Rule X17A-5(g)(3)).

INTERNAL CONTROL CONCEPTS AND OBJECTIVES

The internal control system of any organization acts as a channel of command and as a monitor, assuring that commands are being carried out as required and warning the central decision-making function of changes in circumstances that require new sets of commands. In a corporate organization, management installs whatever internal controls it considers vital and necessary to the continued well-being of the company; the controls exist for and because of management.

The importance of internal control was recognized by the AICPA (1949) when it defined the term as "the plan of organization and all of the coordinate methods and measures adopted within a business to safeguard its assets, check the accuracy and reliability of its accounting data, promote operational efficiency, and encourage adherence to prescribed managerial policies" (AU 320.09). This broad definition recognizes that internal control is concerned with all aspects that contribute to the existence and well-being of the organization. Internal control therefore extends beyond the accounting and financial departments and addresses issues beyond the scope of an audit of financial statements.

In 1958 the AICPA clarified the definition of internal control to emphasize that it was composed of two elements, the first administrative controls, the second accounting controls (AU 320.10); this clarification was most recently repeated in 1972 (SAP 54, now in SAS 1; AU 320.26-.29). The distinctions between administrative and accounting controls are not always clear, and SAS 1 emphasizes that efforts to distinguish them does not mean they are mutually exclusive. Specifically, administrative controls that have an important bearing on the reliability of financial statements are included in accounting controls; nevertheless, auditors are primarily concerned with internal accounting controls.

Accounting and Administrative Control

The AICPA defines *internal accounting control* (AU 320.28) as a system of controls

> ... sufficient to provide reasonable assurance that:
> a. Transactions are executed in accordance with management's general or specific authorization.
> b. Transactions are recorded as necessary (1) to permit preparation of financial statements in conformity with generally accepted accounting principles or any other criteria applicable to such statements and (2) to maintain accountability for assets.
> c. Access to assets is permitted only in accordance with management's authorization.
> d. The recorded accountability for assets is compared with the existing assets at reasonable intervals and appropriate action is taken with respect to any differences.

By contrast, *administrative control* is defined much more broadly (AU 320.27):

> *Administrative control* includes, but is not limited to, the plan of organization and the procedures and records that are concerned with the decision processes leading to

management's authorization of transactions. Such authorization is a management function directly associated with the responsibility for achieving the objectives of the organization and is the starting point for establishing accounting control of transactions.

In this chapter, administrative controls having a strong relationship to accounting controls are often referred to as *corporate-level controls*.

The above definitions were reaffirmed in the AICPA's *Report of the Special Advisory Committee on Internal Accounting Control* (1979r, p. 10) and SAS 30.

When performing an audit, the auditor is interested only in those controls affecting the accuracy and reliability of information to be included in financial statements. Management's responsibilities regarding internal controls are much broader; for example, controls of publicly held companies have come under increasing scrutiny in recent years because of the accounting and internal control provisions of the Foreign Corrupt Practices Act and SEC proposals concerning the reporting of weaknesses in internal accounting controls (both discussed elsewhere in this chapter).

To limit the topic to manageable proportions, this chapter concentrates on the internal accounting controls over information to be included in financial statements —what those controls consist of, how they are used by both management and auditors, and what their inherent limitations are.

Underlying Concepts

Several basic considerations underlie all internal accounting control systems:

- Motivating and controlling people,
- Assessing risk of error or irregularity,
- Assessing probability of error or irregularity,
- Achieving reasonable assurance of prevention or detection of error or irregularity, and
- Recognizing inherent limitations.

Motivating and Controlling People. An internal accounting control system is only as effective as the people who operate it. Thus, even a theoretically perfect system of controls can be rendered ineffective by an inadequate staff. Proper motivation of competent personnel is fundamental and requires that they understand what they have to do, appreciate why they have to do it, and agree that it should be done. Proper motivation usually requires that whenever possible people be allowed to use their own initiative, to increase job satisfaction through the overall feeling of being an important, thinking part of the system. However, unstructured initiative tends toward chaos; a balance has to be struck between those matters where control is more important than individual initiative and those where it is not.

Assessing Risk. All businesses entail risks and therefore need controls. To effectively control the risk, it must first be assessed. Risk can be divided into commercial risk and control risk.

Commercial risk is the risk, inherent in all businesses, that management takes when making or providing a product or service. This risk is controllable only at the point of management's specific or general authorization. Organizations try to assure that the decisions to provide a product or service are made by personnel with the relevant experience and at the correct level, but there is no control—even that of having echelons of review—that can assure a correct decision has been made. Commercial risk, therefore, forms a smaller part of the internal accounting control question for auditors.

This distinction is specifically recognized in SAS 30 (AU 642.05):

In the context of internal accounting controls, *safeguarding of assets* refers only to protection against loss arising from errors [unintentional mistakes] and irregularities [intentional distortions] in processing transactions and handling the related assets. It does not include the loss of assets arising from management's operating business decisions, such as selling a product that proves to be unprofitable, incurring expenditures for equipment or material that later prove to be unnecessary or unsatisfactory, authorizing what turns out to be unproductive research or ineffective advertising, or accepting some level of customer pilferage of merchandise as part of operating a retail business.

Control risk, of much greater concern to auditors, is the risk of having too little or too much control as it relates to management's responsibilities for safeguarding of assets. Once this type of risk has been identified, an assessment has to be made of whether it should or can be controlled. The magnitude and the type of risk differ depending on the asset exposed. For example, different risks are involved when cash and equipment are compared. Cash and items readily convertible into cash are more easily conscripted for personal use, and the controls over cash should therefore reflect this. Other assets and transactions usually have a lower degree of risk, and their controls should be tailored accordingly.

Assessing Probability. The assessment of any risk requires a consideration of *probability* of loss as distinct from *possibility*. Many risks are possible, fewer are probable. Controls can reduce the probability but rarely eliminate the possibility. An internal accounting control system should take into account the possible risks that could materially affect the financial statements. But at the same time, the degree of probability must also be considered when deciding the extent of controls that are necessary and cost-justifiable.

Management's asset-safeguarding responsibilities require that there be adequate protection and control, but management's operating performance responsibilities require that controls always be weighed to see if they will hamper the productivity of any asset. Attempts to increase assets usually involve elements of risk. And usually the extent of potential reward and risk rises concurrently.

Achieving Reasonable Assurance. The balancing act outlined above is solved in the concept of reasonable assurance, based on the premise that the cost of control should not exceed the anticipated benefits. The direct cost of a specific control generally can be estimated—it usually involves known factors such as extra equipment or additional people. However, effectiveness is more difficult to determine—if an error or risk situation arises, will the control under consideration actually prevent or detect that occurrence in a timely manner? Most difficult is weighing the indirect costs and benefits—has the new control restricted operations to the extent that profit losses are greater than the assets at risk prior to installing the control? And some benefits cannot be assigned a monetary value, e.g., a company's image resulting from having (or not having) controls over otherwise minor exposures to off-book accounts.

Thus the evaluation of the net benefit arising from increased controls necessarily involves considerable estimation and judgment. Assessment, however, is valuable to management because it helps emphasize the range of alternative controls and strategies available.

Recognizing Inherent Limitations. Finally, when considering the effectiveness of internal accounting controls, some inherent limitations must be recognized.

People. People are essential to, and form the major limitation in, any system of internal accounting control, because people operate the systems, whether manually or via electronic data processing (EDP). The competence and fallibility of the personnel operating a system must always be a consideration when evaluating that system. Personal performance can be faulty because of a misunderstanding of instructions, a mistake in judgment, distraction, fatigue, or carelessness.

Circumvention or collusion. Whenever internal accounting control relies on the work of one person being checked by the work of another, there is always a risk that circumvention or collusion can reduce or destroy the effectiveness of those procedures. Circumstances that increase the possibility of collusion, such as the formation of personal relationships within the organization or the presence of dominant personalities who can exert their will, should be considered.

Control override. Many procedures can be overridden in certain circumstances. The most notable examples are bypasses by senior management, or by subordinates under their orders, of controls that would otherwise monitor the occurrence of errors or irregularities.

Changing circumstances. The environment in which internal accounting controls operate is constantly changing. Factors external to the organization, such as commercial and political forces, are always in flux, and internal factors such as changes in operations, systems, or the people involved can occur without conscious or complete planning. Thus the effectiveness of controls may be constantly changing, and projecting past evaluations of internal accounting control to future periods is subject to the risks arising from these changes.

Specific Objectives

The AICPA definition of internal accounting control (AU 320.28) states four objectives, but fundamentally these are compressable into two basic ones: (1) the execution of transactions and access to assets should be in accordance with management's general or specific authorization and (2) transactions should be recorded as necessary for the preparation of financial statements and the maintenance of accountability for assets, and the accuracy of this record should be confirmed by comparing it with existing assets at reasonable intervals. Stated another way, the two essential objectives are to permit the preparation of external financial statements and to safeguard assets from loss or abuse.

These objectives contain several ingredients, identified by the Special Advisory Committee on Internal Accounting Control as authorization, accounting, and asset safeguarding (AICPA, 1979r, p. 11). There are also many other ways to subdivide the basic objectives; to integrate this chapter with other auditing discussions in this *Handbook,* seven interrelated objectives are discussed below:

- Authorization,
- Validity,
- Recording,
- Valuation,
- Classification,
- Timing, and
- Summarization.

A review and evaluation of internal accounting controls must assure that these seven objectives have been met in all areas in which the failure to do so could result in a material error in the financial statements.

Authorization. Management should issue guidelines to assure that suitable specific or general authorization procedures exist for the key stages in any series of transactions. For example, in a sales system (see Chapter 18) the key stages requiring suitable authorization procedures would include

- Granting credit,
- Accepting orders,
- Shipping goods or performing services,
- Determining price and terms, and
- Adjusting sales-related balances.

A transaction entered into without proper authorization may, for example, result in a shipment to a bad credit risk.

Validity. This objective deals with the possibility of invalid transactions being included in the record. An example of an invalid transaction is recording a sale when no shipment took place.

Recording. This is the counterpart of the validity objective, and requires that all valid transactions be recorded. An example of a recording error is the shipment of goods without their being billed or otherwise properly included in the accounting records.

Valuation. Even though all transactions are included in the records and are authorized and valid, they may be stated at an incorrect amount. The valuation objective requires that individual transaction quantities, prices, extensions, and footings on sales invoices and other point-of-transaction documents be correctly stated.

Classification. This objective aims to eliminate the possibility of a transaction being improperly classified in the records. Examples of misclassifications include recording a purchase of a fixed asset as an expense or recording a receipt of deposit as a collection on accounts receivable.

Timing. Transactions must be recorded in the proper reporting period. Failure to do so is referred to as a cutoff error, and could result either in the complete omission of transactions because of the loss or mishandling of the basic records or in problems such as an erroneous adjustment for the difference between physical and book inventories (see Chapter 19). In addition, the effectiveness of certain internal accounting controls (e.g., the credit control function) often depends on prompt recording.

Summarization. Individual transactions, which are the source of the balances in the financial statements, must be correctly and appropriately summarized and posted to subsidiary records, the general ledger, and other reports. A defalcation in sales can be concealed, at least for a time, by underfooting the sales journal or posting that incorrect amount to the general ledger. An example of an unintentional error might be recording a sales transaction in the wrong customer's account receivable.

ELEMENTS OF INTERNAL ACCOUNTING CONTROL

Internal control should be conceived in terms of two basic ingredients: the specific system-level controls and the control environment. These are referred to as *primary* and *secondary* controls, respectively, in SAS 30. Specifically:

> Primary control procedures are designed to achieve one or more specific control objectives, and they generally are applied at points where errors or irregularities could occur in the processing of transactions and the handling of assets. Primary control procedures may be applied to transactions and assets individually or at various levels of summarization. . . . [AU 642.23]
>
> Secondary control procedures include any administrative controls or other management functions that achieve, or contribute to the achievement of, specific control objectives and thus are comprehended in the definition of internal accounting control (SAS No. 1, section 320.12). Such procedures are designed primarily to achieve broader management objectives, and they are not a part of the processing of transactions and the handling of assets. . . . [AU 642.24]

To properly set the stage, the control environment is discussed first.

The Control Environment

The control environment, often referred to as *corporate-level controls,* is the general framework within which system-level controls can operate. The four components of the control environment are authorization, communication, segregation of duties, and monitoring of compliance. These factors all reflect management's commitment to achieving the objectives of internal accounting control, and without them system-level controls are at best made less efficient or at worst rendered meaningless. The importance of the internal accounting control environment was addressed by the Special Advisory Committee on Internal Accounting Control, which concluded (AICPA, 1979r, p. 2):

> Internal accounting controls cannot be evaluated in a vacuum. Several factors have a significant impact on the selection and effectiveness of a company's accounting control procedures and techniques.
>
> The committee has found the term *internal accounting control environment* to be a convenient way to describe those factors, including organizational structure, personnel, delegation of authority, communication of responsibility, budgets and financial reports, organizational checks and balances and EDP considerations which contribute to an appropriate atmosphere of control consciousness. It is important to recognize that a poor accounting control environment would make some control procedures inoperative for all intents and purposes because, for example, individuals would hesitate to challenge a management override of a specific control procedure. However, even a strong control environment cannot provide absolute assurance that control procedures will not be circumvented by employee collusion or management override.

Authorization. In conducting any business, even one of modest size, management must make many basic decisions concerning both the exchange of assets with outsiders and the safeguarding of assets within the corporation. Management must determine by whom, under what conditions, and in what manner these activities should be conducted. A key to effective internal accounting control is that management have authorization requirements that are procedurally realistic. Each major aspect of a transaction that relates to safeguarding assets or controlling and processing activities should be covered by management's authorization. Either by types of transactions, by limitation of access to assets, or by amount limitations, management should specify what employees should and should not do, specifically addressing the routine actions of their assigned functions.

This authorization can either be *general* or *specific*. Management employs *general authorization procedures* when it establishes policies for the organization to follow. Subordinates are instructed to implement these general authorizations on transactions within the limits set by the policy. Examples of general authorizations are fixed price lists for sales, credit limits for customers, and automatic reorder points for purchases. For some transactions, however, management is unwilling to establish a general authorization and acts on a case-by-case basis. *Specific authorization* is often required for nonroutine transactions, such as major capital expenditures and the issuance of equity or debt securities. Routine transactions may also be subject to specific authorization when they are of exceptional size, e.g., particularly large sales contracts or the decision to take legal action on, or write off, a large receivable.

Although the matters that must be addressed by authorization procedures will vary from organization to organization depending on their size and the nature of their business, there are certain common items in most companies that normally need to be considered. These are

1. Sales cycle (detailed in Chapter 18):
   a. Granting of credit,
   b. Acceptance of orders,
   c. Shipment of goods or performance of services,
   d. Determination of price and terms, and
   e. Adjustments to sales-related balances.
2. Purchase cycle (detailed in Chapters 17 and 19):
   a. Requisitioning of goods and services,
   b. Selection of supplier, agreement of price and terms, and placing of order,
   c. Approval of purchase invoice, and
   d. Approval of payment and the account to be charged.
3. Wages and salary cycle (detailed in Chapter 19):
   a. Authorization to work,
   b. Number of hours worked,
   c. Rate or salary,
   d. Withholdings,
   e. Payments, and
   f. Allocation of payroll costs.
4. Cost and inventory records (detailed in Chapter 19):
   a. Determination of the type and quantity of goods to be manufactured,
   b. Determination of how goods are to be manufactured, and
   c. Making of adjustments and deductions, or write-offs of inventory-related balances.

To assure the cooperation of subordinates it is important that authorization levels are realistic and consistent with the importance of the matter and with the responsibilities of the people concerned. For example, if a department manager has responsibility for a budget of several hundred thousand dollars, it would be unrealistic and counterproductive to require that manager to seek his superior's approval for all costs in excess of a hundred dollars. Unrealistic authorization levels can suppress initiative and cause creative subordinates to waste time finding ways around the limits. Auditors frequently find instances where check signatory limits are too low, with the result that bills are settled by using several checks, each of which falls below the unrealistic authorization limit.

Communication. This second factor in the internal accounting control environment requires that what has been authorized by management, either specifically or generally, be effectively communicated to all those affected. Essential ingredients for effective communication include such items as

- Organization charts and charts of accounts,
- Clear and effective key forms designed for ease of use and review,
- Forms and records designed for multiple usage wherever possible,
- Procedural manuals that can be easily and promptly updated,
- Effective filing procedures to facilitate the prompt retrieval of key forms and records,
- Adequate training procedures to assure that employees are able to comply with applicable authorizations, and

- A framework that enables employees to report possible violations of management's specific or general authorizations to management at least one level higher than their supervisors.

Segregation of Duties. When the work of one employee is checked by another, and when the responsibility for custody of assets is separate from the responsibility for maintaining the records relating to those assets, there is appropriate segregation of duties. This helps detect errors in a timely manner and deter improper activities, and at the same time it should be devised to promote operational efficiency and allow for effective communications. Segregation can be divided into four basic categories:

- Separation of operational responsibility from financial record-keeping responsibility,
- Separation of the custody of assets from accounting,
- Separation of the authorization of transactions from the custody of related assets, and
- Separation of duties within the accounting function.

Separation of operational responsibility from financial record-keeping responsibility. If operating departments or divisions in an organization were responsible for preparing their own financial records and reports, there could be a tendency to favorably bias the reported performance results. In order to assure unbiased information, financial record keeping is usually included in a separate department under the controllership function. This need not be done for nonfinancial reports, even though the same tendency could exist; for example, sales demography reports not affecting the financial records may properly be maintained by the sales department (but depending on their use, some cross-check with the independent financial records may be advisable).

Separation of the custody of assets from accounting. The reason for not permitting the person who has temporary or permanent custody of an asset, or of documents that govern physical control of an asset, to account for that asset is to protect against the risk of conversion to personal use, covered up by falsified records. Thus, in an EDP system, for example, any persons performing the programming operating function should be denied access to all input records and should not have custody of assets that are accounted for under EDP applications; in cases where this is not feasible, compensating controls must be instituted.

Separation of the authorization of transactions from the custody of related assets. For similar reasons it is desirable, whenever possible, to prevent persons who authorize transactions from having control over the related assets.

Separation of duties within the accounting function. In the least desirable accounting system, one employee records a transaction from its origin to its ultimate posting to the general ledger, maximizing the likelihood that unintentional errors will remain undetected and increasing the opportunity for irregularities.

Simply segregating the recording in original entry journals from the recording in the related subsidiary ledgers provides many automatic cross-checks. As a business becomes larger, it is possible to make many logical separations, and in most cases the simple fact that each person performs his work independently results in a substantial increase in segregation and control without any overall duplication of effort.

In an EDP system, segregation of duties is of a different nature than in manual systems, but it is of equal importance. Frequent cross-checking is unnecessary because of the computer's ability to perform consistently and uniformly, so the emphasis should be on the separation of responsibility for processing of data by computer operators, for custody of transaction and library files, and for programming, all as more fully discussed in Chapter 15.

Monitoring of Compliance. Unless the internal control environment includes compliance monitoring, the effectiveness of the other three elements and of the specific system-level controls is greatly reduced. The knowledge that an organization effectively monitors compliance is a potent spur to obtaining conformity with those guidelines and goals. Monitoring is also an essential part of management's continuing responsibility to assure that the established systems and controls continue to serve the changing needs of the organization effectively. The monitoring process has several facets, both active and passive.

Passive monitoring. These procedures include the manner in which an entity plans its activities—an important part of the overall internal accounting control structure, because to a considerable extent planning determines the overall objectives of, and sets individual goals for elements within, the organization. Effective and realistic planning sets the targets, while system-level controls form part of the sighting mechanism the organization uses to achieve those targets. Provided the targets are well chosen, continual active monitoring of achievement shows whether the system-level controls are operating effectively.

The planning procedures of an organization take place on two scales—strategic and tactical. *Strategic planning* is a long-term process that determines the nature and objectives of a business. Elements include

- Organizational structure,
- Marketing policies,
- Financial policies, and
- Production policies.

Tactical planning, which is sometimes called *management planning,* involves shorter-term, action objectives and includes, for example:

- Formulating profit plans,
- Planning staff levels,
- Planning working capital,
- Formulating advertising programs, and
- Selecting product improvements.

Active monitoring. After setting budgets (a passive element), the first of the active elements is comparing performance to budget. To be effective as a monitoring tool, actual performance must be promptly and regularly scrutinized, variances from budget identified, and explanations sought and questioned.

The second active ingredient is proper supervision. A well-structured organization assures that employees are adequately supervised at all levels, since this is a highly effective method of securing better adherence to management's specific and general authorizations.

A third and increasingly important element of the monitoring framework is the internal audit function. The internal auditor's role, as recently enunciated in *Standards for the Professional Practice of Internal Auditing* (Institute of Internal Auditors, 1978, p. 300-301) covers the following objectives:

- Assuring the reliability and integrity of information,
- Assuring compliance with policies, plans, procedures, laws, and regulations,
- Safeguarding assets,
- Assuring the economical and efficient use of resources, and
- Assuring the accomplishment of established objectives and goals for operations or programs.

The role of the internal auditor can be variable: he operates simultaneously at the specific system control level and as part of the control environment. This is further explained in Chapter 11 and in Appendix 11-B.

Synthesis of Environmental Elements. The control environment forms a vital part of the overall internal accounting control picture. Interaction between the environment and the system-level controls is a key element in the efficient management of any organization. Auditors must take care to understand the degree of control generated by these interactive forces in a particular company. The internal accounting control environment represents management's means of pointing the organization in the desired direction and keeping it on course. Authorization, communication, segregation, and monitoring are the secondary control procedures that strengthen and reinforce the controls operating at the detailed system level.

System-Level Procedures

Primary control procedures are the specific system-level controls exercised over individual transactions and assets. If the internal accounting control environment with its corporate-level controls forms the framework, then system-level controls form the detailed picture. Though there are many different ways of analyzing and classifying system-level controls, they contain the same familiar categories: authorization, communication, segregation of duties, and monitoring of compliance.

Authorization procedures include such controls as the requirement that purchase orders be approved by a senior manager before being sent out or that the seniority of authorized check signers increase with the value of the check. Under communication comes controls over documentation, e.g., the requirement that all key accounting documents (such as sales invoices, checks, and journal vouchers) be prenumbered. Under segregation of duties falls such controls as assuring that the cashier does not have access to sales or receivables records; requiring that customer complaints be routed through a department that is independent of the sales function; restricting access to easily convertible assets, such as cash or inventory; and restricting access to key accounting records, including EDP records and systems. Finally, under monitoring of compliance, there are such controls as the reconciliation of bank statements by someone who is independent of the cashier function; the independent checking of extensions, calculations, and footings; the review of supporting documentation by check signers; and the maintaining of subsidiary ledger accounts and regular reconciliation with control accounts.

A second classification of controls involves their segregation under the broad categories prevention and detection. Detective controls are normally obvious to those involved with them, partly for their deterrent effect (which makes them preventive as well). The concept of detective controls also reaches into the internal control environment; most corporate-level compliance monitoring procedures are detective controls.

Preventive Controls. These are advantageous in that they are often highly cost-effective. They are inconspicuously built in as part of the system and are generally unrelated to the volume of transactions. Since they prevent errors when functioning effectively, they avoid the cost of correcting errors, which can be quite high. Generally, preventive elements include trustworthy personnel, segregation of duties, proper authorization, adequate documents and records, proper record-keeping procedures, and physical controls over assets and important documents that can cause movement of assets.

Detective Controls. While these are more costly than preventive controls, they are nevertheless necessary to measure the efficiency of preventive controls. Also, there are certain types of errors that cannot be controlled preventively in a cost-effective manner. Detective controls must include procedures to assure timely correction of the errors that are revealed, as in the follow-up of overdue accounts receivable, the independent checking of calculations, and the reconciliation of bank and supplier statements.

Types of Controls. While every organization is different and each control is unique in some respect, there are relatively few *types* of controls. Figure 13.1 shows nine basic types of control procedures encompassing both prevention and detection.

Controls in Smaller Enterprises

In smaller businesses, the operating procedures and methods of recording and processing transactions often differ significantly from those used by large enterprises. Indeed, many of the internal controls relevant to the larger enterprise are not possible or even appropriate or necessary. The focus is changed because most small entities are more comprehensible and controllable, and therefore direct management overview is possible and likely. Because there are fewer people, there is less segregation of duties. Management delegates less authority, relies less on environmental controls, and plays a far more direct role in assuring that its objectives are being met. Therefore, in smaller entities, internal accounting con-

Types	Examples
1. Independent approval, review, checking, or recalculation	Specific authorization of purchase or sales invoices, payroll, petty cash, and so on
	Recomputation of arithmetic on vouchers
	Subsequent review of individual transactions
2. Matching of independently generated documents	Matching of sales invoices and shipping documents
	Matching of purchase invoices and receiving reports
3. Prenumbering and sequence checking of key documents	Prenumbered shipping documents, sales invoices, checks, journal vouchers
4. Maintenance of independent control totals	Recording of cash receipts totals before transmitting cash for deposit
	Use of batch controls
	Use of control accounts posted from independent sources
	Use of memorandum records for comparison with accounting totals
5. Comparison with independent third-party information	Bank reconciliations
	Reconciling suppliers' statements
	Matching shipping advices from independent shippers to internal documentation
6. Soliciting independent third-party confirmation	Sending statements to customers
	Routine requests for confirmation of recorded data
7. Cancellation of documentation	Immediate endorsement of incoming checks
	Marking purchase invoices when paid to prevent resubmission
	Defacing spoiled or cancelled checks
8. Segregation of personnel, operations, and assets	Segregation of duties among transaction initiation, approval, and recording functions
	Segregation of cash-handling functions from record-keeping functions
	Segregation of asset custody from record-keeping functions
	Physical controls over easily converted assets
9. Timeliness of operation	Prompt deposit of cash receipts
	Prompt processing of transactions

FIGURE 13.1   BASIC TYPES OF CONTROLS

trol revolves more around individual management and less around systematized approaches. However, the close involvement of management in the details of running the business adds risks, particularly as to overriding controls and manipulating financial statements—although control *by* management may be strong, control *over* management may be weak.

Distinctions in Responsibilities

The board of directors, officers, internal auditors, and outside auditors all have strong interests in the company's internal accounting control system, but for different reasons. Internal accounting control exists for and is created by management; it is designed and maintained to meet the basic objectives of safeguarding assets and providing a basis for management decisions as well as for external financial reporting. By contrast, the outside auditor's interest is utilitarian when viewed solely in an audit framework; it concerns the reliability of the systems for his purpose of formulating an opinion on management's financial statements. In the typical company, management's responsibilities will be exercised at three levels. The board of directors has ultimate responsibility for the adequacy of the systems and controls in operation and must assure that the necessary resources' are available to enable adequate procedures to be put in place. While not responsible for detailed specification and enforcement, the board or its audit committee must be reponsible for basic policies and compliance oversight, as discussed more fully in Chapter 10. To meet its responsibilities, the board should

- Understand in broad outline how the internal accounting control system functions, and judge its sufficiency;
- Broadly monitor compliance, and suggest revisions as needed;
- Review existing policies and whether they are adequately communicated, and consider changes as needed; and
- See that appropriate actions are taken to remedy possible deficiencies, if any, in the system, or possible violations of policy.

Although the board of directors has overall responsibility, tactics are the responsibility of operating management, who must install effective system-level control procedures and create an accounting control environment in which those controls can operate. Operating management must also (1) systematically document the controls, (2) analyze the costs and benefits of possible control revisions, and (3) constantly review the adequacy of controls in light of changing circumstances, to assure their proper operation.

Management relies heavily on feedback from the internal auditor to assure the continued effective operation of internal accounting controls. The internal auditor also has a responsibility to the board of directors, which needs to be assured that operating management is responsive to the board's control requirements.

The outside auditor, unlike the internal auditor, is not a part of the company's internal accounting control system. He has a unique objective in an audit—to form an opinion on the fairness of presentation of the financial statements in conformity with GAAP. To meet this objective under GAAS, the independent auditor plans his examination so that "the financial statements taken as a whole are not materially misstated as a result of errors or irregularities" (AU 327.05). The nature and quality of internal accounting controls can have a significant effect on the nature, timing, and extent of the outside auditor's examination.

The outside auditor must decide the extent to which he will rely on the systems controls when carrying out his examination (the *reliance approach*). This reliance depends both on control adequacy and auditing cost-effectiveness. Performing direct and extensive tests (the *substantive approach*) of the documentation underlying the amounts in the financial statements may be a more direct approach. In most cases the auditor will use a combination of the two approaches. This is discussed in detail in Chapter 12.

Professional standards (AU 320.50) require that the independent auditor gain a general understanding of the systems and the operative controls in the flow of transactions through the business, to the extent these provide the data from which the financial statements are prepared. Should he decide to rely on the systems of internal accounting control, the auditor's understanding of those systems must be thorough, and he must test and evaluate whether those systems serve as intended and can be relied on to produce reasonably accurate data. One area where reliance is virtually inevitable is that of controls that assure completeness of information. It is very difficult to carry out direct testing on information that is not available.

EVALUATING INTERNAL ACCOUNTING CONTROL

Auditing, particularly for larger entities, relies heavily on the study and evaluation of internal accounting control as a basis for reducing the volume of substantive tests of transactions and balances. Although auditors have studied and used evaluations of internal accounting controls for many years, the professionals still debate the best and most effective way to do so.

Two sets of objectives must be kept in mind: (1) the basic objectives of internal accounting controls as to safeguarding assets and controlling transactions and (2) the auditor's objective to provide reasonable assurance, through his opinion report, that there are no material errors in the financial statements. The auditor seeks to reach his opinion in the most efficient and reliable way, and he looks to internal accounting control to aid in this achievement.

The audit process is essentially concerned with evidence. In *The Philosophy of Auditing* (1961), Mautz and Sharaf conclude: "Auditing, in its entirety, is made up of two functions, both closely concerned with evidence. One is gathering evidence, the other is evaluating evidence."

Internal accounting controls are a very important source of evidence for the auditor. Although he has the alternative of placing his audit emphasis on substantive testing of the financial statement balances and transactions, in any large organization it becomes almost essential for audit efficiency to review, evaluate, and test the internal accounting controls in order to establish the degree of reliance (that they will cause the systems to yield reasonably accurate data) that the auditor can place in them. Reliance on control systems minimizes the extent of detail testing of account balances and transactions. And as mentioned earlier, a review is also necessary to establish the effectiveness of those controls that assure completeness of financial information, since this is not really ascertainable through detailed testing of balances and transactions.

Conduct of the Review

A review of an internal accounting control system should be planned and carried out in a logical and systematic way, to assure adequate consideration of all important matters. While control system evaluations are often expressed in generalized terms, systems are made up of a series of interrelated and interdependent controls. Consequently, the evaluation is actually an accumulation of individual determinations ordinarily derived from the following steps:

- Identification of material transactions,
- Allocation of transactions among cycles,
- Determination of transaction characteristics,
- Preliminary review,
- Identification of material error possibilities,
- Preliminary evaluation of controls,
- Completion of control evaluation, and
- Testing to support the control evaluation.

Identification of Material Transactions

Because transactions are the basic components of enterprise operations, they are the primary subject matter and the organizing framework for evaluation purposes. Only transactions that are material individually or in the aggregate, and those that are material because of qualitative factors, can affect the financial report, and these must get the auditor's attention. The initial step, based on the auditor's knowledge of the business and of the industry as a whole, is to determine transaction sources, to assure that no material types are overlooked. The next stage is to consider each type of transaction. There are two levels:

- Transactions that involve the flow of funds with others, and
- Transactions that involve the flow of information or assets internally.

Flow of Funds With Others. Funds flow in and out of an enterprise through, for example, the purchase of raw materials and supplies (payment to vendor), the processing of that material into a product (wages and salaries), and the sale of the product to others (inflow of funds). Business cycles contain a series of interrelated steps that can be used as a framework for determining how transactions are controlled and summarized. For a large proportion of businesses there are three business cycles that encompass the vast majority of all material transactions related to the flow of funds, as shown in Figure 13.2.

Flow of Information and Assets Internally. The business cycles involving flow of funds with outsiders result in an internal information cycle—books and records —that provides information useful in accounting for or safeguarding the company's

Transaction Cycle	Examples of Types of Transactions

1. Sales, Billings, Receivables, and Collections	Sales of:
	  Merchandise
	  Scrap or excess material
	  Investments
	  Fixed assets
	Cash received for:
	  Cash sales
	  Collection of accounts receivable
	  Return on investments
	  Borrowings
	  Investments
	  Cash transfers

2. Purchases, Payables, and Payments	Purchases of:
	  Inventory
	  Fixed assets
	  Recurring services and supplies
	  Nonrecurring services and supplies
	  Investments
	Payments for:
	  Accounts payable
	  Other accrued liabilities
	  Borrowings
	  Investments
	  Dividends
	  Cash transfers

3. Wages and Salaries	Work performed:
	  Accrue salaries
	  Accrue wages
	  Accrue payroll taxes and benefits
	Payments made:
	  Salaries, wages, and benefit plan contributions
	  Payroll and tax returns

FIGURE 13.2   BASIC EXTERNAL TRANSACTION CYCLES

resources. And if it is a manufacturing business, a second cycle will exist—cost, inventory, and warehouse records—to track assets moving to different locations or categories during processing. For example, raw materials in a manufacturing company will be transferred to work in process and ultimately to inventory for sale. These internal cycles are summarized in Figure 13.3.

The books and records cycle is concerned with the functions involved in transferring financial data from the books of original entry to the general or subsidiary

	Examples of Types
Transaction Cycle	*of Transactions*
1. Books and Records	Posting to general ledger, including journal entries
2. Cost, Inventory, and Warehouse Records	Produce goods:
	Record transfers from raw materials to work in process
	Record transfers from work in process to finished goods
	Consume capital assets:
	Record depreciation expense
	Record overhead allocations

FIGURE 13.3   BASIC INTERNAL TRANSACTION CYCLES

ledgers, and with the transfer of financial data within those ledgers. It also deals with the recording of such items as allowance for bad debts; adjustments to the carrying value of property, plant, and equipment (via depreciation); and investments (via reduction to the lower of cost or market). It begins where the other cycles leave off.

Documentation of the books and records cycle should indicate how entries in the books of original entry are summarized, classified, and posted to the general ledger and by whom these processes are carried out. It should detail the types of posting media used, the frequency of posting, the levels of authorization, and the review of such postings. And it should disclose the presence in the system of checks such as the maintenance and reconciliation of control accounts and the regular extraction and review of trial balances.

For a description of the cost, inventory, and warehouse records cycle, see Chapter 19.

Allocation of Transactions Among Cycles

As shown in Figures 13.2 and 13.3, virtually all of a company's transaction types can be allocated among several major business or transaction cycles. The identification of material types of transactions should be a continuous activity throughout the evaluation of internal accounting control, and as the evaluation proceeds, previously unconsidered types of transactions may be identified.

Although the cycles outlined above will normally suffice for commercial and industrial companies, different kinds of cycles may be observed in other companies, such as financial institutions. The cycle concept, however, is normally effective no matter what type of business is under consideration. The AICPA Special Advisory Committee on Internal Accounting Control stated:

The cycle approach transcends the differences in the ways companies are organized and results in an overview of all the effects of a transaction that frequently cross functional lines in a company. [AICPA, 1979r, p. 21]

Determination of Transaction Characteristics

Once all transactions, both external and internal, have been correlated with the basic business cycles, a decision must be made as to the extent of attention different transactions or groupings of transactions should receive. Three key tests are

- Is it an *individually material* transaction?
- Is it a *key* transaction, that is, material from a qualitative (e.g., policy, image, legal) standpoint although not from a quantitative (i.e., financial statement amount) standpoint?
- Is it a *cycle* transaction?

Individually Material Transactions. Auditing concentrates attention on matters that can affect the auditor's report, and hence materiality guidelines apply. But what is material in financial statements has not been answered in professional standards and remains a matter of professional judgment.[2] However, quantitative materiality guidelines could include determination of the appropriate measurement base (e.g., net profit before tax, total stockholders' equity, total assets, or individual components of the financial statements, as appropriate in a specific situation), tempered by consideration of the problems inherent in certain situations (e.g., breakeven or low-margin companies). Because of their significance, material transactions must receive individual attention.

Also in this category are transactions or balances that although less than quantitative materiality guidelines, are significant in relation to the matter under review. In effect, this requires sifting to determine whether a significant portion of an account balance is made up of a few large transactions. Concentration on those few transactions provides a high degree of audit satisfaction about the account for a relatively low effort.

Key Transactions. Auditors devote particular attention to certain transactions not monetarily significant that may nonetheless represent high error opportunities or involve unusual relationships. Characteristics often used to isolate such transactions are shown in Figure 13.4.

Although it is not possible for an auditor to isolate every key transaction, increased audit attention is always appropriate once one is known. The auditor should also be particularly concerned with transactions having both significant financial impact and opportune timing, i.e., occurring around the end of a reporting period.

Cycle Transactions. All transaction types other than individually material or key transactions should be cycle transactions—a logically interrelated series of transactions that flow from source to related asset, liability, revenue, or expense. Unlike individually material or key transactions, cycle transactions need not be tested individually but can be covered within the context of the overall cycle. In

---

[2] The FASB is dealing with materiality in financial accounting and reporting in its conceptual framework project and has approached materiality as a qualitative characteristic, as more fully discussed in Chapters 2 and 3.

- An unusual degree of management involvement in authorization, execution, recording, or accountability
- Direct or indirect economic benefit to management
- Dealings with related parties
- Activities apparently not in the ordinary course of business
- Valuation of transactions or balances that is based to a great degree on judgment
- Risk or probability of involving questionable or illegal matters

FIGURE 13.4   SOME CHARACTERISTICS OF KEY TRANSACTIONS

other words, the auditor can use the total cycle as the basis for evaluating whether the processing properly achieves its objectives.

Preliminary Review

Purpose. Once the sources, types, and characteristics of transactions have been established and the scope of the review determined, the preliminary phase of the evaluation of internal accounting control should begin. It should be designed to provide an understanding of the transaction flow and, for each significant accounting application, the basic structure of accounting controls. This preliminary understanding is necessary to achieve an effective audit, regardless of whether or not the subsequent audit plan will place reliance on controls.

The preliminary understanding can be documented as either a brief narrative or an overview flowchart. Either method is suitable for demonstrating the basic flow of documentation and information through the system and the key controls within that system. This preliminary understanding allows the first-level decision to be addressed: whether more-detailed reviews of internal accounting controls should be undertaken in areas where reliance on them seems proper for audit efficiency, and if so, how the reviews should be structured. Even if it is decided not to place any reliance on controls, the understanding gained from a preliminary review should be sufficient for the auditor to design effective substantive tests of transaction and account balance details.

When portions of an accounting system involve EDP, the review of significant EDP is part of the overall evaluation of internal control. The use of EDP typically results in increased concentration of data and increased integration of processing. This may require new controls to deal with new risks resulting from loss of traditional segregation of duties. As the extent of human involvement declines, new controls may have to be built into the EDP portions of systems in order to maintain satisfactory levels of control. For a more extensive discussion of how EDP affects the review and evaluation of internal accounting control, refer to Chapter 15.

Method. The methods used to obtain this understanding of the flow of transactions through the processing system and their interrelationships in the accounting control structure are

- Referring to available documentation,
- Making knowledgeable inquiries of client personnel,
- Observing job assignments and operating procedures, and
- Tracing transactions through the system.

Available documentation. Normally, the preliminary phase of the study of internal accounting control begins with a review of available system documentation, including the client's flowcharts, narrative descriptions, procedural manuals, organization charts, and so on; also, the auditor's prior working papers will show information gathered in previous audits.

Knowledgeable inquiries. Usually the auditor will have to supplement the available documentation by using questionnaires or checklists and through interviews and discussions with client personnel doing the work.

Observations of job assignments and operating procedures. In addition to reviewing documentation and making inquiries, the auditor must learn by watching. For example, observation of the accounting department during processing can produce valuable information about the flow of transactions and how individuals interrelate. In fact, the auditor should, whenever possible, take a familiarization tour of the company's major facilities to obtain a general understanding of the business, its processes, and the interrelationships between departments and activities. However, although observation helps, it does not constitute a full assessment of performance.

Tracing transactions. This step, often referred to as a *walk-through,* means following a transaction as it moves from one point in the processing stream to another. This is usually done by tracing a transaction from its origin to its final account, or from an account to its source, and is a good way to relate the flow of transactions to control functions and individuals. It can also assure that the auditor's previous understanding of the system was correct.

Identification of Material Error Possibilities

Once the auditor has identified the material, key, and cycle transactions, and has gained a preliminary understanding of the systems and controls, his next step is to consider what risks are inherent in those transactions and systems. The auditor should consider what could materially go wrong, either intentionally or unintentionally. This consideration is usually made for both general and specific factors.

General Factors. Based on his knowledge of the business, the auditor should consider whether general factors would affect the identification of possibly material errors. These factors are considered in four groups:

- General economic and financial conditions,
- Organizational considerations,

- Management integrity, and
- Analytical review of financial data.

General economic and financial conditions. The auditor must consider whether the company is under more strain than normal because of general economic or financial conditions, since this will usually increase the possibility of material errors. Examples of factors and conditions that indicate increased strain include

- Insufficient working capital or credit lines to operate at a profitable capacity;
- Significantly less profitability than other companies in the industry;
- Demands for new capital in excess of availability;
- Dependence on a single (or relatively few) products, customers, or transactions;
- Violations, or possible violations, of debt restrictions or other covenants;
- A depressed industry, perhaps characterized by a large number of business failures;
- Excess capacity and high fixed costs;
- Significant litigation, especially between shareholders and management;
- Rapid expansion of business or product lines;
- Numerous acquisitions, particularly as a diversification move into new and unfamiliar activities;
- A long-term operating cycle for a company's products;
- Overly optimistic sales projections;
- Inadequate funds generated for capital investment;
- Intervention of government agencies; and
- Inadequate supplies of labor, materials, or energy.

Organizational considerations. A company with a positive commitment to good internal accounting control can achieve the objectives of those controls. Evidence of such a commitment is, to a large extent, found in the quality of the internal accounting control environment. Without this commitment, even well-designed systems will ultimately fail. Thus, the auditor cannot possibly give too much attention to the environment in identifying possible exposures to material errors.

Because the key to the control environment is people, both those who establish policy and those who follow it, a significant part of the auditor's evaluation of the effectiveness of an internal accounting control system is assessing the competence and motivation of individuals. While this assessment is subjective and very complex, it is also ordinary (in that the auditor will do some assessment subconsciously) and necessary to reach a conclusion about the propensity of personnel to commit errors and their ability to prevent or detect errors by others.

When performing tests of controls, the auditor will be ascertaining whether or not the controls seem to be operating. This involves identifying the existence of actual errors and judging whether potential errors—those that might have occurred—would have been detected and corrected. The auditor's evaluation process, therefore, considers whether, if an error is presented, an employee will, as intended by the system, actually isolate, correct, and resubmit the transaction into the processing stream.

Some signals that should increase the auditor's concern about possible material errors and the effectiveness of the control environment are

- A management dominated by one or a few individuals, or conversely, a lack of strong leadership;
- High turnover of management positions, especially financial management;
- Failure to develop managerial talent in relation to growth of the business;
- Decentralized operations and record keeping, with a centralized management;
- Diversified activities, each with its own accounting systems;
- Heavy dependence on computer processing for decision making, without the related knowledge of computer operations; and
- Inadequate internal audit.

Management integrity. Although certainly part of the internal accounting control environment, the integrity of management is fundamental to an ability to perform an audit. In identifying possible material errors, auditors must focus on the motives of management and recognize conditions that might cause management to act without integrity or good faith. Conditions that increase concern, aside from questionable reputation and a compulsion to take unnecessary risks, relate to inordinate or unreasonable management desires for

- Favorable earnings (for example, because of the need to support the price of the company's stock or because of management profit-sharing agreements),
- Low taxable income, and
- Power ("empire building").

Analytical review of financial data. Analytical review is an extremely useful and powerful tool. It is used by management, as a significant part of its internal accounting control environment, to monitor performance; it is used by auditors to provide audit evidence and to identify material error possibilities. Analytical review of financial and operating data can show whether account balances and relationships are reasonable in relation to trends and other expectations. Such reviews include the relationship between past, present, and anticipated activity and also comparison with similar companies in the same industry.

The importance of analytical review is emphasized in the *Report of the Special Advisory Committee on Internal Accounting Control:*

> Financial reports that compare budgeted and actual results and analyze variances and the managerial action that results from that analysis may enable management to identify areas where controls may need to be strengthened. They also provide a means for evaluating performance, help provide reasonable assurance that transactions are being executed in accordance with management's authorization, and help develop an attitude of accountability at all levels of the company. [AICPA, 1979r, p. 15]

Available analytical review procedures are, of course, extensive. While they vary between industries, most can be classified into the five distinct types shown in Figure 13.5.

Procedure	Example
1. Comparison of actual results or balances to predicted results or balances	Comparison of actual to budgeted figures and investigation of variances for such activities as sales, costs, and cash flow
2. Comparison of actual results and balances to prior results and balances	Comparison of quantitative data, such as sales, purchases, overhead, receivables, payables, and inventory Comparison of qualitative data, such as principal customers and suppliers
3. Examination of the consistency between interrelated results and balances	Calculating accounts receivable based on sales and receipts; interest expense based on average borrowings; rental income based on rental units; and payroll based on number of employees
4. Comparison of changes in interrelationships between accounts in comparable periods	Examining the ratio of sales to accounts receivable and comparing it to prior-period ratios; examining inventory turnover from period to period
5. Comparison of interrelationships between accounts in other comparable companies	Ratio analysis as above, but comparing results internally (between like branches) or externally (between similar businesses in the same industry)

FIGURE 13.5   TYPES OF ANALYTICAL REVIEW PROCEDURES

In all analytical procedures, the most useful and valid results are obtained when the analysis is done at a detailed level, e.g., by product line or category of expense.

For a more extensive discussion of analytical review, refer to the appendix to Chapter 12, which focuses on use of computer software to develop significant ratios for a business. Chapters 22 and 26 also deal with certain ratios applicable, respectively, to debt and equity.

Specific Factors. Up to this point, the auditor has developed an understanding of the nature, source, and characteristics of transactions, as well as an understanding of the internal accounting control system to the extent needed to provide a focus for his preliminary evaluation. He has also reviewed and assessed the general factors that contribute to material error types. Now he must identify, for each material transaction cycle, those potential error types that could result in a material error in the financial statements. There are two steps:

• Applying general potential error types to transaction cycles, and
• Identifying the possible causes of those potential error types.

Applying general potential error types to transaction cycles. The general error types imply a failure to achieve the basic objectives of internal accounting control, described earlier in this chapter under Specific Objectives. A summary of these problems, together with their remedies, is shown in Figure 13.6.

Applying these general potential error types to specific transaction cycles will identify potential error types in the context of transactions within that cycle, that is, the "points in the processing of transactions and the handling of assets where errors or irregularities could occur" (AU 642.21). For example, the potential error types relating to the sales element of the sales, billings, receivables, and collection cycle (discussed in Chapter 18) are

- Sales recorded but goods not shipped (validity),
- Goods shipped but not invoiced (authorization),
- Goods shipped to bad credit risk (authorization),
- Sales invoiced but not recorded (recording),
- Sales amount recorded incorrectly (valuation),
- Sales invoiced but not properly costed (valuation),
- Sales recorded in wrong period (timing),
- Sales misclassified (classification), and
- Sales journal incorrectly added (summarization).

Identifying the possible sources of potential error types. Once the specific potential error types for the transaction cycle are defined, the auditor should consider the circumstances under which those errors could occur. At the most detailed level, the possibilities are almost limitless, arising whenever a document is prepared, processed, passed from one person to another, or transcribed. There are, however, general causes to keep in mind when assessing whether a system appears to control a specific potential error type:

- Failure to prepare documents,
- Loss of documents,
- Duplication of documents,
- Inaccurate recording,
- Inaccurate processing,
- Incomplete processing,
- Untimely processing and recording, and
- Failure to follow authorization procedures.

Preliminary Evaluation of Controls

The auditor is now able to determine whether additional study of the internal accounting control system is warranted. Although the system has not yet been tested, there should be a sufficient understanding of the transaction flow and primary and secondary control procedures to decide between combinations of the following alternatives:

General Potential Error Types	*Basic Types of Internal Accounting Control*
Transactions are not properly *authorized*	Policy on specific or general authorization at key points (e.g., granting credit)
	Procedures for approvals consistent with policy and requiring documentation (e.g., signatures or attaching supporting documents)
Recorded transactions are not *valid*	Segregation of duties
	Use of prenumbered documents that are accounted for
	Cancellation of documents to prevent reuse
	Monthly reconciliation of subsidiary records and follow-up by an independent person
Existing transactions are not *recorded*	Use of prenumbered documents that are accounted for
	Segregation of duties
	Monthly reconciliation of subsidiary records and follow-up by an independent person
Transactions are improperly *valued*	Internal verification of details and calculations and posting by an independent person
	Reconciliation of details to control totals (e.g., bank reconciliation) by an independent person
Transactions are improperly *classified*	Use of an adequate chart of accounts
	Internal review and verification
Transactions are recorded at the improper *time*	Procedures to assure prompt recording of all transactions
	Internal review and verification
Transactions are improperly included in the subsidiary records and incorrectly *summarized*	Segregation of duties
	Monthly reconciliation of subsidiary records by an independent person
	Internal review and verification

FIGURE 13.6   GENERAL ERROR TYPES AND BASIC REMEDIES

- Does reliance on parts of the internal accounting control system appear to be warranted for some or all of the potential error types?
- Can the audit objectives be accomplished in a more efficient and effective manner without reliance on the internal accounting control system?

In any case, if potential weaknesses have been isolated based on the review of internal controls, their possible impact on the financial report must be assessed; if the weakness is a *material weakness,* it must be communicated to senior management and directors (AU 323).

Reliance Approach. Since no testing has been done, any decision is preliminary; however, the auditor must decide how the study of internal accounting control fits into the audit plan for this enterprise. If the auditor does not intend to rely on internal accounting control, little audit value will be obtained by continuing the study.[3] However, if reliance appears both warranted and efficient, the auditor must decide what controls to use and how the testing and evaluation of those controls should be performed.

Substantive Approach. The auditor may decide that the internal accounting control system does not provide a basis for reliance, or—on the basis of efficiency—he may decide not to rely on it as a basis for designing the nature, scope, and timing of audit tests. In either case no further evaluation or testing of a system would be performed (except as mentioned in fn. 3), and the emphasis shifts to tests of the results of the transaction flow on amounts and balances in the financial statements. These tests are called substantive tests because they aim to directly *substantiate* the reasonableness of individual transactions and balances, determining the presence or absence of monetary errors.

Completion of Control Evaluation

When it has been decided to place reliance on the system of internal accounting control, a more formal study and evaluation of the system is necessary. This involves

- Describing the details of the processing system and the related controls,
- Verifying the system description,
- Testing the controls to be relied on, and
- Reevaluating the controls actually relied on.

Systems Documentation for Cycle Transactions. The objective of documenting the system used to process and control transactions is to establish the appropriate

---

[3] There may be other valid reasons the auditor would proceed with testing a system even though it would be more efficient to use a substantive approach. For example, the company may want a detailed assessment of controls in a department that has had problems; or the auditor may select a certain area or areas to study in depth on a rotating annual basis, as a means of providing incisive comments to management for control improvements that would increase efficiency.

level of reliance. The decision to complete the evaluation requires that the preliminary systems descriptions be augmented, probably in flowchart form but perhaps also or alternatively in narrative. The detailed information should be gathered from a client's existing documentation, from the auditor's prior working papers, and from structured interviews with key employees.

When describing the processing system and control details, the auditor's objective is to identify the existence or absence of specific controls that help to prevent or detect and correct the material potential errors, which have already been identified. The auditor should at the same time collect information relating to the volume of accounting work within that system. This will include such items as the monthly volume of sales orders received; the number of invoices, purchase requisitions, and checks issued; the number of customers and employees in the department; and the number of general ledger accounts. This information provides the basis for determining the timing, nature, and extent of tests to be carried out on the controls as well as on transactions and balances. In addition to volume statistics, it is advisable to obtain or estimate accounting population statistics, such as the range of sales, invoice numbers, and check numbers, since these will be used in planning audit procedures.

The auditor should also gather information about the characteristics of account balances. This would include the number of individual items in those accounts as well as their balance ranges. For example, sales could be to other business enterprises or to individuals, and could be of widely varying magnitudes. All information of this nature will help in designing and planning the audit approach.

Business cycles are usually the most effective way to organize transactions, and usually form the framework for systems descriptions. The major issues that should be addressed for each of the principal business cycles are discussed below. For more complex systems it would be necessary to further classify these transaction cycles into subsystem descriptions and to add other important transactions. For example, it may be appropriate to describe, as a system, the procedures used to manage cash balances, marketable securities, and temporary investments (see Chapter 17). Similarly, the company's operations may require a separate system for transactions relating to fixed assets (see Chapter 20).

Sales, billings, receivables, and collections cycle. The majority of transactions affecting this cycle will arise from the sale of the company's regular products or services, and the systems will be designed primarily to process such transactions. Documentation of the sales cycle should tell how the following basic activities are performed and controlled:

- Recording and invoicing all goods shipped,
- Updating inventory quantity records (when perpetual records are kept) and inventory cost records to reflect goods shipped or returned,
- Approving credit and following up overdue accounts,
- Handling, recording, and depositing cash received for credit sales and cash sales,
- Issuing credit memos for goods returned, adjustments, invoice errors, etc.; and
- Recording miscellaneous income when this is significant.

Other transactions may also result in revenue, receivables, and cash receipts, and these transactions, being of an unusual or infrequent nature, may not be subject to the same systems that apply to regular sales. These miscellaneous sources of income could include such items as the sale of fixed assets or scrap, and, if material, the subsystems that process these transactions should be documented.

Purchases, payables, and payments cycle. In this cycle the majority of the transactions will be purchases of goods and services, setting up of payables to the related creditors, and payments. However, less frequent transactions will include the purchase or construction of fixed assets and the purchase of miscellaneous items such as investments. The documentation of this cycle should address the following basic activities:

- Authorizing the acquisition of goods or services,
- Recording liabilities for all goods or services received,
- Allocating purchases to the appropriate accounts,
- Updating inventory quantity and cost records to reflect purchases or returns to suppliers, and
- Checking, approving, and recording payments.

Wages and salaries cycle. Documentation required for this cycle concerns the following activities:

- Controlling the authorization for and hiring of new employees,
- Controlling the authorization for and implementation of changes in employment conditions,
- Controlling the authorization for and preparation, calculation, and payment of wages and salaries,
- Allocating wage and salary costs to the appropriate accounts, and
- Controlling executive and management payroll.

Cost and inventory records cycle. This transaction cycle will be encountered whenever the company's costing and inventory records are sufficiently complicated that they cannot be adequately described as part of other systems. The cycle is concerned with the recording of inventory movement and changes through labor and overhead in arriving at finished goods. (Costing of sales and relieving of inventory would normally form part of the sales cycle, while direct charges to inventory would normally be covered by purchases and payroll.)

Systems Documentation for Individually Material or Key Transactions. When individually material or key transactions are subject to separate controls and processing systems, these should be documented. However, all material and key transactions must be individually audited using the substantive approach.

Verifying the Systems Descriptions. Having completed the description of a specific system, the auditor must trace each type of transaction through the system to satisfy himself that it is correct. This involves tracing transactions from initiation to final recording, or vice versa. While doing this, the auditor should observe whether permanent and temporary records appear to be up to date and balanced regularly or contain old or irregular items and whether the continuity of documents in the files is complete.

Once the auditor is satisfied that all systems descriptions are complete and accurate, he should proceed to test those controls on which he plans to rely.

Testing the Controls to Be Relied On. To be able to rely on internal accounting controls, the auditor must perform tests to ascertain that the key control procedures were performed properly and independently, as designed. Operating evidence and the nature of the control influence the choice of tests—observation or examination of documentation—and also their timing and extent.

Observation tests. If the performance of a control procedure leaves no documentary evidence, the only method of testing is by observation. Although observation can provide evidence of performance for a wide variety of controls, the reviewer must always consider that the control may not be in operation when he is not there to observe it. Observation tests, therefore, should be supplemented by other evidence, such as inquiry as to the operation of controls at other times.

Examples of controls that usually leave no documentary evidence and must be tested by observation include those over

- Distribution of wages,
- Opening of mail,
- Punching of timecards, and
- Inventory and certain segregations of duties.

In addition, observation supplements tests of documentation by providing evidence of the apparent thoroughness and competence of the person doing the job.

Tests of documentation. When the performance of a control procedure is documented, records can be examined for compliance. Tests should be designed to detect compliance deviations or failures to perform as prescribed.

For example, a test for evidence that all goods shipped have been billed may require comparing sales invoices to shipping documents. Here, the definition of a compliance deviation should include an unmatched shipping document, a shipping document matched to the wrong sales invoice, incorrect recording of quantities shipped, arithmetical errors in extensions and footings, and any other matters important in the specific control situation.

When a control is evaluated as reliable, it is because the auditor is persuaded that (1) the control is effective in achieving its purpose and (2) the persons performing the control are competent and will properly and consistently perform the control. Evidence of the performance of the control is evidence of compliance. If, on the other hand, a negative finding results, the control may not meet the need, and this fact has to be considered in the determination of other audit procedures to be performed to minimize the likelihood of errors in the financial statements.

Timing of tests of controls. The tests should provide the auditor with reasonable assurance that the controls on which he intends to rely are operating as described. For controls whose performance is documented, tests should be applied throughout the period under audit. When controls are tested as part of interim work, additional testing for the period between interim and year-end is necessary. The nature and extent of these "bring-up" tests is influenced by the following factors:

- Results of the interim tests,
- Length of the period between interim and final,
- Responses to inquiries for remaining period,
- Nature and amount of transactions or balances occurring subsequent to interim testing,
- Results of analytical reviews, and
- Results of other tests performed (substantive tests of transactions and balances) that also provide information as to the operation of controls in the remaining period.

The evaluation of internal accounting control is a continuous activity. All the above factors to some extent indicate whether controls are operating as described.

Extent of tests of controls. There are no concrete rules for how much testing is required; it is a matter of judgment. Ideally, the auditor should test as little as is possible within the context of his objective of achieving reasonable assurance that controls being relied on are operating as described. Samples for testing may be selected judgmentally or statistically. For a discussion of how judgmental and statistical sampling concepts apply, see Chapter 14.

Effect of Substantive Tests on Reliance Plans

Substantive tests of transactions and balances will uncover errors; no system can prevent or detect and correct all errors. When an error is discovered, it is important to establish the reason for the error; that is, what control did not operate initially (preventive), and what controls later failed to uncover the error (detective).

The control deficiencies illustrated by the error should be reconsidered to determine whether more work is necessary, either on transactions or amounts or on the evaluation of the controls being relied on. In other words, the auditor's reliance on controls must be reconfirmed in view of the errors found in substantive testing. The important determination is whether the error is so important as to suggest that a total reassessment of a planned reliance on a specific control is necessary. This will depend on the circumstances of the error and the degree of planned reliance on the specific control that failed.

CONCLUSION OF THE EVALUATION PROCESS

The conclusion of the evaluation process is an assessment of the likelihood of a material error occurring and being included in the financial statements. This assessment involves a series of subjective judgments and recognition of the inherent limitations of any internal accounting control system. Essentially, it is a probability analysis, both for errors and for controls. It requires a determination of how much reliance can be placed on a system of internal accounting control and an assessment of other auditing procedures, and it is expressed as a matter of degree rather than an absolute.

In making this assessment, the auditor may identify system deficiencies that would not result in material errors in the financial statements; these matters should be communicated to management, preferably in a letter of comments and recommendations. Of course, material control weaknesses *must* be communicated (AU 323), notwithstanding that substantive procedures have resulted in reasonable assurance of fairly presented financial statements.

Apart from statistically based statements, discussed in Chapter 14, the auditor can express his judgment concerning the reliability of an internal accounting control system (1) in terms of the monetary exposure resulting from the possibility of the controls not operating as designed and (2) in terms of risk (such as high, low, or moderate) that the system will produce undetected errors.

Monetary Error

This approach is based on assessments of both the probable frequency of occurrence and the probable monetary amount involved in any error. The technique was developed to deal with computer controls and security systems, and is based on the use of exponential tables that give deliberately large ranges for both the magnitude and the frequency of error occurrence. Two such tables, adapted from *Security, Accuracy, and Privacy in Computer Systems* (Martin, 1973, p. 14), that can easily be used for such an approach are

Magnitude of Error

0: Negligible (about $1)
1: On the order of $10
2: On the order of $100
3: On the order of $1,000
4: On the order of $10,000
5: On the order of $100,000
6: On the order of $1,000,000
7: On the order of $10,000,000

Frequency of Error

0: Virtually impossible
1: Might happen once in 400 years
2: Might happen once in 40 years
3: Might happen once in 4 years (1,000 working days)
4: Might happen once in 100 working days
5: Might happen once in 10 working days
6: Might happen once a day
7: Might happen ten times a day

After the magnitude and frequency of the error are identified from the tables, they should be factored to develop a general assessment of risk in relation to a specific objective. For example, if the magnitude of an error is on the order of $100 and it might occur once a day, the calculation would be

$$
\begin{array}{ccccccc}
\text{Magnitude} & & \text{Frequency} & & \text{Number} & & \text{General} \\
\text{of} & \times & \text{of} & \times & \text{of days} & = & \text{assessment} \\
\text{error} & & \text{error} & & \text{in year} & & \text{of risk}
\end{array}
$$

or:

$$
\$100 \quad \times \quad 1 \quad \times \quad \frac{250\ \text{business days}}{} \quad = \quad \$25,000
$$

To use these tables on an error of, say, $1,400 estimated to occur every 40th day, the next higher limit would be used in the equation—in this case, $10,000 once every 100 days. The resulting general assessment of risk can then be considered in light of materiality guidelines for the company being audited, and the future audit strategy decided.

Statements of Risk

The auditor can express his judgment concerning the likelihood of risk in more general terms—high, moderate, or low—rather than by attempting to assign a monetary value. Four possible levels of risk are frequently identified:

- Low—the auditor expects few, if any, errors;
- Moderate—the auditor expects errors but has reason to believe they are not likely to be material in relation to the financial statements;
- High—the auditor expects errors and believes they may be material in relation to the financial statements; and
- Unknown—the auditor has not proceeded beyond his preliminary evaluation of the reliability of internal accounting controls and is not relying on these controls. (In this case, the internal accounting controls have not affected the structure of substantive audit procedures, except for dealing with apparent weaknesses noted in the preliminary review.)

Risk assessments, whether words or numbers, relate specifically to individual potential error types. If the concept of evaluating internal accounting controls based on potential error types is being used, all the steps in the review revolve around assessments about specific error types. The conclusions relating to these error types cause additional substantive audit work to assure that potential errors, either singly or in the aggregate, have not resulted in actual material errors in the financial statements.

High Risk. This evaluation indicates that the operation of the systems could cause the financial statements to be materially in error. Because the system is weak the auditor must resolve his uncertainty through substantive tests of transactions and balances. He must seek the most convincing audit evidence available—evidence from physical inspection or outside verification and from a detailed analysis of financial statement amounts.

The timing of the substantive audit procedures would be as of year-end, to directly support the formulation of an opinion on the financial statements. Because the internal accounting control system is considered unreliable, substantive tests at interim dates should only address accumulating balances, i.e., income statement accounts. The substantive procedures used would be extensive and would be directed at obtaining evidence about a significant part of the accounts making up the financial statements. This testing could be done on either a judgmental or a statistical sampling basis and could involve the segmentation of different strata within accounts.

Therefore, for a high-risk assessment, the audit strategy can be summarized as follows (also applicable when risk is unknown because controls were not evaluated):

Nature	To establish existence and amount
	• Physical inspection
	• Confirmation
	• Review of documents from outside the organization
	• Recalculations
Timing	Basically year-end
Extent	Extensive, and concentrated on testing significant parts of affected accounts

Moderate Risk. Here the auditor would use a combination of physical evidence procedures (the most persuasive form of audit evidence) and corroborative procedures, such as analytical review and inquiry, to augment his reliance on the system. The timing, nature, and extent of the tests are interdependent and reflect the nature of the available audit evidence and the practicality of performing substantive tests at different times. If physical audit evidence can be obtained at or near year-end, it will provide a high degree of assurance about the validity of the year-end account balances and reduce the requirements for additional evidence needed to support the audit opinion. This can be summarized as follows:

Nature	Mixed, including
	• Tests to establish existence and valuation
	• Corroborative tests
Timing	Interim and year-end
Extent	Mixed, depending on audit evidence available
	• If physical existence tests are possible and applied, less overall testing
	• If only corroborative procedures possible, more testing

Low Risk. When the quality of the internal accounting control system is such that there is a low risk of material errors in the financial statements, the system carries the major burden of reducing audit uncertainty. Thus, the additional work required need only seek essentially corroborative evidence, which is less extensive and can be spread throughout the year.

In low-risk situations, substantive evidence is gathered to determine whether the evaluation of the internal accounting controls is contradicted or materially altered. Analytical review, intercomparisons with other audit evidence, and limited tests of transactions and balances would be applied.

PUBLIC REPORTING ON INTERNAL CONTROLS

Management Reporting

As mentioned at the outset of this chapter, the SEC had a proposal outstanding that would have required management to report on the achievement of the objectives of internal accounting control. However, well before the SEC release, some companies began such reporting, in less categorical terms, as part of an overall report by management on its responsibility for the financial statements. This development was in response to a recommendation of the Cohen Commission (CAR, 1978, pp. 76-77) and was strongly endorsed by the Financial Executives Institute (FEI).

Shortly after the SEC proposal, a Special Committee on Management Reports issued its report (AICPA, 1979f), encouraging such statements by management, giving examples, and discussing appropriate contents. A typical report is shown in Figure 13.7.

RESPONSIBILITY FOR FINANCIAL STATEMENTS

The Auditors' Report shown below states their opinion as to the reasonableness and consistency of the Company's financial statements viewed in the light of conformity with generally accepted accounting principles. However, it is management's responsibility to see that such financial statements fairly reflect the financial position of the Company and its operating results. In order to meet this responsibility, management maintains formal policies and procedures that are consistent with high standards of accounting and administrative practices, which are regularly communicated to all levels of the organization. In addition, management maintains a comprehensive program of internal auditing within the Company to examine and evaluate the adequacy and effectiveness of established internal controls as related to Company policies, procedures, and objectives.

The Board of Directors reviews the Company's internal controls, auditing, and financial reporting through its Audit Committee, which consists of four members of the Board who are not officers or employees of the Company. The Audit Committee engages the independent auditors, subject to ratification by the stockholders at the annual meeting. The Committee meets periodically with management and the independent auditors, both separately and together, to review and discuss the auditors' findings and other financial and accounting matters. The independent auditors have free access to the Audit Committee.

FIGURE 13.7 TYPICAL REPORT BY MANAGEMENT
SOURCE: United States Gypsum Annual Report, extracted from AICPA, 1979f.

As discussed earlier in the chapter, the response of companies to the FEI's support for the Cohen Commission recommendation was one of the factors that led the SEC to withdraw its proposal.

Auditor Reporting

"Private" reporting—that is, to the company or regulatory agencies—on internal controls has been with the auditing profession for many years. The ground rules were first codified in the early 1970s (SAP 49; AU 640 and SAP 52; AU 641), resulting in a standard report style for public use that contained a lengthy explanation of the objectives and inherent limitations of internal controls. It concluded with the statement that because the auditor's review was for audit purposes, his examination ". . . would not necessarily disclose all weaknesses in the system because it was based on selective tests of accounting records and related data" (AU 640.12). This form of report was heavily criticized because of its lengthy caveats and its failure to address the "adequacy" of a company's systems. Consequently, there was very little publication.

Recommendations of the Cohen Commission (CAR, 1978, pp. 61-62) and constant urgings by the SEC have resulted in the issuance by the Auditing Standards Board of SAS 30 (AU 642). This SAS describes the various types of possible engagements and the procedures an auditor would apply to report on an entity's system of internal accounting control. The auditor could be engaged to

- Express an opinion on the system of internal accounting control, either on a specified date or for a period of time;
- Report on the system for the restricted use of management or other specified third parties based solely on a study and evaluation of internal accounting control made as a part of an audit of financial statements that is not sufficient for expressing an opinion on the system;
- Report on all or part of the system for the restricted use of management or specified regulatory agencies, based on the regulatory agencies' preestablished criteria; and
- Issue other special purpose reports on all or part of the system for the restricted use of management, specified regulatory agencies, or other specified third parties.

SAS 30 points out:

. . . Whether a company is in compliance with those provisions of the FCPA is a legal determination. An independent accountant's opinion does not indicate whether the company is in compliance with those provisions but may be helpful to management in evaluating the company's compliance. [AU 642.12]

The revised form of report in SAS 30 contains the following elements (AU 642.38):

a. A description of the scope of the engagement.
b. The date to which the opinion relates.
c. A statement that the establishment and maintenance of the system is the responsibility of management.

d. A brief explanation of the broad objectives and inherent limitations of internal accounting control.

e. The accountant's opinion on whether the system taken as a whole was sufficient to meet the broad objectives of internal accounting control insofar as those objectives pertain to the prevention or detection of errors or irregularities in amounts that would be material in relation to financial statements.

The revised reporting format (AU 642.39), which isn't much shorter than the form previously sanctioned in AU 640.12, is shown in Figure 13.8. But the words are much more potent and are based on a review beyond that needed for normal audit purposes.

The issue for the 1980s is whether the independent auditor can continue reviewing controls only as needed for his audit satisfaction (as described in this chapter) or whether he will have to revamp his approach for all public companies to directly study and evaluate all controls that bear on the prevention or detection of material errors or irregularities in the financial statements. The infeasibility of going beyond a focus on material weaknesses is, of course, apparent to the Auditing Standards Board, but the test of societal and regulatory pressures is yet to come.

To the Board of Directors and Shareholders of XYZ Company:

We have made a study and evaluation of the system of internal accounting control of XYZ Company and subsidiaries in effect at December 31, 19XX. Our study and evaluation was conducted in accordance with standards established by the American Institute of Certified Public Accountants.

The management of XYZ Company is responsible for establishing and maintaining a system of internal accounting control. In fulfilling this responsibility, estimates and judgments by management are required to assess the expected benefits and related costs of control procedures. The objectives of a system are to provide management with reasonable, but not absolute, assurance that assets are safeguarded against loss from unauthorized use or disposition and that transactions are executed in accordance with management's authorization and recorded properly to permit the preparation of financial statements in accordance with generally accepted accounting principles.

Because of inherent limitations in any system of internal accounting control, errors or irregularities may occur and not be detected. Also, projection of any evaluation of the system to future periods is subject to the risk that procedures may become inadequate because of changes in conditions, or that the degree of compliance with the procedures may deteriorate.

In our opinion, the system of internal accounting control of XYZ Company and subsidiaries in effect at December 31, 19XX, taken as a whole, was sufficient to meet the objectives stated above insofar as those objectives pertain to the prevention or detection of errors or irregularities in amounts that would be material in relation to the consolidated financial statements.

FIGURE 13.8   PROPOSED FORM OF INDEPENDENT ACCOUNTANT'S REPORT ON INTERNAL ACCOUNTING CONTROL

SUGGESTED READING

AICPA. *Report of the Special Advisory Committee on Internal Control.* New York, 1979. Because of the Foreign Corrupt Practices Act of 1977 and the recommendations of the Commission on Auditors' Responsibilities, the AICPA established a committee, made up almost entirely of corporate executives, to define internal controls from the company's perspective. (Most earlier discussions had been framed in the auditor's perspective—what he needs to do as part of his audit.) Although this report suffers from lack of a clear statement on how to judge materiality in the internal control area, it is useful in generally illustrating the approach being used by major audit firms in following transaction cycles.

Arens, Alvin, and Loebbecke, James. "The Study and Evaluation of Internal Control." Chapter 5 in *Auditing, An Integrated Approach.* Englewood Cliffs, N.J.: Prentice-Hall, 1976. This textbook presents one of the first published discussions of auditing concepts using analysis of error types and review for responsive controls.

Touche Ross & Co. *The New Management Imperative.* New York, 1978. The Foreign Corrupt Practices Act of 1977 for the first time made it a matter of law that publicly held companies maintain a satisfactory system of internal accounting control. This booklet explains broadly how management can accomplish this new legal responsibility.

————. *Controlling Assets and Transactions.* New York, 1979. The SEC's proposal to require a management representation on the achievement of the objectives of internal control resulted in many how-to-do-it releases by CPA firms. This publication is perhaps the most straightforward one. Since it was written by the authors of this chapter, it will present similar information stated from management's perspective.

14

Audit Sampling

Ann M. Thornton

SAMPLING PROCEDURE

Any procedure that leads to a conclusion about a complete set of data on the basis of information obtained from only a portion of the set is a *sampling procedure.*

This chapter focuses on the independent auditor's use of sampling, but it of course applies with equal measure to internal or government auditors and corporate financial management seeking adequate answers without looking under every rock. Especially today, with the Foreign Corrupt Practices Act requiring publicly held companies to maintain systems meeting the act's specified objectives of internal accounting control, facing up to sampling as the methodology for achieving compliance is urgent. (See Chapter 13.)

In the early days of the independent audit, it was not unusual for an auditor to examine 100% of the entries and records of the company audited. But companies soon grew so large that complete examination of the tremendous volume of entries became uneconomical. It also came to be recognized as unwarranted, for a 100% examination does not guarantee 100% accuracy; the possibility of not having all factors available for evaluation, of human error in evaluating an item, or of a less than fully effective procedure inevitably leaves some element of uncertainty in any audit conclusion. In practice, an audit undertakes to provide reasonable, not absolute, assurance of its conclusions. (See Chapter 12.) Reasonable assurance can be achieved through examining only a portion of the entries or records subject to audit. Thus, the practice of audit sampling has become widely used and accepted (AU 320B.07).

Necessarily, sampling introduces an element of uncertainty about the audit conclusion, called the *sampling risk*. The element of uncertainty arising from the possibility of less than fully effective performance or procedures is called the *nonsampling risk*.

Sampling risk depends on *sample size:* the larger the sample, the lower the sampling risk. In designing an audit test, the auditor must determine the acceptable degree of sampling risk by considering the length of time (and thus the cost) required to examine the data, the consequences of not detecting an error, and the degree of assurance that he is seeking. When these factors permit the acceptance of only a minimal sampling risk, a relatively larger sample must be examined.

There are two types of sampling: *judgmental sampling,* based on the auditor's judgment, and *statistical sampling,* based on mathematical probabilities. In statistical sampling, it is possible to measure the sampling risk in quantitative terms; in judgmental sampling, the sampling risk can only be evaluated subjectively.

BASIC SAMPLE DESIGN CONSIDERATIONS

In designing any sampling procedure, the basic considerations are (1) the audit objectives, (2) the population, (3) the sampling unit, (4) the sampling risk, (5) the nonsampling risk, and (6) the expectation of errors. Each of these considerations depends to some extent on audit judgment.

Audit Objectives

The most important factor in designing a sampling procedure is defining the objectives of the audit. For each detailed objective there are usually several interchangeable types of procedure that may be performed to achieve it. (See Chapter 12.) The procedure selected, its timing, and its extent should be the most effective and economical of all the procedures available for meeting the audit objectives, not merely adequate. Effectiveness is paramount, for no matter how large a sample is, it cannot compensate for an ineffective procedure.

Population

The results of a sampling procedure are projected upon the whole set of items from which the sample is drawn. This *population,* as the whole set is called, must be carefully defined in a manner consistent with the audit objectives.

In many population definitions, all material transactions or balances are identified and separated, since they will be examined 100%. If the intention is to test population item values, the auditor may also treat, as separate populations, negative and zero-value items (for example, credit or zero balances in the accounts receivable listing). This decision will depend primarily on whether the negative and zero-value items are significant enough to require equal audit consideration with the positive values and whether these items can be audited effectively under a procedure designed for positive values. For example, a confirmation test of accounts receivable balances to determine whether the total is correct may be restricted to positive balances if it is known that there are many zero balances pertaining to closed accounts; those would be tested with a different procedure.

Sampling Unit

The population consists of a set of items from which the sample is to be selected. These items are called *sampling units.* Each sampling unit must be definitely distinguishable, must be individually accessible for sample selection, and must be of such a nature that the selected audit procedure can be applied to it. All the sampling units together must add up to the defined population.

Sampling Risk

Sampling risk is determined by sample size: the larger the sample, the lower the risk. In designing a sampling procedure, therefore, the auditor must strike a balance between cost (as reflected in the number of items tested) and sampling risk. While the evidence to be obtained by the test must be adequate to achieve the audit objectives and must be compatible with other procedures used in the audit, the cost of the test should also be minimized.

Nonsampling Risk

The audit procedure must also be designed to reduce nonsampling risk to a minimum. The two types of nonsampling risk are (1) *procedural risk* (the possibility of inherent ineffectiveness of the audit procedures used), which can be minimized by substituting other procedures to achieve the same audit objectives, and (2) *performance risk* (the possibility of human errors in executing and evaluating the test), which can be controlled through adequate training, supervision, and review.

Expectation of Errors

If errors are known to exist in a population, the objective of the sampling procedure will probably be to estimate the total monetary amount or quantity of error in the population; but if the population is believed to contain no errors, the objective will probably be to confirm the nonexistence of errors. It is important to make this distinction during planning, because it generally takes less audit effort to confirm the nonexistence of errors than to measure or estimate the total amount of error. In deciding whether to expect errors, the auditor should evaluate internal control and consider (1) the results of related audit procedures, (2) the results of previous audits in the same area, (3) the size and makeup of the population, and (4) the materiality to the financial statements of transactions or balances to be examined.

JUDGMENTAL SAMPLING

If a sample is not selected and evaluated using mathematical theorems of probability, the sampling is judgmental. In judgmental sampling, the selection of items to be tested is based on the auditor's knowledge of the population, which enables him to select the items that he believes will yield an accurate conclusion about the whole. Although the sampling risk cannot be mathematically measured, the auditor judges that it will not be excessive.

Sample Design

In judgmental sampling, the criteria for coverage determine the sample size, and the criteria for selection of items to be tested depend on audit judgment. Four factors that often affect sample design are

1. The nature of related audit procedures.
2. The nature of the population. This factor includes the diversity of types of items in the population and the diversity of magnitudes. (Unless it is very small, the size of the population generally has no direct effect on sample design.)
3. The expectation of error, both in terms of frequency and magnitude.
4. Materiality. As a general rule, the smaller the minimum amount that is considered material, the larger the sample must be to provide a result sufficiently precise to make useful audit judgments.

The likely effect of these factors on sample size, both for compliance tests and substantive tests, is shown in Figure 14.1. (For the distinction between these two tests, see Chapter 12.) The chart identifies the components of each factor and shows the effect on sample size of opposing degrees for each component. When designing a compliance test, for example, the lower the planned reliance on internal control, the smaller the sample need be. Conversely, the higher the planned reliance on internal control, the larger the sample should be.

When to Use Judgmental Sampling

The decision to use judgmental sampling should be reached by answering two questions:

1. Is judgmental sampling feasible? It is if the auditor's knowledge of the population is sufficient to justify his belief that the items selected for testing will reflect a reasonably accurate conclusion about the population as a whole.

	QUALITY TENDING TO	
	DECREASE SAMPLE SIZE	INCREASE SAMPLE SIZE
1. NATURE OF RELATED AUDIT PROCEDURES		
For compliance tests		
Planned reliance on internal control	Low	High
Planned substantive procedures		
Implicit effectiveness	Very effective	Less effective
Coverage	Large	Small
Timing with respect to balance sheet date	Near	More distant
For substantive tests		
Results of evaluation of internal control	Good	Less than good
Effectiveness of other substantive procedures	Very effective	Less effective
2. NATURE OF POPULATION		
For compliance tests		
Diversity of types of items	Homogeneous	Diverse
Diversity of magnitude of items	Generally no direct effect	
For substantive tests		
Diversity of types of items	Homogeneous	Diverse
Diversity of magnitude of items	Homogeneous	Diverse
3. EXPECTATION OF ERROR		
For compliance tests		
Frequency	None	Some
For substantive tests		
Frequency	Low	High
Magnitude	Small	Large
4. MATERIALITY		
For compliance tests	No direct effect	
For substantive tests		
Minimum materiality amount apportioned to the specific area being sampled	Large	Small

FIGURE 14.1   FACTORS AFFECTING JUDGMENTAL SAMPLE SIZE

2. Is judgmental sampling more appropriate than statistical sampling? In general, it is if:
   a. A sample that can be evaluated statistically is impossible or very difficult to obtain. This may be the case, for example, when the population is a filing cabinet of un-numbered invoices and there is no obvious way of referencing an individual invoice.
   b. A sample of material balances or transactions is both sufficient to meet the audit objectives and considered more economical than a statistical sample. Whether or not this is the case is a matter of judgment.
   c. The auditor's knowledge of the population allows him to select a sample subjec-

tively that gives him more audit assurance than a sample selected according to the theorems of probability. This may be the case, for instance, when the population contains diverse types of items and specific types are known to be particularly error prone.

Judgmental sampling is *not* appropriate when it is possible to obtain a sample that can be evaluated statistically and either (1) a mathematical determination of sampling risk is required or (2) the auditor has little knowledge of the items in the population.

Illustration

Audit objective: To confirm that the total accounts receivable balance due from 200 customers is materially correct.

Sampling plan: The auditor decides to use judgmental sampling, based on his knowledge that approximately 20 accounts cover 80% of the total value. He samples these accounts 100%, performs separate tests of zero and negative balances, and examines only a few of the remaining accounts on the judgmental grounds that they are not material in total value and that there is no indication they might be incorrect.

Sample evaluation: One large customer disputes his account. After checking the account, the auditor suggests an adjustment, although the amount does not exceed materiality. No other errors are found.

Audit conclusion: The (adjusted) balance is confirmed as being materially correct.

STATISTICAL SAMPLING

A statistical sample, or *probability sample,* is one selected and evaluated in accordance with specific rules based on the mathematical theorems of probability. In a probability sample, it must be possible to determine the mathematical probability that any particular population item will be included in the sample and that any possible combination of items will be selected to constitute the entire sample.

There are many different types of probability sample, but most of them require the random selection of items from the population. This is done with the use of random number tables or computer random number generator programs that are commonly available on timesharing systems.

The Statistical Statement

When statistical sampling is used and evaluated, a statistical statement is incorporated in the auditor's conclusion regarding the achievement of the audit objectives. This statement includes an estimate of the population characteristic being examined, which may be a value characteristic (for example, total population dollar value) or a frequency characteristic (for example, total population error rate), and of the reliability of that estimate. The estimate of the population characteristic is always a range, not a single value. It is called a *confidence interval,* since it is associated with a specific confidence level, or *reliability level* (AU 320A.03). The reliability level, which is usually expressed as a percentage, is the probability that the true population characteristic is somewhere within the stated confidence interval. For example, if an estimate of total dollar value comprises a confidence interval of $150,000 to $180,000 and an associated reliability level of 90%, there is a 90% probability that the true value will lie between $150,000 and $180,000. All other things being equal, the wider the confidence interval, the higher the probability that it contains the true population characteristic. As an interval widens, however, its value in meeting audit objectives will most likely decrease.

The width of the confidence interval is called its *precision:* the smaller the precision, the narrower the confidence interval. At a fixed level of reliability, precision is a function of sample size; specifically, it is inversely proportional to the square root of sample size. By increasing the sample size, the auditor obtains more information about the population, narrowing the confidence interval.

Since the reliability level associated with a confidence interval expresses the probability that the confidence interval contains the true value or frequency, the complement of reliability is the sampling risk. In other words, sampling risk is the probability that the confidence interval does *not* contain the true value or frequency. Thus, if there is a 90% probability that the true value is between $150,000 and $180,000, there is a 10% risk that the value is less than $150,000 or more than $180,000.

Sample Design

In statistical sampling, evaluation and selection methods must be chosen before sample size can be computed or sample items selected. The choice of evaluation method, in turn, depends on the type of statistical statement required. The choice of selection method may be affected by the population's physical characteristics and must be compatible with the evaluation method. Sample size is primarily affected by two judgmental factors: (1) the desired reliability (or its complement, sampling risk) and (2) the desired precision of the statistical estimate at the chosen reliability level.

The practical steps to follow in an application of statistical sampling are to

1. Translate the audit objectives into sampling objectives;
2. Establish the required statistical statement format, i.e., establish the type of estimate required;
3. Determine sampling criteria, i.e., reliability (or risk) and precision;
4. Choose sampling evaluation and selection methods;
5. Determine sample size;
6. Obtain a sample and perform auditing procedures;
7. Statistically evaluate the evidence obtained;
8. Judgmentally review the statistical statement to ensure that it meets the original sampling (and hence audit) objectives; and
9. Arrive at an audit conclusion based on the statistical evaluation plus the results of any related audit procedures.

Translating Audit Objectives Into Sampling Objectives. In this first step, the following factors must be defined:

- Sampling unit and population.
- Population characteristic of interest. (Is it a value or a frequency?)
- How to measure or determine the characteristic in each sampling unit. (This will usually require an exact definition of what constitutes an error.)
- Expectation of errors. (Is the objective to confirm the nonexistence of errors or to estimate the total population error rate or amount?)

Establishing the Statistical Statement Format. In establishing the type of estimate required, the sampling objectives should recognize not only whether the estimate is of dollar magnitude or occurrence rate, but also whether a confidence interval with both a lower and an upper bound is required (a two-sided estimate) or only one of those bounds is important (a one-sided estimate). For example, if a FIFO inventory valuation is being audited and an audit adjustment is likely, the auditor will want to estimate the probable minimum and maximum amount of error in the book value. In other words, he will want to estimate a two-sided interval. A resulting conclusion (statistical statement) might be: We estimate with 95% reliability that an accurate FIFO valuation of inventory is between $950,000 and $1,030,000. For most compliance tests, on the other hand, an auditor is concerned only with the probable maximum error rate in the population; that is, he will be satisfied with a one-sided interval estimate. Then the statement might be: We estimate with 90% reliability that no more than 5% of the purchase orders issued during the year lack evidence of proper approval. The one-sided versus two-sided decision is important because, all other things being equal, a substantially larger sample size is required to produce a two-sided estimate than a one-sided estimate.

Determining Sampling Criteria. The auditor must now judgmentally determine the level of reliability he requires for his estimate (or conversely, the maximum amount of risk he feels is acceptable in the context of the audit objectives and any related audit tests) and the least rigorous precision (i.e., the maximum width of the confidence interval) he can tolerate. If the test is for substantive purposes, precision in terms of dollars will be based on materiality. For compliance purposes, precision in terms of a maximum occurrence rate will depend on the importance of the test relative to the associated substantive tests to be performed in the same audit area. (Chapter 12 explores the meaning of and relationship between substantive and compliance tests.)

Choosing Sampling Methods. Besides indicating which type of statistical evaluation method is most suitable, the sampling objectives should also indicate which modes of sample selection are permissible. The most commonly used evaluation methods for each objective and the corresponding methods of sample selection are shown in Figure 14.2.

Attribute sampling. Attribute sampling is a method of evaluating a probability sample to obtain an estimate of the proportion of population items containing some specified characteristic. Attribute sampling can apply to a single random sample of physical units or to a systematic sample (defined later under Statistical Sampling Techniques) that approximates a simple random sample. Each sample item either has or lacks the characteristic; magnitude of the characteristic is not considered. The resulting statistical statements are of the form: The true occurrence rate in the

Sampling Objective	Evaluation Method *	Sample Selection Method
To estimate an error or occurrence rate	Attribute sampling	Simple (unrestricted) random sample of physical units†
To estimate maximum dollar error amount	Dollar-unit sampling: Simple attribute Combined attribute-variables Multinomial-bound	Simple random sample of dollar units†
To estimate total dollar value or dollar error amount	Variables sampling: Mean-per-unit‡ Difference Ratio	Simple random sample or stratified random sample of physical units
	Mean-per-unit difference	Simple random sample of physical units

* All the listed evaluation methods are estimation methods. Two other methods commonly used in compliance tests are *acceptance sampling* and *discovery sampling,* both forms of attribute sampling that do not provide a confidence interval. Acceptance sampling provides a simple accept-reject decision based on the reliability level and the maximum tolerable error rate specified by the user. Discovery sampling assures, at a specified reliability, the discovery of one error if the true error rate exceeds a specified maximum. These are discussed later under Statistical Sampling Techniques.

† A systematic sample may be used where it approximates a random sample.

‡ The mean-per-unit method can also be used to evaluate a simple random sample of dollar units. (See Statistical Sampling Techniques.)

FIGURE 14.2 COMMON STATISTICAL EVALUATION AND SELECTION METHODS

population is not greater than Y% [or is between X% and Y%] stated at a specified reliability level.

Illustration

Audit objective: To test shipping documents for the year to evaluate the extent to which goods shipped may not have been invoiced.

Sampling plan: The objectives are to test the population of 5,000 consecutively numbered shipping documents to ascertain whether each document has corresponding sales invoices. No errors are expected, and the required statistical statement, to be made with 90% reliability, is: No more than 4% of the documents lack corresponding invoices. Therefore, attribute sampling with a simple random selection of documents is the sampling method chosen. The sample size, ascertained from tables, is 60, based on a reliability of 90% and precision of 4%.

Sample evaluation: No errors are found.

Audit conclusion: The auditor is 90% confident that no more than 4% of the shipping documents do not have corresponding sales invoices.

Dollar-unit sampling. This approach is also known as monetary-unit sampling or sampling with probabilities proportional to size and is based on attribute sampling. In this method, sample units of one dollar are tested to see whether each one is or is not in error. Hence it can only be used to evaluate random samples of monetary units rather than physical units, and only provides estimates of the *maximum* proportion or amount of dollars in error in the population. (Of course, any currency unit other than a dollar may be sampled by this method, but dollar will be used here for convenience.)

Separate evaluations must be made for overstatement errors and for understatement errors. When sample errors are found, various evaluation methods such as *combined attribute-variables* or *multinomial-bound* (in which more than the two outcomes right or wrong are possible for any sampling unit) can be used to modify the simple attribute result, which otherwise would not recognize the magnitude of the errors. However, the estimates become overly conservative and hence less useful as more errors are found, and dollar-unit sampling should be restricted to situations where no or few errors are expected. The statistical statements that result from this method are of the form: There are overstatement errors of no more than $200,000 in the population [or the population is overstated by no more than $100,000 and understated by no more than $80,000] stated at a specified reliability level.

Illustration

Audit objective: To confirm that the total accounts receivable balance of $980,000 is materially correct.

Sampling plan: The auditor's apportionment of audit materiality (see Chapter 12) to this area requires a statistical statement at 90% reliability that the total overstatement does not exceed $30,000. To achieve this objective he chooses the dollar-unit sampling method. A simple attribute sample size of 95 is computed from tables, based on 90% reliability and a one-sided upper precision of 2.5% (a conservative precision level, since a precision of $30,000 in a population of 980,000 dollar units corresponds to a precision of 30/980, or 3%). He selects a random sample of 95 dollar units from the population of $980,000, resulting in a selection of 89 balances (a single customer balance may contain more than one sample dollar). Since dollar-unit sampling biases selection in favor of high dollar balances, a 100% sample of such balances is judged unnecessary.

Sample evaluation: No errors are found in completing the confirmation procedures.

Audit conclusion: The auditor is 90% confident that the total balance is overstated by no more than $24,500 (2.5% of $980,000) and that the balance is confirmed as materially correct.

Variables sampling. Variables sampling methods estimate total dollar amounts from samples of physical units (for example, samples of detail balances). The estimate may be of population total dollar value or of population total dollar error. Unlike dollar-unit sampling estimates, variables sampling can provide a one- or two-sided interval. The resulting statistical statement (two-sided) could be of the form: The true population value is between $1,500,000 and $1,650,000 stated at a specified reliability level. Such estimates are suitable for audit adjustments, but dollar-unit sampling estimates, which provide only an upper bound, are not.

The several variables sampling evaluation methods shown in Figure 14.2 are based on different value characteristics. The *mean-per-unit* method is based on sample item values alone; *difference estimation* is based on the difference between sample item audit value and book value (or on that between any other two defined values relating to one sample item); *ratio estimation* is based on the ratio of two defined values per sample item; and *mean-per-unit difference* is a weighted combination of the first two methods.

For example, consider a population of balances of which a sample has been audited. The mean-per-unit method can be used to estimate the total value of the balances based on the audited values of the sample. The difference method can be used to estimate the total error in the population (where the error equals the difference between the true population value and the book value) based on the differences (audit minus book values) found in the sample balances. The ratio method can be used to estimate the ratio of the true total population value to the book value based on the ratios (audit over book values) of the sample balances. The function of these three methods can be represented symbolically as shown in Figure 14.3. Note that the difference and ratio estimates can both be manipulated to estimate the true population value, X (i.e., $X = D + Y$; $X = R \times Y$).

Sample selection for variables sampling may be unrestricted or stratified and in general must be of physical units. (The exception is that the mean-per-unit method can be applied to a dollar-unit sample.) In *stratified sampling* the population is first formally divided into subpopulations (strata), and then a simple random sample is selected from each stratum. The results for each stratum can be mathematically combined to yield an estimate of the whole population. Stratification is usually done for reasons of sample size efficiency. Other, more sophisticated modes of sample selection include *multistage sample selection* and *cluster sampling;* these are discussed later under Statistical Sampling Techniques.

Method	Estimated Population Characteristics	Sample Characteristic
Mean-per-unit	X	x_j
Difference	$D = X - Y$	$d_j = x_j - y_j$
Ratio	$R = X/Y$	$r_j = x_j/y_j$

where X = estimate of true population value
      Y = population book value
      D = estimate of true population error (difference between X and Y)
      R = estimate of true population ratio of X to Y
      x_j = jth sample item audited value
      y_j = jth sample item book value
      d_j = jth sample item difference between x_j and y_j
      r_j = jth sample item ratio of x_j to y_j

FIGURE 14.3 SYMBOLIC REPRESENTATION OF STATISTICAL SAMPLING METHODS

Illustration

Audit objective: To confirm whether or not the total accounts receivable balance of $980,000 is materially correct.

Sampling plan: The auditor knows that balances exceeding $5,000 total $140,000 but has little knowledge of the rest of the population. Therefore, he decides on 100% confirmation of balances over $5,000 and on statistical sampling to confirm the other balances. He expects errors, so his sampling objective is to estimate whether or not the total dollar error is a material amount ($20,000 is judged material). He therefore requires a statistical statement at a high reliability (say 95%) that the total error amount is between $X and $Y where the range $X to $Y is less than $20,000 (say $15,000). To achieve this objective he chooses the variables sampling method, based on audit differences, with unrestricted random sample selection. Using timesharing, the auditor computes a sample size of 118 based on a reliability of 95% and a precision of ±$7,500 (for a two-sided interval estimate the width of the interval is twice the precision amount, in this case $15,000). The auditor then judgmentally increases the sample size to 130 because his assessment of the expected distribution of errors may be incorrect, which would affect the precision of his estimate, and he cannot expand the sample later. He selects a random sample of 130 balances less than $5,000 plus all the balances over $5,000 and performs appropriate confirmation procedures.

Sample evaluation: The resulting statistical conclusion based on the 130 balances is: We are 95% certain that the total overstatement is between $15,600 and $31,800. The 100% confirmation of high dollar-value balances shows a total overstatement of $9,000.

Audit conclusion: The combined results confirm that the total balance is materially overstated. An audit adjustment of $9,000 (to correct the high dollar balances) plus $23,700 (the midpoint of the estimated overstatement interval) is suggested.

Determining Sample Size. Sample size can be computed mathematically and depends on the specified sampling criteria. In practice, it is usually derived from tables or timesharing programs. However, the computed sample size may need to be increased judgmentally because of special considerations. These considerations include

- The importance of the test in the overall audit context.
- The accuracy of the estimate of expected error rate when attribute sampling or dollar-unit sampling is being used. The sample sizes required to achieve a fixed reliability and precision must be much larger when the error rate is high.
- The accuracy of the estimate of error rate and magnitude when using variables sampling. The effectiveness of the evaluation methods differs according to error rate and error magnitude.
- The possibility of unreliable statistical results when using variables estimation with a small sample size. A minimum sample of 100 items is considered advisable.

A general rule whenever variables sampling is used is to cut off all the high dollar-value items from the rest of the population and to sample them 100%. This often improves the efficiency of the sample required from the rest of the population (i.e., it permits the use of a smaller sample size for fixed criteria) and gives extra audit assurance by confining sampling risk to smaller dollar-value items.

Evaluating the Sample. Selection of the statistical method to be used is determined in part by estimates of error conditions and other factors. Whenever the actual results obtained are found to differ from expectations, the statistical results will also differ. In fact, they may turn out to be unusable for achieving the audit objectives. Therefore fallback plans should be arranged in case of unexpected results. Three basic types of fallback plans can be distinguished, though they are not mutually exclusive. The first is the use of other preconceived audit procedures; this is nearly aways applicable. The second is sample expansion; this is not always possible or advisable, in that a larger sample may not rectify an inappropriate sampling technique. The third is statistical evaluation using another method; this is particularly useful if the estimated error rate was incorrect.

A single probability sample can be evaluated by any method compatible with the method of sample selection used. For example, a simple random sample of physical units can be evaluated using any attribute or variables sampling method but not a dollar-unit sampling method, as Figure 14.2 shows. Evaluation by a different method may even improve the precision of the statistical estimate at a fixed reliability level (i.e., it may reduce the width of the confidence interval). For example, difference estimation results in a narrower confidence interval than does mean-per-unit when errors (differences) are found in a sample. Similarly, multinomial-bound evaluation of a dollar-unit sample produces a narrower estimate of maximum dollar error than does combined attribute-variables evaluation when more than a few errors are found.

When to Use Statistical Sampling

Whether or not to use statistical sampling should be decided by answering two questions:

1. Is statistical sampling feasible? It is whenever a probability sample can be obtained. This is generally easy, in that random numbers can be generated using timesharing programs. However, factors weighing against statistical sampling exist when the correspondence between a group of random numbers and the population is difficult to establish, thus making random selection difficult. Or, there may be practical difficulties in selecting a stratified sample; manual stratification by value, for example, may be excessively time-consuming.

2. Is statistical sampling more appropriate than judgmental sampling? In general, it is if:
   a. Objective results (results that can be defended mathematically) are desired. The size of a statistical sample, its selection, and its evaluation all have a mathematical basis and therefore are objectively defensible before other auditors, client personnel, and a court of law.
   b. The auditor has insufficient knowledge of the population to judgmentally select a sample that will provide a reliable basis for his audit conclusion without being significantly larger than an equally adequate statistical sample.
   c. A representative selection from a population of similar physical units is required, implying use of a probability sample. As a general rule, whenever a probability

sample is selected, it should be evaluated statistically, even when it is also evaluated judgmentally. This eliminates the risk of overlooking a statistical conclusion that contradicts the judgmental conclusion.

Statistical sampling is *not* appropriate when a judgmentally selected sample provides a greater degree of assurance for the audit conclusion, or involves less sampling, or is easier to select than a statistical sample giving equal audit assurance.

Statistical sampling has some inherent advantages. Judgmental sampling can encourage a vague and indefinite approach; there may be little or no attempt to define the population or the basis for selection specifically, and it may be difficult to prove a relationship between the sample results and the whole population. Statistical sampling, on the other hand, forces the auditor to plan his sampling approach carefully and gives him an objective foundation on which to build his audit judgments.

But statistical sampling does not eliminate the need for audit judgment. Judgment is at least as important in planning and evaluating a statistical sample as it is in judgmental sampling (AU 320A.24). With statistical samples, however, it is usually applied discretely to decision factors such as reliability, precision, and expected error conditions, thus simplifying an otherwise aggregate judgment.

Another advantage of statistical sampling is that it reveals past instances of excessive sampling stemming from an overconservative intuition that adequate assurance could be provided only by sampling, say, 5% or 10% of the population.

STATISTICAL SAMPLING TECHNIQUES

Sample Selection

Selection of a probability sample is the essential ingredient of statistical sampling. The three most common methods of sample selection are

1. Unrestricted or simple random selection,
2. Stratified random selection,[1] and
3. Systematic selection when it approximates random selection.

Two more-sophisticated methods are

1. Multistage sample selection, and
2. Cluster sample selection.

Unrestricted Random Sampling. In this method, each sampling unit has an equal chance of being selected as each selection is made, and every possible combination of sampling units has an equal chance of constituting the sample. The sample is usually selected in three steps:

---

[1] These first two methods may be used with or without replacement of an item already selected, since audit populations are usually large enough to negate the impact of replacement on selection.

1. Establishing a correspondence between a set of identifying numbers (or letters) and the sampling units in the population, so that each unit is uniquely identified,
2. Using random-number tables or a random-number generator to obtain a random selection, equal to the required sample size, of numbers (letters) from the complete set of identifying numbers (letters), and
3. Selecting the population units corresponding to the selected identifiers.

The sampling unit may be a physical unit or a dollar (monetary) unit. Physical units can often be identified by using the same means the company uses (for example, voucher number or check number) or by physical location (for example, warehouse row and bin or page number and line number on a computer listing). Dollar units are identified by the cumulative values of the population. That is, whatever the order of physical units containing the dollars, their values are accumulated in dollar increments, and the cumulative value at any point represents the last dollar unit included.

Selection of a dollar-unit sample necessarily implies selecting physical units containing the randomly selected dollars. The probability of selecting a physical unit increases in direct proportion to its dollar value; in other words, the sampling probabilities are proportional to size. Also, one physical unit may contain more than one randomly selected dollar. For example, selection of the 21st and 29th dollar units from three invoices, the totals of which are $12, $8 and $10, results in selection of the third invoice (cumulative value $30) twice.

Stratified Random Sampling. In this method, the population is formally divided into subpopulations, or strata, and then an unrestricted random sample is selected from each stratum. Each sampling unit, therefore, has an equal probability of selection within its own stratum, but across the whole population its chances are weighted by the relationship of sample size and stratum size to the total size of the population. Stratification can not be used for sampling dollar units. There are three main reasons for using stratified random sampling:

1. It can give special attention to a particular subpopulation (e.g., old items),
2. It is sometimes the only practical approach to sample selection (e.g., if units must be sampled at a series of different geographic locations), and
3. It produces subpopulations that are individually more homogeneous, thus decreasing the sample size required to accomplish given statistical objectives (e.g., stratification by value produces subpopulations of similarly valued items).

The key step is the identification of the strata. Any criteria can be used, but each item in the population must fit the criteria for one, and only one, stratum. Then, before sampling, the number of items in each stratum must be determined.

Systematic Selection. This approach is only valid when it approximates a random selection, and therefore requires a relatively homogeneous population, the absence of any correlation (i.e., a built-in bias) between the order of the population units and the sampling objectives, and a fairly uniform error pattern. Since this third constraint is difficult to prove, systematic selection is chiefly recommended when no errors are expected.

To obtain a systematic sample of either physical or dollar units:

1. Determine the selection interval (I) by dividing the total number of units in the population by the required sample size.
2. Select a random number between 1 and I as a starting point.
3. Select units from the population according to their physical sequence in the population, starting with the unit located at the random start position and then selecting every Ith unit following that. For instance, to select 100 units from a total of 1,200, the selection interval (I) will be 12; and if a random start of 7 is determined, then the 7th, the 19th (7 + 12), the 31st (19 + 12), etc., units will be selected, counted in the order with which they physically exist in the population.

To guard against unwarranted correlation between the population sequence and the sampling objectives, more than one random start may be used. This results in as many systematic samples as there are random starts, and the required sample size must be equally divided between them before determining the common interval I.

Multistage and Cluster Sampling. These techniques are generally restricted to samples of physical units where a dollar-value estimate is required. *Multistage sampling* involves sample selection at several levels. For example, the auditor may require a selection of locations, with a further selection of inventory items at each of the selected locations. (The selections at each level can be achieved using any of the methods discussed above.) *Cluster sampling* involves selecting groups of items, rather than individual units, at randomly selected points in the population. For example, it might be a selection of 20 groups of 5 consecutively numbered invoices, starting with each of 20 randomly selected invoices. Both of these methods are used to overcome practical selection difficulties, such as those that occur when a population is dispersed widely over a large geographic area and coverage of the entire area is not economically feasible. These methods usually require larger sample sizes and involve more complex evaluation formulas than do simple or stratified random selection techniques.

The choice of statistical evaluation method largely determines which of these five sample selection methods to use. Figure 14.2 lists the most common choices. Basically, attribute sampling requires an unrestricted random sample of physical units, dollar-unit sampling requires an unrestricted random sample of dollar units, and variables sampling requires a random sample of physical units, either unrestricted or stratified.

How to Obtain Random Numbers

Selection of a probability sample usually involves random numbers. These can be obtained manually, using random number tables (Arkin's 1974 *Handbook of Sampling for Auditing and Accounting* contains a table of 105,000 random digits), or by means of *timesharing,* using a generalized computer program that will create random numbers according to user specifications.

Timesharing. Timesharing is highly preferable to manual determination of random numbers, because manual selection is a tedious and time-consuming process.

In addition to the proprietary software packages of numerous audit firms, the major timesharing vendors (such as General Electric, TYMSHARE, and COMSHARE) have libraries of programs specifically designed for use in accounting and auditing, including programs for statistical sample selection and evaluation. Other common programs include those that

- Compute depreciation,
- Analyze leases in accordance with SFAS 13,
- Calculate loan amortization tables,
- Compute present values of cash flows (e.g., in accordance with APB 21),
- Determine earnings per share in accordance with APB 15,
- Compute financial ratios from financial statement data (including bankruptcy predictors),
- Produce source and application of funds statements,
- Analyze capital investments, including real estate (e.g., a comparison of the financial effect of purchasing versus leasing an asset), and
- Compute the yield on an investment fund.

In general, timesharing programs are simple to use, because they are designed to accept conversational input typed at a computer terminal. Complete information may be obtained from the Computer Services Division of the AICPA.

To illustrate the use of a typical timesharing program for generating random numbers, suppose that random-number selection is required from a population comprising two series of numbers, the first ranging from 1 to 5,000, the second from 1 to 2,600. This can be restated as a requirement for random numbers of five digits grouped into two sets of one and four digits. The first digit must be 1 or 2 to distinguish between the two series; the second set of four digits must be generated from ranges 0001 to 5000 and 0001 to 2600, respectively. The terminal output is shown in Figure 14.4.

Attribute Sampling

Attribute sampling is based on the binomial distribution. It can be used to estimate the probable occurrence rates of specified characteristics in a population where each characteristic has two, and only two, mutually exclusive outcomes (hence the name binomial). Attribute sampling of physical units cannot be used to estimate the total of a variable characteristic such as values.

Techniques Available. *Simple attribute estimation* provides a one- or two-sided estimate of occurrence rate, resulting in one-sided statements such as: We are 95% certain that the error rate in the population does not exceed 5%; or in two-sided statements, with both a lower and an upper bound, such as: We are 95% certain that the error rate in the population is between 1% and 5%. Two related forms of sampling, which do *not* provide an interval estimate, are *acceptance sampling* and *discovery sampling*. *Acceptance sampling* is generally more useful for internal control of error on an ongoing basis than for auditors' test purposes, since it provides only an accept-reject decision and requires a precise advance decision as to

```
THIS PROGRAM GENERATES UP TO 1,000 SINGLE OR
SETTED RANDOM NUMBERS


USER ENTRIES

(1) INPUT THE QUANTITY OF RANDOM NUMBERS
      TO BE GENERATED? 10
(2) ARE THE NUMBERS FORMATTED INTO SETS-YES OR NO?
      YES
(3) SPECIFY GENERATION MODE- 1 = INDIVIDUAL SET
      MODE:   2 = ENTIRE NUMBER MODE? 1
(5) HOW MANY SETS (MAX=7)? 2
(6) INPUT THE HIGHEST NUMBER OF DIGITS IN EACH
      SET: (MAX=6 PER SET)
      SET   1? 1
      SET   2? 4


(7) INPUT THE NUMBER OF RANGES OF VALUES TO BE
      GENERATED (MAX=50)? 2
(8) FOR EACH OF THE   2 RANGES INPUT THE
      LOWER (L) AND UPPER (U) LIMITS. SEPARATE
      SETS, IF ANY, WITH A HYPHEN (-).


      RANGE
      -----
      1 - L? 1-0001
          U? 1-5000

      2 - L? 2-0001
          U? 2-2600


(9) PRINT SELECTION-INPUT 1 FOR NUMERICAL
      ORDER, 2 FOR SELECTION ORDER OR 3 FOR BOTH? 3
```

FIGURE 14.4   USER ENTRIES AND OUTPUT OF RANDOM-NUMBER-GENERATING PROGRAM

the rate of error at which rejection is necessary. For example, a reject decision resulting from an ongoing test check of an internal control system indicates a weakening of the system and instigates an investigation of the system. A reject decision resulting from an external audit test, on the other hand, generally gives insufficient basis for an audit judgment. Alternative procedures, probably including an attribute estimate, have to be used.

Discovery sampling is commonly used in auditing, particularly when the auditor's first interest is whether or not an acceptable population error rate is exceeded. If the error rate is not exceeded, the objective of his test is met and no further work is required. If it is exceeded, he will then apply alternative procedures, possibly

```
OUTPUT

SUMMARY OF NUMBERS SELECTED
- -- -- -- -- -- -- -- -- -- -- -- -- -- -- -- -- -- -- -- -- -- -- -- -- -- -- --


                        TOTAL NUMBER           QUANTITY
    RANGE NO.            OF ITEMS               SELECTED
  - -- -- -- -- --     - -- -- -- -- -- --     - -- -- -- --

        1                   5,000                  7
        2                   2,600                  3
                       - -- -- -- -- -- --     - -- -- -- --


    TOTALS                  7,600                  10
                       ===============       ==========


RANDOM NUMBERS-NUMERICAL ORDER
- -- -- -- -- -- -- -- -- -- -- -- -- -- -- -- -- -- -- -- -- -- -- --

  SEQUENCE
  SELECTED          RANDOM NUMBERS
  - -- -- -- --     - -- -- -- -- -- --

      2             1-1595
      3             1-1795
      7             1-2275
      6             1-2598
      5             1-3327
     10             1-4394
      9             1-4922
      8             2-1773
      4             2-2193
      1             2-2213

          ****RUN FINISHED****
```

FIGURE 14.4   CONT'D

including an attribute estimate. Discovery sampling is based on the minimum sample size that would include at least one error if the population errors exceed a specified rate. Thus, discovery of an error in the sample immediately resolves the test: the error rate is exceeded. Since discovery sampling is based on the minimum sample size necessary to detect only one error, the sample usually must be expanded if a useful attribute estimate (i.e., of the true error rate in the population) is desired.

How to Apply Attribute Sampling. Whichever method is used, the appropriate sample size can be determined from tables, which are available in Arkin's *Handbook of Sampling for Auditing and Accounting*. For attribute estimation, the interval estimate can also be obtained using attribute tables. An alternative method of sample size determination or evaluation is to use timesharing. Several programs dealing with attribute sampling are available from the major timesharing vendors.

Figure 14.5 illustrates the use of attribute estimation tables. It is an extract from a table of one-sided upper precision limits at 95% reliability in an infinite population.

To determine the sample size required for an attribute estimate at 95% reliability:

1. Determine the rate at which the attribute is expected to occur in the population (or sample).
2. Determine the desired precision of the interval estimate. Add this to the attribute occurrence rate to determine the desired upper limit of the estimate (the upper precision limit).
3. Find the column for the expected occurrence rate and go down to the line corresponding to the upper precision limit (interpolation may be required).
4. On the left axis opposite the upper precision limit, find the sample size.

Evaluation of an attribute sample employs the reverse process, starting with sample size and sample occurrence rate to determine the upper precision limit of the interval estimate. For example, a 1% expected occurrence rate and 3.7% precision (or 4.7% [1% + 3.7%] upper precision limit) implies a sample size of 100. Conversely, a sample size of 100 with one error (1% error rate) gives an upper precision limit of 4.7%; i.e., we are 95% certain that there are no more than 4.7% errors in the population.

Obviously, the tables cannot provide exact results for every combination of criteria. Timesharing programs are much more flexible and in general allow entry of most combinations of reliability, occurrence rate, precision, and sample size used in auditing. They also adjust results to recognize that populations are finite in size. The output of a typical timesharing program used to evaluate the above example for a population of 5,000 is shown in Figure 14.6.

Dollar-Unit Sampling

This technique has been described earlier in this chapter. It is generally used when the sampling objective is to confirm that a population value is materially correct, since estimates are of upper bounds only and are unsuitable for audit adjustments.

Techniques Available. The most common evaluation method is *simple attribute estimation* applied to samples of dollar units so as to provide an upper precision limit of the error rate. Assuming that the maximum amount of error (either overstatement or understatement) in any dollar unit is $1.00, this upper precision limit can be directly translated into a dollar amount. For example, an upper precision limit (maximum error rate) of 3% in a population of 120,000 dollars implies a maximum error amount of $3,600 (.03 × $120,000). However, if there is positive indication that the assumption of $1.00 maximum error amount is wrong, the population estimate of the maximum error amount may be amended. For example, assuming the maximum understatement error per dollar unit is $1.50 (e.g., a debt

Occurrence Rate

Sample Size	0.0	.5	1.0	2.0	3.0	4.0	5.0	6.0	7.0	8.0	9.0	10.0	12.0	14.0	16.0	18.0	20.0	25.0	30.0	40.0	50.0
50	5.8			9.1		12.1		14.8		17.4		19.9	22.3	25.1	27.0	29.6	31.6		42.4	52.6	62.4
100	3.0		4.7	6.2	7.6	8.9	10.2	11.5	13.0	14.0	15.4	16.4	18.7	21.2	23.3	25.6	27.7	33.1	38.4	48.7	58.6
150	2.0			5.1		7.7		10.2		12.6		15.0	17.3	19.6	21.7	24.0	26.1		36.7	47.0	56.8
200	1.5	2.4	3.1	4.5	5.8	7.1	8.3	9.5	10.8	11.9	13.1	14.2	16.4	18.7	20.9	23.1	25.2	30.5	35.7	45.7	55.6
250	1.2			4.2		6.7		9.1		11.4		13.7	15.9	18.1	20.3	22.4	24.6		34.8	44.8	54.7
300	1.0		2.6	3.9	5.2	6.4	7.6	8.8	10.0	11.1	12.2	13.3	15.5	17.7	19.8	22.0	24.1	29.1	34.1	44.1	54.1
350	.9			3.7		6.2		8.5		10.8		13.0	15.2	17.4	19.5	21.7	23.6		33.6	43.6	53.6
400	.7	1.6	2.3	3.6	4.8	6.0	7.2	8.3	9.5	10.6	11.7	12.8	15.0	17.2	19.2	21.2	23.2	28.2	33.2	43.2	53.2
450	.7			3.5		5.9		8.2		10.4		12.6	14.8	16.8	18.9	20.9	22.9		32.9	42.9	52.9
500	.6		2.1	3.4	4.6	5.8	6.9	8.0	9.2	10.3	11.4	12.5	14.6	16.7	18.6	20.7	22.6	27.6	32.6	42.6	52.6
550	.5			3.3		5.7		7.9		10.1		12.3	14.4	16.4	18.4	20.4	22.4		32.4	42.4	52.4
600	.5	1.3	2.0	3.2	4.4	5.6	6.7	7.8	9.0	10.0	11.2	12.2	14.2	16.2	18.2	20.2	22.2	27.2	32.2	42.2	52.2
650	.5			3.2		5.5		7.7		10.0		12.1	14.1	16.1	18.1	20.1	22.1		32.1	42.1	52.1
700	.4		1.9	3.1	4.3	5.4	6.6	7.7	8.8	9.9	10.8	11.9	13.9	15.9	17.9	19.9	21.9	26.9	31.9	41.9	51.9
750	.4			3.1		5.4		7.6		9.8		11.8	13.8	15.8	17.8	19.8	21.8		31.8	41.8	51.8
800	.4	1.1	1.8	3.0	4.2	5.3	6.4	7.5	8.7	9.7	10.7	11.7	13.7	15.7	17.7	19.7	21.7	26.7	31.7	41.7	51.7
850	.4			3.0		5.3		7.5		9.6		11.6	13.6	15.6	17.6	19.6	21.6		31.6	41.6	51.6
900	.3		1.7	3.0	4.1	5.2	6.3	7.5	8.5	9.5	10.5	11.5	13.5	15.5	17.5	19.5	21.5	26.5	31.5	41.5	51.5
950	.3			2.9		5.2		7.4		9.4		11.4	13.4	15.5	17.4	19.5	21.4		31.5	41.5	51.5
1000	.3	1.0	1.7	2.9	4.0	5.2	6.3	7.4	8.4	9.4	10.1	11.4	13.4	15.4	17.4	19.4	21.4	26.4	31.4	41.4	51.4
1500	.2		1.5	2.7	3.8	4.9	5.9	6.9	7.9	8.9	9.9	10.9	12.9	14.9	16.9	18.9	20.9	25.9	30.9	40.9	50.9
2000	.1	.8	1.4	2.6	3.7	4.7	5.7	6.7	7.7	8.7	9.7	10.7	12.7	14.7	16.7	18.7	20.7	25.7	30.7	40.7	50.7
2500	.1		1.4	2.6	3.6	4.6	5.6	6.6	7.6	8.6	9.6	10.6	12.6	14.6	16.6	18.6	20.6	25.6	30.6	40.6	50.6
3000	.1	.8	1.4	2.5	3.5	4.5	5.5	6.5	7.5	8.5	9.5	10.5	12.5	14.5	16.5	18.5	20.5	25.5	30.5	40.5	50.5
4000	.1	.7	1.3	2.4	3.4	4.4	5.4	6.4	7.4	8.4	9.4	10.4	12.4	14.4	16.4	18.4	20.4	25.4	30.4	40.4	50.4
5000	.1	.7	1.3	2.3	3.3	4.3	5.3	6.3	7.3	8.3	9.3	10.3	12.3	14.3	16.3	18.3	20.3	25.3	30.3	40.3	50.3

FIGURE 14.5   ATTRIBUTE ESTIMATION TABLE

SOURCE: Arens and Loebbecke, 1976.

USER ENTRIES

ENTER OBJECTIVES - S OR E   ? S ①

                    1U,1L OR 2   ? 1U ②

ENTER REL., EXPD.ERROR RATE, UPPER PRECN.LIMIT,
POP.SIZE ? 95 , 1 , 4.7 , 5000

OUTPUT

SAMPLE SIZE IS 98

USER ENTRIES

ENTER OBJECTIVES - S OR E   ? E ③

                    1U,1L OR 2   ? 1U

ENTER REL., NO. ERRORS, SAMPLE SIZE, POP. SIZE
? 95 , 1 , 100 , 5000

OUTPUT

OCCURRENCE RATE IN SAMPLE IS   1 %

UPPER PRECISION LIMIT IS   4.6 %

USER ENTRY KEY

① Sample size estimate

② One-sided upper limit estimate

③ Evaluation of sample

FIGURE 14.6   USER ENTRIES AND OUTPUT OF A PROGRAM TO EVALU-
ATE AN ATTRIBUTE SAMPLE

with a book value of $100 may be understated by $150), a 3% error rate in a population of 120,000 dollars implies a maximum understatement error amount of $5,400 (.03 × $120,000 × $1.50). Note that both the assumed error amount per dollar and the error rate are maximums. This results in more conservative upper precision limits than those produced by attribute or variables sampling. That is, at a fixed reliability, the stated upper precision limit tends to be higher than the true, but unknown, upper limit. To emphasize this, the estimated maximum error amounts are termed *error bounds*.

The simple attribute estimation method is always applicable, but its usefulness diminishes as errors are found. Other evaluation techniques have been designed to modify the simple attribute estimate on the basis of the error amounts actually found. Most of these methods are based on empirical rather than theoretical research, and one such method is called *combined attribute-variables estimation* (CAV). Instead of assuming that all population dollars in error are misstated by the estimated maximum amount, CAV reasons that the portions of the maximum error rate applicable to the errors found are misstated by the actual amounts of error found in the sample dollar units. This can be illustrated as follows:

A dollar-unit sample of 100 is extracted from a population of $120,000. Two dollar-units are found to be in error by $.10 and $.20, respectively. Simple attribute estimates of the upper precision limits at 95% reliability for a sample size of 100 with zero, one, and two errors are 3%, 4.7%, and 6.2%, respectively, as shown in Figure 14.5. The simple attribute approach thus results in an error bound of $7,440 (.062 × $120,000), assuming a $1.00 maximum error amount per sample unit.

CAV reasons, on the other hand, that the error rate of 6.2% can be split into three portions: 3% errors of assumed maximum amount $1.00; 1.7% (4.7% − 3.0%) errors of maximum amount $.20; 1.5% (6.2% − 4.7%) errors of maximum amount $.10. (The error amounts are taken in descending order to be conservative.) Thus, the CAV upper error bound (at 95% reliability) is $4,188 ([.03 × $120,000 × $1.00] + [.017 × $120,000 × $.20] + [.015 × $120,000 × $.10]).

For a more complete explanation of this bound, see Goodfellow, Loebbecke, and Neter (1974).

The simple attribute method and the combined attribute-variables method are both based on the binomial distribution, which assumes no more than two outcomes for any sampling unit. A different and more complex technique known as *multinomial-bound evaluation* assumes a broader set of possibilities, based on the error information obtained. It often provides tighter precision bounds than CAV, particularly when there are more than a few errors, but the calculations are so complex that it requires computer assistance.

Dollar-unit sampling is designed for use with populations with low error rates. When a dollar-unit sample is found to contain more than a few errors, none of the above methods are likely to give useful results, because the upper error bounds will be too high. In this case, it may be appropriate to evaluate the dollar-unit sample using the mean-per-unit variables estimation method, which will result in a confidence interval estimate of the total dollar error (and thus a statement that the error is between $X and $Y at a certain reliability). Note that mean-per-unit is the only variables sampling method that can be applied to a sample of dollar units.

How to Apply Dollar-Unit Sampling. Sample size for dollar-unit sampling should be determined on the basis of the simple attribute approach. This will involve using attribute tables or an attribute timesharing program, translating the required dollar precision amount into a percentage of population value, and following the steps described above for attribute sampling. When no errors are found in the sample, evaluation can be done in a similar fashion. When errors are found, manual modification of the simple attribute upper precision limit is usually required. To apply combined attribute-variables estimation:

1. Determine the error amount per dollar unit by prorating the error per physical unit (i.e., divide the amount of the error by the number of dollar units represented in the physical unit).

2. Segregate the overstatement errors from the understatement errors, so that separate evaluations can be made. (Overstatement errors do not affect understatement estimates, and vice versa.)

Then, for overstatement and understatement estimates separately:

3. Rank errors in descending order of magnitude.

4. For each error, determine the appropriate portion of the upper precision limit for the total error rate. (That is, for the first error, ascertain the upper precision limit relating to one error and subtract the upper precision limit relating to zero errors; for the second error, ascertain the upper precision limit for two errors and subtract the portion of this precision equal to the upper precision limit for one error; for the third error, ascertain the upper precision limit for three errors and subtract that for two errors; etc. This will require the use of attribute tables or an attribute time-sharing program.)

5. Multiply each error amount (determined in step 1) by its corresponding error-rate portion (determined in step 4), including the assumed maximum error amount by the zero error-rate portion (the upper precision limit for zero errors).

6. Add the multiplication products.

7. Multiply this sum by the total population value to give the modified upper bound of the total error amount.

As an illustration, take the previously described case of a sample of 100 dollar units from a population of $120,000, but suppose that three dollar-units are found to be in error: two are overstated by $.10 and $.20, and one is understated by $1.50. The maximum overstatement per dollar unit is assumed to be $1.00, and the maximum understatement, $2.00. The CAV upper error bound for *overstatement* errors at 95% reliability is $4,188, computed as in the previous example; the CAV upper error bound for *understatement* errors at 95% reliability is $[(\$2.00 \times .03) + (\$1.50 \times .017)] \times \$120,000 = \$10,260$.

Variables Sampling

Variables sampling, also discussed earlier in this chapter, is based on the normal distribution and the related central limit theorem, and provides confidence interval estimates of total population dollar amounts. For an introduction to normal distributions and the central limit theorem see Hays (1973), pp. 316-320.

Techniques Available. The most common variables sampling methods are mean-per-unit, difference, and ratio. They are all based on the same theory, but use different value characteristics to make estimates, as shown in Figure 14.3.

The confidence intervals in variables sampling are based on an estimate of the total population amount and a precision factor that varies according to the reliability required of the confidence interval. For example, for a two-sided confidence interval, the estimate of the population total value will be the midpoint of the interval.

The midpoint estimate is calculated using the average of the sample item characteristic values. For example, using the mean-per-unit method, the population value is estimated from the average of the sample item audited values (x_j). The precision amount is calculated using three factors: reliability, the standard deviation of the sample item characteristic values, and sample size (precision = reliability normal coefficient × standard deviation/square root of sample size). For details of the calculations, including formulae, see Roberts (1978), Chapters 5 and 6, and Appendix 2. In practice, timesharing programs can be used to perform all the calculations.

In selecting the most appropriate variables sampling method in any given audit situation, the following guidelines have been suggested by Neter and Loebbecke (1978):

1. When only one value per sample item is available (e.g., when no book value exists), the mean-per-unit method must be used.

2. If the purpose of the estimate is to compare *two* values per sample item, either to estimate the total difference or the overall ratio, either the difference, ratio, or mean-per-unit method may be used. Difference and ratio methods are preferable when more than a few errors are expected (say 10% or more) or when a large sample size is to be used (more than 300), in that these methods tend to require much smaller sample sizes than mean-per-unit (for fixed precision and reliability). However, difference and ratio methods are likely to be unreliable when few differences exist in the population, i.e., the true reliability level of the estimate will tend to be lower than the stated reliability.

3. When few or no differences are expected, mean-per-unit (or the combined method, mean-per-unit difference) may be used. Mean-per-unit usually has large sample size requirements unless stratification can be used to break the population down into more homogeneous subgroups. For instance, stratification by book value will usually result in a much smaller sample size, but stratification is often impractical unless a computer program is available and the population is maintained on a computer file. When these conditions exist, the computer program can also calculate an optimal stratification plan. The mean-per-unit difference method is the alternative when stratification is not feasible. It combines the two methods, so that sample sizes are smaller than for mean-per-unit yet estimates are still reliable even though few errors are found.

When two values per sample item are available and differences *are* expected, an alternative to the difference or ratio method is *regression estimation,* based on the linear relationship between two values. It can be more efficient in terms of sample size than difference or ratio, but the calculations are slightly more complex. For a brief description of regression estimation, including formulae, see Roberts (1978), pp. 86-92.

How to Apply Variables Sampling. Whichever method is used, sample size can be determined mathematically, based on the sampling criteria. The calculations are tedious if performed manually, so a timesharing program is preferable. The sampling criteria needed are the required reliability level and the precision amount, the population size, and an estimate of the population standard deviation.

The *standard deviation* of the sample item characteristic values is a mathematical measure of their dispersion from their average value. Estimation of standard deviation is often difficult, but is important because sample size increases in proportion to its square. When practical, a preliminary or advance sample may be drawn to estimate the standard deviation. Otherwise, prior sampling experience or judgmental knowledge of the population may be used.

The following four rules should always be observed in sample size determination for a variables estimate:

1. When applicable, pull out all the high-value items and test them 100% to reduce variability of the sampling population.
2. Avoid small sample sizes (less than 100) because they tend to give unreliable results.
3. Consider whether the sample size is large enough to be useful if unexpected results are obtained. (For example, what sample size would be required if an alternative evaluation method had to be used?)
4. Consider whether the sample size seems judgmentally acceptable in the context of the specified audit objectives.

When the sample has been drawn, evaluating it by a variables method is also done with the use of mathematical formulae, most easily through timesharing. The required reliability must be specified and the sample data details must be entered. Figure 14.7 shows the output of a typical timesharing program using difference estimation to evaluate the total error amount in a population of 8,900 items from an audited sample of 160.

Hypothesis Testing

Variables sampling provides support for the statement that at a specific reliability level the estimated value is contained within a specific confidence interval. When the value being estimated is the population audit value, it may be used in hypothesis testing.

There are two possible approaches to hypothesis testing: the positive approach, which hypothesizes that the book value is materially correct, and the negative approach, which hypothesizes that the book value is incorrect by a material amount. Statistical results are then used to support or reject the hypothesis. (See Roberts, 1978, pp. 40-48, for a description of each approach.) Although the two approaches are equivalent, the negative approach is assumed throughout Appendix B of SAS 1 (AU 320B) and is the approach used here.

USER ENTRIES

THIS PROGRAM DETERMINES SAMPLE SIZE OR EVALUATES
        SAMPLE RESULTS USING SIMPLE RANDOM
        SAMPLING METHODS

ENTER PROGRAM OBJECTIVES: ①
        METHOD   ? DA
        PURPOSE   ? E ②
        ESTIMATE OR TEST? E ③
        INTERVAL TYPE   ? 2 ④

ENTER DATA INPUT TYPE? ST ⑤
ENTER TOTALS:
        SAMPLE SIZE REPRESENTED? 160
        SUMS D, D SQR? -33 , 484 ⑥

DO YOU WISH TO CHANGE TOTALS - Y OR N? N

ENTER TOT NUMBER & TOT X & Y VALUES OF 100% ITEMS?
        5 , 21015 , 21015 ⑦
INCLUDE 100% ITEMS IN THE FOLLOWING POPULATION
        PARAMETERS

ENTER PARAMETERS:
        TOTAL POP SIZE   ? 8900
        TOTAL POP BOOK VALUE ? 234615
        RELIABILITY? 90 ⑧

USER ENTRY KEY

① Difference estimation   ④ Two-sided interval   ⑦ Total of material items, sampled 100%

② Evaluation of sample   ⑤ Sample totals

③ Interval estimate   ⑥ Sum of sample item differences and sum of sample item differences squared   ⑧ Reliability level required, in percent

(figure continues)

FIGURE 14.7   USER ENTRIES AND OUTPUT OF A PROGRAM TO EVALU-
ATE ERROR AMOUNT BY THE VARIABLES METHOD

```
OUTPUT
THE ESTIMATED POPULATION STATISTICS FOR A TWO-
      SIDED ESTIMATE WITH A RELIABILITY OF    90%
      ARE AS FOLLOWS:

                              ON THE BASIS OF SAMPLE
                                     DIFFERENCES
          POINT ESTIMATE OF
            THE POPULATION
            DIFFERENCE                    -1835.
          POINT ESTIMATE OF
            THE POPULATION TOTAL    232780.
          STANDARD ERROR OF THE
            ESTIMATES                     1207.
          PRECISION                       1986.
          CONFIDENCE
            INTERVAL FOR
            POPULATION
            DIFFERENCE   -3821. TO         151.
          CONFIDENCE
            INTERVAL FOR
            POPULATION
            TOTAL       230794. TO    234766.


NOTE: NEGATIVE DIFFERENCES REPRESENT AN
      OVERSTATEMENT IN THE BOOK AMOUNT



RERUN - Y OR N? N

          SAMPLE STATISTICS

      MEAN D                   -0.21

                           VAR          STD DEVN
      DIFFERENCES          3.00            1.73
```

FIGURE 14.7   CONT'D

When variables sampling provides a two-sided estimate of a population audit value, a hypothesis test applies two main rules to determine whether the book value is materially incorrect:

1. If the book value is less than a material amount away from both confidence limits of the interval, accept it as not being materially incorrect.

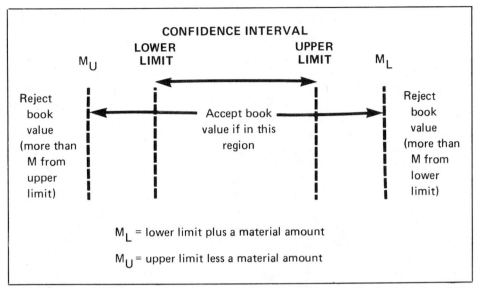

FIGURE 14.8   HYPOTHESIS TEST RULES—TWO-SIDED ESTIMATE OF POP-
ULATION AUDIT VALUE

2. If the book value is a material amount away from the farthest confidence limit, reject
   it. Either an audit adjustment is required or further audit work must be done.

These rules are illustrated in Figure 14.8.

For both the accept decision and the reject decision, there is a risk that it is
wrong. The risk of accepting a materially incorrect book value, known as the
beta risk, is directly related to the reliability level of the confidence interval. The
risk of rejecting a correct book value, known as the *alpha risk,* is a function of
the precision of the confidence interval compared to the materiality amount. (For
precise definitions of the relationships, see Roberts, 1978, p. 41.)

Thus, when the auditor expects the book value to be accepted, a hypothesis test
is the logical way to reach the decision, since this method provides a simple
acceptance decision with a judgmentally acceptable risk level.

How to Apply Hypothesis Testing. Sample size for hypothesis testing can be
determined mathematically, either manually or by using timesharing, in the same
way as for variables sampling. Instead of depending on reliability and precision,
it is based on the beta and alpha risks deemed acceptable and on the amount
deemed material. Evaluation is also based on these factors rather than on reliability.

COMMON USES OF STATISTICAL SAMPLING
IN ACCOUNTING AND TAXATION

There are many opportunities to use statistical sampling to assist in accounting
activities. The more popular uses are

- Directly estimating values in place of 100% detailing. (For example, the dollar value of inventory may be estimated when a full physical count and valuation are not performed.)
- Establishing appropriate values for unexpired subscriptions, allowances for bad debts, or inventory obsolescence.
- Analyzing accounts by age or other category, using estimates of the percentage of accounts in each category. (For example, the aging of accounts receivable or the sales of different products may be estimated by sampling.)
- Controlling bookkeeping and clerical errors and checking on internal control systems. (For example, purchased raw materials can be tested for defects, or purchase disbursements for accuracy, on a sample basis.) In this connection, statistical sampling would seem especially useful for those companies subject to the accounting standards provisions of the Foreign Corrupt Practices Act of 1977 (see Chapter 13).
- Establishing the probable total amounts of payments that were not made in accordance with prescribed regulations. (For example, the extent of welfare payments to ineligible persons can be estimated based on a sample of all payments.)

Statistical sampling may also be used for various income tax calculations, such as (1) analyzing revolving credit accounts of a retailer to determine the portion eligible for the installment method; (2) calculating the provision for redemption of trading stamps and coupons; and (3) determining an index of price level change to be used in calculating a base-period inventory and the value of increments in a LIFO inventory using the dollar value method. Statistical sampling is particularly popular in LIFO, since it makes it unnecessary to keep two complete sets of inventory records. (See Chapter 19.)

SUGGESTED READING

Goodfellow, James; Loebbecke, James; and Neter, John. "Some Perspectives on CAV Sampling Plans." *Canadian Chartered Accountant*, [Part I] October, 1974, pp. 22-30, [Part II] November, 1974, pp. 46-53. This article is a thorough discussion of the combined attribute-variables method of evaluating a dollar-unit sample.

Roberts, Donald. *Statistical Auditing.* New York: AICPA, 1978. This textbook embraces statistical sampling techniques used by auditors.

15

Auditing in an EDP Environment

Kent F. Yarnall

AUDITORS AND THE COMPUTER

The principal groups involved in electronic data processing (EDP) auditing are internal auditors employed by the organization being audited and independent, external auditors. Internal audit emphasis varies with the characteristics and special concerns of a particular company or industry, and independent audits also vary widely in emphasis and approach. However, the maturation of EDP auditing has brought with it an increased awareness that there is no one best approach, and that every audit must be designed to consider specific engagement risks and requirements.

This chapter discusses the audit in an environment that includes EDP. The audit of EDP as performed by the independent auditor is emphasized, but the coverage should also be of interest to management personnel and internal auditors who are responsible for or dependent upon EDP. The total audit process used by independent auditors and the related internal control concepts are covered in detail in Chapters 12 and 13; this chapter builds on those basics with a minimum of repetition.

Beyond the primary purpose of an independent auditor—expression of his opinion on the financial statements—the external audit may include a wide range of computer-related services. These services might include operational audits of data processing operations, or the review of exposures not related to the financial statements, such as invasion of privacy or data center disaster prevention and recovery. Many organizations consider these expanded scope services to be an essential supplement to their overall program of computer control.

Background

EDP has been characterized by constantly changing technology. During the late 1950s and the 1960s, the predominant method of EDP was *batch processing* at a centralized location. Initially, batch applications were designed with few controls, but in time the degree of batch system control reached reasonably high levels. Advances in EDP technology from the late 1960s through the 1970s have resulted in a trend toward on-line, terminal-oriented systems. Since many batch control techniques were not suitable for on-line applications, the development of new systems once again preceded that of control methodology. In the late 1970s, the trend was toward *distributed processing* using terminals linked by telecommunications to a central computer or small computers operating independently at remote locations. The direction today is toward linking these small remote computers to central computers or to other small remote computers. Appropriate control concepts for distributed processing are only now evolving.

Future Trends

Several themes would seem to dominate future EDP trends: decreasing costs, especially for the hardware (the equipment) used for on-line and distributed processing; an exponential growth in the number of small but very powerful computers; a propensity to develop all-new applications (the programs, or software) with on-line terminals; increasingly sophisticated file structures; and a growing awareness of the need for computer controls. For the foreseeable future, EDP will include a mixture of batch, on-line, and distributed processing; and the degree of internal control in any specific EDP situation will probably vary widely.

These trends are resulting in increased concentrations of data, increased integration of processing and controls, and changes in the responsibilities for control. Data, rather than being stored in manual files throughout an organization, are now being physically concentrated in EDP systems. Initially, these data were processed as a series of independent files by independent EDP systems, much as they had been processed manually. However, with increased concentrations of data comes a new sharing of responsibilities. Originally, a single organizational unit had been responsible for creating its own transactions, maintaining its own files, and monitoring its own processing; in many current EDP systems, the responsibilities for these functions involve several departments. The department using the processed data frequently relies extensively on processing performed by others and even on transactions entered by others. Similarly, files once maintained and controlled by a single department are now frequently used and changed by others.

The concentration and sharing of data has been accompanied by the concentration and integration of processing functions. In many EDP systems, a series of functions are automatically performed with nominal human oversight. Some of these functions include initiation, authorization, and execution of transactions; processing of documents that authorize the use or disposition of assets; performance of accounting controls; and the reporting of processing results.

Accounting Impact

Obviously, EDP systems can have significant impact on accounting controls:

- The traditional segregation of duties may be impaired, because a single individual is able to perform incompatible functions, such as making and concealing an error.
- The number of persons who handle a transaction is typically reduced, often to just the individual who enters the data into the computer. As the number of persons involved declines, a consistent level of control can be maintained only if additional controls are included in the EDP system.
- It is frequently difficult to identify the requirements for coordination and control. In a simple environment, a single manager was typically responsible for gathering, processing, and using data; that manager could informally assure the quality of the results. In EDP systems, an individual manager is increasingly only responsible for a portion of the processing and the associated controls. This sharing of responsibility can result in the loss of control, unless control requirements and responsibilities are clearly and formally defined and effectively communicated, monitored, and enforced.

In addition, computer-related exposures and their controls are not sensitive to the size of the computer involved. Highly sophisticated systems can be implemented on small, relatively inexpensive computers. The degree of control needed for any system should be determined by the value and sensitivity of the data and the processing, not by a computer's size or its cost. Accordingly, this chapter applies to all EDP systems, without regard to size or cost.

Although this chapter addresses the auditor's approach to identifying and testing EDP controls and activities, it should not be overlooked that the client bears the responsibility for adequate documentation of its EDP controls and procedures. Indeed, a publicly held company is required by the Foreign Corrupt Practices Act's accounting standards section to maintain systems that provide reasonable assurance of achieving the specific objectives of internal accounting control stated in the act; a demonstration of such achievement should not have to come from the auditor's working paper files because the client neglected to attend to its own documentation needs. In fact, absence of proper client documentation is undoubtedly the threshold sign of significant weaknesses in EDP activities.

EDP EXPOSURES AND CONTROLS

Effective auditing in an EDP environment requires a knowledge of EDP techniques, what can go wrong with these techniques, and what controls can be used to prevent, detect, and correct unintentional errors or deliberate irregularities.

EDP Exposures

EDP techniques vary considerably, depending upon the purpose of the processing, the design of the EDP system, and the type of computer used. Nevertheless, most processing includes

- Conversion of data to machine-readable or electronic media,
- Transmission of data to the computer,
- Initial processing,
- Data retention on magnetic tape or disk files, and
- Subsequent processing to produce output reports or output replies in response to terminal inquiries.

In batch applications, the processing phases are relatively discrete; in on-line applications, two or more phases frequently overlap. For example, in a batch environment, documents are mailed to a central location, converted to punch cards by a keypunch device, physically carried to the computer, and read by a computer card reader. In an on-line application, documents are converted to electronic media using a remote terminal and transmitted directly to the central computer.

In both batch and on-line applications, there are similar exposures:

- Unauthorized transactions may be processed;
- Authorized transactions may be unrecorded, lost, or duplicated;
- Transaction elements (e.g., account number or amount) may be incorrectly converted;
- Files may be lost;
- The wrong file may be used for processing; or
- Processing may be inaccurate or incomplete.

Major EDP application steps and major opportunities for EDP errors at each step are illustrated in Figure 15.1.

PROCESSING STEPS / WHAT CAN GO WRONG	UNAUTHORIZED TRANSACTIONS	TRANSACTIONS UNRECORDED, LOST OR DUPLICATED	INCORRECT VALUES OR CLASSIFICATION	FILE LOST OR WRONG FILE USED	PROCESSING INACCURATE OR INCOMPLETE	OUTPUT INACCURATE OR INCOMPLETE
Convert data to electronic media	●	●	●			
Transmit data to the computer	●	●	●			
Initial processing	●	●	●	●	●	●
Data retention	●	●		●		
Output processing	●			●	●	●

FIGURE 15.1 OPPORTUNITIES FOR EDP ERRORS

EDP exposures may either be specific to an application or apply generally to all applications. For example, an undetected logic error in a computer program will result in errors in only one application, whereas a fire in the data center can destroy files related to all applications. Certain exposures, like fraud, have to be considered in both specific and general terms. For example, a fraud may occur in the user department through the unauthorized submission of an otherwise routine application transaction, or in the data center through the manipulation of data files using unauthorized programs unrelated to the specific application.

The Nature of EDP Controls

Numerous controls can be used to prevent, detect, or correct errors in EDP. For example, transaction counts, control totals, telecommunication controls, and computer hardware and software controls can all be used to prevent or detect the loss of transactions entered at a remote terminal.

Specific controls can be understood best in the context of general types of EDP controls. EDP controls usually relate to a specific processing phase. There are, for example:

- Input controls to prevent or detect lost, inaccurate, or unauthorized transactions;
- Processing controls to assure that processing was performed as intended and that no unauthorized processing was performed; and
- Output controls to assure the accuracy of processing results.

In any processing phase, EDP controls may be specific or general. A specific control, frequently referred to as an application control, relates only to a specific EDP application. General controls, or information-processing facility (IPF) controls, relate to more than one application. For example, keystroke verification procedures can specifically detect transaction conversion errors, whereas data center file library procedures can prevent unauthorized access to all data center files.

Figure 15.2 includes examples of general and application controls that may affect a particular EDP application. As illustrated, controls may be technical or nontechnical and may be implemented at the corporate level, in the user department, in the EDP department, within computer programs, or within computer hardware.

Figure 15.2 also presents the layers of redundant preventive and detective controls that typically exist. For example, key verification to detect data conversion errors, hardware controls to detect an error caused by a hardware failure, batch controls, run-to-run controls, and input-to-output balancing procedures will each prevent or detect inaccurate transaction values. Balancing procedures alone may provide adequate detective control, but EDP operational considerations require preventive controls during early phases of processing. Without such early controls, errors would not be detected until the end of processing, and extensive reprocessing and delays would result.

In addition, controls may be characterized by the span of their effect. For example, both batch controls and overall system-balancing controls detect lost transactions, but batch controls typically monitor less than fifty transactions whereas system balancing may control all the transactions for a day, a month, or a year.

EDP AUDITING STANDARDS

The Effects of EDP on Internal Accounting Control

EDP can have a significant effect on the characteristics of accounting controls. The general structure for a review of internal controls is discussed in Chapter 13, but new types of errors may be caused by EDP. For example, inappropriate accounting or authorization procedures may be included within computer programs, or irregularities may result from routines deliberately included in computer pro-

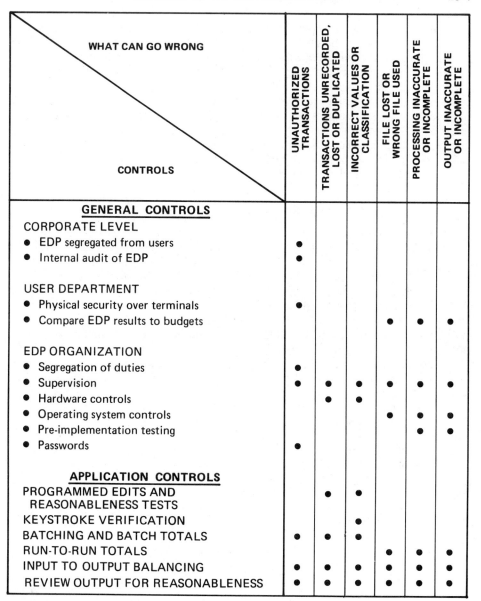

WHAT CAN GO WRONG — CONTROLS	UNAUTHORIZED TRANSACTIONS	TRANSACTIONS UNRECORDED, LOST OR DUPLICATED	INCORRECT VALUES OR CLASSIFICATION	FILE LOST OR WRONG FILE USED	PROCESSING INACCURATE OR INCOMPLETE	OUTPUT INACCURATE OR INCOMPLETE
GENERAL CONTROLS						
CORPORATE LEVEL						
• EDP segregated from users	●					
• Internal audit of EDP	●					
USER DEPARTMENT						
• Physical security over terminals	●					
• Compare EDP results to budgets				●	●	●
EDP ORGANIZATION						
• Segregation of duties	●					
• Supervision	●	●	●	●	●	●
• Hardware controls		●	●			
• Operating system controls				●	●	●
• Pre-implementation testing					●	●
• Passwords	●					
APPLICATION CONTROLS						
PROGRAMMED EDITS AND REASONABLENESS TESTS		●	●			
KEYSTROKE VERIFICATION			●			
BATCHING AND BATCH TOTALS	●	●	●			
RUN-TO-RUN TOTALS				●	●	●
INPUT TO OUTPUT BALANCING	●	●	●	●	●	●
REVIEW OUTPUT FOR REASONABLENESS	●	●	●	●	●	●

FIGURE 15.2 EXAMPLES OF EDP CONTROLS

grams. New types of controls may be required to prevent and detect these EDP-related errors and irregularities. In addition, certain types of EDP controls involve sources of information and evidence that cannot easily be reviewed, and segregation of functions within EDP is different and sometimes difficult. Finally, unfamiliarity with EDP and EDP controls may impede management's responsibility to establish and supervise internal controls over EDP.

Frequently, control weaknesses related to the segregation of functions within EDP are not readily apparent. For example, a computer program that processes purchase orders, receiving reports, vendor invoices, and vendor payments typically verifies prices, quantities, and that the goods have in fact been received. If control weaknesses permit a person to make unauthorized changes to the computer programs or to the purchase order and receiving document files, the program may then be used to process unapproved vendor invoices. In certain situations, complete segregation of incompatible EDP functions may be impossible, impractical, or simply not cost-justified. In such cases compensating controls may be required, including supervision, rotation of personnel, an independent EDP control group, user-department controls, and periodic internal audit review.

Evaluation of EDP Internal Accounting Controls

Although auditing standards in general apply to the audit of electronically processed financial data, SAS 3 (AU 321) specifically considers the auditor's study and evalutation of EDP internal accounting controls when EDP is used to process accounting information that can materially affect the financial statements the auditor is examining (AU 321.03, n. 2). If a client uses EDP in significant accounting applications, the auditor must understand the entire system sufficiently to enable him to identify and evaluate essential accounting control features, and the auditor's review of accounting control should include all significant manual, mechanical, and EDP activities and the interrelationship between EDP and the user department. This requirement holds whether the use of EDP is limited or extensive and whether the EDP facilities are operated by the auditor's client or by a third party, such as a service bureau.

The auditor's review may be done in two phases: a preliminary phase and a completion phase. The *preliminary phase* provides an understanding of the flow of transactions through the accounting system, the extent to which EDP is used in each significant accounting application, and the basic structure of internal accounting controls. This phase normally considers both general and application controls. Since weak general controls often have pervasive effects, the auditor should consider their effect in the evaluation of application controls.

Upon completion of the preliminary phase, the auditor can assess the significance of internal accounting control within EDP in relation to the entire system and determine the appropriate extent of *additional review*.

He has several options. If controls within the EDP portions of an application appear to provide a basis for reliance, the auditor can then complete the review of EDP controls, test controls to determine their effectiveness, and then determine the extent to which subsequent substantive audit procedures may be restricted. Even though EDP controls appear effective, the auditor may conclude that the effort required to complete the control review and to test controls would exceed the resulting reduction in effort related to substantive procedures. In this case, the auditor may decide not to go beyond the preliminary review and would not compliance-test EDP controls. Or, the auditor may conclude that EDP controls appear weak, and therefore decide not to go beyond the preliminary review but to rely on substantive procedures. If the weakness is known to be material, however, the auditor may have a responsibility to advise the management and the board of the deficiencies (see Chapter 13). In all three cases, the auditor assesses the potential impact of identified control weaknesses on the financial statements, and this assessment influences the scope and extent of substantive audit procedures.

EDP AUDIT TECHNIQUES AND TOOLS

The auditor can use a variety of techniques and tools to understand a client's EDP activity, evaluate EDP controls, and evaluate the results of EDP. Figure 15.3 provides a *partial* list of audit techniques and tools related to particular EDP audit tasks, some of which are discussed in this section. Many of these techniques are nontechnical (e.g., checklists and questionnaires) and are useful to auditors who have a general understanding of EDP, its exposures, and its controls. Use of many other EDP tools requires a higher degree of technical expertise. Flowcharting, described in Chapter 13, is another tool commonly employed by auditors to analyze transaction cycles, and its use seems especially applicable to EDP. Of course, these are generalizations, with reality dependent upon the specific engagement and the experience level—general and EDP—of the members of the audit team.

Risk Analysis

Although informal, highly judgmental risk analysis has always been part of auditing, the enormous demands for EDP auditing have caused innovative auditors to experiment with formally assessing EDP-related risks. The results of this formal risk analysis are then used to arrange audit work-schedule priorities. Risk analysis is characterized by an initial survey to gather only that information used in the risk analysis formula. Values are then calculated that represent the degree of risk for specific applications or for all applications serviced by a particular data processing operation. Factors frequently included in the various risk analysis methods are

- Organizational considerations;
- The dollar amount of individual transactions and resulting balances;
- Normal error rates in the various processing phases;
- The susceptibility of assets to theft or fraud;
- The need for confidentiality or privacy;
- The potential for EDP-related business interruption;
- The probable impact of EDP interruptions on income and service levels;
- The stability of the EDP operations (e.g., the number of new or modified applications);
- The complexity of processing;
- Previous audit findings;
- Perceived competency of the EDP and user departments; and
- Preliminary assessments of EDP controls.

A risk analysis methodology developed at Sperry Rand Corporation uses six major categories to analyze EDP application risk. These categories, with their assigned relative weights, are (1) impact of system failure, with a relative weight

AUDIT TASK	TECHNIQUES	TOOLS
Gather and verify application and data center information	Inquiries and observations	Application and data center questionnaires and check lists
	Flowchart transaction flow and controls	
	Review program code and logic	Logic flowcharting software
Test and evaluate controls	Observe controls or control evidence	
	Use test data to test controls	Test decks, audit software, test data generators
	Control analysis	Control evaluation tables
Test transactions for evidence of weak controls	Trace valid and invalid transactions	
	Reasonableness tests	Audit software
Verify processing routines	Manual recalculation	
	Test data, parallel simulation	Test decks, audit software, test data generators
Test transactions and balances for monetary errors	Confirmations, random or key item selection, parallel simulation	Audit software, statistical sampling software
	Analytical review	Analytical software

FIGURE 15.3   EDP AUDIT TECHNIQUES AND RELATED EDP AUDIT TOOLS

of 15; (2) impact on management decisions, with a relative weight of 10; (3) system status, (4) impact on other systems, and (5) application controls, each with a relative weight of 5; and (6) technical complexity, with a relative weight of 2. Within each of these categories, scores related to specific application characteristics have been assigned.

In the system failure category, for example, scores are assigned as follows: 10 if a failure has customer impact; 6 to 8 if the failure has company-wide impact; 2 to 4 if the application has user impact; and 1 if the failure also impacts the management information system. Scoring is on an additive basis, with a maximum system failure score of 23.

In the management decisions category, different scores are assigned for operational systems, financial systems, operational research systems, and statistical systems. In the systems status category, a new system may be assigned a score from 6 to 10, whereas an existing system may be assigned a score from 1 to 5 depending upon the extent of recent modifications. In the impact-on-other-systems category, assigned scores depend upon the degree of system independence or integration with other systems.

Scoring in the application control category is based upon the need for various types of application controls, such as data entry controls, file access security, and run-to-run controls. In the system scope category, local applications are assigned a score of 1 to 4, and divisional or corporate systems may be assigned a score up to 6 or 8, respectively. The technical complexity category considers such characteristics as processing mode (sequential batch, on-line, etc.), the programming language used, the developmental approach used, file data management techniques (sequential, indexed, data base, etc.), and the application recovery mode.

To use this risk evaluation method, scores are first assigned based on system characteristics in each of the six categories; then each category score is multiplied by the relative weight assigned to the category. The sum of these category values represents the degree of risk for the application. (A more detailed description of this risk analysis method appears in Hubbert, 1979.)

Control Analysis

Although the effectiveness of some combinations of controls will always be very judgmental, the use of control evaluation tables to perform a more systematic analysis is gaining increased acceptance. Control evaluation tables used to evaluate application and general (IPF) controls are given in Appendices 15-A and 15-B, respectively, and are extracted from *Computer Control and Audit by* Mair, Wood, and Davis. These tables indicate the relationship of potential errors to controls and suggest the probable strength of each type of control. For example, in an application control, document control counts will typically be a reliable control against lost or duplicated input and, in combination with other controls, may control the risk of processing the wrong file.

The exposure, cause, and control entries of the tables are extensive, and the numeric values have been developed with considerable thought based on actual practice. However, in applying these tables to specific situations, it is the technique that is important, not the specific entries or values. In particular, the effectiveness of a control in dealing with a particular cause can vary significantly according to circumstances. For example, training may be so necessary in complex or technical areas that several years of combined formal and on-the-job training are essential to assure adequate quality of results. Conversely, in simple functions, the usefulness of training may be limited, and other controls thus become much more important.

Test Data

Test data, commonly called *test decks,* are sets of input transactions and master file records that can be used to verify the accuracy of computer routines or the adequacy of computer controls. Test data are a popular technique used by EDP professionals to test new and modified EDP applications and by auditors to test critical routines and controls. Theoretically, test data may be used to test all possible combinations of input and processing. However, in an EDP application of any complexity, such a comprehensive test might require hundreds, perhaps thousands of test decks. Although such a comprehensive approach may be required to test a new EDP application, audit testing is typically restricted to critical routines, perhaps with all other routines tested on a sample basis.

Two examples of how an auditor might use test data follow. In a payroll program that includes a gross pay calculation based on regular hours, overtime hours, and production quotas, test data representing the various combinations of input may be used to test the accuracy of the payroll calculation. In a payroll-check-writing program that has a programmed control to prevent the printing of a check greater than $2,000, test data representing a payment over $2,000 may be used to test the control.

The steps involved in the use of test data are to

1. Define the objectives of the test and identify the specific computer routines to be tested;
2. Prepare test data, including master file records if required;
3. Manually calculate the anticipated processing result;
4. If the system to be tested is already operational, establish test versions of the application computer programs and necessary files;
5. Process the test data through the application computer programs;
6. Compare manually prepared anticipated results to the results of actual computer processing; and
7. Resolve differences between anticipated and actual results.

In most cases, the results of processing will be available on regularly produced computer reports. However, the processing result to be reviewed may only be available within a record in a computer file. In this case, audit software may have to be used to review the processing result.

The use of test data is not technically complex, but the technique does require a thorough understanding of the EDP application to be tested. This understanding is necessary so the auditor can limit testing to only critical routines, develop the necessary test and master-file records, and accurately calculate anticipated results.

When an operational system is to be tested, the auditor must be certain that the results of testing do not become intermingled with the results of actual processing. This is usually achieved by establishing, then testing, nonproduction copies of the application programs and the related files. Extensive cooperation and coordination with the data center staff is necessary to establish copies of computer programs and files and to guard against the accidental inclusion of test data within actual operation files. When this approach is used, the auditor must be certain that the copies of the programs tested are identical to the production versions of the programs.

The risk of introducing test data into actual production results may also be eliminated by using live transactions as test data. This alternative is practical if the required testing involves input transactions and master-file records that are typically found in regular production processing. The approach is similar to using regular test data: test objectives are defined, anticipated results are calculated, and the characteristics of required input and master-file test data are established. However, rather than develop test data, regular production transactions with the required characteristics are identified, and the actual results of processing these transactions are compared to anticipated processing results.

Integrated Test Facility (ITF)

The *integrated test facility,* or ITF, is a refinement of the test data approach that may be used to test operational applications directly. Use of ITF involves the establishment of records that represent "dummy" entities against which test data may be processed. These fictitious entities may be employees or customers, or an entire department or division. The technique is "integrated" because the test transactions are processed with regular production transactions and test master-file records reside on the same files with production master records. Since processing is integrated, the method of separating test transactions from live transactions is critical. Separation may be achieved either by journal or other reversing entries or by the use of production programs that have been designed or modified to automatically perform the separation.

Using ITF involves steps similar to those previously outlined for the use of test data—define objectives, prepare test data, calculate anticipated results, process test data through the system, and compare anticipated and actual results. However, since the ITF approach uses the operational version of programs and files, the auditor must at the end of the test reverse or otherwise eliminate the results of test processing.

Parallel Simulation

Parallel simulation, a powerful and popular EDP audit technique, uses computer programs prepared by auditors to reperform the functions initially performed by an actual computer application. The simulation program reads the same input and the master-file data, and then produces results for comparison with original application processing results. Matching results substantiate the accuracy of the application processing. The auditor may simulate processing for transactions that represent a single processing cycle only or an entire reporting period.

Parallel simulation is most frequently used as an alternative to manual recomputation performed on a sample basis. For example, if a complex depreciation method is used, the auditor might be required to recalculate depreciation on a sample basis; however, by using parallel simulation, the auditor could recalculate complex depreciation for all items.

Parallel simulation requires the use of computer programs written in conventional programming languages, such as COBOL, or the use of generalized computer audit software (GCAS). GCAS is by far the more popular.

Generalized Computer Audit Software

GCAS may be used to perform a wide range of audit tasks, and permits the auditor to use the computer as an audit tool. GCAS consists of a series of computer program routines that can read computer files, select desired information, perform calculations, and print reports in an auditor-specified format. GCAS enables the auditor to have direct access to computerized records and to deal effectively with large quantities of data. Since GCAS can quickly scan, test, and summarize all the data on a computer file, many procedures traditionally performed on a sample basis can be extended to the entire population. In addition, the use of GCAS typically leads to a better understanding of automated systems and EDP operations, can make auditing more interesting and challenging, and is an excellent way to introduce the auditor to EDP.

GCAS can accomplish these six basic types of audit tasks:

1. Examine records for quality, completeness, consistency, and correctness (e.g., review bank demand deposit files for unusually large deposits and withdrawals);
2. Verify calculations and make computations (e.g., recompute interest);
3. Compare data on separate files (e.g., compare current and prior-period inventory files for obsolete and slow-moving items);
4. Select and print audit samples (e.g., accounts receivable confirmations);
5. Summarize, resequence, and analyze data (e.g., resequence inventory items by location to facilitate physical observations);
6. Compare data obtained through other audit procedures with company records (e.g., compare creditor statements with accounts payable files).

The steps in using GCAS parallel those involved in using a conventional programming language. The auditor establishes specific GCAS application objectives; reviews the data files for specific information to be accessed; designs the format of required reports; and develops the logic required to extract, manipulate, and print the required data. Specification sheets that define processing requirements are then prepared, keypunched, and submitted for computer processing. The specifications cause the GCAS to perform the required audit tasks.

GCAS is much easier to learn and use than conventional programming languages. Most GCAS systems require only one week of training, and proficiency may be achieved after several weeks of use. In addition, GCAS specification coding typically requires only a fraction of the coding entries required for conventional programming languages, which permits faster coding and minimizes the opportunity for coding errors.

Figure 15.4 illustrates a report produced by a GCAS package called STRATA, developed and licensed by Touche Ross & Co. Below the report is a portion of the auditor specification coding that defines the data processing elements and the report format.

Sampling

Computer-assisted audit techniques have a two-edged impact on the use of *statistical sampling* by auditors. The availability of a computer for the auditor's use in analyzing masses of data frequently eliminates the need to audit on a sample

STRATA-OS 360/370

RECEIVABLES AGING REPORT

04/05/79
REPORT 1-PAGE 1

CUSTOMER NO.	CUSTOMER NAME	UNDER 30	30 to 50	60 to 80	90 AND OVER	CUSTOMER BAL
04609631	NEW HAVEN STEEL	.00	120.95	42.75	.00	163.70
04610705	AMERICAN STAMP	125.00	5.50	.00	.00	130.50
04611279	MOROW CASTING	36.30	43.88	.00	.00	80.18
04718493	SWIFT-CRAFT	57.98	54.67	.00	38.80	151.45
04719396	ROBBINS & WHITE	54.14	14.11	.00	.00	68.25
04722877	ACME PRODUCTS	.00	.00	.00	215.92	215.92
04738490	SEERO INC.	15.99	.00	.00	.00	15.99
04763028	NAICCO LEASING	.00	73.80	.00	.00	73.80
04769480	ST. PAUL LABS	124.45	46.80	.00	.00	171.25
04791873	GEO-TECH RESEARCH	48.28	57.60	.00	.00	105.88
04800365	S & S TESTING	6.70	.00	.00	.00	6.70
04837173	WINSTON REED INC.	71.90	129.05	.00	.00	200.95
04842671	BIC INDUSTRIES	108.31	97.11	.00	.00	205.42
04866843	ALLEN PRODUCTS	66.73	90.19	87.46	.00	244.38

STRATA product aging report. (Note: Only top of first page is presented.)

	WORK FIELD NUMBER	WORK FIELD NAME	STORAGE FORMAT		
			ALPHA-NUMERIC	NUMERIC	
			LENGTH	Decimal Places	Indicative Y Yes
2	W 01	CUSTOMER NO.	8		
2	W 02	UNDER 30		2	
2	W 03	30 TO 59		2	
2	W 04	60 TO 89		2	
2	W 05	90 AND OVER		2	
2	W 06	CUSTOMER BAL		2	
2	W 07	CUSTOMER NAME	15		
2	W 8				
2	W 9				

Work record specification coding.

PRINT SPECIFICATIONS

REPORT NO. 2 **01**

REPORT NAME RECEIVABLES AGING REPORT

SORT CONTROL FIELDS FOR RECORDS SELECTED
MAJOR → MINOR
W   W   W

LINES TO BE PRINTED (enter Y for Yes)
Details **Y** Major Totals Intermediate Totals Minor Totals Page Totals Grand Totals **Y**

Totals, spacing and breaks are controlled by the corresponding WORK fields specified in Columns 1, 2 and 3 below.

SPACING BETWEEN LINES AND PAGE BREAKS
Details (2) Maj. Breaks Intermediate Breaks (3) Minor Breaks (3) Omit Dashed Lines on Totals (Enter Y for Yes)

CONTENTS OF COLUMN (4)

	CONTROL FIELD FOR MAJOR TOTALS BREAKS			CONTROL FIELD FOR INTERMED. TOTALS BREAKS			CONTROL FIELD FOR MINOR TOTALS BREAKS				
	COL. NO.	FIELD	LOW ORDER POSITION	COL. NO.	FIELD	LOW ORDER POSITION	COL. NO.	FIELD	LOW ORDER POSITION	COL. NO.	FIELD	LOW ORDER POSITION
5	01	W01	15	02	W07	30	03	W02	45	04	W03	60
5	05	W04	75	06	W05	90	07	W06	05	08		

Aging report print specification coding.

FIGURE 15.4 STRATA-PRODUCED REPORT AND RELATED SPECIFICATION CODING

basis. By preparing an audit software application that implements the logic of his audit analysis, the auditor can quickly examine every transaction and every record. In such situations, sampling may be unnecessary.

On the other hand, the computer is a tremendous aid in the selection of random samples and the evaluation of their results (see Chapter 14). Computers may be programmed to select a truly random sample of transactions or records, and thereby eliminate the cumbersome task of manual sample selection. Many of the general-purpose audit software languages provide simple user specifications that result in complex selection calculations. Commercial timesharing services also provide programs that generate random numbers sorted into sequences and within specified ranges of values. These computer-assisted techniques permit auditors to use statistical evaluation techniques that are virtually impossible on a manual basis.

Auditing Around and Auditing Through

There is a long-standing debate as to the merits of two techniques referred to as *auditing around the computer* and *auditing through the computer*. The differences of opinion, to a large extent, arise from imprecise definitions.

"Audit around" can be defined as the use of manual techniques to verify the accuracy of computer processing, without direct auditor involvement in the processing within the computer. Using this definition, audit around would include techniques such as observation of controls, system walk-through, documentation review, transaction tracing, review of processing results, and manual recalculation of processing results. "Audit through" requires auditor involvement in computer processing and may include techniques such as computer code review, the use of program logic flowcharting software, and processing of test data.

A third category of audit procedure, which could be called *automated audit around,* does not fit conveniently into either category. This procedure uses audit software—for parallel simulation, for selection and testing of transactions, or for reasonableness tests of transactions or balances—to detect theoretically impossible values that indicate control weaknesses or processing errors.

There is little to be gained by more precise definitions of audit around and audit through, since communication is more effective when specific audit techniques are identified and explained in the context of their planned use.

Selecting Appropriate EDP Audit Techniques

The extent and availability of audit evidence frequently affects the audit approach and the selection of the most appropriate EDP audit techniques. Certain techniques can only be used if an application or a control produces evidence that can be subjected to manual audit tests. This type of evidence includes documents that initiate automated transactions, documents that indicate that controls are effective, and transaction listings and computer reports that permit manual tracing and manual tests of processing. If this type of evidence is partially or totally unavailable, the auditor may have to test program processing or use the computer to test computer files that contain the results of processing. In practice it is unusual to find a system totally lacking in sources of evidence that can be manually audited. However, systems characterized by high transaction volumes, remote-terminal data entry, complex processing, and limited hard-copy reports may be difficult to audit exclusively by manual techniques.

COMPUTER ABUSE AND CATASTROPHE

General Concerns

Computer abuse includes fraud, embezzlement, theft of assets, invasion of privacy, and malicious destruction of computer hardware, programs, or files. Computer catastrophes include natural disasters, like fire or flood, and the accidental destruction of computer programs or computer files due to operator error, hardware failures, or program errors.

Several factors related to EDP abuse and catastrophes deserve special attention:

1. EDP typically results in great concentrations of data and, correspondingly, great exposures;
2. Manipulation of a computer program or file is much less obvious than corresponding manipulations involving manual procedures and manual records;
3. Data processing professionals, frequently preoccupied with the technical aspects of EDP, may not appreciate the impact of potential EDP abuses or catastrophes;
4. Management outside the data processing organization may not understand or appreciate the risks related to the use of EDP; and
5. As EDP becomes increasingly vital to overall operations, interruptions in service may cripple the overall organization.

The types and estimated frequencies of computer errors, abuse, and catastrophes are included in Figure 15.5. Estimates of the impact of abuse or catastrophes are, however, probably more important. The potential impact of abuse and catastrophes should be considered both for individual applications and for the entire data processing operation. For example, what is the probable impact of the accidental destruction of a payroll program or an accounts receivable file? What is the maximum dollar loss that may result from a theft or fraud related to a purchasing and payables application? What is the impact on profitability and service levels if the entire data center is destroyed by fire?

Controls related to destruction of hardware, programs, and files include conventional physical security controls (e.g., fire detectors) and general controls to prevent or correct the accidental destruction of programs and files (e.g., programmed label checks prior to all processing). Corrective controls typically include offsite storage of duplicate programs, files, and related operating procedures and an arrangement to use a second processing facility if the entire data center is destroyed.

Computer-Related Fraud

Computer-related frauds generally receive dramatic attention whenever discovered; however, most organizations have not addressed these threats in a serious and systematized fashion. This lack of concern and action is usually based on

Exposure	*Estimated Frequency*
Human Carelessness:	
Single record modified	10 times a day
Single record lost	once in 10 days
Wrong file used	once in 4 years
Wrong program used	once in 4 years
Entire file lost	once in 4 years
File damaged	once in 4 years
Hardware and Software Failures:	
Single records modified	once in 10 days
Single records lost	once in 100 days
Entire file lost	once in 4 years
Computer Abuse:	
Invasion of privacy	once in 100 days
Theft of data	once in 4 years
Embezzlement	once in 4 years
Industrial espionage	once in 4 years
Malicious destruction of files	once in 40 years
Acts of God:	
Fire	once in 40 years
Flood	once in 40 years

FIGURE 15.5   ESTIMATED FREQUENCY OF VARIOUS EDP APPLICATION EXPOSURES

ADAPTED FROM: James Martin, *Security, Accuracy, and Privacy in Computer Systems* (Englewood Cliffs, N.J.: Prentice-Hall, 1973), pp. 12 and 13. (The author cautions that the table values are only examples and would have to be evaluated anew for any specific application.)

assumptions that the odds of something happening are low, that the people involved are trustworthy, and that effective controls cost too much or are impossible to implement. There is some truth in all these statements. For example, available statistics indicate that losses related to fire, flood, and routine operational EDP errors far exceed those due to EDP-related fraud or theft, and that most EDP frauds that are discovered (many undoubtedly are not) are discovered by accident, not by controls designed to detect fraud.

Nevertheless, the use of computers frequently involves new and additional risks; and when EDP involves assets that can be manipulated or stolen, the possibility of fraud or theft cannot be ignored. Increased threats may, however, be offset by the increased levels of control that are possible in EDP systems and by techniques that actually use the computer to detect fraud.

The traditional reluctance to discuss computer-related frauds and to conduct aggressive programs of prevention and detection resulted from fears that such efforts might actually provide lessons in how to commit them. Recently, however, both popular and professional publications have discussed the details of specific cases. At this point it can safely be assumed that an active program of prevention and detection will not substantially add to the knowledge level of potential per- petrators. The entire issue, to some extent, may be irrelevant, since available statistics indicate that most acts of computer-related fraud and theft that have been uncovered were committed by first-time offenders who, as part of their routine duties, had or could acquire all the knowledge necessary to commit their illegal acts.

The computer may also process fraudulent records that result from a fraud or theft occurring exclusively outside the computer system. Although this situation is not really a computer-related fraud, controls within the computer system may detect this type of illegal act.

Types of Fraud. In general terms, fraudulent activity has occurred in situations in which

- The computer was used as an instrument to commit the act,
- The computer was used to conceal the act,
- The computer contributed to an environment that fostered and concealed the act, or
- Computer hardware, programs, or files were the object of the act.

Computer-related illegal acts might include, for example, theft of cash, negotiable securities, property, information, or computing resources; inflation of reported earnings or assets; or unauthorized reductions of financial obligations.

Representative Cases. Representative actual computer-related theft and fraud cases are summarized below:

- A computer operator copied, then sold, the customer name and address file.
- A programmer of one company penetrated a competitor's timesharing system and stole a proprietary computer program.
- A bank programmer modified the daily overdraft report program to exclude his own account from the overdraft report.
- An individual not an employee of the company involved penetrated the company's computerized inventory system, entered unauthorized orders for the delivery of equip- ment, then stole and sold the equipment.
- An EDP department employee inflated payroll totals, then forged checks equal to the inflated amount on blank check forms.
- A manager of a data center made unauthorized changes to a program, thereby issuing credits to his own account.
- A head teller, using an error correction routine from a computer terminal, manipu- lated hundreds of customer accounts; one of the techniques used was to reduce the amounts of large deposits so that cash could be withdrawn without detection.
- The management of a company inflated sales by creating unauthorized transactions that were then processed on a computer; the computer printouts, representing to a large extent fictitious transactions, were then used to shield the fraud.

In these cases, indeed in more than half the known cases, collusion and high levels of EDP technical expertise were not involved.

Vulnerable Employment Positions. Computer abuse experts have tried without success to develop a personality profile that might be used to identify the potential perpetrator. However, it is becoming clear that persons in certain positions are more likely to be involved in computer abuse. Individuals who have committed acts of computer theft or fraud frequently occupied positions with the following characteristics:

- A degree of trust and, therefore, exclusion from routine supervision and review;
- The opportunity to understand the total scope of EDP and non-EDP, especially the overall structure of controls;
- The opportunity to initiate transactions, especially adjustments and corrections, without a second-party authorization or review;
- Involvement in the direct flow of a high volume of asset-related transactions;
- The opportunity to both initiate and conceal invalid and unauthorized transactions; or
- The opportunity for unsupervised use of the computer.

Corporate Characteristics. Certain corporate characteristics also appear to be conducive to computer-related theft and fraud. For example:

- Senior management does not maintain high general standards of internal control.
- Record keeping is sloppy.
- Management outside the EDP department is not knowledgeable in EDP and EDP control.
- There are no EDP-qualified internal auditors.
- User departments are neither knowledgeable in EDP nor responsible for the accuracy and integrity of EDP related to their department.
- User-oriented application controls are weak.
- General controls within the EDP department are weak. ("Open shops," i.e., EDP departments with unrestricted access to the computer and to computer files, present an especially high risk.)
- The organization exhibits a high tolerance for computer errors, late processing, EDP reruns, and computer-related confusion and mystique.

Controls. A program to review and improve fraud and theft controls should consider two areas: (1) the general level of implementation of those controls known to prevent or detect computer irregularities and (2) a comprehensive program of threat analysis to identify critical risk areas that should be subjected to a detailed analysis.

Controls that deserve special consideration in both general and specific reviews were identified in an analysis of the relationship between exposures and related preventive or detective controls (Blish, 1978). This analysis first considered the characteristics of 15 representative cases, then identified specific controls that might have prevented or detected the illegal acts. These controls, ranked by the

Percentage of Cases	Controls That Might Have Prevented or Detected the Activity
93	Source document authorization
80	Review by independent control group
66	Segregation of functions within EDP
66	Reconciliation of processing totals to input
66	Reconciliation of output to processing totals
60	Restriction of output to authorized users
53	Review of input for proper authorization
46	Control of document flow between departments
40	Run-to-run processing controls
40	Scan of output for reasonableness
40	Restricted access to files and programs
33	Programmed limit and reasonableness checks
33	Segregation between EDP and users
33	Internal audit review
26	Control over program changes
26	Hardware and operating system controls
26	Restricted access to documentation

FIGURE 15.6   CONTROLS RELATED TO COMPUTER FRAUD AND THEFT
SOURCE: Eugene Blish, "Computer Abuse: A Practical Use of the AICPA Guide," *EDPACS,* September, 1978, pp. 6-12.

percentage of cases in which the control might have been effective, are included in Figure 15.6.

AUDIT IMPLICATIONS OF SYSTEM DEVELOPMENT AND MAINTENANCE

The development of computer applications begins with the definition of new user processing requirements and ends with a new computer system or application. Typically, the process only involves new application programs that run on an existing computer. However, certain types of new systems, such as a new tele-communications network, may involve new computer hardware as well.

System maintenance refers to changes to operational computer programs. Such changes may be necessary to add new program functions, modify existing functions, correct design or coding errors, or permit programs to operate on new computer hardware.

Auditor Concerns

The internal and external auditor share similar concerns related to control over both system development and maintenance. If the system development process is uncontrolled, the new programs may include routines that result in errors or irreg-ularities. If system maintenance is uncontrolled, changes may accidentally modify previously correct routines or may introduce new routines that result in errors or irregularities. In addition, errors may result from inadequate control over con-version from an old to a new system or from the misunderstandings and confusion that frequently characterize the introduction of a new application.

The introduction of a new or modified application may require additional audit procedures or revisions to existing audit procedures. New systems descriptions may have to be developed and verified, new exposures and controls may have to be evaluated, new controls may have to be tested, and the degree of reliance upon controls may change. If a new or substantially modified application is introduced other than at fiscal year-end, the independent auditor's review may have to include the features and controls of the old system, the conversion process, and the new system.

If computer program changes are frequent and uncontrolled, the auditor has no assurance that the findings of previous control reviews still apply to the most recent version of the application. In the extreme, the auditor may not know what version of the system was tested or what version is currently being used. Accordingly, the degree of control over maintenance may influence the auditor's approach and the selection of audit procedures.

System Development and Maintenance Processes

The system development process is similar to the process used to design and build a new automobile in that problems can occur either because of poor design or poor construction. In system development, poor application design (e.g., missing reports or control features) or developmental deficiencies (e.g., incorrect logic introduced by programmer error) may cause EDP problems.

Phases in computer system development projects typically include

1. Initial investigation to determine the nature of a proposed application,
2. Evaluation of technical and economic feasibility,
3. Management review and a decision to continue,
4. Definition of user and technical processing requirements,
5. Definition of control requirements,
6. System design,
7. Development of technical EDP specifications,
8. Development of application program specifications,
9. Programming,
10. Program testing,
11. Development of user procedures,
12. User training, and
13. Conversion from the old to the new system.

Although the phases are generally similar, system development methodologies vary considerably between organizations and between project managers within the same organization. Phases are sometimes consolidated or eliminated, and the developmental effort may proceed in a very formal or informal manner.

System Development Exposures and Controls

During system development, many things can go wrong. Required functions may be overlooked; the characteristics of required functions may be poorly communicated to the designer; or accounting, privacy, fraud, and disaster controls may be ignored or poorly designed. Even if system requirements and design are adequate, unauthorized features or an unauthorized program code may be intentionally introduced while the system is being built; logic and computational errors may be accidentally introduced; and transactions and files may be lost or incorrectly processed during the conversion period. In addition, schedule dates may be missed and developmental cost estimates exceeded. If the new programs are obscure and poorly documented, they may be difficult to understand and expensive to maintain.

Figure 15.7 identifies major system development exposures and related major controls. Although many of these controls, such as project schedules and budgets, are conventional management controls, others, such as technical review for unauthorized codes, require a high degree of EDP technical expertise.

System Maintenance Exposures and Controls

In most respects, the phases, exposures, and controls in system maintenance are similar to those in system development. The inclusion of new or modified program functions may introduce processing errors, accidentally modify routines that were not to be changed, or bypass existing application controls. System maintenance activities also provide an opportunity for the deliberate circumvention of controls or the introduction of unauthorized processing routines.

If maintenance results in major application modifications, all the controls applicable to system development can be used to control system maintenance. If a specific maintenance effort is limited, applicable controls may only include a formal request for the change, a brief narrative description of the change, limited testing, limited technical review, and management's authorization to use the modified program for regular processing.

PLANNING THE EDP PORTION OF THE AUDIT

Relationship of EDP to the Overall Audit

The independent auditor's examination may be conducted in three phases (discussed more fully in Chapter 12). In Phase I, the auditor

- Acquires a knowledge of the business to be audited,
- Appraises auditability,
- Establishes guidelines for materiality,
- Identifies material types of transactions,

WHAT CAN GO WRONG / CONTROLS	DESIGN ERRORS AND OMISSIONS						IMPLEMENTATION ERRORS				OTHER ERRORS	
	USER FUNCTIONS	ACCOUNTING CONTROLS	PRIVACY CONTROLS	FRAUD CONTROLS	ERROR CORRECTION CONTROLS	RECOVERY CONTROLS	UNAUTHORIZED CHANGES	UNAUTHORIZED CODE	CODING ERRORS	START-UP ERRORS	SCHEDULE ERRORS	COST ESTIMATE ERRORS
MANAGEMENT CONTROLS												
• Corporate steering committee	•	•	•	•	•	•					•	•
• Feasibility study	•										•	•
• Appropriate methodology	•	•	•	•	•	•	•		•	•	•	•
• Experienced project management	•	•	•	•	•	•	•	•	•	•	•	•
• Budget and schedules							•			•	•	•
• Periodic status reviews							•				•	•
• Change authorization procedure							•				•	•
STANDARDS												
• Requirements standards	•	•	•	•	•	•					•	•
• Design standards	•	•	•	•	•	•					•	•
• Control standards		•	•	•	•	•					•	•
• Specification standards							•		•		•	•
• Documentation standards	•	•	•	•	•	•	•		•		•	•
• Programming standards							•	•	•			
SIGN OFFS												
• User requirements sign off	•	•	•	•	•	•					•	
• User design sign off	•	•	•	•	•	•					•	
• Auditor design sign off		•	•	•	•	•					•	
ONGOING REVIEWS												
• Periodic user review	•	•	•	•	•	•						
• Periodic auditor review		•	•	•	•	•						
• Periodic technical review			•	•	•	•	•	•	•			
IMPLEMENTATION CONTROLS												
• System testing	•	•	•	•	•	•	•	•	•			
• Conversion plan										•		
• Conversion monitoring										•		
• Pilot or parallel operation	•	•	•	•	•	•	•		•	•		
• Post-implementation monitoring	•	•	•	•	•	•	•			•		

FIGURE 15.7   SYSTEM DEVELOPMENT EXPOSURES AND CONTROLS

- Identifies potential sources of material errors,
- Identifies sources of audit evidence,
- Develops and verifies accounting system descriptions,
- Makes a preliminary evaluation of internal control, and
- Designs the audit approach and supporting audit procedures.

In Phase II, the auditor assesses the likelihood of material errors in the financial statements. The auditor may also test those controls identified in Phase I that appear to prevent or detect material errors. However, if controls appear weak or if the control-testing effort would exceed the expected reduction in Phase III effort, the auditor may proceed to Phase III without testing controls.

In Phase III the auditor performs substantive procedures that lead to the issuance of the auditor's report. These procedures typically include analytical review of account balances, verification of key items, verification of account balances, a post–balance sheet review, and a final review of the financial statements.

The EDP aspects are an integral part of each phase of the overall audit and cannot be considered or performed independently. The overall audit approach and overall materiality guidelines determine the scope and extent of EDP-related procedures. To some degree, the overall audit approach is determined by the extent and complexity of EDP, the degree of control over EDP, and the ease with which EDP-related audit evidence may be obtained. EDP applications without good controls or readily available sources of audit evidence may, in extreme cases, raise questions of auditability. At best, poorly controlled applications will require more extensive audit procedures. In addition, client requests for EDP reviews beyond the scope of generally accepted auditing standards may affect the audit approach and the procedures to be performed.

Developing an Effective and Efficient Approach

Although coordinating and balancing procedures performed in the three audit phases is the key to an optimal audit approach, numerous factors in the EDP audit environment make this difficult. Many EDP applications are well controlled and relatively easy to audit, but certain situations require staff personnel with special technical skills and the use of technically complex audit procedures. The actual degree of audit complexity may not be immediately obvious, yet staff assignments and work plans must frequently be developed based upon preliminary assessments of audit complexity. In addition, the trade-off between control testing and expected reductions in Phase III substantive procedures is frequently difficult to determine.

During Phase I, the auditor must perform a preliminary review for each significant EDP application. The specific scope and extent of these preliminary reviews should, whenever possible, be established to complement tentative plans for Phases II and III. Factors that should be considered when planning Phase I include

- The initial understanding of the client's applications and EDP operations,
- The probable reduction in Phase III procedures that can be achieved if controls are relied on,

- The need to complement Phase III procedures with added assurance obtained from Phase I and Phase II procedures,
- Reporting or other timing constraints that require some degree of control reliance,
- The stability of the systems, and
- The likelihood that computer-assisted audit techniques might be used.

To obtain this type of information, an initial survey is usually required. If the auditor has information obtained during prior-year examinations, it need only be updated by a brief survey. For new clients and for clients with dynamic EDP environments, a more extensive initial survey may be necessary.

When planning information is adequate, the auditor has certain Phase I options. If reliance on controls is planned, the auditor can combine the preliminary and completion phases of application control reviews. If reliance is definitely not planned, the extent of the preliminary review can be restricted. In all cases, the extent of the Phase I audit effort can be established as appropriate to support probable subsequent procedures. Further efficiencies may be obtained by consolidating the review of general controls related to more than one application. Conversely, if the review of general controls is poorly planned, the findings may or may not complement the application reviews and other planned audit procedures.

In designing Phase II procedures, the auditor must consider the effort required to test controls relative to the expected reduction in Phase III procedures. In addition, the auditor should consider whether testing the results of computer processing might be better than testing controls. For example, the auditor might use generalized computer audit software to test transactions for invalid data, rather than test the controls to prevent the entry of invalid data.

In Phase III, the auditor should consider whether the use of the computer could make the audit more effective or economical. For example, the computer might be used for simple but time-consuming tasks such as footing files or for more complex tasks such as the recomputation of interest.

In all three phases, the auditor's appropriate level of EDP audit expertise must be considered. In certain situations, the degree of audit complexity will require the participation of auditors with more advanced EDP audit skills; however, in many situations, participation by auditors with knowledge of traditional manual procedures and less technically complex EDP audit procedures may be sufficient.

Performing Reviews of EDP Internal Controls

Overall materiality guidelines, material types of transactions, and potential material errors are identified early in the audit process. Significant EDP applications are then identified, and an internal control review is completed for each significant EDP application. During such an internal control review, the auditor typically performs the following steps:

1. He conducts a preliminary review of the application to determine the flow of transactions, the extent of EDP use, and the basic structure of internal accounting control.
2. He assesses the significance of internal accounting control within EDP in relation to the entire system of internal accounting control.

3. He conducts a preliminary review of general EDP controls to determine whether weak general controls might affect application controls, or whether general controls might complement the overall control of the application under review.

4. He determines the appropriate extent of additional control review. If no reliance upon controls is planned, he identifies errors and irregularities that could occur; determines the effect of potential errors on the nature, timing, and extent of subsequent audit procedures; and discontinues the control review.

5. If reliance on application or general controls is planned, he completes the control review for the specific controls to be relied upon.

6. If controls still appear reliable, he performs compliance tests of controls.

7. He evaluates internal control, identifying errors and irregularities that could occur, controls that would prevent or detect these errors, and potential errors and irregularities not covered by existing controls. He also determines the effect of potential errors and EDP control strengths and weaknesses on the nature, timing, and extent of subsequent audit procedures.

An AICPA audit and accounting guide, *The Auditor's Study and Evaluation of Internal Control in EDP Systems* (1977a), includes specific points that may be considered during the preliminary phase of an EDP control review:

1. To understand the flow of transactions:
   a. application documentation
   b. activities and source documents that start transaction flow
   c. non-EDP processing applied to source documents
   d. conversion of data into machine-sensible form
   e. flow of machine-sensible transactions
   f. master files that supply additional information
   g. procedures for the correction of errors
   h. output files created, or master files updated
   i. output reports
   j. non-EDP processing of output reports.

2. To understand the extent of EDP utilization:
   a. number and types of transactions processed
   b. total dollar value of each type of transaction
   c. the extent and nature of EDP processing
   d. division of EDP and non-EDP transaction flow.

3. To understand the basic structure of accounting control:
   a. controls that are provided
   b. EDP and non-EDP division of control responsibility
   c. relationships between manual and EDP-based controls
   d. nature, extent, and availability of the audit trail.

The AICPA guide suggests that the following application control review points may be considered during both the preliminary review and in the optional completion review:

4. Input controls, to assure that data are:
   a. properly authorized
   b. accurately converted into machine-sensible form
   c. identified
   d. not lost
   e. not suppressed
   f. not incorrectly added
   g. not duplicated
   h. not improperly changed.

5. Processing controls to assure that:
   a. EDP has been performed as intended
   b. all transactions are processed as authorized
   c. authorized transactions are not omitted
   d. no unauthorized transactions are added.

6. Output controls to assure:
   a. the accuracy of the processing result
   b. that only authorized personnel receive the output.

The AICPA guide suggests that the following general EDP controls may be considered in the preliminary and completion phases of reviews:

7. Organizational controls to provide for:
   a. adequate supervision
   b. segregation of functions within EDP
   c. segregation of functions between EDP and users.

8. Controls over systems development.

9. Controls over access to system documentation.

10. Control over computer operations, including access to data files and programs.

11. Controls to assure completion of file reconstruction and processing recoveries.

12. Internal auditors' involvement in the review and testing of EDP accounting controls.

The AICPA guide recognizes that the controls to be reviewed in any given situation are a matter of audit judgment, and does not identify individual controls that must be considered during either the preliminary or completion phases of the review.

Preliminary review inquiries and observations (e.g., Do there appear to be controls to prevent lost transactions?) typically result in yes-or-no findings. If the review continues into the completion phase, inquiries and observations seek specific information on controls and possible sources of audit evidence (e.g., What are the specific features of the control procedures that prevent or detect lost transactions? What evidence will demonstrate that these controls are in use and effective?). The purpose of the preliminary review is to understand the transaction flow and the extent of EDP use, and to determine if controls over EDP appear to be present. The purpose of the completion phase is to identify the control characteristics and related sources of evidence for specific controls in anticipation of control testing and reliance upon specific tested controls.

During the preliminary review, the auditor gathers information through discussions with data center and user-department staff; through observations; or through the review of system documentation, flowcharts, job descriptions, organization charts, policy statements, operating procedures, or control procedures. The accuracy of this information is typically verified by tracing the flow of a limited number of sample transactions through both the EDP and non-EDP segments of an application. This tracing procedure is often called a *system walk-through*. During the completion phase of the review, the auditor expands the extent of the discussions and observations, and specifically observes controls that might be tested and relied upon.

Both the preliminary and completion phases of an EDP application control review occur in Phase I of the overall audit process. In Phase II, the auditor may or may not perform tests of controls over EDP. During Phase II the auditor may also use audit software or manual techniques to test transactions for evidence of control weaknesses. In Phase III, EDP-related audit procedures shift from control evaluation to the use of the computer as an audit tool. For example, audit software may be used to analyze the accounts receivable file and to select items for confirmation.

Factors That Affect Audit Complexity

Understanding EDP audit complexity and the related levels of skill and effort required to accomplish various EDP audit procedures is critical to the planning process. It is usually not practical to classify EDP audit procedure complexity only in terms of EDP complexity, such as computer size or type of processing. Using this classification approach, an on-line application that operates on a large computer would always be a complex audit situation, but this may not be true. The degree of audit complexity is influenced by many factors, which are presented below.

EDP Complexity. If an application involves complex telecommunications hardware and software, a very large computer, and complex database software, an auditor may require advanced EDP skills just to understand and verify transaction flow and the content of data files.

Application Complexity. If applications involve multiple transaction types, complex calculations, and updates using master files, significant effort may be required to understand the accounting implications of the application.

Decentralization. If source data originate at a variety of remote locations, the auditor is concerned that all data arrive at the processing location. If data conversion is performed at remote locations, the review of conversion procedures and related source documents may be difficult and time-consuming. If processing occurs at multiple locations, the auditor must consider whether the processing and controls are identical.

Nature of Application Controls. If an application is characterized by strong user-oriented application controls, control testing and reliance is typically not technically difficult. For example, in a telecommunications application, lost transactions may be prevented by complex hardware and software controls that are difficult to understand and test. However, lost transactions may be detected by simple user-department control totals that are easy to understand and test.

Strength of General EDP Controls. Even if general EDP controls are excellent, auditors typically will not rely exclusively on them. However, if they are weak, auditors must consider whether they reduce the effectiveness of otherwise strong application controls.

Nature of Compensating Controls. The influence of compensating controls varies considerably. Controls such as supervision and rotation of duties have a positive but general effect. Certain other compensating controls, such as detailed internal audit reviews, can be used to control more specific exposures.

Availability of Audit Evidence. An EDP application can usually be audited by traditional manual procedures if the application is characterized by transaction listings, detailed reports, and documented user-oriented controls. However, if this type of audit evidence is not available, technically complex procedures may be required.

Stability. If there are no new EDP applications and old applications have not been modified, audit procedures used in prior years are probably still effective. However, in a dynamic EDP environment, auditors must always review the extent of change; and they may also have to review system development and maintenance controls, system conversion controls, and possibly, new applications while they are still under development.

Audit Objectives. Specific audit objectives can have a substantial impact on overall audit effort. For example, it is easier to identify and test controls that detect the loss of a transaction than those that should prevent the processing of an unauthorized transaction.

Applications Processed by Computer Service Centers

Many organizations that do not have their own computer use independent computer service centers to process their accounting data. These service centers may be other organizations with surplus computing capacity, subsidiaries of banks, or organizations exclusively devoted to this type of activity.

Neither the nature of EDP nor how the auditor audits is changed if an organization uses a service center. The same EDP errors may occur, and the same types of controls may be used to prevent, detect, and correct errors. The auditor must develop the same level of understanding of the processing, and he has the same option to rely or not rely on EDP controls.

There are, however, practical differences. Generally, the computer user has less influence as to the extent of EDP controls to be employed. If a particular application is designed specifically for the user, the user can and should insist on controls that will address all significant application exposures. Frequently, however, users are only offered existing application packages and do not have the option to add controls. This does not, of course, preclude the implementation of user-oriented controls such as system balancing and reasonableness reviews of processing results. In either case, the user typically cannot influence the degree or type of general controls used within the data center.

Use of a computer service center does not change the independent auditor's responsibilities; AU 321 specifically applies to significant accounting applications processed by service centers. The auditor must understand the flow of transactions, the extent of EDP use, and the basic structure of accounting control. The appropriate extent of the auditor's review of processing and controls depends upon application complexity and the auditor's intention to rely or not rely on controls. In certain cases, an extensive review of service center processing and controls may be required. In most cases, however, processing is not complex, and the auditor does not need to place heavy reliance on service center controls; therefore, extensive reviews at the service center are typically not performed.

When a service center processes applications for many different users, it is inconvenient and expensive for every user's auditor to conduct reviews at the data center independently. In this situation, the service center may retain an independent auditor to review their service center or specific applications and to issue a report that includes the scope and conclusions of this review. This type of review is frequently called a *third-party review*. The requirements for conducting and using third-party reviews are included in the AICPA audit guide, *Audits of Service-Center-Produced Records* (1974b). When auditors are conducting a regular audit for a client who uses a service center and a third-party audit report is available, the auditors must decide whether the contents of the third-party report complement their intended audit approach and to what extent they can rely on the third-party audit report.

SUGGESTED READING

Biggs, Charles; Birks, Evan; and Atkins, William. *Managing the Systems Development Process.* Englewood Cliffs, N.J.: Prentice-Hall, 1979. This book presents practical advice on how to direct and control system development projects.

Institute of Internal Auditors. *How to Acquire and Use Generalized Audit Software.* Altamonte Springs, Fla.: 1979. This book is part of the Modern Concepts in Internal Auditing series and gives practical advice on how to acquire and use audit software.

Mair, William; Wood, Donald; and Davis, Keagle. *Computer Control and Audit.* 2nd ed. Altamonte Springs, Fla.: Institute of Internal Auditors, 1976. This book is a comprehensive reference manual useful to beginning and experienced EDP auditors.

Martin, James. *Security, Accuracy, and Privacy in Computer Systems.* Englewood Cliffs, N.J.: Prentice-Hall, 1973. This book presents in-depth coverage of computer exposures and controls.

Parker, Donn. *Crime by Computer.* New York: Charles Scribner's Sons, 1976. This is interesting and informative coverage of computer fraud and other computer abuses.

Porter, Thomas, and Perry, William. *EDP Controls and Auditing.* 2nd ed. Belmont, Ca.: Wadsworth Publishing Company, 1977. This book is for individuals who are just beginning their study of EDP controls and EDP auditing.

APPENDIX 15-A　　APPLICATION CONTROL EVALUATION TABLES

APPLICATION CONTROL EVALUATION TABLE

RELIANCE ON CONTROLS
3 — Reliably controls applicable cause
2 — Controls cause but should be accompanied by additional controls
1 — Useful but not especially effective
Blank — No significant contribution

EXPOSURES
Erroneous record keeping
Unacceptable accounting
Business interruption
Erroneous management decisions
Fraud
Statutory sanctions
Excessive costs/deficient revenues
Loss or destruction of assets
Competitive disadvantage

APPLICATION CAUSES OF EXPOSURES

PREVENTION CONTROLS	REFERENCE	INPUT — LOST	INPUT — DUPLICATED	INPUT — INACCURATE	INPUT — MISSING DATA	INPUT — TRANSACTIONS NEVER RECORDED	INPUT — BLANKET AUTHORIZE	INPUT — INITIATED INTERNALLY	PROC — WRONG FILE	PROC — WRONG RECORD	PROC — INCOMPLETE	PROC — INCORRECT	PROC — UNTIMELY	PROC — INAPPROPRIATE	PROC — FILE LOST	PROC — PROGRAM LOST	PROC — PEOPLE LOST	OUT — IMPROPERLY DISTRIBUTED	OUT — LATE OR LOST	OUT — ERRONEOUS BUT PLAUSIBLE	OUT — OBVIOUSLY ERRONEOUS	OUT — EXCESSIVE ERROR CORRECTION	OUT — UNSUPPORTABLE	OTHER — SHADOW SYSTEM	OTHER — UNLIMITED ACCESS	OTHER — MANAGEMENT OVERRIDE
Definition of responsibilities		1	2	2	2	2	2	2	1	1	2	2	2	1	2	1	1	1	2	1	2	2	2	2	2	1
Reliability of personnel		1	1	1	2	1			1	1	2	2	2	1	2	1	2	2	1	2	2	2	2	2	2	1
Training		1	2	1	2	2			2	1	2	2	2	2	2	1	1	2	1	2	2	2	2	2	2	2
Competence				2	1	1			1	2	2	2	3	2		1		2	1	2	1	2	1	2	2	2
Mechanization		2	2	2	1			3	1	1	2		1			1		2		1			1	1		
Segregation of duties														2												
Rotation of duties			2	1	2	2			1	1	2		1	2		1	2	2	2	2		1			2	1
Standardization		1	2	1	1				2	1	1		1			2	2	1	1	2	1	1			2	1
Authorization		2	2	2	2	2			2					2		2	2	2		2	2	2			2	2
Secure custody		1													2	2	1	1	1					2	3	1
Dual custody		1				1									2	2		2	1						3	
Forms design		2	2	2	2				2	2	2	2						2		1	2	1	1			
Prenumbered		2	2			2		2			2		2	2		1	2	2	2		1	2	1	1		
Preprinted			3	2					2				2			2	2			1	2	1	2			
Simultaneous preparation		2	2	2	2	1				2		2		2	2		2			1	1	1	1		2	
Turnaround document				2	2								2				2	2					2			
Drum card					1																					
Endorsement		2		2							2	2		2						2						
Cancellation																										
Documentation		2	2	2	2	2			2		2	1	1	2	2	2	2	2	1	2	2	2	3		2	
Exception input							1	2	1		2			2		2				2	1					
Default option							1				2			2												2
Passwords		2	3	3	3	3	2	2	3	3	3	3	3	3	3	3	3	2	2	3	2	2	3	1	3	2

EXPOSURES

		LOST	DUPLICATED	INACCURATE	MISSING DATA	TRANS NEVER REC	BLANKET AUTH	INIT INTERNALLY	WRONG FILE	WRONG RECORD	INCOMPLETE	INCORRECT	UNTIMELY	INAPPROPRIATE	FILE LOST	PROGRAM LOST	PEOPLE LOST	IMPROP DISTRIB	LATE OR LOST	ERRON BUT PLAUS	OBVIOUSLY ERRON	EXCESS ERR CORR	UNSUPPORTABLE	SHADOW SYSTEM	UNLIMITED ACCESS	MGMT OVERRIDE
Erroneous record keeping		2	1	1	1	1	1	1	2	2	3	3	3	3	2	2	2	2	2	3	3	2	2	1	3	1
Unacceptable accounting		1	2	1	1	1	2	2	2	2	1	2	2	3	2	2	2	2	2	2	2	2	2	1	1	1
Business interruption		2	2	2	2	2	1	1	2	2	2	1	1	3	2	3	2	2	2	3	1	2	1	1	2	2
Erroneous management decisions		2	2	2	2	2	1	1	2	2	1	1	2	2	2	2	2	2	2	3	1	2	2	1	2	1
Fraud		2	2	2	1	1	1	2	2	1	2	1	1	1	2	2	3	2	2	2	1	1	3	1	2	1
Statutory sanctions		2	2	2	1	2	1	1	2	2	2	1	1	2	2	3	3	2	2	2	2	3	3	3	1	1
Excessive costs/deficient revenues		2	2	2	2	2	1	1	2	2	2	2	2	2	2	2	1	2	2	2	2	2	1	2	2	1
Loss or destruction of assets		2	2	2	2	1	1	1	2	2	2	1	1	2	2	2	1	2	2	2	1	1	2	1	1	1
Competitive disadvantage		2	2	2	2	1	1	1	3	2	2	1	1	2	2	3	2	2	2	2	2	3	2	2	1	1

3 — Very likely to occur
2 — Likely to occur
1 — May occur
Blank — Generally little effect

Warning: Reliance and impact relationships must be tailored to individual circumstances.

© Touche Ross & Co.

Page 1

APPLICATION CONTROL EVALUATION TABLE

APPLICATION CAUSES OF EXPOSURES

DETECTION CONTROLS	REFERENCE	LOST	DUPLICATED	INACCURATE	MISSING DATA	NEVER RECORDED	BLANKET AUTHORIZE	INITIATED INTERNALLY	WRONG FILE	WRONG RECORD	INCOMPLETE	INCORRECT	UNTIMELY	INAPPROPRIATE	FILE LOST	PROGRAM LOST	PEOPLE LOST	IMPROPERLY DISTRIBUTED	LATE OR LOST	ERRONEOUS BUT PLAUSIBLE	OBVIOUSLY ERRONEOUS	EXCESSIVE ERROR CORRECTION	UNSUPPORTABLE	SHADOW SYSTEM	UNLIMITED ACCESS	MANAGEMENT OVERRIDE
						INPUT					PROCESSING								OUTPUT					OTHER		
Anticipation		3				3					3		1		2	2	2	3	3							
Transmittal document		2	2	2							2							2								
Batch serial numbers		3	3						2						3											
Control register		2	2	2					2		2				2											
Amount control totals		3	3	2					3		3	2														
Document control count		3	3						2			1														
Line control count		3	3						2		2	1														
Hash totals		3	3	2					3		2	1														
Batch totals		3	3	2					3		2	2														
Batch balancing		3	3	2					3		2	2														
Visual verification		1	1	2					2	1	1	1		1				2			3					
Sequence check		2	2	1		2					2	2	2		1											
Overflow check				2							2	2	2	2		2										
Format check				2							2	2														
Completeness check				2							2	2	2	2	1	2				1	2					
Check digit				3							2															
Reasonableness		1	2	2	2			2	2	2	2	2	1	2							2					1
Limit check				2				2	1			2									2					
Validity check				2					2																	
Readback		2		3	2									2							2					
Dating			1			2			2				2	2	2								1			
Expiration			2			2			2					2	1											
Keystroke verification				2	2																					
Approval			1	2	2		2		2		1	2	1	2							3		3	2	3	1
Run-to-run totals									3		3	2			3						3					

IMPACT OF CAUSES

																											EXPOSURES
		3	3	3	3	3	2	2	3	3	3	3	3	3	3			2	2	2	3	2	2	1	1	1	1	Erroneous record keeping
3 — Very likely to occur							2	2				2	2	3				2			2		2			1	Unacceptable accounting
2 — Likely to occur		1	1	1	1		1				1	1	1	1	2	2	2	2	2	2	1	2	1		2	1	Business interruption
1 — May occur		2	2	2	2	2	1	1	2	1	2	2	2	2	2	2	2	2	2	3	1	2	1	1		1	Erroneous management decisions
Blank — Generally little effect			1	1	1	1	1	1		1	1	1		1			1	2	1	1	1	1	2	1	2	1	Fraud
		2		1	1	1	1		1	1	1	1	1	1	1		1	1	1	1	1	1	3		1	1	Statutory sanctions
		2	2	2	2			1	2	2	2	2	1	2	2	3	3	2	2	2	2	3		3	1	1	Excessive costs/deficient revenues
							1	1	2	2		2		2	2		1	1	1						2	1	Loss or destruction of assets
		1	1	1	1	1			1	1	1	1	1	1	1	1	1	1	1	1	1	1			1	1	Competitive disadvantage

RELIANCE ON CONTROLS
3 — Reliably controls applicable cause
2 — Controls cause but should be accompanied by additional controls
1 — Useful but not especially effective
Blank — No significant contribution

Warning: Reliance and impact relationships must be tailored to individual circumstances.

© Touche Ross & Co.

AUDITING IN AN EDP ENVIRONMENT

APPLICATION CONTROL EVALUATION TABLE

APPLICATION CAUSES OF EXPOSURES

RELIANCE ON CONTROLS
3 — Reliably controls applicable cause
2 — Controls cause but should be accompanied by additional controls
1 — Useful but not especially effective
Blank — No significant contribution

Causes legend
3 — Very likely to occur
2 — Likely to occur
1 — May occur
Blank — Generally little effect

EXPOSURES
Erroneous record keeping
Unacceptable accounting
Business interruption
Erroneous management decisions
Fraud
Statutory sanctions
Excessive costs/deficient revenues
Loss or destruction of assets
Competitive disadvantage

DETECTION CONTROLS (continued)	INPUT — LOST	DUPLICATED	INACCURATE	MISSING DATA	NEVER RECORDED	BLANKET AUTHORIZE	INITIATED INTERNALLY	PROCESSING — WRONG FILE	WRONG RECORD	INCOMPLETE	INCORRECT	UNTIMELY	INAPPROPRIATE	FILE LOST	PROGRAM LOST	PEOPLE LOST	IMPROPERLY DISTRIBUTED	OUTPUT — LATE OR LOST	ERRONEOUS BUT PLAUSIBLE	OBVIOUSLY ERRONEOUS	EXCESSIVE ERROR CORRECTION	UNSUPPORTABLE	OTHER — SHADOW SYSTEM	UNLIMITED ACCESS	MANAGEMENT OVERRIDE
Balancing	2	2	2	1	2			3	3	3	2		1							3		2			1
Reconciliation	2	2	2	1	2			3	2	2	2	2	1								2	1		3	
Aging	2	2	1	2	2				2	2	2	2	1								2				
Suspense file	2	2		2	2				2	2	1	2	1						2			1			
Suspense account	2	2		2								2	1									2			
Matching	3	3	3	2	2			3	3	2	2	2	2	2	2		2	2	2	3	2	3	2		
Clearing account	2	2	2	2	1		3			2	1	2	1				2					1			
Tickler file	2	2	3	2				3	2	3	2	2	2	2	2		2	2	2	3	2	3	2	3	1
Periodic audit	2	2		2	2	2					1		2	2										1	
Redundant process		1	2	2				2	2	3				2			2								
Summary process	1	1	1	2	1			3	3	3				2											
Label								2	2																
Trailer record	2	2	1	1				3																1	

CORRECTION CONTROLS	LOST	DUPLICATED	INACCURATE	MISSING DATA	NEVER RECORDED	BLANKET AUTHORIZE	INITIATED INTERNALLY	WRONG FILE	WRONG RECORD	INCOMPLETE	INCORRECT	UNTIMELY	INAPPROPRIATE	FILE LOST	PROGRAM LOST	PEOPLE LOST	IMPROPERLY DISTRIBUTED	LATE OR LOST	ERRONEOUS BUT PLAUSIBLE	OBVIOUSLY ERRONEOUS	EXCESSIVE ERROR CORRECTION	UNSUPPORTABLE	SHADOW SYSTEM	UNLIMITED ACCESS	MANAGEMENT OVERRIDE
Discrepancy reports	2	3	3	3	3	2	2	3	3	3	3	3	3	3	3	3	2	2	3	3	2	2		2	1
Transaction trail		1	1	1		2	2			2	2	2	2	3	3	2	2		2	2	3	2	1	1	1
Error source statistics	2	2	2	2		1	1	2	2	2	2	2	2	2	2	2	1	2	2	2	3	2	1	2	1
Automated error correction		1	2	2		1		2	2	2	2	2	2	1	2	2	1	1	2	2		1			
Upstream resubmission	2	1				1	1			1	1	1	1			1	1	2	1	2	2	2	1	2	1
Backup and recovery	3	2					1	2	2	2	2	2	2	3	3	3	2	2	2	2	2	3	1	2	1

Warning: Reliance and impact relationships must be tailored to individual circumstances.

© Touche Ross & Co.   Page 3

Explanation of Application Controls

Preventive Controls	*Explanations*
Definition of Responsibilities	Descriptions of tasks for each job function within an information processing system that indicate clear beginning and termination points for each job function and cover the relationship of job functions to each other.
Reliability of Personnel	Personnel performing the processing can be relied upon to treat data in a consistent manner.
Training	Personnel are provided explicit instructions and tested for their understanding before being assigned new duties.
Competence of Personnel	Persons assigned to processing or supervisory roles within information systems have the technical knowledge necessary to perform their functions.
Mechanization	Consistency is provided by mechanical or electronic processing.
Segregation of Duties	Responsibility for custody and accountability for handling and processing of data are separated.
Rotation of Duties	Jobs assigned to people are rotated periodically at irregularly scheduled times, if possible, for key processing functions.
Standardization	Uniform, structured, and consistent procedures are developed for all processing.
Authorization	Limits the initiation of a transaction or performance of a process to the selected individuals.
Secure Custody	Information assets are provided security similar to tangible assets such as cash, negotiable securities, etc.
Dual Custody	Two independent, simultaneous actions or conditions are required before processing is permitted.
Forms Design	Forms are self-explanatory, understandable, concise, and gather all necessary information with a minimum of effort.
Prenumbered Forms	Sequential numbers on individual forms printed in advance so as to allow subsequent detection of loss or misplacement.
Preprinted Forms	Fixed elements of information are entered on forms in advance and sometimes in a

Preventive Controls	*Explanations*
	format that permits direct machine processing so as to prevent errors in entry of repetitive data.
Simultaneous Preparation	The one-time recording of a transaction for all further processing, using multiple copies, as appropriate, to prevent transcription errors.
Turnaround Document	A computer-produced document that is intended for resubmission into the system.
Drum Card	Automatic spacing and format shifting of data fields on a keypunch machine.
Endorsement	Marking a form or document to direct or restrict its further use in processing.
Cancellation	Identifies transaction documents to prevent further or repeated use after they have performed their function.
Documentation	Written records for the purpose of providing communication.
Exception Input	Internally initiated processing in a predefined manner unless specifically input transactions specify processing with different values or in a different manner.
Default Option	The automatic utilization of a predefined value in situations where input transactions have certain values left blank.
Passwords	Authorization to allow access to data or processes by providing a signal or "password" known only to authorized individuals.
Detective Controls	
Anticipation	The expectation of a given transaction or event at a particular time.
Transmittal Document	The medium for communicating control totals over movement of data, particularly from source to processing point or between processing points.
Batch Serial Numbers	Batches of transaction documents are numbered consecutively and accounted for.
Control Register	A log or register indicating the disposition and control values of batches or transactions.
Amount Control Total	Totals of homogeneous amounts for a group of transactions or records, usually dollars or quantities.

Document Control Count	A count of the number of individual documents.
Line Control Count	A count of the individual line items on one or more documents.
Hash Total	A meaningless, but useful, total developed from the accumulated numerical amounts of nonmonetary information.
Batch Totals	Any type of control total or count applied to a specific number of transaction documents or to the transaction documents that arrive within a specific period of time.
Batch Balancing	A comparison of the items or documents actually processed against a predetermined control total.
Visual Verification	The visual scanning of documents for general reasonableness and propriety.
Sequence Checking	A verification of the alphanumeric sequence of the "key" field in items to be processed.
Overflow Checks	A limit check based upon the capacity of a memory or file area to accept data.
Format Checks	Determination that data are entered in the proper mode—numeric or alphanumeric—within designated fields of information.
Completeness Check	A test that data entries are made in fields that cannot be processed in a blank state.
Check Digit	One digit, usually the last, of an identifying field is a mathematical function of all of the other digits in the field. This value can be calculated from the other digits in the field and compared with the check digit to verify validity of the whole field.
Reasonableness	Tests applied to various fields of data through comparison with other information available within the transaction or master records.
Limit Check	Tests of specified amount fields against stipulated high or low limits of acceptability. When both high and low values are used, the test may be called a "range check."
Validity Check	The characters in a coded field are either matched to an acceptable set of values in a table or examined for a defined pattern or format, legitimate subcodes, or character values, using logic and arithmetic rather than tables.

Detective Controls	*Explanations*
Read Back	Immediate return of input information to the sender for comparison and approval.
Dating	The recording of calendar dates for purposes of later comparison or expiration testing.
Expiration	A limit check based on a comparison of current date with the date recorded on a transaction, record, or file.
Keystroke Verification	The redundant entry of data into keyboards so as to verify the accuracy of a prior entry. Differences between the data previously recorded and the data entered in verification will cause a mechanical signal.
Approval	The acceptance of a transaction for processing after it has been initiated.
Run-to-Run Totals	The utilization of output control totals resulting from one process as input control totals over subsequent processing. The control totals are used as links in a chain to tie one process to another in a sequence of processes or one cycle to another over a period of time.
Balancing	A test for equality between the values of two equivalent sets of items or one set of items and a control total. Any difference indicates an error.
Reconciliation	An identification and analysis of differences between the values contained in two substantially identical files or between a detail file and a control total. Errors are identified according to the nature of the reconciling items rather than the existence of a difference between the balances.
Aging	Identification of unprocessed or retained items in files according to their date, usually transaction date. The aging classifies items according to various ranges of dates.
Suspense File	A file containing unprocessed or partially processed items awaiting further action.
Suspense Account	A control total for items awaiting further processing.
Matching	Matching of items from the processing stream of an application with others developed independently so as to identify items unprocessed through either of the parallel systems.

Clearing Account	An amount that results from the processing of independent items of equivalent value. Net control value should equal zero.
Tickler File	A control file consisting of items sequenced by age for follow-up purposes. Such files are usually manual.
Periodic Audit	A verification of a file or a phase of processing intended to check for problems and encourage future compliance with control procedures.
Redundant Processing	A repetition of processing and an accompanying comparison of individual results for equality.
Summary Processing	A redundant process using a summarized amount. This is compared for equality with a control total from the processing of the detailed items.
Label	The external or internal identification of transaction batches or files according to source, application, date, or other identifying characteristics.
Trailer Record	A record providing a control total for comparison with accumulated counts or values of records processed.

Corrective Controls

Discrepancy Reports	A listing of items that have violated some detective control and require further investigation.
Transaction Trail	The availability of a manual or machine-readable means for tracing the status and contents of an individual transaction record backward or forward between output, processing, and source.
Error-Source Statistics	Accumulation of information on type of error and origin. This is used to determine the nature of remedial training needed to reduce the number of errors.
Automated Error Correction	Automatic error correction of transactions or records that violate a detective control.
Upstream Resubmission	The resubmission of corrected error transactions so that they pass through all or more of the detective controls than are exercised over normal transactions (e.g., before input editing).
Backup and Recovery	The ability to recreate current master files using appropriate prior master records and transactions.

APPENDIX 15-B   IPF CONTROL EVALUATION TABLES

IPF CONTROL EVALUATION TABLE

RELIANCE ON CONTROLS
3 — Reliably controls applicable cause
2 — Controls cause but should be accompanied by additional controls
1 — Useful but not especially effective
Blank — No significant contribution

CAUSES OF IPF EXPOSURES

PREVENTION CONTROLS	REFERENCE	HUMAN ERRORS				HARDWARE/SOFTWARE FAILURES			COMPUTER ABUSE							CATASTROPHE			
		DATA ENTRY	CONSOLE ENTRY	WRONG FILE OR PROGRAM	FILE DAMAGED	INTERRUPT OPERATION	LOSS OF DATA	LOGIC ERROR	THEFT	EMBEZZLEMENT	FRAUD	ESPIONAGE	INVASION OF PRIVACY	MALICIOUSNESS	MISCHIEVOUSNESS	FIRE	WATER	WIND	CIVIL DISORDER
Definition of duties		1	1	1	1					1	2	1	2						
Segregation of duties		2	2	2	2				2	2	2	2	2						
Reliable personnel		2	2	2					2	2	2	2							
Competent personnel		2	2	1	1				1	2		1				1	1		
Job rotation									1										
Housekeeping				1	1											1			
Equipment maintenance						2	2	3						1	2	1			
Air conditioning						1	1	1											
Scheduling			2	2						2			2						3
Limited physical access									2	2	2	2	2	2	2	2	2		
Restricted knowledge			2	2	1			1		2	2	2	2	2	2	1	1		
File custodian									2	2	2	2	2	2	2	2	2		2
Physical security				1				1	2	2		1				2	2		
External labels			2	2				1		1		1		1	1				
Internal labels			2	2			1	1		1		1		1	1				
Protect rings			2	2			1	1											
Disk enable								1					2		1				1
Containerized operations		2	2	2	2	2	2	1	1	2	2	2	2	1	1	1	1		
Training																			
Authorization						2	2	3		2	2	2	2	1	1				
Manufacturer design		2	1			1	1	1	1	1		2	2	2	1	2	3	3	2
Physical structure						2	2	1	1	1		2	3	2	1	2	2	2	2
Physical location		2																	2

IMPACT OF CAUSES
3 — Very likely to occur
2 — Likely to occur
1 — May occur
Blank — Generally little effect

	DATA ENTRY	CONSOLE ENTRY	WRONG FILE OR PROGRAM	FILE DAMAGED	INTERRUPT OPERATION	LOSS OF DATA	LOGIC ERROR	THEFT	EMBEZZLEMENT	FRAUD	ESPIONAGE	INVASION OF PRIVACY	MALICIOUSNESS	MISCHIEVOUSNESS	FIRE	WATER	WIND	CIVIL DISORDER
Erroneous record keeping	2	2	1	2	1	2	1	1	1				1	1	1	1		
Unacceptable accounting	1	1	2	2	3	2	1						1	1				
Business interruption													3	1	3	3	3	3
Erroneous management decisions													2		1		2	
Fraud									3	3	2	3	2					
Statutory sanctions	2	2	2	2	2	2	2	2	3	2	2	3	3	2	3	3	2	3
Excessive costs	2	2	2	2	2	2	1	2	3	2	1	1	2	1	3	3	2	2
Loss or destruction of assets	2	2	2	2	2	2		2	3	2					3	2	2	2
Competitive disadvantage											2				2			

EXPOSURES
Erroneous record keeping
Unacceptable accounting
Business interruption
Erroneous management decisions
Fraud
Statutory sanctions
Excessive costs
Loss or destruction of assets
Competitive disadvantage

Warning: Reliance and impact relationships must be tailored to individual circumstances.

© Touche Ross & Co.   Page 1

CAUSES OF IPF EXPOSURES

	HUMAN ERRORS				HARDWARE/SOFT-WARE FAILURES			COMPUTER ABUSE							CATASTROPHE			
REFERENCE	DATA ENTRY	CONSOLE ENTRY	WRONG FILE OR PROGRAM	FILE DAMAGED	INTERRUPT OPERATION	LOSS OF DATA	LOGIC ERROR	THEFT	EMBEZZLEMENT	FRAUD	ESPIONAGE	INVASION OF PRIVACY	MALICIOUSNESS	MISCHIEVOUSNESS	FIRE	WATER	WIND	CIVIL DISORDER
DETECTION CONTROLS																		
Supervision	2	2	2	2				2	2	2	1	1	2	2				2
Budgets	2	2	1	2				2	2	1	1	1						
Management reporting	2	2	2	2	1			1	1	1	1	1	1	1				
Operator logs				1		2	1											
Console logs (job journal)	1	2	2		2	1	2	1	2	1	2	2	2	2				
Library logs	2	2	2	2		2	1	1	1	1	1	1	1	1				
Control logs	2	2	3					1	1	1								
Keystroke verification	2																	
Hardware checks	1	2	2	2		2	2											
Operating system checks	1	1	1	2		1		1										
Scan output	1																	
Fire detectors															3			
Application controls	3	2	3	2	2	3	2	2	2	2			2	2		2		2
CORRECTION CONTROLS																		
Recovery plan				2	2	2		1					2	2	2	2	2	2
File histories	2	1	1	1	1	1	1	1	2	2			2	2	2	2		
Error statistics													2	2	2			
Fire extinguishers															2			
On-premises backup	2	3	3	3		3		2					2	2	3	3	3	3
Off-premises backup								2	2	2	1		2	1	2	2	3	3
Discharge personnel	1							2	2	2	1	1	2	2	2	2	2	2
Insurance					2										2			
Uninterruptable power					2	2	1	1					1	1	2	2		2

Warning: Reliance and impact relationships must be tailored to individual circumstances.

© Touche Ross & Co.

Page 2

Explanation of IPF Controls

Preventive Controls	*Explanations*
Definition of Duties	Description of tasks for each job function identifying the responsibilities, functions and relationships of all duties.
Segregation of Duties	Assignment of job responsibilities designed to separate and avoid incompatible duties and conflicts of interest.
Reliable Personnel	Personnel performing their assigned duties can be relied upon to complete their daily tasks in a consistent quality manner.
Competent Personnel	Personnel assigned to operate the computer and control the processing have the technical knowledge necessary to perform their functions.
Job Rotation	Jobs assigned to people are rotated periodically at irregular intervals, if possible, for the processing of sensitive systems.
Housekeeping	Keeping the production areas of a data center neat, tidy, and organized to minimize hazards and the likelihood of confusion.
Equipment Maintenance	Computer hardware is kept in workable condition by qualified personnel on a regular (preventive) and as required (remedial) basis.
Air-Conditioning	The air in the computer room is maintained within limited temperature and humidity ranges as recommended by the computer manufacturer.
Scheduling	Jobs to be run on the computer are identified and placed on a log in priority order.
Limited Physical Access	Avenues of access to the computer room and file library are limited by design and by security measures that prevent unauthorized access.
Restricted Knowledge	Only qualified personnel within the technical data center functions possess knowledge on a need to know basis of run procedure, security, file access, etc.
File Custody	Computer files are maintained in a library and accounted for when they are not scheduled for processing.
Physical Security	The security of the building is sufficient to prevent environmental events that could occur in that location.

External Labels	Visual identification of a file includes file number, volume number, file name, creation date, purge date, and storage location.
Internal Labels	The external label information is also kept on the electronic media itself to be programmatically checked and verified by the application program.
Protect Rings	Write rings are placed into tapes so that the tape drive can copy information onto the tape. Without the ring, the hardware is prohibited by design from the writing function.
Disk Enable	A device on some disk drives that inhibits the write function.
Containerized Operations	The computer room is bounded by sturdy and resistant walls that limit the spread of fire, access, etc.
Training	Personnel are provided explicit instructions and tested for their understanding before being assigned the responsibilities of their positions.
Authorization	Only those persons with a need to know are permitted physical access, file access, or knowledge about operation activities.
Manufacturer Design	Manufacturer controls such as equipment testing that produce a reliable product.
Physical Structure	The computer room and library areas are constructed of durable quality in keeping with the value of the equipment and data that is being protected.
Physical Location	The data center is situated in a geographical location to minimize natural disasters.

Detective Controls

Supervision	Responsibilities of supervising the computer operations area include approving the schedules, monitoring daily operations, observing the activities of initiating and shutting down the equipment, reviewing the daily operations reports (manual and automated) and following up on all problem areas until resolved.
Budgets	Establishment of cost accountabilities for the production aspects of a data center.
Management Reporting	Reporting of accomplishments, activity completed, projected tasks, and outstanding problems to each level of the organizational structure.

Detective Controls	*Explanation*
Operator Logs	Computer operators complete a log indicating the programs that have been run and any abnormal occurrences.
Console Log	A log of computer console messages is maintained in sequential order for review and analysis.
Library Logs	A recording of data file information includes present location of file, file name, volume identification, date created, audit trail to prior data file version, date available for scratching, and serial number.
Control Logs	The input/output control clerk records all items given to and received from the production area. Also control logs state the anticipated and received batches of input from user areas.
Keystroke Verification	A second keypunch operation done by a separate person that checks the keypunched record against the keyed information.
Hardware Checks	Hardware features that identify abnormal occurrences to the operator.
Operating System Checks	System software features that identify abnormal occurrences to the operator.
Scan Output	Visual review of output to catch any gross error in form or content.
Fire Detectors	Devices that provide early recognition of smoke, fire, or heat.
Application Controls	A multitude of control techniques that are specifically incorporated into individual application systems to prevent or detect and correct IPF causes of exposure.

Corrective Controls	
Recovery Plan	A contingency plan that outlines the fallback processing at various levels of disaster. The plan should be formal, modular, and tested.
File Histories	A record of uses of tape files and cleanings to schedule recleaning and certification.
Error Statistics	Records classifying detected errors according to their origin, usually an individual or equipment item for performance measurement.
Fire Extinguishers	Devices to extinguish fire.

On-Premises Backup	File backup (disc, tape, or cards) that is immediately available to reconstruct a file if a data file is unusable.
Off-Premises Backup	File backup (usually tape) that could produce current or near-current data files without using the files available in the computer room.
Discharge Personnel	Removal of a person from his or her assigned duties.
Insurance	A policy that provides recovery of monies lost due to destruction or the theft of computer assets.
Uninterruptible Power	Provision of a backup electrical supply to prevent loss of power on a temporary or continuous basis.

16

The Auditor's Report

Joseph A. Puglisi

SIGNIFICANCE

The product of nearly every audit engagement is the auditor's report, signed in the name of a certified public accounting firm or with the personal signature of an individual practitioner. What is it about this usually brief report that makes it required for publicly held companies and a large proportion of privately held companies, and desired in countless other situations where it is not required?

In Chapter 9, the auditor's role is explored and its importance established in the functioning of our capital-based economic system. This chapter discusses the form in which the auditor reports on an audit examination as well as on the more prevalent engagement variations.

Engagements other than basic audits probably create the most questions concerning the degree of responsibility assumed by the CPA signing the report. Leaving aside controversies about whether an adequate audit has been performed (see Chapter 46), it is popularly assumed that any CPA's signature on almost any kind of report signifies a "certification" or an "O.K." The more recognized the CPA firm's name, the more the degree of responsibility assumed has been exaggerated. However, as more and more specification is codified in the areas of an independent accountant's association, this popular notion is slowly being counteracted.

Because the mere presence of the CPA's signature is so significant, and because a very large proportion of services provided by the accounting profession is in areas other than the auditing of financial statements in accordance with GAAP, this chapter includes reports on unaudited information, aptly referred to as accountant's reports instead of auditor's reports.

Whatever the degree of responsibility the auditor or accountant assumes, it is clear that users of his product—whether the client or third parties—expect enhanced reliability through the association of an independent party's professional expertise and judgment. But users of financial information must evaluate carefully what the auditor or accountant says in his report; though many reports use formula wording, the possible variations are immense. The last section of this chapter explores efforts underway to make these reports less formalistic and more communicative, but changes will be evolutionary rather than revolutionary. Thus, to deal with contemporary practice, the two focal points of this chapter are (1) what type of report should be issued in particular circumstances and (2) what users should understand about the reliance they can place on each of these reports.

REPORTS ON AUDITED FINANCIAL STATEMENTS

Auditor's Standard Report

The auditor's standard report, known as an unqualified report or a "clean opinion," most often consists of formula wording in two paragraphs.[1] The first paragraph, or *scope paragraph,* has several elements. It identifies

---

[1] Price Waterhouse & Co. uses a one-paragraph report with the same elements as the two-paragraph report:

In our opinion the accompanying consolidated balance sheets and the related statements

---

Accountants' Report

Board of Directors
The Mead Corporation
Dayton, Ohio

We have examined the balance sheets of The Mead
Corporation and consolidated subsidiaries as of December
31, 1979 and 1978, and the related statements of earnings,
retained earnings and changes in financial position for the
years then ended. Our examinations were made in accordance with generally accepted auditing standards and, accordingly, included such tests of the accounting records and
such other auditing procedures as we considered necessary
in the circumstances.

In our opinion, the financial statements referred to
above present fairly the financial position of The Mead
Corporation and consolidated subsidiaries at December 31,
1979 and 1978, and the results of their operations and the
changes in their financial position for the years then ended,
in conformity with generally accepted accounting principles
applied on a consistent basis.

Touche Ross & Co.

January 25, 1980
Dayton, Ohio

FIGURE 16.1   EXAMPLE OF AUDITOR'S STANDARD REPORT
SOURCE: The Mead Corporation, 1979 Annual Report.

1. The company whose financial statements the auditor has examined,
2. The specific financial statements examined, and
3. The point in time or the period that each financial statement covers.

The scope paragraph also describes the nature of the auditor's examination—that
the examination was performed in accordance with generally accepted auditing
standards using tests and procedures the auditor considered necessary.

---

of income, shareholders' equity, and changes in financial position present fairly the financial
position of XYZ Manufacturing Company and Subsidiaries as of December 31, 1980 and
1979, and the results of their operations and the changes in their financial position for the
years then ended, in conformity with generally accepted accounting principles consistently
applied. Our examinations of these statements were made in accordance with generally accepted auditing standards and, accordingly, included such tests of the accounting records
and such other auditing procedures as we considered necessary in the circumstances.

The second paragraph, or *opinion paragraph,* expresses the auditor's conclusion that the financial statements are presented fairly in accordance with generally accepted accounting principles. An example of an unqualified opinion is shown in Figure 16.1.

The auditor's standard report represents a professional judgment based on the results of audit procedures complying with broad generally accepted auditing standards. It is not a guarantee or "insurance policy" that the financial statements are correct or that the audited enterprise should be entrusted with the funds of owners, investors, or creditors. What the auditor's report is according to auditors is emphasized in Chapter 9. What it is according to courts acting on charges by plaintiffs—clients, third parties, and regulators—against auditors is explored in Chapter 46.

Issuing the Auditor's Report

The Letter of Engagement. Although professional standards do not require a formal letter of engagement, its use is recommended to ensure that the client and the auditor understand what the auditor is to accomplish and, sometimes more importantly, what the auditor will not accomplish—either by mutual design or because of the inherent limitations in the audit process. The engagement letter should be issued before beginning the audit and should cover

1. The different roles of the company and the auditor;
2. The specific financial statements to be audited, as of what date, and for what period;
3. The objectives, scope, and limitations of the examination;
4. The timetable for issuing the auditor's report;
5. The nature of additional projects to be undertaken by the auditor and other reports and letters he may issue;
6. The scope of assistance to be provided to the auditor by the company; and (usually)
7. Fees and billing intervals.

The engagement letter may also provide that its terms be accepted in writing by the client.

Generally Accepted Auditing Standards. Auditors examine financial statements in accordance with generally accepted auditing standards (GAAS). Of the ten standards, six are concerned with the qualifications of auditors, the quality of their work, and the performance of the audit itself. These six are explored fully in Chapter 11. The other four standards are concerned with the nature of the report issued by the auditors.

The Standards of Reporting. Reporting standards require the auditor to comment in his report on whether (1) the financial statements are presented in accordance with generally accepted accounting principles (GAAP), (2) the accounting principles have been consistently applied from period to period, and (3) the disclosures in the financial statements are reasonably adequate; and then (4) provide his opinion regarding the financial statements—unqualified, qualified, adverse, or that he cannot express an opinion (a *disclaimer*).

Sometimes an unqualified opinion by the auditor is not warranted. Situations (if they are material) ordinarily requiring some modification of the unqualified opinion are: (1) the financial statements depart from generally accepted accounting principles; (2) uncertainties exist as to the effect of a contingency on the financial statements; (3) there are limitations—sometimes client-imposed—on the scope of the auditor's examination; (4) accounting principles have not been consistently applied; (5) other auditors have performed a part of the examination; and (6) the auditor wants to explain or emphasize a particular matter.

Variations From the Auditor's Standard Report

Three broad variations from the auditor's standard report are qualified opinions, disclaimers of opinion, and adverse opinions. Figure 16.2 provides a matrix of causes and effects. In an audit engagement, the distinction between an unqualified opinion, a qualified opinion, a disclaimer of opinion, and an adverse opinion is a matter of degree. Auditor assessment of materiality determines whether the auditor will issue (1) an unqualified opinion because the matter is immaterial; (2) a qualified opinion because the matter is material; (3) a disclaimer of opinion because an uncertainty is so material that its potential effect on the financial state-

CAUSE OF VARIATION	TYPE OF OPINION			
	QUALIFIED	DISCLAIMER	ADVERSE	VARIATIONS NOT AFFECTING OPINION
Departures from GAAP*	●		●	
Uncertainties*	●	●		
Scope limitation*	●	●		
Lack of consistency	●			
Use of other auditors				●
Emphasis comments				●
Degree of materiality determines the nature of the auditor's report.				

FIGURE 16.2   VARIATIONS FROM THE STANDARD AUDITOR'S REPORT

ments is pervasive; or (4) an adverse opinion because a deliberate disregard of GAAP pervades the fairness of presentation.

Qualified Opinions. Qualified opinions, the most common variation from the auditor's standard report, are subdivided into *"except for"* and *"subject to"* opinions. The former relate primarily to departures from GAAP. The latter relate primarily to uncertainties that may have a material impact when resolved.

Disclaimers and Adverse Opinions. When a material uncertainty exists, the auditor cannot simply conclude that the financial statements are not fairly stated; his choice is to issue a qualified "subject to" opinion or a disclaimer of opinion. Similarly, when there is a departure from GAAP, the auditor can issue either an "except for" qualified opinion or an adverse opinion. With a departure from GAAP, the auditor usually knows and can evaluate the effects on the financial statements. If it is major, the auditor can issue an adverse opinion: It's all wrong. In this situation, a disclaimer of opinion is not among the auditor's options.

Causes of Variations

Departures from GAAP. Nonconformity with GAAP, the most clear-cut reason for the auditor to deviate from the standard report, involves (1) the misapplication of accounting principles in the recognition or measurement of amounts in the financial statements or (2) inadequate disclosure in the financial statements of important matters. Examples of misapplication are noncapitalization of capital leases, use of prime costs for pricing inventories, and capitalization of research and development costs. When accounting principles are misapplied, the auditor often can determine the effects on the financial statements and thus will disclose those effects in his report.

Variations from the auditor's standard report have three or more paragraphs instead of two, except for consistency exceptions, discussed below. A middle paragraph (or paragraphs) inserted between the scope and opinion paragraphs explains the reason for the variation from the standard report. The following is an example of a qualified opinion middle paragraph relating to noncapitalization of capital leases (AU 509.36):

> The company has excluded from property and debt in the accompanying balance sheet certain lease obligations, which, in our opinion, should be capitalized in order to conform with generally accepted accounting principles. If these lease obligations were capitalized, property would be increased by ($ amounts), long-term debt by ($ amounts), and retained earnings by ($ amounts) as of December 31, 1980 and 1979, and net income and earnings per share would be increased (decreased) by ($ amounts) and ($ amounts) respectively for the years then ended.

The opinion paragraph then begins with a modification:

> In our opinion, except for the effects of not capitalizing certain lease obligations as discussed in the preceding paragraph, the financial statements referred to above present fairly . . .

The information in the middle paragraph(s) can be briefer if the details are given in a note to the financial statements. At a minimum, the middle paragraph(s) must state the departure from GAAP and refer to the note.

If the departure from GAAP is so great that the financial statements as a whole are not fairly stated, the auditor issues an adverse opinion. After the scope and explanatory middle paragraphs, the auditor presents the final paragraph containing the adverse opinion:

> In our opinion, because of the effects of not capitalizing certain lease obligations as discussed in the preceding paragraph, the financial statements referred to above do not present fairly, in conformity with generally accepted accounting principles, the financial position of XYZ Manufacturing Company as of December 31, 1980 and 1979, or the results of its operations and changes in its financial position for the years then ended.

The third standard of reporting requires the auditor to comment in his report if the financial statements do not contain adequate disclosures involving material matters. In these circumstances, the auditor typically details the omitted information, if he has it available, in a middle paragraph to his report. An example of the applicable portion of a report qualified because of a lack of adequate disclosure follows:

> Certain information with respect to long-term debt of $400,000 at December 31, 1980, has been omitted from the accompanying financial statements. This debt consisted of bank notes payable due December 31, 1986, which bear interest at an 8% minimum rate or 1.5% over the prime rate of interest. All the stock of Sub Corp., a wholly owned subsidiary having net assets of $1,000,000, is pledged as collateral under the terms of the note agreement.
>
> In our opinion, except for the omission of the disclosures contained in the preceding paragraph, the financial statements referred to above present fairly . . .

A key element in an auditor's report that mentions either type of departure from GAAP is the disclosure of the effect of the departure if it is known or readily determinable. Exceptions to this rule are the omission of segment information or of a statement of source and application of funds from financial statements; the auditor is not required to include such omitted data in his reports (AU 435.10 and 545.05).

To avoid a qualified or adverse opinion, clients need only change the financial statements to properly apply the accounting principles or include the adequate disclosure; publicly held companies *must* do so, because the SEC will not accept an auditor's report containing a correctible exception. In practice, unless there is truly a difference of opinion between the auditor and the client or the client does not care to incur the cost of developing the data for correction, changing the financial statements to eliminate the departure is the usual resolution.

Uncertainties. Uncertainties (or *contingencies*) probably are the most frequent cause of variations from the auditor's standard report. They involve matters such as litigation, valuation or realization of assets, the ability of the company to continue (going concern status), and tax or renegotiation liabilities (see Chapter 29). By their very nature, the outcome of certain material uncertainties cannot be evaluated by the auditor or the client.

Normally the auditor issues a qualified opinion regarding a material uncertainty. Under professional reporting standards (AU 509.25), explanation of the uncertainty along with the auditor's qualified opinion is deemed adequate to inform the users of the financial statements about the unresolved problem.

Although the auditor is not precluded from issuing a disclaimer of opinion in cases involving uncertainties, this is no longer frequently done. Prior to 1975 it was common to observe disclaimers when the uncertainties were pervasive, and there will always be those few very serious situations when an uncertainty disclaimer is best.

The following is an example of the applicable portion of a report containing an opinion qualified for uncertainties relating to the effects of litigation:

As discussed in Note 2 to the financial statements, the company is defendant in a lawsuit alleging infringement of certain patent rights and claiming royalties and punitive damages. The company has filed a counteraction, and preliminary hearings and discovery proceedings on both actions are in progress. Company management and counsel believe the company has a good chance of prevailing, but the ultimate outcome of the lawsuits cannot presently be determined, and no provision for any liability that may result has been made in the financial statements.

In our opinion, subject to the effects of such adjustments, if any, as might have been required had the outcome of the uncertainty referred to in the preceding paragraph been known, the financial statements referred to above present fairly . . .

The qualifying words in the above example are based on a 1979 auditing interpretation, *Reporting on an Uncertainty* (AC 9509.29-.32), and do not suggest that when the uncertainty is resolved the financial statements will be reopened for finalization. This was often done prior to issuance of SFAS 16 (AC 2014) in 1977, which virtually eliminated prior-period adjustments that are not corrections of errors or changes in accounting principles. Thus, the auditor's qualification is a "flag" for readers, not an undertaking to later revise the figures.

Scope Limitations. A limitation on the auditor's ability to perform all the procedures he believes necessary to complete the audit is broadly referred to as a *scope limitation*. Clients may impose some limitations (e.g., restricting access to information or withholding permission to confirm certain accounts receivable or to observe physical inventories). External circumstances often impose others; for example, the auditor may not have been able to observe the physical inventory count at the beginning of the year because he was engaged later, or the financial statements may include an unaudited investee carried on the equity method. The auditor cannot report that his scope was limited and then say that he satisfied himself by other means. If he does not complete his normal procedures but uses other procedures to accomplish the same objectives, there is no scope limitation.

Scope limitations are akin to uncertainties in that the auditor cannot evaluate their possible effects on his audit results. When the maximum effect of misstatement in the area of the limitation can be quantified and is not pervasive, a qualified opinion is indicated; otherwise, a disclaimer of opinion is appropriate.

The auditor should always give a client-imposed scope limitation careful attention. In particular, he should be certain to understand the client's reasons for it and should evaluate all of its possible effects on his ability to express any opinion on the financial statements. Usually the auditor will disclaim an opinion; however, depending on the plausibility of the reason for the limitation, he must also evaluate whether continued association with such a client is in his best interest.

A scope limitation in which the auditor did not observe the physical inventory taking at the beginning of the year is expressed in the following example:

> We have examined the balance sheet of XYZ Manufacturing Co. as of December 31, 1980, and the related statements of income, retained earnings, and changes in financial position for the year then ended. Except as explained in the following paragraph, our examination was made in accordance with generally accepted auditing standards and, accordingly, included such tests of the accounting records and such other auditing procedures as we considered necessary in the circumstances.
>
> We did not observe the taking of the physical inventory as of December 31, 1979, since that date was prior to our appointment as auditors for the company, and we were unable to satisfy ourselves regarding inventory quantities by means of other auditing procedures.
>
> In our opinion, the balance sheet of XYZ Manufacturing Co. as of December 31, 1980, presents fairly the financial position of the company as of December 31, 1980, in conformity with generally accepted accounting principles applied on a basis consistent with that of the preceding year.
>
> Because of the matter discussed in the second paragraph, the scope of our work regarding inventories as of December 31, 1979, was not sufficient to enable us to express, and we do not express, an opinion on the statements of income and changes in financial position for the year ended December 31, 1980.

Note that in this example, although the auditor could not express an opinion on the statements of income and changes in financial position because of the pervasive impact on them, he was able to express an unqualified opinion on the balance sheet at the end of the year because (1) he did observe the physical inventory taking at the end of the year and (2) the opening inventory has no impact on the balance sheet at year-end.

Lack of Consistency. The second standard of reporting requires that the auditor state in his report whether the accounting principles used in the preparation of the financial statements have been consistently applied within the periods reported on and in relation to the immediately preceding period. This requirement arises because there are some acceptable alternatives under GAAP. Changing accounting principles, such as from the straight-line to the declining-balance method of depreciation (if the effect is material), impairs the comparability of the financial statements and is therefore important to the reader. Although many other matters, such as changes in estimates used in the application of the accounting principles (e.g., the depreciable lives of fixed assets), may also affect comparability of, and therefore require disclosure in, financial statements, such matters are not ordinarily commented on in the auditor's report because they are not changes in accounting principles.

When making a change in accounting principle, the client must justify that the new principle is preferable. The auditor must evaluate whether (1) the new accounting principle is part of GAAP, (2) the manner of accounting for the change is as prescribed by GAAP, and (3) management's justification of preferability is reasonable. If the auditor cannot satisfy himself as to any of these matters, he would issue a qualified or adverse opinion.

If the auditor is satisfied that the change in accounting principle complies with GAAP, he will modify his report to disclose the lack of consistency. Unlike other variations of the auditor's standard report, a lack of consistency requires only that the auditor modify his opinion paragraph; a middle paragraph is neither necessary nor customary. An example follows of the opinion paragraph of an auditor's report qualified for lack of consistency when the accounting effect of the change is *prospective,* that is, made only in the current year:

> In our opinion, the financial statements referred to above present fairly the financial position of XYZ Manufacturing Co. at December 31, 1980 and 1979, and the results of its operations and the changes in its financial position for the year then ended, in conformity with generally accepted accounting principles consistently applied during the period except for the change, with which we concur, in the method of computing depreciation as described in Note A to the financial statements.

If the accounting change requires *retroactive* restatement of the financial statements of prior periods, the opinion paragraph would read:

> In our opinion, the financial statements referred to above present fairly the financial position of XYZ Manufacturing Co. at December 31, 1980 and 1979, and the results of its operations and the changes in its financial position for the year then ended, in conformity with generally accepted accounting principles applied on a consistent basis after restatement for the change, with which we concur, in the method of valuing inventories as described in Note A to the financial statements.

Retroactive restatement, often prescribed by the FASB as the method of adoption of newly issued standards, should not be confused with now rare prior-period adjustments for matters other than changes in accounting principles.

SEC Preferability Requirements. For SEC companies, the auditor is required to go beyond GAAP and GAAS and state his own conclusion of preferability in a letter filed by the client with the SEC. Because criteria have not been established by the FASB for selecting among the alternatives within GAAP, similar clients of the same auditor will use different methods or variations within methods. Stating that a client's new method is preferable may cast aspersions on a different method used by another client.

The SEC states that a company's business judgment and planning may be considered by an auditor in forming his conclusion of preferability (SAB 14). Although this is more liberal than the initially released SEC position, the auditor must still evaluate

1. The acceptability of the change among the alternatives of GAAP, and
2. The preferability of the new principle in the client's particular circumstances.

An example of a letter (which should be addressed to the client, not the SEC), to be included as an exhibit to Form 10-Q, stating the auditor's conclusion of preferability follows:

> As stated in Note X to the financial statements for the three months ended March 31, 1980, the company changed its method of accounting for (describe the nature of the accounting change) and states that the newly adopted accounting principle is preferable in the circumstances (state the circumstances and elements of business judgment and planning given by the company in the note). At your request, we have reviewed and discussed with you the circumstances and the business judgment and planning that formulated your basis to make this change in accounting principle.
>
> It should be understood that criteria have not been established by the Financial Accounting Standards Board for selecting from among the alternative accounting principles that exist in this area. Further, the American Institute of Certified Public Accountants has not established the standards by which an auditor can evaluate the preferability of one accounting principle among a series of alternatives. However, for purposes of the company's compliance with the requirements of the Securities and Exchange Commission, we are furnishing this letter.
>
> Based on our review and discussion, we concur in management's judgment that the newly adopted accounting principle described in Note X is preferable in the circumstances. In formulating this position, we are relying on management's business planning and judgment, which we do not find to be unreasonable. Because we have not audited any financial statements of the company as of any date or for any period subsequent to December 31, 1979, we express no opinion on the financial statements for the three months ended March 31, 1980.

Use of Other Auditors. Reference to other auditors is neither a qualification of the principal auditor's opinion nor does it signal a report inferior to one that makes no such reference; rather, it is an indication to the user of the divided responsibility between the principal auditor and the other auditors.

If other auditors are examining certain divisions or subsidiaries included in the financial statements, the principal auditor—that is, the auditor who is examining the parent enterprise, auditing the consolidation, and issuing the auditor's report—must decide whether or not to refer in his report to the work of the other auditors. This decision requires an evaluation of the independence and professional reputation and competence of the other auditors and inquiry into the other auditors' examination. Full details are given in the codified standards (AU 543); the principal auditor should in general consider discussing with the other auditors the audit procedures followed and reviewing the audit program and working papers.

If he decides not to refer to the other auditors, the principal auditor assumes full responsibility for the auditor's report on the financial statements. The audit report should be completely devoid of any mention of other auditors, so that there will be no misunderstanding as to the degree of responsibility assumed.

Often, the principal auditor decides to refer to the examination by other auditors, primarily because (1) he is unable to evaluate and review the other auditors' examination or (2) the part of the financial statements examined by the other auditors is very significant to the total. When the principal auditor makes this reference, he should do so clearly in both the scope and opinion paragraphs of the report. The scope paragraph must give the magnitude of the part of the examination performed by other auditors by including the dollar amounts or percentages of total assets, total revenues, or net income, or other appropriate criteria.

While there is no professional rule that an auditor must cover a minimum proportion of the financial statement amounts in order to be the principal auditor, the SEC has informally taken the position that a majority coverage of the total assets, revenues, or net income, as appropriate, is presumed necessary. There are, however, situations where such coverage will not be the case. For example, when there is no principal auditor because the other auditors' proportion is very large, the auditor issuing his report along with the consolidated financial statements sometimes issues a *compilation-only report*; that is, after expressing an opinion on the portions he examined, he adds a paragraph explaining that the portions audited by others have been properly added in. The SEC ordinarily will not accept a compilation-only report in lieu of a required certification, since none of the auditors is taking responsibility for the sum of the parts. Figure 16.3 is an example of a principal auditor's report that refers to a division of responsibility with other auditors.

Emphasis Comments. In some situations the auditor, without qualifying or in any other way modifying his opinion, wants to emphasize an important matter regarding the financial statements, such as (1) the company is a part of a larger company, (2) the company has had significant related-party transactions, (3) there has been a significant subsequent event, or (4) there is an accounting matter that affects

---

STOCKHOLDERS AND BOARD OF DIRECTORS
COMMERCE CLEARING HOUSE, INC.
Chicago, Illinois

We have examined the consolidated balance sheets of Commerce Clearing House, Inc. and subsidiaries as of December 31, 1979 and 1978, and the related statements of earnings, stockholders' investment, and changes in financial position for the years then ended. Our examinations were made in accordance with generally accepted auditing standards and, accordingly, included such tests of the accounting records and such other auditing procedures as we considered necessary in the circumstances. We did not examine the financial statements of C T Corporation System, a consolidated subsidiary, for the years ended December 31, 1979 and 1978, which statements reflect total assets of 14.0% and 13.7% and net earnings of 26.4% and 20.1%, respectively, of the related consolidated totals. These statements were examined by other auditors whose report thereon has been furnished to us and our opinion expressed herein insofar as it relates to the amounts included for C T Corporation System is based solely upon the report of other auditors.

In our opinion, based on our examinations and the report of other auditors referred to above, the consolidated financial statements referred to above present fairly the financial position of Commerce Clearing House, Inc. and subsidiaries as of December 31, 1979 and 1978, and the results of their operations and the changes in their financial position for the years then ended, in conformity with generally accepted accounting principles applied on a consistent basis.

Chicago, Illinois   *Touche Ross & Co.*
February 14, 1980   **Certified Public Accountants**

FIGURE 16.3   EXAMPLE OF RELIANCE ON OTHER AUDITORS
SOURCE: Commerce Clearing House, Inc., 1979 Annual Report.

comparability of the financial statements with those of prior periods (AU 509.27). Though such matters do not affect the auditor's scope or opinion, their inclusion in the auditor's report is often misunderstood to be a qualification by the auditor, and therefore such auditor's reports are not frequently issued. An example of an emphasis comment follows (this one is a separate middle paragraph in an otherwise standard report, though there is no requirement to use a separate paragraph for an emphasis comment):

> As discussed in Note A, the company changed the estimated useful lives of its equipment for purposes of computing depreciation effective January 1, 1979, from 10 to 15 years. Because of this change, depreciation expense in 1979 is $500,000 less than in 1978.

Rule 203 Opinions

Rule 203 of the AICPA Code of Professional Ethics requires compliance with the pronouncements of the FASB and its predecessors; therefore, an auditor must almost invariably issue a qualified or adverse opinion if the financial statements depart from GAAP in a material way. The only exception is when the auditor "can demonstrate that due to unusual circumstances the financial statements would otherwise have been misleading" (ET 203.01).

In ASR 150 the SEC refers to Rule 203 using language stronger than the AICPA intended: "... it is necessary to depart from accounting principles ... if, due to unusual circumstances, failure to do so would result in misleading financial statements." The SEC may accept or require other principles in these cases.

A Rule 203 opinion must

1. Describe the departure from GAAP,
2. State the effects of the departure, if practicable, and
3. State why compliance with GAAP would result in a misleading statement.

Auditors have issued Rule 203 opinions in very few cases, because there is rarely a need to do so, and because they assume a heavy burden of demonstrating that adhering to GAAP is not appropriate. An example of a Rule 203 opinion is shown in Figure 16.4.

LONG-FORM REPORTS AND ADDITIONAL INFORMATION

Purpose of Long-Form Reports

A long-form report consists of the basic conventional financial statements and footnotes plus other financial information. This other information is varied and might include consolidating or combining financial statements, condensed financial statements, schedules or analyses containing explanatory comments, or details of particular financial statement elements. A company may want such additional information because, for example, creditors require it, it may be useful in IRS examinations, or they simply want it as a formal, permanent record. The auditor

Report of Independent Accountants   TOUCHE ROSS & CO.

Board of Directors
Health Industries, Inc.
Columbia, Maryland

We have examined the consolidated balance sheet of Health Industries, Inc. and subsidiaries as of
December 31, 1975 and 1974, and the related statements of operations and deficit and changes in
financial position for the years then ended. Our examination was made in accordance with
generally accepted auditing standards and, accordingly, included such tests of the accounting records and such other auditing procedures as we considered necessary in the circumstances.

As explained in Note B, the Company has changed its method of recording revenues from
recognition at the time of sale to recognition over the membership term and has applied this
change retroactively in the accompanying financial statements. Accounting Principles Board (APB)
Opinion Number 20, "Accounting Changes," provides that such a change be made by including,
as an element of net earnings during the year of change, the cumulative effect of the change
on prior years. Had APB Opinion Number 20 been followed literally, the cumulative effect of the
accounting change would have been included as a charge in the 1975 statement of operations.
Because of the magnitude and pervasiveness of this change, we believe a literal application
of APB Opinion Number 20 would result in a misleading presentation, and that this change
should therefore be made on a retroactive basis.

In our opinion, the aforementioned consolidated financial statements present fairly the financial
position of Health Industries, Inc. and subsidiaries at December 31, 1975 and 1974, and the
results of their operations and the changes in their financial position for the years then ended, in
conformity with generally accepted accounting principles applied on a consistent basis after
restatement for the change described in the preceding paragraph and the changes described in
Note C to the financial statements with all of which we concur.

Touche Ross & Co.

Certified Public Accountants

Los Angeles, California
March 6, 1976

FIGURE 16.4   EXAMPLE OF A RULE 203 OPINION

must take care that none of the additional information is required in the basic financial statements or in any way modifies them.

The basic financial statements should usually be included with the other financial information. When the two parts are separate, the auditor's report on the other financial information, commonly known as additional information, must clearly refer to the basic audit report.

Extent of Auditor's Association

SAS 29, *Reporting on Information Accompanying the Basic Financial Statements in Auditor-Submitted Documents,* states that an auditor has the responsibility to report on all aspects of a long-form report when he submits a document containing audited financial statements as well as other financial information to his client (AU 551.04). However, if the auditor's report on audited financial statements is included in a client-prepared document along with other financial information and the auditor has not been engaged to report on the other information, the auditor's involvement is outlined in SAS 8, *Other Information in Documents Containing Audited Financial Statements* (AU 550), and SAS 27, *Supplementary Information Required by the Financial Accounting Standards Board* (AU 553).

The Auditor's Report on Additional Information

When other financial information is contained in a document the auditor submits to his client or if the auditor has been engaged to report on such information contained in a client-prepared report, the auditor must issue a report. AU 551.06 outlines the content and form of this report:

1. The report should state that the examination has been made for the purpose of forming an opinion on the basic financial statements taken as a whole.
2. The report should identify the accompanying information. (Identification may be by descriptive title or page number of the document.)
3. The report should state that the accompanying information is presented for purposes of additional analysis and is not a required part of the basic financial statements. (The auditor may refer to any regulatory agency requirements applicable to the information presented.)
4. The report should include either an opinion on whether the accompanying information is fairly stated in all material respects in relation to the basic financial statements taken as a whole or a disclaimer of opinion, depending on whether the information has been subjected to the auditing procedures applied in the examination of the basic statements. The auditor may express an opinion on a portion of the accompanying information and disclaim an opinion on the remainder.
5. The report on the accompanying information may be added to the auditor's standard report on the basic financial statements or may appear separately in the auditor-submitted document.

Presented below is the standard form of reporting when the auditor has examined the additional information, as well as several other reporting formats (AU 551.12-.18); these forms of reporting are not appropriate with respect to supplementary information required by the FASB (see next paragraph).

Standard Report

Our examination was made for the purpose of forming an opinion on the basic financial statements taken as a whole. The (identify accompanying information) is presented for purposes of additional analysis and is not a required part of the basic financial statements. Such information has been subjected to the auditing procedures applied in the examination of the basic financial statements and, in our opinion, is fairly stated in all material respects in relation to the basic financial statements taken as a whole.

Disclaimer on All of the Information

Our examination was made for the purpose of forming an opinion on the basic financial statements taken as a whole. The (identify accompanying information) is presented for purposes of additional analysis and is not a required part of the basic financial statements. Such information has not been subjected to the auditing procedures applied in the examination of the basic financial statements, and, accordingly, we express no opinion on it.

Disclaimer on Part of the Information

Our examination was made for the purpose of forming an opinion on the basic financial statements taken as a whole. The information on pages XX-YY is presented for purposes of additional analysis and is not a required part of the basic financial statements. Such information, except for that portion marked "unaudited" on which we express no opinion, has been subjected to the auditing procedures applied in the examination of the basic financial statements; and, in our opinion, the information is fairly stated in all material respects in relation to the basic financial statements taken as a whole.

Report When Opinion on Basic Financial Statements Is Qualified

Our examination was made for the purpose of forming an opinion on the basic financial statements taken as a whole. The schedules of investments (page XX), property (page XY), and other assets (page XZ) as of December 31, 19XX, are presented for purposes of additional analysis and are not a required part of the basic financial statements. The information in such schedules has been subjected to the auditing procedures applied in the examination of the basic financial statements; and, in our opinion, except for the effects on the schedule of investments of not accounting for the investments in certain companies by the equity method as explained in the second preceding paragraph [second paragraph of our report on page 1], such information is fairly stated in all material respects in relation to the basic financial statements taken as a whole.

Report on Consolidating Information Not Separately Examined

Our examination was made for the purpose of forming an opinion on the consolidated financial statements taken as a whole. The consolidating information is presented for purposes of additional analysis of the consolidated financial statements rather than to present the financial position, results of operations, and changes in financial position of the individual companies. The consolidating information has been subjected to the auditing procedures applied in the examination of the consolidated financial statements and, in our opinion, is fairly stated in all material respects in relation to the consolidated financial statements taken as a whole.

SAS 27, *Supplementary Information Required by the Financial Accounting Standards Board* (AU 553), requires that the auditor perform certain limited procedures on supplementary information required by the FASB. The auditor's report on the basic financial statements should be expanded in all situations if (1) the supplementary information required by the FASB is omitted, (2) the auditor concludes that the measurement or presentation of the supplementary information materially departs from the FASB's guidelines, or (3) the auditor is unable to complete the procedures prescribed by the SAS 27 (AU 553.08). When supplementary information required by the FASB is presented outside the basic financial statements in a client-prepared document, the auditor has no specific reporting responsibility on it unless (1) he has been engaged to examine and express an opinion on it or (2) any of the above conditions exist. However, when this information is presented outside the basic financial statements in a document the auditor submits to his client, the auditor should disclaim an opinion on the information unless he has been engaged to examine and express an opinion on it.

An example of such a disclaimer follows (AU 551.15):

The (identify the supplementary information) on page XX is not a required part of the basic financial statements but is supplementary information required by the Financial Accounting Standards Board. We have applied certain limited procedures, which consisted principally of inquiries of management regarding the methods of measurement and presentation of the supplementary information. However, we did not audit the information and express no opinion on it.

ASSOCIATION WITH INTERIM FINANCIAL STATEMENTS OF PUBLICLY HELD COMPANIES

Although annual financial statements are the usual focus in discussions of accounting, reporting, and auditing, interim reporting is needed in almost all enterprises. In privately held companies, it is used principally as information for management and lenders; publicly held companies issue certain interim information to shareholders and are required to provide virtually complete quarterly financial statements in filings with the SEC.

The highest level of auditor association is to perform audits of all interim financial information. This is impractical, because a complete examination would take too long; interim information must be timely to be useful. Also, the cost of interim audits is very high, and ordinarily the related benefits are not commensurate. However, if the client desires a complete audit of interim financial statements (or needs one, such as is common in a first public offering), the auditor can perform it just as he would any annual audit.

Association of a CPA with unaudited statements—interim or annual—of nonpublic companies is discussed in the next section of this chapter. This section concentrates on association with interim financial information published by publicly held companies.

Reviews of Interim Financial Information

SAS 24, *Review of Interim Financial Information* (AU 721), "provides guidance on the nature, timing, and extent of procedures to be applied by the independent accountant in conducting a review of interim financial information and on the reporting applicable to such engagements."

The objective of an accountant's[2] review of interim financial information is to provide him with a reasonable basis for reporting whether material modifications are necessary to obtain conformity with GAAP. A review is not an audit—far from it—and thus there is no assurance the accountant will find problems even if they exist. AU 721 provides suggested review procedures, consisting of inquiries, analytical review, and reading, to the exclusion of the verification procedures and review of internal controls necessary in an audit. AU 721 also guides the account- ant in the extent of review procedures and the use of engagement letters and client representation letters. The accountant's procedures are reviewed in Chapter 5; the following discussion will focus on accountant's reports.

Distinctions in Interim Review Reports

AU 721 provides guidance on one basic type of review report, but there are variations and tangential issues to be considered. The categories covered below are

1. Timely reporting:
   a. Accountant's report on interim financial information of a publicly held company,
   b. Modifications of accountant's review report,
   c. Consent to use of accountant's review report, and
   d. Nonavailability of accountant's review report to underwriters; and
2. Reporting on interim financial information presented in a note to audited financial statements.

Accountant's Basic Interim Review Report. The report on an interim review contains five elements: (1) a statement that a review was conducted in accordance with professional standards for these reviews, (2) the specific interim information reviewed, (3) a description of the review procedures (this can contain variable wording but is likely in practice to be formalistic, as in the example below), (4) a statement that a review is less than an audit and that therefore no opinion is expressed, and (5) a statement on whether the accountant is aware of material modifications that should be made to the financial statements. This report assures users of the interim financial information that the accountant has applied proce- dures under the guidance of the professional literature. The form of the report, given in AU 721.18, follows:

We have made a review of (describe the information or statements reviewed) of XYZ Manufacturing Company and consolidated subsidiaries as of September 30,

---

2 "Auditor" is not the proper technical term for association with any financial information not part of audited financial statements, though it is sometimes used in relation to unaudited data based on audited financial statements; hence, the terms "CPA" and "accountant."

1980, and for the three-month and nine-month periods then ended, in accordance with standards established by the American Institute of Certified Public Accountants.

A review of interim financial information consists principally of obtaining an understanding of the system for the preparation of interim financial information, applying analytical review procedures to financial data, and making inquiries of persons responsible for financial and accounting matters. It is substantially less in scope than an examination in accordance with generally accepted auditing standards, the objective of which is the expression of an opinion regarding the financial statements taken as a whole. Accordingly, we do not express such an opinion.

Based on our review, we are not aware of any material modifications that should be made to the accompanying financial (information or statements) for them to be in conformity with generally accepted accounting principles.

The foregoing is the only form of report to be used, whether there are completed interim financial statements (as in SEC Form 10-Q) or merely excerpts from them (as in quarterly sales and earnings reports sent to shareholders). Also, the format does not distinguish between issuance for internal use (such as for the audit committee or board of directors) or for public distribution. (SAS 10 restricted reporting to boards of directors; SAS 13 removed that restriction, but required standard unaudited disclaimer wording. Both of these SASs have been superseded by SAS 24.)

Modification of Accountant's Interim Review Report. Basically, the accountant is required to modify his report on an interim review only for departures from GAAP. Modification is not required for otherwise adequately disclosed uncertainties or lack of consistency in applying GAAP, because the accountant's report itself is not an expression of opinion. The following are sample third and fourth paragraphs for the report form above for a company that did not record capital leases:

Based on information furnished us by management, we believe that the company has excluded from property and debt in the accompanying balance sheet certain lease obligations that should be capitalized in order to conform with generally accepted accounting principles. This information indicates that if these obligations were capitalized at September 30, 1980, property would be increased by $ . . . . . , and long-term debt by $ . . . . . , and net income and earnings per share would be increased (decreased) by $ . . . . . , $ . . . . . , $ . . . . . , and $ . . . . . , respectively, for the three-month and nine-month periods then ended.

Based on our review, with the exception of the matter described in the preceding paragraph, we are not aware of any material modifications that should be made to the accompanying financial (information or statements) for them to be in conformity with generally accepted accounting principles.

Consent to Use of Accountant's Interim Review Report. A company may request its accountant to perform a limited interim review so that the company may include the report in its filings with the SEC on Form 10-Q. A formal consent is not provided for such use in that the report is not being included in a 1933 act filing.

While it is permissible to include a SAS 24-type report in an SEC 1934 act filing (such as a 10-Q), it has *not* been proper to do so in a 1933 act filing (i.e., a registration statement for issuance of securities). Often such registration statements contain comparative interim information (*capsule data*) or interim financial statements (*unaudited stubs*) as of a date subsequent to the date of the audited financial statements. The accountant associated with the registration statement has been guided instead by SAS 1, *Filings Under Federal Securities Statutes* (AU 710); this guidance recognized the strict responsibilities applying to accountants under Section 11(b) of the 1933 act and the need for review as of the effective date of the registration statement.

Recognizing the incongruity of allowing a SAS 24-type report in an SEC 10-Q while allowing no accountant's report of any kind as to capsule data or stubs in an SEC registration statement, the AICPA Auditing Standards Board reconsidered AU 710. In 1979 the SEC issued ASR 274, which contains rules that would exclude accountants from liability under Section 11(a) of the Securities Act of 1933, in order to permit the SAS 24-type report to be included in registration statements. The SEC issued ASR 274 in part in order to encourage increased auditor involvement with interim financial information. At the time this *Handbook* went to press, an exposure draft (AICPA, 1980g) was pending that would allow the inclusion of a SAS 24-type report in a 1933 act filing; a "consent" would be used even though the report would not be deemed "filed" under Section 11.

Nonavailability of Accountant's Interim Review Report to Underwriters. In SAS 1, *Letters for Underwriters* (see Chapter 26 and AU 630), the accountant is given guidance on what information he may provide to underwriters in connection with underwriters' due-diligence procedures in 1933 act securities offerings. Because underwriters are required to specify the procedures they wish the accountant to perform on their behalf, it is not proper to provide them with a SAS 24-type report; the review procedures followed in a SAS 24 review are the accountant's choice, not the underwriter's. However, reference can be made in the introductory paragraph of the comfort letter to the underwriters that a review of interim financial information has been made; no further mention of or conclusions from such review should be included. The Auditing Standards Board is involved in a reconsideration (see AICPA, 1980g) of the effect of SAS 24 on long-standing comfort letter practices, since underwriters are very interested in the possible augmentation of their due-diligence procedures that may be required by the newer forms of auditor association with unaudited financial statements.

Reporting on Interim Financial Information Presented in a Note to Audited Financial Statements. When any company, whether required by SEC regulations or voluntarily, includes in its annual financial statements or other financial reporting a note on interim financial information, the accountant should perform a limited review following SAS 24; but the procedures need not be done at the time quarterly information is issued. The interim information in an annual footnote is not deemed to be required for a fair presentation of the financial statements, is accordingly not audited, and is labeled unaudited. The accountant should not modify his opinion on the basic financial statements or include a report on a limited review in these circumstances unless one of these three conditions is present (AU 721.27): (1) the scope of the review was restricted, (2) the interim financial information does not appear to be presented in conformity with GAAP, or (3) the accountant did not perform a review (unless this fact is disclosed in the note). An example of a third, final paragraph in an auditor's report on the annual financial statements for which there was a restriction on the scope of the limited review of interim financial information is (AU 721.27):

> Note X, "Unaudited Interim Financial Information," contains information that we did not audit, and accordingly, we do not express an opinion on the information. We attempted but were unable to make a review of such interim information in accordance with standards established by the American Institute of Certified Public Accountants because we believe that the company's system for preparing interim financial information does not provide an adequate basis to enable us to complete such a review.

ACCOUNTING AND REVIEW SERVICES—REPORTS ON UNAUDITED FINANCIAL STATEMENTS

A considerable portion of the practice of many CPAs consists of providing services other than auditing (e.g., tax services, management consulting or advisory services, and record-keeping or data-processing services). Accounting and review services, often referred to as unaudited statement and write-up work, are a major element of such nonaudit services.

Many privately held companies that do not need an audit desire the services of accountants to assist in the preparation of unaudited financial statements and to provide other accounting services.

Statements on Standards for Accounting and Review Services

In December 1978, the AICPA Accounting and Review Services Committee began publishing Statements on Standards for Accounting and Review Services (SSARS). This committee is the senior technical committee with authority to issue pronouncements in connection with unaudited financial statements or other unaudited financial information of a nonpublic entity.

SSARS 1, *Compilation and Review of Financial Statements* (AR 100), provides the accountant with guidance in performing services in connection with unaudited financial statements of a nonpublic entity. This statement replaces the previous practice of an accountant issuing a disclaimer of opinion whenever he was associated with unaudited financial statements. It also divides the accountant's association with unaudited financial statements into compilations and reviews.

Compilations are defined as "presenting in the form of financial statements information that is the representation of management (owners) without undertaking to express any assurance on the statements." *Reviews* are defined as "performing inquiry and analytical procedures that provide the accountant with a reasonable basis for expressing limited assurance that there are no material modifications that should be made to the statements in order for them to be in conformity with generally accepted accounting principles or, if applicable, with another comprehensive basis of accounting." The objectives of these two types of services differ considerably. When an accountant performs compilations, he does not intend to express any assurance; when he performs reviews, his inquiry and analytical procedures should provide him with a basis for expressing limited assurance that there are no material modifications that should be made to the financial statements.

The Intent of the Engagement

The client's intent when engaging the accountant is important in determining the nature and scope of his report. If the accountant engaged to render accounting and review services also performs some audit procedures, this does not make the financial statements audited. Conversely, once an auditor is engaged to perform an audit, clients cannot switch to a compilation or review engagement because the auditor has discovered matters adversely affecting the financial statements. The client can disengage the auditor (see Chapter 46), but an auditor should be wary of midstream shifts by clients, since these may signal problems regarding his association as accountant with the unaudited statements.

When a client requests a change from an audit to an unaudited engagement, the reasons may include new circumstances affecting the requirements for an audit, misunderstanding the nature of an audit, or restrictions on the scope of the audit whether or not client-imposed. Although the first two are usually reasonable bases for agreeing to the change in the engagement, the accountant should pay particular attention to the implications of a scope restriction. One implication is the possibility that the information affected by the scope restriction may be incorrect or unsatisfactory. Such matters may require the accountant to issue an audit report disclosing the scope limitation and its effect on the auditor's opinion (see Scope Limitations above). Whenever the scope restriction is limited to either or both of (1) a prohibition from corresponding with the client's legal counsel or (2) a refusal to sign a letter of representations, an audit report must be issued containing an appropriate disclaimer. Conversely, the accountant engaged to render accounting and review services may be requested to change to an audit. Such a request may usually be complied with, because it involves an expansion of the accountant's work and reporting.

Compilations

Compilations require that the accountant fulfill three basic requirements. First, he must have knowledge of the accounting principles and practices in the client's industry. This does not preclude his undertaking a compilation engagement for an entity in an industry new to him, provided he then obtains the knowledge required. Second, he must have a general understanding of the entity's business transactions and accounting records and of the qualifications of the entity's accounting personnel, as well as an understanding of the accounting basis and form and content of the financial statements. Third, he is not required to make inquiries, obtain verifications or corroborations, or review any information in connection with his engagement. However, if the accountant obtains any information that causes him to believe certain matters are incorrect, incomplete, or unsatisfactory, he must either follow up to a satisfactory resolution or, if the client refuses to provide additional or revised information, withdraw from the engagement.

The accountant's compilation report has three elements (AR 100.14): (1) a statement that a compilation has been performed; (2) a statement that a compilation is limited to presenting management's representations in financial statement format; and (3) a statement that no audit or review has been performed and, accordingly, no opinion or assurances whatever are expressed. The following is the standard form of a compilation report (AR 100.17):

> The accompanying balance sheet of XYZ Company as of December 31, 1980, and the related statements of income, retained earnings, and changes in financial position for the year then ended have been compiled by us.
>
> A compilation is limited to presenting in the form of financial statements information that is the representation of management. We have not audited or reviewed the accompanying financial statements and, accordingly, do not express an opinion or any other form of assurance on them.

Effect of Nonindependence. Although an accountant who is not independent cannot perform an audit, and although SSARS 1 also precludes the accountant who is not independent from issuing a review report, he may issue a compilation report disclosing that he is not independent. He cannot, however, state the specific reasons for nonindependence, since disclosing these may confuse the reader. When the accountant is not independent, he should add as the last paragraph of the above report (AR 100.22): "We are not independent with respect to XYZ Manufacturing Company."

Reviews

When performing a review, the accountant must fulfill the same requirements as when performing a compilation. In addition, he must have knowledge of the entity's production, distribution, and compensation methods; types of products and services; operating locations; and material transactions with related parties. The accountant must also perform inquiry and analytical procedures, which would ordinarily consist of the following as detailed in AR 100.27 and summarized below:

1. Inquiries concerning the entity's accounting principles and practices and the methods followed in applying them.
2. Inquiries concerning the entity's procedures for recording, classifying, and summarizing transactions and accumulating information for disclosure in the financial statements.
3. Analytical procedures designed to identify relationships and individual items that appear to be unusual. The analytical procedures specified in SSARS 1, paragraph 27, are (a) comparison of the financial statements with statements for comparable prior period(s), (b) comparison of the financial statements with anticipated results, if available (for example, budgets and forecasts), and (c) study of the relationships of the elements of the financial statements that would be expected to conform to a predictable pattern based on the entity's experience.
4. Inquiries concerning actions taken at meetings of stockholders, board of directors, committees of the board of directors, or comparable groups.

5. Reading the financial statements to consider whether they appear to conform with GAAP.

6. Obtaining reports from other accountants, if any, who have been engaged to audit or review the financial statements of significant components of the reporting entity, its subsidiaries, and other investees.

7. Inquiries concerning (a) whether the financial statements have been prepared in conformity with GAAP consistently applied, (b) changes in the entity's business activities or accounting principles and practices, (c) questions arising in the review work, and (d) material subsequent events.

The accountant's review report has five elements (AR 100.32): (1) a statement that a review has been performed; (2) a statement that the financial statements are management's representations; (3) a statement that a review consists of inquiries and analytical procedures; (4) a statement that a review is less than an audit and therefore no audit opinion is expressed; (5) a statement that the accountant is not aware of material modifications that should be made to the financial statements except as disclosed. The following is the standard form of a review report (AR 100.35):

> We have reviewed the accompanying balance sheet of XYZ Manufacturing Company as of December 31, 1980, and the related statements of income, retained earnings, and changes in financial position for the year then ended, in accordance with standards established by the American Institute of Certified Public Accountants. All information included in these financial statements is the representation of the management of XYZ Manufacturing Company.
>
> A review consists principally of inquiries of company personnel and analytical procedures applied to financial data. It is substantially less in scope than an examination in accordance with generally accepted auditing standards, the objective of which is the expression of an opinion regarding the financial statements taken as a whole. Accordingly, we do not express such an opinion.
>
> Based on our review, we are not aware of any material modifications that should be made to the accompanying financial statements in order for them to be in conformity with generally accepted accounting procedures.

Additional Responsibilities of Accountants

When engaged to either compile or review financial statements, if the accountant becomes aware of a departure from GAAP, he must evaluate whether this requires mention in his report. Lack of consistency in the application of GAAP and uncertainties do not have to be mentioned in the accountant's report unless appropriate disclosure regarding such matters is not included in the financial statements. Several examples of modifications of reports are given in AR 100.40.

In some situations when the accountant is engaged to perform a compilation, the client may omit substantially all the disclosures that are required by GAAP or another comprehensive basis of accounting. In this case, the accountant should add a third paragraph to his compilation report as follows (AR 100.21):

> Management has elected to omit substantially all of the disclosures (and the statement of changes in financial position) required by generally accepted accounting

principles. If the omitted disclosures were included in the financial statements, they might influence the user's conclusions about the company's financial position, results of operations, and changes in financial position. Accordingly, these financial statements are not designed for those who are not informed about such matters.

Although this form of report is appropriate in a compilation, for which the accountant expresses no assurance, it is not appropriate in a review, in which the accountant's objective is to express limited assurance. The omission of substantially all disclosures required by GAAP is pervasive and certainly inconsistent with the idea of limited assurance. This form of review report cannot be followed even if the statements are marked "for internal use only." Although there is no outright prohibition on internal use reports, it seems the clear intent of the Accounting and Review Services Committee to have obviated them by the two new forms of reporting.

SPECIAL REPORTS

Auditors are often called upon to issue reports on matters that are not financial statements prepared in conformity with GAAP. Four broad areas discussed in detail in SAS 14, *Special Reports* (AU 621), are

1. Financial statements prepared on a comprehensive basis of accounting other than GAAP,
2. Specified elements, accounts, or items of a financial statement,
3. Compliance with aspects of contractual agreements or regulatory requirements, and
4. Financial information presented in prescribed forms.

Another Comprehensive Basis of Accounting

Commonly used comprehensive accounting bases other than GAAP include income tax basis, cash basis, price-level-adjusted basis, and prescribed regulatory basis. These bases may be audited in accordance with GAAS, and the auditor's report (AU 621.05) on such an examination should include three paragraphs:

1. A scope paragraph identifying the financial statements examined and stating whether the examination was conducted in accordance with GAAS,
2. An explanatory paragraph stating (or referring to a note that explains) the comprehensive basis of accounting and how it differs from GAAP, and stating that the financial statements are not intended to be presented in conformity with GAAP, and
3. An opinion paragraph stating whether the financial statements are presented fairly in conformity with the comprehensive basis of accounting, consistently applied.

An example of a report on financial statements prepared on another comprehensive basis of accounting, the cash basis, is as follows (AU 621.08):

We have examined the statement of assets and liabilities arising from cash transactions of XYZ Manufacturing Company and subsidiaries as of December 31, 1980, and the related statement of revenue collected and expenses paid for the year then ended. Our examination was made in accordance with generally accepted auditing standards and, accordingly, included such tests of the accounting records and such other auditing procedures as we considered necessary in the circumstances.

As described in Note X, the company's policy is to prepare its financial statements on the basis of cash receipts and disbursements; consequently, certain revenue and the related assets are recognized when received rather than when earned, and certain expenses are recognized when paid rather than when the obligation is incurred. Accordingly, the accompanying financial statements are not intended to present financial position and results of operations in conformity with generally accepted accounting principles.

In our opinion, the financial statements referred to above present fairly the assets and liabilities arising from cash transactions of XYZ Manufacturing Company and subsidiaries as of December 31, 1980, and the revenue collected and expenses paid during the year then ended, on the basis of accounting described in Note X, which basis has been applied in a manner consistent with that of the preceding year.

Specified Elements, Accounts, or Items

In addition to audit-based reporting on specified elements, accounts, or items, this category of report is designed to cover the results of applying agreed-on procedures to such elements, accounts, or items.

Audit-Based. This type includes reports on matters such as rentals, royalties, a profit participation, or a provision for income taxes. It may be an adjunct to an audit of the basic financial statements or a stand-alone engagement. Either way, the auditor must take into account the fact that the GAAS apply, except for variation in the application of the reporting standards concerning conformity with GAAP and the consistency of applying GAAP. The GAAP standard relates to financial statements and specified elements. Accounts or items are not, per se, financial statements. (The consistency standard applies only if the specified element, account, or item is presented in conformity with GAAP specifically applicable to it.) The reporting format follows the usual guidelines for reporting on audited financial statements. The auditor should not express an opinion on specified elements, accounts, or items if he has either expressed an adverse opinion or denied an opinion on the basic financial statements if such a special report would be equivalent to a prohibited piecemeal opinion (AU 509.48). An example of a report expressing an opinion on a specified financial statement item follows (AU 621.14):

We have examined the schedule of gross sales (as defined in the lease agreement dated March 4, 19XX, between ABC Company, as lessor, and XYZ Stores Corporation, as lessee) of XYZ Stores Corporation at its Main Street store, Littleton, Colorado, for the year ended December 31, 1980. Our examination was made in accordance with generally accepted auditing standards and, accordingly, included such tests of the accounting records and such other auditing procedures as we considered necessary in the circumstances.

In our opinion, the schedule of gross sales referred to above presents fairly the gross sales of XYZ Stores Corporation at its Main Street store, Littleton, Colorado, for the year ended December 31, 1980, on the basis specified in the lease agreement referred to above.

Agreed-On Procedures. A client may ask an auditor to undertake an engagement to render a report based on applying agreed-on procedures that are not a sufficient basis for expressing an audit opinion. The auditor should accept such an engagement only if he and the client have a clear understanding of the procedures to be performed, if distribution of the report is restricted to named parties, and if the financial statements of the client (or another enterprise, such as a company being evaluated for possible acquisition) do not accompany the report. The auditor's report should indicate the specified elements, accounts, or items on which the agreed-on procedures were performed; state the procedures performed and the findings; disclaim an opinion on the specified elements, accounts, or items; state that the report does not extend to the client's financial statements taken as a whole; and specify who is intended to receive the report.

An example of a special report in connection with claims of creditors, based on the results of applying agreed-on proceduers, follows (AU 621.17):

Trustee
XYZ Company

At your request, we have performed the procedures enumerated below with respect to the claims of creditors of XYZ Company as of December 31, 1980, set forth in the accompanying schedules. Our review was made solely to assist you in evaluating the reasonableness of those claims, and our report is not to be used for any other purpose. The procedures we performed are summarized as follows:

a. We compared the total of the trial balance of accounts payable at December 31, 1980, prepared by the company, to the balance in the company's related general ledger account.

b. We compared the claims received from creditors to the trial balance of accounts payable.

c. We examined documentation submitted by the creditors in support of their claims and compared it to documentation in the company's files, including invoices, receiving records, and other evidence of receipt of goods or services.

Except as set forth in Schedule B, we found that amounts claimed by creditors and amounts shown in the company's records were the same. Our findings are presented in the accompanying schedules. Schedule A lists claims that are in agreement with the company's records. Schedule B lists claims that are not in agreement with the company's records and sets forth the differences in amounts.

Because the above procedures were not sufficient to constitute an examination made in accordance with generally accepted auditing standards, we do not express an opinion on the accounts payable balance as of December 31, 1980. In connection with the procedures referred to above, except as set forth in Schedule B, no matters came to our attention that caused us to believe that the accounts payable might require adjustment. Had we performed additional procedures or had we made an examination of the financial statements in accordance with generally accepted auditing standards, other matters might have come to our attention that would have been reported to you. This report should not be associated with the financial statements of XYZ Company for the year ended December 31, 1980.

Compliance With Contractual Agreements or Regulatory Requirements

The auditor may furnish reports concerning compliance with aspects of contractual agreements such as loan agreements, or with aspects of regulatory requirements of government agencies. The auditor may render such reports only in connection with his audit of the client's financial statements by giving *negative assurance* —stating that in performing his examination, nothing came to his attention to cause him to believe the client was not in compliance with the specified aspects of the contractual agreement (or regulatory requirement). If, as is common, the negative assurance is given in a report separate from the basic audit report, the fact that an audit of the basic financial statements (in accordance with GAAS) was performed, and the date of the auditor's report thereon, must be stated in the compliance report. The auditor also may, and usually will, report that his audit was not directed primarily toward obtaining knowledge regarding compliance.

An example of a report based on compliance with a contractual agreement follows (AU 621.19):

> We have examined the balance sheet of XYZ Company as of December 31, 1980, and the related statements of income, retained earnings, and changes in financial position for the year then ended, and have issued our report thereon dated February 16, 1981. Our examination was made in accordance with generally accepted auditing standards and, accordingly, included such tests of the accounting records and such other auditing procedures as we considered necessary in the circumstances.
>
> In connection with our examination, nothing came to our attention that caused us to believe that the company was not in compliance with any of the terms, covenants, provisions, or conditions of sections 1 to 5, inclusive, of the Indenture dated July 21, 1976, with ABC Bank. However, it should be noted that our examination was not directed primarily toward obtaining knowledge of such noncompliance.

Prescribed Forms

Printed forms designated by the party with which they are to be filed often prescribe the wording of the auditor's report. Prescribed forms commonly call for assertions by the auditor that he cannot make. In such situations, or if the auditor has not done everything he deems necessary to express the prescribed opinion, he should either reword the prescribed form or attach a separate report (AU 621.20-.21).

CURRENT ISSUES IN AUDITOR'S REPORTING

Commission on Auditors' Responsibilities

In 1978 the Commission on Auditors' Responsibilities (CAR) issued its *Report, Conclusions, and Recommendations,* in which it stated (p. 71):

Evidence abounds that communication between the auditor and users of his work—especially through the auditor's standard report—is unsatisfactory. The present report has remained unchanged since 1948 and its shortcomings have often been discussed. Recent research suggests that many users misunderstand the auditor's role and responsibilities, and the present standard report only adds to the confusion. Users are unaware of the limitations of the audit function and are confused about the distinction between the responsibilities of management and those of the auditor.

The commission concluded that the standard auditor's report simply does not communicate; it is too brief, and it uses terms that mean something different in common usage and that are essentially the auditor's words of art—in short, it is vague and ambiguous.

Nondescriptive Nature of Auditor's Reports. The most critical charge that the commission made is that the auditor's standard report does not communicate. Although standardization in language developed because the panoply of auditor's reports was confusing, the commission believed this was achieved at the price of losing the character of the report. The commission illustrated this by reciting (CAR, p. 72) the 1903 auditor's report on the United States Steel Corporation. This report said, in part:

1. The statements are correctly prepared from the books;
2. The property account contained only actual additions;
3. Ample provision has been made for depreciation, extinguishment of bad debts, and liabilities;
4. Inventory valuations at approximate cost were accurately made; and
5. Cash and securities were verified and are fully worth the stated amount.

Although today's auditor would find some of the assurances in this report unacceptable, it does describe in greater depth than the current standard report what the auditor did and what his conclusions were.

Proposed Reporting by Auditors. The commission proposed a two-pronged approach to better communication: (1) a report by management and (2) a report by independent auditors.

The report by management would alleviate the erroneous assumption that financial statements are representations of the auditors rather than of management. The recommended report would have these elements (CAR, pp. 76-77):

1. A statement that management has prepared the financial statements in conformity with appropriate GAAP and that in so doing some amounts are based on estimates and judgments.
2. A statement that the company accounting system and related controls provide reasonable assurance that assets are safeguarded and financial records are reliable for preparing financial statements and maintaining accountability for assets, and that all material weaknesses in the accounting and control systems reported by the auditors have either been corrected or the reasons given for their not having been.

3. A statement on the interrelationship among the company's board of directors or audit committee, the internal auditors, and independent auditors.
4. A statement of the company's and its counsel's position in regard to litigation.
5. A statement of the company's code of ethics and the policies and procedures followed to provide reasonable assurance of conduct in accordance with the law as well as with good business practices.
6. A statement on the nature of nonaudit services, if any, performed by the independent auditors.
7. A statement of any disagreements with the independent auditors as to accounting principles, disclosures, or audit scope.

The report by the independent auditor would convey his role and responsibilities with these added elements to the substance of today's auditor's standard report:

1. A statement that the financial statements are management's representations.
2. A statement that other information in the annual report has been reviewed and is not inconsistent with the financial statements and the auditor's knowledge.
3. A statement that interim financial information was reviewed during the year and the scope of such review.
4. A statement that the auditor concurs with management's description of the system of internal accounting controls and material weaknesses.
5. A statement that the company's policy on employee conduct has been reviewed and related internal controls were appropriately designed and applied.
6. A statement that the auditor met with the board of directors or audit committee to discuss audit scope, other services provided, and significant accounting or auditing problems.

An example of the recommended auditor's report is shown on pp. 77-79 of the commission's report.

The commission's proposed reports by management and the auditor would be dynamic, would be different in diverse circumstances, and would call attention to themselves, thus avoiding their contemporary symbolism.

How the profession will respond to all the commission's recommendations remains to be seen. AICPA committees are hard at work on several pieces, and the Financial Executives Institute has endorsed management reporting without complete specification of contents. The SEC generally regards the CAR report as a blueprint for the profession without recognizing its idealistic and declaratory nature. The SEC's thrusts in internal control reporting, which are hinged on the CAR report, are explored in Chapter 13.

Other Current Issues

An accountant is sometimes asked to give opinions on accounting principles and other financial matters. Often these requests come from nonclients and involve disagreements or potential disagreements between the nonclients and their auditor. The accountant should carefully evaluate any requests for opinions on accounting principles and other financial matters.

When there are valid reasons for these requests, such as a complex matter that warrants consultation with a third party, it is appropriate to provide these services. The consulted accountant must discuss the matter with the inquirer's auditor to assure that all salient facts are available for consideration (ET 201.04). In instances when the consulted accountant believes the position taken by the other auditor is incorrect or unsound, it is of course appropriate for him to report this to the inquirer. The accountant must be careful in this process not to assume the role of an advocate for the client. When these matters involve actual or potential litigation, an approach dictated by the specific situation should be used. It is not possible to generalize how the consulted accountant should proceed, if at all. (For a review of accounting issues that have been contested in litigation, see Chapter 45.)

Reporting on uncertainties, internal accounting controls, and illegal acts is in flux and may have considerable impact on future reporting on audited financial statements. These three issues are discussed in greater detail in Chapters 13 and 29. The "auditor of record" concept—that the auditor be involved with all aspects of his clients' financial reporting at all times during the year—may also have a profound impact on future reporting. This concept is discussed in Chapter 9.

SUGGESTED READING

AICPA. *Accounting Trends and Techniques.* New York, 1979. This annual review and compilation contains a section on current auditor reporting practices.

————. *Illustrations of Auditor's Reports on Comparative Financial Statements.* Financial Report Survey 18. New York, 1979. Prior to the issuance of SAS 15 (AU 505) in December 1966, there were varying practices in issuing auditor's reports covering two or more audits. This NAARS survey, based on 8,000 annual reports, shows how practice became more consistent in the issuing of the many different kinds of comparative reports.

————. *Illustrations of Departures from the Auditor's Standard Report.* Financial Report Survey 7. New York, 1975. SAS 2 (AU 509), issued in 1974, represented the first coordinated revision in this area since SAP 33, issued in 1963. Numerous examples are given in the categories of uncertainties, inconsistent GAAP, use of other auditors, emphasis of matters, and other departures.

Carmichael, Douglas. *The Auditors' Reporting Obligation—Meaning and Implementation of the Fourth Standard of Reporting.* Auditing Research Monograph No. 1. New York: AICPA, 1978. The author discusses criteria actually used by auditors in deciding whether an opinion should be qualified or disclaimed when there is a major uncertainty, or qualified or adverse when there is a departure from GAAP.

Commission on Auditors' Responsibilities. *Report, Conclusions, and Recommendations.* New York: AICPA, 1978. Chapter 7 deals extensively with auditors' communication with users, in the context of the auditors' future role.

Part III

Specific Areas of Financial Accounting, Reporting, and Auditing

17

Cash, Marketable Securities, and Payables

John Van Camp

THE LIQUID ASSET CYCLE

Liquid assets consist of cash and marketable securities, and their proper management is essential to the viability of every business organization. The ultimate objective of liquid asset management is to have cash available when and where it is needed. To maximize earnings, cash needs should be borrowed at a minimal interest cost, and excess cash should be invested, since cash itself is not a productive asset. Liquid asset management is often significantly affected by the demands put on the enterprise by its creditors.

In many businesses the cash account is affected by more transactions than any other account because cash is an integral part of the major transaction cycles; also, most business activities begin or end with cash. The accounting concepts for cash and accounts payable are relatively simple, while those for marketable securities are rather complex. Interestingly, this relationship is reversed for the auditing aspects of these accounts.

Investing Excess Funds

Excess funds can be temporarily invested in a number of different securities, depending on the length of time that the cash is expected to be available. Many companies will put money to work temporarily in short-term paper such as certificates of deposit (CDs), commercial paper, or treasury bills. If money is going to be available for a longer period of time, then other security investment options are available, as discussed in this chapter. Usually such transactions are under the control of the senior company management and require the approval of the board of directors for other than routine purchases and sales of high-quality short-term investments.

Cash Sources

The primary source for cash receipts is the revenue cycle—selling merchandise or providing services to a customer and converting the sale or service into a receivable and ultimately into cash. See Chapter 18 for a complete discussion of this cycle, including the important controls.

Other major sources of cash are the sale of an equity interest in the enterprise and borrowings (see Chapters 26 and 22, respectively). These sources of cash can be very large, but for most companies other than financial institutions they are not part of a recurring stream of transactions processed in a major cycle. Cash received in this manner is generally subject to adequate internal control in most enterprises. Larger companies achieve control in these major business transactions through the active participation of the board of directors and top executive officers. Smaller companies generally achieve control through the involvement of the owners.

Less significant sources of cash include the sale of fixed assets and scrap, sale or discounting of receivables, and receipt of investment income. The extent to which such sources fall within a major transaction cycle or are under the control of the company's management is determined by the frequency of receipts and their significance to the enterprise.

Cash Use

The predominant use of cash is to pay for purchases of goods and services, such as raw materials, salaries and wages, supplies, utilities, repairs and maintenance, and research and development. The purchases/payables cycle discussion in this chapter does not include the payroll cycle (see Chapter 19), nor does it include disbursements for capital asset acquisitions, repayment of borrowings and interest, and dividends (see Chapters 20, 22, and 26, respectively).

CASH AND CASH EQUIVALENTS

Cash Management

Objectives. The primary objective of cash management is to ensure that the company has sufficient cash to carry on its operations. Collecting receivables and paying bills have always been functions of cash management; however, with today's high interest rates, the ability to accelerate cash inflows, slow cash outflows, and invest excess funds or reduce costly borrowings has become more important than ever before.

Budgeting. Effective cash forecasting, or budgeting, is the backbone of good cash management. Detailed planning of its receipts and disbursements enables a company to schedule its expected borrowings and cash investments advantageously.

Most short-term cash budgets are designed to indicate the high and low points in a company's cash cycle. Identifying the low points alerts management not to schedule large discretionary payments at these times and can thus preclude the necessity of borrowing. Identifying the high points allows management to plan the company's short-term investment strategy.

The long-term budget shows significant changes caused by acquisitions, the introduction of new products, and the long-term growth of the company. It is used in determining whether to raise funds on a short-term or a long-term basis and how this decision will affect the company's capital structure. The long-term budget also assists in securing funds, since it shows potential lenders a comprehensive cash forecast of both capital needs and means of repayment.

The nature of the firm's business, overall company strategies, and the purpose of the budget are all factors that determine the length of the period the budget covers. Companies whose operations fluctuate widely generally prepare shorter-term operating budgets than companies with more stable operations.

Determining Size of Cash Balances. Enough cash on hand is needed to meet payments arising in the ordinary course of business (e.g., purchases, payroll, taxes, and dividends). A precautionary cushion is also needed to meet unexpected contingencies. The more predictable the cash flows of the business and the more borrowing power available, the less need for a cushion. Not all of the company's funds need be held in cash to meet these requirements; a portion may be held in short-term investments as well. Also, the cash balance may actually be negative on the company's records if float (discussed below) is used effectively.

Compensating Balances. Compensating balances are a part of a company's cash balances. These are amounts a company must maintain pursuant to an informal or formal agreement with a bank that has lent funds or has made a line of credit available. They also effectively pay for bank services rendered to the company for which there is no direct fee, for instance, check processing and lockbox management. By requiring a compensating balance, the bank achieves a higher effective rate on a loan than the stated rate.

The compensating balance requirement can be either an absolute minimum balance below which the cash on deposit according to the bank's records should not fall, or a minimum average balance over some period of time, often a month. The former requirement is more restrictive because the company receives no benefit from its actual balance fluctuating above the required minimum. Funds on deposit to meet a minimum compensating balance are effectively unusable for other purposes. Before it enters a compensating balance arrangement, a company should evaluate the true cost of such an arrangement and compare it with bank charges that might be paid directly for services covered by the balances.

Concentration Banking. For large companies operating in multiple locations, the location of bank accounts is important. The establishment of strategic collection centers will accelerate the flow of funds into the firm by shortening the time between a customer's mailing of a payment and the company's having the use of the funds. The selection of collection centers is based on the geographic areas the company serves and the volume of billings there.

Customers are instructed to remit their payments to a designated collection center. Deposits are made into the collection center's local bank, thus reducing the time required to collect checks, because the customers' banks are generally within the area of the collection center bank. The local bank deposits are then transferred to a major company account in a concentration bank. This is generally accomplished through a wire transfer, which makes the funds immediately available in the concentration account. However, if the amounts to be transferred from the regional account are small, it might be more economical to transfer them by drawing a check on that account.

Concentration banking reduces the size of a company's *collection float,* which is the difference between the amount on deposit according to the company's records and the amount of collected funds according to the bank records. By using regional accounts, amounts deposited clear through the Federal Reserve system more quickly and thus can be drawn against sooner.

Although the operations of many companies are decentralized, cash control works best when centralized under direct corporate management, since less cash is required to support operations, fewer banks are used, balances required to serve as precautionary cushions are reduced, and overall compensating balance requirements may also be reduced.

Types of Bank Accounts. Cash management today has been expanded to a sophisticated financial function, but its original custodial function—cash control and safekeeping—remains significant.

A company can vary the types of bank accounts it uses to obtain desired control objectives. The general cash account is the principal bank account in most companies and the only account in many small companies. Funds are received and cash is disbursed as part of the major transaction cycles through this account; also, deposits from and disbursements to all other bank accounts are made through it.

Imprest accounts. An imprest bank account makes a specific amount of cash available for a limited purpose. For example, it can be used at outlying locations, thus facilitating the disbursement of funds for minor local needs. Authorized personnel disburse these funds at their own discretion, as long as the payments are consistent with company policy. Funds in an imprest account are periodically reimbursed from the general cash account upon receipt of vouchers supporting disbursements made. No other deposits are made into an imprest account.

Imprest bank accounts are often used for disbursing payroll checks. Prior to the disbursement of the payroll checks, the total payroll amount is transferred to the imprest payroll account, whose balance is normally kept at zero or a nominal amount. The account thus acts as a clearing account for a large volume of checks. Separating payroll disbursement from other functions in this manner improves internal control and reduces the time needed to reconcile bank accounts.

The imprest approach is often also used to provide petty cash funds for expenditures that are most conveniently paid in cash. The fund should be sufficiently large to meet the normal need for small payments for a period of two to three weeks.

Branch accounts. A branch account allows a company operating in multiple locations greater local autonomy, since the business branch can deposit and withdraw from an account under its control. A branch account used in this manner functions very much like a general cash account but on a local level. Excesses or deficiencies in cash are periodically adjusted by transfers to or from the company's general cash account. Centralized control over branch accounts requires daily or weekly cash reports and careful monitoring of balances.

Branch accounts can also be used in a slightly different manner wherein separate accounts are maintained for receipts and disbursements. As with concentration banking, a collection account can be established to receive all deposits, which are subsequently transferred to the general cash account. The disbursement account is set up on an imprest basis with a fixed balance.

Lockbox accounts. With a lockbox, payments can be collected and deposited quickly, making the money available in the shortest amount of time for company use. Large, multilocation companies will usually locate lockboxes in cities within regions of heaviest billing. The company rents a local post office box and authorizes its bank in each of these cities to pick up customers' remittances from it. The bank checks the box several times a day and immediately deposits the checks into the company account. The speed of collection and deposit into the account, which thus accelerates the availability of collected funds, is the greatest advantage of this approach.

The bank performs many services in connection with the lockbox: the checks are microfilmed for record purposes and cleared for collection; the company is sent a deposit slip and a list of payments, together with any other material mailed by the customer. Although the lockbox procedure frees the company from handling and depositing the checks, there could be a considerable cost for these banking services.

Because the cost of a lockbox system is almost directly proportional to the number of checks deposited, such arrangements may not be profitable for a company if the average remittance is small. If the income generated from accelerating the receipt of funds exceeds the cost of the system by a large enough amount, it is then considered profitable and worth undertaking. The main factors affecting the degree of profitability are the geographic dispersion of customers, the size of the typical remittances, and the earnings rate on the accelerated funds. Important considerations are whether internal control over cash is improved by a lockbox or whether its use results in a reduction of company personnel otherwise needed to process the receipts.

Electronic Funds Transfer. Part of the effective control of cash balances is the efficient movement of cash—within the company as well as in and out of the company. Businesses use about 12 billion checks annually to pay their obligations. The cost of issuing and mailing a check, receiving it, and clearing it through the banking system is between 55¢ and $1.00 (Hunt, 1978, p. 142) and is rising rapidly with inflation.

Today's electronic technology has made possible another method of transferring funds—electronic funds transfer (EFT). This process uses wire, telephone, or telegraph rather than paper to request a bank to transfer some of the depositor's funds to someone else or to another bank account. Electronic funds transfers can also be made by computer. EFT makes possible the instantaneous transfers of funds, since, unlike checks, they do not require the physical movement of paper. It also promises to be a much cheaper method of transferring funds for both large and small companies.

EFT involves both debit and credit systems. In a debit EFT system the payee has his bank charge the bank account of the payor based on a preauthorized payment instruction the payor has given to his bank; for example, preauthorized payments made by a policyholder to an insurance company, or a customer's authorization to a power company to bill his bank account directly for monthly charges. In a credit EFT system the payor instructs his bank to transfer funds to the bank account of the payee; for example, an employer's automated payroll system generates a magnetic tape containing instructions for the employer's bank to transfer funds from the employer's account to the employees' accounts.

EFT, despite its widespread uses, is not without its drawbacks. Safeguards have been built into EFT systems, but the exposure to massive fraud is increased because of the reliance on computer technology, which transfers funds without personal intervention. See Chapter 15 for a commentary on these exposures and some of the controls used to guard against them.

Float. Another aspect in the control of bank balances is the use of float. There are two types of float, both of which involve a difference between the company's record of cash in the bank account and the bank's record of unrestricted cash in that account.

In the first type of float the company records the cash as soon as it is received and deposited, but cannot draw the funds until the bank has collected them from the banks on which the deposited checks are drawn. Until collected, the deposited checks represent a kind of float. If a company can accurately estimate the size of this float, i.e., the time when funds credited to its bank account will be usable, it can significantly reduce excess cash balances that would otherwise be kept to meet its normal transaction needs.

The second type of float occurs when a company writes a check against its bank balance but the bank has not yet received and paid the check and deducted it from their record of the company's balance. The float is the total amount of such outstanding checks. The company's records can thus show a negative cash balance; however, when the outstanding checks are added to the company's balance, the balance reflected by the bank's records may be positive. By accurately estimating the amount of outstanding checks at a given time, the company can reduce its bank balance to a minimum and keep available only those funds necessary to meet the clearing checks.

Float is eliminated when EFT is used, because the movement of funds is instantaneously recorded.

Bank Relationships. The primary consideration for a company's financial officer is to develop adequate banking facilities to handle present and future financial requirements. The number and distribution of accounts depends largely on the size of the operating balances required, the geographical location of a company's facilities, and the amount of bank credit it may require. In most instances it is wise for a firm to concentrate its bank accounts in a few banks, thus enabling it to maximize its importance to a particular bank. For one thing, banks are generally more inclined to accommodate larger customers; also, if several types of accounts are within one bank, the firm might incur smaller service charges than if they were dispersed among several banks. The company's role in the community, payroll facilities for employees, business relationships, and directorships also play important roles in the development of banking relations.

Temporary Investment Types

In temporarily investing available cash, a firm will have to make decisions regarding the amount of cash to be invested, the types of securities to be purchased, and the timing of security purchases and sales. Most nonfinancial companies do not have elaborate systems for handling marketable securities or short-term paper purchases and sales, because the transactions usually are infrequent and uncomplicated.

Collection and recording of income from dividends and interest is another part of the temporary investments and marketable securities transaction cycle. Checks received as investment income are usually processed as a normal part of the cash receipts system. Companies periodically need to ascertain that all interest and dividend income due has been received and recorded.

Short-Term Paper. A wide range of short-term paper is available for investment. *Certificates of deposit* (CDs) represent formal evidence of indebtedness, issued by a bank, subject to withdrawal under the specific terms of the instrument. CDs are frequently negotiable or transferable. Generally, they are issued in $100,000 denominations and mature in 30 to 360 days. Demand certificates, payable on presentation, seldom bear interest; however, time certificates payable at a fixed date usually do.

Money market savings certificates are issued by banks and savings and loan associations in denominations of $10,000 or more for six-month periods. The interest rate is tied to the 26-week treasury bill rate.

As discussed in Chapter 38, *mutual fund* investment companies provide a service for their stockholders by directly investing in a variety of securities that are compatible with the funds' stated investment objectives. *Open-end funds* have no limit to the number of subscribers. An investment in an open-end fund is made at the fair market value of the fund's assets, determined on a unit basis, plus fees ranging from none to 10% or more. An investment in an open-end fund is disposed of by redeeming the unit at fair market value. Investments in *closed-end funds* are similar to investments in corporate stock, and shares are bought and sold in the over-the-counter market.

In *money market funds,* a relatively recent variation of the mutual fund, the yield is determined by the mix of treasury bills and commercial paper making up the fund's investments. Most money funds require a $5,000 initial minimum investment. Many allow withdrawal by checks or through wire transfers. The former can be advantageous to the investor, since the mutual fund account earns interest until the check clears and is charged against it.

Treasury bills are sold on a discount basis in $10,000 denominations at weekly auctions held by the government. These U. S. government obligations are generally sold with 91- and 182-day maturities; occasionally, nine-month and one-year maturities are available. *Treasury notes* mature in one to ten years. *Treasury bonds* are issued for periods in excess of ten years. Both notes and bonds bear interest at a stated rate.

Commercial paper is a short-term debt (30 to 270 days) issued by large corporations with top credit ratings. These interest-bearing obligations are usually issued in $5,000 and $10,000 denominations. Although they generally yield a higher rate than treasury bills, there is no secondary market for them.

A repurchase agreement, commonly referred to as a "repo," is a short-term sale of securities by a dealer in government securities whereby the dealer agrees to repurchase the securities from the investor at a specified time. The underlying instrument is a U. S. government security; therefore, there is little risk of default. The holding period is tailored to the needs of the investor and can be established for very short periods, even a few days. Interest rates on repurchase agreements are tied to the rate on treasury bills, federal funds, and loans to government security dealers by commercial banks.

Financial Accounting and Reporting

In financial statements the heading "Cash" includes currency on hand and on deposit, demand deposits, and checks drawn prior to the balance sheet date but not released. When certificates of deposit, time deposits, or savings accounts are included in the cash caption, the amount thereof is customarily given either parenthetically on the balance sheet or in a note to the financial statements. Cash should not include funds received after the end of the fiscal period, even though they may have been in transit over the company's year-end.

Some companies issue drafts in payment of purchase obligations; this is frequently done in paying farmers for on-the-spot purchase of agricultural products. The issuing company should ordinarily deduct the amount of such outstanding drafts from cash rather than show them as a liability.

Bank Overdrafts. There are several methods of appropriately reporting a bank overdraft in the financial statements. It is permissible to offset an overdraft in one bank account with *available* funds in other accounts in the same bank or in other banks. Available is defined in this context to require both the existence of a positive cash balance in another account and the unencumbrance of this balance by any arrangements (such as compensating balance requirements or similar restrictions on the use of the cash) that limit its use. Offset is mandatory when there is available cash in another account in the same bank in which the overdraft exists or there is a formal offset arrangement. Overdrafts are not to be offset against certificates of deposit, commercial paper, or other temporary investments.

Overdrafts may be shown as a separate component of current liabilities or combined with accounts payable. If the overdrafts are combined with accounts payable, they must be disclosed (on the face of the balance sheet or in a footnote) if they are material in relation to either the balance in accounts payable (after combination) or to total current liabilities.

The accounting and disclosure for overdrafts as described above appropriately reflect the financial aspects of a company's cash management system. Essentially, where funds are readily available in one account and there is an overdraft in another, financial emphasis is on the ability of the enterprise in the aggregate to liquidate the outstanding claims on cash (checks). To the extent that there is a material cash claim not offset (overdraft) that claim must be disclosed.

Restricted Cash. Cash available for general operations should be distinguished from cash restricted for special purposes. For instance, cash deposited with a trustee for the payment of mortgage interest and taxes should not be included with general cash (although it may be a current asset if the related liabilities are current). Restricted cash funds not available for general operations, such as (1) sinking fund for payment of long-term debt or retirement of capital stock, (2) the proceeds of a construction mortgage that is restricted for use only for construction costs, and (3) funds allocated for special purposes by action of the company's board of directors, should not be shown as unrestricted cash, nor should they be included under current assets, except for any portion relating to current liabilities. For example, cash that has been earmarked for additions to properties should be included under the "Property, plant, and equipment" or "Other assets" heading.

Compensating Balances. Contractual obligations to maintain compensating balances must be disclosed. When it can be specifically determined, the amount of the restricted cash should be segregated. It should be shown as a noncurrent asset to the extent that it relates to the long-term portion of the related debt. A balance sheet caption such as "Cash on deposit maintained as compensating balance" would be appropriate. Footnote disclosure should include the terms of the requirement and details of withdrawal restrictions; if the amount restricted was raised substantially during the year, the average amount restricted during the year and the largest amount so restricted should be disclosed.

Other compensating balances should be disclosed by footnote as follows:

- Where there is a contractual agreement to maintain a compensating balance, but the amount is determined only as an average over a period, the terms of the agreement and the approximate dollar amount affected should be disclosed.
- Where the compensating balance is an acknowledged informal agreement, the footnote should again describe the terms of the agreement and, if determinable, the pattern of voluntary restrictions during the year.

Under ASR 148, which amended Rule 5-02.1 of Regulation S-X, restricted deposits held as compensating balances against short-term borrowing arrangements must be segregated and appropriately described in the balance sheet of an SEC registrant. The rule also requires footnote disclosure of

1. Compensating balances maintained to assure future credit availability, along with the amount and terms of the agreement, and
2. Unrestricted compensating balance arrangements, i.e., those that do not restrict the use of cash shown on the balance sheet.

ASR 148 defines a compensating balance as

that portion of any demand deposit (or any time deposit or certificate of deposit) maintained by a corporation (or by any other person on behalf of the corporation) which constitutes support for existing borrowing arrangements of the corporation (or any other person) with a lending institution. Such arrangements would include both outstanding borrowings and the assurance of future credit availability.

Factors to be considered in deciding whether segregation and disclosure are required are suggested in the ASR and include

1. Relationship to total cash,
2. Total net liquid assets,
3. Net working capital, and
4. The impact of compensating balances on the effective cost of financing.

The ASR defines 15% of liquid assets (current cash balances, whether restricted or not, plus marketable securities) as usually being material.

Compensating balance arrangements with banks usually are expressed in terms of the collected bank ledger balance. The difference between the cash balance reflected in the financial statements and the collected bank ledger balance is *float* (outstanding checks less uncollected funds). Float can be negative if the amount of uncollected funds exceeds the amount of outstanding checks. If the compensating balance arrangement is expressed in terms of the collected bank ledger balance, an adjustment for a float is necessary to state the amount of the balance in book terms. If the compensating balance is fixed or determinable at a given time, the adjustment should be based on actual or estimated float at the date of the balance sheet. If the arrangement calls for an average compensating balance, average float must be used.

Banks customarily credit customer deposits on the date of deposit, not when the funds are collected, so precise information on uncollected funds is seldom readily available. Thus, it will ordinarily be necessary to estimate float. The basis of the estimate should be the method used by the bank in estimating uncollected items; however, a reasonable approximation of that method will suffice. Usually, a company official should discuss the estimation of uncollected items with the banker before calculating the compensating balance. The float adjustment, together with a short statement of criteria used to make the adjustment, are required disclosures under the ASR.

The guidelines and interpretations section of the ASR state that it is not permissible to reduce compensating balance amounts by amounts maintained as minimum balances for operations. However, deposits maintained as compensation for services—bank reconciliations, lockbox arrangements, etc.—need not be considered as compensating balances unless the funds also serve as compensating balances under borrowing arrangements.

ASR 148 recognizes that lines of credit may be offered by financial institutions as a marketing device and that many companies accept them but do not intend to use them. While these lines generally need not be disclosed, they must be considered a part of the company's financing plan and disclosed if the lending institution gets any commitment fee, compensating balance, or other activity of benefit in exchange for the line.

When compensating balances under line of credit arrangements relate to both used and unused portions of the line, the ASR requires disclosure of the compensating balance maintained for each purpose. Nonenforceable compensating balance arrangements present the most disclosure difficulty, particularly if the company has not complied. In nonenforceable arrangements there is some uncertainty; the bank may not renew the loan, may raise the interest, and, generally, may act in a manner not helpful to the company. There is obvious reluctance to detail such problems in writing, by both companies and banks.

Nonetheless, the SEC requires disclosure of such arrangements and of any material sanctions. The determination of any such arrangement is a question of fact. Companies and banks must reach a meeting of minds so that the required disclosures can be made.

SAB 1 (Topic 6.B) includes interpretations of ASR 148 by the SEC staff; Figure 17.1 illustrates a compensating balance disclosure in a published annual report.

Temporary Investments. Savings accounts, time deposits, certificates of deposit, and other temporary investments are sometimes combined with cash in financial statements. More than half the companies reporting savings accounts or time deposits include them under the cash heading; and about half the companies with certificates of deposit include them with cash.

Short-term investments such as commercial paper, bankers acceptances, U. S. treasury notes, and other U. S. securities are generally excluded from the cash caption and separately disclosed using an appropriate descriptive title. However, repurchase agreements are included in cash in most instances.

SHORT-TERM DEBT

During fiscal years 1979 and 1978, lines of credit were maintained at various banks. At December 29, 1979, these lines totaled $2,000,000 and called for interest at the prime rate. Generally, compensating balances, as measured by average collected bank balances, are required equivalent to 10% of each line of credit, increased by 10% of any loans outstanding under such lines. Book cash balances required by lines of credit at December 29, 1979, adjusted for average float, are $1,759,000. Amounts held as compensating balances are legally subject to withdrawal without sanctions and also serve as working capital. In the accompanying financial statements, cash on hand and freely transferable cash in banks, including compensating balances with banks, have been netted for presentation purposes against checks outstanding that have been drawn on another bank account.

During fiscal years 1978 and 1979, there were no short-term unsecured borrowings from banks.

FIGURE 17.1 EXAMPLE OF COMPENSATING BALANCE DISCLOSURE
SOURCE: Nash Finch Company, 1979 Annual Report.

Auditing

General Concepts. The audit philosophy assumed in this section is fully explained in Chapters 12 and 13. The overall audit objective is to determine that cash and cash equivalents are fairly presented in the context of the financial statements as a whole. To meet this objective, the audit must address seven basic questions: existence, ownership, valuation, cutoff, mechanical accuracy, classification, and disclosure.

These seven areas are not entirely congruent with the seven objectives ascribed to internal control in Chapter 13, because internal control systems do not primarily address several substantive audit objectives. The following cross-reference table may be helpful:

Overall Audit Objective, as Shown in This Chapter	Internal Control Objective
Congruent:	
Existence	Authorization
	Validity
	Recording
Valuation—accuracy	Valuation
Cutoff	Timing
Mechanical accuracy	Summarization
Classification	Classification
Not congruent:	
Ownership	
Valuation—changed circumstances	
Disclosure	

Historically, it has been common for cash to be overaudited, both because it comforts the novice auditor who enjoys precision and because cash is the asset most susceptible to theft. It is important that the objective of the audit be kept in mind so as to avoid the use of excessive audit time in this area. At the same time, however, it must be recognized that nearly all transactions affecting the business pass through the cash account at some time, and the alert auditor can, from an unusual cash item, frequently start a train of questioning that leads to important audit findings. This is particularly true in the case of smaller clients with limited accounting sophistication, who may not understand the implications of transactions for financial reporting.

In order to decide between a systems reliance approach and a substantive procedures approach or determine how much of each approach should be blended, the auditor must gain an understanding of the activities of the company that affect its accounting for cash and the potential seriousness of errors. He must also understand the company's preventive and detective internal controls.

Transaction Types. The primary transactions that impact cash and cash equivalents consist of the following:

1. The receipt of cash from the normal liquidation of receivables as well as from sources such as the cash sale of inventory and scrap; the sale of property, plant, and equipment; the sale or discounting of other assets such as receivables; the issuance of debt and equity securities; and the receipt of investment income. The auditor must be familiar with the company's procedures to control the receipt of cash from the varying sources, including controls over the mail, the handling of cash at the point of sale, the processing of cash receipts in the organization, and the depositing of cash into bank accounts.

2. The payment of cash for such items as the purchase of raw materials and property, plant, and equipment; the payment of expenses, including payroll expenses; the purchase of investments; and the payments on indebtedness. The auditor must be familiar with the client's controls over the cash payments system that ensure that payments are authorized and are for valid and approved purchases of raw materials, assets, or services or are in connection with authorized investment decisions.

Audit Approach. The overall design of cash audit procedures for large companies normally involves heavy reliance on the client's system of internal controls, assuming that the controls are assessed as good based on a preliminary evaluation. The reason for this is the large volume of transactions flowing through the cash accounts and the interrelationship of cash with the major transaction cycles.

Much of the transaction testing for the cash component of the financial statements is performed as part of the tests for the sales/receivables, purchases/payables, and payroll cycles. The internal control aspects and systems testing for these cycles are discussed later in this chapter and in Chapters 18 and 19.

Since most of the objectives of the audit of cash can be met through compliance testing procedures, favorable results obtained from such procedures can normally reduce the amount of substantive audit work. Additionally, some of the substantive audit procedures can be performed prior to year-end.

The initial year-end procedures are analytical, and the information derived from them assists in the determination of the type and extent of additional procedures. The analytic procedures are to

1. Review changes in bank balances during the period and consider reasonableness in view of other cash-flow data, such as changes in accounts receivable or accounts payable; and
2. If cash-flow budgets exist, to compare them to cash balances and determine the reasons for variances.

Objectives and Procedures. In addition to analytical procedures, the auditor must devise other substantive or compliance procedures to achieve the objectives of the audit of cash and cash equivalents. Figure 17.2 is a very condensed listing of the interim and year-end audit procedures that are commonly used to achieve these objectives. The procedures shown may be used to satisfy more than one audit objective, but are listed alongside the objective that they most typically satisfy, in order to provide an overview of how the audit objectives are met.

Probably the most common audit procedures in the cash area are obtaining bank confirmations of balances and liabilities using the standard form agreed to by the banking industry and performing *proofs of cash*. In the latter procedure the auditor reconciles deposits and disbursements according to one or more bank statements with the receipts and disbursements shown in the company's books. Also, the auditor may directly obtain *cutoff bank statements* for some accounts; these are bank statements for a short period, say ten days, after period-end, which the auditor receives directly to check out the correctness of the company's period-end bank reconciliation.

Note that for cash equivalents, the audit procedures for marketable securities, discussed later in this chapter, are often applicable.

The increasing use of electronic funds transfer (EFT) will make it more difficult to accomplish the cash audit objectives. With EFT, less paperwork (hard copy) is created to document transactions that have taken place. Computers can now communicate with one another, but unless they are programmed with specific instructions to print out a hard copy of the transactions, a visible audit trail may not be created. Companies should review plans with their internal and external auditors before installing major EFT applications, to ensure that ultimately there is adequate evidence available for required audits.

MARKETABLE SECURITIES

Security Types

Equity securities represent the underlying ownership interest in a business. They encompass common, preferred, and other capital stock and the right to acquire (e.g., warrants, rights, and call options) or dispose of (e.g., put options) ownership shares in an enterprise at fixed or determinable prices. To receive income while holding a stock investment, the equity owner is dependent on the declaration of dividends by the board of directors of the business. The capital invested in an equity security is normally regained by selling the security. Since the sale price is dependent on the fluctuations in the marketplace or in what a private buyer is willing to pay, there is no guarantee that the investor's original cost will be recovered.

Debt securities, such as bonds and notes, are promissory obligations to repay a certain sum (principal) plus interest at a specified rate. Individual certificates state the dates for payment of principal and interest. The rights and obligations of both parties are generally governed by an indenture that places restrictions on the issuing firm for the protection of investors.

Hybrid securities possess both debt and equity characteristics. Convertible debt securities are hybrids because they allow the investor to exchange one type of security—debt—for another—equity. Some preferred stocks are hybrids because by their terms they must be redeemed by the issuing enterprise, thus giving them characteristics of debt.

All types of *marketable* equity and debt securities are covered in this portion of the chapter, except for investments in subsidiaries and equity method investees. The equity method is covered in Chapter 21, as are nonmarketable security investments.

Accounting and Reporting—General

Classification of Securities. Marketable *equity* securities, in accordance with SFAS 12, represent any security (common or nonredeemable preferred stock) for which a quotation is available from a national or over-the-counter market (AC 5132.07). Nonmarketable securities, even though considered a current asset, should not be classified with marketable securities and should be carried at cost, subject to a net realizable value test applied to any asset held for sale. Debt securities are not covered under SFAS 12; however, they would be classified as current assets if they mature within a year or are readily marketable.

Investments that management specifically intends, and evidences an ability, to hold for a year or more from the date of the financial statements should be classified as noncurrent assets. The propriety of classification as noncurrent will take into account the investor's financial position, working capital requirements, debt agreements, and other contractual obligations that bear upon the feasibility of holding the security for at least one year. If a marketable security is expected to be converted to cash within the next 12 months, a current asset classification is appropriate.

Cost of Securities. Like other assets acquired by a firm, securities must initially be recorded at their cost. Cost is considered to be the cash or fair market value of other assets given in exchange for the securities acquired; however, for readily marketable securities, quoted market may be the proper initial valuation, with gain or loss recorded on the exchange of nonmonetary assets therefor. Cost includes all disbursements incident to the acquisition. Incidental disbursements commonly include brokerage fees, taxes, legal fees, and other expenditures necessary to complete the transaction.

Bonds acquired between interest coupon dates are traded on the basis of the market price plus interest accrued since the most recent interest payment. The accrued interest is a separate asset—interest receivable—purchased simultaneously with the bond.

Audit Objective	Sample Year-End Procedures*	Sample Interim Procedures
Existence. Determine whether there are cash and cash equivalent balances supporting the dollar amount shown in the balance sheet and whether all such balances have been properly included.	• Count or confirm petty cash funds. • Obtain directly, from each bank with whom the company had transactions during the period, confirmation of the bank balances, loans, securities held, guarantees given, collateral held and any unused lines of credit available.	• Review bank reconciliations for independent approval. • Test the company's system for controlling payments. • Trace selected daily receipt listings to bank deposit slips and bank statements.
Ownership. Determine whether the cash and cash equivalent balances are owned by the company and whether they are subject to any lien or restrictions.	• Obtain confirmation of each balance direct from each bank, together with details of any collateral held or restrictions or liens over the accounts. • Confirm with employees any cash balances held by them.	• Review the company's procedures for establishing and pledging bank accounts.
Mechanical accuracy. Determine whether the basic mathematical calculations and clerical compilation procedures have been accurately carried out.	• Review reconciliations of bank balances and investigate reconciling items.	• Test the company's procedures for checking the mechanical accuracy of transactions being recorded or posted. • Test the addition and postings of the cash receipts and cash payments records.
Valuation. Determine whether cash and cash equivalent balances are fairly valued in conformity with generally accepted accounting principles.	• Review reconciliation of bank balances and investigate reconciling items. • Check exchange rate and translation calculation of foreign currency balances.	

Disclosure. Determine whether cash and cash equivalent balances disclosure in the financial statements is adequate.

- Agree financial statement disclosures to information noted in performance of the examination.
- Review bank confirmations for details of collateral and liens.

Classification. Determine whether cash and cash equivalent balances are properly classified as an asset or liability and as to liquidity.

- Review bank balances to determine whether there is any setting off of debit (overdraft) and credit balances.
- Confirm with banks the terms (including maturity) of any time deposit.

Cutoff. Determine whether all payments or receipts before and after the year-end are appropriately treated.

- Review cash transactions before and after the balance sheet date.
- Review any interbank and intercompany transfers before and after the year-end date.
- Note numbers of last checks drawn at year-end and trace to cutoff bank statements to ascertain that no subsequent checks cleared before year end.

* May also be performed at an interim date.

FIGURE 17.2 AUDIT OBJECTIVES AND SAMPLE PROCEDURES FOR CASH AND CASH EQUIVALENTS

A new cost basis is established when a security is written down for a permanent decline in value or when there is a transfer between current and noncurrent portfolios at the lower of cost or market, as discussed later.

Stock Dividends and Splits. When an equity owner in a corporation receives additional shares of the same class of stock in the form of either a stock dividend or a stock split, the investor's proportionate stockholding in the issuing company remains unchanged. Therefore, no dividend income should be recognized. The cost basis of the original investment should be allocated among the new shares received and the old shares held.

The same rule applies to dividends distributed in the form of preferred stock, warrants, or rights to purchase common or preferred stock. Again, the original cost is reallocated among the total holdings according to the proportionate relationship of their fair market value shortly after the new securities are issued.

Relieving Cost Upon Disposition of Securities. If only a part of an investment in a security is disposed of and the original investment was acquired in two or more purchases, a problem of cost identification arises. In such situations four possible methods can be used to relieve cost: (1) specific identification, (2) first-in, first-out, (3) last-in, first-out, and (4) average cost.

Critics of the specific identification method point out that the use of that method permits considerable choice in the amount of gain or loss to be recognized if different lots of a security have been purchased at different prices. Advocates of the average cost method believe that once the different lots are purchased they are really fungible in character and that average costs recognize this fungibility. Since the average cost method for security sales is not recognized by the Internal Revenue Service as an acceptable method, those companies that use it create a deferred tax timing difference. The IRS recognizes only the specific identification and first-in, first-out methods for general use. It will allow the use of the last-in, first-out method for entities whose holdings of securities are considered to be equivalent to inventory, such as stockbrokers.

Investment Income. When cash dividends are declared by the investee's board of directors, income is recognized because the investor has a legal right to the dividend. For convenience, companies may record dividends on the ex-dividend date or as received, but at the end of a fiscal period an accrual should be made for dividends receivable, if material. Dividends in kind should be recorded at fair market value; stock dividends and splits are not recorded as income.

Interest income accrues with the passage of time. The income recognized is adjusted for the amortization or accretion of bond premium or discount, which is the difference between the cost and face value of the debt security over its remaining life to maturity. The amortization of premium or accretion of discount using the interest method prescribed by APB 21 (AC 4111.15) results in the recognition of income at the effective interest rate over the remaining period to maturity.

Often the premium or discount on short-term bond investments will not be amortized or accreted, because the holding period is uncertain or will be so short as to make the effect immaterial.

Financial Accounting—Equity Securities

Requirements of SFAS 12. SFAS 12 (AC 5132) requires that marketable equity securities be accounted for by using the lower of aggregate cost or aggregate market value. In order to do this a company must first group its securities into separate portfolios according to the current or noncurrent classification; when the balance sheet is unclassified, the marketable equity securities are treated as noncurrent assets. Next, the aggregate acquisition cost of each of the portfolios is determined; unless a security has been assigned a new carrying amount because of permanent diminution in value or because of a transfer between current and noncurrent classifications, cost is the original cost.

Aggregate market value is the sum of the market price times the number of shares or units of each security in the portfolio. If the company has taken positions involving short sales, sales of calls, or purchases of puts in the same securities as those in the portfolio, these contracts are to be considered in determining market value.

These two aggregates are computed separately for current and noncurrent portfolios. If the aggregate market is less than the aggregate cost for a portfolio, a valuation allowance must be established. Note that under this approach a valuation allowance is required by the depressed market value of a portfolio, not a specific security.

When the valuation allowance for a current portfolio changes, the investor recognizes a gain or loss to be included in net income of the current period. The valuation allowance for a noncurrent portfolio is included in the equity section of the balance sheet and shown separately (the so-called dangling debit).

Affiliated Entities. In determining carrying amount, SFAS 12 (AC 5132.09) requires the current portfolios of entities that are consolidated in the financial statements, excluding those that follow specialized industry accounting practices, to be treated as a single consolidated portfolio with a comparison of aggregate cost and market value. Also, noncurrent and unclassified portfolios of consolidated entities should be combined in the same manner. The portfolios of marketable equity securities owned by entities accounted for by the equity method are not to be combined with the portfolios of any other entity included in the financial statements. However, such an entity must individually apply the rules of SFAS 12.

FASB Interpretation No. 13 (AC 5132-4) clarifies the application of SFAS 12 when the financial statements of a subsidiary are as of a date different from that of its parent but are consolidated with the financial statements of its parent: in order to compute the amount of a valuation allowance in consolidated financial statements, aggregate cost and aggregate market value of the portfolio shall be determined for each consolidated subsidiary as of the date of each subsidiary's balance sheet, and these aggregates shall be combined with aggregate cost and aggregate market value of the parent's portfolio determined as of the parent's balance sheet date. Disclosure should be given to the effect of intervening events that materially affect the financial position or results of operations of a subsidiary, including net realized gains or losses and net unrealized gains or losses applicable to marketable securities arising after the subsidiary's balance sheet date but prior to the parent's financial statement date. However, the subsidiary's financial statements shall not be adjusted for such changes.

Changes in Current/Noncurrent Classification. One of the problems with the accounting promulgated by SFAS 12 is its manipulability based on the classification of securities as current or noncurrent. As an example, if a company has the ability to hold securities on a long-term basis and can demonstrate that ability, the classification of the securities then depends on the company's representation as to its intentions. If a company represents that it will hold a security with a depressed market value on a long-term basis, the changes in the valuation reserve do not affect net income.

If the current or noncurrent classification of a marketable security changes, the security must be transferred between portfolios at the lower of its cost or market value. If market value is less than cost, the market value shall become the new cost basis. The difference between the old and new cost basis must be reflected as a loss in the determination of current net income.

Transfers between current and noncurrent classification are not accounting changes; however, such transfers, if material, may affect the comparability of the financial statements and should be disclosed (AU 9332.12).

Permanent Diminution in Value. Regardless of balance sheet classification, each investment should be evaluated to determine if there are significant factors other than current market conditions that affect the realizability of the carrying amount (AC 5132.21). For example, specific adverse conditions, such as a known liquidity crisis, may affect a particular company's securities, resulting in a permanent diminution in value; a bankrupt investee clearly reflects such a condition, as might a "going concern" qualification on the investee's most recent financial statements. Securities valuations should reflect these conditions by a charge against current operations to reduce the carrying amount to estimated current realizable value. In such a case, current realizable value becomes the new cost basis and is not adjusted for subsequent market recovery.

Keep in mind that the write-down to market of a noncurrent security simply results in a *dangling debit* in the equity section of the balance sheet; whether a permanent diminution in value, chargeable against income, has taken place still needs to be assessed.

In most cases current market quotations may already reflect specific adverse conditions. It is by no means certain, however, that the permanent diminution is the amount of the deficiency of market under cost. Among the relevant factors are the investor's ability to continue holding, the percentage of current market to cost, and the length of time the market for the security has been depressed. Thus the same security, written down to reflect a decline that is other than temporary, could carry a different valuation for different investors.

With respect to "trade relation" investments (e.g., major customer or vendor) in marketable equity securities not accounted for under the equity method of accounting, in addition to the preceding evaluation there must be a current assessment by management of the value of intangible benefits if those benefits are asserted to support an excess of cost over market that might otherwise require write-down. In all other respects, the provisions for noncurrent marketable securities are applicable.

Changes in Market Value After the Balance Sheet Date. FASB Interpretation No. 11 (AC 5132-2) clarifies the accounting necessary when there is a change in the market price with respect to marketable equity securities after the date of the financial statements but prior to their issuance. The interpretation indicates that the subsequent disposition of a security or a change in its market price after the end of the year should be taken into consideration, along with other factors, in making the determination of whether there was a permanent diminution in value of any of the securities held at the balance sheet date. Any loss to be recorded in financial statements is limited to the excess of cost over market value at the balance sheet date; further declines in value should be reported as a loss in the following accounting period.

This interpretation, of course, only affects those noncurrent or unclassified marketable securities for which the effect of a change in the carrying amount is included in stockholder's equity rather than in net income. It would seem that a recordable loss exists *prima facie* when a security is sold just after year-end at an amount that realizes the deferred loss at year-end, since this sale negates the noncurrent classification.

Income Tax Allocation. Unrealized gains and losses on marketable securities, whether recognized in net income or included in the equity section of the balance sheet, are timing differences as described in APB 11 (AC 4091). Since there are certain limitations as to the tax deductibility of investment losses (i.e., they usually must be realized by an offset against capital gains), SFAS 12 prescribes that the tax effect shall be recognized on an unrealized capital loss only when there exists assurance beyond a reasonable doubt that the benefit will be realized (AC 5132.22).

Some interpret the requirement to mean that the tax effect should be recognized when there is assurance beyond a reasonable doubt that the benefit would be realizable if the loss were actually incurred. In this context it is appropriate to take into consideration any usable realized capital gains for the current and preceding three years that could be used to offset the unrealized capital losses if they were to be realized.

Changes in Marketability Status. FASB Interpretation No. 16 (AC 5132-5) states that if the change in the status of an equity security between marketable and nonmarketable is coincident with the change in the classification between current and noncurrent and market value is less than cost, a new cost basis is established. For securities becoming marketable, market value is the first available market price; for securities becoming nonmarketable, market value is the last available market price. Since the accounting for a nonmarketable security is outside the scope of SFAS 12, it should be excluded from the portfolio of marketable equity securities of which it was a part for purposes of applying the statement. Conversely, when a nonmarketable equity security becomes marketable, it should be included in the portfolio at its cost.

Specialized Industry Practices. Certain industries, inc'uding investment companies, brokers and dealers in securities, stock life insurance companies, and fire and casualty insurance companies, apply specialized accounting practices to marketable securities (AC 5132.14-.16). SFAS 12 does not alter previous accounting practices in these specialized industries, except that entities that previously carried marketable equity securities at cost must carry them at the lower of their aggregate cost or market value. This does not preclude the use of the market basis where the industry had formerly allowed for either the cost basis or the market basis. The specialized industry practices for reporting gains and losses, whether realized or unrealized, remain unchanged. Specific reporting requirements are given for enterprises that include entities whose accepted accounting practices differ with respect to marketable securities (AC 5132.18).

Financial Accounting—Nonequity Securities

Classified as Current. SFAS 12 does not apply to marketable debt or similar securities. Nevertheless, there is little conceptual difference between accounting for current debt instruments and accounting for current equity securities, as discussed above. Current asset classification connotes an ability or intention to liquidate the investment within 12 months. Thus, if the valuation concept of lower of cost or market has validity for marketable equity securities, then for the sake of consistency, the concept should have validity for current marketable debt securities. As a result, currently classified marketable securities, whether debt or equity, should be stated at the lower of cost or market; the cumulative amount needed to reduce aggregate cost to aggregate market is considered a securities valuation reserve (valuation allowance); increases or decreases in the allowance are included in current income.

In a lower-of-cost-or-market-basis comparison for debt securities, cost should be amortized cost; therefore, amortization would be recorded prior to making the market comparison.

The computation of the valuation allowance for current marketable nonequity securities should be based on market prices (or, infrequently, on other lower estimates of net realizable value) at the date of the financial statements. In determining aggregate cost and aggregate market for the current portfolio, marketable debt and equity securities could be combined.

Some accountants believe that a write-down to the lower of cost or market is not appropriate for nonequity securities classified as current assets unless there is a permanent diminution in value. For support they cite the words "substantial" and "not due to a mere temporary condition" in ARB 43, Chapter 3A (AC 2031.09), which states:

> ...practice varies with respect to the carrying basis for current assets such as marketable securities.... Where market value is less than cost by a substantial amount and it is evident that the decline in market value is not due to a mere temporary condition, the amount to be included as a current asset should not exceed the market value.

Classified as Noncurrent. Because security investments appropriately classified as long-term carry with them a representation of a later realization date, current market quotations for such securities do not have the earnings impact of current assets. It is appropriate to classify, as part of noncurrent assets, investments in debt securities and in other securities with fixed maturity amounts at amortized cost, even when such amounts are in excess of quoted market, provided there is no indication of permanent diminution in value, it is management's intent to hold such securities until maturity, and there is sufficient evidence that such retention is feasible. Preferred stocks that by their terms are subject to mandatory redemption should be evaluated in the same manner as debt instruments.

Financial Disclosures

Specific disclosure requirements for marketable equity securities are given in SFAS 12 (AC 5132.12), and similar disclosures make sense for nonequity securities as well. The following information, which summarizes SFAS 12 requirements and incorporates nonequity securities, should be disclosed in the body of the financial statements or in the notes thereto:

- Aggregate cost and market value, segregated by current and noncurrent portfolios and between equity and debt securities, with an identification of which is the carrying amount for each balance sheet presented;
- Gross unrealized gains and gross unrealized losses, segregated by portfolio, for the latest balance sheet presented;
- The net realized gain or loss included in income along with the basis used to determine cost (i.e., specific identification, average cost, etc.) for each income statement presented;
- Changes in the valuation allowance accounts included in the equity section of the balance sheet and included in net income, shown separately for each balance sheet presented; and
- The impact of market value changes (realized and unrealized) occurring after the balance sheet date on marketable equity securities held as of the reporting date.

Other required disclosures, if material, are

- The amount of marketable securities pledged as collateral for borrowings,
- The amount of securities reclassified between current and noncurrent,
- Changes in the method of accounting,
- The amount of loss provisions,
- Information concerning specific material investments, and
- Holdings of New York City obligations that exceed 10% of stockholders' equity (ASR 188).

Auditing

General Concepts. The audit of marketable securities follows the same concepts that apply to cash and cash equivalents, as discussed earlier in this chapter.

Transaction Types. The primary transactions affecting marketable securities are

1. The purchase of marketable securities, including the authorization and implementation of security purchases, the recording of the resulting liabilities and assets, and the controls to ensure receipt and safekeeping of the security;
2. The sale of marketable securities, encompassing the authorization and implementation of security sales, the recording of the resulting profit or loss on disposal, and the controls over the transfer of the security to the purchaser;

3. The valuation of marketable equity securities that, because of SFAS 12, are influenced
   by changes in the market values in the following ways:
   a. Securities should be carried at the lower of aggregate cost or aggregate market for
      each portfolio,
   b. A transfer of a security between current and noncurrent classifications will be
      made at the lower of cost or market, which may establish a new cost basis,
   c. When the market value of a noncurrent security is substantially lower than cost
      it may signal a permanent diminution in value, which would result in a charge
      against earnings and a new carrying amount; and
4. The receipt of investment income, including dividends, interest, and the entitlement
   to rights issues, stock options, warrants, etc.

Audit Approach. The nature of marketable securities is such that this segment
is not greatly affected by the major transaction cycles. Unlike cash and accounts
payable, for which much of the auditing can be performed through tests of compliance, it is generally much more efficient to confine the audit of marketable securities to year-end substantive procedures. An exception to this general rule exists
for enterprises that hold large portfolios of marketable securities.

The issue of whether it is sufficient to merely confirm securities held by independent custodians as opposed to physically inspecting and counting them is unresolved. With respect to the audit of investment companies, the auditor is required
to describe in his report how he satisfied himself as to the existence of the securities,
because of their relatively high value in relation to the total assets. The same issue
often exists with respect to marketable securities held by other types of entities;
however, the accounting profession has generally ignored the problem.

In order to focus on possible problem areas, the auditor should initially perform
these analytical procedures:

1. Review changes in balances and value of marketable securities and other investments
   during the period in light of the company's investment policy (considered in relation
   to management of cash), and
2. Compare interest and dividend income to prior years and as they relate to levels of
   marketable security and other investments.

Objectives and Procedures. In addition to carrying out analytical review procedures the auditor must devise other procedures, which will primarily be substantive, to achieve the objectives of the audit of marketable securities. Figure 17.3
is a very condensed listing of the interim and year-end audit procedures that are
commonly used to achieve these objectives. The procedures shown may be used
to satisfy more than one audit objective, but are listed alongside the objective that
they most typically satisfy, in order to provide an overview of how the audit objectives are met.

ACCOUNTS PAYABLE AND ACCRUALS

Functions in the Purchases/Payables Cycle

The purchases/payables cycle involves the decisions and processes for obtaining goods and services to operate a business. There are five primary functions in
the purchases/payables cycle:

1. The internal requisition for goods or services is the starting point for the cycle. The exact form of the request and the required approval depends on the nature of the goods and services and the company policy.
2. The next step is the placement of a purchase order with a vendor for goods or services. The order is often in writing and may become a legal commitment for a specified item at the stated price when it is accepted by the seller.
3. The receipt by the company of goods or services ordinarily establishes a legal liability. Upon receipt the company examines the goods for quantity, condition, and conformity with the specifications of the original order.
4. The company next records its liability in accounts payable, charging the related expense or asset. This recording usually awaits the receipts of an invoice and its matchup with the related purchase order and receiving documents.
5. The final step in the cycle is the extinguishment of the liability through the disbursement of cash.

Financial Accounting and Reporting

In its *Exposure Draft (Revised) on Elements of Financial Statements of Business Enterprises* (1979g), the FASB defines liabilities in this way (paragraph 22):

> Liabilities are probable future sacrifices of economic benefits stemming from present legal, equitable, or constructive obligations of a particular enterprise to transfer assets or provide services to other entities in the future as a result of past transactions or events affecting the enterprise.

The exposure draft points out that "a constructive obligation is created, inferred or construed from the facts"; for example, an accrual for vacation pay or year-end bonuses.

Some liabilities can be definitely determined as to existence and amount. Other liabilities definitely exist but their amounts must be estimated. And still other liabilities are contingent as to both existence and amount (see Chapter 29 for a discussion of contingent liabilities).

Current and Long-Term Classification. Current liabilities include (1) all obligations for which payment will require the use of existing current assets or the creation of other current liabilities and (2) all other obligations that will probably be paid from current assets within the period of one full operating cycle. ARB 43, Chapter 3A (AC 2031.07), contains a more detailed description of current liabilities.

Most companies have an operating cycle of one year or less, and thus it has become common practice to use a 12-month time period to distinguish between current and long-term liabilities. A company may operate on a longer cycle (e.g., several years for long-term construction contractors) and may use that cycle for classification of assets and for certain contract-related liabilities; but most liabilities in such a situation will be classified on the 12-month basis.

Present Valuing. The amount of a liability is the present value of the sum of money or value of goods or services that must be paid to discharge the obligation. However, current liabilities are usually recorded at their face amount, because

Audit Objective	Sample Year-End Procedures*	Sample Interim Procedures
Existence. Determine whether there are marketable securities supporting the amount shown in the balance sheet and whether all such securities have been properly included.	• Inspect securities and investments or obtain direct confirmation where they are held by independent custodians. • Determine reputation of custodian.	• Vouch additions to and disposals of securities and investments to authorization, contract notes and other supporting documentation. Assure that the transaction was at an arm's-length price and that income was correctly accounted for. • Review brokers' advices.
Ownership. Determine whether the marketable securities are owned by the company and whether they are subject to any lien or restrictions.	• Review and inquire as to whether any marketable securities and investments are pledged as collateral. Confirm details.	
Mechanical accuracy. Determine whether the basic mathematical calculations and clerical compilation procedures have been accurately carried out.	• Obtain a schedule of marketable securities and other investments at balance sheet date and trace totals to general ledger, agree opening balances to prior-period financial statements and add and cross-add schedule. • Reconcile the general ledger control account with the detailed investment records.	• For selected periods test the accuracy of the detailed investment transactions by recomputing aggregate sales or market price and commissions based on units sold and per unit prices.
Valuation. Determine whether marketable securities are fairly valued in accordance with generally accepted accounting principles.	• Determine basis for valuing securities and investments and verify market value by reference to published quotations.	• For selected purchases and sales agree cost and sale proceeds to independent sources of market price for reasonableness.

Disclosure. Determine whether marketable securities disclosure in the financial statements is adequate.

- Challenge for permanent diminution in value where cost exceeds market value substantially.
- Verify dates and market values of transfers between current and non-current portfolios.
- Test investment income to determine that interest and dividends are received based on stated rates and published data on dividends.

Classification. Determine whether marketable securities are properly classified as to class of security and liquidity.

- Review and inquire as to whether any marketable securities and investments are pledged as collateral. Confirm details in conjunction with liabilities confirmation procedures.
- Review and inquire as to the proper classification of marketable securities and other investments.
- Review classification of individual purchases based on supporting detail.

Cutoff. Determine whether all marketable security transactions before and after the year-end are appropriately treated.

- Assure that purchases and sales are recorded in the correct period by reviewing purchases and sales immediately before and after the year end to confirm the actual date of the transaction.
- Review timeliness of recording interim transactions.

* May also be performed at an interim date.

FIGURE 17.3   AUDIT OBJECTIVES AND SAMPLE PROCEDURES FOR MARKETABLE SECURITIES

the difference between the present value of the liability and the face amount is generally not significant for the short time period involved. The slight overstatement of current liabilities that results from stating them at face amount seems a justifiable compromise of precision.

Specifically exempted from present-value techniques are those payables arising from transactions with customers or suppliers in the normal course of business that are due in accordance with customary trade terms not exceeding approximately one year (AC 4111.03).

Extent of Disclosure. The details of disclosure vary with the circumstances of the business, but broad categories are generally used. Individual accounts or grouped captions may be shown, such as

- Notes payable to banks,
- Notes payable to trade creditors,
- Accounts payable,
- Income taxes payable,
- Accrued expenses,
- Dividends payable,
- Other liabilities, and
- Current maturities of long-term debt.

Notes are segregated because of their legal status as negotiable instruments and should be identified in the balance sheet or footnotes by type of payee. Collateralized notes should be segregated from noncollateralized notes and cross-referenced to the assets pledged as collateral; alternatively, this information can be given in the footnotes. Generally, accounts payable represent normal recurring trade obligations for which creditors' invoices are received. Income taxes are traditionally segregated, both because of their materiality and because of disclosure rules in APB 11 (AC 4091.53).

Accrued expenses represent provisions for expenses incurred (but ordinarily not yet billed by the seller) during the period as a result of past contractual agreements, past services received, or tax laws. Because there is very little real difference between accounts payable and accrued expenses, the distinction between them has blurred, although for SEC filings any item in excess of 5% of total current liabilities is to be disclosed separately.

At the balance sheet date all trade payables arising from the purchase of goods and services that have been received or that are in transit should be recorded. Trade accounts payable may be recorded net of discounts if the company normally takes cash discounts and has the means of continuing the practice. The company's policy must be followed consistently. Material debit balances due from vendors that are collectible in cash should be reclassified as receivables; amounts that will be applied to future purchases should be reclassified as deposits, which for practical purposes can be combined in receivables.

As a rule of thumb, any single material liability should be separately reported in the current liability section of the balance sheet if it arises from an unusual source, is uncertain in amount, is contingent on a future event, is secured by assets of the business, or is to be paid from an unusual source. The unusual circumstances should be described either in a footnote or parenthetically. Unless they are minor in amount, accounts payable to subsidiaries and other affiliates, officers, directors, and principal stockholders should be shown as separate items.

A uniform, generally accepted ordering of current liabilities does not exist, and uniformity of classification from year to year is often affected by changes in the nature of a company's liabilities. Although current assets can be ordered in relation to their liquidity, a comparable ordering is not as easily made for current liabilities, because the various categories of current liabilities can have many different maturities. Banks overdrafts, which do not appear often, are usually listed first in deference to their priority of maturity.

Vacation Pay. The right to a paid vacation is normally contingent on the employee having worked for a specified length of time, or it may accrue ratably, such as one day per month worked. The length of vacation often increases after an employee has worked for a specified number of years.

Some accountants believe that the liability for vacation pay should be recognized for accounting purposes only to the extent that formally established conditions have been met. Others believe that the liability should be accrued ratably over the employee's work period. According to the latter view, a satisfactory estimate can be made of employee turnover based on experience, and a reasonable accrual can be made. This view holds, too, that the legalities of when vacation pay is earned are less important than the economic reality that the company will have to pay for time not worked and that it is more important to associate the vacation expense with the employee's productive period than to incur a charge based on the time that a legal condition precedent is met.

The SEC stated in SAB 1 that accrued vacation pay should be recorded in the accounts, and the FASB has issued *Exposure Draft on Accounting for Compensated Absences* (1979c), which would require an accrual of the liability during the current accounting period for estimated probable future payments attributable to employees' service during that period.

Taxes Other Than Income Taxes. Real estate, personal property, franchise, and excise taxes should be grouped together under a caption such as "Taxes, other than taxes on income." State franchise and excise taxes based on income should be included in the "Income taxes payable" caption.

In practice, real estate and personal property taxes have been accrued on several different bases, including

1. Year in which payable (cash basis),
2. Fiscal year of governing body levying tax, and
3. Year for which the tax is levied, as shown on the tax bill.

Generally, the most acceptable basis of providing for property taxes is monthly accrual during the fiscal year for which the taxes are levied. However, barring significant changes in the level of taxes, consistency is probably more important than technical accuracy.

Other Accruals. There are numerous accrued liabilities that can be applicable in a given company. Among the more common are

- Interest,
- Payroll taxes,
- Pension expense,
- Price redetermination or renegotiation,
- Professional fees,
- Rent,
- Repairs,
- Royalties,
- Travel,
- Unpaid wages, salaries, and commissions,
- Utilities, and
- Warranties.

Ordinarily the appropriate amounts for a company's usual list of accruals are determined at each period-end and recorded by standard journal entry, which reverses the amount set up at the previous period-end. Under this approach, as actual disbursements are made they are charged to the appropriate asset or expense account, not to the accrual account.

If accruals as a group are material in amount (more than 10% of current liabilities), they are ordinarily shown separately in the financial statements; otherwise, one or more items are separately broken out so as to reduce the remainder to a small amount combinable with accounts payable.

Auditing

General Concepts. There are seven basic audit objectives applicable to accounts payable and accruals, discussed in Chapter 12, and seven not entirely congruent internal control objectives, discussed in Chapter 13. The auditing discussion in this section assumes a familiarity with Chapters 12 and 13. However, to set a framework for the discussion of payables and accruals auditing, the following cross-reference table may be helpful:

Overall Audit Objective, as Shown in This Chapter	Internal Control Objective
Congruent:	
Existence	Authorization
	Validity
	Recording
Valuation—accuracy	Valuation
Cutoff	Timing
Mechanical accuracy	Summarization
Classification	Classification
Not congruent:	
Ownership	
Valuation—changed circumstances	
Disclosure	

Transaction Types. The primary transaction types that impact accounts payable and accruals consist of

1. The purchase of raw materials, supplies, capital assets, and services. The auditor must be familiar with the client's controls over the ordering, receipt, and return of goods and services.
2. The payments of liabilities arising from the above purchases. The auditor must be familiar with the client's controls over cash payments as outlined in the earlier section on auditing cash and cash equivalents.

Audit Approach. As described in Chapter 13, the audit process requires that the auditor obtain an understanding of the client's system of internal control, document his understanding, and analyze the internal control system to ascertain (1) the control points on which he chooses to rely and (2) the effect of systems weaknesses on his audit plan. The auditor must then develop specific audit procedures to test those areas of internal control on which he will rely. As these audit steps must of necessity be geared to the company's system, a cookbook listing of audit steps is not provided here.

Once the auditor is satisfied that the system is operating in the manner that he originally contemplated or he has modified his understanding, he plans the scope and extent of his year-end substantive audit procedures. Depending on the reliability of the client's system of internal control, the auditor might decide to perform some of the procedures prior to year-end.

Listed below are some fundamental analytical procedures generally applied in the audit of accounts payable and accrued liabilities:

1. Compare the current listing of accounts payable and accruals with that of the previous audit date and note any significant changes—e.g., changes in major suppliers, in the number of overdue accounts, or in the proportion of debit balances.
2. Determine whether there are any balances with related companies or with shareholders, directors, or officers. If so, how do these balances compare to similar balances at the last audit date? These types of balances may or may not repesent genuine trade accounts—possibly they should be excluded from the calculation of ratios and other statistics for trade accounts if they are large enough to be distortive. They may also pose particular verification problems (see Chapter 28).
3. Review such statistics as the relationship of accounts payable to purchases (or other meaningful volume relationships), compare to previous periods, and obtain satisfactory explanations for variations in the current figures. It is not sufficient merely to establish that there has been no significant change from the previous period; the important question is, should there be a change, and if so, how much?

Objectives and Procedures. In addition to carrying out analytical review procedures, the auditor must devise substantive and compliance procedures to achieve the objectives of the audit of accounts payable and accruals. Figure 17.4 is a very condensed listing of the interim and year-end audit procedures that are commonly used to achieve these objectives. The procedures shown may be used to satisfy more than one audit objective, but are listed alongside the objective that they most

Audit Objective	Sample Year-End Procedures*	Sample Interim Procedures
Existence. Determine whether the liabilities recorded in the balance sheet exist and whether all such liabilities have been properly included.	• Obtain selected supplier's statements directly and reconcile to accounts. • Review accounts payable control account for the period and investigate any large or unusual entires or any significant increases or decreases in purchases toward the year-end. • Search for unrecorded liabilities by inquiry and examination of post-balance sheet transactions and confirmation as appropriate. • Check validity and accuracy of accruals by reference to supporting documents.	• Check numerical sequence of receiving documents and trace selected receiving documents to supplier's invoices and to purchase journal.
Ownership. Determine whether the liabilities recorded in the balance sheet are valid charges against the company.	• For selected items agree to supplier's invoice, goods receipt advices, copy of purchase orders, and other supporting documents.	• Vouch selected items from the purchase journal and the cash disbursements journal to supporting documentation, including purchase invoices, orders, and receiving documentation.
Mechanical accuracy. Determine whether the basic mathematical calculations and clerical compilation procedures have been accurately carried out.	• Obtain schedule of accounts payable and accruals. Add schedule, agree total to general ledger and agree selected items to subsidiary records or supporting documentation.	• Recompute details on vendor invoices. • Test footings of purchase journal.
Valuation. Determine whether accounts payable and accruals are fairly valued in accordance with generally accepted accounting principles.	• Reconcile supplier's statements to accounts. • Determine that liabilities payable in a foreign currency have been valued at the proper exchange rates.	• Review accounts payable control account for the period and investigate any large or unusual entries or increases or decreases in purchases.

- Determine which liabilities are affected by discounts and ensure that they have been properly handled.
- Ascertain basis of provisions made, check calculations and determine reasonableness.
- Review accounts payable balances and accruals for amounts due to (or from) group and related companies, debit balances, and unusual items.
- Review nature and magnitude of items that are combined for financial reporting purposes.
- Determine that proper cutoff procedures were applied to assure that purchases and supplier debit memos have been recorded at the balance sheet date in the correct accounting period.
- Where there is a lack of substantial internal evidence obtain direct confirmation of account balances from third parties.

- Review agreements underlying various liabilities and accruals (e.g., vendor supply contracts and union agreements).
- Review account classification of initial recording of transactions.
- Test period of recording interim transactions.

Disclosure. Determine whether disclosures included in the financial statements are adequate.

Classification. Determine whether accounts payable and accruals are properly classified in the balance sheet.

Cutoff. Determine whether the liabilities for goods or services received before and after the year-end have been recorded in the correct period.

* May also be performed at an interim date.

FIGURE 17.4 AUDIT OBJECTIVES AND SAMPLE PROCEDURES FOR ACCOUNTS PAYABLE AND ACCRUALS

tory pilferage or other shrinkage. Estimates of bad debts should be periodically recorded among costs and expenses (not as revenue reductions) at the time revenue is recognized, with appropriate adjustments based on ongoing evaluations of accounts outstanding.

In determining the allowance for uncollectible accounts in large volume situations, a methodology may be developed to combine historical experience and current economic considerations in order to generate a future expectation. This may result in reflecting the average experience of the enterprise over time, thus averaging the effect of bad debts into the income statement. Such a method is not useful, however, when a company's receivables comprise a small number of relatively large balances. In these situations, the reserve should reflect the expected loss in the specific receivables at the financial statement presentation date. This loss could be zero, but it could also be large if there is a default by one major customer.

It should be noted, however, that the measurements used for accounting purposes to record bad debts may not be the proper measurements for evaluating the economic cost of granting credit. Bad debt expense is measured by the amount of receivable written off or expected to be written off. The economic cost of such a receivable, however, is generally only the variable cost of the product that was delivered in creating it. Thus, sound credit policy may accept a higher level of credit risk if a product with low variable cost is being sold. Accounting measures may be misleading as to the cost of credit loss in such a case.

Averaging Bad Debts. In an attempt to partly resolve the question of whether averaging was appropriate, the FASB in 1975 issued SFAS 5, *Accounting for Contingencies,* which recognizes collectibility of receivables as a loss contingency (AC 4311.04(a)). SFAS 5 provides the following general guidelines (AC 4311.08):

> An estimated loss from a loss contingency . . . shall be accrued by a charge to income if *both* of the following conditions are met:
> (a) Information available prior to issuance of the financial statements indicates that it is probable that an asset had been impaired or a liability had been incurred at the date of the financial statements. It is implicit in this condition that it must be probable that one or more future events will occur confirming the fact of the loss.
> (b) The amount of loss can be reasonably estimated.

The above conditions seem to suggest an account-by-account evaluation, but the FASB put the matter straight in Appendix A (AC 4311.22):

> Those conditions may be considered in relation to individual receivables or in relation to groups of similar types of receivables. If the conditions are met, accrual [of a loss provision] shall be made even though the particular receivables that are uncollectible may not be identifiable.

Practicing accountants took this to mean status quo in bad debt accounting, but the FASB stirred up matters by stating in SFAS 17, *Accounting for Leases—Initial Direct Costs* (AC 4054.06):

> Accounting for bad debts that are expected to result from leases and other financing activities is a pervasive issue that the Board did not address in *FASB Statement No. 13.*

The Board has not studied that question and did not intend that Statement No. 13 would change existing practices in accounting for bad debts.

What caused the consideration was that numerous leasing companies were treating bad debts as part of initial direct costs, so to say that a proscription against doing so was not a change in existing practices was confusing. The Board chose not to speak further on the subject. (See Chapter 23 for how this has been reconciled in practice.)

If a conclusion can be drawn from the FASB remarks, averaging in the sense of "smoothing" income is prohibited but broad estimations for large numbers of homogeneous accounts is proper. It is often difficult to tell the difference in practice.

Selling Receivables. Individual accounts or groups of accounts receivable can be sold to or factored with unrelated parties under a variety of agreements that may allow recourse against the seller for those accounts ultimately not collected by the purchaser. When the buyer has recourse against the seller for uncollectible items, there is some controversy concerning the appropriate accounting.

SOP 74-6, *Recognition of Profits on Sales of Receivables With Recourse*, discusses current practice in accounting in the income statement for the differential between the recorded amount of the receivable and the price paid by the buyer, generally a financial institution. The SOP identifies three major income recognition methods in current use:

1. *Delayed recognition method*—the differential is spread over the life of the installment receivable or the estimated collection period.
2. *Immediate recognition method*—the differential is recognized when the receivable is sold.
3. *Nonrecourse market method*—the differential is considered to have two components. The first component comes from the sale of the receivable and is recognized immediately. The second, the retention of the credit risk by the seller, is recognized as the risk diminishes over time.

SOP 74-6 concludes that the delayed recognition method is preferable to the immediate recognition method, since receivable sales transactions resemble financing transactions more so than conventional sales transactions. The immediate recognition method was rejected because the seller's risks are not eliminated; the buyer may still look to the seller for ultimate satisfaction. And because practical problems prevent a reasonable allocation of the differential into pieces, the SOP rejected the use of the nonrecourse market method even though it might have been the most conceptually sound.

The balance sheet treatment of sold receivables is as yet an unaddressed problem, and in practice two methods are currently accepted: applying the proceeds against the receivables and, alternatively, recording the proceeds as debt to be repaid as the receivables are collected. These are shown in Figure 18.1.

When receivables are sold without recourse there are no contingencies, and the sale will be recorded as if the receivables were collected in the normal course of business. The discount granted the purchaser will be classified among the company's financial costs.

A. REDUCTION OF RECEIVABLES:
    Caption in balance sheet—

	February 3, 1979	January 28, 1978
Accounts Receivable (net of amounts sold with recourse; $39,900,000 this year and $34,200,000 last year)	$17,035,000	$38,350,000

B. AS A LIABILITY:
    Excerpt from policies footnote—
    (d) *Aircraft Loans Sold to Banks with Recourse*
    Aircraft loans which are originated by the Company and sold to banks, with recourse, are accounted for by the "financing method." These transactions with the banks are reflected on the balance sheets and statements of operations as borrowing from the banks.

FIGURE 18.1 EXAMPLE OF PRESENTATION OF RECEIVABLES SOLD
SOURCE: City Stores Company, 1978 Annual Report (Point A), and Avemco Corporation, 1978 Annual Report (Point B).

Based on an AcSEC issues paper (AICPA, 1980l), the FASB has indicated it will consider whether a project should be added to its agenda regarding transfers of receivables that provide recourse to the transferor in the event of default on the receivables. The central issue is whether they should be accounted for as borrowings or as sales.

Reporting Considerations. Reporting receivables in a company's financial statements is affected by the nature of the originating transactions, the industry involved, and several practical considerations. As a general rule, significant balances should be segregated by type (e.g., lease receivables, trade accounts receivable), and related-party receivables (see Chapter 28), even if originating in the ordinary course of business, should be classified by source (e.g., subsidiaries, affiliates, employees).

If an enterprise presents a classified balance sheet (current assets segregated from noncurrent assets), receivables should be segregated based on whether they will be collected within the next operating cycle (generally one year). There is, however, an exception to this general rule: in enterprises having an operating cycle of more than one year (for instance, distilleries, construction, tobacco, or lumber), accounts collectible within the operating cycle should be considered as current assets. Also, if there is collateral for a receivable, that should be stated where material.

Enterprises often receive revenues from sources other than their primary business activities. These sources may be tangentially related to the main business (e.g., revenues from sales of fixed assets or scrap), or they may be totally unrelated, as with the receipt of dividends or interest on investment of temporarily available funds. When these receipts are not significant, they should be included in the financial statements in whatever manner is most expeditious.

There are two approaches for financial reporting of other revenues: as a separately reported total or as a recovery of cost. The first method aggregates all such miscellaneous items and reports them as one total simply as a practical expedient. The other method recognizes that many receipts actually represent the recovery of a previous expense and should be portrayed as such. The sale of scrap recovers some of the inventory cost previously charged to sales; sublease income actually offsets or recovers rent expense. The reporting method chosen should take such economic realities into account. Additionally, income earned on temporary investment of funds is often classified as an offset to interest expense.

Occasionally, an item of other revenue is very significant to the operations of an enterprise; ordinarily this would be referred to as a gain or loss transaction. If the item fulfills the criteria of being unusual in nature and infrequent in occurrence, as stated in APB 30, *Reporting the Results of Operations* (AC 2012), the gain or loss on the transaction should be presented as an extraordinary item, net of the related income tax effect. If only one of the two criteria is met, the gain or loss may be reported as a separate component of income from continuing operations without a netting of the related income tax effect. (See Chapter 7 for a broader discussion.)

Other Matters

Consignments. Merchandise shipped on a consignment or trial basis should not be considered as a sale, because the consignee is not obligated until he has resold the merchandise or otherwise accepted it. The legal title still rests with the consignor, who has merely relinquished possession of the merchandise. For accounting purposes, the merchandise should remain classified as inventory, separately delineated if the amount is large.

Prepayments, Advance Billings, Deposits, and Unearned Revenue. Occasionally in significant act transactions and more often in proportional performance transactions, funds are advanced by the customer. These can be in the form of contractual prepayments or advance billings, or they may simply be deposits. The seller should account for advance receipts as either unearned (deferred) revenue or as deposits; the nature of the advance will determine the appropriate accounting.

If the advance was made to secure performance under an agreement (e.g., payment of future rents) and is legally refundable, it should be classified as a deposit. As future revenues are recognized, the deposit is not reduced, since it must ultimately be refunded. If, on the other hand, the advance is to be applied as payment (either partial or complete), it should be classified as unearned revenue and credited to revenue when earned within the terms of the agreement.

Differentiation of a deposit from unearned revenue is normally based on the legal provisions of the agreement, since there may be little difference in substance in a particular transaction.

Careful description and disclosure of unearned or deferred revenue is advisable. There have been more than a few instances where amounts labeled deferred profit in the balance sheet have been misunderstood to be assured of inclusion in future income. In fact, many such items are deferred because future events may cause the originating transaction to be undone and the deferred profit simply to be reversed.

Progress Payments. Progress payments may be made as the performance of contracts proceeds. The proper accounting depends on the revenue recognition method being applied to the contract itself. Since the seller receives progress payments to fund his current costs on the remitting customer's order, he should normally record them as an offset to those costs. Under the completed-contract method the contractor accumulates his costs in inventory and thus credits progress payments to inventory accounts. To the extent that progress payments exceed costs, the excess should be classified as a liability.

When the contract is accounted for on the percentage-of-completion method, costs are accumulated in three categories: billed accounts receivable, unbilled accounts receivable, and inventory. Progress payments, especially under fixed-price contracts, are usually applied first to amounts carried in billed and unbilled receivables and then to accumulated costs classified as inventory. Excess payments should be classified as liability.

Nonmonetary Transactions. In the types of transactions discussed above, measurement of revenue has been based on the amount of cash received or expected to be realized. However, some revenue transactions involve an exchange of nonmonetary assets. APB 29, *Accounting for Nonmonetary Transactions* (AC 1041), requires the inclusion in revenues of the fair value of nonmonetary assets received, if the transaction otherwise is a revenue-producing activity. The complex problems associated with recording revenue based on the fair value of a nonmonetary asset received are discussed in Chapter 7.

Service Transactions

Service transactions can be as simple as a car wash or as complex as a contract to provide the plans for a colony on the moon. Over the past few years, the number of businesses providing services or combining services with their products has increased dramatically. The services offered cover a broad spectrum ranging from infant care centers to health spas to retirement homes. Furthermore, the quest for public funds to finance the larger of these organizations, along with a heightened consumerism, has pointed to a need for more definitive GAAP, especially in the area of revenue recognition.

Service transactions are labor intensive and therefore the most significant attendant costs to be accounted for are labor costs and appropriate allocations of overhead. In the performance of certain service transactions, small amounts of material may be used (maintenance contracts). If such materials are incidental to rendering the service and are not separately charged to the customer in a way that would vary the total transaction price, the transaction is a service transaction. If, however, a product and service are combined, and the service is incidental to the product and provided to all product purchasers (e.g., a warranty not separately charged for), the transaction is a product transaction, not covered in the following discussion.

Very little authoritative accounting literature is devoted to the subject of accounting for service revenues and costs, though some aspects are addressed by AICPA industry audit and accounting guides. Because of the paucity of guidance for most service industries, diverse accounting approaches have developed.

Some practices are conservative, delaying revenue recognition until every aspect of the service is performed and deferring only costs directly incurred in providing the specific service. Other practices are very liberal, recognizing all estimated revenues at the inception of the transaction. In the middle are accounting practices that recognize income periodically as the related service is provided and that defer costs associated with the services to be provided and related revenues to be recognized in the future. All approaches are premised on the idea of matching costs and revenues; the debate centers around determining the appropriate period for revenue recognition and identifying the appropriate costs to be deferred or accrued.

In October 1978, the FASB issued *Invitation to Comment on Accounting for Certain Service Transactions* (FASB, 1978e), based on a draft of an AcSEC SOP (published as Section II of the FASB release). The following discussion is based, to a large extent, on the provisions of the draft SOP, since it is the profession's first conceptual attempt at dealing with accounting in the broad area of service transactions. The invitation to comment has not been finalized by the FASB; because of its pervasiveness, this subject has been incorporated into the FASB technical agenda as part of the Board's conceptual framework project on accounting recognition. Meanwhile, the provisions of the SOP are not uniformly followed by nonpublic companies, but SEC reporting companies have a higher compliance likelihood.

Revenue Recognition. APB Statement 4 provides the following generalizations (AC 1026.15):

> Revenue from services rendered is recognized . . . when services have been performed and are billable. Revenue from permitting others to use enterprise resources . . . is recognized as time passes or as the resources are used.

In practice, the latitude implicit in these principles has resulted in the development of a diverse range of accounting methods. In addition to the significant act and proportional performance methods mentioned earlier in this chapter, some service industries utilize an *immediate recognition method,* under which the entire service fee is recognized as revenue at the time the buyer purchases the service even though the service has not yet been rendered. In this method, ordinarily there would be a deferral of at least enough revenue to cover expected future direct costs or, as an alternative, an accrual of those costs. This method typically has been used where customers are irrevocably committed to, or have paid at the inception of the contract, the full purchase price and future *direct* costs to be incurred by the seller were minimal.

The draft SOP concludes (FASB, 1978e), paragraph 10):

> Revenue from service transactions should be recognized based on performance, because performance determines the extent to which the earnings process is complete or virtually complete. Performance is the execution of a defined act or acts or occurs with the passage of time.

This conclusion results in four general revenue recognition methods: the specific performance and completed performance methods (both analogous to the significant act method); the proportional performance method; and the collection method. In applying these conclusions, in particular the proportional performance method, AcSEC confirmed the conceptual soundness of the percentage-of-completion method.

Specific performance accounting. Revenue is recognized when the specific significant act is performed. For example, a real estate sale commission is earned when the real estate sale is consummated.

Completed performance accounting. Where there are an indeterminate number of acts to be performed over an indeterminate period of time, or where the final act is significant in the overall service transaction, revenue is recognized when that final act is performed. For example, a freight transportation company's significant act is delivery to the consignee. The application of this method could be difficult in accounting systems that maintain data primarily based on transaction origination; but most often these are short-term transactions within a single reporting period, and to solve the problem a provision for unearned revenues is estimated and accrued at period-end.

Proportional performance accounting. Revenue is recognized in various ways, depending on the nature of the various acts:

1. If the acts are a series of identical or similar acts, each act should be assigned an equal part of the revenue.
2. If the acts are specifically identified but are not identical or similar, the revenue should be allocated to each specific act on the basis of its direct cost (see Cost Recognition below) if determinable. Otherwise, some other systematic and rational allocation basis, such as using sales values if objectively determinable, should be used. The straight-line method (in 3 below) is applicable if direct costs or sales values are undeterminable.
3. When there are an unspecified number of similar acts (e.g., use of health spa facilities), even if the acts are contingent (e.g., an equipment maintenance contract), revenue should be recognized on a straight-line basis over the term of the contract; there is an exception, however: when the pattern of performance can be shown to differ from that assumed by straight-line amortization (e.g., seasonality or a pattern of usage considerably shorter than the duration of an agreement permitting use of enterprise facilities), the revenue recognition pattern should be modified accordingly.

Collection method accounting. Many services, especially personal services, have a significant degree of uncertainty of ultimate realization. Revenue should therefore be recognized upon collection.

Other problems. Contracts that combine initiation fees and continuing service fees or that relate equipment to services create unusual problems:

1. In the first situation, some objective value must be determined for initiation rights; if none are discernible, those rights should be considered an integral part of the continuing service transaction.
2. In transactions involving equipment installation combined with continuing maintenance, if the customer is able to purchase the installation separately from the service contract, the installation fee is not a service transaction but is a component of the equipment purchase transaction.

Cost Recognition. APB Statement 4 discusses accounting for expenses. The statement indicates:

> Expenses are the costs that are associated with the revenue of the period, often directly, but frequently indirectly through association with the period to which the revenue has been assigned. Costs to be associated with future revenue or otherwise to be associated with future accounting periods are deferred to future periods as assets. [AC 1026.19]

The primary objective of accounting for service transaction costs is to match costs with revenues; this suggests deferral of costs only if such costs are related to expected future revenues equal to or in excess of those costs.

Definitions of the various types of costs related to the performance of service transactions are needed to understand their accounting treatment. There are three basic types of costs.

Initial direct costs. Costs related to the sale but not the performance of the service fall into this category. (See also SFAS 17 (AC 4054) for an expostulation on these costs in leasing transactions.) Examples of such costs are sales commissions, processing fees, and credit investigation costs. Supervisory and administrative expenses do not qualify even if they are directly associated with the sale of the service. Initial direct costs should be deferred and charged to expense in proportion to the revenue recognized in the period except where revenue is recognized on the collection method; in that situation, because of the uncertainties involved, the costs should be expensed as incurred. All initial direct costs associated with unsuccessful attempts to obtain a service sale should be expensed during the period in which incurred and not included or offset against successful efforts in other sales.

Direct costs. Such costs are clearly identifiable with the services performed (e.g., costs incurred in servicing a maintenance contract). Where revenues are recognized on the proportional performance method the direct costs are expensed as incurred, because this should be a close approximation of the degree of performance. For transactions where revenue is recognized under the specific performance or completed performance method the costs are expensed as the related revenue is recognized. Again, where revenue is recognized when collected, the direct costs are expensed as incurred.

Indirect costs. These are all costs that do not specifically qualify as either initial direct costs or direct costs, and they should be expensed as incurred.

Costs in excess of estimated related revenues are not to be deferred but should be recognized as an expense in the period incurred. In addition, if the total estimated future costs combined with the costs incurred to date exceed the total estimated revenue, the estimated loss should be recorded at the earliest date this determination can be made—first reducing the deferred costs already recorded and then recording an accrual for additional loss in excess of the deferral.

Because there are so many possible permutations in the types of service transactions, revenue accounting must be properly correlated with accounting for costs. The preceding discussion on costs can be best understood in the context of the revenue/cost matrix shown in Figure 18.2.

FINANCIAL ACCOUNTING AND REPORTING— OTHER INDUSTRIES

Real Estate Transactions

The unique nature of the primary product, land, combined with the high degree of leverage used in financing its acquisition and development, creates a need for specialized accounting attention. The AICPA issued two responsive industry accounting guides in 1973: *Accounting for Retail Land Sales* and *Accounting for Profit Recognition on Sales of Real Estate* (a second edition, revised and updated, was issued in 1979). The intent of these guides is to account for sales revenues based on evidence of buyer involvement in the property plus seller ability to comply with the agreement. In general, revenue should not be recognized until the significant uncertainties inherent in the transaction have been substantially resolved and the buyer has enough at stake to reasonably assure his continued involvement.

Retail Land Sales. Limited to retail sales of land by subdividers who also finance the sale, the industry accounting guide, *Accounting for Retail Land Sales* (AICPA, 1973c), points out that the typical down payment on these sales is less than that of equivalent sales financed by a bank or savings and loan institution:

> The characteristics of 'sales' in the retail land sales industry—small downpayments, unenforceability of the sales contract by the seller, customer refunds within an established cancellation period—require that criteria be established to determine when a sale should be recorded for accounting purposes. [par. 15]

The key issue to be dealt with in accounting for retail land sales is the uncertainty of ultimate realization of the sales proceeds. Generally, a sale can be recognized when all three following conditions have been met (recognition policies can be established more restrictively by a company if it so desires):

1. The cancellation period has expired and the buyer has made a down payment and each regularly required subsequent payment;
2. Aggregate payments made (including interest) by the buyer are at least 10% of the sales price; and

Method	Criteria	Initial Costs	Indirect Costs	Direct Costs	
				Can Be Reasonably Estimated	Maximum Cannot Be Estimated
Specific performance	Performance consists of a single act	Charged to expense when revenues are recognized	Charged to expense as incurred	Charged to expense when revenues are recognized	(Not applicable)
Proportional performance	Performance consists of more than one act or permitting others to use enterprise resources				
I Identical acts	Specified number of identical or similar acts	Allocated over the term services are provided in proportion to recognition of service revenue		Charged to expense as incurred	Charged to expense as incurred [3]
II Relative direct cost ratio	Specific number of defined but dissimilar acts; direct cost of each act and total can be estimated				(Not applicable)
III Other systematic and rational	If the direct cost method is not practical or performance consists of an unspecified number of similar acts with a fixed performance period; straight-line if no other pattern is more representative of performance[1]				Charged to expense as incurred [3]
Completed performance	Performance occurs on completion of final act because of its significance[2]	Charged to expense when revenues are recognized		Charged to expense when revenues are recognized	Direct costs in excess of realizable revenue charged to expense as incurred
Collection	Revenue realization significantly uncertain	Charged to expense as incurred		Charged to expense as incurred	Charged to expense as incurred

[1] Only the straight-line method may be used for a service that consists of providing facilities for a fixed period.
[2] Also to be used for services that are to be provided in an indeterminate number of acts over an indeterminate period of time.
[3] Cumulative revenues recognized are limited to cumulative costs incurred.

FIGURE 18.2   REVENUE/COST MATRIX FOR SERVICE TRANSACTIONS
SOURCE: FASB, *Invitation to Comment on Accounting for Certain Service Transactions* (Stamford, Conn., 1978), p. 20.

3. The seller is clearly capable of complying with the terms of the contract, especially those promising land improvements and offsite facilities.

Until these conditions are met, revenues collected are to be recorded as deposits. The timing of actual transfer of title is not a factor in accounting so long as there is a contractual obligation to transfer title at some point during or at the end of the contract period. After a sale is recorded, "the method of accounting for the income from it depends on the degree to which it is expected that the resultant receivable will be collected in full" (paragraph 17).

The guide provides for two general income recognition methods:

1. Where there is no undue concern over collectibility of the receivable, the accrual method is to be used. The expected income is recognized upon recording the sales. The accrual method should also be followed for those projects in which collections on contracts are reasonably assured and the following conditions are met:
   a. The land will clearly be useful for residential or recreational purposes and there is little doubt concerning the feasibility of completing the property. It should not be expected that legal restrictions will hamper the development.
   b. The project improvements are well under way and there is evidence the work will be completed according to plan.
   c. The receivable is not subject to subordination, except for construction loans.
   d. Collection experience on the project indicates that collection of receivable balances is reasonably predictable and that 90% of the contracts in force six months after sales are recorded will be collected in full. Increased down payments (20%-25%) constitute an acceptable alternative test.
2. If any of the above conditions is not met, the transaction should be recorded under the installment method (a pro rata portion of the expected net income is recognized as payments are received). Total income should be reduced in each case by discounts and allowances. Further, a portion of the revenue should be deferred and allocated to the cost of any future improvements required by the contract. In lieu of deferring revenue, the cost of the future improvements could be accrued.

Other Real Estate Sales. The industry accounting guide, *Accounting for Profit Recognition on Sales of Real Estate* (AICPA, 1973b), applies to any real estate transaction not covered by the retail guide. As with retail land sales, compliance is required with specific criteria established as a means of supporting the presumption that a specified level of buyer's initial investment in the property plus his continuing investment adequately demonstrates his intent to complete the transaction and thereby reasonably assures the seller's collection of the sales proceeds. The guide emphasizes that the substance, not the legal form, of a real estate transaction is the key to the proper accounting method.

The guide is very complex and provides specific revenue recognition criteria in three areas: buyer's initial investment, buyer's continuing investment, and seller's continued involvement.

A sale should be recorded upon the closing of the transaction (when there has been a transfer of the usual risks and rewards of ownership for consideration). However, the recognition of profit from the transaction must be deferred until all the following criteria have been met:

1. The buyer has made an adequate down payment—the minimum down payment is a specified percentage of the sales price (10% to 25% of the sales price, depending on the nature of the property—see Figure 18.3) or the excess of the sales price over 115% of the loan by the primary lender, if greater than the percentage specified in Figure 18.3.

2. The buyer is committed to a continuing investment—his obligation is to be amortized on a level annual payment basis over a period not to exceed 20 years for land, and normal first mortgage terms for other real estate. Profit recognition should be deferred if the seller's receivable is subject to future subordination.

3. Seller has no continuing commitment for performance—involvement is limited to that of a secured creditor.

If the above conditions are not met, one of the methods described in SOP 78-4, *Application of the Deposit, Installment, and Cost Recovery Methods in Accounting for Sales of Real Estate* (included in Appendix A in the 1979 edition of the profit recognition guide), should be employed.

Deposit method. The profit recognition guide defines the deposit method in the real estate industry in the following manner:

The deposit method postpones recognizing a sale until a determination can be made as to whether a sale has occurred for accounting purposes. Pending recognition of the sale, the seller records no receivable but continues to show in his financial statements the property and related existing debt and discloses the status of the property. Cash received from the buyer is reported as a deposit on the contract except that portions of cash received that are designated by the contract as interest and are not subject to refund may appropriately offset carrying charges (property taxes and interest on existing debt) on the property. [AICPA, 1973b, par. 35]

Under the deposit method, all cash received from the buyer is classified among liabilities until the transaction meets the conditions (Figure 18.3) for recording as a sale. The "sold" property remains carried as an asset during the deposit period, and nonrecourse debt on the property cannot be offset even if assumed by the buyer. Since it remains an asset, depreciation of the property is continued until the sale criteria are cumulatively achieved.

Installment method. In this method the down payment and each subsequent collection of principal from the buyer is apportioned between cost recovered and profit recognized in the same ratio as cost and profit are figured in the entire sale. When the buyer assumes nonrecourse debt, that also is figured into the total sales price for purposes of applying the proration formula.

Unlike the deposit method, a transaction qualifying for use of the installment method is recorded as a sale at the initial transaction date, but the profit portion allocated to later collections is shown as a sales deduction and transferred to deferred revenue. As this deferred profit is later earned it is shown as a separate element of revenue in the income statement.

Type of Property	Minimum Down Payment Expressed as a Percentage of Sales Value
Land:	
Held for commercial, industrial, or residential development to commence within two years after sale	20%*
Held for commercial, industrial, or residential development after two years	25%*
Commercial and Industrial Property:	
Office and industrial buildings, shopping centers, etc.:	
Properties subject to lease on a long-term lease basis to parties having satisfactory credit rating; cash flow currently sufficient to service all indebtedness	10%
Single tenancy properties sold to a user having a satisfactory credit rating	15%
All other	20%
Other Income-Producing Properties	
(hotels, motels, marinas, mobile home parks, etc.):	
Cash flow currently sufficient to service all indebtedness	15%
Start-up situations or current deficiencies in cash flow	25%
Multi-Family Residential Property:	
Primary residence:	
Cash flow currently sufficient to service all indebtedness	10%
Start-up situations or current deficiencies in cash flow	15%
Secondary or recreational residence:	
Cash flow currently sufficient to service all indebtedness	15%
Start-up situations or current deficiencies in cash flow	25%
Single Family Residential Property	
(including condominium or cooperative housing):	
Primary residence of the buyer	5%**
Secondary or recreational residence	10%**

* Not intended to apply to volume retail lot sales by land development companies.
** If collectibility of the remaining portion of the sales price cannot be supported by reliable evidence of collection experience, a higher down payment is indicated and should not be less than 60% of the difference between the sales value and the financing available from loans guaranteed by regulatory bodies, such as FHA of VA, or from independent financial institutions.

FIGURE 18.3 MINIMUM DOWN PAYMENT REQUIREMENTS FOR PROFIT RECOGNITION ON REAL ESTATE SALES
SOURCE: AICPA, *Accounting for Profit Recognition on Sales of Real Estate* (New York, 1979), p. 22-23.

Cost recovery method. Under this method, no profit is recognized until cash collections and existing debt assumed by the buyer exceed the cost of the property sold. Although the total sales price and total cost are reported in the income statement, the entire gross profit is also deducted and carried as a reduction of the related receivable (not deferred revenue as under the installment method).

Changes in method. SOP 78-4 allows the cost recovery method to be used for any transaction qualifying for the installment method. When using either of these methods during the collection period, a switch to the full accrual method should be made if there is evidence that collectibility of the sales price is reasonably assured. One indication might be that the minimum amounts shown in Figure 18.3 have been met on a cumulative basis.

Other SOPs. In addition to SOP 78-4, discussed above, SOP 75-6, *Questions Concerning Profit Recognition on Sales of Real Estate,* is included in the 1979 second edition of the profit recognition guide, and should be consulted in its areas of coverage, which broadly are

1. Buyer's investment in purchased property,
2. Seller's continued involvement with property sold, and
3. Applicability of the guide to non-real estate companies and to different forms of interests sold.

In addition to real estate sales, several SOPs deal with activities within or related to the real estate field:

* Mortgage banking (see Chapter 38):
  ** SOP 74-12, *Accounting Practices in the Mortgage Banking Industry,* and
  ** SOP 76-2, *Accounting for Origination Costs and Loan and Commitment Fees in the Mortgage Banking Industry;*
* Real estate investment trusts (see Chapter 38): SOPs 75-2 and 78-2, *Accounting Practices of Real Estate Investment Trusts;*
* Other:
  ** SOP 78-3, *Accounting for Costs to Sell and Rent, and Initial Rental Operations of, Real Estate Projects,* and
  ** SOP 78-9, *Accounting for Investments in Real Estate Ventures.*

Since mid-1979 the FASB has been deferring action on an AcSEC *Issues Paper on Accounting for Losses on Certain Real Estate and Loans and Receivables Collateralized by Real Estate* (AICPA, 1979p), pending a consideration of the broad subject of whether an allowance for the cost of money (discounting) needs to be provided in determining net realizable values. This matter should be resolved in late 1980 in connection with clearance of a revised AICPA guide on the banking industry (see Chapter 38).

Franchise Fee Revenue

The rapid growth of franchise agreements combined with a difficulty in pinpointing when the earnings process is complete led the AICPA to prepare an industry accounting guide, *Accounting for Franchise Fee Revenue* (AICPA, 1973a). The emphasis in this pronouncement is on accounting for the initial franchise fee, though it contains other selected topics that are unique or important to franchising companies generally.

Initial fees should be recognized when substantial performance has occurred. This concept applies to both individual franchise sales and area franchise sales (the sale of rights to open multiple franchises within specified territorial boundaries). Substantial performance means that

1. The franchisor has no remaining obligation—by agreement, trade practice, or operation of law—to refund any cash received or to excuse payment of notes,
2. Most of the initial services required by contract of the franchisor have been performed, and
3. Any other conditions affecting consummation have been fulfilled.

According to the guide, conservatism justifies the presumption that the franchisee's commencement of operation is the earliest point at which substantial performance can occur; earlier recognition of revenue carries with it a burden of demonstrating that the presumption has been overcome. Whatever the timing of franchise fee revenue recognition, a portion of that initial fee should be deferred if continuing fees are inadequate to cover estimated future costs.

For area franchise fees, when the franchisor must provide initial services in direct relationship to the number of area outlets, it may be necessary to view the franchise agreement as a divisible contract—either by estimating the number of outlets to be opened in a given time period or by referring to maximum or minimum numbers of outlets specified by contract. In such cases the initial franchise fee would be recognized ratably as such units are opened.

Notes are often issued by the franchisee in partial consideration of the initial fee. The guide points out that, except in extreme cases, the preferred method of dealing with bad debts is by valuation allowance. If the payment provisions of a note are such that there remains a significant uncertainty as to ultimate collection, an installment or cost recovery method should be used. The guide also reaffirms the applicability of APB 21, *Interest on Receivables and Payables* (AC 4111), in the imputation of interest on non-interest-bearing notes received on sale of a franchise.

Finance Companies

Sales finance, consumer loan, and commercial finance companies operate somewhat differently than leasing companies and financial institutions in general (Chapters 23 and 38, respectively), even though they follow similar revenue recognition policies. Finance receivables and finance income, the first two chapters of the industry audit guide, *Audits of Finance Companies* (AICPA, 1973f), are highlighted below. The guide also deals extensively with authoritative auditing requirements, which will not be repeated in this chapter.

Finance Receivables. The accounting for consumer finance company receivables generally depends on the nature of the transaction. The four basic types are

1. Retail contracts—receivables result from the purchase by the finance company of a loan receivable from an originating dealer-retailer.

2. Direct cash loans—receivables result from direct cash loans made to individuals, generally repaid on the installment basis.

3. Wholesale and capital loans—receivables result from loans to dealer-retailers to finance their inventory or working capital. These loans are collateralized by the assets financed.

4. Other larger-balance loans to finance equipment, home improvements, or even the revolving charge sales of a retail organization (commercial finance receivables).

Finance receivables can be recorded by net cash advanced or by total gross amount receivable, including interest. When the second method is used, a credit is recorded for the unearned interest income. Most retail contracts and some direct cash loans are recorded at the gross receivable. Other direct cash loans, wholesale and capital loans, and commercial finance receivables are recorded as the net cash advanced.

Finance Income. The recognition of finance income depends, in part, on the nature of the original receivable. For interest-bearing obligations (some direct cash, most wholesale and capital, and most commercial finance loans) finance income is recognized on the effective yield method—as collections are received or scheduled to be received. This method often utilizes a rule-of-78s or sum-of-the-digits amortization of the loan (see Chapter 20 for calculation formula), whereby more interest, relative to the fixed payment, is recognized on the earlier payments than on the later ones.

Finance income from the remaining type of transactions, those recorded on a discount basis, is generally recognized under one of three methods: effective yield, pro rata collection, or fixed percentage. *Discount basis* refers to the deferred finance income, which represents the difference between the cash advanced and the face amount of the note, including interest. In each of the three methods, an initial amount of revenue is often recognized to offset acquisition costs (the cost of acquiring the loan plus a provision for bad debts).

Effective yield method. Income is recognized on an accelerated basis; thus more is recognized in the early periods of the loan, less in the later periods. This procedure can result in a deferred finance income balance in the later periods that is too small to cover the relatively fixed costs of servicing the account. Accordingly, there is some debate over the appropriateness of this method.

Pro rata collection method. This method, also called the *liquidation method,* transfers deferred finance income to operations based on collections; this results in an approximation of straight-line amortization. Under this method equal amounts of income are recognized throughout the term of the loan. This method does not satisfactorily reflect the economic realities of the industry—namely, that income earned should reflect the higher collectibility risks associated with the earlier periods when the loan balance is largest.

Fixed percentage method. Following this approach, deferred finance income is adjusted each month to reflect a fixed percentage return on the receivables balance. This method is probably the weakest conceptually, though frequent revisions in the rate used to reflect changes in cost factors and in receivable volume, term, and yields may provide a satisfactory solution.

Combination method. The guide suggests a fourth method, the combination method, which combines the effective yield and pro rata methods. This method matches costs to revenues by first segregating deferred finance income into three categories reflecting the cost pattern of a finance company:

1. Recognized immediately to offset acquisition costs;
2. Amortized into income on a straight-line basis to offset loan servicing and other operating costs; and
3. Amortized on the effective yield method to offset the cost of borrowed funds and to recognize the profit on the transaction.

Although the combination method is conceptually superior to the others, it is not widely followed in practice because of the high cost of developing accounting systems sophisticated enough to provide the required cost information. Companies that follow it often use periodic tests for making estimates, rather than incorporate the method into their accounting systems.

AUDITING CONSIDERATIONS—REVENUE, RECEIVABLES, AND SERVICE TRANSACTIONS

Objectives and Error Types

The overall objective of the audit of revenue and receivables is to determine whether they are fairly presented in the context of the financial statements as a whole. To meet this objective, the audit must address seven basic areas regarding revenue and receivables: existence, ownership, valuation, cutoff, mechanical accuracy, classification, and disclosure.

The seven basic areas listed above are explained in Chapter 12, and the audit philosophy in this chapter assumes that explanation is understood. However, the seven objectives above are not entirely congruent with the seven objectives ascribed to internal control in Chapter 13, because internal control systems do not primarily address several substantive revenue and receivables audit objectives. The following cross-reference table, along with a review of Chapter 13, may be helpful:

Overall Audit Objective, as Shown in This Chapter	*Internal Control Objective*
Congruent:	
Existence	Authorization
	Validity
	Recording
Valuation—accuracy	Valuation
Cutoff	Timing
Mechanical accuracy	Summarization
Classification	Classification
Not congruent:	
Ownership	
Valuation—changed circumstances	
Disclosure	

Audit Approach

In order to decide between a systems reliance approach and a substantive approach (or how much of each approach should be blended) the auditor must gain an understanding of the activities of the company that affect its revenue and receivables accounting and the potential seriousness of errors. He must also understand the company's preventive, detective, and corrective internal controls, as discussed above.

The company activities that affect revenue and receivables most often and most heavily are

- The shipment of goods or the provision of services to customers for cash or credit,
- Receipt of cash from customers, and
- Return of goods by customers and the issuance of credit memos.

Understanding the Revenue System. With a basic knowledge of internal control objectives and procedures, the auditor must study and review the system to evaluate the adequacy of the internal controls. Every inadequate control (unless it is a redundant control) represents a system weakness and therefore a potential for error.

The auditor performs his analysis in three stages. He

1. Obtains a description of the system,
2. Identifies and evaluates controls in relation to the initial description, and
3. Tests the system to verify how the controls actually operate.

Revenue systems vary significantly from industry to industry; when obtaining a system description, the auditor must understand the nature of the industry and its terminology. Despite detail differences between industries, certain steps and basic documentation are nearly universal, as discussed in the following paragraphs.

Most revenue and receivables systems possess the following types of documents:

- Customer sales orders,
- Credit approval forms,
- Shipping receipts,
- Sales invoices,
- Customer statements,
- Credit memos,
- Remittance advices, and
- Write-off authorization forms.

The foregoing documents are generated in several steps. The first step in a revenue transaction—initiation—results in the generation of customer sales orders or contracts, along with pertinent credit information. These documents can be simple or complex, depending on the nature of the product, the size of the order, and so on. In long-term transactions, contracts usually spell out the terms in considerable detail; these often are the key to identifying the appropriate revenue recognition method. In short-term transactions, initiation documents are usually simple preliminaries to feed basic information into the system. Control must be exercised at the initiation point to ensure that all orders are accurately recognized by the system. Errors here can lead to filling orders with the wrong merchandise or providing the wrong service; such problems ultimately show up in wasted costs and sales returns.

Making goods or services available for transfer is particularly important in long-term proportional performance transactions. When the accounting system is used to document progress toward completion, it does so through the accurate accumulation of cost data. Otherwise, regularly scheduled evaluations of physical progress are used. Though the form of documentation of progress can vary, control over it is critical. In short-term transactions, documentation of progress is less important for revenue recognition than for other internal accounting purposes.

The next step is the exchange of resources; the delivery of the product or service is the significant act that triggers revenue recognition. Shipping documents, customer acceptances, and the like capture the information that, when combined with the original sales order or contract, provides the data to be recorded on the invoice. This invoice is the key document signifying that revenue can be recognized and that an account receivable exists.

The final step is the receipt of cash—either in payment of the receivable balance or as an advance—or the return of goods by the customer and issuance of a credit memo.

Once the auditor has a general understanding of the transactions involved, he must consider the material potential error types to which that system might be exposed and the pertinent controls within the system that deal with those error types. In the context of the revenue and receivables system there are nine basic potential error types. These are illustrated in Chapter 13. Having identified the potential error types, the auditor must consider the pertinent controls within the system. For the revenue and receivables system there are four general control features that form the basis of the system.

Authorization. Authorization can take a variety of forms, ranging from direct approval of individual transactions—such as management approval of new contracts—to implied approval through policy guidelines—such as current price lists approved by management. The basic areas where suitable authorization controls are needed in the revenue and receivables cycle are

1. Granting of credit,
2. Acceptance of orders,
3. Shipment of goods or performance of services,
4. Determination of price and terms, and
5. Adjustments to sales-related balances.

Segregation of duties. Segregation of duties may be the key element of internal control in the revenue cycle. At least two internal control objectives—safeguarding assets and providing reliable information—can be substantially achieved when individual tasks are segregated. The shipping function, for example, should be separated from the billing and invoice-processing function. Invoice processing should be segregated from the recording of accounts receivable, which in turn should be separate from the cash receipts function. In short, documents must be prepared independent of each other, and asset access segregated from record keeping in order to prevent both errors and irregularities.

A key element in the revenue system is the controls that ensure that all goods and services provided are recorded—that is, completeness of data. This requires that the basic provision of goods or services is recorded (e.g., by shipping documents) and that the customer is subsequently billed. While the controls necessary to effect this also draw on such elements as adequate segregation of duties, another fundamental element is the use of prenumbered documents. Once the initial transfer of goods or services is recorded on a prenumbered document, it is then possible to account for all such documents to ensure that all shipments have been billed and also that no billings are duplicated.

Independent verification. The means of independent verification will vary significantly from one organization to another. The use of internal auditors to check on the accuracy of the recording and processing of sales transactions helps fulfill the stated internal control objectives. A periodic independent check can help ensure that company strictures within the revenue system (e.g., credit authorization policies, accounts receivable write-off policies, sales return policies) are being appropriately followed.

Also under the heading of independent verification comes the provision of statements to customers on a regular basis. This provides a key control to confirm both the existence of receivable balances and the recording of all receipts.

Based on the results of the analysis of transactions, potential error types, and controls, an approach will be devised for the audit of the financial statements. Selecting the appropriate audit approach requires both an analysis of the strength of applicable internal controls and an assessment of (1) the level of direct management surveillance of transactions and (2) the significance of individual transactions. Management's direct surveillance can be an invaluable control; the auditor must observe it in context to determine that it does not constitute management override of the system, which can destroy its reliability. And all other things being equal, an error carries a greater risk in a significant revenue transaction than in a small transaction; thus the auditor will plan to devote more of his attention to the individually significant transactions.

The next two stages of the audit of revenue and receivables, identifying and evaluating controls and testing the system, are discussed fully in Chapter 13 and therefore will not be dealt with here.

Objectives and Procedures

Depending on the quality of the system and audit efficiency considerations, a combination of analytical tests and interim and year-end compliance and substantive tests will be selected.

Analytical Procedures. Analytical reviews of related account balances, ratios, trends, and the like provide evidence of the reasonableness of account balances. This approach is particularly suited to audits of revenue and receivable accounts involving estimates. For example, the allowance for bad debts or sales returns may be essentially a projection that can be corroborated through comparison of historical write-off totals to sales and average receivables balances. However, care must be taken in the use of an analytical procedure that employs a historical trend, especially if the enterprise has recently changed on operational policy—less stringent credit-granting criteria, for example. In such an instance, the auditor should evaluate the effect of this change on the results to be expected from the analytical procedures.

General examples of analytical procedures to be applied to revenue include the following:

- Compare sales by product line with budgeted sales and sales of preceding period. Consider whether results are in line with other known information (e.g., expanding/declining markets, changes in sales prices or sales mix, new or discontinued lines). Sales to related companies and sales of an unusual nature should be considered separately.

- Review details of units shipped with sales and production records. Consider whether sales figure appears reasonable compared to level of production.

- Compare gross profit ratio to previous years, and analyze changes. Consider whether the reasons for such changes appear reasonable in light of other sales information.

- Compare sales deductions for the current period, such as discounts as a percent of sales, to prior periods. Consider whether the changes appear reasonable in light of other sales information.

General examples of analytical procedures to be applied to receivables include the following:

- Review the relationship of average receivables to net sales during the period and consider its reasonableness in relation to credit policy, collectibility, etc.

- Compare the aged listing of accounts receivable with that of the previous audit date, and note significant changes—for example, changes in major customers, in the ratio of overdue accounts, in the proportion of credit balances.

- Obtain information as to the bad debts written off during the current period, and compare it with similar information in prior periods and also to the allowance for doubtful accounts established at the last audit date. This information may give some indication of a change in the effectiveness of the company's credit and collection procedures or in general business conditions.

- Determine whether there are any balances with related companies or with officers, directors, or shareholders. If so, compare these balances to similar balances at the last audit date. These types of balances probably should be excluded from the calculation of ratios and other statistics for trade accounts, since they may distort the analysis. These accounts may also pose particular verification and valuation problems.

Year-End and Interim Procedures. In addition to analytical procedures, the auditor will have to conduct a variety of year-end and interim procedures in order to achieve the objectives of the audit of revenues and receivables. Figures 18.4 and 18.5 are condensed listings of audit procedures commonly used to achieve the objectives indicated. The procedures shown may be used to satisfy more than one audit objective, but in order to provide an overview of how the audit objectives are met, each is listed alongside the objective it most directly satisfies.

The majority of these interim and year-end audit procedures involve techniques that are common to audit tests in most areas. These include

- Accounting for the numerical sequence of documents to ensure that all transactions are being recorded;
- Reperforming control operations, such as checking arithmetic, to ensure mechanical accuracy;
- Checking invoices to price lists, agreed-on discount rates, etc., to ensure correct valuation;
- Checking dates of shipment to confirm cutoff;
- Checking receiving documentation for required authorizations, to confirm the validity and propriety of the transaction; and
- Matching independently created documents, such as sales invoices and shipping documents, to ensure existence and accuracy.

However, the interim and year-end procedures for the revenue and receivables cycle also include one technique, the use of confirmations, which, while sometimes encountered in similar forms in other areas (for example bank confirmations), is most prevalent in this area, where it forms a very powerful audit tool.

Confirmation of Receivables

Confirmation of receivables is a standard audit procedure, and the auditor who omits this procedure has the burden of justifying the deviation (AU 331.01). It is probably most often used primarily as a substantive procedure—to obtain direct evidence in support of the recorded receivables—but in large-volume, small-individual-balance situations, it is frequently used primarily as a compliance test—to establish that the client's systems are operating properly.

Omission can be justified on the basis that the confirmation procedures are impractical or impossible and that the fair presentation of the receivables balances can be substantiated through alternative procedures. From a practical standpoint, it is rare that a sample of receivables is not circularized for confirmation when receivables are material, since third-party verification of a company's records provides greater audit assurance than evidence from within the company.

As an audit test it can be very powerful in giving audit evidence with respect to at least seven basic potential error types:

- Sales recorded but goods not shipped,
- Sales invoiced but not recorded,
- Sales amount recorded incorrectly,
- Sales recorded in wrong period,
- Cash receipts not recorded or deposited,
- Cash receipts credited to the wrong account, and
- Cash receipts recorded in the wrong period.

Scope and Timing. The confirmation methodology is left to the auditors' discretion and requires judgment in the following areas:

Audit Objective	Sample Year-End Procedures*	Sample Interim Procedures
Existence. Determine whether there are valid transactions supporting the revenues recorded in the financial statements, and whether all such valid revenue transactions have been properly included.	• Where appropriate, reconcile units shipped with sales, production, and inventory records. • Review sales and gross profit by product line by month and investigate unusual fluctuations.	• Trace selected entries on the sales journal to supporting evidence of shipment/delivery. • Trace dividend income to published information on dividends. • Trace selected shipping documents to billing records to determine that all shipments are billed.
Ownership. Determine whether the revenue shown in the financial statements represents sales of company products or services.	• Confirm sales information with customer.	• Review journal entries, and for unusual items, check to supporting documentation. • Review sales contracts and arrangements to determine if company is a commission agent or broker who should record only fee income and not total proceeds.
Mechanical accuracy. Determine whether the basic mathematical calculations and clerical compilation procedures have been accurately carried out.	• Obtain analyses of sales revenue and sales deduction amounts for the period, check clerical accuracy, and agree to general ledger and analyses of other related accounts.	• For selected periods test postings from the sales and sales returns journals to the general ledger. • Test footings of selected sales journals.
Valuation. Determine whether the revenue balances are fairly valued in accordance with generally accepted accounting principles.	• Where sales are made with a right of return, evaluate the appropriateness of the revenue recognition policy.	• Compare sales prices in selected transactions to price lists.

Disclosure. Determine whether revenue disclosure in the financial statement is adequate.

Classification. Determine whether revenues are properly classified.

Cutoff. Determine whether all revenue transactions before and after the year-end have been appropriately treated.

- Review price adjustments issued for period to determine if errors exist in recorded sales which may not have been corrected by year-end.

- Inquire about sales to related parties and test to assure that they are properly disclosed.

- Ascertain that nonoperating revenues are not included in sales.

- Investigate shipping records immediately before and after balance sheet date and agree to sales records.

- Investigate credit memos issued after the balance sheet date.

- Where appropriate reconcile units shipped with sales, production, and inventory records.

- Test selected sales transactions to determine that stated revenue recognition policy is followed.

- Test input to sales accounts to determine by review of underlying data that entries are properly classified.

- Test cutoff at interim dates to ensure system is working.

* Also often performed at an interim date.

FIGURE 18.4   SAMPLE AUDIT PROCEDURES FOR REVENUE

Audit Objective	Sample Year-End Procedures*	Sample Interim Procedures
Existence. Determine whether there are valid accounts receivable supporting the dollar amount shown in the balance sheet and whether all such accounts receivable balances have been properly included.	• Obtain direct confirmation of selected receivable balances. • Review the accounts receivable control account for the period and reconcile to aged list of receivables.	• For a sample of shipping records, trace details to sales invoices, sales journal and customer account in sales ledger. • For a sample of entries in the sales journal trace to supporting evidence of shipment/delivery.
Ownership. Determine whether the accounts receivable balances are owned by the company and whether they are subject to any lien or restrictions.	• Review receivables for any notation that they have been assigned or discounted. • Review bank confirmations for indications of liens on receivables.	• Review cash receipts journal for evidence of receipts accounts receivable factors. • Review company minutes to see if board of directors has authorized hypothecation of receivables.
Mechanical accuracy. Determine whether the basic mathematical calculations and clerical compilation procedures have been accurately carried out.	• Obtain aged lists of receivables, trace total to general ledger, agree selected items to and from subsidiary records, test the aging, and add and cross-add. • Obtain analyses of the allowance for doubtful accounts and schedule of bad debt expense and check additions, trace total to general ledger, trace individual items to subsidiary records, and agree provisions to the earnings statement.	• For selected periods, test postings from the sales journal, sales return journal, and cash receipts journal to the accounts receivable ledger. • Test footings of various journals.

Valuation. Determine whether the accounts receivable balances are fairly valued in conformity with GAAP.

- Investigate collectibility of account balances.

- If balances are receivable in foreign currency, determine the exchange rate for conversion and check the conversion calculation.

- Test pricing of sales invoices by comparison to price lists and contracts.

Disclosure. Determine whether accounts receivable balance disclosure in the financial statements is adequate.

- Review the accounts receivable control account for the period and investigate any large or unusual entries or entries arising from unusual sources.

- Review receivables for any which have been assigned or discounted, or which are with related parties.

- Test interim entries to receivables to determine that nature of transactions conforms to the description of the business.

Classification. Determine whether accounts receivable are properly classified.

- Review lists of balances for amounts due from group or related companies, employees, etc., credit balances, and unusual items.

- Test entries to receivables control account to determine they represent sales in the normal course of business.

Cutoff. Determine whether all sales and cash receipts before and after year-end have been appropriately treated.

- Review sales and credit memos issued before and after year-end to test if recorded in the correct accounting period.

- Check serial continuity of shipping/delivery records and trace selected items to sales invoices for timeliness of recording transactions.

* Also often performed at an interim date.

FIGURE 18.5 SAMPLE AUDIT PROCEDURES FOR ACCOUNTS RECEIVABLE

- Confirmation date,
- Form of confirmation request, and
- Number of accounts circularized.

Confirmation date refers to the timing of the confirmation procedures. Whether confirmations are requested as of year-end or as of some other date will depend on the overall design of the audit approach; the audit will consider the efficiency of the examination and whether client deadlines need to be met. A confirmation date other than year-end can be justified when the internal control system is sufficiently reliable to produce reasonably accurate revenue and collection data between the confirmation date and year-end. Otherwise, confirmation must be performed at or very near to the balance sheet date. If there is a gap between confirmation date and year-end, some level of substantive procedures will be applied to intervening transactions.

In making judgments as to the *form of confirmation* and the *number of accounts to be circularized,* the auditor will consider the strength of the internal controls, the nature of the receivables population, and the results of the previous year's procedures. Statistical sampling selection and evaluation methods, described in Chapter 14, are frequently used.

Please examine the accompanying statement carefully and either confirm its correctness, or report any differences to our auditors

[Name and address
of auditors]

who are making an examination of our financial statements.

Your prompt attention to this request will be appreciated. An envelope is enclosed for your reply. Please do not send your remittances to the auditors.

[Name of client]

_____

Confirmation:
The balance receivable from us of [amount] as of [date] is correct except as noted below:

_____

_____

_____

_____

[Name of customer]

Date _____   By _____

[Respondent's signature]

FIGURE 18.6   POSITIVE CONFIRMATION REQUEST

The circularization of individual accounts can be accomplished by using a *positive request* or a *negative request* or a combination of both. A positive request (see Figure 18.6) asks the debtor to respond and state whether the information is or is not correct. A negative request (see Figure 18.7) requires action only if the information is incorrect. The positive confirmation is considered more reliable because it requires affirmative action on the part of the debtor, but it requires considerable effort in following up on nonreplies. Negative requests, though perhaps less conclusive, serve a useful purpose given both reasonably reliable internal controls and a relatively large number of homogeneous accounts. Due to the possibility of nonreply when the balance is incorrect and the lack of follow-up on nonreplies (since the presumption is that the balance is correct), negative procedures require more requests than positive confirmation procedures for the same degree of auditor assurance. Also they should not be used should the auditor feel that the debtor would for some reason ignore negative requests.

Generally, the existence of a reliable control system will tend to reduce the number of confirmation requests required. And these requests would usually be limited to positive confirmation of large accounts or, where there is a large number of small accounts, negative confirmation of a relatively small sample of accounts. When the auditor deems the system unreliable or chooses to not test related internal controls as a matter of audit efficiency, he must perform more extensive confirmation procedures.

The auditor must be alert to the uncertainties inherent in confirmation procedures. There is the possibility that the debtor might not be conscientious and thus might verify an incorrect balance. Furthermore, a confirmation is an acknowledgment of indebtedness but not an indication of a debtor's ability or inclination to pay; thus a satisfactory confirmation does not ensure a properly valued receivable.

Follow-Up Procedures. The use of alternative procedures is required on significant positive confirmation requests for which the auditor receives no replies (AU 331.08). In addition to the use of second or third requests as appropriate, the alternative procedures could include

- Examination of shipping documents,
- Review of customer order documentation,
- Review of duplicate copies of sales invoices,

Please examine this statement carefully. If it does NOT agree with your records, please report any exceptions directly to our auditors

[Name and address
of auditors]

who are making an examination of our financial statements. An addressed envelope is enclosed for your convenience in replying.

Do not send your remittance to our auditors.

FIGURE 18.7 NEGATIVE CONFIRMATION REQUEST

- Examination of subsequent cash receipts, and
- Confirmation of subsequent cash receipts.

Each of the above procedures carries a different level of significance and should be considered in light of the company's particular accounting procedures and system of internal control.

If a customer responds to a confirmation request and reports a difference, it is necessary to determine the nature of and the reason for the difference. Timing differences, for example, are a very common reason for respondent complaints of error; these result when a delay in recording transactions affects balances in the customer's or the client's records. Examples of differences and some of their possible causes are shown in Figure 18.8.

When all confirmation procedures have been completed, the auditor evaluates the results in the context of the results of other relevant auditing procedures, including analytical procedures and tests of revenue transactions.

New Developments in Conformation Procedures. The failure of customers to reply to positive confirmation requests and the subsequent need to adopt alternative procedures is the principal drawback of the confirmation process. Doubt has also been cast on the accuracy of replies received. This has led to some new research in this area; it is possible that, in time, new versions of the receivable

Difference	*Some Possible Causes*
Payments not recorded on company records	• postal delays • payment applied to wrong account • embezzlement (kiting, lapping, etc.)
Goods or services not received by customer	• delivery delays • service not completed • invoice sent to wrong customer • goods delivered to wrong customer • fictitious invoice
Goods returned by the customer for credit	• delivery delays • returned goods received, but credit memo not issued
Clerical errors	• wrong quantity • wrong price • duplicate invoice recorded • discounts calculated incorrectly • errors in recording invoices, payments or credits
Disputed amounts	• goods received in damaged condition • quality or price of goods or services disputed by customer

FIGURE 18.8   SELECTED CAUSES OF CONFIRMATION DIFFERENCES

confirmation will be added to the armory of audit techniques. One technique being explored is that of the use of an *expanded field confirmation* (Sorkin, 1979).

Essentially, this technique involves including several account balance figures in the confirmation, with the request that the customer indicate which one is correct. Sorkin found in his research that respondents were less likely to confirm an incorrect balance when confronted by an expanded field request rather than the usual positive confirmation.

Recent research (Krogstad and Romney, 1980) has also investigated the effectiveness and efficiency of confirming individual invoices rather than account balances. This technique is already used in certain industries (e.g., insurance companies) where confirmations sent to brokers are often based on open items rather than balances (which can be almost impossible to agree, due to timing differences between the broker collecting premiums from policyholders and forwarding them, sometimes net of commission or claims, to the insurance company). The results of initial research indicate that the use of such *open invoice confirmations* can save audit time by being both easier to organize and effect and by requiring less time for alternative procedures, due to improved response rates.

Provision for Bad Debts

Determining validity, ownership, and existence are essential, but the inability to collect a receivable obviates the fact that someone actually owes money to the company. Valuation thus is a key factor in the audit of receivables, and it is also one of the most subjective of audit judgments.

The auditor uses a variety of approaches to evaluate collectibility, including

- Historical experience,
- State of the economy and its effect on the client's customers,
- Aging of the receivables,
- Financial stability of the company's customers, and
- Credit-granting policies.

Ultimately, the auditor must be satisfied that the amount presented as receivables, after deducting an allowance for uncollectible accounts, is a reasonable presentation, in the context of the financial statements taken as a whole, of future realizable amounts.

Additional Audit Issues

Due to the typically large volume of revenue transactions and related number of individual accounts, the system encompassing the revenue cycle is often the first to be computerized. The risks inherent in the use of EDP in the revenue cycle can create an additional burden for the auditor; this subject is fully discussed in Chapter 15.

When a system problem exists, the great speed at which computers operate tends to compound simple problems at alarming rates. Accordingly, it is important that the auditor understand the computer system and evaluate the attendant controls if he plans to rely on them in limiting the extent of his substantive audit tests.

There are also legal considerations associated with granting credit. For example, an enterprise may find itself subject to various penalties resulting from violations of state or federal regulations barring discriminatory practices in credit granting. Further, individual customers are entitled to know the rates of interest being charged on outstanding balances. Another issue is the rate of interest that may be changed. The auditor should be alert to evidence of violations and should make appropriate inquiry of management and company counsel in this area. (See SAS 17, AU 328.08-.09 for additional guidance.)

Auditing Service Revenue

The objective of the audit of the wide variety of service transactions is to reflect as revenues only those amounts that are earned through performance and to determine that all related costs are either expensed or deferred in keeping with the method of revenue recognition applicable to the company.

The auditor must determine the nature of the company's service agreements, generally by observing operations and by reading descriptive brochures and company contracts. Additionally, the auditor must understand the risks of the business and the type of customers serviced by the company. Based on this knowledge, the auditor must assess the acceptability of the company's revenue recognition procedures.

Auditing Service Costs

The auditor must obtain an understanding of the company's system for accumulating costs of service transactions. A review of the cash disbursements, accounts payable, and payroll systems (including appropriate tests of these systems) will facilitate this understanding. Once the auditor has made a determination that the company has classified costs into the proper categories, his next concern will be the company's system of cost allocation for individual transactions or kinds of services.

The auditor should review the company's accounting system for the transfer of costs from the cost accumulation centers to the income statement. Costs are allowed to be deferred as long as the total of costs incurred to date plus future anticipated costs does not exceed anticipated future revenues. The auditor should audit the company's estimates and be satisfied that they are reasonable.

The company's method of identifying service transactions that ultimately may result in a loss to the company should be challenged, and the auditor should discuss this area with the appropriate personnel and perform general reasonableness tests on the data supplied. In particular, new types of service transactions entered into during the current year should be studied; the company might be erroneously estimating revenues and costs because of lack of sufficient historical background.

Since there are numerous types of service transactions, it is difficult to identify specific procedures. These will need to be determined by the auditor, depending on the attendant circumstances.

AUDITING CONSIDERATIONS—REAL ESTATE TRANSACTIONS

In general, the audit concepts discussed in Chapter 12 apply to real estate transactions. Likewise, the internal control review and reliability considerations apply, but a control reliance audit approach is improbable when considering large individual transactions. Thus, retail land sales company audits will tend more towards control reliance, and audits of large individual real estate transactions will be substantive.

There are almost endless variations in real estate transactions. Thus the sections that follow deal with some of the more complex areas of concern to auditors.

Retail Land Sales

Land development has historically been regulated primarily by local governments, which impose a battery of building and mechanical codes, zoning ordinances, and subdivision regulations, although more recently there has been some trend toward regional, state, and federal control of real estate development. The emphasis on environmental concerns in many cases has resulted in requirements for the filing of environmental impact statements and related increases in regulation by the various government agencies. The auditor must obtain an understanding of these industry features in order to recognize problems in the course of his audit.

Provision for Uncollectibles. In order for financial statements to be fairly stated under generally accepted accounting principles, adequate allowances for contract cancellations must be provided. The auditor should be concerned with the adequacy of the amount provided and satisfy himself that it covers all foreseeable losses.

The audit of the allowance should include confirmation of a significant portion of contracts outstanding. An aging of current amounts due should be analyzed, along with the effects that the client's credit-granting policies and economic conditions might have on each receivable balance.

Frequently, the number of receivables accounted for by the company is disproportionately large compared to the other accounting requirements of the company. Therefore, careful consideration should be given in evaluating the internal control over this area. Furthermore, it is not unusual for a land developer to have sold his accounts receivable with the buyer still maintaining a right of recourse on those notes. This means that the buyer may still look to the land developer for collections on the receivables he has acquired, and the land developer must therefore continue to fully analyze and maintain an adequate reserve on those accounts.

In addition, since the better receivables are usually the ones sold, the sale of notes with recourse will establish the minimum discount rate to be applied to the remaining receivables. If the company carries and sells paper with recourse, consideration should be given to some type of limited review of the quality of the remaining paper to help in the evaluation of the allowance for cancellations.

One criterion for the accrual method relates to collection experience of receivables. This requirement, 90% collection of contracts in force six months after sales are recorded, effectively limits the cancellation reserve to a maximum of 10% of *those* sales except for sales less than six months old. If the receivable aging deteriorates to the point where bad debts greater than 10% are experienced after six months from date of sale, one of the requirements for accrual accounting is not being met. Because of this, a thorough review should be made to determine the reasons for collectibility declining below 90%. The auditor should concern himself with the severity of the decline—how long the decline is expected to continue and the extent of the decline. If the company has been experiencing 90% or better collectibility for its entire existence and then dips temporarily to 87% or 88% collectibility, a critical problem may not exist. If, however, factors that produced the decline are expected to exist for an indefinite period, causing even further declines in collectibility, a decision is necessary as to whether the company can continue to qualify under the accrual method. If not, a change to the installment method should be made.

Future Performance Costs and Development Risks. In both the accrual and installment methods it is necessary to determine the cost of completing a project once a lot sale is recognized. If the developer has not completed the project, it is necessary to use cost forecasting to arrive at total anticipated cost, which should include a factor for anticipated inflation. For the past few years the construction field has been experiencing one of the highest inflation factors of any industry. This fact, plus the normal construction risks such as environmental problems, zoning, local and state ordinances, personnel requirements, equipment, and material shortages, plus the current energy shortage, makes a meaningful future evaluation of anticipated costs difficult. The most reliable means of determining future improvement costs is through engineering studies provided by an outside consultant. When this is not possible, management estimates must suffice. In analyzing either outside engineering studies or management estimates the auditor should consider use of outside experts.

Other Real Estate Sales

The auditor should obtain and study the documents related to the real estate transaction and corroborate their authenticity. Because of the complexity usually encountered in this area, other experts—especially lawyers—may be called on to assist in reducing to a statement of their essential ingredients the voluminous contracts having a variety of legal names.

The existence of minimum down payment requirements (see Figure 18.3) should also cause the auditor to focus on certain aspects critical to meeting those requirements.

Notes, Mortgages, and Contracts. Substantially all transactions involving the transfer of land and buildings are financed by notes, mortgages, or contracts because of the large dollar amounts involved. These notes, mortgages, and contracts usually provide that a relatively small portion of the total value of the property transferred be paid in cash, either at execution of the agreement or upon the occurrence of some event that transfers title to the property or possession of the property. The balance of the purchase price, with interest, is usually payable over future years with acceleration upon the occurrence of certain events, such as financial difficulties of the buyer or resale.

In addition to the standard terms for principal and interest payments, these agreements may contain options for the lender or seller to buy or repurchase portions of the property transferred at fixed prices or at appraised amounts. Other provisions may require the payment of additional sums to the lender or seller if net income or cash flow exceeds specified levels or if the resale price of the property exceeds specified levels. An agreement might also contain restrictive covenants with respect to use or resale of the property, amount of debt the buyer is permitted to incur, parties to whom the property may be resold, or various other activities of the buyer. Other agreements may specify additional obligations of the seller, such as agreements to provide funds for future operations, provide improvements not available at time of transfer, or buy the property back upon the occurrence of certain events or the completion of certain items; guarantees of specific return on amounts invested; or other items of continued involvement.

There may also be side agreements containing various commitments by a buyer or seller; these agreements may contain any of the items described above or any other item the buyer and seller agree on.

Briefly, the auditor should obtain copies of purchase or sale agreements for all major transations and review the documents, including all related side agreements, to determine whether there are any commitments by the buyer or seller that might have continued impact on the financial statements. These documents must be carefully evaluated to be sure the transactions contain no unrecognized financial aspects. The rules with respect to recognition of profit must be considered in this review. The potential for liability for improvements of property sold must be carefully considered. The auditor should be alert for any indication of seller participation in the buyer's financing and for any other indication that the transfer of property was not an arm's-length transaction.

In light of the potential for revision of the original terms of these agreements or of various side agreements, the auditor must ascertain whether there have been any changes in the documents from year to year and must evaluate the impact of any changes. Also, each agreement should be reviewed each year to determine that all terms and covenants have been complied with. To accomplish this continued review process, the auditor should obtain and retain a file of all documents relating to each major transaction. Each year the auditor should review incomplete major transactions from the previous year to determine that the accounting for disposition or changes in status was proper.

Notes, mortgages, and contracts receivable, including those receivables arising from transactions that are not recognized as sales for accounting purposes, often represent a significant portion of the assets of a development company. In many instances, these documents are readily convertible into cash through discounting or other sales. The auditor must recognize this characteristic of these assets and determine that they are actually valid assets of the client by applying procedures comparable to those applied to marketable securities, including physical inspection or other verification of the existence and safekeeping of the original receivable documents.

Option agreements must also be carefully evaluated to determine if the asset and liability must be recorded (e.g., are circumstances such that the company in substance *must* exercise the option?).

Funds Provided Indirectly by Seller. It is clear that funds loaned directly to the buyer by the seller for the down payment should be deducted from the down payment for purposes of determining its adequacy.

Funds provided indirectly by the seller must also be deducted from the down payment for purposes of determining adequacy. Funds indirectly provided by the seller would include loans made by affiliated financing institutions of the seller, including real estate investment trusts, savings and loan associations, and mortgage companies, and loans outstanding from the seller to the buyer or their affiliates at the time of sale (or loans expected to be made in the future) unless fully secured by completely unrelated properties.

Capital contributions made by the seller to the buyer or required to be made in the future would also be considered funds provided by the seller. Also included would be loan guarantees or collateral support to induce third parties to make loans to the buyer.

Finally, this prohibition would include any other situation where the seller is subject to loss as a result of funds borrowed by a buyer. Related purchases of property by the seller from the buyer or from third parties who, in turn, have bought from or will make loans to the buyer should be carefully evaluated to determine if the substance of the transactions includes funds provided indirectly by the seller to the buyer.

Receivables Subject to Subordination. In some circumstances a buyer may use his newly acquired property as collateral for loans from third parties. The proceeds from these loans may help the buyer in maintaining cash flow sufficient to pay his debt to the seller. If the loans from third parties are subordinate to the seller's receivable, no profit recognition problems would arise.

If, however, the seller's receivable were subject to subordination to (or to equal status with) such future loans, it is obvious that the realization of the seller's receivable from the buyer may be sufficiently uncertain as to require use of the cost recovery or installment method of accounting for the sale.

The auditor should satisfy himself, therefore, that no agreements, understandings, commitments, or other side agreements exist that would permit the future subordination of the seller's receivable. He should do this by obtaining confirmations from the buyer and from other parties who might have knowledge of such agreements or understandings. The letter of representations should contain representations from the seller to this effect.

Certain types of situations involving future subordination do not jeopardize the ultimate realization of the seller's receivable and do not, therefore, preclude profit recognition; these situations are as follows:

1. Subordination to a primary lien on the property that existed at the date of sale,
2. Subordination agreements requiring that the proceeds of the loan from third parties be applied first toward payment of the seller's receivable, and
3. Situations where the seller has obligations for construction on the property and the seller's receivable is subordinated to a construction loan for construction to be performed by the seller.

Subordination to all other types of construction loans would require the cost recovery method.

The auditor should be alert to the above provisions. For example, the sale from seller to buyer might be financed with a 60% down payment and a 40% unsecured note from the buyer to the seller. The buyer would obtain the cash required for the 60% down payment with a loan from a third party, using the property as collateral. The transaction would not qualify for profit recognition, however, because the loan obtained from the third party, having a superior lien to the seller's receivable, would in effect subordinate the seller's receivable to the new loan, and in substance the buyer has no investment in the property. The cost recovery method would therefore be appropriate.

Installment and Cost Recovery Accounting. The auditor should exercise special care in analyzing the substance of certain types of transactions being accounted for under the installment or cost recovery methods. In such instances, a schedule should be prepared showing the expected balance of the note due from the buyer, the balance of the underlying note payable, if any, and the deferred income at the end of five-year intervals over the terms of the seller receivable. The net of these amounts will represent the net asset arising from the sale at each of these intervals. This net asset amount should then be compared to the depreciated cost of the property had the property not been sold. If the depreciated cost is significantly less than the net asset amount arising from the sale, the substance of the transaction may be such that an accounting sale has not occurred or that losses have been eliminated through a thin sale. Accounting for the transaction as a financing arrangement, rather than as a sale, would be preferable in these circumstances. In any case, a provision for losses eliminated by the transaction should be made.

The auditor should make a similar analysis for all subsequent years in which the transaction has a material effect on financial statements being presented.

Fee Income. Accounting for fee income is not well defined in accounting literature. Fees should be audited to determine their substance and accounted for accordingly. Generally speaking, revenue recognition policies for fees should follow the guideliness for real estate sales set forth in the AICPA profit recognition guide (AICPA, 1973b), because the same substance questions are applicable.

The question of fees is being studied by several AICPA committees. In general it appears that commitment fees can be recognized over the commitment period if the commitment is to make the loan at determinable market terms at the time the loan is made and over the combined commitment and loan period if at terms fixed when the commitment is made. Other fees are to be recognized as the services are performed. If a client has a substantial fee during the period under examination, the auditor should confirm all the details of the transaction with all parties. In complex situations, the auditor may want to discuss the details of the transaction with a real estate industry expert to determine a reasonable accounting approach.

Overriding Caution. The auditor must look at the environment in which the client operates and the client's methods of doing business, to determine the inherent checks created by both. He must evaluate these checks and the client's system of internal controls to ascertain the degree to which the client is susceptible to management involvement in material transactions (see Chapter 28) and illegal payments (see Chapter 13).

SUGGESTED READING

Accountants International Study Group. *Revenue Recognition.* New York: AICPA, 1978. The AISG, comprising representatives from Canada, the United Kingdom and the United States, began in 1966 to issue booklets describing accounting thought and practice in their countries. Many of the topics discussed in this chapter are interestingly and informatively reviewed in this particular booklet.

Bohan, Michael. "Service Enterprises and the Accounting Standards Executive Committee." *Journal of Accounting, Auditing and Finance,* Fall, 1978, pp. 76-80. This article is a summary of the position of the Accounting Standards Executive Committee on accounting for service transactions, how it would have been applied if issued, and an identification of some affected industries.

FASB. *Invitation to Comment on Accounting for Certain Service Transactions.* Stamford, Conn., 1978. At a time when the operating relationship of AcSEC to FASB was most unsettled and the FASB agenda overcrowded, AcSEC was encouraged to work on service transactions—a topic scarcely mentioned in the accounting literature. The resulting exposure draft of an SOP was deemed too pervasive to be issued by AcSEC, so FASB incorporated it in its first invitation to comment. Strong resistance showed in responses to the FASB, and the project thus became part of the FASB's conceptual framework project. Until the subject again emerges, this invitation to comment is as concise a summary of service transaction accounting recommendations as can be found.

Peat, Marwick, Mitchell & Co. *Revenue Recognition for Long-term Contracts.* New York, 1976. This accounting research paper presents a point of view on accounting for contracting transactions (services as well as products) where revenue recognition at the time the contract is entered into is not appropriate. Although it does not change GAAP, it is helpful in describing perennial problem areas.

19

Inventories, Cost of Sales, and Construction Contracts

Michael P. Bohan
Michael J. Styczenski

FINANCIAL ACCOUNTING AND REPORTING FOR INVENTORY AND COST OF SALES

Inventory consists of

those items of tangible personal property which (1) are held for sale in the ordinary course of business, (2) are in process of production for such sale, or (3) are to be currently consumed in the production of goods or services to be available for sale. [AC 5121, Statement 1]

The object of inventory management is to have adequate quantities on hand to meet production and customer demands but at the same time not to maintain excess quantities or obsolete items.

In a financial statement, a major objective of accounting for inventories is "the proper determination of income through the process of matching appropriate costs against revenues" (AC 5121, Statement 2). To accomplish this matching in the existing accounting framework, inventories and costs of sales must be measured, generally on the basis of historical costs:

The primary basis of accounting for inventories is cost, which has been defined generally as the price paid or consideration given to acquire an asset. As applied to inventories, cost means in principle the sum of the applicable expenditures and charges directly or indirectly incurred in bringing an article to its existing condition and location. [AC 5121, Statement 3]

In addition to accomplishing this matching, the accountant and auditor must also be concerned with such questions as

- Will the company be able to sell the product?
- Will the company be able to sell the product it has on hand for at least as much as it cost to make and to hold in inventory?
- What future purchase commitments has the company made? Will it be able to recover these amounts through subsequent sales?
- Did the company order everything it received?
- Did the company pay for something it did not receive?
- Did the company bill for what it shipped?

In general, financial accounting for inventory reports on the flow of inventory cost. This is done by first accumulating the costs to purchase and manufacture the product in the inventory balance sheet account and then transferring these costs to the income statement as cost of sales or cost of products sold when the sales are recorded. This is the cost-of-products-sold/inventory cycle. It does not require that an accounting entry be generated every time there is physical movement or change in the inventory: summary entries that cover aggregate changes in a period are often used instead. Financial accounting allocates costs either to the balance sheet (to associate them with the inventory units that are still on hand) or to the income statement (showing the cost of inventory sold or consumed during the period) at such time as the financial statements are prepared.

In the historical cost context, the primary results of the cost-of-products-sold/ inventory cycle are shown in two of the basic financial statements:

1. *Balance sheet.* Here the objective is to report inventories either at the cost to acquire them or at market, whichever is lower. In this way, inventories will be reported at an amount that does not exceed the estimated amount the company can expect to recover if the inventory units are disposed of in an orderly fashion—i.e., other than in a forced liquidation sale.

2. *Income statement.* Here the objective is to report the cost of products sold, as determined in accordance with the matching concept. This cost includes all the costs of acquiring and manufacturing the products and excludes costs that are allocable to the unsold inventory presented in the balance sheet. In other words, the cost of sales shows the excess of the sum of the inventory at the beginning of the period plus the costs to acquire and manufacture the products during the period over the amount of such costs allocated to the ending inventory. While accounting for the cost of products sold attempts to match the costs of acquiring and manufacturing a product with the revenue derived from its sale, the cost of sales is actually a residual amount. It includes in varying amounts the costs of pilferage, theft, damage to goods, and other losses affecting units that are not themselves sold.

This chapter discusses product-related transactions. Service transaction costs and revenues are discussed in Chapter 18.

Cost Components of Inventory

There are two basic types of costs associated with inventory: prime or direct costs and indirect costs. *Prime costs* are the costs of direct material and direct labor.

Direct material cost includes the invoice price less any discounts (accounting for cash discounts may differ in practice; some accountants show them as a part of finance income, others as an adjustment of product cost); vendor charges for design, tooling, and fabrication; and the costs incurred by the manufacturer in obtaining the product from the vendor (transportation, import duty, etc.). Direct labor represents that portion of the labor expended by manufacturing personnel that directly results in the manufacture of the product. For a company that does not manufacture or process inventory for sale (for instance, a retailer), its prime inventory valuation basis is direct material cost.

Indirect manufacturing costs (sometimes called manufacturing overhead, burden, or factory burden) are nonprime manufacturing costs. Some are fixed and some are variable. Fixed indirect manufacturing costs, such as real estate taxes and operating lease rentals on a manufacturing facility, are incurred regardless of the level of production. Variable indirect manufacturing costs vary with the level of productive activity; charges for electricity, for instance, increase as production increases.

A major phase of accounting for the cost-of-products-sold/inventory cycle is the assignment of direct and indirect manufacturing costs to particular inventory units. Prime costs are assigned on the basis of direct association with the unit. The assumptions and conventions used in accomplishing this are described below. Indirect manufacturing costs, on the other hand, cannot be associated directly with the unit, and many different methods of accounting for them are possible, as discussed later under Allocating Indirect Costs.

Cost-Flow Assumptions and Conventions

Financial accounting is a cost accumulator that uses cost-flow assumptions and conventions to develop financial statement presentation of inventories and cost of products sold. A comprehensive example of the results that can be obtained by applying the various cost-flow assumptions and conventions is presented in the appendix to this chapter and should be referred to for illustrations for the methods described below.

Assumptions. After costs have been determined for inventory purchased and produced during the current period, certain assumptions must be made about the flow of these costs, so that the company can allocate the cost of inventory available for sale (which is the total of the cost of beginning inventory plus the cost to acquire and produce new inventory during the period) between ending inventory and the cost of products sold during the period. For example, should cost of products sold be based on the cost of the actual units sold, the cost of the oldest units available for sale, or the cost of the most recently acquired units? Should the ending inventory reflect the actual cost of the units on hand, the most recent cost incurred in obtaining the quantity on hand, or the earliest cost incurred in obtaining and sustaining the quantity on hand? The selection of a cost-flow assumption is not easy, for any of the following approaches can be argued as meeting the requirement of matching costs with revenues.

Specific identification. Presenting the cost of products sold at the actual cost of the units sold is known as the specific identification method. Use of this method provides an exact match of cost to revenue when a unit is sold, because the cost of acquiring that very unit is known. But keeping records that identify individual units is impractical when the number of inventory transactions is large and when most inventory items are fungible, so this method is not widely used.

First-in, first-out. Presenting the cost of products sold at the cost of the oldest units available for sale during the period is known as the first-in, first-out (FIFO) cost-flow assumption. Under the FIFO assumption, inventory costs follow what normally is the physical movement of inventories; that is, the first goods purchased (oldest on hand) are the first goods to be sold, leaving the last goods purchased (newest) in inventory. This method provides a practical way of matching the cost of products sold to current revenues, but critics point out that it results in charging old costs against current revenues.

Last-in, first-out. Presenting the cost of products sold at the cost of the most recent inventory acquisitions is known as the last-in, first-out (LIFO) cost-flow assumption. LIFO produces dramatically different results from those obtained with FIFO when price levels are changing rapidly, because the cost of products on hand at the beginning of the period or purchased early during the period may differ considerably from the cost of products purchased late in the period. Supporters of LIFO argue that it provides a better measure of current profits because it uses current, not old, costs as the measure. The use of LIFO has grown recently, not only for this reason, but because it is an acceptable method for income tax purposes (provided it is also used for the financial statements). In periods of rising prices, LIFO produces substantially lower taxable income than does the FIFO method. Critics of LIFO point out, however, that it does not reflect the normal physical movement of inventory and that it presents inventories in the balance sheet at an amount that almost never approximates the current cost of the physical units on hand.

Conventions. Various conventions are used for assigning costs to inventory units when either the FIFO or the LIFO assumption is applied. Their objective is to assign to inventory amounts that approximate its historical cost. Applications of these conventions are described in the appendix to this chapter and are summarized below.

Specific identification. Invoices and other specifically identifiable unit costs for the actual items of inventory on hand are the source for the prices assigned to the inventory.

Average cost. Average costs of inventory units for the period of time associated with the inventory on hand are used to price the inventory.

Retail method. First the inventory is valued in terms of its normal selling price. Then this amount is reduced to a cost amount by applying the ratio of the cost of inventory available for sale during the period (beginning inventory plus purchases) to the selling price of this inventory. This is discussed more fully later in this chapter.

Standard cost. Costs are assigned to inventory on the basis of a predetermined norm or standard for each unit, as discussed later in this chapter.

Market value. In certain cases inventories may be stated at their market value, even if this exceeds cost:

> For example, precious metals having a fixed monetary value with no substantial cost of marketing may be stated at such monetary value; any other exceptions must be justifiable by inability to determine appropriate approximate costs, immediate market-ability at quoted market price, and the characteristic of unit interchangeability. Where goods are stated above cost, this fact should be fully disclosed. [AC 5121, Statement 9]

Market value is presently also used for reporting certain agricultural commodities, but its use in this area is currently being rechallenged by the AICPA Agribusiness Committee.

Inventory Existence and Valuation

Inventory Quantities. Inventories typically represent a significant asset to a manufacturing company. Thus it is important for the company to periodically conduct accurate and documented physical counts of inventories to determine the quantities of goods on hand. The counts also assist management in determining how well the inventory control and reporting system is working by providing a comparison of the physical count to the company records, either on a unit basis or in terms of aggregate dollars.

As noted in the next subsection, the company may count inventories on a cyclical basis, performing counts at different locations on different dates; or it may count everything at the same time. Either way, adequate instructions should be prepared for the counting operation. These instructions may include many procedures; typical ones are shown in Figure 19.1.

In determining its inventory quantities, the company should look not only to its own materials on hand, but also to any units it may have out on consignment, stored in outside warehouses, or left with outside processors. Goods being held on consignment from another entity, customer materials on hand for processing, and units being warehoused for others should be excluded from the company's inventory, but these units may also be counted to make sure there is adequate control over all materials on hand that belong to others.

Inventory Date. The amount presented as inventories in the balance sheet is in theory the aggregate historical cost (determined using the cost-flow approach discussed above) of physical units on hand at the reporting date, adjusted for certain economic and physical factors such as market conditions, excess stock, damaged stock, and obsolete stock. There are two basic approaches to the determination of the historical cost:

1. The inventory quantities are determined as of the reporting date and are valued at historical cost using the selected cost-flow conventions. The quantities are determined

- Provision for the counts to be performed by personnel familiar with the inventory. (Total responsibility for a count, however, should rest with those who are charged with safeguarding the inventory.)
- Provision for adequate supervision of the counts.
- Identification of the individuals who will test the counting.
- Control of the inventory tags issued and used.
- Orderly arrangement of inventory to facilitate counting.
- Limited production and movement of inventory during the counting, preferably none at all.
- Accumulation and identification of inventory at outside locations or held for others (consignments).
- Identification of scrap.
- Identification of obsolete or other items that are not to be included in the count.
- Accumulation of appropriate cutoff information.
- Treatment of shipments and receipts during the count.
- Treatment of items received in sealed trailers or railroad cars.
- Treatment of orders on shipping dock but not yet picked up.
- Identification of items returned by customers.

FIGURE 19.1 TYPICAL PHYSICAL INVENTORY CONSIDERATIONS

either by physical count as of the reporting date or by reference to perpetual inventory records for each inventory item.

2. The inventory quantities are determined by physical count at a date other than the reporting date and valued at their historical cost using the selected cost-flow conventions. This amount is then updated to the reporting date by adjusting for the cost of interim transactions such as purchases, cost of goods sold, scrapped material, and estimated shrinkage.

A company's selection of an approach to determining inventory quantities should be based on the relative costs and benefits of the alternatives. A physical count at the close of the reporting period provides the most accurate determination of period-end units because it is not exposed to the updating errors that can result from interim determination. Though the period-end approach obviates the need for a sophisticated system to account for intervening transactions, it often delays the release of financial statements because of the time required to compile the data.

However, a company often must shut down its entire operation at one time to carry out the physical inventory, so the company must choose an opportune time, which may have to be an interim date. It may also be possible to cycle its physical inventory counting so that not all operations are shut down at the same time. Based on its systems and controls, a company may use either approach, or both, for different types of inventory.

Book-To-Physical Difference. When a company has an accounting system designed to adjust inventory and cost of products sold for transactions throughout the year, a good indication of the performance of this system is to compare the inventory shown in the general ledger to the physical inventory at the same date priced out at the old standard costs (assuming standard costs, discussed later, are in use). If the amounts are substantially the same, the system probably adequately reflects the application of the company's cost-flow assumption and costing conventions to the physical movements of inventory, though it is also possible that there may be offsetting errors. If the amounts differ substantially, this could be caused by several factors, including the common reasons that follow.

Inventory cutoff errors. The inventory general ledger balance may not reflect shipments that have been removed from the physical inventory, or may not reflect receipts of merchandise that are included in the physical inventory. The general ledger balance may also reflect receipts of merchandise that have been excluded from the physical inventory, or may reflect shipments of merchandise that have not yet been removed from the physical inventory.

Unreported standard cost variances and adjustments. A standard cost system has failed to use consistently the same standard for reporting inventory transactions. This results in standard cost differences remaining in inventory and becoming part of the physical inventory adjustment. (See the Standard Costs—Accounting for Variances section.)

Unreported scrap. Units of inventory have been scrapped, but their cost has not been removed from the inventory accounts.

Pilferage and theft. Units of inventory have been stolen, but their cost has not been removed from the inventory accounts.

Failure to cost out sales properly. The cost used to reduce the inventory accounts for units sold is not the same as the cost at which these units are carried in the inventory accounts.

Improper reporting of production. Reported production (the basis for inventory cost input) is not the same as actual production.

Updating the Interim Inventory Determination. Identification of the causes of inventory adjustments is always valuable to management because it provides information that can be used for operating control. But it is even more important for companies that take their physical inventory at an interim date and wish to rely on their system to update the inventory accounts for the amount to be presented in the year-end financial statements.

To the extent that the physical inventory difference can be traced to specific system flaws (for instance, improper costing of sales), the effect of each flaw on inventory transactions between the inventory date and year-end can be quantified, and the year-end inventory adjusted. If the reasons for material differences cannot be identified and quantified, there is prima facie evidence that the inventory accounting system cannot be relied on to adequately update the inventory accounts and cost of products sold from the interim date to the reporting date, unless some form of modification is applied to allow for deficiencies in the system that have repeatedly given rise to physical inventory adjustments. The modification that is normally employed is a provision for inventory shrinkage based on the book-to-physical differences that occurred in the past. The amount of the provision is normally quantified on some measure of volume of productive transactions, since production is generally the cause of shrinkage.

For instance, the past relationship of inventory adjustments to direct labor input might provide a ratio that could then be applied to direct labor incurred between the interim inventory date and the reporting date. Using such an approach, the cost of sales for the interim period would be the standard cost of sales adjusted by reported variances and the estimated shrinkage factor. This factor would adjust the inventory and cost of sales figures generated by the accounting system for the applicable portion of adjustments expected at the next inventory date.

Lower of Cost or Market. GAAP normally requires the use of historical cost, but

a departure from the cost basis of pricing the inventory is required when the utility of the goods is no longer as great as its cost. Where there is evidence that the utility of goods, in their disposal in the ordinary course of business, will be less than cost, whether due to physical deterioration, obsolescence, changes in price levels, or other causes, the difference should be recognized as a loss of the current period. This is generally accomplished by stating such goods at a lower level commonly designated as *market*. [AC 5121, Statement 5]

This is generally described as the *lower-of-cost-or-market principle*. A layman would probably interpret the term *market* to mean the amount that could be realized if the unit were sold, but in a technical accounting sense market is somewhat different. The authoritative literature (AC 5121, Statement 6) defines it as follows:

As used in the phrase *lower of cost or market* the term *market* means current replacement cost (by purchase or by reproduction, as the case may be) except that:

(1) Market should not exceed the net realizable value (i.e., estimated selling price in the ordinary course of business less reasonably predictable costs of completion and disposal); and

(2) Market should not be less than net realizable value reduced by an allowance for an approximately normal profit margin.

The upper and lower limits placed on replacement cost as an equivalent of market are intended to prevent the inventory from being stated at an amount above the net proceeds that can be expected from the disposition of the item or at an amount below the net proceeds less normal profit margin. From a practical standpoint, at least for finished goods, the accountant has generally looked to the upper limit of the test in defining market, both because that number is often more available than the replacement cost figure, and because that number must be determined even if a replacement cost figure is determined, since it is the upper limit of market.

The lower-of-cost-or-market determination can be made based on individual items or by inventory groupings. The authoritative pronouncement dealing with this subject (AC 5121, Statement 7) states:

> Depending on the character and composition of the inventory, the rule of *cost or market, whichever is lower* may properly be applied either directly to each item or to the total of the inventory (or, in some cases, to the total of the components of each major category). The method should be that which most clearly reflects periodic income.

Grouping is allowed because the utility of the inventory may be best judged not on the basis of individual inventory items, but on the basis of the products in which those items are combined. The company can make the lower-of-cost-or-market test on an item-by-item basis, or on some logical aggregation of inventory items (account groupings, product line, production location, geographic location, or company wide). The selection of an approach should take into consideration the nature of the inventory items in the grouping and should provide the best reflection of income. For instance, refrigerators and high-fashion clothing would not be put in the same group for purposes of determining the lower-of-cost-or-market adjustment. Whatever system the company adopts, it must be applied consistently from year to year. Once the inventory carrying amount is written down to market because it is less than cost, the new carrying amount becomes the cost from that point forward (AC 5121, fn. 2).

Excess and Obsolete Inventory. In addition to comparing the carrying amount of inventory to its market, a comparison must also be made of the actual volume of inventory with the demand for it or the ultimate products into which this inventory is to be converted. Inventory on hand may exceed future demand either because the product is now outdated (obsolete) or because the amount on hand, whether of materials or finished products, is more than can be used to meet future need (excess). The excess or obsolete portion of the inventory should be reduced to an amount not less than its net realizable value. Such reserves may be established on some formula basis (for instance, everything over two years' supply might be fully reserved) for financial statement purposes if justified by historical or present conditions. A formula-type approach, however, is not acceptable for determination of excess stock provisions for income tax purposes; but the carrying amount of inventory can be reduced for tax purposes if supported by objective evidence, such as having the items scrapped or offered for sale at a reduced price.[1]

The physical inventory listings should carefully identify units that are obsolete or have previously been written off. Although these units may have no operating value to the company for its current production requirements, the company should institute controls over them to ensure that they are not misused. These controls should also ensure that these units are not carried at more than recoverable value or at an amount higher than that at which they were recorded in prior periods.

---

[1] *Thor Power Tool Co. v. Commissioner,* 79-1 USTC 9139 (Sup. Ct.) 439 U.S. 522 (1979); Revenue Procedure 80-5, as amended by Internal Revenue News Release 80-48 (4/8/80); and Revenue Ruling 80-6.

LIFO

The LIFO cost method has been used with IRS approval for almost 40 years, yet virtually nothing in the authoritative accounting literature states precisely how it should be applied. Instead, the literature simply describes the LIFO cost-flow assumption and the general benefits that can be derived from using it in periods of rising prices. LIFO may be applied to the material, labor, and manufacturing elements of inventory cost, but for the sake of simplicity the discussion in this chapter generally refers only to material cost.

A great deal has been written about LIFO, however, in IRS pronouncements. Because they provide more guidance, and because of the IRS conformity rule discussed below, IRS releases have dominated the establishment of practices in financial reporting using the LIFO inventory assumptions. This has given rise to the circular proposition that "whatever is good for tax is good for accounting is good for tax. . . ." See Chapter 43 for a discussion of the IRS approaches in the LIFO area. Illustrations of the various applications of LIFO are given in the comprehensive example in Appendix 19.

LIFO Requirements. With the rapid inflation of the 1970s, which shows no sign of slowing, many users of financial statements are questioning the appropriateness of the FIFO method for determining the cost of products sold. Many companies consequently have changed to the LIFO method, which shows lower earnings in a period of rising prices and stable or rising inventory levels. Not only does LIFO address the demand for an income measurement approach that takes better account of inflation, it is also an acceptable method for income tax reporting and results in considerable savings of tax dollars. But in order to use LIFO for income tax purposes, a company must also use LIFO to determine income for financial statement purposes. In other words, a company cannot avail itself of the tax savings offered by LIFO without applying the same method to report earnings in its financial statements. This is known as the conformity requirement, and it is part of the law passed by Congress in 1938.

Historically, the IRS has interpreted the conformity rule to extend beyond the income statement. The rule generally applied to other disclosures that the company made to shareholders and outsiders regarding the effect of LIFO on reported earnings. Until recently, the IRS interpretations prohibited supplemental disclosure of the effect of LIFO on earnings, such as what earnings would have been had FIFO been used.

LIFO Supplementary Disclosures. On July 17, 1979, the IRS proposed (Proposed Regulation 1.472-2(e)) liberalizing the conformity rule to permit use of a method other than LIFO for purposes of determining supplemental disclosures (such as those required under SFAS 33 (AC 1072); see Chapter 8) regarding a taxpayer's income and to allow the taxpayer to use a non-LIFO method for internal management reports. The proposal (which is actually in effect) states that supplementary or explanatory non-LIFO disclosures do not violate the conformity requirement causing the loss of a LIFO election. Permissible disclosures include footnotes, news releases, letters to shareholders, etc., but information (other than footnotes to the statement) "on the face of a taxpayer's financial income statement is not considered a supplement or explanation," and would violate the conformity

rule. The proposed regulations specifically would not permit a parenthetical statement included on the face of the income statement and presumably also would not
permit a two-column statement, one LIFO and one FIFO. However, the proposal
would permit supplemental disclosures using a non-LIFO method to

1. Provide supplemental information about or explanation of the taxpayer's primary
   presentation of income in the financial statements,
2. Ascertain the value of the taxpayer's inventory for balance sheet purposes,
3. Ascertain information contained in internal management reports, and
4. Determine income for a single continuous period of operations that is less than a year.

Although the SEC had originally supported some relaxation of the requirement,
it balked at the extent of the IRS liberalization. The SEC is concerned that the
disclosure of earnings on a FIFO basis might give the impression that earnings
information based on FIFO is more representative of actual operating performance,
i.e., the "true earnings." The SEC indicated it would seriously object to such
disclosure in the case of a company that might have recently changed to the LIFO
method, because the change was presumably to a preferable method. However, if
LIFO is used, the SEC requires that the excess of replacement cost (FIFO cost can
be used if not materially different) over the stated LIFO value be disclosed (Regulation S-X, Rule 5-02.6(c)).

The SEC staff has indicated that its primary concern is the risk of user confusion, which would be mitigated if registrants give users a proper perspective
for evaluation of the supplemental material being presented by (1) stating clearly
that the use of LIFO results in a better matching of costs and revenues and (2)
indicating the reasons FIFO disclosures are appropriate (generally because some
users want to have the information to compare operating results with those of companies not on LIFO). The SEC staff has also indicated that such disclosures are
not to be made in financial highlights, president's letters, or press releases, since
supplemental analytical data is not generally included in those places.

LIFO Inventory Groupings. The IRS regulations require that if LIFO is not to
be calculated unit by unit (a rare practice), there must be some common basis
for grouping inventory "cost pools" in making LIFO cost determinations. There
are many approaches for determining this commonality, including source of supply
and use of the various items in a similar finished product. It is fairly obvious that
the use of a pool representing all the wood products at a given location would
be an acceptable cost pool; it is probably equally obvious that a company cannot
pool wine at its winery with the stone it has at a tombstone-producing segment.
Many cases, however, are not so clear-cut. The general guidance is to use a rational
and consistent approach.

Valuation of LIFO Layer. When there are more units than at the previous year-
end (which are valued at the previous year's amount), how should LIFO costs
for a given period be assigned to units in inventory? The IRS allows three methods:

1. The most recent purchase cost during the current year. Essentially this is a FIFO
   approach.

2. Purchase cost at the beginning of the current year. Some view this as the approach most harmonious with the basic LIFO concept.
3. Average unit cost for the current year.

LIFO Indexing Methods. Since LIFO is rarely applied item by item, the application may be based on indices that represent the relationship between current cost and base-year cost of the inventory. The current cost basis of the inventory is divided by the relationship of the current costs to the base-year costs, in order to restate the current inventory in terms of base-year dollars. The excess of the current inventory in base-year dollars over the inventory at the beginning of the year in base-year dollars is the LIFO layer for the year in base-year dollars. Multiplication of the current-year LIFO layer in base-year dollars by the index for the current year yields the current-year LIFO layer in current-year dollars. The index can be determined by one of the following methods.

Double-extension method. The index is the relationship of the aggregate of the current-year cost of the ending inventory units to the base-year cost of the ending inventory units. (See description of link-chain method below for a variation of this approach.)

Direct index method. The index is determined by extending a representative portion of the ending inventory at the current-year layer cost and at the base-year layer cost. The link-chain method described below is also used in a variation of this approach.

Externally generated index. Companies sometimes use an index provided by an outside source to avoid double-extending the inventory either in total or on a sample basis. One commonly used index is the Bureau of Labor Statistics Index, issued semiannually by the U.S. Department of Labor, which is often applied by general purpose retailers. With constantly changing styles and models in fashions, appliances, and furniture, it would be extremely difficult to double-extend an existing inventory using a prior-period's price for the same item, since the identical item probably did not exist in the past even if a similar one did. Companies that encounter this situation frequently use an externally generated index, though such an index should not be used for inventory items that are not generally included in its determination. For instance, the Department Store Price Index should not be used by a metal fabricator to adjust the current year's prices; an index related to that industry would be more appropriate if double extension is not feasible. The company must be ready to demonstrate to the IRS the appropriateness of the external index used.

Applying the Index. The two most common ways of applying indices are the *dollar value* LIFO approach and the *link-chain* LIFO approach. The dollar value approach uses an index based on the relationship of current-year cost to base-year cost to determine if there has been an increment or decrement in the LIFO layers. The link-chain method uses an index based on the relationship of the current cost to the beginning-of-year cost. This index is then converted to reflect the relationship of current-year cost to base-year cost by multiplying the current-year index by the prior-year index to obtain a cumulative index.

Addition of New Item to LIFO Cost Pool. A common problem encountered when using an internally generated index is how to assign a prior-period cost to a unit that was not in inventory during the prior period. Two basic approaches have been used in practice. The first approach assigns the current-year cost to the new item as if it were the prior-year cost. The reasoning is that since the item was not in inventory during the prior year, it should figure in the index only in relation to the year in which it entered the pool. The second approach assumes that although a new item was not previously in stock, it would undoubtedly have carried a lower cost basis (assuming a rising price level) if it had been the current-year cost; it should therefore be factored down to reflect an equivalent prior-year cost. This factoring can be accomplished either by direct reference to vendor price lists for like items in existence but not on hand in the prior year, or by applying an index to the current-year cost in order to restate the item in terms of prior-year dollars.

If the prior-year cost is to be estimated on the basis of an index, the index can be generated by double-extending the quantity of items on hand in the current year and similar items available from vendors in the previous year. Alternatively, it can be based on a double-extended index of prices for all inventory items that were in the same cost pool during the prior year and the current year using the current-year quantities, or a representative externally generated index can be used.

Lower of LIFO Cost or Market. Under IRS rules, LIFO is a cost method, and companies are prohibited from applying the lower-of-cost-or-market principle to inventories carried at LIFO. In fact, in the year in which a company adopts LIFO for income tax purposes, the carrying basis of its beginning inventory becomes the base-year LIFO regardless of which cost-flow assumption was previously used, except to the extent that the inventory at the beginning of the year was reduced to market because it was lower than historical cost. This problem exists mostly in the retail industry. Any market reserves deducted for income tax purposes existing at the beginning of the initial LIFO year must be reversed, effectively restoring those amounts to taxable income in the first LIFO year. Then, from that point forward, market reserves can no longer be established for income tax purposes.

The application of the lower-of-cost-or-market principle, however, is not suspended for LIFO financial reporting purposes. Companies must make a determination of the relationship of the carrying basis of the inventory at LIFO to the appropriate market, as described earlier. To the extent that the carrying basis exceeds market, a provision must be made to reduce it to market. From a practical standpoint, this will only occur in the first, and perhaps the second, year in which a company employs LIFO; since LIFO is usually adopted on the presumption that prices will continue to rise, the market prices of the inventory can be expected to increase, while the LIFO carrying basis will generally reflect earlier-period costs (the costs of the base-period layer and the subsequent layers by year).

From a theoretical standpoint the provision of a market adjustment must be recorded as a permanent adjustment of the cost basis of the inventory for financial reporting purposes (AC 5121, fn. 2), but from a practical standpoint most companies using LIFO create a separate allowance account for the market adjustment in the years in which it is needed and reverse that reserve in subsequent periods; in this manner the tax and financial statement cost basis of LIFO inventory are identical, while the amount shown in the financial statements is the cost basis reduced by the reserve. IRS regulations, however, do permit the LIFO inventory for financial reporting purposes to differ from the LIFO inventory for income tax purposes by the amount of lower-of-cost-or-market reserves provided for financial reporting purposes.

LIFO Layer Liquidation. When a company's LIFO inventory value is lower at the end of the fiscal year than it was at the beginning, LIFO does not achieve its desired results, because old costs—i.e., the carrying amounts of prior-period layers —rather than current costs are charged to costs of products sold. In a period of rising prices, this will result in more profit being reported than would normally be expected with the use of LIFO—indeed more than would have been reported using FIFO.

In SAB 1 the SEC indicates that reporting companies should disclose the effect on earnings of a LIFO layer liquidation. The conformity rule notwithstanding, the IRS has agreed that disclosure of the effect of a LIFO layer liquidation will not jeopardize a company's LIFO election. In practice, however, there has been some uncertainty about how that "profit effect" should be computed. Two approaches for making this computation have been supported: the *current layer* approach and the *deferred* approach.

Under the current layer approach, the effect on cost of products sold of penetrating a LIFO layer is the difference between the LIFO cost of the inventory sold and the current cost of that inventory. Current cost is the cost that would have been used to price a layer had it been added during the year. Though there is some theoretical debate about this (see below), current cost is determined by the company's LIFO pricing convention (beginning-of-year costs, average costs, or end-of-year costs). The net income effect should reflect the impact for nondiscretionary costs (for example, profit sharing) and should be net of taxes at the company's incremental tax rate.

Those who support the current layer approach believe that the disclosure is intended to tell the reader what would have happened if LIFO had worked as theoretically intended—i.e., if current costs had been matched against current revenues. They reason that this matching is the prime justification for the use of LIFO. On the other hand it is argued that the current layer approach is an "as if" computation—it assumes purchases during the year that were not made.

As an alternative, the effect of the layer erosion can be computed by subtracting the LIFO cost from the prior-year-end FIFO cost for the layers liquidated. Under this line of reasoning, the disclosure is intended to tell the reader how much of the profit that was "deferred" in the prior year has been recognized in the current year. This approach has considerable practical appeal because of its relationship to tax deferral benefits; however, it has little to do with LIFO's theoretical rationale.

Another debate deals with how current cost should be determined under the current layer approach. Some have argued that the lowest price paid in the current year is an appropriate base. Others have suggested that the average price paid during the year is a better measure. Each of these alternatives has merit, but the simplest method is to determine current cost in the same way the company would cost a new layer, since this must normally be determined in order to adjust the inventory to LIFO whether or not there has been a layer liquidation.

As a practical matter, the current layer approach is required by paragraph 3 of Rev. Proc. 76-7, which states:

The computations made to determine the income effect of a penetration of a LIFO layer must be made on the same basis employed by the taxpayer in actually valuing its LIFO increments. For example, if the taxpayer actually values inventory increments on the basis of the average cost method, such method must also be used in determining the effect on income as a result of the penetration for purposes of the financial statement footnote.

Figures 19.2 and 19.3 are examples of the applications of the current layer approach.

Purchase Business Combinations. In a purchase business combination, authoritative literature (AC 1091.88(c)) requires that the inventories of the acquired company be valued on the basis of their fair value. If a purchase business combination meets certain tax regulations, the company can use a different LIFO basis for tax purposes than that used for financial statement purposes, as long as it employs LIFO on a consistent basis in determining LIFO layers from then on. See Chapter 30 for a further discussion.

Interim LIFO. The use of LIFO creates unique problems in interim financial reporting, primarily because it is a calculation made once a year to comply with income tax regulations and cannot be conclusively computed for interim financial reporting. Most enterprises that report on a LIFO basis maintain their accounts on a FIFO or average cost method, and provide a LIFO reserve to reduce the carrying amount to a LIFO amount. For interim reports, some companies merely account for costs of products sold on a FIFO basis and retain the prior year's LIFO reserve without adjustment until year-end. This has worked reasonably satisfactorily when inflation has not been extreme. Other companies go through LIFO computations considering the interim period as if a year-end or looking forward to assess what the LIFO impact will be for the entire year.

Companies that apply an externally generated index do so also to an inventory of current cost amount generally equivalent to FIFO. Companies using the double-extension approach may be able to estimate the effect of LIFO in the interim period by estimating an index on a sampling basis and applying it to the inventory maintained on a FIFO or average cost basis.

Authoritative literature provides limited guidance on interim accounting for inventories, stating that

> those costs and expenses that are associated directly with or allocated to the products sold or to the services rendered for annual reporting purposes (including, for example, material costs, wages and salaries and related fringe benefits, manufacturing overhead, and warranties) should be similarly treated for interim reporting purposes. [AC 2071.13]

This would suggest that the effect of rising prices should be reflected in the interim period in which they occur. Some have argued, however, that the inflation effect that LIFO measures should be related to the year as a whole by using the integral approach rather than the discrete approach normally used for inventories. They hold, therefore, that the LIFO effect should be allocated to the current and future interim periods of the current year. Others contend that a discrete approach is intended, and the effect of LIFO should be shown on a current basis as if the interim-period-end were the close of the year, since the LIFO effect is a cost or benefit associated with current revenue for the interim period.

Another problem with applying LIFO in interim financial reporting arises in accounting for the effect of a LIFO layer liquidation on an interim basis when that layer is expected to be replaced by the fiscal year-end. As noted above, LIFO is regarded as an annual calculation. If a layer liquidated on an interim basis is reinstated by the fiscal year-end, it will be accounted for at the same cost as that at which it was carried at the beginning of the year. This conflicts with what happens if a layer is liquidated at the end of a fiscal year and replaced in a subsequent year, for in that case the replacement is valued at the LIFO layer cost rate in effect in the year of replacement rather than at the rate of the layer when it was liquidated. APB 28 provides guidance in handling this problem:

> Companies that use the LIFO method may encounter a liquidation of base period inventories at an interim date that is expected to be replaced by the end of the annual period. In such cases the inventory at the interim reporting date should not give effect to the LIFO liquidation, and cost of sales for the interim reporting period should include the expected cost of replacement of the liquidated LIFO base. [AC 2071.14(b)]

Where applicable, procedures for determining whether there has been a LIFO layer liquidation on an interim basis are virtually identical to procedures used to determine the effect of a LIFO layer liquidation in annual financial statements.

For a further discussion of LIFO in interim financial statements, see the FASB's *Discussion Memorandum on an Analysis of Issues Related to Interim Financial Accounting and Reporting* (FASB, 1978b).

Retail Method

A shopping tour of any department store on a busy Saturday afternoon will suggest the staggering problems faced by the retailer in accounting for so many types of merchandise and such a large volume of transactions. The goods stocked range from toothpicks and greeting cards to major appliances and diamond rings; there are hundreds of thousands of individual items on the racks and shelves, and the separate sales transacted number in the millions during the course of the year. How does a store keep track of all its inventory and all its transactions? How are sales costed out? How is inventory controlled and valued?

Computers are rapidly coming to the point of being able to handle all these details automatically, and a complete perpetual record may be within the realm of practicality. The costing of inventory items sold at purchase cost is an overwhelming task and, except in the most sophisticated database computer systems, does not provide sufficiently timely information. While an annual physical inventory does produce a cost-of-sales figure for the fiscal period and a year-end inventory valuation, management must of course have current information both for control purposes and for the day-to-day decisions required to run the business. This is the need that the retail inventory method was developed to meet. It evolved shortly after the turn of the century and was accepted by the IRS in 1941.

FACTS

	Layer	Units in Inventory	Beginning-of-Year Unit Cost	LIFO Value	Year-End FIFO Value	Reserve
At December 31, 19X4	19X2	100,000	$1.00	$100,000		
	19X3	40,000	1.20	48,000		
	19X4	30,000	1.40	42,000		
		170,000		$190,000	$255,000	$65,000
At December 31, 19X5	19X2	100,000	$1.00	$100,000		
	19X3	20,000	1.20	24,000		
		120,000		$124,000	$204,000	$80,000

Unit value LIFO is used. There is only one pool. There are no variable nondiscretionary costs, and the beginning-of-year convention is used. Purchases during 19X5 were:

Month	Units	Price	Amount
Jan.	30,000	$1.60	$ 48,000
June	50,000	1.65	82,500
Dec.	120,000	1.70	204,000
			$334,500

SOLUTION

Units Sold		Unit Cost	Charged to Cost of Products Sold	Current Cost	"As If" Computation
19X5: Jan.	30,000	$1.60	$ 48,000	$1.60	$ 48,000
June	50,000	1.65	82,500	1.65	82,500
Dec.	120,000	1.70	204,000	1.70	204,000
19X4	30,000	1.40	42,000	1.60	48,000
19X3	20,000	1.20	24,000	1.60	32,000
Total			$400,500		414,500
					400,500
Pretax impact of layer erosion					$ 14,000

FIGURE 19.2   EXAMPLE OF LIFO LAYER LIQUIDATION UNDER UNIT LIFO

FACTS	Layer	Base-Year Cost	Index*	LIFO Value	Year-End FIFO Value	Reserve
At December 31, 19X4	19X2	$10,000,000	100	$10,000,000		
	19X3	1,000,000	110	1,100,000		
	19X4	1,000,000	120	1,200,000		
		$12,000,000		$12,300,000	$14,400,000	$2,100,000
At December 31, 19X5	19X2	$10,000,000	100	$10,000,000		
	19X3	500,000	110	550,000		
	19X4	—	120	—		
	19X5	—	130	—		
		$10,500,000		$10,550,000	$13,650,000	$3,100,000

Dollar value LIFO is used. There is only one pool, no variable nondiscretionary costs, and the average cost convention is used.

* Average cost to base year.

SOLUTION

Old costs charged to cost of products sold:

December 31, 19X4 LIFO inventory	$12,300,000	
Less December 31, 19X5 LIFO inventory	10,550,000	
Old costs in 19X5 cost of sales		$1,750,000

If there had not been a liquidation of a LIFO layer, these old costs would have been charged at current costs:

Determine base-year value of layer liquidation:

Base-year value at: December 31, 19X4	12,000,000	
December 31, 19X5	10,500,000	
Base value of layer liquidation	1,500,000	
Ratio of current-year costs to base-year costs	1.3	
Current-year cost of liquidated layer		1,950,000
Pretax impact of layer liquidation		$ 200,000

FIGURE 19.3 EXAMPLE OF LIFO LAYER LIQUIDATION UNDER DOLLAR VALUE LIFO

	(1)	(2)	(3)	(4)
			Mark-On	Cost Complement
	Cost	Retail	(Percent)	(Percent)
			(2-1) ÷ 2	1 ÷ 2
Beginning inventory	$13,000	$20,000	35.0%	65.0%
Total purchases	12,000	20,000	40.0	60.0
Available for sale	$25,000	40,000	37.5	62.5
Net sales		25,000		
Ending inventory at retail		$15,000		
Ending inventory at cost ($15,000 × 62.5%)	$ 9,375			

FIGURE 19.4   ILLUSTRATION OF THE BASIC RETAIL METHOD

Principles and Operation. The retail method is essentially an averaging method that results in a valuation at cost or market, whichever is lower. The basic principle for determining inventory is the relationship between the cost and retail values of the merchandise. Figure 19.4 illustrates this principle. As the table shows, the opening inventory had a mark-on of 35%, or a dollar mark-on of $7,000 on a retail value of $20,000. (Percentages in retail statistics always use the retail value as the base.) Purchases during the period, however, were marked up 40%. This increased the final cumulative mark-on percentage to 37.5% and reduced the cost complement to 62.5%.

Thus, the cost of the ending inventory can be determined without reference to detailed purchase information such as suppliers' invoices and without the necessity of a physical inventory at cost.

Basically, the only requirement is the computation of the relationship of cost to retail price and the application of this percentage to the retail inventory as indicated by the company's inventory records, periodically verified by actual count. Of course, records that accurately show the cost of all purchases and sales data must be maintained.

Serious distortions can result if the various items being accounted for have substantially different mark-on rates. High-mark-on items, which tend to turn over more slowly, often constitute a larger portion of the inventory than low-mark-on goods. Under these circumstances, the averaging process would tend to equalize the mark-on percentage and result in an overstatement of inventory value. To obtain a reasonably accurate inventory value, therefore, the method must be used for groups of merchandise items that have approximately the same mark-on percentage. This is easily done in department stores, because the operations are divided into separate departments that handle similar items.

The simple illustration shown in Figure 19.4 can now be expanded in Figure 19.5 to consider further aspects of the method. The cost figures in Figure 19.5 are

	Cost	Retail	Mark-On (Percent)	Cost Complement (Percent)
Beginning inventory	$13,000	$20,000	35.0%	65.0%
Purchases less returns	11,000	20,000 } 40.0		60.0
Transportation costs	1,000	—		
Markups, less markup cancellations	—	500		
Available for sale	$25,000	$40,500	38.3	61.7
Less:				
Net sales		25,000		
Markdowns, less markdown cancellations		500		
		25,500		
Ending inventory at retail		$15,000		
Ending inventory at cost ($15,000 × 61.7%)	$ 9,255			

FIGURE 19.5   FURTHER ASPECTS OF THE RETAIL INVENTORY METHOD

ultimately the same as in Figure 19.4, though purchase cost has been broken down into the elements of actual material cost as shown on suppliers' invoices and the transportation costs—freight, cartage, etc.—that were incurred in conjunction with the purchases. The retail figures in Figure 19.5 are also the same as in Figure 19.4 for net sales and ending inventory at retail, but ending inventory at cost has been changed by markups over, and markdowns from, the initially established retail prices.

After a selling price has been established for an item and the original mark-on set, factors of supply and demand sometimes lead the retailer to increase his selling price. These increases, or markups, cause no problems with the retail method other than accounting control. The aggregate amount of the markups is added to the inventory and to the purchase total at retail, and becomes a portion of the retail balance for determining the cost-to-retail relationship.

Markdowns, or reductions from the originally determined retail price, are more common than markups. Figure 19.5 shows how markdowns are handled in the retail method. If markdowns were used to offset markups, merchandise available for sale in this example would have a retail value of $40,000. But instead, markdowns are computed only as retail reductions from the goods available for sale, and thus do not affect the cost-to-retail relationship. This causes the mark-on percentage to be higher than actual cost would indicate, and the cost complement percentage to be somewhat lower. The application of the lower cost complement is what produces a valuation at cost or market, whichever is lower. Rather than the inventory value of $9,375 obtained in Figure 19.4, the value has now been reduced in Figure 19.5 to $9,255 because of the markdowns.

The reason for computing ending inventory in this way can best be seen by taking the example of one inventory item. Suppose a retailer buys a pair of shoes for $10 and originally tries to sell them for $20. However, time passes, and the shoes are damaged or go out of style, requiring a markdown to $15. Thus, the retail value of this item of inventory is $15. If the cost-to-retail relationship were computed with the markdown taken into consideration, the cost complement would then be 66⅔% ($10/$15), which, when applied to the retail value, would yield the original cost of $10. But would this be an adequate value to assign to this item? There is no market quotation for shoes damaged or out of style, but if the retail price has depreciated, it is reasonable to assume a proportionate decrease in the "market" value of the article. This is why the retail method applies the original cost-to-retail relationship of 50% to the final retail inventory, to obtain what is considered a lower-of-cost-or-market inventory valuation of $7.50.

This writedown to market value is automatic in the operation of the retail method. It reduces the valuation from cost to market for goods that have been marked down in retail value and remain in inventory at the inventory date. Essentially, the adjustment results in maintaining the gross margin percentage relationship.

The retail method also creates a book valuation that can be compared against the inventory physically on hand. Normally, physical counts are taken once or twice a year. The retail method greatly simplifies compilation of the total valuation by using the readily available retail prices in extending the physical quantities. A shortage can quickly be determined at retail by comparing physical inventory on hand with the book amounts; and the cost of the extended physical inventories can be computed by applying the cost complement percentage.

Advantages and Limitations. The advantages of the retail inventory method are that

- Periodic inventory and gross margin determinations can be made without performing a physical inventory;
- Marking and stockkeeping are less expensive because marking or ticketing is done at retail only;
- The taking of physical inventories is simplified;
- An accurate determination of any inventory shortage is possible without resort to actual cost values;
- All merchant-oriented inventory information is expressed in terms of retail dollars only, so that the buyer or merchandising manager can plan sales, stock levels, gross margin, markdowns, desired merchandise turnover, and open-to-buy in an intelligent manner; and
- Its use results in an ending inventory that is essentially at cost or market, whichever is lower, by using current retail prices as the basis for determining cost.

The limitations of the retail inventory method are that

- Additional record keeping is required because all invoices must be marked with the retail price of each article and all retail price changes must be recorded when taken.

- Manipulations are possible because deferred markdowns may overstate inventories. Unrecorded markdowns may overstate book inventories and may ultimately be buried in shortages. Conversely, fictitious markdowns may understate shortages and undervalue book inventories, while fictitious markups may overvalue book inventories and overstate shortages.

- When goods at different mark-ons are handled in the same department but are not sold in the same proportion as that in which they were bought, the closing inventory may be overstated or understated.

- The cost and retail values at which goods are transferred out of one department must be the same as that at which they are transferred into another department, for it is essential that the retail relationships agree. For instance, when goods are moved out of a department because they fail to sell there, that department should take the loss by recording the markdown before the transfer. This requires some extra bookkeeping effort.

Payroll and Personnel

The payroll and personnel function of a company encompasses hiring, timekeeping, and paying wages and salaries, including any related taxes and fringe benefits. From an operations standpoint the company wants to hire the right people at the right price. From an accounting standpoint the company wants to ensure that employees are paid only for appropriate service and that the related payroll costs are recorded in the appropriate accounts.

Payroll costs are allocated to the accounts based on the assignment of the individual. Generally, these costs are included in either production, sales, or administrative categories, although they are sometimes capitalized as part of property, plant, and equipment if the individual is involved in the construction of equipment for the company's own use.

Payroll costs in a manufacturing concern are first allocated to production and then allocated to inventory, either as part of direct labor to the extent the individual works directly on the production of the product (e.g., an assembly line worker) or as part of manufacturing overhead to the extent the individual works in the manufacturing area but not directly on the product (e.g., a plant maintenance worker).

In the case of manufacturing employees, timecards generally record not only the hours worked but the nature of the work performed, for use in allocating these costs to inventory. In the case of a standard cost system, engineering studies are used to determine the "normal" amount of time devoted to an operation, and that time is priced out at the hourly pay rate of the employee doing the work to determine the standard cost. See the Standard Costs—Accounting for Variances section for a discussion of the accounting for differences between standard labor costs and costs actually incurred.

A further discussion of the payroll, or salaries and wages, cycle is provided in the auditing section later in this chapter.

Allocating Indirect Costs

One way, known as *prime costing,* to allocate indirect manufacturing costs is to charge all indirect manufacturing costs to expense when incurred. But the treatment of *all* manufacturing overhead costs as a period expense is not in accordance with generally accepted accounting principles (AC 5121.05). The opposite approach, known as *full absorption costing,* allocates them all to units produced. A compromise method, known as *direct costing,* allocates *variable* indirect manufacturing costs to units of production and *fixed* indirect manufacturing costs as a period expense. The income tax regulations (Sec. 1.471.11) include specific guidelines as to which indirect manufacturing costs must be allocated to inventory and which may be excluded for income tax purposes.

The formula selected for apportioning indirect costs to various production units will have the amount of the indirect costs to be allocated as the numerator and the allocation base as the denominator. All indirect costs do not have to be allocated on the same basis. For instance, vacation pay expense may be allocated on the basis of direct labor assigned to units of production, whereas maintenance expense might be allocated on the basis of machine time. Furthermore, overhead may be applied to production on a departmental basis or on a plant-wide basis.

In practice, direct labor is often used as the allocation basis because it provides a measure of productive effort per unit that is readily available in most companies' records. Another factor in determining this denominator is the level of utilization of the manufacturing facility in relation to its capacity.

If the dollar amount of direct labor is chosen as the denominator for allocating indirect manufacturing costs, the accountant must then determine how the direct labor dollar base is to be established. Some of the ways in which the direct labor dollar base is established in practice are

- Actual—the direct labor dollars *incurred* during the same period that the indirect manufacturing costs were incurred;
- Expected—the direct labor dollars that the company *planned* to incur during the period in which the indirect manufacturing costs were incurred;
- Normal—the historical *norm* of direct labor dollars incurred during such a period; and
- Practical capacity—the direct labor dollars that would be incurred during the period if the company sustained *maximum* manufacturing output with a given number of workshifts per day for an extended period.

The income tax regulations essentially require full absorption of indirect production costs, with some specific exceptions. The regulations place indirect production costs into three categories, and provide the guidance for their allocation to inventory, as discussed below.

Category one. These costs must be allocated to inventory for tax purposes regardless of financial statement treatment, as long as they are incident to and necessary for the production operations or processes. They include

- Repair expenses,
- Maintenance,
- Utilities,
- Rent,
- Indirect labor and production supervisory wages, including overtime, payroll taxes, and some payroll-related costs,
- Indirect materials and supplies,

- Tools and equipment not capitalized, and
- Costs of quality control and inspection.

Category two. These costs need not be allocated to inventory for tax purposes regardless of financial statement treatment. They include

- Marketing expenses,
- Advertising expenses,
- Selling expenses,
- Other distribution expenses,
- Interest,
- Research and development,
- Losses on sales, exchanges, or destruction of property,
- Percentage depletion in excess of cost depletion,
- Depreciation and amortization reported for federal income tax purposes in excess of depreciation taken for financial statement purposes,
- Income taxes attributable to income received on the sale of inventory,
- Pension contributions to the extent that they represent past service cost, and
- General and administrative expenses (including officers' salaries) that are necessary for the company's activities as a whole, not just for its production operations or processes.

Category three. These costs must be treated in the same way for tax purposes as they are for financial statement purposes if the financial statement treatment is in conformity with GAAP. They include

- Taxes other than income taxes,
- Depreciation and cost depletion,
- Some employee benefits,
- Costs attributable to strikes, rework labor, scrap, and spoilage,
- Factory administrative expenses,
- Officers' salaries to the extent that they are related to production processes, and
- Insurance costs.

To the extent that a cost is incident to the manufacturing process and is not similar to the types of costs included in categories one and two, it is considered a category three cost. (See Other Inventory Audit Areas, Category Three Letters, for the auditor's involvement in this area.)

Accounting for Product Warranty Costs

Additional accounting considerations arise when products are sold subject to product warranties. SFAS 5 defines a warranty as "an obligation incurred in connection with the sale of goods or services that may require further performance by the seller after the sale has taken place" (AC 4311.24). A warranty may be explicit in the sales agreement, or it may be implicit. It may be direct (e.g., when the manufacturer sells directly to the end user), or it may be indirect (e.g., when the sale is made by an automobile dealership). Examples include agreements to provide repair services or to furnish replacement parts for a given period of time after the sale of a product.

The objective of accounting for warranty costs is to match revenues with related costs. In discussing the matching principle regarding product warranties, Accounting Research Study No. 7 (Grady, 1965) states:

> When a sale of merchandise is accompanied by a warranty or service guarantee, a cost or expense is incurred at the time of the sale. The amount of the expense and accompanying liability are unknown at the time of sale and are therefore estimated on the basis of past experience. When the liability is subsequently paid, it may be paid in labor and materials rather than cash.

The warranty is considered one of the costs of making the sale, and the matching of costs with revenues is normally accomplished at the time of sale by accruing as an operating expense or as part of cost of sales the estimated future costs related to the warranty. Alternatively, although less commonly, revenue in amounts approximating the future warranty costs may be deferred. Normally, there is not a separate source of revenue related to the warranty, but where a special fee is paid for such warranty, it would be appropriate to defer such income over the warranty period, as is done for service contracts. If the estimated warranty costs exceed the separate fee, the excess cost would be accrued at the time of the sale.

Because warranties involve uncertainties as to the amount of costs to be incurred, the accounting for warranty obligations is covered by SFAS 5, *Accounting for Contingencies* (AC 4311). Under SFAS 5, contingencies are to be accrued if it is probable that a liability has been incurred at the date of the financial statements *and* the amount of the liability can be reasonably estimated.

The most common basis for estimating future warranty costs is past experience with the same or similar product or product line. Often, a reasonable estimate of warranty costs can be obtained by applying a predetermined rate to a measure of sales volume. For instance, future warranty costs might be reasonably estimated as a percentage of sales or as a fixed dollar amount per unit sold.

The rate might be obtained by calculating the average of the actual rates for a given number of prior years, or if the historical rates indicate a definite trend, the appropriate rate might best be obtained by extrapolation. As an example, if the current-year sales were $10,000,000 and the estimated rate of warranty cost was 1.5% of sales, the warranty cost accrual would be $150,000. If the warranty period was one year, the entire accrual would be included in current liabilities. Otherwise, an allocation of the obligation would be made between current and noncurrent liabilities, based on estimates as to the timing of warranty claims. For tax purposes warranty costs are deductible only when paid, often by means of supplying repair services or replacement parts, so their accrual will give rise to timing differences.

Where there is no directly related past experience, the experience of other companies in the industry or of other related product lines might be used as a guide. Results of preproduction tests, either in the laboratory or in the field, and a review of quality control procedures might provide a basis on which warranty costs could be estimated. Where there is no way of obtaining a reasonable estimate of the warranty costs, no accrual may be made (AC 4311.25). Where there exists a possibility of significant warranty costs, that fact "may raise a question about whether a sale should be recorded prior to expiration of the warranty period or until sufficient experience has been gained to permit a reasonable estimate of the obligations" (AC 4311.25). Where no accrual is made, the nature of the contingency and the range of potential loss or the fact that such an estimate cannot be made should be disclosed in the financial statements (AC 4311.10). Given the inherent uncertainties, judgment is necessary in arriving at a reasonable estimate of future warranty costs.

Standard Costs—Accounting for Variances

A standard cost system is a management tool that predetermines what unit costs are expected to be for inventory items. These costs are then used to account for the inventory transactions from inception through the time of sale. Because the system predetermines the cost for a given period, this standard cost usually differs from the actual cost incurred. The difference for a given item is called a variance. An *unfavorable variance* results when actual cost exceeds standard cost; *a favorable variance* results when standard cost exceeds actual cost.

When the actual amount paid differs from the amount at standard, the variance is described as a *price, rate, or spending variance*. For direct material and direct labor, these variances are differences between the actual per-unit cost and the standard per-unit rate. For overhead, they are the difference between the actual overhead incurred and the expected aggregate overhead. When the actual input quantity required to produce a given unit differs from the input anticipated by the standard, *volume and yield variances* arise. For instance, the quantity of material, number of direct labor hours, or number of machine hours actually incurred to produce a given unit of product may differ from the predetermined standards for these inputs.

Since GAAP requires that inventories be stated at cost (unless cost exceeds market), the occurrence of a variance indicates that standard cost should be adjusted to approximate historical cost. The analysis of standard cost variances should look not only to the differences between unit prices and volumes but also to the combined impact of the two. Because variances indicate that standard costs may differ from historical costs, the variances, if material, must be allocated in an appropriate manner between inventory and cost of sales.

Choosing the Approach. The choice of a variance reallocation approach depends in part on the cost allocation convention used by the company. For instance, if the company uses the average cost convention, it would be appropriate to consider the total of purchase price variances for the year in allocating between inventory and cost of sales, since the average cost should reflect the total purchase price for the year (purchase price equals standard cost plus variance). If a FIFO cost assumption were used, on the other hand, it would be more appropriate to allocate to inventory only the portion of the purchase price variance that is related to purchases near the end of the year, perhaps based on inventory turnover, to determine which variances should be allocated to ending inventory. Whatever approach is adopted, it should be rational, systematic, and consistent from year to year.

Allocating Variances to Inventory. If it is necessary to allocate variances to inventory, care must be taken to ensure that, in making the lower-of-cost-or-market test, the cost figures used include not only the standard cost but also the allocated cost variance. Similarly, when making LIFO calculations using a standard cost system, the LIFO current-year cost should reflect not only the standard cost but also any variances properly allocable to inventory.

An immaterial ending balance in a variance account should not lead the accountant to conclude that the variance need not be considered for allocation to inventory. In some cases, favorable variances early in the period and unfavorable variances later may net to an immaterial amount, but there may still be a need to allocate a portion of the unfavorable variances incurred late in the period to inventory in order to adjust that inventory from standard cost to historical cost. If the company uses a FIFO inventory valuation approach, it would be necessary to allocate a portion of the unfavorable variances incurred near the end of the year to ending inventory.

Costing of Transactions. In addition to the variances derived from the inventory and cost-of-products-sold accounting system, the accountant must be concerned with whether the standard cost of a given item is used consistently throughout the application of the costing system. Improper costing of transactions may be caused by human error or by failure of the system to account for physical conversions, substitutions, or scrap. There may also be a failure to adjust the carrying amount of inventory to new standard costs at the time new standards are put into effect. Unreported differences between input and output standards, and failure to recognize the effect on the inventory of a change in standards, result in unreported variances that remain in the inventory account.

At the time a physical inventory is taken and costed at the old standard, the book-to-physical difference will reflect unreported physical shrinkage and the effects of failure to use the same standards consistently in reporting input, conversions, substitutions, and interim changes in standards. If the effect of these unrecorded factors in the book-to-physical difference cannot be reasonably estimated, a major financial reporting benefit of applying a standard cost system is lost: the auditor will not be able to observe an interim physical inventory and rely on the standard cost system to determine a reasonable amount at which to state year-end inventory on a historical cost basis. Thus, the physical inventory will have to be taken at or near the fiscal year-end. Additionally, such failures in the standard cost system may cause interim financial reporting to be incorrect.

Changing Standard Costs. A company will often institute a change in its standard cost at the same time it takes its physical inventory. This enables the company to quantify the effect of the change by valuing inventories at both the old and new standards. Any difference should be recorded as a separate inventory reserve (when the new standard exceeds the old; in rare cases where the old standard exceeds the new, this may signify the need for a downward adjustment of inventories valued at the old standard). After adjusting for the book-to-physical inventory difference, the financial statements will reflect an inventory balance comprising the inventory at the new standard less the reserve for the excess of the new standard over the old standard (this step effectively states the inventory at old standard) and adjusted for any other inventory provisions based on the old standard (this step adjusts the inventory from the old standard to the lower of historical cost or market).

In subsequent periods, as costs of sales are charged based on the new standard, the reserve for the excess of the new standard over the old is credited to earnings, usually on an estimated turnover basis.

Financial Reporting Issues

Valuation Methods. In the historical cost framework, the objective of accounting for inventories that receives the most attention is the proper matching of costs with revenues (AC 5121, Statement 2); to achieve this matching, one of several cost-flow assumptions can be used.

FIFO and LIFO are the two most commonly used cost-flow assumptions. FIFO presents inventories at an amount that is fairly close to the replacement cost of the inventories at the balance sheet date (assuming a fairly frequent turnover of inventories), whereas the gross profit reported in the income statement presents the excess of selling prices over costs that lag behind replacement cost equivalents. On the other hand, the inventory amount presented in the balance sheet on a LIFO basis does not even closely approximate replacement cost (assuming the condition of rising prices and the use of the LIFO cost-flow assumption over an extended period), but LIFO does report a gross profit that more closely reflects replacement cost of inventories sold.

For both the balance sheet and the income statement to reflect current conditions, accounting will have to step away from the historical cost framework and look to some other approach, one that accounts for inflation or changes in value, or one that allows the balance sheet and the income statement each to use different valuation bases (i.e., nonarticulation). The approaches presently receiving the most attention are current cost and constant dollar accounting (see Chapter 8).

Financial Reporting and Changing Prices. In September 1979 the FASB issued SFAS 33, *Financial Reporting and Changing Prices* (AC 1072), which requires large companies (public companies with over $125 million in inventories *and* gross plant before deducting depreciation, or total assets in excess of $1 billion after deducting depreciation) to present income from continuing operations and related information on the basis of both current cost and constant dollars. These requirements are discussed in Chapter 8. For inventory and cost of sales, SFAS 33 requires disclosure of

- The current cost of inventory or lower recoverable amounts (AC 1072.030(b)).

- Income from continuing operations on a constant dollar and on a current cost basis, including the effects of inflation on the cost of sales (AC 1072.029(a) and AC 1072.030(a)).

- Increases or decreases for the year in the current cost of inventory net of inflation (AC 1072.030(c)). Increases or decreases in current cost amounts shall not be included in income from continuing operations (AC 1072.030).

- Significant types of information used to calculate the current cost of inventory and cost of goods sold (AC 1072.034(a)).

- The Consumer Price Index used for the measurement of income from continuing operations (AC 1072.035).

Classification of Inventories. Current assets are defined as assets that are "reasonably expected to be realized in cash or sold or consumed during the normal operating cycle of the business or within one year if the operating cycle is shorter than one year" (AC 1027.25). Since inventories are acquired for production or sale and the acquisitions should not often exceed the quantity of inventory needed for the company's current operating cycle, inventories are generally classified as current assets.

Inventory is usually subclassified in terms of its stage of completion (raw materials, manufacturing supplies, work in process, or finished goods) or in terms of the types of cost components of the inventory (raw materials, direct labor, or manufacturing overhead) or as a combination of both. Generally accepted accounting principles do not address whether the various components of inventory need be disclosed. Regulation S-X, Rule 5-02.6, requires that the major classes of inventory be disclosed in terms of their stage of completion. In practice, this approach is applied by all public companies and many nonpublic ones. The disclosure is made either on the face of the balance sheet or in a note.

Inventory is often used as collateral for loans obtained by the company. Authoritative literature requires disclosure of assets pledged as security for loans (AC 4311.18), and Regulation S-X, Rule 4-08(b), requires that the carrying amount of inventories being used as security be disclosed in the notes to the financial statements.

Capitalization of Interest. Generally, interest has not been capitalized on goods held for sale except in unusual cases when the goods are held for an extended maturation period, as with tobacco and liquor. In October 1979 the FASB issued SFAS 34, *Capitalization of Interest Cost* (AC 5155), which limited the capitalization of interest on inventories to discrete projects that are not part of the repetitive inventory production cycle. When interest is capitalized in inventory, the accountant must look not only to the basic cost of the inventory unit but must consider all cost factors included in the inventory account, including capitalized interest, in making the lower-of-cost-or-market test. (For a full discussion of interest capitalization, see Chapter 22.)

Purchase Commitments and Hedges. Purchase commitments and purchase hedges are transactions entered into primarily to secure the acquisition of needed materials and to protect against unfavorable price fluctuations. They represent contracts and agreements for the future purchase of specified quantities of materials at a specified price. In financial reporting, they should be evaluated in the same fashion as inventory on hand for the purpose of determining any lower-of-cost-or-market adjustment. GAAP requires that

> accrued net losses on firm purchase commitments for goods for inventory, measured in the same way as are inventory losses, should, if material, be recognized in the accounts and the amounts thereof separately disclosed in the income statement. [AC 5121, Statement 10]

Similarly, agreements requiring the sale of goods in the future for a specified price should be used in making the lower-of-cost-or-market evaluation for existing inventory and should be viewed in the context of whether the cost to acquire and produce the product will exceed the agreed selling price. If firm agreements have been made for future sales, that selling price should usually be used in establishing net realizable value for the product on hand subject to the sales commitment. If the carrying amount of the inventory on hand (or the estimated cost to produce inventory) needed to meet the future sales agreements exceeds such net realizable value, losses should be recognized currently in the financial statements.

Product-Financing Arrangements. Product-financing arrangements are transactions in which a company sells a portion of its inventory to another entity with the intent to reacquire that inventory in the future. In SOP 78-8, *Accounting for Product Financing Arrangements,* inventory repurchase arrangements meeting certain criteria (primarily those in which the seller retains the risks and rewards of ownership) are viewed as financing transactions. The SOP recommends that the merchandise covered by the arrangement should be included with the inventory of the company and should be valued in accordance with the cost-flow assumption and pricing convention employed by the company, with the proceeds from the sale to be treated as debt. (See Chapter 23 for further discussion of product financings.)

Changes in Accounting—Consistency. AC 5121, Statement 8, says:

> The basis of stating inventories must be consistently applied and should be disclosed in the financial statements; whenever a significant change is made therein, there should be disclosure of the nature of the change and, if material, the effect on income in accordance with section 1051, *Accounting Changes.*

Under AC 1051, accounting changes for inventory should be reflected in the financial statements in a fashion similar to other accounting changes (cumulative catch-up approach at the beginning of the current period) that are adopted when alternatives exist, and their application is not mandated by authoritative literature, except as follows:

- A change from another cost-flow assumption to LIFO does not result in a cumulative catch-up adjustment, because the company cannot determine what the inventory would be at the date of change on a LIFO basis as if LIFO had been adopted at the inception of the company (AC 1051.26). The inventory at the beginning of the first period in which LIFO is adopted is considered its base-period LIFO inventory regardless of the prior cost-flow assumption and pricing convention.
- A change from LIFO to another cost-flow assumption is to be reflected in the financial statements by retroactive restatement for all periods presented, and the cumulative effect of the change at the beginning of the first period presented is included as an adjustment of retained earnings of that period (AC 1051.27). This is one of the few changes in acceptable alternative accounting principles for which authoritative literature requires retroactive restatement. The pervasiveness of the differences between the two methods makes such restatement necessary and the availability of information make this restatement practical.

AUDITING INVENTORY AND COST OF SALES

The audit philosophy assumed in this section is fully explained in Chapters 12 and 13. The overall objective of the audit of inventory and cost of sales is to determine whether inventory and cost of sales are fairly presented in the context of the financial statements as a whole. To meet this objective, the audit must address seven basic questions regarding inventory: its existence, ownership, valuation, cutoff, mechanical accuracy, classification, and disclosure.

These seven areas are not entirely congruent with the seven objectives ascribed to internal control in Chapter 13, because internal control systems do not primarily address several substantive inventory audit objectives. The following cross-reference table may be helpful:

Overall Audit Objective, as Shown in This Chapter	Internal Control Objective
Congruent:	
Existence	Authorization
	Validity
	Recording
Valuation—accuracy	Valuation
Cutoff	Timing
Mechanical accuracy	Summarization
Classification	Classification
Not congruent:	
Ownership	
Valuation—changed circumstances	
Disclosure	

Audit Approach

In order to decide between a systems reliance approach and a substantive procedure approach, or how much of each approach should be blended, the auditor must gain an understanding of the activities of the company that affect its inventory accounting, and the potential seriousness of errors. He must also understand the company's preventive and detective internal controls.

The company activities that affect inventory and cost of sales most often and most heavily are

- Purchasing and accounts payable activities for the acquisition of inventory materials and overhead items. The auditor must be familiar with the client's procedures to control the ordering, receipt, payment for acquisition, and returns of materials and overhead.
- Personnel activities that apply to labor costs allocated to inventory (direct labor, indirect labor, and fringe benefits). The auditor must understand how individuals are hired and terminated, how payroll data are accumulated, how payroll and fringe benefit costs are determined, and how costs are allocated among periods and products.
- Capital asset activities that affect the production of inventory. The auditor must understand how property, plant, and equipment acquisitions, utilization, and disposals

are controlled, and how the costs of these assets are allocated to periods and products (see also Chapter 20).

- Inventory transfer activities within the company and scrap disposals. The auditor must understand how inventory movements are initiated, approved, effected, and recorded.

- Product sales activities. The auditor must understand the company's procedures to control the order acceptance, shipment, recording of sales of inventory, and customer returns (see also Chapter 18).

- Inventory quantity and value determination procedures. The auditor must understand how and when the company physically determines the units of inventory it has on hand, what cost convention is used to assign a carrying amount to the units, how costs are mechanically assigned to inventory, how market and economic considerations impact inventory costs, and how inventory amounts (units or dollars) are updated from the date of the physical inventory to the reporting date if the dates differ.

Regardless of the approach selected, the auditor is required to perform analytical review procedures in accordance with SAS 23, *Analytical Review Procedures* (AU 318), but an initial assessment of the adequacy of the client's internal controls will assist the auditor in deciding whether to proceed with a systems reliance or a substantive procedure approach.

Objectives and Procedures

Under either approach, the auditor needs to plan procedures to satisfy the inventory audit objectives. Figure 19.6 is a very condensed listing of the interim and year-end audit procedures that are commonly used to achieve these objectives. The procedures shown may be used to satisfy more than one audit objective, but are listed under the objective that they most typically satisfy in order to provide an overview of how the audit objectives are met. The procedures are discussed in more depth in the material following the figure.

Using the Computer. Companies now commonly use EDP to control and compile their inventories. When auditing these companies, the auditor should consider using the computer himself to audit aspects of the inventory, for instance:

- Testing clerical accuracy,
- Tracing in test counts,
- Accounting for inventory tags used,
- Identifying and aggregating dollar concentrations of inventory,
- Aging the inventory (if the company uses stock numbers or codes that make this practical),
- Identifying overstock conditions,
- Performing lower-of-cost-or-market tests, and
- Selecting perpetual inventory items for test counting.

As with all audit procedures, the auditor must determine whether using the computer is the most cost-effective method. For example, while the company's

Audit Objective	Sample Year-End Procedures*	Sample Interim Procedures
Existence. Determine whether there are physical goods supporting the dollar amount of inventory in the balance sheets, and whether all such goods have been properly included.	• Observe inventory at year-end. • Review inventory instructions. • Tour facilities before count. • Recount selected items. • Record test counts for subsequent tracing to the inventory compilation. • Note items that appear to be slow-moving or obsolete. • Test control over inventory count tags and record for future testing. • Determine if any items were not included in the count.	• Observe inventory at an interim date. • Test perpetuals.
Ownership. Determine whether inventory owned by the company is included and whether inventories of others are properly identified and excluded from the inventory amounts.	• Confirm quantities and ownership of merchandise at outside locations. • Confirm with outsiders the merchandise identified as theirs. • Request vendor statements.	• Test company's system for controlling the receipt, movement, and shipment of merchandise belonging to others or shipped to others on consignment or for processing.
Mechanical accuracy. Determine whether the basic mathematical calculations of the physical inventory are proper, and whether data gathered during the observation are properly used.	• Agree test counts to quantities included in the compilation. • Test tag control. • Test mathematical accuracy of extensions and footings of inventory compilation. • Test company's method of accumulating unit costs and assigning them to physical inventory units.	• Test extensions, footings, and postings of transactions between physical inventory date and period-end.

Valuation. Determine whether inventory quantities are fairly valued in conformity with generally accepted accounting standards.

- Review update of interim inventory to year-end and test it.
- Review components of book to physical adjustment.
- Perform analytical review procedures:
  — Gross margin percentages.
  — Inventory turnover ratios.
- Review and test the company's method for determining and adjusting for lower-of-cost-or-market situations and providing for allowances needed for obsolete or slow-moving items.
- Test updating system to ensure that inventory transactions after the physical inventory are recorded on same basis as physical inventory was valued.

Disclosure. Determine whether disclosures included in the financial statements are adequate.

- Agree financial statement disclosures to information noted in performance of the examination.

Classification. Determine whether inventory is properly classified as raw materials, work in process, or finished goods.

- Review inventory compilation for proper classification of inventory.
- Test the updating system to ensure that interim inventory transactions are properly recorded by class of inventory.

Cutoff. Determine whether all inventory items received or shipped before and after the reporting date are appropriately considered.

- Obtain receiving or shipping cutoff documentation at time of inventory.
- Test recording of purchases and sales for a period before and after the reporting date.
- Test recording of purchases and sales for a period of time before and after the inventory date *and* before and after the reporting date.

* Also often used at an interim date.

FIGURE 19.6 INVENTORY AUDIT OBJECTIVES AND PROCEDURES

inventory may be compiled on a computer, it may consist of so few items as to make automated testing more expensive than manual testing. On the other hand, use of the computer can often add to the efficiency of an audit of a large inventory. In fact, in some circumstances the auditor may decide that although the company did not use a computer to compile the inventory, the most efficient audit method would be to enter the inventory data onto a computer file for analysis and audit testing. (See Chapter 15 for a discussion of auditing in a computer environment.)

Existence

SAS 1 (AU 331.09-.13) indicates that the auditor should observe the taking of the physical inventory and be satisfied with the effectiveness of the counting procedures used. The observation may take either of two forms, or some combination of them may be best:

1. In the systems reliance approach, the perpetual inventory records maintained by the client are tested. Companies that maintain perpetual inventory records may test them continually throughout the year, never taking a complete shutdown physical inventory. The auditor should review the results of the company's cycle tests to make a preliminary assessment of the reliability of the system. If the system appears reliable, the auditor should test it himself. His tests will typically include a selection of items from the perpetual records for tracing to the inventory and a selection from the physical inventory items for tracing to the perpetual records. These tests can be performed either on an interim or a year-end basis. If the system does not appear reliable, the company may have to take a full physical inventory at year-end.
2. The auditor observes and tests the count of the full physical inventory taken at an interim date or at year-end. This observation can be used as a systems test at an interim date to assess the accuracy of the client's perpetual records or the aggregate inventory balance accumulated in the general ledger, or it can serve as a substantive procedure at year-end to test the company's determination of final inventory quantities. The timing of the inventory will be influenced by the company's operating cycle (a company generally prefers to count its inventory during low-production periods or when inventory quantities are at their lowest levels) and by the quality of internal controls.

As part of his observation of the taking of inventory, the auditor should go on a tour of the plant, should be familiar with the inventory instructions, should be aware of any inventory not stored on the premises, and should give indications of areas of concern to the company before the count begins. Members of the audit team assigned to the inventory observation should be familiar with the type of inventory and the procedures to be followed in case difficulties arise that require immediate resolution. Even if members of the audit team have previously participated in an observation of the company's inventory, it is usually beneficial for them to have a tour of the facilities to identify the critical areas in the plant (shipping, manufacturing, receiving, etc.). The auditors should also become aware at the outset of the location and identity of the major dollar items of inventory.

Control of Counting Procedures. To facilitate an accurate count of the inventory, the auditor should ascertain that

- The inventory is arranged to allow for easy access and counting.
- No production is scheduled. If production must go on, the departments should be segregated from other areas.
- No movement of goods occurs during the count. If movement is necessary, the auditor and the company personnel in charge of the inventory must be previously informed so as to control the goods and avoid double counting.
- The counting teams will take a systematic approach, and will not skip around their assigned area.
- Inventory tags (which often are EDP cards) are used sequentially and systematically in each department and throughout the inventory.
- Inventory tags are not removed (pulled) before the auditor observing the count or a designated in-charge employee gives clearance, area by area.
- All inventory tags are accounted for.
- Personnel are available to identify parts and units of work in process.

Although these procedures will not guarantee an accurate count, they will assure that the count is well organized.

Accuracy of Counts. The auditor observes the company's count to determine whether the inventory instructions are being followed. Thus, the auditor need not record all test counts made to confirm that the physical count was accurate. To allow him to make subsequent tests of the compilation of the physical inventory, he should record some test counts made during the observation. Tying in these test counts enables the auditor to evaluate whether the physical counts have been properly included in the company's subsequent inventory compilation. The auditor should know which inventory items have a high value, because an error in the counting of these items is more likely to have a significant effect on the inventory.

Condition of Inventory. During the observation the auditor should be alert for merchandise that appears to be slow-moving or of impaired value. An accumulation of rust or dust, for example, may indicate valueless or slow-moving items, and a discussion with the counting teams may elicit the comment that the same items were counted in last year's inventory. While none of this is conclusive evidence for inventory valuation, it may point to a need for evaluation studies after the count is completed.

Stage of Completion. Counts of raw materials and finished goods may be relatively easy to test, because their quantities and classification are easily ascertained; but work-in-process inventories present another problem. The last operation completed on the work-in-process inventory must be identified to assist in valuing it after the count. The inventory tags should be reviewed to ascertain that the last operation has been identified, and if possible the auditor should obtain a routing sheet or other document to confirm that the last operation performed is appropriately identified on the inventory tag. To facilitate subsequent compilation procedures, some companies gather all the material necessary to complete the in-process inventory in one place. In such cases the last operation recorded applies only to the labor and overhead components of the in-process inventory.

Cutoff Data. To ensure an accurate physical inventory as well as proper recording of purchases and sales, it is important that the auditor test the company's cutoff procedures. The shipping cutoff should assure that no order shipped after the inventory count is included as a sale in the period before the count, and that an item sold before the count has been removed from the inventory compilation. The auditor can test this during the observation by referring to sequentially numbered shipping documents and obtaining the number of the last shipping document before the count. He should also make sure that no orders preceding the last shipping advice number have yet to be shipped. This can be done by observing the shipping area, inquiring of the counting personnel, and later reviewing freight bills.

The receiving cutoff is equally important, so the auditor should test the appropriateness of the company's recording of receipts of merchandise to be included in the book inventory and compare it to the physical inventory. Again, the auditor should make sure that subsequent receipts have not been included in the inventory count or recorded as a purchase and related liability.

The following information also should be obtained at the physical inventory count:

- Goods returned by the company to the manufacturer,
- Customer returns for rework or replacement,
- Interplant shipments, and
- Goods on consignment or out for processing.

Inventories being held on consignment, being stored at outside locations, or being processed outside the plant should be confirmed. If significant, they should be observed in conjunction with the physical inventory.

Although the physical inventory observation would tend to support the ownership of the inventory, it is possible that merchandise on hand includes inventory owned by others. Ownership of the inventory can be ascertained during the tests of the purchasing system, which will include a review of the documentation supporting the purchases. Requests for information from vendors regarding consigned goods will also support the ownership of inventory.

Use of Specialists. If the auditor is unfamiliar with the identification or measurement of quantity or quality of the inventory (paintings, diamonds, drugs, coal piles, etc.), he may find it necessary to obtain the services of specialists in determining whether the inventory actually is as represented by the company. The use of outside inventory services is discussed in detail later in this chapter. SAS 11 (AU 336) describes the appropriate procedures to be followed when using specialists.

Valuation

The main purpose of valuation procedures in the audit of inventory is to test the appropriateness of pricing of the physical inventory, or in the absence of a complete physical count to otherwise corroborate the recorded inventory balances. The alternative cost-flow assumptions and conventions for the valuation of inventory were discussed at the beginning of the chapter. While it is management's responsibility to decide which assumption the company will use, the auditor still must determine whether the method chosen is generally accepted and is properly and consistently applied.

Compilation—Quantities. A significant portion of the audit of inventory is to determine whether the physical compilation of the inventory quantities is reasonably accurate and whether these quantities are fairly priced. The information gathered during the physical inventory observation is used to check the accuracy of the recording of the physical counts. This is done by means of test counts and tag controls.

Test counts. Some (or all, if the controls seem weak) of the test counts taken during the observation should be agreed to the inventory compilation, and any adjustments or differences should be satisfactorily reconciled.

In recording test counts for tracing to the compilation, the auditor makes his own record of the data on the inventory tag. In tracing the amounts to the compilation, the auditor must take particular care to make sure that the unit of measure used in the compilation is the same as that recorded in the inventory test count; for instance, counts based on numbers of units should not be recorded as pounds without appropriate conversions.

Tag control. The auditor must satisfy himself that the inventory compilation includes only tags actually used to record the inventory unit counts. In other words, he must be alert that no additional tags were written and that none of the tags used were omitted. This is done by comparing the tags included in the physical inventory compilation to the tag control prepared by the company and verified by the auditor at the time of the physical inventory. He should obtain satisfactory explanations for any differences between the control established during the taking of inventory and the tags actually used in the inventory compilation.

Similar procedures should be applied if the company uses count sheets or their equivalent in its counting procedures instead of tags or EDP cards.

Compilation—Dollars. Probably the most time-consuming phase of the inventory audit is the testing of clerical accuracy and the accuracy of unit costs used in pricing the inventory quantities. The test of clerical accuracy is basically a mechanical test of the various multiplications (e.g., units times price) and additions (e.g., summation of dollar amounts of the individual items) made to arrive at a total inventory figure, and is often done using computer software applied to a client's EDP-prepared compilation. The procedures for testing unit valuation, on the other hand, depend on the type of cost records maintained by the company— i.e., on whether the company uses a standard cost system, the retail inventory method, or actual costs.

Standard cost system. A standard cost system probably allows for the easiest testing of unit cost. When the company has standard costs for all units at all stages of production, it is a simple clerical task to trace these costs from the company's records to the inventory compilation. The audit scope for agreement of standard costs to those used in the inventory compilation should concentrate on large dollar items and include a selected number of smaller items. This selective scope will enable the auditor to cover a large dollar portion of the inventory with a relatively small sample size.

To substantiate that the standard costs approximate actual costs will require more work, for it involves a test of the company's standard cost system. The method of testing and the scope of items to be tested must be decided by the auditor, but these tests should include a review of cost buildups—material costs, labor costs, and manufacturing overhead—for a representative number of standards.

The *material* components of the inventory item are tested by a review of the engineering bill of materials (see Figure 19.7 for an example). Inspection of the inventory item at some time during the manufacturing process is necessary to determine that all components included on the standard cost card (see Figure 19.8 for an example) are used during production. Agreement of the material cost to suppliers' invoices will determine the relationship of the material costs used in the standards to actual cost. (If the company takes cash discounts, they should be regarded as a reduction of inventory standard costs. The same holds true if freight costs are invoiced separately from unit costs.)

The *labor* components are tested by a review of industrial engineering estimates, timecards, and pay rates. When labor represents a significant portion of the inventory cost, the auditor must review the payroll system and test the development of payroll data. Companies usually use some type of individual timecard to account for the employee's time on the project or task. After these timecards are completed, the total hours worked by individuals are paid for at an authorized wage rate. The total payroll is then allocated to the inventory based on data collected from the timecards, production records, and engineering time studies. The auditor should test the company's method of accumulating time by individual and project worked on. He must also test the labor rates used and the method of allocating the total payroll (i.e., inventory-direct, inventory-overhead, administrative).

Manufacturing overhead (burden) is tested by a review of the company's method of overhead allocation, to satisfy the auditor of its reasonableness and its consistency with the method used in prior periods. The auditor should also determine whether the components of overhead are appropriate and consistent with those of prior periods.

The degree of adequacy of the company's internal control system will influence the auditor in deciding whether the review of the standard costs should be performed at an interim date or at period-end. Although detailed tests of the standard

Part No.	Quantity	Description
1-123	2	$\frac{1}{2}$" diameter rod—8" long
2-234	3	$\frac{1}{2}$ horsepower motor
3-345	6	Electrical assemblies
4-456	2	Clamps

FIGURE 19.7 SAMPLE BILL OF MATERIALS FOR MOTOR ASSEMBLY

Part No.	Quantity	Unit Material Cost	Total Cost
1-123	2	$1.50	$ 3.00
2-234	3	3.00	9.00
3-345	6	9.00	54.00
4-456	2	.50	1.00
Total material			67.00
Assembly labor			5.00
Burden application (200% of assembly labor dollars)			10.00
Standard cost			$82.00

FIGURE 19.8   SAMPLE STANDARD COST BUILDUP FOR MOTOR ASSEMBLY

cost components may indicate that the standard cost approximates actual cost, the auditor should review variances generated throughout the period, as well as those generated after the physical inventory, to determine whether to consider some of the variances for adjustment of the inventory and, if so, the proper method of applying the variances (to individual products or to the total inventory).

Retail inventory method. The retail method depends heavily on properly accounting for the relationship of cost to retail selling price at acquisition and for subsequent adjustment of the selling price for markups and markdowns. The auditor should review the company's system for calculating the mark-on percentage and cost complement. This review will include making sure that the percentage has been properly accumulated for all categories of inventories. The auditor should also perform tests to ascertain that the retail selling price used in the cost complement calculations is the actual selling price; this can be done by reference to company catalogs, sales slips, and prices shown on the merchandise.

Actual costs. When a company uses actual cost for its compilation, the auditor's procedures for testing material, labor, and overhead costs depend on the company's cost-flow assumption. To test material costs for a company using FIFO, the auditor must refer to current-period invoices for the purchase of inventory materials and verify that actual costs have been properly applied. The review should also determine that current-period invoices contain sufficient quantities to be compared with the quantities and prices used in the inventory compilation; if current purchase quantities are less than the quantities in inventory, the auditor must look to purchases in prior periods to determine whether the unit prices used in the inventory compilation reflect the actual cost of the inventoried quantities.

(If ending inventory quantities for a given item exceed the aggregate quantity of that item purchased during the current year, this is a signal to the auditor that there may be excess or obsolete inventory on hand.)

To test labor and overhead costs, the audit procedures previously described for use with a standard cost system may be used with the actual cost system.

If the company uses LIFO, the auditor must review the application of prior-period costs to inventory quantities and make sure that any adjustments of LIFO layers resulting from inventory increments or decrements are properly applied. If the company uses a unit cost LIFO approach and the quantities of individual items have not increased since the end of the preceding fiscal year, the auditor has no need to refer to current-period invoices to review the application of historical costs; but he should examine these invoices as part of his lower-of-cost-or-market evaluation, and should test the company's supplemental disclosure of the inventory at FIFO or replacement cost. If the company uses some form of index approach for the determination of LIFO cost, the auditor must review the application of both current- and prior-period unit costs used in developing the individual year's total cost, as well as making tests of the mathematical accuracy and consistency of the approach used. (See the appendix to this chapter for illustrations of dollar value calculation.)

If a decrement occurs under LIFO, the auditor must be satisfied that the most recent layer costs are the first ones removed in determining the aggregate LIFO costs of the ending inventory. Further, if a LIFO decrement occurs and the company must disclose the income effect of a material layer liquidation, the auditor should make sure that this effect has been properly calculated.

Payroll and Personnel. An auditor must rely heavily on the internal controls of a company in the area of payroll. There is generally a segregation of duties between the personnel function (hiring, maintenance of employee records, and terminations) and the payroll function (timekeeping, preparation of payroll, and payments). This segregation is imposed principally to guard against fictitious employees being added to the payroll. There often is a further segregation of duties within the payroll functions between timekeeping, payroll preparation, and distribution of payroll checks, to avoid fictitious or erroneous payments.

The auditor should review hiring practices, concentrating on controls used to ensure that only real employees are placed on the payroll. Audit procedures may include a search for "ghosts" (nonexistent employees) by observing the distribution of payroll checks and having employees present identification in order to receive their checks; a review of the control over timecards; and a determination that manufacturing department heads are aware of the identities of all employees who are charged to their departments.

The above procedures, coupled with clerical tests of the mechanical accuracy of the payroll preparation, provide the auditor with a basis to evaluate the company's determination of payroll cost and its departmental allocation. For payroll costs charged to inventory the auditor must review the cost allocation approach to determine that it is reasonable. This will include a review of the methods used to assign labor to inventory (e.g., engineering studies and job cost tickets) and a test of the manner in which the labor is valued (actual cost or standard cost). The manner of labor valuation under a standard cost system was covered in a preceding section of this chapter, Compilation—Dollars.

For a thorough discussion of the audit of payroll and personnel, see Chapter 13 of *Auditing—An Integrated Approach* (Arens and Loebbecke, 1976).

Inventory Valuation Allowances. The auditor must make sure that the company has consistently followed an appropriate policy in establishing valuation allowances for inventories whose market is lower than cost and for obsolete or excess inventory quantities. Such allowances are more commonly used than direct reductions of unit values in a standard cost system, as this permits dollar controls to be maintained at regular standard cost. Sufficient tests must be performed to assure that the preestablished company policy is appropriate and is being applied accurately. Such tests include review of past product turnover, future engineering plans, and sales forecasts.

Reconciliation of Book Inventory to Physical Inventory. Typically, the physical inventory compilation total differs from the amount of inventory recorded on the general ledger. The company should find the reasons for this difference if it is more than negligible, and the auditor should review these reasons to assure that they make sense and that all the necessary adjustments are made to present the inventory in conformity with GAAP in the financial statements.

The auditor should review and understand all the differences making up adjustment of book inventory to physical inventory—transaction costing errors, actual shrinkage, and so on—to gain a better understanding of the inventory system. And if the inventory was taken as of a date other than year-end, this review will assist in determining whether the client has made appropriate adjustments in the update period.

Inventory Update. The auditor should review the transactions recorded during the period from the count date to the reporting date, testing the standard costs to ensure they are the same as those used to record the physical inventory. Otherwise, the ending inventory will include unreported variances, and it will be difficult to determine the adjustment required so that the inventory approximates historical cost. If the auditor has performed systems tests throughout the year and has established the reliability of the systems, he can review the updated inventory by agreeing the individual general ledger entries to books of original entry, and he may not need to perform other detailed tests of these items. If any material intervening items look unusual compared with similar items noted in prior periods, he should obtain satisfactory explanations for them.

If the adjustment of the book inventory to physical inventory at an interim date is attributed to physical shrinkage or to some problem in the accounting system that remains uncorrected (e.g., failure to report the use of substitute materials), the auditor must be satisfied that the company has made adequate provision for the probable recurrence of similar events between the date of the physical inventory and year-end.

Typically, a company will change its standard costs at the time the physical inventory is counted, and the inventory is compiled using both the old and the new standard costs. The old standard cost is used to compare the compilation amount to the general ledger accumulated inventory totals, and provides the basis for determining how well the standard cost system performed. When the standard costs are changed at the time of an interim inventory, the auditor should review the company's system to ascertain that all transactions after the change use the new standards rather than the old ones.

The auditor must also become satisfied that the aggregate difference between old and new standards is properly considered in determining whether standard costs at year-end approximate historical costs. The audit approach is similar to that used to review the reallocation of standard cost variances to ending inventory at standard.

Analytical Procedures. The two basic types of analytical procedures applicable to inventories are general procedures, which apply to the final inventory totals, and compilation review procedures.

General. Some examples of general analytical review procedures the auditor should consider are to

- Compare dollar amount of inventory by major class to prior years. This procedure may show undercosting/overcosting, excess quantities, or counting errors.
- Compare gross margin percentages in total and by product groups with margins of prior years and periods within the current year. This procedure may produce evidence of lower-of-cost-or-market concerns or costing problems.
- Review inventory turns compared to prior years. This procedure may uncover slow-moving or obsolescent inventory or lower-of-cost-or-market or costing problems.
- Compare individual unit costs between years. This procedure may produce evidence of clerical errors or production cost problems.
- Compare quantities on hand with sales forecasts. This procedure may yield signs of slow-moving or obsolescent inventory or lower-of-cost-or-market problems.

Compilation. Some examples of compilation analytical review procedures are to

- Review the entire inventory compilation for large-quantity items with small total extended values or small-quantity items with large total extended values. These items could be signs of errors in unit prices or recorded quantities.
- Identify any items with negative quantities or costs. Such items generally indicate clerical errors or problems with the inventory updating system.
- Compare unit sales for the current year with quantities on hand to estimate the turnover period of ending inventory. Slow-moving inventory may indicate obsolescence or lower-of-cost-or-market problems.
- List all items with a unit price or extended value over a certain desired level. Such items may indicate clerical errors.

These procedures should help the auditor uncover unusual items in the compilation for further review. Depending on the company's inventory and compilation system, the auditor will devise additional analytical procedures. The above list includes only a few of the many possible procedures that the auditor should consider. Note that many analytical tests can be performed using the computer.

Disclosure

At the completion of the audit of inventory, the auditor must ascertain that all the required disclosures have been made and consider if any other items noted during the audit should be disclosed (e.g., pledge of inventory). One of the objectives of the audit of inventory is to determine the propriety of the balance sheet classification of inventory as a current or noncurrent asset, and of the presentation of the raw material, work in process, and finished goods components of inventory. The auditor should review the components of the company's inventory to see if any should be classified as noncurrent because they will not be used in the company's normal operating cycle; this is normally done by reviewing turnover statistics and operating plans. At the time of the inventory compilation, the auditor should review the type of items the company categorizes as raw materials, work in process, and finished goods. If an interim inventory is taken, the update should be reviewed to determine how transfers between these categories are recorded and controlled.

Other Audit Areas

Inventory at Public Warehouses. The auditor is expected to physically observe at least a portion of the inventory, either when a usual physical inventory is taken or alternatively by making test counts at other times and comparing them to the perpetual records (AU 331.09-.13). As to inventories held at public warehouses, the auditing of quantities of such inventories is most often handled through confirmation, with additional work where amounts are material. The provisions of AU 331.14 state:

> In the case of inventories which in the ordinary course of business are in the hands of public warehouses or other custodians, direct confirmation in writing from the custodians is acceptable provided that, where the amount involved represents a significant proportion of the current assets or the total assets, supplemental inquiries are made to satisfy the independent auditor as to the bona fides of the situation.

The AICPA Committee on Auditing Procedure further considered the internal controls and auditing procedures applicable to goods held in public warehouses, and suggested that the auditor make the following supplemental inquiries where amounts are significant (AU 331.15):

a. Discussion with the owner as to the owner's control procedures in investigating the warehouseman, and tests of related evidential matter.

b. Review of the owner's control procedures concerning performance of the warehouseman, and tests of related evidential matter.

c. Observation of physical counts of the goods wherever practicable and reasonable.

d. Where warehouse receipts have been pledged as collateral, confirmation (on a test basis, where appropriate) from lenders as to pertinent details of the pledge receipts.

A special report of the Committee on Auditing Procedure, *Public Warehouses— Controls and Auditing Procedures for Goods Held* (AU 901), deals with the internal controls at the warehouse, how such businesses operate, and what the auditors of the warehouse and of the client whose goods are stored there might do. This report was written in reaction to the "great salad oil swindle."

Outside Inventory Services. Many retail and some other types of companies engage outside inventory services to perform their physical inventory counts and compilation procedures. Not all of these services use the typical inventory tag system. Instead, they may use calculators and tape recording machines to accumulate totals of the inventory at retail without identifying specific subtotals. Typically, these services will submit an inventory certificate showing the total amount of inventory, either by class or in total. If there are no inventory tags for the auditor to test, he must understand the inventory counting procedures followed by the service and must observe the actual making of the counts. He may also have to accumulate totals of inventory for selected test areas and agree these to totals counted by the service.

Detailed tests of the compilation may prove difficult, but if the outside inventory service is an independent contractor, the auditor should recognize that probably fewer tests of its compilation are necessary than would be the case for a compilation done by the company itself. Of course, the auditor must determine whether the service is truly independent of the company, just as he would in employing the services of a specialist (AU 336). Both the auditor and the company should review adjustments of book inventory to physical inventory to see if the adjustment appears reasonable in view of current facts and the prior years' physical inventories. Typically, a given retail unit will have a known approximate capacity for inventory. Results that are out of line for the location or the industry in general should be challenged, and a recount of the inventory should be performed if necessary.

Alternative Procedures for Opening Inventories. On a new engagement, the auditor usually is engaged after the beginning of the year. If requested to issue an opinion on a full set of the current year's financial statements, he will need to be satisfied with the opening balance sheet in order to issue an unqualified opinion on the income statement and statement of changes in financial position.

If the prior year was reported on by another auditor, the new auditor should discuss the results of the prior examination with the previous auditor, and should review his working papers to become satisfied that the opening inventory balance is appropriate. If this is not feasible or if no other auditor observed the prior year's inventory, the current auditor will have to devise other procedures to test the opening inventory balance. The nature and the extent of these tests will again depend on the company's inventory system. If the system proves to be reliable, the auditor may be able to work back from the results of the current year's observation to the end of the prior year. If the company's systems are not sufficiently reliable, the auditor may not be able to perform satisfactory alternative procedures and may have to disclaim an opinion on the current year's statements of income and changes in financial position. This type of scope limitation disclaimer is discussed in Chapter 16.

Information on Changing Prices. Companies meeting certain size tests are required by SFAS 33 (AC 1072) to include specified current cost and constant dollar supplementary information as discussed earlier in this chapter. SAS 27 (AU 553) discusses procedures to be performed by the auditor regarding the unaudited supplemental information. Basically, the standard requires

- Inquiring of management as to whether the information has been prepared and presented in accordance with FASB guidelines on a consistent basis with prior periods. This includes inquiring as to the significant assumptions or interpretations underlying the measurement and presentation.
- Comparing the supplementary information for consistency to management's responses to the above inquiries, to the audited financial statements, and to other knowledge obtained during the audit.
- Giving consideration to obtaining a letter of representations on the information.
- Making additional inquiries if the above procedures cause the auditor to question whether the supplemental information meets the FASB guidelines.

The auditor has no obligation to perform any procedures to corroborate management's responses concerning the unaudited supplementary information. Furthermore, the auditor need not expand his report on the audited financial statements to refer to the supplemental information unless the necessary information is omitted or is found to depart materially from the FASB guidelines, or the auditor is unable to complete the prescribed procedures.

Category Three Letters. Revenue Procedure 75-39 (September 29, 1975) describes the procedure that a taxpayer must follow to change his treatment of category three costs. Category three costs, those which must be included in inventory cost for tax purposes if they are part of inventory cost for financial statement purposes, are discussed in an earlier section, Allocating Indirect Costs. The revenue procedure requires that a taxpayer requesting permission to change the treatment of a category three cost must provide a letter to the IRS stating that the proposed treatment conforms to GAAP, without regard to materiality. The taxpayer may also request his CPA to furnish a similar letter supporting the conclusion.

The authoritative accounting literature does not contain a definitive list of the elements of overhead costs. As discussed in FASB Interpretation No. 1 (AC 1051-1.05) and APB 20 (AC 1051.09), a change in the elements of inventory cost is considered an accounting change and must be justified on the basis of preferability. If the change is material, the auditor must ascertain that the change is in conformity with generally accepted accounting principles, and must express his concurrence in the audit report. The reason given for the change cannot be only that it will produce an income tax benefit. The reasons most often given are that there will be a better matching of costs with revenues or that the switch is to a method more commonly used in the industry. While the auditor may concur with the change itself, the reasons for it may not be sufficiently auditable to enable him to issue the kind of letter the IRS wants concurring with the change, because GAAP provides very little definitive guidance regarding components of inventory.

Unusual LIFO Concerns. LIFO presents some unique audit questions, since it is possible for a company to influence its earnings significantly by managing its LIFO inventories. Maintaining its LIFO layers for tax purposes so as to forestall large tax payments on the earnings results of layer liquidations may also be a reason for a company to manage its LIFO inventory. Consequently, significant purchases or sales of inventory may be consummated near the end of the fiscal year. By themselves, these transactions do not present any special problem for recording inventories or cost of sales (though they may require footnote disclosure), but the auditor should review them, along with transactions after year-end, to assure that the purchases or sales were not accommodation transactions made only to be later reversed or rescinded.

The auditor must be concerned with substance, not form. Accommodation transactions predicated on buy-back or sell-back of the inventory after year-end may in substance be a loan of the inventory and not a transfer of the ownership risks.

In some such transactions, the inventory never even moves, because the sole purpose of the transaction is simply to attempt to qualify the transaction for tax purposes by establishing that the buyer is "at risk," if even for a brief period. Analyzing such transactions often becomes circular, with the auditor asking the tax associate if the transaction is good for LIFO tax accounting, and the tax associate responding that its probably good for tax if it's good for financial accounting. The SEC is planning (as of October 1980) to issue admonitions and guidance on these transactions; the commission has already prosecuted several cases involving management of earnings through LIFO transactions.

To identify the substance of purchase or sale transactions around the year-end accounting periods may be difficult, but the auditor should discuss the possibility of accommodation transactions with the company's management and, if necessary, obtain management representations not controverted by evidence or clues that the purchases or sales represented bona fide transactions and were not entered into for accommodation purposes. If the company is prone to this type of LIFO transaction, it would be wise to have an advance discussion among the auditor, tax person, and management in order to avoid a major disagreement after the fact.

Product Warranty Costs. The auditing of product warranties entails determining the existence of the warranty obligation and obtaining satisfaction as to the valuation and recording of the estimated liability. Normally, existence is determined by reading the sales agreement; however, implicit warranties are often determined by common industry practice, company practice, or legal opinion. Valuation of the estimated liability is normally based on past history, which should be updated for the most recent experience and for any changes in current conditions. For instance, a valuation based only on historical experience might be affected by known or anticipated quality changes or changes in warranty policy. An example would be results of laboratory field tests on new automobile tires that demonstrate improved performance and durability. In any case, when historical basis is used it is necessary to recognize and challenge the assumption that current conditions are similar to past conditions.

FINANCIAL ACCOUNTING AND REPORTING FOR CONSTRUCTION CONTRACTS

Two features generally distinguishing long-term construction projects from other projects of producers and manufacturers are that a longer period of time is required to complete the production process and that contracts for performance are ordinarily invoked. The existing professional literature on accounting and reporting in the construction industry is found in ARB 45, *Long-Term Construction-Type Contracts* (AC 4031), and two industry audit guides, *Audits of Construction Contractors* (AICPA, 1965a), and *Audits of Government Contractors* (AICPA, 1975b). In January 1980 the AICPA issued an exposure draft of a proposed *Audit and Accounting Guide for Construction Contractors* intended to update the existing construction contractors audit guide. And in December 1979 the AICPA issued an exposure draft of a proposed SOP, *Accounting for Performance of Construction-Type and Certain Production-Type Contracts,* intended to provide additional guidance in accounting for contracts.

The accounting and reporting requirements discussed in ARB 45 (AC 4031) relate to long-term contracts. However, the proposed SOP and proposed guide do not distinguish on the basis of length of the contracts. In short-term projects, revenue is typically recognized when the facilities are substantially complete and accepted, as with any typical significant act transaction. Such accounting treatment is permitted based on the assumption that the resulting revenue and cost, in the aggregate, would not be materially different from the results using the percentage-of-completion method. If the circumstances are such that a material difference would result at the close of a reporting period, the percentage-of-completion method should then also be used for the short-term contracts.

The objective of accounting for construction contracts is the fair presentation of accumulated contract costs in the balance sheet at net realizable value and the fair presentation of contract revenues and costs in the income statement, appropriately matching costs with the revenue recognized.

Types of Construction Contracts

Construction contracts differ by the type of pricing arrangement or method of determining total revenues they use. Four basic types of arrangements are currently in use, (1) fixed price, (2) time and materials, (3) cost plus a fee, and (4) unit price:

1. In a *fixed price* or *lump sum* contract, total revenues are predetermined by the contract. Normally they are not subject to change even if costs should differ from those initially estimated, but sometimes the agreement may provide for additional payments based on inflation adjustments or performance incentives, to name only two factors. Further, if the contract provides for multiple unit deliveries, the contracts are often subject to renegotiation after a certain number of deliveries.

2. Time-and-materials contracts are generally structured in such a way that the contractor is reimbursed at a fixed hourly rate for labor hours incurred and for the direct cost of materials or other specified costs. The reimbursement rate is estimated in such a way as to cover the direct costs of labor and overhead and to provide a profit as well.

3. Cost-plus-a-fee contracts generally provide for the reimbursement of allowable or defined costs plus a fee that represents the contractor's profit. The amount of the fee can vary, depending on the terms of the contract; for example, the fee is often subject to incentive adjustments.

4. The unit price contract is one in which the price of each unit is fixed but the total number of units to be supplied is not. These contracts are subject to the same variations as other fixed price contracts.

Contract Revenues

Revenue Measurement. Two generally accepted methods are currently used in accounting for construction contracts: (1) percentage of completion (or, proportional performance), and (2) completed contract. The selection of the appropriate method depends on the type of contract and any inherent uncertainties. As a general rule, the percentage-of-completion method is preferable to the completed-contract method when estimates of costs, revenues, and progress toward completion are reasonably reliable. Thus, the accounting method should be selected contract by contract, and the choice should be based on factual considerations. Different accounting methods should not be applied to substantially similar circumstances, however.

Many construction contracts provide for incentive payments or penalties—i.e., revenue adjustments depending on future events. They often also allow for contract changes resulting from change orders or other adjustments to basic specifications. These provisions introduce a degree of uncertainty that must be made an integral part of the accounting treatment afforded these transactions. The total revenue to be recognized is continuously estimated by a process similar to that for projecting costs to complete the contract. As contracts progress, estimates of revenue to be earned will become more and more accurate. Changes in recorded revenue and costs that result from refinements of the original estimates should be reflected in the financial statements in the same manner as other changes in estimates in accordance with APB 20, *Accounting Changes* (AC 1051.31-.33).

The relationship between the contractor and the customer in a cost-plus contract will determine what items of reimbursable costs are to be included in revenue. In some situations the contractor serves as nothing more than an agent who supervises the work of the subcontractors who actually provide the materials and perform the work. In such situations, the contractor's revenue should include only his fee, regardless of whether he acts as a paying agent for the subcontractors or vendors. In other situations the contractor has discretionary responsibility with regard to materials, labor, and subcontract work, and he should include in revenue all reimbursable costs for which he was at risk or on which his fee was based at the time the contract was negotiated. On large or complex projects the customer may do the purchasing of materials because they have greater leverage with the suppliers, but if the contractor has the responsibility for deciding on the nature, type, and characteristics of such material, it is then properly includible in revenues.

Aggregation or Segmentation of Contracts. There is a general presumption that the basic unit for estimating revenues, expenses, and progress toward completion is the individual contract. However, since contracts vary significantly in scope and complexity, occasionally it becomes desirable either to aggregate a number of similar contracts or, if one contract covers several different tasks, to segment the contract into smaller profit centers. Each approach is acceptable under certain circumstances. In general, contracts should not be aggregated unless they were negotiated as a package with the same customer at approximately the same time and are performed concurrently or continuously on the same project. Contracts should not be segmented unless the tasks are clearly separable (e.g., perhaps they were proposed as separate components and could have been awarded to varying contractors, carry different levels of risk and reward, or have a history of being covered by separate contracts). Another justification of segmentation is that the difference between the price of the project and the total price of the component tasks is attributable to the cost savings of the combined performance of the tasks. The decision to aggregate or segment contracts must be based on careful evaluation of the substance of the contracts, not on convenience. The proposed SOP lists certain criteria that must be met if a contractor either aggregates or segments contracts.

Contract Costs

The method of cost accumulation depends on the type of contract. It should be noted that this chapter discusses contract costs in the context of GAAP; these costs are not always the same as allowable costs under contracts covered by the pronouncements of the Cost Accounting Standards Board (see Chapter 42).

Contract Method. Contract costs generally include all direct material and direct labor costs and indirect costs identifiable with contracts but exclude selling costs which are charged to expense as incurred. The authoritative accounting literature requires costs to be considered period costs if they cannot be clearly related to production, either directly or by an allocation based on their discernible future benefits. General and administrative costs are usually treated as expenses of the current period if the percentage-of-completion method is used. When the completed-contract method is used and there is an uneven pattern of jobs being completed from year to year, it may be appropriate to allocate general and administrative costs to individual contracts, provided they are recoverable from future revenues. ARB 45 states:

> When the completed-contract method is used, it may be appropriate to allocate general and administrative expenses to contract costs rather than to periodic income. This may result in a better matching of costs and revenues than would result from treating such expenses as period costs, particularly in years when no contracts were completed. [AC 4031.10]

The method of assigning costs to contracts should be disclosed in the notes to the financial statements, and the major types of costs included in contract costs should be identified.

Many contractors incur costs that they describe as precontract costs. Some examples are costs incurred in anticipation of a specific contract but which will have no future benefit unless the contract is won, and learning and start-up costs incurred for unidentified contracts. Most precontract costs may be deferred if their recovery from future contracts is probable. Learning and start-up costs, however, should be charged to existing contracts unless they qualify for program accounting treatment (as described below). Any precontract costs that are deferred should ordinarily be classified in the balance sheet apart from other contract costs.

Program Cost Method. Sometimes contractors will enter into contracts where it is not economically feasible for them to produce the required quantity without incurring a loss; they bid on such contracts when they expect to receive follow-on contracts for production of essentially similar units from the same or different customers and the economics are such that they will be able to make a profit, taking into consideration the spread of the tooling and start-up costs over a larger number of units and the anticipated benefits of the learning curve effect. The justification for spreading currently incurred costs over future contract sales is that it is a better matching of the revenues and expenses.

Before program accounting was eliminated from its scope, the proposed SOP indicated that program accounting should be used only when a contractor can demonstrate all the following:

1. The investment in the production effort cannot be recovered from the initial firm contracts for production of units;
2. Except for inflation, the selling price of each unit will be relatively level;
3. The costs of the units produced early in a program are expected to be substantially higher than the costs of those produced later, because of production efficiency gains (the learning curve effect);
4. Reasonable estimates can be made of the number of units to be produced, the associated production costs, and the length of the period involved;
5. He has the ability to finance and produce the product; and
6. The product is in an identifiable market with a limited number of competitive buyers.

ASR 173 points out that in program accounting the use of estimates "requires strong accounting controls with constant monitoring and the recording of variances between estimates and actual experience."

This section was deleted from the proposed SOP because of the need for further study of its unique treatment of long-term production costs. There is likely to be considerable controversy about the appropriate resolution of this accounting issue.

Disclosure in the financial statement should include a description of the program, the estimated number of units in the program, the number of units covered by the contracts or conditional orders, and a discussion of the risks associated with the program.

In establishing costs to be regarded as program costs, the contractor may not include any costs that would qualify as research and development by the FASB definition (AC 4211.08).

Computation of Revenues Using Percentage of Completion

There are a number of acceptable methods of determining the extent of progress toward completion of a contract. Measurements related to output, such as yards of pavement laid for highway contracts, units produced, or specified contract milestones, are considered to be the best measure of progress where available; in other circumstances it is more appropriate to use input measures that relate elements of effort, such as labor hours incurred, to the total estimated labor hours on the project or that compare costs incurred to date (eliminating uninstalled materials purchased) to total estimated costs. Whatever the method of measurement, it should be used consistently for all projects having the same characteristics.

At the end of each accounting period the contractor will reestimate the aggregate revenues and costs associated with each significant contract to determine the estimated gross profit. The percentage of completion is applied to the estimated gross profit to arrive at the estimated gross profit earned to date, and any previous gross profit earned on the contract is deducted to yield the gross profit earned in the current period.

There are two alternative but acceptable methods of determining the revenues and costs to be reported. Under one method the percentage of completion will be applied to the estimated revenue and costs, yielding the cumulative amounts to be recognized. Under the other method, the total costs incurred on the contract will be added to the earned gross profit, and the sum will be the cumulative revenues to be recorded on the contract. The former method yields a more consistent gross profit percentage in the various accounting periods; the latter method records the actual costs incurred on a contract without creating accrued costs. The gross profits earned for the period would be the same under either method.

Anticipated Loss Contracts

Under any contract accounting method, an additional charge to current earnings will be necessary if the company expects to incur a loss on any individual contract. The loss should be charged to the earnings statement when its amount is first determinable, and an accrual for contract losses reflected in the balance sheet should either be included among liabilities or applied as a reduction of contract-related assets. If the company aggregates several contracts with one customer and establishes what it believes to be a reasonable profit margin percentage for the group, losses on any individual portion (project) of the contract need not be accrued unless the contract as a whole incurs a loss.

Methods for Adjusting Estimates

The accounting for contractors is based on estimates that are continuously being revised as the contract progresses and more information becomes available. Under the percentage-of-completion method, revisions to the estimates for contract revenues and costs and the extent of the contract's progress toward completion are recorded as a change in estimate and are reflected in the current-period financial statements as changes in estimates.

Both the cumulative catch-up (revising the cumulative amounts from contract inception) and the prospective methods (the "to go" approach—not revising prior amounts but spreading remaining revenues and gross profit over the remainder of the contract) have been used in practice. The proposed SOP selects only the cumulative catch-up method, in order to bring more uniformity to accounting practices followed under percentage-of-completion accounting.

Some accountants believe that under the program method of accounting, the effect on the amortization of costs for adjustments in estimates is generally viewed as being similar to the effect of a change in estimated useful lives of depreciable assets, and is recorded on the prospective method (the "to go" approach). Others believe that the cumulative catch-up approach should be used, since the underlying

20

Property, Plant, and Equipment

Florence L. Haggis

CAPITAL ASSET CYCLE

Investments in property, plant, and equipment—those long-lived tangible assets used for the production of other goods and services—often are a substantial portion of the total assets of many companies. Acquisition, control, expiration of assigned carrying amounts, and disposal are the transactions that make up the capital asset cycle, and these phases are highlighted briefly below. They are discussed in greater detail in the accounting and auditing sections that constitute the remainder of the chapter.

The acquisition of property, plant, and equipment may require a major use of funds and may represent a commitment for a relatively long period of time. Accordingly, acquisition is generally the object of long-term decision making, and major acquisitions must be ratified by the board of directors in most larger companies.

Capital Budgeting

The planning, analysis, evaluation, and final decision regarding major expenditures for long-term investments and their financing are all encompassed in *capital budgeting*. Major investments in property, plant, and equipment are typical examples, but major research and development or advertising programs may also call for similar budgeting approaches.

In evaluating capital expenditures, the most important and most difficult task is the estimation of cash flows relating to a project. First, the incremental cash outflows must be measured. This is sometimes straightforward, but often the task of calculating the total incremental cash to be invested requires knowledge of trade-in values, construction costs, and working capital investment associated with a project that are far from certain at the crucial decision point. It is particularly common for a capital budgeter to omit consideration of the investment in credit granted to customers and inventory requirements that may be implied by the building of a new plant or major project.

By far the most significant problem, however, is the estimation of future cash inflows that a project may bring. These incremental inflows may be based on additional revenues, cost savings, or a combination thereof. Often several alternative means of achieving a business objective must be considered, and incremental calculations will have to be made sequentially rather than simply compared to the present condition. In addition, the attribution of cash inflows to particular decisions may be difficult, and there is great uncertainty where cash flows must be estimated over a period of several years. In fact, future estimates can only accurately be described by probability distributions, while most of the techniques used in present-value analysis are applied to single point estimates as illustrated below.

Nevertheless, it is useful to develop approaches that allow estimates, however imperfect, to be analyzed.

There are many profit-ranking methods (called *return-on-investment* techniques) that are used in capital budgeting, but the most common are (1) *payback*, (2) *unadjusted rate of return,* and (3) *internal rate of return.*

Initially, these factors should be kept in mind:

- All return-on-investment techniques require estimation. It is rare that a company can precisely determine all the effects and cash flows of any business transaction.
- Return-on-investment analysis is essentially a quantifying process. However, there are also always qualitative factors, which cannot be quantified. The corporate decision maker must always evaluate the qualitative factors in conjunction with the quantitative analysis.

- The internal-rate-of-return method is superior to other methods presented in this chapter. Although it was once difficult and expensive to apply, electronic technology has made it easy and cheap. It is the one method that considers all relevant information.

Payback Method. As its name implies, the payback method computes the amount of time it takes for a company to get back its investment. In computing annual cash flow, taxes must be considered. The computation is: Payback Method = Cost of the Investment ÷ Annual Cash Flow.

To illustrate the method, assume that a company is considering purchasing a fleet of trucks for $200,000. The company estimates the trucks will have a useful life of ten years and will generate additional revenues of $60,000 per year. The annual cash flow is computed as shown in Figure 20.1. With this information, the payback period may now be computed:

$$\frac{\text{Cost of the Investment}}{\text{Annual Cash Flow}} = \frac{\$200,000}{\$\ 40,000} = 5 \text{ years.}$$

This means that it will take the company five years to get back its initial investment in the trucks.

Often a capital investment will not yield constant annual cash flows. This occurs for many reasons. For example, a fleet of trucks may require greater amounts for maintenance in later years than in earlier years. Similarly, other investment decisions may have varying cash flows. For example, a new product in a highly innovative industry may sell more in its first several years than in later years. Figure 20.2 illustrates four investments with equal costs and total cash flows over the life of the investment but differing annual cash flows.

Additional cash revenues	$60,000
Less depreciation*	20,000
Additional pretax increase	$40,000
Increase in taxes**	$20,000
Cash flow:	
Additional cash revenues	$60,000
Less increase in taxes	20,000
	$40,000

* Straight-line method used, minimum salvage value, computed as $\dfrac{\$200,000 \text{ cost}}{10 \text{ years}}$.

** For simplicity, a 50% tax rate is used.

FIGURE 20.1 PAYBACK METHOD—COMPUTATION OF ANNUAL CASH FLOW

	Varying Cash Flows			Constant Cash Flow
	Investment A	Investment B	Investment C	Investment D
Cost	$200,000	$200,000	$200,000	$200,000
Expected annual cash flow*				
1980	$125,000	$ 75,000	$ 20,000	$ 40,000
1981	35,000	75,000	20,000	40,000
1982	35,000	50,000	40,000	40,000
1983	30,000	50,000	50,000	40,000
1984	30,000	30,000	60,000	40,000
1985	30,000	30,000	70,000	40,000
1986	30,000	30,000	50,000	40,000
1987	30,000	20,000	40,000	40,000
1988	30,000	20,000	30,000	40,000
1989**	25,000	20,000	20,000	40,000
Total	$400,000	$400,000	$400,000	$400,000
Payback period	3.2 years	3 years	5.1 years	5 years

* Assumed to be received evenly throughout the year.
** Should include any salvage value of the investment.

FIGURE 20.2   PAYBACK METHOD—CONTRASTING CONSTANT AND VARY-
ING CASH FLOWS

For all the investments in Figure 20.2, average annual cash flow is $40,000; if
this number were used in the computation, the payback period would be five years.
But it is wrong to use an average cash flow. On closer examination, investment B
provides the *fastest* payback. When there are varying cash flows, the cumulative
payback from the earliest date determines the payback period. With investment A
there is a large cash flow in 1980, but substantially smaller cash flows are estimated
for 1981-1989. Investment C has smaller cash flows in the early and later years,
with larger cash flows in the middle years. Investment D has constant cash flow
in each year (it is the same example as Figure 20.1). Investment B has large cash
flows in the first two years, which drop substantially in the third year and continue
dropping from there. Cumulatively, investment B pays back most quickly.

The payback method has two big advantages: (1) it is very easy to understand
conceptually—a company makes an investment in fixed assets, a new product, or
whatever, and instinctively wants to know how long will it take to get the money
back; and (2) it is very easy to compute—since the amount of the investment and

	Investment D	Investment E
Cost	$200,000	$200,000
Expected annual cash flow	$ 40,000	$ 50,000
Payback period	5 years	4 years

FIGURE 20.3   PAYBACK METHOD—PROFITABILITY ANALYSIS I

the cash flows are known or estimated, computation is a matter of simple arithmetic.

But the payback method does have disadvantages. It ignores two critical factors that are necessary for all capital investment purposes—profitability and the time value of money.

All business decisions should ideally generate a profit. The payback method ignores profitability. In the examples in Figures 20.1 and 20.2 each of the investment possibilities yielded a cash flow greater than the investment's cost. Accordingly, they are all potentially profitable. However, the payback method itself did not give this information; only the knowledge of each investment's useful life indicated the profitability. Consider the investments in Figure 20.3. The payback method demonstrates that investment E is the better choice because its payback period is four years whereas investment D's is five years. (Again, investment D is the same as in Figures 20.1 and 20.2.) However, investment E has a useful life of four years, whereas investment D has a useful life of ten years. Clearly then, investment E would not add to the company's profit—its cost is $200,000 and its total cash flow is $200,000. Investment D—although it has a longer payback period—has total cash flows of $400,000; it is the only appropriate choice (Figure 20.4).

The payback method also ignores the time value of money. A dollar received today is worth more than a dollar received a year from now, and that dollar is worth progressively more than one received two, five, or ten years later. More will be said about this later.

	Investment D	Investment E
Cost	$200,000	$200,000
Estimated annual cash flow	$ 40,000	$ 50,000
Payback period	5 years	4 years
Useful life	10 years	4 years
Total cash flow	$400,000	$200,000
Profit	$200,000	—0—

FIGURE 20.4   PAYBACK METHOD—PROFITABILITY ANALYSIS II

Cost	$200,000
Estimated salvage value	20,000
	$220,000
Divide by	2
Average investment	$110,000

FIGURE 20.5   UNADJUSTED RATE OF RETURN—COMPUTATION
OF AVERAGE INVESTMENT

Unadjusted Rate of Return. The unadjusted-rate-of-return method goes beyond the payback method in that it considers profitability. The unadjusted rate of return is computed by dividing the estimated annual cash flow less depreciation by the average investment. The equation is: Unadjusted Rate of Return = Annual Cash Flow Less Depreciation ÷ Average Investment.

Figure 20.1 already indicated how to compute annual cash flow. The average investment is computed by adding to the initial cost of the investment its salvage value (the value at the end of its life) and dividing by two. Figure 20.5 illustrates this.

An investment that continually depreciates over time will always have an average investment equal to its cost less straight-line accumulated depreciation at the end of half its useful life. This is what the formula for unadjusted rate of return computes. Figure 20.6 illustrates the application of the unadjusted rate of return using the same investment possibilities as those of Figure 20.4, but with an estimated salvage value of $20,000.

Like the payback method, the most serious disadvantage of the unadjusted rate of return is that it does not consider the time value of money.

	Investment D	Investment E
Cost	$200,000	$200,000
Salvage value (estimated)	20,000	20,000
Average investment	110,000	110,000
Expected useful life	10 years	4 years
Annual depreciation*	18,000	45,000
Annual cash flow	40,000	50,000
Annual cash flow less depreciation	22,000	5,000
Unadjusted rate of return	20%	4.5%

* Straight-line method used.

FIGURE 20.6   ILLUSTRATION OF UNADJUSTED RATE OF RETURN

Internal Rate of Return. Internal rate of return (IRR) is one of the most appropriate and valid techniques for computing return on investment. It eliminates all the disadvantages of the payback and unadjusted-rate-of-return methods, because it considers both profitability and the time value of money. Internal rate of return can be described as the interest rate that equates the cash outflows and cash inflows for a given investment.

It was previously difficult to compute internal rate of return; it had to be done either by sophisticated computer software or by trial and error using present-value tables. In the last few years inexpensive hand-held financial calculators have made it possible to compute internal rate of return directly. Figure 20.7 repeats the four investment alternatives in Figure 20.2. The internal rate of return on investment A is the highest rate.

	Varying Cash Flows			Constant Cash Flow
	Investment A	Investment B	Investment C	Investment D
Cost	$200,000	$200,000	$200,000	$200,000
Expected annual cash flow*				
1980	$125,000	$ 75,000	$ 20,000	$ 40,000
1981	35,000	75,000	20,000	40,000
1982	35,000	50,000	40,000	40,000
1983	30,000	50,000	50,000	40,000
1984	30,000	30,000	60,000	40,000
1985	30,000	30,000	70,000	40,000
1986	30,000	30,000	50,000	40,000
1987	30,000	20,000	40,000	40,000
1988	30,000	20,000	30,000	40,000
1989**	25,000	20,000	20,000	40,000
Total	$400,000	$400,000	$400,000	$400,000
Payback period	3.2 years	3 years	5.1 years	5 years
Internal rate of return	24.70%	23.98%	14.72%	15.86%

* Assumed to be received evenly throughout the year.
** Should include any salvage value of the investment.

FIGURE 20.7 CONTRASTING INTERNAL RATE OF RETURN WITH PAYBACK METHOD

Figure 20.7 indicates certain significant factors:

- The payback method does not indicate the best investment. Investment B is the best under the payback method, whereas A yields the largest return.
- The payback method does at least give some indication of yield, because earlier cash flows are worth more than later cash flows. By focusing on the cash flows closest to the investment's inception there is some built-in—though not highly accurate—consideration of the time value of money.
- The internal rate of return will directly consider all relevant financial factors, including profitability and the time value of money.
- The internal rate of return can be computed just as easily for the irregular cash flows of investments A, B, and C as for the constant cash flow of investment D. This is significant because most investments will not generate a constant cash flow.

The IRR is computed by determining the point at which the present value of future cash flows exactly equals the value of the investment. The computer or calculator does this automatically. Figure 20.8 illustrates how this works for the cash flow of investment A—the best alternative. Notice that at a 25% rate of return the present value of cash flows is less than $200,000—this means that the rate of return is less than 25%. At a 24% rate the present value is greater than $200,000 —this means that the rate of return is greater than 24%. Thus the actual rate is between 24% and 25%—the computer or calculator determines it to be 24.7%.

Using Return on Investment for Capital Budgeting. Companies make decisions all the time—not only in the acquisition of plant assets—selecting a particular action over possible alternatives. For example, a decision of the Acme Tool Manufacturing Company to sell 1,000 hand tools to the Friendly Retail Store at $19.90 per unit may represent many decisions:

- Certainly when Acme sells to Friendly a decision on price has been made and the sale will be made at $19.90 per unit, not at any other price;
- Depending on inventory levels, selling 1,000 units to Friendly may eliminate (in the short run) any opportunity to sell to others; and

	Actual Cash Flows	Present Value of Cash Flows at a 25% Rate of Return	Present Value of Cash Flows at a 24% Rate of Return
Cost	$200,000	$200,000	$200,000
Expected total cash flow	$400,000	<$200,000	>$200,000

FIGURE 20.8   PRESENT VALUE OF FUTURE CASH FLOWS

• Selling the units to Friendly will probably require production of more hand tools to meet future needs.

What does all this have to do with using return-on-investment techniques? If Friendly is a recurring customer of Acme and customarily buys hand tools at the prevailing price, and if the combination of market forces and Acme's costs has already set the price at $19.90, what return-on-investment analysis is necessary?

While most business transactions, such as the one between Acme and Friendly, are routine, the underlying elements can always be determined by return-on-investment techniques. These include

• What products (or services) the company should produce (or offer),
• How these products (or services) should be produced,
• To whom the company should sell,
• What the sales terms should be—the creditworthiness of customer and length of time he should be given to pay, and
• What the price should be.

These elements need to be considered carefully and reevaluated regularly. The routine phases of most business transactions can then be allowed to proceed.

Of course, there are many business transactions that are not routine; they involve long-term decisions that have a high cost and will affect the company for a long time (e.g., a plant expansion). Return-on-investment techniques must be applied to these transactions as well. Return on investment quantifies the investment alternatives for the company. Company officials can then consider this quantitative analysis along with the qualitative characteristics, and a decision can be made.

Return-on-investment techniques should be used for the following types of business decisions:

1. Capital expenditure decisions
   a. Fixed asset acquisitions (and dispositions)
      • Plant expansion
      • Purchase of equipment
      • Buy/lease alternatives
   b. Patents and copyrights
2. Investment decisions
   a. Financing
      • Short-term borrowing
      • Long-term borrowing
      • Selling stock
      • Making payments to vendors
   b. Acquiring other companies
      • Which ones
      • Level of control to exercise
   c. Investing cash
      • Marketable securities
      • U.S. treasury or government obligations
      • Bank certificates of deposit and commercial paper

3. Production decisions
   a. Product types
   b. Quantities
   c. Introduction of new products
   d. Expansion or contraction of plant facilities
4. Sales decisions
   a. Intended customers
   b. Sales quantities
   c. Sales prices.

Alternatives to Acquisition for Cash

Lease Financing. An important alternative to buying and owning assets is leasing them, either by taking a lease from the original owner of the asset or by purchasing the asset, selling it, and leasing it back from the buyer.

In order to choose between leasing or buying, company management must compare the cost of leasing with the cost of ownership. Figure 20.9 shows how such a comparison is made for a building that has ten years of economic life remaining. In this example, although the total payments to the bank ($97,640) are more than the total lease payments ($97,000) and the total cost of owning ($48,820) is more than the total cost of leasing ($48,500), there is still an advantage to owning the asset, because a dollar saved or spent ten years in the future is not the equivalent of a dollar saved or spent today. The example takes the time value of money into account in column 13, which shows that when the present-value factor is applied, the advantage of owning in the earlier years outweighs the advantage of leasing in later years. Discounted cash flow automatically weighs near dollars more heavily than distant dollars.

In the analysis of a lease-or-buy decision, accelerated depreciation, the investment tax credit, and salvage value should also be taken into account, as these factors will change the outcome of the calculations. They are not shown in Figure 20.2, which simplifies the analysis to point out the use of present-value methodology.

Self-Construction. Another possibility in the acquisition of a capital asset is for the company itself to build the asset. The costs assigned to self-constructed assets are handled in much the same way as those for purchased assets: all the costs of putting the asset into the condition and location for use are capitalized.

Purchase Business Combinations. Long-lived assets may also be acquired through a purchase business combination. Chapter 30 gives a full description of business combinations and discusses accounting for assets acquired in that way. The carrying amount applied to the assets acquired through a purchase business combination depends on the allocation of the total cost of the purchased business to the individual assets and liabilities included in it.

Depreciation

Depreciation has been defined as

. . . a system of accounting which aims to distribute the cost or other basic value of tangible capital assets, less salvage value (if any), over the estimated useful life of the

	(1)	(2)	(3)	(4)	(5)	(6)
Year	Payment to Bank	Interest on Loan	Repayment of Principal	Balance of Loan	Depreciation Expense*	Expenses for Tax Purposes (2 plus 5)
1	$ 9,764	$ 6,000	$ 3,764	$56,236	$ 6,000	$12,000
2	9,764	5,623	4,141	52,095	6,000	11,623
3	9,764	5,209	4,555	47,540	6,000	11,209
4	9,764	4,753	5,011	42,529	6,000	10,753
5	9,764	4,252	5,512	37,017	6,000	10,252
6	9,764	3,700	6,064	30,953	6,000	9,700
7	9,764	3,094	6,670	24,283	6,000	9,094
8	9,764	2,428	7,336	16,947	6,000	8,428
9	9,764	1,694	8,070	8,877	6,000	7,694
10	9,764	887	8,877	—	6,000	6,887
	$97,640	$37,640	$60,000		$60,000	$97,640

(7)	(8)	(9)	(10)	(11)	(12)	(13)
Tax Saving	Net Cost of Owning (1 minus 7)	Lease Payments	After-Tax Cost of Leasing	Advantage of Owning (10 minus 8)	Present-Value Factor**	Present Value of Advantage of Owning (11 times 12)
$ 6,000	$ 3,764	$ 9,700	$ 4,850	$ 1,086	.909	$ 987
5,812	3,952	9,700	4,850	$ 898	.826	742
5,605	4,159	9,700	4,850	691	.751	519
5,376	4,388	9,700	4,850	462	.683	316
5,126	4,638	9,700	4,850	212	.621	132
4,850	4,914	9,700	4,850	(64)	.564	(36)
4,547	5,217	9,700	4,850	(367)	.513	(188)
4,214	5,550	9,700	4,850	(700)	.467	(327)
3,847	5,917	9,700	4,850	(1,067)	.424	(452)
3,443	6,321	9,700	4,850	(1,471)	.386	(568)
$48,820	$48,820	$97,000	$48,500			$1,125

Assumptions:
  Investment in building = $60,000.
  Remaining economic life of asset = 10 years (of a 40-year life).
  Firm's average cost of capital = 10%.
  Firm borrows $60,000 to be repaid in 10 equal annual payments computed using a present-value table:
    Interest factor for 10 years at 10% = 6.145.
    Annual payment to bank = 60,000/6.145 = $9,764.
  Lease payments, if leased, would be $9,700 per year for 10 years.
  No salvage value at the end of 10 years.
  Tax bracket is 50%.
  Straight-line depreciation.
  Leased building would revert to the lessor at the end of the lease term, and there is no bargain purchase option.

* For the sake of simplicity, the investment tax credit is ignored.
** Present-value factor is calculated at the firm's average cost of capital — 10%.

FIGURE 20.9   LEASE-OR-BUY ANALYSIS

unit (which may be a group of assets) in a systematic and rational manner. It is a process of allocation, not of valuation. *Depreciation for the year* is the portion of the total charge under such a system that is allocated to the year. Although the allocation may properly take into account occurrences during the year, it is not intended to be a measurement of the effect of all such occurrences. [AICPA, 1953, par. 56]

Depreciation is a systematic means of charging operations with the cost of capitalized assets, less their estimated salvage value, over the estimated useful life of the asset. Depreciation recognizes that most assets physically deteriorate and decrease in market value over time. Land is not included in the depreciation calculation because land can never be physically consumed (though certain land uses may cause deterioration requiring an accrual of cost of restoration).

Since depreciation can be so simply described, accounting for it would presumably be a straightforward matter. Yet few topics in accounting have been so controversial. Some of the factors giving rise to dispute are the costs to be included in the depreciable amount, estimation of useful life and salvage value, evaluation of obsolescence, varying methods of allocating depreciation to product costs, treatment of constant dollar and current cost changes, and appreciation of property values.

Since depreciation is not a means of asset valuation but a process of cost allocation, it is fundamentally an unreliable indicator of asset expiration. The objective of this process of allocation is basically to distribute the cost, less salvage value, over the estimated useful life of the asset. But in order to estimate the useful life and salvage value of an asset, management must predict the effects of numerous economic and physical factors.

Projections into the future always involve uncertainties. In some cases the estimated physical life can be based on past experience with similar assets, but in other cases there is no past history. Also, unforeseen events, such as the sudden obsolescence of an asset due to revolutionary changes in technology, unsalability of the goods being produced due to changes in fashion, losses resulting from governmental edict, or catastrophic destruction, may end an asset's usefulness long before its originally estimated useful life expires. On the other hand, an asset may appreciate in value rather than depreciate. For example, a building may double in value simply because it stands in an area that has become a prime business location.

Management is responsible for estimating useful lives that reflect economic circumstances as closely as possible. Because of the uncertainties of estimation, many companies simply adopt the useful lives published by the IRS, since these guidelines purport to reflect the actual experience of taxpayers. But situations that make a particular guideline unrealistic should not be ignored. For example, if a machine is purchased to produce goods that will be obsolete in five years and the machine will have no other useful purpose after that time, it should have an estimated economic life of five years even though its physical life might well be ten years.

The estimation of salvage value gives rise to similar problems. Some companies ignore salvage value if it is considered immaterial to the cost of the asset. Others, for the sake of simplicity, assume it to be a certain percentage of the cost of the asset. Estimates of salvage value should be based on conditions at the time of the purchase of the asset.

Disposal

The final transaction in the capital asset cycle is disposal. Ultimately, property assets will be retired, either by sale, exchange, abandonment, or scrapping. If detailed records of property, plant, and equipment have been maintained, the accounting treatment for retirements is well defined. Since depreciation is merely an allocation of the cost of the asset, gain or loss on disposal of the asset will probably occur.

FINANCIAL ACCOUNTING AND REPORTING CONSIDERATIONS

The objective of accounting for property, plant, and equipment is to state these assets at cost less an allowance for depreciation aimed at allocating cost over the useful lives of the assets. An important quality for capitalization *and depreciation* criteria is consistency. Whatever methods are chosen, they should be consistently applied.

Acquisition

Property, plant, and equipment may be acquired through purchase (with or without trade-ins), self-construction, leasing, donation, or a business combination. The accounting for each type of acquisition other than through lease is described below. Leasing is discussed in Chapter 23.

Criteria for Capitalization. An asset should be capitalized if it is expected that it will be useful for more than the current period. It is usually not difficult to determine whether a particular asset should be capitalized or expensed. For some items (e.g., portable tools), however, the decision may be less obvious, so a company should set up rules that define the capitalization criteria. One expedient guideline for many companies is the amount of the expenditure: assets costing less than a specified amount, say $500, are expensed, those costing more are capitalized.

In some cases it may not be advisable to capitalize an item, even if it meets these criteria, because it is difficult to control. With small tools, for example, it may be better practice simply to record the item as a current expense.

Purchase for Cash. Capital assets should be recorded at cost plus any expenditures necessary to place those assets into readiness for use. Costs of acquisition thus include not only the invoice price but also installation, freight, testing, legal fees to establish title, and any other costs of putting the asset in the condition and location for use. Purchase discounts should be applied to reduce the cost. In the case of land, demolition costs of a preexisting structure may properly be included in the land acquisition cost.

Purchase on Contract. Costs of properties acquired under a conditional sale or other installment contract should include the same basic elements as those for cash purchases. However, interest charges included in the purchase payments are not part of the cost of the asset; they should be accrued as interest expense. If the installment contract does not state the interest and the principal separately, a determination of the two parts should be made.

Generally speaking, the cost of the asset should approximate the present value of the payments required, using the stated interest rate if that rate is reasonable or the current interest rate used for similar borrowings if the stated rate is unreasonably high or low. The amount included in the face value of a note or installment payable that is in excess of the present value of the payments is interest and should be recorded in accordance with APB 21 (AC 4111).

Basket Purchase. If assets are purchased in groups (frequently called a *basket purchase*), the total purchase cost should be allocated among the individual assets in the group on the basis of their respective fair values. If the aggregate of the fair values is greater than the total cost, the cost should be allocated proportionately.

For example, if three assets are purchased together for $56,000 and the fair value of the three assets at time of purchase is $16,560, $48,240, and $7,200, respectively, the cost would be allocated as follows:

	Fair Value	Proportion	Cost Allocation
Asset A	$16,560	(23%)	$12,880
Asset B	48,240	(67%)	37,520
Asset C	7,200	(10%)	5,600
	$72,000	(100%)	$56,000

This approach is not used in a purchase business combination, except when there is an overall excess of fair values over purchase price (see Chapter 30).

Purchase for Equity Securities. If assets are acquired through a business combination that meets all the conditions for a pooling of interests, the recorded historical cost of the assets of the separate companies becomes the recorded amount in the combined corporation. If, however, the acquisition is treated as a purchase for accounting purposes, the recording of the acquisition would follow the rules in APB 16 (AC 1091.67-.68); that is, assets acquired by exchanging equity securities are still recorded at the purchaser's cost. Cost in this situation is usually defined as the fair value of the assets acquired. Business combinations are discussed in Chapter 30.

If a company's equity securities are used to pay for capital assets apart from a business combination, the cash that would have been obtained from a sale of the securities for cash should be determined. If that is not possible, the fair value of the asset should be used. Par or stated value of the security is not an acceptable valuation.

Trade-Ins. When certain types of depreciable assets (such as automobiles or machinery) are purchased, part of the consideration is frequently a similar asset being traded in. The trade-in allowance granted by the seller usually differs from the net carrying amount of the old asset. If greater, it would appear that a profit is being realized on the exchange, but the seller may also have an inflated list price for the new asset. Therefore, other reasonably objective evidence of a profit is required in order to account for the trade-in as if it were an unrelated asset disposal.

Because it is often difficult to determine separately the economic substance of the purchase price and the trade-in allowance, the cost of the new asset is commonly recorded at the amount of the monetary consideration paid plus the unexpired cost of the trade-in surrendered.

Suppose, for example, that a delivery truck was acquired four years ago at a cost of $10,000 and depreciated on a straight-line basis over an estimated useful life of five years. Now the old truck is traded in for a new model having a list price of $12,000, but the dealer allows a trade-in value of $2,400 for the old truck. The cost of the new truck would be computed as follows:

Cost of old truck	$10,000
Less accumulated depreciation ($2,000 × 4)	8,000
Unexpired cost of trade-in	2,000
Monetary consideration paid for new truck ($12,000 − $2,400)	9,600
Recorded cost of new truck	$11,600

However, if a gain or loss is clearly indicated, the entire gain or loss on the exchange should be recognized. Thus, if independent appraisals determined that the net realizable value of the old truck is $2,500, a gain of $500 (the difference between that value and the net carrying amount) should be recognized. The new truck would then have a cost of $12,100 (cash paid of $9,600 plus market value of old truck of $2,500).

The cost and accumulated depreciation of an asset traded in should be removed from the accounts in conjunction with recording the acquisition cost of the new asset.

Self-Construction. The principle for recording costs of self-constructed plant and equipment is similar to that for purchased assets: record the cost to place the assets in condition and location for use. The practical problems in determining self-construction costs, however, are more like those encountered in determining the cost of goods manufactured for sale. Costs of material and direct labor are usually readily identified, but the treatment of indirect overhead and its apportionment between construction activity and the enterprise's normal production operations are not so simple in companies that do not normally construct their own assets.

Indirect costs not specifically identifiable with the construction project are usually allocated on the incremental cost method. This limits the capitalized overhead to the increase in overhead reasonably attributable to the construction work. Many companies do not assign any overhead to construction, because they reason that indirect costs are fixed in nature and that assets are frequently constructed during slack periods. Thus, the absorption of overhead into construction costs is, in their view, an understatement of expenses. The extent of deductibility of overhead for income tax purposes during a period of self-construction often has a considerable influence on the approach used for financial accounting.

Capitalization of interest is another issue in accumulating costs of a self-constructed asset. Most companies (other than public utilities) have traditionally treated interest as a period expense. Other nonutility companies have capitalized interest but have limited it to interest incurred during the construction period on amounts borrowed specifically for construction purposes. (Utilities also capitalize an allowance for equity funds; see Chapter 36.)

Beginning in 1980, SFAS 34, *Capitalization of Interest Cost,* requires capitalization of interest cost as part of the historical cost of "assets that are constructed or otherwise produced for an enterprise's own use (including assets constructed or produced for the enterprise by others for which deposits or progress payments have been made)" (AC 5155.09). The rate to be used for capitalization may be ascertained in this order (AC 5155.13): (1) the rate of specific borrowings associated with the asset and (2) if borrowings are not specific for the asset, or the asset exceeds specific borrowings therefor, a weighted average of rates applicable to other appropriate borrowings. Alternatively, a company may use a weighted average of rates of all appropriate borrowings regardless of specific borrowings incurred to finance the asset. Interest capitalized may not exceed total interest costs for any period, nor is imputing interest cost to equity funds permitted. (See Chapter 22 for a discussion of interest capitalization.)

Additions and Betterments to Existing Assets. There are fine distinctions between additions, betterments, improvements, alterations, and rearrangements—just as there are between costs of assets and costs of repairs. Regardless of how they are described, expenditures that extend the useful life of capital assets or increase their productivity should be capitalized as an addition to the individual or composite asset account. If a related asset is retired, its cost and accumulated depreciation is removed from the appropriate individual accounts; if composite accounts (described later) are used, the cost of the retired asset should be charged to accumulated depreciation.

Donated Assets. Assets donated by unrelated parties should be recorded at fair value, using either the applicable market price or an appraisal value in the absence of a readily determinable market value. The offsetting credit should be to paid-in capital, reduced by any costs incurred in the acceptance of the asset, such as installation costs, transportation expense, or legal fees.

Depreciation

Depreciation is a systematic method of charging operations with the cost of a capitalized asset, less salvage value, over its estimated useful life—but estimates of the useful life of assets are seldom accurate. An asset may be capable of lasting a long time, but obsolescence or other factors may abbreviate its usefulness to a company. Because of this uncertainty, the general guideline lives promulgated for tax purposes by the IRS are frequently used in financial accounting as well. The asset depreciation range (ADR) guidelines are contained in Revenue Procedure 77-10 and in the Commerce Clearing House *1980 U.S. Master Tax Guide* at paragraph 1168N.

Salvage value is also difficult to predict. Therefore, it is often ignored in depreciation computations if it is estimated to be less than 10% of the cost of the asset.

Depreciation Methods. There are several kinds of depreciation methods.

Straight-line method. Under this method, the cost (less salvage value) of the capitalized asset is spread in equal periodic portions over its estimated useful life. Straight-line depreciation is calculated by simply deducting the estimated salvage value from the cost of the asset and then dividing the remaining depreciable cost by the estimated years of useful life. It is acceptable to record a half-year's depreciation in the year the asset is acquired and another half-year's depreciation in the year it is retired. Companies that calculate depreciation on a monthly basis generally begin depreciating at the beginning of the month closest to the acquisition date. Other practical variations are acceptable, provided the criteria adopted are consistently applied.

Declining-balance method. Under the declining-balance method of depreciation, relatively larger amounts of depreciation are recognized in the earlier years of the asset's use, smaller amounts in later years. The conceptual reasons for adopting such a method are that the utility derived from a productive asset will often be greater in the early years and that repairs and maintenance will often be more costly in the later years. Thus, the sum of depreciation and repairs and maintenance expenditures is more likely to be fairly constant over the asset's life. In this light, an accelerated method of depreciation seems more realistic than the straight-line method.

Declining-balance depreciation is computed by applying a constant rate (generally double the straight-line rate for new assets, one and a half times for used assets) to the remaining undepreciated balance. In theory, there will always be a small balance remaining, since a constant rate is being applied to successively smaller amounts of undepreciated cost. Therefore, depreciation stops when the asset has been written down to salvage value; or, at an appropriate point, depreciation is switched to the straight-line method for tax purposes.

For example, for a machine that has an estimated useful life of ten years, costs $8,000, and has an estimated salvage value of $1,500, the double declining-balance depreciation would be calculated as shown in Figure 20.10.

Sum-of-the-years'-digits method. Another method of allocating a larger portion of the cost of an asset to its early years of use is the sum-of-the-years'-digits method. Each year's depreciation is calculated by using the sum of the total years of life as a denominator of a fraction of the depreciable base (cost of the asset less estimated salvage value). Thus, for a machine with a ten-year useful life, the denominator would be 55 (10 + 9 + 8 + 7 + 6 + 5 + 4 + 3 + 2 + 1); the numerator is always the remaining years of life.

Year	Net Undepreciated Cost	Depreciation for the Year
1	$8,000	$ 800*
2	7,200	1,440
3	5,760	1,152
4	4,608	922
5	3,686	737
6	2,949	590
7	2,359	472
8	1,887	377
9	1,510	10
10	1,500**	—

* Depreciation taken for a half-year in the year of acquisition.
** The machine is depreciated to salvage value in a little more than nine years.

FIGURE 20.10   DOUBLE DECLINING-BALANCE DEPRECIATION

A simple formula for determining the denominator for the sum of the years' digits for any useful life is

$$n \left(\frac{n+1}{2} \right)$$

where n signifies the estimated useful life.

Using the same data as the preceding example, yearly depreciation would be calculated on a depreciable base of $6,500 ($8,000 cost − $1,500 salvage value). Figure 20.11 shows the calculation of sum-of-the-years'-digits depreciation. (For simplicity, it ignores the half-year convention.)

Units-of-production method. The useful lives of some assets, such as machinery, can be estimated in terms of units produced or hours of operation rather than years, since this measure may provide a more equitable allocation of asset cost. In this case depreciation is computed as the ratio of the actual number of units produced or hours operated during the period to the total number of units or hours in the estimated useful life.

For example, if a machine with a depreciable cost of $8,000 is estimated to produce 200,000 units of a product over its estimated life, and 10,000 units have been produced during the period, depreciation would be calculated as follows:

$$\frac{10,000 \text{ units}}{200,000 \text{ units}} \times \$8,000 = \$400 \text{ depreciation.}$$

The difficulties involved in estimating the hours of operation or units of production for a particular asset or in keeping track of actual utilization generally deter most companies from using this method.

Year	Depreciation for the Year Fraction	Depreciation for the Year Amount
1	10/55	$1,182
2	9/55	1,064
3	8/55	945
4	7/55	827
5	6/55	709
6	5/55	591
7	4/55	473
8	3/55	355
9	2/55	236
10	1/55	118
	Total depreciation for ten years	$6,500

FIGURE 20.11   SUM-OF-THE-YEARS'-DIGITS DEPRECIATION

Variations Within Methods. The methods described above can be used to compute depreciation on an individual asset basis or on a group basis. Since depreciation accounting depends on estimates and judgments, the differing results derived from the use of various methods and bases are acceptable as long as the methods chosen are applied consistently. Thus, a company can use different methods to depreciate different assets; also, some assets can be depreciated individually, others in groups.

Unit basis. On the unit basis, each asset is recorded, depreciated, and retired individually. Very often the individual assets are recorded on asset cards that show the cost of the asset, the depreciation expense for the period, the accumulated depreciation, and the net undepreciated cost, as well as any other necessary information. Whatever the recording form, the unit basis is helpful in arriving at the net undepreciated cost when the asset is sold or retired. It is also valuable for purposes of physical accountability of individual items. EDP systems reduce the effort required to maintain a unit record system.

Composite accounts. In composite accounts, assets of the same general class are grouped together even though their individual estimated useful lives are different. A single composite life, generally a weighted average of the lives of the individual assets in the group, must be applied to the entire group. Composite accounts work best when the assets are segregated into appropriate groups by classification or function. If the "mix" of the group changes substantially, the composite life should be redetermined.

Composite accounts have the advantage of being simple, since they eliminate the necessity for computing depreciation accruals for individual assets. In addition, the asset lives recommended by the IRS are composite lives, so composite accounts can be used for both income tax and financial statement purposes. But if the net undepreciated cost of an individual asset is needed, the depreciation applied to the asset would not be computed at the composite rate. Instead it must be computed as if the asset had been depreciated on an individual basis.

Lapse schedules. Lapse schedules are worksheets showing all the assets of a similar class and life that were acquired during a given period. Depreciation is calculated on a group basis and recorded to show the "lapsing" of the cost of each group over its assigned life.

Changes in Methods and Lives. APB 20, *Accounting Changes,* says:

> . . . in the preparation of financial statements there is a presumption that an accounting principle once adopted should not be changed in accounting for events and transactions of a similar type. Consistent use of accounting principles from one accounting period to another enhances the utility of financial statements to users by facilitating analysis and understanding of comparative accounting data. [AC 1051.15]

However, companies sometimes voluntarily change to a different generally accepted accounting principle to improve the matching of revenue and expense, to adopt a method prevailing in the industry, or for other reasons.

A change from one method of depreciation of previously acquired and depreciated assets to another equally acceptable method is a change in accounting principle that should be accounted for as any other nonretroactive change (AC 1051.19); financial statements for prior periods should be presented as previously reported, and the cumulative net-of-tax effect of the change to the new depreciation method on beginning retained earnings should be included in the net income of the period of the change. Related per share amounts should also be included. For all periods presented, income before extraordinary items and net income should be shown on a pro forma basis on the face of the income statements as if the newly adopted accounting principle had been retroactively applied.

Because changes in depreciation methods have proven to be complex calculations in practice, the APB singled them out for specific recitation of steps (AC 1051.22) and included an extensive example in Appendix A of APB 20 (AC 1051A.01-.03). The "bottom end" of the APB's sample income statement is shown in Figure 20.12.

A company may decide to depreciate newly acquired assets by a different method than that used for old assets. For example, a company may continue to depreciate all old machinery by the straight-line method and depreciate all new machinery by the double declining-balance method. For this type of change there is no cumulative effect on beginning retained earnings, since all assets prior to the date of change continue to be depreciated on the old (straight-line) method (AC 1051.24).

If it is determined that a change in the estimated life of an asset or a change in the estimated salvage value is proper, this constitutes a change in accounting estimate. If the change will affect several future periods, current-period disclosure of the effect of the change in estimate is required in relation to income before extraordinary items, net income, and related per share amounts (AC 1051.33).

Amortization of Leasehold Improvements. Leasehold improvements are additions or improvements made to a leased asset. Because they revert to the owner of

	19X1	19X0
Income before extraordinary item and cumulative effect of a change in accounting principle	$1,200,000	$1,100,000
Extraordinary item (description)	(35,000)	100,000
Cumulative effect on prior years (to December 31, 19X0) of changing to a different depreciation method (Note A)	125,000	—
Net Income	$1,290,000	$1,200,000

Per share amounts:
  Earnings per common share assuming no dilution:

	19X1	19X0
Income before extraordinary item and cumulative effect of a change in accounting principle	$1.20	$1.10
Extraordinary item	(0.04)	0.10
Cumulative effect on prior years (to December 31, 19X1) of changing to a different depreciation method	0.13	—
Net income	$1.29	$1.20

Earnings per common share assuming full dilution:

	19X1	19X0
Income before extraordinary item and cumulative effect of a change in accounting principle	$1.11	$1.02
Extraordinary item	(0.03)	0.09
Cumulative effect on prior years (to December 31, 19X0) of changing to a different depreciation method	0.11	—
Net income	$1.19	$1.11

Pro forma amounts assuming the new depreciation method is applied retroactively:

	19X1	19X0
Income before extraordinary item	$1,200,000	$1,113,500
Earnings per common share assuming no dilution	$1.20	$1.11
Earnings per common share assuming full dilution	$1.11	$1.04
Net income	$1,165,000	$1,213,500
Earnings per common share assuming no dilution	$1.17	$1.21
Earnings per common share assuming full dilution	$1.08	$1.13

FIGURE 20.12   INCOME STATEMENT PRESENTATION OF CHANGE IN DE-
PRECIATION METHOD
SOURCE: AC 1051A.03.

the property on termination of the lease, they should be amortized by the lessee over the economic life of the improvement to the asset or the life of the lease, whichever is shorter. In determining the amortization period, the likelihood that renewal options will be exercised should be considered.

Income Tax Allocation. Companies often use one depreciation method (usually straight-line) for financial reporting and another (usually accelerated) for tax purposes. Other timing differences, such as in depreciable life, also occur. The purpose of such arrangements is to increase the company's cash flow by minimizing taxes currently payable, deferring them to a future period. The difference between book and tax depreciation gives rise to deferred taxes, determined by calculating the tax on income both before and after the deduction of the depreciation timing difference using the current tax rate. The difference between the two tax amounts is the deferred tax attributed to the timing difference. Most often this calculation is made on a net change basis (AC 4091.36), which combines prior timing differences that reverse in the current period with timing differences that originate in the current period. For further discussion of income tax allocation, see Chapter 25.

Obsolescence. Occasionally it is found that an asset built or purchased for a particular purpose can no longer be used because of sudden style changes, improved technology, or unforeseen reduction of demand. When an asset suddenly becomes obsolete and has no remaining useful life, the undepreciated cost, less salvage value, should be charged to operations. Incipient obsolescence may be dealt with by shortening depreciation lives.

Disposals and Retirements

As units of plant and equipment wear out or become obsolete, they must be sold, scrapped, traded in, exchanged, or abandoned. When an asset is disposed of or retired from use, the cost and related accumulated depreciation should be removed from the accounts. Since depreciation expense charged over the estimated useful life of the asset was only an allocation of the cost based on an estimate, a gain or loss will probably be realized on disposal of the asset.

These gains or losses, adjusted for the costs of removal or disposal, are recognized as income or expense in the period of the disposal, except when the asset disposed of was part of a composite account.

Sale. When a unit of property is sold, the cost should be removed from the appropriate asset account, and the related depreciation removed from the accumulated depreciation account. The difference between the net undepreciated cost and the proceeds received on the sale will be the gain or loss. If assets are recorded on lapse schedules, it is necessary to determine the acquisition-year group in which the asset is included on the lapse schedule, the original cost of the individual asset, and its accumulated depreciation based on the number of periods it has been depreciated as part of the group.

In composite account situations, the cost of the asset should be removed from the appropriate asset account and charged to the accumulated depreciation account. Proceeds received on disposal should be credited to the accumulated depreciation account. No profit or loss should be recognized on a composite account asset disposal unless it is abnormal or unusual; this makes it necessary to determine the accumulated depreciation based on the individual life of the asset. Gains or losses should then be recognized as if the assets were not composites, based on the proceeds received.

Trade-ins are sometimes accounted for as outright disposals but perhaps more frequently as a reduction of the cost of new assets acquired. Trade-in accounting is discussed under Acquisition earlier in this chapter.

Involuntary Conversion. Assets may be lost or destroyed through fire, casualty, condemnation, or other involuntary events. Generally, the gains or losses resulting from these events are measured by the difference between the insurance proceeds received and the net undepreciated cost of the asset.

Federal income tax rules allow deferral of the gain resulting from an involuntary conversion if the owner of the asset uses the funds received to replace the asset. In other words, the cost of the newly acquired replacement asset, adjusted for the gain, becomes the recorded cost of the asset for future tax depreciation purposes.

FASB Interpretation No. 30, *Accounting for Involuntary Conversions of Non-monetary Assets to Monetary Assets* (AC 1041-1), requires that gain or loss must be recognized in all involuntary conversions of nonmonetary assets to monetary assets. This is so even though an enterprise may have to reinvest in similar nonmonetary assets to continue its business.

Retirement. When a property asset has become fully depreciated and no salvage value has been assigned to it, the asset and the related accumulated depreciation should be removed from the accounts if the asset is being retired. If it remains in use, the asset and the accumulated depreciation accounts should, as a matter of control, continue to be carried on the balance sheet.

Abandonment. Abandonment of an asset is essentially the disposal of it without receiving any consideration except perhaps salvage. Abandonment presumes that the property has no more usefulness to its present owners. Accounting for an abandoned asset is the same as accounting for a retirement: the cost and the related depreciation are removed from the accounts, and a loss is realized if the asset has not been fully depreciated to zero.

Transfer. When an asset is transferred from one unit of a company to another, its original cost and accumulated depreciation to date of transfer should be recorded on the acquiring unit's books. Depreciation may continue according to the original plan, or the new unit may relife the asset. If the method is changed, this is dealt with as described earlier under Changes in Methods and Lives. Similarly, transfers of property assets between account classifications within the same company unit should be recorded using original cost and depreciation rather than net undepreciated cost.

Other Matters

Appraisals. Property, plant, and equipment should not be written up to reflect appraisal values, because appraisals do not reflect cost (except in rare situations—

mostly donated assets). Appraisal valuations can be useful for other purposes, however, such as determining insurance values, salvage values, and tax assessment figures; allocating cost to a finished product for the establishment of a selling price; allocating costs of a group purchase of properties; and preparing supplementary financial statements to show the effects of changing prices and values (see Chapter 8).

If appraisal values are used in the preparation of the basic financial statements, accountants should be sure to disclose the fact that the financial statements are not presented in conformity with GAAP. Concomitantly, depreciation should be computed on the written-up amounts (AC 4072.01) if appraisals are recorded in disregard of GAAP rules.

Investment Tax Credit. As an incentive to businesses to invest in productive assets, a tax credit equal to a specified percentage of the cost of certain productive assets placed in service during the period is made available under tax laws. For companies, the amount of the credit that may be used in the current year is limited to the first $25,000 of the federal income tax payable, plus 70% for 1980, 80% for 1981, and 90% for 1982 and thereafter of the remaining federal income tax payable. Investment tax credits are subject to recapture if the property is not held for the required length of time. The recapture becomes part of the current year's tax provision.

Although the APB expressed a preference for deferring the investment credit and amortizing it ratably over the expected life of the property (the deferral method), businesses (except most direct finance leasing companies) usually follow the flow-through method of recognition and reduce income tax expense by the full amount of the tax credit realized in the current year.

If investment credit is material, disclosure should be made in the financial statements of the method of accounting for it, the amount of the credit, and the amount of any unused portion of the credit to be carried forward to other periods. Income tax timing differences often give rise to questions about the appropriate period and amount in which the investment credit should be recorded; this complex subject is discussed in Chapter 25.

Tax Basis Differentials. If a company uses one accounting method for tax purposes and another for financial statements, differences may arise in the recording of assets and liabilities as a result of a purchase business combination. APB 16 requires that all identifiable assets acquired and liabilities assumed be assigned a portion of the cost of an acquired company equal to their fair values at date of acquisition (AC 1091.87). However, the fair values of the individual assets and liabilities recorded on the books may differ from their income tax bases, which will not change in an acquisition of the stock of the purchased company.

The tax effect of these differences depends on numerous factors. APB 16 (AC 1091.89) states that the differences between assigned amounts and the tax bases are not timing differences, and deferred tax accounts should not be recorded at the date of acquisition. Instead, the new carrying amounts are adjusted for the expected tax effects of the differences, and the assets are effectively carried net of tax. In many situations, however, tax basis differentials in excess of purchase cost are not assured of realization, and therefore their potential tax effects are not recorded as a reduction of the carrying amount of assets purchased in a business combination.

This situation occurs frequently in connection with purchases of computer-leasing companies that earlier had written down their computer portfolios without sufficient tax loss carryback absorption and that may subsequently have sold out at even lower values. The utilization by the purchasing company of the two basis differential layers presents a very complex accounting allocation problem that finally results in enhancing postcombination net earnings, assuming a high probability that the depreciability of the high depreciation basis is sustained with the IRS. For more information, see Chapters 25 and 30.

Asset Impairment Write-Downs. When management decides that some element of property, plant, and equipment is to be disposed of, its net realizable value should be estimated; if this is less than the net carrying amount, a write-down should be recorded in order to place the asset on a realizable value basis. If the asset is expected to be sold within 12 months, it should be carried as a current asset.

A more difficult problem arises in considering whether a company has the ability to fully recover the carrying amount of long-lived assets from future operations. As indicated in APB Statement 4:

> In unusual circumstances persuasive evidence may exist of impairment of the utility of productive facilities indicative of an inability to recover cost although the facilities have not become worthless. The amount at which those facilities are carried is sometimes reduced to recoverable cost and a loss recorded prior to disposition or expiration of the useful life of the facilities. [AC 1027.09]

This problem, often referred to as *impairment of value,* is described this way in SFAS 5:

> In some cases, the carrying amount of an operating asset not intended for disposal may exceed the amount expected to be recoverable through future use of that asset even though there has been no physical loss or damage of the asset or threat of such loss or damage. For example, changed economic conditions may have made recovery of the carrying amount of a productive facility doubtful. The question of whether, in those cases, it is appropriate to write down the carrying amount of the asset to an amount expected to be recoverable through future operations is not covered by this Statement. [AC 4311.31]

In practice, there have been limited write-downs and disclosures of impairment in value of assets not to be sold or otherwise disposed of; part of this problem is attributable to the difficulty of forecasting how much future realizable value an asset really has.

This matter was debated by AcSEC, which proffered certain advisory conclusions to the FASB; however, the problem was not included in the FASB's agenda. The AcSEC advisory conclusions (AICPA, 1980k) were that

1. The inability to fully recover the carrying amount of long-lived assets should be reported in financial statements;

2. The concept of *permanent decline* (see, for example, AC 5132.21) is unsatisfactory, but the *probability test* in SFAS 5 (AC 4311.08(a)) is a workable alternative;

3. Judgment is necessary in selecting the asset measurement that best predicts future economic benefits, and it is difficult to select one measurement that would be appropriate in all circumstances; and

4. If the inability to fully recover the carrying amounts of a long-lived asset is recorded in the accounts, future upward adjustments to the asset's historical cost would be permitted if evidence indicates a recovery.

Financial Statement Presentation

Balances of major classes of depreciable assets should be disclosed at cost at the balance sheet date (AC 2043.02(b)). Nondepreciable property (e.g., land) should be presented separately from depreciable assets. Property not used in the business, idle equipment, assets held for resale, and construction in progress should also be segregated if material in amount.

Property, plant, and equipment should not be written up to reflect appraisal, market, or current values; but if its components *are* shown at values in excess of cost, this fact should be disclosed in the financial statements until the effect has become insignificant through successive application of depreciation. If the effect is material, a qualified or even adverse auditor's opinion would be required.

Accumulated depreciation, either by major classes of depreciable assets or in total, should be disclosed either in the balance sheet or in a note to the financial statements; in addition, depreciation expense for the period and a general description of the methods used in computing depreciation for financial statement and tax purposes should also be disclosed (AC 2043.02(a), (c) and (d)).

As discussed in Chapter 23, *lessors* should include leased property under operating leases as noncurrent assets within or near the property, plant, and equipment caption; and property leased under capital leases should be recorded by a *lessee* as an asset and an obligation in an amount equal to the present value of the minimum lease payments during the term of the lease.

AUDITING CONSIDERATIONS

Objectives of the Audit

The overall objective of the audit of property, plant, and equipment and the related depreciation provision and accumulated depreciation accounts is to evaluate whether these accounts are fairly presented in the context of the financial statements taken as a whole.

Chapter 12 discusses the audit process and its implementation, and Chapter 13 discusses internal control and its impact on the audit. To obtain an understanding of the audit philosophy utilized in the following discussion of the audit of property, plant, and equipment, those chapters should be consulted.

There are seven basic audit objectives to be satisfied while performing the audit of property, plant, and equipment; they are existence, ownership, valuation, cutoff, mechanical accuracy, classification, and disclosure.

These seven areas are not entirely congruent with the seven objectives ascribed to internal control in Chapter 13, because internal control systems do not primarily address several substantive audit objectives applicable to property, plant, and equipment. The following cross-reference table may be helpful:

Overall Audit Objective, as Shown in This Chapter	*Internal Control Objectives*
Congruent:	
Existence	Authorization
	Validity
	Recording
Valuation—accuracy	Valuation
Cutoff	Timing
Mechanical accuracy	Summarization
Classification	Classification
Not congruent:	
Ownership	
Valuation—changed circumstances	
Disclosure	

Controls Over Capital Assets

Most larger firms have formal procedures for determining capital budgets and monitoring capital expenditures for property, plant, and equipment. However, after the assets have been acquired, it sometimes seems that control over them receives little attention. One of the reasons for this may be that the bookkeeping required for these assets is not elaborate; thus management's attention may be focused on the capital asset accounts only a few times a year. Also, auditors do not often require periodic physical inventories to be taken of these assets. The accounting standards provisions of the Foreign Corrupt Practices Act of 1977 require publicly held companies to have adequate internal accounting controls over all assets (see Chapter 13); this law will undoubtedly cause increased physical and accounting controls over long-lived assets in those companies that are covered by the act.

Proper control of capital assets provides many benefits, such as optimization of cash flow by claiming the maximum depreciation allowed for income tax purposes; appropriate determination of current cost enabling product pricing to include full costs of production; accurate measurement of return on investment; ability to evaluate the reasonableness of property tax assessments; and accurate evaluation of losses for insurance purposes.

Control over long-lived assets involves (1) control over the physical asset itself and (2) control over each phase of the transaction cycle, from introduction in the capital budget through acquisition to expiration and, finally, disposal.

Existence Controls. A property record system should be maintained for all property, plant, and equipment. Control accounts should be established in convenient categories, supported by individual records maintained on cards or sheets (for manual systems) or on computerized records. Each asset should be assigned an identification number, and periodic physical counts of the assets should be made by personnel (such as internal auditors) not having responsibility for their acquisition, use, or disposition.

Cycle Controls. A company's policy governing property acquisitions should be well defined. The system of internal control should provide for the authorization of all capital expenditures, whether they consist of purchases from outside parties or of construction using the company's own materials and labor.

Routine or recurring purchases are normally processed through the purchasing department and are subject to the same controls as other purchases. Acquisitions of more technically specialized assets would probably be handled by engineers or other specialists, and major acquisitions might be handled by top management.

A written policy should be established for rates and methods of depreciation. Forms or schedules for manual systems or EDP software for computing entries for depreciation should be set up. Standardized procedures should be initiated for periodically reviewing depreciation calculations, estimated lives, estimated salvage values, and depreciation methods. Documentation of this review should be required.

Controls over the disposition of property, plant, and equipment should be established in order to preserve the accuracy of the accounting records and to safeguard the assets. For example, no property should be removed or released without a properly authorized order. Retirement orders should be reviewed by a management-level employee, who will evaluate the reason for the disposition and take steps to have the asset disposed of and removed from the accounting records.

Audit Approaches

Systems Tests. The basis for evaluation of internal control includes two phases: (1) a knowledge and understanding of the company's prescribed methods and procedures and (2) a reasonable degree of assurance that these controls are in use and operating as planned. These two phases are referred to as review of the system and tests of compliance, respectively (AU 320.50).

In its simplest form the system for the acquisition of capital assets can be reviewed in conjunction with the purchasing system, especially if there are a large number of homogeneous units (e.g., a fleet of automobiles). In most situations, however, an auditor will decide to test some of the controls over property, plant, and equipment, because acquisitions will not occur frequently enough to assure satisfactory audit coverage merely through auditing the purchasing system. The applicable controls would include

- Authorization and approval of major purchases and the extent of capital-budgeting activities,
- Purchase orders for major acquisitions,
- Evidence of receipt,
- Reviews to assure compliance with accounting policies for determining costs and capitalizing or expensing transactions,
- A check on the regularity and accuracy of depreciation computations,
- A work-order system for plant additions,
- Controls over disposals and retirements, and
- Physical protection and accountability for assets owned.

If a client's system does not include some of these controls, the auditor will locate alternative controls or he will expand his substantive testing of property, plant, and equipment transactions and balances. In addition, an auditor should review and test controls that may exist over reevaluation of useful lives, net realizable values, and salvage values.

Analytical Tests. The nature of analytical tests depends on the individual nature of each client's operations. Some suggested analytical review procedures are listed below:

1. Review changes in the accounts during the period and consider reasonableness in view of other available information, such as cash-flow data, changes in accounts payable or long-term debt, and level of production.
2. Review capital budgets (if used), compare amounts spent with amounts authorized, and determine whether differences were properly approved.
3. Consider the likelihood of property, plant, and equpiment becoming idle during the period. Has there been a significant drop in production at one of the plants? Has there been a change in product lines that might render some machinery idle?
4. Review repairs and maintenance expense accounts for the period and compare with previous period to ascertain whether there are any material items that should have been capitalized.
5. Compare the ratio of depreciation to categories of property, plant, and equipment (exclusive of land) for the period with that of previous periods to evaluate the adequacy of the annual depreciation expense and whether a uniform policy of recognizing depreciation is in effect. Obtain satisfactory explanations for any unusual items noted.

The following tests illustrate the type of ratio and trend analysis that could be performed relating specifically to manufacturing equipment (Arens and Loebbecke, 1976, p. 474):

Ratio or Trend	Use as It Relates to Manufacturing Equipment
Depreciation expense to gross manufacturing equipment cost	Possibility of a material error in computing depreciation
Accumulated depreciation to gross manufacturing equipment cost	Possibility of an error in accumulated depreciation
Monthly or annual comparison of repairs and maintenance, supplies expense, small tools expense, and similar accounts with previous years	Indication of expensing of a capital item or the increasing deterioration of the quality of the equipment.
Gross manufacturing equipment cost to some measure of production	Possibility of idle equipment that has been disposed of

Of course, this type of ratio and trend analysis may be tailored to an analysis of other capital assets as well.

Substantive Procedures

An auditor reporting on a client's financial statements for the first time may find it necessary to extend the examination of property, plant, and equipment to prior periods. Since the long-lived assets are apt to constitute a substantial part of the assets of a company, verification of the authenticity of those assets could be an important part of a first audit. On subsequent audits, the auditor may simply agree the prior year's ending balances to the current year's beginning balances as a starting point. He would then audit current-year additions, which are important because of their long-term effect on the financial statements. Failure to record an asset properly can affect the balance sheet and the income statement (through depreciation) for the entire life of the asset.

Using the results of the analytical review procedures previously mentioned, the auditor should select the nature and extent of the remaining audit procedures required to satisfy the property, plant, and equipment audit objectives. Figure 20.13 identifies some interim and year-end procedures commonly used to achieve those audit objectives; no attempt has been made to provide an exhaustive list, since the procedures must be tailored for each engagement. The listed procedures may satisfy a number of the audit objectives, but each is shown alongside the objective it most directly satisfies.

Information on Changing Prices

Companies that meet certain size parameters are required by SFAS 33 (AC 1072) to disclose specified current cost and constant dollar supplementary information as discussed in Chapter 8.

SAS 27 (AU 553) discusses procedures to be performed by the auditor regarding such information, and this SAS has been specifically augmented by SAS 28 (AU 554). Basically, the two standards require an inquiry of management as to whether the supplementary information has been prepared and presented in accordance with FASB guidelines on a basis consistent with prior periods. This includes inquiring as to the significant assumptions or interpretations underlying the measurement and presentation. SAS 28 adds specific items on which the auditor's inquiries should focus (AU 554.03):

1. The sources of information presented for the latest fiscal year and for the five most recent fiscal years, the factors considered in the selection of such sources, and the appropriateness of their application in the circumstances;
2. The assumptions and judgments made in calculating constant dollar and current cost amounts (such as the methods and timing of acquisition and retirement of assets and the classification of assets and liabilities as either monetary or nonmonetary); and
3. The need to reduce the measurements of inventory and of property, plant, and equipment from (a) historical cost/constant dollar amounts or (b) current cost amounts to lower recoverable amounts and, if reduction is necessary, the reason for selecting the method used to estimate the recoverable amount and the appropriateness of the application of that method.

Audit Objective	Sample Year-End Procedures*	Sample Interim Procedures
Existence. Determine whether there is property, plant, and equipment to support the dollar amount shown in the balance sheet and whether all such property, plant, and equipment has been properly included.	• Check physical existence of property, plant, and equipment, or participate in client's cycle counts of assets and check reconciliation to detailed asset records. • Review leases and determine that the leased assets and the related lease obligations have been properly accounted for.	• Vouch additions and disposals to supporting documentation using summaries showing detailed movements.
Ownership. Determine whether the property, plant, and equipment is owned by the company and whether it is subject to any lien or restrictions.	• Examine, or obtain direct confirmation of, deeds or documents of title where appropriate. • Ascertain whether any items are pledged as collateral.	
Mechanical accuracy. Determine whether the basic mathematical calculation and clerical compilation procedures involved in maintaining the records of property, plant, and equipment costs and the related depreciation have been accurately carried out.	• Obtain schedule of property, plant, and equipment showing cost, depreciation, additions, and disposals. Check adds and cross-adds, agree totals to general ledger, etc. • Test depreciation calculations.	• Test posting and clerical accuracy of general ledger accounts.
Valuation. Determine whether the property, plant, and equipment is fairly stated at cost less an allowance for depreciation in accordance with generally accepted accounting principles.	• Review capitalization policy to assure that all significant capital expenditures are properly capitalized. • Review depreciation policy.	• Vouch additions and disposals to supporting documentation.

* Also often performed at an interim date.

FIGURE 20.13 SAMPLE AUDIT PROCEDURES FOR PROPERTY, PLANT, AND EQUIPMENT

In addition, a comparison should be made of the supplementary information for consistency with (1) the responses obtained from inquiries directed to management, (2) the audited financial statements, and (3) other knowledge obtained during the audit.

The auditor has no obligation to perform any procedures to corroborate management's responses concerning the unaudited supplementary information. Furthermore, the auditor need not expand his report on the audited financial statements to refer to the supplemental information unless the necessary information is omitted or found to depart materially from the FASB guidelines or he is unable to complete the prescribed procedures. This is also discussed in Chapter 8 and SAS 18 (AU 730).

SUGGESTED READING

Grady, Paul. *Inventory of Generally Accepted Accounting Principles for Business Enterprises.* Accounting Research Study 7. New York: AICPA, 1965. This analysis of all generally accepted accounting principles, which became the foundation for APB Statement 4, includes a discussion of property, plant, and equipment.

Lamden, Charles; Gerboth, Dale; and McRae, Thomas. *Accounting for Depreciable Assets.* Accounting Research Monograph No. 1. New York: AICPA, 1975. This monograph analyzes the problems in treatment of depreciable assets including those caused by the differing methods of depreciation.

21

Other Assets and Research and Development

Dane W. Charles

Royalties and license fees entitling the licensee to use an intangible for a future period of time or number of units should be carried as assets to the extent of the unexpired time period or in proportion to the number of units permitted or reasonably estimated to be produced in the future.

Taxes. Refundable income taxes arise from recognition of the tax effects of operating loss carrybacks or other claims for payments made under protest. Though these items are receivables, they are sometimes grouped in prepaid expenses if minor in amount. Offsets to future taxes as a result of recognition of operating loss carryforwards are usually carried in prepaid expenses, if current, or as a noncurrent other asset; where the amount is material it should be set out separately.

Property, franchise, and similar taxes may also be prepaid, with the unexpired asset amount usually being based on the future portion of the period to which the tax is applicable.

Deferred Charges

APB Statement 4 did not define a deferred charge. It said: "Assets also include certain deferred charges that are not resources but that are recognized and measured in conformity with generally accepted accounting principles" (AC 1025.19). Although Statement 4 was not an authoritative standard, it did purport to describe practice as it was at the time (1970). The discussion has broadened over ten years, but the solution regarding which specific costs may be deferred as assets does not appear near.

The *Exposure Draft (Revised) on Elements of Financial Statements of Business Enterprises* (FASB, 1979g) talks about this problem thus:

Incurring costs results in assets only if an enterprise acquires or increases future economic benefits available to it in exchange transactions or through production. Once that conceptual point is made, however, it is also obvious that cost incurred (acquisition cost or sometimes "historical cost") is commonly the attribute that is measured in financial reporting for many assets. Thus, . . . a host of other future economic benefits are now represented in financial statements by some variation of costs incurred to acquire or make them. [par. 166]

Other "deferred costs" that are not themselves assets may be costs of the kinds of assets of an enterprise described in the preceding paragraph. For example, . . . the legal and other costs of successfully defending a patent from infringement are "deferred legal costs" only in the sense that they are part of the cost of retaining and obtaining the future economic benefit of the patent. [par. 167]

. . . [E]nterprises that incur relocation, repair, training, advertising, or similar costs usually receive services (that is, something of value) in exchange for cash paid or obligations incurred. The question that needs to be answered to apply the definition of assets is whether the economic benefit received by incurring those costs was used up at the time the costs were incurred or shortly thereafter or future economic benefit remains at the time the definition is applied. Costs such as those of relocation, repair, training, or advertising services do not *by themselves* qualify as assets. . . . The reason for considering the possibility that they might be accounted for as if they were assets stems from their possible relation to future economic benefits. [par. 168]

The examples do not, of course, preclude accounting for the kinds of costs involved as expenses of the period in which they are incurred, and many, perhaps most, will not be shown as assets at all for practical reasons stemming from considerations of uncertainty or measurement. However, they are not automatically excluded from being considered for a place among the assets. . . . [par. 171]

Accordingly, there are many types of items that might be found in the other asset types of deferred charge category in financial statements; some of the more common ones are discussed below, including those described in the FASB's discussion memorandum (1973a) as costs similar to R&D—marketing research, promotion, start-up, and relocation and rearrangement.

Organization Costs. Organization costs usually represent those costs incurred in forming a business: legal services, filing fees, and stock issuance record costs are representative. The costs are either expensed as incurred or deferred and amortized over a reasonably short period. Since organization costs are deductible for income tax purposes over a 60-month amortization period, this period is also generally used for convenience in financial reporting. Some contend that organization costs should be retained intact as long as the organization exists. However, this is not often done in practice, because the costs are rarely significant.

Generally, an accumulated amortization account is not maintained or presented in financial reporting, and the asset account is usually reduced directly by the periodic amortization.

Debt Issuance Costs. Debt issuance expenses are legal fees, commissions, and printing and other costs incurred in the process of issuing debt instruments. Commonly, these expenses are deferred and amortized, along with the premium or discount, if any, over the life of the debt issue using the interest method (AC 5361.01) to calculate the amount applicable to each period. Less commonly, the straight-line method of amortization is used.

When bonds or other forms of debt are sold with warrants (which entitle the holder to acquire other securities), the warrants usually have value and are recognized as an element of debt issuance expenses. Valuation and other aspects of warrants attached to debt issues are discussed in Chapter 22.

Costs to issue capital shares are applied in reduction of the proceeds from the sale of the securities (see Chapter 26).

Marketing Research. The FASB's R&D discussion memorandum (1973a, p. 18) defines marketing research as an information-gathering activity aimed at:

a. the acceptance by customers of a company's products,
b. the possibility of increasing sales of its products to existing or to new customers, and
c. the possibility of attracting customers for new products which will either replace its current products or lead to new areas of enterprise.

Even before 1973, it was rare to find a deferral of marketing research costs; where it did occur, it was usually based on the cost of research performed by an outside specialist organization. The fact that the FASB neglected to include it by name in the examples in the elements exposure draft (1979) cited at the outset of this section further reinforces the current practice of charging these costs to expense as incurred.

Advertising and Promotion. In this category are various sales promotion activities that disseminate information about a company's products in order to create a favorable emotional response. Most such activities are short-lived and thus as a practical matter are simply expensed. A major campaign, however, sometimes gives rise to questions of whether the cost is deferrable, but in practice deferral was and continues to be infrequent. In the R&D discussion memo, the FASB implied that such costs would be subjected to whatever treatment might apply to R&D (FASB, 1973a, p. 19). Thus the matter was left at rest by the FASB's conclusion to write off all R&D (AC 4211.12). The FASB has again raised the question by listing advertising as a deferral candidate in the elements exposure draft (FASB, 1979g, par. 168).

Of course, unused advertising and promotional supplies, catalogs, and the like—tangible items to be used or already in use by customers—may be deferred if material. Also, advance payments for advertising yet to be run is not expensed until run. An example of deferred promotion costs that contain a mixture of types is shown in Figure 21.4.

Start-Up and Preopening Costs. Start-up costs are often seen in financial statements of companies involved in major new undertakings that involve a *learning*

SALES RECOGNITION AND RELATED PROMOTION COSTS*

Revenue is recognized on sales of products at the time of shipment. Depending on the contractual agreement between the company and the customer, shipments are made either as single mailings, as a series over a number of months, or as single mailings of the remaining issues in a series program. Advance payments from customers are received with the sales order on certain programs.

The company's principal method of selling its products is through direct mail and newspaper or magazine advertisements. Printing and mailing costs of direct mail advertising, the cost of media advertisements and the cost of the collector albums or chests shipped to a customer at the beginning of a series are deferred and charged against income over the shorter of the shipment period or fifty months. For programs where promotion costs are amortized over the shipment period, adjustments are made to the deferred balances by additional charges to expense whenever the company makes downward revisions to series fulfillment expectations. Costs incurred by company personnel in the development of sales programs, including salaries, wages and other administrative expenses, are charged to expense in the period incurred.

* Presented under Summary of Significant Accounting Polices.

FIGURE 21.4   FINANCIAL STATEMENT DISCLOSURE OF DEFERRAL OF PROMOTIONAL COSTS
SOURCE: Franklin Mint Corporation, 1979 Annual Report.

curve—the excess costs, especially of labor, in a new facility that is expected to produce similar or identical products over an extended period. The concept is that, based on engineering studies, the expected normal cost will stabilize at a lower figure than initial costs, which are severely affected by testing, "debugging," training, and so on. When a particularly large program is involved, the deferred costs are often called *program costs* and may be included in the inventory classification if the program will be completed within the business cycle of the contractor, even though that may be several years. (See Chapter 19 regarding program costs.)

Preopening costs are sometimes deferred by retailers, and finance companies may defer costs in excess of revenues during initial periods of a new unit, amortizing them against subsequent profits. A relatively short amortization period, say 12 months, is normal for preopening costs.

There are many similarities between start-up costs in an established enterprise and preoperating costs in a development stage enterprise, and it is puzzling why the FASB did not extend the write-off accounting required in the latter situation. They clearly did not intend to, based on the recognition that while a development stage subsidiary had to write off preoperating costs in its separate financial statements, this write-off could be reassessed and qualify for reinstatement in consolidated financial statements (AC 2062-1.04).

At least one FASB member was displeased with the Board's failure in 1975 to pronounce on other similar costs—and in a way he expressed the disappointment of practicing accountants who were looking forward to much needed guidance in this area:

> Although he agrees with the basic conclusions in this Statement [SFAS 7] that development stage enterprises should use the same accounting principles and prepare the same basic financial statements as established operating enterprises, Mr. Schuetze dissents because he believes that the Board should have addressed the question of accounting for start-up costs before issuing this Statement.... A substantial portion of the costs incurred by many development stage enterprises falls into a broad category that most persons would regard as start-up costs. In Mr. Schuetze's view, neither this Statement nor any other authoritative pronouncement furnishes adequate guidance as to how the recoverability of start-up costs should be assessed or as to how those start-up costs that are capitalized or deferred should be accounted for thereafter. Mr. Schuetze believes that until such a pronouncement is issued the accounting practices of development stage enterprises will vary significantly.... [FASB, 1980d, p. 767]

Relocation and Rearrangement. The costs of changing the location of a plant or office or of rearranging production facilities in a plant—in all instances intended to significantly enhance future profitability and productivity—have occasionally been recognized as deferred charges and amortized against subsequent operations for a relatively short time period, say 3 to 5 years. The justification is the same as that used for deferring any kind of cost: there is a demonstrable probability of obtaining a future economic benefit against which the costs thereof should be matched.

Other Deferred Charges. If it can be claimed and is reasonably evident that a current expenditure has an economic benefit obtainable in a future period, someone somewhere will possibly defer it in a financial statement. There is no way to name the various items that have been deferred from time to time, but the FASB mentioned several in the elements exposure draft (1979, pars. 167-168) that were not described in the above discussion:

- Legal costs,
- Repair, and
- Training.

It can be said that such items are less visible in publicly held corporations, either because the deferral approach is not used, or because the amounts are not consequential and are therefore included within broad captions such as "other assets," without delineation. The former reason is the more likely, given the SEC's traditional skepticism about the realizability of such "assets" out of future operations.

Operating Assets Other Than PP&E

There are several types of business that use information bases as the operating asset enabling the performance of their primary activities. Though these are tangible, they usually have little intrinsic value but may have a substantial value if sold as a unit. Only a few of the many possible types are highlighted below.

Computer Software in Service Bureaus. As indicated earlier in this chapter under Computer Software as R&D, computer software development cost is sometimes deferred by service bureaus and software houses (i.e., companies in the business of preparing software for sale or license to others). The conceptual formulation of software or the translation of knowledge into the design of software is to be expensed (AC 4211-3.07), but other developmental costs may qualify for capitalization. The FASB points out:

> Because the term *product* also encompasses services that are sold, leased, or otherwise marketed to others, this paragraph applies, for example, to costs incurred in developing software to be used by a data processing service bureau or a computer time-sharing company. [AC 4211-3.07]

Educational Programs. Correspondence and residency schools dealing with technical, paraprofessional, self-improvement, and similar subjects have sometimes deferred the costs of course development, amortizing them over the expected useful life of the course program. Because of the SFAS 2 indication that "conceptual formulation and design of possible product or process alternatives" is an R&D activity (AC 4211.09) to be expensed, it is probable that the current practice generally is to write off course development costs when the production costs are not material.

However, there are several companies that produce video and audio cassettes for sale or term use by customers. Production costs are material and are deferred and amortized. An example of a disclosure in this area is shown in Figure 21.5.

Title Insurance Plant. For a long period, accountants could not agree whether the title plant—an integrated and indexed collection of title records covering all

---

DEFERRED EDUCATIONAL PROGRAM PRODUCTION COSTS

Costs incurred by the Company in the original production of, and improvement to, educational courses are capitalized and amortized by the straight-line method over four years.

FIGURE 21.5 DISCLOSURE OF CAPITALIZED PRODUCTION COST OF EDUCATIONAL VIDEOTAPES
SOURCE: URS Incorporated, 1979 Annual Report.

parcels of real estate within a specific geographic area—was a tangible or an intangible asset. Nor could they agree whether it was deemed to have a limited life and therefore subject to amortization. Finally, in SOP 80-1, *Accounting for Title Insurance Companies,* AcSEC put the debate to rest. It resolved that

1. A title plant is a unique tangible asset. If properly maintained it has an indeterminate life and does not diminish in value over time.
2. Costs to construct or purchase a title plant should be capitalized up to the point that the plant can be used to conduct title searches and issue title insurance policies.
3. The title plant should not be depreciated or amortized.
4. After reaching operating status, maintenance costs should be expensed. However, costs of computerizing a title plant or otherwise modernizing the storage and retrieval system—though not part of title plant—may be separately deferred and amortized in a systematic and rational manner.

Auditing Considerations

A systems approach to auditing prepaid expenses, deferred charges, and similar costs generally is not practicable because the volume of transactions is small and control over the transactions is often limited, except as these amounts may arise from basic operating cycles such as purchasing and cash disbursements.

In general, the auditor must establish the reasonableness of the amounts and the likelihood that the costs are properly deferrable as benefits of future periods. It is difficult to obtain assurance that untried and unproven operations will be profitable when commenced, let alone that there will be sufficient margin to absorb such items as deferred start-up costs. In a similar vein, knowing that program costs are deferred on the basis that the learning curve will be achieved (causing unit costs to decline), the auditor must satisfy himself that the program appears realizable. The auditor must test actual experience to see that unit costs do decrease. He may have to use the experience under previous contracts or programs if the current program is in its early stages.

The audit of operating assets such as computer software, educational program costs, and title plant is similar to the audit of self-constructed plant and equipment. (See Chapter 20.)

Analytical Procedures. The auditor will have to deduce the appropriate procedures to fit the specific asset, and he will use certain analytical procedures as a guide to where his audit attention is needed. Typical analytical procedures might be to

1. Compare the account balances to similar items at the previous audit date and determine whether the figures seem reasonable in relation to other information (e.g., increase in level of expenses over the previous year, changes in operations);

2. Review reasonableness of deferral of expenditure in relation to operating results, prevailing economic conditions, immediate industry prospects, client's going concern status, etc.; and

3. Consider appropriateness of deferral under GAAP; sometimes this requires searching for analogies and precedents and could include discussion with other accounting firms or specialists who have experience with the matter.

Substantive Procedures. Results from the analytical procedures guide the auditor in selecting the nature and extent of other substantive procedures. Such other procedures should reflect in their design the likelihood of errors in the financial statements for each transaction/error type affecting the account balance. An interrelationship matrix as described in Chapter 12 is a useful tool for this purpose.

A sample of substantive procedures is given in Figure 21.6. Each procedure may serve more than one purpose in assuring the auditor that all error types are adequately covered.

It must be emphasized here that, as with the audit of cash, there is a tendency for younger audit assistants to overdo the substantive procedures in analyzing and obtaining evidence for items that are relatively minor in relation to the overall financial statements, such as prepaid insurance and prepaid rent. The in-charge accountant should monitor this area to ensure that efforts are focused on the real issues, which invariably deal with the propriety of deferring a cost that is material.

INTANGIBLE ASSETS

Intangibles is a collective term useful to accountants, but the nature of intangibles makes them impossible to define in any categorical way; indeed, the preceding section on deferred charges and similar costs contains some items that could as readily have been discussed in this section. A generally satisfactory concept is that intangible assets lack physical substance and possess economic value. Their value depends on, and varies with, many circumstances. It may rise, fall, disappear, reappear, or be extinguished forever; it all depends.

A list of assets that most accountants would call intangibles at least some of the time includes the following:

Copyrights	Licenses	Operating rights
Trademarks	Patents	Covenants not to compete
Trade names	Franchises	Future interests
Secret processes	Goodwill	Record masters

1. Obtain schedules of prepaid expenses and deferred charges showing, where applicable:
   - Description of item,
   - Asset balance at beginning and end of period,
   - Accumulated amortization at beginning and end of period,
   - Additions giving date of purchase or acquisition and identifying vendor,
   - Amounts amortized or written off in period,
   - Sales proceeds and profit or loss on disposal,
   - Lapsed items, renewal fees, and amounts written off, and
   - Any other relevant information.
   a. Check accuracy of information on schedule.
   b. Add and cross-add schedules.
   c. Trace totals to the general ledger.
   d. Trace balances at beginning of period to prior period's working papers.
   e. Check calculations where appropriate.
2. Obtain direct confirmation of material account balances, if feasible given the nature of the item.
3. Examine underlying documents in support of account balances. Vouch selected items to evidence of authorization required by company policy.
4. Determine whether balances are collectible or otherwise realizable or, alternatively, whether expectations of future benefits are reasonable in relation to prepayments and deferrals.
   a. Ascertain that adequate provision has been made for any items that are overdue or appear doubtful.
   b. Where applicable, ensure all suspense accounts not cleared are fully analyzed and represent amounts that are properly carried as other assets.
   c. Consider management's policy with regard to prepayment and deferral of expenses to evaluate that only those costs attributable to future periods are being carried forward, and that there is reasonable support for retaining such amounts as assets (e.g., continuing value, no adverse change in conditions or expectations).
   d. Where deferred charges are being systematically amortized, ascertain that the method has been consistently applied and that no events have occurred that might lead to a reduction in the write-off period.

FIGURE 21.6   PREPAID EXPENSES AND DEFERRED CHARGES— SUBSTANTIVE TESTS OF BALANCES

Accounting Standards

APB 17, *Intangible Assets* (AC 5141), governs in this area. It was issued in 1970, contemporaneously with APB 16, *Business Combinations* (AC 1091), to resolve in the first instance what to do with goodwill resulting from a business combination (discussed in Chapter 30); however, the APB properly decided to cover all intangibles at the same time. Research and development costs, which were then being capitalized by some companies as intangibles, were specifically excluded from APB 17 (and since resolved in SFAS 2; AC 4211, discussed earlier in this chapter).

Characteristics of Intangibles. A useful way of classifying or thinking about intangibles is presented below (AC 5141.10).

Identifiability. Some intangibles are specifically identifiable, perhaps represented by a legal title that may be used to defend against infringement or other unlawful usage by others. Other intangibles may not be specifically identifiable; goodwill is not, and a purchased business territory may not be (see, for example, AC 1091-1.08(c)-.09).

Manner of acquisition. Intangibles may be purchased from others or may be developed internally. Purchased intangibles may or may not be specifically identifiable, whereas by definition internally developed intangibles will be specific.

Expected period of benefit. Some intangibles have a duration limited by law or contract; others have an indeterminate or indefinite life. For example, a copyright is valid for the life of the author plus 50 years.

Separability from the enterprise. An intangible with a legal title is separable and thus may be salable. The general goodwill of an enterprise is not separable, but it may be salable in a sense through franchising.

Capitalizable Costs. When intangibles are purchased from others, they are recorded at purchase cost. Costs of developing specific intangibles such as patents are also capitalized, but only out-of-pocket items such as legal fees and application and filing fees are included. The more basic costs of development, which are akin to research and development, are expensed as incurred. Of course, self-developed intangibles that are not specifically identifiable and are inherent in a continuing business as a whole are not capitalized (AC 5141.24).

Amortization. APB 17 postulates that all intangibles eventually lose their value and thus must be reduced by systematic charges to income over the estimated benefit period. For specific intangibles, legal, regulatory, or contractual provisions may set a maximum useful life, but certain other factors also need to be taken into account (AC 5141.27):

- Provisions for renewal or extension may alter a specified limit on useful life;
- Effects of obsolescence, demand, competition, and other economic factors may reduce a useful life;
- A useful life may parallel the service life expectancies of individuals or groups of employees;
- Expected actions of competitors and others may restrict present competitive advantages;
- An apparently unlimited useful life may in fact be indefinite, with benefits incapable of reasonable projection; and

- An intangible asset may be a composite of many individual factors with varying effective lives.

To put a limit on the variety of answers obtainable under the above guidelines by different evaluators, APB 17 specifies that the maximum amortization period for any intangible is 40 years (AC 5141.29). The method of amortization is to be straight-line unless it is demonstrated that some other method is more appropriate (AC 5141.30).

Periodic Reassessment. As with any asset, intangibles must be assessed periodically to ascertain whether any permanent diminution in value needs to be recognized in addition to normal amortization. Also, each intangible right must be assessed periodically by management to see if the amortization term continues to be reasonable. If not, adjustment of the term may be necessary based on the actual facts and circumstances. As a practical matter, diminution in value often is recognized through shortening the amortization term. Every so often, an intangible balance could be completely written off based on the occurrence of a single event. (For example, see the problem with operating rights in Chapter 36.)

Auditing Considerations

The auditing problems with and procedures for intangibles are like those described earlier in this chapter for prepaid expenses, deferred charges, and similar items. A systems approach is not practicable, because the volume of transactions invariably is small and internal control systems are not often designed specifically to embrace intangibles.

Substantive Procedures. Sample procedures in addition to those discussed earlier might include the following:

1. For additions and disposals, vouch to
   a. Independent supporting evidence, and
   b. Appropriate authorizations or board minutes.
2. Scrutinize unusual items and obtain satisfactory explanations for them.
3. For disposals:
   a. Check calculation of profit or loss on disposal and trace to earnings statement accounts, and
   b. Determine that proper reductions of carrying amounts have been made.
4. For amounts amortized or written down, vouch to appropriate authority. Determine whether policy is consistent with prior year.
5. Confirm title or ownership rights:
   a. Inspect renewal receipts or payments as evidence of title at date of renewal, and
   b. Consider obtaining direct confirmation of title.
6. Consider, discuss with responsible personnel, and document in working papers the reasonableness of amounts at which intangibles are carried in the financial statements. Intangible rights that have been allowed to lapse or are no longer used should be considered for write-off. Where book amounts appear excessive, discuss with management and evaluate management's decision regarding the write-off of any excess amount.

NONMARKETABLE SECURITY INVESTMENTS

Very broadly, all assets employed in the pursuit of profit are investments. This generalization is not very helpful; in fact, there is a host of definitions and interpretations that characterize the accounting for investments. In this chapter the discussion will focus on nonmarketable security investments in 50%-or-less-owned companies. (Marketable equity and debt securities are covered in Chapter 17, and more-than-50%-owned companies are discussed in Chapter 31.)

Investments in the form of securities display a marvelous variety. There are many kinds of debt instruments, preferred and common stocks, and numerous combinations of warrants, voting rights, convertibility, and other special conditions. All of these complicate the accounting.

Investments can be passive or can bring a measure of influence over the investee. Generally, this influence comes with equity investments of 20% to 50% ownership. At more than 50%, control is presumptively established and the rules change.

General Accounting Standards

Marketable, as applied to an equity security in SFAS 12 (AC 5132.07(b)), means an equity security for which sales prices or bid and ask prices are currently available on a national securities exchange or in the over-the-counter market publicly reported by the National Association of Security Dealers Automatic Quotations System (NASDAQ) or the National Quotations Bureau, Inc. *Nonmarketable,* as applied in this chapter, means any security—equity, debt, or hybrid—that does not meet the FASB's definition of marketable. This includes stock that is restricted from sale by governmental or contractual requirements for longer than one year from the financial reporting date. And of course it includes securities changing classification from marketable to nonmarketable as discussed in FASB Interpretation No. 16, *Clarification of Definitions and Accounting for Marketable Equity Securities that Become Nonmarketable* (AC 5132-5).

Nonmarketable investments are recorded at their acquisition cost, which includes commissions, transfer fees, and legal fees. Premium or discount on the acquisition of debt investments is a part of the security cost and is amortized on the interest method (AC 5361). When a marketable security becomes nonmarketable, its carrying amount will be the lower of cost or market at the date it changes status.

If purchases are made at differing costs, a consistent method of determining cost for individual units should be followed, so that a proper matching can be made upon sale. Possible methods include specific identification; average cost; first-in, first-out; and last-in, first-out.

Assessment of Value. When value falls significantly below cost, an evaluation of whether or not the impairment is temporary is necessary. If the investment is scheduled for redemption at a fixed date and price, if the security holder intends and is financially able to hold to maturity, and if there are no reservations regarding the ability of the debtor to pay, the temporary impairment is ignored, and there is no write-down. Otherwise it is necessary to examine clues from the performance of similar securities, through information obtained from analyzing the investee's financial statements, cash-flow potential, security market conditions, industry conditions, economic conditions, and other relevant factors.

If the security holder determines that impairment is not temporary, a write-down will be reflected in the financial statements, and a new cost (i.e., carrying amount) established for the investment.

Good Faith Valuations. Since there is no established market for nonmarketable investments, it is often necessary for value to be determined by the investor or by a specialist engaged by the investor. The goal is to arrive at the amount that a willing buyer would pay a willing seller, for purposes of determining whether a write-down is needed and, if so, how much.

While no single standard has been established, factors that should be considered can be drawn from ASR 118, *Accounting for Investment Securities by Registered Investment Companies* (1970). The main factors include (1) analytical data relating to the investment, such as earnings multiples, market value of a similar freely traded security, and yield to maturity, (2) the nature and duration of restrictions (if any) on disposition of the security, and (3) the forces that influence the market where the securities would be purchased and sold. Other considerations might include the type of security, financial standing of the issuer, availability of current financial statements, size and period of holding, discount from market value of similar but unrestricted securities at the time of purchase, special analysts' reports, and any transactions or offers with respect to such restricted or nontraded securities.

ASR 118 was aimed at Small Business Investment Companies (SBICs), which are licensed by the Small Business Administration and generally used to provide venture capital to small businesses. The investments of SBICs are usually active and in small, start-up situations (often involving combinations of debt, convertibles, warrants, and preferred and common shares with special rights).

Such investments are generally carried at cost until there is evidence that value is other than cost. The investor in an SBIC generally encounters the same situation as the SBIC itself in valuing the investment and likewise carries it at cost until there is evidence that value is other than cost. Evidence is thus a matter of good faith valuation, as discussed above.

Valuation problems are discussed at length in the industry audit guide, *Audits of Investment Companies* (AICPA, 1973g, pp. 35-37), which should be referred to for a more detailed discussion of the valuation process. Also see the discussion in Chapter 38 regarding investment companies.

Other Valuation Approaches. For investments in securities based on future cash flows, such as real estate, it may also be necessary to obtain the opinion of independent experts. When real estate is an operating property leased to others, a common approach is to determine the present value of the future rent amounts and adjust the aggregate so determined by the estimated residual value, if any, at the end of the lease term.

With respect to "trade relation" investments (e.g., major customer or vendor) in securities not accounted for under the equity method, in addition to the evaluations discussed above there must be a current assessment by management of the value of any intangible benefits asserted to support the excess of cost over market or other indicator of current value.

Disclosure

Nonmarketable securities carried at cost should be separately identified among other assets if amounts are material, with an indication that cost is the basis used. Where premium or discount is being amortized, that fact may be disclosed by a caption phrase such as "at cost adjusted for amortization of premium and discount." If there is some indication of a temporary impairment in value, disclosure (usually by footnote) is required for material amounts.

Equity Investees Other Than Joint Ventures

If an investment in voting stock gives the investor the power to exercise significant influence over operating and financial policies of the investee, the investment must be accounted for on the equity method. Under APB 18, *The Equity Method for Investments in Common Stock* (AC 5131), there is a presumption that ownership of 20% or more of the voting stock delivers significant influence and that less does not. In each case, evidence may exist to support application of the equity method when less than 20% is owned or not to support the equity method when more than 20% is owned. Kennecott Copper, a recent example, is 14.3% owned by Curtiss-Wright, which discloses that it has significant influence and thereby includes 14.3% of Kennecott's earnings in its consolidated earnings under the equity method.

Under the equity method broadly, the investment is initially recorded at cost, is increased by the investor's share of the investee's net income and antidilutive capital transactions, and is reduced by dividends, share of investee's net losses and dilutive capital transactions, and amortization of a difference between cost at acquisition and the then-proportionate share of fair-valued net assets of the investee.

In the investor's income statement, the proportionate share of the investee's results of operations is shown as a single-line item (except where the investee has extraordinary items that would be material in the investor's income statement). Taxes must be provided by the investor as to his share of investee income, as discussed later.

Figure 21.7 summarizes features in applying the equity method, based on AC 5131.19 and 4096. Some of these matters are discussed below, while others are covered in Chapter 31.

Applicability. Although APB 18 applies to investments in common stock of corporations and does not expressly apply to investments in partnerships and unincorporated joint ventures, its provisions (except those relating to income taxes) are applicable in accounting for investments in noncorporate investees (AC U5131.008-.012). Income taxes should be provided on the profits accrued by investor-partners regardless of the tax basis employed in the partnership return. The tax liabilities applicable to partnership interests relate directly to the partners, and the accounting for income taxes generally contemplated by APB 11 (AC 4091) is appropriate.

The equity method should only be used by business enterprise investors. This requirement excludes estates, trusts, individuals, investment companies and eleemosynary organizations, but includes business partnerships and unincorporated joint ventures.

a. Intercompany profit and loss must be eliminated.

b. Where there is a difference between cost and underlying equity at acquisition, the fair-valuing principles in APB 16 (AC 1091.88) should be followed.

c. The investment is shown as a single amount in the investor's balance sheet; likewise for the income statement, except for extraordinary items.

d. Extraordinary items of the investee that are material in the investor's income statement are shown by the investor as extraordinary.

e. Investee capital transactions are accounted for by the investor as he would account for them in a subsidiary—no gain or loss.

f. Gain or loss on sale is based on carrying amount at the sale date.

g. The investor's share of earnings may be recorded based on the investee's most recent available financial statements; the time lag should be consistent from period to period.

h. A loss in value that is other than temporary should be recognized by the investor.

i. The investor should not reduce the investment account below zero as a result of losses of the investee unless he has an obligation to provide further financial support.

j. The investor should provide for income taxes on his share of investee net income based on which is more probable—distribution in the form of dividends or realization on disposal (AC 4096.07). This *does not* apply to subsidiaries and joint ventures.

k. The investor's share of investee earnings is based on earnings less preferred dividend requirements.

l. When ownership falls below 20%, the investment account is carried forward as cost, without subsequent or retroactive adjustment.

m. When an investment first reaches 20%, the equity method is applied retroactively as in a step acquisition.

n. Goodwill or negative goodwill must be amortized based on APB 17.

FIGURE 21.7   EQUITY METHOD APPLICATION FEATURES

Attributes of Significant Influence. Evidence of ability to exercise a significant influence (AC 5131.17) includes representation on the board of directors, participation in policy-making processes, material intercompany transactions, interchange of managerial personnel, and technological dependency. The absence of concentration of other shareholdings is also a positive factor, but the use of the equity method is not negated simply because someone else has a substantial or majority interest in the investee.

APB 18 (AC 5131.17) states that there is a presumption the investor has the *ability* to exercise significant influence *in the absence of evidence to the contrary* if he owns 20% or more of the investee. It should be emphasized that the opinion does not require the investor to actively display significant influence but only to have the *ability* to exercise such influence. Examples of evidence to the contrary might be that

1. The investor is legally prohibited from exercising influence,
2. Hostile investee stockholders are effectively able to keep the investor from participating in investee policy decision making,
3. The investee is a regulated company, and legal or practical problems make it impossible for the investor to impact the investee, or
4. There are overriding exchange restrictions, controls, or other uncertainties with regard to foreign investments.

Examples of the ability to exercise significant influence where less-than-20% ownership exists could be where the investor is also a primary creditor (or guarantor) or the principal customer and, as a result, exercises a practical influence much greater than his stock ownership percentage.

In the fall of 1980 the FASB added to its agenda a project to address certain aspects of the equity method, including how litigation between an investor and an investee affects the propriety of the investor using the equity method. In particular, an interpretation is planned to explain that the numeric presumptions in APB 18 do not eliminate the need to apply judgment to determine whether an investor has the ability to exercise significant influence over operating and financial policies of an investee.

Adjustment of Equity Investment Carrying Amount. Investments that are appropriately valued on the equity method must be adjusted periodically to reflect the change in the investor's proportionate equity in net assets of the investee. Thus, the investment account is to be revised each reporting period to reflect the investor's equity in the results of operations of the investee, the dividends received from the investee, and any changes in the investee's capital structure that affect the investor's proportionate interest.

Any difference at the acquisition date between the cost of the investment and the equity in net assets of the investee is required to be accounted for as if the investee were a consolidated subsidiary. If the cost exceeds the investor's proportionate equity and is not attributable to specific accounts of the investee, the excess (goodwill) is required by APB 17 (AC 5141) to be amortized over a reasonable period not to exceed 40 years. An excess of equity over cost (negative goodwill) would be amortized over a lesser period, say 5 to 10 years.

The investor's share of an investee's losses may exceed the investor's cost. Ordinarily, the investor's financial statements would stop reflecting these losses when the investment account is reduced to zero. Equity in losses would still be recognized, however, if the investor is committed to provide further financial support to the investee, such as through legal obligations or voluntary assumption of liabilities. Also an investor should not provide for additional losses when the return to profitable investee operations seems assured. For example, a nonrecurring loss may reduce the investment below zero while the profitable operating pattern of the investee is unimpaired.

Intercompany Profits and Losses. In applying the equity method, APB 18 requires intercompany profits and losses to be eliminated until realized by the investor or investee (AC 5131.19(a)). Although ARB 51 (AC 2051.13) provides for complete elimination of intercompany profits or losses in consolidation, it also states that the elimination of intercompany profit or loss may be allocated proportionately between the majority and minority interests. Whether all or a proportionate part of the intercompany profit or loss should be eliminated under the equity method depends largely on the relationship between the investor and investee.

From the perspective of the minority investor in a nonsubsidiary investee, it is not necessary to eliminate 100% of the profit. Instead, he must eliminate intercompany profit in relation to his proportionate common stock interest. The elimination is the same whether the transaction is "downstream" (i.e., a sale by the investor to the investee) or "upstream" (investee to investor). The following two examples taken from an unofficial APB staff interpretation (AC U5131.006-.007) illustrate how these eliminations might be made. Given: an investor owns 30% of the common stock of an investee; the investment is accounted for under the equity method; and the income tax rate for both investor and investee is 40%.

Downstream. The investor sells inventory items to the investee. At the investee's balance sheet date, the investee holds inventory for which the investor has recorded a gross profit of $100,000. The investor's net income would be reduced $18,000 to reflect a $30,000 reduction in gross profit and a $12,000 reduction in income tax expense. The elimination of intercompany profit might be reflected in the investor's balance sheet in various ways: one is that the investor might present $12,000 as a deferred tax charge (a timing difference under APB 11; AC 4091) and $30,000 as a deferred income credit.

Upstream. The investee sells inventory items to the investor. At the investor's balance sheet date, the investor holds inventory for which the investee has recorded a gross profit of $100,000. In computing the investor's equity "pickup," $60,000 ($100,000 less 40% of income tax) would be deducted from the investee's net income and $18,000 (the investor's share of the intercompany gross profit after income tax) would thereby be eliminated from the investor's equity income. Usually, the investor's investment account would also reflect the $18,000 intercompany profit elimination, but the elimination might also be reflected in various other ways, such as by reducing the investor's inventory $18,000.

Income Tax Allocation. APB 24, *Accounting for Income Taxes—Investments in Common Stock Accounted for by the Equity Method (Other than Subsidiaries and Corporate Joint Ventures* (AC 4096), requires that investors provide income taxes on their share of investee's undistributed earnings either as if the earnings had been received as dividends or as if the investment had been disposed of based on all available facts and circumstances. The APB reached this conclusion on the premise that only control—more-than-50% ownership—can justify that undistributed earnings are invested indefinitely (AC 4096.07).

Additional guidance is also provided (AC 4096.10) regarding income taxes when investments cease to be accounted for by the equity method.

In situations where an investment in a particular security of a nonsubsidiary is of such a magnitude that it is appropriately accounted for under the equity method, and it is also a marketable security, APB 18 requires:

A loss in value of an investment which is other than a temporary decline should be recognized the same as a loss in value of other long-term assets. Evidence of a loss in value might include, but would not necessarily be limited to, absence of an ability to recover the carrying amount of the investment or inability of the investee to sustain an earnings capacity which would justify the carrying amount of the investment. A current fair value of an investment that is less than its carrying amount may indicate a loss in value of the investment. However, a decline in the quoted market price below the carrying amount or the existence of operating losses is not necessarily indicative of a loss in value that is other than temporary. All are factors to be evaluated. [AC 5131.19(h)]

Thus, the investment should be specifically evaluated to determine whether particular adverse factors require a reduction in the carrying amount. The potential for maintaining the investment indefinitely, and the investor's holding intentions, should be considered. If there is substantial uncertainty as to ultimate realization, and if it is deemed inappropriate to recognize this by a provision through income for the estimated permanent diminution in value, a qualification of the auditor's report may be required.

Income Statement Presentation of Equity in Earnings. There are several ways in which investors reflect their equity in earnings of 50%-or-less-owned companies. Where the investee has no extraordinary, unusual, or similar-type items that would be proportionately material in relation to the investor's financial statements, the investor's share of the investee's after-tax net income is most often shown after arriving at operating income (before taxes). For example the investor's income statement might show:

Revenues (listed)	$ XXX
Less costs and expenses (listed)	XXX
Income from operations	XX
Equity in earnings of XYZ Co., 27% owned	XX
Income before taxes	XX
Provisions for income taxes	X
Net earnings	$ X

It is also common for investors to include the equity amount as a separately delineated item within revenues. Where the equity investee exists to provide products or services to the investor, the equity in earnings may be offset (with parenthetical or footnote disclosure, if material) against the line item, grouped in costs and expenses, that contains the investee's product or service charges.

In all the above presentations, the investor's income tax provision will include an amount for taxes on the undistributed portion of the equity in earnings, as required by APB 24 (AC 4096). Such amount is not to be offset against the equity in earnings, as it is the investor's tax provision, not the investee's.

When the investee's financial statements contain extraordinary items (AC 2012.20), prior-period adjustments (AC 2014.10-.12), or the cumulative effect of a change in accounting principles (AC 1051.19(b)), and the investor's proportionate share of any of these would be material in the financial statements of the investor, such amounts are to be similarly presented in the investor's financial statements. This situation creates complexities in the investor's income tax provision; unlike the approach described in the preceding paragraph, the investor would apportion the income tax amount required to be provided under APB 24 (AC 4096) to these investee items that fall below after-tax income from operations.

Another problem sometimes encountered is caused by the investee having an unusual item *or* an infrequently occurring item that is separately reported in its financial statements (AC 2012.26). Where the investor's proportionate share of this amount is material in the investor's financial statements, it may (but is not required to) be set out parenthetically in the investor's earnings statement. For example:

Equity in earnings of XYZ Co., 27% owned (including $25,000,000 pretax gain on disposal of certain oil producing properties).

Unusual items may not be shown net of tax on the face of the income statement. Thus it is especially problematic to set out a material proportionate share of an investee's unusual item in the investor's financial statements in any manner other than parenthetically. Of course, footnote discussion may be the best solution, as there are no proscriptions there against tax netting.

It must be kept in mind in all of these presentational variations that the determination of what is extraordinary, unusual, or infrequently occurring is determined for each party—the investee and the investor—by reference to its own circumstances. Thus an item that qualifies as extraordinary for the investor, for example, might be ordinary for the investee, and vice versa. This does not change whatever the relationship of the parties. The result could be the same type of transaction showing up as ordinary and extraordinary in a single income statement, but there may be enough breadth in the definition of extraordinary, unusual, and infrequent to avoid this somewhat ludicrous occurrence.

Financial Statement Disclosures. Required disclosures with respect to equity investees, if material, include (AC 5131.20)

- The accounting policies of the investor with respect to investments in common stock;
- The name of each investee and the percentage ownership;
- The reasons any significant less-than-20% investment (to be named) is valued by the equity method;
- The reasons any significant 20%-or-more investment (to be named) is not valued by the equity method;
- The difference between the carrying amount of an investment and the underlying equity in net assets, and the accounting treatment of the difference;

- The aggregate quoted market price of the investment, if available;
- Summarized information as to investees' assets, liabilities, and operating results, if the investments are material in relation to the investor; and
- Material effects of possible conversions, exercises, or contingent issuances of investees' securities.

Advances and loans are often made to equity method investees, and these are usually combined in the balance sheet under a caption such as "investment in and advances to XYZ Company." The footnote details conforming to the above list will then provide the breakout of advances and loans for material investees.

Joint Ventures

An investment may be made in a particular situation in the form of a joint venture (this discussion includes 50%-owned companies), which is defined as an entity that is owned, operated, and jointly controlled by a small group as a separate, specific business project for the mutual benefit of the ownership group (AC 5131.03(d)). Each venturer commonly participates in the overall management, and significant decisions commonly require the consent of each of the *venturers* (regardless of ownership percentage) so that no individual *venturer* has unilateral control (AICPA, 1980i, p. 1). The venturers will not necessarily have equal ownership interests, and a venturer's share could be as low as 5% or 10%, and as high as 70% or 75%. These situations differ from what is encountered in the normal application of equity method or consolidation accounting, in that joint venturers have special rights and obligations assuring their significant influence even at ownership percentages less than 20%.

A joint venture may be organized as a corporation, partnership, or undivided interest. If organized as a corporation, APB 18 applies, and the investment in the corporate joint venture would be accounted for following the equity method. (However, income tax allocation is done differently, as discussed later.) If the investment is in a joint venture in partnership or unincorporated form, an AICPA staff interpretation of APB 18 says that many of the provisions of that opinion are appropriate in accounting for such investments (AC U5131.008-012).

Other than APB 18 and the unofficial interpretation, there is almost no definitive guidance in the professional literature about accounting by investors for their investments in joint ventures. Recently this void has been receiving some attention by an AcSEC task force on joint venture accounting, which has prepared an issues paper (AICPA, 1979q) and submitted it to the FASB for further consideration. The major problems identified in that paper, and AcSEC's advisory conclusions are discussed below.

Defining a Joint Venture. There are conflicting definitions of joint venture if one looks beyond the authoritative definition given in APB 18 (AC 5131.03(d)). The legislative record of APB 18 shows that the APB had a difficult time reaching a definition, but the members were no doubt impelled to reach some conclusion given the lack of any definition in the professional literature and the increasing use of joint ventures including 50%-owned companies. The end result of the APB's effort, however, limited the definition to a corporate joint venture, given the APB's primary focus on the equity method of accounting for investments in common stock.

AcSEC reached the advisory conclusion that *joint venture* should be defined very broadly to encompass all entities, regardless of legal form, that have certain characteristics—with the central distinguishing characteristic being point control of major decisions. AcSEC specifically recommends adoption of the definition used in the Canadian Institute of Chartered Accountants Handbook (Section 3055):

> A joint venture is an arrangement whereby two or more parties (the venturers) jointly control a specific business undertaking and contribute resources towards its accomplishments. The life of the joint venture is limited to that of the undertaking which may be of short or long-term duration depending on the circumstances. A distinctive feature of a joint venture is that the relationship between the venturers is governed by an agreement (usually in writing) which establishes joint control. Decisions in all areas essential to the accomplishment of a joint venture require the consent of the venturers, as provided by the agreement; none of the individual venturers is in a position to unilaterally control the venture. This feature of joint control distinguishes investments in joint ventures from investments in other enterprises where control of decisions is related to the proportion of voting interest held.

Accounting for Investments in a Joint Venture. AcSEC arrived at the following advisory conclusions in this area (AICPA, 1979q, par. 52):

a. The portion of APB 18 dealing with investments in joint ventures should be reexamined.
b. The one-line equity method as described in APB 18 should be required for investments (other than off–balance sheet financing arrangements[11]) in joint venture entities (whether incorporated or unincorporated) that are subject to joint control, except that the cost method should be permitted for investments not material to the investor.
c. If an entity that otherwise meets the definition of a joint venture is, in fact, controlled by majority voting interest or otherwise, the entity should be required to be accounted for as a subsidiary of the controlling investor and to be fully consolidated by that investor.
d. If an entity that otherwise meets the definition of a joint venture is not subject to joint control, by reason of its liabilities being several rather than joint as in some undivided interests, investments in the entity should be required to be accounted for by the proportionate consolidation method.
e. The use of the same method in the balance sheet and income statement should be required.
f. Disclosure of supplementary information as to the assets, liabilities, and results of operations should be mandatory if the investments in the aggregate are material.

Although AcSEC did not conclude how an investor should account for a difference between carrying amount and valuation for assets contributed to a venture, it did conclude, by narrow majorities, that from the standpoint of the venture itself (par. 53):

---

1 See Chapter 23.

a. The creation of a joint venture establishes a reporting entity separate from its owners that requires a new basis of accounting for its assets and liabilities.
b. Assets contributed to the venture should be recorded at the amount agreed on by the parties, which is assumed to be determined by reference to fair market value, but not in excess of the assets' fair market value.

In an addendum to the issues paper, AcSEC pointed out the need for consideration of the problem of investor accounting when cash distributions from a venture exceed the investment carrying amount, but could not reach an advisory conclusion. (When such an excess results from tax benefits, it is often referred to as the *negative basis problem*—see Chapter 27.)

Financial Statement Presentation. The AcSEC issues paper identifies seven possible approaches in displaying joint ventures in the investor's financial statements, as briefly described below. While four of these approaches are considered acceptable in the advisory conclusions above, they are not interchangeable, and each is applied where the specified circumstances exist.

One-line equity method. This is the approach discussed in APB 18 (AC 5131.11) and described in the preceding investment section of this chapter. This would remain the prevalent method (see advisory conclusion b above).

Expanded equity method. Though there are several variations, the essence of this proposal is to include a proportionate share of the assets and liabilities in the venturer's statement, but without combining directly. For example, the last item in current assets might be "share of current assets of joint venture." (See Dieter and Wyatt, 1978.) This approach was not recommended by AcSEC.

Proportionate consolidation. Under this method the investor's proportionate share of the venture's assets, liabilities, income, and expenses is combined with the similar items in the investor's financial statements. This method has been in use for some time in the real estate and oil and gas industries, and has received approbatory mention in an unofficial AICPA staff interpretation (AC U5131.012). It is recommended by AcSEC (advisory conclusion d) to be limited to those situations where the venture's liabilities are several, not joint (i.e., the investor is obligated for a specific portion of the venture's debt).

Full consolidation. When a venturer has control, AcSEC concluded that he should fully consolidate as if the venture were a subsidiary (advisory conclusion c).

Cost method. This approach is to be permitted only for immaterial investments in ventures, as has been the case in practice thus far.

Fair market value method. This method is not recommended, because it would change the historical cost measurement basis underlying present GAAP. Essentially, it carries the investment (presumably on a one-line basis) at its fair market value; changes therein would be income or loss. Apart from the probable difficulty of arriving at market value in all but those few cases where a venture's shares are publicly traded, this approach would be akin to accounting for marketable securities classified as current assets (AC 5132.11).

Combination of methods. One method might be used in the investor's balance sheet and another in the income statement. For example, see Figure 21.8. As a practical matter, in the relatively few instances where this has been used, only two of the foregoing methods—one-line and proportional consolidation—are involved. AcSEC specifically recommended against this method (advisory conclusion e).

Income Tax Allocation. In APB 23, *Accounting for Income Taxes—Special Areas* (AC 4095), the APB reached a conclusion on income tax allocation for investments in joint ventures (in AC 4095.15-.18) different from that prescribed in APB 24 (AC 4096) for other equity method investments. Specifically, for ventures that are essentially permanent in duration, the investor should not provide for income taxes on undistributed earnings of joint ventures when there is sufficient evidence that the venture has invested or will invest the undistributed earnings indefinitely or that the earnings will be remitted in a tax-free liquidation. This is the same rule used for subsidiaries.

For limited life ventures, the timing difference approach in APB 11 (AC 4091) is required, but the rates used for tax allocation would be based on those used for APB 18 investees as described in AC 4096.08.

Auditing Investments

The auditor's purpose in applying procedures to investments (see also Chapter 17) is to obtain evidential matter to corroborate the amounts at which the investments are stated, whether at cost, realizable value, or equity in net assets. If the investment is carried on the equity method, the auditor must also examine evidential matter to corroborate the amounts reported as the investor's share of earnings or losses and other transactions of the investee.

In order to accomplish the audit objectives discussed in Chapter 12, the auditor must be satisfied as to existence, ownership, classification, cost or carrying amount of investments, periodic income or loss attributable to the investments, and the adequacy of any related disclosures. The brief comments that follow are based on AU 332, *Evidential Matter for Long-Term Investments,* which should be referred to for an expansion on these subjects.

Existence and Ownership. These can ordinarily be established by either physical inspection or written confirmation from an independent custodian of the securities. If loans or advances are involved, the written confirmation should be obtained from the debtor or trustee for bondholders.

Classification. An investment is nonmarketable and noncurrent based partly on management's investment objectives as documented by management for the auditor in the representations letter. In addition to securing the representations letter, the auditor looks at minutes of board of directors' meetings and investment committee meetings and considers whether the classification is appropriate in light of the company's financial position, working capital requirements, debt agreements, and

NOTE C—ADVANCES TO AND EQUITY IN CONSTRUCTION JOINT VENTURES

Assets of the construction joint ventures consist primarily of operating funds, progress payments due under contracts and construction equipment. Liabilities are primarily trade payables and notes payable guaranteed in certain instances by the Company and the other coventurers. A condensed combined balance sheet for the joint ventures follows:

	December 31,	
	1979	1978
Assets	$79,290,000	$100,970,000
Liabilities	52,587,000	46,167,000
Net Equity	26,703,000	54,803,000
Equity Applicable to Other Coventurers	19,271,000	41,247,000
Equity Applicable to Company	7,432,000	13,556,000
Less Notes Payable to Joint Ventures	1,500,000	9,172,000
Advances to and Equity in Construction Joint Ventures	$ 5,932,000	$ 4,384,000

Notes payable to construction joint ventures consist of demand notes at interest rates from 5% to 7%. These notes represent advances of excess funds and a consequent reduction in the Company's investment in the joint ventures. The notes normally remain outstanding until near the completion of the contracts at which time they are retired through the distribution of earnings. The 1978 Balance Sheet has been reclassified to conform to the 1979 format.

The Company's proportionate share of joint venture revenues and costs included in the Consolidated Statements of Earnings follows:

	Years Ended December 31,	
	1979	1978
Contract Revenues	$21,540,000	$23,705,000
Contract Costs	20,819,000	22,929,000
Earnings Before Taxes	$ 721,000	$ 776,000

FIGURE 21.8 EXAMPLE OF JOINT VENTURE ACCOUNTING—EQUITY METHOD IN BALANCE SHEET, PRO RATA CONSOLIDATION IN INCOME STATEMENT
SOURCE: Arundel Corporation, 1979 Annual Report.

the like. If the company's needs imply that an investment will have to be sold to provide operating capital, it should be reclassified as a current asset and stated at net realizable value.

Carrying Amount. Evidential matter pertaining to the carrying amount of APB 18 equity investments, income and losses attributable to the investments, and other transactions of the investee may be obtained from audited financial statements of the investee. Or, if these are not available, unaudited financial statements, regulatory examination reports, and the like may be useful. However, the auditor for the investor may need to perform, or have performed by the investee's auditor, audit procedures to supplement the unaudited information (see AU 543). In some circumstances, as with real estate, mineral rights, and other natural resources, the auditor may need to use the work of a specialist (AU 336) in obtaining satisfaction.

The auditor must obtain information relating to intercompany transactions so as to ascertain that intercompany profit eliminations are properly made, and he will obtain by inquiry and through other evidence an indication of management's intent with respect to holding, obtaining dividends from, or reinvesting earnings in an investee; this is necessary to determine the proper method for income tax allocation.

The auditor has a difficult task in satisfying himself that the investor does or does not have the ability to exercise significant influence. The criteria for this determination were described earlier in this section and have been most problematic when a client asserts that it has overcome the presumption that the ability to exercise significant influence does not exist below 20% ownership. Problems also exist when there are signs that influence does not exist above 20%, such as litigation between the parties. The auditor must in the end do sufficient work to be satisfied that the basis for valuing the investment is supported and that appropriate disclosures as specified earlier are reflected in the investor's financial statements.

Cutoff. Differences in investor's and investee's year-ends are often encountered. The condition often results in a time lag in reflecting equity by the investor. A time lag is acceptable but must be consistent from period to period. The auditor for the investor also needs to make inquiry as to events and transactions from the date of the investee's financial statements to the date of the investor auditor's report to see whether any material events or transactions have occurred that require reflection or disclosure in the investor's financial statements.

When unaudited interim financial statements of a material investee are used to coincide with the investor's year-end, audit or review procedures will need to be applied by either the investor's or investee's auditor to corroborate the appropriateness of the amounts included in the investor's financial statements.

Auditors' Report—Valuation Uncertainties. In the case of securities for which market quotations cannot be obtained, current values would ordinarily be determined by management or the board of directors. The independent auditor does not function as an appraiser and is not expected to substitute his judgment for that of management; rather, he is to review all information considered by management and ascertain that the procedures followed appear to be reasonable and adequate.

If the independent auditor is unable to satisfy himself as to the reasonableness of

Board of Directors
ABC Investment Co.

We have examined the statement of net assets of ABC Investment Co. as of December 31, 19X1, and the related statement of changes in net assets for the year then ended.

Except as explained in the following paragraph, our examination was made in accordance with generally accepted auditing standards and, accordingly, included such tests of the accounting records and such other auditing procedures as we considered necessary in the circumstances.

As discussed in Note B to the financial statements, securities amounting to $7,285,000 (24% of net assets) have been valued at current value as determined by the directors. We have reviewed the procedures applied by the Board of Directors in valuing such securities and have inspected underlying documentation; while in the circumstances the procedures appear to be reasonable and the documentation appropriate, determination of current values involves subjective judgment which is not susceptible to substantiation by auditing procedures.

In our opinion, subject to the possible effect, if any, on the financial statements of the valuation of securities determined by the Board of Directors as described in the preceding paragraph, the financial statements referred to above present fairly the net assets of ABC Investment Co. at December 31, 19X1 and the changes in its net assets for the year then ended, in conformity with generally accepted accounting principles applied on a basis consistent with that of the preceding year.

FIGURE 21.9   EXAMPLE OF AN AUDITOR'S REPORT FOR VALUATION UNCERTAINTIES

the amounts at which such investments are stated, appropriate qualification of the auditor's opinion should be made, as discussed in Chapter 16.

The example of the auditor's report in Figure 21.9 assumes satisfaction with the existence of assets and all other matters except valuation of securities. Usually, investments are not material, and the example, taken in part from ASR 118, is rarely appropriate for enterprises other than investment companies.

SUGGESTED READING

AICPA. *Illustrations of Accounting for Joint Ventures.* Financial Report Survey 21. New York, 1980. This book, based on a NAARS survey of over 8,000 published annual reports, illustrates the application of various methods of accounting for joint ventures in the financial statements of ventures.

Dieter, Richard, and Wyatt, Arthur. "The Expanded Equity Method—An Alternative in Accounting for Investments in Joint Ventures." *Journal of Accountancy,* June, 1978, pp. 89-94. In addition to describing several variations of the expanded equity method approach possibility, the authors effectively describe the range of other methods used in joint venture investment accounting.

Gellein, Oscar, and Newman, Maurice. *Accounting for Research and Development Expenditures.* Accounting Research Study No. 14. New York: AICPA, 1973. This study, which was extensively referred to in the discussion memorandum that preceded SFAS 2, recommended segregating R&D into *continuing research* and *substantial development projects.* The former would be currently expensed, whereas under specified circumstances the latter could be deferred, at least in part. Should R&D accounting be reconsidered, ARS 14 may become a significant influence.

International Accounting Standards Committee. *Accounting for Research and Development Activities.* International Accounting Standard 9. New York: AICPA, 1978. This standard, which *does not* take precedence over SFAS 2 in the U.S., would allow deferral of R&D costs if (1) the project is clearly defined and the costs are separable; (2) the product or process is technically and commercially feasible; (3) the company has the intent and the resources available to complete the project and market the product or process; and (4) there is a clear indication that the product or process can be marketed or its usefulness to the company can be demonstrated.

22

Debt and Interest

Robert N. Waxman

THE NATURE OF LIABILITIES

The issues of whether every credit in the balance sheet (except shareholders' equity) is a liability as is suggested by *Accounting Terminology Bulletin 1* (AC 1025.19, fn. 5), and whether every liability (e.g., executory contracts) is to be recorded, have been the subjects of constant debate both at the FASB and among accountants. The meaning of *liability* has been discussed in accounting literature over the years and has been described in various ways.

APB Statement 4 says that liabilities are "economic obligations of an enterprise that are recognized and measured in conformity with generally accepted accounting principles. Liabilities also include certain deferred credits that are not obligations but that are recognized and measured in conformity with generally accepted accounting principles" (AC 1025.19). This latter category would comprehend items such as unearned revenue, deferred income taxes, negative goodwill, and deposits. APB Statement 4 goes on to say that economic obligations of an enterprise are "its present responsibilities to transfer economic resources or provide services to other entities in the future" (AC 1023.19); that liabilities "are recorded when obligations to transfer assets or provide services in the future are incurred in exchanges" (AC 1027.07); and that a "liability is measured at the amount of cash to be paid discounted to the time the liability is incurred" (AC 1027.07).

In its *Exposure Draft (Revised) on Elements of Financial Statements of Business Enterprises,* the FASB defines liabilities as "probable future sacrifices of economic benefits stemming from present legal, equitable, or constructive obligations of a particular enterprise to transfer assets or provide services to other entities in the future as a result of past transactions or events affecting the enterprise." Further, the draft says that "an enterprise commonly settles or satisfies liabilities by paying cash, transferring goods, or providing services according to the terms of the agreement in which the liability arose, but some liabilities are satisfied by using assets or incurring other liabilities" (FASB, 1979g).

When the FASB issues its final statement on elements of financial statements, a uniform and authoritative definition of the term "liability" should at last be available. The placement of financial statement elements within the conceptual framework project can be observed in Chapter 2.

Obligations With Debt Characteristics

The FASB rejected the concept of "legal debt" as a determinant for lease capitalization. In SFAS 13 (see Chapter 23), the Board noted "that the determination of whether a lease obligation represents debt in the strict legal sense would of necessity rest primarily on court decisions, and that such decisions have arisen almost entirely from litigation involving bankruptcy, reorganization, or taxation" (AC 4053.071).

. Whether a capital lease is legal debt or not, the lessee records it both as an asset and as a liability. The obligation is required to be separately identified in the balance sheet as "obligation under capital lease," and is subject to the same considerations as other obligations when classifying them as either current or noncurrent in classified balance sheets. In adopting SFAS 13, the FASB settled on the right to use the property concept rather than an economic obligation concept.

Although capitalized leases may not necessarily be debt in the legal sense, they have many of the same characteristics as debt, and the financial obligation recorded for a capitalized lease is as real and as burdensome as a note due to a bank.

After the passage of ERISA in 1974, some financial analysts considered unfunded pension liabilities as accrued liabilities that were not funded, and they factored these unfunded amounts into the various ratios they use in evaluating a company.

ERISA notwithstanding, unfunded prior service costs (supplemental actuarial value), unfunded vested benefits, and insured unfunded vested benefits are not recognized by employers as liabilities. Nonrecognition in the financial statements is based on the assumption that the employer is a going concern and has no plans to terminate the pension plan.

Under APB 8 (AC 4063) (see Chapter 24), prior service costs are required to be recognized in the income statement over a reasonable period, using a rational and systematic actuarial method, after the inception or amendment of a pension plan. It was the view of the APB that prior service costs do not represent expenses of any prior period. They represent the cost of prospective retirement benefits and relate to periods after the date that a pension plan was established or amended.

Ways to Raise Money

Among the possible ways to raise intermediate and long-term debt funds are

1. Public debt offering through an underwriter (see Chapter 26 for a general discussion of letters to underwriters for public financings);
2. Private placements with banks, pension funds, insurance companies, private venture capital firms, or investment management companies;
3. Financing with a Small Business Investment Company;
4. Domestic and/or international project financings;
5. Public sector financing (e.g., industrial revenue bonds, housing authority bonds, general obligation bonds, and special tax and revenue bonds);
6. Factoring with banks and finance companies; and
7. Mortgaging property.

Typical sources of short-term funds may be (1) commercial banks, (2) commercial paper, (3) factors and finance companies, and (4) customers and suppliers.

Debt Classifications

Classifying debt can be complicated, since to accommodate the changing business environment over the years, financial institutions and their lawyers have created debt instruments with many combinations of characteristics. As a result, notes and bonds take various forms. Debentures, floating rate notes, convertible bonds, equipment trust certificates, income bonds, and participating bonds are only a few of the common types.

To add to the complexity of financing, some debt may be secured and some may not (e.g., debentures). If secured, debt can be further classified by the type of assets pledged as security. Debt can be secured by a mortgage or by company-issued collateral trust bonds and notes, guaranteed bonds, or equipment trust certificates.

Debt can also be categorized by the purpose of the issue and the issuing agency. For example, the purpose of a debt issue can be classified into those with a prior lien, a refunding issue, or a purchase-money mortgage. The issuing agency may be a commercial enterprise, railroad, utility, municipality, or quasi-government agency (e.g., toll road, sewer and water district).

Adding to the complexity of classifying debt are an enormous number of descriptive features such as denomination of the principal, interest rate, interest payment dates, repayment terms, whether issued with warrants, if subordinated, and many others.

Municipal Bonds

While this chapter deals primarily with the debt issued by business enterprises, a very significant portion of the debt issued annually in the United States is issued by government bodies. The federal government and federal government agencies issue huge amounts of paper backed by the credit of the United States government. Such debt has few accounting problems that will concern the professional accountant and it will therefore not be discussed in this volume.

The debt of municipalities and other nonfederal government entities is generally encompassed by the term *municipal bonds;* these bonds create special accounting problems. Such bonds, whose interest is tax exempt to the holder, are generally recorded in a separate set of municipal accounts titled the long-term debt accounts, in which the debt is shown as a liability and offset by an entry titled "proceeds from future taxation" or an equivalent. The bonds are usually issued on a serial basis, and principal repayments and interest payments are treated as a budgetary charge (and a charge in the statement of general fund operations) in the year paid. Such debt is further discussed in Chapter 34.

SHORT-TERM DEBT

ARB 43 defines current liabilities as those whose liquidation "is reasonably expected to require the use of existing resources properly classified as current assets, or the creation of other current liabilities" (AC 2031.07). That paragraph goes on to say that the current liabilities classification "is intended to include obligations for items which have entered into the operating cycle . . . and debts which arise from operations directly related to the operating cycle. . . ." In ASR 148, however, the SEC says that commercial paper and other short-term debt should be classified as a current liability even though the issuer's intention is to roll over the debt at maturity, unless (1) the borrower has a noncancelable binding agreement from a creditor to refinance the debt, (2) the refinancing extends the maturity date beyond one year (or current operating cycle, if longer), and (3) the borrower's intention is to exercise this right.

Obligations Expected to Be Refinanced

In 1975, SFAS 6 (AC 2033) was issued as a response to the inconsistencies between ARB 43 and ASR 148 and to the diverse accounting that was found in practice concerning short-term obligations that were expected to be refinanced on a long-term basis. These obligations were included in the balance sheet in several ways: as current liabilities, as long-term liabilities, or as a class of liabilities distinct from both current and long-term (i.e., *interim* or *intermediate* debt).

For purposes of understanding this statement, certain definitions are in order (AC 2033.02). *Short-term obligations* are those scheduled to mature within one year after the balance sheet date. For those enterprises that use the operating cycle concept of working capital, debt related to assets within an operating cycle that is longer than one year is considered short term if the assets are classified as current. *Long-term obligations* are those scheduled to mature beyond one year (or the operating cycle, if applicable) from the balance sheet date. *Refinancing a short-term obligation on a long-term basis* means either replacing it with a long-term obligation or equity securities, or renewing, extending, or replacing it with short-term obligations for an uninterrupted period extending beyond one year (or the operating cycle, if applicable) from the balance sheet date. Thus, despite the fact that the short-term obligation is scheduled to mature during the ensuing fiscal year (or operating cycle), it will not require the use of working capital during that period.

SFAS 6 requires that short-term obligations arising from transactions in the normal course of business and to be paid in customary terms be included in current liabilities (AC 2033.08). Examples are accounts payable; collections received in advance of the delivery of goods or performance of services; accruals for wages, salaries, commissions, rentals, and royalties; and income and other taxes.

Short-term obligations such as commercial paper, construction loans, the currently maturing portion of long-term debt, short-term obligations arising from the acquisition or construction of noncurrent assets, and notes given to a supplier to replace accounts payable that originally had arisen in the normal course of business and been due in the customary terms may be excluded from current liabilities, but only on two conditions: (1) the entity must intend to refinance the obligation on a long-term basis (AC 2033.10) and (2) the intent to refinance must be supported by an ability to consummate the refinancing (AC 2033.11). The ability to consummate the refinancing can be demonstrated by

1. Issuing a long-term obligation or equity securities after the balance sheet date, but before the balance sheet is issued, for the purpose of refinancing the short-term obligation on a long-term basis (AC 2033.11(a)), or

2. Before the balance sheet is issued, entering into a financing arrangement that clearly permits the enterprise to refinance the short-term debt on a long-term basis on terms that are readily determinable. In this case, however, all the following conditions must also be met (AC 2033.11(b)):
   a. The agreement may not expire within one year (or operating cycle) from the balance sheet date;
   b. The agreement may not be cancelable by the lender, prospective lender, or investor, except for violation of a provision with which compliance is objectively determinable or measurable;

c. The obligations incurred under the agreement may not be callable within one year;
d. No violation of any provision in the financing agreement may exist at the balance sheet date;
e. There may be no available information indicating that a violation has occurred between the balance sheet date and the date of issuance; or if one has occurred, it must have been cured or a waiver obtained; and
f. The lender, prospective lender, or investor with whom the agreement has been made must be expected to be financially capable of honoring the agreement.

When long-term debt or equity securities are issued after the balance sheet date, the amount of short-term debt excluded from current liabilities must not exceed the proceeds of the debt or equity securities issued. When there is a financing agreement, the amount of short-term debt excluded from current liabilities must be reduced to the amount available for refinancing under the agreement (when this amount is less than the amount of the short-term obligation). The amount must be further reduced if there are restrictions (e.g., as to transferability of funds) and other agreements or if the funds obtainable under the agreement will not be available to liquidate the short-term obligation.

If the amount obtained under the agreement fluctuates in relation to the entity's needs or in proportion to the value of collateral, the amount excluded from current liabilities must be limited to a reasonable estimate of the minimum amount expected to be available at any date from the scheduled maturity of the short-term debt to the end of the fiscal year or operating cycle. If no reasonable estimate can be made, the entire outstanding short-term debt should be included in current liabilities.

Gaps in Ability to Finance Long-Term. FASB Interpretation No. 8 (AC 2033-1) states that a short-term obligation would be classified as current if it is repaid after the balance sheet date by using current assets, even though long-term financing is subsequently obtained before the issuance of the balance sheet. However, debt is considered noncurrent if the long-term debt is issued prior to the repayment of the short-term obligation.

Replacing a short-term debt with another short-term debt between the balance sheet date and the date the balance sheet is issued is not, by itself, evidence of the enterprise's ability to refinance a short-term debt on a long-term basis. Examples indicating an ability to refinance on a long-term basis are (1) a replacement made under the terms of a revolving credit agreement that provides for renewal or extension of a short-term obligation for an uninterrupted period extending beyond one year from the balance sheet date and that meets the other ability-to-refinance conditions and (2) a replacement made by a roll-over of commercial paper accompanied by a standby credit agreement that meets the other ability-to-refinance conditions.

Subjective Acceleration Clauses. SFAS 6 creates some uncertainty in practice. It prohibits the long-term classification of short-term debt that is in existence at the balance sheet date but is to be replaced under a long-term financing agreement entered into before the balance sheet is issued, when the agreement is "cancelable for violation of a provision that can be evaluated differently by the parties to the agreement" (AC 2033.11, fn. 4). This statement does not, however, address the question of the classification of preexisting long-term debt, or debt initially issued as long-term, that is subject to similar cancelation provisions. Since some long-term loan agreements contain such *subjective acceleration clauses* (which could result in acceleration of principal payments), a question arises whether the full amount of such a loan must be classified as a current liability, notwithstanding long-term scheduled maturities. In practice, the mere presence of such a clause in a long-term agreement does not require that the amounts payable thereunder be classified as current. (See Figure 22.1 for an example of subjective acceleration clause disclosure.)

Revolving Credit Agreements

Assume the following situation. An enterprise borrows under a revolving credit agreement expiring in more than one year. After the balance sheet date, the company repays the entire amount. Should the amount borrowed be classified as long-term in the balance sheet? Although authoritative literature is not conclusive on this matter, SFAS 6 (AC 2033) specifically addresses the classification of short-term obligations that are expected to be refinanced with long-term obligations; and ARB 43 defines *current liabilities* as "obligations whose liquidation is reasonably expected to require the use of existing resources properly classifiable as current assets...." (AC 2031.07). In current practice, some companies classify such debt as current liabilities, some classify it as long-term. The long-term liability advocates say that although the corporation uses current assets to pay down the borrowing after the balance sheet date, the fact that it may borrow at its discretion mitigates the requirements of ARB 43.

The loan agreement contains certain restrictive covenants relating to, among other things, payment of dividends and incurrence of additional indebtedness. Further, the Company's ratio of total liabilities to tangible net worth (as defined in the agreement and including oil and gas properties at the present worth of future net income) must not, at any time, be more than 1 to 1, and the Company must maintain a current ratio of at least .8 to 1. The loan agreement also contains a subject acceleration clause which, if exercised by the bank, could cause an acceleration of the due date. However, the bank has advised that such clause will not be evoked during the year ended May 31, 1979, unless the Company is in default of any of the remaining covenants of the loan agreement.

FIGURE 22.1   EXAMPLE OF SUBJECTIVE ACCELERATION CLAUSE DISCLOSURE
SOURCE: Galaxy Oil Company, 1978 Annual Report.

Disclosures Under GAAP

Short-term debt, notes, or loans payable are usually listed as the first item in the current liabilities section of the balance sheet. Revolving obligations, such as demand notes or commercial paper, should be classified as current debt unless the criteria of SFAS 6 for exclusion from current liabilities are met. Current maturities of long-term obligations, although usually the last item under current liabilities, are sometimes grouped with short-term notes under a suitable caption. Short-term notes payable should be itemized in the balance sheet (or footnoted) by type of payee—bank, finance company, trade, affiliates, directors, officers, stockholders. They may also be itemized by their significant terms—demand loans, notes against which assets are pledged.

The balance sheet (or footnotes) should clearly indicate the nature and amount of collateral supporting notes or loans and the seniority/subordination status of the debts. Obligations endorsed or guaranteed by others, or collateralized by assets belonging to others, should be disclosed. The disclosures required by SFAS 6 are (AC 2033.15):

1. Total of current liabilities if a classified balance sheet is used; and
2. If a short-term obligation is excluded from current liabilities, the notes to the financial statements must include a general description of the financing agreement and the terms of any new obligations incurred or expected to be incurred, or equity securities issued or expected to be issued, as a result of the refinancing.

Companies that issue drafts in payment of debts should deduct the amount of such outstanding drafts from cash, rather than show them as a liability. If the total of drafts or checks outstanding exceeds the cash balance, a bank overdraft is deemed to exist for accounting purposes. Current practice permits the offsetting of an overdraft in one bank account with a balance in another bank account if the balance available to offset the overdraft is not in any way restricted, and is not part of a minimum balance requirement of a loan or other agreement. If any portion of an overdraft is not offset by a free balance in another bank account, it should be presented as a current liability.

Disclosures Required by SEC

The SEC's disclosure requirements (for both accounts payable and short-term notes payable) are found in Rule 5-02-19 of Regulation S-X, essentially as follows:

(a) Disclose the amounts payable to (1) banks for borrowings; (2) factors or other financial institutions for borrowings; (3) holders of commercial paper; (4) trade creditors; (5) related parties; (6) underwriters, promoters, and employees, other than related parties; and (7) others.

(b) Footnote the amount and terms (including commitment fees and conditions under which lines may be withdrawn) of unused lines of credit for short-term financing. Identify the amount of these lines supporting commercial paper arrangements.

Requirements relating to short-term debt also include Schedule IX, *Short-term borrowings* (Regulation S-X, Rules 5-04 and 12-10):

(a) Information required by this schedule may be presented in Management's Discussion and Analysis of Financial Condition and Results of Operations—Item 11 of Reg. S-K.

(b) Schedule requires the following information for each period for which an income statement is required to be filed: Aggregate short-term borrowings (ASTB) at the balance sheet dates categorized by amounts payable to banks, factors or other financial institutions, and holders of commercial paper. State (i) general terms (also formal provisions for the extension of the maturity) of each category of ASTB, (ii) the weighted average interest rate, (iii) the maximum amount of ASTB outstanding at any month-end during the period, (iv) the average ASTB outstanding during the period, and (v) the weighted average interest rate for such ASTB during the period. Describe the means used to compute the average ASTB outstanding and the average interest rate.

See Figure 22.2 for an example of short-term borrowing information disclosure.

When an SEC filing includes both consolidated and parent-company-only financial statements, the disclosures relating to the consolidated financial statements are usually sufficient. When a filing includes separate financial statements of an unconsolidated subsidiary, such as a finance subsidiary, the disclosures should be made for the subsidiary. If, however, the filing includes financial data of a subsidiary in a note to the consolidated financial statements, the disclosures relating to the consolidated financial statements usually suffice. The disclosures apply to arrangements with both domestic and foreign lending institutions.

SHORT-TERM BORROWINGS

Short-term borrowings consist principally of commercial paper issued in the United States and bank loans of foreign subsidiaries. The Company entered the commerical paper market on November 1, 1979.

Domestic borrowings at December 31, 1979 were $137,122,000; the weighted average interest rate on such borrowings was 13.8 percent. There were no domestic borrowings in 1978.

At December 31, 1979, unused domestic bank lines of credit, all of which were in support of commerical paper borrowings, were $70,000,000. Commercial paper borrowing arrangements do not require compensating balances; however, an average commitment fee of $\frac{1}{4}$ percent annually is required.

At December 31, 1979, the Company's foreign subsidiaries had available approximately $57,000,000 in unused lines of credit. Generally, these credit lines call for interest rates ranging from five percent to 64 percent; however, arrangements relating to certain currencies are subject to floating rates. In connection with credit availability, and in support of outstanding bank loans, the Company maintains nominal amounts on deposit with lending banks. For the most part, these credit lines do not require commitment fees and are cancelable at the option of the Company or the banks.

FIGURE 22.2   DISCLOSURE OF SHORT-TERM BORROWING INFORMATION
ADAPTED FROM: Schering-Plough, 1979 Annual Report.

Credit lines and commitments that may be offered by financial institutions as a marketing device, and accepted by corporations without any intention of their use and not as part of their financial plan, do not require disclosure. Unused lines of credit disclosed as supporting commercial paper or other debt arrangements should include only usable lines. Usable lines are those used to support commercial paper less lines needed to meet clean-up provisions (i.e., provisions that require borrowers to retire credit extended at a bank at some specified interval, for a specified period). Total lines outstanding are, therefore, not necessarily a measure of the total credit available on a continuing basis. Similarly, if a corporation has lines arranged with several banks that in total exceed borrowing levels permitted under existing lending agreements, disclosure should be limited to the usable amounts.

LONG-TERM DEBT

Bonds and Notes

When an enterprise issues a bond or note, it promises two kinds of future payments: the payment of principal—a fixed sum—at specified dates and the payment of interest at specified dates. Interest on bonds is expressed as a percentage of the face amount. This is known as the *nominal or coupon rate.* But the interest expense actually incurred on bonds is determined by the price at which the bonds are sold. This is known as the *effective interest rate or yield,* and it depends on the current money market. If the money market prices the bonds to yield an amount identical to the coupon rate, the bonds will sell at face amount. If the bonds are sold with a greater yield than the coupon rate, they will sell for less than face amount, or at a *discount.* Conversely, if the bonds are sold with a yield that is less than the coupon rate, they will sell for more than face amount, or at a *premium.*

For example, suppose an entity issues a $300,000 term bond due in ten years, and the coupon rate is 9%, paid annually. At current money market conditions, the bond must yield 12%. The selling price and discount are computed as follows:

Present value of $300,000 due in ten years at 12%	$ 96,592
Present value of $27,000 per year for ten years at 12%	152,556
Bonds sold for	$249,148
Discount on bond	$ 50,852

Serial Bonds

The bond discussed in the above example had a single fixed maturity date. Another type of bond, the *serial bond,* provides for the repayment of principal in a series of periodic installments. As with term bonds, serial bonds may sell at a discount or a premium because of differences between the coupon rate and the yield demanded in the money market. The proceeds of a serial bond issue are a little more difficult to compute, but the approach is essentially the same.

For example, suppose an entity issues a $300,000 serial bond to be repaid in the amount of $60,000 per year. The coupon rate is 9%, paid annually, but the bond is sold to yield 12%. The selling price and discount are computed as follows:

End of Year	Principal and Interest Due			Present Value of 1 (12% table)	
1	$60,000	+	$27,000	× .892857	$ 77,679
2	$60,000	+	$21,600	× .797194	65,051
3	$60,000	+	$16,200	× .711780	54,238
4	$60,000	+	$10,800	× .635518	44,994
5	$60,000	+	$ 5,400	× .567427	37,110
	Bonds sold for				$279,072
	Discount on bonds				$ 20,928

Convertible Bonds

Simply put, a *convertible bond* is one that may be exchanged for an agreed-on number of shares of stock. Suppose a company sells a 6.5% subordinated debenture that is convertible at the holder's option into common stock at $29 per share. No fractional shares will be delivered on conversion of each bond, but a cash payment will be made in lieu thereof. Thus, the holder of each bond with a $1,000 face value will receive 34 shares of common stock and $14 cash. Further, the debentures have a call provision—that is, they are redeemable at the company's option, in whole or in part, at an initial redemption price of 106.5% plus accrued interest, with declining premiums thereafter. In this example, the issuance and conversion is recorded as follows:

	Dr.	Cr.
Cash	$98,693,000	
Deferred debenture costs	1,307,000	
6.5% convertible subordinated debentures		$100,000,000
To record the sale of 25-year debentures at beginning of year one.		
6.5% convertible subordinated debentures	45,000,000	
Cash		630,000
Deferred debenture costs		541,098
Common stock, $1 par value		1,530,000
Additional paid-in capital		42,298,902
To record the conversion of debentures into 1,530,000 shares of common stock and write off 45% of unamortized debenture costs at end of year two.		

When the bonds are redeemed pursuant to a call provision, the accounting should follow that prescribed in APB 26 (AC 5362) and SFAS 4 (AC 2013), discussed later in this chapter.

The terms of convertible bonds generally include (1) an interest rate that is lower than the issuer could establish for nonconvertible debt, (2) an initial conversion price that is greater than the market value of the common stock at the time of issue, and (3) a conversion price that does not decrease, except to prevent dilution. In most cases the bonds are also callable at the option of the issuer, and are subordinated to nonconvertible debt.

Convertible debt offers a number of advantages to both the issuer and the purchaser. For the issuer, it provides a lower interest rate than nonconvertible debt. Further, the issuer may view convertible debt as essentially a means of raising equity capital. If the market value of its common stock should increase, the issuer can force conversion of the convertible bonds into common stock by calling the issue for redemption. Thus, the issuer can effectively terminate the conversion option and eliminate the debt. If the market value of its common stock does not increase sufficiently to make conversion of the debt attractive, the issuer will still have received the benefit of the cash proceeds to the scheduled maturity dates at a relatively lower interest cost. For the purchaser, convertible debt provides both the status of a creditor and the opportunity to gain from price appreciation of the common stock.

APB 14 holds that "no portion of the proceeds from the issuance of . . . convertible debt securities . . . should be accounted for as attributable to the conversion feature [because of the] inseparability of the debt and the conversion option . . . [and] practical difficulties" (AC 5516.10).

Previously, authoritative accounting literature (APB 10, pars. 8 and 9) had assigned a value to this conversion feature, in effect debiting discount on convertible bonds payable and crediting additional paid-in capital. This feature was measured by the difference between the price at which the debt was issued and the estimated price for which it would have been issued without the conversion privilege.

When convertible bonds are issued, a portion of the proceeds is logically attributable to the conversion feature. This factor is reflected in a lower coupon rate of interest. But unlike stock purchase warrants for which a market price based on arm's-length trading can be determined, the value of the conversion feature cannot be established in the marketplace. Therefore, the APB reversed their position and suspended (in APB 12, pars. 11-15) the requirements of APB 10 while it studied the problem. Its solution was APB 14.

Many accountants continue to feel that the position taken in APB 14 is theoretically unjustified. They believe the conversion option is so important that it cannot simply be ignored, and that there is not enough difference between convertible debt and debt issued with warrants to support a different accounting treatment.

Debt With Stock Purchase Warrants

Unlike convertible debt, debt issued with detachable warrants to purchase stock is usually issued with the expectation that the debt will be repaid when it matures. The detachable warrants often trade separately from the debt itself. Thus, the two elements of the security exist independently and may be treated as separate securities. For example, a corporation may issue $50,000,000 of 10.5% subordinated debentures with warrants to purchase 3,750,000 shares of common stock. Each $1,000 debenture might have 75 warrants attached, with the debentures and warrants being separately transferable. The warrant may entitle the holder to purchase one share of common stock by tendering cash (or an equal principal amount of debentures) and may be exercisable for a period of ten years. If the market value of each common share at the time of issue is, say, $6.50, the warrant price for the share might be around $10 (depending on market conditions and the identity of the issuer).

APB 14 provides that the

> portion of the proceeds of debt securities issued with detachable stock purchase warrants which is allocable to the warrants should be accounted for as paid-in capital. The allocation should be based on the relative fair values of the two securities at the time of issuance [which is generally the date when an agreement as to terms has been reached and announced, even though there may be further actions, such as directors' or stockholders' approval]. Any resulting discount or premium on the debt securities should be accounted for [using the interest method]. The same accounting treatment applies to issues of debt securities (issued with detachable warrants) which may be surrendered in settlement of the exercise price of the warrant. [AC 5516.14]

When stock purchase warrants are not detachable and the debt security must be surrendered in order to exercise the warrant, the two securities taken together are considered substantially equivalent to convertible debt, and no portion of the proceeds is considered attributable to the nondetachable warrant feature.

Some corporations issue "units" composed of, for instance, a $1,000 principal amount of subordinated convertible debenture, 100 shares of common stock, and 20 warrants. Here, too, an allocation should be made to additional paid-in capital for the portion of the proceeds of the debenture issue attributable to the detachable stock purchase warrants.

When warrants are exercised, the consideration tendered (cash or the debt security) is considered as proceeds from the issuance of common stock. When warrants are repurchased, additional paid-in capital is charged for the full purchase price.

Bond Sinking Fund

Some bond indentures require that a sinking fund be established for the retirement of the bonds. The indenture may require the company to periodically redeem a fixed amount of principal. The price for all redemptions through the sinking fund is usually the principal amount of the bonds redeemed plus the interest accrued to the redemption date. Most companies have the privilege of purchasing bonds on the open market to cover their future sinking fund requirements. Bonds so purchased and held in treasury to satisfy future sinking fund requirements are shown as a deduction from the related long-term debt.

Bond Issue Costs

A variety of costs are incurred in preparing and selling a bond issue. They may include underwriting discounts, legal fees, accounting fees, other professional fees, engraving, printing, registration fees, and others. APB 21 (AC 4111.15) says that issue costs should be reported in the balance sheet as a deferred charge. When costs treated in this way are material, the total amount is generally amortized on a straight-line basis over the period the debt is outstanding.

Periodic Interest Payments

Most interest payments are made semiannually, quarterly, or in a few instances monthly. Accounting for the interest expense in these situations presents no special accounting problems. When a bond is sold between interest dates, interest at the coupon rate is sold from the last interest payment date until the sale date. The buyer pays the seller for the accrued interest, since the debtor is obligated to pay the full amount of interest to the bondholder when due.

Disclosures Under GAAP

Long-term debt is itemized by lender (or by groups when there are a number of similar lenders, e.g., "banks") in the same manner as indicated earlier for short-term debt. The important features and provisions of the debt should also be disclosed, including (1) interest rate; (2) due dates and amount of debt installments; (3) collateralized property, partial or full; (4) maintenance of working capital requirements; (5) dividend restrictions; (6) convertible features; (7) defaults in principal, interest, or other covenants of the debt agreement; and (8) subordination.

Long-term debt should be segregated between the current and the long-term portions. As to unearned discounts or premiums, APB 21 (AC 4111.15) provides that the discount or premium be reflected in the balance sheet as a direct deduction from, or addition to, the face amount of the debt; further, when there is a discount or premium, the description of the note should include the effective interest rate.

Treasury bonds held but not retired are not an asset, and should be deducted from bonds payable shown in the balance sheet.

An example of a long-term debt footnote is shown in Figure 22.3.

Disclosures Required by SEC

Certain long-term debt disclosures in addition to those mentioned above are specifically required by the SEC. The following may be used as a reference to the pertinent Reg. S-X rules and schedules:

1. Bonds, mortgages, and similar debt: Rule 5-02-22.
2. Significant changes in bonds, mortgages, and similar debt: Rule 4-08(f).
3. Reacquired indebtedness: Rule 4-06.
4. Indebtedness to related parties, noncurrent: Rule 5-02-23.
5. Schedules to be filed in support of most recent audited balance sheet: Schedule XII (Rule 12-29)—mortgage loans on real estate.
6. Schedule to be filed for each period for which an income statement is filed: Schedule IV (Rule 12-05)—indebtedness of and to related parties.

5. Long-Term Debt
The major components of long-term debt are as follows:

	1979	1978
8½% notes payable to banks (due in equal quarterly installments from 1980 to 1984)	$23,438,000	$25,000,000
10% subordinated debentures due in 1999 (annual sinking fund payments required beginning in 1990)	3,212,000	3,159,000
11% subordinated debentures due in 2004 (annual sinking fund payments required beginning in 1989)	29,672,000	
6⅝% to 7⅞% capitalized industrial revenue bonds due in varying amounts to 2001)	4,349,000	4,582,000
Other	2,652,000	2,459,000
	$63,323,000	$35,200,000

The 8½% notes payable represent funds borrowed under a $25,000,000 term loan agreement with several banks.

The subordinated debentures are subordinate in right of payment to all senior indebtedness of the company and are redeemable at the company's option at face value. The debentures are stated net of discount, which is being amortized over the life of the debentures. The discount for the 10% debentures amounted to $1,113,000 and $1,166,000 at June 30, 1979 and 1978, respectively. The 11% debentures were issued as of May 1, 1979 in exchange for 754,208 shares of the company's common stock, and are net of discount totaling $487,000 at June 30, 1979.

Maturities of long-term debt during the five years ending June 30, 1984 are $2,221,000, $6,833,000, $6,841,000 $6,770,000 and $5,188,000, respectively.

Property with a depreciated cost of $4,887,000 (primarily related to capitalized revenue bonds), and real estate sold for which the company holds all-inclusive trust deed notes receivable of $2,288,000 are pledged as collateral for long-term debt at June 30, 1979.

Certain of these loan agreements contain provisions that limit the amount of long-term debt, creation of liens and guarantees, redemption of capital stock, and payment of cash dividends. Under the most restrictive of these provisions, approximately $16,400,000 was available at June 30, 1979 for the payment of cash dividends and for the redemption, purchase or other acquistions of capital stock.

FIGURE 22.3   DISCLOSURE OF LONG-TERM DEBT INFORMATION
SOURCE: Monogram Industries, Inc., 1979 Annual Report.

Distinguishing Between Debt and Stockholders' Equity

In some situations, the dividing line between debt and stockholders' equity may be very thin. Certain equity securities look exactly like debt; conversely, since interest is tax deductible and a dividend is not, there may be situations where debt has all the characteristics of an equity security, but is legally considered a liability.

Mandatory Redemption Preferred Stock. Some forms of preferred stock are very similar to debt, but legally are equity securities. In ASR 268, the SEC amended Regulation S-X to require the separate balance sheet classification of redeemable preferred stock subject to mandatory redemption requirements or whose redemption is outside the control of the issuer. The SEC believes that because of the required redemption, "such securities have characteristics similar to debt and should . . . be distinguished from permanent capital."

The SEC requires, in filings made with it, balance sheet segregation of amounts attributable to redeemable preferred stocks, nonredeemable preferred stocks, and common stocks. The general heading "stockholders' equity" is not to be used, and the presentation of a combined total for equity securities, including redeemable preferred stocks, is prohibited. ASR 268 did not address any possible income statement consequences (e.g., whether dividend payments should be charged to operations similar to interest expense, how to account for extinguishments) or the conceptual question of whether redeemable preferred stock is a liability (current in the case of payments to be made in the ensuing year).

See Chapter 26 for further discussion and an example of presentation.

Subordinated Debt Classification. The SEC, in SAB 1 (Topic 4A), stated that subordinated debt may not be included in the stockholders' equity section of the balance sheet. Furthermore, any caption representing the combination of stockholders' equity and subordinated debt is not acceptable. The SAB was issued in response to the emerging practice in financial institutions of combining subordinated capital loans with equity (see Chapter 38).

EXTINGUISHMENT OF DEBT

Gain or Loss Recognized

Early extinguishment is the reacquisition (except through conversion by the holder) of any debt before its scheduled maturity, regardless of whether the debt is terminated or held in treasury. All open-market or mandatory reacquisitions of debt to meet sinking fund requirements are considered early extinguishments. In accounting for extinguishment of debt, the *net carrying amount* is the amount of debt that would have been due at maturity, adjusted for unamortized premium, discount, and issue costs; whereas the *reacquisition price* is the amount paid on early extinguishment. It includes call premiums and the costs of reacquisition. If early extinguishment is achieved by a direct exchange of new securities, the reacquisition price is the total present value of the new securities. A general term for the replacement of debt with other debt is *refunding*.

The appropriate accounting for the difference between the reacquisition price and the net carrying amount is covered in APB 26 (AC 5362). This opinion applies to all debt retirements, including concurrent borrowings or refundings, but not to (1) debt that is converted according to conversion privileges of the holder, (2) payment at maturity, or (3) settlement after maturity. The extinguishment of debt in troubled debt restructurings is discussed later in this chapter.

APB 26 (AC 5362.20) concludes that the difference between the reacquisition price and the net carrying amount of extinguished debt should be recognized as a gain or loss in the income statement in the period of extinguishment. The gain or loss should not be amortized to future periods. If on extinguishment of debt the parties also exchange rights or privileges (stated or unstated), the portion of the consideration exchanged should be allocated to those rights or privileges and treated as an asset or expensed as appropriate. Note that an extinguishment transaction between related parties may in essence be a capital transaction.

Extraordinary Treatment. SFAS 4 (AC 2013.08) requires that, except for sinking fund purchases, a material aggregate gain or loss from extinguishment of debt (whether earlier than, at, or later than the scheduled maturity date), be classified as an extraordinary item, net of related income tax effect. Sinking fund purchase gains or losses cannot be shown as extraordinary.

Some obligations to acquire debt have the essential characteristics of sinking fund requirements, for instance debt that is required to be purchased before its scheduled maturity at a certain percentage of the total amount outstanding each year. Gains or losses on such transactions are not required to (but may) be classified as an extraordinary item. However, debt maturing serially does not have the characteristics of a sinking fund, and any resulting gain or loss from the extinguishment of serial debt is to be presented as extraordinary (AC 2013.08, fn. 2).

Disclosures

APB 26 has no special disclosure requirements; however, the disclosures required by SFAS 4 (AC 2013.09) are (1) description of extinguishment transaction, including source of funds; (2) income tax effect; and (3) per share amount of aggregate gain or loss, net of related income tax effect.

Problems

APB 26 does not apply to debt that is tendered to exercise detachable warrants originally issued with that debt under the original terms of the debt agreement. The tendering of the debt is considered a conversion "pursuant to the existing conversion privileges of the holder" (AC U5362.002). The carrying amount of the debt, including any unamortized premium or discount, is credited to the shareholder equity accounts upon conversion to reflect the issue of common stock, and no gain or loss is recognized (AC U5362.003).

The opinion statement that "all early extinguishments of debt . . . are fundamentally alike" (AC 5362.19) is based substantially on the belief that only the change in the general cost of money causes a gain or loss in a nontroubled extinguishment. It ignores other factors in an entity's economic situation; e.g., where convertible debt is involved, there is, APB 14 (AC 5516) notwithstanding, an equity element. Ignoring the equity element causes peculiar things to happen. For instance, if convertible debt is reacquired, the difference between the cash acquisition price and its net carrying amount is required to be recognized currently in income. When the debt is equity in substance (because the value of the securities into which it is convertible is higher than the conversion price), the acquisition of such debt is in reality an acquisition of treasury stock. However, an extinguishment of convertible debt is never considered an acquisition of treasury stock. The opinion requires the unnecessary process of first converting the debt to common shares and then reacquiring the shares in order to reflect the financial reality inherent in the transactions—the purchase of treasury stock.

For example, assume the following facts: $3 million of convertible debentures due 1985, convertible at the option of the holder into common stock at $10.75 per share, current fair market value $14 per share. If the holder converts, he will get 279,000 common shares; if he then sells those shares back to the company, the company will recognize no gain or loss and will record the shares purchased as treasury shares. However, if the company extinguishes the $3 million of debentures, it would have to pay $3,906,750 and would reflect a $906,750 charge to operations for the difference between the conversion price and the fair market value ($3.25 × 279,000 shares). (See example in Figure 22.4.)

APB 26 does not discuss using nonmonetary assets to extinguish debt; however, this topic is covered in the context of troubled debt restructurings by SFAS 15 (AC 5363.013 and .014).

Tax Effects

Ordinarily, gains arising from the extinguishment of debt are taxable. However, Section 108 of the Internal Revenue Code allows a taxpayer to postpone the gain and reduce the basis of property as explained by Section 1017. When the taxpayer decides to postpone such a gain, a difference between accounting income and taxable income results. This difference is a timing difference under the provisions of

---

On February 17, 1977 the Company called its 8% convertible subordinated debentures for redemption on March 22, 1977 at 106.34% of their principal amount. Of the $20,000,000 principal amount outstanding, $364,000 was converted into 24,000 shares of common stock and the remaining $19,636,000 was redeemed on March 22, 1977.

On June 21, 1977 the Company called its 7% convertible subordinated debentures for redemption on July 22, 1977, at 104.96% of their principal amount. Of the $10,477,000 principal amount outstanding, $3,234,000 was converted into 175,000 shares of common stock and the remaining $7,234,000 of such debentures was redeemed on July 22, 1977. As a result of these redemptions, the Company recognized an extraordinary charge of $1,100,000 (net of income tax benefits of $1,300,000) reflecting the redemption premium and other costs related to the redemption of the debentures, which reduced primary earnings per share by $.12 ($.11 fully diluted).

FIGURE 22.4   DISCLOSURE OF EXTINGUISHMENT OF CONVERTIBLE SUBORDINATED DEBENTURES
SOURCE: Itel Corp., 1977 Annual Report.

FASB Interpretation No. 22 (AC 4091-1). Prior to 1978, it was often treated as a permanent difference. (This is further discussed in Chapter 25.)

Refunding of Bonds

For reasons such as declining interest rates, a more favorable payment schedule, extended maturity dates, or the removal or modification of restrictive debt covenants, companies undertake programs to replace old debt with new debt. However, when the preexisting debt does not allow for immediate retirement, companies may incur additional new debt and use the proceeds to establish a fund to retire the old debt. The fund invests in risk-free securities until the old debt can legally be retired.

A typical *advance refunding* situation involves major capital improvements of a company financed by government agencies. These government agencies obtain funds by issuing tax-exempt bonds, use the proceeds to purchase the capital improvements, and then lease them (or sell them subject to mortgage) to the company. The company pays rent (or mortgage payments) sufficient to permit the government agency to service the underlying debt. Title to the capital improvements usually passes to the company when all the outstanding bonds have been paid.

The key terms in advance refunding are

1. *Advance refunding.* Refunding debt (new debt) to replace refunded debt (old debt) at a specified future date(s), with the proceeds placed in trust or otherwise restricted to replacing the refunded debt.

2. *Defeasance provision.* A provision in the old debt instrument that provides the terms by which the debt may be legally satisfied and the related lien released without the debt necessarily being retired.

3. *Crossover advance refunding.* An advance refunding in which the proceeds from the new debt, the additional cash deposits, if any, and the income on the related investments are sufficient to pay the principal and any call premium of the old debt and the interest on the new debt until the date of crossover. Crossover occurs when the proceeds from the new debt are used to retire the old debt and the entity becomes obligated to service the new debt. In a crossover, the old debt is never defeased at the time of advance refunding.

4. *Qualifying securities.* Direct U.S. Treasury obligations, securities backed by the U.S. government, or securities collateralized by U.S. government obligations (risk-free securities).

Tax-Exempt Debt. There are two authoritative pronouncements that provide guidance in accounting for refundings of tax-exempt debt. They are SFAS 22, *Changes in the Provisions of Lease Agreements Resulting from Refundings of Tax-Exempt Debt* (AC 4055) (an amendment of SFAS 13), and AICPA SOP 78-5, *Accounting for Advance Refundings of Tax-Exempt Debt.* SFAS 22 resolves to some extent the contradiction that existed in the accounting literature between APB 26 and SFAS 13 (AC 4053).

APB 26 (AC 5362.19) states that "all extinguishments of debt before scheduled maturities are fundamentally alike" and requires uniform accounting for these transactions, i.e., current recognition of a gain or loss. SFAS 13, which avoided the use of the word "debt" in favor of "obligations under capital leases," originally stated that all changes in lease terms must be accounted for prospectively. SFAS 22 resolves this contradiction by requiring that changes in lease terms of tax-exempt debt be accounted for pursuant to APB 26.

According to SFAS 22, when there is a change in the provisions of a lease made prior to the expiration of the lease term resulting from a refunding by the lessor of tax-exempt debt (including an advance refunding), when the perceived economic advantages of the refunding are passed through to the lessee, and when the revised agreement is classified as a capital lease by the lessee or a direct financing lease by the lessor, the change is accounted for as follows:

- *Lessee accounting* (AC 4053.014, as amended by AC 4055.12(a)(i)). The lease obligation is adjusted to the present value of the future minimum lease payments under the revised lease using the effective interest rate applicable to the revised agreement. Resulting gain or loss is recognized currently as a gain or loss on early extinguishment of debt pursuant to APB 26, and classified in accordance with SFAS 4 (AC 2013).

- *Lessor accounting* (AC 4053.017, as amended by AC 4055.12(b)(i)). Gain or loss is recognized currently and consists of two components: (1) the adjustment to the balance of the minimum lease payments receivable and the estimated residual value (gross investment in the lease), if affected, and (2) the adjustment of unearned income in the amount required to adjust the net investment in the lease to the sum of the present values of the two components of the gross investment based on the interest rate applicable to the revised agreement.

If the provisions of the lease are changed in connection with an advance refunding by the lessor of tax-exempt debt that is not accounted for as an early extinguishment of debt at the date of the advance refunding, and the lessee is obligated to reimburse the lessor for any costs related to the debt to be refunded that have been or will be incurred (such as unamortized discount or issue costs or a call premium), the following accounting applies:

- *Lessee accounting* (AC 4055.12(a)(ii)). Debt costs are accrued by the interest method over the period from the date of the advance refunding to the call date of the debt to be refunded.

- *Lessor accounting* (AC 4055.12(b)(ii)). Any reimbursements to be received from the lessee for debt costs are systematically recognized as revenue over the period from the date of the advance refunding to the call date of the debt to be refunded.

SOP 78-5 provides that for issuers other than state and local governments, an advance refunding in which the refunded debt is defeased is viewed as an early extinguishment, and gains or losses should be recognized. The old debt is legally satisfied, and it should be removed from the balance sheet. A nondefeased advance refunding meeting all the following criteria should be accounted for as a defeased refunding (an *in substance defeasance*):

1. The issuer must be irrevocably committed to refund the old debt;
2. The funds used to complete the refunding must be placed in an irrevocable trust to satisfy the old debt at a specified future date(s) and invested in "qualifying securities"; and
3. The invested funds may not be subject to lien for any purpose other than in connection with the advance refunding.

An advance refunding that does not meet the above criteria is not an early extinguishment; therefore, two liabilities (both the old and new debt) should be presented in the balance sheet.

In a crossover advance refunding, since by definition the defeasance never occurs, there is no in substance defeasance, and no gain or loss is recognized. The call premium, unamortized issue premium or discount, and deferred issue costs of all old debt should be amortized to operations over the remaining life of the old debt in all advance refundings that are not initially accounted for as a defeasance.

Non-Tax-Exempt Debt. Not covered by the authoritative literature are advance refunding transactions of non-tax-exempt debt involving leases. These may be accounted for in accordance with the provisions of either SFAS 13 (prospectively) or APB 26 (immediately). SFAS 13 generally provides that a change in lease terms, including lease payments, must be accounted for over the life of the lease rather than recognized immediately. To satisfy himself that the legal form of the transaction is a lease, the auditor should obtain an opinion from the company's lawyer.

Although in economic substance an advance refunding of non-tax-exempt debt involving a lease is the same as an advance refunding not involving a lease, current accounting literature allows a distinction between the two.

DEFAULT

Definitions

Debt agreements often include many covenants. The violation of any covenant constitutes an event of default, usually giving the lender the option of declaring the loan immediately due and payable. Several key terms are defined below:

1. *Debt agreement.* The contract between the borrower and the lender containing the specific terms under which the loan was made.
2. *Covenant.* A specific agreement or promise made to the lender that the borrower will perform in a designated manner. Covenants may refer to specific events or transactions or to conditions that require compliance over a period of time. For example, a specific covenant might stipulate that the company will not declare or pay any dividend, or make any distribution on its capital stock to its stockholders; or a covenant might require the company to maintain a certain amount of working capital or certain ratios (conditions requiring compliance over a period of time).

3. *Event of default.* A failure of the borrower to comply with a covenant.

4. *Waiver.* A document that evidences the intentional relinquishing or abandoning of a known right, claim, or privilege by the lender when a default has occurred. The waiver may specify the time during which it is effective.

5. *Cross covenant.* One that specifies that a default or event of default under one debt agreement constitutes a default or event of default under another debt agreement.

6. *Subjective covenant.* One in which the requirements are vague or cannot be objectively measured. Covenants calling for "no adverse changes," or for continued favorable increases in ratios or earnings, are examples. (Subjective acceleration clauses were discussed under Short-Term Debt.)

SEC Rules on Defaults

The SEC, in Rule 4-08(c) of Regulation S-X, requires the disclosure of the facts and amounts concerning any default in principal, interest, sinking fund, or redemption provision, or any breach of covenant of an indenture or agreement, if the default or breach existed at the most recent balance sheet filed and has not been subsequently cured. If a default or breach exists, but acceleration of the obligation has been waived for a stated period of time beyond the date of the most recent balance sheet being filed, disclosure is required of the amount of the obligation and the period of waiver.

ACCOUNTING FOR TROUBLED DEBT RESTRUCTURINGS

Granting a Concession

The nature of real estate investment trusts and real estate development operations is usually such that the assets are highly leveraged with debt. This debt may be restructured, depending on the success of a particular project. In the mid-1970s the largest number of restructurings to help debtors avoid bankruptcy occurred in the real estate industry. In 1977 the FASB issued SFAS 15, *Accounting by Debtors and Creditors for Troubled Debt Restructurings* (AC 5363), in response to the lack of guidance in authoritative literature. SFAS 15 supersedes FASB Interpretation No. 2, *Imputing Interest on Debt Arrangements Made under the Federal Bankruptcy Act,* and amends APB 26 to exclude troubled debt restructuring from that opinion.

A *troubled debt restructuring* is one in which "the creditor for economic or legal reasons related to the debtor's financial difficulties grants a concession to the debtor that it would not otherwise consider. That concession either stems from an agreement between the creditor and the debtor or is imposed by law or a court" (AC 5363.002). Thus, SFAS 15 prescribes accounting for restructuring if the concession is agreed to by the creditor and debtor, if it is imposed by a court, or if it involves repossessions or foreclosures. The statement does not deal with changes in lease agreements, creditors' delays in taking legal action to collect overdue receivables, and quasi-reorganizations.

Troubled debt restructurings are generally divided into three broad groups (AC 5363.005):

1. Those in which the debtor transfers receivables, real estate, or other assets to the creditor to fully or partially satisfy a debt. This group includes transfers resulting from foreclosure or repossession.
2. Those in which the debtor transfers an equity interest to the creditor to fully or partially satisfy a debt.
3. Those in which the debt is continued but the terms are modified to defer or reduce cash payments that the debtor is required to make to the creditor. This group includes reduction of the stated interest rate for the remaining original life of the debt, extension of the maturity date or dates at a stated interest rate lower than the current market rate for new debt with similar risk, reduction of the face or maturity amount of the debt as stated in the instrument or other agreement, and reduction of accrued interest.

Many other situations are not regarded as troubled debt restructurings and are not covered by SFAS 15. Here are a few examples (AC 5363.007):

1. Those in which the fair value of cash, other assets, or an equity interest accepted by a creditor in full satisfaction of its receivable at least equals the creditor's recorded investment in the receivable.
2. Those in which the fair value of cash, other assets, or an equity interest transferred by a debtor in full settlement of its payable at least equals the debtor's carrying amount of the payable.
3. Those in which the creditor reduces the effective interest rate on the debt to reflect a decrease in risk. This reduction is made in order to maintain a relationship with a debtor who can readily obtain funds from other sources at the current market interest rate.
4. Those in which the debtor refunds the old debt by issuing new marketable debt having an effective interest rate that approximates current market interest rates of debt with similar maturity dates and interest rates issued by nontroubled debtors.

Accounting by Debtor

The accounting by the debtor in a troubled debt restructuring is as follows (AC 5363.013-.019):

1. If the debtor transfers assets to fully settle a payable, the difference between fair value of the assets and the carrying value of the assets transferred is a gain or loss on the disposition of assets (see APB 30; AC 2012), and the difference between the carrying amount of the payable less the fair market value of the assets transferred is a gain on restructuring.
2. If the debtor issues an equity interest to fully settle a payable, the debtor should account for the equity interest issued at its fair value. The excess of the carrying amount of the payable over the equity at fair value is a gain on restructuring.

3. If a restructuring involves a modification of terms, the debtor should account for it prospectively. The carrying amount of the payable is not adjusted (with the exception discussed below), and the effect of the changes in cash payments is reflected in future periods.

If the future cash payments (principal and interest) exceed the carrying amount of the payable, no gain or loss results. The interest expense for future periods is computed using the *interest method,* by which a constant effective interest rate is applied to the payable at the beginning of each period between the restructuring and maturity. The effective rate is the discount rate that equates the present value of the future cash payments required by the modified agreement, excluding amounts contingently payable, with the carrying amount of the payable.

An exception to the nonrecognition of gain or loss is the situation in which the payable exceeds the total future cash payments based on the new terms. Here a gain is recognized on the restructuring equal to the excess of the carrying amount of the payable over the future cash payments. Since the cash payments are less than the carrying amount of the payable, there is no interest expense recognized in the future. Each payment is considered to be principal.

4. If the debt is restructured by partial settlements (transferring assets and/or granting an equity interest) and modified terms, the debtor must first account for the asset and/or equity issuance as described above, then account for the modified terms.

Repossessions, contingent payments, and costs of a restructuring are also prescribed by SFAS 15 (AC 5363.020-024):

1. A repossession or foreclosure is accounted for in the same manner as the transfer of assets and the restructuring by partial settlement.
2. Contingent payments on restructured debt are recognized as a payable in accordance with SFAS 5 (i.e., when it is probable that liability has been incurred and the amount can be reasonably estimated) (AC 4311.08).
3. Legal fees and other direct costs of a debt restructuring involving an equity issuance should reduce the amounts credited to the equity accounts. All other direct costs to effect a debt restructuring reduce the gain recorded, or are expenses of the period if no gain is recognized.

Disclosures by Debtor

Disclosures required by the debtor (AC 5363.025-.026) include a description of the principal changes in terms, the major features of settlement, or both. In addition, gains from restructured debt are aggregated and, if material, classified as an extraordinary item, net of related income tax effect. Also required are disclosures of the aggregate net gain or loss on transfers of assets recognized during the period; the per share amount of the aggregate gain on restructuring of payables, net of related income tax effect; and in financial statements for periods after restructuring, the extent to which amounts contingently payable are included in the carrying of the amount of. restructured payables.

If required by SFAS 5 (AC 4311.08), the total amounts that are contingently payable on restructured payables, and the conditions under which those amounts would become payable or would be forgiven, should be given.

Debtor/Creditor Symmetry

In most matters, the accounting for troubled debt restructurings by debtors and creditors is symmetrical. However, there are a few important exceptions, including the following situations:

1. The required classifications are different, i.e., the debtor considers gains and losses recognized at the time of restructuring as extraordinary, but the creditor treats income items as ordinary.
2. The debtor includes contingent cash payments in the total future cash payments specified by modified terms to the extent necessary to prevent recognizing a gain at the time of restructuring that may be offset by future interest expense, but the creditor excludes contingent receipts from the total future cash receipts unless subsequent realization is probable and the amount can be reasonably estimated. Contingent cash payments not included in the total future cash payments at the time of the restructuring are recorded as interest when the contingency is removed. This same principle also applies to other future cash receipts that may have to be estimated. For example, if the number of interest receipts is flexible because the face amount and accrued interest is collectible on demand or becomes collectible on demand at a certain point in time, estimates of total future cash receipts should be based on the minimum number of periods possible under the terms of the restructuring.
3. Future interest receipts may fluctuate, in which case estimates of the total future cash payments are based on the interest rate in effect at the time of the restructuring. For example, if the terms of the restructure specify that interest will be paid at the prime rate, the rate at the date of the restructure is used to calculate the total future cash payments. Fluctuations are accounted for as changes in estimate. However, if the interest rate decreases below the initial interest rate, a loss is recognized for the difference between the total future cash payments based on the lower current interest rate and the recorded amount of the receivable.

Any allowances for uncollectible amounts at the time of the restructuring should be offset against the losses determined by SFAS 15's provisions (AC 5363.027-.039).

Disclosures by Creditor

At each balance sheet date a creditor must disclose for each receivable whose terms have been modified the aggregate recorded receivable, the interest income that would have been recorded if the restructuring had not taken place, and the amount of interest income recorded for the period. These disclosures do not have to be made if the creditor would have been willing to accept a new receivable with comparable risk for an interest rate equal to or less than the effective rate of the restructured receivable. A creditor must also disclose the amount of commitments to lend additional money to debtors whose receivables have been restructured (AC 5363.040-.041).

INTEREST ON RECEIVABLES AND PAYABLES

Imputation Requirements

When recording a transaction involving debt, the face amount and interest rate of a note should be realistically stated. For example, because of the different tax rates on interest income and capital gains, parties to debt agreements may attempt to maximize capital gains and minimize interest income. In such situations, it may be necessary to determine a realistic interest rate rather than simply to record the note at its face amount.

For tax purposes, this can sometimes be simple. When property that is subject to capital gains treatment is sold in a deferred payment sale (payments due more than one year from the date of sale and a sale price of more than $3,000), and the stated interest rate is less than 6% simple interest each year, interest income or expense must be imputed for tax purposes at the rate of 7%, compounded semi-annually.

But determining a realistic interest rate is not always so simple. The process of making the determination is called *imputation,* and the interest factor determined in this way is known as the *imputed interest rate.* When it was issued, APB 21 (AC 4111) pointed out that the imputation process was not a new accounting principle and that the purpose of the opinion was merely to refine the manner of applying existing accounting principles.

One problem addressed by APB 21 (AC 4111.11) is the appropriate accounting for the exchange of notes for noncash consideration (property, goods, or services) when the face of the note does not reasonably represent the present value of the consideration. This situation exists when the note is non-interest-bearing, or when its stated interest rate is materially different from the prevailing interest rate at the date of the transaction. In such a situation, if reasonable present values are not used in recording the notes given or received, the financial statements of both buyer and seller will, in part, be misstated, and the financial statements will not be in conformity with GAAP (assuming, of course, that material amounts are involved). It should be recognized that even a small difference in rate may significantly affect the financial statements if the note is large and long-term.

Imputation of the interest is required when the stated rate of the note is "unreasonable" (AC 4111.11(2)). Determination of whether the stated interest rate of a note is unreasonable should be based on the effect of imputation on income before extraordinary items or on net income of the company, and on the trend of earnings—again, assuming the effect is material.

The major items to which APB 21 does *not* apply are (AC 4111.03-.04)

1. Receivables and payables arising from transactions with customers or suppliers in the normal course of business that are due in customary trade terms not exceeding approximately one year.

2. Receivables or payables to be paid in property, goods, or services.

3. Deposits, progress payments, or other amounts that do not require repayment in the future, but rather will be applied to the purchase price of the property, goods, or services involved.

4. Security deposits, retainages on contracts, or other amounts intended to provide security for one party to an agreement.

5. The customary cash lending activities (and demand or savings deposit activities) of financial institutions whose primary business is lending money.

6. Transactions in which interest rates are affected by the tax attributes or legal restrictions prescribed by a government agency.

7. Transactions between parent and subsidiary companies and between subsidiaries or a common parent. (The fact that the APB deferred consideration of transactions between related parties when it issued APB 21 should not be interpreted to mean that imputation in these circumstances is inappropriate. Transactions between affiliates should be evaluated to determine whether imputation is required for a fair presentation of the results of operations in the particular circumstances (e.g., subsidiaries with minority interests).)

8. Accounting for convertible debt.

9. Warranties for product performance or other estimates of contractual obligations assumed in connection with sale of property, goods, or services.

Measurement of Interest in Noncash Transactions

When a note is issued for property, goods, or services in a noncash, arm's-length transaction, the note contains two elements: (1) a principal factor, which is equivalent to a bargained exchange price, and (2) an interest element, which is equivalent to the interest that would have been earned by the seller had he received cash instead of a note (AC 4111.07).

If a transaction is at arm's length, there is a presumption that the stated rate of interest is fair to the seller. To determine fairness, a "form vs. economic substance" test is required, which takes the following form: the interest rate is not appropriate or fair if (1) there is no stated interest, (2) stated interest is not reasonable, or (3) the stated face of the note is materially different from current cash sales price for the same or similar items or the market value of the note at the transaction date (AC 4111.11).

In these circumstances, the implicit discount or premium should preferably be measured as follows:

1. Face of note,
2. Less the value of
   a. Property, goods, or services at the established exchange price (or cash sale price), or
   b. The notes as determined by the market rates of interest and the market value of the notes (when the notes are traded in an open market), whichever is more clearly evident,
3. Equals the discount or premium, which will be amortized by using the effective interest rate.

The market value of a note will generally be equivalent to the proceeds the maker could have received had he issued a note payable with identical terms and collateral to a bank. This market value would also be equal to the amount the holder would have been entitled to had the note receivable been discounted without recourse at the time it was received.

APB 21 says that "if an established exchange price is not determinable and if the note has no ready market, the problem of determining present value is more difficult" (AC 4111.09). In this case, an imputed interest rate must be used to determine the appropriate discount or premium.

The imputed interest rate should be determined at the time the note is issued, assumed, or acquired. Any subsequent changes in the prevailing interest rate should be ignored. This eliminates fluctuations in the cost of money that would, if recognized, result in future income or expense.

Amortization of Discount or Premium

The discount or premium should be amortized to interest expense or income over the term of the note under the *interest method*. The objective of this method is to arrive at a periodic interest cost that will result in a constant (level) effective rate on the face amount of the note, plus or minus the discount or premium, at the beginning of each period (AC 4111.14). Other methods of amortization may be used if they produce results that are not materially different from those obtained from using the interest method. Some of the other methods of amortization (none of which results in a level effective rate) are the straight-line method, the bonds-outstanding method, and the dollar-year method. Any difference between the financial statement accounting and tax return accounting because of the amortization is considered a timing difference giving rise to deferred taxes.

Unamortized debt discount or premium, either imputed or actual, should be shown as a direct deduction from or addition to the face of the note on the balance sheet. Further, the payable or receivable must show the effective interest rate and the face amount of the note, either in the balance sheet or in footnotes.

Calculations Involving Imputed Interest

The concept of present value pervades many business decision-making processes; consequently, the theory underlying compound interest, present values, and annuities must be understood. At the very least, the auditor must understand how to use a handheld calculator designed to solve interest problems. The calculator should be able to determine values when the payments are constant, decrease by a constant amount, increase by a constant amount, do not begin in the current period, are due in a single sum, and involve a stated interest rate change. Also, the auditor should not overlook the assistance offered by the various timesharing computer services. These services have many programs that can solve the most complicated problems involving interest.

Capitalization of Interest

Background. Prior to 1973 or 1974, the practice of capitalizing interest cost was found mostly in regulated utilities (see Chapter 36). However, companies then began using it in numerous other situations in which funds were invested for a relatively longer-than-normal time. To avert proliferation of the practice without accounting standards guidance, the SEC placed a moratorium on interest capitalization in new areas. Specifically, the SEC announced in ASR 163 that publicly held companies other than electric, gas, water, and telephone utilities; retail land sales companies; and savings and loan associations that had not, as of June 21, 1974, publicly disclosed an accounting policy of capitalizing interest costs were prohibited from following such a policy.

SFAS 34 Standards. In October 1979, the FASB issued SFAS 34, *Capitalization of Interest Cost* (AC 5155). The basic issue addressed in the earlier *Discussion Memorandum on Accounting for Interest Costs* (FASB, 1977a) was to determine which of three accounting alternatives should be followed: (1) account for interest on debt as an expense of the period in which it is incurred; (2) capitalize interest as part of the cost of an asset when certain conditions are met; or (3) capitalize interest on debt *and* imputed interest on stockholders' equity as part of the cost of an asset when certain conditions are met.

The FASB did not in any event intend to adopt the proposal for comprehensive recognition of imputed equity interest in its final statement on accounting for interest costs, because that could involve fundamental changes in the measurement of earnings and asset values—a subject that properly belongs in its conceptual framework project. For that reason, the issues related to imputed interest costs were identified as "advisory" issues.

The FASB chose (by a narrow margin of four to three) to require interest capitalization as part of the cost of an asset in certain circumstances. The Board believes this practice conforms with the principle of stating assets at historical cost, and recognizes that in theory every asset that requires time in which to be prepared for use should qualify. However, even as to qualifying assets (described below), the FASB emphasized that capitalization is not *required* if the effect would not be material (AC 5155.08). This commentary was aimed at business community critics of the Board's exposure draft (FASB, 1978d), who felt that the effort involved in the proposal was not worth the result. Of course, SFAS 34 additionally contains the standard legend that "the provisions of this statement need not be applied to immaterial items."

In response to SFAS 34, the SEC issued ASR 272 and rescinded the moratorium on interest capitalization. While SFAS 34 is prospective for years beginning after December 15, 1979, amended Rule 4-08(j) of Regulation S-X has been conformed to follow the disclosures required by the SFAS. Thus, for income statements reported in the future SEC filings, the disclosure requirements of SFAS 34 must be followed, thereby effectively making the SEC's disclosure requirements retroactive.

By making SFAS 34 prospective only, the FASB provided a short-run income benefit that will gradually disappear as the future amortization of capitalized interest costs gradually increases to the amount of interest currently being capitalized. In the meantime, however, users of statements should be wary of material gains in income arising from capitalization of interest that do not reflect an increase in the fundamental earning power of the business.

Qualifying assets. Interest is to be capitalized on assets that are constructed or otherwise produced for an enterprise's own use, and on assets intended for sale or lease that are constructed or produced as discrete projects (such as ships or real estate developments) (AC 5155.09). Specifically excluded are inventories produced routinely regardless of the production period length (e.g., whiskey), any assets in use or ready for use in earnings activities, and assets not in such use nor in preparation therefor (AC 5155.10).

Amount capitalizable. Only "real" interest cost (actually incurred or imputed on debt or applicable to capital leases) can be allocated to qualifying assets. The rate to be used for capitalization may be ascertained in this order (AC 5155.13): (1) the rate of specific borrowings associated with the qualifying asset and (2) if borrowings are not specific for the qualifying asset, or the asset amount exceeds specific borrowings therefor, a weighted average of rates applicable to other appropriate borrowings. Alternatively, a company may use a weighted average of rates of all appropriate borrowings regardless of specific borrowings incurred to finance the qualifying asset. However, the amount capitalized in an accounting period (presumably one year) cannot exceed the total interest cost incurred (AC 5155.15), lest the effect be capitalization of an allowance for the use of equity funds. The "allowance for funds used during construction" (AFUDC), which includes equity costs, is not affected in the case of enterprises regulated for rate-making purposes (AC 5155.05) (see Chapter 36 on AFUDC).

The expenditures to which the interest rate is applied are those, generally, that are normally capitalized in the asset cost, provided cash has been paid or an interest-bearing obligation incurred. The FASB emphasizes the need to use approximations here to avoid a computational monstrosity (AC 5155.16).

Time parameters. Interest capitalization starts when money is spent, asset preparation activities are underway, and interest cost is being incurred (at least somewhere in the consolidated group). If activity is suspended more than briefly, capitalization of interest stops during the suspension. When the asset is ready for its intended use, or separable parts are ready, interest capitalization is concluded (AC 5155.17-18).

Since interest cost is considered an integral part of the total cost of acquiring a qualifying asset, its disposition must be the same as that of other components of asset cost, i.e., as part of the charge to depreciation or to cost of sales.

SFAS 34 requires certain disclosures: (1) for an accounting period in which no interest cost is capitalized, the amount of interest charged to expense during the period and (2) for an accounting period in which interest is capitalized, the total amount of interest incurred during the period, and the amount that has been capitalized (AC 5155.21).

AUDITING

Objectives

In performing his examination, the auditor must keep in mind his audit objectives. For debt, these may include ascertaining that

1. Internal controls over debt are adequate,
2. All debt has been recorded,

3. Debt is properly valued and classified in the financial statements,

4. All significant disclosures have been made,

5. Interest expense, including interest payable and amortization of premium or discount and expense, is properly stated and all significant disclosures relating to interest expense have been made, and

6. The company has met all the requirements and restrictions imposed by long-term debt covenants.

Internal Control

An evaluation of the company's internal control system will assist in attaining these objectives. Accordingly, the auditor should review the internal control systems to determine (1) whether they reliably prevent or detect and correct potential errors, (2) whether the controls are still in operation, and (3) among other things, whether new or additional assets have been pledged. If the systems prove reliable, the auditor may limit the extent of his substantive (year-end balance) tests. An adequate system of internal control for debt might include the following:

1. A record of notes payable is maintained.
   a. A note register controls unissued, issued, reacquired, and cancelled notes.
   b. There are supporting records and documentation.
2. Totals are reconciled periodically with general ledger control accounts.
3. Note register and supporting records are maintained independently of records relating to authorizations, issuance of notes, and payments of notes.
4. Notes are prenumbered and accounted for, and there is limited access to blank forms.
5. There is written authorization of borrowings by the board of directors.
6. There are minutes authorizing designated officers to borrow up to a fixed limit.
7. There are minutes that specifically name the banks or other financial institutions from which funds may be borrowed.
8. Notes are signed by two authorized officials.
9. A checklist is maintained of restrictions under articles of incorporation, loan agreements, bylaws, and corporate minutes, and the checklist is regularly reviewed to be certain the company is in compliance with all restrictions.
10. Accrued interest is recorded monthly and rechecked for accuracy.
11. If interest payments are made by an independent agent, i.e., a bank:
    a. Control accounts are maintained.
    b. Periodic reports from the agent are checked.
    c. Reports are reconciled with control accounts.
12. If the company makes disbursements, there is proper control over the preparation, signing, mailing, and reconciling of checks.
    a. Payments are authorized or checked to original loan agreements.
    b. Unclaimed interest checks are accounted for.
13. There is an adequate record of the company's assets pledged as security.
14. Paid notes are cancelled, retained in files, and in the custody of an authorized official.

15. There is control over and safekeeping of all reacquired treasury notes.

16. A trustee represents bondholders (Trust Indenture Act of 1939) and/or there is a sinking fund.

17. An independent registrar maintains a record of registered bondholders.

Substantive Approach

If debt financings are infrequent, as is common, a substantive approach is usually more efficient than relying on internal controls. Substantive auditing procedures will include some of the following steps, as appropriate to the engagement:

1. Perform analytical procedures:
   a. By reference to repayment requirements, determine whether the change in long-term debt for the year seems reasonable. Factor in additional borrowings.
   b. Test overall reasonableness of interest expense. Calculate the approximate interest expense by multiplying the average interest rate on notes by the average monthly balance.

2. Prepare or obtain an analysis of notes and/or bonds payable and accrued interest showing:
   a. Payee
   b. Date made
   c. Date due
   d. Interest rate
   e. Date interest paid to
   f. Original amount of note
   g. Collateral
   h. Opening balance
   i. Additions
   j. Payments
   k. Ending balance
   l. Interest accrued or prepaid at beginning
   m. Interest accrued
   n. Interest paid
   o. Interest accrued or prepaid at end
   p. Cross-reference to loan agreement and/or abstract.
   If there are numerous transactions, consider preparing a schedule of only that debt with an unpaid balance at the end of the year. In this event the analysis worksheet above should be appropriately modified.

3. Verify addition of the analysis, and compare totals to general ledger.

4. Check interest calculations by recomputation.

5. Corroborate interest expense for the period by reference to the amount of debt outstanding during the period. (See analytical test in 1b above.)

6. Verify computation of amortization of debt premium or discount and expense.

7. Examine supporting documentation (i.e., bond, note, and loan indentures and agreements) for all debt and related expenses; examine corporate minutes for authorizations.

8. Examine agreements for restrictive covenants (see Auditing Debt Covenants below).

9. Ascertain the receipt of funds from borrowings and account for their disposition.

10. Confirm balances and collateral by direct communication with creditors (see Chapter 17 on compensating balances); if independent trustee is used, confirm transactions and balances.

11. Examine cancelled or paid notes and/or bonds and uncancelled bonds purchased (treasury bonds).

13. Review notes paid or renewed since balance sheet date; determine whether there were any unrecorded liabilities at year-end.

14. Account for all unissued bonds.

15. Review sinking fund activity.

16. Determine that mortgages have been recorded, and confirm liens on property (see Uniform Commercial Code below).

A matrix approach for visualizing substantive procedures applicable to long-term debt can be found in Chapter 12, Figure 12.2, where it is used as an example for understanding the overall audit process.

Guarantees

When the client acts as guarantor for another or endorses a negotiable instrument, the auditor may follow these procedures:

1. Determine whether, and the instances in which, the client is a guarantor by reviewing bank confirmation replies and loan payable confirmations.

2. Confirm terms of guarantees that are mentioned in agreements or are disclosed through inquiry.

3. Determine whether it is probable, reasonably possible, or remotely possible that the client will be called upon to perform under the guarantee.

4. Be alert to "concealed" guarantees and the possibility of a forebearance. (An example of a forebearance is the failure of a lender to foreclose on defaulted debts when there is some commonality of management between the debtor and lender. Another example is the failure to enforce a guarantee given by a company whose management also exercises management authority over the party who is the beneficiary of the guarantee.)

5. Determine that the client has included in its representation letter the fact that "related-party transactions and related amounts receivable or payable, including sales, purchases, loans, transfers, leasing arrangements, and guarantees," have been properly recorded or disclosed in the financial statements (see Chapter 28).

6. Determine that the financial statements contain the appropriate disclosures concerning guarantees.

SAS 6 (AU 335) requires that an auditor obtain an understanding of the nature of related-party relationships; accordingly, all identified related-party guarantees must be reviewed, and the auditor should obtain reasonable satisfaction that such guarantees do not lack substance and are properly disclosed (see AC 4311.12, AU 335.16-.18, and Chapter 28).

Auditing Debt Covenants

The client should have procedures designed to detect events of default, to measure the effect of any proposed transactions on restrictive debt covenants, and to notify the lender about transactions and events as required. The auditor should obtain an understanding of the client's debt compliance determination procedures.

To evaluate the client's internal controls and to be reasonably sure that all restrictions are footnoted or otherwise adequately disclosed in the financial statements, the auditor should gather certain documents into his working papers, including a conformed copy of the debt agreement and all amendments, a summary of the calculations supporting the compliance with restrictive covenants, correspondence with the lender, and waivers of any defaults.

The auditor should inspect the documentation produced by the client's procedures. He should review the calculations and compliance checklists and compare these checklists with the underlying debt agreements. He should also obtain from the lender (or the client's lawyer) a written opinion as to the proper interpretation of subjective covenants.

If there are any events of default, they must be carefully assessed. If violations of the restrictive covenants are not waived by the lender and the loan is in default, it is immediately due and payable. In this case, the auditor must consider what financial statement classification and disclosures will be required and how the default will affect his opinion.

Waivers and Cures. The auditor must exercise care in evaluating a waiver of default to be sure that the waiver is applicable. A single waiver may be sufficient for a specific event of default, but if the default is or may be of a continuing nature, a waiver should be obtained for at least 12 months from the balance sheet date. Otherwise it may be necessary to classify the debt as current.

When the client corrects a default, it may be considered "cured." In this case, the auditor should determine that either the terms of the debt agreement or the lender have specified the corrective action to be taken, and that the action taken to cure the default is complete and in accordance with the agreement. If the corrective action is not complete at the date of the auditor's opinion, the auditor may not be able to satisfy himself that the debt is properly classified as long-term; he may then express a qualified or adverse opinion (see Chapter 16).

When an event of default has occurred and he has not given notice of acceleration, the lender may indicate prior to the reporting date whether or not he intends to exercise his rights under debt agreement. If the lender does not indicate his intentions and the violation has not been cured, the debt should be classified as short-term.

Debt Compliance Letters. Many debt agreements require the auditor to provide the lender with assurance as to the existence or nonexistence of certain conditions. For example, the debt agreement may require the maintenance of a certain amount of working capital at specified points in time, a limitation on investments, and an accountant's letter as to compliance with these requirements.

SAS 14 (AU 621) says that the auditor may only be requested to furnish assurance that the borrower has complied with those covenants of the loan agreement that deal with accounting and auditing matters. The scope of this assurance should exclude legal matters, items beyond the expected expertise of the auditor, and those financial matters that are not covered in the normal scope of an audit. Covenants that may be considered unauditable include, for example, restrictions on business activities and uses of property; title to property; continuation of licenses or franchises; obtaining of all appropriate permits, licenses, and other authorizations; commissions of acts of bankruptcy; obtaining of legal opinions; lack of defaults in other agreements; "compliance with loan restrictions to the extent feasible through examination of books and records" (language too broad); and "review of loan agreement" (language too broad).

A timely discussion with the client, lender, and counsel as to exactly what the terms to be used in the loan agreement mean, and how the various covenants will be measured, is essential. Only then can the auditor be assured that the final debt agreement will be worded in a manner that recognizes the boundaries of his expertise as an auditor.

See Chapter 16 for examples of special reports by auditors on a client's compliance with contractual provisions of a debt agreement.

UNIFORM COMMERCIAL CODE

In addition to confirming with lenders the amount of debt outstanding and the existence of any security interest in the company's properties, the audit of debt has the objective of ensuring that the financial statements contain adequate disclosure of all assets pledged as collateral. To determine the existence of security interests and become familiar with their details, the auditor can examine the client's copies of security agreements and financing statements.

A search for debt is facilitated by the Uniform Commercial Code (UCC). Under Article 9 of the UCC, any lender, in order to establish his interest in collateral, must either take possession of the collateral or give public notice of his interest in it by filing a financing statement or a security agreement with the appropriate filing officer. The UCC applies to any transaction intended to create a security interest in personal property (tangible or intangible) or fixtures but not to transactions involving real property. Definitions of some of the key terms used in UCC are given below.

A *secured interest* is an interest in personal property or fixtures that secures the payment or performance of an obligation. A security interest cannot exist until three conditions are met: (1) there must be an agreement that a security interest attaches to the collateral, (2) value must be given by the creditor, and (3) the debtor must have rights to the collateral.

A *security agreement* is an agreement that creates or provides for a security interest. It must be signed by the debtor and must contain a description of the collateral. Article 9 provides that "any description of personal property . . . is sufficient whether or not it is specific if it reasonably identifies what is described." For example, the collateral may be broadly described as accounts receivable or inventory. The agreement can provide for a *future security interest*; this is a typical clause found in agreements when the debtor is using inventory or accounts receivable as collateral in a revolving loan agreement. A security agreement may also contain a *future advance clause,* and/or an *acceleration clause.*

A *financing statement* is the document used to perfect a security interest in property by giving public notice. It gives the secured party enforceable rights in the collateral against third parties.

In every first audit, in any audit where the client is in liquidation, and in any case where the client's financial condition or borrowing ability is deteriorating, it may be advisable to search for public filings of security interests. Other situations in which a search should be considered occur when the client has recently completed a new or complex financing program, or when there is a possibility of concealed management involvement in material transactions.

It is not necessary for the auditor to go in person to the various filing offices to search for financing statements or recorded security agreements. Instead, he may mail a confirmation to the UCC Division of the Office of the Secretary of State of the state in which the pledged property is located. (Accounts receivable are "located" where the applicable receivable records are kept.) The request to the secretary of state to search the files is made using the standard Form UCC-11.

While most filings are made with the secretary of state, filings for the following types of collateral are made with county offices: fixtures (personal property that is attached to real property); consumer goods (household items in the hands of the ultimate consumer); and farm-connected collateral (farming equipment, crops, and farmers' accounts receivable). Purchase-money contracts (e.g., installment sales) are generally excluded from the public filing provisions of the code, but are covered by all of the code's other provisions.

The UCC cannot be relied on to disclose certain transactions, notably those involving real property and those involving liens against goods purchased for purchase-money contracts. Also, Louisiana has not adopted the UCC, and some states have made textual changes. Therefore, the auditor should continue to rely on other audit procedures to search for liens against any assets located in Louisiana, or against excluded assets in any state.

BANKRUPTCY PREDICTORS

There have been a number of articles written about financial statement ratios and their use in determining liquidity. Obviously, such ratios are of interest to auditors. Some of these ratios are discussed in "How to Figure Who Is Going Bankrupt" (Hershman, 1975) and "Evaluation of a Company as a Going Concern" (Altman and McGough, 1974).

The ratios used in bankruptcy evaluation are the so-called *long-term liquidity* and the *short-term liquidity* trend ratios. They are used to indicate whether a company may have liquidity problems within the next five years. The development of these trend ratios stems from the fact that other widely used ratios depicting financial health (e.g., the current ratio and the debt-to-equity ratio) are effective only as very short-range predictors of illiquidity.

The *long-term liquidity trend ratio* uses a mathematical technique known as the *gambler's ruin prediction*. Simply put, a mathematical model is used to determine the nature of the year-to-year change in the liquidity of a company during the years prior to the evaluation date. From this, the model determines the probability that future negative trends could occur at a magnitude significant enough to absorb the net assets of the company, thus making the company illiquid.

Since the model deals with liquidity, assumptions must be made regarding the liquidation value of the various assets. For instance, cash and marketable securities would be recorded at face value, other current assets would be deflated to 70% of their recorded value, and net tangible long-term assets would be deflated to 50% of their recorded value upon liquidation.

The *short-term liquidity trend ratio* uses the technique of discriminant analysis with five key ratios: working capital to total assets; retained earnings to total assets; earnings before interest and taxes to total assets; market value of equity to book value of total debt; and sales to total assets.

The long-term liquidity trend ratio is expressed as a decimal fraction. If there is very little indication that the company could become illiquid within the ensuing five years, the ratio will be close to zero. If there is a serious indication that it could, the ratio will be close to one. In the short-term liquidity trend ratio, all five key ratios are mathematically combined to produce a *score value*. The score value can then be compared to a set of standard score values that have been empirically developed as indicators of short-term bankruptcy predictors. (One timesharing program that will compute the long-term and short-term liquidity trend ratios is the Touche Ross program FINALY, written in BASIC and available through Tymshare, Inc. See Chapter 14 and Appendix 12 for a further exploration of timesharing of this type.)

RATIO OF EARNINGS TO FIXED CHARGES

Basic Requirements

Conceptually, a company's ability to pay interest on long-term debt should be demonstrated by a ratio that compares earnings to fixed charges; in fact, the SEC requires the inclusion of this ratio in certain of its registration and annual report forms. For example, Form S-1 says that if debt securities are being registered, the ratio of earnings to fixed charges is to be disclosed for each year. If appropriate, the ratio must be disclosed on a total enterprise basis, in a position of equal prominence with the ratio for the registrant or for the registrant and its consolidated subsidiaries. In addition, for the most recent year or 12 months, pro forma disclosure must be made of the ratio of earnings to fixed charges, adjusted to give effect to the issuance of securities being registered; to any issuance, retirement, or redemption of securities during the period; or to any issuance, retirement, or redemption of securities taking place or presently proposed to take place within one year after the current period.

Form S-1 requires that earnings be computed after all operating and income deductions except fixed charges and taxes based on income or profits, and after eliminating undistributed income of unconsolidated subsidiaries and 50%-or-less-owned persons. Fixed charges include interest and amortization of debt discount and expense, and premium on all indebtedness; a portion of rentals that can be demonstrated to be representative of the interest factor in the particular case; and in case consolidated figures are used, preferred stock dividend requirements of consolidated subsidiaries, excluding items eliminated in consolidation (see Figure 22.5).

1. Net income   _____

2. Income taxes   _____

3. Minority interests   _____

4. Total   _____

5. Fixed charges:
   • Interest and amortization of debt discount and
     premium on all indebtedness   _____

   • "Appropriate" portion of rentals   _____

   • Preferred stock dividend requirements of
     consolidated subsidiaries   _____

   Total fixed charges   _____

6. Earnings before income taxes, minority interests,
   and fixed charges (total of line 4 plus line 5)   _____

7. Ratio (line 6 divided by line 5)   =======

FIGURE 22.5   COMPUTATION OF RATIO OF EARNINGS TO FIXED
CHARGES

If long-term debt or preferred stock is being registered using Form S-1, the annual interest requirements of the debt or the annual dividend requirements on the preferred stock must be disclosed. To the extent that an issue represents refunding or refinancing, only the additional annual interest or dividend requirements must be stated. If preferred stock is being registered, there must also be disclosure in tabular form, for each year or other period, of the ratio of earnings to combined fixed charges and preferred dividend requirements (see Figure 22.6). The registrant must file as an exhibit the computations of all the required ratios. When the interest rate has not yet been fixed, an assumed maximum interest rate on the securities may be used for the purpose of this exhibit and the pro forma ratio. If this is done, the assumed rate must be disclosed.

In ASR 119, the SEC indicated that for the purpose of computing the ratio, it is unacceptable to reduce fixed charges by (1) amounts representing investment income earned or interest (either actual or imputed) on funds raised or being raised that are in excess of the company's requirements for working capital and (2) gains on retirement of debt.

Consolidated Ratio

In ASR 122, the SEC says that the ratio for the registrant must be accompanied by disclosure (by presenting the ratio for the total enterprise in equivalent prominence with the other ratios) of the significance of fixed charges of other companies included in the enterprise, whether or not the revenues and expenses of such

1. Net income _____
2. Income taxes _____
3. Minority interests _____
4. Total _____
5. Fixed charges:
   • Interest and amortization of debt discount
   and premium on all indebtedness _____
   • "Appropriate" portion of rentals _____
   Total fixed charges _____
6. Earnings before income taxes, minority interests,
   and fixed charges (total of line 4 plus line 5) _____
7. Total preferred dividend requirement _____
8. Effective tax rate _____
9. Total preferred dividend "grossed-up" _____
10. Total fixed charges and preferred dividends
    (total of line 5 plus line 9) _____
11. Ratio (line 6 divided by line 10) _____

FIGURE 22.6 COMPUTATION OF RATIO OF EARNINGS TO FIXED
CHARGES AND PREFERRED DIVIDENDS

companies are set forth in the registrant's financial statements. This is necessary, the SEC holds, because some registration statements were filed with a ratio of earnings to fixed charges computed on financial statements that excluded significant amounts of fixed charges incurred by a substantial portion of the business operation carried on by the registrant.

For instance, some issuers operated large affiliated credit companies, or *supplier companies,* that were obligated for substantial amounts of fixed charges on debt, leases, or other contractual obligations. In addition, the registrant may have guaranteed the debt of a supplier company that is not a subsidiary of the registrant, or may have entered into contracts with a supplier that provided for payments designed to service debt of the supplier. Since the fixed charges of these related companies generally are not taken into account in computing the ratio, this ratio by itself may be misleading when inclusion of the fixed charges of the total enterprise would produce a materially different result.

Interpretations of ASR 155 (AICPA, 1974h, pp. 95-97) state that when registrant-only income statements as well as consolidated statements are presented, the ratio is generally required only for the consolidated statements. However, the ratio may be required in some registrant-only statements, such as those for savings and loan association holding companies and bank holding companies.

Interest Factor in Rentals

Other interpretations of ASR 155 pertaining to the ratio of earnings to fixed charges are:

1. The SEC staff stated that one third of rentals in the fixed-charge component was allowed in the past because it was considered a reasonable approximation of the interest portion of rentals. Although they feel that this approximation may not be the most appropriate now, they will not automatically disallow it simply because SFAS 13 (AC 4053) provides a different answer. One third is still acceptable if it represents a reasonable approximation of the interest factor.

2. If practical, the computations of the ratio for prior years should be revised retroactively when a new method of estimating interest costs in rentals is used in the current year's ratio. In this way, all years will be presented on a consistent basis.

SUGGESTED READING

AICPA. *Illustrations of Accounting for Debt Under FASB Pronouncements.* Financial Report Survey 17. New York, 1978. This NAARS survey, based on 8,000 annual reports, illustrates the application of APB Opinion No. 26 and FASB Statements Nos. 4, 6, and 15.

Bernstein, Leopold. *Financial Statement Analysis: Theory, Application, and Interpretation.* Rev. ed. Homewood, Ill.: Richard D. Irwin, 1978. This book covers the framework of statement analysis, the raw materials of analysis, and various tools for analyzing financial statements.

Brauns, Robert A. W. Jr., and Slater, Sarah. *Bankers Desk Reference.* Boston: Warren, Gorham & Lamont, 1979. This is a reference work on commercial banking, including commercial lending from banks' point of view.

Frascona, Joseph. *CPA Law Review.* 5th ed. Homewood, Ill.: Richard D. Irwin, 1977. This book introduces the Uniform Commercial Code and covers it sequentially.

Sherwood, Hugh. *How Corporate and Municipal Debt is Rated.* New York: John Wiley & Sons, 1976. This is a look at the Standard & Poor's rating system, the factors that are assessed, and how they are weighted.

Thorndike, David. *The Thorndike Encyclopedia of Banking and Financial Tables.* Boston: Warren, Gorham & Lamont, 1980. This book provides tables for commercial loans, mortgages, bonds, simple interest, compound interest, present worth, sinking funds, annuities, and others.

23

Leases and Off-Balance Sheet Financing

Eugene G. Taper

EXECUTORY TRANSACTIONS AS ASSETS AND LIABILITIES

Leases and other executory transactions give rise to rights and obligations on the part of the parties involved, but not all the rights or obligations rest in a single party. This causes a major problem for preparers, auditors, and users of financial statements. In fact, accounting does not yet have a conceptual definition of assets and liabilities, though the FASB's conceptual framework project is well along. (See Chapter 2.) A lease is one of the most elusive transactions to evaluate in terms of whether it gives rise to assets and liabilities.

Despite the FASB's attempted resolution of the problem by the issuance of SFAS 13 (AC 4053) and a multitude of amendments and interpretations, there is still unending debate over economic resources and property rights. Are they assets in an accounting sense, and perhaps more importantly, are the associated obligations liabilities?

Lease Financing Arrangements

The use of leasing as a financing vehicle is continuously expanding, and other off-balance sheet financing arrangements have emerged as major financing devices. The usual arrangements—other than leases—involve inventories and accounts receivable. These arrangements can be as complex and diverse as the imaginations of the experts who make them. They run the gamut from simply selling accounts receivable to a bank to creating a trust to build a factory whose output will go into the company's production process. Unless lease financing arrangements are recorded as assets and liabilities in a company's financial statements—and many, perhaps most, are not—they are considered off-balance sheet financing. In these situations, only certain use rights required by the user are transferred, but not enough rights are transferred to be deemed a transfer of outright ownership.

Lessee Advantages. Because debt has overshadowed equity as a major source of capital in recent years, financial institutions have increased their attention to the financial strength ratios and liquidity indicators in borrowers' balance sheets. Since a balance sheet looks stronger without big liabilities on it, transactions that do not create balance sheet liabilities are thought of as useful. Another advantage is that leasing typically gives the lessee the ability to finance 100%; he can get his truck or factory or whatever with no down payment.

Lessor Advantages. The ability to lease the property gives its manufacturer or a dealer an added marketing dimension—he can offer his customer a choice. And because of accelerated depreciation, investment tax credits, and interest expense deductions, a lessor is in a position to obtain significant tax shelter benefits from leasing. Finally, if leased property appreciates, the residual value is often a bonus to the lessor or creditor or is shared by the parties in some predetermined manner.

Nonlease Financing Arrangements

Virtually everything in codified GAAP and in other pronouncements of the accounting profession or the SEC that deals with off-balance sheet financing arrangements focuses on leases. But there has been a surge of "other" transactions, and that subject also deserves accounting pronouncements. The AICPA has been thinking about off-balance sheet financing for several years, via a task force appointed to identify areas of concern, kinds of transactions, and approaches to solutions. AcSEC has dealt with this matter on a piecemeal basis, and the first tangible result was SOP 78-8, *Accounting for Product Financing Arrangements.* A previous SOP (74-6) dealt with receivables sold with recourse, but omitted any consideration of balance sheet implications.

Parties in Off-Balance Sheet Financing

In general, the parties to an off-balance sheet financing transaction are the beneficiary, financier, equity participant, and underwriter. The *beneficiary* is the consumer. For example, he is the user of the leased property or the originator/owner of the accounts receivable being sold. The *financier* assumes a moneylending role for interest. The *equity participant* is involved primarily for tax benefits and residual values and often also to generate sales of his product inventory and cash inflow. The *underwriter* is the broker who brings the parties together; he typically is compensated by fees. One party may play several of these roles, and the attributes of these four parties can be divided among them in many ways.

Any business can be a beneficiary of off-balance sheet financing. Perhaps the most consistently involved group are retailers, who often lease their facilities, sell their receivables, and have complex arrangements for obtaining merchandise for retail sale. Equipment manufacturers, equipment dealers, real estate developers, and leasing companies serve as financiers and equity participants. Banks and insurance companies, pension funds, and other *portfolio investors* are significant in the financier role. Lease underwriters, investment bankers, and tax shelter syndicators play the deal-making role, while the existence of tax-shelter-motivated investors, who are often wealthy individuals willing to provide the equity participation, creates a viable off-balance sheet financing industry.

HISTORICAL PERSPECTIVE

Early Pronouncements

The evolution of lease accounting principles began with the AICPA Committee on Accounting Procedure's ARB 38, which was issued in October 1949, and included unchanged in the ARB 43 restatement and revision. The concern of this bulletin was almost totally with disclosure, although the committee did say that "where it is clearly evident that the transaction involved is in substance a purchase, the 'leased' property should be included among the assets of the lessee with suitable accounting for the corresponding liabilities . . ." (ARB 43, Chapter 14, par. 7.) As interpreted, leases were capitalized only if (1) the term was very short in relation to the useful life of the property and (2) the lessee had the right to acquire the property for a pittance.

Accounting Principles Board Efforts

The APB, perceiving shortcomings, superseded the ARB provisions by issuing APB 5, *Reporting of Leases in Financial Statements of Lessees,* and APB 7, *Accounting for Leases in Financial Statements of Lessors.*

APB 5, Lessees. APB 5, which was issued in 1964, tried to provide a better definition of when a lease was in substance a purchase. The notion continued to exist that only those leases that were in essence purchases should be capitalized. Of interest here is that one member of the Board dissented, saying "a liability (discounted to present value) should be recorded for all material amounts payable under noncancellable leases, which are in fact 'take or pay' contracts representing a present liability payable in the future."

APB 5 established that leases between related parties should be capitalized; this was aimed at dummy leasing companies, which were established solely to lease property to their sponsors and that had obtained the property by some access to the sponsors' creditworthiness. Another common situation affected by APB 5 was the lessor corporation owned by the sole or principal stockholder of the lessee company.

APB 7, Lessors. APB 7, which was issued in 1966, covered the lessor. It dealt with the accounting distinction between an *operating lease* (where the lessor accounted for the leased assets in the same manner as fixed assets) and a *financing lease* (where the lessor accounted for the leased assets in two segments—a receivable for rental payments, and the residual value). The basic distinction between the two was whether the lessor's risks lay in owning the property or in having granted credit. APB 7 did not require symmetry between the lessee and lessor, even though it specifically addressed the question. The lessee did not have to capitalize a lease that was to be accounted for as a finance lease under APB 7. This conclusion was very useful to lessors, who generally preferred financing leases, while still permitting lessees to avoid putting abhorrent capital leases on their balance sheets. Even though several other APB opinions addressed the leasing question, APBs 5 and 7 were the authoritative word on lease accounting until the issuance of SFAS 13 in late 1976. APB 10 (1966) established the requirement that subsidiaries be consolidated if their principal business activity was to lease property to their parent or other members of the affiliated group. APB 18 (1971) reaffirmed APB 10 and, in a cryptic footnote, admonished: "The Board is giving further consideration to the accounting treatment of lease transactions." This footnote went on to say the Board didn't know what to do with a new breed of dummy leasing companies, thus demonstrating the sieve-like nature of APB requirements for related-party lease capitalization. (See SEC Involvement.)

APB 27, Manufacturer-Dealer Lessors. APB 27 (1972) clarified the provisions of APB 7 as they related to lessors who were manufacturers or dealers and ended its rather prevalent abuse. Manufacturers and dealers had been interpreting it very liberally in order to accommodate finance method accounting in situations in which it was not at all clear that the risks and the rewards of property ownership had been transferred to the buyer. At that time, required remarketing or first-priority remarketing was common in financing leases. APB 27 established a checklist of rather specific tests that had to be met in order for a seller to recognize a profit in a leasing transaction.

APB 31, Lessee Disclosures. APB 31 (1973) expanded the disclosure requirements for lessees, basically requiring enough information so that the knowledgeable financial statement user could rough out what the effect would be if the company capitalized leases. However, the Board made optional that part of the disclosure that had to do with the discounted present value of lease commitments (the liability). But the SEC, in ASR 147, shortly mandated those disclosures for public companies for 1973 and later year-ends, using this unusual introductory wording: ". . . disclosure of the present value of financing leases and of the impact on net income of capitalization of such leases, neither of which is required by Opinion No. 31, are essential to investors." For a time there was confusion about whether the SEC was taking over the establishment of GAAP, and some firms required clients to make the APB 31 optional disclosures. ASR 150 cleared up this confusion. (See Chapter 40.)

SEC Involvement

Before ASR 147, the SEC had dealt with leasing only in ASR 132, which dealt with *see-through* or *conduit leases.* In these leases, a lessor with no substance was merely a pipeline so that a lessee might obtain debt financing. ASR 132 expanded the concept of related-party leases to include see-through lessors, even though the lessee might not have any equity ownership in the lessor.

The more noticeable see-through leases were large transactions by publicly held companies, and they usually involved an investment banking firm acting as a lease underwriter. Now that ASR 132 required lessors to have economic substance in order to have something at risk, some investment banking firms established (at least nominally) nonsubsidiary lessor entities through capital contributions of certain of their partners. This paid-in capital ranged from $500,000 to $1,000,000, and the lessor so capitalized would act as owner/lessor in numerous highly leveraged leases. In an exchange of correspondence between Goldman Sachs & Co. and the SEC's chief accountant, John C. Burton, the SEC admitted that such initial capitalization constituted economic substance, provided in a given lease transaction such capital was indeed at risk. Thus auditors not only obtained representation from these satellite lessor companies as to the capital, but they also went through many discussions with the lease parties about the sufficiency of the extent to which hypercomplex provisions placed the capital at risk. (According to ASR 132, sufficiency meant 5% of the amount of real property or 15% of personal property.)

With the enactment of SFAS 13 (AC 4053), ASR 132 was rescinded, and the auditor's need for a carry-along lawyer diminished somewhat.

LEASE ACCOUNTING UNDER SFAS 13

One of the very first FASB projects was accounting for leases. It took the Board over two years to issue its pronouncement, and in November 1976, SFAS 13 was released. SFAS 13 (AC 4053), as amended and interpreted, represents GAAP for lease accounting.

In an appendix to SFAS 13, the Board provides the conceptual basis for its opinion: ". . . the view that a lease that transfers substantially all of the benefits and risks incident to the ownership of property should be accounted for as the acquisition of an asset and the incurrence of an obligation by the lessee and as a sale or financing by the lessor" (AC 4053.060). This conceptual rationale is logically justifiable and hardly arguable; it is not a part of the statement, which consists of a series of specific rules.

The Board apparently believed these rules would result in more companies capitalizing more leases. Not surprisingly, even before SFAS 13 was issued, its very specific rules were under the microscope of the leasing industry, which by and large found ways of avoiding capitalization for parties so inclined. The new rules were tighter, but their dependence on clearly defined equations made up of fuzzy factors made it easy to work close to the edge. The FASB reacted by patching SFAS 13. As of October 1980, there had been seven amendments and six interpretations. Still, SFAS 13 and its various amendments and interpretations make up a very complex and highly technical, specific, and rigid rule book.

It appears that the Board may be tiring of devoting a substantial portion of its resources to heaping rules on top of rules in an attempt to legislate proper accounting for lease transactions. In 1979, the Board (whose membership had changed since the enactment of SFAS 13) said that if the lease issue were reopened, a majority might opt for capitalizing all except immaterial leases (FASB *Action Alert* No. 79-10, March 8, 1979). Another hint was the withdrawal in 1979 of exposure drafts of two more amendments. In a way, this was a warning to the loopholers that they should desist or be faced with no alternative to capitalization. However, interest in the possibility gathered some momentum in the business community and the accounting profession, both of which were weary of the steady stream of time-consuming rules. Thus the Board has begun staff work on the conceptual underpinnings of SFAS 13; a fundamental change in approach might be a genuine possibility.

SFAS 13 establishes a rather narrow universe for itself; it covers agreements that convey the right to use property, plant, or equipment consisting of land and/or depreciable assets. This definition of a lease is less inclusive than many accountants had previously used. For example, the definition excludes agreements covering the use of intangibles. Although it does include certain agreements that are not nominally leases (e.g., heat supply contracts), it excludes many other similar agreements (e.g., take or pay agreements, which are described later in this chapter). In a way, the narrow scope of SFAS 13 chartered the "other off-balance sheet financing" boom of recent years. The issuance of SFAS 13 superseded all the APB opinions mentioned above, and the SEC rescinded ASRs 132 and 147.

Classification of Leases

The essence of SFAS 13 is that there are three kinds of leases: capital, operating, and leveraged. *Capital leases* apply to both the lessor and lessee, but for the lessor they are either sales-type leases or direct financing leases, depending on whether there is a seller's profit. *Operating leases* are leases that fail to meet any of the tests for a capital lease. *Leveraged leases* are relevant only to the lessor, because they have to do with special treatment for the lessor if he has financed the leased property with a significant proportion of nonrecourse debt.[1]

Distinguishing Capital Leases From Operating Leases. The conceptual basis for lease accounting lies in evaluating who has the risks and rewards of ownership (AC 4053.060). If substantially all the risks and rewards of ownership of the property reside with the lessee, he has "bought" that property; if they do not, he has not. From this simple thread of conceptual truth come four tests for distinguishing capital leases from operating leases (AC 4053.007):

1. If the lease *transfers ownership of the property* to the lessee, either during its term or at its end, it is a capital lease.
2. If the lease has *a bargain purchase option,* it is a capital lease.
3. If the lease term (including any bargain renewal periods) is equal to at least *75% of the estimated economic useful life* of the property, it is a capital lease.
4. If the present value of the minimum lease payments is equal to at least *90% of the fair value* of the leased property minus the lessor's investment credit, the lease is a capital lease.

If none of these tests is met, the lease is an operating lease. An exception to the third provision occurs when the property is very old at the beginning of the lease term (three quarters of the way through its estimated economic useful life). In this situation, the economic life rule and the present value rule should be ignored.

The fourth classification rule—the 90% test—is the one that is most complex and most difficult to apply. It is also the test that most often results in a capital lease classification, because if the lessor is essentially providing financing, he wants to recover his investment with an appropriate return through lease payments.

From the lessor's standpoint, there are two additional criteria that must be met before a lease can be called a capital lease (AC 4053.008):

---

[1] It is interesting to note that one Board member dissented to the issuance of SFAS 13 because he believed that, since the leasing business is a leveraged business, there should not be a difference between lessor accounting for leveraged leases and for direct financing leases. While his dissent was slanted against including tax benefits in the income recognition stream, it could as easily be argued that all lessor accounting should be like leveraged lease accounting. See Appendix 23 for an example of an incongruity resulting from not considering after-tax consequences in lessor accounting.

1. Collectibility must be reasonably assured; that is, there must be no unusual uncertainties about the credit risk.
2. Any unreimbursable costs yet to be incurred by the lessor must be estimable within reasonable limits.

Types of Capital Leases. A *sales-type lease* is a capital lease that gives rise to a manufacturer's or dealer's profit for the lessor. This profit is recognized immediately and is measured by the difference between the fair value of the property and its cost (or other carrying amount) to the lessor.

A *direct financing lease* is a capital lease in which the lessor's cost is the fair value of the property. Typically, a direct financing lease results where the lessor is a financial institution purchasing the property specifically for the lessee's use, i.e., the lessee has arranged for the lessor to buy the property.

Leveraged Leases. *Leveraged lease* accounting applies only to the lessor. Lessees get only two choices: operating and capital. A leveraged lease is probably intended to be a tax shelter vehicle, and it has these characteristics (AC 4053.042):

1. It would be a direct financing lease if it were not a leveraged lease.
2. It involves at least three parties: the lessee, a long-term creditor, and a lessor.
3. The long-term creditor provides financing that is nonrecourse as to the general credit of the lessor.
4. The amount of the financing is a significant percentage of the cost of the property. (This percentage is not defined, but it is interpreted to mean more than 50%.)
5. The lessor's investment (net of investment tax credit and benefits of tax deductions) in the property declines after the original investment has been made, often turns negative, and then increases during later years of the lease before it finally is realized.
6. The investment credit on the leased property is to be deferred and amortized along with the rest of the lease income.

Accounting for leveraged leases is very complex, typically requires computer assistance for the necessary calculations, and follows two basic premises:

1. Leveraged lease accounting is an after-tax concept and is based only on the lessor's net equity in the property.
2. Income after tax from a leveraged lease should represent a constant rate of return on the lessor's net investment. During those periods when the net investment is below zero, no income is to be recognized.

Definitions

The foregoing criteria would be inapplicable without definitions of the terms, summarized here from the AICPA's Professional Standards (AC 4053.005). The vulnerability of some of these definitions is what keeps the FASB staff busy.

1. *Related parties in leasing transactions* have the ability to exercise significant influence one over the other, or a third party can exercise significant influence over both.

2. *Inception of the lease* is the date of the lease agreement or, if earlier, the date of the written commitment specifying the significant terms of the deal. Originally, the inception of the lease for property to be constructed was the date of completion, but SFAS 23 (AC 4056) specified the inception as the time when all of the significant provisions of the lease were agreed to.

3. *Fair value of the leased property* is the price at which the property is (or could be) sold in an arm's-length sale. Cost is often used as an approximation of fair value if the property is reasonably new.

4. *Bargain purchase option* is an option price so low that at the inception of the lease predictability of purchase is almost certain. The definition is cast so that the presence of a bargain should be very obvious; if it is not, there is no bargain.

5. *Bargain renewal option* makes renewal rents so cheap that exercise is reasonably assured at the inception of the lease. Again, if the existence of the bargain is not clear, there is none.

6. *Lease term* is the noncancellable period of the lease plus bargain renewal periods, periods during which failure to renew would cause a penalty high enough that renewal is reasonably assured, periods during which the lessee has guaranteed the lessor's debt on the property, ordinary renewal periods up to the point of a bargain purchase option, and periods during which lessor may enforce renewal.

   The bargain purchase option and the lease term can interact. For example, suppose a five-year lease has a five-year renewal option. If he exercises the renewal, the lessee can buy the property for a dollar at the end of the tenth year. The dollar price clearly is a bargain, but the option is available only if the renewal option is exercised. If the lessee concludes at the inception of the lease that he is likely to exercise the renewal option and the purchase option, the term of the lease is ten years. If he concludes that this action is not reasonably assured, the term of the lease is five years, and there is no bargain purchase option.

   This definition also specifies when a lease is *noncancellable*. A lease that is cancellable only upon a remote contingency, or with the permission of the lessor, or provided the lessee enters a substitute lease with the same lessor, or only on payment of a prohibitive penalty is really a noncancellable lease.

7. *Estimated economic life of leased property* means the period when the property is expected to be economically usable by one or more users for the purpose originally intended. This definition is vague and has caused some interpretational problems. For example, the lessor of a freestanding one-story building may view his property as being usable by any number of tenants for any number of purposes, while the retail grocer who leases that property views it only as a supermarket. If the intended use is that which is viewed by the lessee, the useful life may be a relatively short period, perhaps no more than 15 or 20 years. On the other hand, if the intended use applies to the lessor, the property may be usable as long as it stands. Neither of these extreme positions is really justifiable. The use of a retail property after the primary lease term should be considered in light of general retail businesses, not the particular retail business of the lessee.

8. *Estimated residual value of leased property* is the expected fair value at the end of the lease term. In a May 1979 exposure draft, the Board would have ended a controversy by requiring that this value be figured in today's dollars, not those expected

at the end of the lease term after years of inflation rate compounding. However, that exposure draft has been withdrawn, so the question has been reopened.

9. *Unguaranteed residual value* of the leased property is not guaranteed to the lessor, either by the lessee or by a third party such as a lease broker.

10. *Minimum lease payments* are payments the lessee is required by contract to make, excluding executory costs (e.g., insurance, taxes, maintenance) and a profit thereon to the lessor. The lessee eliminates executory costs whether or not they are separately stated. If the executory costs are not separately stated and he does not know what they are, he makes an estimate. These minimum lease payments include any guarantee by the lessee of a residual value and any penalty he has to pay if he does not renew the lease. If the lessor has the right to require the lessee to purchase the property at the end of the lease term for a determinable amount, that amount is the same as a lessee guarantee.

    If the lessee agrees to make good on any deficiency in residual value of the property below a stated amount, that stated amount should be included as part of the minimum lease payments. From the lessor's standpoint, minimum lease payments include all of these things plus any guarantee of the residual value made by a third party not related to the lessor.

11. *Interest rate implicit in the lease* is the discount rate that causes the sum of the minimum lease payments and the unguaranteed residual value to have a present value equal to the fair value of the property at the beginning of the lease term minus any investment tax credit (ITC) that the lessor keeps and expects to realize. This formula considers ITC dollars equal to cost dollars and rental income dollars, even though an ITC dollar is worth more than a regular dollar because it is a tax credit, not a tax deduction. This flaw in the formula results in a significantly different implicit rate when the lessor keeps the investment tax credit rather than (a) passing it on to the lessee and (b) increasing the rent to produce an equal number of after-tax dollars over the term of the lease. The example in Appendix 23 shows that in a hypothetical situation, the implicit rate is 10% where the lessor passes the investment tax credit (ITC) and only 8% where he keeps it. Under both alternatives, the lessor is left with the same after-tax yield.

    SFAS 13 (AC 4053.007(d)) requires that the lessee use the rate implicit in the lease if (a) it is practicable for the lessee to find out what it is and (b) if it is lower than the lessee's incremental borrowing rate. When SFAS 13 was first released, the immediate reaction of lessors was not to disclose the rate; and lessees wouldn't ask the rate because the lessors wouldn't disclose it if they did. This left the auditor a bit incredulous, especially in those cases where the property was being made to order for the lessee. The FASB has withdrawn its November 1978 exposure draft proposing that the lessee be required to estimate the interest rate implicit in the lease. The economics of leasing often induce the lessor to accept an interest rate lower than the straight borrowing rate the lessee could obtain as a debtor. The Board's withdrawal of its proposal to put teeth into the implicit rate rule (and the attendant residual value) tacitly approved the lessee's incremental borrowing rate as the lease discount rate.

12. *Lessee's incremental borrowing rate* is the going rate at which the lessee could borrow to buy the leased property and repay over the term of the lease.

13. *Initial direct costs,* as first defined, were the incremental costs the lessor incurred directly in negotiating and closing specific deals. But SFAS 17 (AC 4054) broadened this to include costs "directly associated" with making and closing deals. The new definition encompasses costs that vary with either specific leasing transactions or with the general level of leasing activity. The costs do not necessarily have to be incremental for each lease. The significance of the change was to include salaries of lawyers and salespersons working for leasing companies, thereby improving the front-end income of these companies. (See Accounting by Lessors in this chapter.)

14. *Contingent rentals* were not defined in the initial release, but are now defined by amendment to mean those increases or decreases in lease payments that result from changes occurring subsequent to the inception of the lease in certain factors on which lease payments are based. Thus, payments based on machine hours or sales volume are contingent rentals excluded from the determination of minimum lease payment.

Accounting by Lessees

Operating Leases. For the lessee, accounting for an operating lease is relatively straightforward. Rental payments are charged to operations when they are due. The only variation occurs when payments are irregular in amount but not contingent; then the rent must be expensed on a straight-line basis without discounting over the term of the lease. Contingent rentals are any rentals that are based on something other than the passage of time and are to be charged against operations as they are incurred. SFAS 29 (AC 4048) amends this to remove from the definition of contingent rents amounts that are based on factors outside the control of the parties, such as prime interest rates or price levels.

Capital Leases. Capital lease accounting by the lessee is more complex. The lessee records the present value of the minimum lease payments (calculated when making the 90% test under the fourth classification rule) as an asset under property, plant, and equipment and as a liability under long-term debt.

If the discounted present value exceeds fair market value, only the fair market value is recorded in the accounts. This limitation increases the discount rate for the liability, since the total obligation equals that stated in the lease. As rental payments are made, a portion of each payment is applied against the obligation and a portion is charged as interest expense. The amount to be charged as interest is the amount determined by applying the discount rate used in establishing the asset and liability accounts to the remaining unpaid liability. The asset is depreciated over its estimated economic useful life, or amortized over the term of the lease if shorter and if the property reverts to the lessor at the end of the lease term.

Accounting by Lessors

Operating Leases. From the lessor's standpoint, accounting for an operating lease is straightforward. As the rents are earned, they are credited to income. The property under lease is part of property, plant, and equipment and is depreciated over its estimated useful life down to its estimated residual or salvage value.

Sales-Type Capital Leases. Accounting for capital leases is more complex. The lessor's accounting for sales-type leases involves calculating these elements:

- *Gross investment in the lease*—minimum rentals (excluding executory costs) plus unguaranteed residual value.
- *Sales*—present value of minimum lease payments less executory costs included in them (discounted at lessor's implicit rate in the lease).
- *Cost of sales*—carrying amount of property (usually cost) plus initial direct costs minus present value (at implicit rate) of unguaranteed residual.
- *Unearned income*—gross investment in the lease minus the sum of the present value of the minimum lease payments and the unguaranteed residual value.

An example of accounting for a typical sales-type lease transaction follows.

Assumptions

Minimum rental payments—gross	$4,050
—present value	3,517 *
Unguaranteed residual—gross	2,000
—present value	1,483 *
Equipment fair value	5,000
Equipment cost	4,750
Initial costs	100

* Based on fair value using rate implicit in lease

Computations

Sales, equal to present value (PV) of minimum rental payments		$3,517
Cost of sales:		
Equipment cost	$4,750	
Less PV of residual	(1,483)	
Plus initial costs	100	3,367
Gross margin		$ 150
Asset:		
Net investment in sales-type lease		$5,000
Made up of:		
Minimum rental payments	$4,050	
Plus residual	2,000	
Less unearned income	(1,050)	
	$5,000	

For balance sheet presentation, note that (1) unearned income is classified as an offset to the gross investment in the lease and (2) the net amount is carried like a receivable and classified according to the usual current/noncurrent criteria. (Most leasing companies, however, do not use classified balance sheets.) The unearned income is amortized by the interest method, using the rate at which the present values were discounted. Initial direct costs are charged immediately to cost of sales. The estimated residual value is reviewed periodically, and if the new estimate is lower than the recorded residual value, an immediate write-down is required. (The write-down is calculated by present valuing the new residual estimate at the interest rate implicit in the lease and comparing that to the present value of the residual as accreted upwards since the beginning of the lease.) No write-up is permitted.

Direct Financing Capital Leases. For a direct financing lease, the lessor's accounting is similar to that for a sales-type lease, with a few exceptions. First, there is no immediate profit to be recognized, so there are no entries for sales or cost of sales. Second, unearned income is calculated simply as the difference between gross investment in the lease and the carrying value of the leased property, which is usually its cost. Third, initial direct costs are offset against unearned income. This offset is accomplished by an immediate transfer of unearned income to realized income in an amount equal to the initial direct costs. An example of accounting for a typical direct financing lease transaction follows.

Assumptions

Minimum rental payments—gross	$4,050
—present value	3,517 *
Unguaranteed residual—gross	2,000
—present value	1,483 *
Equipment cost fair value	5,000
Initial costs	100

* Based on fair value using rate implicit in lease

Computations

Earned income (revenue)	$ 100	
Initial costs (expense)	$ 100	
Asset:		
Net investment in direct financing lease		$5,100
Made up of:		
Minimum rental payments	$4,050	
Plus residual	2,000	
Less unearned income, after offset		
of initial costs	(950)	
	$5,100	

The classification of gross investment and unearned income, the amortization method, and the periodic review of the residual value for direct financing capital leases are the same as the methods used for sales-type leases.

Under both sales-type leases and direct financing leases, any contingent rentals are credited to revenue as they are earned. For example, contingent rentals might relate to levels of sales (for a retail store), excess mileage (for an automobile or truck), or an increase in prime interest rates (for a lease where the payment fluctuates in parallel). Contingent rentals and their relationship to lease classification and accounting are discussed later in this chapter.

Leveraged Leases. The first step in accounting for a leveraged lease is to calculate the cash flows over the term of the lease. These cash flows include the income tax effect of tax deductions to the lessor (FASB Technical Bulletin 79-16 states that because of the importance of the lessor's tax rate in accounting for leveraged leases, the income effect of a change in the tax rate should be recognized in the first accounting period after the change (AC B4053.023)), the investment credit, the lessor's initial investment in the property, rental receipts net of debt service, and proceeds estimated to be obtained from the sale of the residual. The cumulative net cash inflow is the total income from the lease; this is the amount allocated in proportion to the lessor's positive net investment in the lease.

The second step is to calculate the rate to be used to allocate income. If possible, a computer should be used in this calculation. When applied to the net investment in the years in which that net investment is positive, this rate will exactly distribute the net income to those years. The rate is determined through trial and error, using successive iterations within the computer.

Nonrecourse debt financing is not recorded in the balance sheet; the "investment in lease" asset consists of only the excess of the present value of rental payments and estimated residual value over debt service requirements. The "unearned income" credit consists of the investment tax credit and the *pretax* component of the total income.[2]

Appendix E of SFAS 13 (AC 4053.123) presents a detailed example of the steps required to account for a leveraged lease. That example is indispensable to anyone who has to deal with a leveraged lease.

Disclosures in Financial Statements

SFAS 13 specifies in minute detail the required disclosures in the financial statements or footnotes thereto related to leases. The overall intent is to obtain a description of leasing activities, the flow of lease income or expense, and the future cash flows related to leasing. Some recent examples of lease disclosure are shown in Figures 23.1, 23.2, and 23.3.

A general description of leasing arrangements and a brief summary of disclosure requirements follows.

Lessees. (See AC 4053.016.) For capital leases, these items must be disclosed:

- The gross amount of assets capitalized,
- Aggregate future minimum lease payments,

---

[2] Note that the Board went "conceptual" on the income recognition by including tax benefits as an element thereof, but remained "traditional" in financial statements. Deferred tax balances related to leveraged leases are classified as such in balance sheets; and in income statements, the tax effects of leveraged leases are included with the usual tax provision. See AC 4053.123, "Illustrative Partial Financial Statements Including Footnotes."

Lease Commitments

Company as lessee:

The Company and its subsidiaries and joint ventures are lessees under noncancelable lease commitments on land and office buildings with varying lease periods to 2065. In addition to specified rents, most of these leases require the payment of property taxes, insurance and additional rentals based on a percentage of revenues. Certain of the lease agreements provide for renewal options. At February 28, 1979, the aggregate rental commitments under these leases, discounted to present value at interest rates from 6% to 11%, were $24,517,000.

The minimum rental commitments under these operating leases aggregated $106,811,000. Payments required during the next five years (including the Company's pro rata portion for joint ventures) are as follows (in thousands):

Year ending February 28 (29),	Amount
1980	$2,316
1981	2,307
1982	2,322
1983	2,322
1984	2,330

Rent expense was $2,955,000 and $2,050,000 for the years ended February 28, 1979 and 1978, respectively.

Company as lessor:

The Company leases space to tenants in its retail centers for which the Company charges minimum rents; the terms of the leases vary with the tenants. The majority of these leases also provide for additional rents during any year that the tenants' gross sales exceed an amount stated in the tenants' leases; the tenants are also obligated to reimburse the Company for certain operating expenses. Revenues from the shopping centers and other operating properties are summarized below (in thousands):

	Year Ended February 28,	
	1979	1978
Minimum rents	$28,128	$23,618
Overage rents	3,227	2,311
	$31,355	$25,929

Minimum rents receivable from tenants under leases executed at February 28, 1979, are as follows (in thousands):

1980	$ 29,243
1981	29,629
1982	29,606
1983	29,371
1984	29,033
Thereafter	250,955
	$397,837

FIGURE 23.1   LEASE DISCLOSURES—LESSEE AND LESSOR

SOURCE: Ernest W. Hahn, Inc., 1979 Annual Report.

Note A — Investment in Financing Transactions:

Greyhound Leasing is engaged in the financing of general industrial and commercial equipment principally as lessor under direct financing leases. The carrying amount of equipment leases, installment contracts and other loans, including the estimated residual value of equipment upon lease termination at December 31, 1979 (before allowance for doubtful accounts) was $701,487,000, of which 30 per cent was represented by aircraft and related equipment, 25 per cent by railroad cars, locomotives and other railroad equipment, 12 per cent by automotive vehicles and trailers, 4 per cent by tugboats, barges and oceangoing ships, and the remainder by various other commercial and industrial equipment. Approximately $90,485,000 of the above carrying amount relates to business outside the United States of which 53 per cent is in Latin America (including 24 per cent in Mexico), 19 per cent in Africa and 18 per cent in Canada.

The leases and contracts outstanding at December 31, 1979 had initial terms ranging from 1 to 16 years, and the average initial term weighted by carrying amount at inception was 12 years. The weighted average of the remaining terms is 6 years. One customer accounted for 14 per cent of earned income and represented 14 per cent of the carrying amount of related receivables at December 31, 1979.

Equipment leases, installment contracts and other loans at December 31, 1979 are due in installments during the years ending December 31, 1980 to 1995, approximately as fol-

lows: $159,690,000 (1980), $135,342,000 (1981), $116,708,000 (1982), $106,990,000 (1983), $93,932,000 (1984), $79,953,000 (1985), $67,005,000 (1986), $52,489,000 (1987), $43,080,000 (1988), and $69,380,000 thereafter.

Greyhound Leasing has a substantial number of leases and contracts with income fluctuating with changes in bank prime interest rates. Periodic adjustments are made to receivables and unearned income for changes in interest rates. The investment in equipment leases and contracts with fluctuating interest rates at year-end was as follows:

	1979	1978
Receivables	$368,854	$376 037
Estimated residual value	43,433	45 305
Less unearned income	(176,241)	(158 836)
	$236,046	$262 506

Earned income on leases and contracts with fluctuating rates was $29,419,000 and $21,854,000 in the years ended December 31, 1979 and 1978, respectively. The adjustments arising from changes in bank prime rates can have a significant effect on earned income; however, the effects on net income are reduced by related debt expense which also fluctuates with bank prime rates.

Earned income includes $1,412,000 and $897,000 in 1979 and 1978, respectively, transferred from unearned income to offset incremental initial direct leasing costs charged to expense.

FIGURE 23.2   LEASE DISCLOSURES—LESSOR

SOURCE: Greyhound Leasing & Financial Corporation, 1979 Annual Report.

Leases and Commitments

The Company leases most of its real estate. The typical lease period is 25 years and most leases contain renewal options. Exercise of such options is dependent on the level of business conducted at the location. In addition, the Company leases certain equipment. Most leases contain contingent rental provisions based on sales volume for retail units and miles traveled for trucks.

All leases and subleases with an initial term greater than one year are accounted for under Financial Accounting Standards Board Statement No. 13, Accounting for Leases. These leases are classified as capital leases, capital subleases, operating leases and operating subleases.

Assets under capital leases are capitalized using interest rates appropriate at the inception of each lease. Contingent rents associated with capital leases in 1978 and 1977 were $1,590,697 and $1,149,298. Following is an analysis of the Company's assets under capital leases:

	February 1, 1979	January 28, 1978
Real estate	$132,547,027	$123,687,641
Equipment	4,180,775	4,436,293
	$136,727,802	$128,123,934
Accumulated amortization	$ 25,600,202	$ 23,111,335

Future minimum lease payments for the above assets under capital leases at February 1, 1979 are as follows (in thousands):

	Real estate	Equipment	Total
1979	$ 13,942	$ 857	$ 14,799
1980	14,397	831	15,228
1981	14,359	653	15,012
1982	14,278	612	14,890
1983	14,217	327	14,544
Remainder	235,395	693	236,088
Total minimum obligations	306,588	3,973	310,561
Less executory costs	(1,628)		(1,628)
Net minimum obligations	304,960	3,973	308,933
Less interest	(183,759)	(1,109)	(184,868)
Present value of net minimum obligations	121,201	2,864	124,065
Less current portion	(1,844)	(499)	(2,343)
Long-term obligations at February 1, 1979	$119,357	$2,365	$121,722

Minimum obligations have not been reduced by minimum capital sublease rentals of $6,097,000 receivable in the future under noncancellable capital subleases. Executory costs include such items as property taxes and insurance.

Rent expense under operating leases is as follows:

	1978	1977
Minimum rent	$ 17,462,557	$ 11,968,063
Contingent rent	3,283,759	2,763,312
	20,746,316	14,731,375
Less sublease rent	(2,971,968)	(2,489,742)
	$ 17,774,348	$ 12,241,633

Future minimum lease payments for all noncancellable operating leases and related subleases having a remaining term in excess of one year at February 1, 1979 are as follows (in thousands):

	Real Estate	Equipment	Subleases
1979	$ 12,867	$ 4,233	$ (2,271)
1980	13,894	4,216	(1,816)
1981	13,620	4,157	(1,440)
1982	13,365	2,809	(1,348)
1983	13,062	1,576	(1,204)
Remainder	210,317	1,658	(7,878)
Total minimum obligations (receivables)	$277,125	$18,649	$(15,957)

At February 1, 1979, the Company was committed under contracts and purchase orders for approximately $21,775,000 for property held for resale and for land, buildings and equipment.

FIGURE 23.3 LEASE DISCLOSURE—LESSEE AND SUBLESSOR
SOURCE: Albertson's Inc., 1979 Annual Report.

- Minimum lease payments for each of the next five years,
- Executory costs and imputed interest, each as included in the aggregate and five years' minimum payments,
- Minimum sublease rentals receivable, and
- Contingent rents incurred, included in income statements presented.

For operating leases written for longer than a year, these items must be disclosed:

- Aggregate future minimum lease payments,
- Minimum lease payments for each of the next five years, and
- Minimum sublease rentals receivable.

For all operating leases, the total rental expense included in income statements presented, classified into minimum rents, contingent rents, and sublease rentals, must be disclosed.

Lessors. (See AC 4053.023.) For capital leases, these components of net investment must be disclosed:

- Future minimum lease payments receivable,
- Executory costs, including profit, included in lease receivables,
- Accumulated allowance for uncollectible lease receivables,
- Unguaranteed residual values, and
- Unearned income.

For capital leases, in addition to net investment components, these items must be disclosed:

- Minimum lease payments for each of the next five years,
- Initial direct costs offset against unearned income on direct financing leases for each income statement presented, and
- Contingent rentals earned in each income statement presented.

For operating leases, these items must be disclosed:

- Asset and accumulated depreciation amount by major classes,
- Minimum future rentals in the aggregate and for each of the next five years, and
- Contingent rentals earned in each income statement presented.

Special Types of Leases

Real Estate. The most important of the special kinds of leases covered by SFAS 13 are those involving real estate (AC 4053.024-.028). Not only are real estate leases typically more complicated than leases for personal property, but they can also involve huge sums of money, particularly in industries such as retailing. The Board observes that if the ownership of land (which is eternal and so does not depreciate) does not pass to the lessee either directly or through a bargain purchase option, a land lease is always an operating lease. If a lease covers a *building and the land* it sits on, it should be treated as two leases—one for the land and one for the building—based on the relative fair values of each. If the land element of the lease is small, however, the total package is treated as a building lease and classified accordingly. ("Small" is less than 25% of the total value of the property under lease.) If a real estate lease also involves *personal property,* the personalty element must be carved out and treated as a separate lease regardless of the relative value of the equipment.

Another factor in real estate leases is the lease for *part of a building.* Quite commonly a tenant will occupy a suite of offices in a high-rise, or a storeroom in a shopping center, or some other portion of a building. The parties to these leases may not be able to determine the fair value of the property under lease or, in the case of the lessor, the cost. In those circumstances, the lessee is to look to the estimated useful life of the property, and if his lease is for 75% or more, it is a capital lease. The lessor should consider these leases operating leases regardless of how long they run. (See commentary below on FASB Interpretation No. 24 (AC 4053-4).)

Related-Party Leases. Although SFAS 13 retained the APB 10 requirement that subsidiaries must be consolidated if their principal activity is to lease property to the parent or other affiliates, the Board retreated from APB 5's notion that leases between related parties probably should be capitalized. SFAS 13 (AC 4053.029-.031) states that a lease is a lease and that it does not matter whether it is between related parties except "where it is clear that the terms of the transaction have been significantly affected by the fact that the lessee and lessor are related" (AC 4053.029). Then the accounting must follow the substance rather than the form.

Accounting for arm's-length equivalence can be a difficult process. (See Chapter 28 for a full discussion.) In many instances, the owner of a company will buy property and lease it to his company on a short-term basis. If the company and the auditor conclude that similar property would not be available for lease from unrelated lessors on a short-term basis or that the company would not risk being deprived of the property by leasing from a person who was not also the company's owner, appropriate accounting must alter the term of the lease to make it reasonable. One way to alter the term of the lease is to deem that the lease terms have been extended so that the present-valued rents equal the owner's cost.

Another commonly encountered situation involves the owner of the company buying property and leasing it to his company at a rental higher than market rate. This situation can exist for many reasons, but usually it is tax motivated. If the lease is an operating lease, the accounting problem is troublesome. Rent expense could be overstated, and some other expense or dividend could be understated. If it is a capital lease, the problem is more than troublesome. The leased asset cannot be capitalized at more than fair value, which presumably is the cost to the owner, and the liability cannot be discounted at more than the incremental borrowing rate of the company. These leases must therefore be altered for proper accounting. Because there are several practical problems that complicate that process, it may be best to adopt the technique of issuing combined financial statements, i.e., combining the company's accounts with the leasing operation of the company's owners. This combination not only provides a neat solution to a vexing problem, it also makes sense from a financial reporting standpoint, because the combined financial statements then account for the economic impact of the company's use of the property.

Sale and Leaseback Transactions. The lease part of a sale and leaseback transaction is treated the same as any other lease for classification and accounting purposes. SFAS 13 (AC 4053.032-.034) said, however, that the lease part of the transaction cannot be separated from the sale part, because the two are interdependent. Therefore, any gain or loss on the sale transaction should be deferred and amortized to income, using the straight-line method if the lease is an operating lease, and in tandem with the depreciation or amortization of the leased asset if the lease is a capital lease. But when the fair value of the asset is demonstrably less than its carrying value at the time of the sale and leaseback, the transaction is considered closed, and the loss is recognized.

The Board amended SFAS 13 with SFAS 28 (AC 4047). This amendment essentially says that if the leaseback is minor in relation to the property sold, either as to the duration or portion of the property leased back, then the sale transaction and the leaseback transaction are separate and should be accounted for separately.

The sale and leaseback technique has become a very important financing vehicle for many companies. Often these arrangements are facilitated by lease brokers or underwriters, whose role—and the accounting problems they generate—is discussed later in this chapter.

Subleases. SFAS 13 provisions for sublease accounting (AC 4053.035-.040) were initially taken to imply that future losses on lease-sublease transactions (e.g., if a retailer were to close a store and sublease the premises for an amount short of the rent payable on the primary lease) need not be currently recognized. FASB Interpretation No. 27 (AC 4053-6) corrects that impression, however, and states that the FASB does not intend to prohibit timely recognition of a loss on a sublease. But this does not say exactly what to do, so there are still debates about whether a sublease shortfall needs to be accrued as a loss. Ordinarily, a sublease of property no longer usable in the business means loss accrual, and property being banked for future use through short-term subleases militates against loss accrual.

Transition Period for Adoption of SFAS 13. The effective-date provisions are detailed in AC 4053.048-.051. SFAS 13 was effective for new leases beginning January 1, 1977, but did not have to be applied to preexisting leases until January 1, 1981. The delay was intended to permit companies to work out any problems caused by existing loan covenants or other contractual agreements. Of course, earlier implementation on all pre-1977 leases is permitted and encouraged. The SEC did its share to encourage earlier application by requiring in ASR 225 that public companies retroactively adopt SFAS 13 beginning with calendar year 1978.

Implementation of SFAS 13 will be accomplished by the retroactive restatement of financial statements for all periods presented (or at least as many as is practicable). If the restatement goes back through the earliest period presented, the net effect on the beginning of that earliest period should be included as an adjustment to retained earnings at the beginning of that period. If the restatement goes only partway back, the cumulative effect on income should be presented in net income of the earliest restated period.

CHANGES TO SFAS 13

As of October 1980, the FASB had issued seven amendments and six interpretations of SFAS 13. Because of the number of changes to SFAS 13, in May 1980 the Board published a codification titled *Accounting for Leases,* which incorporates all of the amendments and interpretations until then. (An *interpretation* simply clarifies or provides additional guidance to a Statement of Financial Accounting Standards. An *amendment* is itself a Statement of Financial Accounting Standards; it releases changes to the existing SFAS.) The following text is a very brief synopsis of what each changes or tries to change.

Amendments

Initial Direct Costs. SFAS 17, *Accounting for Leases—Initial Direct Costs* (AC 4054, amending 4053.005(m)), broadens the definition of initial direct costs to include those costs that are not necessarily incremental to a specific lease but are related to the general level of leasing activity.

Leases With Tax-Exempt Debt. SFAS 22, *Changes in the Provisions of Lease Agreements Resulting from Refundings of Tax-Exempt Debt* (AC 4055, amending 4053.014 and .017(f)), is very narrow. It deals with the advance refunding of municipal bonds underlying leased property. Often a municipal authority acts as a financing conduit for a company that wants to build a factory or other productive facility, or the authority owns the facility and leases it to the company. Typically, these leases are absolutely tied to the outstanding bonds. The rent is exactly enough to pay the debt service. As soon as the bonds are paid off the rent stops, and the property belongs to the company.

Before SFAS 13, these arrangements were almost universally accounted for by the company as property ownership, with a liability for the bonded debt. But under SFAS 13, these arrangements are accounted for as capital leases. A problem arose in applying one of the SFAS 13 provisions, which said that if a capital lease is changed so that the amount of rents changes, the asset and liability should be recalculated using the original interest rate. APB 26 (AC 5362) says, however, that where debt is extinguished before its maturity, any difference between the extinguishment price and the carrying amount of the debt is current profit or loss. Because there is no substantive difference between a see-through lease by an industrial development authority and the direct debt of the company, SFAS 22 treats them the same; it requires recognition of profit or loss at the time of the advance refunding.

Lease Inception. SFAS 23, *Inception of the Lease* (AC 4056, amending 4053.005(b)), redefines inception for property that must be constructed or manufactured or that involves a significant delay between negotiation of the lease and availability for the lessee's use. SFAS 23 says that the inception of the lease occurs when its significant terms are agreed to. This statement also closes a loophole covering new construction. Often the parties would negotiate the terms of a lease based on the expected cost of a building or shopping center not yet constructed. By the time the property was finished and ready for occupancy, the lessee could argue convincingly that the property's fair value had increased to an extent that the present value of rentals would now be less than 90% of the new fair value, even though the lease might have been negotiated on the basis of the lessor recovering all of his cost.

This amendment gave rise to another interpretation problem: minimum lease payments are to be present valued at the beginning of the lease term for purposes of making the 90% test required by AC 4053.007(d). If the present value is taken back to the inception of the lease, that value will be lower, perhaps under 90%. The FASB informally advised inquirers that discounting should not be taken further than the beginning of the lease term.

Sales-Type Real Estate Leases. SFAS 26, *Profit Recognition on Sales-Type Leases of Real Estate* (AC 4057, amending 4053.008), conforms to the requirements of the AICPA industry accounting guide, *Accounting for Profit Recognition on Sales of Real Estate* (1974a). SFAS 13 sanctioned recognition of profit on sales of real estate even though the buyer made no down payment, as long as the parties structured the transaction in the form of a sales-type lease. SFAS 26, however, prohibits profit recognition unless the buyer, at the inception of the lease, has made an investment adequate to assure that he is economically bound to the acquisition. Percentages of investments deemed adequate and therefore required are given in the industry accounting guide.

Renewals or Extensions. SFAS 27, *Classification of Renewals or Extensions of Existing Sales-Type or Direct Financing Leases* (AC 4046, amending AC 4053.017, fn. ii), permits classification of these renewals or extensions as a sales-type lease if they meet the criteria in SFAS 13. Previously, such classification and the attendant profit were precluded the second time around.

Leasebacks. SFAS 28, *Accounting for Sales with Leasebacks* (AC 4047, amending 4053.032), provides that if a leaseback is minor, the profit on sale may be recognized. Even if a major part is leased back, profit can be recognized to the extent it exceeds the present value of the minimum leaseback payments. SFAS 13 mandated complete deferral of sales profit, which could result in the ludicrous situation of negative future rental expense.

Contingent Rents. SFAS 29, *Determining Contingent Rentals* (AC 4048, amending 4053.005), says that even though SFAS 13 excludes them from the calculation of minimum lease payments, certain contingent rentals that are tied to uncontrollable variables such as interest rates or price levels should be included in the calculation.

Interpretations

Residual Value of Leased Property. Interpretation No. 19, *Lessee Guarantee of the Residual Value of Leased Property* (AC 4053-1), clarifies questions related principally to automobiles and trucks under lease. It states that a surcharge for excessive wear and tear or for damages does not constitute a guarantee of residual value. It also states that where the lessee guarantees only a portion of the residual value, the balance is unguaranteed and is not to be included in minimum lease payments for purposes of testing against the capital lease criteria. This split residual guarantee was invented to cope with SFAS 13. Previously, it was customary for the lessee to guarantee any residual realization shortfall. Under the split arrangement, however, the economic risk to the lessor is negligible because the lessee's guarantee covers the top dollars.

Business Combination Leases. Interpretation No. 21, *Accounting for Leases in a Business Combination* (AC 4053-2), states that leases acquired in a purchase business combination keep their old classification under SFAS 13, so they are regarded as capital leases or operating leases based on the factors present at the inception of the lease. Even though the leases are fair valued as part of the purchase price allocation, they are not retested as new leases against the classification rules at the date of the business combination.

Government Property Leases. Interpretation No. 23, *Leases of Certain Property Owned by a Governmental Unit of Authority* (AC 4053-3), clarifies the narrow question caused by the language in SFAS 13, paragraph 28, which had been interpreted to mean that all such leases were automatically operating leases. The interpretation establishes four rules that must be followed if a lease is to be eligible for the special operating lease provisions of paragraph 28.

Partial-Building Leases. Interpretation No. 24, *Leases Involving Only Part of a Building* (AC 4053-4), attempts to resolve another paragraph 28 problem by telling how to calculate the fair value of part of a building. Paragraph 28 provides that if a lease covers only part of a building and the fair value of the premises is not *objectively determinable,* the lessee should look only to the useful life in order to classify the lease. This practice led retailers (particularly large retailers operating in numerous shopping centers) to conclude that their leases were operating leases. Interpretation No. 24 reaffirms that it is possible to establish fair value even if there are no sales of similar property. It has had very little practical impact, however, because it provides very little guidance on how the fair value may be established.

Leased Asset Purchased by Lessee. Interpretation No. 26, *Accounting for Purchase of a Leased Asset by the Lessee during the Term of the Lease* (AC 4053-5), requires that any difference between the purchase price and the remaining liability on the lease obligation be an adjustment of the basis of the asset.

Sublease Loss. Interpretation No. 27, *Accounting for a Loss on a Sublease* (AC 4053-6), simply clarifies that a current loss really can result from entering into a sublease. The wording in SFAS 13 implied that no loss could be recognized except over the term of the sublease. (See earlier discussion of subleases.)

Implementation of Changes

Implementation of the various amendments and interpretations is selective, depending on whether a company has yet adopted SFAS 13 by a retroactive restatement of its financial statements. One restatement is enough; if the company has already restated for SFAS 13 and an amendment or interpretation that has an impact on an existing lease is issued, that lease can be left alone. An identical lease created later, however, would be included under the pronouncement. This undermines the Board's intention of getting all preexisting leases evaluated under consistent criteria by 1981. On the other hand, the Board recognized that earlier leases might have been written differently if the new criteria had been in effect, so they decided against double restatements.

CONTEMPORARY ISSUES IN LEASING PRACTICE

The major contemporary issue related to lease accounting is that the FASB has mandated a series of mechanistic rules with no underlying conceptual framework by which to decide whether a particular transaction has resulted in the acquisition of recordable resources and obligations by lessees. The Board has compounded the frustrations of those trying to figure out appropriate and consistent accounting for leases.

Structuring to Avoid Capitalization

The existence of SFAS 13 and its satellites along with the emphasis on projecting financial strength in the balance sheet and the continuing reluctance by management to accelerate charges against income creates the challenge of avoiding capitalization for prospective lessees. These same factors have created a problem for lessors because, to accommodate their customers, they may have to forego the sales-type or direct financing accounting they prefer. In some cases, structuring close to the line results in operating leases for lessees and capital leases for lessors (e.g., auto and truck leases through lessee guarantee of the top layer of residual). (See Interpretation No. 19; AC 4053-1.)

SFAS 13 provides any number of ways to avoid capitalization, although some are more expensive for the lessee because they require that the lessor assume risks for which he wants to get paid. By laying down precise rules for capitalization of leases, SFAS 13 provides a detailed design for structuring leases that qualify as operating leases. Lessees and lease brokers are imaginative and resourceful in creating sophisticated leasing arrangements that use the SFAS 13 rules to their advantage. The useful life provisions, the contingent rental provisions, and the residual value guarantee provisions provide ample opportunity for people intent on avoiding capitalization of leases to do so.

As an extreme example, suppose a retailer leases a store building for 20 years (less than 75% of the useful life) with the rent stated in terms of sales, such as 100% of the first $250,000 annual sales. It is clear that as long as the store remains open, the sales figure will be met and the rent will be paid. But because the lessee can close the store, the entire rent is contingent, so it is not included in minimum lease payments. Thus the lease becomes an operating lease, since zero is not 90% of anything. Although other considerations, such as investment in leasehold improvements, agreements with employee unions, or operating history, might make it highly unlikely that the lessee will close the store, that fact is of no consequence.

Disclosure Reductions

An unintended result of SFAS 13 was to reduce in some instances the amount of disclosure provided in financial statements. The ASR 147 disclosure requirements included the present value of minimum lease payments (or the liability) on finance-type leases. In practice, many companies considered real estate leases for 20 years or more to be finance-type leases. Though ASR 147 was not a GAAP pronouncement, public companies (and many nonpublic companies) gave the information. Under SFAS 13, no similar disclosure requirement exists for operating leases.

The SEC staff has been concerned about this lack of a disclosure requirement for operating leases and has challenged the frequent interpretation of capital leases in SFAS 13 as being far narrower than ASR 147 financing leases. A group of large retailers discussed their interpretations with the FASB at the SEC's request. The Board agreed that the retailers were in compliance with SFAS 13, but this only left less information available than before.

Although the Board agreed that the retailers were within the literal requirements of SFAS 13, the SEC did not publish any retraction of its indicting statement, reported in the March 1979 *Journal of Accountancy* (p. 24), that "the retailers' interpretation . . . exaggerates the useful life of the leased facility (and) could result in understatement of debt and overstatement of earnings."

F. W. Woolworth Co. presents an interesting example of the "before and after" disclosure in Figure 23.4. For the year ended January 31, 1978, the footnote states that had SFAS 13 been adopted, the capitalized lease liability at February 1,

January 31, 1977

Note 10 – Leases

At January 31, 1977 the Company was obligated under more than 5,000 leases, principally for store properties. Many of the store leases contain renewal options and provide for additional rental payments based on a percentage of store sales. Under certain leases additional payments are required of the Company for real estate taxes, insurance and other expenses.

Total rental expense in 1976 of $176,000,000, net of sublease income of $48,300,000 was charged to income (1975 – $166,900,000 net of sublease income of $43,800,000). Rental payments based on a percentage of sales included in total rental expense amounted to $20,500,000 (1975 – $17,300,000). Minimum rental commitments under noncancellable leases less sublease income, to which the Company is committed at January 31, 1977 are as follows: 1977, $176,600,000; 1978, $176,500,000; 1979, $176,100,000; 1980, $173,300,000; 1981, $167,800,000; 1982-1986, $741,600,000; 1987-1991, $577,000,000; 1992-1996, $243,700,000 and $143,100,000 thereafter.

The aggregate present value of minimum rental commitments, less sublease income, of financing leases, as defined by the Securities and Exchange Commission, at January 31, 1977 was $1,043,600,000 (January 31, 1976 – $996,500,000). If these leases had been capitalized, and the related property right amortized on a straight-line basis and interest expense computed on the basis of the present value of the declining outstanding balance of the lease commitments, net income would have been decreased $1,500,000 in 1976 and $2,400,000 in 1975.

In late 1976 the Financial Accounting Standards Board adopted Statement No. 13, "Accounting for Leases," which establishes standards of financial accounting and reporting by lessees and lessors. In accordance with this Statement, leases meeting certain criteria, similar in many respects to the SEC's definition of financing leases, would be considered capital leases and recorded at their present value as an asset and an obligation in the financial statements. Other leases not meeting the criteria of a capital lease would be considered operating leases and not capitalized. The provisions of the Statement must be applied to all lease transactions entered into after December 31, 1976 and by December 31, 1980 must be applied retroactively to all then existing lease agreements.

January 31, 1978

Note 9 – Commitments

At January 31, 1978 the Company was obligated under more than 5,000 leases, principally for store properties. Many of the store leases contain renewal options, ranging from five to ten years, and provide for additional rental payments based on a percentage of store sales. Certain leases provide that the Company shall pay for real estate taxes, insurance and other expenses. Management expects that in the normal course of business, leases that expire will be renewed or replaced by other leases.

Rental expense charged to income was comprised of the following:

	1977	1978
	(in thousands of dollars)	
Minimum rentals	$212,000	$203,800
Percentage rentals, including $100 on leases capitalized in 1977	20,700	20,500
Sublease income	(49,000)	(48,300)
Total	$183,700	$176,000

Leases entered into after 1976 and capitalized in accordance with Financial Accounting Standard No. 13 (Accounting for Leases) consists of the following, expressed in thousands of dollars:

Land and buildings	$20,000
Furniture, fixtures and equipment	8,400
	28,400
Less accumulated amortization	1,000
	$27,400

The effect on net income in 1977 of capitalizing these leases was not material.

FAS No. 13 includes a requirement, not yet effective, that the present value of capitalized leases be retroactively recorded as an asset and an obligation in the financial statements. If those capital leases entered into prior to 1977 were capitalized, the Company estimates that assets and liabilities would have increased approximately $287,800,000 (1976 – $307,300,000) and $322,000,000 (1976 – $339,600,000), respectively. Income of consolidated companies would have decreased by $1,900,000, or $.07 per share (1976 – $2,300,000, or $.08 per share).

Future minimum lease payments due under capital and operating leases are, in thousands of dollars, as follows:

	Capital	Operating	Total
1978	$ 5,500	$ 196,400	$ 201,900
1979	5,500	192,500	198,000
1980	5,300	186,600	191,900
1981	5,100	177,200	182,300
1982	4,900	166,400	171,300
Thereafter	52,100	1,434,800	1,486,900
Total minimum payments	78,400	$2,353,900	$2,432,300
Less estimated real estate taxes, insurance and other expenses	13,500		
Net minimum lease payments	64,900		
Less imputed interest	36,600		
Present value of net minimum lease payments	$28,300		

Minimum lease payments have not been reduced by minimum sublease rentals of $45,100,000 due in the future under noncancellable subleases. They also do not include percentage rentals which may be paid under certain store leases where sales exceed stipulated amounts.

The Company is constructing a $26 million (1.3 million square foot) distribution center in Junction City, Kansas. The funds are expected to be raised in a private placement of industrial revenue bonds.

FIGURE 23.4   FEWER CAPITAL LEASES THAN FINANCING LEASES
SOURCE: F. W. Woolworth Co., 1977 and 1978 Annual Reports.

($ in thousands)	SFAS 13 Capital Leases		ASR 147 Non-Cap Financing Leases	% SFAS 13/ ASR 147 Liability
	Asset	Liability		
Sears Roebuck & Co.*	$ 115,523	$ 149,000	$ 359,000	41.5%
K-Mart	1,007,476	1,174,540	1,630,338	72.0%
J.C. Penney Company, Inc.	300,000	300,000	1,005,300	29.8%
F. W. Woolworth	307,300	339,600	1,043,600	32.5%
Federated Department Stores	119,700	142,700	213,400	66.8%
May Department Stores*	32,983	39,288	103,000	38.1%
Dayton Hudson	38,237	44,247	35,971	123.0%
Allied Stores	68,255	81,907	174,049	47.0%
Carter Hawley Hale Stores	221,400	239,100	295,000	81.0%
Mercantile Stores Co. Inc.	14,631	17,437	56,576	30.8%

*Retroactive capitalization provided in January 1978 financial statements.

FIGURE 23.5   CAPITAL LEASES VS. NONCAPITALIZED FINANCING
LEASES
SOURCE: Francis Phalen, "The Impact of SFAS 13 on the Retail Industry," *Financial Executive,* November, 1978, p. 54.

1977, would have been $339,600,000. The similar 1977 footnote says, however, that noncapitalized financing leases at January 31, 1977, totalled $1,043,600,000. Thus, two thirds of the financing leases under ASR 147 became operating leases under SFAS 13. Another interesting feature of this 1978 lease footnote is the tabulation of future minimum lease payments due under capital leases and operating leases. The comparison between capital leases ($78 million gross undiscounted lease payments) and operating leases ($2,354 million) shows clearly that Woolworth does not have many capital leases under the precise definitions of SFAS 13.

Woolworth is not alone, however. As shown in Figure 23.5, in only one of ten cases studied did the disclosed capital leases under SFAS 13 exceed the noncapitalized financing leases reported under ASR 147. For those such as the SEC who may have thought the definitions were consistent, their dismay is understandable.

Lease Underwriters/Brokers

Another contemporary issue related to the leasing industry is accounting for lease underwriters and brokers, an industry group burgeoned by the advent of SFAS 13. Lease underwriters bring sellers and lessees together with financiers and equity participants. Their deals are often very complex. They may buy a property, sell it to a third party, lease it back, and then sublease it to the user, with different lease durations and leveraging in the various stages. Regardless of the many layers of paper involved, their compensation typically consists of a fee up front and an interest in the residual value of the property. At the end of the lease term, the underwriter takes possession of the property, either selling it to the lessee or someone else or re-leasing it to the lessee or someone else. The underwriter keeps all or part of the proceeds. Because SFAS 13 does not deal with these transactions directly, accounting practices by lease underwriters for income recognition at the outset of a deal have taken three divergent routes:

1. There is no accounting for the residual value until the property is sold or re-leased;
2. The discounted present value of the estimated residual is recognized, and the discount to income over the term of the lease is accreted; or
3. The discounted present value of the estimated residual is recognized, but the discount is not accreted.

The first two approaches can be justified conceptually. If the residual value can be reasonably estimated, it should be recorded; otherwise it should not. Some accountants believe the third approach does not have conceptual underpinning. Since the discount is supposed to represent the time value of money, this value should increase as time passes. The rationale for not accreting the discount is presumably to build in a cushion for conservatism in order to recognize the frailties of the residual estimating process.

Virtually nothing comprehensive has been published on the very complex subject of lease broker accounting for fees, residuals, and subleases. For a technical excursion into the problems, 1977-78 correspondence between the FASB, AcSEC, Touche Ross & Co., and Arthur Andersen & Co. may be inspected at the FASB. AcSEC is presently studying this area with the intention of submitting a comprehensive issues paper to the FASB.

Lessors—Bad Debts

Before SFAS 13, most financing lessors estimated bad-debt expense as a percentage of leases written, and applied that percentage to reduce their unearned revenue at the time the lease was recorded. In effect, the amortization of the remaining smaller amount of unearned revenue into earned revenue resulted in recognition of bad-debt expense on a declining basis over the term of the lease.[3] When the Board issued SFAS 17, *Initial Direct Costs* (AC 4054), it said its intent was that initial direct costs would not include a provision for bad debts. Since lessors have accounted for bad debts the same as for initial direct costs, these lessors face a dilemma. This dilemma is compounded by another statement in SFAS 17 that the Board did not intend to change present accounting for bad debts. The problem is presumably being solved on an ad hoc basis by each affected lessor in his own way. Some have concluded that no change in accounting is required because, while they treat bad debts *like* initial direct costs, they do not treat them *as* initial direct costs.

---

[3] For large leasing companies with thousands of leases, use of a percentage provision is a sensible alternative to periodic evaluation of each lease. Mechanically, there are various ways to accomplish this result. For example, applying the estimated bad-debt percentage to the periodic amount transferred from unearned to earned revenue accomplishes the same income statement result as initial set-up, but on the balance sheet unearned revenue would then include a hypothetical bad-debt reserve equal to the bad-debt provision percentage. Whether the allowance for uncollectible accounts is set out separate from, or included within, unearned revenues makes no real difference except when offering securities. Some underwriters feel "soundness" is conveyed by lowering unearned revenues and setting out separately the allowance for uncollectible rentals.

OTHER OFF-BALANCE SHEET FINANCING ARRANGEMENTS

Off-balance sheet financing transactions other than leases range from the very simple to the highly complex and innovative. They involve all sorts of assets, particularly property, plant, and equipment, inventory, and accounts receivable. The thread that runs through all of these transactions is that they involve the company with a financier, and the result (perhaps the objective) is that liabilities slide off the balance sheet.

Property, Plant, and Equipment

Financing arrangements for property, plant, and equipment (see Chapter 20) take many forms but have certain common elements. The company agrees to do enough business with a facility to provide funds sufficient to service the debt on the facility. Someone else arranges to acquire or build a facility, obtaining the financing to do so. The financier is then lending money on the company's ability to perform.

Some examples of this kind of arrangement are through-put agreements, in which the company agrees to run a specified amount of goods through a processing facility; take or pay arrangements, in which the company guarantees to pay for some specified requisite volume of goods, needed or not; and long-term charter of barge or vessel space or contract for warehouse storage space, in which the company agrees to provide the requisite amount of goods for service or pay a minimum fee.

A recent and very sophisticated technique for acquiring use of facilities involves the beneficiary's creation of entities for ownership and financing. The common characteristic of these entities (joint ventures, limited partnerships, trusts) is that they are not consolidated with the company's financial statements, and the debt they incur is therefore not included among the company's liabilities.

Inventory

Inventory (see Chapter 19) also provides numerous opportunities for getting liabilities off the balance sheet. One device, the product repurchase arrangement, works like this: the company manufactures a product, sells it to a third party, and agrees to buy it back. The third party, using the sales agreement and the buy-back agreement as collateral, borrows money to carry the inventory. The AICPA's SOP 78-9 covers simple product repurchase arrangements of this sort. But there are more subtle and less direct arrangements, such as a company arranging financing for its suppliers or a company issuing guaranteed purchase contracts to an intermediary who bought merchandise from the company's supplier. These are some of the hard cases that will not be satisfactorily resolved until the basic conceptual question of accounting for resources and obligations is answered.

Although SOPs are not the only generally accepted accounting principles, the staff of the SEC has indicated that it believes product financing arrangements of the type covered by SOP 78-9 should be displayed on the balance sheet. In fact, the staff indicated that in its judgment, such arrangements have always required recording in the accounts. In practice, however, some of these arrangements have been treated as off-balance sheet financing.

Accounts Receivable

Accounts receivable (see Chapter 18) historically have provided a vehicle for off-balance sheet financing. The sale of receivables with recourse to a financing institution is common. In some situations, a company creates an unconsolidated finance subsidiary that borrows money (usually guaranteed directly or indirectly by the company) and buys the company's accounts receivable. The company's balance sheet then shows the residual cash rather than displaying accounts receivable and debt (either long-term or short-term). This is a far more appealing presentation from a liquidity standpoint.

Prognosis

Those who argue against off-balance sheet financing are hindered by the absence of a conceptual distinction between an economic obligation and an accounting liability. Companies are reluctant—indeed unwilling—to record the obligations arising from these transactions. They point to the presence of practical precedents and the absence of authoritative prohibition. Some argue that forcing them to record these obligations would be a disadvantage to them in the money markets, because it would impact their present credit ratings or affect their future credit limits. In extreme cases, existing credit agreements or debt limitations would be violated by recording these obligations. Until the concepts are clear, off-balance sheet financing arrangements will probably continue to create practical problems. In March 1980 the FASB issued an exposure draft that would require—as a stop-gap—disclosure of these arrangements, including the amounts involved. A revised exposure draft calling for disclosure of unconditional guarantees is expected late in 1980, along with a proposed interpretation on disclosure of indirect guarantees.

AUDITING CONSIDERATIONS

For the auditor to understand off-balance sheet financing arrangements (leases and other types) he must be aware of their economic substance and know what risks and rewards his client will obtain in the transaction. In addition to obtaining information from the client's counsel and management, this process may involve communicating with parties to the lease transaction and outside parties such as suppliers to obtain the information necessary for audit judgments. When he understands the transactions, the auditor must determine that the accounting and disclosure reflect the substance of the transaction. One of the more difficult aspects is auditing assets and obligations recorded by nonclient parties to the transaction, which might be necessary to evaluate the propriety of the client's accounting treatment. The following discussion focuses on leases, whose prevalence results in groups of identified problems.

Objectives

The auditor's primary objective in examining leasing transactions must be to ensure that the financial statements are in strict compliance with SFAS 13 as amended. The transactions must also make economic sense to the auditor. He must determine whether the transaction he is looking at is really a lease in accordance with the SFAS 13 definition and not in substance a transaction requiring a different accounting treatment. He must be satisfied that strict compliance with the rules does not result in the absence of fair presentation. Beyond the accounting issues, the auditor must evaluate the adequacy of disclosure of leasing transactions.

Auditing Procedures

The auditor must consider a number of procedural issues when planning and conducting his examination. The accounting requirements for leases impose some important audit procedural problems in themselves and imply that much evidence is needed to support the accounting treatment for complex leases. Proper lease accounting also requires that the parties make a number of estimates, and proper auditing requires that the auditor challenge these estimates and their underlying documentation.

Lessee. For the lessee, leases are often material transactions. Misclassification of a lease could have a material effect on the financial statements. The typical purchase, accounts payable, and cash disbursements control systems do not usually encompass the lease transaction, so the auditor needs a substantive approach for searching out the features of these transactions.

The auditor should take the simple but nonetheless important step of asking whether leases exist. A review of expense accounts, including the rent account, for recurring periodic charges can uncover new leases. When reading the minutes of the meetings of the board of directors and other senior groups in the company, the auditor should remain alert to discussion of lease arrangements. Typically, an auditor will scrutinize lawyers' invoices to became aware of matters to which they are attending, which also helps uncover leases. After he has become aware of the leases, the auditor should read them and understand the rights and obligations they convey. He should consider requesting confirmation of the terms of the lease from the other party or parties.

Lessor. If he is auditing a lessor, the auditor has the same kinds of procedural concerns plus some new ones. For example, he is concerned over the existence, effectiveness, and functioning of internal control systems covering multilease transactions. If contingent rentals are involved in leases, the auditor must satisfy himself that the company has an effective means of determining and monitoring compliance with the terms of those contingent rental arrangements. Lessors' accounting for bad debts is also of concern to the auditor. He must be concerned not only with the propriety of the bad debt provision amount, but also with the timing of charges against income. Finally, the auditor must be concerned with the general area of revenue recognition. Lease classification is only one element of this problem. Continuing involvement by the lessor, costs to be incurred, and executory cost estimates are all problems with which the auditor must deal.

Lease Classification in Computer-Assisted Auditing

As to both the lessee and the lessor, the auditor is confronted with auditing the classification of leases. When there are many leases, this can be very complicated and extremely time-consuming. Many lessors have developed computer software routines to help them structure lease packages so they get classified correctly. Auditors can use these routines to test the classifications. Some accounting firms have also developed similar software routines accessible through timesharing terminals.

Lease Classification Through Lessor Certification

Sometimes the lessor will certify to the lessee that from the lessor's standpoint, the lease is an operating lease. Given that both the lessor and lessee use the same classification criteria in SFAS 13, the lessee should probably conclude that the lease is an operating lease from his standpoint as well. Although this certificate does constitute an item of audit evidence, it does not relieve the lessee's auditor of the need to test the classification under SFAS 13; there is sufficient latitude in how the criteria are read to result in asymmetrical accounting by the parties.

Potential Lessee Audit Problem Areas

When dealing with lease classification by the lessee, the auditor needs to substantiate a number of estimates, including the fair value of property at the inception of the lease, the residual value at the end of the lease term, the interest rate implicit in the lease, and the economic useful life. The auditor is also confronted with some difficult judgmental decisions. For example, when is a purchase option or a renewal option a "bargain"?

Related-Party Leases. Related-party leases continue to provide potential audit problems, just as any other related-party transactions do. The first obvious problem is to determine whether there is related-party involvement, which is difficult, since leases typically are outside the company's regular transaction cycles. Once a related-party lease is identified, the auditor has the very difficult task of determining whether the lease terms have been significantly affected, i.e., is the lease equivalent to what could have been arranged with an unrelated party? If not, the auditor must convince the company of the need to account for it as though it were. And while the required disclosure of the related-party nature of these transactions is often difficult for the client to accept, the auditor must insist on it.

Implicit Interest Rate. SFAS 13 requires that the lessee use the interest rate implicit in the lease if it is known and it is lower than the lessee's incremental borrowing rate. SFAS 13 implies that the only way for the lessee to determine that rate is to ask the lessor and be told by him. If the lessor will not tell, the auditor must then decide what his obligation is to encourage communication between the lessee and the lessor. And if the lessor announces an interest rate, the auditor is faced with the problem of evaluating that rate.

Potential Lessor Audit Problem Areas

Bad Debt. Bad debts could be of significant concern to the auditor for the lessor. Typically, the lessee is financing 100% and has no equity in the property. The credit exposure to the lessor also goes beyond the unrealized profit in the transaction.

Sales-Type Lease Profit. The recognition of profit on sales-type leases is another source of possible audit difficulties. The existence, measurement, and accounting for potentially unreimbursable costs to the lessor over a long lease term can be a significant problem. Sometimes customers will tend to lease, rather than buy, new untried or innovative products. This may imply a requirement on the part of the lessor to provide technical support, product maintenance, or other services on a continuing basis, and the costs must be identified, estimated, and considered for their accounting impact.

Residuals. Residual values present one of the biggest problems in auditing lessors. The economics of leasing are such that leasing companies' fortunes are significantly impacted by the residuals. The residual is an asset of the leasing company. If the leveraged financing and the lease receivables are looked on as an offset, then the residuals are probably the most significant *real* asset of the leasing company. It is incredibly difficult for the lessor to estimate at the beginning of the lease term what the property is going to be worth at the end of the term. It is even more difficult for the auditor to reach a satisfactory level of comfort with that estimate.

At least as difficult as the initial estimate of residual value is its periodic evaluation and rechallenge. The residual must be written down if its previously determined value has been impaired, but it may not be written up if the first estimate was too low or if market factors have increased the value.

A dramatic example of the difficulty of estimating residual values is provided by the Lloyds problem, which has received significant coverage in the business press. Some computer lessors assumed a residual value risk by giving short-term cancellation rights to their customers desiring to qualify the lease as an operating lease. To qualify for capital lease accounting, the lessors attempted to hedge the cancellation risk by insuring the residual values with Lloyds of London. Obviously, Lloyds needed to estimate the residual values in order to decide how to price the insurance; the leasing companies had to make a similar estimate in order to determine whether the insurance was economically justified. When IBM subsequently announced significant new computer technology and greatly lowered per-unit processing cost, the estimates of residuals for older existing equipment were no longer appropriate. Lloyds stands to lose an enormous amount of money on these policies and has in fact brought suit to rescind the contracts. The lessors and their banks are trying to collect on their policies, and some have sued Lloyds. Eventually, someone's auditors will be named in a related suit.

SUGGESTED READING

AICPA. *Illustrations of Accounting for Leases.* Financial Report Survey 16. New York, 1978. This survey, based on 8,000 annual reports included in the NAARS database, illustrates the application of SFAS 13 in financial reporting.

Blum, James. "Accounting and Reporting for Leases by Lessees: The Interest Rate Problems." *Management Accounting,* April, 1978, pp. 25-28. This is a detailed review of the difficulty of determining the rate implicit in the lease.

Bohan, Michael. "New Directions in Lease Accounting." *Journal of Accounting, Auditing and Finance,* Spring, 1980, pp. 264-269. This article is a forecast of how the FASB might deal with the conceptual problems inherent in SFAS 13.

Collins, William. "Accounting for Leases Flowcharts." *Journal of Accountancy,* September, 1978, pp. 60-63. To help decipher the plethora of definitions and tests, the author organizes SFAS 13 in decision flowcharts.

Fogelson, James. "The Impact of Changes in Accounting Principles on Restrictive Covenants in Credit Agreements and Indentures." *Business Lawyer,* January, 1978, pp. 769-783. The author explores a major concern about SFAS 13, which was that lease debt would cause numerous debt covenant violations and acts of default, even though the imperiled covenants were written at a time when SFAS 13 was not seriously in prospect.

Grant, Edward. "A Look at Leveraged Leases under SFAS No. 13." *Management Accounting,* February, 1979, pp. 49-52. This subject is discussed in an understandable manner, despite the hypercomplexity of the SFAS 13 provisions.

Malernee, James Jr. and Witt, Robert. "Equipment Price Insurance: An Emerging Market." *Best's Review* (Property/Casualty Insurance Edition), June, 1978, pp. 22, 26, 96-97. With some residuals not holding up, the authors' evaluation of this type of insurance is interesting.

Phalen, Francis. "The Impact of SFAS 13 on the Retail Industry." *Financial Executive,* November, 1978, pp. 52-56. The author demonstrates that SFAS 13 and ASR 147 do not mean the same thing in the retail industry, perhaps the largest user of leases.

APPENDIX 23   EXAMPLE OF EFFECT OF INVESTMENT TAX CREDIT (ITC) ON LEASE STRUCTURE

Assume a company manufactures a product:

Normal selling price	$12,000
Cost	9,000
Gross profit	3,000
Tax at 48%	1,440
Profit less tax (before any operating expenses)	$ 1,560

The company is also willing to *lease,* with lease terms that provide $1,560 after-tax profit on the lease plus 10% pretax interest to cover credit risk and additional administrative costs. Assume a residual value of $1,000; a lease term of eight years; and that the lessee pays executory costs.

Lessor needs to recover:

Net lease income	$ 1,560
Cost:	
From lessee	$ 8,000
From residual sale	1,000
	$ 9,000

	If lessor passes ITC	If lessor keeps ITC
Net lease income	$ 1,560	$ 1,560
ITC	—	900
After-tax profit	1,560	660
Tax at 48%	1,440	610
Pretax profit to yield $1,560 after-tax profit	$ 3,000	$ 1,270
Need to recover:		
Pretax profit	$ 3,000	$ 1,270
Cost—from lessee	8,000	8,000
Total from lessee	11,000	9,270
Cost—from sale of residual	1,000	1,000
Total principal recovery	$12,000	$10,270
Total recovery of principal from lessee	$11,000	$ 9,270
Annual payment to amortize $1 at 10% for eight years	.187444	.187444
Annual rental, to amortize	$ 2,062	$ 1,738
Add: Interest at 10% on residual value	100	100
Total rental payment	$ 2,162	$ 1,838

Formula, based on FASB 13 (AC 4053.5(k)):

$$PV_r(MLP) + PV_r(RV) = FMV - ITCR$$

where

$PV_r(MLP)$ = present value of minimum lease payments
$PV_r(RV)$ = present value of residual
FMV = fair market value of property at inception of lease
$ITCR$ = investment tax credit retained by the lessor

	Pass ITC	Keep ITC
MLP	$ 2,162	$ 1,838
RV	1,000	1,000
FMV	12,000	12,000
ITCR	—	900

Calculation of present value of return:

Pass ITC: (at $r = 10\%$) : $(2162 \times 5.334) + (1000 \times .467) = 11,999 = 12,000$.
Keep ITC: (at $r = 8\%$) : $(1838 \times 5.746) + (1000 \times .540) = 11,101 = 11,100$.

As shown, the implicit rate calculation results in a two percentage point difference, depending on whether the lessor passes or keeps ITC, when in fact the lessor is *indifferent,* because his return is identical in either situation.

24

Employee Benefit Plans

R. Scott Miller

INCREASED SIGNIFICANCE

The Accounting Issue

Financial accounting and reporting of employee benefit plan costs and financial reporting by employee benefit plans are two subjects about which there continues to be many more questions than answers. Articles in the popular press, such as that appearing in the August 14, 1978, issue of *Business Week* entitled "Unfunded Pension Liabilities: A Continuing Burden," exemplify questions surrounding this subject. The article's central issue might best be stated as follows: What accounting is appropriate to clarify the meaning of pension liabilities that appear on the footnotes to the financial statements of America's major corporations? In order to focus this concern, the article included a table, reproduced here as Figure 24.1.

ERISA

Much of the reason that accounting, reporting, and auditing of employee benefit plans, particularly pension benefit plans, and of the related sponsor costs and obligations in the company's financial statements and footnotes have taken on increased significance can be found in the Employee Retirement Income Security Act of 1974 (ERISA). ERISA is mentioned throughout this chapter, and the last section gives a more complete discussion of its technical aspects.

The stated purpose of ERISA is to protect employee benefit rights by

	THE 12 LARGEST IN DOLLARS...		...AND AS A PERCENT OF NET WORTH	
	Unfunded Vested Benefits			
	Millions of Dollars	*Percent Change From Prior Year*		*Percent*
General Motors	$3,500	+17%	Lockheed	184.6%
Ford Motor	1,290	+33	LTV	121.4
Chrysler	1,260	+15	Bethlehem Steel	55.6
Bethlehem Steel	1,212	− 6	National Steel	44.1
Du Pont	693	+56	TWA	43.7
Westinghouse	692	− 8	Chrysler	43.1
U.S. Steel	600	+50	Republic Steel	41.1
General Electric	596	+ 5	Bendix	32.5
National Steel	565	+21	Westinghouse	30.2
AT&T	560	−18	Alcoa	22.9
Alcoa	555	+33	General Motors	22.2
Republic Steel	548	+10	Goodyear	22.1

FIGURE 24.1   MEASURING INDUSTRY'S UNFUNDED PENSION LIABILITIES
SOURCE: "Unfunded Pension Liabilities: A Continuing Burden," *Business Week*, August 14, 1978, p. 63, © 1978 by McGraw-Hill, Inc., New York, N.Y. 10020. All rights reserved.

- Requiring reporting to participants and beneficiaries,
- Establishing the obligations of and standards of conduct for fiduciaries, and
- Providing a means to enforce the provisions of the law.

The law also establishes minimum standards for participation, vesting, and funding, and requires plan termination insurance. Important, too, is the requirement for the filing of an annual report with the Internal Revenue Service. The annual report for plans that have more than 100 participants but that are not fully insured must include the independent auditor's opinion on the financial statements of the plan for the year of the filing.

From the company's viewpoint, accounting for pension benefit plans is principally a matter of expensing currently, in the period in which the company benefits from the employee's services, costs that are to be paid in the future. The principal operating considerations to the company are the impact of costs on earnings and the impact of funding on cash flow. From the viewpoint of the employee benefit plan, accounting consists of the proper recording of funds received or receivable, valuation of investments at current value, and recording of benefits paid. The plan's operating considerations made more important by ERISA relate generally to administration and compliance.

Many issues concerning accounting, reporting, and auditing of employee benefits derive from actuarial considerations. Changes in the actuarial cost method or in actuarial assumptions about covered employees or return on investment assets, for example, can have a significant impact on the company's current expense and unfunded vested benefits and on the timing and manner of funding the plan.

This chapter does not discuss employee stock ownership plans (ESOPs) and stock-based executive compensation arrangements, including stock appreciation rights (SARs) and stock option arrangements; these are discussed in Chapter 26.

ATTRIBUTES OF EMPLOYEE BENEFIT PLANS

Benefits

Employee benefit plans may be of three types: defined benefit, defined contribution, and health and welfare benefit.

Plans that specify the benefit (or the method used to determine the benefit) to be received at retirement are referred to as *defined benefit plans*. The most common example is a pension plan that calculates benefits as a function of final salary or years of service. The sponsor's annual contribution to the plan is determined by actuarial valuation. Many defined benefit plans are integrated with government social security (FICA) benefits, so that the total calculated benefit is reduced by FICA benefits received.

The *defined contribution plan* specifies the amount of periodic contribution to be paid by the sponsor, rather than the benefits to be received by the participant. A participant's benefits, when he becomes eligible to receive them, are usually based on the amount credited to his individual account. Sponsor contributions are determined by applying a specified rate against a variable such as labor hours worked or wages earned (in the case of retirement savings plans) or by a formula applied to defined earnings of the sponsor (in the case of profit-sharing plans).

The employer-sponsored *health and welfare benefit plan* provides medical, dental, or other health benefits; or unemployment, vacation, legal, or some other form of welfare benefits. Informal welfare benefit plans to which sponsor contributions are made on a pay-as-you-go basis are not unusual. (Voluntary health and welfare organizations, i.e., not employer-sponsored, are discussed in Chapter 35.)

Sponsorship

Employee benefit plans also fall into categories by sponsor—single-employer or multiemployer plans. A *single-employer plan* is usually established unilaterally because the employer desires to provide certain benefits for his employees, although some may be collectively bargained. The plan is normally administered by the employer, who may also act as trustee for the plan or who may arrange for a bank or insurance company to act as trustee.

Multiemployer plans are normally established within an industry and are collectively bargained. This type of plan is jointly administered by union and employer representatives. Generally, plan assets are maintained in a bank trust arrangement or an insurance company contract. Such a plan usually provides pension or health and welfare benefits to the participants. Multiemployer pension plans often have characteristics of both defined benefit and defined contribution plans in that the specified contribution rate is expected to produce a promised benefit. Employer contributions to multiemployer pension plans are usually based on a formula such as a fixed rate times employee hours or employee wages paid. Benefits, however, are calculated in a manner similar to defined benefit plans. Multiemployer plans usually require the services of an actuary to value plan obligations and establish the contribution rate employers should use. In practice, the contribution rate is normally determined through union negotiations and may not really be related to promised benefits.

Funding Provisions

Employee benefit plans are identified as contributory or noncontributory, depending on whether participants do or do not contribute to the plan. *Noncontributory* plans receive contributions only from the employer or employers. *Contributory* plans also receive mandatory or voluntary contributions from the participants.

Vesting

Most pension plans stipulate that a plan participant must remain in service for a certain number of years to earn benefits under the plan. Usually vesting is incremental over the specified period of time and is expressed as a percentage, but in some plans a participant has no vested rights until a specified period has elapsed, at which point he is vested 100%. For example, the plan may specify that a participant is 50% vested at the end of eight years of participation and that vesting increases 10% for each year of participation beyond eight years until fully vested (100%); or it may specify that a participant has no vested rights until he has completed ten years of service, at which time he becomes fully vested.

COMPANY PENSION COSTS AND OBLIGATIONS

At retirement, employees with vested pension rights are entitled to receive a stream of benefit payments called an *annuity*. These rights have been accruing to the individual over his employment term. Under GAAP, the cost of this annuity should be expensed over the period of the individual's employment.

Actuarial valuation of the pension plan has two purposes. The first is to estimate the amount of contributions necessary to pay to each employee the earned pension annuity when due. The second is to provide for systematic allocation of the contribution cost over the period of the individual's employment. To accomplish these two purposes the actuary must (1) select the appropriate actuarial cost method for the plan and (2) make relevant assumptions about the nature of the work force and the expected interest rate to be earned by the assets held by the plan.

Prior to December 31, 1966, the effective date of APB 8 (AC 4063), the methods for recognition of pension expense varied widely, even among actuarially valued plans. The effect of APB 8 was to narrow the alternatives for recognition of pension expense and to improve comparability in reporting.

Actuarial Valuation

An actuarial valuation produces several kinds of information:

1. *Value of vested benefits,* the present value of accrued vested benefits under the plan;
2. *Unfunded accrued liability,* the unamortized portion of costs assignable to the period prior to the date of the actuarial valuation (also called unfunded past service cost); and
3. *Normal cost,* the annual cost of the plan assignable to years subsequent to the inception of the plan or subsequent to a particular valuation date.

The following discussion should provide a general understanding of how this information is calculated.

Cost Methods. An actuarial cost method is a technique for determining the total cost of future benefits under the plan and for assigning those costs to successive years. Examples of actuarial methods include the accrued benefit (unit credit) method, the entry age normal method, the frozen initial liability method, and the aggregate method. All these cost methods except the last result in separate identification of the employer's contribution for unfunded accrued liability and normal or current cost. The aggregate cost method calculates only a single cost amount that includes a portion of the unfunded accrued liability.

Cost methods affect the rate at which assets accumulate. That is, the relative dollar valuation of assets of the plan under some cost methods tends to be higher than under other cost methods. Also, certain cost methods produce little variability from year to year in the recognition of pension costs, while others generate relatively more variability as can be seen in Figure 24.2.

In determining which method to use, the actuary considers the company's growth potential and cash-flow expectations, among other things. If a company is in a period of growth when cash is scarce, a method that provides for smaller contributions

Selected Years	Accrued Benefit Method	Entry Age Normal Method	Frozen Initial Liability Method	Aggregate Method
1	$622	$753	$875	$1,107
2	638	753	856	1,055
3	651	753	839	1,007
4	661	753	823	961
5	670	753	808	918
10	695	753	745	744
15	704	753	701	620
20	714	753	669	534
25	730	753	648	474
30	737	753	632	431
31	473	317	368	424
40	450	317	349	377
50	453	317	341	354

Notes: 1. All four methods were applied to the same plan using the same assumptions. Differences in funding streams result from the cost methods used.
2. No inflation assumptions have been used to make these calculations in order to avoid distortion of the effects caused by differing cost methods.

FIGURE 24.2   COMPARISON OF CONTRIBUTIONS IN SELECTED YEARS RESULTING FROM DIFFERING COST METHODS
ADAPTED FROM: C. L. Trowbridge and C. E. Farr, *The Theory and Practice of Pension Funding* (Homewood, Ill.: Richard D. Irwin, 1976), pp. 45, 53, 59, 66.

currently and larger contributions in later years might be more appropriate. Conversely, for some companies it might be more appropriate to apply a cost method that results in relatively stable contributions.

Assumptions. *Actuarial assumptions* are estimates of the likelihood of occurrence of future events. Examples of assumptions include mortality (the probability of death in each future year for each member of the employment population); salary scale (the expected rate at which salaries will increase); employee turnover (the termination rate of the employee population); and interest (the expected growth rate of investment assets resulting from appreciation and earnings on investments). The actuary must exercise his professional judgment in making the proper assumptions for a particular plan.

Of the assumptions mentioned above, probably the most important is the interest assumption, since the interest rate affects not only the expected growth rate of plan assets but also the discount rate used to calculate the present value of the unfunded accrued liability and the present value of vested benefits. Because relatively small changes in the discount rate have a large inverse effect on the results of present value calculations, a relatively small increase in a plan's anticipated earnings, from

7% to 8.5% for example, will cause a large reduction in the unfunded future liability and the present value of vested benefits.

A complication of the interest rate assumption is introduced if inflation is considered. During periods of inflation, the interest rate is normally higher. If benefits are a function of pay rate or salary in later years of employment, then the salary scale assumption must also be adjusted for inflation.

Changes in this assumption cause an increase in the future value of benefits to be paid. Therefore, when higher expected future benefits are discounted to present value, the result will not be the same as that which would have resulted from a simple increase in expected interest on assets. Further, the direction of change (that is, increase or decrease) of the present value of the unfunded accrued liability and the present value of vested benefits is ambiguous unless the effect of inflation on benefits is assumed to be the same or smaller than the effect on interest.

In practice, actuaries maintain a constant differential, often 2%, between interest rate assumptions and salary scale to avoid unwarranted fluctuations of the present value calculations and, therefore, the company's annual cost. Thus, for example, if the interest rate assumption is 9% and the salary scale is 7%, the results are comparable to an interest rate assumption of 6% and salary scale of 4%.

One final important observation about actuarial assumptions is that consistency is very important. When assumptions are made, the implications of those assumptions must be applied in a consistent manner to all appropriate assumptions. It would be inappropriate to assume inflation for interest rate purposes but not to assume inflation for salary scale purposes.

Gains and Losses. The only real certainty about actuarial assumptions is that they will diverge from actual experience under the plan. This divergence, referred to as actuarial gain or loss, arises because actual experience under the plan differs from the actuarial assumptions and because assumptions about future events change. Actuarial gains and losses may be averaged (including both past and expected gains and losses) and recognized over future periods; this will result in a different future cost pattern than would exist if future actuarial gains and losses are not anticipated. The particular treatment of actuarial gains and losses is determined by the cost method chosen.

One example of a circumstance in which an actuarial gain or loss might occur is a plant closing. A gain may well result in this circumstance, because the turnover assumption for the plan may prove to be too low. A second example is actual mortality verses expected mortality. The plan's mortality experience might deviate from the expected mortality for many reasons. On a statistical basis, deviation from the population norm is expected, since the randomly selected sample of employees only approximates the total population. Further, in some industries the work force may be exposed to environmental factors that alter mortality for that segment of the population. As actuarial gains or losses from such events occur, they must be considered in the actuary's periodic valuation of the plan.

Funding Pension Obligations

Funding refers to the employer's contribution of assets, usually cash, to a pension plan. While ERISA established legislative rules providing for a minimum contribution level, with the funding standard account as the mechanism for testing compliance with that minimum, tax rules for many years have provided a maximum deductible amount that effectively limits the company contribution. The tax rules also provide that in order for the contribution to be deductible, it must be paid by the filing date, including extensions, of the company's federal income tax return.

The actuarially calculated contribution that the company must make is determined as of a certain date. Normally, the company does not contribute to the plan at that date. When the contribution is made, it must be increased by the amount of interest that it would have earned if it had been contributed on the date used by the actuary to make his calculations. The proper interest rate to use is the assumed interest rate used by the actuary in his cost calculations.

The employer must consider such matters as cost of money to the company, the company's rate of return on assets, and tax deductibility in deciding when to fund the pension obligation. The question, however, is larger than just the company's own maximization of return on investment.

Questions have been raised concerning the inhibiting effects of the substantial aggregate value of pension assets on capital formation in the United States. One such question focuses on the effect of pension funding on venture capital. ERISA emphasizes fiduciary responsibility to manage plan assets solely for the interest of the participants and also requires diversification of investments in order to protect plan assets. For these reasons, it has been argued that high-risk venture capital is not available from pension plans, since the fiduciary may be liable under ERISA for not fulfilling his responsibility to the participants. Recent regulations issued by the Department of Labor (DOL) have attempted to alleviate this situation by identifying circumstances where such investments might be appropriate.

A second question concerns removal of assets from the company, where they earn a higher return, to a pension plan, where they earn a lower return due to risk aversion. Some have suggested that rather than fund the pension liability, the employer should accrue it on the financial statements. Assets that otherwise would be used to fund the plan would then be available to the company. The higher return that the company earned would then be shared with the plan; funds for internal financing and venture capital would also be more readily available. This type of proposal has a number of difficulties. Among the more obvious are the tax deductibility of an unfunded cost and the liquidity to pay plan benefits. The Presidential Commission on Pension Policy has included in its agenda the investigation of the effects of pension plans on capital formation in the Unted States (*CCH Pension Plan Guide,* 1978, pp. 11-12). In a recently released interim report, the commission states that the country should give top priority to a balanced system of private pensions, social security, and retirement savings programs for all workers. It recommended a universal minimum advance-funded pension system (mandatory private plans) to supplement social security. This commission is expected to present its findings in late 1980.

Taxation and Qualified Pension Plans

Pension plan arrangements are attractive in part because of the favorable tax treatment that results when the plans are qualified as tax exempt. Plan activities, including investment earnings and contributions, are tax exempt. The company contribution is deductible by the company as an ordinary and necessary business expense; the participants receive deferred compensation and, accordingly, deferred taxation.

A plan is qualified as tax exempt if it meets certain technical requirements and if it is nondiscriminatory in operation. Through a formal application, a plan may request a determination letter from the IRS stating that the plan document meets the requirements for qualification. The IRS reviews the plan document for technical compliance with participation, vesting, funding, and benefit standards. The process of securing IRS approval may be accelerated by adopting a model or pattern plan that the IRS has precleared as a qualified plan. Once the IRS is satisfied that the plan document meets technical requirements, a determination letter is issued. In the event that the plan does not qualify, the IRS provides explicit information concerning modifications needed to secure a favorable ruling for the plan.

Final determination of a plan's tax-exempt status, however, is based on actual operation of the plan. If the plan is found in practice to be discriminatory, for example by excluding from participation individuals who should be included, it will be ruled not to be a qualified plan. Generally, the penalties for such unfavorable rulings on plans already in operation are brought against the employer rather than against the plan or the participants. This is done to avoid the depletion of plan assets and hence the loss of benefits to participants, who cannot control plan operations.

FINANCIAL ACCOUNTING AND REPORTING OF PENSION COSTS

Professional Pronouncements

Principles governing financial accounting and reporting of employee benefit obligations by a company are included in APB 8 (AC 4063), APB 16 (AC 1091.88(h), fn. 14), and FASB Interpretation No. 3 (AC 4063-1). There is currently outstanding an FASB exposure draft (discussed below) that would modify some of the disclosure requirements of APB 8.

APB 8. APB 8 requires that the actuarially calculated annual cost of the pension plan be accrued and expensed by the sponsor. Actuarial assumptions and method of calculation are to be consistent from year to year. APB 8 also establishes minimum and maximum limits for the annual company accrual and expense. The minimum limit is the sum of normal cost, plus an amount equivalent to interest on any unfunded prior service cost, plus a provision for vested benefits (if vested benefits exceed the total pension fund plus any balance sheet pension accruals less any balance sheet prepayments or deferred charges, and such excess is not at least 5% less than the comparable excess at the beginning of the year). The maximum limit is the sum of normal cost, plus 10% of past service cost, plus or minus 10% of any increase or decrease in prior service cost arising from amendments of the plan, plus interest equivalents on the difference between amounts accrued and amounts funded.

APB 8 also requires footnote disclosure concerning pension plan arrangements, including

1. A statement that the plan exists and a description of the employee groups covered;
2. A statement of the company's accounting and funding policies;
3. The amount provided for pension costs for the period;
4. The excess, if any, of the actuarially computed value of vested benefits over the total of the pension fund and any balance sheet pension accruals less any pension prepayments or deferred charges; and
5. The nature and effect of any significant matters that affect comparability for all periods presented in the financial statements. (Examples include changes in actuarial cost methods, amortization periods, actuarial assumptions, amendment of the plan, or adoption of a new plan.)

SFAS 36. This statement (AC 4065) requires revised disclosures about defined benefit pension plans in employers' financial statements. Under the new standard, effective for annual financial statements for fiscal years beginning after December 15, 1979, and for complete sets of financial statements for interim periods within those fiscal years *issued after June 30, 1980,* employers are required to disclose the following data determined in accordance with SFAS 35, *Accounting and Reporting by Defined Benefit Pension Plans* (AC 6110). The data must be presented as of the most recent benefit information date for which the data is available. Although SFAS 35 is not applicable until plan years beginning after December 15, 1980, the data is substantially available in Schedule B of Form 5500 and includes the following:

1. The actuarial present value of vested accumulated plan benefits;
2. The actuarial present value of nonvested accumulated plan benefits;
3. The plan's net assets available for benefits;
4. The assumed rates of return used in determining the actuarial present value of vested and nonvested accumulated plan benefits; and
5. The date as of which the benefit information was determined.

The data may be reported in total for all plans, separately for each plan, or in such subaggregations as are considered most useful. For plans for which the above data is not available or not applicable, the employer should continue to comply with the disclosure requirements originally contained in APB 8 (AC 4063), namely, the excess, if any, of the actuarially computed value of vested benefits over the total of the pension fund and any balance sheet pension accruals, less any pension prepayments or deferred charges; and the reasons why the information required by 1 above is not provided. The new standard retains requirements 1, 2, 3, and 5 as described under APB 8 above.

Early application of this pronouncement is encouraged. The disclosures required by SFAS 36 need not be included in financial statements for periods beginning before the effective date of this statement that are being presented for comparative purposes with financial statements for periods after the effective date, but if included, that information should be presented in conformity with the provisions of this statement.

The FASB states that SFAS 36 represents a temporary approach to the overall problem of accounting for defined benefit pension plans. A comprehensive project, now underway, to consider all aspects of accounting by employers for pensions and related benefits is to be completed in 1982.

APB 16. Brief reference is made in APB 16 (AC 1091.88(h), fn. 14) to accounting for pension obligations in business combinations (for a comprehensive discussion, refer to Chapter 30). Purchase accounting requires the fair valuing of all purchased assets and liabilities, including the pension obligation. The fair value of the acquired pension obligation is "the greater of (1) the accrued pension cost computed in conformity with the accounting policies of the acquiring corporation for one or more of its pension plans or (2) the excess, if any, of the actuarially computed value of vested benefits over the amount of the pension fund." The pension obligations as valued above are then recorded as a liability in the financial statements of the acquiring company. Pension obligations for business combinations treated as a pooling of interests would only be recorded on the balance sheet of the surviving company to the extent they appeared on the balance sheets of the companies prior to the pooling of interests. Accounting methods may be conformed if the change would have been appropriate for the separate companies and if it is applied retroactively.

FASB Interpretation No. 3. FASB Interpretation No. 3 (AC 4063-1) modifies the requirements of APB 8 based on the effects of ERISA. The interpretation states that the provisions of APB 8 continue to be applicable; it discusses the proper accounting and disclosure for the effects of technical amendments required by ERISA (notably matters related to participation, funding, and vesting). Besides the requirements in APB 8 and APB 16 for recording pension liability on the financial statements of the company, two additional standards are set by the interpretation for recognition of liability: it must be recognized (1) when the company fails to meet the minimum funding standards established by ERISA and a waiver of the requirement has not been secured from the secretary of the treasury and (2) when the plan is to be terminated and there is company liability for benefits in excess of plan assets as defined by ERISA (AC 4063-1.05).

Financial Statement Disclosure Examples

Often the only reference in the financial statements to pension plan matters will be a discussion of such arrangements in the footnotes. Figure 24.3 is a typical example of such a footnote. The note contains the disclosures required by APB 8 for defined benefit pension plans. This example does not comply with the requirements of SFAS 36. Figure 24.4, taken from the appendix of SFAS 36, would comply.

Current Accounting and Reporting Issues

Unfunded Liability. Probably the most important issue related to the company's accounting and reporting for pension obligations is whether to record a liability for

Much of the controversy surrounding ERISA relates to the heavy burden of reporting requirements. Many believe that these requirements have led to the substantial increase in plan terminations, particularly among small plans. Current federal legislation, if passed in its present form, will eliminate some reporting requirements and substantially reduce the frequency of others. The IRS and the Department of Labor are also reviewing reporting requirements with an eye toward simplification or some elimination.

ERISA and Case Law

ERISA's provisions relating to fiduciary responsibility, improved benefit security, and preemption of state law have led to significant litigation. Current questions are discussed below.

Fraud. The single most important suit in the area of fraud was the *Daniel* case (*International Brotherhood of Teamsters v. Daniel*, [Current Binder] Fed. Sec. L. Rep. (CCH) par. 96,714), now decided by the Supreme Court. The case involved benefits lost under a mandatory, noncontributory defined benefit plan due to an involuntary break in service. Suit was brought under SEC antifraud provisions and was based on the argument that pension benefits represented a security interest. Although the plaintiff won the case in the lower courts, the Supreme Court reversed the lower courts' decisions and found that a pension under such a plan is not a security. Hence, the antifraud provisions of the securities acts do not apply. However, state statutes that provide for action based on fraud would appear to remain as grounds on which to base a suit.

Sex Discrimination. In *Manhart* (*Manhart v. City of Los Angeles, Department of Water and Power*, 577 F.2d 98 (1978)), suit was brought because, under the plan in question, female participants were required to make higher contributions than male participants. Since women tend to live longer than men, female participants in a plan require a higher absolute contribution than male participants in order to receive the same benefit entitlement. The Supreme Court found that higher contribution based on sex was discriminatory. In another case, the courts also found benefit arrangements that provide lower benefits to women than to men as a result of the mandatory purchase of annuities to be discriminatory. The Supreme Court stated that when the only form of benefit available to the participants is an annuity, there can be no discrimination in monthly benefit payments that is based solely on sex.

Multiemployer Plans. In the *Connolly* case (*Connolly v. Pension Benefit Guarantee Corp.*, 581 F.2d 729 (1978)), it was argued on a technicality that multiemployer defined contribution plans with employee benefits determined by formula (as single-employer defined benefit plans are) were more like defined contribution plans than defined benefit plans. Therefore, they should be exempt from termination insurance premiums payable to the PBGC and, by extension of logic, exempt from other PBGC jurisdiction, including employer liability to the PBGC in the event of termination. The appeals court reversed the lower court decision and found this type of multiemployer plan to come under PBGC jurisdiction. The decision stands as final, because the Supreme Court declined to hear the case. Additional legal challenges dealing with the same issue are still under appeal in the sixth circuit court (CCH Pension Plan Guide, 1979, pp. 5-6). Consequently, this legal issue is not fully resolved, and an auditor may need to consult with legal counsel to ascertain what the obligations of the company may be under such a plan.

SUGGESTED READING

AICPA. *Illustrations of Accounting for Employee Benefits.* Financial Report Survey 14. New York, 1977. This NAARS survey provides numerous examples of accounting and disclosure in the areas of pensions, stock issuances, and cash payments.

Pomeranz, Felix; Ramsey, Gordon; and Steinberg, Richard. *Pensions; An Accounting and Management Guide.* New York: Ronald Press, 1976. This comprehensive discussion of legal, operational, and financial accounting and reporting aspects of pensions considers both sponsor and plan views. It is an excellent book for those desiring a broad, single-volume discussion of the subject.

Trowbridge, C. L., and Farr, C. E. *The Theory and Practice of Pension Funding.* Homewood, Ill.: Richard D. Irwin, 1976. This text is a comparative summary of actuarial costing methods. Although the text is intended for actuaries, the interested layman will find it to be a readable source to expand his knowledge of the subject.

Wiesen, Jeremy, and Eng, Richard. "Corporate Perks: Disclosure and Tax Considerations." *Journal of Accounting, Auditing and Finance,* Winter, 1979, pp. 101-121. This article surveys the current status of perquisites.

25

Income Taxes

Raymond E. Perry

A PERSPECTIVE

Accounting for income taxes is one of the most complex aspects of financial accounting, in concept as well as in practice. It is also vitally important, for federal income tax rates for corporations generally range from 40% to more than 50% of reported pretax earnings. In addition to the federal income tax, most corporations pay state and local income taxes. Not surprisingly, therefore, accounting for income taxes has given rise to much contention in the profession and to numerous official pronouncements and interpretations. Many pronouncements dealing with other matters in financial accounting, such as leveraged leases, interim financial reporting, and translation of foreign currency transactions, also discuss the related income tax aspects.

Much of the controversy and complexity arises because certain important items of revenue and expense are reported in one period's financial statements and in another period's income tax determinations. Perhaps the most important example of these *timing differences* is depreciation expense; many companies use the straight-line method for financial reporting and an accelerated method for income tax purposes. There are also some items of revenue and expense that are reported for financial accounting purposes but never subjected to taxation. The best-known example of these *permanent differences* is interest earned on state and local government securities, which is exempt from federal income taxation. Still other sources of complexity and controversy are the special items that reduce tax liability directly, such as the investment tax credit, foreign tax credits, and carryovers of operating losses.

Financial reporting determines net earnings for a given period by matching expenses to revenue. Thus, different ways of matching income tax expense to revenue and other expenses for the period can result in significantly different determinations of net earnings reported in conformity with GAAP.

HISTORICAL OVERVIEW

Until the mid-1950s, the amount shown for income tax expense in an annual statement was almost always the amount of tax indicated as payable on the income tax returns for the year. The few exceptions were the result of material and nonrecurring expenses recognized in one year for financial purposes but not allowable as a tax deduction until a succeeding year. For example, if a company decided to dispose of a plant, its financial reports would show the estimated loss in the year the decision was made; but a tax deduction for the loss could not be claimed until the discontinued plant was actually sold. In these circumstances it was considered appropriate to reduce the income tax expense in the year of loss recording. Similar approaches were also occasionally applied to unusual revenue items recognized in one period for financial accounting purposes and in another as taxable income.

The first official pronouncement on income tax accounting, ARB 23 (AICPA, 1944), dealt with these unusual and nonrecurring differences, and discussed the disclosures appropriate when operating loss carryforwards arose or income tax refunds were realized as a result of the carryback of current income to an earlier loss year.

Accelerated Depreciation

The Internal Revenue Code, adopted in 1954, allowed companies to use accelerated methods of tax depreciation even if the straight-line method was used for financial reporting. (See Chapter 20 for a discussion of depreciation methods.) Some accountants argued that the use of accelerated depreciation methods for tax purposes should not result in timing differences, because companies should also use the same accelerated method for financial reporting. However, the practice of using different methods for taxes and financial reporting gained wide acceptance as many companies took advantage of accelerated methods for tax purposes, and resulted in recurring timing differences.

Hence, many accountants advocated that during the early years of the useful life of a depreciable asset an amount equal to the taxes saved should be recorded as an expense, with an offsetting deferred credit. The deferred credit could then be amortized to income during the later years of useful life, when the timing difference reversed. This procedure was often called *normalization,* particularly in the public utility industry (see Chapter 36), since the result was to normalize net income—that is, to eliminate the variations in reported income resulting from depreciation timing differences.

The opponents of normalization advocated just as strongly that providing such deferred taxes was improper, because most continuing or growing companies would make expenditures for depreciable assets each year. Thus the excess of reported income over taxable income would never reverse, or would reverse only in the indefinite future—so many years hence that recognizing it currently would be misleading. The deferred tax liability that resulted from such accounting, they argued, was not a true liability but a subdivision of retained earnings. Simply taking the actual tax liability as it appears on the income tax return and recording it as the income tax expense for that year in financial reports is often called *flow-through accounting.* It may also be called *partial allocation* if it requires deferred income taxes for nonrecurring differences but does not provide them for recurring differences. A third approach—providing deferred income taxes in all cases of timing differences—is called *comprehensive tax allocation.* The AICPA Accounting Research Committee considered these rival views and issued ARB 44 (AICPA, 1954a). That bulletin adopted the partial allocation method.

SEC Actions

Since accounting research bulletins were not mandatory at that time, some companies still provided deferred income taxes for recurring timing differences;

others, following ARB 44's recommendations, did not. The chief accountant of the SEC publicly expressed the view that failure to provide the deferred taxes could mislead investors by resulting in the reporting of inflated net earnings; in several cases SEC used its authority to require companies filing registration statements to provide deferred taxes. The most frequent targets of this action were companies with histories of large annual increases in net earnings that were going public for the first time.

In the public utility industry, the controversy involved the question of whether deferred tax provisions should be allowed as an expense in rate determination. As explained in Chapter 36, the traditional practice for public ultility companies had become one of conforming deferred tax accounting for financial reporting purposes with that allowed or required for rate-making purposes, whatever method was followed.

To reduce the confusion resulting from the alternative accounting methods, and in response to pressure from the SEC, the Accounting Research Committee reconsidered the matter and issued ARB 44, Revised (AICPA, 1958). It required the provision of deferred income taxes for depreciation timing differences, except for regulated companies whose regulatory authorities specified flow-through accounting for rate-making purposes. Since the SEC fully supported this revision and required all registrants to follow it, the practice became mandatory.

In the years that followed, many companies also provided deferred taxes on other recurring differences between financial reporting income and taxable income, but such practices varied. Even when companies chose to provide deferred taxes, the methods of computing them and the manner of their presentation in financial statements were diverse.

Investment Tax Credit

The Revenue Act of 1962, which reduced income taxes through an investment tax credit (based on a percentage applied to expenditures for designated depreciable assets), gave rise to still more variations. The initial rate was 7% for items with a useful life of more than seven years, and lower rates for shorter-lived assets. (Currently the maximum rate is 10%.)

On the principle that income can be earned only by the profitable employment of depreciable assets, not simply by purchasing them, the Accounting Principles Board (APB) decided that tax benefits from the investment tax credit should be reflected over the life of the related assets. Called the *deferral method* of accounting for the investment tax credit, this practice was adopted in APB 2 (AC 4094), issued in 1962. However, most companies believed the tax benefits should be reflected in income immediately in the year for which the investment tax credit reduced income taxes, a practice called the *flow-through method.*

The SEC decided, perhaps as a result of pressures from the Treasury Department, to accept either the deferral method required by APB 2 or the flow-through method. The APB subsequently recognized this divergence of practice by amending its opinion. In APB 4 (AC 4094), it expressed a preference for the deferral method but said the flow-through method was also acceptable.

Then in 1967, the APB sought to reduce variations in practice by issuing the hotly debated APB 11 (AC 4091), which installed comprehensive tax allocation using the deferral method. The public exposure draft of this opinion required the use of the deferral method for the investment tax credit and prohibited the flow-through method (AICPA, 1967a). About 1,000 letters of comment, most of them opposing the deferral method, were received. The SEC's chief accountant supported the exposure draft, but opposition from industry was so intense that the APB and the SEC reversed their positions and permitted alternatives to continue in accounting for the investment credit.

By 1971 the APB was reconsidering the question of the investment tax credit, and many companies brought their opposition to the attention of Congress. The result was an accounting provision in the Revenue Act of 1971 (Section 101(c)) stating:

> ... notwithstanding any other provision of law ... no taxpayer shall be required to use, for purposes of financial reports subject to the jurisdiction of any Federal agency or reports made to any Federal agency, any particular method of accounting for the [investment] credit [and] shall disclose, in any such report, the method of accounting for such credit ... and ... shall use the same method of accounting ... in all such reports made by him, unless the Secretary of the Treasury or his delegate consents to a change to another method.

No further pronouncements on the investment credit were issued. Many believe this debacle was most significant in the decline of confidence in the ability of the APB to deal effectively with financial accounting matters that led to its replacement by the Financial Accounting Standards Board in 1973 (see Chapter 40).

INTERPERIOD TAX ALLOCATION

Having concluded that some form of accounting recognition must be given to all timing differences, not just accelerated depreciation, the APB considered, prior to the adoption of APB 11, three different approaches. These three approaches to comprehensive *interperiod income tax allocation* are the deferral method, the liability method, and the net-of-tax method.

The *deferral method* focuses on the effects on income for the period in which the tax timing differences originate. For financial accounting purposes, deferred taxes applicable to the timing differences are computed using the tax rates then in effect and are not adjusted for subsequent tax rate changes or for new taxes later imposed. If loss carryback situations are ignored for the moment, the tax effects of transactions that reduce taxes currently payable are treated as deferred tax credits though classified among liabilities in the balance sheet. Conversely, the tax effects of transactions that increase taxes currently payable are treated as deferred tax charges though classified among assets in the balance sheet. Such deferred credits and charges are amortized to income tax expense in future years as the timing differences reverse.

Under the *liability method* of accounting for tax timing differences, income tax expense shown in the financial statements represents the taxes paid or to be paid on pretax income for the period shown in those statements. Differences between the tax expense shown and taxes currently payable resulting from timing differences are deemed (and presented in the balance sheet as) liabilities (for taxes payable in the future) or assets (for prepaid taxes). Deferred taxes are computed at the rates expected to be in effect when the timing differences are expected to be included in taxable income. Adjustments of the liability or prepaid accounts for deferred taxes are made whenever tax rates change or new taxes are imposed.

Under the *net-of-tax method,* tax allocation for timing differences (whether computed by the deferral method or the liability method) explicitly recognizes that taxability or tax deductibility are factors in the valuation of assets and liabilities and the related revenues and expenses. Thus, deferred tax accounts are not presented separately in the balance sheet but instead are applied as reductions of the related assets and liabilities. Under a variation of the net-of-tax method, revenue and expense amounts in the income statement are adjusted by the related effects of tax allocation.

The majority of the APB preferred the deferral method because it does not require deferred tax charges and credits to be deemed receivables and payables. Thus, the deferral method has the practical advantage of not requiring assumptions as to future taxes, does not require adjustments of prior deferred tax balances when tax rates change or new taxes are imposed, and avoids the issue of the need for discounting a long-term tax liability to reflect its present value. Finally, the effects of applying interperiod tax allocation are more simply presented by showing deferred taxes as separate items in the financial statements than by showing them net-of-tax as adjustments of related asset, liability, revenue, and expense accounts.

Though the APB adopted the deferral method in APB 11, certain aspects of the liability method are implicit in provisions dealing with operating losses. And in two later pronouncements, APB 23 (AC 4095) and APB 24 (AC 4096), which deal with special areas of income tax accounting not resolved in APB 11 (AC 4091), the liability method is, in effect, the method used.

Objectives

Comprehensive interperiod income tax allocation regards each transaction giving rise to revenue or expense reported in the financial statements during a period as having an associated income tax effect: an income tax charge related to each revenue item and an income tax credit or benefit related to each expense item. Thus, the total income tax expense reported during the period is the sum of the individual tax charges and tax benefits associated with the specific revenues and expenses reported during the period, regardless of when those specific revenues and expenses are taxable. The only items to be excluded from determining income tax expense for a period are (1) revenues that will never be subjected to taxation, because of exemptions provided in the law and (2) expenses that will never be deductible, because they are disallowed under the law. These are permanent differences that do not enter into determining taxable income for any period.

There are four general categories of timing differences. Listed below are the four categories and some common examples of timing differences in each (adapted from Appendix A of APB 11; AC 4091A):

1. *Revenues or gains* taxed *after* being reported in financial statements:
   a. Profits on installment sales are reported at date of sale, but included in tax returns when collected.

   b. Revenues on long-term contracts are reported on the percentage-of-completion method, but included in tax returns under a completed-contract method.

   c. Revenues from capital leases are reported in the lessor's financial statements as sales-type or direct financing leases, but are included in tax returns under the operating method.

   d. Earnings of foreign subsidiary companies are reported in financial statements currently, but included in tax returns when later remitted.

2. *Expenses or losses* deducted for tax purposes *after* being reported in financial statements:

   a. Estimated costs of guarantees and product warranty contracts are reported at date of sale, but deducted in tax returns when later paid.

   b. Expenses for deferred compensation, profit sharing, bonuses, and vacation and severance pay are reported when accrued for the applicable period, but deducted in tax returns when later paid.

   c. Anticipated losses on inventories and purchase commitments are reported when reasonably estimable, but deducted in tax returns when later realized.

   d. Anticipated losses on disposal of facilities and discontinuing or relocating operations are reported when estimable, but deducted in tax returns when losses or costs are actually incurred.

3. *Revenues or gains* taxed *before* being reported in financial statements:

   a. Rents, royalties, fees, dues, and service contracts are taxed when collected, but deferred in the financial statements to later periods when earned.

   b. All profits on intercompany transactions are taxed when reported in separate returns, but the profits on assets remaining within the group are eliminated in consolidated financial statements.

   c. Gains on sales of property leased back are taxed at date of sale, but if material are deferred in the financial statements and amortized over the term of lease.

   d. Proceeds of sales of oil payments or ore payments (carve-outs) are taxed at date of sale, but deferred in the financial statements and reported as revenue when the oil or ore is produced.

4. *Expenses or losses* deducted for tax purposes *before* being reported in financial statements:

   a. Depreciation deducted in tax returns exceeds financial statement amounts because of accelerated methods of computation in early years or shorter lives for tax purposes.

   b. Unamortized discount, issue cost, and redemption premium on bonds refunded are deducted in tax returns, but deferred and amortized in the financial statements.

   c. Interest and taxes during construction are deducted in tax returns when incurred, but included in the cost of assets reported in the financial statements.

   d. Preoperating expenses are deducted in tax returns when incurred, but may be deferred and amortized in the financial statements.

When timing differences exist and interperiod tax allocation procedures are applied, the tax expense reported in the income statement is composed of two elements: (1) the taxes currently payable as shown on the income tax return for the year and (2) a change in the deferred taxes resulting from providing deferred taxes on originating differences and amortizing deferred taxes on reversing differences. The deferred tax element can be positive, raising the tax expense above the amount currently payable, or it can be negative, reducing the expense below the amount currently payable.

The effect of interperiod tax allocation is to normalize the rate that reported income tax expense bears to income before taxes. Ideally, the effective tax rate would be equal to the statutory tax rate, but the ideal is not often achieved, because of

- The effect of changes in tax rates,
- Special rates applying to capital gains and certain other classes of transactions,
- The use of foreign tax credits and the investment tax credit,
- The presence of revenues and expenses that are exempt from taxation, and
- The effects of state and local income taxes.

For a large corporation with a variety of transactions, the reasons for the difference between the effective tax rate and the statutory rate can be complex. Therefore, the SEC requires (in ASR 149, as amended by ASR 280 in September 1980) that public companies under the commission's jurisdiction include a note to the financial statements explaining variations from the statutory rate.

Basic Provisions of APB 11

APB 11 says that "the tax effect of a timing difference should be measured by the differential between income taxes computed with and without inclusion of the transaction creating the difference between taxable income and pretax accounting income" (AC 4091.35). This is commonly referred to as the *with-and-without computation*. The tax effect computed on an originating timing difference is included as an addition to or reduction of income tax expense, with an offsetting deferred tax credit or charge recorded in the balance sheet. As noted above, accountants who argued in favor of comprehensive income tax allocation believed that the deferred tax credits and charges that appear in the balance sheet should be treated as liabilities and receivables. Some further argued that especially for timing differences that reverse over a relatively long period of time (as those for long-lived assets do), the deferred tax liabilities and receivables should be discounted to present value. This suggestion was specifically considered, and APB 11 did not change the prohibition contained in APB 10 (AC 4092) against discounting deferred taxes.

Gross Change Method. When the timing differences reverse, the deferred tax previously recorded in the balance sheet reenters the income statement and is eliminated from the balance sheet. This can be seen in a simplified illustration. Assume that in year 1, depreciation expense deducted for tax purposes exceeded the amount reported in the financial statements by $100, and that in year 2 the timing difference completely reversed so that depreciation expense reported in the financial statement exceeded the amount deducted in the tax return by $100. The computations and related effects on the financial statements are shown in Figure 25.1.

The effective rates if interperiod tax allocation had not been applied and taxes currently payable had simply been reported as the tax expense for each of the

YEAR 1

Pretax income for financial reporting purposes	$1,000
Additional depreciation expense deductible on income tax return (i.e., originating timing difference)	(100)
Taxable income	$ 900
Tax currently payable on taxable income (50% of $900)	$ 450
Tax computed on reported income (i.e., income without the timing difference—50% of $1,000)	500
Difference representing tax effect and recorded as a deferred tax credit on the balance sheet	$ 50

The income statement for the year will show:

Income before income taxes		$1,000
Income tax expense:		
Currently payable	$450	
Deferred	50	500
Net income		$ 500

YEAR 2

Pretax income for financial reporting purposes	$1,000
Reduction in depreciation deductible on income tax return (i.e., reversing timing difference)	100
Taxable income	$1,100
Tax currently payable on taxable income (50% of $1,100)	$ 550
Tax computed on reported income (50% of $1,000)	500
Difference representing tax effect recorded as amortization of deferred tax credit recorded on balance sheet in year 1	$ (50)

The income statement for the year will show:

Income before income taxes		$1,000
Income tax expense:		
Currently payable	$550	
Deferred	(50)	500
Net income		$ 500

FIGURE 25.1 COMPUTATION OF DEFERRED TAXES (GROSS CHANGE METHOD)

two years are shown in Figure 25.2. Without interperiod tax allocation, the apparent tax rate would have increased from 45% in year 1 to 55% in year 2, even though the statutory rate remained unchanged at 50%. This is the kind of distortion that interperiod income tax allocation is designed to avoid.

The simplified illustration in Figure 25.1 assumes that the entire timing difference reverses in one year—effectively a nonrecurring timing difference. Actually, for most businesses, reversing timing differences that result from use of accelerated depreciation for tax purposes are usually more than offset each year by originating differences on newly acquired depreciable assets and by depreciable assets still in the earlier years of their useful life, when accelerated depreciation exceeds straight-line depreciation. Thus, the deferred tax credits that appear in the balance sheet from applying interperiod tax allocations tend to grow continually, and in the aggregate do not reverse.

This can be illustrated by a variation of the first example. Assume that in year 2 not only is there a reversal of the $100 timing differences originating in year 1, but there is also a new originating difference of $150. Also, assume that the statutory tax rate has declined from 50% in year 1 to 40% in year 2. Figure 25.3 shows the results of these conditions.

The effective tax rate in Figure 25.3 is 39%, even though the statutory rate for year 2 is 40%. This apparent lack of normalization results because deferred taxes provided in year 1 on the additional depreciation deducted that year were based on the then-prevailing 50% rate. When the additional taxable income appeared in the year of reversal, the tax rate was only 40%; hence, the tax actually paid was $10 lower than the amount that had been deferred. And that $10 "correction" in the deferred taxes was in effect recorded in year 2, reducing the tax from that year below the $400 that would have resulted if the normalized tax rate of 40% had been applied to the $1,000 income before taxes for that year. This illustrates that when tax rates change, interperiod income tax allocation procedures do not provide the normal tax rate.

The method of computing deferred taxes illustrated in Figures 25.1 and 25.3 is known as the *gross change method* and is consistent with the conceptual basis of the deferral method of tax allocation. The gross change method illustrates the idea that deferred tax accounts continually "roll over." Although the aggregate balance of deferred taxes reported in successive balance sheets may remain stable or grow, the composition of the balance is continually changing as additions are made for originating differences at the same time reductions are made for reversing differences.

Net Change Method. An alternative method for computing deferred taxes is the *net change method.* In computing deferred taxes under the net change method for a particular timing difference such as depreciation, it is not necessary to make separate computations for the originating depreciation differences and the reversing depreciation differences. Instead, a single computation can be made for the net change in the cumulative difference between depreciation recognized for financial reporting purposes and depreciation deducted for tax purposes. The net change method does not permit a single computation for *all* types of timing differences, however. For example, in addition to timing differences stemming from depreciation, a company may have differences stemming from estimated provisions for warranty expenses, or from using the installment method for recognizing sales for tax

YEAR 1

Pretax income for financial reporting purposes	$1,000
Income tax expense (equal to tax currently payable)	450
Net income	$ 550
Effective tax rate ($450/$1,000)	45%

YEAR 2

Pretax income for financial reporting purposes	$1,000
Income tax expense (equal to tax currently payable)	550
Net income	$ 450
Effective tax rate ($550/$1,000)	55%

FIGURE 25.2 EFFECTIVE TAX RATES WITHOUT INTERPERIOD TAX ALLOCATION

purposes while using the accrual method for financial reporting purposes. Separate computations must be made for these timing differences. The net change method is illustrated in Figure 25.4, using the same assumptions as in Figure 25.3.

As can be seen by comparing the results in Figure 25.4 with those in Figure 25.3, the provision for deferred taxes in year 2 obtained by applying the net change method is $10 higher than that obtained by applying the gross change method with the same facts. The reason is that the deferred taxes provided under the net change method are at the 40% rate assumed to be in effect for year 2 and no effect is realized because of the change in rates. Of course, the deferred tax credits shown in the balance sheet will also be $10 higher under the net change method.

Unlike the gross change method, the net change method does not "correct" the balance sheet amount to the new rate; therefore, the balance sheet amount of deferred tax credits will not represent the current rate of 40% times the aggregate net timing difference. However, even under the gross change method, the effective restatement of the balance sheet accrual for deferred taxes to the new statutory rate will not necessarily be achieved in one year. In the illustration it was achieved in one year because we assumed that the timing difference that arose in year 1 under the old rate entirely reversed during year 2. In a realistic situation involving different depreciation methods, originating differences that occur under the old rate will probably take many years to reverse. Thus, it may take many years before the gross change method achieves a balance sheet accrual equal to the new tax rate times the aggregate amount of net timing differences; as a practical matter, this may in fact never occur. APB 11 (AC 4091) mandated comprehensive income tax allocation but did not require that its provisions be adopted retroactively. For example, many companies did not provide deferred tax for specific recurring timing differences (other than differences in depreciation methods covered in ARB 44, Revised), since no existing pronouncement required comprehensive allocation for all recurring timing differences. If such a company had chosen to apply compre-

Pretax income for financial reporting purposes	$1,000
Depreciation differences:	
Reversal of year 1 additional tax depreciation (i.e., taxable income is higher than reported income by this amount)	100
Origination of new additional tax depreciation	$ (150)
Taxable income	$ 950
Tax currently payable (40% of $950)	$ 380
Taxable income (as above)	$ 950
Add originating difference	150
Taxable income without the originating difference	$1,100
Tax thereon ($1,100 × 40%)	$ 440
Tax currently payable (as above)	380
Differential representing deferred tax to be recognized on the originating difference	$ 60

The income statement for the year would appear as follows:

Income before taxes		$1,000
Income tax expense:		
Currently payable	$380	
Deferred (see note)	10	390
Net income		$ 610

Note: The $10 increase in tax expense attributable to deferred taxes is the net result of a reversal of $50 in deferred taxes recognized in year 1 on timing differences that reversed in year 2, and the recognition of $60 in deferred tax on timing differences originating in year 2.

FIGURE 25.3 COMPUTATION OF DEFERRED TAXES (GROSS CHANGE METHOD) WITH REPETITIVE ORIGINATING DIFFERENCES

hensive interperiod allocation for a timing difference under the net change method, the balance sheet accrual for deferred income taxes would never have reached the level it would have under the conceptually sound gross change method, as long as the cumulative amount of a specific type of timing difference remained level or increased after the adoption of the net change method.

Thus, the net change method is usable only if balance sheet accruals for deferred taxes have been retroactively adjusted to the amounts that would have been determined if the net change method had always been used during any period when presently existing timing differences originated (AC 4091.36). Accordingly, companies adopting APB 11 in 1968 could either use the net change method with retroactive restatement or use the gross change method with or without retroactive re-

---

YEAR 1

Same as in Figure 25.1

YEAR 2

Pretax income for financial reporting purposes	$1,000
Net increase in depreciation for tax purposes (originating difference of $150 less reversing difference from year 1 of $100)	50
Taxable income	$ 950
Tax currently payable (40% of $950)	$ 380
Taxable income (as above)	$ 950
Net increase in timing differences	50
Taxable income without net change in timing differences related to depreciation	$1,000
Tax thereon (40% of $1,000)	$ 400
Tax currently payable (as above)	380
Differential representing net change in deferred taxes to be recognized for year 2	$ 20

The income statement for the year would appear as follows:

Income before income taxes		$1,000
Income taxes:		
Currently payable	$380	
Deferred	20	400
Net income		$ 600
Effective tax rate ($400/$1,000)		40%

FIGURE 25.4 COMPUTATION OF DEFERRED TAXES (NET CHANGE METHOD)

statement. Because some timing differences take many years to reverse, there are a small number of companies that, more than a decade after the adoption of APB 11, have not yet achieved a theoretically full balance sheet accrual for deferred taxes. In practice, most companies have chosen to follow the net change method because it is simpler. But financial statement users are often not sure which method a company is using, or whether the net change method is properly being applied separately for each kind of timing difference or improperly being combined into a single aggregate computation for all timing differences. In the absence of changes in rates or other complicating circumstances (e.g., the effect of the investment tax credit or operating loss carryover), shortcuts may be acceptable because the differences are not material. Of course, these shortcuts can create problems if they are mechanistically applied when circumstances change.

Operating Losses

When a company incurs operating losses, tax benefits may be available either from refunds of taxes paid in prior profitable years—that is, by *carrybacks of losses* —or as reductions of taxes otherwise payable in future profitable years—that is, by *carryforwards of losses*.

Loss Carrybacks. Refundable taxes arising from carrybacks of operating losses to prior years should be recognized during the loss year (AC 4091.43). Since the refund is assured, no problem of realization arises. Uncollected refunds should be reported in the balance sheet as current assets. The refund should be computed at the amount actually refundable, regardless of current tax rates.

An illustration of the presentation of an operating loss carryback, assuming that pretax income for financial reporting purposes and taxable income are identical, is shown below:

Loss before refundable income taxes	$1,000
Refund of prior years' income taxes arising from carryback of operating loss	485
Net loss	$ 515

If a loss carryback occurs when net deferred tax credits exist, adjustments of such net deferred tax credits may be necessary. The tax effects of the loss carryback included in the income statement should be based on the loss for financial reporting purposes rather than for tax purposes. The objective is to report the carryback refund that would have existed if there had been no timing differences. The difference between this amount and the amount currently refundable should be added to or deducted from the appropriate balance sheet deferred tax account. This is accomplished by recomputing the net deferred tax amounts for the carryback periods and the current period on a cumulative basis.

Loss Carryforwards. Loss carryforwards are handled much differently than carrybacks. Although a carryforward may be elected for tax strategy reasons even when a carryback is available, for the most part a carryforward is resorted to when a company has incurred operating losses that exhaust all benefits available from a carryback. Often such a company is undergoing financial difficulties so serious that the future realization of the carryforward is doubtful. Such a company may not have shown a profit in any recent year, or even in its entire history. Reporting the tax benefit of a loss carryforward as an asset during the loss year under such circumstances would be contrary to the accounting concept that revenues or gains should not be recognized if realization is not reasonably assured.

APB 11 thus requires that the realization concept should prevail over the matching concept—the future tax benefit of a loss carryforward should be recorded as an asset during the loss year only in cases where realization is assured beyond any reasonable doubt (AC 4091.44). Usually, the future tax benefit of a loss carryforward is reported as it is realized in years subsequent to the loss year (i.e., as the reduction in taxes otherwise payable is actually achieved as a result of the loss carryforward). If the future realization of a carryforward should become assured

Income before income taxes and extraordinary items		$1,000
Income tax expense:		
Currently payable	$200	
Tax effect of loss carryforward	300	500
Income before extraordinary item		500
Extraordinary item—reduction of income taxes arising from carryforward of prior years' operating losses		300
Net income		$ 800

FIGURE 25.5   RECOGNITION OF LOSS CARRYFORWARD BENEFIT IN YEAR REALIZED

beyond any reasonable doubt in a period subsequent to the loss year, it is not permissible to then recognize the future tax benefit. Recognition is permitted only in the loss year or when realized.

When a loss carryforward is realized and recognized subsequent to the loss period, income statement presentation is a problem. Under the matching concept, the benefit applies to the loss period and not to the period of realization. This suggests retroactive adjustment of the loss period, but such retroactive adjustment of prior years is not permitted under GAAP. Because it seems illogical to consider such a credit to be part of ordinary income, APB 11 (AC 4091.60) requires that it be presented as extraordinary in the year of realization. This is illustrated in Figure 25.5.

Assurance Beyond Any Reasonable Doubt

Since the future tax benefit of a loss carryforward should be recognized as an asset during the loss period if realization is "assured beyond any reasonable doubt," the meaning of this phrase is important. APB 11 (AC 4091.46) says:

> Realization of the tax benefit of a loss carry*forward* would appear to be assured beyond any reasonable doubt when both of the following conditions exist: (a) the loss results from an identifiable, isolated and nonrecurring cause and the company either has been continuously profitable over a long period or has suffered occasional losses which were more than offset by taxable income in subsequent years, and (b) future taxable income is virtually certain to be large enough to offset the loss carry*forward* and will occur soon enough to provide realization during the carry*forward* period.

The SEC has stated that both conditions (a) and (b) above must be met in order to record the future tax benefit of a loss carryforward during the loss year (SAB 8). Meeting only condition (b) is not sufficient.

Two examples of loss carryforwards that may qualify for recognition during the loss period are

1. Losses resulting from the expropriation of a foreign subsidiary or from the abandonment of one of several operations where the continuing operations are and have been profitable and are virtually certain to be profitable enough to offset the loss carryforward.

2. Losses (meeting the "identifiable, isolated and nonrecurring" test) of one or more subsidiaries of a profitable parent company where the carryforward will be used as an offset against other taxable income by claiming a bad debt deduction or by some other means. (But it would not be appropriate to record a loss carryforward of a subsidiary company, even though the parent and other subsidiaries are profitable, if there are no specific plans to obtain the tax benefit from the loss).

If a subsidiary has recurring losses *and* a consolidated return is filed, and if the consolidated tax entity has taxable income, it is appropriate to recognize the tax benefit of the subsidiary loss without reference to the conditions in AC 4091.46 mentioned above. In such a case no loss carryforward occurs; the subsidiary loss is simply an element of the net consolidated taxable income.

In those infrequent cases where operating loss carryforwards are expected to be realized beyond any reasonable doubt as offsets against future taxable income, the potential tax benefits should be reported in the balance sheet as assets and classified as current or noncurrent depending on when realization is expected to occur.

Recognition of Carryforwards as Offsets to Deferred Tax Credits. An operating loss carryforward may arise when net deferred tax credits exist because of prior timing differences. Even though the realization of the operating loss carryforward is not assured beyond any reasonable doubt, it may be appropriate to recognize all or a portion of it as an offset to net deferred tax credits. APB 11 (AC 4091.47) says:

> . . . net tax credits should be eliminated to the extent of the lower of (a) the tax effect of the loss carry*forward,* or (b) the amortization of the net deferred tax credits that would otherwise have occurred during the carry*forward* period. If the loss carry*forward* is realized in whole or in part in periods subsequent to the loss period, the amounts eliminated from the deferred tax credit accounts should be reinstated (at the then current tax rates) on a cumulative basis as, and to the extent that, the tax benefit of the loss carry*forward* is realized.

The limiting factor in the amount of loss carryforward that may be recognized by way of offset against net deferred tax credits is indicated in clause (b) above. When making a computation of the amortization of deferred tax credits during the carryforward period, no estimate of the tax effects of timing differences expected to arise during that period is to be taken into account.

Offsetting of loss carryforwards against deferred tax credits is justified because it is unrealistic to require recognition of deferred tax credits while at the same time denying recognition of deferred tax charges in the form of loss carryforwards. This is true because both the deferred credits and the deferred charges will reverse during the same future accounting periods. However, net deferred credits that will not be amortized until after the expiration of the loss carryforward period cannot be offset by loss carryforwards.

As the loss carryforward benefit is realized, the net deferred credits eliminated to give recognition to the carryforward, as well as credits related to originating timing differences of the loss year (net of any amortization that would otherwise have occurred), should be reinstated at the then current rates (i.e., at the rates at which the loss carryforward is realized) before an extraordinary tax credit is shown for any remaining loss carryforwards.

Deferred Tax Charges Existing When Loss Carryforward Arises. A loss carryforward may arise at the same time that there are unamortized net deferred tax charges representing the tax effects of additional expenses not recognized for tax purposes but recognized for financial reporting purposes, or a tax benefit of a new carryforward not yet realized may be recorded. If the realization of the tax benefit of the arising carryforward is not assured beyond any reasonable doubt, the propriety of continuing to carry the remaining deferred tax charges as assets must be questioned. In such situations the prior net deferred tax charges should be evaluated for realizability in the same manner as are other assets, but assurance of realizability beyond a reasonable doubt—the strict criterion applicable to initially recording the tax benefit of an operating loss carryforward—is not required.

In other situations companies may incur losses creating additional carryforwards that, because of the nature of timing differences, are larger for accounting purposes than the losses carried forward for tax purposes. When there is no assurance of future realization of the tax benefits of such *accounting loss carryforwards,* no recognition is given to the tax effects (deferred tax charges) of such timing differences (additional accounting loss carryforwards), inasmuch as the tax effects would be zero under the with-and-without computation.

Therefore, when these timing differences reverse, the tax benefits realized will not be offset by the amortization of deferred charges that would otherwise have been provided. Accordingly, in these situations the tax benefits realized from these timing differences (additional accounting loss carryforwards) should be included in the income statements as extraordinary credits in the same manner as benefits obtained upon future realization of tax loss carryforwards.

In a few situations the accounting loss carryforward will meet the conditions stated in AC 4091.46, that is, the loss results from an isolated and nonrecurring cause and future income is virtually certain to be large enough to offset the loss. The complication, of course, is the need to evaluate *when* the accounting loss carryforward will become tax deductible; in some situations, such as major plant realignment provisions, it may be years before estimated costs are expended or tax deductible losses incurred. When the accounting loss carryforward meets the conditions in AC 4091.46, the deferred tax debit applicable to the timing difference is properly recordable.

Loss Carryforwards Arising Before Bankruptcy or Quasi Reorganization. A company that goes through a reorganization under bankruptcy, or a quasi reorganization that includes the elimination of a deficit against contributed capital, is likely to be in a loss carryforward position. The proper accounting for the future tax benefit of such a loss carryforward poses a problem because the loss occurred prior to reorganization or quasi reorganization but the tax benefit from the carryforward is available as an offset against subsequent taxable income. Normally, it would be inappropriate to recognize the potential future tax benefit from the carry-

Note O – Taxes on Income

The provisions (credits) for taxes on income (loss) from continuing operations are as follows (in thousands):

	Year Ended December 31,	
	1978	1977
LTV:		
Currently payable	$ —	$ —
Due (from) subsidiaries for taxes on income includible in consolidated return	(3,798)	—
Deferred taxes (credit) with respect to items offsetting deferred taxes of subsidiaries	(5,788)	27,533
	$(9,586)	$27,533
Consolidated:		
Currently payable		
Federal	$ 1,653	$ —
State	4,484	610
Foreign	569	685
Deferred (credit):		
Federal	—	(5,331)
State	(2,606)	36
Total	$ 4,100	$(4,000)

The income tax effects of the factors accounting for the differences between the statutory federal income tax rate of 48% and the actual provisions (credits) on income (loss) from continuing operations are as follows (in thousands):

	Year Ended December 31,	
	1978	1977
Theoretical tax expense (credit) at 48%	$ 11,560	$(18,714)
Increases (decreases) resulting from:		
State income taxes, net of related federal income tax benefit	977	336
Depletion	(4,911)	(4,146)
Permanent differences between tax and book, primarily depreciation	(3,642)	(4,451)
Dividends received deduction	(1,354)	(2,373)
Unrecognized operating loss carryforward	—	24,705
Investments tax credit reversals	—	3,406
Minimum tax	1,653	—
Other items, net	(183)	(2,763)
Income taxes (credits) as recorded	$ 4,100	$ (4,000)

Federal income tax benefit of $5,331,000 has been reflected for the year 1977 as a reduction of deferred income tax credits previously provided. No benefit has been provided in 1978 as all available benefits were exhausted in 1977.

At December 31, 1978, a loss carryforward of approximately $68,000,000 generated in 1977, expiring in 1984, is available for financial reporting purposes. Investment tax credits of $60,000,000 generated in the five years ended 1978 have not been recognized in the income tax computations for financial reporting purposes for such periods and are available as carryforwards to the years 1979 through 1985.

For income tax reporting purposes, LTV had available net operating loss carryforwards of approximately $255,000,000 at December 31, 1978. Of this amount $145,000,00 is from tax years prior to the merger with Lykes on December 5, 1978 and is restricted to offsetting future taxable income of the respective companies which generated the losses. Of this restricted carryforward, $28,000,000 expires in 1979, $57,000,000 in 1982, and $60,000,000 in 1983. The balance of the tax loss carryforward amounting to $110,000,000, of which $55,000,000 relates to the Lykes merger, is not restricted as to use and expires in 1985. Use of these loss carryforwards is dependent on future taxable income.

At December 31, 1978 LTV had available approximately $105,500,00 of investment tax credit carryovers for tax reporting purposes. Of this amount $69,500,000, expiring in 1979 to 1985, is from tax years prior to the merger with Lykes and is restricted to offsetting future taxes of the respective companies which generated the credits. The balance of the investment tax credit carryovers amounting to $36,000,000 which relate to the Lykes merger and are not restricted as to use, expire from 1979 to 1985. Use of these tax credits is dependent on future taxable income.

Income tax returns for LTV through 1973 and for Lykes through 1972 have been examined by the Internal Revenue Service. The net effect of unagreed adjustments made by the Service to the LTV returns is to reduce overall net operating loss carryforwards by an amount which will not have a material effect upon LTV. Adjustments to the Lykes returns made by the Service with which the company does not agree are being protested. Adequate provision has been made for taxes and interest relating to possible disallowances.

FIGURE 25.7 EXAMPLE OF INCOME TAX INFORMATION DISCLOSURE
SOURCE: LTV Corporation, Form 10-K, 1978.

Note I — Income Taxes:
The consolidated provision for income taxes for 1978 and 1977 consists of the following:

	1978	1977
Currently payable:		
Federal	$12,228	$40,878
Canadian	8,555	8,610
Other, principally state	7,070	7,638
	27,853	57,126
Deferred	(16,507)	(8,224)
Provision for income taxes	$11,346	$48,902

Deferred income taxes relate to the following principal timing differences:

	1978	1977
Federal:		
Plant closing and relocation costs	$ (21,267)	$ (8,966)
Depreciation	9,949	7,087
Uninsured loss accruals	(4,293)	(4,328)
All other	675	(1,601)
Canadian, principally depreciation	836	605
State, related to plant closing and relocation costs	(2,407)	(1,021)
Total deferred income taxes	$ (16,507)	$ (8,224)

The Financial Group domestic subsidiaries, as well as eligible consolidated subsidiaries of Greyhound, are included in the consolidated federal income tax returns of Greyhound.

Source: The Greyhound Corporation, 1978 Annual Report

As a result, certain amounts of tax losses, investment tax credits and foreign tax credits have been utilizable by Greyhound which could not have been utilized by the Financial Group on a separate return basis. These amounts, aggregating $13,041,000 in 1978 and $13,833,000 in 1977, have not been reflected as a reduction of the provision for federal income taxes currently payable, since the reductions in Greyhound's tax liability are paid to the Financial Group when realized by Greyhound.

A reconciliation of the provision for income taxes and the amount that would be computed using the statutory federal income tax rate of 48 per cent is set forth below:

	1978	1977
Taxes on income before income taxes at statutory federal income tax rate	$16,551	$50,558
Investment tax credits	(8,116)	(6,633)
Minority interests	2,328	2,994
State income taxes	1,392	2,983
Foreign income taxes at rates higher than 48%	1,610	478
Refund of prior years' taxes	(1,454)	
Other, including effects of capital gains and foreign tax credits	(965)	(1,478)
Provision for income taxes	$11,346	$48,902

At December 31, 1978, retained income includes $19,702,000 of undistributed net income of foreign subsidiaries and DISC companies on which no federal taxes have been provided because management considers that such income has been permanently invested.

Note E—Income Taxes Greyhound pays to Greyhound Leasing an amount equal to the tax reductions realized by Greyhound as a result of the inclusion of Greyhound Leasing's tax losses in Greyhound's consolidated federal income tax returns.

The consolidated provision for income taxes for 1978 and 1977 consists of the following:

	1978	1977
Currently payable - Canadian	$ 849	$
Federal:		
Benefits from inclusion in Greyhound's consolidated return	(4,376)	(7,438)
Deferred	8,992	13,146
Provisions for Income Taxes	$ 5,465	$ 5,708

Deferred taxes arise from the principal timing differences set forth below:

	1978	1977
Lease and other contract income and related depreciation	$10,150	$16,333
Gains on disposals of equipment	(538)	(2,581)
Provision for doubtful accounts	(720)	(674)
Other	100	68
	$ 8,992	$13,146

In addition to the tax losses set forth above, investment and foreign tax credits utilized in Greyhound's consolidated federal income tax returns, and the benefits therefrom due Greyhound Leasing by Greyhound, were $5,382,000 and $3,792,000, respectively, during the years ended December 31, 1978 and 1977. Since Greyhound Leasing reported losses for federal income tax purposes, such credits would not have been available to Greyhound Leasing as a reduction of federal income taxes on a separate return basis.

The effective federal income tax rates of Greyhound Leasing reflected in the financial statements approximates the statutory rate of 48 per cent of income before federal income taxes after deducting from pre-tax income the amortization of investment tax credits of $5,237,000 and $4,902,000 and the lower effective rate applicable to dividends received on preferred stocks of $2,290,000 and $593,000 included in earned income in 1978 and 1977, respectively.

At December 31, 1978, retained income includes approximately $14,833,000 of undistributed net income of foreign subsidiaries on which no deferred federal income taxes have been provided because management considers that such income has been permanently invested.

FIGURE 25.8   EXAMPLE OF INCOME TAX DISCLOSURE IN CONSOLIDATED AND SEPARATE SUBSIDIARY REPORTS
SOURCE: The Greyhound Corporation, 1978 Annual Report and Greyhound Leasing & Financial Corporation, 1978 Annual Report.

are necessary because the transactions giving rise to their effects are reported as discrete items of the specified interim period in which they occur, not apportioned over the entire year. The specific tax effect associated with each of these excluded items is reported during the same interim period as the related transaction.

The computation of an effective annual rate and its application to interim reporting is illustrated in the following simplified examples. Assume the following facts:

- The company expects annual pretax income for financial reporting purposes of $1,000,
- The company anticipates investment tax credits of $100, and
- The statutory tax rate (federal and state rates combined) is 50%.

The effective annual tax rate would be computed as follows:

Expected annual pretax income for financial reporting purposes	$1,000
Expected annual income taxes before investment credit at 50%	500
Investment credit	100
Expected annual income tax	$ 400
Estimated annual effective tax rate	40%

The company will pay income taxes, considering all credits available to it, at the rate of 40% of its reported pretax income. The 40% effective tax rate would then be applied to the interim financial reported pretax income. Accordingly, if in the first quarter the company had pretax income of $300, its interim financial statements would appear as follows:

Income before taxes	$ 300
Taxes on income (40% effective tax rate)	120
Net income	$ 180

Cumulative Calculation

Any changes in the estimated annual effective tax rate are accounted for on a prospective basis. To illustrate, assume that during the second quarter the company revised its estimate of its annual income from $1,000 to $1,250. Its new effective annual tax rate would be computed as follows:

Expected annual pretax income for financial reporting purposes	$1,250
Expected annual income taxes before investment credit at 50%	625
Investment credit	100
Expected annual income taxes	$ 525
Revised estimated annual effective tax rate	42%

In the second quarter, the company would apply a revised effective annual tax rate of 42% to its cumulative pretax reported income for the first two quarters and subtract the income tax expense reported on the first quarter's earnings to determine the tax expense for the second quarter. To illustrate, assume that the company had cumulative pretax income for the first two quarters of $500 ($300 for the first quarter, as above, and $200 for the second quarter). At an effective tax rate of 42%, the income tax expense for the first six months would be $210. Since the company had already reported $120 of income tax expense in the first quarter, it would report the difference—$90—on the $200 of pretax income of the second quarter. The interim financial statements would appear as follows:

	First Two Quarters Combined	Second Quarter	First Quarter (as previously reported)
Income before income taxes	$ 500	$ 200	$ 300
Taxes on income	210	90	120
Net income	$ 290	$ 110	$ 180

The tax reported for the second quarter includes taxes at the new revised rate of 42% on second quarter pretax income of $200, which equals $84, plus an additional 2% on the first quarter pretax income of $300, or $6, for a total of $90. The difference between the 42% revised effective tax rate and the 40% original effective tax rate applied to first quarter income is reported in the second quarter.

Interim Losses

Losses during the year also complicate the determination of interim tax expense. It is appropriate to provide a tax benefit in an interim period with a loss if it is anticipated that the loss will be offset by income in later periods of the year, or if it can be offset against income in earlier periods of the year. For example, continuing the above illustration, assume that in the third quarter the company had a $100 pretax loss. Also assume that the company anticipated this loss and took it into consideration in estimating the annual tax rate. In this case it would be appropriate to record a tax benefit in the third quarter using the 42% rate. The financial statements for the third quarter would appear as follows:

	First Three Quarters Combined	Third Quarter
Income (loss) before income taxes	$400	$(100)
Taxes on income (refundable taxes)	168	(42)
Net income (loss)	$232	$ (58)

If a loss is expected for the full year, or if a loss is experienced in an interim period and it is not known whether profits in other periods will offset it, refundable taxes may be recorded, provided the company can also carry back the loss to earlier profitable years. Should carrybacks not be available, refundable taxes can be recorded only if a carryforward of the loss is assured beyond any reasonable doubt. The rules for accounting for such carrybacks and carryforwards as discussed for annual financial reporting earlier in this chapter also apply to interim reports. There are numerous other examples of accounting for income taxes in interim periods shown in FASB Interpretation No. 18 (AC 2071-1).

INTERCORPORATE TAX ALLOCATION

When a company files a consolidated tax return with its subsidiaries, and separate financial statements for the parent or a subsidiary are to be prepared, the consolidated tax expense must be allocated among the affiliated companies. Special procedures for intercorporate tax allocation are required, because the consolidated tax expense usually differs from the summation of what the tax expense for the companies would be on the basis of separate returns.

Internal Revenue Code Methods

The Internal Revenue Code (Section 1552) and related regulations provide specific methods of apportioning a consolidated tax among the affiliated companies for tax purposes. Consolidated groups can also devise any other method of apportionment, though only with the prior approval of the IRS. In the absence of authoritative financial accounting pronouncements, the methods of apportionment provided in the tax law are also acceptable for financial reporting purposes, provided full disclosure of the method used is made in a note to the separate financial statements of the parent or the subsidiary. Companies often use the same method of apportionment for financial reporting purposes as they use for tax purposes in order to minimize the number of allocations required, which can become quite complex.

The first alternative method of intercorporate allocation provided in the Internal Revenue Code apportions the consolidated tax currently payable to profitable component corporations based on their respective taxable incomes. The second alternative apportions the consolidated tax currently payable to each component corporation on the basis of the aggregate of taxes payable on a separate return basis. A third method is set forth in the Internal Revenue Code, but is rarely used. For an excellent detailed discussion of these methods, see Mertens's *Law of Federal Income Taxation,* Volume 8A, Section 46.61.

Other Financial Reporting Methods

Variations of the methods of apportionment set forth in the Internal Revenue Code are also acceptable for financial reporting purposes. These are briefly described below.

Separate Return With Differences Allocated to Parent. Under this method, taxes are reported in the financial statements for each subsidiary as if it filed a separate return. The difference between the total taxes so reported for the subsidiaries and the consolidated expense is reported as part of the parent company's tax expense. The parent therefore receives the benefit of or charge for any difference between the consolidated tax provision and separate return provisions.

Ratio of Individual Company Income to Consolidated Income. Under this method, each member of the consolidated group obtains an income tax charge or credit based on the ratio of its pretax income or loss to the consolidated group's pretax income or loss. For example, if the consolidated pretax income is $1,000, consolidated taxes on income are $500, the parent company's income is $600, subsidiary A has income of $500, and subsidiary B has a loss of $(100), the tax provision would be allocated as follows:

	Consolidated	Parent	Sub. A	Sub. B
Income (loss) before income taxes	$1,000	$ 600	$ 500	$ (100)
Taxes on income (refund of taxes)	500	300	250	(50)
Net income (loss)	$ 500	$ 300	$ 250	$ (50)

Since subsidiary B had a loss, it would have a negative tax provision.

Marginal Contribution. Under this method, the provision for income taxes is first computed for the consolidated group. Then the provision is computed with one member of the group excluded. This amount is subtracted from the consolidated tax provision, and the difference is taken as the tax provision for the excluded member. The tax provision for each remaining member is computed in the same way. If there is any difference between the total of the provisions for all the members and the consolidated provision, it is added to or subtracted from the parent company's provision.

Allocation of Deferred Taxes

Deferred income taxes arising from timing differences should be allocated to the component members of a consolidated group on a basis that is consistent with the allocation of income tax expense. Generally, the deferred tax attributable to a specific timing difference should be allocated to the component in which the timing difference occurs. The computational procedures are generally less involved when separate return methods of allocation are used, and such approaches will most often accomplish the objective of normalizing the total tax expense of an individual component with timing differences. (For an example, see Figure 25.8.)

AUDITING

Objectives

Conceptually, the auditing objectives for income taxes are the same as for other costs and liabilities. In other words, auditors must evaluate the reasonableness of the reported amounts. Auditing income taxes, however, is often more challenging than other areas, both because the amounts involved are usually a significant portion of income and are significant to the balance sheet and because a thorough knowledge is required of the many specific tax rules that apply to the company under audit. The auditing of income taxes has these three objectives:

1. To conclude that the income tax amounts presented in the balance sheet fairly represent, in the context of the financial statements taken as a whole, the amounts that are currently payable or receivable and the amounts that must be shown as deferred taxes according to interperiod income tax allocation procedures. Also, income tax items should be properly classified in the balance sheet among current or noncurrent assets and liabilities.
2. To conclude that the amounts of income tax expense (or credit) presented in the income statement are fairly stated, including the separation between amounts currently payable and amounts deferred, in the context of the financial statements taken as a whole.
3. To conclude that disclosures in the financial statements about income taxes are appropriate in context—that they adequately explain the important aspects of the company's income taxes, including significant amounts of deferred taxes, amounts of tax carryforwards available, and (for publicly held companies) differences between the statutory rate and the company's effective tax rate.

Substantive Approach to Auditing

Before the auditor can be satisfied as to the reasonableness of the reported income tax amounts, he must understand in considerable detail the specific tax rules that apply to the company under audit. The approach to auditing income taxes is substantive, rather than one of reliance on the internal accounting control system. Thus the auditor will obtain and review (or prepare) an analysis of all transactions affecting the income tax accounts for the year. The auditor must evaluate the company's computations and calculations of the income tax expense and the related balance sheet accrual and deferrals. Where there is the possibility of a material assessment of additional taxes, the auditor, with his tax adviser, will consider the adequacy of accrual and disclosure under the rules covering accounting for contingencies (see Chapter 29).

In addition to checking tax computations, the auditor should review tax returns and any correspondence between the company and tax authorities relating to questions or open items on the company's tax returns. The auditor must understand and evaluate the status of any examinations by taxing authorities that are in process. Often, the auditor will need to seek precedent to evaluate a particular tax question or to draw analogies between the company's tax problems and similar problems of other companies, and to obtain advice from tax specialists. (For a detailed discussion of the relationship between auditor and tax adviser, and the contributions of tax specialists to an audit, see Chapter 43.)

In principle, there are no differences between the auditing approach for federal income taxes and that for state and local taxes. An important aspect of auditing state and local taxes is to determine if the company is appropriately providing for taxes in all jurisdictions in which it is subject to income tax.

Difficult Areas

Assessing Realizability of Net Operating Loss Carryforwards. As discussed earlier, the future tax benefit of a loss carryforward cannot be recognized during the loss year unless it is assured beyond any reasonable doubt. This is one of the most exacting realization tests applied in financial accounting. The "reasonable assurance that an asset will be realized" test generally applied in other aspects of financial statements is not as exacting.

In order to meet the prescribed test, (1) the loss carryforward must result from "an identifiable, isolated and nonrecurring cause" and (2) sufficient future taxable income must be virtually certain. Those few cases where loss carryforwards are recognized during the loss year require that the auditor obtain sufficient evidence to provide him with a high degree of assurance that these conditions have been met. In order to be assured that sufficient future taxable income is a virtual certainty, the auditor must accumulate and evaluate considerable information as to the future prospects of the company. A careful analysis must also be made to see that the reason for the loss is clearly identifiable, isolated, and nonrecurring. This ultimately requires careful exercise of professional judgment by the auditor, since specific guidelines as to the quantity and nature of the required audit evidence applicable in all cases cannot be set forth.

Sustaining Management Intent With Respect to Undistributed Earnings of Subsidiaries and Joint Ventures. A company is not required to provide deferred taxes on its share of the undistributed earnings of subsidiaries or joint ventures if the presumption that such earnings will be distributed and subjected to taxation can be overcome. In practice, the provisions for overcoming the presumption of distribution have been generally interpreted to require a documented position that is reasonable in the light of both statutory requirements and prevailing economic circumstances. For example, it may be that the company plans a tax-free liquidation of the subsidiary so as to effectively distribute the earnings without incurring any tax. The auditor must be satisfied, through the advice of a tax expert if necessary, that the relevant provisions of the tax laws, regulations, rulings, and decided court cases have been studied, analyzed, and properly interpreted to support the planned tax-free liquidation. Alternatively, the company may plan to overcome the presumption by reinvesting in new facilities all funds generated internally by the subsidiary or the joint venture. In such a case, the auditor must be satisfied that the plans for reinvestment have actually been formulated and that they are reasonable in the light of the past practices and the potential of the organization. Also, he must be satisfied that there are sound business reasons for carrying out the reinvestment plans.

The presumption of distribution of earnings cannot be overcome with respect to investments in investees that are not subsidiaries or joint ventures. This sometimes requires a judgment as to whether or not a particular investee qualifies as a subsidiary or joint venture. Ordinarily a subsidiary would be a company in which the investor owns a majority of the voting stock. However, there are cases (see Chapter 31) where the investor can demonstrate control without having a majority voting interest. For example, an investor with a 49% interest may by contract have a right to elect a majority of the board of directors, whereas the holders of the remaining 51% of the voting stock can only elect a minority of the board of directors. In such cases, it could be appropriate to conclude that the 49%-owned investee was a subsidiary; then, assuming that the presumption as to distribution could be overcome, it would be appropriate to omit the provision for deferred taxes on unremitted earnings.

Questions can also arise as to whether an investee qualifies as a joint venture. A common example of a joint venture is one owned 50% by each of two investors and operated jointly for their common benefit. Obviously, a venture can have more than two holders, or have one venturer with more than a 50% interest, and still qualify as joint, provided it is clear that all the joint venturers are involved in the management of the operation at least at a policy-making level. However, as the number of joint venturers grows, a point is reached where the investee is simply a corporation with a lot of minority holders and no longer qualifies as a joint venture; it would then be necessary for the investor to record deferred taxes on undistributed earnings regardless of the ability to overcome a presumption that distribution will be made. These are examples of borderline cases in which the auditor must carefully accumulate and analyze evidence. A complete understanding of all the facts and the exercise of professional judgment are necessary, because again, specific rules and guidelines are not available for determining when a corporation can be considered a joint venture.

Differentiating Between Permanent and Timing Differences. In most cases, the distinction between a permanent difference and a timing difference is rather clear-cut. A timing difference will reverse in a future period; a permanent difference will never reverse, because it involves revenue exempt from taxation or an expense that is simply never deductible. In some cases, however, an originating difference may or may not reverse depending on future occurrences, for example, undistributed earnings of subsidiaries. Prior to the adoption of FASB Interpretation No. 22 (AC 4091-1) in April 1978, companies and auditors had to determine if the indefinite reversal criteria described in APB 23 (AC 4095) also applied to situations not explicitly mentioned in that opinion.

An example of such a situation not explicitly covered by GAAP is the extinguishment by a corporation of debt for less than its carrying amount. The result is reported as income for financial statement purposes, but for tax purposes the company may be able to postpone the recognition of the income by adjusting the tax basis of certain assets. However, FASB Interpretation No. 22 says that indefinite reversal criteria apply only to situations explicitly covered in an APB opinion (such as those discussed earlier in this chapter) or in an FASB statement.

Accordingly, at present the only areas that require judgments of this type relate to interpreting the provisions of the law to determine whether a specific revenue qualifies for exemption from taxation or whether a specific expense is never deductible. In such situations the auditor must be satisfied, through the advice of a tax expert if necessary, that a thorough-enough study has been made of the relevant tax law and regulations to determine if the company's position is appropriate.

Tax Allocation of Consolidation Adjustments. In most cases the parent company and each subsidiary company of a consolidated group file separate tax returns. Accordingly, taxable income of the various components may include gains or losses resulting from transactions with other components. Since intercompany profits and losses are required to be eliminated in consolidated statements (see Chapter 31), the tax effects, if any, of such eliminated transactions must also be determined and eliminated. Such elimination could give rise to deferred taxes in the consolidated financial statements that do not appear in any of the separate financial statements of the component companies.

An even more difficult problem arises with respect to transactions that are included in the consolidated statements but do not appear in separate financial statements of any of the components. For example, when a company has foreign subsidiaries, its foreign currency financial statements must be translated into dollars for consolidation purposes. In most cases the translation process gives rise to gains or losses. It is necessary to ascertain whether these gains or losses are timing differences, and if so, an appropriate deferred tax change or credit must be provided in consolidation (see discussion in Chapter 31).

In any consolidated group with a number of companies where transactions occur among the separate companies, the allocation of taxes on consolidating adjustments can become quite complex. Auditors are often required to spend a great deal of time in study and analysis to determine that the allocations are all properly handled.

THE FUTURE

Accounting for income taxes is an extremely complex subject and has been very contentious over the years. Many had hoped that when the APB intensively studied accounting for income taxes and issued APB 11 in 1967, dealing with the subject in practice would be simplified because of the availability of comprehensive and universal guidelines. However, APB 11 explicitly recognized its own shortcomings in setting forth the five areas deferred for future consideration. Additionally, the adoption of the deferred method, with its emphasis on mechanical calculations rather than on concept, has created numerous interpretation problems over the years. This has been aggravated by the virtually universal adoption of the flow-through method for the investment credit, which often impacts the determination of deferred taxes.

APBs 23 and 24, in dealing with a number of the special areas left open in APB 11, found it necessary to depart from a strict interpretation of the deferred method. And in the years since APB 11 was adopted, differences between reported income and taxable income have proliferated. Very often these differences involve the recognition of credits against taxes otherwise payable rather than simply the timing of deductions. Each set of credits gives rise to a complex set of rules for entitlement to the credit, not to mention carryover and carryback provisions. Applying all of these complications under the with-and-without computation required by the deferred method under APB 11 can create a nightmare of computational difficulties and give rise to varying interpretations. In addition to being extremely complex, these interpretations can also have very significant effects on reported income.

Accordingly, it will probably be necessary for the patchwork of income tax accounting pronouncements and interpretations that now exist to be reconsidered by the FASB in the early 1980s.

SUGGESTED READING

Accountants International Study Group. *Accounting for Corporate Income Taxes.* New York: AICPA, 1971. This booklet is one of a series of comparisons of important accounting and auditing matters in the United States, the United Kingdom, and Canada, and is highly informative for those who want an international perspective on tax allocation evolution.

AICPA. *Exposure Draft on Proposed APB Opinion: Accounting for Income Taxes.* New York, 1967. This is the exposure draft that preceded the issuance of APB 11.

————. *Illustrations of Interperiod Tax Allocation.* Financial Report Survey 4. New York, 1974. This booklet, fourth in a series, is a survey of applications of APBs 11, 23, and 24 and SEC ASR 149. Based on research of published reports using the National Automated Accounting Research System (NAARS), it contains many useful examples.

Bevis, Donald, and Perry, Raymond. *Accounting for Income Taxes—An Interpretation of APB Opinion 11.* New York: AICPA, 1969. This is an extensive unofficial interpretation of the opinion, based on initial experience with APB 11.

Schlag, Rene. "Accounting for Taxes of Foreign Subsidiaries—a Simplified Approach." *Management Accounting,* December, 1979, pp. 15-19. This is a summary of APBs 11, 23, and 24 and also discusses taxes of foreign subsidiaries.

26

Equity Capital and Earnings Per Share

Irwin Goldberg

OVERVIEW OF EQUITY CAPITAL

A business enterprise requires capital to procure the assets and services it needs to start and to remain in operation. It can raise initial capital by borrowing funds or selling a part of itself. The result of the latter method is commonly called *equity capital.*

This chapter discusses stockholders' equity accounting, reporting, and auditing as it is presently practiced. However, there are many conceptual issues involved, which are discussed at length in Accounting Research Study No. 15, *Stockholders' Equity* (Melcher, 1973). Appendix 26 contains a synopsis of ARS 15, and comments throughout the chapter suggest some of the conceptual anomalies covered by the study.

Two categories of initial equity capital, *preferred stock* and *common stock,* are distinguished by their respective rights. Two additional categories usually appearing in the equity section of the balance sheet are *paid-in capital* and *retained earnings.*

Preferred Stock

The rights of preferred stock usually consist of a preference in the distribution of earnings (dividends) and a preference in the distribution of assets upon liquidation; hence, the term *preferred.* In addition, most preferred stocks have a fixed face value (par value) and the right to a fixed rate of dividend distribution, stated as either a percentage of par value or a fixed dollar amount (for example, 8% preferred stock or $2.50 preferred stock). Individual preferred stocks often have various other rights determined at issuance. For example, preferred stocks that must receive dividend distribution payments for all years prior to any common stock dividend payment are described as cumulative; those without this right are noncumulative. Preferred stocks may have voting rights in the election of directors; those without this right are nonvoting. Some are redeemable optionally, some have mandatory redemption features, some have no redemption features, and some can be converted into common stock. Because preferred stocks can vary widely in their terms, some business enterprises have several classes of preferred stock, each with distinct rights.

Common Stock

Common stock almost always includes voting rights as to directors and major changes in the activities of the enterprise (such as sale of the whole enterprise or a major division). It may or may not have a par or stated value. However, common stock does not usually have a fixed dividend rate but receives dividends only as declared by the board of directors. Sometimes there are separate classes of common stock having differing rights, such as voting versus nonvoting.

Paid-In Capital

When preferred or common stock is sold by an enterprise to outsiders to raise operating capital, it may be at a price above par or stated value. This premium is known as additional paid-in capital, capital contributed in excess of par or stated value, or something similar. Depending on individual state law, dividends may be declared out of paid-in capital. These dividends are commonly called *liquidating dividends,* since they are a return of capital to the shareholders (though not necessarily to the same shareholders who invested it). A company with no par stock need not have a paid-in capital account, though most do. The excess can simply be carried in the capital stock account.

Retained Earnings

When net earnings of an enterprise are not distributed to its shareholders through dividends, they are retained by the enterprise; hence, *retained earnings.* (They are also known as accumulated earnings, earnings retained or reinvested in the business, or earned surplus.) Some enterprises organized for a profit may incur cumulative losses; the amount by which invested capital is diminished through losses is called a *deficit.*

Meaning of Earnings Per Share

In SFAC 1 (AC 1210.47), the FASB, when speaking about the information needed by users of financial statements, said that investors and creditors "may use earnings information to help them (a) evaluate management's performance, (b) estimate 'earning power' or other amounts they perceive as 'representative' of long-term earnings ability of an enterprise, (c) predict future earnings, or (d) assess the risk of investing in or lending to an enterprise." Among the numerous financial ratios used in analyzing investment decisions, the most prominent is probably earnings per share (EPS). In its simplest form, EPS is the earnings for the period divided by the weighted average number of shares outstanding; but there are many variations discussed later in this chapter.

UNDERWRITERS' INVOLVEMENT

General

Underwriters are almost always involved in a securities offering to the public, whether the securities are debt, equity, or some hybrid of the two. They assess the marketability of the security, the price that should be expected, and the conditions under which a public offering can or could be made. Various arrangements can exist between an underwriter and the company regarding a particular offering (e.g., a "firm" underwriting, in which all securities are taken by the underwriter and resold or retained as permitted by market conditions or as otherwise desired, or an "all-or-nothing best efforts" underwriting, in which failure to achieve the resale of the securities effectively aborts the offering).

Underwriters are experts in securities valuation, and their advice is often needed by accountants (in determining the allocation of proceeds of a hybrid security or the valuation of a warrant, to mention only two situations).

Section 11 of the Securities Act of 1933 (Securities Act) invests underwriters with a responsibility for "due diligence" as to the appropriateness of information contained in the offering documents up to the effective date (issuance date upon clearance by the SEC).

Of course, an essential ingredient in any SEC-registered offering (and in most intrastate or small issues exemption offerings) is financial and operating information—mostly in the form of audited financial statements for five years, unaudited subsequent interim data, and supplementary data derived from the enterprise's accounts and records. The traditional manner by which the underwriter augments his own due-diligence procedures with respect to financial data is through the obtaining of a *comfort letter* from the enterprise's accountants.

Although many securities offerings, probably most if taken individually, are not underwritten, this chapter also applies to them.

Comfort Letters

Underwriters invariably request the enterprise's accountants to aid them in exercising their due-diligence requirements by issuing a comfort letter as to certain procedures. Various auditing pronouncements have been issued on comfort letters in an attempt to clarify the nature and scope of the accountants' procedures, the most recent and comprehensive being SAP 48, now codified in AU 630. But since the due-diligence criteria for underwriters have never been authoritatively established, accountants cannot give assurance as to whether the procedures performed at the request of the underwriters are sufficient for establishing such due diligence.

The underwriter is required to specify the steps he wants the accountant to perform. These procedures traditionally encompass unaudited changes in financial statement items and a review of statistical and tabular data.

The desired procedures and conclusions to be expressed in the comfort letter are usually specified in the underwriting agreement. Therefore, the accountant must read the underwriting agreement prior to its finalization to ascertain whether the stipulations are within the scope of his services as defined by professional standards.

A comfort letter concludes with negative assurance as to fairness of presentation of unaudited financial data in conformity with GAAP. An examination in accordance with GAAS is required for a positive opinion (auditor's standard report); since comfort letter procedures are limited, only negative assurance ("nothing came to our attention . . .") is permitted in a comfort letter.

Model comfort letters (AU 630.44-.53) were developed by the accounting profession to help accountants comply with the underwriters' requests. However, not every situation could be illustrated, and some letters will have to be modified for specific situations. Comfort letters usually meet the following criteria:

1. *Dating.* The letter is ordinarily dated at or shortly before the date the sale of securities is consummated (closing date). Another important date is the one on which the procedures are to be concluded (the cutoff date). The letter should specify that no procedures were performed after the cutoff date. A letter may also be requested at the date the registration statement becomes effective.

2. *Addressee.* The letter is usually addressed to the underwriter or the client. A request to address the letter to any other person should cause the accountant to consult legal counsel.

3. *Independence.* The Securities Act requires that an expert (the accountant) disclose any interest in the client. The underwriter usually requests confirmation of the accountant's independence.

4. *Compliance with SEC requirements.* A request to give an opinion concerning compliance as to conformity of the financial statements with the pertinent published rules and regulations of the SEC is usual.

5. *Unaudited financial statements and subsequent changes.* Comments with respect to unaudited financial statements, changes in capital stock and long-term debt, decreases in other specified financial statement items, and pro forma financial statements should be given with care. Comments should always be made in the form of negative assurance. AU 630.16-.20 should be consulted as to the matter of complying with a request for comments on unaudited data.

   Subsequent changes in financial statement items should concern only increases or decreases. The use of the term "adverse change" is not acceptable, as this term is not defined in authoritative accounting literature and is subject to misinterpretation. A detailed discussion of appropriate wording is contained in AU 630.21-.26.

6. *Tables, statistics, and other financial information.* Accountants should not comment on matters to which their competence as accountants is not related. They should comment only with respect to information (a) expressed in dollars or percentages derived from dollar amounts that have been obtained from accounting records subject to the internal accounting controls of the enterprise or (b) derived directly from the accounting records by analysis or computation. The accountant should not comment on matters concerning management's exercise of business judgment or dollar amounts not subject to internal accounting control. The information should be covered in precise language by page, paragraph, and sentence.

7. *Concluding paragraph.* This should contain a statement restricting use of the comfort letter to the underwriters and the client.

8. *Miscellaneous.* More than one accountant can be involved in the examination of the financial statements; subsidiaries, branches, or equity investees may be audited by other accountants. In such instances, the principal accountant should request a letter from the other accountant(s) on all significant units.

Comfort letters are now also commonly issued in business combinations (see Chapter 30), even though no party professes to be an underwriter subject to the rigors of Section 11 of the Securities Act. This expansion of negative assurance in a profession that grudgingly gave it only to underwriters by tradition happened slowly until recent governmental and social demands for more degrees of auditor assurance than all or none.

As the original beneficiaries of negative assurance, underwriters have been asking that the various forms of permitted negative assurance, based on procedures outlined in professional pronouncements, be given also to them. Thus far, the profession has sustained the premise that due-diligence procedures for an underwriter under the Securities Act are his choice; for example, if he requests performance of an SAS 24 (AU 721) interim review, comfort letter comments thereon cannot be directed to him unless he specifies sufficient criteria for all the procedures so that there is no implication that the responsibility for the sufficiency of the agreed-on procedures has been assumed by the accountants.

EXCHANGE LISTING PROCEDURES

An enterprise that has wide public distribution may want to increase the market for its stock. The usual way to do so is to obtain listing on a *stock exchange*.

There are many exchanges, the most important of which are the New York Stock Exchange and American Stock Exchange. The National Association of Security Dealers Automated Quotation (NASDAQ) System also operates effectively as an exchange. It is important to note that the exchange listing requirements are imposed by the exchanges themselves, not the SEC, although the commission must approve all changes in them. The original listing of a security on an exchange also requires the filing of a registration statement under the Securities Exchange Act of 1934 (Exchange Act). The exchanges have a substantial number of requirements, but only those concerning accountants will be briefly covered here. Both the New York and American Stock Exchanges have manuals to guide and assist enterprises and their accountants in preparing both original and subsequent listing applications.

New York Stock Exchange

Financial Statements—Original Listing. The New York Stock Exchange (NYSE) requires the following financial statements or data to be included in an original listing application:

1. A summarized consolidated earnings statement for the last ten years, at a minimum detailing sales, earnings before depreciation, interest, taxes, and net earnings.

2. Audited financial statements for the last two years and the related accountant's opinion.

3. Any interim consolidated statement of earnings from the audited balance sheet to a current date if available, and a balance sheet at the close of the current interim period statement of earnings if available. Such statements shall be certified by either the enterprise's accountants or its principal accounting officer.

4. A pro forma balance sheet giving effect to a completed or contemplated recapitalization, acquisition, reorganization, or major financing.

5. Separate financial statements of equity investees if the investment or proportion of earnings (equity pickup) is substantial.

6. Parent company financial statements as required.
7. If shares are to be issued in an acquisition, financial statements of a potential acquiree. In addition, pro forma financial statements may be appropriate.

Although a manually signed accountant's report is required, the NYSE became aware that accountants were not always notified that a listing application was being filed. Therefore a letter is required from the independent accountants acknowledging that the financial statements and their report are being used in a listing application.

Financial Statements—Subsequent Listings. Subsequent listings require the following principal items:

1. Latest available certified financial statements.
2. If the period covered in item 1 above is less than a full year, the previous year's certified earnings statement must be included.
3. If a more recent earnings statement than item 1 above has been released for publication in any form, it shall be included, certified by the enterprise's principal accounting officer.
4. Requirements similar to items 5, 6, and 7 under Financial Statements—Original Listing.

If previous applications contain any of this data, incorporation by reference may be used in the current application.

The NYSE provides that the financial statement data required for original or subsequent listings may at the company's option be incorporated by reference to a Securities Act prospectus (not more than 30 days old) or proxy statements issued under the Exchange Act. This is a commonly used approach.

Annual and Interim Financial Statements. In the NYSE listing agreement, the company also agrees to

1. At least once a year, publish consolidated financial statements of the enterprise for that year and submit them to shareholders at least 15 days in advance of the annual shareholders' meeting and not later than three months after the close of the preceding fiscal year. These financial statements should disclose the details of certain data regarding unconsolidated subsidiaries and the existence of any defaults by the company or any of its subsidiaries (consolidated or unconsolidated).
2. Submit the opinion of certified public accountants covering the financial statements in 1 above. The NYSE must be notified of a change in accountants.
3. Publish quarterly statements of earnings disclosing substantial items of an unusual or nonrecurring nature, net earnings, and either taxes or earnings before taxes.
4. Refrain from making any substantial charges to capital surplus without notifying the exchange.
5. Refrain from making any substantial change in its accounting methods or policies as to depreciation and inventory valuation without notifying the exchange and disclosing the effect of any such change in the next succeeding interim and annual report to shareholders.

6. Maintain an audit committee in accordance with NYSE requirements (see the NYSE Manual and Chapter 10 for details).

Pooling Letter. The NYSE requires a special letter from the outside accountants before it will process a listing application that authorizes shares to be issued in a pooling-of-interests transaction. This letter should set forth, in detail, the compliance with the criteria specified in APB 16 (AC 1091). The letter should be tailored to meet the individual circumstances of the transaction, rather than generalized. (See Chapter 30 for further discussion.)

American Stock Exchange

Financial Statements—Original Listing. The American Stock Exchange (Amex) requires the following independently audited financial statements in an original listing:

1. Balance sheet at latest fiscal year-end.
2. Comparative earnings statements, retained earnings and surplus analysis, and changes in financial position for each of the last three fiscal years.
3. Manually signed report of independent accountants covering the above financial statements.
4. If the financial statements are more than 90 days old, corresponding interim statements as of a date not more than 90 days prior to the filing of the listing application, with comparative statements of the preceding year. These supplementary financial statements are to be certified by either independent accountants or the chief accounting officer of the enterprise.
5. Five-year summary of earnings, with latest comparative interim periods if also required.

Financial Statements—Subsequent Listings. Subsequent listing applications require the following principal items:

1. Independently audited annual report to shareholders for latest year.
2. Financial statements as of a date not more than six months prior to the date of the filing of the listing application, certified by independent accountants or by the chief accounting officer.
3. If shares are to be listed on an acquisition, the balance sheet of the acquired company as of a recent date and earnings statement and surplus analysis to that date— usually the latest annual financial statements and latest available interim statements. A report of independent accountants should be included if available; if not, certification by the chief accounting officer of such acquired company may be acceptable.

The Amex also accepts the incorporation by reference of a prospectus under the Securities Act or proxy statements under the Exchange Act as appropriate to fulfill the financial statement requirements of original or subsequent listings applications.

Annual and Interim Financial Statements. The requirements of the Amex as to annual and interim financial statement reporting are virtually identical to those of the NYSE. They differ in that the Amex requires submission to shareholders of the annual report only ten days in advance of the shareholders' meeting; also, the publication may be four months after the end of the fiscal year.

NASDAQ System

The requirements for listing under the NASDAQ System are much simpler than the NYSE or Amex requirements. An enterprise must be registered under the Exchange Act and have at least 300 holders of record and total assets of $1 million. Thus, the NASDAQ System contains all securities listed on national exchanges and a large number of the over-the-counter stocks, warrants, rights, convertibles, and bank securities that are registered with the FDIC, Federal Reserve, or the Office of the Comptroller of the Currency but not with the SEC. Further, certain insurance company and closed-end investment company securities are included in the NASDAQ System.

There is no formal application for inclusion in the NASDAQ System; an informal letter will suffice. The letter should be accompanied by the latest available financial statements filed with the appropriate regulatory agency.

ACCOUNTING VALUATION OF EQUITY TRANSACTIONS

The Equity Capital Cycle

The equity cycle starts with initial equity capital, is increased by further equity capital infusions or earnings, and is decreased by dividends, reacquisition of stock, or losses from operations. Other kinds of transactions (such as poolings, transfers, and exchanges) also cause changes in equity capital directly. All the methods by which equity capital can increase involve the issuance of an equity security for some type of consideration. The increase in equity capital arises from recording the consideration received. If the consideration is cash and the security is a simple stock, no particular problems arise. If stock is issued in exchange for property or services, however, valuation of consideration received is often complex. Also, expenses may be incurred in the issuance of stock. Although in the past these costs were sometimes deferred and amortized over a specific period as if they were organization costs, in current practice they are deducted from the related proceeds, and the net proceeds are recorded as equity capital.

Issuance for Cash

The amount of net cash proceeds determines the valuation for stock issued. Net proceeds in excess of par or stated value are included in additional paid-in capital. If the net cash proceeds are less than the par or stated value, the stock may not be fully paid or may be assessable, matters requiring the attention of legal counsel. When stock is issued at a discount, even though not less than par or stated value, it is not appropriate to carry the discount as an asset; it is a reduction of proceeds. In those infrequent situations of stock discounted for services or other value deemed received, the systematic amortization of the discount through earnings will result in eventually restoring the capital to what it would have been had no discount been granted.

In addition to the straightforward sale of capital stock for full cash payment, there are several other common forms of issuance. Stock options granted to officers and employees bring in cash upon exercise; there are so many complexities in options that there are described in a separate section later in this chapter. Rights and warrants are discussed below.

Issuance of Rights and Warrants. *Rights* are issued to existing shareholders and enable them to purchase additional common stock (sometimes other company equity securities) at a stipulated price for a stated time period. The rights are usually separable from the underlying stock ("detachable"), and some company rights are publicly traded. In some cases, rights can be exercised only as part of the financing package in which they were issued.

Warrants are usually issued as part of a debt financing package (see Chapter 22) and entitle the holder to obtain equity securities for a stated duration and price. Some warrants are detachable and may be exercised by surrendering the warrant and the cash payment required for the common stock. For nondetachable warrants, the debt security must be turned in for exercise—effectively a conversion of debt into common stock. Detachable warrants may also be publicly traded.

Because warrants may also be issued separately from another security, it is often not possible to make a distinction between a right and a warrant—each can now have identical features.

The value of warrants is attributable solely to the conversion feature. When warrants are sold by themselves, their value is determined by the cash proceeds. However, detachable warrants issued in conjunction with debt have a separate fair value that must be measured. Accordingly, as stated in AC 5516.13, when debt is issued with detachable warrants, the proceeds should be allocated between warrants and debt based on relative fair values. The portion allocated to the warrants increases paid-in capital. (See Chapter 22.)

When rights or warrants are issued to shareholders as a dividend (no cash paid or received by the issuing company), there are no accounting entries made unless a value must be placed on the right or warrant (e.g., when there is a significant reduction in exercise price below market price at time of issuance of the right or warrant). In such cases, the accounting is similar to that for stock dividends or stock options. If the issuance is in an offering for cash, the net proceeds from sale of rights or warrants is credited to paid-in capital.

Exercise of Rights and Warrants for Cash. Because rights and warrants effectively constitute options to buy stock, they have no accounting significance upon exercise, except in the sense of setting the price. Cash received is credited to common stock (to the extent of the par or stated value) and paid-in capital (for the excess).

Subscriptions

An investor can subscribe for the purchase of stock, but plan not (nor be required) to make payment until a later time. Such transactions are common in the formation of corporations and are often part of special transactions with officers, major shareholders, and other related parties (see Chapter 28). Recording a subscription involves setting up the receivable and crediting capital stock subscribed. For financial reporting, however, the amounts are offset, because capital not paid in (cash or other value received) is not deemed to be capital. This is clear for publicly held companies; in SAB 1, the SEC specified that subscriptions receivable from officers and employees may be shown as an asset only if collected prior to the publication of the financial statements. Private companies should also now be adhering to the practice of offsetting unpaid subscriptions against the related capital account.

Issuance for Other Than Cash

Ordinarily, noncash (nonmonetary) transactions are to be valued at the fair value of the consideration received or of the consideration given, whichever is more clearly evident (APB 29, *Accounting for Nonmonetary Transactions*; AC 1041.18). Although there is a specific exception stated in AC 1041.04(c) to this general principle for noncash equity transactions (APB 29 does not apply to acquisition of nonmonetary assets or services on issuance of capital stock), it is nonetheless generally regarded as applicable to equity transactions unless more specific principles exist, as they do for business combinations and stock option plans. When the stock issued has a quoted market price, that is usually the more clearly evident value.

There are numerous purposes and methods involved in the issuance of stock for other than cash. Two of these are discussed in other chapters—for property (Chapter 20) and in business combinations (Chapter 30)—and will be omitted here. Situations covered below are (1) stock issued for services, (2) stock dividends and splits, and (3) conversions of other securities. (Stock issued in stock appreciation rights plans is dealt with in a separate section.)

Issuance for Services. Smaller companies, often in the formative stages, will issue stock for services. The company may lack the cash with which to pay, or the provider of services may desire the opportunity for capital growth instead of cash payment. Valuation is simple if the service is one readily available commercially at prices not widely varying. The general rule of valuing on the basis of the more clearly evident—the service value or the stock value—can be followed. But most stock-for-service transactions involve a unique or special service whose value will be problematic and stock that ordinarily has indefinable values. Thus, the usual resolution is establishment of valuation by the issuing company's board of directors or management at an amount that they consider fair and that is not controverted by available evidence.

When stock for services is issued to officers, directors, or employees, the valuation process is complicated further by the relationship of the parties (see Chapter 28).

Stock Dividends and Splits. Stock dividends and stock splits are similar in that both involve issuance by an enterprise of its own common shares to its common shareholders without additional consideration. A *stock dividend* is usually intended to give the shareholders a distribution of earnings without expending cash. A *stock split* is usually intended to increase the number of outstanding shares and reduce the current market price per share to obtain wider distribution and improve marketability. A split is a distribution of shares in excess of 20% to 25% of currently outstanding shares, a dividend is a distribution of less than 20% to 25% (AC 5561.16); this conforms with the New York and American Stock Exchange rules. Neither stock dividends nor splits result in an increase in total equity capital, only in reclassifications within the equity section.

Stock dividends should be accounted for at fair value. The New York Stock Exchange position is that the fair value of stock dividends may be computed by (1) multiplying the quoted market price of the underlying stock at the declaration date by the number of shares to be issued or (2) dividing the current market price by the aggregate of outstanding shares plus shares to be issued and multiplying the result by the number of shares to be issued. In either case, the fair value of the stock dividend should be charged to retained earnings and credited to common stock (as to par or stated value) and paid-in capital (as to the excess of fair value over par or stated value).

When rights or warrants are issued to shareholders without any consideration, if they have a value attributable to a bargain price for future stock purchases, that value should be charged to retained earnings and credited to paid-in capital.

Convertible Securities. Convertible securities benefit both the holder and the issuer: the holder obtains some of the benefits of common stock, such as participation in the earnings growth of the enterprise and possible gains from rising stock prices, and the issuing enterprise usually obtains a lower rate of interest or dividend requirement than could be obtained on a nonconvertible security. Further, if the convertible security can be called at the option of the issuer, the enterprise can under rising market conditions force conversion into common stock, thereby eliminating interest or preferred dividend payments.

Although there is an economic value to the conversion feature of a convertible debt security, no accounting recognition is given to the conversion feature because of its "inseparability" (AC 5516.05). The choices of the holder of convertible debt are mutually exclusive: either the security is converted into common stock or held until redeemed for cash. (See Chapter 22 for factors involved in issuance accounting.)

A conversion of convertible preferred stock into common stock will not affect total shareholders' equity, although the elements thereof will change. The preferred stock classification is reduced for the par or stated value of the shares converted, common stock is increased for the new shares issued, and the difference adjusts paid-in capital.

A conversion of a convertible debt security into common stock reduces the debt classification and increases shareholders' equity by the carrying amount of the converted debt. Debt with nondetachable warrants is the equivalent of convertible debt and is treated identically.

Decreases by Payment of Cash

There are relatively few methods of decreasing equity capital; reacquisitions, dividends in cash, and liquidation are the major ones.

Reacquisitions. The acquisition by an enterprise of its own shares reduces its equity capital. This reacquired stock, which can be common or preferred, is called *treasury stock.* Why does an enterprise perform this transaction and thereby reduce its equity base? Management of the enterprise may decide that it can more greatly increase the earning power of its remaining shares outstanding by utilizing cash resources for a partial liquidation than by investing in operating assets or holding the cash in liquid investments. This might often be a sensible strategy when a management does not wish to expand its business. Also, the enterprise may wish to use the treasury stock in the future, for example in stock option plans or business combinations. Because common treasury stock reduces the outstanding shares, it may mechanically cause an increase in EPS, which may in turn bring about an increase in market price, thus causing the treasury stock to be worth more when used in an acquisition. This is circular, it is true, but it does happen. The SEC recognized in SAB 29 that this situation occurs. The SAB states that when there are material changes in the amount of EPS from factors other than changes in net income, those changes should be explained in management's discussion and analysis of the summary of earnings. Since there are complex rules relating to treasury stock, such transactions are treated in a separate section later in this chapter.

Dividends in Cash. The declaration and payment of a dividend decreases an enterprise's retained earnings. The dividend may be required by the terms of a preferred stock or simply represent the return to common shareholders of accumulated earnings. Dividends may be paid as a method of preventing an unfriendly takeover. It reduces equity and assets and thus may make the target company less attractive, or it may make shareholders less susceptible to the blandishments of the proposed acquirer. Dividends from paid-in capital (where legal) are technically a partial liquidation.

Liquidation. The management of an enterprise may decide to cease business, dispose of assets, and declare a liquidating dividend. A liquidation usually occurs over a span of years, because assets need to be disposed of in an orderly manner to realize the greatest proceeds (e.g., at Merritt Chapman & Scott Corporation the liquidation process has lasted over ten years). In this process, equity is reduced by each liquidating dividend and eventually disappears.

Sometimes the decision to cease business is taken out of management's hands by creditors. When a creditor is concerned about recovery of its receivable because of an enterprise's financial difficulties, the creditor may petition a court to appoint a trustee under the Federal Bankruptcy Act. Until October 1, 1979, this involuntary bankruptcy petition was filed under Chapter X of the act. A voluntary petition under Chapter XI of the act was filed when management requested the court's protection from creditors. Under a Chapter XI bankruptcy, management, as a debtor-in-possession, continued to run the day-to-day operations while trying to restructure the enterprise into a profitable entity and avoid liquidation; under Chapter X, an independent trustee was appointed to oversee current operations. The Bankruptcy Reform Act of 1978, which applies to all cases filed after October 1, 1979, contains substantial changes in many areas of bankruptcy practice, among them the replacement of Chapters X and XI of the old act by one new chapter that encompasses all business reorganizations.

Mandatory Redemption Preferred Stock. A preferred stock with a sinking fund or a mandatory redemption requirement has traditionally been classified as an equity security, although it has some aspects of debt. The FASB reinforced the debt concept in its statement on marketable securities (AC 5132.07), which indicated that a preferred stock that must be redeemed by the issuing enterprise or is redeemable at the holder's option is not, from the standpoint of the holder, an equity security. The SEC considered the issue and responded in SAB 1, stating in part that preferred stock with mandatory redemption provisions should be shown on the balance sheet at not less than the aggregate redemption price. If there is a premium paid in on the issuance of such stock over par or stated value, it is acceptable to reflect the premium amount as a separate account in the equity section as "Excess of Redemption Value Applicable to Preferred Stock Required to be Redeemed." SAB 1 further states that if preferred stock with mandatory redemption is issued for consideration having a fair value less than the aggregate redemption price, the difference between fair value and the redemption amount must be accreted on the interest method. The periodic accretion amount, like cash dividends, should be considered as a reduction of income applicable to common shareholders on the income statement and in computing EPS and fixed-charge ratios. Figure 26.1 shows an example of accretion to the redemption price. (Effective September 15, 1979, the SEC took another step—ASR 268—requiring segregation of mandatory redemption preferred stocks. This is discussed later under Presentation and Disclosure.)

Payments into sinking funds administered by outside trustees are accounted for as stock reductions unless there is a nonsynchronization between cash payments

---

CONSOLIDATED STATEMENTS OF STOCKHOLDERS' EQUITY
YEARS ENDED DECEMBER 31, 1978 AND 1977

	Series A preferred stock—at redemption value (A)	Series B convertible preferred stock (A)	Junior preferred stock—at redemption value (B)
Balance, January 1, 1977	$1,100,000		$250,000
Issuance of 1,565 shares of Series B convertible preferred stock, in exchange for Medallion Group common stock (Note 10)		$1,200,000	
Accretion of discount on Series B convertible preferred stock		55,089	
Exercise of stock options			
Payment of dividends on Series A and B preferred stocks			
Net earnings			
Balance, December 31, 1977	1,100,000	1,255,089	250,000
Adjustment for 40% common stock dividend (Note 8)			
Accretion of discount on Series B convertible preferred stock		82,632	
Exercise of stock options			
Tax benefit relating to exercise of stock options			
Payment of dividends on Series B preferred stock			
Net earnings			
Balance, December 31, 1978	$1,100,000	$1,337,721	$250,000

FIGURE 26.1   ACCRETION TO MANDATORY REDEMPTION PRICE OF PRE-FERRED STOCK

SOURCE: Health-Chem Corporation, 1978 Annual Report.

and stock acquisitions and retirements by the trustee. Advance cash payments constitute a segregated asset. Most sinking funds permit the company to acquire stock on the market and tender the shares to the trustee.

Decreases Other Than by Payment of Cash

Dividends in Kind. Dividends need not be in cash. Tax or other benefits are often associated with dividends in kind. Assets such as marketable securities can be distributed to shareholders, the difference between carrying amount and market value entered into earnings, and the dividend charged to retained earnings at market value.

Accounting for the distribution of nonmonetary assets to owners in a complete or partial spin-off (whether of a subsidiary or a division) or other form of reorganization, in a liquidating dividend, or in a rescission of a business combination is to be based on the recorded amount (reduced if appropriate for an impairment in value) of the assets distributed. Other kinds of nonmonetary assets distributed to shareholders should be valued at fair value if that is objectively measurable and clearly realizable; otherwise, carrying amount is used (AC 1041.23).

Other Decreases. Under SFAS 12 (AC 5132), marketable equity securities are required to be carried (except by industries having specialized practices) at the lower of cost or market. The aggregate excess, if any, of cost over market is classified as a *dangling debit* in shareholders' equity (refer to Chapter 17). A similar dangling debit can result from an employee stock ownership trust (ESOT), discussed separately below.

Other Transactions Affecting Equity Capital

Some transactions do not increase or decrease equity capital but do affect the classifications within the equity categories. Transactions of this type that have already been discussed include conversion of preferred stock into common stock, and stock dividends and splits.

Recapitalizations. An enterprise in its formative years or experiencing operating and financial difficulties may have accumulated large losses and thus may decide to reorganize. One type of reorganization, other than those of the Federal Bankruptcy Act, that is occasionally encountered is *quasi reorganization*. In essence, the management, with shareholder approval, revalues assets and eliminates the deficit (increased by asset devaluations if any) by charging it to other equity accounts. Although a charge to paid-in capital may be all that is required, a reduction in par or stated value may also be required to create additional paid-in capital sufficient to absorb the charge. The general rules describing quasi reorganizations are enumerated in AC 5581 and ASR 25. The entire procedure must be made known to all persons entitled to vote on matters of general corporate policy, and their appropriate consents to the particular transactions obtained in advance, in accordance with the applicable law and charter provisions. A quasi reorganization accomplishes, with respect to the accounts, substantially what might be accomplished in a reorganization by legal proceedings. Retained earnings accumulated after a quasi reorganization must be "dated" for a period of ten years; that is, the fact that a deficit was eliminated via a quasi reorganization must be stated (AC 5582).

Another type of reorganization is a *reverse stock split.* Total outstanding shares are reduced by issuing a smaller number of new shares for existing shares (for instance, two new shares for three old shares). This does not affect total equity but may affect other equity accounts by a concurrent change in par or stated value.

Transfers Between Equity Accounts. A change in the par or stated value of stock may affect other equity accounts. For example, a change from $1 par value to $2 par value causes an increase in the stock account and a corresponding decrease in paid-in capital or, sometimes, retained earnings. Conversely, a decrease in par value from $2 to $1 may cause a decrease in the common stock account and an increase in paid-in capital.

Exchanges. Although an enterprise may decide that a change in par value is not feasible, it can accomplish the same result through an exchange. An exchange among different classes of preferred stock and common stock does not increase or decrease total equity, but it does cause an adjustment of the respective equity accounts.

STOCK OPTIONS AND SIMILAR PLANS

General

A stock option is the right granted to an employee to receive stock upon payment of a specified price (the *option price*). Although the primary purpose usually is not to raise equity capital, the payment (*exercise*) of the option price does increase equity in the same way as a sale for cash.

Instituting a stock option plan usually requires shareholder approval. Stock option grants, or *awards,* usually contain restrictions as to when the option may be exercised. Restrictions are designed to achieve the objectives of the enterprise—specifically, to retain and motivate the employee. When the restrictions placed on the exercise of any or all options awarded are met, the option is said to be *vested.* Restrictions may include a predetermined length of future service (e.g., five years), performance restrictions (e.g., the enterprise must achieve 5% compounded growth in EPS over a defined period, say five years), or a combination of both (e.g., vesting based 80% on length of service and 20% on EPS growth). If an employee leaves the employ of the enterprise, the unvested options are forfeited. Antidilution and merger/sale provisions are common. There are certain tax ramifications attendant on stock options; under current tax law, the recipient of the option award is not required to report income until the shares are vested.

Stock options have been used for many years to motivate, retain, or attract desired officers and employees. In recent years many variations of the basic stock option have developed, and the more common ones are discussed in this section. The main accounting issue is whether a stock-based plan results in a compensation cost to the sponsor and, if so, how it is measured and what the measurement date is. The APB addressed these questions in APB 25 (AC 4062) in December 1972.

In the conventional stock option and purchase plans, an employer grants employees the right to buy a fixed number of shares at a fixed price over a specified period. If the options are made exercisable in installments, the awards are usually contingent only on continued employment. Although more complex forms of option plans require a more detailed analysis, these plans have one concurrent theme: there is a variable, in that either the number of shares or the option price is not fixed. The accounting issues—compensation expense, its measurement, and the measurement date—are fundamentally the same.

The basic requirement regarding compensation expense is that it be measured at grant date, not date of exercise. Some accountants believe that current practice is inappropriate because options granted at current market price are not valued nor is compensation recorded, although the option intends to give officers and employees something of value. Both the recipient and the enterprise hope and expect the value of the stock to rise, and in theory, at least a part of any value increase is attributable to favorable company results achieved with the help of the grantee/employee. Therefore, it can be said that a bonus has been incurred that can only be measured by the excess of the market price at exercise date over the option price. This is the premise stated in Accounting Research Study No. 15, *Stockholders' Equity* (Melcher, 1973).

Measurement

There are four general criteria for measuring whether a plan is to be treated for accounting purposes as noncompensatory:

1. Substantially all full-time employees meeting limited employment qualifications may participate,
2. The stock is offered to eligible employees equally or as a uniform percentage of salary (although there may be a maximum number of shares restriction),
3. Exercise is limited to a reasonable period, and
4. A discount from quoted market, if any, is no greater than would be expected in an offering to shareholders or others.

Plans not meeting these four criteria are considered compensatory. However, a compensatory plan does not necessarily require the recording of compensation, as discussed below.

Measurement Date. The measurement date is the first date on which both the number of shares granted and the option price are fixed. It is usually the grant date; however, in complex (variable) plans, it may be as late as the exercise date.

Renewal of an option arrangement establishes a new measurement date, but a reduction in the number of granted shares because of early termination does not affect this determination. For grants of convertible stock, the measurement date is normally the date the ratio of conversion is fixed. Compensation is measured using the higher of either the quoted market price of the convertible stock or the market price of the security obtainable upon conversion.

Measurement Principle. Compensation is measured as the difference between the option price and the quoted market price at the measurement date. Thus, if options are granted at market (and there are no other complicating features as mentioned below), there is no compensation, even though the plan is a compensatory plan. If treasury stock is used to fulfill the share requirements, its cost may be used to measure the amount of compensation only if it is acquired during the fiscal period in which the awards are made and the awards are made shortly thereafter.

Cash paid to settle an earlier award of stock should measure compensation. This has, however, caused various problems. If the enterprise also grants the employee a "put" exercisable at quoted market price when the shares are issued (for example, to avoid the costs of registration), does the exercise of the put entail cash paid to settle an earlier award and thereby cause compensation to be measured at the exercise date, presumably at a higher quoted market price? Some accountants believe that it does. Many others view the put as a mechanism to save costs of registration or to provide the employee with the wherewithal to pay the income taxes on the appreciation gain, not as cash paid to settle an option award, since presumably the employee could sell the shares on the open market and receive the same proceeds. The FASB needs to deal with plans that effectively allow cash in lieu of exercise of the option.

Compensation. Compensation expense related to stock options should be accrued and amortized over the periods the employee performs services. When the measurement date has not yet passed, compensation should be accrued by charges to expense based on the quoted market price at the end of a period. This estimation will cause adjustments of compensation expense in future periods through fluctuations in the quoted market price.

In plans not resulting in the accrual of compensation expense, the enterprise usually receives a tax deduction for the appreciation gain when taxable to the employee deemed to have received the income. The tax benefit of the excess deduction, when realized, should be credited to paid-in capital, since it is similar to profits in treasury stock transactions. In those rare instances where the tax deduction is less than the recorded compensation expense, the charge to paid-in capital is limited to the amount of previous credits for excess deductions, with any remainder included in income tax expense.

Variable Terms

There are plans in which events that may affect either the number of shares to be issued or the option price are not known or determinable at the grant date (e.g., market performance criteria or earnings level attainment). Accordingly, the measurement date has not yet arrived. In addition, there are combination or *tandem plans*; for example, alternative plans where the employee has a choice in exercising options under either plan but not both. One type of tandem plan may have a fixed number of shares at a fixed option price coupled with another option plan with variable terms; and it may also have a cash payment option. The compensation expense accrued should be based on the alternative the employee is most likely to choose at the date of accrual (end of period).

Stock-based plans are plans whose value is derived from the market price movement in the underlying security, although there may be no intent to issue a security or its issuance may be delayed, discretionary with the company, or optional with the employee. These plans are sometimes called "phantom" stock option plans. Some common examples of these plans are stock appreciation rights (SARs) and employee stock ownership plans (ESOPs).

Stock Appreciation Rights. Stock appreciation rights plans are a relatively new phenomenon in employee benefit plans. They are awards of rights, usually granted in combination with compensatory stock option plans but sometimes granted separately, entitling the recipient to receive cash, stock, or a combination of both in an amount equivalent to the increase in quoted market price over an option price for a fixed number of shares. The option price is usually the quoted market price at date of grant. When granted in combination with other stock option plans, the SARs usually provide that the rights of each are mutually exclusive; that is, employees may elect benefits under one plan or the other but not both (see Figure 26.8). Accounting for SARs is dealt with in FASB Interpretation No. 28 (AC 4062-1), which contains computation illustrations.

For stock appreciation rights and other variable option plans, compensation should be measured as the amount by which the current quoted market price of the underlying stock exceeds the option price, subject to maximum limitations, if any, in the plan. Accordingly, changes in the quoted market price change the measure of compensation. Compensation should be accrued, as in other plans, over the period of the employee's service. This accrual is adjusted in subsequent periods for changes in the quoted market price (either up or down) calculated under a method commonly known as the *liability method.*

For combination or tandem plans, the choice that the employee is most likely to make determines the manner of computing compensation for the period. However, if an enterprise has been accruing compensation based on the SAR alternative and circumstances change, the compensation previously accrued is not adjusted down.

Employee Stock Ownership Plans. Another compensation arrangement that achieves the objectives stated previously is an employee stock ownership trust (ESOT). The ESOT borrows money from a bank and purchases the enterprise's stock. The loan is frequently guaranteed, formally or as a practical matter, by the enterprise, and thus should be shown as such on the sponsor enterprise's financial statements with a corresponding decrease in shareholders' equity. Both the SEC (in SAB 8) and AICPA (in SOP 76-3) take the position that since the ESOT has no substance independent of its sponsor's undertaking to make future cash contributions, the sponsoring enterprise should record the cash received from the ESOT for the stock purchase as a loan. Further, payments by the ESOT on its bank debt should be recognized by the sponsor to reduce the "loan," and the equity offset shown in its financial statements. All shares held by the ESOT are to be treated as outstanding and included in EPS calculations.

TREASURY STOCK

Accounting and Presentation

Treasury stock is carried at cost of acquisition. If the enterprise purchases treasury stock as part of a systematic method of fulfilling its requirements to issue shares for employee stock options, it may be (but usually is not) shown as an asset; otherwise, treasury stock should be shown as a deduction from total share-holders' equity. If treasury stock is to be shown as an asset by a publicly held enterprise, preclearance by the staff of the SEC is advised.

Retained earnings are usually restricted from payment of dividends by the cost of treasury stock on hand. Disclosure of this restriction is required where material. Whether retained earnings are in fact restricted and by how much is primarily a legal question, and counsel should be consulted.

Other Matters

An interesting issue not dealt with in accounting literature is the presentation of the stock of a parent company held by its subsidiary (i.e., a *reciprocal investment*). The presentation in the parent enterprise's balance sheet of its stock held by a sub-sidiary is clear—treasury stock. The presentation on the subsidiary's balance sheet, however, is unclear. Some accountants believe that the parent's stock should be shown on the subsidiary's balance sheet as treasury stock at cost. Other accoun-tants believe that the parent's stock should be shown as a long-term investment at cost or at equity in the parent's net assets. Intracorporate investments of this na-ture lead to complex reciprocal equations to calculate earnings, EPS, and equity ownership.

A purchase of treasury stock may, under the rules in ASRs 146 and 146A, affect an enterprise's ability to enter into a pooling transaction. Depending on the ma-teriality of the treasury stock acquisition, it may preclude entering into an otherwise valid pooling business combination. Care should be exercised prior to entering into major treasury stock acquisitions. (This subject is covered in depth in Chapter 30.)

Reissuance. Subsequent sale of treasury shares creates a charge or credit to paid-in capital. An enterprise is not allowed to record profits from trading in its own stock; therefore, any difference between cost and proceeds adjusts paid-in capital.

Retirement. There are two types of retirements, actual and constructive. Cancel-lation through formal application to the secretary of state's office in the state of issue is an *actual retirement*. *Constructive retirement* is effecting the retirement on the financial statements by the authorization of the board of directors without for-mal cancellation through the secretary of state. The accounting and presentation (AC 5542.13) are the same for constructive and actual retirements.

When the cost of the treasury stock is in excess of par or stated value of the stock, the excess should be allocated to paid-in capital and retained earnings, or it may be charged entirely to retained earnings. The allocation is made first to paid-in capital to the extent it arose from that issue or to the extent paid-in capital is avail-able from that issue's previous retirements. Any remaining excess is then allocated between paid-in capital and retained earnings on a proportionate basis. Practically, it is much simpler to allocate the excess of cost over the par or stated value to paid-in capital based on the per share amount of paid-in capital for all shares, with the excess charged to retained earnings. The only method not sanctioned by GAAP or by the SEC is to simply charge paid-in capital for the excess. However, if the purchase price is. less than par or stated value, the excess credit must be to paid-in capital.

PRESENTATION AND DISCLOSURE

General

The disclosure requirements for equity accounts (AC 2042) include a description of the changes in each account as well as the changes in the number of shares for at least the annual period(s) for which financial statements are presented. Thus, a two-year comparative statement would contain a two-year analysis of changes. In addition, Regulation S-X, Rule 5-02.30, requires disclosure of the title of each security; the number of shares authorized, issued, or outstanding; and the total dollar amount of issued or outstanding stock.

In practice, a statement of shareholders' equity is provided for each period for which an income statement is given. Though this is an SEC rule, most enterprises comply, and such presentation has become generally accepted.

Mandatory Redemption Preferred Stock. In ASR 268, the SEC amended Regulation S-X, effective for financial statements for periods ending on or after September 15, 1979, to modify the financial statement presentation of preferred stocks subject to mandatory redemption or redeemable at the option of the holder. When a company has such a preferred stock outstanding, it may no longer show a combined heading of "Stockholders' Equity," but instead must show separately (1) mandatory redemption preferred stock, (2) other preferred stocks, and (3) common stocks. Remaining elements of stockholders' equity (paid-in capital and retained earnings) would be classified under the general heading "Other Stockholders' Equity." These rules do not, of course, apply to privately held companies and would not apply to public companies that have no outstanding mandatory redemption preferred stock; they would continue to use the broad category "Stockholders' Equity."

In ASR 268, the SEC expresses its concern about the need to distinguish obligations similar to debt from "permanent capital," deferring, however, to the FASB for an ultimate determination of whether such a preferred stock is a liability. The ASR (incorporated in Regulation S-X, Rule 5-02.28) requires footnote disclosure of redemption features, combined aggregate amount of redemption requirements for the ensuing five years, and changes in such stock for periods presented in the financial statements. This footnote requirement is additional to any statement presentation that may incorporate some or all of the disclosure features. An example of ASR 268 compliance is shown in Figure 26.2.

Typical Statement Presentations

Figure 26.3 provides an example of the typical balance sheet equity section classifications that would be supplemented by presentation of activity for the period and by footnote disclosures.

To comply with the detailed disclosure requirements, many enterprises present a statement of shareholders' equity for each period (Figure 26.4) and incorporate share changes instead of cramming all the information into the balance sheet captions. Other enterprises prefer two statements, one for paid-in capital and another

INVESTED CAPITAL, LIABILITIES, AND DEFERRED CREDITS	Thousands Of Dollars	
	December 31, 1978	December 31, 1977
COMMON SHARE OWNERS' EQUITY		
Common shares (Includes excess of proceeds over $16⅔ par value) (I)........	$ 20,846,632	$19,571,994
Authorized shares: 750,000,000		
Outstanding shares: at December 31, 1978—669,549,000;		
at December 31, 1977—647,632,000		
Reinvested earnings—see page 27 (E).............................	19,771,576	17,699,401
	40,618,208	37,271,395
PREFERRED SHARES CONVERTIBLE TO COMMON SHARES (J)		
(Includes excess of proceeds over stated value)......................	501,205	593,703
PREFERRED SHARES SUBJECT TO MANDATORY REDEMPTION (J)........	1,600,000	1,625,000

FIGURE 26.2 EXCLUSION FROM SHAREHOLDERS' EQUITY OF MANDA-
TORY REDEMPTION PREFERRED STOCK

SOURCE: American Telephone & Telegraph Company, 1978 Annual Report.

for retained earnings (Figure 26.5) (changes in the number of shares of stock may be disclosed therein or given elsewhere). A variation of this presentation method is to use a combined statement of earnings and retained earnings. Each of these activity presentation techniques is considered as meeting the disclosure requirements of GAAP (AC 2042) and the SEC.

There are other variations of these presentations, all of which are acceptable as long as all necessary disclosure requirements are met either in tabular or narrative form.

Footnotes

General. As indicated previously, changes or activity in the equity accounts are frequently disclosed in footnotes. Typical disclosures are (1) shares issuable upon and/or reserved for conversion or exercise of convertible securities, options, war-

	Dec. 31, 1979	Dec. 31, 1978
Liabilities and Shareowners' Equity		
Shareowners' Equity:		
Preferred stock—authorized, 10,000,000 shares without par value, issuable in series; outstanding, 158,181 shares in 1979 and 185,112 shares in 1978; involuntary liquidation preference, $35 per share, or an aggregate of $5.5 in 1979 and $6.5 in 1978	0.3	0.4
Common stock—authorized, 100,000,000 shares, par value $2 each; issued, 36,978,084 shares in 1979 and 36,976,516 shares in 1978..	73.9	73.9
Additional contributed capital	652.9	651.5
Reinvested earnings	2,102.3	1,892.5
	2,829.4	2,618.3
Less common stock in treasury, at cost (946,916 shares in 1979 and 786,653 shares in 1978)	47.6	38.9
	2,781.8	2,579.4
	$5,539.1	$5,035.7

FIGURE 26.3 TYPICAL BALANCE SHEET EQUITY CLASSIFICATION

SOURCE: Monsanto Company, 1979 Annual Report.

**Statement of
Consolidated Shareowners' Equity**

Monsanto Company and Subsidiaries

(Dollars in millions, except per share)	Preferred Stock	Common Stock	Additional Contributed Capital	Reinvested Earnings	Treasury Stock
Balance, January 1, 1978	$0.6	$73.7	$650.6	$1,705.3	$(29.3)
Net income				302.6	
Dividends:					
Preferred—$2.75 per share				(0.6)	
Common—$3.175 per share				(114.8)	
Conversion of $2.75 Preferred					
Stock to common stock	(0.2)	0.2			
Shares issued under employee stock					
ownership and option plans			0.8		3.2
Shares purchased					(12.8)
Other			0.1		
Balance, December 31, 1978	0.4	73.9	651.5	1,892.5	(38.9)
Net income				331.0	
Dividends:					
Preferred—$2.75 per share				(0.5)	
Common—$3.35 per share				(120.7)	
Conversion of $2.75 Preferred					
Stock to common stock	(0.1)		(1.3)		1.4
Shares issued under employee stock					
ownership and option plans			0.3		4.5
Shares issued upon conversion					
of Monsanto Limited convertible					
loan stock			0.2		2.0
Shares reclassified from					
Miscellaneous Investments					(4.4)
Shares purchased					(12.4)
Other			2.2		0.2
Balance, December 31, 1979	$0.3	$73.9	$652.9	$2,102.3	$(47.6)

FIGURE 26.4   COLUMNAR STATEMENT OF SHAREOWNERS' EQUITY
SOURCE: Monsanto Company, 1979 Annual Report.

rants, and rights; (2) features of preferred stock (i.e., voting, cumulative, redeemable, liquidation preference); (3) restrictions on retained earnings; and (4) dividends per share and in the aggregate.

An example of footnote disclosure of equity account transactions, highlighting a stock split and change in authorized shares and par value, is given in Figure 26.6.

Consolidated Retained Earnings

	(Thousands of dollars except per share data) Year ended December 31	
	1979	1978
Amount at beginning of year	$1,685,900	1,653,600
Net income	347,500	118,000
Cash dividends paid (per share: 1979—$3.40; 1978—$3.10)	(94,200)	(85,700)
Amount at end of year	$1,939,200	1,685,900

Consolidated Capital Surplus

	(Thousands of dollars) Year ended December 31	
	1979	1978
Amount at beginning of year	$164,000	163,200
Credit arising from issuance of Common Stock at market values under employee plans	2,700	800
Amount at end of year	$166,700	164,000

FIGURE 26.5 TYPICAL SEPARATE EQUITY STATEMENTS
SOURCE: Cities Service Company, 1979 Annual Report.

Options and Stock-Based Plans. Since the terms of stock-based plans require disclosure, including number of shares, option prices, and number of shares exercisable, these types of footnotes appear regularly in annual reports (see Figures 26.7 and 26.8). In addition, SOP 76-3 recommends that certain disclosures relating to obligations of ESOTs be made.

Until the overhaul of Regulation S-X in September 1980, Rule 3-16(n) covered SEC requirements with respect to stock option disclosures. These disclosure requirements were in excess of those required by GAAP and, in order to avoid wasting space in the annual report, were normally given as additional financial information in the Form 10-K. The SEC disclosure requirements included (1) options outstanding at period-end by year of grant, detailing both option price

(11) Common stock:

A two-for-one split of common stock was effected on September 22, 1978. Common stock authorized was increased to 15,000,000 shares and the par value was changed to $.50 a share. The number of shares and all per share amounts as presented in the consolidated balance sheet, consolidated statement of earnings, consolidated statement of stockholders' investment, and accompanying notes have been restated to give effect to the split as if it took place on May 1, 1977.

At April 30, 1979, 134,860 shares of common stock were reserved for issuance on conversion of the $3.50 cumulative convertible preferred stock. In addition, 879,698 common shares were reserved for issuance under the Company's stock option and employee stock purchase plans.

FIGURE 26.6 TYPICAL EQUITY FOOTNOTE
SOURCE: Scott, Foresman and Company, 1979 Annual Report.

8. Stock Options

Under the qualified "Stock Option Plan for Officers and Key Employees (1972 Key Plan)", the Company authorized the issuance of 66,000 shares (adjusted to reflect the 10% stock dividend on April 28, 1978). The following tabulation summarizes certain information relative to stock options.

	Options Granted—Fiscal Year Ended	
	April 28, 1979	April 29, 1978
Balance beginning of year	39,600	47,300
Options granted	—	16,500
Options exercised	(4,750)	(22,000)
Options expired (unexercised)	—	(2,200)
Balance end of year	34,850	39,600
Options exercisable at end of year....	23,850	4,400

The options outstanding are exercisable at prices ranging from $4.545 to $7.386 per share. The options become exercisable at the rate of one third each year beginning one year after date of grant and expire five years from date of grant, or earlier in the event of death or other termination of employment by the optionee. From the inception of the plan through April 28, 1979, options for 28,950 shares have been exercised and 2,200 shares expired unexercised.

FIGURE 26.7   TYPICAL STOCK OPTION FOOTNOTE
SOURCE: Blessings Corporation, 1979 Annual Report.

and market value, per share and in total; (2) per share and in total amounts for option price and market value of shares that became exercisable during the year; (3) number of shares, option price, and fair value, per share and in total, for exercised shares; and (4) basis of accounting for option arrangements and any resulting charges in income. Though Regulation S-X now omits this requirement, an example of the old disclosure, which will be seen in all Forms 10-K filed prior to September 1980, is shown in Figure 26.9.

EARNINGS PER SHARE

EPS data are considered an important tool in making investment decisions and are required to be shown on the face of the income statements of publicly held companies for all periods presented. During 1978, the FASB considered the applicability of certain required disclosures (among them EPS) to small or closely held enterprises and, after due deliberation, decided that such information was not

8. Stock Option and Incentive Share Plans

At December 31, 1978, there were options outstanding to purchase 98,932 shares (90,457 exercisable) of the Company's common stock at prices ranging from $8.67 to $10.84 per share (market prices at dates of grant) under the Company's 1967 Stock Option Plan. During fiscal 1977 options to purchase 13,650 shares were granted at a market price of $10.00. In 1978 and 1977, respectively, options to purchase 1,266 and 23,386 shares were exercised at prices ranging from $5.34 to $8.00. The Company's obligations under options to purchase an aggregate of 4,687 shares and 10,778 shares were discharged in 1978 and 1977, respectively, as a result of the exercise of stock appreciation rights. Options for 56,061 shares and 5,371 shares were forfeited or cancelled in 1978 and 1977, respectively. Options under the 1967 Plan expire five years from the date of grant and 25% per year become exercisable after the first year.

In December, 1976, the Company adopted the 1976 Stock Option and Stock Appreciation Plan and resolved that no further options would be granted under the 1967 Plan subsequent to December 31, 1976.

The 1976 Stock Option and Stock Appreciation Plan permits the granting of stock options and stock appreciation rights in connection with any stock option plan approved by the stockholders. Rights covering options to purchase 71,296 and 108,324 shares under the 1967 Plan were outstanding at December 31, 1978 and December 25, 1977, respectively. Rights covering options to purchase 68,654 shares under the 1976 Plan were outstanding at December 31, 1978. The option price may be less than fair market value. Upon exercise of a stock appreciation right, an optionee is entitled to receive a number of shares of stock having an aggregate fair market value equal to the amount of appreciation between the option price and the market value on the date of exercise or, at the option of the committee that administers the Plan, to settle such obligations in whole or in part for an equivalent amount of cash. To the extent that a stock appreciation right is exercised, the Company's obligation with respect to the related stock option is deemed to be discharged. The terms and conditions of options and stock appreciation rights including optionees, option prices, and the option period is determined by the committee. No grants may be made subsequent to December 31, 1986 and options granted will expire no later than 10 years from the date of grant. Not more than 500,000 shares of the Company's common stock is issuable under this Plan.

At December 31, 1978, there were options outstanding to purchase 215,034 shares (148,125 exercisable) of the Company's common stock at prices ranging from $7.00 to $9.00 (market prices at dates of grant) under the 1976 Plan. Upon achievement of specified earnings levels, options to purchase 103,000 shares may be exercised at prices below fair market value at date of grant. During 1978 and 1977 options to purchase 217,354 shares and 1,500 shares, respectively, were granted at market prices ranging from $7.00 to $10.00. Options for 2,820 and 1,000 shares were forfeited or cancelled in 1978 and 1977, respectively. At December 31, 1978 options to purchase 284,966 shares were available for future grants under this Plan.

Compensation expense of $153,000 in 1978 was recognized in connection with stock appreciation rights and options with exercise prices deemed to be below fair market value at date of grant. When options are exercised, the excess of the option price over the par value of the stock issued is credited to paid-in capital.

The Company also has an Incentive Share Plan which provides for granting of performance shares (units equivalent to one share of common stock) and sale (at $1 per share) of a maximum of 281,250 restricted shares to key executives. There is no limit on the aggregate number of performance shares that may be granted during the life of the Plan although no more than 281,250 performance shares may be outstanding at any one time. Under the terms of the Plan, no grantee is eligible to receive performance shares or retain restricted shares unless the Company achieves a stipulated growth in earnings per share over a specified period commencing with the year of grant.

With respect to performance shares, payment may be made in cash, common stock or a combination of both, at the option of the committee administering the Plan. However, payment shall not exceed 200% of the average fair market value of a share of common stock during the 30 days preceding the year of grant.

At December 31, 1978, 233,000 restricted shares and 19,888 performance shares were outstanding, leaving 48,250 and 261,362 respectively, available for future grant.

The potential cost of rights granted under the Incentive Share Plan is considered to be compensation, measured by the market value at the end of each year, and is amortized over the period of restriction from the year of grant. The cost of this Plan was not significant in 1978 or 1977.

Amortization applicable to restricted shares is charged or credited to paid-in capital. At December 31, 1978, unamortized deferred compensation amounted to $291,000 after applicable tax benefit.

FIGURE 26.8   STOCK OPTION FOOTNOTE INCLUDING SAR PLAN
SOURCE: Kane-Miller Corporation, 1978 Annual Report.

THE FOLLOWING SUMMARIZES ADDITIONAL INFORMATION WITH RESPECT TO THE STOCK OPTIONS REFERRED TO IN NOTE F.

	Number of Shares	Option Price Per Share	Total	Market Value (1) Per Share	Total
Shares under option at December 31, 1978:					
Year of grant:					
1974	2,265	$4.26	$ 10,000	$4.26	$ 10,000
1975	54,548	4.56	248,000	4.56	248,000
1976	18,800	4.79-5.07	90,000	4.79-5.07	90,000
1977	20,596	5.79	119,000	5.79	119,000
	96,209		$467,000		$467,000
Shares as to which options became exercisable during the periods ended:					
December 31, 1978	21,466	$4.56-$5.79	$109,000	$ 9.63-$12.88	$230,000
December 31, 1977	36,416	4.25- 5.08	167,000	4.25- 9.00	194,000
Shares as to which options were exercised during the periods ended:					
December 31, 1978	23,144	$4.26-$6.13	$111,000	$10.50-$19.00	$308,000
December 31, 1977	4,213	3.56	15,000	6.00	25,000

(1) At date options were granted, became exercisable, or were exercised, adjusted for subsequent stock dividends. No charges or credits have been made to income with respect to options granted or exercised.

FIGURE 26.9   SEC STOCK OPTION FOOTNOTE
SOURCE: W. R. Berkley Corporation, 1978 Form 10-K.

required for such businesses. Accordingly, the FASB in SFAS 21 suspended the EPS reporting requirements for nonpublic enterprises (AC 2083).

A nonpublic enterprise is defined as "an enterprise other than one (a) whose debt or equity securities trade in a public market on a foreign or domestic stock exchange or in the over-the-counter market (including securities quoted only locally or regionally) or (b) that is required to file financial statements with the Securities and Exchange Commission" (AC 2083.13). However, when EPS data are presented for a nonpublic enterprise, the presentation must be in conformity with APB 15 (AC 2011). Other entities for which EPS data are not required are mutual companies that do not have outstanding common stock or equivalents (mutual savings banks, cooperatives, credit unions, and similar entities).

Per Share Amounts Other Than EPS

The SEC indicated in ASR 142 that per share data should be limited on the face of the income statement to those EPS calculations required by GAAP. However, some enterprises believe that conventional financial statement data and presentation do not adequately reflect business economics, and in the past some gave presentations to highlight certain data, such as cash flow per share. Presentation in a "Financial Highlights" section accentuated this disclosure. Some enterprises even presented sales per share data. The SEC has ruled that such a presentation is not acceptable in that unsophisticated investors could misinterpret the data and be misled. Accordingly, only earnings per share data recognized by GAAP may be presented in SEC filings, and this restriction is observed for private companies as well.

AUDITING

The objectives of auditing the equity accounts are verification that the securities exist (that they are valid and properly recorded), that they are accurately valued and properly classified, and primarily, that there is adequacy of disclosure. The approach most commonly used is substantive, since the number of equity transactions with outside parties is usually not large. EPS calculations are also audited on a substantive basis, since this calculation requires individual analysis.

In a few instances, a public company may act as its own registrar or transfer agent. Such a situation is not contemplated in the brief coverage of auditing in this chapter. The matrix in Figure 26.14 summarizes the basic substantive procedures applicable to the equity accounts, and these procedures are described in a sample skeleton audit program in Figure 26.15. (The integration of this type of matrix into the overall audit is discussed in Chapter 12).

Of course, the auditor will take into account the results of other procedures in the audit, including his evaluation of internal control systems, to the extent such procedures apply to the equity accounts. General internal control considerations that may be applicable to equity transactions are discussed in Chapter 13.

TRANSACTION — ERROR TYPE	MECHANICAL ACCURACY	EXISTENCE		ACCURACY	CLASSIFI-CATION	ADEQUATE DISCLOSURES
		VALIDITY	RECORDING			
Books and records Posting or addition errors in ledgers	1, 2, 6					
Incorrect journal entries	1, 2, 6					
Audit procedures with no specific error type		3, 5, 7	3, 5, 7	3, 5, 7	1	4, 18

FIGURE 26.14   SHAREHOLDERS' EQUITY AUDITING MATRIX

1. Obtain a schedule of all equity accounts, showing:
   a. Nominal unit values and authorized number of shares,
   b. Number of shares issued and balances at beginning and end of period,
   c. Changes during the period,
   d. Any other relevant information, and
   e. Identification of distributable and nondistributable balances.

2. Ascertain by review of general ledger and register of shareholders (by examining the sequence of unissued shares) whether there have been any changes in capital stock during the period.
   a. Request confirmation of the issued stock from the registrar and transfer agent where used and reconcile reply to schedule of shares outstanding.
   b. Examine documents supporting treasury stock transactions during the period.
      (1) Ascertain propriety of their recording.
      (2) Account for and inspect treasury stock certificates, noting that they are in the name of the company or are properly endorsed.

3. Examine supporting documents for increases in issued shares.
   a. Agree to board/shareholder minutes.
   b. Ascertain that amounts issued do not exceed those authorized.
   c. Vouch receipt of proceeds of issue.
   d. For issuances other than for cash inspect documents supporting the assets acquired or services received.

4. Review agreements and contracts for effect on equity accounts.

5. Inquire as to the existence of any stock options, warrants, rights, or conversion privileges existing at the balance sheet date.
   a. Ascertain shares required for options, warrants, rights, or conversions at year-end.
   b. Ascertain options granted, canceled, lapsing and exercised during the year. Vouch authorization to board minutes, option agreements, receipts, and similar support.

6. Determine that dividend payments/liabilities have been correctly recorded.
   a. Review extracts of board minutes for dividends declared and paid.
   b. Confirm calculation of total dividends and trace total dividends to retained earnings statement.

7. Examine all changes in paid-in capital, retained earnings, and other capital accounts.
   a. Vouch to appropriate authorizations and supporting evidence.
   b. Determine propriety.

8. Review computation of earnings per share.

FIGURE 26.15   SAMPLE AUDITING PROCEDURES FOR EQUITY ACCOUNTS

In companies where there are a substantial number of stock options or similar transactions, or extensive treasury stock transactions, the applicable basic procedures listed in Figure 26.15 will be spelled out in more detail. Also, auditors' procedures in a Securities Act offering, including procedures for underwriters' letters, are omitted from Figure 26.15, but may be found in *Accountants SEC Practice Manual* (Poloway and Charles, 1980).

SUGGESTED READING

AICPA. *Illustrations of Accounting for Employee Benefits.* Financial Report Survey 14. New York, 1977. This NAARS survey provides numerous examples of accounting and disclosure in the areas of pensions, stock issuances, and cash payments.

————. *Illustrations of the Disclosure of "Pro Forma" Calculations.* Financial Report Survey 11. This NAARS survey provides examples of pro forma calculations made in financial statements for such topics as earnings per share, business combinations, and accounting changes.

Landsittel, David. "SEC Commentary, New Developments in Comfort Letters to Underwriters." *CPA Journal,* February, 1978, pp. 69-72. A review of certain interpretations by the accounting profession and matters that have not been dealt with.

McDaniel, Lloyd. "Problems Involved in Compensation Costs Due to Stock Options." *National Public Accountant,* March, 1977, pp. 15-17. The author argues, contrary to the views expressed in this chapter, that accountants should stop efforts to ascribe compensation to options and that APB 25 should be rescinded.

Melcher, Beatrice. *Stockholders' Equity.* Accounting Research Study No. 15. New York: AICPA, 1973. This is a comprehensive study of the then-current status of accounting for stockholders' equity, recommendations for solving the accounting and presentation problems, and implementation considerations. ARS 15 is the last of the ARS series, but remains current because little has been implemented since 1973. (See synopsis in Appendix 26.)

Poloway, Morton, and Charles, Dane. *Accountants SEC Practice Manual.* Chicago: Commerce Clearing House, Inc., 1980. Chapter III provides extensive discussion of letters to underwriters. Chapter V gives a complete discussion of exchange-listing procedures and the NASDAQ System, and refers to specific portions of exchange manuals and NASDAQ bylaws for precise citation of rules and requirements.

Weygandt, Jerry. "Valuations of Stock Option Contracts." *Accounting Review,* January, 1977, pp. 40-51. Weygandt posits that options can be valued with a high degree of confidence and describes models for use with nonqualified options. He recognizes that additional research is needed to model qualified option plans.

APPENDIX 26   SYNOPSIS OF ARS 15, STOCKHOLDERS' EQUITY

Several of the treatments recommended in ARS 15 would change net income reported under present practices, although total stockholders' equity would not differ. Some of the significant changes recommended in the study are:

1. When there is an increase in outstanding equity securities that changes stockholders' proportionate interests:
    a. The consideration received when restricted stock is issued at a large discount should be measured by the fair value of such stock at the date issued. Related financing costs should be deducted from retained earnings.
    b. The consideration received when stock is issued on exercise of employee stock options should be measured by the fair value of the stock at the date issued. Related compensation expense should be deducted from net income.
    c. The consideration received when stock is issued on conversion of other securities should be measured by the fair value of the stock at the date issued. Related financing expenses should be deducted (1) from net income for debt securities converted and (2) from retained earnings for equity securities converted.
    d. When the consideration is contingent on future events, some distinction should be made between those contingencies that result from the unresolved measure of the fair value of the consideration received and those that result from the fair value of the stock issued for that consideration.
    e. The consideration received when stock is issued on exercise of purchase warrants should be measured by the fair value of the stock at the date issued. Related financing costs should be deducted from net income or retained earnings according to the nature of the transaction in which the stock purchase warrants are issued.
2. When there is an increase in outstanding equity securities that does not change stockholders' proportionate interests, the additional number of shares of stock issued should be recognized without changing equity components.
3. When there are decreases in outstanding equity securities:
    a. An expenditure to acquire stock for retirement should be allocated between the two sources of equity: reduce contributed equity by the pro rata portion applicable to the number of shares retired, and reduce or increase retained earnings by the difference between that portion and the expenditure.
    b. Capital stock acquired for reissuance and held as treasury stock should be accounted for as retired shares.
4. Presentation of equity:
    a. A major conclusion is that the readers of financial statements are primarily interested in the sources of stockholders' equity—contributions by stockholders and earnings retained by the corporation. The components of the equity section should be classified by source rather than by legal definition.
    b. A separate category of contingent equity financing should be provided to include obligations and nonequity securities that carry a right to exchange for equity interests.
    c. Stockholders' equity should exclude any consideration received by the corporation that does not apply to shares of stock.

27

Partnerships

Richard A. Nest

FEATURES OF PARTNERSHIPS

When a few sole proprietors of business enterprises first realized that by banding together they might operate more efficiently and profitably, they brought into being the oldest form of business combination that has come down to the modern era— the partnership. Corporations, by contrast, are a relatively new form of business combination, having developed principally during the last two hundred years. For all their antiquity, however, partnerships continue to be a very popular method of operating a business with more than one owner.

The *Uniform Partnership Act* is a model statute that has been adopted by most states to govern the creation and operation of partnerships. A partnership is defined in the act as "an association of two or more persons to carry on as co-owners of a business for profit." The act defines a person as either an individual, a business corporation, or any other entity having the same rights, privileges, and responsibilities as an individual. This general definition is modified in various ways for special kinds of partnerships such as limited partnerships, joint ventures, and professional corporations or associations.

Partnership advantages differ from corporate advantages. A corporation is recognized as a legal entity apart from its owners. Thus, shareholders are with rare exceptions liable only to the extent of their investment, a feature important to the public investor. In general, a partnership does not limit liability for the partners. But an advantage is that a partnership is easy to create. A written or even oral agreement is all that is necessary; no special approval is required by any governmental unit. A partnership can also be formed with a specified limited existence and can provide tax advantages when, in certain circumstances, the partners reflect on their income tax returns ordinary and capital losses in excess of the cost of the partnership (see Negative Tax Basis later in this chapter).

The Partnership Agreement

Although a partnership can be created by oral agreement, misunderstandings are avoided by setting forth the terms of the partnership in a written agreement. A brief listing of the basic matters the agreement should cover follows:

1. Partners' names and the name of the partnership.
2. Date of formation and the length of time the partnership is to exist—for an indefinite period, or until a specific date or completion of a project.
3. Capital to be invested by each partner.
4. Methods to be used in valuing noncash capital investments and the penalties for not contributing or maintaining required capital investments.
5. Discretionary authority to be vested in each partner and the related rights, responsibilities, and duties of each.
6. Accounting period to be used and the plan for sharing profits and losses, including cash distributions to partners.
7. Salaries and drawings allowed to partners and the penalties, if any, for excessive withdrawals.
8. Insurance to be obtained on the lives of partners.
9. Provisions for the arbitration of disputes, the liquidation of the partnership at the end of the specified term of the contract, or the liquidation or continuance of the partnership on the death or withdrawal of a partner. (Technically, a partnership ceases with a change in partners, but this problem can be handled by covering such an eventuality in the agreement.)

Considerable thought should be given to the partnership agreement. All foreseeable contingencies (except those very remote) should be discussed, and a method of handling them should be stipulated. For example, potentially costly disputes may be avoided by agreeing on procedures for valuing assets and for settling with the estate of a deceased partner. See Rabkin and Johnson (1979, pp. 1001-1006) for a sample partnership agreement.

Methods of Sharing Net Income and Losses

A major advantage of a partnership is the unlimited variation it allows in the sharing of net income and losses. The partners may share on any basis or method on which they agree. The most commonly used method is the *capital ratio method,* by which each partner shares in net income and losses in the same proportionate relationship that his capital account bears to total capital. Among the variations of this method are

1. Sharing all income or loss in proportion to each partner's capital at year-end;
2. Sharing all income or loss in proportion to the average capital balance maintained by each partner during the year;
3. Paying agreed-on salaries to the partners and dividing the remainder on one of the bases of capital; and
4. Paying salaries and interest on capital to the partners and then dividing the remainder on one of the bases of capital.

Another method is simply to divide net income and losses equally.

Cash Distributions

Whether the partnership is operating as a private company or as a public limited partnership, the availability of cash for distribution is an important consideration. There is generally less need for cash accumulation in a partnership than in a corporation, since most partnerships are service organizations, thus having a greater emphasis on labor than on capital. Also, although partnerships are not subject to federal income taxes, the individual partner is taxed on his share of the partnership taxable income, and he needs cash to meet his tax obligations. Thus the partnership tends to distribute cash to the partners as soon as it is available. Cash flow is also an important factor in tax shelter partnerships, though very often the cash flow does not come from the partnership but from the reduction in the individual partners' income taxes that results from the partnership's loss for tax purposes.

Privately Held Partnerships

The typical partnership is organized by individuals to operate a private business. Partnerships formed for a specific limited objective usually have a limited term of existence, while those formed to operate an ongoing business or profession are likely to be of indefinite duration. Typically, the number of partners is small; but there is no legal limitation, and some professional partnerships—accounting firms and legal firms, for example—have hundreds.

The nonincorporated *joint venture* is a form of partnership composed of a limited number of parties with a specific business purpose. Most joint ventures are of short duration, though when they are formed to handle a large project that will take years (such as building a dam or port) or to exploit a natural resource deposit, they remain in existence until their purpose is achieved.

The *limited partnership* is composed of one or more general partners plus a number of limited partners. The limited partners assume no responsibility for the obligations of the partnership beyond the capital they have paid in or have promised to pay, while the general partners assume the unlimited liability characteristic of partnerships. A general partner (which often is a corporation syndicating a series of limited partnerships) typically is active in the management of the company and is recognized as a principal agent of the company. In most instances, such a partnership can permit the transfer of limited partnership interests without a termination of the partnership. Public offerings made in real estate, oil and gas exploration, and other tax shelters are often in the form of limited partnerships.

The *professional corporation* or professional association is used by doctors, lawyers, CPAs, and other professionals to form an association of their practice that will provide all the features of a corporation except limited liability. These associations are recognized as a corporate entity for income tax purposes.

Partnerships must file an information return with the IRS but are not liable for federal income taxes. Under the Internal Revenue Code, certain corporations electing to be treated as partnerships for income tax purposes are known as *Subchapter S corporations*. The tax regulations for Subchapter S corporations limit the number of shareholders to no more than ten. Also, no more than one class of stock may exist; all shareholders must be individuals or estates; and no more than 20% of the corporation's income can come from nonoperational sources such as interest, dividends, rents, or royalties. In all respects other than for tax purposes, the company operates as a corporation.

Since the cash aspects of the businesses are of prime interest, it is not uncommon for private partnerships to maintain their books essentially on a cash basis, with some modification to recognize noncash expenses such as depreciation and amortization. Such an approach facilitates the preparation of the income tax return and the determination of the individual partners' taxable income or losses. As partnerships grow in size and number of partners, however, the need for additional financial data for operations and planning purposes also increases; a transition to the accrual basis of accounting for other than income tax purposes may fulfill this need.

Publicly Held Partnerships

Virtually all publicly held partnerships are engaged in tax-sheltering operations. The public investor anticipates that the partnership will distribute cash from its operations while creating tax losses for him through depreciation and cash basis expenses. The tax losses are, of course, used to reduce (shelter) his taxable income.

Under the Securities Act of 1933, the syndication of limited partnership interests is considered the sale of a security. Accordingly, either the offer and sale must be registered with the SEC or an exemption must be applicable. The only exemptions available are the intrastate offering exemption, the Regulation A exemption, and the private placement exemption. (These exemptions apply generally to any securities offering, not only to limited partnership interests.)

The qualifications that an offering must have to meet the *intrastate exemption* are described in SEC Rule 147. In general, this exemption applies when the offering is made only within one state and sold only to that state's residents. The partnership must be organized and doing business in that state, and its project must also be located in the same state. Caution should be taken in applying these rules, however, as there are many restrictions and numerous specific conditions that must be met.

A *Regulation A exemption* is available for offerings currently raising a maximum of $1,500,000 in a 12-month period. The limited partnership must meet the information requirements stipulated in SEC Rules 251 through 263 and the 1933 act. However, certified financial statements are not required in the "Reg A" offering if the limited partnership has not otherwise filed certified statements with the SEC. Under Rule 254 of Regulation A, a series of offerings is permitted by the same general partner, each up to $500,000, without violation of the 12-month period maximum amount limitation.

The *private placement* or *private offering exemption* is provided under Section 4(2) of the 1933 act. SEC Rule 146, which establishes objective criteria for the availability of this exemption, permits an unlimited number of offers, but there can be no more than 35 purchasers in any offering. Those who purchase $150,000 or more are not included in the count. Another requirement is that the syndicate must have grounds to believe that the offeree, alone or with a representative, has the basic business experience and knowledge to evaluate the investment and the accompanying risk. The rule also requires each offeree to be furnished with the information normally obtained in a registration statement, if one were to be filed.

For example, in accordance with Rule 146, the following information would normally be included in a basic private real estate offering:

1. A certified balance sheet of the partnership.
2. A certified balance sheet of any corporate general partner.
3. A personal financial statement and disclosure of the current net worth of the general partner.
4. A track record of the general partner or sponsor along the lines set forth in Table II of Guide 60. (See illustration in Figure 27.1.)
5. A five-year financial information backup on the particular property planned to be acquired with the net proceeds of the offering.
6. A description of annual financial statements and tax information that would be provided to the investor after the offering. When necessary, unaudited statements will be acceptable if audited statements are not available.

Rule 146 is not an easy set of guidelines to follow. The facts of a proposed offering should, with the advice of counsel, be scrutinized carefully against the details of Rule 146 before deciding that an exemption is available.

For federal income tax purposes, most partnerships report on a cash basis. However, limited partnership financial statements included in annual reports filed with the SEC must meet the requirements specified in ASR 162—they must be presented in conformity with GAAP and certified (accompanied by an auditor's opinion). ASR 162 takes the position that tax basis financial statements do not contain sufficient data to satisfy the information needs of the investors. Tax data may be given in footnotes and other supporting schedules, however. See Accounting Basis for Form 10-K for an example of such footnote information.

The SEC's attitude toward the need for GAAP basis financial statements of tax shelter partnerships has been questioned by many accountants. Investors in these ventures are looking to the tax consequences, and accrual accounting not consistent with the tax return could be more confusing than enlightening. It is likely that the investors pay attention primarily to the individual tax return data they are given by

TABLE II
(To be used for each prior partnership)

Name of Partnership

	Year	Year	Year	Year	Year
SUMMARY OF OPERATIONS - GAAP Basis *					
1. Gross Revenues	$				
1(a) Gain (Loss) on Sale of Property	$				
2. Less:[1] Operating Expense	$				
Interest Expense	$				
Depreciation	$				
3. NET INCOME (LOSS) - GAAP BASIS	$				
Computation To Tax Basis					
4. Less:[2]	$				
5. Plus:[2]	$				
6. TAXABLE INCOME (LOSS)	$				
Computation of Cash Generated					
7. *Plus:* Capitalization of Loan Fees Depreciation	$				
8. *Less:* Mortgage Reduction	$				
9. CASH GENERATED (DEFICIENCY)[3][7]	$				
10. Cash Distributions to Partners[4]	$				
11. CASH GENERATED (DEFICIENCY) AFTER DISTRIBUTION (BEFORE SPECIAL ITEMS)	$				
12. Special Items[5]	$				
13. Cash Generated (Deficiency) after Special Items	$				
Tax and Distribution Data Per $1,000 Investment					
Federal Income Tax Deductions[6]					
Ordinary Income (Loss)	$				
Capital Gain (Loss)	$				
Cash Distributions to Partners[4]					
Investment Income	$				
Return of Capital	$				

Instruction: The foregoing tabulation should include: (a) Summary Income and Expense Data prepared on the basis of Generally Accepted Accounting Principles (GAAP), (b) adjustments necessary to GAAP Net Income (Loss) to compute Taxable Income (Loss) (c) adjustments necessary to Taxable Income to compute Cash Generated (Deficiency) and (d) Tax Deductions and cash distribution data both on an income and cash basis (see Guide 25, Release 33-4936).

* Generally Accepted Accounting Principles.

[1] Should include all operating and other appropriate deductions from revenues necessary to arrive at a calculation of net income on a GAAP basis.

[2] Lines 4 and 5 should include any differences between GAAP (line 3) and Taxable Income (Loss). Detail major items and aggregate all others.

[3] Explain any cash deficiency (line 9). If distributions are made to partners in excess of the amount of cash generated (line 9), appropriate disclosure should be made of the sources and amount of the funds used in making the distribution shown in line 10.

[4] See Guide 25 of Release 33-4936.

[5] All sources and uses of cash from refinancings, purchase and sales of properties, loans and other similar items not directly associated with partnership operations, which result in a material cash effect, should be individually disclosed in line 13 for those periods in which such transactions occur.

[6] Any expense items challenged by IRS should be indicated in a footnote.

[7] In any interim period (fiscal quarter), subsequent to that shown above, where a deficit cash flow occurs, such deficit should be reflected in a note with the corresponding interim period of the preceding fiscal year.

FIGURE 27.1　GUIDE 60—PREPARATION OF REGISTRATION STATEMENTS RELATING TO INTERESTS IN REAL ESTATE LIMITED PARTNERSHIPS

SOURCE: Release No. 33-5692, April 26, 1976; also available in SEC Docket, March 30, 1976, and Poloway and Charles, 1980, ¶ 2375.

the general partner, and the 10-Ks with their GAAP basis statements are regarded as bureaucratic.

One benefit, if it may be called that, resulting from ASR 162 is the SEC's greater ability to prosecute syndicators (auditors, too) through the medium of alleged violations of GAAP reporting and disclosure requirements. Though these are often as murky as income tax basis reporting, at least they are within the SEC's S-X bailiwick.

FINANCIAL ACCOUNTING AND REPORTING FOR PARTNERSHIPS

Because of partners' interest in cash flow, it is common to find the financial statements of partnerships presented on a cash basis. SAS 14, *Special Reports,* recognizes that "in some circumstances ... a comprehensive basis of accounting other than generally accepted accounting principles may be used" (AU 621.03). Such a basis may be "the cash receipts and disbursements basis of accounting, and modifications of the cash basis having substantial support, such as recording depreciation on fixed assets ..." (AU 621.04 (c)). Also recognized as a comprehensive basis of accounting is the basis used by the reporting entity to file its income tax return for the period covered by the financial statements (AU 621.04 (b)). How the auditor reports on such statements is discussed in Chapter 16.

Sale of Interest in a Partnership and the Admission and Withdrawal of Partners

There are several ways of accounting for the sale of a part or all of the interest in a partnership, or for the admission or withdrawal of partners. Legally, any such event constitutes a termination of the partnership, unless the partnership agreement provides for continuation, with or without a special accounting, beyond the date of the event.

Admission. One approach in accounting for the admission of a new partner is to revalue the partnership at fair market value. The current partners are allocated their shares of increase or decrease in value, and the new partner is then admitted to the partnership either by purchase of a proportion of the rights of another partner or by joining the partnership through a cash capital contribution. By this accounting approach, the newly organized partnership will begin with net assets stated at fair market value, thereby averting a future "windfall" profit (or detriment) to the new partner from realization of fair value excesses (or deficiencies) unrecorded at the date of his admission.

Note that this approach, supported in advanced accounting textbooks (see Suggested Reading at chapter end), may be useful for internal partnership accounting purposes, but will not be appropriate for financial statements prepared in conformity with GAAP (see, for example, AC 4072). Use of fair market or appraisal values in excess of historical cost in basic financial statements is not acceptable, even when the partnership is technically terminated and the old partners form a new one by contributing the assets "distributed" in the termination. (See Chapter 28 for a discussion of the accounting basis of property contributed to a partnership by a partner.)

An alternative approach that complies with GAAP is to retain preadmission net assets at historical cost and simply record the new partner's cash contribution as his capital. To the extent there are unrecorded excess values, it may be specified that the newly admitted partner will not share in them upon realization; or more commonly, the capital contribution required will be disproportionately high in relation to the new partner's income-sharing percentage. Even when cash basis (non-GAAP) accounting is used, the above approaches may be followed to prevent the new partner from sharing in the unrecorded assets, such as accounts receivable.

As stated at the outset of this chapter, the partners can agree on *any* method of sharing among themselves as long as it can be computed with reasonable objectivity. And if the agreed-on method is based on something other than accounting that conforms with GAAP, the financial statements can still be presented using GAAP.

Of course, if there is a sale by a partner of his interest to a third party acceptable to the remaining partners, this does not affect the carrying amounts of assets or liabilities, because the transaction is made outside the partnership. Thus, the price may be influenced by many factors other than the financial position or results of operations of the partnership as determined under GAAP or some other comprehensive basis of accounting.

Withdrawal. Similar considerations arise when a partner withdraws from the firm. If the retiring partner's distribution is predicated on the fair market value of the firm's assets and liabilities rather than on historical cost, he will receive a payment that may be either greater than or less than the amount shown as his current invested capital. One way of recording such a transaction is to revalue the entire partnership at fair market value and then to allocate the new valuation to the capital accounts of the partners according to their participation. (As noted previously under Admission, this approach is not appropriate for financial statements conforming with GAAP.)

Another approach is to recognize in the accounts only the proportionate excess amount applicable to the retiring partner. Some favor the latter method as a conservative one that essentially maintains the records at historical cost; others criticize it as being piecemeal. When a retiring partner is paid more than his stated capital and no revaluation in whole or in part is made, the excess payment is ordinarily allocated to the remaining partners according to their profit and loss ratios and regarded as essentially a bonus payment to the withdrawing partner.

Financial Statements

Formal Statements. The financial statements of a partnership presented in conformity with GAAP are essentially the same as those prepared for a corporation, except for the equity section of the balance sheet and the income statement with regard to partners' salaries and other items paid to partners. The footnote disclosures required under GAAP are also applicable to the financial statements of a partnership.

It is not uncommon for a partnership's financial statements to be prepared and presented on a comprehensive basis of accounting other than GAAP, such as the cash basis or the income tax basis. Such presentations are accepted by the accounting profession as useful and relevant to the particular interests of partners. However, an accountant associated with such statements would have to mention non-conformity with GAAP (see Chapter 16).

Changes in partners' equity during the period should be disclosed in the financial statements. If there has been little change, the details may be incorporated on the face of the balance sheet rather than in a separate schedule. Ordinarily, however, a statement of changes in partners' equities will be presented. An example is shown in Figure 27.2.

THE ASJ COMPANY
(A Limited Partnership)
STATEMENT OF CHANGES IN PARTNERS' EQUITY
YEAR ENDED DECEMBER 31, 1979

		Limited Partner	*General Partners*	
	Total	*Robert E. Anderson*	*Thomas A. Smith*	*John W. Jones*
Balance, January 1, 1979:				
Permanent capital (Note A)	$11,000	$ 7,000	$ 2,000	$ 2,000
Capital subject to withdrawal	9,000	3,000	3,000	3,000
	20,000	10,000	5,000	5,000
Net income after partners' salaries of $40,000 each (Note B)	48,000	1,000	23,500	23,500
	68,000	11,000	28,500	28,500
Less withdrawals	48,000	1,000	22,000	25,000
Balance, December 31, 1979	$20,000	$10,000	$ 6,500	$ 3,500
Consisting of:				
Permanent capital	$11,000	$ 7,000	$ 2,000	$ 2,000
Capital subject to withdrawal	9,000	3,000	4,500	1,500
	$20,000	$10,000	$ 6,500	$ 3,500

Note A—Permanent capital is the initial capital contribution of each partner in accordance with the partnership agreement.

Note B—Income is allocated in the following manner:

Robert E. Anderson	10% return on his capital account at the beginning of the year.
Thomas A. Smith and John W. Jones	50% each after deducting the amount allocated to Robert E. Anderson.

FIGURE 27.2 SAMPLE STATEMENT OF CHANGES IN PARTNERS' EQUITIES

funded as accrued; prior service costs, where applicable, are amortized over 30 years. (The U.S. firm has a formal plan for active partners and principals. The market value of plan assets was approximately $3,000 in excess of the actuarial value of vested benefits at the latest valuation date, July 1, 1978.)

Arthur Andersen & Co.

5. Partner Resignation, Retirement and Death Benefits

All eligible partners are required to participate in the United States Partners' Profit Sharing Plan (Keogh plan) or equivalent plans outside the United States. Such plans are administered by a committee of partners, and benefits are paid by the trusts.

The firm makes basic retirement payments to retired partners and the estates of deceased partners. Such payments were made at the annual rate of $14,400 in 1979 and $13,500 in 1978, commencing at mandatory retirement age (62) for life or for 10 years certain in case of death. Such payments may begin at an earlier age at reduced amounts. The amounts payable are subject to annual adjustment, based upon a price index. Such payments aggregated $1,524,000 in 1979 and $1,150,000 in 1978. An actuarial determination of retirement amounts payable to partners as of August 31, 1979 (being amortized over 30 years), was approximately $27,901,000, of which approximately $15,917,000 was applicable to partners already retired. These basic retirement payments may be rescinded at any time by a two-thirds vote of the partners.

Supplementary retirement benefits are payable upon resignation, retirement or death to partners with more than one year of service as a partner as of July 1, 1974. As of August 31, 1979, the aggregate amount payable was $32,048,000, which is being allocated from annual earnings over 10 years ending in 1984. Payments of $4,217,000 were made in 1979 and $4,056,000 in 1978.

Payments and allocations of earnings for partner retirement aggregated $11,200,000 in 1979 and $10,250,000 in 1978.

The surge of inflation during 1978 and into 1980 caused two of the firms to include footnote disclosures as to the effect of changing prices, while Price Waterhouse & Co. included adjusted figures in its highlights. The disclosures are as follows:

Arthur Andersen & Co.

10. Adjustments for the Effects of Inflation (Not Audited)

Earnings for the year, adjusted for the effects of inflation, reflect the decline in purchasing power of partners' capital for the years ended August 31, 1979 and 1978 (resulting from the increase in the general price level), net of the impact of inflation upon the firm's nonmonetary assets (property and equipment). To determine the impact of inflation on partners' capital, the U.S. rate of inflation (12.0% in fiscal 1979 and 7.9% in fiscal 1978, as determined by the change in the U.S. Consumer Price Index for All Urban Consumers) was applied to partners' capital at the beginning of the years (adjusted for the effect of distributions to partners during the years) and to property and equipment at the beginning of the years (adjusted for the impact of prior years' inflation).

The adjustments of $3,109,000 in 1979 and $2,342,000 in 1978 to historical-cost depreciation and amortization provisions were based on the inflation-adjusted amounts of property and equipment.

Peat Marwick International

7. Effect of Changing Prices

Substantially all of the firms' net assets are monetary in nature. Because the active partners and principals in the various countries finance the operations of the various firms by capital not withdrawn, they suffer a loss in purchasing power as the prices of goods and services in their respective countries increase. The increase of prices varies from country to country and on a weighted average basis approximated 10% in 1979 and 7½ % in 1978 in all countries; as a result, the active partners and principles lost purchasing power of approximately $7,500 and $5,700 in 1979 and 1978, respectively.

After many years of no public disclosure, it is not unexpected that much attention is focused on the question of partners' earnings. However, just as with the corporate variable of earnings per share, the average earnings figure for a partner in an accounting firm can be misleading. Earnings per partner of firms with similar earnings may be drastically different because of the different numbers of partners sharing in the profit. The number of partners depends on the firm's philosophy regarding its objectives, its mix of client services, its office locations, and other factors. Thus, the average earnings of partners are generally not comparable from firm to firm. Coopers & Lybrand addressed this matter in its notes to the financial statements, stating:

Earnings for a year attributable to active partners are not net profit in the usual corporate sense, but rather constitute the total available to the partners for current compensation which is subject to taxation and is before consideration of return on capital, retirement benefits and normal executive fringe benefit costs. Partners' earnings depend on the income of the individual member firm of which they are partners, and not on the combined income shown in this summary.

Focusing on growth and quality would undoubtedly provide better criteria for evaluating a partnership. However, competition and the desire to understand and learn what the partners in the Big Eight are earning has tended to distract attention from this factor, although the current-year reports do not stress earnings per partner as directly as in 1978.

All the annual reports disclosed in their footnotes on litigation or contingent liabilities that any net liabilities arising from uninsured risks were either immaterial or had been adequately accrued. Arthur Andersen & Co., in addition to accruing for its uninsured risks, had allocated an undisclosed portion of its capital to cover such risks. In several instances, total cost of legal liabilities costs were disclosed.

As the large public accounting firms continue to publish financial statements and other operating data, the format and basic financial data and related disclosures should become more structured and uniform. In view of the complexity of the subject, the AICPA has evidenced an interest in the matter, but to date evolution has been the only active factor.

AUDITING AND AUDIT REPORTING FOR PARTNERSHIPS

Privately Held, Non-Tax-Oriented Partnerships

The independent auditor of the financial statements of a private partnership faces the same kind of auditing problems he would encounter if the entity were operating as a corporation. Furthermore, the disclosure requirements under GAAP are essentially the same.

The partnership agreement is the basic document under which the partnership has been organized and operates. The independent auditor must read this document carefully to understand the partnership's organization and to identify the aspects of the agreement that bear upon financial and accounting matters; he must be alert to any evidence that does not conform to the partnership agreement or that may have been omitted despite being required by the partnership agreement.

In reporting to the company, any material omissions or deviations from the agreement should be brought to the attention of management for review and possibly for revision and adjustment. If management does not make the necessary revisions or disclosures, the auditor will consider the effects on the financial statements and, if necessary, modify his report. Typically, contentious items may be found in the payment of salaries and interest on capital, accounting for admission and retirement of partners, distribution of earnings, minimum capital accounts, and withdrawal limitations. The auditor should also be alert to partnership agreement requirements that are not in conformity with GAAP (or another comprehensive basis of accounting used in the financial report), so that necessary adjustments can be made.

In reporting on his examination, the independent auditor's opinion language may vary, depending on whether the financial statements are presented on the basis of GAAP or on another comprehensive basis of accounting (see Chapter 16).

When the basis of accounting used in reporting by the partnership is not GAAP but another comprehensive basis of accounting (AU 621), the independent auditor ordinarily includes a middle paragraph describing the basis of accounting. An example of such a middle paragraph is as follows:

> As described in Note 1 it is the policy of the partnership to prepare its financial statements on the accounting basis used for income tax purposes; consequently, certain revenue and related assets are recognized when received rather than when earned, and certain expenses are recognized when paid rather than when the obligation is incurred. Accordingly, the accompanying financial statements are not intended to present financial position or results of operations in conformity with generally accepted accounting principles. [AU 621.08]

Once the independent auditor has clearly established the basis of accounting, his opinion then reads the same as a standard opinion except that he substitutes alternative wording for the phrase "in conformity with generally accepted accounting principles." An example of such wording is:

> In our opinion, the financial statements referred to above present fairly the assets, liabilities and capital of STV partnership as of September 30, 1979 and its revenue,

expenses and changes in its partners' capital accounts for the year then ended, on the basis of accounting described in Note X, which basis has been applied in a manner consistent with that of the preceding year. [AU 621.08]

In reporting on partnership financial statements on a cash or income tax accounting basis, the auditor must be alert that the financial statements do not obscure significant matters. If they do, the auditor should consider the need to modify his opinion concerning adequate disclosure, or should recommend that the statements be prepared on an accrual basis if that would solve the problem.

Publicly Held, Tax-Oriented Partnerships

Independent CPAs usually play an active role in tax shelter offerings to the public. They provide advice on the applicability of tax methods to be used, audit the financial statements, and may review the financial projections for the venture (see Chapter 33).

The tax shelter prospectus usually contains an offering memorandum that discusses the financial information provided, the projections made, the tax aspects of the investment, and the many risk factors involved. The CPA's special concern is with the tax and financial projections presented in the prospectus, since the historical financial statements of the new partnership itself show virtually nothing, no activities except formation having occurred. In some instances, the offering does not involve specified properties, but only a *blind pool,* that is, a general indication of the type of assets to be acquired with the proceeds of the offering. Though the regulations stipulate a level of sophistication by those who may invest in such ventures, this type of professional service carries a high risk for the independent auditor. The high-risk nature of these offerings is recognized by accountants in the manner described below.

Knowing the Client and His Integrity. A tax shelter offering is substantially predicated on future occurrences. In some instances, a track record of the developer's or general partner's activities may not be available to provide the offeree with relevant information. Thus, it is common for the independent auditor, before accepting the engagement, to assure himself of the client's integrity and reputation in the marketplace by reviewing his prior ventures in other fields, searching for past or pending actions alleging violations of SEC regulations or state laws, and making inquiries of bankers, attorneys, and other knowledgeable business persons.

Some Infamous Frauds. Some publicly held limited partnership tax shelters have caused investors to suffer significant financial losses through fraud. Two interesting cases are Geotek and Homestake Production.

Geotek. The SEC case against Geotek, its auditors, and others arose out of the sale of interests in limited partnerships organized to explore and drill for oil and gas. There were 1,600 participants, and over $30,000,000 was invested in four limited partnership programs. Independent auditors were engaged to perform audits of receipts and disbursements of the limited partnerships and to audit the GAAP financial statements of the corporate general partner.

Criminal indictments were handed down against the 80% stockholder in the general partner corporation alleging fraud in the sale of securities, mail fraud, and filing false statements. He admitted that in certain prospectuses and filed financial statements he had failed to make required disclosures of certain prior business associations, his affiliation with certain persons dealing with the partnerships, and transactions inconsistent with the provisions of the limited partnership agreements.

There appeared to be no direct evidence that the limited partnership investors suffered losses from unfair dealings, but the promoter (the 80% stockholder) profited by indirect means through related-party activities and by his violations of limited partnership provisions. The SEC also commenced a civil enforcement proceeding, primarily against the promoter and his associates but also against the independent auditors.

The SEC's allegations provide an insight into its view of the auditor's responsibility to limited partners. The SEC asserted that the auditors failed to revise their opinion properly after learning of the disclosures made by the promoter, and that they failed to discover certain disbursements made to undisclosed affiliated persons in violation of the partnership agreements. Furthermore, the SEC said that the auditors failed to discover and disclose secret affiliations, which resulted in misstatements about drilling contracts, property transfers, classifications of properties, and the allocation and estimation of general and administrative expenses among the partnerships.

Pointing to the improper pledge of certain properties of one program against the obligations of another, the SEC charged the auditors with failing to change their reports retroactively after these transactions had been disclosed. Several allegations involved the auditors' failure to ascertain that the partnerships complied with partnership documents and statements in the public offering materials. In some instances the independent auditors had obtained opinions from counsel to the partnerships to the effect that various transactions were in compliance.

The promoter pleaded guilty to the criminal charge of filing false statements with the SEC and was fined and sent to prison. In addition, the court found against the promoter and others on certain civil charges. However, all the SEC's charges against the independent auditors were rejected by the courts because there was insufficient proof or legal basis to support the allegations that the auditors knew or should have known of the misrepresentations. The court held that the independent auditors did their work in good faith, in accordance with GAAS.

The SEC appealed the lower court's rejection of these allegations, but the decision was affirmed that the auditors had met their legal duty in accordance with GAAS.

Homestake. The Homestake Production Company case involves the sale of participation units of undivided interest in programs for the exploration and development of oil leases. Many prominent investors put millions of dollars into these programs. Programs for a fixed number of units were sold annually through operating subsidiaries of Homestake, which owned portions of the oil property and was responsible for all production and other operating activities. The parent company guaranteed investors that each operating subsidiary would perform its obligations to the investors under the investment contracts.

Independent auditors were engaged to audit the consolidated financial statements of the parent and its subsidiaries for the calendar year 1966 and the balance sheet of the 1967 operating company for inclusion in a registration statement covering the units of participation to be sold that year. The Homestake company was in fact operating a Ponzi scheme; proceeds from sales of units of participation in later years were not being used for the lease exploration and operations as stated in the registration statement, but were used to make payments to holders of participation units sold in prior years, as if such payments were the operating profits from those earlier investments.

The auditors were charged with aiding and abetting this scheme by failing to determine and disclose that funds received from the sale of units of participation were not being used as required by the registration statements, and that the funds were not properly segregated as required but were commingled with other general funds. In addition, the auditors were charged with knowledge that Homestake consistently oversold the units in each program but failed to disclose this fact in the audited financial statements. The litigation is still pending against the company's management and the auditors.

Tax Opinions by CPAs. A tax shelter raises numerous questions significant to a potential limited partner. He must know, for example, the extent to which the partnership is entitled to claim depreciation, whether the methods of depreciation to be used will be acceptable, whether the useful lives are appropriate, which expenses may be deducted and which deferred and amortized, and what might happen if those methods were challenged by the IRS. Thus, relative to making an offering of a tax shelter partnership, a CPA may be requested to express an opinion on the tax accounting methods proposed for use in the partnership's federal and state income tax returns. In a typical situation, the independent CPA may issue a tax opinion that would read somewhat as follows:

General Partner and Prospective Limited Partners
Flareup Co.
Brooklyn, New York

Gentlemen:

We have reviewed the tax accounting methods listed below, which are proposed to be used in the federal income tax return of Flareup Co. These methods, which are described in the attached "Proposed Federal Income Tax Methods," are

- Accounting basis and tax year,
- Net lease of property,
- Deductions for expenditures allocated to various specific periods,
- Depreciation, and
- The proposed transfer of partnership interest.

Our review was limited to evaluating the appropriateness of using these tax methods in preparing federal income tax returns under the assumed conditions described and referred to in "Proposed Federal Income Tax Methods."

In our opinion, the aforementioned proposed tax methods are appropriate for use in preparing federal partnership income tax returns under stated conditions. Our opinion is based upon existing provisions of the Internal Revenue Code, certain regulations proposed or adopted thereunder, current public rulings, and court decisions. There are many factual and legal questions involved concerning the availability and timing of specific deductions that have not been the subject of such provisions, regulations, rulings, or decisions. Future legislative or administrative changes and court decisions may require that different methods be used. There can be no assurance that such methods will be allowed. These matters are discussed under "Risk Factors" and "Federal Income Tax Consequences" in the private placement memorandum. Moreover, determination of the tax methods that will be used in preparing future federal partnership income returns must be made based on actual conditions, which may vary from those in the periods covered by the returns.

It should be noted that many factors in addition to a partner's allocable share of partnership income enter into the determination of his personal federal and state income taxes. While not addressed herein, such considerations are discussed elsewhere in the offering memorandum. Because of the complexity of the federal and state tax laws that may be applicable to an individual partner, each prospective limited partner should consult with his personal tax adviser.

/signed/

Certified Public Accountants
New York, New York

The attachment mentioned in the specimen letter above is reproduced below:

FLAREUP CO.
(A Limited Partnership)
Brooklyn, New York

PROPOSED FEDERAL INCOME TAX METHODS

ACCOUNTING BASIS AND TAX YEAR

The partnership plans to use the accrual basis of accounting and to file its federal income tax returns on a calendar year basis.

NET LEASE OF THE PROPERTY

The partnership considers itself subject to a net lease under Section 163 of the Code.

DEDUCTIONS FOR EXPENDITURES ALLOCATED
TO VARIOUS SPECIFIC PERIODS

The partnership plans to deduct the general partner service fee over periods that the offeror believes are the periods for which they are ordinary and necessary expenses.

DEPRECIATION

The partnership plans to elect to compute depreciation of the building and equipment as follows:

- Building shell basis—125% declining balance.
- Rehabilitation basis—Section 167(K) 60-month amortization for qualified low-income rental housing units, to a maximum of $20,000 per rental unit.

- Excess rehabilitation building cost and new equipment basis—200% declining balance.

THE PROPOSED TRANSFER OF PARTNERSHIP INTEREST

In offering for sale 49.5% of the partnership interests, the partnership anticipates that the investor limited partners will obtain a basis adjustment for partnership assets under Internal Revenue Code Section 743(b) as the result of an election by the partnership under I.R.C. Section 754.

The partnership further anticipates that the basis adjustment for partnership assets allowable under I.R.C. Section 754 will be allocated to the underlying partnership assets using the above-mentioned depreciation methods. However, it should be noted that the basis adjustment allocated to the rehabilitation costs will not be depreciated using the Section 167(K) 60-month amortization, but rather by componentizing the assets using the 200% declining balance method.

Tax Information Transmittals by CPAs. In addition to providing auditing services and tax opinions on offerings, independent CPAs may also prepare the income tax returns for tax shelter partnerships. Such an engagement ordinarily includes preparation of the partnership income tax Schedule K and submission to the partnership of each partner's taxable income and other tax return information. The tax return information for each partner is usually submitted in the form of a Schedule K-1 setting forth the partner's applicable share of the partnership items. Schedule K-1 is shown in Figure 27.4.

When this information is submitted to the general partner, other matters are normally included in the CPA's transmittal letter to dispel any ambiguity concerning his responsibility for the individual data. The transmittal letter would ordinarily include the following:

1. Reference to audited financial statements or a comment that the financial information has not been audited.
2. Specification of the source of the information; for example, federal and the named state partnership income tax returns for the year specified.
3. Reference to the fact that the individual partnership information has been prepared by the general partner and is being submitted to the other partners by the general partner in fulfillment of the partnership agreement.
4. Identification of any positions taken by the partnership that are currently being challenged by the IRS. It is important that the participants in the partnership be made aware of any such challenge.
5. A comment as to whether or not the IRS has approved changes in accounting made by the partnership.

Negative Tax Basis. Occasionally, partners find themselves in a negative tax basis situation because the losses reflected on a tax basis are in excess of the cash capital invested. This occurs most frequently when there is nonrecourse financing by the partnership, with the individual partner being considered at risk for his share of such borrowings. In such cases it is important for all the partners to recognize the situation and its potential future tax and accounting effects, because it imposes

SCHEDULE K-1
(Form 1065)
Department of the Treasury
Internal Revenue Service

Partner's Share of Income, Credits, Deductions, etc.—1979
For calendar year 1979 or fiscal year
beginning ...., 1979, and ending ...., 19........

Copy A
(File with Form 1065)

Partner's identifying number ▶   Partnership's identifying number ▶

Partner's name, address, and ZIP code   Partnership's name, address, and ZIP code

	Yes	No
A (i) Date(s) partner acquired any partnership interest during the year ▶...............		
(ii) Did partner have any partnership interest before 1/1/77? .		
B Is partner a nonresident alien?		
C (i) Is partner a limited partner (see page 2 of Instructions)? .		
(ii) If "Yes," is partner also a general partner?		
D (i) Did partner ever contribute property other than money to the partnership (if "Yes," complete line 21)? . .		
(ii) Did partner ever receive a distribution other than money from the partnership (if "Yes," complete line 22)? . .		
(iii) Was any part of the partner's interest ever acquired from another partner? . .		
E (i) Did partnership interest terminate during the year? . .		
(ii) Did partnership interest decrease during the year? . . .		

Time devoted to business . . . . %
G IRS Center where partnership return filed ▶....................................
H What type of entity is this partner? ▶....................................
I Partner's share of liabilities (see page 8 of Instructions):

	(i) Incurred before 1/1/77	(ii) Incurred after 12/31/76
Nonrecourse . .	$.................	$.................
Other	$.................	$.................

J Enter total amount of liabilities other than nonrecourse for which the partner is protected against loss through guarantees, stop loss agreements, or similar arrangements of which the partnership has knowledge:

Incurred before 1/1/77 . . . . . . $.................
Incurred after 12/31/76 . . . . . . $.................

K Partner's share of any pre-1976 loss(es) from a section 465(c)(1) activity (i.e. film or video tape, section 1245 property leasing, farm, or oil and gas property) for which there existed a corresponding amount of nonrecourse liability at the end of the year in which loss(es) occurred . . . . $.................

F Enter partner's percentage of:	(i) Before decrease or termination	(ii) End of year
Profit sharing	...............%	...............%
Loss sharing	...............%	...............%
Ownership of capital		...............%

M Reconciliation of partner's capital account:

a. Capital account at beginning of year	b. Capital contributed during year	c. Ordinary income (loss) from line 1b	d. Income not included in column c, plus non-taxable income	e. Losses not included in column c, plus unallowable deductions	f. Withdrawals and distributions	g. Capital account at end of year

a. Distributive share item	b. Amount	c. 1040 filers enter col. b amount as shown
1 a Guaranteed payments to partner: (1) Deductible by the partnership . . .	....	Sch. E, Part III
(2) Capitalized by the partnership	....	Sch. E, Part III
b Ordinary income (loss) (see instructions for your tax return for loss limitations) . .	....	Sch. E, Part III
2 Additional first-year depreciation	....	Sch. E, Part III
3 Gross farming or fishing income	....	Sch. E, Part IV
4 Dividends qualifying for exclusion	....	Sch. B, Part II, line 3
5 Net short-term capital gain (loss) a After 10/31/78	....	Sch. D, line 2
from transactions entered into: b Before 11/1/78	....	Sch. D, line 7
6 Net long-term capital gain (loss) a After 10/31/78	....	Sch. D, line 10
from transactions entered into: b Before 11/1/78	....	Sch. D, line 19
7 Net gain (loss) from involuntary a After 10/31/78	....	Form 4797, line 1
conversions due to casualty or theft: b Before 11/1/78	....	Form 4797, line 1
8 Other net gain (loss) under section a After 10/31/78	....	Form 4797, line 4
1231 from transactions entered into: b Before 11/1/78	....	Form 4797, line 4
9 Net earnings (loss) from self-employment	....	Sch. SE, Part I or Part II
10 a Charitable contributions: 50% ...., 30% 20%	....	Sch. A, line 21 or 22
b Other itemized deductions (attach list)	....	See Sch. A
11 Expense account allowance	....	
12 Jobs credit	....	Form 5884, line 9
13 Taxes paid by regulated investment company	....	Line 61, add words "from 1065"
14 a Payments for partner to a Keogh Plan (Type of plan ▶................)	....	Line 26
b Payments for partner to an IRA or Simplified Employee Pension (SEP) . .	....	Line 25
15 a Foreign taxes paid (attach schedule)	....	Form 1116
b Other income, deductions, etc. (attach schedule)	....	(Enter on applicable lines of your return)
c Oil and gas depletion. (Enter amount (not for partner's use) ▶................)		
16 Specially allocated items (see attached schedule): a Short-term capital gain (loss) . . .	....	Sch. D, line 2
b Long-term capital gain (loss)	....	Sch. D, line 10
c Ordinary gain (loss)	....	Form 4797, line 10
d Other	....	Sch. E, Part III

FIGURE 27.4 SCHEDULE K-1 (FORM 1065), PARTNER'S SHARE OF IN-COME, CREDITS, DEDUCTIONS, ETC.—1979

17 Items of tax preference: a Accelerated depreciation on real property—

    (1) Certified historic structure rehabilitation (167(o) or amortization under 191) . . .. Form 4625, line 1(a)(1)

    (2) Low-income rental housing (167(k)) . . . . Form 4625, line 1(a)(1)

    (3) Other government assisted low-income housing . . . . Form 4625, line 1(a)(1)

    (4) Other real property . . . . Form 4625, line 1(a)(2)

  b Accelerated depreciation on personal property subject to a lease . . . . Form 4625, line 1(b)

    Amortization: c................., d................., e................., f................. .... Form 4625, line 1(c) thru (f)

  g Reserves for losses on bad debts of financial institutions . . . . Form 4625, line 1(g)

  h Depletion (other than oil and gas) . . . . Form 4625, line 1(i)

  i (1) Excess intangible drilling costs from oil, gas or geothermal wells . . .. See Form 4625 instr.

    (2) Net income from oil, gas or geothermal wells . . . .

18 Interest on investment indebtedness: a Investment interest expense—

    (1) Indebtedness incurred before 12/17/69 . . . . Form 4952, line 1

    (2) Indebtedness incurred before 9/11/75, but after 12/16/69 . . . . Form 4952, line 15

    (3) Indebtedness incurred after 9/10/75 . . . . Form 4952, line 5

  b Net investment income (loss) . . . . Form 4952, line 2 or line 10(a)

  c Excess expenses from "net lease property" . . . . Form 4952, lines 11 and 19

  d Excess of net long-term capital gain over net short-term capital loss from investment property .... Form 4952, line 20

19 Property qualified for investment credit:

Basis of new investment property	a 3 or more but less than 5 years	Form 3468, line 1(a)
	b 5 or more but less than 7 years	Form 3468, line 1(b)
	c 7 or more years	Form 3468, line 1(c)
New commuter highway vehicle	d 3 or more years	Form 3468, line 1(d)
Qualified progress expenditures	e 7 or more years 1974 through 1978 . . .	Form 3468, line 1(e)
	f 7 or more years 1979	Form 3468, line 1(f)
Cost of used investment property	g 3 or more but less than 5 years	Form 3468, line 1(g)
	h 5 or more but less than 7 years	Form 3468, line 1(h)
	i 7 or more years	Form 3468, line 1(i)
Used commuter highway vehicle	j 3 or more years	Form 3468, line 1(j)

20 Property used in recomputing a prior year investment credit (enter in corresponding column of Form 4255):

(1) Description of property (also state whether new or used)	(2) Date placed in service	(3) Cost or basis	(4) Estimated useful life	(5) Applicable percentage	(6) Original qualified investment (column 3 × column 5)	(7) Date item ceased to be investment credit property	(8) Period actually used	(9) Applicable percentage	(10) Qualified investment (column 3 × column 10)
a									
b									

21 a Basis to partner of contributed property (other than money) at time(s) of contribution to partnership . . ..

  b Value of contributed property in line 21a as reflected in the partner's capital account . . . .

22 a Basis to partnership of distributed property (other than money) at time(s) of distribution to the partner . . ..

  b Value of distributed property in line 22a as reflected in the partner's capital account . . . .

	Yes	No			Yes	No
23 Partnership information on international boycotting. For partner's reporting requirements see Form 5713.			b Did partnership participate in or cooperate with an international boycott?			
a Did partnership have operations in a boycotting country? .			c Did partnership file Form 5713?			

FIGURE 27.4 CONT'D

on the individual partners a deferred tax that at some time they will have to settle, perhaps even without cash flow from the partnership to offset it.

Changes in Tax Shelters. The 1976 Tax Reform Act significantly reduced the benefits to be obtained from tax-sheltered investments, and the regulations were further tightened in 1978. One of the major changes made by the 1976 act was a new "at-risk" rule. It provided that the tax loss deduction from certain activities cannot exceed the amount a taxpayer is personally at risk to lose at the close of the activity's taxable year. The amount a taxpayer is at risk includes the money and other property (on an adjusted basis) contributed by the taxpayer to the activity, plus any amounts borrowed for use in the activity to the extent that the taxpayer is personally liable to repay the debt from his personal assets, plus the net fair market value of the taxpayer's other assets that secure nonrecourse borrowing. If a taxpayer is protected from a loss through guarantees, stop-loss agreements, or repurchase agreements, such borrowing is not regarded as being at risk.

The at-risk limitation applies to the following four types of activities: (1) farming, except farming operations involving trees other than fruit or nut trees (thus the growing of timber is not affected); (2) oil and gas exploration or exploitation; (3) holding, producing, or distributing motion pictures or videotapes; and (4) equipment leasing. Each activity within a classification (such as each farm or each oil or gas property) is treated as a separate activity. However, a partner's interest in a partnership, or a shareholder's interest in a Subchapter S corporation, is regarded as one activity no matter how many activities the investee enterprise operates.

Failure to obtain the full benefits of a deduction in any one year because of the at-risk limitation does not necessarily mean it is lost forever. The undeducted amounts carry over to future years and may be deducted when the taxpayer's at-risk amounts increase or the activity becomes profitable.

The 1976 act did not materially affect investments in real estate, though it did bring a few changes in the taxation of real estate. The capitalization and amortization of construction period interest and taxes, extension of five-year amortization for low income housing rehabilitation costs, and real estate depreciation recapture were the areas affected.

Because of the 1976 clampdown on the four activities listed above, other forms of investment (e.g., coal mining, books, master phonograph records) were structured to replace the lost tax shelters. But then the 1978 act extended the specific at-risk rule to *all* activities except real estate and repealed the partnership at-risk rule as redundant.

The repeal of the partnership at-risk rule provided an unexpected, if narrow, benefit to some corporate partners. Corporate partners (other than Subchapter S and personal holding companies) were exempted by the 1976 act from the at-risk rule on the four specified investment activities, but were made subject to the rule if their partnership invested in activities other than these four and real estate. The repeal of the partnership at-risk rule thus eliminated the at-risk rules for widely held corporations investing in partnerships.

The government's increasing concern over the tax shelter activities of closely held corporations that were neither Subchapter S nor personal holding companies (already subject to the at-risk provisions) led in the 1978 law to the extension of the at-risk rule to all corporations in which five or fewer individuals own more than 50% in value of the corporate stock at any time during the last half of a taxable year. Subchapter S corporations are still subject to the at-risk rule. Specifically excluded are closely held companies actively engaged in the leasing business—that is, those having at least 50% of gross receipts from the leasing and selling of tangible personal property (other than recordings, tapes, books, lithographs, etc.).

Accounting Basis for Form 10-K. Under the Securities Act of 1933, registration statements are filed with the SEC for the public sale of interests in limited partnerships formed in connection with activities involving tax shelter opportunities. Pursuant to Rule 15d-1 under the Securities Exchange Act of 1934, registrants are required to file an annual report on Form 10-K for the fiscal year in which a registration statement becomes effective and for each fiscal year thereafter, unless the registrant is exempt under Section 15(d) from such subsequent filings. (Many limited partnership registrants qualify for this exemption when the securities concerned are held by less than 300 persons at the beginning of the fiscal year.)

As previously noted in discussing publicly held partnerships, in ASR 162 the SEC mandated GAAP as the only acceptable basis for the presentation of a publicly held limited partnership's financial statements. However, financial data presented on a tax basis may still be necessary in footnotes or supporting schedules to provide disclosures regarding tax aspects of the investments. An example of such a footnote is as follows:

RECONCILIATION OF NET EARNINGS PER FINANCIAL STATEMENTS (ACCRUAL BASIS) TO TAX REPORTING (CASH BASIS)

The financial statements of the Partnership are prepared on the accrual basis of accounting whereas the partners are taxed individually on the cash basis of accounting. A reconciliation of net earnings on the accrual basis to the cash basis of accounting is as follows:

	Year ended December 31	
	1978	1977
Net earnings per financial statements (accrual basis)	$598,887	$393,748
Minimum lease payments received, net of income earned on leases accounted for under the financing method	40,778	30,918
Difference between expense accruals net of income accruals at beginning of year and end of year	11,626	156,365
Difference in losses for tax purposes on sale or reconveyance of properties	(23,282)	(51,835)
Depreciation for tax purposes in excess of that for financial statement purposes due to leases accounted for under the financing method	(367,834)	(242,299)
Taxable income to partners (cash basis)	$260,175	$286,897

ACCOUNTING BY INVESTORS FOR PARTNERSHIP INTERESTS

The accounting for an investment by one corporation in another corporation has received considerable attention in the accounting literature, whereas the treatment of a corporation's investment in a partnership has not been discussed nearly so extensively.

The investor's percentage of ownership is the principal determinant of the accounting method to be used. ARB 51 (AC 2051.02) states that consolidated financial statements are generally considered more meaningful when an entity has a controlling financial interest (more than 50% of the voting interest).

Ownership of 20% to 50% of an entity's common stock ordinarily presumes that the owner is able to exercise significant influence over that entity; and this, according to APB 18 (AC 5131), requires the use of the equity method of accounting. APB 18 also requires the use of the equity method for investments in corporate joint ventures. An AICPA interpretation, *Investments in Partnerships and Ventures* (AC U5131.012), generally recommends the equity method of accounting for investments in partnerships and unincorporated joint ventures, in accordance with the provisions of APB 18.

Many corporations have significant interests in publicly held partnerships or unincorporated joint ventures, particularly in real estate construction or oil and gas exploration. Original cost is not an acceptable method of accounting for such an investment, but three other basic methods are in use, as discussed below. Income accounting results for the investor are the same under all three methods, but individual financial statement amounts will vary significantly depending on which method is used. Full disclosure of the method applied is required.

Accounting Methods

The *equity method* requires that the investor record its share of the partnership income or loss, determined on a GAAP basis, for the period, and adjust the carrying value of its investment in the partnership. Any distribution of net income would also require the carrying value of the investment to be reduced. Deferred taxes for the investor's income tax purposes would be provided on income tax timing differences resulting from the use of non-GAAP accounting.

Under the *full consolidation method,* a partnership more than 50% owned is treated as a subsidiary. Other partners' interests in the partnership are presented in the consolidated financial statements as a minority interest.

The *proportional consolidation method* lies between the equity method and full consolidation method. Under this approach, the corporate investor reflects in its financial statements its pro rata share of the assets, liabilities, and operations of the partnership. This method differs from full consolidation in that no minority interest is presented in the financial statements. It is founded on the concept that all partners have an undivided interest in all assets and liabilities equal to their capital ratio.

The proportional consolidation method is used by investors to record their interest in partnerships and unincorporated ventures in certain industries, primarily oil and gas. This method is sanctioned by an interpretation to APB 18 (AC U5131.008-.012), which states that the equity method is generally appropriate in accounting for such investments, but that if "the investor-venturer owns an undivided interest in each asset and is proportionately [i.e., severally] liable for its share of each liability, the provisions of [AC] section 5131.19c [equity method] may not apply in some industries" and the proportionate consolidation method may be appropriate.

For a more thorough discussion of accounting by investors in partnerships and joint ventures, see Chapter 21. See also Chapter 31 for a further discussion of proportional consolidation.

SUGGESTED READING

Commerce Clearing House. "SEC vs. Geotek et al." *Federal Securities Law Reports, New Court Decisions,* 12/1/76, pp. 70719-70728. A detailed description of background of the case and final decision is given in this writeup.

Fischer, Paul; Taylor, William; and Leer, J. Arthur. *Advanced Accounting.* Cincinnati: South-Western Publishing Co., 1978. A review of the organization of a partnership and of changes occurring after organization is included in Chapters 13 and 14.

McKee, William; Nelson, William; and Whitmore, Robert. *Federal Taxation of Partnerships and Partners.* Boston: Warren, Gorham & Lamont, 1977. This is a two-volume service, updated by a looseleaf text focusing on the peculiar problems of a closely held corporation and its shareholders, for the generalist who must deal with a diversity of tax problems in the context of a much larger area of responsibility.

Meigs, Walter; Mosich, Andrew; and Larsen, E. John. *Modern Advanced Accounting.* 2nd edition. New York: McGraw Hill Book Company, 1979. Chapter 1 contains a discussion of partnership changes such as admission and withdrawal of partners, and the several alternatives in accounting for and valuation of such changes.

Orbach, Kenneth, and Strawser, Robert. "Public Disclosure Requirements for CPA Firms?" *CPA Journal,* February, 1979, pp. 15-21. The authors review several 1978 CPA firm reports and conclude that pressures on the profession may cause all firms, small and large, that have public clients to publish annual reports.

Palmer, Robert, publisher. "Peat Beats Coopers in Operating Statistics. How Does Your Firm Compare?" *Public Accounting Report.* Atlanta: Professional Publications, August, 1979, pp. 7-8. This privately circulated monthly newsletter reviewed the published financial statements of the five Big Eight firms that released such information for the 1978 fiscal year.

28

Related-Party Transactions

James I. Konkel
Thomas B. Wall

PERSPECTIVE

In 1973 the New York Stock Exchange (NYSE) released a "white paper" reaffirming its long-standing policy of "precluding the continuation of conflict-of-interest situations" and suggesting that such situations could be eliminated through a policy of disclosure. The exchange said (p. 10):

> A publicly owned company . . . should be free from any suspicion that can stem from transactions with insiders.
>
> Conflicts, when they occur, usually center on business transactions with affiliates or related parties, including officers or directors. Information about such conflicts is required in corporate proxy and 10-K reports. However, investors should have ready access to this information and the annual report would appear to provide the most appropriate vehicle for providing it.
>
> We believe that when such transactions or relationships exist, and are material, the circumstances—i.e., the nature and volume of transactions—should be described in the notes to the financial statements. Ideally, adequate disclosures will prompt the elimination of arrangements which might be interpreted as questionable, and we believe this to be in the interest of the investing public.

The NYSE used the terms *transactions with insiders* and *conflict of interest,* and those terms convey a general message of what this chapter is all about. Though there are many different terms used to describe such transactions and situations, and there are many different types, they are all generically referred to as *related-party transactions.* Their common characteristic is that one party (whether a person or an enterprise) is in a position to control the effect of a transaction or situation on another party; hence, a conflict of interest exists unless the two parties have identical beneficiaries.

For example, a parent company can control the results of its transactions with a wholly owned subsidiary. If consolidated financial statements are issued (assuming a consolidated income tax return and no other outside-party consequences), it is irrelevant whether transactions between the two companies meet any kind of objective standards. For purposes of all users of the financial statements the two companies are looked on as one.

But if there is a reason to issue separate financial statements of either party, questions quickly arise as to the objectivity of intercompany transactions. Even if special care is taken to base such transactions on verifiable external criteria, most users of the separate financial statements would, at the least, be justified in wondering whether the two companies could separately exist as is suggested by the appearance of separate reports. Of course, all these situations are a matter of degree, and very often the potential for concern is quite low (e.g., when a separately reporting subsidiary has no transactions with its holding company parent).

What has been described in the simple example above is the basic issue in presenting the financial statements of a *component of a business enterprise.* But the concept of controllability of the effect of transactions can also be seen in numerous similar situations, such as:

- An officer or director in relation to his responsibility to the company,
- A stockholder in relation to the company in which he owns stock, and
- A partner or joint venturer in relation to the partnership or venture.

Various kinds of related parties and transactions will be defined below. However, an initial review of the environment will be helpful in understanding why related-party transactions are such a hotly debated issue.

Nature of the Issues

The phrase *related-party transactions* emerged quite actively as part of the accounting scene during the mid-1970s, as the result of several highly publicized business frauds. Concealed relationships and hidden ownerships were used by corporate managements to facilitate deceptions of the auditor and the public, usually to produce artificially inflated earnings reports and stock values. Related-party transactions thus took on an odious flavor and have since frequently been perceived by reformers such as legislators and prosecutors as evils to be exposed (frequently by the use of extended audit techniques), laid bare by punitive disclosure requirements, and finally eradicated.

The existence of business dealings between persons or parties who bear some relationship or mutual economic interest is as old as commerce itself. Indeed, major segments of legitimate commerce are dependent on transactions between related parties. But the focus of attention has led to an unfortunate misapprehension about the role that related-party transactions play in commerce, because they provide circumstances susceptible to at least two kinds of abuses:

1. In the absence of proper identification and disclosure that relationships exist between parties to a business transaction, the hidden relationships can be used to obscure the "true" financial condition and results of operations of one or more of the related parties. Such abuses clearly occurred in certain of the major fraud cases of the 1970s.
2. The relationships may be used to improperly divert to one entity the economic benefit of a transaction from another entity to which it rightfully belongs. An example of such an abuse would be the sale of personally owned raw land by an officer of a corporate real estate developer to the corporate entity at unnaturally inflated prices.

Related-party transactions may be strongly criticized from time to time, but no one is seriously attempting to eradicate them. Underwriters may have done more than anyone else, including the SEC and the public accounting profession, to discourage these transactions in public companies. They have done this by withholding support of new securities issues until high-profile related-party transactions, whether abusive or not, were stopped or adequately disclosed. But only a few of the countless related-party transactions are abusive, and most inure to the benefit of society. They seem likely to increase in number and complexity as the economic environment grows more complex.

The obligation to preclude related-party abuses falls primarily on corporate management and directors. The auditor is expected to make reasonable inquiry to ascertain that all material relationships are identified and disclosed and that such relationships do not appear to have been used to violate fiduciary responsibilities.

The accounting profession and the FASB cannot, of course, prohibit any business operating method such as dealing with related parties—nor should they. They could effectively discourage it by making the accounting and disclosure requirements painfully onerous, but so far they properly have not done so. Indeed, no one has made a persuasive case that all related-party transactions ought to be prohibited.

In the understandable climate of public skepticism concerning related-party transactions, managements are well advised to establish definitive policies and procedures governing such transactions. The sensibilities of the public regarding business conduct should be carefully considered, even in proper pursuit of the shareholders' interests.

Government Action

The Watergate investigations of 1973-74 demonstrated a point of great interest to auditors. Though the investigators had unlimited powers of subpoena, unlimited financial resources, and no deadlines, they found it difficult and often impossible to disprove deceptive representations by high officials. Like the Watergate investigations, an audit is essentially a process of either supporting or disproving management's representations. An audit, however, operates under time pressures, financial limitations, and a total lack of subpoena power. Thus, when certain kinds of deceptive representations by management—known in the vernacular as "cooking the books"—escape exposure by the auditor, as can be arranged with a good deal of cleverness when all parties to a transaction are related, it seems hardly fair to blame the auditor.

Recognizing that a management lacking integrity can do a great deal to deceive the auditor, the SEC has supported legislation to prohibit such deception. In response to the SEC's efforts, and to the illegal payments and bribes brought to light by the post-Watergate investigations, Congress passed the Foreign Corrupt Practices Act of 1977 (the FCPA). This law requires publicly held companies to "make and keep books . . . which, in reasonable detail, accurately and fairly reflect the transactions and dispositions of the assets of the [company]." To promote compliance, the SEC adopted rules (Release 34-15570) effective March 23, 1979, that prohibit falsifying books and records of publicly held companies, making a false or misleading statement to the auditor, or omitting a statement of fact essential to the integrity of the financial statements. (See Chapter 13 for a further discussion of the FCPA.)

It is much too early to evaluate the effectiveness of these rules in forcing disclosure of previously concealed related-party transactions contrived by management, but the SEC's rules are at least a first step in providing some basis for argument by an auditor who becomes the victim of fraudulent management representations.

The SEC has never adopted any regulation that would actually ban related-party transactions. It has only required that transactions involving persons related to the management of a filing corporation be specifically disclosed to the commission and to public investors and has noted that the presence of transactions between affiliates should raise broader questions about the reliability and completeness of the information provided.

Other federal and state laws and regulations have, at various times, tried to curb abuses in transactions with related parties. One example is the federal prohibition of certain types of loans to stockholders and other affiliates of savings and loan associations and banks.

Definitions

Viewed from the perspective of the financial statements of an enterprise, a *related party* may be any of the following:

- Affiliates,
- Principal owners and close kin,
- Management and close kin,
- Parents and subsidiaries,
- Equity method investors and investees, or
- Any other party that has the ability to significantly influence the management or operating policies of the reporting enterprise, to the extent that it may be prevented from fully pursuing its own separate interests.

This listing is based on SAS 6, *Related Party Transactions* (AU 335.02), and its brevity belies the extensiveness of the possible relationships, as indicated in the broader definitions that follow.

Affiliates. An affiliate is a party that directly or indirectly, through one or more intermediaries, controls, is controlled by, or is under common control with a specified party; *control* means the possession, direct or indirect, of the power to direct or cause the direction of the management and policies of a specified party through ownership, by contract, or any other way (AU 335.02, fn. 2). These definitions, though appearing in SAS 6, are based on SEC definitions contained in Regulation S-X, Rule 1-02(b). This definition is quite obviously cloaked in "fuzzy" words, such as *direct or indirect* and *any other way*, prompting critics of related-party transactions to interpret the definition as "you'll know 'em when you see 'em."

Principal Owners. SAS 6 defines *principal owner* as the owner(s) of record or known beneficial owner(s) of more than 10% of the voting interests of the reporting enterprise (AU 335.02, fn. 3). This definition is also based on Regulation S-X, Rule 1-02, which contains the broader provision that determination is based on any class of equity securities, not only voting stock. At a minimum, this would encompass nonvoting convertible securities, where a determination should be made on an "if converted" basis.

By and large, this definition of principal owners also encompasses *promoters,* who are defined by Regulation S-X, Rule 1-02(r), as

(1) Any person who, acting alone or in conjunction with one or more other persons, directly or indirectly takes initiative in founding and organizing the business or enterprise of an issuer;

(2) Any person who, in connection with the founding and organizing of the business or enterprise of an issuer, directly or indirectly receives in consideration of services or property, or both services and property, 10 percent or more of any class of securities of the issuer or 10 percent or more of the proceeds from the sale of any class of securities. However, a person who receives such securities or proceeds either solely as underwriting commissions or solely in consideration of property shall not be deemed a promoter within the meaning of this paragraph if such person does not otherwise take part in founding and organizing the enterprise.

Two or more shareholders may be known or presumed to operate in concert through a voting trust or informally; it is often difficult to identify such situations in the absence of a representation asserting them. When these circumstances exist, the group may, in the aggregate, be a principal shareholder. If a group is able to control the policies of a company, it is considered a *control group.*

Management. Persons having responsibility for achieving the objectives of the organization, and the concomitant authority to establish the policies and make the decisions by which these objectives are to be pursued, are deemed to be management. This definition would normally include members of the board of directors, the president, secretary, treasurer, any vice president in charge of a principal business function (such as sales, administration, or finance), and any other person who performs similar policy-making functions (AU 335.02, fn. 3).

Close Kin. Members of the immediate families of principal owners and management are also to be considered, *ipso facto,* as related parties. This has long been recognized for income tax purposes and also shows up as part of SEC definition; for example, the definition *associate* in Regulation 14A, Rule 14a-1(3), includes

any relative or spouse of such person, or any relative of such spouse, who has the same home as such person or who is a director or officer of the issuer or any of its parents or subsidiaries.

As a practical matter, close kinships do not become an active audit concern unless circumstances or information become known that bring these relationships into question.

Parents and Subsidiaries. A parent company is one that controls a subsidiary directly, or indirectly through one or more intermediaries (based on Regulation S-X, Rule 1-02(o)). By inference, ARB 43, Chapter 1A, defines a parent as a company that "directly or indirectly has a controlling financial interest" in a subsidiary company (AC 2051.02), further defining *controlling financial interest* as "ownership of a majority voting interest," that is, "ownership by one company, directly or indirectly, of over fifty per cent of the outstanding voting shares of another company . . ." (AC 2051.03).

Equity Method Investors and Investees. Under APB 18 (discussed at length in Chapter 21), an investor who owns 20% or more or the voting stock in a company but not more than 50% is presumed, in the absence of evidence to the contrary, to have the ability to exercise a significant influence over that investee and should therefore use the equity method of accounting (AC 5131.17). Thus, a person or enterprise owning 20% to 50% of another company is deemed a related party of the investee company.

Significant influence is described (AC 5131.17) as

> . . . representation on the board of directors, participation in policy making processes, material intercompany transactions, interchange of managerial personnel, or technological dependency. Another important consideration is the extent of ownership by an investor in relation to the concentration of other shareholdings, but substantial or majority ownership of the voting stock of an investee by another investor does not necessarily preclude the ability to exercise significant influence by the investor.

The FASB has added to the above list in SFAS 13 (AC 4053.005(a)) guarantees of indebtedness, extensions of credit, ownership of warrants, debt obligations or other securities, and common officers or directors.

Other Parties. Significant influence can come from one party having a relationship with two or more otherwise separate transacting parties—that is, the transacting parties do not have a direct parent-subsidiary or investor-investee relationship. SAS 6 concerns itself with this relationship "to the extent that one or more of the transacting parties might be prevented from fully pursuing its own separate interests" (AU 335.02). A related party could also include, where this kind of constraint exists, one on which an enterprise is economically dependent, such as a sole or major customer, supplier, franchisor, franchisee, distributor, general agent, borrower, or lender (AU 335.05). *Economic dependence* in and of itself does not create a related-party situation, but *economic interdependence,* discussed as a transaction type below, may cause it.

SEC Definition. The SEC has not defined a related party in its own rules and regulations, but in 1980 it adopted the SAS 6 definition (ASR 280). The SEC's definition of affiliate already could have been interpreted quite broadly, since it recognizes the possession of indirect power in ways other than through ownership or by contract. Thus, it is reasonable to conclude that the narrower term *affiliate* has expanded to become synonymous with *related party.* That the SEC applies both terms broadly is demonstrated in ASR 173 (1975), in which the commission says that related-party transactions are not limited to any particular type of classification but can take an infinite number of forms.

It is, perhaps, salutary that the SEC has adopted parts of SAS 6, since this may give better guidance to preparers and auditors of financial statements than the practice sometimes used by the SEC of deciding on proper accounting for and disclosure of related-party transactions after the fact. Another benefit of the SEC's adoption of SAS 6 disclosures is that it has catalyzed AcSEC (at the time this *Handbook* went to press) into pushing the FASB to include these parts of SAS 6 in authoritative *accounting* literature, where they belong—not in SEC rules or in *auditing* literature.

Public Versus Private Companies

The SEC and some regulatory agencies have long required stringent accounting and disclosure standards for publicly held and otherwise-regulated companies (e.g., banks), but these standards have not been automatically applied in reporting on privately held companies. That different accounting standards might apply to privately held companies has also been acknowledged by the FASB. For example, in SFAS 21 (AC 2083), the FASB exempts those companies from the requirement to report earnings per share and segment information.

Should the auditing, accounting, and reporting on related-party transactions also be different for privately held companies? No authoritative pronouncement has yet addressed this question. As discussed in Chapter 4, a major complaint of smaller and/or closely held companies has been the propensity of SASs to be written in reaction to the problems of larger, public companies, and this is all somewhat true with respect to SAS 6. The SAS does not offer any exceptions to its applicability, and it can be easily argued that no conceptual basis exists in this area for a dual standard regarding large and small companies or privately held and publicly held companies.

Privately held companies may draw less attention for abuse of related-party transactions than do publicly held companies: related-party transactions are less likely to be questioned or attacked by shareholders or the general public in privately held companies. But privately held companies are often controlled by a few individuals, increasing the opportunities for such transactions. Thus, while readers may associate much of the discussion in this chapter with publicly held company situations, most is applicable to all companies and should be considered in the preparation, auditing, and review of financial statements.

RELATIONSHIP AND TRANSACTION TYPES

The preceding definition section might lead one to the conclusion that a related party is a chameleon; the same party can be defined variously depending on the relationship assumed in a specific situation. This is indeed so, and this chapter will not attempt to maintain any stringent distinctions between related parties, management, affiliates, or other terms of similar meaning.

The same may be true of attempts at specification of relationship and transaction types, because there are infinite gradations and overlaps. To provide a further focus, some broad generalizations may be useful.

Overt/Covert Distinction

Most related-party transactions are quite visible in relation to the financial statements of a reporting enterprise. Usually a parent-subsidiary relationship is obvious; or a material recorded transaction between an investor and equity method investee will at least become visible through inquiries. Management perquisites may be less observable, but for public companies the disclosure requirements are such that there is every likelihood the data will be complete. Further, the various SEC forms require information on remuneration of officers and directors, principal holders of equity securities, any material interest of management, directors and principal holders in the company's transactions, indebtedness of officers and directors to the company, and other similar items.

At the opposite end of the spectrum are the related-party transactions of notoriety—those that have been deliberately concealed, most often by collusion among the parties. Most cases involving management fraud have been based on concealed relationships, side deals, and gross misrepresentations of fact corroborated by coconspirators who were allegedly independent. It is these situations that lead regulators, who are representatives of the general public, into rhetoric clamoring for an absolute prohibition of related-party transactions. In reality all that they want outlawed are related-party transactions concealed with fraudulent intent—and indeed such transactions are; fraud is a crime. Keep in mind, however, that there is nothing *intrinsically* wrong with an above-board related-party transaction that is not specifically prohibited by law or regulation.

Relationships

The introductory section of this chapter discussed a variety of situations that by broad definition qualify as related-party relationships. Some of these relationships are easily identified. Others present greater challenge, either because they are difficult to distinguish from arm's-length dealings and other conventional business practices or because their nature makes them easily concealable.

Conflict of Interest. Webster defines the term *conflict of interest* as a conflict between private interests and the official responsibilities of a person in a position of trust. Today the term has a broader application, as if any interest not at arm's length were a conflict of interest. It need not be an actual conflict; the mere presence of the ability to bias a transaction is an adequate basis for describing it as a conflict relationship.

An illustrative situation would be ownership of a supply company by an officer or employee of another company that purchases its supplies from the supply company. Many companies have policies and internal controls that aim to identify such situations in order that the conflict-of-interest situation can be reviewed to ascertain that no special benefits resulted from it.

Of greater concern is an active conflict of interest in the form of bribes and kickbacks to officers, directors, stockholders, or employees. No record will exist on the payee side, since the payment will have gone directly to the individual. Thus, the likelihood of identification from that company's records is remote. The extent to which such payments are illegal is addressed in SAS 17, *Illegal Acts by Clients* (AU 328).

Though some reasonable chance of identification exists in the records of the company paying the bribe or kickback, note that a conflict-of-interest situation does not exist in that company, presuming the payoff was to obtain favorable treatment only for the company. If the paying company is publicly held, however, it may be in violation of the Foreign Corrupt Practices Act if such payments are not properly recorded. The SEC may interpret the act to require all bribery and kick-backs to be so recorded in the company records.

In order for a conflict of interest to exist, a related party must be in a position to exercise a significant influence. All the related parties listed under Definitions earlier in this chapter have such an ability to a greater or lesser degree.

Absence of Transactions. In some cases the relationship among the parties is such that the person or entity having a conflict of interest causes transactions *not* to occur. Typical examples of nontransactions are

- Loss of business opportunity. Where two or more businesses perform the same basic function under common management control, management has the choice of ascribing basically indistinguishable transactions to one company rather than another.
- Forebearances. A party does not foreclose on a defaulted debt or enforce a guarantee made by a related party of the debt of a third party.

Failure to enter into a transaction with a related party when the effects of that transaction rightfully or properly should inure to the related party can readily result in presenting a misleading picture in the financial statements of the related party. While a material transaction that did not occur cannot be recorded, disclosure of conditions under which this situation could occur, such as common ownership, may be necessary.

Components of a Business Enterprise. Components include identifiable segments, such as parent companies; majority-owned subsidiaries; divisions, branches, or other parts of a corporation; and brother-sister companies under common control. The status of a component as a member of a broader enterprise is in itself sufficient to deem it a related party, regardless of its apparent autonomy.

Authoritative literature pertaining to components other than the parent-subsidiary relationship is limited, and deals mostly with the exclusion of components from applicability of such authoritative pronouncements as those related to income taxes (AC 4091.05) and interest on receivables and payables (AC 4111.03). SFAS 14, *Financial Reporting for Segments of a Business Enterprise* (AC 2081), covers a narrower subject, though principles and concepts expressed therein may be useful in a consideration of component relationships.

A component may be economically dependent on its parent or another component for its continued existence, or a company in a controlled group may operate independently of its parent with respect to products and customers but still be wholly dependent on its parent for financing. Although this dependence might not distort the balance sheet, its disclosure is vital to suppliers and vendors who could suffer losses if the parent company were to stop financing the subsidiary. Disclosure of these relationships is required in the financial statements and may need to be emphasized in the auditor's report, as discussed later.

When the component is less intimately connected with the parent, simple disclosure of its controlled status should suffice.

Other Relationships. The composite definition of significant influence (from AC 5131.17 and 4053.005(a)) comprises several types of relationships that suggest an ability to exercise significant influence. These include

- *Technological dependency,* such as a royalty arrangement with an otherwise unrelated party, when such arrangement is essential to a company's operation;
- *Guarantees of indebtedness,* such as a guarantee of a debt of an otherwise unrelated company by one of its suppliers; and
- *Common officers and directors,* e.g., one director having significant influence on the boards of directors of two otherwise unrelated companies.

SAS 6 states that such parties should not be considered related parties unless one of them clearly exercises significant management or ownership influence over the other. However, technological dependency, guarantees, and commonality of officers and directors may need to be disclosed in order to present a party's financial position in conformity with generally accepted accounting principles (AU 335.05).

Transactions

Ordinary/Nonordinary Transactions. In this chapter related-party transactions fall into two categories—ordinary and nonordinary. The distinction is not official, but is made based on APB 30, *Reporting the Results of Operations* (AC 2012).

Related-party transactions made in the ordinary course of business are generally entered into because they offer some economic benefit to both parties involved, such as the retention of profits within the related group. For example, a petroleum refinery may sell gasoline and other products to a retail service station chain in which the refinery owns 50% of the stock, but it must do so at the same prices charged to all the refinery's other customers. These prices will also approximate those paid by the retail chain for products purchased from unrelated refiners.

Nonordinary related-party transactions may be made for the same reason—or they may not. Often, instead of economic benefit to the group as a whole, the reason is to benefit only one of the parties. For example, a sale of real estate or investment securities may be made to a related party at or near year-end to increase the earnings of one of the parties. Or operating properties may be leased from a related party, such as a stockholder, mainly to increase the stockholder's compensation or improve his tax position. The less ordinary a related-party transaction is, the more obscure the reason for it is likely to be. Sometimes, the auditor, the SEC, the IRS, and the stockholders all have their own theories about the reason for such a transaction, and none of them believes the reason given by management.

Suppose, for example, that an executive buys a jet airplane and leases it to a corporation he manages. The official reason for this arrangement is to benefit the corporation, perhaps by keeping the debt for the airplane off the books or by supplementing the corporation's already-strained borrowing capacity or by avoiding violation of a restrictive covenant in a debt agreement. Others may wonder, however, if the corporation benefits as much as the executive. Maybe he simply wants the "perk" of an airplane that the corporation does not need. Perhaps he will receive direct additional compensation by way of excess net rental income or indirect additional compensation by way of investment tax credits and depreciation deductions. This result will seem all the more likely if the corporation retains all the risks of ownership through guarantees and noncancelable lease terms.

Beneficial Transactions. Some related-party transactions may appear to improve the reporting company's financial position. In these cases, some executives may also benefit personally, perhaps because their bonus participation is based on corporate earnings or because they own or have an option to acquire stock that presumably rises in price when the improvement is reported. This is to be expected: good performance should result in proper rewards. Even when the transaction is of benefit to the reporting company exclusively, primarily, or mutually, the transaction must be disclosed if material.

Related-party transactions are often used to obtain real benefits for the company through tax savings. Tax laws tend, more than accounting conventions, to follow the legal form of transactions, thus affording some opportunity to structure transactions that will produce tax savings. The use of foreign affiliates, for example, is a popular means of minimizing taxes; and the government encourages the use of domestic international sales corporations, which have a tax rate advantage.

Another example may be seen in a principal owner's contribution of stock to a charity as of year-end, followed early in the next year by purchase of the stock from the charity by the corporation for its treasury. In legal form these two transactions are a personal contribution of securities and a purchase of treasury stock. Assuming, however, that the tax benefits are achieved by the stockholder, these transactions in substance may be some or all of a cash dividend to the stockholder, a contribution to the corporation's capital by the stockholder, or a cash contribution by the corporation to the charity.

Interdependent and Reciprocal Transactions. In some situations two or more companies may engage reciprocally in material transactions. These relationships may arise out of an economic interdependence of the two parties or may be simply a means of exaggerating recorded worth on financial statements of both parties. For example, "if you'll buy my three cats, I'll buy your two dogs."

By a strict interpretation of SAS 6, the reciprocal buy/sell transaction can be considered a related-party transaction. When the parties have a history of reciprocal transactions, the auditor must decide whether a particular transaction, represented to be complete, is actually linked to prior or prospective buy/sell transactions. Where such reciprocal transactions are in substance nonmonetary exchanges, APB 29, *Accounting for Nonmonetary Transactions* (AC 1041), offers appropriate guidance. Usually, they do not culminate in an earning process (AC 1041.21).

Accommodations. One party may participate in a transaction as an accommodation for another, sometimes receiving a fee or commission for the service. Such direct compensation is not always apparent, but in practice it is advisable to assume the existence of a quid pro quo. Accommodations can look very real on paper, but their usual substance is commonly summed up in such descriptors as *swap, sham, parking, laundering,* and *straw man.* The party being accommodated usually conceals the transaction. The need to record fee income makes concealment by the accommodator less likely.

Executive Compensation and Perquisites. Yachts, private jet airplanes, and hunting lodges are examples of items in the perquisite category. Although these transactions may have economic benefit to a recipient, they are usually a bigger boost to the person's ego than to his income. The SEC has issued a release pertaining to disclosure in proxy statements of the personal benefits accruing to officers and directors from use of company assets (Release 33-6003). The broader issue —whether these assets were acquired for an essential business purpose—has received little scrutiny.

A conflict of interest may exist in transactions covering the compensation and expense reimbursements of management. Ordinarily, sufficient controls can be established to assure arm's-lengthness (for example, approval of significant salaries by the board of directors and review of expense reimbursements by management at a level senior to that being considered) and thus eliminate such transactions from the related-party category. But difficult questions arise when the management personnel basically sets its own compensation or other monetary rewards (for example, by domination of the board of directors).

No-Charge Transactions. Especially in situations involving a component of a business enterprise, a related component—often the parent company—may provide products or perform valuable services without charge. In theory, the going price for (or perhaps the performer's cost of) the product or service should be imputed in the benefiting company's statements and the opposite effect imputed in the providing company's statements. Most often, however, only disclosure of the situation is provided.

QUALITATIVE CHARACTERISTICS

Form Versus Substance

Many related-party transactions have form/substance problems because substance depends so much on the intentions of the parties and it is most difficult to probe those intentions when the parties are not at arm's length.

Legal Form. Related-party transactions can be described by their legal form, such as profit-sharing plan, stock bonus, or other fringe benefit; a purchase or sale of products or services or of property, securities, or receivables; a lease; a loan; a sale and leaseback; or a financing service, guarantee of debt, maintenance of a compensating balance, and so on. They can also be described by their economic substance, which may be different from their legal form. For example, what is legally a lease may in economic reality be a purchase; a sale in legal form may in economic reality be a borrowing. Just what the economic substance of a transaction is may also be subjective and controversial. To identify it usually depends on understanding the reasons for the transaction.

The *Report of the Study Group on Objectives of Financial Statements* (AICPA, 1973j) has this important comment on the question of substance:

The substantive economic characteristics, not the legal or technical form, should establish the accounting for transactions and other events. For example, this subordination of legal formality may affect the accounting for transactions between affiliated or related parties. [p. 57]

SFAC 2, *Qualitative Characteristics of Accounting Information,* subsumes *substance over form* into the qualities of reliability (AC 1220.059) and representational faithfulness (AC 1220.063). SFAC 2 says (AC 1220.160):

> Substance over form is an idea that . . . is not included because it would be redundant. The quality of reliability and, in particular, of representational faithfulness leaves no room for accounting representations that subordinate substance to form. Substance over form is, in any case, a rather vague idea that defies precise definition.

Accounting Qualities. The accountant's basic concern is to achieve fair presentation in the financial statements. The information given in the statements cannot be fairly presented unless it reflects the substance and not just the form of the transactions underlying the information. Unless notified to the contrary, the reader normally assumes that the economic activity of an entity is a result of transactions with nonrelated parties. In fact, it is a fundamental assumption that financial statements represent the results of arm's-length transactions between independent parties influenced by normal market conditions. Even when related-party transactions are fully disclosed, therefore, they may cast some doubt on the financial statements; when these transactions are material or their purpose is questionable, users may well doubt both the existence and the amounts of the economic activity presented in the statements.

In addition to the need to recognize substance as mentioned above, financial statements need the following matters considered.

Freedom from bias. To be useful, financial statements must be free of bias. The *Report of the Study Group on Objectives of Financial Statements* (AICPA, 1973j) reported that absence of bias, which may be characterized as neutrality and fairness, has long been recognized in accounting.

In SFAC 2, these qualities are included under the broad heading of *reliability*— the faithfulness with which a measure represents what it purports to represent (AC 1220.059). Further:

> Bias in measurement is the tendency of a measure to fall more often on one side than the other of what it represents instead of being equally likely to fall on either side. Bias in accounting measures means a tendency to be consistently too high or too low. [AC 1220.077]
>
> Accounting information may not represent faithfully what it purports to represent because it has one or both of two kinds of bias. The measurement method may be biased, so that the resulting measurement fails to represent what it purports to represent. Alternatively, or additionally, the measurer, through lack of skill or lack of integrity, or both, may misapply the measurement method chosen. In other words, there may be bias, not necessarily intended, on the part of the measurer. [AC 1220.078] . . .
>
> Accounting information cannot avoid affecting behavior, nor should it. If it were otherwise, the information would be valueless—by definition, irrelevant—and the effort to produce it would be futile. It is, above all, the predetermination of a desired result, and the consequential selection of information to induce that result, that is the negation of neutrality in accounting. To be neutral, accounting information must report economic activity as faithfully as possible, without coloring the image it communicates

for the purpose of influencing behavior in *some particular direction.* [AC 1220.100; emphasis in original]

Related-party transactions, by their very nature, cannot be free of bias. They present an obvious problem of measurement, and further difficulties in deciding on the extent of adequate disclosure.

Verifiability. The verifiability of financial statements is the duplicability of their results from a given set of assumptions or facts by independent means using the same measurements (AC 1024.18). This definition is repeated in SFAC 2 (AC 1220.082). Information that is unverifiable and, therefore, unauditable generally justifies less confidence. With many related-party transactions there may be no independent means of measurement, and so their verifiability is difficult at best.

Business Purpose. Practice has identified a number of related-party transactions in which the business purpose or economic substance called for different accounting from that suggested by the legal form of the transaction.

Third-party benefit. A third party with management influence over both of the transacting parties is discovered to be the beneficiary of the transaction. Examples of this kind of transaction have involved executives of reporting companies who also own all or a portion of other companies that transact with the reporting company. Additional compensation or contribution to capital seems to be involved here, but the appropriate accounting to follow in such cases is not settled in practice.

Accommodation and sham transactions. These transactions were mentioned above, under Accommodations. If an accommodation or sham can be identified, the accounting to follow is usually apparent.

Structured leases. Month-to-month leases of major facilities from related parties have been used to avoid capitalization. Also, leases have been structured between related parties to avoid capitalization; for example, where lease terms result in a present value of minimum lease payments equal to 89.9% of the fair value of leased property, rather than 90%, which would require capitalization. Unfortunately SFAS 13 (AC 4053.029) condones this kind of structuring.

Artificial pricing. For income tax or other reasons, two related entities may deal with each other at prices that cannot be supported in terms of economic substance. To change the accounting to acknowledge the artificial pricing often defeats the purpose of the transaction. The appropriate accounting to follow in such cases is not settled in practice. SAS 6 (AU 335) does not speak to the issue, and segment reporting under SFAS 14 specifically requires use of the prices charged without qualification (AC 2081.023).

Materiality

Materiality is a term connoting economic significance. Although the concept is essential to the preparation of financial statements, it is a highly subjective form of measurement, depending as much on the preparers' and auditors' viewpoints as it does on current practice and the facts of the specific situation. Although authoritative bodies address the issue of materiality from time to time, the only official concepts that have been produced are contained in SFAC 2 (AC 1220.123-.132), summed up as follows:

> The magnitude of an omission or misstatement of accounting information that, in the light of surrounding circumstances, makes it probable that the judgment of a reasonable person relying on the information would have been changed or influenced by the omission or misstatement. [AC 1220.171]

Authoritative Guidance. Authoritative literature generally does not discuss the materiality of related-party transactions. Disclosure of material related-party transactions is required (AU 335.17), and an auditor's opinion may need to be modified to an extent, depending on materiality, if satisfaction is not obtained regarding management representations on the equivalence issue (AU 335.18). But materiality itself is not defined for these contexts.

The SEC has offered a general definition of materiality by stating that publicly held companies may limit their disclosure of information "to those matters about which an average prudent investor ought reasonably to be informed" (Regulation S-X, Rule 1-02(n)). This definition is nearly a tautology, however, and does not extend specifically to related-party transactions.

Regulation S-K, Item 4, describes materiality in relation to nonfinancial disclosures of transactions with management:

> The materiality of any interest or transaction is to be determined on the basis of the significance of the information to investors in light of all of the circumstances of the particular case. The importance of the interest to the person having the interest, the relationship of the parties to the transaction to each other and the amount involved in the transaction are among the factors to be considered in determining the significance of the information to investors.

The SEC extended its definition of materiality to include managerial integrity in a 1964 decision, *In re Franchard Corp.* (Fed. Sec. L. Rep. ¶ 77,113). This position was underscored during later investigations in which the SEC enforcement staff stated that the size of disclosed illegal payments was irrelevant in comparison to the potential damage done to investors by doubts about the integrity of management.

Quantitative Materiality. In the absence of standards or workable guidelines, current practice occasionally provides some small assistance. In some areas of accounting and reporting, materiality is pegged to a given minimum percentage. For example, in reporting on dilution in earnings per share, any reduction of less than 3% can be ignored (AC 2011.14, fn. 4). On the other hand, a business combination will fail to qualify for pooling-of-interests accounting if more than 10% of the stock of a combining company is acquired in exchange for consideration other than common stock (AC 1091.47). About ten years ago, when considering materiality in relation to the need for a consistency exception, a range of 10% to 20% was considered material. Today that percentage would likely be much lower.

For related-party transactions, even a 3% test of materiality may be unsatisfactory. Authoritative literature does not support such a generalization, but the SEC has sometimes applied more rigid criteria for materiality than the 3% test. For example, amounts that would change an upward trend in earnings to a downward trend, even if less than 3% of earnings, might be considered material. The same has been true when a questionable or illegal payment is being measured for purposes of disclosure. The SEC has also been observed to allow items of more than 3% to be considered immaterial, e.g., the 10% test permitted in the definition of a significant subsidiary (Regulation S-X, Rule 1-02(v)). Because abuses have made related-party transactions suspect, a prudent course to follow until standards are established would be to use a more rigid standard of materiality for disclosure and auditing and reporting of such transactions.

Qualitative Materiality. Materiality does not depend entirely on relative size: the concept involves qualitative as well as quantitative judgments. The qualitative characteristics of materiality are discussed further in Chapter 3, but an example related to the components area can be seen in SAS 21, *Segment Information* (AU 435), issued in 1977. The SEC, in ASR 236 (1977), also on segment information, adopts the SAS 21 comments on materiality and states that a company should take into account such qualitative factors as the significance of the matter to the company (e.g., whether a matter with a relatively minor impact on the company's business is represented by management to be important to its future profitability), the pervasiveness of the matter (e.g., whether it affects or may affect numerous items in the segment information) and the impact of the matter (e.g., whether it distorts the trends reflected in the segment information). When qualitative materiality significantly alters the apparent immateriality of a matter, the pertinent information must be disclosed.

Equivalence

When the goods or services rendered in a related-party transaction are commonplace or easily replicated, the standard of equivalency may be met without difficulty because the values can easily be determined in a nonrelated environment. But when the goods or services are more nearly unique, comparisons to transactions in an arm's-length environment become more difficult and the recording will therefore be more subjective and less verifiable.

Equivalence is a problem primarily with regard to transactions beyond the normal course of business. It asks, essentially, whether the related-party transaction would have taken place had the parties not been related and, if so, what the terms and manner of settlement would have been in the equivalent arm's-length transaction. The AICPA, the SEC, and auditors have divergent views on how to deal with the question.

Authoritative Guidance. The only authoritative direct reference to equivalence is the SAS 6 warning that, except for routine transactions, it is generally impossible to judge whether an arm's-length transaction could have taken place or what the terms and manner of settlement would have been (AU 335.18). The statement concludes that if the financial statement includes a representation to the effect that terms are no less favorable than terms for an unrelated party and the auditor cannot find any substantiation for that remark, the auditor should consider including a comment to that effect in his report, along with a qualified opinion or disclaimer. If the auditor believes that the representation is misleading, he should give a qualified or adverse opinion, depending on materiality.

SAS 6 does not describe audit procedures for resolving the equivalence issue, leading some auditors to conclude that no judgment on the issue is required. Such an interpretation would seem at variance with the expectations of the SEC. In ASR 227 the commission contended that the auditors had failed to conduct sufficient tests to establish the value of an inventory repurchase between related parties. In ASR 241 it pointed out that a footnote failed to disclose that charges for management fees by a related company bore no necessary relationship to the value of the services provided, the auditor having determined previously that such charges were practically impossible to verify.

Nonequivalent Transactions. SAS 6 (AU 335) does not discuss cases known to be nonequivalent. Common examples of these include

• Administrative services without charge,
• Guarantee of debt without charge,
• Agreement with third parties to support the operations of a related company or to maintain that company's income at specified levels through product purchases or otherwise, usually without charge,
• Income tax concessions, such as payment for use of investment tax credits that the related party is unable to use or failure to charge a component its share of consolidated income taxes, and
• Cash advances with nominal or no interest charges.

In these situations the state of the art is unsettled. The transaction itself is often disclosed as a related-party transaction, but the disclosure seldom deals with the lack of equivalence and the auditor seldom modifies his report with respect to this nonequivalence. In fact, some related-party transactions do not have any arm's-length equivalent.

AUDITING CONSIDERATIONS

In this chapter the usual sequence—accounting before auditing—is reversed, because the challenge of identifying and evaluating transactions that may be related-party transactions is necessary before the proper accounting or disclosure can be determined. If a suspected material transaction turns out not to be with a related party, the accounting treatment will then be something other than indicated later in this chapter.

Audit Approach

The guidance given in SAS 6 (AU 335) regarding identifying, auditing, and reporting on related-party transactions should serve as a sound basis for the audit approach. Because the procedures set out are not all-inclusive (AU 335.01), auditors should consider whether additional procedures are necessary.

For example, SAS 6 advises auditors that if they do not fully understand a particular transaction they should consider confirming the amount, terms, guarantees, and other significant data with the other party (AU 335.15). One might add that the auditor ought also to be alert for any further written agreements or oral understandings that might modify the terms outlined in the agreements and documents at hand.

Of course, if both related parties intend to deceive the auditor, no confirmation, regardless of what points are covered, is likely to produce reliable information on which he can base his opinion. Therefore, a confirmation reply from a related party is in some cases more akin to a representation by management than to an outside confirmation.

Preliminary Evaluations. At the outset of the audit the auditor should evaluate the extent of known relationships and related-party transactions to decide whether his client is an auditable entity. An auditability assessment requires cautious judgment; it cannot simply be assumed. Related-party involvements may be too pervasive or nonsubstantive to allow a valid audit. Inevitably, the auditor will need to weigh the integrity of management. The Commission on Auditors' Responsibilities pointed out in their *Report, Conclusions, and Recommendations* (1978): "... when management is untrustworthy, there is a significant chance that a valid independent audit cannot be performed" (p. 38). "Chance" seems a rather soft choice of words; seasoned auditors would substitute "probability."

Since related-party involvements can present significant problems, the auditor must consider whether he is capable of taking special action to resolve these problems. He may conclude, for example, that uncertainties can be diminished to an acceptable level by audit procedures designed to provide sufficient audit evidence for that purpose. (A number of Accounting Series Releases suggest, however, that sufficient procedural safeguards have not yet been found.)

Should the auditor conclude that he will proceed, a number of further preliminary evaluations are called for. These are summarized in SAS 6 and include an examination of management responsibilities and the relationship and business purpose of each component; an evaluation of internal control over management's activities; and an examination of other factors (AU 335.10). If the client still appears trustworthy and auditable, the auditor must then determine the scope of the audit and choose appropriate procedures for identifying and auditing the related-party transactions.

Identifying Related-Party Situations

SAS 6 gives audit procedures for determining the existence of related parties (AU 335.12) and for identifying transactions with those related parties (AU 335.13). However, these procedures may not uncover every situation the auditor wishes to examine. Because of the relative informality with which related parties can make agreements, the ensuing transactions may be poorly recorded or even overlooked by management. Worse, they may be deliberately concealed. The auditor will at some point need to draw on his own practical experience and judgment in deciding how to proceed.

Concealment of related-party relationships and transactions has resulted in several lawsuits against auditors, alleging that an auditor is expected to be consummately thorough in his attempt to identify concealed related-party transactions or management involvement that has a material effect on the financial statements. Though the procedures in the auditor's power cannot guarantee the discovery of all concealed management involvement, the auditor must not resign himself to nondiscovery for that reason. SAS 6 recognizes that an examination made in accordance with GAAS cannot be expected to ensure that all related-party transactions will be discovered; thus the SAS develops an *awareness* responsibility for the auditor and sets forth specific procedures for related-party transactions.

Conducive economic factors (AU 335.11) that often lead to the concealment of related-party transactions are listed in Figure 12.2. Figure 28.1 summarizes SAS 6 procedures for identifying related parties and transactions with them. Comments on certain of these procedures follow.

Deliberate Concealment. Attempts to deliberately conceal relationships or transactions with related parties will influence, if not change, the auditing, accounting, and possibly the disclosures. Deliberate concealment, which may be fraud if done with an intent to mislead, may also affect the auditor-client relationship, for the auditor must now decide whether to continue his professional relationship with the company.

The auditor's legal counsel should be consulted in concealment situations. Auditor-client relationships can be continued despite the concealment *if* the client takes satisfactory action, such as firing the involved officials or transferring them to less sensitive positions. For an auditor to expect such actions is compatible with measures taken by the SEC. For example, the SEC has said that officers involved in fraud or concealment could not serve as chief executive or chief financial officers of SEC-reporting companies, at least for a period of time.

DETERMINING EXISTENCE

1. Evaluate the company's procedures for identifying and properly accounting for related-party transactions.

2. Inquire of appropriate management personnel as to the names of all related parties and whether there were any transactions with these parties during the period.

3. Review filings with the SEC and other regulatory agencies for the names of related parties and for other businesses in which officers and directors occupy directorship or management positions.

4. Determine the names of all pension and other trusts established for the benefit of employees and the names of the officers and trustees thereof.

5. Review stockholder listings of closely held companies to identify principal stockholders.

FIGURE 28.1 PROCEDURES FOR IDENTIFYING RELATED PARTIES AND TRANSACTIONS WITH THEM
SOURCE: AU 335.12-.13.

6. Review prior years' audit working papers for the names of known related parties.

7. Inquire of predecessor, principal, or other auditors of related entities as to their knowledge of existing relationships and the extent of management involvement in material transactions.

8. Review material investment transactions during the period under examination to determine whether the nature and extent of investments during the period created related parties.

IDENTIFYING TRANSACTIONS

1. Provide audit personnel performing segments of the examination or examining and reporting separately on the accounts of related components of the reporting entity with the names of known related parties so that they may become aware of transactions with such parties during their examination.

2. Review the minutes of meetings of the board of directors and executive or operating committees for information as to material transactions authorized or discussed at their meetings.

3. Review proxy and other material filed with the SEC and comparable data filed with other regulatory agencies for information as to material transactions with related parties.

4. Review conflict-of-interest statements obtained by the company from its management. (Conflict-of-interest statements are intended to provide the board of directors with information as to the existence or nonexistence of relationships between the reporting persons and parties with whom the company transacts business.)

5. Review the extent and nature of business transacted with major customers, suppliers, borrowers, and lenders for indications of previously undisclosed relationships.

6. Consider whether transactions are occurring but not being given accounting recognition, such as receiving or providing accounting, management, or other services at no charge or a major stockholder absorbing corporate expenses.

7. Review accounting records for large, unusual, or nonrecurring transactions or balances, paying particular attention to transactions recognized at or near the end of the reporting period.

8. Review confirmations of compensating balance arrangements for indications that balances are or were maintained for or by related parties.

9. Review invoices from law firms that have performed regular or special services for the company for indications of the existence of related parties or related-party transactions.

10. Review confirmations of loans receivable and payable for indications of guarantees. When guarantees are indicated, determine their nature and the relationships, if any, of the guarantors to the reporting entity.

FIGURE 28.1 CONT'D

Information Normally in Auditor's Files. In continuing engagements, the auditor's permanent files, audit programs, the preceding year's working papers, and (if he is auditing a recently accepted publicly held client) his documentation of new client investigation as required by the rules of the AICPA SEC Practice Section may contain applicable information. To the extent they do, the matter should be extracted for the current year's audit working papers, to ensure appropriate consideration. The existence in the past of nonrecurring material related-party transactions may, in some instances, be indicative of current opportunities or propensities.

With respect to new clients, the auditor will be amassing his information foundation, and thus, apart from the predecessor auditor's working papers (discussed below), there may not be a great deal of prior information to review. However, if the client is publicly held there may be a substantial amount of information gathered as part of the new-client investigation procedure.

In a majority of situations, audit clients engage the services of the audit firm's tax personnel to prepare, or advise in connection with the preparation of, income tax returns. Also, client executives often engage the audit firm's tax department to prepare their income tax returns. Accordingly, a direct inquiry should be made of the partner responsible for tax services to the client and its executives (or other tax personnel he designates as being knowledgeable with respect thereto) as to whether they have found any evidence (not already known) concerning material related-party transactions. Recognizing that tax return preparation almost invariably postdates the audit completion, tax personnel should be asked to bring to the audit partner's attention relevant information arising after completion of the audit. This interchange of information is permitted under IRS Reg. § 7216.

If the audit firm also provides management consulting services to the client, the partner responsible for such services (or others he designates as being knowledgeable with respect to those consulting engagements) should be asked whether, during the course of the consulting engagement, any information came to their attention concerning material related-party transactions that may not already be known to the auditor.

Information Available From External Sources. It is a recognized audit procedure that minutes of meetings of the board of directors and its important committees be reviewed. In performing this review, the auditor should be alert to indications of material related-party transactions.

If the company has recently had a first SEC registration (or a registration has recently occurred after several years during which no registrations were filed) the company's counsel (special SEC counsel, if engaged) will have performed a circularization of management for purposes of disclosures that had to be made in the registration statement. Where these circumstances exist, the auditor should obtain, with the authorization of his client, access to the counsel's circularization files.

Also, recurring registration statements, proxy statements, stock exchange listing applications, and the nonfinancial portions of Forms 10-K, 10-Q, and 8-K may contain information concerning related-party transactions. It is generally understood that the auditor reviews the complete text of all such documents sometime during the course of the audit engagement. There may be instances, however, where voluminous exhibits accompany some of these filings. Accordingly, the auditor should consider whether there is a need to peruse the exhibits.

A rather obvious source of external information is represented by trade news-paper and magazine articles about the client. Occasionally, such publicity will describe operating practices or innovations that may point to possible related-party transactions.

Timing of Material Transactions. Material transactions entered into at or near year-end or quarter-end are often designed to bolster the earnings of the company. The auditor should pay special attention to any transactions timed toward the end of a reporting period, questioning whether there is related-party involvement, as might be suggested by transactions closed in haste or documentary material that may have been backdated.

In a business involving a large volume of small transactions, the auditor expects to see a relatively level, seasonally adjusted transaction volume. In instances where the business comprises a small number of large transactions, it may be credible that the closing of transactions clusters near year-end or quarter-end. However, such circumstances require more thorough audit certainty to establish the appropriateness of the timing of transactions—certainly a problem not unique to related-party transactions.

It may also be determined by the auditor that documentation was executed subsequent to the period-end but intended by the parties to be effective as of the period-end. In these cases, legal advice may be required as to whether the transaction is binding on (thus legally impacting on the assets and liabilities of) the company on the "as of" date. Enforceable agreements in principle or oral agreements are sometimes considered acceptable, pending "completion of the paper work."

Conflict-of-Interest Programs. If a client has a policy of performing a circularization of its management group for conflicts of interest, the auditor should review the results.

Many major corporations have such procedures, but it is relatively uncommon in small organizations. In those instances where it is used, the auditor is often engaged to receive the completed questionnaires and decide which should be brought to the attention of the designated committee or individual in the client's organization. When the auditor is involved in the client's circularization program, he may be aware of possible related-party transactions from screening of the answers. A major drawback of such a program is that it does not, of course, have any means of ensuring that the respondents answer truthfully. Further, such questionnaires are not likely to cover all related parties as defined earlier (e.g., principal stockholders).

Management Representations. Where the auditor assesses that conditions exist that afford the opportunity for related-party involvement in a material transaction, he should obtain specific representations from the persons so situated that (if such is the case) they have no direct or indirect involvement in the transaction. Further, such a letter might well repeat representations made to the auditor concerning the identity of the parties to the transaction, the purpose of the transaction (if not evident), and its terms.

Management personnel could, of course, have personal reasons for diverting further inquiries if they should be asked to provide specific representations concerning a material transaction. However, the mere fact that representations are not satisfactory evidence per se in such situations does not eliminate their usefulness as a starting point and as documentation of what the auditor was told.

There may be significant client relations problems created if the auditor indiscriminately adopts an "affidavit" of sorts, even on a fairly limited basis. For example, it would be rare that the auditor would ask for representation from individual family members of the management individual; where there is a concern of this nature, he would ordinarily have the management party express such representation for his family members.

Oral representations as to the absence of related-party transactions should be acceptable only if the auditor is fully satisfied with his other audit procedures.

Consultation With Company Attorneys. The auditor may find consultation with company legal counsel useful in identifying related parties. In theory, at least, legal counsel of the client should be the auditor's staunchest ally. Both should have as their objective the rendering of financial statements of a quality that will keep the mutual client out of difficulty—both operating difficulty and legal difficulty. In a few cases, however, some attorneys have supported their client against the auditor in accounting for and disclosure of related-party transactions lacking substance. Auditors often need to rely on the expertise of legal counsel in related-party matters; that such reliance may have been misplaced in certain situations is, of course, unfortunate.

The responsibilities of the auditor and those of the attorney can also conflict. An attorney might state that the existence of material related-party transactions represents a contingency on which he does not wish to report because of possible breach of the attorney-client privilege. Should the auditor be informed that the attorney is aware of material related-party transactions concerning which he will give no further information, he must impose on the client to cause the attorney to identify the relationships and transactions and to describe the circumstances. The auditor should assume as a matter of course that an attorney's refusal to discuss an acknowledged transaction is indicative of the attorney's serious concern. (See Chapter 29 for a discussion of attorneys' letters.)

In at least two instances the disciplinary arm of the SEC has taken a position that the auditor must substantiate legal counsel's opinion regarding the date of a transaction (ASRs 173 and 241). Authoritative auditing literature has not supported this position. However, the prudent auditor should have his own counsel study a legal opinion on which his client has based the accounting for and disclosure of a material related-party transaction when there is some question about the persuasiveness of the legal opinion.

Change of Auditors. Clients sometimes change auditors because of disagreements over the treatment of related-party transactions. A change of auditors where nonordinary related-party transactions are prevalent can indicate unauditable or nonsubstantive related-party transactions. Strong disagreements will be made public if they come within SEC regulations (ASR 165) and requirements of the SEC Practice Section of the AICPA. But the issue may never come to light if it never reaches the disagreement stage (as defined by the SEC) or does not involve a publicly held company. For this reason, a succeeding auditor in an environment of material and complex related-party transactions should attempt to determine any disagreements through consultation with the previous auditor (see SAS 7; AU 315).

Examining Related-Party Transactions

Once he has determined that some kind of related-party transaction has taken place, the auditor's next concern is a practical one. He must judge whether the transaction will make enough of a difference on the client's financial statement to merit the time and attention of detailed audit procedures. Closely intertwined with this question of materiality is the determination of economic substance. (The *qualitative* characteristics of materiality and substance were described earlier in this chapter.) The auditor looks at the bare economic facts of the transaction and asks, What kind of agreement was this—a sale, a lease, a fair exchange of assets, or perhaps something else? When assessed for economic substance, a transaction often turns out to be something quite different from what it seems to be on paper, as discussed further below.

To help determine substance, the auditor can try to compare the available facts to what they would have been in an equivalent transaction between nonrelated parties. For obvious reasons, the nature of the related-party relationship itself often invalidates the comparison. Nevertheless, the concept of equivalence (discussed further in the accounting section below) can be a useful guide in helping the auditor determine the proper method of accounting for a transaction. It can also cue the auditor to the possibility that his client has not recorded certain facts that may need to be disclosed in the financial statement.

Figure 28.2 identifies SAS 6 procedures for examining related-party transactions, separated into basic procedures (those to be considered as normal) and extended (those to be considered when necessary to fully understand a particular transaction). Note that SAS 6 (AU 335.14-.15) does not *mandate* these procedures—it suggests them. In particular AU 335.15 points out that the extended procedures are not normally called for by GAAS and that advance arrangements may need to be made with the client.

Challenging Substance. There are no assured methods for determining the substance of a related-party transaction. Not only do informed practitioners disagree among themselves on the substance of a given transaction, but the auditor can find himself in complete disagreement with management on the question of substance. Present auditing standards require auditors to obtain certain written representations from management (AU 333.01). Ordinarily, these would include information concerning related-party transactions and related amounts receivable or payable (AU 333.04(e)). Of course, the auditor cannot rely solely on these representations but must also perform whatever inquiries, confirmations, and other procedures are appropriate under the circumstances. All too often, however, there is not much conclusive evidence available about the intentions of the parties.

Thus a considerable burden is placed on the auditor seeking to determine a transaction's substance by the flexibility and informality inherent in the related-party relationship. The pricing and terms of related-party transactions are readily changeable under circumstances that seldom arise in arm's-length dealings. Sometimes a related-party agreement that seems to convey the substance of a transaction is quickly revised or revoked when an auditor points out that it would produce

NORMAL

1. Obtain an understanding of the business purpose of the transaction. (Until the auditor understands the business sense of material transactions, he cannot complete his examination.) If he lacks sufficient specialized knowledge to understand a particular transaction, he should consult with persons who do have the requisite knowledge.

2. Examine invoices, executed copies of agreements, contracts, and other pertinent documents, such as receiving reports and shipping documents.

3. Determine whether the transaction has been approved by the board of directors or other appropriate officials.

4. Test for reasonableness the compilation of amounts to be disclosed, or considered for disclosure, in the financial statements.

5. Arrange for the audits of intercompany account balances to be performed as of concurrent dates, even if the fiscal years differ, and for the examination of specified, important, and representative related-party transactions by the auditors for each of the parties, with an appropriate exchange of relevant information.

6. Inspect or confirm and obtain satisfaction as to the transferability and value of collateral.

EXTENDED

1. Confirm transaction amount and terms, including guarantees and other significant data, with the other party or parties to the transaction.

2. Inspect evidence in possession of the other party or parties to the transaction.

3. Confirm or discuss significant information with intermediaries, such as banks, guarantors, agents, or attorneys, to obtain a better understanding of the transaction.

4. Refer to financial publications, trade journals, credit agencies, and other information sources when there is reason to believe that unfamiliar customers, suppliers, or other business enterprises with which material amounts of business have been transacted may lack substance.

5. With respect to material uncollected balances, guarantees, and other obligations, obtain information as to the financial capability of the other party or parties to the transaction. Such information may be obtained from audited financial statements, unaudited financial statements, income tax returns, and reports issued by regulatory agencies, taxing authorities, financial publications, or credit agencies. The auditor should decide on the degree of assurance required and the extent to which available information provides such assurance.

FIGURE 28.2   PROCEDURES FOR EXAMINING RELATED-PARTY TRANSACTIONS
SOURCE: AU 335.14-.15.

undesired financial results or reporting requirements. Such an abrupt about-face makes it doubtful that the planned transaction has an auditable substance. Clearly, such an arrangement is only tentative though not initially represented as such.

Also, transactions that would otherwise require extensive description of terms and conditions are often reduced to a page or two when the contracting parties are related. Simple agreements covering complex related-party transactions may be appropriate in some circumstances, but auditors should always consider the need for extended audit effort to ascertain substance in such cases.

When an auditor has doubts about the substance of a related-party transaction or about management's representations regarding it, he is expected to modify his report accordingly (AU 335.18). Note, however, that present-day literature is misleading on this subject. To (1) assume that management's representation is truthful (AU 333.03 and AU 327.12) and (2) consider transactions with related parties to be within the ordinary course of business (AU 335.11) are both acceptable practices as long as the audit reveals no evidence to the contrary. But these GAAS assumptions have not been fully accepted by the SEC, which has maintained in disciplinary proceedings against auditors that reliance on management representations was obviously unacceptable in situations where those representations later turned out to be false.

The SEC has thus underscored the auditor's need to understand the economic substance of related-party transactions. Present auditing practice for public companies generally aims toward the attitudes of the SEC in maintaining more skepticism about management representations concerning material related-party transactions than might be considered necessary under SAS 6 (AU 335) and SAS 19 (AU 333).

Audit of All Parties. When related parties are dealing among themselves, the auditor should try to audit, or at least review, the records of all the parties. Authoritative literature does not address the problems of an auditor engaged for only one or a few of the entities involved. Yet some managements controlling several companies make it a policy to engage a different auditor for each company. Since an auditor in that position has a reduced chance of understanding any related-party transactions, such a policy should warn him of the possibility that transactions may not be what they appear.

Suppose, for example, that the company under audit makes a material cash advance to another company whose accounts are not audited. How the other company uses the money will be impossible to determine. An executive could represent that the advance was for working capital when in fact he used it to cover margin calls on his own commodities trading. Even if the auditor reviewed, but did not audit, the accounts of the other company, the true use of the money could be obscured through a series of nonsubstantive transactions called *laundering*.

This example illustrates the point that in situations where material transactions occur with related companies or parties that are not audited, the auditor should recognize that he may be confronted with an "unauditable entity." This may be true even if the related company is audited by another firm. Depending on his analysis of the situation, he can try to persuade the client to use only one audit firm for all related parties, or he can insist on reviewing the work of the other auditors in accordance with AU 543.12-.13. If the client refuses, the auditor must decide whether he can obtain sufficient evidence through review and inquiry procedures. He may even decide to resign if he concludes that a single entity in such a situation is an unauditable entity.

The situation is exacerbated when material transactions involve individuals such as stockholders or officers, for the financial affairs of individuals are seldom subject to audit or open to review and the other side of a transaction may forever remain obscured from the auditor.

Approval by Directors. It is common practice that a known material related-party transaction is a subject of resolution at the board of directors level. Of course, discovery of concealed management involvement is unlikely to gain board approval, but rather precipitate some other action by the board or its representatives.

It is also a common audit procedure that an auditor having doubts about whether a company's business purpose has been furthered, or at least not hampered, by a material related-party transaction obtains the board of directors' approval of such transaction. The auditor might encounter some reluctance from directors who are not accustomed to taking such positions; a discussion with the company's legal counsel as to the nature of the auditor's concern may be helpful so that legal counsel could then advise the board as to the need for approval. In any event, where the auditor believes such approval is required and it is not forthcoming, he will have to consider the material transaction as unauthorized, and therefore unacceptable, for financial reporting purposes.

Care must be taken not to demand the board of directors' attention to insignificant items—for example, a question concerning the amplitude of an executive's expense allowance that in and of itself is not a material figure in the financial statements. (Such matters, of course, may be brought to the attention of the appropriate levels of management, including the board, but the auditor should not insist on formal resolution except in cases that have a material impact on the financial statements.)

In some organizations the board of directors may substantially or completely comprise officers of the company. Thus, approval of a material transaction in which there was management involvement may not really be substantive. In the case of publicly held companies there will at least be some number of outside directors. In major publicly held companies there will be a substantial proportion of outside directors, who will clearly bring a strong measure of independence to the board. If the company is a NYSE company, it will have an all-outsider audit committee that can be responsive in these situations.

If a related-party transaction occurs in a segment of a larger entity, it will often be more appropriate to ask for approval of the board of directors of the parent company.

Confirmation of Material Transactions. Material transactions and balances (especially those suspected of being, or known to be, related-party transactions) should be considered for confirmation with the other parties to the transactions. The inquiry should specify the documents involved in the transaction and ask whether there are any other documents or understandings. Admittedly, such a procedure is unlikely to detect deliberately collusive practices between the parties to a transaction, but it could disclose a "side deal" or perhaps a guarantee by a member of management, thus making the transaction acceptable to an independent party.

In some cases, components for example, the auditor knows in advance that a balance confirmed by a component would rarely constitute independent evidence. When the confirmation would be sent to a component of the entity and the auditor is auditing both components, he may be able to obtain the needed information by direct reference to the component's records. When the auditor is the principal auditor but does not audit the component, he usually has the right to look into the component's records and may want to do so (AU 543.13).

It is important to keep in mind that there may be industry practices (such as a small group of buyers and sellers) that defeat successful confirmation efforts.

Equivalence. Though the SEC and plaintiffs against auditors would assert otherwise, it is not possible to determine whether a transaction would have taken place if the parties had not been related; usually, what the terms would have been in an arm's-length transaction cannot be determined either (AU 335.18). Therefore, when considering equivalence the auditor is often concerned with finding the substance of a transaction rather than disclosing arm's-length equivalence in the financial statements. For example, an auditor may obtain independent appraisals of the fair value of the property or services involved in a transaction. Such appraisals establish neither an arm's-length price nor whether the transaction would have taken place, but they help to indicate whether the transaction differs in substance from an arm's-length exchange.

Some material transactions with related-party involvement can easily be compared with arm's-length transactions—for example, the sale of readily marketable securities. However, equivalence should be judged in the light of all relevant circumstances, since seemingly minor differences can have a major effect on terms and conditions.

The auditor should ask the client whether a comparison has been made and what the results were. Although generally the auditor is not required to make a comparison when the company has not done so, he may decide that a significant portion of the evidence he requires in connection with the transaction can only be provided by making or attempting such comparison. In those situations, he will pursue the matter.

Further, because disclosure of a material transaction in which there is related-party involvement will usually be required or otherwise may be given in the client's financial statements, management may wish to state therein that (if a comparison were feasible) the terms of the transaction were substantially equivalent (or were not substantially equivalent and the reasons therefor) to what would have been arrived at as a result of arm's-length negotiation between independent parties. If the client does not make such a representation in the financial statements, the auditor must be satisfied that the comparison, if it were actually made by the client, resulted in a conclusion of substantial equivalence; in any event, the auditor must not otherwise hold the opinion that substantial equivalence does not exist where a comparison was not made even though it may have been feasible.

ACCOUNTING CONSIDERATIONS

For the most part, the accounting treatments to be given to related-party transactions are the same as those for unrelated parties. SAS 6 states (AU 335.06):

Until such time as applicable accounting principles are established by appropriate authoritative bodies, the auditor should view related party transactions within the framework of existing pronouncements, placing primary emphasis on the adequacy of disclosure of the existence of such transactions and their significance in the financial statements of the reporting entity. He should be aware that the substance of a particular transaction could be significantly different from its form.

These comments may be interpreted as saying that accounting for related-party transactions should follow the accounting appropriate for the same type of transactions occurring between unrelated interests, provided the substance is not significantly different from the form. However, the SEC has on occasion required deferral of profit or carryover of seller's cost in related-party transactions brought to its attention for preclearance. ASRs involving proceedings against auditors have often taken a similar position—but after the fact.

Related-Party Sales and Purchases

Of all the issues pertaining to related-party transactions, perhaps the most crucial are those involving sales and purchases between the parties. Since authoritative literature is limited, custom and usage must serve as a guide.

For purposes of illustration, assume a situation in which a sale of real property is made to a related party and the auditor is satisfied that it is not a sham or fraudulent transaction and that it meets the tests of the industry guide for profit recognition on sales of real estate as discussed in Chapter 18. The key issues are discussed below.

Price Structure. Setting a sale or transfer price is not the function of financial accounting; the contracting parties are expected to arrive at the price. (Of course, accounting requirements have been influential in determining transfer prices.) If profit cannot be recognized for accounting purposes, or valuations in excess of seller cost cannot be recorded by the buyer, cost rather than fair value is often used. But when fair value is the price intended to be used, the parties must try to determine what the fair value would be in an equivalent arm's-length relationship.

Minority Interests. The presence of a minority or public interest in either of the related parties raises questions about the fair and equitable treatment of those other interests. To the extent that public or minority interests are not identical in each entity in a related-party transaction, a sale at any price other than fair value will either be a disadvantage or an advantage to those interests.

Profit Recognition/Deferral. Neither professional literature nor Regulation S-X prohibits the recognition of profit in sales transactions between related parties. Profits have been recognized historically, but the deferral of profit recognition seems to have gained considerably during the last five years.

Full deferral, or elimination, of profit is followed when the reporting entity owns a majority interest in the purchasing or selling entity. But proportionate elimination would seem acceptable under the equity method of accounting for non-subsidiaries (AC U5131.005-.007).

In practice, profits have been both recognized and deferred when the parties are related but neither owns a portion of the other. There is no authoritative guidance for choosing between full or partial profit recognition or profit deferral in these situations, although it is clear that profit is not to be recognized in sham or fraudulent transactions.

Where the sale price is at fair value and the seller is not justified in recording a profit, the selling entity also might consider the profit as a contribution to capital. This accounting is most often confined to situations in which the buyer has direct ownership interest in the seller.

Asset Valuation. On the buyer's side, when fair value is used for the price, at least three methods of asset accounting have been observed in practice. In some instances the acquired property has been recorded at the price paid. In other instances the difference between the seller's cost and the price paid has been accounted for as (1) a so-called *dangling debit,* deducted from the total of stockholders' equity, or (2) a constructive dividend. Constructive dividend accounting seems to be confined to situations in which the buyer has a direct ownership interest in the seller.

Authoritative guidelines do not exist that would aid in arriving at uniform accounting solutions for either the buyer or seller in such situations. Thus a variety of solutions might occur in practice for similar related-party transactions.

Accounting After the Transaction. If the seller appropriately recognized profit and the buyer appropriately recorded the purchased asset at his cost, these amounts are simply carried over into subsequent periods. Otherwise, further accounting may be necessary.

Consider a situation in which the seller has sold at fair value and deferred the profit or credited contributed capital and the buyer has accounted for the difference between his own purchase price and the seller's historical cost as a constructive dividend or as a dangling debit. Deferred income and the dangling debit will presumably be adjusted at resale or some other time. But accounts probably will not be adjusted for an item carried as a contribution to capital or a constructive dividend.

A further complication will arise if the buyer and seller record differently. For example, the buyer may record the purchased property at the price paid while the seller credits contribution to capital. Or the buyer may charge a constructive dividend while the seller defers income. Either way, one party may have subsequent gain or loss while the other will not.

Resales. If property is sold at seller's cost that is less than fair value, the buyer may realize a profit upon subsequent sale. This happens occasionally in practice— and sometimes is even planned, perhaps to bolster sagging earnings by buying appreciated property from a related party at less than fair value and then selling it to an unrelated party. Is profit recognition by the middleman appropriate, or does it belong to the initial seller? If the middleman can recognize profit, is a minimum holding period required? Or can a company buy property from a related party one day at that party's cost and sell it at a fair value and record a sizable gain the next day? These and other questions on subsequent accounting remain unanswered, and the accounting treatment used should best attempt to reflect the substance of the series of transactions.

Stock Issuances

Transactions involving issuance of stock (or other ownership interests) in exchange for nonmonetary assets or services are numerous and often involve material amounts. The question of the appropriate accounting to follow is pertinent to both the company involved and to the stockholder or owner. APB 29, *Accounting for Nonmonetary Transactions* (AC 1041), gives some guidance on certain transactions with stockholders and owners, but consideration of accounting for stock issuance transactions was deferred at the time (1973) APB 29 was issued and has yet to be concluded.

Some accountants would prefer to record the received assets or services at their fair value, thereby permitting the owner to record profit to the extent that there are outside interests. For example, a sale of real estate at its fair value of $200,000 less a cost basis of $100,000 would result in a $60,000 profit recognition by a 40% owner-seller. The more common practice, and the one required by the SEC, is to record such transactions in the receiving company at the owner-seller's cost. The latter practice is indirectly supported by SOP 78-9, *Accounting for Investments in Real Estate Ventures,* which says that the owner should not recognize profit on a transaction that is in economic substance a contribution to capital of an entity. However, he may recognize profit if the transaction looks like a contribution but is a sale in economic substance.

DISCLOSURE

Some managements seem generally reluctant to disclose related-party transactions, though the degree of reluctance is somewhat dependent on the nature of parties to the transaction. Some accountants intuitively follow the belief that the stronger the objection of management to disclosure, the greater the need for disclosure—though this is perhaps too categorical an approach.

An important 1970 release, APB Statement 4, observes that non-arm's-length transactions are commonly disclosed (AC 1027.26). SAS 1 contained, until 1980, the comment that the generally accepted accounting practice was to contemplate disclosure of the existence of affiliated or controlling interests and the nature and volume of transactions with such interests, but this language was removed by SAS 32 (AU 430). ARB 43 contains a few references (AC 5111.01 and AC 2031.04) to required disclosure of receivables from officers and other minor matters. By consolidating these few disclosure matters and considering the SEC's attitudes as evidenced in ASRs sanctioning public accounting firms, SAS 6 sets the stage for greater uniformity in disclosure of related-party transactions. The FASB so far has not dealt comprehensively with the subject; its only specific requirement is the disclosure of the nature and extent of related-party leases (AC 4053.029).

SAS 6 Requirements

The effect of SAS 6 disclosure requirements has been a gradual improvement in disclosures. SAS 6 (AU 335.17) requires financial statement disclosure of the following in material related-party situations:

1. The nature of the relationship(s);

2. A description of the transactions (summarized when appropriate) for the period reported on, including amounts, if any, and such other information as is deemed necessary to an understanding of the effects on the financial statements;

3. The dollar volume of transactions and the effects of any change in the method of establishing terms from that used in the preceding period; and

4. Amounts due from or to related parties and, if not otherwise apparent, the terms and manner of settlement.

The noticeable increase in disclosure of related-party transactions may be occurring because managements as well as accountants have been increasingly sensitized by the continued appearance of this problem in ASRs, by changes in SEC proxy disclosure rules, and by the current environment, in which the concept of qualitative materiality seems prominent. Despite the continuing progress, a number of issues remain unresolved, as discussed below.

Profit or Loss Disclosure. SAS 6 makes no provision for disclosure of profit or loss to the selling related party. In practice, the profit or loss is often disclosed by the seller, but this information is infrequently disclosed in the financial statements of the buying related party. It would seem that such information is equally important to the users of both sets of financial statements.

The SEC requires disclosure of profit or loss. If, however, this cannot be determined without unreasonable effort or expense, an estimate or explanation is acceptable (Regulation S-X, Rule 3-16).

Duration of Disclosure. When balance sheet amounts of the purchasing party include capitalized profits of the selling party, the amount of profit may have been disclosed by the purchaser in the year of purchase, as noted above. Continuing disclosure would seem to depend on the general principle of making the financial statement meaningful. In practice, however, an initial disclosure is typically abandoned in subsequent years.

Recognizing Substance. SAS 6 places emphasis on disclosure of transactions between related parties (AU 335.16-.18). When such transactions have been recorded in the accounting records by form that differs materially from substance, the transactions must be restated in the financial statements to comply with GAAP, and the profit or loss effect must be deferred until the involved asset has either been sold to an unrelated party or otherwise consumed. Often the fact that the substance differs from form should be disclosed even where the substance has been reflected in the financial statements.

There may be occasions when disclosure is not enough even if the profit has been deferred; the auditor may need to address the matter in his report. Guidelines are needed for these situations.

Equivalence. SAS 6 cautions against representing the terms of a transaction to be no less favorable than those that would have been obtained from an unrelated interest (AU 335.18). This position is understandable, inasmuch as it is generally impossible to determine whether the transaction would have taken place at all had the parties not been related or, assuming that it had taken place, what the terms and manner of settlement would have been.

However, the frequent practice of remaining silent on the issue may not be supportable. The users of the financial statements may find lack of disclosure hampers their understanding.

It is interesting to note that information submitted by a chief executive officer to the Council on Wage and Price Stability under the voluntary wage and price control program adopted in 1978 is to be accompanied by a statement from that officer that transfer prices between divisions, subsidiaries, and profit centers treated as a separate company have been valued as if they were arm's-length transactions. Although this requirement does not pertain to financial statements, it may presage a federal government attitude that silence on the equivalence issue is unacceptable. Should this position extend to other areas of reporting, including financial statements, auditors may be placed in a position of having either to support such management representations or to cover the matter in their report.

Components of a Business Enterprise

One of the most frequent types of related-party disclosures is that occurring between entities bound together by complete or partial ownership—either ownership of one entity by another or ownership of the entities by a third party. Such transactions as those between a subsidiary and its parent, between two companies under common control, or between a company and its shareholders all fall into this category. As the following subsections indicate, the need for additional disclosure guidelines is apparent.

Component Disclosure. Disclosures required in separate financial statements of a component generally should closely follow SAS 6 disclosure requirements for related-party transactions. Some additional disclosures for components have been seen in practice, primarily because of the interdependence of the component. Such additional disclosures often include (1) the basis of intercompany transactions; (2) the dollar effect of any significant change in the basis of pricing intercompany transactions; and (3) any material amount of unrealized intercompany profit remaining in inventories or in property, plant, and equipment.

Where the intercomponent relationships are significant, disclosures may flow from one component to another. For example, a contingent liability or a major lawsuit against one component may have to be disclosed in the separate statements of another related component; or use of proceeds of a significant intercompany advance for extraordinary purposes (e.g., loan to an officer) may have to be disclosed in the statements of the component making the initial advance.

When going concern problems of one component are alleviated by the parent's or another component's guarantee of debt, the separate statements of the component should disclose all relevant terms of the guarantee. A firm, legally enforceable guarantee usually is necessary to satisfy the auditor that a going concern qualification in his report is unnecessary.

Nothing is inherent in a component that requires an exception to the standard audit report. An unqualified opinion should be appropriate on a component statement, provided intercomponent transactions are "not unreasonable." However, if intercomponent transactions have been recorded at unreasonable prices, some auditors believe that the auditor's report should describe the circumstances in an intermediate paragraph and that a qualified or adverse opinion should be expressed.

Transfer Pricing. A problem can result from arbitrary product pricing between components, as might occur in attempts to both comply with and avoid foreign currency transfer restrictions or to minimize income taxes in countries having very high tax rates. ASR 236, *Industry Segment Reporting,* issued in 1977, called for disclosure and discussion of intersegment and intraenterprise sales, transfers, or purchases when (1) transactions were made at prices substantially higher or lower than prevailing market prices for similar products or services to unaffiliated entities and (2) the effect of such pricing practice on the segment was quantitatively or qualitatively material to an understanding of the enterprise as a whole. This SEC requirement ran only to the text of filings with the SEC, not to the financial statements. Because SFAS 14 (AC 2081.023) does not require such extensive disclosures regarding transfer pricing, the SEC dropped these extra requirements in September, 1980, but still generally asks for disclosure of segment matters that are qualitatively material (Regulation S-K, Item 1(b)(1)).

SAS 21, *Segment Information* (AU 435), is confined to intersegment information and avoids the broader concept of component information. Because it is aimed at SFAS 14, it has little guidance for auditing in accordance with the implied requirements of ASR 236. It requires the auditor only to (1) ask for the bases of accounting for sales or transfers and (2) test to see if the sales or transfers conform to those bases (AU 435.07(b)). No testing is required for equivalence (or prevailing market prices to unaffiliated entities).

AUDITOR'S REPORT

The standard report without qualification may be the norm where related-party transactions are involved; however, the modifications discussed in this section occur with varying degrees of frequency.

Emphasis of a Matter

SAS 2 offers general guidance on issuing various types of reports (AU 509), but it does not deal with related-party transactions, except for making an explanatory intermediate paragraph available to emphasize a matter regarding the financial statements without the necessity of qualifying the opinion. For example, an auditor may use such an intermediate paragraph to point out that the entity reported on is a component of a larger business enterprise or that it has had significant transactions with related parties (AU 509.27). In practice, the use of an intermediate paragraph to add emphasis is common, but by no means preponderant. When it appears, it is usually innocuous, such as:

As more fully described in Note 1, the Company is a wholly owned subsidiary of ABC Company and purchases receivables from and conducts certain other business transactions with its parent.

The notes would, of course, contain the information required by SAS 6 (AU 335.17).

Qualified Opinion

An auditor's report may sometimes need to be qualified with regard to related-party transactions (e.g., if there is a material uncertainty regarding the collectibility of receivables from related parties). Other qualifications can stem from such items as the carrying amount of investments in joint ventures and other investee companies and the related equity in earnings or loss of the investee companies, which at times may be unaudited. Less common are qualifications regarding the validity of related-party transactions and the validity of management's representations. When uncertainties are this grave, the auditor will more likely furnish a disclaimer of opinion, render an adverse opinion, or even resign from the audit.

There is a considerable need for guidelines to help the auditor cope with such uncertainties. Some accountants believe that pervasive qualifications are really tantamount in the reader's eyes to a disclaimer of opinion and that the all-inclusive disclaimer is therefore preferable. Other accountants insist that since a disclaimer of opinion "tells no one anything," it is better to furnish an opinion on the whole and note that inaccuracies or errors may exist because certain related-party aspects, internal control aspects, or management representations could not be audited.

Disclaimer

A disclaimer of opinion in connection with related-party matters can be offered for numerous reasons, but nearly always stems from problems so grave that an intermediate paragraph explanation or a qualification in the auditor's report would not convey the impact on the financial statements as a whole. Most disclaimers of opinion in related-party situations probably are issued because the auditor could not perform sufficient work to permit him to form an opinion (AU 509.46), but, as suggested above, they are sometimes prompted by cases involving broad uncertainties (AU 509.25 and AU 335.18). For example, if a representation as to equivalence is included in the financial statements and the auditor is unable to reach a conclusion as to the propriety thereof, he should, if the matter is material, include in his report a comment to that effect and express a qualified opinion or a disclaimer of opinion.

Whether the disclaimer is said to result from uncertainties or from insufficient audit work is often a distinction without a real difference. In cases involving material amounts, when the auditor is unable to understand the economic substance of a related-party transaction, he may have arrived at a point where a disclaimer of opinion is his own proper response. That lack of understanding may be phrased in terms of audit scope (lack of competent evidential matter); in terms of an uncertainty about the effect on the financial statements (recovery of investments in a related party); or in terms of an inability to reach a conclusion (the transaction simply does not make sense, even though revenue has been realized and audit scope seems to have been sufficient).

A disclaimer of opinion thus may be appropriate when the auditor is uncertain about the substance of a transaction. Should he be certain that the substance of a material transaction has not received proper accounting treatment, a disclaimer would be inappropriate—an adverse opinion is called for.

Adverse Opinion

An auditor should express an adverse opinion, depending on materiality, when he believes that a representation pertaining to equivalence is misleading (AU 335.18). Further guidance is not given in SAS 6 regarding the use of adverse opinions in relation to related-party transactions; hence the general rules of usage of that type of opinion would seem to apply.

An adverse opinion would be used in a circumstance in which disclosures of material related-party transactions are inadequate or are omitted altogether or where their legal form rather than economic substance is accounted for in the financial statements.

SUGGESTED READING

AICPA. *Illustrations of the Disclosure of Related Party Transactions.* Financial Report Survey 8. New York, 1975. Though it predates SAS 6, this practice aid of the AICPA furnishes still-useful illustrations of the extent and type of related-party disclosures.

Benke, Ralph, and Edwards, James Don. *Transfer Pricing: Techniques and Uses.* New York: National Association of Accountants, 1980. This study was based on information on transfer pricing practices determined by surveying large U.S. companies, along with a survey of current literature. The authors arrive at the general rule that transfer price should equal standard variable cost plus lost contribution margin. The book is helpful to accountants in illustrating the wide variety of approaches in use and their ramifications in the taxation area.

Mason, Alister. *Related Party Transactions.* Toronto: Canadian Institute of Chartered Accountants, 1980. The author uses a research study to gather information concerning measurement and disclosure criteria in the related-party area and summarizes current requirements, with emphasis on transfer pricing. Effective audit techniques are also discussed.

29

Uncertainties

Ronald A. Berman

UNCERTAINTIES IN BUSINESS

Final results do not necessarily match original expectations. Uncertain outcomes clearly apply to economics, and that fact should be understood in reading reports on economic activities. Accounting is called the language of business, and various aspects of accounting are discussed throughout this *Handbook*. Auditing adds reliability to that accounting information and is therefore linked to the *Handbook's* accounting discussions. Thus, it is inevitable that uncertainties are brought up in numerous other chapters; this chapter tells how to understand accounting and auditing uncertainties.

Uncertainty was postulated by APB 4. The APB also noted that certain elements of economic dealings reduce uncertainty, i.e., those that provide continuity and stability:

> The framework of law, custom, and traditional patterns of action provides a significant degree of stability to many aspects of the economic environment. In a society in which property rights are protected, contracts fulfilled, debts paid, and credit banking and transfer operations efficiently performed, the degree of uncertainty is reduced and the predictability of the outcome of many types of economic activities is correspondingly increased. [AC 1023.16(2)]

Types of Uncertainties

Changing Social Values. In business, changing social values have tended to reduce the value of property rights versus the rights of society as a whole. Thus, contracts are more frequently broken, as exemplified by

1. The Westinghouse refusal to perform under what it deemed oppressive uranium delivery contracts when uranium market prices increased dramatically.
2. Foreign government nationalization, seizure, or nonnegotiated price increases.
3. An increasing number of businesses seeking the protection of the courts against their creditors or the assistance of the federal government in financing.

Remote Uncertainties. Benjamin Franklin said that nothing in the world is certain but death and taxes. However, for a business enterprise, not even death and taxes are certain. Corporate entities do not necessarily have the limited lives of individuals. The financial accounting framework includes a basic feature called the *going concern* concept, which assumes more or less indefinite continuation of operations in the absence of intention or evidence to the contrary. Still, abrupt cessation caused by major and remote uncertainties does threaten the existence of many going concerns, as was dramatized by the nuclear "accident" at Three Mile Island.

Tax Liabilities. The IRS's aggressive interpretation of the Internal Revenue Code and the regulations (see Chapter 43) has made it clear that no taxpayer can determine tax liability with precision. The IRS challenges, interprets, and changes tax liability through an active program of examinations. Although payment of taxes may be certain for a profitable enterprise, the amount due is usually not certain for a long time.

Macroeconomic Matters. SFAC 1 recognizes that "the outcome of economic activity in a dynamic economy is uncertain and results from combinations of many factors" (AC 1210.20). Events beyond the control of the enterprise that affect the world and economy as a whole create uncertainties about the future environment in which the enterprise will operate. Such macroeconomic matters include outbreak of war, an oil embargo, inflation, recession, high interest rates, tight credit, the unavailability of capital funds, and a myriad of other events.

Industry Uncertainties. Every enterprise is also subject to uncertain future events that may affect only it or its industry. Inventory may be rendered worthless or worth less by a new product that operates more effectively and less expensively, e.g., electronic calculators and digital watches. Other major business uncertainties may include litigation and governmental regulation. And although a business may be very successful, its nature or management structure may be severely affected if key management personnel leave unexpectedly.

Controlling Uncertainty

An enterprise usually has some control over routine uncertainties. For example, collectibility of receivables cannot be a concern if there are no credit sales. If credit sales are made, the enterprise can control its type of customer, such as selecting only AAA-rated companies, in an effort to limit bad-debt losses. An enterprise that wants to minimize the chance of interruption in fuel or other supplies can arrange for alternate sources of supply.

Business is concerned with profits, however, and minimizing risks and uncertainties is not always good business policy and will not necessarily maximize profits.

Implications for Financial Accounting and Reporting

Financial accounting and reporting attempt to interpret economic operating events such as sales, production, purchasing, and collections. Some operating events are quite easy to account for because the transaction is completed in a short time and has few uncertainties. For example, a purchase and sale for cash, all in one day, is easily measurable and does not require estimates. But most operating events are not so clear-cut. As a result, two of the basic features of financial accounting listed in APB 4 are approximation and judgment (AC 1022.17). Financial statements prepared under GAAP must reflect many factors. As the operations of an enterprise become more complex, the need to make estimates increases. The present accounting model permits only a single-valued approach to the presentation of a probabilistic reality, so the alternative of presenting a range of measurements reflecting alternate possible outcomes rather than a single point estimate does not exist. Uncertainties therefore must be dealt with by footnote or other supplemental disclosure rather than by direct incorporation into financial statements.

FINANCIAL ACCOUNTING AND REPORTING

Definitions

Three overlapping terms frequently used in this chapter are uncertainty, contingency, and estimate.

1. An *uncertainty* is any matter that may affect the financial statements or the disclosures required therein whose outcome is not susceptible of reasonable estimation (AU 509.22).
2. A *contingency* is an existing condition, situation, or set of circumstances involving uncertainty that will ultimately be resolved when future events occur or fail to occur (AC 4311.01).
3. An *estimate* is a nonexact measurement used to assign an amount to the effects of business transactions and events (AC 1022.27). "Estimates resting on expectations of the future are often needed, but their major use, especially of those formally incorporated in financial statements, is to measure financial effects of past transactions or events or the present status of an asset or liability" (AC 1210.21).

Thus, uncertainties include all contingencies and some estimates. A contingency is always an uncertainty, but some uncertainties are not narrowly defined as contingencies (e.g., general business risks). An estimate made of a future outcome is an uncertainty, but an estimate made to approximate amounts that could be determined nearly exactly if inordinate effort were expended is not an uncertainty.

Objectives

To be consistent with the overall objectives of financial accounting and reporting, information on uncertainties reported in financial statements should be useful to the reader who is considering making, retaining, or disposing of an equity investment in or a loan to an enterprise. Thus, for uncertainties that probably will have a material effect on financial position or results of operations, an estimate of the effect of the uncertainty should be recorded in the current financial statements, or in cases where reasonable estimates cannot be made, their existence should be disclosed.

When estimates are routine, such as expected future warranty costs for normal adjustment to a product, current operations are charged based on prior experience (factual data), and details could confuse rather than enlighten the reader. However, when management is not able to reasonably estimate the effect of a material uncertainty, it may be more useful to disclose the circumstances—and perhaps the inapplicability of past experience or other factual data. This might be the case, for example, when an unusual lawsuit is brought against an enterprise. With proper disclosure the user of the financial statements can then factor the potential effect into his own perception of financial condition and prospects and, depending on his purpose, decide on the extent, if any, to which the uncertainty should affect his business decision.

Trueblood Committee. The *Report of the Study Group on the Objectives of Financial Statements* (the Trueblood Committee) concluded that full factual disclosure is important to a user because the user can then make his own assessment. The Trueblood Committee also concluded that it would be useful to state assumptions, interpretations, and predictions and to estimate both a single value and a range of possible results. Classification of information by relative risk based on the assessment of uncertainties would permit the user to compare the information and make decisions based on his own risk preferences (AICPA, 1973j, pp. 33–34).

The Commission on Auditors' Responsibilities supported these conclusions (1978, pp. 23–30).

FASB. The FASB's conceptual framework project (see Chapter 2) parallels the recommendations of the Trueblood Committee; financial information should be useful to investors and lenders, should be classified on a range from most factual to most interpretative, should disclose assumptions, and should consider changing values. SFAC 1, *Objectives of Financial Reporting by Business Enterprises,* concludes that users are aided in evaluating estimates and judgmental information by explanations of underlying assumptions and methods used (AC 1210.54).

All the various study groups and the SEC (ASR 166)[1] seem to agree on the need for more definitive guidelines regarding materiality measurements and required disclosures. The profession must be concerned with whether there are detrimental effects of disclosure—such as litigation whose disclosure might cause damage or proprietary information whose disclosure might affect competitive position. In some cases disclosure detriments may outweigh user benefits, but this argument is becoming less and less compelling as disclosure requirements proliferate.

Cohen Commission. Following a recommendation of the Commission on Auditors' Responsibilities (CAR, 1978, p. 29), the accounting profession is considering whether to require the placement of all information on uncertainties in a single note to the financial statements, as contrasted with the current practice of dispersing such information throughout the notes to the financial statements. AcSEC has recommended the use of a separate note similar to that on accounting policies, but its members cannot agree on what uncertainties to include in the note. Some AcSEC members believe that a single note would lead to more boilerplate, and they want more useful specific disclosures. Others believe that only by placing all uncertainty disclosures in one note and agreeing on the rules for its content can the auditing profession accomplish the needed removal of uncertainty qualifications from auditors' reports. The FASB will review this issue in conjunction with a postreview of SFAS 5 (AC 4311) upon completion of the Conceptual Framework Project's elements of financial statements and accounting recognition criteria segments.

Measurement and Disclosure Standards

One of the FASB's early projects resulted in SFAS 5, *Accounting for Contingencies* (AC 4311), which contains accounting and disclosure requirements for loss contingencies. It also incorporates the guidance of ARB 50 on accounting for and disclosure of gain contingencies; it precludes the accrual by charges against

---

[1] ASR 166 calls for management to disclose unusual risks and uncertainties facing the enterprise. The SEC recognizes that many estimates are required in preparing financial statements. What is said about uncertainties may be so voluminous—buried in such boilerplate—that it is not very useful. The SEC believes that when investors are already aware of general uncertainties it is useful to be specific. In ASR 166, the SEC gives examples of disclosure they believe may be required in specific areas of uncertainty, e.g., loan loss reserves for a bank. The point is that disclosure should be as specific as possible without clouding the issues with too many details.

income of any reserves for general contingencies, self-insurance, and castastrophe losses for insurance companies.

SFAS 5 defines a contingency as "an existing condition, situation, or set of circumstances involving uncertainty as to possible gain . . . or loss . . . to an enterprise that will ultimately be resolved when one or more future events occur or fail to occur" (AC 4311.01). The future event or nonevent will establish the actual amount of the asset or liability. Because the amount is not known when earlier financial statements are issued, an estimate is recorded if sufficient evidence is available to set an amount. For example, a suit for $1 million against an enterprise for a breach of contract (existing condition) may result in an ultimate liability of $250,000 determined by adjudication or settlement (future events) with the plaintiff. If this is deemed to be the probable result, $250,000 will be accrued currently.

Uncertainties, because they include the broad area of accounting estimates, are not always contingencies as contemplated by SFAS 5. For example, amounts owed to others for services rendered but not yet billed may require an estimate in the accounting process, but a contingency is not involved; the cost does not depend on a future confirming event. An obligation has been incurred, although the amount of the obligation requires estimation.

Accrual. Accrual of an estimated loss contingency by a charge against earnings is required if—and only if—two conditions are met: (1) it is probable an asset has been impaired or a liability has been incurred and (2) the loss can be reasonably estimated (AC 4311.08). FASB Interpretation No. 14 (AC 4311-1) requires accrual of the most likely estimate of the loss if a range of loss is possible, and requires recording at least the lowest point in that range when no amount within the range is a better estimate than any other amount. Ability to estimate a range of loss when the loss is probable indicates that a reasonable estimate can be made; therefore, accrual is required.

In applying these accounting requirements, certain definitions are needed (AC 4311.03):

1. *Probable.* The future event or events are likely to occur.
2. *Reasonably possible.* The chance of the future event or events occurring is more than remote (slight) but less than likely (probable).
3. *Remote.* The chance of the future event or events occurring is slight.

These definitions turn out to be quite vague in practice. One of the problems in applying SFAS 5 is the absence of guidelines for the judgment required in determining what is meant by "likely to occur." And the statement does not give specific parameters to measure "probable" or "remote."

Disclosure. Disclosing the *nature of an accrual* made for a loss contingency is required, but the amount of the accrual sometimes need not be disclosed. When to disclose the amount accrued is open to judgment; however, it seems prudent to make such disclosure whenever the accrual is unusual or material to current earnings or materially affects the trend of earnings. Many enterprises make no disclosure regarding litigation or other contingencies if the amounts involved are not material and an unfavorable outcome is less than reasonably possible.

Disclosure of the existence of a material *unaccrued loss contingency* is required when a reasonable possibility exists that a loss may have been incurred. If a reasonable estimate of the amount or range of loss can be made, disclosure of the amount is necessary; otherwise, inability to estimate should be disclosed.

Unasserted Claims. Unasserted claims or assessments are given special consideration in SFAS 5. An unasserted claim or assessment is one in which the injured party or potential plaintiff has not manifested an awareness of a possible claim or assessment. For example, suppose X claimed that Z used sales practices that were in restraint of trade and damaging to X. The court awarded damages to X, which Z has recorded as a charge against earnings. Z believes Y might win a similar damage award, but since Y has been silent, Y's potential claim against Z is an unasserted claim.

Another example of an unasserted claim involves a patient who may have wrongly died in a hospital operating room because of negligence by the medical staff. The distraught family of the patient may not even think about potential legal action against the hospital for months. The hospital's fiscal year may end, and financial statements may be released for the period in which the event occurred. Because the injured parties (the family members) have not mentiond or threatened litigation, this is an unasserted claim at the financial statement date.

Disclosure of an unasserted claim or assessment is not required unless it is probable that the claim will be asserted and there is a *reasonable possibility* that the outcome will be unfavorable. If it is probable that the assertion will be made and *probable* that the outcome will be unfavorable, accrual is necessary if the amount can be estimated reasonably, just as with an asserted claim.

Unasserted claims have been given this special treatment because (attorneys have argued) disclosure could cause the injured party to recognize the injury and assert the claim; in other words, the disclosure tends to be self-fulfilling. Attorneys were also concerned with the loss of attorney-client privilege if certain disclosures were made regarding unasserted claims. These problems and the compromise worked out between accountants and lawyers are discussed later in this chapter. A matrix summarizing accrual and disclosure requirements is presented in Figure 29.1.

Subsequent Events. Information becoming available after the balance sheet date but before issuance of the financial statements may indicate that an asset became impaired or a liability was incurred *after* the date of the financial statements. Disclosure of such losses or loss contingencies may be necessary to keep the financial statements from being misleading. SFAS 5 (AC 4311.11) gives some guidance, not very specific, as to what would make such disclosure necessary. It seems prudent to disclose any matter that could have a material effect on financial position or operations or could materially affect the trend of operations.

If disclosure is deemed necessary, the nature of the loss or contingency and the amount or range of the possible loss should be disclosed. If the effect on financial position is extremely material, supplemental pro forma financial data giving effect to the loss as if it had occurred at the date of the financial statements may be useful. Of course, if the material loss contingency existed at the date of the balance sheet, accrual is necessary when the loss is probable and the amount can be reasonably estimated.

Gain Contingencies. The principle of conservatism was reflected in ARB 50, which specified that gain contingencies, unlike loss contingencies, usually are not

Loss Is ⟍ Loss Can	Probable	Reasonably Possible	Remote
Be Estimated	Accrue and Disclose Nature	Disclose Nature ①	No Accrual or Disclosure
Not Be Estimated	Disclose Nature	Disclose Nature	No Accrual or Disclosure

① *Disclosure of amount or range is also required or a statement that an estimate of the amount cannot be made.*

Note — AC 4311.10 adds another dimension for unasserted claims or assessments. These should be disclosed only where it is probable that a claim will be asserted. When assertion is probable, the above matrix applies.

FIGURE 29.1   SFAS 5—ACCRUAL AND DISCLOSURE REQUIREMENTS FOR LOSS CONTINGENCIES

to be reflected in the accounts. The FASB incorporated this approach into SFAS 5 (AC 4311.17) without passing judgment on the continued usefulness of conservatism as a principle. Thus, gain contingencies are not to be recognized prior to realization, but adequate disclosure of potential material gain contingencies is required under SFAS 5. This disclosure should not lead to overly optimistic estimates of the likelihood of realizing a gain. Some accountants question the inconsistency of only disclosing, rather than accruing, gain contingencies whose realization may be as predictable as recorded loss contingencies.

Guarantees. Disclosure of guarantees of indebtedness of others, obligations of commercial banks under standby letters of credit, and guarantees to repurchase receivables or property sold or otherwise assigned is required even though the probability of loss may be remote. Disclosure should include the nature and amount of the guarantee and might also state, or be net of, the value of any expected recovery from an outside party (AC 4311.12). The FASB has proposed a rule that would extend existing disclosure requirements relating to guarantees to include indirect guarantees and unconditional obligations.

Self-Insurance. Before SFAS 5, many enterprises that did not carry insurance against certain risks, such as property damage from fire or explosion, charged earnings in a systematic fashion (e.g., as an insurance premium would have been) to set up an insurance reserve against which actual losses could then be charged. Charges in lieu of insurance are no longer permitted. Lack of insurance may be considered a loss contingency, because a future event, if it occurs, will confirm the fact and amount of loss (AC 4311.27-.28).

Charges against earnings for unspecified business risks, sometimes known as *general contingency reserves,* also are prohibited. An appropriation of retained earnings for such contingencies and for uninsured risks remains permissible (AC 4311.15). This involves segregating retained earnings, but not by a charge to earnings. When losses occur, they cannot be charged against the appropriated retained earnings, but must be charged against current earnings. Disclosure of uninsured or underinsured risks is not required (AC 4311.14), because of the difficulties in developing criteria; however, when the risk of loss appears reasonably possible, disclosure seems appropriate.

Catastrophe Losses. One of the most controversial prohibitions in SFAS 5 relates to catastrophe losses of property and casualty insurance companies. When an insurance company issues a policy, it assumes a risk that a catastrophe (e.g., a hurricane) might occur within the policy coverage period. It has been argued that insurance companies are able to predict the occurrence rate of catastrophes, and amounts of losses from them, using actuarial methods based on past occurrences. Insurance companies use such methods for rate-setting purposes; therefore, such reasonably estimated losses should be accrued.

The FASB concluded that catastrophe reserves fail to satisfy SFAS 5's conditions for accrual, because losses over the relatively short periods of time covered by policies in force cannot be estimated reasonably. Therefore, unless the catastrophe occurs within the policy period, no asset is impaired and no liability is incurred at the balance sheet date, so no accrual for a catastrophe loss should be made (AC 4311.40-.42).

Claims resulting from catastrophes often are not made until a long time after the catastrophe occurs. This happens for various reasons, e.g., some damages may take time to discover or people who are dislocated may have other concerns to consider before filing an insurance claim. A property and casualty insurer is required to accrue losses from catastrophes that occurred before the date of the financial statements but have not yet been claimed by the policyholders if the claims are probable of being made and if a reasonable estimate of the loss can be made (AC 4311.43).

Interim Financial Statements. Interim financial statements usually contain more estimates than annual financial statements and thus may be less reliable. For example, claims or assessments against the enterprise may be given careful consideration by inside and outside counsel at year-end but not at an interim date. APB 28, *Interim Financial Reporting* (AC 2071.22), briefly covers the reporting of contingencies and other uncertainties in interim financial reports. It says they are to be disclosed in the same manner as in annual financial statements; however, materiality is to be judged in relationship to the annual financial statements, not the interim figures. Required disclosures are to be repeated in each interim report until the contingency has been removed, resolved, or determined to be immaterial.

Estimates

Nearly all financial statement amounts require some degree of estimation. Collectibility of current accounts receivable must be evaluated to present the accounts at estimated net realizable value; inventories stated at cost must be measured against estimated market value less an estimate for disposal costs; various accrued liabilities require estimation of services received or amounts due; even accounts payable are subject to future adjustment due to such possibilities as improper billing or inadequate product performance. Cash is possibly the only asset recorded with no uncertainties surrounding it, and then only if denominated in the currency of the country in which the reporting entity resides. Perhaps the only liabilities with no uncertainties surrounding them are notes and loans payable based on amounts previously borrowed (as opposed to payment for goods or services), and again, only if denominated in the currency of the country in which the reporting entity resides.

In some cases the impact of estimates on financial statements is necessarily pervasive, and special kinds of disclosure may be required. In the 1974 accounts of Lockheed Aircraft Corporation, for example, the net income could have been anywhere from $50 million to a loss of $500 million, depending on the company's estimate of the number of L-1011 TriStar aircraft that would ultimately be sold. In this case, the SEC required Lockheed to label the net income figure on the face of the income statement and anywhere else it was presented as "Net income based on the assumptions of a 300-airplane TriStar program" and to include a full description of the uncertainty in the footnotes.

See Figure 29.2 for a listing of various types of accounting estimates. An AICPA Accounting Standards Executive Committee task force, established to consider accounting for changes in estimates because of a concern that practitioners are not consistently applying APB 20 (AC 1051) on accounting changes, produced this listing to illustrate that estimates are necessary in many situations and are pervasive in financial statements.

In dealing with the many estimates required in preparing financial statements, the auditor must judge in each case whether amounts have been or can be estimated reasonably. Neither SFAS 5 nor any other authoritative literature contains definitive guidelines on measuring the difference between uncertainties that can and cannot be estimated reasonably. (For a general discussion, see AC 4311.22-.32). Though estimates are always uncertainties, they are not necessarily loss contingencies. Thus, estimates regarding normal course of business events are generally included in the financial statements without specific disclosure, unless a reasonable estimate cannot be made and the effect could be material.

Asset Realization. Assets are generally valued on a balance sheet at historical cost amounts; however, they may be written down if future utility clearly does not warrant a recovery of the cost through future utilization or realization of revenues. Future events affecting asset values include collectibility of specific receivables, salability of inventories, recovery of deferred costs (including start-up and pre-opening costs), recovery of investments, assurance beyond a reasonable doubt of

I. BALANCE SHEET AMOUNTS EMPHASIZED
   A. *Future events directly involved*
      • Future selling prices of and future costs involved in inventories carried at net realizable value
      • Earnings of a subsidiary that will be distributed to its parent in a taxable transaction
      • Loss on disposal of a segment of a business
      • Effective tax rate for full fiscal year for interim reporting
      • Losses of property and liability insurance companies
      • Recoverable cost of productive facilities less than historical cost
   B. *Estimate of present condition confirmed by future events*
      • Uncollectible receivables
      • Obsolete inventory
      • Defective goods sold under warranty
II. INCOME STATEMENT AMOUNTS EMPHASIZED
   A. *Future events directly involved*
      • Revenue to be earned, costs to be incurred, and extent of progress toward completion of a contract accounted for by percentage of completion
      • Gross profit rates under the program method of accounting
      • Life in years or units of output and salvage value of depreciable asset
      • Life of intangible asset subject to amortization
      • Residual value of a sales-type, direct financing, or leveraged lease
      • Actuarial assumptions involved in pensions
      • Estimated gross profits from a motion picture film
   B. *Estimate of present condition confirmed by future events*
      • Recoverable reserves of natural resources

FIGURE 29.2   AcSEC TASK FORCE LISTING OF NECESSARY AND PERVASIVE ACCOUNTING ESTIMATES

realizing net operating loss carryforwards, and threat of expropriation by foreign governments.

Liability Determination. Liabilities may also be affected by future events that determine the amount of the liability. Although prior experience or other factors may allow a reasonable estimate for financial statement purposes, future events may prove the estimate to be inaccurate. For example, in the Firestone Tire and Rubber Company case, government intervention forced Firestone to "voluntarily" recall tires of a certain model and replace them with new tires because of what the government said was a faulty product. Although Firestone may not have believed its warranty covered such alleged defects, government action created an "implied warranty."

An enterprise theoretically should accrue all future costs, including product recall cost, in the period of sale to obtain a proper matching of revenues and expenses. The cost of the recall would be accrued in the period of sale if the company could foresee all costs that would be incurred. However, since a company cannot, almost by definition, be aware of a recall at the time of sale, the actual costs are charged in the period or periods in which they become known.

Other examples where future events may change an estimated liability include costs to complete a long-term contract, ultimate determination of tax liability, policy reserves of a life insurance company if the mortality rates and other assumptions change from those used to estimate the liability, and costs required to restore strip-mined property to original condition.

Other Estimates. Many other cases exist where amounts may be estimated based on reasonably reliable data. Although it is recognized that estimates can and probably will be changed based on actual results, the estimates are considered reliable enough to record in the financial statements. Examples include depreciation based on estimated service lives of assets, collectibility in total as opposed to specific receivable collectibility, and written-off costs based on geological estimates of proved oil and gas reserves.

Estimates and contingencies such as endorsements, guarantees of debt, and assignment of receivables with recourse may require disclosure only, not accrual, because of the remoteness that future events will cause a liability to accrue. On the other hand, most lawsuits that may create material liability are not recorded; they are disclosed, not because of the uncertainty of the confirming future event, but because of the inability to make a reasonable estimate of the outcome.

Litigation and Government Action. One of the major uncertainties facing every business is the risk of litigation. Class and derivative actions and individual suits and actions taken by government agencies are numerous. And the effect, the possible outcome, may require current accounting or disclosure of the contingent liability, i.e., the potential future obligation of an uncertain amount resulting from past activities. There are many different types of litigation in which an enterprise may become involved, and it seems that new ones are constantly invented (see Chapters 44, 45, and 46).

Figure 29.3 lists a few types of litigation an enterprise may face. (See AC 4311.33-.34 for a more complete discussion.) This sample list illustrates the wide areas that may be covered in litigation or a regulatory action against the business entity. Consequences to the business enterprise could include payment of damages however determined, payment of fines and penalties, repayment of revenue previously received, and even discontinuation of certain operations.

The entire nature of the entity may change as a result of the uncertainty. For example, the government's antitrust action against IBM has been in progress for approximately ten years and may take another ten. The outcome is unknown, but presumably could result in dissolution of IBM into two or more separate entities; the potential effect cannot be comprehended at this time.

Because the cost of defending a lawsuit or fighting a government action can be prohibitive, an enterprise may agree to a settlement despite belief in its innocence. Of course, not all actions are harmful to an enterprise; for a plaintiff in litigation, the outcome could be beneficial.

Incongruities

GAAP is not consistent as to treatment of the various types of estimates and uncertainties in financial accounting and reporting. For example, the FASB has

CIVIL LITIGATION
- Antitrust
- Restraint of trade
- Breach of contract
- Patent infringement
- Product liability
- Violation of federal securities laws

GOVERNMENT ACTIONS
- Discrimination—racial, sex, age, etc.
- Environmental protection
- Antitrust
- Restraint of trade
- Violation of federal securities laws
- Violation of wage and price guidelines or controls
- Renegotiation of government contracts
- Income tax disputes
- Violation of other laws and regulations, e.g., Foreign Corrupt Practices Act

FIGURE 29.3   EXAMPLES OF TYPES OF LITIGATION

decided it is inappropriate to allow financial statement preparers to estimate general research and development recoverability. Since any such estimates are considered too subjective, all such costs must be expensed. However, estimates as to the future utility of other assets, including those that appear to be very similar to research and development expenditures (e.g., preoperating expenses and start-up costs), may still be deferred based on estimates of future utility. The FASB simply has not followed through on this final phase of R&D-type costs—hence, the incongruity. (See Chapter 21 for a full discussion of this area.)

There are numerous other examples of incongruity in financial accounting and reporting principles, but after the FASB completes its conceptual framework project (see Chapter 2) systematic attention can be directed to all prior statements of GAAP to assess their consistency with the chosen concepts.

AUDITING

Objectives

Management must estimate the outcome of future events to determine the appropriate amounts and disclosures to include in the financial statements. Estimates that tend to recur over the normal business cycle may be based on prior experience (e.g., useful lives of depreciable assets and collectibility of customer accounts).

Management may rely on outside experts for advice on the outcome of unusual contingencies such as litigation.

The auditor's objective is to be satisfied (if possible) that management's estimates are reasonable. In reaching this overall conclusion, the auditor obtains and evaluates evidential matter relevant to the existence of the contingency or estimate and the appropriateness of financial accounting, reporting, and disclosure. The auditor must distinguish between uncertainties that can be reasonably estimated and therefore should be accrued and uncertainties that are inestimable in amount and thus should not be accrued. As to the latter, the auditor may modify his opinion for material uncertainties where a reasonable estimate of amount cannot be made. (See Chapter 16.)

Evidential Matter

Procedures. When dealing with uncertainties, the auditor is assessing "soft" data that cannot be measured until a future event occurs or fails to occur. Accordingly, a substantive approach to auditing, rather than a reliance-on-systems approach, is usually followed. In auditing the reasonableness of management's estimates for normal recurring items, the auditor may be able to rely somewhat on past experience of the enterprise or the industry. However, for nonrecurring contingencies each matter may be unique, so past experience is not useful. The auditor often must place a great deal of reliance on management representations (SAS 19; AU 333) and must form an opinion that management is capable of making informed estimates and has the requisite integrity to report objectively those known contingencies as required by SFAS 5 (AC 4311).

In performing all auditing procedures, the auditor should remain alert to evidence that may indicate an uncertainty or contingency that requires specific attention. Procedures such as confirming cash balances, accounts and notes receivable, and accounts and notes payable and reviewing contracts may disclose specific uncertainties or contingencies.

Substantive procedures specifically designed to bring contingencies to the auditor's attention might include the following:

1. Obtaining oral representations (through discussion with upper and middle level management) and written representations (as part of the overall audit letter of representations) indicating that management has disclosed all known contingent liabilities and has, to the best of its knowledge, appropriately accounted for the contingencies and appropriately disclosed them in the financial statements. (See AU 333.)
2. Reviewing minutes of meetings: board of directors, committees of the board, and shareholders. Important obligations, contracts, lawsuits, and related matters are likely to be discussed by management at these meetings. (See Chapter 10.)
3. Reviewing income tax liability status, tax returns, and revenue agent reports. Income tax liability is determined through filing of tax returns for the current liability and by accruing deferred taxes. The Internal Revenue Service has the option, very often exercised for business enterprises, to subject the tax return to an examination. The revenue agent's report gives the auditor information on whether there are additional tax accruals that should be considered. (See Chapter 43.)
4. Obtaining information on guarantees and letters of credit at balance sheet date and confirming with the outside party.

5. Reading contracts, loan agreements, leases, and correspondence from government agencies to determine what commitments the enterprise may have.

Other substantive procedures include inquiring of responsible company officials whether client has complied with applicable laws, controls, and regulations imposed by various government agencies. Specific areas of concern should include the Foreign Corrupt Practices Act, wage and price controls, employee safety regulations, environmental regulations, and filing requirements of the SEC and other government agencies. The auditor should discuss these potential liabilities with company officials and determine, consistent with his normal range of expertise, the details of any contingent liabilities, including an estimate of the maximum potential liability, whether any security has been pledged to secure payment, and the likelihood of a contingency becoming an actual liability.

The opinion and advice of the company's legal counsel often will be necessary to evaluate whether there has been noncompliance with laws and regulations and to estimate the potential effects of noncompliance. Legal expense should be analyzed and lawyers' invoices reviewed for an indication of areas of professional services suggesting possible contingent liabilities. As billings from attorneys often are itemized, matters not previously known to the auditor may bring to his attention contingencies that could become actual liabilities. A key audit procedure has the auditor inquire of and obtain a written response from the company's lawyers as to the status of certain litigation. (This is discussed later in this chapter.)

Estimates and Uncertainty. SAS 2 says that "matters are not to be regarded as uncertainties . . . unless their outcome is not susceptible of reasonable estimation. . ." (AU 509.21). Once the auditor is aware of the existence of uncertainties, he must then evaluate them as to their effect on the financial statements. In addition to the auditing procedures and evidential matter considered above, the auditor must utilize his knowledge of general business conditions and specific knowledge of the entity being audited. In determining whether a reasonable estimate can be made or whether an uncertainty exists, the auditor uses inductive reasoning to reach conclusions. Certain matters, e.g., collectibility of normal customer receivables and useful lives of assets, are within management and auditor expertise and should be subject to reasonable estimation and evaluation.

In evaluating evidence to determine the appropriateness of management's estimates, the auditor must consider the objectivity of such evidence. Can the potential effect truly be measured within reasonable limits? How imminent is the possibility of the contingent future confirming event? How material is the potential effect on the financial statements? What independent expert advice has been used in arriving at the conclusion?

For instance, in the familiar situation of determining whether the allowance for doubtful receivables is appropriate, consideration is given to the entity's prior history of collection. Also important, however, is knowledge as to whether the company has changed its method of doing business with customers. Has there been a change in the type of customer? A change in customer base, for example, from major Fortune 500 companies with high credit ratings to many small, fledgling businesses that have a higher degree of business failures indicates an increase in the allowance might be necessary. Even if the company being audited has no prior experience with a particular type of customer, reasonable estimates can usually be made by referring to external information such as statistics from other companies doing business with comparable customers and by obtaining credit information on nonestablished customers.

The potential effect of other far less common uncertainties may be exceedingly difficult to estimate. For example, consider an enterprise operating in a country where threat of expropriation may endanger both the assets and the continuing business in that country. Useful information would include whether the country has openly indicated its intention to expropriate property of the enterprise or other enterprises and what the country has done in the past. It may be known that although the country has a recent history of expropriation, payments have equaled or exceeded the carrying amounts of assets taken; therefore, the potential effect on the enterprise may be only the loss of continuing business in that country. All other factors being equal, disclosure would be the only requirement in such a case. However, if it appears that expropriation is imminent and sufficient payment by the country is not likely, a current provision charged against income for asset impairment may be necessary.

Attorney Letters

Evidential Matter. When dealing with uncertainties, especially contingent liabilities resulting from litigation, potential litigation, and government regulation, the auditor must communicate with the entity's outside counsel and, where applicable, house counsel. Although attorneys are experts at law, many factors limit their ability to opine accurately on the outcome of litigation: proliferation of litigation, the increasing impact of current judgments and settlements in similar cases, and a proclivity to settle are three. Attorneys are the first to admit they cannot accurately predict the outcome of unasserted claims. In a world where manufacturers may be deemed liable for defects in material or workmanship long beyond the express warranty period and the amount of the ultimate liability may extend beyond previously imagined proportions (Ford Motor Company's alleged failure to correct safety deficiencies in gasoline tanks in certain Pinto automobiles is just one example), no one can be expected to foresee the future and accurately predict the ultimate liability. And consider the judgments against pharmaceutical manufacturers for effects of drugs taken decades ago where the specific manufacturer is not even known.

Crowded court dockets, delaying tactics by both plaintiff and defendant, and other factors also increase the difficulties in trying to estimate potential outcome. It is beyond comprehension to estimate the consequences of the federal government's antitrust litigation against American Telephone & Telegraph and International Business Machines; both have been in process for many years, the IBM case for approximately ten, with no end in sight. Much litigation ends in settlement between the opposing parties for amounts well below damages originally sought. Countersuits by a defendant may result in damages being assessed against the original plaintiff. Even in cases where legal arguments and common sense may indicate a particular outcome, jury perceptions may differ. A change in the social environment may occur over the lengthy period of the litigation, adding more uncertainty. And the appeal process also adds to uncertainty of outcome.

Background. Auditors seek opinions of outside experts such as geologists, actuaries, and appraisers to support information supplied by management. The auditor views outside legal counsel as an expert in legal matters and seeks his expertise and knowledge of the company to help him reach a conclusion as to appropriateness of accounting for and disclosure of litigation and other contingent liabilities. A standard auditing procedure requires that company management write to outside legal counsel requesting counsel's opinion on the status and the potential outcome of litigation and other contingent liabilities.

Prior to 1976, auditors requested management to ask for information on any pending litigation and any other contingent liabilities, such as unasserted claims, of which counsel had knowledge. Although attorneys responded to client requests, many were silent as to unasserted claims. Auditors were generally satisfied with replies being received from outside counsel and generally were unaware of limitations being put on such responses. Many attorneys who previously responded to auditors' requests became reluctant to respond to general requests, because they were aware of the increasing amount of litigation and believed that the less information available to outsiders, including auditors, from whom information could be "discovered" by a potential plaintiff, the better they could protect their clients from adverse consequences of litigation.

The attorney-client privilege does not extend to information disclosed to an auditor, because the auditor legally does not have such privileged communication with his clients. Attorneys were concerned that disclosing an evaluation of potential effects of a claim might be viewed in court as an admission of guilt, and they were adamant about giving potentially damaging information to auditors that could then be caught by "fishing" plaintiffs. Attorneys were also concerned with their own exposure to litigation if they were held responsible for damages arising from an inaccurate estimate of a client's potential liability.

Compromise. The problem between auditors and attorneys centered around the auditors using the attorney letters to *discover* unasserted claims and the attorneys' reluctance to jeopardize privilege.

In late 1975 a compromise was agreed on by the American Bar Association and the AICPA. From the auditor's point of view, SAS 12 (AU 337) contains the essence of the compromise—guidance to the auditor on procedures to follow to identify and satisfy himself as to the accounting and reporting for litigation, claims, and assessments.

Under SAS 12 (337.02-.05), it is management's responsibility to adopt policies and procedures to identify, evaluate, and account for litigation, claims, and assessments. The auditor should obtain evidential matter to determine the existence of the uncertainty, the period in which the underlying cause occurred, the probability of an unfavorable outcome, and the amount and range of potential loss. Since management is the primary source of information on contingent liabilities, the auditor's procedures should include

1. Discussing with management their policies and procedures for identifying, evaluating, and accounting for litigation, claims and assessments;
2. Obtaining from management a description and evaluation of the contingent liabilities existing at date of the balance sheet and subsequent thereto, including identification of matters referred to legal counsel;
3. Obtaining assurances from management that all matters required to be disclosed by SFAS 5 (AC 4311) have been disclosed;

4. Examining documentation in the client's possession, including correspondence and invoices from attorneys; and

5. Obtaining management's assurance that they have disclosed all unasserted claims the lawyer has advised the client are probable of assertion and required to be disclosed in accordance with SFAS 5. (The attorney should be informed that the auditor has received such assurance.)

A difficulty facing the auditor in the area of unasserted claims is that the ABA Statement of Policy and the ABA Code of Professional Responsibility call for an attorney to resign an engagement when a client does not follow the attorney's advice to disclose material unasserted claims. SAS 12 restates this responsibility as a reminder that the auditor should consider the need for inquiries as to the reasons the attorney is no longer associating himself with the enterprise (AU 337.11). This solution, worked out between auditors and lawyers and approved by the SEC, attempts to give the auditor assurances from the enterprise, corroborated by their attorney, that all disclosures required under SFAS 5 have been made; at the same time the attorney-client privilege has not been breached.

However, the legal profession's policy statement is not binding on a lawyer. The auditor should therefore determine whether the attorney understands and follows the ABA Statement of Policy. Some attorneys may specifically dissociate themselves from the ABA statement, making the gathering of evidential matter by the auditor much more difficult. In such cases, the auditor must assure himself that he has obtained sufficient information to be able to determine that management and counsel are not aware of material matters that should be but are not disclosed in the financial statements. Perhaps the attorney will agree to another procedure; discussion will be necessary if the auditor is to become satisfied that he has received the necessary information.

Inquiry of Attorney. The audit inquiry letter to outside counsel is the auditor's primary means of corroborating information on contingencies furnished by management. SAS 12 (AU 337.09) lists specific matters to be covered in an audit inquiry letter, including information regarding unasserted claims as agreed to in the compromise between auditors and attorneys, as follows:

• Listing of pending and threatened litigation,
• Listing of unasserted claims and assessments considered by management to be probable of assertion with unfavorable outcome reasonably possible,
• A request of the attorney to describe and evaluate the outcome of each pending or threatened matter listed, including a request for additions to the list,
• A request of the attorney to comment on unasserted claims where his views differ from management's evaluation,
• A statement by client's management acknowledging an understanding of the lawyer's professional responsibility involving unasserted claims or assessments,
• A request that the attorney confirm whether the client's understanding of the attorney's professional responsibility is correct,
• A request of the attorney to indicate whether his response has been limited and reasons for such limitation, and
• A description of materiality levels agreed upon for purposes of the inquiry and response.

Materiality Guidelines. It may be appropriate for management to limit the letter of inquiry to contingencies that are considered to be material. It is important that such a materiality judgment be agreed to by the enterprise, the auditor, and the attorney.

In a few instances, suits can be classified as clearly immaterial by any aspect: the amount, the nature, and the anticipated impact on the financial statement. However, in today's litigious climate, most suits are instituted for amounts far in excess of the damages incurred and are clearly material to the financial statements if settled for the amount of the action. The enterprise may believe certain of these suits to be frivolous, having no material impact on the financial statements, and accordingly omit them from the listing sent to their attorney. It may be difficult for the auditors to obtain the necessary "other" corroborative evidence to agree to the omission of these actions as immaterial. If there is a particular reason to be concerned in this regard, the auditor should request management to prepare a listing of pending or threatened litigation that it feels will have no material impact on the financial statements and include that listing with the standard letter of inquiry. This procedure is recommended not only to assure the validity of management's evaluations but to assist the attorney in responding. The attorney would be responsible for corroborating the completeness of the listing.

Sample Inquiry Letter. An example of an inquiry letter to an attorney is presented in Figure 29.4 (see also AU 337A for a general form of inquiry letter). It mentions a few matters that perhaps require further articulation:

1. *Judgments rendered or settlements made.* Include in this listing the following information with respect to any material judgment or settlement involving the company: the nature of the judgment or settlement, the amount incurred, and the implications, if any, for the company and its financial statements.

2. *Pending or threatened litigation.* Include in this listing the nature of the litigation, how management is responding or intends to respond (for example, to contest the case vigorously or to seek an out-of-court settlement), the progress of the case or negotiations to date, an indication of the likelihood of an unfavorable (favorable) outcome, and an estimate (if one can be made) of the amount or range of potential loss (gain).

3. *Unasserted claims and assessments.* Include in this listing the following information with respect to those matters considered by management to be probable of assertion and that, if asserted, would have at least a reasonable possibility of an unfavorable outcome: the nature of the matter, how management intends to respond if the claim is asserted, an indication of the likelihood of an unfavorable outcome, and an estimate (if one can be made) of the amount or range of potential loss.

4. *Other matters.* The auditor may request the enterprise to inquire about other matters, e.g., specified information on certain contractually assumed obligations of the company such as debt guarantees of others. Requests pertaining to unpaid legal fees should be covered in a separate statement.

Attorney's Response. As part of the compromise between attorneys and auditors, in December 1975 the American Bar Association issued *Statement of Policy Regarding Lawyers' Responses to Auditors' Requests for Information* (reprinted in

Inability to evaluate litigation. Management or its representatives are responsible for evaluating the degree of probability of an unfavorable outcome as well as the amount or range of potential loss for financial statement purposes. The letter of inquiry to the lawyer requests corroboration of management's estimate. The lawyer may decline to corroborate management's estimate because he is unable to for one reason or another, e.g.: "The matter is in discovery stage" or "The issues are not yet sufficiently defined." Further, a lawyer may respond with statements that are clearly not acceptable for the auditor's purposes, such as: "The litigation is being defended vigorously and the client has meritorious defenses"; "From what we presently know, it appears that the company has a good chance of prevailing"; "We believe the claim is grossly exaggerated from the evidence available"; or "We are unable to express an opinion but the company believes. . . ." These statements do not corroborate the probability of outcome or the amount or range of loss. An auditor receiving such a response may review the matter with the attorney and the client and attempt to obtain a more complete and acceptable response.

Other corroborating evidential matter can be obtained by reviewing with management their procedures and the documentation, scanning related files, reviewing results of similar actions, and discussing the matter with inside counsel and, in certain circumstances, other outside counsel who gave substantive attention to the matter. If the auditor cannot obtain satisfaction from the attorney and there is insufficient other corroborating evidential matter to support management's estimate, a "subject to" qualified opinion should be rendered. (See Chapter 16.)

Lawyer as a director/officer. The ABA statement (AU 337C, commentary on par. 2) advises that

> . . . a lawyer who is also a director or officer of the client would not include information which he received as a director or officer unless the information was also received (or, absent the dual role, would in the normal course be received) in his capacity as legal counsel in the context of his professional engagement. Where the auditor's request for information is addressed to a law firm as a firm, the law firm may properly assume that its response is not expected to include any information which may have been communicated to the particular individual by reason of his serving in the capacity of director or officer of the client.

A reply limiting the response in the above manner is acceptable if it does not exclude the lawyer/director entirely. The ABA position was meant to exclude only knowledge the individual might have obtained outside of his professional engagement. The law firm is responsible for including in its response any knowledge the director might have learned in his professional capacity as attorney.

Lawyer's professional responsibility. Before discussing information that would disclose a confidence or require evaluation of a claim, the attorney must discuss with his client the consequences of disclosure, recognizing that an adverse party may assert that any evaluation is an admission of liability. The client should request attorney responses regarding unasserted claims only if the client believes that such claims are probable of assertion and a material loss is reasonably possible. In this regard, the ABA's Statement of Policy (AU 337C, par. 6) provides:

> The auditor may properly assume that whenever, in the course of performing legal services for the client with respect to a matter recognized to involve an unasserted possible claim or assessment which may call for a financial statement disclosure, the lawyer has formed a professional conclusion that the client must disclose or consider disclosure concerning such possible claim or assessment, the lawyer, as a matter of professional responsibility to the client, will so advise the client and will consult with the client concerning the question of such disclosure and the applicable requirements of SFAS 5.

The auditor should recognize that the undertaking quoted above does not require an attorney to go out of his way to obtain information regarding unasserted possible claims unless they are apparent to him in performance of legal work for which he is retained and is engaged by a client. The lawyer's responsibilities are to consider an unasserted possible claim if he realizes one exists and to recognize there may be a requirement for financial statement disclosure; he does not commit to devoting substantive attention to searching for such claims.

Because a lawyer is not considered an expert as to detailed disclosure requirements under SFAS 5, he should notify a responsible client officer or employee of an unasserted possible claim that the lawyer has concluded must be considered for disclosure to the auditor and should satisfy himself that the officer or employee understands the requirements of SFAS 5. Having done this, the lawyer has fulfilled his commitments unless he has concluded that the unasserted possible claim is probable of assertion; such a claim, if material, must be disclosed in the financial statements.

The ABA Statement of Policy, in referring to disclosure, applies to whether or not the unasserted claim or assessment must be brought to the auditor's attention, and does not refer to the requirements of disclosure under SFAS 5. It is the client's responsibility to evaluate whether financial statement disclosure is required, and the auditor's responsibility to evaluate the appropriateness of that disclosure.

Documentation. Responses from attorneys should be retained in the audit working papers. They should be annotated to indicate disposition of significant matters, e.g., an item of litigation may be indicated as having been disclosed in the notes to the financial statements, as not material enough to consider for disclosure, or as the cause of a "subject to" opinion. Where conversations with attorneys either supplement or substitute for an attorney's letter, a memorandum documenting the conversations should be prepared and included in the working papers, and a copy should be sent to the attorney for his confirmation—preferably in writing. The standard audit letter of representations (AU 333) should include assurances from management that disclosure has been made to the auditor of contingent or other possible liabilities that are probable of assertion (and that must therefore be disclosed in the financial statements in accordance with SFAS 5) or that counsel otherwise has advised should be disclosed.

AUDITORS' REPORTING ON UNCERTAINTIES

Uncertainties are among the leading reasons that auditors qualify their opinions. The auditor must evaluate evidence concerning management's accounting and reporting of the uncertainties to determine the appropriate type and form of opinion. If an uncertainty is not appropriately disclosed, an exception may be required in the auditor's report. If the disclosure is in conformity with GAAP, the auditor must still determine whether the effect of the uncertainty is sufficiently material to financial position to require a qualified ("subject to") opinion or, in extreme cases, a disclaimer of opinion. The types and forms of auditor's reports are described in Chapter 16.

Materiality

SFAS 5 (AC 4311.08) requires accruing for a contingency if a material liability is probable and the amount may be reasonably estimated. If the liability is reasonably possible (i.e., more than remote but less than likely), footnote disclosure is required; if it is remote, neither provision nor disclosure is necessary (AC 4311.10). Although specific materiality measurements are not discussed in SFAS 5, the base against which to measure materiality is a factor in determining the type of report to be issued by the auditor.

A 1979 auditing interpretation, *The Materiality of Uncertainties* (AU 9509.25-.28), takes the position that because most uncertainties are unusual in nature or infrequent in occurrence, they are only indirectly related to the normal recurring activities affecting earnings. The interpretation concludes that "the auditor should ordinarily evaluate the materiality and uncertainty by comparing the potential outcome to shareholders' equity and also to other relative balance sheet components such as total assets, total liabilities, current assets or current liabilities."

However, when an uncertainty is closely related to normal recurring activities, such as in the case of public utility revenues collected but subject to refund, materiality may be measured in relation to the potential effect on both income and financial position. Because future resolution of the uncertainty will not result in a retroactive adjustment of the income being currently reported (SFAS 16; AC 2014.10), current income is not exposed to adjustment; net worth is exposed to the future charge against future earnings. Assuming appropriate footnote disclosure is used, the auditor's opinion on the financial statements is usually a "subject to" qualification when the effect on net worth may be material.

Another 1979 auditing interpretation, *Reporting on an Uncertainty* (AU 9509.29-.32), recognizes this fact. It states that it is normally preferable to word a qualified opinion "subject to the effects, if any, of such adjustments as might have been required had the outcome of the uncertainty been known . . ." rather than "subject to the effects, if any, on the financial statements of the ultimate resolution of the matter. . . ." The former language is preferable because it does not imply that the statements may be adjusted in the future.

If the effect of the contingency may be pervasive as opposed to being isolated and measurable, the auditor may disclaim an opinion on the financial statements. SAS 2 permits such disclaimer, but makes it clear that appropriate disclosure and a "subject to" opinion are enough to adequately inform financial statements users (AU 509.25, fn. 8).

Disclosure criteria are more stringent than criteria to determine whether a report qualification is necessary, because the financial statements should inform the user of a potentially material charge to future earnings. Thus, for footnote disclosure, the appropriate materiality base may be income from continuing operations or net income. If disclosure is insufficient, an exception for failure to follow GAAP should be taken in the auditor's report.

Going Concern

Underlying financial accounting and reporting is the *going concern* concept. Unless otherwise stated, it is assumed that the reporting entity will continue for a sufficient time to realize its assets in the normal course of business; therefore, use of liquidation values is not appropriate. However, businesses do fail, especially in recessionary times. Perhaps the most fundamental uncertainty the auditor must evaluate is whether an entity seems able to continue. Factors usually leading to failure are continuing losses and inability to obtain adequate financing. Operating problems may manifest themselves as continued losses, doubtful prospective revenues, impairment of operating ability (possibly through legal proceedings or unavailability of essential materials), or seriously ineffective management control over operations. Financing problems may be reflected by a deficiency in working capital, a deficiency in assets, or debt defaults.

The auditor uses the enterprise's earnings and financing history as predictors, with other evidence, to gauge the potential success of future operations and financings. Other evidence includes the liquidity of assets, the prior reliability of budgets and forecasts, and whether the enterprise's current situation will affect its access to credit or equity markets. How long a company might be able to hold out in the face of adversity is also crucial.

The auditor may conclude that a disclaimer of opinion should be issued when the going concern assumption is in question, failure may be imminent, and the effect of failure on the financial statements would be pervasive. Technically, the auditor need not disclaim an opinion in this situation, but he may do so, depending on the risk that the financial statements and his relationship thereto may be misunderstood if he issues a less onerous report.

The imminence of the uncertainty, as the auditor sees it, is one of the important factors in determining the type of opinion to issue. For example, when it is evident that the entity cannot operate indefinitely if the losses of the last several years continue, but it can withstand another year of such losses without going out of business, the auditor may determine that a going concern qualification is not necessary.

The Auditing Standards Board is currently considering a pronouncement giving guidance to the auditor when a question arises about an entity's continued existence.

The SEC prohibits a "subject to" going concern opinion for financial statements that are to be included in a registration statement under the Securities Act of 1933 unless the offering is a firm underwriting or an "all or none" best efforts offering (ASR 115). The auditor must be satisfied that the contemplated proceeds of the offering will be adequate to remove the "immediate threat" to the continuation of business. The problem of immediate threat can also be solved by firm commitments from other sources, such as loans, providing they permit the enterprise to continue as a going concern.

ASR 115 deals with the problem of a company selling securities, using the proceeds to pay off existing creditors, and then going out of business. Such offerings would surely be deceptive to the public. Because the SEC did not want to preclude companies with pressing problems from selling securities, it made it clear that the accountant's report could meet the certification requirements of the 1933 act if the accountant is satisfied there is no immediate threat to continuation as a going business. The staff of the SEC has informally supported an interpretation by some accountants that "immediate" covers a period of one year from the date of the accountant's report contained in the registration.

SUGGESTED READING

AICPA. *Illustrations of Accounting for Contingencies.* Financial Report Survey 10. New York, 1976. In this survey of the application of SFAS 5, the AICPA staff searched NAARS computer files containing over 6,000 annual reports. The examples shown in the report are classified into various categories of contingencies and are useful in understanding many of the matters discussed in this chapter.

Commission on Auditors' Responsibilities. *Report, Conclusions, and Recommendations.* New York: AICPA, 1978. In Section 3 (pp. 23-30) the commission discusses "Reporting on Significant Uncertainties in Financial Presentations" in a manner that will be easily understood by presenters, auditors, and users of financial information. In some respects, the recommendations in this report point to the future direction of accounting, auditing, and reporting standards for uncertainties.

Goshay, Robert. *Impact on Corporate Risk and Insurance Management.* Statement of Financial Accounting Standards No. 5. Stamford, Conn.: FASB, 1978. In this research report, the effect of SFAS 5 on companies that had self-insurance reserves was studied by comparison with companies that did not. Professor Goshay concludes that SFAS 5 did not affect the way firms make risk and insurance management decisions.

30

Business Combinations

Bruce N. Willis

THE BUSINESS OF MERGING BUSINESSES

Businesses have combined as long as man has been involved in some form of organized commercial activity. One reason such transactions are the subject of special attention is that their magnitude is generally much greater than that of most other transactions. Selling a bar of soap does not have the same economic importance as selling the whole soap business. In any particular industry, the sale of a whole company can have significant repercussions—on competition, the market mechanism, and industry practice.

Another reason is that the modern system of absentee ownership gives the millions of shareholders in publicly traded companies a right to "sell" their businesses or "buy" other businesses with no more knowledge of what they are "selling" or "buying" than the financial information that must be supplied to them under the securities acts. Thus the public has a significant interest in business merger or combination activity, and the absentee owners have a particular need for some sort of reporting yardstick by which they can assess such activities. These two reasons necessitate the special accounting and auditing attention given business combinations and covered in this chapter.

Commonly Used Terms

Discussants of business combinations often frame their remarks in terms of strict definitions. In a purchase business combination, the purchaser is referred to as the *acquiring company* or the *acquirer,* while the seller is referred to as the *acquired company,* the *acquired,* or the *acquiree.* But when the business combination is accounted for as a pooling of interests, one company does not, in concept, *acquire* another, so different terms are used. A pooling of interests represents a *combining* of shareholder interests, the companies to be *pooled* are termed *combining companies,* the resulting entity is the *combined company,* and the formerly separate entities after the combination are the *combinee companies.*

Such hairsplitting is mostly a matter of semantics. Whether a business combination is a purchase or a pooling of interests is based on the precise circumstances attendant to the combination; the facts dictate the accounting method. This is so even when Goliath acquires David in a pooling. In this chapter, when a combination is discussed, it will often be in terms of a larger company acquiring a smaller one. It should *not* automatically be assumed that use of "acquire" in any of its forms means that purchase accounting is in order.

The Merger Movement[1]

In the United States, the first large number of mergers to be recorded followed passage of the Sherman Act in 1890 (which, curiously, was designed to discourage combinations by prohibiting those in restraint of trade). Most of these early mergers were achieved through an exchange of stock recorded at its par value and resulted in the creation of numerous vertical, fully integrated corporate complexes, such as Standard Oil Company and the United States Steel Corporation.

Shortly after the turn of the twentieth century another merger surge took place, though not among the existing corporate giants excluded by tough antimonopoly laws. Unfortunately, some of these combinations were "watered" through being accounted for at the par value of the issuer's stock and "dried up" during the Depression of the early 1930s. The par value accounting had not yet changed from the earlier era.

The current merger period, which introduced the phrase *pooling of interests,* started shortly after World War II and has been more or less continuous up to the present time. Relatively few mergers since World War II have combined two major corporate entities. Rather, most of them have involved two corporations so greatly disproportionate in size that the resulting company was not much different from the larger company before the merger.

Pooling of Interests. The earliest apparently official use of the phrase occurred in hearings before the Federal Power Commission (FPC) in connection with rate base cases. In a 1943 case (*Niagara Falls Power Co.,* 137 F.2d 749 (1943)) the FPC ruled (quoted in Wyatt, 1963, p. 22):

> ...while it may be tolerable to allow a buyer to capitalize the purchase price he may have paid, ... there is surely nothing to be said in favor of allowing two companies mutually to pool their interests, and from that time forward to treat as vested the values they happen then to have.

In a case shortly afterward involving two parties that had been previously related (*In re The Montana Power Company,* Opinions and Decisions, Vol. 4, p. 235), the FPC followed the logic of its 1943 ruling and required the companies to pool their interests. The FPC ruled (quoted in Wyatt, 1963, p. 23):

> It was not a sale by which one party disposed of an interest and another acquired that interest. Just as clearly, actual legitimate cost cannot be increased by a transaction which does not result in parting with property.

Thus the phrase was used to describe a type of transaction, not the accounting. The accounting simply followed the type of transaction.

The notion of pooling of interests first appeared in unofficial correspondence of the AICPA in late 1945 (Wyatt, 1963, p. 23). In this reference a pooling of

---

[1] See Wyatt, 1963, pp. 1-3.

interests was considered to have occurred in a merger between two previously unrelated companies of comparable size. However, no accounting standard resulted. It was not until the latter part of 1950 that the AICPA Committee on Accounting Procedure (CAP), the forerunner of the APB, issued ARB 40. That bulletin distinguished between the accounting for a purchase (involving enterprises disproportionate in size and in postmerger ownership interest and having a discontinuity of management and dissimilarity in operations) and the accounting for a pooling of interests (involving a stock-for-stock exchange between two previously unrelated companies of comparable size). This distinction failed to be sufficiently definitive, because numerous mergers did not fit easily into either category.

The CAP tried again in January 1957 with ARB 48. But this bulletin merely reiterated the earlier criteria, and was really no more than a rewording of ARB 40.

The Conglomerate Era

A significant increase in merger activity occurred during the early 1960s, the so-called conglomerate era. During this period the size test criterion was so stretched that combinations of 100 to 1 were treated as poolings, and the practice of part-purchase, part-pooling accounting developed. This type of accounting was popularly applied to combined stock and cash (or other forms of securities) mergers—literally, part of the combination was accounted for as a purchase, the balance as a pooling of interests.

Pooling Abuses. Certain abuses also became evident. The successor of two pooled enterprises would occasionally sell off a significant operating asset of the smaller predecessor entity and obtain a dramatic boost in earnings. There is certainly nothing abusive about such a transaction normally, but when such sales occurred soon after a pooling was consummated and the profits from the sale sustained a continued earnings growth by the combined company, there was a good deal of skepticism to say the least.

Earnings increases were also obtained by *retroactive pooling,* in which companies could merge after the year-end of the principal company and retroactively pool their income before the combined annual report for that year was issued. In at least one such arrangement a June merger in the year subsequent to that being reported on was treated as if the merger had occurred on or before the previous December 31, and financial statements were then issued for the combined enterprise. This practice provided an opportunity to locate a pooling partner after it was determined that the results of operations for the year were poor and needed augmentation. In the view of many, this was the most serious pooling abuse.

Still another procedure was to provide an earnings or market price contingency in the merger agreement, under which additional consideration would be received by the merged company's shareholders at a future date if certain earnings levels of the merged company, or market prices of the successor company's stock, were subsequently achieved. Some believed that this kind of transaction did not represent the marriage underlying a true pooling; it was more like a conditional dowry.

With the pooling criteria of ARB 48 eroded, abuses occurring, and criticism coming from the SEC, investment analysts, and financial writers, the APB decided to act. Thus, the present accounting rules, APB 16, *Business Combinations* (AC

1091), and APB 17, *Intangible Assets* (AC 5141), were issued in August 1970. By then, however, the conglomerate era, at which the opinions had been aimed, was practically over.

THE THEORY

A business combination involves an economic transaction in which there is an exchange of some form of consideration between two or more economic units (businesses) so that control of all units rests with all or part of the previous owners of the units. For example, if corporation A bargains with corporation B and corporation B's shareholders receive corporation A's equity securities, debt securities, notes, or cash in exchange for corporation B shareholders' voting common stock or the net assets of the corporation, a business combination has occurred. Note that the shares of corporation B could remain outside the exchange transaction. All that is required is that corporation B's former owners receive something of value for their ownership interest.

Business combinations are normally complex transactions. Although there appears to be no conceptual difference between the purchase of an asset and the acquisition of a business (which some view as simply the purchase of a basket of assets), in practice the acquisition of a business creates a host of problems and decision points. Among the things acquired are operating or manufacturing processes; management, staff, and line employees; a marketing, manufacturing, and administrative structure; and a company and product names. One problem is that some of these assets are not recorded in the accounts of the acquired business. Further, some of these assets are not directly valued even when they specifically have been purchased. This aspect of GAAP frequently results in the creation of an intangible asset that accountants call *goodwill,* discussed later in this chapter. These are some of the problems that attend a business combination when it is accounted for as a purchase.

But under certain circumstances, business combinations are accounted for as poolings of interests. Although there are many features that can be argued, most of the theoretical debate has focused on medium of exchange and on size of the companies.

Medium of Exchange

Some accountants argue that the medium of exchange used in a business combination affects the nature of the transaction. They contend that paying cash results in a net outflow of resources, since the cash goes to the shareholders of the acquired corporation and thus ends up outside the combined corporate entity. However, if the same combination is consummated by the issuance of common stock, no net resources are disbursed outside the combined corporate entity. Thus the second example would be a pooling of interests without a new basis of accounting.

This argument may put form over substance and is not particularly persuasive. Indeed, ARB 48 stated that the distinction between a purchase and a pooling rested on the circumstances of the combination, not its legal form. Nonetheless, when previously voting common shareowners exchange their stock for voting common stock of another entity, there is continuity of ownership by both sets of shareowners, and this notion is the theoretical justification for pooling-of-interests accounting.

Size of the Companies

Some accountants believe the size of the two components is critical in the purchase or pooling question. By one definition, a pooling of interests can only occur between entities of roughly equal size. The notion of pooling views the combining companies as if nothing had changed other than joining them; neither supposedly has become dominant in the combined company. If near equality of size were a criterion, the combining of General Motors with a small corporate parts supplier could hardly be considered a pooling of interests, since General Motors would obviously be the dominant company. Yet these kinds of combinations have been and still are accounted for as poolings of interests.

Current Accounting Standards

In spite of sharp criticism, multiple interpretations, and some fine tuning by the APB, FASB, and SEC, APBs 16 and 17 (AC 1091 and 5141) remain the authoritative literature[2] on business combinations. They represent an arbitrary, "cookbook" approach. Abuses of pooling accounting were thought to be rampant, and the APB felt compelled to act, without being able to agree on the underlying concepts.

The introductory text of APB 16 describes the nature and acceptance of both methods of accounting: purchase and pooling. It was generally understood in practice that certain transactions qualified as poolings and anything else had to be a purchase. Thus, the problem APB 16 addresses is how to identify a pooling of interests. By making the definition rigorous, the APB also eliminated part-purchase, part-pooling accounting.

A Perspective

As background for this chapter, it must be constantly kept in mind that the APB set a series of criteria for the use of pooling accounting. Failure to meet those criteria results in purchase accounting. The APB began work in the late 1960s, when there were serious pooling abuses; however, by the time the APB finished in 1970, business combinations as a whole had substantially subsided. As has happened with other major APB releases, the rules were established after their greatest need had passed. By failing to focus on purchase accounting, the APB neglected the possibility that companies might favor it because it could benefit subsequent results of operations in numerous situations.

---

[2] The FASB has issued two amendments to APB 16—SFAS 10 (AC 1092), extending the "grandfather" provisions of APB 16 (AC 1091), and SFAS 38 (AC 1093), dealing with later accounting for preacquisition contingencies—and two fairly narrow interpretations (AC 4211-1 and 1091-1). However, the AICPA issued over 100 unofficial interpretations of APBs 16 and 17 between 1970 and 1973, which may be found in the codification series AC U1091 and AC U5141. Some are mentioned in this chapter, and all are in fact regarded as reasonably "official."

This is not to suggest that there ought to be criteria that if not met would cause an intended purchase not to be accounted for as such; this would result in transactions not qualifying for either treatment, which is ludicrous. However, valuation practices in purchases fail to take into account the severe effects of different price/earnings multiples, whereby an otherwise sound company earning a modest rate of return allows the creation of an excess credit (*negative goodwill*) because the company acquiring it has a higher price/earnings multiple for its stock. Of course, the excess credit will not likely end up as negative goodwill, but will instead be applied to reduce noncurrent assets. This has a substantial benefit on near-term future operations, because there are lower bases, if not elimination, of assets that are otherwise amortized against future income. And if there is negative goodwill, it is usually amortized over a relatively few years, also enhancing near-term future earnings.

The problem, therefore, seems to be the predominant practice of using the value of the consideration given (as it is deemed more clearly evident for a publicly traded security) to establish the purchase price, when in fact the value of the consideration received may often be a better indicator. This would seem particularly appropriate with respect to companies being acquired whose quoted market value is below book value, assuming those book values are not below current cost. Often they are substantially above current cost.

A highly theoretical approach might be that each company should record the goodwill or negative goodwill reflected by the stock market's evaluation of its stock. If, for example, all companies valued their net assets in as close a manner as possible to discounted future cash flow[3] and identified in their equity sections the difference between the amount of revalued net assets and the stock market price as goodwill or negative goodwill, then presumably an exchange of securities among companies having substantially different proportionate amounts in this category (assuming a relatively efficient market—see Chapter 47) should result in a post-merger equalization of market valuations, without the goodwill games now played. A hypothetical and quite esoteric example is shown in Figure 30.1.

POOLING ACCOUNTING

A business combination, to be accounted for as a pooling of interests, must meet all the conditions in AC 1091.46-.48. Those conditions are grouped into (1) attributes of the combining companies, (2) manner of combining interests, and (3) absence of planned transactions. Each group is supported by two or more criteria.

Attributes of the Combining Companies

A pooling of interests must bring about the combination of two or more unrelated groups of shareholder interests having separate operations. This condition is fulfilled by meeting two criteria, autonomy and independence.

---

[3] For a good explanation of this approach see Ronen and Sorter, 1972.

Entities Under Common Control. When parties to a business combination are controlled by one entity, person, or group, the rules in APB 16 do not apply (AC 1091.05). For example, when the net assets of a wholly owned subsidiary are transferred to the parent company and the subsidiary is left holding treasury stock of the parent, only the legal organization is changed. The same is true of a parent company that transfers its interest in several partially owned subsidiaries to a new wholly owned subsidiary. A third example is a parent company exchanging its ownership or the net assets of a wholly owned subsidiary for additional stock issued by a subsidiary that is partially owned by the parent company. Although this increases the parent's share of ownership in the partially owned subsidiary, it leaves all existing minority interest outstanding.

Not all cases are as clear-cut as the examples above. Consider two publicly held companies in which family interests directly own, say, 60% of each. That's probably clear enough, but if smaller percentages are owned and that ownership is less direct, the classification becomes murky. Historically, for publicly held companies, the SEC has insisted that such mergers be accounted for *as poolings,* though technically they are not poolings of interests and do not meet the pooling criteria.

Manner of Combining Interests

The pooling concept contemplates the merging of separate stockholder interests of two or more companies into one combined group of stockholders. This condition is fulfilled by meeting seven criteria under the topics of (1) single transaction, (2) exchange of shares, (3) change in equity interest, (4) treasury stock, (5) ratio of shareholder interest, (6) proportionate voting rights, and (7) contingencies.

Single Transaction.

The combination is effected in a single transaction or is completed in accordance with a specific plan within one year after the plan is initiated. [AC 1091.47(a)]

A revision in a major term of the plan, such as the ratio of exchange, would create a new plan and initiate a new one-year period. If shares exchanged in accordance with the terms of the old agreement are not adjusted to the new terms and more than 10% of the shares of the company to be acquired have already been exchanged, pooling accounting simply may not be used. The acquiring company must obtain 90% of the *total* shares to be exchanged, in accordance with the new terms, in order to use pooling accounting.

If a delay in consummation beyond the one-year limit is caused by government proceedings, such as an antitrust suit or the need for regulatory agency merger approval, the time limit criterion is deemed not violated. Delays caused by the need for SEC registration of securities, on the other hand, are not acceptable as a reason for waiver of the one-year limit.

APB 16 does not clearly define what constitutes consummation. As a result, in December 1970 the AICPA issued an interpretation that states:

A plan of combination is consummated on the date the combination is completed, that is, the date assets are transferred to the issuing corporation. The quantitative measurements specified in sections 1091.46b and 1091.47b are, therefore, made on the date the combination is completed. If they and all of the other conditions specified in sections 1091.46-.48 are met on that date, the combination must be accounted for by the pooling of interests method. [AC U1091.012]

There is no theoretical reason for the one-year criterion as a condition of pooling. The time limit was probably included because of the concern that consummation might be delayed until certain market conditions exist, in effect guaranteeing a market price. Such a guarantee, directly given, would invalidate a pooling.

Exchange of Shares.

A corporation offers and issues only common stock with rights identical to those of the majority of its outstanding voting common stock [the class that has voting control] in exchange for substantially all of the voting common stock interest of another company at the date the plan of combination is consummated. [AC 1091.47(b)]

Substantially all means 90%. The 90% minimum also applies to common stock investments in the acquiring company held by the acquired company. Depending on the relationship of the outstanding shares of the two companies and the exchange ratio, it is possible that an investment in less than 10% of the shares of the acquiring company could prohibit the use of pooling accounting. An example is shown in Figure 30.2.

When 90% or more of the voting common stock of the acquired corporation is obtained, the 10% or less not exchanged may remain outstanding as a minority interest, or these shareholders may be eliminated with cash or other securities.

	Company A	*Company B*
Shares outstanding	1,000,000	500,000

Assume company B holds 75,000 shares of company A. Assume company A is acquiring company B in a common-stock-for-common-stock exchange, one share of A for one share of B. For company B, the following computation must be made:

1. Company A shares held by company B in terms of company B share (at ratio of 1 to 1) = 75,000

2. Total company B shares — 500,000
   Less: share equivalent above — 75,000

   Number of shares of company B considered as exchanged — 425,000

3. 90% of company B shares — 450,000

The number of company B shares considered as exchanged must equal or exceed the number representing 90% of all company B shares outstanding. Since it does not, pooling accounting may not be used.

FIGURE 30.2   EFFECT OF INTERCORPORATE INVESTMENT BY ACQUIRED COMPANY IN ACQUIRING COMPANY

However, a single shareholder may not exchange shares for part of his interest and accept cash for the remainder (a *partial dissenter*) (AC U1091.092).

Prior to consummation, one shareholder may privately buy out another for cash or other consideration. As long as this agreement is separate from the merger contract and is not a condition of the merger, it will not upset a pooling. Such agreements have occasionally been negotiated to take care of a potential dissenter who holds more than 10% of the shares of the company to be acquired.

The acquiring company may issue restricted shares. In the view of some accountants, there need not be a promise of future registration of shares that are restricted because of nonregistration with the SEC. However, even though they can "dribble" the shares onto the market, it would be wise to provide recipients of restricted shares with an opportunity to "piggy-back" (i.e., be carried along) the first time the acquiring company subsequently registers and sells securities following the pooling. Any resale restriction other than SEC registration of common stock issued in a merger will most likely invalidate a pooling.

The acquiring company has a number of options for dealing with securities of the acquired company other than voting common stock. They may remain outstanding, they may be redeemed for cash, or they may be exchanged for similar or other equity or debt securities. In the normal case, they have no effect on a pooling transaction. However, if the acquired company had exchanged its voting common stock for other equity or debt securities within two years of initiation of the merger or between initiation and consummation dates, voting common stock must be issued by the acquiring company. When equity securities (such as preferred stock) or debt securities remain outstanding after the pooling and they are publicly traded, the acquired company remains an SEC registrant and must file reports required under the 1934 Securities Exchange Act. This is a great deal of work, but it is often worthwhile to maintain capital less expensive than might currently be available.

In making a tender offer for the voting common stock of another company, the tendering company frequently cannot be assured of obtaining 90% of the stock. As a result, the tendering of at least 90% of the shares is made a condition of the offer if the acquirer intends to achieve pooling accounting.

The AICPA has interpreted the *exchange of shares* criterion as summarized below:

- The phrase "rights identical to those of the majority of its outstanding voting common stock" pertains to voting, dividends, liquidation, etc. Restrictions on rights to sell the exchanged stock, except in compliance with government regulations (such as SEC registration), would cause the rights to be different from those of the issuing company's stockholders and thereby preclude pooling-of-interests accounting (AC U1091.036-.039).

- Only common stock may be exchanged. Thus, pro rata distribution of warrants of the issuing corporation to stockholders of a combining company would ordinarily require the combination to be accounted for as a purchase. However, warrants (or cash or debt) could be used to acquire up to 10% of the common stock of the combining company as long as the other conditions for the 90% test are met. Warrants may also be issued in exchange for warrants, but the issued warrants may not permit purchase of a greater number of shares than could be obtained if the original warrants were exercised (AC U1091.040-.044).

- More than two companies may be involved in a business combination, but if pooling accounting is contemplated, the 10% and 90% tests must be met by all companies. In applying the 90% test, all intercompany investments are treated as outstanding but not as exchanged (AC U1091.147-.150).

Change in Equity Interest.

None of the combining companies changes the equity interest of the voting common stock in contemplation of effecting the combination either within two years before the plan of combination is initiated or between the dates the combination is initiated and consummated; changes in contemplation of effecting the combination may include distributions to stockholders and additional issuances, exchanges, and retirements of securities. [AC 1091.47(c)]

This criterion relates to voting common stock transactions and other net worth changes between the companies and their shareholders before consummation.

A dividend paid in cash or other assets by the acquired company to its shareholders before consummation will not invalidate a pooling as long as the dividend follows its own *normal* historical pattern. A company to be acquired might determine *normal* by looking to the dividend equivalent that the acquiring company paid, before consummation, to its own shareholders. Extreme care must be used in applying this provision, since the APB could not have intended that a company, perhaps a closely held company that has never paid a dividend, could be allowed to disburse half of its assets to pay that dividend equivalent. Yet, taken literally, this criterion would seem to permit such an action. The SEC would very likely challenge pooling accounting if this were the case.

In a pooling, those assets used in the operation of the business would seem to be most important. Thus the liquidation of the acquiree's significant portfolio of short-term investments representing a temporary use of funds would not preclude pooling treatment nor would a provision in the merger agreement that the sole stockholder of a combining company receive the cash surrender value of insurance on his life. However, a company's assets are presumed to be for use in the operation of the business, and it will be difficult to overcome this presumption.

This criterion (AC 1091.47(c)) was originally included to prevent companies from adjusting their outstanding stock to meet a size test. Later the APB abandoned any size test, but it neglected to remove the criterion. Some have suggested that the criterion was retained to prevent acquired companies from "cashing out" dissenters before consummation.

Treasury Stock.

Each of the combining companies reacquires shares of voting common stock only for purposes other than business combinations, and no company reacquires more than a normal number of shares between the date the plan of combination is initiated and consummated. [AC 1091.47(d)]

"For purposes other than business combinations" means for stock option and compensation plans and other recurring distributions, provided a systematic pattern of reacquisition has been established at least two years before the plan of combination is initiated. This has been the most interpreted criterion in APB 16. Treasury shares that do not meet this criterion are *tainted*. This criterion was originally demanded by SEC to govern situations in which the consideration paid is treasury stock, since the SEC tends to view such consideration as the equivalent of cash.

Treasury stock acquisitions by acquired companies to avert the need for buy-outs of potential dissenters to a merger transaction is another target of this rule. An AICPA interpretation (AC U1091.067-.073), approved by the APB and the SEC, permits a company to hold up to 10% tainted shares. The tainted shares are measured against the total shares to be issued in any combination to be accounted for as a pooling. The 10% test applies to all merger parties. For the acquired company, the test is applied by restating treasury shares in terms of the acquiring company's stock using the combination ratio of exchange. If the merger parties individually have 10% or less tainted shares, but more than 10% in the aggregate, the merger may not be accounted for as a pooling.[4]

Tainted shares held for two years or more become untainted. Other than by passage of time, a tainted share problem can only be cured by resale of the shares or the issuance and sale of an equivalent quantity of new shares. Formal retirement does not constitute a cure.

A systematic pattern is evidenced by the orderly, but not necessarily equal, acquisition of shares over a period of time. Such acquisition should relate in some manner to the anticipated requirements for an acceptable purpose, but this relationship need only exist at the date the shares are purchased. At a subsequent date there need only be a reasonable expectation that the shares will eventually be issued.

Acceptable purposes, according to the SEC,[5] include purchases to meet share requirements for stock option plans, stock purchase plans, stock compensation plans, convertible debentures, convertible stock, and warrants. Another acceptable purpose for acquiring shares is to meet stock dividend requirements (paid, declared, or planned) considered to be a recurring distribution. A paid, declared, or planned stock dividend is considered *recurring* when at least one stock dividend similar in amount was paid in each of the two preceding years.

The SEC further states that it is not necessary to meet the systematic pattern

---

[4] The 10% catch-all rule discussed later permits use of tainted treasury shares in a pooling in a limited way.

[5] The rules on treasury stock acquisition, tainting, and untainting are very convoluted as a result of the SEC's issuance of ASR 146 in 1973. Arthur Andersen & Co. became so concerned over the SEC's adding rules to the professional literature that it filed suit against the SEC.

Although the suit never came to trial, the SEC issued ASR 146A in 1973, which retained the rigid requirements of ASR 146, gave a few interpretations in sensitive areas, and passed the problem to the FASB, which by then had placed business combinations on its agenda.

After this skirmish with the accounting profession, the SEC thought it advisable to inform the world of its overall support of the FASB and issued ASR 150. This ASR said, in effect, that the SEC regards promulgations of the FASB as GAAP. Instead of assuaging the profession's feelings, this brought another lawsuit from Arthur Andersen, alleging that the SEC was violating the Administrative Procedures Act in the wholesale adoption of all FASB rules as SEC rules. This lawsuit failed to achieve the injunction sought, and ASR 150 stands. See Chapter 40 for more information on ASR 150.

test for purchase business combinations, or for existing contingent share agreements from a prior business combination, or to meet contractual obligations. To the extent reissued, such as in a purchase business combination, tainted treasury shares are cured on a *last-in, first-out (LIFO) basis.*

Under certain conditions, tainted shares purchased subsequent to a pooling combination may upset the pooling. The number of shares that may be acquired increases as the pooling consummation date becomes more remote. For a detailed evaluation of this complex criterion, readers should refer to "Implementing SEC Rules on Effect of Treasury Stock Transactions on Accounting for Business Combinations—ASR Nos. 146 and 146A," issued by the SEC in conjunction with the AICPA (*Journal of Accountancy,* November 1974, pp. 76-82).

The rules on the treasury stock criterion are almost pharisaical and in many respects extremely arbitrary. If future mergers are contemplated and pooling accounting desired, all treasury stock transactions should be scrutinized. Orderly resale of tainted treasury shares, depending on their age, should be seriously considered.

Ratio of Shareholder Interest.

The ratio of the interest of an individual common stockholder to those of other common stockholders in a combining company remains the same as a result of the exchange of stock to effect the combination. [AC 1091.47(e)]

Each shareholder of the prospective merging companies must receive the same exchange terms. A problem occasionally arises when a control group[6] exists in a publicly held company to be acquired. Normally, the control group will negotiate the merger agreement, and then a tender offer is made by the acquiring company to the noncontrolling group of shareholders. To encourage the noncontrolling group to tender, they may be offered a better ratio of exchange than is offered the control group. Although this is in no sense an abuse, it precludes the use of pooling accounting. To meet this criterion, all stockholders must be offered the same ratio of exchange.

Proportionate Voting Rights.

The voting rights to which the common stock ownership interests in the resulting combined corporation are entitled are exercisable by the stockholders; the stockholders are neither deprived of nor restricted in exercising those rights for a period. [AC 1091-.47(f)]

No special voting provisions, such as the transfer to a voting trust of shares issued in a merger, are permitted. Each shareholder must have the same proportionate voting rights after the merger as before.

---

[6] See SEC "No Sell-Off" Rule for commentary on control groups.

Contingencies.

The combination is resolved at the date the plan is consummated and no provisions of the plan relating to the issue of securities or other considerations are pending. [AC 1091.47(g)]

Neither earnings contingencies nor market price contingencies nor any combination of the two are permitted to exist at or after the consummation date. Contingency provisions in which shares issuable in a business combination are reserved or escrowed to back up *general management warranties* are acceptable. For example, a warranty by the management of an acquired company that the assets exist and are carried on a specified basis and that all liabilities and their amounts have been accrued and/or otherwise disclosed is a general representation.

An AICPA interpretation permits up to 10% of the shares that are to be issued in a pooling to be held in escrow for a period not extending beyond the date of the first auditor's report following consummation. Such an escrow may also be invoked for unspecified contingencies. Reservations of stock in addition to the 10% general provision are accepted in practice if specific asset valuation or potential liability problems exist. Examples are suspected inventory obsolescence problems or additional income taxes that may be payable as a result of an IRS review of income tax returns. The additional percentage of shares reserved must relate to the amount of the asset valuation problem or the additional liability that may be incurred. Some contingencies, such as income tax or legal matters, may not be resolved for years. Thus, the period for specific contingencies is permitted to extend beyond the date of the first subsequent auditor's report.

Employment contracts for acquired company personnel may be a condition in a merger to be accounted for as a pooling. If such plans are for stockholder employees who hold some nominal company position, they would probably be viewed as a form of earnings contingency and would likely invalidate a proposed pooling. Furthermore, bonus arrangements based on future results are not ruled out, as long as the compensation is not a camouflage for additional consideration under the plan of combination. Since fringe benefits are normally included in any compensation package, pension plans, profit-sharing plans, retirement plans, and other similar arrangements do not automatically rule out pooling accounting.

However, an agreement that calls for payments even though the individual should die is another matter. This links the bonus arrangement with the consideration under the plan of combination, because it will be paid in any event. Such a bonus would probably violate the pooling criterion that requires the combination to be resolved at the date the plan is consummated.

Since employment agreements take many forms and are limited only by the imagination of those involved in the negotiations, precise rules cannot be given for determining whether they are genuine compensation or disguised additional consideration. Among the factors that will influence this determination are (1) compensation of other executives of the combined companies with similar responsibilities, (2) previous compensation, and (3) compensation of executives in other companies engaged in similar businesses.

The contingencies criterion attempts to prevent the use of the *earnout* in a pooling of interests (which was one of the allegedly serious abuses of the period prior to APB 16), and it has been the subject of a considerable amount of interpretation. Though the rules regarding such contingencies seem to have become more flexible in recent years, the SEC and New York Stock Exchange (discussed later in this chapter) can be expected to scrutinize contingency provisions in specific transactions.

Absence of Planned Transactions

The third condition required for a pooling of interests is the absence of planned transactions. Holding that certain transactions after merger may raise doubts about whether a true combining of existing shareholder interests occurred, the APB specified three types of postcombination transactions that were presumed to proscribe pooling treatment. The SEC later added a fourth.

Reacquisition of Pooling Consideration.

The combined corporation does not agree directly or indirectly to retire or reacquire all or part of the common stock issued to effect the combination. [AC 1091.48(a)]

Any condition in a merger agreement that requires a shareholder of the combined company to sell or not sell shares is a violation of this criterion. Subject to restrictions inherent in the stock itself, such as a need for SEC registration, any shareholder should be able to arrange for the sale of his securities to another party after consummation, or hold them, as he wishes. (But see SEC "No Sell-Off" Rule below.)

Other Financial Arrangements.

The combined corporation does not enter into other financial arrangements for the benefit of the former stockholders of a combining company, such as a guaranty of loans secured by stock issued in the combination, which in effect negates the exchange of equity securities. [AC 1091.48(b)]

Under certain circumstances, an acquiring company may make a loan to an acquired company prior to consummation. Such a loan must be in accordance with normal commercial terms, i.e., not unusually liberal. Basically, any form of special benefit to a shareholder of a combining company is precluded, e.g., selective stock option or compensation plans, as noted above.

Asset Dispositions.

The combined corporation does not intend or plan to dispose of a significant part of the assets of the combining companies within two years after the combination other than disposals in the ordinary course of business of the formerly separate companies and to eliminate duplicate facilities or excess capacity. [AC 1091.48(c)]

Asset dispositions to comply with orders of governmental or judicial bodies are acceptable. Some asset sales before consummation are also acceptable, but sale of a subsidiary, division, or production process would probably violate the pooling, although no specific criterion in APB 16 can be cited. The reasoning is that such a sell-off would probably be viewed by the SEC as changing the entity in contemplation of pooling, which would be analogous to the provisions of AC 1091.47(c) discussed earlier.

The 10% Catch-All Rule

Because APB 16 was written in categorical terms, many questions were immediately raised about whether *any* deviation could be permitted while still achieving a pooling. For example, if an acquiring company makes a special arrangement for the benefit of a few shareholders of the acquired company (a prohibited transaction under 1091.48(b)), can it never qualify as a pooling? Practice quickly settled into using the *10% catch-all rule,* whereby any kind of transaction inimical to pooling has to be equated in terms of the number of shares of issuing company stock; the total of all such "negatives" cannot be more than 10% of the amount of stock the issuing company would issue to acquire 100% of the outstanding voting stock of the company to be acquired. The 10% comes, of course, from the fact that the APB required the acquiring company to achieve 90% of the acquiree's voting common stock to have a pooling, so it seems obvious that whatever happens with the other 10%, whether it is unacquired or in some other way not supportive of pooling, seems of little concern. However, the 10% cushion generally cannot be used to do partial special deals for shareholders. There can be no such thing as a *partial dissenter,* e.g., a 20% shareholder who tenders three-fourths his stock like everyone else, but gets a special deal on the remainder.

SEC "No Sell-Off" Rule

Although APB 16 theoretically permits the sale of any shares immediately after consummation of a business combination (as long as the sell-off is not a condition of the merger), the SEC decided that this condition is not acceptable for pooling accounting by a registrant. The commission views this as a *bailout* if the selling shareholder is part of a *control group.*[7]

To clarify its views, the SEC issued ASRs 130 and 135. Under these rules, a pooling transaction can be made subject to obtaining registration with the SEC of the issuable or issued shares, but the control group shareholders of the acquired company must nevertheless hold the stock they receive (be *at risk*) for a minimum holding period of thirty days of combined operations. Further, the results of combined operations must be published in a posteffective amendment to a registration statement, a Form 10-Q or 8-K, a quarterly earnings report, or any other public statement that includes combined sales and net income for at least the minimum period.

ASR 130 originally imposed the holding requirement on all shareholders of the acquired company. ASR 135, however, recognized the impracticality of that re-

---

[7] Neither ASR 135 nor any other SEC release defines *control group.* However, an *affiliate* as defined by Regulation S-X is considered a controlling shareholder. In general, the control group should be assumed to include officers, directors, and any direct or beneficial owner of 10% or more of the outstanding voting shares.

quirement and said only that *affiliates* of the acquired company would have to hold their new shares at risk for the holding period. It appears that "affiliate" was used in the release in the same sense as in Regulation S-X, i.e., only members of a clearly recognized control group are considered affiliates.

The fact that the stock ownership is widely dispersed over a large group does not necessarily mean that there are no affiliates. Other factors, such as relationships among some of the shareholders, would be considered. Clearly, though, the casual investor having a few hundred shares in a public company can do whatever he wants.

Applying Pooling-of-Interests Accounting

If all of the pooling criteria are met, a business combination *must* be accounted for as a pooling of interests. Combining companies who want to account for a business combination as a purchase need only violate a pooling criterion. However, when the merger appears to require purchase accounting, it is difficult, and sometimes impossible, to restructure negotiations to meet the pooling criteria. Because APB 16 is designed to prevent pooling abuses, it provides no real way to prevent the arranged use of purchase accounting when the parties find it more advantageous in accounting.

Pooled Financial Statements. When companies combine in a pooling, the accounting basis for the assets and liabilities of all the combined companies remains virtually unchanged—previous balance sheets and statements of income are simply added together. There are a few exceptions to this:

1. The combined capital structure of the surviving company will not be the same as the components of the individual companies. This occurs because new capital shares are issued in exchange for the shares of one or more combining companies. Because it is necessary to show the new shares at their par or stated value, which is highly unlikely to be exactly the same as such amounts in the balance sheet of the acquired company, a different total for common stock will occur.

   As to the sequence of this capital combination accounting, all the retained earnings of the previously separate companies are added to form a combined retained earnings. Then, if the total dollar amount at par or stated value of shares of stock outstanding after the pooling exceeds the total amount of capital stock of the separate combining companies, the excess should be deducted first from the combined additional paid-in capital, and if that is not sufficient, then from the combined retained earnings. If there is an excess of the individual company's capital stock accounts over the new par or stated value, that becomes added to combined additional paid-in capital.

2. Any significant amount of purchases and sales between the combining companies prior to the combination should be eliminated (along with the profits thereon) from the combined financial statements by the usual intercompany eliminations procedure performed in normal consolidations. To the extent the balance sheet is affected by intercompany profits in inventory or property, plant, and equipment, these should also be eliminated.

3. If the separate companies have recorded assets and liabilities under differing methods (for example, depreciation), they may be conformed retroactively (AC 1091.52 and

1051.35). But they need not be conformed and very often are not. See Figure 30.3 for an example of a combining balance sheet in a pooling.

Pooling Disclosures. The combined corporation should disclose in notes to the financial statements that a pooling-of-interests business combination has occurred during the period, and provide the following specific disclosures (summarized from AC 1091.64):

- Names and descriptions of the combined companies,
- Type and number of shares issued in the combination,
- A summary of the results of operations of the combining companies prior to the combination,
- Adjustments to conform accounting methods necessitated by the combination and their effects, if any, on net income of the previously separate companies,
- Details of an increase or decrease in retained earnings due to a change in fiscal year of a combining company, and
- Reconciliation of revenues and earnings previously reported by the company issuing the shares with currently reported amounts.

Retroactive poolings of interests, i.e., recording in the previous year a business combination consummated shortly after a company's year-end, are prohibited by APB 16 (AC 1091.61). However, a business combination initiated after the date of the financial statements but consummated before the financial statements are issued or incomplete at that date must be disclosed (AC 1091.65).

PURCHASE ACCOUNTING

This section deals with acquisition in a single transaction of a majority interest in an acquiree. See Chapter 31 for consideration of step-by-step acquisitions, including those that start well below 50% ownership.

Any business combination that does not meet all the pooling criteria must be accounted for as a purchase. The consideration given can be in any form—cash or any other kind of monetary asset, stock, debt, warrants, or nonmonetary assets. Determining the fair value of consideration given is quite easy when the consideration is cash or readily marketable monetary assets. When it is something else, valuation problems will ensue, as discussed in later paragraphs.

Acquiring Assets or Stock

When a business combination is formed by acquiring all the stock of the acquiree company, all its assets and liabilities come in through the transaction; if there are particular assets or liabilities that are subject to future reevaluation, such as possible uncollectible receivables or lawsuit contingencies, those matters may be dealt with by some sort of escrow and warranty. However, business combinations (whether pooling or purchase) can also be formed by acquiring assets rather than stock. In a pooling, of course, the assets tendered must be substantially all the

**PEPSICO, INC. AND SUBSIDIARIES AND TACO BELL AND SUBSIDIARY
CONDENSED PRO FORMA COMBINED BALANCE SHEET** (Unaudited)

(Pooling of Interests Basis)

(in thousands)

The following condensed pro forma balance sheet combines the consolidated balance sheet of PepsiCo and subsidiaries as of December 31, 1977 and the consolidated balance sheet of Taco Bell and subsidiary as of February 28, 1978, on a pooling of interests basis, after giving effect to the pro forma adjustments set forth in notes (a) and (b) below. This balance sheet should be read in conjunction with the separate consolidated financial statements and the related notes thereto of the respective companies included elsewhere herein.

	PepsiCo, Inc.	Taco Bell	Pro forma Adjustments	Pro forma Combined
ASSETS				
Current assets:				
Cash and marketable securities	$ 256,336	$ 10,323		$ 266,659
Notes and accounts receivable — net ...	372,035	1,646	$ 613 (a)	374,294
Inventories	314,314	1,465		315,779
Prepaid expenses	37,336	485		37,821
Total current assets	980,021	13,919	613	994,553
Property, plant and equipment — net	840,096	29,680	16,924 (a)	886,680
Other assets	227,174	8,405	15,082 (a)	250,661
	$2,047,291	$ 51,984	$ 32,619	$2,131,894

LIABILITIES AND SHAREHOLDERS' EQUITY

	PepsiCo, Inc.	Taco Bell	Pro forma Adjustments	Pro forma Combined
Current liabilities:				
Notes payable including current maturities on long-term liabilities	$ 47,039	$ 307	$ 1,294 (a)	$ 48,640
Accounts payable and accruals	401,619	4,071		405,690
Accrued taxes including taxes on income	115,470	2,187		117,657
Total current liabilities	564,128	6,565	1,294	571,987
Long-term liabilities and deferred credits	511,316	11,854	32,708 (a)	555,878
Shareholders' equity:				
Capital stock — 5¢ par value — PepsiCo, Inc.	4,343		247 (b)	4,590
Common stock — $.10 per value — Taco Bell		345	(345)(b)	—
Capital in excess of par value	161,339	3,115	98 (b)	164,552
Retained earnings	806,165	30,105	(1,383)(a)	834,887
Total shareholders' equity	971,847	33,565	(1,383)	1,004,029
	$2,047,291	$ 51,984	$ 32,619	$2,131,894

(a) Reflects the early application of Statement of Financial Accounting Standards No. 13 for Taco Bell's capital and direct financing leases to conform to PepsiCo's accounting policy (see Note 1 to PepsiCo's Consolidated Financial Statements and Note 7 to Taco Bell's Consolidated Financial Statements).

(b) Reflects the issuance of 1.43 shares of PepsiCo Capital Stock (a total of 4,938,000 shares as of February 28, 1978) in exchange for each of the outstanding shares of Taco Bell Common Stock.

FIGURE 30.3   EXAMPLE OF A COMBINING BALANCE SHEET IN A POOLING

Source: Pepsico, Listing Application to New York Stock Exchange, June 15, 1978.

operating net assets of the acquiree company, and this is accomplished by the acquiree company tendering assets and receiving the stock; it may or may not then
liquidate by distributing the stock to its shareholders. In a purchase business combination some of the assets may be held back, e.g., the acquiring company may
want only certain operations, or it may wish to leave the acquiree company with
certain problem assets or liabilities instead of handling these through a warranty
and escrow.

In this case, the consideration is distributed to the acquiree company in exchange
for the agreed-on net assets, and the acquiree company remains in existence pending resolution on the assets not exchanged, having as one of its (presumably) major
assets some or all of the consideration received (usually stock) of the acquiring
company.

Valuation of Net Assets Purchased

In a purchase, the value of acquired assets and assumed liabilities is based on
the consideration given or received, whichever is more clearly evident. Normally,
the value of the consideration given (such as cash, common stock, preferred stock,
debentures) is more clearly evident; the consideration given becomes the new cost
of the net assets in almost all cases. The acquisition of a group of assets and
liabilities requires that the new cost be assigned to the individual assets and liabilities. General guidelines for the specific assignment of the purchase price are given
in AC 1091.88 and are summarized in Figure 30.4. In effect, all the assets and
liabilities are to be recorded at their fair values as of the consummation date or a
nearby accounting cutoff date. Certain of the items in Figure 30.4 are discussed in
more detail in the paragraphs that follow.

Inventories. The LIFO inventory valuation of an acquired company may not be
carried forward after the purchase. AC 1091.88(c), through its valuation guidelines, requires appropriate assignment of the new cost. For federal income tax
purposes, LIFO may be continued (in an acquisition of stock rather than assets);
thus, the excess of cost assigned to LIFO inventories over LIFO amount in a
purchase acquisition will be added to inventories (or goodwill) in all balance
sheets after the acquisition, as if it were a discrete LIFO layer. Having such a
difference does not violate the LIFO conformity rule, based on IRS pronouncements (see Chapters 19 and 43). If this quasi layer is penetrated and the difference has been classified for balance sheet reporting as an element of goodwill, the
appropriate portion of the goodwill will be charged off to cost of sales. It is not
appropriate to deem that LIFO has been reestablished for that purpose at new
cost at the purchase date and then to carry that amount forward as the initial
layer for future LIFO computation purposes (unless this has actually happened
through an acquisition of the assets rather than the stock of the acquiree).

As to the assignment of purchase price to inventories, APB 16 (AC 1091.88(c))
takes the position that, in effect, part of the profit derived from inventories is earned
in the manufacturing process; not all of it comes from their sale. This method of
valuation is also based on the belief that, should the same inventories, in exactly
the same state of completion, be acquired in a bulk transaction, the least that the
seller would expect is a profit for manufacturing efforts. Thus, finished goods and
work in process reflect this in the valuation, raw materials do not.

Acquired Asset or Liability	Valuation
Marketable securities	Net realizable value
Receivables	Present value
Inventories	Finished goods: selling price less disposal costs and profit
	Work in process: estimated selling price less completion and disposal costs and profit
	Raw materials: replacement cost
Property, plant, and equipment	To be used: replacement cost
	To be sold: net realizable value
	To be used temporarily: net realizable value less future depreciation
Intangible assets	Appraised value
Other assets	Appraised value
Accounts and notes payable, long-term debt	Present value (determined at current interest rates)
Other liabilities and accruals	Present value (determined at current interest rates)

FIGURE 30.4 ASSET AND LIABILITY VALUATION BASES IN A PURCHASE BUSINESS COMBINATION

Identifiable Intangibles. AC 1091.88 states that identifiable intangible assets should not be included in goodwill but should be recorded at their own fair value. An example would be a favorable operating lease in which the facilities could presently be rented only at a higher cost (also considering nonmonetary terms of the lease). The intangible asset to be recorded in this situation represents the present value of this cost differential, which would be written off over the remaining lease term. Note that as to leases capitalized by the acquired company, the fair-valuing process must also be applied, but the value differential will affect the capitalized balances rather than being carried as an intangible asset. (See fn. 3 to AC 4053-2.15.)

Any goodwill carried in the accounts of an acquired company before acquisition should not be carried forward as such. However, as a practical matter, it may end up in the goodwill account of the acquiring company if the purchase price exceeds the fair values of the assets acquired less liabilities assumed, as discussed later.

Pensions. Another difficult problem exists if the acquired company has a pension plan in which the actuarially computed value of vested benefits exceeds the amount of the pension fund. As explained in AC 1091.88(h), fn. 14, the acquiring company must record the greater of the accrued costs calculated as if based on its own accounting policies or the actuarially computed vested benefits of the acquired company. This accounting is generally based on the theory that in a purchase acquisition there cannot be a carryover unaccrued liability for *past* service; but, in finalizing the opinion, the APB relented from the pure theory and allowed the same (but no more) relative unaccrual as that of the acquiring company.

Tax Effects as Assets and as Determinants of Fair Value. Tax benefits of loss carryforwards should be recorded as assets (receivables) in the acquisition if their realization subsequent to the acquisition date is assured beyond a reasonable doubt. Such loss carryforward tax benefits are generally not carried in the accounts of the acquired company, because of the stringent rules in APB 11 (AC 4091.44-.46); but they may be "good assets" because of tax opportunities available through the acquiring company or simply because their realizability has improved over time. When recording is not appropriate at the acquisition date, the tax benefits of loss carryforwards should be recorded when realized and should reduce the acquired goodwill (or increase negative goodwill) retroactively (AC 1091.88). In effect, such a tax benefit is viewed as an adjustment of the purchase price of the acquisition.

A determinant of the fair values of the assets acquired and liabilities assumed is the difference between such fair values and their tax basis (AC 1091.89). When a *tax-free purchase* occurs and the prior tax basis thus continues for tax purposes, the difference must be taken into account in determining fair value to be recorded. These differences are not considered timing differences (AC 4091.14), and therefore the purchasing company should not set up any deferred tax accounts to reflect these effects, nor should deferred tax accounts of the acquired company (which could relate to a part of these basis differences) be carried as such into the acquiring company's financial statements (AC 1091.88). Instead, these differences are handled as described in the following paragraphs.

The excess of fair value assigned to depreciable property assets over their tax basis signifies that depreciation in the future financial statements relating to such assets will not be fully deductible for tax purposes. Accordingly, the valuation excess would be halved (assuming a 50% corporate tax rate), taking this non-deductibility into account. Further, the halved excess should be discounted to reflect the probable timing of expiration of the difference. Many accountants refer to such treatment as *net-of-tax accounting,* proscribed by APB 11 (AC 4091.20) and readdressed in APB 16. In theory, the tax netting done under AC 1091.89 is based on the liability method (AC 4091.19) and thus is rationalized as not being an inconsistency between APBs 11 and 16.

Note that if the acquired company had deferred tax credits because of accelerated depreciation, they would be subsumed in this calculation and transmuted into a valuation credit. Although discounting of deferred taxes is prohibited, discounting of tax as a valuation factor is proper. The example in Figure 30.5 illustrates this calculation.

Accounting for tax basis differentials is more difficult when the deferred taxes of the acquired company arise from timing differences not directly related to assets or liabilities on the balance sheet. For example, the construction contractor who follows the percentage-of-completion method for financial statement purposes and the completed-contract method for tax purposes will have deferred tax accounts relating to the excess of profits reported for book purposes over those reported for tax purposes. It is conceivable, however, that some or all of the profits reported for financial statement purposes but not yet taxed have already been collected. If the untaxed profits have already been collected, the applicable deferred tax will

Depreciable property assets:	
Net book amount before acquisition	$1,000,000
Tax basis before acquisition	$ 800,000
Deferred tax credits applicable thereto	$ (100,000)
Fair value in acquisition without considering tax differentials	$1,500,000
Calculation:	
Excess of fair value over tax basis	$ 700,000
Tax effect at 50%	$ 350,000
Discounted to take into account the timing of expiration	$ 200,000*
Fair value at acquisition to be stated at:	
Gross amount	$1,500,000
Less discounted tax effect	200,000
Recorded in balance sheet as an asset	$1,300,000

* The amount shown is hypothetical. The interest rate, timing incidence, and depreciation method need to be factored into determining the discounted amount in a specific situation.

FIGURE 30.5   EXAMPLE OF TAX BASIS DIFFERENTIALS IN RECORDING PURCHASED ASSETS

have to be treated as a current liability for income taxes, since there seems no other appropriate place to put it. (It certainly cannot be deducted from cash!)

Preacquisition Contingencies

A difficult and complex problem in purchase accounting has been the finalization of the values to be placed on assets, liabilities, and contingencies of a purchased enterprise. For example, if certain segments or assets of the acquiree are to be sold off, an estimate of their realizable value is needed when allocating purchase price, but actual realization may turn out to be far different. Or accrued liabilities and outstanding lawsuits may be easy to identify but difficult to value, and later actual settlement amounts can vary tremendously, especially for contingencies.

When the actual realization or settlement amounts vary substantially from estimates at the acquisition date, many companies use retroactive accounting, especially in the first year following acquisition, but often also in the second and later years. The purchase goodwill is effectively revised and current operations are not affected.

The issuance of SFAS 16 in June 1977 (AC 2014) disallowed most prior-period adjustments, thus closing off the "holding open" valuation practices. The final opening was closed by the FASB with SFAS 38 (AC 1093) in September 1980, in that preacquisition contingencies are now also required to be estimated within a short time, say one year, after the acquisition date, and later differences must be included in operations of the period of reestimation or settlement. This accounting is all based on the theory that changes in estimates (which are not errors in the original estimation) are current-period events.

Earnings and Market Price Contingencies

One of the determinants in the purchase price of a business combination may be an earnings contingency, or *earnout*. Such arrangements typically provide for the payment of additional consideration based on the acquired company maintaining or achieving a specified earnings level in future periods. If the level is achieved and the additional consideration becomes payable, the acquiring corporation must record the then current fair value of the additional consideration as additional purchase cost (AC 1091.80). This additional cost must be spread among the affected assets acquired. Since the tangible and identifiable intangible assets would already have received, at the acquisition date, an allocation of purchase cost up to their fair values, the additional cost of the earnout would be added to goodwill and amortized over its remaining life.

A market price contingency (AC 1091.81-.82) may also be part of a purchase agreement. It could result in the issuance of additional consideration by the acquiring company to the former shareholders of the acquired company if the price of the security initially issued as consideration to the acquired company's shareholders does not at least equal a specified amount at a specified future date(s). When this occurs, the acquiring company must record the then current value of the additional consideration, at the same time reducing the recorded amount of the security paid when the combination was consummated. In this situation, the total cost of the purchase combination does not change; simply stated, more units of the security at a lower per-unit value are deemed to have been issued to accomplish the purchase acquisition. However, if the consideration originally issued is a debt security, a later reduction to a lower fair value results in a debt discount that must be recorded and amortized from the date additional consideration is issued.

Of course, there can be combination earnout and market price contingencies in a single deal, and the series of simultaneous equations required in these contingent payout deals can become computational horrors.

"Push-Down" Accounting

Although APB 16 requires the allocation of the purchase price based on the fair values of the net assets acquired (AC 1091.87), it is silent as to the physical disposition of the excess over (or decrement under) the historical cost of the net assets acquired. The question is, then, should the fair value increments (or decrements) be held in consolidation, held in the accounts of the acquiring company, or "pushed down" to the accounts of the acquired company? Obviously, in a situation in which consolidated reporting is always the practice, the question is academic. But frequently, parent-only and separate subsidiary financial statements are presented. To some accountants, the increment or decrement is properly held at the parent level. After all, it is the disposition of the parent's acquisition cost that is in question. Other accountants believe it is fallacious to present separately a subsidiary at the historical cost of the net assets acquired when a purchase has occurred and the subsidiary's accounts have been fair valued.

Those accountants supporting the push-down approach face an interesting dilemma when the subsidiary is not wholly owned.[8] Because the parent company obviously didn't purchase it, the minority interest must be maintained on its previous historical cost basis. The minority shareholders do not share in the additional capital resulting from the restatement, nor do they share in the depreciation, amortization, or any other charges or credits based on the differences between restated amounts and historical cost. As a result, when the purchase cost is to be allocated to the net assets of the subsidiary, a question arises whether to allocate only a percentage of the fair value increment or decrement based on the parent's ownership percentage or to allocate 100% of it. Obviously, the allocation of 100% could result in a total fair value assignment in excess of the purchase price, since the parent acquired less than 100% ownership of the subsidiary. (As further discussed in Chapter 31, the allocation is done on a proportional basis.)

In theory, there are many variations possible in recording a push-down where there is a minority interest. In practice, however, there are relatively few push-down examples available, and none with a large minority interest percentage.

Acquisition Date

The date of acquisition of a purchased company should ordinarily be the date the net assets are received and other assets (such as cash) are disbursed or securities are issued. For convenience, the effective date may be at the end of an accounting period between initiation and consummation of the combination. In this case, however, the written agreement transferring control should contain no restrictions except those required to protect the stockholders of the acquired company—for example, permission to pay dividends equal to those regularly paid before the effective date.

An effective date other than the date assets or securities are transferred requires adjustment of the consideration cost and net income of the acquired company to compensate for the period between the actual acquisition date and the effective date of recording (AC 1091.93). For example, if a purchase acquisition is consummated on May 5 and the parties agree to the convenience of effectively recording it as of the preceding April 1 (the beginning of a quarter), the income of the combined companies, which will include income of the acquired company from April 1, will have to be reduced by imputing interest at a current rate on the consideration given for the period April 1 to May 5.

Purchase Presentation and Disclosure

The statement of income for the combined companies for the year in which the purchase acquisition occurs should include the operations of the acquired company

---

[8] Even though all an acquiree's voting common stock may be obtained, the subsidiary may have publicly held preferred stock or debt outstanding and thus have to publicly issue financial statements. Push-down accounting is used in some of these situations. The discussion in this section focuses on a minority interest in common stock.

commencing with the date of acquisition. For purchase combinations, certain footnote disclosures are required for the period in which the combination occurs (AC 1091.95-.96):

- Name and description of the acquired company,
- Identification that the purchase method of accounting was used,
- Results of operations for the acquired company from the date of acquisition to the end of the period,
- Cost of the acquired company and, if applicable, the number and value of shares issued,
- Goodwill amortization plan, method, and period,
- Proposed accounting treatment for contingencies specified in the acquisition agreement, and
- Pro forma presentation of the results of operations as though the combination had been effected at the beginning of the period and, if comparative financial statements are presented, the same presentation for the preceding period.

GOODWILL

Positive Goodwill

Some of the intangible assets an enterprise acquires in a business combination are clearly identifiable; but in most cases there remains a balance of purchase cost in excess of the fair values assigned to all identifiable net assets. This excess is *goodwill,* though it is often described in lengthier terms. In concept it is considered that portion of the purchase price paid for earning power in the future, but in reality it is the product of the bargaining process between parties to a business combination. The imponderables of negotiation make it generally impossible to determine the worth of goodwill by direct valuation approaches.

Since ordinarily a direct valuation for goodwill cannot be made nor can its useful life be determined, it is a reasonable compromise, admittedly arbitrary, to define goodwill as the excess of purchase cost over fair value of all identifiable net assets and assign it a finite life. In constructing APB 17 (AC 5141), the APB concluded that goodwill and other intangible assets have neither the "infinite" life of such assets as land nor the finite life of such assets as machinery (AC 5141.22-.23). Goodwill must therefore be amortized systematically to income over the period estimated to be benefited, but not more than 40 years.

Although it is impossible to predict at the outset how long goodwill will last, it is sometimes easy to recognize that its value has diminished or expired. A company that reorganizes a purchased subsidiary and introduces substantially new product lines in place of previous lines or a purchased subsidiary that has produced a string of operating losses is generally demonstrating that the related purchased goodwill has significantly diminished in value and that part or all of the unamortized asset amount should be currently written off against income. The answer is not categorical, however. All the factors have to be considered, including what was expected of the purchased company at the date of purchase (for example, realigning product lines or experiencing losses for a time may have been contemplated, with the goodwill still resulting through the arithmetic of the net asset valuation). Note that a company may not write off goodwill when the purchase combination is consummated, even if it isn't possible to identify attributes of the purchased company that would justify it as an asset; this is an accounting anomaly that presumes no one would pay good money for nothing.

In arriving at the position that all intangibles diminish in value, the APB suggested factors to be considered in estimating useful lives. Among them are legal, regulatory, or contractual provisions that may limit the maximum useful life; provisions for renewal or extension that may alter a specified limit on useful life; effects of obsolescence and other economic factors that may reduce a useful life; the expected service life of individuals or groups of employees; and expected actions of competitors and others that may restrict present competitive advantages (AC 5141.27).

Negative Goodwill

The term *negative goodwill* is logically impossible but nevertheless widely used. When there is an excess of the fair value of net assets received in a purchase business combination over the fair value of the consideration paid, i.e., a *bargain purchase,* the excess must be allocated proportionately to reduce all noncurrent assets except marketable securities. After all such noncurrent assets are reduced to a zero value any remaining amount should be separately classified as a deferred credit, or *negative goodwill.* This negative goodwill should be amortized (as an addition to income) in a systematic manner over a period not exceeding 40 years. From a practical standpoint, the amortization period is never extended to the maximum. Most frequently the period extends from 3 to approximately 15 years, depending on the nature of the business acquired and its operating record after acquisition.

There is a presumption in APB 16 (AC 1091.91) that negative goodwill will rarely exist, and thus the net assets being valued in a purchase should have an inherently lower valuation close to the purchase price. However, there will still be some bargain purchases, such as the listed company whose stock is selling considerably below book value. In a purchase business combination brought about through an exchange of equity securities, when the acquired company has a low price/earnings ratio and and the acquiring company has a high price/earnings ratio, a considerable amount of negative goodwill could arise. The amount would, of course, depend on whether the low price/earnings ratio represented market recognition of unrecorded depreciation in net book values, but often it is the result of being in an industry faced with a low, but not negative, rate of return on invested capital. If net book values are in need of reduction to fair values, presumably little or no excess credit or negative goodwill should result.

APB 16 suggests that there may be cases where the quoted market price is not fair value of the stock issued, and that the net assets received should be estimated even though it would be difficult to measure their fair values directly (AC 1091.75). One meaning attributed to this paragraph is that it was intended to cover a particularly significant purchase by issuing stock, e.g., one in which the issuing company doubles its stockholders' equity. There could be a drastic effect, perhaps upward, in the market value of the issuing company's stock after acquisition, and this possibility should be considered when valuing the shares issued. It would be wrong in such a case to record negative goodwill when in fact positive goodwill may be involved. (See discussion under The Theory, A Perspective, earlier in this chapter.)

SEC REQUIREMENTS

Regulations

Because of their importance, business combinations involving publicly held companies are subjected to a myriad of SEC regulations designed to protect the interests of existing and prospective shareholders. Many business combinations are accomplished by the issuance of additional securities, either unissued or treasury shares, and if the newly issued shares are to be unrestricted, they must be registered under the Securities Act of 1933.

Many combinations involving the issuance of securities require the preparation of a proxy solicitation under Section 14 of the Securities Exchange Act of 1934 requesting existing shareholders to approve the combination. If two publicly held companies are involved, each can use the same proxy with separate covers. Frequently, the SEC registration requirements are met by preparation of a 1933 act Form S-14, which incorporates or "wraps around" the proxy materials.

A popular vehicle for accomplishing a business combination is the tender offer by one corporation inviting the shareholders of another corporation to tender or sell their shares for cash (or less frequently, for debt or equity securities or a combination thereof). SEC regulations controlling tender offers are contained in Sections 13 and 14 of the 1934 act, and require substantial information about the tender offer and financial data about the tendering company to be filed with the SEC and sent to the target company shareholders. Many publishers have services that describe in detail the ever-changing SEC requirements in the business combination area. (For an accounting and auditing viewpoint, as contrasted with the usual legal slant, see Poloway and Charles, *Accountants SEC Practice Manual.*)

In the fall of 1980, the SEC made available a new, short-form registration statement—Form S-15—for stock to be issued (by a company meeting Form S-7 eligibility requirements) in a business combination. The new form can be used where the company to be acquired would not cause a change of more than 10% in gross sales and operating revenues, net income, total assets and total shareholders' equity, and where the purchase price does not exceed 10% of the acquirer's total assets. The major ingredient in an S-15 will be the issuer's latest annual report to security holders, and the S-15 may serve as the proxy statement required under Section 14, mentioned above. For further information see Release 33-6232.

Accounting

Generally, the SEC rigorously enforces the provisions of APBs 16 and 17. Over time, the SEC has interpreted and expanded these provisions, especially the ones relative to the pooling-of-interests criteria. Some of these more important developments have been discussed previously in the chapter. However, a brief summary of published SEC interpretations follows; there are, of course, numerous SEC decisions or approvals that can only be observed by looking at effective SEC filings.

Operating Entity Rule. In a specific case involving the stock-for-stock acquisition of a company owning valuable natural resources and having only nominal sales, the SEC insisted on the application of purchase accounting (*CPA Journal,* June, 1974, p. 16). However, the SEC did not generalize on what constitutes the acquisition of an operating entity versus the acquisition of an asset. APB 16 (AC 1091.46(a)) is silent on whether a combining company in a business combination must be an operating entity.

Cash Exchanged for Warrants. Although APB 16 (AC 1091.47(b)) is silent on the matter, the SEC believes that the exchange of cash or cash equivalents like debt securities for the warrants of a combining company is a pooling-of-interests violation, since the warrants are viewed as similar to voting common stock (Arthur Andersen, 1978, p. 29).

Sale of Significant Assets Before Consummation. Although APB 16 does not address the subject (in AC 1091.47(c)), the SEC believes that the sale of significant assets of a combining company prior to consummation of a business combination is a pooling-of-interests violation, since it would be presumed that such action is in contemplation of the pooling. Such transactions are prohibited after consummation (AC 1091.48(c)), and the SEC apparently believes registrants should not be permitted to do before consummation what they cannot do after (Arthur Andersen, 1978, p. 35).

Treasury Stock Transactions. ASRs 146 and 146A and the unofficial AICPA/ SEC interpretation services discuss in considerable detail what treasury stock transactions may or may not be permitted without violating the pooling-of-interests criterion in AC 1091.47(d).

"No Sell-Off" Rule. ASRs 130 and 135 require a period of combined operations by pooled companies before securities received in a combination may be registered and sold. APB 16 invokes no such sales restriction.

Identifying an Acquiring Company. APB 16 (AC 1091.70) states that unless there is clear contrary evidence, the acquiring company in a purchase transaction is the company whose shareholders hold a majority of the voting stock after the purchase is consummated. In a specific case detailed in SAB 24, the SEC identified what it considered clear evidence that the smaller shareholder group was the acquirer. The SAB states that the decision as to which company was the acquirer was based on these considerations:

1. There would be restrictions on the ability of the former chairman of the board of the larger shareholder group company to solicit proxies or to participate in an election contest;

2. Top management and the board of directors of the combined corporation would substantially be individuals currently holding such positions in the smaller shareholder group company;

3. The assets, revenues, net earnings, and current market value of the smaller shareholder group company significantly exceed those of the larger; and

4. The market value of the securities (common and preferred) to be received by the former common shareholders of the smaller shareholder group company significantly exceeds the market value of the securities (common only) to be received by the former common shareholders of the larger.

The decision is not an obvious one, but it is a judgmental call that could be invoked by the SEC at a later date.

Pro Forma Financial Data. For a purchase business combination, AC 1091.96 requires the presentation of pro forma *combined results of operations*—revenue, income before extraordinary items, net income, and earnings per share—for the current year and preceding year if comparative financial statements are presented. The SEC continues to insist on the additional disclosure of the *contribution* to combined net sales and net income of material acquisition in the year of acquisition (Arthur Andersen, 1978, p. 115).

AUDITING

The companies involved in a business combination are most often audited by different CPA firms. Thus, the first challenge faced by the auditors is to establish a working arrangement with each other. For the *lead* auditor who decides to express reliance on the auditor of the company to be acquired, a business combination presents no special problems other than the usual reliance considerations discussed in Chapter 16. Even if reliance is not expressed by the lead auditor, he should satisfy himself as to the financial statements and the *secondary* auditor following the guidance in AU 543.

The material that follows is written mostly from the perspective of the auditor for the acquiring company, but by reversing the focus, it is equally applicable to auditors of the acquiree.

Pooling Versus Purchase

The critical factor in the audit of a business combination is the degree of assurance the auditor achieves in determining that the proper accounting method has been used, either pooling-of-interests or purchase accounting. To confirm that all the criteria have been met for a pooling of interests, the auditor must assess the terms of the business combination agreement, the history of the capital structure of all combining companies, the financial transactions of all the companies (both prior transactions and those that are probable after the combination is consummated), and the terms of any other possibly related contract, agreement, or arrangement coming to his attention that might affect the accounting for a combination.

Once there is a breach of any one pooling criterion, adherence to the other criteria is academic; purchase accounting must be applied. In a purchase the auditor is no longer concerned with the pooling criteria, but instead faces a whole series of valuation problems.

Depooling. When the pooling method has been used, the auditor must be particularly alert to the possibility that one of the combining companies, either inadvertently or intentionally, has performed some act after the combination was consummated that violates the criteria. If so, the combining companies could be faced with the very complex problem of unwinding the accounting, i.e., a retroactive *depooling*. This could even result in unwinding the combination itself, for some business combinations are consummated on the condition that pooling accounting is available.

As a practical matter, subsequent acts of this kind do not show up until quite some time after combination and can usually be justified on the basis of business developments occurring substantially after the pooling date. Such "current events" do not result in retroactive depooling. This treatment is consistent with SFAS 16 (AC 2014) proscribing prior-period adjustments, except that errors should be rolled back if material. Thus, if it should be determined by a preponderance of evidence that a major violative act was contemplated at the pooling date but not disclosed to the auditor, this is an error (AC 1051.13) requiring the auditor to follow SAS 1, *Subsequent Discovery of Facts Existing at the Date of the Auditor's Report* (AU 561); the treatment would be retroactive depooling or other accounting that currently accomplishes the same net result that would have been obtained if the transaction had been initially treated as a purchase.

Valuation of Consideration in a Purchase

The total purchase price is either the value of the consideration given or of that received, whichever is more clearly evident. In a combination in which all of the consideration given is cash, there is probably no question that this is the more clearly evident value and that it establishes the outside limit on the fair value of the net assets received. Also reasonably clear, granting that there may be some blockage involved, is the issuance by the purchaser of a relatively small proportion (in relation to amounts outstanding) of freely traded, marketable equity or debt securities of the purchasing company. Generally, the value of such marketable securities should also establish the outside limit on the fair value of the net assets received.

However, an audit challenge is necessary when the consideration given is an operating asset of the purchaser, thinly traded equity or debt securities of the purchaser, the equity securities of a closely held company, or a large block of securities whose issuance may upset the market. Sometimes an investment banking concern is engaged to establish a security's value (particularly where blockage may be involved), but apart from actively traded public companies, the fair value of the consideration received may often be the more clearly evident value. In this case, the appraised (or otherwise determined) fair values of the net assets received become crucially important. When the purchase price is determined in this way, the combination will not result in any goodwill. The auditor must assess management's decision on what is more clearly evident, and be concerned that undesired goodwill is not being improperly disposed of. When the assets received are comprised substantially of natural resources (petroleum reserves, hard minerals, standing timber), their values are more easily obtained and are readily usable as the fair value of the consideration received.

The problem may be much more difficult if, as is often the case, long-term assets (other than marketable investments) are involved. As responsible as an appraisal may be, to a large degree the total purchase price depends on the vagaries of the appraisal process. With the availability of replacement cost data under ASR 190 and current cost data under SFAS 33 (AC 1072; see Chapter 8) for some companies, the problem should have become easier. However, the large companies subject to these rules are not sellers, except perhaps of divisions and subsidiaries.

Negative Goodwill. In determining whether negative goodwill exists, the auditor should carefully consider whether stock being exchanged really has a value more readily determinable than the assets being acquired. The services of investment bankers could be used to evaluate the probable effect on the issuing company's stock as a result of making the offer, especially if the total amount of stock to be exchanged is much larger than the outstanding stock of the issuing company.

The action in the market of both companies' stocks before and after the announcement of exchange would also be significant in setting valuation. The auditor must be alert to the creation of negative goodwill, whereby the fair value of assets received is considerably in excess of the fair value of consideration given. The credit is first applied, of course, to noncurrent assets (except marketable securities), and if these amounts should be wiped out, the future operations of the acquired company will not be burdened with charges such as depreciation. This is said to caution that there can indeed be abuses of purchase accounting, as there were in the late 1960s in pooling accounting. (See The Theory, A Perspective, earlier in this chapter.)

SEC Releases on Securities Valuations. The SEC has issued two instructive documents, ASR 113, *Problems of Investment Company Ownership of Restricted Securities,* and ASR 118, *Accounting for Investment Securities by Registered Investment Companies,* which deal indirectly with the various factors involved in the valuation of all securities investments. ASR 118 points out that a wide variety of factors determines fair value, since in the final analysis, fair value is a free-market notion. If a security is not freely and widely traded, fair value must be estimated by some substitute method—a multiple of earnings, a discount from market value of a similar but freely traded security, yield to maturity (in the case of debt issues), or a combination of these and other methods.

Some general factors the SEC believes should be considered include (1) the fundamental analytical data relating to the investment, (2) the nature and duration of restrictions on disposition of the securities, and (3) factors that influence the market in which these securities trade. Some specific factors include the type of security, financial statements, cost at date of purchase, size of holding, discount from market value of unrestricted securities of the same class at time of purchase, special reports prepared by analysts, information as to any transactions or offers with respect to the security, the existence of merger proposals or tender offers affecting the securities, and the price and volume of public trading in similar securities of the issuer or comparable companies. For securities for which market quotations are available, the auditor should independently verify the quotations

the acquisition review, the reviewing auditor must nonetheless acquire his own understanding of the business, the major risks, and the basic reasons for the acquisition, and know the probable form of the transaction.

When a review rather than an audit is sufficient, the auditor's inquiries are generally aimed at the accounting principles employed, and he will use various analytical procedures (see Chapter 12) to evaluate the reasonableness of the account balances. Typically, supporting documentation would be reviewed (e.g., accounts receivable agings, excess and obsolete inventory analyses), but verification of balances with outside parties would be omitted or not be extensive. SSARS 1, *Compilation and Review of Financial Statements* (AR 100), and SAS 23, *Analytical Review Procedures* (AU 318), provide examples of inquiry and review procedures that are also appropriate ingredients in acquisition reviews.

Working With Attorneys. In an acquisition, attorneys for the parties perform a significant role in drafting the letter of intent, actual or definitive agreements, and supporting documents. The acquirer's attorney will aim to reduce the risk of his client through requiring more of the sellers and their attorneys and auditors. Likewise, the attorney expects the acquiring company's auditor to help reduce the risks. Naturally, the mergee's attorneys have the same objectives for their client. It is therefore important that each client, his attorneys, and his auditors work together on a timely basis to properly assemble a feasible overall acquisition audit or review plan and merger agreement. The auditor must understand the timing sequence, which often will include a letter of intent, a definitive agreement, the signing of the definitive agreement, and the closing.

Unrealistic expectations of auditors by attorneys often result from an unclear understanding or communication of the audit or review process or of what work the auditor is actually performing. They can also result from the use of vague or imprecise language in the merger. Such terms as "sound accounting principles and practices," used in place of "generally accepted accounting principles," can subsequently be used to argue in court that an accounting principle may not be sound even though generally accepted. Indeed, it has been suggested that terminology is sometimes used with a private knowledge of its vagueness and imprecision, just so that all options are kept open. Therefore, let the auditor beware!

Other conditions of closing the agreement will commonly be based on the expectation of acceptable reports from the auditor. These may also involve qualitative aspects relating to one or both companies' financial statements discussed below. Another common contingency relates to the accounting treatment of the merger, typically the acceptability of the pooling method. Because the auditor obviously must stay within the boundaries of professional standards in determining both the scope of his work and the report that he may issue, he should ensure at the outset that his plan is acceptable to the parties. He may wish to draft the type of report he would expect to issue upon satisfactory completion, to make sure it is acceptable to the attorneys.

Qualitative Financial Statement Considerations. During the period between the date of signing the merger agreement and the closing, developments can occur that would make the acquisition substantially less desirable. Depending on the nature of the merger candidate's business, operations could perhaps decline markedly, or adverse government regulation or litigation could drastically impact the original evaluations. It is the client's responsibility to anticipate such possibilities.

Although the auditor may be requested to perform an update review covering the period from signing to closing, he should not permit the agreement to require that he report the occurrence of an unquantifiable development, such as a "material adverse change" compared with an earlier date. Such matters are rarely susceptible to subsequent agreement in the event of a dispute between the buyers and sellers, and the buyer's auditor is in an impossible situation if he in effect defines, by his report, what the parties did not adequately define in the merger agreement itself. The auditor must insist that any such report he would be expected to issue would address only quantitative standards, such as increases or decreases of recorded or otherwise readily determinable amounts.

Assisting in Recognition of Business Risks. The auditor can be of considerable assistance to his client in recognizing exposure areas for which additional escrow may be warranted, as indicated in the illustrative list below:

• Uncollectible accounts receivable because of returns, allowances, or bad debts;
• Overvalued inventory because of mispricing or excess, obsolete, or nonexistent quantities;
• Obsolete or missing equipment or furnishings; and
• Unrecorded liabilities to vendors, litigants, or tax authorities.

Subsequent operations and audits may disclose such matters; however, there is no assurance that all such matters that could affect the escrow, if any, would be noted by management or even reported to the purchaser. This is particularly true if the former owners continue as management of the acquired company.

Large inventory adjustments subsequent to acquisition are particularly troublesome, because it is usually difficult if not impossible to establish when or why a loss occurred. Although this risk does not necessarily mean that a complete physical count and pricing must be made of all inventory and equipment in conjunction with the closing, the auditor should ensure that his client understands the room for argument in other alternatives. The client must make these and other decisions (and compromises) based on materiality, available escrows, and effect on morale of the parties involved. Absolute assurance is never practical.

Comfort Letters

The acquiring company should attempt to obtain a comfort letter from the proposed mergee's auditor on any unaudited period subsequent to the last audit. Ordinarily, that auditor is able to issue a "negative assurance" letter comparable to that provided to underwriters in a 1933 Securities Act filing (see Chapter 26). For acquisitions, such letters are sanctioned by SAS 26 (AU 504.20). The proposed mergee's auditor is the proper party to issue the letter, because he undoubtedly has more audit experience with his client than is obtainable by the review. At the same time, the acquirer's auditor may be asked to issue a comfort letter about his client's unaudited period, addressed to the acquiree company. These letters are called cross-comfort letters when both auditors issue them.

The Auditor in a Takeover Attempt

The auditor is often active in situations in which his client is a target in an unwanted takeover attempt, a frequent occurrence in recent years. He will work with his client in professionally acceptable ways to attack the insufficiency of the offer or the undesirability of the transaction at any price. The defensive efforts may encompass projections of the undervalued target company's operations (see Chapter 33) as well as analysis of the unconservative accounting principles of the proposed acquirer.

New York Stock Exchange Pooling Letters

Ever since the issuance of APB 16, the New York Stock Exchange has required that auditors provide a letter to the exchange regarding the conformity of a particular business combination with each and all of the criteria for pooling-of-interests accounting. Auditors at first complained that this was "painting the lily," since the auditor could not approve the transaction as a pooling unless it met all of the criteria of APB 16. However, the exchange received its share of criticism from the public regarding high-flying stocks used for poolings prior to 1970, and therefore the NYSE felt it wanted to check the details to aid in preventing a recurrence of the problem. (Remember, however, that the glamour was over by 1970.)

After issuing the early NYSE pooling letters, auditors found that the exchange asked many questions, particularly about escrows for future contingencies, and the result was a number of interpretations adopted by the AICPA. Thus, the NYSE did have, and continues to have, an impact with respect to some of the fuzzy areas in APB 16. (An example of a NYSE pooling letter is shown in Poloway and Charles, ¶ 3541.)

THE FUTURE OF BUSINESS COMBINATION ACCOUNTING

In the past, many companies involved in business combinations painstakingly avoided purchase accounting, because the resultant goodwill must be amortized and can be a significant deduction on the income statement without being deductible for income tax purposes.

In purchase transactions, when the consideration paid is a publicly traded security, its valuation for accounting purposes is normally based on the traded price of the security. Yet the traded value of the security has not always been the crucial value that closes the deal. In some respects, after all, the purchaser is giving up no more than paper, and he may be willing to give up more paper than he is cash.

The sellers' view of the paper in the transaction has also tended to exacerbate the problem. Although the seller can see the current market price of the security received, he has no certain method of forecasting that security's prospects. He may demand more paper as insurance against a potential downturn. The measurement base may again be ignored, thus exerting further upward pressure on the total price of the combination.

As a result, goodwill has often risen to illogical levels, at least for measurement purposes, making purchase accounting aversive. The strong desire to avoid this problem by using pooling-of-interests accounting is generally disruptive of orderly business combination accounting. In the view of many accountants, it is thus goodwill for which a solution is needed.

Widespread discontent with APBs 16 and 17 led the FASB to place accounting for business combinations on its agenda very early—November 1973. The task force appointed to the project took up the question of whether to attack the entire existing framework of business combination accounting or simply to perform a "patch job." The task force recommended a full reconsideration of the subject, and the Financial Accounting Standards Advisory Council concurred. Concluding that tampering with a problem area would only make the problem worse, the FASB adopted this recommendation and devoted a considerable amount of staff effort to identifying and analyzing the issues. The results were published in a discussion memorandum (FASB, 1976a) that identified 38 issues and alternative solutions, covering all aspects of business combinations, within the framework of historical cost accounting.

But no public hearings on the subject have been held. The FASB concluded that a statement on the elements of financial statements (see Chapter 2), possibly including new definitions of assets, liabilities, owner's equity, earnings, revenue, expenses, and gains and losses, must precede further action on the business combinations project, since the answers to the elements questions are crucial to many business combination accounting decisions. For example, if the Board were to conclude that goodwill is not an asset or that it should be determined by some direct means, it would be useless to have developed accounting standards for a purchase business combination that defines goodwill the same as at present.

After the FASB finalizes its elements statement, the business combinations project must go through a public hearing, consideration of comments, issuance of an exposure draft, another comment and evaluation period, and development of a final statement. Thus it is likely that APBs 16 and 17, despite the inadequacies that many observers find in them, will continue at least until the end of 1981.

Though it is difficult to predict how business combinations will be accounted for in the future, it does seem logical that the growing emphasis on current value concepts could have a dramatic effect. For if the historical cost basis for financial statements recedes, so must the long-standing notion of pooling of interests.

SUGGESTED READING

Briloff, Abraham. *Unaccountable Accounting.* New York: Harper & Row, 1972. This book is a highly critical assessment of accounting and accountants over a more than 30-year period. A part of the criticism relates to pooling and purchase accounting abuses generally during the 1960s.

Burton, John C. *Accounting for Business Combinations.* New York: Financial Executives Research Foundation, 1970. The study deals extensively with the theory of accounting for business combinations and the alleged accounting abuses of the conglomerate era of the 1960s. Burton draws heavily on corporate responses to questionnaires used in the study.

FASB. *Discussion Memorandum on Analysis of Issues Related to Accounting for Business Combinations and Purchased Intangibles.* Stamford, Conn., 1976. This publication discusses conceptual and pragmatic issues concerning business combination and intangible asset accounting, drawing on a wide body of literature. It is an excellent source for readings on these subjects.

Poloway, Morton, and Charles, Dane. *Accountants SEC Practice Manual.* Chicago: Commerce Clearing House, 1980. This service, which is updated monthly, describes SEC accounting requirements. The material relative to business combinations is presented from an accounting and auditing point of view instead of from the more usual legal view.

Wyatt, Arthur. *A Critical Study of Accounting for Business Combinations.* Accounting Research Study 5. New York: AICPA, 1963. The study provides complete coverage of the history of, economics of, and accounting for business combinations up through the early 1960's.

31

Consolidated Financial Statements and Foreign Currency Translation

Robert J. Sack

CONSOLIDATED FINANCIAL STATEMENTS

The purpose of consolidated statements is to present the results of operations and the financial position of a parent company and its subsidiaries as though they were a single company (AC 2051.02). According to ARB 51, a consolidated presentation is presumptively more meaningful than presenting each company's statements separately; but it goes on to say that the presumption can be overridden. It concludes that a company's consolidation policy should be designed to produce the most meaningful financial presentation in the circumstances (AC 2051.02-.04).

Despite the latitude suggested by the "meaningful" criterion, current practice seems much more rigid. Except for the exclusions mentioned in the following subsection, material majority-owned subsidiaries are almost always consolidated.

Underlying Theory

The theory behind the preparation of consolidated financial statements may be stated quite simply: when a parent company has a controlling financial interest in a subsidiary, permitting it to direct the subsidiary's policies and its management—and in particular to direct the subsidiary to pay a dividend—the assets, liabilities, and operations of the two companies should be presented in one set of consolidated financial statements as though they had operated as a single company. This general approach was articulated originally by the American Institute of Accountants (forerunner of the AICPA) in 1929, and 30 years later it was formally promulgated in ARB 51 (AC 2051), which with few amendments is still the authority for today's practice.

The theory, however, is often difficult to apply, because the parent-subsidiary relationship can be a complex one. For example, it is fair to question whether a parent should consolidate its wholly owned subsidiary when the creditors have de facto control as a result of restrictions in the subsidiary's lending agreements, or conversely whether a parent should deconsolidate an operationally integrated subsidiary just because it owns a shade less than a majority of the voting stock. These complexities make it difficult enough to apply the consolidated rules fairly, but other accounting standards add to the complications. For example, as leasing rules under SFAS 13 (AC 4053) have tightened up, some companies have attempted to push otherwise capitalizable leases and other off–balance sheet financing (discussed further in Chapter 23) into an independent financing company, nominally controlled by an outsider. Also, because SFAS 2 (AC 4211) requires expensing the costs of research and development activities, there has been a temptation to have those activities performed as contract research by a company owned by technically unaffiliated parties but financed by the contract with the beneficiary company (see Chapter 21).

No matter what the *form* of the association might be, the consolidation rules should be applied based on the *substance* of the relationship. The underlying consolidation theory requires consolidation of any company *substantively* controlled by its parent, but consolidation of companies not more than 50% owned is almost never permitted in practice.

Control Defined. There is no original definition of "control" in the authoritative accounting literature, but the SEC has provided one in Rule 1-02 of Regulation

S-X, incorporated for accountants' use in SAS 6: "*Control* means the possession, direct or indirect, of the power to direct or cause the direction of the management and policies of a specified party whether through ownership, by contract, or otherwise" (AU 335.02, fn. 2).

As a general rule, a parent may consolidate only those controlled subsidiaries in which it has a voting stock interest in excess of 50%. There are many ways one company can exercise control over another, of course. For practical purposes, a company could find itself controlled by a major customer, a major supplier, or a major creditor. However, for consolidation purposes, control is defined in strict quantitative terms under ARB 51: ". . . a controlling financial interest . . . [results from] ownership directly or indirectly of over fifty percent of the outstanding voting shares . . ." (AC 2051.03).

Even though the SEC definition of control is not limited to majority stock ownership, when it comes to consolidation the SEC insists on it. Rule 3A-02 of Regulation S-X deals with consolidation practices and provides that "no subsidiary shall be consolidated which is not majority owned." Here, again, ownership of the subsidiary is measured in terms of the voting stock of the subsidiary.

There have been exceptions to the majority ownership rule, but very few. For example, a large multinational company had a 48% interest in a foreign subsidiary it clearly controlled. The parent provided all of the management and technical know-how and was assured a majority of the seats on the subsidiary's board of directors. Under local law, a majority of the subsidiary's voting stock had to be owned by nationals, and such stock was widely distributed. Consolidation of the subsidiary was justified by the substance of the parent's control and because of the unique circumstances that required an outside majority ownership. But other apparently similar situations use the equity method (see Chapter 21), so it cannot be said there is only one way to account for such companies.

Unconsolidated Subsidiaries

The statistics available in *Accounting Trends and Techniques* (AICPA, 1979c) demonstrate that consolidation is the norm for publicly held companies—but they also identify a few well-established exceptions, as shown in Figure 31.1.

Most of the unconsolidated subsidiaries identified in Figure 31.1 are financial companies of some kind, and most are affiliated with a manufacturing or retailing parent. Subsidiaries in a unique or specialized business are usually not consolidated with other subsidiaries in different businesses. That exclusionary practice has a practical basis: a financial statement that consolidated the activities of a manufacturing company and an insurance company, for example, might be a hodgepodge of significant numbers—inventories and investments, mortgage debt and insurance reserves—and there is serious concern that a consolidated presentation could obscure the true picture of the overall enterprise position and results.

The idea that subsidiaries in fundamentally disparate businesses should be excluded from a consolidation has long been part of the profession's thinking. The very first version of Regulation S-X in 1940 included rules prohibiting the consolidation of any subsidiary in insurance, banking, or the investment business. In addition to the concern about commingling different kinds of assets, there was apparently some feeling that the special legal status of those heavily regulated businesses should be a factor in the decision that they should not be consolidated.

Total companies sampled	600
Companies consolidating all significant subsidiaries	428
Companies consolidating certain significant subsidiaries	163
Nature of subsidiaries not consolidated:	
Finance entities:	
Credit	94
Insurance	31
Leasing	18
Banks	6
Real estate	25
Foreign	33
Companies not presenting consolidated statements	9

FIGURE 31.1   1978 CONSOLIDATION PRACTICES
SOURCE: AICPA, *Accounting Trends and Techniques* (New York, 1979), adapted from Table 1-9.

In 1974 the SEC adopted a more contemporary view in ASR 154, which repealed that part of Regulation S-X prohibiting the consolidation of finance-type subsidiaries. ASR 154 said that such subsidiaries *could* be consolidated, as long as their financial statements were also presented separately as footnotes to the consolidated statements. That permissive release has so far had little impact on practice, however. Many companies seem reluctant to contradict tradition by extending their consolidation policies. Perhaps more importantly, many companies hesitate to consolidate their finance-type subsidiaries simply because this would result in the consolidated statements including the normally large outstanding debt of those subsidiaries.

Real Estate and Credit Subsidiaries. It was the debt presentation problem that led to dealing with real estate subsidiaries in APB 10 (1966). This *omnibus opinion* provision (later transferred to APB 18 and then to SFAS 13; AC 4053.031) requires consolidation of any subsidiary whose principal business is leasing real estate or other property to other members of the corporate group. Prior to APB 10 some companies had created separate real estate subsidiaries to hold the property required for the companies' businesses and to carry the related debt. They argued that their real estate subsidiaries were in dissimilar businesses, and thus kept the property-related debt out of the consolidated statements. APB 10 maintained that the real estate subsidiaries were not in dissimilar businesses but were in fact integral pieces of the consolidated group, and that only consolidated statements could fairly present that integrated relationship.

Based on the theory presented in APB 10, it would seem reasonable that captive credit companies should also be consolidated, but that has not been the case. Typically, a captive credit company borrows money in its own name, using long-term notes and short-term paper (sometimes guaranteed by the parent). The credit subsidiary may then use the proceeds of its borrowings to purchase its parent's trade accounts on a recourse basis. In other situations the credit subsidiary extends credit directly to the ultimate customer and assumes all credit risk.

In theory, consolidation practice should follow the substance of that risk. When the parent company remains responsible for the ultimate credit risk (because it has sold its accounts on a recourse basis or guaranteed the subsidiary's debt), it should consolidate its credit subsidiary. However, even when the parent has the ultimate credit risk, present accounting permits a parent to treat its credit subsidiary as a "diverse" business and to include its operations as a single-line item in the overall financial statements, using the equity method. If it is a material subsidiary, a summary of its financial statements would, in any event, be presented in a foot-note or supplement to the consolidated financial statements.

Temporary or Ineffectual Control. ARB 51 indicates that a subsidiary should not be consolidated if there is some uncertainty as to the effectiveness or the per-manency of the parent's control (AC 2051.03). For example, a parent should not consolidate a subsidiary's statements when the subsidiary is in bankruptcy, when a foreign subsidiary's funds are blocked because of currency exchange restrictions, or when the subsidiary's debt covenants prevent the parent from exercising its legal control.

These traditional requirements for excluding subsidiaries can be observed in practice, but they are not invoked as often as one might expect. For example, the foreign subsidiary exclusion based on ARB 43 (AC 1081.08), a 1953 codification of earlier rules, has not been revised, because most foreign countries still have exchange control restrictions that make it difficult—in some cases impossible—for a local company to remit dividends to a parent outside the country. And most loan agreements in which the subsidiary is the obligor restrict the payment of dividends from the subsidiary to its parent. Despite the fact that many subsidiaries are burdened with one or both of these obstacles, in practice most are consolidated.

A parent might feel justified in consolidating an apparently burdened subsidiary because the subsidiary is an important manufacturing facility or sales outlet or because it is in some other way significant to the enterprise as a whole. As long as the parent is in a position to control the deployment of the subsidiary's assets or its operating policies, the subsidiary's financial statements may (and should) be consolidated, even when there may be some restrictions on the parent's total latitude. If the distribution of the subsidiary's earnings is blocked in some way, that fact, and the dollars involved, should be disclosed in the notes to the con-solidated statements.

Consolidation Procedure

Conceptual Approaches. There are several ways of looking at a consolidated company, and each point of view suggests a different accounting. Some argue that a consolidated company should be seen as a *single entity,* without real separation between its components. Therefore, they would argue that there could never be a minority interest, only a different kind of stockholder. However, those who look at a consolidated company from the viewpoint of the parent's shareholders have a *proprietary* perspective. They see the subsidiaries as separate legal companies. They therefore insist that a minority interest is not a part of the parent's capital structure but a simple, mathematical by-product of the consolidation process.

There are other accounting issues that separate the *entity theory* from the *proprietary theory*, and strong arguments abound on both sides. Unfortunately, current consolidation practice has evolved with little regard to these theoretical arguments, and in fact without much regard for a conceptual basis. The remainder of this section on consolidation, therefore, presents procedures as they exist today in practice, whether or not practice is logically consistent in all its aspects.

Formation of a Subsidiary. If the parent forms a subsidiary, its investment will be represented by the subsidiary's net assets. As long as transactions between the parent and the subsidiary are recorded at cost, the consolidation process will usually consist simply of substituting the details of the subsidiary's net assets for the aggregate of the parent's investment. Any intercompany advances or purchases and sales are offset and eliminated from the consolidated statements. The details of the subsidiary's assets and liabilities, third-party sales, and costs and expenses are combined with those of the parent.

Acquisition of a Subsidiary. If the parent acquires a subsidiary in a pooling transaction, the same accounting result is obtained as if the subsidiary were newly formed. The parent's investment in the subsidiary is presumed to be equal to the subsidiary's net assets, based on the subsidiary's historical costs. Upon consolidation the intercompany accounts are eliminated and the details of the two companies' financial statements are simply combined.

However, if the parent acquires the subsidiary in a purchase transaction, the accounting will be more complicated. At the date of the purchase, the subsidiary's balance sheet will be restated to reflect the fair value of all its identifiable assets and liabilities. The resulting net fair value may be more or less than the parent company's purchase price, and different accounting rules apply in different situations:

- When the parent's purchase price exceeds the fair value of the subsidiary's net assets, the difference is accounted for separately as goodwill. This is an asset of the parent, attributable to the newly purchased subsidiary, to be amortized over the period of its estimated benefit but in any event not in excess of 40 years.
- When the parent's purchase price is less than the fair value of the subsidiary's net assets and liabilities, that difference should be allocated first to the subsidiary's noncurrent assets (except marketable securities); any remainder should be amortized to income over a period not in excess of 40 years. (In practice, this *negative goodwill* is amortized much more rapidly.)
- When a parent acquires a majority of, but not all, the subsidiary's stock, the accounting can be more complicated. In allocating the purchase price, the buyer must first establish the fair value of 100% of the net assets acquired and then determine goodwill as the excess of purchase price over the proportion of fair-valued net assets actually acquired by the parent. It is not proper to assign 100% of the excess of fair values over carrying amounts of the subsidiary's assets to the parent's cost of purchasing less

than a 100% interest, except where the effect would be immaterial (such as with a very small proportionate minority interest). For example, if company A paid $100,000 for a 75% interest in company B, which had net assets of $50,000 at previous carrying amounts and $80,000 at fair values, the goodwill is $40,000 ($100,000 cost less 75% of $80,000), not $32,500 ($100,000 cost less 75% of $50,000 plus $30,000 full fair value excess). The correct approach properly allocates more of the purchase price to the parent's goodwill and less to specific subsidiary assets.

The purchase-date fair values can be recorded directly in the subsidiary's books; but where it may be necessary to maintain separate records for the subsidiary reflecting its historical costs, fair values can alternatively be recognized on a worksheet basis as part of the consolidation process. However, the parent will need the acquisition-date fair value information to enable it to consolidate the subsidiary at its purchase cost basis. Even when the subsidiary's books and its financial statements reflect the original historical cost, the consolidated statements must reflect the parent's cost.

See APB 16 (AC 1091), APB 17 (AC 5141), and Chaper 30 for a detailed discussion of accounting for business combinations, particularly the section in Chapter 30 on "push-down" accounting detailing the factors to be considered when presenting the separate financial statements of a purchased subsidiary.

Intercompany Transactions and Balances. Seen from a consolidated perspective, transactions between a parent and its subsidiaries must be considered incomplete. Because such transactions and the resulting balances do not reflect arm's-length business dealings, they should be eliminated in consolidation. The consolidation process is facilitated when each component records intercompany transactions and balances in separate, easily identified accounts so that on cross-addition in the combination they are eliminated automatically.

Some companies record all intercompany transactions at cost. However, those companies who see a need to measure profitability by component record intercompany transactions at fair values; and sometimes the intercompany price is set at an arbitrary figure, perhaps to generate taxable profits in low- rather than high-tax-rate jurisdictions. In either event the intercompany profits not realized through transactions with third parties are to be eliminated upon consolidation. For example, if products are sold between a parent and a subsidiary at a price in excess of the cost to the transferor, the unrealized intercompany profit in the transferee's inventory must be eliminated upon consolidation.

Typically, the amount of intercompany profit included in inventory is determined from an analysis of inventory on hand at period-end. The parent must be able to determine how much and what items of intercompany inventory remain within the corporate system at the reporting date. It must then be able to calculate with reasonable accuracy the amount of intercompany profit included in the inventory, and eliminate it in consolidation.

If there are charges between a parent and subsidiary for management services or for interest on intercompany advances, those charges must also be eliminated in consolidation. Intercompany charges capitalized in fixed assets or included in overhead in inventory should not be eliminated, however, if the charge is simply a pass-through of an item that would have been considered an asset in the accounts of the originating company.

Minority Interests. When a parent owns a majority (but less than 100%) of a subsidiary's stock, the consolidated financial statements must reflect the minority's interest in the subsidiary. The minority interest will be equal to the minority's proportionate share of the subsidiary's net assets, based on the subsidiary's historical costs. When a parent purchases a controlling interest in a subsidiary, only the parent's proportionate interest should be fair valued in consolidation. Even if the subsidiary's assets and liabilities are fully fair valued individually (see earlier discussion under Acquisition of a Subsidiary), that increase or decrease must be proportionally allocated only to the parent's interest, and the minority interest must be retained based on the historical costs recorded by the subsidiary.

The minority interest will be increased and decreased for its share of the subsidiary's historical basis income and losses, and its share of the dividends paid out. Occasionally, a subsidiary will suffer losses to the extent that it incurs a deficiency in net assets. In most situations the minority interest will bear its share of losses only to the extent of its share of net assets. It will not be appropriate to reflect a minority interest as a debit balance (in effect, a receivable) in the consolidated statements unless the minority owners have guaranteed the subsidiary's debt or have committed to provide additional capital. When a subsidiary's loss would completely eliminate the minority interest, only a portion of that loss sufficient to bring the minority interest to zero should be allocated to the minority (AC 2051.14). The balance of the loss should be reflected as a part of the consolidated net loss attributable to the controlling parent.

Balance sheet presentation. If the minority's interest in the subsidiary's net assets is material to the consolidated statements, that balance should be presented in the consolidated balance sheet as a separate-line item just above stockholders' equity. It should not be subtotaled with consolidated debt or with consolidated equity. The SEC further requires that when the minority interest is material the balance be separated between equity and retained earnings; this may be given on the face of the balance sheet or in a footnote. Very often the minority interest is immaterial to the consolidated balance sheet and is simply aggregated within long-term debt.

Income statement presentation. If the minority interest in the subsidiary's net earnings is material to the consolidated statements, it should be presented as a single-line item just before net earnings and just after the deduction for income taxes. (The subsidiary's income taxes on its total earnings will thus be included in the consolidated tax provision—the minority interest is, in effect, presented net of tax.) If the minority interest in the earnings of the subsidiary is of lesser materiality, it may be presented (net of tax) in the consolidated statements among the costs and expenses, either as a single-line item or combined with other miscellaneous expenses.

Intercompany profit elimination against minority interest. Accountants have argued for years about the elimination of intercompany profit on transactions within a corporate group when there is a significant minority interest. Some contend that the profit on an intercompany transaction that would accrue to the minority should not be eliminated, because that portion of the transaction is a third-party transaction. From the standpoint of the minority interest, that intercompany profit could be considered to have been realized. However, others argue that the parent's control over the group makes it impossible for any intercompany transaction to be at arm's length, and they therefore insist that all intercompany profit be eliminated. The latter view is required in practice. The full amount of intercompany profits is eliminated regardless of the size or the nature of a minority interest, but if the intercompany profit is "earned" by the subsidiary, a proportion of it equal to the minority ownership percentage is applied as a reduction of minority interest in consolidation (AC 2051.13).

Income Tax Allocation. Income taxes become a problem when some units of a consolidated group issue separate financial statements. In many situations the parent and its eligible domestic subsidiaries will file a single consolidated tax return, and the subsidiary will have tax expense only as the parent allocates the total consolidated tax liability among the components. If there is a minority interest in the subsidiary, or if the subsidiary enjoys a statutory tax benefit (as in the case of a savings and loan association), that allocation of total tax expense should preferably be based on the taxable income of the individual components, computed as though they were filing separately.

It may be that there will be a difference between the aggregate "as if" tax computations of the individual components and the total tax liability, because some of the components may have tax credits that would be unusable if they were filing on their own. That difference may be treated in many different ways—for example, absorbed by the parent, allocated to the unit that benefits from the credit usage, or spread pro rata to the separate subsidiaries.

Whatever allocation methods are used, they should be formalized and perhaps even documented by a resolution of the boards of directors of the respective companies. And where there is a minority interest in a subsidiary, the allocation decision should not disadvantage the cash flow of that subsidiary simply because it files with the consolidated group.

If the components in the consolidated group file separate tax returns, and if there are intercompany profits eliminated in the preparation of the consolidated financial statements, there will be a difference between consolidated net income and the aggregate of the components' taxable income. That timing difference should be tax allocated, following the provisions of APB 11 (AC 4091.35). The allocation process will produce a deferred tax debit, which must be evaluated for realizability. For example, the deferred tax debit relating to the elimination of intercompany profits in inventory should be included as part of the inventory cost when performing the lower-of-cost-or-market test on the related inventory.

In addition to the taxes that may be assessed against the individual components, the parent may be faced with taxes on the earnings of its subsidiaries, should they be distributed. It may or may not be necessary to provide for those taxes in the consolidated financial statements. See APB 23, *Accounting for Income Taxes— Special Areas,* which contains a section on undistributed earnings of subsidiaries (AC 4095.07-.14); and see Chapter 25.

Subsidiaries With Differing Fiscal Years. There will be situations where a subsidiary will have a fiscal year different from that of its parent. For example, the subsidiary may be in a seasonal industry in which most of the companies use a specific fiscal year. The advantage of having data that is suitable for comparison with the competition may outweigh the disadvantages of having differing fiscal periods internally. Also, some parents have established their foreign subsidiaries with earlier fiscal year-end dates, to facilitate consolidation. For example, a calendar-year parent may ask its foreign subsidiary to use a November 30 year just to be sure that the foreign company's data is fully analyzed and available to include with the parent's quick closing.

If the parent and the subsidiary have different fiscal years, the consolidation should use the best available data from the subsidiary. There are two aspects to determining the "best available data"—timely, current information is always better than stale data, but there are situations in which year-end data is often better than interim data. Therefore, it is better for consolidation purposes to use the subsidiary's data as of its interim date coinciding with the parent's balance sheet date unless the subsidiary's system for producing interim data is considered unreliable.

If the parent concludes that the trade-off between timeliness and reliability forces it to use the subsidiary's data as of the subsidiary's year-end, the data for the subsidiary's 12 months should be combined with that of the parent, just as though they had the same year-end. Significant transactions in the subsidiary between its year-end and the date of the consolidated financial statements should be recorded or disclosed according to the professional guidelines regarding subsequent events (see AU 560).

It should be noted that the SEC will not accept consolidated financial statements if the subsidiary's data is more than 93 days old. That SEC requirement has become broadly accepted in practice.

Accounting for Unconsolidated Subsidiaries. When it is determined that a subsidiary's financial statements should not be consolidated, the parent's investment will ordinarily be accounted for using the equity method. APB 18 explains that the equity method should produce the same results as full consolidation, except for the level of detail presented (AC 5131.19).

In consolidation, the subsidiary's assets, liabilities, revenue, and expenses are combined, line by line, with those of the rest of the consolidated group. Under equity accounting, the parent's investment in the subsidiary, increased or decreased by earnings, losses, and dividends, is shown as a single-line item in its balance sheet. Similarly, the parent's share of the subsidiary's current net earnings or losses is shown as a single-line item in its income statement (except where the investee has, in amounts proportionately material to the investor, extraordinary items and cumulative effects of a change in accounting principle that should be specifically segregated as required by AC 5131.19(d)).

All the other aspects of consolidation accounting apply when accounting for a subsidiary using the equity method: intercompany profit included in transactions between the parent and the subsidiary must be eliminated, and where the subsidiary is purchased, the fair values of its assets and liabilities must be determined and any resultant goodwill must be amortized.

See Chapter 21 for a detailed description of the application of the equity method to *nonsubsidiary* investees, and see Chapter 28 for matters affecting presentation of the separate financial statements of components such as unconsolidated subsidiaries or subsidiary groups.

Change in Reporting Entity. The decision to consolidate a subsidiary or present it on the equity method must be made based on the facts existing at the end of each reporting period. If the status of the subsidiary changes, its status at period-end will determine the accounting treatment, and that accounting usually will be applied retroactively. The several situations discussed below are included in the overall summary shown in Figure 31.2. This figure does not depict accounting for a business combination accomplished in a single transaction (see Chapter 30). Note, however, that the accounting for a step acquisition *at such time as* a majority voting equity position is achieved is the same as accounting for a single-transaction purchase business combination. Also, many of the situations shown in the figure will require or benefit from the presentation of pro forma statements. See Chapter 30 for a discussion of pro forma statements in purchase business combinations.

Step acquisitions. Assume, for example, that (1) a company acquires a 10% interest in another company during the first quarter, (2) during the second quarter it acquires an additional 5% interest, (3) during the third quarter it acquires an additional 10%, and (4) in the fourth quarter it acquires a 30% interest, giving it a 55% controlling interest in the subsidiary at year-end. In its interim reports for the first two quarters, the parent would reflect its less-than-20% investment in the subsidiary at cost; the cost of the investment would be shown as an asset, and income would be recognized only to the extent of dividends received. In the third quarter statement the parent would begin accounting for its investment on the equity method, reflecting its aggregate cost plus or minus its proportionate share of the earnings or losses in the prior quarters. It would reflect 10% of the subsidiary's earnings for the period when it owned 10%; 15% of the subsidiary's earnings for the period when it owned 15%; and 25% of the subsidiary's earnings for the period when it owned 25%.

At year-end the subsidiary's balance sheet would be consolidated with the parent's (unless consolidation is not required as discussed at the beginning of this chapter, in which case the equity method would continue). Prior financial statements usually would not be consolidated, because of the absence of a majority interest at those dates; but pro forma statements of operations as if fully consolidated for the current and preceding year would be provided. In the pro forma prior income statements the minority interest amount would reflect the interests of the outsiders (who for all periods prior to acquisition would actually represent a majority ownership) in the subsidiary's earnings.

Disposal of all or part of a subsidiary. When part of an investment in a subsidiary is sold during the reporting period, the status of the subsidiary (if it still is that) at period-end should determine the accounting followed:

1. If a parent sells a portion of its investment in a subsidiary but still retains a controlling interest, the consolidated financial statements at the period-end should include the assets, liabilities, and operations of the subsidiary—and of course the new minority interest. The minority interest in results of operations would be calculated for the period from date of disposition of the interest to the reporting date.

2. If a parent sells a controlling interest in its subsidiary but still retains an investment of 20% or more, that remaining investment should be reflected in the period-end balance sheet as a single-line item, using the equity method; the subsequent results of operations should also be recast on a one-line basis (AC 2051.11). In prior periods' comparative financial statements the subsidiary may be deconsolidated and restated using the equity method presentation; however those prior-period statements may also be left unchanged, and footnote disclosure given as to the later deconsolidation.

Transaction	Accounting Treatment at the Time of Transaction	Accounting Presentation in Prior Periods' Financial Statements	Comment Required in Auditor's Report [a]
ACQUISITIONS			
1. Initial purchase of less than 20%. [b]	Use cost as the basis of accounting for the investment.	None.	No
2. Subsequent purchase of a layer that results in owning from 20% [b] to 50% inclusive.	Use the equity method of accounting.	All prior periods financial statements are to be restated on the equity method of the percentages of ownership in effect.	No
3. Subsequent purchase of a layer that results in ownership greater than 50%:			
a. If subsidiary is to be consolidated.	Consolidate operations from date of purchase of layer.	Generally do not restate as consolidated for earlier periods, but give pro forma information (AC 1091.96). However, if not previously on the equity method restate to equity method for prior periods, using the percentages (even if below 20%) of ownership in effect in those periods.	No
b. If subsidiary is to be carried on the equity method.	Same accounting as in 2 above.	Same accounting as in 2 above.	No
DISPOSITIONS			
4. Complete disposal of a subsidiary or disposal of such portion as results in retaining an investment less than 20%:			

a. Not qualifying as a segment under a segment under APB 30 (AC 2012.13):			
i. If previously consolidated.	Cease consolidating results of operations at disposal date; switch to cost method for less-than-20% portion retained.	Recast predisposition financial statements to show the subsidiary on the equity method, providing a footnote reconciliation of previously reported amounts (AC 2051.11);	Yes
		or	
		Leave consolidated for all prior periods but give footnote information as to amounts included in predisposition operations.	No
ii. If previously carried on the equity method.	Cease pickup of equity in earnings at disposal date; switch to cost method for less-than-20% portion retained.	No change	No
b. Qualifying as a segment under APB 30 (AC 2012.13) for situations where subsidiary was either consolidated or carried on the equity method.	Reclassify as a discontinued operation in all financial statements presented.		No

[a] A comment regarding lack of consistency (consistency exception) is required in the auditor's report if a material change is made in the companies selected by management for inclusion in the consolidated financial statements. See AC 1051.34-.35 and AU 420.07-.10.

[b] 20% of voting equity is used as the cutoff for equity accounting in this figure. APB 18 (AC 5131) establishes rules that may cause this figure to vary in certain situations. See Chapter 21.

(*figure continues*)

FIGURE 31.2 ACCOUNTING FOR STEP ACQUISITIONS AND STEP DISPOSITIONS

Transaction	Accounting Treatment at the Time of Transaction	Accounting Presentation in Prior Periods' Financial Statements	Comment Required in Auditor's Report[a]
5. Disposal of a portion of a subsidiary resulting in retention of a majority interest (cannot qualify as a disposal of a segment):			
a. If previously consolidated.	Continue consolidation but set up minority interest from date of transaction.	No change.	No
	If a change from consolidation is justified, switch to equity method.	Recast to equity method.	Yes
b. If previously carried on the equity method.	Reduce equity percentage pickup.	No change.	No
6. Disposal of a portion of a subsidiary resulting in retaining an ownership of 20% to 50% inclusive (cannot qualify as disposal of a segment):			
a. If previously consolidated.	Recast to equity method for all periods presented; *or* Commence equity method at date of transaction.	Leave consolidated in prior periods and give footnote disclosure of operations later deconsolidated.	Yes No
b. If previously carried on the equity method.	Reduce equity percentage pickup.	No change.	No

[a] A comment regarding lack of consistency (consistency exception) is required in the auditor's report if a material change is made in the companies selected by management for inclusion in the consolidated financial statements. See AC 1051.34-.35 and AU 420.07-.10.

FIGURE 31.2 · CONT'D

If the sale of a subsidiary qualifies as a disposition of a segment (AC 2012.13), all its results of operations up to the date of sale are condensed and shown as a single-line item in the consolidated income statement as discontinued operations, following the subtotaling of income from continuing operations (AC 2012.08). This treatment is required for any prior period's income statement presented that includes any portion of that subsidiary's operations.

If the subsidiary that has been disposed of does not qualify as a segment, its operations need not be condensed into a single-line item. Its sales and expenses (up to the date of the sale) may be fully consolidated as they would have been had the disposition not taken place. When this is done, it is usually appropriate to include a footnote disclosing the sales and expenses and net results attributable to the subsidiary that are included in the consolidated income statements. It is also permissible to compress the subsidiary operations into a one-line equity presentation (AC 2051.11), but when this is done, the equity in earnings of the subsidiary must be shown before arriving at income from continuing operations.

Continuing Involvement in a Sold Business. There are circumstances when disposal of a subsidiary should not be recognized as a sale. In SAB 30 the SEC specifies the accounting treatment when a seller sells a subsidiary or other business operation but retains a continuing involvement in the business sold. Continuing involvement is retained if

- The seller has effective veto power over major contracts or customers,
- The seller has significant voting power on the company's board,
- The seller has continuing involvement in the company's affairs, with risks and managerial authority similar to ownership,
- The buyer does not make a significant financial investment in the company (e.g. a minimal down payment),
- The buyer's repayment of debt that constitutes the principal consideration in the acquisition is dependent on future profitable operations, or
- The seller continues to guarantee debt or contract performance.

In these circumstances the seller should not account for the transactions as a divestiture and may not recognize any gain—even a deferred gain. The seller should segregate on its balance sheet the assets and liabilities of the sold subsidiary or business operation under captions such as "assets of business transferred under contractual arrangements" and "liabilities of business transferred." If the seller's realization of the consideration is contingent on future profits, and if losses are incurred after the transaction, the seller should reflect these losses by recording a valuation allowance on its balance sheet with a corresponding loss on its earnings statement.

Consolidation Disclosures

Policies. APB 22 recommends a footnote comment with any set of consolidated financial statements, outlining the consolidation policies followed: "Examples of disclosures by a business entity commonly required with respect to accounting policies would include, among others, those relating to basis of consolidation . . ."

Principles of Consolidation—The consolidated financial statements include the accounts of the Company and its significant majority owned subsidiaries other than its wholly-owned finance subsidiary and Times Fiber Communications, Inc., a joint venture in which the Company's 51% control is expected to be temporary. Investments in the finance subsidiary, joint ventures and other associated companies are accounted for using the equity method, except for two companies (not significant) recorded using the cost method.

FIGURE 31.3   DISCLOSURE OF EXCLUSIONS FROM CONSOLIDATION
SOURCE: Insilco Corporation, 1978 Annual Report.

(AC 2045.13). Practice follows that guideline. The theory is that a company should disclose the accounting principles it follows in any situation in which there might be some confusion as to what principles were used.

Inasmuch as the consolidation guidelines are generally well understood, it would not seem necessary for a company to comment specifically on its consolidation policy unless that policy deviates from the norm. Most companies that might be expected to have a material subsidiary of any kind include a standard, innocuous statement in their accounting policies footnote, such as:

The consolidated financial statements include the accounts of the company and its wholly owned subsidiaries. All material intercompany profits, transactions and balances have been eliminated.

Whenever a company follows a consolidation policy that is a little out of the ordinary, the details should be outlined in the policies footnote, as illustrated in Figures 31.3 and 31.4.

Subsidiary Details. Generally speaking, the consolidated financial statements need not provide any details from the statements of the consolidated subsidiaries.

Consolidation—The consolidated financial statements include the accounts of all majority-owned subsidiaries except a wholly-owned domestic finance subsidiary, which is accounted for under the equity method, and a wholly-owned Brazilian subsidiary which is carried at cost due to economic uncertainty. Intercompany transactions have been eliminated in the consolidated financial statements. Financial statements of certain consolidated subsidiaries, principally foreign, are included on the basis of their fiscal years ending July 31 through September 30. Such fiscal periods have been adopted by the subsidiaries in order to provide for a timely consolidation with the Corporation.

FIGURE 31.4   SUBSIDIARY EXCLUDED DUE TO ECONOMIC UNCERTAINTY
SOURCE: Harnischfeger Corporation, 1979 Annual Report.

Once the decision has been made that a consolidated statement best presents the combined activities of the group, it would be inconsistent to encumber the notes accompanying the consolidated statements with details from the statements of the component entities. There are some exceptions to the general rule, however.

First, when the assets of a subsidiary are not available for the use of the corporate group, either because of a government regulation, a business restriction, or a loan requirement, the details of the restricted assets should be spelled out in a footnote. The assets themselves should be classified in the consolidated balance sheet so as to properly reflect the restriction; in effect they may be noncurrent assets. Second, consolidated statements filed with the SEC must include separate statements of significant subsidiaries engaged in insurance, securities brokerage, finance, savings and loan, and banking. It may be appropriate to present combined statements for several subsidiaries in the same business. (See ASR 175 and SAB 2 for specific requirements.) Third, SFAS 14 (AC 2081) requires disclosure of assets and earnings on a segment basis and on a geographic basis. (See Chapter 32 for a detailed discussion of segment reporting.)

Changes in Consolidated Group. When there is a material change in the makeup of the consolidated group, the effect of the change must be detailed in a footnote in the year of the change. APB 20 requires a footnote describing the nature, reason for, and effect of the change, if any, on income before extraordinary items, on net income, and on related per share amounts (AC 1051.35). The footnote in Figure 31.5 illustrates a situation in which a previously consolidated operation is now accounted for on the equity method.

Changes in the makeup of a consolidated group resulting from acquisitions or dispositions also require certain disclosures. APB 20 specifically says that the disclosures required by the "change in entity rules" apply to subsidiaries acquired during the period that are accounted for as a pooling of interests (AC 1051.12). But in fact APB 16 requires even more detailed disclosures for any change in the entity that occurs because of a pooling of interest (AC 1091.63-.65) or a purchase (AC 1091.95-.96). Similarly, APB 30 requires special disclosures in the notes whenever a segment of the business is disposed of during the period (AC 2012.18).

Auditor reporting. From the viewpoint of the auditor reporting on financial statements, changes in the consolidated group constitute a change in the application of the consolidation accounting principle (AU 420.07). Therefore, in any of the

---

... In recognition of the decreasing significance of the land development segment, the investment in homebuilding operations is carried at equity and the results of its operations are shown separately in the statements of consolidated income. The accompanying 1978 financial statements have been restated to reflect the deconsolidation of the homebuilding operations; previously the land development segment was fully consolidated.

FIGURE 31.5   DISCLOSURE OF CHANGE IN ENTITY
SOURCE: Foremost-McKesson, Inc., 1979 Annual Report.

following situations the auditor's report must include a statement calling attention to the lack of consistency (misnamed a *consistency exception*):

* Presenting consolidated or combined statements in place of statements of individual companies,
* Changing specific subsidiaries comprising the group of companies for which consolidated statements are presented,
* Changing the companies included in combined financial statements (discussed later in this chapter), and
* Changing among the cost, equity, and consolidation methods of accounting for subsidiaries or other investments in common stock.

A consistency exception is not required when a consolidation is changed because a subsidiary is created, purchased, dissolved, or sold (AU 420.09). A consistency exception is not to be used when pooling-of-interests accounting is properly applied in comparative statements, but is required when comparative statements for prior years are not restated for a pooling or when comparative statements are not presented and the footnotes do not disclose specified comparative summary data (see AU 546.12-.13 and Chapter 30).

Other Matters

Parent Company Statements. In filings with the SEC, consolidated financial statements must be accompanied by parent-company-only financial statements unless (a) the parent company is primarily an operating company (SAB 1) and minority interests in subsidiaries and long-term debt of the subsidiaries held by any person other than the parent or other subsidiaries of the parent are less than 5% of consolidated total assets or (b) the parent's total assets and gross revenues (exclusive of investments in and advances to consolidated subsidiaries, interest and dividends from the consolidated subsidiaries, or equity in income from consolidated subsidiaries) are 75% or more of the consolidated assets and revenues.

If the corporate structure is complex, it is often difficult to prepare meaningful financial statements for the parent company, standing by itself. (See Chapter 28 for a discussion of the difficulties in reporting on a component.) To be sure that the reader of the financial statement reads the parent statements in the proper context, the statements required by the SEC are often prepared on a multicolumnar basis; the amounts for the consolidated group and the parent by itself appear side by side. Footnotes accompanying that multicolumn presentation are designed to deal first with the consolidated statements. Additional footnotes that may be required to understand the parent company's statements follow. The parent company's notes should describe generally the nature of the transactions with subsidiaries and the basis used to account for those transactions.

Combined Statements. To justify the preparation of consolidated financial statements, there must be a majority voting equity interest held by a parent in its subsidiaries. However, in some situations companies are effectively linked together because they are under common management or common control (such as "brother-sister" companies, i.e., subsidiaries of a common parent), but there is no controlling equity interest of one in another. In those situations it may be appropriate to present combined statements.

Although ARB 51 makes quite a point of distinguishing between consolidated statements and combined statements (AC 2051.21), the difference is mostly semantic. The principles and procedures used to prepare combined statements are virtually the same as those used to prepare consolidated statements: all intercompany transactions, balances, and profit must be eliminated in the combination (AC 2051.22). To the extent there is any intercompany investment, it is offset against the related equity. If there is no intercompany investment, the individual company equities are combined.

The combined statement approach is useful to present the financial statements of a group of subsidiaries that are all in a similar business. It is also used to present the financial statements of separate companies controlled by one individual or a family.

In recent years some of the larger international CPA firms have published combined financial statements, in order to include individual international practice units that do not have equity interests in each other. The firms justify the preparation of the combined statements because the individual practice groups are under common management. (See Chapter 27 for further discussion of CPA-firm published statements.)

Proportionate Consolidation. Some accountants have argued in favor of proportionate consolidation for a company owning a substantial, but less than controlling, interest in another company. In other words, if a company has a one-third interest in a noncorporate joint venture, that investor company would include in the consolidated financial statements one third of each of the assets, liabilities, revenues, and expenses of the venture. That form of accounting was first developed for those situations in which the investor had a true joint venture interest in a project. And some accountants carried that thinking further, extending it to the corporate-venture-type investment.

In its *Issues Paper on Joint Venture Accounting* (AICPA, 1979q) the AICPA asked the FASB to consider a project on accounting and reporting for investments in joint ventures, and what the basis of accounting should be for a joint venture entity. (The project has been dormant at the FASB, with no decision on whether to add it to the agenda.)

The issues paper (AICPA, 1979q, p. 25) contains a summary of a NAARS search of 4,071 annual reports from 1977, indicating that of 415 companies reporting investments in 50%-owned companies, joint ventures, partnerships, or undivided interests, 65 companies used the proportionate consolidation method; these are enumerated in Appendix B of the issues paper (AICPA, 1979q, pp. 57-63). This survey suggests that proportionate consolidation of joint ventures is used principally in the real estate and construction, oil and gas, and utilities industries. The SEC generally is not in favor of proportionate consolidation and therefore expansion of this practice to other industries is constrained (Poloway and Charles, 1980, par. 4330 at page 3391). And it should be noted that as to *corporate* joint ventures in the real estate industry, the usual full consolidation or equity accounting rules apply, as discussed in SOP 78-9, *Accounting for Investments in Real Estate Ventures.*

Auditing Considerations

Audit Objectives. The audit of a client's consolidation process has several objectives. First and most importantly, the auditors must challenge the consolidation policy to be sure that it meets the requirements of ARB 51 (discussed above), good contemporary practice, and, where applicable, the rules of the SEC. The objective established in ARB 51 provides the benchmark for this challenge: "In deciding upon consolidation policy, the aim should be to make the financial presentation which is most meaningful in the circumstances" (AC 2051.04).

The client's consolidation policy will be stated in the accounting policy footnote, although that statement will not deal with procedures. Most companies will find that a more detailed statement in their internal policy manual will be helpful for their own purposes; this policy statement should be the reference for the auditors' challenge. The audit committee also will want to refer to that policy statement as it makes periodic challenges of the company's various accounting policies.

A second audit objective, to ascertain that the consolidation policy is consistently and correctly applied, will obviously be critical when new components join the group. In addition, there must be a regular, ongoing challenge that the companies included in or excluded from the consolidated group in prior years still warrant that treatment.

As a third objective, the auditor must be concerned that the detailed consolidation eliminations, adjustments, and combinations have been properly made. A good audit of the individual components could be for nought if the final audit of the consolidation mechanics is handled improperly or carelessly.

Finally, the auditors must be satisfied that the total consolidation presentation is appropriate. They must not only be satisfied that the detailed disclosures are adequate, but they must also be satisfied that the overall picture presented in the consolidated statements does not obscure significant information about individual units.

Audit Approach. Generally speaking, the audit approach will be substantive (see Chapter 12). A challenge to the consolidation policy requires an analysis of all the factors involved in the choice of the policy and in its application. Two substantive challenges warrant specific consideration here.

First, when evaluating the measure of control the parent exercises over its subsidiaries, the substance of the intercompany arrangement must prevail. For example, when a subsidiary is not consolidated because the parent does not own more than 50% of the outstanding voting stock, it will be important for the auditor to know the identity of the other owners to understand what relationships they might have to the corporate group. The auditors must be alert to relationships that produce indirect control as well as to those that produce direct control.

Second, while the auditors search for the nature of the intercompany relationships, they must be alert to legal or business restrictions that influence the substance of the parent-subsidiary relationship, especially the possibility that the assets, earnings, and funds of the subsidiary are not available to the corporate group even though the parent owns a majority of the voting stock. If there is a concern about the parent's ability to control the subsidiary's funds, it may be that the subsidiary should not be consolidated. In those situations, the auditors should also consider whether the parent's investment in (and advances to) the subsidiary should be subjected to a net realizable value test.

In addition to substantively challenging the consolidation policy, the audit must cover the consolidation process itself. This aspect can follow a substantive approach or a systems reliance/compliance testing approach (see Chapter 12), depending on the strength of the company's system for performing the consolidation. As the auditor reviews and tests the system, he should determine that it properly

1. Identifies intercompany transactions and balances for elimination purposes,
2. Calculates intercompany profit in inventory or fixed assets,
3. Combines like balances with like balances, and
4. Accounts for changes in the consolidated group.

In order for the auditor to rely on the system, there must be sufficient controls to prevent or detect and correct errors in the above areas. If the auditor believes the substantive approach is more efficient, or if he is concerned about weaknesses in consolidation controls, he will adopt a substantive approach to the audit of the consolidation process and will extend his detailed testing accordingly.

FOREIGN CURRENCY TRANSLATION

This section deals primarily with the *translation of foreign currency financial statements* that are to be consolidated into financial statements denominated in another currency. It also deals with the translation of *foreign currency transactions,* because the basic accounting is the same under SFAS 8, *Accounting for the Translation of Foreign Currency Transactions and Foreign Currency Financial Statements* (AC 1083).

In SFAS 8 the FASB concluded that financial statements of a foreign subsidiary should be translated just as though its transactions had been entered into by a domestic branch.

Historical Perspective

Prior to the adoption of SFAS 8, companies could select from several acceptable alternatives to account for foreign currency transactions and to translate foreign currency financial statements of subsidiaries and branches.

Current/Noncurrent Approach. Many companies followed the current/noncurrent approach, which was first promulgated in 1939 in ARB 4, and codified in ARB 43, Chapter 12 (AC 1081). Under this approach, all a foreign subsidiary's current assets and current liabilities were translated at the exchange rate in effect at the balance sheet date, and all noncurrent assets and liabilities were translated at the exchange rates in effect when the assets were acquired or the debt incurred. Realized exchange gains and losses were recognized immediately. Unrealized translation losses were also recognized immediately, but unrealized translation gains were deferred in a suspense account to be absorbed by future translation losses. The accounting standards that sanctioned this approach were prepared at a time when there was general concern about the stability of foreign investments; yet there was also a feeling that the dollar would always appreciate. Therefore, it seemed prudent or conservative to maintain the lower exchange rate for those assets that would be realized over a longer term, but reasonable to use the current rate for those assets that were to be turned over promptly.

Monetary/Nonmonetary Approach. Some companies were following the monetary/nonmonetary approach, effectively approved in paragraph 18 of APB 6, *Status of Accounting Research Bulletins* (1965). When the APB reviewed ARB 43, Chapter 12, they apparently decided that the distinction between current and noncurrent items was too simplistic. APB 6 was conceptually different, because the translation rate to be used was to be determined by the characteristics of the item to be translated, not by its balance sheet placement. The APB concluded that monetary items, including long-term receivables and payables, were to be translated at current rates "in many circumstances" (which in practice meant always). All nonmonetary items, including inventory, were to be translated at historic rates.

It should be noted that the dollar was still appreciating in the mid-1960s, and many companies with substantial foreign debt were happy to adopt the new method. The implied translation gain in their long-term debt appeared to provide a significant cushion against any potential foreign losses.

Cover Concept. Some companies were following an approach considered by the APB in a 1971 exposure draft (described in AC 1083.064) but never formally endorsed in an opinion. The *cover concept* permitted deferral of losses on the translation to the extent that the company had operations in the foreign country that would apparently generate sufficient foreign funds in subsequent years to offset the losses. That idea was eagerly accepted in 1971 because the U.S. dollar had experienced its first devaluation, and U.S. parents with large foreign debt found that the monetary/nonmonetary approach would have caused them to report substantial unrealized translation losses.

Early FASB Attention. In 1973 the United States formally devalued the dollar again, and consideration of the translation method became critical. It seemed unreasonable that there should be such widely divergent practices in such an important area, and the profession turned to the newly formed FASB, asking which of these approaches was most appropriate. After some study, the Board concluded, in SFAS 1, *Disclosure of Foreign Currency Translation Information* (FASB, 1973b), that the subject was far too complex to deal with on an emergency basis. SFAS 1 simply asked companies to be consistent in their accounting for foreign operations, and to include a footnote describing the procedures followed and the effect on the financial statements. The FASB promised to study the question further and issue a definitive pronouncement at a later date. Two years later, in October 1975, SFAS 8 (AC 1083) was issued, which eliminated all the previously acceptable alternatives and specified the *temporal method*.

Temporal Method. The FASB called its approach the temporal method rather than the monetary/nonmonetary method to emphasize an important new concept in the statement. The temporal method is not concerned with the balance sheet placement of the item or the character of the item itself, but with the nature of the accounting basis used for that item. For example, fixed assets are to be translated at the rates in effect at the acquisition date, not because fixed assets are nonmonetary items, but because under GAAP they are carried in the financial statements at historic costs. SFAS 8 says: "The temporal method generally translates assets and liabilities carried at past, current, or future prices expressed in foreign currency in a manner that retains the accounting principles used to measure them in the foreign statements" (AC 1083.123). That difference is more conceptual than practical, however.

The principal practical difference between the monetary/nonmonetary method and the temporal method is that the latter requires current-rate translation for those few nonmonetary items carried at market, such as investments or, in some cases, inventories. For example, inventory carried in the subsidiary's statements at cost must be translated at exchange rates in effect during the acquisition period; however, inventory carried in the foreign currency statements at market (because of a lower-of-cost-or-market adjustment) should be translated at current rates. Appendix A to SFAS 8 contains an extended discussion of how the temporal method is to be applied to a wide variety of assets and liabilities.

Underlying Theory of SFAS 8

Consolidated financial statements and the translation of foreign financial statements are combined in this chapter because in practice the latter process is usually an adjunct of the former; also, current translation theory is tied directly to the consolidation theory expressed in ARB 51. The FASB explained the basis for its conclusions this way:

> The procedures adopted by the Board are consistent with the purpose of consolidated financial statements. The foreign currency transactions of an enterprise and the local and foreign currency transactions of its foreign operations are translated and accounted for as transactions of a single enterprise. [AC 1083.094]

In accordance with that theory, a parent company must translate every element of its foreign subsidiaries' financial statements as though it owned the individual assets and liabilities itself and had entered itself into all of the subsidiaries' transactions. To determine an appropriate translation rate, each item is considered separately. Financial statement items carried by the subsidiary at realization values —cash, receivables, payables, debt—are translated at current exchange rates. Foreign subsidiary financial statement items carried at historical costs—inventory and fixed assets—are translated at the exchange rates in effect when the assets were acquired.

It is generally agreed that SFAS 8 is conceptually consistent within itself and with ARB 51. However, some feel that traditional consolidation theory does not reflect the nature of a modern company's international operations and that the related translation theory therefore must also be obsolete. They believe that a foreign subsidiary should not be seen as an equivalent to a domestic branch, arguing that most companies that expand internationally view their foreign investments as self-supporting entities. They would, accordingly, translate the parent company's aggregate investment in those subsidiaries—its net exposure overseas—at the current rate. Reexamination of the theory of SFAS 8 is well under way, as discussed at the end of this chapter. It will also be interesting to see how the theoretical basis for the preparation of consolidated financial statements might be affected by a new approach to the translation of foreign subsidiary financial statements.

Requirements of SFAS 8

The accounting and reporting requirements of SFAS 8 (other than hedging, discussed separately in the next section) are briefly summarized below. The points outlined in the first two subsections present the basics, but there are several subtleties that deserve extra emphasis, described in further subsections.

Foreign Transactions. A sale (or purchase) denominated in a foreign currency must be seen as two transactions. The first transaction is the sale itself, and that transaction should be translated at the rate in effect at the date of the transaction (AC 1083.007(a)). The collection of the related receivable (or the payment of the payable) is a separate transaction, and if the settlement produces (or requires) more or less dollars than were anticipated in the original transaction, that difference should be accounted for as an *exchange* gain or loss. The difference may not be netted against (or combined with) the first part of the transaction.

The translation rate to be used for foreign transactions at any balance sheet date will depend on the nature of the accounting used for the item to be translated. Currency, receivables, payables, and balance sheet items carried at market prices, if denominated in foreign funds, must be translated at the rate in effect at the balance sheet date (AC 1083.007(b) and (c)). If the adjusted dollar amounts differ from the dollars recorded as a result of the originating transaction, that difference should be recognized as an exchange gain or loss.

Translation of Foreign Financial Statements. Accounts that the foreign subsidiary carries at prices in past exchanges (historic costs) must be translated at the exchange rate in effect at the acquisition date (AC 1083.012(a)). That originating exchange rate must be used whether the asset (such as plant or inventories) was acquired for cash or debt and whether the settlement of the debt was at the same exchange rate or at a vastly different one.

The foreign subsidiary's cash, cash-type items such as receivables and payables, and other assets or liabilities that are carried at current prices must be translated at the exchange rate in effect at the balance sheet date (AC 1083.012(b)). Any change since the last reporting date in the difference between those translated balances and the translated balances as originally recorded must be recognized as translation gain or loss and included in current income.

All revenue and expense transactions should be translated at the rates in effect when the transactions took place. To be practical, however, revenues and expenses may be translated at a weighted average rate covering the reporting period (AC 1083.013).

Recognition of Gains and Losses. The requirement to apply the temporal method was, for most companies, not nearly as important as the requirement for immediate recognition of translation gains and losses. In SFAS 8 the FASB rejected the cover concept because it was implicitly inconsistent with the theory underlying the preparation of consolidated financial statements. Consolidation assumes that the subsidiary's individual assets are available to the consolidated group and that the individual liabilities are the responsibility of the consolidated group. The cover concept assumes that the consolidated group has only a net equity position in the foreign subsidiary. Further, the FASB considered all the other arguments that had been advanced for deferring translation gains and losses and rejected each. The Board concluded its explanation for requiring immediate recognition of exchange gains and losses this way: "Exchange rates fluctuate; accounting should not give the impression that rates are stable" (AC 1083.199).

Application to Interim Statements. SFAS 8 specifically precludes the deferral of translation gains or losses at year-end, and the Board concluded that the same treatment was required at interim reporting dates. Translation adjustments are specifically defined as "gains and losses" and SFAS 8 (AC 1083.017) points out that APB 28 (AC 2071.15(d)) requires immediate recognition in an interim report of any "gain or loss" that would not be deferred at year-end.

Use of Rate at Balance Sheet Date. Those balance sheet items that are to be translated at the current rate must be translated at the rate in effect on the balance sheet date. The translation process is not aimed at valuation, and therefore the use of any judgmental adjustment of the rate at the balance sheet date or of any average rate—even when the rate at the balance sheet date has been subject to unusual fluctuations—is precluded (AC 1083.034). This is so even if a devaluation or revaluation occurs shortly after the balance sheet date. Footnote disclosure (or even pro forma statements) might be required to spell out the effect of such a rate change, but the applicable amounts in the basic financial statements must be translated at the rate in effect at the balance sheet date.

Many times a U.S. company will consolidate the results of its foreign subsidiaries on an early cutoff basis. For example, a calendar-year parent will often consolidate its foreign subsidiaries' financial statements as of November 30. A foreign subsidiary's statements must be translated at the rate in effect at *its* balance sheet date (AC 1083.031).

Disclosures Required. It is generally not necessary to mention the company's translation policies in the accounting policies footnote. A company that prepares its financial statements in accordance with GAAP will presumably have followed SFAS 8 in its entirety. And since SFAS 8 leaves almost no room for interpretation or alternative application, there is nothing unique a company can say about its translation policy.

However, any interim or year-end financial statement must disclose the aggregate translation and exchange gain or loss included in the net income for the period (AC 1083.032). Also, when the exchange rate has changed after the period-end, disclosure of the amount of the change and the effect on the financial statements, if material, may be necessary (AC 1083.034). A pro forma statement could be appropriate if the effect is very significant.

The FASB stepped beyond the usual bounds of historical financial statements and suggested that companies might want to describe in a footnote how a rate change during the year affected the reported results of operations. In fact, that disclosure is required (AC 1083.033), but the requirement is qualified by a statement that it should be given if practicable. In Appendix D of SFAS 8 (AC 1083.223-.224) the FASB explains that they intended to encourage disclosure of those operational effects that, in the judgment of management, provide useful information. However, that kind of disclosure has thus far not been extensively given.

Hedging Foreign Currency Exposures

Faced with foreign currency fluctuation risks, many companies have elected to hedge their exposure by buying or selling a forward contract in the foreign currency. For example, assume that a company has assets in France from which it expects to realize 100,000 francs at the end of 12 months. If the currency market is expected to be turbulent, management may want to protect the current position with regard to those assets. They therefore enter into a contract to sell French francs, equal to the realization value of the French assets, at the date those assets are expected to be realized, and at the exchange rate in effect today. For the purposes of this example, assume that the exchange rate was four francs to one dollar at the date of the contract, but has fallen to five to one at the date the assets are realized. The ideal hedge would then look like this:

Beginning value: FF100,000 @ 4:1 = $25,000
Realized asset value: FF100,000 @ 5:1 = $20,000
Realized contract value: FF100,000 sold @ 4:1 = $25,000

If the company decides to bring those realized French assets home, they will simply use the FF100,000 realized from the transaction to settle the forward contract: they would deliver the FF100,000 and receive $25,000 in cash, which was the original value of the French assets. In all likelihood, however, the company will not want to remit the proceeds of the French transaction, but will keep those assets employed in France. In order to maintain their original status, they could close out the forward contract by buying FF100,000 at five to one (a cost of $20,000), delivering them, and collecting $25,000. They could then convert the $5,000 gain back into francs at the five-to-one exchange rate and realize an additional FF25,000 to be reinvested in the French operation. Upon translation, this would restore their original *dollar* position.

The settling of the forward contract rarely goes through the complete process described above. Most often a forward contract can be settled without buying and reselling the foreign currency, which of course would produce the same net gain or loss result.

A forward contract always has a cost, of course. The cost of the contract has been ignored in the above discussion, but in real life it can be significant. The cost of a forward contract is usually a factor of the prime interest rates prevailing in the two currencies.

Accounting for Hedges. If a forward exchange contract is outstanding over a reporting sheet date, the contract must be accounted for in accordance with the provisions of SFAS 8 that deal with hedging (AC 1083.022-.028). Though these seem complicated, the accounting is in fact straightforward—it follows the accounting used by commodity dealers to account for futures contracts. Generally speaking, a contract in effect at a balance sheet date must be valued at the then-current rate, and any unrealized gain or loss at that date must be recognized currently in the income statement.

There is an exception, however. The gain or loss on a forward exchange contract should be deferred if the foreign asset (or liability) that the forward contract is intended to protect is an *identifiable foreign currency commitment* (AC 1083.024) and if the hedge meets certain conditions:

1. The life of the forward contract must extend from the date when the original commitment was made to or beyond the date when the commitment is to be settled (AC 1083.027(a)),
2. The forward contract must be denominated in the same currency as the commitment that is to be settled in the foreign currency and for an amount on a net-of-tax basis that is the same or less than the amount of the foreign currency commitment (AC 1083.027(b) as amended by AC 1084.13), and
3. The original commitment itself must be firm and uncancelable (AC 1083.027(c)).

For example, if the French asset in the above example is a contract for services to be performed by the company for which it will receive French francs, it might then be possible for the company to defer any unrealized gain or loss on the related foreign exchange forward contract at an intervening balance sheet date.

It is important to emphasize that SFAS 8 does not permit deferral of gains or losses on forward exchange contracts intended to hedge receivables, payables, inventory, or fixed assets (AC 1083.023(a)). That fact is of no real consequence when a hedge is intended to protect a receivable or a payable, because the contract and the receivable or payable will both be translated at the current rate, and the resulting gains and losses will offset each other. However, that offsetting process does not work when a forward contract is purchased to hedge inventory. In that situation, the inventory will be translated at its historical rate, and no exchange gain or loss will be recognized in the income statement. The forward exchange contract will be valued at the current rate, however, and any unrealized gain or loss must be taken into income.

That result seems unusual, but the FASB argues that it follows naturally from the nature of the transaction. Following the logic of SFAS 8, the inventory must be translated at its historical rate because it is carried at past prices (cost). Its realization in a specific foreign currency amount is not yet assured, and will not be assured until it is sold for a specified foreign currency amount. The hedge, however, is a forward contract, which must be valued at market and therefore translated at the current rate.

Long-Term Hedges. With exchange rates as unsettled as they are, it is often difficult to buy a forward contract for an extended period. Forward contracts can be purchased from international banks in most major currencies, but generally not for periods of more than two years. Nevertheless, gains or losses on forward contracts, realized *and* unrealized, may be deferred over the life of the commitment, as long as successive contracts are purchased—that is, as long as the first forward contract date coincides with the date of the original commitment and as long as successive contracts are rolled over without interruption through the settlement date of the commitment.

One company entered into a contract to purchase several supertankers from a Japanese shipbuilder and committed themselves to make installment payments in yen over eight years. They were unable to purchase a forward contract for the eight-year period and so began purchasing successive six-month contracts equal to the unpaid commitment. As the contracts were rolled over, the cumulative gain on the hedge was deferred. As installment payments were made, a pro rata portion of the deferred gain was offset against the payment entry, so that the recorded net dollar cost of the ships was equal to the cost at the original rate even though the installment payments in yen required more dollars than had been anticipated.

Other Aspects of Translation

Applying the Lower-of-Cost-or-Market Rule. SFAS 8 (AC 1083.014) requires that the lower-of-cost-or-market test from ARB 43 (AC 5121.08-.10) be applied in the translated dollar statements. That particular requirement is discussed in some detail in SFAS 8, Appendix A (AC 1083.046-.049). It is a narrow point, and one that could easily be overlooked, but it could have a material effect on a foreign subsidiary's translated financial statements.

SFAS 8 requires that the inventory be measured at its historic cost *in dollars* and, compared against the current market, also translated *in dollars*. The discussion in Appendix A to SFAS 8 points out that an inventory item could have a lower-of-cost-or-market problem in dollars but not in local currency, and of course the reverse might also be true. As long as the dollar market exceeds the dollar cost, no market write-down is required, even if an adjustment would seem to be indicated in the local currency. FASB Interpretation No. 17, *Applying the Lower of Cost or Market Rule in Translated Financial Statements* (AC 1083-2), contains an expanded discussion of this requirement.

Realizability of Investment in Plant. Before the translation to dollars can begin, the foreign subsidiary's financial statements should be reviewed carefully, and cash, receivables, and payables denominated in a currency that is foreign to the subsidiary should be translated into the subsidiary's local currency at the current rate (AC 1083.011). That intermediate process may indicate a potential *valuation* loss that should be recognized in the dollar financial statements.

For example, in 1975 Mexico devalued its peso. Some Mexican subsidiaries of U.S. companies had outstanding bank debt payable in U.S. dollars. The devaluation produced a loss in the peso statements, because the dollar debt was translated at the current rate; therefore, the peso amount of the debt was increased. There would be no exchange loss in the dollar statements, because its plant would be translated at historic (predevaluation) rates and its debt would be translated into original dollars. On investigation, however, there were indications in some companies of potentially serious realization problems.

The situation above is illustrated in the hypothetical example presented in Figure 31.6. The U.S. parent may or may not be faced with a loss, depending on the business situation of the foreign subsidiary:

1. If the foreign-based plant produces products that are shipped to the United States and sold for dollars that can be used to pay off the bank debt, no economic loss will have been incurred, and the dollar statements prepared in accord with SFAS 8 will reflect the subsidiary's economic circumstances.

2. If, however, the subsidiary produces items that are sold in Mexico for pesos, the parent may have a loss in the dollar statements. It is clear that more pesos will be required to pay off the bank debt; if product prices (in pesos) can be raised so that sales from the plant produce enough dollars (purchased with pesos) to retire the dollar debt, no dollar loss will have occurred. However, if it cannot be demonstrated that the plant's production will produce enough dollars, a realization write-down of the plant may be necessary in the translated dollar statements.

Tax Allocation. Generally, U.S. income tax regulations do not permit recognition of exchange gains or losses resulting from translation until they become re-

---

FOREIGN SUBSIDIARY
BALANCE SHEET BEFORE THE DEVALUATION

In Local Currency		*In Dollars*
LC 100,000 *	Plant (translated at historic rates)	$25,000
LC 80,000	Bank debt (denominated in dollars)	$20,000
LC 20,000	Equity	$ 5,000

   * LC 4 = $1

FOREIGN SUBSIDIARY
BALANCE SHEET AFTER THE DEVALUATION

In Local Currency		*In Dollars*
LC 100,000 *	Plant (translated at historic rates)	$25,000
LC 120,000	Bank debt (denominated in dollars)	$20,000
LC (20,000)	Equity	$ 5,000

   * LC 6 = $1

FIGURE 31.6 EFFECT OF FOREIGN CURRENCY DEVALUATION ON SUBSIDIARY'S ECONOMICS

alized through a consummated transaction. Because there will be a timing difference between tax and financial accounting for exchange gains and losses, tax
allocation rules apply.

SFAS 8 (AC 1083.020) says that tax allocation of translation gains or losses
will be determined based on the guidelines expressed in APB Opinions 23 and 24.
In essence, APB 23 says that U.S. taxes need not be provided on the undistributed
earnings of foreign *subsidiaries* if it can be demonstrated that the undistributed
earnings are permanently (indefinitely) invested or can be repatriated tax free
(AC 4095.12). Following that same line of thinking, it may not be necessary to
tax-allocate unrealized exchange gains or losses pertaining to foreign subsidiaries
when it can be demonstrated that those exchange gains or losses relate to amounts
indefinitely invested overseas or amounts that can be repatriated tax free.

The substance of APB 24 is that the undistributed earnings or losses of nonsubsidiary foreign *investees* must be tax-allocated. The APB reasoned that if the
investor does not have absolute control over the investee (by definition) and therefore cannot be sure that the undistributed earnings will be permanently invested,
the investor cannot demonstrate that the earnings will be remitted tax free (AC
4096.07-.09). That theory also applies to gains and losses resulting from translation, namely, gains or losses resulting from translating the financial statements of
foreign investees must be tax-allocated, because the investor cannot be sure he can
control their eventual realization.

It is important to note that, as to a given subsidiary, SFAS 8 (AC 1083.020)
does not require that exchange gains or losses resulting from translation be tax-
allocated in the same way as unremitted earnings. It follows from the logic of
APB 23 that a company might tax-allocate a loss resulting from the translation of
a subsidiary's financial statements, but might not provide for U.S. taxes on that
subsidiary's unremitted earnings. That disparate treatment could be appropriate,
but only if the company can demonstrate that it could realize the foreign exchange
losses for tax purposes without having to realize the unremitted earnings for tax
purposes. Of course, the reverse could also be true.

Translations for Convenience

When the financial statements of a foreign subsidiary are to be consolidated (or
combined), the statements must be translated in accordance with the requirements
of SFAS 8. However, if the financial statements of a foreign company are to be
presented separately, standing alone, they may be translated using the current rate
for all balance sheet and income statement amounts. For example, a foreign company reporting to its shareholders in the United States may find that its financial
statements will be more meaningful to readers in the U.S. if a version of the statements are shown in U.S. dollars. All years' statements shown should be translated
at the exchange rate in effect at the date of the most current balance sheet. Such
translations for convenience are specifically exempted from the requirements of
SFAS 8 (AC 1083.002).

Auditing Considerations

Audit Objectives. The objective of the audit of the translation process is to
ensure that the requirements of SFAS 8 have been met. To accomplish that objec-

tive, auditors must have a working familiarity with the requirements of the statement, and they also must have in-depth understanding of the nature of the company's business. They must know what is included in the foreign subsidiary's accounts, so that they can be sure that the nuances of SFAS 8 have been properly considered.

Audit Approach. The audit of the translation process requires a substantive approach (see Chapter 12). Auditors will want to be satisfied that the appropriate exchange rate has been used, and they will test the application of the rates to the larger foreign subsidiary balances.

CPA firms have on occasion had internal arguments as to where the audit of the translation process should be performed. In a widespread company, different auditors will be responsible for different pieces of the work, although most often they will be part of the same firm or group of firms. Because the auditor must have a thorough understanding of the makeup of the subsidiary's accounts, it makes most sense for the translation tests to be performed by the individual who is responsible for the audit of the subsidiary in the field.

Most auditors, however, will refuse to give a "fairly presents" opinion on a subsidiary's translated financial statements because of the artificialities introduced by the translation process. They argue that they can only express a "fairly presents" opinion on the subsidiary's local currency financial statements, because that is the currency used by the subsidiary to transact its business and keep its records. Further, the auditors responsible for the audit of the subsidiary will point out that the translation process is really part of the preparation of the consolidated financial statements, and therefore tests of the translation should logically be the responsibility of the auditor who is to audit the consolidation. In turn, the individual responsible for the audit of the parent and the consolidation will argue that he may not have sufficient familiarity with the subsidiary's accounts and that if he attempts to test the translation he may overlook a significant problem area.

A possible way to deal with this problem is to present the subsidiary's statements in two columns, one in local currency and one translated into dollars. Thus, the subsidiary's auditors should be asked to express their opinion as to the fair presentation of the financial statements of the subsidiary expressed in local currency and to add a third paragraph to their report expressing an opinion as to whether the translation complies with the requirements of SFAS 8. This approach still requires a good deal of coordination between the two auditors to make sure an important matter is not overlooked.

Evolving Translation Standards

Ever since its adoption in October 1975, SFAS 8 has been controversial. Currency rates have become more volatile, and the critics of SFAS 8 have accordingly become more vocal. The more reasonable of the critics have attacked the statement in the following ways.

First, translating inventory at historic rates can produce significant swings in gains and losses if there is an inventory buildup at a period-end. If a company liquidates this inventory in a subsequent period, an implied translation gain or loss is deferred while the inventory is being accumulated but is then recognized in a rush when the inventory is sold. Critics argue that such timing of the recognition of a gain or loss required by SFAS 8 is artificial and that it distorts gross margin measures.

The distortion from inventory buildup is magnified when the inventory is financed by current trade payables. In those situations, the inventory is effectively hedged, and the company is not likely to incur any real exchange gain or loss, overall. And yet, under SFAS 8, the company is required to recognize a gain or loss on the payable in the current period but is not able to recognize the concomitant gain or loss on the inventory until the subsequent period when the inventory is sold.

In the same way, some real estate companies object to the provisions of SFAS 8 because it forces them to recognize a gain or loss on foreign debt, even though that debt is fully collateralized and fully supported by revenue-producing property in the foreign country. In many cases the companies have been able to demonstrate that the noncancellable lease revenue would be more than enough to service the debt, resulting in the debt being effectively hedged. The real estate companies do not object to translating debt at the current rate, but they ask for the right to translate the property—or a least noncancelable rents under long-term leases—at the current rate as well. They argue that the translation rate to be used should be determined by the business nature of the asset, not by its accounting basis.

Finally, there are those who argue that a currency exchange rate at any one date is an artificial measure and should not be used for translation purposes. They argue that a moving average rate or a weighted rate should be used, particularly for translating interim-period financial statements. They point out that unusual market activity at any quarter-end can have a dramatic effect on that quarter's financial statements, which may well be reversed in the subsequent quarter when order is restored to the currency market. In some situations very material translation gains or losses were "gone" by the time of publication of the quarterly statement in which they were being reported.

Research Projects. The FASB has been sensitive to these concerns, and in 1977 it decided to look at them in several different ways, including the sponsorship of two research projects.

The first was designed to determine whether the securities market had been affected by the requirement to charge all translation gains and losses to earnings immediately. That study, conducted independently by an academic consultant to the Board, concluded that "the issuance and implementation of FASB Statement 8 does not appear to have had significant detectable effects on the security returns of multinational firms" (Dukes, 1978, p. 3).

The second was designed to determine whether the actions of multinational corporations and their officers had been influenced by the requirements of SFAS 8. That research project, also completed by independent consultants to the Board, concluded that these firms took unusual protective steps during the period after SFAS 8 was issued, apparently influenced at least in part by the belief that the market price of their companies' securities would be affected by the income statement effect of the translation procedures (Evans et al., 1978, pp. 15-20).

In addition to these two research projects, the Board in early 1979 decided to reconsider SFAS 8 and appointed a 14-member task force to advise it on this project. This action came after 200 comment letters were received by the Board on its project to evaluate SFAS 1 through 12. Nearly 90% of these letters addressed SFAS 8.

Tentative Changes. Based on the input described above and on further research by the FASB staff, the Board decided some change was in order. The FASB has issued an exposure draft of a revised statement on foreign currency translation, to be effective for fiscal years beginning after December 15, 1981 (FASB, 1980b). If the exposure draft proceeds as planned:

- Unrealized *translation* gains and losses would *not* be reflected in income, but would be shown (tax-allocated if appropriate) as a separate component of stockholders' equity (in a manner similar to the treatment of unrealized losses on marketable equity securities (AC 5132.11 and .12(c)(iii)));
- Gains and losses from foreign currency *transactions* would be reflected in income, unless they are a result of a hedge or unless they result from parent-subsidiary transactions;
- Assets and liabilities (not capital) would be translated at the rates in effect at the balance sheet date, in other words, under the all-current-rate method;
- An analysis of the accumulated translation adjustment classified in stockholder's equity would be presented separately, together with other disclosures analyzing the foreign exchange exposure of the enterprise; and
- Hedge accounting in SFAS 8 would be liberalized so as not to require specific initiation and conclusion dates.

The exposure draft is sure to be controversial. Some will see it as the specific answer to the concerns expressed ever since SFAS 8 was published. Others will see it as a betrayal of traditional accounting, especially traditional consolidation accounting. It would be a mistake to assume that the exposure draft will be routinely finalized into a new set of accounting rules. The Board will have to do still more research and study. In the meantime, SFAS 8 remains in effect.

SUGGESTED READING

Dukes, Roland. *An Empirical Investigation of the Effects of Statement of Financial Accounting Standards No. 8 on Security Return Behavior.* Stamford, Conn.: FASB, 1978. This research report relates to the reaction of investors in common stocks to the issuance and implementation of SFAS 8. The study results demonstrate that SFAS 8 has not noticeably affected the market values of multinational firms.

Evans, Thomas; Folks, William Jr.; and Jilling, Michael. *Research Report on the Impact of Financial Accounting Standards No. 8 on the Foreign Exchange Risk Management Practices of American Multinationals: An Economic Impact Study.* Stamford, Conn.: FASB, 1978. This research report is an analysis of the effects of SFAS 8 on the foreign exchange risk management practices of multinational companies. It describes the state of the art on foreign exchange risk management and thus is a way for a multinational company to compare its management practices with those of other companies.

FASB. *Discussion Memorandum on an Analysis of Issues Related to Accounting for Foreign Currency Translation.* Stamford, Conn.: 1974. Published before SFAS 8, this discussion memorandum covers in depth 26 issues relating to foreign currency translation. Appendices cover a summary of relevant accounting literature, causes and economic effects of changes in exchange rates, and alternatives to exchange rates.

Lorensen, Leonard. *Reporting Foreign Operations of U.S. Companies in U.S. Dollars.* Accounting Research Study No. 12. New York: AICPA, 1972. This study deals with translating financial statements of foreign subsidiaries into U.S. dollars. It contrasts the current/noncurrent method and the temporal method and advocates the use of the temporal method, which was eventually adopted in SFAS 8, for translating foreign currency financial statements.

32

Business Segments

James A. Johnson

SEGMENT REPORTING

As discussed in Chapter 31, it has long been presumed that a company's consolidated financial statements are more meaningful for investors and creditors than are separate financial statements of the parent company and each of its subsidiaries. However, many users still find financial information on a less than total enterprise basis valuable in assessing a company's standing, its past results, and its future prospects. When a company presents such data, usually as a supplement to its basic consolidated financial statements, it is reporting *segment information.*

What segment information a company reports depends on (1) the *specific items disclosed,* such as sales, operating profit, assets, and so on, and (2) the *basis* the company uses to determine what constitutes a segment. Profit centers, geographic locations of operating units, legal subsidiaries, even branches under the supervision of various managers are all bases a company could conceivably use. However, in December 1976, the FASB issued SFAS 14, *Financial Reporting for Segments of a Business Enterprise* (AC 2081), which established the appropriate bases for segment information presented in accordance with GAAP and required extensive disclosures about a company's segment operations.

The Benefits of Segment Reporting

Useful segment information enhances a reader's ability to understand a diversified company. For example, a portion of a company's operations may be conducted in an industry whose products will soon be in great demand; as a result, investors and creditors might conclude that the future bodes well for increased cash flows to the company. On the other hand, a company might derive a significant portion of its consolidated income from operations in a politically unstable part of the world; as a result, investors and creditors would conclude that their expectation of future cash flows was riskier than it otherwise might have been.

Segment information gives investors and creditors the opportunity to make these types of evaluations. Financial analysts, for example, have advocated segment reporting because this information improves their ability to forecast earnings and dividends. Analysts recognize that growth cycles, profit characteristics, and capital requirements differ among a company's business segments and that an adequate forecast comprehends the variability of these factors. (See Chapter 6.) Segment information may also identify a company's strengths and weaknesses, which helps other users understand its operations.

Growing Need for Segment Reporting

Prior to SFAS 14, presentation of selected business segment information had been required or encouraged by generally accepted accounting principles (GAAP) and regulatory agencies such as the SEC. The need for more extensive segment disclosure has been the result of many factors, the most important of which follow.

Growth of Conglomerates. The business environment of the 1960s was characterized by aggressive merger and acquisition activity. Frequently, takeover candidates were not selected on the basis of common or linked products and markets;

rather, they were chosen because the accounting results of complex business combinations maximized earnings per share at the time the merger was effected. More often than not, the subsequent operating results of the resulting conglomerates disappointed investors, who also complained they were unable to understand the complexities of the companies' operations.

Growth of Foreign Activity. As the U.S. economy matured in this same period, many companies found that the growth prospects of foreign economies offered more opportunities to realize a higher rate of return on their investment than was available domestically. Increased rates of overseas marketing activity and direct foreign investment followed. Investors and creditors required information about a company's foreign markets to analyze its future prospects and to evaluate the risk of the company's doing business in politically less stable climates.

Acquisition and Diversification. The end of the conglomerate era has not meant an end to ongoing merger activity. Current business combinations are stimulated largely by the availability of companies at prices substantially less than the cost of acquiring equivalent operating assets individually. Also, many companies have added to their traditional lines of business to benefit from higher rates of return or to reduce undue concentration in a single industry. Today's conglomerates are as difficult for investors and creditors to assess as those of an earlier era.

In short, many modern corporations are large, complex, heterogeneous structures. Segment reporting enables investors to evaluate the building blocks of the structure as a basis for their assessment of its future prospects.

Opposition to Segment Reporting

In spite of the important information provided by segment reporting, many companies have opposed adoption of segment requirements by rule-making bodies. To support their position, opponents have reasoned that

1. Many financial statement users would compare segment results between companies. The fact that companies determine their segments in various ways could make such a comparison dangerously misleading.
2. Many users would not understand the inherent limitations of segment reporting. Judgmental allocations of common costs to segments and artificial (i.e., not arm's-length) pricing of intersegment transfers of goods and services hamper the usefulness of segment data.
3. A basis of segmentation other than by type of economic activity would provide more useful information. Economic activity (similar goods or services), the basis now used, has been the one most frequently advocated, but some opponents argue that segmenting, if required at all, should be on an organizational unit basis (divisions, subsidiaries, etc.) because this would enable investors to evaluate the performance of divisional management.
4. Presenting the results of segment operations could lead to competitive damage. A company would be forced to reveal its strengths as well as its weaknesses, possibly attracting new entrants to the segment's market. Furthermore, all companies would

not be treated equally. For example, foreign companies not subject to U.S. accounting standards would not have to make these types of disclosures.

Although these arguments have been considered, the history of segment reporting indicates that they have been outweighed by the benefits segment information provides.

HISTORY OF SEGMENT REPORTING REQUIREMENTS

AICPA

In 1967 the Accounting Principles Board urged companies to voluntarily disclose supplemental financial information about their industry segments. APB Statement 2 did not specify the type of information required; instead, it urged companies to experiment with segment disclosure so that the APB would have a sound basis for ultimately issuing a definitive pronouncement. Few companies complied with the APB's request, and not until almost a decade later did the APB's successor, the FASB, finally mandate segment reporting.

Specific elements of segment information were required by GAAP even before the FASB's release of SFAS 14. These elements, required by pronouncements still in effect, are listed below.

Foreign Operations. ARB 43, Chapter 12, requires adequate disclosure of foreign operations by United States companies (AC 1081.04-.06 and .08). This requirement is reaffirmed in SFAS 8 (AC 1083.004).

Equity Method Investees. APB 18 requires companies to disclose various information about their significant investments carried by the equity method, including summarized assets, liabilities, and results of operations (AC 5131.20). (See Chapter 21.)

Discontinued Operations. APB 30 requires companies to disclose various types of information about discontinued business segments, including operating profit or loss and data about assets and liabilities (AC 2012.08-.09 and AC 2012.18). (See Chapter 7 for additional discussion.) Note that the FASB defines business segments differently than did APB 30.

In December 1977, SAS 21, *Segment Information* (AU 435), was issued. This guides the auditor in planning the scope of the audit to include the segment disclosures required by SFAS 14. These auditing guidelines are discussed later in this chapter.

SEC

In 1977 the SEC issued ASR 236, which conformed its industry segment reporting requirements to SFAS 14, although the commission requires certain additional disclosures regarding sales or transfers between business segments. Prior to ASR 236, the SEC had required companies to disclose, apart from the financial statements, their material "lines of business." Included in the information required by the old SEC rules were

- A five-year breakdown, in dollars or percentages, of sales, revenue, and pretax income before extraordinary items by material lines of business;
- Revenue, in dollars or percentages, by class of similar products and services;
- Information about customers on whom the company was materially dependent; and
- Information about foreign operations.

A line of business was considered material if its sales, revenue, or profit contribution exceeded a *percentage limit*. The SEC required companies to consider profitability, risk, and growth opportunities in determining a line of business, but did not specify how a company should actually segment its operations.

The SEC's rules for registration statements filed with the commission were adopted in 1969. In 1970 the commission applied the rules to Form 10-K filings, and it extended them in 1974 to shareholder annual reports.

In the September 1980 overhaul of its integrated disclosure system, the SEC substantially retained the ASR 236 requirements (which remain in Item 1(b) of Regulation S-K) but dropped the requirement for information about whether intersegment transaction prices were substantially different from prevailing market prices or prices in transactions with unaffiliated parties.

Federal Trade Commission

In 1970, the Federal Trade Commission (FTC) first proposed collecting information from major companies on their lines of business. The need for the line-of-business (LB) survey grew out of the FTC's "recognition that large corporations engaged in manufacturing were becoming increasingly diversified and, as a consequence, their consolidated financial reports were becoming less helpful in determining conditions in particular industries" (Long, 1979, p. 1). The FTC feared that much of the nation's aggregate economic data, based on information supplied by individual corporations and used by policy makers in various federal agencies, were potentially misleading. Besides giving the FTC a clearer picture of economic activity, the LB statistics could help it identify unusually high or low profit areas of the economy, information which could be used in investigations concerning unfair trade practices or possible antitrust violations.

The first LB survey, requiring 345 manufacturing companies to submit 1973 financial data, was mailed in 1974. Based on the experience gained from this survey, the FTC expanded the required information on the survey of 1974 financial data and ordered 440 companies to submit LB data.

Because the FTC needs information about defined markets, its rules concerning the data it collects are quite specific. The categories, which range from "abrasive products" to "X-ray apparatus and tubes, electrical equipment and supplies," are based on combinations of standard industrial codes. The 1973 survey, for example, included 228 reporting categories, mostly in manufacturing industries.

To determine its lines of business, a company groups establishments that fall under the same reporting category. An *establishment* is a plant or other economic unit where manufacturing operations or other services are performed, generally at a single location. If the establishment manufactures products falling into two or more categories, it is classified by the category accounting for the largest percentage of its sales or receipts. A company does not have to report LB information for foreign activities or for domestic activities monitored by regulatory agencies other than the FTC, such as the Interstate Commerce Commission.

A furor developed when the 1973 rules were issued, and many of the companies subjected to the survey began a series of administrative and judicial challenges to the program. A similar controversy erupted when the rules were expanded for the 1974 survey. The FTC brought multiple enforcement actions against companies that refused to comply and eventually decided to concentrate its enforcement efforts on the 1974 survey. These legal wrangles are covered in more detail in the last section of this chapter.

Because of the legal dispute, only 1973 data have so far been published in a staff report. An example of the aggregate data by various lines of business falling under the broad category "food and kindred products" is shown in Figure 32.1.

As Figure 32.1 shows, the 1973 survey collected LB data on five items: (1) sales, (2) direct cost of sales, (3) direct media advertising expense, (4) direct research and development expense, and (5) direct net plant, property, and equipment. In the expanded 1974 survey, companies had to report additional information, including costs allocated (not directly traceable) to individual lines of business. The FTC's staff cautions readers of the 1973 report that the data represent the initial efforts of a complex program that was subsequently refined. The data may also not be representative, because 120 (generally the larger and more diversified) of the original 345 companies contacted refused to comply with the 1973 rules.

Financial Accounting Standards Board

The project that culminated in SFAS 14 was first put on the Board's agenda in 1973. In 1974, the FASB issued *Discussion Memorandum on an Analysis of Issues Related to Financial Reporting for Segments of a Business Enterprise* to "examine whether information about segments of a business enterprise should be included in financial statements, and, if so, ... to determine what information should be included and how it should be presented" (FASB, 1974a, p. vii). An exposure draft of a proposed statement was issued in 1975, after public hearings. The Board received extensive comments at each stage. Finally, in December 1976, the Board released SFAS 14. All companies, in their financial statements for fiscal years beginning after December 15, 1976, were required to follow SFAS 14 rules. The FASB did not require companies to include this information in comparative financial statements of earlier periods that were presented with financial statements issued after the effective date.

SFAS 14 is a complex pronouncement and will be analyzed later in this chapter. After it was released many companies objected to the high cost of following its rules. The FASB considered these objections and issued several responsive amendments.

THE SCOPE OF SFAS 14

When originally issued, SFAS 14 applied to annual financial statements prepared in conformity with GAAP and to those interim statements "expressly described" as being in accordance with GAAP. The rules covered virtually all businesses, and many companies objected to these broad-ranging requirements. The meaning of

CODE	RELATED SIC'S	INDUSTRY CATEGORY TITLE	NO. OF COS.	SALES	DIRECT COST OF SALES	DIRECT ADVER- TISING	DIRECT RES. & DEV.	DIRECT PR., PLT. & EQUIP.	PART. RATIO	SPEC. RATIO	COV. RATIO
20.01	201	MEAT PRODUCTS	14	10385670	9693558	33485	(D)	578909	28	95	100
20.02	2026	FLUID MILK	7	1546561	1303980	9051	(D)	145965	16	92	100
20.03	202, x 2026	DAIRY PRODUCTS EXC. FLUID MILK	10	1337136	1097770	15831	3297	152304	19	90	84
20.04	2032	CANNED SPECIALITIES	(2)	(2)	(2)	(2)	(2)	(2)	(2)	(2)	(2)
20.05	203, x 2032	PRESERVED FRUITS AND VEGETABLES, EXC. CANNED SPECIALITIES	(3)	(3)	(3)	(3)	(3)	(3)	(3)	(3)	(3)
20.06	2043	CEREAL BREAKFAST FOODS	4	404674	251849	43892	4124	82581	36	86	90
20.07	2047	DOG, CAT, AND OTHER PET FOOD	8	1097895	802055	78002	9026	277594	58	98	98
20.08	204, x 2043,7	FLOUR AND OTHER GRAIN MILL PRODUCTS, RICE MILLING, BLENDED AND PREPARED FLOUR, WET CORN MILLING, PREPARED FEEDS, NEC	19	3016686	2620137	23447	13605	314146	24	96	96
20.09	2051	BREAD, CAKE, AND RELATED PRODUCTS	10	1731523	1144591	32504	2001	356139	30	96	104
20.10	2052	COOKIES AND CRACKERS	4	464496	309965	6503	311	91703	27	98	90
20.11	2065	CONFECTIONERY PRODUCTS	9	440484	289574	11889	760	44688	18	95	93
20.12	2066	CHOCOLATE AND COCOA PRODUCTS	(2)	(2)	(2)	(2)	(2)	(2)	(2)	(2)	(2)
20.13	2067	CHEWING GUM	(2)	(2)	(2)	(2)	(2)	(2)	(2)	(2)	(2)
20.14	2061-3	RAW CANE SUGAR, CANE SUGAR REFINING, BEET SUGAR	6	1624795	1457060	3629	1535	250592	45	95	100
20.15	207	FATS AND OILS	7	3483106	3195037	12972	1972	102310	36	99	96
20.16	2082,3	MALT BEVERAGES, MALT	4	1457355	1105751	68328	2235	490919	32	100	100
20.17	2084,5	WINES, BRANDY, BRANDY SPIRITS, AND DISTILLED LIQUOR	6	1076706	678402	92958	(D)	219149	42	100	100
20.18	2086	BOTTLED AND CANNED SOFT DRINKS	5	571540	369407	11707	(D)	113094	12	99	93
20.19	2087	FLAVORING EXTRACTS AND SYRUPS, NEC	4	453223	199174	48706	2690	43343	27	93	98
20.20	2095	ROASTED COFFEE	(2)	(2)	(2)	(2)	(2)	(2)	(2)	(2)	(2)
20.21	209, x 2095	MISC. FOODS AND KINDRED PRODUCTS, EXC. ROASTED COFFEE	(3)	(3)	(3)	(3)	(3)	(3)	(3)	(3)	(3)
20.51		COMBINATION OF 20.04 AND 20.05	21	1855287	1405848	51028	3932	258957	16	97	92
20.52		COMBINATION OF 20.12, 20.13, 20.20 AND 20.21	22	3536044	2372116	164183	16683	577691	33	95	97

FIGURE 32.1 1973 LINE-OF-BUSINESS DATA FOR FOOD AND KINDRED PRODUCTS

SOURCE: William Long, *Statistical Report: Annual Line of Business Report, 1973* (Washington, D.C.: Federal Trade Commission, 1979), p. 3.

"expressly described" was questioned; the usefulness of the disclosures for certain types of companies, especially parent companies and consolidated subsidiaries, was challenged; and the burden of compliance for smaller privately held companies was held to be especially onerous. As a result, the FASB issued three amendments to the original standard, narrowing its applicability. The requirement to include segment data in interim financial statements was suspended, and applicability was restricted to

- Consolidated financial statements of publicly held companies;
- Separately issued financial statements of publicly held parent companies, and the following investees if they themselves are publicly held: subsidiaries, corporate joint ventures, and 50%-or-less-owned investees; and
- Financial statements of a significant publicly held investee accounted for by the cost or equity method that are included in the financial report of another publicly held entity.

According to the FASB, a *public company* is one: "(a) whose debt or equity securities trade in a public market on a foreign or domestic stock exchange or in the over-the-counter market (including securities quoted only locally or regionally) or (b) that is required to file financial statements with the Securities and Exchange Commission" (AC 2083.13). If a company's financial statements are issued in preparation for the sale of securities in a public market, it is also public.

Separately issued refers to the manner in which financial statements are released by a company. Consolidated financial statements are often accompanied in the same publication by the financial statements of subsidiaries or other investees. If these financial statements are published apart from the consolidated financial statements, they are said to be separately issued.

Figure 32.2 describes the three financial accounting standards that amend the scope of SFAS 14. A fourth amendment, SFAS 30 (AC 2085), modifies certain disclosure requirements rather than the scope of SFAS 14 and is discussed later in this chapter.

DISCLOSURE OF SEGMENT INFORMATION

Under SFAS 14, as amended, companies must disclose a great deal of information about their operations in different industries, foreign operations, export sales, and major customers. However, the most complicated task companies face is determining how to group their operations into segments. SFAS 14 permits the exercise of considerable judgment in the critical area of determining segments, in contrast, for example, with the rigid lease accounting rules of SFAS 13 (AC 4053).

Companies may present segment information as part of their basic financial statements, with explanatory footnotes; entirely in the footnotes; or in a separate schedule that is clearly referenced to and incorporated in the financial statements.

Objectives and Accounting Principles

The purpose of SFAS 14 is "to assist financial statement users in analyzing and understanding the enterprise's financial statements by permitting better assessment of the enterprise's past performance and future prospects" (AC 2081.005).

SFAS No.	Title and Summary
18	*Financial Reporting for Segments of a Business Enterprise—Interim Financial Statements* • Eliminates any requirement to report information required by SFAS 14 in interim period financial statements pending completion of the Board's interim financial reporting project (deferred in 1979 pending further progress on the conceptual framework project).
21	*Suspension of the Reporting of Earnings per Share and Segment Information by Nonpublic Enterprises* • Suspends the requirements of SFAS 14 (and APB 15) for separately issued financial statements of nonpublic enterprises pending completion of the Board's conceptual framework project. • Does *not* suspend SFAS 14 requirements for financial statements of nonpublic companies presented in the financial report of another public company.
24	*Reporting Segment Information in Financial Statements That Are Presented in Another Enterprise's Financial Report* • Exempts financial statements from SFAS 14 requirements when they are presented in another company's financial report if: •• The financial statements are consolidated or combined, •• The financial statements are for a foreign investee that is not a subsidiary (unless the foreign investee prepares separately issued financial statements with SFAS 14 disclosures), or •• The other company's financial statements are exempted under SFAS 21. • Does *not* otherwise exempt separate financial statements presented in another company's financial report from SFAS 14 disclosures, unless they fail to meet certain tests of significance.

FIGURE 32.2   SCOPE AMENDMENTS TO SFAS 14

Differences in companies' operations and their accounting systems prevented the Board from developing the highly specific rules that would be necessary if different companies were expected to report comparable information. The Board warns users that segment information "may be of limited usefulness" (AC 2081.076) in comparing similar segments of two companies.

SFAS 14 does not introduce new accounting principles to be applied to individual transactions. Instead, the consolidated financial information is "disaggregated" into segments of similar products and services and, if appropriate, among geographic areas. To disaggregate is not to deconsolidate; the latter would suggest an allocation on the basis of companies legally constituted as subsidiaries. Because segment data are a disaggregation of consolidated financial information, they should reflect the same accounting principles the company used in preparing its basic finan-

cial statements, with one exception—significant intercompany transactions are eliminated in the consolidated financial statements (see Chapter 31), but transactions
between segments are included in the information required by SFAS 14.

An example of the segment disclosures required by SFAS 14 is shown in Figure
32.3. The Mead Corporation has five significant or reportable segments: paper;
pulp; packaging products and paperboard; consumer and distribution; and industrial products. The data segregate sales to unaffiliated customers and reflect other
adjustments so that the segment information in total agrees to Mead's consolidated
balance sheet and income statement.

Determining how to disaggregate operations into industry segments requires considerable judgment; determining which of these industry segments qualify as reportable involves the application of numerical tests. Both of these matters are described below.

Reportable Industry Segments

Grouping Products and Services. A company first analyzes the goods and
services produced by each of its *profit centers,* which the FASB defines as "com-

---

L. Industry Segments

The company operates principally in five segments. The *Paper* segment includes the manufacture and sale of printing, writing, carbonless copy, publishing, and specialty paper. The *Pulp* segment includes the manufacture and sale of pulp. The *Packaging Products and Paperboard* segment involves the manufacturing and marketing of beverage and food packaging materials, corrugated shipping containers, paperboard, and other paperboard products. The *Consumer and Distribution* segment includes the manufacture and distribution of school and office products and home furnishings and the distribution of a full line of paper products, industrial supplies, pipe, valves, fittings, and electrical supplies. Mead's *Industrial Products* segment consists primarily of the manufacture and distribution of small and medium size castings, coal, and rubber products.

Information concerning the company's operations in different industry segments for the years ended December 31, 1978 and 1977, is as follows:

(All dollar amounts in millions)	Sales (1) 1978 Unaffiliated	Sales (1) 1978 Intersegment	Sales (1) 1977 Unaffiliated	Sales (1) 1977 Intersegment	Operating Earnings 1978	Operating Earnings 1977	Identifiable Assets 1978	Identifiable Assets 1977
Industry segments:								
Paper	$ 463.9	$ 85.6	$ 406.9	$ 77.6	$ 76.1	$ 45.5	$ 366.9	$ 340.6
Pulp	39.2	27.3	36.3	37.5	7.4	18.2	64.3	63.3
Packaging Products and Paperboard	513.6	10.2	454.3	9.6	60.2	61.7	250.6	228.8
Consumer and Distribution	1,020.7	2.9	656.5	2.7	43.6	29.7	311.2	280.6
Industrial Products	261.1		250.5		29.4	25.9	117.6	108.6
Other	23.6		17.3		3.5	.4	6.4	4.2
Intersegment elimination		(126.0)		(127.4)			(11.6)	(7.1)
	$2,322.1		$1,821.8		220.2	181.4	1,105.4	1,019.0
Equity in earnings before taxes of jointly-owned companies and non-consolidated overseas operations (2)					67.1	51.7		
Investments in and advances to jointly-owned companies and non-consolidated overseas operations (3)							248.9	209.5
Corporate and other non-segment items (4)					(72.6)	(53.3)	169.5	145.5
Earnings before income taxes					$214.7	$179.8		
Total assets							$1,523.8	$1,374.0

(1) Intersegment sales are made at the same prices and terms as to unaffiliated customers.
(2) Amounts applicable to vertically integrated jointly-owned companies are (Paper) $2.9–1978, $2.5–1977; (Pulp) $6.6–1978, $8.1–1977; and (Packaging Products and Paperboard) $13.5–1978, $11.9–1977. Operations of these companies are conducted within the United States except for those of Northwood which operates in Canada. These amounts are included as a reduction of cost of products sold.
(3) Amounts applicable to vertically integrated jointly-owned companies are (Paper) $8.5–1978, $7.7–1977, (Pulp) $39.8–1978, $34.5–1977, and (Packaging Products and Paperboard) $91.5–1978, $79.0–1977. Investments in and advances to non-consolidated overseas operations amount to $10.6 in 1978 and $10.5 in 1977.
(4) Corporate assets consist primarily of cash and temporary cash investments and property, plant, and equipment.
    For information on capital expenditures and depreciation for 1978 and 1977, see "Capital expenditures (excluding capital leases)" and "Depreciation and cost of timber harvested" on page 41.

FIGURE 32.3   EXAMPLE OF SFAS 14 SEGMENT DISCLOSURES
SOURCE: Mead Corporation, 1978 Annual Report.

ponents of an enterprise *that sell primarily to outside markets* and *for which information about revenue and profitability is accumulated*" (AC 2081.013). But profit centers may cross industry lines. For example, a company might operate a division that manufactures small metal consumer appliances and, as a sideline, fabricates metal parts as a service to other manufacturers. Even if the company does not maintain separate accounting records for each operation, it should nonetheless develop the financial information through special analysis in order to disaggregate the profit center along industry lines for purposes of determining segments.

After the company has identified the various industries in which it operates, it groups related industry lines into segments. No hard-and-fast rules apply to this step; as a result, companies have considerable flexibility and must exercise careful judgment in order to make the reported information meaningful. Although no rules are given to guide companies in this judgment, the FASB suggests the following factors should be among those considered by a company in determining which of its products and services are related (AC 2081.100):

a. *The Nature of the Product.* Related products or services have similar purposes or end uses. Thus, they may be expected to have similar rates of profitability, similar degrees of risk, and similar opportunities for growth.

b. *The Nature of the Production Process.* Sharing of common interchangeable production or sales facilities, equipment, labor force, or service group or use of the same or similar basic raw materials may suggest that products or services are related. Likewise, similar degrees of labor intensiveness or similar degrees of capital intensiveness may indicate a relationship among products or services.

c. *Markets and Marketing Methods.* Similarity of geographic marketing areas, types of customers, or marketing methods may indicate a relationship among products or services. For instance, the use of a common or interchangeable sales force may suggest a relationship among products or services. The sensitivity of the market to price changes and to changes in general economic conditions may also indicate whether products or services are related or unrelated.

A company may use an existing *business classification system* such as Standard Industrial Classification (SIC) or Enterprise Standard Industrial Classification (ESIC) to help group its products and services. However, such classification systems, designed to gather national economic data, have important limitations: their narrowest classifications include a wide variety of products, and alternatively, similar products are often included under different classifications. The use of business classification systems alone will usually not result in business segments that fulfill the objectives of SFAS 14.

Selecting Reportable Segments. After a company has grouped its related products and services into segments, it must select which of these segments are important enough to be included separately in the information reported. Some segments may not be of interest to investors and creditors because they historically have not had nor are they expected to have a significant impact on the company's operations. Returning again to the Mead Corporation example (Figure 32.3), operations with 1978 sales totaling $23.6 million did not fit in any of Mead's five reportable segments. Because of the insignificance of these operations (less than 1.1% of consolidated sales), they have been reported simply as "other" in the Company's segment information. SFAS 14 provides the following tests to determine if a segment is reportable (AC 2081.015):

a. Its revenue (including both sales to unaffiliated customers and intersegment sales or transfers) is 10 percent or more of the combined revenue (sales to unaffiliated customers and intersegment sales or transfers) of all of the enterprise's industry segments.
b. The absolute amount of its operating profit or operating loss is 10 percent or more of the greater, in absolute amount, of:
   i. the combined operating profit of all industry segments that did not incur an operating loss, or
   ii. The combined operating loss of all industry segments that did incur an operating loss.
c. Its identifiable assets are 10 percent or more of the combined identifiable assets of all industry segments.

In general, if a segment meets any of these tests, it is reportable. However, a company should also evaluate the results of these tests for unusual aberrations. For example, if a company reports abnormally low combined operating profits in a given year, a historically insignificant segment may qualify as reportable because the segment's results satisfy the operating profit or loss test. If it is unlikely that the segment will again meet one of the significance tests in the forseeable future, the company may choose not to consider that segment reportable, although the company must explain these circumstances in its segment disclosures. Conversely, a historically significant segment expected to so continue should be considered reportable if, in an aberrant year, it happens to fail the three tests.

Reportable segments must explain a significant part of a company's operations without confusing the reader with overly detailed information. Guidelines to achieve this are listed below:

1. Segment data must explain a significant part of the company's operations. Until the combined sales to unaffiliated customers of all reportable segments equal or exceed 75% of the combined sales to unaffiliated customers of all segments, additional segments must be reported.

2. If the segment information is too detailed, it may not be useful. The FASB suggests that this point may be reached when a company has more than ten reportable segments. If this occurs, a company might consider combining the most closely related reportable segments, although the 75% test above must still be met.

3. Many companies are not diversified or only diversified to a very limited extent. A company has a dominant industry segment if a single segment's revenue, operating profit or loss, and identifiable assets are more than 90% of these items totaled for all the company's segments and no other segment would qualify in its own right as reportable. The financial statements must identify the dominant industry, but segment reporting of revenue, profitability, identifiable assets, and certain other information is not required in this situation.

Information About Operations in Different Industries

SFAS 14 requires information about the revenue, profitability, and identifiable assets of a company's operations in different industries.

Revenue. Sales of products and services to unaffiliated customers and intersegment sales (sales to other segments) consisting of products and services similar to those sold to unaffiliated customers should be separately presented for each segment. In the case of Mead Corporation (Figure 32.3), "intersegment sales are made at the same prices and terms as to unaffiliated customers" (Footnote (1)). Frequently, however, a company prices such sales on a different basis than it uses for pricing sales to outside customers; SFAS 14 tells companies to report intersegment sales or transfers on the actual basis the company used in recording the transaction. Financial statement users should be aware of this provision and not equate non-arm's-length intersegment sales or transfers with arm's-length outsider transactions. Chapter 28 discusses the ramifications of related-party transactions. Interest earned by the segment, except on loans to other segments,[1] is generally included in revenue.

Operating Profit or Loss. Operating profit or loss, which is revenue less all operating expenses and is reported for each segment, is computed before any provision for income taxes. It also excludes general corporate expenses, interest expense,[2] income or loss from unconsolidated subsidiaries, and other items. Again, a segment's operating profit or loss may reflect revenue from intersegment sales or costs from intersegment purchases.

A company often incurs expenses that benefit the operations of two or more segments. For example, a company may operate a computer facility that processes records for different segments. SFAS 14 requires that companies allocate common operating expenses on a reasonable basis to those segments that derive benefits. One problem is distinguishing general corporate expenses from common operating expenses; the nature of the expense rather than the location incurred is the determining factor. A more significant problem is that financial data that incorporate judgmental allocations are usually less reliable than financial data based solely on arm's-length market transactions.

Most diversified companies have, over the years, allocated common operating expenses for internal financial reports and have developed a wide variety of allocation methods. Some methods are sophisticated, involving the use of formulas and narrow categories of common expense; others are simpler—common expenses are pooled and allocated on a single-factor basis (such as sales). Because of the diversity of methods employed, cross-company comparisons of similar segments are likely to be misleading, and the reliability of segment operating results varies depending on how closely the basis of allocation approximates results that would have been produced by market transactions. Figure 32.4 illustrates four different bases (revenue, operating profit before allocation of common operating expenses, tangible assets, and number of employees) that a company might use for allocating common oper-

---

[1] Special rules apply to segments in financial industries such as banking, insurance, or leasing.
[2] See fn. 1.

ating expenses among segments. As the figure shows, each segment reports a different operating profit or loss depending on the basis used to allocate operating expenses. Furthermore, the difference between each segment's resulting highest and lowest operating profit can be a significant percentage of consolidated income.

Companies must disclose the methods used for allocating common operating expenses. The methods should be consistent from period to period; however, if they are changed, companies must indicate the nature of the change and the effect on segment operating results in the period the change occurred.

In addition to operating profit and loss, SFAS 14 allows a company the option of presenting additional profitability information about its operations in different industries. For example, in 1978 Standard Oil Company (Indiana) reported net income by industry segment in addition to operating profit (Figure 32.5). A company may disclose segment contribution to operating profit and loss (a segment's sales less costs directly identified with the particular segment), net income or loss by segment, or some profitability measure between operating profit or loss and net income or loss. Standard Oil's footnote illustrates two related requirements: if a company chooses to present a profitability measure other than operating profit and loss, it must (1) consistently report this measure for each comparative year shown in the financial statements and (2) identify differences between operating profit and loss and the alternative profitability measure.

Identifiable Assets. Each segment must disclose the carrying amount of its tangible and intangible assets, including an allocated portion of assets used jointly with other segments. Goodwill is included in identifiable assets, but general corporate assets not used in the operations of any industry segment are excluded. Also excluded are loans to other segments of the company.[3]

Other Information. Other information required about operations in different industries includes

1. Basis of intersegment sales or transfers and nature of change in basis, if any, and its effect on segment's operating profit or loss in period of change.
2. Nature and amount of any unusual or infrequently occurring items included in operating profit. (See Chapter 7.)
3. Types of products and services for each reportable segment.

Information About Foreign Operations and Export Sales

The information about industry segments helps financial statement readers evaluate a company's prospects based on the types of products and services it provides. To further their understanding, readers may also be interested in knowing the extent of a company's foreign operations. For this reason, SFAS 14 contains another set of requirements that stipulates the presentation of segment information based on the geographic areas in which a company operates. Thus, a manufacturer producing a variety of products in locations around the world would report two disaggregations of its consolidated operations, one on the basis of related products and one on the

---

[3] See fn. 1.

	Segment 1	Segment 2	Segment 3	Total
(000's Except No. of Employees and %)				
Selected Financial and Operating Data:				
Revenue	$ 825	$1,000	$1,000	$2,825
Operating profit before allocation of common operating expenses	$ 250	$ 75	$ 175	$ 500
Tangible assets	$1,250	$1,500	$1,000	$3,750
Number of employees	75	82	78	235
Common Operating Expenses*				
Centralized research and development				$ 75
EDP operation				100
Noncorporate legal and accounting				50
Other				50
Total				$ 275
Operating Profit (Loss) After Allocation of Common Expenses; Allocation Based On:				
Revenue	$170	$(22)	$ 77	$225
Operating profit before allocation of common expenses	$112	$ 34	$ 79	$225
Tangible assets	$158	$(35)	$102	$225
Number of employees	163	(22)	84	225
Range of segment income as a percentage of consolidated operating income depending on allocation method used	50%-76%	(16%)-15%	34%-45%	

* All segments derive benefits from listed operating expenses.

FIGURE 32.4 EFFECT ON SEGMENT OPERATING PROFIT OF VARIOUS BASES USED TO ALLOCATE COMMON OPERATING EXPENSES

basis of geographic areas. A company with significant foreign operations would disaggregate its consolidated operations on the basis of geographic area even if all locations produced an identical product or service.

Figure 32.6 shows the geographic information Dow Chemical Company reported in its 1978 annual report. SFAS 14 requires companies to separate foreign opera-

Statement of Information by Industry Segment and Geographic Area

Standard Oil Company (Indiana) and Subsidiaries

For the Years 1978 and 1977

(Dollars in thousands)	Petroleum Industry — Exploration and Production	Petroleum Industry — Refining, Marketing, and Transportation	Chemical Industry	Other Industries	Unallocated Corporate Amounts	Consolidated[1]
Industry Segment — Year 1978						
Revenues other than intersegment sales	$1,736,836	$12,677,274	$1,766,219	$ 14,541	$ 154,884	$16,349,754
Intersegment sales	3,052,443	427,965	65,412	—	—	—
Total revenues	$4,789,279	$13,105,239	$1,831,631	$ 14,541	$ 154,884	$16,349,754
Operating profit	$2,383,968	$ 364,021	$ 71,821	$ (51,927)		$ 2,767,883
Equity in earnings of others	(2,080)	21,709	374	1,471		21,474
General corporate amounts	49,025	21,114	15,015	890		86,044
Interest expense	(105,742)	(67,337)	(50,000)	(2,961)		(226,040)
Income before income taxes	2,325,171	339,507	37,210	(52,527)		2,649,361
Income taxes	(1,453,589)	(153,959)	8,258	26,341		(1,572,949)
Net income	$ 871,582	$ 185,548	$ 45,468	$ (26,186)		$ 1,076,412
Depreciation, depletion, amortization, etc.	$ 604,594	$ 146,752	$ 149,900	$ 2,611	$ 8,298	$ 912,155
Capital expenditures	$1,241,667	$ 259,315	$ 228,339	$ 1,432	$ 13,285	$ 1,744,038
Identifiable assets	$6,097,305	$ 4,219,323	$2,224,690	$116,277	$1,668,412	$13,926,892
Equity investments	$ 34,746	$ 64,155	$ 62,529	$ 20,942		182,372
Total assets						$14,109,264
Year 1977*						
Revenues other than intersegment sales	$1,544,097	$11,040,268	$1,568,968	$ 11,653	$ 98,244	$14,263,230
Intersegment sales	2,805,803	381,727	57,746	—	—	—
Total revenues	$4,349,900	$11,421,995	$1,626,714	$ 11,653	$ 98,244	$14,263,230
Operating profit	$2,324,667	$ 390,699	$ 89,101	$ (67,997)		$ 2,736,470
Equity in earnings of others	2,102	19,014	2,112	1,266		24,494
General corporate amounts	19,195	4,776	3,269	219		27,459
Interest expense	(98,645)	(65,438)	(37,542)	(2,523)		(204,148)
Income before income taxes	2,247,319	349,051	56,940	(69,035)		2,584,275
Income taxes	(1,386,191)	(160,904)	(17,326)	12,364		(1,552,057)
Net income	$ 861,128	$ 188,147	$ 39,614	$ (56,671)		$ 1,032,218
Depreciation, depletion, amortization, etc.	$ 550,023	$ 148,533	$ 100,108	$ 6,304	$ 6,188	$ 811,156
Capital expenditures	$ 908,778	$ 280,943	$ 269,840	$ 5,035	$ 8,867	$ 1,473,463
Identifiable assets	$5,728,370	$ 3,979,494	$2,054,520	$114,361	$1,589,890	$12,796,192
Equity investments	$ 10,503	$ 65,091	$ 43,492	$ 18,793		137,879
Total assets						$12,934,071

* Restated – (Refer to Financial Review).
[1] After elimination of intersegment transactions.

FIGURE 32.5   EXAMPLE OF SEGMENTED NET INCOME REPORTING
SOURCE: Standard Oil Company (Indiana), 1978 Annual Report.

tions from domestic operations. Dow Chemical further separated its total foreign operations into more detailed geographic areas: Europe/Africa, Canada, Pacific, Latin America, and Brazil.

The information about (and the identification of) significant foreign operations required by SFAS 14 is similar to the information a company provides on its industry operations. Important differences are explained below.

Profitability. A company may present operating profit or loss (as defined earlier) for each geographic area, or elect to report net income, or use another measure of

R. GEOGRAPHIC AND INDUSTRY SEGMENTS The Company conducts its worldwide operations through separate geographic area organizations which represent major markets or combinations of related markets. Brazil was designated as a new area and the operating results reported separately in 1978. The Latin American Area was restated for 1977 to separate the Brazilian operations on a comparable basis. The results for all areas for 1978 and 1977 were (in millions):

	United States	Europe/ Africa	Canada	Pacific	Latin America	Brazil	Elim. & Corp. Assets	Consoli- dated
Twelve months ended December 31, 1978:								
Sales to unaffiliated customers	$3,645.7	$1,813.1	$438.5	$404.4	$336.5	$249.4		$6,887.6
Transfers between areas	605.5	123.0	24.9	.6	2.4	9.2	$(765.6)	
Total sales and transfers	$4,251.2	$1,936.1	$463.4	$405.0	$338.9	$258.6	$(765.6)	$6,887.6
Operating income	$ 682.5	$ 211.7	$ 44.1	$ 55.3	$ 40.7	$ 17.1		$1,051.4
Profit (loss) before income taxes	$ 616.6	$ 218.2	$ 27.6	$ 73.1	$ 38.5	$ (5.9)		$ 968.1
Identifiable assets at December 31, 1978	$4,329.7	$2,058.6	$922.1	$536.1	$260.7	$625.1	$ 56.8	$8,789.1
Twelve months ended December 31, 1977 (Restated):								
Sales to unaffiliated customers	$3,456.8	$1,618.6	$396.4	$294.7	$277.1	$190.7		$6,234.3
Transfers between areas	534.8	77.7	25.4	.2	2.8	2.6	$(643.5)	
Total sales and transfers	$3,991.6	$1,696.3	$421.8	$294.9	$279.9	$193.3	$(643.5)	$6,234.3
Operating income	$ 664.2	$ 200.5	$ 63.3	$ 38.0	$ 50.1	$ 3.9		$1,020.0
Profit (loss) before income taxes	$ 621.5	$ 194.1	$ 46.0	$ 43.1	$ 46.7	$(20.1)		$ 931.3
Identifiable assets at December 31, 1977	$4,028.7	$1,932.5	$698.4	$362.3	$228.3	$458.5	$ 43.8	$7,752.5

Transfers between areas are valued at cost plus a markup. There were no direct sales to foreign customers from domestic operations.

Aggregation of products into industry segments is generally made on the basis of process technology and channels of distribution. The Chemicals/Metals segment embodies chemicals, hydrocarbon intermediates and the Company's magnesium business. The Plastics/Packaging segment includes large volume polyethylene and polystyrene products as well as a variety of plastic coatings, films and foams. The Bioproducts/Consumer Products segment encompasses human, animal and plant health care products, in addition to household films and cleaning chemicals.

FIGURE 32.6 EXAMPLE OF GEOGRAPHIC SEGMENTATION
SOURCE: Dow Chemical Co., 1978 Annual Report.

profitability between these two. The same measure must be used for all geographic areas, although the company, at its option, may report additional profitability information for some or all of its geographic areas. Dow chose to report both "operating income" (operating profit) and "profit (loss) before income taxes" for each geographic area.

Export Sales. Export sales are those made by a company's domestic operations to unaffiliated customers in foreign countries. If export sales exceed 10% of the company's consolidated revenues from sales to unaffiliated customers, the amount of export sales in total and by geographic area (as appropriate) must be reported. A company must report export sales meeting this test regardless of whether it is necessary to provide the other information required by SFAS 14. Export sales are not to be combined with foreign operations located in the foreign countries in which export sales are made.

Identification of Foreign Operations. The basic distinction a company must make is between *foreign and domestic operations.* Foreign operations are located outside the company's home country and generate revenue either from sales to unaffiliated customers or from intraenterprise sales or transfers between geographic areas.

At first glance this appears straightforward. But in applying the requirements of SFAS 14, companies with *mobile assets* (offshore drilling rigs, ships, cargo containers leased out for ocean transport, etc.) have experienced difficulties. To determine whether operations using mobile assets are foreign or domestic, a company should consider with which area the assets are normally identified.

A company presents information about foreign operations only when its foreign operations are significant. According to SFAS 14, this occurs when either of the following conditions is met (AC 2081.032):

   a. Revenue generated by the enterprise's foreign operations from sales to unaffiliated customers is 10 percent or more of consolidated revenue as reported in the enterprise's income statement.
   b. Identifiable assets of the enterprise's foreign operations are 10 percent or more of consolidated total assets as reported in the enterprise's balance sheet.

Unlike the tests for determining reportable segments, there is no operating profit or loss test for determining significant foreign operations.

Determination of Geographic Areas. A company may be required to further segregate its foreign operations into *geographic areas*—countries or groups of countries—if any area alone meets the significance tests in the preceding paragraph. The unaffiliated sales of Dow Chemical's Europe/Africa operations and the identifiable assets of its Canadian operations in 1978 (Figure 32.6) satisfy the related percentage tests. It is interesting to note that Dow Chemical segregates its Brazilian operations from others in Latin America, although neither area alone meets SFAS 14's significance tests; most likely the company judged that readers would find this presentation informative. Each company must evaluate its own unique circumstances to determine appropriate geographic areas; the FASB suggests consideration of the following factors: ". . . proximity, economic affinity, similarity in business environments, and the nature, scale, and degree of interrelationship of the enterprise's operations in the various countries" (AC 2081.034).

Information About Major Customers

SFAS 14 requires information about significant customers so users of financial statements can assess a company's degree of dependency on these customers. For example, if an aerospace contractor derives a significant portion of its business from weapon sales to the U.S. Department of Defense, a user is alerted that the company's near-term future performance will largely depend on factors affecting defense spending. These factors may be complex and difficult to assess, but they cannot be ignored in considering the company's prospects.

SFAS 14 defined a *major customer* as one who provides 10% or more of a company's revenues from sales to nonaffiliates and held that several customers under common control should be treated as a single customer. It required companies to aggregate sales to domestic government agencies and to aggregate sales to foreign governments for purposes of the 10% test. Many held that such aggregation was meaningless. The Board considered this point of view and concluded, in SFAS 30, that the original SFAS 14 approach "has limited usefulness" (AC 2085.03). Accordingly, the FASB amended the major customer definition to include: "The federal government, a state government, a local government (for example, a county or municipality), or a foreign government shall each be considered a single customer" (AC 2085.06, amending AC 2081.34). If sales are concentrated in a particular government agency, however, SFAS 30 encourages companies to disclose that fact and the amount of revenue derived.

A company subject to SFAS 14 rules must report information about major customers even if it is required neither to disclose industry segments (for lack of diversification) nor to provide information about foreign operations (for lack of nondomestic activities).[4] The FASB allayed fears of disclosing competitively damaging information by not requiring companies to identify by name their major customers (including domestic government agencies or foreign governments).

Information About Equity Method Investees

Companies that have unconsolidated subsidiaries and other investees carried by the equity method of accounting do not have to include these operations or assets in their segment information. However, the investor company must identify the industry and the geographic area in which the equity method subsidiary or other investee operates. SFAS 14 encourages disaggregation of equity investee financial information if this would help a user better understand the investor's overall operations.

Special rules apply to *vertically integrated investees,* which are those whose products or services are sold primarily to other components of the company. A petroleum refinery whose product is sold entirely to its owner's retail gas operation is an example of a vertically integrated investee. Rules requiring disclosures for vertically integrated investees are as follows:

1. For each reportable segment, disclose equity in net income from, and investment in net assets of, unconsolidated subsidiaries and other equity method investees whose operations are vertically integrated with the operations of the segment.
2. Disclose geographic areas in which such vertically integrated investees operate.

Footnote (2) of Mead's industry segment information (Figure 32.3) illustrates the rules for vertically integrated investees.

---

[4] A company exempt from SFAS 14 requirements may nonetheless be required to report similar information if it is "economically dependent on one or more parties with which it transacts a significant volume of business . . ." (AU 335.05). (See Chapter 28.)

Other Disclosures Required by SFAS 14

In addition to the broader areas described above, other disclosures required include

- Accounting policies relevant to segment information to extent not adequately explained in the accounting policies footnote.
- Aggregate depreciation, depletion, and amortization expense for each reportable segment.
- Capital expenditures for each reportable segment.
- Effect on operating profits of reportable segments of a change in accounting, for the period of change.
- Retroactive restatement of prior-period information (at least as far back as SFAS 14's effective date) and disclosure of effect and nature of restatement when
  - •• Financial statements of the company have been retroactively restated (e.g., because of a change in accounting principle or a pooling of interests), or
  - •• A company decides to change the method of grouping industry segments or geographic areas. (See Figure 32.6; Dow Chemical decided to separately disclose its operations in Brazil and restated 1977 geographic segments.) If reported industry groups or geographic areas change due to a change in the underlying nature of a company's operations or because of the results of segment percentage tests, no retroactive restatement is required.

AUDITING SEGMENTS

As mentioned earlier in this chapter, a company may report segment information directly in the financial statements, with explanatory footnotes; entirely in the footnotes; or in a separate schedule incorporated in the financial statements. Whichever option a company chooses, segment disclosures are an integral part of the financial statements. If auditors are examining the financial statements with the objective of expressing an unqualified opinion, they must also consider the reasonableness of the segment information reported by their client.

Segment disclosures present auditors with two major problems. First, because SFAS 14 permits companies to exercise considerable judgment, the grouping a company selects as a basis for segmenting its operations is most likely not the only one possible. Therefore, to what extent should an auditor investigate a company's methods for grouping related industries and to what extent should the auditor explore alternatives? Second, consolidated revenues, profits, and assets are now addressed as segmented amounts. In his tests, therefore, should the auditor incorporate a smaller materiality level appropriate to the smaller segment amounts or retain a materiality level appropriate for the consoliated financial statements? Because of these and other problems, the Auditing Standards Division of the AICPA issued SAS 21, *Segment Information* (AU 435), in December 1977. This section will discuss the auditor's objectives, audit procedures, and reporting considerations presented in SAS 21.

Objectives and Materiality

The auditor reviews segment information with the objective of obtaining "a reasonable basis for concluding whether the information is presented in conformity with FASB Statement No. 14 . . . *in relation to the financial statements taken as a whole*" (AU 435.03; emphasis added). Auditors should treat segment information like other informative disclosures. That is, they do not apply audit procedures to the extent required if they were to issue an opinion on the segment information alone.

Materiality is critical in determining the extent of an auditor's procedures. According to SAS 21, the auditor must make quantitative judgments primarily, and qualitative judgments secondarily, in determining the materiality of segment information.

Quantitative Judgments. The auditor's *quantitative judgments* relate the dollar magnitude of the segment information to the consolidated financial statements taken as a whole. For example, if during an audit the auditor concludes that 5% of consolidated operating income is an appropriate cumulative materiality level, he does not have to apportion this amount to segments. In a ten-segment company, a 5% consolidated materiality does not become 0.5% at the segment level.

Qualitative Judgments. Though quantitative materiality considerations are useful to the auditor as rules of thumb, the auditor must also consider *qualitative factors*. A misstatement of the segment information may cause a company's financial statements taken as a whole to be misleading even if the magnitude of the misstatement is below the dollar materiality level the auditor judges is appropriate for the consolidated statements. The auditor should insist that the segment information be corrected to eliminate the misstatement or appropriately modify his report. (See Chapter 16.)

For example, consider a segment of a company whose operating profit has grown at an exceptional rate in recent years. The auditor is aware through analysts' reports that investors and potential investors believe the growth rate will continue in the future and that the market price of the company's stock incorporates the investors' evaluation. During his examination the auditor discovers that the current year's joint operating expenses have been misallocated and understated for the segment in question; as a result, the trend in earnings continues. Although the consolidated income is correct (a misallocation would not affect total expense), the auditor must assess whether the segment's misstated profit, in light of the probable importance of the trend, makes the financial statements taken as a whole misleading. If in his judgment the statements are misleading, the misstatement in segment information is material even though the dollar impact on consolidated income was zero.

SAS 21 tells auditors to consider the following when evaluating whether a qualitative segment matter is material to the financial statements taken as a whole:

1. The significance of a matter to a particular entity,
2. The pervasiveness of a matter, and
3. The impact of a matter.

The previous example of the segment with understated operating expenses illustrates the first and last points above. A company that misapplies the guidelines of

SFAS 14 in grouping its products and services into segments illustrates the second.

The impact of qualitative factors is difficult for an auditor to assess. If in the example the historical growth rate of operating earnings has been 15% and the actual growth rate for the segment when joint expenses are correctly allocated is 14%, is the 1% difference significant? Is 5%? Is 0.5%?

Auditors have traditionally grappled with similar qualitative considerations in assessing the materiality of various matters. But many auditors objected to SAS 21 because it formally introduced qualitative materiality considerations into professional auditing standards without adequately articulating them. Auditors believe this may extend their legal exposure. The FASB continues to search for an appropriate definition of materiality. (See Chapter 2.)

Audit Procedures

Because the profession has decided that segment information does not require a different quantitative materiality standard, an auditor theoretically does not have to increase the overall level of auditing procedures during his examination. As a practical matter, however, segment information will require additional effort on the auditor's part. In general, segment information affects the audit plan and must be considered throughout the engagement.

Auditors should consider segment information when planning the audit. For example, in the absence of segment information, an auditor might plan to have staff persons observe physical inventory counts of items representing 50% of the dollar value of the consolidated inventory balance. If the same company is reporting segment information, the auditor would probably still plan to cover 50% of the inventory, but would locate his observations on the basis of the company's segments. He may emphasize a reportable segment encompassing several divisions over another segment with a single operation and a single accounting system.[5] In the words of SAS 21, segment information may cause the auditor to "modify or redirect selected audit tests to be applied to the financial statements taken as a whole" (AU 435.06). The auditor considers the following when deciding whether or not to redirect or modify his tests (AU 435.06):

a. Internal accounting control and the degree of integration, centralization, and uniformity of the accounting records.
b. The nature, number, and relative size of industry segments and geographic areas.
c. The nature and number of subsidiaries or divisions in each industry segment and geographic area.
d. The accounting principles used for the industry segments and geographic areas.

Auditors should also consider segment information when performing their normal tests of the underlying accounting records. Auditors should challenge whether revenue, operating expenses, and identifiable assets are properly classified among industry segments and geographic areas.

---

[5] The auditor would consider many factors in determining the percentage of consolidated inventory he should observe. In this simple example, the only factor isolated is the effect of segment operations on internal control.

SAS 21 lists a number of specific procedures auditors should perform to determine if a company's segment information is presented in conformity with SFAS 14. These procedures (summarized below from AU 435.07) cover the segmenting procedures followed by the company when grouping related products and industries, the bases used for intersegment sales and transfers, the disaggregation of the company's financial statements, and other matters. The auditor should

1. Inquire concerning the company's method of determining segment information. Evaluate the reasonableness of the method in relation to SFAS 14 guidelines.
2. Inquire as to the basis for sales and transfers between segments and areas. Test whether the basis conforms to recorded transactions.
3. Test the disaggregation of the financial statements into segment information.
   a. Evaluate the application of SFAS 14 percentage tests. Check if the data are properly summarized and recompute as necessary.
   b. Analytically review the segment data and inquire if items or relationships appear unusual.
      (1) Compare current-year data to prior-year and current-year budgeted data.
      (2) Consider the interrelationship of elements that should correlate based on the company's experience.
      (3) Consider matters that have required adjustment to segment information in the past.
4. Inquire about, evaluate reasonableness of, and mathematically test as necessary the allocation of operating expenses and jointly used assets.
5. Determine whether segment information has been consistently presented. If not, determine that appropriate disclosures and restatements, if appropriate, are being made.

Auditor's Report

Although segment information rarely affects the auditor's report (see Chapter 16), in some situations (if material) the report should be modified. A brief description of those situations follows.

Misstatement or Omission of Segment Information. The auditor should issue either a qualified or an adverse opinion. The auditor should describe the effects of the misstatement, but he is not required to provide omitted information regarding segments. An auditor will rarely encounter omitted segment information, because SFAS 14, as amended, applies only to public companies. However, in 1978, Sony Corporation, a Japanese company, omitted segment information in its annual report. The auditors reported (see Figure 32.7) that Sony's consolidated financial statements were presented fairly in accordance with accepted United States accounting principles "except for" the omission of segment information.[6]

---

[6] Sony's reluctance to provide segment information is not unusual for some foreign companies. *Keidanren,* a prestigious Japanese association of businesses of which Sony is a member, strongly objected to SEC proposals to expand the financial statement disclosure of foreign companies whose securities trade in U.S. markets. *Keidanren* maintained that "the imposition of additional disclosures such as replacement cost data and segment report [sic] . . . would go so far as to affect the corporate management system of Japanese enterprises" (letter from Messrs. Shibuya and Yoshii to Harold Williams, SEC chairman, October 2, 1978).

REPORT OF INDEPENDENT ACCOUNTANTS

PRICE WATERHOUSE & CO.

AOYAMA BUILDING, 2-3, KITA-AOYAMA 1-CHOME
MINATO-KU, TOKYO

To the Stockholders and Board of Directors of   December 17, 1979
Sony Corporation (Sony Kabushiki Kaisha)

We have examined the consolidated balance sheets of Sony Corporation (Sony Kabushiki Kaisha) and its consolidated subsidiaries as of October 31, 1979 and 1978, and the related consolidated statements of income and retained earnings and of changes in financial position for the years then ended, expressed in yen. Our examinations were made in accordance with generally accepted auditing standards and accordingly included such tests of the accounting records and such other auditing procedures as we considered necessary in the circumstances.

The company has not presented segment information for the years ended October 31, 1979 and 1978. In our opinion, presentation of segment information concerning the company's foreign operations and export sales is required by accounting principles generally accepted in the United States of America for a complete presentation of the consolidated financial statements.

In our opinion, except for the omission of segment information as discussed in the preceding paragraph, the consolidated financial statements examined by us, expressed in yen, present fairly the financial position of Sony Corporation (Sony Kabushiki Kaisha) and its consolidated subsidiaries at October 31, 1979 and 1978, and the results of their operations and the changes in their financial position for the years then ended, in conformity with accounting principles generally accepted in the United States of America consistently applied.

Price Waterhouse & Co.

FIGURE 32.7   AUDITOR'S REPORT—OMISSION OF SEGMENT DATA
SOURCE: Sony Corporation, 1979 Annual Report.

Scope Limitation. A scope limitation occurs when a company requests that the auditor not examine its segment information. SAS 21 also discusses the situation of an auditor not being sure which provisions of SFAS 14 (existence of reportable segments, export sales, major customers, etc.) apply to his client. If the company refuses to develop information to this end, the auditor also faces a scope limitation. It is difficult to imagine an auditor not being familiar enough with his client's operations to conclude he faced an omission of segment information rather than a scope limitation. Conceivably, the SAS includes this situation in order to help auditors convince reluctant clients that it is the clients' responsibility to assemble the information required by SFAS 14. The auditor should explain a scope limitation and qualify his opinion.

Separate Reports. Occasionally an auditor will be asked to issue a separate report on his review of financial information prepared in accordance with SFAS 14 for one or more of the diversified company's segments. The auditor's procedures will be more extensive than the procedures he would direct to those same segments in an examination of the company's financial statements, because the auditor must base materiality on the particular segment information itself.

SAS 21 refers the auditor to AU 621.10-.13 (special reports expressing an opinion on one or more specified elements, accounts, or items of a financial statement) for guidance in this type of examination and also instructs the auditor to state in his separate report whether or not segment information is presented fairly in accordance with GAAP.[7]

The separate reporting requirements of SAS 21 are ambiguous. When the auditor reports that segment information is presented fairly in accordance with GAAP, does this mean that only the disclosures required by SFAS 14, no more or no less, have been made? Or does it mean that the auditor should consider whether additional informative disclosures required by GAAP other than SFAS 14 are necessary so that the segment information is not misleading?

The auditing literature does not resolve the dilemma. But because segment information provides a broad view of one or more components of a diversified company (information about revenue, profitability, assets, etc.) the auditor must seriously consider whether potential users might consider the information misleading unless accompanied by disclosures beyond those required in SFAS 14. For example, when the enterprise as a whole is faced with a material uncertainty, he might conclude that the disclosures required by SFAS 5, *Accounting for Contingencies* (AC 4311), are also necessary for a fair presentation of the segment information.

Consistency. As summarized in Figure 32.8, a company may change an accounting practice that in turn affects the way segment information is prepared or presented. According to SFAS 14, a company must disclose the nature and effect of a change in the period the change occurs, and for certain changes the segment information must be retroactively restated.

If an auditor is reporting on the consolidated financial statements taken as a whole, the effect of the change on the segment information would not cause him to modify his report. Certain changes, such as a change in the basis of pricing intersegment sales, affect only the segment information, and the auditor would not mention such changes in his report. On the other hand, if a company changes accounting principles as discussed in APB 20 (AC 1051), the change also affects the consolidated financial statements, and for that reason the auditor would mention the change in his report.

Qualified opinions. However, if a company did not disclose the nature and effect of a change or make the retroactive restatements as required by SFAS 14, the auditor would issue a qualified (in rare instances an adverse) opinion, because the company's failure to provide this information constitutes a departure from GAAP. The auditor may also consider including the nature and effect of a change in an explanatory paragraph in his report. Unlike segment information that is omitted

---

[7] If the segment constitutes a separable entity whose complete financial statements are presented in conformity with GAAP, usual audit considerations apply, not the guidance in this section.

in its entirety, the nature and effect of a change may be readily ascertainable and compactly presented.

If an auditor is reporting separately on segment information, he should mention any of the changes listed in Figure 32.8.

CURRENT ISSUES

A number of issues have emerged as companies grow more experienced in reporting segment information. These issues and a look to the future conclude this chapter.

The SEC and One-Segment Companies

As previously mentioned, the SEC has largely conformed its line-of-business requirements to SFAS 14. In March 1978, the SEC released ASR 244 "to assist registrants with the implementation of the segment reporting requirements." This ASR confirms the approach recommended by the FASB for determining appropriate segments and presents examples of appropriate (and in the SEC's view, inappropriate) segmentation in a number of industries. ASR 244 also warns that if the SEC's staff finds a company's segment decisions unacceptable, the company will be required to amend its filings with the SEC and "to communicate this additional information to shareholders in some appropriate manner." The "penalty" of the additional shareholder communication could be as extreme as a revised annual report.

What has caused concern among many accountants is the industry examples included in ASR 244: electrical and electronic products, forest products, chemicals, drugs, and property/casualty insurance. Those concerned believe that the SEC's stance communicated in certain of these examples requires companies to define segments more narrowly than intended by SFAS 14.

The nature and effect of the change must be disclosed in the period of change when

- The basis for recording intersegment sales is changed.
- The method of allocating common operating expenses or identifiable assets among segments is changed.
- The method of determining or presenting segment profitability is changed.
- An accounting principle as discussed in APB 20 is changed.
- The financial statements of the company as a whole have been retroactively restated.*
- The method of grouping industry segments or geographic areas is changed.*

* Prior-period segment information must be retroactively restated.

FIGURE 32.8   CAUSES OF INCONSISTENT SEGMENT INFORMATION

Insurance Companies. The example of property/casualty insurers best illustrates both viewpoints. Property/casualty insurers offer various products and services: workmen's compensation, automobile, homeowner's, commercial fire, other commercial liability, and professional malpractice coverage. The SEC believes that if companies properly assessed these products keeping in mind factors such as relative profitability, risk, and growth, they would disaggregate their operations into multiple segments.

The AICPA Insurance Companies Committee interprets the guidelines of SFAS 14 differently. It says the guidelines "do not support the view that insurance companies should generally group their products and services into more than two industry segments, that is, a life insurance segment and a property/liability [i.e., property/casualty] insurance segment." The committee did not question the SEC's authority to require further segmenting of property/casualty companies; it believed, however, that this would constitute product-line disclosure that "goes beyond the requirements of FASB Statement No. 14 as it relates to insurance companies." [8] The committee asked the FASB to resolve the disagreement by issuing an interpretation of SFAS 14; the Board demurred because it wanted further time to observe the implementation of SFAS 14.

Electrical and Electronic Products. A second industry mentioned in ASR 244 is electrical and electronic products. Several companies considered their various products to be one line of business and concluded that they operated in a single industry segment. Furthermore, electrical and electronic products constituted a single industry group in the SIC code and were all dependent on semiconductor and circuitry technology. The SEC disagreed, saying that the industry "may be too imprecise or may include too many disparate products to be considered one industry segment" (ASR 244). The commission held that the products had different markets and different production facilities, factors that outweighed the companies' arguments.

Differing views on segments will continue while the SEC and registrants gain familiarity with SFAS 14. However, public companies should carefully evaluate an initial conclusion on their part that they operate in a single segment. Unless there is little room for doubt, such companies should consider obtaining approval of their single-segment decision with the staff of the SEC.

The Cost of Segment Reporting

Among the reasons accountants object to the SEC's interpretation of SFAS 14 is the cost of accumulating the information. The narrower the definition of a segment, the more discrete are segments likely to be identified and reported on, and the higher the cost of gathering the information.

Cost Factors. Many companies' accounting systems will not routinely accumulate all of the information required by SFAS 14. Thus, much of the data must be

---

[8] The quoted remarks in this paragraph are taken from a letter written by John Hart, Chairman of the AICPA Insurance Companies Committee, to Donald Kirk, Chairman of the FASB, on March 21, 1978. The full text of the correspondence is available for inspection at the FASB, file number 1001.

33

Prospective Financial Information

Norman A. Lavin

PUBLISHED FORECASTS

Advantages of a Forecast-Based Disclosure System

Making today's activities yield future economic benefits has always been the goal of the free-market businessman, and this has always involved some form of prediction of customer preferences, cost changes, and other developments. But in former times, each businessman knew most of his customers and suppliers personally and thus could predict the economic consequences of his actions with the help of information obtained directly from them.

Today's manager operates in a totally different environment. He cannot readily communicate directly with his numerous and widely dispersed customers and suppliers, and yet he needs information from them as much as ever. In addition, he must communicate with other members of the management team and with the owners of the business—who may also be numerous and widely dispersed—to obtain the information on which to base his plans.

Because of these new demands and difficulties, the businessman has increasingly come to rely on recent developments in transportation, communications, management science, and computer technology—which have reduced the costs and delays in generating, obtaining, and disseminating information—to devise new predictive techniques and refine old ones. Using statistical inference and sophisticated modeling techniques, today's manager may evaluate formal market analyses and studies to measure the effects of change on his business. Many businesses routinely use advanced forecasting techniques to estimate operating requirements and results and to develop budgets for alternative plans.

External users—investors, creditors, and government—also need information to assess business performance and future prospects. Private-sector standard-setting bodies, regulatory officials, and our judicial system have specified information disclosure requirements, but differences in their perspectives have resulted in expansive and overlapping disclosures. There is growing recognition that more is not necessarily better, since users have increasing difficulty finding the particular information they need in voluminous corporate disclosures. Thus, the search is on for a practical system of providing users with needed information on a timely basis without burdening them with massive amounts of extraneous data that might be useful only to a few. Furnishing financial forecasts, updating them promptly to reflect important changes in future performance expectations, and periodically reporting on actual performance may prove to be such a system.

A forecast-based disclosure system would be responsive to some of the criticisms of present financial disclosures by facilitating

1. Realistic measurement of underlying economic values, with recognition of tangible and intangible assets and operating performance;
2. Continuous rather than periodic disclosure;
3. Making material information available to all shareholders and investors equally, not just to insiders; and
4. Evaluation of management performance and predictability of future financial performance and inherent risk.

But the benefits of future-oriented information advances made by businessmen and used for internal management have not been made directly available to investors. Most companies have withheld their future estimates from the public, carefully disclosing this data only on a selective basis.

Impediments to Publication of Forecasts

Companies say little about the future for several reasons. In our litigious climate, managers and their professional advisers have staunchly held that only "hard" information is suitable for release to the public. *Hard information* can be described as reasonably factual data prepared using high standards of care. Some hard information, e.g., financial statements, real estate appraisals, and actuarial presentations, is frequently accompanied by reports prepared by independent outside parties. (See Chapter 4 for a further discussion of hard versus soft data.)

Management information systems are designed to produce the information needed for day-to-day decision making. Although some data are gathered under rigorous procedures to enhance accuracy, much must be produced in too short a time, and management decisions often cannot be postponed to allow for additional accuracy checks. Information, like money, has a time value, and data used internally by management (who understand the limitations on its reliability and usefulness) are often not documented and verified to the extent customary with information released to the public. Thus, predictive information developed for internal use has recognizable limitations on its usefulness for other purposes.

Most managers do not want to risk finding out whether the courts will recognize more lenient standards for predictive information than they do for hard data if it turns out to be erroneous or incomplete. Theoretically, it might be possible to modify management information systems to provide a very high level of assurance on soft data, but such modifications even if feasible would be very costly, especially because of the delays invariably involved. It might also be necessary to incur costs for third-party reviews; and since prospective financial information probably will not soon be recognized as reducing presently applicable disclosure requirements, the costs would all be extra.

Investors, meanwhile, do not seem to be demanding prospective financial information from company management. Starting in the mid-1970s, for example, Fuqua Industries published portions of its forecast of the ensuing year's operations, but this caused hardly a ripple of public acknowledgement. Fuqua stopped the practice after only a few years.

Deeply entrenched attitudes also stand in the way of disclosure of prospective financial information. Some have argued that publication of management forecasts would fundamentally change the investor's function by shifting risk taking away from the provider of capital (Kapnick, 1972, p. 3). Nor has public forecasting had any strong advocates historically. The FASB has consistently ignored forecasting, despite the Trueblood study group's conclusion that "an objective of financial statements is to provide information useful for the predictive process. Financial forecasts should be provided when they will enhance the reliability of users' predictions" (AICPA, 1973j, p. 46).

The SEC has also been a potent force inhibiting the publication of prospective financial information. Elements of its long-standing policy of prohibiting publication of predictive information stood until February 1973, when it published a release

(Securities Act Release 5362) stating that projections would be permitted; only in 1979 did it move to a position of encouraging forecasts and providing a "safe harbor" rule covering them, as discussed later in this chapter.

Forecasts in Special Areas

These impediments have not, however, kept companies from using internally prepared budgets, projections, and forecasts in negotiations with bankers, other potential credit granters, and selected investors. This prospective financial information may be highly summarized, but additional detail is usually provided through informal discussion. Also, many projections or forecasts have been included in certain types of public offerings: it is common practice to include prospective financial information in offerings of limited partnership tax shelter equity investments (discussed in Chapter 27) and debt offerings of hospitals, sports arenas, and other quasi-governmental entities.

The providing of prospective financial information is prevalent in certain types of securities offerings despite the obstacles that impede similar practices by publicly held companies, because these private offerings have not been subject to the jurisdiction of SEC. Another reason is that a few states require disclosure of specified prospective financial information in certain circumstances. California, for example, requires that certain projections be included in real estate tax shelter offerings.[1] The Pennsylvania Securities Commission requires that third parties report on such information if optionally included in filings.[2] The Michigan Hospital Financing Authority goes even further; administratively, it requires a comment by the third party on the reasonableness of the assumptions. Even when providing prospective financial information is not required, doing so has become so widespread in these specialized offerings that promoters and underwriters seem to insist on it.

Future-oriented information about publicly held companies is also available today, though much of it must reach investors through professional analysts who evaluate the potential return on investment of particular securities and the related levels of risk. In preparing their analyses, analysts obtain forecasts from management through company presentations at luncheons, meetings, or private sessions.

A large proportion of the respondents to a recent survey indicated that they provide forecast and other information not published in their annual reports to analysts on request. Almost 71% of the respondents indicated that their companies have no written guidelines stipulating what information officers and others in the company are authorized to provide to analysts or others, and almost 53% indicated that their companies do not have written policies indicating which executives may talk to members of the financial community about company operations (Miller, 1978). These practices suggest that management is less wary about providing information to analysts and others who are expert in digesting and appraising the information and comparing it with data obtained from other sources if the information is provided informally and not given directly to the general public.

Most companies today routinely develop estimates of their expected future operations and prospects, but only for internal use. Companies that publicly disclose

---

[1] California Administrative Code Section 260.14.117.4, Chapter 3, Title 10.
[2] Pennsylvania Securities Code Section 401.010.

future estimates give only very limited information. The disclosures range from nods or remarks like "That's in the ball park," signifying concurrence with a statement made by an analyst, to comprehensive presentations in the form of financial statements, including a statement of the principal underlying assumptions.

This uneven distribution of prospective financial information in the marketplace was the principal factor persuading the SEC to modify its policy prohibiting the inclusion of prospective data in filings with the commission. This is discussed after the next section, which delineates the several types of prospective data.

TYPES OF PROSPECTIVE FINANCIAL INFORMATION

Qualitative Features

The most important qualitative features of prospective financial information are (1) the purpose for which the information is intended, (2) the degree of uncertainty, and (3) the extent of disclosure. These features are interrelated. For example, the reader's ability to evaluate the likelihood that predicted results will be achieved (degree of uncertainty) may depend on the extent of disclosure of pertinent information.

Intended Purpose. Some future estimates are intended to predict expected transactions and events, whereas others are intended only to facilitate an assessment of the effect of particular events that may or may not happen. In either case, estimates may deal only with some, not all, of the factors that bear on the company's future economic performance. For example, an estimate could be made of the impact of specified raw material cost levels on selling prices, sales volume, and profitability.

The most useful type of prospective financial information is that directly meeting the user's particular needs. When these needs are not specified, however, a future operations estimate made by a publicly held company is generally expected to show how the most likely events will affect the company's financial statements.

Degree of Uncertainty. Any prognostication is inherently uncertain, and the degree of uncertainty can vary widely. In some cases, like predicting the chance of rain, it may be possible to express uncertainty mathematically, but in other cases such precision is beyond reach. Often, in fact, it is impossible to identify all the factors that will influence the outcome in question. In such cases the best way to convey the degree of uncertainty may be simply to disclose the assumptions that underlie the predicted results and let the reader judge for himself. At present, however, estimates of future performance are commonly presented with very little information on the degree of uncertainty or on the underlying assumptions.

Extent of Disclosure. The extent of disclosure of prospective financial information varies over a broad range, from general statements of factors expected to affect future operations and summaries of management's plans and objectives, to estimates of the dollar amounts of one or more key financial indicators, and even to condensed statements of future operating results and financial position. Each of these disclosures may be accompanied by a description of the underlying assumptions and other useful evaluative information; then again, there may be no evaluative information.

The prospective financial information disclosed may be of a general nature, but often it concerns only certain factors bearing on a special purpose. Privately held companies, for example, often provide bankers and other creditors with their estimates of future performance and the related rationale. As mentioned earlier, hospitals, sports stadiums, and other public-service-oriented projects frequently provide comprehensive estimates of their future prospects when they seek financing through state financing authorities; and projections of future operations and the income tax consequences to investors are included in prospectuses that offer interests in tax-oriented investments.

Public companies generally have been more guarded in formally disclosing information about their future prospects, but they sometimes provide additional, more specific prospective information to professional financial analysts, who use it to develop their views of the merits of investments in the company. Analysts' predictions, frequently widely disseminated, are based in part on opinion and estimates beyond the analysts' control, and may not have been subjected to the discipline and full-disclosure conventions applied to the information that companies formally publish. As a result, the ultimate user has no way to evaluate the quality of the analyst's predictions and assessments available to him.

Generally, the more limited a company's disclosure, the more difficult the assessment of its quality and hence its reliability. The information may respresent no more than the pro forma effect of a hypothetical condition on actual results reported for a past period—for example, disclosure of what the effect on bank borrowing costs of a 1% variation in the prime rate would have been in last year's financial statements. In other cases of limited disclosure, the information may have been extracted from a comprehensive estimate of expected future results—for example, the effect of a 1% variation in the assumed prime rate on next year's expected operating results, including how that would affect the prices charged by suppliers.

AICPA Definitions

The AICPA has developed definitions (discussed in SOP 75-4) that distinguish financial forecasts from several other types of prospective financial information, based on intended purpose, degree of uncertainty, and extent of disclosure. These definitions have not yet been widely adopted in practice—presumably because of lack of familiarity with them, not disagreement.

Financial Forecast. "A financial forecast for an enterprise is an estimate of the most probable financial position, results of operations and changes in financial position for one or more future periods" (SOP 75-4, par. 6). *Enterprise* refers to any entity (including an entity to be formed in the future) for which financial statements could be, but not necessarily will be, prepared in accordance with GAAP. A financial forecast can be prepared for a company that actually uses or will use a comprehensive basis of accounting other than GAAP (such as the income tax basis) because such a company would still be *able* to apply GAAP in preparing its financial statements. *Most probable* means that the forecast is based on "management's judgment of the most likely set of conditions and its most likely course of action."

Financial Projection. "A financial projection for an enterprise is an estimate of financial results based on assumptions which are not necessarily the most likely" (SOP 75-4, par. 7). Financial projections are often developed to explore what would happen if certain hypothetical conditions were to occur.

Feasibility Study. "A feasibility study is an analysis of a proposed investment or course of action" (SOP 75-4, par. 8). When a feasibility study involves preparation of financial projections or a financial forecast, it is referred to as a *financial feasibility study*.

Other Types. The AICPA does not individually define *budgets, plans, goals, and objectives*. They all involve ". . . elements of predicting the future. However, each tends to have elements which distinguish it from a financial forecast although, in some situations, each may be identical to a forecast" (SOP 75-4, par. 9). To a certain extent, budgets, plans, goals, and objectives represent targets, and "budgets especially involve motivational, control, and performance evaluation considerations." The SOP also does not define *prospective financial information, prediction, predictive information, forward-looking information* and *future estimate*. These terms are used in this chapter to designate any or all forms of future financial information, as applicable in context.

Distinguishing Characteristics

What are the features that distinguish one type of prospective financial information from another? *Financial forecasts* are different from other types of prospective financial information in two respects. First, financial forecasts are estimates of what is expected to occur. They describe the most probable results, whereas other types of prospective financial information take no position on the probability that the depicted results will actually occur. Second, financial forecasts include all the GAAP elements of financial position, results of operations, and changes in financial position that historical financial statements include. Thus, a financial forecast is a specific type of financial projection, but not every projection is a forecast.

A hypothetical assumption used in a *financial projection* may be selected without considering evidence as to probability of occurrence. Unless there is disclosure to the contrary, the identified hypothetical assumptions in a projection are treated as givens, and the other assumptions are presumed to be the most likely. Also, projections need not comprehend all the elements of financial position, results of operations, and changes in financial position. They can be prepared for any entity (e.g., a cost center), without regard to whether financial statements for such an entity could be prepared in accordance with GAAP.

In contrast to both financial projections and financial forecasts, a *feasibility study* need not involve financial considerations at all, though it normally would if a possible investment were the action being analyzed. Unlike financial projections and forecasts, financial feasibility studies are always prepared for a special purpose, and they invariably include nonfinancial as well as financial analysis. A financial feasibility study usually involves the preparation of financial projections while it is being conducted, and the findings of the study may be summarized in the form of a financial forecast after the decision has been made to proceed with the proposed investment or course of action.

For example, a financial feasibility study may be conducted to explore a proposal to build a bridge over a river at a particular location. Normally, before financial analysis is begun, a study would be made of traffic patterns and existing roadways that might provide access to the completed bridge. The next step might be to prepare rough projections of the cost of constructing the bridge and approach roads. Then projections of toll revenues might be prepared based on various toll-rate and traffic-level assumptions. An analysis might also be made of the broader effects of the proposed bridge, such as the alleviation of traffic overloads and lower toll revenues for existing bridges on alternate routes. An engineering study might be made to consider whether physical characteristics of the bridge site—geological properties of the riverbed, swiftness of the current—would support the type of structure planned.

If the findings of the initial engineering, traffic, and other studies, as well as the financial projections, appear favorable, specific plans would be made, and projects undertaken. The sensitivity of traffic volume to toll rates, gasoline costs and availability, and other factors would have to be explored. Legislative or other legal authorizations may be required, rights-of-way may have to be obtained, and private property may have to be obtained through condemnation proceedings. A detailed design would have to be developed for the bridge itself, and arrangements made for financing the activities involved.

Financial projections would ordinarily be prepared to reflect development and refinement of plans concerning all aspects of the project, and ultimately contracts would be signed for the construction and financing of the facilities. After all these plans are completed, a financial forecast might be prepared for the entity that would be formed to own and operate the bridge. This forecast would reflect management's assumptions concerning the events and conditions most likely to prevail during the forecast period. If financing is to be obtained through the sale of bonds to the public, the financial forecast might be included in the official offering statement.

EVOLVING VIEWS OF THE SEC

Traditional Prohibitions

Basic Policy on Projections. In 1969 an internal study headed by SEC Commissioner Francis Wheat set out "to examine the operation of the disclosure provisions of the Securities Act of 1933 and the Securities Exchange Act of 1934 and the commission rules and regulations thereunder." The group concluded that no change was called for in the commission's policy on projections, and stated its reasons in these words:

> Because of their conjectural and rapidly changing character, projections would—if included in prospectuses—raise difficult questions of civil liability. Moreover, projections in filed documents might become traps for the unsophisticated who would be prone to attach more significance to such projections than they deserve. [SEC, 1969, p. 12]

Thus the SEC's long-standing policy generally not to permit projections in filings with the commission remained firmly entrenched. Reconsideration of this policy was signalled in speeches by William Casey, appointed SEC chairman in December

1971. Then, late in 1972, the SEC's Division of Corporation Finance conducted extensive public hearings on the use of estimates, forecasts, or projections of economic performance by publicly held companies. On February 2, 1973, the commission issued a statement (Release 33-5362) recognizing that its policy prohibiting projections in filings did not prevent their being widely sought by, disclosed to, or relied on by investors. In its statement the commission also expressed concern because not all investors have equal access to material projection information and announced its intent to permit disclosure of projections in a manner that would even out the accessibility of projection information within the securities markets.

Gamble-Skogmo Case. The commission's public role in the case of *Gerstle, et al. v. Gamble-Skogmo, Inc.,* 478 F.2d 1281 (2nd Cir. 1973), suggested that in adopting the new positions described above it had not abandoned its concern for the unsophisticated investor who might be misled by projection information.

Shortly after Gamble-Skogmo issued its 1963 proxy statement, an SEC branch chief met with representatives from the company and from a brokerage firm that had raised objections to the adequacy of the proxy statement disclosures. At the meeting, the brokerage firm's representatives demonstrated that using information contained in the proxy statement concerning previous plant sales, an investor could deduce that considerable profits might be realized on the sale of the remaining plants. They argued that the disclosure deficiency could be remedied by including disclosure of appraised fair market values of the remaining assets or projections of anticipated profits in the event the remaining plants were sold. The branch chief replied that because such profits were subject to a variety of contingencies, SEC policy was to prohibit their inclusion.

When the issue that there were disclosure deficiencies in the proxy statement because this information had been omitted was subsequently litigated, the SEC filed an *amicus curiae* brief, arguing that appraisals of current liquidation value made by a qualified expert and sufficiently based on fact must be disclosed. The brief acknowledged that because appraisals, in the commission's experience, were "often unfounded" and unreliable, the staff had generally requested their deletion on a case-by-case basis. The SEC asserted that the branch chief's statements were merely a recitation of the commission's general policy, not a definitive ruling that appraisals or projections could not be included in Gamble-Skogmo's proxy statement. The court disagreed, concluding that

> the SEC's brief attempts to . . . clothe its long-standing policy against disclosure of appraisals with an appearance of flexibility and case-by-case analysis. . . . However desirable such a policy may be, we do not believe this is what it was in 1963. The Commission's examiners are trained to strike at appraisal values as unacceptable whenever they read them in documents filed with the Commission.

Recent SEC Activities

In April 1975 the commission published proposals (Release 33-5581) to implement its 1973 policy statement of intent. Designed to even out the flow of projection information, these proposals defined specific types of selective disclosures that would trigger a requirement to make broader disclosure through filings with the commission. They also called for comprehensive information to be filed to reduce the likelihood that readers might be misled.

One year later, in April 1976, the commission amended its standing rule (14a-9) by deleting the reference to earnings predictions as possibly misleading (Release 33-5699). However, citing important legal, disclosure policy, and technical issues raised in 420 letters commenting on its proposals, it withdrew all the other 1975 rule and form proposals. Still remaining neutral and "neither encouraging nor discouraging the making and filing of projections because of the diversity of views on the importance and reliability of projections," the commission noted that "investors appear to want management's assessment of a company's future performance and some managements may wish to furnish their projections through Commission filings." The commission said it would not object to disclosure in filings with the commission of projections that are made in good faith and have a reasonable basis, provided they are presented in an appropriate format and accompanied by information adequate for investors to make their own judgments.

In this release the commission generalized its concern about the problem of selective disclosure of material nonpublic information, and reminded issuers of their responsibilities to make full and prompt disclosure of material facts—adding that management's assessments of the company's future performance may frequently be material. The SEC also proposed new guides (instructions to be followed by the corporate finance division staff in reviewing filings that contain projections). Release 33-5699 implied that finalization of the guides would await the recommendations of the Advisory Committee on Corporate Disclosure, chaired by former commissioner A. A. Sommer.

Advisory Committee Recommendations. The Advisory Committee on Corporate Disclosure finalized its report in November 1977, recommending that the commission encourage voluntary disclosure of management projections and permit companies considerable latitude on specific disclosure (SEC, 1977a). A year later, the commission announced its intent to adopt this recommendation (Release 33-5992), and issued final guides for staff use in reviewing projections. At the same time, it reiterated its view that projection information should not be made available on a selective basis. The SEC also admonished issuers to make full and prompt disclosure of material facts concerning situations in which previously disclosed projections no longer have a reasonable basis.

Finally, the SEC exposed for comment a safe harbor rule excluding registrants generally from liability under the federal securities laws for reasonably based projections, made in good faith, that were subsequently proven to have been erroneous. And most importantly, the burden of proof would fall to the plaintiff, unlike the usual situation in certain types of actions under the securities laws.

Safe Harbor Rule. In June 1979 the commission issued the long-heralded safe harbor rule (Release 33-6084). It covers only projections included in SEC filings or in the annual report to shareholders and, accordingly, offers a degree of legal protection only to companies that disclose their future performance estimates broadly rather than selectively. The commission thus allows registrants to disclose, in a straightforward manner, estimates of future economic performance in order to provide investors with information they would not otherwise have. That the commission would offer legal protection to companies under these conditions seems totally consistent with its regulatory role.

The safe harbor rule applies to more than just projections of financial items and disclosed underlying assumptions. It also applies to statements of management's plans and objectives and to management's discussion and analysis of future performance prospects and the related assumptions. (The SEC's new integrated disclosure system, announced in September 1980, provides for major changes in management's discussion and analysis, including much more data that would be usable, at least by a financial analyst, to build a rough forecast model for the company. See ASR 279.)

Safe harbor protection is available to noninvestment company registrants, new registrants that include forward-looking disclosures in an initial registration statement, and third parties retained to review projections. Management (or the third party) is protected as long as the plaintiff does not succeed in showing that the covered statement had no reasonable basis or was made or reaffirmed in bad faith. A summary of SEC releases dealing with future economic performance is shown in Figure 33.1.

DEVELOPMENT OF STANDARDS

Most outside users have only limited additional information available to evaluate prospective financial information, whereas management personnel, their advisers, and a few active investors or lenders usually bring some previous knowledge to their evaluation and also know how to obtain more information directly. Standards are needed to provide a basis for communication between the preparer and the outside user in view of the widening public dissemination of prospective financial information.

The SEC's reversal of its forecast embargo has added impetus to the development of new standards and has focused attention on the extent of progress made to date. Reexamination and refinement of the older standards implicit in federal court decisions and in early guidance developed by the private sector, both discussed below, have resulted in today's standards.

The Public Sector

State regulatory bodies have required disclosure of specified prospective financial information in some circumstances, but have not provided comprehensive criteria to be employed in meeting the requirements. The California, Pennsylvania, and Michigan regulations mentioned earlier are examples. Similarly, SEC Staff Guides 5 and 62 provide only the broadest guidance:[3]

1. Management should have the option to present its reasonably based, good faith assessment of a registrant's future performance;

---

[3] Guide 62 is identical to Guide 5, except that the former applies to filings under the Securities Act of 1933, the latter to filings under the Securities Exchange Act of 1934. The full text of these general releases may be found in the *CCH Federal Securities Law Reporter,* paragraphs 3765 (Guide 5) and 3822 (Guide 62), and in Poloway and Charles, *Accountants SEC Practice Manual,* paragraph 2375.

Release No.	Date	Summary
33-5362	February, 1973	Announcement of a policy change to allow (but not encourage) companies that so choose to disclose their future performance estimates in filings with the commission.
33-5581	April, 1975	Issuance for public comment of rule and form proposals for implementing the policy change announced in 1973. Under the proposals, disclosure of future economic performance estimates would not have been made mandatory, but once disclosed, extensive reporting requirements would have been triggered.
33-5699	April, 1976	Proposal of Guides 4 and 62 on disclosure of projections of future economic performance, deletion of Rule 14a-9 reference to projections as possibly misleading, and withdrawal of other 1975 rule and form proposals relating to future performance estimates.
33-5992 and 33-5993	November, 1978	Issuance of final Guides 5 and 62 on disclosure of projections of future economic performance, and proposal for public comment of a safe harbor rule for projections that would have placed the burden of proof on the defendant. In these releases, the commission first adopted the recommendation of the Advisory Committee on Corporate Disclosure to encourage rather than merely permit the disclosure of future economic performance estimates.
33-6084	June, 1979	Adoption of a safe harbor rule for reasonably based projections issued in good faith. The burden of proof is on the plaintiff.

FIGURE 33.1 SUMMARY OF SEC RELEASES DEALING WITH FUTURE PERFORMANCE

2. The information should be presented in an appropriate, nonmisleading format; and
3. Accompanying disclosures should facilitate investor understanding of the basis for and limitations of the data.

Federal Court Decisions. Federal courts have provided only a few decisions pertaining to financial projections and forecasts, but they are important. The courts have not imposed liability just because actual results differed significantly from forecasted or projected results. Instead, the courts have upheld prospective financial information having a rational basis and including disclosure of material facts. In many ways the decisions seem to be the foundation for the reasonable basis and good faith requirements for protection under the SEC safe harbor rule, but there are also some areas in which the earlier decisions are at variance with the new rule.

Federal securities laws make it unlawful to defraud or deceive a purchaser in the offer to sell, or sale of, securities. Section 17 of the 1933 act and Sections 10 and 17 of the 1934 act require proof of willfulness (scienter) to sustain the plaintiff's position. Under Section 11 of the 1933 act, however, an issuer is subject to liability if it is proved that a registration statement contained any material misstatement or omitted any material fact as of its effective date, unless the issuer can prove that the plaintiff knew of the defect. In effect, the safe harbor rule would appear to make the liability standard set forth in Sections 10 and 17 applicable as a basis for establishing liability relating to forward-looking information disclosures under all sections of the federal securities laws.

The discrepancy between the SEC safe harbor rule and certain sections of the 1933 act makes it likely that legal challenges will eventually be raised to the SEC's authority to administratively alter the act's provisions. To sustain its posture in court, the SEC will presumably cite statutory authority delegating it the power to adopt a rule on forecasts and will demonstrate that it has complied with the Administrative Procedure Act. Beyond that, it will be up to the court. A look at earlier decisions may suggest the attitude of the courts.

Douglas Aircraft. In this 1972 case (*Beecher v. Able,* 374 F. Supp. 341 (S.D.N.Y. 1974)) a statement in a prospectus of Douglas Aircraft Company read: ". . . it is very likely that net income, if any, for fiscal 1966 will be nominal." The court held that this was a prediction that Douglas would break even, and not, as the defendant claimed, a warning that more than nominal profits were unlikely for the year. The court would not construe the statement as a warning, because it failed to put investors on notice of the possibility of substantial losses, which in fact ensued. (It is interesting that the court construed this very generalized statement as a prediction, since in 1966 the SEC policy of not allowing projections to be disclosed in commission filings was firmly established and had not begun to shift; apparently the SEC had not thought of it as a projection.)

The U.S. District Court for the Southern District of New York noted: ". . . plaintiffs concede that an earnings forecast is not actionable merely because the facts do not turn out as predicted. Additionally, projections, unlike other statements contained in prospectus, will not often be clearly true or false." In finding for the plaintiffs under Section 11 of the 1933 act, the court held that

> . . . an earnings forecast must be based on facts from which a reasonably prudent investor would conclude that it was highly probable that the forecast would be realized. Moreover, any assumptions underlying the projection must be disclosed if their validity is sufficiently in doubt that a reasonably prudent investor, if he knew of the underlying assumptions, might be deterred from crediting the forecast.

But the plaintiffs were suing Douglas under Section 10(b) of the 1934 act as well as under Section 11, and in this action (435 F. Supp. 397 (S.D.N.Y. 1975)) the court held for the defendant:

> . . . the evidence presented does not permit, and the court's prior findings preclude, a finding here that the defendant's conduct constituted reckless misrepresentation and

stemmed from a conscious purpose to avoid learning the truth. Although the prediction was unreasonable, in that a reasonably prudent investor would not have concluded that it was highly probable that the forecast would be satisfied, the existence of some basis in fact for making the prediction indicates that the defendant's conduct was not so highly unreasonable as to constitute recklessness or fraud. Plaintiffs have failed to sustain their burden of proof with regard to the fraudulent nature of defendant's representations concerning the likelihood that Douglas would break even in 1966.

The court added, however, that ". . . although plaintiffs need not under Section 10(b) meet the very stringent requirements under Section 11, they must sustain a significantly greater burden of proof."

One might conclude that if the courts sustain and interpet the safe harbor rule in the manner in which the court in the *Douglas* case interpreted Section 10(b), a registrant would only need to demonstrate that it had not consciously avoided learning the truth and that it had some basis—however meager—for its prediction. As a matter of prudence, it would be unwise to presume the courts will interpret the reasonable basis and good faith standards quite so leniently.

Monsanto. In *Dolgow v. Anderson,* 53 F.R.D. 664 (E.D. N.Y. 1971), the plaintiff shareholders asserted that various publicly reported statements by Monsanto spokesmen concerning past results, current developments and problems, and anticipated prospects were made as part of a conspiracy to inflate the price of Monsanto stock. Of the 37 items cited by the plaintiffs, 20 referred to anticipated sales and earnings projections for the years 1965, 1966, and 1967. Many of these estimates were substantially realized, and for those that were not, full and contemporaneous disclosure of supervening developments and estimates had been made.

In finding for the defendants, the court said:

> Monsanto's reporting to its shareholders, to the public and the financial community was a fair and accurate reflection of the facts and the best estimates available to the Monsanto management. Moreover, Monsanto timely reported events which materially affected Monsanto's estimates and prospects and indicated the changes in Monsanto's estimates and prospects that could be expected.

The court decided that Monsanto's internal documents "were appropriately prepared and extensively reviewed, at all levels of Monsanto, for the purpose of fairly and realistically reflecting Monsanto's results and informed estimates of its future prospects." The most crucial factor appears to have been the company's ability to demonstrate that its officials' public statements were consistent with and well supported by informed judgments based on thorough analysis. Also, the company continued to analyze the principal factors on which its predictions had been based, and management promptly disclosed changes in these factors and their anticipated effects.

As a matter of fact, the court did not require Monsanto to have foreseen the especially severe impact of the general business and stock market recession in late 1966 on the chemical industry. In the court's words:

Plaintiffs cannot show any substantial possibility that the statements complained of by the plaintiffs concerning Monsanto's results, prospects, developments and problems contained any untrue statement of a material fact, or were misleading, deceptive, manipulative or in any way fraudulent.

Perhaps the message of the *Monsanto* case is that it pays to keep the public well informed of changes in forecasts.

Computer Sciences Corporation. The U.S. Court of Appeals, 9th Circuit, clarified managements' disclosure obligations under Section 10(b) in *Marx v. Computer Sciences Corporation,* 507 F.2d 485 (9th Cir. 1974). The president of Computer Sciences had publicly announced expected earnings two months before the end of the year without describing certain problems that already existed in the company's development activities. Shortly afterward, the project under development was abandoned, and accumulated development expenses were written off.

The court said, in holding for the plaintiffs:

... an earnings forecast is a shorthand description of the general financial well-being of a company; it creates an influential impression of the condition of the company in the eyes of the investing public. Under the statute and rule when an earnings forecast is made, such facts should be disclosed as are necessary to allay any misleading impression thereby created.

Thus, another message is: tell it all, the good and the bad.

Green v. Jonhop. Companies that do not publish their own forward-looking estimates will still have to be concerned about representations concerning their future prospects made by others. In the case of *Green v. Jonhop,* 358 F. Supp. 413 (D. Ore. 1973), where an underwriter had published a prediction of the company's future earnings, the court decided that the company was not responsible for all omissions or representations made about its financial condition and future prospects by every brokerage or securities salesman. A company is, however, obligated to act when it (1) learns of such misstatements or incomplete statements and (2) is aware that their publication will be misleading. Under such conditions, a company's failure to act would be tantamount to tacit agreement with the representations.

The Private Sector

Much information dealing with prospective financial information has been developed and published in the private sector. Most of these texts and articles address narrow technical issues, such as how to use particular techniques, and thus are useful only in special cases, but comprehensive guidelines are given in AICPA pronouncements.

AICPA Guidelines. The AICPA has been wrestling for many years with the difficult issue of whether and how CPAs should become associated with their clients' published prospective financial information. When the AICPA committees could not reach a consensus on the whole issue, the subject was broken down into separate aspects. In 1975 the AICPA Management Advisory Services Division issued MAS 3, *Guidelines for Systems for the Preparation of Financial Forecasts*. Also in 1975 the Accounting Standards Division published SOP 75-4, *Presentation and Disclosure of Financial Forecasts*. And finally in 1980 the AICPA Auditing Standards Division issued a guide, *Review of a Financial Forecast*.

The AICPA has benefited from the experience of its members in advising clients about and performing reviews of forecasts and other types of prospective financial information. Because of the wide variety of reporting practices followed by CPAs reporting on engagements involving prospective financial information, the AICPA is also considering the development of guidelines that would apply to types of prospective financial information other than financial forecasts and to engagements other than reviews.

Before 1975 the only AICPA pronouncement dealing with forecast engagements was that contained in the Rules of Conduct. It is still in force, and it states: "... a member shall not permit his name to be used in conjunction with any forecast of future transactions in a manner which may lead to the belief that the member vouches for the achievability of the forecast" (ET 201.01). There is also an interpretation of Rule 201 indicating that members should presume that forecasts with which their names are associated may be used by parties other than the client. Therefore, the sources of the information supporting the major assumptions used in the statements, the character of the work performed by the member, and the degree of responsibility a CPA is taking must all be fully disclosed (ET 201.03).

PREPARATION AND PRESENTATION

This section parallels AICPA guidelines for preparation, presentation, and disclosure of financial forecasts; interpretive comment is also included. These guidelines were developed for financial forecasts but can often be adapted to other types of prospective financial information.

The general philosophy underlying both MAS 3 and SOP 75-4 (summarized in Appendix 33) is that a financial forecast should provide the reader with management's best estimate of what future financial statements will show. A forecast prepared on this basis allows comparisons with the results of earlier periods and, later, with those actually achieved in the period covered by the forecast. Thus, the prospective data should be consistent with the generally accepted accounting principles or other comprehensive accounting basis (AU 621.04) expected to be used in the historical financial statements that will cover the forecast period. As a consequence, the data must be developed in sufficient detail to permit application of the enterprise's accounting methods, as many assumptions will actually have to be made at the transaction level.

The AICPA also recommends that financial forecasts be presented in the same format as the historical financial statements to be issued (although a forecast may be summarized or condensed) and that at a minimum, if the data is to be described as a financial forecast, specific information obtained from it should be disclosed as follows:

- Sales or gross revenues,
- Gross profit,
- Provision for income taxes,
- Net income,
- If applicable, disposal of a segment of the business and extraordinary, unusual, or infrequently occurring items,
- Primary and fully diluted earnings-per-share data for each period presented, and
- Significant anticipated changes in financial position.

If a change in accounting principles is expected during the forecast period—because new financial accounting standards are coming into effect on a certain date, for example—the change should be reflected in the forecast for that later period just as it would be if it were a historical financial statement. Allocation methods for interim perods in forecast years should also be the same as those that would have been used in historical interim financial statements.

As estimates of what the annual financial statements will show, a forecast should be expressed in single monetary amounts representing the most probable result. For key measures, this single amount may be supplemented by ranges, probabilistic statements, or other means of conveying degrees of uncertainty.

Assumptions and Preparation

Forecasts are based on assumptions about circumstances and events that have not taken place and are subject to variation. The assumptions reflect management's judgments, based on present circumstances, of which conditions and events are most likely to occur and of its own most likely course of action. After formulating the assumptions and preparing the forecast based on them, management must decide which of these assumptions to disclose along with and as an integral part of the forecast presentation.

Key Factors Affecting the Business. The formulation of assumptions begins with explicit identification of the key factors on which the financial results of the business depend. Once these key factors have been identified, appropriate assumptions for each can be developed.

Although all the key factors for which assumptions must be developed should be made explicit, it is not feasible to explicitly identify all the assumptions involved. Many of the most basic assumptions, those with enormous potential effect on results, are implicit ones that often posit the continuation of present or past conditions or patterns. Examples include natural or social phenomena such as the absence of world war and the repetition of seasonal climate patterns.

Implicit assumptions always concern matters that are beyond management's control. If asked, any reasonably prudent, informed person would be expected to make the same assumptions. For example, it is implicitly assumed that domestic assets of U.S. companies will not be condemned or expropriated by the local government, but this assumption would have to be made explicit for assets in countries without stable political institutions.

Explicit Assumptions. The explicit assumptions most significant to the forecast should be disclosed. The following categories typify these assumptions:

1. Those reasonably open to variations that could significantly affect the forecast results, and
2. Those that assume conditions significantly different from current conditions, if the change would not otherwise reasonably be expected.

Of course, any other key factors should be disclosed in addition to the specific assumptions, and the forecast should ordinarily give some indication of the basis or rationale by which management selected these assumptions from among the alternatives. The amount of detail given need not be so great as to divulge valuable proprietary information.

The disclosure of assumptions should be captioned "significant assumptions" and should include a summary of the significant accounting policies used in preparation of the forecast, just as historical financial statements do. When historical financial statements are included along with the financial forecast, disclosure of the forecast accounting policies may be accomplished by cross-referencing the historical financial statements.

The explicit assumptions are based on information reasonably available inside or outside the organization at the time the forecast is prepared, plus management's judgment of its relevance. Management must, of course, consider the cost of obtaining information in view of the anticipated benefits of using it; but information should not be dismissed just because getting it is expensive. The cost factors include not only the direct costs of obtaining or developing the information but also the cost of considering it and the cost associated with delays in obtaining it.

Frequently, time constraints and cost considerations preclude obtaining the best information to support an assumption. For instance, signed order acknowledgments from vendors specifying the price of new equipment on delivery provides better evidence than does a manufacturer's suggested price list, but as an extreme example, it would surely be imprudent to place purchase orders for capital equipment expected to be acquired during the forecast period just to have a firm price commitment to use in a forecast. In such cases, the reasonably persuasive price list is adequate to support the assumptions and is usually available on a timely basis.

Support for assumptions should meet two tests, relevance and validity:

1. The *validity* test applies to the factual data that are used in formulating assumptions. Historical financial information, demographic data, and statistics such as units sold or produced are examples. Corroborative data obtained from alternative sources may be a satisfactory adjunct or even a substitute. Obviously, the nature of the data influences the type and amount of support that must be obtained.
2. The *relevance* of factual data gathered to support assumptions is more difficult to establish than their validity. Ordinarily, a logical argument or theory is developed to explain the link between the present facts and the assumed future conditions. Informed opinion is often a major source of support for the relevance of data. When logic alone is not sufficiently persuasive to explain why specified facts may be expected to lead to a particular forecast result, it may be possible to establish suitable support through statistical inference. For instance, while a retailer will not be able

to support specific assumptions about sales to be made to individual charge customers, he may be able to develop excellent support for aggregate charge sales on the basis of past spending habits in relation to age, sex, annual income, interest rates, and other available demographic factors.

Not all the evidential matter itself will be consistent, so the rationale used in selecting assumptions must be based on the preponderance of evidence. Inconsistencies may cause more work to be done until the preponderance level is achieved. For example, if estimated sales exceed the company's production capacity, support will be needed for assumptions concerning procurement of additional products from alternative sources. Conversely, the known financial distress of a long-time supplier of readily available raw materials would not necessarily cast doubt on the assumption that adequate supplies of raw materials will be available under normal trade terms.

Assumptions Involving Management Plans. The assumptions should incorporate management's objectives and strategies, programs, and plans for achieving them— though this information need not be disclosed in a way that could self-inflict competitive damage. For example, management's decision to manufacture rather than purchase a product component may require further assumptions, such as a development project and the acquisition of new property, plant, and equipment. Similarly, personnel policies affect assumed payroll costs. For example, a policy to maintain peak production capacity even during economic downturns would require that work force levels not be treated as variable.

Since each member of the management team has some degree of autonomy in his area of responsibility, all members of management authorized to make operational decisions that might be material to the forecast should participate in its development.

Appropriate Care. MAS 3 recommends that financial forecasts be prepared with appropriate care by qualified personnel and adequately reviewed and approved by management at the appropriate levels (guidelines 3 and 10). Appropriate care requires the exercise of due diligence and proper attention. It entails not only integrity and objectivity in the preparation process but also procedures for raising appropriate challenges to the validity and relevance of supporting data. In addition, it requires appropriate procedures to facilitate detection and correction of calculation and other mechanical errors.

Qualified personnel are those who have both the authority within the organization and the technical competence relevant to their particular tasks in the forecasting process. No one should be asked to substantively participate in the preparation of a forecast in areas outside the scope of his ordinary organizational and operational responsibilities. Technical determinations involving marketing, operations, finance, research and engineering, and other skills should ordinarily be performed by persons working in those areas. Middle managers should review and approve input to the forecasting process by others reporting to them organizationally. Top management will ordinarily be competent to interpret the data produced by each participant in relation to his area and level of responsibility.

Forecast preparation often involves technical methodologies not regularly used in the business. These techniques should be reviewed by competent experts, and management should be satisfied that the assumptions to which the techniques apply are consistent with the other forecast assumptions.

Documentation. There should be adequate documentation of both the forecast and the forecasting process to facilitate

1. Management review, and participation in the forecasting process by all appropriate persons,
2. Maintaining the discipline necessary for effective forecasting as well as preparing a framework useful for future forecasting efforts, and
3. Comparison of the forecast with results actually attained to assure that the forecast can be updated on a timely basis.

Documentation involves recording the assumptions made, the factual data used in developing them, and the rationale and support of relevant determinations. Moreover, it involves organizing the details so as to demonstrate that the forecast indeed has been prepared based on the underlying assumptions and that any inconsistencies have been exposed and eliminated.

Publication

In addition to the usual factors that apply to publishing historical financial statements, there are five more factors in publishing forecasts that warrant attention: (1) distinguishing forecasts from historical financial statements, (2) a general description of the nature of a forecast, (3) the period to be covered, (4) updating the forecast, and (5) special purpose situations.

Distinguishing Forecasts From Historical Financial Statements. SOP 75-4 recommends that financial forecasts be clearly distinguished from historical financial statements. Separate presentation or clear segregation of forecasts, clear labeling of statement titles (e.g., Forecast Balance Sheet), and clear line captions help accomplish this purpose.

Historical information may be presented in a column parallel to a financial forecast to facilitate comparison, but audited financial statements, which include more detail and technical disclosures than forecast statements, generally should not be used for side-by-side comparison. In any comparative statement, the historical financial information and the forecast should be plainly labeled, so that the reader can always tell one from the other.

General Description of a Forecast. Many of those who testified at the SEC's public hearings on forecasts discussed earlier in this chapter expressed the concern that readers might give too much credence to forward-looking statements. To counter this danger, SOP 75-4 recommends that each forecast include a general description of the forecasting process, a statement on the nature of forecast information, and a notice that not all the assumptions used or implicit in forecast preparation are disclosed. The AICPA recommends that the statement of assumptions be captioned with a descriptive phrase such as "summary of significant forecast assumptions," and that the summary be prefaced by an introductory statement similar to the following:

> This financial forecast is based on management's assumptions concerning future events and circumstances. The assumptions disclosed herein are those which management believes are significant to the forecast or are key factors upon which the financial results of the enterprise depend. Some assumptions inevitably will not materialize and unanticipated events and circumstances may occur subsequent to (date), the date of this forecast. Therefore, the actual results achieved during the forecast period will vary from the forecast and the variations may be material. [SOP 75-4, paragraph 25]

In some circumstances, such as those in which certain of the significant assumptions are highly sensitive, the introductory statement should be expanded to specifically explain these matters.

Period to Be Covered. The AICPA recommends that in determining the period to be covered by the forecast, management should consider both its ability to forecast and the needs of users. Management's ability to prepare a forecast depends on the general economic situation, the nature of the industry involved, and many other factors, including its own aptitude. Although uncertainty generally increases with time, no fixed outside limit can be specified for a forecast period. Certainly it should not extend beyond the point at which the assumptions can no longer be reasonably supported or the criteria specified in the MAS 3 guidelines (see Appendix 33) can no longer be met.

The length of the forecast period may depend on the needs of particular users. A banker considering a mortgage loan to the owner of an office building in a metropolitan area with a relatively stable economic history, for example, may find a one-year forecast suitable for his purposes, whereas a prospective buyer of the same building may need information covering a much more extensive period so as to assess the income tax effects on his investment decision. If a user needs information covering a period beyond that for which management is able to prepare a forecast—that is, beyond that for which the assumptions can be reasonably supported —the forecast may be supplemented by projections.

The nature and anticipated effect of significant changes in operations or conditions that are expected to take place after the forecast period, and significant contingencies (e.g. major litigation in progress), should always be disclosed.

Updating the Forecast. Without a statement to the contrary, there is a presumption that management will update its outstanding forecast to reflect changed assumptions, variations in actual results, or unanticipated events and circumstances if they are significant. Unless the historical financial statements covering the forecast period are to be imminently released, an updated forecast including a description of the new condition that made it necessary should be issued promptly. If an updated forecast cannot be issued on a timely basis, notification that the outstanding forecast is no longer to be used should be issued. The notification should include a description of the new condition and state whether an updated financial forecast is in preparation. If management decides that an updated forecast is not necessary, this decision and the reasons for it should be disclosed. Of course, this should not be done in order to suppress negative information.

Management can always decide to discontinue the issuing of forecasts and tracking of attained results, but companies subject to SEC jurisdiction should be aware that SEC Guides 5 and 62 state: "Companies should not discontinue or resume making projections in Commission filings without a reasonable basis for such action."

In some cases, such as in certain debt or equity offerings, forecasts are prepared one time only, with no intention to issue updated or revised forecasts. The AICPA recommends specific disclosure of that fact, and it might also be advisable to disclose the reasons no update is to be expected. The disclosure might be worded as follows:

> The following financial forecast statements were prepared to assist the prospective bondholder in estimating whether the operations of XYZ Company during the forecast period may be expected to support a proposed $10 million bond issue. Because it is contemplated that all of the related bonds will be sold within 90 days hereafter, management does not intend to update or otherwise revise this forecast to reflect changes from present circumstances or the occurrence of unanticipated events.

The importance of internally tracking actual financial results, key assumptions, and other leading performance indicators used in developing the forecast cannot be overemphasized, for any failure to promptly disclose significant deviations from key forecast assumptions (unless the information is publicly available) might be construed as failure to disclose a material fact, thus exposing the company to liability under federal securities laws and other laws and regulations.

Special Purpose Situations. Certain disclosure practices have become widely used in special purpose situations where prospective financial information is included in offering materials. In bond offerings of quasi-governmental organizations, for example, it has become customary to include extensive demographic data and market analysis. Normally, the additional information bears directly on the development of the forecast or provides additional details concerning the enterprise, though it is more detailed than necessary for understanding the forecast itself. It is also customary to include debt service coverage calculations; there are variations in practice in the methods used to make the calculations, and the method used should therefore be disclosed.

Forward-looking information, most often a projection, is included in offerings of a wide variety of tax shelter investments, the most common probably being those involving the rental of residential and commercial real estate properties, whether existing or planned. Another common type is that of entities engaged in the extractive industries in which the properties to be mined or drilled have not been acquired at the time of the offering. Other offerings are those of enterprises engaged in breeding horses, making master recordings, raising agricultural products, and operating bowling alleys and (more recently) racquetball courts.

In some cases, laws or regulatory requirements specify the information that must be disclosed. Generally, these requirements include projections covering an extended period of time, since the tax deferral features of the investment and the time value of money are essential factors in assessing economic return. For real estate ventures and certain other situations, the effect of sale of the property, normally at the point at which the tax advantages of accelerated depreciation "turn around," is often projected. In some of these cases, it is assumed that the property will be abandoned, in others, that the property will be sold for cost; in still others, the assumed selling price reflects an estimated gain. It is not unusual to find calculations of return on investment that reflect an assumed sales price.

Interpreting the SEC Guides

SEC Guides 5 and 62 acknowledge the existence of the AICPA definitions contained in SOP 75-4 for prospective financial information but then proceed to state that the guides pertain to projections. This should not be interpreted as an SEC rejection of the AICPA guidelines for the preparation, presentation, and disclosure of financial forecasts.

The SEC guides do not specify minimum disclosures, but they clearly warn that insufficient disclosures might be considered misleading. The AICPA presentation and disclosure guidelines provide an objective benchmark for measurement of disclosure adequacy, and therefore should be valid for preparing projections that will qualify for the SEC's safe harbor rule.

Preparation. To avail himself of protection under the SEC's safe harbor rule, an issuer must successfully defend himself against specific evidence offered by the plaintiff that the issuer's forward-looking statement did not have a reasonable basis or was disclosed other than in good faith. It would appear likely that a plaintiff, who has the burden of proof, could show that an issuer did not have a reasonable basis for his projections, or disclosed them in bad faith, by demonstrating that MAS 3 guidelines had not been met. In this regard, the following questions might be considered:

1. If management neglected to consider the best reasonably available and timely information in developing its estimate of the most probable result, could it possibly meet the commission's charge in Guides 5 and 62: "Management should disclose what in its opinion is the most probable specific amount or the most reasonable range ... "?

2. Could management demonstrate that it was not misleading to fail to disclose the effect of preparing its projections using accounting principles different from those expected to be used to record the transactions when they later occur?

3. Could a plaintiff successfully argue that management had acted in bad faith if he showed that management did not consider the relative effect (which turned out to be material) of variations in the major underlying assumptions used in formulating projections?

4. Could a plaintiff demonstrate that management had not met the good faith and reasonable basis criteria by showing that management failed to accumulate adequate documentation to be able to suitably support the assumptions made?

5. Could a plaintiff show that when management failed to make regular comparisons of attained results with its projections, it failed to comply with the reminder (included in Guides 5 and 62) of management's responsibility "to make full and prompt disclosure of material facts, both favorable and unfavorable ... [that] may extend to

situations where management knows or has reason to know that its previously disclosed projections no longer have a reasonable basis"?

6. If a plaintiff were able to demonstrate that management had not adequately reviewed or approved a projection at the appropriate levels, how might management convince the court that its projection had been disclosed in good faith?

At the same time, it does not seem likely that a plaintiff could sustain the burden of proof that a forward-looking statement did not have a reasonable basis, or was disclosed in bad faith, if management clearly asserted it had not determined which conditions were most likely to occur with respect to one or more dichotomous assumptions, and gave the reasons for these circumstances.

Presentation and Disclosure. The SEC guides allow companies that choose to include projections in commission filings considerable latitude in the extent of information to be provided. While the guides suggest that sales, earnings, earnings per share, and significant assumptions would ordinarily be disclosed, they merely discuss factors to consider if, as is the present practice of many companies, less is disclosed to the public. The considerations include some of the case law discussed earlier in this chapter and the commission's general reminder of companies' obligations to promptly and fully disclose material information.

THE CPA'S ROLE

AICPA Rules of Conduct do not prohibit a member from preparing, or helping a client prepare, forecasts of the results of future transactions. They govern only the disclosure required when a CPA's name is associated with such forecasts. However, in 1980 the AICPA issued a guide, *Review of a Financial Forecast*. This guide does not apply if the CPA is engaged to perform services other than a review or if the engagement involves a type of prospective financial information other than a financial forecast. However, the AICPA is also considering the development of guidance for CPAs on engagements that are not covered by the guide.

In the meantime, CPAs will presumably continue to serve as preparers, advisers, or attestors, covering a scope of work ranging from consultation on specific questions to formal reporting on financial forecasts and projections. When engaged to review and report on financial forecasts, CPAs will probably adhere quite strictly to the recommendations contained in the guide; because it is the only authoritative guidance available, it would be risky not to have the protection afforded by following it.

Review of a Financial Forecast

The guide introduces general review guidelines that appear similar to generally accepted auditing standards applicable to audits of financial statements prepared in conformity with GAAP. The guidelines cover adequacy of technical training and proficiency, independence, professional care, planning and supervision, review scope determination, informative disclosure, and the nature of the report to be issued.

The purpose of a forecast review is to establish a basis for the accountant's belief that the assumptions used provide a reasonable basis for management's forecast, that the forecast is indeed based on the stated assumptions, and that it is presented in conformity with the AICPA's recommendations in SOP 75-4. The review process involves definition of the scope of the review, evaluation of assumptions, and evaluation of the preparation and presentation of the forecast.

The CPA can conclude that the assumptions provide a reasonable basis for management's forecast when he is persuaded that management has explicitly identified the key factors on which the financial results of the business depend, has developed assumptions about the state of these factors in the forecast period, and has suitably supported these assumptions. The CPA can conclude that the forecast is presented in accordance with the SOP 75-4 guidelines, and thus with the MAS 3 guidelines, when he is satisfied that the forecast is presented in an appropriate format, expresses the results in specific monetary amounts compiled on the basis of the historical accounting principles used by the company, and contains adequate informative disclosure.

To define the appropriate scope of the review, the CPA must have adequate knowledge of the business, evaluate management's forecasting experience, determine the length of the forecast period, and understand the forecasting process used. The term *forecasting process* is defined in the guide as either a formal forecasting system, a work program, or the documented procedures, methods, and practices used in preparing the forecast. Regardless of the type of forecasting process employed, MAS 3 guidelines are the yardstick by which the CPA evaluates the adequacy of the process in determining the scope of his review.

Evaluation of assumptions involves reviewing the key factors identified by management for completeness, and evaluating the suitability of support for the assumptions made about these factors. To evaluate the suitability of support, the CPA considers the sufficiency, pertinence, reliability, and comparability of important matters; the appropriateness of the logic used; and the consistency of the assumptions with the underlying support and with each other.

Evaluation of the preparation and presentation of the forecast involves considering whether that forecast was properly compiled from the assumptions, whether it is internally consistent and mathematically accurate, and whether it is presented in conformity with the guidelines in SOP 75-4.

The guide would not require an audit base as a condition for acceptance of a forecast review engagement, but historical financial statements covering a part of the forecast period should be subjected to not less than a review (see Chapter 16). It is advisable for the CPA to have performed an examination or review of the past financial statements that serve as the source of historical financial and statistical data used in preparation of the forecast.

Reporting on the Review

The guide lists the following elements of a CPA's report on the review of a financial forecast:

1. Identification of the forecast and a description of what it is intended to represent,
2. Description of the review and a statement that it was made in accordance with AICPA guidelines,

3. A denial of responsibility to update the CPA's review,

4. A statement of the accountant's belief concerning his evaluation of the assumptions and the presentation of the forecast, and

5. A caveat on the ultimate attainment of the forecast results.

In the standard case, the concluding paragraph would be worded as follows:

Based on our review, we believe that the accompanying financial forecast is presented in conformity with applicable guidelines established by the American Institute of Certified Public Accountants for presentation of a financial forecast. We believe that the underlying assumptions provide a reasonable basis for management's forecast. However, some assumptions inevitably will not materialize and unanticipated events and circumstances may occur; therefore, the actual results achieved during the forecast period will vary from the forecast, and the variations may be material.

In some circumstances it would not be appropriate to issue the standard form of report. If the CPA believes that one or more significant assumptions does not provide a reasonable basis for the forecast or that the forecast fails to conform with AICPA guidelines in any other way, his report should indicate that he believes the forecast is not presented in conformity with applicable guidelines developed by the AICPA. He may be unable to determine whether the assumptions provide a reasonable basis for management's forecast because of limitations on the scope of his review imposed by the client or because he believes the assumptions are insufficiently supported. If the effect might be material, he should express no conclusions about the preparation and presentation of the forecast. Similarly, he should not express a conclusion if he lacks independence.

The CPA may extend his report to (1) state that (if applicable) his evaluation of the financial forecast is based in part on another accountant's report, (2) indicate the nature of his association with historical information presented with the forecast for comparative purposes, and the extent of responsibility he is taking for it, or (3) emphasize a matter he believes important.

THE FUTURE OF FORECASTING

A significant impetus may be given to publishing forecasts by the SEC revision (ASR 279, September 1980) of the management discussion and analysis of financial position and results of operations required to be included in annual reports for shareholders and on Form 10-K. For example, the new rules for 1980 calendar-year reporting ask for analysis of and commentary on short- and long-term liquidity factors that might have an impact on the sufficiency of cash for future needs, and on material commitments for capital expenditures and the anticipated sources thereof. ASR 279 encourages but does not actually require the provision of forward-looking data. However, as practice develops, managements may find it preferable to include formal financial forecasts complying with the safe harbor rule rather than take a chance that analysts' forecasts based on more eclectic data will be satisfactory.

With time, forecasting systems will probably become more integrated with systems for recording past transactions. Computers may analyze historical data as soon as it is recorded to determine its implications for the ongoing forecast. As management becomes more accustomed to these systems, confidence in the ability to forecast and, more importantly, to revise forecasts promptly will grow. Forecasts will probably be published more frequently, and the investing public will become accustomed to accepting forecast results until they are revised. This process may gradually reduce the importance of historical financial statements relative to forecasts, projections, and other types of financial disclosure.

Forecasting can be used as an approach to continuous disclosure, in which information is assumed to be current but subject to modification. With continuous disclosure, investors will better be able to measure management performance, and economic values can be compared more closely to reasonable performance goals and cash-flow considerations.

But such integrated financial information systems, though not unrealistic, are still in the future. The immediate future of forecasting depends on the willingness of the regulatory and financial communities to modify their perspectives and remove the existing impediments to progress in forecasting.

SUGGESTED READING

AICPA. *Presentation and Disclosure of Financial Forecasts.* Statement Of Position 75-4. New York, 1975. This SOP contains guidelines for presenting financial forecasts, including disclosure ef assumptions. It recommends that the forecasts be presented in the format of historical financial statements and specifies disclosure minimums.

————. *Guidelines for Systems for the Preparation of Financial Forecasts,* Management Advisory Services Guideline Series, No. 3. New York, 1975. The guidelines contained in this document pertain to forecast preparation and forecasting systems. This document initially distinguished financial forecasts from other types of prospective financial information.

————. *Review of a Financial Forecast.* New York, 1980. This guide covers a CPA's review of, and reporting on reviews of, financial forecasts. It includes illustrative review procedures and other aids to conducting review engagements.

Kidd, Robert. *Earnings Forecasts.* Toronto: Canadian Institute of Chartered Accountants, 1976. This research study contains a comprehensive review of the state of the art of publicly disclosing earnings forecasts in the U.K., U.S., and Canada in 1976; in large measure it is pertinent today.

Reiling, Henry, and Burton, John C. "Financial Statements: Signposts as well as Milestones." *Harvard Business Review,* November-December, 1972, pp. 45-54. This article presents the case for forecast disclosure and outlines the authors' expectations about both forecasts and the legal liability therefor.

APPENDIX 33   SUMMARY OF AICPA FORECAST PREPARATION AND PRESENTATION GUIDES

In this chapter, AICPA guidance as to forecast preparation (from MAS 3) and presentation and disclosure (from SOP 75-4) has been presented in an integrated manner. For reader convenience, the documents are summarized below.

MAS 3, Guidelines for Systems for the Preparation of Financial Forecasts

The ten guidelines, listed below, apply to enterprises that prepare recurring financial forecasts that may need to be updated. They also apply to the preparation of forecasts that are not recurring, or that are not based on a formal forecasting system but do use a formal work program and an appropriately constituted forecasting project team.

1. A financial forecasting system should provide a means for management to determine what it considers the single most probable forecast result, generally supplemented by ranges or probabilistic statements.
2. The financial forecasting system should provide management with the means to prepare financial forecasts using the accounting principles that are expected to be used when the events and transactions envisioned in the forecast occur.
3. Financial forecasts should be prepared with appropriate care by qualified personnel.
4. A financial forecasting system should provide for seeking out the best information, from whatever source, reasonably available at the time.
5. The information used in preparing a financial forecast should reflect the plans of the enterprise.
6. The assumptions utilized in preparing a financial forecast should be reasonable and appropriate and should be suitably supported.
7. The financial forecasting system should provide the means to determine the relative effect of variations in the major underlying assumptions.
8. A financial forecasting system should provide adequate documentation of both the forecast and the forecasting process.
9. A financial forecasting system should include the regular comparison of the forecast with attained results.
10. The preparation of a financial forecast should include adequate review and approval by management at the appropriate levels.

SOP 75-4, Presentation and Disclosure of Financial Forecasts

The SOP recommends that financial forecasts be presented in the format of the historical financial statements expected to be issued covering the forecast period, to facilitate comparisons with results of prior periods and actual results (when known) for the forecast period. However, in order to allow for experimentation in communicative formats as companies gain experience in forecasting, the SOP says that financial forecasts should at least include the following information (as applicable):

- Sales or gross revenues,
- Gross profit,
- Provision for income taxes,
- Net income,
- Disposal of a segment of a business and extraordinary, unusual, or infrequently occurring items,
- Primary and fully diluted earnings-per-share data for each period presented, and
- Significant anticipated changes in financial position.

Financial forecasts should be prepared on a basis consistent with the generally accepted accounting principles expected to be used in the historical financial statements covering the forecast period. They should contain specific monetary amounts representing the single most probable forecast result.

The forecasts should state those assumptions management considers most significant to the forecast (i.e., the key factors) and the rationale for these assumptions. It is also desirable to state the relative impact of variations in assumptions that could significantly affect the forecast results. But basic assumptions—about war or peace, for example, or the absence of natural disasters—need not be discussed unless there is a reasonable likelihood of change.

In determining the period to be covered, the committee concluded that managements should perceive user needs and consider whether they are able to forecast for the full duration. Forecasts should be clearly distinguished from the historical financial statements, and should be updated to reflect significant changes in assumptions, actual results, or unanticipated events and circumstances unless (1) the original forecast indicated that it would not be updated or (2) issuance of historical financial statements covering the forecast period is imminent.

Part IV

Specialized Industries

34

Governmental Units

Gerald W. Hepp

THE GOVERNMENTAL ENVIRONMENT

Today most private financial dealings are significantly influenced, whether directly or indirectly, by the presence of government. But there is also an ever-expanding interest in government in general and governmental financial affairs in particular. Governmental units are constantly facing a financial management problem. On one side there is a constant demand for more and better services; on the other is constant demand for reduced taxes.

The service demands and the resulting problems are perhaps best illustrated by the financial crises experienced by New York City and Cleveland. The demand for reduced taxes is illustrated by Proposition 13 in California and the Headley Amendment in Michigan. The total problem is illustrated by the forces at work in Cleveland. For the period from 1975-1977 the city's assessed property valuation reportedly increased 15% while its general fund spending increased 25%.

An analysis of the climate in the country for tax limitation is available in a publication entitled *Tax and Expenditure Limitations, 1978,* which was published by the National Governors Association Center for Policy Research. A good publication for reviewing the fiscal problems of U.S. cities is entitled *Urban Fiscal Stress* (Howell and Stamm, 1979), published in 1979 by the First National Bank of Boston and Touche Ross & Co.

These problems have brought about a greater interest in governmental accounting. Interested parties—citizens who are paying for the cost of government and looking for services in return; employees providing services to the governmental unit and looking to it for current income and retirement security; creditors who provide goods and services; creditors who provide money by purchase of the governmental unit's debt instruments; and governing and oversight bodies that are responsible for setting policies and appraising managerial performance—are more concerned over whether governmental financial statements are providing adequate information as to the financial health of governmental units.

For many years, government bonds and other securities were sold on the public market, with little or no financial information provided by the governmental units that issued the securities. For the most part, purchasers simply accepted the governmental unit's pledge of full faith and credit, feeling that their investment was secure because of the governmental unit's taxing power. More recently, however, public awareness of the financial stress experienced by many governmental units has led to concern about their ability to meet the debt service requirements on their outstanding obligations, and to a demand for adequate information on those putting new security issues on the market. A vivid example of the problem can be found in Chapter 2, "Report on Accounting Practices and Financial Reporting," of the 1977 *SEC Staff Report on Transactions in Securities of the City of New York,* which concluded:

The results of our investigation indicate that New York City's accounting and reporting practices effectively served to obfuscate the City's real revenues, costs, and financial position and that substantial weaknesses in the City's system of internal accounting control caused published financial information to be inherently unreliable. [SEC, 1977b, p. 1]

A similar outcome developed from the financial plight of Cleveland. On December 18, 1979, *The Wall Street Journal* reported:

Yesterday, the first bomb of the war was dropped, as private accountants disclosed that the city's treasury account is deeply in the red. As of Nov. 11, the day before Mr. Voinovich [new mayor] took office, the accountants said Cleveland had a $111 million deficit, in its treasury account.... Of the $111 million deficit, the accountants said $30 million resulted from commingling much of the city's cash. Funds designated for capital projects, grants, and other restricted uses were improperly spent for general fund operating purposes.... The analysis of the city's treasury account wasn't labeled an audit, but rather "a review of certain records and accounts." From a practical standpoint, Cleveland is unauditable...." [Alsop, 1979, p. 13]

In 1975 the Securities Exchange Act of 1934 was amended to provide for the registration of municipal securities dealers and establish the Municipal Securities Rule-Making Board, a self-regulatory organization that formulates rules regarding the activities of municipal securities dealers. A major purpose of the amendments was to establish requirements for adequate disclosure in connection with the sale of municipal securities. These requirements apply only to brokers and dealers, and prohibit the board or the SEC from directly or indirectly prescribing the information to be made available by the governmental unit issuing the securities. Nevertheless, by increasing the responsibility of underwriters and dealers in municipal securities, the board has contributed to an improvement in municipal disclosure.

Because issuers are subject to the antifraud provisions of the federal securities laws, governmental units themselves have grown concerned about the adequacy of their financial disclosures, and the Municipal Finance Officers Association (MFOA), a voluntary membership organization, has established committees to study the question of what information should be made available. In 1976 the MFOA issued disclosure guidelines for offerings of municipal securities; in 1978 it issued guidelines for the preparation of yearly information to be made available to security holders.

Congress is considering further legislation to amend the securities acts as they apply to governmental units. One proposal would simply remove the exemption for municipal securities from the federal securities laws. Should this provision be enacted, governmental units will become subject to all the rules and regulations that govern the securities of publicly held companies. Other proposals would set up special rules for municipal securities. Generally, these proposals have recommended that the SEC be given wide latitude in establishing the nature and extent of financial information that must be made available.

The governmental accounting model differs from its commercial counterpart. A governmental unit reports its financial activities in a series of separate financial statements rather than in consolidated financial statements designed to measure the overall results of operations. Because the governmental accounting model is primarily concerned with the flow of funds, costs are generally reported at the time of expenditure instead of being allocated to the time period benefited.

These and other variations present in the governmental accounting model are discussed in this chapter. Although the principles are presented primarily in terms of a municipal unit, they are applicable to all types of governmental units. Municipalities generally are like any other governmental unit and provide a good model for comprehension.

Levels of Government

Federal Government. All governmental units have the power to levy taxes and borrow money, but only the federal government can create money and thus avoid the immediate discipline of balancing cash outflows with inflows. This unique feature, plus the sheer size of the federal government, makes the preparation of financial statements an enormous task. Nevertheless, the secretary of the treasury, with the help of the comptroller general and the General Accounting Office (GAO), first prepared a set of consolidated financial statements for the United States government for the fiscal years June 30, 1974 and 1975, and released them in late 1976; consolidated financial statements have been prepared annually ever since. These financial statements are still at the prototype stage. The secretary of the treasury recognizes that many conceptual and methodological issues are yet to be resolved before these statements can be represented as conforming to GAAP, but they do represent a useful summary of the activities of the government.

State Government. Most states, like the federal government, comprise a wide variety of commissions, boards, and agencies. Gathering all the financial data from these agencies and presenting them on comparable terms is a difficult task. In most cases financial data is gathered in connection with the budget process and is not necessarily in the form required to prepare comprehensive financial statements on a generally accepted accounting principles basis.

Local Government. These units are creatures of the state and subject to statutes that sometimes dictate rules on accounting for and reporting of financial information. However, several local governmental units may overlap; for example, a given geographical area may be under a county government, a city government, a school district, and a sewer district, each with taxing power and the power to borrow money. In order to evaluate the ability of a particular community to support debt, therefore, a prospective investor must consider the amount of overlapping debt of all the governmental units with jurisdiction over the area. Unfortunately, most local governments do not provide this information in their financial statements.

Special Purpose Units. In some cases these are merely segregated funds for discrete functions of a single governmental unit. In other cases they are partly or fully independent. They may be the creation of two or more governmental units subject to the agreement between them, or they may be established by specific state legislation, either with or without the involvement of local governments. Examples of special purpose governmental units are port authorities, airports, industrial development districts, libraries, sanitation districts, and mosquito abatement districts.

To the extent that these special districts, authorities, or commissions provide services to the general public on the basis of charging for the basic value of the service, their accounting will usually be on a full accrual basis, like that of a commercial enterprise. Otherwise the unit will follow governmental accounting principles. When the unit is the creation of an individual local government, its financial statements usually are included with all the other financial statements of the local government. Otherwise its financial statements are issued separately.

School Districts. In some states, school districts are independent governmental units with many of the same taxing powers as municipalities. In other states the school district is effectively an arm of the municipal unit and must look to that unit for its resources. In almost all cases, the financial statements of the school district follow the same principles as other governmental units, though it is common to find variations in their terminology.

Sources of Accounting Principles

Municipal Finance Officers Association. Several important publications on governmental accounting have been issued by the MFOA. Most MFOA members are government officials (predominantly in the accounting area), but many independent CPAs and management consultants active in government finance also participate.

The National Council on Governmental Accounting (NCGA), one of MFOA's committees, has written a number of publications on governmental accounting over the years. NCGA's most significant publication, *Governmental Accounting, Auditing and Financial Reporting* (GAAFR), was originally issued in 1968 and its most recent update was issued in 1980. This book, often called the "blue book," was written primarily for use by financial management and accounting personnel of governmental units, as it contains procedural and management matters integrated into the discussion of accounting principles.

In 1979 the NCGA issued *Statement 1—Governmental Accounting and Financial Reporting Principles* to update, clarify, amplify, and reorder GAAFR and to recognize the effect of the AICPA industry audit guide, *Audits of State and Local Governmental Units* (AICPA, 1975c). Also in 1979 the NCGA published *Statement 2—Grant, Entitlement, and Shared Revenue Accounting and Reporting by State and Local Governments.* The NCGA plans to continue this series of statements.

Other committees of MFOA have also issued publications dealing with accounting and financial reporting matters. Three significant documents by MFOA are

1. *Procedural Statements in Connection with the Disclosure Guidelines for Offerings of Securities by State and Local Governments and the Guidelines for Use by State and Local Governments in the Preparation of Yearly Information Statements and Other Current Information* (1978);
2. *Guidelines for Use by State and Local Governments in the Preparation of Yearly Information Statements and Other Current Information* (1978); and
3. *Disclosure Guidelines for State and Local Governments* (1979).

AICPA. The industry audit guide, *Audits of State and Local Governmental Units* (AICPA, 1975c), deals with accounting and financial reporting by governmental units as well as with how they are to be audited. Instead of providing a complete treatment of accounting and reporting, however, the guide recognizes the principles set forth in GAAFR as GAAP except as modified by the guide.

Subsequently, the AICPA has issued SOPs 75-3, 77-2 and 78-7, which modify the audit guide. SOP 75-3 deals with the accrual of revenues and expenditures by state and local governmental units, SOP 77-2 clarifies accounting for transfers, and SOP 78-7 provides that government-operated hospitals should follow the AICPA *Hospital Audit Guide* (1972e) rather than the industry audit guide, *Audits of State and Local Governmental Units* (AICPA, 1975c).

In 1980, AICPA issued SOP 80-2, which further amended the basic audit guide. The purpose of this SOP was to give effect to the provisions in NCGA Statement 1 regarding general purpose financial statements necessary for GAAP and to eliminate the option to treat encumbrances (described later in this chapter) as the equivalent of expenditures. It also revises the financial statement reporting concept from a focus on individual funds to one on the governmental unit taken as a whole; several reporting examples are given.

The AICPA is presently undertaking an experimental project designed to evaluate concepts of consolidated financial statements for governmental units with regard to their usefulness to citizens, government securities holders, and other parties. An experimentation booklet (AICPA, 1979i) has been widely distributed, and the data gathered in this project will aid the further development of GAAP applicable to governmental units.

Financial Accounting Standards Board. Though the FASB is the private sector's recognized authority for establishing GAAP, many accountants who work for governmental units maintain that the FASB's authority should not extend to governmental accounting, and that their own association should establish accounting principles in their area. On the other hand, CPAs who audit and report on governmental financial statements are presently required to recognize the FASB as the authoritative body to establish GAAP; this applies across the board—in government, in other nonprofit areas, and in the business enterprise arena.

Many pronouncements by the FASB and its predecessors are written so as to be applicable only to profit-seeking business enterprises, and some pronouncements specifically mention their inapplicability to nonprofit organizations. But pronouncements that are neither obviously limited to business enterprises nor specified as being inapplicable to nonprofit organizations are fully applicable to governmental units. Thus SFAS 5, *Accounting for Contingencies* (AC 4311), for example, applies to governmental units. In addition, many pronouncements that seem applicable only to business enterprises apply to governmental enterprise funds, which follow commercial accrual accounting. Of course there are obvious exceptions, such as not reporting earnings per share.

The FASB has undertaken a project to establish the conceptual framework of financial accounting and reporting, and a part of it deals with the objectives of financial reporting by nonbusiness organizations. As a first step in identifying these objectives, the FASB commissioned a research report, *Financial Accounting in Nonbusiness Organizations* (Anthony, 1978). Next issued was the FASB *Discussion Memorandum on Conceptual Framework for Financial Accounting and Reporting: Objectives of Financial Reporting by Nonbusiness Organizations* (FASB, 1978a). Among other things, the discussion memorandum asks whether the objectives of financial reporting by nonbusiness organizations are the same as or different from those of business enterprises. A subsidiary question is whether the objectives of financial reporting are the same for all nonbusiness organizations or are different for various types, such as governmental units and private nonprofit organizations.

Continuing in the concept direction, the FASB subsequently published *Exposure Draft on Objectives of Financial Reporting by Nonbusiness Organizations* (FASB, 1980c), which states that the financial reporting of all nonbusiness organizations including governmental units should provide

- Information useful in making resource allocation decisions,
- Information useful in assessing services and ability to provide services,
- Information useful in assessing management stewardship and performance,
- Information about economic resources, obligations, net resources, and changes in them, and
- Managers' explanations and interpretations.

This exposure draft states that in contrast to business enterprises, nonbusiness organizations have no indicator of performance comparable to business profits and that, accordingly, information about the sources and uses of resources and their relationship, and about service efforts and accomplishments, is needed in the financial statements.

Proposed Government Accounting Standards Board. Since government accountants have been unwilling to recognize the authority or the ability of the FASB to set standards for governmental entities, a group of their organizations have entered into a series of negotiations with the AICPA, the trustees of the Financial Accounting Foundation, and the FASB, hoping to achieve a new organization that would be recognized as the authoritative body for the establishment of government accounting standards. At the end of 1980 a proposal for the creation of a Government Accounting Standards Board was in the process of development, although the problems of conflicting "authoritative" standards were far from resolved. (See further discussion later in this chapter.)

General Accounting Office. The GAO, under the comptroller general of the United States, is the auditing arm of Congress. In addition to its primary responsibility with respect to the federal government, the GAO has involved itself with state and local governmental units both indirectly through federal programs and directly by providing leadership and guidance. Its most significant influences upon state and local government have been its recommendations of audit standards and its sponsorship of cooperative auditing programs between government agencies.

The GAO has published *Standards For Audit of Governmental Organizations, Programs, Activities and Functions* (Comptroller General of the United States, 1972), sometimes called the "yellow book." This publication endorses GAAP promulgated by the AICPA and provides further detail on financial compliance matters. In addition, the "yellow book" recommends auditing by the government for program compliance, which is described as including a determination as to whether financial operations are properly conducted. The "yellow book" also prescribes auditing for efficiency and economy in the use and management of resources and for program results—i.e., whether the objectives established for the program are being met. The GAO does not expect every audit to encompass efficiency, economy, and program-results auditing, but believes that governmental auditing should move toward these goals.

ACCOUNTING PRACTICES

Most qualitative characteristics of accounting information (discussed in Chapter 3) apply to governmental units just as they do to any other type of enterprise, but there are some practices peculiar to governmental accounting. Perhaps the most notable of these is fund accounting: in a governmental unit, the basic accounting entity is not the unit as a whole; instead, the individual funds that make up the unit are considered separately. Governments set up separate funds to record different kinds of activity, and their financial statements traditionally do not consolidate these funds.

The funds of a governmental unit fall into three classes: governmental funds, proprietary funds, and trust and agency funds. Governmental funds record activities that are unique to governmental units and are supported by taxation. Proprietary funds record activities that are self-supporting and resemble commercial activities. Trust and agency funds record amounts the governmental unit is holding as a trustee or agent. In addition to these three types of funds, there are two account groups, one for fixed assets and one for long-term debt.

Governmental Funds

Separate fund accounting can be prescribed in a variety of ways. For local governments, a requirement is often written into state law. For grant programs, the federal government may specify that funds be accounted for separately. And governmental units often pass their own resolutions that specifically provide for the establishment of separate funds, or the resolutions at least suggest it. Special tax levies for specific purposes, such as public safety services, are frequent examples. In addition, bond ordinances usually have provisions for the maintenance of separate funds designated for specific purposes.

The laws, ordinances, and documents that provide for the establishment of separate funds may be either mandatory or permissive, but in either case there is cause for questioning the meaning of the term *funds* as used in these requirements. Traditionally, having a separate fund meant that there must be a separate accounting unit with a separate bank account and that it would be improper for the individual accounting unit to combine its financial information with that of other accounting units of the governmental unit. Recently, however, some officials have interpreted a separate fund as requiring a separate accounting unit but permitting the pooling of actual cash resources, as long as the portion attributable to each pooled fund is properly identified and maintained. Others have interpreted it as necessitating a strict segregation of cash resources but not requiring a separate accounting unit.

Totally apart from the physical arrangements above, many accountants believe that while separate accounting records and segregation of monies may be necessary for compliance with laws or agreements, this should not in any way affect the preparation of consolidated financial statements. They reason that the restriction of assets to a particular purpose can readily be disclosed within a single set of financial statements rather than being disclosed through a cumbersome set of separate statements.

General Fund. The general fund is the accounting entity that is used for the general operations of the governmental unit. It includes the financial transactions for all activities not required to be accounted for in separate funds.

Special Revenue Funds. Special revenue funds ordinarily are used to account for the receipt of proceeds from specific revenue sources and for their disbursement for legally restricted purposes. In some cases such disbursements should be accounted for in other funds, necessitating a transfer (discussed later). In practice, the legal restriction is often broadly interpreted. Thus, if a community has a special tax levy to provide for the cost of public safety, that levy and the related cost may be accounted for in a special revenue fund though literally there is no legislation or regulation requiring this handling. A common example of a discretionary separate special revenue fund is a federal general revenue-sharing fund. This fund may actually be used to transfer monies to other funds, or it may have direct expenditures as its ultimate purpose.

Consequently, many governmental units will report the cost of general governmental operations in several such funds when all of these activities normally should have been reported in the general fund. When analyzing general fund financial statements for any governmental unit, therefore, or when trying to make comparisons with other governmental units, activities that have been segregated at the governmental unit's discretion into special revenue funds must be identified.

Debt Service Funds. Debt service funds are used to account for the receipt of monies (usually specifically designated tax revenue) restricted for the payment of long-term debt, most often general obligation bonds. Some debt is accounted for in special assessment funds and enterprise funds as discussed below, and some long-term debt service may be accounted for in the general fund. This would often be the case when items are acquired on an installment purchase basis, such as a five-year contract for the acquisition of fire-fighting equipment.

Some jurisdictions have a separate debt service fund for each general obligation long-term debt outstanding. In other jurisdictions it is considered sufficient to have one all-inclusive debt service accounting entity. Regardless of the number of accounting entities, it is necessary to earmark the resources intended for the servicing of each individual bond issue.

Capital Projects Funds. These funds are used for the acquisition or construction of major capital projects, especially if there is a restricted revenue source—e.g., a bond issue designated for a construction project such as a new city hall or a new school. An individual project is sometimes considered a separate fund, but often the projects are regarded as separate accounts within a single fund. In some cases capital projects are accounted for in the general fund.

Special Assessment Funds. Special assessment funds are similar to capital project and debt service funds. They are used to account for the cost of improvements or services that are deemed to benefit particular properties, against which assessments are levied to recoup the costs. Sometimes a portion of the cost is to be paid by other governmental funds, which then transfer the needed amounts into the special assessment fund.

A common example of a special assessment is one levied against homeowners for the construction of local streets. It is common to permit property owners to pay special assessments over a period of five to ten years, but since the actual cost of construction must be paid immediately, the governmental unit will normally issue special assessment bonds, which are recorded as liabilities in the special assessment fund. These bonds are secured by the unpaid special assessments and backed by the *full faith and credit* of the governmental unit; that is, an undertaking that the governmental unit will pay the debt service if for some reason the earmarked revenues are not adequate. (The value of this guarantee depends, of course, on the fiscal condition of the guarantor unit, which, as in the case of the New York City problem mentioned at the chapter's outset, is not always as solid as might be expected.)

Like other funds, special assessment funds sometimes are set up separately for individual assessment districts and sometimes merely pooled within a single fund.

Proprietary Funds

Enterprise Funds. The principal feature of an enterprise fund is its similarity in purpose to a commercial entity, and it generally follows accrual accounting principles, including the recording of depreciation as an expense, a practice not currently followed by the governmental funds described above. An enterprise fund is used when the cost of particular services is to be paid through usage charges designed to recover the cost, including depreciation. Examples are water supply and sewage disposal systems.

When the governmental unit does not intend to recover its service costs through specific user charges, the activity is often accounted for in special revenue funds. The main distinction here lies in the accounting for fixed assets: an enterprise fund records fixed assets and depreciates them, while a special revenue fund does not.

In Statement 1 (1979a) the NCGA recommends that, even though a service is not funded primarily by user charges, an enterprise fund should be established wherever the governing body has decided that periodic determination of net income is appropriate for such reasons as capital maintenance, public policy, management control, and accountability.

Internal Service Funds. Internal service funds, called *intragovernmental service funds* in GAAFR, are used to account for goods or services provided on a cost reimbursement basis by one department or agency of a governmental unit to other departments, agencies, or governmental units. The cost of goods or services provided should include depreciation if it is to be reimbursed; otherwise depreciation is omitted. For example, a motor pool may record as assets the cost of both vehicles and a garage. However, if charges to users include only an allowance for depreciation of the vehicles, vehicle depreciation will be recorded in the accounting records of the internal service fund, but there will be no depreciation recorded for the garage.

Trust and Agency Funds

Generally speaking, trust and agency funds are used to account for those assets that a governmental unit holds in trust for other governmental units or private individuals. Such funds can be classified as *expendable, nonexpendable, pension,* or *agency* funds. When the monies placed in trust are to be used for a particular purpose, they are classified as either expendable (if the principal can be spent) or nonexpendable (if only income earned on the principal can be expended).

In an agency fund, the governmental unit serves purely as custodian—e.g., one governmental unit acts as the tax collecting agent for another. Such monies are placed in the fund as collected and paid over to the other governmental unit periodically.

Account Groups

The *general fixed assets account group* is, in effect, a listing of the governmental unit's fixed assets, excluding those employed in enterprise or internal service funds. Further, it is common practice not to include certain immovable assets such as streets and bridges. Fixed assets are listed either at cost or, if actual cost is unknown, at estimated cost. Some governmental units compute and show an allowance for depreciation, but there is no depreciation expense charged to any fund.

The *general long-term debt account group* is a listing of the long-term debt that is not included as a liability in any other fund of the governmental entity. This debt is balanced, for double entry bookkeeping purposes, by an "asset" reflecting the commitment of future taxing power to repay the debt.

FINANCIAL STATEMENTS

In the past, many accountants took the position that it was mandatory to present a separate financial statement for each individual fund. With the publication of GAAFR (NCGA, 1968) and the AICPA government industry audit guide (1975c), however, it became common practice for funds to be put together by type. Thus, financial reports show a single set of statements (balance sheet and statement of revenues and expenditures) for all the funds of a given type—combined special assessment funds, for example. However, variations are found in the handling of interfund balances within a given type of fund, such as between two special assessment funds. In some cases these balances are eliminated; in others they are shown gross, as both assets and liabilities.

It is accepted practice for governmental units to present what are called combined financial statements, though these are not literally single amounts aggregating all funds. A governmental unit's combined financial statements comprise a balance sheet and a statement of revenues and expenditures, both having a separate column for each of the eight fund types and two account groups, all on a single sheet of paper. Under current practice, if there is a column showing a total of all the other columns, it is labeled "Memorandum Only," and there are no eliminations of interfund balances and transactions.

According to NCGA Statement 1, "financial statements necessary to fairly present financial position and operating results in conformity with GAAP are referred

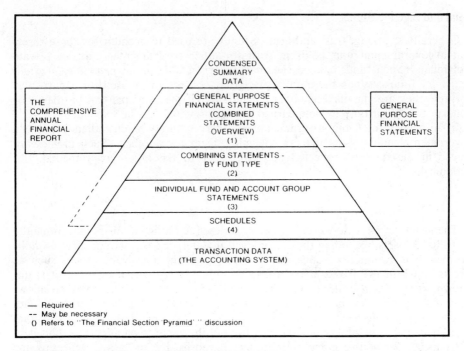

FIGURE 34.1   THE FINANCIAL REPORTING PYRAMID FOR A
GOVERNMENTAL UNIT

SOURCE: National Council on Governmental Accounting, *Statement 1—Governmental Accounting and Financial Reporting Principles* (Chicago: Municipal Finance Officers Association, 1979), p. 20.

to as basic statements" (NCGA, 1979a, p. 18). "Basic statements" are defined (p. 25) as "general purpose financial statements" such as might be used in "official statements" for securities offerings, and are considerably condensed or summarized from a governmental unit's comprehensive annual financial report, as depicted in Figure 34.1. Essentially, the difference lies in omitting from the basic statements the combining statements by fund type, individual fund and account group statements, and supporting schedules of details.

The basic statements consist of

1. A combined balance sheet for all fund types and account groups (Figure 34.2);
2. A combined statement of revenues, expenditures, and changes in fund balances for all five types of governmental funds (Figure 34.3);
3. A combined statement of revenues, expenditures, and changes in fund balances, budget and actual, for all general and special revenue funds, and similar fund types for which annual budgets have been legally adopted (Figure 34.4);
4. A combined statement of revenues, expenses, and changes in retained earnings (or equity) for all proprietary funds;
5. A combined statement of changes in financial position for all proprietary funds;

6. Separate trust and agency fund financial statements if not included as appropriate in 2, 4, and 5 above; and

7. Notes to the financial statements.

Figures 34.2, 34.3, and 34.4 have been taken from NCGA Statement 1 to illustrate the format of the basic financial statements; the full examples, along with those applicable to proprietary funds, are found on pages 29 to 39 of NCGA Statement 1. When reviewing matters that follow in this chapter, it may be useful to refer to these illustrations, which will provide the proper context. As noted earlier, SOP 80-2 recognized NCGA Statement 1 in place of GAAFR, and thus the illustrated financial statements, as detailed as they are, are in conformity with GAAP.

Modified Accrual Accounting

The principles followed for governmental funds are generally described as modified accrual accounting, because the starting point of accrual accounting is subjected to some significant modifications. In past years, the term *modified accrual accounting* was used in many cases to justify almost anything that accounting executives in governmental units wished to do, but actual accounting practices have tended to stabilize since the publication of GAAFR (NCGA, 1968) and the AICPA government industry audit guide (1975c).

Accrual accounting is, of course, required for the presentation of financial statements in conformity with GAAP, so it may seem that *modified* accrual accounting would not conform with GAAP. Actually, governmental accounting is considered no differently than accounting for other special industry situations; the governmental modifications are regarded as industry variations that are acceptable because of the practices that have grown up in the area over many years.

Budgetary Accounting

Most governmental units adopt an annual budget for general fund expenditures, and some also have budgets for special revenue funds, debt service funds, and other funds. Some also have long-term (e.g., three-year) capital budgets. Budgeting is the method used by legislative bodies to control the expenditures of a governmental unit. Budgets normally cover revenues as well as expenditures, but the revenue budget is only an estimate of revenue used to determine the amount that will be available for spending.

For financial reporting purposes, GAAP requires presenting a comparison between amounts budgeted and actual amounts spent. This comparison gives a reader some information about how successfully the administration of the governmental unit has adhered to budget limitations and how closely actual spending has approximated the original plan. In order to use budget information as an evaluative tool, however, it is necessary to understand the level at which budget control operates. In the budget preparation process, a great amount of detail is usually developed, but the official budget document will contain only a portion of it, the rest being relegated to background data. The level of detail remaining in the official budget largely determines the extent of authority that the administration has in deviating from the projections, for the administration normally has authority to change the amounts presented as background data, whereas amounts

Combined Balance Sheet — All Fund Types and Account Groups

December 31, 19X2

ASSETS	Governmental Fund Types					Proprietary Fund Types		Fiduciary Fund Type	Account Groups		Totals (Memorandum Only)	
	General	Special Revenue	Debt Service	Capital Projects	Special Assessment	Enterprise	Internal Service	Trust and Agency	General Fixed Assets	General Long-Term Debt	December 31, 19X2	December 31, 19X1
Cash	$258,500	$101,385	$43,834	$431,600	$232,185	$257,036	$29,700	$216,701	$ —	$ —	$1,570,941	$1,258,909
Cash with fiscal agent	—	—	102,000	—	—	—	—	—	—	—	102,000	—
Investments, at cost or amortized cost	65,000	37,200	160,990	—	—	—	—	1,239,260	—	—	1,502,450	1,974,354
Receivables (net of allowances for uncollectibles)												
Taxes	58,300	2,500	3,829	—	—	—	—	580,000	—	—	644,629	255,400
Accounts	8,300	3,300	—	100	—	29,130	—	—	—	—	40,830	32,600
Special assessments	—	—	—	—	646,035	—	—	—	—	—	646,035	462,035
Notes	—	—	—	—	—	2,350	—	—	—	—	2,350	1,250
Loans	—	—	—	—	—	—	—	35,000	—	—	35,000	40,000
Accrued interest	50	25	1,557	—	350	650	—	2,666	—	—	5,298	3,340
Due from other funds	2,000	—	—	—	—	2,000	12,000	11,189	—	—	27,189	17,499
Due from other governments	30,000	75,260	—	640,000	—	—	—	—	—	—	745,260	101,400
Advances to Internal Service Funds	65,000	—	—	—	—	—	—	—	—	—	65,000	75,000
Inventory of supplies, at cost	7,200	5,190	—	—	—	23,030	40,000	—	—	—	75,420	70,900
Prepaid expenses	—	—	—	—	—	1,200	—	—	—	—	1,200	900
Restricted assets:												
Cash	—	—	—	—	—	113,559	—	—	—	—	113,559	272,968
Investments, at cost or amortized cost	—	—	—	—	—	176,800	—	—	—	—	176,800	143,800
Land	—	—	—	—	—	211,100	20,000	—	1,259,500	—	1,490,600	1,456,100
Buildings	—	—	—	—	—	447,700	60,000	—	2,855,500	—	3,363,200	2,836,700
Accumulated depreciation	—	—	—	—	—	(90,718)	(4,500)	—	—	—	(95,218)	(83,500)
Improvements other than buildings	—	—	—	—	—	3,887,901	15,000	—	1,036,750	—	4,939,651	3,922,200
Accumulated depreciation	—	—	—	—	—	(348,944)	(3,000)	—	—	—	(351,944)	(283,750)
Machinery and equipment	—	—	—	—	—	1,841,145	25,000	—	452,500	—	2,318,645	1,924,100
Accumulated depreciation	—	—	—	—	—	(201,138)	(9,400)	—	—	—	(210,538)	(141,900)
Construction in progress	—	—	—	—	—	22,713	—	—	1,722,250	—	1,744,963	1,359,606
Amount available in Debt Service Funds	—	—	—	—	—	—	—	—	—	210,210	210,210	284,813
Amount to be provided for retirement of general long-term debt	—	—	—	—	—	—	—	—	—	1,889,790	1,889,790	1,075,187
Total Assets	$494,350	$224,860	$312,210	$1,071,700	$878,570	$6,375,514	$184,800	$2,084,816	$7,326,500	$2,100,000	$21,053,320	$17,059,911

(Continued)

FIGURE 34.2 EXAMPLE OF A GOVERNMENTAL UNIT COMBINED BALANCE SHEET

SOURCE: National Council on Governmental Accounting, *Statement 1—Governmental Accounting and Financial Reporting Principles* (Chicago: Municipal Finance Officers Association, 1979), pp. 30-31.

Combined balance sheet — all fund types and account groups (continued). Columns are grouped as: Governmental Fund Types (General, Special Revenue, Debt Service, Capital Projects, Special Assessment); Proprietary Fund Types (Enterprise, Internal Service); Fiduciary Fund Type (Trust and Agency); Account Groups (General Fixed Assets, General Long-Term Debt); Totals (Memorandum Only) (December 31, 19X2 and December 31, 19X1).

LIABILITIES AND FUND EQUITY	General	Special Revenue	Debt Service	Capital Projects	Special Assessment	Enterprise	Internal Service	Trust and Agency	General Fixed Assets	General Long-Term Debt	Totals December 31, 19X2	Totals December 31, 19X1
Liabilities												
Vouchers payable	$118,261	$33,850	—	$29,000	$20,600	$131,071	$15,000	$3,350	—	—	$351,132	$223,412
Contracts payable	57,600	18,300	—	69,000	50,000	8,347	—	—	—	—	203,247	1,326,511
Judgments payable	—	2,000	—	22,600	11,200	—	—	—	—	—	35,800	32,400
Accrued liabilities	—	—	—	—	10,700	16,870	—	4,700	—	—	32,270	27,417
Payable from restricted assets												
Construction contracts	—	—	—	—	—	17,760	—	—	—	—	17,760	—
Fiscal agent	—	—	—	—	—	139	—	—	—	—	139	—
Accrued interest	—	—	—	—	—	32,305	—	—	—	—	32,305	67,150
Revenue bonds	—	—	—	—	—	48,000	—	—	—	—	48,000	52,000
Deposits	—	—	—	—	—	63,000	—	—	—	—	63,000	55,000
Deposits	—	—	—	—	—	—	—	680,800	—	—	680,800	200,000
Due to other taxing units	24,189	2,000	—	1,000	—	—	—	—	—	—	27,189	17,499
Due to other funds	—	—	—	—	—	—	—	1,850	—	—	1,850	1,600
Due to student groups	15,000	—	—	—	—	—	—	—	—	—	15,000	3,000
Deferred revenue	—	—	—	—	—	—	—	—	—	—	—	—
Advance from General Fund	—	—	—	—	—	—	65,000	—	—	—	65,000	75,000
Matured bonds payable	—	—	100,000	—	—	—	—	—	—	—	100,000	—
Matured interest payable	—	—	2,000	—	—	—	—	—	—	—	2,000	—
General obligation bonds payable	—	—	—	—	—	700,000	—	—	—	2,100,000	2,800,000	2,110,000
Revenue bonds payable	—	—	—	—	—	1,798,000	—	—	—	—	1,798,000	1,846,000
Special assessment bonds payable	—	—	—	—	555,000	—	—	—	—	—	555,000	420,000
Total Liabilities	215,050	56,150	102,000	121,600	647,500	2,815,492	80,000	690,700	—	2,100,000	6,828,492	6,456,989
Fund Equity												
Contributed capital	—	—	—	—	—	1,392,666	95,000	—	—	—	1,487,666	815,000
Investment in general fixed assets	—	—	—	—	—	—	—	—	7,326,500	—	7,326,500	5,299,600
Retained earnings												
Reserved for revenue bond retirement	—	—	—	—	—	129,155	—	—	—	—	129,155	96,975
Unreserved	—	—	—	—	—	2,038,201	9,800	—	—	—	2,048,001	1,998,119
Fund balances												
Reserved for encumbrances	38,000	46,500	—	941,500	185,000	—	—	—	—	—	1,211,000	410,050
Reserved for inventory of supplies	7,200	5,190	—	—	—	—	—	—	—	—	12,390	10,890
Reserved for advance to Internal Service Funds	65,000	—	—	—	—	—	—	—	—	—	65,000	75,000
Reserved for loans	—	—	—	—	—	—	—	50,050	—	—	50,050	45,100
Reserved for endowments	—	—	—	—	—	—	—	134,000	—	—	134,000	94,000
Reserved for employees retirement system	—	—	—	—	—	—	—	1,426,201	—	—	1,426,201	1,276,150
Unreserved:												
Designated for debt service	—	—	210,210	—	46,070	—	—	—	—	—	256,280	325,888
Designated for subsequent years expenditures	50,000	—	—	—	—	—	—	—	—	—	50,000	50,000
Undesignated	119,100	117,020	—	8,600	—	—	—	(216,135)	—	—	28,585	106,150
Total Fund Equity	279,300	168,710	210,210	950,100	231,070	3,560,022	104,800	1,394,116	7,326,500	—	14,224,828	10,602,922
Total Liabilities and Fund Equity	$494,350	$224,860	$312,210	$1,071,700	$878,570	$6,375,514	$184,800	$2,084,816	$7,326,500	$2,100,000	$21,053,320	$17,059,911

The notes to the financial statements are an integral part of this statement.

FIGURE 34.2   CONT'D

**Combined Statement of Revenues, Expenditures, and Changes in Fund Balances —
All Governmental Fund Types and Expendable Trust Funds
For the Fiscal Year Ended December 31, 19X2**

	General	Special Revenue	Debt Service	Capital Projects	Special Assess-ment	Expend-able Trust	Decem-ber 31, 19X2	Decem-ber 31, 19X1
	Governmental Fund Types					Fiduciary Fund Type	Totals (Memorandum Only) Year Ended	
Revenues:								
Taxes	$ 881,300	$ 189,300	$ 79,177	$ —	$ —	$ —	$1,149,777	$1,137,900
Special assessments levied	—	—	—	—	240,000	—	240,000	250,400
Licenses and permits	103,000	—	—	—	—	—	103,000	96,500
Intergovernmental revenues	186,500	831,100	41,500	1,250,000	—	—	2,309,100	1,258,800
Charges for services	91,000	79,100	—	—	—	—	170,100	160,400
Fines and forfeits	33,200	—	—	—	—	—	33,200	26,300
Miscellaneous revenues	19,500	71,625	7,140	3,750	29,095	200	131,310	111,500
Total Revenues	1,314,500	1,171,125	127,817	1,253,750	269,095	200	4,136,487	3,041,800
Expenditures:								
Current:								
General government	121,805	—	—	—	—	—	121,805	134,200
Public safety	258,395	480,000	—	—	—	—	738,395	671,300
Highways and streets	85,400	417,000	—	—	—	—	502,400	408,700
Sanitation	56,250	—	—	—	—	—	56,250	44,100
Health	44,500	—	—	—	—	—	44,500	36,600
Welfare	46,800	—	—	—	—	—	46,800	41,400
Culture and recreation	40,900	256,450	—	—	—	—	297,350	286,400
Education	509,150	—	—	—	—	2,420	511,570	512,000
Capital outlay	—	—	—	1,625,500	313,100	—	1,938,600	803,000
Debt service:								
Principal retirement	—	—	60,000	—	—	—	60,000	52,100
Interest and fiscal charges	—	—	40,420	—	28,000	—	68,420	50,000
Total Expenditures	1,163,200	1,153,450	100,420	1,625,500	341,100	2,420	4,386,090	3,039,800
Excess of Revenues over (under) Expenditures	151,300	17,675	27,397	(371,750)	(72,005)	(2,220)	(249,603)	2,000
Other Financing Sources (Uses):								
Proceeds of general obligation bonds	—	—	—	900,000	—	—	900,000	—
Operating transfers in	—	—	—	64,500	10,000	2,530	77,030	89,120
Operating transfers out	(74,500)	—	—	—	—	—	(74,500)	(87,000)
Total Other Financing Sources (Uses)	(74,500)	—	—	964,500	10,000	2,530	902,530	2,120
Excess of Revenues and Other Sources over (under) Expenditures and Other Uses	76,800	17,675	27,397	592,750	(62,005)	310	652,927	4,120
Fund Balances — January 1	202,500	151,035	182,813	357,350	293,075	26,555	1,213,328	1,209,208
Fund Balances — December 31	$ 279,300	$ 168,710	$ 210,210	$ 950,100	$231,070	$ 26,865	$1,866,255	$1,213,328

The notes to the financial statements are an integral part of this statement.

FIGURE 34.3   EXAMPLE OF A GOVERNMENTAL UNIT COMBINED
STATEMENT FOR ALL FUND TYPES

SOURCE: National Council on Governmental Accounting, *Statement 1—Governmental Accounting and Financial Reporting Principles* (Chicago: Municipal Finance Officers Association, 1979), p. 33.

considered part of the official budget can be changed only by the legislative body.

It is also necessary to understand the basis for budget preparation. Some governmental units prepare cash basis budgets, which are not comparable to accrual basis statements. A cash basis budget can meaningfully be compared only with a statement of cash receipts and disbursements.

Combined Statement of Revenues, Expenditures, and Changes in Fund Balances—Budget and Actual—General and Special Revenue Fund Types
For the Fiscal Year Ended December 31, 19X2

	General Fund			Special Revenue Funds			Totals (Memorandum Only)		
	Budget	Actual	Variance – Favorable (Unfavorable)	Budget	Actual	Variance – Favorable (Unfavorable)	Budget	Actual	Variance – Favorable (Unfavorable)
Revenues:									
Taxes	$ 882,500	$ 881,300	$ (1,200)	$ 189,500	$ 189,300	$ (200)	$1,072,000	$1,070,600	$ (1,400)
Licenses and permits	125,500	103,000	(22,500)	—	—	—	125,500	103,000	(22,500)
Intergovernmental revenues	200,000	186,500	(13,500)	837,600	831,100	(6,500)	1,037,600	1,017,600	(20,000)
Charges for services	90,000	91,000	1,000	78,000	79,100	1,100	168,000	170,100	2,100
Fines and forfeits	32,500	33,200	700	—	—	—	32,500	33,200	700
Miscellaneous revenues	19,500	19,500	—	81,475	71,625	(9,850)	100,975	91,125	(9,850)
Total Revenues	1,350,000	1,314,500	(35,500)	1,186,575	1,171,125	(15,450)	2,536,575	2,485,625	(50,950)
Expenditures:									
Current:									
General government	129,000	121,805	7,195	—	—	—	129,000	121,805	7,19¹
Public safety	277,300	258,395	18,905	494,500	480,000	14,500	771,800	738,395	33,405
Highways and streets	84,500	85,400	(900)	436,000	417,000	19,000	520,500	502,400	18,100
Sanitation	50,000	56,250	(6,250)	—	—	—	50,000	56,250	(6,250)
Health	47,750	44,500	3,250	—	—	—	47,750	44,500	3,250
Welfare	51,000	46,800	4,200	—	—	—	51,000	46,800	4,200
Culture and recreation	44,500	40,900	3,600	272,000	256,450	15,550	316,500	297,350	19,150
Education	541,450	509,150	32,300	—	—	—	541,450	509,150	32,300
Total Expenditures	1,225,500	1,163,200	62,300	1,202,500	1,153,450	49,050	2,428,000	2,316,650	111,350
Excess of Revenues over (under) Expenditures	124,500	151,300	26,800	(15,925)	17,675	33,600	108,575	168,975	60,400
Other Financing Sources (Uses):									
Operating transfers out	(74,500)	(74,500)	—	—	—	—	(74,500)	(74,500)	—
Excess of Revenues over (under) Expenditures and Other Uses	50,000	76,800	26,800	(15,925)	17,675	33,600	34,075	94,475	60,400
Fund Balances — January 1	202,500	202,500	—	151,035	151,035	—	353,535	353,535	—
Fund Balances — December 31	$ 252,500	$ 279,300	$26,800	$ 135,110	$ 168,710	$33,600	$ 387,610	$ 448,010	$ 60,400

The notes to the financial statements are an integral part of this statement.

FIGURE 34.4   EXAMPLE OF A GOVERNMENTAL UNIT COMBINED STATEMENT FOR GENERAL AND SPECIAL REVENUE FUND TYPES
SOURCE: National Council on Governmental Accounting, *Statement 1—Governmental Accounting and Financial Reporting Principles* (Chicago: Municipal Finance Officers Association, 1979), p. 34.

Encumbrance Accounting

An encumbrance is defined in GAAFR as an obligation in the form of purchase orders, contracts, or salary commitments chargeable to an appropriation, and for which a part of the appropriation is reserved. They cease to be encumbrances when paid or when the actual liability is recorded. Encumbrances are commitments that will turn into liabilities, and eventually expenditures, in the future.

On the subject of bookkeeping entries for encumbrances, GAAFR states:

. . . the *Reserve for Encumbrances* account . . . represents an earmarked reservation of the Fund Balance to liquidate the contingent obligations of goods ordered but not yet received. In the following fiscal year, this *Reserve for Encumbrances* account is charged, by means of a specially designated *Expenditures* account, with the actual expenditures when they occur. If the expenditures so charged differ from the comparable amounts encumbered during the preceding year, the difference is debited or credited, as appropriate, to *Fund Balance*. [NCGA, 1968, p. 19]

In short, GAAFR called for treating the establishment of encumbrances as if they were expenditures, and for directly adjusting the fund balance to show the difference between estimated amounts set up at the close of a period and actual amounts expended thereafter. But in Statement 1, the NCGA reversed the earlier GAAFR position. Accordingly, outstanding encumbrances should be disclosed, either in a footnote or in a segregation of fund balance, but should not be treated as expenditures.

Some governmental units are still using the encumbrance method of accounting. Since this system creates expenditures simply by issuance of purchase orders, financial statement analyses and comparisons can be misleading if the user fails to note this fact.

Other Variations

While proprietary funds generally follow accounting principles applicable to commercial entities, and while many aspects of accounting for governmental funds are also identical to commercial accounting, there are some significant differences.

Fixed Asset Accounting. Amounts paid for fixed assets by governmental funds are recorded as expenditures in the fund making the payment, and the assets are then usually recorded in the general fixed assets account group. Expenditures that might not be recorded as assets include such items as street and sidewalk costs.

Assets recorded in the general fixed assets account group should be removed from the account group when they are disposed of, though some governmental units have merely accumulated cost information, improperly failing to relieve the accounts for dispositions. The effect may not be material, but usually that can be determined only by taking an inventory of fixed assets, feasible only if detailed records have been maintained or are developed.

The cost of fixed assets will generally not appear in a municipality's general fund operating statement, either when acquired or when used (through a depreciation charge). (An exception would be expenditures funded out of current revenues, which might appear as a current charge.) Rather, the repayment of the debt incurred to purchase assets will be reflected in the general fund accounts. The relationship of the repayment of debt to the use of assets is seldom direct.

The fixed assets of a proprietary (or enterprise) fund, on the other hand, are normally accounted for under the commercial model, with depreciation being charged over the lives of the assets.

Inventories. Inventory items may be entered as expenditures either at the time they are purchased or at the time they are used. If treated as expenditures when purchased, it is considered acceptable to show inventories as an asset in the balance

but are reluctant to rely on a third party's auditing if the other auditor has not issued a public report. Outside CPAs usually feel reliance is valid only if the other auditor has made his own opinion explicit.

CURRENT DEVELOPMENTS

Standard Setting

Some accountants consider the MFOA, through the NCGA, to be the authoritative standard-setting body for governmental accounting principles. Others argue that the only authoritative body for establishing accounting principles is the FASB, pointing out that the MFOA is a trade association and does not possess the independence necessary for a standard-setting body. Still other accountants believe that the federal government should become involved in the process of setting standards for governmental accounting, and legislation to establish an independent body for this purpose has been suggested. Some bills introduced in Congress to provide for regulation of government bond issues would give the SEC authority for setting governmental accounting standards.

The appropriate structure for setting governmental accounting standards was discussed in 1979 and 1980 at meetings of representatives of the GAO, MFOA, NCGA, Financial Accounting Foundation (FAF), FASB, AICPA, National Association of State Auditors, Comptrollers and Treasurers (NASACT), and U.S. Department of Housing and Urban Development. These meetings did not resolve the issue but did yield two proposals:

1. A separate meeting of those employed in government produced a proposal for a small full-time board financed 75% by federal appropriations. This proposal called for the NCGA to continue as an advisory council to the board, which would be supported by an independent oversight body; federal legislation would be the method used to ensure compliance with promulgated standards.
2. The other proposal, issued by the Financial Accounting Foundation, recommends that the NCGA sever its ties with the MFOA, revise its name to something like Governmental Accounting Standards Board, reduce its size, and become the standard-setting body. This proposal calls for an oversight board composed of one representative each from the GAO, MFOA, NASACT, AICPA, FAF, and Public Securities Association (or a rating agency or other user group).

A steering committee was established early in 1980 made up of one member from each organization in 2 above and from the NCGA. It is the responsibility of this steering committee to develop a final plan for setting government standards and the necessary implementation.

Accounting Issues

The principle that governmental units must establish separate accounting records and financial statements for each fund is based on the theory that the legal obligations of the separate funds prohibit any commingling of accounting information.

Separate fund accounting demonstrates the governmental unit's stewardship and legal compliance. It also provides a means of control over legal compliance matters. Some accountants believe that stewardship and legal compliance are the very essence of governmental units and, therefore, that it would be improper to permit accounting or reporting on any basis other than that of separate funds.

An alternative view is that the primary objective of governmental financial reporting should be to present the cost of government, deemphasizing the government's stewardship and legal compliance. This issue of fund versus cost gives rise to many other much-debated issues in governmental accounting, six of which are discussed below.

The Accounting Entity. Under the fund theory each individual fund of a governmental unit constitutes an accounting entity with its own financial statements. It is usually considered inappropriate to group accounting entities together for purposes of preparing financial statements.

Under the cost theory, on the other hand, the governmental unit as a whole constitutes the accounting entity. Legal restrictions may exist and must be complied with, but all the financial activities of a governmental unit should be consolidated into a single set of financial statements. Only in this way can the governmental unit's financial position be usefully presented.

Matching Principle. In commercial accounting it is a basic principle to match costs against the income to which the costs relate, but in accounting for governmental funds this is not done. Those who support the fund theory usually say there is no matching principle whatsoever in governmental accounting. To them the aim of governmental accounting is to demonstrate stewardship, so they argue, for example, that revenues should not be recognized until the cash is received.

Those who advocate the cost theory contend that there is a relationship of income to expense. It is not, they agree, quite the same type of relationship as that represented by the matching principle in accounting for profit-oriented businesses, but they maintain that it should nevertheless be observed because a government's scarce revenues must be allocated among the various services being provided. To the extent that the costs of one period are not covered by revenues, the governmental entity is either drawing on past resources or creating obligations for the future. This is useful information to citizens and investors alike. Accordingly, they lean toward the position that revenues and expenses should be recognized on substantially the accrual basis.

Expenditures Versus Expenses. A consequence of the fund theory is that expenditures—the actual outflow of funds—not expenses, are recorded in a governmental unit's operating statement. The ultimate application of the recording of expenditures is the use of encumbrance accounting. This fixes the stewardship responsibility at the time the commitment is made to use the money.

The cost theory calls for the recording of expenses rather than expenditures.

The principle would be substantially the same as that applied in commercial entities.

Budget Application. Under the fund theory, the budget is a controlling document that affects the accounting of a governmental unit. Whether to record an item in the operating statement thus often becomes a question of whether it is required to be budgeted. This position is based on the belief that the necessity for a budget, like the demonstration of stewardship, is fundamental to a governmental unit.

Cost theory advocates agree that the budget is important to a governmental unit, but maintain that it should not determine the financial reporting in general purpose financial statements.

Debt Service Versus Depreciation. Under the fund theory, principal paid on debt is treated as an expenditure. Supporters of the fund theory believe this is the appropriate way to account for expiration of the cost of assets that were acquired with debt proceeds.

Advocates of the cost theory argue that the cost of assets should be allocated to various programs over the time periods of usage. To them the function of the operating statement is not to reflect the method of financing but to show the cost of providing governmental services by recording depreciation.

Financial Statement Presentation. Under the fund theory, separate financial statements are prepared for each fund, and the funds may not be mixed. Under the cost theory, financial statements are prepared to show cost in a commercial sense, regardless of the type or number of governmental funds that may be involved.

A common criticism of the cost theory is that this practice is geared to a determination of net income and is inappropriate here inasmuch as government ideally should break even. Cost theory advocates answer that if, in the case of governmental units, the net income objective is zero rather than some positive amount, the principle is not thereby invalidated. The objective is to measure costs so that choices can be made between the various services that compete for the limited resources available.

Figures 34.2, 34.3, and 34.4 illustrate financial statements prepared under the fund theory. Figures 34.5 and 34.6 illustrate financial statements prepared under the cost theory.

Prospects for Change

Many of the accounting principles used in governmental accounting today have remained unchanged since the turn of the century. NCGA Statement 1 represents a modest improvement in standards, but much more is needed, including standards for full accrual accounting and consolidation. This is the primary aim of the AICPA experimental project and an integral part of the FASB project on the conceptual framework for nonbusiness organizations. The old standards are not adequate for present needs, but before these problems can be attacked, the question of what body will have standard-setting authority in governmental accounting must be settled.

City of Example
Consolidated Balance Sheet
September 30, 1978 and 1977
(in thousands of dollars)

Assets	1978	1977
Unrestricted assets		
Cash and certificates of deposit	$ 45,875	$ 44,802
Receivables (net of uncollectibles)	7,551	6,471
Notes receivable	12	13
Inventories at cost	1,629	1,426
Total unrestricted assets	55,067	52,712
Restricted assets (primarily for construction purposes, debt service requirements, and equity in regional airport)		
Cash and investments, at cost approximating market	150,816	147,511
Receivables (net of estimated uncollectibles)	14,788	18,005
Notes receivable	4,480	3,916
Inventories	2,308	2,987
Other assets	1,197	1,401
Equity interest in regional airport	89,889	85,372
Total restricted assets	263,478	259,192
Property, plant, and equipment, at cost		
Land and rights	150,077	158,314
Buildings	191,530	196,015
Improvements other than buildings	733,636	740,522
Other	172,175	163,397
	1,247,418	1,258,248
Less accumulated depreciation	289,350	330,934
Net property, plant, and equipment	958,068	927,314
Total assets	$1,276,613	$1,239,218
Liabilities and Municipal Capital		
Liabilities		
Accounts payable	$ 3,313	$ 4,005
Accrued interest expense	2,530	2,832
Accrued pension expense	5,000	—
Other accrued expenses	10,331	16,439
Other liabilities	6,610	7,304
	27,784	30,580
General obligation bonds payable	293,923	301,576
Revenue bonds payable	185,302	193,205
Total liabilities	507,009	525,361
Municipal Capital		
Restricted	735,949	669,933
Unrestricted		
Appropriated	19,526	23,345
Unappropriated	14,129	20,579
Total unrestricted	33,655	43,924
Total municipal capital	769,604	713,857
Total liabilities and municipal capital	$1,276,613	$1,239,218

FIGURE 34.5   ILLUSTRATIVE BALANCE SHEET PREPARED UNDER THE COST THEORY

SOURCE: AICPA, *An Experiment in Government Accounting and Reporting* (New York, 1979), p. 10.

City of Example
Consolidated Statement of Financial Activity
Years Ended September 30, 1978 and 1977
(in thousands of dollars)

	Total Costs	Inter-Governmental	Customer Charges and Other	Net Costs	1977 Net Costs
		1978			
		Related Revenues			
General government					
Mayor and Council	$ 230	$ –	$ –	$ 230	$ 165
City manager	404	–	–	404	354
Support activities	42,505	158	5,173	37,174	34,400
Public safety					
Police	47,154	3,337	265	43,552	41,825
Fire	30,544	4	385	30,155	29,257
Other	2,987	57	–	2,930	2,811
Public works					
Public works	8,677	–	15	8,662	8,125
Streets	15,138	–	934	14,204	13,812
Sanitation	10,120	–	7,602	2,518	3,125
Human resources					
Public health	3,291	180	524	2,587	2,725
Environmental health	2,396	–	51	2,345	2,750
Human development	9,208	8,409	503	296	259
Culture and recreation					
Parks and recreation	18,660	159	1,629	16,872	14,625
Library	6,202	630	2,184	3,388	4,287
Convention center	5,913	–	1,962	3,951	4,125
Radio	933	–	707	226	250
Urban redevelopment					
Housing	4,239	13	1	4,225	3,975
Community center	2,614	–	–	2,614	2,247
Planning and zoning	1,160	–	134	1,026	1,121
Public utilities					
Water utilities	40,429	–	52,785	(12,356)	(8,711)
Utilities regulation	300	–	–	300	275
Transportation					
Aviation	5,485	–	7,558	(2,073)	(2,125)
Transportation terminals	832	–	162	670	635
Transit	21,497	2,638	15,331	3,528	2,985
TOTAL	$280,918	$15,585	$97,905	167,428	163,297

	Net Costs	1977 Net Costs
Financed by		
Taxes		
Ad valorem	112,498	104,299
Sales	34,610	30,555
Franchise	17,333	14,172
Hotel-motel	2,009	1,717
Other	1,348	1,514
Total taxes	167,798	152,257
Licenses and permits	3,061	2,335
Intergovernmental revenues (unallocated)	13,973	17,319
Fines and forfeitures	5,856	5,564
Interest	8,689	4,983
Other	2,760	840
Total financing	202,137	183,298
Excess of current revenues over costs of current operations	34,709	20,001
Equity in earnings of consolidated regional airport	4,517	3,885
	39,226	23,886
Contributions from contractors and customers	16,521	14,211
Municipal capital (beginning of year)	713,857	675,760
Municipal capital (end of year)	$769,604	$713,857

See Notes to Financial Statements.

FIGURE 34.6   ILLUSTRATIVE STATEMENT OF FINANCIAL ACTIVITY
PREPARED UNDER THE COST THEORY
SOURCE: AICPA, *An Experiment in Government Accounting and Reporting* (New York, 1979), pp. 8-9.

SUGGESTED READING

Council of Arthur Young Professors. *Improving the Financial Discipline of States and Cities, Proceedings of the Arthur Young Professors' Roundtable—1979.* Reston, Va., 1980. This book summarizes issues in public sector accountability which were covered in a conference held at the Wharton School. Included are papers dealing with the need for an operating approach to municipal accounting, including one by a co-editor of this *Handbook.*

Davidson, Sidney, et al. *Financial Reporting by State and Local Government Units.* Chicago: University of Chicago Center for Management of Public and Nonprofit Enterprise, 1977. This book analyzes the problems in governmental accounting and recommends solutions.

Hay, Leon. *Accounting for Governmental and Nonprofit Entities.* 6th ed. Homewood, Ill.: Richard D. Irwin, 1980. This textbook provides a good amplification of the basic accounting principles and concepts in government.

Holder, William. *A Study of Selected Concepts for Governmental Financial Accounting and Reporting.* Chicago: Municipal Finance Officers Association, 1980. This book explores and formulates a suggested conceptual framework for financial accounting and reporting by governmental units.

Howell, James, and Stamm, Charles. *Urban Fiscal Stress.* Lexington, Mass.: D. C. Heath, 1979. A review of the fiscal problems of U.S. cities is discussed in this book, which is the product of a project jointly performed by the Economics Department of The First National Bank of Boston and Touche Ross & Co. The book concentrates on a comparative analysis of 66 U.S. cities.

International City Management Association. *The Local Elected Officer's Handbook Series.* Washington, D.C., 1977. This series was developed by the International City Management Association, the National League of Cities, and the National Association of Counties under a contract with the Office of Policy Development and Research, U.S. Department of Housing and Urban Development. These publications, which give insights to good operating policies in government, include "Use of Advisory Committees," "Evaluating the Chief Administrator," "Intergovernmental Relations," "Money—How to Raise It and How to Spend It," and "Goal Setting By the Governing Body."

National Governors Association Center for Policy Research. *Tax and Expenditure Limitations, 1978.* Washington, D.C., 1979. This study analyzes the climate in the country for tax limitation.

Pomeranz, Felix; Cancellieri, Alfred; Stevens, Joseph; and Savage, James. *Auditing in the Public Sector.* Boston: Warren, Gorham & Lamont, 1976. This book has information on auditing for efficiency, economy, and program results.

University of Texas at Austin. *Municipal Accounting and Reporting Issues for Research.* Chicago: Alexander Grant & Company, 1976. This report of a conference at the University of Texas at Austin on November 11-12, 1976, presents issues in governmental financial reporting identified by the nationally recognized participants in the conference.

35

Nongovernmental Nonprofit Enterprises

Emerson O. Henke[1]

---

[1] The author acknowledges with appreciation the assistance of Bruce D. Rand of Touche Ross & Co. in several aspects of this chapter.

TYPES OF ENTERPRISES

Nonprofit enterprises are sometimes called not-for-profit or nonbusiness organizations. Their one common characteristic is that *they are not organized to realize a profit on the goods or services they provide as their basic activity.* Technically, a company organized to make a profit is a nonprofit business if it has an operating loss during a year. Some believe, therefore, that using the term *nonprofit* for those not having a profit motive is inappropriate. The FASB differentiates by using the term *nonbusiness.* But a hospital, for example, *is* a kind of business. Though unwieldy, perhaps the correct terminology should be *businesses not organized for a profit.* In this chapter the various terms are used interchangeably.

Nonprofit organizations may also be referred to as tax-exempt organizations. In fact, it is common for an organization to refer to itself according to the Internal Revenue Code section under which it receives exempt status, for example a 501(c)(3) organization. Despite the common misconception, tax-exempt organizations do pay taxes on income from an activity unrelated to their basic purpose. Furthermore, exemption from federal income taxes usually does not automatically exempt an organization from state income taxes. Because the term *tax exempt* is not an appropriate descriptor, it is generally not further used in this chapter.

This chapter considers nongovernmental nonprofit enterprises, which are among the most prominent and socially visible organizations in the United States. The most recent statement by the Internal Revenue Service (based on exemption data) indicates that there are almost 800,000 such organizations (Webster, 1979), and this is without considering the countless chapters of many national organizations that may be counted as only one in the IRS list. Though not exhaustive, the following list suggests their broad scope of activities:

- Botanical societies,
- Cemetery organizations,
- Child care organizations,
- Civic organizations,
- Condominium and residential management associations,
- Eleemosynary organizations,
- Fraternal organizations,
- Hospitals,
- Labor unions,
- Libraries,
- Museums,

- Performing arts organizations,
- Philanthropic organizations,
- Political parties,
- Private and community foundations,
- Private elementary and secondary schools,
- Professional associations,
- Public broadcasting stations,
- Religious organizations,
- Research and scientific organizations,
- Schools, colleges, and universities,
- Social, recreational, and country clubs,
- Trade associations,
- Voluntary health and welfare organizations, and
- Zoological societies.

Social Environment

Nonprofit organizations exist *pro bono publico,* providing goods or services considered socially desirable by and for the general public, a community, or its members. In the case of a membership organization, its philosophical or ideological purpose may be the main reason it gains and retains members. Of course, the rationale for one organization may directly conflict with that for another, even though both groups of members would consider their organizations to be socially desirable.

Nonprofit organizations compete not only for individuals, groups, or other organizations to support their purpose, but also for funds; this competition is fierce.[2]

Obtaining Funds. Charitable giving is big business in the United States. In 1979 contributions received by U.S. charities totaled $43.24 billion, 83% of this amount from individual donors (National Information Bureau, 1980, p. 1).

Funds may come from federated fund-raising campaigns (such as the United Way of America), from foundations (such as the Rockefeller Foundation and the Ford Foundation), and from business corporations. In 1978 the United Way of America, a federation of 2,300 local chapters that raise and distribute funds, allocated more than $1 billion to 39,000 agencies throughout the United States. In 1979 foundations made grants totaling $2.24 billion; corporations, led by the oil companies, contributed $2.3 billion (*New York Times,* April 15, 1980). Still other funds come from membership dues, fees for services, subscriptions for publications, bequests and legacies, investments, and grants for specific projects or research from various sources.

Watchdog Agencies. Because these funding sources represent limited resources, it is not surprising that the worthiness of a nonprofit organization may be constantly

---

[2] *The Touche Ross Survey of Business Executives on Non-Profit Boards* (New York, 1979) found that 50% of the respondents considered the ability to solicit funds as a necessary qualification for membership on a nonprofit board.

challenged. Claims of mismanagement and misuse of funds can lead to lawsuits, fines, or harsher punishment.

This challenge comes from so-called watchdog agencies on behalf of the general public. The most evident of these is the Internal Revenue Service, which regularly examines the tax or information returns of nonprofit enterprises. If an organization fails to maintain its tax-exempt purpose, the IRS may impose taxes as if the organization were a business enterprise. On a state level, an organization is also subject to this type of supervision and could lose its state tax exemption.

Certain nongovernmental agencies also perform a "watchdog" service. One of the largest and most influential organizations is the National Information Bureau, Inc. (NIB), headquartered in New York City. Monthly, the NIB publishes the *Wise Giving Guide,* which rates national nonprofit organizations other than religious, fraternal, or political organizations and single institutions such as hospitals or colleges. The NIB's ratings of the main social welfare activities supported through national solicitations from the general public are grounded in these "Basic Standards in Philanthropy" (National Information Bureau, 1980, p. 20):

1. Board: an active and responsible governing body, holding regular meetings, whose members have no material conflict of interest and serve without compensation.
2. Purpose: a clear statement of purpose in the public interest.
3. Program: a program that is consistent with the organization's stated purpose and its personnel and financial resources and that involves interagency cooperation to avoid duplication of work.
4. Expenses: reasonable program, management, and fund-raising expense.
5. Promotion: ethical publicity and promotion excluding exaggerated or misleading claims.
6. Fund-raising: solicitation of contributions without payment of commissions or undue pressure, such as mailing unordered tickets or merchandise, general telephone solicitation, and use of identified government employees as solicitors.
7. Accountability: an annual report available on request that describes program activities and supporting services in relation to expenses, and includes financial statements (1) employing uniform accounting standards showing all support revenue and expenses in reasonable detail and (2) accompanied by a report of an independent public accountant. National organizations operating with affiliates should provide combined or acceptably compiled financial statements prepared in the foregoing manner.
8. Budget: detailed annual budget approved by the governing body in a form consistent with annual financial statements.

Ratings based on these standards are available for use by potential contributors. Two of the standards, accountability and budget, are directly affected by the quality of the accounting function in the organization. Another standard, expenses, is affected by the proper accounting classification of managerial and fund-raising costs.

Accounting Environment

Nonprofit organizations tend to have specialized accounting and reporting practices, often differing from those of profit-oriented enterprises. Some types of organizations follow practices not followed by any other type of nonprofit organization. The most obvious contrast with business organizations shows up in financial statements. Typically, nonprofit organization statements are not widely distributed, going to a limited number of governing bodies, creditors, resource providers, and oversight agencies. Furthermore, the statements are often designed as special purpose reports to meet the informational needs of users and thus may not be too informative to casual readers.

Among the reasons that minimal attention has been given to the widespread diversities in accounting and reporting for nonprofit enterprises has been the orientation of the standard-setting organizations themselves. The FASB and its predecessor organizations have had to concentrate on principles used by business enterprises. ARB 43, issued in 1953, says it as well as later statements:

> The committee has not directed its attention to accounting problems or procedures of religious, charitable, scientific, educational, and similar non-profit institutions, municipalities, professional firms, and the like. Accordingly, except where there is a specific statement of a different intent by the committee, its opinions and recommendations are directed primarily to business enterprises organized for profit. [AC 510.05]

Accounting and reporting by nonprofit enterprises evolved gradually over the years, influenced by interested industry groups. In the 1970s the AICPA became active in the area, publishing pronouncements such as SOP 78-10, *Accounting Principles and Reporting Practices for Certain Nonprofit Organizations* (1978), and audit guides for several types of nonprofit organizations. Although the accounting and reporting principles in AICPA pronouncements are to some degree consistent, they occasionally diverge. These similarities and differences are discussed later in this chapter. Most recently, the FASB (1980c) issued a proposed Statement of Financial Accounting Concepts, *Objectives of Financial Reporting by Nonbusiness Organizations,* also discussed later.

Similarity to Business Enterprises

A nonprofit organization has much in common with a business enterprise:

1. *Both provide goods or services to segments of the economy.* Although the nature of the goods and services provided may (but need not) be different, it is the public or some specific sector of the economy that ultimately receives the goods or services. For example, some hospitals may be operated for profit, but a nonprofit hospital provides the same service—health care.

2. *Both obtain resources from external sources.* For a business enterprise, the external sources would include equity capital from owners. For a nonprofit enterprise, the external sources may include donations or dues from members. Both may obtain resources from trade creditors, bank loans, or debt securities.

3. *Both are accountable to the resource providers.* The stockholders and other resource providers of a business enterprise are interested in the company's profitability and future cash-flow prospects (among other matters). Resource providers of a nonprofit enterprise are interested in the organization's performance—how well the resources provided were spent. One way to account for the use of resources is, of course, to prepare financial statements and to distribute them to the resource providers.

4. *Both must obey applicable laws and regulations.* This includes paying all taxes for which they are liable, filing annual returns with the Internal Revenue Service and state agencies to maintain their exempt status, and observing limits in some states as to the amount that may be spent for fund raising or on noncharitable purposes.

Differentiation From Business Enterprises

There are three characteristics that distinguish nonprofit organizations from business enterprises (based on FASB, 1980c):

1. *Many resource providers do not expect to receive repayments or economic benefits from a nonprofit enterprise that are proportionate to resources provided.* In a business enterprise, the prices charged for goods or services are meant to cover costs and allow a profit. But nonprofit enterprises have no "owners" with an interest similar to equity shareholders in a business enterprise. Dues-paying members, contributors, and grantors provide needed capital without necessarily receiving or even expecting commensurate benefits. And most often they do not receive even a measure of control of the organization's policies. Providers may expect *some* return on their "investment," but not a *proportionate* return. It often happens that the benefit received is disproportionately small (e.g., Christmas seals) or disproportionately large (e.g., education at a college or university where the tuition charge covers only a portion of the actual costs).

2. *Nonprofit enterprises have accounting and reporting differences that stem from not primarily aiming for profit.* Most notably, the nonprofit enterprise's financial statement shows no counterpart to earnings or profits as found in a business enterprise. In fact, many do not earn revenue because they do not have exchange transactions. Instead of a statement of earnings, information is provided on resources received and used. Further, the financial statement classification of expenses by object (salaries, general and administrative expenses, etc.) is less meaningful for the typical nonprofit organization; thus a different categorization of expenses—by activity or service—is often provided.

3. *Nonprofit organizations do not have defined ownership interests that can be sold, transferred, or redeemed, and there are no owners.*

These three basic differences are not always apparent. In fact, some companies start out as profit-seeking ventures but later obtain tax-exempt status and become nonprofit enterprises. (An example is *Ms.* magazine, which was founded in 1972 and changed status in 1979.) Other companies have started as nonprofit enterprises and later switched to a business status.

Users of External Financial Reporting

The proposed SFAC, *Objectives of Financial Reporting by Nonbusiness Organizations* (FASB, 1980c), discusses the types of users of externally reported financial information. A comparison of these users with those identified for business enterprises in SFAC 1 (AC 1210.25) is shown in Figure 35.1. These lists appear different partly because the users have been grouped differently, but actually the users are quite similar.

Nonbusiness *Organizations*	*Business* *Enterprises*
Resource providers	Investors
Constituents	Lenders
Governing and oversight bodies	Suppliers
Managers	Employees
	Customers
	Managers

FIGURE 35.1   USERS OF FINANCIAL INFORMATION

For nonbusiness organizations, users are defined as follows (FASB, 1980c, pp. 12-14):

- *Resource providers:* those who are directly compensated for providing resources—lenders, suppliers, and employees—and those who are not directly and proportionately compensated—taxpayers, members, and contributors.
- *Constituents:* those who use and benefit from the services rendered by the organization. Sometimes resource providers are also constituents.
- *Governing and oversight bodies:* those responsible for setting policies and for overseeing and appraising managers of nonbusiness organizations. Governing bodies may include boards of directors, boards of trustees, boards of overseers and regents, and other similar groups. Their responsibilities include reviewing for conformance with laws, restrictions, or guidelines. Oversight bodies include oversight committees of legislatures, governmental regulatory agencies, national headquarters of organizations with local chapters, accrediting agencies, and agencies acting on behalf of contributors and constituents. In membership organizations, governing bodies are commonly the elected representatives of a constituency that is largely composed of resource providers. In organizations such as charities, hospitals, and private colleges, governing bodies may be self-perpetuating through the election of their own successors.
- *Managers:* those responsible for carrying out the policy mandates of governing bodies and controlling the day-to-day operations of the organization.

These users have varying needs for financial information. Resource providers need information to assess how well the organization has met its objectives, whether managers have carried out policy mandates, and whether to continue their support. For managers and governing bodies, the information may suggest new policy strategies for the organization.

In addition to the users described above, there are external (as well as internal) users who can prescribe the information they want. External users in this category include donors and grantors who restrict the use of resources for a specific purpose, governmental authorities who by regulation can prescribe the manner and form of requested information, and some creditors. Internally, managers and governing bodies may need additional information such as comparisons of actual results with budgeted amounts, evaluations of spending proposals, or detailed information about compliance with donor and grantor restrictions.

An investor in a business enterprise may be either a resource provider or constituent or both. An employee is a resource provider and may also be a constituent, a member of the governing body, a manager, or a combination of these. A customer of a business enterprise is a constituent of that enterprise.

Accounting Differences

To an accountant unfamiliar with them, financial statements of nonprofit organizations may at first seem bewildering. However, he should have little trouble interpreting them once he understands the accounting differences between nonprofit and business entities. These differences fall into five general areas:

1. Terminology,
2. Fund accounting,
3. Cash versus accrual basis,
4. Treatment of fixed assets, and
5. Pledges and noncash contributions.

Some of these differences are endemic to nonbusiness enterprises, coming about through practice rather than purpose. Some have been modified or changed in recent years or are now being challenged as to their propriety. The state of the art for nonprofit accounting is evolving, and this evolution will continue.

The discussion that follows is only a brief overview of the issues relating to nonprofit organizations. For a more thorough discussion, refer to the FASB research report, *Financial Accounting in Nonbusiness Organizations* (Anthony, 1978), which is discussed later in this chapter.

Terminology. Some of the mystery relating to nonprofit financial statements stems from terminology. What for a business enterprise is known as an income statement has no direct nonprofit entity counterpart, because the nonprofit entity does not operate to earn net income. For a nonprofit entity, the bottom line is more frequently called the operating excess (deficit), or excess of receipts over expenses (expenses over receipts), or excess of revenues over expenditures (expenditures over receipts). Likewise, the financial statement that includes this final result may be called an operating statement; a statement of activity; a statement of revenues and expenses and changes in unrestricted fund balances; a statement of revenues and expenditures; a statement of support, revenues and expenses, and changes in fund balances; or a statement of cash receipts and disbursements. These terminology differences should not intimidate the financial statement reader once the terms are understood. Figure 35.2 shows the terms selected nonprofit organizations used in their recently published annual reports in place of the business enterprise balance sheet, income statement, and net earnings.

Other terminology used by nonprofit organizations is different simply because there is no equivalent for a business enterprise. Examples are:

Organization	Balance Sheet	Income Statement	Net Earnings (Loss)
AICPA	Balance Sheet	Statement of Revenues and Expenses	Excess of Revenues over Expenses
American Cancer Society	Combined Balance Sheet	Combined Statement of Support, Revenue and Expenses and Changes in Fund Balances	Support and Revenue in Excess of (Less Than) Expenses
CARE and CARE Canada	Consolidated Balance Sheet	Consolidated Statement of Support, Revenue and Costs and Changes in Fund Balance	Excess (Deficiency) of Support and Revenue over Costs
Girl Scouts of the United States of America	Consolidated Balance Sheet	Consolidated Statement of Revenue and Expenses	Excess (Deficiency) of Revenue over Expenses
Metropolitan Opera Association	Balance Sheet	Statement of Activity	Excess of Revenues over Expenses
Muscular Dystrophy Association, Inc.	Consolidated Balance Sheet	Consolidated Statement of Support, Revenue and Expenses and Changes in Fund Balance	Excess of Support and Revenue over Related Expenses
The Rockefeller Foundation	Statement of Assets, Obligations and Principal Fund	Statement of Operations and Changes in Principal Fund	Excess of Grants Announced and Program Costs and General Administrative Expenses Incurred over Net Investment Income

FIGURE 35.2 TERMINOLOGY IN FINANCIAL STATEMENTS OF NONPROFIT ENTERPRISES

- Contributions,
- Bequests and legacies,
- Receipts from federated campaigns,
- Pledges receivable,
- Endowment funds,
- Program services (or expenses), and
- Fund balances.

Finally, still other differences in terminology derive solely from the nature of the organization itself. A hospital will show patient service revenues on its financial statements, while a religious organization will show parish revenues. A zoological society's statements will detail the expense of paying curators and keeping animals, a museum's will be concerned with paying curators and maintaining art.

Fund Accounting. Of all the accounting differences between nonprofit organizations and business enterprises, fund accounting is the most prominent and perhaps the most widely misunderstood. It is an accounting practice reflected in nonprofit financial statements as a method of accounting for resources that have been (1) restricted by a donor or other outside party for a specific purpose or use or (2) identified by the organization for a specific purpose or use. These resources are set up in a separate set of accounts and accounted for separately. For example, if John Jones gives a college $100,000 to be used as a scholarship fund, the college might establish the Jones Scholarship Fund and account for all the transactions in the fund as if it were a separate economic entity.

Some accountants view fund accounting as a method to obfuscate the financial statements and make them nearly incomprehensible to the average financial statement reader. However, a greater number of accountants defend the fund accounting concept, convinced that it is the proper method for the organization to demonstrate stewardship of resources entrusted to it. Because of the importance of fund accounting in nonprofit organizations, a separate section of this chapter is devoted to it, and further discussion of fund accounting concepts in the context of governmental units is found in the preceding chapter.

Cash Versus Accrual Basis. Although the accrual basis of accounting underlies GAAP for business enterprises, the cash receipts and disbursements method of accounting is frequently used by nonprofit organizations. There is also a hybrid of the cash basis and the accrual basis—the modified cash basis or modified accrual basis. Under the modified cash (accrual) basis, some transactions are recorded on a cash basis and others on an accrual basis, although different organizations do not necessarily account for the same transactions in the same way. Many organizations record transactions on a cash basis during the year and convert to the accrual basis at year-end for reporting purposes. The main advantage of the cash basis lies in its simple, like-a-checkbook recording requirements. In many nonprofit organizations, simplicity is important because of the lack of a sufficiently large accounting staff. And for many organizations no significant difference results from using the cash versus the accrual method, so the cash method is likely to be chosen.

Treatment of Fixed Assets. Accounting for fixed assets (property, plant, and equipment) is one of the more controversial nonprofit subjects. Many organizations capitalize fixed assets; others do not. Some organizations that capitalize fixed assets record depreciation; others do not. Some organizations expense fixed asset additions, then capitalize the assets in the balance sheet (the write-off, then-capitalize method). The fact that GAAP requires the capitalization and depreciation of fixed assets in business enterprises has not done much to silence the controversy in nonprofit organizations.

The broader issue in fixed asset accounting is whether the resources received (revenues) should be matched against resources spent (expenditures) or against expenses incurred. Those favoring the expenditures approach say that the amounts spent for the acquisition of fixed assets are derived from resources received during the year and that the proper matching is expenditure against revenue. Also, they say that capitalizing the asset would make it appear that the organization made money, when, in fact, the funds it received were spent.

For example, assume that a nonprofit organization showed that its net revenue over expenditures for a year was $0, including a deduction of $10,000 for acquisition of fixed assets. If the fixed assets were capitalized instead, the organization would show an excess of $10,000. Some proponents of the expenditure approach fear that this apparent excess would dissuade financial statement users from making donations.

The controversy regarding depreciation runs along similar lines. Those in favor of not depreciating say that resource providers during the current period should not be expected to pay for acquisitions made in a prior period. Also, they point out that if an organization spent all the funds it received during the year on that year's operations and then included a depreciation charge, it would show a deficit.

Pledges and Noncash Contributions. Business enterprises do not receive pledges. For a nonprofit organization, a pledge of a contribution may or may not be legally enforceable. Hence, there is the accounting question of whether pledges should be recorded. Many organizations record amounts pledged based on their experience in collecting them. Others do not record pledges, because of uncertainty over how much will be collected, or because the financial statements are not significantly affected by nonrecording.

Noncash contributions include donated securities, facilities, materials, and services. Business enterprises rarely receive such contributions. The most significant measurement problems arise when services are donated. Many nonprofit enterprises simply could not exist without the level of donated services they receive. However, because it is often impossible or impractical to measure the value of such services, many organizations do not record them.

FUND ACCOUNTING

Fund accounting is a *separate* accounting for restricted resources that are either *legally* restricted by a donor or another outside party or *designated* by the board for a specific purpose or use. When such resources (together with the related liabilities) are accounted for separately, the separate set of accounts constitutes a *fund,* and the net assets in the fund are called the *fund balance.* Some resources, of course, are not restricted, and these are included in *unrestricted funds.* A single nonprofit organization, therefore, may have several separate funds.

To use a simple example, assume that a newly formed nonprofit organization receives two cash donations on December 31—$100,000 that the donor specifies is only to be used to purchase a headquarters building and $10,000 that may be used for the general operations of the organization. In the organization's balance sheet as of December 31, there are three presentation possibilities, shown in Figure 35.3:

1. Separate funds in a layered format (Example 1),
2. Separate funds in a multicolumn format (Example 2), or
3. A single balance sheet with the restricted assets identified (Example 3).

Depending on the type of organization or the nature of the restrictions on an organization's assets, all three formats are used in actual practice.

In the *layered format* the balance sheet could be quite lengthy if the organization has many restricted funds. This format does not provide for an aggregation of the various assets, liabilities, and fund balances to display the financial position of the whole organization. Thus, common criticisms of this presentation are that (1) the financial statements become very complex and nearly incomprehensible unless it is made crystal clear exactly what the various restricted funds represent and (2) it is quite a challenge to determine the financial position of the organization as a whole, especially if the numerous funds have receivables from and payables to each other.

In *multicolumn format* statements there often is no total column, since many preparers of financial statements believe that presenting a total column is mixing apples and oranges. For example, showing total cash may give the false impression that the organization can use all that cash in its operations. Thus, a common criticism shared with the layered format is that it can be difficult to determine the financial position of the organization as a whole.

The *restricted asset identification format* is most like that used for a business enterprise and is used by many nonprofit organizations that classify assets as current or noncurrent. Without this classification, the format can be cumbersome. Some relief can be provided by classifying assets and liabilities as restricted or unrestricted by type of fund, but this presentation does not work well when there are many funds.

Types of Funds

Funds are classified in one of three ways: by type of restriction if any, simply by whether they are unrestricted or restricted, or by whether they are expendable or nonexpendable.

Type of Restriction. There are six general fund categories based on the type of restrictions placed on the fund's resources:

1. Current unrestricted fund,
2. Current restricted fund,

EXAMPLE 1—LAYERED FORMAT

UNRESTRICTED FUNDS

	Assets		*Liabilities and Fund Balances*	
Cash	$ 10,000	Fund Balance	$ 10,000

RESTRICTED FUNDS

Building Fund:			
Cash	$100,000	Fund Balance	$100,000

EXAMPLE 2—MULTICOLUMN FORMAT

	Unrestricted Fund	*Building Fund*	*Total*
Assets			
Cash	$10,000	$100,000	$110,000
Liabilities and Fund Balances			
Fund Balances:			
Unrestricted	$10,000	$ —	$ 10,000
Restricted	—	100,000	100,000
	$10,000	$100,000	$110,000

EXAMPLE 3—RESTRICTED ASSETS IDENTIFIED

Assets	
Current assets:	
Cash	$ 10,000
Noncurrent assets:	
Cash held for building fund	100,000
	$110,000
Liabilities and Fund Balances	
Fund Balances:	
Unrestricted	$ 10,000
Restricted	100,000
	$110,000

FIGURE 35.3   SIMPLIFIED NONPROFIT BALANCE SHEET

3. Land, building, and equipment fund,

4. Endowment fund,

5. Custodian fund, and

6. Other funds—loan fund, annuity fund, life income fund.

Current unrestricted fund. This fund may also be called the *general fund, current fund, current general fund, undesignated unrestricted fund,* or *operating fund.* These terms are descriptive of the fact that the fund's resources can be used to carry out the day-to-day operations of the organization. In some organizations unrestricted investments in property, plant, and equipment are set up in a separate fund.

The current unrestricted fund also includes *board-designated funds,* which are sometimes referred to as *appropriations* or *allocations.* The purpose of board-designated funds is to set aside resources for a specific use or purpose even though there is no legal restriction. Because the board has the authority to change or reverse its designations, such funds should not be shown in financial statements as restricted. It is not uncommon for nonprofit organizations to provide with their financial statements a list of unexpended board-designated funds included in the current unrestricted fund, stating the purposes for which the resources have been set aside.

Current restricted fund. Also called the *donor-restricted fund* or *fund for specified purposes,* this category consists of operating funds restricted by donors and grantors who specify the permitted use. For example, $1,000 given to a local hospital to be used for reading materials for patients would be included in the current restricted fund. Usually the unexpended balances in the fund are relatively small, since these gifts and grants are generally used shortly after receipt. When the amounts are not to be used currently for a normal activity of the organization, they are usually included in another fund. A list of restricted donations, including the name of the donor or the activity for which the donations are restricted, is sometimes provided with the financial statements.

Land, building, and equipment fund. Sometimes referred to as the *plant fund, capital asset fund,* or *fixed asset fund,* this fund is used to segregate investments in and contributions specifically designated for the acquisition of land, buildings, and equipment. Its purpose is to segregate capital assets not expendable for current operations. Generally there is no need for such a fund, and these investments may be included in the unrestricted fund balance; doing so will communicate the fact that (1) the fixed assets are not legally restricted and (2) they are used to carry on the day-to-day activities of the organization.

Endowment funds. These funds represent gifts and bequests accepted with the donor stipulation that (1) the principal be maintained (a) intact in perpetuity or (b) until the occurrence of a specified event or (c) for a specified period and (2) only the income from investment of principal should be expended, either for general purposes or for purposes specified by the donor. Technically, the fund is an *endowment fund* only if the principal amount is to be maintained intact in perpetuity. If the principal is to be maintained until the occurrence of a specified event or only for a specified period, the fund is a *term endowment fund.*

If the governing board of an organization determines that certain resources are to be retained and invested, the fund is a *quasi endowment fund.* This type of fund is actually a board-designated fund, and many organizations include the resources with other unrestricted funds. Some other organizations, principally colleges and universities, include quasi endowment funds with other endowment funds under the caption "endowment and similar funds."

Custodian fund. Sometimes called an *agency fund* or *funds held in trust (or custody) for others,* this fund simply represents resources received by an organization to be held or disbursed only on instructions of the person or organization from whom they were received. For example, a college or university may hold funds belonging to the student government association, to be disbursed only on the association's instructions.

Other funds. These include *loan funds, annuity funds,* and *life income funds* and are most often associated with colleges and universities. A *loan fund,* as its name implies, represents resources restricted for loans (to students or faculty for example). An *annuity fund* represents gifts of money or other property with the restriction that the organization make periodic payments to the donors or other specified individuals for a specified period of time. A *life income fund* represents gifts of money or other property with the restriction that the organization periodically pay the income earned by the donated assets. Such payments may be to the donors (or other specified individuals) for the lifetime of the income beneficiary. The primary difference between an annuity fund and a life income fund is that the principal amount of the life income fund will remain intact, whereas the payments from the annuity fund might not leave the principal amount intact.

Unrestricted or Restricted. This classification recognizes that from the viewpoint of the governing board there only two types of funds—those over which it has total control and those over which it has limited control. Therefore, the types of funds previously mentioned would be grouped for financial statement purposes according to whether the funds are unrestricted or restricted.

An example of this presentation is shown in Figure 35.4; note that unrestricted funds are categorized into three types—undesignated, board-designated, and invested in capital assets (the capital assets are shown among the noncurrent assets). The assets of the one restricted fund grouping, endowment funds, are included in noncurrent assets.

Expendable or Nonexpendable. This classification is based on the expendable or nonexpendable nature of the resources available to an organization for current activities. Therefore, current unrestricted funds and current restricted funds would be classified as *expendable.* Endowment funds and the land, building, and equipment fund would be classified as nonexpendable, because they are generally not available for the organization's current operations.

SPECIALIZED INDUSTRIES

	July 31,	
	1979	1978
Unrestricted funds:		
Undesignated	4,233	3,981
Board-designated	1,833	2,097
Invested in capital assets	1,114	511
	7,180	6,589
Endowment funds	2,291	2,062
Total fund balances	9,471	8,651
Total liabilities and fund balances	$28,191	$24,731

FIGURE 35.4 FUND BALANCE PRESENTATION SHOWING RESTRICTION
GROUPINGS IN BALANCE SHEET
SOURCE: Metropolitan Opera Association, Inc. (New York), Annual Report 1978–1979
Season.

Need for Separate Fund Presentation

There are differences of opinion regarding the need for fund accounting. Knowledgeable accountants honestly disagree on its merits. However, the differences of opinion are a symptom of the evolution of accounting for nonprofit organizations, which has occurred more slowly than it has for business enterprises.

Recent years have seen increasing discussion of the need for continuation of fund accounting as opposed to a single set of financial statements presenting the assets and obligations of the entire organization. The following discussion presents the arguments for and against fund accounting, based on the FASB research report, *Financial Accounting in Nonbusiness Organizations* (Anthony, 1978, pp. 104-112).

Arguments for Fund Accounting. Arguments for fund accounting are based primarily on these points:

• Because there are legal restrictions on resources, it is necessary to report compliance with those restrictions; fund accounting is a convenient way to do so.
• An aggregated statement is misleading because restricted resources are not interchangeable with unrestricted resources.
• Aggregated statements are not adequate to represent what is really a complex situation. Because of restrictions on resources or spending, statements prepared as if the organization were a business enterprise are inappropriate.
• Although there may be abuses of fund accounting in some organizations, these abuses are not inherent attributes of fund accounting.

Arguments Against Fund Accounting. Arguments against fund accounting are based primarily on these points:

- Separate financial statements for each fund group fragment the overall organization instead of presenting the activities and financial position of the organization as a whole.
- Separate accounting by different funds is difficult to understand and tends to confuse the reader. Therefore, a single set of financial statements is more understandable; also, readers familiar with financial statements of business enterprise are used to that format.
- It is possible for management to manipulate the financial statements by using its discretion as to the fund or funds in which costs should be included.
- Because there are transfers and reimbursements among funds, it can appear that revenues are being counted twice.
- The existence of restrictions on resources and whether these restrictions have been complied with can be disclosed in footnotes to financial statements.

INTERNAL USE OF ACCOUNTING DATA

External financial reports of nonprofit organizations are organized to disclose the accountability of upper-level managers to the governing board, constituents, creditors, and other outside interested parties. Within the organization, of course, lower-level managers are accountable to upper-level managers. Therefore, the accounting system should be organized to provide appropriate feedback regarding the activities of subordinates in their particular areas of responsibility. The relationships of upper-level managers to externally interested parties and to subordinates can be seen in Figure 35.5.

In monitoring and controlling the activities of subordinates, upper-level managers should expect the accounting system to be governed by an effective system of internal control and to provide

1. An effective departmental budgeting program;
2. Measurement of departmental contributions toward the operating objectives of the organization, including the disclosure of operational accountability data for departmental managers; and
3. A system of cost allocation that can be used in establishing prices for services to be fully or partially recovered from user fees.

Effective Budgeting

The budgetary process expresses the operating plans of the organization in dollars. Most outflow budgets involve a combination of amounts appropriated for specific purposes and formula-related items. Thus, appropriation-type budgets are used by enterprises that rely on taxes and/or contributions for resource inflows and that provide services on the basis of need. On the other hand, the budgets of profit enterprises include mostly formula-related outflow items (outflows related to anticipated volume of operations). Between these two limits are organizations that depend on user fees for some of their operating revenues and whose outflow budgets typically include both appropriation and formula-controlled items.

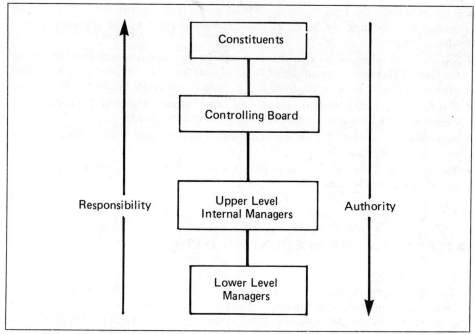

FIGURE 35.5   RESPONSIBILITY/AUTHORITY FLOW IN A NONPROFIT
ORGANIZATION

Internally, nonprofit organizations usually have lower-level supervisory responsibility divided along the lines of departments or service functions provided by
the organization. From the point of view of internal managers, it is therefore
important that the overall outflow budget be appropriately subdivided according
to subordinate manager responsibilities. Such an arrangement has the effect of
setting outflow standards for each of the individual subordinate managers and, in
that way, holds each lower-level manager accountable for his or her segment of
operations.

Contributing to Operating Objectives

It is important, in evaluating the effectiveness of departmental managers, that
the accounting system be organized so as to relate actual outflows to the same
specific areas of responsibilities as were used in the budgetary system. This allows
measurement of their adherence to budgetary allocations and of the units of service
provided by their departments. Functional unit costs or expenditures per unit of
service provided can be developed and compared with the budget on a departmental
basis. In effect, this is a responsibility accounting system for the purpose of evaluating the efficiency and effectiveness of lower-level managers in carrying out their
responsibilities.

Cost Allocations

It is always important for managers to know the cost of converting resources into various services and products. In the nonprofit area a system for allocating costs to functions performed allows management and external users to determine functional unit costs over different periods of time. Such costs can then be compared with budgeted unit costs, with unit costs incurred in other periods, and/or with functional unit costs incurred by other enterprise units in providing similar services. Such comparisons can be useful in evaluating operational efficiency.

Appropriate allocation of costs is especially important for nonprofit organizations that depend on user fees for the recovery of part or all of their operating costs. In such instances it is important to divide the various departments within the organization into *revenue-producing* and *supporting activity* categories for both budgetary and accounting purposes. The accounting system should include procedures to allocate supporting activity costs to revenue-producing departments. After such allocations have been completed as part of the budgeting process, the anticipated cost per unit of billable service can be determined by dividing total cost by the anticipated number of units of services to be provided. Such cost allocation procedures have been used for many years by hospitals in arriving at billing rates for the various services provided. Logically, a similar system of cost allocation could be used in establishing college and university tuition and fee schedules.

Internal Controls

Managers of nonprofit organizations depend on internal control procedures just as much as managers of profit-oriented enterprises do. Ordinarily this requires that the accounting system, the organization chart, and the procedures manual include these characteristics:

1. A work assignment arrangement that provides for an appropriate separation of custodial and record-keeping responsibilities;
2. An organization chart and procedures manual that specifically places various operational responsibilities on specific persons within the organization;
3. Adequate records, forms, and authorization procedures;
4. A personnel policy ensuring that all personnel will be appropriately qualified for the responsibilities assigned to them;
5. Provision for a periodic check of actual procedures being followed against those prescribed in the procedures manual; and
6. Appropriate provisions for the physical protection of assets such as cash and securities.

In the process of assuring compliance (see item 5 above) it is important to use an internal auditor when an organization becomes large enough to preclude the top-level manager from personally checking compliance. The internal auditor has the responsibility of seeing that lower-level supervisors and employees comply with managerial directives and the procedures spelled out in the procedures manual. (See also Appendix 11-B's discussion on the relationship of internal and outside auditors).

FASB CONCEPTUAL FRAMEWORK PROJECT

As part of its conceptual framework project for financial accounting and reporting (see Chapter 2), the FASB has been concerned with the broad fundamentals, not the detailed standards, of general purpose external financial reporting. The Board's initial pronouncement (1978) on this subject was SFAC 1, *Objectives of Financial Reporting by Business Enterprises* (AC 1210). The Board has also focused attention on nonbusiness organizations.

Research Report

In August 1977 the FASB engaged Robert N. Anthony of the Harvard Business School to prepare a research report, *Financial Accounting in Nonbusiness Organizations,* dealing with the conceptual issues involved. Although the final report was the responsibility of Anthony, he was assisted by an advisory group of 53 members. The project represented two "firsts" for the FASB—the first time that the subject matter had been addressed by the Board and the first independently authored research study to be issued by the Board. Also, the advisory group of 53 members was the largest group put together to assist in the preparation of an FASB publication. Yet the research report was completed in the relatively short span of nine months and was published in May 1978.

The research report dealt with governmental as well as nongovernmental organizations, and it identified 16 issues relating to financial accounting in nonbusiness organizations. The issues are summarized in Figure 35.6, and some are discussed further below.

Operating flows (issue 3), as defined in the research report, are resource inflows related to operating activities of the *current* period. There are two types of operating flows:

1. *Revenues*—amounts realized in exchange for goods and services during the current period; and
2. *Other operating inflows*—nonrevenue inflows, including contributions, appropriations made by another entity, and grants.

Capital flows are inflows of resources that are intended to benefit activities of *future* periods rather than the current period. Otherwise, the sources of capital flows are the same as for other operating inflows identified above.

An *operating statement* (issue 4), as defined in the research report, is a financial statement that reports operating inflows, expenses, and the difference between them during the current period.

A *financial-flow statement* (issue 6) is defined as one that reports some or all of the financial resource inflows (operating flows and capital flows), expenditures, and/or asset conversions (transactions that convert an asset or liability into another asset or liability but do not result in a change in the organization's equity) during a current period. Given this definition, the issue is whether the financial-flow statements should report encumbrances (contractual commitments to acquire goods or services) as well as or instead of expenditures (amounts actually spent to acquire goods or services).

USERS AND THEIR INFORMATIONAL NEEDS

1. Is the following list of primary users of financial report information adequate for the purpose of identifying needs for such information: governing bodies, investors and creditors, resource providers, oversight bodies, and constituents?

2. Is the following list of the types of financial report information needed by users adequate as a basis for deciding how best to meet these needs: financial viability, fiscal compliance, management performance, and cost of services provided?

USER NEEDS RELATED TO FINANCIAL STATEMENTS

3. Do users need a report of operating flows that is separate from a report of capital flows?

4. Do users need an operating statement?

5. Do users need a report of cost of services performed?

6. Should financial-flow statements report encumbrances as well as, or instead of, expenditures?

7. Do users need a single aggregated set of financial statements for the organization rather than separate financial statements for each fund group? If the latter, what criteria should determine the composition of fund groups?

8. Are there conceptual issues related to the balance sheet?

SELECTED ISSUES

9. How should the nonrevenue operating inflows of an accounting period be measured?

10. How should endowment earnings be measured?

11. Under what circumstances, if any, should a charge for the use of capital assets be recorded as an item of spending?

12. Should pension costs be accounted for as spending in the period in which the related services were rendered?

13. Under what circumstances, if any, should donated or contributed services be reported as an item of expense at their fair value?

BOUNDARIES FOR NONBUSINESS ACCOUNTING CONCEPTS

14. How, if at all, should business organizations be distinguished from other organizations for the purpose of developing accounting concepts?

15. Should the federal government and/or the state governments be excluded from the applicability of financial accounting concepts for nonbusiness organizations?

16. Should a single set of concepts apply to all types of nonbusiness organizations or should there be one set for governmental organizations and one or more additional sets for nongovernmental, nonbusiness organizations?

FIGURE 35.6   ISSUES RELATING TO FINANCIAL ACCOUNTING IN NONBUSINESS ORGANIZATIONS

SOURCE: Robert Anthony, *Financial Accounting in Nonbusiness Organizations* (Stamford, Conn.: FASB, 1978), pp. xi and xii.

As to the appropriate way to measure *endowment fund earnings* on investments (issue 10), the research report identifies five possibilities:

1. Report only investment income (interest, dividends, rents, royalties, and similar items) as operating inflows. Exclude gains or losses, whether realized or not.
2. Report investment income plus realized gains as operating inflows.
3. Report investment income and both realized and unrealized gains as operating inflows.
4. Report a prudent percentage of average market value of the endowment portfolio as operating inflows. This approach is commonly referred to as *the total return concept* in practice.
5. Select the preferred alternative among the first three alternatives, then allow that alternative or the total return approach, whichever one the organization's management decides is the more appropriate.

In issue 12, the question is whether organizations that do not follow the provisions of APB 8, *Accounting for the Cost of Pension Plans* (AC 4063), may record pension costs when payments are made (the cash basis) or when the current liability is incurred (the budgetary expenditure basis).

An alternative *classification of organizations* (issue 14) is graphically displayed in the research report, as shown in Figure 35.7. As can be seen, a major problem is the treatment of Type A nonprofit organizations, which have some of the attributes of profit-oriented businesses.

Presently, there are separate and *differing pronouncements* for colleges and universities, hospitals, voluntary health and welfare organizations, and other not-for-profit organizations. Issue 16 questions the continued propriety of this situation.

The research report does not identify any conceptual issues relating to the *balance sheet*. However, issue 8 is listed in the event readers might perceive some conceptual issues not recognized in the research report.

Discussion Memorandum

The FASB's 1978 *Discussion Memorandum on an Analysis of Issues Related to a Conceptual Framework for Financial Accounting and Reporting: Objectives of Financial Reporting by Nonbusiness Organizations* was a direct result of Anthony's research report. On the issues listed in Figure 35.6, all are included in the discussion memorandum except issues 9-13, which the Board excluded because they deal more with specific accounting standards than with objectives.

After issuance of the discussion memorandum, three public hearings were held in October and November 1978—in Washington, D.C., San Francisco, and Chicago. The Board reviewed 87 written responses, and 48 oral presentations were made at the public hearings.

After the public hearings, the Board discussed the issues at ten meetings open to the public. During these discussions, the Board decided that issues 6 and 7 listed in Figure 35.6 should also be excluded from the scope of this project.

Exposure Draft

The resulting exposure draft (FASB, 1980c), planned for finalization late in 1980, makes these major points:

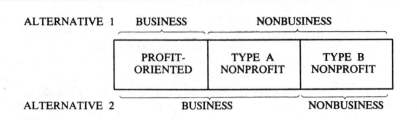

TYPE A Nonprofit: A nonprofit organization whose financial resources are obtained, entirely, or almost entirely, from revenues from the sale of goods and services.

TYPE B Nonprofit: A nonprofit organization that obtains a significant amount of financial resources from sources other than the sale of goods and services.

FIGURE 35.7   ALTERNATIVE CLASSIFICATIONS FOR ORGANIZATIONS
SOURCE: Robert Anthony, *Financial Accounting in Nonbusiness Organizations* (Stamford, Conn.: FASB, 1978).

1. The general purpose of external financial reporting is to meet the common interests of external users who generally cannot prescribe what they want from an organization;
2. The objectives of external financial reporting are largely determined by the economic, legal, political, and social environment within which nonbusiness organizations function in the United States;
3. The objectives of financial reporting by nonbusiness organizations are to provide information that is useful in
   a. Making resource allocation decisions,
   b. Assessing the services provided by the organization and its ability to continue to provide those services, and
   c. Assessing management stewardship and performance;
4. Financial reporting should provide information about
   a. Economic resources, obligations, and net resources of an organization,
   b. The service efforts and accomplishments of the organization,
   c. The amounts and kinds of inflows and outflows of resources during a period, including the identification of inflows and outflows of restricted resources;
5. Accrual accounting generally provides a better indication of an organization's performance than the cash basis of accounting; and
6. Financial reports should include explanations and interpretations to help users understand the financial information.

Excluded from the scope of the exposure draft are organizations that do not possess all the distinguishing characteristics of nonbusiness enterprises, e.g., membership clubs with transferable equity interests, investor-owned hospital and educational institutions, mutual insurance companies, and other types of mutual and cooperative organizations that directly provide dividends, lower costs, or other economic benefits to their owners, members, or participants. These types of organizations are said to be covered by SFAC 1, *Objectives of Financial Reporting by Business Enterprises* (AC 1210). This exclusion is likely to be the source of some controversy, because the Board is basically saying that some nonprofit organizations are really business enterprises (see Figure 35.7).

The exposure draft does not include criteria for determining the appropriate reporting entity for purposes of financial reporting. Financial statements of nonprofit organizations typically specify by footnote which affiliated organizations or activities are included in the data, but it is often unclear precisely which organizations ought to be included. For example, if a membership organization has both a national headquarters and local affiliates, should the headquarters report its financial data alone or in combination with that of its affiliates? Likewise, some organizations (e.g., large religious bodies)—have lower-level units that are essentially autonomous but ultimately answerable to the national organization. Other nonprofit entities, notably hospitals and universities, have separate foundations whose sole purpose is to raise money for the parent organization. In all of these instances it is unclear whether and when to combine the financial statements of the affiliated organizations with those of the central or parent institution. Though certainly a critical question, this was excluded from consideration in both the exposure draft and the research report.

PRESENT ACCOUNTING AND REPORTING PRINCIPLES

A common misconception about accounting by nonprofit organizations is that GAAP does not apply and that therefore such organizations do not have to follow any authoritative pronouncements by the FASB or its predecessors. This idea is, of course, incorrect; possibly it results from a statement in ARB 43: "... except where there is a specific statement of a different intent by the committee, its opinions and recommendations are directed primarily to business enterprises organized for profit" (AC 510.05).

Authoritative Literature

The most far-reaching pronouncement affecting nonprofit organizations was issued in 1979 as SFAS 32, *Specialized Accounting and Reporting Principles and Practices in AICPA Statements of Position and Guides on Accounting and Auditing Matters* (AC 1052). It amends APB 20 (AC 1051.16, fn. 5) as follows:

> The specialized accounting and reporting principles and practices contained in the AICPA Statements of Position and Guides on accounting and auditing matters listed in Appendix A of FASB Statement No. 32 [Section 1052.13] are preferable accounting principles for purposes of justifying a change in accounting principle.

Because APB 20, *Accounting Changes,* prohibits a change in accounting principle unless the enterprise justifies the new alternative principle as preferable (AC 1051.16), what SFAS 32 has done is grant authority to the many SOPs and guides issued by the AICPA in the past. Several of these publications deal specifically with nongovernmental nonprofit entities, as listed in Figure 35.8. This means that

- There is no requirement for an organization to change accounting in order to adopt the accounting and reporting practices in the SOPs and guides if it is currently using other accounting and reporting practices.
- If an organization does change, the principles in the SOPs or guides are considered to be the preferable accounting principles.
- If an organization changes to an accounting principle other than one specified in the applicable SOP or guide, the organization has the burden of proof to demonstrate that the new principle is preferable. In this case, the auditor reporting on the financial statements with the objective of rendering an unqualified opinion would also have a burden of proof to be satisfied that the organization has demonstrated the preferability of the new principle before he renders an opinion that the financial statements are prepared in conformity with GAAP. As a practical matter, therefore, it is likely that the organization will adopt the principles and practices included in the SOPs and guides when changing accounting principles.

COLLEGES AND UNIVERSITIES

- Industry audit guide, *Audits of Colleges and Universities* (1973)
- Statement of Position 74-8, *Financial Accounting and Reporting by Colleges and Universities*

VOLUNTARY HEALTH AND WELFARE ORGANIZATIONS

- Industry audit guide, *Audits of Voluntary Health and Welfare Organizations* (1974)

HOSPITALS

- Industry audit guide, *Hospital Audit Guide* (1972)
- Statement of Position 78-1, *Accounting by Hospitals for Certain Marketable Equity Securities*
- Statement of Position 78-7, *Financial Accounting and Reporting by Hospitals Operated by a Governmental Unit*

OTHER NONPROFIT ORGANIZATIONS

- Statement of Position 78-10, *Accounting and Reporting Practices for Certain Nonprofit Organizations*

FIGURE 35.8   AICPA NONPROFIT SOPs AND GUIDES GIVEN AUTHORITY UNDER SFAS 32

Continuing FASB Involvement

SFAS 32 is only an interim solution. Definitive authoritative pronouncements for accounting and reporting practices by nonprofit organizations still need to be established. To quote SFAS 32:

> ... the Board [has] agreed to exercise responsibility for all the specialized accounting and reporting principles and practices in the existing AICPA SOPs and Guides by extracting those specialized principles and practices from the SOPs and Guides and issuing them as FASB Statements after appropriate due process. [AC 1052.02]

Of course, this is a formidable task. The FASB plans to appoint task forces for those principles and practices relating to health care, colleges and universities, and other not-for-profit entities. These task forces will include knowledgeable individuals from the affected industries and the public accounting profession and other interested individuals. Their work will ultimately result in exposure drafts, and the "due process" of the FASB is likely to include public hearings at which interested parties can present their views. For those interested in accounting and reporting practices of nongovernmental nonprofit organizations, this process will be a stimulating period during which the accounting profession will focus on an important sector of the economy.

In the interim the guidance given in certain guides and SOPs forms a basis for much of current practice, as discussed in the next section.

Distinctive Accounting Practices

In this section the major distinctive elements of presently accepted accounting practices for colleges and universities, hospitals, voluntary health and welfare organizations, and other nonprofit organizations are summarized, with a brief discussion of the following areas in each category:

- Accounting basis,
- Typical funds,
- Budgetary practices,
- Accounting for fixed assets, and
- Financial reporting.

Appendix 35-B presents the accounting and reporting practices recommended in SOP 78-10 for other nonprofit organizations, since this SOP is the most current and complete pronouncement on the subject; the appendix also provides information about differences found in the other three audit guides discussed in this section of the chapter.

The discussion that follows is only a *summary* of major distinctive accounting practices. The audit guides and SOP 78-10 contain much more detailed information.

Colleges and Universities. Colleges and universities can be subdivided into state-supported and private. Both receive a major portion of their revenues from user

charges. State-supported institutions receive most of their fees from state allocations based on some measure of enrollment, but they usually require some direct
payment by the student in the form of tuition and fees. The private university
receives all its user-based fees directly from students, the parents of students,
alumni, or scholarship funds. Both types of institutions also typically receive a
significant amount of gifts, contributions, and grants.

In accounting for resource inflows, colleges and universities distinguish between
operating revenues and *nonoperating revenues.* All operating revenues, such as
tuition and fees, unrestricted gifts, and endowment income, should flow through
the operating statement. Resource inflows that are externally restricted to specified
nonoperating uses (such as endowment or the acquisition of fixed assets) are
recorded in designated fund groups (such as "endowment and similar funds" or
"plant funds").

Accounting basis. The AICPA audit guide (1973e) states that the accounts
should be maintained on the accrual basis (p. 7), except that depreciation is not
recognized as an element of expense in the operating statement (p. 9).

Typical funds. Colleges and universities use fund accounting extensively, allowing the college or university to depict its adherence to the restrictions placed on the
uses of specific resource segments. The following fund groups are typical:

• Current funds,
• Loan funds,
• Endowment and similar funds,
• Annuity and life income funds,
• Plant funds, and
• Agency funds.

Because of the number of funds typically presented and the detail of accounts
within each fund, the balance sheet of a college or university is usually quite
lengthy. Examples may be found in Exhibit A in the audit guide (pages 60-61) or
in Exhibit 1 in SOP 74-8.

Current funds include spendable resources—those available to be used directly
in carrying out the operations of the institution; the current obligations required
to be satisfied with those resources are also included. Current funds are divided
into two subcategories: *unrestricted current funds* include those resources that
(within the limits of budgetary constraints) may be used at the discretion of management, *restricted current funds* include spendable resources restricted to specified
operating uses by donors or other outside agencies.

Loan funds are used to account for loans to faculty, students, or staff. The
agreements under which these funds operate usually specify the loan-granting
restrictions. Cash not committed for loans is generally invested, in order to add
resources.

Endowment and similar funds include resources to be invested for the purpose
of producing operating revenue. *Regular endowment funds* are externally restricted
from use for any purpose other than investment purposes, and the revenue is used

for general operating purposes. The revenues from *designated endowment funds* can be used only for the purposes specified in the endowment agreement, such as scholarships or individual schools within the university.

Term endowment funds are similar to regular endowment funds except that after the passage of a stated period of time or the occurrence of a particular event, all or part of the principal may be expended.

Quasi endowment funds represent resources designated by the governing board of the institution for use as endowment. Since they are internally designated, the governing board has the right to rescind its action and allow the principal to be expended.

Most colleges and universities accept contributions subject to donor claims, such as the right of the donor to receive an annuity for a specified period of time (or for life) or the right of the donor to receive the income from the contribution for the remainder of his or her life. Upon termination of these annuity or life income agreements, the assets remaining in the fund become the property of the college or university. The accounts of an annuity fund will include an actuarially determined liability for annuities payable.

Plant funds are used to carry the acquisition costs of fixed assets. Obligations (such as bonds payable) relating to those assets, plus resources restricted to debt retirement or capital expenditures, are also included in the plant fund.

Agency funds are used to account for resources held by the college or university as custodian or fiscal agent for others, such as student organizations, faculty organizations, or perhaps even individual students or faculty members. In the financial statements the total of the agency funds may be grouped under "deposits held in custody for others"; however, the accounting records would show the obligations to the specific depositors of funds.

Budgetary practices. All effectively managed resource conversion enterprises plan future operations through the medium of budgets and measure operational results against them. Colleges and universities are no exception.

Earlier in this chapter budgets were distinguished between governmental appropriation-type budgets (discussed in the preceding chapter) and profit enterprise budgets designed to be adjusted as levels of operations changed. College and university budgets fall somewhere in between. Generally, a college or university will establish an operation budget prior to the beginning of a period; implicit in it is a specific level of operations. If operations later deviate from the anticipated level, many schools (especially private ones) will revise their outflow projections, insofar as possible, to those allowed for the actual level of operations achieved.

Accounting for fixed assets. Most fixed asset expenditures are acquired using resources in the plant fund. As assets are acquired, they are capitalized in the plant fund, with an offsetting credit to cash or a liability account. Current fund outlays for fixed assets are recorded as expenditures in the operating statement rather than being capitalized as assets, but they may then be transferred to the plant fund and capitalized there.

Colleges and universities do not recognize depreciation as an operating expense. The AICPA industry audit guide states, however, that accumulated depreciation may be reported in the balance sheet, with the depreciation provision reported in the statement of changes in the plant fund balance (AICPA, 1973e, pp. 9-10).

Financial reporting. Colleges and universities present three basic statements: balance sheet, statement of changes in fund balances, and statement of current fund revenues, expenditures, and other changes. In addition, supporting schedules show the financial position and activities of various auxiliary enterprises (such as intercollegiate athletics, student health services, dormitories and housing systems, and the college bookstore) and the various individual fund entities.

Hospitals. Hospitals can be classified as voluntary, governmental, or proprietary. Proprietary hospitals are owned by private investors and therefore are profit-oriented, so this discussion will cover only voluntary and governmental institutions. Voluntary hospitals typically receive most of their operating revenue through user-based fees, whereas governmental hospitals partially cover their operating costs through federal, state, county, or city appropriations.

A large part of the cost of hospital services is paid by third-party payors such as Medicare, Medicaid, Blue Cross, and private insurance carriers. Settlement with some third-party payors requires cost data in support of charges to patients, and this need has caused hospitals to develop sophisticated techniques to allocate total operating expenses among the various service billing centers.

Hospitals receive both externally restricted and unrestricted contributions. Hospital accounting systems therefore distinguish between operating and nonoperating resource inflows. Unrestricted contributions represent one form of nonoperating revenue and should be included in the operating statement. Externally restricted contributions, however, should be entered directly in the appropriate fund entities (such as plant replacement and expansion funds, specific purpose funds, or endowment funds), depending on the restrictions placed on their use.

Accounting basis. Hospitals use *accrual basis accounting,* requiring capitalization of assets and recognition of depreciation. Therefore, accrued and prepaid items, inventories, and accumulated depreciation are reflected in the balance sheet.

Typical funds. Because hospitals receive resources that are externally restricted, fund accounting procedures are incorporated into their accounting systems. All fund entities fall into one of two major categories: *unrestricted funds* and *restricted funds.* The assets of these funds may include cash, investments, and pledges receivable net of estimated uncollectible amounts.

Unrestricted funds include all assets and obligations related to general operations. This includes property, plant, and equipment and the obligations relating to those assets.

Restricted funds are subdivided into three categories. *Specific purpose funds* are used to account for resources restricted for such uses as research projects. *Plant replacement and expansion funds* are used to account for resources designated for plant replacement and expansion. The fund balance section of this fund is designed to disclose more specifically the types of plant replacement or expansion activities for which the funds may be used. *Endowment funds* are used to account for resources required by donors to be invested for the purpose of producing endowment income. The accounting procedures and account names are similar in most respects to those found in college and university endowment funds. However, hospitals show no quasi endowment funds in their statements. Instead, they list these internally restricted resources as investments included within unrestricted funds.

Budgetary practices. Voluntary hospitals, which depend on user fees for most of their revenues, generally follow the flexible budgetary approach used by profit-seeking enterprises. Governmental hospitals, which receive most of their operating revenues from federal, state, or local governmental units, are controlled through appropriation-type budgets similar to those used for governmental units (see Chapter 34).

Accounting for fixed assets. Fixed assets are usually paid for out of a restricted plant replacement and expansion fund. Thus, when a fixed asset is acquired, its cost must be entered both in that restricted fund (reducing the fund balance) and the unrestricted fund (increasing the fund balance). Otherwise, the accounting procedures for hospital fixed assets are the same as those followed in business enterprises.

Financial reporting. The financial reports for hospitals normally include four statements: balance sheet, statement of revenues and expenses, statement of changes in fund balances, and statement of changes in financial position. The statement of revenues and expenses typically presents those activities affecting the unrestricted resources of the hospital. The remaining transactions are shown in the statement of changes in fund balances. Sample financial statements are shown in the AICPA's *Hospital Audit Guide* (1972e).

Voluntary Health and Welfare Organizations. The AICPA industry audit guide (1974c) defines voluntary health and welfare organizations as entities that "derive their revenue primarily from voluntary contributions from the general public to be used for general or specific purposes connected with health, welfare, or community services" (p. v). Note that this definition has two parts: the revenue must be derived primarily from voluntary contributions from the general public, and it must be used for purposes connected with health, welfare, or community services. There are many organizations that meet one part of this definition but not the other.

Accounting practices of health and welfare organizations varied significantly in the past, because the industry had no generally accepted publication defining those procedures. In 1964 the National Health Council published *Standards of Accounting and Financial Reporting for Voluntary Health and Welfare Organizations.* That publication (sometimes referred to as the "black book") was subsequently revised in 1974 to incorporate most of the procedures set out in the 1974 AICPA industry audit guide. Those two publications now constitute the best available descriptions of GAAP for voluntary health and welfare organizations.

Accounting basis. The accrual basis of accounting, with capitalization of assets and recognition of depreciation, is followed.

Typical funds. Health and welfare organizations often receive restricted contributions for the creation of endowment funds, purchases of fixed assets, and other specified uses. Therefore, fund accounting procedures are often used to demonstrate compliance with those externally imposed constraints. These organizations will always have *a current unrestricted fund* and may have one or more of five restricted-type funds. These include *current restricted funds; land, building, and equipment fund; endowment funds; custodian funds;* and *loan and annuity funds.*

The *current unrestricted fund* is used to account for all resources over which the governing board has discretionary control in carrying on the operations of the organization except for amounts invested in land, buildings, and equipment. It is the operating fund of the organization, obtaining its resources from contributions, bequests, program service fees, dues, investment income, and, in some cases, the sale of goods and services.

The board of a health and welfare organization may designate current unrestricted fund resources for specific purpose projects, or it may choose to invest some of the resources to earn investment income. These designated assets should not be included with donor-restricted funds. Instead, they are reflected as elements of the unrestricted fund balance.

As in other organizations, *current restricted funds* are used to account for resources that are expendable only for externally specified operating purposes.

The *land, building, and equipment fund* is used to account for resources externally designated for acquiring or replacing land, buildings, and equipment, and it includes, of course, currently owned land, buildings, and equipment. Any liabilities associated with the assets in this fund, such as mortgages payable, are also carried here. Unlike accounting for college and university plant funds, depreciation is recognized on depreciable assets, and accumulated depreciation is shown as a reduction of the buildings and equipment accounts in this fund.

Endowment funds are used to account for resources externally restricted for a specific purpose. Revenues earned from investing such funds are expended either for general purposes or as specified by the donor of the endowment.

Custodian funds are used to account for assets received by the organization with the stipulation that they be held or disbursed on instructions from the person or organization providing them.

A *loan fund* represents resources restricted to loans for specified purposes of the organization, and an *annuity fund* represents gifts of money or other property, with the restriction that the organization make periodic payments to the donors or other specified individuals for a specified period of time.

Budgetary practices. Health and welfare organizations convert resources into various types of services. The choices in planning operating activities involve the development of a system of priorities among the services to be rendered and the establishment of the most effective ways of providing those services. That, in turn, calls for the establishment of budgetary procedures correlating those priorities and the operating procedures with the consumption of resources. Ideally, the budgetary operating plan should be used as one element in the solicitation of contributions. A condensed budget of anticipated expenses can be used to help potential donors understand what the real service objectives of the organization are.

The initial expense budget often must be modified to accommodate a higher- or lower-than-anticipated level of contributions. Here again, particularly if expenses must be adjusted downward, it is important for the governing board, in cooperation with internal managers, to review the system of priorities developed during the initial planning of operations. Capital expenditure programs often may involve a significant sales effort on the part of the governing board, as well as a separate solicitation campaign. Generally speaking, this will call for a soundly based estimate of the probable costs of assets to be acquired, as well as a justification, in terms of future service potential, of the need for such facilities.

Accounting for fixed assets. Health and welfare agencies capitalize and depreciate fixed assets. Such assets are sometimes accounted for in a land, buildings, and equipment fund and will most often be acquired using resources received for that specific purpose. When assets are purchased with the current fund, a transfer must be made from the current fund to the plant fund; this will directly reduce the fund balance in current unrestricted funds and increase the fund balance in the land, buildings, and equipment fund. Depreciation of fixed assets will also be recorded in the land, buildings, and equipment fund. Depreciation expense, in turn, is allocated to the different services being performed by the organization and is included as an expense in the statement of functional expenses.

Financial reporting. Three financial reports are usually prepared for health and welfare organizations, and they should be presented in such a way that comparisons can be made with preceding periods. The first financial report should include a balance sheet subdivided by fund entities. The second report, a statement of support, revenue and expenses, and changes in fund balances, is the basic operating statement. In that statement, it is important to show the amount of resource inflows realized from public support separately from revenue realized from membership dues, investment income, etc. It is also important that expenses be subdivided by services performed and that expenses for supporting services be separated from those for program services. The third report, a statement of functional expenses, shows how various expense items are allocated to the various service categories. This statement essentially is a supporting schedule for the operating statement; an example is shown in Figure 35.9.

Other Nonprofit Organizations. In December 1978 the AICPA issued SOP 78-10, *Accounting Principles and Reporting Practices for Certain Nonprofit Organizations.* This statement is intended to be applicable to all categories of nonprofit organizations except those that are already covered by existing audit guides —colleges and universities, hospitals, and voluntary health and welfare organizations. Therefore, many types of organizations are covered by SOP 78-10; for example, see the list at the outset of this chapter.

Because SOP 78-10 was issued at the time the FASB had already taken onto its agenda a project on objectives of financial accounting by nonbusiness organizations, the AICPA did not state an effective date for the SOP, in the event its conclusions conflicted with the FASB's. However, some nudge towards adoption was made in the form of providing for voluntary adoption, with transitional procedures stated.

Some may wonder at the anomaly of not stating an effective date for a pronouncement not enforceable under the accounting profession's ethical rules (ET 203.01, Appendix B); but SFAS 32 (AC 1052), discussed earlier under Authoritative Literature, has since granted SOP 78-10 the status of preferable accounting principles for the purpose of making changes in accounting principles.

CONSOLIDATED STATEMENT OF FUNCTIONAL EXPENSES FOR THE YEAR ENDED DECEMBER 31, 1978
(WITH COMPARATIVE TOTALS FOR 1977)

	Program Services				Supporting Services		1978 Total	1977 Total
	Research	Medical Services	Professional Education and Training	Public Health Education	Fund Raising	Management and General		
Awards and grants	$12,661,999						$13,085,499	$12,229,052
Postdoctoral fellowships	3,007,971						3,007,971	2,280,103
Disbursements made on behalf of individuals		$11,160,959					11,160,959	8,027,284
Costs reimbursed for telethon network production, preempted time, and facilities					$1,707,704		$ 1,707,704	$ 1,726,382
Contribution to Theatre Authority, Inc.					300,000		300,000	300,000
Salaries	313,269	7,288,111	487,773	$1,162,604	414,866	$ 771,181	10,437,804	8,902,138
Payroll taxes	21,073	556,765	44,642	95,883	38,447	70,334	827,134	685,121
Employee benefits—Note 4	36,583	753,697	50,782	116,383	35,668	83,752	1,076,865	704,597
Occupancy—Note 5	59,490	754,609	94,668	225,341	82,193	127,163	1,343,464	1,065,057
Telephone and telegraph	31,977	1,242,961	82,765	161,761	1,610,955	56,723	3,187,142	2,757,544
Travel, meetings, and related expenses	126,052	2,416,058	259,266	323,578	276,043	243,583	3,644,580	2,890,318
Office supplies and equipment	23,601	653,849	67,258	166,263	251,675	66,618	1,229,264	827,552
Printing, visual aids, etc.	4,609	1,188,209	22,939	363,806	1,347,439	9,524	2,936,526	2,317,871
Postage and shipping	42,430	443,257	23,748	34,473	862,448	17,357	1,423,713	1,051,980
Professional fees	31,057	238,219	18,500	44,398	146,645	260,945	739,764	512,714
Miscellaneous expenses	14,088	597,854	39,018	70,397	556,748	119,945	1,398,050	846,429
Total expenses before depreciation	16,374,199	27,294,536	1,614,859	2,764,887	7,630,831	1,827,125	57,506,439	47,124,142
Depreciation of fixed assets	445	13,689	1,496	3,377	1,052	12,287	32,346	13,564
Total functional expenses	$16,327,644	$27,308,227	$1,616,355	$2,768,264	$7,631,883	$1,839,412	$57,538,785	$47,137,706
Percentage to total functional expenses	28.5%	47.4%	2.8%	4.8%	13.3%	3.2%	100%	
	-------- 83.5% --------				-------- 16.5% --------			

See notes to consolidated financial statements.

FIGURE 35.9 SAMPLE STATEMENT OF FUNCTIONAL EXPENSES

SOURCE: Muscular Dystrophy Association, Inc., 1978 Annual Report.

Accounting basis. SOP 78-10 provides that the accrual basis should be used in the financial statements in order to comply with GAAP (p. 10). However, it does recognize the possibility that cash basis financial statements may not be materially different from those prepared on the accrual basis.

Typical funds. If the organization does not report on a fund accounting basis, the financial statements should disclose all material restrictions. Otherwise, fund accounting may be used for reporting purposes when it is necessary to disclose the nature and amount of significant externally restricted resources.

The *unrestricted fund balance* will include

1. Amounts designated by the board for specific purposes,
2. Undesignated amounts, and
3. Amounts invested in fixed assets (however, the plant fund may be reported separately).

A departure from financial reporting permitted for other nonprofit organizations is that *current restricted resouces* and *resources restricted for future acquisition of fixed assets* should be reported as deferred revenue until the restrictions are met.

Budgetary practices. Because of the diversity of organizations covered by SOP 78-10, it is difficult to generalize about their budgetary practices. It is not uncommon, however, for the budgets to be quite detailed and prepared on a monthly or quarterly basis. For many organizations the level of contributions, dues, or other support received can be very volatile and thereby affect the level of services provided by the organization. Because of this constraint on spending, it is common for these organizations to monitor expenses and expenditures several times during a year.

Accounting for fixed assets. SOP 78-10 requires the capitalization of fixed assets, but recognizes the practical problem of obtaining historical cost information by organizations that have not previously capitalized the assets. If historical cost records are not available, another basis may be used to value the assets, including cost-based appraisals, insurance appraisals, replacement costs, or property tax appraisals adjusted for market value.

In addition to capitalizing fixed assets, the statement also requires that exhaustible fixed assets be depreciated over their estimated useful lives. Inexhaustible assets— landmarks, monuments, cathedrals, historical treasures, and collections owned by museums, art galleries, botanical gardens, libraries, and similar entities—need not be depreciated.

Financial reporting. The three financial statements required are a balance sheet, a statement of activity, and a statement of changes in financial position. The statement of activity reports the support, revenue, capital or nonexpendable additions, and expenses classified into functional categories. This statement may have a different title, such as statement of support, revenue, expense, capital additions, and changes in fund balances or statement of changes in fund balances. The SOP presents examples of financial statements, including representative footnote disclosure, for 13 types of organizations (SOP 78-10, Appendix C).

AUDITING CONSIDERATIONS

Generally accepted auditing standards apply to examinations made for the purpose of expressing an opinion on the fairness of presentation of financial statements in conformity with GAAP. In addition, the auditor may be engaged to

1. Review or compile (rather than audit) the financial statements (Statements on Standards for Accounting and Review Services (SSARSs) provide guidance); or
2. Issue special reports (AU 621.01) in connection with
   a. Financial statements that are prepared in accordance with a comprehensive basis of accounting other than generally accepted accounting principles,
   b. Specified elements, accounts, or items in a financial statement,
   c. Compliance with aspects of contractual agreements or regulatory requirements related to audited financial statements, or
   d. Financial information presented in prescribed forms or schedules that require a prescribed form of auditor's report.

In these cases, SAS 14 (AU 621) provides guidance on the appropriate wording of the auditor's report. If an organization prepares its financial statements using the cash basis or modified accrual basis, for example, SAS 14 should be referred to. (See also Chapter 16.)

If the special report is to be audited, GAAS applies; if unaudited, SSARSs apply. The purpose of this section of the chapter is to refer to some auditing considerations peculiar to nonprofit organizations, many of which will also be applicable to audits of nonprofit special reports.

Knowledge of the Organization

In addition to the obvious need to be familiar with the operating structure, accounting practices, and activities of the specific organization, the auditor should be familiar with the industry in which the organization operates. For example, the auditor should be knowledgeable about

1. The applicable industry audit guide and statement(s) of position,
2. The tax laws that affect the organization,
3. The applicable laws or regulations that affect specific activities of the organization, such as regulations relating to grants received from the federal government or other sources, and
4. Provisions of documents restricting the use of resources received by the organization.

Internal Controls

Internal controls for a nonprofit organization may be relatively weak compared to those of a business enterprise because

1. The governing body (board of directors, board of trustees, or similar group) may be fairly large, comprising volunteers who are relatively inactive in the day-to-day affairs of the organization;

2. There may be a limited availability of resources that can be used to strengthen controls;

3. The accounting function may receive relatively little attention either because of a lack of staff or because the organization places most of its emphasis upon its operating activities or programs; or

4. There may be a small staff, so that a desired segregation of duties is difficult to attain.

Budgets. For many organizations, the budget is a key element of internal control if it is frequently compared to actual results. The budget is usually prepared by the staff and approved by the governing body. If the actual results are carefully reviewed and deviations challenged by the executive director or treasurer, the timely detection of errors and irregularities may be augmented.

Audit Committees. Many organizations audited by independent public accountants have audit committees made up of board members not involved in the day-to-day activities. The audit committee may meet with the auditors prior to the audit to discuss the audit scope, internal controls, or particular areas or activities that the committee believes should be stressed during the audit. After the audit is complete, the auditors may again meet with the audit committee to discuss the results of the audit and areas where internal controls or operating procedures may be improved. (See Chapter 10.)

Cash Receipts. Nonprofit organizations receive cash from many sources—direct mail campaigns, door-to-door solicitation, radio and television solicitation, special events, and contributions from noncontrolled organizations and groups. It is of great concern, of course, that all contributions are received by the organization. Although control over cash contributions can never be absolute, it should be sufficient to reasonably assure the auditor that contributions are not materially misstated. Otherwise, a qualified auditor's report would be required that would limit the auditor's opinion to recorded receipts.

Certain Revenues

Grants. An organization may receive grants from such outside organizations as the federal government or private foundations, requiring a determination that the resources are being used in accordance with the grant provisions. Federal agency grantors publish audit guides that govern the accounting for supported programs. Organizations receiving federal grants should follow the procedures prescribed by the guide as well as those specified in the grant agreement.

The audit concern is that if the grant is being used or accounted for improperly, the grantor may disallow certain costs and require the organization to make refunds. Many grants, especially from federal or state agencies, specify that the accounting records of the grantee organization are subject to audit by the grantor or a designated party.

Restricted Gifts. The auditing considerations for restricted gifts are somewhat similar to those for grants received by the organization. Investments received may also have restrictions placed on the use of the investment income. The auditor should read the original documents relating to the gifts, examine evidence supporting the amounts spent and the unexpended balance, and review reports sent to the donors. Because it is sometimes difficult to determine that the funds have been used for their restricted purpose, the auditor in those cases may need to obtain the opinion of legal counsel. Also, the auditor should be aware that restricted gifts are often refundable to the grantor if not essentially usable for the purpose intended or if the purpose of the gift has been attained without expending the entire gift.

Pledges. The major audit concern is whether pledges represent accounts receivable or whether they are contingent assets not to be recognized until actual receipt. The industry audit guides and SOP 78-10 (see Appendix 35-B) are not in agreement on the appropriate accounting treatment; refer to the appropriate pronouncement for specific guidance. If pledges are properly considered to be assets, audit procedures applicable to accounts receivable should be followed.

Donated Services. If the value of donated services is recorded in a nonprofit organization's financial statements, it can alter such key ratios as that of supporting services (general management expenses) to total contributions. However, the several pronouncements discussed in this chapter restrict the circumstances in which the value of these donations may be recorded. The auditor will want to review the nature and valuation of the donated services and perhaps confirm significant amounts with the donors.

Cost Reimbursement Programs. Some organizations, particularly hospitals, receive reimbursements of costs incurred for services provided. In many cases, receivables are recorded for these reimbursements, subject to final adjustments based on audit. The auditor should be familiar with the contractual arrangements with third-party payors. For reimbursements to hospitals, for example, the auditor should be familiar with the provisions of the *Medicare Audit Guide* (AICPA, 1969b), which discusses the unusual problems inherent in the auditing and reporting on statements of reimbursable costs.

The federal Office of Management and Budget (OMB) also issues circulars giving requirements for determination of costs under any federal grant or contract in which costs are used in pricing, administration, and settlement. Circular A-122, issued and effective on July 8, 1980, covers all nonprofit organizations except hospitals, colleges and universities (which are covered by Circular A-21), and state, local, and federally recognized Indian tribal governments (which are covered by Circular A-74-4).

In addition, the circular excludes from coverage over 30 specific nonprofit organizations that because of their size and nature of operations are considered similar to commercial concerns and are subject to cost principles included in either the Defense Acquisition Regulations (DAR) or the Federal Procurement Regulations (FPR), as appropriate.

The new cost principles are to be incorporated into new grants and contracts made after the start of the nonprofit organization's next fiscal year. Included in the principles are criteria for determining direct and indirect costs and allowability, allocability, and reasonableness of costs. In addition, 50 select items of frequently incurred costs are discussed as to the nature and circumstances of allowability.

Membership Dues. In a membership organization, dues usually are paid for a period of one year or longer, and this membership period may not coincide with the organization's fiscal year. Thus, part of the revenue from dues should be deferred until the period in which earned. In addition, some organizations have several membership levels, each requiring different dues amounts. All of this can create a formidable accounting task, particularly if the amount of deferred dues is material. In smaller organizations, the accounting may be accomplished by using a lapse schedule based on the period over which the dues are to be recorded as revenue. In larger organizations, the accounting may be done by computer, and the calculations can be tested by using statistical sampling techniques (see Chapter 14). This typically will involve reviewing the documents supporting the amount paid and the membership period and testing the amount deferred or, alternatively, the amount recorded as revenue.

Fixed Assets

Because nonprofit organizations have followed varied practices in capitalizing or not capitalizing fixed assets, many organizations may have maintained inadequate fixed asset documentation. If fixed assets have not been capitalized, initial capitalization often requires a physical inventory and valuation and the establishment of adequate internal controls. If historical costs of fixed assets are unknown, a specialist may be needed to appraise them. The auditor's responsibility in such a situation is outlined in SAS 11, *Using the Work of a Specialist* (AU 336).

Interfund Borrowings

Borrowings between funds, especially from a restricted fund to an unrestricted fund, can create auditing problems. If, for example, a borrowing violates legal prohibitions against interfund loans, the auditor may need to modify his report. The auditor should make sure that all interfund borrowings are disclosed and have been approved by the governing board.

Sometimes the collectibility of interfund loans is in doubt. For example, funds may have been "loaned" to a plant fund that has no ability to repay (except by disposing of the assets in the fund). The auditor might also question why a separate plant fund was created in the first place.

Functional Presentation of Expenses

The audit guides and SOP 78-10 generally require or encourage the presentation of expenses on a functional basis. For this purpose, the organization's cost accounting techniques should be sufficient to reasonably satisfy the auditor. However, the auditor should be aware that definitive guidelines for allocation procedures by nonprofit organizations are not included in the audit guides or SOP 78-10, and therefore a variety of allocation procedures will be encountered in practice.

Financially Interrelated Organizations

If a reporting organization controls another financially interrelated organization, it is presumed that the financial statements of the two organizations should be combined or consolidated. This issue has particular importance in relation to third-party reimbursements and allocations from federated fund-raising organizations, legislatures, and other groups. The key word is *control,* "the direct or indirect ability to determine the direction of the management and policies through ownership, by contract, or otherwise" (SOP 78-10, par. 42). For example, a separate fund-raising organization may have as its sole purpose raising money for a single charitable organization or hospital. The audit problem arises when there is no professed control over the fund-raising organization; the auditor may require access to the books and records of the legally separate organization in order to reach a satisfactory conclusion.

Taxes and Regulatory Reporting

Because (1) nonprofit organizations *may* be subject to taxes on certain types of income, (2) receiving tax-exempt status from the Internal Revenue Service does not automatically exempt the organization from state income taxes, (3) the organization must file periodic returns with regulatory authorities, and (4) the organization's returns filed with the IRS are subject to audit, the auditor should be alert to these matters during the examination.

Form 990, discussed in Appendix 35-A, calls for an accountant's signature. Because this form is available for public inspection, it has to be treated as a special report, and a separate accountant's report should be attached (AU 621.20-.21).

Single Audit Concept

In Circular A-102, the OMB prescribed uniform audit requirements for grantee organizations. These requirements are referred to as the *single audit concept* because they ensure that audits are made on an organization-wide basis rather than on a grant-by-grant basis. According to the circular (Attachment P):

Such audits are to determine whether (a) financial operations are conducted properly, (b) the financial statements are presented fairly, (c) the organization has complied with laws and regulations affecting the expenditure of Federal funds, (d) internal procedures have been established to meet the objectives of federally assisted programs, and (e) financial reports to the Federal Government contain accurate and reliable information. Except where specifically required by law, no additional requirements for audit will be imposed unless approved by the Office of Management and Budget.

Grantee audits are to be conducted in accordance with the GAO standards as described in Chapter 11.

Audit Guide for Certain Nonprofit Organizations

In July 1980 the AICPA released an exposure draft of a proposed guide, *The Audits of Certain Nonprofit Organizations*. Expected to be finalized early in 1981, the proposed guide parallels the accounting matters discussed in SOP 78-10 (see Appendix 35-B).

The earlier AICPA industry audit guides covered both accounting and auditing matters, since they were issued at a time when the AICPA had authority to establish GAAP. With this role now filled by an independent organization—the FASB—the AICPA can only recommend accounting standards to the FASB (this in fact is the status of SOP 78-10); but it can and does establish GAAS. Hence the separate publication of the proposed audit guide.

Certain of the subjects covered in the guide have been mentioned in the preceding paragraphs in this auditing section. The guide itself provides amplification on these and many other auditing matters peculiar to nonprofit organizations.

SUGGESTED READING

Batzer, R. Kirk. "Auditing Nonprofit Organizations." *CPA Journal,* August, 1979, pp. 21-25. This brief article gives a quick overview of some of the unique audit problems in nonprofit organizations.

Greif, Joseph, ed. *Managing Membership Societies.* Washington, D.C.: Foundation of the American Society of Association Executives, 1979. This booklet is a practical handbook for people who manage individual membership societies.

Gross, Malvern, and Warshauer, William. *Financial and Accounting Guide for Non-profit Organizations.* 3d ed. New York: John Wiley & Sons, 1979. This book is probably the most current and comprehensive reference in the field and has been updated to incorporate SOP 78-10.

Henke, Emerson. *Introduction to Nonprofit Organization Accounting.* Boston: Kent Publishing Co., 1980. This book presents a thorough overview of accounting practices, including practical uses of accounting data.

"Nonprofit Boards Under Fire." *Dun's Review,* October, 1979, pp. 108-113.

APPENDIX 35-A INCOME TAX EXEMPTIONS

There are currently 28 Internal Revenue Code classifications of organizations that *may* qualify for exemption from federal income taxation. These classifications, and the types of organizations included, are shown in this appendix. It should be remembered that

1. *Tax-exempt status is not automatic.* For most organizations, a form must be filed with the Internal Revenue Service, and each category has its own set of rules governing how the organization must operate. Also, as stated earlier, federal exempt status

does not automatically exempt the organization from state taxes, for which a separate application is ordinarily required.

2. *There are likely to be restrictions on the activities of the organization.* For example, there may be restrictions on (a) providing services at reduced rates to an individual when the reduced rates are not available to others receiving the service, (b) lobbying activities, or (c) participating in political campaigns.

3. *Taxes may be payable by a tax-exempt organization.* Although this may seem contradictory, a tax-exempt organization must pay taxes on income derived from activities not related to the organization's exempt purpose. Based on the type of organization, taxes *may* be payable for such *unrelated business income* as investment income, net advertising revenues, or income derived from debt-financed property.

4. *Most tax-exempt organizations are required to file annual returns with the Internal Revenue Service and state agencies.* For example, returns are required to be filed with the IRS on Form 990 for most organizations, Form 990-C for a farmers' cooperative, Form 990-PF for a private foundation, or Form 990-BL for Black Lung Benefit Trusts. Also, Form 990-T is used for exempt organizations with unrelated business income.

In addition to tax exemption, organizations *may* also qualify for low postal rates or for exemption from paying local sales taxes, and contributions received by the organization *may* be tax deductible by the contributor. However, these factors do indicate the obvious need for competent legal and tax advice by nonprofit organizations, and both accountants and auditors should be aware of these factors.

Federal Tax Exemption Classifications[3]

Code	Section	Type of Organization
501	(c)(1)	Corporation organized under act of Congress as a U.S. instrumentality
501	(c)(2)	Corporation organized for the exclusive purpose of holding property, with its net income turned over to an exempt organization
501	(c)(3)	Corporation and any community chest fund or foundation organized and operated exclusively for religious, charitable, scientific, testing for public safety, literary, or educational purposes; to foster national or international amateur sports competition (if none of its activities involve the providing of athletic facilities or equipment); or for the prevention of cruelty to children or animals.
501	(c)(4)	Civic league, an organization not organized for profit but operated exclusively for the promotion of social welfare, or a local association of employees whose members are employees of a particular municipality
501	(c)(5)	Labor, agricultural, or horticultural organization
501	(c)(6)	Business league, chamber of commerce, real estate board, board of trade, or professional football league

[3] Taken from Commerce Clearing House, Inc., *1980 U.S. Master Tax Guide* (Chicago, 1979).

Code	Section	Type of Organization
501	(c)(7)	Club organized for pleasure, recreation, and other nonprofit purposes
501	(c)(8)	Fraternal beneficiary society, order, or association
501	(c)(9)	Voluntary employees' beneficiary association
501	(c)(10)	Domestic fraternal society or association
501	(c)(11)	Teachers' retirement fund association
501	(c)(12)	Benevolent life insurance association, mutual ditch or irrigation company, or mutual or cooperative telephone company
501	(c)(13)	Cemetery company
501	(c)(14)	Credit union without capital stock
501	(c)(15)	Mutual insurance company or association other than life or marine
501	(c)(16)	Corporation organized by an association under Code Section 521 for the purpose of financing the ordinary crop operations
501	(c)(17)	A trust or trusts forming part of a nondiscriminatory plan providing for the payment of supplemental unemployment compensation benefits
501	(c)(18)	Nondiscriminatory employee pension trust or trusts created before June 25, 1959
501	(c)(19)	War veterans' organization or post
501	(c)(20)	Organization or trust forming part of a qualified group legal services plan under Code Section 140
501	(c)(21)	A trust established by coal operators for claims of compensation under the black lung acts
501	(c)(22)	Exempt function income of condominium and residential real estate management associations
501	(c)(23)	Political organization
501	(d)	Religious or apostolic association if it has a common or community treasury
501	(e)	Cooperative hospital service organization
501	(f)	Cooperative service organization for the collective investment of funds of operating educational organizations
527		Political action committees
530		Farmers' or fruit growers' cooperative

APPENDIX 35-B SUMMARY OF NONPROFIT ACCOUNTING PRINCIPLES

Entire books have been devoted to the accounting practices of particular types of nonprofit organizations, as well as to the practices of nonprofit organizations as a group. Although such detailed discussion is not possible here, it may be useful to summarize the accounting principles specified in AICPA SOP 78-10, which currently is the most comprehensive document dealing with accounting principles for nonprofit organizations.

This appendix presents the SOP content, contrasted with that of the three other audit guides discussed in this chapter, in the following categories; therefore the paragraph references do not always follow consecutively:

1. Financial statements
   a. General
   b. Comparative
   c. Combined
2. Assets
   a. Fixed assets
   b. Pledges
   c. Investments
3. Liabilities
4. Fund accounting
   a. General
   b. Interfund borrowings
   c. Annuity and life income funds
   d. Agency funds
   e. Funds held in trust by others
5. Revenues
   a. General
   b. Donated services, materials, and facilities
   c. Investment income
6. Expenses
   a. General
   b. Fund-raising costs
   c. Grants

SOP 78-10 does not alter the principles stated in the AICPA audit guides for hospitals, colleges and universities, and voluntary health and welfare organizations (or those for state and local governmental units covered in Chapter 34). In many respects the accounting in the guides and the SOP is the same, but in some important respects there are differences—the treatment of investments, fixed assets, and current restricted resources for example—requiring that the earlier guides be consulted for those kinds of organizations.

Many topics in SOP 78-10 are not discussed in the three other audit guides discussed in this chapter; for other topics SOP 78-10 and one or more of the audit guides differ. While certain variations might be expected because of the nature of the organization, it is possible that the FASB, as it extracts the accounting and principles from the various pronouncements for issuance as Statements of Financial Accounting Standards, will decide the appropriate practice to follow, so that standards will be uniform where there are no substantive differences.

In addition to the above guides and SOP 78-10, other SOPs deal with nongovernmental nonprofit organizations:

• SOP 74-8, *Financial Accounting and Reporting by Colleges and Universities,*
• SOP 78-1, *Accounting by Hospitals for Certain Marketable Equity Securities,* and
• SOP 78-7, *Financial Accounting and Reporting by Hospitals Operated by a Governmental Unit.*

These should be consulted in their specific topical areas.

SOP 78-10's Accounting Principles and Reporting Practices for Certain Nonprofit Organizations[4]

Topic	SOP 78-10 Par. No.	Key to Audit Guides
Financial Statements-General		
Accrual basis of accounting required for GAAP financial statements.	11	
Use cash basis statements for special purpose; report accordingly.	13	2, 3
Basic financial statements:	16, 25	5, 6, 7
1. Balance sheet		
2. Statement of activity		
3. Statement of changes in financial position		
4. Separate statement of changes in fund balance acceptable.	25	
Flexible format allowed.	18	
Use classified balance sheet if not otherwise indicated.	24	1
Totals of all fund groups is preferable, but not required.	40	5, 6, 7
Comparative Financial Statements		
Comparative statements encouraged, but not required. If information summarized, sufficient disclosure is required.	41	1
Combined Financial Statements		
Combined financial statements required for financially interrelated organizations if *control* and any of the following exist:	44	5, 6, 7
1. Separate entities solicit funds in the name of and with the approval of the reporting organization and funds are intended for the reporting organization.		
2. Reporting organization transfers some of its resources to another separate entity whose resources are held for the benefit of the reporting organization.		
3. The reporting organization assigns functions to a controlled entity whose funding is primarily derived from sources other than public contributions.		

---

[4] The numbers in the Key to Audit Guides column represent the following:
1—This topic is not discussed in any of the three industry audit guides.

This topic is not discussed in the industry audit guide for
2—Hospitals
3—Colleges and Universities
4—Voluntary Health and Welfare Organizations

This topic is treated differently in the industry audit guide for
5—Hospitals
6—Colleges and Universities
7—Voluntary Health and Welfare Organizations

If no reference is made to the audit guides, the guides and SOP 78-10 are substantially in agreement.

Topic	SOP 78-10 Par. No.	Key to Audit Guides
Disclose basis for combining and describe interrelationship of organization.	44	4
If related organizations hold unrestricted resources that are restricted to the reporting organization, it may be appropriate to present the resources as restricted in combined financial statements.	45	1
If affiliated organizations are not combined, disclosure should be made by the reporting organization of affiliation and relationships.	46	
If a religious organization concludes that meaningful financial information would not result from combined financial statements, they need not combine.	48	2, 4

Fixed Assets

Topic	SOP 78-10 Par. No.	Key to Audit Guides
Capitalize purchased fixed assets at cost; donated fixed assets at fair value at date of gift.	105	
Retroactively capitalize fixed assets at historical costs; if not available, use another basis (but only to adopt SOP).	105	
Depreciate exhaustible fixed assets over estimated useful lives and disclose depreciation.	107, 110	6
Nonexhaustible assets need not be capitalized or depreciated if cost records or values do not exist, but should be described in note.	108, 113	1
Depreciation need not necessarily be included in basis for grants, allocations, or reimbursements.	109	2, 3
Disclose the cost, or contributed value, of current additions and disposals.	114	1
Exhaustible collections that have a limited life should be capitalized and amortized over life.	115	1

Pledges

Topic	SOP 78-10 Par. No.	Key to Audit Guides
Record legally enforceable pledges as assets at their estimated realizable value, and recognize as "support" in period designated by donor and as "deferred support" if period extends past balance sheet date.	64, 65	5, 6, 7
Record pledges and restricted contributions and specifically related costs as deferred if related to succeeding periods.	95	3

Investments

Topic	SOP 78-10 Par. No.	Key to Audit Guides
Investments should be reported as follows:	116	5, 6, 7

1. Marketable debt securities (if ability and intention to hold to maturity) at amortized cost, market value, or lower of amortized cost or market value.
2. Marketable equity securities and marketable debt securities not expected to be held to maturity at either market value or lower of cost or market.
3. Other investments at fair value, or lower of cost or fair value.

Topic	SOP 78-10 Par. No.	Key to Audit Guides
4. Investment pools should equitably allocate realized and unrealized gains and losses on investments using market value unit method.		
If investments are carried at other than market, disclosure should be made of market value.	79	2, 3
Recognize adjustments due to unrealized gains or losses of a noncurrrent investment account as a direct addition or deduction to fund balance if account is carried at lower of cost or market.	80	6, 7
Reflect adjustments to current investment account due to unrealized gains and losses in the statement of activity if account is carried at lower of cost or market.	80	6
Reflect increases or decreases in investments carried at market in the period in which they occur.	81	3
Record interfund sales or exchanges involving restricted funds at fair value and the difference between the carrying amount and fair value as realized gains and losses.	82	
Disclose in notes a summary of total realized and unrealized gains and losses and income from investments by all funds, except life income and custodial funds.	83	
Liabilities		
Encumbrances are not liabilities.	12	2, 4
Significant commitments should be disclosed.	12	2, 4
Fund Accounting-General		
Fund basis of accounting acceptable to segregate restricted and unrestricted resources. If not fund basis, disclose restricted resources.	15	5, 6, 7
Board-designated amounts should be included in the unrestricted fund balance. Total of all unrestricted fund balances required.	20	
Plant fund may be reported separately or combined with *either* unrestricted or restricted fund as appropriate.	22	5, 6, 7
Current restricted resources and resources restricted for acquisition of fixed assets should be reported as "deferred revenue" until the restrictions are met.	21	5, 6, 7
Reflect other restricted resources (endowments) separately in fund balance. If significant, disclose nature of restriction on fund balances and deferred revenues.	22	
Changes in fund balance should include	25	4, 6
1. Excess or deficiency of revenue and support over expenses after capital additions.		
2. Adjustments in carrying amounts of noncurrent marketable securities and other investments.		
3. Interfund transfers.		
Noncurrent restricted gifts, grants, and bequests (including restricted investment income and gains and losses on investments)		

Topic	SOP 78-10 Par. No.	Key to Audit Guides
to endowment, plant, and loan funds should be recorded as "capital additions" or "nonexpendable additions."	28, 29	5, 6, 7
Interfund Borrowings		
Interfund transfers should be considered permanent, recorded as transfers, and disclosed when evident that repayment is not likely.	118	4, 5
Disclose material interfund borrowings when restricted funds have been loaned or if there is a liquidity problem.	119	2, 4
Interfund borrowings may be legally prohibited.	118	2, 4
Annuity and Life Income Funds		
Record annuity gifts as	121	2, 6, 7
1. Asset—not stated.		
2. Liability—present value of actuarially determined liability at date of gift.		
3. Difference—if expendable, support in year of gift; if not expendable, deferred revenue.		
The principal of life income gifts should be recorded as deferred support in the balance sheet when received.	121	4, 5, 6
Record annuity or life income gifts as support or capital additions when specified terms are met.	121	4, 5, 6
Agency Funds		
Separate or combined disclosure of agency funds.	123	4, 5, 6
Funds Held in Trust by Others		
Funds held in trust by others, not controlled by the organization, and for which the organization is not the remainderman, should not be included in the balance sheet even though income is derived from the funds. Disclosure should be made of the funds and any significant income derived from them.	122	4, 6
Revenue-General		
Statement of activity should have an "excess (deficiency) of revenues and support over expenses" line. If presenting "capital additions," use two "excess" lines, one before and one after.	30	5, 6, 7
Record unrestricted gifts, grants, and bequests in the statement of activity above "excess" line before capital additions.	63	5, 6, 7
Separate disclosure not necessary of contributions to organizations by governing board members, officers, or employees if contributor receives no reciprocal economic benefit.	49	1
Current restricted gifts, grants, bequests, and other income should be recognized based on the following concepts:	59	
1. Economic events.		
2. Donor restrictions are complied with when organization incurs an expense in the manner specified in donative instrument.		

Topic	SOP 78-10 Par. No.	Key to Audit Guides
3. Unexpended restricted funds should be reported in a manner reflecting restrictions.		
Current restricted gifts, grants, bequests, and other income should be accounted for as revenue and support to the extent that expenses have been incurred for donor-specified purpose. Present "deferred revenue or support" in the balance sheet, outside the fund balance section, until restrictions are met.	62	5, 6, 7
Recognize subscriptions and revenues from services and sales of goods in period provided.	84	
Recognize membership dues in period to which dues relate.	84	1
Recognize nonrefundable initiation and life membership dues as revenue in period it is receivable, *if* future fees will cover future services. If not, amortize fees to future periods based on average membership duration, life expectancy or other appropriate method.	84	1

Donated Services, Material, and Facilities

Topic	SOP 78-10 Par. No.	Key to Audit Guides
Donated or contributed services should not be recorded as contribution and expense unless	63	
1. The services are a significant, integral part of the organization that would otherwise be performed by salaried personnel.		
2. The organization controls and influences duties of the service donors.		
3. There is a clearly measurable basis for the recorded amount.		
4. The services are not intended principally for the benefit of members.		
Disclosure is required of methods used in valuing, recording, and reporting donated services and of those donated services not recorded or reported.	70	5
Record, at fair value, only significant donated materials and facilities that are clearly measurable and that are not passed on to another group.	71	

Investment Income

Report investment income as follows:

Topic	SOP 78-10 Par. No.	Key to Audit Guides
1. Unrestricted—revenue when earned.	72	
2. Restricted—deferred in balance sheet.	73	5, 6, 7
3. Endowment—if required to be added to principal, capital addition; if expendable, deferred amounts.	73	5, 6, 7

Report investment gains and losses as follows:

Topic	SOP 78-10 Par. No.	Key to Audit Guides
1. Unrestricted and current restricted—in statement of activity before "capital additions."	72	5, 6, 7
2. Endowments—as "capital additions" or "deductions" if required to be added to principal; if utilized, record as transfer from endowments to other.	73, 76	5, 6, 7
3. Other restricted—as deferred amounts in balance sheet.	72	5, 6, 7
If endowment gains or losses are transferred to a restricted fund to which investment income is reported as deferred revenue, gain should be transferred to deferred revenue.	76	5, 6, 7

Topic	SOP 78-10 Par. No.	Key to Audit Guides
Account for net gains on investments in quasi endowment funds the same as for current funds.	76	2, 4, 6

Expenses-General

Topic	SOP 78-10 Par. No.	Key to Audit Guides
A summary of the cost of providing services on a functional basis in the statement of activity is required when the public contributes; if services are not presented on functional basis, notes should describe programs.	85	
Functional classification should include program services describing activities and supporting services.	86	2, 3
Costs should be presented separately for each significant program and supporting activity.	87	
Local organizations that are collecting agents for a state or national organization should report the remittance as a deduction from support and revenue; otherwise, such remittances are program expenses.	90	2, 3
Costs pertaining to various functions should be allocated if applicable.	98	2
Interperiod allocation of taxes should be made if timing differences exist between the income base for tax and financial reporting purposes.	103	3, 4

Fund-Raising Costs

Topic	SOP 78-10 Par. No.	Key to Audit Guides
Fund-raising costs, including cost of merchandise sold, should be disclosed; if paid directly by a contributor, report as support and expense.	92	2, 5
Special fund-raising events should be reported net of direct benefit costs, with disclosure of costs.	93	3, 5
Total of all fund-raising activities should be disclosed; fund-raising costs should be expensed when incurred.	94	6

Grants

Topic	SOP 78-10 Par. No.	Key to Audit Guides
Costs incurred in solicitation of grants from foundations or governments and cost of membership development should be shown in separate categories of supporting expense.	96	4, 6
Grants made to others should be recorded as expenses and liabilities when recipient is entitled to it.	101	1
Grants subject to periodic renewal should be recorded when renewed.	102	1
If the grantor reserves the right to revoke the grant regardless of the performance of the grantee, unpaid grants should not be recorded as an expense and liability.	102	1

36

Regulated Industries

Arthur L. Litke

REGULATION IN THE U.S. ECONOMY

The economy of the United States has become increasingly subject to regulation by all levels of government—federal, state, and local—through a bewildering variety of regulatory agencies. Though each agency has its own scope and statutory purposes, a study by the Congressional Budget Office (1976) recognized three broad types of regulation (pp. 15-16): (1) that which affects the operating business environment of broad sectors of private enterprise, including market entry and exit; rate, price, and profit structures; and competition; (2) that which affects specific commodities, products, or services through permit, certification, or licensing requirements; and (3) that which involves the development, administration, and enforcement of national standards. Such national standards, if violated, are grounds for the imposition of civil or criminal penalties.

Most regulation is justified on one of two grounds: to alleviate the effects of market failure or to meet social policy objectives. Natural monopoly, destructive competition, and inadequate information in the marketplace are examples of market failure. Providing air, bus, or public utility services to small communities is a typical social policy objective.

To carry out their mission, many regulatory agencies have been given the authority to require specific accounting or financial reporting practices by the industries they regulate. The financial information yielded by these practices is frequently used to determine the cost of services provided by the regulated companies and the adequacy of their return on investment. This is the basis of rate regulation, the main focus of this chapter. Prominent among the rate-regulated industries are public utilities and common carriers, discussed generally in this chapter, and financial institutions, discussed extensively in Chapter 38. More specifically, the following nonfinancial institutions are usually rate regulated at the federal, state, and/or local level:

1. Communication
   a. Radiotelephonic carriers
   b. Telephone
   c. Wire telegraph and ocean cable carriers
2. Energy
   a. Electric power
   b. Gas distribution
   c. Natural gas pipelines
   d. Natural gas production
   e. Oil pipelines
   f. Oil production
3. Transportation
   a. Air carriers
   b. Common and contract water carriers of passengers
   c. Freight forwarders
   d. Inland and coastal waterway carriers
   e. Maritime carriers
   f. Motor freight carriers
   g. Railroads
   h. Refrigerator car lines
   i. Taxis
4. Other
   a. Health care
   b. Sewerage
   c. Water supply.

The principal federal regulatory agencies that prescribe specific accounting or financial reporting requirements, whether for rate-setting or other purposes, are

1. *Civil Aeronautics Board* (CAB). Established under the Civil Aeronautics Act of 1938 for the purpose of regulating the civil air transport industry within the United States and between the United States and foreign countries. Numerous modifications in its authority were made by the Airline Deregulation Act of 1978.

2. *Commodity Futures Trading Commission* (CFTC). Created in 1974 to regulate all agricultural and other commodities traded on commodity exchanges.

3. *Economic Regulatory Administration* (ERA). Created in 1977 as part of the Department of Energy. Regulates oil pricing.

4. *Energy Information Administration* (EIA). Created in 1977 as part of the Department of Energy. Collects and processes financial information of energy-producing companies.

5. *Federal Communications Commission* (FCC). Established by the Communications Act of 1934 and given expanded jurisdiction by the Communications Satellite Act of 1962. The scope of regulation includes radio and television broadcasting, telephone, telegraph, cable television, and satellite communications. Accounting jurisdiction applies only to telephone, wire telegraph, ocean cable, and radiotelephonic carriers. Congress is currently considering revision of the various communications-related acts.

6. *Federal Energy Regulatory Commission* (FERC). Established in 1977 as an independent agency within the Department of Energy, succeeding the former Federal Power Commission (FPC) established in 1920. FERC inherited FPC's regulatory responsibilities for the electric power and natural gas industries, while responsibility for oil pipelines was transferred to FERC from the Interstate Commerce Commission.

7. *Federal Maritime Commission* (FMC). Created in 1961 to regulate the waterborne foreign and domestic offshore commerce of the United States.

8. *Federal Trade Commission* (FTC). Created in 1914 to enforce antitrust laws. In its surveillance of industry, the FTC requires the filing of certain financial information, such as line-of-business reports (see Chapter 32).

9. *Interstate Commerce Commission* (ICC). Established in 1887. Broadly regulates surface transportation economics and service, including trucking companies, bus lines, freight forwarders, water carriers, transportation brokers, and railroads. Regulatory responsibilities were modified by the Motor Carrier Act of 1980 and the Staggers Rail Act of 1980. The latter act established the Railroad Accounting Principles Board.

10. *Rural Electrification Administration* (REA). Created in 1935 to finance electric and telephone facilities in rural areas of the United States.

11. *Securities and Exchange Commission* (SEC). Created in 1934 to provide the fullest possible disclosure to the investing public and to protect the interest of the public and investors against dishonesty in the securities and financial markets. The Public Utility Holding Company Act of 1935 provides for regulation by the SEC of the purchase and sale of securities and assets by electric and gas utility holding companies. These companies generally follow the FERC uniform system of accounts. SEC also promulgates accounting rules and disclosure requirements that must be followed by companies registered with the commission (see Chapter 41).

All the states, and some local governments, have also established agencies to regulate the intrastate or local aspects of the federally regulated industries. In addition, state and local governments regulate some industries not regulated by the federal government, such as sewerage, taxi, and water supply companies. The number of commissioners per state varies from one to seven, with most states having three; they serve staggered terms of from three to ten years. About one third of the states elect their commissioners; in other states they are appointed by the governor with the consent of the state senate.

To reduce conflict between the federal and state regulatory agencies and to promote coordinated regulatory efforts, federal enabling legislation requires or encourages communication between agencies at both levels (e.g., 47 U.S.C. 221(1) telegraphs, telephones, and radiotelegraphs). For regulated public utilities and common carriers, this function is performed by the *National Association of Regulatory Utility Commissioners* (NARUC). Established in 1889 by the commissioners of the federal and state agencies responsible for the regulation of these enterprises, NARUC promotes, among other things, uniformity of regulation and cooperation among the agencies. The NARUC Committee on Accounts, and its staff subcommittee composed of selected chief accounting officials of various regulatory bodies, specifically aim for common understanding of the accounting, and occasionally of the rate treatment, appropriate for specific kinds of transactions.

ACCOUNTING FOR REGULATED COMPANIES

Uniformity

Uniformity in accounting and financial reporting was considered important early in the development of economic regulation. In 1866, for example, Massachusetts directed its Board of Railroad Commissioners to prescribe a system in which the accounts of corporations operating railroads of street railways would be kept in a uniform manner.

Companies had followed their own diverse accounting and financial reporting systems prior to regulation. This diversity made it difficult to determine, on a national basis, that reliable and consistent financial information was available for regulatory purposes. Thus, most regulatory agencies were given authority to prescribe both a *uniform system of accounts* (USOA) and reporting requirements. Where authority has not been given for a USOA, a uniform reporting system with detailed instructions, as required by the EIA, may indirectly result in a uniform accounting system.

Since each state has one or more regulatory commissions that have responsibilities similar to those of the federal agencies but on an intrastate level, the state commissions also prescribe USOAs. In many instances the state USOA is identical to that issued by a federal regulatory agency or by NARUC. When an industry is regulated by both federal and state agencies, the required financial reporting and accounting is frequently coordinated but may differ in some ways. For reporting to federal agencies and for external reporting, the federal position prevails. The FERC (FPC) asserted jurisdiction over financial reporting to the public by requiring financial reports to conform to its USOA. This position was affirmed by the U.S. Court of Appeals in *Appalachian Power Company vs. Federal Power Commission,* 328 F.2nd 237 (4th Cir. 1964), *cert. denied,* 379 U.S. 829 (1964). Under certain provisions of the Railroad Revitalization and Regulatory Reform Act of 1976 (4-R Act), the SEC asserted jurisdiction over financial reporting to the public by all regulated companies. The FERC has neither admitted nor denied SEC jurisdiction in this area. Reporting by FERC-regulated companies has not changed since passage of the 4-R Act.

Some federal agencies, such as the ICC, require companies to explain, in stockholders' reports, differences between the financial reporting to stockholders and that in accordance with the agency's USOA. However, the ICC has revised its general regulations to semiautomatically adopt the accounting profession's authoritative GAAP. Apart from depreciation versus betterment accounting for railroads, discussed later, there now are few differences between ICC requirements and GAAP for nonregulated industries.

Relationship to Rate Making

The accounting processes and procedures prescribed by the USOA supply information about the financial position and operating results of a company, including the cost of its property, its revenues and expenses, its capital structure, its return on investment, and data on its nonregulated operations. In addition, most USOAs provide for accumulating data necessary to develop the basis for rates that regulated companies can charge their customers and data used to support petitions for rate changes. This is particularly true for companies whose rates are regulated on an individual basis (such as electric or gas utilities) and to a lesser degree for companies whose rates are set on a group basis (e.g., buses).

According to most authorities, the primary aim of the rate-making process is to determine the minimum rate of return that will permit a utility to pay its legitimate operating expenses, compensate its existing investors, and attract new capital. To carry out this function, federal and state agencies have been granted what is often described as *legislative authority.* This implies that rate determinations are not subject to review in the courts unless they are unconstitutional or clearly unsupported by the evidence.

For individual enterprises, rate making is usually approached from a return-on-investment concept. This concept involves determining the company's *cost of service* (also known as revenue requirements). Cost of service includes all expenses *necessary* to provide the required service, including operation and maintenance, depreciation, amortization expenses, taxes, and an allowance for the use of capital. The allowance for capital is calculated by applying a rate of return to the *rate base,* which usually consists of the original cost of the tangible fixed properties used in serving the public plus operating materials and supplies and an allowance for working capital less accumulated depreciation and deferred taxes.

The *rate of return* is a composite rate that reflects the cost of capital and includes cost of debt, preferred stock, and provision for a return on common equity securities or their equivalents. *Original cost* is the amount expended up to the time property and plant are *first* placed in public service. If the same property is purchased by another utility, the purchaser must record the property at the seller's depreciated original cost, with any excess being recorded as an acquisition adjustment (Suelflow,

1973, pp. 28, 165-167, and 196). Depending on the circumstances, this adjustment can be amortized and included in the cost of service or written off as a non-
recoverable cost for rate-making purposes.

By a process known as *rate design*, the cost of service is translated into rates,
which are usually prospective, for specific services. For companies subject to group
rate making, rates are approved or established for a particular type or class of
service on an industry-wide basis. The rates are designed to cover the industry's
cost in general.

The rate-making process is an adversary proceeding, and all elements of the cost
of service are subject to challenge and judicial review. Normally the most controversial element is the determination of the rate of return. Judicial review of many
cases has established the general guideline that the rate of return must be just and
reasonable, which, to a large degree, is a matter of considered judgment. This
principle was first established by the U.S. Supreme Court in the *Bluefield* case[1]
(and reaffirmed in the *Hope* case[2]), in which the court stated that "return . . . should
be commensurate with risks on investments in other enterprises having corresponding risks [and] should be sufficient to assure confidence in the financial
integrity of the enterprise, so as to maintain its credit and to attract capital."

Accounting Principles

Companies subject to rate regulation account for certain transactions differently
than unregulated companies do. Most of these differences can be attributed directly
to circumstances peculiar to the rate-making process, in which government agencies
have the authority to permit, defer, or deny the recognition of revenues and costs
in establishing rates.

The statutes authorizing the establishment of USOAs by regulatory agencies
usually do not refer to GAAP, but accounting prescribed by USOAs conforms, for
the most part, to the financial accounting standards issued by the FASB. The CAB
and ICC have revised their general regulations to provide for semiautomatic adoption of FASB statements as part of their USOAs. Other federal agencies go through
rule-making procedures before modifying their USOAs to incorporate new accounting pronouncements.

Differences in the application of GAAP between regulated and nonregulated
enterprises, though relatively few in number and generally resulting from the time
at which certain elements of revenues and costs are recognized, often have a very
material impact on the financial statements of regulated companies. The unique
aspects of applying accounting principles to companies whose rates are established
by government agencies were formally recognized by the accounting profession
more than 20 years ago; since 1962, such problems have been subject to the broad
guidance provided by the APB in its addendum to APB Opinion No. 2, *Accounting
Principles for Regulated Industries* (AC 6011).

---

[1] *Bluefield Water Works and Improvement Co. v. Public Service Commission of West Virginia*, 262 U.S. 679 (1923).

[2] *Federal Power Commission v. Hope Natural Gas Co.*, 320 U.S. 591 (1944).

The APB 2 Addendum. In substance, the addendum (AC 6011) provides that

- GAAP pertains to business enterprises in general, including "public utilities, common carriers, insurance companies, financial institutions and the like," that are subject to government regulation.
- Differences may arise in the application of GAAP because of the rate-making process. "Such differences usually concern mainly the time at which various items enter into the determination of net income in accordance with the principle of matching costs and revenues."
- To reflect the results of a rate-making process, a cost "may be deferred in the balance sheet [but] only when it is clear that the cost will be recoverable out of future revenues, and it is not appropriate when there is doubt, because of economic conditions or for other reasons, that the cost will be so recoverable."
- The imposition by regulatory agencies of accounting requirements not directly related to the rate-making process does not necessarily mean that those requirements conform to GAAP.
- "The financial statements of regulated businesses other than those prepared for filing with the government for regulatory purposes preferably should be based on generally accepted accounting principles (with appropriate recognition of rate-making considerations . . .)."
- "In reporting on the financial statements of regulated businesses, the independent auditor should . . . deal with material variances from generally accepted accounting principles (with appropriate recognition of rate-making considerations . . .), if the financial statements reflect any such variances, in the same manner as in his reports on nonregulated businesses."

These broad guidelines have been interpreted in different ways, leading to confusion in their application. A source of concern has been the vagueness regarding the specific industries to which the guidelines should apply. Also, a difference of opinion still exists as to the appropriate accounting principles to be followed in presenting general purpose financial statements for external use. The question is: Do financial statements prepared in conformity with accounting principles prescribed by regulatory agencies—principles that differ materially in some respects from those followed by nonregulated enterprises—provide sufficient information for external users (i.e., financial analysts and investors) who lack the authority to require specific financial information? Or should GAAP be followed in all instances in financial statements intended for use by the public?

Effect on GAAP for regulated industries. Under provisions of the addendum, regulated businesses are required to follow GAAP in financial reporting to the public and in filings with the SEC. Apart from a relatively uniform format within each regulated industry, influenced no doubt by the USOAs, the only variations that can be in conformity with GAAP are

1. The deferral under the addendum of an expense or a benefit that would otherwise be included in income determination under GAAP but it is clear the regulatory authority will match with future revenue or expense, and

2. Intercompany profit not eliminated as to manufacturing or construction subsidiaries, "to the extent that such profit is substantially equivalent to a reasonable return on investment . . ." (AC 2051.07).

The question of deferral of expense or benefit under the addendum—a seemingly minor point in the volumes of accounting literature—has caused much debate about GAAP accounting for matters discussed in the next section of this chapter. The addendum is considered applicable to all codified accounting pronouncements, though it is not specifically mentioned in all of them (e.g., generally where the subject matter seems unrelated). The basis for the addendum and its scope have come under increasing discussion because of varying interpretations of its applicability as well as of the circumstances in which it will be used. For example, in Release No. 33-5812, the SEC stated that the effect of the addendum on disclosure of capital leases is not clear. The SEC added that some believe the addendum relates solely to the income statement and that leases should be capitalized on the balance sheet, while others believe the addendum applies to all financial statements and that lease capitalization is not required.

FASB Discussion Memorandum. As a result of this and other questions concerning the addendum, the FASB began an in-depth study of accounting for rate-regulated industries. The FASB issued *Discussion Memorandum on Effect of Rate Regulation on Accounting for Regulated Enterprises* (FASB, 1979b), which was designed to

- Determine whether there are circumstances that would support a different application of GAAP by regulated enterprises in general purpose financial statements.
- Identify any such circumstances, principally those resulting from rate making, and determine any impact they should have on the identification and measurement of assets, liabilities, revenues, and expenses.
- Establish criteria for recognizing circumstances that should be reflected in the application of GAAP by regulated enterprises.

To determine whether additional interpretation or clarification of the addendum or a new pronouncement on accounting for regulated enterprises is needed, the FASB solicited views on nearly 40 specific issues set forth in the discussion memorandum. The threshold issue is whether accounting prescribed by regulatory agencies should, in and of itself, be considered "generally accepted" for purposes of presenting general purpose financial statements by rate-regulated enterprises. The discussion memorandum explores certain circumstances in which an economic dimension introduced by rate regulation might affect the application of GAAP to rate-regulated enterprises.

A public hearing on the discussion memorandum was held in May 1980. After the FASB has considered the views of interested parties on the issues, it will release an exposure draft recommending the accounting principles to be followed and the manner in which they should be applied. The FASB plans an exposure draft in late 1981 and a final statement in 1982.

ACCOUNTING ISSUES IN REGULATED INDUSTRIES

Among the most significant accounting issues that result from the regulation of rates are deferred taxes, allowance for funds used during construction, intercompany profits, fuel cost adjustment clauses, betterment accounting, operating rights, leasing, reacquired long-term debt, original cost and acquisition adjustments, research and development costs, and the effects of inflation. Each of these issues is discussed in the following pages.[3]

Deferred Taxes

One of the most complex and controversial of all regulated industry accounting issues is deferred taxes. (See Chapter 25 for a broad discussion of income tax accounting; this section focuses on regulated industry aspects.) Tax timing differences resulting from the use of accelerated depreciation for tax purposes and straight-line depreciation for accounting purposes, and other differences, such as the tax deduction of capitalized interest, are the usual causes of deferred taxes. Regulated utilities are generally required to use straight-line depreciation for accounting and rate-making purposes. Accelerated depreciation is a tax provision designed to help expand and modernize the nation's productive facilities by providing an economic benefit through the time value of money made available by the postponement of tax payments. The investment tax credit is another tax feature enacted for the same purpose, but instead of postponing tax payments, it provides permanent tax savings.

The controversy surrounding deferred taxes centers on rate making and the debate over *normalized* versus *flow-through* treatment of tax timing differences. The question is: Should utilities include in the cost of service only those taxes payable in a certain year (flow-through), or should the cost of service reflect the accrual (normalization) of taxes as based on recorded revenues and expenses, including book depreciation? Also at issue is the manner in which permanent tax savings, such as the investment tax credit, are treated for rate-making purposes.

The term *timing difference* is defined in APB 11 (AC 4091.12(e)) as

differences between the periods in which transactions affect taxable income and the periods in which they enter into the determination of pretax accounting income. Timing differences originate in one period and reverse or "turn around" in one or more subsequent periods.

The total amount of plant cost that can be depreciated is not increased by the tax incentives giving rise to tax timing differences; only the timing of the depreciation of tax basis and the timing of tax payments are changed.

---

[3] Other accounting issues not commented on here include depreciation, unbilled revenues, consolidated taxes, off–balance sheet financing (other than leases), extraordinary losses, prior-period adjustments, projections, extractive industry accounting, pension costs, investments in common stocks, deferred excess plant capacity, and deferred maintenance.

Accounting for Normalization. The accounting for the normalization of tax timing differences, as adopted in APB 11, calls for an accounting provision for income tax expense at the statutory tax rate, based on pretax accounting income. APB 11 (AC 4091.33) states:

> The tax effects of those transactions which enter into the determination of pretax accounting income either earlier or later than they become determinants of taxable income should be recognized in the periods in which the differences between pretax accounting income and taxable income arise and in the periods in which the differences reverse.

The difference between income tax expense and income taxes that are currently payable is accounted for in a balance sheet account for deferred taxes.

Some regulated industries account for accelerated tax deductions by recording the deferred tax provisions as additional book depreciation, with a corresponding credit to the reserve for accumulated depreciation. This practice has no different effect on net income and properly recognizes the consumption of the asset's tax-reducing ability. The Wisconsin Public Service Commission has prescribed this method for many years.

The accounting for the normalization of the investment tax credit, as adopted in APB 2 (AC 4094), called for establishing a deferred credit and amortizing it to income over the service life of the related property. APB 4 (AC 4094) reaffirmed the accounting profession's preference for amortization, but also permitted the flow-through of the credit in the year taken. In 1975, Congress increased the maximum investment tax credit for utilities from 4% to 10%, and forbade regulatory agencies from requiring utilities to flow through the additional 6% credit.

Conceptual Basis for Normalization. Proponents of normalization for rate-regulatory purposes argue that inherent in an asset are its abilities to generate revenues by producing a product and, through depreciation or amortization, to reduce income taxes otherwise payable. When an asset's tax basis is consumed more rapidly, as through accelerated depreciation, an additional cost is incurred equal to the tax effect of the tax deferral. This cost is recognized through normalization as an expense for cost-of-service purposes during the period in which the tax basis is consumed more rapidly. Proponents also argue that the economic substance of a utility or business transaction should be distinguished from the timing of cash payments for related taxes. The economic substance of transactions is realized by applying the statutory tax rate to all transactions passing through an income statement for a given period, including accounting depreciation.

Proponents of normalization further argue that the flow-through of tax timing differences to current customers will increase revenue requirements in the future. This increase occurs when accounting depreciation exceeds tax depreciation (a reversal of the timing difference), resulting in increased taxable income. This presumes that regulatory commissions will permit utilities to charge future users for the higher revenue requirements needed to pay the additional taxes then flowing through as a result of the increased taxable income. Companies and their auditors have learned that prior flow-through practices of a commission cannot be relied on, particularly in view of the extreme rate-making pressures brought about by escalating energy costs.

Effect of Normalization on Cash Flow and Capital Costs. Through normalization of tax timing differences (and deferral and amortization of the investment credit), utilities are, in effect, provided an increase in funds available for construction and other purposes. This increase in interest-free funds reduces the requirements for other sources of capital, thereby reducing capital costs. Moreover, the rate base is usually reduced by the amount of deferred taxes, thereby reducing revenue requirements from customers. The Tax Reform Act of 1969 and the Revenue Act of 1971 affirmed the intent of Congress to make funds available for plant construction and modernization by prohibiting utilities from flowing through, for ratemaking purposes, the tax benefits of accelerated depreciation, the asset depreciation range (ADR,) and the investment tax credit. These acts also prevented the loss of tax revenues to the Treasury that would occur from the combined effects of accelerated depreciation and ADR for tax purposes and reduced utility revenue under flow-through; it was deemed unlawful for utilities to take advantage of tax benefits such as liberalized tax depreciation if regulatory authorities required utilities to flow through the benefits to current customers. Only utilities that were already using flow-through were allowed to continue this method. Almost all federal and state regulatory authorities currently allow some degree of tax normalization for rate-making purposes, with a limited number of authorities allowing normalization of all tax timing differences.

In a case that may ultimately have broad national significance, the California Public Utilities Commission ruled in September 1977 that two major telephone companies in California must flow through to customers some of the benefits of certain federal tax provisions and refund certain overcollections from customers in prior years.[4] The two telephone companies began using accelerated tax depreciation and taking the investment tax credit following the Tax Reform Act of 1969 and the Tax Revenue Act of 1971. The commission's decision was upheld by the courts, and the two companies began refunding overcollections to customers in 1980. The U.S. Department of Treasury believes the refunds defeat the objectives of the Tax Reform Act of 1969 and the Revenue Act of 1971. As a result, the Internal Revenue Service is assessing back taxes that potentially could approach $2 billion for the two companies combined.

Accounting for Flow-Through. The flow-through method of accounting for tax timing differences and the investment tax credit recognizes as a cost only the amount of taxes that is currently payable. The funds provided by the deferral or reduction of current taxes are passed or flowed through to current customers by means of a reduction in cost of service, which is reduced further by the lowered tax effects of the lowered revenue requirements. Assuming an income tax rate of 50%, revenue requirements are reduced in the earlier years of a utility plant's life by twice the reduction in taxes payable resulting from accelerated tax depreciation or from claiming the investment tax credit (see Figure 36.1).

Flow-through proponents principally hold that current reductions in income taxes payable represent a permanent tax savings because utilities will never pay the amount of the current tax reduction. This argument is based on the historical

---

[4] Decision No. 87838, September 13, 1977 (82 Cal. PUC 549).

record of continual increase in the plant expenditures of many utilities and on the assumption that such growth will continue, even without considering inflation. The accumulated deferred taxes will not decline so long as plant expenditures continue to increase and tax laws are not changed or tax rates reduced. Thus, advocates of flow-through accounting argue that current customers should not be charged for a provision for deferred taxes. To charge current customers for income taxes that are never paid, they say, is tantamount to charging customers for phantom costs.

The argument that current reductions in income taxes payable actually represent permanent tax savings is challenged by flow-through's critics on the grounds that this conclusion ignores the recording of depreciation deductions and accruals for deferred taxes by vintage year of property addition. Although the accumulated deferred taxes may increase in the aggregate, the accruals applicable to earlier vintages of property are declining while the accruals for later vintages of property are increasing.

Normalization Versus Flow-Through: Comparison of Effects. The effects of normalized and flow-through treatment of liberalized tax depreciation are compared in Figure 36.1. It is assumed that an asset was purchased at the beginning of the year for $100 million, that its estimated life is ten years, and that no salvage value is expected. The sum-of-the-years'-digits method of accelerated depreciation is used for tax purposes. Figures are for the first year only.

As Figure 36.1 shows, revenue requirements in the first year are $7,551,000 less under flow-through than under normalization or straight-line tax depreciation. The combined effects of accelerated depreciation and reduced utility rates under flow-through are illustrated in the calculations of federal income tax. The tax is $3,927,000 less under normalization, and $7,551,000 less under flow-through, than under straight-line tax depreciation. It is this loss of tax revenue, occasioned by the combined effects of accelerated depreciation and reduced utility rates under flow-through, that led Congress to make it unlawful for utilities to take advantage of tax benefits if regulatory authorities require utilities to flow through the benefits to current customers.

Regulatory Treatment of Several Income Tax Differences. The rate-making treatment by state regulatory authorities and the accounting treatment by federal regulatory authorities for various income tax provisions are summarized in Figure 36.2. The FCC's rate-making treatment for liberalized depreciation and the investment tax credit is the same as the accounting treatment. Rate-making treatment for the asset depreciation range is still pending. The FERC's accounting treatment requires that normalization be followed to the extent that normalization is followed in rate making.

Continued Congressional Interest. The Oversight Subcommittee of the House Ways and Means Committee held hearings in 1979 on various tax-related issues, including a review of whether normalization or flow-through of the investment tax credit and tax benefits of accelerated depreciation is the most appropriate for public utilities. Representatives of NARUC testified in favor of flow-through, while representatives of the Edison Electric Institute (an electric power industry trade group), the American Gas Association (a gas industry trade group), and the U.S. Department of Energy and Department of the Treasury testified in favor of nor-

Cost of Service	Straight-Line Tax Depreciation	Accelerated Tax Depreciation		
		Normalized	Flow-Through	Difference
Operating income:				
Return and taxes	$53,290,000	$53,290,000	$45,739,000	$7,551,000*
Federal income				
taxes, actual	(15,290,000)	(11,363,000)	(7,739,000)	(3,624,000)
Net operating				
income	38,000,000	41,927,000	38,000,000	(3,927,000)
Less provision				
for deferred				
income taxes	—	(3,927,000)	—	(3,927,000)
Return	$38,000,000	$38,000,000	$38,000,000	$ —
Federal income tax				
calculation:				
Operating income	$53,290,000	$53,290,000	$45,739,000	$7,551,000
Less regular				
income tax				
deductions,				
excluding				
depreciation	(11,408,000)	(11,408,000)	(11,408,000)	—
Subtotal	41,882,000	41,882,000	34,331,000	7,551,000
Less straight-				
line depre-				
ciation	10,000,000	—	—	—
Less accelerated				
depreciation	—	18,180,000	18,180,000	—
Taxable income	31,882,000	23,702,000	16,151,000	7,551,000
Income tax				
at 48%	15,303,500	11,376,500	7,752,500	3,624,000
Less surtax	(13,500)	(13,500)	(13,500)	—
Federal income tax	$15,290,000	$11,363,000	$7,739,000	$3,624,000

* $3,927,000 ÷ .52 = $7,551,000

FIGURE 36.1 COMPARISON OF THE EFFECTS OF NORMALIZATION VS. FLOW-THROUGH

	Liberalized Depreciation	Asset Depreciation Range	Investment Tax Credit	Pollution Control Facilities
CAB[a]	N	N	E	U
FCC[b]	E	E	E	U
FERC[c]	N	N	N	N
ICC[b]	N	E	E	U
States:[d]				
Normalized	28	20	32	22
Actual or				
flow-through	5	10	3	3
Either	15	15	13	8
Not addressed				
or not				
decided	3	6	3	19

KEY: N = Normalized; E = Either normalized or actual; U = Undecided or not addressed.

[a] Effective 1 January 1978.
[b] Effective 1 October 1977.
[c] Effective 1 April 1978.
[d] Statistics from National Association of Regulatory Utility Commissioners, *1978 Annual Report on Utility and Carrier Regulation*, edited by Geneva Beierlein, Washington, D.C., 1979.

NOTE: Some authorities have allowed, on a case-by-case basis, exceptions to prescribed rules of treatment. As a result, statistics may be only generally correct.

FIGURE 36.2   REGULATORY TREATMENT OF SEVERAL INCOME TAX DIFFERENCES

malization. NARUC testified that normalization leads to phantom taxes and is substantially more expensive to customers than flow-through. The proponents of normalization argued, among other points, that customers are not adversely affected by normalization, because capital costs and plant expenditures are lower and because the rate base is reduced by the amount of deferred taxes. Congressional interest is expected to continue.

Allowance for Funds Used During Construction

For many years regulatory authorities have held that today's utility customers should not pay for the costs of financing construction that will benefit only future users. A basic regulatory principle is that current customers should pay a return only on assets that are currently performing a useful service. As a result, many regulators have withheld major plant construction costs from the rate base until the new plants are "used" and "useful." To offset the loss of return on their investment, utilities have been allowed to recover the cost of construction funds from future users by capitalizing an allowance for funds used during construction (AFUDC), also known as interest during construction, as part of construction work in progress (CWIP) or charged directly to the appropriate property account. The AFUDC is subsequently recovered through depreciation and effects a return through its inclusion in the rate base as part of plant. (For a broad discussion of capitalization of interest, see Chapter 22.)

Although there is general agreement among the regulatory agencies that AFUDC is an appropriate regulatory accounting concept, there are considerable differences in its application. The agencies agree that cost of debt funds should be capitalized, but differ on whether imputed interest on equity funds should be included as part of the total AFUDC. The agencies also differ on other matters, such as the determination of the appropriate AFUDC rate and the capitalization period.

An example of a published report discussion of AFUDC is shown in Figure 36.3.

Construction Work in Progress. Considerable concern has been expressed in recent years over the quality of utility earnings in view of the sizable increase in the amount of the AFUDC—a noncash revenue item—in relation to net income. Utility companies generally have substantial funds tied up in construction work in progress. Because property is by far the largest item in most utility companies' balance sheets and because the companies do much of their own construction, the effect of capitalizing a return on their equity funds used in construction in addition to capitalizing interest on debt funds so used is frequently material to both the balance sheet and the statement of income. In some cases AFUDC has exceeded 50% of net income.

This concern has prompted many regulatory authorities to reconsider their practice of disallowing CWIP costs in the rate base. They have noted the frequent increases in construction programs, the long construction periods, and the consequent drain on utilities' cash flow. Nuclear generating stations, for example, generally cost in excess of a billion dollars and may take ten or more years to build. Some contend that current customers would benefit from placing CWIP costs into the rate base, even though CWIP may not be "used" or "useful" in the traditional sense of those terms. The benefits to current customers, it is claimed, would include (1) assurance that their growing energy needs will be met, (2) achievement of air- and water-pollution and safety standards, and (3) reduction in revenue requirements over the plant's life, since the rate base on which customers pay a rate of return would be lower (because of absence or minimization of AFUDC). Moreover, according to the U.S. General Accounting Office,

... the CWIP issue is really part of a larger issue, namely, the determination by regulators that electric utility companies need rate relief. When regulators determine that a utility company needs rate relief to maintain financial integrity and to finance necessary construction programs, they have several alternatives to achieving that goal— one of which is inclusion of CWIP in the rate base. Regardless of the alternatives chosen, the result will be the same—higher utility bills. Thus, the CWIP issue must

NOTES TO FINANCIAL STATEMENTS

1. Significant Accounting Policies:

Allowance for Funds Used During Construction (AFUDC): AFUDC is defined in the applicable regulatory system of accounts as "the net cost for the period of construction of borrowed funds used for construction purposes and a reasonable rate on other funds when so used." AFUDC is recorded as a charge to construction work in progress (CWIP) and the equivalent credits are to "Interest Charges" for the cost of borrowed funds, excluding the related income tax benefits, and to "Other Income" for the cost of other funds. For income tax purposes, AFUDC is not included in taxable income nor is the depreciation of capitalized AFUDC a tax deductible expense. The rate used for capitalizing AFUDC, which averaged 7.2% in 1978, is computed under a new method prescribed by the regulatory authorities which provides for its application to the CWIP base including prior AFUDC and is compounded semi-annually. The AFUDC in 1978 amounts to approximately the same under the new method as the amount which would have been accrued under the previous method utilizing a higher average rate (8.65% in 1977) applied to the CWIP base, excluding prior AFUDC, and without compounding. The rates are "net after-tax rates" whereby the current income tax reductions arising from interest charges associated with debt used to finance construction, $28,346,000 in 1978 and $26,237,000 in 1977, were allocated from "Operating Expense" to "Other Income."

FIGURE 36.3 EXAMPLE OF ALLOWANCE FOR FUNDS USED DURING CONSTRUCTION
SOURCE: Philadelphia Electric Company, 1978 Annual Report.

be viewed in the context of the effects that other alternatives for providing rate relief would have on utility bills. [U.S. General Accounting Office, 1980, p. 17]

As of mid-1980, about two thirds of the state public utility commissions allowed certain CWIP costs in the rate base (U.S. General Accounting Office, 1980, p. 17). Among federal regulatory commissions, the FCC allows construction projects with expected timeframes of less than one year to be included in the rate base, while the CAB and the ICC, which generally apply the group rate-making process to a particular type or class of service on an industry-wide basis, do not necessarily review individual enterprise cost of service for rate-making purposes. The FERC limits the inclusion of CWIP costs in the rate base to expenditures for pollution control and to individual cases where the utility is judged by the FERC to be in "severe financial difficulty." FERC is currently reviewing its policy with respect to the inclusion of CWIP costs in rate base.

Allowance on Equity Funds. The practice of capitalizing an allowance on equity funds is generally accepted in regulated industries but not followed in nonregulated industries. The FASB, in SFAS 34, *Capitalization of Interest Cost* (AC 5155), states that imputing interest cost on equity funds should be prohibited. Although recognizing that the use of equity funds entails an economic cost, the FASB holds that the amount is not reliably determinable. However, companies that for rate-making purposes are regulated on an individual cost-of-service basis are governed by the APB 2 addendum. Thus the FASB has left prior practice unchanged for such companies, to be reconsidered when the discussion memorandum of APB 2, discussed earlier, is being dealt with by the FASB.

In nonregulated industries, there is no limitation on the amount that stockholders may earn on their investment. With this prospect of unlimited earnings, stockholders may be willing to forego current returns during periods of construction in anticipation of higher returns in later years. Regulated industry, on the other hand, cannot offer the same potential. Utility commissions limit the prospective amount that stockholders of regulated industry may earn on their investment. Retroactive rates, moreover, are not allowed. In recognition of this peculiar situation, utility commissions have normally allowed AFUDC to be computed on both debt and equity funds (the ICC, however, does not allow it on equity). It is argued that the cost of capital is not measured by interest payments alone, but rather by all the economic costs of an entire financing arrangement. This point is supported by the difficulty of differentiating between the use of debt and equity funds in a going concern.

Determining the AFUDC Rate. The FASB, in SFAS 34, stipulates that "the amount of interest cost to be capitalized for qualifying assets is intended to be that portion of the interest cost incurred during the assets' acquisition periods that theoretically could have been avoided . . . if expenditures for the assets had not been made" (AC 5155.12). (See Chapter 22.) SFAS 34 can be contrasted with regulatory agencies' determinations of an AFUDC rate. The FERC prescribes (in Order 561, February 1977) formulas for determining AFUDC rates, thus providing a uniform method that gives recognition to the interrelationship between capital utilized for rate-base purposes and the capital components of AFUDC. These formulas permit a utility to achieve a rate of return on its total utility operations, including its construction program, at about the rate that would be allowed in a rate base.

Other federal regulatory agencies are not as specific as FERC in their instructions for computing AFUDC rates. For the FCC, the AFUDC rate includes the cost of both debt and equity funds. The FCC requires only that "reasonable amounts for interest during the construction period . . . on general funds expended for the acquisition or construction of . . . plant shall be charged to the . . . plant accounts and credited to . . . 'interest income.' " [5] Criteria for determining reason-

---

[5] 47 CFR 31.2-22 (10i), October 1, 1979.

ableness can include such factors as the cost of embedded debt, the cost of recent borrowings, the prime interest rate, borrowing costs of comparable companies, and previous commission rate orders. In cases where funds are specifically acquired and used for plant construction, the FCC requires that the expense—total interest plus discount or premium on debt less interest earned on such funds—is the amount to be included in the cost of plant and to be credited to interest income.

The ICC requires that only the expense on debt incurred for the acquisition or construction of specific property is to be capitalized, with exceptions recognized for motor carriers of freight and freight forwarders, which require specific ICC interpretation for interest capitalization. The ICC permits only debt funds to be capitalized. The CAB permits capitalization of interest on both debt and equity funds, the computation of which is based on the weighted average of rates being paid on all long-term debt outstanding. The FMC also allows capitalization of interest on both debt and equity funds transferred to construction projects. The computation, however, is based on the prime rate on borrowed funds. Other federal and state regulatory authorities either require or permit capitalization of interest on construction projects—both debt and equity funds—but differ widely as to how and at what rate the amount capitalized shall be computed.

Other AFUDC Application Problems. In SFAS 34 the FASB states: "If the enterprise suspends substantially all activities related to acquisition of the asset, interest capitalization shall cease until activities are resumed" (AC 5155.17). Most regulatory agencies have adopted similar rules. Some, however, are more specific. The FERC, for example, has stated in its Accounting Release AR-5 (FPC, January 1, 1968) that "interest during construction may be capitalized starting from the date that construction costs are continuously incurred on a planned progressive basis" and that the "capitalization of interest stops when the facilities have been tested and are placed in or ready for service."

Interest may not be capitalized during periods of intentional delay or interrupted construction if the interruption is deemed unreasonable. Labor strikes, for example, have been deemed unreasonable by the FERC. In the case of multiunit generating plants, an average in-service date or offset method can be used. Under this method, the days of nonproduction attributable to construction are offset against the days of production in the period to arrive at an average in-service date. The AFUDC on all common plant facilities ceases when the first unit of a multiunit generating plant goes into operation. The FCC has limited interest capitalization during periods of suspended construction to six months for whatever cause.

Related Tax Treatment. A separate issue involving AFUDC is that of the federal income tax effect of the debt component of AFUDC. Interest on debt will, of course, be deducted for income tax purposes, though capitalized for accounting purposes. Capitalized interest is often a major element in the origination of deferred taxes, discussed above.

Many state regulatory authorities have determined that current utility customers should not benefit from the related income tax reduction. Two methods are used to normalize the tax effects, a net-of-tax method and a deferral method. Both methods require a charge to cost of service to restore the tax benefit already removed. Under .the net-of-tax method, AFUDC is reduced and other income is increased. Under the deferral method, AFUDC remains the same and deferred tax is increased. The FERC prescribes the deferral method for utilities whose state regulatory authorities have not ruled on treatment of the tax benefits of the debt component of AFUDC.

Intercompany Profits

ARB 51 (AC 2051.07) provides that

> in a regulated industry where a parent or subsidiary manufactures or constructs facilities for other companies in the consolidated group, . . . the elimination of intercompany profit to the extent that such profit is substantially equivalent to a reasonable return on investment ordinarily capitalized in accordance with the established practice of the industry [is not required].

For nonregulated enterprises the elimination of such profits is always required. Some utility companies, particularly in the telephone industry (see Figure 36.4), often purchase property and materials and supplies from affiliated or subsidiary vendors, usually manufacturers. In accordance with the rate making generally followed (which allows the capitalized or "uneliminated" profits to be included in the purchaser's rate base) and the provisions of ARB 51, they do not eliminate intercompany profits from their consolidated financial statements. Thus, depending on the extent and type of affiliations and purchasing practices, the effect on the consolidated financial statements of companies following this practice can be significant.

Fuel Cost Adjustment Clauses

Electric and gas utility tariffs may include adjustment clauses that allow companies to modify customer rates to reflect changes in the cost of fuels used to produce electricity and of purchased gas needed for natural gas pipelines and gas distribution. These utilities will often establish a deferred charge in their financial statements for increased fuel and gas costs not currently recovered through customer rates, and later match the increased costs with additional revenue collected through surcharges on customer bills. In nonregulated industries, costs of this type would ordinarily be charged to expense as incurred, since the physical items or assets have been consumed and the service rendered to customers. However, regulated industries may defer such items if they meet the criterion of the addendum to APB 2: ". . . when it is clear that the cost will be recoverable out of future revenues . . ." (AC 6011.02).

During periods of rapidly rising fuel prices, such adjustment clauses help prevent earnings erosion. Conversely, they could reduce customer bills if fuel costs should decrease. Administratively, adjustment clauses reduce the need for rate proceedings, thereby decreasing the burden on the commissions and diminishing the cost of regulation to consumers.[6]

---

[6] The Congressional Research Service reported (December 21, 1978, p. CRS-18) that during 1977 more than 80% of the $13 billion in electric and gas utility price increases were flowed through to customer rates by adjustment clauses.

Consolidation —The consolidated financial statements include the accounts of the Company and its telephone subsidiaries. The consolidation process eliminates the effects of all significant intercompany transactions except as discussed below under "Purchases from Western Electric." The investment in Western Electric Company, Incorporated ("Western Electric"), an unconsolidated subsidiary, and certain other investments (where it is deemed that the Company's ownership gives it the ability to exercise significant influence over operating and financial policies) are included at equity (cost plus proportionate share of reinvested earnings). All other investments are included at cost. See also Note (I).

Purchases from Western Electric —Most of the telephone equipment, apparatus and materials used by the consolidated companies have been manufactured or procured for them by Western Electric. Contracts with the telephone companies provide that Western Electric's prices shall be as low as to its most favored customers for like materials and services under comparable conditions. The consolidated financial statements reflect items purchased from Western Electric at cost to the companies, which cost includes the return realized by Western Electric on its investment devoted to this business.

FIGURE 36.4   DISCLOSURE OF INTERCOMPANY PROFITS NOT ELIMINATED
SOURCE: American Telephone and Telegraph Company, 1979 Annual Report.

A study of electric and gas utility adjustment clauses (NARUC, 1978) indicates that commission policies and utility operating characteristics contribute to the great variety among the fuel adjustment clauses of the several states. Differences exist both in the type of items that are eligible as a basis for a rate adjustment—fuel costs, transportation and handling costs, taxes—and in the basis of the application, such as actual or estimated costs. Also, some adjustment clauses are *automatic* and some are *nonautomatic,* depending on whether the state commission requires a formal hearing when a utility requests a change in the surcharge. Utilities allowed automatic adjustment clauses do not have to participate in formal hearing proceedings—notice of hearing issued, testimony from interested parties taken, and commission order issued—but are subject to various audit review procedures, such as verifying the arithmetical accuracy of computation, reviewing fuel invoices, studying the relationship between fuel suppliers and the utility, comparing published market prices and amounts actually paid for fuel, and insuring that gas price changes or refunds approved by the FERC are recognized in the adjustment calculations.

The FERC allows regulated utilities to maintain the deferred charge resulting from unrecovered cost increases on their financial statements as long as the state commission allows it. (See Figure 36.5.) However, the value of uncollected fuel

BALANCE SHEET

ASSETS	December 31,	
	1979	·1978
Utility Plant at Original Cost:		
Plant In Service and Held for Future Use:		
Electric	$335,971,000	$310,584,000
Gas	36,848,000	34,205,000
Water	55,194,000	51,683,000
Common	11,759,000	11,317,000
	439,772,000	407,789,000
Less Accumulated Provision for Depreciation	90,946,000	79,322,000
	348,826,000	328,467,000
Construction Work in Progress	92,393,000	62,606,000
	441,219,000	391,073,000
Deferred Debits:		
Deferred Energy Costs	12,438,000	3,840,000

Deferral of Energy Costs:
The Company utilizes an energy cost adjustment provision with respect to the Company's retail electric and gas operations. The provision includes accounting procedures whereby the Company defers all changes in costs incurred for fuel, purchased power and gas for resale from the base costs as defined until such time as the Company will recover or refund those cost differentials. The provision calls for prescribed deferral periods of not less than six months with recovery or refunding of these costs through billing surcharges or credits over a six to twelve month period.

FIGURE 36.5   EXAMPLE OF DEFERRED ENERGY COSTS
SOURCE: Sierra Pacific Power Company, 1979 Annual Report.

and gas costs recorded as deferred charges can be undermined by utility company action (e.g., applying for a rate increase); by state commission decision (e.g., subsequently ruling that deferred charges are not allowed); or by audit (e.g., detection of improper items included in the adjustment determination).

The audit process can also result in disallowance of costs included in adjustment clauses because of imprudent management actions. For example, in one case, the FERC ruled that a utility incurred fuel costs imprudently because the company made spot coal purchases instead of enforcing its contractual right to purchase coal from its supplier. Therefore the additional cost could not be recovered through the fuel adjustment clause.[7]

Although widespread use has been made of adjustment clauses, there are indications that increased stability of fuel costs and continued criticism of adjustment clauses may diminish their use. Fuel and purchased gas adjustment clauses have been criticized, in part because they single out one cost element subject to dramatic increases, as experienced in 1974 and again in 1979, without recognizing possible

---

[7] Docket No. ER 76-285, Phase II.

reductions in other cost elements. Furthermore, the capability to pass on increased costs to consumers may reduce incentives to be fuel efficient. The use of adjustment clauses may change as a result of planned FERC and state commission reviews of adjustment clauses.

For example, one state commission eliminated its automatic fuel adjustment clause in favor of semiannual public hearings for individual companies. Each hearing considers historical and projected fuel cost information, and results in an order establishing the fuel component of base rates for the ensuing six months. The difference between actual fuel costs and fuel charges in base rates is considered in the next hearing (South Carolina Public Service Commission, 1980). This could be a trend for the future.

Rate Increases Subject to Refund

A rate increase, once granted, may be challenged in court and may result in a temporary condition on the new rates. In such cases, the rates may be placed into effect, with a notification to customers that some or all of the increase may be subject to refund depending on the outcome of the court challenge. (See Figure 36.6 for a typical disclosure.) This occurred, for example, when the FERC (FPC) issued its Opinion No. 770 (July 27, 1976) permitting a national rate of $1.42 per MCF for natural gas, up by a substantial margin. The final approval of the rate did not come until 1977, and the proper accounting for material amounts was in question for many natural gas producers at the 1976 year-end. It was not entirely clear that SFAS 5, *Accounting for Contingencies* (AC 4311), was applicable, with the result that some companies did not recognize any increased revenue, some recognized part, and some recognized all—in each instance with appropriate disclosures.

Betterment Accounting

Retirement-replacement-betterment (betterment) accounting is the method railroads have been required to use for track structures in reports to the ICC since adoption of the first Uniform System of Accounts for railroads in 1914. Although many utilities used methods similar to betterment accounting until the 1930s, betterment is now unique to railroads. Under betterment accounting, the initial cost of track structures is capitalized and no systematic depreciation is taken. The cost of equal-quality replacements is charged to expense as they occur. "Betterments" occur when improved quality components are installed. An amount equal to the current cost of the component replaced is expensed, and the excess amount, which represents the betterment portion, is capitalized. Capitalized amounts are recovered when the asset is retired.

Historically, betterment accounting has been the subject of much debate. Proponents have principally argued that betterment accounting accurately reflects economic reality, particularly during periods of inflation, because income is charged with current replacement costs rather than with depreciation based on understated historical costs. This argument is similar to arguments for the LIFO method of accounting for inventory. Critics of betterment accounting contend that it fails to recognize properly the cost of capital used or consumed in operations, particularly during periods when maintenance is postponed or accelerated. Income is

Operating Revenues

Total revenues for system companies in 1978 amounted to almost $1.9 billion, an increase of 14.6 per cent over the prior year. The increase mainly reflects the pass-through of higher purchased gas costs by the regulated companies, the addition of coal sales through the acquisition of Industrial Fuels, and rate increases placed into effect on December 1, 1977, on a conditional basis by Natural.

These rates remain subject to final approval by FERC and are subject to possible refund. They would provide an annual increase in revenues of approximately $106.1 million over the last approved rates, which became effective December 1, 1976. Pending resolution of this rate proceeding by FERC, Natural has provided a reserve for a possible rate refund to its customers, before income taxes, of $70.7 million as of September 30, 1978, based on a 13.25 per cent rate of return on common equity, the last rate allowed Natural.

On June 30, 1978, Natural filed an amended request for an additional rate increase designed to increase annual revenues by an amount subsequently modified to about $49 million when compared to the rates presently in effect. On July 28, 1978, FERC accepted this revised filing and approved Natural's request that the new rates be made effective December 1, 1978, subject to possible refund pending final determination by FERC.

FIGURE 36.6   EXAMPLE OF RATE INCREASES SUBJECT TO REFUND
SOURCE: Peoples Gas Company, 1978 Annual Report.

overstated during periods of postponed or deferred maintenance because operating expense is inadequately charged for the costs of capital consumed. In addition, the decline in the service value of assets is not recognized through depreciation charges to operations. The opposite is true during periods of accelerated maintenance; income is understated because operating expense is charged with the full cost of replacements that will benefit future periods.

The SEC and ICC each issued an Advance Notice of Proposed Rulemaking, in April 1977 and October 1978, respectively, questioning the appropriateness of betterment accounting. Although the ICC has stated its preference for depreciation accounting, neither agency has concluded its administrative rule-making process. The SEC has deferred to the ICC, while the ICC is postponing further action until tax-related issues are resolved.

Meanwhile, several railroads have begun to use depreciation accounting for their

> **a) Principles of Consolidation.** The consoli-
> dated financial statements reflect the operations
> of the Company and all majority-owned sub-
> sidiaries. All significant intercompany transac-
> tions have been eliminated.

FIGURE 36.7   RAILROAD DEPRECIATION ACCOUNTING DISCLOSURE
SOURCE: Chicago and North Western Transportation Co., 1979 Annual Report.

track and roadbed structure in their reports to stockholders. Figure 36.7 illustrates
this approach and shows the required reconciliation to ICC reporting.

Operating Rights

Motor carriers regulated by the ICC must obtain *operating rights*—certificates
or permits authorizing transportation of commodities over defined routes or areas—
before they can engage in interstate or foreign commerce. Carriers can either
obtain operating rights directly from the ICC or purchase another carrier's rights.
The costs of operating rights include either regulatory agency fees and related legal
fees, or the purchase price, if acquired separately from other carriers. If an entire
carrier is acquired, the purchase price of the operating rights may be the price
stated in the contract. For many years the ICC did not require these intangible
assets to be amortized. Under APB 17 (AC 5141), intangible assets are required
to be amortized over a period not to exceed 40 years. Although the trucking
industry strenuously challenged the FASB on the issue of whether operating rights
were intangibles subject to amortization, no amendments to the opinion were made.
Part of the industry's argument was the applicability to APB 17 of the addendum
to APB 2.

Enactment of the Motor Carrier Act of 1980 significantly decreased the value
of intangible operating rights. The act makes it easier for carriers to enter a market
because it requires the ICC to grant certificates unless "the transportation to be
authorized by the certificate is inconsistent with the public convenience and necessity." Diversion of revenue on traffic from an existing carrier is not in and of
itself justification for denying a certificate. The problem facing the trucking industry and the accounting profession is how to account for the diminished value of
operating rights.

Some carriers believe the operating rights, equal to a significant amount of
stockholders' equity, are worthless and have written them off as an extraordinary
item. One large trucking company, Consolidated Freightways, Inc., wrote off the
entire carrying value of its U.S. motor carrier operating rights of $32 million in
the third quarter of 1980 (*Wall Street Journal,* October 21, 1980). Other carriers
recognize that the market value of the rights has declined but believe they represent
goodwill and therefore should be amortized over 40 years in accordance with
APB 17 (AC 5141).

The ICC had not normally required the cost of operating rights, obtained from
the ICC or purchased from other carriers, to be amortized, because they historically
appreciated in value. The ICC issued Accounting Series Circular No. 182 in
August, 1980, announcing its intention of working with the accounting profession

port facilities (such as living quarters or field power plants) or processing facilities (such as natural gas processing plants) have value that is primarily dependent on the value of the reserves in the field, the cost of these facilities is also considered a development cost.

Production costs are incurred in lifting oil and gas from subsurface reservoirs, gathering, treating, field processing, field storage, and operating and maintaining field equipment. These costs may include severance taxes and other taxes on the assets in the field; costs to repair field equipment; labor costs incurred in maintenance, operation, and inspection of production facilities; insurance; and any necessary equipment, materials, supplies, fuel, or other items required for production. Production activities are usually regarded as terminating at the point where product is delivered from a production storage tank into a refining or main transporting facility, known as the *point of custody transfer* in the field.

Several theories have been sustained concerning the presentation of periodic results of operations and financial statement classification of costs arising from the activities of oil and gas producing enterprises. The greatest diversity in practice appears in the accounting for preacquisition, acquisition, and exploration costs. Two distinguishable accounting methods have evolved as generally accepted, and others are under consideration as discussed later in this chapter. The two methods are *full cost* and *successful efforts* and were developed based on differing views of the circumstances that should result in the capitalization (or deferral) of costs incurred.

Full Cost. Under the broadest form of the full cost concept (not currently acceptable for SEC companies, as discussed later), all costs incurred in prospecting, acquisition, exploration, and development activities, generally including those portions of general and administrative costs that are associated with these activities, are capitalized. Cost centers established are usually not defined by the existence of contiguous oil and gas bearing geological formations. In the broadest application of this method, a single company-wide cost center may be established, regardless of the location of an enterprise's properties. Traditionally, it has been more common for individual continents, countries, or large geographic regions within countries to be adopted as cost centers. Offshore properties are normally included with onshore properties in a cost center.

Capitalized costs are amortized as production occurs from the reserves in a cost center. If no recoverable reserves are discovered in a cost center within a reasonable period of time after expenditures have been made, capitalized costs in that center are written off as a loss. If capitalized costs exceed the estimated present value of net revenues from future production of reserves in a cost center, the costs are written down to that estimated value that is their allowable ceiling.

There are two areas in full cost accounting that have been subject to modification in practice. One is the selection of the cost center, as described above. The other is the timing of transfer of preproduction costs into a producing center. Some companies assign preproduction costs to the cost center as they are incurred, whereas others defer the transfer until a determination is made of whether the related undeveloped properties will be productive or nonproductive. This affects the timing of amortization.

The major premise underlying the full cost concept is that the value of reserves discovered should be related to the total of all direct and indirect costs incurred in their finding and development. Exploration costs, including the drilling of dry holes, are considered prerequisites of production from developed reserves.

Successful Efforts. Capitalized under the successful efforts concept are only those acquisition, exploration, and development costs directly associated with properties where commercially recoverable reserves are discovered. Here, cost centers generally have been established on the basis of specifically identified reserves. The *field* is the predominant cost center used in practice, although some successful efforts companies have accounted on a lease, district, or division basis.

In general, the costs of geological and geophysical studies, the costs of carrying undeveloped properties, and general and administrative costs are charged to expense as incurred. All acquisition, exploration, and development costs associated with properties where commercially recoverable reserves are not discovered are written off at the time the property is determined to be nonproductive. Capitalized costs are amortized as production from reserves within a cost center occurs.

Prior to standardization through SFAS 19 (AC 6021), variations occurred in the application of the successful efforts method in practice. Some companies amortized the costs associated with nonproductive properties based on an experience factor rather than recording a loss when the properties were determined to be worthless. Some capitalized a portion of geological and geophysical costs instead of expensing them as incurred. Nonproductive development costs, such as development dry holes, were expensed as incurred by some, capitalized to the productive cost center by others. And, as mentioned previously, there have been variations in the cost centers selected.

The successful efforts concept rests largely on the premise that only costs directly identifiable with future benefits should be recorded as assets. Thus, finding costs should be associated only with the reserves toward which exploratory and development efforts are specifically directed. This approach has been deemed by the FASB to achieve a matching of revenues with the cost of reserves from which the revenues are derived.

Move to Standardization. It took an act of Congress to provide the incentive to limit the methods currently practiced. This act, the Energy Policy and Conservation Act of 1975 (EPCA), mandated the development of uniform practices by December 22, 1977.

Thus in 1975 the FASB undertook this project, ultimately producing SFAS 19, *Financial Accounting and Reporting by Oil and Gas Producing Companies* (AC 6021), in December 1977. This pronouncement, originally effective for fiscal years beginning after December 15, 1978, mandated the use of a specified method of successful efforts accounting.

The SEC, however, did not agree with the Board's conclusions. In general terms, the SEC believed that none of the currently followed accounting and reporting practices based on historical cost, including the SFAS 19 approach, provided sufficient useful information. Accordingly, they proposed an alternative approach, termed *reserve recognition accounting* (RRA), which is a form of current value accounting. Further, because of the time expected to be required to develop a new accounting method, the SEC has deemed acceptable either the successful efforts method as prescribed by SFAS 19 or a full cost method as prescribed by the SEC.

As a result of the SEC position, the FASB amended SFAS 19 with the issuance of SFAS 25 (AC 6022), indefinitely suspending the effective date for application of most of the provisions of SFAS 19.

Current Accounting Requirements—Public Companies

The SEC has prescribed standardized accounting, reporting, and disclosure rules, under both the full cost and the successful efforts methods, for oil and gas producing companies within its jurisdiction.

The SEC requirements have been prescribed in a series of releases that will be mentioned as appropriate in this chapter. These are summarized in Figure 37.1.

One of the two specified methods must be or have been adopted for fiscal years ending after December 25, 1979, with retroactive restatement of prior-period financial statements. In ASR 261 the SEC stated that although a company would be expected to elect the method that more closely corresponds to its current practices, preferability[4] need not be demonstrated in making the initial election between the two methods. Specifically:

> If conforming the company's present accounting method to the specified version of that method will have a significant impact on the company's financial statements, the Commission has concluded that the company may then change to either of the specified forms of accounting.

Changes made in accordance with the above provision could only be made once, but there was one general exception to the above rule. If a company previously following the full cost method elected early implementation of SFAS 19 (prior to the publication of ASR 253), the company was allowed the one-time change to the full cost method as prescribed by ASR 258. Figure 37.2 summarizes the plethora of change options that were available to a public company.

Definitions. The SEC adopted the definitions of acquisition, exploration, development, and production costs and activities specified by SFAS 19 (AC 6021.015-.024). Reserve definitions, however, were conformed by ASR 257 to those contained in the Department of Energy's *Financial Reporting System* (*FRS*). The FASB subsequently adopted these definitions in SFAS 25 (AC 6022.34), where the full definitions are given.

Although there are numerous intricacies within the definitions that affect classifications of reserves, there are three criteria that should be given particular attention:

1. The SEC rules specify that reserves may be classified as proved if economic producibility is supported by either actual production or conclusive formation tests. This

---

[4] Preferability of a newly adopted accounting principle is required to be justified by management (AC 1051.16). The SEC also requires the independent accountant's representation of such preferability (see Chapter 16). Thus the abeyance of these requirements by the SEC represents not only a variation in SEC rules, but also a fracture of GAAP.

AUGUST 31, 1978

- *ASR 253*—adopts requirements for financial accounting and reporting practices for oil and gas producing activities
- *Release 33-5967*—proposes disclosure of oil and gas reserves and operations (amendment to Regulation S-K)
- *Release 33-5968*—proposes full cost accounting practices of oil and gas producers
- *Release 33-5969*—proposes supplemental earnings summary for oil and gas producing activities (RRA preliminary specifications)
- *SAB 23*—rescinds SAB 16 (which required disclosure of the impact of SFAS 19) and provides guidance regarding costs to be classified as mineral assets with respect to the replacement cost disclosure rule

DECEMBER 19, 1978

- *ASR 257*—amends ASR 253 regarding successful efforts accounting
- *ASR 258*—provides final rules for full cost accounting practices of oil and gas producers
- *Release 33-6008*—amends Regulation S-K concerning disclosure of oil and gas reserves

FEBRUARY 23, 1979

- *ASR 261*—discusses accounting changes resulting from above SEC actions
- *Release 33-6029*—deletes requirement for full costers to disclose as-if successful efforts information

SEPTEMBER 24, 1979

- *ASR 269*—requires supplemental disclosures on the basis of reserve recognition accounting
- *ASR 270*—provides that the supplemental data in ASR 269 need not be audited for years ending before December 26, 1980

DECEMBER 17, 1979

- *SAB 36*—for limited partnerships, provides relief from disclosure of estimated future net revenues, present value and changes therein, and the ASR 269 supplemental data; allows Canadian registrants to use Canadian GAAP provided a footnote reconciliation is given

APRIL 17, 1980

- *ASR 277*—postpones the audit requirement for reserve information until a decision is made on the adoption of RRA

FIGURE 37.1   SEC PRONOUNCEMENTS ON OIL AND GAS ACCOUNTING

	Methods Available in ASR 261	
	SE* Per	*FC* Per*
Current Method Followed	*SFAS 19*	*ASR 258*
SE similar to SFAS 19	Yes	No**
SE differs substantially from SFAS 19	Yes	Yes
FC similar to ASR 258	No**	Yes
FC differs substantially from ASR 258	Yes	Yes
Companies previously using FC who early adopted SFAS 19	Yes	Yes

* SE = successful efforts; FC = full cost.
** Not absolutely proscribed by SEC, but unlikely in view of SEC statements in ASR 261.

FIGURE 37.2   ACCOUNTING CHANGE OPTIONS

element emphasizes the judgmental nature of reserve classification and implies the high degree of reliance that often must be placed on engineering interpretations.

2. The SEC rules require that proved reserves must be recoverable with reasonable certainty under "existing economic and operating conditions," specifying that current prices must be applied in determining future production revenues. Consideration of changes in current prices may be made only to the extent provided for by contractual arrangements. Announced future changes in regulated pricing are not to be taken into consideration, nor are known or anticipated future changes in posted prices. In no event may consideration be given to estimated inflation factors.

3. Production is to be classified and priced under existing regulatory requirements. Estimated future oil production is to be reclassified as appropriate under phased decontrol and priced by applying prices being received for the applicable categories of oil at the date of the valuation. The related impact of the windfall profit tax is to be included in determining future net revenues.

Full Cost. The SEC-mandated full cost accounting rules were prescribed in ASR 258, for the express purpose of conforming "existing practice to a relatively standardized method that, in the Commission's view, is generally consistent with the conceptual basis of full cost accounting." The SEC rules are to be applied to all oil and gas producing operations of a registrant and its subsidiaries. However, the requirements do not apply to investees accounted for under the equity method, unless they are directly subject to SEC requirements.

Basis for capitalization. Cost centers are to be established on a country-by-country basis only. All costs associated with acquisition, exploration, and development activities, including preacquisition costs, are to be capitalized within each cost center. Internal costs directly identified with those activities may be capitalized.[5] Production (lifting and workover) costs, general and administrative costs (such as corporate overhead), all costs reimbursed by other persons, and all costs related to drilling arrangements on which income is recognized are to be charged to expense.

Costs to be amortized. All capitalized costs included in a country's pool, including those that are unevaluated and in the process of being evaluated, must be depleted based on proved reserves. The costs to be amortized should also include estimated future expenditures to be incurred in developing proved reserves and estimated dismantlement and abandonment costs, net of estimated salvage values.

Unusually significant investments in unevaluated properties and major development projects may be excluded from the amortization computation until proved reserves can be attributed to the properties. (Examples of such costs are the acquisition of major offshore leases, installation of offshore drilling platforms, and improved recovery projects.) Such properties are subject, however, to impairment evaluations (described below under Successful Efforts), and if impairment is indicated, the amount of impairment should be added to the costs to be amortized.

Amortization. Amortization is computed by the unit-of-production method over the proved reserves attributable to each cost center. Oil and gas are to be converted to a common unit of measure (equivalent units) based on physical units, unless computation on the basis of monetary units of current gross revenues is more appropriate. As a practical matter, conversion to equivalent units based on physical measures of energy content is usually computed at the rate of six MCF (MCF = thousand cubic feet) of gas to one barrel of oil. Amortization computations are to be made on a consolidated basis, with investees accounted for on the equity method treated separately.

Limitation on capitalized costs. For each cost center, aggregate capitalized costs less accumulated amortization and related deferred taxes may not exceed a defined ceiling. The ceiling is equal to the sum of (a) the present value of future net revenues from production of proved reserves in the center plus (b) the cost of properties not being amortized plus (c) the lower of cost or fair value of unproved properties included in costs being amortized less (d) income tax effects related to book/tax basis differences of the properties involved. Any amounts in excess of the computed ceiling should be written off and not reinstated for any subsequent ceiling increases.

Property conveyances. The rules for accounting for mineral property conveyances were established by SFAS 19 (AC 6021.042-.047) as adopted by the SEC, and are discussed in greater detail under Successful Efforts. In the SEC version of full cost accounting, there are some exceptions to those rules:

---

[5] The FASB has on its agenda a project to interpret SFAS 34 (AC 5155) regarding appropriateness of capitalization of interest by oil and gas producing enterprises that use the full cost method of accounting. The Board tentatively concluded that only unusually significant investments in unimproved properties and major development projects not being amortized are qualifying assets for purposes of applying SFAS 34 to such enterprises.

1. No gains or losses are recognized on sales or abandonments of properties unless treatment as an adjustment of capitalized costs would significantly alter the relationship between those costs and proved reserves in a cost center. A significant alteration would not be expected for sales involving less than 25% of the reserve quantities of a cost center.
2. If cash consideration received from the sale of unproved properties or drilling arrangements either exceeds total cost of the properties plus exploration and development costs to be incurred subsequently, or represents reimbursement for amounts currently charged to expense, then income should be recognized.
3. Significant purchases of properties with lives substantially shorter than the composite life of the cost center should be accounted for separately.

Interest capitalization. Capitalization of interest by oil and gas companies following the full cost method must conform with standards of SFAS 34 (AC 5155) and FASB Interpretation No. 33 (AC 5155-1). Interest must be capitalized on unusually significant investments in unproved properties and major development projects that are not being depreciated, depleted, or amortized currently, and on significant properties and projects in cost centers with no production, provided that exploration or development activities on such assets are in progress.

Successful Efforts. Successful efforts accounting requirements prescribed by the SEC in ASR 257 are identical to those stated in SFAS 19 (AC 6021).

Asset classification. Under successful efforts accounting, the assets involved in oil and gas producing activities are broadly classified into four categories. The first, *mineral interests in properties,* consists of the rights to extract oil and gas, and is subdivided into *unproved properties* and *proved properties.* The other three categories are *wells and related equipment and facilities; support facilities and equipment;* and *uncompleted wells, equipment, and facilities.* The costs of assets included in the four categories are to be capitalized as incurred.

Basis for capitalization. Under successful efforts accounting, cost centers are to be established on a field basis. In general, only those costs directly related to the acquisition, exploration, and development of proved reserves in an individual field may be capitalized.

Preacquisition G&G costs are expensed as incurred, as are the costs of carrying undeveloped properties. Certain contingent exploratory costs, such as dry-hole contributions and bottom-hole contributions, are also treated in this manner.

Property acquisition costs and postacquisition exploratory costs are initially capitalized to the appropriate unproved property and uncompleted well accounts, pending evaluation of the property. If proved reserves are discovered in the field, the costs are transferred to proved properties and to wells and related equipment and facilities. If proved reserves are not found, the costs are charged to expense. This determination can be made in two ways. First, if an exploratory well is completed as a dry hole, all costs accumulated for that field should usually be written off. Second, if a conclusive determination has not been made as a result of drilling, costs related to unproved properties are annually subject to an impairment test, as discussed below.

Development costs are capitalized as incurred, even if a specific development well is unsuccessful. All development costs are included in the category of wells and related equipment and facilities.

Production costs are charged to operations when incurred, and include the direct overhead that can be traced to production activity. Costs such as maintenance of production office facilities, record keeping, and similar overhead items are to be charged to period expense as incurred. The depreciation, depletion, and amortization of proved property costs and related equipment are considered production costs.

Amortization. Amortization is computed on the unit-of-production method. Conversion to equivalent units is made on the basis of physical units of energy content (usually six MCF of gas to one barrel of oil).

Capitalized acquisition costs of proved properties are to be amortized on the basis of proved reserves, whereas capitalized development costs and the costs of exploratory wells and exploratory-type stratigraphic test wells that have found proved reserves are amortized on the basis of proved developed reserves. Costs of development wells in progress are carried without amortization until the development well is completed. Costs of large capital investment programs associated with several development wells, such as offshore platforms, should be assigned to completed or uncompleted wells on some reasonable basis, such as the number of wells expected to be completed in the program. Those proved developed reserves that will be produced only after significant future expenditures are made should also be excluded from amortization computations.

Amortization may be computed on a property-by-property basis or on the basis of a reasonable grouping of properties with a common geological structure, such as a field or reservoir. As a practical matter, amortization is usually computed on a field basis, because costs are aggregated within cost centers in that manner.

Estimated salvage values and anticipated future dismantlement, restoration, and abandonment costs are to be provided for in determining amortization rates.

Impairment of unproved properties.[6] Unproved properties must be assessed periodically to determine if they have suffered an impairment in value. If so, a valuation allowance is to be provided. In general, impairment occurs when it becomes doubtful that the carrying value of the property will be recovered.

Impairment would be indicated if a dry hole is drilled on an unproved property and there are no firm plans for further drilling or if an unproved property has been held for a major portion of the initial lease term without commencement of drilling activity. The assessment for impairment should be done on a property-by-property basis if the acquisition costs are individually significant. If they are not, the allowance may be determined, in the aggregate or by groups, on the basis of experience factors such as exploratory well success rates on similar types of properties and average holding periods for unproved properties.

---

[6] In general, these comments concerning impairment also apply to unusually significant investments by full cost companies in unevaluated properties and major development projects excluded from the amortization base.

The impairment test is also relevant when an exploratory well is completed and has located reserves but a substantial capital expenditure, such as installation of a trunk pipeline, is required before production can begin. Here, classification of the reserves depends on whether the expenditure can be justified. This often requires the drilling of additional exploratory wells. In this situation, capitalized costs may be retained if the discovered reserves are sufficient to justify the expenditure and additional exploratory drilling is in progress or firmly planned. If both conditions are not met, the costs of the exploratory well are to be expensed. As a general rule, exploratory drilling costs may not be carried for longer than one year after well completion without a determination that proved reserves have been found.

The requirement for impairment assessment does not change the current practice of using realization tests for impairment determination of proved properties.

Surrender or abandonment. Capitalized acquisition costs related to the surrender or abandonment of unproved properties should be charged against the allowance for impairment to the extent that such an allowance has been provided, with a loss being recognized for any excess. If only a portion of a proved property is abandoned or retired, such as an individual well or item of equipment, no loss shall be recognized. Rather, the asset being abandoned or retired shall be deemed fully amortized and charged to accumulated DD&A, unless the abandonment or retirement was the result of catastrophic event or other major abnormality.

When the last well of the proved property ceases to produce and the entire proved property or proved property group is abandoned, a loss should be recognized if the carrying value of the property differs from the salvage value net of any reclamation costs.

Property conveyances. Oil and gas financing and conveyance arrangements take on a wide variety of complex forms. The following discussion deals with the general concepts embodied in SFAS 19 (AC 6021.042-.047) governing the accounting for these transactions and, although pointing out a few of the more common forms of such arrangements, is not intended to address all the special situations that may occur. A careful reading of the rules adopted by the SEC in ASR 257 is required when considering a specific conveyance transaction.

The rules governing the accounting for mineral property conveyances and related transactions focus on the substance of the arrangement: is it a transfer of rights and responsibilities of operating a property or is it a financing arrangement? If a transaction is in substance a borrowing repayable in cash or its equivalent, it is to be accounted for as a borrowing, with no recognition of gain or loss.

For example, if cash advances are made to an operator to finance exploration in return for the right to purchase oil or gas discovered, and if the advances are repayable in cash should insufficient oil or gas be discovered to offset them, the transaction should be accounted for as a receivable by the lender and a borrowing by the operator. This treatment must also be used if the funds advanced are repayable in cash from the proceeds of a specified share of future production until the advance, plus interest, is repaid in full.

When a transaction results in a true conveyance, the key considerations in determining whether gain or loss recognition is appropriate relate to liquidity of proceeds, certainty of cost recovery, obligation for future performance, and the nature of the property. No gain or loss may be recognized at the time of conveyance when there is a transfer of assets used in oil and gas producing activities for other assets used in those activities, such as in a carried interest, free well, or overriding royalty transaction, or in a pooling of assets under a joint venture or unitization.

A loss (but not a gain) may need to be recognized if part of an interest in a property is sold, but recovery of costs applicable to the retained interest is highly uncertain if the seller has substantial obligation for future performance.

A gain may usually be recognized on the sale of all or part of a property if the proceeds are in cash or its equivalent, collectibility is reasonably assured, and the seller has no obligation for substantial future performance. Otherwise, proceeds are generally considered a recovery of cost.

Current Accounting Requirements—Nonpublic Companies

The FASB's decision in SFAS 25 (AC 6022) to indefinitely suspend the requirements of SFAS 19—a virtually unavoidable one with the SEC sanctioning both full cost and successful efforts—resulted in a large number of alternatives for nonpublic companies compared with those for SEC registrants. Though there is no specified form of either full cost or successful efforts accounting that nonpublic companies must follow, they must apply the same definitions of proved reserves adopted by the SEC, disclose their method of accounting in the financial statements, and provide the same disclosures of reserve quantities, costs incurred, and capitalized costs as SEC companies.

Certain of the mineral conveyance and related transaction provisions of SFAS 19 were also adopted by the SEC for full cost companies and thus affect all public companies. Since the SEC adopted these provisions, it is reasonable to expect that even those conveyance rules not imposed on private companies will be extended to all companies, public and private.

Interest capitalization for full cost companies applies to public and nonpublic companies alike, since there is an FASB standard (SFAS 34). Finally, the income tax allocation requirements of SFAS 19 (AC 6021.260-.264), as discussed below under Income Taxes, have been retained, and thus apply to nonpublic companies.

Disclosure Requirements

Because the SEC concluded that traditional accounting methods failed to provide sufficient information regarding the financial position and results of operations of oil and gas producing enterprises, extensive supplemental financial and operating disclosure is required regardless of the accounting method employed. The specific requirements are based on SFAS 19 as adopted by the SEC, plus the requirements added through the numerous SEC releases indicated in Figure 37.1.

Originally SEC-required disclosures generally were to be made in financial statements for full fiscal years ending after December 25, 1978, contained in filings that included fiscal years ending after December 25, 1979. SFAS 19-required disclosures became effective for fiscal years beginning after December 15, 1978. ASR 277 (April 1980) revised the SEC requirements to permit disclosure outside the financial statements.

The required disclosures can be grouped into three categories, which are cumulative: all companies; public companies; and public companies using full cost.

Thus, public companies using full cost accounting must give the most extensive disclosures.

All Companies. SFAS 19 required certain disclosures that were explicitly continued in SFAS 25. These are applicable to all companies.

Method of accounting. The accounting policies for costs incurred in oil and gas producing activities and the manner of disposing of capitalized costs must be given (AC 6022.08).

Estimated quantities of proved reserves. Net quantities of proved reserves and proved developed reserves are to be reported as of both the beginning and end of each year for which the financial statements are presented (AC 6021.050). Changes in those net quantities should be disclosed under the following categories (AC 6021.051):

1. Revisions of previous estimates,
2. Improved recovery,
3. Purchases of minerals-in-place,
4. Extension, discoveries, and other additions,
5. Production, and
6. Sales of minerals-in-place.

The FASB specified that these reserve disclosures may be made outside the financial statements (AC 6022.06), and the SEC finally agreed, for public companies, in ASR 277.

The net quantities and their changes are to be shown by the enterprise's home country and by each foreign geographic area in which significant reserves are located. Such disclosure requirements do not include oil or gas reserves subject to purchase under long-term supply, purchase, or similar agreements and contracts unless the enterprise participates in the operation of the properties or otherwise serves as the "producer" of those reserves. Any important economic factors or significant uncertainties that may affect the components of the proved reserves must also be explained.

These disclosures are illustrated in Figure 37.3. Normally, a petroleum engineer's report of reserve quantities and changes therein form the basis for this information.

Capitalized costs. The aggregate amount of capitalized costs and related accumulated DD&A amounts and valuation allowance relating to oil and gas producing activities must be disclosed. Such disclosure should be reported as of the end of each period for which a balance sheet is presented. The disclosure of capitalized costs is to be made by asset category (i.e., mineral interests, equipment).

Costs incurred in producing activities. The following types of costs, whether capitalized or expensed, including certain depreciation expenses (see AC 6021.058), must be disclosed:

	Total Worldwide		United States		Foreign Geographic Area A		Foreign Geographic Area B		Other Foreign Geographic Areas	
	Oil	Gas	Oil	Gas	Oil	Gas	Oil	Gas	Oil	Gas
Proved developed and undeveloped reserves:										
Beginning of year	X	X	X	X	X	X	X	X	X	X
Revisions of previous estimates	X	X	X	X	X	X	X	X	X	X
Improved recovery	X	X	X	X	X	X	X	X	X	X
Purchases of minerals-in-place	X	X	X	X	X	X	X	X	X	X
Extensions, discoveries, and other additions	X	X	X	X	X	X	X	X	X	X
Production	(X)	(X)	(X)	(X)	(X)	(X)	(X)	(X)	(X)	(X)
Sales of minerals-in-place	(X)	(X)	(X)	(X)	(X)	(X)	(X)	(X)	(X)	(X)
End of year	X	X	X	X	X	X	X	X	X	X
Proved developed reserves:										
Beginning of year	X	X	X	X	X	X	X	X	X	X
End of year	X	X	X	X	X	X	X	X	X	X
Oil and gas applicable to long-term supply agreements with foreign governments or authorities in which the company acts as producer:										
Proved reserves at end of year	X	X			X	X	X	X	X	X
Received during the year	X	X			X	X	X	X	X	X
Company's proportional interest in reserves of investees accounted for by the equity method, end of year	X	X	X	X	X		X		X	

FIGURE 37.3 DISCLOSURE FORMAT FOR RESERVE QUANTITIES AND CHANGES IN QUANTITIES

Source: SFAS 19 (AC 6021.050-.056).

1. Property acquisition,
2. Exploration,
3. Development, and
4. Production (lifting).

This disclosure is to be made for each period for which an income statement is presented and for each geographic area for which reserve quantity information is disclosed.

All Public Companies. In addition to all the disclosures listed in the preceding subsection, the extensive disclosures discussed below, based on ASR 257, are required.

Description of method. The method is to be disclosed on the face of the balance sheet.

Estimated future net revenues. The reserve quantity information specified above for all companies must be augmented by providing estimated future net revenues, calculated by using current prices and current costs. The amounts applicable to each of the first three succeeding fiscal years should be presented separately, with the remainder as a single amount, as illustrated in Figure 37.4.

Disclosure shall also be made of the present value of estimated future net revenues (using a 10% discount rate) as of each period for which an income statement is required, in the aggregate and for each of the following categories:

1. Proved reserves,
2. Proved developed reserves,
3. Proved reserves applicable to long-term supply agreements with foreign governments, and
4. The company's share of proved reserves of equity method investees, in the aggregate.

This presentation is illustrated in Figure 37.5.

Costs incurred. In addition to disclosure of acquisition, exploration, development, and production costs, DD&A (depreciation, depletion, and amortization) and valuation provisions are to be disclosed, also by geographic area. Disclosure of the company's share of the costs incurred by an investee accounted for under the equity method is also required.

Revenues from oil and gas production. For each full year for which an income statement is required, ASR 257 also requires disclosure of net revenues related to the following activities (by geographic area):

1. Proved developed reserves,
2. Long-term agreements with foreign governments where the company is producer, and
3. Proportional share of net revenues of equity method investees.

**ESTIMATED FUTURE NET REVENUE FROM
PROVED OIL AND GAS RESERVES**

DECEMBER 31, 19X1

	Proved Developed and Undeveloped	Proved Developed	Long-term Supply Agreements With Foreign Governments (Company Operated)	Equity Investees (Proportional Share)
Total Worldwide				
19X2	$ X	$ X	$ X	$ X
19X3	X	X	X	X
19X4	X	X	X	X
Remainder	X	X	X	X
	$ X	$ X	$ X	$ X
United States				
19X2	$ X	$ X		$ X
19X3	X	X		X
19X4	X	X		X
Remainder	X	X		X
	$ X	$ X		$ X
Foreign Geographic Area A				
19X2	$ X	$ X	$ X	$ X
19X3	X	X	X	X
19X4	X	X	X	X
Remainder	X	X	X	X
	$ X	$ X	$ X	$ X
Foreign Geographic Area B				
19X2	$ X	$ X	$ X	$ X
19X3	X	X	X	X
19X4	X	X	X	X
Remainder	X	X	X	X
	$ X	$ X	$ X	$ X
Other Foreign Geographic Areas				
19X2	$ X	$ X	$ X	$ X
19X3	X	X	X	X
19X4	X	X	X	X
Remainder	X	X	X	X
	$ X	$ X	$ X	$ X

FIGURE 37.4   SAMPLE FORMAT FOR DISCLOSURE OF ESTIMATED FUTURE
NET REVENUES
SOURCE: AICPA, Proposed Audit and Accounting Guide, *Oil and Gas Reserve Information
Required by Regulation S-X* (1980n), p. 12.

Public Companies Using Full Cost. In addition to the requirements in the two
preceding subsections, ASR 258 requires that full costers make the disclosures
below.

Amortization per unit. The total amount of amortization expense per unit used
for each cost center for each year that an income statement is required must be
disclosed.

Properties not being amortized. Companies must disclose on the face of the
balance sheet the aggregate capitalized costs of unproved properties and major
development projects that are not being amortized. A description in the notes to
the financial statements should include

**PRESENT VALUE OF ESTIMATED FUTURE NET REVENUE
FROM PROVED RESERVES OF OIL AND GAS**

	Total Worldwide		United States		Foreign Geographic Area A		Foreign Geographic Area B		Other Foreign Geographic Areas	
	December 31, 19X1	19X0	December 31, 19X1	19X0	December 31, 19X1	19X0	December 31, 19X1	19X0	December 31, 19X1	19X0
Proved developed and undeveloped reserves (1)	$ X	$ X	$ X	$ X	$ X	$ X	$ X	$ X	$ X	$ X
Proved developed reserves	$ X	$ X	$ X	$ X	$ X	$ X	$ X	$ X	$ X	$ X
Long-term supply agreements with foreign governments (company operated)	$ X	$ X			$ X	$ X	$ X	$ X	$ X	$ X
Equity investees (proportional share)	$ X	$ X	$ X	$ X	$ X	$ X	$ X	$ X	$ X	$ X

Basis for Present Value of Estimated Future Net Revenue

a. Oil prices used were based on prices at December 31, 19X1 and 19X0, with no escalation. Gas prices used were based on current contracts adjusted for contractual escalations.

b. Development and production costs were estimated on the assumption that existing economic conditions will continue.

c. A 10 percent discount rate was used.

d. Income tax effects were not considered.

(1) The requirement to segregate reserves added in the current year from those added in prior years was deleted by ASR 269 for years ending after December 26, 1979.

FIGURE 37.5   SAMPLE FORMAT FOR THE DISCLOSURE OF PRESENT VALUE OF ESTIMATED FUTURE NET REVENUES
SOURCE: AICPA, Proposed Audit and Accounting Guide, *Oil and Gas Reserve Information Required by Regulation S-X* (1980n), p. 43.

1. Current status of the properties and projects involved, including anticipated timing of the inclusion of such costs in the amortization calculation and the potential future impact on the amortization rate; and
2. The nature of the costs by category, and the approximate date that such costs were first incurred, with respect to each property or project.

Interim Financial Statement Disclosures. Disclosure of aggregate capitalized costs by geographic area as required by SFAS 19 (AC 6021.049) and ASR 257 is to be made in complete sets of interim financial statements that present financial position, results of operations, and changes in financial position in conformity with GAAP. Disclosure of reserve quantities and property acquisition, exploration, development, and production costs is not required in interim financial statements.

Supplemental RRA Summary. In ASR 269 the SEC adopted a requirement that all public oil and gas producing companies present a supplemental summary of activities based on reserve recognition accounting. The next section of this chapter is devoted to the methods to be employed in the development of information under reserve recognition accounting.

Reserve Recognition Accounting

The SEC concluded in ASR 253 that traditional historical-cost-based accounting methods provide inadequate information about the economic activities of oil and gas producers. Thus, the commission proposed the adoption of the reserve recognition methods, a value-oriented approach that would require income recognition on the basis of the value of proved reserves added during a period.

RRA is not a true current value approach, however, in that only proved reserves are considered and value measurement would be made under the definitions adopted for disclosure purposes. An estimate of current value would require consideration of known or reasonably estimable future economic conditions and of additional reserve categories. Because of the additional imprecision that would be introduced by consideration of these factors, the SEC opted to include only those reserves whose existence was reasonably certain and whose valuation rested on present economic circumstances. Moreover, since the marketability of proved properties and of the hydrocarbons to be produced may be considered almost certain under the present demand and supply situation, traditional tests for revenue recognition are largely met.

Within this framework, then, it may be appropriate to recognize revenue from exploration and development activities at the time reserves enter the proved category. Under reserve recognition accounting, the balance sheet will show two accounts for oil and gas properties:

1. Unproved properties, which are stated at the cost of the unproved properties less any allowance for impairment, and
2. Proved properties, which are recorded at the net present value of the properties.

One of the SEC-suggested formats for the RRA income statement, presently a supplemental disclosure, is shown in Figure 37.6. Other forms, such as cash-flow statements, are presently allowable. See, for example, the SEC's second illustrative format in Figure 37.7. Presumably, if RRA should become required for the primary statements, formats similar to Figures 37.6 and 37.7 would no doubt be specified by the SEC. The value of proved reserves is the critical component of this statement. Reserve values added in the period, and changes in these values, comprise the revenues recognized from exploration and development activities.

Reserve Valuation. Proved reserves are periodically evaluated by reservoir engineers. These evaluations are considered of primary importance in determining reserve purchase or sales prices and in determining the amount and repayment terms for loans secured by reserves. Thus, it is this report that becomes the basis for the reserve valuation proposed in RRA. To standardize the application of RRA and thus to provide for comparability across firms, the SEC has proposed several assumptions that are to be employed in preparing the value estimate:

1. The estimate is to be based on proved reserves only, as defined previously, using a current economic conditions concept under which future price changes are not anticipated but are recognized in the income statement as they occur.

SUMMARY OF OIL AND GAS PRODUCING ACTIVITIES ON THE BASIS OF RESERVE RECOGNITION ACCOUNTING

YEAR ENDED DECEMBER 31, 1979

(THOUSANDS)

Additions and revisions to estimated proved oil and gas reserves:	
Additions to estimated proved reserves, gross	$1,110
Revisions to estimates of reserves proved in prior years:	
Changes in prices	683
Other	(239)
Accretion of discount	749
Subtotal	2,303
Evaluated acquisition, exploration, development and production costs:	
Costs incurred, including impairments	577
Present value of estimated future development and production costs	873
Subtotal	1,450
Additions and revisions to proved reserves over evaluated costs	853
Provision for income taxes	356
Results of oil and gas producing activities on the basis of reserve recognition accounting	$ 497

CHANGES IN PRESENT VALUE OF ESTIMATED FUTURE NET REVENUE FROM PROVED OIL AND GAS RESERVES

YEAR ENDED DECEMBER 31, 1979

(THOUSANDS)

Increases:	
Additions and revisions	$2,303
Less related estimated future development and production costs	873
Net additions and revisions	1,430
Purchase of reserves in place	483
Expenditures that reduced estimated future development costs	337
Subtotal	2,250
Decreases	
Sales of oil and gas and value of transfers, net of production costs of $231	967
Sales of reserves in place	238
Subtotal	1,205
Net increase	1,045
Beginning of year	7,490
End of year	$8,535

FIGURE 37.6 SUGGESTED FORMAT FOR RRA INCOME STATEMENT
SOURCE: ASR 269.

SUMMARY OF OIL AND GAS PRODUCING ACTIVITIES ON
THE BASIS OF RESERVE RECOGNITION ACCOUNTING
(INCLUDING FUNDS FLOW AND DEFERRED COSTS)
YEAR ENDED DECEMBER 31, 1979
(Thousands)

	Funds Flow	Deferred Costs	Net Present Value of Proved Reserves	Results of Oil and Gas Producing Activities
Additions to estimated proved reserves, gross			$1,110	$1,110
Revisions to estimates of reserves proved in prior years:				
Changes in prices			683	683
Other			(239)	(239)
Interest factor			749	749
Subtotal			2,303	2,303
Evaluated acquisition, exploration, development and production costs:				
Costs incurred, including impairments	$(435)	$(142)		(577)
Present value of estimated future development and production costs			(873)	(873)
Expenditures that reduced estimated future development costs	(337)		337	
Sales of oil and gas and value of transfers, net of production costs of $231	967		(967)	
Sales of reserves in place	238		(238)	
Purchase of reserves in place	(675)	192	483	
Subtotal	(242)	50	1,045	853
Provision for income taxes	(38)			(356)
Net change or amount	$(280)	50	1,045	$ 497
Balance -beginning of year		621	7,490	
Balance - end of year		$671	$8,535	

FIGURE 37.7   SUGGESTED ALTERNATE FORMAT FOR RRA INCOME
STATEMENT
SOURCE: ASR 269.

2. Unproved properties are to be carried at historical cost, subject to a valuation allowance.

3. The engineer's scheduled future production from the company's proved properties and the cash flow estimated by using the current cost and price assumptions are to be discounted to the present using a 10% discount rate. The rate was selected by SEC for several reasons:

   a. There is no set of conceptual rules that would permit computation of a consistent and defensible rate for all companies.

   b. The rate should reflect only the risks of producing proved reserves, plus a normal return on capital. Since prices and costs are not to be inflated in the reserve value estimates, the SEC's rate is not intended to compensate for inflationary effects.

   c. The 10% rate is consistent with studies on the rates of return earned on oil and gas operations.

Revenue Recognition. The exploration revenues to be recognized in any period reflect the net present value of reserves added to the company's proved reserves.

These additions may result from new discoveries (including upgrading of probable reserves to proved reserves), improved recovery systems, revisions of previous estimates, changes in decline rates or other production rate changes, and price and cost changes that affect economic recoverability of reserves. The change in value that occurs from the passage of time is also recognized in the period (as accretion of discount), as are revisions to estimates of reserves proved in prior years.

Production revenue is not recognized, but is an element of changes in proved reserves based on the sale price of gas and liquids sold to outsiders. The market price of gas and liquids transferred to downstream segments of an integrated company is included in the statement of changes in the period when the transfer takes place.

Expense Recognition. All exploration and development costs are to be written off as expense in the period in which they are incurred, except that costs of exploratory wells in progress and acquisition costs of unproved properties are capitalized. Acquisition costs of unproved properties are written off against exploration and development revenue at the time the property is evaluated or abandoned. Exploratory well costs are written off when the well is completed. When a large capital investment program (such as an offshore platform) is in progress but only part of the reserves expected from the property are considered proved, the costs of the project are to be prorated between proved and unproved properties on some percentage-of-completion basis.

The values of proved oil and gas reserves as computed under the RRA assumptions are not subject to amortization, because neither income from production nor amortization of reserve values is considered relevant in the context of this method.

Income Tax Allocation. When reserve recognition accounting information is disclosed, interperiod tax allocation under the liability method (see Chapter 25) is required by ASR 269, based on the difference between the discounted future net revenues and the income tax basis of the properties at the beginning and end of the period, net of any future investment tax credits to be earned from the incurrence of future development costs included in the RRA computations. The SEC believes that the liability method is more consistent with discounted cash-flow concepts and, therefore, is preferable to the deferred method for purposes of the RRA presentation.

ASR 269 requires that income taxes be computed at the *effective incremental rate* and discounted to a present value amount. Specifically, aggregate taxable income from the production of proved reserves may be approximated by subtracting from the present value of estimated future net revenues the current tax basis of the properties involved (including any carryforwards of operating losses and other deductions). The statutory income tax rate at the end of the current period is applied to this amount, and applicable investment tax credits and permanent differences considered. The total tax provision then consists of the currently computed amount less the similarly computed amount as of the beginning of the period plus the current tax provision based on oil and gas producing activities during the period.

Status of RRA. Late in 1980, RRA was still in the proposal stage. The rules summarized in this section represent the beginning of an evolutionary process. The

SEC has expressed the belief that disclosure of supplemental RRA information required by ASR 269 will be meaningful and will provide information relevant to the development and implementation of RRA as a basis for financial statement presentation; the SEC also admits that the feasibility of RRA is not assured. At present, RRA disclosures are supplemental only. Whether they will be required for primary financial statement presentation is an open question.

Meanwhile, the 1979 supplemental reports in Form 10-K have shown striking differences between RRA and conventional earnings. In a *Forbes* article (Greene, September 29, 1980) these results were compared for eight major companies, as indicated in Figure 37.8. For 1980 this kind of information will have to be in annual shareholder reports, undoubtedly accompanied by considerable disclaimers about the genuine tenuousness of the figures. It is therefore somewhat comforting to reporting companies that the safe harbor provisions of ASR 257 covering the disclosure of information relating to future net revenues from estimated production of proved oil and gas reserves has been extended by the SEC, in ASR 269, to cover RRA disclosures.

Department of Energy Requirements

The Energy Policy and Conservation Act of 1975 (EPCA) provided the initial impetus for the development of uniform accounting practices. One of its purposes was to provide a means for developing a comprehensive energy database. In accordance with this objective, the Department of Energy (DOE) developed its *Financial Reporting System* (*FRS*), with which certain major companies must comply. The requirements of *FRS* will be extended to most major producers and a sample of smaller companies in coming years. The DOE has the authority to require reporting by virtually all companies in the industry.

The DOE has not prescribed an accounting method and has indicated that it does not advocate any particular method, although a preference for development of a form of reserve value accounting has been expressed. The *FRS* does include numerous definitions, including those of proved reserves, which have been adopted

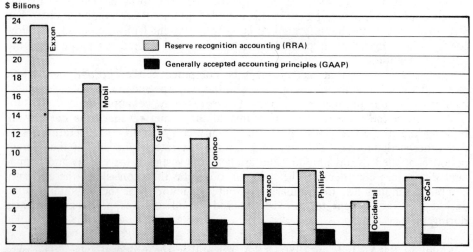

FIGURE 37.8   COMPARISON OF RRA AND GAAP EARNINGS
ADAPTED FROM: "Buried Treasure," *Forbes,* September 29, 1980, p. 113.

by the SEC and conformed to by the FASB in SFAS 25 (AC 6022.07). *FRS* also requires separate reporting for individual segments of integrated operations that are not required under generally accepted accounting principles or SEC rules.

Inflation Accounting

As a result of the issuance of SFAS 33, *Financial Reporting and Changing Prices* (AC 1072), certain large companies must disclose supplemental information on the effects of changing prices.

SFAS 33 initially exempted oil and gas reserves from current cost disclosures for years ended before December 25, 1980. SFAS 39, *Financial Reporting and Changing Prices: Specialized Assets—Mining and Oil and Gas* (AC 1073), issued in October 1980, lifted this exemption for years ending on or after December 25, 1980.

For mining and oil and gas reserves, "current cost" may be measured using one or more of the following methods (AC 1073.02):

- Current market buying prices,
- Current cost of finding and developing reserves,
- Historical cost adjusted by an index of the changes in specific prices of the inputs concerned, and
- Other statistical evidence of the cost of acquisitions (for example, engineering or other cost assessments).

The method chosen "should reflect whatever method of acquisition would currently be appropriate in the circumstances of the company" (AC 1072.058).

For many companies, the appropriate method would be to determine the cost of finding and developing reserves. On the other hand, the FASB recognized that there is currently no generally accepted method for measuring this finding cost. In reality, the finding cost would be a guess at best, and therefore would be an unreliable estimate of current cost. This is so because

1. There is usually a long lead time to explore for and develop new reserves;
2. There is presently no satisfactory method to determine the current prices that would be paid to carry out the exploration and development to obtain the resources;
3. For oil and gas reservoirs that are fully depleted, there are simply no other reservoirs that are identical to those depleted;
4. It may not be possible to find existing quantities at any cost; and
5. If the cost could be determined it would probably be impossible to estimate the quantity that might be found.

Because of these and other factors, it is unlikely that companies will use the finding cost of reserves. Other estimates of current cost, although perhaps more reliable, may not reflect the method of acquisition that would currently be appropriate in the circumstances. The FASB recognized this difficulty, stating that a measure of current cost "is preferable to the alternatives of making no adjustment to historical cost or of using historical cost adjusted for changes in the general price level" (AC 1073.02). Further, "the Board believes that there is an urgent need to provide information about the effects of specific price changes on enterprises that use mineral resource assets. There is a serious gap in public understanding of income levels that may appear large under historical cost measures and yet be inadequate to provide for the maintenance of operating capability. Current cost measures, even if they are subject to difficulties of estimation, are likely to be a useful supplement to historical cost measures by contributing to the development of public understanding" (AC 1073.45).

Income Taxes

Provisions in the income tax law permit treatments for many of the costs of oil and gas exploration and development that differ from the accounting methods specified for financial reporting. Under SFAS 19 (AC 6021.060-.062) and ASR 253, the need for comprehensive interperiod tax allocation for differences in timing between tax and financial income has been firmly established. Income tax accounting procedures are discussed at length in Chapter 25; aspects applicable to the oil and gas producing industry are discussed briefly here.

Timing differences for oil and gas exploration and development activities arise from two primary sources: (1) *intangible drilling costs* and (2) *amortization of tangible equipment* when cost depletion is used. Under tax regulations, expenditures for intangible drilling costs (IDC) may be deducted in the year incurred, or capitalized and amortized over the productive life of the property. If capitalized, IDC on wells in progress may be deducted when the well is found to be nonproductive. Although tax rules provide for the recapture of certain IDC in the event of sale of the property, and treat IDC as a tax preference item under certain circumstances, in many cases the benefit of the immediate deduction outweighs these disadvantages. When IDC is deducted for tax purposes and capitalized for financial reporting purposes, interperiod tax allocation must be followed.

Under tax regulations, tangible property employed in producing oil and gas may be depreciated under the same depreciation rules used for similar property employed in other kinds of activities. For example, costs of machinery, tools, equipment, pipes, and related installation not deducted as IDC may be capitalized and depreciated over the useful life of the equipment using accelerated depreciation methods, rather than the unit-of-production method required for financial reporting under either full cost or successful efforts accounting. Interperiod tax allocation must, of course, be followed for these timing differences.

For tax purposes, certain small producing companies may be permitted to use percentage depletion rather than cost depletion on their oil and gas properties. The primary benefit of percentage depletion is that a taxpayer may deduct an amount greater than the capitalized cost of the property. The lower the capitalized cost (e.g., through immediate deduction of IDC), the greater the potential tax savings through the use of percentage depletion. However, the amount of percentage depletion allowable is limited to the lesser of 50% of the taxable income from the property to which it has been applied or 65% of the taxpayer's taxable income from all sources before the percentage depletion deduction and certain other items. Percentage depletion in excess of the 65% limit may be carried over to the next year. In most circumstances, the difference between income under financial-reporting-based rules and under percentage depletion for tax purposes is expected to be permanent. Usually, therefore, no interperiod tax allocation is required.

When using percentage depletion, it may be expected that in future years, when accumulated percentage depletion exceeds the cost of the properties, the use of percentage depletion will reduce tax payments that would otherwise be payable from other sources. Although this *interaction* between financial depletion and percentage depletion has, in many cases, been treated as permanent, SFAS 19 (AC 6021.062) holds that it should not be anticipated in computing deferred taxes, but that it should be recognized in the year for which the excess deduction is actually taken. The FASB issued a proposed interpretation of SFAS 19 in August, 1980, however, which would require the excess of percentage depletion over cost depletion to be treated as a timing difference (on which deferred taxes are to be provided) to the extent the percentage depletion reduces the tax basis of a property. Percentage depletion in excess of tax basis would be treated as a permanent difference (FASB, 1980f).

Auditing Considerations

The auditor must gain a thorough understanding of industry practices, accounting and reporting requirements, and the nature of the client's systems and transactions. Then, because of the complexity, volume, and variety of transactions that usually recur in the operations of oil and gas producing companies, the auditor must subject pertinent systems of accounting and internal control to appropriate testing.

Compliance with contractual agreements is a highly pertinent attribute, since seemingly minor differences in the terms of operating or other agreements may have significant effects on how a transaction should be recorded.

The functions of the land, geological, and operating departments must also be understood, and their records should be tested. In general, test points must be established for every phase of information flow in which generation or approval of data or its ultimate entry into the accounting system takes place. As the foregoing discussion of current requirements implied, classification of costs is often a matter of substantial concern.

Examination of reserve data presents a unique set of considerations. The SEC had expressed the intent that the extensive disclosures required by ASRs 253 and 257 be considered a part of the financial statements covered by the auditor's opinion for years ending on or after December 26, 1980. Thus, the Oil and Gas Committee of the AICPA issued a proposed audit and accounting guide, *Oil and Gas Reserve Information* (AICPA, 1979d). In April of 1980, however, the SEC withdrew the proposed audit requirement, and it would appear that the Auditing Standards Board will not move to release a final guide because of a debate over its strong implication that an audit could not succeed without the CPA's engagement of a reservoir engineer.

The AICPA has since issued SAS 33, *Supplementary Oil and Gas Reserve Information* (AU 555), to be applied in conjunction with SAS 27, *Supplementary Information Required by the Financial Accounting Standards Board* (AU 553). Further general guidance is provided in SAS 28, *Supplementary Information on the Effects of Changing Prices* (AU 554).

Reserve Value Disclosures. The auditor's association with the supplemental reserve value disclosures has the objective of determining whether the information contained in the disclosures complies with the SEC's requirements in relation to the financial statements taken as a whole. Since the process of reserve estimation and valuation is complex and beyond the expertise of auditors, who are not trained reservoir engineers, the guide requires that the auditor obtain either a consulting engineer's *opinion* on the enterprise's reserve information or a consulting engineer's *reserve estimates* for substantially all the company's reserves.

A consultant's opinion would normally be sufficient if a company has adequate records and an internal staff of reservoir engineers. Otherwise, an engineer's reserve estimates would probably be required. In either event, the auditor must be satisfied that the engineer is independent of the entity and that the engineer's work covers all properties with significant potential for material adjustment.

If a consulting engineer's opinion is used, the auditor must ascertain that the engineer has surveyed a representative cross section of the company's properties. The auditor is responsible for testing the data submitted to the engineer on which the engineer's opinion will be based. Tests of the listing of properties, production, cost, price and discount factors, and ownership interest proportions should be made by the auditor.

Although the exposure draft guide does not discuss the matter, the auditor may find it useful to integrate the consulting engineer's report in assessment of both the adequacy of allowances for impairments and the base of costs related to proved properties used for DD&A.

Neither the SEC nor the FASB require these reserve value disclosures as part of the financial statements, so lesser tests may suffice to determine that reported book values do not exceed the appropriate limits (i.e., the net present value "lid") and that amortization rates are proper. At the least, an auditor should test the information supplied to the company's engineers to observe that sufficient evidence exists to support the reported book values and amortization. The reserve quantity data (see Figure 37.3) is required, however, for all companies, even though SFAS 25 permits placement outside the financial statements (AC 6022.06), as does ASR 277. The proposed audit and accounting guide, *Oil and Gas Reserve Information* (AICPA, 1979d), though it will probably not be finalized, aims at the disclosures made in the audited financial statements, as mentioned above. Current standards applicable to supplementary information require that the auditor perform certain analytical procedures and make specified inquiries about the reserve quantity information, and report on them explicitly only if he has concerns about the data presented (see SAS 33; AU 555).

Windfall Profit Tax

In 1979 the President elected to phase out the domestic crude oil price controls established in the early 1970s, but at the cost of what many have described as the largest tax ever imposed on a single industry. The so-called windfall profit tax is an excise, or severance, tax on the first sale of domestic crude oil. Producers, defined as holders of the economic interest in the oil, are the taxpayers under the law. Certain royalty owners (state and local governments, and interests owned by charitable institutions before January 22, 1980, and by Indian tribes) are exempt from the tax.

The tax is levied on excess revenues from sales at a price above a statutory base price, and is withheld from gross receipts by either the first purchaser of the oil or the operator of the property. The excess revenues (i.e., the windfall profit) from a barrel of oil that is subject to tax cannot exceed 90% of the net income attributable to the barrel of oil.

The tax structure is correlated with the price control program, from which it has adopted the tier system for classification of oil. There are, however, some significant differences between the two programs. One example is the definition of a property that is treated in the Department of Energy sense for pricing and tax calculations, but which follows the Internal Revenue Code definition for determination of the net income limitation and calculation of percentage depletion.

There are numerous considerations and variables that come into play in calculating the tax and determining record-keeping requirements. An in-depth reading of the regulations is necessary to gain a complete understanding of all requirements, which are not covered here. (For further information see Touche Ross & Co., *HR 3919: The Crude Oil Windfall Profit Tax Act of 1980.*)

Tier Structure. The windfall profit tax program established a three-tier system of taxable oil and a fourth category of exempt oil. Tax rates vary according to their structure and the status of production according to law.

Tier 1 oil includes most categories of oil from fields in production before 1979. Specifically, Tier 1 consists of the DOE classifications of *upper tier, lower tier, released upper tier,* and *heavy (20°)* oil. *Tier 2* oil consists of *stripper* and *national petroleum reserve* oil. *Tier 3* oil comprises *newly discovered, incremental tiertiary,* and *heavy (16°)* oil. *Front-end tertiary* and *north slope Alaskan* oil are exempt.

Tax Structure. The tax is imposed on the excess of the removal, or sales, price over an adjusted base price (after deducting severance taxes paid on the windfall profit element). The base prices for each tier are determined by formulae specified by the regulations. Although all base prices vary according to grade, quality, and location and are adjusted for inflation, typical base prices approximate $12.81 for Tier 1, $15.20 for Tier 2, and $16.55 (plus an annual 2% "kicker") for Tier 3.

Tax rates for all producers, including royalty owners, are 70% for Tier 1, 60% for Tier 2, and 30% for Tier 3. The first 1,000 barrels of production per day are taxed at the reduced rates of 50% (Tier 1) and 30% (Tier 2) for independent producers. The 1,000 barrels of production are prorated between Tiers 1 and 2. Within a tier, the reduced rate is applied first to the highest priced oil.

Phaseout. The crude oil windfall profit tax became effective as of March 1, 1980, and will be phased out over a period of 33 months beginning the later of January of 1988 or one month after $227.3 billion in revenue has been collected. The phaseout will begin no later than January of 1991.

THE HARD MINERALS INDUSTRY

Accounting for hard mineral extraction has been less complex and less subject to public review than has oil and gas accounting. Nevertheless, similar issues arise in the application of accounting rules to the hard minerals industry.

Mineral Reserves

The principal asset of a mining company is generally the rights it holds to extract natural resources. In some cases, these rights are valuable because of the intrinsic value of the resource. In other cases, notably sand and gravel operations, the value of the rights derives from governmental permission obtained by the company to extract the resources in an area where they can be marketed at a profit. In either case, the commercially recoverable reserves are the focus of operations and of the accounting system.

Since there are wide variations in geologic structures, marketability, costs, and other economic determinants of the value of hard minerals, the accounting principles and related definitions must be viewed as general guides, and must be adapted to the circumstances existing for each specific type of resource. Definitions of reserves vary, but they are generally considered to be those resources that are commercially recoverable under current economic conditions. When mineral prices vary widely, the use of current prices and costs for reserve definition purposes can result in wide period-to-period variations in estimated reserves. This occurs, for example, when marginal ore deposits (*gangue*) become sufficiently valuable to be recovered in times of high prices but their recovery becomes uneconomic as prices fall.

If reserve quantities are used as a basis for amortization of capitalized costs, a large base results in smaller amortization charges during periods of high prices, because more reserves are considered economically recoverable; the reverse occurs in periods of low prices. To minimize this problem, and to relate amortization of costs of reserves to the generally long-run nature of mining operations, it is probably most reasonable to use an estimate of longer-term economic conditions for reserve estimates. Reference to past price and cost behavior in the specific mineral may be used as a basis for assessment of future conditions in the absence of major shifts that would require separate consideration. Disclosure of the economic basis used for reserve determination may be necessary to enable a reader to evaluate the company's operations.

In certain circumstances, reserve quantities may be so large relative to annual production that exhaustion of the reserve may not occur until long after the benefits of the rights acquired are exhausted. In such cases, reserves may be limited to those quantities estimated to be recovered over some reasonable period (e.g., 40 years. Reserves recoverable after that time may be treated separately for amortization and disclosure purposes.

Cost Classifications

The four types of costs likely to arise in the hard minerals extractive industry are (1) exploration, (2) acquisition, (3) development, and (4) production. These classifications are similar to those used in the oil and gas industry.

Exploration. Exploration costs are normally incurred prior to acquisition of the right to extract resources. For most hardrock mining activity, exploration costs consist of the relatively fixed costs of the company's exploration and scouting department. They include salaries of geologists, incidental expenditures for mapping, and the cost of studies of geologic structures, together with the direct overhead for these activities. Costs incurred to obtain shooting rights on properties are also a part of exploration costs.

Because these costs are usually ongoing and tend to be low relative to the total costs of any particular extractive operation, it has been predominant practice to expense these costs as incurred. This treatment is also consistent with the approach usually taken for tax reporting purposes.

Some companies, however, believe that the practice of expensing exploration costs as incurred understates the balance sheet costs of mineral properties and may understate current income while overstating future income through smaller amortization charges during the productive cycle. These companies, therefore, capitalize exploration costs identified with successful prospects.

Because of the wide variety of minerals and related geologic structures, of success probabilities, and of exploration costs relative to total costs of the mine or other facilities, support may be found for each method of recording exploration costs. To minimize the likelihood of misunderstanding, disclosure of the method used for recording exploration costs is necessary when these costs are material. Disclosure of balances of capitalized exploration costs would also be helpful for comparisons across companies.

Acquisition. Acquisition costs may be incurred either as fee interests or as leasehold interests. Contrary to the practice in the oil and gas industry, acquisition costs are usually incurred only if there is a high degree of certainty about the existence of natural resources on the property. It is common practice to capitalize property acquisition costs under either fee or leasehold interests. Capitalizable costs would include the purchase price of fee interests; lease bonus costs; surveying, legal, and recording fees; and other related costs of acquisition. Costs of in-house legal and surveying staff that are directly related to the acquisition, together with associated overhead, may also be capitalized. Typically, though, in-house costs are expensed, whereas the costs for identical services from outside suppliers are capitalized. (In theory, the treatment of similar costs should be the same, whether the services are obtained from within or from outside the company.) Time records or other source documents may be used to provide an allocation basis for salaries, out-of-pocket costs, and related overhead.

Capitalized acquisition costs may be written off if the property is found not to be commercially productive. Technological or governmental restrictions are more likely to be the cause of nonproductivity than is the nonexistence of ores or other minerals on the property.

Development. Development costs include site access and preparation, removal of overburden, mining equipment, support facilities, and the installation of these facilities. Many mining companies classify postacquisition costs as development costs. These costs are normally subdivided into *intangible development costs* (IDCs) and *the costs of tangible (depreciable) property* at the site of extractive operations, since tax provisions make separate accounting for these two types of costs necessary. In most cases, following tax practice, IDCs are expensed as incurred, but in a few cases they are capitalized. The costs of tangible equipment, buildings, and other related depreciable property items are capitalized. Normally, disclosure is made of the accounting method employed for IDCs.

Production. Production costs include costs to operate the mine and the costs that arise from the extraction of minerals or other natural resources. In many cases, once a mine has started producing, all further development costs are regarded as production costs rather than as capitalizable along with preproduction development costs. Production costs are inventoried as the products are extracted and charged to cost of goods sold as the products are sold. The depreciation, depletion, and amortization of exploration, acquisition, and development costs are also considered part of the inventoriable costs of the extracted product.

Impairment

Because typical practice in the mining industry calls for immediate expensing of exploration costs and IDCs, there is little likelihood that the capitalized cost balance for mining properties will be more than the net realizable value of the property. However, in those few cases where accounts include capitalized exploration and intangible development costs, a net realizable value limitation is a distinct possibility. If the balance in the property account exceeds the net realizable value of the properties, a valuation allowance should be provided.

The value limitation may be determined either on a property basis or on the basis of each country in which the company holds mining interests. In some instances, it may be appropriate to aggregate company-wide costs and net realizable values in determining whether impairment has taken place, although the separate-country basis is probably the most common.

The value of mining properties may be determined either through the use of data on sales of similar properties and equipment or by the use of discounted cash-flow techniques. If mineral prices fluctuate widely, an expectation of future average prices may give more consistent valuation results than the use of current (spot) prices. Once a property has been written down for valuation purposes, subsequent write-ups, although occasionally found in practice, may result in inconsistent reporting results. The FASB recommended against such subsequent write-ups for oil and gas properties, thus setting a precedent that may be considered applicable to other extractive operations.

Amortization

The capitalized cost balances for a particular property are usually amortized over the expected production from the property on a unit-of-production basis. Some variations arise because of the different types of extractive operations and different philosophical approaches to the amortization question.

Tangible equipment costs may be depreciated over production from the mine or over the life of the equipment, whichever is shorter. A unit-of-production method may be employed, or, consistent with tax regulations, these assets may be depreciated on a time basis.

Acquisition costs and capitalized exploration and development costs are generally amortized on a unit-of-production basis over the total production from the property. When properties are acquired in fee, it is necessary to ascertain the portion of the acquisition cost that derives from extractive rights and the portion that derives from the land itself. Land costs are, of course, not amortized.

Indefinite Life. In the past it was common practice not to amortize any of the capitalized acquisition or intangible costs. This treatment was supported on the basis that mine lives were generally indefinite and more similar to land than to amortizable assets. Support for no amortization was also provided by the frequency with which book value equaled the salvage value of a property. Contemporary practice and literature suggest, however, that these costs should be amortized. In part, this may be because of changes in technology and regulation and other factors that tend to limit the economic life of an extractive operation. Moreover, regulations calling for the restoration of properties at the end of extractive operations may result in a negative salvage value.

Still, the indefinite life of many mining properties causes some problems in the determination of amortization rates. When the productive life of the property is indefinite or so long as to be irrelevant for amortization purposes, an arbitrary time limit is usually set for amortization. Although no standard time limit has been established either in practice or in specific recommendations for mining operations, the amortization of goodwill bears many similarities to that of some mining properties. Thus, the 40-year maximum for goodwill, given in APB 17, *Intangible Assets* (AC 5141), although somewhat arbitrary for tangible minerals, may provide a useful benchmark. In practice, many companies amortize these costs over the lesser of the productive life of the property or some set time period.

Restoration Costs. In many cases, environmental regulations call for extensive restoration of properties on completion of extractive operations. These future costs are associated with all production from the property. Thus, a liability may be assumed to arise that should be provided for over the production period, yet practice varies. The FASB has held that for oil and gas operations, these expected future costs must be considered in determining the depreciation and amortization rates (AC 6021.037), but no such rules have been established for the hard minerals extractive industry. In fact, when the productive life of a property is indefinite, the present value of any restoration liability may be immaterial. An assessment of the facts and circumstances for each extractive operation is necessary to support the chosen treatment of these costs. When a performance bond has been made to provide for restoration costs, the portion of the bond that is expected to offset restoration costs may be used as a basis for recognizing the current portion of those costs. This may be accomplished through a valuation allowance against the performance deposits, through establishment of a liability account, or through expensing current performance-bond payments as may be appropriate in the circumstances.

Amortization Basis. Separate amortization bases may be called for when an acquired property has been only partially developed. Capitalized acquisition costs and capitalized exploration costs may be assumed related to all the minerals on the property, whether developed or undeveloped. The appropriate amortization basis for acquisition costs would, therefore, be the total reserves on the property. Development costs may be associated only with those reserves that are developed. For this reason, it is common practice to amortize development costs over the related proved developed reserves.

Joint Products

In many extractive processes, several products may be derived from the same extracted ore. When this happens, accounting may be based on either a by-product or a joint product approach. With the by-product method, a primary product is identified. The primary product is charged with all the production and amortization costs less the net realizable values of the by-products. The by-products are carried at their net realizable value. Under the joint costing approach, the production and amortization costs are prorated to each of the jointly produced items on some reasonable equivalence basis. In most cases, the relative sales value of the products is used as a basis. Thus, for example, if one product accounts for 60% of the net revenues to be received from sale of the products from a specific quantity of ore, the cost assigned to that product would equal 60% of the total costs of the extracted ore. Other bases for allocation include weight and energy content. Except for the oil and gas industry, in which relative energy content has been specified as the basis for proration, the preference is for equivalent market values. This preference arises because market value may be the only common element for diverse products and use of market values provides identical gross margins at the point of product separation for each of the joint products.

Income Taxes

Accounting for the effects of provisions in the tax law gives rise to a number of analyses that must be conducted to minimize the effective tax levels and to provide for appropriate interperiod tax allocation in the financial statements. Tax law permits the use of percentage depletion for virtually all natural resources without the production restrictions imposed on oil and natural gas. Rates range from 22% for sulfur and uranium and for U.S. deposits of bauxite, lead, nickel, and other listed minerals, down to 5% for gravel, peat, sand, and stone. Oil shale is permitted a 15% rate; other shales are allowed 5%. Rates are applied to the defined gross profit from the property. This gross profit is computed at the point of sale on the property, generally after benefication processes that are considered mining in nature, and may include the price received at plants or mills where such processing takes place, provided such mills are within 50 miles of the property.

Tax law permits certain aggregations of mines that may enable a mine owner to obtain a greater allowance than would be obtained if each property were treated separately, but the depletion allowance is limited to 50% of the taxable income from a property. Percentage depletion may be taken even if accumulated allowances exceed the tax basis of the property. However, depletion in excess of the basis may be subject to minimum tax provisions.

Tax regulations also permit the immediate write-off of most exploration expenditures, subject to recapture when the property is disposed of. IDCs and certain costs of tangible equipment necessary to maintain production may be deducted as incurred. Because percentage depletion is computed regardless of recorded cost, and may be taken in excess of cost, maximum tax benefits are usually obtained by deducting exploration and intangible IDCs as incurred and employing percentage depletion. Tangible equipment may be depreciated using acceptable methods for nonmining equipment.

Except for the benefits of percentage depletion, differences between tax income and income for financial reporting purposes are considered timing differences. Interperiod tax allocation is required for these differences. It has been pointed out that when percentage depletion exceeds the financial reporting basis for the property, the benefits of percentage depletion may serve to offset taxes that would otherwise be payable. This *interaction* between percentage depletion and financially reported income has been discussed by a number of authorities. Some feel the interaction should be anticipated when computing the deferred tax provision on the grounds that because of these tax provisions, the ultimate amount of tax payable will be reduced. Others suggest that the interaction benefits are subject to substantial uncertainty, and therefore should only be recognized as realized. The latter position was adopted by the FASB and the SEC in their oil and gas industry rules. Practice varies in the hard minerals extractive industry.

Disclosure

Traditional Disclosure. It is common practice to disclose quantities of minerals produced, subdivided by types of mineral or other natural resource. In addition, when there are significant operations in a particular mine or nation, companies often make disclosure of the production and, in some cases, the revenues for those mines or nations.

Disclosure of quantities of coal reserves held is usually made for companies with significant coal operations. Practice is mixed with respect to the disclosures of estimated reserves of other hardrock minerals. The portions of financial statements that are unique to the hard minerals industry and the related disclosure and explanatory notes are illustrated in Figure 37.9.

Many mining companies enter into long-term purchase agreements with buyers of the mine output. Often these agreements are required if the company is to obtain financing for development costs at a particular mine site. The contract assures the extractive operator that there will be a sufficient market for the production to make mine development an economically viable project. If purchases under such contracts are necessary to make the mining operation economically viable, disclosure of the contract and related details may be necessary for assessment of the risks involved in company operations. In some cases the contract prices, increased-cost recovery provisions, minimum purchases, cancellation terms, and even the names of the other party to any substantial contract are disclosed.

Current Cost and Constant Dollar Information. The FASB finalized SFAS 33, *Financial Reporting and Changing Prices* (AC 1072), in September 1979, requiring large public companies to provide current cost and constant dollar information for fiscal years ending after December 25, 1979, as supplementary information (not part of the primary financial statements). See Chapter 8 for a detailed discussion of SFAS 33.

The FASB initially exempted unprocessed mineral ore reserves from the current cost disclosures for years ending before December 25, 1980. If the company voluntarily elected to present current cost information, it measured the assets and related expenses at their historical cost/constant dollar amounts or by reference to an appropriate index of specific price changes (AC 1072.053).

In October 1980, SFAS 39, *Financial Reporting and Changing Prices: Specialized Assets—Mining and Oil and Gas* (AC 1073), was issued. This statement lifted the exemption from current cost disclosures for unprocessed mineral ore reserves for years ending on or after December 25, 1980. The current cost of these assets is to be determined using one or more of the methods discussed earlier for determining the current cost of oil and gas reserves. The implementation difficulties, as well as the FASB's basis for requiring these disclosures, is also discussed earlier in this chapter.

In addition to the current cost information for mineral reserves, companies will also have to disclose the following quantity and price information (AC 1073.13):

PORTION OF BALANCE SHEET

Receivables:
Mineral sales $2,000

Inventories:
Mine supplies   100
Mineral product   10

Property, plant, and equipment:
Land and mineral rights   500
Plant and equipment   5,000
                                                                   5,500
Less accumulated depreciation and depletion   1,500
                                                                   4,000

PORTION OF STATEMENT OF INCOME

Mineral sales   10,000

Costs and expenses
Cost of minerals produced $7,500
Depreciation and depletion   800
Selling, administrative and general   700   9,000

Earnings before taxes (etc.) $1,000

PORTION OF NOTES TO FINANCIAL STATEMENTS

SUMMARY OF ACCOUNTING POLICIES

Property, Plant, and Equipment

Property, plant, and equipment carried at cost includes expenditures for new facilities and expenditures that substantially increase the productive lives of existing plant and equipment. Maintenance and repair costs are expensed as incurred. Mineral rights are depleted at a rate based on the cost of the mineral properties and estimated recoverable tonnage. Depreciation of plant and equipment is determined by the straight-line and accelerated methods over the estimated useful lives of the assets. Exploration and development costs are capitalized during the construction and preoperating stage. These costs are amortized against production after commercial operations are commenced.

Income Taxes

Deferred taxes are provided for the income tax effect resulting from timing differences between financial statement pretax income and taxable income. The investment tax credit, to the extent allowable, is applied as a reduction of the provision for income taxes. Deferred taxes related to mineral resource activities are provided on the excess of tax deductions for development and exploration costs over the amount of such costs charged to income in the financial statements.

FIGURE 37.9 EXAMPLE OF FINANCIAL STATEMENT ELEMENTS UNIQUE TO THE HARD MINERALS INDUSTRY

1. Estimates of significant quantities of proved, or proved and probable, reserves (whichever is used for cost amortization purposes) at the end of the year or at the most recent date during the year for which estimates can be made;

2. The estimated quantity, expressed in physical units or in percentages of reserves, of each mineral product that is recoverable in significant commercial quantities if the mineral reserves include deposits containing one or more significant mineral products;

3. The quantities of each significant mineral produced during the year, including the quantity of each significant mineral product produced by the milling or similar process;

4. The quantity of significant proved, or proved and probable, mineral reserves purchased or sold in place during the year; and

5. For each significant mineral product, the average market price, or, for mineral products transferred within an enterprise, the equivalent market price prior to use in a manufacturing process.

These disclosures are not required by SFAS 39 to be made for oil and gas reserves, since information on quantities of oil and gas reserves is currently required by SFAS 19. Although the FASB initially had proposed that the fair value (the exchange price that could be reasonably expected in an arm's-length transaction between a willing buyer and a willing seller) be disclosed for each mineral reserve, the Board decided that the reliability of such measurements was currently inadequate for the disclosure to be required at the present time.

Auditing Considerations

Although auditing the hard minerals industry has many similarities to auditing the oil and gas producing industry, the auditor needs to develop an understanding of the unique practices and accounting and reporting in hard minerals and of the internal accounting controls and systems his client has established. In addition, he must evaluate those controls and systems through review and testing.

One of the unique problems in this industry relates to mineral reserves, which must be estimated to determine the cost of minerals produced. The auditor will need to understand the work of mineral engineers, and he may need to use the work of a specialist in accomplishing this assessment. SAS 11 (AU 336) provides professional guidance for the auditor under these circumstances.

It is also necessary to review the details of the mineral properties to see that mineral rights are included in the ownership rights of the land, that options for rights have not expired or been forfeited, and that advance royalty payments are expected to be recoverable from future operations based on existing economic conditions.

TIMBER RESOURCES

The Industry

One characteristic of the forest products industry is unique: the raw material—timber—used in the manufacture and processing of forest products is renewable. Oil, gas, and hard minerals, once extracted, are gone forever. Admittedly, agricultural products are also renewable, but the short planting-to-harvest cycle allows reasonably accurate projection of yield quantities. This is not true with timber. The shortest timber cycle from planting to harvest is about 20 years, and the longer cycles are commonly 50-80 years. Return on investment is not at all certain, because of potential loss of timber resources through natural disaster, fire, insect infestation, and disease. Further, prediction of market conditions so many years into the future is all but impossible.

Accounting for and auditing of the timber segment of the forest products industry presents some unusual problems, which are discussed in this section. Once lumber and pulp have been produced, traditional accounting methods are applicable.

Accounting Considerations

Cost Capitalization. Timber and timberland are acquired through (1) purchase of the land and timber thereon, (2) lease of the land with assumption of timber-cutting rights, or (3) purchase of timber-cutting rights on land owned by private interests or the federal government. In addition, cut timber is often purchased on the open market.

When the forest-products company maintains an economic interest in the land as well as in the timber on that land, that interest is called fee timber and is classified as a fixed asset. Economic interest applies both to purchased and leased land and timber, even though the lease agreement may provide that the deforested land reverts to the original landholder upon termination of the lease rights (i.e., upon completion of the logging operation). Timber leases generally meet the capitalization criteria and are, likewise, classified as fixed assets.

Fee timber acquisition costs, such as surveys, purchase price, brokerage costs, and legal fees, are also capitalized. Development costs such as road construction, temporary lodging facilities, and land-clearing activities are also capitalized, generally as land improvements. Carrying costs such as interest and taxes on the timberland and overhead costs related to the development period may be capitalized, but only if incurred prior to the start of harvesting operations. However, most companies treat interest, taxes, and overhead as operating expenses. Similar acquisition and development costs related to timber-cutting rights on leased land are capitalized.

Even after cutting has begun, it is proper to capitalize costs attributable to future harvests, e.g., land clearing, reseeding or planting, and forest management. Costs associated with research and development related to new growing techniques or improving trees genetically are expensed.

Often, timber-cutting rights are purchased from land owners under long-term contracts. The deposits required under such contracts are capitalized and depleted as timber is harvested from the land. Costs related to purchase of timber on the open market are treated the same as the purchase of raw materials in any industry, that is, capitalized as raw material inventory and expensed as used.

Depletion. Just as oil, gas, and hard mineral reserves are depleted over time, so too are timber resources. Thus, some portion of the total cost of the fee timber should be depleted based on the proportion of timber harvested during the year to timber available for cutting. Many companies adjust depletion rates on an annual basis.

Generally, small and medium-sized firms use a single average depletion rate for all the timber, regardless of its geographic location or grade. Larger companies frequently break down the rate by tract (i.e., geographically) or by species and grade of timber, which results in a more precise depletion calculation.

The actual method used to calculate depletion is disclosed in notes to the financial statements, and the depletion charge itself is separately disclosed only when it is material. If timber harvesting is a significant part of a company's operations, timber assets are shown on the balance sheet as a separate line item, typically "Timber and timberlands at cost, less cost of timber harvested."

Modern forest-products companies subscribe to sustained-yield forestry, that is, replacement of the amount of timber cut by an equal or greater amount of timber growth. The effect is that total timber available for harvest remains about the same or is increased. In certain hardwood areas, natural regeneration occurs on the former sites of standing timber. Seeds that have dropped to the forest floor over time and remained dormant are later exposed to adequate sunlight and water. These seedlings naturally grow to maturity with little actual forest management expense warranted. Softwoods, e.g., southern pine, do not naturally regenerate as easily. Extensive forest management efforts must be expended in cutting seed stock from mature trees, growing and planting the seedlings, and managing the growth process. The cost of naturally regenerated stands of timber on owned or leased land permitting more than one-rotation cutting may be small compared to original acquisition costs.

Inventories.

Physical measurement. Forest-products companies vary greatly in size and operations. A few are large, complex entities with vertically integrated operations in many or all aspects of the forest-products industry—from growing and harvesting timber through processing, distributing, and retailing. The medium-sized and smaller companies are engaged in one or two of these activities. Our concern here is with the growth and harvesting of timber and the processing and manufacturing of lumber and pulp. The distribution and sale of these products are similar to those processes for products in other manufacturing and retailing entities, so they are not discussed here. Rather, we will consider the methods used to physically count standing timber (a fixed asset) and harvested wood (inventory).

It would be very difficult to measure accurately the quantity, species, and grades of standing timber. Therefore, the determination of quantities must depend on estimation formulas developed by the forestry industry and sampling surveys performed by foresters. Standard volume tables have been developed over the years, and the forester uses them to measure volumes of available timber. Aerial surveys may be used to verify generally the acreage and species quantities carried on the company's books.

Measurement of harvested wood (in log or chip form for use in pulp production, in log or finished lumber form at sawmills) also requires the services of an expert, and the auditor can observe the estimation process. Standard scales are used to measure quantities, and frequently an experienced auditor can ascertain species and grades. Pulpmill wood is generally measured in terms of cords and converted to tons or vice versa. Sawmill inventories of raw logs are counted at the boom ponds or cold decks of mills in terms of cords and are converted to board feet. Finished lumber may be measured and counted, and board feet determined therefrom.

Valuation. Standing timber constitutes the reserves of the forest products industry, and it is in this area that the accounting practices peculiar to the industry are most evident. Unlike oil and gas reserves or hard mineral deposits, timber supplies can be replenished. But unlike agricultural products, the growth cycle occurs over extended periods of time, from 20 years to as long as 80 years. The problem then becomes one of valuing a resource that is simultaneously being depleted and regenerated. As mentioned previously, standing timber is valued at cost less accumulated depletion.

Valuation of many forms of harvested timber is made in conjunction with the estimation of physical inventories. Most companies use lower of cost (determined by the LIFO method) or market, but it is rare that market value of timber is lower than cost. That conclusion is easily verified by examining recent sales records of various species and grades of lumber. Periodical publications of the industry and industry associations present up-to-date market values.

Cost Accounting. One of the difficulties in determining actual costs is the matching of logs processed to the cost of the standing timber. Ordinarily, as mentioned, acreages of timberland are purchased and depletion rates established based on estimates of cords or board feet contained thereon, regardless of species or grade. Yet when the timber is cut into finished boards or plywood at sawmills or processed into pulp, cost is assigned to the timber by quality. For example, the unit purchase price for the timber in a given tract may turn out on average to be $20 per cord. However, the more valuable species may have a unit cost substantially higher.

Overall, however, gross costs do tend to average out; thus average costs are reflected in the accounting records. Few companies attempt to determine unit costs per species or grade in the felling, transporting, milling, and processing states. If a company replenishes its standing timber on a sustained-yield basis without natural regeneration, cost per unit may be more accurately determined, since companies predetermine species to be harvested eventually and maintain continuing records of site preparation, seeding, planting, pruning and thinning, spraying, and similar costs.

Income Taxes

Under the Internal Revenue Code (Section 1231), timber is considered an asset used in a trade or business, and under Section 631, gains on timber harvested are treated as capital gains, whereas losses are treated as ordinary deductions. However, the taxpayer must elect the advantages of Section 631, and once made, the Internal Revenue Service only rarely permits reversal.

The provisions of Section 631 apply only to companies that have an economic interest in the timberland, and that interest must have been held for a specified period of time (which differs somewhat from that of other capital gain sections) before the timber is harvested.

One of the provisions of Section 631 involves companies that harvest timber for use in their own mills. The fair market value of the timber harvested is added to cost of sales and is an ordinary deduction. The fair market value then also becomes a theoretical sales price—in that the timber itself has not been sold—which is netted against the historical cost basis; the resultant amount is taxed at capital gain rates. Another provision of Section 631 deals with entities that sell timber to others. Assuming the timber has been owned for the statutory time period and at the time of sale the seller retains an economic interest in the timber, any gain on the sale would be treated as a capital gain. The buyer who mills and then sells the lumber, however, may not treat gains as capital gains.

Disclosure

Traditional Disclosure. The portions of financial statements that are unique to the timber resources industry and the related disclosure and explanatory notes are illustrated in Figure 37.10.

Inflation-Oriented Disclosure.

Replacement cost. Many forest-products companies were required under ASR 190 to disclose replacement costs for assets used to achieve present productive capacity. ASR 190 does not apply once the company fully adopts both the constant dollar and current cost information required by SFAS 33, discussed below.

Of primary interest in replacement costing was the disclosure of costs to replace standing timber, the unique asset in the industry; disclosures of replacement cost for other property, plant, and equipment, for inventory, and for cost of sales generally followed the disclosure practices used in other industries.

Typically, the historical cost of a company's fee timber includes the undepleted amount of timber available plus the initial acquisition costs; forestry management costs that are expensed as incurred are not included. In arriving at replacement

---

PORTION OF BALANCE SHEET

Timber resources, at cost less cost of timber harvested $100,000

PORTION OF NOTES TO FINANCIAL STATEMENTS

- Fixed Assets—
  Timber and timberlands, which includes original costs, road construction costs, and reforestation costs. . . .

- Depletion—
  The rates used to determine cost of timber harvested are based on estimated quantities of timber available for cutting.

- The cost of timber harvested is determined by calculating that portion of the investment in timber corresponding to the proportion of the current year's cut to the total standing timber.

- Timber and timberlands, which includes original costs, road construction costs, and reforestation costs such as site preparation and planting costs, is stated on the balance sheet at the unamortized cost balance.

- Forestry management expenses such as pest and fire control and other costs such as property taxes are charged to expense as incurred.

- Cost of timber harvested is based on the estimated quantity of timber available during the growth cycle and is credited directly to the asset accounts.

FIGURE 37.10 EXAMPLE OF FINANCIAL STATEMENT ELEMENTS UNIQUE TO THE TIMBER RESOURCES INDUSTRY

costs, companies disregarded initial acquisition costs and include instead reforestation costs, certain forestry management costs, and estimated property taxes that will be incurred until the timber reaches an average state of maturity. Some companies assumed, however, that the total fee timber holdings were to be grown from seedlings to the present state of maturity. As a result of the various subjective judgments used in the computations, there was considerable variation in these replacement costs.

Replacement costs for cost of sales were generally more uniform, as most companies use the LIFO method, which often approximates current costing in cost of sales. Other methods, such as indexing or specific price quotations, were also used.

Calculation of replacement costs for inventories was generally based on FIFO, current-year average costs or year-end costs, average manufacturing costs, indexes, and combinations thereof.

Current cost and constant dollar information. The FASB finalized SFAS 33, *Financial Reporting and Changing Prices* (AC 1072), in September 1979, requiring large public companies to provide current cost and constant dollar information for fiscal years ending after December 25, 1979, as supplementary information (not part of the primary financial statements). ASR 190 has been rescinded for those companies subject to SFAS 33 upon initial publication of current cost data. See Chapter 8 for a detailed discussion of SFAS 33.

Initially, SFAS 33 exempted timberlands and growing timber (including timber held under cutting contracts) from current cost disclosures for years ending before December 25, 1980. If a company voluntarily disclosed current cost information for years ending before December 25, 1980, the assets and related expenses were measured at their historical cost/constant dollar amounts or by reference to an appropriate index of specific price changes.

SFAS 40, *Financial Reporting and Changing Prices: Specialized Assets—Timberlands and Growing Timber* (AC 1074), was issued in November 1980. This statement lifted the exemption from the current cost disclosures for years ending on or after December 25, 1980. SFAS 40 is an *interim* solution to the measurement of the current cost of timberlands and growing timber, since the current cost of the assets and related expenses may still be measured at their historical cost/constant dollar amounts. However, the FASB now allows a company to use other methods of determining current cost. SFAS 40 states:

> If an enterprise estimates the current cost of growing timber and timber harvested by adjusting historical cost for the changes in specific prices, those historical costs may either (a) be limited to the costs that are capitalized in the primary financial statements or (b) include all costs that are directly related to reforestation and forest management, such as planting, fertilization, fire protection, property taxes, and nursery stock, whether or not those costs are capitalized in the primary financial statements. [AC 1074.07]

Therefore, the FASB is allowing companies to use various means of determining current cost, including methods similar to those used for ASR 190 replacement cost disclosures as discussed above. Unfortunately, at least until the FASB decides

Statements of Income The Hibernia Bank
_____ **15**

Years ended December 31, 1979 and 1978 (in thousands)	1979	1978
Interest income:		
Interest and fees on loans	$38,819	30,226
Interest on Federal funds sold	1,558	490
Interest on deposits with banks	386	142
Interest and dividends on investment securities:		
U.S. Treasury securities	2,369	2,136
Securities of other U.S. Government agencies and corporations	2,964	1,527
Obligations of states and political subdivisions	3,495	3,175
Direct lease financing income	1,014	27
Total interest income	50,605	37,723
Interest expense:		
Interest on deposits (note 7)	27,095	19,013
Interest on borrowings	1,351	62
Total interest expense	28,446	19,075
Net interest income	22,159	18,648
Provision for loan and lease losses (note 3)	715	600
Net interest income after provision for loan and lease losses	21,444	18,048
Other operating income:		
Trust income	818	735
Service charges on deposit accounts	1,212	931
Other	648	479
Total other operating income	2,678	2,145
Other operating expense:		
Salaries	8,589	7,193
Employee benefits (notes 10 and 11)	1,214	1,019
Occupancy expense, net	1,267	1,182
Furniture and equipment expense	740	914
Provision for loss on sale of loans (note 13)	451	—
Other	6,406	5,202
Total other operating expense	18,667	15,510
Income before income taxes and securities transactions	5,455	4,683
Provision for income taxes (note 9)	779	715
Income before securities transactions	4,676	3,968
Net securities losses after tax effect of $253 in 1979 and $191 in 1978	(231)	(158)
Net income	$ 4,445	3,810
Earnings per share (note 12):		
Income before securities transactions	$3.65	3.10
Securities transactions, net of income tax effect	(.18)	(.12)
Net income	$3.47	2.98

FIGURE 38.3   EXAMPLE OF NET INTEREST INCOME STATEMENT FORMAT
Source: The Hibernia Bank, 1979 Annual Report.

sum of the parts does not equal the whole, and both the parts and the whole comply with GAAP. This distinction is brought out in the following listing of important differences:

1. _Goodwill._ The regulatory authorities will not allow goodwill to be capitalized and amortized on individual bank statements. The Federal Reserve Board allows it on the statements of bank holding companies as a consolidation entry. GAAP requires its recognition and amortization, if material, on individual bank statements.
2. _Capital notes._ These notes are essentially debt, except that the rights of the note holders are subordinated to depositors. Notes issued by a parent holding company do

	Comptroller of the Currency	Federal Reserve Board	Federal Deposit Insurance Corporation
National bank	X		
Member state and trust banks		X	
Nonmember insured state and trust banks			X

FIGURE 38.4   REQUIRED CALL REPORTING TO COMMERCIAL BANK REGULATORY AGENCIES

not provide the note holder with a claim on the subsidiary banks' assets; but if the proceeds are invested in the capital stock of subsidiary banks, they are also classified in the holding company financial statements as capital notes. Although these notes are debt under GAAP, regulatory authorities permit inclusion of these amounts under the capital funds caption. This issue is being studied and regulatory authorities may in the future require that capital notes be classified as debt.

3. *Stock dividends.* Bank holding companies observe the GAAP requirement that stock dividends be capitalized at fair value. Regulatory authorities require banks to capitalize the legal (par or stated) value.

4. *Property and other assets.* Certain bank assets, primarily real estate and stock acquired as a result of foreclosure, cannot be carried indefinitely by a bank at cost or at market value. National banks, for example, have a definitive formula for amortization to zero over a five-year period for assets acquired in foreclosure, whether or not they actually decline in value below the resulting carrying amount. State requirements are similar, but may vary. If as a result a material amount of assets is, in effect, not reflected in the financial statements, they will not be in conformity with GAAP.

Internal Controls and Internal Auditing. The effectiveness of internal controls takes on special significance in a commercial bank because

- The banks are in the public trust, heavily regulated, and expected to be strong;
- Considering the inherent high volume of transactions, requirements for daily balancing of the general ledger and frequent balancing of the detail ledger to the general ledger would not be possible without strong internal controls; and
- The typical automation of a bank operation would not function without the discipline of internal controls.

All banks have a proof department to perform the balancing procedures and, except for small banks, have an internal audit function to monitor the overall operations of the bank (including internal controls) throughout the year.

Bank examining committees frequently prefer selected *surprise audit procedures,* especially at cash-handling points. Arrangements should be made without the knowledge of management. The importance of surprise audits appears to be fading, except for agency banks with foreign parents.

Most commercial banks have organized their accounting activities into transaction cycles with associated transaction types. (See Chapter 13 for a general discussion of transaction cycles and types.) For instance, the loan-granting cycle might be composed of the following transaction types:

- Commercial loans,
- Real estate and construction loans,
- Loans to financial institutions,
- Consumer loans,
- Acceptance financing,
- Loans for purchasing or holding securities, and
- Leasing.

The most efficient approach in satisfying the auditor's requirement that there be a proper study and evaluation of the existing internal control is to first study, test, and evaluate the activities of the proof department and the internal auditors within these cycles. Then, regular compliance testing on other significant cycles and transaction types can be designed to augment reliance on what will typically be an adequate system. (See also Electronic Data Processing later in this chapter.)

For transactions that are few in number or that are for large amounts, such as opening and closing significant loans and deposit accounts and purchasing and selling securities, the operation of internal controls should be tested throughout the entire year.

The quality of the internal audit function is often relative—the size of the bank and the emphasis placed on internal auditing by top management are the determinants. Larger banks usually have staffs of sufficient size and ability to use audit tools such as flowcharting, statistical sampling, and computer audit programs. Small banks normally have a much more restricted internal audit function. Still, the internal audit staff is normally a significant part of the internal controls within any bank.

Professional standards recognize that the existence and effectiveness of the internal audit function affects the nature, timing, and extent of the external auditor's tests. SAS 9, *The Effect of an Internal Audit Function on the Scope of the Independent Auditor's Examination* (AU 322), provides guidance on this matter. (See also Chapter 11, Appendix 11-A.)

Bonding. Because of their constant access to large amounts of liquid assets, bank employees require bonding. The ABA Preferred Group Bonding Plan allows the participation of CPAs in performing certain required procedures, but the AICPA Banking Committee has cautioned that the procedures, which do not constitute an audit in accordance with GAAS, may not provide sufficient overall CPA services for banks. For CPAs who want to participate in the ABA plan, suggested guidelines have been issued (AICPA, 1980q) explaining how the ABA plan should be modified to allow CPAs to conform to professional standards.

Multinational Transactions. Multinational banks have recognized the importance of internal controls and tight supervision of foreign operations in the past few years, after experiencing well-publicized fraud losses.[3] Preventive controls and accurate, timely documentation are important in foreign transactions.

Open letters of credit generally are recorded in memorandum accounts. Actual accounting entries are made when the transaction cycle is completed. Foreign exchange transactions are usually recorded on a *position report,* which in effect is a perpetual inventory record. SFAS 8 (AC 1083), discussed in Chapter 31, has helped to establish uniform accounting principles.

As a result of the use of memorandum accounts until a transaction cycle is complete, controlling incoming mail for several days to verify proper recording is an important audit procedure. All significant detail accounts should be reconciled and confirmed on a test basis. Positive confirmation requests should be sent to regular respondent banks to ascertain the accuracy of memorandum accounts.

Loan Accounting and Auditing

The auditor and bank supervisory authorities spend a significant amount of time on loans outstanding, since these loans comprise the largest portion of the assets at risk. Numerous lending limitations and requirements are imposed by the supervisory agencies. These include

- Maximum individual borrower lending limits, based on the bank's capital and liquidity;
- Specific limits on loan types considered to be more risky, such as real estate and building construction;
- Loans to purchase or carry securities; and
- Loans to directors, executive officers, and other insiders.

The loan function is organized to promote internal controls and specialization, although the extent of specialization depends on the size of the bank. The auditor should devote considerable time to evaluation of controls, compliance with regulations and proper accounting, assessment of risk and loss reserves, and verification of balances. The accounting and auditing requirements within each of these tasks depend somewhat on the type of loans. The following discussion outlines some of the unique characteristics for the major lending classifications.

Commercial Loans. The chief characteristic of commercial loans is that they are large. Loans are made on the basis of the financial responsibility of the maker or endorser, and may be either unsecured or collateralized. Each is approved by the board of directors or a delegated committee or officer—larger loans by formal resolution in the minutes, and smaller loans by periodic review and ratification. For

---

[3] For example, the substantial losses of the Union Bank of Basel are intriguingly described in a novel by Paul Erdman, *The Billion Dollar Sure Thing* (New York: Simon and Schuster, 1976).

qualifying customers, many banks will open a *line of credit,* and periodic loans may then be granted within the established limit without further formal approval. This line may be renegotiated periodically. Normally, a certain loan official is assigned responsibility for each loan.

Record keeping. The flow of most direct loans is relatively simple. As each new loan is disbursed, the amount to be repaid is posted at the end of the business day to a subsidiary ledger known as a *liability ledger.* This ledger is updated as payments are made or new loans are advanced, and thus a record of all an obligor's borrowings from the bank is shown. Since there is a ledger sheet for each borrower, a trial balance of the liability ledger should equal the general ledger totals of commercial loans and discounts (loans where initial proceeds are reduced by the interest charge).

Some banks have an additional subsidiary ledger known as an *indirect liability ledger,* showing obligations for which a borrower is indirectly or secondarily responsible as a guarantor or endorser.

The general ledger loan account balances are supported either by the notes or by loan cards. When the notes are used, partial payments are entered directly on the note, and in these cases the notes serve as the subsidiary record. Demand notes usually are filed alphabetically, whereas time notes are usually arranged in maturity date order. In either case, a further breakdown is often made between secured and unsecured loans.

If loan cards are used, there is one for each loan. (A computer report in an automated system is another form of loan card.) This record reflects the loan balance and the status of pledged collateral. When loan cards are used, payments are seldom recorded on the notes themselves. When the collateral is withdrawn for any reason, the borrower's signature is obtained to signify receipt.

Noncomputerized banks use *maturity ticklers* for commercial notes—numbered forms on which descriptive information is typed. Systems differ but typically will include copies for note register, maturity notice, interim payments due (if any), and audit copy. The maturity tickler, the note notice, and any interim payment ticklers are filed by due date, the note notice being mailed a certain number of days in advance as notice to the customer of his forthcoming due date.

A credit file is maintained for each borrower. For unsecured loans, this file usually contains financial statements, memoranda regarding financial or personal status, financial statements of guarantors (individual or corporate), loan applications, designated officer or loan committee approval, copies of supplementary agreements between the bank and the borrower, and other applicable correspondence and memoranda. In the case of borrowers whose loans are fully secured, the credit file may be meager.

Audit procedures. Commercial loan examination procedures usually require the largest single portion of the time expended in the examination of a bank's financial statements. The examination of commercial loans generally should be performed at an interim date that is no more than 90 days before the examination date, because the composition of the commercial loan portfolio may substantially change during a longer period.

Audit procedures should include

- Agreeing the loan subsidiary ledgers (liability ledgers) to the general ledger on a surprise basis;

- Confirming directly with debtors a substantial percentage of outstanding loan dollars, using positive confirmations (requiring a response)—less than 20% of the number of loans outstanding will usually result in high dollar coverage;

- Reviewing the credit files for the loans confirmed, inspecting related collateral on a sample basis (including collateral at customer's place of business), and price testing collateral to see if it meets bank limits;

- Reviewing past-due reports and testing their accuracy, and discussing past-due loans or potential problem loans with loan officers; and

- Determining whether loans to directors and officers are in excess of the bank's policy or in violation of regulatory limitations (see Article 9-02 of Reg. S-X for special disclosure rules).

Real Estate and Building Construction Loans. These loans are usually subdivided into three groups: conventional; Federal Housing Authority (FHA) insured; and Veterans Administration (VA or GI) insured. Loans on commercial and residential improved property are based on a percentage of the appraised value and are secured by first mortgage liens. During periods of rising property values, lending activity may occur in the form of junior mortgages (second liens or trusts) or *wraparound* mortgages. The latter form consolidates prior mortgages and servicing in one bank without disturbing the original terms.

Fees for making a mortgage loan (primarily FHA loans) can be charged to the mortgagor. These *points* in actuality represent an adjustment of yield on the loan and should be amortized over the average life of the mortgage loan portfolio, which is usually about 7 to 10 years.

Mortgage loans may originate directly with bank customers or by purchase from other banks or mortgage banking companies. Similarly, mortgage payments may be made directly to the bank by mortgagors or may be collected by the servicing agent who originally sold the mortgage to the bank. Repayment terms are customarily based on level monthly payment amortization schedules of principal and interest. Frequently, the monthly payments include escrow deposits for payments of insurance and real estate taxes (ordinarily required in FHA and VA loans).

Banks also grant loans to finance building construction, but generally only after long-term financing (a *takeout commitment*) has been arranged. Though these construction loans are also usually secured by real estate, they are considered more risky because of the volatility of construction costs.

Record keeping. Generally, an individual mortgage loan record is maintained for each mortgagor, showing unpaid mortgage principal balance and other pertinent information, such as escrow fund balances. To avoid duplication of effort, most banks do not record principal payments on the mortgage notes, so only the ledger cards (which are often computer records) reflect the mortgage balances. If mortgage loan ledger cards are used, they are frequently kept in a separate real estate loan department, but if volume is small the commercial loan department may maintain them.

Customarily a mortgage document folder is maintained for each loan. The basic documents in this folder are

- The note,
- A mortgage, with evidence of recording as a lien against the property,
- An assignment (if the bank has purchased the mortgage loan from a prior mortgagee),
- A title policy or certificate of title,
- An appraisal (a loan insured by the VA or the FHA will also have an appraisal by one of their representatives),
- Insurance policies providing fire coverage, extended coverage, and mortgage coverage (the bank will usually maintain a separate tickler file of insurance policies, arranged in expiration date order),
- FHA and VA guarantees, and
- Other documents required under state statutes (the auditor should be familiar with the applicable state requirements).

Audit procedures. The two principal audit procedures are loan confirmation and loan file review. Because of the homogeneous nature of most residential mortgage and building construction loans, both of these procedures may be applied on a limited test basis if the bank has adequate internal control. Large residential and commercial mortgage loans usually should be audited in greater detail. Because of the slow turnover of mortgage portfolio, it is feasible to perform the majority of the audit procedures at an interim date. Audit procedures should include

- Agreeing the subsidiary ledgers, including escrow balances, to the general ledger on a surprise basis;
- Confirming a portion of the loans directly with the mortgagor (debtor), using both positive and negative confirmation forms;
- Testing the accuracy of past-due reports and reviewing loans in foreclosure or that have been written off, to evaluate the extent of possible losses;
- Reviewing a small sample of credit files (loan folders); and
- Confirming purchased mortgages, including participation in mortgage pools, using positive requests.

Retail Credit and Consumer Loans. Installment loans made directly to consumers are called *direct paper;* those made through dealers are called *indirect paper.* The loan contract will normally call for monthly repayments, and the bank will ordinarily hold a security agreement on the purchased consumer goods as collateral.

In the case of direct paper, the customer makes an application, and if the application is approved, the funds are disbursed according to the customer's directions. For indirect paper, the customer deals with a third party, who takes the initial application (called a conditional sales contract) and submits it to the bank. The bank follows its routine procedure in determining creditworthiness; if the loan is granted, the proceeds (less any dealer reserve if so arranged) are credited to the dealer.

Recourse, or the practice of holding the dealer responsible for defaulted payments on sales contracts discounted by the bank, is not always available to the bank, since the merchant may not be willing to agree to it. Some banks do not seek recourse as a matter of policy; others arrange recourse according to the stability and character of the merchant.

In larger banks, the consumer loan function may be segregated into several specialized departments. There may be persons who only handle direct transactions with the public; others may limit their activities to dealer paper. The latter may be divided further, e.g., automobile dealers and appliance dealers.

Dealer reserves and floor plan loans. Dealer reserves represent a holdback agreement between the dealer and the bank whereby the bank will retain part of the proceeds on indirect loans made through a dealer to protect the bank from possible losses. Some banks will not hold back the proceeds, but will reclassify some of the "add-on" interest (described below) as a dealer reserve and not as unearned income.

Banks also make *floor plan* loans to finance dealers' inventories. These loans have a single date maturity, with or without a renewal option and agreed holdback terms. As items are sold from inventory, payment is required.

Credit cards and other consumer credit. Credit card financing has increased in importance in the last few years. The credit card essentially sets up a line of credit on issuance, and the associated short-term loans are initiated by cardholder purchases from merchants or through cash advances. Processing of the purchases and subsequent billings has been automated in virtually all banks. The merchant submits charge slips through its own bank to the bank granting the line of credit or to an affiliate. The bank receiving the charge slips immediately credits the merchant's account, less a negotiated discount, part of which may be refunded to the bank granting the line of credit.

The issuing bank must exercise strict controls over issued cards and must monitor accounts with high balances, excessive activity, and delinquencies. These controls should be documented by the bank, and their adequacy evaluated by the auditor.

Banks may also offer customers other forms of revolving credit loans, under names such as "ready credit" and "no-bounce checking." The controls over these loans are similar to those on credit cards and should be audited in the same way.

Record keeping. Installment loans are primarily made using the *add-on method* —the interest, creditor's life insurance premium, and other charges are added to the amount advanced to arrive at the face amount of the note. The note is repayable in installments, usually in equal monthly amounts.

The add-on method of applying interest charges is different from that of the *discount method* (usually used on commercial loans). Under the add-on method, the interest charges are computed by multiplying the periodic interest percentage times the amount to be given the customer. The result is then multiplied by the number of periods comprising the life of the loan. For example: for a loan of $1,000 at 8% per annum to be repaid over a period of two years, interest would be computed as $1,000 \times .08 = \$80.00 \times 2 = \$160$. The customer would pay for having used the entire $1,000 for all of the two years, whereas principal is in fact being repaid over that period. Unearned interest income normally is credited to an unearned discount account and transferred to income on the *rule-of-78ths* (sum-of-the-months' digits) method.[4]

In a manual system each installment loan is recorded on a separate ledger card. These are serially numbered to correspond with the notes receivable and may be filed alphabetically, by payment due date, or by loan number. In addition to borrower information, the ledger card usually shows the amount of the original loan, total discount and other charges, monthly payment due, and the current unpaid balance. If collateral has been supplied, such as the title to an automobile, it is also described. The collateral, which is usually nonnegotiable, is placed in the vault with conditional sales contracts and notes. Separate files are also maintained for (1) borrower applications for personal loans and (2) credit information on individuals or on dealers from whom the bank has purchased paper.

Various methods of posting ledger cards are used, the majority of which involve automated accounting equipment. Generally, payments are not posted on the notes or conditional sales contracts. Many banks use coupon payment books, which permits all tellers to accept installment loan payments. The coupons are assembled in the proof department for posting to the ledger cards, frequently on the day following the transactions.

In banks using computerized equipment, coupons may be in the form of tabulating cards or may have MICR (i.e., magnetic ink character recognition) capability. Under these circumstances, the ledger card is usually eliminated, and all records of each individual loan are stored in the data processing system.

Audit procedures. The two principal phases of the examination of consumer loans will normally be balancing and confirming ledger balances and determining the reasonableness of the unearned discount account. Other phases are far less time-consuming. Installment loans are usually homogeneous, and the audit procedures can be applied on a very limited test basis if the bank has adequate internal control. But because of the large number of individual loans, the sample to which audit procedures are to be applied will normally be larger, in absolute terms, than the accounts sampled in either commercial or real estate mortgage loans.

Loan Loss Reserves. Before 1976 accounting for loan loss reserves was influenced by IRS requirements for concurrence on method and amounts between the books and the tax return. Changes in the tax regulations have eliminated this requirement and transferred responsibility for the book reserves onto management's judgment.

Because federal tax regulations provide for formula determination of the tax deductible provision for loan losses (see Income Taxes, Loan Loss Reserves), this tax basis allowance is comprised of three pieces spread on the balance sheet: the GAAP basis valuation allowance is deducted from loans; the deferred tax portion

---

[4] The sum of 12 months' digits, $12 + 11 + 10$, etc., is 78. In the first month, 12/78ths is amortized; in the second month, 11/78ths; and so on. This method approximates the *interest method* (AC 5361.01) for short-term loans.

is included with other deferred taxes; and the remainder is shown as appropriated retained earnings.

Auditing the judgment of management on loan loss reserves as required under GAAP is not a simple task, since the recommended procedures amount to a critical challenge of the evidence used by, and the intent of, management in reaching their decision. A suggested checklist of evidence to be weighed by the auditor is described in Chapter 8 of the *Exposure Draft on the Audit and Accounting Guide for Banks* (AICPA, 1980b).

Several controversial accounting matters continue to be debated by the banking industry and accounting practitioners. The majority of these disagreements are concerned with the proper method of recognizing losses on troubled loans; some of this debate has been resolved by the issuance of SFAS 15 (AC 5363).

Sales To and From Other Financial Institutions. Commercial banks sell loans to and buy loans from other financial institutions to improve liquidity, to gain an operational advantage, and for other reasons, such as diversification of the portfolio. If the loans are sold along with servicing rights, a gain or loss should be recognized for the difference between the selling price and the carrying amount of the loan. If servicing rights are retained, the recognized gain or loss should be adjusted by the present value of the difference between estimated future servicing revenues and servicing costs.

Another form of transaction among financial institutions is loan participation. The purchase and sale of portions of a loan help to spread the risk as well as broaden the client base. The major accounting consideration is whether such a transaction is in substance a borrowing or a sale. For example, repurchase agreements and "sale" of only a small percentage of the loans tend to make the transaction a borrowing that does not result in immediate recognition of gain or loss.

Audit procedures for loan participations are similar to direct loans except that

- Confirmation requests on participations purchased should be sent to the managing or lead bank, and
- Confirmations on participations sold should cover the participating amount for each of the participating banks.

Troubled Debt Restructurings. As a result of SFAS 15 (AC 5363), uniform accounting was prescribed for restructurings, many of which were entered into by banks as creditors of REITs and other distressed debtors. Accounting by debtors and creditors for troubled debt restructurings is discussed in detail in Chapter 22.

Investments Accounting and Auditing

Most banks purchase securities for investment purposes. Some banks also purchase and hold securities for resale as dealers, and set up trading accounts for the transactions. The investment or trading philosophy is to maximize income within conservative liquidity and safety requirements. Common stocks are not considered appropriate investments by the regulatory agencies except in unusual circumstances, such as repossessed collateral.

Although the auditing procedures are similar between investment and trading accounts, the accounting policies are distinctive.

Hedging transactions in interest rate futures contracts are engaged in by financial institutions—primarily banks, S&Ls, and mortgage bankers—to minimize risks in trading and investment security portfolios, debt securities issued, and mortgage portfolios. This complex activity is not discussed in this chapter, but a good overview can be obtained from a two-part article by Schrott, Casciani, and Bernstein (1980).

Accounting for Investment Securities. Marketable equity securities held for investment are accounted for under the provisions of SFAS 12 (AC 5132); ordinarily these securities are not predominant in a commercial bank. The significant accounting policies for investment securities not covered by SFAS 12 (typically bonds) are that

1. Investment securities are recorded at cost, which may include a premium or be net of a discount. Premium or discount should be amortized using the interest method (AC 5361.01) over a period extending from the purchase date to the maturity date, unless there is an earlier call date. Regulatory authorities require that the interest method be used for accretion of discount in banks with total resources of more than $25 million.
2. Estimated average life of the contract should be used as the amortization period in the case of premiums or discounts related to Government National Mortgage Association (GNMA) modified pass-through securities and similar instruments.
3. Investment security gains and losses should be recognized on the completed-transaction basis. Transfer of the risks and opportunities of ownership for a reasonable period of time constitutes a completed transaction.

Shadings of meaning in the definition of a completed transaction make the accounting for *wash sales* and *short sales* somewhat difficult.

Wash sales. Wash sales occur when securities are "sold" with the intent to acquire the same or substantially similar securities in a short period of time for tax or other reasons. Sometimes broker's advices are the only evidence of such transactions. If a commercial bank "sells" a security and acquires the same or substantially similar securities in a reasonably short period of time, no sale should be recognized. What constitutes a reasonably short period of time is a matter of judgment.

To qualify as "substantially similar," a security should meet the following criteria:

- It should be a security of the same entity or same division of government; and
- If it is a debt security or an equity security with debt characteristics:
  - The securities should carry comparable yields based on the market value at the time of disposition of the securities sold and the market value at the time of acquisition of the securities purchased and
  - Both securities should have approximately the same maturity date, call date, and prospects for redemption if the security agreement calls for some form of serial redemption.

Short sales. Short sales occur when the seller does not own the securities at the time of sale and must acquire and deliver them later. A completed transaction in an investment account security should receive gain or loss recognition at the time of the original sale. Whether the bank uses borrowed or its own securities to effect delivery at a later date is not relevant to accounting for the transaction.

Valuation reserves for investment securities should be clearly described as allocations of undivided profits. Realized gains and losses must run through income; they cannot be absorbed by this reserve.

Investment securities should be written down to market value when the bank cannot demonstrate an ability to hold the obligations to maturity or when there is evidence of permanent impairment. Once such a writedown is made, no reinstatement is allowed. Investment securities subject to troubled debt restructuring should follow SFAS 15 (5363.027 *et seq.*)

An example of investment securities reporting and disclosure is shown in Figure 38.5.

Accounting for Trading Securities. At the date of acquisition, securities should be designated as either trading or investment, and that designation should be documented.

Banks' trading account securities do not come within the main coverage of SFAS 12, since trading accounts fall within the rules included in *Enterprises in Industries Having Specialized Accounting Practices with Respect to Marketable Securities* (AC 5132.14-.17). Instead, accounting for trading transactions should follow the AICPA industry audit guide, *Audits of Brokers and Dealers in Securities* (AICPA,

	1979	1978
Investment securities (Note C):		
U.S. Treasury securities	15,501	14,012
Securities of other U.S. Government		
agencies and corporations	6,804	5,875
State and municipal securities	3,600	3,896
Other securities	1,301	1,247
Total Investment Securities	27,206	25,030

Note C—Investment Securities The estimated market values of investment securities at December 31 are as follows:

	1979	1978
U.S. Treasury securities	$15,046,000	$13,378,000
Securities of other U.S. Government		
agencies and corporations	6,484,000	5,733,000
State and municipal securities	3,244,000	3,613,000
Other securities	1,173,000	1,072,000
	$25,947,000	$23,796,000

Securities carried at approximately $4,712,000 at December 31, 1979 ($9,422,000 at December 31, 1978) were pledged to secure public deposits and for other purposes.

FIGURE 38.5   EXAMPLE OF INVESTMENT SECURITIES REPORTING BY A COMMERCIAL BANK
SOURCE: Security National Bank, 1979 Annual Report.

1975a). In general, the guide recommends the market value concept, although the supervisory authorities have allowed more flexibility. Adjustments for market value should be made whenever financial results are made public.

Transfers of securities from the trading account to the investment account should be at market value, and the appropriate gain or loss recognized. Transfers of investment securities to the trading account should also be at market value, but gains should be deferred until final disposition.

Wash sales discussed in the investment securities section should receive similar treatment in the trading account. However, open short sales should be shown as a liability and "marked to market value" at any financial reporting date. Borrowed securities should not be shown on the balance sheet, but disclosed. Long and short positions in the same security should be netted.

Auditing. Audit procedures for securities are not unique to banks. However, the relative volume and high negotiability of securities in banks require significant controls by the bank and assumption of control by the auditor during examination. The majority of the work in this area can and probably should be done before year-end, with an updated review of transactions, yields, etc., through year-end. For further commentary, see Chapter 17.

Electronic Data Processing

In the banking environment, with its huge transaction volume, it frequently is convenient for the auditor to categorize the automated systems into two dimensions, as shown in Figure 38.6.

The accounting transaction systems have already been considered; the system elements (data entry, processing, and reporting) and other audit aspects will be mentioned briefly below. General guidelines for the audit of EDP can be found in Chapter 15.

Data Entry. The auditor should understand and document the data entry procedure for each system. Vulnerability to errors and dishonesty are greatest at this

Transaction Systems	System Elements		
	Data Entry	Processing	Reporting
Cash		Typical questions:	
Loans		1. System documented?	
Investments		2. Compliance with accounting	
Payroll		policies and bank regulations?	
Capital		3. Existence and adequacy of	
General Ledger		internal controls?	
Other			

FIGURE 38.6 EDP ACCOUNTING TRANSACTION SYSTEMS

stage. Results of tests of compliance with the documented procedures and controls should be reported to bank management.

Compliance with the institution's accounting policies and with regulatory requirements is critical at the data entry points. Once data is entered, the processing steps usually comprise relatively straightforward, standardized computations and manipulations of large volumes of data.

Processing. Processing steps in most automated systems have been refined to the most efficient routines. The auditor should document these steps and search in particular for the adequacy of preventive controls, to assure that all changes to these processing steps are properly authorized. Computer audit software can be used to analyze, test, and verify processing steps.

Reporting. The product of the data entry and processing elements of an accounting transaction system is a series of generated forms and reports. The auditor should be concerned with report accuracy, appropriate distribution, and integrity of underlying data. Computer audit software can also be used to audit this element.

Income Taxes

Leasing and Leveraged Leases. Many commercial banks are extensively involved in direct leasing, and the leases often qualify as financing transactions under SFAS 13 (AC 4053). Complicated options and other contractual relationships may cause the same leases to qualify as operating leases for tax purposes. The timing differences created by this book-to-tax difference should follow the usual accounting described in APB 11 (AC 4091.33-.36).

Banks have also acted as equity participants (owners) in leveraged leases, and some banks have treated the investment tax credit related to leveraged leases as a component of operating income rather than as part of the income tax provision. They justify this presentation method with the concept that the tax credit is part of the yield. SFAS 13 (AC 4053.123) takes the contrary position: the accounting for investment tax credits should be a part of the income tax provision; thus, if the amounts were material, an auditor's GAAP exception might be needed for nonconforming presentations.

Loan Loss Reserves. Federal tax regulations provide for a transition period in which to reach a standard formula by 1987 based on a six-year moving average loss experience. However, supervisory agencies ceased supporting a formula basis such as a moving average in 1976, when management's judgment was established as the proper determinant for regulatory purposes. The audit difficulties associated with assessing the adequacy of "management's judgment" has been discussed in previous sections. In any event, the result may be a book-to-tax difference that should follow the usual accounting prescribed in APB 11 (AC 4091.33-.36).

Bank Holding Company Taxation. Special rules allow opportunities for extensive tax savings through proper planning. The highly technical nature of these rules puts the subject beyond the scope of this *Handbook,* but tax accountants should be alert to the potential for savings.

Financial Futures

Financial institutions use financial futures markets to hedge against volatile interest rate movements. The hedge may be entered into to protect the yield of a given investment or loan portfolio or to lock in a yield or interest cost on a future investment or indebtedness. A diversity of accounting practices exist because there is virtually no authoritative accounting guidance provided. Because of this lack of accounting guidance in a significant area, the AICPA formed a task force on Forward Commitments and Interest Rate Futures.

In September 1980 AcSEC approved, subject to positive clearance, the submission to the FASB of the task force's issues paper, *Accounting for Forward Placements and Standby Commitments and Interest Rate Futures Contracts.* The essential conclusion of the issues paper is that there are two types of futures or forward transactions—hedges and speculative transactions. Unrealized gains and losses are to be recognized currently on speculative transactions but may be deferred on hedges, to be recognized in conjunction with the recognition of income or loss on the hedged transaction. For a transaction to be considered a hedge under the issues paper

- The purpose should be specifically identified and documented at the time it is entered into;
- The transaction intended to be hedged must be specified;
- There should be a "high degree of correlation" between the market price movement of the hedging transaction and the transaction intended to be hedged; and
- For an anticipatory hedge (a hedge of a planned future transaction), there must be a reasonable expectation that the anticipated transaction will take place.

Transactions not meeting the preceding criteria are deemed to be speculative.

SAVINGS AND LOAN ASSOCIATIONS

A savings and loan association (S&L), while much like a commercial bank, differs in two basic respects: S&L loans are primarily for residential properties and S&L funds sources are principally interest-earning savings deposits. However, these historical differences are gradually disappearing. Electronic funds transfer systems, for example, permit depositors to move funds out of savings accounts to pay bills and permit borrowers to make automatic payments on loans with funds in other banks. In addition, some states permit S&Ls to provide Negotiable Order of Withdrawal (NOW) accounts, which have many demand deposit characteristics. (Recently, commercial banks also have been authorized to offer NOW savings accounts.)

Charters and Equity Structure

Savings and loan associations are chartered (licensed), either by the states in which they operate or by the Federal Home Loan Bank Board (FHLBB). Associations chartered by the FHLBB are federal, and state-chartered associations that insure their accounts with the Federal Savings and Loan Insurance Corporation (FSLIC) are subject to both FSLIC and state regulations.

An S&L is either a mutual or a capital stock association; the FHLBB licenses both, as do many states. As with any corporation, the capital stock represents equity ownership, generally cannot be withdrawn, and is not insured. Mutual associations have no capital stock. They are owned by the savers, who, together with the borrowers, are entitled to vote at annual meetings and govern the association.

Capital stock associations may be owned by holding companies that are not otherwise involved in savings and loan operations. Such holding companies are regulated, and the acquisition of savings and loan associations by a holding company must be approved by various regulatory authorities.

Regulation and Supervision

The FSLIC was created by Congress during the 1930s to insure S&L depositor accounts, just as the FDIC insures bank deposits. The FSLIC charges premiums, invests them, and generates reserves for use should the insured institution fail or encounter other severe liquidity problems. In order for an S&L to have account insurance it must comply with the FSLIC's regulations; one of those conditions is membership in the Federal Home Loan Bank system.

The Federal Home Loan Bank (FHLB) system was also created by Congress in the 1930s. It is a central banking system that provides resources for lending expansion or for funding withdrawals in excess of a member association's liquidity. Stock in the local FHLB must be purchased by a member institution in proportion to its size and the amount it has borrowed from the FHLB.

State-chartered S&Ls are governed by the state's laws. Normally, a state commissioner oversees the operations of state-chartered associations, but the degree of regulation varies considerably from state to state; in some areas it is more stringent than the federal regulations.

Stock savings and loan associations that are publicly held (500 or more shareholders) are required to file annual and quarterly reports with the Federal Home Loan Bank Board (FHLBB). Publicly held holding companies file annual and quarterly reports with the SEC. The FSLIC's insurance regulations have adopted the SEC's Regulation S-X by reference. FSLIC regulations also include accounting requirements unique to the savings and loan industry, and they specify the form and content of financial statements to be filed in connection with the conversion of a mutual association to a stock association, the issuance of subordinated debt, and periodic filings.

Some S&Ls have diversified their activities. Federal and state laws have permitted real estate development on a limited basis, and many associations have entered this activity, some by hiring experienced personnel and others through joint ventures with established building companies. Mortgage banking activities by S&Ls—buying and selling loans through secondary mortgage market operations—

have arisen in response to the uneven demand for lendable funds around the country.

Accounting Considerations

AICPA Guide. In 1979 the AICPA issued a revised audit and accounting guide, *Savings and Loan Associations* (AICPA, 1979e). Some of the more significant changes included in the new guide are detailed below.

GNMA futures transactions. Associations may buy or sell futures contracts to offset transactions in the cash market, as a means of hedging. Except for recording margin deposits, no accounting entry is generally required until the futures contract is closed; and the gain or loss then realized should be matched with the related cash market transaction. In other words, the gain or loss from the futures contract should be reflected as part of the gain or loss on the loans sold in the cash market.

However, gains or losses from futures contracts should be deferred and amortized over the expected life of the related loans if entered into to hedge against price fluctuations in originating or purchasing loans for investment. Since savings and loan associations are only permitted to engage in hedging, rather than futures speculation, contracts should be treated as closed at any time it becomes known that the expected cash transactions will not occur; the futures contract should be carried at market thereafter (AICPA, 1979e, pp. 23-24).

Loan commitment fees. Loan commitment fees are divided into two general categories, floating rate commitments and fixed rate commitments. A *floating rate commitment* is an agreement by the S&L to make loans in the future at the then-market interest rate. Fees received for this type of commitment may be amortized over the term of the commitment, since at the time the loan is funded it will bear interest at the current market rate.

A *fixed rate commitment* is an agreement by the association to make loans at some time in the future at an interest rate agreed to at the time the commitment is made. In this case, fees must be deferred and amortized over the combined commitment and loan term. If at the time the loans are funded the current market interest rate is the same as (or lower than) the rate committed, the remaining unamortized deferred fees may be recognized as income.

In the case of both fixed rate and floating rate commitments, the guide permits the current recognition of that portion of the fee income that represents a recoupment of the cost of making the commitment, including cost analyses, feasibility studies, appraisals, etc. (AICPA, 1979e, pp. 68-74).

Service corporations. Savings and loan associations are permitted to invest a limited amount of money in the stock of service corporations. A service corporation may be wholly owned or may be owned by a group of associations. Service corporations may engage in real estate development, mortgage banking operations, data processing centers, the holding of loans secured by junior liens, and other similar activities. The usual accounting principles for consolidation (see Chapter 31) should be applied in accounting for the activities of service corporations (AICPA, 1979e, pp. 45-46).

Sales of real estate. When associations sell real estate, they usually originate loans to finance the sale. Recognition of gains and losses on such sales is governed by two AICPA industry accounting guides, *Accounting for Profit Recognition on Sales of Real Estate* (AICPA, 1973b) and *Accounting for Retail Land Sales* (AICPA, 1973c). In addition, the provisions of APB 21, *Interest on Receivables and Payables* (AC 4111), must be observed. Thus, if an association sells real estate and takes back a loan that bears interest at a rate lower than the current market rate, the sales price must be discounted, and the discount amortized to income over the expected life of the loan. The effect of this is to record a realistic gain or loss in the year of sale, and provide a yield on the note taken back equivalent to current market yields (AICPA, 1979e, pp. 42-43).

Loan Fee Income. Recognition of loan fee income is related to the recovery of costs incurred in the loan origination process. Thus, fees that exceed origination costs should be deferred and amortized over the composite estimated life of loans originated (usually ten years). The savings and loan guide (AICPA, 1979e, p. 74) provides: "Since determination of origination cost is difficult, fees other than commitment fees allowed to be recognized as current income by FSLIC regulations may be recorded as income at loan closing. Fees based on such amounts generally do not exceed origination costs."

Until December 1979, FSLIC regulations had permitted current recognition of amounts not in excess of 1% of the loan plus $200 on nonconstruction loans, and of 2% of the loan plus $200 on construction loans. In December 1979 the FSLIC regulations were amended to provide that fees equal to 2% of the loan plus $400 on nonconstruction loans and $2\frac{1}{2}$% plus $400 on construction loans may be recognized as current income. There is general agreement that this new schedule allows income in excess of the recoupment of origination costs.

Accordingly, associations should continue to recognize income based on the old schedule, unless a study of origination costs substantiates the fact that costs are higher. If so, recognition should be in an amount equal to origination costs.

Once this cost recovery method is adopted, it must be consistently applied based on actual costs of each year. The industry may undertake a study to estimate an overall appropriate cost recovery approach, to spare each association the considerable effort of estimating on its own.

Business Combinations. The principal problem area involves the valuation of the loan portfolio, the major asset of savings and loan associations. It had been argued that the loan portfolio must be viewed together with the principal liability —the savings portfolio—and if the spread (the difference between the average yield on the loan portfolio versus the average cost of money in the savings portfolio) was comparable to other savings and loan associations in similar market areas, then no premium or discount need be computed on the loan portfolio. However, if the literal requirements of APB 16 (AC 1091.88(b)) are adhered to, a loan portfolio must be valued based on current interest rates at the time of a purchase business combination. This procedure could result in increasing the goodwill resulting from acquisition (which could be amortized over a period as long as 40 years) while amortizing the discount on the loan portfolio to income over the estimated loan portfolio life (usually 10 years or less), thus "front ending" a significant amount of income.

This controversy resulted in the issuance of FASB Interpretation No. 9 (AC 1091-1), which required the valuation of the individual assets and rejected the spread approach. The potential acceleration of income recognition described above can be eliminated by shortening the period of amortization of goodwill to the same period as the estimated loan life.

Variations Between Regulatory Accounting and GAAP. Because of regulations, certain types of transactions must be accounted for in a manner not in accordance with GAAP. Normally these differences are not material, and usually the association will report to the FHLBB on the regulatory basis and make the appropriate adjustments so that published financial statements are in accordance with GAAP. Important differences are described below.

Recognition of gains on sales of real estate. Regulatory accounting permits recognition of gains on sales of real estate on a dollar-for-dollar matching of principal collected. For example, if an association sold a parcel of real estate resulting in a gain of $20,000, and the association received a downpayment of $5,000, regulatory accounting would permit the immediate recognition of a gain of $5,000. As additional principal was collected, gain would be recognized on a dollar-for-dollar basis until the entire $20,000 was recognized. Under GAAP, criteria to be met are described in two AICPA industry accounting guides, *Accounting for Profit Recognition on Sales of Real Estate* (AICPA, 1973b) and *Accounting for Retail Land Sales* (AICPA, 1973c). If these criteria are not met, no profit may be recognized; when they are met, the profit is recognized in its entirety.

Commitment fees. The regulations provide for recognition of commitment fee income on a formula basis related to the term of the commitment. GAAP distinguishes between fixed rate and floating rate commitments, as discussed above under AICPA Guide.

Valuation allowances. Federal regulations require the establishment of valuation allowances, but permit those allowances to be established by charges either against current period earnings or against equity reserves. GAAP requires that valuation allowances be established only by charges against current income.

Valuation of Real Estate Owned Through Foreclosure. Prior to foreclosure, a delinquent loan may be modified by the lender as to terms, interest rate, monthly payment, etc., but as long as the terms of the modification provide that the principal balance will be repaid in entirety, no gain or loss results under SFAS 15 (AC 5363.030). However, upon foreclosure, the property acquired in satisfaction of the debt must be fair valued based on the requirements of SFAS 15 (AC 5363.028). From this point on, the property must be looked on as inventory, and the book value may not be increased even if the property appreciates in value. In addition, if after the property has been foreclosed an extended holding period is encountered, or if there is a decline in the value of the property, an additional allowance for losses must be established taking into consideration the estimated net realizable value of the property.

Fair value of real estate is the amount that can reasonably be expected to be reduced by the estimated costs of improvements or completion and the estimated value. *Estimated net realizable value* is defined as the anticipated sales price reduced by the estimated costs of improvements or completion and the estimated direct holding costs, which include a provision for the average cost of all capital, taxes, maintenance, and other items, as well as the cost of disposition.

For a further discussion of accounting by debtors and creditors for troubled debt restructurings, see Chapter 22.

Capitalization of Interest. Under SFAS 34, *Capitalization of Interest Cost* (AC 5155), interest must be capitalized on qualifying assets that are constructed or otherwise produced for an enterprise's own use, and on assets intended for sale that are being constructed or otherwise produced as discrete projects. Many savings and loan associations are involved in real estate developments, but not all have capitalized interest. SFAS 34 requires a uniform accounting treatment beginning in 1980.

Repurchase Agreements. Associations enter into agreements from time to time to sell pools of loans and concurrently agree to repurchase those pools of loans at a specified price. AcSEC has concluded that if the loans sold and repurchased are substantially identical, the transaction is a financing, and no gain or loss should be recognized. Otherwise, gain or loss must be recognized on the sale, and a new basis established upon the repurchase of the new pools. It is anticipated that an SOP will be issued dealing with this subject.

Auditing

Federal associations are subject to examination by the Office of Examinations and Supervision of the FHLBB. State-chartered associations, when insured by the FSLIC, are subject to examination by both federal and state authorities, who in some instances may perform joint examinations. Regulatory examinations generally concentrate on compliance with regulations and are not substitutes for independent audits. In addition to regulatory examinations, the FHLBB requires insured institutions to be audited annually in a manner satisfactory to the FSLIC. This audit requirement is usually satisfied by an independent public accountant, though sometimes it is done by internal auditors. FHLBB audit regulations are described in Bulletin PA-7, which includes rules and regulations relating to audits of savings and loan associations and sets forth criteria for an acceptable audit. The bulletin deals with qualifications of independent public accountants, independence, audit report requirements, scope requirements, provisions required to be included in engagement letters, a required review of the system of internal control, and numerous other matters. Amendments to Bulletin PA-7 specify the minimum requirements for the audit of EDP installations, both in-house departments and outside service bureaus. Public accountants who audit S&Ls must be thoroughly familiar with these specific requirements. The FSLIC and the states also issue audit-related bulletins and regulations.

Some associations keep records and report financial results in accordance with regulatory requirements, while others follow GAAP. Because the differences may be material, the auditor may require adjustments in order to issue an unqualified opinion; the auditor's report on regulatory-based statements must follow the provisions of SAS 14, *Special Reports,* dealing with compliance with regulatory requirements related to audited financial statements (AU 621.18-.19).

A difficult audit problem in the savings and loan industry is the evaluation of the adequacy of allowances for losses on loans and real estate. When there is a strong real estate market, or when inflation causes real estate values to be high, rising prices ease the evaluation burden; but in a falling or depressed real estate market, difficult audit judgments are required; for example, the auditor must be satisfied that the method of appraisal used by the appraiser is proper, that adequate documentation is included in the appraisal (including comparable sales), that formulae generally accepted in the appraisal profession are used, and so on. In addition, when extended holding periods are contemplated, it is necessary to determine the reasonableness of the estimated holding time, the anticipated costs of holding and disposing of the property, and the valuation of unique or single-purpose properties.

The audit of savings accounts includes, on a test basis, examining direct mail requests (which may be positive or negative) for confirmation of balances, the association's accounting and internal control systems to determine that subsidiary ledgers are in balance and that controls exist over the withdrawal of funds, changes in address, and required signatures. Good controls are especially important for inactive savings accounts, which are more vulnerable to improper transactions.

In the construction area, the auditor must ascertain that appropriate controls exist with respect to cost classifications on properties being built, that the disbursement of funds is in accord with such cost breakdowns and is being properly documented by inspections and lien releases, and that funds are being disbursed to the proper contractors, subcontractors, or suppliers.

Income Taxes

Savings and loan associations meeting certain tests (Internal Revenue Code, Section 593) enjoy a tax shelter in the form of a statutory bad debt deduction. The tests include limitations on the type of loans that may be in the loan portfolio, the nature of the S&L's income sources, and the proportionate relationship of accumulated bad debt deductions to the loan portfolio. Under current tax law, this bad debt deduction is 40% of net income. Accordingly, savings and loan associations are taxed on 60% of income, which means an effective federal tax rate of approximately 28% versus a normal corporate tax rate of 46%.

Special tax disclosures are necessary in the financial statements. Most savings and loan associations use a modified cash basis for income tax purposes and the accrual basis for financial statement reporting, resulting in timing differences in such areas as loan fees, the special bad debt deduction allowed for tax purposes, and recognition of real estate profits. Normally, the footnotes will contain an analysis of the related deferred income taxes. The differences between unappropriated retained earnings based on regulatory requirements and retained earnings available for dividends in accordance with tax regulations must also be described.

Evolving Savings Instruments and Lending Practices

Disintermediation is a condition of net shrinkage caused when savings are with-drawn by depositors seeking higher-yield investments. When short-term deposits are withdrawn the associations must replace those funds with borrowings from the FHLB, commercial banks, or other sources. Since this occurs when interest rates are high, it can lead to a situation in which the S&L's cost of money exceeds the yield on portions of its loan portfolio, thus reducing profits or in some instances creating losses.

Prior to the mid-1970s, the principal economic problem of the savings and loan industry was borrowing short and lending long. Deposits were generally with-drawable on demand, whereas loans were for periods up to thirty years. Accord-ingly, associations were quite vulnerable to money market conditions and disin-termediation. Since the mid-1970s, associations have been permitted to issue higher-rate savings instruments with longer-term maturities and substantial interest penalties for early withdrawal.

In 1978 the *money market certificate* was introduced. With this instrument, savings deposits made on terms comparable to those of treasury bills (usually six months) are paid treasury bill interest rates, thus insulating the industry against disintermediation caused by high U.S. government yields.

There have also been innovations on the lending side of the business. Secondary markets for the sales of loans have expanded, and participating interests in loans are now common.

Pass-through certificates guaranteed by the Government National Mortgage Association (GNMA) and the Federal Home Loan Mortgage Corporation (FHLMC) are also available. *Pass-through certificates* are instruments tying together groups or "pools" of loans for sale to one investor. Generally the asso-ciation continues to receive the payments on these loans, do the bookkeeping, send delinquency notices, etc. As monies are received they are remitted to the purchaser of the certificate.

The FHLMC and FNMA conduct periodic auctions to sell loans they own to individual purchasers. FNMA deals in government-insured loans, the FHLMC deals in loans not so insured. The FHLMC also sells forward commitments. This means that an association can purchase the right to sell a given amount of loans to the FHLMC at a specified interest rate.

All of these possibilities make the management of an association's lending operation more complex than ever before, but they also give associations a great deal of flexibility in the management of their assets.

SAVINGS BANKS

Savings banks generally share the advantage that savings and loan associations have over commercial banks, i.e., they are allowed to pay higher interest rates on savings accounts and time certificates of deposit. Although far less numerous than S&Ls, they are also a significant source of home mortgage funds. At December 31, 1978, total assets of all 465 mutual savings banks approximated $158 billion, with deposits of $143 billion. (National Association of Mutual Savings Banks, 1979,

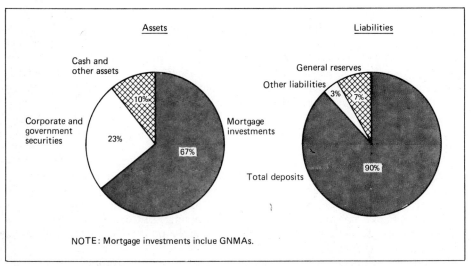

FIGURE 38.7 PERCENTAGE DISTRIBUTION OF ASSETS AND LIABILITIES
OF MUTUAL SAVINGS BANKS, JUNE 30, 1979
SOURCE: National Association of Mutual Savings Banks, *1979 National Fact Book of Mutual Savings Banking* (New York, 1979), p. 9.

pp. 9-10). Figure 38.7 shows the distribution of assets and liabilities at June 30, 1979.

Equity Structure

Although a few stock savings banks were formed many years ago in the New England states, most are *mutuals*. Mutual savings banks operate in 18 states, with a concentration in the Mid-Atlantic and New England region, primarily Massachusetts, New York, and Connecticut.

Legally, ownership of the mutuals resides with the board of trustees, for the mutual beneficial ownership of the depositors. No public market exists for a mutual savings bank's equity interests.

The board of trustees is essentially a self-regulatory body generally precluded from actions that might enrich its members. In most instances, there is a prohibition against trustees being affiliated with other financial institutions. The board is installed at the inception of the savings bank, and among its responsibilities is the election of successive members. By contrast, in a mutual savings and loan association the depositors are considered shareholders for purposes of voting for directors.

Regulation and Supervision

Title XI of the Financial Institutions Regulatory and Interest Rate Control Act of 1978 makes provisions for conversion of state mutual savings banks to federal mutual savings banks under the Homeowners Loan Act of 1933. These associations are subject to federal law except where the Federal Reserve Board decides that state laws and regulations impose more stringent requirements.

Most savings banks deposits (about 70%) are insured by the FDIC. The balance are insured by state-sponsored funds, such as the Mutual Savings Central Fund, Inc. in Massachusetts, or are in savings banks that are members of the FHLB system. All savings banks are subject to regulation, including periodic examination by both the chartering state and the insuring agency.

Accounting Considerations

The financial statements of most savings banks conform to GAAP. Some savings banks, however, deviate from GAAP in accounting for allowances for losses on mortgage loans and for losses on equity securities. GAAP requires the allowances for such losses to be presented as reductions of the related assets. A few savings banks, however, still follow the old practice of treating these allowances as a segregation of retained earnings, thus inflating the ratio of net worth to deposits.

As shown in Figure 38.7, mortgage loans represent the major assets of savings banks—67% of all savings bank assets at June 30, 1979 (National Association of Mutual Savings Banks, 1979). Prior to the real estate problems of the early 1970s, loss experience in the industry had been minimal. However, many of the "nonspeculative" commercial mortgages proved to be less than adequately secured, and significant losses occurred. Savings banks now must comply with SFAS 15, *Accounting by Debtors and Creditors for Troubled Debt Restructurings* (AC 5363), and with other authoritative accounting literature, such as the accounting and auditing guide, *Savings and Loan Associations* (AICPA, 1979e), with respect to reserves for losses.

Savings banks in some states are permitted, within certain guidelines, to invest a portion of their funds in marketable equity securities (usually preferred stocks). Given a decline in market values of such securities (even if deemed temporary) under original cost, and a material effect on net worth, some states require a specific appropriation of undivided profits, much as is required by SFAS 12 (AC 5132). However, there is no overall regulatory requirement to follow SFAS 12, under which a valuation allowance against the related investment is offset as a reduction of net worth (AC 5132.11).

Auditing Considerations

The auditor must be aware that each state has unique requirements for trustees' examinations, and the auditor should obtain and read any such requirements. The adequacy of the reserve for possible losses on mortgages, loans, and investment portfolios must be challenged; also, there must be a proper maintenance of net worth accounts, and an adequate ratio (as defined by state law) of net worth and subordinated debentures to deposits.

In general, there is no requirement for savings banks to be audited by independent accountants; subordinated debenture agreements, however, often call for this. In practice, many boards of trustees of the larger institutions retain independent accountants to assist them in complying with their statutory obligation to perform a trustee's examination, especially as the regulations, tax laws, and accounting systems become more and more complex.

One motive for an outside audit, for example, is a result of massive volume: many savings banks have on-line EDP systems for processing savings transactions, and auditors must have the requisite EDP audit expertise.

Income Taxes

Savings banks enjoy favorable tax treatment under the Internal Revenue Code (Section 593, 1954, as amended) in the form of an arbitrary bad debt deduction equal to a fixed percentage (40% in 1979) of net income as defined (if certain criteria are met), as more fully discussed in the S&L section of this chapter. The accountant must know the facts regarding this rather complex area to perform a competent audit. In addition to this provision, other accounting options available to commercial banks under the Internal Revenue Code are available to savings banks.

Life Insurance Sold by Savings Banks

Savings banks in Massachusetts, New York, and Connecticut have the authority to write life insurance. Among the restrictions are that (1) there are dollar limitations on the maximum coverage of an individual policy, (2) the assets related to the policies must inure only to the benefit of the policyholders, and (3) any earnings must be used to reduce insurance premiums. Within limits, the bank can allocate certain of its operating expenses to the department. Because of the different nature of the insurance function, the bank carries its initial investment therein at cost and maintains separate records for the life insurance department.

MORTGAGE BANKS

Mortgage banks, or mortgage companies as they are often called, are engaged primarily in originating, marketing, and servicing real estate mortgage loans for profit. A mortgage bank finances its portfolio, or inventory, with short-term bank borrowings (the *warehouse line*) collateralized by the mortgages; it differs from a real estate broker, who simply acts as agent to secure a loan commitment for a borrower. The mortgage loan portfolio is usually the largest asset, and it has an average holding period of 60 to 180 days. A mortgage banking company's equity structure is essentially the same as that of other commercial enterprises.

The major functions of a mortgage bank are

1. Originating loans—locating borrowers, processing loan documents, and disbursing funds;
2. Selling mortgages—finding permanent investors to purchase long-term mortgages; and
3. Servicing loans—collecting monthly payments, maintaining escrow accounts for taxes and insurance, and bookkeeping.

Generally, the mortgage banker is either originating or purchasing loans to fill a commitment to a permanent investor for a specific package of mortgage loans at a guaranteed yield, or is investing in a portfolio while negotiating with potential investors seeking such a package. Mortgage bankers originate two types of loans, residential and commercial (or income). Since a residential loan is relatively small, mortage bankers will generally originate these without a commitment from a permanent investor. They seek block commitments from investors for a large dollar amount of residential loans meeting broad criteria. In the case of commercial loan originations (shopping centers, office buildings, etc.), there is usually a commitment from a permanent investor to finance the project after construction is completed.

Rather than directly originate loans, mortgage bankers can acquire them for resale to permanent investors from a variety of sources, including the FHA or VA; these guaranteed or insured loans reflect market rates and often are acquired at a discount. At times, nonguaranteed or noninsured loans are also acquired.

Mortgages are normally sold to various permanent investors, such as insurance companies, savings banks, commercial banks, savings and loan associations, the Federal Home Loan Mortgage Corporation ("Freddie Mac"), the Federal National Mortgage Association ("Fannie Mae"); or they are used as collateral for mortgage-backed securities (MBS) guaranteed by the Government National Mortgage Association ("Ginnie Mae") and sold to the same kinds of customers.

Earnings Sources

Mortgage origination seldom results in a profit, because the costs associated with the process (applications, appraisals, etc.) almost always exceed the income from fees paid by the mortgagor. In a competitive market the mortgage bank even may absorb those fees.

Instead, income is derived from servicing the loans and from related businesses: (e.g., insurance, property management, and appraisal services). Loan servicing generates revenues at a fixed percentage of the outstanding principal balance of the mortgage. During the holding period, the mortgage banker assumes the primary risk for the collectibility of the loan but has the benefit of the interest income (also the risk, and resultant gain or loss upon sale, from fluctuations in interest rates).

The mortgage banker utilizes the available escrow funds from loans in its inventory and servicing portfolios as compensating balances for its warehouse borrowing, thereby reducing its interest expense.

Regulations

The Department of Housing and Urban Development (HUD) has responsibility for administering housing programs under the National Housing Act. Mortgage bankers operate as approved mortgagees under the act when they originate mortgages insured by HUD. When a mortgagee is not subject to supervision by a government agency it falls within the scope of the audit guide for HUD-approved nonsupervised mortgagees. While this audit guide suggests certain compliance tests, it is not intended to supplant the auditor's judgment. The audit steps are similar to those in *Uniform Single Audit Program for Mortgage Bankers* (described later under Auditing Considerations), but are structured around various HUD handbooks relating to mortgagees. Coverage includes

- Escrow account review,
- Branch office operations,
- Loan origination,
- Loan settlement,
- Loan servicing, and
- Mortgage-backed securities.

There are numerous other regulations, both federal and state, to which mortgage bankers could be subjected:

- State usury laws and laws covering interest on escrow balances,
- State mortgage finance agency requirements if originations are funded through such agencies,
- Federal Home Loan Mortgage Corporation requirements for serviced loans, and
- S&L requirements imposed by the FHLBB.

Tax Considerations

Depending on a mortgage banker's practices, deferred income taxes could arise from different accounting and tax treatment of

- Purchase price of certain bulk purchases,
- Fees paid,
- Discounts and fees for loans originated,
- Provision for loan losses, and
- Gains or losses on sales of mortgages.

The tax considerations become extensive if the mortgage banker is involved in construction, operation of real estate owned, or tax shelters.

Accounting Considerations

AcSEC has issued two SOPs directed specifically to mortgage banking. The first, SOP 74-12, *Accounting Practices in the Mortgage Banking Industry,* is concerned primarily with the valuation of mortgage portfolios, transactions with affiliates, and classification of balance sheets. The second, SOP 76-2, *Accounting for Originating Costs and Loan and Commitment Fees in the Mortgage Banking Industry,* suggests that it is not acceptable to defer costs of originating mortgage loans in-house; however, portions of the cost of acquiring loans by other means (bulk purchase of government-insured portfolios, for example) may be deferred subject to specific limitations. In addition, AcSEC believes that loan and commitment fees should be recognized based on an analysis of the nature and substance of the related transactions, as discussed below under Current Accounting Practices.

An FASB *Invitation to Comment on Accounting for Certain Service Transactions* (FASB, 1978e) addressed, among other things, the question of revenue recognition by mortgage bankers. The intent was to narrow the range of accounting alternatives for recognition of revenue and costs related to service transactions. The industry is opposed to this proposal, which would require that mortgage servicing income be amortized on a straight-line basis, rather than on a percentage of outstanding principal as is now done. The FASB has decided to defer the project by incorporating it into the recognition part of the conceptual framework project.

An issues paper, *Accounting for Bulk Purchases of Mortgages Between Mortgage Bankers* (AICPA, 1979o), was prepared in 1979 by the AcSEC Task Force on Mortgage Banking. The advisory conclusions propose, as an interim measure, that paragraph 15 of SOP 76-2 be revised to indicate that a portion of the purchase price of any bulk purchases (not only GNMA, FNMA, and other government-insured loans) be deferred as the cost of acquiring the right to receive future servicing revenue. Also, gains arising from sales of loans to mortgage bankers would be used to offset amounts deferred on purchases, and additional financial statement disclosures would be required. The task force believes that a complete review of the issues of revenue and expense recognition is necessary for the mortgage banking industry, and expects to present its final conclusions during 1980.

Current Accounting Practices. The principal accounting areas addressed in the two SOPs, and the recommended accounting treatment, are summarized below.

Valuation of mortgage loans owned. Loans held for sale and loans held for market recovery should be valued at the lower of cost or market. Loans intended to be held as long-term investments, not a frequent practice in the industry, should be transferred to that category at the then-lower of cost or market, and the carrying value reduced as necessary at the time of transfer to reflect permanent impairment in value. Any difference between the face amount of these loans and their carrying value should be amortized to income over their estimated life.

Transactions with affiliates. The unique nature of transferring (or selling) loans to an affiliate requires a departure from the accepted practice of ARB 51 (AC 2051.07), that of eliminating intercompany profit or loss. SOP 74-12 observes that intercompany sales of loans whose market value is less than the cost basis, or whose agreed-on sales price is more closely akin to a capital contribution or dividend, do not reflect the substance of the transaction. Therefore, as to whether gain or loss should be recorded or eliminated, accounting should follow the specific treatment recommended in the SOP for specific situations.

Classification of balance sheets. The Mortgage Bankers Association believes that classified balance sheets do not reflect the economic reality of the industry's investing and financing activities. AcSEC agrees but indicates that classified balance sheets are acceptable. In either case, the mortgage banker's balance sheet should distinguish between mortgages held for sale and those held for investment.

Origination costs. All the costs of originating loans in-house (including warehousing and/or marketing) are to be expensed as incurred. Costs of certain bulk purchases of mortgage loans may be partially deferred as the cost of acquiring rights to receive future servicing revenue; however, the amount deferred should generally not exceed the excess of the purchase price of the loans over the market value of the loans at date of purchase. Some deferral is permitted for other types of acquisition or sale, namely costs to issue certain GNMA mortgage-backed securities and costs of purchasing the rights to service mortgage loans.

Loan and commitment fees. There is a wide variety of fees charged to borrowers in conjunction with the origination and sale of mortgage loans, including

- A fee that in reality is an adjustment of the interest rate,
- Fees received for committing funds to a borrower,
- Fees to guarantee a borrower an interest rate at or near market at the time a commitment is issued,
- A fee for underwriting and processing the loan, and
- A fee to provide a construction lender assurance that he will be repaid.

Deferral or expensing of fees received varies with the substance of the transaction. For example, as discussed in SOP 76-2, paragraph 33:

- *Residential loan origination fees* are essentially a reimbursement for the costs of the underwriting process of obtaining appraisals, processing the loan application, reviewing legal title to the real estate, and other procedures. Reimbursement fees should be recognized in income as collected, because the costs of these services are charged to expense as incurred. Excess fees should be treated as commitment fees, below.
- *Residential loan commitment fees* are often charged to the borrower or to a builder/ developer to guarantee the later funding of loans. And the mortgage banker often pays committment fees to permanent investors to ensure the ultimate sale of the funded loans. These fees may relate to blocks of loans for a specified total dollar amount, and should be deferred and recognized in operations on completion of the prearranged sale of the loans or when it is evident that the commitment to a borrower will not be used.
- *Commercial loan placement fees* are received for arranging a commitment directly between a lender and a borrower. In these transactions or others that are in substance loan placement transactions, the mortgage banker is serving only as a conduit between lender and borrower. Accordingly, the fees become income when the mortgage banker has no remaining significant performance obligations.
- *Commercial loan commitment fees* relating to income-producing or commercial property frequently have longer terms and involve larger dollar amounts than those for residential loans. They also vary more widely as a percentage of the loan. Such fees received and paid should be deferred until completion of the sale of the loan to the permanent investor.
- *Land acquisition, development, and construction loan fees* should be deferred and recognized as income over the combined commitment and loan period. Straight-line amortization should be used until funding begins; the interest method should be used for the remaining unamortized balance during the loan period. The commitment and loan period is affected by many variable factors, so the best estimate should be utilized,

and revisions in the original estimate should be amortized ratably over the revised period.

- *Standby and gap commitment fees* are collected because of the potentially volatile nature of the market for real estate loans. Such fees should be amortized into income over a combination of the commitment period and the standby or gap period— straight-line method during the commitment period, and interest method for the unamortized balance if the loan is funded.

- *Fees solely for services rendered* with respect to the origination of a loan, such as appraisals, should be recognized in operations when the services have been performed.

In recognizing noncash loan fees as income, there must be evidence that collectibility of the fee is reasonably assured. Unamortized loan fees should be recognized in operations when commitments expire without being funded or when loans are repaid prior to the estimated repayment date.

Auditing Considerations

The Mortgage Bankers Association of America, in cooperation with the Auditing Standards Division of the AICPA, has prepared the *Uniform Single Audit Program for Mortgage Bankers* (Mortgage Bankers Association of America, 1975). The purpose of this program is to establish an efficient method of auditing the mortgage banker on behalf of each of the permanent investors. As its name implies, the single program followed by the mortgage banker's auditors should be adequate to forestall each investor from sending in his own auditors. The audit tests include a review of trust funds, mortgage principal, interest and amortization, escrow accounts, insurance policies and fidelity bonds, and error-and-omissions policy.

Current Industry Trends

Mortgage bankers have begun using sources other than the warehouse line to fund their lending operations. These sources include

- *Mortgage-backed bonds,* i.e., a long-term promissory note against which the issuer has pledged mortgages as security. These bonds generally have a fixed interest rate paid semiannually. Principal repayment is either lump sum or sinking fund. The earnings from mortgages purchased with the proceeds of the bonds are offset by bond interest and other costs, and the difference is added to net income.

- *Conventional mortgage pass-through certificates,* which are an undivided interest in a pool of conventional mortgages. The issuer of the pass-through is simply changing the form of the asset held. Under the pool servicing agreement, the issuer collects interest and principal monthly, deducts a fixed service fee plus all scheduled principal payments and prepayments, and passes the remainder to the holder of the certificate.

- *90-day commercial paper* collateralized by mortgage-backed securities.

- *Hedging,* i.e., futures contracts with the Chicago Board of Trade. The purpose of all futures trading is to shift the risk of significant market fluctuations from holders (hedgers) to individuals who seek profits from taking risks. The mortgage hedger who is short in the cash market (investor commitments exceed inventories of mortgages) purchases futures contracts. A hedger who has mortgages without investor commitments is said to have a long cash position and, therefore, sells futures contracts. Mortgage hedging means taking a position in the futures market equal and opposite to the position in the cash market, thereby shifting the risk. The question of accounting for hedges is under study by AcSEC. See the discussion of financial futures in the Commercial Banks section of this chapter.

INSURANCE COMPANIES

There are two major types of insurance: life, and property and liability. Other types insure titles and guarantee mortgages. Though all are termed insurance, the underlying risks differ substantially. For life insurance, given a large enough population, the risks can be easily determined by actuarially prepared mortality tables. Using mortality rates and interest and expense assumptions, the life insurer can determine a proper premium to charge. The risks associated with property and liability insurance are much more difficult to determine and can only be based on past experience of a large group of similar risks. Consequently, the pricing of property and liability premiums is more difficult. Even though the risks are different, essentially all insurance companies accumulate large sums of money, which are invested to cover future benefit and claim payments.

Life Companies and Their Products

Life insurance companies market three basic kinds of products:

1. *Life insurance,* distinguished from other forms of insurance by the long period of risk coverage and by risk that increases with age. There are three types of life insurance:
   a. *Whole life* insurance provides coverage over the insured's entire life and is paid only upon the death of the policyholder. The premiums are usually level and are either payable over a certain period of time (e.g., 20 years) or over the life of the insured.
   b. *Endowment* insurance provides coverage over the term of contract and is paid either to the beneficiary or, if still living at the maturity date, to the insured.
   c. *Term* life insurance provides death-benefit coverage for only a specified period of time. This is the least expensive form of life insurance and the policyholder often has the option to renew this policy for an additional period (at increased premiums) up to a stipulated maximum age.
2. *Pension contracts,* probably the fastest-growing product offered by life companies. There is a wide array of contracts tailored for group and individual pension plans, including fixed and variable annuities.
3. *Health and accident insurance,* offered by both life insurance and property and liability companies, largely through group plans. There are two basic types: one protects against loss of income when disabled, the other reimburses for medical expenses when ill.

Property and Liability Company Products

Property insurance indemnifies against the loss of insured property. Liability insurance indemnifies the insured against damages caused both by the insured to others or by others to the insured. Property insurance and liability insurance are often so intertwined that they are written under one policy.

The property and liability industry is much more regulated than the life insurance industry. The premium structure is regulated by state insurance departments. One consequence of this regulation is the *underwriting cycle,* whereby rate increases lag behind the effect inflation has on the cost to settle claims. As rate increases become effective, underwriting profits increase until inflation catches up and new rates are requested. While some companies file for rate adjustments on their own, most file collectively through a rating organization.

Reinsurance

Reinsurance is usually an insurance contract between two insurance companies. The *assuming* company, for consideration, agrees to indemnify the *ceding* company against loss or liability arising under a contract (life or property and liability) in which it insured a third party.

Reinsurance contracts between companies may be facultative or treaty agreements. *Facultative* agreements provide that each insurance contract is individually underwritten and insured. *Treaty* agreements provide that the assuming company will accept a stated amount or percentage of a certain type or line of insurance written by the ceding company. In most instances, the assuming company receives only a monthly settlement statement that shows the amount of premiums written and the losses paid. Reinsurance business has traditionally been transacted on the basis of full faith and credit among the parties.

Other Insurance Products

A *title insurance company* indemnifies against loss arising from defects in title of real estate or from liens or encumbrances on the property. This is a unique kind of insurance, since it represents a policy with an indefinite term and since the risks, if any, pertaining to title policies exist at the time the policies are issued. Title insurance companies have low loss ratios. Their costs relate basically to the title search and record-keeping activities. Title insurance companies have a unique asset called a title plant, which is an indexed collection of title records covering all parcels of real estate within a geographic area. For accounting purposes the cost to purchase or construct a title plant has traditionally not been amortized. This has been challenged over the years, and the SEC has informally taken a position on title plant amortization, saying it is an amortizable intangible. In 1980 the issue appears to have been settled by the FASB's acceptance of SOP 80-1, *Accounting for Title Insurance Companies,* which states that title plants should not be amortized.

A *mortgage guaranty insurance company* insures lenders against nonpayment by borrowers. Policies are written for a specified time period and are commonly required by lenders who finance greater than 80% of property value. Mortgage guaranty insurance is the same as that offered by the federal government under the FHA or VA. Loss ratios are low except in times of severe recession. Approximately 15 companies are in this business; however, there are presently many diverse methods of premium revenue recognition in use. The Insurance Companies Committee has published a draft issues paper, *Accounting for Mortgage*

Guaranty Insurance (AICPA, 1980a), which recommends the straight-line, pro rata method for recognizing income. The FASB has reviewed the issues paper and instructed the committee to prepare an SOP.

Captive insurance companies provide popular tax advantages for industrial companies that have both a need for risk management and significant insurance costs. With a captive company, a company can pay premiums to its own insurance subsidiary and either retain or reinsure its risks. Another approach is to insure with a nonrelated insurance company and reinsure (i.e., take back) a portion of the risk through its captive. There are obvious tax advantages if the company can effectively be self-insured and still get tax deductions for the "premiums" (see Self Insurance in Chapter 29).

Equity Structure

Insurance organizations are either mutuals or stock companies. A stock company operates like an ordinary corporation and is organized to generate a profit for its stockholders. Conceptually, mutual life insurance companies are owned by the aggregation of individuals who are both the insured and the insurer. Reciprocal and interexchange insurance companies represent basically a slight variation of the mutual insurance company form of organization.

Today, the life insurance industry is dominated by a handful of giants. Almost half the insurance in force has been written by the top ten life insurance companies. Six of these life companies are mutuals. In the property and liability insurance business, the ten largest companies (three are mutuals) represent approximately 37% of the premium volume of the industry.

Regulation and Supervision

Prior to 1945 insurance companies were for the most part unregulated. Then the McCarran Act was passed, stipulating that the regulation of insurance companies was the responsibility of the states in which the insurance company conducted its business. As a result, each state formed a state insurance department, and large insurance companies may therefore be regulated by up to 50 departments.

The primary objectives of these state insurance departments are (1) monitoring and promoting the companies' solvency to ensure payment of claims, (2) enforcing fair dealings with the policyholders, (3) developing uniform financial reporting to ensure the correct monitoring of each company, and (4) determining the premium rates that property and liability insurance companies may charge to policyholders.

The insurance commissioners of various states organized the National Association of Insurance Commissioners (NAIC) to provide a forum and to coordinate reporting and examination requirements among the states. While the recommendations and findings of the NAIC are not binding, they are highly regarded and usually adopted by the states. One result is that each insurance company files uniform financial statements as prescribed by the NAIC.

Another major NAIC development is the uniform examination procedures for insurance companies. Under these procedures, the country is divided into six zones. Insurance company examinations are performed every three to five years, and representatives from each zone (insurance examiners employed by the state insurance departments) participate. The NAIC procedures contain two key elements:

- An "early warning system," which applies a series of tests to the published financial statements and provides a warning to the state insurance department that a company may be in financial difficulty; and
- An *Examiners Handbook* (NAIC, 1976), which contains the "Financial Condition Examiner's Handbook" as well as the "Market Conduct Examination Handbook" and provides guidance for scheduling, planning, and conducting an examination of an insurance company.

Recently there has been a trend toward CPA annual audits in place of, or supplemental to, the NAIC zone examinations. Several states already require CPA-audited statements for insurance companies conducting business in, or domiciled in, their domain, and others are proposing this approach. The NAIC has developed a model CPA audit rule, but has not endorsed its adoption by the states.

Accounting and Auditing Considerations

There are several major users of financial statements of insurance companies—policyholders, regulators, and stockholders. The policyholders and regulators are primarily concerned with the solvency of the insurer, whereas the stockholders are primarily concerned with the value of their existing or potential investment. Statutory and GAAP financial statements are intended to meet the diverse needs of these users.

Statutory Accounting. Statutory accounting practices, which differ from those of normal commercial accounting, are primarily concerned with serving and protecting the needs of the policyholders, and consequently emphasize financial strength, liquidating value, and solvency of the insurance company. Operating results are less important. Statutory accounting practices are prescribed or permitted by state insurance authorities and only recently have they been codified by the NAIC in *Accounting Practices and Procedures for Life and Accident and Health Insurance Companies* (NAIC, 1979).

Some financial rules are unique to statutory insurance accounting:

1. Acquisition costs such as commissions, premium taxes, and other items are charged to current operations as incurred, whereas related premium income is taken into earnings over the period covered by the policy;
2. Certain assets (furniture and equipment and certain receivables) are not permitted to be reported on the balance sheet in the annual statement and are referred to as *nonadmitted assets* based on the theory that they are not sufficiently liquid;
3. There is no provision for deferred taxes; and
4. The mortality and interest assumptions for life insurance reserves are dictated by the (home) state insurance department and are generally conservative.

GAAP Accounting. Insurance industry GAAP has been established for the most part by two industry audit guides prepared by the AICPA Insurance Companies

Committee. The first, *Audits of Fire and Casualty Insurance Companies* (AICPA, 1966), was effectively updated as to accounting principles in 1978 by AcSEC SOP 78-6, *Accounting for Property and Liability Insurance Companies.* The other is *Audits of Stock Life Insurance Companies* (AICPA, 1972b).

The major features of GAAP are that

1. Revenues and expenses are matched through deferral and amortization of acquisition costs against the related premium revenue;
2. For life insurance companies, policy reserves are based on most likely assumptions as to interest and mortality (the assumptions are more realistic than those dictated by statutory authorities); and
3. Deferred income taxes are provided.

Some of the more significant disclosure requirements under GAAP include

1. For life company reserves, actuarial assumptions for mortality, interest, and lapses;
2. The effect of material reinsurance transactions such as premiums ceded, losses recovered, and the amount of reinsurance credit taken against reserves and unearned premiums; and
3. The nature of the acquisition costs deferred and the method of amortizing the costs.

Also, in SEC filings, Article 7 (property and liability companies) and Article 7A (life companies) of Regulation S-X require that a reconciliation of statutory income and capital to GAAP income and capital be presented as supplementary data or in the footnotes to the financial statements. Many companies include this reconciliation in their shareholder reports although it is not required by GAAP. Figure 38.8 gives an example of disclosure of accounting policies along with a reconciliation of net income and stockholders' equity from a statutory basis to a GAAP basis for a life insurance company.

The industry audit guide, *Audits of Stock Life Insurance Companies* (AICPA, 1972b), reserved decision as to the applicability of the same accounting principles to mutual and stock life insurance companies. The nature of the mutual life operations and the purpose of the mutual life financial statements were the principal considerations. Presently, mutual life insurance companies publish general purpose financial statements on a statutory basis. Many believe that this is equivalent to GAAP for mutual life companies, and auditors' opinions are expressed accordingly. Others believe that GAAP for life insurance companies, as spelled out in *Audits of Stock Life Insurance Companies,* should be applied to mutuals. The issue has been deliberated by a task force of the AICPA Insurance Companies Committee ever since 1972, and still agreement has not been reached. As a result there are various forms of auditors' opinions being expressed on the financial statements of mutual life insurance companies.

Establishing Reserves. Actuaries are an integral part of the insurance industry, particularly in the life insurance industry, in which the largest liability is the actuarially calculated policy reserve. Actuaries also have significant involvement in the development and particularly the pricing of products marketed by life insurance

NOTE 1—BASIS OF FINANCIAL STATEMENTS

The accompanying consolidated financial statements have been prepared in conformity with generally accepted accounting principles as defined in the AICPA guide, *Audits of Stock Life Insurance Companies*. Such basis of presentation differs from statutory accounting practices permitted or prescribed by insurance regulatory authorities primarily in that

(a) policy reserves are computed according to the Company's estimates of mortality, investment yields, withdrawals, and other benefits and expenses, rather than on statutory valuation bases;

(b) certain expenditures, principally for furniture and equipment and agents' debit balances (nonadmitted assets) are recognized as assets rather than being charged to stockholders' equity;

(c) commissions and other costs of acquiring new business are recognized as deferred charges and are being amortized over the premium-paying period of policies and contracts rather than being charged to current operations when incurred;

(d) deferred federal income taxes have been provided for timing differences between financial statements and tax filings relating primarily to policy reserves and acquisition expenses;

(e) the statutory mandatory securities valuation reserve has been reclassified to stockholders' equity;

(f) realized investment gains/losses are included in net income rather than charged/credited to stockholders' equity.

The following is a reconciliation of net income and stockholders' equity for the Company as reflected in the accompanying financial statements, to the reports filed with insurance regulatory authorities (in thousands of dollars).

	Year Ended December 31— Net Income	At December 31— Stockholders' Equity
As reported to statutory authorities	$5,500	$29,000
Additions:		
Increase in deferred policy acquisition costs	2,600	30,000
Decrease in policy reserves	250	3,700
Mandatory securities valuation reserve	—	2,900
Nonadmitted assets	—	375
	2,850	36,975
Deductions:		
Deferred federal income taxes	920	9,500
Realized investment losses	150	—
	1,070	9,500
In conformity with generally accepted accounting principles	$7,280	$56,475

FIGURE 38.8   EXAMPLE OF LIFE INSURANCE COMPANY ACCOUNTING POLICY DISCLOSURE AND STATUTORY RECONCILIATION

companies. In the audit of a life insurance company, the auditor may need the services of a qualified consulting actuary when auditing life insurance reserves. SAS 11, *Using the Work of a Specialist* (AU 336), provides guidelines that generally apply when the auditor relies on an actuary.

Property and liability companies establish loss reserves for the estimated amount of reported and unreported claims. The estimation is very subjective, and, depending on the type of insurance, it may take many years before settlement is made. Property and liability insurance companies attempt to establish an accurate database of loss development and other experience statistics; yet even with a reliable database, many unknowns remain, such as inflation, economic conditions, and the courts. The difficulty in establishing loss reserves is related to whether the loss involves property or liability. For example, it is much easier to estimate the loss on an automobile collision claim than to estimate the ultimate damages relating to a product liability or medical malpractice claim. That there are many unknowns with respect to ultimate reserves can be found in the footnotes of many property and casualty insurance companies; reserves are described as estimates, and, if those estimates vary from actual, differences will be charged to operations in the period in which they are resolved.

Reinsurance Transactions. There are inherent difficulties in auditing reinsurance transactions, because so little evidence of transactions reflected in the financial statements even exists and there are customarily only limited controls. The shortage of evidence is based on a tradition of good faith among the parties, and the SEC has challenged the auditing profession to do more. In a July 1979 letter to the chairman of the Auditing Standards Board, the SEC's chief accountant said: "... based on investigations of insurance companies ... we have concluded that audit practices with regard to certain aspects of reinsurance transactions may be less rigorous or comprehensive than desirable." The SEC has also expressed concern over accounting for certain reinsurance transactions that enhance statutory surplus even though actual risk of loss does not pass to the reinsurer. The SEC evidently believes the problem is the absence of appropriate guidance, and the AICPA Insurance Companies Committee has formed a task force to study reinsurance accounting and auditing and publish an issues paper.

Other Issues Under Study. The AICPA Insurance Companies Committee is very active and continually deals with current events, issues, and pronouncements that affect the industry. Recent committee projects in addition to those mentioned above are summarized below.

Life insurance purchase accounting. A task force has been studying the application of APB 16, *Accounting for Business Combinations* (AC 1091), to life insurance companies.

Revision of the industry guide for audits of fire and casualty insurance companies. This is a long-term project in process since 1973. The property and liability insurance company SOP (78-6) and the reinsurance accounting and auditing project mentioned above will be significant areas in the revised guide. The committee considers this its primary project.

Discounting loss reserves. This is a very controversial concept, supportable from a theoretical standpoint but encountering considerable resistance from industry. AcSEC is also studying the subject of the application of present value techniques to loss reserves.

Medical malpractice self-insurance. A joint task force from the AICPA Health Care Committee and the Insurance Companies Committee is studying this complex accounting and auditing problem.

Accounting for insurance brokers and agents. The main issues here are revenue recognition and accounting for premium funds.

Key-man life insurance. Life insurance salesmen have been trying to sell key-man insurance on the basis that there is little or no cost to the company because in the long run and in later years cash value increases exceed the premiums paid. Some major life companies are proponents of the ratable charge accounting method and have attempted recently to gain support for it.

Under the *ratable charge method* the net cost (total premiums to be paid minus total cash surrender value for a paid-up policy) of the policy is amortized over the life of the policy on a straight-line basis, resulting in a level annual charge to the income statement. This would result in a deferred charge in the early years for premiums paid, which would only be offset against future operations if the policy was not cancelled. The *cash value method,* supported by a 1970 AICPA unofficial interpretation (AC U4064), charges the income statement with the difference between the premium paid each year and the increases in cash value that year. Under this method the cash value would be the only asset recorded. This issue is broad (in that it encompasses accounting for compensation plans) and will be presented in a committee issues paper.

Income Taxes

Both stock and mutual life insurance companies are taxed under provisions of the Life Insurance Income Tax Act of 1959. Compared to other companies, the tax computation and special provisions are complex. Income is segmented into three interrelated phases: taxable investment income, gain from operations (which includes investment income), and policyholders' surplus. Policyholders' surplus represents 50% of the gain from operations and is only taxed if certain events occur, such as payment of dividends beyond a certain amount, or if the company is no longer qualified as a life insurance company. Underwriting and investment income of property and casualty insurance companies is taxed in the same manner as income of other corporations.

The application of deferred income tax accounting to life insurance companies under GAAP is unique. Depending on a company's tax position and its ability to maintain this position, it is appropriate not to provide deferred taxes for timing differences that will reverse without a tax effect. (This is more fully described in Appendix C of *Audits of Stock Life Insurance Companies* (AICPA, 1972b).)

INVESTMENT COMPANIES

Investment companies provide professional investment management for a pooling of funds obtained from shareholders or other equity interests. Included are management investment companies, unit investment trusts, face amount certificate companies, and various other forms of investment vehicles. Investment management companies include exchange, dual purpose, hedge, and special purpose funds; venture capital investment companies; and small business investment companies.

Equity Structure

Management investment companies are either open-end or closed-end. Open-end companies have no fixed capitalization, make continuous share offerings at net asset value, and agree to redeem shares on demand; closed-end companies do the opposite in these areas. Small business investment companies (SBICs) are closed-end companies licensed by the Small Business Administration (SBA). SBICs are normally venture capital companies, but some may be essentially finance companies.

A unit investment trust is an arrangement under a trust indenture or similar instrument concerning a specified portfolio of securities. It only issues redeemable securities, each of which represents an individual interest in a unit of the portfolio.

Face amount certificate companies issue securities representing an obligation to pay a stated amount at a future date in exchange for funds received in either periodic installments or in a lump sum.

Regulation and Supervision

Investment companies are subject to both state and federal regulations, particularly the Investment Company Act of 1940. Section 3 of that act provides generally for the registration with the SEC of every investment company with more than 100 security holders. Unregistered companies may not conduct interstate business and are denied the use of the mails for purchases or sales of securities.

Companies offering shares to the public are also subject to the Securities Act of 1933, and closed-end companies with publicly traded securities must comply with the Securities Exchange Act of 1934. Intrastate sales of shares also require registration with state securities commissions under state "blue sky" laws. Such laws generally deal with the distribution of securities rather than company operation and management.

Federal Regulations. Several of the major provisions of the Investment Company Act, together with important SEC requirements, are that

1. The initial registration filed with the SEC must describe officers' backgrounds, the terms of management advisory contracts, and the company's intended investment policies and mode of operation. This information must be kept current by periodic revision.
2. Management investment companies must have minimum capital of $100,000 before stock may be publicly offered.

3. Closed-end companies may issue funded debt or incur a bank loan only if the amount issued is covered three times by assets; preferred stock must be covered twice. Only one class of bonds and one class of preferred stock may be issued, and preferred stock must have voting rights. Open-end companies may not issue senior securities, and any bank loans must be covered three times by assets. Face amount certificate companies must have minimum capital of $250,000 and may not issue preferred stock.

4. Semiannual reports, including financial statements (frequently, audited), must be issued to stockholders.

5. Dividends to stockholders from sources other than undistributed net income must be accompanied by a written statement disclosing the source, so that stockholders may distinguish income from capital gains distributions.

6. Sales practices, largely self-regulated, must follow the rules of fair practice of the National Association of Securities Dealers (NASD). Under the 1940 act, all sales of new securities must be made in compliance with the Securities Act of 1933. Sales promotion literature is governed by the SEC's Statement of Policy issued in 1950, which deals with methods of stating performance results, claims in regard to management ability, and other items.

Other provisions of the Investment Company Act cover standards of operating conduct, including intercompany investments, self-trading, dealings with sponsors, and custody of assets. Also, at least 40% of the directors must be persons who are not officers or employees of the investment company, its investment adviser or principal underwriter.

Certain regulations governing the sales practices, financing and operations of fixed trusts, installment plans, and face amount certificate companies are also included in the Investment Company Act. Under 1970 amendments to that act, significant regulations regarding management fees and sales commissions were adopted.

Prospectuses are prepared by closed-end companies when offering new securities; open-end companies must issue new prospectuses regularly, because they are continually offering new shares. In addition to financial statements, the prospectus must contain information about the history, functions, investment policies, capitalization, management, provisions for purchase and redemption of shares, price of shares, and dividend record of the company, together with a complete listing of the portfolio of investments shown at both cost and market values.

SBICs are regulated by the SBA, especially Part 107 of the SBA Rules and Regulations, and by a series of SBA Policy and Procedure Releases. Release 2012 is an examination guide that specifies audit procedures and reporting requirements (e.g., Form 468); Release 2014 contains a prescribed system of account classification; and Release 2006 deals with standards related to techniques to be used by SBICs for valuation of investment portfolios.

A real estate investment trust (REIT), depending on the nature of its investment portfolio and the nature of the securities it issues, may come within the definition of an investment company. REITS are discussed in the next section of this chapter.

Reporting and Record-Keeping Requirements. The registration statements and annual reports of regulated investment companies contain detailed financial statements that must be certified by an independent accountant. Whether the investment company's securities and investments are in the custody of the company or of a member of a national securities exchange, the independent accountant must periodically examine the securities, occasionally without advance notice to the custodian, and must report his findings to the SEC.

Annual reports to the SEC are required to be filed on Form N-1R by all management investment companies other than (1) those that issue periodic payment plan certificates and (2) SBICs, which file annual reports on Form N-5R.

The annual report on Form N-1R (or N-5R) is intended to update information in the registration statement (Form N-8B-1), describing in detail the company's objectives, policies, management, investment restrictions, and similar matters, and to provide audited financial statements. It also aims to have the company demonstrate compliance with provisions of the 1940 act.

The registration of fund securities to be offered under the Securities Act of 1933 is filed on Form S-5 for open-end funds, on Form S-4 for a closed-end company. As required under Form N-8B-1, each SEC form consists principally of the prospectus describing the fund's objectives, policies, management, and investment restrictions, and includes audited financial statements.

Registered management investment companies also have to file quarterly reports with the SEC describing significant events occurring within the preceding quarter and giving information on purchases and sales during the quarter and holdings of portfolio securities at quarter-end.

SBICs are required to file semiannual financial reports (on Form 468) with the SBA. The fiscal year-end report includes audited financial statements.

The Investment Company Act of 1940 (Section 30(d)) and the SEC's rules require registered investment companies and unit investment trusts to send reports, at least semiannually, to their stockholders. The fiscal year-end report must cover the entire year and must include audited financial statements.

Financial statements included in reports filed with the SEC are generally required to conform to Article 6 of the SEC's Regulation S-X (Article 5 for SBICs). Financial statements included in reports to stockholders should generally conform with those in reports filed with the SEC, and should include (1) statements of assets and liabilities, operations (investment income and expense, realized and unrealized gains and losses), and changes in net assets and (2) a schedule of investments (*Audits of Investment Companies*, AICPA, 1973g, Chapter 7). In addition, the aggregate purchases and sales of security investments during the period covered and the remuneration paid to officers, directors, and advisers must be reported.

Rules under the Investment Company Act prescribe the accounting records that an investment company must maintain (Section 31(a)). These records are examined periodically by SEC representatives (Section 31(b)).

The 1934 act specifies the records that must be maintained by the principal underwriter of the fund, the period for which the records must be preserved, and the reports that must be filed with the SEC (Section 15(b)). These records are also examined periodically by SEC representatives.

Accounting and Auditing Considerations

An independent accountant reports in Form N-1R on his review and evaluation of a registered investment company's internal accounting controls, and must describe any material inadequacies. The report must also indicate any corrective action taken or proposed (AICPA, 1973g, Chapter 8).

Form N1-R specifies audit requirements for the independent accountant. Certain of these, including the financial information, issuance-and-redemption-of-securities data, and monthly sales-of-shares data, are of a statistical nature and are easily incorporated into normal audit tests and procedures. Others, such as information on underwriting commitments, descriptions of services provided by investment advisers, and procedures followed upon receipt of orders for purchase, repurchase, or redemption of shares by the investment company, require audit procedures beyond the scope of a normal financial statement examination.

The statement of assets and liabilities must include not only securities on hand or held by a custodian, but also securities purchased but not yet received. Securities sold but not delivered are to be excluded. In ordinary transactions through a broker, the trade date rather than the settlement date determines when securities have been purchased or sold.

Securities held by the company or its custodian should either be seen or confirmed in writing by the custodian. Securities purchased and not yet received should also be confirmed. In addition, all investments in the portfolio should be considered in relation to compliance with the provisions of the Investment Company Act, state law, or the company's investment policy; a written legal opinion may be required in questionable situations.

Valuation of Securities. Investment companies should, in general, report security investments at market value (AICPA, 1973g, p. 16).

For listed securities the last, or closing, sales price is appropriate. If traded on more than one exchange, the closing sales price on the exchange on which the security is principally traded should be used. If there is no exchange transaction on the valuation date, the valuation should be within the range of closing bid and asked prices, if available. Some companies use the bid price and others use the mean of the bid and asked prices (AICPA, 1973g, p. 34).

For over-the-counter securities there are several possible sources of market prices. A company may use a mean of the bid prices or bid and asked prices from several transactions, or an average from within a range of bid and asked prices that is considered best to represent value in the circumstances. Any of these policies is acceptable if consistently applied (AICPA, 1973g, p. 34).

If market quotations appear to be questionable, or if the number of quotations indicates a thin market, perhaps a "market quotation" is really not available. In this case, the securities should be fair valued by the board of directors considering all the relevant factors (ASR 118 and AICPA, 1973g, p. 35).

The valuation of venture investments is often difficult, because the investee companies generally are closely held, immature, and illiquid. Absent indications of market values, the investment company directors must establish fair values for such investments, frequently with advice from experts.

The SEC has specified factors that should be considered in valuing a security (ASR 118). They include (1) the fundamental analytical data relating to the investment, (2) the nature and duration of restrictions on dispositions of securities, and (3) an evaluation of the forces influencing the market in which the securities are traded. The information considered by the directors and the judgmental factors applied should be documented in the board minutes, and supporting data retained for inspection by the independent auditors.

In auditing securities valuations made by the board of directors, the independent accountant should review the information considered by the board, read relevant minutes of directors' meetings, and ascertain their procedures. If the independent accountant is unable to express an unqualified opinion because of the uncertainty inherent in the valuation of the securities based on the directors' subjective judgment, he should nevertheless state in his certificate whether in the circumstances the procedures were reasonable and the underlying documentation was appropriate (ASR 118 and AICPA, 1973g, Chapter 8).

Income Taxes

Under Subchapter M of the Internal Revenue Code, an investment company registered under the Investment Company Act can elect to be a "regulated investment company" and is then relieved of income taxes on distributed investment income and realized gains. To qualify, the company must (1) distribute as taxable dividends not less than 90% of net investment income (interest and dividends less expenses) for any taxable year, (2) derive at least 90% of gross income from dividends, interest, and gains from sales of securities, and (3) comply with other percentage limitations regarding both (a) gains on securities held less than three months and (b) composition of investment assets.

If realized security gains are retained, the investment company may elect to pay the federal income tax on such gains for the account of its shareholders. Such taxes would then be deemed to be distributed to the shareholders, and the basis of their holdings would be adjusted as if the net after-tax gain had been distributed and reinvested.

Nonregulated investment companies are required to pay normal corporate taxes on net income and realized gains. Special provisions applying to SBICs are the availability of a 100% deduction on qualifying dividends received, and ordinary loss rather than capital loss treatment on the sale or exchange of investments in convertible securities or on stocks acquired under conversion privileges.

For all investment companies subject to income taxes, the financial statements should show the provision for federal, state, and foreign taxes applicable to net investment income and gains or losses on investments, including unrealized gains or losses; amounts should be apportioned to investment operations and security gains and losses (realized and unrealized). This is shown in Figure 38.9.

Investment Adviser Companies

The Investment Advisers Act of 1940 requires certain persons in the business of advising others about securities to register with the SEC. The application for registration must describe the investment adviser's background and business associations, authority with respect to clients' funds and accounts, and basis for compensation (which cannot provide for a sharing of gains or appreciation).

The law prohibits fraudulent practices by advisers, and describes specific books, records, papers, and memoranda that he must maintain and preserve. If an investment adviser has custody of any funds or securities in which a client has a beneficial

CONSOLIDATED STATEMENT OF OPERATIONS

Investment Income

Revenues (principally interest)	$ 800,000
Costs and expenses	600,000
Income before income taxes	200,000
Income taxes	100,000
Net investment income	100,000
Extraordinary item—income tax benefit	
from operating loss carryover	100,000
Net income	$ 200,000

Realized and Unrealized Gains (Losses) on Investments

Realized gains	
Net gains on sale of securities	$ 570,000
Less related income taxes	170,000
	400,000
Extraordinary credit—income tax benefit	
from capital loss carryover	170,000
Realized gain	570,000
Unrealized gains (losses), less applicable	
deferred income taxes	
Balance at beginning of year	$1,260,000 (1)
Balance at end of year	980,000 (1)
Increase (decrease) in unrealized	
appreciation of investments, less	
applicable deferred income taxes	
of $120,000	$ (280,000)
Net realized and unrealized gains	
on investments	$ 290,000

(1) Unrealized appreciation has been reduced by deferred income taxes of $540,000 and $420,000 at the beginning and end of this year, respectively.

FIGURE 38.9   ILLUSTRATION OF PRESENTATION OF INVESTMENT COMPANY INCOME TAX APPORTIONMENT

interest, such funds or securities must be properly segregated and be verified by actual examination at least once each calendar year by an independent accountant on an unannounced basis. The independent accountant's statement that he has made such an examination must be filed with the SEC promptly after each such examination. In addition, any material inadequacy in the books and records and safekeeping facilities must be identified, and any corrective action taken or proposed must be indicated (ASR 103).

REAL ESTATE INVESTMENT TRUSTS

A real estate investment trust (REIT) is a trust organization that obtains funds by issuing shares to obtain equity capital and by borrowing from banks, insurance companies, and other financial institutions. It then invests the funds in real estate, either as an equity owner or as a lender. REITs, which are passive owners, not operators, began to grow when the Internal Revenue Code was amended in 1961 to give small investors better real estate investment opportunities.

Few other financial intermediaries have experienced the heady growth that the REITs had in the 14 years between 1961 and 1975. In 1961 total industry assets were estimated at $300 million; by year-end 1974 assets totaled about $21 billion (according to *REIT Fact Book, 1979*, published by the National Association of Real Estate Investment Trusts (NAREIT), source of all data not otherwise referenced in this section). The REITs' fall from prominence was almost as dramatic; by year-end 1978 the value of industry assets was approximately $12.5 billion. These massive swings shook the nation's financial system and were accompanied by unique accounting problems.

Equity Structure

By meeting certain requirements of the Internal Revenue Code, a REIT is exempt from most state and federal income taxes. It acts as a conduit, passing its earnings along to shareholders. In this regard a REIT is like a mutual fund; however, its capital structure is better likened to that of a closed-end investment company. A REIT does not redeem shares on demand. An investor must sell his shares in the marketplace—where the price is only rarely equal to net asset value per share if known. Since most REITs are publicly held entities, they must meet the registration and filing requirements of the SEC.

A REIT's shareholders elect trustees, who determine its broad investment strategy and act much like a corporation's board of directors. The day-to-day operations of most REITs are administered by external advisers who also advise the trustees on investment opportunities and alternatives. The adviser is often a subsidiary of another financial institution such as a commercial bank, mortgage banker, or insurance company, and typically the adviser or its parent is the REIT's original sponsor. Because advisers charge for their services and because there is no legal or regulatory requirement for external management, many REITs have dispensed with the services of a separate adviser.

Income Taxes

The impetus for the expansion of REITs was an amendment to the Internal Revenue Code (Section 856-858) effective January 1, 1961, subsequently amended, most recently in 1976. A trust qualifies for tax treatment as a REIT if it meets IRS requirements in four major areas: "(1) it must follow rules and regulations that generally prevent it from taking a direct role in the development, operation and sale of property; (2) its income must be derived mostly from real estate; (3) its assets must be mostly real estate-related; and (4) it must distribute almost all of its income to its shareholders" (NAREIT, 1979, p. 60). Prior to 1961 the illiquid nature of traditional real estate investments and sizable cash requirements precluded small investor participation. The amendment was designed to distinguish REITs from other financial intermediaries and forestall real estate developers and other types of companies from converting to REITs for their tax advantages.

Types of REIT Investments

A REIT can be categorized by the type of investment it makes: an equity trust owns income-producing properties and derives its earnings mostly from rents; a mortgage trust finances real estate projects owned by others and derives its earnings mostly from interest; a hybrid trust combines both types of investments.

Equity Trusts. Equity trusts, which dominated the industry in its early years, offered the small investor the advantages associated with sound real estate investments, including

- The increase in economic value of assets that are indestructible (land) or durable (buildings).
- The benefits of leverage. Real estate investments are often financed largely by borrowings, and as long as the project's assets are earning in excess of its cost of money the equity holder with a proportionately small investment receives a higher rate of return.
- Protection against inflation.
- The availability of accelerated depreciation and other tax shelter benefits.

Equity trusts invest in industrial, commercial, and residential properties, including hotels, shopping centers, apartment buildings, office buildings, and warehouses. They lease their properties to others (usually on a long-term net lease basis), or they hire an independent property manager.

Mortgage Trusts. According to the NAREIT, REITs made approximately 300 public offerings totaling over $6 billion during the four-year period starting in 1969. And by 1973 mortgage loans represented 75% of REIT industry assets. New REITs were formed because many financial institutions viewed REIT sponsorship as advantageous; trusts would be sources of loans "that were beyond the legal or policy limits of highly regulated banks, savings and loans, insurance companies or other real estate-oriented financing institutions. Because their lending policies were relatively unregulated and because they had access to public securities markets, mortgage trusts were in a position to fill a great void in the real estate financing market" (Hoagland, Stone, and Brueggeman, 1977, pp. 469-70). The sponsors also hoped to benefit from advisory fees and loan service fees.

The 1974 Recession and Aftermath. REITs were major victims of the 1974 economic recession. According to *Fortune,* of the 20 stocks showing the greatest percentage decline on the New York Stock Exchange in 1974, 18 were REITs and included the industry's 5 largest trusts (Robertson, 1975, p. 113).

Hardest hit were the mortgage trusts specializing in construction and development loans. The 1974 recession was characterized by tight money markets; as interest rates climbed, mortgage trusts incurred losses because many REITs had previously committed themselves to lending funds below their now-prevailing cost of money. The recession struck at property developers too: increasing costs of construction and falling demand for completed projects forced many to default on their obligations to REITs. As the risk of default increased, REITs found that an important source of funds, the commercial paper market, dried up; REITs were forced to rely on bank lines of credit.

Equity trusts generally fared better during the recession, although the value of their publicly traded shares also declined sharply. Profits were reduced or eliminated as inflation drove up property operating costs and deteriorating economic conditions caused higher vacancy rates.

While the impact of the recession on REIT operations cannot be overstated, other factors contributed to their setback in the mid-1970s. *Fortune* summarized the industry's mistakes as follows:

REITs proliferated far more rapidly at the end of the sixties than the supply of talent needed to run them. Thereafter, seized by a naive euphoria about the size of the market for condominiums, motels and office buildings in many cities, scores of REITs began a competitive scramble to put to work the easy money flowing into their coffers. The inevitable result was overbuilding and a frightening vacancy rate.

Bankers, who might have injected an element of prudence along the way, didn't. Indirectly, through the REIT mechanism, they made loans for projects they would never have financed directly, and they permitted some REITs to build a giant pyramid of debt on what was often a thin foundation of equity capital. [Robertson, 1975, p. 113]

The REIT crisis inevitably affected commercial banks, which as a result faced "their most crucial period since 1936" (Green, 1976, p. 24). At the end of 1974, REITs owed banks $11.8 billion (56% of REIT assets). Many of these loans were in default, and REITs had suspended paying interest on $1 billion. To prevent wholesale bankruptcy of REITs, which would have severely strained the nation's financial system, commercial banks and trusts renegotiated their loan terms in a variety of ways, including the following:

- Commercial banks extended many REITs large unsecured lines of credit,
- Interest rates were reduced, interest payments suspended, and maturity dates extended, and
- Banks swapped their loans for assets owned by REITs or acquired those assets through foreclosure.

In more recent years, the outlook for REITs has improved as real estate demand has increased. The current trend in the industry is towards equity investments, because of their sounder performance during the 1974 recession. Beginning in 1977, REITs were again able to attract new equity capital although on a vastly reduced scale. Of $12.5 billion in REIT assets at year-end 1978, over $7 billion was in equity investments.

Accounting and Auditing Considerations

Professional Pronouncements. As REITs and their creditors struggled to cope with the financial problems of the mid-1970s, so did the accountants. In 1975 the AcSEC issued SOP 75-2, *Accounting Practices of Real Estate Investment Trusts,* to encourage REITs to adopt uniform accounting methods. Although SOPs are not authoritative (in the sense of binding CPAs to adherence under the AICPA's Code of Professional Ethics), the accounting practices recommended by SOP 75-2 have become generally accepted.

In 1977 the FASB, responding to both the REIT crisis and financial difficulties of major municipalities, issued SFAS 15, *Accounting by Debtors and Creditors for Troubled Debt Restructurings* (AC 5363; discussed in Chapter 22). To conform SOP 75-2 with the FASB's rules, AcSEC issued SOP 78-2 in 1978.

Losses From Loans. Since the release of SOP 75-2, REITs can use a single approach "when it appears that an original borrower will be unable to make the payments required by the terms of his loan agreements" (SOP 75-2, paragraph 10). In this approach

- The allowance for losses should be based on an evaluation of *individual* loans rather than on an overall, "systematic" provision such as a percentage of net income;
- The carrying amount of individual loans (including accrued interest) should be compared to the *estimated net realizable value* of the property collateralizing the loan; and
- Individual loans should be evaluated at annual and interim reporting dates.

The estimated net realizable value of the collateral property, rather than the credit standing of the borrower, determines the amount to be allowed for loan losses, because it is realistic; only rarely would a borrower from a REIT be able (or willing) to repay a loan from other sources (SOP 75-2, paragraph 12).

Net realizable value is defined as the sales price a property could command on the open market, allowing a reasonable time to find a purchaser and reduced by estimated costs (1) to place the property in salable condition, (2) to dispose of the property, and (3) to hold the property to the point of sale, including interest, property taxes, and other cash requirements.

The requirement to include holding costs—especially interest—in the determination of net realizable value was and remains very controversial. Interest has traditionally been accounted for as a period cost, but AcSEC concluded that "the principle of providing for all losses when they become evident" (SOP 75-2, paragraph 18) requires that estimated future interest costs be anticipated when losses on loans appear likely. SOP 75-2 also discusses factors to be considered in determining a property's estimated net realizable value, stipulates the method for determining the rate for interest costs during the holding period, and concludes that the following items be separately disclosed on the balance sheet of a REIT: loans, earning; loans, nonearning; foreclosed properties held for resale; and allowance for losses.

39

The Accounting Profession

Russell E. Palmer

EVOLUTION OF U.S. PUBLIC ACCOUNTING

"Accountant" can include a number of occupations: bookkeeper, auditor, preparer of financial statements and tax returns, financial and tax consultant, controller or other financial executive, researcher, and teacher. An accountant may be engaged in public practice, doing work for other companies as clients; in private practice, on the internal accounting, financial, or audit staff of a corporation or organization; or as an educator in accounting at a business school or university.

The focus of this chapter is the public practice of accounting. The most important function performed for society by the practicing CPA is the independent audit of financial statements, a function essential to the operation of the nation's economic system (see Chapter 1). And it is the public accountant's ability to perform this function that has been the subject of almost continuous controversy.

As this author said recently in the London *Financial Times:*

> There is no easy explanation for the current challenge to the profession in the United States. It is certain that we are paying the price today for the amorphous accounting . . . principles which we allowed to prevail in the early 60s. . . . And we are paying today for our past failure to challenge the business practices of some of our clients—too many assumed that questionable payments made by clients were a normal way of life, until that kind of corporate conduct became a national issue. However, it may also be that we accountants are now faced with a dramatic challenge because we have been successful in our efforts to convince the public that we are a profession. Today, the public is asking that we live up to that promise.
>
> The challenge to the profession touches on many issues, but perhaps the most critical is directed to the regulation of the profession. Congress has been sceptical of the profession's self-regulation efforts, and the most serious legislative proposals have been directed towards imposing a governmentally sponsored regulatory scheme.
>
> Practically speaking, the public accounting profession in the U.S. is regulated more by outside forces than by its own regulatory efforts. [Palmer, 1978]

The evolutionary story that follows is useful in understanding where the profession is today and how it will cope with the challenges of the 1980s. (For a detailed review of the auditor's role, see Chapter 9.)

Early Factors

During the years following the Civil War, the American economy expanded rapidly. European investors, especially the British, saw the opportunity and began to invest heavily in this country.

In the late 1800s an accounting profession as such did not exist in the U.S.—there was no professional organization to standardize procedures or enforce ethical behavior. Many English and Scottish accountants were sent to the U.S. to examine the financial condition of British-owned companies. These early accountants were part of a well-disciplined and organized profession. Not only did they establish accounting firms here (many of the present U.S. firms trace their beginnings to English and Scottish accountants in the late 1880s), but they helped the American accountants establish, in 1887, the first national professional organization, the American Association of Public Accountants. The association grew slowly. Starting with only 31 members, by 1896 it had grown to only 45, most of whom were in the New York City area (Chatfield, 1977, p. 151).

Accountants were first licensed as professionals in this country in 1896, when the state of New York passed a law that permitted the issuance of a license to practice as a "certified public accountant" to qualified persons (those who passed an examination) and prohibited the use of the title by others. Licensing laws were soon adopted in other states; however, the statutes passed were not uniform. Even today the lack of consistent requirements is a problem, as mentioned later in this chapter.

Changing Roles

Besides European investors, U.S. commercial banks were also among the early clients of public accountants. At the turn of the century, companies financed operations mostly through short-term loans, and bankers hired accountants to check their customers' records. Companies rarely needed what today would be recognized as an audit of their financial statements. Instead, companies hired accountants to perform a variety of other services—for example, setting up clients' books, advising on recording transactions and closings, and consulting on general business matters. Accountants also spent a great deal of time verifying the clerical accuracy of the books; they pored over the details of transactions searching for misappropriations of cash and other employee irregularities.

A milestone was reached in 1903 when the United States Steel Corporation became the first American company to publish financial statements accompanied by an auditor's report (described further in Chapter 16) and a number of large corporations followed suit. Other developments affected the profession's future during the first third of the twentieth century:

1. *Developing governmental involvement* came with the concentration of certain industries into monopolies and trusts. This led President Theodore Roosevelt to enforce the Sherman Anti-Trust Act of 1890, to establish the Department of Commerce and Labor, and to expand the authority of the Interstate Commerce Commission. Early on, government executives recognized the need for improved reporting by companies of their business affairs.

2. *Corporate income taxes* were levied under laws passed in 1909 and 1913, and companies needed the help of accountants to prepare returns. An interesting side note is that the 1909 law mandated that companies base their taxes on calendar-year (rather than natural fiscal-year) results. Although the 1913 law lifted this requirement, many companies had already adopted the calendar fiscal year, the taproot of the accountant's hectic busy season.

3. *Public equity financing* was used by more and more businesses in the 1920s. Companies believed that permanent capital, rather than bank debt, made them less vulnerable to cyclical vagaries. Consequently, auditors had to face the problem of attesting to financial data for distribution to stockholders, who generally had little accounting knowledge.

Professional Responsibilities

Public accountants faced these early challenges largely without the benefit of professional guidelines. Not only were examinations of corporate accounts conducted without a set of uniform standards, but also the variety of corporate accounting and reporting practices was virtually unrestricted. Bankruptcies of widely known concerns and other signs of financial abuse compounded the problems. The profession's early leaders recognized that unless accountants took an active role in solving these problems, federal regulation was inevitable.

The American Institute of Accountants, predecessor of today's AICPA, became the focal point for the profession's reform efforts. Itself a combination of several professional organizations, including the American Association of Public Accountants, the institute began efforts to evaluate and explain accounting practices and to establish appropriate standards for the conduct of audit examinations. In fact, the AICPA functioned as the standard setter in the accounting principles area until 1973, when this responsibility was transferred to the FASB (see Chapter 40); generally accepted auditing standards continue to be very much in the AICPA's bailiwick (see Chapter 11).

LICENSING PROCESS

Accountants are licensed by the state boards of accountancy. To receive a license, an applicant must pass the four-part uniform CPA examination developed by the AICPA and adopted by all 54 licensing jurisdictions. Nearly all jurisdictions participate in a system of reciprocity: a CPA in good standing in one jurisdiction will be certified, upon application, by most other jurisdictions. And an applicant who has passed ("conditioned") parts of the examination in one jurisdiction is often not required to pass them again in another.

There is, unfortunately, a lack of uniformity in education and experience requirements. Most jurisdictions require a bachelor's degree, but some require only two years of college study; a very few require none at all. There is even greater variety in experience requirements. Many jurisdictions require two to four years of public accounting experience, but some accept other accounting experience, and a few accept advanced education as a substitute for all or part of the experience requirement.

An *Exposure Draft on Proposed Model Accountancy Bill,* released by the AICPA in 1980, represents a revision of the 1974 model bill. The current draft catches up with major changes in the profession and aims to establish greater uniformity in state requirements. When a state legislature is considering accountancy legislation, efforts are made to recognize the model bill.

Beamer Committee

The AICPA has long sought to establish uniformity in the licensing requirements of all jurisdictions, and in 1969 a special AICPA committee (the Beamer Committee) recommended that a minimum of five years of study (with no qualifying experience) should be required in all jurisdictions (AICPA, 1969c, p. 6). Even though the AICPA endorsed the Beamer Committee's recommendations, the five-year requirement has not been adopted by the state boards and has not met with much implementation in the academic community.

The AICPA had greater success, however, with a different approach urging that the states require CPAs to demonstrate they are continuing their professional education as a condition for continued licensing. The AICPA council adopted a resolution to that effect in 1971, with the support of the National Association of State Boards of Accountancy (NASBA). As a result, by early 1980, 36 out of 54 jurisdictions had instituted a requirement for some form of continuing professional education. More are establishing continuing education requirements each year.

Professional Schools of Accounting

In 1970 the AICPA and NASBA sponsored a Committee on Professional Recognition and Regulation to study the feasibility of separate professional schools of accounting. The committee recommended, in 1973, that such schools be established at "qualified and receptive colleges and universities," and that the AICPA, NASBA, other professional accounting associations, the American Assembly of Collegiate Schools of Business (AACSB), and the American Accounting Association determine accreditation procedures (AICPA, 1973i, p. 5).

The AICPA generally supports the establishment of separate professional schools of accounting modeled after the schools for other professions—the law school, for example. But among practicing professionals there is no consensus on their desirability. Supporters claim that the low prestige of the profession is a result of the low status of accounting education and that schools of accounting will abet professional identity. Critics argue that establishment of separate schools will result in vocationalism.

THE PRACTICE OF PUBLIC ACCOUNTING

Forms of Practice

Public accounting firms take three basic forms: the sole proprietorship, the partnership, and the professional corporation. The CPA sole proprietor, though he may or may not hire others, is the sole owner of the practice. His exposure to liability for debts and professional performance extends to all personal assets.

Two or more persons may join together to form a partnership; in fact the larger public accounting firms number their partners high in the hundreds. All partners are jointly liable for debts and professional performance of the partnership. Partnerships are governed in most states under the Uniform Partnership Act, and the few states that have not adopted this act have similar laws. (See Chapter 27.)

Some accounting firms have elected to organize as professional corporations. Even though professional corporations do not afford their owners a limitation on liability for professional performance, there are advantages of incorporation that are useful to some practitioners—for example, the ease of transfer of ownership and the deductibility of premiums for most insurance programs covering owner-employees. According to the AICPA's *Management of an Accounting Practice Handbook:*

While the state statutes vary in many respects, common features are limitation of stock ownership to licensed practitioners of one profession and no limitation on liability with respect to professional acts. Most state statutes provide considerable limited liability for acts other than professional. [AICPA, 1976d, Section 109.01]

Types of Firms

Accounting firms vary considerably in their size and the types of services they offer. The largest *international firms* having their major operations in the United States form a group known as the Big Eight: Arthur Andersen & Co.; Coopers & Lybrand; Deloitte Haskins & Sells; Ernst & Whinney; Peat, Marwick, Mitchell & Co.; Price Waterhouse & Co.; Touche Ross & Co.; and Arthur Young & Company.[1] The Big Eight accounting firms offer extensive services, and they all maintain offices throughout the world. (See Chapter 27 for further details.)

About the next 25 largest accounting firms are characterized as *national firms*. Though less widespread than the Big Eight, national firms have offices throughout the U.S., and many have offices or affiliates in other countries as well. There are also about 30 *regional firms,* concentrated in specific sections of the country and having few offices outside those areas. The *local firms,* too numerous to count, have offices within a limited area—in a single state, in neighboring cities, or just one office.

Range of Services

Depending on the size and resources of the firm and the needs of its clients, an accounting firm's services fall into three general categories: accounting and auditing, tax, and management consulting.

Accounting and Auditing. Accounting and auditing services include such activities as designing reliable record-keeping systems, assisting in the preparation of financial statements, and auditing financial statements to report whether they have been prepared in conformity with generally accepted accounting principles.

Companies also frequently need expert accounting advice on complex transactions. For example, a company interested in acquiring another business may ask its accounting firm to help evaluate the financial aspects of the proposed merger and to explain the financial statement effects of the combination. Similar advice is sought when companies contemplate a public offering of their securities, decide to expand into new industries or markets, or engage in activities such as leasing or real estate development, where accounting standards are constantly evolving.

The range of the CPA's accounting and auditing services has greatly expanded in recent times. By all indications the trend will continue, affecting first the traditional media in which companies report their affairs: annual and quarterly shareholder reports. As public companies respond to requirements that more extensive financial information be given, greater auditor association is inevitable.

---

[1] A 1979 confederation has, in effect, created a Big Nine internationally: Klynveld Main Goerdeler, comprising large European firms, includes Main Hurdman & Cranstoun in the United States.

Growing federal regulation also causes companies to seek the help of their outside accountants. The 1974 Employee Retirement Income Security Act (ERISA) requires that financial statements of certain defined-benefit pension plans be examined by CPAs (see Chapter 24). More recently, the Foreign Corrupt Practices Act of 1977 has caused companies to turn to CPAs as experts qualified in evaluating the effectiveness and reliability of internal control systems (see Chapter 13).

While firms of all sizes can provide a limited or a full range of services depending on the technical resources they decide to gather, the larger accounting firms generally serve the more complex businesses—diversified companies with widespread operations, heavily regulated companies, and public companies monitored by the SEC. In 1979, the Big Eight firms audited the financial statements of about 75% of the companies listed on the New York Stock Exchange. National firms also provide accounting and auditing services to many public companies.

The type of accounting and auditing services provided may also vary depending on the type of accounting firm. Sole practitioners and smaller local firms may only rarely be engaged to audit their clients' financial statements. But they may frequently provide bookkeeping assistance, help compile or perform limited reviews of their client's business and personal financial statements, and advise on installing or improving accounting systems. Perhaps the most valuable service offered by a smaller CPA firm is providing accounting and financial expertise that less sophisticated clients cannot afford to maintain internally. At the other end of the spectrum, the largest accounting firms derive a substantial portion of their revenues from audits of financial statements.

But the largest and the smallest firms are alike in that they offer their expertise whenever a client, large or small, encounters financial and accounting challenges. Regardless of the size of the accounting firm or the client, the relationship all CPAs hope to cultivate is captured when a businessman boasts that he never makes a major business decision without consulting his CPA.

Tax. Accounting firms offer tax services in varying degrees to the individual as well as the corporation. For the individual, tax services include the preparation of returns, and may include estate planning and executive financial counseling. For the corporation, the accounting firm can prepare or review tax returns, but a more significant contribution is tax planning—the legitimate avoidance or deferral of taxes. CPAs may also become qualified to represent their clients before the Internal Revenue Service or in Tax Court. (See Chapter 43 for an extended discussion of this phase of practice.)

Management Consulting. The management consulting services offered by major accounting firms cover a wide range of activities, and some of these activities are indeed the same as those involving advice and counsel to clients in connection with accounting and auditing services. Often the distinction lies in the complexity of the project, not in its nature. Of course, there are numerous management consulting services requiring special expertise, and firms providing those services must have appropriately qualified personnel.

Although this *Handbook* expressly deals with accounting and auditing, a general listing of the kinds of management consulting services available (in varying degrees) from CPA firms may provide a useful perspective of the environment in which firms practice:

- *Management Information Systems Services:*
  - •• Assistance in planning, design, and implementation of management information systems;
  - •• Evaluation of data processing equipment and software;
  - •• Review of data processing operations and controls; and
  - •• Assistance in implementing changes and improvements in existing systems.

- *Financial Services:*
  - •• Evaluation and assistance in improvement of general accounting, financial planning, budgeting, capital expenditures, cash management, cost accounting, and related systems and procedures;
  - •• Assistance in preparing financial projections for managements' planning purposes;
  - •• Review of financial forecasts and reporting on the reasonableness and appropriateness of the underlying assumptions;
  - •• Assistance in the analysis and financial evaluations of specific business practices or operations; and
  - •• Assistance in the analysis and evaluation of alternate financing sources.

- *Operations Services:*
  - •• Assistance in developing and improving production planning, scheduling, and inventory management policies and procedures;
  - •• Assistance in developing and implementing changes for improving the control and efficiency of operations; and
  - •• Assistance in developing and implementing changes for improved transportation and distribution methods.

- *Marketing Services:*
  - •• Assistance in the analysis of marketing plans and programs, product profitability, pricing, and performance measurement; and
  - •• Evaluation and improvement of marketing controls and procedures.

- *Human Resource Services:*
  - •• Assistance in management development and training programs;
  - •• Assistance in the analysis and development of executive compensation programs; and
  - •• Assistance in review and development of personnel practices and procedures.

- *General Services:*
  - •• Review and analysis of policies, objectives and goals, profit opportunities, and business plans;
  - •• Development of procedures for strategic planning and control;
  - •• Assistance in the analysis and development of organization plans and structure;
  - •• Assistance in developing merger and acquisition programs;
  - •• Analysis and evaluation of prospective business acquisitions; and
  - •• Assistance in government contracting matters.

Most of these services may be performed for nonaudit clients as well as audit clients, and the major accounting firms compete on a broad front with large and well-known management consulting firms. The SEC has shown a great interest in whether the performance of such services for publicly held audit clients might affect the audit firm's independence, in appearance if not in fact. This is explored in the last section of this chapter.

PROFESSIONAL INSTITUTIONS

Within the accounting profession, four institutions are responsible for establishing the standards of the profession and for regulating and disciplining its practitioners: the American Institute of Certified Public Accountants (AICPA), the Financial Accounting Standards Board (FASB, discussed in Chapter 40), state societies of certified public accountants, and the state boards of accountancy as represented by their organization, the National Association of State Boards of Accountancy (NASBA).

American Institute of Certified Public Accountants

The AICPA's objectives, as stated in its bylaws, are to

unite certified public accountants in the United States; to promote and maintain high professional standards of practice; to assist in the maintenance of standards for entry to the profession; to promote the interests of CPAs; to develop and improve accounting education; and to encourage cordial relations between CPAs and professional accountants in other countries. [BL 101.01]

Membership in the institute is open to "those who are in possession of valid and unrevoked certified public accountant certificates issued by the legally constituted state authorities" (BL 220.01), that is, the state boards of accountancy. As of March 1980 the AICPA had about 156,000 individual members, of whom 86,000 were in public practice, 5,000 were academicians, 5,000 were in government, and 60,000 were in industry.

The Division for CPA Firms, established in recognition of the fact that almost all services CPAs render are performed by firms rather than individuals, as of March 1980 had 2,026 members, 29 in the SEC Practice Section, 1,451 in the Private Companies Practice Section, and 546 in both.

Organization. The governing body of the institute is its council—about 250 members who have the power to prescribe policies and procedures of the institute and to enact resolutions binding on the board of directors, officers, divisions, committees, boards, and staff. The council comprises six groups of members: the officers of the institute; representatives of each state (elected by the members in the state); members at large (elected by the council); members of the board of directors, with the exception of the secretary; past presidents and past board chairmen of the AICPA; and designated representatives of the state societies, usually the president of each society. The full council meets twice a year; additional council meetings are held by regions.

The board of directors is the Executive Committee of the council. In this capacity, the board controls and manages the property, business, and activities of the institute, including the establishment of policies for the conduct of the institute's affairs. Board members include the chairman, vice chairman, vice presidents, treasurer, and immediate past chairman; the institute's president and secretary; nine present or former council members; and three representatives of the public who are not members of the institute. The board meets five time a year and reports to the council at least semiannually.

The officers of the institute are the chairman and vice chairman of the board of directors, three vice presidents, and a treasurer, all of whom are members of the institute and volunteer their time. In addition, the president and the secretary (who needs not be a CPA) are full-time officers of the institute. Five staff vice presidents are appointed by the board of directors to perform specific duties assigned to them by the president, as indicated in Figure 39.1.

Within the institute's organization there are numerous divisions, boards, executive committees, special committees, and other committees, subcommittees, and task forces. Selected ones are briefly described below.

Professional Ethics Division. The Professional Ethics Executive Committee develops standards of ethics and promotes understanding and voluntary compliance with such standards. The committee also has responsibility for identifying apparent violations and presenting them to the Joint Trial Board for disciplinary action. There are three subcommittees—behavioral standards, independence, and technical standards.

Joint Trial Board. The Joint Trial Board hears disciplinary charges against members of the institute. Its powers are exercised through a system of regional trial boards and the National Review Board. The regional trial boards hear complaints made under the ethics codes. The National Review Board is the final adjudicator of matters brought before and ruled on at the regional level.

Executive Committees. These committees have responsibility for policy setting in their designated areas, and are authorized to make public statements and issue authoritative and binding professional pronouncements without having to obtain the approval of council or the board of directors. Some of the executive committees are

- Education,
- Continuing Professional Education,
- Federal Government,
- International Practice,
- Accounting Standards,
- Computer Services,
- Federal Taxation, and
- Management Advisory Services.

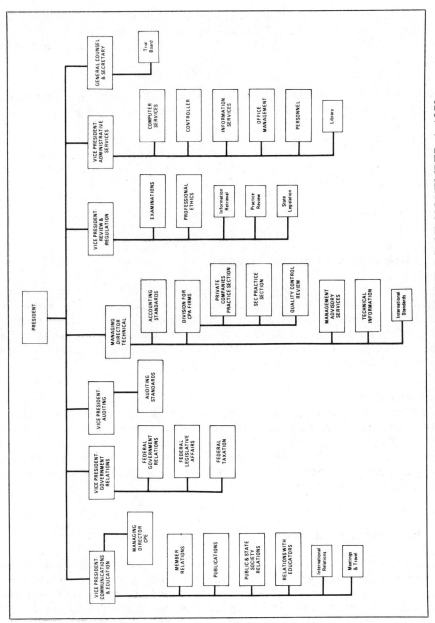

FIGURE 39.1 AICPA STAFF ORGANIZATION CHART AS OF NOVEMBER 1, 1979

SOURCE: AICPA, *Committee Handbook, 1979/1980* (New York, 1979), p. 146

Though not designated as an executive committee in the AICPA organization, the Auditing Standards Board (ASB) operates in much the same manner. The ASB and the Accounting Standards Executive Committee (AcSEC) are mentioned frequently throughout this *Handbook*.

Quality Control Committees. In the late 1970s, quality control and peer review committees emerged in the AICPA structure because of the focus of outside pressures described later in this chapter.

The Quality Control Standards Committee issues broad standards, such as SQCS 1 (QC 10), *System of Quality Control for a CPA Firm,* and it administers compliance reviews that may be requested by firms that are not members of the AICPA Division of Firms. As described later, each of that division's sections has a peer review committee for performing and reporting on such reviews and for monitoring adherence to the section's membership requirements.

State Societies of Certified Public Accountants

Each state and territory of the United States (as well as the District of Columbia) has a CPA society. A primary activity of state societies evolving in the past decade is to provide members with continuing professional education courses. State societies are also active in lobbying on state legislative bills affecting the licensing of CPAs, and members of state societies are frequently active on their state boards of accountancy.

State Boards of Accountancy. All states and territories and the District of Columbia have boards of accountancy, charged with the responsibility for administering the public accountancy laws. The state boards award the license to practice to each person who successfully completes the uniform CPA examination and meets the education and experience requirements imposed by the state statutes. State boards also have been very active in establishing and enforcing continuing professional education requirements.

Other Professional Organizations

Many other professional organizations have had a pronounced effect on the profession and the development of accounting and auditing standards. Often these organizations conduct related research, and they interact heavily with standard-setting and other rule-making bodies. Notable among these organizations are the American Accounting Association, National Association of Accountants, Financial Executives Institute, Robert Morris Associates, Association of Government Accountants, and the Institute of Internal Auditors.

American Accounting Association. The AAA is the national organization of academic accountants. Its Committee on Financial Accounting Standards repre-

- The firm's quality controls over its accounting and auditing practice are to be subjected to peer review every three years, and at any other time as may be imposed as part of a disciplinary action.
- All partners and members of the professional staff resident in the USA must complete at least 120 hours of continuing professional education over three years, but not less than 20 hours in any given year.
- The audit partner in charge of an SEC engagement can serve in that capacity for a maximum of five consecutive years.
- A preissuance concurring review of an audit report for an SEC client must be made by a partner other than the audit partner in charge.
- The firm must provide specified information annually about its operations for inclusion in files open to the public.
- The firm must fulfill certain requirements set by the Executive Committee with regard to its independence (discussed below).
- Total fees for management consulting services, and a description of their types, must be reported annually to the audit committee or board of an SEC client. Disagreements with management on material financial accounting and reporting matters and auditing procedures must likewise be reported.
- A firm must promptly report to the Special Investigations Committee any litigation against it or its personnel, or publicly announced investigations by regulatory agencies, where these matters allege deficiencies in auditing and reporting on SEC clients or former clients.

FIGURE 39.2 SUMMARY OF MAJOR REQUIREMENTS FOR SEC PRACTICE SECTION MEMBERSHIP

Independence. The profession's critics have been deeply concerned about the independence of auditors. To protect the independence of firms auditing SEC clients, many of the SEC Practice Section's membership requirements listed in Figure 39.2 are designed to enhance independence.

In addition, member firms are not allowed to perform certain consulting services for audit clients that are SEC registrants that may impair the auditor's appearance of independence. The services specified by the Executive Committee so far are

1. Psychological testing,
2. Public opinion polls,
3. Merger and acquisition assistance for a finder's fee,
4. Executive recruitment for managerial, executive, or director positions with audit clients, and specified related services,
5. Actuarial services to insurance companies where the client does not have (or obtain from third parties) the primary actuarial capability, and
6. Any other service inconsistent with the firm's responsibilities to the public.

The scope-of-services issue is a *cause celebre,* as discussed later under Evolving Issues.

Executive Committee. The SEC Practice Section is governed by its Executive Committee. Composed of representatives of at least 21 member firms, the committee is responsible for establishing general policies for the section and overseeing its activities, including the initial selection of members of the Public Oversight Board and the imposition of sanctions.

The Executive Committee has authority to impose sanctions on errant firms either on its own initiative or on the recommendation of the Peer Review Committee. For a firm's failure to comply with the requirements of membership in the section, which includes adherence to the standards issued by the Quality Control Standards Committee, the Executive Committee may

- Require corrective action by the firm, including appropriate action with respect to individuals on the firm's staff;
- Impose additional continuing professional education requirements for firm members;
- Require special peer reviews;
- Impose fines;
- Suspend or expel the firm from membership; and
- Admonish, censure, or reprimand the firm.

In late 1979 the section formed a Special Investigations Committee, charged with investigating facts relating to alleged audit failures (reported under the membership requirements as above) to ascertain whether the firm needs to take corrective measures or whether changes in GAAS or quality control standards need to be considered. It will make recommendations to the Executive Committee for such actions, including sanctions, as it deems appropriate. This committee aims to speed up the fact-finding process without prejudicing rights of the firms in litigation. Whether this arrangement is a sufficient response to the criticism that disciplinary actions remain unresolved for many, many years depends on its acceptability to the SEC, which in turn undoubtedly depends on how the committee performs and on the cooperativeness of the firm being investigated.

Task Force on the Auditor's Work Environment. During 1979 the SEC's chief accountant also expressed concern that nothing was being done about the Cohen Commission's recommendation that firms perform their own internal surveys of whether audit steps are being "signed off" without actual performance. The SEC Practice Section Executive Committee established a Task Force on Certain Aspects of the Auditor's Work Environment, whose position paper (AICPA, 1980m) identified "certain profession-wide developments [that] have occurred since the publication of the Cohen Commission's report [and] that should have the effect of enhancing audit quality: issuance of SAS No. 22 on planning and supervision, actions by the AICPA Division for CPA Firms with related membership requirements, measures taken by the AICPA to discipline its individual member CPAs, and the inauguration of separate authoritative pronouncements on quality control standards" (p. 7-8).

After discussing the incisiveness of these actions and recognizing that competition and time pressures are a fact of life in the profession, the task force made a number of recommendations aimed at the Cohen Commission's criticisms, specifically excluding any recommendation that firms conduct their own internal surveys. The task force concluded that its recommendations, in light of new professional standards and programs, were applicable whether or not a firm chose to conduct a survey.

Peer Review Committee. The 15-member Peer Review Committee is responsible for establishing standards of performance of, and reporting on, peer reviews. It administers the program and recommends sanctions to the Executive Committee. The objectives of the peer review program are to determine that member firms maintain quality controls satisfying the standards established by the AICPA's Quality Control Standards Committee and that the firms meet the SEC Practice Section membership requirements.

Public Oversight Board. The Public Oversight Board evaluates the effectiveness of both the Peer Review and Executive Committees and makes recommendations to the Executive Committee, the SEC, congressional committees, or conceivably the public at large. The board consists of five individuals from outside the profession with established reputations for integrity and concern for public interest. Board members have access to all files, meetings, and other activities of the section and the authority to employ their own staff, and they are compensated from dues charged to the member firms. In addition, the POB monitors the peer review program by postreviews of working papers and observations of reviews in process.

Private Companies Practice Section

The Private Companies Practice Section is similar to the SEC Practice Section in structure, but the requirements for membership reflect the different needs of the clients served by the members of this section. Not appropriate to this section are the various reports SEC Practice Section members are required to make to their clients' audit committees and to the SEC, and there is no POB installed nor is there a special investigations committee. The principal objectives of the Private Companies Practice Section are to improve the performance of practitioners in their audits of smaller firms, to facilitate participation by smaller firms in the affairs of the profession, and to tailor technical standards to fit the circumstances of small and privately owned businesses. The section also has an extensive *Peer Review Manual* (AICPA, 1979g) that parallels the SEC section's manual.

EVOLVING ISSUES

SEC Reports to Congress

The Moss and Metcalf Subcommittees, though advocating direct regulation of the profession, perhaps achieved their real goals—getting the SEC in the posture of exercising forceful surveillance over the accounting profession. One of the clear strengths in the SEC oversight process is the current SEC chairman, Harold M. Williams, who aggressively believes the profession can and should do more; at the same time he acknowledges that considerable strides are being made.

In mid-1978 the SEC began issuing a comprehensive annual report to Congress on how the accounting profession is doing. And each January, at the AICPA-sponsored SEC Conference, Chairman Williams and members of the SEC staff emphasize their thoughts on what needs to be done.

The potency of the SEC should not be underestimated. For example, their posture on the scope-of-services issue has effectively told the Public Oversight Board that the POB was not properly "sensitized" on the issue. This issue is explored later in this section.

In July 1978 the SEC issued its first report (SEC, 1978) to Congress on the profession's efforts to improve its self-regulation process and the results of the commission's involvement in that process during the period July 1977 through June 1978. The SEC stated it was then too early to determine whether legislation or regulation by a governmental body would be necessary in the future. The SEC explicitly disagreed with Congressman Moss's proposed legislation that would establish NOSECA. The SEC did suggest, however, that certain areas mentioned below require the further attention of the profession.

In mid-1979 the SEC released its second annual report to Congress regarding the accounting profession. The SEC continued its conditional support of self-regulation, with admonitions that in certain respects it was still too early to determine whether future possible legislation or regulation would be necessary.

Important elements of the SEC's second report (SEC, 1979) were that

• Progress had been sufficient to merit continued opportunity for the profession to pursue self-regulation.

• The SEC had been active during the year in overseeing the profession's initiatives concerning the independence of auditors and the accounting and auditing standard-setting processes, giving specific attention to maintaining the momentum for progress in such areas as reporting on internal accounting control and scope of services performed by auditors. (These terms are SEC euphemisms; see ASR 264 on scope of services, discussed later in this chapter, and Release 34-15572 proposing mandatory reporting on internal control, discussed in Chapter 13.)

• The profession and the SEC must continue their commitment to demonstrating that accountants themselves rather than government should (1) retain primary authority to regulate the profession, (2) ensure and instill confidence in professionalism and objectivity, (3) maintain control over the quality of the work of the profession's members and discipline those who fail to adhere to its standards, and (4) formulate appropriate accounting and auditing standards.

In a third report to Congress (SEC, 1980), the major new item discussed was the SEC's expressed intention to have sufficient access to peer review working papers, as discussed below. The release of the SEC's third report was delayed until an accord was reached with the AICPA. Otherwise, the 1980 report continues the SEC's conditional support of self-regulation, using new phrases—"an interim assessment and endorsement of the profession's current activities and commitment for the future" (SEC, 1980, Transmittal Letters, p. 3).

Audit Committee Requirement

By 1978 many companies had already installed audit committees either because the New York Stock Exchange requires listed companies to have them or because of other pressure from government and activist groups (see Chapter 10). Nonetheless, the SEC wanted the AICPA to establish a standard requiring public companies to have independent audit committees, as a means of assuring auditor independence from management. An AICPA special committee studied the feasibility of a requirement that CPAs refuse audit engagements with publicly held companies that do not have audit committees, and recommended that such a standard not be adopted, because of the demands it would place on many smaller and medium-sized companies. Perhaps most importantly, the special committee concluded that audit committees were not essential to assure an auditor's independence.

Peer Review Strengthening

According to the SEC's 1978 report, the peer review program also needed to be strengthened. Thus, the commission recommended that (1) the AICPA establish a performance review panel to determine the acceptability of each firm-on-firm peer review and issue its own report on the review; (2) the public have access to the results of each peer review, including the reviewing firm's letter of recommendation and the reviewed firm's letter of response; (3) the reviewing team, with the oversight of the POB, should determine which engagements can be excluded from the review, taking into consideration whether the firm's personnel and the procedures it uses can be adequately examined in other ways; and (4) reviewers directly consider the quality of engagements performed outside the U.S. in audits of U.S. companies.

What has evolved is a quality control panel of not more than three individuals selected from various firms, who use the work of the firm that is doing the peer review. The panel must reach its own conclusion on the quality control system of the reviewed firm. This is done to guarantee to the public that no "backscratching" occurs when a major firm selects another major firm to do a firm-on-firm peer review, the only viable approach according to the POB in these large situations. This hierarchy is expensive, though probably useful in maintaining public credibility.

Although peer review reports are now available to the public, the SEC has been concerned about not having access to peer review working papers. The SEC strongly felt that it should be in a position to evaluate whether a satisfactory review has been performed and did not see how its congressionally mandated oversight responsibilities could be fulfilled without doing some kind of investigation. Although there was no conceptual objection to the SEC review in this regard, there was a concern whether the SEC would use entry into these papers for a "fishing expedition"—totally apart from uncertainty about whether the intervention by the SEC into peer review might make the whole process more discoverable, given the Freedom of Information Act requirements under which the SEC operates.

As to being able to reach into work performed on U.S. registrants by non-U.S. offices, affiliates, or correspondents, in early 1980 a tentative accord has been reached whereby the U.S. auditors' procedures and documentation relating to supervision and control of work performed by the non-U.S. auditor would be subjected to peer review to ascertain that there was reasonable compliance with professional standards (AU 543). The peer reviewers would not go into other aspects of the foreign office's or affiliate's professional practice. There were strong objections from the professional societies in other countries that the SEC had no business looking into their non-SEC and non-U.S. practices.

In connection with completion of the 1980 report to Congress, the SEC and the AICPA, with the participation of the Public Oversight Board, agreed on the extent of SEC access to peer review working papers. The substance of this agreement is as follows:

1. Access would be through the Public Oversight Board;
2. Access would begin with 1981 reviews;
3. With respect to member firms that have one or more SEC clients, the SEC chief accountant's staff will have access to the following peer review working papers:
   a. Firm-wide summary memorandum,
   b. Summary memorandum for each office for a multioffice firm,
   c. Combining working papers showing the trail from the office memoranda to the firm-wide memorandum for a multioffice firm,
   d. Working papers relating to the review of functional areas, and
   e. Working papers of the quality control review panel;
4. With respect to member firms that have a permanent seat on the AICPA SEC Practice Section Executive Committee, at the chief accountant's option, his staff may have access to the following peer review working papers in lieu of the summary memorandum for each office for a multioffice firm and combining working papers showing the trail from the office memoranda to the firm-wide memorandum for a multioffice firm:
   a. All matters-for-further-consideration (MFC) forms,
   b. Firm-wide summary MFCs, and
   c. Firm-wide summary of answers to engagement checklists.

Public Oversight Board Role

The Public Oversight Board needed to be strengthened, in the 1978 view of the SEC. As indicated earlier, the POB was created to oversee the activities of the SEC Practice Section. However, it does not have any direct authority to require the section to do anything—though the profession has assumed that if the POB spoke, there could be no question that attention would be given. The SEC wanted the POB to have direct authority, despite the fact that the POB is separate from the Institute—the POB has no official status in the AICPA, and none of the POB members is a member of the AICPA. They are, just as their title suggests, representatives of the public.

The SEC also said the POB must be more actively involved in the disciplinary process and in the peer review process and its results, rather than having only a recommendation role (see above).

In its 1978 report to Congress the SEC took cognizance of the criticisms of the Moss and Metcalf Subcommittees and the Cohen Commission, noting that the AICPA SEC Practice Section Executive Committee had asked the Public Oversight Board to study the issue of whether the furnishing of any particular types of services might impair the auditors' independence, in appearance if not in fact. Even though the Cohen Commission said it had not found more than one instance where an auditor's independence was in fact compromised by an audit firm doing management consulting services (CAR, 1978, p. 102), the SEC felt there was enough controversy on the point that it ought to be laid to rest.

The POB studied the issue and in 1979 released its report, *Scope of Services by CPA Firms* (POB, 1979). The POB said that there could be no valid reason to restrict the scope of services of CPA firms beyond the restrictions already installed in the profession, and that there were many positive factors in favor of having a broad range of services.[5]

The POB took due note of the fact that the SEC had released ASR 250, which requires that registrants

- Describe each professional service provided by the auditor.
- State the percentage relationship that the aggregate of the fees for all nonaudit services bears to the audit fees.
- State the percentage relationship that the fee for each nonaudit service bears to the audit fee, except where the fee for the specific service is less than 3%.
- Indicate whether before each professional service provided by the auditor was rendered, it was approved by, and the possible effect on the independence of the accountant was considered by, the audit committee or the board of directors.
- Describe the circumstances and give details of any services provided by the registrant's auditor that were furnished at rates and terms that were not customary.
- Describe any existing direct or indirect understanding or agreement that places a limit on current or future years' audit fees, including fee arrangements that provide fixed limits on fees that are not subject to reconsideration if unexpected issues involving accounting or auditing are encountered. Disclosure of fee estimates is not required.

The POB concluded by cautioning that the scope-of-services matter should be under continual surveillance, considering future developments in public accounting practice.

The AICPA received the POB report in earnest, with the SEC Practice Section promptly adopting the specific recommendations made by the POB. The AICPA, of course, continued its study of whether any detailed services, such as the ones listed under SEC Practice Section earlier in this chapter, should be identified as not falling within the appropriate range of services by a CPA firm to its SEC audit clients.

Given ASR 250 and the POB report, there was a tremendous shock when the SEC, in mid-1979, issued ASR 264, *Scope of Services by Independent Accountants*. Simply put, the SEC observed that the POB report was not sufficiently responsive to the concerns voiced by the commission, and while the SEC did not ask

---

[5] It did recommend (POB, 1979, p. 53) that professionals should not provide primary actuarial services for life insurance clients; those clients must have this capability, directly or through their own consulting actuaries.

any company not to hire its auditors for management consulting work, the SEC's independence concerns were so strongly stated that registrants were being swayed from obtaining management consulting services from their audit firms. In a way it was a feeling of, Why should we bother with all that red tape when there are plenty of other firms around that can provide such a service?

Despite the considerable protests of the accounting profession and suggestions that the SEC acted to restrain trade without due process, no legal battles have ensued. The SEC has spoken in terms of issuing some interpretive release, but none existed as of October 1980. Chairman Williams has spoken on this subject a number of times, stating that the SEC has no intention of putting CPA firms out of the management consulting business, and the profession is simply adjusting to the existence of ASR 264, hoping to regain the valid business opportunities that were lost.

Disciplinary System Changes

As indicated earlier, the SEC Practice Section has inaugurated a Special Investigations Committee to look immediately into alleged wrongdoings by CPA firms with respect to audits of SEC clients performed by members of the section.[6] The committee will generally operate as an "oral court" by looking at whatever evidence the CPA firm has to show with regard to the problems alleged, and the committee will conclude, in private, whether some immediate remedial action has to be taken, either as to professional standards or as to the CPA firm. Having determined that, the committee will back off and let litigation and disciplinary action take its normal (and usually elongated) course. It is important to note, however, that the public interest aspect will be immediately investigated and addressed.

As also mentioned earlier, in order to avoid duplicate investigations, 44 of the 54 licensing jurisdictions have joined in the Joint Ethics Enforcement Program, whereby an advance determination is made of whether the state society or the AICPA will pursue the investigation. If prosecution is required, the matter will be heard by the Joint Trial Board, and the decision of that board will be binding on both the AICPA and the state societies. This has removed at least some of the red tape that has frustrated the disciplinary machinery in the past.

Immediately after the Metcalf Subcommittee remonstrations, the profession began to remove the veil of secrecy in disciplinary actions, and now regularly publishes the names of offenders found guilty by trial boards. There is still a catatonic wail heard from professional gadflies that all the disciplinary actions seem to involve smaller firms and, by innuendo, that the larger firms are immune. This line of reasoning presumes that the bigger firms, who of course have more than their share of alleged audit deficiencies merely because of the larger bull's-eye painted on their treasuries, are involved in work that should be disciplined. In other

---

6 In theory, this places outside the committee's reach such a situation involving an SEC client audited by a nonmember of the section; however, a strong campaign is underway to make sure all these smaller SEC audit firms sign up, lest the SEC take some remedial administrative or regulatory action.

words, the very fact that the larger firms are common targets of litigation causes some to presume that they are guilty of many misdeeds. The Special Investigations Committee will hopefully eliminate this myth.

The SEC has shown a new awakening in this area, as it is obviously pursuing an aggressive enforcement course by calling for formal investigations of accounting, auditing, and reporting practices its staff simply doesn't like. In other words, where alternative accounting practices exist in certain areas, the SEC can't believe that the audit firm would have accepted one that the SEC staff does not believe to be the preferred practice. Some of these "revelations" coming to the SEC staff have turned into very time-consuming proceedings because of the SEC's crusading zeal. Apart from using regulatory authority in an overbearing manner, this approach is a waste of taxpayers' as well as investors' money.

THE FUTURE

The accounting profession has faced up to many problems in the last several years, albeit with some prodding by the SEC and Congress. Much of this was caused by litigation; even though the auditing firm performed the audit in conformity with GAAS and issued a report on financial statements prepared in conformity with GAAP, the plaintiffs and courts pushed harder, in effect saying, Your standards aren't high enough. This is, of course, a way to further the responsibility of professionals, even though it hurts. The severe difficulty is that under the present federal securities laws, audit firms and other experts can be held responsible for damages out of proportion to fees, for example, the entire offering price of a securities issue or the entire decline in market value of all of a company's shares. This could amount to, say, $50 million or $100 million. Overhaul of the federal securities laws, placing a limitation on damages and allowing assessment of costs against unsuccessful plaintiffs, is long overdue.

SEC Chairman Harold Williams, in a speech before the AICPA's Seventh National Conference on Current SEC Developments in January 1980, underscored the role he believes the profession must play in the future:

> While the profession can justifiably derive a sense of confidence and satisfaction from its ability to conceive and implement significant changes, it must guard against the tendency to become complacent, or to develop an attitude that enough, or too much, has been done, and that much of what is being done is not substantively necessary or cost justifiable, but rather a mandatory tithe to keep powerful, but misguided, forces at bay. This must not happen.

In many ways the accounting profession has stepped up to the issues. The FASB now works at a brisk pace to provide accounting principles needed in major situations; and they are, at last, creating a conceptual framework that is getting results—something all predecessor bodies have talked about but have never succeeded in doing. The profession has attended to the recommendations of the Cohen Commission, judiciously selecting those that will work and installing them, though it complicates life for the practicing professional. Though there will never be a time we can stop improving, this is a great profession, with a solid future. The free enterprise system is based on the ability to place reliance on financial and related information, and the accounting profession is ready to provide this reliability through its attest function.

In addition, through the expanding services audit firms provide with respect to financial information (as contrasted with financial statements), and through the additional management consulting and tax services that assist companies in the accomplishment of their just objectives, all parties benefit: the client, the public accountant, and in the end, the public—the profession's only client.

SUGGESTED READING

Bernstein, Peter. "Competition Comes to Accounting." *Fortune,* July 17, 1978, pp. 88-96. This article is a study of the competitive philosophies and techniques of the large, national accounting firms.

Burton, John C. "The Organization of the Public Accounting Profession." *National Public Accountant,* November, 1974, pp. 8-12. Long before the establishment of the AICPA Division for Firms, the then chief accountant of the SEC addressed the need for regulation of the accounting profession, including a method for accrediting firms that practice before the SEC.

————. "The Profession's Institutional Structure in the 1980s." *Journal of Accountancy,* April, 1978, pp. 63-69. This article is an analysis of shortcomings of the regulatory structure within the profession, and presents recommendations for a new self-regulatory body that would have congressional authorization for its establishment.

————. "A Critical Look at Professionalism and Scope of Services." *Journal of Accountancy,* April, 1980, pp. 48-56. This article takes a position opposed to the 1979-80 thrust of the SEC aimed at restricting the scope of nonaudit services provided by audit firms to publicly held audit clients.

Carey, John. *The Rise of the Accounting Profession.* 2 vols. New York: AICPA, 1969 & 1970. These volumes chronicle the accounting profession's development from its beginning to its current status as *the* profession in the fields of finance and management.

Commission on Auditors' Responsibilities. *Report, Conclusions and Recommendations.* New York: AICPA, 1978. Refer to the suggested readings list in Chapter 9 for a complete description of this important work.

McRae, T. W. *AICPA Policies and Programs for Regulating the Auditing Profession and Maintaining the Quality of Practice.* New York: AICPA, August, 1976. This book is a study of the profession's regulatory mechanism prior to the Cohen Commission report.

Miller, Herbert, and Davidson, Sidney. "Accreditation: Two Views." *Journal of Accountancy,* March, 1978, pp. 56-65. This article presents two separate discussions of the issue of accreditation, including discussion of the Joint AAA/AICPA Committee charged to develop an accreditation mechanism for the profession.

Olson, Wallace. "How Should a Profession be Disciplined?" *Journal of Accountancy,* May, 1978, pp. 59-66. This article examines the layers of discipline imposed on practitioners and the various bodies that impose it, with arguments favoring continuation of self-regulation applied more stringently.

————. "The Accounting Profession in the 1980s." *Journal of Accountancy,* July, 1979, pp. 54-60. This article is a forecast by the president of the AICPA of the responsibilities the profession will have in the 1980s, focusing on the CPA's role, organizational structure and education, technical standards, and regulation.

Palmer, Russell. "The American Profession: Facing a Growing Challenge." *Financial Times* (London, England), October 11, 1978. This article is a summary of actions taken by the accounting profession and governmental groups to improve professional standards.

40

The Financial Accounting Standards Board

Marshall S. Armstrong

HISTORY OF STANDARD SETTERS

Correspondence With the New York Stock Exchange

The phrase *generally accepted accounting principles,* used throughout this book, is part of the standard lexicon of today's financial community. Its origin is found in early correspondence between the American Institute of Accountants (now the AICPA) and the New York Stock Exchange. Prior to this correspondence, enforceable rules of accounting simply did not exist. Leading accountants and others in the business community grew increasingly uneasy with deficiencies in financial reporting practices observed during the boom economy of the mid-1920s. A joint effort by the institute and the New York Stock Exchange to remedy accounting abuses and better define the role of the auditor was first proposed in 1926, although the dialogue did not begin until 1930, following the stock market crash.

The result of the joint effort was a pamphlet, *Audits of Corporate Accounts,* published by the institute in 1934 and distributed to all members.

The SEC

The significance of *Audits of Corporate Accounts* was overshadowed by the Securities Act of 1933 and the Securities Exchange Act of 1934. As discussed in Chapter 41, the latter act created the Securities and Exchange Commission, which was given the authority to "prescribe, in regard to reports made pursuant to this title, . . . the methods to be followed in the preparation of reports, in the appraisal or valuation of assets and liabilities, in the determination of depreciation and depletion, in the differentiation of investment and operating accounts, and in the preparation . . . of separate and/or consolidated balance sheets or income accounts" (Section 13(b)).

With the passage of those acts, some thought that the debate over the creation of enforceable standards appeared to be resolved. Why, then, has the search for an appropriate method of standard setting continued? In 1938, the commission voted (three to two) to accept, in filings, financial statements prepared according to accounting principles for which there was "substantial authoritative support" (ASR 4). In effect, the SEC turned to the accounting profession to provide leadership in establishing accounting standards. Without this decision, today's accounting standards (for publicly held companies at any rate) would likely be a set of rules established by an agency of the federal government. Although some prefer the clarity of rules—you either follow them or violate them—others see significant dangers in the fact that too often the rules established by many government agencies are arbitrary and the result of political pressure. The 1938 decision of the SEC was both a watershed and a challenge for the accounting profession. The SEC did not abdicate its authority, since at any time it can recast itself as the standard setter, but chose instead to oversee accounting standards as they developed.

The Committee on Accounting Procedure

The AICPA's Committee on Accounting Procedure (CAP) was revitalized and enlarged in 1938. Thereafter, the committee issued its pronouncements as Accounting Research Bulletins. The committee examined specific accounting topics, a procedure criticized as the *piecemeal approach*. Given the economic and social crises of the 1930s, it is doubtful whether the CAP could have developed a broad conceptual framework.

Beginning with the fourth, each ARB contained a proviso that it represented "the considered opinion of at least two-thirds of the committee. . . . Except in cases in which formal adoption by the Institute membership has been . . . secured, the authority of the bulletins rests upon the general acceptability of opinions so reached." What little teeth the proviso contained was in these phrases: "It is recognized also that any general rules may be subject to exception; it is felt, however, that the burden of justifying departure from accepted procedures must be assumed by those who adopt other treatment" (ARB 4, p. 36).

Fifty-one ARBs were issued by the committee before its 1959 demise, including ARB 43, which restated and revised those previously issued. In spite of their ambiguous authority, the bulletins did achieve general acceptability.

The Accounting Principles Board

Formation. By the mid-1950s, it was becoming increasingly clear that the process of standard setting needed change. Alvin Jennings, as president of the Institute, summarized the criticism of the profession as follows:

> We are told that the public finds reports inadequate and insufficient; that stockholders have need for more quality and less quantity; and that it is our responsibility that it is not possible to compare operating results of companies within a given industry or one industry with another because of the wide choices in accounting methods which are available. [1958, p. 28]

To the extent that Jennings believed such criticisms were valid, he felt that they should be aimed at financial statement preparers as well as attestors. Nonetheless, he did believe that improvements could be made. Thus, a special committee, called the *Powell Committee,* was formed, and it proposed and obtained the creation in 1959 of an Accounting Principles Board and an accounting research staff.

Evolving Authority of the APB. Problems beset the APB and the research function from the beginning, and unfortunately, a framework was not forthcoming. The pronouncement coming closest to being the elusive accounting framework, APB Statement 4, *Basic Concepts and Accounting Principles Underlying Financial Statements of Business Enterprises* (AC 1021-1029), was not issued until October 1970. As the one dissenting board member assessed it, the statement "fails to provide what purports to be a 'basis for guiding the future development of financial accounting.' . . . The Accounting Principles Board is looking backward to what has occurred rather than forward to what is needed" (APB Statement 4, p. 105).

In 1964 the Institute's council adopted recommendations that departures from promulgated accounting principles should not only be justified, but should also be *disclosed* in the financial statements or in the auditor's opinion thereon. Three other recommendations also then adopted by the council were:

1. "Generally accepted accounting principles" are those principles which have substantial authoritative support.

2. Opinions of the Accounting Principles Board constitute "substantial authoritative support."

3. "Substantial authoritative support" can exist for accounting principles that differ from Opinions of the Accounting Principles Board. [APB 6, Appendix A]

What remained unclear was what constituted principles that have "substantial authoritative support" but were not set forth in APB opinions.

Suggested as an interim solution at the time (Armstrong, 1969) was a two-level hierarchy: class one consisted of APB opinions, ARBs, SEC rules, AICPA industry audit guides, and, in the absence of these other items, industry practice; class two items (not all of equal weight) ran the gamut from industry regulatory authorities to speeches of prominent spokesmen. Nothing in class two was alone sufficient evidence of authoritative support, but these items could help an accountant make a case.

Rule of Conduct 203. In 1973, to complete the 1964 council resolutions by making adherence to the disclosure requirements an ethical standard, the AICPA adopted Rule of Conduct 203:

A member shall not express an opinion that financial statements are presented in conformity with generally accepted accounting principles if such statements contain any departure from an accounting principle promulgated by the body designated by Council to establish such principles which has a material effect on the statements taken as a whole, unless the member can demonstrate that due to unusual circumstances the financial statements would otherwise have been misleading. In such cases his report must describe the departure, the approximate effects thereof, if practicable, and the reasons why compliance with the principle would result in a misleading statement. [ET 203.01]

Thus, substantial authoritative support, which had never been successfully pinned down, was removed from the profession's official literature as a basis for departure from authoritative pronouncements. In the period since Rule 203 has taken effect, rarely has an auditor issued an unqualified report stating that adherence to an authoritative pronouncement would have resulted in misleading financial statements.

ASR 150: The SEC Reaffirms the Private Sector's Role. When Rule 203 was adopted, standard setting was in the process of passing from the hands of the APB to the FASB, the subject of the next section. In reaffirming the profession's role originally encouraged by ASR 4 in 1938, the commission said: "... principles, standards and practices promulgated by the FASB in its Statements and Interpretations ... will be considered by the Commission as having substantial authoritative support, and those contrary to such FASB promulgations will be considered ... to have no such support" (ASR 150). Oddly enough, just when the profession expunged "substantial authoritative support," the SEC chose to preserve it, because of its ASR 4 genesis as the commission's rationale for private-sector standard setting.

Although ASR 150 is generally viewed as the contemporary underpinning of private-sector standard setting, Arthur Andersen & Co. disagreed. In 1976 it filed a petition asking the SEC to revoke ASR 150, claiming that the commission exceeded its statutory authority by mandating that anything contrary to professional pronouncements is misleading. Andersen called it "the most significant and sweeping rule relating to accounting principles ever issued by the Commission" (Arthur Andersen & Co., 1976, p. 1).

The profession's reaction to the petition—and Arthur Andersen & Co's. subsequent court challenge to the SEC—was incredulity. The Andersen position appeared to strike at the heart of private-sector standard setting and SEC oversight. Andersen vehemently denied this and asserted their action was designed to strengthen the private sector's role and encourage a clarification of the muddle of confused authority and responsibility that had evolved in the preceding half-decade. In March 1978 the firm's legal challenge failed to win an injunction preventing the SEC from enforcing ASR 150.

THE CONCEPT OF THE FASB—STUDY ON ESTABLISHMENT OF ACCOUNTING PRINCIPLES

In March 1971, the AICPA appointed a distinguished group of seven to "find ways for the American Institute of Certified Public Accountants to improve its function of establishing accounting standards" (AICPA, 1972c, p. 87). The group, chaired by Francis M. Wheat, a former Securities and Exchange commissioner, investigated the accounting standard-setting process then in effect and concluded that the AICPA could best improve its role by relinquishing it. Thus was born the Financial Accounting Standards Board, which began operations in 1973, charged with promulgating and maintaining the standards governing financial accounting and reporting.

Composition and Methodology of the Study Group

The Study on Establishment of Accounting Principles, initiated by the AICPA in 1971, was undertaken to examine the standard-setting process and determine "what changes are necessary to attain better results faster." No holds were barred; the study group was asked to evaluate then-existing suggestions for improvement but also to consider "entirely new approaches," always keeping in mind "the public interest . . . [because] the function of setting accounting principles affects the public" (AICPA, 1972c, p. 87).

In addition to the chairman, Francis Wheat, the study group consisted of three CPAs, an investment banker, an accounting professor, and a financial executive.

The study group met with numerous individuals and organizations, and public hearings were held. Participants in the hearings were asked to consider the major questions, which had been included in the notice of public hearings. (These questions are listed in Figure 40.1.)

Recommendations for a New Standard-Setting Structure

The study group's final report, *Establishing Financial Accounting Standards,* proposed the structure for standard setting that is in effect today. The FASB is actually one arm of the Financial Accounting Foundation, a nonprofit corporation

1. ESTABLISHING ACCOUNTING PRINCIPLES: SCOPE OF THE TASK.

   What is meant by the term "accounting principles"? Would it be more accurate and useful to refer to "financial accounting and reporting standards"? Should the body with primary responsibility for formulating such standards limit itself to fundamentals, should it develop detailed standards, or should it undertake to do both?

2. SHOULD THE PRIMARY RESPONSIBILITY FOR ESTABLISHING ACCOUNTING STANDARDS RESIDE IN A GOVERNMENTAL BODY OR A NONGOVERNMENTAL BODY?

   Should the SEC or another government agency take over the basic task? Or should it remain with a nongovernmental body, such as the Accounting Principles Board? If a nongovernmental body, what should be its relationship to the AICPA? To the SEC? What is the nature of its authority and by what means can its pronouncements be enforced?

3. COMPOSITION OF A NONGOVERNMENTAL STANDARDS BOARD.

   Who should serve on the board? Should they all be CPAs? Members of the AICPA? What is the optimum size? In lieu of the present volunteer board, would it be preferable if the chairman, or chairman and some members, or all of the members were paid and served full time? If so, what should be their term of office? What needs to be done about staffing? How should the board be financed?

4. METHODS OF OPERATION OF A NONGOVERNMENTAL STANDARDS BOARD.

   The procedures of the Accounting Principles Board have evolved to the point where the board now holds public hearings on subjects for proposed opinions. Are these proceedings satisfactory? How could they be improved? By what vote of its members should a nongovernmental standards board act? Majority? Two thirds? Other? What procedures would enable such a board to take swift action on developing problems? Is the present procedure for obtaining unofficial interpretations of APB opinions satisfactory? If not, how should it be changed? Should there be an appeal procedure? To whom?

5. ACCOUNTING RESEARCH SUPPORT FOR A NONGOVERNMENTAL STANDARDS BOARD.

   What sort of research is necessary as a prelude to the establishing of financial accounting standards? Who should conduct it? What guidelines for research studies would improve their quality and shorten the time for their completion? How should accounting research be financed?

FIGURE 40.1   STUDY ON ESTABLISHMENT OF ACCOUNTING PRINCIPLES: MEMORANDUM OF PERTINENT QUESTIONS

SOURCE: AICPA, *Establishing Financial Accounting Standards, Report of the Study Group on Establishment of Accounting Principles* (New York, 1972), pp. 95-96.

independent of other business and professional organizations. The other arm is the Financial Accounting Standards Advisory Council (FASAC). The foundation is governed by a board of trustees, who appoint members of the FASB and raise funds for its operations. The FASB has full responsibility for the establishment of standards of financial accounting and reporting. FASAC members, also appointed by

Other Acts

During the 1920s, interlocking holding companies controlled a large part of the country's utility investment through complex pyramidal structures. The economic depression of the 1930s resulted in chaos in utility financing, and the pyramidal structures accentuated the impact. Thus, in 1935, the *Public Utility Holding Company Act* gave the commission the authority to oversee the reorganization and simplification of public utility holding companies. Nearly half the commission's staff was devoted to simplification of the pyramidal structure, but by the 1940s this task was largely complete, and the remaining regulatory responsibilities of the commission in this area are not major.

In 1939 the *Trust Indenture Act* was passed, which established certain requirements for trustees under indenture agreements between security issuers and holders of the securities; the commission was given authority to administer this statute.

In 1940 the commission's authority was extended to include investment companies and investment advisers. The *Investment Company Act of 1940* gave the commission direct regulatory authority over all investment companies, including their organization, business practices, and financial reporting. At the same time, the *Investment Advisers Act* gave the commission power to require the registration of investment advisers and certain very limited regulatory authority over such advisers.

In addition to the responsibilities set forth in the securities laws, the commission is given certain responsibilities and authority under *federal bankruptcy laws*. The SEC may enter bankruptcy proceedings to protect public investors, and may advise the court on the fairness of reorganization plans in major bankruptcies.

ORGANIZATION OF THE COMMISSION

Commissioners and Staff

The commission is made up of five commissioners appointed by the President and confirmed by the Senate. Each commissioner is appointed for a five-year term, and one term expires on June 5 each year. If a commissioner does not serve out his term, his successor is appointed to complete the unfilled term. No more than three commissioners may be members of the same political party at any time.

One of the commissioners is designated as chairman by the President and serves as chairman at the President's pleasure. His term as commissioner, however, is not subject to termination by the President. Thus when there is a change of administrations, a change in the chairmanship is common, but there is not a complete turnover of commissioners.

While all commissioners have an equal vote on matters before the commission, the chairman exercises a disproportionate influence in most cases both through his control of the commission's agenda and by the power he has as presiding officer at meetings. In addition, the chairman serves as chief executive officer of the commission and hence maintains control over budgets and staff appointments.

It has been common for one or more commissioners to be appointed to the commission from senior positions on the staff. In 1980, for example, two commissioners (Loomis and Pollack) were former senior staff members. An overwhelming majority of commissioners have been lawyers by training, while remarkably few have been accountants. In 1980, only Commissioner John Evans, an economist, lacked a legal background.

The regulatory activities of the commission are carried on through five operating divisions, three staff offices, nine regional offices, and two offices concerned with the commission's judicial activities. These groups are collectively known as the staff. Approximately three fourths of the staff are located in Washington, D.C.; the rest are spread among the nine geographical regions.

Operating Divisions

Corporation Finance. The Division of Corporation Finance has the basic responsibility for administering the disclosure policy of the commission. It is this division with which registrants most often deal, since it is responsible for maintaining the files of registration statements and 1934 act reports (e.g., Form 10-K), which are the basic raw materials of the commission's responsibility to assure adequate disclosure.

The division was reorganized in 1980 into ten processing branches, each headed by a branch chief and staffed by attorneys, accountants, and analysts. An assistant director supervises every two branches, and registrants are assigned to branches according to industry code. Each assistant director is responsible for seven industry codes. This reorganization recognizes industry specialization, which was largely lacking in the previous 15-branch approach. The division expects to achieve increased efficiency and industry expertise with this framework. The division also has a chief counsel and a chief accountant, who deal primarily with registrant problems.

In addition to processing filings, the Division of Corporation Finance, through its Office of Disclosure Policy, has the responsibility for maintaining the commission's disclosure rules, with the exception of the ones pertaining directly to financial statements; those are the responsibility of the commission's chief accountant. The Office of Disclosure Policy handles both changes in the basic reporting forms and general disclosure requirements.

Additionally, there are a few groups in the division that handle specialized projects and problems, e.g., disclosure for oil and gas industries and disclosure problems of small business (reflecting the commission's concern that its requirements not represent a major detriment to small business in raising capital in the public markets).

Enforcement. The Division of Enforcement has responsibility for surveillance over the capital markets and the investigation of possible violations of law. When the division, based on a preliminary investigation, believes that a violation has occurred, it may obtain from the commission an order of investigation, which permits it to subpoena records and take testimony under oath. After completing its investigation, the enforcement division reports to the commission with a recommendation as to what action if any should be taken, and the Commission determines the next step.

In its enforcement actions in court, the commission normally seeks an injunction prohibiting both the continuation of current violative behavior and similar violations in the future. Such an injunction, if granted, exposes violators to both civil and criminal contempt actions if they continue their behavior. In addition, the commission may obtain, as part of a settlement, other forms of "ancillary relief" to assure that the public will be protected from future violations and that violators will not profit from their activities.

While the commission frequently prosecutes civil actions to their conclusion, far more commonly the defendants seek a settlement with the commission. In such cases, the commission enters into *consent decrees,* under which those accused, without admitting or denying the violation, agree not to engage in proscribed activities and frequently also agree to specific sanctions. These may include the refund of profits made in connection with the activity in question, the agreement to surrender control of an enterprise, the secession from practice before the commission, and other remedies as appropriate in particular cases.

The Division of Enforcement also investigates and brings actions against companies in the securities markets, where the commission has the right to suspend persons from the securities business for a period of time or bar them permanently. Often these activities are carried out jointly with the self-regulatory bodies of the securities industry: the stock exchanges and the National Association of Securities Dealers.

The enforcement division also investigates possible deficiencies in the performance of professionals practicing before the commission. In recent years there has been considerable attention given to enforcement activities against lawyers and independent accountants, which have usually resulted in settlements, major sanctions, and statements of commission policy. Under Rule 2(e) the power to suspend a professional from practicing before the commission represents a major threat to the professional's practice. Though there recently has been considerable debate and some legal action about the rights of the commission to impose 2(e) sanctions, to date the courts have upheld its legality (but see Chapters 44 and 46). The commission's enforcement program and philosophy regarding professionals are discussed in more depth below.

While the SEC's ability to impose severe enforcement sanctions is limited, it must be recognized that the securities laws have placed in the hands of private litigants the right to obtain damages from those who violate the law. Whenever the commission brings an enforcement action, the private bar is (if not well ahead) normally not far behind in filing a civil lawsuit for damages.

The commission does not have the power to bring criminal actions under the law. When investigations suggest that there are violations of law sufficiently serious to warrant a criminal action, the commission normally refers the case to the Department of Justice for prosecution. Staff of the enforcement division commonly work with U.S. attorneys when the Department of Justice decides to prosecute.

Market Regulation. The Division of Market Regulation is responsible for regulating the securities trading markets. The 1975 amendments to the Securities and Exchange Act mandated the establishment of a national market system, bringing into the forefront the commission's efforts to develop a single national market system for trading of securities.

In fulfilling this responsibility, the division must work closely with the registered stock exchanges and with the National Association of Securities Dealers, whose rules currently define practices in the market areas of the exchanges. Any rules passed by these organizations must be approved by the commission, and the commission has the authority to impose rules on these bodies.

In recent years the commission's decision to eliminate minimum commission rates on the New York Stock Exchange had a dramatic effect on the structure of the securities industry. Similarly, its proposals in regard to the elimination of exclusive rights for trading enjoyed by the New York Stock Exchange (Rule 390) promise significant changes in the marketplace as well.

Investment Management. The Division of Investment Management has the responsibility for regulating the mutual fund industry and investment advisers. It processes filings by these kinds of companies, and it establishes rules covering business practices in this industry.

Corporate Regulation. The Division of Corporate Regulation fulfills the commission's obligations under the Federal Bankruptcy Act and the Public Utility Holding Company Act of 1935. It reviews all bankruptcy filings affecting public companies, and it enters into court procedures when it feels a substantial matter of public investor interest is involved. It advises judges on the fairness of reorganization plans and on such other matters as the appropriateness of attorneys' fees charged to the bankrupt estate..

The division's responsibility under the Public Utility Holding Company Act requires that it approve financing plans of public utility holding companies as well as contemplated major changes in their corporate structure. Since the number of public utility holding companies in the United States today is small, this activity is not a major part of the SEC's duties.

Staff Offices

Chief Accountant. The chief accountant of the SEC has the basic responsibility of advising the commission on all accounting matters and has direct responsibility for Regulation S-X, which describes the form and content of financial statements filed with the commission. He also has primary responsibility for accounting series releases (ASRs) and for maintaining liaison with the accounting profession and with the Financial Accounting Standards Board. He advises the commission on enforcement matters relating to professional accountants and accounting and reporting matters, and he also serves as a spokesman for the commission's accounting policies in public forums.

The chief accountant serves as a consultative resource on specific questions relating to registrants' accounting and auditing problems referred to his office by the Division of Corporation Finance and the Division of Enforcement, and he will sometimes deal directly with unusual accounting matters brought directly to his attention by registrants.

General Counsel. The general counsel is the SEC's chief legal officer and adviser. Because most of the commission's rule-making initiatives have legal implications, he is deeply involved in virtually all of them. In addition, the general counsel provides legal advice to other divisions and offices, and he is the principal litigator of the commission, although representatives of the Division of Enforcement also handle litigation matters. The general counsel is responsible for developing statements of the SEC's legal position that are filed by the commission as *amicus curiae*.

Economic and Policy Research. The Directorate of Economic and Policy Research is directed by the chief economist of the commission. His role is to advise the commission on economic policy matters. While this is potentially a highly significant office, in practice it has not played a major role. The directorate gathers and regularly publishes economic data about the marketplace, and it has participated in numerous studies of the commission's policies.

Regional Offices

The SEC has nine regional offices, located in New York, Boston, Atlanta, Chicago, Fort Worth, Denver, Los Angeles, Seattle, and Arlington, Virginia. The regional offices play an important role in surveillance over securities activities in their areas. Their largest function is to decentralize enforcement; they conduct investigations, bring injunctive actions, and generally undertake the same activities as the Division of Enforcement does on a national basis. The regional offices also supervise and review broker-dealers and investment companies, and process certain limited registration statements (generally those filed under Regulation A, which provides for more limited disclosure by small companies).

Judicial Offices

Opinions and Review. The Office of Opinions and Review drafts the commission's formal opinions in the cases brought before it. This office also must explain the commission's reasoning and relate current decisions to previously established precedents.

Administrative Law Judges. The Office of Administrative Law Judges comprises the commission's nine administrative law judges, who hear cases presented by the Division of Enforcement and other divisions. The administrative law judge is the first level of judicial review for most cases, and he makes the initial findings of fact and decisions on legal issues. The judges' decisions may be appealed to the commission, and subsequently to the Federal Court of Appeals.

SEC POLICY ON ACCOUNTING MATTERS

Specific Accounting Authority

The Securities Act of 1933 gives the commission specific statutory authority to prescribe principles of accounting and reporting. Section 19 of the act provides:

Among other things, the Commission shall have authority . . . to prescribe the items or details to be shown in the balance sheet and earning statement, and the methods to be followed in the preparation of accounts, in the appraisal or valuation of assets and liabilities, in the determination of depreciation and depletion, in the differentiation of recurring and non-recurring income . . . and in the preparation . . . of consolidated balance sheets or income accounts.

In addition, the commission has been given authority in Section 13 of the Securities and Exchange Act (the 1934 act) to prescribe procedures for periodic accounting and reporting to the commission.

Responsibility in the Private Sector

While the commission has virtually unlimited statutory authority to set accounting principles, as a matter of policy it has used this authority sparingly. The SEC's basic policy decision not to undertake the establishment of accounting principles was made in 1938 with the issuance of ASR 4. This release provided that financial statements filed with the commission that were prepared in accordance with accounting principles for which there was no *substantial authoritative support* would be presumed to be misleading. The concept of *substantial authoritative support* was used to encourage the accounting profession to establish standards narrowing the areas of difference in accounting practices. The American Institute of Accountants (later renamed the AICPA) created the Committee on Accounting Procedure in response to this initiative, followed in turn by the Accounting Principles Board in 1958 and the Financial Accounting Standards Board in 1972. More about the history and activities of these standard-setting bodies is provided in the preceding chapter.

In 1972 the commission reiterated its policy of reliance on the private sector, in ASR 150. Noting its long-standing policy of looking to bodies designated by the accounting profession to provide leadership in establishing and improving accounting principles, the SEC endorsed the establishment of the FASB "in the belief that the Board would provide an institutional framework which will permit prompt and responsible actions flowing from research and consideration of varying viewpoints." ASR 150 acknowledged the experience and expertise of the members of the FASB and the commitment of resources to the Board as "impressive evidence of the willingness and intention of the private sector to support the FASB in accomplishing its task" and noted that the SEC intended to "continue its policy of looking to the private sector for leadership in establishing and improving accounting principles and standards through the FASB with the expectation that the body's conclusions will promote the interests of investors."

The conclusion of ASR 150 was the expression of a policy that "principles, standards and practices promulgated by the FASB in its statements and interpretations will be considered by the Commission as having substantial authoritative support and those contrary to such FASB promulgations will be considered to have no such support." This policy was subsequently challenged in court by Arthur Andersen & Co. on the grounds that the policy constituted an illegal delegation of authority to the FASB. The court rejected Andersen's request for a temporary injunction, noting that the plaintiff had little likelihood of succeeding on the merits of the case, and subsequently dismissed the case for lack of standing. While this is less than a complete judicial endorsement of the commission policy, one court certainly was not convinced that the commission's policy was illegal.

Subsequent to the issuance of ASR 150, substantial questions were raised as to the desirability of the commission's policy in hearings before the Metcalf and Moss Subcommittees of Congress (further described in Chapter 39). Neither of these committees in the end formally criticized the commission's judgment, and in its annual reports to Congress on its oversight role, the SEC has reiterated its policy as being responsive to the interests of investors.

Oversight and Occasional Overruling

While the commission has steadfastly maintained its general policy of reliance on the private sector for accounting standard setting, it has nevertheless not adopted a totally passive role. The commission's oversight responsibilities necessitate a close working relationship with standard-setting bodies so that each is fully aware of the views of the other. Both organizations seek to avoid confrontation that could result in the deterioration of the relationship.

The degree of cooperation between the bodies has varied substantially over time. On occasion, the standard-setting body has worked virtually as a partner with the commission staff in drafting opinions, so the input of the SEC staff was direct and substantial. At other times, the private-sector standard-setting body has kept the SEC at a distance, discussing pronouncements with the staff only in general terms prior to their issuance. The relationship between the bodies sometimes has been less than cordial, but on the whole a satisfactory *modus operandi* has been established.

On a few occasions the commission has expressed itself strongly on what accounting principles it would consider acceptable in certain areas, and in most cases the standard setter has accepted this judgment. In addition, on a few occasions the SEC has requested a solution to a particular problem, and both parties knew the result would be commission action if the standard setter did not act.

There have also been a few occasions in which the commission overruled the actions of the standard-setting body. The first of these occurred when the SEC declined to support the APB's 1962 decision (APB 2) on how to account for investment credit (AC 4094.11-.12). More recent and more significant was the commission's determination to overrule SFAS 19 (AC 6021) on accounting in the oil and gas industry.

When Congress directed the SEC in 1975 to determine the best method of accounting in the oil and gas producing industry, the commission asked the FASB to develop its conclusions on the matter. These were issued in 1977 in SFAS 19, in which the FASB opted for successful efforts historical cost accounting. But the commission concluded in ASR 263 that it could not support this approach, and it proposed a solution called reserve recognition accounting, intended to reflect revenues when oil and gas reserves became proven rather than when their sale took place. (See Chapter 37 for an extended discussion.)

While the commission took pains to point out that it had a special congressional mandate in this area, its action was a blow to the FASB's prestige. Nevertheless, since that time the FASB and the commission have largely worked in harmony and seem to be communicating effectively in an atmosphere of mutual nonsurprise.

Though the FASB recognizes that it cannot sustain positions that are directly contrary to the expressed judgments of the SEC, at the same time the commission recognizes that if it attempts to overrule the Board regularly, this would destroy the standard-setting mechanism it believes to be the most effective. Accordingly, both parties seem to see the benefit of working together rather than at cross purposes.

Meetings With Registrants and Their Auditors

While the commission's formal authority in the area of accounting principles and practices is considerable, in many ways this is eclipsed by its informal influence, for it also has substantial impact through its interaction with registrants and independent public accountants in particular cases. Ultimately, it is the commission that must decide whether or not the accounting treatment used by registrants is in conformity with its rules and regulations. While evaluation of conformity with GAAP is primarily the responsibility of the independent accountant, the commission will on some occasions disagree with him when it comes to appropriate accounting for a particular set of facts. In such circumstances, there normally are meetings between the registrant, the SEC staff, and the independent accountant to discuss and resolve the issue.

Where an intended accounting or disclosure treatment is unusual, the registrant and its independent accountant will confer with the commission staff before the financial statements are filed. Through discussion and decisions reached in such cases, the commission staff may exercise a substantial influence on the development of accounting practices, because it is generally understood that a staff conclusion to which the independent accountant accedes is to be used by the accountant's entire firm in future and other situations having the same facts.

One conspicuous example is the set of guides arising in the late 1960s as registrants sought to use pooling-of-interest accounting in widely varying circumstances. The commission's chief accountant developed a number of guidelines which, through conferences with accountants and registrants, came to be well known.

In numerous instances, the commission's chief accountant has concluded that the form of transactions differed from their substance, which governed the accounting treatment. For example, a "timber-cutting contract" was in substance the purchase of timberland; or the "sale" of inventory that remained on a company's premises was deemed to be a financing device.

In most cases the staff advises the registrant of its view regarding the substance of the transaction and the proper accounting to be followed. If the registrant and the staff cannot reach agreement, the issue may be referred to the commission for its consideration. The commission usually has the last word in such cases, since its potential authority over registrants is enormous. For example, it can refuse to accelerate the effectiveness of a registration statement, issue a stop order barring trading in a security, or bring an enforcement action.

Despite this substantial authority, the commission and its staff only rarely seek to impose their judgment on registrants and their independent accountants. In most cases the staff will raise questions about the accounting treatment of a particular event, the registrant will fully explain its basis for choosing the accounting used, and the staff will accept it. This policy properly places on the registrant and its independent accountant the responsibility for achieving a fair presentation. Thus the comment letters, or so-called deficiency letters, issued by the staff with regard to a preliminary 1933 act or a 1934 act report filing are usually resolved by explanation rather than confrontation.

Accounting Pronouncements

Regulation S-X. The basic accounting regulation of the commission is Regulation S-X, which prescribes rules for the form and content of financial statements filed with the commission. Figure 41.1 lists the major sections of this regulation; of the specialized rules, Article 5 relating to commercial and industrial companies is by far the most used.

The commission attempts to keep Regulation S-X up to date with FASB pronouncements as well as with its own other disclosure requirements. Accordingly, it is amended frequently and periodically undergoes major revisions. The most recent of these revisions was issued in the fall of 1980.

Regulation S-K. This is a recently published generalized regulation covering the content of non-financial statement portions of registration statements and certain periodic filings under the Securities and Exchange Act. For example, it notes the basic requirements in a filing document, such as description of business, description of property, identification of directors, identification of executive officers and their current remuneration, related-party transactions, and legal proceedings.

While the individual forms for both registration and continuing disclosure (see Figure 41.2) still exist and spell out specific requirements, Regulation S-K will increasingly be utilized to provide general instructions applicable to all filings.

Accounting Series Releases. These releases are official statements of policy approved by the commission and issued under the jurisdiction of the Office of the Chief Accountant. Frequently they are exposed for comment before final issuance, under the requirements of the Administrative Procedures Act. They have the force of rules and except for those dealing with enforcement are incorporated by reference into Regulation S-X. By October 1980, 281 of these releases had been issued.

While the releases are not officially categorized, they can be divided into several major types: (1) matters of accounting principle, (2) specific disclosure requirements, (3) auditing standards and practice matters, (4) independence of accountants, and (5) enforcement proceedings. In an appendix to this chapter the more important ASRs are briefly described.

Staff Accounting Bulletins. For many years the staff followed the procedure of offering informal interpretations to registrants and their independent accountants concerning both the rules of the commission and the accounting principles and practices the staff considered acceptable in filings with the commission. Since only a relatively small number of accountants represent substantial numbers of SEC registrants, an informal information system grew up that communicated these interpretations and allowed registrants to be aware of the policies being followed.

In 1975 the commission decided it would be desirable to put in writing all these informal interpretations and practices followed by the staff in administering the

---

RULES OF GENERAL APPLICATION

Article 1	Definition of terms used in Regulation S-X
Article 2	Qualifications of accountants and the form and content of accountant's report
Article 3	Uniform requirements for financial statements and periods to be covered in essentially all filings
Article 3A	Consolidated financial statements of registrants and principles of consolidation
Article 4	Rules of general application to all financial statements, including such matters as required general notes to financial statements and accounting and reporting for oil and gas producing activities; provides that GAAP must be followed in order for financial statements to be not misleading

SPECIALIZED RULES APPLICABLE TO FINANCIAL STATEMENTS

Article 5	Various financial statement categories for commercial and industrial companies
Article 5A	Additional information required in financial statements by companies in the development stage
Article 6	Management investment companies; unit investment trusts; face-amount certificate investment companies; and employee stock purchase, savings, and similar plans
Article 7 and 7A	Insurance companies
Article 8	Committees issuing certificates of deposit
Article 9	Banks and bank holding companies
Article 10	Natural persons (proposed to be changed to provide guidance for interim financial statements)

CONTENT OF STATEMENTS AND SCHEDULES

Article 11	Statements of other stockholders' equity
Article 11A	Requirement for the inclusion of a source and application funds statement in published financial statements
Article 12	Various detailed schedules required to be filed as supplements to the financial statements.

FIGURE 41.1   MAJOR SECTIONS OF REGULATION S-X

securities laws, so that all registrants could be aware of them without relying on a totally informal system. Accordingly, it authorized the creation of a series of Staff Accounting Bulletins (SABs). These bulletins are issued jointly by the Office of the Chief Accountant and the Division of Corporation Finance without the commission's official approval; thus they are not official rules or interpretations of the commission. Occasionally, controversial bulletins are shown to the commission on an informal basis before publication. By October 1980, 40 SABs had been issued.

1933 ACT

S-1   General form for registration of securities

S-7   Abbreviated registration form covering the sale of securities by companies with a previous record of registration and that meet certain size tests

S-8   Registration statement for a company's shares to be offered to its employees pursuant to an employee benefit plan

S-15   Abbreviated prospectus for small business combination acquisitions; to be accompanied by user's latest annual report

S-16   Registration statement covering securities issued in business combinations and other special transactions

1934 ACT

8-K   Filing form covering current transactions required to be disclosed promptly

10-K   General form for annual reports filed with the commission by registrants

10-Q   General form for quarterly reports

FIGURE 41.2   MAJOR SEC FILING FORMS

SEC OVERSIGHT OF AUDITING AND THE PROFESSION

General Auditing Authority

The 1933 act provides that financial statements filed with the commission shall be audited by independent public accountants and that the commission may prescribe the form and content of the auditor's report. The 1934 act does not prescribe an auditor's report, but Section 13(a)(2) gives the commission the authority to require auditor's reports, which it has done. At the time the securities laws were enacted, Congress is reported to have considered the possibility of government auditors, but ultimately accepted the counsel of a number of witnesses from the profession that audits by independent public accountants would achieve the same result more efficiently and effectively. The degree of SEC authority over auditing standards and procedures, and for that matter the organization of the accounting profession, has been a subject of dispute in recent years. The commission's view is that its authority to prescribe the form and content of the auditor's report gives it sufficient authority to prescribe auditing standards, since it may indicate what the auditor says about what he does. In addition, the SEC has devoted substantial attention to a broad definition of what constitutes auditor independence and believes that it thus has substantial influence over the way an auditing firm may operate. Finally, the commission has enforcement powers to investigate accounting firms and issue staff reports on their practices when it feels them to be deficient, or to commence enforcement actions.

This combination of powers gives the SEC substantial de facto authority over the accounting profession, and to date the profession has not chosen to litigate the commission's authority in most of these areas. One attempt was made to question the commission's authority to discipline accountants under Rule 2(e); in this circumstance the Circuit Court of Appeals generally upheld the commission's authority. This case[2] was not appealed to the Supreme Court.

The commission has used its influence in this regard to encourage the auditing standard-setting bodies to adopt standards consistent with the SEC's view of auditor responsibility. While there have been disputes about the extent of SEC authority, in large part the profession and the commission have reached accommodation on most of the crucial issues. In one case, where the commission was uncertain whether the Auditing Standards Executive Committee (AudSEC) would adopt a standard covering limited review of interim financial statements, the SEC proposed a rule that would have specified the commission's expectations as to auditor association with such data. But it indicated that it would withdraw this proposed rule if AudSEC developed appropriate standards, and that development promptly occurred. Thus the SEC has followed the same basic policy that they adopted in the accounting area—namely, urging by various means a change in performance by the accounting profession rather than seeking an affirmative role of its own.

In the drafting of the proposed Unified Securities Code introduced in Congress in late 1979, there was a substantial dispute between the SEC and the accounting profession as to whether the code should make explicit the authority that the commission believed it already possessed. At that time the authority was left in essentially its current state, but as the commission comments on the code while it is further being considered by Congress, the possibility of a more specific SEC authority over the auditing function is likely to come up again.

The commission's activities in the auditing area have been principally of three sorts, discussed below.

Releases and Rules. A number of releases and rules have been issued that directly affect auditing practices, primarily by indicating what reports will be acceptable to the commission. In 1962, for example, ASR 90 was issued, in which the commission indicated that it would not accept an opinion qualified as to audit scope as meeting certification requirements. In 1970 a similar release, ASR 115, banned going concern qualifications on registration statements. In 1975 the commission expanded auditors' responsibilities for quarterly data and the preferability of accounting changes in ASR 177. (See Chapters 5 and 16.)

Auditors' Independence. A second major dimension has been the establishment of guidelines regarding the independence of auditors. Twelve ASRs (starting with ASR 2 in 1937) have summarized SEC conclusions regarding independence of certifying accountants and have been the principal means of promulgating the guidelines. In general, the commission's policies in this regard have been issued earlier than those of the accounting profession, although in substantive respects the accounting profession has gradually incorporated the commission's independence requirements in its own rules of conduct.

In addition, the commission has fostered the independence of accountants, both by supporting them in individual circumstances when a client seeks to have the auditor's judgment overruled by the SEC staff and by imposing general require-

---

[2] *Touche Ross & Co. v. SEC,* CCH Fed. Sec. L. Rep. ¶ 96,854 (2d Cir. 1979). See Challenges of SEC Authority in Chapter 44 for a fuller description.

ments that make it difficult for clients to obtain more palatable answers to accounting issues by changing auditors. In 1971 the commission imposed a requirement for disclosure on Form 8-K whenever an auditor change took place, including the filing of letters by the registrant and the displaced auditor giving a description of any disagreements on matters of accounting and disclosure that preceded the change. This was further strengthened and proxy statement disclosures about auditors mandated in ASR 165 (1974).

Investigation and Enforcement. The final way in which the commission has taken an active role in the auditing area is through its investigatory and enforcement powers. Over the years following the commission's first investigation (described below), it has frequently issued ASRs detailing the results of its investigation of auditing performance that it considered deficient and expressing its views on the practices about which it was concerned and on what those practices should be. In addition, in some of the enforcement actions resulting from these investigations, the commission has obtained as part of a settlement agreement an undertaking from the accounting firm involved to perform research activities of various sorts, which have contributed to the development of auditing standards. A later section of this chapter explores the enforcement philosophy in depth, and the major releases are summarized in Appendix 41.

McKesson-Robbins case. The first and probably the most famous of the commission's investigations resulted from the McKesson-Robbins fraud, which culminated in the issuance of a report summarized in ASR 19 in December 1940. ASR 19 contained a number of observations regarding independence, the auditor-client relationship, the quality of Price Waterhouse's audit, and the implications for a number of the auditing procedures used. By the time the release was issued, the accounting profession had already taken steps to deal with the fraud, which had been uncovered nearly two years before. The American Institute of Accountants mandated the circularization of accounts receivable and observation of physical inventory as two required auditing steps, and the commission endorsed these actions in ASR 19.

The release also noted the need for greater investigation of new clients, a more comprehensive evaluation and review of systems of internal control, and the need for additional work on intercompany accounts. Although ultimately the commission did not take action against Price Waterhouse or impose new standards in its rules, it did reach the judgment that

> the audits performed by Price Waterhouse & Co. substantially conformed in form as to the scope and procedures employed to what was generally considered mandatory during the period of the Girard-McKesson engagements. Their failure to discover the gross overstatement of assets and of earnings is attributable to the manner in which the audit work was done. In carrying out the work, they failed to employ that degree of vigilance, inquisitiveness and analysis of the evidence available that is necessary in a professional undertaking and is recommended in all well-known and authoritative works on auditing.

At the end of its release, the commission articulated its policy on auditing standards, which it has largely continued to the present time:

We have carefully considered the desirability of specific rules and regulations governing the auditing steps to be performed by accountants in certifying financial statements to be filed with us. Action has already been taken by the accounting profession adopting certain of the auditing procedures considered in this case. We have no reason to believe at this time that these extensions will not be maintained or that further extensions of auditing procedures along the lines suggested in this report will not be made. Further, the adoption of the specific recommendations made in this report as to the type of disclosure to be made in the accountant's certificate and as to the election of accountants by stockholders should insure the acceptable standards of auditing procedures will be observed, that specific deviations therefrom may be considered in the particular instances in which they arise, and that accountants will be more independent of management. Until experience should prove the contrary, we feel that this program is preferable to its alternative—the detailed prescription of the scope of and procedures to be followed in the audit for the various types of issuers of securities who file statements with us—and will allow for further consideration of varying audit procedures and for the development of different treatment for specific types of issuers.

Organization of the Profession

The commission has at various times exerted substantial pressure on the profession to make changes in its approach and organization. The most noteworthy example is the commission's action in urging the creation of a new section of the AICPA made up of firms in SEC practice and the development of an extensive program of peer review within that section.

The establishment of the SEC Practice Section of the AICPA Division for Firms arose in part through the initiatives of Congress, whose hearings conducted by Senator Metcalf, Congressman Moss, and Senator Eagleton foreshadowed a significant threat of greater government involvement (see Chapter 39). As a result of these hearings the commission undertook the preparation of an annual report to the Congress on its oversight of the accounting profession; the first of these was submitted in 1978. In its second report to the Congress, submitted in June 1979, the commission described its regulation and oversight responsibility as follows (SEC, 1979, pp. 28-29):

In response to the urgings and recommendations for self-initiated reform under the oversight of the Commission, the AICPA established the Division for CPA Firms and, within that Division, an SEC Practice Section. As stated in the 1978 Report, the Commission regards the creation of the Section as a major accomplishment and its establishment formed the primary basis for the Commission's conclusion that there is promise for successful voluntary self-regulation.

The progress of the formulation and development of the Section has been closely monitored by the Commission and its staff. The Commission's oversight is directed toward assuring that the profession makes progress in achieving the objectives that the Commission believes the self-regulatory structure must meet in order to be effective. These objectives were outlined in the 1978 Report as follows:

- Regulation of the practice of public accountancy is thoroughly involved with the public interest, and therefore, should not be left exclusively to those engaged in the profession.

- The self-regulatory structure must have available to it the capability and resources necessary to anticipate, address and resolve accounting and professional issues needed to assure quality performance.
- The self-regulatory structure must be firm, timely, even-handed and fair in both its administration and disciplinary procedures.

One year ago, several factors were identified which could hinder the Section's ability to meet these objectives. During the past year, both the profession and the Commission have addressed these issues and progress has been made. Although the task of assuring the viability of the self-regulatory structure has not been completed, the Commission is encouraged by the progress to date.

It seems that as long as the profession functions effectively under this oversight, the commission is unlikely to take further action to impose regulation.

SEC ENFORCEMENT PROGRAM AND PHILOSOPHY

The SEC enforcement program aims to maintain the integrity of the marketplace and deter fraud rather than to punish wrongdoers. While its statutory authority is clear and its authorizations broad, the commission has limited resources and finds it impossible to investigate and prosecute every possible violation. Consequently, the commission has sought in recent years to focus its enforcement efforts at key points where maximum impact can be achieved. For this reason enforcement efforts involving professionals, such as accountants and lawyers, have been important, even though the number of cases in which professionals were involved has not been large.

The reasoning of the commission is simple: these professionals are an essential element in providing access to the marketplace, since the sale of securities cannot take place without their involvement. It is hoped that holding the professional responsible at these points of access can prevent many questionable activities before they occur. By insisting on high standards of performance by accountants and increasing them where the commission deems it necessary, more reliable and meaningful financial information for the investing public should be assured.

Quality Control in CPA Firms

The commission's enforcement program deters substandard performance by increasing the risk to an accounting firm of a commission injunctive action and of private actions for money damages. As a result it becomes desirable for individuals and firms to devote greater resources and more care to the avoidance of such performance. Although professionals in general have a desire to do a good job, excellence is costly, and in a world of competing claims and equities a program that raises the cost of deficient work should have the impact of improving performance—though the equation between these is not crystal clear. The threat of an enforcement action and the costs of an adverse determination by a court—unfavorable publicity, possible civil judgments, the financial burden of litigation, and perhaps ultimately a loss of professional stature with a consequent decline in business—all combine to reduce the likelihood of substandard professional performance.

In response to commission actions, actions by private litigants, and some public concern about the adequacy of audits, accounting firms have been substantially increasing their commitment of resources to more extensive quality controls. This should result in better auditing judgments and perhaps minimize the frequency of future enforcement actions. In those cases in which erroneous judgments occur, quality control procedures should lessen the likelihood that they will go undetected and result in the auditor's acceptance of financial statements that are not fairly presented. While quality review procedures are important, they should not be overemphasized. It is not productive to load a mountain of review on a pinhead of audit field work. The qualified and alert auditor in the field is still the first line of defense.

Highlighting Problem Areas

In addition to encouraging better quality controls, enforcement actions may be beneficial in directing attention to areas in which auditing standards may be more effectively articulated and applied. Although commission actions are based on the facts of particular cases, in some situations the facts may be typical of general problem areas; commission opinions, orders, and complaints may therefore emphasize matters that require profession-wide attention.

In ASR 154, for example, the commission set forth in considerable detail its view that an audit that failed to uncover concealed transactions with related parties was deficient. Comments in the ASR also dealt with communications between predecessor and successor auditors that the commission believed were inadequate in the particular case. Both of these situations received treatment in subsequent SASs.

In addition, the commission's emphasis in a number of cases on "overall fairness" in financial reporting has communicated to the profession the commission's expectation that accountants' responsibilities go beyond the mechanical application of defined accounting principles. This approach has not met with approval by the profession, however.

Decision to Take Enforcement Action

In deciding whether to institute an enforcement action, the commission considers each case in light of several major factors, including the seriousness of the perceived professional deficiency and the extent to which the auditor had knowledge of what was happening. The commission also considers the degree to which the auditor appeared to be an active participant in a scheme to mislead the public through artful or incomplete disclosure or through the creative selection of accounting principles designed to present a picture inconsistent with reality.

There are many enforcement actions brought by the commission involving deficient financial reporting in which auditors are not named as defendants. The commission does not have a policy of pursuing every possible professional deficiency it can find simply for the joy of the hunt. Selectivity in the use of resources and attention to the more serious cases are keys to an effective program.

It is, of course, important that the SEC's enforcement program be a fair one to specific firms and individuals affected in each separate case. Safeguards to ensure fairness do exist in the procedures followed by the staff and the commission, and although various parties may disagree with conclusions reached, the judgments made are based on a full consideration of the facts, including any written presentations from the proposed defendant, known as *Wells submissions* (after the name of the advisory committee that recommended this procedure).

Before a case involving an accountant is sent to the commission, it is submitted to the chief accountant for review on the merits. The assistant chief accountant (investigations) in the Office of the Chief Accountant generally reviews the testimony and other evidence and reports his conclusion to the chief accountant. In many cases the proposed defendant will request a meeting with the chief accountant to discuss the case, and this meeting is generally held before any recommendation is forwarded to the commission. After careful review of the evidence, the chief accountant then makes his recommendation, which is submitted to the commission along with the recommendation of the Division of Enforcement. Cases against accountants have seldom been brought without the concurrence of both the chief accountant and the Division of Enforcement. If the case involves novel or particularly difficult questions, the commission's Office of General Counsel will also review the recommendations.

After recommendations have been sent to the commission together with Wells submissions by proposed defendants, the commissioners and their legal assistants review the case with great care, frequently asking questions of the staff about details in the case. Then the case is discussed at the commission table before any decision is reached, and these discussions are substantive in nature. The staff is subjected to vigorous questioning, and the principles and objectives underlying the proposed action are considered in depth.

All of these procedures normally occur prior to an action being brought by the commission, since it is recognized (though there have been lapses) that such an action against a professional has a substantial impact on his reputation even before any judicial determination is made. After the action is brought and 2(e) proceedings if any are concluded, the normal due process of the legal system is, of course, still available to provide protection against unjust actions.

While virtually all commission cases are civil in character, on rare occasions it is concluded that a case is sufficiently serious to be referred to the Department of Justice for possible criminal prosecution. Referrals in regard to accountants have only been made when the commission and the staff believed that the evidence indicated a professional accountant certified financial statements that he knew to be false when he reported on them. The commission does not make criminal references in cases that it believes are matters of professional judgment, even if the judgments appear to be bad ones.

Enforcement Remedies

In most cases the sanctions imposed in commission proceedings serve the remedial purpose of improving the quality of an accounting firm's work. In other cases the performance of particular individuals or firms is found to be so deficient that their continued practice before the commission in the public marketplace carries too great a risk and hence is unacceptable. While small firms have more commonly been involved in such cases, a consistent pattern of deficient work by a large firm might lead to a similar conclusion. Three forms of sanctions have been used with some frequency:

1. *Temporary or permanent suspension of right to practice before the commission.* In cases involving unacceptable performance, the commission has the authority under Rule 2(e) of its Rules of Practice to bar an individual, and may have the right to bar a firm, from practice before the commission. It may also suspend the professional from commission practice until there is an appropriate showing of fitness to resume. The ultimate sanction of a permanent bar is not frequently used, since the commission usually believes that a professional firm can take actions to bring its performance up to an acceptable level and can provide the commission with assurance that such a level is being maintained. Even when an accountant has been barred from practice before the commission, his right to practice may be reinstated after the passage of time, upon a proper showing of fitness.

2. *Quality control review and inspection.* Over the years the commission has attempted to use sanctions that will meet the needs presented in each particular case. New sanctions have been developed in consent situations that the commission believes hold some promise. When cases raise questions concerning the adequacy of an accounting firm's quality control procedures, the commission may require the firm to submit its procedures for review by the commission's staff or by a group of outside professionals. As a result of this review, the firm and the commission may agree on certain additional quality control and audit procedures to be followed. Such procedures may emphasize particular areas of practice that relate to the specific enforcement action, but they are generally not limited to such areas. If the peer review report is not satisfactory to the SEC, further action will be required.

   In the recent past the SEC has been relying on the peer review program, established as a requirement for membership in the SEC Practice Section of the AICPA Division for Firms to accomplish SEC-sanctioned reviews. In those particular instances where the AICPA peer review is performed as a "firm on firm" review, the SEC delegates to the AICPA's appointed panel (which the SEC refers to as "The Committee for the [XYZ] Review") the additional responsibility to act as a review committee for the SEC. The panel accordingly is responsible to report not only to the AICPA but also the SEC on the results of the review. Even in these instances, the SEC will occasionally request the panel to review certain areas of a firm's practice that are beyond the scope of the peer review program and report to the SEC on those specific areas. The movement by the SEC to accept the profession's peer review program is clearly evident in sanctions used in the more recent ASRs involving accountants.

3. *Limiting the firm's new business.* In some cases the commission has imposed a partial or complete limitation on new SEC business for a firm, either for a prescribed period or until such time as a peer review group is able to inspect a practice and report to the commission. In this way the commission feels it has obtained outside evidence that the program has been effectively implemented before the firm is allowed to grow, either in the aggregate or in the areas that are affected most.

Impact on Public Opinion

A major objective of the enforcement program is to increase the level of public confidence in financial reporting. If this is to be achieved, there must be greater confidence in the accounting profession and in the reporting environment. The investor must also be assured that redress will be achieved in situations where deficiencies are found to exist. While some accountants suggest that confidence in the public accounting profession would be enhanced if all actions against accountants were kept private and only a few actions were brought, this is a shortsighted view. The public must be persuaded that an overwhelming majority of public accountants do a good job and that in those cases where they do not, vigorous action is taken by public agencies to call them to task.

Confidence in the SEC is an important part of this total package. If investors are satisfied that the commission, as the principal regulatory agency in the area, is alert and effective in discovering significant abuses and obtaining effective sanctions against those involved, there will be an increase in the level of investor confidence in financial reporting. At the same time, the SEC's need for public confidence serves as a deterrent against the commission bringing enforcement actions in marginal cases where the auditor involved was guilty of a simple error in judgment that was not particularly egregious. It is neither practical nor desirable for the commission to bring an enforcement action every time it may conclude that an auditor has made a mistake.

MAJOR DISCLOSURE THRUSTS

In the past decade there have been several major thrusts to the commission's disclosure policy. These can be seen in a number of rule-making initiatives and in speeches of commissioners and senior staff members. These are discussed below.

Continuous Reporting

One of the major efforts of the commission in recent years has been to make the disclosure process a continuous one rather than one focusing on periodic filing. Shares are traded continuously, and it is important to ensure that current information is readily available in the marketplace. The commission also recognizes that businesses operate in a continuum rather than in a series of discrete segments, and a meaningful disclosure policy must take this into account.

Form 8-K was the first clear evidence of this approach. Designed for reporting significant events on a timely basis, the form identifies certain major classes of events (changes of control of registrant, acquisition or disposition of a significant amount of assets other than in the ordinary course of business, bankruptcy, changes in accountant, and resignations of directors) that must be described in a filing within 15 days of their occurrence. The form includes another item (other materially important events), which offers to registrants the option of reporting the occurrence of other events "which the registrant deems of material importance to security holders."

In addition, in recent years there has been a substantial increase in the amount of disclosure required in quarterly reports (10-Q) filed with the commission: a narrative analysis of the balance sheet and income statement explaining material changes in financial position and results of operations is required, along with substantially a full set of financial statements.

Historically, the commission had substantial additional requirements for disclosure when new shares were issued. In keeping with the recommendations of both the Wheat (SEC, 1969) and Sommer (SEC, 1977a) reports on disclosure policy, the increasing integration between disclosure requirements under the 1934 act (securities currently outstanding) and the 1933 act (new issues of securities) is another evidence of the commission's thrust in continuous reporting (for example, see ASRs 278, 280 and 281). It seems likely that eventually companies rather than securities will be registered, and that registration will imply a mandate to have continuously updated information available in the marketplace to security buyers and sellers.

Future-Oriented Disclosure

In its earlier years the SEC was extremely cautious about any forms of disclosure that did not reflect exclusively historical fact. It steadfastly refused to allow discussions about the future in documents filed with it, on the grounds that this was speculative and nonobjective. Forecasts and projections were a particular anathema.

In the past decade, however, this policy has been radically revised, and the commission has increasingly moved in the direction of requiring registrants to make disclosures that are relevant to future expectations.

In 1971 Chairman William Casey, in a public speech, indicated that the commission's historic prohibition of forecasts and projections was "not cast in stone." In that same year the commission filed a brief in a court case in which it took the position that under certain circumstances forecasts were required in order to make disclosure complete. In 1972 the commission held hearings on projections and forecasts, and in 1973 it issued a release formally abandoning its policy of prohibiting projections in filings with the commission. (See Chapter 33 for an extended discussion of these developments.)

In 1974 the commission adopted a requirement (ASR 159) mandating a management discussion of analysis of the summary of operations; this called for a better description of the reasons for the changes in operating results and imposed a specific requirement that management discuss "material facts whether favorable or unfavorable" that might "make historical operations or earnings as reported in the summary of operations not indicative of current or future operations or earnings."

In 1977 the Advisory Committee on Corporate Disclosure (SEC, 1977a) recommended that "the Commission actively and generally encourage the publication of forward looking and analytical information in company reports" (CCH Fed. Sec. L. Rep. ¶ 81,357 at p. 88,667). It also recommended an expansion of the management analysis and a policy of encouraging forecast disclosure, although it stopped short of recommending a mandate.

In response to these recommendations, the SEC adopted safe harbor rules for forecasts filed with the commission, in an attempt to protect registrants from liability for good faith projections; at the same time it expressed encouragement for the filing of forecasts. In early 1980 a major revision of management's analysis was proposed (Release 33-6176), further emphasizing the future orientation of the disclosures that would be expected; this was adopted in the fall of 1980.

The commission's adoption of this new approach has been consistent with the actions of standard setters in the accounting profession. The FASB, in SFAC 1, *Objectives of Financial Reporting by Business Enterprises,* identified as the primary objective providing information useful to investors in predicting the amounts, timing, and uncertainty of future cash flows to the corporation (AC 1210.37).

While both the FASB and the commission have so far indicated that they have no plans to mandate explicit forecasts, the direction of both their policies seems to be moving more and more toward requiring some form of explicit disclosure of future expectations.

Auditor of Record

Related to the continuous reporting concept is the development of a policy associating the auditor on an ongoing basis with all public financial reporting of his client.

The commission has taken several steps to encourage the ongoing association of the auditor with company financial reports. In ASR 138 a requirement was imposed for an auditor's letter evaluating (without audit) the accounting followed for major unusual charges of credit to incomes at the time the charge or credit was made. This was later related to the 10-Q requirements. In ASR 177 a very controversial provision required the auditor, in connection with an accounting change, to express his judgment as to the preferability of the new accounting principle.

In 1974 the commission expanded proxy statement disclosures relating to auditors and their relationships to their client (ASR 165). One of the disclosures required was the name of the principal accountant selected for the current year. The commission noted that the purpose of this was "to make stockholders aware of the identity of the independent accountant of record for the current year." Disclosure was also required of the name of the principal accountant for the previous year if different (or if no accountant has been selected for the current year), once again "to inform the stockholder when a change in accountant has occurred and who the independent accountant of record is in cases where no action has been taken to select an accountant for the current year." While the commission used the term, it did not formally define the responsibilities of the auditor of record.

In 1975 the commission further expanded the auditor's ongoing role by involving him in quarterly reporting by the registrant. ASR 177 did not explicitly identify an obligation for timely involvement in quarterly financial statements, but it did require, in a note to annual financial statements, a recapitulation of quarterly results; and the SEC spelled out its expectations regarding the auditor's role in reviewing these data. Though the note in the annual statements may be labeled "unaudited," the SEC expressed its view that certain review procedures were required, and it ultimately accepted SAS 10 (since incorporated into SAS 24; AU 721) spelling out this responsibility. Since management does not want auditors revisiting previously published quarterly results on a fresh basis at year-end, it often involves them on a current basis.

The combination of commission exhortation and requirements and the increasing recognition by directors of the responsibility associated with interim reports has led to a substantial expansion of auditor involvement with reporting on an ongoing basis. The auditor-of-record concept is not specified in legal terms, but the commission's clear interest in this area has had a significant impact on public accounting practice.

Disclosure of the Effects of Inflation

During the past decade the commission has also been deeply involved in the problem of appropriate accounting for and disclosure of the impact of inflation. This was initially evidenced in an exhortatory 1974 release (ASR 151) calling for the disclosure of "inventory profits." The adoption of ASR 190 in 1976 brought required disclosure of certain replacement cost information in notes to financial statements filed with the commission. Subsequently, the commission has worked closely with the FASB to develop appropriate measures of the impact of inflation. It was the commission's strong position that it could not abandon ASR 190 unless the FASB adopted a current cost approach, which contributed in part to the final requirements in SFAS 33 (AC 1072) for both current cost and constant dollar supplemental disclosures. The development of accounting for the impact of inflation is fully described in Chapter 8.

Differential Disclosure

One of the ongoing problems faced by the commission in designing disclosure requirements is to whom the disclosures are aimed. The SEC feels an obligation to ensure that disclosure is available to everyone, but it recognizes the need of certain sophisticated users of financial data for more detailed information than is readily usable by the average investor. The struggle between meeting the needs of the sophisticated investor while communicating effectively with the average investor has been a continuing problem not yet fully resolved.

The thrust of the commission's disclosure policies in recent years seems to be aimed at a policy that meets the needs of both sophisticated and average investors through techniques that might be described as *differential disclosure*. Certain requirements are identified in commission releases as being primarily of interest to the sophisticated investor; these data are required to be filed with the commission and available to all, but they need not necessarily be included in documents sent to the entire investment community. At the same time the commission has attempted to encourage the use of summaries for the average investor that try to simplify complex disclosure documents by extracting the most important elements in an introductory statement or section.

In September 1980 the SEC adopted new rules to integrate the annual report to stockholders with Form 10-K. This was seen by many commentators as a step away from differential disclosure concepts, a step that would make the annual report a less effective communications device to average investors. The commission reflected the concern expressed in these comments in its final rule, in which it made many elements of the integration voluntary and reaffirmed its commitment to effectively communicate with the unsophisticated investor. This task of management is as important as the supplying of analysts and professional users with sufficient data to perform their tasks.

In the final analysis the commission must be primarily concerned with meeting the needs of the financial analyst, who plays the largest role in making markets efficient. If comprehensive disclosure is made and absorbed by the marketplace, the small investor is ultimately protected by the fact that the price is a fair reflection of value based on current knowledge. Direct service to the small investor is probably more important politically than it is in making the market work more effectively in the allocation of capital.

SUGGESTED READING

Commerce Clearing House. *SEC Accounting Rules.* Chicago. This service presents in regularly updated loose-leaf form the basic accounting disclosure requirements of the commission: Regulations S-X and S-K, Accounting Series Releases, Staff Accounting Bulletins, guides for preparation of SEC filings, and currently pending rule proposals.

Poloway, Morton, and Charles, Dane. *Accountants SEC Practice Manual.* Chicago: Commerce Clearing House. This loose-leaf service sets forth the basic accounting and reporting requirements of the commission with explanations of SEC policy and practices. It is aimed at the professional.

Rappaport, Louis. *SEC Accounting Practice and Procedure.* 3rd ed. New York: Ronald Press, 1972. This comprehensive volume describes SEC history, practices, and procedures in the accounting area. It is aimed at the professional and difficult reading for someone without a detailed interest in the area.

Securities and Exchange Commission. *Report of the Advisory Committee on Corporate Disclosure.* 2 vols. Washington, D.C.: U.S. Government Printing Office, 1977. This report is a comprehensive analysis of SEC disclosure policy and recommendations for change, many of which have since been adopted. It includes a summary of findings formally approved by the committee and a detailed report of the disclosure process and how the recommendations might improve it (in Volume 1) and a set of appendices (Volume 2) that include both research data and background papers prepared by the staff and outsiders.

————. *Report to Congress on the Accounting Profession and the Commission's Oversight Role.* Washington, D.C.: U.S. Government Printing Office, 1978, 1979, and 1980. These annual reports provide substantial insight into the commission's activities and the activities of professional bodies during the periods covered.

APPENDIX 41 MAJOR ACCOUNTING SERIES RELEASES OF THE SEC

Accounting Principles

ASR 4 (1938)   Maintained that disclosure in place of revision of financial statements in dispute between registrant and commission is acceptable only where substantial authoritative support existed for practices followed by the registrant. This statement was significant in that it represented the commission's acceptance of standards developed in practice and gave notice to the accounting profession that the commission did not intend to prescribe accounting principles by rule.

ASR 95 (1962)   Specified accounting for real estate transactions where circumstances indicate that profits were not earned at the time the transactions were recorded.

ASR 96 (1963)   Accepted either the deferral or flow-through approach for accounting for the investment credit, undercutting APB 2.

ASR 102 (1965)   Required that balance sheet classification of deferred income taxes arising from installment sales be consistent with the classification of the receivable arising from the sales.

ASR 113 (1969)   Discussed the problems of valuation and disclosure in connection with the holding of restricted securities by investment companies.

ASR 118 (1970)   Discussed accounting by investment companies for portfolio securities, with particular emphasis on securities valued by the board of directors in good faith at fair value. A letter to the AICPA discussing the appropriate auditor's report in such cases was attached to the release.

ASR 124 (1972)   Discussed stock dividend accounting practices, and cautioned that stock dividends could be misleading if there is inadequate accounting or disclosure.

ASR 130 (1972)   Interpreted APB 16 to require risk sharing by stockholders of combining companies if combination is to qualify as a pooling of interests.

ASR 142 (1973)   Discussed disclosures of cash flow and use of cash flow as a proxy for income, and prohibited disclosure of cash flow per share.

ASR 145 (1973)   Imposed a moratorium on changes in accounting for catastrophe reserves until the FASB resolved the accounting and disclosure issues.

ASR 146 (1973)   Interpreted APB 16 to preclude pooling-of-interests accounting if
and   treasury shares were acquired within two years of the combination.
ASR 146A (1974)   ASR 146 was challenged procedurally and suspended pending comments, then readopted in essentially unchanged form.

ASR 150 (1973)   A statement of policy that reiterated the commission's support for private-sector accounting standard setting, identified the FASB as the private-sector body with this responsibility, and noted that the commission would treat FASB standards as representing "substantial authoritative support" and contrary principles as having no such support.

ASR 163 (1974)   Imposed a moratorium on the capitalization of interest by most companies other than public utilities and referred the accounting issue to the FASB for final determination.

ASR 244 (1978)   Outlined the commission's interpretation of appropriate segmentation for purposes of segment disclosure under SFAS 14.

ASR 253 (1978),   Unfurled the commission's policy on accounting for oil and gas
ASR 257 (1978),   producing companies. They rejected SFAS 19, which mandated
ASR 258 (1978),   successful efforts accounting, and proposed in its place reserve

ASR 261 (1979), and ASR 269 (1979)	recognition accounting (RRA). They also (1) adopted a standardized approach to full cost accounting for those companies using it during the RRA development period, (2) permitted accounting changes reflecting the commission's methods, and (3) adopted rules covering supplemental RRA disclosures.
ASR 268 (1979)	Required a separate balance sheet presentation apart from stockholders' equity category for preferred stocks subject to mandatory redemption requirements.

Disclosure Requirements

ASR 133 (1972)	Cautioned registrants of the possible need for disclosure of contingent liabilities that might arise under price control legislation.
ASR 134 (1973)	Required disclosure of the method of accounting for catastrophe reserves and their impact on reported results.
ASR 138 (1973)	Required substantial timely disclosure regarding material unusual charges and credits to income.
ASR 147 (1973)	Required disclosure of the present value of financing leases and the income effect if such leases were treated as capitalized leases.
ASR 148 (1973)	Required increased disclosure for short-term borrowing arrangements, including compensating balances.
ASR 149 (1973)	Required increased disclosure of income tax expense, including disclosure of the sources of tax deferrals and a reconciliation of the effective tax rate to the statutory rate.
ASR 151 (1974)	Noted the impact of inflation, and urged registrants to disclose the magnitude of "inventory profits" arising from increase in prices between the time goods were acquired and sold.
ASR 159 (1974)	Required management's discussion and analysis of the summary of earnings, including a discussion of significant changes from year to year and disclosure of factors that would indicate historical earnings were not indicative of present and future earnings.
ASR 164 (1974)	Required additional disclosures in financial statement footnotes regarding long-term contracts.
ASR 166 (1974)	Noted the need for disclosure of unusual risks and uncertainties in financial reporting, with specific examples relating to loan loss reserves of banks, marketable securities, and cases in which a small number of projects may have a dominant effect on financial results.
ASR 169 (1975)	Presented an exchange of correspondence regarding LIFO disclosures and the IRS position on conformity.

ASR 177 (1975)   Adopted substantially expanded quarterly reporting requirements, including a requirement for increased involvement of auditors in quarterly results and a controversial requirement that auditors express their judgment on the preferability of accounting changes.

ASR 188 (1976)   Required disclosure of certain information regarding New York City securities. (This was an interpretative statement.)

ASR 190 (1976)   Adopted rules requiring disclosure of replacement cost data on inventories, cost of sales, fixed assets, and depreciation in the notes to financial statements filed with the SEC.

ASR 194 (1976)   Required disclosure of the impact of using accounting principles that were the subject of disagreement with prior auditors.

ASR 203 (1976)   Adopted a safe harbor rule for replacement cost information (ASR 190).

ASR 236 (1977)   Conformed SEC rules with segment disclosure under SFAS 14, and expanded disclosure requirements somewhat further.

ASR 279 (1980),   Integrated securities acts disclosure systems and generally revised
ASR 280 (1980),   Regulation S-X. Under these newly adopted rules, uniform finan-
ASR 281 (1980),   cial disclosure requirements for virtually all documents covered by
ASR 284 (1980)   either the 1933 or the 1934 acts have been formulated.

Auditing Standards and Practices

ASR 19 (1940)   Summarized the finding and conclusions resulting from the McKesson & Robbins fraud case, commenting on auditing deficiencies and noting existence of new standards.

ASR 62 (1947)   Discussed the circumstances under which auditors could express an opinion on summary earnings tables and the form such opinion should take.

ASR 90 (1962)   Stated that the commission will not accept auditor's certificates that contain "subject to" or "except for" statements that refer to the scope of the audit and indicate that the accountant has not been able to satisfy himself on some significant element in the financial statements.

ASR 115 (1970)   Stated that the certification requirement is not acceptable for auditor's reports containing a going concern qualification in which the opinion is subject to the registrant's ability to obtain financing and/or acheive profitable operations.

ASR 165 (1974)   Increased the requirements for timely 8-K and proxy disclosure of relationships between registrants and auditors when changes in auditor occur; delineated the commission's auditor-of-record concept.

ASR 242 (1978)   Called the attention of auditors and registrants to the requirements imposed by the Foreign Corrupt Practices Act of 1977.

ASR 247 (1978)   Adopted a requirement that disclosure be made as to whether any change in auditors was recommended or approved by the audit committee.

ASR 250 (1978)   Required that nonaudit services be disclosed in proxy statements, including the percentage of the cost of those services as a proportion of the total audit fee and whether the audit committee approved each such service.

ASR 264 (1979)   Interpretatively discussed the issues involved in the scope of services rendered by auditors and their possible impact on independence.

ASR 274 (1979)   Limited the liability of auditors for reports on unaudited interim financial information incorporated by reference in 1933 act filings.

ASR 278 (1980)   Indicated the desirability of statements by management on internal accounting control, but withdrew specific rule proposals in that connection as a result of its perception of voluntary development and presentation of such statements.

Independence of Accountants

ASR 2 (1937)   Found an accountant not independent when value of a partner's investment in client securities exceeded 1% of partner's net worth.

ASR 22 (1941)   Prohibited an indemnity agreement that protected accountant against loss.

ASR 44 (1943)   Noted that the commission would consider all relationships between the auditor and his client in determining independence.

ASR 47 (1944)   Summarized several commission determinations as to auditor independence.

ASR 81 (1958)   Summarized commission administrative rulings regarding independence.

ASR 126 (1972)   Discussed independence guidelines and summarized commission administrative rulings regarding independence.

ASR 234 (1977)   Summarized commission interpretations and administrative rulings regarding independence.

ASR 251 (1978)   This interpretative release dealt with the problems of auditor independence when the auditor and the client are involved in litigation or threatened litigation.

Enforcement Proceedings

ASR 28 (1942)   Suspended Kenneth Logan from practice for 60 days for concealing improper trading practices and failing to be independent.

ASR 48 (1944)   Permanently barred C. Cecil Bryant from practicing before the commission for signing an audit certificate without making an audit or in fact ever seeing the books.

ASR 64 (1948)   Found that financial statements of Dreyer-Hanson Inc. were materially misleading because of inventory errors in work-in-process inventory and that Barrow, Wade, Guthrie & Co. had failed to audit these statements properly. No disciplinary action taken because the firm was "sufficiently impressed with the inadequacy of their former policies and has revised them."

ASR 68 (1949)   Suspended firm of F. G. Masquelette & Co. for 30 days and Cassel, a partner, for one year for signing a certificate as an independent accountant when Cassel was in fact a promoter of his client and the financial statements were materially misstated.

ASR 73 (1952)   Suspended Haskins & Sells and Andrew Stewart, a partner, for ten days for permitting Thomascolor to "grossly overstate intangible assets by the arbitrary use of par and stated value of stock issued to acquire the assets."

ASR 78 (1957)   Suspended Touche, Niven, Bailey & Smart and two partners of the firm from practice for 15 days for audit failures in connection with the evaluation of the reserve for losses on receivables of Seaboard Commercial Corporation.

ASR 88 (1961)   Permanently barred Myron Swartz from practicing before the commission for providing his client with a blank letterhead for the client to fill in, falsely stating he had performed audit work, and falsely testifying before the commission on the matter.

ASR 105 (1966)   Accepted the withdrawal of H. E. Kerlin from practice before the commission because he failed to discover the fraudulent misstatement of inventories of the Olen Co. and subsequently the Olen Division of H. L. Green.

ASR 144 (1973)   Imposed new remedial sanctions on Laventhol, Krekstein, Horwath and Horwath in the Takara Partners case. The firm consented to submit to a peer review by an AICPA committee that would report its findings to the commission. In addition, the firm was prohibited for a year from merging with another accounting firm without submitting evidence to the commission that its newly adopted procedures on mergers were complied with and from accepting any new SEC business for 30 days.

ASR 153 (1974)　　Issued in response to Touche Ross & Co.'s failure to detect frauds perpetrated by the management of U.S. Financial (primarily in structured related-party transactions), amplified by failure of adequate communication between predecessor and successor auditors. Touche Ross consented to a sanction that included a censure, the development and adoption of procedures to examine related-party transactions in the absence of such guidance in the professional literature, and more frequent internal office review procedures. In addition, the firm accepted a peer review, a one-year suspension of new SEC business for the office responsible for the audit, and a firm-wide suspension of acceptance of new real estate clients where the firm's report would be required in an SEC filing within one year.

ASR 153A (1979)　　Censured Touche Ross & Co. in connection with audit procedures followed in the Giant Stores audit, in which an undetected fraud based on false credits for advertising and merchandise returns and understated accounts payable resulted in material errors in the financial statements.

ASR 157 (1974)　　Censured Arthur Andersen in connection with auditing the inventory of Whittaker Corporation and failing to make full disclosure in meetings with the commission staff of the circumstances surrounding the settlement of Whittaker's litigation against the firm.

ASR 167 (1974)　　Censured Westheimer, Fine, Berger & Co. for the nature of its auditing work regarding certain non-arm's-length transactions affecting the financial statements of Realty Equities Corp. and for accepting an agreement to employ a special consultant to review certain audits by the firm prior to the issuance of the firm's report.

ASR 173 (1975)　　Peat, Marwick, Mitchell & Co. consented to sanctions in five cases: National Student Marketing, Talley Industries, Penn Central, Republic National Life, and Stirling Homex. The ASR recited problems in the planning of initial audits, the failure to emphasize substance over form, the need to consider the aggregate impact of accounting issues on financial statements, the dangers of the misapplication of percentage-of-completion accounting, and the dangers of accepting the representations of management without obtaining independent verification. The sanctions included two annual peer reviews, a prohibition on new SEC business for six months, and the revision of certain of its audit review procedures.

ASR 174 (1975)　　Censured Harris Kerr Forster & Co. in connection with the audit of Stirling Homex.

ASR 176 (1975)　　Described the auditing performance of Hertz, Herson and Co. in the audit of Drew National Corp. relating to an inadequate provision for doubtful accounts. The auditors consented to employ two consultants to review their procedures and report thereon to the commission and to accept no new public clients until one month after the consultants' report.

ASR 196 (1977)   Described the auditing practices followed by Seidman & Seidman and a predecessor firm in connection with the examinations of Equity Funding, Omni-Rx, SaCom, and Cenco. The firm agreed to a peer review, a four-month ban on the acceptance of new SEC audit clients, and a second review to verify the implementation of the peer review recommendations.

ASR 209 (1977)   Discussed the audit examination by S. D. Leidesdorf & Co. of the financial statements of Tidal Marine International Corporation. Leidesdorf consented to a peer review and a sixty-day suspension on the acceptance of new SEC clients.

ASR 227 (1977)   Analyzed the audit by Laventhol & Horwath of Cosmopolitan Investors Funding, Western Properties, and Co-Build. L&H consented to a peer review and to a suspension of the acceptance of new SEC clients for sixty days.

ASR 238 (1978)   Criticized the audits by Price, Waterhouse & Co. of National Telephone and Continental Mortgage Investors. PW agreed to return $120,000 in audit fees and to review its own audit procedures in specified areas. The firm also consented to a peer review of its practice.

ASR 241 (1978)   Criticized the Haskins & Sells audits of FISCO, Falstaff Brewing, Oceanography Mariculture, and Ampeco Securities. Haskins & Sells agreed to a peer review and to a temporary suspension of the acceptance of new SEC audit engagements in one office.

ASR 248 (1978)   Reviewed the commission's long investigation of the Westec case under Rule 2(e). Ernst & Ernst was censured, and one of the firm's partners was suspended from practice before the commission for a year.

ASR 255 (1978)   Criticized the financial reporting of SCA Services, Inc., and, under rule 2(e), censured Gerald J. Flannelly, SCA's chief financial officer. In addition, Flannelly consented to supply full facts to any auditor in the future, and to satisfy himself by consultation as to financial statements being filed with the commission. This represented the first significant SEC enforcement action against a CPA not in public practice.

ASR 267 (1979)   Analyzed the deficient financial statements prepared by ISC Financial Corporation, of which Martin Davis was chief financial officer. The commission suspended Davis for two years from practice before the commission.

42

The Cost Accounting Standards Board

Gordon Shillinglaw
Nelson H. Shapiro

THE CASB ROLE IN DEFINING COST

The U.S. government and its agencies, in contracting for necessary goods and services, often use cost as a basis for negotiating price or establishing payment. But cost can be defined in many ways. One definition may be used for financial accounting, another for tax accounting, and still another for managerial planning and control. From 1971 to 1980 the Cost Accounting Standards Board (CASB) had the authority to develop standards that specify how the costs of individually negotiated defense contracts should be measured. This chapter explains why the CASB was formed, its scope and purposes, how it operated, and the standards it issued.

Origin and Termination of the Board

For generations the government has set the definitions of cost by requiring adherence to various regulations, notably the Defense Acquisition Regulation (DAR), previously called the Armed Services Procurement Regulation (ASPR). Individuals and firms using cost information in their contractual dealings with the federal government generally have to accept these definitions. In the post–World War II period, however, Congress became increasingly concerned about the possibility that the existing regulations allowed contractors too much flexibility in defining cost. In 1969, therefore, Congress asked the General Accounting Office (GAO) to study the feasibility of establishing uniform cost accounting standards for negotiated defense contracts.

Both the AICPA and the National Association of Accountants maintained a neutral attitude toward this idea; most industry representatives opposed it. For its part, GAO concluded that such standards were both feasible and desirable, and Congress agreed when it passed Public Law 91-379 establishing the CASB. The law was signed by the President on August 15, 1970, funds were appropriated, and the board was organized in January 1971. It issued the first standards on February 29, 1972.

The board continued to operate until September 1980. Its budget authorization expired at the end of that month, Congress decided not to authorize funds for the next fiscal year beginning October 1, 1980, and the board therefore ceased to function. The board's cost accounting standards remain in force, however. As this *Handbook* went to press in the fall of 1980, Congress was considering various aspects of a proposal to transfer to the Office of Management and Budget the authority to keep the standards up to date.

Organization of the CASB

The CASB was responsible to Congress. The board had five members, with the comptroller general of the United States as chairman. The comptroller general appointed the four other members, two from the accounting profession, one from industry, and one from the federal government. Board members were appointed for concurrent four-year terms and served on a part-time basis. The board was assisted by a staff of professional accountants and attorneys headed by an executive secretary. Like the board itself, the staff represented various backgrounds and interests, being recruited from government, industry, academia, and public accounting. (About half the 1979 staff had been recruited from other government agencies.)

The staff carried out research, developed and tested proposed cost accounting standards, and analyzed data supplied to the board.

OBJECTIVES AND JURISDICTION

The objective of the CASB, as stated in Public Law 91-379, was "to achieve uniformity and consistency in the cost-accounting principles followed by defense contractors and subcontractors under Federal contracts" (Sec. 719, par. (g)). The CASB's procedures for attaining this objective were initially outlined in a 1973 board document entitled *Statement of Operating Policies, Procedures and Objectives*. This statement described the framework of CASB operations, including how it develops standards, rules, and regulations. A revised version of this statement, *Restatement of Objectives, Policies and Concepts*, was published in 1977. This statement reemphasized the objectives of uniformity and consistency. It expressed the board's conclusion that development of cost allocation standards includes definition and measurement of costs, determination of the accounting period to which costs are assignable, and assignment of costs to cost objectives. It also described the beneficial or causal concept for cost allocation, set up a hierarchy of principles for cost allocation, and pointed out that the board's procedures included reviewing proposed standards for comparisons of costs and benefits.

The CASB's finished products are *cost accounting standards*. The cost accounting practices of contractors subject to CASB rules must follow these standards. The CASB defined a cost accounting standard (CAS) as

a statement formally used by the Cost Accounting Standards Board that (1) enunciates a principle or principles to be followed, (2) establishes practices to be applied, or (3) specifies criteria to be employed in selecting from alternative principles and practices in estimating, accumulating, and reporting costs of contracts subject to the rules of the Board. [CASB, 1977, p. 1]

Applicability of the Standards

As soon as the board adopted a standard, it submitted it for publication in the *Federal Register* and sent it to Congress. Congress then had 60 days of continuous session to pass a concurrent resolution disapproving the standard; otherwise the standard became effective. Congress never took action to disapprove any of the board's standards.

The board's standards must be used by all relevant federal agencies and by defense contractors and subcontractors in estimating, accumulating, and reporting costs in connection with the pricing, administration, and settlement of all negotiated national defense procurements (both prime contract and subcontract) with the United States in excess of $100,000, except for the following three kinds of contracts and subcontracts:

1. Those in which the negotiated price is based on established catalog or market prices of commercial items sold in substantial quantities to the general public;
2. Those in which the negotiated price is based on prices set by law or regulation; and
3. Those that the board has exempted from the application of the new standard.

According to government records, approximately $39 billion in government contracts awarded during fiscal year 1978 were subject to cost accounting standards.

Exemptions

Public Law 91-379 authorized the board to prescribe rules and regulations exempting individual contracts or classes of contracts from the provisions of some or all standards. The board used this authority mainly to exempt from the standards each contract or subcontract awarded to any of the following:

1. A contractor awarded a contract or subcontract of $500,000 or less who is not already performing under a covered contract;
2. A small business concern, as defined by the Small Business Administration;
3. An educational institution (unless the contract is to be performed by a unit within the university classified as a federally funded research and development center);
4. A contractor or subcontractor in an area that has been designated as a labor surplus area, if the contract or subcontract has been awarded as part of an authorized program to give preferential treatment to potential contractors or subcontractors in labor surplus areas; or
5. A foreign government.

In addition, the board exempted two classes of contracts or subcontracts from the application of all standards except 401 and 402. A contract is subject to this limited coverage if it is awarded to

1. A foreign business enterprise; or
2. A contractor or subcontractor who in the preceding accounting period received less than $10 million in awards of contracts, and for whom such awards were less than 10% of total sales.

These two exemptions were established to relieve problems experienced by the Department of Defense and by industry. The Department of Defense had advised the board that "the requirement to apply some standards had become a significant impediment to efficient, successful contracting with foreign concerns. . . ." Business organizations in the United States indicated that implementation of standards required some effort and that the cost of implementation was excessive when only small amounts of covered contracts were concerned. In addition, several companies stated a belief that the imposition of cost accounting standards had caused some companies to avoid government contracts requiring compliance with these standards.

Administration of the Standards

The CASB did not negotiate contracts. Contract negotiation was and is the responsibility of the procurement officers in the various federal departments and agencies whose contracts are subject to the standards. The CASB has the responsibility to ensure compliance with the standards, but it looked to other government agencies to carry out reviews of compliance with the standards. In most cases, this task is performed by the Defense Contract Audit Agency (DCAA), an arm of the Department of Defense.

The CASB required that every major defense contractor within its jurisdiction (i.e., those with contract awards of more than $10 million in the most recent fiscal year) file a disclosure statement describing its cost accounting system in considerable detail. The CASB used these disclosure statements to identify areas in which standards appeared to be necessary. Their primary purpose, however, was to ensure compliance with Public Law 91-379, which mandated that contractors disclose their accounting practices and follow those disclosed practices consistently in pricing contract proposals and in accumulating and reporting costs of contract performance. As of September 30, 1979, reporting units of 288 companies had filed 1,674 disclosure statements with the board.

PROCEDURES

The CASB operated under a fairly well defined set of procedures. Among the most important ones were (1) the stages through which a proposal for a new standard passed before it emerged as a cost accounting standard, (2) the procedures used by the board to monitor the work of the staff and the operation of the standards, and (3) the criteria used by the board and the staff in determining the need for and applicability of proposed new standards.

Stages in the Development of a New Standard

The promulgation of a cost accounting standard was the final step in a long process. Typically this process included the following steps:

1. With the approval of the board, a staff work-project was launched. Subjects were selected in view of the significance of emerging problems and their relationships to other standards or current projects.
2. The staff reviewed prevailing concepts and practices. This step included review of existing practices, disclosed problems, current literature, and appeals board and court decisions.
3. The staff prepared and circulated a questionnaire, an issues paper, or both requesting information on the issues identified by the staff.
4. The staff prepared and circulated a preliminary draft of a proposed cost accounting standard. This staff draft was generally accompanied by questions on the probable costs and problems of implementation.
5. The board prepared a proposed standard, which was formally published in the *Federal Register* with a call for comments and suggestions. (The *Federal Register* publication process sometimes was repeated if the comments and suggestions led the board to make major and extensive changes in the proposed standard.)
6. The standard in its final form was adopted at an open meeting of the board. The adopted standard was then published in the *Federal Register*, along with a descriptive preamble that analyzed the major issues raised by commentators on the earlier draft and that presented the board's position on each of these issues.
7. The standard was submitted to Congress as required by law.

Public comment and interest were invited because the board regarded these as vital elements of the developmental process. Some of the proposed standards elicited several hundred letters. The standard dealing with depreciation was even the subject of a congressional hearing. The required 60 days of continuous session had already been completed and the standard had been formally adopted when the hearings took place. These hearings took the form of a review, and Congress found no objection to the requirements of the standard.

Board Review Procedures

The members of the board served on a part-time basis. For this reason they did not participate actively in the day-to-day operations of the CASB staff, but they did review the work of the staff on individual projects at each major step in the developmental process.

The board usually met once a month. Before each meeting, the staff provided the board with proposals for questionnaires, issues papers, staff-drafted standards, and draft standards for *Federal Register* publication. The board was also provided with staff papers analyzing the proposals. Whenever necessary, members of the staff visited with board members before the monthly meetings to provide background information on topics scheduled for discussion.

The board also attempted to monitor the effect of standards already in force. There was an established process for government agencies to report to the board annually on the operation of standards. Evaluation conferences with industry and professional organizations to obtain their observations on standards in operation were held about every two years. In addition, the board occasionally used consultants to evaluate particular issues of concern to the CASB.

As a result of this evaluation process, the board issued several interpretations of standards and CASB regulations. This continuous evaluation also helped the board exercise its responsibility to provide exemptions from standards where appropriate.

Criteria Applied by the Board

Public Law 91-379 provided that

> ... the Board, in promulgating standards, [shall] take into account ... the probable costs of implementation, including inflationary effects, if any, compared to the probable benefits, including advantages and improvements in the pricing, administration, and settlement of contracts. [CASB, 1977, p. 19]

The law established uniformity and consistency as the primary benefits to be derived from cost accounting standards. The board stated that it believed additional benefits could be derived by obtaining accounting data that are representative of the facts, thereby reducing controversy and simplifying negotiation, administration, audit, and settlement procedures (CASB, 1977, p. 19).

In evaluating proposed standards, the board considered the costs of implementation both to industry and to government agencies. Cost estimates were usually requested when the staff draft was circulated for comment. The board then evaluated proposed changes in the light of their expected effects on costs and benefits. This evaluation of the costs and benefits of each change affected the board's final deliberations on whether the potential benefits of a proposed standard as a whole would outweigh the expected costs of implementing it. The comments provided with each approved standard summarized the board's findings on costs and benefits.

Allocability Versus Allowability

The board's standards were designed only to identify the costs that are assignable or *allocable* to individual contracts or subcontracts. The board did not decide which costs are *allowable*—that is, reimbursable by the federal government. The board emphasized this point in these words:

> Allocability is an accounting concept involving the ascertainment of contract cost; it results from a relationship between a cost and a cost objective such that the cost objective appropriately bears all or a portion of the cost.
> Allowability is a procurement concept affecting contract price and in most cases is determined by regulatory or contractual provisions. . . . The use of Cost Accounting Standards has no direct bearing on the allowability of individual items of cost which are subject to limitations or exclusions set forth in the contract or which are otherwise specified as unallowable by the government. [CASB, 1977, p. 2]

In other words, a cost may be allocable to a contract, but allocability may be a determinant of contract price only if the regulations or the particular contracts permit the allocable cost to be classified as an allowable cost.

BASIC MEASUREMENT CONCEPTS

Shortly after issuing its first standards, the board outlined its basic approach to the measurement of contract cost. It made three basic points (CASB, 1973, pp. 16-18):

1. Contract cost is to be based on full costing;
2. The primary criterion for assigning costs to contracts is traceability; and
3. For costs not readily traceable to individual contracts, the board provided a hierarchy of alternative criteria to be applied one after the other—that is, the first criterion would be applied first; if it could not be implemented, the second would be applied; and so on.

Figure 42.1 provides the official definitions of several key CASB terms.

Full Cost

Full cost, as defined by the board, includes a share of all the costs necessary to support or fulfill the contracts for which costs are to be estimated or accumulated. The costs of overall corporate administration are just as necessary to the completion of the contract as direct labor costs are; they differ primarily in that the causal or beneficial relationship of such costs to individual contracts is much less clear.

Traceability

The preferred basis for assigning costs to contracts and other final cost objectives is traceability. Costs are supposed to be assigned to the cost objectives that have caused them or made them necessary. Traceability implies that this beneficial or causal relationship is clear and exclusive.

The only situation in which the cost of the specific resources traceable to a cost objective may not be properly assignable to that cost objective arises when the resources used are interchangeable with others. In such cases, an average may measure the relationship between cost and the cost objective more appropriately.

Every cost can be traced to a specific cost objective. Costs that cannot be traced to individual *final cost objectives* can be traced to *intermediate cost objectives,* such as home offices, service centers, or support centers. A particular intermediate cost objective may serve or support other intermediate cost objectives, final cost objectives, or a combination of both. The board developed a concept of relation-

---

ALLOCATE. To assign an item of cost, or a group of items of cost, to one or more cost objectives. This term includes both direct assignment of cost and the reassignment of a share from an indirect cost pool.

BUSINESS UNIT. Any segment of an organization, or an entire business organization that is not divided into segments.

COST OBJECTIVE. A function, organizational subdivision, contract, or other work unit for which cost data are desired and for which provision is made to accumulate and measure the cost of processes, products, jobs, capitalized projects, etc.

FINAL COST OBJECTIVE. A cost objective that has allocated to it both direct and indirect costs and, in the contractor's accumulation system, is one of the final accumulation points.

HOME OFFICE. An office responsible for directing or managing two or more, but not necessarily all, segments of an organization. An organization that has intermediate levels, such as groups, may have several home offices that report to a common home office. An intermediate organization may be both a segment and a home office.

INDIRECT COST POOL. A grouping of incurred costs identified with two or more objectives but not identified specifically with any final cost objective.

SEGMENT. One of two or more divisions, product departments, plants, or other subdivisions of an organization reporting directly to a home office, usually identified with responsibility for profit and/or producing a product or service.

FIGURE 42.1 OFFICIAL DEFINITIONS OF KEY CASB TERMS
SOURCE: Cost Accounting Standard 400.

ships between intermediate and final cost objectives that requires a contractor to choose a method of allocating the costs of particular intermediate cost objectives on the basis of the following hierarchy of techniques:

1. If the intermediate cost objective provides services or operating capacity to other cost objectives and if the *inputs* used in the intermediate cost objective can be identified with those other cost objectives, the costs should be allocated on the basis of the average cost per input unit in the intermediate cost objective. For example, the costs of a computer programming department might be distributed in proportion to the number of programming hours identified with other cost objectives serviced.

2. If the intermediate cost objective provides service or operating capacity to other cost objectives but the inputs used in the intermediate cost objective cannot be identified readily with those other cost objectives, the contractor should look for a measure of the *output* of the intermediate cost objective and allocate its costs in proportion to the number of units of output provided to other cost objectives. For example, the costs of a print shop might be allocated on the basis of the number of printed pages prepared for other cost objectives.

3. When neither the inputs nor the outputs of an intermediate cost objective can be identified with other specific cost objectives, a *surrogate* should be sought that seems likely to vary in the long run with the cost of services provided by the intermediate cost objective. This surrogate is usually some other measure of the activity in the cost objectives receiving service or support from the intermediate cost objective. For example, the number of employees in the departments served by a personnel department may be a useful basis for assigning the costs of maintaining personnel records to the cost objectives identified with those departments.

4. Any costs for which no homogeneous measure of input or output or a surrogate can be identified with the cost objectives they serve or support should be allocated among those cost objectives in proportion to their shares of the *total activity* of all the cost objectives as a group. For example, the costs of a plant manager's office might be allocated to final cost objectives in proportion to the total of all other factory costs assigned to those final cost objectives.

Figure 42.2 shows how costs might flow through a contractor's cost objectives. This contractor has a home office serving two or more segments. Each segment has two or more final cost objectives. Costs traceable to the home office are divided among the segments it serves and administers. The costs of the segments are then divided among the final cost objectives.

BOARD PRONOUNCEMENTS

The standards, rules, and regulations of the CASB are contained in Title 4, Chapter III, Code of Federal Regulations. Each standard constitutes a part of Chapter III, identified by a three-digit number starting with 401. Part 400 is reserved for definitions of technical terms, and is revised each time a new definition is adopted.

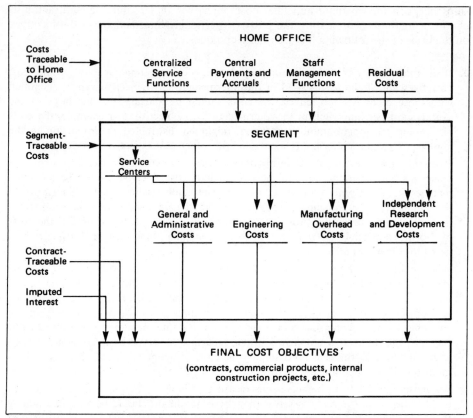

FIGURE 42.2   IMPLICIT STRUCTURE OF COST FLOWS IN COST ACCOUNT-ING STANDARDS

SOURCE: Gordon Shillinglaw, *Managerial Cost Accounting,* 4th ed. (Homewood, Ill.: Richard D. Irwin, 1977), p. 904.

The three-digit identifying numbers were assigned to the standards at the time they were adopted. Neither the sequence nor the identifying number indicates any relationship among the standards. The following classification system is unofficial and imperfect, but may provide some help to a person approaching these standards for the first time:

1. System constraints:
    a. CAS 401, *Consistency in Estimating, Accumulating, and Reporting Costs*
    b. CAS 402, *Consistency in Allocating Costs Incurred for the Same Purpose*
    c. CAS 405, *Accounting for Unallowable Costs*
    d. CAS 406, *Cost Accounting Period.*
2. Assigning costs to accounting periods:
    a. CAS 404, *Capitalization of Tangible Assets*
    b. CAS 408, *Accounting for Costs of Compensated Personal Absence*
    c. CAS 409, *Depreciation of Tangible Capital Assets*

d. CAS 411, *Acquisition Costs of Material*
e. CAS 412, *Composition and Measurement of Pension Cost*
f. CAS 413, *Adjustment and Allocation of Pension Cost*
g. CAS 415, *Accounting for the Costs of Deferred Personal Compensation*
h. CAS 416, *Accounting for Insurance Costs*
i. CAS 417, *Cost of Money as an Element of the Cost of Capital Assets Under Construction.*

3. Assigning costs to cost objectives within a period:
a. CAS 403, *Allocation of Home Office Expenses to Segments*
b. CAS 407, *Use of Standard Costs for Direct Materials and Direct Labor*
c. CAS 410, *Allocation of Business Unit General and Administrative Expenses to Final Cost Objectives*
d. CAS 414, *Cost of Money as an Element of the Cost of Facilities Capital*
e. CAS 418, *Allocation of Direct and Indirect Costs*
f. CAS 420, *Accounting for Independent Research and Development and Bid and Proposal Costs.*

System Constraints

Consistency. The first two standards to be issued, 401 and 402, set forth the fundamental criteria for consistency. They were designed to meet some of the strongest criticism of the cost accounting practices that had been adopted by some contractors based on the principles set forth in ASPR.

CAS 401 requires the contractor to accumulate and report costs on the same basis it uses in preparing cost estimates for contract-bidding purposes. In flexibly priced contracts, this prevents the contractor from bidding low on the basis of one cost accounting practice and then charging higher amounts to the government on the basis of some other practice. CAS 401 also requires the contractor to prepare cost estimates on the same basis it expects to use in accumulating costs. For fixed price contracts, this prevents the contractor from preparing a cost estimate based on one practice when it expects to account for its costs through some other practice that would allocate fewer costs to that contract. An example of a cost accounting practice that is inconsistent with CAS 401 is the estimation of labor costs by function—assembly, machining—when such costs will be accumulated in a single account without distinguishing between functions.

CAS 402 forbids double counting:

> . . . each type of cost is [to be] allocated only once and on only one basis to any contract or other cost objective. . . . All costs incurred for the same purposes, in like circumstances, are either direct costs only or indirect costs only with respect to final cost objectives.

An example of double counting is the charging of any kind of cost such as travel, supervision, or quality control directly to a contract when other travel, supervision, or quality control costs incurred in like circumstances are treated as indirect costs.

Unallowable Costs. CAS 405 deals with the identification of costs that are not allowable. The unallowable items should be identified and excluded from costs in preparing cost proposals, billings, or claims under covered contracts. The unallowable costs should be subject to the same cost accounting principles governing cost allocability that allowable costs are. Therefore, unallowable costs that are part of an indirect allocation base should remain in that base. Associated indirect costs that would be allocated on that base can be determined through the regular allocation process and then classified as unallowable.

Cost Accounting Period. CAS 406 is primarily concerned with the determination of an accounting period for the allocation of indirect costs. The standard generally requires that the company use its own accounting year as the cost accounting period for accumulating costs in an indirect cost pool and for determining the allocation base for that pool. The standard also requires that appropriate annual deferrals, accruals, and other adjustments be made in determining the cost accounting period to which costs should be assigned.

Assigning Costs to Accounting Periods

Capitalization of Tangible Assets. CAS 404 deals with the capitalization of acquired resources for amortization during future periods of expected use. The standard requires the acquisition cost of tangible capital assets to be capitalized if significant. Acquisition cost includes the purchase price of the asset and the costs necessary to prepare it for use. The contractor should prepare and adhere to a written policy designating the economic and physical characteristics associated with the assets to be capitalized, including a minimum service life and a minimum acquisition cost. This policy must be reasonable and consistently applied.

Compensated Personal Absence. CAS 408 provides that the costs of compensated personal absences (vacation, holiday, and sick pay) be assigned to the cost accounting period in which they are earned. The compensation is earned in the period in which the company becomes obligated to provide the compensation. The costs of compensated personal absences should be allocated to contracts on an annual basis.

Depreciation. CAS 409 deals with assigning the cost of capital assets among the cost accounting periods in which the assets are expected to be consumed. The standard establishes that (1) the cost to be assigned is the capitalized cost of assets less their estimated residual value, (2) the assignment should begin in the period in which the assets are ready for use in a normal or acceptable fashion, (3) the cost should be prorated over the expected useful life of the assets, (4) the cost should be assigned to individual accounting periods based on the expected pattern of asset usage, and (5) any gain or loss recognized on disposition of the assets should be assigned to the period in which it is recognized.

Many industry representatives objected to this standard's provision requiring the use of estimated useful life as the amortization period. They generally preferred the use of tax life or the life estimate used for company financial statements; these life estimates are often shorter than the actual lives of depreciable assets. They expressed concern that longer life estimates would delay cash receipts, reduce incentives for modernization, increase administrative record-keeping costs, and create differences between the depreciation amounts determined for contract costing and those used in financial statements. The CASB took the position, however, that cost for contract-costing purposes should be based on cost accounting concepts and not on tax lives, which may be artificially shortened to achieve various nonaccounting goals. In the hearings it conducted on this standard, Congress accepted the board's position.

Acquisition Cost of Material. CAS 411 provides that the cost of material may be allocated directly to a cost objective, provided the cost objective was specifically identified at the time of purchase or production of the material. If the cost objective was not specifically identified at this time, the cost of each category of material must be accounted for in material inventory records. The standard requires that the same inventory-costing method be used for similar categories of materials within a business unit.

Composition and Measurement of Pension Cost. CAS 412 establishes the amount of the cost of pension benefits earned in the current and prior cost accounting periods the contractor is to assign to the current period. For a defined-benefit pension plan, it provides that pension costs of the current period are (1) the normal cost of the period, (2) an appropriate part of any unfunded actuarial liability plus interest on the unamortized portion, and (3) an adjustment for any actuarial gains and losses (see CAS 413). For defined-contribution pension plans, the net contribution in a cost accounting period is the pension cost for that period.

Adjustment and Allocation of Pension Cost. CAS 413 provides the basis for determining actuarial gains and losses and requires that the calculation be made annually. In determining actuarial gains and losses, a valuation method is used that assesses the increases and decreases in value of all fund assets. The pension cost for a period, including actuarial gains and losses, is allocated to each segment having participants in the pension plan. Allocation may be made on a composite basis to two or more segments, unless circumstances indicate that a materially different result would be obtained through separate calculation of pension cost for each segment.

Deferred Compensation. CAS 415 provides that the cost of deferred compensation be assigned to the cost accounting period in which the contractor incurs an obligation to compensate a specific employee. If no obligation is incurred before payment, the cost of deferred compensation is the amount paid, and is assigned to the cost accounting period in which the payment is made. The cost of deferred compensation is the present value of the future benefits to be paid by the contractor.

Insurance Costs. CAS 416 provides that the amount of insurance cost to be assigned to a cost accounting period is the projected average loss for that period plus insurance administration expenses. The allocation of insurance costs to cost objectives is based on the factors that determine the cost, except that insurance costs may be allocated along with other indirect costs if the resulting allocation to cost objectives is substantially the same.

Cost of Money as an Element of the Cost of Capital Assets Under Construction. CAS 417 provides for the capitalization of interest as part of the cost of capital assets. This standard requires the capitalization of interest on the total cost of assets under construction, not just the part financed by specific borrowing. The interest rate to be used is calculated periodically by the secretary of the treasury. (See discussion of CAS 414 in the next section for more detail on the interest calculation.)

Assigning Costs to Cost Objectives Within a Period

Allocation of Home Office Expenses to Segments. CAS 403 deals with home office expenses, which consist mainly of (1) the costs of centralized service functions, including staff management functions, (2) central payments and accruals, and (3) residual expenses. Note that the word "expense" was used by the CASB to describe an operating cost. This may not equal the amount reported as an expense on the company's income statement.

Centralized service functions are functions that, but for the existence of a home office, would be performed or acquired by some or all of the segments individually. Examples include centrally performed personnel administration and centralized data processing. If these costs can be traced directly to a specific segment, they must be charged to that segment. If they are not traceable to a segment, the standard prescribes the use of the hierarchy of allocation bases described earlier.

Similarly, *central payments and accruals* are those that, but for the existence of the home office, would be accrued or paid by the individual segments. Common examples are group insurance costs, local property taxes, and payrolls paid by a home office on behalf of its segments. The standard provides that these payments and accruals are to be assigned directly to individual segments if they can be traced to the segments. Otherwise, they are to be assigned to segments "using an allocation base representative of the factors on which the total payment is based."

Residual expenses are all those not falling in either of the first two categories. A typical example is the salary of the chief executive officer. It is to be allocated to the segments on a base representing the segments' total activity. The standard prescribes a formula to be used for this purpose if the amount exceeds specified limits.

It should be noted that the term "beneficial or causal relationship," first used by CASB in this standard, has a different connotation in these standards than when used for other cost accounting purposes. For managerial accounting purposes, "causal" often applies to the relationship of *variable* indirect costs to cost objectives, while "beneficial" applies to the relationship of *fixed* indirect costs to cost objectives. Because of the full-costing approach used for negotiated government contracts, cost accounting for these contracts has generally ignored the different relationships of fixed and variable costs, and for cost-estimating and reimbursement purposes, it has attributed to fixed costs the same relationship to product as variable costs. Therefore, the term "beneficial or causal relationship" as used by the CASB must be understood as describing a relationship between cost objectives and the costs necessary to achieve those objectives under the full-costing approach.

CAS 403 has been challenged by a number of contractors, particularly in connection with its application to the allocation of various kinds of taxes to individual segments. In the first administrative law proceeding arising from a dispute on this standard, the Armed Services Board of Contract Appeals (ASBCA) rejected the Boeing Company's challenge and ruled that the company's method of allocating state and local taxes on a per capita basis was not permissible under the standard. The ASBCA concluded that the company's method did not reflect the bases on which the taxes were assessed (ASBCA, No. 19224). Boeing appealed this ruling to the Court of Claims in 1979.

Standard Costs for Direct Material and Direct Labor. CAS 407 provides a basis on which standard cost systems for direct labor and direct material can be used in determining the cost of covered contracts. The standard describes the organizational level at which a company may group its costs and account for variances from standard cost. The standard also requires that variances, when significant, be allocated to covered contracts at least annually and on the same basis as the standard costs previously charged.

Allocation of General and Administrative Overheads. CAS 410 contains two main provisions:

1. Each business unit is to have a pool of general and administrative (G&A) costs, and this is to be allocated directly to final cost objectives; and
2. General and administrative costs of any business unit are to be allocated by means of a cost input basis.

Cost input may mean all the operating costs of the business unit other than general and administrative costs, or it may mean costs other than materials, or it may mean a single cost element, such as direct labor. General and administrative costs cannot be allocated as a percentage of sales or cost of sales (output measures). Instead, they must be assigned to contract work in process before it is ready for delivery to the government. In the prefatory comments to CAS 410, the board explained its reason for precluding the use of an output base:

> The Board's position is that the measurement of a cost of sales base is representative, in part, of the productive activities of prior periods and is subject to fluctuations which can distort the allocation of G&A expenses to activities of the current period. Although the measurement of cost of sales is based on a recorded date of sale, that is not necessarily an index of the activities of a period.

CAS 410 has given rise to a good deal of controversy, centering on whether the standard established a hierarchy of cost input measures starting with total cost input and working down to a single input index applicable in specified circumstances. Many contractors argue that the standard allows them to choose among the available cost input indexes.

Imputed Interest on Facilities Capital. CAS 414 plowed new ground. For the first time, imputed interest was recognized as an element of contract cost. The amount of imputed interest is computed by applying a long-term commercial borrowing rate to the individual contractor's investment in facilities. Neither actual interest incurred nor the contractor's actual borrowing rate is a consideration in determining the amount of imputed interest. The standard requires the following:

1. Interest must be imputed to individual contracts.

2. The amount to be imputed must be based on the amount of facilities used to support work on individual contracts. (Investments in working capital are specifically excluded from the provisions of this standard.)

3. The interest rate must be based on an average of long-term commercial borrowing rates calculated periodically by the secretary of the treasury.[1]

4. Imputed interest assignable to an indirect cost pool must be allocated to final cost objectives in proportion to the number of *allocation base units* (direct labor hours, and so on) identified with the contract.

Allocation of Direct and Indirect Costs. One of the board's most difficult tasks was the development of CAS 418, covering the allocation of the costs of a business unit to final cost objectives. After several years of intensive staff work, the board published a proposed set of five standards in March 1978. After reviewing the comments, the board published a revised proposal in July 1979 calling for the issuance of three standards on the subject. The single standard that emerged was finally adopted in May 1980.

CAS 418 provides guidance in general terms for handling indirect costs of a business unit other than those covered by CAS 410 or CAS 420. It requires that each business unit have a written statement of accounting policies and practices for classifying costs as direct or indirect. It also requires that the pools of indirect costs should be homogeneous.

This standard distinguishes between (1) indirect cost pools containing a material amount of the costs of management or supervision of activities involving direct labor or direct materials costs and (2) other indirect cost pools. Costs in pools of the former type are to be allocated on bases that are representative of the activity being managed. For example, direct labor might be used as a base for allocating manufacturing overhead costs. Costs in indirect cost pools of the latter type, mostly the costs of service centers, are to be assigned to the cost objectives served (1) on the basis of inputs in the pool whose use can also be traced to specific cost objectives, (2) on the basis of the amount of service provided by the activities in the pool (the output of the pool), or (3) on the basis of a surrogate for service inputs.

Research and Development and Bid and Proposal Costs. CAS 420, *Accounting for Independent Research and Development (IR&D) and Bid and Proposal (B&P) Costs,* became effective in March 1980. IR&D is defined as effort in basic and applied research, development, systems, and other concept formulation activities that are not performed under contract or grant. B&P is defined as effort in preparing and submitting any bid or proposal that is not required under the terms of an existing contract or grant. IR&D and B&P costs are to be accumulated by individual projects. They are to include the direct costs incurred solely for the particular projects plus an appropriate share of all indirect costs except general and administrative costs.

---

[1] The secretary of the treasury is required by Public Law 92-41 to establish a rate semiannually that takes "into consideration current private commercial rates of interest for new loans maturing in approximately five years."

Relationship to Financial Accounting Standards

As explained under Objectives and Jurisdiction, cost accounting standards cover definition and measurement of cost, determination of the accounting period to which costs are assignable, and assignment of costs to cost objectives. Some companies have expressed concern that the requirements of standards will differ from financial accounting standards (GAAP), which govern the measurement and reporting of financial information in financial statements prepared primarily for use outside the organization.

Some standards do differ from GAAP. CAS 414, requiring the allocation of imputed interest to contracts, is a case in point. The board stated, however, that it would carefully consider situations in which conflict might exist and that its pronouncements would differ only when departures were necessary to help the board meet its objectives under Public Law 91-379.

In some cases, standards provide for alternative accounting treatments, one or more of which are acceptable under GAAP while one or more others are not. In other situations, the standards are more restrictive than GAAP, narrowing the list of accounting alternatives that are permitted. Only two standards require the assignment of costs to accounting periods on a basis different from the assignment provided under GAAP. CAS 416 provides that insurance cost for an accounting period be based on the risk of loss rather than on the actual loss identified during the period. CAS 417 provides that implicit interest rather than interest paid shall be capitalized.

APPLICABILITY TO NONDEFENSE CONTRACTS

The future effect of cost accounting standards on nondefense contracts was also under consideration early in 1980—the Office of Federal Procurement Policy (OFPP) was developing the Federal Acquisition Regulation (FAR). Designed to provide guidance in all federal procurement matters, this regulation was to replace both the Defense Acquisition Regulation and the nondefense Federal Procurement Regulation.

Regarding the application of cost accounting standards to nondefense agencies, OFPP proposed to exempt nondefense contracts awarded to business units that are not currently performing any defense contracts covered by the standards. Also, in the interest of uniformity, OFPP proposed that nondefense contracts subject to the standards should have the same type of coverage (i.e., either modified coverage subject to only CAS 401 and 402, or full coverage subject to all standards) as the most recently awarded defense contract currently being performed by the same business unit of the company.

SUGGESTED READING

Anderson, Henry. "The G&A Overhead Pool: Accounting Tool or Cop-Out?" *Management Accounting,* October, 1977, pp. 37-42. This article reviews the treatment of general and administrative costs and includes a discussion of the treatment of state income taxes.

Anderson, Lane. "Influencing the Work of the CASB." *National Contract Management Journal,* Summer, 1979, pp. 50-54. In this article, a former staff member of the board writes about interpersonal relationships between CASB staff and the regulated public. He presents an interesting point of view on how the staff may be influenced in the development of standards to be presented to the board.

Cost Accounting Standards Board. *Restatement of Objectives, Policies and Concepts.* Washington, D.C., 1977. This is the board's latest official summary of the guidelines it observed and the basic conceptual structure underlying the standards.

Everett, Ronald. "Cost Accounting Standards: Boon or Burden?" *National Contract Management Journal,* Summer, 1979, pp. 91-100. This article discusses the advantages and disadvantages of cost accounting.

Greenough, Donald. *Basic Cost Accounting Considerations in Government Contracting.* New York: Touche Ross & Co., 1979. This 86-page pamphlet provides an extensive summary of the standards, the legislative background, and the contracting environment in which the cost standards are applied.

Huefner, Ronald. "Analysis of CASB Disclosure Statements." *Management Accounting,* June, 1976, pp. 45-48. This article summarizes the practices followed by defense contractors as the first cost standards began to go into effect.

Lynn, Bernard. "Auditing Contractor Compliance with Cost Accounting Standards." *Journal of Accountancy,* June, 1975, pp. 60-70. This article is a good statement of the role of the DCAA and a summary of early experience with the first three standards.

Mautz, Robert. "Living with the Cost Accounting Standards Board." *Financial Executive,* February, 1973, pp. 38-41. In this article, a member of the CASB suggested some ways industry could contribute to the work of the board.

Mautz, Robert. "The Other Accounting Standards Board." *Journal of Accountancy,* February, 1974, pp. 56-60. In this article, a board member writes about the potential impact of the CASB, particularly in regard to its relationship with other authoritative bodies engaged in establishing accounting standards. He also discusses the board's research process.

National Association of Accountants, Management Accounting Practices Committee. *Concepts for Contract Costing.* Statement No. 1. New York, 1971. This statement was prepared while the legislation establishing the board was being considered and was issued and submitted to the board shortly after it was formed.

Schoenhaut, Arthur. "CASB—Past, Present and Future." *Financial Executive,* September, 1973, pp. 28-32. In this article, the executive secretary of the CASB describes the establishment of the board and its then-current operations from an insider's point of view.

Staats, Elmer. "The History of Standard No. 409." *Management Accounting,* October, 1975, pp. 21-26. In this article, the chairman of the CASB discusses the reasons for issuing the standard on depreciation of fixed assets. He also explains the board's view of the relationship between depreciation and profit.

U.S. General Accounting Office. *Study of Feasibility of Adopting Uniform Cost-Accounting Standards: Analysis of Responses on the Suitability of Using Section XV of the Armed Services Procurement Regulation in Developing Uniform Cost-Accounting Standards.* Washington, D.C., 1969. This is one of a number of reports prepared by the GAO as part of its study of the feasibility of adopting uniform cost accounting standards.

Wright, Howard. "Uniform Cost Accounting Standards: Past, Present and Future." *Financial Executive,* May, 1971, pp. 16-23. In this article, a long-time authority on government contract costing places the work of the board in its institutional context.

APPENDIX 42 MEMBERS OF THE CASB

Elmer B. Staats, chairman (served 1971-1980). Mr. Staats is comptroller general of the United States. He became comptroller general in 1966, after twenty-six years' service with the Bureau of the Budget. A graduate of McPherson College, he also has an M.A. degree from the University of Kansas and a Ph.D. from the University of Minnesota.

Herman W. Bevis (served 1971-1980). Mr. Bevis served with Price Waterhouse & Co. from 1933 to 1969 and became their senior partner in 1961. He was executive director of the Banking and Securities Industry Committee from 1970 to 1974. He is a graduate of Southwestern at Memphis and the Harvard Graduate School of Business Administration.

Charles R. Dana (served 1971-75). Mr. Dana is the director of government accounting controls of the Raytheon Company. He has been with Raytheon in various capacities for a number of years, and has been active in industry associations concerned with government contracting. He is a graduate of Boston University and the Harvard Graduate School of Business Administration.

Robert K. Mautz (served 1971-78). Mr. Mautz was a partner in the firm of Ernst & Ernst at the time he served on the board. He is now with the University of Michigan. Before his service with Ernst & Ernst, he was professor of accountancy at the University of Illinois, where he taught from 1948 to 1972. He is a graduate of the University of North Dakota and the University of Illinois.

Terence E. McClary (served 1975-77). At the time of his membership on the board, Mr. McClary was assistant secretary of defense (comptroller). He is now with the General Electric Co. Before his service with the Defense Department he had been with Sanders Associates for four years as vice president—controller, and previously had spent 20 years with the General Electric Co. Mr. McClary is a graduate of the University of Nebraska.

Robert C. Moot (served 1971-75). At the time of becoming a member of the board, Mr. Moot was assistant secretary of defense (comptroller), occupying this position from 1968 to 1973. In 1973, he became vice president—finance of Amtrak. He has since retired. Mr. Moot's previous government service was as assistant secretary of defense for logistic services and as administrator of the Small Business Administration. Before his government service, Mr. Moot held accounting and marketing positions in private industry.

Gordon Shillinglaw (served 1978-1980). Mr. Shillinglaw is professor of accounting at the Graduate School of Business at Columbia University. He received his A.B. degree at Brown University, his M.S. at the University of Rochester, and his Ph.D. at Harvard University.

Fred P. Wacker (served 1977-1980). Mr. Wacker is assistant secretary of defense (comptroller). He has been with the Defense Department since 1951. A graduate of American University, he also received an M.S. degree from George Washington University.

John M. Walker (served 1975-1980). Mr. Walker is senior vice president and corporate treasurer of Texas Instruments, Inc. He has been with Texas Instruments and predecessor companies since 1955, previously having served with Westinghouse Electric Co. He is a graduate of the Georgia Institute of Technology and the Harvard Graduate School of Business Administration.

43

The Internal Revenue Service and CPA Tax Practice

William L. Raby
Eli Gerver

TAX ORIGINS

The accounting profession may have its origins in the attest function, but the income tax has been a major factor in its growth.

First enacted simply as a revenue measure, the income tax has become a major instrument of U.S. domestic and foreign policy.[1] Today its role in society is pervasive, and its effectiveness is due not only to the efficiency of the government and the generally law-abiding character of the American public, but also to the diligent services of tax practitioners, among whom accountants have been particularly active. As the application of the income tax laws expanded to affect most people in virtually every aspect of life, it was only natural for taxpayers to turn for assistance to the profession that had established its expertise in income determination. Although the accounting profession does not by any means have the field of tax advice and practice solely to itself, it provides the bulk of such services to American business, and there are few, if any, tax issues in which accountants are not involved.

Taxes are, of course, levied at all levels of government in this and other countries, but this chapter will concentrate on the role of the accountant in federal taxation, with particular emphasis on the income tax.

SOURCES OF TAX RULES

Most of the tax law is not new. Many provisions of the present Internal Revenue Code can be traced to earlier tax legislation, but this does not make them any easier to understand. Even where the statute has never been changed, an endless process of interpretation has adapted it to the ever-changing circumstances of our society. As it might have been said, age cannot wither nor custom stale the infinite variety of our tax laws.

Congress

Under the Constitution, tax laws must originate in the House of Representatives, which in effect means the Ways and Means Committee. While a proposed law is under consideration, however, amendments may be proposed by any member of Congress. Specific amendments that are incorporated into the tax law often arise in the Senate Finance Committee, or even from the floor of the Senate or the House. The staffs of the Ways and Means Committee and the Senate Finance Committee probably do much of the actual drafting of tax legislation. The Joint

---

[1] The Sixteenth Amendment to the Constitution was formally ratified in 1913, but there was a corporate excise tax in 1909 measured by net income over $5,000. Even that early law, although it referred to actual payments, was interpreted by the Treasury to permit use of accrual concepts. The Revenue Act of 1916 authorized a corporation to "make its return upon the basis of which its accounts are kept." Regulations under the 1918 Act stated: "... the law contemplates that each taxpayer shall adopt such forms and systems of accounting as are in his judgment best suited to his purpose."

Committee on Taxation, which consists of five members from each of these two committees, is most influential in the development of tax legislation, although it does not report to Congress on specific legislation. Economists, attorneys, and usually at least one accountant make up the Joint Committee's staff, which provides information on problems to be approached through legislation, prepares drafts of suggested language to incorporate Congressional decisions, and develops projections of the probable results of specific provisions.

The Treasury Department is the administration's representative in seeking tax legislation. It provides recommendations to Congress, projections, and "evidence" on the existing tax system. Most tax bills emerge from Congress looking very little like the proposals submitted by the administration.

Information on problems and issues is also submitted by industry organizations, individual companies, public interest groups, individuals, and professional organizations such as the AICPA. The effort to relieve the problems of taxpayers often leads to tax law provisions that are considerably more detailed than they might otherwise be.

Treasury and IRS

The Treasury Department issues regulations and procedures interpreting the tax laws, both in its own name and through its subunit, the Internal Revenue Service. In performing its primary job of collecting taxes, the IRS also designs forms and develops procedures that inevitably constitute an interpretation of the law. The IRS district offices audit returns filed by taxpayers and deal with their refund claims, resolving ambiguities and uncertainties in the course of this activity and thus providing further interpretation. Also, the IRS is willing to provide taxpayers with formal opinions (rulings) on the tax consequences of specific transactions or events, which is the occasion for still more interpretation.

The Courts

Since the job of the IRS is to collect taxes, it tends to resolve doubts against the taxpayer, while taxpayers and their advisers naturally tend to take the opposite view. There generally is a presumption in any administrative or judicial proceeding in favor of the correctness of an IRS determination that additional tax is due. Litigation may go as high as the Supreme Court. Of all the cases that are taken to court, however, most are settled before they actually come to trial. All decisions of the courts are published, and the interpretations of the law that these decisions constitute are usable by other taxpayers and by the IRS as precedent.

THE INTERNAL REVENUE SERVICE

The Internal Revenue Service has the day-to-day responsibility for administration of the tax law. It is the agency with which taxpayers and practitioners must deal.

The head of the IRS is the Commissioner of Internal Revenue, who is appointed by the President. In addition to its national office in Washington, D.C., the IRS has regional and district offices throughout the country. The commissioner appoints assistant commissioners to take national responsibility for specific areas of tax administration, regional commissioners to take responsibility for the regional offices, and district directors to take local responsibility. It is through the local office that the IRS provides taxpayer information, tax forms, and facilities for the employees who audit tax returns.

The initial step in the collection of tax is the filing of a return by the taxpayer. The returns are filed with service centers in key locations throughout the country, where large data processing installations select some returns for review. The selected returns are forwarded to the district level for possible audit. An administrative organization has been established for resolving disputes that arise in the process of auditing returns. When a dispute cannot be resolved through these administrative procedures, the taxpayer's ultimate recourse is the courts.

Audits of Returns

Office Audits. Audits of individual returns (other than those related to business returns under audit) are normally handled through the *office audit* procedure. The taxpayer receives a letter from an IRS employee requesting that he appear at the local IRS office at a particular time. The taxpayer may appear alone, may be accompanied by a representative, typically the accountant who prepared the return, or may send the representative in his stead. This representative should be authorized in writing to appear on behalf of the taxpayer.

IRS office auditors tend to have less training and experience than field auditors. They handle a relatively large workload of returns, but these returns involve few complex tax issues. Thus, the office auditors tend to be arbitrary and mechanical in applying the tax law to any unusual situation.

Field Audits. Audits of business returns, as well as of related individual returns, are conducted outside IRS offices, usually at the taxpayer's place of business. As with office audits, taxpayers may handle the examination themselves, may be assisted by an authorized representative, or may have the representative handle the examination completely. Typically, the accountant who handles the examination has prepared the return, but it is also common for accountants to assist a client in the examination even though the return was prepared by the client himself.

Revenue agents engaged in field audits view themselves as professionals engaged in an activity comparable to the work of the audit professional in a CPA firm. They tend to focus their work on areas of the tax return that offer the most potential for additional tax revenue.

Settlement of Disputes

Agent Level. Disagreement with the office auditor or the revenue agent conducting a field audit is not unusual. The taxpayer or representative who can document a version of the facts that is favorable to the taxpayer's case can often persuade the IRS people involved that that version is "true." Similarly, well-reasoned arguments reflecting a grasp of the tax law and dealing with the questions of interpretation raised by the revenue agent often succeed in persuading the agent to change his position.

However, the agent is not the only person who must be convinced. IRS procedures include a review function within the district office. If the agent is to agree to the taxpayer's position, there may have to be sufficient documentation and supporting memoranda to help the agent write a report that will be accepted by the reviewer.

The agent may accept an issue that is part of a case, particularly when it is a question of reasonable compensation, unreasonable accumulation of earnings, travel and entertainment, or capitalization versus expensing of repairs. These are matters of judgment in which the agent has a fair amount of discretion in deciding the adequacy of support. But this agreement on an issue should not be confused with settling a whole case. Agents are not permitted to settle cases by making compromises. That authority belongs to the appeals officer, who will be discussed shortly.

If as a result of the audit the IRS agent feels an additional amount of tax is due, the taxpayer will usually be asked to agree to the assessment. He can do so by signing a Form 870, which states the *amount* of additional tax (usually called a deficiency) but not the *basis* for it. The effect of signing Form 870 is to waive the taxpayer's statutory right to receive a "90-day letter" (described later) before the tax can actually be billed. If the taxpayer does not plan to contest the issue further, the advantage of signing Form 870 is to limit the period for which interest will be charged on the deficiency. While Form 870 contains language indicating that the taxpayer agrees that the deficiency is correct, this does not prevent filing a claim for refund and even bringing a suit in court to get it.

Appeals Office. If the taxpayer does not sign a Form 870, procedure calls for the IRS to send a "30-day letter" setting forth the details of the proposed deficiency and offering an opportunity to protest that proposed deficiency to the appeals office of the IRS within 30 days. The "30-day letter" is the starting point of the depiction of the appeal procedure in Figure 43.1.

The appeals office is part of the regional structure of the IRS, but it includes additional branch offices scattered throughout each region. As with the agent-level examination of the returns, taxpayers may represent themselves. But it is far more usual for an accountant or lawyer to appear on behalf of the taxpayer at this level. If the amount in dispute does not exceed $2,500 for any single year involved, a case can be brought to the appeals office through a simple letter requesting that it be forwarded from the district office to the appeals office and that a hearing with an appeals officer be granted. If the amount in dispute for any year is over $2,500, a *written protest* must be filed. The protest must set forth the facts, the IRS position, the taxpayer's position, and such supporting arguments and citations as seem appropriate and should end with a request for an appeals-office conference on the matter.

The function of appeals officers is to settle cases. They have the authority to compromise issues on the basis of the probable outcome should the issues be taken to court. They are usually receptive to an offer of settlement submitted for the taxpayer that seems to reflect realistically the relative strengths of the taxpayer's and IRS's positions. The appeals office conference is expected to be a quasi-judicial hearing in terms of the attitude of the appeals officer, but it is conducted informally, with no formal record of the exact words said by either side.

Appeals officers are more experienced revenue agents, by and large, than those

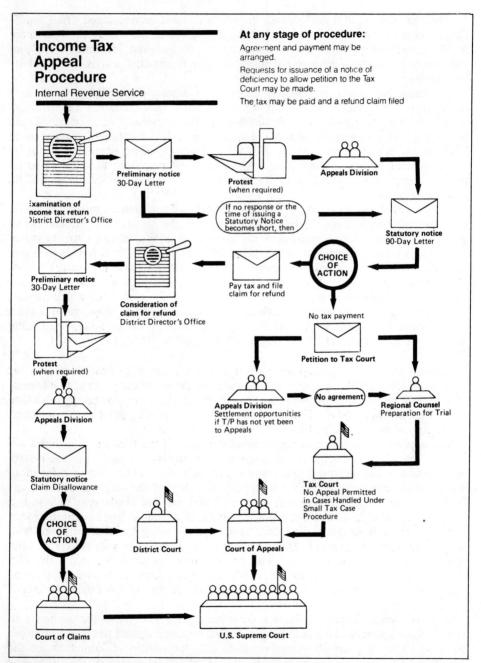

FIGURE 43.1   INCOME TAX APPEAL PROCEDURE

SOURCE: Internal Revenue Service, Publication 566, *Examination of Returns, Appeal Rights, and Claims for Refund* (1979).

engaged in field audits. As a result, the appeals officer is frequently more willing than the revenue agent to see the taxpayer's side when the taxpayer has a meritorious case. On the other hand, it is not unknown for an appeals officer to identify issues that may have escaped the notice of the field agent. While the appeals officer's instructions are not to raise new issues unless they are substantial in nature, the possibility of new issues being raised is one of the risks to consider when bringing a matter to the appeals-office level. The accountant representing the taxpayer at this level needs technical ability and advocacy skill.

If the taxpayer fails to file a protest, or if the protest does not resolve the issue, a "90-day letter" will ultimately be issued by the IRS. This informs the taxpayer that unless a petition is filed with the Tax Court within 90 days, the IRS will proceed to assess the tax and take whatever actions may be necessary to collect it.

Tax Court. If the taxpayer is unable to reach a satisfactory resolution of the controversy with the appeals office, but does not want to pay the tax before seeking further settlement opportunities or ultimate judicial review, the next step is to file a petition with the U.S. Tax Court. Cases are tried before the Tax Court in cities throughout the United States. The Tax Court judges travel individually from city to city to hear cases. At the time of filing a petition, the taxpayer indicates the city in which he would like to have the case tried. The case will be heard in either that city or one close to it where the court plans to hold sessions.

The taxpayer may still represent himself before the Tax Court, but it is much more usual to be represented by a lawyer or an accountant. Lawyers, generally, can appear for taxpayers before the Tax Court, but accountants who are not also lawyers must take a special examination to perform this function.

Cases submitted (docketed) before the Tax Court are handled for the government by IRS lawyers who are part of the regional counsel's office. If an appeals-office conference was not held before the taxpayer docketed the case, such conferences will probably be scheduled now. If the appeals office has considered the case already, the management of the case will normally be in the hands of regional counsel's office, and the appeals officer involved may work closely with regional counsel.

Through discussions and negotiations with either the appeals officer or regional counsel, the majority of Tax Court cases are settled without any trial. Even those that go to trial normally have most of the facts stipulated (agreed to by the government and the taxpayer) in advance, so that the actual trial before the Tax Court frequently takes no more than a few hours. After the hearing, the taxpayer and the government file briefs setting out their separate views of the facts and the applicable law.

The decision of the court is appealable, either by the taxpayer or by the government, to the U.S. Circuit Court of Appeals, but if there is no appeal, the Tax Court's decision is a complete and final determination of the issues.

The Tax Court also has a relatively informal (and frequently speedier) procedure for handling cases in which the amount at issue is not over $5,000 for any one year. Under this procedure there is no right of appeal from the Tax Court's decision, nor can the decision be used as precedent in any other cases. The trial judges who handle these small cases generally appear to give the taxpayer's case equitable consideration.

Other Courts. In the procedure noted above, an issue is presented to the Tax Court without the taxpayer first paying the deficiency. But if the taxpayer prefers to have his case heard by some other court, he must first pay the deficiency and may then go either to the U.S. district court, where a jury trial may determine the facts, or to the U.S. Court of Claims. The taxpayer may represent himself in these courts, but is not likely to do so. If he wishes to be represented, it must be by a lawyer admitted to practice before the specific court.

The Tax Court, the district court, and the Court of Claims may follow different precedents in deciding tax issues that have not been reviewed by the Supreme Court. A decision in the Tax Court or the district court is appealable to the judicial circuit in which the taxpayer resides, but an opinion of the Court of Claims is appealable only to the Supreme Court. To complicate matters further, different circuits do not necessarily agree with one another, and may hold different views on similar issues until the matter is finally resolved by the Supreme Court. Because of these complications, and because the tax must be paid before going to the district court or the Court of Claims, any decision to litigate in court requires the active participation of legal counsel.

Collections and Refunds

Collection Enforcement. Taxpayers who ignore IRS notices of tax due will normally have their salaries garnisheed, liens filed against their bank accounts, or their property seized. The taxpayer or his representative can discuss notices of tax due with the IRS collection personnel to get errors corrected and, in legitimate hardship situations, to arrange for payment terms or even some compromise of the amount due. The IRS employs awesome power to seize property and collect taxes. Taxpayers who do not take that power seriously can be seriously damaged.

Refund Procedures. A taxpayer who has filed a tax return normally has three years from the due date of the return or the date filed, whichever is later, to file a claim for refund of the tax involved in that return. As with a return, a refund claim may be prepared by the taxpayer alone or with the assistance of a professional. After the taxpayer has paid a deficiency, a refund claim for the amount paid can be filed during the two years following the date of payment. The IRS typically either honors the claim or audits it.

When a revenue agent contacts the taxpayer in connection with a refund claim, the procedure is somewhat similar to the audit of a tax return. This audit focuses mainly on the refund claim, but agents may also find other issues to offset the amount claimed as a refund and may even discover additional tax due. Because of this risk, taxpayers generally seek professional assistance with refund claims. If the claim is disallowed, the taxpayer can bring a refund suit in either a district court or the Court of Claims.

As noted above, a taxpayer who has agreed to a deficiency by signing Form 870 may still bring suit to recover the tax paid. Thus, an action in a district court or the Court of Claims after denial of a refund claim is an alternative route to the Tax Court in the examination and settlement process.

Interest and Penalties. Taxpayers pay interest on tax deficiencies from the due date of the return to the date of payment. Various additions to the tax, usually called penalties, may be imposed for late filing of a return, failure to pay tax due, or underpayment of estimated tax. Interest is deductible, but penalties are not. Penalties for late filing may be avoided by obtaining permission to file at a later date, but interest still is charged on the unpaid balance.

If any part of a deficiency is attributable to negligence or intentional disregard of tax rules by the taxpayer, there can be a penalty of 5% of the entire deficiency. (See Regulations for Preparers and Representatives for a discussion of penalties for negligence on the part of tax return preparers.) If any part of a deficiency is attributable to fraud, there can be a civil penalty of 50% of the total deficiency. Criminal fraud penalties may be imposed as well.

Pronouncements of the Treasury and IRS

Treasury Regulations. Treasury regulations are issued only after they have been published in the *Federal Register* as proposed regulations and taxpayers have been given an opportunity to comment in writing. In many instances a public hearing is also held. There are no fixed rules on when the Treasury Department will issue regulations or even propose them. In fact, regulations have not yet been proposed for several tax provisions enacted years ago. Without regulations it may be difficult for taxpayers to apply the tax statute to a specific situation, and in these cases the advice of a skilled tax practitioner is especially important.

Some laws contain a provision directing the Treasury Department to establish rules. For example, the law that authorizes the last-in, first-out (LIFO) method of inventory valuation contains such a provision, and so does the law permitting the filing of a consolidated return. Such Treasury regulations are called *legislative regulations* and may have more authority than others.

Revenue Procedures. Revenue procedures are issued by the IRS and describe various procedures and practices. They set out guidelines on a wide range of matters, such as depreciation, leases, corporate reorganization, change of accounting, and the use of magnetic tape. They are important in dealing with the IRS. For example, if a revenue procedure requires certain information for a private ruling on a corporate reorganization, then the information must be supplied or the ruling will not be issued.

Private Rulings. Taxpayers proposing to engage in transactions that are significant to them can apply for, and frequently receive, private rulings from the IRS national office on the tax treatment that will be given the transaction. In some cases a ruling is actually required, as when a company changes its accounting method or period, undertakes certain transactions with foreign corporations, or changes from consolidated returns to separate returns.

Ruling requests may be submitted by the taxpayer or by a duly appointed representative. Accounting firms often handle such requests for clients. Many larger firms maintain an office in Washington, D.C. and process requests not only for their own clients but also on behalf of other firms' clients. If a conference with IRS personnel is necessary, the accountant representing the taxpayer can appear and argue every aspect of the case. A ruling request will not be considered by IRS unless considerable information is supplied, including the names of the taxpayers and all other interested parties, details of the transaction, and copies of contracts, if any. Financial information also may be appropriate. The written statement advocating the position that the taxpayer would like the IRS to take should be supported by references to cases and rulings.

Private rulings are not binding on the IRS in a formal sense, but accepted practice for many years has given them a high degree of certainty for the taxpayers to whom they are issued. In fact, a ruling is the closest thing to insurance a taxpayer can obtain. In complex transactions involving substantial sums and tax consequences, a ruling may be a "must" before taxpayers proceed. However, taxpayers cannot rely on a ruling issued to others.

Technical Advice. The IRS national office provides a *technical advice* process, similar to the rulings process, in connection with audits of tax returns. When an issue raised by an audit cannot be resolved, and the taxpayer or the revenue agent feels that an opinion from the IRS national office is warranted, either party may request that the issue be submitted to the national office for technical advice. The taxpayer cannot veto a request for technical advice made by the revenue agent, but the revenue agent can deny the taxpayer's request. The taxpayer can, however, appeal this denial.

Private rulings and technical advice are released to the public by the IRS after deletion of identifying data. Since private rulings are issued without any high-level review in the IRS, it can be dangerous to rely on them as a definitive statement of IRS policy. They can, however, be helpful in considering the consequences of a transaction.

Published Rulings. Every year, the IRS formally publishes hundreds of rulings known as *revenue rulings* for the guidance of IRS personnel and taxpayers. Revenue rulings are frequently based on private rulings and technical advice, but are considerably reviewed and rewritten before publication. Although they may be viewed as merely the opinion of one party (the IRS) to a tax controversy, a taxpayer or preparer who takes a position contrary to an applicable ruling must have some support for his position or risk a penalty. Citing an applicable ruling in support of a position, on the other hand, will usually dispose of any IRS challenge.

PROFESSIONAL TAX PRACTICE

Tax Practitioners

Law Firms. Some large law firms provide a wide range of legal services, including those of a sizable tax department; some small firms express no knowledge of or interest in tax practice. There are also firms of various sizes that do practically nothing but tax work. Law firms tend to be less involved with compliance work than accounting firms, but many law firms do prepare numerous individual, partnership, fiduciary, and small corporation returns, commonly using accountants or paralegal personnel to handle most of the work involved.

Law firms compete directly with many accounting firms in tax planning and in handling tax controversies, including revenue agent examinations and, more frequently, conferences at the appeals-office level. But whether or not they represent clients at the administrative levels, lawyers in tax practice do handle tax litigation in the Tax Court, the Court of Claims, the district courts, courts of appeals, and the Supreme Court; accountants, on the other hand, unless qualified to represent taxpayers in Tax Court, would not be involved with litigation at the judicial level except as they might assist the lawyers.

Return Preparers. As returns have become more complicated, more and more taxpayers have turned to preparers. Returns are prepared by a wide range of people, including professionally qualified CPAs, people licensed by the states as public accountants, former IRS employees, and employees of commercial tax return preparation organizations. Banks, insurance companies, and brokerage houses also prepare returns, sometimes using their own personnel and sometimes in association with a commercial preparer. Commercial tax return preparation organizations usually do only individual returns.

Some of these return preparers can come to the taxpayer's aid when the IRS examines a return they have prepared, while others can do very little. Commercial return preparers may accompany the taxpayer on his visit to the IRS and explain items in the return, but they are rarely well equipped—and frequently not permitted under IRS rules—to argue the taxpayer's case on his behalf before the IRS agent. They can never represent the taxpayer above the agent level. CPAs, former IRS employees, and practitioners who have passed a special examination enrolling them to practice before the IRS can represent a taxpayer at all levels within the IRS. Many of them can also offer tax planning services.

The IRS does not regulate the preparation of tax returns. Rather, it regulates the conduct of all tax return preparers. This is not a play on words, since anybody is free to prepare any federal tax return for a fee. However, preparers must comply with several rules. (See generally IRC Secs. 6694, 6695, and 7701(a)(36) and related regulations.) Some of these govern mechanical matters; for example, the client must be given a copy of the return before he signs the original. Other rules impose a penalty on the preparer whose negligence in preparing a return results in an understatement of tax liability. The IRS can obtain injunctions against further tax return preparation practice if a preparer is guilty of negligent preparation, misrepresentation of experience or education, or guaranteeing refunds to taxpayers (IRC Sec. 7407). These rules and penalties are described in detail under Regulations for Preparers and Representatives.

At least two states, California and Oregon, license preparers who are not CPAs, attorneys, or persons enrolled to practice before the IRS. The purpose of this licensing is to provide an additional level of professional and financial responsibility, not to establish technical qualifications for the persons licensed.

Accounting Firms. A limited number of smaller accounting firms specialize in tax practice. They offer tax planning advice and represent taxpayers in tax disputes through the level of the Tax Court. In most smaller firms, however, tax practice is handled by each person along with all the other services provided by the firm. Everyone is more or less a jack-of-all-trades.

As firms grow, they tend to departmentalize. A tax department is usually the first to be set apart. Before long the senior tax people have developed their own relationships with clients, and the tax department has begun to operate somewhat autonomously, though in close cooperation with the audit people. This is as much a reflection of the growing complexity of professional practice as it is of the firm's size or the number of its offices. The range and level of knowledge required for competence in any one of the disciplines that make up the practice of an accounting firm today are such that it is a rare audit partner who feels comfortable in dealing with the specifics of a complex tax problem.

With the establishment of a separate tax department, the need for coordination of tax work with accounting and auditing services becomes apparent. Customarily, the staff people who are rendering accounting and auditing services to the client prepare the client's tax returns, and the tax department reviews them. The tax department also handles questions raised by the accounting and auditing people, and it takes the initiative in pointing out, both to the auditors and the client, any tax planning opportunities that may advance the client's interests. The tax provision and liability disclosed in the financial statements are reviewed by both audit and tax people. (The relationship between audit and tax functions is described in detail under Relationships With the CPA's Audit Function.)

Tax Engagements

Advocacy in Tax Practice. When a tax practitioner requests a private ruling on behalf of a taxpayer, he not only presents the facts and reasons for granting a ruling, but presents them in such a way that a favorable ruling is suggested. The practitioner is not an impartial observer but an advocate for the taxpayer's cause.

Similarly, a tax return should present the results of a taxpayer's affairs in the light most favorable to the taxpayer. The preparation of a return can be viewed as the first step toward a dispute that could go to the courts. A dispute actually begins, of course, when the revenue agent raises issues or suggests deficiencies. Then the practitioner who prepared the return customarily handles the examination of it by the IRS. (To do this, he must be authorized in writing to represent the taxpayer.)

Initially, the practitioner may only explain how figures were combined or reclassified for the return. But when he starts to explain why the figures were treated as they have been, argues the taxpayer's cause with the agent, and continues with the protest to the IRS appeals office, he is forthrightly advocating his client's cause. Depending on his capabilities and established scope of practice, he may go on to docket cases before the Tax Court, negotiate settlements in such cases, and even try cases before that court.

Though acting as an advocate throughout the engagement, the CPA in tax practice is nevertheless an objective professional. That is, he does not substitute the client's judgment of what is proper for his own. He will assist the client in taking a position, and will advance an argument on behalf of the client, only if there is *reasonable support* for it. Reasonable support can be found in relevant case law, in the published writings of recognized tax authorities, in informed concurring opinion of legal counsel, and (for partners of larger accounting firms) in the concurring opinion of another tax partner. Professional practice does not countenance lying or misrepresentation, but neither does it require the CPA to volunteer information detrimental to his client or to point out the weaknesses of his client's position. The client's value system must be given consideration. The CPA must ensure that the client understands the positions taken on his behalf and the available alternative positions, as well as their possible consequences, and fully acquiesces in what is being done.

The AICPA's Statements on Responsibilities in Tax Practice, discussed later in this chapter, provide guidance in this area.

Tax Planning. Sometimes tax planning takes the form of an answer to a question raised by the taxpayer: the taxpayer first identifies his problem and then asks a question. Sometimes the tax practitioner takes the initiative, suggesting tax-saving possibilities based on his knowledge of the client's affairs. Sometimes the taxpayer's question leads to an initiative action on the part of the practitioner. For example, a question about a specific charitable contribution and the limits on deduction may simply be answered yes or no, but discussion of related aspects may trigger the practitioner to review the feasibility of a foundation to be used by the corporation and to study the estate plans of its principal shareholders.

In tax planning, the practitioner frequently answers inquiries about the tax consequences of a proposed transaction, and even about how to structure a transaction so as to solve not only the client's tax problem but that of the other party as well. Tax planning includes research to support recommendations. In many instances it is desirable (and sometimes necessary) to obtain advance assurance in the form of a ruling from the IRS that the desired tax consequences will be achieved. CPAs can and do represent clients in obtaining such rulings from the IRS.

Tax planning also includes writing letters to clients explaining new tax legislation, directing attention to specific administrative rulings or court decisions, or suggesting an innovative tax interpretation. There may also be oral presentations to groups at client meetings, or seminars to which many clients are invited.

Tax Returns. Accounting firms prepare tax returns for corporations, partnerships, and individuals, often as a service incidental to other engagements, such as the annual audit, the review of unaudited financial statements, or a compilation (write-up) of financial statements. The preparation of a business tax return requires access to detailed information, and because this is facilitated by a thorough understanding of the client's business, the preparation is often done by the auditors. If they and the tax people work together on the planning of the audit or other engagement, tax people are available to answer questions that arise during the engagement, not just when the return is prepared. The auditor-prepared return can then be reviewed by qualified tax people familiar with the client's situation.

The accounting firm typically prepares the tax returns of smaller clients, but larger clients often maintain tax departments of their own, thus reducing the firm's involvement in return preparation and other compliance work. For such clients, the firm is used primarily in tax planning. It may also be asked to review the client's tax department for efficiency of organization and effectiveness in handling the company's tax affairs.

When the firm prepares tax returns for an individual, this quite often involves returns such as trust returns, partnership returns for investment activities, and returns for other members of the individual's family.

Accounting firms prepare returns not only for people associated with business clients, such as owners, executives, and other key personnel, but also for individuals in the community who have no other client relationship with the firm. Corporate executives, lawyers, bankers, doctors, brokers, other professionals, and government officials all need professional tax service. By serving them well, the firm hopes to be kept in mind when these individuals become aware of others, whether businesses or individuals, who need the professional services of a CPA firm.

Tax return engagements do not require an audit of the information furnished by the client, but they do require sufficient contact with the taxpayer to satisfy the preparer that the return will be prepared in accordance with the tax law. For example, a CPA preparing a return does not have to see receipts of canceled checks for charitable contributions, but he should believe, either from his knowledge of the taxpayer or by asking him, that the amounts can be substantiated if the IRS challenges the return. Nor does the CPA have to ascertain that each donee is qualified for deductible contributions, but if an organization's name indicates it might not be qualified, he should verify its status. Other aspects of the need to consider the reasonableness of the return data are discussed under Qualitative Penalties.

Tax Fraud. A CPA should not help a taxpayer defend a charge of criminal tax fraud except under the direction of an attorney. It is not uncommon for an attorney who is defending a taxpayer on tax fraud charges to engage a CPA to assist in the development of information necessary to the defense. Even if the fraud charge itself cannot be refuted, the CPA can help in the defense of issues that are not related to the fraud, since the 50% civil fraud penalty would apply to the entire deficiency. (Note that a criminal fraud case is normally disposed of before a civil fraud matter proceeds.)

In the process of a tax return examination, the revenue agent may introduce another IRS representative as a special agent from the Criminal Investigation Division. At this point the CPA should stop work in connection with the examination of the return, advise the client to obtain legal counsel, and then proceed only with the authorization or at the direction of legal counsel. The problem, in part, is that information learned by the CPA is not privileged. Thus, unless he is acting on behalf of counsel, his involvement may well result in his having to give evidence against the taxpayer that otherwise might not be obtainable by the IRS.

Also, the experience of the CPA, even one who devotes all his time to tax matters for business clients, may not be helpful in a criminal fraud situation. In a typical tax examination, the aim is to determine the tax liability. From the viewpoint of the CPA and the client, the less tax the better, allowing for recognition of the need to compromise and settle issues. In a fraud examination, on the other hand, the IRS's first goal is to determine whether or not to prosecute the taxpayer criminally. Only after this has been resolved will the IRS turn its attention to the amount of tax due. The attitudes of the parties in a criminal tax investigation are totally different, and the adversary atmosphere is very clearly present. The leadership and advice of an attorney is necessary if the taxpayer is to have the benefits of the rights available under the Constitution.

It must be emphasized that the instigation of a criminal investigation does not mean that the taxpayer is guilty. Of the many criminal investigations begun, only a small fraction actually proceed to indictment, trial, and conviction. Nevertheless, the risks for the taxpayer (and his advisers) are far too heavy to permit using any but the most skilled and knowledgeable practitioners in this uncertain area.

Some accounting firms regularly work under the direction of an attorney in criminal tax fraud matters and render outstanding service in that capacity. These firms usually have continuing relationships with attorneys who specialize in criminal tax fraud, and have the attorney rather than the taxpayer as client. Other firms will not accept tax fraud engagements except when the taxpayer being investigated is already a client of the firm. Under the best of circumstances, a tax fraud investigation is a difficult assignment that occupies a disproportionate amount of partners' and managers' time, including possible courtroom appearances.

Tax Research Materials. In comparison to other fields of accounting practice, research on tax matters is relatively easy. In addition to the Commerce Clearing House, Prentice-Hall, and RIA loose-leaf tax services, there is a large body of published material that is well organized and easily accessible to all practitioners. Selected items are listed in the Suggested Reading at the end of this chapter.

Client Relationships

Investigation of Clients. Typically, an accounting firm will receive requests for services, particularly the preparation of individual returns, from many people. It is thus necessary to decide whether to accept each opportunity presented. The problem is not much different from deciding whether to accept an audit engagement, although fees and available personnel are less likely to be a problem with a tax return than an audit. If these considerations are no obstacle, the firm must decide whether it wants the new client.

There is no requirement that a firm must provide services to anyone with whom it does not want to be associated. Accepting a disreputable person as a tax client can cause image problems, fee problems, and even problems in the relationship between the firm and the IRS. Thus, every prospective tax client should be investigated to ascertain that the firm will feel comfortable with him. Most firms do not want as clients people who have criminal records or engage in unethical business or financial operations. To some extent, a client may be evaluated on the basis of his professional advisers, and thus may seek to be associated with a reputable accounting firm. By the same token, the firm can be evaluated on the basis of its clients. It should not lend its name or reputation for a fee to those who do not warrant it.

Engagement Letters. Engagement letters or memoranda are used to ensure a meeting of the minds on what services the firm will render, how it will charge for these services, when bills for these services will be paid, and any other matters that have been or should be agreed on between the client and the firm. They should be worded with some care. For example, it might not be advisable to undertake to "prepare all required tax returns" for a multistate business when, in fact, what is intended is the preparation of only the federal income tax returns and certain state returns. The returns for other states may be prepared by the client's personnel or may not be prepared at all because the client believes it is not taxable there.

Fee Policies. Engagement letters should also be cautious when discussing fees. When tax work is intended to produce beneficial results that can be measured, the fee arrangement should normally be described in such a way that the minimum charge will be time at standard billing rates, with the door open for additional amounts to be charged on the achievement of certain results.

The accounting and auditing services of CPAs may not be offered on the basis of a fee that is contingent on the results of the services, but in tax work this type of fee is permissible if based on the results of court action or the findings of government agencies. Thus, in an engagement to represent the taxpayer in a specific tax controversy, it would be proper either to make the amount of the fee entirely dependent on the results or to base the fee on time but also make provision for an additional amount to be paid when results beyond a certain minimum are achieved. The Professional Ethics Division of the AICPA has held, however, that basing a fee for *preparing* a tax return on the amount saved in taxes would violate the rules against contingent fees (ET 391.023-.024). If this were viewed as guaranteeing the client a refund, the IRS could use it as grounds for enjoining a preparer from engaging in the preparation of tax returns.

Legal Liability. The accountant may be liable to his client for negligent tax work. As is true of the dollars-and-cents value of good results, the dollars-and-cents cost of negligent work can very easily be demonstrated. The liability to the client will normally be the amount of loss actually sustained by the client, which may include an allowance both for interest and for the fees and expenses of other professionals incurred as a result of the accountant's negligence.

Contested services. It may be instructive to describe some situations in which an accountant's negligence in tax services could result in a loss to the taxpayer. Many taxpayers are required to make payments of estimated taxes and are subject to penalties if these payments are not made in accordance with the law. The taxpayer may allege that the accountant was instructed to prepare a "safe" estimate, but the IRS may feel that not enough was paid and assess a penalty. Then the taxpayer would expect the accountant to reimburse him for the penalty.

It is unlikely that an accountant will be held liable for suggesting a course of action to a client if the risks as well as the benefits of that course of action, and the available alternative approaches, have been explained to the client and the client acquiesces in the position taken. On the other hand, suppose an accountant incorrectly advises a client that the sale of stock of one of his controlled corporations to another of his controlled corporations will produce capital gain results. Upon examination of the return, IRS treats the transaction as a dividend to be taxed as ordinary income. In this case the accountant may be liable to the taxpayer both for the difference in tax and for the related expenses incurred.

The CPA's exposure. Compared to that in audit work, the CPA's liability exposure in tax work is almost nominal. Meticulous attention to the details of tax return preparation and filing will normally eliminate most, if not all, of the mistakes that can result in small amounts being owed the client by the accountant. However, even these small amounts can damage the accountant's credibility and affect his reputation with that client and possibly in the business community at large. The best method of controlling liabilities resulting from tax practice may be to routinely evaluate the risk to the client of wrong advice and, when that risk is large, to double-check the conclusions reached.

It goes without saying that whether or not the accountant will be found liable for the taxpayer's deficiency or penalty, he will first make every effort to reduce if not eliminate the amount involved. For example, there are a number of ways to calculate estimated tax payments, and one of the exceptions may apply. The dividend issue might be attacked from several angles. Perhaps it can be demonstrated that the requisite control was not present, or perhaps the corporation's earnings and profits should be recalculated to make certain there are sufficient earnings to support the dividend treatment. In short, the presumption that IRS findings are correct is by no means conclusive. Frequently, they can be rebutted with careful work. Of course, it is always better to make these efforts when the service is first provided to the taxpayer, not later when the IRS mounts its attack.

Third parties. Except for the preparer penalties discussed in the following section, the accountant has no liability to the IRS or to third parties who are not affected by the return for negligence in preparation of the return. However, third parties who *are* affected by a return can claim that the accountant is liable to them. Such parties would include stockholders of certain corporations, partners in partnerships, and beneficiaries of trusts or estates, among others.

Liability to third parties may also be alleged where no return is prepared. For example, suppose the accountant gives a categorical opinion on the tax consequences of a proposed tax shelter, the opinion is made available to prospective investors, and the described tax results are not achieved. The investors, whether they are the accountant's clients or not, may seek restitution. In some instances, the SEC or a state regulatory authority may consider action against the accountant, either because of the tax opinion itself or because of an alleged failure to comment on the uncertainty of the tax problems when giving an opinion on the financial statements of the shelter. As with other possible liability matters, the best defense is careful work before a position is recommended or an opinion given.

Relationships With the IRS

Regulations for Preparers and Representatives. In general, income tax return preparers are persons who prepare returns for a fee or who hire persons to prepare returns for others. The term *preparer* includes not only the person who signs the return, but also anyone who prepares a substantial part of it or decides how it is to be prepared. Further, the preparer of a Subchapter S return or a partnership return can be deemed also responsible for certain items in a stockholder's or partner's return.

Penalties for rule infractions. Penalties are imposed on preparers and their employers for a variety of acts or failures to act. The penalties vary in amount, depending on the offense. For example, the failure to give a taxpayer a copy of the return brings a $25 penalty, and so does the failure to sign a return or include the preparer's social security number. These penalties are largely mechanical in operation and application. The IRS probably recognizes that an occasional omission of a social security number or an inadvertent failure to give a taxpayer a copy of his tax return is not an act requiring a penalty.

Qualitative penalties. There are also penalties relevant to the quality of the prepared return. A penalty of $100 is imposed if any part of an understatement of liability in a return is due to the preparer's negligent or intentional disregard of rules and regulations. If there is a willful attempt to understate the tax, the penalty is $500.

These penalties mean that the return preparer is responsible for the *reasonableness* of tax information. Although a preparer may, as noted above, rely on information furnished by the taxpayer, he may not, as the regulations put it, "ignore the implications of information furnished." In other words, the preparer is expected to make reasonable inquiries if the information furnished appears to be incorrect or incomplete. He may also be required to make inquiries of the taxpayer to determine the existence of facts and circumstances that may be necessary for the claiming of deductions.

The regulations illustrate the need for inquiry with an example of a tax return preparer who used the amounts of medical expense and travel and entertainment expenses furnished by a taxpayer. Though the taxpayer had, in fact, paid smaller amounts, the preparer calculated the deductions using the information supplied, which resulted in an understatement of liability. The preparer had no reason to believe that the information given was incorrect or incomplete. He asked for no documentation of medical expenses, but did inquire about the records to support the travel and entertainment expenses. The representations made to him by the taxpayer were satisfactory. In this example, the IRS concluded that the understatement of liability was not due to the preparer's willful attempt to understate liability and, accordingly, that no penalty applied.

In any situation where the examination of a return results in the assessment of a deficiency, it is likely that the examining agent will consider whether or not the understatement of liability was due either to the preparer's negligence or to willful intent. If a penalty is imposed, appeal rights within the IRS are limited. The preparer who wants to challenge the penalty first has to pay it and then bring a refund action in district court. Unfortunately, this guarantees a maximum amount of damaging publicity.

The $100 and $500 penalties are not the IRS's sole weapons; it also has the right to go to court to obtain an injunction against specific actions, including the preparation of tax returns. The best defense against assertion of penalties is to document the support for a position taken in a return, particularly when the position is one that may be contrary to rules or regulations.

Circular No. 230. A substantial part of a CPA's tax practice is the representation of taxpayers before taxation authorities. The rules governing this service are set forth in the Treasury Department's *Circular No. 230 Revised, Regulations Governing the Practice of Attorneys, Certified Public Accountants, and Enrolled Agents before the Internal Revenue Service* (1979). Except for the preparation of returns, this circular covers just about all activities connected with any presentation to the IRS on behalf of a client and its tax affairs.

If a charge is made that a practitioner has behaved improperly, there are appeal procedures. The bulk of the actions to reprimand, suspend, or permanently disbar practitioners tend to be connected with complicity in tax fraud or the practitioner's failure to file his own returns or pay his own tax.

Working Paper Availability. The *Internal Revenue Manual* is the official compilation of policies, procedures, instructions, and guidelines followed by the IRS in its audit functions. It provides that in the examination of a return, an agent may have access to audit working papers of the independent accountant. The manual states (IRM Sec. 4024.2(1), June 11, 1979):

> Examiners will not request access to such work papers as a matter of standard examining procedure in every case. The access sought should be only to the portion of the work papers *believed to be material and relevant to the examination* [emphasis added]. In determining materiality and relevance in this context, the examiner should keep in mind that the taxpayer's records are the primary source of information and the accountant's work papers should be used as a collateral source, access to which should be requested with discretion.

Cooperation by the CPA. It is normal for the practitioner to make available to the revenue agent any and all working papers that deal with the compilation of data entered on the return. This would include schedules showing the reclassification and combination of trial balance items to fit the tax return categories, as well as detailed schedules dealing with such matters as property, plant, and equipment, depreciation, and investment credit calculations. Many firms separate those tax files that contain working papers of this sort, which can then readily be made available to revenue agents, from those that contain papers and internal memoranda in which the pros and cons of various positions are discussed, which are to be withheld.

Contested availability. It is not uncommon for revenue agents making a routine audit to request access to working papers that the practitioner is unwilling to make available. Some of these papers may be so essential to the audit planning process that the accountant would not be willing to make them available even to the client. In this case, he should be firm in refusing to make them available to the revenue agent as well.

Other papers might not be so critical, but could direct the revenue agent's attention to approaches, theories, or transactions that he otherwise might not investigate. Normally, the accountant would also resist making these working papers available, although some degree of judgment may be required here. With the concurrence of the client, for example, the accountant may occasionally take a calculated risk. He may make such papers available in order to get the tax audit completed expeditiously. This may be especially worth the risk when the papers seem unlikely to lead the agent down undesirable trails.

Refusal of access. But when there is little to gain and much to lose by releasing these papers, and particularly if they contain speculation and unsupported views on tax consequences, the accountant and client may refuse to turn them over. At this point, the revenue agent has the recourse of proposing a deficiency in certain items. This challenge will, of course, involve material that has already come to his attention, but it may also net some of the material discussed in the papers denied him.

The agent can also serve a summons on the accountant for the papers. He will probably resort to a summons only when there is some suspicion of fraud. That is not invariably the case, however, and agents do serve summonses to obtain working papers in connection with routine audits. When served with a summons, the accountant should, of course, consult his own legal counsel. The taxpayer must be notified by the IRS that a summons is being served on the accountant, and must be given an opportunity to intervene. Whether or not the taxpayer intervenes, the accountant, guided by his own legal counsel, will take steps to protect his position.

Let us assume that the accountant, after discussion with his client and with counsel, concludes that the papers sought are not relevant to the IRS inquiry and refuses to comply with the summons. In that circumstance, the IRS may take the accountant to court to enforce the summons. If a criminal fraud investigation is involved, the accountant is likely to find that the IRS will ultimately get access to the working papers. Even if the IRS believes the documents are only relevant to its inquiry into the liability for tax, it may still go to court to enforce the summons.

Court challenges. The IRS attitude is that if a document "may be relevant," it should be subject to the summons authority granted by the Internal Revenue Code. There are limitations to this authority, and in addition to the need for relevance, the IRS does acknowledge the requirements established by the Supreme Court (*U.S. v. Powell,* 64-2 USTC 9858 (Sup. Ct.)):

1. There must be a legitimate purpose for the inquiry,
2. The information sought must not be in the possession of the IRS already, and
3. The IRS must follow its prescribed administrative rules.

In at least one case, *U.S. v. Coopers and Lybrand* (77-1 USTC 9216 (10 Cir.)), the courts have refused to enforce an administrative summons, but the IRS takes the position that the case is wrong as a matter of law. In the *Coopers* case, the papers sought by the IRS were described as the tax pool analysis, and probably included an analysis of the tax provision and accrual of liabilities. The Tenth Circuit Court was impressed by the fact that the papers had not been used in preparing the taxpayer's return. Also, the analysis was not a record of any actual transactions. Finally, the taxpayer, not the accountant, had prepared the return. In a similar case where the CPA *had* prepared the return, however, the bankruptcy court ordered production of various memoranda prepared by the company's outside auditors (*In re Co-Build Companies, Inc.* 77-2 USTC 9735).

However, the official IRS position as set forth in its manual is that IRS authority to issue a summons to obtain access to working papers is not affected in any way by the fact that the accountant whose papers are sought did not prepare the return. Hence, the IRS believes that the *Coopers* decision is wrong, a belief that had some measure of support from a decision in the Second Circuit Court. In *Noall* (78-2 USTC 9822 (2 Cir.)), that court held that internal audit reports, also not used in the preparation of returns, should be made available to IRS through an administrative summons, since the papers could be relevant. Further, although this was not necessary to reach its conclusions, the Second Circuit Court specifically stated that it disagreed with the reasoning in the *Coopers* case—i.e., permitting working papers to escape administrative summons because they were not used for the preparation of a return.

The Second Circuit Court believes that the IRS has very broad powers. In another recent case, *U.S. v. Arthur Andersen* (79-1 USTC 9249 (2 Cir.)), a summons was served seeking the release of three sections of a two-page document concerning a corporation of which the taxpayer was president and principal shareholder. The accounting firm resisted turning over portions of the document that pertained solely to the corporation, but the court saw no reason to deny the IRS the opportunity to see the entire document, since even though the material was primarily concerned with the corporation, it might possibly throw light on the tax liability of the taxpayer.

An interesting policy argument was raised in the *Coopers* case, but not considered fully there because the court was able to base its conclusions on the irrelevance of the documents. The argument is that the relationship between the independent CPA and the client makes it necessary for taxpayers to be completely open with their auditors, and that such openness may be impossible if information given to auditors may then become subject to IRS summons. There is, however, no federal law recognizing privileged communication between CPA and client, and even if there were, it is understood that the IRS would seriously question its application to accountants' working papers developed for purposes of reaching an opinion on information to be included in a published financial statement. The IRS has successfully argued that since these statements are intended for third-party use, any privilege that might otherwise attach should be considered waived (*U.S. v. Arthur Andersen & Co.,* 80-2 USTC 9515 (CA-1)).

It would be foolish optimism to assume that the IRS will not use its summons power whenever it thinks this necessary to accomplish its goals. Both the IRS and the taxpayer use all the weapons at their disposal, including not only the summons but also the right to resist compliance with the summons. However, the tax practitioner should not act in this area without advice of his own counsel.

Relationships With the CPA's Audit Function

Preparation of Returns. Most CPA firms prepare more individual returns than business returns. Since most individual taxpayers file their returns on the basis of the calendar year, this preparation is concentrated in the early months of the year, and even with extensions and the use of computers, this concentration presents a scheduling problem. Thus, although individual returns are usually prepared in the tax department, audit personnel may assist the tax personnel, and the firm may also use paraprofessionals.

Business returns, i.e., returns for corporations or partnerships, are fewer in number, but are more likely to present complex preparation problems. Much of the audit work done in connection with financial statements is closely related to the work necessary for preparing business tax returns, so audit personnel generally play a large role in the preparation of these returns. If time schedules permit, it is usually more efficient for the business return to be prepared at the time of the audit than at a later date. Simpler returns may be handled entirely by audit personnel, with specific questions or problems referred to the tax department. A final review of such a return could be done by an audit manager or the audit partner in charge of the engagement, who is familiar with the client. Even with simple returns, however, it is probably wise to have a tax person review the return.

Complex returns may be prepared by audit people and thoroughly reviewed by tax people. Even when tax people prepare the returns, some assistance from the auditors is usually necessary. Clients with their own tax departments will prepare their own returns, but may ask the CPA firm's tax people to review them. (Tax provision review is discussed under Tax Provision and Accrual Review.)

Tax return preparers must sign the returns. In the typical accounting firm, several people are involved in the preparation of the return, but only one signs it. For many years, before the adoption of stricter tax return preparer rules, it was not unusual for auditors to sign tax returns. Now the regulations clearly state that when more than one person prepares a return, it should be signed by the one who has the ultimate responsibility for its accuracy. This probably results in more returns being signed by tax partners and managers.

Finding Tax Problems. A tax problem can be a tax opportunity in disguise. In reviewing the details of a client's operations, an auditor can discover problems in completed and contemplated transactions that will have tax implications. He should therefore be familiar enough with tax matters to recognize these problems, even though his knowledge may be insufficient to solve them.

Many firms assign a tax person to each client to work with the audit people as the audit is being planned, answering questions, solving problems, and identifying opportunities for service. This tax person is also responsible for reviewing the tax provision, tax liability, and tax return.

Accounting and Auditing Problems. Conversely, a review of a company's affairs from a tax point of view frequently raises accounting questions. For example, a company may be assuming that the change in financial accounting it is contemplating will be used for tax accounting as well. The tax person reviewing the change, however, will consider whether it requires special permission, and even whether it is advantageous for tax purposes at all. A change in the accounting period may result in a net operating loss carryover, and this consequence, overlooked at first, will involve an unexpected cost affecting the financial statements. The tax person's review may also uncover situations with audit implications, such as payments made but not deductible for tax purposes, that the auditor must consider.

Recommendations made to the company for tax planning may also have accounting or auditing implications. For example, a recommendation that the company adopt the LIFO method of inventory valuation has significant accounting implications (which will be discussed later in this chapter). Other changes that could produce tax savings may depend on using a different accounting method from that used for financial reporting purposes, and this in turn may require a calculation of deferred taxes. Again, when a company acquires another business, it is most important that both the tax people and the auditors consider the differences between the tax rules governing tax-free acquisitions and the accounting rules governing the treatment of a transaction as a purchase or pooling. An aggressive position taken in a tax return provides yet another example. Tax personnel and auditors must consider such an action within the framework both of the tax rules and of the accounting rules governing the treatment of a contingency, as set forth in SFAS 5 (AC 4311).

Tax Provision and Accrual Review. The government is a significant partner in business operations. The calculation of its share, taking into account timing adjustments as required by APB 11 (AC 4091), has a substantial impact on the financial statements. This calculation, whether done by the company or by the auditors, should be reviewed by the tax people from at least two points of view.

First, the potential for tax controversy must be assessed, with regard both to the year being reviewed and to any prior years that are open under the statute of limitations, even if the returns are not being examined by the IRS. Exposure to tax deficiencies may range from "probable" to "remote." Based on the auditor's findings as to the facts of transactions, tax people can consider the issues that may be raised and the likely outcome if they are. The proper application of SFAS 5 (AC 4311) to this evaluation of possible issues is done by auditors, but they need the assistance of tax people to understand the issues.

Second, the tax calculation must be reviewed for compliance with tax regulations. In an opinion on financial statements, the auditor may determine that the effect of an error is not material and therefore may not insist on its correction. In tax matters, however, immateriality is not grounds for treating an item of income or deduction in any manner other than that prescribed by law.

In addition to reviewing tax calculations, the tax department should examine financial statement footnotes that describe or explain the company's tax expense or liability. .

Some companies, particularly large corporations, have the opinion of their own counsel on their current tax issues. This is useful in reviewing the tax provision, but since the auditor must pass judgment on income tax questions, a legal opinion of company counsel does not relieve CPAs of the responsibility of reaching their own conclusions on the tax issues and their effect on the financial statements. In some instances, the auditor will consult his own counsel as to the merits of company counsel's position.

The involvement of the tax department does not mean that the audit partner has delegated his responsibility for the treatment of the tax accounts in the financial statements. The tax department's participation in the audit—to review the tax provision and related deferred charge or deferred credit accounts—provides the audit partner with the benefit of the tax department's expertise, but the audit partner still decides how the tax consequences of the year's events will be reflected in the financial statements.

AICPA PRONOUNCEMENTS AND OTHER GUIDES

In addition to the rules they must follow under the revised Circular 230 and the tax return preparer regulations, members of the AICPA are bound by their organization's Code of Professional Ethics. However, the AICPA does not extend to tax practice those rules that clearly apply only to the examination of financial statements. In tax practice, a member or associate must observe the same standards of truthfulness and integrity he is required to observe in any other professional work. This does not mean, however, that a member or associate may not resolve doubt in favor of his client, as long as there is reasonable support for his position (ET 102.01). This is consistent with the advocacy role of the CPA in tax practice.

Statements on Responsibilities in Tax Practice

The AICPA Federal Tax Division has issued eleven Statements on Responsibilities in Tax Practice, listed in Figure 43.2. The primary effect of these statements is educational.

The first substantive statement, issued in September 1964, dealt with the deceptively simple question of when a CPA is required to sign a return as its preparer (TX 111). It specified that "a CPA should sign as preparer any Federal tax return which requires the signature of a preparer if he prepares it for and transmits it to the taxpayer or another, whether or not the return was prepared for compensation" (TX 111.02). Twelve years later, Congress enacted a statute imposing a penalty on *any* preparer who prepared a return for compensation and failed to sign it as preparer.

Other statements have dealt with such matters as providing answers to questions on tax returns (TX 131), the use of estimates (TX 151), the actions to be taken when it appears that an error has been made in a prior year's return (TX 161), and what to do when an error is caught in an administrative proceeding such as the examination of a tax return (TX 171). Statements that contain standards of responsibility more restrictive than those established by the Treasury Department or by the AICPA's Code of Professional Ethics depend for their authority on the general acceptability of the opinions expressed.

Under Statement 9 (TX 191), the CPA is told that he may ordinarily rely on information furnished by the client, but does have an obligation to ask questions when the material furnished seems to be incorrect or incomplete. This statement also preceded the issuance of tax return preparer regulations imposing the same requirement.

The most recent statement, issued in 1977, deals with the question of disclosure in tax returns (TX 201). It states that a CPA can take positions that are contrary

No.	Title
—	*Introduction* (TX 101)
1	*Signature of Preparer* (TX 111)
2	*Signature of Reviewer: Assumption of Preparer's Responsibility* (TX 121)
3	*Answers to Questions on Returns* (TX 131)
4	*Recognition of Administrative Proceeding of a Prior Year* (TX 141)
5	*Use of Estimates* (TX 151)
6	*Knowledge of Error: Return Preparation* (TX 161)
7	*Knowledge of Error: Administrative Proceedings* (TX 171)
8	*Advice to Clients* (TX 181)
9	*Certain Procedural Aspects of Preparing Returns* (TX 191)
10	*Positions Contrary to Treasury Department or Internal Revenue Service Interpretations of the Code* (TX 201)

FIGURE 43.2   AICPA STATEMENTS ON RESPONSIBILITIES IN TAX PRACTICE

to Treasury or IRS interpretations of the law without making any disclosure of that fact. However, he must have reasonable support for the position he takes. If a position is taken that is clearly contrary to a specific section of the Internal Revenue Code (a highly unlikely event), then there must not only be reasonable support for the position, but there should be disclosure of the treatment given the item in the return.

Disclosure

Disclosure may be advisable even when a regulation or standard of practice does not require it. Sometimes disclosure of relevant information improves and protects the taxpayer's position. For example, if a taxpayer has omitted from gross income an amount that exceeds 25% of the gross income shown on the return, the statute of limitations for assessing additional tax is six years from the date of filing the return instead of the usual three years. However, if there is a statement in the return disclosing the amounts omitted, these amounts are not included in measuring the 25% omission.

It is reasonably clear that adequate disclosure generally will prevent the imposition of fraud penalties. While it is not so clear that disclosure will prevent the imposition of a negligence penalty, it could certainly be a factor in determining whether or not there were reasonable grounds for the position taken in the return.

Where disclosure seems appropriate, its nature will depend on the circumstances. It is not necessary to cite authorities for the position taken. In some cases, the very mechanics of reporting the transaction will constitute disclosure. On occasion a footnote may be necessary, but in other cases the identification of a line item in a tax return may be sufficient.

SOME PHILOSOPHICAL ISSUES

Conformity

Tax accounting's dependence on (not subservience to) financial accounting is a logical consequence of any tax based on or measured by income. Different tax accounting methods have been developed to meet special needs without seriously interfering with the improvement of financial accounting. While these different accounting methods usually result in a figure for taxable income that is lower than that for financial income, deferred tax accounting prevents this discrepancy from distorting the financial statements (see Chapter 25).

It has been suggested from time to time that the tax laws could be simplified, and their administration facilitated, if tax accounting were to conform to GAAP. For some years, in fact, the IRS has permitted a change in tax accounting only on the condition that the same change be reflected in the taxpayer's books and financial statements. This provides the IRS some additional procedures for deciding whether to allow the change. The determination that the new methods are acceptable for financial accounting purposes is based on an independent review, and apparently this simplifies the processing of requests by the IRS. Unfortunately, however, this approach discriminates in favor of companies that do not need the association of a CPA with their financial statements, because they usually can make any change in book accounting and financial reporting that would permit the use of a different (and more advantageous) tax method.

A policy of strict conformity as a condition for the use of a tax accounting method would inhibit improvements in financial reporting. As new tax concepts developed that offered more favorable treatment, there would probably be considerable pressure on the accounting profession to approve the new methods for financial statement purposes. This could hinder efforts toward sounder accounting and weaken the profession's ability to develop principles governing appropriate financial reporting.

LIFO

The problems that would be raised by enforced conformity are clearly illustrated by many companies' experience with the LIFO method of inventory valuation. This is probably the only situation in which the statute requires that the taxpayer using one accounting method for tax purposes may not use any other method to ascertain income "for the purpose of a report or statement . . . (1) to shareholders, partners, or other proprietors, or to beneficiaries, or (2) for credit purposes" (IRC Sec. 472(c)). Some obvious problems with respect to this sweeping requirement were resolved by regulations, but other perhaps not so obvious problems continued to arise. Until recently they caused considerable confusion and uncertainty about the right to use or continue to use the LIFO method.

For tax purposes, LIFO is strictly a cost method. (An accounting discussion of LIFO is contained in Chapter 19.) When this flow-of-cost assumption is used for tax purposes, inventories must be valued at cost only, not at the lower of cost or market. This is squarely in conflict with GAAP, which requires the use of the lower of cost or market. The conflict was resolved only by a clear statement in the income tax regulations that the use of market value instead of cost in a company's financial statements would not be considered a violation of the LIFO conformity requirement (Reg. Sec. 1.472-2(e)).

Less obvious problems came to light as the SEC, APB, and FASB issued pronouncements on particular accounting issues. To the extent that any of these pronouncements required that inventories be restated, or that the effect of accounting changes be described in detail, they created a conflict with the statutory requirement that no method other than LIFO be used in financial reporting. For example, the financial accounting for the purchase of a business requires that its assets be valued at the purchase price; but for tax purposes, such a purchase may qualify as a nontaxable exchange, in which event inventories may not be restated. If these inventories had been valued at LIFO, would the difference in values between the financial statements and the tax returns mean that the taxpayer had violated the conformity requirement? After much debate, IRS decided that it would not (Rev. Proc. 72-29).

For another example, a company that changes to LIFO must in the year of change indicate the effect on earnings. This disclosure of results under an accounting method other than LIFO may be a literal violation of the conformity requirement; but once again, the IRS agreed that since it was the result of accounting pronouncements, it would not be regarded as a violation that called for termination of the LIFO election (Rev. Proc. 76-3).

To appreciate the seriousness of these episodes, it is necessary to understand that the IRS did not promptly advise affected taxpayers of the consequences of the conformity requirement. On the contrary, it was with considerable reluctance and delay that the IRS agreed not to press the conformity requirement, provided the "violation" resulted from compliance with an official pronouncement of the SEC, FASB, APB, or some equivalent authority. And then this allowance was applied quite literally. Late in 1978, for example, the IRS announced that there would be a violation of the LIFO conformity requirement if a taxpayer that was not subject to SEC jurisdiction decided to disclose information on replacement cost of inventories, as the SEC requires in some circumstances (Rev. Proc. 78-39).

The LIFO conformity issue could have grave effects on a company. A violation of the rule could result in a substantial additional tax cost on the difference between LIFO and FIFO cost. While a company may not be permitted to explain specifically what its earnings would have been on FIFO, it is allowed to explain what its inventories would have been, and a reasonably knowledgeable reader of the financial statement could quickly calculate FIFO earnings. It is also interesting to note that the IRS, except for statements in rulings, does not seem inclined to take action to assess a deficiency because of a violation of the conformity rule.

As concern grew in recent years about paper profits in inventory, and more and more companies began to use LIFO, the straitjacket effect of the conformity rule became apparent. Finally, during the summer of 1979, the IRS issued regulations to permit the use of LIFO with an explanation in supplementary information of its effect on the financial statements (Prop. Reg. Sec. 1.472-2(e)). This was 25 years after the enactment of the 1954 Code. Any conformity rule for other tax provisions should not have to wait that long before it is made workable.

Scope of Services

As professionals in the determination of income, auditors have always been involved in income taxes. If they were not permitted to continue providing tax services to audit clients, business's cost of compliance would increase significantly. Someone else would have to again do the review and analysis of income that had already been performed by the accountant.

Independence. But when an accountant or a firm provides tax services for a client, is its independence impaired in auditing the same client? This question has been studied by Congress, AICPA committees, individual CPAs and CPA firms, the Commission on Auditors' Responsibilities, the AICPA's Public Oversight Board, and the SEC itself. Published articles on the subject are numerous.

The Commission on Auditors' Responsibilities (1978) and the Public Oversight Board (1979) both concluded that tax and audit services are compatible. A role as tax planner and adviser does not interfere with that of auditor in reviewing tax provisions and liabilities. It is also instructive to note that in all the years of the present income tax, going back to 1912 and the Sixteenth Amendment, and even to its predecessor, the 1909 Corporation Excise Tax Act, no cases have come to light in which an auditor's independence has been compromised because of his assisting a company in its tax affairs.

Perhaps the reason for this record is that the tax practitioner operates in a special technical and professional environment created by the IRS and the courts. In accounting and auditing, the regulatory environment created by the SEC and similar state agencies affects only a small number of companies, whereas the tax environment affects every company and individual. Even nonprofit organizations and government agencies must be concerned with the preservation of a tax exemption and the control over any tax liability that may arise from unrelated business activities. Every professional decision and every action taken by a tax practitioner is subject to detailed scrutiny by the IRS. Its technical standards are uniform and voluminous, and the sanctions at its command—preparer penalties, injunctions, disbarment from practice before IRS, prosecution for conspiracy—are awesome. Thus, even though the practitioner serves as advocate for his client, he acts in an environment that keeps him acutely aware of his professional responsibilities.

Independence is valued because it promotes integrity. No one has charged that the CPA in tax practice lacks integrity. After all, he observes the same ethical rules as any other CPA and, in addition, shoulders the responsibilities imposed by the rigorous technical and professional environment of tax practice.

In much the same vein, the possible conflict between the tax advocate and independent auditor roles should not cause concern. The long-standing identification of the CPA with tax practice, and the unquestioning acceptance by the public of this role, makes it unlikely that the propriety of tax services to audit clients will be seriously challenged.

SEC Thrusts. The SEC requires that registrants disclose information on non-audit services provided by the registrant's auditor. These requirements, set forth in ASR 250, do not call for the disclosure of specific dollar amounts, but the proportion of total nonaudit services to audit fees must be indicated. If nonaudit services amount to 3% or more of audit fees, they must be briefly described. In addition, it is necessary to state whether, before the nonaudit services were provided, the audit committee or the board of directors approved the engagement and considered the possible effect on the auditor's independence. This disclosure to shareholders of the extent of nonaudit services provided by an auditor should suffice to remove any doubt or misunderstanding about the auditor's independence. Since tax services can be provided at less cost and with greater efficiency by the CPA firm that acts as a company's auditors than by a third party, this disclosure to the stockholders seems a far better way to protect independence than a prohibition of tax services motivated by a misguided concern about a theoretical conflict.

In its latest release (ASR 264) on the subject of scope of services, the SEC expressed the belief that public confidence in auditors would be weakened if auditors were to engage in activities and services that the public perceives as foreign to the auditor's expected role. The traditional association of accountants with taxes has existed for so long, virtually paralleling the growth of the profession and the significance of taxes in society, that the withdrawal of accountants from their client's tax affairs might be more disturbing to the public than their continued involvement.

The involvement of the auditor in the client's tax planning provides the possibility for interim review by the auditor of the financial statement implications of tax planning as well as of the tax implications of financial transactions. The IRS review, shareholder notice of auditor involvement under ASR 250, and other controls described above are sufficient to ensure the independence of the CPA who, as an auditor, must pass on a tax provision (or liability) that may be based on tax advice given either by the CPA himself or by a member of his firm.

Unauthorized Practice of Law

From time to time, though probably less frequently in recent years, local bar associations have tried to enjoin CPAs in some aspect of their tax practice. Also, CPAs who have sued for their fee have occasionally been met with the defense that they may not collect the fee because it was charged for services that were the unauthorized practice of law.

These efforts to trim the practice of a CPA in tax matters are unwarranted and not likely to meet with much success in the future. The U.S. Justice Department has taken a dim view of any attempts to establish a monopoly of practice that might prevent qualified people from serving the public. This seems particularly true in all matters pertaining to federal tax practice. At the federal level, the CPA is authorized to represent taxpayers before the IRS as a result of congressional action. The scope of this practice is described in the revised Circular 230 of the Treasury Department. The CPA who is engaged in practice under federal law (which overrides any contrary state laws) is not engaged in the unauthorized practice of law.

Proper scope of practice certainly includes representation of taxpayers before the IRS, and probably includes opining on the tax treatment of items under the jurisdiction of the IRS, but it does not authorize expressing an opinion on federal nontax law, state probate or property law, or any other state law.

It is accepted practice for CPAs to represent their clients in connection with state and local as well as federal taxes, but the question of what would constitute unauthorized practice of law in connection with state and local taxes must be decided by each state. At the moment, there do not seem to be any state efforts to restrict representation of taxpayers to attorneys, but it is not clear what would happen if such an attempt were made. The U.S. Justice Department has expressed some concern about the efforts of the organized bar to obtain a monopoly for its profession in certain areas. For example, it has been held that "unauthorized practice of law" may not be used as a reason to prohibit someone who is not a member of the bar from performing a title search for compensation (*Surety Title Insurance Agency, Inc. v. Virginia State Bar,* 431 F. Supp. 298 (1977)). The decision seems based on the comparatively ministerial aspect of the function performed, but there is running through recent decisions and Justice Department pronouncements a thread of unwillingness to permit the formation of a monopoly to prohibit any qualified professional from participating in the legitimate aspects of his practice.

While the courts may not look kindly on attempts to prevent accountants from participating in state tax practice, the threat of a challenge to tax practice based on unauthorized practice of law can nevertheless act as a deterrent.

Conflict of Interest

When an accountant is auditing a corporation as well as doing tax work for shareholders and executives, there is a possibility that he will become aware of information in his tax consultant capacity that he may want to use as an auditor. For example, he may be preparing a tax return for the purchasing vice-president of an audit client and learn that this individual is a stockholder of a Subchapter S corporation that is selling services or materials to the audit client. This is important information that he should immediately disclose to his associates responsible for the audit. Can he?

The Internal Revenue Code imposes significant sanctions, including penalties and jail sentences, for the unauthorized disclosure of tax return information (Sec. 7216). However, an accountant who prepares a tax return for a taxpayer is permitted by the regulations under Sec. 7216 to disclose the tax return information to others in his firm for use in connection with their audit or taxwork. Tax clients should be informed that there may be such disclosures. Otherwise, the CPA is breaching the implied promise of confidentiality inherent in his relationship with the tax client, in order to carry out his responsibilities in dealing with his audit client. As a practical matter, when any tax work is done for an employee of a company that is an audit client, the practitioner should thus always ask in advance for permission to disclose any information learned in the process of preparing the return that might be relevant to the firm's work for the audit client. When the purpose of this request is explained to the employee, objections are unlikely. After all, the accountant has no intention of advising the employer about the individual's financial standing, but only wants to ensure that the employer is protected against the possibility of improprieties or conflicts of interest between the employee and his company.

It is most important that the employee feel fully assured that, unless there is some evidence of impropriety or conflict of interest, his tax return information will never be disclosed. Any reluctance on the part of the employee to give his accountant all the information necessary for the preparation of his tax return will affect the accountant's ability to be effective as a tax consultant, and may raise questions for the auditor as well.

A PROPER BALANCE

The CPA, like any other tax practitioner, works for the taxpayer. His aims are to help the taxpayer comply with the law and to minimize his tax burden. There is no doubt that these two aims are perfectly compatible. As one of this country's great judges, Learned Hand, observed:

> Over and over again courts have said there's nothing sinister in so arranging one's affairs as to keep taxes as low as possible. Everybody does so rich or poor; and all do right, for nobody owes any public duty to pay more than the law demands: taxes are enforced exactions, not voluntary contributions. To demand more in the name of morals is mere cant. [Dissenting opinion in *Newman*, 47-1 USTC 9175 (2 Cir.)]

Our tax laws are extremely complex and grow more so every day. A bare list of tax laws enacted since 1954 would fill many pages, and we can confidently expect more legislation in the future. Legislation, in turn, begets regulations, administrative pronouncements, judicial decisions, and professional articles. Thus, the taxpayer faces an increasingly awesome and mysterious tax system. No matter how intelligent he may be, he badly needs professional help in dealing with it. And in providing that help, the CPA in tax practice helps make the system work, for without the assistance of knowledgeable practitioners, it would probably collapse of its own weight.

SUGGESTED READING

Bittker, Boris, and Eustice, James. *Federal Income Taxation of Corporations and Share-holders.* 4th ed. Boston: Warren, Gorham & Lamont, 1979. This is a technical treatise on federal income taxation of corporations and shareholders that is often used as a textbook in an advanced course on taxation. It is documented with citations of cases, code sections, regulations, and rulings.

Frankel, Paul. *Tax Court—Forum; Pleadings* (152-3rd T.M.). Washington, D.C.: Tax Management, Inc. (Division of Bureau of National Affairs, Inc.), 1974. This is a portfolio prepared for practical use by attorneys, accountants, and corporate executives who are involved in tax controversies with the IRS. It provides assistance for handling the disposition of tax controversies through both administrative and judicial procedures that may be used by the taxpayer.

McKee, William; Nelson, William; and Whitmire, Robert. *Federal Taxation of Partnerships and Partners.* Boston: Warren, Gorham & Lamont, 1977. This is a loose-leaf text focusing on the peculiar problems of a closely held corporation and its shareholders and is excellent for the generalist who must deal with a diversity of tax problems in the context of a much larger area of responsibility.

Ness, Theodore, and Vogel, Eugene. *Taxation of the Closely Held Corporation.* 3rd ed. Boston: Warren, Gorham & Lamont, 1975. This book is a treatise on federal taxation of partnerships and partners that can be used by the nonspecialist who is wise enough to recognize that partnership taxation, though a most difficult area, offers many opportunities for tax planners. It is also useful for the partnership tax specialist because of its comprehensive coverage of the problems and authorities, and its imaginative and novel insights.

Raby, William. "Advocacy vs. Independence in Tax Liability Accrual." *Journal of Accountancy,* March, 1972, pp. 40-47. This article examines the relationship of tax practice to auditing and the advocacy role adopted by a CPA for a tax client versus an independent opinion on the presentation of financial statements that show income tax expense as a liability.

———. *Tax Practice Management.* New York: AICPA, 1974. This working manual is for the CPA in public accounting practice who finds that taxes have become an essential element of his practice and who wants to manage this aspect with the same care that he gives to his clients' other affairs.

———, and Tidwell, Victor. *Introduction to Federal Taxation.* Englewood Cliffs, N.J.: Prentice-Hall, 1981. This one-volume text for collegiate schools of business covers the entire range of federal taxes and has a unique orientation to tax planning. A new edition is published every year.

Sacks, J. Mason. *Modern Tax Planning Checklists.* Boston: Warren, Gorham & Lamont, 1977. This book gives accountants, attorneys, corporate officers, and others concerned with tax matters a timely collection of checklists covering a wide range of tax planning topics for both businesses and individuals.

Sommerfeld, Ray, and Streuling, Fred. *Tax Research Techniques.* New York: AICPA, 1976. This guide for nonspecialists helps them develop their tax research skills. Using specific examples and step-by-step techniques, the book explains how to approach and research tax problems.

Surrey, Stanley; Warren, William; McDaniel, Paul; and Ault, Hugh. *Federal Income Taxation: Cases and Materials.* 2 vols. Mineola, N.Y.: The Foundation Press, 1973. This casebook on federal income taxes highlights judicial decisions in major cases; it is theoretically oriented for use in law schools.

Touche Ross & Co. *Accounting Principles: Conformity or Creativity.* New York, 1971. This pamphlet explores the separate developmental channels for tax and financial accounting, and argues against any requirement that the two channels must conform.

West Publishing Co. *West's Federal Taxation: Corporations, Partnerships, Estates and Trusts.* St. Paul, Minn., 1980, pp. 1-37. This federal taxation textbook is a sequel to one on taxation of individuals. It includes an introduction to tax research and discusses the treatment of property transfers that are subject to gift and death taxes. A new edition is published every year.

————. *West's Federal Taxation: Individual Income Taxes.* St. Paul, Minn., 1980, pp. 1-46. This is a textbook for an introductory course on the federal income taxation of individuals, but can also be used as a tool for self-study. A new edition is published every year.

Part VI

The Legal Environment

44

The Legal Framework[1]

Harvey L. Pitt
James H. Schropp

---

[1] *Editors' note.* This chapter begins a trilogy of sorts dealing with how the accounting and auditing issues discussed throughout this *Handbook,* and those parties involved in them, are viewed in a legal sense. (Indeed, for the party under assault, the often bizarre developments and the seemingly endless number of plaintiffs and lawyers sometimes take on a Tolkienesque character.) Chapter 44 describes the court system, which is basically trilevel both in the states and federally. The legal process, including discovery and investigations (which are all too prevalent for accountants), and accountant-client privilege (of which accountants seem to have little) are also covered. This chapter closes with the important topic of the accountant as expert witness, a process increasingly involving accountants. Chapter 45 examines accounting principles in the eyes of the law, and Chapter 46 deals with the broad spectrum of auditor liability. There are some unavoidable overlaps among the three chapters as needed to round out a topic, and there may even be differing perspectives on the same issues among the three chapters; such is the ever-evolving nature of the legal environment. In order to harmonize as much as possible with the overall thrust of the *Handbook* and hopefully to present the legal issues in a style appropriate for nonlawyers, a large proportion of the citations and discussion of relevant cases that would appear in a presentation for lawyers has been omitted in these three chapters.

THE SETTING

Auditors (and accountants in industry, on whom the burden of financial reporting most directly falls) properly suggest that financial accounting, reporting, and auditing questions should be resolved by appropriate pronouncements of the professional standard-setting bodies. Because of the high volume of litigation in this country's current financial environment, however, these questions are instead often resolved by nonaccountants in either a judicial or quasi-judicial forum.

Although not startling or unique, this fundamental fact is of great importance—and potential concern—to the accounting profession. To the extent litigation ensues over an accounting or auditing matter, accountants and auditors will ineluctably find themselves part of the process—either as witnesses, called on to explain the events, the principles applied, and the justifying reasons, or as the subjects of formal proceedings, called on to defend their conduct (or, perhaps, their failure to have prevented the adverse developments complained of) in a variety of formal and informal contexts. The accounting profession, therefore, has an important need to know and understand the *legal framework* within which accounting and auditing issues will be resolved.

Particular attention is focused in this chapter on the operations of the Securities and Exchange Commission (SEC), since that agency has been given explicit statutory authority directly affecting the practice of accounting (at least insofar as it relates to publicly held companies); the SEC has long asserted—in the face of considerable controversy regarding its authority to do so—the power to discipline accountants (and attorneys) who appear or practice before the agency and who do not, in the commission's view, meet acceptable standards of competence or ethics.

This chapter also examines the so-called accountant-client privilege in judicial and other proceedings and the increased use in litigation of accountants as expert witnesses. The complexity of the financial issues raised in court cases, many of which are decided by juries of nonexperts, has led to a greater use of witnesses who can explain the facts and provide an authoritative opinion.

THE JUDICIAL SYSTEM

The structure of the U.S. judicial system reflects the divisions of authority inherent in our federal form of government. Each state has its own independent and comprehensive system of courts, able to adjudicate most types of controversies and, ordinarily, not subject to federal judicial authority. A system of federal courts has also been created, which, in theory at least, adjudicates matters identified as being of federal, or national, concern.

The federal courts are established by a brief constitutional provision—Article III, Section 1—that gives Congress extensive power to create (or eliminate) courts and to grant (or take away) their jurisdiction. The types of cases to which federal judicial power extends essentially fall into two major classes: (1) those cases involving the Constitution and the federal laws (the so-called federal-question cases) and (2) cases involving controversies between citizens of different states (the so-called diversity cases). The Constitution gives the Supreme Court original jurisdiction in a very limited number of cases, with Congress having the power to determine the appellate jurisdiction of the Supreme Court.

To a considerable degree, state and federal courts exercise concurrent jurisdiction. But, in interpreting the Constitution or federal law, the federal courts are supreme, just as federal law is supreme over state laws that may conflict with the Constitution or federal statutes.

Federal Courts

District Courts. In 1789 Congress made the fundamental determination to create lower federal courts to decide cases involving federal matters in the first instance. While the organization of the federal court system has varied since then, the present federal court of first resort (or general jurisdiction) is the District Court of the United States; thus, litigants with claims that are cognizable in a federal court generally (but not always) must first bring their claims to a district court.[2] District courts are often referred to as *trial courts* because matters requiring a trial, whether before a jury or a judge, must be heard in those courts.

Except in unusual cases involving very important constitutional issues, a single judge presides over litigation in federal district court. The country is divided into 88 judicial districts, each district having at least one courthouse. Depending on such factors as population and caseload, some districts are further divided into divisions. Each courthouse has at least one judge and usually considerably more than that. In all, there are 396 judges currently authorized to preside over federal district court litigation.

Although in theory the judicial process is designed to clarify the application and operation of various federal laws, the large number of district judges virtually assures that conflicting views will be rendered in connection with the interpretation of particular statutes and administrative rules. While this is more likely to occur in different districts, conflicts arise even within the *same* district.

Appeals Courts. In order to minimize conflicts, the 88 judicial districts are, in turn, grouped into 11 judicial circuits, each having one court of appeals with jurisdiction to review the decisions of the various district courts within its territory. The courts of appeals, or appellate courts, conduct no trials themselves; rather, they review the results of litigation in the trial courts.

The jurisdiction of each appellate court spans several states, with the exception of the Court of Appeals for the District of Columbia Circuit; that court reviews only the decisions of a single district court and has jurisdiction to review the decisions of a number of federal agencies headquartered in Washington, D.C. Unlike the district courts, which normally have only one judge presiding over any case, three judges normally preside over each case heard by an appellate court. With few exceptions, either party to a district court proceeding has a right to appeal a partially or completely adverse final district court decision to the court of appeals. In some rare cases, the issues involved are so significant (e.g., a three-judge appel-

---

[2] Congress has also created certain specialized courts, such as the Court of Claims, the Court of Customs and Patent Appeals, and the Tax Court.

late decision that conflicts with decisions of other circuits) that a circuit court may agree to rehear a case *en banc,* with *all* the active judges of the circuit participating.

The jurisdiction of the courts of appeals is limited, by statute, to final decisions (28 U.S.C. § 1291 (1976)) and a very few interlocutory, or nonfinal, decisions (28 U.S.C. § 1292 (1976)). Thus, a court of appeals may review interlocutory orders granting or denying an injunction, and certain other orders that have a direct and immediate effect on the litigants. In addition, a district judge may certify a "controlling question of law" for immediate appellate review, if that procedure will "materially advance the ultimate termination of the litigation" (28 U.S.C. § 1292b). The appellate court has broad discretion whether to accept a certified question for review.

In addition, the courts of appeals are often given statutory jurisdiction to hear appeals on the decisions of various federal regulatory agencies; in those situations, the agency functions in a manner analogous to a district court, but may combine other functions, such as its investigatory and rule-making authority, with its quasi-judicial powers. An agency regulation is binding on all persons subject to the agency's jurisdiction and has the force and effect of law.

The distinction between a trial court and an appellate court is quite significant. In those cases involving disputed facts, the district court must conduct a trial for the purpose of reaching a series of required factual conclusions. Once the facts of a case have been determined, the appropriate legal principles are applied. Because appellate courts may not retry a case, and because the district judge who presides over a trial is able to observe the demeanor and character of the witnesses and thus make a judgment as to their credibility, a district judge's factual conclusions are generally binding unless an appellate court can find that the district judge's factual findings were clearly erroneous. Thus, on appeal, a court of appeals must usually accept the *factual* findings of the district court, but is free to review the *legal* principles applied and the *legal* conclusions reached by the district court. The same appeal process is utilized as to hearings initially conducted before administrative agencies.

Once an appellate court has interpreted a federal statute or agency regulation, the district courts within that appellate court's circuit are bound by the legal principles enunciated by the appellate court. But the other ten appellate courts (and the scores of other district courts throughout the country) are not *required* to accept the legal principles articulated by a different appellate court. This means that, on occasion, conflicts between the various courts of appeals will occur.

Supreme Court. If the full complement of appellate judges in a circuit declines to review a conflicting decision rendered by a three-judge panel, there are only two ways such conflicts can be resolved: either the Supreme Court must review the appellate decision or Congress must revise the statute in question to undo the effect of an appellate decision.

The Supreme Court, standing at the pinnacle of this country's judicial system, was established expressly by the Constitution, which grants it limited jurisdiction. Congress has, by statute, conferred additional jurisdiction on the Supreme Court, consisting largely of discretionary jurisdiction (referred to as *certiorari* jurisdiction) to review decisions of the federal appellate courts (28 U.S.C. § 1254 (1976)) and limited jurisdiction, also largely discretionary, to review certain state court decisions involving an interpretation of the federal Constitution (28 U.S.C. § 1257 (1976)).

By contrast, the Supreme Court held in *Hochfelder* (425 U.S. 185 (1976)) that the precise language of Section 10(b) of the Securities Exchange Act—proscribing "deceptive" and "manipulative" conduct—dictated the Court's holding that mere negligence is not enough to sustain a private damage action under Rule 10b-5. The Court left open the questions of (1) whether its ruling was applicable to the commission's *injunctive* actions under Rule 10b-5, (2) what showing beyond mere negligence would suffice in a private damage action under Rule 10b-5, and (3) whether the holding in *Hochfelder* would be applicable to actions alleging violations of other antifraud provisions of the federal securities laws.[4]

As a result of the *Hochfelder* decision, there is some indication that the commission may view it as "appropriate . . . to place greater reliance upon Rule 2(e) in the future as a means of preventing a recurrence of unethical or improper conduct" (Pitt, 1976, p. 1472, n. 3).

How Rule 2(e) Is Applied. Under certain circumstances, the SEC may suspend the right of an individual to practice pursuant to Rule 2(e) without a hearing. Such a suspension may occur if some other forum has made a determination on the basis of which the SEC decides that the individual is, in effect, not fit to practice his profession or is a danger to the public; the commission relies on such findings rather than instituting *de novo* proceedings. Thus, Rule 2(e)(2) provides that, upon the entry of judgment or order by the cognizant tribunal, any accountant, attorney, or other expert

> whose license or practice . . . has been revoked or suspended in any State . . . or any person who has been convicted of a felony, or of a misdemeanor involving moral turpitude, shall be forthwith suspended from appearing or practicing before the Commission.

The commission also can *temporarily* suspend, without a preliminary hearing, any professional who, in an action for misconduct brought by the commission, has been permanently enjoined from violating or aiding and abetting the violation of the federal securities laws and related rules and regulations. Similar authority exists with respect to findings entered in administrative proceedings, unless the violation is found not to have been willful. In each of these cases the commission may provide a subsequent hearing on request of the persons suspended.

In the SEC staff memorandum referred to above (Pitt, 1976), it was noted that the practice of accountancy before the SEC is substantially carried on by the larger accounting firms and that such firms have an obligation as practicing entities to design adequate quality control and review procedures. The staff noted that the problems that have come to the commission's attention during private investigations

---

[4] In a recent case (*Aaron v. SEC*, CCH Fed. Sec. L. Rep. ¶ 97,511, June 2, 1980), the Supreme Court has now ruled that Section 10(b) of the 1934 act requires the SEC to prove fraudulent intent when seeking an injunction to prohibit violations of the securities laws. The Court held that the same condition required to sustain a private damage action must apply in cases brought by the SEC seeking injunctive relief based on violations of the securities laws. The decision sustained the AICPA position, stated in an *amicus curiae* brief, that the SEC is not entitled to an injunction under Section 10(b) "in the absence of a showing of scienter."

of such large firms have involved a fairly small portion of the personnel of those firms and that, very often, the shortcomings that led to the institution of a proceeding were rooted in poor supervision by persons with positions high in the firm, lack of adequate quality controls, or insufficient enforcement of those controls that did exist. In addition, the staff memorandum expressed the views that, in some instances, personnel training was not commensurate with the complexity of the tasks undertaken and that personnel were required by the firm to assume responsibility beyond their competence.

Thus, if the problem sought to be remedied appears to result more from organizational defects than from wrongdoing on the part of particular individuals, the SEC has deemed it appropriate to name accounting firms as respondents in proceedings instituted under Rule 2(e), and in some cases the commission has recognized that it is not necessary to name individual accountants as respondents to accomplish the remedial purposes of a Rule 2(e) proceeding.

Not pointed out in the staff memorandum, but implicit in it, is the fact that smaller firms reflect more directly the operations of their individual members and that when the SEC finds violations involving a small accounting firm it is more likely to be necessary to name the individual partners it deems responsible for the objectionable conduct. The staff memorandum noted that the flexibility in Rule 2(e) permits the commission to fashion remedies appropriate to the circumstances involved; thus the commission has, in certain circumstances, required that there be an investigation by a qualified group of outside professionals, at the respondent accounting firm's expense, designed to review and make recommendations with respect to the firm's overall practice.

Factors in Choice of Remedy. Finally, the staff memorandum set forth guidelines applied by the SEC in determining the appropriate remedy in a particular case. Although the commission adheres to an *ad hoc* approach to selecting an appropriate remedy, the factors considered include (Pitt, 1976, p. 1476)

1. The gravity of the misconduct or other professional deficiency involved;
2. Whether the misconduct or deficiency arose in connection with appearing or practicing before the commission;
3. Whether the problems that led to the proceeding appear to result more from institutional faults than individual failings;
4. The degree to which the misconduct or other deficiency casts doubt on an individual's ability or willingness to perform competent and reliable professional services in the future;
5. Whether the individual or firm involved has been the subject of any previous enforcement action or Rule 2(e) proceeding brought by the commission; and
6. The experience of the commission's staff in conducting the investigation that led to institution of a proceeding.

Challenges of SEC Authority. The predicate for the SEC's adoption of Rule 2(e) is the rule-making authority contained in the statutes it administers—the Securities Act of 1933, Securities Exchange Act of 1934, Public Utility Holding Company Act of 1935, Trust Indenture Act of 1939, Investment Company Act of 1940, and Investment Advisers Act of 1940. In 1979 the commission's disciplinary authority with regard to accountants was confirmed in a suit that was the first direct challenge to that authority and was brought about by the SEC's stated intention to hold the Rule 2(e) hearing in public for the first time.

The court of appeals in *Touche Ross & Co. v. SEC,* 609 F. 2d 570 (2d Cir. 1979) held that Rule 2(e) was a valid exercise of the agency's general rule-making powers because the rule protects both the integrity of the administrative process and the public in general. Prior to this decision only a relatively small number of courts had had occasion to deal with the disciplinary authority of other agencies or, inferentially, with the SEC's authority. The court accepted the SEC's principal arguments, noting that the SEC relies heavily on the legal and accounting professions to perform their tasks diligently and responsibly and that "breaches of professional responsibility jeopardize the achievement of the objectives of the securities laws and can inflict great damage to the public." However, the court did express doubt that the commission's rule could be applied to suspend from practice an entire national accounting firm based on the conduct of certain partners or of one of its offices, a power that the SEC had been exercising without challenge for many years. In both the principal and concurring opinions the appeals court said:

> Nothing [i.e., that must be decided prior to time of exhaustion of administrative remedies] purports to raise the question of the extent to which the Commission has the power, in a disciplinary action, to hold Touche Ross and its 525 partners vicariously liable to the extent of permanent revocation of the right to practice for the acts of its erstwhile partners. It may be argued, for example, that the Commission may not proceed against Touche Ross on a theory of *respondeat superior* without first establishing that Congress has delegated such authority and that the Commission has, through a rulemaking proceeding, set standards for such an adjudication, including a definition of "willful conduct" by organizations. See generally Fuller, "The Forms and Limits of Adjudication," Harv. L. Rev. 353, 373 (1978). We express no view on this question, but it is one that the Commission might want to consider.

Thus, the staff noted that to bar a large accounting firm from all appearance or practice before the SEC, either temporarily or permanently, would have the effect of penalizing many individuals whose conduct was in no way culpable or responsible for the problems that led to the proceeding and could require the clients of that firm to bear the great expense and trouble of finding new independent accountants. Further judicial review of the question was avoided when, shortly after the appellate court decision, a Rule 2(e) order was issued (supplementing a 1974 order) in which Touche Ross consented to an SEC censure. No new sanctions were imposed.

THE PROCESSES OF THE LAW

Initiation of Litigation

Litigation is the process by which facts are determined—not in the scientific sense, of course, but for purposes of applying the law. It is the method by which legal rights are enforced. Litigation in United States courts is, in most cases, an adversarial process; that is, a proceeding having opposing parties rather than being initiated by an *ex parte* application. The efficiency of the adversarial process has often been called into question; probably overshadowing that question, however, are the resource problems that plague the system—a shortage of judges, other court personnel, and courtrooms—and procedural rules that frequently permit, if not encourage, delay.

In addition, the expeditious processing of civil cases is often sacrificed by statute in the interest of providing speedy trials to those accused of criminal offenses. When these opportunities for delay occur in a situation in which at least one party to the litigation believes delay is in his interest, the progress of litigation can quickly be brought to a virtual standstill.

In most systems litigation is classified as either *civil* or *criminal*. The procedural distinctions between civil and criminal litigation are significant—so much so that they can have a decidedly substantive effect on the outcome of litigation. Criminal litigation involves only lawsuits instituted by the government—by various of the state or municipal governments through each state's or city's attorney general or district attorney, or by the federal government through the Department of Justice. Depending on the nature of the case and its location, prosecutions for the federal government are handled either by the attorney general or by the United States attorney in the district where the litigation is to be instituted.

In a criminal case the focus of the lawsuit is generally conduct by the defendant that allegedly violates some statute or administrative rule adopted pursuant to a statutory grant of authority. The moving party is always the government, and the result sought is the imposition of either a prison term or monetary fine (or both). Under the Sixth Amendment to the Constitution, criminal cases must be tried before a jury unless a jury is waived by the defendant, and the prosecution must prove the facts of its case beyond a reasonable doubt. Separate Federal Rules of Criminal Procedure (following 28 U.S.C.) apply to criminal prosecutions, and the defendant may not be *compelled* to testify against himself.

Civil litigation is generally different from criminal prosecutions, but there are circumstances under which the distinctions between the two forms of litigation are more conceptual than real. Thus, civil lawsuits may be instituted by either the government or a private citizen. In most circumstances civil litigation requires either an express statutory grant of permission to bring a lawsuit or a well-recognized common-law cause of action. Nevertheless, on occasion the courts have implied remedies for private parties, although the incidence of such implied remedies has been drastically curtailed by the Supreme Court since 1975. (See, for example, *Transamerica Mortgage Advisors, Inc. v. Lewis,* 444 U.S. 11 (1979) and *Touche Ross & Co. v. Redington,* 442 U.S. 560 (1979), which is also discussed in Chapter 46.)

When the government is the moving party, it may seek either equitable relief—for example, an order enjoining the defendant from commencing, continuing, or repeating conduct believed to violate some statutory or regulatory command, or an order requiring a defendant to correct the effects of prior unlawful conduct, such as by disgorging illegally obtained funds—or some other prescribed remedy, such as a civil fine or the disqualification of a professional. Agency administrative procedures are most analogous to, and are generally classified with, civil proceedings; but it is important to note that agency disciplinary proceedings, which can result in a personal loss or serious sanction (such as being barred from an occupation or profession), are sometimes classified as quasi-criminal in nature, with the result that the government is subject to a variety of heavier burdens.

In a civil case, litigation is usually begun by the filing of a complaint, which sets forth the nature of the claim being asserted. In some states (e.g., New York), however, a complaint can be filed *after* a lawsuit has been instituted. The complaint generally is required to set forth a concise statement of the alleged facts on which the claim is based, a specification of the law or legal duty that is asserted to have been violated by the defendants, and a statement of the relief the plaintiff seeks. In criminal proceedings the case is begun by the filing of an indictment or its equivalent.

Administrative agencies are often authorized to enforce the specialized laws committed to their respective jurisdictions by bringing administrative proceedings that are generally initiated by an order for proceedings; this document is analogous to a complaint or indictment, usually setting forth the nature of the agency's allegations and specifying the relief sought—that is, the sanctions or penalties.

Discovery

After the suit is initiated, most litigation proceeds to a discovery phase. In federal civil litigation, extensive discovery rights are provided by the federal rules of procedure. Thus, the parties to the litigation may obtain documents, require written answers to questions, and take testimony before a court reporter from the other parties and (subject to certain restrictions) from persons who are not parties to the litigation. A failure or refusal to provide discovery can result in a court order requiring compliance with valid discovery requests, and a failure to abide by such orders may be punished as a contempt of the court or by a default judgment. Discovery in criminal and administrative cases has typically been less extensive than that available in civil cases, although the trend has been toward more liberalized discovery rights. In some of the state courts, a more restrictive standard is applied in the discovery phase.

It is during the discovery stage of litigation involving commercial or financial matters that information is frequently sought from accountants. These requests for information may seek access to an accountant's working papers or, indeed, any other documents in an accountant's possession concerning the subject of the litigation. They may also take the form of requests for oral testimony from the accountant concerning his knowledge of the matters in dispute. If the accountant is properly subject to the jurisdiction of the court hearing the case, the only valid objections to requests for discovery are that the information is not relevant or is privileged. The privileges afforded to information in an accountant's possession are treated later in this chapter.

In federal litigation the relevance requirement is interpreted very liberally in favor of permitting discovery; indeed, the breadth of permissible discovery (and the resulting length of time that discovery can require) is the basis of frequent criticism of the discovery process in the federal courts. To be relevant, it is not necessary that the information sought ultimately be admissible into evidence; rather, it is only necessary that the information sought *may* lead to the discovery of admissible evidence—a very loose standard. (Further coverage of discovery is found in Chapter 46.)

Trials and Administrative Proceedings

Following the completion of discovery, litigation proceeds to the trial stage, in which the parties present their evidence before the judge and jury. (Some cases are not tried by a jury, either because there is no constitutional right to a jury trial or because the parties waive their right to a jury.) Again, an accountant may be called to testify to matters within his personal knowledge, subject to the objections that were relevant during discovery. Certain additional objections are made during trial, generally designed to eliminate from evidence matters that are, by their nature, less probative or insufficiently trustworthy. For example, hearsay testimony is generally excluded, as is information that is deemed to be unnecessarily prejudicial to one of the parties, especially if the information is also considered to be less probative of the truth.

Proceedings before an administrative agency are governed by the procedural rules established by the legislature or by the agencies themselves. Discovery is, as noted, frequently more abbreviated (and sometimes virtually nonexistent) in agency proceedings than it is in federal court actions. While the rules of practice in effect at the different agencies vary considerably, often being tailored to the specific type of proceedings they govern, the evidence in an agency proceeding will typically be heard by a judicial officer bearing a title such as administrative law judge. His decision is generally reviewable in the first instance by the members of the agency, who may, but usually do not, hear evidence first-hand. However, many of the objections to the admission of evidence that might be sustained in a court proceeding are inapplicable in an agency proceeding. Appeal from the decisions of the agency is generally to the courts, typically to a court of appeals in the federal system.

Right to a Jury Trial. In commercial litigation—particularly litigation under the antitrust and securities laws—financial and accounting issues often must be considered in determining both liability and damage issues. The complexity of these issues and the length of time a trial to decide them requires have led some courts to deny jury trials in some cases, despite the provision in the Seventh Amendment to the Constitution granting a jury trial in civil cases. The Seventh Amendment provides: "In suits at common law, where the value in controversy shall exceed twenty dollars, the right of trial by jury shall be preserved. . . ." The basic purpose of this provision was to preserve the right to jury trial in all cases where it existed when the amendment was adopted in 1791. The phrase "suits at common law" was thus meant to distinguish cases traditionally heard in courts of equity and admiralty, where there was no right to a jury.

There are several examples of cases denying jury trials: the court in *In re Boise Cascade Securities Litigation,* 420 F. Supp. 99 (W.D. Wash. 1976) struck a demand for jury trial because of the complexity of accounting and securities issues involved; the court in *Bernstein v. Universal Pictures, Inc.,* 79 F.R.D. 59 (S.D.N.Y. 1978) on its own motion struck plaintiff's demand for a jury trial in an antitrust suit brought by composers and lyricists; and the court in the antitrust case *ILC v. Peripherals International Business Machines,* 458 F. Supp. 423 (N.D. Cal. 1978), after dismissing a deadlocked jury, entered a directed verdict in favor of defendant and entered an order striking a demand for jury trial in the event the case was reversed and remanded.

The legal reasoning of these courts is twofold. First, some courts have concluded that complex financial suits are not suits of law at all, but are really in the nature of actions at equity for an accounting. Support for this theory is drawn from *Dairy Queen, Inc. v. Wood,* 369 U.S. 469, 478 (1962), in which the Supreme Court rejected a plaintiff's attempt to bring a suit in equity for an accounting, thereby negating the defendant's right to a jury trial, and stated that a plaintiff may bring an action for an equitable accounting only when it can be shown "that the 'accounts between the parties' are of such a 'complicated nature' that only a court of equity can satisfactorily unravel them." Second, some courts have reasoned, in a somewhat circular fashion, that since the case is too complex for a jury, there is no adequate remedy at law; that cases where there is no adequate remedy at law come within the jurisdiction of courts of equity; and that there is, therefore, no right to a jury trial in any complex case. For example, in the recent Third Circuit Court case, *Matsushita Electric Industrial Co., Ltd. v. Zenith Radio Corp.,* 49 USLW 1013 (July 7, 1980), the court held that due process precludes a jury trial when the jury would be unable to understand the evidence and the relevant legal standards. Support for this theory is drawn from a footnote in another Supreme Court case, *Ross v. Bernhard,* 396 U.S. 531, 538 n. 10 (1970), in which the Court stated that one of the factors used in determining whether a case was legal or equitable was "the practical abilities and limitations of juries."

But other courts have concluded that the right to a jury trial cannot be dispensed within a complex case. In the only appellate case in which this issue has been raised (*In re U.S. Financial Securities Litigation,* 609 F.2d 411 (9th Cir. 1979), *cert. denied* 48 USLW 3698 (1980)), the right to a jury trial was soundly reaffirmed. The district court judge had struck demands for a jury trial, stating that "complicated accounting problems are not generally amenable to jury resolution." He also ruled that in this particular case a jury was not capable of understanding or rationally reconciling the mass of data involved, the variety of legal theories, and the number of parties involved in the case. Moreover, it was estimated that the trial would require two years and that it would accordingly be difficult to find a jury to hear the case.

The appellate court stated it did not believe that "any case is so overwhelmingly complex that it is beyond the abilities of a jury," but the court nevertheless agreed that some of the points raised by the critics of the jury system "should not be summarily dismissed." Nevertheless, the court felt that the argument that jurors could not understand complicated matters "improperly demeans the intelligence of the citizens of this Nation," and that "jurors, if properly instructed and treated with deserved respect, bring collective intelligence, wisdom, and dedication to their tasks, which is rarely equalled in other areas of public service." Rejecting the premise that a "single judge is brighter than the jurors collectively functioning together," the court pointed out that it is the function of trial counsel, aided by expert witnesses and special masters, to "educate the uninitiated" about the complex accounting, financial, and other matters presented in the case.

Eventually, this disagreement between the courts will have to be resolved by the Supreme Court in an appropriate case.

Investigations

Investigations are generally conducted by means of investigative subpoenas, which are, in turn, usually enforceable by a court through its contempt powers. Investigations are also classified as civil or criminal, and the subject of a criminal investigation has rights that do not inure to the subject of a civil investigation. As a general rule, civil and criminal investigations are conducted by different administrative units (*U.S. v. LaSalle National Bank,* 554 F.2d 302 (7th Cir. 1977) *cert. denied* 434 US 996 (1977)). But information compiled in a civil investigation may, and often does, become the basis for a referral of a case to a criminal law enforcement agency and may be used in a criminal investigation or prosecution (*U.S. v. Kordel,* 397 US 1 (1970)). Thus, from the earliest stages of a civil investigation, subjects of an investigation, witnesses, and their attorneys must evaluate their potential *ultimate* liability in determining whether to assert applicable privileges, such as the Fifth Amendment privilege against self-incrimination.

Investigations are perhaps most readily analogized to the discovery phase of civil litigation. There are, of course, important distinctions: an investigation is discovery that occurs in advance of the initiation of proceedings, and it is a decidedly one-sided form of discovery, with the subject of the investigation having only a very limited right, if any, to adduce evidence in his defense. And the scope of permissible inquiry during an investigation is subject to even fewer restrictions than the discovery that occurs in litigation between private parties.

In *United States v. Morton Salt Co.,* 338 U.S. 632 (1950), the Supreme Court compared an inquiry conducted by an administrative agency to that of a grand jury, which can investigate merely on suspicion that a law has been violated, without a showing of probable cause:

> Because judicial power is reluctant if not unable to summon evidence until it is shown to be relevant to issues in litigation, it does not follow that an administrative agency charged with seeing that the laws are enforced may not have and exercise powers of original inquiry. It has a power of inquisition, if one chooses to call it that, which is not derived from the judicial function. It is more analogous to the Grand Jury, which does not depend on a case or controversy for power to get evidence but can investigate merely on suspicion that the law is being violated, or even just because it wants assurance that it is not. When investigative and accusatory duties are delegated by statute to an administrative body, it, too, may take steps to inform itself as to whether there is probable violation of the law. . . . [338 U.S. at 642-643]
>
> Even if one were to regard the request for information in this case as caused by nothing more than official curiosity, nevertheless law-enforcing agencies have a legitimate right to satisfy themselves that corporate behavior is consistent with the law and the public interest. [338 U.S. at 652]

Thus, investigations are limited only by a liberally interpreted requirement that the evidence sought be relevant to the matter under investigation, that the information sought not already be in the hands of the investigating body, and that the prescribed formal requirements relating to the issuance of subpoenas have been satisfied. As one court recently summarized the restrictions on an investigative subpoena, it is only required that "the inquiry is within the authority of the agency, the demand is not too indefinite and the information sought is reasonably relevant" (*SEC v. Arthur Young & Co.,* 584 F. 2d 1018 (D.C. Cir. 1978), *cert. denied* 439 U.S. 1071 (1979)).

Generally speaking, it is not a defense to a subpoena to attempt to prove that a violation of the law has not occurred—that is a question that must await the completion of the investigation and the investigatory body's decision as to whether the institution of a proceeding is warranted. Even an allegation that the investigator lacks jurisdiction over the subject matter of the transactions being investigated is generally, although not always, insufficient. The target of the investigation must await the day when it is formally charged, if ever, in order to have an opportunity to prove that it should never have been investigated in the first place (*SEC v. Wall Street Transcript Corp.,* 422 F.2d 1371, 1375 (2d Cir.), *cert. denied,* 398 U.S. 958 (1970)).

Of course, there are some narrow exceptions. Thus, investigations can be restricted when they are being conducted patently outside the investigatory body's proper sphere (*Leedon v. Kyne,* 358 U.S. 184 (1958)); when the investigator is acting with biased or improper motives as held by the lower court in *SEC v. Wheeling-Pittsburgh Steel Co.,* 482 F. Supp. 555 (W.D. Pa. 1979), *rev'd on appeal,* 3rd Cir., No. 80-1735, August 27, 1980 (CCH Fed. Sec. L. Rep. ¶ 97,619); or when an investigation would in some manner constitute an ongoing violation of constitutional rights involving irreparable damage (*Breen v. Selective Service Board,* 396 U.S. 460 (1920)). And, if the subpoena would place an unreasonable expense on any person, the investigating agency may be required to bear or alleviate the financial burden of complying with the subpoena.

Privilege

General Concepts. Privileges, which have the effect of making the search for the truth more difficult, are not favored by the law. Recently, in the celebrated case of *United States v. Nixon,* 418 U.S. 683, 709, the Supreme Court had occasion to note again the "ancient proposition of law . . . that 'the public has a right to every man's evidence,' except for those persons protected by a constitutional, common-law, or statutory privilege." As this statement indicates, privileges may have their origin in the Constitution, such as the provision of the Fifth Amendment that no man "shall be compelled in any criminal case to be a witness against himself." Privileges may also be derived from the common law or created by a statute. The attorney-client privilege is the only privilege derived from the common law, having been recognized as early as 1577 (*Berd v. Lovelace,* Cary 62, 21 Eng. Regs. 22 (Ch. 1577)), and thus does not depend on the existence of a statute. Of course, a common-law privilege may be modified (or abolished) by statute, and most states do have a statute governing the attorney-client privilege. These statutes are collected in 8 J. Wigmore, Evidence § 2292, n.2 (McNaughten Rev. 1961) (hereafter cited as Wigmore).

Wigmore noted that privileges are "an exception to the general liability of every person to give testimony upon all facts inquired of in a court of justice . . ." (Wigmore, § 2285 at 527). Because any privilege acts in derogation of a court's search for truth, it has often been observed that privileges ought to be reluctantly conferred and, once conferred, narrowly construed. And these principles are frequently invoked by the courts when the scope of any privilege must be evaluated.

As the Supreme Court has stated in the *Nixon* case (418 U.S. at 709): "The need to develop all relevant facts in the adversary system is both fundamental and comprehensive. The ends of criminal justice would be defeated if judgments were to be formed on a partial or speculative presentation of the facts. The very integrity of the judicial system and public confidence in the system depend on full disclosure of all facts, within the framework of the rules of evidence." The Court added that "when the ground for asserting privilege . . . in a criminal trial is based only on generalized interest in confidentiality, it cannot prevail over the fundamental demands of due process of law in the fair administration of criminal justice."

Accordingly, the day of judge-created privileges is probably past, and the federal courts have generally shown great reluctance to adopt state statutory privileges in federal court or administrative proceedings where those privileges lack support in federal law; this has generally been true with respect to the accountant-client privilege, discussed below.

Accountant-Client Privilege. While excessive recognition of privileges is cautioned against, four conditions have been suggested that justify the recognition of a privilege for certain communications. These conditions are that (1) the communications must be made in confidence, (2) the confidentiality must be essential to the satisfactory maintenance of the relationship, (3) the relationship must be one which, in the opinion of the community, should be fostered, and (4) the injury that would be caused the relationship by the disclosure of the communications must be greater than the benefits gained for the correct disposition of litigation by refusing to recognize the privilege (Wigmore, § 2285 at 527).

Needless to say, a respectable argument can be advanced that the accountant-client privilege satisfies each of the criteria mentioned above. Nevertheless, opinion on the subject remains divided, even among the professional groups that speak for accountants. Those who feel a privilege is inappropriate with respect to accountant-client communications generally emphasize the independent role of the auditor and argue that a privilege for communications between such accountants and their clients would operate to destroy that independence. There is a competitive implication inherent in this issue, however, and some large law firms are marketing their services in the tax area by suggesting to corporate clients that only lawyers can give them privileged tax consultation and advice.

On the other hand, those who favor a privilege are more likely to point to the accountant's role as a tax adviser, arguing that a privilege will foster the communication of complete and accurate information concerning the client's financial affairs to the accountant, thus enabling better-informed tax advice without the danger that the communications will have to be divulged to the tax authorities. With this divergence in views within the profession, the accountant-client privilege understandably has achieved far from universal acceptance.

State-based recognition. The accountant-client privilege is unknown at common law and therefore exists only by virtue of specific statutes, which have been enacted in 18 jurisdictions. The privilege has never been endorsed by the AICPA, and on occasion the AICPA has taken a position against recognition of the privilege.[5] More recently, however, the AICPA has recognized that the accounting profession itself is divided on the question of the desirability of accountant-client privilege statutes:

---

[5] For example, see letter from William C. Doherty, Director of Professional Ethics and Legislation, AICPA, to the *Yale Law Journal,* November 28, 1961, cited in Comment, *Functional Overlap Between The Lawyer and Other Professionals: Its Implication for the Privileged Communication Doctrine,* 71 Yale L.J. 1226, 1248 n. 147 (1962).

The Institute has not adopted a position either in favor of or in opposition in legislation creating a privileged status for confidential communications between CPAs and their clients. . . .

The primary interest of most CPAs who desire the creation of a statutory accountant-client privilege is to promote full disclosure of information necessary for the preparation of income tax returns. This interest in the creation of a privilege for tax matters, however, is not necessarily compatible with the primary function of public accountants—auditing. Reconciling the interests of these two functions is not always achieved in privilege legislation.[6]

At the same time, some state CPA societies have sponsored privilege legislation; indeed, the state organizations have undoubtedly been the strongest supporters of privilege legislation in the state legislatures, whereas the absence of support from the AICPA on the national level is likely a major reason there have been no major initiatives with respect to federal legislation.

Despite this lack of national support, the accountant-client privilege nevertheless enjoyed a modest growth until the mid-1950s, and it may have been on the verge of acquiring truly significant status in the 1960s by virtue of being enacted in a major commercial jurisdiction, New York. In 1967 both houses of the New York legislature passed an accountant-client privilege statute (Senate Bill No. 1965-A) by substantial margins—49 to 7 in the Senate and 115 to 0 in the House. But the bill was vetoed by then-Governor Rockefeller, who was of the view that the legislation did not contain needed safeguards for third parties.

At present, no new accountant-client privilege statutes have been enacted since the 1969 Indiana statute, and the privilege was on the verge of extinction in the federal courts in 1973, when new rules of evidence proposed by the Supreme Court would have recognized only certain enumerated privileges, *excluding* the accountant-client privilege. But Congress did not adopt the proposed evidence rules relating to privilege, providing instead that in federal cases where state law provides the "rule of decision"—generally, in the so-called diversity cases—state privilege law will apply (P.L. 93-595, 88 Stat. 1926). This rule ensures recognition, in certain federal proceedings, of the state accountant-client statutes. At the present time, the legislatures of 17 states and the Commonwealth of Puerto Rico have enacted a statutory accountant-client privilege. Figure 44.1 sets forth the citation of each of these statutes.

Since the accountant-client privilege is wholly a creature of statute, it is necessary to examine the specific statutory words to determine the scope of any applicable privilege. Of course, no statute can anticipate all problems that may arise with respect to its application, so the courts must frequently attempt to discern what the legislature would have intended had it contemplated the specific situation before the court. In doing so, the more defined parameters of the attorney-client privilege (as often construed in the courts) sometimes become surrogates, since many of the principles in these cases are capable of being applied by analogy.

---

[6] Letter from Timothy T. McCaffrey, Manager, State Legislation, AICPA, to the *Michigan Law Review,* cited in Note, *Privileged Communications—Accountants and Accounting—A Critical Analysis of Accountant-Client Privilege Statutes,* 66 Mich. L. Rev. 1264 (1968).

Arizona: ARIZ. Rev. STAT. ANN. § 32-749 (1976)
Colorado: COLO. Rev. STAT. ANN. § 13-90-170(1)(f) (1974)
Florida: FLA. STAT. ANN. § 473.15 (1965)
Georgia: GA. CODE ANN. § 84-220 (1979)
Illinois: ILL. Rev. STAT. CT. 110-1/2, § 51 (1977)
Indiana: IND. CODE tit. 25 § 3 (1971)
Iowa: IOWA CODE § 116.15 (1966)
Kentucky: KY. Rev. STAT. § 325.440 (1972)
Louisiana: LA. Rev. STAT. ANN. § 37.85 (1974)
Maryland: MD. ANN. CODE CT. § 9-110 (Supp. 1979)
Michigan: MICH. COMP. LAWS ANN. § 338.2120 (Supp. 1979-80)
Missouri: MO. ANN. STAT. § 326.151 (Supp. 1979)
Montana: MONT. CODE ANN. § 37-50-402 (1978)
Nevada: NEV. Rev. STAT. § 49.185 (1975)
New Mexico: N.M. STAT. ANN. § 38-6-6(c) (1978)
Pennsylvania: PA. STAT. ANN. tit. 63, § 9.11a (1968)
Puerto Rico: P.R. LAWS ANN. tit. 20, § 990 (1961)
Tennessee: TENN. CODE ANN. § 62-114 (1976)

FIGURE 44.1   STATE STATUTES CREATING AN ACCOUNTANT-CLIENT
PRIVILEGE

In the frequently cited case of *United States v. United Shoe Machinery Corp.,*
89 F. Supp. 357, 358-59 (D. Mass. 1950), Judge Wyzanski stated the circumstances under which the attorney-client privilege is applicable:

The privilege applies only if (1) the asserted holder of the privilege is or sought to
become a client; (2) the person to whom the communication was made (a) is a member of the bar of a court, or his subordinate and (b) in connection with this communication is acting as a lawyer; (3) the communication relates to a fact of which the
attorney was informed (a) by the client (b) without the presence of strangers (c) for
the purpose of securing primarily either (i) an opinion in law or (ii) legal services or
(iii) assistance in some legal proceeding, and not (d) for the purpose of committing
a crime or tort; and (4) the privilege has been (a) claimed and (b) not waived by
the client.

Most, if not all, of the same requirements can be transposed to the accountant-
client context. Thus, in order for the privilege to be applicable, the parties must
bear the relationship of accountant and client. Most of the state statutes specify
that only communications between a client and a "certified public accountant" or
"public accountant" will qualify for the privilege; other accountants, including
accountants not in public practice, are excluded. In this respect, the accountant-
client privilege differs from the attorney-client privilege; the latter applies even to
communications with employed or "in-house" counsel. Moreover, the accountant
must have been engaged or consulted by the client for the purpose of obtaining
services that the accountant may give in his capacity as an accountant.

The 18 statutes currently in effect range from very broadly worded provisions that contain no express limitations to statutes that are quite narrowly drawn. The broadest statutes are those in effect in Illinois, Kentucky, and Puerto Rico. For example, the coverage of the Illinois statute (cited in Figure 44.1) is limited only by the requirement that the communication must originate in confidence. It provides, in its entirety: "A public accountant shall not be required by any court to divulge information or evidence which has been obtained by him in his confidential capacity as a public accountant."

Accountant's privilege or client's privilege? The federal courts in Illinois have repeatedly held that the Illinois statute creates an "accountant's privilege" that can be claimed only by the accountant, not the client; see, for example, *Baylor v. Mading-Dugan Drug Co.,* 57 F.R.D. 509 (N.D. Ill. 1972). If correct, this would be a rather startling departure from the law generally applicable to privileges, which normally provides that the privilege is for the benefit of the client, not the professional.

That the federal court's view of the Illinois statute is not correct is indicated by an Illinois state court decision (*Kunin v. Forman Realty Co.,* 157 N.E. 2d 785 (Ill. App. 1959)). The court here held, in litigation instituted by a director seeking access to a copy of an auditor's report addressed to the directors of a corporation, that the report could not be withheld. The director caused a subpoena to be served on the auditors who prepared the report. The auditors interposed a claim of accountant-client privilege based on the Illinois statute. The court disposed of the auditors' claim caustically:

> It is argued that under the existing Illinois statute, a report is privileged. Privileged for whom? Not the accountant. It is privileged for his client. While the company probably pays the accountant's fee, the report itself, as we have said, was addressed to the board of directors, and it is to them, rather than to the executive officers, that the report was made. Thus, plaintiff is in that respect the client of the accountant.

The federal courts in Illinois, seemingly oblivious to this state court precedent, have continued to interpret the Illinois statute in accord with their own notions of accountant's privilege. This anomalous situation was recently surveyed by an Indiana state court in *Ernst & Ernst v. Underwriters National Assurance Co.,* 381 N.E. 2d 897, 905 n.6 (Ind. App. 1978), which dismissed the federal court's attempts to interpret state law as entitled to no weight, noting that "in such a situation the federal court's interpretation is not controlling." The court went on to hold that the Indiana statute created a privilege that was "personal to clients," a conclusion it found to be supported "by the fundamental purpose for which the accountant-client privilege was created...." The court's conclusion is consistent with those reached by numerous other jurisdictions.

Features of privilege in some states. The typical accountant-client privilege is more narrowly drawn than the Illinois statute and contains a variable number of explicit limitations; the most frequently occurring limitations are that (1) the privilege is limited to communications made in the course of the accountant's professional employment; (2) the privilege may be waived by consent of the client; and

(3) the privilege can be waived by the accountant when the information is material to the accountant's defense of an action brought against him by the client. These limitations are generally equally applicable to other privileges, including the attorney-client privilege. Other limitations imposed by certain accountant-client privilege statutes, however, are not common to other privileges and serve to narrow the accountant-client privilege even further in some state statutes.

In some states, for example, the privilege may not be invoked in criminal or bankruptcy proceedings or against a person who relied on an accountant's audit or report. These are, of course, among the situations in which both the client and the accountant are likely to feel the greatest need for the privilege shield.

The Pennsylvania statute (cited in Figure 44.1) is an example of a very restrictively drawn accountant-client privilege that preserves virtually all of the limitations on the privilege found in the various statutes. It provides:

> Except by permission of the client or person, firm or corporation engaging him or the heirs, successors or personal representatives of such client or person or firm or corporation, a certified public accountant or a person employed by a certified public accountant shall not be required to, and shall not voluntarily, disclose or divulge information of which he may have become possessed relative to and in connection with any professional services as a certified public accountant other than the examination of, audit of or report on any financial statements, books, records or accounts, which he may be engaged to make or requested by a prospective client to discuss. The information derived from or as the result of such professional services shall be deemed confidential and privileged: Provided, however, that nothing herein shall be taken or construed as modifying, changing or affecting the criminal or bankruptcy laws of this Commonwealth or of the United States.

And, curiously, the Montana privilege statute is limited by a provision that it "shall not apply to the testimony of a public accountant given pursuant to subpoena in a court of competent jurisdiction," leaving it potentially effective only in a narrow range of circumstances and hardly a "privilege" in the usual sense of the word.

Application of privilege statutes. Judicial interpretations of these various statutory provisions by state courts have been very few. When the state courts have been called on to construe these statutes, however, they have tended to do so narrowly, even when the statutory language could support a broader reading.

Moreover, as might be expected, the reception given state accountant-client privilege statutes in federal court has not been hospitable. Generally, the claim of privilege has been rejected on the ground that it is recognized neither at common law nor in federal statutory law. Another reason given by federal courts for their rejection of the privilege is the need to ensure uniformity in the litigation of federal questions.

In *Fisher v. United States,* 425 U.S. 391 (1976), the Supreme Court settled a question (which had long divided the lower courts) concerning the standing of an attorney (and presumably of an accountant as well) to assert a Fourth or Fifth Amendment privilege when served with a subpoena calling for documents relating to the client. In the case an attorney was served with an IRS summons directing the production of documents prepared by the client's accountants and relating to the accountants' preparation of tax returns. The Court held that the documents would be privileged from production, or exempt, if the attorney having possession of them had received them from the client for the purpose of providing legal advice. The Court further held that if the documents could have been obtained from the client while in his possession they could be obtained by the IRS directly from the attorney, the agent of the client.

In a criminal case the provisions of Rule 26 of the Federal Rules of Criminal Procedure (which provide that "the admissibility of evidence and the competency and privileges of witnesses shall be governed . . . by the principles of the common law as they may be interpreted by the courts of the United States in the light of reason and experience") have been held to be dispositive, since that rule refers the court to the common law. State privilege laws have also been held to be inapplicable in administrative or investigatory inquiries conducted by federal agencies such as the Federal Trade Commission, the Interstate Commerce Commission, the National Labor Relations Board, and the Internal Revenue Service.

While the grounds for applying state privilege law in diversity cases have varied in the past, the rationale of the 1973 Rules of Evidence (mentioned earlier under State-based recognition) would appear to be that state evidentiary rules of privilege are to be treated as substantive state law and thus will continue to be applied in diversity cases.

Arranging for Privilege. Because of the inherent limitations in the applicability of the accountant-client privilege, especially in federal proceedings, it is often advisable to seek to protect an accountant's work product or work processes by other means wherever appropriate. One of the most effective ways of doing this is to extend the protection given to the attorney-client relationship to the accountant. This generally requires that the accountant be working at the request or direction of an attorney and that the client have a relationship with the attorney that makes the invocation of the attorney-client privilege appropriate. In addition, if legal and accounting services are being provided in connection with pending or contemplated litigation, the work product of the accountant may also be protected by the attorney work-product doctrine, which is, in certain respects, broader in coverage than the attorney-client privilege.

The vital element that serves as a basis for the privilege is that the communication to the accountant must be made in confidence for the ultimate purpose of obtaining legal advice from the attorney. (See *United States v. Judson,* 322 F. 2d 460 (1963) and *Bauer v. Orser,* 258 F. Supp. 338 (D.N.D. 1966).) It must also be remembered that any information that is disclosed to others may destroy the element of confidentiality necessary for the maintenance of the privilege.

Work-product doctrine. The work-product doctrine generally applies to documents prepared in contemplation of litigation, whether or not the matters concern a communication between the attorney and client. The purpose of the doctrine, as set forth in the leading Supreme Court case, *Hickman v. Taylor,* 329 U.S. 495 (1947), is to protect against the disclosure of the mental impressions, conclusions, opinions, or reasoning of an attorney or other representative of a party concerning the litigation; the rationale for the doctrine is that without this protection thorough preparation for trial by attorneys would be discouraged, since the attorney would fear disclosure of his sensitive work product to his adversary in litigation. Thus, under the work-product doctrine, documents prepared by an accountant working at the direction of an attorney in connection with pending or contemplated litigation will normally be protected.

The work-product doctrine has been codified in Rule 26(b)(3) of the Federal Rules of Civil Procedure. Under that rule, documentary materials prepared under the direction of an attorney may be subject to discovery only on showing that the party seeking discovery has substantial need of the materials and is unable, without substantial hardship, to obtain the equivalent of the materials by other means. But even when this fairly stringent test is met, only factual materials may be disclosed, and disclosure may never be made in a manner that reveals the mental impressions, opinions, or legal theories of the attorney.

Engagement letters. Whenever it is contemplated that a privilege claim may be asserted with respect to the work product of an accountant, care should be taken to record the fact that the accountant will be working at the direction of an attorney. If the professional is both an attorney and an accountant, it should be specified that he is being consulted principally as an attorney, to provide legal advice. On occasion, it may be necessary to categorize the type of tasks performed, extending the privilege only to communications involving legal services. Otherwise, a potential factual dispute concerning the role of the professional will exist, which will engender an element of uncertainty defeating the very purpose of the privilege—to enable the client to make full disclosure of relevant facts with confidence that there will be no public disclosure.

To help eliminate this element of uncertainty, an engagement letter should be prepared spelling out the legal duties to be performed by an accountant-attorney whenever it is contemplated that the communications between such a professional and the client should be made and kept in confidence. The engagement letter should specify that the accounting services to be performed are incidental, or subsidiary, to the legal services, since, as the discussion in the rest of this section indicates, accounting services performed at the request or direction of an attorney often do qualify for confidential treatment under the rubric of the attorney-client privilege.

It is particularly important to have an engagement letter if the accountant has rendered accounting services for the client in the past and it is desired to retain him in connection with a new matter to which the attorney-client privilege is intended to attach, since a court may otherwise make the determination as to whether the matter in question is an accounting matter or a legal matter based on the mechanistic test of which professional was first consulted by the client.

THE ACCOUNTANT AS EXPERT WITNESS

Because the accounting and auditing issues that courts and juries are called on to address are becoming increasingly complex, an accountant often will be called by the parties to litigation as an expert witness, to lend support to the accounting theories or auditing practices favored by that party. Sometimes an accountant may be appointed an expert witness by the court, in which case the accountant will perform duties specified by the court and will be available for examination by both parties. Finally, in a somewhat different context, accountants may be appointed by the court as a special agent of the court, to carry out some function, such as the performance of an audit, under the terms of a court order.

The expert witness who is able to reduce complex, technical issues to a level that can be understood by the layman (i.e., the person not steeped in the discipline in which the expert has been trained), can be an invaluable aid in any litigation and is perhaps indispensable in a trial before a jury.

Expert Witnesses Generally

In the federal courts the framework for the receipt of expert testimony is established by Article VII of the Federal Rules of Evidence, in particular by Rules 702 through 706. These rules were enacted by Congress in 1975 as part of an extensive revision of the Federal Rules of Evidence. Although the rules regarding expert witnesses are broad and represent a considerable liberalization of the use of expert testimony, they did not generate much controversy and were enacted in 1975 in much the same form they were first proposed in 1969.

Rule 702, the basic rule regarding expert testimony, provides that if "scientific, technical, or other specialized knowledge will assist the trier of fact to understand the evidence or to determine a fact in issue," a witness who is "qualified as an expert by knowledge, skill, experience, training, or education" may testify as to his specialized knowledge "in the form of an opinion or otherwise." Under this rule, two questions must be answered in the affirmative before an expert will be permitted to testify: (1) will expert testimony assist the trier of fact to understand the issue or to determine a fact in issue? and (2) does the witness qualify as an expert?

Usefulness of Expert Testimony. Courts have distinguished between those subjects that are within the grasp of the ordinary untrained finder of fact through common experience and understanding and those subject matters that are beyond the sophistication of the ordinary jury. Under this standard the use of expert testimony in cases involving medical issues of fact is commonplace; on the other hand, courts have refused to let experts take the stand when the issue involves something more within the normal experience of the average juror, such as the cause of an automobile or household accident. Indeed, Mr. Justice Stewart once observed, with respect to obscenity, that "I know it when I see it;" in cases comprehensible to the average person, there is no need for expert guidance (*Jacobellis v. State,* 378 U.S. 184, 197 (1964)).

Generally, of course, specialized knowledge regarding accounting issues is not within the scope of the average juror's expertise; thus, the admission of expert accounting testimony should presumptively be favored whenever accounting issues are involved. However, it is necessary to distinguish between cases in which the issue to be determined is in fact an accounting or financial issue and those cases in which expert accounting testimony is offered for its purported relevance as to other issues. In the latter case the court may exclude expert testimony if it concludes that the ultimate issue is within the jury's experience or if the expert testimony would have no relevance to a determination concerning the ultimate issue.

For example, in *Fineburg v. United States,* 393 F.2d 417 (9th Cir. 1968), the defendant offered the expert testimony of an accountant to rebut evidence of his intent to defraud. The accountant was prepared to testify, based on his examination of the defendant's financial records, that it was possible that the defendant's business could have improved to the point that he could have repaid his debts. Since criminal intent is an issue that juries are normally expected to evaluate, however, the court excluded the accountant's testimony.

Qualification as an Expert. The second question pertaining to the admissibility of expert testimony is whether the witness offered as an expert qualifies as such. Like the question whether expert testimony will assist the trier of fact, this is a question as to which the trial judge is given wide latitude, and it is rare that a determination, whether it be to admit or exclude expert testimony, will be reversed on appeal.

The rule states that a person may qualify as an expert on the basis of "knowledge, skill, experience, training or education." Normally, a party who offers an accountant as an expert will want to establish the witness's credentials as to as many of these facts as possible before asking the trial court to rule on the admissibility of the witness's qualifications. In general, the trial court must be satisfied that the expert's "education and experience demonstrates a knowledge of the subject matter." If the witness demonstrates a command of his subject matter, he will generally be permitted to testify, even if his area of specialized expertise is different from the particular area that is the subject of the suit.

Weight Ascribed to Expert Testimony. A question related to the permissibility of expert testimony is the weight to be ascribed to expert testimony once it is elicited. With respect to factual issues, if *all* the evidence introduced on a question of fact is consistent, the trier of fact is not free to find the facts contrary to all the evidence. But expert testimony may be subject to a different rule. By its nature, expert testimony does not relate to questions of fact; rather, it usually relates to the opinions of the experts. The Supreme Court long ago articulated the distinction between factual testimony and opinion testimony:

> While there are doubtless authorities holding that a jury . . . has no right arbitrarily to ignore or discredit the testimony of unimpeached witnesses so far as they testify to facts, . . . no such obligation attaches to witnesses who testify hereby to their opinion; and the jury may deal with it as they please, giving it credence or not as their own experience or general knowledge of the subject may dictate. [*The Conquerer,* 166 U.S. 110, 131 (1897)]

Thus, the weight to be given to any expert testimony must be determined by the trier of fact (i.e., the jury or, if there is no jury, the judge), who cannot surrender his own function by giving controlling influence to the experts. Rather, the trier of fact must weigh all the evidence, and "the testimony of an expert witness may be disregarded if it conflicts with the sound judgment" of the trier of fact "based on his evaluation of all the evidence" (*Barry v. United States,* 501 F.2d 578, 584 (6th Cir. 1974)).

Nevertheless, experts are now permitted to testify to more than just their opinion, and the old rules may have to take account of the changing nature of expert testimony under the new Federal Rules of Evidence. Much of the concern about the use of expert testimony relates to the proffer of opinion testimony as to the ultimate issues of the case. While the new federal Rule 704 unequivocally recognizes the right of a party to offer such evidence, even if it goes to the ultimate issue in the litigation, the Advisory Committee on the new rules of evidence, in its notes on Rule 702, nevertheless recommended that expert testimony in *nonopinion* form be used "when counsel believes the trier can itself draw the requisite inference."

Thus, the preference is that the expert limit his testimony to relevant principles, leaving the trier to apply the principles to the facts of the case. In the case of an accounting expert, for example, the expert might testify as to the generally accepted auditing standards at the particular time in question or the standards relating to the presentation of financial information. Though the expert might also be allowed to testify as to whether, in his opinion, the actual conduct in question met those standards, the court as the trier of fact is free to apply the stated principles to the facts and to arrive at conclusions other than those expressed by the expert.

When an expert testifies as to a factual issue (e.g., the operative accounting principles in a certain period) and that testimony is left uncontradicted, either by other expert testimony or otherwise, it may, in effect, be conclusive. However, when the expert ventures into areas in which he states his opinion (e.g., whether certain conduct was consistent with generally accepted principles), the testimony, if admitted at all, may be accorded such weight as the trier of fact deems appropriate and may be completely disregarded, even if it is uncontradicted on the record. This is borne out by important cases discussed below.

Exemplary Cases. A 1978 case (commonly referred to as the *Westec* proceeding) involving disciplinary proceedings against accountants pursuant to Rule 2(e) of the SEC's Rules of Practice provides a good example of the distinction between opinion and nonopinion expert testimony concerning accounting matters (ASR 248, *In the matter of Ernst & Ernst, et al.*). In this case, the SEC considered the weight to be given to expert testimony from "an impressive array of leaders of the [accounting] profession," including professors of accounting, a former president of the AICPA, a former chief accountant of the SEC, and the chief accountant at the time of the hearing. The administrative law judge gave little weight to all the expert testimony, which was, for the most part, uncontradicted, stating that while the testimony was "helpful," in the final analysis the SEC had to determine for itself what was sound accounting practice.

On appeal to the SEC, the commission held that the administrative law judge had failed, in certain respects, to give the experts' testimony the weight it deserved. Specifically, with respect to the question of defining the pertinent accounting principles that were generally accepted in the mid-1960s when the case arose, the SEC held that the accountants' testimony should have been given "considerable" weight. But with respect to the crucial question—whether the accountants named as respondents in the Rule 2(e) proceeding had conducted a sufficient audit—the SEC was willing to give but "relatively little" weight to the experts' testimony. The commission explained this distinction by noting:

> While the experts gave their opinions regarding audit procedures with respect to some of those transactions, they also stated or indicated that considerations had to be given to the total "audit environment." This point, which seems self-evident, was most cogently made by Robert M. Trueblood, former AICPA president. Respondents'

counsel asked Trueblood, with reference to a lengthy statement of assumed facts concerning one of the transactions at issue, what further accounting steps he would have taken. Trueblood replied as follows: "That is a difficult question for me to answer. All auditing procedures are judgmental to a degree. They involve being there. They involve relationships with people. They involve prior relationships with the entities involved in the transactions. I simply cannot reconstruct what, in my opinion, I might have felt required to do had I been there under the described circumstances."

The distinction made by the SEC in this case (although not articulated in these terms) is the distinction between nonopinion expert testimony and opinion testimony.

The same distinction is implicit in the decision of the court of appeals with respect to the expert accounting testimony adduced by the defendant in a case commonly referred to as the *Continental Vending* action (*United States v. Simon,* 425 F.2d 796 (2d Cir. 1969), *cert. denied,* 397 U.S. 1006 (1970)). Rejecting the defendant's argument that the jury was bound to accept the uncontradicted expert testimony of several accountants, the court stated:

We think the judge was right in refusing to make the accountants' testimony so nearly a complete defense. The critical test according to the charge was the same as that which the accountants testified was crucial. We do not think the jury was also required to accept the accountants' evaluation whether a given fact was material to overall fair presentation, at least not when the accountants' testimony was not based on specific rules or prohibitions to which they could point, but only on the need for the auditor to make an honest judgment and their conclusion that nothing in the financial statements themselves negated the ... [facts]. [425 F.2d at 806]

Court-Appointed Experts

Rule 706 of the Federal Rules of Evidence permits the court to appoint one or more expert witnesses, either on its own motion or on the motion of a party. The court may ask the parties to submit nominations and may appoint either an expert agreed on by the parties or a witness of the court's own selection.

If a person appointed by a court agrees to serve as an expert witness, his duties are either set forth in writing and filed with the clerk or agreed on at a conference at which all parties have a chance to participate. The expert then conducts whatever inquiry is appropriate and advises the parties of his findings, if any. After that, the expert's deposition may be taken by any party, and he may be called to testify at trial by the court or by any party.

A court-appointed expert's compensation is set by the court. In criminal cases and cases involving a determination of just compensation under condemnation proceedings, there may be appropriated funds to pay the expert; in civil proceedings, however, the expert must be paid by the parties, although the court may apportion the fee among the parties in whatever manner it deems just. The expert's fee may also be taxed as costs to the losing party.

The court may or may not authorize disclosure to the jury of the fact that the court appointed the expert witness. Normally, of course, the party whom the court-appointed expert supports will want to bring to the attention of the jury the fact that the expert was appointed by the court and is, presumably, more impartial than a witness offered by a party. In the view of one commentator on the federal rules, there may be instances in which disclosure that the expert is court-appointed may work an unfairness to one or more of the parties by affording additional weight to the witness's testimony that may not be warranted. In effect, court-appointed experts may, if their appointment is disclosed, acquire an aura of infallibility to which they are not entitled.

Finally, even if the court does appoint an expert, the parties themselves are not prohibited from calling expert witnesses of their own selection. The power of courts to appoint experts has long been recognized, but except for the area of expert medical testimony, which has been the subject of various formal plans and programs, the power has largely been unused. In view of the increasing frequency with which complex financial issues are taken to the courts for resolution, however, this situation may change. The courts often find themselves in need of assistance in understanding financial and accounting issues, and the expert accountant witness may often be a key figure in that regard.

SUGGESTED READING

Burton, John C. "SEC Enforcement and Professional Accountants: Philosophy, Objectives and Approach." *Vanderbilt Law Review,* Vol. 28 (January, 1975), pp. 19-29. This article presents views by the SEC chief accountant (at time of writing).

"Foreign Corrupt Practices Act of 1977 and the Regulation of Questionable Payments." Program, *Business Lawyer,* Vol. 34 (January, 1979), pp. 623-664. This article is a discussion of the nature, scope, culpability standards, and administration of the foreign corrupt payments prohibitions of the Foreign Corrupt Practices Act and other criminal laws and the relationship of accounting records and controls to the act's provisions.

Mathews, Arthur. "SEC Civil Injunctive Actions." *Review of Securities Regulation,* Vol. 5 (February 18 and March 22, 1972), pp. 949-956, 969-976. This article is, as its subtitle indicates, a "Primer on [Their] Nature and Consequences."

U.S. Congress, Senate Subcommittee on Reports, Accounting and Management of the Committee on Government Operations. *The Accounting Establishment, A Staff Study.* Washington, D.C.: U.S. Government Printing Office, 1976. This staff study of the accounting profession contains a lengthy appendix dealing with the SEC. Of particular interest are the inquiries of Senator Metcalf concerning Rule 2(e) and *Hochfelder* and the responses thereto, at pages 1467-1508.

45

Accounting and the Law

Ronald D. Greenberg

BASIC CONSIDERATIONS

An accountant must follow at least two sets of accounting rules. One is that body of professional standards and practices referred to as generally accepted accounting principles (GAAP). The other is that area of law pertaining to accounting, whether formulated in custom, governmental regulations, court decisions, or statutes. Where these two systems overlap they often agree—accounting principles are sometimes embodied in law, and some legal restrictions are incorporated into GAAP—but they frequently conflict.

This disagreement is seldom a simple collision between a principle of law and a principle of accounting. It arises almost entirely within the legal system itself. There are many legal rulings that from a purely juristic point of view seem harmonious and even complementary to each other but from the accountant's standpoint may seem grossly incompatible.

Lacking means of enforcement and adjudication similar to those enjoyed by law, accounting principles have had to evolve through adaptation (to legal statutes, court rulings, and other regulations) and by consensus (in that the applicability of an accounting standard promulgated by a standard-setting body depends ultimately on its general acceptance by accountants and businessmen or at least by acceptance of the standard-setting body's right to set standards). Under our adversary system of law, an accounting principle or practice usually is brought under scrutiny only when it figures in litigation. Even then the court is interested only in resolving the case between the disputing parties, not in broadly interpreting the accounting principle. The questions of concern to the accountant—whether or not the approach at issue is a generally accepted accounting principle, whether the principle is inappropriate to the case at hand, whether there are specific points of fact or law that distinguish this case from other instances in which the same principle is applied—are usually ignored.

The ingredients that enter into accounting/legal differences are described below.

Judicial Approach

Legal Method. Legal method provides the framework by which courts adjudicate disputes. There are several schools of thought on what forms legal method should take so that judges can arrive at just and equitable decisions in accounting matters.

There is the *analytical approach,* for those who think that law is the embodiment of perfect reason or logic. One of its hallmarks is distinguishing cases that differ in one or more material ways. Based on the principle of *stare decisis* (the adherence to precedent), by which an earlier case may dictate the decision in the case in question (assuming that the earlier case has not been overturned), similar cases are supposedly decided by the courts similarly. Thus, if the case in question can be shown to differ from a judicial precedent (that is, to be *distinguished* from it), the earlier case would not apply.

Cases can be distinguished *on their facts,* when the surrounding circumstances are materially different. And cases may also be distinguished *on the law* (e.g., the statute may have been amended or is shown not to have been intended to apply to the case in question). The analytical approach might best be summarized as follows: similar situations should be disposed of similarly by the courts.

A second legal method or school of thought is one grounded in *history.* This school would emphasize the historical *trend* of jurisprudence. Thus, what was once good law may no longer be. For example, laws that applied in the days of the horse and buggy may not be appropriate in a more advanced technological age.

A third school is based on *sociology.* This school looks at how humans act in relation to one another. It views the laws *as they are* and asks if the laws are *as they should be.* Consumerism is an outgrowth of this kind of thinking; increased product liability of manufacturers and truth in lending are examples.

A fourth school is grounded in *economics.* The courts will look at economic statistics such as share of market in deciding an antitrust case, for example. In the tax field the economic impact of various tax measures would be considered by Congress when enacting new statutory provisions or amending old ones.

A fifth school, traced to Plato, looks at the *purpose* behind the laws. Here the emphasis is on the usefulness of the laws in furthering the particular legislative purpose that concerns the lawmakers.

Sources of Law. An outline of some of the major *sources of law* might also shed some perspective. One source is the United States *Constitution.* Here basic rights are set forth in general terms. For example:

- No person shall be deprived of life, liberty, or property without due process of law (5th Amendment);
- No state shall deprive any person of life, liberty, or property without due process of law (14th Amendment);
- The right of trial by jury shall be preserved (7th Amendment);
- No state shall pass any law impairing the obligation of contracts (Article 1, Section 10, clause 1); and
- The powers not delegated to the United States by the Constitution nor prohibited by it to the states are reserved to the states respectively or to the people (10th Amendment).

Another source is *statutes.* In the federal tax area, the Internal Revenue Code is the controlling law. The courts are often called upon to construe what Congress intended to do in enacting the law in question. The courts will usually try merely to decide Congressional intent, not the wisdom of the law. Courts generally decide controversies, but the controversy may be either about the facts (the court decides *what happened*) or about the meaning of the words in a statute (the court interprets *what the statute means*).

A third source is *court cases.* These may involve statutory interpretation or may simply resolve a dispute regarding the facts. The "common law" is the significant body of judge-made law established in the course of deciding cases.

A fourth source is *administrative regulations, rulings, and orders* developed by regulatory agencies such as the FHLBB, Comptroller of the Currency, ICC, DOE, and SEC with respect to various accounting matters within the agency's jurisdiction. For example, in the accounting area the Securities and Exchange Commission issues Regulation S-X, among others. Before an executive can be confident of a particular accounting presentation in an SEC filing he may need to consult with accountants and lawyers to be advised of the latest relevant rulings and regulations.

A fifth source of law is *custom.* What is customary in a trade for industry (if it is not thought by a court to be a practice against the public interest, community morals, or the like) may influence either a court in its decision of a case or a legislature in its enactment of a law.

A sixth source is the writings of various *scholars*. Lawyers, professors, accountants, executives, and others who write articles appearing in law reviews and journals and in accounting or other journals may be influential in what direction the law takes.

A seventh source might be the so-called *natural law*. Some legal thinkers describe it as a preexisting, perfect, universal set of rules. Other legal scholars suggest that it is more dynamic in character—that it is susceptible to purposeful growth. A formulation somewhere between these views might be that the natural law constitutes a process of maximum fulfillment of man's equitable principles through the use of reason.

Additional sources might include treaties, canon law, and anything else uncovered in an exhaustive catalogue of the various sources of law. In any event, law is not a mechanical subject. There is much in the law that appears technical, but law is much more. It involves many aspects of such disciplines as history, economics, philosophy, sociology, logic, accounting—perhaps even poetry. In short, the many rules of law are merely tools with which to accomplish a task on behalf of society.

Accounting Approach

Unlike legal rules, accounting principles are not generally the product of a legislative body or a judicial system whose statutes and decisions are enforceable through the exercise of state and federal power in their respective jurisdictions. Thus judges will often prefer to consult a dictionary for definitions of accounting terms of art. Some cases admit this; in others it's plainly obvious.

Legal rules have been developed with a certain degree of uniformity and finality. GAAP, however, incorporates a consensus and depends on notions such as general acceptance and substantial authoritative support (AC 1026.01). Generally accepted accounting principles are therefore conventional—that is, they become generally accepted by agreement (often tacit agreement) rather than by formal derivation from basic concepts. These principles have been developed on the basis of experience, reason, custom, usage, and practical necessity (AC 1026.03).

Authoritative and Other Sources. Opinions of the Accounting Principles Board (APB), statements of the Financial Accounting Standards Board (FASB), and accounting research bulletins (ARBs) are *authoritative* sources of GAAP for members of the AICPA. So are certain AICPA industry and accounting guides and statements of position (see SFAS 32; AC 1052). Pronouncements of the SEC, and sometimes of other regulatory agencies, are another important source, but these are regulations and technically are not GAAP. Nonetheless, they have the force of law within the scope of the agencies' jurisdictions.

Actual accounting practices not covered by authoritative sources and publications of professional organizations are additional sources of GAAP. Surveys that disclose either predominant or preferred accounting practices may provide guidance, as might accounting textbooks and other accounting writings. For example, the consensus of a number of writers may be a good indication of existing accounting principles not specified in authoritative accounting sources.

Rule 203 of the Rules of Conduct of the AICPA (AC 510.08) requires compliance with accounting principles formulated by the body (currently the FASB) designated by the council of the AICPA to establish such principles. In ASR 150 the SEC declared that, for its purposes, financial statements prepared in accordance with accounting practices for which there was no substantial authoritative support were presumed to be misleading (see ASR 4). The principles, standards, and practices promulgated by the FASB in its statements and interpretations will be considered by the SEC as having substantial authoritative support and those contrary to these FASB promulgations will be considered to have no such support.[1]

Accounting principles are thus developed through a consensus. Although they are generally not enforceable pursuant to a court order, as legal rules can be, accounting principles that enjoy general acceptance and substantial authoritative support would appear, in effect, to have a persuasive influence on accounting matters, perhaps tantamount in many ways (e.g., through various ethics and disciplinary proceedings—see Chapter 39) to the force of law.

The actions of the APB and FASB have been likened to those of a legislature. Like legislatures, they have been subjected to many political and lobbying pressures with respect to some of their pronouncements. The chairman of the FASB acknowledged this pressure in speaking to the American Petroleum Institute in 1978 after release of SFAS 19 (AC 6021) on oil and gas accounting. (See Kirk, 1978.) Three months later the SEC abrogated SFAS 19.

Accounting Court Proposal. There have been proposals from time to time for the establishment of an accounting court designed to solidify the development of accounting principles and to eliminate the frailties of a consensus-based system. Leonard Spacek (1958) made perhaps the most detailed suggestions for such a court, which would have operated as a professional body within the AICPA; thus "its decisions would not affect the laws nor the administration of the laws by the regulatory bodies" (p. 378). Spacek recommended a definition of *accounting principle* as

> ... one which can be specifically but separately demonstrated as resulting in a fair reporting of income from a business transaction for:
> a. Management, as a statement of accountability to stockholders.
> b. Stockholders or equity owners, as a fair determination of income.
> c. Labor, as a fair determination of the stockholders' income and capital devoted to a corporation's activities.
> d. Consumers, as a fair determination of corporate income from the prices they paid. [pp. 377-378]

These criteria are close in many respects to those a court of law might look to in resolving an accounting dispute, and it is perhaps for just that reason that the idea has not taken hold. The immense subjectivity of the definitional criteria was simply overwhelming to a practicing accountant. One can only speculate how the

---

[1] This blanket adoption of FASB rules without subjecting each to a rule-making proposal under the Administrative Procedures Act was challenged in a petition and a lawsuit by Arthur Andersen & Co. The SEC partially responded in ASR 193, which exposed the questions for public comment, but no further releases have been issued. The lawsuit was dismissed by the court. Thus ASR 150 and ASR 193 stand as written.

existence of an accounting court would have affected current pressures for governmental establishment of accounting principles.

Accounting in the Law

The accountant views financial statements as an impersonal source of facts whose purpose is to furnish useful information. The courts view financial statements as a source of evidence in the determination of justice between two conflicting claims and, accordingly, will accept as proper rules for financial statements only those rules that aid in the resolution of the controversy at bar.

The law of accounting consists of legal concepts formed by judicial decisions and statutory enactments. The courts are not a forum for deciding what are or are not correct or generally accepted accounting principles, although courts do establish accounting principles on occasion for certain purposes (e.g., corporate franchise taxes, dividends, and mergers). Cases also take accounting principles and cast them into rules of law; in some instances case law has accepted (or rejected), through the submission of accounting literature as evidence, a large number of accounting principles. Thus the body of case law contains, in effect, principles of the law of accounting.

Judicial opinions on various accounting matters may not be useful, however, because either accounting principles were inaccurately applied by the judges or accounting thought has advanced beyond the particular judicial application. Though an analysis from an accounting point of view has aided many courts in understanding the controversy and in stating relevant rules of law, there are many cases in which the court's reasoning is obscure and unsatisfactory. It was argued as long as a half-century ago that many rules of law can be profitably restated and new problems can be solved more readily and confidently if counsel and the courts have an understanding of fundamental accounting principles (Graham and Katz, 1938, pp. 3-4), but this has not occurred in any large measure.

The corporate lawyer generally recognizes that in drafting a contract the insertion of "in accordance with generally accepted accounting principles" may not be especially useful, because the phrase by itself does not add any certainty to the agreement, and that the phrase could indeed be harmful, because it often serves to delude the parties into failing to foresee what their accounting problems may be and how these problems can be properly provided for in the agreement.

Thus, courts, counsel, and accountants will acknowledge that judicial rules on accounting matters may vary considerably according to the particular problems at issue. Although GAAP may meet the needs of certain users of financial statements, these principles may not be appropriate in other contexts (e.g., in determining whether an executive is entitled to incentive compensation).

Because of the possible interest of the court in a problem apart from the accounting principle involved, courts on occasion have reached different interpretations of the same accounting principle. Many times a court will be called on to interpret the meaning of a statutory provision that may bear on an accounting principle, but in construing a statute the court seeks to determine what the statutory wording means in light of the legislative intent, not whether or not that interpretation is in accordance with generally accepted accounting principles. As the court stated in *Randall v. Bailey,* 23 N.Y.S. 2d 173 (1940), in dealing with a question of divi-

before he has received the funds if he has earned the right to receive them; but if he has already received them, even though he may be required to return them later, under the claim-of-right doctrine he probably must report them as income in the year of receipt unless he has agreed in the year of receipt to repay excess income, and adjusts his books accordingly.

Taxation, in sum, is a very practical subject, and the courts in determining what constitutes income for tax purposes do not give much weight to GAAP. Congress, in its tax laws, is presumed to have used words in their usual, ordinary, and everyday sense and not necessarily as defined in accounting theory or under GAAP. For further comment on the absence of conformity between tax and financial accounting see Chapter 43.

State Regulation. An important area has been the regulation by state laws of corporate dividends, distributions and stock redemptions, and repurchases. The Model Business Corporation Act provides protection for directors who rely on certified financial statements in these areas and, since its amendment in 1974, reflects the broader range of situations in which a director can rely on others (such as public accountants). It also reflects the range of materials (such as financial statements prepared by public accountants as to matters that the director reasonably believes to be within the accountants' professional or expert competence) on which a director can rely.

In New York and Delaware the statutory provisions that pertain to accounting can be classified as follows: (1) provisions related to definitions of accounting concepts and terms, such as *stated capital, surplus,* and *net assets* and (2) provisions related to the application of accounting definitions, such as those dealing with determination of the proper amounts of stated capital and various surplus accounts for regulating dividends and other purposes.

The Blue Sky laws of various states provide rules and regulations on accounting matters. For example, the Indiana Securities Division has issued rules and regulations on the form and content of all financial statements required to be filed. The Pennsylvania Securities Commission has issued regulations providing that financial statements shall be prepared in conformity with generally accepted accounting principles applied consistently with past periods or noting any changes. The Pennsylvania Securities Act provides that the accountant's report shall state clearly the opinion of the accountant with respect to (1) the financial statements covered by the report and the accounting principles and practices reflected therein, (2) the consistency of the application of the accounting principles, and (3) any changes in such principles that have a material effect on the financial statements.

New York Blue Sky regulations provide that financial statements of investment advisers shall be prepared in accordance with GAAP. The California Blue Sky law provides that the Commissioner of Corporations may prescribe by rule or order the form and content of financial statements required; and the commissioner has prescribed that all financial statements shall be prepared in accordance with GAAP.

Regulations of the Washington Administrator of Securities provide that all financial statements required to be filed shall be in the form and content specified by Regulation S-X of the SEC. Financial statements meeting the requirements of the SEC will be deemed to have met the financial disclosure requirements of the Washington Blue Sky law.

For further details in this area, refer to the *CCH Blue Sky Law Reporter.*

COURT APPROACH TO MAJOR ACCOUNTING CONCEPTS

If GAAP and the body of law affecting accounting principles used the same words to mean the same things, presumably there would be little conflict between accounting principles and the law. Accountants could depend on the courts to interpret accounting terminology in a manner consistent with professional usage. Courts and legislatures could avoid the ambiguity they now encounter when interpreting or formulating a legal judgment or statute. As it happens, confusion abounds and is made all the more striking by the many interpretations that have been handed down concerning some of the most common accounting terms.

It must be understood that much of the court controversy over accounting is found in tax cases; although this chapter does not attempt to deal with a comparison of tax and GAAP approaches, the topic is unavoidable in dealing with some of the areas below.

Fair Presentation

The terms *fair presentation* or *fairly presents* can be construed countless ways. These interpretations, among others, appear in accounting and legal literature: (1) generally accepted accounting principles imply fairness, so presentation is fair *to the extent* GAAP are fair; (2) fairness is conformity with generally accepted accounting principles, thus presentation is fair *because it is in accordance* with GAAP; (3) the phrase *fairly presents* emphasizes that financial statements are matters of estimation and judgment; (4) fairness involves something beyond mere conformity with generally accepted accounting principles—a presentation must be fair *and* accord with GAAP; (5) fairness implies, among other things, a selection of appropriate (not merely acceptable) principles and a reasonable disclosure of underlying events; and (6) fairness means full disclosure of all material facts of the enterprise in order to protect investors so that they can make informed investment decisions and not be misled.

Accountants' and SEC Views. Simply to set the stage for contrast with court views, the accountant's view contained in SAS 5 (AU 411.04) predicates a fair presentation of financial statements on whether

a. the accounting principles selected and applied have general acceptance;
b. the accounting principles are appropriate in the circumstances;
c. the financial statements, including the related notes, are informative of matters that may affect their use, understanding, and interpretation;
d. the information presented in the financial statements is classified and summarized in a reasonable manner, that is, neither too detailed nor too condensed; and
e. the financial statements reflect the underlying events and transactions in a manner that presents the financial position, results of operations, and changes in financial position stated within a range of acceptable limits, that is, limits that are reasonable and practicable to attain in financial statements.

The AICPA's Auditing Standards Board is engaged (in late 1980) in an attempt to remove the word *fairly* from the auditor's standard report (AICPA, 1980h). This has been tried before, but has met, and may still meet, resistance from the SEC.

In the SEC arena, several general conclusions have been stated by the previous chief accountant of the SEC (Burton, 1975b), and these seem to still be the SEC's prevailing view:

1. "Fairness" seems to be related in some way to "truth," which has some meaning beyond generally accepted accounting principles;
2. The courts appear to believe that generally accepted accounting principles are a set of defined rules and conventions and that following these rules does not give complete absolution from the possibility of either civil or criminal liability;
3. The overall impression left by the financial statements must be considered in appraising fairness; and
4. The courts seem to view fairness as something that can be interpreted by the layman as well as the sophisticate.

Accountants have frequently stated that accounting is an art, not a science, for a number of reasons. First, the financial statements, although expressed in numbers, do not measure financial data with mathematical exactness. Second, in numerous instances the reporting of financial information depends on a subjective determination that will vary from accountant to accountant. Third, even where accounting principles are well defined, if permissible alternative principles are available, the accountant must exercise judgment. For these and other reasons, accountants have disagreed with the SEC's requirement that the CPA express his concurrence concerning the preferability of a client's new accounting method when there is a change in accounting (see Chapter 16).

Perhaps implicit in the SEC's preferability requirement is that there is a lack of uniform accounting principles; this observation has also been made by the courts. For example, the court in *Burroughs International Co. v. Datronics Engineers, Inc.,* 255 A.2d 341, 351 (1969), concluded its opinion with the comment: "More than ample support can be found for the proposition that generally accepted accounting principles (GAAP) are nebulous in concept and almost incredibly elastic."

Some writers go so far as to state that fair presentation on a financial statement means that the principles used in preparing the statement conform to sound accounting doctrines and that, where more than one accounting principle would be generally acceptable, one of these principles has been used so that "erratic notions have been avoided" (Faris, 1975, p. 410).

Judicial and State Regulatory Views. The purpose behind the securities laws is to protect investors. To ask whether or not GAAP has been followed does not answer the question of whether or not investors received full disclosure of material facts as required under the securities laws enacted for their protection. Fair presentation to accountants may mean, among other things, presentation in accordance with GAAP; fair presentation under the securities laws means full disclosure. It is possible that the terms could in some circumstances mean the same thing but not necessarily in other circumstances.

Judicial view. The question of what constitutes fair presentation would appear to have been subdivided by the courts into two questions: first, whether GAAP constitutes a standard of fair and adequate disclosure, and second, if these principles are not deemed to be a sufficient standard, whether to extend the parameters of accountants' (auditors') liability. (The three case excerpts below are limited to the first question. For a discussion of the second, see Chapter 46.)

In *United States v. Simon*, 425 F.2d 796, 805-808 (2d Cir. 1969), *cert. denied*, 90 S. Ct. 1235 (1970), a case involving the allegedly false and misleading financial statements of Continental Vending Machine Corporation, many prominent accountants testified that the disclosure in a certain footnote conformed with GAAP. Nonetheless, Judge Friendly said that

> the "critical test" was whether the financial statements as a whole "fairly presented the financial position of Continental as of September 30, 1962, and whether [they] accurately reported the operations for fiscal 1962." [at 805]
>
> Generally accepted accounting principles instruct an accountant what to do in the usual case where he has no reason to doubt that the affairs of the corporation are being honestly conducted. [at 806]
>
> The jury could reasonably have wondered how accountants who were really seeking to tell the truth could have constructed a footnote so well designed to conceal the shocking facts. [at 807]

In *SEC v. Bangor Punta Corp.*, 331 F. Supp. 1154 (S.D. N.Y. 1971), *modified*, 480 F.2d 341 (2d Cir. 1973), *cert. denied*, 414 U.S. 924 (1973), the court held that if the disclosure required under generally accepted accounting principles was different from fair disclosure required by the securities act, the applicable standard was the securities act, for the protection of investors. In a nice gesture, the court added that disclosure under the securities laws is the responsibility of management, not the certifying accountants.

In *Feit v. Leasco Data Processing Equipment Corporation*, 332 F. Supp. 544, 549, 565-566 (E.D. N.Y. 1971), the court deemphasized GAAP and talked about a double-edged disclosure mandate:

> ... the objectives of full disclosure can be fully achieved only by complete revelation of facts which would be material to the sophisticated investor or the securities professional, not just the average common shareholder. But, at the same time, the prospectus must not slight the less experienced. They are entitled to have within the four corners of the document an intelligible description of the transaction.

The courts' guidance on fair presentation is far from unified and clear, as the above three cases illustrate.

State regulatory view. New York State in its Security Takeover Disclosure Rules provides that required financial statements shall be prepared in accordance with GAAP consistently applied and shall include opinions by "independent public accountants as to the fairness of presentation of the financial statements" (Reg. § 12.5, 2 *CCH Blue Sky L. Rep.* ¶ 35,655). The Illinois Securities Law regulations operate with the same effect.

The Indiana securities regulations provide that any change in accounting principle or practice or in the method of applying any accounting principle or practice made during any period for which financial statements are filed that affects the comparability of such financial statements with those of either prior or future periods and the effect thereof on the net income for each period for which financial statements are filed shall be disclosed in a note to the appropriate financial statement. Pennsylvania, on the other hand, simply calls for disclosure in an appropriate manner.

Results of Operations

Various methods of reckoning income have been recognized by the courts, including the cash method and the accrual method. Although the courts have recognized that different methods may be appropriate in different circumstances, on occasion the courts have disapproved a method as not being in accordance with GAAP.

Definition of Income. The courts have long tried to define and to distinguish the terms *income, earnings,* and *profit(s)* as these terms appear in statutes, corporate documents, and contracts.[3] Although sometimes these terms have been held to be synonymous, each seems to be legally significant and to have a separate meaning when standing alone; and the courts have not applied a uniform meaning. The meaning of these terms may vary depending on the intent of the parties, the context in which the terms are used, and other circumstances.

In the courts, *income* generally means all that comes in. It does not include that which might have come in but did not, nor an amount that a person is saved from paying. Income may be derived from capital; from labor; through the exercise of skill, ingenuity, or judgment; or from a combination of these sources.

It has been said that *profit* has perhaps received a greater variety of judicial interpretation than any other one word known to law. It is an elastic and relative term, and it is often properly used in more than one sense. Some courts have held that it is ambiguous, some have held the opposite.

There are also many court decisions that make the distinction between operating and nonoperating income for various purposes. For example, a federal court stated that upon the sale or exchange of an investment, any resulting gain does not represent "earnings" and should not appear on the income statement for the accounting period (*Associated Elec. Co. v. U.S.,* 97 F. Supp. 821, 826 (Ct. Cl. 1951)).

Net Income. There appears to be similar lack of uniformity among the courts regarding the terms *net income, net earnings,* and *net profits.* Neither a single definition of the terms, nor one of general applicability, has been stated by the courts. The court in each instance has based its opinion on the specific problem at bar. Some examples follow.

A New Jersey court in 1907 set up two tests for net profits: first, an excess of earnings over operating expenses of the current year, and second, an excess of the value of the present assets over the value of the assets with which the company began business (*Goodnow v. Amer. Writing Paper Co.,* 66 A. 607, 69 A. 1014, 1015). The first test was used in a Missouri case (*Morrow v. Missouri Pac. Ry.,*

---

[3] See, e.g., *Eisner v. Macomber,* 252 U.S. 189 (1920).

123 S.W. 1034 (Mo. 1910)), in which the court said profit is the benefit remaining after all costs, charges, and expenses have been deducted from the income. The second test was used in a Massachusetts decision, in which the court said that net profits represented the difference between the value of the receipts and assets at the end of the year and the value of similar items at the beginning of the year, deducting reasonable depreciation of the plant (*Stein v. Strathmore Worsted Mills,* 221 Mass. 86, 108 N.E. 1029 (Mass. 1915)).

In *Tooey v. Percival Co.,* 182 N.W. 403, 405 (1921), the court said that the principles of bookkeeping restrict the net profits of any business to those profits that have been reduced to actual possession in the form of either cash or its equivalent by completed sales.

These very early cases are mentioned to illustrate that some things never change: accountants are still looking for the elusive definition of income (see Chapter 7). It has even been said recently that most accountants would be hard pressed to explain its precise meaning (Vickery, 1976).

Gross Margin

Gross margin, the difference between revenues and cost of goods sold, is utilized for a number of purposes in the law as well as in accounting. For example, a computation of royalties, or a determination of percentage rentals for a retail store, may by contract be based on gross margin.

Discounts, Returns, and Allowances. Trade discounts, allowances on goods sold, and refunds on returned goods are generally considered by both accountants and the courts as direct subtractions from gross revenues. Cash discounts are sometimes treated as a financial expense but are more usually treated as an offset to the sales price.

Cost of Goods Sold. Cost of goods sold, for businesses that sell goods, are deducted from gross revenues to arrive at gross margin or gross profit. The courts agree that cost of goods sold comprises direct material cost, direct labor cost, and factory or other relevant burden (including depreciation).

The courts have faced two major questions with regard to direct materials to be included in cost of goods sold: what materials are to be included and how their cost is to be computed. With regard to the first question, for example, the courts have held that the cost of incoming freight and packaging are to be included in materials cost. However, the courts have held that such items as office and factory supplies, small stores, and advertising material are not inventory under the federal tax law but are assets that represent deferred charges to future operations (even though accountants might carry them as inventory). Courts recognize that shrinkage and waste are normal aspects of the manufacturing process and are properly included as costs of materials. However, administration charges incurred in procuring materials are operating expenses and are not part of inventory cost.

Direct labor cost, long recognized by the courts as a fundamental element of cost of goods sold, is not limited to wages paid; it generally includes the various economic benefits that workers receive from the employment relationship.

The courts and accountants have not used the term *overhead* with any semblance of uniformity. Whether a particular expense should be treated as either a directly chargeable cost or part of general plant overhead must be determined in accordance with recognized commercial accounting practices applied on an objective basis. The impossibility of precise allocation is generally recognized, and the law does not require mathematical certainty.

Other Costs and Expenses

Various deductions from gross margin recognized by accounting and legal authority may be taken to compute net income: selling, general and administrative expenses, other operating expenses, and income taxes.

Selling and General and Administrative Expenses. The courts have recognized that selling expenses are a proper cost in the determination of net income. For example, expenditures for advertising, a species of selling expense, are a proper charge against current revenues, but courts have held that some portion of advertising should be deferred as an expense of future periods if it is probable that it will influence sales for succeeding years. (Such deferrals are rare under GAAP; see Chapter 21.) The costs of sales personnel, such as commissions and travel expenses, are recognized by the courts as direct selling expenses.

In the general and administrative expense category, compensation paid to an officer is a proper operating expense, whether the compensation is fixed or is in whole or part dependent on earnings or sales. The reasonableness of executive compensation has been held to be a question of fact and also to be a matter for the courts, not the accountants. Most executive compensation adjudications are in the tax deductibility area.

Other Operating Expenses and Taxes. Profit is the excess of income that remains after deducting "not only the operating expenses and depreciation of capital but also interest on the capital employed" (73 C.J.S. Profit 2 (1951, 1978)). Many courts have had occasion to decide what is an operating expense; in general, they appear to agree with GAAP. For example, courts have included costs such as production, commercial, and general expenses; inward freight; supplies; rent; insurance; labor; officers' salaries; lawyers' and accountants' fees; experimental costs; repairs and maintenance; compiling and publishing expenses; the cost of training employees; interest on borrowed money; and amortization of the expense of procuring a lease.

In contrast, brokers' commissions on the purchase of securities, contributions to a bond sinking fund, principal amortization payments on a mortgage debt, imputed interest, and imputed rent have been held not to be valid operating expenses or deductions from gross income. The need for expense imputations usually stems from accounting requirements (see, for example, Chapter 22 regarding imputed interest and Chapter 28 regarding expenses not charged); thus conflicts between accounting and law do occur in this area.

Various taxes other than federal income taxes are considered by the courts to be operating expenses. But federal income taxes are not deductible as operating expenses in computing taxable income, though in contract cases income taxes have been held to be ordinary and necessary expenses of a business and thus deductible in arriving at net income.

Assets

The courts take a broad approach in defining *assets;* as stated in 6A C.J.S. Assets at 574 (1975, 1979), the meaning of the word *assets* must be determined by the context in which it is used.

Under GAAP (AC 2031.04) classification as a current asset depends on whether the asset is reasonably expected to be realized in cash or sold or consumed within one year or within a short-term operating cycle; the courts generally agree. (See Thompson et al., 1978, Chapter 8, for a lawyer's view of classifying balance sheet items.)

Cash and Securities. Legally, the use of the term *cash* does not necessarily mean only the physical dollars represented by currency or by bank deposits; and a bank account is cash unless there is a restriction on its use. Courts have specifically eliminated outstanding checks, IOUs, and demand notes receivable from the cash account. Temporary investment of an enterprise's cash in marketable securities is usually classified as current assets, both in the courts and under GAAP (see Chapter 17).

Investment in securities of another corporation made for the purpose of control or other continuing advantage should, if material, be clearly identified in the balance sheet and distinguished from current assets. Whether the investment should be recorded either at cost or at cost plus the investor's share of postacquisition earnings or losses (equity method) has been a question on which various opinions can be found in court cases. Although accountants have been primarily concerned with distinguishing long-term investments from those that are short-term, the courts have been concerned primarily with the definition of *security* for the purpose of various federal and state regulatory statutes.

Notes and Accounts Receivable. An important question faced by the courts is whether a note receivable should be classified as a current asset or whether it is a less liquid kind of asset. The value and classification of a note receivable is a question of fact, not one of law. Where notes are secured by collateral or pledged, court and administrative decisions are in accord with GAAP that this fact must be disclosed as to material amounts. Similarly, notes receivable due from or owed to directors, officers, and principal shareholders must be separately stated, if material.

Accounts arising from selling goods to customers on credit in the ordinary course of business are properly shown in current assets as trade accounts receivable, assuming that there is no undue question of their collectibility, whereas accounts receivable not so arising have been questioned. If a question exists as to whether there is an open account receivable, a court will interpret the contract between the parties in reaching a decision. It has been deemed misleading to fail to show in the balance sheet that accounts receivable have been pledged as collateral security for a loan (see Uniform Commercial Code, § 9-106).

Notes and accounts receivable known to be uncollectible should be excluded from the assets as well as from the reserve accounts.

Inventory. Inventory includes merchandise held for sale to customers or material otherwise used in the ordinary course of a trade or business. Whether property is to be included in inventory has depended in the courts on various factors, such as whether title to the property has passed to the company and whether the property is tangible and is, or will become, salable in the ordinary course of business. The courts have generally based the determination of either actual or fair value of inventories on cost or on the lower of cost or market. Courts have also held that a proper inventory, in some circumstances, must be sufficiently itemized to show the kinds and numbers or quantities thereof. Under IRC Section 472(c), those companies electing to use the last-in, first-out (LIFO) method of inventory valuation for federal income tax purposes must also use it for purposes of reporting to shareholders and for credit and other external purposes.

Property, Plant, and Equipment. The courts and accountants have generally agreed that property, plant, and equipment assets should be shown on the balance sheet at cost. Chapter 20 contains a detailed description of applicable GAAP, but there are two matters deserving mention here.

Unrealized appreciation. Whether a surplus arising from a write-up of fixed assets will form the basis for a declaration of dividends depends on the law of the state of incorporation. *Randall v. Bailey,* 288 N.Y. 280, 43 N.E. 2d 43 (1942), is perhaps the only significant decision permitting unrealized appreciation of fixed assets to enter into the measurement of funds available for dividends.

According to one authority the trial court paid no attention to accounting practice that prohibited recording unrealized appreciation; in the court's view, the question was not one of sound economics, of proper accounting practice, or even of what the law ought to be; the problem was one of statutory construction. Herwitz (1979, pp. 326-327) describes it this way:

> Of course this view overlooks the fact that the words of a dividend statute are typically terms of accounting art, not legal art, and their meaning comes primarily from the accounting background from which they spring.
>
> This is not to say that the proper construction of the dividend statute as to unrealized appreciation . . . should be entirely controlled by accounting views or practice. There is as much danger in giving too great weight to accounting implications as giving too little. Unless the accounting significance of a term is so clear that no other meaning would rationally be attributed to the legislature—and such complete freedom from ambiguity is as rare in accounting as in the law—the accounting implications simply represent one factor to be taken into account. Thus the difference between the policy underlying dividend regulation, to accommodate fairly the interest of creditors as well as the interests of shareholders *inter se,* and the primary purpose of financial accounting to disclose meaningfully the financial condition of an enterprise, might well lead to different views on unrealized appreciation. But certainly as a first step in interpreting the statute it is essential to know whether accounting encourages, simply permits, or actually condemns the recognition of unrealized appreciation in financial statements.

In a majority of jurisdictions, statutory and case law prohibit using unrealized appreciation in determining the funds available for dividends. Courts taking the minority position, however, have stated that this fund should be based on "actual values." *Randall v. Bailey* is the case usually cited in support.

Because dividends are paid out of corporate profits that are often overstated

are tax cases. The courts have reasoned that once an obligation's existence is established it should lose its contingent liability classification regardless of whether the actual amount or time of payment is fixed. This difference between the law and GAAP is further discussed in Fiflis and Kripke, 1977, pp. 321-326.

Deferred Income. Though almost all the legal controversy has been in the tax area, a few remarks are in order because of the significance of the problem.

Under the tax law, an accrual basis taxpayer as a general rule will be required to report income before it has been received if he has earned the right to it. This issue has been sufficient to generate three United States Supreme Court decisions, all leading to government victories (that is, the taxpayers were not allowed to defer recognition of the advance receipt as income). The last of these was *Schlude v. Commissioner, 372 U.S. 128 (1963).* Subsequently, however, various legislative and administrative actions have limited these cases' scope, and there have been judicial decisions distinguishing these cases and their progeny. Some of the reasons for the failure of *Schlude* to win broad acceptance can be seen in the economic issue it deals with and in the circumstances related to legislation it complements. Some examples of the legislative, administrative, and judicial reactions to *Schlude* follow.

In 1957 Congress added IRC Section 455, which permits accrual basis publishers to elect to exclude from current year income prepaid subscription income to a newspaper, magazine, or other periodical that applies to subsequent years. This section was passed largely to codify a decision favorable to the taxpayer-publisher in *Beacon Publishing Co. v. Commissioner, 218 F.2d 697 (10th Cir. 1955).* In like manner Congress in 1960 enacted Section 456, which allows for the deferral of prepaid dues income of various membership organizations over the period (not to exceed 36 months) during which these organizations are obligated to render services for which members have paid dues. In 1980, IRC Section 453 was significantly amended to make the treatment of installment sales more in keeping with commercial practice.

At the administrative level, Revenue Procedure 71-21 provides that in connection with advance receipts for services to be rendered by an accrual taxpayer before the end of the year following the year of receipt, the taxpayer must perform the services by the end of the following year, in which event the recognition of income may be deferred until the advance receipt is earned. The amount of income deferred is in proportion to the services remaining unperformed at the end of the year of receipt. The deferred amount must, however, be recognized as income in the year following the year of receipt whether or not all of the remaining services are performed in the following year.

Special rules also permit the deferral of income with respect to advance receipts even when no agreement requires the taxpayer to perform the services prior to the end of the year following the year of receipt. For example, the recognition of income from the sale of transportation services (involving tokens and tickets) can be deferred in accordance with GAAP for the industry but for no longer than to the end of the year after the year of receipt. And Treasury Regulation §1.451-5 provides that advance receipts with respect to the sale of goods by an accrual basis taxpayer may be deferred from recognition as income until the taxpayer would normally accrue it (such as when earned by delivery pursuant to the sales contract). This rule would apply as well to various transactions for construction and for manufacturing.

The courts too have found ways to circumvent *Schlude*. For example, *Artnell Co. v. Commissioner*, 400 F.2d 981 (7th Cir. 1968), ostensibly dealt with the question of the level of proof demanded of the taxpayer. In that case the taxpayer, who was the owner of the Chicago White Sox baseball club, wanted to defer income from prepaid tickets until after the majority of home games had been played and, *ipso facto*, until after the end of the taxpayer's fiscal year. On remand, the tax court found that the allocation proposed by the commissioner was no more reasonable or economically sound than the taxpayer's equally inadequate allocation system. The court nonetheless found that since neither party had provided the necessary proof to give the court an acceptable standard, judgment should be entered for the taxpayer.

Whether the *Artnell* court was expressing a dissatisfaction with the system left in the wake of *Schlude* is a matter for speculation. It appears, however, that there is a definite division of authority on the lower court level in cases falling into what would seemingly be *Schlude* terrain.

Owners' Equity

APB Statement 4 (AC 1027.25) categorizes *capital* for accountants: "Owners' equity of corporations is conventionally classified into categories including par or stated amount of capital stock, additional paid-in capital, and retained earnings." In the law, however, *capital* takes on various meanings depending on context, and appears to include only the contributed capital and not the undivided profits or *surplus* unless that becomes a part of capital by means of a formal capitalization.

Corporate Capital. The accounting treatment of corporate capital by a business corporation must meet the standards of the state of incorporation. While some early court decisions spoke of corporate capital as a "trust fund" for creditors, it is generally understood that legal paid-in capital is not an actual fund held in trust for creditors, even though it does represent a limit below which corporate assets may not lawfully be distributed to shareholders until the corporation is liquidated. There is also a prohibition on capital impairment.

The term *stated capital* is employed by the Model Business Corporation Act (MBCA, § 2) to avoid the ambiguity that has sometimes arisen from using the terms *capital* and *capital stock*. Under the MBCA (§ 2(j)) *stated capital* means, at any particular time, the sum of

1. the par value of all shares of the corporation having a par value that have been issued,
2. the amount of the consideration received by the corporation for all shares of the corporation without par value that have been issued, except such part of the consideration therefor as may have been allocated to capital surplus in a manner permitted by law, and
3. such amounts not included in clauses (1) and (2) as have been transferred to stated capital of the corporation, whether upon the issue of shares as a share dividend or otherwise, minus all reductions from such sum as have been effected in a manner permitted by law.

Other significant definitions of the MBCA include *authorized shares,* which means the shares of all classes that the corporation is authorized to issue (§ 2(g)); *net assets,* which means the amount by which the total assets of a corporation exceed the total debts of the corporation (§ 2(i)); and *treasury shares,* which are those shares issued that have been subsequently acquired by and belong to the corporation and have not been cancelled or restored to the status of authorized but unissued shares (§ 2(h)). Treasury shares are deemed to be issued shares but not outstanding shares.

The Model Business Corporation Act definitions do not cause any conflicts with GAAP. The New York Business Corporation Law, however, requires that surplus (excess of net assets over stated capital) be charged for the full cost of the shares upon their acquisition and immediate retirement and that stated capital then be charged, and capital surplus credited, with par or stated value (§§ 513, 515(d)). ARB 43, Chapter 1B, provides that where the laws of some states govern the circumstances under which a corporation may acquire its own stock and prescribe the accounting treatment therefor, and where such requirements are at variance with GAAP, the accounting should conform to the applicable law (AC 5542.14). When state laws relating to acquisition of stock restrict the availability of retained earnings for payment of dividends or have other effects of a significant nature, these facts should be disclosed in the financial statements. (For more discussion, see Stanger, 1968).

Stock Dividends and Splits. A share dividend, unlike a dividend in cash or property, does not constitute a distribution of assets to shareholders.

Legally, the amount of surplus to be capitalized on the issuance of a stock dividend should be not less than the aggregate par value of dividend shares having a par value. In the case of shares without par value, the amount to be capitalized should be not less than the aggregate stated value.

GAAP calls for an accounting treatment that will in most cases result in a capitalization of earned surplus in excess of that required by the laws of the state of incorporation. Where the additional shares issued are less than, say, 20% or 25% of the number previously outstanding, the corporation should transfer, from earned surplus to the category of permanent capitalization, an amount equal to the fair value of the additional shares (ARB 43, Chapter 7B, as amended; AC 5561.10). A greater proportion of shares distributed signifies a stock split, which does not result in a capitalization of surplus (AC 5561.15). (See Chapter 26 and the New York Stock Exchange *Company Manual* (1979, § A13).)

Undivided Profits. The somewhat archaic term *surplus* is used extensively in law even though it is not preferred for accounting. The MBCA defines *surplus* as the excess of the net assets of a corporation over its stated capital (§ 2(k)) and *capital surplus* as the entire surplus of a corporation other than its earned surplus (§ 2(m)). The meaning of surplus (in its various forms) under the various corporate statutes is not necessarily in accordance with accounting concepts.

Earned surplus is defined as the portion of the surplus of a corporation equal to the balance of its net profits, income, gains, and losses from the date of incorporation, or from the latest date when a deficit was eliminated by an application of its capital surplus or stated capital or otherwise, after deducting subsequent distributions to shareholders and transfers to stated capital and capital surplus to the extent such distributions and transfers are made out of earned surplus (MBCA,

§ 2(1)). The act adds that earned surplus shall include also any portion of surplus allocated to earned surplus in mergers, consolidations, or acquisitions of all or substantially all of the outstanding shares, or of the property and assets, of another corporation, domestic or foreign.

The accounting profession has for 40 years recommended that the term *earned surplus* be replaced by one that will indicate the source, such as *retained earnings, retained income, accumulated earnings,* or *earnings retained for use in the business* (AICPA, 1953, ¶ 65, referring to a 1941 recommendation). Courts, however, have continued to distinguish net earnings from other types of surplus in their interpretation of state laws governing the payment of dividends and in construing contracts, bylaws, and charters containing dividend clauses.[4]

Whether and to what extent the funds of a corporation legally may be distributed to shareholders from the various surpluses is regulated by the corporate laws of the states. The fiduciary and contractual relations of a corporation with its shareholders and creditors are thus derived from applicable corporate laws, not from GAAP. The accounting features of corporation laws, at least the recent enactments, usually embody generally accepted accounting principles, although corporation laws containing prohibitions against the payment of dividends out of capital long antedate modern concepts of corporate accounting. The case law in this area focuses on the distinction between capital and surplus for the protection of creditors from unlawful withdrawals of capital by shareholders.

A PERSPECTIVE

Increased Scrutiny of Accounting

In recent years there has been increasing controversy regarding the role of legislative and regulatory bodies in the process of determining accounting standards and whether there should be greater uniformity (see Merino and Coe, 1978). Legislators and regulators have also increasingly scrutinized the accounting profession. Examples are the Moss and Metcalf reports and the SEC's three annual reports to Congress, all discussed in Chapter 39.

Among the many issues raised in these detailed scrutinies of the accounting profession is whether accounting principles should be established in the private sector (i.e., the FASB) or in the public sector (e.g., the SEC). The SEC has the authority under the securities acts to set the rules for publicly held companies, but has been somewhat restrained in exercising this right. However, the SEC can usually get its way on how a rule should look simply by withholding its support of an FASB or AICPA proposal or by effectively countermanding an FASB standard (as was done in oil and gas accounting; see Chapter 37).

One can only speculate how the courts would react if all accounting standards were embodied in government regulations. While arguments against the propriety of specific regulations are possible and are occasionally successful in achieving a

---

[4] On the question of whether uniform terminology between accounting and law is desirable for shareholder equity accounts or other areas, see ABA Committee on Corporate Law and Accounting, "Corporate Responsibility in The Financial Accounting and Disclosure Areas: Who Makes And Who Implements The Rules?", *Business Lawyer,* July, 1979, pp. 1979-2020.

change in the regulations, it would seem likely that the courts might pay more heed to actual accounting regulations than they now do to the more than 2,000 pages of fine print it takes to contain the present authoritative accounting rules (e.g., those promulgated by the FASB).

Based on the assumption that accounting standard setting will remain in the private sector, it is hardly possible that the courts can ever become harmonized with the accountant's burgeoning definitions of accounting principles. Perhaps accountants and the courts could get closer if the tomes of rules were jettisoned in favor of a concise listing of broad concepts (as has been suggested by Catlett, 1980). At least both parties would have less to read and digest.

Accounting Rules as Law

Court cases come up one at a time, and there is no mechanism for a canvass of all undecided cases outstanding at any one time to ascertain whether there are common accounting issues. The availability of LEXIS (see Chapter 49) has immensely improved the searchability of decided cases so as to enable jurists (if they wished) to synchronize decisions on a more timely basis; however, this is not likely to happen to any significant extent, because the legal system (see beginning of this chapter) simply is not structured to incorporate an accounting rule that is not also a law or formal regulation.

Looking at the brighter side, there has been no case in recent years that has the effect of outlawing (i.e., in *all* instances) a generally accepted accounting principle formally adopted by the accounting profession's rule-making body. This could happen if accounting were law.[5]

It would not be fair to accountants to leave this chapter without acknowledging that the tomes of accounting rules are making some accountants operate legalistically, at least in the larger CPA firms. There is so much to know and more to research that the effects occasionally can be seen in accounting rule applications that seem to make little sense, though totally in conformity with prescribed GAAP. As lawyers have their LEXIS and case precedents, so too have accountants their NAARS and microfiche (see Chapter 49). Whether the accountant is becoming

---

[5] A sample of what happens when accounting is law is shown in the following article, which appeared in *In Perspective,* a publication of Touche Ross & Co., New York, on June 6, 1980:

Honi soit qui mal y pense

A recent United Kingdom tax case (*Shearer* [Inspector of Taxes] v. *Bercain Ltd.*) (March 1980) involved the valuation process when one company acquires the shares of another company in a common share-for-share exchange. Based on these facts alone, it would appear that under U.S. standards, pooling-of-interests accounting would be proper.

In his judgment, Mr. Justice Walton of the High Court held that the directors of the company issuing shares must estimate the value of the shares received and that any excess over the par or stated value of the shares issued is a credit to share premium (paid-in capital in U.S. parlance). Judge Walton also held, effectively, that the accumulated earnings of the acquired company are not accumulated earnings of the combined company, and are therefore not available for distribution after the business combination.

All this sounds suspiciously like purchase accounting, which is consistent with Justice Walton's decision. Reading on, we find his final judgment held that the pooling-of-interests concept is illegal!

Although the underpinning of the U.S. legal system is English common law, this is one English decision American business might prefer not to import.

much like a lawyer in a special area of practice is, at least, a question not to be dismissed. And if he is, what does that portend for the relationship between law and accounting in the future?

SUGGESTED READING

Fogelson, James. "The Impact of Changes in Accounting Principles on Restrictive Covenants in Credit Agreements and Indentures." *Business Lawyer,* January, 1978, pp. 769-782. Restrictive covenants commonly contain reference to generally accepted accounting principles, and there is often no placement of the date at which that term should be reckoned. Accordingly, changes in accounting standards, occurring at a constantly accelerating pace, can create significant technical problems and occasionally result in a dilemma: violate the restrictive covenant or accept a nonstandard auditor's report for failure to adopt a newly mandated principle (which in itself might be a violation of a restrictive covenant). A prime example lies in SFAS 13, *Accounting for Leases* (AC 4053), in which the FASB granted a five-year period during which companies might rearrange their restrictive covenants so as to not be in automatic violation thereof by the capitalization of leases existing at the effective date of SFAS 13. The author provides useful suggestions for both accountants and lawyers to cope with this problem.

Hills, George. *The Law of Accounting and Financial Statements.* Boston: Little, Brown & Co., 1957. Although this is an older book, it is extremely complete and an invaluable reference for the accountant or lawyer who wishes to research matters up to its publication date. Each item of assets and liabilities in the balance sheet and each item of income and expense in the income statement is described in conformity with legal decisions as well as with accounting authorities (as they then existed) on the subject.

McClure, Melvin. "Diverse Tax Interpretations of Accounting Concepts." *Journal of Accountancy,* October, 1976, pp. 67-74. The author reviews the ever-widening breach between income tax and financial accounting, pointing out that the breach was never originally intended. Although part of the problem lies in the use of income tax regulations and administrative philosophies to achieve social goals, the courts have contributed by misunderstanding underlying accounting principles and concepts or by a reluctance to be bound by or to evaluate those concepts.

Solomons, David. "The Politicization of Accounting." *Journal of Accountancy,* November, 1978, pp. 65-72. The author likens accounting to cartography, pointing out that every map is in fact a special purpose map; it all depends on what the cartographer is trying to present. The author argues that the accountants cannot appear indifferent to national objectives in setting accounting standards that have economic consequences, but at the same time they cannot endanger the integrity of measurement techniques by skewing an accounting standard so as to produce the appearance of a desirable economic result. Accountants should prepare the best maps they can, but it is for others, or for accountants acting in a different capacity, to use those maps to steer the economy in the right direction.

Thompson, George, et al. *Accounting and the Law—Cases and Materials.* 4th ed. Mineola, N.Y.: The Foundation Press, 1978. This law school text is basically designed for students who have not had previous training in accounting. It covers the interrelationship of law and accounting, accounting concepts in a legal and business setting, the equity section of the corporate balance sheet, and employment of capital. In addition, several special areas of interest to the lawyer are reviewed. The book is quite useful for accountants as well, since it has benefited from the participation of a senior technical partner in a Big Eight CPA firm.

46

Auditing and the Law[1]

R. James Gormley

[1] This chapter consists of excerpts from the author's book, *The Law of Accountants and Auditors: Rights, Duties and Liabilities* (New York: Warren Gorham & Lamont, 1981), including a few portions adapted from the author's article, "Accountants' Professional Liability—A Ten-Year Review," 29 Bus. Law. 1205 (1974), © 1974, with permission of the American Bar Association and its Section of Corporation, Banking and Business Law.

PERFORMANCE STANDARDS

An auditor may be subjected to a formidable array of private, governmental, and professional proceedings questioning the quality of his work. They flow from

1. Common law,
2. Federal securities laws,
3. State blue sky laws,
4. Federal and state criminal laws,
5. Governmental authorities (e.g., IRS, SEC),
6. State accountancy authorities, and
7. Professional associations.[2]

When the quality of an auditor's work is questioned in a legal sense, the performance standard is one of *adequacy*—did the professional possess and exercise the skill, judgment, and knowledge generally possessed by members of his profession? Lapses in performance may lead to misrepresentation by the auditor and may create financial liability to clients, nonclients, or both, as well as professional penalties and criminal liability. Distinctions among lapses in performance may be drawn by considering an audit opinion on financial statements that later prove to have been unfairly presented. Any such opinion is a misrepresentation by the au-

---

[2] Points 5, 6, and 7 are not discussed in this chapter; see Chapters 39, 41, 42, and 43.

ditor, as the financial statements themselves are a misrepresentation by the client. The auditor's responsibility depends on a judgment of his state of mind at the time of issuance of the opinion, which may be

- *Innocent*—believed with adequate basis,
- *Negligent*—believed without adequate basis,
- *Constructively fraudulent*—without belief in its truth, or
- *Fraudulent*—known to be false.

The range of misrepresentation—from innocent to fraudulent—consists of infinite gradations of fact. Distinctions can be made only by individual judgment, and in litigation such judgment must be made by the trier of fact. Judgments, however, must proceed from legal definitions of professional responsibility (or the character and degree of lapses therein).

Legal Definitions for Auditors

Due Care. Due care is the performance of, and reporting on, professional engagements with at least the degree of care, competence, learning, and experience commonly possessed by members of the profession and required by professional standards.

Negligence. Negligence (i.e., ordinary negligence) is the failure of an accountant to perform or report on an engagement with the due care and competence expected of members of his profession. Negligence connotes an intention to exercise due care but some inadequacy or shortcoming in fulfillment.

Gross Negligence. Gross negligence is an extreme, flagrant, or reckless departure from standards of due care and competence in performing or reporting on professional engagements. *Recklessness* or reckless conduct has been defined as a highly unreasonable omission or misrepresentation, involving not merely simple, or even inexcusable, negligence, but an extreme departure from the standards of ordinary care, that presents a danger of misleading others that is either known to the defendant or is so obvious that the actor must have been aware of it. Gross negligence and recklessness are largely synonymous. The term *recklessness* has been used prevalently in recent years in civil cases, and the term also appears in criminal cases. As to either term, there is no easily stated distinction from the oversight, inattention, or error of judgment or perception that amounts to ordinary negligence.

Constructive Fraud. Constructive fraud is a deceit that involves a false representation of a material fact, with lack of reasonable ground for belief, in expectation of reliance by another, that is then justifiably relied on by the other and results in his damage. Constructive fraud may be inferred from evidence of gross negligence or recklessness, although they are not necessarily constructive fraud in and of themselves.

Fraud. Actual fraud differs from constructive fraud in that instead of "lack of reasonable ground for belief," there is conscious knowledge of the falsity with deliberate intent to deceive.

In discussing constructive and actual fraud, lawyers speak of *scienter*. In the more liberal of current definitions, scienter embodies conduct evidencing (1) an intent to defraud or an intent to deceive, (2) actual knowledge (of a misstatement or omission), or (3) conduct amounting to gross negligence or recklessness. More conservative definitions omit (3), and sometimes (2) as well. Clause (1) appears to coincide with actual fraud, and clauses (2) and (3) appear to relate to constructive fraud.

Law in Practice

Facts affect the state of mind of the trier of fact, judge or jurors, and influence him or them toward personal convictions that the auditor did or did not do as much as should have been expected of him in the circumstances. From this conviction, the applicable rule of law may tend to suggest itself—from facts to law in practice, rather than from law to facts as in theory.

The trier of fact may often be guided to a sound decision by expert accounting and auditing testimony (see Chapter 44) and reference to the professional rules and literature. Like all persons, however, triers of fact will be influenced by their own values, backgrounds, and experience. Some may begin the fact-finding process with ignorance, or even a serious misconception, of the professional issue. Some members of the jury might wrongly assume that *any* error in an audited financial statement is the responsibility of the auditor.

Moreover, a trier of fact has no objective means of detecting what specific acts of human behavior will transform due care into negligence, negligence into gross negligence/recklessness, or gross negligence/recklessness into fraud. In any close question (and most questions litigated to a conclusion are close), the outcome of the case depends on the judge's or the jury's decisive reaction to and interpretation of the evidence presented, and their understanding and evaluation of the rules of law to be applied to the facts as they find them.[3]

Sources of Legal Responsibility

Common Law. The traditional source of professional responsibility is the (non-statutory) common law. An accountant or auditor may be held liable, to all persons whose reliance on his accounting work or audit opinion should have been foreseen by him, for a professional lapse that is so reckless as to amount to a constructive fraud. For ordinary negligence, the accountant-auditor's liability is mainly to his client, but occasionally and increasingly extends to nonclients who can prove

---

[3] A reader with a deep interest in the thought processes of triers of fact and with uncommon patience might examine the closely printed 105-page opinion in *Pacific Acceptance Corp. Ltd. v. Forsyth,* 92 N.S.W. W.N. 29-133 (1970), a protracted and bitterly fought client-against-auditor negligence litigation under Australian common law. The opinion is essentially an *abridged* transcript of the detailed analysis of facts and law by the trial judge, sitting without a jury, in oral remarks from the bench over much of two days, in which the judge seemed almost to be thinking aloud.

that his services were performed primarily for their benefit or, according to more recent and liberal formulation, to persons whose specific reliance he should have foreseen.

Federal Securities Laws. Some provisions of the federal securities laws impose standards of responsibility more stringent than those of common law on persons associated with securities transactions, including secondary defendants such as accountants and auditors. In public offerings of securities registered under the Securities Act of 1933, Section 11 imposes a stern liability (for purchasers' losses resulting from a material misstatement or omission) on issuers, and on associated persons, including auditors, unless they can prove that they exercised due care, i.e., were not negligent. Under the Securities Exchange Act of 1934, Section 18(a) imposes liability on issuers and secondary persons, including associated auditors, for losses by reliant purchasers or sellers of securities based on a materially false or misleading statement, unless a defendant can prove good faith and no knowledge of the deficiency. All of the states also have so-called blue sky or securities laws, which contain liability and other provisions generally similar to those in the federal acts.

Dissatisfaction with the limited scope of common-law liability generally—not only as to accountants—has resulted in development of the law of liability in litigation under the federal securities laws. The development has not been limited to the express liability provisions, such as Section 11 of the 1933 act, but has extended to the acceptance by the courts of theories of implied liability.

Implied liability is best known in connection with Rule 10b-5 under Section 10(b) of the 1934 act, which contains generally worded prohibitions against misrepresentations, omissions, and fraud in connection with purchases and sales of securities. In 1976 the Supreme Court of the United States resolved a long controversy by ruling (in *Ernst & Ernst v. Hochfelder,* 425 U.S. 185 (1976)) that the standard of culpability in Rule 10b-5 is not negligence but *scienter,* or fraudulent conduct. The full ramifications of that holding are gradually being developed in federal court opinions.

After almost a decade of effort, a proposed official draft of the federal securities code was issued in 1978 for submission to the Congress. The code would integrate all seven statutes now administered by the SEC. Whether or when the code will be enacted by the Congress cannot be predicted with confidence; there are many who believe it will not be. If enacted, the code would differ from the presently proposed form, perhaps substantially. For the immediate future, probably all of this decade, it will cast shadows. Even if not enacted, portions of the code may influence judicial and administrative interpretation of the securities laws and the substance of future amendments to them, and to some extent SEC rule revisions concerning filings and other procedures.

Federal Criminal Law. The federal mail fraud statute contains a broadly interpreted prohibition against use of the mail in fraudulent schemes. The securities laws and some more-general statutes prohibit fraud and the filing of false information with the SEC and other government bodies. Charges of aiding and abetting, and of conspiracy, can be made against other persons, such as accountants and lawyers, allegedly involved with the primary violations.

Governmental Authorities. Broad governmental supervisory authority of the SEC (Chapter 41), the Internal Revenue Service (Chapter 43), and other federal and state authorities (e.g., state securities commissioners) also affects accountants. These supervisory authorities, given evidence suggesting possible violation of law, conduct investigations and issue orders compelling accountants and others to testify and submit records on broadly defined matters. They may sue accountants, among others, for injunction against continuance of alleged violations of law. The SEC has asserted the right, largely with success heretofore but recently under challenge, to conduct administrative proceedings against professionals, primarily accountants and lawyers, to determine whether they should be disqualified or suspended from practice before the SEC or otherwise disciplined for alleged violations of its Rule of Practice 2(e). The SEC refers some matters to the Department of Justice for consideration of possible criminal prosecution.

A Multicount Complaint Against Accountants

The impact of private litigation against accountants may be illustrated by a hypothetical merger of two publicly owned companies, and subsequent financial disaster to the merged company with large losses to investors. Amidst other recriminations, there is a challenge to the fairness of the audited and unaudited financial statements contained in the combined prospectus-proxy statement circulated to obtain shareholder approval of the merger. A complaint is filed in a federal district court against issuer, directors, officers, underwriters, auditor, and perhaps counsel, containing a series of separate charges or counts, on behalf of an alleged class of purchasers of securities and derivatively on behalf of the issuer (and thus indirectly for the benefit of its investors and creditors). The auditor is a codefendant because he expressed his audit opinion on the audited financial statements and was allegedly associated with the unaudited financial statements by advising or participating in their preparation or by reviewing them.

The complaint may include alleged violations of law and derelictions of legal duty on a number of legal grounds:

1. Section 14(a) of the 1934 act—misstatements or omissions in the merger proxy statement; conspiracy with, or aiding and abetting of, the primary defendants (the managements who solicited proxies) by auditors, lawyers, and other secondary defendants (who furnished professional and other assistance);
2. Section 11 of the 1933 act—misstatements or omissions in the prospectus or elsewhere in the registration statement required for the sale (issuance) of the securities in the merger (and additionally for any ensuing related distributions of the securities issued);
3. Section 12(2) of the 1933 act—misstatements or omissions in written (e.g., prospectus) or oral communications in the sale (issuance) of the securities in the merger, again containing allegations of conspiracy with, or aiding and abetting of, the primary defendants by the same secondary (nonselling, nonbuying) defendants as those named in count 1;
4. Rule 10b-5 under Section 10(b) of the 1934 act and Section 17(a) of the 1933 act— fraud in connection with the sale (issuance) of the securities in the merger;

5. Section 18(a) of the 1934 act—false or misleading statements in applications, reports, or other documents filed with the SEC relating to the merger (e.g., Forms 8-K or 10-K, both containing or incorporating financial statements); and

6. Charges against the auditors alleging breach of contract, negligence, or fraud under applicable state common law or securities statutes, over which the federal court has "pendent jurisdiction" because the claims are based, in whole or in part, on some or all of the same facts as those in the federal questions in the above counts.

This multiplicity of counts is not complete, but it is not redundant, because there are a variety of technical legal differences, both substantive and procedural, among the counts.

The Impact of Liability

Once a defendant is found to have violated the law, the court may award damages by selecting from a variety of damage theories and formulations. The most important single truth in damages under the securities laws is that damage theories are fluid. Second most important is that damages may far outrun any fee or benefit received by a defendant auditor from its engagement.

Under the securities laws, the courts' concern is to stimulate diligence and penalize indifference. "Thus, the question of who pays . . . is of as great concern as the issue of whether the plaintiffs are compensated at all" (*Gould v. American-Hawaiian Steamship Co.,* 387 F. Supp. 163, 168 (D. Del. 1974)). Accordingly, a court may impose on a defendant the burden of disproving damages—according to the court's view of the factual details, nature of the violation, extent of defendant's culpability, statutory context, and other qualitative considerations of fairness and equity. The court may apply rules of mitigation when it considers a reduction in damages to be equitably justified. Similarly, the court may avoid damages by allowing idemnification from others, or may apportion the damages by awarding contribution from others.

Although the courts continually search for general principles and common approaches, they cannot find them in complicated and confused areas such as damages, indemnification, and contribution in securities law cases. Courts decide controversies one at a time, and their judicial opinions reflect the unsettled nature of this aspect of the law. Because of the complexity of any thorough legal analysis of damages, including indemnification and contribution, these comments are merely an observation on the subject.

PROFESSIONAL PERFORMANCE PROBLEMS

Fraud of Client Personnel

Responsibility for Detection. Earlier in this century there was a universal understanding, including among auditors themselves, that detection of individual fraud by client employees was among the most important, if not *the* most important, objectives of an audit of financial statements. But a number of judicial opinions on

Other Illegal and Questionable Acts

Financial statements were traditionally conceived of as presentations of economic and financial data, not as critiques of business morality. In those circumstances, an auditor becoming aware of illegal or questionable payments or other dubious behavior within the audited entity had an understandable responsibility of defined and limited scope. First, had the payments or activities been approved, if necessary at the board level, on behalf of the enterprise? Second, were the payments or activities material for any reason (not limited to quantitative measures) in relation to financial position or results of operations? If the answers to these questions were satisfactory, the audit inquiry could be concluded.

During the mid-1970s, in the aftermath of Watergate, investigations by the SEC and others revealed evidence of illegal political contributions, bribery of foreign government officials, and other illegal and questionable payments by businesses. In many instances such misbehavior was compounded by deliberate falsifications of accounting records (e.g., off-book slush funds) or other accounting deficiencies (e.g., misleading or inadequate description or documentation). The SEC understandably ascribed a qualitative materiality regardless of amount, because of the implications concerning the credibility of financial data and accounting controls and the integrity of management.

These events led to a new audit standard, SAS 17 (AU 328), in early 1977, which (1) pointed out that although an auditor should be aware that some client acts might be illegal, evaluations of illegality in general are outside an auditor's expertise; (2) discussed procedures for detection and evaluation of illegal acts; and (3) considered the particular response required by the auditor:

> If the client's board of directors, its audit committee, or other appropriate levels within the organization do not give appropriate consideration . . . to the illegal act, the auditor should consider withdrawing from the current engagement or dissociating himself from any future relationship with the client. The auditor's decision . . . is ordinarily affected by (a) the effects on his ability to rely on management's representations and (b) the possible effects of continuing his association with the client. [AU 328.18]

Congress and the SEC seized on the developed investigative talents of auditors, and directed them to diverse functions at most tangentially related to their normal field of endeavor. Thus, as detailed in Chapter 13, Congress in 1977 enacted the misnamed Foreign Corrupt Practices Act (FCPA); the SEC in 1979 adopted Rules 13b2-1 and -2 under provisions added to the 1934 act by FCPA; and the SEC in 1979 proposed (and in 1980 withdrew) a requirement that (1) managements report annually on their companies' internal accounting controls and (2) the companies' auditors report on the management reports.

The FCPA contains disparate provisions prohibiting foreign corrupt payments and requiring specified accounting records and internal accounting controls, essentially internal corporate matters. As such, they give the SEC, and in particular its enforcement division, a broad new jurisdiction over management misconduct, from which the SEC had previously been largely excluded, and may also broaden the responsibilities and potential liability of independent auditors as well as of accounting executives. Chapter 13 contains a detailed discussion of how a practical and effective demonstration of compliance with the new accounting provisions can be developed.

Accountants' Working Papers

Working papers (see Chapter 12 and AU 338.01-.05) are evidence prepared or assembled by an auditor to support his audit or nonaudit report and the adequacy of his performance, in conformity with GAAS, of the audit procedures underlying the opinion. They include audit programs; work sheets and other analyses of accounting data; confirmations, legal opinions, and other affirmations and correspondence; documents concerning the charter, bylaws, and transactions; and audit memoranda that record the conduct of the audit. If an auditor's audit opinion or performance is challenged, an audit that was adequate in fact may be ruled inadequate in law because of a failure of proof through lack of documentation.[4]

Once a suit is filed, it is frequently followed by subpoena of working papers (among other things) and a painstaking examination of the papers by plaintiff's legal-accounting team. Particular attention is given to familiar sources of trouble in audit performance and to defects in the paper trail that indicate possible failure to perform steps in the audit program, gaps in information, conflicts, contradictions, junior staff queries and comments without documented resolution, unreconciled data, negative confirmation responses not disposed of in writing, and inadequate supervisory memoranda, some of which might be exploited by skilled plaintiff's counsel and his expert accountants.

Ownership, Possession, and Access. Accounting records of a client on which an accountant performs accounting or bookkeeping services remain the property of the client. But all papers, including copies of client records, prepared or obtained by the accountant for professional examination and documentation in expressing an audit opinion or performing accounting services become the property of the accountant as a nonemployee independent professional (see AU 338.06).

However, the accountant's ownership of working papers might more accurately be thought of as a right to possession. The confidential nature of the information obtained in the professional relationship prohibits the accountant from disclosing or disposing of the papers as ordinary property, and may require him to grant access to others, notably the client and successor auditors, on appropriate occasion (ET 501.02).

Access by third persons neutral to accountant. To the extent that information in an accountant's working papers appears relevant to issues raised in litigation involving the client, the information is obtainable by the litigating parties by legal process upon the nonparty accountant.

The information in auditors' working papers that is sought by genuinely neutral parties is almost always substantive accounting data rather than audit information, and the primary source is the client's own accounting records. But, as a matter of convenience, laziness, disorganization of client records, or client resistance, some

---

[4] See *Adams v. Standard Knitting Mills, Inc.,* 623 F.2d 422, 434-435 (6th Cir. 1980) (holding auditors not liable). "The District Court found that Peat's testing of the standard cost build-up was not documented in its work papers, and concluded that Peat never audited the standard cost at all." Also: "The District Judge evidently inferred from Peat's failure to document such testing in its work papers, that the testing [of inventory work-forward] did not occur. The record also establishes adequate foundation for this inference."

litigants attempt to obtain their information through the auditor's working papers, in the often well-founded belief that the auditor has organized the information in a suitable manner. The auditor should resist the inclination of such litigants, and of some courts, to think of audit working papers as a convenient free lending library, and should insist that parties exhaust their efforts to meet their needs from primary sources.

However, if a party specifies the particular accounting (nonaudit) information desired and offers compensation, it may be in the auditors' interest to agree to furnish excerpts or abstracts of relevant accounting information, eliminating information on audit procedures performed. This should not be voluntary but under subpoena, and subject in any case to court order if objected to by the auditors' client. The furnishing of piecemeal accounting information diminishes the danger that someone is likely to perceive an alleged grievance over audit performance. The auditor cannot hope that the agreed compensation would cover the additional cost of careful review.

Access by third persons adverse to accountant. Adversaries to auditors in litigation are habitually granted a right by subpoena to examine and to obtain copies of the working papers. The first concern of auditors' counsel is obtaining a reasonable limitation of its commonly overbroad scope. Among other things, counsel is concerned with arguable lack of relevance or materiality of particular papers to the issues in litigation. He also considers whether individual papers are protected by an attorney-client, attorney work product, or other privilege from having to be produced, and subsequently informs the adversary's counsel of any papers, identified by general description, withheld from production on grounds of privilege.

Examinations of auditors' papers by adversary's counsel and accountants are usually made in the auditors' offices, and are attended *at all times* by a person from the auditors' staff or counsel's firm. The auditor arranges for copies (at the adversary's expense) of papers requested by the adversary and usually orders an additional copy (at his own expense) for identification and defensive use.

Courts occasionally have acknowledged that auditors' internal and confidential "proprietary" accounting and auditing manuals, guides, and checklists "are in the nature of *trade secrets* [emphasis added], and as such are only discoverable upon the higher showing of actual need or necessity," on the ground that divulgence could impair the integrity of the audit processes (*Rosen v. Dick,* CCH Fed. Sec. L. Rep. ¶ 94,989 (S.D. N.Y. 1975)) and the auditors' competitive economic position. The courts have also excluded training and other manuals considered not demonstrably relevant to the auditors in issue.

Also, courts have issued "protective orders" intended to confine access to the materials to actual participants in the litigation—judge, jury, and representatives of and counsel to the litigating parties and their experts. Such orders may contain provisions as to confidentiality and restricted access, use solely at the trial and appeal, exclusions and other limitations, and return at the conclusion of litigation.

Accountant-Client Privilege. In considering the privilege of communication between accountant and client, the most important thing to be aware of is how little there is of it. Since invocation of a privilege may obstruct the introduction of material and relevant evidence, it is justifiable only in "the protection of interests and relationships which, rightly or wrongly, are regarded as of sufficient social importance to justify some incidental sacrifice of sources of facts needed in the administration of justice" (McCormick, 1938, pp. 447, 448). In a recent opinion, the United States Supreme Court said: "Whatever their origins, these exceptions to the demand for every man's evidence are not lightly created nor expansively construed, for they are in derogation of the search for truth" (*United States v. Nixon,* 418 U.S. 683, 710 (1974)).

To be privileged from production, evidence concerning a communication, e.g., between client and accountant, either written (auditor's working papers) or oral (auditor's testimony), must be (1) confidential (and not waived by disclosure to others, initially or subsequently, intentionally or unintentionally) and (2) critically important to the well-being of a professional relationship (a) that is socially so valuable that it should be protected and (b) in which the injury from disclosure would outweigh the benefit in administration of litigation. For a further discussion of accountant-client privilege, see Chapter 44.

Disclosure of Auditor Changes and Disagreements

The SEC has rules "designed to strengthen accountants' independence by discouraging the practice of changing accountants in order to obtain more favorable accounting treatment" (ASR 165). Those rules require disclosures, to be made by companies registered under the 1934 act, in connection with changes of independent auditors—on Form 8-K, under Schedule 14A, and under Regulation S-K.

Form 8-K. The language adopted by the SEC creates some difficult problems of interpretation and application for the company, the former auditor, and possibly the new auditor. Identification and description is required by ASR 165 as to

[1] any disagreements with the former accountant [2] on any matter of [a] accounting principles or practices, [b] financial statement disclosure, or [c] auditing scope or procedure, [3] which disagreements if not resolved to the satisfaction of the former accountant would have caused him to make reference in connection with his report to the subject matter of the disagreement(s) . . .

regardless of whether or not resolved to the accountant's satisfaction. It also requires a statement as to whether the termination was recommended or approved by an audit committee or, if none, by the board.

Although the company is also required to ask the former auditor for a letter as to whether he agrees or disagrees with the company's disclosure of the termination, no SEC rule requires the former auditor to furnish such a letter. Many auditors, however, regard this as at least a professional duty, and letters are customarily furnished. A former auditor is responsible for the contents of any letter that he does furnish, and the consequences could be serious if it is determined that he exceeded the scope of Form 8-K to the injury of his former client or if his letter does not adequately disclose a reportable disagreement.

Disagreements are "those which occur at the decision-making level; i.e., between personnel of the registrant responsible for presentation of its financial statements (e.g., chief accountant, financial vice president, or chief executive officer or officers) and personnel of the accounting firm responsible for rendering its report" (ASR 165). On the auditor's side, the audit partner in charge of the engagement, who has the authority of the partnership to release the audit opinion, clearly is the decision maker; the restraints on him within his firm—by policy, rules, reviewers, technical specialists, and committees—are an internal firm matter.

Normally, a position taken by a chief accounting officer, chief financial officer, or chief or vice chief executive officer after a full exposition and exchange of views regarding the relevant facts and reasoning would constitute a decision by a decision maker. At the same time, there could be an honest difference of opinion, and conflicting testimony and other evidence, as to whether or not a disagreement occurred during an intensive debate of a problem between company and auditor decision makers, or whether the process of argumentation and persuasion led to a resolution without a reportable disagreement.

Reportable Disagreements. Matters of reportable disagreement concern (1) accounting principles or practices, (2) financial statement disclosure, or (3) auditing scope or procedure. They do not concern fees, personality clashes, antagonism or noncooperation on the part of company management, and dissatisfaction with professional attentiveness or quality of performance, except in a case in which a company disputes the adequacy (or overadequacy) of scope or audit performance.

Suppose, for example, that the auditor finds evidence of a material misstatement of financial statements or of irregularities at a high level of management. The auditor must extend his examination to the extent feasible and make preliminary and subsequent reports to the board of directors or its audit committee. An attempt by officers to resist the examination would be a limitation of audit scope and, even though eventually abandoned, would be reportable in the event of a subsequent change of auditors (see AU 327.14). Other forms of management resistance also may constitute interference with scope or procedure.

Reference in Audit Opinion. Form 8-K further requires disclosure of those disagreements that the auditor would have reported if they had not been resolved to his satisfaction. That standard contains some elements similar to those of the materiality concept, because the auditor would not have been required to take exception if the disagreement had been unimportant. But the auditor must ask and answer: What, if any, exception would have had to be taken in the audit opinion if something had happened that in fact did not happen? Even to identify the question, the auditor and his crews must search their recollections and their files of two prior audits and recent interim work, which might run for two and one-half years or so.

Company management, on whom the responsibility for disclosure falls directly, has a correlative duty to make its own review of the audit relationship to identify relevant matters of disagreement that the auditors may either have overlooked in their review or, occasionally, may not have been aware were disagreements in the view of the management.

Reflecting on the indefinite nature of a disagreement, the SEC said, in ASR 165, that a reportable disagreement occurs if the auditor resigned or was dismissed after informing his client that ". . . he had concluded that internal controls necessary to develop reliable statements did not exist . . ." or ". . . that he had discovered facts which led him no longer to be able to rely on management representations or which made him unwilling to be associated with statements prepared by management. . . ." The inclusion of these examples within the meaning of disagreement is tenuous.

Whether even the SEC could enforce such an interpretation in a court may be arguable, but it certainly can in its own office through its wide variety of formal and informal commission and staff actions. It thus appears that to the SEC, disagreement means more, as well as less, than the conversational meaning of the term.

In fact, it includes any disagreement that *would have caused* him "to make reference in connection with his report," that is, *if* he had had occasion to issue an audit report at the time of the disagreement, even though he did not have such occasion. This has obvious repercussions for interim reviews and other nonaudit engagements.

Schedule 14A. In proxy statements that relate to elections of directors or include financial statements, Item 8 of Schedule 14A requires a description of any disagreements with a former auditor disclosed in a Form 8-K report, with an advance copy to the former auditor, in response to which the former auditor may, if he regards the description as incorrect or incomplete, within ten days of receipt deliver to the issuer a brief statement of his own view for inclusion in the proxy statement. The proxy statement must indicate whether a change of auditors was recommended or approved by an audit committee or, if none, by the board.

Regulation S-K. Under Item 12, Regulation S-K, disclosure accompanying financial statements included in Form 10-K, for the year of the change of auditors and the subsequent year, is required if the effect of any material transactions or events "were accounted for or disclosed in a manner different from that which the former accountants *apparently* [emphasis added] would have concluded was required." The company may have to make assumptions and resort to conjecture in disclosing the apparent effect of the former auditor's position, unless it already knows or can determine the former auditor's views.

Purchase Audits and Reviews

The term *purchase audits and reviews* is an overly narrow description of a broad variety of professional accounting and auditing services (1) performed in connection with some type of substantial change or proposed change in the ownership, control, or management of a business (referred to in this discussion as a *business sold*), such as (a) a sale of all or a substantial part of its securities or assets, (b) a statutory merger, or (c) a recapitalization, reorganization, or separation of a portion of the business, and (2) allegedly relied on by persons interested in or affected by the transaction or proposed transaction. In some cases (e.g., sales of assets, mergers) the business sold is the actual seller. In others the actual sellers are the owners of controlling shares. In this discussion they are both referred to as sellers. (See Chapter 30 for a discussion of accounting and auditing aspects of business combinations; and see Gormley, 1980, for a more extensive discussion of purchase audits and reviews.)

A purchaser is sometimes misled by inadequate or controversial accounting (and occasionally misrepresentation) by the officers or principals of the business sold, and by inadequate performance by an independent auditor in a purchase audit or review. Although the performance of a purchase audit might normally be expected to inform a purchaser adequately concerning the significant accounting principles and methods employed by the business sold, the purchaser still might discover after completion of the purchase that the *application* of those methods to such items as doubtful receivables, excess or obsolete inventory, and unprofitable contracts has in his view been unsatisfactory, and that the accounting adjustments that he considers to be required will reflect losses of values or operating results that make the acquisition appear disadvantageous, at least as interpreted by accounting conventions.

In an ordinary professional engagement, the content of financial statements or data of an enterprise to be audited or reviewed by an accountant are determined by the enterprise as the client of the auditor. But in many cases in which a business is sold, the professional relationship is confused by contractual provisions or by understandings and especially misunderstandings among the contracting parties (if not the auditors) concerning who the auditor's client or clients are, and whether the financial statements to be audited or reviewed are to be determined by the seller or by the purchaser or are subject to the concurrence of both the seller and the purchaser.

In assigning responsibility, a remorseful purchaser may overlook his own shortcomings, limitations, and errors of judgment and blame others, such as an accountant associated with financial data of the business sold. Courts sometimes conclude that the sellers have defrauded the purchaser and, as an incident to doing so, also defrauded the codefendant accountant, or that the demise of the business subsequent to its purchase has actually been caused by the purchaser's own mismanagement.

Purchase Price Related to Net Worth or Earnings. Among the riskiest of all purchase audits to accountants are those in which the purchase price of a transaction is linked by formula to net worth or earnings reflected in audited financial statements of the business sold. The soft numbers in financial statements—e.g., allowances for doubtful receivables, excess and obsolete inventory, and unprofitable contracts—which are determined by management judgments as to which there may be reasonable difference of opinion, become hard money, transferable between pockets of buyer and seller. Under these circumstances, the materiality threshold may be almost anything.

Audit by Auditor of Business Sold. The most common type of lawsuit against accountants arising from a business sold is by a purchaser against the regular auditor of the business sold because of an audit or review opinion allegedly relied on by the purchaser. Auditors of businesses sold also have occasionally been charged by purchasers with misrepresenting the viability of the purchased business.

Like the purchaser, the seller may, by related reasoning, charge its auditor with liability, and for negligence, not only for fraud. The sellers may claim indemnification for the costs of having warranted the financial statements audited or reviewed by the accountants, even though sellers' warranties were much broader than a standard audit opinion or the auditor had made a review without audit.

Audit by Purchaser's Auditor. When a purchaser's regular auditor audits a business to be bought, and the audit is to be relied on by the purchaser in completing the purchase, the auditor exposes himself to significant potential risks both as to purchaser and to seller.

Liability to purchaser. Such an engagement has all the problems encountered by an auditor in a first audit—familiarization with the system, policies, procedures, and business of the business sold; in addition, the auditor and his new "client" (the seller) are strangers in reality. Under those conditions, and possibly with less than normal cooperation from the audit "client," the hazard of a misunderstanding, deception by the seller, or other lapse is increased.

For example, an owner-management, especially of a private company, that has understated inventory during prior periods for income tax reasons cannot afford to reveal such behavior to purchaser's auditor, and causes the inventory to be fully accounted for and valued in the audited financial statements for the most recent period of the business sold. If the auditor fails to discover the understatement of inventory at the start of the period under audit, net income for the most recent period, and therefore the earnings trend, will be overstated and for some (undetermined) prior periods will be understated, to the possible prejudice of the purchaser.

Liability to seller. The seller may believe that the purchaser's auditor, who has had no previous professional relation with the business sold, is at least overcritical of seller's accounting, and perhaps is biased in favor of his regular client, the purchaser.

On the one hand, the one-time audit client (the business sold) is entitled to an auditor's opinion that supports such client's financial statements within limits of GAAP and fairness. On the other hand, the auditor's regular client (purchaser) may expect, and the auditor may believe that he should furnish, information on details of accounting valuations and other applications of accounting methods by the business sold. The furnishing of such information to the purchaser cannot be justified without any possible question as something to which the regular client is entitled in the purchase audit, except to such extent, if any, as may be expressly authorized by the business sold in the agreement or otherwise. The result may be a genuine, and possibly dangerous, conflict of interest on the part of the auditor. In principle such conflicts are not improper, but in practice they may expose the practitioner to charges that he neglected or otherwise prejudiced one interest in favor of another.

The danger in a conflict of interest on the part of a conscientious person is one of inadvertence—arising from a limitation, proven by experience, in the ability of a human mind to analyze fully, and to reconcile or otherwise resolve equitably, all the ramifications of diverging points of view. This suggests that accountants should consider declining purchase audit and review engagements in which there are substantial inherent conflicts of interest, even though there is no lack of independence.

Audit by Joint Auditor. Purchase audits undertaken for *both* purchaser and the business sold expose the auditor somewhat differently, and even more broadly. The auditor owes a duty of care to both, and may be held liable for negligence to either (or both). Such an engagement involves a conflict of interest by its very definition. Auditors also find themselves in a position similar to that of joint auditors of buyer and seller, though not expressly so engaged, when performing an audit in connection with a buy-out within a control group of one member by another.

Each party may claim and expect the concurrence of the auditor in the client's determinations of values and choice of methods, within limits of GAAP and fairness, to which the client has become accustomed in more conventional engagements. If the clients give conflicting directions or disagree on such matters as valuations or applicable GAAP, it may be difficult if not impossible for the auditor to decide, in the special circumstances, which of them is entitled to determine the financial statements to be audited or to demand detailed information.

For example, in *Franklin Supply Co. et al. v. Tolman,* 454 F.2d 1059 (9th Cir. 1972), the United States purchaser of a Venezuelan oil well supply company, despite its negotiation from the seller of a reduction in the purchase price of the business, sued the audit firm that had been engaged (and whose fee had been shared equally) by both buyer and seller. The court found that the auditor owed a duty of care to the purchaser as well as seller and had committed negligence, though not fraud, in nondisclosure that (1) the oil well equipment inventory had been valued by regular prices of normal suppliers (ruled by the court on expert testimony to be an acceptable method of valuation) rather than by lower prices of surplus suppliers and (2) defendant's Venezuelan auditor was an alternate director of the seller and during the audit period had been a director of the company sold (without ruling on the effect on independence of defendant). The court also ruled, based on expert testimony, that GAAP did not require recording of a liability in connection with a trade practice of crediting customers for the value of reusable diamonds salvaged from drill bits returned for rehabilitation, because the diamonds had an inventory value equal to the credit. The court of appeals reversed an award of punitive damages and of damages in connection with inventory that the seller had already compensated in the price adjustment, and awarded damages limited to certain out-of-pocket costs.

The selection and application of accounting principles, and valuation decisions, may and often do involve matters of judgment and discretion for which the engagement by the contracting parties of an accountant as arbitrator may be appropriate. By alertness and attentiveness in stipulating and clarifying the terms of a purchase audit or review, an auditor may avoid not only the risk and expense but also the embarrassment of becoming entangled with the principal parties to a ridiculous spectacle.

Instructions as to Particular Accounts. When audits are performed in connection with a specific transaction such as a merger or other business acquisition, the contracting parties not infrequently take a special interest in particular data or accounts because of their comparative importance, unresolved questions, or other information. Auditors have had rather poor success in maintaining their contention that their audit opinion relates only to the financial statements as a whole, not to individual elements, and they have no hope at all of maintaining that proposition as to a matter in which they accept an instruction to give special attention to particular accounts (such as accounts payable or accounts receivable) or other designated matters. Rather surprisingly, from the opposite tack, a special instruction of *inattention* to particular accounts may also be a source of trouble.

Implications. Published information does not reveal that the problems of purchase audits and reviews have received the degree of professional attention they deserve. The authoritative audit pronouncements directed to the distinctive characteristics of such engagements consist of

1. One narrow illustration of a report on nonaudit procedures performed on certain accounts of a company in connection with its acquisition (AU 621.17),
2. A perfunctory acknowledgment of the appropriateness of an engagement for the issuance of a comfort letter relating to unaudited financial statements of a public entity in connection with its proposed acquisition, if the standards that would be applicable to a comfort letter to underwriters are fulfilled (AU 504.20), and
3. A warning in 1956 by a former professional committee on accounting definitions that book value formula prices in sales of businesses "have given rise to misunderstandings and can easily develop into controversies when the intention of the parties is not clear" (AICPA, 1956, par. 8).

It is suggested that audit firms consider creating for the guidance of their professional personnel special forms of engagement letters for purchase audits and reviews that attempt to anticipate abnormal problems and risks in such engagements and that are designed to override obtuse purchase contract provisions that, if read literally as they sometimes are, distort a professional engagement into a task impossible to perform. Ideally, such a letter would disclaim any undertakings not contained within the engagement letter and would specifically disclaim any undertakings contained in the purchase-sale agreement. The letter should identify the auditors' client as the business sold (regardless of who is to pay the audit fee) and should specify that the presale management of the business sold should be the sole determiner of the financial statements or data that the auditor is obliged to recognize. Any special provisions in the engagement letter, including any variations from GAAP and GAAS, should be examined carefully in advance, and suitable disclaimers included concerning possible effect upon fairness of presentation.

If an auditor cannot avoid assuming professional responsibility to both the purchaser and the business sold, he should attempt to stipulate that as to all matters in which he is required to exercise professional judgment and discretion, he is entitled to the immunities of an arbitrator (i.e., with no liability for acts performed in good faith even though negligently).

COMMON-LAW LIABILITY

Liability to Clients for Negligence

Clients may sue allegedly negligent auditors either for breach of contract in failing to perform the audit with the due care implied in undertaking the engagement, or in tort, which is a civil (noncriminal) breach of a duty to another, in this case for failure to exercise due care. Clients ordinarily sue on both grounds.

"Those who hire [public accountants] are not justified in expecting infallibility, but can expect only reasonable care and competence. They purchase service, not insurance . . ." (*Lindner v. Barlow, Davis & Wood,* 27 Cal. Rptr. 101, 104 (App. 1962)). Thus, an auditor should not ordinarily be held negligently responsible for the breakdown of an apparently satisfactory system of internal control because of collusive fraud among top client people (who can subvert *any* system). Even if an auditor were negligent, he should be relieved of liability to the client (though not necessarily to certain reliant third persons) that, through its own top personnel, committed the greater fault of fraudulent deceit.

The AICPA's Statements on Auditing Standards (see Chapter 11) are a compact summation of the general audit standards of field work and reporting currently in force in the United States (AU 150.02). Lapses from those standards are the stuff from which negligence litigation is fashioned. But perhaps the most illuminating example of negligence issues in client-against-auditor cases of the recent generation is the 1970 opinion of a New South Wales trial court in *Pacific Acceptance Corp. Ltd. v. Forsyth,* 92 N.S.W. W.N. 29 (1970), which reveals an unusually keen comprehension by the judge of professional audit standards, procedures, and performance. An audit firm was held liable to its client for failure to detect a massive fraud committed on a branch office of the finance company client by a loan customer. The court said (at pp. 50-51):

> Whatever task the auditor expressly or impliedly contracts to perform, he is obliged to do so exercising that degree of skill and care which is reasonable in the circumstances. . . . [W]hatever the precise content of his audit duty [i.e., engagement], the auditor promises, first, to conduct an audit of some description and, second, to provide a report of his opinion based on his audit work, which report has to comply with the *Companies Act* and the articles, and also impliedly agrees to exercise reasonable skill and care in the conduct of the audit and in the making of the report.

In an elaborately detailed examination of the conduct of the audits, the court was severely critical of the auditors' performance, and concluded that they had committed negligence. The court cited a failure to pay due regard to the possibility of fraud, which was in fact being committed by a borrower from the client, and to make adequate tests of security documents by physical examination or where necessary by obtaining adequate confirmation from independent sources. The court also cited unwarranted reliance of the auditors on the client's branch manager without making their own examination.

Contributory Negligence of Clients. Generally, a defendant may avoid liability if he can prove that the plaintiff's own negligence contributed to the injury, yet the courts have rarely been willing to allow this defense to accountants. (See, e.g., *1136 Tenants' Corp. v. Max Rothenberg & Co.,* Index No. 10575/1965 (N.Y. Sup. Ct. N.Y. County, June 16, 1970).) Most of the cases have involved embezzlement or other alleged fraud of client personnel, with which an audit engagement is in part, though not primarily, concerned. There are three main lines of contributory negligence.

Failure to supervise personnel. The pattern was set by the disallowance of a contributory negligence defense in *National Surety Corp. v. Lybrand,* 9 N.Y.S.2d 554, 563 (App. Div. 1939), in which the court said that "negligence of the employer is a defense only when it has contributed to the accountant's failure to perform his contract and to report the truth." The court purported, unconvincingly, to distinguish an earlier opinion in a similar case (*Craig v. Anyon,* 208 N.Y.S. 259 (App. Div. 1925)) as holding that the employer in that case had held its employee out to the auditors as a person to be trusted, although actually the opinion had concluded that the employer's assumption of the employee's honesty and the lack of supervision were the actual causes of the loss.

A recent opinion, *Shapiro v. Glekel*, 380 F. Supp. 1053 (S.D. N.Y. 1974), observing the irreconcilable conflict in the precedents, chose to follow the *National Surety* rule in denying the defendant auditor's preliminary motion for summary judgment on the negligence count. The auditors had asserted that the plaintiff, the bankruptcy trustee of an audit client, had conceded that the two top officers (who were also directors) of the client had known or should have known of overstatements of income and financial position. The court ruled that their knowledge did not prevent the auditors from performing their engagement and did not as a matter of law preclude recovery for the client because of contributory negligence.

Disregard of auditor's recommendations. Negligent auditors have occasionally escaped liability when they have proved that the client had neglected to act on auditors' recommendations that could have avoided or diminished subsequent loss, even though the auditors were, or had previously been, negligent.

Independent knowledge. In some instances a client should realize, because of knowledge of the facts in question or of other information, that reliance on the auditor's opinion is unjustified; in such cases the client's alleged reliance is a form of contributory negligence. However, the decisions are not uniform, and some of them reflect the *National Surety* point of view.

Liability to Nonclients for Negligence

Until well into this century, accountants were liable at common law only to their clients for negligence in the performance of their professional engagements. This was an application of an old English common-law rule that a person who was not a party to a contract had no right of recovery for its negligent performance.

The Primary Benefit Rule. The basic U.S. pronouncement on auditors' liability to third persons was made by Judge Cardozo in 1931, in the famous case of *Ultramares Corp. v. Touche*, 174 N.E. 441 (N.Y. 1931), a suit against auditors who issued an opinion based on an allegedly negligent audit, brought by a creditor who, without the knowledge of the auditors, had made a loan to the audit client in reliance on the report and had suffered loss when the client proved to have been insolvent. The court ruled in favor of the auditor on the negligence charge.

First, the court dealt with the pragmatic question of the relation between degree of fault and exposure to liability:

If liability for negligence exists, a thoughtless slip or blunder, the failure to detect a theft or forgery beneath the cover of deceptive entries, may expose accountants to a *liability in an indeterminate amount for an indeterminate time to an indeterminate class* [emphasis added]. The hazards of a business conducted on these terms are so extreme as to enkindle doubt whether a flaw may not exist in the implication of a duty that exposes to these consequences. [174 N.E. at 444]

Second, the court ruled that auditors should not be liable for negligence to creditors and investors if their report "... was *primarily for the benefit of the [client]* [emphasis added] ... for use in the development of the business, and only incidentally or collaterally for the use of those to whom [the client] and his associates might exhibit it thereafter" (174 N.E. at 446). This is the *primary benefit rule*. It is based on the premise that a company ordinarily needs or desires audited financial statements for many purposes—for management guidance, taxes, debt and equity investors, lenders, suppliers, customers—and that there may be no single decisive reason for having financial statements audited.

A few years later, a court said that even an unreasonable belief of a defendant accountant was not fraud if the belief was honest (*O'Connor v. Ludlam,* 92 F.2d 50, 54 (2d Cir. 1937)). The "honest belief" test of *O'Connor* and of *Ultramares* is still being employed in distinguishing between negligence and scienter (*McLean v. Alexander,* 599 F.2d 1190, 1198 (3d Cir. 1979)).

The primary benefit rule proved to be a powerful defense for auditors against liability for negligent misrepresentations to persons other than clients, and it may have been applied against third persons more literally than anyone, including Judge Cardozo, would have expected. As sometimes happens, a reaction set in in two forms. One was a frontal assault on the primary benefit rule, the other a resort to the federal securities laws in lieu of the common law.

Foreseen Persons and Classes. In 1963, *Hedley Byrne & Co., Ltd. v. Heller and Partners, Ltd.,* [1963] 2 All E.R. 575, was decided by the highest court of England. *Hedley Byrne* did not involve auditors, but rather a negligently stated accommodation credit report by a bank, on which a third person relied to its damage. In their opinions the justices spoke variously of "special," "particular," "direct," and "proximate" relationships between defendant and plaintiff, and said that "where [as here] there is a relationship equivalent to contract [but for the absence of consideration] there is a duty of care." But the justices did not synthesize in a general principle their conception of the circumstances that create a "special relationship."

By 1965 the American Law Institute (ALI), in its Restatement (Second) of Torts (Section 552, tentative draft 12, p. 14 (1966)), citing *Hedley Byrne* among other authorities, was interpreting the law of negligent misrepresentations by professionals to third persons to mean that liability of a professional for negligence in supplying false information is

    . . . limited to loss suffered
    (a) by the person or one of a limited group of persons for whose benefit and guidance he intends to supply the information or knows that the recipient intends to supply it; and
    (b) through reliance upon it in a transaction that he intends the information to influence or knows that the recipient so intends or in a substantially similar transaction. [Final form, 1977, with slight changes]

The ALI notes (Section 552, tentative draft 11, p. 56 (1965)) state that its objective is to express the interpretation in "language which will eliminate liability to the very large class of persons whom almost any negligently given information may *forseeably* [emphasis added] reach and influence, and limit the liability, not to a particular plaintiff identified in advance, but to the comparatively small group whom the defendant expects and intends to influence"—i.e., foreseen persons and classes.

The generalities of the restatement, however, are not discrete principles; they are attempts to classify factual distinctions that vary by infinite gradations of detail. Like all such attempts, the classifications overlap and blur, according to differing usages of key words and individual interpretations, inconsistent precedents and authorities, and views of counsel with cases to press or defend. What follows is one attempt at such a classification:

1. *Primary beneficiary*—the identified person whose reliance is the "end and aim of the transaction" (*Glanzer v. Shepard*, 135 N.E. 275 (N.Y. 1922)) and who with rare exceptions was only the client, prior to *Hedley Byrne* and the Second Restatement.

2. *Foreseen person*—one or more specifically identified persons or entities known by the auditor to be intended recipients, directly or indirectly, of the audit opinion for the purpose of reliance in a particular business transaction known to the auditor, including a primary beneficiary and others as well.

3. *Foreseen class*—a particular defined group, of any size, sometimes very large, specifically identified to the auditor by class, though not known to him individually, any one or more of whom rely on the auditor's opinion. According to the Second Restatement, each member of such a foreseen class is entitled to the same rights against the auditor as a foreseen person. A class might include a group of banks formed by a lead bank or a group of underwriters to be organized by a managing underwriter.

4. *Foreseeable persons and classes*—the potentially very large numbers of persons, not identified as specific persons or a specific class in a specific transaction, who may foreseeably be expected to receive an auditor's report when published by the client and in some way to act or forebear to act in reliance on it. Foreseeable persons have some form of business relationship to or interest in the client that makes such reliance plausible. Such persons may include public investors in equity or debt securities of the client, purchasers or suppliers of goods or services under substantial or continuing contracts, and possibly such persons as employees and taxing bodies. According to the Second Restatement (Section 531, 1977), an auditor would not be liable to such persons for loss from reliance on his audit opinion if it were a negligent misrepresentation, but *would* be so liable if the audit opinion were a fraudulent misrepresentation, actual or constructive, to the extent, as determined by the trier of fact, that he should expect their conduct to be influenced by his deceit.

5. *General public*—anyone who might *possibly* see the auditor's opinion and rely on it in some act or forebearance. These people are not within the group whose reliance is considered foreseeable, and the auditor does not have a duty or liability to them. Examples might include retail customers, trade creditors, and regulatory and other government bodies or jurisdictions to which the client is subject. The differentiation between the general public and foreseeable persons is even more indistinct than between other classifications, if only because there has not yet been a great need to try to make the distinction.

Primary benefit contrasted with foreseen persons and classes. Some courts have affirmed or reaffirmed the primary benefit rule of *Ultramares*, including the Court of Appeals of New York in which the rule was first announced. Plaintiff in the New York case of *White v. Guarente*, 372 N.E.2d 315 (N.Y. 1977), who was one of approximately 40 limited partners, alleged that defendant auditors of the partnership had known or should have known of the general partners' withdrawals of funds in violation of the partnership agreement, and that the auditors had been negligent in not citing the violations. The court made a reasoned statement of adherence to *Ultramares*. In addition, however, it said in Second Restatement idiom (without citing it): "Here, plaintiff was a member of a limited class whose reliance on the audit and [tax] returns was, or at least should have been, specifically foreseen" (372 N.E.2d at 319). Several other courts have also adhered to the primary benefit rule, though in some cases with reluctance, because they considered themselves bound by controlling precedents.

Other courts have accepted the Second Restatement, but have softened their conclusions with alternative rulings that the third-person plaintiffs were primary beneficiaries of the audit services—although those kinds of third persons had not previously been found to be primary beneficiaries. Some of the opinions express a preference for the Second Restatement rule. The most prominent of such opinions, *Rusch Factors, Inc. v. Levin*, 284 F. Supp. 85, 91, 93 (D. R.I. 1968), contained dicta disparaging the *Ultramares* rule, but held for plaintiff on the ground that "plaintiff is a single party whose reliance was actually foreseen by the defendant"; in further dicta, the court said that such liability should extend to "actually foreseen and limited classes of persons."

However, several of the most recent opinions have clearly applied the Second Restatement to auditors without reliance on the primary benefit rule. The third persons in these opinions would not have qualified as primary beneficiaries in the interpretations of earlier years. The first such case was *Rhode Island Hospital Trust National Bank v. Swartz, Bresenoff, Yavner & Jacobs*, 455 F.2d 847, 851 (4th Cir. 1972), 482 F.2d 1000 (4th Cir. 1973), in which defendant auditor knew and acknowledged that plaintiff bank required annual financial statements of the audit client borrower under the loan agreement. Capitalized leasehold improvements that had purportedly been constructed by the audit client with its own labor and materials were in fact totally fictitious. The auditors, who had identified some of the purported labor costs, were held negligent in not having searched for materials costs.

Another opinion, *Bonhiver v. Graff*, 248 N.W.2d 291, 299, 303 (Minn. 1976), stretched the foreseen class concept beyond all reason in finding that the general agents of an insurance company (which had been looted by its officers) were members of a foreseen class and were entitled to damages for the negligence of the outside accountants, on whom the state insurance commissioner, as a supposed "agent" of the general agents, had relied. A dictum in the opinion was even more extreme, suggesting that by similar reasoning the policyholders themselves might also have been a foreseen class.

Potential liability to primary beneficiaries and to foreseen persons and classes for negligence is an inevitable consequence of audit attestations to financial statements. In large part it is not competitively feasible for a public practitioner to attempt contractually to avoid or limit such third-person liability. When a particular person, directly or through legal or financial advisers, attempts during negotiations to insinuate himself into the role of a foreseen person by direct communications with the auditor or by contractual stipulations, an auditor very occasionally has sufficient bargaining position to expressly disclaim responsibility for negligence, depending largely on his client relationship and the particular circumstances.

Potential for Extension to Foreseeable Classes. If the primary benefit of *Ultramares* is indeed being supplanted by the Second Restatement, it can at least be said that a stable Restatement rule carefully applied and thoughtfully limited should be acceptable, though the size of the foreseen class and transaction is sometimes very large.

However, there is the same infinite gradation of factual differences, and the pressures that may be changing the test from primary benefit to foreseen class would continue to operate in an attempt to make a further change to foreseeable class. The foreseen class test would tend to protect powerful and sophisticated lenders, businesses, and institutions, whose personnel and counsel would make certain that the auditor foresaw their reliance and knew of their transaction, and to exclude from its scope the less powerful and less sophisticated. This could prove distasteful to a judge, and to the public, and could lead to semantic stretching by counsel for plaintiffs. The law changes with thought and sentiment, and how courts will weigh fault and liability in the future is uncertain.

Liability to Nonclients for Fraud

Although in most instances an auditor is not liable at common law to persons other than his client for ordinary negligence, he may be held liable to nonclients if there are deficiencies or lapses in his professional work of such magnitude that the issuance of his opinion constitutes a fraudulent deceit—actual or constructive. The line of distinction between ordinary negligence and constructive fraud is blurred and inconsistent. The best description of the relationship of gross negligence to fraud continues to be the following graphic statement from *State Street Trust Co. v. Ernst*, 15 N.E.2d 416, 419 (N.Y. 1938):

> A representation certified as true to the knowledge of the accountants when knowledge there is none, a reckless misstatement, or an opinion based on grounds so flimsy as to lead to the conclusion that there was no genuine belief in its truth, are all sufficient upon which to base liability. A refusal to see the obvious, a failure to investigate the doubtful, if sufficiently gross, may furnish evidence leading to an inference of fraud so as to impose liability for losses suffered by those who rely on the balance sheet. In other words, heedlessness and reckless disregard of consequence may take the place of deliberate intention.

The fraud of deceit has also been construed to include the failure of an auditor to disaffirm an opinion on which others are still relying if he becomes aware of facts demonstrating that the financial statements and opinion are erroneous (see, e.g., AU 561.05-.07). An auditor who commits a deceitful misrepresentation in an audit opinion may be held liable to the persons or class of persons whom he should have reason to expect may act or refrain from acting in reliance on his deceit; the extent of liability is for economic loss suffered through reliance in the types of transactions in which he should expect their conduct to be influenced by his deceit (ALI, Restatement (Second) of Torts, Section 531 (1977)).

Such liability is not limited to particular persons or classes whose reliance in particular transactions is *foreseen* by the auditor, but extends beyond that to all persons whose reliance is *foreseeable* by him. It could therefore include the potentially large numbers of present and prospective investors, suppliers, customers, contractors, and others.

LIABILITY UNDER FEDERAL SECURITIES LAWS

Securities Act—Section 11

Negligent misrepresentations and omissions in connection with sales of securities are expressly subject to two liability provisions of the federal securities laws, Sections 11 and 12(2) of the 1933 act. Section 12(2) is mentioned later in connection with aiding and abetting.

Section 11 gives purchasers of registered securities a right of recovery against the issuer and other specified persons for resulting losses if the registration statement contains any misstatement of a material fact or any omission of a material fact required to be stated or necessary to make the statements not misleading. The purpose is to stimulate the efforts of the responsible persons toward making accurate and adequate disclosures.

An auditor who has examined and expressed his opinion on financial statements in a registration statement, and has consented to the use of his opinion in the registration statement, is subjected by the section to heavy responsibility for his opinion. The responsibility is imposed because of the auditor's training and experience as an expert in accounting and auditing and because of the reliance of investors on his opinion.

Burden of Proof. Under Section 11(a), unlike common law, a plaintiff need *not* prove

1. Negligence or fraud by the auditor in auditing the financial statements,
2. Reliance on the auditor's opinion (unless plaintiff acquired his securities after the registrant made generally available an earnings statement for a period of at least twelve months beginning after the effective date of the registration statement),
3. A causal relationship between the omission or misstatement and plaintiff's loss, or
4. Any contractual relationship between plaintiff and the auditor, issuer, sellers, or underwriters; thus, even a stranger purchasing the registered security in the open market subsequent to the offering is entitled to recover under the section.

Plaintiff must prove only that he has suffered a loss by investing in a security registered under the act and, in suing the auditor, must prove that, contrary to the audit opinion, the audited financial statements contained an omission or misstatement of material importance. Although plaintiff may be required to post security for defendants' costs under Section 11(e), the courts have been hesitant to require such security, because it seems to call for clairvoyance as to the merit of the litigation.

The auditor may escape liability if he is able to bear successfully the burden of proving affirmatively by a preponderance of the evidence that

1. After making reasonable investigation (i.e., exercising "due diligence"), he had reasonable ground to believe, and did in fact believe, that the statements in his audit opinion were true; in effect, the auditor will be held liable unless he can prove that he exercised due care, i.e., was not negligent either in the performance of his audit or in the expression of his audit opinion (which is indeed a rigorous standard though not insurmountable),

2. There was no causal relationship between an untruth in his audit opinion and plaintiff's loss, or

3. Plaintiff knew of the untruth in the audit opinion when he acquired the security.

Who may sue. Section 11 provides that the suit may be brought on a material misstatement or omission in a registration statement by "any person acquiring such [registered] security."

The courts have limited this remedy to purchasers of the particular shares or other securities registered under the 1933 act. Purchasers of other classes of securities, or of securities of the same class but other than those registered for sale, are precluded from recovery under this provision.

Materiality. The opinion in *Escott v. BarChris Construction Co.,* 283 F. Supp. 643 (S.D. N.Y. 1968), the first definitive interpretation under Section 11 concerning auditors' responsibility, contains a sobering reminder of the elusive quality of the term *materiality.* The court attempted its own definition of materiality by saying (at 681):

> The average prudent investor is not concerned with minor inaccuracies or with errors as to matters which are of no interest to him. The facts which tend to deter him from purchasing a security are facts which have an important bearing upon the nature or condition of the issuing corporation or its business.

The court's analysis of the facts led it to conclude (at 682) that overstatements of 1960 sales and net operating income, by approximately 14% in the case of net income, were "comparatively minor errors. . . ." The court reasoned (at 681) that investors would have been attracted to the registered convertible debentures, which were rated as speculative, "primarily by the conversion feature, by the growth potential of the stock." The court considered (at 682) that investors would not have been deterred if they had known that sales had increased 256% over the previous year, rather than 276% as reported, or that earnings had approximately doubled, rather than more than doubled. Had this growth figure been substantially lower, the court might possibly have found a 14% overstatement of earnings to be material.

However, as to balance sheet data, the court ruled that a misstatement leading to computation of a current ratio overstated by less than 15% *was* material. The conclusion is surprising. In an otherwise meticulous opinion there seems to be a lapse in the analysis of this crucial issue, because the opinion contains only a single unilluminating remark (at 682):

> There must be some point at which errors in disclosing a company's balance sheet position become material, even to a growth-oriented investor. On all the evidence I find that these balance sheet errors were material within the meaning of Section 11.

This illustrates the degree of hazard to which auditors and others are exposed in the opinions and predelictions of finders of fact, judge (as in *BarChris*), or jury.

Accountants are accustomed to living and working with materiality (see Chapter 3) as a general concept (e.g., AU 150.04; AU 411.04(e); AU 509.16). However, materiality means different things to different people when applied to particular facts, and accordingly accountants are exposed to the risk that a court might analyze the information differently. Materiality may be a sword in its generality rather than the shield that accountants tend to assume it is.

Defenses Against Liability. Having traced his security to those covered by the registration statement, and also having proved a loss and that contrary to the audit opinion, audited financial statements in that registration statement contained a material misstatement or omission, a plaintiff in a Section 11 action has satisfied his burden of presenting a prima facie case to the finder of fact. The burden then shifts to the auditor-defendant to vindicate his opinion and establish one of three defenses provided by the statute.

Lack of reliance. Liability will not be incurred if the auditor can prove facts showing that the particular plaintiff knew of the untruth or omission or that plaintiff's decision to purchase did not depend on the opinion. But there is almost no way of establishing such a proof in class actions.

Lack of causation. A lack-of-causation defense may be asserted under Section 11(e). As applied to an auditor, the section provides that damages may not be recoverable by plaintiff if and to such extent as the auditor can prove that plaintiff's damages were caused by factors other than the auditor's defective audit opinion. It is unlikely that all damages can be avoided, if only because a part of the loss of value is likely to be traceable to disclosure of the proved misrepresentations and omissions. However, the defense might relieve an auditor from damages compensating a decline in value prior to disclosure because of market or industry conditions, and may reduce his liability for the decline in market value subsequent to disclosure that is directly attributable to factors such as a general market decline.[5]

Exercise of due diligence. A defense of due diligence in Section 11(b) requires proof of freedom from negligence in connection with the misstatement or omission, i.e., an adequate basis for belief in the representations in his audit opinion. Defendant's posture is much more unfavorable than in common-law cases, in which plaintiff has the burden of proving negligence.

It is standard practice for underwriting agreements in securities offerings to specify that one of the conditions precedent to the obligation of the underwriters to accept and pay for the securities is the delivery of a "comfort letter" (containing limited negative assurances) from the auditors to the underwriters in partial support of the underwriters' burden of diligence (see Chapter 26). In *BarChris* the comfort letter contained the invariable stipulation that it was furnished for the information of the underwriters and was not to be referred to in the registration statement or the offering. Accordingly, the court held that "plaintiffs may not take advantage of any undertakings or representations in this letter," particularly as to the responsibility for unaudited financial statements (283 F. Supp. at 698).

---

[5] In *Feit v. Leasco Data Processing Equip. Corp.,* 332 F. Supp. 544, 586 (E.D. N.Y. 1971), the court took "judicial notice of the very drastic general decline in the stock market in 1969," which continued after discovery of the material error, and deflated the damages by deducting the degree of decline in the Standard & Poor's daily stock price index during the period.

Section 11(a) is unique in continuing the audit opinion responsibility to the effective date of the registration statement, rather than only to the date of the audit opinion. It is possible that the information available to the auditor at the audit opinion date might *justify* one audit opinion, but that additional information available to the auditor at or near the effective date might then *require* a different audit opinion. However, as to the post-balance sheet period, investigation cannot be as intensive and conclusive as the audit examination (see AU 710.08-.11).

In *BarChris* the court, perhaps without realizing it, rewrote a bit of GAAS; authoritative pronouncements since then require identification and evaluation of two types of subsequent events:

1. Events that provide evidence of conditions existing at the balance sheet date, which perhaps should affect the estimates reflected in the audited financial statements (AU 560.04).
2. Subsequent events not related to conditions existing at the balance sheet date, which should not require adjustment of the financial statements although they may require disclosure "*to keep* the financial statements *from being misleading* [emphasis added]" (AU 560.05)—the italicized words are almost identical to those in the quotation from *BarChris*. Prior to 1960 this type of event was said to "have no direct effect on and ... not require adjustment of the financial statements of the prior period but their effects may be such that disclosure is advisable" (AICPA, 1954b, par. 10).

The only prudent conclusion is that despite the language of Section 11, which purports to limit an auditor's responsibility under that section to the defensibility of his opinion on the audited financial statements, a subtle process of interpretation may be producing substantial audit responsibility for the post-balance sheet period.

Exchange Act—Section 18(a)

Section 18(a) of the 1934 act could subject an auditor to liability for loss sustained by purchasers or sellers of securities in reliance on a materially false or misleading audit opinion on financial statements contained in an application, report, or other document "filed" by a client with the SEC or a securities exchange as required under the 1934 act. Section 18(a) liability does not apply to unaudited interim financial statements and to reports sent directly to shareholders but not filed (see, e.g., *Rich v. Touche Ross & Co.*, 415 F. Supp. 95, 102 (S.D. N.Y. 1976)).

At first glance, Section 18(a) liability for filed documents appears to resemble Section 11 liability for 1933 act registration statements. However, a closer look reveals additional obstacles to recovery by plaintiff:

1. Plaintiff must prove "eyeball reliance," i.e., that he actually knew of and relied on the allegedly false or misleading statement in making his investment decision, and that at the time of his action he was not aware that the information was false or misleading.
2. Plaintiff must also prove causation, i.e., he must demonstrate
   a. That his damages were caused by his reliance on the false or misleading statement, and
   b. That the purchase or sale *price* was affected by the false or misleading statement.

3. Section 18(a) absolves a defendant who can prove that he had acted in good faith and had not known at the time of the filing that his opinion was false or misleading, i.e., he had not acted with scienter (i.e., guilty knowledge, or possibly recklessness), even though he may have been negligent. It should logically follow that such a defendant is not liable in any event for negligence, a view supported in *Hochfelder*, 425 U.S. 185 (1976), though in dicta not essential to the rationale of the holding.

Although multicount complaints against auditors and others have commonly contained a count alleging violation of Section 18(a), the decisive issues have tended to be resolved by application of other liability provisions. However, the recent decline in importance of implied remedies such as Rule 10b-5 (discussed below) may revive the efforts of plaintiffs to obtain favorable interpretations of express liability provisions such as Section 18(a).

Exchange Act—Section 10(b)

Adoption and Evolution. As a result of an expansive judicial and SEC interpretation, SEC Rule 10b-5, adopted under Section 10(b) of the 1934 act, has become a formidable legal hazard to accountants and others. The creation of Rule 10b-5 was prompted in 1942 (SEC Release 34-3230) by a report that a corporate president was purchasing his company's shares at depressed prices by circulating falsely pessimistic information. The rule was conceived and drafted by the SEC staff, submitted to and adopted without discussion by the SEC, and announced with a 79-word explanation, all during a single day (Freeman, 1967b).

Section 17(a) of the 1933 act and Rule 10b-5 under Section 10(b) of the 1934 act contain substantially identical prohibitions, stated in Rule 10b-5 as follows:

1. to employ any device, scheme, or artifice to defraud,
2. to make any untrue statement of a material fact or to omit to state a material fact necessary in order to make the statements made, in the light of the circumstances under which they were made, not misleading, or
3. to engage in any act, practice, or course of business which operates or would operate as a fraud or deceit upon any person.

In Section 17(a), discussed later, the prohibitions are "in the offer or sale of any securities," in Rule 10b-5 "in connection with the purchase or sale of any security." The SEC adopted Rule 10b-5 as a disciplinary weapon for its own enforcement purposes, to "make applicable to the purchase of securities the same broad antifraud provisions" imposed by the Congress on sales in Section 17(a). Unlike the express liability provisions of the 1933 act, it may be invoked by sellers as well as purchasers. The SEC did not comprehend the ramifications of its new rule, and did not foresee the weedlike growth of the rule through judicial interpretation. The impact of Rule 10b-5 has been magnified by the great increase in recent years of class actions on behalf of large groups of purchasers and sellers of securities.

Rule 10b-5 prohibits securities fraud with a generality almost to the point of vagueness. The first and third clauses of the rule are palpably fraud provisions, although in *Hochfelder*, 425 U.S. 185, 212 (1976), the SEC, as amicus curiae, unsuccessfully attempted an argument that if the effect (operation) of the misstatement or omission were to deceive investors, the rule was violated even if the culpable conduct were only negligent.

Since the question was first litigated in 1946, the courts have ruled that investors injured by violations of Rule 10b-5 have an implied private right of action for damages, despite the fact that some qualified observers had believed that the Supreme Court might conclude otherwise.

Liberal Interpretation of Purchaser-Seller Requirement. In general, the courts have interpreted the language of Rule 10b-5 as authorizing a private right of action only for actual purchasers or sellers of securities, and have excluded holders of securities and other nonpurchasers and nonsellers, including a holder dissuaded from selling and a nonholder dissuaded from buying. However, the opinions have interpreted the terms *purchase* and *sale* broadly (as they are defined in the 1933 and 1934 acts), to include transactions that are not regarded as purchases or sales in the common-law sense. Among them are unconsummated agreements to purchase or sell; short-form and other statutory mergers, consolidations, and liquidations; original issuances by a corporation of its shares; fraudulent dissuasion from sale; and pledges of securities. In addition, even though a nonselling shareholder claiming irreparable injury may not sue for damages, he may sue for an injunction under Rule 10b-5, because the elements of suits for injunction are different from those in suits for damages.

No Privity Requirement. A purchaser or seller of securities injured by violation of Rule 10b-5 is not limited to suing the seller from whom he purchased or the purchaser to whom he sold, but is also entitled to sue others alleged to have participated in the violation. As a result, auditors whose opinions are circulated in connection with a sale or purchase of securities are exposed to potential liability in private suits under Rule 10b-5, even though they did none of the purchasing or selling and realized no profit in any securities transaction.

Meaning of "In Connection With." The scope of Rule 10b-5 was broadened radically in the 1968 opinion in the famous injunction suit of *SEC v. Texas Gulf Sulphur Co.,* 401 F.2d 833 (2d Cir. 1968) (en banc), *cert. denied,* 394 U.S. 976 (1969), in which the court held that Rule 10b-5 had been violated by defendant company in issuing a misleading press release that would foreseeably influence the investing public in the purchase and sale of the company's securities. The company was held responsible even though it had not been engaged in purchasing or selling its securities (other than sales in employee programs). The court interpreted the phrase "in connection with the purchase or sale of any security" in Section 10(b) of the statute as requiring only that misrepresentations by defendants be likely to cause reasonable investors to purchase or sell the company's securities in reliance on the misrepresentations, not that the defendants be purchasers or sellers or involved with them. Since 1968, therefore, the term *in connection with* has been construed broadly enough so that audit opinions and audited or unaudited financial statements with which auditors become associated may, along with other corporate statements and information, be statements *in connection with* purchases and sales of the corporation's securities.

Expansive Definition of Security. The liberality and flexibility of the federal securities laws encourage attempts by plaintiffs to avoid the heavy burden of proving common-law mismanagement (Jacobs, 1978) by drafting complaints that purport to characterize essentially commercial controversies as misbehavior in connection with a purchase or sale of securities. In this effort they have been partially successful. The definition of *security* has undergone considerable expansion, especially in cases under Rule 10b-5, so that it now includes many things one would not ordinarily call a security.

The term *security* includes an "investment contract" to derive income or gain from the efforts of others in a common enterprise. Because of the broad interpretation of an investment contract, auditors may find themselves falling within the scope of the 1933 and 1934 acts for services in connection with sales of breeding cattle, orange groves, variable annuity policies, country club memberships, and self-motivation courses.

Some types of financing involve securities, while others do not. The more general the nature of the financing—e.g., a money borrowing rather than indebtedness for the purchase price of goods or services—and the longer the term, the more the financing may appear to be of an investment rather than a commercial character. The dividing line is indistinct, and the legal difference may be important to the auditor. (Compare the factual conclusions in *Exchange National Bank of Chicago v. Touche Ross & Co.,* 544 F.2d 1126 (2d Cir. 1976) and *Tri-County State Bank v. Hertz,* 418 F. Supp. 332 (M.D. Pa. 1976)—security in former, commercial loan in latter.)

Materiality, Reliance, and Causation. In common-law fraud or misrepresentation, a plaintiff must prove that (1) defendant misrepresented or omitted a *material* fact, (2) plaintiff justifiably *relied* on the misrepresentation or omission, *and* (3) such reliance *caused* damage to plaintiff. Initially, the same elements of proof were required under Rule 10b-5 and other fraud provisions of the securities laws. However, more recent cases under Rule 10b-5 have increasingly permitted reliance and sometimes causation to be presumed merely from a showing of materiality.

Materiality has been applied by the courts with substantial consistency. Misrepresented or omitted facts are considered of *material* importance if a reasonable investor would attach importance to them in determining his choice of action in the transaction in question.

Reliance is directed more toward the individual plaintiff. Having found that a reasonable man would have acted on the material fact that was misrepresented or omitted, a parallel requirement is added that the individual plaintiff must be shown to have acted on such misrepresentation or the adequacy of the representations made.

Causation, in this context, refers to the relationship of cause and effect between the misrepresentation or omission and plaintiff's damages.

Materiality, reliance, and causation are not entirely distinct and independent. For example, reliance of plaintiff on a misrepresentation is an element of causation although not alone conclusive of such. Court opinions have shown a lack of clarity regarding the relation of materiality, reliance, and causation.

For example, the test of *reliance* in a misrepresentation case is whether the defendant's misrepresentation was a "substantial factor" in determining the course of conduct that resulted in the plaintiff's loss. A court or jury analyzing the question looks to specific conduct and determines whether an identified misrepresentation or omission was a substantial factor in bringing such conduct about. However, in an omissions case the judge or jury testing for reliance must imagine the form that the proper disclosure would have taken and hypothesize what effect it would have had on plaintiff's choice of alternative courses of conduct. In such circumstances, reliance may be telescoped into materiality, which looks to the reasonable investor rather than to the individual plaintiff, as both determinations involve speculation as to how others might have acted. This telescoping may particularly be true when the suit is a class action, given the tendency of courts to expedite these complex and cumbersome cases by minimizing individual issues. Such an analysis is evident in the recent district court opinion in *Seiffer v. Topsy's International, Inc.*, 487 F. Supp. 653, 666 (D. Kan. 1980), in which the opinion states that "[w]hen it is, as a practical matter, impossible to demonstrate reliance, resort must be had to materiality . . . [especially] when the action involves communications disseminated to thousands of investors."

The United States Supreme Court decided, in *Affiliated Ute Citizens of Utah v. United States*, 406 U.S. 128, 153-154 (1972), that a plaintiff who can establish materiality in an omission case under Rule 10b-5 need not prove reliance. The plaintiffs were former shareholders who had not been told by the defendant bank appointed as stock transfer agent that a secondary market existed in which the price exceeded that paid by the bank. There was no affirmative proof that individual plaintiffs had relied on material omissions by the bank, and the court of appeals thus ruled there was no violation of Rule 10b-5. In reversing that portion of the decision, the Supreme Court stated:

> Under the circumstances of this case, involving primarily a failure to disclose, positive proof of reliance is not a prerequisite to recovery. All that is necessary is that the facts withheld be material in the sense that a reasonable investor might have considered them important in the making of this decision.

The holding of *Affiliated Ute* is somewhat unclear. Although it makes reliance a less important element in Rule 10b-5 actions, it has left unresolved a number of questions as to when proof of reliance is or is not required, and how the presumption of reliance operates, with resulting variance among lower federal court interpretations. The following tendencies have been appearing among court opinions:

1. For a host of reasons, only occasionally identified or expressed by the courts, reliance tends to be presumed more often
   a. In omission cases than in misrepresentation cases, although a given deficiency may often be alleged as either,
   b. In impersonal market transactions than in face-to-face transactions,
   c. In class actions than in individual actions, and
   d. In cases alleging fraudulent schemes including other conduct as well as misrepresentations and omissions;
2. In some jurisdictions the plaintiff is relieved only of proving reliance on specific omissions or misrepresentations, and must still prove general reliance on financial statements or other communications;

3. A presumption of reliance or causation may be rebuttable by evidence, although the opinions are unclear, and some might be read to imply that the presumption is conclusive; and

4. Some courts seem to presume reliance as an element of materiality, others seem to presume reliance as an element of "causation in fact," and still others seem to presume *both* reliance *and* causation as an element of materiality.

In short, confusion has been created by the *Affiliated Ute* decision's loosening of the reliance requirement in what was previously an understandable three-part test. The result is that recognized defenses are often being extensively, though nonuniformly, eroded by judicial precedents having the apparent, though unarticulated, purpose of enabling plaintiffs to win previously unprovable claims.

Scienter. Scienter, roughly meaning *guilty knowledge,* is one of that discredited and diminishing group of Latin phrases, words, and derivatives that obscure legal analysis by substitution of a seemingly profound expression that in fact is only a disguise for vagueness and ambiguity.

Hochfelder. Prior to the 1976 decision of the United States Supreme Court in *Ernst & Ernst v. Hochfelder,* 425 U.S. 185 (1976), there was a long struggle over whether defendants in Rule 10b-5 cases, especially nonpurchaser, nonseller defendants such as auditors, could be held liable for negligent (i.e., without scienter) misrepresentations or omissions. *Hochfelder* held that there is no private cause of action under Rule 10b-5 for negligent conduct, but left unresolved exactly what level of culpability should result in liability.

In this case, the president-majority shareholder of a small brokerage firm had induced customers to invest in high-yield escrow accounts. Investment checks were made payable to the president or to a designated bank for his account. The escrow accounts were fictitious, and the president converted the money to his own use. He concealed this scheme by insisting that he alone personally open mail addressed to him or to his attention. The auditors were accused by plaintiffs of "inexcusable negligence" (but not "deliberate, intentional fraud") in failing to discover the lapse of internal accounting controls that would have revealed the fraud.

The court of appeals held that one who breaches a duty of inquiry and disclosure owed another is liable for aiding and abetting a third party's violation of Rule 10b-5 if the fraud would have been discovered but for the breach, and that in undertaking a statutory audit of the broker under the 1934 act, the auditors had assumed a statutory (though not a common-law) duty to plaintiffs of exercising due care.[6]

The Supreme Court reversed the court of appeals on the grounds that

1. The use of the words *manipulative, device,* and *contrivance* in the rule connotes "intentional or willful conduct" rather than negligence (at 199);

---

[6] In a subsequent case, *Touche Ross & Co. v. Redington,* 442 U.S. 560 (1979), the Supreme Court held that customers of broker-dealers have no implied private right of action under the broker-dealer audit provision (Section 17(a)) of the 1934 act (*not* of the 1933 act).

2. Legislative history supports the conclusion that "§10(b) was addressed to practices that involve *some element* [emphasis added] of scienter and . . . [not] negligent conduct alone" (at 201);
3. In adopting Rule 10b-5, the SEC evidenced an intention of applying it only to activities involving scienter; and
4. The extension of Rule 10b-5 to cover negligence would nullify
    a. The procedural limitations on the express remedies for negligence in Sections 11, 12(2), and 15 of the 1933 act, and
    b. The scienter requirements of the express liability provisions in the 1934 act (other than Section 16(b), which is a self-contained accountability provision).

Hochfelder thus bears significantly on the degree of culpability that constitutes scienter in damage and injunction suits.

Damage suits. The Supreme Court in *Hochfelder* decided only that "negligent conduct" did not violate Rule 10b-5, apart from stating a corollary that "some element of scienter is required" and mentioning an array of possibilities as to what level that might mean:

1. *Deliberate intent.* "In this opinion the term 'scienter' refers to a mental state embracing intent to deceive, manipulate, or defraud." (at 194 n.12)
2. *Willfulness.* Willfulness was defined as "willful conduct designed to deceive or defraud investors." Under the 1934 act, "willfully" has been construed to mean "intentionally committing the act which constitutes the violation," and does not require the actor to be aware that he is violating the acts or rules. (at 199)
3. *Knowledge.* It was suggested that Section 10(b) prohibited "knowing or intentional misconduct." (at 197)
4. *Recklessness.* "In certain areas of the law recklessness is considered to be a form of intentional conduct for purposes of imposing liability for some act." (at 194 n.12)

The court left the range of possibilities open by saying that since *Hochfelder* was an action in damages for negligence, the court need not consider "whether, in some circumstances, reckless behavior is sufficient for civil liability under §10(b) and Rule 10b-5." (at 194 n.12)

Although deliberate intent, willfulness, knowledge, and recklessness are all descriptions of states of mind, the available relevant evidence usually consists primarily of behavior. Consequently, those terms commonly serve as symbols for classifying culpable behavior by degree. In any case, the burden of proof in the scienter issue is on the plaintiff (*McLean v. Alexander,* 599 F.2d 1190, 1196-1197 (3d Cir. 1979)).

Lower court decisions on the degree of scienter applicable in private actions for damages under Rule 10b-5 have reflected the Supreme Court's reaffirmation (in *Hochfelder*) of *Ultramares* and the common-law approach. Whether referring to the common-law underpinnings or not, the post-*Hochfelder* trend has been to predicate Rule 10b-5 liability on some kind of recklessness standard. This trend is also marked with some disagreement among the courts as to the precise formulation of what constitutes recklessness. One prevalent definition from *McLean* is as follows:

Reckless conduct may be defined as . . . highly unreasonable [conduct], involving not merely simple, or even inexcusable negligence, but an extreme departure from the standards of ordinary care, and which presents a danger of misleading buyers or sellers that is either known to the defendant or is so obvious that the actor must have been aware of it. (at 1197)

This definition emphasizes the more culpable *character* of recklessness from that of negligence, and the kinship of recklessness to guilty knowledge. An indication of this closer proximity is the number of recent decisions in which plaintiff has not shown the required scienter to have been met. In *McLean* the court applied literally the maxim in *Ultramares* that an accountant is not liable if he honestly believes, *whether reasonably or unreasonably,* that the statements made are true.

However, other post-*Hochfelder* cases define recklessness in a manner closer to negligence than to knowledge. One line of aiding and abetting cases attaches Rule 10b-5 liability for reckless behavior only when a fiduciary duty is owed, and otherwise requires more serious culpability. Discussion of fiduciary concepts has led another court to base primary liability on "gross negligence" and "wantonly ignor-[ing] evidence of the unfairness," and yet another to announce that the degree of culpability required varies with the duty owed. If a concept of recklessness close to negligence becomes established in this area, it might spread to other areas by the elimination of the fiduciary duty element.

Injunction suits. Recently, the Supreme Court resolved the question, left open by *Hochfelder* and much disputed in the lower courts, of whether scienter must be proved in an SEC action for injunction under Rule 10b-5 (*Aaron v. SEC,* 446 U.S. 680 (1980)). The Court relied heavily on *Hochfelder's* discussion of the language of Rule 10b-5 in holding that scienter was, indeed, required in such cases. (*Aaron* also held that scienter was required in SEC injunction actions under Section 17(a)(1) of the 1933 act, though *not* under Sections 17(a)(2) and (3), on similar "wording" analysis.)

Private Suits

Class and Derivative Actions. The risk of liability in securities law litigation has been magnified by the development of two types of collective adjudications of controversies involving interests of large numbers of persons.

A *class action* is a suit on behalf of a defined group of purchasers, sellers, or (in some cases) holders of shares or other securities, instituted by one or more members of the class, to enforce a right of, or to recover for a loss sustained by, the class members directly as purchasers, sellers, or holders.

A *derivative action* is a suit by one or more shareholders, on behalf of the corporation itself (in which the corporation is theoretically the plaintiff), to enforce a right of, or to recover a loss by, the corporation.

Plaintiffs generally favor a class action over a derivative action, because any recovery is paid directly to the members of the class; in a derivative action the recovery is paid to the company in which the shareholders have underlying pro rata interests, not to the shareholders themselves. Some suits are maintainable as either class or derivative actions, sometimes as both. (See, e.g., *Ernst & Ernst v. United States District Court,* 439 F.2d 1288 (5th Cir. 1971) (Westec Corp.).)

As applied to securities law cases, the federal class action rule requires not only that there must be questions of law or fact common to the class, but that such common questions must *predominate* over individual questions. In practice the rule has been bent. Plaintiffs gloss over the disparities, claiming that the alleged misrepresentations are interrelated, interdependent, and cumulative, and the courts tend to accept the claims, even in doubtful cases. The federal courts have preponderantly appeared receptive to class actions, both to reduce duplicative litigations and to support the interests of multitudes of small investors who would not sue individually. The result has been coercive pressure on defendants to buy peace by settlement, and auditors and other defendants may be victimized.

Proposed congressional legislation sponsored by the Department of Justice to "reform" class action proceedings would further prejudice the rights of defendants by permitting a "class compensatory action" for injuries to all persons arising from a single series of occurrences with a *substantial* question of law or fact common to all persons. According to the proposed bill, the common question need no longer *predominate* over other questions, and the claims of the class representatives need no longer be *typical* of those of the other class members.

Implied Private Rights of Action. Although the Supreme Court has on a number of occasions found a private right of action to be implicit in statutes containing no express liability provision, it has been applying more restrictive criteria in recent years. In its 1979 opinion in *Touche Ross & Co. v. Redington,* 442 U.S. 560, 575 (1979), the court said that "the central inquiry remains whether Congress intended to create, either expressly or by implication, a private cause of action."

Redington alleged dereliction on the part of the defendant accountant in auditing financial statements of a broker-dealer filed with the SEC. The statements were subsequently determined to contain misleading information in violation of a 1934 act provision concerning records, financial statements, and audits of broker-dealers. Of the plaintiffs' claim to an implied private remedy, the court said that "the fact that a federal statute has been violated and some person harmed does not automatically give rise to a private cause of action in favor of that person." (at 568) The court concluded that "there is no basis in the language of [the section] for inferring that a civil cause of action for damages lay in favor of anyone." (at 571)

More recently the Supreme Court held that a private action was not sustainable under Section 206 of the Investment Advisers Act (similar to Rule 10b-5); lower federal courts had previously upheld suits under the section that charged defendant accountants as being aiders and abettors. The current question is whether implied private rights of action may be denied under other securities law provisions, especially those that may arguably be construed to relate more to SEC supervision than to disclosure to investors, e.g., the accounting records and internal accounting control provisions of Section 13(b)(2) of the 1934 act added in 1977 by the Foreign Corrupt Practices Act, various provisions of the Investment Company Act, and Section 7 of the 1934 act relating to Federal Reserve margin rules.

Courts have allowed private rights of action against broker-dealers under rules of stock exchanges and of the National Association of Securities Dealers, and in one case against an issuer of listed securities under the issuer's listing agreement with the stock exchange. In such cases the particular rules and agreement provisions were construed to be designed for the direct protection of investors. In one recent opinion (*Jablon v. Dean Witter & Co.,* 614 F.2d 677 (9th Cir. 1980)), the court was admittedly influenced, in deciding to deny a private action under stock exchange and NASD rules, by the recent opinions of the Supreme Court restricting implied rights of action.

Section 17(a) of 1933 Act. Of various statutory provisions under which the existence or nonexistence of a private right of action is not clearly resolved, the most important is Section 17(a) of the 1933 act, the prototype of Rule 10b-5 (though applying only to violations by sellers, not purchasers, of securities). Although conflicting positions have been taken on that question among several federal courts of appeal, the Supreme Court has not thus far accepted a petition to review the question.

Plaintiffs see two potential advantages to suit under Section 17(a) (and possibly a third):

1. A possibility of convincing the courts that the standard of culpability in the second clause of Section 17(a) should be negligence, rather than scienter as in the post-*Hochfelder* Rule 10b-5.
2. The right to sue under the 1933 act in a state court, rather than only in a federal court as under the 1934 act. Defendants would then have to face fragmented litigations of a nationwide controversy, with possible nonuniformity of result, local prejudice, and lack of expertise in this sophisticated area.

It is possible that a Supreme Court ruling would confirm that Section 17(a) is redundant as a private liability section, essentially as it has been heretofore. In the past, a number of courts have allowed Section 17(a) counts in private actions to stand in tandem with Rule 10b-5 counts, because, as Judge Friendly said in *SEC v. Texas Gulf Sulphur Co.,* 401 F.2d 833, 867 (2d Cir. 1968), "once it had been established . . . that an aggrieved buyer has a private action under §10(b) of the 1934 Act, there seemed little practical point in denying the existence of such an action under §17—with the important proviso that fraud, as distinct from mere negligence, must be alleged."

It has also been said that the express provision for civil remedies in Sections 11 and 12 of the 1933 act "creates the reasonable inference that the absence of such a remedy in §17 was not an oversight or the product of inartful draftsmanship" (*Reid v. Mann,* 381 F. Supp. 525, 526 (N.D. Ill. 1974)). If a private remedy for negligence were implied under Section 17(a) without restriction, the short statute of limitations and other conditions attaching to the express remedy of Section 12 would tend to lose meaning. Thus, despite the similarity in language between Section 17(a) and Rule 10b-5, the justifications for implying a private remedy under Rule 10b-5 are not necessarily applicable to Section 17(a).

Particularity in Alleging Fraud. Federal Rule of Civil Procedure 9(b) has been construed to require fraud allegations that set forth the particular financial statements and audit opinions giving rise to the cause of action, the nature of alleged omissions and misstatements, and the facts on which plaintiff alleges belief that the auditor has committed fraud. Since plaintiffs are routinely permitted to amend their complaints to cure inadequacies under Rule 9(b), dismissal of a complaint on a motion under Rule 9(b) may seem like a narrow and transitory procedural victory for a defendant. However, auditors have found such warfare of attrition worthwhile, because the motion may result in

1. Identifying specific issues to which defendant may file a response and prepare a defense,
2. Forcing plaintiff to allege a claim that may be difficult or impossible to prove at trial, or
3. Revealing the emptiness of a claim filed simply to conduct discovery proceedings in a search for a genuine claim.

Plaintiffs' Due-Diligence Requirement. In third-party cases under Rule 10b-5 and other federal securities laws, courts have recognized a defense of lack of plaintiff's "[d]ue diligence [which] imposes on the plaintiff the duty to act with the caution expected of a reasonable person in his position . . . as would a person similarly possessed of his degree of business expertise" (*Wachovia Bank & Trust Co. N.A. v. National Student Marketing Corp.,* 461 F. Supp. 999 (D. D.C. 1978)).

The basis for a due-diligence defense may be doubtful against a claim by a rank-and-file investor, but

the securities laws were not enacted to protect sophisticated businessmen from their own errors of judgment. Such investors must, if they wish to recover under federal law, investigate the information available to them with the care and prudence expected from people blessed with full access to information. [*Hirsch v. duPont,* 553 F.2d 750, 763 (2d Cir. 1977)]

In one case (*Shahmoon v. General Development Corp.,* CCH Fed. Sec. L. Rep. ¶ 94,308 (S.D. N.Y. 1973)), a court found that plaintiff's expertise and sophistication so discredited his alleged reliance on a technical misrepresentation that the court concluded: "This litigation is a sham."

Conspiracy—Aiding and Abetting

Civil conspiracy is an agreement to commit a wrongful act, and some overt act by any one of the conspirators toward accomplishing the wrongful act, plus, in private litigation, injury to the plaintiff. *Criminal conspiracy* is an agreement to commit a crime, and some overt act by any one of the conspirators toward accomplishing the crime, even though the objective is never accomplished.

Civil aiding and abetting is the unilateral performance by a secondary party (e.g., auditor, lawyer) of an act of knowing and substantial assistance of what he knew was a wrongful act by another (e.g., issuance of misleading financial statements by a client), without proof of agreement or concert between the parties. *Criminal aiding and abetting* is assistance in similar circumstances of a *criminal* act of another.

Both conspiracy and aiding and abetting originated in criminal law and were subsequently extended to civil common law. Because of their similarity, the same occurrences commonly constitute both offenses. The key distinction is that conspiracy is *agreement,* and aiding and abetting is *action.*

If financial statements or other data prove to have been unfairly presented, the element of agreement between auditor and client, plus an audit opinion on, or other association with, the statements or data, provides at least a superficial basis for charges that the auditor conspired with, or aided and abetted, the client—or both. It is common for charges against auditors to include such allegations, even though the auditor obviously took no part in the overt act that caused the injury, such as an allegedly fraudulent purchase or sale of securities. Among other things, conspiracy charges may enable plaintiffs or prosecutors to obtain admission in trial of some otherwise inadmissible testimony. Although such charges are an additional threat, the opinions thus far are believed to justify a conclusion that accountants have by and large been judged on the defensibility of what they did (and did not do) in the performance of their professional engagements.

Analyzed objectively, there is no way in which ordinary negligence can be equated with aiding and abetting. A negligent failure to make the inquiry that might have revealed a deficiency is still negligence, not the equivalent of the knowledge required in aiding and abetting (Ruder, 1974).

Scienter Standard. Traditionally, courts have held that Section 12(2) liability of a seller is limited to a purchaser in privity, and does not extend to a person less closely related to the seller than an agent acting for the seller. The "agency" issue arose in a case in which the defendant public accountant in the employ of a certified public accounting firm "prepared" (examined?) annual financial statements of a client corporation, under the supervision of a CPA. After leaving that employment, he kept in touch with the president, and as a favor and without compensation, persuaded the plaintiff, who was then his personal client, to invest in the corporation. The district court concluded on these narrow facts that defendant was not an agent of the corporation or its president, and hence was not liable under Section 12. The court also concluded that defendant was not a coconspirator or an aider and abettor, for which "plaintiff would have to establish that defendant had knowledge of a fraudulent scheme of [or] acted so recklessly that knowledge may be imputed to him" (*deBruin v. Andromeda Broadcasting Systems, Inc.,* 465 F. Supp. 1276, 1280 (D. Nev. 1979)). The accountant's victory was a close one, and should serve as a warning to professionals not to solicit from one client investment in tax shelters or other interests in another client.

The elements of aiding and abetting are *knowledge of the violation* and *knowing assistance of a substantial nature,* but the meaning of the knowledge requirement is not easily generalized, because the rulings are expressed in a diversity of factual situations.

In a recent Rule 10b-5 case, *Seiffer v. Topsy's International, Inc.,* 487 F. Supp. 653, 679, 707 (D. Kan. 1980), plaintiffs claimed that auditors were liable for certain proved deficiencies in the narrative portion of a prospectus because of a note to audited financial statements, "Note (11), Subsequent Events" (i.e., subsequent to the date of the audited balance sheet) that read, "For information relating to the subsequent acquisition of all the outstanding stock of SaxonS Sandwich ShoppeS, Inc. see 'SaxonS Sandwich ShoppeS, Inc.' under 'Business' elsewhere in this Prospectus." Plaintiffs argued that the note incorporated by reference the indicated portion of the business description of the prospectus into the audited financial statements. The court held significantly "that [defendant auditor] has no *direct* responsibility for the SaxonS narrative as a result of note (11). The footnote does not serve to incorporate that portion of the narrative into the certified financial statements. *This does not, of course, mean that [the auditor] may not be liable secondarily, as an aider-abettor, for misrepresentations in or omissions from narrative portions of the prospectus*" (emphasis added). The court concluded from its detailed examination "that while plaintiffs have shown that there were securities laws violations, they have not proven that [defendant auditors] *knew* of the violations and of its possible implication in the scheme or that [the auditors] *knowingly* aided and assisted substantially in the violations" (emphasis added).

Lack of any element of the triple *knowledge* by an auditor—of (1) the securities law violation, (2) his role in it, and (3) his substantial assistance of it—is a complete defense to a Rule 10b-5 abetting charge, even if his ignorance was the result of negligence.

Careful auditors examine the entire contents of every prospectus (and all proxy statements) containing their audit opinion or their name in association with financial data, with benefit of their usually intimate knowledge of the business and access to information on its affairs. They also participate in prospectus drafting meetings, which alerts them to additional matters that they should be considering in connection with their audit and leads them to mention matters that should be considered by those responsible for preparing the narrative of the prospectus.

Solicitors of Proxies. Under Section 14(a), solicitors of proxies are analogous to sellers of securities under Section 12(2). Auditors should therefore be excluded from the scope of Section 14(a) as nonsolicitors, in the same sense that they have been excluded from the scope of Section 12(2) as nonsellers. However, again as in the case of Section 12(2), auditors may be subject to charges of conspiracy or of aiding and abetting a misleading proxy solicitation. However, proof of scienter would be required:

> To subject [the auditor] to liability under §14(a) for aiding and abetting, the plaintiffs must prove [the auditor] knowingly and substantially assisted in the wrongdoing which resulted in the injury to plaintiffs. [*In re Clinton Oil Co. Securities Litigation,* CCH Fed. Sec. L. Rep. ¶ 96,015 (D. Kan. 1977)]

In the complaint in *SEC v. National Student Marketing Corp.,* CCH Fed. Sec. L. Rep. ¶ 93,360 (D. D.C. 1972), an SEC suit for injunction charged a firm of auditors and a partner and professional employees, together with a corporate client and director-officers and counsel, with violating, and with aiding and abetting violations by the corporate management of, Section 14(a) and Rules 14a-3 and 14a-9 (and of Section 17(a) of the 1933 act and Section 13(a) of, and Rule 10b-5 under, the 1934 act). The complaint alleged that audited annual and unaudited interim financial statements in a merger proxy statement materially overstated outstanding contracts, and therefore sales, earnings, and assets, and that they understated liabilities. The complaint alleged further that the auditors had failed at the time of completion of the merger to insist on revision of the financial statements or to withdraw from the engagement and to make their position known to the SEC or to the shareholders of the merging companies. The audit firm and its partner and employees, as well as most of the other defendants, subsequently consented to judgments of permanent injunction without trial (ASR 173). In one of the related private suits for damages, the auditors were charged as conspirators in a violation of Section 14(a) (*Wachovia,* 461 F. Supp. at 999). In a related criminal proceeding, *United States v. Natelli,* 527 F.2d 311 (2d Cir. 1975), the court of appeals affirmed a criminal conviction of the audit partner.

In *Adams v. Standard Knitting Mills, Inc.,* 623 F.2d 422, 428, 446-447 (6th Cir. 1980), defendant auditors were absolved from liability in connection with a merger proxy statement in which they had committed negligence but had acted without scienter. The court did not discuss their status in terms of nonsolicitor and of aiding and abetting, but held that *outside* accountants, unlike the company and its management, should not be held liable for proxy statements in the absence of scienter. In support of plaintiffs' unsuccessful petition for rehearing *en banc,* the SEC argued that accountants should be liable as primary violators for negligence in connection with proxy statements.

SEC ENFORCEMENT

Together with others affected by the exercise of SEC authority, accountants must be concerned with a range of SEC activities called *enforcement.* Enforcement is conducted when the SEC determines, or has reason to believe, that there is or was, or may be or have been, a violation or potential violation of laws or its rules, and includes

• Investigations,
• Suits for injunction,
• Administrative disciplinary proceedings, and
• Criminal references.

SEC enforcement is also covered in Chapter 44, in the context of the adjudicatory system. The following description approaches enforcement from the viewpoint of those subject to the process.

Investigations

General. From the outset, an accountant should regard any involvement in any SEC investigation as potentially dangerous. The most direct unfavorable results could be (1) publication of the SEC's findings, (2) an SEC injunction suit, and (3) a disciplinary or other SEC administrative proceeding. Others include so-called parallel non-SEC proceedings such as (4) reference by the SEC to the Department of Justice for possible grand jury investigation and criminal indictment, (5) investigation and possible action by other federal agencies, such as IRS, (6) disciplinary proceedings by state securities or other governmental authorities and by national and state professional bodies, and (7) instigation or aggravation of related civil litigations by or on behalf of investors for damages (in which the SEC sometimes appears as a "friend of the court" to support its view of matters of law and administration, but not of the facts as such).

A professional practitioner before the SEC, such as an auditor or lawyer, is expected to respond as a professional rather than an adversary by cooperating, not in the sense of capitulating, but of being willing to respond straightforwardly to appropriate substantive inquiries. Generally speaking, a professional must largely rely on the persuasive influence of the facts, the merits of his position and performance, and mitigating circumstances, presented as favorably as honesty permits. Resistance would be prejudicial.

Informal Preliminary Investigations. SEC enforcement personnel may make a "preliminary investigation" of a possible violation without specific commission authorization, but with no subpoena power. Cooperation by auditors with such inquiries is ordinarily advisable. However, except as waived by the client, an auditor must decline an SEC request for information obtained in a confidential professional relationship. Since any noncooperation by the client with the SEC changes the prospect of a formal investigation from likely to nearly certain, the client often consents to voluntary disclosure by the auditors.

It may prove vital for the auditor to examine the implications, sense the issues and direction of the inquiry, and identify his own potential problems (with counsel). Although the scope of voluntary response is less binding than that of response to subpoena, the auditor must carefully avoid giving any knowingly false or inaccurate information, either oral or written, to personnel of the SEC—a federal crime under the federal false statement statute.

Private Formal Investigations. The SEC is authorized to investigate "whether any person has violated, is violating, or is about to violate" federal securities laws, to decide whether to take enforcement action, and to obtain evidence for the action. A witness or other interested person has no appeal, because of a legal fiction that an SEC investigation is a nonadversary fact-finding inquiry in which there are no parties, i.e., no *accused,* no penalties, and no (stated) issues. An investigation is almost always conducted in private.

There is conflict between the SEC's disclosure mandate and its suppression of material disclosures in its investigatory processes. The conflict is illustrated by the fact that the SEC has declined, during the investigations, to furnish any information even to independent, uninvolved auditors, despite the fact that the information would have been relevant in deciding on the scope, direction, and performance of an audit, and would have altered the contents of and disclosures in financial statements and the audit opinions expressed. In recent years the SEC has said that the privacy of its own procedures and information is not relevant to disclosure in financial statements. A company and its auditors must judge materiality of an SEC investigation as in actual and threatened litigation. Perhaps for this reason, there has been a substantial increase in the number of disclosures of SEC investigations.

Orders of investigation. A formal order of investigation identifies statutes and rules that may have been violated; but the areas of inquiry are typically stated very broadly, making it difficult for counsel both to assert that a line of interrogation is outside the scope and authority of the investigators and to identify the direction and significance of an inquiry to the witness.

Preparation for response. Relevant papers should be assembled as quickly as possible and fully reviewed by experienced audit personnel under instructions from counsel. Findings, a critique of any apparent professional problems, and other relevant information should be presented to counsel for legal advice. The purpose of that procedure is to preserve the privilege of confidentiality between client and attorney. Otherwise there would be an obligation under subpoena to testify and to produce the papers concerning the review itself.

Apart from removing misfiled and other clearly extraneous papers, auditors should not alter a closed file, an act violating the subpoena. Even before receipt of a subpoena, such an act could seriously damage the auditors' credibility (see ASR 196).

Supplementary working papers appended to photocopies of the original working papers may be useful in filling working paper gaps, or as an aid in correcting other inadequacies with testimony or by introduction of the supplemental papers into evidence.

Testimony, common counsel. A person subpoenaed to give testimony is entitled by SEC rule to be accompanied, represented, and advised by counsel, which has been construed to imply the concomitant right to the lawyer of one's choice.

The hearing officer allows admission of evidence inadmissible in a court of law, hearsay evidence, leading questions, and conjectural questions, but there is no cross-examination, no rebuttal testimony, and no right to attempt an affirmative case by eliciting testimony from counsel's own witness that exceeds the scope of questioning by the SEC investigatory personnel. Since testimony may be admissible in subsequent proceedings, it is important for auditors to have practice interrogations with their counsel under simulated conditions. The objective is to be, and to appear to be, poised, forthright, and credible.

Under ordinary circumstances, it is normal for audit personnel to prefer (and have) common representation. However, common counsel must continually consider whether there appears to be any potential adverse interests among his several witness clients (e.g., evidence of a possible fault of one or more but less than all of them) that would require him to decline or terminate common representation.

Transcripts and disclosures of information. By rule, a witness and his counsel have an unqualified right to "inspect" the transcript of his testimony but not that of others. The witness may also purchase a copy, *unless* his request should be denied by the commission "for good cause," presumably that the transcript would be used to subvert the investigation. In practice, copies have been readily obtainable by auditor witnesses. Witness and counsel should make every effort to detect errors and submit corrections.

The SEC has full discretion to furnish information obtained in private investigations to other government agencies, to state securities and accountancy authorities, to the AICPA and state professional societies, and private litigants, if consistent with its enforcement objectives. An auditor should assume that under the Freedom of Information Act and related SEC rules, all testimony and other statements made by or for him, all of his working papers, and all other evidentiary information concerning him, with certain rather narrow exceptions, will become publicly available upon application by any person after enforcement action is completed or a determination has been made that no enforcement action will be taken.

Wells Committee submissions. Formerly, SEC procedures had provided no opportunity for arguments in opposition to the recommendations of the enforcement staff. In partial acceptance of one of the recommendations made by the Wells Committee for improving enforcement procedures, the SEC now authorizes nonbinding "informal procedures" permitting, and hopefully encouraging, the investigatory staff to advise prospective defendant-respondents "of . . . indicated violations," and indicating the time available to submit a statement. If the staff recommends enforcement proceedings, the target's Wells Committee submission accompanies the staff recommendation.

A Wells Committee submission has numerous possible uses for auditors: to distinguish their role as a secondary target of enforcement from more central targets; to distinguish their behavior, performance, and motivations as professionals; to suggest that the public interest to be served by the proposed action does not require their involvement; to argue issues of law and fact that might vindicate them in an adversary proceeding; and to present equitable considerations and matters in mitigation, such as remedial actions already accomplished or initiated. (For further comment, see Kronstein, 1979.)

Offers of settlement. The SEC is likely to seriously entertain a realistic proposal for the sake of effective allocation of its limited enforcement resources. If serious negotiations develop, it may be possible to narrow the charges, eliminate some of the prospective parties (e.g., individual auditors as contrasted with the firm), and modify the allegations in a statement of charges and in a consent opinion and findings. Otherwise, an adverse proceeding might contain all this information, with opinions, and be prejudicial to the accountant in private damage suits or other parallel proceedings. However, the settlement order should be expected to contain prohibitions, restrictions, obligations, and burdens.

Suits for Injunction

Issues. The grant or denial of an injunction to the SEC is subject to broad discretion of the individual judge, so there is no reason to expect uniformity of result in relation to comparable facts. SEC enforcement personnel believe in effect that proof of a violation should alone routinely be sufficient to justify an injunction: the existence of improper conduct implies more of such conduct, and mere resistance to SEC efforts should add support for a grant of injunction.

By contrast, defendants cite court opinions that require a proper showing by the SEC, as a condition to issuance of an injunction, of a reasonable likelihood that the wrongdoing will recur or sometimes, more strongly, of a "propensity or natural inclination to violate the securities law" (*SEC v. Bangor Punta Corp.*, 331 F. Supp. 1154, 1163 (S.D. N.Y. 1971)). Court judgments against different types of defendants have varied. In several cases in recent years, courts have shown an unwillingness to enjoin professionals of good reputation when the SEC could not prove, nor the courts observe, any inclination to commit future violations.

Consequences of Injunction. The consequences of an injunction against a professional in an SEC securities lawsuit may be much more far-reaching than a simple prohibition against violating the law. A subsequent violation may result in a criminal, as well as civil, prosecution for contempt, in which defendant has no right of jury trial unless the SEC requests imprisonment for longer than six months. Also, by SEC order without hearing, the professional may be temporarily suspended from SEC practice, and the suspension becomes permanent unless within 30 days the suspended person petitions the SEC to lift it. The SEC may then (1) lift or, after a hearing, (2) censure or (3) disqualify the petitioner temporarily or permanently. In the hearing, petitioner (a) may not contest the findings and (b) has the burden to show cause.

An injunction in an SEC case may also have burdensome ancillary features, which require the defendant to do something or submit to something, such as peer review or establishment of internal practice review committees.

Recent Suits. Prior to the 1970s the SEC had evidently filed suits for injunction against accountants only when it thought that accountants were committing intentional fraud in league with clients. But beginning in 1970 the SEC named auditors as codefendants with clients and management in a series of major injunction suits. Names familiar to accountants will be *SEC v.*

- *Liberty Equities Corp.,*
- *Utilities Leasing Corp.,*
- *Everest Management Corp.,*
- *National Student Marketing Corp.,*
- *Geotek,*
- *Talley Industries, Inc.,*
- *Republic National Life Insurance Co.*
- *Penn Central Co.,* and
- *Koracorp Industries, Inc.*

There have also been a whole series of ASRs relative to this phenomenon—more than 30 since 1970.

The principal merit in an injunctive rather than an administrative proceeding is speed. But speed is seldom vital in a proceeding against an accountant, in which the issues usually involve a retrospective examination of past events and their consequences. In *SEC v. Arthur Young & Co.,* 590 F.2d 785 (9th Cir. 1979), *aff'g SEC v. Geotek,* 426 F. Supp. 715, 731 (N.D. Cal. 1976), the district court had bypassed the issue of the auditors' alleged culpability, concluding "that even if a violation . . . were found, the evidence is insufficient to show a reasonable likelihood or expectation that AY would commit further violations in the future." Upon appeal by the SEC in the *Geotek* case, the court—in choosing between the auditors' argument that compliance with GAAS should immunize it from liability and the SEC argument that the law requires that the audit function reveal to the ordinary investor the financial risk of investment—said:

> To accept the SEC's position would go far toward making the accountant both an insurer of his client's honesty and an enforcement arm of the SEC. We can understand why the SEC wishes to so conscript accountants. Its frequently late arrival on the

scene of fraud and violations of securities laws almost always suggests that had it been there earlier *with the accountant* it would have caught the scent of wrong-doing and, after an unrelenting hunt, bagged the game. What it cannot do, the thought goes, the accountant can and should. The difficulty with this is that Congress has not enacted the conscription bill that the SEC seeks to have us fashion and fix as an interpretive gloss on existing securities laws. 590 F.2d at 788 [Emphasis in original]

Administrative Disciplinary Proceedings

Rule 2(e). SEC Rule of Practice 2(e)(1) provides that the SEC may temporarily or permanently disqualify from practicing before it any person found by the SEC after a hearing

(i) not to possess the requisite qualifications to represent others, or

(ii) to be lacking in character or integrity, or to have engaged in unethical or improper conduct, or

(iii) to have willfully violated, or willfully aided and abetted the violation of any provision of the federal securities laws . . . , or the rules and regulations thereunder.

The proceeding is governed by the SEC Rules of Practice, and is prosecuted by the SEC Division of Enforcement before an administrative law judge, who presents his initial decision to the SEC for final determination. It is generally similar to a non-jury judicial litigation, though with some important differences, especially the fact that the proceeding is prosecuted, and the initial and final decisions are made, by personnel of the same agency.

Enforcement program against professionals. A few years ago, the SEC conceived an aggressive enforcement "program" of administrative and injunctive actions and criminal references. In the words of the chief accountant of the SEC at that time:

The reasoning of the Commission is simple: these *professionals are an essential element in providing access to the market place,* since the sale of securities cannot take place without their involvement. Professional responsibility at these *points of access* can prevent many questionable activities before they occur. [Burton, 1975c, pp. 19-20; emphasis added]

The existence of a concerted SEC campaign against "points of access" was confirmed by Stanley Sporkin (director of the SEC Division of Enforcement), and by Milton Freeman (a practicing lawyer and at one time an SEC staff counsel) who said: "[The SEC] can't trace all the crooks so they have to have accountants' and lawyers' help. If the accountants and lawyers don't catch the crooks, *then the Commission will catch the accountants and lawyers.* It is the Commission's theory that you can make *policemen out of accountants and lawyers,* and that is wrong" (Guzzardi, 1974, p. 194; emphasis added).

The only sanctions mentioned in Rule 2(e) are temporary and permanent disqualification from practice before the SEC and censure (in the provision relating only to summary sanctions after an injunction or an administrative finding of violation). Nevertheless, beginning in 1973, the SEC began to negotiate various affirmative or "mandatory" sanctions, including

1. Peer reviews and inspections of a firm's auditing standards and procedures,
2. Restrictions for specified periods against mergers with other firms,
3. Prohibitions for specified periods against undertaking new engagements likely to result in filings with the SEC,
4. Requirements to develop and implement auditing procedures for certain types of transactions,
5. Censure of firms, other than following permanent injunctions or criminal convictions,
6. Imposition of continuing education programs, and
7. Requirements to give notice of the commission's findings to potential new SEC clients.

Advantages to the SEC. In a Rule 2(e) proceeding, the SEC enforcement division may avoid standards that would apply if it sued for injunction in court:

1. It may proceed on a theory of negligence, whereas a court might apply a theory of scienter under *Hochfelder;*
2. It is not required to make a "proper showing" of a likelihood of future violation or wrongdoing, as it might be in a suit for injunction; and
3. The burden of proof may (in its view) be satisfied by a "preponderance of the evidence" rather than the more rigorous "clear and convincing evidence" standard of an injunctive proceeding.

Challenges of the SEC's authority under Rule 2(e), and particularly of its intention to hold such hearings in public, are discussed in Chapter 44. (See *Touche Ross & Co. v. SEC,* CCH Fed. Sec. L. Rep. ¶ 96,415 (S.D. N.Y. 1978), *aff'd* 609 F.2d 570 (2d Cir. 1979).)

Stop-Order Proceedings. Of various other SEC administrative proceedings, the one most likely to affect auditors adversely is a "stop-order" proceeding under Sections 8(b) or (d) of the 1933 act against an allegedly materially deficient registration statement containing an audit opinion. An order under Section 8(b) prohibits a pending registration statement from becoming effective, and an order under Section 8(d) suspends an effective registration statement, in either case until amended as required. The importance of these provisions lies mainly in their sheer existence, and in the substantial leverage that they give the SEC in dealing with allegedly deficient registration statements.

Criminal References

The SEC does not administer criminal enforcement of the federal securities laws but refers matters that it regards as meriting consideration of criminal proceedings to the Department of Justice. SEC enforcement personnel customarily assist in a grand jury proceeding and a subsequent prosecution.

In discussing criminal referrals concerning accountants, a former chief accountant of the SEC said that they "have only been made when the Commission and the staff believed that the evidence indicated that a professional accountant certified financial statements that he knew to be false when he reported on them . . . not . . . simply [in] matters of professional judgment, even if the judgments appear to be bad ones" (Burton, 1975c, p. 28).

Apart from a standard warning at the commencement of investigatory testimony, the SEC does not disclose a possible referral. Since decisions concerning criminal prosecution are within the discretion of the Department of Justice, SEC enforcement personnel have no authority to promise to make any recommendation concerning possible criminal proceedings.

The Weight of SEC Enforcement on Professionals

The machinery constructed by the SEC for enforcement against professionals is awesome in its power, the more so because of the inadequate tools with which the SEC was required to work in building it. One essential factor has been a general, though recently diminishing, deference on the part of the courts.

The SEC's principal instrument has been the consummately skillful employment of the age-old technique of judges and legal advocates in changing law by transforming a concept, principle, or rule from its traditional context into a different and sometimes alien one, resulting in its alteration to accomplish the objective desired. When performed by judges, such alchemy is denounced by some and accepted by others. But many who are willing to accept the handiwork of the judges vested with "the judicial Power of the United States" by Article III of the Constitution disapprove of similar behavior by administrative creations of the Congress to which the Congress has delegated some quantum of authority.

Because of the unimpeachable worthiness of the SEC's ends, the SEC has enjoyed broad support for (or despite) the excess of zeal with which it has fashioned its means and coercively employed its superior power upon professionals. The result has been a mixture of administration of law and exertion of muscle.

CRIMINAL LIABILITY

In recent years accountants have been shocked to realize that they could be subjected to criminal prosecution, fine, and imprisonment for charges arising out of the regular course of their professional practice.

Criminal Statutes

The federal statutes under which accountants are most likely to be prosecuted on charges of criminal deficiencies in their professional work are

- The general *mail fraud* statute, prohibiting use of the United States mail, and the misnamed *wire fraud* statute, prohibiting transmission of interstate or foreign communications by wire, radio, or television, in any scheme to defraud or to obtain money or property by false or fraudulent representations.
- A *securities fraud* and *false filing* statute, Section 24 of the 1933 act, prohibiting willful violation of any provision of the 1933 act or SEC rules under it, and the willful

making of a material misstatement or omission in a registration statement filed under the act.

- A second *securities fraud* and *false filing* statute, Section 32(a) of the 1934 act, prohibiting willful violation of any provision of the 1934 act or SEC rules under it, and the willful and knowing making of a false or misleading statement of any material fact in any application, report, or document required to be filed with the SEC or a securities exchange under the act or related SEC rule.

- The general *false statement* statute, prohibiting knowing and willful falsification or concealment of any material fact, or the making of a "false, fictitious or fraudulent" statement or representation, orally or by use of a false writing or document, with knowledge of the falsehood, to government personnel in any matter within the jurisdiction of any department or agency of the United States.

- The *false statement to bank* statute, prohibiting the knowing making of any false statement, or willful overvaluation of any property, for the purpose of influencing in any way the action of a wide variety of banking and other financial institutions on any application for a loan or other extension of credit.

- *Aiding and abetting* and *conspiracy* in the commission of crimes described above. Not untypically, there is ample proof of a primary crime such as preparation and circulation of deceptive financial statements, and charges of conspiracy and of aiding and abetting widen the group that may be indicted and convicted for guilty involvement, e.g., the auditors of Continental Vending (*United States v. Simon,* 425 F.2d 796 (2d Cir. 1969)).

There are also a number of state crimes with which accountants might be charged, to which state statutes on criminal *conspiracy* and criminal *aiding and abetting* apply, as discussed above. These include Section 409 of the Uniform Securities Act, state criminal fraud statutes (mostly of a general nature), and unauthorized-practice laws.

Proof of Willfulness. Many cases have involved egregious financial falsifications by corporate managements, and one typical issue has been whether the evidence established beyond a reasonable doubt that the accountant knew he was participating in a crime and therefore was acting willfully. The concept of willful conduct permeates criminal prohibitions and sanctions, though its meaning varies among statutes, some of which are interpreted as requiring conscious intent to defraud and some not.

In *United States v. Benjamin,* 328 F.2d 854, 862 (2d Cir. 1964), affirming the conviction of an accountant on securities fraud charges, the court said that in proving willfulness, "the Government can meet its burden by proving that a defendant deliberately closed his eyes to facts he had a duty to see . . . or recklessly stated as facts things of which he was ignorant." In the absence of conclusive direct evidence, prosecutions against accountants have been based primarily on circumstantial evidence.

Commenting on the fraud in Equity Funding Corporation of America, which involved massive overstatement of net income and assets, the bankruptcy trustee said:

Responsibility for failing to detect the fraud rests primarily with the accounting firms. . . . Aside from the perpetrators themselves, only the auditors, as part of their annual examinations, had regular opportunities to review these books and records. . . . [H]ad the auditors properly discharged their obligations, the fraud would have been caught years ago. . . . There is strong evidence that several of the accountants in charge of these audits were aware of or suspected the fraud and cooperated in its concealment. Such a conclusion seems irresistable. . . . Performance was so manifestly incompetent . . . to be inexplicable on any other basis.[7]

United States v. Weiner, 578 F.2d 757 (9th Cir. 1978), affirmed the conviction of Equity Funding's principal audit personnel. The court of appeals found the evidence sufficient to support the jury verdict that the auditor defendants were guilty of willful and knowing violation of the securities laws under the false filing charges concerning their audit opinions and the financial statements filed with the SEC.

In another criminal litigation, arising from Four Seasons Nursing Centers of America, Inc., the government failed to prove that the auditors knew of alleged management falsifications. The issue involved a type of percentage-of-completion accounting, and the indictment alleged that the auditors acquired knowledge of, and accepted, "false, fictitious and non-existent construction costs" for a particular fiscal year, which resulted in an overstatement of earnings for the year. The auditor defendants denied knowledge of any alleged false construction costs, defended their audit examination and audit judgments, cited their rejection of management's proposed percentage-of-physical-completion test that would have yielded higher earnings than the cost percentage test, and asserted that although percentage-of-completion accounting for construction contracts is recognized in GAAP, the uncertainties inherent in the earnings results on eventual future completion of construction necessarily affect an audit evaluation of results for any fiscal year during the construction period.

Responsibility for Disclosure of Known Facts. The above discussion shows that an auditor who obtains knowledge of a client's illegal acts in the regular performance of professional services may become criminally implicated if he does not take appropriate steps to disassociate himself from the illegality.

Although it cannot be drawn directly from the words of the opinion, *United States v. Simon,* 425 F.2d 796 (2d Cir. 1969), shows that an auditor has an obligation in issuing his opinion to require that the financial statements adequately disclose known management irregularities that significantly affect the financial condition and operating results of the company. Such disclosure is required to assure fairness of presentation, which is a professional standard.

In *United States v. Natelli,* 527 F.2d 311 (2d Cir. 1975), the court of appeals affirmed a criminal conviction of the audit partner under the false filing provision of the 1934 act. In connection with a merger proxy statement

---

[7] Report of the trustee of Equity Funding Corporation of America, pursuant to Section 167(3) of the Bankruptcy Act 141; *In re Equity Funding Corporation of America,* No. 73-03467 (C.D. Cal. Oct. 31, 1974).

1. The auditor prepared and proposed to the client retroactive adjustments that had the effect of concealing a currently discovered prior-period discrepancy and that failed to conform to professional accounting standards of adequate disclosure of prior-period adjustments to income; and

2. Long after the close of a period, the auditor acquiesced, without requiring supporting evidence, in the recording by management under suspicious circumstances of a sale that increased net income (and later proved to be fictitious).

The court said that "circumstantial evidence, particularly with proof of motive, where available, is often sufficient to convince a reasonable man of criminal intent beyond a reasonable doubt" (at 318), and upheld the jury verdict. The case is a stark warning to auditors that although an audit error may (or may not) be an act of negligence, a failure to take appropriate action upon its discovery by the auditors may be interpreted as an act of willfulness within the meaning of criminal law.

False Statements to Federal Personnel. The false statement statute applies generally to any statements to government personnel in their official capacities in matters within the authority of their agencies. For accountants, violations could include responses to inquiries and investigations by government personnel, and to statements in support of or relating to applications or other requests for rulings, interpretations, and other government actions or decisions concerning clients.

The statute has been applied in connection with voluntary oral falsehoods in conversations with a government employee in a matter within the scope of his employment; falsehoods in testimony elicited by SEC investigators; and voluntary submission of altered documents to SEC investigators in an informal preliminary SEC investigation.

False Statement to Financial Institutions. It is a crime to knowingly make any false statement or to willfully overvalue any property in connection with an application for a loan or other extension of credit from federal government banks or other financial institutions; federally insured banks, home loan banks, and savings and loan associations; federal or state-chartered credit unions; or small business investment companies.

Persons responsible for such statements and data, including the accountants who prepare them and the auditors who examine or are professionally associated with them, are within reach, sometimes directly and sometimes under theories of conspiracy or of aiding and abetting. The same is true as to certain documents required under the Employee Retirement Income Security Act (ERISA).

Criminal Responsibility of Accounting Partnerships

There is no existing precedent that determines whether or not an accounting partnership could be indicted for alleged felony under the federal securities laws or, if it could, whether it could be convicted if fewer than all of the partners were indicted and convicted. In practice, accounting partnerships have been charged as unindicted coconspirators in criminal proceedings in which individual partners have been indicted. Such an accusation is painfully frustrating to the collective partnership, because there is no way in which it may contest the merits of such a charge, which is entered in a public record forever.

Even if it should eventually be determined that an accounting partnership can be indicted, the partnership could not be held criminally responsible for criminal derelictions of its audit partners or staff unless it were proved by some means that the firm directed, counseled, approved of, or otherwise participated or acquiesced in what the auditors had done, with knowledge of the nature of the act. Whether an individual partner's criminal conduct would result in criminal responsibility to the firm without the knowledge and acquiescence of other partners should depend on the partner's position; in most accounting partnerships of medium and larger size, only a few of the partners have authority to commit the firm as a whole.

SUGGESTED READING

Adams v. Standard Knitting Mills, Inc., CCH Fed. Sec. L. Rep. ¶ 95,683 (E.D. Tenn. 1976), *rev'd,* 623 F.2d 422 (6th Cir. 1980), *cert. denied, Adams v. Peat, Marwick, Mitchell & Co.,* 101 S.Ct. 795 (1980). Plaintiff's motion for rehearing by the court of appeals *en banc,* supported by the SEC as amicus curiae, was denied, one judge dissenting both from opinion and from denial of rehearing. The district court opinion and the dissent on appeal are illustrations of how far wrong a court can go in a litigation against an auditor, rectified in this case by reversal by majority of judges on appeal.

Bialkin, Kenneth J. "Sanctions Against Accountants." *Review of Securities Regulation,* Vol. 8 (November 26, 1975), pp. 823-831. This article is a critical discussion of mandatory SEC sanctions.

Bucklo, Elaine E. "The Supreme Court Attempts to Define Scienter under Rule 10b-5: *Ernst & Ernst v. Hochfelder." Stanford Law Review,* Vol. 29 (January, 1977), pp. 213-240. This article is a thorough examination of alternative interpretations of the culpability standard in Rule 10b-5.

"Criminal Liability of Public Accountants: a Lurking Nightmare?" Law Student Comment, *Journal of Criminal Law and Criminology,* Vol. 67 (March, 1976), pp. 32-45. This article is a discussion of federal criminal statutes and judicial opinions.

"Development in the Law—Class Actions." Law Student Comment, *Harvard Law Review,* Vol. 89 (June, 1976), pp. 1318-1644. This is a massive study of class action theory and practice and of difficulties in applying the requisite elements of class actions in management, in administration, in settlement, and in professional conduct of class counsel. The article also discusses alternative reforms, by amendment to the class action rule or by congressional legislation on class actions.

Fiflis, T. J. "Current Problems of Accountants' Responsibilities to Third Parties." *Vanderbilt Law Review,* Vol. 28 (January, 1975), pp. 31-145. This article is an extensive academic comment on accountants' functions, duties, problems, and liabilities.

Gormley, R. James. "Professional Risks in Purchase Audits and Reviews." *Journal of Accounting, Auditing and Finance,* Summer, 1980, pp. 293-312. This article, which is part of the larger work referred to in footnote 1 to this chapter, outlines types of risks encountered by accountants, with examples of actual cases and suggestions on how accountants may protect themselves from liability in this area of practice.

Guzzardi, Walter Jr. "Those Zealous Cops on the Securities Beat." *Fortune,* December, 1974, pp. 144-147, 192, 194, 196, 198, and 202. A business writer views SEC enforcement.

Hawkins, Carl S. "Professional Negligence Liability of Public Accountants." *Vanderbilt Law Review,* Vol. 12 (June, 1959), pp. 797-824. This article is a classic piece on legal theories of common law liability.

Jaenicke, Henry R. *The Effect of Litigation on Independent Auditors.* The Commission on Auditors' Responsibilities, Research Study No. 1. New York: 1977. This is a wide-ranging discussion by a CPA of the "litigation explosion" against auditors—influences on the legal environment; auditor liability under common law and the federal securities acts; class actions and contingent legal fees; criminal, injunctive, and SEC administrative proceedings; the proposed federal securities code; and the benefits and costs to society of (and proposals for change to) the legal environment.

Kay, Robert S. "Disagreements under Accounting Series Release No. 165." *Journal of Accountancy,* October, 1976, pp. 75-82. This article contains a discussion of the many ramifications of the SEC's requirements for reporting disagreements between auditors and publicly held clients.

Marsh, Harold Jr. "Rule 2(e) Proceedings." *The Business Lawyer,* Vol. 35 (April, 1980), pp. 987-1019. This article is a critical examination of history, SEC administration, statutory authority, and constitutionality of Rule 2(e).

Mathews, Arthur F. "Effective Defense of SEC Investigations: Laying the Foundation for Successful Disposition of Subsequent Civil, Administrative and Criminal Proceedings." *Emory Law Journal,* Vol. 24 (Summer, 1975), pp. 567-638. This article is a comprehensive discussion of the subject.

McLean v. Alexander, 420 F. Supp. 1057-1086 (D. Del. 1976), *rev'd,* 599 F.2d 1190-1202 (3d Cir. 1979). These opinions are an excellent example of differences in the evaluation and legal characterization of facts by judges; in a litigation involving Rule 10b-5 and Delaware common-law fraud, the district court found, on extended review of factual details of the audit, that defendant auditor had committed recklessness (which the court interpreted as constituting scienter within *Hochfelder*); the court of appeals reversed the decision because, on review of the same facts, it found probable negligence but not recklessness.

Merrifield, Lewis B. III. "Investigations by the Securities and Exchange Commission." *The Business Lawyer,* Vol. 32 (July, 1977), pp. 1583-1631. This article is a thorough and excellent description of SEC investigations.

Miller, Richard L. "The Distortion and Misuse of Rule 2(e)." *Securities Regulation Law Journal,* Vol. 7 (Spring, 1979), pp. 54-75. The author of this article launches a frontal assault on SEC administrative enforcement proceedings.

Morrison, Peter H. "SEC Criminal References." *Review of Securities Regulation,* Vol. 11 (January 15, 1978), pp. 991-996. Criteria, methods, discretion, and disclosure of SEC criminal investigations are discussed in this article.

Ruder, David S. "Multiple Defendants in Securities Law Fraud Cases: Aiding and Abetting, Conspiracy, *In Pari Delicto,* Indemnification and Contribution." *University of Pennsylvania Law Review,* Vol. 120 (April, 1972), pp. 597-665. This is a fundamental text on issues important to secondary defendants such as accountants.

————, and Cross, Neil S. "Limitations on Civil Liability under Rule 10b-5." *Duke Law Journal,* February, 1972, pp. 1125-1152. This article is a good survey of the origin of the rule and its coverage, purchaser-seller requirement, materiality, reliance, causation, scienter, and statutes of limitation. However, the scienter discussion is pre-*Hochfelder;* for a post-*Hochfelder* discussion of scienter, see "Bucklo" above.

"SEC Civil Injunctive Actions" (program). *The Business Lawyer,* Vol. 30 (July, 1975), pp. 1303-1340. A critical discussion among lawyers and an SEC commissioner.

Seiffer v. Topsy's International, Inc., 487 F. Supp. 653-709 (D. Kan. 1980). A reading of this opinion conveys some of the Armageddon-like atmosphere of massive multi-count class actions under federal and state securities laws against multiple defendants, including auditors. For reported opinions in earlier phases, see 64 F.R.D. 714 (D. Kan. 1974), *appeal dismissed,* 520 F.2d 795 (10th Cir. 1975), *cert. denied sub nom.*

Touche Ross & Co. v. Seiffer, 423 U.S. 1051 (1976) (class certified); 69 F.R.D. 69 (D. Kan. 1975) (partner of defendant audit firm "specially employed" by firm as expert in anticipation of litigation held immune from giving testimony to plaintiffs); 70 F.R.D. 622 (D. Kan. 1976) and 80 F.R.D. 272 (D. Kan. 1978) (approval of settlement by most defendants other than auditors).

Septimus, Judah. "Accountants' Liability for Negligence—A Contemporary Approach for A Modern Profession." *Fordham Law Review,* Vol. 48 (December, 1979), pp. 401-421. This article is an instructive example of one type of academic criticism that conceives standards of responsibility for others with inadequate understanding of or regard for reasonable expectations of performance. The author would abrogate *Ultramares* on the specious analogy of products liability, with disregard of professional liability standards generally, and on a bland assumption concerning availability of insurance, and would propose to mitigate the impact with an unworkable formula for limiting accountants' negligence liability to third persons.

Siegel, Mary. "The Implication Doctrine and the Foreign Corrupt Practices Act." *Columbia Law Review,* Vol. 79 (October, 1979), pp. 1085-1117. This article is a broad review of recent Supreme Court decisions concerning the criteria by which private rights of action should and should not be implied from statutes; the author also applies the emerging criteria in this rapidly changing subject to the antibribery and accounting provisions of the FCPA.

Sonde, Theodore. "The Responsibility of Professionals under the Federal Securities Laws—Some Observations." *Northwestern University Law Review,* Vol. 68 (March-April, 1973), pp. 1-23. This article reflects the views of an SEC enforcement attorney on responsibilities of accountants and lawyers under the securities laws.

Part VII

Research in Accounting and Auditing

47

Accounting Information and Efficient Markets

A. Rashad Abdel-khalik
Bipin B. Ajinkya

THE EFFICIENT MARKET HYPOTHESIS

An organized capital market such as the New York Stock Exchange (NYSE) can be perceived as a machine that distills information to constantly revise expectations about competing investment opportunities. The outcome of this processing of information is redistribution of capital (when equity capital shares change hands); and the assignment of new prices represents a constant, market-wide re-ordering of investment preferences.

No one, of course, knows all the considerations entering the decisions of all the buyers, bidders, and sellers of even one actively traded stock on any day, but academicians can make a systematic evaluation of events and information from which inferences may be drawn. The efficient market hypothesis facilitates this process. The hypothesis (often called EMH) is that the market is informationally efficient in that it processes information instantaneously and reflects it in security prices. The manner and speed with which the market processes information are essential elements of this hypothesis.

It is vital to distinguish informational efficiency from economic efficiency (input/output ratios, etc.) and to emphasize that the EMH refers directly to the *processing* of information, not to the economic utilization of resources. Most of the EMH evidence has been accumulated using common stocks traded on the New York Stock Exchange. But recently other markets and financial instruments have been used with not too dissimilar findings.

There are three main variants of the EMH—the strong, semistrong and weak forms. These forms are functions of information categories identified as (1) private and (2) public, either (a) embedded in stock prices or (b) all other.

When Mayer-Sommer (1979) surveyed users of financial statements, he found that few understand or believe in the efficient market hypothesis. He reported:

> *Fortune* 500 controllers and Big Eight partners showed the greatest lack of understanding of the EMH; . . . almost two-thirds of the controllers and Big Eight partners did not understand the EMH in any of its forms. This compares with half of the responding academicians. [p. 97] . . .
>
> . . . only one in 20 responding accounting academicians accepted the research findings relating to the EMH in its weak, semi-strong, and strong forms. The corresponding figures for chartered financial analysts are one in 25, and for partners in Big Eight firms, one in 100. [p. 99] . . .
>
> Based on the responses of accounting information preparers and users, low levels of understanding of the EMH and its accounting implications as well as extremely low levels of acceptance of EMH research findings were inferred. [p. 103]

This chapter surveys the evidence relative to the EMH and considers its implications for accounting.

GENERAL SUMMARY

As a preview of what will be found in this chapter, a summary of certain general statements about accounting information and efficient markets, given the current state of the art, seems in order.

Economic Effects

1. Economic consequences may be assessed as the redistribution effects caused after the fact by the adoption of accounting policies and regulation.
2. No research evidence (or skill) has yet been developed to satisfactorily evaluate economic consequences prior (ex ante) to adopting certain accounting policies.
3. The tenor of the debate concerning the role of the FASB seems to endorse the proposition that accounting policies must be based on and guided by accounting issues and considerations, not by the desire to effect certain types of economic changes.
4. Decisions about accounting policies should guard against leading to severe adverse economic consequences for any affected group.

Capital Markets

1. The redistribution of capital in the capital market is a part of the economic consequences mentioned above.
2. Redistribution of capital is judged by observing capital shares change hands at changing prices.
3. Accounting systems (for external reporting) provide only a portion of the information set used by capital markets to effect redistribution.
4. Evidence concerning the association between security prices and accounting information, announcements, alternatives, and disclosures has been accumulating rapidly.
5. Early evidence was highly consistent with the concept of the semistrong form of informational efficiency, suggesting that all accounting information and events (that are not primarily cosmetic) are impounded in security prices as soon as they are made public.
6. Recent evidence has raised some doubts about the earlier findings and sometimes appears inconsistent with the accumulated evidence.
7. No evidence has been found to support the strong form of the EMH.

Accounting Standards

1. Most authors agree that the choice among competing accounting alternatives cannot be guided by the capital market theories and evidence developed to date.
2. Only the after-the-fact consequences (redistribution of capital) of accounting policies and standards could be assessed to a reasonable degree.

INFORMATIONAL EFFICIENCY AND ITS FORMS

The market is considered efficient if it processes information instantaneously and reflects it in security prices. Under these conditions, a trading strategy based on information available to the market could not be used to consistently earn above-average returns. Economic efficiency is not automatically studied as a consequence of studying informational efficiency. But to emphasize the difference between informational and economic efficiency, three elements will be highlighted: (1) the rapid speed with which the market processes information; (2) the effect of processing information captured by observing prices and volumes; and (3) the effect of processing information on the profitability of traders.

The form of the informational efficiency of the market depends on the category—private or public—of the information being processed. Public information is available to every interested person, while private information is monopolized by a few, as with inside information known only to the board of directors or top management. Public information is further subdivided into information (a) embedded in past security prices and (b) all other. According to this classification, the securities market is said to be informationally efficient if it processes the information set (call it set X) in such a manner that no market trader can use the knowledge of information set X to consistently earn above-normal returns:

1. If information set X consists only of the historical pattern of prices, the efficiency is said to be of the *weak form;*
2. If information set X consists of all publicly available information, the efficiency is said to be of the *semistrong form;* and finally
3. If information set X consists of all information, public and private, the efficiency is said to be of the *strong form.*

Capital Asset Pricing Model

The technical nature of EMH analysis requires a brief review of the underlying stock valuation models. The model underlying most of the studies is the capital asset pricing model (CAPM), which states that the expected rate of return of a single security or a portfolio is equal to the risk-free rate plus a risk premium. The risk premium of a security is generally a function of the operating risk and the financial risk of the firm. The former captures the expected profitability of the firm, whereas the latter captures the risk associated with leverage (Rubinstein, 1973). The functional form of the risk premium (of a single security or a portfolio) is estimated by the risk premium of the market portfolio weighted by a measure of risk unique to each firm called *systematic risk* or *market risk* and is commonly referred to as *beta.*

The CAPM model is stated as

$$R_{jt} = R_{ft} + B_j(R_{mt} - R_{ft}) + u_{jt},$$

where

R_{jt} = the rate of return of stock j in time t as measured by the change in price over the period plus dividends divided by the initial price;

R_{mt} = the rate of return for the market portfolio (such as the Standard and Poor's index) for period $t;$ and

R_{ft} = the risk-free rate of return for period t.

Thus,

$(R_{mt} - R_{ft})$ = the risk premium on market portfolio;

B_j = the systematic risk or the weight assigned to the market risk premium for the stock j, also called market risk or relative risk; and

u_{jt} = the deviation of observed from expected rate of return at time t, also called residual or abnormal return.

Deviation. If the CAPM is a "true" model for forming the expected value of a security, then the *deviation* between the rate of return of a security as observed in the market and the expected rate of return as estimated by the model should be random (without a systematic pattern). These deviations are sometimes referred to as *residual* or *abnormal* and, over time, should average zero. Also, this randomness of the residuals implies that the deviations are not related to each other from one period to another in a systematic way. The properties of the deviation (u_{jt}) are important for all the analysis to follow. The most important property is that, in the absence of any significant information or event, the average of the deviation over time should be zero, and the deviations should also not be correlated over time. The implication of these two properties in a semistrong form of EMH is that no one can use public information to consistently earn above-normal returns (i.e., to have a positive average u_j).

CAPM Surrogates. Other forms of linear models have been used as CAPM surrogates. All models use the ex post data generated by security prices in the market to estimate the weight of the risk premium (beta) and to estimate the expected rate of return for the purpose of generating the measurements of the residuals. Rates of return are sometimes called *price relatives* or, as used in the forthcoming sections, simply *prices*.

The objectives of using linear models to estimate the expected rates of return are (1) to observe any significant deviations of average residuals from zero (expected mean) and (2) to evaluate any changes in the systematic risk (beta). Much of the analysis deals with the behavior of the residuals (or with the differences between total returns as will be explained later). In essence, the average of residuals accumulated over time provides a measure of the market effects of information.

Cumulative Average Residuals. To simplify the presentation, the term *cumulative average residuals* (CAR) essentially means the average of the residuals for a sample of stocks accumulated over a period of time. If there is no informational effect, the value of CAR should not deviate significantly from zero. Another metric, the *abnormal performance index* (API), is obtained by multiplying residuals; it functions almost exactly like the CAR measure. In any case, the analysis of accounting information or events in this area uses various statistical methodologies to analyze and draw inferences from the abnormal or unusual behavior of rates of return.

Definitions

The remainder of this chapter discusses the empirical evidence generated by these methodologies. Some facts and definitions need to be kept in mind:

1. The terms *abnormal* or *residual* mean the deviation of observed rate of return (or price) from the return (or price) expected by the valuation model.

2. The term *abnormal performance* means the presence of residuals significantly different from the market expectations in either direction; therefore, a qualification usually follows, such as *positive* or *above the market.*

3. Abnormal performance is measured either by the average accumulation of the residuals (CAR) or by the multiplicative form (API); in most cases, the results of using both methods are equivalent.

4. The above discussion of models, residuals, and abnormal returns applies to individual securities as well as to portfolios of any size. Inconclusive arguments abound as to which model, level of analysis, or methodology is more desirable.

EARNINGS ANNOUNCEMENTS

Issues discussed here relate to the association between earnings announcements and security prices; the association between earnings announcements and trading volume; the similarities between the findings concerning annual and interim reporting; the extent to which the results are generalizable to different markets and different capital instruments; and the role of earnings expectations (i.e., what the market expected in the report relative to what was actually reported) in analyzing the information content of earnings. These issues will be presented under three subheadings:

1. Earnings expectations not considered;
2. Earnings expectations considered; and
3. Anomalous findings.

Earnings Expectations Not Considered

Research on Earnings Announcements and Stock Prices. An early systematic evaluation of the association between annual earnings announcements and common stock prices and volumes was reported by Beaver (1968). Using a sample of weekly data from 143 firms, Beaver evaluated the behavior of the volume of transactions and of security prices for a period of 17 weeks surrounding the announcement week in which the annual earnings announcement was made. An analysis was made of the behavior of average volume, both adjusted and unadjusted for overall market movement; rates of return were analyzed after isolating market-wide effects. As shown in Figure 47.1, the level of activity and unexpected rates of return were high during the week of the announcement. Beaver observed that the mean volume (adjusted for market-wide effects) was about 40% higher during the week of the announcement than it was for the preceding eight weeks (p. 76). A comparable change in rates of return amounted to 67% (p. 81). This analysis prompted Beaver to conclude that the results are consistent with the "contention that earnings announcements possess information content" (1968, p. 77 and p. 82).

Beaver's analysis of the association between earnings announcements and stock prices was replicated by May (1971) and Kiger (1972), with these differences: (1) both May and Kiger examined quarterly earnings announcements, (2) May

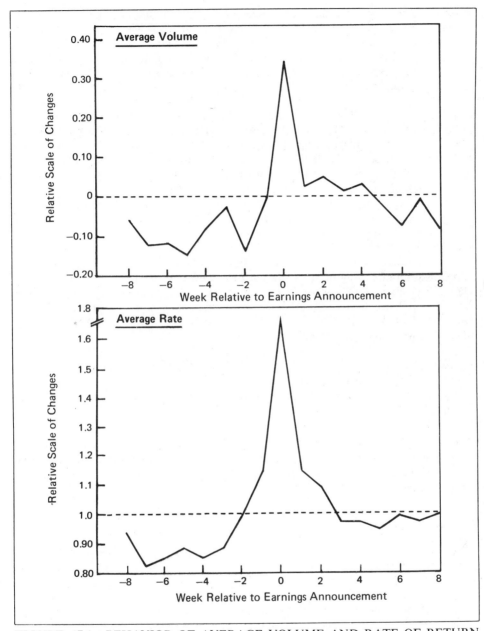

FIGURE 47.1 BEHAVIOR OF AVERAGE VOLUME AND RATE OF RETURN
AFTER FILTERING OUT MARKET-WIDE EFFECTS (RESIDUALS)
ADAPTED FROM: Beaver, 1968.

also examined annual earnings announcements, (3) May used a sample of common stocks listed on the American Stock Exchange, whereas Kiger used a sample of common stocks listed on the New York Stock Exchange, (4) Kiger used price and volume analysis, whereas May used only price data, and (5) Kiger used price/earnings ratios, whereas May used the ratio of market rates of return during the week of the announcement to average rates of return during nonannouncement periods.

The findings reported by both May and Kiger were in general agreement with those obtained in the 1968 study by Beaver. Essentially, they both reported that price revisions took place during the week of the announcement of interim reports, and Kiger reported similar findings on volume changes. In addition, May reported that his findings showed that the "relative price-change response to quarterly earnings was less than response to annual earnings, but with one exception, not significantly less" (p. 150). He interpreted this to be due to the perceived differences in the reliability of interim reports, which led him to suggest that "any significant improvement in the quality of the quarterly data themselves might lead to significant social benefits" (p. 151).

Application of Common Stock Research to the Bond Market. A recent study by Davis, Boatsman, and Baskin (1978) attempted to extend this type of common stock research to the bond market. The association between the annual earnings announcements and the rates of return on bonds was examined for 85 firms. The results showed two distinct findings:

1. A significant price revision of bonds was observed during the announcement period only for convertible bonds, and
2. No consistent findings of price revisions of any sort were observed for nonconvertible bonds.

Davis, Boatsman, and Baskin believed that the second result was the result of a model misspecification, and they generally concluded that their results were consistent with earlier findings reported by Beaver and May for common stocks. However, such a conclusion should not be accepted without adequate replication.

Earnings Expectations Considered

All four studies reported above have one thing in common: they ignore market expectations about accounting earnings. If information is defined as a variation from expectations (or a surprise element), then earnings announcements should convey information only to the extent by which they deviate from expectations.

One of the pioneers in recognizing the importance of prior expectations was Benston (1967), who incorporated only the "unexpected" elements of income statement information as the relevant independent variables in studying the impact on stock prices. The design of the study also simultaneously controlled for "unexpected" dividends and used a surrogate for information contained in interim reports. (In view of the taxonomy adopted in this chapter, this study by Benston more appropriately falls under the category "Basic and Broad Disclosure Rules," and hence is reviewed later under that heading.)

Forecasting Models. Another early classic study that incorporated earnings expectations only was by Ball and Brown (1968), in which they relied on naive mechanical models to forecast annual earnings. Forecasting errors (differences between reported earnings and the numbers predicted by these mechanical models) were used to classify the sample into positive forecast errors (actual higher than forecast) and negative forecast errors (actual lower than forecast). Each class was considered a portfolio for which abnormal rates of return were computed on a monthly basis beginning with the 12th month prior to the announcement. Ball and Brown's findings (Figure 47.2) show that

1. Mean positive abnormal returns (above the market level) were observed for the portfolio with positive earnings forecast errors;
2. Mean negative abnormal returns (below the market level) were found for the portfolio with negative earnings forecast errors;
3. A very high percentage of the value of the informational content of annual income announcement (estimated to be no less than 85%) appears to have been anticipated prior to the month of the announcement; and
4. The stock market progressively increased its discrimination between the two portfolios (of positive and negative forecast errors), starting almost a year prior to the announcement and continuing only up to and including the announcement month.

Ball and Brown did not verify the quality of their mechanical forecasting models. Although the results were positive, the question still remained as to the effects of the choice of the forecasting model. The consistency of their results with their a priori conception about the efficiency of the market led them to consider the mechanical forecasting models adequate.

Testing the quality of forecasting models. To attest the quality of the mechanical forecasting model, Gonedes (1973) used several mechanical models with both scaled and absolute levels of earnings as variables. The results of the association between the announcement of earnings and the behavior of security prices were consistent with those of Ball and Brown.

Correlation between forecasting models and security prices. An improvement in the use of the mechanical forecasting models was provided by Brown and Kennelly (1972), who in essence replicated the study of Ball and Brown using different mechanical models to forecast earnings, some of which were based on quarterly data. Though the objective of their study was the opposite—to evaluate the quality of forecasting models by the strength of their correlation with security prices—their findings shed some light on models based on quarterly data. Using four mechanical models to generate annual forecasts for a sample of 93 firms, portfolios were formed on the basis of the differences between reported earnings and predictions obtained by the mechanical models along the lines of "good," "bad," and "indifferent" news, depending on whether the reported results were higher, lower, or equal to forecasted numbers. Abnormal rates of return (deviations from the expected rates of the return using the market model) were computed for 11 months preceding and for 6 months following the announcement of annual earnings. Brown and Kennelly found that higher abnormal returns were associated with

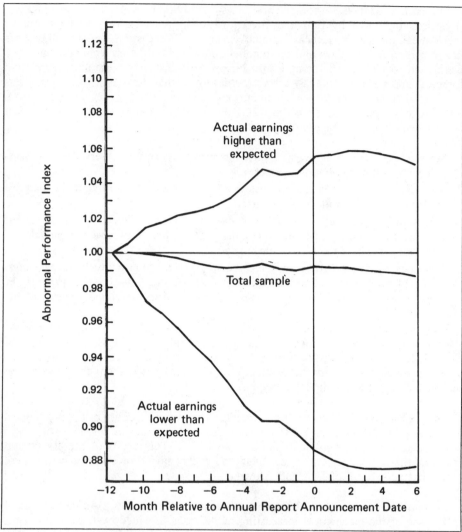

FIGURE 47.2 PERFORMANCE OF PORTFOLIOS HAVING POSITIVE AND
NEGATIVE EARNINGS FORECAST ERRORS
ADAPTED FROM: Ball and Brown, 1968.

the portfolios when mechanical models based on quarterly data were used to form
earnings expectations. They estimated that these models improved the predictive
content of forecasts by 30% to 40% over the models using annual data only.

Correlation between unexpected earnings and security prices. In a later study,
Foster (1975) used two mechanical models, one with absolute earnings and one
with changes in earnings, to forecast insurance companies' earnings, categorized
into underwriting, investment, and capital gains or losses. Rates of return on com-

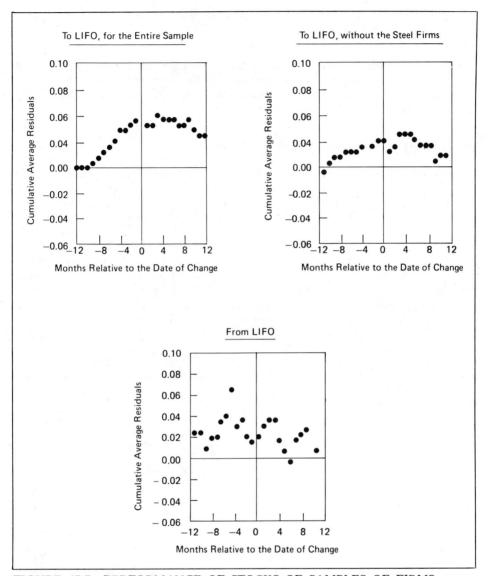

FIGURE 47.7   PERFORMANCE OF STOCKS OF SAMPLES OF FIRMS
THAT SWITCHED TO OR FROM LIFO
ADAPTED FROM: Sunder, 1975.

suggest that changes in market prices are conditional on forecasted near-term profitability. In particular:

1. Abnormal positive market returns were observed for firms that made the switch to LIFO at the time their earnings were forecasted to be higher than last year's.
2. Abnormal negative market returns were observed for firms that made the switch to

LIFO at the time their expected earnings were projecting a downward trend, independent of the change.

These results imply that the decision to switch to LIFO could convey an alternative meaning (i.e., financial stress) for some of the firms making the switch (i.e., firms for whom analysts had projected a downward trend). Additional work is being done to evaluate this hypothesis.

Discretionary Versus Nondiscretionary Changes

Harrison (1977) observed that different managerial motivation could be associated with different accounting changes, depending on whether or not they are made at the discretion of the management. He used 346 accounting changes made by 280 firms during the period 1968-1972. Of these changes, 74 were nondiscretionary (i.e., they were required by the issuance of a professional pronouncement), and the rest were made at the discretion of the management. The sample and a comparison sample were partitioned according to whether the change increased or decreased reported income and according to the level of market risk. Differences between average total market returns for each subsample that made accounting changes and those of its control sample were graphed and statistically analyzed. Results of the 1977 study by Harrison are depicted in Figure 47.9.

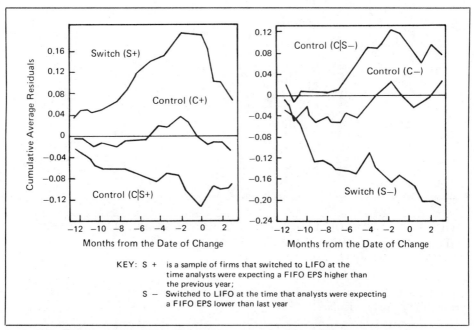

FIGURE 47.8   PERFORMANCE OF SAMPLES OF FIRMS THAT HAD
    SWITCHED TO LIFO COMPARED TO NO-SWITCH SAMPLES
    ADAPTED FROM: Abdel-khalik and McKeown, 1978.

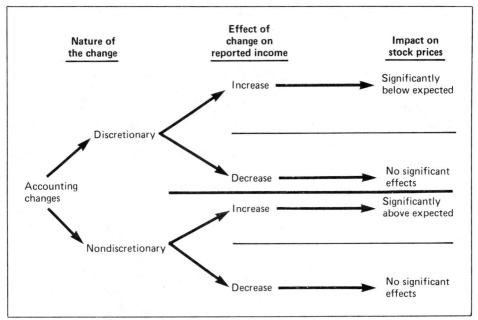

FIGURE 47.9 COMPARISON OF MARKET EFFECTS OF DISCRETIONARY VS. NONDISCRETIONARY CHANGES
SUMMARIZED FROM: Harrison, 1977.

Foreign Currency Translation. A controversial nondiscretionary accounting change relates to the method of translating foreign currency transactions and financial statements as required by SFAS 8 (AC 1083). Several market studies have been performed to assess the effect on security prices of the change to the temporal method of translation. A comprehensive study conducted by Dukes (1978) used a sample of 479 firms. His analysis adopted several classifications based on

1. The pre-SFAS 8 translation method;
2. Periods of stable versus volatile currency exchange markets; and
3. Magnitude of foreign operations based on measures of income, assets, and sales.

A control sample of firms that were not classified as multinationals was selected for comparison purposes. Dukes used several types of analyses involving (a) differences resulting from comparisons of total risk-adjusted returns and (b) evaluation of abnormal returns. His findings are summarized as follows:

1. No significant differences were observed between the mean market rate of return for multinational firms and that of control firms.
2. No effect of pre-SFAS 8 methods of translation was discerned.
3. Firms with larger foreign operations (as defined by Dukes's measures) experienced average lower market rates of return as compared to other multinationals, but none can be directly attributed to the implementation of SFAS 8.

4. No change in financial structure or risk measures could be attributed to SFAS 8. Dukes concluded that "the number of firms whose security returns were measurably affected by Statement No. 8 is small, if indeed can be identified at all" (p. 7).

Figure 47.10 depicts Dukes's conclusions. Other studies dealing with the same problem are summarized by Griffin (1979).

Leases. Another example of a nondiscretionary accounting change is the reporting of noncapitalized financing leases required in 1973 financial statements by ASR 147. (See Chapter 23.) A cash-flow schedule and the present value of noncapitalized financing leases (along with the assumptions underlying their compu-

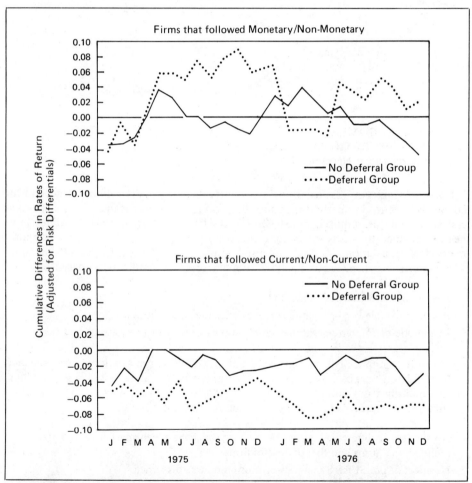

FIGURE 47.10   CUMULATIVE DIFFERENCE IN MARKET RETURNS OF STOCKS OF MULTINATIONAL AND DOMESTIC FIRMS
ADAPTED FROM: Dukes, 1978.

tations), not previously reported by many firms, were to be disclosed in a footnote. At least two published studies attempted to evaluate market reactions to this non-discretionary change concerning disclosure.

The study by Ro (1978) analyzed two independent variables: the disclosure of present values and cash-flow commitments for noncapitalized financing leases, and the would-be effect on net income of capitalization and amortization of such leases. Ro used a sample of 99 firms affected by ASR 147, of which a subset disclosed a material (3% or greater) effect on net income if the financing leases were capitalized. The test firms were classified into two risk classes, high and low beta. After adjusting for differences in market risk (beta) measures between the test and the comparison sample of similar but unaffected firms, differences in total rates of return were measured at several dates relative to ASR 147: proposal announcement date, SEC adoption date, effective date, and the date of the first required disclosure. Ro concluded (see Figure 47.11) that

1. No significant difference between risk-adjusted means of rates of return was observed for the entire sample disclosing present value;
2. A significant difference was observed between the means of rates of return for the firms disclosing material effects on income when capitalization was used, suggesting the market reacted negatively to the disclosure of income effect;
3. Thus the market reacted to the income statement information and did not react to the balance sheet information; and
4. Comparing the effects of income disclosure on the high- and low-risk firms suggested that the high-risk firms were more sensitive to the income effect.

In another study, Abdel-khalik, Thompson, and Taylor (1978) evaluated the effects of ASR 147 on risk premiums for a sample of 84 bonds issued by firms disclosing present values of noncapitalized financing leases as required by ASR 147. A comparison sample was selected by pair-matching each bond in the test sample with another bond having a similar bond rating, date-to-maturity, and coupon rate. Based on these matching criteria and on the evidence provided by earlier studies dealing with determinants of bond risk premiums, Abdel-khalik, Thompson, and Taylor hypothesized that differences between the bond risk premiums of the test and the comparison samples would be due to ASR 147.

Analysis of the data concentrated on evaluation of the significance of deviations of mean risk premiums of the test sample from those of the comparison sample (for each risk class). These differences in means were then accumulated over the period of time covering the significant implementation events of ASR 147. The results showed no significant differences in risk premiums between the test and comparison samples. The authors suggested that

1. The disclosure had no significant effect on the assessment of risk of default;
2. The bond market might have impounded the information content of the new disclosures through information obtained independently by the bond-rating agencies but not included in the financial statements; or
3. The research methods utilized were too insensitive to capture the variations in risk premiums associated with ASR 147 disclosures.

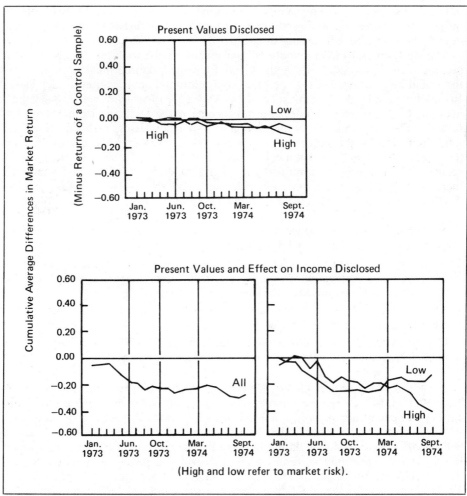

FIGURE 47.11   PERFORMANCE OF STOCKS OF FIRMS DISCLOSING
ASR 147 INFORMATION
ADAPTED FROM: Ro, 1978.

Anomalous Findings

In general, the anomalous findings vis-a-vis accounting changes are not of the
severity and magnitude of the recent anomalous evidence vis-a-vis earnings announcements. One explanation of this difference is that there has been a greater
number of research studies done on earnings announcements, and for a much
longer period of time. Given the constraints imposed on making accounting
changes by APB 20 (AC 1051) and SEC preferability requirements (ASR 177
and SAB 14), it is unlikely that the number of research studies on this subject
can proliferate.

To summarize some of the possible conflicts in conclusions:

1. Kaplan and Roll (1972) observed a downward drift in the cumulative abnormal residuals of firms switching to straight-line from accelerated depreciation for accounting purposes, a result not consistent with the concept of rapid processing of information under the semistrong EMH.

2. Sunder (1975) observed that after correcting for changes in betas (systematic risk), the behavior of residual rates of return for a small sample of firms switching from LIFO to FIFO was almost random; the semistrong EMH would call for a negative reaction.

3. Tom Harrison (1977) and Walter Harrison (1978) studied accounting changes not having cash-flow effects; their results suggest that the stock market was reacting to cosmetic accounting changes that increased income—negatively if the change was discretionary and positively if the change was nondiscretionary. The semistrong EMH postulates that the market sees through cosmetic accounting changes.

4. Abdel-khalik and McKeown (1978) disclosed a drop in cumulative average residual rates of return of firms that switched to LIFO in the month following the disclosure period. The semistrong form of EMH is postulated to discriminate between real and cosmetic events, which implies that cumulative residuals should not change significantly in the period following the disclosure.

5. Ro (1978) disclosed a downward drift in the mean return differences of firms after they disclosed (under ASR 147) the would-be effect on income of capitalizing financing leases. This raises questions about the speed with which the market processed the information.

DISCLOSURE RULES

This section deals with the effects on security prices (or rates of return) of disclosure rules (1) under the Securities Exchange Act of 1934, (2) for extraordinary and special items, and (3) for line-of-business (segment) reporting.

Many of the results obtained in the studies that follow are conspicuously inconsistent, and no definitive line of thought has yet emerged. The inconsistencies are due both to the wide variation of the research methods adopted and to the small number of studies covering the area.

Basic and Broad Disclosure Rules

In a series of papers, Benston (1967, 1969, and 1973) focused on assessing the association of general disclosure rules with changes in security prices. Emphasis on the 1934 SEC act dominated the latter two studies.

In the 1967 study, Benston used a sample of 483 NYSE firms to evaluate the effect of three accounting measures on the stock prices of the reporting firms. After estimating these measures, Benston regressed the residual market rates of return for time periods coinciding with (a) the month of filing annual reports with the SEC and (b) the month of the announcement of earnings. Reviewing the results of this 1967 study, Benston concluded that except for commencement of disclosure of sales figures, "this evidence is not consistent with the underlying assumption of the [1934 act] legislation, that the financial data made public are timely or relevant, on average" (1973, p. 139).

In his 1973 study, Benston concentrated on the period extending from 1926 through 1941. Building on the results of his earlier study, Benston hypothesized that the disclosure of sales was the most important requirement mandated by the 1934 act. Benston identified 193 firms of the 508 firms listed on NYSE in 1934 as the sample of firms that had not earlier disclosed sales and revenues.

Capital Asset Pricing Model. Residual market rates of return were computed (as described in the studies reviewed earlier) by comparing observed and expected rates of return obtained by a linear regression (the capital asset pricing model). For each of the two samples (the 193 and the remaining 314 firms), the distribution of residuals showed a smaller dispersion in the postact period; but no significant *difference* was observed between the disclosure sample and the nondisclosure sample. Since the nondisclosure firms started to disclose sales revenues in 1934 under the law, these results were interpreted by Benston as being consistent with the hypothesis that disclosure provisions of the 1934 act "were of no apparent value to investors" (1973, p. 149). Figure 47.12 represents some basis for this conclusion. Evidently, these 1973 study findings are inconsistent with Benston's 1967 findings that sales are important in determining equilibrium prices. However, it should be noted that Benston was among the pioneers of this research approach and some anomalies are natural in early, pathbreaking efforts (in fact, a decade later, similar anomalies abound).

Effects of Mandatory Disclosure. Hagerman (1975) evaluated mandatory (general) disclosure requirements by studying the effects of requiring banks to issue financial statements to shareholders. The requirements became effective in 1964 for state banks, in 1968 for national banks. Hagerman hypothesized that differences in risk-adjusted market rates of return between state and national banks during 1965-1967 could be attributed to the 1964 disclosure regulation. Analysis of residual market rates of return of a sample of 55 national and 42 state banks led Hagerman to conclude that (1) for both bank groups there were significant price changes around the date of the release of annual reports for the period 1965-1967 and also for the earlier period 1961-1964 and (2) no significant *differences* were observed for residuals between state and national banks during 1965-1967, which suggests minimal impact of the differential disclosure.

Effects of 10-K Requirements. Finally, a recent study by Foster III and Vickrey (1978) concerning data required by the 10-K but not reported in the annual report showed somewhat positive results. For a sample of 96 firms in nine industries, the residuals of market rates of return were evaluated during the week of filing the 10-K with the SEC. When the mean of weekly residuals were rank ordered, the week of filing with the SEC had the fifth highest residual rate of return. Statistical analysis showed a small significant difference between the mean residual during that week and the mean residual during nonreporting weeks. They concluded that the results "seem to imply that incremental information contained in the 10-K produced greater than average unexplained price variability" (p. 930), and "that investors, in the aggregate, use the incremental information in the 10-K

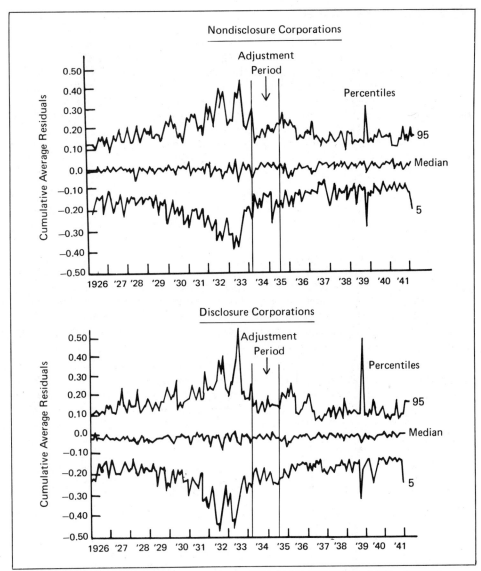

FIGURE 47.12   DISTRIBUTION OF RESIDUALS BEFORE AND AFTER
1934 SECURITIES EXCHANGE ACT
ADAPTED FROM: Benston, 1973.

in setting equilibrium security prices" (p. 921). The Foster III and Vickrey study provided evidence that does not constitute very strong support for their conclusion. As in all studies reported here, it has its methodological weak side. (Note that the SEC's requiring substantial conformity of 10-K and annual report financial statements effective for 1980 calendar year-ends provides opportunity for new research in this area.)

Extraordinary and Special Items

Accounting rule-making bodies have spent considerable effort in determining the degree of emphasis and distinctive reporting to be accorded transactions that are atypical of a firm's normal operations. In 1967, APB 9 (AC 2010) reclassified the "special items" of ARB 41 into the finer categories of extraordinary items, prior-period adjustments, and regular operating items. In 1973, APB 30 (AC 2012) further restricted the definition of extraordinary items but maintained the idea of separate and distinctive disclosure.

Conclusions of three major studies on the relationship between extraordinary items and security prices are presented in brief below:

1. Gonedes (1975) concluded that special items, on average, do have informational content pertinent to establishing securities prices, but segregation by type does not provide incremental information to market agents (earnings expectations not considered; data for 510 firms for 1962-1966).

2. Eskew and Wright (1976) argued that aggregating different types of extraordinary items may mask their separate impacts, especially if some extraordinary items have implications for future cash flows (real consequences) while others are merely bookkeeping (cosmetic) adjustments. Based on their sample of 332 firms that had at least one extraordinary item during the 1967-1972 period, they concluded that classification of extraordinary items by type provides information useful in setting market-equilibrium prices.

3. Using data for the period 1952-1972, Gonedes (1978) considered simultaneously the impact of unexpected earnings (before extraordinary items), unexpected dividends, and unexpected extraordinary items (not segregated as to type) and concluded that "the evidence presented ... is uniformly inconsistent with the view that dividend or extraordinary-item signals reflect information beyond that [already] reflected in contemporaneous income signals" (p. 71). Gonedes added the qualification that these results do not imply that extraordinary or special items have no informational content, but simply that extraordinary items *may have only substitute informational content;* that is, their information may have already been reflected in existing information or in contemporaneous (overall) earnings information.

Line-of-Business Reporting

The SEC began requiring line-of-business (LOB) breakdowns for revenues and earnings in the narrative section of registration statements in late 1969, and in 1970 extended such disclosure to its annual Form 10-K for certain diversified firms. In 1974, the Federal Trade Commission commenced its own line-of-business reporting program, and finally in 1976, the FASB issued SFAS 14 (AC 2081), which requires disclosure of industry-segmented information (see Chapter 32).

Intuitively, information disaggregated by major product lines will lead to forecasts of future earnings (or security investment decisions based on such forecasts) that cannot be any worse than forecasts based only on consolidated information. Hence, the studies of the effect of mandatory LOB disclosure on security prices essentially test *only* (1) whether the mandated disclosure provides information not

Kaplan, Robert. "The Information Content of Financial Accounting Numbers: A Survey of Empirical Evidence." *The Impact of Accounting Research on Practice and Disclosure.* A. Rashad Abdel-khalik and Thomas F. Keller, eds. Durham, N.C.: Duke University Press, 1978. The author surveys empirical research on the informational content of annual accounting numbers, interim reports, and earnings forecasts; the time series properties of accounting earnings; and the evaluation of the effects of choice among accounting alternatives on security prices. He also summarizes the accounting research on business failure. He is pessimistic about the ability of empirical research to give many insights to the accounting profession, especially in current debates over issues which involve costly disclosure.

Foster, George. *Financial Statement Analysis.* Englewood Cliffs, N.J.: Prentice-Hall, 1978, Chapters 7-12. This book is a brief but reasonably complete, well-written introduction to the use of research in capital markets and financial information and risk assessment, capital asset prices and financial information, and implications of evidence to investment decisions. At the end of each chapter, an excellent set of exercises is provided for classroom discussion.

Dyckman, Thomas, and Smith, Abbie. "Financial Accounting and Reporting by Oil and Gas Producing Companies." *Journal of Accounting and Economics,* March, 1979, pp. 45-75. This study examines the joint hypothesis of market efficiency and informational content with respect to the release of the exposure draft on SFAS 19, which recommended the use of the successful efforts (SE) method for oil and gas companies. Concerns were raised that a change would have a negative impact on the ability of full cost (FC) firms to raise capital. The study used two methods to test for difference in the distribution of security returns between FC and SE firms around the date of issuance of the exposure draft. The results indicate a relatively insubstantial negative impact on the returns of FC firms compared to those of the SE firms.

Collins, Daniel, and Dent, Warren. "The Proposed Elimination of Full-Cost Accounting in the Extractive Petroleum Industry." *Journal of Accounting and Economics,* March, 1979, pp. 3-44. This article indicates that the proposal to eliminate FC accounting was associated with a negative shift in the level of returns for FC firms relative to the level of returns for SE firms. The authors attribute this result not to market inefficiencies but rather to certain possible consequences that this accounting change must have on managerial behavior and to increased costs that may have to be borne by the affected companies.

Lev, Baruch. "The Impact of Accounting Regulation on the Stock Market: The Case of Oil and Gas Companies." *Accounting Review,* July, 1979, pp. 485-503. In contrast to the several weeks of returns used in other studies, Lev used daily price reaction for a more sensitive test of market reaction around the issuance date of the SFAS 19 exposure draft. Results indicate a relevant decline of about 4.5% in the stock prices of FC companies during a three-day period after the release of the exposure draft.

48

Academic Research in Accounting and Auditing

Miklos A. Vasarhelyi

HISTORICAL BACKGROUND

In 1916 academic accountants founded the American Association of University Instructors in Accounting, later renamed the American Accounting Association (AAA). Initially serving as a means to facilitate communication among accounting educators, permit discussion of subjects of interest in the field, and promote curriculum improvements (Zeff, 1966), AAA soon became a major force in the development of accounting research.

It was for this purpose that AAA launched *The Accounting Review* in 1926, with William Paton as editor. The early years of the *Review* emphasized accounting, law, and economics, to the detriment of auditing and taxation. The lack of legislative bodies in this field allowed authors to suggest a wide range of possible solutions to accounting problems. Eric Kohler, editor of the *Review* from 1928 to 1943, began an editorial column promoting the development of accounting principles, and in 1936, AAA published *A Tentative Statement of Accounting Principles Underlying Corporate Financial Statements.* Chatfield (1975) states that "*Review* articles of the late thirties laid the conceptual foundation for most of the Accounting Research Bulletins which appeared during the next two decades" (p. 4).

Before the mid-1950s, the literature of accounting research consisted mainly of opinion and internal logic. During the 1950s and early 1960s, however, scholarly work in accounting turned toward empiricism and interdisciplinary approaches.

The 1950s saw considerable attention given to accounting valuation, electronic data processing, and the need for scientifically supported assertions and theories. Cases and empirical data began to appear in the literature, introducing more scientific approaches to accounting research. The early 1960s brought other disciplines into the field, techniques from mathematics and economics being the most frequent imports. In 1963, the University of Chicago began publication of the *Journal of Accounting Research,* which emphasized empirical research and brought about considerable change in the nature of the support of accounting theories. It has had a major impact on the formulation of contemporary accounting thought.

In the 1970s, accounting research borrowed still more from other disciplines, including statistics (audit sampling and the empirical testing of theories), psychology (behavioral hypotheses and theories), sociology (contingency theory and agency theory), and economics (efficient market studies). *The Accounting Review* and the *Journal of Accounting Research* became more academic and theoretical, presenting major difficulties for lay comprehension, while the many professional journals sponsored by public and management accountants seldom if ever presented major research contributions. Today the gap between these two types of publications is wide, though a few new publications such as the *Journal of Accounting, Auditing and Finance* are attempting to bridge it. The aim of this chapter is to provide a framework enabling practitioners to comprehend the current status of accounting research and its prospectives.

Early accounting researchers were either practicing accountants with little formal training or economists who approached accounting problems with an interest in economic valuation and resource allocation issues. The first uses of empirical methods in accounting research were made by accountants trained in schools of commerce or business. They focused on the relationships between accounting and economic events and attempted to improve and simplify accounting measures. The present generation of researchers usually comes from doctoral programs in business administration that encourage the use of an interdisciplinary approach to problem solving and point out the need for supporting fields of specialization. Researchers are often well versed in quantitative methods, the behavioral sciences, econometrics, and social issues. More and more accounting research is being conducted jointly— by accountants and economists, by accountants and behavioral scientists (e.g., Driver and Mock, 1975), and by accountants and mathematicians. The keen demand for accounting academics has attracted many academics from other disciplines to accounting problems and to collaborations with accountants.

Accounting researchers have been using the tools imported from other disciplines very creatively, often contributing technology to the original field. Many accounting researchers currently publish in behavioral, statistical, and economic journals, using the theories, approaches, and results developed under interdisciplinary methods.

STATE OF THE ART

Buckley (1976) has classified the methodologies of contemporary research into four main categories: analytic, archival, empirical, and opinion. As shown in Figure 48.1, the selection of a methodology or strategy for investigating a given research problem leads to further choices of domain (i.e., the setting in which the research will take place) and research technique.

Methodology can be defined as the sequential decision process used for the selection among alternative paths in a research process. Mock (1972) described the methodological decision process as a sequential, but interactive, decision tree. In more common day-to-day use, the word *methodology* refers to the principal approach adopted for the resolution of a particular research problem. Intrinsic to the notion of research is the concept of scientific method, whereby knowledge is advanced through logical thinking and experimentation. Two basic approaches (Buckley, 1976) may be used for the development of scientific evidence: (1) *induction,* whereby new theories are developed, and (2) *deduction,* whereby new theories are tested. Deduction therefore is implemented through the hypothetic-deductive method, in which theory-based hypotheses are formulated and methodologies used for their testing.

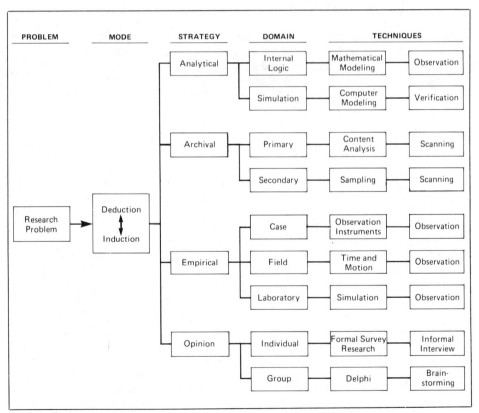

FIGURE 48.1   METHODOLOGIES FOR ACCOUNTING RESEARCH
ADAPTED FROM: Buckley, 1976.

Prior to the 1950s, scholarly research emphasized individual opinion and internal logic. Current research has almost abandoned the individual opinion approach, favoring more empirical and analytical methodologies. This chapter discusses these potential methodologies and their principal characteristics.

Research Methodologies

Analytic. Analytic research uses mathematical representations, economic theory, and logic for the analysis of accounting phenomena. In an internal logic study, this methodology entails extensive mathematical development from a set of postulates; in a simulation study, it uses electronic data processing for the representation of economic and accounting phenomena. The newly developed field of information economics has produced several studies that use the analytic approach. Originally introduced by Marschak (1969) and Marschak and Radner (1972), information economics has found a large number of applications in accounting (e.g., Demski and Feltham, 1976).

Simulation, though still in its infancy, has great promise. Once the cost and complexities of using computers in simulation have been overcome, this approach will be fully incorporated into the researcher's arsenal of tools. One use of simulation in accounting is the comparison of different multiple-ranking criteria as applied to management accounting (planning) by Lin (1978).

Archival. Archival research is basically a variation of empirical research that works with data already recorded and prepared for the researcher or with data recorded by another source and gathered by the researcher.

Primary archival research utilizes prerecorded data of research databases (such as those provided by COMPUSTAT and the Center for Research in Security Prices) for hypothesis testing. This type of research is called *ex post facto* research, because the collection of data and the study design come after the occurrence of the data-producing events. Typical examples of primary archival research can be found in the efficient market research discussed in Chapter 47 (e.g., Ball and Brown, 1968; Basu, 1978).

Secondary archival research deals with literature surveys and summarizations of the literature (e.g., Hofstedt, 1976). Papers that summarize prior research often serve as a basis for model building and internal logic developments. For example, Libby and Lewis (1977) surveyed the human information processing (HIP) literature in accounting, and classified existing studies into three main approaches: (1) the lens model, (2) probabilistic judgment, and (3) cognitive style. Such surveys provide an assessment of the state of the art in a particular area of accounting and suggest paths for future research, but they seldom propose or test new theories.

Empirical. Empirical research, one of the main accounting research approaches, uses case studies, field research, and laboratory studies.

A *case study* usually involves no experimental design and no explicit control features (i.e., there is no attempt to separate external effects from the effects being studied). Instead, the researcher introduces a particular method into a real-life setting and then carefully monitors the results. For example, Mason (1969) introduced a new method for corporate planning and monitored its implementation in a corporate situation. No control groups were set up to perform the same tasks by traditional methods; it was simply assumed that the changes observed after the introduction of the new method were its effects.

Field research involves experimental design, with at least one experimental and one control group, but no explicit environmental control, since it is maintained in a real setting. Thanks to the control group, the results of a field study may be valid and even applicable to other situations, but many field studies show mixed results because of the interference of exogenous factors. Another difficulty is that many firms and corporations are reluctant to become the subject of field studies because the experiment may produce adverse effects. However, Stedry (1960) and Stedry and Kay (1966), in a field study of the effect of budget participation on employee performance, demonstrated one way of removing this difficulty by using a large manufacturing firm with several subsettings in which they found different levels of managerial budget participation.

Laboratory studies have experimental design and environmental controls, allowing the researcher to determine the sources and effects of the experimental treatments. These studies may yield significant results in a laboratory setting, but it may not be valid to extrapolate them to real life. In a typical example, Mock (1976) used a business game to examine the effects of the timeliness of information on decision makers. Both managers and graduate students were subjects. A variation is shown in a recent study by Newton (1977), who, rather than bring partners of CPA firms into the laboratory, performed a laboratory study by taking fictitious cases to the partners. She asked them to evaluate the cases in terms of materiality and discuss issues and rules for materiality judgments.

One of the key problems in laboratory studies is that of surrogation. A laboratory experiment may feature any or all of the following: (1) a surrogate problem or case representing a real-life problem, (2) a surrogate environment representing a real-life situation, or (3) surrogate decision makers representing real-life decision makers. Inadequate surrogation along any of these lines may render the results of a study invalid or decrease their generalizability.

In recent years an increasing number of laboratory studies have been performed, but their focus has been on research issues and theories imported from other disciplines, not on current practical accounting problems. The standard-setting organizations and accounting firms could greatly benefit by using the laboratory method for examining disclosure issues and their impact on decision makers.

Opinion. Individual opinion research basically consists of an expert (e.g., Paton, 1922) expressing his opinions on particular accounting procedures or theories and presenting some logical support for these opinions. The line that separates individual opinion research from internal logic research is a fine one. Early accounting research, which usually did not explore the internal logic of its postulates or perform analytic development to any great extent, belongs more clearly to the individual opinion category (Smith, 1954), but modern research in scholarly journals tends to emphasize internal logic and linkages with the literature even if the message is really individual opinion. Individual opinion articles are still prevalent in professional journals (e.g., *The Journal of Accountancy*), despite a trend toward more articles devoted to practical solutions to problems rather than advocacy. Scholarly journals generally restrict opinion research to the opinions of established academics or practitioners.

Group opinion research served as the link between the classical phase of accounting research and the empirical phase. Several studies of the opinions of practicing CPAs served as the basis for rule making. A variation of the traditional opinion survey has been used recently by researchers who manipulate hypothetical or real situations to examine particular issues through cases or questionnaires. This approach has the advantage of using real decision makers in their normal surroundings to deal with a laboratory problem. Such studies may be classified as empirical field research, as laboratory studies, or as group surveys, depending on the nature of the task, the experimental design, and the controls on the questionnaire.

Research Techniques and Concepts

Accounting research, like many other specialized fields of endeavor, has its own vocabulary for the techniques and concepts it uses. Here are definitions and explanations of the most frequently used terms in the research vernacular.

Modeling. A *model* is a symbolic or physical representation of a particular phenomenon or system. *Modeling* is the construction of such a representation. Models are called *stochastic* when probabilities are used to describe events, and *deterministic* when events are assumed to be certain if logical conditions are satisfied. Models are the essence of any theory. They may be completely abstract, mathematical representations, or iconic (physical) representations. An airplane, for example, may be represented by an abstract term such as flying machine, as a set of equations, or as a piece of metal to be tested in a wind tunnel. Models that prescribe behavior are called *normative,* and those that simply represent phenomena are called *descriptive*.

Most research defines an area of study and states a set of axioms about that area. These axioms constitute a model that may be as theoretical or abstract as the researcher desires.

Simulation. Simulation entails the use of models to test particular conditions or hypotheses. A simulation may be either behavioral or computer-based. Examples of behavioral simulation are role playing, the use of computer models to test individual decision making, war games, and scenarios. Computer-based simulations use electronic data processing for the representation of phenomena and their testing under different conditions.

A simulation must, in most instances, define the starting conditions (e.g., empty system, average-loaded system, or overloaded system) and the length of the period being simulated, which can range from microseconds in some instances to decades in others. A simulation must also define the statistical distributions of the events being considered and potential rules (heuristics) to be used in conjunction with the model. Many computer languages, such as DINAMO, Symscript, and SIMULA, specialize in computer simulation.

Statistical Measurement. Many different statistical techniques are used for empirical research, but they can be classified into two main categories: *parametric,* in which a statistical distribution is assumed, and *nonparametric,* in which few distribution assumptions are made. The ability to assume a statistical distribution, such as a normal distribution of values, is contingent on the measurement scale used (Stevens, 1959).

Events may be measured in increasingly powerful scales, depending on the nature of the process being measured. According to the basic principles of measurement theory (Mock, 1976; Sterling, 1970), economic events (transactions for example) occur in what is called the empirical relational system (ERS), the system of relationships in the real world. But these events are measured through a numerical relational system (NRS), in which events are placed into categories and implicit relationships between these numbers exist. Depending on the nature of the ERS, different measurement scales are used. The four main types of measurement scales are nominal, ordinal, interval, and ratio.

A *nominal* scale is used when events can only be classified into discrete categories with no perceptible dimensional relationships among them. For example, a nominal scale is used to identify different persons if their characteristics and relationships are not comparable.

An *ordinal* scale allows for the establishment of dimensional relationships among the different categories, though the magnitudinal relationships have no meaning. For example, if a housewife is asked to rate five cereals in terms of her preference, it does not mean that the cereal rated first is twice as good as that rated second. Measurements in ordinal scales are not additive; they only present ordering characteristics. For example, it is safe to assume that if cereal number 1 is preferred to cereal number 2, and number 2 is preferred to number 3, then number 1 is preferred to number 3.

An *interval* scale is a more powerful scale than the ordinal because the intervals between the elements have relational meaning. For example, if yesterday's temperature was 20°F and today's temperature is 40°F, it cannot be said that today is twice as warm as yesterday. But if tomorrow's temperature is 80°F, it may be said that the difference (interval) between the temperatures of yesterday and today is half of the difference between today's temperature and tomorrow's.

A *ratio* scale is the most powerful scale of measurement. It is discrete, its categories can be ranked, their intervals have meaning, a zero exists and has meaning, and there is meaning to the measurement's absolute value. For example, a plant purchased for $1 million is twice as expensive as one bought for $500,000.

Different measurement scales apply to different accounting issues. Since a firm with $20,000 in cash has twice as much cash as one with $10,000, a ratio scale can be used. But firm A with $400,000 recorded in goodwill cannot be said to have twice as much in goodwill (in the abstract sense) as firm B with $200,000 recorded. It can only be said that firm A has more goodwill recorded than firm B, and an ordinal scale is being used.

Statistical analysis is considerably less powerful in weak measurement scales than in strong ones. Nominal and ordinal scales only allow the use of nonparametric statistics, whereas interval and ratio scales allow the use of both parametric and nonparametric statistics. There are nonparametric versions of most statistical tests, but they are considerably weaker in deriving inferences.

In addition to classical statistics, where events are considered in their ex ante (a priori) statistical distribution, business is increasingly using Bayesian statistics (Winkler, 1972). Bayesian statistics allow for the revision of a priori probabilities in view of posterior events. This permits more realistic assessment of the probability of the occurrence of a particular event.

Statistical Hypothesis Testing. A *research hypothesis* is usually a theory-based statement about a particular phenomenon. It is tested in a null form, the form that states that the phenomenon does not exist. If the test shows that the null hypothesis must be rejected, an effect has been found.

Statistical testing of a hypothesis either succeeds or fails to yield results that are *significant* at a certain level. The significance level indicates the probability that the results were due to chance. A significance level of 5%, for example, means that if an effect is found, there is a 5% probability that it was found by chance. Suppose that 100 partners of CPA firms are told of a particular audit situation and asked if they agree that a real problem exists. Sixty partners say that a problem exists and forty say there is no problem. From a statistical table that appropriately represents the distribution, the researcher finds that in only 5% of such cases would these numbers occur by chance. Thus, if the null hypothesis stated that no more than half of the partners would find the situation problematic, the null hypothesis could be rejected at a 5% level of significance.

The statistical tests most commonly used in accounting research are (1) descriptive statistics, (2) regression analysis, (3) analysis of variance, (4) factor analysis, and (5) mathematical programming approaches. The general objectives, prospective uses, and strengths and weaknesses of these tests are examined below.

Descriptive statistics. This is the simplest form of statistical test and involves description of populations, subpopulations, or population parameters. It usually involves frequencies (counts) of elements belonging to the different categories being considered, means, cross-breaks (cross-tabulations), modes, and chi-square tests. Descriptive statistics are commonly used for nominal scales, survey studies, and studies in human resource and social accounting. In these types of research, theory is not highly developed.

Regression analysis. The behavior of one variable, called the *dependent variable,* on the basis of another, called the *independent variable,* is explained through regression analysis. The relationship between the two variables, if any, can often be described by a *linear regression.* A simple linear regression can be represented by a formula of the type

$$Y = a + bX$$

where Y = dependent variable, X = independent variable, and a and b = constants derived in the analysis. For example, if fixed costs in a small hospital are $2,000,000 a year and variable costs $300 per patient-day, the hospital total costs could be represented by

$$TC = \$2,000,000 + (\$300 \times PD)$$

where TC = total costs and PD = number of patient-days.

Figure 48.2 plots the total costs of a hospital against the number of patient-days for 12 different months. With this data, regression analysis can be used to construct an equation representing total costs as a function of a constant and a slope (variable cost per unit) multiplied by the number of patient-days (dependent variable).

Several statistics are used in connection with regression analysis. R^2 is an index that shows what percentage of the variation of the dependent variable is explained by the independent variable. R^2 ranges from 0, signifying that none of the variation is explained by the independent variable, to 1, signifying that all of the variation is explained by the independent variable. F values are used to measure the goodness of fit, or in other words, the significance of the quality of fit.

Regression analysis is basically an attempt to find a straight line through a set of observations with a reasonable fit. The regression line is the most likely estimator of a linear representation of the phenomenon under study.

An extension of simple regression is *multiple regression,* which is still linear but has multiple independent variables. With multiple regression, an F test can be used not only to establish the quality of the fit but also to test the significance of a particular variable as a part of the explanatory model. For example, if regression is used to construct an explanatory model of uncollectibles, bad debts will be the dependent variable, and aging of receivables, macroeconomic factors, and other factors may be independent variables. The overall F statistic serves to evaluate goodness of fit. As a rule of thumb, the higher the F the better the fit. An F value can be calculated for each independent variable to decide whether it should be included in the overall model. If the F value is too small, showing no significance, the variable can be left out of the model. Another rule of thumb is that for each independent variable included in the model, there must be about ten observations of all variables. Thus, if the researcher wants to construct a model with three independent explanatory variables, he may need 30 or more observations to ensure model stability.

Analysis of variance. Analysis of variance, as Kerlinger points out, "is not just a

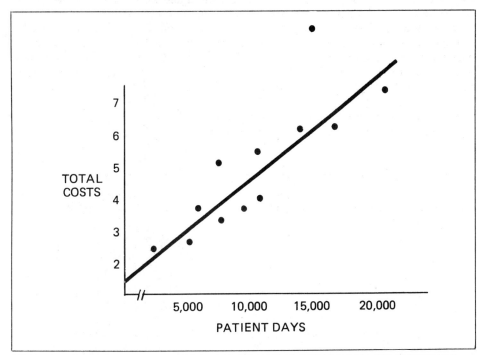

FIGURE 48.2   HOSPITAL COST ALLOCATION EXAMPLE—REGRESSION LINE AND TOTAL

statistical method. It is an approach and a way of thinking" (1973, p. 216). It is probably the most frequently used method of hypothesis testing and data analysis. By this method, the total variance of all measurements is broken down to the variance between groups and the variance within a group. If the variance between groups is wider than the variance within a group, there may be evidence of a particular effect, but if the variance within a group is wider than that between groups, the results are probably not significant.

The simplest form of analysis of variance is the comparison of two groups. Suppose that a CPA firm decides to test a new approach for staff training using new educational materials. They divide the trainees into two similar groups and train one with the new method and the other (the control group) with the old method. Scores on the old final exam are used to test the efficacy of both. Analysis of variance is used to test the effect of the new training method. A common statistic used in this situation (one way, two groups) is the *Student t* test. Computer programs are used to calculate the *t* value, and the significance of the result can be looked up in a statistical table. If several educational methods were being tested, then a one-way, multiple-group situation would arise, calling for use of an *F* statistic.

If the firm suspects that the different results of the two training programs may be due not only to the training method but also to the program instructors, it may use analysis of variance with four groups of trainees. The first group is trained with the new method and instructor 1, the second group with the old method and instructor 2, the third group with the new method and instructor 2, and the fourth with the old method and instructor 1. This design, called *factorial design,* separates the effect of the instructor from the training method and from the interaction of the two variables. These approaches are shown in Figure 48.3.

When sample sizes are small or the data being considered is ranked ordinal, parametric statistics are not applicable. Several nonparametric tests are available, such as the Kolmogorov-Smirnov test for goodness of fit and the Kruskal-Wallace and Friedman analysis-of-variance tests. These nonparametric tests can be found in Siegel (1956) or any good nonparametric statistics text.

Factor analysis. Factor analysis has become much more widely used in accounting research with the ready availability of computers (e.g., Milani, 1975), for its

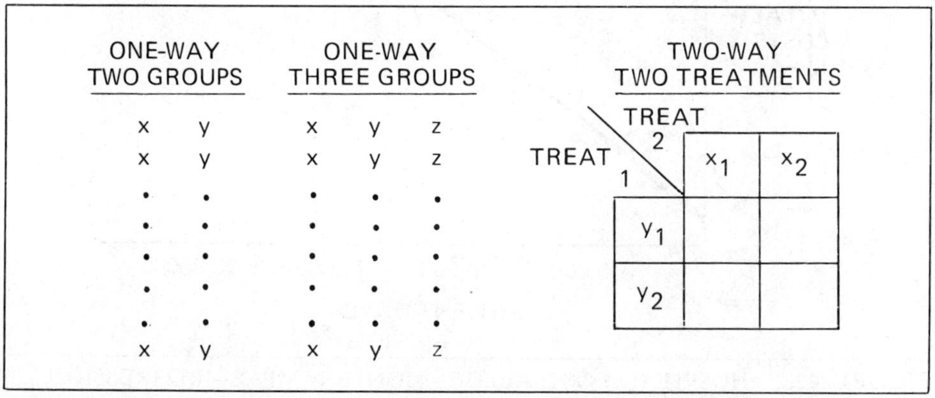

FIGURE 48.3   ANALYSIS OF VARIANCE

inherent mathematical complexity makes it difficult to apply by manual methods. It is a technique for determining the number and nature of underlying variables within a larger set of information. Suppose for example, that a researcher wants to investigate the factors that influence auditor performance. He may measure such variables as auditor behavioral characteristics, auditor training, nature of the engagement, timing of the engagement, budget of the engagement, and many others. With factor analysis he can reduce this large set of variables to a considerably smaller number. The variables identified in this way are the factors that have the greatest influence on variations in auditor performance. In research designed to test an existing theory through the behavior of experimental groups, analysis of variance remains a powerful method of assessing the results. But in studies that measure a great many variables and produce masses of numbers, it can be very difficult without factor analysis to pinpoint the factors that underlie the phenomenon under investigation and to arrive at theories describing its behavior. Many applications of factor analysis are currently being made in accounting research, notably in the areas of capital markets and human information processing. Its potentialities are wider still, particularly for use in audit research.

Mathematical programming. This term is an overall description for many techniques, including *linear programming, dynamic programming, integer programming,* and *optimal control.*

Linear programming, the workhorse of operations research, has been used widely in the literature and in practice (Charnes and Cooper, 1961; Summers, 1972). Dynamic programming has been used sporadically in auditing and information economics. Integer programming, optimal control, and other mathematical programming techniques are still infrequently used as tools in accounting research. For most of these techniques, elaborate software packages are already available, thus enabling users to avoid extensive computation.

Linear programming may be useful to the practitioner as well as to researchers. It always entails an objective function such as a maximization (of profits for example) or a minimization (of costs or audit hours) and is subject to a series of constraints. These constraints may reflect the production capabilities of a firm, the limitations of the skills of its components, or the limitations in cash available for a particular period. The linear programming formulation also contains parameters related to particular features of the process, such as units of contribution margin or number of production hours.

Figure 48.4 shows a small linear programming problem for the profit maximization of a small CPA practice in a particular month. X stands for hours of audit work, Y for hours of tax work, and Z for hours of consulting work. Substituting the functions in Figure 48.4 into a linear programming package would lead to an optimal allocation of staff efforts. The optimal allocation is the one that leads to the highest profit possible, subject to the constraints.

Optimal solutions often contain fractional results. Unfortunately, some types of problems do not permit fractions, as when a capital-budgeting linear program suggests the solution of building two thirds of a steel mill. But *integer programming* algorithms have been developed for such situations, and may be applicable as well to CPA engagement planning. Integer programming would accept engagement planning as a profit maximization problem and provide an integral solution.

Dynamic programming, another mathematical programming technique, is used for dynamic situations where the optimal solution at a particular point is contingent

istration, and ease of external and internal validation. But unless the questions are very carefully worded, ambiguity and misinterpretation will invalidate the survey findings.

A recent survey (Rhode, 1977) was based on a questionnaire distributed to audit partners and staff in an attempt to determine the influence of certain aspects of the auditor's work environment on his professional performance. Of 4,888 CPAs screened in the original sample, 2,770 (56%) responded to a request to participate and 2,016 (41.2%) met all the criteria for participation and were mailed questionnaires. Of this sample, 41% filled out and returned the questionnaire, which asked 91 questions on many of the critical issues in the quality of audits. The conclusions were basically positive toward the profession, but the survey disclosed instances of substandard performance.

Several questions may be raised that cast doubt on the validity of these results. First, how candid were the auditors, all CPAs, in a survey sponsored, in effect, by the AICPA? Also, how accurate were the auditors' self-perceptions? How biased were the questions? Were all the key areas covered? And finally, was the responding sample representative?

Isaac and Michael (1971) list the following potential shortcomings of questionnaires in general: (1) other techniques may be more appropriate to the investigation of specific research questions, (2) they may not have been given a pretest, (3) they may be too long, (4) they may be given a bad format and presentation, and (5) the researchers may fail to check for respondent bias.

Panels. Groups or panels of people may be used as representatives of larger populations. Some panels consist of experts who are better informed or more insightful than the larger population. A currently popular method of panel survey is the *Delphi method* (Helmer, 1966), in which experts forecast events or explain phenomena through a complex set of controlled interactions that are monitored and moderated by the researcher.

Controlled observation. In this survey method, either an artificial setting is created or careful controls are placed in the real setting to gather observations on a particular process. In one example, Baker (1976) used participant observation to examine the behavior and activities of a partner of a CPA firm. This technique, imported from anthropology, may allow considerable insight into some basic questions. However, a more usual form of controlled observation in accounting research is the laboratory method.

Research Databases. Large computer-readable databases on corporate financial statements and stock market prices have markedly facilitated research in many areas, particularly security price research. Two particularly useful databases are provided by COMPUSTAT and the University of Chicago's Center for Research on Security Prices (CRSP). CRSP tapes contain data on daily security prices from the major stock exchanges and facilitate studies on the effect of accounting announcements on the market valuation of stocks. COMPUSTAT tapes include annual and other reports in addition to high, low, and closing stock prices for the period reported, but do not provide daily prices.

Another database is the National Automated Accounting Research System (NAARS), developed jointly by the AICPA and Mead Data Central Inc. NAARS contains data from annual reports, prospectuses, and other releases of thousands of publicly traded companies. This database is supplemented by a literature file containing such material as APB opinions and Accounting Research Bulletins, FASB statements and interpretations, CASB statements, and AICPA Technical Practice Aids. (See Chapter 49 for a detailed discussion.)

Other databases of great potential value to researchers await development. Despite the currently surging interest in auditing research, audit data have been difficult to obtain, because public accounting firms are reluctant to disclose information about audit engagements, particularly working papers. The development of a large audit database could do for audit research what CRSP and COMPUSTAT have done for security price research. A limited database was recently developed by Kinney (1979) from the working papers of 44 audit engagements; using the auditor's requested adjustments shown in the working papers, the researcher tested the effectiveness of proposed models of analytical review. Another database has been developed by Neter and Loebbecke (1975), with data on four actual audit populations.

MAJOR RESEARCH CONTRIBUTIONS

In a literature survey concentrating on academic research and dealing only tangentially with the professional accounting literature, Vasarhelyi and Berk (1980) studied nearly twelve hundred articles published in five major American accounting journals during the 15 years from 1963 to 1978, classifying them by area of research. They found that although the areas of research are not mutually exclusive, each article could be fairly categorized by its research emphases. Security price research, the major application of empirical methods in the last decade, is discussed in Chapter 47. The other areas, discussed below, are (1) accounting theory, (2) behavioral accounting research, (3) audit research, (4) institutional studies, and (5) accounting information systems.

Accounting Theory

The changes in accounting theory that have occurred over two decades were examined by the AAA Committee on Concepts and Standards for External Financial Reports in a study entitled *Statement on Accounting Theory and Theory Acceptance* (1977b). This study concluded that "a single universally accepted basic accounting theory does not exist at this time. Instead a multiplicity of theories has been and continues to be proposed. . . ." The committee proceeded to identify three prominent approaches to the construction of accounting theory: (1) classical models, (2) decision usefulness, and (3) information economics.

The classical approach is taken by two schools. The true-income school, which includes Paton (1922), Sweeney (1936), and Edwards and Bell (1961), advocates current accounting practice, and its explanation is mixed with missionary zeal and suggestions for reform. The inductive school, which is represented by Hatfield (1927), Gilman (1939), Littleton (1953), and Ijiri (1975), attempts to rationalize and sometimes even to justify major elements of current accounting practice with the use of normative deductive reasoning.

Human Information Processing. Behavioral accounting research is a general category. In recent years one of its branches has evolved into what is called human information processing (HIP) research. Libby and Lewis (1977) have classified HIP research into three main approaches or paradigms: (1) the lens model, (2) probabilistic judgment, and (3) cognitive styles.

The *lens model* (Brunswik, 1952, 1956), as adopted by information processing researchers such as Dudycha and Naylor (1966), Tucker (1964), and Ashton (1974b), is used to analyze situations where individuals make decisions about real events based on imperfect information. Regression equations, correlation, and ANOVA have been used to model the individual's decision-making process. In many respects, the lens model is similar and complementary to the information economics approach. A combination of these approaches (e.g., Mock and Vasarhelyi, 1978) presents interesting prospects for research.

The *probabilistic judgment* approach focuses on the stochastic nature of events and their sequentiality. According to this approach, each information cue is considered in the decision model, and its probability is revised upon the outcome of events. Two main lines of thought evolved from probabilistic judgment studies, one of which dealt with Bayesian revisions (Barefield, 1975; Dickaut, 1973; and Kennedy, 1975) and the other with decision-maker heuristics and biases (Swieringa et al., 1976; Tversky and Kahneman, 1974; and Uecker and Kinney, 1975). Probabilistic judgment models seem to indicate that humans are not particularly good Bayesian probability revisers nor are they really rational decision makers.

Cognitive style studies basically deal with human decision-maker characteristics and their effect on the use of information cues in decision making (Mock, Estrin, and Vasarhelyi, 1972; Dermer, 1973; Driver and Mock, 1975; and San Miguel, 1976). These studies may serve to identify, explain, and describe human decision-making heuristics and biases. The cognitive style approach illustrates the nature of interindividual differences and the possibility of their classification into categories of similarly behaving decision makers. But these categories, in spite of often being statistically discriminant in terms of decision-maker behavior, fail to present the stability and consistency necessary for the potential development of information systems related to decision makers.

Libby and Lewis (1977) conclude that "although human information processing research is receiving research attention by accountants, such research in accounting contexts is still in its infancy" (p. 263). Most HIP studies satisfactorily replicated psychologists' findings, with some interesting exceptions still to be explored in the accounting literature. Lens studies now need expansion toward more elaborate settings, environments, and feedback effects.

Another survey of the HIP literature, conducted by the HIP Committee of AAA (1977a), classified the research into the same three main categories as did Libby and Lewis, but also added a fourth: process tracing (Hogarth, 1975; Payne, 1976; Clarkson, 1962; and Mock and Biggs, 1978). Without recognizing process tracing as a separate paradigm, Libby and Lewis (1977) stated that

it shows great promise for providing more detailed descriptions of the way in which information is combined. Such models are not subject to the insensitivity of the linear model to alternative weighting schemes as are the traditional lens model approaches. [p. 264]

An entirely different classification of the HIP literature has been suggested by Driscoll and Mock (1976). This classification is illustrated in Figure 48.6.

In sum, the HIP literature provides insight into the actual ways in which accounting data is used by decision-makers. Although the mapping of cognitive processes is still not complete, and basic thought processes are far from understood, aggregate patterns and probabilistic tendencies have been recognized. Potentially, this work can lead to basic paradigms describing information needs to be met by corporate disclosure. Such questions as the level of aggregation of cost information in income statements, the desirability of disclosing contingencies in the body of statements rather than in footnotes, and the frequency of reporting may be resolved by HIP paradigms.

Budget Research. Another field of behavioral accounting research investigates organizational budgeting. Vasarhelyi and Mock (1977) have divided budget research into three areas: (1) organizational research, (2) behavioral research in budgeting, and (3) information and human information processing research in budgeting.

The organizational studies include Bruns and Waterhouse (1975), Mock (1973), Holstrum (1971), Ijiri et al. (1968), and Cyert and March (1963). These studies relate organization, organizational structure, and organizational performance to mode of and approach to budgeting.

The behavioral studies of budgeting deal with motivation, participation, attainability of goals, reinforcement of achievement, and employee attitudes toward the budget and the organization. Among them are Stedry and Kay's (1966) classic field study of foreman task-difficulty perception; Milani's (1975) field study of budget participation in relation to on-the-job performance; Cherrington and Cherrington's (1973) laboratory experiment on different budget situations and controlled rewards (reinforcement contingencies); and Ronen and Livingstone's (1975) elegant conceptual work applying the expectancy model to a set of disjointed behavioral budget research findings.

The budget studies that focus on informational issues (e.g., Mock, 1972; Welsch, 1973; and Vasarhelyi and Mock, 1977) basically deal with ways to present information, the type of variance information to be presented, and types of budget reports.

The conclusions of the behavioral research on budgeting confirm that participation in budgeting decisions is important to most employees, but even more so is the communication of valid information on the budget-reward process. Subjects of the Cherrington and Cherrington study (1973), for example, performed well and were reasonably satisfied under autocratic budget-setting methods as long as their performance was measured basically on their output and not on budget variance. Once budget variance was part of the evaluation process, budgetees were very dissatisfied if they could not participate in formulating the budget under which they would work.

Audit Research

The criticism by congressional subcommittees in 1976 and 1977 aimed at the public accounting profession and its standard-setting process has prompted new research efforts in several areas. Criticism of the audit practices of large firms in

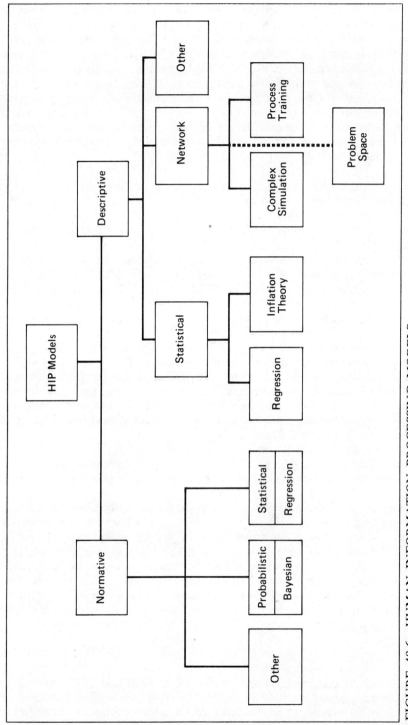

FIGURE 48.6 HUMAN INFORMATION PROCESSING MODELS
ADAPTED FROM: Driscoll and Mock, 1976.

particular, and of the firms' influence on standard-setting bodies such as the FASB, the AICPA, and the SEC, has motivated new research interest in the auditing field and in institutional matters.

Lin et al. (1980) surveyed the auditing literature and attempted to identify its underlying theories and domains. This survey dealt exclusively with the academic literature, to the exclusion of professional literature, authoritative pronouncements, and literature dealing with the use of electronic data processing in auditing. The studies surveyed were found to fall into three main categories: (1) classical theories of auditing, (2) decision theory and decision models, and (3) auditors as decision makers. Classical audit theory has been the subject of four major studies: Mautz and Sharaf (1961), AAA (1973), Toba (1975), and Kissinger (1977). These are mainly normative works and are based on philosophical rules of evidence and a priori arguments. They provide broad guidance on the audit function, but a homogeneous and comprehensive basis for audit work has still not been achieved.

Decision theory and models. A large number of studies were classified by Lin et al. (1980) as being concerned with decision theory and decision models. They were subdivided into the areas of (1) overall audit planning and information economics, (2) statistical sampling, (3) internal control evaluation and compliance tests, and (4) substantive tests.

Studies on *audit planning and information economics* include Ijiri and Kaplan (1971), Demski and Swieringa (1974), Scott (1973, 1975) and Kinney (1975b). This approach seems to provide the tools for the formulation and analysis of auditor environment and task relationships. Insights gathered from these studies are valuable and generalizable but provide little direct, long-term application to audit practice.

The numerous studies on *statistical sampling* are mainly concerned with proposed sampling plans, sampling objectives, and sampling risk. Among them are Loebbecke and Neter (1975), Teitlebaum and Robinson (1975), Kaplan (1975), Kinney (1975a), and Hansen and Shaftel (1977). This extensive literature represents the most notable direct influence of research on the audit profession. Statistical sampling (see Chapter 14) is rapidly becoming integrated into auditing practices, but more research is still needed, particularly on the costs and benefits of alternative sampling plans, their relationships with different sampling objectives, the nature of accounting error distributions, and the nature of general population distributions and biases.

Internal control evaluation has been the subject of considerable study by Brown (1962) and King (1964). These studies used many different theories, approaches, and methodologies, but had little effect on the profession or the practice of auditing. Studies by Cyert and Davidson (1963) and Arkin (1974) dealt with the issue of internal control compliance tests, and this research has found its way into audit practice; but the works by Sorensen (1969), Smith (1972), and others using the Bayesian approach have not yet had any impact. Other studies such as Cushing (1974) and Burns and Loebbecke (1975), which used analytical methods and computer simulation, respectively, to evaluate internal controls, seem promising but are still very far from widespread applicability. Another promising approach, the assessment of prior probability distributions by auditors, has been explored by Corless (1972), Chesley (1975), and Felix (1976).

In the area of *substantive tests and analytical review,* researchers have studied stochastic processes, decision theory, and regression analysis in estimating errors and intervals, dollar value of accounts, and error distributions. For example, regression analysis, statistical theory, and the time-series models were used by Stringer (1975), Albrecht and McKeown (1977), and Kinney (1979), respectively, in studies of the analytical review process. Surprisingly enough, this area, despite its practical importance, has generated little scholarly research. Substantive testing often makes use of statistical sampling, which has been extensively explored, but the processes of source document selection, identification, and validation have not been researched at all. The area of analytical review still needs considerable research on its objectives, its interrelationship with the other parts of the audit process, and its techniques to predict potential areas of adjustment (Kinney, 1979).

Auditors as decision makers. The third major research category identified by Lin et al. (1981) is that concerning auditors as decision makers. This area, which overlaps the HIP research discussed above, identifies a particular issue of auditor decision making and applies a laboratory methodology to study the processes that come into play. As with other HIP research, audit decision-making studies focus either on the individual decision maker or on groups of auditors in situations requiring decisions.

Among the studies focusing on individuals, Ashton (1974a, b), Corless (1972), and Joyce (1976) described the audit decision models used by individual judges. Ashton, for example, used a lens-type model to represent the auditor's judgment of the quality of internal controls of a particular firm. His findings indicate that a linear model performed well. Individual differences in judgment were significant, while interjudge ratings were highly correlated, indicating some degree of consistency and a considerable amount of self-insight on the part of the judges.

The *group approach* (e.g., Hofstedt and Hughes, 1977) attempts to construct a joint model of auditors in audit decisions and test the model's predictive power. Boatsman and Robertson (1974) used a field experiment to model materiality judgments based on environmental (company-related) cues and found that the aggregate model, developed using discriminant analysis, was reasonably accurate in predicting individual judgments.

Lin et al. (1981) concluded that "a tentative integrated model is needed to integrate the key phases and theories underlying audit research related to decision theory/decision models" (p. 31). They also suggested that the area of internal control evaluation holds great potential for research and proposed a set of more creative research approaches, such as the use of pattern-recognition techniques, the representation of audit biases in auditor reliance, the use of factor analysis for the analytical review process, and the subclassifying of individual audit decisions.

Institutional Studies

Institutional studies deal with problems in the establishment of accounting legislation (e.g., FASB, 1978c; AAA, 1978), the processes of public reaction to such legislation (Sutton, 1979), and the incorporation of contemporary accounting thought into accounting legislation (AAA, 1978).

"Concern about the economic consequences of financial accounting standards," the FASB has noted, "is not new. It plagued the Accounting Principles Board and has permeated responses to FASB discussion memoranda and exposure drafts since the Board's inception" (FASB, 1978c, p. i). In 1978, the FASB sponsored a conference, coordinated by Dr. George Staubus, to obtain academic input regarding these consequences and the methods to examine them. Staubus (FASB, 1978c, p. vii) summarized current research on the subject by asking six questions:

1. Can standard-setting bodies, ex ante or ex post facto, determine the methods that yield the greatest benefits to society?
2. Can standard-setting bodies rely on market efficiency to minimize the economic consequence of financial accounting standards?
3. Can financial reporting affect the allocation of resources?
4. Should standard-setting bodies consider the macroeconomic impact of their decisions and make decisions on their perception of public values?
5. Should accounting standards favor others besides the users of data?
6. Should standard-setting bodies deliberately mandate what they believe to be an inferior accounting method?

Six papers were presented at the FASB conference, most of them attempting ex post facto evaluations of the effect of particular accounting rulings or the opinion of a particular audience. The most interesting approach was that of Abdel-khalik et al. (in FASB, 1978c), who used Moody's bond rating to evaluate changes in market risk perception due to SFAS 13 on leases.

Ex post facto analysis can only provide insight into the effect that regulations have had in the past. There is no guarantee that the same effects can be expected of proposed rules. AAA (1978) states: "...'a priori' problems are those for which solution frameworks or heuristics already exist. The value of having an 'a priori' policy procedure is to be able to deal generically with problems which have common attributes..." (p. 34). Methodologies are needed to provide forms of a priori evaluation of proposed accounting rules other than individual opinion and visionary forecast.

Accounting Information Systems

Despite the rapid development of computer technology and its enormous effect on corporate accounting systems, research on information systems is still an emerging field. Until now, it has concentrated on only three aspects of this vast field: (1) the relationships between accounting and accounting information structures (Mock, 1969), (2) the behavioral effect of computerized accounting information (Vasarhelyi, 1977, and Libby, 1976), and (3) the use and audit of computer systems (Cash et al., 1977).

Major changes in the electronic data processing environment such as distributive processing, minicomputers, wire transfers, macrodatabases, and the dramatic decrease in data processing costs will have long-term, drastic effects on the way accounting information is measured, coded, organized, transmitted, and displayed. These factors need considerable research.

CONCLUSIONS

Accounting research is still in the preparadigmatic phase in the sense that there are no generally accepted comprehensive accounting theories that students, professors, practitioners, or standard setters may fall back on for performing their duties. Even though many of the most important societal functions are contingent on consistent, reliable, and unbiased reporting, accounting is a *pragmatic* science (or art) and will continue even without a well-based set of accounting paradigms or axioms.

The evolution of accounting thought and research allows the identification of a few common threads: methodologies, subject matter, contributing disciplines, and general findings.

Methodologies

Most traditional accounting thought was based on empirical practices and justified through academic treatises. These slowly evolved into normative studies that can be classified as a priori research, and then into a priori inductive studies attempting to integrate practical evidence and normative statements into a general framework. The early to mid-1960s witnessed the development of empirical studies consisting mainly of opinion surveys. Development of the security price databases led to increased emphasis on archival studies.

In the early 1970s, a considerable percentage of scholarly studies of an a priori nature were still observed, but there was also a marked increase in empirical studies of an archival nature and in laboratory and field studies. The late 1970s have yielded a multitude of studies utilizing diverse methods and approaches leading to the expectation that accounting research will be more and more scientific in nature, will use many different methodologies, and will search for empirically based unifying theories.

Subject Matter

Traditional accounting research dealt almost exclusively with accounting theory issues and normative procedural topics in the search for correct accounting methods. Historical analogy and a priori arguments were slowly evolving into studies of the impact of accounting events on the value of securities. This area of security price research expanded once the CRSP and COMPUSTAT databases became available for use in examining the effect of specific information on security prices. Another area of development was behavioral research, which slowly evolved into a series of different paths, such as the modern HIP research. Modern security price research is now moving toward the development of time-series econometric models and the use of the developing field of agency theory (Ng and Stoeckenius, 1979, and Ross, 1973). This field deals with information asymmetries to explain auditor and market behavior through the use of analytic modeling.

Auditing studies have become more and more popular, using both security price methodologies and behavioral and HIP approaches. A particular type of a priori research that entails analytical modeling and study of the properties of accounting error distributions has also been emphasized, leading to major contributions in the area of substantive testing and sampling. Institutional studies using the principles of agency theory are becoming a popular field. In addition, there is a resurgence of special schools of thought in accounting, emphasizing particular accounting settings such as not-for-profit and regulated industries; accounting history works are also flourishing. Special interest sections of the AAA in areas such as audit, not-for-profit, history, and management advisory services have been conducive to these developments.

Contributing Disciplines

Early accountants were economists and brought with them the influence of classical economics and the use of the scientific method. The field of finance combined with accounting in developing security price research, which imported technologies from neoclassical economics, econometrics, and statistics. Modern behavioral research heavily utilizes psychology and, to a lesser extent, also relies on imports from other social sciences. The tendency seems to be toward continued reliance on these fields and also towards increased imports from mathematics, statistics, and decision theory.

Accounting researchers have been using these tools very creatively and often contribute new and creative technology to the originating field. Many accounting researchers currently publish in behavioral, statistical, and economic journals.

General Findings

Accounting researchers understand the nature of the accounting profession's audiences and how accounting information is used. They realize that their heuristics are somewhat conservative, that decision processes are rather linear, and that decision makers have basic biases and poor self-insight. They are also aware that many of the disclosure decisions are dependent on context and that the change in value of currencies is a major reporting obstacle.

Accounting researchers theoretically tend to prefer value methods for inflation accounting but, for reasons of practicality, offer variations of the historical method as a solution, realizing that the standard-setting process is not one of theoretical optimization but of practical compromise with theoretical validity as a basis. They know that although accounting information does not have an effect on individual decision making, it does have a limited effect on the market on an aggregate basis.

The auditing field has accepted sampling and has incorporated a scientifically integrated approach to audit planning, internal control evaluation, and substantive testing. It understands the need for analytical reviews and the establishment of defensible audit practices. It realizes the need for controlling risk and minimizing legal exposure.

FUTURE RESEARCH

In the 1980s, accounting research will become still more interdisciplinary, more empirical, and more quantitative. With the increasing use of tools from management science, research will expand in the field of auditing. Researchers will study not only the performance and planning of audit tasks but also the management of CPA firms in such areas as staff scheduling, audit budgeting, the optimal allocation of audit procedures, and the minimization of audit costs while maximizing evidence search.

Research on information systems will also expand, and it will affect the quantities of information presented to users and the ways it is presented. Microfiche and the development of mass memories will alter the economics of the reporting process and its cost-to-benefit factors, leading to further-increased disclosures, multilayered reporting systems, and perhaps some type of stochastic reporting. The use of large databases will become part of the everyday activity of accountants and managers as they cope with immense quantities of legislation, legal precedents, and potential accounting and audit problems.

The accountant's universe is rapidly growing more complex. As a result, the 1980s will bring the need for further specialization and for expansion of the scope of accounting education and practice. Financial attestation will interact with legal attestation, with economic attestation in terms of valuation, and with statistical attestation in terms of probability-estimation reporting and sampling, all on a day-to-day basis.

SUGGESTED READING

American Accounting Association. *Report of the Committee on Human Information Processing.* Sarasota, Fla., 1977. This report reviews the developments in the study of human information processing in accounting. Studies are classified into four basic approaches: probabilistic judgment, lens model, cognitive style/cognitive complexity, and other. These are explained, literature examined, and the paths for future research suggested.

Burns, William, and DeCoster, Don, eds. *Accounting and Its Behavioral Implications.* New York: McGraw-Hill, 1969. This collection of readings has great historical value in the establishment of behavioral accounting as a respectable area of research.

Demski, Joel, and Feltham, Gerald. *Cost Determination: A Conceptual Approach.* Ames, Iowa: Iowa State University Press, 1976. This book is a major classic of the information economics approach. Its major contribution is in the area of analytical formulation of managerial accounting/cost issues.

Dopuch, Nicholas, and Revsine, Lawrence. *Accounting Research 1960-1970: A Critical Evaluation.* Urbana, Ill.: Center for International Education and Research in Accounting, University of Illinois, 1973. This set of readings from a conference on accounting research held at the University of Illinois provides discussions of developments in three accounting research areas.

Hofstedt, Thomas. "Behavioral Accounting Research, Pathologies, Paradigms and Prescriptions." *Accounting, Organizations and Society,* Vol. 1, No. 1 (1976), pp. 43-58. This paper compares the developments, paradigms, and theories of securities price research (SPR) with those of behavioral accounting research (BAR). The primary technique used is quotation analysis.

Lin, W. Thomas; Mock, Theodore; Newton, Lauren; and Vasarhelyi, Miklos. "A Review of Audit Research." *Accounting Journal,* forthcoming 1981. This article surveys the academic auditing literature for common trends and underlying theories.

Sterling, Robert, ed. *Research Methodology.* Lawrence, Kan.: Scholars Book Co., 1972. This book contains the papers and responses presented at the second Arthur Young Accounting Colloquium held at the University of Kansas in May, 1971. Seven of its papers also constitute the report of the American Accounting Association Committee on Research Methodology. Papers deal with security price research, accounting theory and methodology, behavioral accounting research, and other subjects.

49

Professional Research

Dowlan R. Nelson[1]

[1] The author acknowledges with appreciation the assistance of Andrew P. Gale, Touche Ross Research Associate, in the discussion of research tools and how research is performed.

PURPOSE AND OBJECTIVES

When the term *research* is used in the context of accounting or auditing, the image of a scholarly paper often comes to mind. However, academicians are not the sole source of accounting research and are probably not the major source of auditing research. Of course, that depends on how research is defined.

The purpose of this chapter is to describe the research performed outside academia.[2] This chapter highlights the needs for research within the practicing part of the accounting profession, discusses some of the products of the research effort, and examines research tools and methods currently used.

Some accounting and auditing research efforts are published and distributed, frequently as monographs or booklets. Other research consists of gathering factual background in order to reach an informed conclusion on a practice issue. This research is not always formally published, although its findings may result in the issuance of a professional standard or an authoritative document. Research of this kind may be performed or sponsored by the organization charged with the dissemination of the standard, or it may be performed by a group obviously interested in the development of a standard in a certain direction. Background information is increasingly being made public, as a result of the movement toward rule making in the open.

Some research, seldom available to the public, is directed toward problem resolution in a professional environment. Performed by individual companies or CPA firms, this research attempts to solve specific accounting or auditing problems related to the company or a client. Although the findings themselves are kept private, they often result in new or revised firm policies or guidelines, or in communications to standard-setting bodies describing practice problems resulting from new types of transactions or implementation problems arising from the application of existing authoritative literature. This kind of research may also enable a practice firm to comment effectively on a proposed standard.

In addition to performing their own research, companies, organizations, and CPA firms encourage research by funding or sponsoring academic research.

Most of the major accounting firms have established foundations to fund research projects in accounting and auditing theory and practice. Generally, the sponsoring firm agrees to contribute a certain amount each year to the foundation, to be used for research projects. The foundation's board must then select appropriate proposals for research projects that appear to have potential for expansion of knowledge about a particular aspect of accounting or auditing.

Many professional organizations also provide funds to support academic accounting and auditing research. The AICPA has long been an active sponsor, funding the Accounting Research Studies and, subsequently, the Auditing Research Monographs. The Planning Executives Institute and the Financial Executives Institute have also been active in sponsoring accounting and financial and business-planning research, publishing the results of that research. The National Associa-

---

[2] Some of this research is performed by academics engaged by CPA firms and associations, but it will be oriented generally to current professional practice issues as determined by its sponsors.

tion of Accountants has sponsored extensive research, concentrating on management accounting.

ACCOUNTING STANDARD SETTING—THE FASB

By its very nature, the FASB is a research organization because it sets standards for financial accounting and reporting. The FASB needs and depends on its own research activities as well as those of outsiders, and much of this research culminates in the issuance of authoritative pronouncements.

A formal research group within the staff acts as a focal point for the development of standards. As projects arise, a project manager and team are assigned to develop a proposal for consideration by the Board. In conceiving and designing the proposal, the project team draws on its fundamental knowledge and the results of prior research.

If the Board accepts the proposal, the project team carries on with its research efforts throughout the due-process procedures for developing a new standard (see Chapter 40). The writing of the discussion memorandum requires a detailed analysis of existing relevant literature. The project team may need to research existing practice or schedule discussions with individuals experienced in the project area. Other important research information may be uncovered in responses to the discussion memorandum or in documents and comments obtained in the public hearing.

Two members of the Board's staff advise the project team throughout their research. The first is the project consultant, whose primary assignment is another study; he can thus bring an outside perspective to the project development. The other is the in-house research specialist. Like an internal auditor, the research specialist draws on his technical knowledge to review the project approach and suggests improvements. The in-house research specialist reports periodically to the Board on the quality of the ongoing projects and recommends ways of making the research program more effective.

The research specialist also edits the *FASB Research Report* series and advises the Board on results of studies and their implications for FASB policy decisions. The research specialist may suggest new investigations into topics discussed in research reports.

Influencing Standard Setting

To provide the standard-setting group with input in developing standards and to protect the interests of their memberships, some professional organizations have established a formal mechanism to respond to proposals issued by the FASB (and other groups).

Professional Organizations. Between 1959 and 1973 the APB functioned as the primary accounting standard-setting group. Its technical research arm, the Accounting Research Division of the AICPA, was created in the hope that its studies would be adopted by the APB. Although this did not happen directly, the research activities proved to be useful in the formulation of APB pronouncements. The

Accounting Research Division ultimately issued fifteen Accounting Research Studies, authored by different individuals.

Currently the Accounting Standards Executive Committee of the AICPA (Ac-SEC) carries on accounting research, issuing statements of position on accounting issues that are often industry-related.

These statements are recommendations to the FASB and do not have the authority of an FASB pronouncement. However, under SFAS 32 (AC 1052) most SOPs are deemed to establish preferability for purposes of making accounting changes (AC 1052.10).

The National Association of Accountants (NAA) has designated their Management Accounting Practices (MAP) Committee as the mechanism for communications with the FASB. The MAP Committee has also met with the FASB to discuss the standard-setting process and how the NAA can contribute more directly to the process, beyond its role of providing research data through responses to proposed pronouncements. The MAP Committee also comments on proposals by the SEC and the AICPA.

The comments of the Financial Executives Institute to the FASB are developed by its Committee on Corporate Reporting. Similarly, the Financial Analysts Federation has designated its Financial Accounting Policy Committee to comment on FASB proposals and the proposals of other bodies.

These and many other organizations also influence standard setting by alerting their members to proposed standards. This stimulates direct commentary to the standard-setting group by those whose accounting or reporting may be directly affected.

CPA Firms. CPA firms are vitally concerned with the standard-setting process. Since the CPA firm will be, ultimately, the initial interpreter of any new standard (and perhaps the only one if the standard deals with auditing), the firm will want the new standard to be as clear as possible and will therefore comment on proposals.

Once standards have been issued, the CPA firm becomes involved with implementation. Generally, firms issue internal policies and guidelines concerning new standards, and these necessarily require a degree of research. Later, as both clients and the firm become more familiar with the standard and have had experience applying it, the firm may wish to modify the initial policies and guidelines. Research efforts will again play an important role in the formulation of the revisions. All along, the firm may be commenting to the FASB about the need for standards revisions or formal interpretations.

A number of large industrial corporations also maintain research staffs to respond to standard-setting and regulatory initiatives and to test the impact of new accounting proposals on their operations.

AUDITING STANDARD SETTING

The establishment of auditing standards (discussed in Chapter 11) has traditionally been vested in the AICPA. Since these standards apply only to those who practice in the auditing profession, interest by those outside the profession arose only infrequently in the past. In recent years greater concern has been expressed by those not directly affected, partly because of increased audit fees that have accompanied the implementation of new audit standards. Some concern also stems from the belief that business failures ought to be predictable through adequate auditing.

During the past decade, disclosures of massive fraud, which often led to the ultimate collapse of an entity, have helped make the public more aware of auditing issues. Congress and the SEC specifically have taken an intense interest in the development of auditing standards. Finally, the proliferation of professional accounting pronouncements during the last few years has required the development of additional auditing procedures and new auditor reporting standards.

AICPA

Although the promulgation of auditing standards is one of the most important functions of the AICPA, the amount of effort devoted to auditing research has not been significant. In 1969 the AICPA established an auditing research function, which provides research to support the activities of the group promulgating auditing standards, now called the Auditing Standards Board. The auditing research function has also published two monographs, *The Auditor's Reporting Obligation* (Carmichael, 1978), and *Behavior of Major Statistical Estimators in Sampling Accounting Populations* (Neter and Loebbecke, 1975).

Other Groups

Additional auditing standards research has been provided by accounting firms, both through participation in the Auditing Standards Board and its predecessors and through responses to auditing standards proposals. The firms' contribution to auditing standard setting is described in a subsequent section.

The Commission on Auditors' Responsibilities, popularly known as the Cohen Commission, evaluated the auditing standard-setting process and recommended improvements (CAR, 1978). The commission drew from many different sources, including a number of research projects that it commissioned. Some of these projects were never completed (e.g., the project to study the effectiveness of auditor reporting on uncertainties). Others were only analytical approaches, designed to highlight areas of future study.

AREAS OF RESEARCH

Perhaps the most complex research task is the resolution of accounting, auditing, and reporting problems that are not specifically dealt with in authoritative pronouncements. These issues may be specific to a given company or common among many companies, and can arise from many different sources. For example, a new professional pronouncement invariably generates application questions and problems. Or changes in business practices and shifts in the general economic environment may bring about a new emphasis in the reporting area and cause new accounting problems. All of these issues must be dealt with initially by the reporting enterprise and by its CPA firm.

ample SFAS 5, *Accounting for Contingencies* (AC 4311). Others are written very much like a rule book, for example SFAS 13, *Accounting for Leases* (AC 4053).

Because these pronouncements are subject to differing interpretations, many CPA firms prepare material to help their staffs and clients apply them. Preparing interpretive material always requires a degree of research. Initially, the preparers may study background material that was used by the standard-setting body. Comments by the members of the standard-setting group may also aid in explaining the application or intent of a particular part of the standard; and comments to the standards group can alert them to problems that may have to be dealt with formally. Finally, the firm can confer with its own members, particularly specialists in an industry the standard directly affects.

Standards change, and professional practice firms have to update their interpretive materials. In doing so they will rely heavily on the firm's experience in applying the standard. Thus the firm's own past decisions regarding its clients, as well as precedents derived from public financial statements, will be drawn on. The firm may very well choose to discuss these internal decisions with other major firms in order to assure a degree of interfirm consistency or to resolve an intramural debate.

Lack of Authoritative Literature. Many areas in accounting are not directly discussed in authoritative or semiauthoritative literature. The professional practice firm must study these areas to provide timely guidance to its staff. Often the firm expresses only a preference, and may acknowledge that other accounting methods are acceptable; but sometimes a treatment is mandated, with no other accounting acceptable.

In formulating its position, the firm must study current practice to analyze alternative treatments and distinguish among fact patterns that call for dissimilar accounting. Analogies may also be drawn between the issue under consideration and similar transactions already encompassed by authoritative literature. Discussions of the issue appearing in professional journals and other firms' position papers may be used in reaching a conclusion.

The maintenance of these internal positions on an ongoing basis is important to a CPA firm. Where no specified GAAP requirements exist, practice tends to change more readily and therefore should be monitored closely; this should include a review of technical journals.

Consultation. Where the professional practice firm has been able to maintain an up-to-date reference system, engagement management can often resolve a specific client question or problem by combining the materials prepared by their firm with their own knowledge and experience. Sometimes, however, the engagement management will consult with others in accordance with their firm's established consultation policies, especially if the transaction is unusual, if they cannot locate any relevant material, or where the accounting principle is rapidly evolving. This last situation is exemplified in accounting for leases: companies are structuring the terms of their leases to achieve a desired result under SFAS 13 (AC 4053) at the same time the FASB is interpreting and amending that statement in response to questions and problems raised.

In order to fill this need, CPA firms have established groups and designated individuals devoted solely or primarily to research and consultation. The large firms have some type of centralized research group,[4] although the responsibilities and functions of the groups vary. In some firms, the research group itself only provides examples on request—other firm members work with engagement management in finding a solution to the accounting or reporting problem. In other firms, the research group participates coequally with engagement management to the extent that in designated matters neither can mandate a solution without the concurrence of the other. The types of research tools utilized by these groups are described in a subsequent section.

For a more extensive discussion of the functioning of these groups, see the article by Boley and Danos (1980), "Centralized Research in CPA Firms."

Auditing Procedures Problems

Generally, the research effort in specific audits on the proper application of audit procedures is kept internal, and the client may not even be aware that an auditing problem is under discussion. However, there is no reason clients cannot involve themselves in the audit research if they wish.

Industry Audit Approach Consultation. When first engaged by a client in a new industry, particularly one with unusual characteristics, the engagement management may not be familiar with the characteristics and peculiarities of the industry and therefore may first have to research both the industry and the client. For background material, engagement management can examine relevant books and other reference materials. If this material contains detailed audit procedures specifically tailored to the industry, these procedures can provide a foundation on which to build the audit approach appropriate to the new client. If additional guidance is necessary, engagement management usually finds it useful to obtain the help of a firm member who has experience with similar clients in the industry.

Central research groups also can be of some assistance in developing an approach to a specific audit, but the need for continual on-site consultation during the first audit tends to argue against the use of a central research group member in such a situation. When members of the central research group do not have a depth of current experience in the specific industry being considered, they may call on the services of an otherwise uninvolved practice office partner or manager to work with the engagement personnel. Alternatively, the central research group may consult several experienced practice office partners or managers, and then synthesize their ideas and suggestions for use by the engagement management.

Specific Audit Consultation. Problems may arise in the application of specific audit steps because of conditions in the client's records, client reluctance to have certain procedures performed, or the need to issue a special report. These situations frequently require consultation outside the practice office.

In some firms, auditing and accounting consultation occurs within the same central group. In other firms, a specialized group may be established to deal ex-

---

[4] These central groups generally cover a wide range of technical areas, not only research, and in some firms they are also located regionally.

clusively with various auditing issues. Regardless of the structuring of the firm, the discussions tend to move rapidly away from the generalities of GAAS and focus on the specifics of the audit situation. In such cases, the application of mature judgment and experience becomes of paramount importance.

In establishing unified audit procedures and practices, some firms have mandated the application of certain procedures that are not specifically detailed by generally accepted auditing standards. When a client objects to the performance of such proprietary procedures, firm policies often require consultation with a designated group, usually the central technical group. This central group will usually have sufficient experience and authority to consider the problem in light of previous decisions and, if warranted, to modify the prescribed procedure. Such mandatory consultation has the advantage of facilitating communication of alternative approaches that have proved effective in parallel situations. It also makes possible the maintenance of a consistent audit approach should the firm decide to modify its current audit procedure requirements.

Application of Sophisticated Audit Tools. Encompassed in this category are statistical sampling procedures and timesharing (Chapter 14), procedures to audit in a computer environment, and utilization of computer software to perform certain audit procedures (Chapter 15). Firms generally have a department devoted to the development of sophisticated audit tools. In some firms, problems in applying these tools in a specific audit situation are directed to the firm units responsible for their development; in others, such questions may be directed to designated individuals in the central research group. The more likely research consultants will be practice office personnel experienced in the application of such tools. Because of the specialized problems that can arise during an audit in a computer environment, it is imperative that the individuals consulted be more than computer technicians understanding only the hardware and software; the techniques and objectives of the audit itself must be understood.

The application of statistical sampling to specific audit situations may again require consultation with others who have particular expertise in the sampling field. For problems encountered by auditors in sampling accounting populations, see Auditing Research Monograph No. 2, *Behavior of Major Statistical Estimators in Sampling Accounting Populations* (Neter and Loebbecke, 1975). This monograph underlines the scarcity of empirical research on certain statistical areas as well as the lack of systematic information about the characteristics of accounting populations. The auditor using statistical sampling should take note of these comments as well as the consultation process within his firm.

Accounting Theory Research

Research into the theory of accounting has traditionally been considered the province of academics. This conclusion is probably due to the lack of publicity about accounting firms' efforts in the area. Actually, there is a great deal of theoretical and a priori research being conducted by accounting firms.

Theoretical Research. Theoretical research by accounting firms has been spurred to some extent by a general inquiry into the objectives of financial statements and the conceptual framework for accounting and reporting (see Chapter 2). For example, in the early 1970s an analysis of this area led one firm to develop pioneer guidelines for information that would be more relevant to the users. The purpose of *"Relevant Accounting"* was to remedy many of the weaknesses in the historical cost accounting model by building a framework that would describe risk and return. This research project was carried out by the firm's central research staff in collaboration with two academicians, and resulted in an accounting model that utilized both exit values and use values. (For details, see Ronen and Sorter, 1972.)

Although this research project did not result in radical changes, it was a precursor of significant theoretical accounting research projects undertaken in the late 1970s by many of the major accounting firms. Galvanized by a significant increase in the rate of inflation, and recognizing that the historical cost model may no longer be valid in an inflationary era and in fact may produce misleading results, several firms tried to devise alternative accounting and reporting models that would realistically portray the financial condition and results of management decisions. Some firms also sought to encompass a new information model that would be more predictive than the historical cost model. Although the stimulus for the research arose from a common source, there was a lack of unanimity in the conclusions.

Some firms built on the prior research on "Relevant Accounting" and espoused forms of current value accounting and reporting. Others, reacting to inflationary conditions, advocated a price-level adjustment form of accounting. Significant experimentation by accounting firms has been conducted in the attempt to design a workable supplemental or alternative accounting model, and the results have been provided to the FASB to help them define a logical conceptual framework.

Other Research. Professional practice firms also undertake research projects in order to prepare responses to FASB discussion memoranda and exposure drafts. These commentaries bring the current working experience of the firm relative to the issues under consideration by the FASB. Necessarily, the responses reflect an a priori bias based on previous decisions regarding the situations addressed in the discussion memorandum. The bias is not all bad, however, because the responding firm may be able to describe specific implementation problems foreseen in the suggested approach. Thus, the research efforts in writing such papers necessarily focus on determining the current state of accounting in the particular area and commenting on the appropriateness of one or more of the suggested alternatives proposed by the discussion memorandum. The firm may also want to assess the reasonableness of the proposed accounting treatments by determining what effect they would have on the financial statements of clients—the does-it-make-sense approach.

The professional practice firm may also need to prepare position papers when the accounting methods used in a client's financial statements are challenged by an outside body such as the SEC or the AICPA's Practice Review Committee or when a client asks to have an accounting treatment explained. These situations almost invariably arise because the accounting literature is unclear or because alternative treatments seem to be available. In such cases, it is frequently necessary to draw analogies and to describe the probable results of alternative approaches, demonstrating that the firm's conclusion is the appropriate one.

Auditing Theory Research

Professional practice firms conduct significant research in the area of audit techniques. Yet, because much of this research is directed toward improved audit techniques for internal use, the results are not widely publicized.

New Audit Approaches. It has been said that the primary output of an audit— the auditor's report on the financial statements—has a relatively low level of utility to the client. Audits are frequently conducted because of government (principally SEC) mandates or because of outside demands from creditors and potential creditors. A prime example of this exists in government. Until the passage of the Revenue Sharing Act, the vast majority of municipalities felt no need for an audit of their financial statements. The act, however, mandated an audit as a condition of receiving revenue-sharing funds. When the audit is looked on simply as an expedient regulatory obstacle, the professional practice firm is constantly being pressured to reduce the cost of the audit and, hence, the fee.

In recent years, recognizing that an evaluation of audit techniques and approach was overdue, several of the major firms undertook projects to reevaluate their audit approach and documentation requirements and devise different methods of performing an audit. The mandates for accurate accounting and control contained in the Foreign Corrupt Practices Act stimulated the development of new audit approaches. In some instances, the reevaluation process resulted in the conclusion that one could audit more effectively by applying risk evaluation to the various elements of the financial statements. This research project eventually led to a redesigned overall audit approach and defined a revised audit process comprising a series of logical sequential steps.

Of course, when the research group decides to make significant changes in the audit approach, they must run rigorous field tests of their proposed methodology before attempting to implement it. Should they decide to implement the new approach, their next objective will be writing a set of guidelines so that firm members will understand how to audit under the new system and why this new approach is more accurate and logical than the old one.

As an aside, some firms believe that the development of an improved audit approach is important for their image; advertising material has been built around how the firm approaches an audit. Thus, the audit approach has been used as a way for a firm to differentiate its services from those of its competitors.

Professors in Residence. Several firms have found an academically related program an effective means of accomplishing audit methodology research. This program brings the talents of an academician, called a professor in residence or professorial research associate or something similar, together with those of the members of the firm. If properly administered, this arrangement can produce extensive research. From the viewpoint of the academician, it provides an opportunity for fresh insight into the problems of the practice and allows him to test theoretical approaches in a real-world environment. From the viewpoint of the firm, the program can provide an independent challenge to their thinking. At a more practical level, the program also allows the firm to exploit talents that would be unavailable on a full-time basis and to secure the manpower needed for specific tasks to which the firm might have been unable to devote adequate time.

This program must be carefully structured in order for it to succeed and to provide an enriching and satisfying experience for the professor in residence. Before starting such a program, a firm must ask itself what it wishes to achieve and carefully outline how it plans to achieve it. These objectives should be discussed with candidates for the program in order to see whether the project is feasible and of interest to the academicians. The background and talents of a prospective candidate should be reviewed and matched with the objectives. Finally, the firm should be prepared to set aside sufficient personnel time for working with the academician. It must be kept in mind at every stage of the program that close interaction is vital to both the success of the research and the morale of the professor in residence.

Results of Audit Research Projects. The results of audit research projects can take many forms. As indicated above, one type of project may result in a significant change to the way in which the firm performs its audits and documents its results. More often, however, audit research projects are undertaken to explore certain aspects of the audit process in depth, reinvestigate the efficacy of certain procedures, or review past conclusions reached because a particular procedure was used. Frequently the results of this research are published in books or articles. A collaboration between the researcher and a practicing accountant (auditor) often synergistically results in a conclusion or model that has a practical application or raises effective challenges to current audit processes. Auditing Research Monograph No. 2 (Neter and Loebbecke, 1975) is an example of this type of collaboration.

As previously suggested, the extent of research in auditing has not been overwhelming. In recognition of this gap, in 1976 Peat, Marwick, Mitchell & Co. published a booklet, *Research Opportunities in Auditing,* describing in some depth various areas in which research would be of benefit. The range of topics included an expression of a need for research to better understand the fundamental role of auditing in our society as well as a need to examine in depth the various functions encompassed by contemporary auditing. The study also examined current trends, and projected such trends into the future to suggest priorities within the lengthy listings of opportunities in audit research.

The Peat, Marwick study suggested that auditing research cannot be performed by either practicing auditors or academicians alone. Rather, it strongly urged that audit research be interdisciplinary, using the knowledge and skills of law, statistics and other quantitative methods, economics, the behavioral sciences, and engineering.

Another very important result of audit research was the *Report, Conclusions, and Recommendations* of the Commission on Auditors' Responsibilities (CAR, 1978). Accounting firms took part in research projects to assist the commission in fulfilling its assignment; this research, in almost every instance, suggested that a significant fertile field remained to be explored by audit researchers.

Business Problems Research

In recent years, professional practice firms have conducted research projects or studies in areas of general business problems. In some respects the firms are uniquely qualified to perform such research: they have professional standing, a lack of ostensible bias, and an attitude of independence.

Many of these projects involve surveys to obtain and summarize factual information. To the extent that such information is not public, the practice firms may be able to obtain it more readily because of confidence by business that the information will be kept confidential. In addition, the experience of the firms in analyzing business and financial trends adds credibility to the conclusions drawn from the data and hence increases the willingness of business to provide needed data.

The types of problems included in such research projects are varied. For example, a project may measure the economic health of specific municipalities and identify characteristics predictive of future financial problems, or survey corporate boards of directors to find out how board members view their responsibilities and how such responsibilities might be changed. These types of projects, focused as they tend to be on matters directly relevant to how businesses operate, also tend to improve the quality of audits in providing additional information to aid the auditor in understanding his clients and the environment in which they operate.

RESEARCH TOOLS

In the preceding sections there have been several references to the need for the researcher to clearly understand and analyze appropriate professional literature and to utilize precedent. There are a number of tools, some of them created only in the last few years, that have greatly enhanced the ability of the researcher to locate examples and retrieve data.

National Automated Accounting Research System

One of the most exciting developments in research in the past decade has been the implementation of the National Automated Accounting Research System, or NAARS. NAARS comprises the accounting and auditing segment of a computer system known as LEXIS, which also has extensive legal and tax research information. NAARS was developed in 1972 through the joint efforts of the Information Retrieval Committee of the AICPA and Mead Data Central, Inc. Contained within the system, and accessible through terminals located in a subscriber's office, is a continually updated file of financial statements, notes thereto, and auditors' reports taken from the published annual reports of some 4,000 major public companies. In addition, the database contains most of the authoritative accounting and auditing pronouncements of the FASB, the AICPA, the Cost Accounting Standards Board, the SEC, and the International Accounting Standards Committee.

Unlike most other systems for information retrieval, NAARS research does not depend on the use of an index. Rather, the full text of the document is included in the database and is searchable by the researcher. In order to retrieve or locate a particular item, the researcher inputs the words or phrases that he expects would be used in the relevant documents. The computer then searches the database and produces a list of documents that contain those words or phrases. Even more important, the NAARS system is interactive, i.e., the researcher can review the results of his initial search (the full text of the retrieved material is shown on a video display screen (cathode ray tube—CRT)—see Figure 49.1—

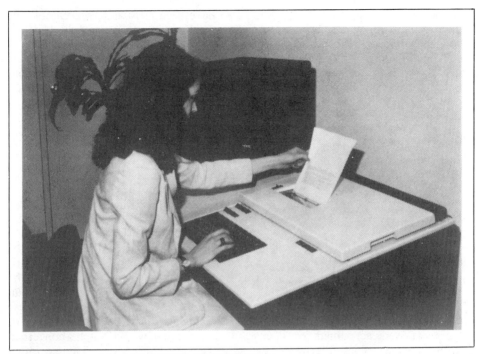

FIGURE 49.1   NAARS/LEXIS CONSOLE

which is part of the unit in the subscriber's office), modify it, and obtain a revised search. This procedure can be repeated as often as needed.

NAARS is available for specific research requests through the AICPA. Rates charged depend on the amount of computer time expended and are very reasonable, particularly in relation to the vast volume of material available for searching.

Illustration of NAARS Research. A U.S. company has an investment of 40% in a foreign joint venture, accounted for on the equity method; the government of the foreign country owns the other 60%. The foreign country controls the board of directors of the joint venture, which has recently reduced the amount of dividends from at least 50% of the joint venture's earnings to less than 25%. The U.S. company believes it is no longer in a position to exert "significant influence" over the joint venture and that, even though it owns at least 20%—the point at which APB 18 (AC 5131) deems "significant influence" exists—it should now account for its investment at cost rather than on the equity method. The U.S. company wants to locate other companies that account for investments greater than 20% on the cost method.

NAARS search strategy. It was decided to search the annual report (AR) file, which includes all annual reports in the NAARS database from July 1, 1977, through June 30, 1979. (At the publication date of this book, the database for the year July 1, 1979, through June 30, 1980, was in the process of being created and was not fully operational.) It would also have been possible to search only the annual reports for either July 1, 1977, through June 30, 1978, or July 1, 1978, through June 30, 1979.

NAARS attempts to include in its AR files all companies traded on the New York and American Stock Exchanges as well as a substantial sample of companies traded over the counter. In total there are about 8,000 annual reports included in the AR files—approximately 4,000 for each of the last two years.

Most NAARS searches of the AR file will be directed to the notes to the financial statements. These are searched and designated by the segment term "FTNT." Other components of the annual report are segmented on NAARS as shown in Figure 49.2.

The advantage of having these components segmented is that the research may focus on one or two components of the reports in which the desired information is likely to occur rather than on the whole report. This reduces computer time, the time the researcher spends in interpreting the data, and the chances for irrelevant responses.

The next step is to decide which words or phrases most likely describe the situation being researched. For this problem the researcher chose several elements, having decided that (1) either the term "cost method" or "cost basis" would be included in the footnotes along with (2) the terms "at least 20%," "greater than 20%" or "more than 20%," or "over 20%" or "above 20%." Together, these elements would describe situations where investments of from 20% to 49% of an investee were accounted for at cost. The researcher would not be concerned with investments of less than 20%, because these are ordinarily accounted for at cost. Similarly, the researcher would not be concerned with investments of greater than 50%, because these would be subsidiaries that would almost invariably be either consolidated or carried on the equity method, and also because control is almost always present where ownership is greater than 50%. The search request is illustrated below in Figure 49.3. Notice that the search request starts with FTNT. This directs NAARS to search only the notes to the financial statements, not any other components. W/15 tells NAARS that the terms immediately preceding and following it within the parentheses should be within 15 words of each other. This "connector" is used to further limit the search and provide the researcher only with material which is potentially useful. The researcher could, of course, increase the number of words to 20 (W/20), 30 (W/30), or any other number, or decrease them; this is a matter of judgment. Also notice that the percentages from 21 to 29 are individually cited, whereas the percentages from 30 to 39 and 40 to 49 use the "universal character" (*). This tells NAARS to include all examples with a two-digit percentage that starts with either a 3 or a 4. (The same technique could have been used for percentages from 20 to 29 but was not, because the researcher felt this would have retrieved statements including such phrases as "owned less than 20% accounted for on the cost method," which would have been irrelevant and may have been numerous. The researcher decided not to try to retrieve companies exactly 20% owned that are accounted for on the cost method, both because he considered these to be marginal situations that would not prove the point of the research and because he wanted to avoid the irrelevant items this search strategy would have retrieved.) A similar character is available to provide words with any ending. For example, if the researcher wanted the search request to include the terms "consolidate," "consolidated," "consolidating," or

Components	NAARS Segment Term Code
General information	
Name of company	CO
SIC code	SIC
Stock exchange	EXCH
Type of document	DOC
Date of balance sheet	DB/S
Auditor	AUD
Total assets	ASET
Net worth	N/W
Total sales	SALS
Net income or loss	N/I
Comments	COM
Type of financial statements	TYP
Fortune index	FORTN
Balance sheet	
Balance sheet	B/S
Title (balance sheet)	TITLE-B/S
Current assets	CURA
Noncurrent assets	NCURA
Unclassified assets	UNCLA
Total assets	TASET
Current liabilities	CURL
Noncurrent liabilities, credits, and minority interests	NCURL
Unclassified liabilities	UNCLL
Total liabilities	TLIAB
Stockholders' equity	EQUIT
Total liabilities and stockholders' equity	TLSE
Statement of income	
Statement of income	I/S
Title (income)	TITLE-I/S
Income before extraordinary items	IBEI
Extraordinary items and accounting changes	EXTOR
Net income or loss	INC
Earnings per share	EPSH
Capital changes	
Statement of capital changes	CAPCHG
Funds statement	
Funds statement	F/S
Title (funds statement)	TITLE-F/S
Funds provided	PROV
Funds used	USD
Components of change	COMP
Footnotes	
Footnotes (Also, Note 1 thru Note 40)	FTNT
Title of notes to financial statement or financial review	TITLE-FTNT
Auditor's report	REPRT
Realized and unrealized losses on investments	INVGN

FIGURE 49.2   NAARS ANNUAL REPORT COMPONENTS

```
YOUR SEARCH REQUEST IS:
FTNT ((COST METHOD OR COST BASIS) W/15 (GREATER THAN 20%
    OR MORE THAN 20% OR OVER 20% OR ABOVE 20% OR 21% OR 22%
    OR 23% OR 24% OR 25% OR 26% OR 27% OR 28% OR 29% OR 3X%
    OR 4X%))
AND FOREIGN OPERATIONS
```

FIGURE 49.3 ILLUSTRATIVE NAARS SEARCH REQUEST

"consolidation," he would input "CONSOLIDAT!" The "super universal character" (!) directs NAARS to include any words that begin with "consolidat" no matter how they end. (NAARS automatically searches the plural of a word if the plural is formed by either "s" or "ies").

NAARS will next tell the researcher how many examples from the AR file satisfy the search request. In this case there were 32. This is a remarkable feature of NAARS. The researcher now knows with certainty that only 32 of over 8,000 annual reports have the combination of words that he considers likely to disclose instances of an investment of at least 20% and less than 50% accounted for at cost rather than on the equity method as is customary under AC 5131. Similarly, he also knows that the remaining companies do not meet this search criteria. The researcher can justifiably state that he has performed a search of over 8,000 reports—a volume that would be almost impossible to tackle manually.

Of course, there may be other ways to phrase this disclosure in an annual report. Here the skill of the researcher becomes vital, because he must use his expertise in reporting and his knowledge of the accounting issue to come up with the best search strategies.

After NAARS tells the researcher that it has 32 reports that satisfy the search request, the researcher has several options. He may direct NAARS to display on the CRT cites of the 32 companies, which include the company's name, SIC code, where its stock is traded, the date of the financial statements, and the name of the company's auditors. The researcher can then obtain hard copy of some or all of the reports or use NAARS to generate further information. The researcher has three options:

1. FULL. The full text of the annual report is displayed on the CRT. This option is seldom used, because it requires the researcher to review too much information—most of which will be irrelevant. Even with only 32 reports out of 8,000, the researcher wants to make optimal use of his time.
2. SELECT. This enables the researcher to direct NAARS to display a particular segment of the financial statements. These are the same as the components of the annual reports that may be searched as shown in Figure 49.2. When using the SELECT feature, the researcher will almost always want to direct NAARS to display the segment that it has searched—in this case, the notes to the financial statements.
3. KWIC. This enables the researcher to direct NAARS to display the words from the report that satisfied the search request as well as a few words before and after. KWIC can be expanded to include as many as 999 words before and after those satisfying the search request.

KWIC is by far the most widely used of the NAARS options, because it enables the researcher to quickly review the relevant part of each of the 32 reports and the context in which each disclosure is made. Figure 49.4 illustrates four examples that satisfied the search request that the researcher—after reviewing the material displayed by NAARS—believed would be of interest to the U.S. company. These were printed immediately by the hard-copy printer of the NAARS console.

Each of these reports discloses an investment of greater than 20% accounted for on the cost method. The researcher may go to hard copy or microfiche of the annual report for further information or expand the NAARS disclosures using FULL or SELECT.

Financial Report Surveys

From time to time the AICPA publishes *Financial Report Surveys,* primarily based on information filed in the NAARS database. These are a quick and handy source of reference in specific areas and might obviate the need for a complete NAARS search in resolving a problem. Topics covered include such matters as accounting for uncertainties, disclosure of related-party transactions, and examples of reports by management on its responsibility for financial statements. A complete listing of the 21 surveys released through early 1980 can be found in the consolidated bibliography in this *Handbook.*

Accountants' Index

For many years, the *Accountants' Index* was the only good index to accounting literature. This publication, prepared by the AICPA, indexes articles from many professional journals, books, and other material of interest to accountants under fairly broad subject headings. Like all indexes, its usefulness depends to a great extent on the skills of the indexer and the ability of the user to review fairly large amounts of data in order to locate material of interest. This index has been in existence for at least 40 years and is probably the most widely known of all non-computerized accounting research tools.

AICPA Index

In 1977 the Information Retrieval Committee of the AICPA, recognizing that the explosion of literature had made it increasingly difficult to locate all pertinent data, undertook a project to explore various systems for indexing. The goal of the committee was to produce an index that would encompass all authoritative and semiauthoritative literature, a document that heretofore had not existed.

After exploring various systems, the committee determined that a system developed by Price Waterhouse & Co. for internal use was the most useful system in existence. The basis of the system is a form of coordinate indexing, in which material is indexed under a string of terms and additional explanatory material can be added to the index string itself to further describe the contents of a particular item. A cross-referencing of index terms is also included, so the user is directed to other terms that are narrower or broader than the term with which he begins.

LEVEL 1 - 3 OF 32 REPORTS

THE WILLIAMS COMPANIES 331 NYSE ANNUAL REPORT DEC. 31, 1978 ARTHUR YOUNG & COMPANY 201

NOTE-1:
...SUBSIDIARIES. COMPANIES ENGAGED IN REAL ESTATE ACTIVITIES AND COMPANIES IN WHICH WILLIAMS AND ITS SUBSIDIARIES OWN 20% TO 50% OF THE VOTING COMMON STOCK ARE ACCOUNTED FOR UNDER THE EQUITY METHOD, EXCEPT FOR A 25% OWNED FERTILIZER COMPANY IN THE REPUBLIC OF KOREA WHICH IS ACCOUNTED FOR UNDER THE COST METHOD. THE COST METHOD IS USED BECAUSE WILLIAMS DOES NOT HAVE THE ABILITY TO EXERCISE SUFFICIENT INFLUENCE OVER OPERATING AND FINANCIAL POLICIES OF THE COMPANY TO WARRANT APPLICATION OF THE EQUITY METHOD.

LEVEL 1 - 9 OF 32 REPORTS

QUESTOR CORPORATION 371 NYSE ANNUAL REPORT FOR DEC 31, 1978 PEAT, MARWICK, MITCHELL & CO. 411

NOTE-10:
...SPANISH ASSOCIATED COMPANIES AND INSTALLED NEW MANAGEMENT. AS A RESULT OF THE INCREASE IN OWNERSHIP AND NEW MANAGEMENT, THE COMPANY NOW HAS BOTH FINANCIAL AND OPERATING CONTROL OF THESE COMPANIES. THE PREVIOUS INVESTMENT IN THESE COMPANIES RANGED FROM 38% TO 85% AND WAS ACCOUNTED FOR BY THE EQUITY METHOD FROM 1975 TO 1977 AND BY THE COST METHOD PRIOR TO 1975. BECAUSE OF THE 1978 INVESTMENT CHANGES (OWNERSHIP NOW RANGES FROM 60% TO 100%) AND THE ATTAINMENT OF OPERATING CONTROL, THESE COMPANIES ARE CONSOLIDATED FOR THE FIRST TIME IN 1978.

LEVEL 1 - 25 OF 32 REPORTS

EG & G, INC. 366 NYSE ANNUAL REPORT JAN 1, 1978 ARTHUR ANDERSEN & CO. 578

NOTE-7:
(CONSPOL, RECLAS)

(7) OTHER ASSETS

THE PRINCIPAL ITEMS INCLUDED IN OTHER ASSETS ARE INVESTMENTS.

THE COMPANY OWNS 24% OF THE COMMON STOCK OF NIPPON SEALOL CO., LTD. DURING 1977, THE COMPANY ADOPTED THE COST METHOD OF ACCOUNTING FOR THIS INVESTMENT. AS A RESULT OF ADOPTING THAT METHOD, THE COMPANY DID NOT RECOGNIZE ITS EQUITY ($219,000) IN THE EARNINGS OF NIPPON SEALOL IN 1977. THE COMPANY'S EQUITY IN THE REPORTED NET ASSETS OF NIPPON SEALOL AS OF SEPTEMBER 30, 1977 EXCEEDS THE CARRYING VALUE (APPROXIMATELY $1,500,000) OF THE INVESTMENT AT JANUARY 1, 1978.

THE COMPANY HAS AN $865,000 INVESTMENT IN MEDICAL INFORMATION TECHNOLOGY, INC. WHICH CONSISTS OF CONVERTIBLE PREFERRED STOCK. (IN DECEMBER, 1977, THE COMPANY AGREED TO SELL ITS ...

LEVEL 1 - 32 OF 32 REPORTS

INTERNATIONAL RECTIFIER CORPORATION 366 NYSE ANNUAL REPORT JUL. 2, 1978 COOPERS & LYBRAND

NOTE-1:
... EACH COUNTRY. INTERCOMPANY TRANSACTIONS BETWEEN MARCH 31 AND THE COMPANY'S FISCAL YEAR-END ARE ELIMINATED. EFFECTIVE JANUARY 2, 1978 THE INVESTMENT IN THE JAPANESE ASSOCIATE COMPANY, IN WHICH THE COMPANY OWNS A 33% INTEREST, IS REPORTED ON THE COST BASIS OF ACCOUNTING. PRIOR TO JANUARY 1978, THE INVESTMENT HAD BEEN REPORTED ON THE EQUITY BASIS. (SEE FOREIGN OPERATIONS NOTE FOR FURTHER DISCUSSION.)

FIGURE 49.4 EXAMPLE OF KWIC CITES PRINTED OUT

A major advantage of this system is that a software package has been developed to process the material prepared by the indexer and to explode entries so that a single indexing by the indexer will result in several entries in the final index. In addition, the index can be carried in a briefcase and thus can serve as a reference tool for the auditor working in the client's office.

Some of the major firms have found this indexing system to be very useful in indexing their own internal literature. Using the AICPA's computer software, it is possible to produce a combined index to both internal and external literature. In addition, the software allows for the inclusion of additional index terms, so an individual firm can add terms to fit its needs.

A large proportion of the index references are to codification numbers in the *AICPA Professional Standards* series, a four volume work published in bound and loose leaf form by CCH. Most references in this *Handbook* to the codified literature use these AICPA codification numbers. The *Professional Standards* service and *Index to Accounting and Auditing Technical Pronouncements* can be purchased from the AICPA.

Disclosure Journal

A reference tool that has had a somewhat unstable career is the one produced by Disclosure, Inc. This company has a contract to produce microfiche copies of documents filed with the SEC for use in the SEC's reference rooms, and these fiche may be purchased on specific request or by bulk subscription. Disclosure, Inc. believed that a need existed for a way to access these documents other than by company name, and indexed these documents, including the financial statements, using fairly broad terms. Thus, accounting researchers were provided with another tool, prepared and issued monthly, for obtaining access to examples of accounting treatments and disclosures.

As with any index, the usefulness of the *Disclosure Journal* depended on the abilities of the indexers to properly identify and categorize the information in the filing. However, the index did include all companies filing with the SEC, making available a much larger population than could otherwise be used.

In 1976 production costs forced Disclosure, Inc. to discontinue its indexing efforts. Although no longer current, the index still serves as a valuable tool, particularly for researching in litigation situations where information concerning accounting or reporting practices extant during the time period may be available in the *Disclosure Journal.*

Disclosure, Inc. has indicated that revival of the index is under consideration. However, they propose to make it available in a computer database rather than in printed form. The database would be accessible through various timesharing services, possibly including Mead Data Central, and a user would thus need access to a computer terminal. The amount of information to be made available is not yet determined, nor is the extent of the indexing. Initially, it is expected that the file will include only a portion of the companies filing with the SEC. In addition, Disclosure, Inc. has made available a computer file that lists companies and the filings they have made with the SEC—10-Ks, 10-Qs, 8-Ks, registrations, etc. This is also a somewhat limited file.

Other Databases

In addition to the NAARS and Disclosure databases, there are other databases available on a subscription basis to accounting researchers through various time-sharing services. As mentioned earlier, Mead Data Central also has available a legal research library that includes tax law and cases (LEXIS). And news releases from wire services, magazines such as *Newsweek,* and newspapers such as the *Washington Post* are available on NEXIS. The *New York Times* Data Bank contains abstracts from many publications, including business and finance journals. The ABI/INFORM Library also contains a large number of abstracts from some 350 magazines and newspapers. This library encompasses a greater number of technical and professional journals than does the *New York Times* Data Bank. All of these databases except ABI/INFORM are accessible using the NAARS terminal (Figure 49.1). CCH also makes excerpts of important articles available through its *Accounting Articles* loose leaf service.

Firm Manuals and Guides

The practice firm researcher often has at his disposal significant research material in the form of manuals and guides, research papers, position papers, and documentation of decisions reached by his firm's central research groups, but accessing it may be difficult. As previously noted, some firms have prepared an index to internal materials using the AICPA Index. Other firms, however, recognizing the power of a full-text retrieval system, have utilized the system available through Mead Data Central, creating a private library that is an integral part of the total NAARS/LEXIS system. Thus, on a single search, the researcher can review not only public material but also the proprietary material of his own firm.

Consultation With Other Firms

Another research tool, which may not be widely known, is the process of consultation with other firms. This process is often a necessity when one firm wishes to follow an accounting treatment that appears in financial statements prepared by another practice firm.

Consultation can uncover data and audit peculiarities not appearing in the financial statements and will enable the firm to decide whether the original case is sufficiently comparable to serve as precedent.

Consultation with other firms is also useful when a firm is developing guidance for its members in areas not clearly covered by authoritative accounting literature. Exploring alternative treatments may shed additional light on a particular treatment. In addition, certain firms are recognized within the profession as having a particular expertise in a specific area of accounting theory or in a particular industry. For example, one firm has been recognized as having a unique familiarity with the theory underlying the tax allocation concepts expressed in APB 11 (AC 4091). Another firm is recognized as an authority in the savings and loan industry because it has many clients in that industry and many members active in industry committees and professional committees dealing with problems of that industry. Still other firms are recognized as having unique expertise in other specialized industries, such as oil and gas and public utilities.

HOW ACCOUNTING RESEARCH IS PERFORMED IN A CPA FIRM

The primary research function at Touche Ross & Co. is carried out by the firm's Research Associate, who reports to a partner of the National Accounting and Auditing Staff located in the Executive Office. An accountant working in a practice office may contact the Research Associate directly, or indirectly through a partner assigned to the National Staff, if he needs information within the Research Associate's domain of resources.

Request for Research

The Research Associate logs in the request by assigning it an identification number consisting of the year followed by the sequential number of the request during that year. He then elicits the inquirer's name and office and the client's name, for charging his own time and computer time. The researcher then asks the inquirer to describe his problem and to suggest terms or "buzz words" the inquirer feels might appear in the text, for possible use in a NAARS search. He also asks the type of information to be developed, such as literature or examples from annual or other reports, and how many examples are necessary. Finally the researcher and inquirer agree on a time for the research results to be made available, so the researcher can organize request priorities as well as meet the inquirer's time constraints.

The researcher then fills out a special summary form that, when typed, becomes the top sheet of the completed request, which eventually includes copies of all the information developed during the course of research on this problem. The Research Associate makes several decisions at this point:

1. Is this a bona fide request for research? Examples of nonresearch requests are those in which (a) the inquirer wants a particular filing of a given company, a specific article, or something not within the research domain of resources, such as a NAARS search of 8-Ks or annual report president's letters (these do not exist in the NAARS data bank) or (b) the inquiry is not related to accounting and auditing matters in a broad sense. In this case, the Research Associate may order reports from the firm's library to be delivered to the inquirer or inform the inquirer that the research cannot be done as formulated.

2. Is prior research available on this problem? If a search of prior research requests retrieves helpful information, these requests are loaned to the inquirer for his evaluation. He may decide that these prior results are sufficient, need updating, or are not germane.

3. Is the information requested unusual, or does it pertain to a sensitive area, such as litigation, potential mergers, or fraud? If the Research Associate feels uncertain as to

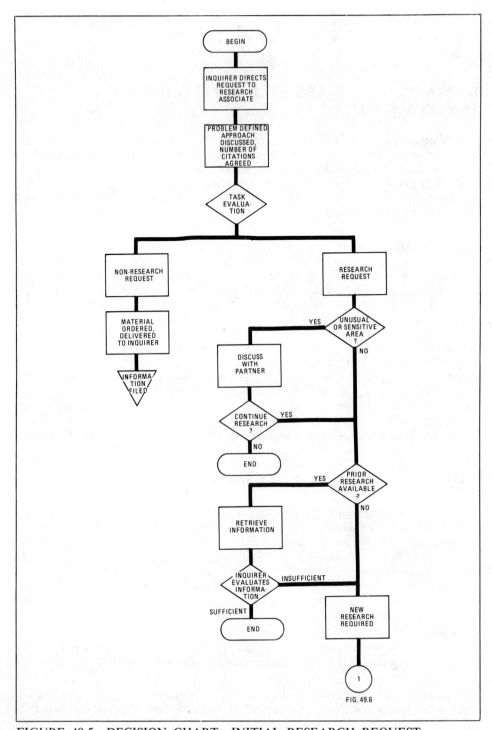

FIGURE 49.5   DECISION CHART—INITIAL RESEARCH REQUEST

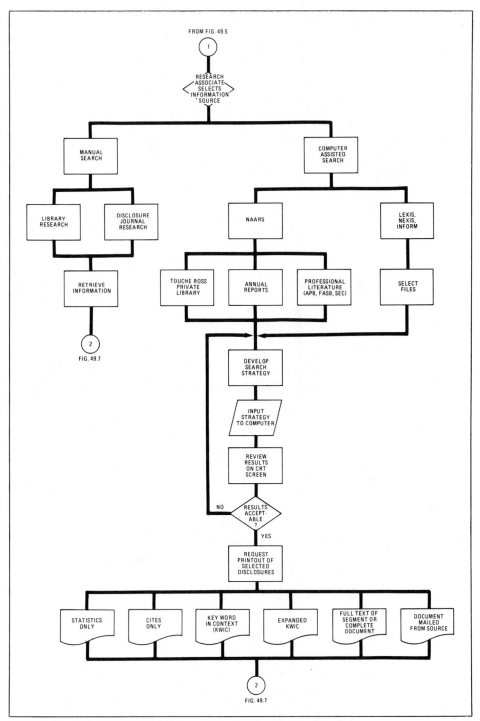

FIGURE 49.6   FLOWCHART—NEW RESEARCH

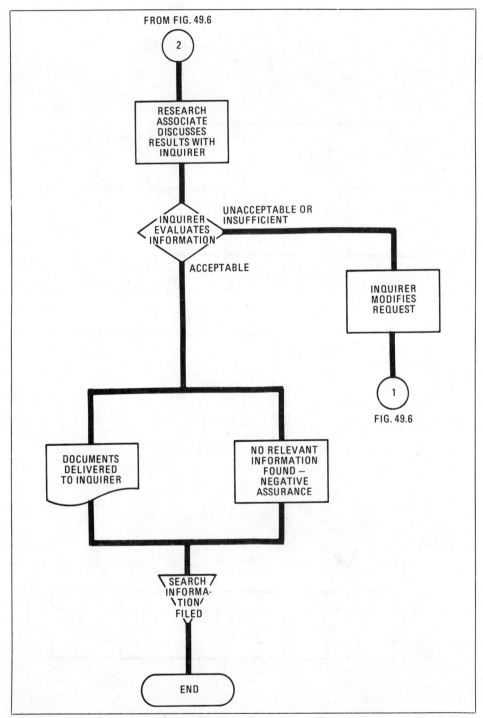

FIGURE 49.7   EVALUATING RESEARCH RESULTS

the propriety of doing this research, he may discuss the problem with a partner and obtain his approval.

Performing the Research

If new research is required, either because the problem has not been researched previously or because prior results are old or inadequate, the Research Associate then decides which resources to use. These may include any of the following:

1. NAARS, for disclosures from annual reports, authoritative accounting literature or proxies, or the firm's private information, in the manner previously described in this chapter;
2. *Disclosure Journal,* for examples from annual reports, 10-Ks, 8-Ks, prospectuses, or proxies from 1972 through 1975 (10-Ks through 1976);
3. LEXIS, for court cases, tax regulations, etc.;
4. INFORM, for articles from 350 periodicals;
5. NEXIS, for news releases from the wire services, magazines such as *Newsweek,* or newspapers such as the *Washington Post*; and
6. Library research, for information on company history, subsidiaries, indexes (e.g., *Wall Street Journal Index, Business Periodicals Index, Accountants' Index*), periodical articles, microfiche on all companies filing with the SEC, textbooks, authoritative literature, etc.

In performing *Disclosure Journal* research, the researcher determines the subject headings listed in the *Disclosure Journal* thesaurus that are pertinent and examines entries under a particular subject heading. These consist of the names of companies and associated other subject headings. The researcher determines which companies meet the criteria originally specified and then reviews microfiche or hard copy of the indicated reports to see if the indexed disclosure is relevant.

A LEXIS search of law and tax materials is performed in a manner similar to NAARS. An INFORM or NEXIS search is also performed by connecting key words likely to appear in the text of articles, inputting the search strategy to the computer, and reviewing the retrieved documents. The strategy may be modified or narrowed, and new results retrieved. The abstracts, articles, or cites may be printed at the console, or the entire article copied from the relevant periodical. INFORM and NEXIS actually are limited automated versions of the traditional library references, the *Business Periodicals Index* and the *Accountants' Index.*

Evaluating Findings

After the research results have been obtained to the satisfaction of the Research Associate, the final step is to discuss them with the original inquirer. The extent of the discussion is dependent on the complexity of the original problem, the uniqueness of descriptive wordings, the numbers and quality of disclosures retrieved, the materiality of the original problem, and the time pressures inherent in the problem.

Often the inquirer will accept NAARS printouts if they sufficiently describe the transaction or method or provide the necessary statistics. If nothing relevant is found, the researcher will explain the strategy to the inquirer to make sure that no alternative wordings were overlooked. This provides the inquirer with assurance that no disclosures of the type he has sought exist in the database (*negative assurance*).

The inquirer may be favorably impressed with the results and search the firm's microfiche files for the complete documents, including financial statements, footnotes, and auditor's report. Or sometimes the inquirer asks that the original criteria be modified (e.g., if he finds no examples for companies that are in the Fortune 500 or audited by Big Eight firms, he will accept smaller firms instead). Sometimes the inquirer comes up with new terminology describing the event or finds that the original objective was modified during discussions. Sometimes further information is needed to give the complete picture for a statistical presentation.

In any case, the inquirer has the final say as to whether the results are acceptable and whether modifications are necessary. However, when a search has not retrieved any examples, he should carefully examine and understand the search criteria. If the Research Associate as well as the inquirer cannot think of new possible wordings, the research is ended. Difficulties can also occur when the event can be described only by using wordings that appear very frequently; this provides huge numbers of retrieved documents, many of which may be irrelevant. In such circumstances, the inquirer and the researcher should agree on the number of documents to be reviewed, perhaps limiting the number to no more than 150.

Upon completion of the research, the Research Associate assembles copies of all the material behind the top sheet previously described and files the folder numerically. A summary of each request is entered in the firm's private library on NAARS, where the request can be searched by key words should a similar problem arise. Finally, a monthly list of research summaries is distributed to interested parties within the firm.

A PROGNOSIS ON RESEARCH

Professional research by academic and practicing accountants is essential to solving the many complex problems involved in communicating economic phenomena to users of financial information. The academic should continue dealing with the longer-range issues, of course, as the practicing professional is not likely to carve out the time necessary to do that. The practicing professional will undoubtedly continue his focus on solving client-related problems and on providing input to standard-setting bodies.

For both academic and practicing professionals, the explosion in data needing consideration will mean much more use of sophisticated research tools, databases, and methodologies. Failure to cover all the sources could mean, for the auditor, exposure to allegation of "error" by not following what might otherwise have been considered an obscure precedent or analogy.

SUGGESTED READING

AICPA. *NAARS—National Automated Accounting Research System.* New York, 1979. This book is an overview of NAARS, including recent articles on NAARS, a system summary, the NAARS library contents, other available services, and user costs.

Boley, Richard, and Danos, Paul. "Awareness and Usage of LEXIS by Accounting Educators: A Survey." *Accounting Review,* January, 1980, pp. 102-106. This article describes the results of a survey of accounting educators as to their awareness, access to, and usage of the LEXIS and NAARS document retrieval system.

Gale, Andrew. "A Breakthrough in Disclosure Retrieval." *Journal of Accountancy,* September, 1978, pp. 86-90. This article discusses how NAARS aids CPAs in research.

Leonhardi, Willis, and Neumann, Robert. "NAARS and LEXIS: Research Tasks." *CPA Journal,* September, 1977, pp. 33-37. This article describes and gives examples of how computerized information retrieval systems help solve accounting, auditing, and tax problems.

Major Accounting Pronouncements

PROMULGATED GENERALLY ACCEPTED AUDITING STANDARDS

Statements on Auditing Standards

1   *Codification of Auditing Standards and Procedures* (a codification of all previous Statements on Auditing Procedures, superseded in part by subsequent pronouncements)
2   *Reports on Audited Financial Statements*
3   *The Effects of EDP on the Auditor's Study and Evaluation of Internal Control*
4   *Quality Control Considerations for a Firm of Independent Auditors* (superseded by SAS 25)
5   *The Meaning of "Present Fairly in Conformity With Generally Accepted Accounting Principles" in the Independent Auditor's Report*
6   *Related Party Transactions*
7   *Communications Between Predecessor and Successor Auditors*
8   *Other Information in Documents Containing Audited Financial Statements*
9   *The Effect of an Internal Audit Function on the Scope of the Independent Auditor's Examination*
10 *Limited Review of Interim Financial Information* (superseded by SAS 24)
11 *Using the Work of a Specialist*
12 *Inquiry of a Client's Lawyer Concerning Litigation, Claims, and Assessments*
13 *Reports on a Limited Review of Interim Financial Information* (superseded by SAS 24)
14 *Special Reports*
15 *Reports on Comparative Financial Statements*
16 *The Independent Auditor's Responsibility for the Detection of Errors or Irregularities*
17 *Illegal Acts by Clients*
18 *Unaudited Replacement Cost Information*
19 *Client Representations*
20 *Required Communication of Material Weaknesses in Internal Accounting Control*
21 *Segment Information*
22 *Planning and Supervision*
23 *Analytical Review Procedures*
24 *Review of Interim Financial Information*
25 *The Relationship of Generally Accepted Auditing Standards to Quality Control Standards*
26 *Association With Financial Statements*
27 *Supplementary Information Required by the Financial Accounting Standards Board*
28 *Supplementary Information on the Effects of Changing Prices*

Statements on Auditing Standards (cont'd)

PROMULGATED GENERALLY ACCEPTED ACCOUNTING PRINCIPLES

Accounting Research Bulletins (ARBs)

Accounting Principles Board (APB) Opinions

1969. *Disclosure to Investors—A Reappraisal of Administration Policies Under the '33 and '34 Acts.* Washington, D.C.: U.S. Government Printing Office.

Shillinglaw, Gordon. 1977. *Managerial Cost Accounting.* 4th ed. Homewood, Ill.: Richard D. Irwin.

Siegel, Sidney. 1956. *Non-Parametric Statistics for the Behavioral Sciences.* New York: McGraw-Hill.

Simon, Herbert, and Newell, Allen. 1971. "Human Problem Solving: The State of the Theory in 1970." *American Psychologist,* February, pp. 145-159.

Simonds, Richard, and Collins, Daniel. 1978. "Line of Business Reporting and Security Prices: An Analysis of a SEC Disclosure Rule: Comment." *Bell Journal of Economics,* Autumn, pp. 646-658.

Smith, C. Aubrey. 1954. "Accounting: Circa 2000 A.D." *Accounting Review,* January, pp. 64-71.

Smith, Kenneth. 1972. "The Relationship of Internal Control Evaluation and Audit Sample Size." *Accounting Review,* April, pp. 260-269.

Sorensen, James. 1969. "Bayesian Analysis in Auditing." *Accounting Review,* July, pp. 555-561.

Sorkin, Horton. 1979. "Third Party Confirmation Requests: A New Approach Utilizing an Expanded Field." In *Proceedings of the 1978 Touche Ross University of Kansas Symposium on Auditing Problems.* Lawrence, Kansas: University of Kansas Printing Service.

Sorter, George. 1974. "Accounting Income and Economic Income." In *Objectives of Financial Statements,* Vol. 2, *Selected Papers,* ed. Joe Cramer, Jr. and George Sorter, pp. 104-109. New York: AICPA.

South Carolina Public Service Commission. 1980. *Public Utility Fortnightly,* June 19, pp. 95-97.

Spacek, Leonard. 1958. "The Need for an Accounting Court." *Accounting Review,* July, pp. 368-379.

Sprouse, Robert, and Moonitz, Maurice. 1962. *A Tentative Set of Accounting Principles For Business Enterprises.* Accounting Research Study No. 3. New York: AICPA.

Stanger, Abraham. 1968. "Comparative Accounting Treatment Mandated by the Model Business Corporation Act and the New York Business Corporation Law Regarding Share Reacquisitions and the Related Effect on Surplus." *The Business Lawyer,* November, pp. 115-123.

Staubus, George. 1954. "An Accounting Concept of Revenue." Ph.D. Dissertation, Graduate School of Business, University of Chicago.

Stedry, Andrew. 1960. *Budget Control and Cost Behavior.* Englewood Cliffs, N.J.: Prentice-Hall.

————, and Kay, Emanuel. 1966. "The Effect of Goal Difficulty on Performance: A Field Experiment." *Behavioral Science,* November, pp. 459-470.

Sterling, Robert.
1972. "Decision Oriented Financial Accounting." *Accounting and Business Research,* Summer, pp. 198-208.
1970. *Theory of the Measurement of Enterprise Income.* Lawrence, Kan.: University Press of Kansas.

Stevens, S. S. 1959. "Measurements, Psychophilosophies and Utility." In *Measurement: Definitions and Theories,* ed. C. W. Churchman and P. Ratoosh. New York: John Wiley & Sons.

Stringer, Kenneth. 1975. "A Statistical Technique for Analytic Review." *Studies on Statistical Methodology in Auditing: Journal of Accounting Research,* Annual Supplement, pp. 1-9.

Suelflow, James. 1973. *Public Utility Accounting—Theory and Application.* East Lansing, Mich.: Michigan State University Public Utilities Studies.

Summers, Edward. 1972. "The Audit Staff Assignment Problem: A Linear Programming Analysis." *Accounting Review,* July, pp. 443-451.

Sunder, Shyam.
    1975. "Stock Price and Risk Related to Accounting Changes in Inventory Valuation." *Accounting Review,* April, pp. 305–315.
    1973. "Relationship Between Accounting Changes and Stock Prices: Problems of Measurement and Some Empirical Evidence." In *Empirical Research in Accounting: 1973,* pp. 1-45. Chicago: Institute of Professional Accounting, Graduate School of Business, University of Chicago.

Sutton, Timothy. 1979. "Corporate Management and the Setting of Accounting Standards: An Analysis and Empirical Tests." Dissertation Proposal, University of Washington.

Sweeney, Henry. 1936. *Stabilized Accounting.* New York: Harper Brothers.

Swieringa, Robert; Gibbins, Michael; Larssen, Lars; and Sweeney, Janet Lawson. 1976. "Experiment in the Heuristics of Human Information Processing." *Journal of Accounting Research,* Annual Supplement, pp. 159-187.

Teitlebaum, A. D., and Robinson, C. F. 1975. "The Real Risks in Audit Sampling." *Journal of Accounting Research,* Supplement, pp. 70-91.

Thompson, George; Whitman, Robert; Phillips, Ellis Jr.; and Warren, William. 1978. *Accounting and the Law—Cases and Materials.* 4th ed. Mineola, N.Y.: The Foundation Press.

Toba, Yoshihide. 1975. "A General Theory of Evidence as the Conceptual Foundation in Auditing Theory." *Accounting Review,* January, pp. 7-24.

Touche Ross & Co.
    1980a. *HR 3919: The Crude Oil Windfall Profit Tax Act of 1980.* Houston.
    1980b. *Roundtable on Inflation Accounting.* New York.
    1979a. *Controlling Assets and Transactions.* New York.
    1979b. *Financial Reporting and Changing Prices—A Guide to Implementing FASB Statement 33.* New York.
    1979c. *The Touche Ross Survey of Business Executives on Non-Profit Boards.* New York.
    1979d. *What's New in Accounting.* Toronto.

Treynor, Jack. 1972. "The Trouble With Earnings." *Financial Analysts Journal,* September-October, pp. 41-43.

Trowbridge, C. and Farr, C. 1976. *The Theory and Practice of Pension Funding.* Homewood, Ill.: Richard D. Irwin.

Tucker, Ledyard. 1964. "A Suggested Alternative Formulation in the Developments by Hammond and Hursch and by Hammond, Hursch and Todd." *Psychological Review,* November, pp. 528-530.

Tversky, Amos, and Kahneman, Daniel. 1974. "Judgment Under Uncertainty: Heuristics and Biases." *Science,* September, pp. 204-222.

Uecker, W., and Kinney, William. 1975. "Judgmental Evaluation of Sample Results: A Study of the Type and Severity of Errors Made by Practicing CPAs." Working Paper, University of Iowa.

U.S. Congress.
    1977. Senate Committee on the Judiciary. *The Role of the Shareholder in the Corporate World.* Washington, D.C.: U.S. Government Printing Office.
    1976a. House of Representatives, Subcommittee on Oversight and Investigations of the Committee on Interstate and Foreign Commerce. *Federal Regulation*

and Regulatory Reform. Washington, D.C.: U.S. Government Printing Office.

1976b. Senate Subcommittee on Reports, Accounting and Management of the Committee on Government Operations. *The Accounting Establishment, A Staff Study*. Washington, D.C.: U.S. Government Printing Office.

U.S. General Accounting Office. 1980. *Construction Work in Progress Needs Improved Regulatory Response for Utilities and Consumers*. Washington, D.C. (EMD-80-75).

U.S. Treasury Department. 1979. *Circular No. 230 Revised, Regulations Governing the Practice of Attorneys, Certified Public Accountants, and Enrolled Agents before the Internal Revenue Service*. Washington, D.C.: U.S. Government Printing Office.

Vasarhelyi, Miklos.

1978. "Staff Scheduling in Large Offices of National CPA Firms." *CPA Quarterly* (California), September, pp. 28-33.

1977. "Man-Machine Planning Systems: A Cognitive Style Examination of Interactive Decision Making." *Journal of Accounting Research*, Spring, pp. 138-153.

————, and Berk, Joel. Work in Progress. "The Multiple Taxonomies of Accounting Research."

Vasarhelyi, Miklos, and Mock, Theodore. 1977. "An Information Processing Analysis of Budget Variance Information." Department of Accounting, University of Southern California.

Vasarhelyi, Miklos, and Pearson, Edward. 1979. "Studies in Inflation Accounting: A Taxonomization Approach." *Quarterly Review of Economics and Business*, Spring, pp. 9-27.

Vickery, Don. 1976. General-Price-Level-Adjusted Historical-Cost Statements and the Ratio Scale View. *Accounting Review*, January, pp. 31-40.

Wall Street Journal. 1980. "Rights of Consolidated Freightways Written Off, Resulting in Loss." October 21, p. 4.

Watts, Ross. 1978. "Systematic Abnormal Returns After Quarterly Earnings Announcements." *Journal of Financial Economics*, pp. 127-150.

Webb, Eugene; Campbell, Donald; Schwartz, Richard; and Sechrest, Lee. 1966. *Unobtrusive Measures—Nonreactive Research in the Social Sciences*. Chicago: Rand, McNally & Co.

Webster, George. 1979. *The Law of Associations*. New York: Matthew Bender.

Welsch, Glenn. 1973. *Budgeting: Profit Planning and Control*. Englewood Cliffs, N.J.: Prentice-Hall.

————, and Deakin, Edward. 1977. *Measuring and Reporting the "Replacement" Cost of Oil and Gas Reserves*. Austin, Tex.: University of Texas.

Wiesen, Jeremy, and Eng, Richard. 1979. "Corporate Perks: Disclosure and Tax Considerations." *Journal of Accounting, Auditing and Finance*, Winter, pp. 101-121.

Wilcox, Jarrod. 1971. "A Gambler's Ruin Prediction of Business Failure Using Accounting Data." *Sloan Management Review*, Spring, pp. 1-10.

Winkler, Robert. 1972. *Introduction to Bayesian Inference and Decision*. New York: Holt, Rinehart & Winston.

Wright, William. 1977. "Financial Information Processing Models: An Empirical Study." *Accounting Review*, July, pp. 676-689.

Wyatt, Arthur. 1963. *A Critical Study of Accounting for Business Combinations*. Accounting Research Study No. 5. New York: AICPA.

Zeff, Stephen. 1966. *The American Accounting Association: Its First 50 Years*. Sarasota, Fla.: American Accounting Association.

Index

Chapter numbers are indicated in boldface and are followed by a dot; the lightface numbers after the dot refer to pages within the chapter.

Audit committees (*cont'd*)
nonprofit enterprises, **35**•36
reports, **10**•23-24
responsibilities, **10**•5-6,30-31
Killearn Properties, Inc., **10**•7,30-31
Securities and Exchange Commission, **10**•2-3,27-28
Stirling Homex case, **10**•6
Audit evidence
defined, **12**•2-3
types, **12**•3-5
comparison, **12**•4-5
confirmation, **12**•3, **18**•31
documentation, **12**•3-4
observation, **12**•4
physical examination, **12**•3
recomputation and posting, **12**•4
representations by client, **12**•4
Audit objectives
capital assets, **20**•27
consolidated financial statements, **31**•20
debt, **22**•30-35
covenants, **22**•34
debt compliance letters, **22**•34-35
waivers and cures, **22**•34
foreign currency translation, **31**•30-31
interest, **22**•30-35
representation by management, **12**•2
revenue and receivables, **18**•26
Audit planning
accounting policies, **12**•11-12
accounting research, **48**•21
client relations, **12**•12
electronic data processing, **15**•23-26
elements of audit plan, **12**•15
GAO standards, **11**•15
internal control, **12**•11
evaluation, **12**•14
reliance on, **12**•15
materiality, **12**•14-15
shared materiality, **12**•15
professional risk, **12**•9-10
segment information, **32**•22
special expertise, **12**•11
Audit research
accounting research, **48**•19,21-22
Audit sampling, **9**•9, **12**•5, **14**•1-30
See also Statistical sampling
definition, **14**•1-2
error in financial statements, expectation of, **14**•3
judgmental sampling, **14**•2
nonsampling risk
performance risk, **14**•3
procedural risk, **14**•3
performance risk, **14**•3
population, **14**•3
procedural risk, **14**•3
sample size, **14**•2

sampling risk, **14**•2
statistical sampling, **14**•2
Audit scope
audit committee meetings, **10**•13-16
audit committees, review by, **10**•10,13-15
Audit scope limitation
segment information, **32**•24
Audit supervision
GAO standards, **11**•15
Auditing
categories
financial, **9**•2-3
operational, **9**•3-4
social, **9**•4
debt and interest, Uniform Commercial Code, **22**•35-36
development in United States, **9**•4-5
Auditing procedures
See also Auditing standards
audit planning, **12**•7
accounting policies, **12**•11-12
client relations, **12**•12
internal control, **12**•11
professional risk, **12**•9-10
special expertise, **12**•11
cash, **17**•12-14
changing prices, capital assets, **20**•30
consolidated financial statements, **31**•20-21
credit unions, **38**•62-63
debt, substantive, **22**•32-33
electronic data processing, **12**•6-7, **15**•10
audit around, **15**•16
audit through, **15**•16
extractive industries, **37**•39
foreign currency translation, **31**•31
governmental units, **34**•21-23
health and welfare plans, **24**•24-25
insurance companies, **38**•46
internal control,
evaluation, **12**•13-14
Foreign Corrupt Practices Act, **9**•15-16
investment companies, **38**•53
leases, **23**•29-31
marketable securities, **17**•23-24,26-27
off-balance sheet financing, **23**•29-31
partnerships
publicly held, tax-oriented, **27**•17-24
privately held, **27**•16
pension costs, **24**•14-15
pension plans, **24**•18-22
real estate investment trusts, **38**•60-61
related-party transactions, **28**•18-19
research, **49**•9-10,12-13
professors in residence, **49**•12-13
reserves, oil and gas industry, **37**•29
savings and loan associations, **38**•32
savings banks, **38**•36
segment information, **32**•20-26
substantive debt, **22**•32-33

I-8

INDEX

Auditing procedures (*cont'd*)
systems testing, 12•7
timber industry, 37•43-44
verification, 12•7
analytical tests, 12•17
detailed tests of balances, 12•17
Auditing requirements
purchase audits and reviews, 46•18-19
Auditing research
American Institute of CPAs, 49•4-5
Commission on Auditors' Responsibilities, 49•5
CPA firms, 49•5
Auditing standards
See also Auditing procedures; Auditing Standards Board
Accounting Series Releases, 41•28-29
adequacy, 46•2
audit planning, 11•15
audit supervision, 11•15
auditor's report, 16•4
due professional care, 46•3-4
electronic data processing, 15•6-9
fraud, 46•3-5
actual fraud, 46•4
constructive fraud, 46•3-4
future development of, 11•23-24
governmental auditors, 11•4,14
illegal acts, 46•10
internal auditors, 11•5,14
internal control, 11•16
negligence
gross negligence, 46•3-4
ordinary negligence, 46•3-4
recklessness, 46•3-4
Securities and Exchange Commission, 41•13-15,18,28-29
Auditing Standards Board
See also Auditing standards; Auditing standards setting
composition, 11•3-4
history of, 11•3-4
Auditing standards setting
See also Auditing Standards Board; Auditing standards
American Institute of CPAs, 49•4-5
Commission on Auditors' Responsibilities, 49•5
Auditor
audit committee meetings, 10•13-27
change of, 46•13-15
Form 8-K, 46•13-14
independence, 46•13
Auditor of record, 9•22-23
degree of assurance, 9•23
Auditor's report
additional information, 16•15-17

adverse opinion, 12•20, 16•6-7
related-party transactions, 28•37
segment information, 32•23
auditing standards, 16•4
components of a business enterprise, 28•34-35
consistency, 16•9
consolidated financial statements, consistency exception, 31•17-18
critique of auditor's report, 16•29
current issues, 16•30-31
departure from GAAP, 16•6-7,13,24-25
disagreements, 46•14
disclaimer of opinion, 12•20, 16•6,16
related-party transactions, 28•36-37
elements, 9•6-8
emphasis of a matter, 16•12
exception in opinion, 12•20
extent of association, 16•15
financial reporting standards, 11•21
generally accepted auditing standards, 11•5
interim financial statements, 16•17-18
interim review report, 16•18
consent, 16•19
modification, 16•19-20
underwriters, 16•20
long-form report, 16•13-14
middle paragraph, 16•7
opinion paragraph, 16•4,7
other auditors, 16•11
pension plans, 24•20-21
preferability, 16•10
proposed, 16•29-30
qualified opinion, 12•20, 16•6-7,16
except for, 16•6
litigation, 29•22,24-25
related-party transactions, 28•35-36
segment information, 32•23,25-26
subject to, 16•6
related-party transactions 28•27,35-36,36-37
reporting standards, 16•4
Rule 203 report, 16•13
scope paragraph, 16•3
limitations, 16•8-9
standard report, 16•2-4
types, 16•5
additional information, 16•15-17
adverse opinion, 16•6-7
consistency, 16•9
departure from GAAP, 16•6-7,13,24-25
disclaimer of opinion, 16•6,16
emphasis, 16•12
other auditors, 16•11
preferability, 16•10
qualified opinion, 16•6-7,16
uncertainties, 16•7
uncertainties, 16•7, 29•24-26
valuation, 21•35-36

Realization
revenue recognition, **18**•3
Reasonable assurance
concept of, in auditing **13**•7-8
Recapitalizations
equity capital, accounting valuation, **26**•15
Receivables
accounting principles and the law, **45**•18
Receivables and payables
interest, **22**•26-29
Receivership. *See* Bankruptcy
Reciprocal transfer
definition, **7**•35
nonowners, **7**•35
owners, **7**•35
Recision, business combination
nonreciprocal transfer, **7**•37
Recklessness, 46•3-4,35
Recognition
conceptual framework, definition, **2**•15-16
Recovery method, 18•7
Regression analysis
research techniques, **48**•8
Regression estimation
statistical sampling, **14**•25-26
Regulated industries, 36•1-37
accounting policies, **36**•4-32
acquisition adjustments, **36**•27
betterments, **36**•22
construction, **36**•14-18
decommissioning costs, **36**•31
deferred taxes, **36**•9-12,18
fuel cost adjustment, **36**•19
inflation, **36**•32
intercompany profits, **36**•19
leases, **36**•25
operating rights, **36**•24
original cost, **36**•27
rate increases, **36**•22
reacquired long-term debt, **36**•25-27
research and development, **36**•30
commercial banks, **38**•4-27
credit unions, **38**•62-64
deregulation, **36**•33
financial institutions, **38**•1-64
insurance companies, **38**•43-50
investment companies, **38**•51-56
management audits, **36**•35
mortgage banks, **38**•37-42
Public Utility Regulatory Policies Act, **36**•34
real estate investment trusts, **37**•57-61
regulatory agencies
Civil Aeronautics Board, **36**•3
Commodity Futures Trading Commission, **36**•3
Economic Regulatory Administration, **36**•3
Energy Information Agency, **36**•3
federal, **36**•3

Federal Communications Commission, **36**•3
Federal Energy Regulatory Commission, **36**•3
Federal Maritime Commission, **36**•3
Federal Trade Commission, **36**•3
Interstate Commerce Commission, **36**•3
local, **36**•4
National Association of Regulatory Utility Commissioners, **36**•4
Rural Electrification Administration, **36**•3
Securities and Exchange Commission, **36**•3
state, **36**•3
savings and loan associations, **38**•27-34
savings banks, **38**•34-37
types, **36**•2
utilities, management audits, **36**•35
Regulation S-K
disagreements, **46**•15
1980 amendments, **4**•4-5,7-9
Securities and Exchange Commission, **41**•11-13
Regulatory accounting
accounting issues, **36**•9-35
accounting principles, **36**•4-8
Allowance for funds used during construction (AFUDC), **36**•14
AFUDC rates, **36**•17,18
allowance on equity funds, **36**•17
APB guidance, **36**•6-8
capitalization of interest, **36**•17
commercial banks, **38**•4-27
construction, **36**•14-15
construction work in progress (CWIP), **36**•15
credit unions, **38**•62-64
deferred taxes
congressional interest in, **36**•12-13
flow-through, **36**•11,13
normalization, **36**•10-11
financial institutions, **38**•1-64
insurance companies, **38**•43-50
investment companies, **38**•51-55
mortgage banks, **38**•37-42
rate-making process, **36**•5-6
original cost, **36**•5
rate base, **36**•5
rate design, **36**•6
rate of return, **36**•5
reacquired long-term debt, **36**•25-27
real estate investment trusts, **38**•57-61
regulated industries, **36**•4-32
savings and loan associations, **38**•27-34
savings banks, **38**•34-37
Uniform System of Accounts, **36**•4
railroads, **36**•34
telephone companies, **36**•34
utilities, **36**•34
utility plant, **36**•27-31

Regulatory agencies
American Bankers Association, **38**•3
Central Credit Union, **38**•3
Central Liquidity Facility, **38**•3
Civil Aeronautics Board, **36**•3
Commodity Futures Trading Commission, **36**•3
Department of Housing and Urban Development, **38**•3
Economic Regulatory Administration, **36**•3
Energy Information Agency, **36**•3
federal, **36**•3
Federal Communications Commission, **36**•3
Federal Deposit Insurance Corporation, **38**•3,10
Federal Energy Regulatory Commission, **36**•3
Federal Home Loan Bank, **38**•3
Federal Home Loan Bank Board, **38**•3
Federal Home Loan Mortgage Corporation, **38**•3
Federal Housing Authority, **38**•3
Federal Maritime Commission, **36**•3
Federal National Mortgage Association, **38**•3
Federal Reserve System, **38**•3
Federal Savings and Loan Insurance Corporation, **38**•3
Federal Trade Commission, **36**•3
Government National Mortgage Association, **38**•3
Interstate Commerce Commission, **36**•3
local, **36**•4
Mortgage Bankers Association of America, **38**•3
National Association of Insurance Commissioners, **38**•3
National Association of Mutual Savings Banks, **38**•3
National Association of Regulatory Utility Commissioners, **36**•4
National Association of Real Estate Investment Trusts, **38**•3
National Association of Securities Dealers, **38**•3
National Credit Union Association, **38**•3
Office of the Comptroller of the Currency, **38**•3,10
Rural Electrification Administration, **36**•3
Savings and Loan Association, **38**•3
Securities and Exchange Commission, **36**•3, **38**•3,10
Small Business Administration, **38**•3
Small Business Investment Company, **38**•3
state, **36**•4
Veterans Administration, **38**•3
Reimbursed costs
nonprofit enterprises, auditing considerations, **35**•37-38

Reinsurance
insurance companies, **38**•44
Related party
close kin, **28**•6
definition, **28**•5-6
equity method investors and investees, **28**•7
financial statements, **28**•5
leases
accounting, **23**•17-18
auditing procedures, **23**•30
capitalization, **23**•4-5
management, **28**•6
parents and subsidiaries, **28**•6-7
SEC definition, **28**•7-8
Related-party transactions
accommodations, **28**•12
accounting principles, **28**•29-32
asset valuation, **28**•31
minority interests, **28**•30
nonmonetary transactions, **28**•32
price structure, **28**•30
profit recognition and deferral, **28**•30-31
resales, **28**•31
subsequent period accounting, **28**•31
approval by directors, **28**•28
asset valuation
constructive dividend, **28**•31
dangling debit, **28**•31
auditing procedures
Commission on Auditors' Responsibilities, **28**•19
identification, **28**•19
auditor's report, **28**•27
adverse opinion, **28**•37
disclaimer of opinion, **28**•36-37
emphasis of a matter, **28**•35-36
qualified opinion, **28**•36
beneficial transactions, **28**•12
tax savings, **28**•12
common officers and directors, **28**•11
components of a business enterprise, **28**•10
disclosure, **28**•34-35
wholly owned subsidiary, **28**•2-3
confirmation, **28**•28-29
conflict of interest
bribes and kickbacks, **28**•9-10
Foreign Corrupt Practices Acts, **28**•9-10
illegal payments, **28**•9-10
controllability of transactions, **28**•3
deliberate concealment, **28**•20
disclosure
components of a business enterprise, **28**•34-35
duration of disclosure, **28**•33
equivalence, **28**•33-34
profit/loss, **28**•32-33
recognizing substance, **28**•33

S

Unaudited financial statements
compilations, **16**•22
  independence, **16**•23
review services, **16**•21,23
standards, **16**•21
Unbilled receivables
construction contracts, auditing procedures, **19**•57
Uncertainties
accrual, **29**•6
  catastrophe losses, **29**•9
  general contingency reserves, **29**•9
  product recalls, **29**•11-12
auditing procedures, **29**•13
  going concern, **29**•25-26
  management representations, **29**•17-18
  reasonability, **29**•15-16
auditor's report, **16**•7, **29**•24-26
valuation, **21**•35-36
Commission on Auditors' Responsibilities, **29**•5
contingency, **29**•3-4
definition, **29**•3-4
disclosure, **29**•3
  assessments, **29**•7
  estimates, **29**•9
  gain contingencies, **29**•7-8
  interim financial statements, **29**•9-10
  subsequent events, **29**•7
  unasserted claim, **29**•6-7
documentation, auditing procedures, **29**•23
estimate, **29**•3-4
evidential matter, **29**•14
Financial Accounting Standards Board, conceptual framework, **29**•5
gain contingencies, disclosure, **29**•7-8
legal counsel of client, inquiry letter, **29**•20
litigation, **29**•12-13
  auditor's report, **29**•24-26
materiality, auditing procedures, **29**•19
qualified opinion, **29**•22,24-25
reporting standards, **9**•21-22
revenue recognition, **7**•25
subsequent events, disclosure, **29**•7
types
  changing social values, **29**•2
  industry uncertainties, **29**•3
  macroeconomic matters, **29**•2-3
  remote uncertainties, **29**•2
  tax liabilities, **29**•2
Uncollectible accounts receivable, 18•9-11
Unconsolidated subsidiaries, 31•3-4
Underwriters
comfort letters, **26**•4
equity capital, **26**•3-4
leases, accounting for, **23**•25-26
related-party transactions, **28**•3-4
Undistributed earnings
income taxes, **25**•19-20

Unearned revenue, 18•13-14
Uniform Commercial Code, 22•35-36
accounting standards, **45**•21
Uniform Partnership Act, 27•1
Uniform System of Accounts
regulatory accounting
  Federal Communications Commission, **36**•34
  Federal Energy Regulatory Commission, **36**•34
  Interstate Commerce Commission, **36**•34
  rate-making, **36**•5-6
  uniformity, **36**•4-5
Unit value LIFO approach
inventory, **19**•18
Unit-of-delivery method
revenue recognition, **18**•5
United Nations
financial reporting, standards, **1**•7
United States General Accounting Office
compliance auditing standards, **11**•14
financial auditing standards, **11**•14
financial reporting standards, **11**•21-22
management audit standards, **11**•14
United States government obligations
treasury bills, **17**•8
treasury bonds, **17**•8
treasury notes, **17**•8
Unrestricted random sampling
statistical sampling, **14**•14-15
Unusual items, 3•18
security analysis, **6**•5-6
Utilities
Uniform System of Accounts **36**•4
Utility industry
accounting policies, Uniform System of Accounts, **36**•4
National Association of Regulatory Utility Commissioners, **36**•4
regulatory accounting, APB guidance, **36**•6-8
Utility plant
acquisition adjustments, **36**•27-29
  regulatory accounting, **36**•22-27
decommissioning costs, **36**•31
  regulatory accounting, **36**•31
original cost, **36**•27-29

V

Vacation pay, 17•29
Validity
forecasts—preparation and presentation, **33**•18
internal control, **13**•9
qualitative characteristics, earnings recognition, **7**•28